Encyclopedia of the

Romantic Era,

1760–1850

ENCYCLOPEDIA

OF THE

ROMANTIC ERA,

1760–1850

VOLUME 2

L–Z

Index

Christopher John Murray, General Editor

Fitzroy Dearborn

An Imprint of the Taylor & Francis Group

New York   London

Published in 2004 by
Fitzroy Dearborn
An Imprint of the Taylor & Francis Group
29 West 35th Street
New York, NY 10001

Published in 2004 by
Fitzroy Dearborn
An imprint of the Taylor & Francis Group
11 New Fetter Lane
London EC4P 4EE

10 9 8 7 6 5 4 3 2 1

Library of Congress Cataloging-in-Publication Data

Encyclopedia of the romantic era, 1760–1850/volume editor, Christopher John Murray.
     p. cm.
   Includes bibliographical references and index.
   Contents: v. 1. A–K – v. 2. L–Z.
   ISBN 1–57958–361-X (hb: set : alk. paper)-ISBN 1-57958-423-3 (hb: vol. 1: alk. paper)-ISBN 1-57958-422-5 (hb: vol. 2: alk paper)
   Romanticism—Encyclopedia. I. Murray, Christopher John.

   NX452.5.R64E53 2003
   700′.4145′03—dc21
                                                                                        2003042406

ISBN 1-57958-361-X (2-volume set)
ISBN 1-57958-423-3 (Volume 1)
ISBN 1-57958-422-5 (Volume 2)

TABLE OF CONTENTS

L

THE LADY OF SHALOTT 1832

Poem by Alfred, Lord Tennyson

This 171-line poem, divided into four parts and consisting of nineteen nine-line stanzas with a rhyme scheme of *aaaabcccb*, is one of the most famous and effective works of Alfred, Lord Tennyson's early career. He started writing it in October 1831, and finished it in May of 1832. It was published in *Poems* (1832) but revised fairly extensively for the two-volume edition of *Poems* (1842). The subject of this Arthurian ballad is Elaine, who fell in love with Sir Lancelot, King Arthur's greatest knight. She was known as "the lily maid of Astolat," from which Tennyson derives the name "Shalott." He later claimed not to have read Thomas Malory's prose collection of Arthurian writing *Morte D'Arthur* (1485) until after writing this poem, and said he had found the story in a fourteenth-century Italian romance called "La Donna di Scalotta" (the actual title is *Quì conta come la Damigella di Scalot morì per amore di Lancialotto de Lac*). He changed "Scalotta" because "Shalott was a softer sound than Scalott." In 1868 Tennyson told F. J. Furnivell that "I met the story first in some Italian *nouvelle*: but the web, mirror, island, etc., were my own. Indeed, I doubt whether I should ever have put it in that shape if I had been then aware of the Maid of Astolat in *Mort Arthur*."

The protagonist of the poem lives a sequestered life, occupied only with weaving a beautiful web; she may not look directly upon the outside world for fear of a curse, but has a mirror through which she can observe goings-on. She has grown miserable with her condition, declaring "I am half sick of shadows." "Shadows" here means the reflected images in her mirror; but it also suggests the shadowy half-life that she is living. The landscape outside her tower is based on the flat worlds of Tennyson's Lincolnshire, the evocation of the natural world tending paradoxically to stress the isolation of the lady.

> Willows whiten, aspens quiver,
> Little breezes dusk and shiver,
> Through the wave that runs forever
> By the island in the river (10–14)

"The Lady of Shalott" as a whole makes poetry out of precisely this sort of finely observed monotony. Monotony is described, but monotony also emerges in its form—for instance in the deliberately limited rhyme scheme, as well as the standard patterning of the ballad meter. It is, for all its brightly colored cod-medieval trappings ("a troop of damsels glad, / An abbot on a shambling pad . . . Or long haired page in crimson clad . . . and sometimes through the mirror blue / The knights come riding two by two"), a poem about the repetitive boredom of life. In its static and colorful medievalism it anticipates many Pre-Raphaelite paintings: and Tennyson was indeed a major influence on this 1850s and 1860s artistic movement. (There are famous paintings of this poem by William Holman Hunt, John Everett Millais, and John William Waterhouse.) In fact, Margaret Lourie argues that with poems such as this one, "between 1830 and 1833, Tennyson had essentially invented Pre-Raphaelitism." The strength of the pre-Raphaelites was their capturing of moments of Romantic intensity in scintillating but static images; and for Tennyson's Lady of Shalott nothing *can* happen. The "event" of the poem, if we can call it that, is the intrusion of Lancelot into the world of the lady. His shining armor is so mirror-like that it doubly reflects the world outside, the protection afforded by the mirror is canceled and it cracks from side to side. The reduplication is caught by the repetition where there should be rhyme ("river" / "river"), although this is also an effect that underlines the monotony of the Lady's existence:

> From the bank and from the river
> He flashed into the crystal mirror,
> "Tirra lirra" by the river
> Sang Sir Lancelot.

The lady and the knight never meet; nothing happens between them. In fact, in this poem nothing happens at all (the only exception to this is the crack that opens in the mirror). We are not given a description of the lady leaving her tower—she simply appears in a barge, floating down the river chanting a mournful carol until "her blood was frozen slowly, / And her eyes were darkened wholly." Such action as there is, in other words, is described in a passive way. As with much early Tennyson (most notably "Mariana," "The Kraken," and "The Lotus Eaters"), this is a poem very much about impotence and monotony.

This is a reading at odds with the conventional critical responses to the poem. As Elaine Jordan puts it, most "modern criticism has interpreted the Lady in psychoanalytic terms, as imprisoned libido unable to find expression in a utilitarian age." In other words, as a Romantic icon dying because unable to find a place in a Victorian world. Such readings ignore both the detailed Romantic intertextuality that pervades and gives life to the piece and the mystic obliqueness of the Lady's position and demise. Critics have seen in the poem allusions to Percy Bysshe Shelley's *Witch of Atlas* and to John Keats's repeated theme on the immiscibility of life in art and life in the world (the lady in her tower, devoted to her aesthetic object, the web, represents the former; she dies when she tries to embody the latter). "The Lady of Shalott" is undeniably a profoundly Keatsian poem, but it owes less to the formal argumentation of the great odes, especially "On a Grecian Urn" and "To a Nightingale," with which this thesis is particularly associated, and owes more to a piece of fairy Arthuriana like "La Belle Dame Sans Merci." In a sense we might read Tennyson's poem as a self-conscious inversion of the gender alignments of that poem; instead of knight falling thrall to Lady and pining away, it is the other way around. But the mood and timbre of both works is of a piece, and this more than anything explains the continuing popularity of "The Lady of Shalott."

ADAM ROBERTS

See also **In Memoriam A.H.H.; Poetry: Britain; Tennyson, Alfred, Lord**

Selected Works

Ricks, Christopher, ed. *The Poems of Tennyson*. 2nd ed., 3 vols. London: Longman, 1987.
Roberts, Adam, ed. *Tennyson: The Oxford Authors*. Oxford, U.K.: Oxford University Press, 2000.

Bibliography

Armstrong, Isobel. *Victorian Poetry: Poetry, Poetics and Politics*. London: Routledge, 1993.
Bloom, Harold. *The Ringers in the Tower: Studies in Romantic Tradition*. Chicago: University of Chicago Press, 1971.
Jordan, Elaine. *Alfred Tennyson*. Cambridge: Cambridge University Press, 1988.
Lourie, Margaret. "Below the Thunders of the Upper Deep: Tennyson as a Romantic Revisionist." *Studies in Romanticism* 18 (1979): 3–27.
Ricks, Christopher. *Tennyson*. 2d ed. London: Macmillan, 1989.
Sinfield, Alan. *Alfred Tennyson*. Rereading Literature series. Oxford, U.K.: Blackwell, 1986.
Tennyson, Hallam. *Alfred, Lord Tennyson: A Memoir*. 2 vols. 1897.

LAMARCK, JEAN BAPTISTE PIERRE ANTOINE DE MONET, CHEVALIER DE 1744–1829

French biologist and paleontologist

The famous event of Jean Baptiste Pierre Antione de Monet Lamarck's youth occurred shortly after his arrival at Willinghausen, Westphalia, on a cheap horse; he had just left the theological path his late father had set him on to fight in the Seven Years War. Within hours his company was all but obliterated. The new recruit, however, refused to retreat without orders and so took command over the other thirteen survivors. The act promptly earned him a promotion to officer.

If such a start to a military career was resplendently comic, Lamarck's discharge eight years later was tragicomic: a fellow soldier had inadvertently caused a neck injury by picking him up by the head. Lamarck nonetheless did not leave his preferred vocation empty-handed for, during his garrison duty at Toulon and Monaco, he had acquired an interest in botany. Further encouraged by the friendship of Bernard de Jussieu and, by chance, Jean-Jacques Rousseau, he soon found work under the former at the Jardin du Roi (Royal Gardens) and was to assist him for the next eighteen years.

Thus began a career that would prove central to the development of the concept of evolution, from the transformisms of Benoît de Maillet and Georges de Buffon, which described how one species became another, to Darwinism. Lamarck's *Flora française* (*French Flora*, 1778), based on more than a decade of flora study, brought him universal acclaim and he was swiftly appointed to the Académie Royale des Sciences. The Jardin des Plantes (botanical gardens) secured him as assistant botanist and, after the French Revolution, as professor of invertebrate zoology at its Musée National d'Histoire Naturelle (National Museum of Natural History). Above all, Lamarck worked on what eventually became four colossal volumes for the *Encyclopédie méthodique* (*Methodical Encyclopaedia*, 1783–1817), a project begun by Denis Diderot and Jean le Rond d'Alembert and later completed by Jean Louis Marie Poiret.

Lamarck's popularity at that time resided in his departure from the Swedish botanist Carolus Linnaeus's artificial taxonomy; he had devised a dichotomous method of classifying plants by genus and species which both regarded real structures and was practical for laymen. It soon led to his construction of a series organizing plants on six levels—polypetalous, monopetalous, composite, incomplete, unilobed, and cryptogamous—and this, in turn, inspired a series for the animal kingdom, one stretching in decreasing complexity from man or mammals to unicellular organisms. His *Philosophie zoologique* (*Zoological Philosophy*, 1809) produced the first important diagram of evolutionary movement.

By the time of his *Histoire naturelle des animaux sans vertèbres* (*Natural History of Invertebrate Animals*, 1815–22), Lamarck was already specifying four laws of organic change; this massive work on invertebrates itself vindicated the use of museum collections to revise systematic biology. Lamarck's first law states that life force tends to increase a body's volume and enlarge its parts while his second law asserts that new needs and their demands produce new organs. His third goes on to state that these organs develop in proportion to their use. The last, which claims that heredity preserves what is acquired and passes it on to progeny, is called "the inheritance of acquired characteristics" and has since been commonly, but erroneously, thought to be the crux of Lamarckianism.

It is extraordinary that Lamarck had arrived at all these ideas without much systematic proof for the processes he described. Underlying such a theory of active regeneration was, in fact, a generalizing belief with Romantic overtones: Lamarck had assumed that life possessed a transcendental principle that worked through "excitations," "subtle and ever-moving fluids," and "inner feeling" to perfect each creature. He even hinted that God was the evolutionary force and, as such, there could be no extinction of species since all were preserved by continual transformation in line with the perfect nature of divine creation. Such a formulation kept in balance the ideas of species variation behind evolution, of immutable species behind conservative biology, and of special creation behind Christianity in a way that Charles Darwin after him could not repeat.

To go deeper, Lamarck's vision of life drew heavily from an integrative perspective on forms of knowledge such as biology, physics, chemistry, geology, and meteorology; his interest in heat and electricity, for example, stemmed from a conviction that these were used by higher life forms to effect self-determination and transcend lower mechanistic behavior. So strong was his conviction on this that he disagreed—crucially but lamentably—with Antoine Lavoisier and Antoine de Fourcroy, whose chemistry, he thought, generated a widening field of unstable particularities without "grand knowledge." His related meteorological study ended abruptly in 1810 when Napoleon publicly ridiculed his attempt to predict weather through the classification of clouds.

In geology, Lamarck contributed what was to become an important scientific concept, the paradoxical idea of geologic or extended time. "Time," he famously said, "is insignificant and never a difficulty for Nature" and so, in *Hydrogéologie* (1802), geological history was organized in terms of successive global inundations which, in shoring up distinguishable organic deposits, allowed biotic continuity to be read out of the stratigraphic record. This posed an immediate challenge to Georges Cuvier's paleontology, which had depended on catastrophes as the fracturing force bringing extinction and renewal to a region's organic life; Lamarck's stress on the obstinacy of life processes and time's "insignificance" contradicted catastrophic disruptions and would converge with the emerging uniformitarian approach that had just begun with James Hutton's *Theory of the Earth* (1797).

Lamarck, however, made a powerful enemy in Cuvier, who went on to use his influence not only to turn scientific attention away from Lamarck, but also to viciously misrepresent and mock his theories in his eulogy following Lamarck's death. Poor and scoffed at in his later years, his ideas misunderstood and either neglected or dismissed by those—such as Erasmus Darwin,

Johann Wolfgang von Goethe, and Étienne Geoffroy Saint-Hilaire—who actually advocated transformism, Lamarck died every inch a tragic genius; his grave was rented, his body later misplaced and lost. Lamarck's importance was nonetheless readily acknowledged by Honoré de Balzac, Henry de Blainville, Samuel Butler, Auguste Comte, Ernst Haekel, and Arthur Schopenhauer; Charles Lyell, who criticized Lamarckianism in his *Principles of Geology* (1830–33), ironically made the idea of evolution accessible to his English readers, among whom was the young Darwin.

GWEE LI SUI

Biography

Born in Bazentin-le-Petit, Picardy, on August 1, 1744; educated at the Jesuit College at Amiens, 1755–59; military career, 1760–68; settled in Paris after resignation, where he soon befriended Jussieu, Buffon, and Rousseau, 1769; published *Flora française*, 1778; elected into the Académie Royale des Sciences, 1779; made Royal Botanist, 1781; traveled in central Europe as tutor of Buffon's son, 1781–82; made professor of invertebrate zoology at the Musée National d'Histoire Naturelle, 1793; made secretary of the Assembly of Professors in 1795, and director, three years later; published *Hydrogéologie*, 1802; refused chair of zoology in the Faculty of Sciences of the Sorbonne, 1809; published *Philosophie zoologique*, 1809; published *Histoire naturelle des animaux sans vertèbres*, 1815–22; became totally blind by 1818; died in Paris on December 18, 1829.

Selected Works

Flora française. 3 vols., 1778.
Recherches sur les causes des principaux faits physiques, et particulièrement sur celles de la combustion. 2 vols., 1794.
Réfutation de la théorie pneumatique, ou de la nouvelle doctrine des chimistes modernes. 1796.
Annuaires météorologiques. 11 vols., 1799–1810.
Système des animaux sans vertèbres, ou tableau général des classes. 1801.
Hydrogéologie, 1802. Translated as *Hydrogeology* by Albert V. Carozzi. Urbana: University of Illinois Press, 1964.
Recherches sur l'organisation des corps vivants [*Research on the Organization of Living Bodies*], 1802.
Philosophie zoologique, 2 vols., 1809. Translated as *Zoological Philosophy* by Hugh Elliot. London: Macmillan, 1914.
Histoire naturelle des animaux sans vertèbres. 7 vols., 1815–22.
Système analytique des connaissances positives de l'homme. 1820.

Bibliography

Bathélemy-Madaule, Madeleine. *Lamarck: ou le mythe du précurseur*. Paris: Éditions du Seuil, 1979.
Berthelot, René. *Science et philosophie chez Gœthe*. Paris: Félix Alcan, 1832.
Burkhardt, Richard W. *The Spirit of System: Lamarck and Evolutionary Biology*. Cambridge, Mass.: Harvard University Press, 1977.
Butler, Samuel. *Evolution, Old and New; or, The Theories of Buffon, Dr. Erasmus Darwin, and Lamarck, as compared with that of Mr. Charles Darwin*. London: Hardwicke and Borgue, 1879.
Cannon, H. Graham. *Lamarck and Modern Genetics*. Manchester: Manchester University Press, 1959
Corsi, Pietro. *The Age of Lamarck*. Berkeley and Los Angeles: University of California Press, 1988.

Gizycki, Georg von. *Philosophische Conseqeunzen der Lamarck-Darwin-'schen Entwicklungstheorie.* Leipzig, 1876.

Hutton, Frederick Wollaston. *Darwinism and Lamarkism: Old and New. Four Lectures.* London: Duckworth, 1899.

Jordanova, Ludmilla J. *Lamarck.* Oxford, U.K.:: Oxford University Press, 1984.

Lyell, Charles. *Principles of Geology.* Ed. and introduced by James A. Second. Harmondsworth, England: Penguin, 1997.

Packard, Alpheus S. *Lamarck: The Founder of Evolution. His Life and Works.* London: Longman, 1901.

Tschulok, Sinai. *Lamarck. Eine kritische-historische Studie.* Zürich, 1937.

LAMARTINE, ALPHONSE MARIE-LOUIS PRAT DE 1790–1869

French poet and statesman

While as a Romantic poet Alphonse Marie-Louis Prat de Lamartine's achievement clearly pales when measured against that of his compatriot, the incomparable Victor Hugo, his place in the history of French poetry remains indisputably secure to this day. With the publication of the *Méditations poétiques* (*Poetic Meditations*, 1820), Lamartine revitalized French verse, rescuing it from the thematic banalities of his neoclassical predecessors in the eighteenth century and investing it with fresh and personal emotion, powerfully expressed, as the poet wrote of his own love experience. It is true that Lamartine was not able to sustain, in his subsequent poetic production—with occasional exceptions, such as the remarkable poem of his advanced years "La Vigne et la maison" ("The Vine and the House," 1857)—the admirable originality of the first *Méditations*. It is also true that once poetic fashion moved beyond the conventionalities of the Romantic mode, succeeding generations of poets in the nineteenth century, the Parnassians and Symbolists among them, would judge Lamartine with considerable severity, condemning the excesses of his sentimentality and the imperfections of his style. Nor, generally, would their progeny in the twentieth century veer far from this criticism. But a fair evaluation of Lamartine's contribution as a poet must necessarily take into account the historical significance of his ability to orient French poetry in the direction in which Jean-Jacques Rousseau, and François-Auguste-René, Vicomte de Chateaubriand before him, had oriented French prose—namely, toward the direct incorporation of personal sentiment and a communion, at once lyrical and religious, with the wonders of nature. Their disclaimers notwithstanding, it is not in the least excessive to maintain that the representatives of post-Romantic poetic movements are substantially indebted to Lamartine to the degree that his rejection of many, if not all, of the stereotypes of neoclassical poetry opens the way to their more intrepid experimentations with theme and form.

If one is tempted to underestimate Lamartine's poetic contribution, one is even more tempted to discount his impact on French political life. Admittedly, a quick glance at his political activity yields the conclusion that, in spite of his extraordinary, if short-lived, ascendancy during the convulsions of 1848, an ascendancy that propelled him to the post of minister of foreign affairs in the provisional government, Lamartine's unrealistic refusal to choose sides, his unavailing attempt to placate all the opposing factions, led to his humiliating undoing—and to the eventual coup d'état of Louis-Napoleon. But a more penetrating examination of his political thought and his political action results in a more favorable assessment of both. If the essential Lamartine—whose early political thinking was theocratic—

would always be hard-pressed to indict systematically the monarchy and the church, the mature politician of the 1840s was a republican and a progressive proponent of the separation of church and state, of freedom of the press, of expanded voting rights. In addition, he was against the institution of slavery, and for the abolition of the death penalty—almost a worthy forerunner of the liberal practitioners of Third Republic politics, except for his insistence on a strong executive branch.

Published anonymously, the twenty-four poems comprising the *Méditations poétiques* made Lamartine, the as-yet-unemployed aristocrat, an overnight sensation. The poet's touchingly sincere and emotional evocation in "Le Lac" ("The Lake") of his love affair with the married Julie Charles, whom he had met at Aix-les-Bains in 1816, and whom he had hoped to meet again there in 1817—gravely ill, she would not come and would die of consumption in December of that year—struck a vibrantly responsive chord in a generation hungry for such sentimentality, wedded as it was to a typically Romantic communion with nature. Neither Lamartine's religious fluctuations, as evidenced in the contrasting poems "Le D'ésespoir" ("Despair") and "La Providence de l'homme" ("Providence for Humanity"), nor his heavy debt to Chateaubriand and Rousseau, among others; nor his reproduction of many features of neoclassical poetry, such as the Alexandrine, and a generally abstract vocabulary even in the description of nature diminish the charm of his poetry. He brilliantly blends all these elements in an original work exemplifying the potential of poetic subjectivity and graced with a subtle but enchanting musicality.

Lamartine was never again to experience such dizzying literary success. The *Nouvelles Méditations poétiques* (*New Poetic Meditations*, 1823), the creation of a man now happily married (to the Englishwoman Marianne Eliza Birch), and now gainfully employed (he had been named attaché to the French embassy in Naples), reproduced for the most part the same themes of the earlier work, but without their elegiac authenticity. One of the few merits of the book is the evidence of the poet's emerging social consciousness: in "Bonaparte" and "La Liberté, ou une nuit á Rome" ("Liberty, or a Night in Rome"), Lamartine defends liberty against Napoleonic or Roman tyranny; yet, in the latter poem in particular, he also inveighs against the excesses of liberty in modern times, and it is not clear whether he is championing a republican form of liberty or merely the freedom of aristocracies from the exactions of the tyrant. The *Harmonies poétiques et religieuses* (*Poetic and Religious Harmonies*, 1830), an expression of the firmness of Lamartine's Christian faith despite occasional moments of doubt, was no more a poetic triumph than the prior publication, although in it there is an arresting innovation: Lamartine's religious beliefs, increasingly eschewing dogma, are characterized by a growing tolerance and a recognition of Islam. As for *Jocelyn* (1836), the tale of a seminarian in love, and *La Chute d'un ange* (*The Fall of an Angel*, 1838), in which the angel Cédar falls for the mortal Daïdha, they were, as to both substance and style, seriously flawed fragments of the poet's project for an epic poem retracing humanity's social evolution. In Lamartine's last book of poetry, the *Recueillements poétiques* (*Poetic Contemplations*, 1839) the poet once again failed to re-create the magic of the landmark publication of 1820. But the work's preface, suggesting a more republican spirit than before, reflects Lamartine's ardent advocacy of political liberty and social progress worldwide. With regard to the poems themselves, "Utopie" ("Utopia") displays the expansion of the poet's religious thought to include the hope of a universal cult, and "À Monsieur Félix Guillemardet forthrightly expresses the poet's realization that he must no longer speak just for himself but for humanity in general.

After the *Receuillements poétiques*, Lamartine's evolving preoccupation with social causes took the more concrete form of active participation in France's political life: having been elected to the Chamber of Deputies in 1833, he would represent his constituents until 1851. Lamartine's ambitions in this area were not unrelated to his subsequent emergence as a gifted prose writer. Confirming the existence of a talent already suggested in 1835, *Souvenirs, impressions, pensées et paysages, pendant un voyage en orient (1832–1833)* (*A Pilgrimage to the Holy Land: Comprising Recollections, Sketches, and Reflections Made during a Tour in the East in 1832–1833*), Lamartine won praise, at least initially, for the historical prose of his *Histoire des Girondins* (*History of the Girondists*, 1847). Before long, however, the factual inaccuracies, the general omission of detail related to the state of the French economy at the time of the Revolution, and the partiality of the portrait of the royal family provoked sharp criticism. But today one tends to appreciate in this work—perhaps intended by the author to favor his political career by extolling the progressive fruits of the French Revolution while deploring its savage treatment of the monarchy—the purely literary merits not entirely discredited by a propensity for melodrama: vivid portraits of major historical figures and engaging descriptions of the masses in revolt.

Ironically, much of Lamartine's subsequent prose was historical hack work that he felt obliged to undertake when, after his humiliating defeat at the hands of Louis-Napoleon in the presidential election of 1848, he had to write to survive. Among these publications were the largely unreliable histories of Turkey and Russia, published in 1854 and 1855, respectively. But similarly mediocre works of fiction were also flowing from the writer's pen: undistinguished novels like *Raphael* (1849), the implausibly idealized account of his love for Julie Charles, and *Geneviéve* (1851), a laudable but unpersuasive foray into the domain of the social novel—Lamartine portrayed the misery of a peasant woman. One of the rare gems in Lamartine's extended literary drought between 1847 and 1869, the year of his death, was, appropriately enough, a poem. "La Vigne et la maison" appeared in the fifteenth *entretien* (conversation) of the third volume of a publication called *Cours familier de littérature* (*Informal Course on Literature*, 1856–69). The latter, part of the hack work of this period, although intended by the author to instruct the

Théodore Chassériau, *Alphonse de Lamartine*. Reprinted courtesy of AKG.

masses, was a collection of poorly researched writings on a wide variety of subjects, including history, biography, and literary criticism, which appeared in monthly installments. In "La Vigne et la maison," Lamartine returns to the personal mode of the *Méditations*, this time writing nostalgically of his happy childhood, as old age and approaching death weigh heavily on his mind. In poignant and unaffected language, the poet expresses a renewed faith in a merciful God, and, consequently, is able to close on a note of consolation and hope.

As far as literary achievement is concerned, when all is said and done, it is the lyrical Lamartine that has survived, the creator of the *Méditations poétiques* and "La Vigne et la maison," whose subjective approach to love and life allowed the poets who followed him to give freer reign to their imagination in the exploration of all things, justifying the praise, however conditional, of one of those poets, Arthur Rimbaud, who recognized Lamartine, in spite of the latter's outmoded style, as a *voyant* (visionary).

NORMAN ARAUJO

Biography

Born in Mâcon, October 21, 1790. Enrolled in the Puppier boarding school in Lyons, 1801. Attended the school in Belley run by the Fathers of the Faith, 1803. Named attaché to the French embassy in Naples, married Marianne Eliza Birch, 1820. Birth of son Alphonse, 1821. Birth of daughter Julia, death of Alphonse, 1822. Elected to the Académie Française, 1829. Trip to the Middle East, death of daughter Julia, 1832. Elected as representative to the Chamber of Deputies by the voters of Bergues, 1833. Became Minister of Foreign Affairs, defeated in the presidential election by Louis-Napoleon, 1848. Left public life after Louis-Napoleon's coup d'état, 1851. Died in Paris, February 28, 1869.

Selected Works

Collections

Mélanges Poétiques et discours. 1840.
Livres complétes de Lamartine publiées, et inédites. 41 vols., 1860–66.

Poetry

Méditations Poétiques, 1820; enlarged, 1820; enlarged edition, 1823. Translated as *The Poetical Meditations of M. Alphonse de La Martine*, by Henry Christmas. 1839.
Nouvelles Méditations Poétiques, 1823; enlarged edition, 1830.
Le Dernier Chant du pèlerinage d'Harold, 1825. Anonymously translated as *The Last Canto of Childe Harold's Pilgrimage.* 1827.
Harmonies Poétiques et religieuses. 1830.
Jocelyn: Épisode Journal trouvé chez un curé de village, 1836. Translated as *Jocelyn, an Episode: Journal Found in the House of a Village Curate*, by Robert Anstruther, 1844. Translated by Hazel Patterson Stuart, New York: Exhibition Press, 1954.
La Chute d'un ange: Épisode, 1838; revised, 1839.
Recueillements Poétiques. 1839.
La Vigne et la maison. 1857.

Fiction

Raphaël, pages de la vingtième année, 1849. Translated as *Raphael; or, Pages of the Book of Life at Twenty.* 1849.
Les Confidences, 1849. Translated as *Confidential Disclosures*, by Eugene Plunkett, 1849.
Geneviève, histoire d'une servante, 1850. Translated as *Geneviève; or, The History of a Servant Girl*, by A. R. Scoble, 1850.
Le Tailleur de pierres de Saint-Point, Écrit villageois, 1851. Anonymously translated as *The Stonemason of Saint-Point: A Village Tale.* 1851.

Drama

Toussaint Louverture: poème dramatique. 1850.

Other

Sur la politique rationnelle. 1831.
Souvenirs, impressions, pensées et paysages, pendant un voyage en Orient (1832–1833), ou notes d'un voyageur, 1835. Anonymously translated as *A Pilgrimage to the Holy Land: Comprising Recollections, Sketches, and Reflections Made during a Tour in the East in 1832–1833.* 1835
Histoire des Girondins, 1847. Translated as *History of the Girondists; or, Personal Memoirs of the Patriots of the French Revolution from Unpublished Sources*, by Henry T. Ryde, 1847.
Histoire de la Révolution de 1848, 1849. Translated as *History of the French Revolution of 1848.* by Francis A. Durivage and William S. Chase, 1849.
Histoire de la Turquie, 1854–55. Translation *History of Turkey.* 1855–57.
Histoire de la Russie. 1855.
Cours familier de littérature: un entretien par mois. 1856–69.

Bibliography

Araujo, Norman. *In Search of Eden: Lamartine's Symbols of Despair and Deliverance.* Brookline, Mass.: Classical Folia, 1976.
Birkett, Mary Ellen. *Lamartine and the Poetics of Landscape.* Lexington, Ky: French Forum Monographs, 1982.
Calmettes, Gérard. *Lamartine: voix de la république.* Paris: L'Armanèon, 1998
Croisille, Christian, ed. *L'Année 1820, année des 'Méditations'.* Paris: Nizet, 1994.
Guillemin, Henri. *Lamartine.* Paris: Le Seuil, 1987.
Lombard, Charles M. *Lamartine.* New York: Twayne, 1973.
Luppé, Marquis de. *Les Travaux et les jours d'Alphonse de Lamartine.* Paris: Albin Michel, 1952.
Toesca, Maurice. *Lamartine ou l'amour de la vie.* Paris: Albin Michel, 1969.
Unger, Gérard. *Lamartine: poète et homme d'État.* Paris: Flammarion, 1998.

LAMB, CHARLES 1775–1834

British critic and essayist

Charles Lamb was a critic and essayist whose literary career successfully spanned both generations of British Romanticism: his first published work, four sonnets in Samuel Taylor Coleridge's *Poems on Various Subjects*, came in 1796; his most famous, the *Essays of Elia* (published initially in the *London Magazine* between 1820 and 1823), arrived in book form more than a quarter of a century later, in 1823.

In many respects, Lamb was typical of his period; in others, he was something of an eccentric exception to it. He was serious and humorous, intellectual and sentimental, a writer who fused the personal and the social and tried his hand at many artistic forms, turning from his initial love of philosophy, through poetry, drama, and criticism, to the essays with which he would make his name. His oeuvre, especially the "informal" (to use Lamb's word) essays, was intimately connected with the remarkable life that he lived. The lighthearted persona Elia that he created was a response in art to the limitations of his character

in life: alternating between innocence and experience, this voice authorized Lamb to confront and express aspects of his personal life in ways that he felt unable to in his actual relationships.

Lamb was admired as an author, and valued as a personality, by the Cockney school of poetry and the "lake poets" alike, even if he was not always equally generous, in return. In the 1790s, Lamb, Samuel Taylor Coleridge, and Robert Southey were cast as seditious radicals by artists such as James Gillray (in "The New Morality," 1798) and progovernment journals such as the *Anti-Jacobin*. Lamb's political beliefs and associations gained him a profile as a leading liberal author of his day. Coleridge (who had been his schoolmate at Christ's Hospital), published his first poems. Southey, William Wordsworth, and, with a brief hiatus, William Hazlitt, were intimates. William Godwin commissioned *Tales from Shakespeare* (1807). His friendship with Leigh Hunt brought him into contact with several members of the Cockney school of poetry.

Despite this almost universal acceptance, Lamb was an outsider. Writing was not his occupation (he worked for almost all his adult life as a clerk for the East India Company), even if it was his passion, a fact that is symptomatic of his individualistic path. It offered him a valuable distance from the concerns of his contemporaries, and allowed him to assess them with a disinterested, and often satirical, eye: the mundane practicalities of professional life, for example, add a different perspective to Lamb's musings on the escapist possibilities of art that preoccupied his peers.

Lamb delighted in flouting expectation, finding his aptest outlet in wit and humor: when scolded by a superior at the East India Company with "You arrive late, Mr Lamb," his instant response was "But see how early I leave." Thomas Carlyle believed that Lamb's addiction to punning showed him to be "in some considerable degree insane." Lamb's friend Valentine Le Grice perceived a more urgent reason: "His wit [flashed] out of melancholy . . . a pun may discharge a whole load of sorrow: the sharp point of a quibble or a joke may let out the long-gathered waters of bitterness." His sense of humor, as light as it was cutting, was indeed a reaction to a troubled personal life; it was a mask, like that of Elia, with which he could protect himself from sorrow and liberate himself from weakness. When his farce *Mr. H_____* (1806) was booed off the stage at Drury Lane on its first night, Lamb joined in, hissing his own production. Comedy helped him to transcend his own deficiencies and ward off demons: he had an incurable stammer; his sister Mary (for whom he cared until his death) had murdered their mother "in a fit of insanity;" he had a failed romantic life, and a delicate temperament that played a role in his being committed to an asylum in 1795. His essay "On the Artificial Comedy of the Last Century" (in *The Essays of Elia*, 1823) suggests how his irreverence was put to personal, political, and creative effect: "I wear my shackles more contentedly for having respired the breath of an imaginary freedom." When his sense of humor failed him, Lamb found that alcohol and tobacco (as he admits in "Confessions of a Drunkard" (in *The Last Essays of Elia*, 1833) provided alternative solace.

Such sensational biographical details have inevitably overshadowed Lamb's eclectic literary contribution to Romanticism. Moreover, like Hunt and Thomas Love Peacock, Lamb has become at least as famous for his influential friendships with the great Romantic artists of his time as for anything that he wrote. His name is preserved, for example, by his walk-on part in Coleridge's 1797 poem "This Lime-Tree Bower My Prison," and by his drunken sending-up of Wordsworth, so enjoyed by John Keats, at the "Immortal Dinner" given by Benjamin Haydon. His poetry, plays, and fiction (the didactic, sentimental tale *Rosamund Gray*, 1798) have mostly been forgotten by the reading public. Even his criticism and essays have not warranted the scholarly attention paid to those of Coleridge and Hazlitt: fusing quirky comic passages with pathos after the style of Joseph Addison, Michel Eyquem de Montaigne, and Richard Steele, they have been attacked for lacking Coleridge's intellectual ambition and Hazlitt's political and critical acerbity.

If the circumstances of Lamb's life have conspired to make him an awkward, misunderstood, and marginalized figure in the Romantic canon, then it is partly an image that he seems to have fostered actively. He upbraided Coleridge for making him seem ridiculous by terming him "gentle-hearted in print" in "This Lime-Tree Bower My Prison." With the self-mocking caveat "I never was more serious," Lamb preferred that Coleridge should substitute "drunken dog, ragged-head, seld-shaven, odd-eyed, stuttering, or any other epithet which truly and properly belongs to the gentleman in question." Hazlitt's largely affectionate portrait in *The Spirit of the Age* (1824) notes that: "Mr. Lamb has succeeded, not by conforming to the Spirit of the Age, but in opposition to it. He does not march boldly along with the crowd, but steals off the pavement to pick his way in the contrary direction."

The gentle contrariness that Hazlitt identifies is central to understanding Lamb's contribution to Romanticism. Hazlitt detects the same impulse for genial subversion that defines his character in the "quaintness and singularity" of Lamb's prose style, which is the direct descendant of Robert Burton, Thomas Fuller, and Laurence Sterne. Although he moved freely in the social circles of these writers, Lamb was always on the margins. As Hazlitt suggests, Lamb's primary literary passion was for productions of a "more remote period": the *Edinburgh Review* ridiculed Lamb's play *John Woodvil* (1802) by saying that it was a work by "a man of Thespis." In combination with his amateur status, this remoteness from his time helped Lamb to survey the artistic scene that he encountered with skeptical acuity. Indeed, literary criticism proved to be Lamb's first public triumph: his short critical notes to *Specimens of English Dramatic Poets Who Lived About the Time of Shakespeare* (1808) formed the basis of his reputation as an author.

One of the first great commentators on Romanticism, Lamb's attraction to obscure authors made him one of the earliest critics to approve of William Blake ("a real name . . . and a most extraordinary man"), John Clare (who deserved to be "generally tasted"), and Keats (who, Henry Crabb Robinson averred, Lamb believed second only to William Wordsworth in poetic greatness). The amused tone of his assessments could be cruel as well as kind (especially in his letters); less congenial to Lamb's palate were Lord Byron and Percy Bysshe Shelley (the latter of whom "nobody was ever wiser or better for reading").

Lamb's comic lightness of touch does not make him a lightweight. As Lamb wrote half-seriously in the preface to *The Last Essays of Elia*, "Elia has been accused of trying to be witty, when in truth he was struggling to give his poor thoughts articulation." In the same way that reading, drinking, and smoking all provided spiritual respite from the cares of his life, however briefly, the whimsical tone of his writing revealed a highly individual critical and creative intelligence that is without peer.

JAMES KIDD

Biography

Born in London, February 10, 1775, the son of a scrivener who worked for a lawyer in the Temple. Attended Christ's Hospital school, where he was a near contemporary of Samuel Taylor Coleridge, 1783. Left school and began work in the counting-house of Joseph Paice, 1783. Became a clerk in the South Sea House, along with his elder brother John, 1791(?); moved in 1792 to East India House, where he remained until retirement in 1825. In September 22, 1796, his sister Mary murdered their mother in a fit of insanity (Mary died in 1847.) Lamb, who had himself been committed briefly in 1795, became her guardian in 1799 to save her from life in an asylum, and continued to care for her until his death. Contributed to the *Morning Post*, 1803. Contributed to Leigh Hunt's *The Reflector*, 1810. In 1820, essays published in the *London Magazine*, later to be the *Essays of Elia*. Proposed to, and was rejected by, actress Fanny Kelly, 1819. Died December 27, 1834 due to an attack of erysipelas brought on by a fall.

Selected Works

Collections
The Works of Charles and Mary Lamb. Edited by E. V. Lucas. 7 vols. London: Methuen, 1903–5.
The Letters of Charles and Mary Lamb. Edited by E. V. Lucas. 3 vols. London: J. M. Dent and Sons/Methuen, 1935.
The Letters of Charles and Mary Anne Lamb. Edited by E. W. Marrs. 3 vols. Ithaca, N. Y.: Cornell University Press, 1975.

Individual and Selected Works
Poetry for Children. With Mary Lamb. Edited by R. H. Shepherd. 1876.
Poems, Plays and Miscellaneous Essays of Charles Lamb. Edited by Alfred Ainger. London: Macmillan, 1902.

Essays of Elia. Edited by Alfred Ainger. London: Macmillan, 1903.
The Elian Miscellany: A Charles Lamb Anthology. Edited by S. M. Rich. London: Herbert Joseph, 1931.
Lamb as Critic. Edited by Roy Park. London: Routledge and Kegan Paul, 1980.

Bibliography

Blunden, E. *Charles Lamb: His Life Recorded by his Contemporaries*. London: Hogarth Press, 1934.
Cecil, David. *A Portrait of Charles Lamb*. London: Constable, 1983.
Courtney, W. F. *The Young Charles Lamb: 1775–1802*, London: Macmillan, 1982.
Lucas, E. V. *The Life of Charles Lamb*. 2 vols. London: Methuen, 1905.
Monsman, Gerald, *Confessions of a Prosaic Dreamer: Charles Lamb's Art of Autobiography*. Durham, N.C.: Duke University Press, 1984.
Riehl, Joseph R. *Charles Lamb's Children's Literature*. Atlantic Highlands, N.J.: Humanities Press, 1980.
Riehl, Joseph R. *That Dangerous Figure: Charles Lamb and the Critics*. Columbia, S.C.: Camden House, 1998.

LAMENNAIS, FÉLICITÉ DE 1782–1854

French priest and writer

If the underlying coherence of the Romantic movement is to be sought in the cultural response—sanguine or circumspect—to historical awakening to independent selfhood, then (together with kindred spirits such as Louis de Bonald and Joseph de Maistre) Félicité de Lamennais belongs to that branch of the movement that regarded the liberated self as an abhorrent deviation from a previous order characterized by its reverence for the sublime and the spiritual. Such men were in tune with the Romantic age in its revived taste for things spiritual, but uncomfortable in the vestments of subjectivity in which the spiritual was now clothed. The early, royalist Lamennais, who welcomed the return of the Bourbons, the ultramontanist Lamennais who championed the Papacy above nation state, and the later Lamennais who supported the popular uprising of 1848, have in common a belief in obedience to supreme authority, be it that of hereditary monarchy, of universal Catholicism, or of the people in its sovereign voice. Christian fundamentalist to the point of abandoning formal Christianity, Lamennais is the troubling ghost at the Romantic celebration of the severing of the contract subordinating mankind to God, and the prophet of its redrafting in ever more radical terms. One of three renowned Bretons who would make a major contribution to the religious life of the new century, Lamennais was, in his militant transcendentalism, as much a stranger to the sentimental religiosity of François-Auguste-René de Chateaubriand as to the refined impieties of Ernest Renan.

From start to finish, Lamennais's career is governed solely by the demands and strategies of his own polemic until it reaches an inevitable, tragic crescendo in isolation and obsession. It is conventional to divide this career into several phases, each marked by a pronounced shift in his political position as opposed to his religious one, which remains—broadly speaking—consis-

tent. For Lamennais, the error of European society, starting with the Reformation and culminating in the French Revolution, had been its claim of God's infinite authority for itself. In the place of the humility of belief, men had erected the principle of the sovereignty of their own judgement, thereby exposing successive societies to the arbitrary abuse of power in the name of the false god of reason. "Religion as a belief," he declares in the first volume of his seminal *Essai sur l'indifférence* of 1817, "was everywhere, and its absence has made itself felt everywhere . . . Man has been told Religion is an invention of man; then all appeared to him to be human inventions, even society, even justice; and feeling himself great enough to obey God only, he contemptuously rejected the yoke of man." Lamennais's supporting argument, deriving originally from Jean: Jacques Rousseau, is that religious belief, whatever its precise form, is a natural human condition endorsed by common experience, an inalienable summons to the mind, securing morality from license and ensuring true liberty for all in the universal observance of its laws. Far from being an arbitrary construct of human devising, it is the sine qua non of human society itself and of the psychological well-being of its members. In place of the Cartesian cogito, corrosively centered on the individual, mankind's true identity resides for Lamennais in the assent of faith.

It is, however, when he adds doctrinal substance to this ontological matrix that his controversial impact on a century struggling to come to terms with the legacy of Enlightenment skepticism is most keenly felt. If his first step is to proclaim the supremacy of the Catholic church as the unique instrument of the general religious will, his second, conceived in an age of Napoleonic tyranny, was to acknowledge the Pope in Rome as the unrivalled representative of divine authority. By the same token, he sided initially with the restored monarchy of Louis

XVIII as the rightful temporal government of a Catholic France. In 1824, Leo XII lent the weight of the Vatican to Lamennais's views and, for a moment, there were rumors he would be named a cardinal. Lamennais was encouraged to the point of founding a school of his own doctrines at his family home in Brittany. More and more, however, he found himself at odds with a Restoration regime which, contrary to his own uncompromising stance, regarded the Church as an organ of the state and, with the first issues of the periodical *L'Avenir* following the fall of the Bourbons in July 1830, a regenerate Lamennais began proclaiming the alliance of the church with the groundswell of the democratic will. The Pope this time recognized the threat posed to political stability by his intemperate champion. Lamennais was snubbed on his return to Rome in 1831 and the politics of *L'Avenir* were condemned. His response was to publish, in 1834, his hypnotic *Paroles d'un croyant* in which, in tones reminiscent of the *Book of Revelation*, he visualizes the establishment of a radically egalitarian Christian society.

Lamennais was never formally excommunicated, but his new Christianity, on which he elaborated in his later *Livre du people* (1838), owed little to Catholic orthodoxy. Ironically, his appeal to popular consensus, as the yardstick of religious conviction in the face of sophistry and skepticism, had led him back to something very close to Voltairean Deism. Lamennais's excesses alienated many a would-be sympathizer, but he correctly predicted the inevitable rupture between church and state and he gave currency to a fruitful new alliance between Christianity and emergent socialism. Though he was more a highly gifted vulgarizer than an original thinker, he sensed, through his theory of "indifference," the threat posed to his own and future societies by the mental and emotional disorientation engendered in a religious vacuum.

DAVID LEE

Biography

Born Hughes-Félicité-Robert de la Mennais in Saint-Malo June 19, 1782. He was the fourth son of a wealthy shipowner ennobled in 1788 for services to his native town. He was brought up by his uncle and his older brother, Jean, after destitution of family during Revolution. He developed a growing interest in theology following Jean's ordination in 1804, and the brothers collaborated to publish *Réflexions sur l'état de l'Eglise en France pendant le XVIIIe siècle et sur sa situation actuelle* (1808), which was subsequently seized by police. Lamennais took his first step toward Holy Orders in 1816, and published the first volume of *Essai sur l'indifférence en matière de religion* (1817) to universal acclaim. Warmly received by Pope Leo XII on first visit to Rome

in 1824. Established school for dissemination of "Mennaisian" doctrines at family estate of La Chênaie to which are attracted Lacordaire, Montalembert, Gerbet, and others. *De la religion considérée dans ses rapports avec l'ordre politique et civil* (1825–26) promotes ultramontanist principles against Restoration Gallicanism. Following the Revolution of July 1830, published the of first issue of *L'Avenir* (October 1830) under the slogan "Dieu et la liberté." Cold reception from Pope Gregory XVI on second Roman visit in December 1831 and implicit censure of doctrines of *L'Avenir* in encyclical *Mirari vos* of following year. Appearance of *Les Paroles d'un croyant* in April 1834 provoked direct papal condemnation. Separation from Catholic Church by the year of the publication of *Le Livre du peuple* (1838), in which he propounds his own natural religion divorced from all orthodoxy. Condemned to a year's imprisonment by Louis-Philippe government for sedition (1840–41). Founded *Le Peuple Constituant* in February 1848 in support of the Second Republic and is elected to Constituent Assembly as a representative of the extreme Left, but retires from active political life after *coup d'état* of December 1851. Died February 27, 1854 and was buried without religious rites.

Selected Works

Réflexions sur l'état de l'Eglise en France pendant le XVIIIe siècle et sur sa situation actuelle. 1808.
Essai sur l'indifférence en matière de religion. 4 vols. 1817–23, trans. Lord Stanley of Alderley. 1895.
De la religion: considérée dans ses rapports avec l'ordre politique et civil. 1825–26
Les Paroles d'un croyant, 1833, 1834. Translated by William G. Hutchison, 1905, and by Cuthbert Reavely. 1943
Le Livre du peuple, 1838. Translation: J. H. Lorymer, 1838.
Esquisse d'une philosophie. 4 vols. 1840–46

Bibliography

Derré, Jean-René. *Lamennais, ses amis et le mouvement des idées à l'époque romantique, 1824–1834.* Paris: Klincksieck, 1962.
Le Guillou, Louis. *L'Evolution de la pensée religieuse de Félicité de Lamennais.* Paris: Armand Colin, 1966.
Mourre, Michel. *Lamennais ou l'hérésie des temps modernes.* Paris: Amiot-Dupont, 1955.
Reardon, Bernard. *Liberalism and Tradition: Aspects of Catholic Thought in Nineteenth-Century France.* Cambridge, U.K.: Cambridge University Press, 1975.
Roe, W. G. *Lamennais and England: The Reception of Lamennais' Religious Ideas in England in the Nineteenth Century.* London: Oxford University Press, 1966.
Vidler, Alec R. *Prophecy and Papacy: A Study of Lamennais, the Church and the Revolution.* London: S. C. M. Press, 1954.

LAMIA, ISABELLA, THE EVE OF ST. AGNES, AND OTHER POEMS 1820

Edition by John Keats

Lamia, Isabella, The Eve of St. Agnes, and Other Poems, published by Taylor and Hessey in 1820, established John Keats's poetic reputation both in his own time (Percy Bysshe Shelley, in particular, was greatly impressed by "Hyperion") and for generations to follow. The volume shows a wide reading of the poetry of Keats's immediate predecessors, especially such purveyors of Romantic medievalism as Walter Scott and Samuel Taylor Coleridge. However, it also establishes itself as something new, offering its own updated and sophisticated version of the Romantic concern with art, its possibilities, limits, and responsibilities.

Whereas Coleridge and William Wordsworth's *Lyrical Ballads* (1798), seeks to deploy "the real language" spoken by ordinary people, Keats's 1820 volume is unabashedly a work written by a poet: concentrated, musical, and suggestive.

While claims are frequently made for the fineness of his earlier poems, felt to have a life-enhancing or, more recently, politically radical "vulgarity," it is the 1820 volume that displays Keats's poetic genius. Simply to list the volume's contents in their order of appearance is to recognize the achievement it represents: "Lamia," "Isabella," "The Eve of St Agnes," "Ode to a Nightingale," "Ode on a Grecian Urn," "Ode to Psyche," "Fancy," "Ode (Bards of Passion and of Mirth)," "Lines on the Mermaid Tavern," "Robin Hood," "To Autumn," "Ode on Melancholy," and "Hyperion: A Fragment." In the volume, one finds evidence not only of Keats's ability to write both narrative and lyrical poems, but also of the readiness of his imagination to dwell in uncertainty, doubt, and paradox. If he shows a Shakespearean capacity for imaginative surrender, he couples this capacity with an ironic awareness that poetic inventions may be no more than cheating tricks. Self-forgetful "negative capability" goes hand in hand with his sense of the inescapability of the "sole self." In the act of investing his hopes in art, he recognizes the cost of such an investment; trying to imagine a libertarian politics in "Hyperion," he sympathizes with the death throes of the old order. Keats repeatedly explores the contraries that make up existence; he is at once an entranced participant in, and self-aware spectator of, his own poetic vision.

"Lamia" opens the collection. The poem tells the story of Lamia, a serpent transformed by Hermes into a woman before securing the affections of Lycius, a young Corinthian. Lamia is treated ambivalently, but with considerable sympathy, especially when Lycius risks their happiness by making their relationship public, insisting that they get married. At the wedding feast, Apollonius, a philosopher and Lycius's former mentor, exposes Lamia's former existence as a serpent; she vanishes and Lycius dies. The worldly poise and detachment of the poem's Drydenesque couplets make a sharp contrast with the more leisurely and seemingly uncritical use of romance in two narrative poems that follow, "Isabella," written in *ottava rima*, and "The Eve of St. Agnes," composed in Spenserian stanzas. Yet there are connections as well as differences between "Lamia" and its successors in the volume. All three narrative poems counterpoint reality and romance. In "Isabella," a story derived from Giovanni Boccaccio's *Decameron* (1348–53) the two collide as the heroine obsessively tends a basil-plant covering the decapitated head of her lover, Lorenzo, murdered by her brothers. "The Eve of St. Agnes" is set in medieval times. In it, the heroine Madeline, in accord with superstitious belief, has gone to bed without supper in the hope of dreaming of a future lover. Porphyro, who is hated by the inhabitants of the castle, gains access to Madeline's bedchamber. She wakes; then, in a semi-awake, dreamlike state, she and Porphyro make love. Afterwards, with sleet pelting the castle, they leave together. Madeline's fantasy that "dream" can merge with reality is fulfilled when she wakes to find Porphyro. Still, the beauty with which their lovemaking is imagined ("Into her dream he melted") coexists with a sense of the forces opposed to the consummation of that "dream": the icy cold prefiguring illness and death, the possibility that she will be deserted, voiced by Madeline, and, above all, the sophistication with which Keats ushers the reader out of, as well as into, the magical world of romance. In "Lamia," Keats's

quarrel with the desires of his own imagination takes on a near-tragic and yet coolly ironic power. The hapless Lycius is caught between the reductive rationalism of Apollonius and the bewitching illusoriness of Lamia; if the poem's heart sides with the latter, its head reinforces the judgment of the former.

Each of the great odes has its own unique life, but in each Keats's imagination shows itself to be at home with dialectic turns and counter-turns. Though "Ode to Psyche" is the most programmatic, its development is full of fascinating surprises, such as the assertion that "I see, and sing, by my own eyes inspired" and the emergence of "some untrodden region of my mind" as the poet's true subject. The poem ends, though, by renegotiating a relationship with "the warm Love" (a reference to the poem's underlying myth of Cupid and Psyche), and Keats's desire to escape the self gives vivid and poignant life to "Ode to a Nightingale." The poet may return, at the close, to his solitary self, but only after he has engaged in remarkable voyages into other states and possibilities as he tracks the nightingale's song. "Ode on a Grecian Urn" shifts its focus from music to the visual arts, exploring with stealthy intentness the link yet gap between "breathing human passion" and the "Cold Pastoral" of art. Whatever one makes of the identification of beauty with truth at the close, there is no denying the poem's clear-sighted view that art will not put a stop to "other woe than ours." Suffering and mortality are the price that is paid for being alive and aware.

The coexistence of pain and pleasure becomes a major theme in "Ode on Melancholy," a poem that values "the wakeful anguish of the soul" but transcends a poetry of statement through its transitions and hauntingly depicted personifications. In "To Autumn," drama derives from the serenity of acceptance that suffuses Keats's descriptions: there is no repining over individual "anguish" or collective suffering, even as temporal pressures make themselves felt. Responsive though they are to thematic explication, the odes live as poetry through the intensity with which they plot their individual imaginative trajectories. For example, in stanza 6 of "Ode to a Nightingale," Keats moves between celebrating the freedom from death of the nightingale (as symbol) to imagining the song's passage "Through the sad heart of Ruth, when, sick for home, / She stood in tears amid the alien corn." These lines convert the biblical character into a representative of us all.

"Hyperion" represents the conclusion and aftermath of the overthrow of the Titans by the Olympians. In book 1, Keats shows how the fallen Saturn and the not-quite-fallen Hyperion respond to their experience. In book 2 he depicts the Titans debating different ways of coping with their fall: views range from acceptance (Oceanus) to war-mongering (Enceladus). In book 3 we meet the figure of Apollo, god of the sun and of poetry, a young figure on the verge of assuming his responsibilities as a god. After his encounter with the muse-like Mnemosyne, the poem stops, unfinished. The poem is, among other things, Keats's magnificent attempt to rival John Milton's *Paradise Lost* (1665), and like Milton's poem, Keats's fragment begins with an account of fallen immortals. But whereas Satan is charismatic, if evil, Saturn is confused yet benign, and "Hyperion" is both enriched and complicated by Keats's division of sympathies. Keats's poem, in part about historical change, also seeks to be a modern epic of poetic growth, the Wordsworthian "egotistical sublime" of Saturn and Hyperion giving way to the "negative capability" of Apollo. The poem breaks off just after Apollo has asserted, "Knowledge enormous makes a God of me," as if Keats recognized that the assertion was merely assertion. In "The Fall of Hyperion," unpublished until 1857, he would attempt to situate the poem more openly in the territory of subjective consciousness; this territory was mapped with great tact and poetic skill in the 1820 volume.

MICHAEL O'NEILL

See also **Keats, John; Poetry: Britain**

Text

The volume was first published in 1820. The poems can be found in the best modern editions, which are *The Poems of John Keats*, edited by Miriam Allott (London: Longman, 1970); *The Poems of John Keats*, edited by Jack Stillinger (London: Heinemann, 1978); *John Keats: The Complete Poems*, 3d ed., edited by John Barnard (Harmondsworth, England: Penguin, 3rd ed., 1988); and *John Keats: Selected Poems*, edited by Nicholas Roe (London: Dent, 1995).

Bibliography

Aske, Martin. *Keats and Hellenism*. Cambridge, U.K.: Cambridge University Press, 1985.

Barnard, John. *John Keats*. Cambridge: Cambridge University Press, 1987.

Bate, W. J. *John Keats*. Cambridge, Mass.: Harvard University Press, 1963.

Bayley, John. "Keats and Reality," *Proceedings of the British Academy* 48 (1962): 91–125.

Bennett, Andrew. *Keats, Narrative, and Audience*. Cambridge, U.K.: Cambridge University Press, 1994.

Cox, Jeffrey N. *Poetry and Politics in the Cockney School: Keats, Shelley, Hunt and their Circle*. Cambridge, U.K.: Cambridge University Press, 1998.

Levinson, Marjorie. *Keats' Life of Allegory*. Oxford, U.K.: Blackwell, 1988.

McFarland, Thomas. *The Masks of Keats: The Endeavour of a Poet*. Oxford, U.K.: Oxford University Press, 2000.

O'Neill, Michael. *Romanticism and the Self-Conscious Poem*. Oxford, U.K.: Oxford University Press, 1997.

———, ed. *Keats: Bicentenary Readings*. Edinburgh: Edinburgh University Press, 1997.

Ricks, Christopher. *Keats and Embarrassment*. Oxford, U.K.: Oxford University Press, 1974.

Roe, Nicholas. *John Keats and the Culture of Dissent*. Oxford, U.K.: Oxford University Press, 1997.

———, ed. *Keats and History*. Cambridge, U.K.: Cambridge University Press, 1995.

Ryan, Robert M. and Ronald A. Sharp, eds. *The Persistence of Poetry: Bicentennial Essays on Keats*. Amerherst: University of Massachusetts Press, 1998.

Sperry, Stuart M. *Keats the Poet*. Princeton, N.J.: Princeton University Press, 1973.

Vendler, Helen. *The Odes of John Keats*. Cambridge, Mass.: Harvard University Press, 1983.

Waldoff, Leon. *Keats and the Silent Work of Imagination*. Urbana: University of Illinois Press, 1985.

Wolfson, Susan J. *The Questioning Presence: Wordsworth, Keats, and the Interrogative Mode*. Ithaca, N.Y.: Cornell University Press, 1986.

Woof, Robert, and Stephen Hebron. *John Keats*. Grasmere, England: Wordsworth Trust, 1995.

LANDON, LETITIA ELIZABETH 1802–1838

English poet and novelist

The tragic death of Letitia Elizabeth Landon labels her a Romantic heroine in the popular, modern sense. However, it is also correct to claim her as a literary Romantic, in view of her focus on the nature and function of the poet. She was undoubtedly influenced by William Wordsworth (whom she met), as by her poem "On Wordsworth's Cottage, near Grasmere Lake." Her working life coincided with a period when the Romanticism instigated by Wordsworth and Samuel Taylor Coleridge had become the poetic norm. Landon has also been viewed as a transitional writer, in the sense that the critical reception of her work reflected wider developments in society: in the 1820s her writings were considered morally unobjectionable, but by the second half of the 1830s both her life and work were subjected to generally unfavorable inspection.

Landon was the eldest child in a middle-class family that was sliding down the social scale. Her early exposure to some degree of want may have helped to determine her willingness to accede to the commercial demands of the literary market place. With the money she earned she maintained her mother in a separate dwelling and paid for her brother's education, and later also purchased a clerical living for him. Her own education was minimal. For a few months at the age of five she attended Miss Rowden's Chelsea School, where Lady Caroline Lamb and Mary Russell Mitford had formerly been pupils. Otherwise she was largely self-taught, reading voraciously at home.

Landon began publishing in her teenage years; she was thus exposed to public scrutiny from a very young age. She first published in *The Literary Gazette*, edited by William Jerdan, under the initials "L.E.L.," and her work rapidly became popular. In 1822, *The Literary Gazette* published forty-seven of her poems, and this figure rose to ninety in 1823. Landon's literary debut coincided with a period in which poetry was immensely popular and women poets in particular were sought after. Joanna Baillie, Elizabeth Barrett, Felicia Hemans Hannah More, and Helen Maria Williams, all published in Landon's lifetime. However, the general critical perspective on women poets was not enlightened. They were held to embody a reductive Romanticism in which the Wordsworthian "spontaneous overflow of powerful feelings" was not translated by a mediating intellect. Landon's first book of poetry, *The Fate of Adelaide*, was published in 1821, but was not given a wide circulation, as the publisher had gone bankrupt. Her first long poem, *The Improvisatrice*, was published in 1824 and was very successful both commercially and critically, going through six editions in a year. Landon never fully repeated the success of *The Improvisatrice*, though her poetry continued to be popular for a time. She published *The Troubadour* in 1825,

The Golden Violet in 1826, and *The Venetian Bracelet* in 1829. Landon's poems tend to be set in exotic locations (reflecting the taste for the exotic which was typical of the second generation Romantics) and are peopled by historical and mythical figures. Landon also published three novels: *Romance and Reality* (1831), *Francesca Carrara* (1834), and *Ethel Churchill* (1836). In addition, from 1831 she edited the annual *Fisher's Drawing Room Scrap Book* and contributed to *Heath's Book of Beauty*, a forerunner of the coffee-table book. Landon also wrote critical essays, notably "On the Ancient and Modem Influence of Poetry" (1832) and "On the Character of Mrs Heman's Writings" (1835). She also wrote an unsuccessful drama, *Castruccio Castrucani*, which was not published in her lifetime, and a selection of poems and tales for children, *Traits and Trials of Early Life* (1836).

In the preface to *The Venetian Bracelet*, Landon presents something of an artistic manifesto: "I have ever endeavoured to bring forward grief, disappointment, the fallen leaf, the faded flower, the broken heart, and the early grave." This is an accurate, if reductive, summary of her work; speakers in Landon's poems are often characterized by a sense of loss and alienation. However, in many respects both publishers and critics constructed this role for Landon: the grief-stricken, lovelorn female was a marketable commodity. The speed with which Landon wrote, and the diversity of her writing (particularly with regard to form), reflects her status as a professional writer dependent upon publication for her livelihood. Allegations surrounding Landon's private life provided ample fuel for contemporary gossip columnists. She was rumored to have had improper relationships with her publisher William Jerdan, the writer Edward Bulwer-Lytton, painter Daniel Maclise, and journalist William Maginn. *Romance and Reality* provoked widespread controversy, as it featured thinly-veiled portraits of Edward Bulwer-Lytton and his wife Rosina Lytton, who terminated her friendship with Landon because of concerns about Landon's closeness to her husband. Landon's letters to Maginn, commencing "My Dearest William," were released to the press in 1834 and 1835 by Maginn's wife, causing great scandal. None of the allegations were proven, but the damage to Landon's reputation was considerable. The rumors resulted in Landon's fiancé John Forster (a friend and later biographer of Charles Dickens) terminating his engagement to her.

In 1838, Landon married George Maclean, governor of Cape Coast Castle. Two months after their arrival in Africa she was dead from an overdose of prussic acid, which was quite commonly prescribed as a cough suppressant, notwithstanding the fact that it contained cyanide. The inquest into Landon's death was not at all satisfactory; it was characterized by haste and insufficient rigor, with no autopsy performed. The possibilities surrounding this unsolved mystery are that either she died of an accidental overdose, she committed suicide, she was murdered by her husband's mistress, or by her husband himself.

With hindsight, Landon can be viewed as one of the first media-created celebrities, her life being the constant source of speculation in the popular press. She did influence other women poets, with Elizabeth Barrett publishing "Stanzas Addressed to Miss Landon," which itself was a response to Landon's poem "Stanzas on the Death of Mrs. Hemans," written upon the death of Felicia Hemans. There is a risk that Landon's poetry could become lost in her life story, but the best of her verse stands the test of time. "Lines of Life," one of her most enduring poems, is bitter and self-condemning. It also directs some of its anger against the role cast for her by society, and voices despair at her own unavoidable acquiescence thereto:

> I live among the cold, the false,
> And I must seem like them;
> And such I am, for I am false
> As those I most condemn.
>
> I teach my lip its sweetest smile,
> My tongue its softest tone;
> I borrow others' likeness, till
> Almost I lose my own.

MICHAEL FLAVIN

Biography

Born August 14, 1802 at 25 Hans Place, Chelsea, to John Landon and Catherine Jane Bishop. Started attending boarding school in 1807, but after a short while the family moved to Hertfordshire. The family returned to London in 1815. Engaged briefly to John Forster, then editor of *The Examiner*, 1835. Met George Maclean, governor of Cape Coast Castle, October 1836, married June 7, 1838 at St Mary's, Bryanston Square. Sailed for Africa, July 1838; arrived in August. Died October 15, 1838 at Cape Coast Castle.

Selected Works

Poetical Works of Letitia Elizabeth Landon. 1850.
The Complete Works of L. E. Landon. 1856.

Bibliography

Blain, Virginia. "Letitia Elizabeth Landon, Eliza Mary Hamilton, and the Genealogy of the Victorian Poetess," *Victorian Poetry* 33 (1995): 31–51.
Greet, Germaine. *Slip-Shod Sibyls: Recognition, Rejection and the Woman Poet*. London: Penguin, 1995.
Stephenson, Glennis. "Letitia Landon and the Victorian Improvisatrice: The Construction of LEL," *Victorian Poetry* 30 (1992): 1–17.
Sypher, F. J., "The Magical Letters of L.E.L.," *Columbia Library Columns*, 39 (1990): 3–9.

LANDOR, WALTER SAVAGE 1775-1864

English writer

The defining feature of Walter Savage Landor's long career as a poet, dramatist, essayist, and activist is his commitment to republican principles. From the 1790s when he and his contemporaries among the "first generation" of Romantic era writers shared a youthful enthusiasm for the French Revolution, to the 1840s and 1850s, when he and liberal Victorians looked with sympathy on uprisings across the European continent, Landor imbued his works with reflections on the benefits of constitutional rights and the dangers of arbitrary power.

The prominence of political and historical references in Landor's works has sometimes been thought to diminish their literary merit. Until recently, scholarship attached greater importance to Landor's adaptations of classical forms, language, and style than to the contexts for his writing. He was generally considered a minor and derivative writer. The historical turn in Romantic era studies, however, has prompted new interest in Landor's situation.

The greatest attention has been paid to *Gebir*, a poem about its title character's failed attempt to take control of Egypt, which appeared in 1798, coinciding with Napoleon Bonaparte's Egyptian campaign. *Gebir* is sufficiently critical of imperialist ideology to warrant classification as a Jacobin poem, though the first edition included a note of praise for Napoleon that Landor revoked in the second edition of 1803. In that year, he also brought out an edition of the poem in Latin, a language in which he wrote and published throughout his career. It has been argued that Landor used Latin strategically to make statements that might have invited legal action if made openly in English.

Reviews of *Gebir* in its own time did not all echo the praise bestowed upon it by Robert Southey, with whom Landor maintained a lifelong friendship despite their political differences; nevertheless, the reception was encouraging enough to prompt Landor to publish several other volumes in close succession. Most of the pieces in these collections tried obviously to exploit the themes and setting of *Gebir*, but the poems in *Simonidea* (1806) included more personal lyrics, such as the still-admired and anthologized epitaph for Rose Aylmer ("Ah what avails the sceptred race") and epigram from Sappho ("Mother, I cannot mind my wheel").

During this first decade of the 1800s, Landor was involved in political conflicts on both local and global scales. Having penned a pamphlet in support of a tax protest in Warwick, he cultivated Whig and radical acquaintances in London with the apparent intention of writing on their behalf in the periodical press. Although Landor did not become a frequent contributor to such journals as the *Examiner* until much later, he did in 1812 draft a book-length *Commentary on the Memoirs of Mr. [Charles James] Fox*. In addition to a positive presentation of the Whig leader, the study carries a dedication to U.S. President James Madison and offers strong criticism of the Tory government in general and George Canning in particular. Publication was aborted by fears of prosecution for libel; an edition was finally printed in 1907. Landor took an active role in the Peninsular War, fighting with the Spanish army against Napoleon. His experience of this conflict, and his conflicting attitudes toward King Ferdinand, whose commitment to constitutional government he questioned, influenced *Count Julian* (1812), a play about the struggles of competing leaders for control of Spain.

Back in England, Landor exhausted his resources attempting to turn Llanthony Abbey into a liveable estate. His inability to manage his tenants, workers, and finances drove him out of the country by 1814. He settled in Italy, where he remained until 1835. Although Landor's position on revolutionary activity in Italy and Greece was compatible with the views of Lord Byron and Percy Bysshe Shelley, personal antipathies kept any camaraderie from developing between him and these fellow English poets and exiles. During his first years abroad, Landor wrote in Latin and cultivated Italian publishers, but by the 1820s, he was writing a series of "imaginary conversations" in English prose and intended for publication in England. Five volumes of *Imaginary Conversations of Literary Men and Statesmen* were published between 1824 and 1829. These works are Landor's most characteristic achievement.

The *Imaginary Conversations* consist of invented discussions among characters drawn from all eras of history. They are not sequential or connected by narrative. Except for some *Imaginary Conversations of Greeks and Romans* excerpted for publication in 1853, Landor did not organize the pieces by speakers, nationalities, or eras as some later editors have done. While structurally episodic, the *Conversations* are thematically repetitive. They center on the criticism of authoritarian rule and the endorsement of republican principles. Landor's correspondence indicates that his wish to expatiate on such a theme was a motive for this composition. Scholarship on the *Conversations* has often treated the combination of fact and fiction as a weakness. It has been revalued as a strength in studies of the work as an exercise in historical construction. Because they portray the past as filled with the questioning of authority and debating of issues that sustain republican government, the *Conversations* shape history into a precedent for the kind of behavior that Landor wanted to encourage in his present.

Landor continued to work with dialogic structures, historical sources, and republican themes in many of the works he published after his return to England. In *Pericles and Aspasia* (1836), invented letters from ancient Greeks provide a springboard for a discussion of democracy; in the *Pentameron and Pentalogia* (1837), conversations between Giovanni Boccaccio and Petrarch likewise allow reflections on political issues. A cycle of tragedies—*Andrea of Hungary*, *Giovanna of Naples*, and *Fra Rupert* (1839–1940)—dramatizes and criticizes the allure of power. The collected edition of Landor's works that appeared in 1846 contained many new "imaginary conversations" written after the publications of the original volumes.

Given the extent of Landor's publications after the 1820s, the rise of his reputation during the 1830s and 1840s, and the friendships he developed with Charles Dickens, Robert Browning and Elizabeth Barrett Browning, and other Victorian writers, readers have sometimes regarded Landor as more of a Victorian than a Romantic writer. Landor's career, however, resists periodization and testifies to the vital influence of Romantic era figures well into the nineteen century. Landor's enthusiasm for the early French Revolution and his abhorrence of Napoleon's Bonaparte and William Pitt's power plays have their counterparts in his support for Lajos Kossuth, the Hungarian revolutionary leader whom he praised in poems and whose activities he tried to fund; in his anger over Louis Napoleon's alliance with Pope Pius IX against Giuseppe Garibaldi, which he expressed in Latin pamphlets; and in his opposition to British interference with uprisings in Portugal, over which he launched a petition that reached Parliament.

Many of Landor's later works were collected in *Last Fruit Off an Old Tree* (1853) and *Dry Sticks, Fagoted* (1858). The latter volume occasioned his second and final flight from England, for it included poems deemed libellous against a neighbor with whom Landor had a personal quarrel. To avoid financial ruin from the litigation, Landor spent his final years in Italy, where he remained a writer and activist to the end.

REGINA HEWITT

Biography

Born in Warwick, England, January 30, 1775. Attended Trinity College, Oxford University, 1793–94. Married Julia Thuillier, May 24, 1811; they had four children: Arnold Savage, born March 5, 1811; Julia Elizabeth Savage, born March 6, 1821; Walter Savage, born November 13, 1822; Charles Savage, born August 5, 1825. Died in Florence, Italy, September 17, 1864.

Selected Writings

Collections

The Works of Walter Savage Landor. 2 vols., 1846.
Last Fruit Off an Old Tree. 1853.
Dry Sticks, Fagoted. 1858.
The Works and Life of Walter Savage Landor. 8 vols. Edited by John Forster. 1876.
Imaginary Conversations. 6 vols. Edited and annotated by Charles G. Crump. 1891.
The Longer Prose Works. 2 vols. Edited and annotated by Charles G. Crump. 1892.
Poems. 2 vols. Edited and annotated by Charles G. Crump. 1893.
The Complete Works of Walter Savage Landor. 16 vols. Edited by T. Earle Welby and Stephen Wheeler. London: Chapman and Hall, 1927–36
Selected Imaginary Conversations of Literary Men and Statesmen. Edited by Charles L. Proudfit. Lincoln: University of Nebraska Press, 1969.
Selected Poetry and Prose. Edited by Keith Hanley. New York: Persea, 1981.

Plays

Count Julian. 1812.
Andrea of Hungary, and Giovanna of Naples. 1839.

Fra Rupert. 1840.

Poetry

Gebir, 1798. Revised edition, 1803. Latin edition (*Gebirus*). 1803.
Poems from the Arabic and Persian. 1800.
Poetry, by the Author of Gebir. 1802.
Simonidea. 1806.

Prose

Commentary on the Memoirs of Mr. Fox, written 1812. Published as *Charles James Fox: A Commentary on his Life and Character.* Edited by Stephen Wheeler. London: J. Murray, 1907.
Imaginary Conversations of Literary Men and Statesmen. 5 vols. 1824–29.
Pericles and Aspasia. 1836.
The Pentameron and Pentalogia. 1837.

Bibliography

Bainbridge, Simon. *Napoleon and English Romanticism.* Cambridge: Cambridge University Press, 1995.
Bicknell, Titus. "*Calamus Ense Potentior Est*: Walter Savage Landor's Poetic War of Words," *Romanticism on the Net* 4 (November 1996), at http://users.ox.ac.uk/~scat0385/landor.html.
Cronin, Richard. *The Politics of Romantic Poetry: In Search of the Pure Commonwealth.* Basingstoke, England/Macmillan, New York: St. Martin's Press, 2000.
Hanley, Keith. Introduction to in *Selected Poetry and Prose of Walter Savage Landor.* Edited by Keith Hanley. New York: Persea, 1981.
Hewitt, Regina. "Landor, Shelley, and the Design of History," *Romanticism on the Net* 20 (November 2000), at http://users.ox.ac.uk/~scat0385/20hewitt.htm.
———. "On Reconciling Past and Future: Some Effects of Landor's *Imaginary Conversations*," *Studies in Symbolic Interaction* 24 (2001): 273–97.
Kestner, Joseph. "The Genre of Landor's *Gebir*," *Wordsworth Circle* 5, no. 1 (1974): 41–49.
Proudfit, Charles L. Introduction to *Selected Imaginary Conversations of Literary Men and Statesmen.* Lincoln: University of Nebraska Press, 1969.
———. *Landor as Critic.* Lincoln: University of Nebraska Press, 1979.
Roberts, Adam. " 'Geborish': A Reading of Landor's *Gebir*," *English* 18 (1996): 32–43.
Ruoff, A. La Vonne. "Landor's Conception of the Great Leader," *Wordsworth Circle* 8, no. 1 (1976): 38–50.
Sharafuddin, Mohammed. *Islam and Romantic Orientalism: Literary Encounters with the Orient.* London: Tauris/New York: St. Martin's Press, 1994.
Super, R. H. *The Publication of Landor's Works.* London: Bibliographic Society, 1954.
———. *Walter Savage Landor: A Biography.* New York: New York University Press, 1954.
Vitoux, Pierre. "*Gebir* as an Heroic Poem," *Wordsworth Circle* 8, no. 1 (1976): 51–57.

LANDSCAPE AND GARDEN DESIGN

It would be a mistake to characterize the early part of the mid-eighteenth century in Britain as a period of rigidly formal garden design in contrast to a later, freer Romantic ethos. Many of the features associated with Romantic gardens—for example, Chinese-inspired buildings and Gothic towers—can all be found in early eighteenth-century garden designs. Where Romantic commentators show a marked difference from earlier eighteenth-century views is in their celebration of what lies beyond a garden's or estate's furthest bounds: a responsiveness to the picturesque and the sublime becoming touchstones of good taste in the Romantic era. Before examining the Romantic response to landscape on a large scale, it will be useful to consider the key design elements in the Romantic garden.

The late seventeenth century in Britain had seen a vogue for the "Williamite" style of formal garden, epitomized by William of Orange's estate at Het Loo, which he purchased in 1684. The garden contained trees planted regularly in *allées*, giving height to a pattern already established on the ground by low-lying evergreen shrubs such as box arranged in embroidery-style patterns or *parterres de broderie*. Water was plentiful on the estate and could be channeled into formal canals and symmetrically arranged fountains. This was a northern interpretation of the French formal gardening style most evident in the palaces of Louis XIV and his court, such as Vaux-le-Vicomte, and which would reach its zenith in André le Nôtre's transformation of the gardens at Versailles. In the first half of the eighteenth century, British garden designers were already rejecting such formal layouts as a distortion of nature. Alexander Pope's "Epistle to Burlington" (1731) specifically contrasts "proud Versailles" with what he considers a greater garden "to wonder at—perhaps a Stow." The "wonder" of William Kent's design for Stowe gardens in Buckinghamshire (the seat of Richard Temple, Viscount Lord Cobham) was that Kent made it impossible to gain an overview of the garden's many features from any single vantage point. Here was a design that demanded to be walked or ridden through to be appreciated, and that could not be surveyed from one monarchical position of authority. To walk around Stowe in search of its classically inspired temples, monuments, and statuary is to be greeted by a constantly changing series of vistas rather than to have the eye drawn along a grid of straight lines or formally patterned blocks of greenery. In his work for Lord Cobham at Stowe, and with his invention of the ha-ha or sunken fence that abolished the division between the formal garden and the landscape around, William Kent became one of the single greatest influences on Romantic garden design.

All eighteenth-century garden designers sought to emulate what were believed to have been the designing principles of gardens in the classical world. From such Roman writers as Pliny the Younger, descriptions of gardens were eagerly digested and "Roman" design emulated in Hanoverian Britain. From Latin texts, British designers believed they had sanction for a mixture of formal and informal gardening practice, and works such as Robert Castell's *Villas of the Ancients Illustrated* (1728) enjoyed popularity long after its first publication. The classical model and works such as Virgil's *Georgics* seemed to imply that good taste and good sense alike called for areas of *ruris imitatio* or "wilderness" in the garden. But classical Rome was not the only model cited as giving authority to modern developments away from Williamite and French formal gardens. Chinese gardens had been described by a number of Jesuit writers (engaged in missionary work there in the late seventeenth century) and their descriptions explicitly highlighted garden features reminiscent of the imagined Roman model. William Chambers's *Designs of Chinese Buildings* (1753) merely cemented an existing vogue for *chinoiserie* in the garden: Chambers's Chinese pagoda at Kew Gardens being only the most famous example of a fondness for bridges, temples, and mock-Oriental interiors, resplendent with handpainted wallpapers.

Like the century's enduring love affair with chinoiserie, the taste for elements of Gothic design in the garden predates the Romantic era. When Kent built Esher Place, Surrey, for Henry Pelham from 1729–39, his design had to accommodate existing fifteenth-century structures. The result is a fusion of Palladian and Gothic styles. And already at Kew in 1735, we see in Kent's Merlin's Cave, built for Queen Caroline, a realization of the Gothic grotto that would become a staple of Romantic gardens.

Since gardens are constantly evolving, and the lines of sight afforded a visitor today will rarely correspond exactly with those enjoyed by a Romantic traveler, the evolution of a garden's design is often best appreciated on a ground plan before experienced—partially—on the ground. Romantic garden features are however still visible in many places, most notably Claremont in Surrey, Stourhead in Wiltshire, Stowe in Buckinghamshire, and Studley Royal in Yorkshire. When visiting Studley Royal today, the visitor should remember that the original "Gothic" ruins of the Cistercian Fountains Abbey that sit within its grounds were only incorporated into the estate in 1768, prior to which the estate's early-eighteenth-century owner, John Aislabie, had longed to be able to make them part of his grounds but had been unable to secure their purchase. Early-eighteenth-century visitors to Studley Royal therefore had to content themselves with partial views of these fashionable Gothic features, looking down on them from a Gothic designed viewing platform known as "Anne Boleyn's seat." Since Henry VIII's divorce from Catherine of Aragon had resulted in a split between the English Church and Rome, Henry's Dissolution of the Monasteries—of which the ruins of Fountains Abbey are evidence—is here attributed to Anne Boleyn's sway over the British king. The Romantic garden and its associated design features may encode political meanings as well as represent aesthetic movements.

In the preceding discussion of the Studley Royal estate, it will be apparent that an object outside the estate and its formal gardens (here a Cistercian Abbey) may, in a sense, be incorporated into a visitor's horizons by providing vantage points and vistas from within the estate to a point or points outside its recognised boundaries. With the publication of Edmund Burke's *A Philosophical Inquiry into the Origins of Our Ideas of the Sublime and the Beautiful* (1756), we see a distinctive Romantic innovation in landscape design take its cue from Burke's text: the view that one seeks from within the confines of one's estate or—preferably travelling outside its bounds—should be as imposing as possible and ideally evince aspects of the sublime. Uvedale Price criticized the garden landscapes of Lancelot (Capability) Brown on the grounds that they were unvarying and predictable, calling for the introduction of a variety of rugged effects that he termed "picturesque." Together, the terms *sublime* and *picturesque* exerted a huge influence on Romantic views of landscape. Within Britain, the moorland scenery of Derbyshire, the glaciated landscape of the Lake District and the granite splendour of Scotland quickly became prospects that any well-traveled person of taste should have experienced. Armed with guidebooks by writers such as William Gilpin, tourists understood the awed reaction expected of them when confronted by natural features (unlike those designed as part of a garden's attractions), and a distinctly modern vogue for tourist literature had begun.

GLYNIS RIDLEY

Bibliography

Barrell, John. *The Dark Side of the Landscape: The Rural Poor in English Painting 1730–1840.* Cambridge, U.K.: Cambridge University Press, 1980.

Jacques, David, and Arend Jan van der Horst. *The Gardens of William and Mary.* London: Christopher Helm, 1988.

Mosser, Monique, and Georges Teyssot, eds. *The History of Garden Design.* London: Thames and Hudson, 1991.

Schama, Simon. *Landscape and Memory.* London: Harper Collins, 1995.

Worsley, Giles. *Classical Architecture in Britain: The Heroic Age.* New Haven, Conn.: Yale University Press, 1995.

LANDSCAPE PAINTING: BRITAIN

British landscape painting exhibited a Wordsworthian impulse to return to nature and a thirst for knowledge about natural phenomena in the post-Enlightenment era, thereby developing along aesthetic modes of inquiry that took cues from seventeenth-century Dutch painting and eighteenth-century discourse on the beautiful, the picturesque, and the sublime. Landscape artists championed the countryside as not only a background or setting, but as a worthy artistic subject in and of itself, enabling the canvas or page to become a locus for interpretation where discussions on nature, individuality, politics, God, and country could be framed. Dreamily bucolic landscapes such as the garden urban designs of Capability Brown or Humphrey Repton, rational categorization of skies and clouds, antiquarian-inspired topographical views, and indeterminate panoramic vistas that invoke the sublime collectively define the genre of landscape painting in Britain.

Related to patterns of collecting, the emergence of a British landscape school exhibited a fondness for Dutch landscape artists' views from the seventeenth century, many of which were based upon direct observation. Such artists included Aelbert Cuyp, Jan van Goyen, Meindert Hobbema, Rembrandt Van Riju, and Jacob van Ruisdael, who provided a model for British artists to follow as a way to purposely elevate landscape painting, (up to that point a minor genre in England). Philosophy provided a theoretical framework upon which to build this new pictorial model, as the terms beautiful, sublime, and picturesque form part of the vocabulary of representations of Romantic landscape. Edmund Burke reintroduced into modern consciousness the notion of an actual, visual experience that was aweinspiring. In contrast, William Gilpin published many essays that celebrated raw, varietal settings organized by no rational principals. Richard Payne Knight, connoisseur, author, and garden enthusiast, defended painting as a private art form of visual sensation and his poem *The Landscape, a Didactic Poem* (1794) extolled the beauty of the picturesque. Uvedale Price, theorist of the picturesque, published his treatise *An Essay on the Picturesque as Compared with the Sublime and the Beautiful; and on the Use of Studying Pictures for the Purpose of Improving Real Landscape* (1794).

Pictorial models and philosophical and aesthetic reasoning guided the artists during their time; their works that bear witness to a variety of media (watercolor and oil painting), level of execution (from the hastily sketch to the highly finished), scope (detailed glimpses or panoramic views), and approach (idealized views, realistic portrayals, or abstracted visions).

The first artists to characterize a decidedly British school of landscape were John Robert Cozens, Thomas Gainsborough, Philipp Jacque de Loutherbourg, and Richard Wilson. Any discussion of British landscape painting should begin with Wilson, who sought to create landscapes on the level of Grand Style emu-lating the landscape in the classical tradition of Niaolas Poussin and Claude Lorrain. Gainsborough admired the Dutch approach to nature and his idyllic landscapes inspired a generation of artists including J. M. W. Turner and John Constable. Although known for his etchings, Cozens method of sketching on location and added washes in ink capture the spontaneity of nature as well as urgency to document its fleeting effects. Alsatian by birth, Philipp Jacque de Loutherbourg adopted England as him home where he proclaimed his legacy in another variety of landscape painting, that of the stage, as a scenographer for David Garrick at Drury Lane. There, he captivated audiences with themes of the picturesque and the sublime: babbling brooks, quiet streams, and impending falls, gorges, and threatening clouds.

John Crome, founder of the Norwich school, created evocative landscapes such as *Slate Quarries* (c. 1802–5) that bring to the fore the awe-inspiring sublimity of the mountainscape. Crome's colleague, John Sell Cotman, was undeniably the Norwich school's most talented watercolorist. His works were inspired by a number of sketching tours around Britain in 1800 and 1802. Enamored of the idea of touring and, in turn, sketching outdoors, John Constable and J. M. W. Turner shared a preoccupation with landscape, yet differ in their approach, manner, and style. Constable, taking his cues from Gainsborough, celebrated the beauty of his native Suffolk. Known for his meteorological sky studies of the early 1820s as well as his large six-foot canvases celebrating the countryside that came to bear his name, he championed the landscape of England as superior to that of the Continent. Although a Grand Tour to Italy and the Continent was part of an artist's training, Constable found in England subjects enough for his work. Turner, on the other hand, traveled to Italy and the Continent to explore the grandness of nature. Trained as both an archi-

Philip James (Jacques) de Loutherbourg *Coalbrookdale by Night.* Reprinted courtesy of Bridgeman Art Library.

tectural draftsman and a topographer, his landscapes range in scope from realistic, topographic portrayals, as guides to the countryside on the one hand, and expressive, emotive, visionary dreamscapes that invoke the sublime.

Art-historical discourse has considered British landscape paintings and watercolors, whether hasty but thoughtful sketches or panoramic views, within the modernist construct furthering the development of landscape painting as a distinct art form in Europe that ushered in the outdoor sketching pursued by the Barbizon school and the impressionists in France. Recent studies of English landscape painting, however, have analyzed property relations, social practices, and national identity as created by and through depictions of the land and those who inhabit it. Representations of cultivated land and uncultivated nature, it has been argued, promoted a view of British society that was usually ordered and harmonious. John Barrell, Ann Bermingham, and Michael Rosenthal have studied to what extent agrarian landscapes articulate class relations. Andrew Hemingway has analyzed the naturalist landscapes to explore the landscape's relationship to the urban and provincial middle class. Stephen Daniels has explored the ways in which English landscape painters sought to represent a particularly English form of landscape via sites, industries, and activities that have nationalist implications. For Kay Dian Kriz the discourse shifts again from artists encoding a landscape to an image encoding an artist as characteristically English.

JUILEE DECKER

Bibliography

Barrell, John. *The Dark Side of the Landscape: The Rural Poor in English Painting, 1730–1840*. Cambridge: Cambridge University Press, 1980.

————. *The Political Theory of Painting from Reynolds to Hazlitt: the Body of the Public*. New Haven, Conn.: Yale University Press, 1986.

Bermingham, Ann. *Landscape and Ideology: The English Rustic Tradition, 1740–1860*. Berkeley and Los Angeles: University of California Press, 1986.

Binyon, Laurence. *Landscape in English Art and Poetry*. London: Cobden-Sanderson, 1931.

Daniels, Stephen. *Fields of Vision: Landscape Imagery and National Identity in England and the United States*. Princeton, N.J.: Princeton University Press, 1993.

Grigson, Geoffrey. *Britain Observed: The Landscape through Artists' Eyes*. London: Phaidon, 1975.

Helsinger, Elizabeth. *Rural Scenes and National Representation: Britain, 1815–1850*. Princeton, N.J.: Princeton University Press, 1997.

Hemingway, Andrew. *Landscape Imagery and Urban Culture in Early Nineteenth-Century Britain*. Cambridge: Cambridge University Press, 1992.

Kriz, Kay Dian. *The Idea of the English Landscape Painter: Genius as Alibi in the Early Nineteenth Century*. New Haven, Conn.: Yale University Press for the Paul Mellon Centre for Studies in British Art, 1997.

Rosenthal, Michael, Christiana Payne, and Scott Wilcox, eds. *Prospects for the Nation: Recent Essays in British Landscape, 1750–1880*, New Haven, Conn.: Yale University Press for the Paul Mellon Centre for Studies in British Art, 1997.

Schneider, Norbert. *Geschichte der Landschaftsmalerei, vom Spätmittelalter bis zur Romantik*. Darmstadt: Primus, 1999.

Sloan, Kim. *Alexander and John Robert Cozens: The Poetry of Landscape*. New Haven, Conn.: Yale University Press in Association with the Art Gallery of Ontario, 1986.

LANDSCAPE PAINTING: FRANCE

The Académie Royale de Peinture et de Sculpture, an important regulator of artistic practice and theory in eighteenth-century France, ranked landscape well below the most prestigious genre, history painting, in its hierarchy. Only history painting was deemed to have *âme* (soul, or what nowadays might be called imagination), and thus artists practicing other genres were seen as mere copyists of nature. As happens so often, however, the theory did not entirely reflect reality. Claude-Joseph Vernet, one of the most admired eighteenth-century landscapists, was singled out for special praise by the critic Denis Diderot at the Paris Salon exhibition of 1767. Diderot described Vernet's paintings as though they were sites which he came across on an imaginary walk with a fictitious companion. The critic has his corambler say "You can say, Vernet, Vernet all you like, but I won't abandon nature to run after an image of it; however sublime a man may be, he's not God." Diderot then asks whether a mountain or a pyramid is the more remarkable phenomenon and answers rhetorically that it is the pyramid, because "nothing coming from God, the mountain's author, is astonishing, while the pyramid would be an incredible human phenomenon." Vernet is thus revealed as a creative force, far more than a mere copier of nature, in a manner akin to that promoted by Jean-Jacques Rousseau of man as godlike in his free will. Landscape painting could be perceived as essentially inventive, and therefore arguably Romantic, by those sufficiently sophisticated to see beyond academic rules.

The Académie Royale was, unsurprisingly, swept away along with the royal family in the wake of the 1789 Revolution. Previously unexhibited landscape painters, such as Georges Michel, could thenceforth show their work at the Salon, made open to all artists. His views of the environs of Paris, with windmills depicted beneath leaden skies, have a robust naturalism which might seem to consign him to the copyist tradition promoted by the erstwhile Académie Royale, but he (and others like him) can also be seen as a Romantic alternative to the neoclassical tradition of landscape promoted from within the Académie des Beaux-Arts, the eventual successor to the Académie Royale. Pierre-Henri de Valenciennes published an important artistic treatise, *Eléments de perspective pratique* (*Aspects of Practical Perspective*, 1799 or 1800), the first to deal substantially with landscape. His view of the genre was that it would progress best by allying itself with history painting, depicting scenes with significant human interest, usually taken from classical antiquity. In 1816 his efforts, abetted by others, resulted in the creation of a competitive scholarship for landscape painters. This might be seen as an impediment to the development of a Romantic sensibility in French landscape painting, but Valenciennes was important in putting the genre on the map.

Treatises written in the wake of Valenciennes' pioneering efforts moved the debate onward, and the mere fact that landscape painting began to develop a theoretical basis indicates its rise in importance. C. J. F. Lecarpentier's *Essai sur le paysage* (*Essay on Landscape*, 1817) strikes a marked note of Romantic reverie: "Anyone who has the innate gift of observation and that slight touch of melancholy that can find happiness in solitude . . . is a born landscapist." Practice followed theory, particularly after 1830, which saw the replacement of the restored Bourbon regime with that of Louis-Philippe, the so-called bourgeois monarch. The rise of landscape painting is often linked with the rise of the bourgeoisie to political and social prominence. The middle class might not have had the education to comprehend the sometimes recondite stories illustrated by history paintings but they liked to adorn their homes with evocative rural scenes that provided an imaginative alternative to the reality of their industrialized and urbanized existence.

As it developed after 1830, French landscape painting deserves the epithet *Romantic*, in distinction to the classically based art of Pierre-Henri Valenciennes and his followers, but it varies significantly from its European counterparts. It lacks, for example, the intensely contemplative and specifically religious dimension of works by German painters such as Caspar David Friedrich and Philipp Otto Runge. It does not approach the apocalyptic visions of the British artist J. M. W. Turner. The example of England was, however, crucial for developments in France. John Constable exhibited the ubiquitously illustrated *Hay Wain* in Paris in 1824, to the delight of, among many, Stendhal. "The *truth* of these charming works instantly strikes and delights us," he wrote in his review of the 1824 Salon, setting the naturalist aspect of the agenda for the development of French Romantic landscape painting after 1830.

The Barbizon school, so named from a village in the forest of Fontainebleau much frequented by landscape painters and also known as the school of 1830, relied considerably on its perceived closeness to nature for its effect and its appeal. But artists such as Jules Dupré, Narcisse Diaz de la Peña, and most notably Théodore Rousseau relied on adding a significant dose of the imaginative to this naturalism. Rousseau's *Effet de givre* (*Morning Frost, Uplands of Valmondois*, 1845) shows a banal motif of grass and sandy soil punctuated only by ramshackle wooden fencing beneath a contrasting sunrise of almost sublime intensity. The supremely subtle critic and arch-Romantic poet Charles Baudelaire characterized Rousseau in 1846 as "a naturalist, ceaselessly swept toward the ideal." In 1846, Rousseau's work was not part of the Salon exhibition that Baudelaire was reviewing, having been consistently refused by the jury for some years

previously. After the 1848 revolution, his reputation grew but Baudelaire increasingly withdrew his support from Rousseau and from Rousseau's colleagues. By 1859, he was convinced that painters were privileging the real over the imaginative: "Those artists who want to express nature *minus* the feelings which she inspires are submitting to an odd sort of operation which consists in killing the reflective and sentient man within them." Baudelaire arguably sounded the death knell of Romantic landscape painting in France too early, since Camille Corot was in the middle of his most imaginative phase, with paintings collectively called *Souvenirs*, but 1859 also saw the first public exhibition of the work of Camille Pissarro, a man soon to be called, with others, an impressionist, and with a mentality far removed from Romanticism.

ED LILLEY

Bibliography

Adams, Steven. *The Barbizon School and the Origins of Impressionism.* London: Phaidon, 1994.

Baudelaire, Charles. *Oeuvres complètes.* Paris: Gallimard, 1961. Translated as *Art in Paris 1845–1862,* by Jonathan Mayne. Oxford, U.K.: Phaidon, 1965.

Champa, Kermit S. *The Rise of Landscape Painting in France: Corot to Monet.* Manchester, N.H.: Currier Gallery of Art, 1991.

Diderot, Denis. *Salons.* 4 vols. Oxford, U.K.: Oxford University Press, 1957–67. Published as *Diderot on Art: II The Salon of 1767.* Translated by John Goodman. New Haven, Conn.: Yale University Press, 1995.

Dorbec, Prosper. *L'Art du paysage en France: essai sur son évolution de la fin du XVIIIe siècle à la fin du Second Empire.* Paris: Henri Laurens, 1925.

Green, Nicholas. *The Spectacle of Nature: Landscape and Bourgeois Culture in Nineteenth-Century France.* Manchester, U.K.: Manchester University Press, 1990.

Lecarpentier, Charles-Jacques-François. *Essai sur le paysage.* Paris: Treuttel et Wurtz, 1817.

Miquel, Pierre. *L'Ecole de la nature.* 10 vols. Maurs-la-Jolie: La Martinelle, 1975–87.

Stendhal, *Oeuvres complètes.* 50 vols. Geneva: Cercle du Bibliophile, 1968–1974. (vol. 47 *Mélanges III-Peinture*, 1972). Translated as *Stendhal and the Arts* by David Wakefield. London: Phaidon, 1973.

Valenciennes, Pierre-Henri. *Eléments de perspective pratique.* 1799 or 1800.

Wenzel, Carol R. *The Transformation of French Landscape Painting from Valenciennes to Corot, 1787 to 1827.* Ann Arbor, Mich.: University Microfilms International, 1981.

LANDSCAPE PAINTING: GERMANY

It was in a new conception of landscape that German painting found its greatest achievement in the first half of the nineteenth century, despite the consensus long held in the academies and by many critics that history painting was the most significant of all the genres. Rejecting academic rules that allowed for the representation of nature only in certain categories (the heroic, the pastoral, or the picturesque, for example), Romantic artists developed a new type of landscape picture: the landscape of mood or emotion. The most original German contribution to the genre was the image, at times bordering on the abstract, of an

infinite nature that alone conveyed moral, historical, or religious meaning. That nature itself could act as allegory, that it could be bearer of idea without the intervention of human agency, was a radical break with tradition.

The artist Philipp Otto Runge's famous conclusion about the inevitable path of art's development, that "es drängt sich alles zur Landschaft" ("everything strives toward landscape") sums up the position of the genre in Germany especially well. The importance assumed by landscape painting in the Romantic era is revealed by the quantity of theoretical writings that sprang up to interpret it, as a host of writers and artists such as Carl Gustav Carus, Carl Ludwig Fernow, Wilhelm Basilius von Ramhdor, and Christian August Semler, and attempted to define its primary goals, debated the proper relationship between the ideal and the real in the depiction of the natural world, and strove to map out the position of the human figure within it.

A variety of concerns pressed upon landscape painting practice in Germany: the era's myriad scientific and philosophical inquiries into nature by writers like Johann Wolfgang von Goethe and Gotthilf Heinrich von Schubert; the aesthetic discourses surrounding the sublime and the beautiful especially as formulated by Immanuel Kant and Johann Christoph Friedrich von Schiller; newly aroused religious and spiritual attitudes that theologians like Friedrich Ernst Daniel Schleiermacher promoted, the cult of nature unleashed by Jean-Jacques Rousseau's writings; a burgeoning national consciousness, especially in the wake of the Napoleonic conquest; and a growing bourgeoisie within German society that looked to the countryside for edification as well as recreation. In many respects, then, German Romantic landscape painting addressed issues similar to those elsewhere in Europe and the United States, where the taste for the sublime, the direct observation and naturalistic rendering of nature, and the revaluation of the native countryside were also important trends. But the German emphasis on the transcendental, spiritual quality of nature was matched in intensity perhaps only by American attitudes. Stylistically, much of German Romantic landscape painting is set apart from its English and French counterparts, for until the loose brushwork of Carl Blechen and Carl Rottmann made its appearance, its most innovative practitioners employed a Clarity of form and a lucid structure aligned more to neoclassical tradition than to the dramatic swirls of J. M. W. Turner or Eugène Delacroix.

Already in the late eighteenth century, hints at the undermining of traditional aesthetics had begun to surface, and no clean break separating the neoclassical and Romantic formulation of nature can be identified. Sublime mountain and volcanic scenery proved to be exceptionally popular material, and a new pathos of the natural found its way even into the work of an artist like Jakob Philipp Hackert, the most celebrated German landscape painter of his time (and revered by Goethe), who was firmly entrenched in the ideal landscape tradition of Claude Lorrain and Nicolas Poussin. Hackert's great concern for a naturalistic rendering of a variety of trees in a work like *Ideal Land Schaft Mit Juno-Tempel aus Agrigent* (*Ideal Landscape with a Temple from Agrigento*, 1794) suggests this new feeling for nature, matched also by others of his generation, such as Adrian Zingg, whose sunlit, poetical (but highly detailed) drawings of the Saxon countryside (such as *Prebischkegel in Saxon Switzerland*, c. 1800) are a direct predecessor to the landscapes of the Dresden Romantics.

Truly revolutionary ideas about landscape came out of Dresden in the early 1800s, where the previous decades' sentiment toward nature evolved into full-blown mystical reverence, primarily in the work of Runge and Caspar David Friedrich. Friedrich Wilhelm Joseph von Schelling's *Naturphilosophie*, in particular his conception of the spiritually expressive potential of nature and of the function of art as "ein tätiges Band zwischen der Seele und der Natur" ("the active bond between the soul and nature"), was instrumental in shaping the development of this transcendental image. Friedrich, at his most extreme, pro-

duced pictures radical in their sheer emptiness, divesting them of diversions for the eye, as in *Der Mönch am Meer* (*Monk by the Sea*, 1810). But other artists inspired by his work, especially his circle of followers in Dresden (Carus, Friedrich Oehme, August Heinrich), eschewed this extreme and instead adopted his quotable pictorial vocabulary (Gothic ruins, solitary trees, contemplative backward figures, dramatic moonrises and sunsets) constructing a recognizable vision of mood and spirit that reverberated throughout the century.

Carus's postulation that landscape painting should be concerned not with the mere reflection of the outward appearance of objects, but with a particular state in the natural process that would correspond to state of mind in the viewer, relates to the Romantic interest in the passage of time, manifest in the frequent portrayal of the symbol-laden themes of the four seasons and times of day, as in Runge's *Der Morgen* (*Morning*,). But it also points to the scientific interest in nature that stood alongside quasi-pantheistic attitudes. Cloud studies, depictions of different atmospheric conditions, and topographical cataloging of vegetal and geological forms were practices all related to a belief in a living earth whose geological history played an important role in cultural history.

Landscape painting flourished especially in cities, where it addressed a growing taste among the bourgeoisie for experiencing the wonders of nature. Besides Dresden, the other major centers of landscape painting included Berlin (Carl Blechen, Karl Friedrich Schinkel), Düsseldorf (Ferdinand Theodor Hildebrandt, Karl Lessing), and Munich (Johann Georg von Dillis, Wilhelm von Kobell, and Carl Rottmann). The native countryside beyond the city walls became the visual material for many of these artists, and although there is no one unifying aesthetic among them, in general the growing interest and pride in all things German that is indicative of the new sense of national identity sparked the trend for regional exploration.

Throughout the Romantic era, the heroic landscape remained a staple of landscape painting production, although it, too, was modified by various concerns of the day. The Deutsch-Römer (German Romans) in Italy still took inspiration from the past to produce grand paintings of an arcadian world. Yet in the work of Joseph Anton Koch and Johann Christian Reinhart, the heightened sensitivity toward nature that had been set in motion by Romanticism can also be felt; often the power of the highly described scenery overwhelms whatever figures have been added to it, as in Koch's *Heroische Land Schaft Mit Regenbogen Heroic Landscape with Rainbow*, 1815). Other artists, such as Lessing, Ludwig Richter, Schinkel, and the Nazarenes, reworked the heroic genre by turning to the German middle ages instead of classical antiquity for narrative content, in a nostalgic search to uncover the country's lost golden age in order to present a paradigm of German society, as in Schinkel's *Mittel alterliche Stadt an einem Fluss* (*Medieval City on a River*, 1815).

This complex mixture of objective investigation and subjective feelings, played out in a variety of styles, characterizes the German reaction to nature during the Romantic era. Few German artists were unaffected. By mid-century, a realist aesthetic had begun to tip the balance back toward the objective. However, the Romantics' engagement with the metaphysical forces of nature endured, a persistent subtext in German landscape painting through to the end of the 1800s and beyond.

MARGARET DOYLE

Bibliography

Börsch-Supan, Helmut. *Die Deutsche Malerei von Anton Graff bis Hans von Marées 1760–1870*. Munich: Beck and Deutscher Kunstverlag, 1988.

Décultot, Élisabeth. *Peindre le paysage: discours théorique et renouveau pictural dans le romantisme allemand*. Tusson: Du Lérot, 1996.

Eschenburg, Barbara. *Landschaft in der deutschen Malerei*. Munich: Beck, 1987.

Geismeier, Willi. *Die Malerei der deutschen Romantik*, Stuttgart: Kohlhammer 1984.

Hartley, Keith, ed. *The Romantic Spirit in German Art*. London: Thames and Hudson, 1994.

Mitchell, T. F. *Art and Science in German Landscape Painting 1770–1840*. Oxford, U.K.: Clarendon Press, 1993.

Rosenblum, Robert. *Modern Painting and the Northern Romantic Tradition*. New York: Harper and Row, 1975.

Roters, Ebehard. *Jenseits von Arkadien. Die romantische Landschaft*. Cologne: DuMont, 1995.

Vaughan, William. *German Romantic Painting*. 2nd ed. New Haven, Conn.: Yale University Press, 1994.

LANGUAGE

The Romantic period saw the consolidation of Standard British English in both speech and writing, and the basis of this developing idiom was the language of London and its periphery. Elite officials of the church, the state, and the academic establishment succeeded the courts in deciding lexical norms from about 1700. Conformity to standard British English became the hallmark of the educated classes, as the employment of Latin diminished. Codifying and enforcing the standard became grist for lexicographers, grammarians, and public authorities such as Archbishop Richard Chenevix Trench, from whose high pulpit correct linguistic practice would be equated with personal morality.

The hundred years commencing with Samuel Johnson's *Dictionary* (1755) and concluding with Trench's *On the Study of Words* (1851) is characterized by the dissemination of this new linguistic contract with the public. The need for new conventions had already been evident to Sir Francis Bacon, who wrote of "the cheating slights and charms of words, which many waies abuse us, and offer violence to the understanding." *Abuse* is a key word for grasping Enlightenment animus against existing habits of communication. John Locke's *Essay Concerning Human Understanding* (1690) included an important chapter on "The Abuse of Words." A century later, Samuel Taylor Coleridge would aim "to expose the Folly & the Legerdemain of those, who have thus abused the Blessed Organ of Language" (1803). This note recalls the squib of William Shakespeare's clown in *Twelfth Night*, for whom "wordes are grown so false, I am loath to prove reason with them." Bacon, Coleridge, and the Romantic company at large are instigators of the modern drive for communicative adequacy that would later motivate Jürgen Habermas and Raymond Williams.

Social dissolution was a source of their attacks on the abuse of language. Polemics surrounding the English Civil War had dramatized a national crisis of representation. A common basis for ideas went missing; words had drifted perilously from distinct reference. This crisis is the background to the development of the new social contract, and of the new standard English in, and through which, it would be realized. Settling on the meaning of words was the instrument of a general reformation of the national mind. Among Locke's inheritors, Johnson defines the word *ballad* simply as "a song." A simplification of a notoriously complex term, this equation distills the word's associations down to a simple idea. Johnson follows Locke's emphasis on the force of simple ideas, and on the value of naming them unmistakably. The point was to create a common vocabulary in the interest of clarity. Coleridge, in 1805, would find in his own mental habits the rationale for simple signification, writing, "It is worthy of notice, the instinctive passion in the mind for a one word to express a one act of feeling."

With William Wordsworth, Coleridge would turn such simplification to the fresh poetic ends essayed in the Preface to their *Lyrical Ballads* (1800) and explored in some of their verse. Here were poetic experiments in "the real language of men," with an emphasis on what the two writers argued was the best part of language. For Wordsworth, this would not be Standard British English at all, but something rustic, reflecting the settled habits of nonurban speakers. The lyrical ballad links him with Thomas Percy, who had led the way in adopting antique diction in popular balladic recensions. Percy's *Reliques of Ancient English Poetry* (1765) can be read as a Romantic challenge to the cultural authority of the new standard English. These set the stage for writers with regional (especially northern British) and antiquarian tastes. Robert Burns would employ Scots dialect in his popular songs and verses, and John Clare and William Barnes adapted regional diction to poetic purposes. Walter Scott made a successful career writing verse and prose romances full of local history and dialect. All were enlisted in a struggle to keep older forms of language and custom alive in the face of linguistic and cultural nationalization. This reactive turn is an essential feature of literary Romanticism throughout Europe.

For Coleridge, the best part of language was not simple in this sense at all, but the product of the mind's reflection on its own activity. In fact, as he practiced it, English was complex to a fault. Locke and his follower David Hartley (*Observations on Man*, 1749) had tried to account empirically for linguistic practice. Hartley's association psychology made language acquisition a matter of the accumulation of related ideas, a reasonable proposition which Coleridge (and later I. A. Richards) would promote. It foundered on the doctrine of mental vibrations which Hartley had picked up from Etienne Bonnot de Condillac's *Essai sur l'origine des connaissances humaines* (*Essay on the Origin of Human Knowledge*, 1746). More important was Horne Tooke's manic *Epea Pteroenta* (*The Diversions of Purley*, 1786–98), the strange production of a radical simplifier whose influence was registered throughout the period. Tooke dominated Coleridge's thinking about words, but did not limit the scope of his understanding of the whole range of linguistic phenomena. Coleridge coined new words to introduce modern concepts—"psychosomatic" and "neuropathology" are two still that are current. He rationalized the language of poetry in ways that would later be extended by Cambridge English. He developed a cognitive approach to language that was at odds with Hartley, Locke, and Tooke, in the tradition of Cartesian linguistics later elaborated by Noam Chomsky. Chomsky has acknowledged Coleridge's significance for his own approach to language, which remains current in cognitive science. Coleridge looks ahead to modern ideas of language like no other writer of the period.

Yet Coleridge's contribution lay outside the new philology being developed by Franz Bopp and others in Germany. Scientific philology was inspired by earlier speculations on the origin and nature of language by Etienne Bonnot de Condillac, Johann Georg Hamann, and Johann Gottfried von Herder. Hamann wrote of onomatopoesie, the way that sounds of the voice make up the "root and stem, sap and life spirit of language." The organic idea is characteristic of his approach; he compares human with animal organization, concluding that the origin of language is as natural as the human capacity for learning. Poetry was the mother tongue of the species, Hamann maintained, conceiving language itself as an art. He took speech to be a translation of thoughts into words, of things into names, of images into conventional signs. The translation that was speech he compared to the underside of a rug, which "shows the stuff but not the workman's skill." Wrapped in turgid biblical parlance, Hamann's speculations intimate the difficulty of bridging the world of scripture and the observed world as it had been considered since Bacon, whom he mentions in passing.

Herder's *Abhandlung über den Ursprung der Sprache* (*On the Origin of Language*, 1772) followed Condillac's (and Jean-Jacques Rousseau's) emphasis on speech as an immediate expression of human nature. Original languages as Herder conceived them (and as Coleridge followed him in calling them) included vestiges of natural expression: interjections, and the roots of substantives and verb stems. The elegiac tones of such languages harked back to primitive mourning. Herder's search for an original principle of language, and his way of thinking about language as a national institution, are often called Romantic. Herder inspired Johann Wolfgang von Goethe, among many others, to reflect on speech as the hallmark of national identity. At the end of his life, Herder challenged Immanuel Kant's critical philosophy on the grounds of its failure to address the problem of language.

In 1808 the Romantic writer and critic Friedrich von Schlegel published a study of the language and culture of ancient India, *Über die Sprache und Weisheit der Indier* (*On the Language and Wisdom of India*). Bopp pursued it in a treatise on the comparative conjugations of Sanskrit, Greek and Latin, Persian, and German verbs (1816). Sanskrit's kinship with European languages had been observed by Sir William Jones, the English orientalist, from about 1790 on. Bopp demonstrated the case conclusively, and the discipline of comparative philology was born. The discovery of the Indo-European language system was a spur to the development of scientific philology. Bopp went on to apply his comparative method to all parts of grammar, and to produce a six-part *Vergleichende Grammatik* (*Comparative Grammar*, 1833–52) that widened the scope of his research to include other tongues as well as other features of the Indo-European linguistic family. Bopp was especially interested in reconstructing the original grammatical forms concerned. Herder's Romantic quest for a principle of origination remains alive in this form in Bopp's science of language.

Karl Wilhelm von Humboldt's treatise of 1836 on the linguistic forms of Javanese Kawi, Barmanic, and Sanskrit, among others, took Bopp's approach in other directions. The character of languages was the issue here: what grammar had to tell us about cultural and national identity. Humboldt proposed to measure the intellectual development of human groups on a scale calibrated by the complexity of the grammatical forms provided by their native tongues. The Indo-European family, rich in complexity, became the effective standard by which more primitive languages (and cultures) were measured. Language and mind were one thing in his treatment, intimately related through learning and modification in response to changing conditions. Humboldt's cognitive linguistics is an important prototype of cognitive science, but its Indo-European standard has attracted criticism from linguistic anthropologists. It remains a monument of speculative philology, and the most imposing document on the subject of language in the period.

A. C. GOODSON

Bibliography

Aarsleff, Hans. *From Locke to Saussure: Essays on the Study of Language and Intellectual History*. Minneapolis: University of Minnesota Press, 1982.
Bacon, Francis. *Of the Advancement of Learning or the Partitions of Sciences*. Aldburgh, England: Archival Facsimiles, 1987.
Bailey, Richard W. *Nineteenth-Century English*. Ann Arbor: University of Michigan Press, 1996.
Chomsky, Noam. *Cartesian Linguistics: A Chapter in the History of Rationalist Thought*. New York: Harper and Row, 1966.
———. *Coleridge's Writings*. Volume 3, *On Language*. London: Macmillan, 1998.
Goodson, A. C. "Romantic Theory and the Critique of Language," in *Questioning Romanticism*. Edited by John Beer. Baltimore, Md.: Johns Hopkins University Press, 1995.
Görlach, Manfred. *English in Nineteenth-Century England: An Introduction*. Cambridge, U.K.: Cambridge University Press, 1999.
Hamann, Johann Georg. *Sämtliche Werke*. Edited by J. Nadler. Vienna: 1950.
Herder, Johann Gottfried. *Sprachphilosophische Schriften*. Edited by Erich Heintel. Hamburg: Felix Meiner, 1960.
Humboldt, Wilhelm von, *The Diversity of Human Language-Structure and its Influence on the Mental Development of Mankind*. Translated by Peter Heath. Cambridge, U.K.: Cambridge University Press, 1988.

LAPLACE, PIERRE-SIMON DE 1749–1827

French mathematician, astronomer, and physicist

Being popularly thought of as the French Newton may have led to the belief that Pierre-Simon de Laplace and Isaac Newton had more in common than a lifelong interest in the complementary fields of mathematics, astronomy, and physics. One may perhaps note that both possessed personalities strong enough to subsume precursors, overshadow peers, and command younger or more malleable scientists. Traditional sources also tell of how, like Newton, Laplace had a peasant birth and owed his education to some personage; this part of the story was really romantically fabricated after Louis XVIII made him a marquis in 1817.

Reliable scholarship suggests as well that Laplace's love for mathematics neither began in his university days at Caen nor under Christophe Gadbled's tutelage, but went farther back to the early influence of a clerical uncle. It also seems that, before the age of twenty, Laplace was already in contact with the mathematician and astronomer Joseph Louis Lagrange. It is certain that, Laplace came to the attention of the reigning scientific figure of the time, Jean le Rond d'Alembert, after composing a memoir on mechanics for him. He then dazzled the scientific community in 1773 by solving a notoriously difficult Newtonian puzzle: the relation between Jupiter's shrinking orbit and Saturn's expanding one.

Laplace achieved this by rendering extremely precise the approximate values involved; it led to his discovery that the terms in the final expression for the effect of Jupiter's action on Saturn's mean motion actually negated each other. That the observed eccentricities were not secular—that is to say, accumulative—meant that they were self-correcting or periodic, although this period was too long for human observation. Laplace's calculations of 1784 showed it amounting to 929 years; that year, he completely solved the equation for all mutual gravitational interactions within the solar system. Such a solution was previously unthinkable and Newton himself had resorted to God's periodic intervention as a means to overcome the impasse and keep his own theoretical system in equilibrium.

Laplace's proof allowed him to formulate theorems relative to both the positions of planetary orbits and the oscillations in their forms; he also solved the curious mathematical relations of Jupiter's satellites and furnished theorems on their libration. Climactically, Laplace explained a lunar phenomenon that neither Leonhard Euler nor Lagrange before him could account for, and his success led to the moon becoming his popular poetic emblem, as the rainbow was Newton's. The puzzle involved the moon's accelerating mean motion which, in closing its mean distance from the earth, suggested a future terrestrial precipitation. Laplace'demonstrated how the planets' changing action on the earth made the earth's orbit more circular by retarding its acceleration; this, in turn, altered the sun's action on the moon which then accelerated the moon's mean motion. Because the earth's orbit would in time become elliptical again and so reverse this whole process, the inequality was shown to be periodic but stretching into millions of years.

The solution broke up the last threat to a completely Newtonian universe exactly a century after the publication of Newton's *Principia Mathematica* (1687). Laplace's astronomical findings are documented in his five-volume *Traité de mécanique céleste* (*Treatise on Celestial Mechanics*, 1798–1827), which further carries a black hole theory, a theory on Saturn's rings consisting of small particles, later mathematically proven by James Clerk Maxwell, and an evolutionary theory on how the universe began, also called the Kant-Laplace nebular hypothesis since Immanuel Kant had earlier proposed something similar. In physics, Laplace's study on spheriod and mass-particle attractions formed the mathematical basis for future investigations into heat, magnetism, and electricity. He also correctly identified Newton's failure to distinguish between gaseous flow at constant temperature and at constant entropy (the measure of "useless" thermal energy) and, with Antoine Laurent Lavoisier, made some of the first thermochemical explorations; they had invented an ice calorimeter in 1780 to show respiration as a form of combustion. To pure mathematics he gave a very effective expansion of determinants and a transformation of functions for solving difference equations, both of which still bear his name; his *Théorie analytique des probabilités* (*Analytical Theory of Probabilities*, 1812) argues for the use of probability to interpret scientific data.

Laplace is therefore central to the gradual rise of deterministic beliefs built on the evidence of exact science; his probabilistic approach and achievements in astronomy culminate in a conviction that nature is utterly rational and that all events are predictable in relation to how much is known in the present. Laplace himself goes so far as to cheerfully undermine the notion of free will by extending the limits of knowability into the realm of personal moral choices; his celebration of the quasi-divine power of an existential human mind nonetheless gives back to individualism what he has only just taken away. Such a fundamental paradox must be read into Jean Baptiste Joseph Fourier's proclamation that, unlike Newton and Euler, Laplace knew every perfection of the world: Laplacean perfection draws from a rare kind of agreement between the often antithetical demands of Enlightenment and Romantic thought. His well-known reply to Napoleon Bonaparte's query about the absence of God in his work—"I have no need for that hypothesis"—not only sums up the exigency of pure and progressive science but also mirrors the iconoclastic spirit of a revolutionary age and attests to a faith in the self-sufficiency of the human to the task of grasping and overcoming an externally given reality.

As such, Laplace's ideals fit the goals of Napoleon's empire perfectly, though it must be noted that Laplace was remarkably buoyant during the turbulent period from the French Revolution to the Bourbon Restoration. Perhaps a masterful combination of personal genius and powerful connections ensured that he stayed at the center of the French scientific community for the rest of his life, asserting much influence on high-level committees such as those for finding the longitude and for fixing the metric system; he was also a pillar of the illustrious Society of Arcueil, which he and the chemist Claude-Louis Berthollet had filled with their own supporters. At the height of his flirtation with the empire, he was greeted with an appointment as Napoleon's minister of the interior, which nonetheless ended six weeks later after Napoleon complained that he calamitously "carried the spirit of the 'infinitely small' into administration."

GWEE LI SUI

Biography

Born in Beaumount-en-Auge, Normandy, on March 23, 1749; studied at the University of Caen, 1766–68; taught mathematics at the École militaire in Paris, 1769–76; made associate member of the Académie des sciences after solving the puzzle involving Jupiter's and Saturn's orbits, 1773; presented his great memoir on a fully Newtonian solar system to the Académie des sciences, 1784; appointed examiner of cadets in the Royal Artillery, 1784; promoted to the Section of Mechanics, 1785; Napoleon's examiner, 1786; married Marie-Charlotte de Courty de Romanges, 1788; published Exposition du système du monde, 1796; six-week appointment as minister of the interior by Napoleon, 1799; made a count by Napoleon, 1803; published Théorie analytique des probabilités, 1812; elected into the Académie Française, 1816; made a marquis by Louis XVIII, 1817; died in Paris on March 5, 1827.

Selected Works

Théorie du mouvement et de la figure elliptique des planètes. 1784.
Exposition du système du monde. 2 vols., 1796. Translated as The System of the World by John Pond. London: Richard Phillips, 1809.
Traité de mécanique céleste. 5 vols., 1798–1827. Translated as Celestial Mechanics, 4 vols. by Nathaniel Bowditch, Jerzy Neyman, Lucien M. Le Cam. Boston, Mass.: Hillard, Gray, Little, and Wilkins, 1829–1839.
Théorie analytique des probabilités. 1812.
Essai philosophique sur les probabilités, 1814. Translated as A Philosophical Essay on Probabilities by Frederick L. Emory and Frederick W. Truscott. New York: John Wiley and Sons, 1902.

Bibliography

Andoyer, Henri. L'oeuvre scientifique de Laplace. Paris: Payot, 1922.
Bell, E. T. Men of Mathematics. London: Victor Gollancz, 1937.
Crosland, Maurice. The Society of Arcueil: A View of French Science at the Time of Napoleon I. London: Heinemann, 1967.
Fourier, Jean Baptiste Joseph. An Historical Eulogy of M. Le Marquis De Laplace. Translated by Rosswell W. Haskins. Buffalo, N.Y.: 1830.
Gillispie, Charles Coulston. Pierre-Simon Laplace, 1749–1827: A Life in Exact Science. Princeton, N.J.: Princeton University Press, 1997.
Hahn, Roger. Laplace as a Newtonian Scientist. Berkeley and Los Angeles: University of California Press, 1967.
Pearson, Karl. "Laplace," Biometrika 21 (1929): 202–16.
Todhunter, I. A History of the Mathematical Theory of Probability from the Time of Pascal to That of Laplace. 2 vols. London: Macmillan, 1865.
Whittaker, Edmund T. "Laplace," Mathematical Gazette 33 (1949): 1–12.

LARRA, MARIANO JOSÉ DE 1809-1837

Spanish journalist and satirist

Mariano José de Larra never identified formally with classicism or Romanticism, wishing to remain independent of schools of thought. However, he saw Alexandre Dumas père and Victor Hugo as manifestations of changing times, and was influenced toward the end of his life by Heinrich Heine and Félicité Robert de Lamennais. He shared with other Spanish left-liberal contemporaries a hope for a new literature for the new age, but also joined in prevailing uncertainties about the violence done to ethical and literary needs. The former issue, seen in the varying treatment of adultery in his review of Anthony and his two versions of the story of Macías—Macías and El doncel de don Enrique (The Page of Don Enrique)—doubtless reflects his own personal plight, having become unhappily involved with a married woman and separated from his wife.

His main concern was that literature should be based on genuine insight into feelings and the imagination, the truths of humanity that would be apparent in the new age. That led him not just to admire Dumas over Hugo, but to share his contemporaries' enthusiasm for Augustin Eugène Scribe's so-called "well-made" plays. As he explains in a brief introduction, his own play Macías (1834) is not a classical tragedy, a golden-age Spanish play, nor a drama in the style of Dumas and Hugo. It is, he tells us, the story of a man in love. It focuses not on multiple plot lines or audacious probing of the sublime and grotesque, but on mounting passions culminating in a death.

An admirer of Hugo's blending of good and evil, Larra said humanity should be portrayed in a mixed state. That concern is exemplified in his novel El doncel de don Enrique (1835), where the tragic outcome is in part a peculiar and ironic result of this fact. Further ironies in that novel derive from the supposed truths of the imagination when producing a historical fiction.

True insight also meant, an awareness that different societies were at different stages of development. While sharing wider enthusiasm for a rebirth of Spain's past literary success, Larra aligned with those who rejected basing the renewal on past forms that lacked freedom of thought or solidity. Writers should express philosophically the new realities of specifically Spanish life on its way to universal progress, a view expounded in "Literatura" (1836). Sharing the preoccupations of other Spanish political writers, Larra felt that Spain lagged behind France, that French influence could prove alienating, and that the full awfulness of truth that French writers exposed was not for Spain.

In a world of unchanging passions, literature was to capture the ever-changing reality of social customs. In this, Honoré de Balzac in France and Mesonero Romanos in Spain were models for the difficult task of reconciling a superficial phenomenon with deep insight. Such literary preoccupations relate closely to Larra's main achievement in his periodical articles about mores and politics, which helped contribute to the erosion of distinctions between high and low forms of writing. Larra was a master of the ephemeral. Much of his writing is made up of literary reviews and occasional political polemic rather than systematic analysis of Spanish society, with the forces of conservatism frequently his target. The variations in his style and views can partly be related to his ephemeral vocation as a journalist. Larra self-consciously reinvented himself on successive occasions as a different character with a different name, from the innocently talkative Pobrecito Hablador (Poor Little Talker) to the waspish weeping clown Fígaro, a fact he attributes to his own search for novelty, expressed in "Las casas nuevas" ("The New Houses," 1833). On one occasion, in "Antigüedades de Mérida" ("Antiquities of Mérida," 1835), he refers to "mi carácter el cual podría muy bien venir a ser el de no tener ninguno" ("my character which might well come down to not having one"). Ultimately, as John R. Rosenberg has commented, even his double is doubled by the use of an accusing servant who takes the form of his conscience in "Nochebuena de 1836" ("Christmas Eve, 1836"). This persona is at times treated with an element of irony, perhaps because of its eccentric behavior, the autobiographical origin of the views expressed, or because it is implicated precisely in the society and language it criticizes. Larra was explicit about the problem of addressing a heterogeneous and less than moral public through newspapers, yet saw that as inherent in what he was doing. Many of his articles are described specifically as originating from a contingent event that Larra observes or which causes him to dream or imagine. Influenced by Étienne de Jouy and Joseph Addison, as well as Mesonero Romanos, Larra often depicts himself wandering around Madrid spying, or viewing things as through a magic lantern. Anecdotal observations thus provide a loose structure for several articles, where behavioral patterns, modes of thought, and ways of talking are the basis for comic accounts, in a way later echoed in Leonardo Alenza y Nieto's art. Larra was not least concerned with the deceptive role of language and especially political discourse used around him in society (and on newspaper pages) as a basis of satire. In a different vein, in several later political articles, he accumulates multifaceted jokes through comparison and metaphor, sometimes revealing an alienation from the discourse of all political parties, as in "Los tres no son más que dos" ("The Three Are Just Two," 1834). This is part of a preoccupation, derived from seventeenth-century satire (in particular that of Francisco Gómez de Quevedo y Villegas), with dispelling illusions by seeing one set of ideas and words in terms of another. Such tendencies converge on his most impressive article, "Nochebuena de 1836," which culminates when his drunken servant double accuses him of inventing words and then being disappointed that they do not exist, but offers as a sole alternative a base material existence.

Larra's influence as a writer stretches to the present day. His suicide has helped color a (rather biased) legend of him as a voice in the desert. Many of his contemporaries rejected his partially unjustified political despair, and it is perhaps best to see him principally as a literary rather than a political figure.

ANDREW GINGER

Biography

Born in Madrid, 1809, to a doctor working on the side of the Bonapartist forces. Goes with his family into exile in France, 1812. Returned to Spain, 1817. Studied in Reales Estudios de San Isidro and began to work as clerk at Junta Reservada de Estado, joined absolutist militia, 1825. First article in *El Duende Satírico del Día*, 1828. Member of the *Parnasillo* in early 1830s. Publication of *Pobrecito Hablador* began August 1832; started to write for *Revista Española*. In 1833 also worked for *El Correo de las Damas* (*The Ladies' Mail*), and in 1834 with *El Observador*. Separated 1833, from wife, and around the end of 1834 or start 1835 temporarily separated from his long-time mistress Dolores Armijo. In April 1835 traveled to Badajoz, Lisbon, London, and Paris where he met leading figures including Heine. Returned to Madrid, December 1835. From January 1836 onward worked on *El Español*. Despite radical progressive statements (including prologue to translation of Lammenais), joined with other former *exaltado* liberals in supporting the moderate leader Francisco Javier de Istúriz in 1836. Larra's election as member of parliament was frustrated by the progressive uprising at La Granja. Final split with Dolores Armijo in 1837. Committed suicide February 13, 1837.

Selected Works

Collections

Fígaro: Colección de artículos dramáticos, literarios, políticos, y de costumbres, 1835.
Obras completas de Fígaro, 1843.
Artículos completos. Edited by Melchor de Almagro San Martín, Madrid: Aguiler, 1944.
Obras. Edited by Carlos Seco Serrano. Madrid: Rivederneyn/Real Academic, 1960.
Artículos. Edited by Carlos Seco Serrano. Barcelone: Plarneta, 1990.

Articles

"El café," *El Duende Satírico del Día*, February 26, 1828.
"¿Quién es el público y dónde se le encuentra?" *El Pobrecito Hablador*, August 17, 1832.
"El mundo todo es máscaras: Todo el año es carnaval," *El Pobrecito Hablador*, March 4, 1833.
"Las casas nuevas," *La Revista Española*, September 13, 1833.
"Las palabras," *La Revista Española*, May 8, 1834.
"El hombre-globo," *Revista Mensajero* March 9, 1835.
"La diligencia," *Revista Mensajero*, April 16, 1835.
"Las antigüedades de Mérida," *Revista Mensajero* May 30, 1835.
"Cuasi: Pesadilla política," *Revista Mensajero*, August 9, 1835.
"Literatura: Rápida ojeada a la historia e índole de la nuestra. Su estado actual. Su porvenir. Profesión de fe," *El Español*, January 18, 1836.
"Dios nos asista," *El Español*, April 3, 1836.
"Antony," *El Español* April 23–25, 1836.
"Panorama matritense (Cuadros de costumbres, por un Curioso Parlante)," *El Español*, June 19–20, 1836.
"El día de difuntos de 1836: Fígaro en el cementerio," *El Español*, November 2, 1836.
"La Nochebuena de 1836: Yo y mi criado—Delirio filosófico," *El Redactor General*, December 26, 1836.

Other

Macías. 1834.
El doncel de don Enrique. 1834.

Bibliography

Benítez Rubén, ed. *Mariano José de Larra*. Madrid: Taurus, 1979.
Dérozier, Albert, and A. Gil Novales. *Revisión de Larra (¿Protesta o revolución?)*. Besançon: Annales Littéraire de l'Université, 1983.
Fontanella, Lee, *La imprenta y las letras en la España romántica*. Berne: Peter Lang, 1982.
Ginger, Andrew. "Larra in Context." In *Political Revolution and Literary Experiment in the Spanish Romantic Period*. Lampeter, Wales: Mellen, 1999.
Goytisolo, Juan. "La actualidad de Larra," in *Furgón de cola*. Barcelona: Seix Barral, 1976.

Ilie, Paul. "Larra's Nightmare," *Revista Hispánica Moderna* 38 (1974–75): 153–56.

Kirkpatrick, S. *Larra: El laberinto intextricable de un romántico liberal*. Madrid: Gredos, 1977.

Ríos-Font, Wadda C. "From Romantic Irony to Romantic Grotesque," *Hispanic Review* 65 (1997): 177–98.

Rosenberg, John R. "Between Delirium and Ethical Luminosity," *Hispanic Review* 3 (1993): 379–89.

Ullman, Pierre L. *Mariano José de Larra and Spanish Political Rhetoric*. Madison: University of Wisconsin Press, 1977.

LATIN AMERICA, THE CARIBBEAN, AND THE WEST INDIES: CULTURAL SURVEY

Two major approaches have traditionally characterized the way in which the cultural production of the region now known as Latin America has been understood for the period from 1760 to 1850. One general approach has been to study the extent to which certain European ideas and movements fared in the New World. A second perspective has looked has looked for specific influences that the American landscape and experience might have had on these European models. While different in focus, the two approaches share a basic assumption: the central role of European critical traditions and sensibilities as a starting point to understand and assess the Latin American cultural experience in the second half of the eighteenth century and first half of the nineteenth. A great deal has been written in the last few years exploring the difficulties and obstacles to genuine self-expression of a people living under the colonial control of another, of which Latin America until the 1820s is a prime example. Regrettably, a full-scale reassessment from this promising perspective has yet to take place. As a consequence, when historians and literary critics write about this stage of Latin American culture, they focus on the works of that small minority schooled in institutions founded to replicate Spanish models aimed at training local elites to serve the needs of colonial authorities. Aside from this obvious shortcoming, the publicly recognized writers and artists of the time were never more than a small group. They catered to their own kind, another small minority, and espoused the views of the official culture that sponsored their work.

What gave this otherwise bleak cultural landscape some life was the growing tension between the American-born elites (*criollos* or *americanos* in the parlance of the day) and the Spaniards (variously known as *peninsulares, chapetones*, or *gachupines*). When the first group began to express opposition to policies that excluded them from major roles in the three most important institutions of the age (government, the army, and the church), a new period was due to begin.

The creoles' disaffection manifested itself in a number of ways. In 1753, for example, Juan José de Eguiara y Eguren wrote the first volume of the *Bibliotheca mexicana* (A to C) to highlight the intellectual contributions of American-born authors as a way of demonstrating the intellectual accomplishments and parity of the creoles. The popularity of the Freemasons among the American elites is a second example: through the proliferation of this secret society in the second half of the eighteenth century in cities like Havana, Veracruz, and Caracas, Americans eagerly explored the latest European theories, engaging in discussions about the role of science and reason in society and the inherent equality and perfectability of mankind. It goes without saying that these ideas would later be used by these same Americans to reject their historical present and undermine the foundations of Spain's colonial control.

The notions of freedom and equality discussed in salons in the New World are inseparable from the period of the European Enlightenment during which they were popularized. Charles III of Spain deserves much of the credit for introducing these ideas into the New World, as for his many efforts to reform and modernize colonial administration. Whether, as some have claimed, Spanish America witnessed a period of great intellectual production during this period or not, the fact remains that European ideas influenced American thinkers, such as Antonio de León y Gama, José Celestino Mutis (born in Spain), and Francisco José de Caldas, individuals whose intellectual endeavors left a permanent mark on the cultural life of the continent. It is also clear that in the second half of the eighteenth century, Spanish America accepted the aesthetic principles of neoclassicism associated with the European Enlightenment—a presence nowhere more evident than in architecture, in such buildings as the Palacio de Minería in Mexico City and the Palacio de la Moneda in Santiago. The spirit of the Enlightenment also made itself felt in the proliferation of newspapers, of which the *Diario Erudito* in Lima and the *Primicias de la cultura* in Quito are the most important.

When José Joaquín Fernández de Lizardi published his best-known work in 1816, *El periquillo sarniento* (*The Itching Parrot*), he was echoing a different continental tradition, the picaresque novel. A well-known social critic and prolific writer, Lizardi adopted the genre to condemn slavery and expose the hypocrisy and corruption of Mexican society; by using popular language and characters from everyday life, in what has been called an "emancipatory gesture," Lizardi is credited with having written the New World's first novel. The Argentine writer Bartolomé Hidalgo also captured in his works the language and preoccupations of the noncultured elites.

The frequent equation of liberalism in politics with Romanticism in art (first attributed to Victor Hugo) has been amply studied in reference to the New World. As a result, most scholars acknowledge the influence of such canonical figures as Lord Byron, François-Auguste-René de Chateaubriand, Victor Hugo, and Mariano José de Larra on Spanish-American letters, all the while noting the difficulties of charting a clear and unambiguous trajectory of their collective influence on the evolution of American letters in the nineteenth century.

One of the major difficulties in this endeavor is the fact that the early nineteenth century was the period during which the Spanish colonies declared their political independence from Spain. Notions of individualism and the need for the proper outlet for the gamut of human emotions, historical circumstances, and the rejection of neoclassical rationalism, associated with continental Romanticism, all played a part in these emancipatory efforts. On the other hand, the newly established republics that fought for their political independence in the 1820s faced the task of refashioning themselves in light of political inexperience, economic ruin, regional divisiveness, and an obsolescent yet powerful class and race structure, all overwhelming obstacles to a bright future. Only a few prescient individuals, however, could see this coming. Simon Bolívar's "Carta de Jamaica" (1815) captures better than any contemporary text the plight of those seeking political independence. Only at the end of the nineteenth century would Spanish Americans fully realize, thanks to José Martí and others, the sense in which the declaration of political independence which Bolívar risked so much to achieve guaranteed so little.

Andrés Bello is generally singled out as one of the most illustrious voices of independence in America; in his *silvas americanas* (1823–26), the distinguished intellectual praises the multiple merits of the continent, a sentiment captured in the poetry of the Ecuadorian José Joaquín de Olmedo, the Cuban José María de Heredia, and the Colombian Gregorio Gutiérrez González.

No survey of Spanish-American letters in the period under discussion would be complete without mention of accomplished figures such as the Argentine Esteban Echeverría, whose story "El matadero" (The Matador, 1823) has become a classic indict-

ment of oppression, and Gertrudis Gómez de Avellaneda, the Cuban-born writer whose poetic, narrative, and dramatic works have attracted attention in the last few years.

Last, but not least, is the figure of Domingo Faustino Sarmiento, author of *Civilización y barbarie: vida de Juan Facundo Quiroga* (*Life in the Argentine Republic in the Days of the Tyrants*, 1845), president of Argentina from 1868 to 1874, and a tireless advocate for an America whose merits should be measured by the extent to which they resemble his own, narrow definition of civilization. In Sarmiento's case, civilization was associated with urbanism, technology, the taming of nature, and other features since rejected as valid markers and determinants of culture.

CLARA ESTOW

Bibliography

Arroyo, Anita. *América en su literatura*. Puerto Rico: Editorial Universitaria, 1978.

González Echevarría, Roberto. *The Voice of the Masters: Writing and Authority in Modern Latin American Literature*. Austin: University of Texas Press, 1985.

Martin, Gerald. "The Literature and Art of Latin America from Independence to c. 1870." In *The Cambridge History of Latin America*. Vol. III. Edited by Leslie Bethell. Cambridge, London, New York: Cambridge University Press, 1986. 797–839.

Williams, Lorna. *The Representation of Slavery in Cuban Fiction*. Columbia/London: University of Missourri Press, 1994.

LATIN AMERICA, THE CARIBBEAN, AND THE WEST INDIES: HISTORICAL SURVEY

The period between 1760 and 1850 was of fundamental importance in the development of what would eventually be known as Latin America, in particular those regions under the colonial control of Spain. The opening date, in the mid-eighteenth century, coincides with efforts on the part of the Spanish Bourbons, Carlo III in particular, to reform and modernize colonial administration with the aim of reducing inefficiency and increasing crown revenues. As a consequence, Spain's American colonies underwent a profound transformation. By 1850, colonial bonds had been broken for a generation through a series of wars of independence, after which all former Spanish possessions in continental America had reconstituted themselves as politically autonomous republics. Spain's control of Cuba and Puerto Rico, however, would linger nearly another half century, until 1898.

Portuguese Brazil followed a different trajectory, due to several historical and economic factors—chiefly, Portugal's looser administrative and bureaucratic control over the colony. Given an insufficiency of human and material resources at home to commit to its vast possessions overseas, Portuguese crown policy in Brazil was largely aimed at collecting revenues from exports, thereby minimizing intrusive legislation and excessive interference with local markets. The potential for animosity and competition between colonial elites and metropolitan interests—often cited as one of the principal causes of the wars of independence in Spanish America—was consequently reduced. A second distinguishing feature was the presence in Brazil of King Dom Joao and the Braganza royal family, exiled in the colony since the

Napoleonic invasion of Portugal in 1807. During this crisis, the king took a series of measures aimed at reducing the colony's ties with Portugal. After the French were driven from Portugal the following year and the king returned to Lisbon, Dom Pedro, Prince Regent, stayed behind. When Brazil eventually declared its independence in the 1820s, it did so as an independent monarchy under Dom Pedro.

In the Caribbean basin, a vast region once monopolized by Spain, the eighteenth century brought important changes as other European powers, chiefly the Dutch, English, and French, profiting from Spain's decline, solidified their presence, which dated back to the 1620s. A century after this process began, Spain could claim only Cuba, Puerto Rico, the eastern part of Hispaniola (today's Dominican Republic), and Trinidad. The British and, to a lesser degree, the French controlled much of the Lesser Antilles and a significant area of the Greater Antilles— namely, British Jamaica and French Saint Domingue (today's Haiti). Meanwhile, the Dutch settled in Curaçao and Aruba.

Following the end of the War of the Spanish Succession (1700–1713), during which Spain ceded to Britain rights to the slave trade in its colonies, those who controlled the production of and trade in sugar throughout the Caribbean enjoyed a long period of peace and prosperity. With almost exclusive reliance on African slaves for most aspects of sugar-cane cultivation and production, the sugar industry thrived and was inextricably linked to the institution of slavery. While Caribbean sugar accounted for 80–90 percent of Western Europe's consumption, slaves made up some 90 percent of the population of the islands that produced it. Though unprecedented in history, this slave-dependent plantation system became the dominant agricultural model in the entire region. It also established the basis for a monoculture economy throughout much of the Caribbean, a precedent that would have dire economic consequences for the future prosperity of the region. In the Spanish Caribbean, on the other hand, a sugar-based system flourished only in Cuba.

The independence movements in Spanish America at the close of the eighteenth and beginning of the nineteenth century ended three centuries of colonial rule. The length of this period notwithstanding, Spanish control coexisted with widespread dissatisfaction, which manifested itself in a variety of ways. Throughout the eighteenth century, the region was never without turmoil. A series of revolts against Spain broke out in Paraguay in the 1730s, Perú in the 1740s, Caracas in the 1750s, and Perú and Bogotá in the 1780s. For much of the colonial period, the creole and *mestizo* elites resented a social order that discriminated against them. Economic reforms enacted by Carlos III, which included lowering trade barriers, inspired the colonists' sense of economic freedom. Unfair taxes, mistreatment of local populations, and complaints against corrupt officials all found outlets in various uprisings against Spanish authorities. In 1780, in one of the more dramatic examples, a revolt protesting the mistreatment of Indians in the mines started in Cuzco and spread, developing a poignant political agenda along the way. Led by José Gabriel Condorcanqui, claiming to be a direct descendant of the last of the Inca and taking the name of Tupac Amaru II, the movement added to the serious economic grievances of the exploited Indian populations the desire to expel the Spanish and restore legitimate Inca rule. It took fifteen thousand Spanish troops to suppress the rebellion.

External factors also contributed to the wars of independence. The United States and French revolutions, the latter in particular, had loud echoes throughout the Americas. The slaves in Haiti rose in open rebellion using the words of the French Revolution and in 1804 declared independence. Spanish-American colonists reacted to the events in Europe in at least two important ways. Ideologically, the creole elites sympathized with the revolutionary call for liberty, equality, and fraternity; independence

from Spain would help redress centuries of discrimination against the American-born. Yet it was Napoleon's occupation of Spain in 1807, and the forced exile of the Spanish king to France, that offered the colonists the ideal opportunity to take up arms against Spain.

Rebellions broke out simultaneously in various places; by 1810 La Plata, La Paz, Santiago, Quito, Bogotá, Caracas, and Querétaro, among others, had witnessed some sort of uprising. The momentum continued to grow, and a series of charismatic leaders emerged to command the colonists' cause: Simón Bolívar, Miguel Hidalgo, José Morelos, Antonio Nariño, Bernado O'Higgins, and José de San Martín. By 1830, the wars were over and sixteen new nations sprung up to fill the political void left by Spain.

The long years of war had devastated the economy, ruined the administrative apparatus, interrupted communications, and caused great hardship. The task of rebuilding and filling the void left by Spain fell largely into the hands of the leaders of the independence movements, many of whom failed miserably at the task. In fact, most newly independent republics struggled for at least another generation settling tensions and conflicts generated around political questions, all of which delayed even further, with the exception of the abolition of slavery in all the independent republics, the fulfillment of the hopes for freedom and expectations of equality that were the ideological underpinnings of the wars of independence.

CLARA ESTOW

Bibliography

Andrien, Kenneth J., and Lyman L. Johnson, eds. *The Political Economy of Spanish America in the Age of Revolution.* Albuquerque: University of New Mexico Press, 1994.

Bukholder, Mark A., ed. *Administrators of Empire.* Aldershot: Ashgate, 1998.

Burkholder, Mark A., and Lyman L. Johnson. *Colonial Latin America.* 3rd. ed. New York: Oxford University Press, 1998.

Halperin Dhongi, Tulio. *Reforma y disolución de los imperios ibéricos, 1750–1850.* Madrid: Alianza Editorial, 1985.

Rodríguez, O. and E. Jaime. *The Independence in Spanish America.* Cambridge: Cambridge University Press, 1998.

Rogozinski, Jan. *A Brief History of the Caribbean.* New York: Meridian, 1992.

LAVATER, JOHANN CASPAR 1741–1801

Swiss theologian and physiognomist

Johann Caspar Lavater, a Swiss theologian and physiognomist, was born on November 15, 1741 in Zurich, to Regula (Escher) Lavater and Hans Heinrich Lavater, a physician. Throughout his life, the dual concerns of science and religion would be central in forming his thought and guiding his public career.

From early childhood, Lavater had Swiss Protestantism ingrained in his thinking by his parents. This led to Lavater's early conviction that he was touched by god and therefore understood the secrets of life, a notion that would inform the religious fervor and scientific interest of his adult life. He entered the Collegium Carolinium in 1756, at a moment of ferment in Swiss culture. He received a classically based education, and was introduced

to the work of such writers as Dante Alighieri, Homer, and John Milton. In particular, two professors at the university, Johann Jakob Bodmer and Johann Jakob Breitlinger, influenced him heavily; aside from introducing Lavater to the classical literary canon, they instilled in him a lifelong interest in modern ideas ranging from the "sublime" and bourgeois liberalism to the Sturm und Drang (storm and stress) movement and Swiss nationalism.

More specifically, Lavater's education was one that forwarded ideas regarding religion that deviated from traditional Protestant orthodoxy. Deriving from John Locke and Gottfried Wilhelm Leibniz, the notion of "natural religion" was one that was central to contemporary theological debates throughout Europe. Basically, this notion entailed the merging of a traditional belief in god's creation of the universe with a strong sense of empirical observation. In this sense, modern Enlightenment conceptions of reason and scientism were merged with faith in the metaphysical.

Following his graduation from the university, Lavater was ordained a pastor in 1762. This was also an important year in Lavater's political development. He and a group of friends, among them the future artist Henry Fuseli, drafted a protest tract titled "The Unjust Bailiff, or The Complaint of a Patriot". This was Lavater's first published writing and his first venture into public political debate. It was drafted as an anonymous protest against one Felix Glebel, then the bailiff of Zurich. Lavater and friends alleged that Glebel, a powerful man in Zurich, was extorting money out of and harassing the city's poorer citizens. The text contained moralizing arguments that appealed to a sense of justice and national pride in the ruling class of Zurich. Lavater eventually took responsibility for the tract, and was punished in court. However, he was successful in having Glebel removed and thus made a name for himself throughout the city.

In the years following this episode, Lavater traveled around Europe, especially Germany, and embarked on his famous intellectual career. During his travels he met and began correspondences with the most famous intellectuals of the day, including Johann Wolfgang von Goethe and Jean-Jacques Rousseau. His correspondences often revolved around questions of religion, morality, health, and science. At one point, Lavater is said to have attempted to convert the Jewish philosopher Moses Mendelssohn to Christianity by arguing for the superiority of that religion. However, Lavater's uncompromising positions on questions of religion and science often made him the target of critical attacks from the likes of Goethe, Georg Christopher Lichtenberg, and eventually the German philosophers G. W. F. Hegel and Immanual Kant.

It was during the 1760s and 1770s that Lavater wrote his most well-known books. After marrying Anna Schinz on June 3, 1766 (with whom he later he had eight children), Lavater published *Swiss Songs* in 1767. This text highlights Lavater's aforementioned love of an independent Swiss cultural tradition and proclaims the virtues of famous Swiss citizens. In 1768, he began writing *Views of Eternity*, which he would publish in a series of volumes between 1768 and 1778 and which would become one of his more noted writings. In it, Lavater conducts a series of correspondences with Johann Zimmerman, a physician and friend. The correspondence covers a wide range of topics relating to physical and moral well being. Indeed, it is this insistence on the correspondence between the physical and the moral, the body and the soul that characterizes Lavater's conceptions of religion and science.

This connection would be explored in greater depth with his two most famous books, *Journal of a Self-Observer*, originally published in 1771, and *Physiognomical Fragments to Promote the Knowledge and Love of Mankind*, originally published in 1775. *Journal of a Self-Observer* is an intensely introspective diary of Lavater's day-to-day existence. In it, he painstakingly details his state of mind in seemingly trivial situations. Throughout, the commonplace is endowed with a sense of metaphysical significance, as if each interaction were a manifestation of a celestial order. Lavater continually critiques himself and others for lapses

G. B. Bosio, *Johann Kasper Lavater*. Reprinted courtesy of the Mary Evans Picture Library.

in religious and moral focus, and offers suggestions for greater connection with god through one's daily actions and thoughts.

Physiognomic Fragments (or, *Essays on Physiognomy*) is undoubtedly Lavater's most well known and important writing. With this text, he attempts to systematize his perception of a necessary correlation between the appearances of nature and metaphysical truth. Lavater posits physiognomy, a "science" which would prove influential for many aspects of nineteenth century European culture, as the science of determining the relative connection between the exterior appearance of human beings and their interior moral state. Focusing on facial features, Lavater's physiognomy attempted to categorize on a large scale all possible character types based on differences in the proportion and appearance of the face. By so doing it was believed that one could gauge the moral character and internal abilities of any other individual human being. Facial features were indicative of morality for Lavater because of his belief that god intentionally created humanity in such a way. Thus, facial features become a divine language that one could read through empirical observation. While many of his contemporaries, especially Lichtenberg and Kant, found physiognomy unsystematic, unreliable, and irrational, it nevertheless would prove influential on art, literature, criminology, medicine, and science throughout the nineteenth century.

While writing his famous texts, Lavater continued to travel and preach at churches throughout Switzerland. His fame grew, but his belief in a theological and physiognomic determinism never endeared him with the advanced guard of the intelligentsia during the Enlightenment, which steadfastly insisted upon political change based on the equality and unlimited potential of human beings. This difference of opinion on the question of human potential has caused many historians to label Lavater a political reactionary. He nonetheless remained vocal about his political views, especially the sovereignty of Switzerland. This led to an altercation with occupying French soldiers in Zurich in 1799, during which Lavater sustained a gunshot wound. His health never fully recovered, and he died on January 2, 1801.

PETE MAURO BIO

Biography

Born November 15, 1741 in Zurich, to Regula (Escher) Lavater and Hans Heinrich Lavater. Enters the Collegium Carolinium in 1756. Graduated from college and ordained a pastor in 1762. Drafted his first published work, "The Unjust Bailiff, or The Complaint of a Patriot." Married Anna Schinz June 3, 1766. Published *Swiss Songs* in 1767. Published *Journal of a Self-Observer* in 1771. Published *Physiognomical Fragments to Promote the Knowledge and Love of Mankind* in 1775. Died on January 2, 1801.

Selected Works

Aphorisms on Man. Translated by Henry Fuseli. 1789.
Essays on Physiognomy: Calculated to Extend the Knowledge and the Love of Mankind. Translated by C. Moore. 1797.
Journal of a Self-Observer. Translated by Peter Will. 1795.

Bibliography

Graham, John. *Lavater's Essays on Physiognomy: A Study in the History of Ideas.* Bern: Land, 1979.
Heisch, P. I. *Memoirs of Johann Caspar Lavater.* London: Samuel Bagster and Sons, 1842.
Huppert, Otto. *Humanismus und Christentum: Goethe und Lavater; die Tragik einer Freindscaft.* Stuttgart: Loepthien, 1949.
Jaton, Anne Marie. *Lavater.* Lucerne: Rene Coeckelberghs, 1988.
Moffitt, John F. "The Poet and the Painter: J. H. W. Tischbein's 'Perfect Portrait' of 'Goethe in the Campagna' (1786–7)," *Art Bulletin* 65, no. 3 (1983): 440–55.
Schmidlin, Johannes. *Scheizerlieder mit Melodieen.* Zurich: D. Burkli, 1796.
Stafford, Barbara. " 'Peculiar Marks': Lavater and the Countenance of Blemished Thought," *Art Journal* 46, no. 3 (1987): 185–92.
Tytler, Graeme. *Physiognomy in the European Novel: Faces and Fortunes.* Princeton, N.J.: Princeton University Press, 1982.

LAWRENCE, THOMAS 1769–1830

English painter

Sir Thomas Lawrence was probably the last great portrait painter in the eighteenth-century classical tradition. In many other respects Lawrence was a Romantic, both as a man and as an artist. His early career has been described in terms of the Romantic view of the artist as child prodigy; as a boy in the mid 1770s, Lawrence drew pencil portraits of the travelers who stayed at his father's inn.

Even as a young man, Lawrence was supremely confident of his own talent, and his move to London in 1787 was determined by his ambition to follow in the footsteps of the eminent portraitist Joshua Reynolds. Lawrence's earliest oil paintings show a dependence on Reynolds in the way the sitter is presented and, to some extent, in the lighting. Lawrence's instant success in London was the result of his particularly expressive treatment of his sitters, achieved with dramatic lighting which was reminiscent of the theater.

Lawrence's use of light was sometimes criticized because it was regarded by some as inappropriate for many of his conventional sitters, but this technique proved popular with the exhibition-going public. This reflected the artist's own sense of the theatrical; he was almost acting the role of artist as he painted his subject. Therefore it is not surprising that many of his sitters seem to also be playing a part in a play, whether that of an exotic Byronic hero (*John Lord Mountstuart, MP*, 1794) or of a young Regency dandy with brooding forthright gaze (*Arthur Atherley, MP*, c. 1791–92).

Lawrence, in true Romantic fashion, has been described as a man divided. He was hard working but had no business sense. He was often in debt because he spent too much and was always prepared to lend to others. He regretted being unable to pursue his dream of painting in the Grand Style, but managed to imbue his portraits with an emotive element that expressed much of the same sensibility as traditional history painting. In 1797 he exhibited a vast work at the Royal Academy entitled *Satan Summoning his Legions* (1796–97). Lawrence considered this his masterpiece but it was badly received by the critics and public.

Lawrence also suffered in his personal life, when he fell passionately in love with the daughters of his friend, the actress Sarah Siddons. Her eldest daughter, Sally, rejected the artist. Lawrence's attachment to her second daughter, Maria, was ended when the girl died of consumption in 1798. Sally later declared that she did not think she had ever loved anyone as she had him but she said, "I seriously believe that he is, at times, quite mad."

The Prince Regent's patronage of Lawrence, which lasted from 1814 until 1830, brought the artist even greater acclaim. He was asked by the prince to paint the portraits of the allied heads of state and military leaders who had helped defeat Napoleon Bonaparte. Each of these paintings portray the subject as if on the battlefield; plumes of black smoke contrast with a reddish glow, suggesting that the heat of battle has not yet abated. The subjects hold center stage in splendid dress uniforms covered in awards and medals.

If Lawrence had come to epitomize the notion of the regency hero in both style and personality then his sudden death and public funeral helped to promote the notion of the artist as

Romantic martyr. Although he was deeply in debt, Lawrence's funeral was a national event (in honor of his status as president of the Royal Academy), and extensive details of it, including descriptions of the coffin and funeral coach, were printed in the national papers. His pall bearers included several peers, and there were sixty-four carriages in attendance; he was buried alongside French war heroes in St. Paul's Cathedral.

CHERRY SANDOVER

See also **Art; Britain: Cultural Survey; British Romanticism: Approaches and Interpretations; Byron, Lord George Noel Gordon; Dandy; Genius; Géricault, Jean Louìs André Théodore; History Painting: Britain; Individualism; Portraiture: Britain; Siddons, Sarah; Southey, Robert**

Biography

Born April 13, 1769 in Bristol. Father was an innkeeper who, in 1773, moved his family to Devizes where he was employed as landlord of a coach inn: Lawrence began sketching pencil portraits of guests at about the age of five: received little formal education. In 1783 he moved to Bath and charged three guineas a head for portraits; received instruction from William Hoare, portrait painter, in techniques of painting in pastel and oil. In 1787, admitted as a student at the Royal Academy Schools in London, but only spent a few months in attendance. Had six works accepted for the Royal Academy Exhibition; 1788. Summoned to Windsor to paint Queen Charlotte, 1789. Elected Associate of the Royal Academy, 1791. Elected painter to the Dilettanti Society and painter-in-ordinary to the King, 1792. Elected full academician, at the earliest permitted age, 1794. Love affairs with the Siddons sisters and financial problems adversely affected the quality of his work, 1797–1807, in 1807, William Etty was pupil for one unsatisfactory year. Knighted in anticipation of a visit to Europe to continue with the series of portraits of the allied sovereigns and military leaders, 1815. Gave evidence to the Committee of the House of Commons in favor of buying the Elgin marbles for the nation, 1816. In Europe to continue the series of portraits of allied leaders, commissioned to paint Pope Pius VII, 1818. Elected president of the Royal Academy on the death of Benjamin West, 1820. Received Gericault as a visiting artist to London, 1820. Awarded Chevalier de l'Ordre Royal de la Legion d'Honneur by Charles, 1825. Lawrence's death on January 7, 1830 in London was attributed to "ossification of the heart."

Selected Works

John Lord Mountstuart, MP, 1794. Oil on canvas, 238.8 × 147.3 cm. Private collection.
Arthur Atherley, MP, c. 1791–92. Oil on canvas, 125.8 × 100.3 cm. Los Angeles County Museum of Art, William Randolph Hearst Collection.
Sarah Siddons, 1804. Oil on canvas, 254 × 148.6 cm. Tate Gallery, London.
Karl Philipp, Prince Schwarzenberg, 1818–19. Oil on canvas, 313.7 × 241.9 cm. Her Majesty the Queen, Windsor Castle.
George IV, 1822. Oil on canvas, 270.5 × 179.1 cm. Wallace Collection, London.
Charles William Lambton, 1825. Oil on canvas, 137.2 × 111.8 cm. The Lord Lambton.

Bibliography

Farington, Joseph. *Diary 1805–1821*. Edited by Kathryn Cave. New Haven, Conn.: Yale University Press, 1982.
———. *Collection for a King: Old Masters from the Dulwich Picture Gallery*. Edited by Giles Waterfield. London: Dulwich Picture Gallery, 1994.
Garlick, Kenneth. *Sir Thomas Lawrence*. Oxford: Phaidon, 1989.
Valentine, Helen. *From Reynolds to Lawrence: The First Sixty Years of the Royal Academy of Arts and its Collections*. Edited by MaryAnne Stevens. London: Royal Academy of Arts, 1991.
Vaughan, William. *Romantic Art*. London: Thames and Hudson, 1978.

LEAVES OF GRASS

Edition by Walt Whitman

Walt Whitman's first volume of poetry, the 1855 edition of *Leaves of Grass*, stands out as one of the most remarkable and revolutionary literary achievements of the nineteenth century. A homemade-looking volume of only ninety-five pages, published in Brooklyn by an out-of-work journalist, *Leaves of Grass* nevertheless launched Whitman's career and dramatically redefined American poetry at the end of the Romantic era. Many scholars have seen *Leaves of Grass* in the context of American literary consciousness; Whitman published the work on the Fourth of July, and he conceived himself specifically as a new American poet on the grand nationalistic model provided by Ralph Waldo Emerson. However, *Leaves of Grass* also has many features of a Romantic masterwork: a sprawling and sublime scale, a mystical vision of nature, a sustained passionate intensity, and a heroic conception of the poet. Whitman's achievement, in fact, was in his revitalizing and recasting of many of the literary, philosophical, and political ideals of the Romantic era in a new and dynamic American form.

Leaves of Grass was to go through many editions and revisions, but the 1855 version is arguably the most Romantic, in large part because of Whitman's profound absorption of Emerson's brand of transcendentalism. Whitman had heard Emerson lecture on his ideal of American poetry as early as 1842; by the early 1850s, Whitman experienced a mystical awakening inspired by Emerson's philosophy. The characteristic mixture of memoir and dream-vision in the first edition of *Leaves of Grass* owes much to transcendentalist notions of the divine intimations of nature and the powerful spiritual prerogatives of the individual, in this case the poet. The title *Leaves of Grass* suggests the transcendentalist implication of nature (here common and ubiquitous nature, as represented by grass) as a microcosm and symbol of divinity.

In this respect, the most important of the twelve untitled poems that make up the 1855 edition is the first one, later (in 1881) called "Song of Myself." In this poem of more than thirteen hundred lines, often regarded as the poet's finest, Whitman celebrates a transcendentalist self that, though based on autobiography, includes all of humanity in its democratic diversity, as well as nature. Whitman adopts multiple points of view with a unifying sympathy; he glorifies individualism in the context of a profound and mystical collective, represented in the abstract by American democracy and in the concrete by Whitman's local world of Long Island, Brooklyn, and Manhattan. Whitman matches his acceptance of all social levels with his valorization (which many of his contemporaries found scandalous) of the body as well as the soul. Such themes strongly define other parts of the collection, particularly the poems later titled "The Sleepers" and "I Sing the Body Electric." The poem afterward known as "There Was a Child Went Forth" touches on the Romantic theme of ecstatic childhood vision and is likewise one of Whitman's best. Other poems in the 1855 edition, however, have been regarded as less successful, and Whitman eliminated or else shifted some of these to minor positions in his subsequent revisions.

It is important, in fact, to understand *Leaves of Grass* not as a single static volume but as a work in progress throughout Whitman's career, his further expansions and additions broaden his poetic range and his vision of *Leaves of Grass* as his central work. In this respect, the second and third editions are especially important. The 1856 edition, as well as featuring Emerson's adulatory letter to Whitman, added twenty new poems, notably "Crossing Brooklyn Ferry." The 1860 edition included darker poems that reflected the inevitability of change and death, such as "Out of the Cradle Endlessly Rocking" and "As I Ebb'd with the Ocean of Life." The 1860 edition also incorporated his homoerotic "Calamus" poems as well as his heterosexual "Children of Adam" poems: the latter contributed to Whitman's reputation as an indecent poet. Subsequent editions of *Leaves of Grass* appeared in 1867, 1871, 1881–82, 1888, 1889, and 1891–92. Many of these were mere rearrangements of poems, although some of them incorporated material from Whitman's other books, notably *Drum-Taps*, his 1865 collection of Civil War poems, and *Passage to India*, his 1871 orientalized epic of poetic prophecy.

It was in the 1855 edition of *Leaves of Grass* however, that Whitman initially and in some ways most profoundly forged his revolutionary poetics: his free and expansive lines, democratically inclusive catalogues, vernacular rhythms, and tones ranging from sublime public oratory to startling personal intimacy. In the first edition he powerfully expressed many of his most important themes; *Leaves of Grass* was daring in its confidence in democracy, its celebration of the body, its faith in nature, its fascination with common (often working-class) life, and its vision of a comprehensive and divine self. Some of these themes recalled the idealistic philosophy and individualistic literature of the Romantic era, as translated and interpreted through American transcendentalism, but in his 1855 edition, Whitman put a strong personal and American stamp on such ideas. He dramatized Emerson's notion that "small and mean things serve just as well as great symbols" and created in his "leaves of grass" one of the most characteristic and enduring of Romantic metaphors.

PAUL FISHER

See also **American Romanticism: Its Literary Legacy; Art and Politics; Artist, Changing Conceptions of the, Emerson, Ralph Waldo;** *Essays: First Series;* **Gay Approaches to the Romantic Period; Transcendentalism; United States: Cultural Survey; Whitman, Walt**

Text

Leaves of Grass: Reproduced from the First (1855) Edition. Edited by Clifton Joseph Furness. New York: Columbia University Press, 1939.

Leaves of Grass: A Comprehensive Reader's Edition. Edited by Harold Blodgett and Sculley Bradley. New York: New York University press, 1965.

Bibliography

Allen, Gay Wilson. *New Walt Whitman Handbook.* New York: New York University Press, 1975.

Crawley, Thomas Edward. *The Structure of Leaves of Grass.* Austin: University of Texas Press, 1970.

Hollis, C. Carroll. *Language and Style in Leaves of Grass.* Baton Rouge: Louisiana State University Press, 1983.

Killingworth, M. Jimmie. *The Growth of Leaves of Grass: The Organic Tradition in Whitman Studies.* Columbia, S.C.: Camden House, 1993.

Miller, Edwin Haviland. *Walt Whitman's "Song of Myself": A Mosaic of Interpretations.* Iowa City: University of Iowa Press, 1989.

Miller, James E., Jr. *A Critical Guide to Leaves of Grass.* Chicago: University of Chicago Press, 1957.

Moon, Michael. *Disseminating Whitman: Revision and Corporeality in Leaves of Grass.* Cambridge, Mass.: Harvard University Press, 1991.

Stovall, Floyd. *The Foreground of Leaves of Grass.* Charlottesville: University of Virginia Press, 1974.

LEBENSOHN, ABRAHAM (DOV BER BEN CHAYYIM) 1789–1878 AND MICAH JOSEPH 1828–1852

Lithuanian Jewish writers

Abraham Lebensohn was a Litvak (a Lithuanhian Jew) and was born in the Judaic center of learning, Vilna, in the Russian Pale of Settlement. Married shortly after his bar mitzva, he moved to his wife's home in nearby Michailishok. He was known familiarly as the "Mikhailishker," and his *nom de plume* Adam ha Cohen is an acronym for "Abraham ben Dov Mikhailishker." ("Lebensohn" is merely the German translation for ben Chayyim"—that is, "son of life)." Lebensohn's names, then, signified his membership in the generation that saw its Jewish tradition become Europeanized.

This transformation was as true of his literature as it was of his name. Like many *Haskalah* literary figures, Abraham Lebensohn began his career as a rabbi trained in Talmud. He developed an interest in grammar early on, and began to write Hebrew poems.

This led him to write what is termed "neo-Hebrew" literature; that is, literature written in the formerly sacred tongue Hebrew (*leshon ha kodesh*), but employing more colloquial diction and putting to novel use the literary forms of the gentile nations of Europe. This was not the first use of Hebrew for literary ends, but it marked a sharp departure from the received culture of askenazic Judaism in east central Europe.

His earliest poetic work was the "Shir chabibim" ("Song of the Beloved Ones") in 1822, a poem in honor of the marriage of a powerful local nobleman. It was his 1825 elegy on the death of Rabbi Saul Katzenellenbogen, however, that established his reputation as a Hebrew poet. These works, and in particular the collection of his Hebrew poems *Shirei sefat kodesh* (*Songs in the Holy Tongue*), established him as a leader in the Lithuanian Haskalah, though he also wrote biblical commentaries (from 1848 to 1853) and taught, from 1848 to 1867, in the rabbinical school at Wilna. There, too, he wrote his most famous work, the allegorical drama *Emet ve-Emunah* (*Truth and Belief*). In this work, protagonists such as "Wisdom" and "Reason" fight opponents including "Ignorance" and Superstition." Lebensohn's program sought to align Judaism and modern high culture, not to abandon Judaism. Therefore, his final religious works in prose did not mark an abandonment of his his program as a *maskil*, that is, an advocate of Jewish Enlightenment.

Abraham Lebensohn influenced the writing of his son, who developed his father's ideas and practices in a tragically brief career. Micah Joseph Lebensohn, known as "Mikaele" in the Yiddish diminutive, poetically surpassed his father's work in a life cut short by consumption. Since rabbinic traditionalism in Eastern Europe frowned upon delight in natural beauty, Micah's poetry was both subversive and innovative in its loving description of nature. It is often charged with his consciousness of his approaching death. At the same time, however, he was introducing a Jewish Romanticism which also sought inspiration in the brightest periods of the Jewish past in agrarian Judaea or the Spanish Golden Age of the tenth through the thirteenth centuries. In a way that illustrates how one emerging literature inspires another, Micah's first book of poetry, *Harisut Troya* (*The Destruction of Troy*) was a poetic translation into neo-Hebrew of Johann Christoph Friedrich von Schiller's previous poetic translation into German. In his *Shirei bat Tsiyyon* (*Songs of a Daughter of Zion*) Micah went further and wrote Jewish epic poetry with naturalistic description. He thus prepared the way for the work of Abraham Mapu (1808–67) who, with his first novel *Ahavat Zion* (*Love of Zion*, 1853), wrote the first modern Hebrew novel.

ROBERT SOUTHARD

Bibliography

Lebensohn, Adam ha-Cohen. *Emet v'Emunah*. Jerusalem, 1994.
———. *Shir S'Fat kodesh*. 1870.
Lenensohn, Micah Yosef. *Shirim*. Berlin, 1924.
Waxman, Meyer. *A History of Jewish Literature*. Vol. 3. New York, 1960.
Zinberg, Israel. *A History of Jewish Literature*. Vol. 11. Cincinnati, 1978.

LELEWEL, JOACHIM 1786–1861

Polish historian, politician

Joachim Lelewel is the preeminent representative of Polish Romantic historical writing. Nevertheless, his education and early academic career at the University of Vilna were heavily influenced by the ideals of the Enlightenment. His first writings addressed some of the most popular themes of Enlightenment historiography: the origins of nations and universal history, especially the history of ancient India, Rome and Greece. Lelewel was also fascinated with Northern mythology and epic poetry. His early book on the *Edda* served as an inspiration for Maurycy Mochnacki's studies in this field. Lelewel also wrote about idolatry, which he identified as the religion of the pagan Slavs. The most significant achievement of the historian's early career lay in the *Historyka* (*Historica*, 1815) which was the first Polish book dedicated to the theoretical and methodological problems of history. Furthermore, a critical review on Nikolai Karamzin's *Istorija Gosudarstvo Rossiskiego* (*History of the Russian State*), brought him to the attention of various Russian scholarly societies.

Lelewel's charisma made him popular among the younger generations. Adam Mickiewicz dedicated his poem "Dziejepis" ("History") to the scholar on the occasion of his inaugural lecture of 1821. Three years later, Lelewel was accused of contributing to the unrest at the university in Vilna and was ordered to return to Warsaw. There he engaged in fervent political activity, which culminated in his participation in the uprising of 1830–31. After the failure of the uprising he emigrated to France, and after his expulsion from Paris in 1833 he settled in Belgium. He remained involved in political life and became the spiritual leader of the democratic wing of the Polish emigration.

Lelewel's historical activities are characterized by a blend of scholarship and nationalism. He argued that originality is to be found in the primitive but democratic communities of the early Slavs. His theory of dual development contrasts the freer conditions of the Slavs and Scandinavians with those of the Southern peoples whose society developed on the foundations of the despotic Roman Empire. He endowed the prehistoric Slavic communities, especially early Polish society, with the virtues of freedom, citizenship, and responsibility. Lelewel believed that foreign intervention, Christianity, and feudalism ended this equality and, as a consequence, social inequalities arose. But, at the same time he also claimed that some values of the early community survived throughout Polish history, especially in the democratic institutions of the gentry. He saw the role of the Diet as the embodiment of the nation and the manifestation of the qualities of the early, idyllic society.

Lelewel identifies the golden age of Polish history as the years between 1333 and 1588, and more specifically, in the Polish-Lithuanian commonwealth. In his view, this was the time when gentry democracy reached its peak, when freedom and citizenship were most fully developed. Lelewel's verdict about Poland's glorious past sought to boost the national ego and intended to provide a consolation for Poland's tragic fate: at the end of the eighteenth century, Russia, Prussia, and Austria partitioned Poland and as a consequence, the country disappeared from the map of Europe. As a devoted republican, Lelewel did not agree with those scholars who claimed that the principle of unanimity in the Diet contributed to the anarchy and subsequently the failure of the Polish state. Rather, he tended to ascribe the misfortunes of the country to the abuse of a basically healthy system and to the conquering appetite of neighboring powers. At the beginning of his emigration Lelewel hoped to gain the assistance of European powers in Poland's restoration. After his disappointment with traditional diplomacy, he propagated the belief that the Poles should rely on their own powers.

Lelewel's democratic conviction manifested itself in his departure from the traditional equation of the nation with those who enjoyed political rights, (i.e., the ruling classes). He repeatedly stressed the necessity of social reform and the extension of political rights to the masses. He envisioned those changes not as novel developments, but as a return to the ancient freedom of early Polish society. These democratic principles were also evident in Lelewel's historical works. In keeping with a general trend of Romantic historiography, he wanted to write the history of the common, unprivileged people who had been ignored by traditional historical accounts and scholarship. According to the scholarly demands of his age, Lelewel also stressed the importance of archival research and the use of original sources in history writing.

In the 1830s, Lelewel was influenced by the messianist world view of Adam Mickiewicz. In a Romantic fashion, he understood history as a resurrection and argued that Poland sacrificed itself for the cause of humanity, but as Christ, will one day resurrect from its grave. Interestingly, Lelewel's Romantic-nationalist narrative complemented his meticulous and serious research in the field of auxiliary sciences. After the revolutions of 1848, Lelewel retired from political life and devoted his time to the study of numismatics and geography. His five-volume *Géographie du moyen Age* (*Geography of the Middle Ages*), was an outstanding achievement.

MONIKA BAÁR

Biography

Born in Warsaw, March 22, 1786. Studied at the University of Vilna as a candidate for a career in teaching 1804–8; university lecturer in Vilna 1815–18; professor of bibliography and curator of university library, Warsaw 1818–21. Professor of universal history, Vilna 1821–24. Leading politician in the uprisings of 1830–31 and minister of education in a short-lived revolutionary government. Émigré to France 1831–33, to Brussels 1833–61; active in the democratic wing of the Polish émigré organizations. After 1848, retired from politics. Died in Paris, May 24, 1861.

Selected Works

Collections
Listy emigracyjne Joachima Lelewela. 5 vols. Edited by Helena Wieckowska. 1948–56.
Dzieła. 5 vols. Edited by Marian Serejski et al. 1957–69.

Historical Works
Dzieje Polski potocznym sposobem opowiedziane. 1828.
Historyczna Paralela Hiszpanii z Polską w XVI, XVII, XVIII wieku. 1831.
Panowanie Stanisława Augusta. 1831. Final version 1888, as *Geschichte Polens unter Stanislaus August.*
Historia Polski do końca panowania Stefana Batorego. 1841.
Uwagi nad dziejami Polski i ludu jej. 1846. Later edition as *Histoire de Pologne* [History of Poland], 1844.
Géographie du moyen age. 5 vols. 1850–57.

Bibliography

Julkowska, Violeta. *Retorika w narracji historycznej Joachima Lelewela.* Poznań: Instytut Historii VAM, 1998.
Pajewski, Janusz, ed. *Z badań nad pracami historycznimi Joachima Lelewela.* Poznań: Uniwersytet im. Adama Mickiewicza, 1962.
Serejski, Marian Henryk. *Koncepcja historii powszechnej Joachima Lelewela.* Warsaw: Państwowe Wydawnictwo Naukowe, 1958.
Skurnewicz, Joan S. *Romantic Nationalism and Liberalism: Joachim Lelewel and the Polish National Idea.* New York: Columbia University Press, 1987.

LENAU, NIKOLAUS 1802–1850

Austrian poet

Nikolaus Lenau (pseudonym of Franz Nikolaus Niembsch) is often taken as a melancholic representative of late Romanticism. Of all early-nineteenth-century German authors, he was especially and rigorously committed to the concept of self-expression. He expressed himself most vibrantly through verse, with the result that even his dramas, most notably *Faust* (1835), are predominantly lyrical. His work inspired compositions by Hector Berlioz, Franz Liszt, and Richard Strauss.

Lenau's early verse is typical of the late eighteenth century, with its preponderance of conceits and tendency toward sentimental posing. Where he struck a new note was in his many depictions of the world of the deracinated gypsies of the Hungarian steppes, and (having crossed the Atlantic in pursuit of authentic experience) in his sympathetic portrayal of the indigenous peoples of North America. In this respect he was at once profoundly Romantic, in his Rousseauesque admiration of the primitive but natural human being, but also modern, in his pragmatic approach to the causes of poverty and to the deleterious effects of colonialism. Lenau's gypsies and Native Americans are not the weakly-sketched or stereotypical constructs one encounters in Clemens Brentano, Joseph von Eichendorff, or Novalis; they are the plausible products of close observation. This clear-sighted authenticity, combined with a powerful poetic flair, made Lenau appealing to a public that, having been brought up on fables and romances, was beginning to reject artifice and contrived fantasy. Lenau could write about unknown, remote, and exotic worlds from personal knowledge. An intense musicality (Lenau was an accomplished violinist and composer) was another asset that helped to assure his success as a poet.

Unlike his predecessors, Lenau did not write novels or novellas. Apart from his poetry, he completed several verse epics, *Savonarola* (1837), *Johannes Zizka* (1838–42), *Die Albigenser* (*The Albigensians*, 1842), and the fragmentary *Don Juan* which, like his *Faust*, was to have been a "dramatic poem." These longer works contain strong elements of social criticism, and several of them revolve around revolutionary subjects. Lenau is best contextualized as being on the fringes of Romanticism, pointing forward not so much toward the Biedermeier movement as to the politically aware Junges Deutschland group. Yet, as with Heinrich Heine, his personal political stance remains controversial, and his importance extends far beyond his promulgation of progressive ideas.

Lenau's *Faust* was written as a direct challenge to what many perceived to be Johann Wolfgang von Goethe's restrictive monopoly of the theme, and, more particularly, to its ethos of enlightened optimism, as implied in Goethe's version. Like many other Romantic Fausts, Lenau's hero fails to achieve the synthesis of spiritual endeavor and sensual yearning that is the apparent outcome of Goethe's exemplary work. In twenty-four discontinuous episodes (some dramatic, some narrative), Faust, perpetually torn between pantheism and nihilism, remains frustrated by a shallow world no less than by his ever-cynical companion. The only escape from isolation appears to be a complete retreat into the inner recesses of the imagination, where a mere dream of suicide is enough to ensure that the devil obtains his reward.

The epic poems *Savonarola* and *Die Albigenser*, which deal with the dissident friar Savonarola and the heretical Albigensians, enabled Lenau to develop the anticlerical themes that were glimpsed in several earlier poems, and in *Faust*, into a veritable litany of grievances against the Roman Catholic church. Savonarola's life is chronicled in terms of the bitter indictments of Papal frivolity which he delivered from the pulpit to his eventual death at the stake. Visions of the plague, monstrous prophesies of desolation, and the turbulent vices of both the Borgia clan and Lorenzo d'Medici give this epic work an apocalyptic dimension. *Die Albigenser* ends with a celebration of the revolutionary spirit that proceeded to gain momentum from the Middle Ages, through the time of Luther and the Reformation, and up to the storming of the Bastille in the French Revolution.

It was the muted tones of Lenau's *Weltschmerz* ("World Pain," a characteristic mood of the Romantic era), rather than his diatribes against present and historical injustices, that ensured the success of his slim volume of poetry, *Gedichte* (*Poems*, 1832). It was reprinted seven times during his life and supplemented by *Neuere Gedichte* (*Newer Poems*) in 1838. These poems combine the otherworldliness of Novalis with the passion of Brentano and the social awareness of Adelbert von Chamisso, Heinrich Heine, and Ludwig Uhland. For Lenau, there can be no joy in nature, but only the choking awareness of an isolated, internal existence, which is why Lenau concentrates not on the promise of spring, as Eichendorff and Goethe had done, but on autumnal scenes, where dark colors and rising mists mirror the poet's solitude and pessimism. Groups of itinerant musicians, defiant Native Americans, and even thieves and brigands are portrayed realistically and without false sentimentality. One poem that caught the mood of the age was "Farewell. An Emigrant's Song," with its bitter indictment of German subservience to despotic masters. Another, "By the Grave of a Minister,"

attacks Metternich's legacy in the years following the Vienna Congress. These aggressive and perceptive pieces reveal a fervor that is far from otherworldly; Lenau's somewhat wooden, mechanical, and rhetorical style can be justified on the grounds that it shatters the familiar conceit of the omniscient, vatic poet who alone can plumb the mysteries of art and the universe.

Lenau's reputation remains controversial. By the end of his life, he had few friends, having ruthlessly questioned the sincerity of his fellow poets, whom he regarded as well-meaning but ineffective. He displayed disdain for philistine burghers, grasping clerics, and despotic politicians. The Roman Church objected to his many attacks on its corruption and went so far as to place *Die Albigenser* on its official index of prohibited books. The progressive faction in German politics, which had originally welcomed his constructive approach to Polish and Hungarian causes as well as his indictment of social oppression, was unable to respond positively to the mysticism of *Savonarola* and to Lenau's increasing preoccupation with ecclesiastic history. He has been praised for his uncompromising sincerity and cited as a product of the terminally decadent stages of the Romantic movement. Lenau's life and works were fraught with paradoxes; for example, this sympathetic chronicler of the marginalization of Native Indians was not above joining forces with their exploiters by purchasing 400 acres of virgin land in Lisbon, Ohio, in 1832.

OSMAN DURRANI

Biography

Franz Nikolaus Niembsch was born August 13, 1802 in Csatád (renamed Lenauheim in his honour) near Timisoara in present-day Romania; his father died in 1807 and he was brought up by his grandparents. On the death of his grandfather he inherited the latter's honorary title "Edler von Strehlenau," the last five letters of which became his *nom de plume*. Lenau spent his youth in Hungarian-speaking areas of the Austrian Empire and attended school in Budapest before studying Law, Philosophy, Agriculture, and Medicine in Vienna between 1819 and 1831. Supported by a modest private income, he traveled restlessly in Europe and the New World. His verse started to appear in journals in 1828, and his first collection of poems was accepted for publication, on the recommendation of Gustav Schwab, by the much-respected firm of Cotta in 1832. His work found favor and enabled him to travel, and he was for some time engaged to Schwab's niece, Lotte Gmelin, in Tübingen. But in the end, his frenetic impulses got the better of him and the engagement was summarily broken off. From 1832 until his collapse in 1844 he raced across Europe from Vienna to Stuttgart and back again, spending as much as 160 hours per month in stage coaches. He attempted to start a new life in America, but soon returned in disillusionment, commenting that he preferred wine to cider and nightingales to mockingbirds. His attachments to various women brought him more despair than joy; he gave his all to art and saw his personal life as inconsequential. Several subsequent authors (Härtling, Kürnberger) were moved to write imaginative biographies of his tormented, Byronesque career. He collapsed in September 1844 and never regained his sanity. Died August 22, 1850 in a mental hospital at Oberdöbling near Vienna.

Selected Works

Gedichte. 1832.
Faust. 1834.

Savonarola. 1837.

Neuere Gedichte. 1838.

Die Albigenser. 1842.

Waldlieder. 1843.

Nikolaus Lenau. Sämtliche Werke und Briefe. Kritische Ausgabe seiner Dichtungen und Briefe. 6 vols. Edited by Eduard Castle. Leipzig: Hesse, 1910–23.

Nikolaus Lenau. Sämtliche Werke und Briefe. 2 vols. Edited by Walter Dietze. Leipzig: Insel, 1970.

Nikolaus Lenau. Briefe und Werke; Historisch-kritische Gesamtausgabe. Edited by Helmut Brandt. Internationale Lenau-Gesellschaft. Vienna: Deuticke, 1989–(in progress).

Translation: *Poems and Letters of Nikolaus Lenau.* Translated, with an introduction, by Winthrop H. Root. New York: Frederick Ungar, 1964.

Bibliography

Butler, Michael. "Nikolaus Lenau." In *German Men of Letters.* Vol 6. Alex Natan, and Brian Keith-Smith, eds. London: Wolff, 1969.

Dickens, David Bruce. *Negative Spring: Crisis Imagery in the Works of Brentano, Lenau, Rilke and T.S. Eliot.* New York: Lang, 1989.

Dove, Richard. "The Rhetoric of Lament. A Reassessment of Nikolaus Lenau." *Orbis Litterarum* 39 (1984): 230–65.

Eke, Norbert O., and Karl J. Skrodzki, *Lenau-Chronik 1802–1851.* Stuttgart: Klett-Cotta, 1992.

Gibson, Carl. *Lenau. Leben—Werk—Wirkung.* Heidelberg: Winter, 1989.

Hammer, Jean-Pierre. *Nikolaus Lenau. Poète, rebelle et libertaire.* Paris, 1987; German ed.: *Dichter und Rebell.* Wiener Neudorf: Berenkamp, 1989; 2d ed., 1993.

Härtling, Peter. *Niembsch oder Der Stillstand. Eine Suite.* Stuttgart: Goverts, 1964; reprinted Munich, 1994.

Hochheim, Rainer. *Nikolaus Lenau. deutschsprachige Personalbibliographie (1850–1981).* Budapest: Loránd-Eötvös-Universität, 1983 (*Budapester Beiträge zur Germanistik*, vol. 12); 2d ed., Frankfurt: Lang, 1986.

Korninger, Siegfried. "Lord Byron und Nikolaus Lenau," *English Miscellany* 3: 61–123.

Kürnberger, Ferdinand. *Der Amerikamüde.* Vienna: Lowit, 1855 reprinted Berlin/GDR: Volk und Welt, 1985; Frankfurt/Insel, 1986.

Mádl, Antal. *Auf Lenaus Spuren. Beiträge zur österreichischen Literatur.* Vienna: Österreichischer Bundesverlag. 1982.

Mulfinger, George A. "Lenau in Amerika," *Americana-Germanica* 1 (1897): No. 2, 7–61; No. 3, 1–16.

Rocek, Roman. *Dämonie des Biedermeier. Nikolaus Lenaus Lebenstragödie.* Vienna: Böhlau, 2001.

Schmidt, Hugo. *Nikolaus Lenau.* Twayne World Authors Series no. 135. New York: Twayne, 1971.

Schmidt-Bergmann, Hansgeorg. *Ästhetismus und Negativität. Studien zum Werk Nikolaus Lenaus.* Heidelberg: Winter, 1984.

Sengle, F. "Nikolaus Lenau." In *Ibid.*, *Biedermeierzeit. Deutsche Literatur im Spannungsfeld zwischen Restauration und Revolution.* 3 vols. Stuttgart, Metzler: 1980. III, 640–690.

Steinecke, Hartmut. "Nikolaus Lenau." In *Deutsche Dichter des 19. Jahrhunderts.* Benno von Wiese, ed. Berlin: E. Schmidt, 1969. 403–27.

———, ed. *Nikolaus Lenau heute gelesen,* Vienna: Braumüller, 2000.

Stillmark, Alexander, and Fred Wagner. *Lenau zwischen Ost und West. Londoner Symposium.* Stuttgart: Heinz, 1992.

Turóczi-Trostler, Jószef. *Nikolaus Lenau.* Budapest:1955; Berlin/ GDR: Rütten, 1961. *Neue Beiträge zur Literaturwissenschaft.* Vol. 12.

LENZ, JAKOB MICHAEL REINHOLD 1751–1792

German writer

Jakob Michael Reinhold Lenz was, along with the young Johann Wolfgang von Goethe, the key member of the most distinctive form of German pre-Romanticism, the short yet important Sturm und Drang (storm and stress) movement, which is usually dated from 1770 to 1778. The important earmarks of the movement—the critique of social strictures and a consequent idealization of subjective feeling and spontaneity, the glorification of genius and creativity, and a cult of (male) friendship—are the themes that also characterize Lenz's works. The works of the Sturm und Drang aggressively rejected French neo-Classicism and its formal constraints. With chaotic plots and unconventional subject matter, Lenz strove for a nationally specific aesthetic and authentic unmediated linguistic expression in the vernacular, which often set out to shock in its strong language.

Lenz's period of greatest creativity came after he left his studies in theology at the University of Königsberg and moved to Strasbourg. He began to write fiction and met the important literary young talent of the time: Johann Wolfgang von Goethe, Franz Christian Lerse, Heinrich Jung-Stilling, and Heinrich Leopold Wagner. Literary historiography later grouped these writers together as the Sturm und Drang movement. In 1775, the literary and social exchange between the members had reached its greatest intensity; they exchanged their ideas at the Tischgesellschaft (dinner society) which soon became the more formal Society of the German Language organized by Johann Daniel Salzmann.

In 1774 Lenz published some of his most important texts: the plays *Der Hofmeister* (*The Tutor*, 1772) and *Der neue Menoza* (*The New Menoza*, 1774), the treatise *Anmerkungen übers Theater* (*Observations on the Theater*, 1774), and translations of William Shakespeare's *Love's Labour's Lost* and of five Plautus comedies. These were followed by the play *Die Soldaten* (*The Soldiers*, 1774). In *Pandämonium Germanikum* (1775), Lenz, in an attempt to guide the audience's reception of his aesthetics, affirms his position as author vis-à-vis Goethe. He insists on his own individuality and on the originality of his works, while at the same time affirming their realistic portrayal of social conditions. The artistic conflict is about how a work of art that does not simply imitate a negatively perceived reality should look. In 1776, Lenz hoped to continue his literary and personal friendship with Goethe, who had joined the court of Weimar. However, Goethe, who was working on finding his place in courtly society, distanced himself from Lenz after several incidences of inappropriate behavior on the part of Lenz. Lenz's works, the "dramolet" *Tantalus* and the novel fragment *Der Waldbruder* (*The Hermit*), written in 1776 during his stay in Berka, near

Weimar, deal with events at the court. Goethe's dismissive attitude was ascribed to his own psychological fear that he could become like Lenz if he released his watch over himself. Critics have speculated that Lenz's break with Goethe contributed to his mental breakdown, which, in essence, ended his successful literary career. As he became isolated from his literary community, Lenz's later works, such as *Myrsa Polagi* and *Die sizilianische Versper* (*The Sicilian Vespers*), both published in 1782, lacked a proper distribution network and became more obscure.

While Lenz produced in all genres (poetry, prose, drama, and moral, philosophical, aesthetic, and theological writings) he is mostly known today for his dramatic works—in particular *Der Hofmeister* and *Die Soldaten*, and to a lesser degree *Der neue Menoza*.

The anonymously published drama *Der Hofmeister* was mistaken for a play by Goethe, who with his *Götz von Berlichingen mit der eisernen Hand* (*Götz von Berlichingen with the Iron Hand*, 1773) fired the first shot against French neoclassicism and the bourgeois tragedy of Gotthold Ephraim Lessing (in which tragic events take place in the social and psychological context of a middle-class setting and are no longer limited to the heroic deeds of the nobility). *Der Hofmeister*, with its many scene changes, multiple plots, coincidences, and mixed characters, and its unstable designation as a comedy—depending on the audience's affinity to the new movement—delighted or shocked his contemporaries, and anticipated the works of Georg Büchner. In several more or less independent plots Lenz creates the world of the bourgeois intellectual who is faced with the abuses of power within the feudal system. The protagonist, Läuffer, accepts a position as a tutor in Major Berg's household, where he is treated like a servant rather than as instructor of the son and daughter. In the absence of the daughter's (Gustchen) beloved, Fritz, who is away at school (and in a separate plot line gets into all kinds of trouble in the university town) Läuffer and Gustchen have a rather clumsy affair. If the Gustchen-Fritz plot is conceived as a Romeo and Juliet plot, the Läuffer-Gustchen plot is reminiscent of Abélard and Héloïse; both love affairs are portrayed as clichéd. Civilization has spoiled love as a natural feeling.

While the attack on the abuses of power inherent in the feudal system is essentially a radicalization of an Enlightenment theme, what is new is that the emerging bourgeoisie is implicated in its precarious position. Thinking and speaking in clichés undermines the sincerity of their positions and convictions. Often gestures undercut the dialogue that they are presumed to support. Demonstrating how the emerging bourgeoisie was itself both self-contradictory and oppressive, Lenz radically highlights the flaws of the Enlightenment's model for self-emancipation.

A similar overall position can be claimed for his other famous play *Die Soldaten*. In a convoluted, fast-paced plot with many scene changes, Marie, the daughter of a fancy-goods dealer, engages in a dalliance with Desportes, an officer, who cynically deserts her. Stolzius, Marie's middle-class fiancé avenges her by poisoning Desportes and himself. Unlike the fathers in bourgeois tragedy, Marie's father forgives his destitute daughter.

While the theme of the seduction of a middle-class girl by a member of the nobility is hardly new, the portrayal of bourgeois complicity radicalizes the theme in Lenz's plays. Marie is initially wooed by Desportes with gifts—from her father's store, no less. While Desportes accumulates debts with her father, the latter's business flourishes. The officers, as members of the nobility,

purchase luxury items there (often, we can assume, for the express purpose of seducing women of the lower classes). While outwardly scolding his daughter, the father suggests that if she plays her cards right and is discreet she could wind up marrying. In the brilliant opening scene of *Die Soldaten*, in which we see Marie composing a letter striving for elegance, the author exposes the ridiculousness of her striving for a higher social position. He unmasks the role of language in the construction of identity. Her attempts at a linguistic register that she does not master becomes clichéd and inauthentic. The play refers to the tragic elements of bourgeois tragedy while at the same time critiquing its characters as caricatures. By allowing reformist Enlightenment positions to clash with the pessimistic portrayal of character as inauthentic, Lenz vacillates between idealism and materialism, between confidence in the subject to control his or her fate and the disillusioned assessment that the individual is a mere cog in the wheels of his or her social environment, which determines language and actions.

His important essay *Anmerkungen übers Theater*, presented at the Salzmann table in 1771–72, is a rhapsodic, loosely argued, associative elliptic piece of poetics. It argues for a theater that will educate the spectator to become a participant in the creative process by making organizational decisions (and sense) out of the chaotic multilinear plots and the ambiguous positions offered. The Romantics Clemens Brentano and Ludwig Tieck recognized Lenz's avant-garde contribution to dramatic theory and practice, his challenge to literary and social norms. The latter edited the first edition of Lenz's oeuvre.

As his theoretical works claim and his fictional works demonstrate, Lenz's writing invites the reader or spectator to participate in the construction of the open and discontinuous texts; this participation enables textual destruction and reconstruction.

KARIN A. WURST

Biography

Born in Sesswegen, Livonia, January 23, 1751. Studied theology at the University of Königsberg 1768–71. Tutor in the services of the brothers von Kleist in Strasbourg, 1771–74, visit in Weimar (Goethe) and Berka, 1776. Psychological breakdown, placed in the care of Pastor Oberlin in Waldersbach, 1777–78, then care with various friends and relatives until he moved to Petersburg in 1780, then to Moscow in 1781, where he worked as tutor, teacher, writer, and translator until his death on May 23 or 24, 1792.

Selected Works

Drama
Der Hofmeister, 1774. Published with *Die Soldaten* as *The Tutor, The Soldiers*. Translated by William E. Yuill. 1972.
Der neue Menoza, 1774. Translated as *The New Menoza* by Meredith Oakes. In *Lenz: Three Plays*. 1993.
Die Soldaten, 1776. Published with *Der Hofmeister* as *The Tutor, The Soldiers*. Translated by William E. Yuill. 1972.

Poetry
Ausgewählte Gedichte. Edited by Erich Osterheld. 1909.

Fiction
Zerbin oder die neuere Philosophie. 1776.
Der Landprediger. 1777.
Der Waldbruder, ein Pendant zu Werthers Leiden. 1797.

Theoretical Writings

Anmerkungen übers Theater. 1774.

Bibliography

Damm, Sigrid. *Vögel die verkünden Land.* Weimar: Aufbau, 1985.

Duncan, Bruce. *Lovers, Parricides, and Highwaymen: Aspects of Sturm and Drang Drama.* Columbia, S.C.: Camden House, 1999.

Harris, Edward P. "J. M. R. Lenz." In *German Writers in the Age of Goethe, Sturm und Drang, and Classicism.* Edited by James Hardin and Christian Schweitzer. Detroit, Mich.: Gale, 1990. 167–76.

Hill, David. *Jakob Michael Reinhold Lenz: Studien zum Gesamtwerk.* Opladen: Westdeutscher Verlag, 1994.

Leidner, Alan C., and Helga Madland, eds. *Space to Act: The Theater of Lenz,* Columbia, S.C.: Camden House, 1993.

Leidner, Alan C., and Karin A. Wurst, eds. *Unpopular Virtues: The Scholarly Reception of J. M. R. Lenz.* Columbia, S.C.: Camden House. 1999.

Osborne, John, *J. M. R. Lenz: The Renunciation of Heroism.* Göttingen: Vandenhoeck and Ruprecht, 1975.

Stephan, Inge, and Hans-Gerd Winter. *"Ein vorübergehendes Meteor?" J. M. R. Lenz und seine Rezeption in Deutschland.* Stuttgart: Metzler, 1984.

———. *"Unaufhörlich Lenz gelesen . . .": Studien zu Leben und Werk von J. M. R. Lenz.* Stuttgart: Metzler, 1994.

Winter, Hans-Gerd. *J. M. R. Lenz.* Stuttgart: Winter, 1987.

Wurst, Karin, ed. *J. M. R. Lenz als Alternative? Positionsanalysen zum 200. Todestag.* Cologne: Böhlau, 1992.

LEOPARDI, GIACOMO 1798-1837

Italian poet and writer

Giacomo Leopardi's critical and polemical attitude toward contemporary trends in poetry is set out in his *Discorso di unitaliano intorno alla poesia romantica* (*An Italian's Discourse on Romantic Poetry*, 1818), his contribution to the ongoing literary debate, which was not, published until after his death. His argument that the simplicity and naturalness of the poetry of antiquity remain unsurpassed was not a token gesture to classicism, but a conviction stemming as much from his mastery of Greek and Latin as his distrust of the excesses of modern practitioners. Yet in his own writings he would combine the rigor and clarity of traditional form with a thoroughly modern sensibility.

Born in a remote corner of the papal states of a noble but impecunious family, Leopardi's prodigious talents as a philologist were encouraged by his father, even to the extent of obtaining a papal dispensation for the fifteen-year-old to read banned books. His adolescence was spent in what he described as "seven years of mad and desperate study," which produced several precocious erudite essays and the ruination of his health. This biographical fact has preoccupied many critics, to the point of ascribing what has been seen as his "philosophy of despair" to his physical ills, a simplistic correlation denied by Leopardi himself and which overlooks the fact that, however personal the point of origin of his poetry, the ramifications have universal validity. What is remarkable is not so much the speed with which Leopardi outstripped his tutors, but the ideological distance that this period of intense activity created between him and the reactionary outlook of his father.

By 1817 Leopardi had turned his attention from philology to literature, and had made his first attempts at poetry. In the same year he began his correspondence with Pietro Giordani, a liberal intellectual and writer, to whom he confided his literary ambitions and the growing sense of cultural claustrophobia in parochial Recanati, and especially in the repressive atmosphere of Palazzo Leopardi. Between 1817 and 1823 Leopardi continued to write poetry, some of which, such as the civic and patriotic odes, is reminiscent of the style of Vittorio Alfieri and Ugo Foscolo. But he was also developing his own distinct poetic voice in a type of composition he rather misleadingly called an idyll, as it consisted of a fusion of lyricism and thought, in which the landscape does not function simply as a backdrop but is intimately linked to the poet's state of mind.

In 1825 the need to escape from his birthplace led him to take on various commissions for the editor Antonio Stella in Milan, including anthologies of poetry and prose and a commentary of Petrarch that was to become a benchmark for the century.

Portrait of the painter [Giacomo Leopardi], painted postmortem, by Domemico Morelli Reprinted courtesy of the Museum G. Leopardi by Centro Nazionale Studi Leopardiani, Recanati, Italy.

It was during this period that he turned his attention from poetry to prose, and in 1827, the same year that saw the publication of Alessandro Manzoni's *I promessi sposi* (*The Betrothed*), he published his *Operette morali* (*Little Moral Works*). The preoccupations of his poetry are presented in tones of irony and satire, mainly in dialogue form, though the interlocutors rarely represent contrary positions and tend to follow the same line with an inexorable logic and tenacity. The unflinching gaze at the reality of the human condition characterizes the *Operette*, which are generally unrelieved by the lyrical celebration of the natural world that runs through his poetry. In fact, the representation of nature in the prose writings signals a marked shift in Leopardi's position, as he had previously inclined to Jean-Jacques Rousseau's notion of a former harmony between humanity and nature that was ruptured by the process of civilization, akin to the classical idea of a lost golden age. The concept of nature as benign and maternal gives way to the notion of a force that is at best indifferent, if not actively hostile, to the needs of humanity, outlined most vividly in the "Dialogue between Nature and an Icelander."

The interlocutors of the dialogues range from the fantastic creatures—an elf and a gnome, the earth and the moon—to historical characters such as Christopher Columbus and Torquato Tasso. Leopardi felt a particular affinity with Tasso, the archetypal figure of the artist at odds with his times, and adopted this persona to explore key concepts in the "Dialogue between Torquato Tasso and His Familiar Spirit." The discussions on truth and pleasure reach startling conclusions which derive from the dialectical tension between reason and imagination informing all of Leopardi's writings. The consoling effects of fantasy and memory are infinitely preferable to the starkness of reality, and pleasure is both the ultimate goal of human existence and forever elusive, as it belongs either to the past or the future, never the present.

Some of Leopardi's greatest poetry was written after 1828, such as "Canto notturno di un pastore errante dell' Asia" ("Night Song of a Nomadic Asian Shepherd" 1829), in which a series of questions is addressed to the moon on the meaning of existence and the purpose of the universe. The character of the shepherd is projected into a time and space that is indefinite, almost abstract, and his existential isolation is accentuated by the silence of the moon. While the element of reflection in these later poems is pronounced, the lyrical nucleus of his poetry remains, as indicated by the title of *Canti* (*Songs*) Leopardi gave to his collected poems.

The formation and development of Leopardi's ideas can be charted in the pages of the *Zibaldone* (*Miscellany*), a journal kept from 1817 until 1832, which comes to over 4,500 pages. The entries include annotations and comments on literature and philology, as well as Leopardi's thoughts on a wide variety of topics, from his reflections on poetic inspiration to the relationship between nature and reason.

Leopardi's radical views aroused suspicion in some of his contemporaries, and critics are still exercised by the mixture of uncompromising honesty, imagination, and compassion in his works. Combining a classical education, Enlightenment influences, and a sensibility with Romantic aspects, Leopardi remains a figure who defies and transcends classifications and categories.

LYNNE PRESS

Biography

Born in Recanati, near Ancona June 29, 1798. Educated privately, his precocious writings include a *History of Astronomy* (1813) and *Essay on the Popular Errors of the Ancients* (1815). Extended stay in Rome, first time outside Recanati, 1822–23. Worked in Bologna and Milan for the editor Stella, 1825–26. After five months in Recanati, left for Bologna, Milan, Florence, and Pisa, where poetic inspiration was revived in 1828. Final return to Recanati 1828–30, then to Florence, which he left in 1831 for Rome. To Naples in 1833 in company of Ranieri. Died of cholera in Naples, June 14, 1837.

Selected Works

The Poems of Giacomo Leopardi. Translated with introduction and notes by Geoffrey L. Bickersteth. 1923.
Tutte le opere di Giacomo Leopardi. 5 vols., 1973.
Giacomo Leopardi: Moral Essays. Translated by Patrick Creagh. 1983.
The Letters of Giacomo Leopardi, 1817–1837. Translated by Prue Shaw. 1998.

Bibliography

Bini, Daniela. *A Fragrance from the Desert: Poetry and Philosophy in Giacomo Leopardi.* Saratoga: Anma Libri, 1983.
Carsaniga, Giovanni. *Giacomo Leopardi: the Unheeded Voice.* Edinburgh: Edinburgh University Press, 1977.
Damiani, Rolando. *Vita di Giacomo Leopardi.* Milan: Mondadori, 1992.
Origo, Iris, *Leopardi, a Study in Solitude.* London: Hamish Hamilton, 1953.

LERMONTOV, MIKHAIL YURIEVICH 1814–1841

Russian poet, dramatist, and novelist

Mikhail Yurievich Lermontov's best works are commonly recognized as masterpieces of Russian Romantic literature, for they exhibit the most significant features of Romanticism as a literary school and method. Although Lermontov borrowed rather heavily from his Russian predecessors (such authors as Evgenii Baratynskii, Kondratii Ryleev, and Vasilii Zhukovskii) various Western writers (notably Johann Wolfgang von Goethe, Victor Hugo, Alphonse-Marie-Louis de Lamartine, Walter Scott, Johann Christoph Friedrich von Schiller, and Alfred de Vigny,) also played a significant role in his development as a poet. In general, Lermontov's outlook was extremely tragic and individualistic; all contradictions in his works were proclaimed unresolvable, and a poet's personality was presented as an arena for the eternal fight between good and evil.

At the very beginning of his literary career in the late 1820s, Lermontov fell under the influence of a number of movements—

in particular, a philosophical program issued by the circle of the so-called liubomudry-writers (wisdom lovers) under the leadership of Nikolai V. Stankevich, and personalities such as Konstantin Batiushkov and Aleksandr Pushkin. Since he began writing very early, at the age of fourteen, Lermontov had managed to write a large number of works (about two hundred verse pieces of various lengths) before he became a mature, well-known, and popular author. As shown by the Russian critic Boris M. Eikhenbaum, the young poet was working as an apprentice, using the poetic lines of Batiushkov, Aleksandr A. Bestuzhev-Marlinskii, Ivan I. Dmitriev, Ivan I. Kozlov, Pushkin, Zhukovskii, and even Mikhail Lomonosov as foundations for his own poems. His first romantic poems, written in 1828–29—"Korsar" ("The Corsair"), "Kavkazskii plennik" ("The Prisoner of the Caucasus"), "Dva brata" ("Two Brothers"), and "Prestupnik" ("The Criminal")—exhibit these influences. These first works of Lermontov were written in the genre of the narrative poem, identified in the Russian tradition as "Byronic." The young author was attracted to this style as it was the most popular and developed genre at this time. According to the standards of this genre, a poem should be centered around a strong character, a romantic hero, who is meant to be in conflict with the world, society, and himself. He ignores all social and ethical rules and usually commits a crime, although his extensive suffering wins him readers' sympathies. The narration in such a poem is lyrical and depicts primarily the story of a spiritual development of a main character, rather than an account of his doings. Later in life, Lermontov returned to this genre in "*Demon*" (*The Demon*, 1829–39) and *Mtsyri* (*Novice*, 1839). In the latter, the Byronic hero is transformed into a naive and sincere man of nature, whose only credo is to fight for his individual freedom. A different way of developing the Byronic poem is found in "*Pesnia pro tsaria Ivana Vasil'evicha, molodogo oprichnika i udalogo kuptsa Kalashnikova* (*The Story of Tsar Ivan Vasilievich, the Young Oprichnik, and the Starthearted Merchant Kalashnikov*," 1838), where the main character embodies the most valuable features of a nation and his antithesis, who represents the cult of individuality, is vanquished.

By 1830 Lermontov had started a new period of his apprenticeship. He became disappointed with Russian literature as a source of inspiration and turned to foreign authors. His poetic exercises written in 1830 and 1831—the narrative poems *Dva raba* (*The Two Slaves*), *Ispoved* (*A Confession*), and *Poslednii syn vol'nosti* (*The Last Son of Freedom*); and the verse pieces *K Sushkovoi* (*To Sushkova*), *Noch* (*A Night*), and *Podrazhanie Baironu* (*Imitation of Byron*)—demonstrate that Lord Byron had captivated the imagination of the young poet and occupied a very special place in Lermontov's personal development. Byron's creative writings influenced the character of Lermontov's work, philosophy, and lifestyle for the rest of the younger poet's life. According to the memoirs of Ekaterina A. Khvostova (Sushkova), "Lermontov declaimed Pushkin and Lamartine, and was inseparable from the great Byron." The cult of Byron, as well as the cult of Napoleon, each representative of "a great man," was a phenomenon of Russian culture in the epoch of Romanticism. In Eikhenbaum's opinion, this phenomenon "must be distinguished from the literary influence of Byron and English poetry in general." Trying to find meaningful similarities with Byron's own life, Lermontov asserted his personal originality as a poet in "Net, ia ne Bairon, ia drugoi" ("No I Am Not Byron, I Am Another," 1832).

Lermontov's lyric verse was also marked by the influence of the narrative poem, as its philosophical framework was based on the concept of an exceptional character who had liberated himself from any social or ethical laws. Love in Lermontov's verses takes extreme forms and often takes over the entire life, while the loss of love means death. Moreover, love is never portrayed as harmony, and women as addressees of Lermontov's lyric are usually presented by means of his favorite techniques, antithesis and juxtaposition, as a source of evil beauty that can be mistaken for the angelic. Women in Lermontov's verses cannot be faithful, sincere, or grateful, and essentially do not deserve the romantic passion of the lyrical "I"; see, for example, "Ia ne liubliu tebia: strastei" ("I Do Not Love You: Passion," 1830), "L Ia ne unizhus' pred toboiu . . ." (I Will Not Abase Myself in front of You . . . 1830), Net, ne tebia tak pylko ia liubliu . . . ("No, This is Not You Whom I Am Loving so Passionately . . .," 1841). Mutual misunderstanding and solitude are also strong themes in Lermontov's meditative verses, in which the author reveals his feelings through pictures of nature: "Kogda volnuetsia zhelteiushchaia niva" ("When the Yellowing Cornfield Waves," 1837), "Vykhozhu odin ia na dorogu" ("I Step Out onto the Road Alone," 1841), "Tri pal'my" ("Three Palms," 1839), "Vetka Palestiny" ("The Branch from Palestine," 1837), "Na severe dikom stoit odinoko . . ." ("In the Wild North It Stands Alone . . .," 1841).

Having become well known for his poem "Smert' poeta" ("Death of a Poet," 1837), inspired by Pushkin's death, Lermontov continued to discuss the question of the place of a poet and poetry in society. In such poems as "Zhurnalist, chitatel' i pisatel' " ("A Journalist, a Reader, and a Writer," 1840), and especially in "Prorok" ("The Prophet," 1841), Lermontov proclaims that poets are out of place in society, and suggests that as a poet he should run from people rather than come toward them, as was proposed by Pushkin. Lermontov's image of loneli-

Mikhail Yurievich Lermontov. Reprinted courtesy of AKG.

ness extended also to his generation, which he defined as "lost" in the poem "Duma" ("The Meditation," 1839). The ideas of this poem found their further development in Lermontov's innovative novel *Geroi nashego vremeni* (*A Hero of Our Time*, 1840). Compared to this novel, Lermontov's other exercises in prose— *Vadim* (1832–34), and the unfinished *Kniaginia Ligovskaia* (*Princess Ligovskaia*, 1836) and *Shtoss* (1841)—are not so refined. Lermontov's dramatic works, the best known of which is *Maskarad* (*Masquerade*, 1836), were strongly dependent on Shakespearean theater and early plays by Johann Christoph Friedrich von Schiller.

Although Lermontov's creative life lasted for only thirteen years, his literary works represent a turning point in the development of Russian Romanticism.

EKATERINA ROGATCHEVSKAIA

Biography

Born in Moscow, October 3 (or 15), 1814; a descendant of Captain George Learmont, a Scotsman in the Russian service; was brought up by his grandmother. Student of the Moscow University's Boarding School for the Nobility, 1828–30; studied at the University of Moscow, 1830–32. Studied at the School of Ensigns of the Guards and of Cavalry Cadets, 1832–34; started his military service in Tsarskoe Selo, 1834. Sent into exile from Saint Petersburg to the Caucasus to continue his military service, 1837. Back in service in Tsarskoe Selo, 1838. Punished for participation in a duel and sent to the Caucasus, 1840. Killed in another duel, July 15 (27), 1841.

Selected Works

Poetry

Demon, 1829–39. Translated as *The Demon* by Archibald Cary Coolidge, with an introduction by Prince D. S. Mirsky. London: School of Slavonic Studies at the University of London, 1925.

Pesnia pro tsaria Ivana Vasil'evicha, molodogo oprichnika i udalogo kuptsa Kalashnikova, 1838. Translated as *The Story of Tsar Ivan Vassilyevich, the Young Oprichnik, and the Stouthearted Merchant Kalashnikov* by Irina Zheleznova. Moscow: Raduga, 1983.

Mtsyri, 1839. Russian text with introduction, notes, and vocabulary by J. D. Duff. Cambridge: Cambridge University Press, 1919. Translated as *The Novice* by E. W. Morgan. Scotland: E. W. Morgan, 1975.

The Demon and Other Poems. Translated by Eugene M. Kayden, with an introduction by Sir Maurice Bowra. Yellow Springs, Ohio: Antioch Press, 1965.

Plays

Iunosheskiia dramy. 1890.
Maskarad, Moscow: Khudozhestvennaia literatura. 1956.

Prose

Geroy noshego vremeni, 1840. Translated as *A Hero of Our Time* by Eden and Cedar Paul. London: Oxford University Press, 1958. Also published as *A Hero of Our Time*. Edited by Neil Cornwell. New York: Everyman, 1995.
Vadim. Translated and edited by Helena Goscilo. Ann Arbor, Mich.: Ardis, 1984.

Collections

Polnoe sobranie sochinenii. Moscow: Pravda, 1953.
Sobranie sochinenii. Moscow: Khudozhestvennaia literatura, 1984.
Polnoe sobranie sochinenii v desiati tomakh. Moscow: Voskresen'e, 1999–.

Bibliography

Barratt, Andrew, and A. D. P. Briggs. *A Wicked Irony: The Rhetoric of Lermontov's "A Hero of Our Time."* Bristol: Bristol Classical, 1989.

Briggs, A. D. P., ed. *Mikhail Lermontov: Commemorative Essays (1991)*. Birmingham Modern Languages Publications 7. Birmingham: University of Birmingham, 1992.

Eikhenbaum, Boris M. *Lermontov*. Translated by R. Parrott and Harry Weber. Ann Arbor, Mich.: Ardis, 1981.

Etkinda Efim, ed. A symposium dedicated to M. Khail Lermontov, 1989. Efim Etkinda. Northfield, Vt.: RussKaia shkola Norvichskogo Universiteta, 1992.

L'Ami, C. E., and Alexander Welikotny. *Michael Lermontov: Biography and Translation*. Winnipeg: University of Manitoba Press, 1967.

Lavrin, Janko. *Lermontov*. London: Bowes and Bowes/New York: Hillary House, 1959.

Russian Literature 33, no. 4 (1993). Special issue on Lermontov.

Shchegolev, Pavel E. *Lermontov: vospominaniia, pis'ma, dnevniki*. Moscow: Agraf, 1999.

Williams, Jessica. *From Lermontov to Dostoevsky: a Study in the Development of Psychological Realism in Russian Literature*. Birmingham, U.K.: University of Birmingham, 1991.

Vatsuro, Vadim E., "*M. Iu. Lermontov.*" In *Russkie pisateli 1800–1917, biograficheskii slovar'*. Moscow: K-M, 1994.

Zakharov, Vladimir A. *Zagadka poslednei dueli: dokumental'noe issledovanie*. Moscow: Russkaia Panorama, 2000.

LESSING, GOTTHOLD EPHRAIM 1729–1781

German dramatist, critic, and aesthetician

Sometimes hailed as the first important aesthetician or as co-founder of modern German letters with Johann Wolfgang von Goethe, and certainly recognized as the first important professional German writer, Gotthold Ephraim Lessing presides over the German Enlightenment as one whose writings both direct and mirror its central developments. We may, in fact, trace his development through a phase dominated by admiration for French classical models, through a stage of conscious experimen-

tation influenced primarily by English writers and thinkers, to, eventually, the arrival at an original style defined in part by his speculations on a German ideal.

The young Lessing had at first adhered to the cult of emulation led by the Francophile Johann Christoph Gottsched, and his aspiration to become the "German Molière" drove him to fashion his comedies on human failings and the value of good character, after the French. These early plays include the first to be performed, *Der junge Gelehrte* (*The Young Scholar*, 1747), which mocks his own bookishness, and two more noteworthy ones: *Der Freigeist* (*The Freethinker*, 1749) and *Die Juden* (*The Jews*, 1749), which respectively criticize the small-mindedness of the anticlerical thinkers and the anti-Semites of his day.

Lessing's preference for realism and rationalism soon compelled him to break with the norm. He famously rose to the task of portraying a bourgeois heroine in a way previously reserved for aristocracy, that is, in terms of the heroic and the tragic. If *Miss Sara Sampson* (1755), which drew from his reading of Samuel Richardson's sentimental novels, went on to become the first great *bürgerliches Trauerspiel* (domestic tragedy), his next grand but unfinished project, the depiction of a Faust characterized not by evil but by an inquiring spirit, was to pave the way for Goethe's more famous and complex version. Lessing then proceeded to establish modern German comedy with *Minna von Barnhelm* (1763), a play set at the end of the Seven Years War, which raised the issue of an inherent German oneness.

All these plays may be evaluated not only on their own merits or in relation to Lessing's other plays, but alongside the volumes of articles and reviews he wrote on the theater. The late tragedy *Emilia Galotti* (1772)—called "a great example of dramatic algebra" by Friedrich von Schlegel—plainly illustrates the principles of dramatic balance, clear action and movement he proposes in a series of 104 essays written for the short-lived National Theater in Hamburg, and collected as *Hamburgische Dramaturgie* (*Hamburg Dramaturgy*, 1767–69). His reinterpretation of Aristotelian catharsis as arousing pity and fear not for the tragic characters but for "ourselves" or "someone like ourselves" reinforces his dislike for the ceremonial nature of French classicism; it escalates his attack on Gottsched and, more significantly, on French dramatists like Pierre Corneille and Voltaire but not Denis Diderot, whose bourgeois realism he finds commendable.

Lessing's critical writings also frequently express support for original German writers and thinkers, among them Herder and the proto-Romantic poets Friedrich Gottlieb Klopstock and Christoph Martin Wieland. Today, the main value of his critical writings lies in their advocacy of Shakespeare's preeminence, an evaluation preceding the bardolatry of the emerging Sturm und Drang movement. In addition, he produced polemical works in the field of antiquarian studies that sought, on the one hand, to defy the overriding influence of arrogant scholars such as Christian Adolf Klotz and Samuel Gotthold Lange, and, on the other, to rescue misunderstood writers and thinkers like Horace and the medieval heretic Hieronymus Cardanus. In the newly formed field of aesthetics, Lessing cowrote with Mendelssohn a controversial pamphlet called *Pope ein Metaphysiker!* (*Pope a Metaphysician!*, 1755) that dissected the subject of a contest at the Prussian Royal Academy, the philosophical system of Alexander Pope's *Essay on Man* (1733–34), a contest that a young Immanuel Kant himself had intended to join.

This discussion of the incompatibility of poetry and philosophy was, in fact, a precursor to the most famous of all Lessing's writings on aesthetics, his *Laokoon, oder über die Grenzen der Malerei und Poesie* (*Lacoön, or On the Limits of Painting and Poetry*, 1766), which began as an attack on the art historian Johann Joachim Winckelmann. Famously challenging Winckelmann's interpretation of Lacoön's suppressed cry in the Greek sculpture similarly named, Lessing reenvisions it as not a cry of the noble Greek soul but rather of beauty delineated by the rules of a static art form. From here, he proceeds to denounce the nondistinction of method for art and literature promoted by the Comte de Caylus and Joseph Spence and, to systematically differentiate between the principles of the visual and the aural arts. Poetry, he insists, is "articulated sounds in time" while painting is "figures and colours in space," representing only "the most pregnant moment"; as neither can take on the other's work, the genre of descriptive poetry, like the earlier-criticized genre of philosophical poetry, is pronounced as a contradiction in terms and thereby rejected.

In theology, one of Lessing's main contributions was his courageous publication of the writing fragments of Hermann Samuel Reimarus, the German deist whose works reject the truth of the Gospels and present Jesus as a mere human with messianic delusions. In his ensuing battle against Johann Melchior Goeze, the chief pastor of Hamburg, Lessing argues that, while he does not share Reimarus's views, the common search for truth must uphold the right to open discussion on issues of religion and history and not fall back on the merciless arm of orthodoxy. This astonishingly modern sentiment is expressed again in *Nathan der Weise* (*Nathan the Wise*, 1779), a dramatic poem in which the central characters, as representatives of Judaism, Christianity and Islam, discover at long last that they are blood relatives; the themes of religious tolerance and peaceful coexistence here are obvious enough.

Lessing himself would in fact formulate his own theory of the Gospels, which was published posthumously. In it he offers a purely literary approach to biblical study, as opposed to an archeological one, and this clearly anticipates the highly controversial retelling of Jesus's life by David Friedrich Strauss. He crucially turns the attention of biblical research to two problematic areas: the chronological and cultural gap between the historical Jesus and the Gospels (Lessing being the first to point to this disparity between the Jesus of his own time and of orthodox religion) and the idea that similarities across the Gospels may suggest a lost primary source on which they were based.

GWEE LI SUI

Biography

Born in Kamenz, Saxony, on January 22, 1729; entered the famous *Fürstenschule* (prince's school) of St. Afra in Meissen, 1741; studied theology at the University of Leipzig, 1746–48. Caroline Neuber's company performed *Der junge Gelehrte*, 1748; fled from his creditors in Leipzig and enrolled to study medicine at the University of Wittenberg, 1748; began journalistic work in Berlin under the guidance of Christlob Mylius, 1749; launched the periodical *Beiträge zur Historie und Aufnahme des Theaters* (*Contributions to the History and Reception of the Theater*), 1750; awarded master's degree, 1752; published six volumes of his works, including *Miss Sara Sampson*, 1753–55; began the periodical *Theatralische Bibliothek* (*Theatrical Library*), 1754. befriended Moses Mendelssohn, the Enlightenment publisher Friedrich Nicolai and poet Karl Wilhelm Ramler, and conducted the famous *Briefwechsel über das Trauerspiel* (*Correspondence on Tragedy*) with them, 1755. Stayed in Leipzig for three years before moving back to Berlin, 1758. Worked in Breslau as secretary to General Bogislaw Friedrich von Tauentzien, the military governor of Silesia, 1760–65; turned down for a post as royal librarian in Berlin due to an earlier feud with

Voltaire, 1765; published *Laokoon*, 1766; worked as critic of the National Theater in Hamburg, 1767–68; worked as librarian to the Duke of Brunswick in Wolfenbüttel, 1770; published Reimarus's work as *Fragmente eines Ungenannten* (*Fragments of an Unknown*); 1774–77; married Eva König, 1776 (she died, 1778). Died in Braunschweig, Brunswick, on February 15, 1781.

Selected Works

Miss Sara Sampson. 1755.
Laokoon, oder über die Grenzen der Malerei und Poesie, 1766. Translated as *Lacoön: An Essay on the Limits of Painting and Poetry* by Edward Allen McCormick. Indianapolis: Bobbs-Merrill, 1962.
Minna von Barnhelm, oder das Soldatenglück, 1767. Translated as *Minna von Barnhelm, or A Soldier's Luck* by Patrick Maxwell. London: The University Press, 1899.
Hamburgische Dramaturgie, 1767–69. Translated as *Hamburg Dramaturgy* by Helen Zimmern. New York: Dover, 1962.
Emilia Galotti, 1772. Translated as *Emilia Galotti: A Tragedy in Five Acts* by Charles Lee Lewes. London: Sampson Low, Son, and Marston, 1868.
Nathan der Weise, 1779. Translated as *Nathan the Wise: A Dramatic Poem in Five Acts* by William Taylor. London: Sampson Low, Son, and Marston, 1868.
Die Erziehung des Menschengeschlechts, 1780. Translated as *The Education of the Human Race* by Frederick W. Robertson. London, 1858.

Bibliography

Allison, Henry E. *Lessing and the Enlightenment: His Philosophy of Religion and its Relation to Eighteen-Century Thought*. Ann Arbor: University of Michigan Press, 1966.
Brown, Andrew F. *Gotthold Ephraim Lessing*. New York: Twayne, 1971.
Cassirer, Ernst. *Die Philosophie der Aufklärung*. Tübingen: Paul Siebeck, 1932.
Danzel, Theodor W., and Gottstalk E. Guhrauer. *Gotthold Ephraim Lessing. Sein Leben und seine Werke*. 2 vols. 2d ed. Revised by Wendelin von Maltzahn and Robert Boxberger. Berlin: Theodor Hofman, 1880–81.
Garland, Henry B. *Lessing: The Founder of Modern German Literature*. 2d ed. London: Macmillan, 1962.
Guthke, Karl S., and Heinrich Schneider. *Gotthold Ephraim Lessing*. Stuttgart: Metzler, 1967.
Ilse, Graham. *Goethe and Lessing: The Wellsprings of Creation*. London: Paul Elek, 1973.
Kofink, Heinrich. *Lessings Anschauungen über die Unsterblichkeit und Seelenwanderung*. Stassburg: Trübner, 1912.
Rilla, Paul. *Lessing und sein Zeitalter*. Berlin: Aufbau, 1981.
Robertson, John G. *Lessing's Dramatic Theory: Being an Introduction to and Commentary on His Hamburgische Dramaturgie*. Edited by Edna Purdie. Cambridge, U.K.: Cambridge University Press, 1939.
Schmidt, Erich. *Lessing: Geschichte seines Lebens und seiner Schriften*. 2 vols. Berlin: Weidmann, 1884–92.
Wellbery, David E. *Lessing's Laocoon: Semiotics and Aesthetics in the Age of Reason*. Cambridge: Cambridge University Press, 1984.

LETTERS: BRITAIN

Out of the wealth of letters produced at any point in history, the selection of a handful as being representative of the age is obviously fraught with problems. Selections from the letters of two of English Romantic poets, Lord Byron and John Keats, are a staple of anthologies of British Romantic writing, since both are capable of giving a poet's perspective on the creative process in the most hauntingly memorable terms. Yet recent anthologizers are mindful of the charge that, for all their differences, Byron and Keats articulate essentially the same voice, one that is educated, male and intensely self-reflective. Beyond the canonical names of English literature, letters survive from the period that reflect a range of class and gender experience, that respond to contemporary events now deemed key to an understanding of the time, and that show no engagement with the wider world but which open up a range of local socioeconomic concerns to us. Alongside the letters of leading Romantic writers, we now have the opportunity to hear other voices from the time and consider the form of the letter outside its construction by educated men.

Undoubtedly the greatest influence on letter writing in the Romantic era is the popularity of epistolary fiction during the eighteenth century. As developed by Samuel Richardson in *Clarissa* (1747–48), the artifice of "writing to the moment" encouraged a fictitious letter form in which characters describe external events and resulting inner turmoil in a stylistically distinctive fusing of action and emotion. It is impossible to read the letters of Byron, for example—three thousand of which have survived—without being convinced of the near simultaneity of the thought and the act of committing it to paper. Byron's letters range from frank discussion of sexual desire to abstract reflections on the meaning of art and the life of the artist.

Despite the quantity of Byron's letters, however, it is those of Keats that are cited most frequently as an unparalleled exploration of the meaning of art and life. Precisely because Keats uses the letter form to express the latest state of his thinking, the reader shares a sense of exploration of questions to which there can be no earthly resolution. No matter how our views of literature and literary merits change, Keats's letters seem unlikely to lose their preeminent position among Romantic letters.

While the quality of Keats's letters deserves special mention, literary historians are growing increasingly interested in the works of British radical writers during the Romantic period. When the radical in question is also a woman, her letters may provide a gendered as well as a political challenge to received ideas about Romantic writing. Helen Maria Williams uses the letter form in a distinctive manner in her *Letters Written in France in the Summer of 1790* (1790) and *Letters Containing a Sketch of the Politics of France* (1795). Where the first volume is suffused with a visitor's optimism about the French Revolution, the second describes the daily reality of house arrest during the Terror. Throughout, Williams retains her belief in the perfectibility of the state and uses the letter form to write the "testimony of a witness" to "future times." The use of a volume of letters written to posterity, to help a writer reflect upon her own immediate experience, is clearly seen in the work of Mary

Wollstonecraft. Her *Letters Written during a Short Residence in Sweden, Norway, and Denmark* (1796) are an extraordinary blend of the private and public, and the style is a mixture of the confessional and the didactic.

All of these writers were acutely aware of literary conventions and a world of political and artistic possibilities around them. But with the recovery of previously unheard voices from the Romantic period come letters that offer snapshots of lives where political ideology and daily necessity meet with urgency and despair. Alongside the *Letters of the Late Ignatius Sancho, an African* (1782), we can set another African's experience: a single surviving plea from one James Harris petitioning a leading slave trader, James Rogers, for work: "Mr Hicks did promise me when I quitted his Service that he would give me my freedom that I might go to any Part of the world unmolisted and I have applyd several times to Him by Letters and have never receivd an answer from either of the Letters. . . ." If Keats and Wollstonecraft write to the future,

Harris writes in a desperately urgent present in which an answer to his letter may bring the only means he has to live. In future years, it is likely that more letters like these will be published— letters that lie outside traditional conceptions of the literary and political spheres but nevertheless form a vital part of our understanding of Romantic letter writing and reading.

GLYNIS RIDLEY

Bibliography

Favret, Mary A. *Romantic Correspondence: Women, Politics, and the Fiction of Letters.* Cambridge: Cambridge University Press, 1993.

Kitson, Peter J., and Debbie Lee, eds. *Slavery, Abolition and Emancipation: Writings in the British Romantic Period.* Vol. 1. *Black Writers.* Edited by Sukhdev Sandhu and David Dabydeen; Pickering and Chatto, 1999.

Potkay, Adam. *The Fate of Eloquence in the Age of Hume.* Ithaca, N.Y.: Cornell University Press, 1994.

LETTERS: GERMANY

At the end of the eighteenth century, when German Romanticism emerged, the letter was already firmly established as a favored literary genre. Publications of travel letters such as Georg Christoph Lichtenberg's *Briefe aus England*, (1776/78), and Karl Philipp Moritz *Reisen eines jungen Deutschen in England im Jahre* (*The Travels of a Young German in England*, 1782, 1783) and literary critical letters such as Gotthold Ephraim Lessing's *Briefe die neueste Litteratur betreffend* (*Letters Concerning the Newest Literature*, 1759–65) owe their popularity to the conception of the letter as a widely suitable didactic medium, as well as to its qualities of matching the communicative needs of the developing bourgeois society, therefore of privacy and subjectivity, and the values attributed to the individual's feelings. The literary response to the emerging cult of friendship, as an aspect of eighteenth-century sentimentalism, subsequently promoted the letter as an apt medium for expression of individuality and subjectivity. Within the cult of friendship, letters were seen not only as an intimate and exclusively private form of communication, but also as semipublic, since letters were read, copied, and circulated among large groups of friends. Other letters were written for publication (such as those of Christian Fürchtegott Gellert, Gleim, and Johann Wolfgang von Goethe). Furthermore, the rise of the early form of the bourgeois novel, the epistolary novel, which seemed to provide truthfulness and intimacy of communication and allowed subjectivity and social relationships to be publicly explored (Sophie de la Roche's *Geschichte des Fräuleins von Sternheim* [*The History of Lady Sophia S.*, 1771–72] and Goethe's *Leiden des jungen Werthers* [*The Sorrows of Young Werther*, 1774]), rooted the letter as a literary genre firmly within the literary discourse of the time. Moreover, since attempts at a theory of letter writing such as Gellert's *Praktische Abhandlung von dem guten Geschmacke in Briefen* (*Practical Treatise on Good Taste*, 1751) praised naturalness and individuality as well as its affinity to the spoken word as the key properties of the letter, the letter as a literary genre enabled even women to enter the literary world.

During the Romantic period, the letter was no longer primarily valued for its educational qualities but became valued more for its subjective qualities, its dialogic structure, and its resemblance to spoken conversation. The high esteem attributed to the letter by Romantic writers is to be seen within the context of the early Romantics' aesthetic theory, which reunites all literary genres and proclaims the interchangeability of art and life. Friedrich von Schlegel's reflections on poetry show dialogue in particular as the underlying principle of Romantic thinking, comprising life as well as literary production, according to which dialogue is regarded as a major contributor to the process of creating totality via multiple perspectives. Therefore, dialogically structured forms of the spoken and written word become to play a central part in Romantic theory and practice, which are inseparably interconnected.

Schlegel and other Romantic writers' reflections on the letter establish it as a highly regarded genre. The letter's reputation among the Romantics is based on its versatility as well as on its quality as an open, unsystematic form of writing, both much preferred by Romantic writers to established genres. As a highly versatile genre, the letter appeals in manifold contexts. Schlegel's *Athenaeum's-Fragment 77* reflects on the affinity between letter and fragment, on the basis that both genres initiate dialogue, the core principle of creating totality. Novalis states the similarities between letter and essay and Schlegel claims that in transgressing its own genre, the letter can transform even into a novel. Consequently, a great number of the early Romantic novels are, as a whole or partially, epistolary novels (Ludwig Tieck's *William Lovell*, [1796] Schlegel's, *Lucinde* [1799]; and Clemens Brentano's *Godwi oder das steinerne Bild der Mutter* [*Godwi, or the Image of the Mother in Stone*, 1802]). Others are structured as a dialogue, with interspersed letters (Tieck's *Franz Sternbalds Wanderungen* [1798] or Wilhelm Heinrich Wackenroder and Ludwig Tieck's, *Herzensergießungen eines kunstliebenden Klosterbruders* [*Outpourings of an Art-Loving Friar, 1797*]). Sophie Mereau published epistolary novels based on her correspondence with a former lover. Brentano excelled in mingling letters and poetry in his works as well as in his correspondences. As a consequence of the decades of warfare throughout Europe increasing use was made of personal letters, often manipulated and coded as newspaper articles.

All in all, the popularity of letters did not wane during the Romantic period; in contrast, collections of letters, edited and often mixed with other forms of autobiographical writings, gained in popularity, and women writers such as Rahel Varnhagen von Ense and Bettina von Arnim created new forms of fiction. Bettina von Arnim drew on letters and memories in her fictionalized autobiographical epistolary novels *Die Günderrode* (1830), Goethe's *Briefwechsel mit einem Kinde* (*Goethe's Correspondence with a Child*, 1835), and *Clemens Brentanos Frühlings Kranz* (*A Vernal Wreath for Clemens Brenlano*, 1844). An extraordinary success was the 1834 edition of Rahel Varnhagen von Ense's letters, *Rahel: Ein Buch des Andenkens für ihre Freunde* in three volumes. Together with her husband Karl August Varnhagen von Ense, Rahel Varnhagen had put together and prepared this collection of letter fragments, which, organized in chronological order, aimed at an comprising portrait of Berlin's most renowned Salonière, who corresponded with three hundred partners and whose posthumous letters count more than six thousand documents. The success of Rahel Varnhagen's literary portrait as well as her enormous productivity in writing letters highlight important aspects of the culture of letters during the Romantic period: the interdependence of the intellectual Salon society's communication and its continuation in the written correspondence, and the interdependence of life and art. The letter seemed to have been the aesthetic medium best suited to express the Romantic concept of "life as art."

URSULA HUDSON-WIEDENMANN

Bibliography

Blackwell, Jeannine, and Susane Zantop, eds. *Bitter Healing. German Women Writers from 1700 to 1830: An Anthology.* Lincoln: University of Nebraska Press, 1990.

Ebrecht, Angelika, Regina Nörtemann, and Herta Schwarz, eds. *Brieftheorie des 18. Jahrhunderts. Texte, Kommentare, Essays.* Stuttgart: Metzler, 1990.

Feilchenfeldt, Konrad. " 'Berliner Salon' und Briefkultur um 1800," in *Der Deutschunterricht* 36, no. 4 (1984): 77–99.

———. "Öffentlichkeit und Chiffrensprache in Briefen der späteren Romantik." In *Probleme der brief-edition.* Edited by Wolfgang Frühwald, Hans-Joachim Mähl, and Walter Müller-Seidel. Bonn: Bad-Godesberg, 1977.

Francke, Kuno, and W. G. Howard, eds. *The German Classics of the Nineteenth and Twentieth Centuries.* 20 vols. New York: AMS Press, 1969.

Habermas, Jürgen. *Strukturwandel der Öffentlichkeit. Untersuchungen zu einer Kategorie der bürgerlichen Gesellschaft.* Darmstadt: Luchterhand, 1962.

Hahn, Barbara. *"Antworten Sie mir!" Rahel Levin Varnhagens Briefwechsel.* Berlin: Stroemfeld/Roter Stern 1990.

Nickisch, Reinhard M. C., *Brief.* Stuttgart: Metzler, 1991.

LETTERS: UNITED STATES

The apparent truism that letters are designed primarily with *either* public *or* private consumption in mind is true only up to a point in the study of American letters in the Romantic era. As the period encompasses the American Revolution, the letter format finds itself employed in broadsheets for the purposes of political debate; yet, even as a public dialogue is invited, the writer reveals his own passionate conviction (for example, in *The Federalist*). At the same time, private correspondence may be both true to its ostensible purpose and yet hint that its writers recognize that their lives and beliefs are already of importance in a rapidly changing public sphere (for example, the letters of John and Abigail Adams). Finally, in a century in which the possibilities of epistolary fiction were systematically extended by Choderos de Laclos, Samuel Richardson, and J. Hector St. John de Crèvecoeur's *Letters from an American Farmer* would succeed where novelists had failed in sustaining the illusion that his "letters" were a true account of life at the frontier. Yet in truth, they illustrate the full potential of the letter format to allow the creation of an imagined letter writer whose apparent sincerity masks the fact that he is a fictional construct, creating one of the iconic explorations of eighteenth-century American life in letters.

The history of the letter as an instigator of, and vehicle for, American public debate on constitutional matters begins outside America and just outside the widest chronological definition of the Romantic era. From 1720 to 1724, the London-based writers Thomas Gordon and John Trenchard wrote for the Whig *London Journal* a series of letters under the pseudonym of Cato.

Cato's recurring interest in the politics of empire (believing that imperial expansion increases commerce for the benefit of all) ensured *Cato's Letters* a high profile in the American colonies, long after their original production. The argument of letter number 106, "Of plantations and colonies" (December 8, 1722), was to be frequently cited by leading revolutionaries. Cato writes that "there can be but two Ways in Nature to hinder [colonies] from throwing off their Dependence; one to keep it out of their Power, and the other out of their Will. The first must be by Force; and the latter by using them well. . . ." The argument that Cato develops from this was interpreted by many later American writers as justification for the equal treatment of colonists, whose commerce benefits both themselves and their mother country. In *Cato's Letters* we see a literary and political model for those at the forefront of American revolutionary politics, and the pattern for one of the most important texts in American political theory: James Madison's tenth letter from *The Federalist*.

In the political debate out of which the American Constitution was born, James Madison was of the Federalist party: favoring the Constitution rather than supporting those who already had reservations about the power it envisaged for national government. As Alexander Hamilton embarked upon a series of letters to be published in New York papers seeking ratification of the Constitution by that state, he sought the aid of both Madison and John Jay. Writing together under the pseudonym of Publius, the three men produced eighty-five letters from October 1787 to August 1788 that have been collected as *The Federalist*. Unquestionably one of the most important of these letters is the tenth, ascribed to Madison. With the models of ancient Athens and Rome firmly in view, Madison invites the people of New York to support a greater and as yet untried vision of republican government, one in which the sheer size of the nation will demand that its elected representatives think beyond their electors' local concerns, balancing them against the potentially competing interests of a much larger state.

While the letter form was being employed for the purposes of public constitutional debate, it naturally continued to be used as a vehicle for the most private exchanges. One of the greatest collections of private letters from the period is that of John Adams and his wife, Abigail. From 1774 to 1783, over three hundred letters passed between the man who would be second president of the United States and his unschooled wife, to whom fell the management of their farm and raising of four children during John Adams's frequent absences. When their grandson published the correspondence of John and Abigail Adams in the mid-nineteenth century, it became apparent that the letters revealed not only the writers' extreme happiness in a fifty-four-year marriage, but that they touched upon the key issues informing the creation of the American nation, giving readers an unparalleled insight into the reactions of two people to the extraordinary events in which they played such a key part. That Abigail Adams lacked a formal education and that her letters preserve an idiosyncratic spelling only adds to the richness of these letters as a source of information about American life at this time. For the reader wishing to trace contemporary responses to the Declaration of Independence or to gain a firsthand account of figures such as Benjamin Franklin, the Adams correspondence will not disappoint.

Situated both chronologically and stylistically between Madison's public letters and the intimate correspondence between the Adams, events in America generate one of the most distinctive uses of the letter form in a text that resists easy classification. Crèvecoeur's *Letters from an American Farmer* (1782) is simultaneously one of the great investigations of what it means to be an American as well as an astonishing blend of fact and fiction that has frequently passed for unadulterated truth. Crèvecoeur

was born in France, and lived in both Britain and Canada before spending a period of time farming in New York, beginning in 1769. The American Revolution saw him embark for France, where he remained until 1783. Returning to America as French consul to New York, Connecticut, and New Jersey, he learned of the death of his wife and loss of his farm in an Indian raid. The twelve letters that constitute Crèvecoeur's text were begun in 1769 and completed in 1780, before being sold to the London bookseller Thomas Davies. Crèvecoeur's cosmopolitan background and diplomatic role are worth knowing simply in order to appreciate the degree of fictional construction separating Crèvecoeur's American farmer, James, from Crèvecoeur himself. In Crèvecoeur's text, we confront one of the paradoxes of letter writing: that the minute we commit our views to paper, we shape them for an intended audience, whether an audience of one that is known, or an audience of many beyond our immediate geographical and temporal confines.

Many more letters and letter writers of this period deserve mention, the correspondences of Franklin, Jefferson and Washington being only the most obvious. The letters discussed, however, serve to show the differing uses to which the letter may be put, and between their poles of public and private engagement, we see the way in which letters may shape not only the mood of an individual, but of a nation in the making.

GLYNIS RIDLEY

Bibliography

Norton, Mary Beth. *Liberty's Daughters: The Revolutionary Experience of American Women, 1750–1800*. Boston: Little, Brown, 1980.

Regis, Pamela. *Describing Early America: Bartram, Jefferson, Crèvecoeur, and the Rhetoric of Natural History*. De Kalb: Northern Illinois University Press, 1992.

Shields, David S. *Civil Tongues and Polite Letters in British America*. Chapel Hill: University of North Carolina Press, 1997.

Warner, Michael. *The Letters of the Republic: Publication and the Public Sphere in Eighteenth-Century America*. Cambridge, Mass.: Harvard University Press, 1996.

Wood, Gordon S. *The Creation of the American Republic, 1776–1787*. Chapel Hill: University of North Carolina Press, 1969.

LEWIS, MATTHEW GREGORY 1775–1818

English novelist, playwright, and poet

Matthew Gregory Lewis did not on the face of it seem destined to become more than a peripheral figure in the intellectual life of his time. Born into a well-to-do family, he obediently followed the path set out for him by his father, a government official. He received a classical education at Oxford and was sent to the continent to perfect his French and learn German before embracing, without passion, a diplomatic career with the British embassy in The Hague from 1794. Later on he became an unenthusiastic member of parliament. Despite his rather dull character (both his friend Walter Scott and Lord Byron described him as "a good man" but "a bore"), in 1796 Lewis suddenly gained

notoriety and found himself at the forefront of public life with the publication of *The Monk*, a long romance written in the space of only ten weeks.

The novel instantly won him an enduring reputation and a nickname. "Monk Lewis" became universally known as an immoral writer and possibly a plagiarist. Byron's romantic apostrophe gives a sense of the image that was constructed around Lewis: "Even Satan's self with thee might dread to dwell / And in thy skull discern a deeper hell . . ." (*English Bards and Scotch Reviewers*, 1809). Samuel Taylor Coleridge, in the *Critical Review* (1797), condemned the novel as "a poison for youth and a provocative for the debauchee." When in the second edition Lewis included with his name on the title page the initials "MP", his name became anathema. Lewis became known as the "author of *The Monk*," and all his subsequent work was judged in reference to the literary merit and the moral standard of the romance.

Beyond the scandal created by its overt sexual allusions and sometimes blasphemous character, Lewis's text must be seen as a landmark in Romanticism. Whether it created "an epoch in our literature," as Scott wrote, or simply documents certain literary tendencies of its time, *The Monk* is linked to the arrival of German Romantic drama and fiction in England, and Lewis is associated with the introduction of German material to the English Romantic movement. Lewis knew German very well; he was a proficient and avid reader of German literature and a very capable translator. He is said to have translated parts of Johann Wolfgang von Goethe's *Faust* aloud for Byron, and he published translations of several German Romantic pieces, such as Johann Christoph Friedrich von Schiller's *Kabale und Liebe* (*The Minister*, 1798), for instance. His *Tales of Wonder* (1801) give a sense of the importance of German literature in his work. Scott describes *The Monk* as "a romance in German taste," not so much because it is filled with references to German works—most of them so unconscious that his reputation as a plagiarist is hardly justified—but because of its dark atmosphere and the intensity of the emotions it unleashes. *The Monk* draws on the Sturm und Drang (storm and stress) movement, on shock and horror rather than sentimentality. But Lewis's contribution to the Gothic tradition amounts to a redefinition of the genre. Unlike the traditional villain, Ambrosio, the monk, is not a prototypical, recognizable embodiment of evil. He is an outstanding individual inhabited by conflicting qualities and destroyed by the impossibility of fulfilling his complex potential as both true saint and perfect rake.

As a traditional Gothic text, *The Monk* shows how younger generations are victimized by parental figures, here religious figures of authority. But far from simply staging the terrifying traps awaiting the young heroes and uncovering the dangers lurking beneath the smooth surface of a familiar world, *The Monk* concentrates on the exploration of an ego that, unable to comply with the rules and at the same time to break them, is thus condemned to madness and alienation. Such madness and excess are in fact the very mark of a turning point in the tradition of the Gothic. Horror has replaced terror as the dominant literary impulse, and Lewis does not strive to present a world in which rationality and high moral intentions ultimately triumph. Virtue, order, and morality are no longer attainable goals in an age in which man preys on man. *The Monk*, as the Marquis de Sade wrote (*Idées sur les romans*, 1878), was "the inevitable result of the revolutionary shocks which all Europe had suffered."

Although Lewis's other works have for the most part failed the test of posterity, *The Castle Spectre*, an absurd and highly successful melodrama, made him a popular dramatist. Conceived in the vein of Horace Walpole's *Mysterious Mother*, Lewis's Gothic drama is notable for its sensationalism and its stage effects more than its intrinsic literary qualities. Despite its stock characters and a rather involved plot, the play is notable for the spectacular appearance on stage of a ghost in blazing light. Once again, Lewis exerted a considerable influence on the taste and literary tendencies of his time. Lewis wrote or translated a total of eighteen plays, and the theater seems to have been the medium most suited to his literary temperament, his sense of the spectacular, and his love of effects.

Lewis was a very prolific writer, but if, as Eino Railo remarks, "one searches in vain for what might truly denote a development in a literary sense," one cannot help wondering, with André Parreaux, whether "the obvious dwindling of Lewis' creative power" was not to be ascribed to the constantly renewed charges of immorality and plagiarism which accompanied the critical reception of his works, regardless of their actual content. Lewis never developed a persecution complex. Yet, it is symptomatic that the only work Lewis did not write to conciliate or provoke public opinion is the one which in Coleridge's eyes, and in the view of most critics, is considered his best work. *Journal of a West India Proprietor*, which was not meant for publication and appeared sixteen years after Lewis's death, is an "unaffected, delightful" book of travels that "shows the man himself, and not an inconsiderable man, certainly a much finer mind than I supposed before from the perusal of his romance," Coleridge concludes. It seems that Lewis was, in a way, the victim of his dark literary persona "Monk Lewis."

CHRISTINE BERTHIN

Biography

Born on July 9, 1775 in London. Spent the last half of 1792 in Weimar, met Goethe and Weiland. Received bachelor's degree in 1794, Christ Church, Oxford. Arrived in The Hague in May. *The Monk* completed in September. Obtained a seat in parliament in 1796. In 1797, Coleridge's review of *The Monk* led the way for future attacks. Met Walter Scott in 1798. Inherited a sizable fortune in 1812 at the death of his father. Met Lord Byron in 1813. In 1815 first journey to Jamaica to institute humanitarian reforms in slave treatment. In 1816, began a year and a half long tour of the continent. Met Percy Bysshe Shelley and stayed with Byron. Second journey to Jamaica, 1817; died on the way back, in 1818. Buried at sea.

Selected Works

The Monk: A Romance. 1796.
Village Virtues: A Dramatic Satire. In Two Parts. 1796.
The Minister: A Tragedy in Five Acts. 1797.
The Castle Spectre: A Drama, in Five Acts. 1798.
The Love of Gain: A Poem. 1799.
The East Indian: A Comedy in Five Acts. 1800.
Tales of Wonder. 1801.
Aldermon, the Outlaw: A Romantic Drama, in Three Acts. 1801.
Alfonso, King of Castile: A Tragedy, in Five Acts. 1801.
The Bravo of Venice, A Romance. 1805.
Adelgitha; or, The Fruits of a Single Error. A Tragedy, in Five Acts. 1806.
Feudal Tyrants; or, The Counts of Carlsheim and Sargans. A Romance. 1806.
He Loves and He Rides Away: A Favourite Ballad. 1808.
Romantic Tales. 1808.
Venoni; or, The Novice of St.Mark's. A Drama, in Three Acts. 1809.
Timour the Tartar: A Grand Romantic Melo-Drama, in Two Acts. 1811.
One O'Clock! or, The Knight and the Wood Daemon. A Grand Musical Romance, in Three Acts. 1811.
Rich and Poor: A Comic Opera, in Three Acts. 1812.

Poems. 1812.
Journal of a West India Proprietor. 1834.

Bibliography

Botting, Fred. *Gothic.* London: Routledge, 1996.
Kiely, Robert. *The Romantic Novel in England.* Cambridge, Mass.: Harvard University Press, 1972.
Kilgour, Maggie. *The Rise of the Gothic Novel.* London: Routledge, 1995.

Parreaux, André. *The Publication of The Monk: A Literary Event 1796–1798.* Paris: Librairie Marcel Didier, 1960.
Peck, Louis. *A Life of Matthew G. Lewis.* Cambridge, Mass.: Harvard University Press, 1961.
Punter, David. *The Literature of Terror: A History of Gothic Fictionss from 1765 to the Present Day.* London: Routledge, 1980.
Railo, Eino. *The Haunted Castle, A Study of the Elements of English Romanticism.* London, 1927.

LIBERTY

"O Liberty, how many crimes are committed in thy name!" Madame Roland's final words before submitting to the guillotine of the French Revolution have come, for many, to highlight the gulf that often opens between the pursuit of a political ideal or individual goal and the means used to achieve its implementation. In framing the *Declaration of Independence* (1776), Thomas Jefferson would shrewdly choose a word order that recognized all men's right to "life, liberty, and the pursuit of happiness"; in this formulation, the preservation of life is given primacy over an individual's right to pursue his own notion of liberty at any cost. Throughout the Romantic era, across Europe and the United States, writers and artists would test notions of individual liberty, often against a turbulent political backdrop where claim and counter-claim was made for the defense of the ideal of liberty itself. Moving chronologically through the period and ranging across Britain, the United States, Ireland, and France, the definition of liberty may be seen to evolve and shape itself in accordance with surrounding social and political pressures.

Liberty became a rallying cry in both Britain and France in 1763. In London, the writer John Wilkes was tried for seditious libel for his outspoken criticism of the government and "Wilkes and Liberty" demonstrations first convulsed the capital (ending only in 1774). If Wilkes's supporters were seeking greater political freedom, then religious liberty was at issue in France where, in 1763, Voltaire (1694–1778) published his Treatise on Tolerance. Responding to the brutal execution of a French Protestant father accused of murdering his son (who, it was rumored, was going to convert to Catholicism), Voltaire's text sought to demonstrate that liberty of worship was not a threat to any state. In challenging the supposed benefits of religious and political conformity, many writers of the 1760s and beyond were inspired by Jean-Jacques Rousseau's famous assertion in *The Social Contract*, 1762 that "man is born free but everywhere is in chains." That is, established political and religious systems were envisaged as mental prisons, any challenge to which might result in actual physical imprisonment, or worse.

The first systematic attempt to enshrine individual liberties in law and to uncouple religious conformity from full citizenship of the state was made by those who challenged the British government in the American War of Independence (1776–83). For over a decade before the official declaration of hostilities, American residents had been requesting the same liberties (however limited) as their British counterparts—chiefly the right to some representation at Westminster. But while Jefferson's original framing of the Declaration of Independence recognized that liberty could not be partial and, if extended to all men, must include

recognition of the plight of America's African slaves, his references to slavery had ultimately to be struck from the Declaration before it was acceptable to all signatory states. As the meaning of liberty was debated and tested during the Romantic era, it should be remembered that slavery was not abolished in the British empire until 1807, and that the American Civil War would be fought before Jefferson's original conception of liberty could begin to be imagined for many inhabitants of North America.

The victory of American forces against British imperial might was to be an inspiration to many at the beginning of the French Revolution in 1789. The fall of the Bastille on July 14, 1789, was quickly followed by the Declaration of the Rights of Man on August 4. Yet in this new republic, its leaders committed to "liberté, égalité, fraternité," it quickly became apparent that the concept of liberty for the many was being used to sanction the state's brutalizing treatment of a few. What was being done in the name of liberty was, as Madame Roland realized, quite at odds with the political rhetoric that surrounded the ideal. In part 1 of the *Rights of Man* (1791), Thomas Paine would enthusiastically insist that the rights of men, including equality and individual liberty, took primacy over man-made forms of government. Paine's willingness to extend this sentiment to the plight of the imprisoned Louis XVI led to his imprisonment as a traitor. Deprived of his own individual liberty, Paine must have been in a better position than many to reflect on the gulf between the ideal of liberty and the *realpolitik*.

In Britain, Paine's ideas informed the creation of the London Corresponding Society (founded in 1792 by shoemaker Thomas Hardy). The commitment of its members to constitutional reform led to much informed political debate. Horrified that the pursuit of liberty by what Edmund Burke termed "the swinish multitude" might lead to the overthrow of the political establishment, the British government imprisoned and tried leading radicals whose only crime was to question what words such as *rights*, *constitution*, and *liberty* actually meant. That the Treason Trials of 1794 saw the upholders of Paine's ideology walk free was for many a triumph of the individual's right to pursue liberty of speech. Four years later, in 1798, discussion of liberty in Ireland (the attempted freeing of Ireland from British rule) would culminate in an uprising of Catholic and Protestant Irishmen against the British crown. The United Irishmen's pursuit of liberty was not of the liberty of the individual within the state, but of one state from another: not liberty *within* empire but liberty *from* empire. Powerful though the idea of liberty was for the United Irishmen, the lack of substantial support from France dealt their campaign a crushing blow.

That France failed to provide all the support the leaders of the United Irishmen required in 1798 is, with hindsight, unsurprising, since Napoleon Bonaparte (1769–1821) was less interested in the liberty of Ireland than in the aggrandizement of France. The rise of Napoleon and the terrifying march of his rapacious armies across Europe was to deprive many individuals and states of their right to self-determination. Defeated by the Russian winter in 1812 before he was more decisively defeated by allied forces under the command of the Duke of Wellington at the Battle of Waterloo, Napoleon came to symbolize, for many, the archoppressor of liberty. And yet, within France itself, his reform of the legal system and mechanisms of government would in no small way enshrine the original principles of the French Revolution in the nation's constitution. When the Orleanist monarchy was overthrown in France in 1848, the leaders of the revolution had no qualms about seeing the republican flag that had so terrified Napoleon's conquests as a "symbol of equality, of liberty, and of fraternity," but most of all as a "symbol of order." The need for the pursuit of liberty to be in accord with the rule of law and not in conflict with it was again restated, over seventy years after Jefferson had sought the right order of words to express the relationship between individual freedom and public responsibility.

GLYNIS RIDLEY

LIBERTY LEADING THE PEOPLE 1830

Painting by Eugène Delacroix

During the 1820s, Delacroix sought to establish and then consolidate his career by producing large-scale paintings on literary and contemporary subjects to be shown at the biennial salons. This trend continued when, following the July Revolution, he painted *Liberty Leading the People*.

On July 25, 1830, Charles X signed four proclamations with the intention of crushing liberal opposition and securing an ultraconservative government. These measures, which included the abolition of the freedom of the press, the dissolution of an unfavorable National Assembly, and a new electoral system that favored the aristocracy, were greeted with scorn and anger, and in three days (July 27–29, 1830), the so-called Trois Glorieuses, a coalition of the middle classes and workers, swept him from power and forced his abdication on August 2, 1830. In his place, the constitutional monarch Louis-Philippe, the Duc d'Orléans, was installed.

Although he took no part in the uprising, Delacroix quickly produced a tribute to the heroes of the barricades: *Liberty Leading the People* (also known as *Liberty on the Barricades*). On October 12, 1830, he wrote to his brother Charles, "I have undertaken a modern subject, a barricade, and if I have not fought for my country, at least I will paint for her." He worked on the canvas from October until early December, eventually signing two of the spars of wood at the right with his name and the date of 1830.

Delacroix showed his *Liberty* at the salon of 1831 with about thirty-five other drawn and painted commemorations of the Trois Glorieuses and the burials that followed. In the Salon's catalog it appeared as *28 July: Liberty Leading the People*, indicating that the action took place during the day of fiercest fighting around the Hotel de Ville. However, the painting was not the action of a partisan of the Revolution; Delacroix wrote to his nephew Charles Verinac, "A simple stroller like myself ran the same risk of stopping a bullet as did the improvised heroes who marched on the enemy with pieces of iron lashed to broom sticks," a comment by which he clearly disassociated himself from the participants. Alexandre Dumas recalled meeting Delacroix and saw that he was much alarmed by the sight of the unruly, working-class mob. But, as Dumas recounted, memories of his Bonapartist upbringing were stirred by the sight of the tricolor fluttering from Notre Dame, and enthusiasm soon took the place of fear.

Liberty was visually striking, capturing the excitement and energy of the event, and was a potent symbol of the struggle for freedom. Silhouetted against a backdrop of cannon smoke, the personification of *Liberty* is a combination of the real and the ideal, the palpable and the ephemeral. On her head she wears the red cap of liberty, as popularized during the first French Revolution and derived from the ancient Roman Phrygian cap, the emblem of freed slaves. Bare breasted and holding the tricolor in one hand and an infantry musket in the other, she appears as half goddess and half woman of the people. Delacroix's knowledge of classical art shaped her appearance and she is based partially on the Venus de Milo and on ancient personifications of Victory, though now lacking wings. Such sculptural references did not prevent *Liberty* from also becoming apparition-like, and she is perhaps the last ecstatic vision of the dying man at her feet. Many stories and poems about the bravery of women emerged in the aftermath of the revolution, and Auguste Le Barbier described *Liberty* as "a strong woman with powerful breasts." Numerous other visual sources have been proposed for *Liberty*, such as Le Barbier the Elder's painting of Jeanne Hachette (1778) and Pierre-Narcisse Guérin's mythological paintings *Aurore and Céphale* (1810), and *Iris and Morpheus* (1811). However, Delacroix's figure of *Liberty* was primarily the product of his own imagination and, as preliminary drawings show, built on the example of his *Greece Expiring on the Ruins of Missolonghi* (1826).

Liberty is accompanied by figures from all classes of society: a bereted street urchin brandishing a pair of pistols, a white-shirted, saber-wielding factory worker, and a blue-shirted day laborer from the country who is on his knees. The top-hatted figure has been variously identified as a student, Delacroix himself (which it certainly is not), Delacroix's friend Fréderic Villot, and Etienne Arago, an ardent Republican and director of the Vaudeville Theater with whom Delacroix seems to have had little or no contact. It seems unlikely that this figure is meant to be a known individual, and probably represents an artisan or chief of a workshop rather than someone of the middle classes. The main figures surge forward victorious over the corpses of a Royal Guardsman and a Carbinier. For the dead figures in the

(Ferdinand Victor) Eugène Delacroix, *Liberty Leading the People*. Reprinted courtesy of the Bridgeman Art Library.

foreground Delacroix took his cue from Théodore Géricault's *Raft of the Medusa* (1819) and Antoine-Jean Gros's two great works of Napoleonic propaganda, *The Plague House at Jaffa* (1804) and *The Battle of Eylau* (1808). The action is set on the right bank of the River Seine, probably close to the Hotel de Ville, but no precise topography is suggested and Delacroix invented the view of the towers of Notre Dame since no such vista was possible in 1830.

Some critics were unnerved by the sight of the rebellious rabble that Delacroix had depicted, and complained that Liberty was too ugly and common to portray such a lofty ideal, disturbed by the seeming contradiction of a realistic allegorical personification. Others found no such difficulties and concluded that Delacroix was employing artistic license and had created a new idiom: a simultaneous history painting and allegory that had universal significance because he had avoided references to specific locations and actions.

Delacroix saw the arrival of the July Monarchy as a return of the opportunity to paint substantial historical works, subjects that the Bourbon government had denied him. But *Liberty* was not simply a deliberate and perhaps cynical attempt to ingratiate himself with the new regime, and Delacroix invested it with a spirited optimism and belief in the righteous self-determination

of the French. However, *Liberty*'s content was too inflammatory for Louis-Philippe and the painting was not purchased by the royal household. Instead, it was bought by the Ministry of the Interior for the modest fee of three thousand francs and Delacroix was awarded the Legion of Honor. The painting entered the Luxembourg Gallery immediately but was displayed only until 1832 and then put into storage for fear of it either inspiring further insurrection or becoming a permanent and divisive reminder of defeat for supporters of the Bourbons. It was again briefly displayed following the 1848 Revolution and entered the Louvre in 1874.

During the last 120 years, Delacroix's *Liberty* has become intermingled with personifications of the French Republic and ultimately the work has come to embody the authority of the French state. From 1979 until 1994, it was placed on the back of the hundred-franc note, and since 1982 *Liberty*'s head has appeared on postage stamps.

SIMON LEE

See also **Delacroix, Eugène**

Work

Liberty Leading the People, 1830. Oil on canvas, 259 cm × 325 cm, Louvre, Paris.

Bibliography

Agulhon, M. "Marianne into Battle: Republican Imagery and Symbolism in France, 1789–1880," Cambridge: Cambridge University Press, 1981. 38–42.

Gaudibert, P. "Delacroix et le romantisme révolutionnaire," *Europe* 41, no. 408 (1963): 4–21.

Hadjinicolaou, N. "La Liberté guidant le peuple de Delacroix devant son premier public," *Actes de la recherche en sciences sociales* 28 (1979): 3–26.

Hamilton, G. H. "The iconographical origins of Delacroix's *Liberty Leading the People*," in *Studies in Art and Literature for Bella da Costa Greene*. Edited by Dorothy Eugenia Miner. Princeton, N.J.: Princeton University Press, 1954. 55–66.

Johnson, L. *The Paintings of Eugène Delacroix*. Vol. 1. Oxford: Oxford University Press, 1981.

Marrinan, M. *Painting Politics for Louis-Philippe: Art and Ideology in Orléanist France 1830–1848*. New Haven, Conn.: Yale University Press, 1988.

Toussaint, H. *La Liberté guidant le peuple de Delacroix*. Paris: Réuniion des Musées Nationaux, 1982.

Trapp, F. "The Attainment of Delacroix." Baltimore, Md.: Johns Hopkins University Press, 1971. 93–104.

LICHTENBERG, GEORG CHRISTOPH 1742–1799

German physicist and satirical writer

Georg Christoph Lichtenberg, the hunchbacked physicist from Göttingen, was a complex character who cannot easily be subsumed under Enlightenment values, even though he never faltered in his allegiance to reason. His writings are multifarious, ranging from poems to scientific articles, but they are all part of a single confession. He attempted to write a history of his mind as well as his wretched body, his "own natural history,"

with a "sincerity which, in some, may cause a kind of sympathetic embarrassment." J. P. Stern has called Lichtenberg's thought a "doctrine of scattered occasions," and this characterization befits Lichtenberg's life as well. Some time between 1768 and 1771, according to his diary, we find him studying Isaac Newton and reflecting on his mood, which would push him toward melancholy and self-degradation were it not for two compasses which steer him through this sea of trouble: friendship and wine. He feels elevated by the fact that his mind can follow that of the great Newton, until his two chambermaids enter and distract him from his lofty intellectual pursuits towards the material side of existence: "The two of us, me and my body, were never before so divided; at times, we don't even recognise the other, and then we run into each other in such a fashion that we both don't know where we are." Perhaps there was a chance of greater unison when he was about to marry Maria Dorothea Stechard, who had joined his household as a maid at the age of thirteen but who died of a sudden illness at seventeen. Lichtenberg later married and had children; however, marriage was never easy for him.

Lichtenberg's life was uneventful, and his reputation as one of the best physicists did not rest on any groundbreaking scientific discovery. His contemporaries acknowledged his range of knowledge, but above all his experimental skill. Lichtenberg had a way with instruments and mechanical devices that he was said to lift out of their delivery boxes like babies out of the cradle. And he was also a practical man who could be trusted to determine the exact geographical position of the towns of Hannover, Osnabrück, and Stade on behalf of the English king, who improved the electrophorus (a device for generating static electricity) and discovered the basic principles of modern xerographic copying, who almost invented the hot air balloon while experimenting with hydrogen bubbles, and who paved the way for the lightning conductor. As a testament to his work, a lunar crater was named after him in 1802.

His name as a scientist remains associated with the *Lichtenberg'schen Figuren*; Lichtenberg's "figures" were an accidental discovery. Dust settling on his electrophorus showed star- and branch-shaped patterns that indicated the distribution of otherwise invisible electrical forces. Lichtenberg refined the accidental phenomenon and wrote about it in 1777. This was interesting at the time but would not have made his posthumous fame, nor would the fact that in 1784 he became editor of Johann Erxleben's much respected journal *Anfangsgründe der Naturlehre* (*Foundations of the Natural Sciences*).

The Lichtenberg best remembered now is Lichtenberg the writer, aphorist, and keeper of diaries (*Sudelbücher*), the essayist and correspondent, the man of boundless wit whose imagination was able to see a connection among even the most remotest of things, yet who never relinquished positivism and empiricism, and the psychologist and social critic. His commentary on William Hogarth's copper plates bears witness to all of this.

As the editor of the *Göttingischer Taschenkalender* (*Göttingen Pocket AlmanacI*, 1777–), his aim was to enlighten the public in a scientific spirit. Due to Lichtenberg's talent for illustration of principle by way of the fantastic, it is easy to lose sight of this. In a text titled *Ein Traum* (*A Dream*), a physicist is asked by a higher being to analyze a kind of marble which turns out to be a miniature earth. It is destroyed by the scientific investigation (which finds nothing but the most basic minerals) before the physicist realizes what it is. Lichtenberg's point is not how mysterious transmutations in nature are, but how prone to massive error our methods of investigation are if interpreted in a simplistic way. The same point lies behind his criticism of Johann

Kaspar Lavater's physiognomy. It is not the project as such—the attempt to draw conclusions about psychological traits from the physical—that Lichtenberg rejects, but the primitivism of the method which compensates for lack of empirical detail by prematurely establishing laws of correlation that are both too simple and make the wrong connections. In *Amintor's Morgenandacht* (*Amintor's Morning Prayer*, 1783) we find the same attitude: a pure, natural, and pantheistic curiosity which takes the world and experience exactly as it finds them and also accepts religious elements in so far as they are grounded in experience. At the point where the empirical limits are reached, the text concludes that no more can be said because "it is like that: philosophy, if it is to be more than a collection of subject matters for discussion, can only be taught indirectly."

DANIEL STEUER

Biography

Born July 1, 1742, in Oberramstadt, the seventeenth child of Johann Conrad and Henrike Catharine Lichtenberg. He was educated at the Darmstädter Pädagogium, and then the Georgia Augusta University in Göttingen, which had been founded by George II in 1737. From 1763 to 1767 he studied mathematics, astronomy, and natural history, and at the end of this period was appointed second professor of mathematics and teacher of English at the University of Giessen but preferred to stay in Göttingen. Two journeys to England in 1770 and 1775 left a lasting impression on Lichtenberg, and he remained a lifelong anglophile. He was appointed to a personal chair in philosophy at Göttingen in 1770, and in 1775 finally became ordinary professor. After a violent illness in 1789, his hypochondriacal streak gained in strength. In 1795 he declined a prestigious position at the University of Leiden. He died, after a short illness, on February 24, 1799 at the age of fifty. "Our life," he wrote, "may be compared to a winter's day, we are born between 12 and 1 at night, it is not before 8 o'clock that daylight breaks, and it is not even four in the afternoon when it begins to darken again, and at midnight we die."

Selected Works

Briefe aus England. 1776–78.
Göttinger Taschenkalender. 1778–, editor.
Göttingisches Magazin der Literatur und Wissenschaft. 1780–82. Editor, with J. G. A. Forster.
Über die Pronunciation der Schöpse des alten Griechenlandes. 1782.
Amintor's Morgenandacht. 1783.
Ausführliche Erklärung der Hogarthschen Kupferstiche. 1794–99.

Bibliography

Benjamin, Walter. "Lichtenberg. Ein Querschnitt." In *Gesammelte Schriften*, vol. 4. Edited by Rolf Tiedemann and Herman Schweppenhäuser. Frankfurt: Suhrkamp, 1972.
Hofmann, Gert. *Die kleine Stechardin.* München: Hanser, 1994.
Lichtenberg, Georg Christoph. *Schriften und Briefe.* 5 vols. Edited by Wolfgang Promies. München: Hanser, 1968.
Promies, Wolfgang. *Lichtenberg.* Reinbek: Rowohlt, 1964.
Schöne, Albrecht. *Aufklärung aus dem Geist der Experimentalphysik. Lichtenbergsche Konjunktive.* München: Beck, 1982.
Stern, J. P. *Lichtenberg: A Doctrine of Scattered Occasions.* London: Thames and Hudson, 1963.

LIEDER

The German Romantic Lied (plural: *Lieder*), or art song, flourished during the nineteenth century as a result of the close interaction between the literature and music of the time. The Romantics embraced the open texture of a single voice accompanied by a solitary piano for its ability to provide not only greater emotional expressiveness than instrumental music, but also more intimacy than the *bravura* style of opera. The Lied as a genre is specific to the Romantic era, unlike, for example, the symphony or opera. Symphonies arose in the mid-eighteenth century and are still composed to this day; the opera spans much of music history from the late sixteenth century through to the present. By contrast, the Lied did not appear until early in the eighteenth century and had faded by the end of that century, with the advent of "modern music." Thus, while many Romantic symphonies and operas exist, there are also numerous non-Romantic representatives. Conversely, all Lieder are Romantic, and probe such characteristic Romantic themes as death, night, dreams, unfilled longing, or wanderlust. The brevity of the Lied provides for the intensification of these concepts, placing the German art song among the defining manifestations of Romanticism in music.

Originally, the German word *Lied* referred to a poem, either with or without music. But in the nineteenth century, an extraordinary cultural commingling of poets, novelists, and musicians was seeking to erase the boundaries between the branches of art and to achieve an artistic synthesis. Whereas poets had traditionally considered their works complete, the early Romantic German poets now found that the addition of music turned their poems into "art songs" or Lieder. The concurrent emergence of German lyric poetry, especially that of Johann Wolfgang von Goethe, provided a wealth of poetic material for composers to set. Social conditions of the time also contributed to the Lied's rise in popularity. With the middle class growing and most homes owning a piano, the performance of art song became a favorite pastime in the bourgeois salons of Europe. An explosion in the mass publishing of music provided the consuming public with inexpensive sheet music to buy.

The roots of the German Romantic Lied date back to the eighteenth-century *Volkstümliches* Lied, a national or popular song, simple in composition, with sources in folk music. Emerging from the poetic ballad, the words were strophic in form, that is, consisting of several repeated stanzas, each sharing the same poetic meter and rhyme scheme, and usually dealing with such themes as nature, romantic love, heroism, or the supernatural. The Romantics' admiration of the primitive and their call for simplicity and naïveté in art and literature led to a renewed interest in this form of poetry. The *Volkstümliches* Lied was frequently presented as an ordinary piano solo, since the text was usually de-emphasized by being inscribed between the two staves of the piano.

The Lied first materialized in northern Germany, late in the eighteenth century. Contemporary theoretical descriptions of the new genre describe the Lied as a lyrical poem of several stanzas united by a melody that is repeated for each stanza. According to the description, it should be similar to folk music, carefully expressive of the mood and meaning of the text, set to a simple accompaniment, and easily sung by an average voice, with or without formal training. The typical setting was musically unambitious, syllabic (one note per syllable of text), and pretentiously simple.

Ludwig van Beethoven, who composed over sixty lieder, wrote mostly in the *Volkstümliches* mode. In his early Lieder, the style is instrumental, the voice superfluous; words yield to the musical exigencies. Musical and not textual demands determine the repetition of lines and even of individual words. Gradually, Beethoven infused this simple genre with operatic traditions such as the *recitative* (speechlike declamation) and the *arioso* (songlike melody), but forms generally remained strophic with straightforward melodic lines.

Franz Schubert was the first great master of the Romantic Lied, having written over 600 settings during his brief lifetime. Schubert explored and expanded the genre with haunting melodies, complex modulations, chromaticism, unexpected shifts between tonic major and minor, and a pictorial piano accompaniment suggested by the text. His earliest examples continued to reflect the ballad style, which, in Schubert's hand, became an extended piece with dramatic shifts in texture and tonality, between recitative and arioso, and among several different illustrative keyboard configurations. However, Schubert gradually lost interest in these rambling, sectional songs. A Schubert Lied, although usually strophic in form, might have only two or three strophes and sometimes only one. Schubert employed repetition of words and even phrases for textual rather than musical emphasis. The Schubertian Lied was not intended for concert performance, but rather for private salon gatherings (known as "Schubertiads") of Schubert's own friends, often with Schubert himself at the piano.

Most of the Romantic composers dabbled in Lieder, but the first important successor to Schubert is Robert Schumann. Although Schumann initially believed Beethoven's large instrumental forms to be the foundation of Romanticism in music, he eventually turned to the wave of the future and concentrated on miniatures. Schumann brought to the genre the sensibilities of the concert pianist, introducing a flexible accompaniment independent from pictorial images in the poem. He saw the voice and accompaniment as equal partners in the interpretation of the poetry, using both to reflect minute shifts in meaning in the text. Schumann's piano, rather than presenting a literal illustration of the text, enters into a dialogue with the voice, interrupting, commenting, and adding more than merely harmonic support. Instrumental preludes, postludes, and interludes gained prominence in his settings. Schumann wrote many strophic songs, but he preferred to avoid sectionalization by masking breaks between strophes. Schumann's harmonies are most often open, that is, lacking a distinct tonal center, full of sudden modulations to remote keys, and often ending, seemingly, in midphrase. Schumann also experimented with the suspension of the rhythmic expectations of the barline. Schumann's demanding vocal lines with their extended range and wide leaps removed the Lied from the realm of the amateur singer.

The late-Romantic Lied culminated at the end of the nineteenth century in the songs of Johannes Brahms, Hugo

Wolf, and Gustav Mahler. By this time, the Lied had become an established musical form. Brahms's Lieder looked backward to the old ballad style with strophic forms complemented by dramatic, somewhat pictorial, accompaniments. Wolf wrote intense, piano-dominated songs, filled with rich harmonies and chromaticisms, anticipating the breakdown of traditional tonality. He avoided regular phrasing and never wrote a strophic Lied. Mahler turned the simple Romantic Lied into a symphonic genre, not only by providing orchestral accompaniments, but by expanding the scale and elaborateness of the composition.

NANCY F. GARF

Bibliography

Ivey, Donald. *Song: Anatomy, Imagery, and Styles*. New York: Free Press, 1970.

Hall, James Husst. *The Art Song*. Norman: University of Oklahoma Press, 1953.

Landau, Anneliese. *The Lied: The Unfolding of its Style*. Washington, D.C.: University Press of America, 1980.

Meister, Barbara. *Art Song: the Marriage of Music and Poetry*. Wakefield, N.H.: Hollowbrook, 1992.

———. *An Introduction to the Art Song*. New York: Taplinger, 1980.

Stevens, Denis, ed. *A History of Song*. New York: W. W. Norton, 1960.

LIEDER CYCLE

The *Lieder* cycle (song cycle), a grouping of individually complete songs linked by one of several unifying factors, flourished in the Romantic era. The genre resists precise definition, since the distinction between a song cycle and a song collection can be cloudy. Whereas the song cycle is an assortment of interrelated, self-sufficient songs, the song collection is a group of self-sufficient songs that are independent of one another. Generally, the poems of the cycle predate the music and are usually the output of a single poet. The task of the poet is to create a sequence of poems unified in subject matter yet diverse in mood, and organized to achieve a gradual intensification of emotion. The composer then follows the design of the poet and emulates, in music, the intensity and variety of the texts.

The defining factor in the song cycle is the presence of some identifiable element that provides cyclical coherence. This element may appear either in the text, in the music, or in both. The earliest texts related a story, providing cyclical coherence through the narrative itself. Sometimes, absent a narrative thread, the poems might share a textual relationship to one another in that they all treat a central idea or theme. In other examples, instead of a textual relationship, the sole evidence of cyclicism among the songs might be a musical coherence, which might manifest itself in any of several ways, including the use of instrumental interludes, a recurring melodic motive or harmonic progression, or the presence of a tonal plan.

The Lieder cycle was the next step in the late eighteenth-century rise of the uniquely Romantic genre, the German art song or Lied, a piece written for a single voice with piano accompaniment. The Lied was a result of the German poetic renaissance and the concomitant close interaction between the literature and music of the time. Social gatherings devoted to the arts were legendary; activities included eating, drinking, and dancing, along with singing, writing poetry, and composing melodies. Whereas the Lied is illustrative of the Romantic predilection for a blurring between the arts, the further emergence of the Lieder cycle reflects the Romantic penchant for the merging of the classic forms of the epic, lyric, and drama. The Lieder cycle, presenting a dramatic episode in verse set to music, was considered a prime example of this synthesis. Furthermore, the Romantics embraced two essentially incompatible scales of form: miniatures (in their songs, poems, and short piano works), and the grand gesture (in their lengthy novels and symphonies). The song cycle was thus a hybrid genre, a combination of several miniatures into an oversized whole. As the nineteenth century progressed, the song cycle gained even more momentum as the individual songs grew shorter.

Ludwig van Beethoven composed the first recognized Lieder cycle, *An die ferne geliebte*, (*To the Distant, Beloved*, 1815–16) a setting of six poems by Aloys Jeitteles. Beethoven achieves cyclic coherence both textually and musically. The textual connection is an essential factor, as the poetry is a narrative based on the daydreams of a lover separated from his beloved. Beethoven also links the poems musically, both tonally, and through transitional passages between the songs. Further musical coherence takes place when the cycle comes to an end with the return of musical material from the opening song.

Franz Peter Schubert's well-known cycle, *Die schöne Müllerin* (*The Lovely Miller Maid*, 1823; twenty poems by Wilhelm Müller) depicting the fortunes and misfortunes of a wayfaring young miller, was often acted out in the private salon gatherings of artists drawn to Schubert (Schubertiads). In addition to the textual cohesion provided by the story, Schubert unites several of the songs musically with related accompanimental figures to suggest the nearby brook beside which the narrative unfolds. Schubert's other great cycle, *Winterreise* (*Winter Journey*, 1828; twenty-four poems, also by Wilhelm Müller), in the absence of an explicit narrative thread, combines the predominant Romantic literary themes of wandering, alienation, nature, and unrequited love. Neither of Schubert's song cycles evidence tonal coherence.

Robert Schumann, by contrast, felt that key relationships between songs in a cycle were paramount. Schumann organized the major portion of his songs into cycles, grouped by such components as poet, subject, mood, or key association. The sixteen songs of his crowning achievement, the well-known cycle *Dichterliebe* (*Poems of Love*, 1840; poetry by Heinrich Heine), while distinct, are tonally linked, with adjacent songs in the cycle set in related keys. Furthermore, recurring motives, melodic figures, and harmonic progressions infuse the cycle, in the face of jarring mood shifts between songs.

The late nineteenth-century composers continued the Romantic tradition of the Lied, but the Lieder cycle, having already seen its pinnacle, became less precisely defined as exclusive from the song collection. The distinction between the cycle and the collection is most blurred in the work of Johannes Brahms. Brahms combined most of his Lieder into "collections." Even though Brahms never used the term *cycle*, he was precise about the ordering of his songs within the collections. Hugo Wolf, whose entire output consists almost exclusively of songs, grouped his Lieder according to individual poets. The song cycles of Gustav Mahler belong as much to the history of the symphony as of the Lied. Mahler took a genre that had begun as one of the most private and personal, and by substituting a full Romantic-sized symphony for the accompanying piano, transformed it into one of the most public.

NANCY F. GARF

Selected Works

Beethoven, Ludwig van. *An die ferne Geliebte, Op. 98*. New York: Schirmer, 1902.
Schumann, Robert. *Dichterliebe*. Edited by Sergius Kagan. New York: International Music, 1959.

Schubert, Franz. *Schöne Müllerin*. Edited by Sergius Kagan. New York: International Music, 1962.
———. *Winterreise*. Edited by Sergius Kagan. New York: International Music, 1962.

Bibliography

Gorrell, Lorraine. *The Nineteenth-Century German Lied*. Portland, Ore.: Amadeus, 1993.
Hallmark, Rufus, ed. *German Lieder in the Nineteenh Century*. New York: Schirmer, 1996.
Lewis, Christopher. "Text, Time and Tonic: Aspects of Patterning in the Romantic Cycle," *Intégral* 2 (1988): 37–73.
Turchin, Barbara. "The Nineteenth-Century *Wanderlieder* Cycle," *Journal of Musicology* 5 (1987): 498–525.
———. "Schumann's Song Cycles: the Cycle Within the Song," *Nineteenth Century Music* 8 (1984–85): 231–44.

LIND, JENNY (JOHANNA MARIA) 1820–1887

Swedish singer

One of the most gifted and renowned sopranos of her age, Jenny Lind gave acclaimed performances of the leading roles of Romantic opera and oratorio. Though universally known as Jenny, she was baptized Johanna Maria; in later life, she strongly preferred to be called by her married name, Mrs. Lind-Goldschmidt. These are but minor contradictions in a performer who fascinated audiences in the middle decades of the nineteenth century. She was born in Stockholm on October 6, 1820 to unmarried parents. From her twenty-two-year-old father she may have inherited some of her musicality; perhaps her intelligence came from her mother, a rather older and somewhat wealthier divorcee who was the proprietor of a girls' school. Lind passed her earliest years under the care of Carl Fendal, parish clerk and organist of Ed-Sollentuna, a country town fifteen miles from Stockholm. Early biographers dwell on this period as idyllic, and there can be little doubt that when the public called her the Swedish Nightingale they were to some degree responding to the notion of the singer as a child of nature coming from what were envisaged as distant Nordic locations. It was not long, however, before Lind returned to Stockholm. At first she was a pupil in her mother's school, but when she was still only nine the promise of her voice was noticed and, despite her mother's reservations about a stage career, she was admitted to the Stockholm Royal Opera School in 1830.

In 1838, after gaining stage experience by taking juvenile parts in a number of plays (such as Swedish translations of August Friedrich Ferdinand von Kotzebue's *Das Testament* and of Ducange's *Trente Ans dans la Vie d'un Joueur*), Lind made her operatic debut as Agathe in Carl von Weber's *Der Freischütz*. Her success in this demanding role, with its combination of colaratura and youthful exuberance, soon led to further opportunities in the works of Wolfgang Amadeus Mozart (as Pamina in *Die Zauberflöte* and Dona Anna in *Don Giovanni*) as well as in more recent works of a Romantic character, such as Gaetano Donizetti's *La straniera*, *Norma*, and *Lucia di Lammermoor*, Giacomo Meyerbeer's *Robert le Diable*, Gasparo Luigi Pacifico Spontini's *La Vestale*, and Weber's *Euryanthe*. Though the roles assigned to Lind in these operas call for a wide soprano range, confident breath-control, and great accomplishment in the performance of coruscating scales and arpeggios, she did not have to confront the vocal demands that Giuseppe Verdi and Richard Wagner would later make of their heroines. Nonetheless, by 1841 it was evident that Lind's voice was failing.

She therefore went to Paris and took lessons with Manuel Garcia, the son of the famous tenor and the most distinguished singing teacher of the century. After prescribing a period of rest for her vocal chords, he reconstructed her singing technique. A triumphant appearance in *Norma* in Stockholm on October 10, 1842 gave ample proof not only of Lind's recovery of form but of a marked improvement in both her voice and her interpretative powers. Though her midrange notes remained relatively weak, her register now extended even higher and had exceptional brilliancy. Her singing voice extended from B below middle C, up no less than two and a half octaves to G *in alt*. She had at her command not only a chromatic scale across this wide range, but also the complete control over dynamics and trills then required of sopranos.

Lind next embarked on the relatively short busy middle period of her career. With a repertory enlarged to include Donizetti's *Anna Bolena* and *La Fille du Régiment* and Giacomo Meyerbeer's *Les Huguenots*, she moved on from Stockholm to Berlin and Vienna. In 1846 she made a deep impression on Felix Mendelssohn at his ambitious Lower Rhine Festival in Aachen, when she distinguished herself in oratorio by her performance of the soprano solos in George Frideric Handel's *Alexander's Feast* and Franz Joseph Haydn's *Creation*. She returned to opera in May 1847 in a triumphant visit to Her Majesty's Theatre in London, where Queen Victoria and Prince Albert were as thrilled by her performance as was the British public. Francis Palgrave, the future editor of the *Golden Treasury*, provides an account of Jenny Lind in *I Puritani*: "admired her acting more than ever—the simplicity of a great soul, who never *acts*, but shows her thoughts in the action:—the singing perfection, as before. [Arthur Stanley] rather shocked at the intense reality of the madness—delighted with the joyous, irresistibly winning, cheerful parts." At the same time, her performance in Mendelssohn's *Elijah* at London's Exeter Hall established her reputation in oratorio.

Next came a prolonged tour of the United States: in eight months she visited ninety-three cities. Returning exhausted to Europe, Lind fulfilled her resolution to give up opera. She had long had doubts about the propriety of appearing on stage, the life of a traveling artist had no attractions for her, and her career had been marred by squabbles over contracts. In addition, she felt the attractions of respectability. Visiting Norwich while on tour in 1847 she had, for instance, felt honored to be received by the bishop. In 1852 she married Otto Goldschmidt, a gifted pianist who had become her accompanist three years earlier. Though he was ten years younger, the marriage was a great success; it provided her with the security she needed, while he enjoyed his wife's support as he became a force in English musical life, acting as vice principal (under Sterndale Bennett) of the Royal Academy of Music. When he contributed to the Bach revival in England by forming the Bach Choir, she trained the sopranos and led them in the epoch-making 1876 performance of the B-minor Mass. Though Lind firmly resisted all attempts to persuade her to perform again in opera, she continued with recital tours on the Continent and in England, where she sometimes disappointed the public by singing in German. She was a willing supporter of good causes, from the foundation of children's hospitals to the endowment of the Mendelssohn scholarships. Living her final years in London, the child who had become the Swedish Nightingale achieved her desired metamorphosis into eminent Victorian.

CHRISTOPHER SMITH

Biography

Born Stockholm, October 6, 1820, of unmarried parents. From age of six or seven began training for stage, taking children's roles. First operatic role, 1836. Success as Agathe in Weber's *Freischütz*, 1838. After near vocal breakdown, traveled to Paris to train with Manuel Garcia, 1841. Great success in Berlin in *Norma* and *La somnambula*, 1844. Debut at Gewandhaus in Leipzig, 1845. acquaintance with Mendelssohn and Joachim. Operatic roles in Germany, 1846. To England, appearing first as Meyerbeer's *Robert le diable*, 1847, tours in provinces. Last operatic performances, 1849. Singing tour in United States, 1850. Married Otto Goldschmidt, a pianist, 1852. Settled in London, 1853; concentrated on oratorio repertory, especially Mendelssohn's *Elijah*; became a professor of singing at Royal College of Music (of which Goldschmidt was deputy principal). Last stage appearance, as soloist in Goldschmidt's oratorio *Ruth*, 1870. Died at Malvern, on November 2, 1887.

Bibliography

Bishop, S., J. Buist, and M. Flynn. *Jenny Lind in Norwich: A Centenary Celebration*. Norwich, England: Norfolk and Norwich Hospital.

Black, A. F. "Two Virtuoso Performers in Boston." In *New Perspectives on Music: Essays in Honor of Eileen Southern*. Edited by J. Wright and S. A. Floyd Jr. Detroit Monographs in Musicology/Studies in Music no. 11. Warren, Mich.: Harmonie Park, 1992.

Bulman, J. *Jenny Lind*. London: Barrie, 1956.

Holland, H. Scott, and W. S. Rockstro. *Jenny Lind the Artist (1820– 51)*. 1893.

———, eds. *Memoir of Madame Jenny Lind-Goldschmidt: Her Early Life and Dramatic Career*. 2 vols. 1891.

Maulde, J. M. C. *The Life of Jenny Lind*. London: Cassell, 1926.

Pleasants, H. *The Great Singers*. London: Macmillan.

Wagenknecht, E. "Jenny Lind: The Nightingale as Avatar and Angel." In *Seven Daughters of the Stage*. Norman: University of Oklahoma Press, 1964.

LISZT, FRANZ 1811–1886

Hungarian pianist and composer

One of the most fascinating and controversial musicians of the Romantic era, Franz Liszt defies categorization. The label *pianist* would have been the most likely choice to be made by his contemporaries, but it fails to encompass his range of activities as composer, conductor, teacher, writer, and polemicist. Liszt lived three quarters of a century while redefining himself repeatedly to stay at the forefront of musical innovations. That his enemies reviled him with an intensity rivaling that of his followers' devotion is testimony to his influence.

A chronological approach to his life illustrates the evolution of his aesthetic views, his art, and his career. His early life was dominated by a desire to become a virtuoso pianist. His progress was so rapid that his father took him to Vienna, where he studied with Ludwig van Beethoven's pupil Carl Czerny.

By age twelve Liszt was established in Paris, where his youthful appearance and impressive playing allowed him to carve out a niche for himself among the numerous aspiring virtuosos flocking to the French capital. By his late teens he had enjoyed so many successes that he entered a period of despondency that was ended, by his own testimony, by the guns of the July Revolution in 1830. Musically, the defining event in his awakening was hearing the renowned violinist Niccolò Paganini. Upon hearing the Italian virtuoso in 1832, Liszt set out to reinvent his technique and stage persona, with the purpose of emulating Paganini's feats on the piano. The result was a series of monumentally difficult works (most notably the six *Études d'execution transcendante d'après Paganini* and the twelve *Études d'execution transcendante*) that redefined piano technique. These works were not only the result of Liszt's fertile imagination but were also the result of his contact with Sebastien Érard's recently invented repetition action, an innovation that allowed unprecedented speed in the piano mechanism. To match his virtuosity, Liszt created an audacious stage persona that captured the imagination of Romantic audiences. The frenzy over his visit to Berlin in 1842 led Heinrich Heine to coin the term *Lisztomania*, which could be applied in a broader sense to the ten-year period of relentless touring from 1838 to 1847, also known to Liszt scholars as the "Glanzzeit" (golden age). At the height of his fame, Liszt abandoned the concert stage, playing his last public concert for pay in the Ukrainian town of Elisabetgrad in September

1847. He had set new standards for virtuosity and showmanship, had set precedents as a touring artist, and had introduced the solo recital, an institution that continues to be a central part of the culture of art music today. Having attained the pinnacle of his profession, he abruptly turned to other challenges.

In February 1848 he took up residence in Weimar, accepting a long-standing offer to serve as kapellmeister to the Grand Duke Carl Friedrich and later Carl Alexander. The city had been home to Johann Wolfgang von Goethe, Johann Gottfried von Herder, Johann Nepomuk Hummel, Johann Friedrich Chistoph von Schiller, Christoph Martin Wieland, and other intellectual luminaries of the previous generation, and both Liszt and his employer saw his move there as an opportunity to rekindle the glory days of Carl August. The appointment aroused skepticism among musicians, though, since Liszt had no experience as a conductor and seemed unsuited temperamentally to life in a provincial German town. During his thirteen years of residence there, he proved the critics wrong and continued to be an innovator in a different arena. Despite a continual struggle to enlarge the orchestra and hire competent players, Liszt managed to stage a number of important works in the court theater, including the premiere of Wagner's *Lohengrin*. In his repertoire choices he emphasized modern works, which soon made Weimar synonymous with musical progressivism but did not please the taste of the local audiences. When he finally resigned his position, it was because of a negative response to the premiere of *Der Barbier von Bagdad*, a comic opera by his protégé Peter Cornelius.

The thirteen years in Weimar saw the development of Liszt's most influential musical innovations, as he became the acknowledged leader of a group of progressives labeled the New German school. Together with Richard Wagner and a small group of students and followers, he opposed the classicism associated with musical life in Leipzig and set about creating *Zukunftsmusik* (music of the future). The primary obstacle he faced as a composer was lack of credibility, since many in the musical world associated him with empty virtuosity designed to show off his pianistic skills. This perception plagued him for the rest of his career and slowed the reception of his most innovative works. Symbolic of this lack of respect for Liszt as a composer is the famous story of the twenty-year-old Johannes Brahms falling asleep during a private performance of Liszt's monumental Sonata in B Minor in 1853. The work's structural ambiguities and extensive use of thematic transformation make it one of the seminal works of the era, but to contemporary listeners it seemed formless and lengthy. The same is true of Liszt's principal innovation of this period, the symphonic poem. This new orchestral genre was typically shorter than a symphony but longer than an overture or a single movement of a symphony. The formal structure was derived from an extramusical program rather than one of the traditional classical forms, allowing for an infinite number of formal structures. The inherent flexibility of the genre as well as the expressiveness allowed by the programmatic organization made it extremely influential, as every major composer of art music between 1850 and 1920 tried his hand at it, with the exception of Brahms. As the battle between the progressives and conservatives became increasingly heated, Liszt found himself at the center of the controversy. To Brahms, Joseph Joachim, Clara Schumann, and other conservative musicians, his ideals were anathema to all they valued most in music. To Germany's

Heinrich (Henri) Lehmann, *Franz Liszt*. Reprinted courtesy of AKG.

young radicals, Liszt represented the spirit of innovation. Once again, Liszt's symbolic value made him seem larger than life.

In 1861 Liszt moved to Rome, where he spent eight years in study and contemplation. He studied church music in depth and completed many works on sacred themes, notably the oratorios *Die Legende von der heiligen Elisabeth* and *Christus*. He became friends with Pope Pius IX and in 1865 took minor orders of the priesthood. This apparent change in his life was actually the culmination of a lifelong devotion to the Catholic faith, and in fact he had begged to become a priest as a teenager, only to be forbidden by his father. Liszt produced a significant amount of piano music on religious themes during this period of his life, little of which has been performed extensively. Alan Walker notes that during this period Liszt suffered the death of two of his three children and had a number of other disappointments that made him age quickly. His appearance for the last two decades of his life was of a tall man with long gray hair, whose sparkling eyes provided the only clue to his youthful spirit.

Starting in 1869, Liszt returned to Weimar in the summers, where he taught a steady stream of students from around the world. His fame as a teacher grew so great that he was besieged by aspiring pianists, forcing him to teach in large groups of twenty or more. The new format, known today as the masterclass, is still practiced by master teachers. For Liszt, the masterclass was an opportunity to work exclusively on musical interpretation while ignoring technical details. He expected his students to be technically proficient when they arrived and to be prepared to play pieces at or near performance level. Under these circumstances, he could hear a selected piece and critique one or two aspects of it, perhaps demonstrating his own interpretation at the piano. Liszt's genius in this situation was extrapolating from the individual composition to universal truths that would benefit all those present. Numerous students left descriptions of these sessions; that of the American student Amy Fay is among the most entertaining and perceptive.

The restless Liszt called this final period of his life his *vie trifurquée* (three-pronged life), as he divided his time among Weimar, Rome, and Budapest, where he was also active as a teacher. As he saw his life approaching its end, he was determined to "throw my spear as far as possible into the future." His compositions indeed anticipated many aspects of twentieth-century harmonic practice while eschewing the virtuoso technique for which he had earlier been famous. Contemporaries scratched their heads over compositions such as the *Bagatelle sans tonalité* a work that is not truly atonal but clearly points toward Arnold Schoenberg's revolutionary technique of a generation later. In other works, Liszt explored the ramifications of the whole-tone scale, the augmented triad, and the diminished-seventh chord, all of which consist of equal intervals and therefore have no inherent tonal implications. These pieces were viewed by most contemporaries as the senile ramblings of an old man but provided challenge and inspiration to subsequent generations of composers.

This chronological discussion shows the evolution of Liszt's ideas and activities, but it does not fully capture the tremendous symbolic power that he held for the Romantic era. By attaining an unprecedented level of virtuosity and turning the public concert into a showcase for personal magnetism, Liszt fundamentally altered the role of the performer in musical life. This aspect of his career was undoubtedly the most widely known, despite his early retirement from the concert stage. His subsequent role in the polemics between conservatives and progressives in Germany, his far-reaching compositional innovations, and his dedication to teaching kept him at the center of musical Romanticism until his death.

The fascination he inspired in his contemporaries and in later audiences derives in part from the paradoxes in his character. His famous romantic liaisons, including a love affair with Countess Marie d'Agoult that produced three illegitimate children, seem irreconcilable with his lifelong devotion to the Catholic faith. His self-designation as a Hungarian musician is belied by the fact that he never learned to speak the Hungarian language fluently; his music is essentially cosmopolitan in style, yet he produced fifteen Hungarian rhapsodies that are perhaps the most popular evocations of the musical style of that country. He was known throughout his career as a musical modernist for his innovative compositions, but he admired the music of Bach and Beethoven deeply. He was one of the great improvisers of musical history, yet he admonished his students to play the music of past composers with absolute fidelity to the score. These contradictions reflect the complexity of a musical character who fascinated and challenged his contemporaries throughout a long and fruitful career.

E. DOUGLAS BOMBERGER

Biography

Born in Raiding, Hungary, October 22, 1811. Settled in Paris, 1823. Heard Niccolò Paganini, 1832. Toured Europe as a pianist, 1838–47. Served as kapellmeister to the court of Weimar, 1848–61. Lived in Rome, 1861–69, taking the minor orders of the priesthood in 1865. Divided his time among Weimar, Rome, and Budapest from 1869. Died in Bayreuth, July 31, 1886.

Selected Works

Piano
Douze Études d'exécution transcendante, 1826. Revised 1837–38 and 1851.
Années de pèlerinage. 1835–55.
Six Études d'exécution transcendante d'après Paganini, 1838–40. Revised 1851.
Tre sonetti del Petrarca. 1843–46.
Rhapsodies hongroises. 1847–53.
Sonata in B Minor. 1852–53.

Orchestra
Piano Concerto No. 1 in E-flat. 1835–56.
Piano Concerto No. 2 in A. 1839–61.
Ce qu'on entend sur la montagne. 1847–56.
Les Préludes. 1849–55.
Mazeppa. 1851–54.
Eine Faust-Symphonie in drei Characterbildern. 1854–57.
Eine Symphonie zu Dantes Divina Commedia. 1855–56.

Oratorios
Die Legende von der heiligen Elisabeth. 1857–62.
Christus. 1866–72.

Writings
Frédéric Chopin. 1852.
Des Bohèmiens et de leur musique en Hongrie. 1859.

Bibliography

Bernstein, Susan. *Virtuosity of the Nineteenth Century: Performing Music and Language in Heine, Liszt, and Baudelaire*. Stanford, Calif.: Stanford University Press, 1998.
Burger, Ernst. *Franz Liszt: A Chronicle of His Life in Pictures and Documents*. Translated by Stewart Spencer. Princeton, N.J.: Princeton University Press, 1989.
Dahlhaus, Carl. "Virtuosity and Interpretation." in *Nineteenth-Century Music*. Translated by J. Bradford Robinson. Berkeley and Los Angeles: University of California Press, 1989.
Fay, Amy. *Music-Study in Germany*. Chicago, 1880. Reprint New York: Da Capo, 1979.
Johns, Keith T. *The Symphonic Poems of Franz Liszt*. Stuyvesant, N.Y.: Pendragon Press, 1997.
Legany, Dezso. *Ferenc Liszt and His Country, 1874–1886*. Translated by Elizabeth Smith-Csicsery Ronay. Translation revised by Paul Merrick. Budapest: Occidental Press, 1992.
Liszt, Franz. *An Artist's Journey: Lettres d'un bachelier ès musique*. Translated and annotated by Charles Suttoni. Chicago: University of Chicago Press, 1989.
Merrick, Paul. *Revolution and Religion in the Music of Liszt*. Cambridge: Cambridge University Press, 1987.
Searle, Humphrey. *The Music of Liszt*. London: Williams and Norgate, 1954. 2d rev. ed., New York: Dover, 1966.
Walker, Alan. *Franz Liszt*. Rev. ed. 3 vols. Ithaca, N.Y.: Cornell University Press, 1987–97.

LITERARY CRITICISM: BRITAIN

In late eighteenth- and early nineteenth-century Britain, writers and critics abandoned the neoclassical literary tradition. Rejecting the tenets that had guided Alexander Pope, Jonathan Swift, and the other Augustans, they turned to new sources of inspiration, theories, and practices.

The term *Augustan Age* reveals the debt that early eighteenth-century British writers felt toward first century Roman figures. Alexander Pope took Horace as his primary model, while Samuel Johnson, in his poems *London* (1738) and *The Vanity of Human Wishes* (1749), adapted Juvenal. The Romantics did not reject the classical world, but they turned from Rome to Greece. According to Thomas Love Peacock's "The Four Ages of Poetry" (1820), the first golden age of literature was the period of Homer, Aeschylus, and Pindar. The early Roman Empire was an age of silver, the later empire one of brass. That Lord Byron was prepared to fight for Greek independence (and die in the process) reflects the power that ancient Greece held for English writers and critics of his generation.

Peacock maintained that the cycle of literary growth and decline had repeated itself in more recent centuries. The modern golden age was that of William Shakespeare. The cult of Shakespeare had been growing throughout the eighteenth century, but the full flowering of bardolatry coincided with the beginning of the Romantic "rebellion."

John Dryden, a founder of English neoclassicism, admired William Shakespeare but regarded him as crude and Gothic. Therein lay much of Shakespeare's appeal for the Romantics, for whom Gothic now became a term of praise rather than opprobrium. Robert Southey edited the fourteenth-century *Morte d'Arthur*, which appealed to him for its depiction of a medieval, chivalric world. Thomas Percy collected and published a collection of traditional ballads and folk songs dating back to the Middle Ages (*Reliques of Ancient English Poetry*, 1765). Thomas Chatterton found an eager audience for his forgeries, which he attributed to the fifteenth-century poet-monk Thomas Rowley, as did James Macpherson for the work that he ascribed to the third-century Celtic bard Ossian. The early nineteenth century witnessed the first English translation of Dante Alighieri's *Commedia*. Horace Walpole invented the Gothic novel with *The Castle of Otranto* (1764), and his successors were legion.

The Gothic appealed to the Romantic sensibility because it involved the supernatural and the irrational. Dethroning reason and realism, Romantic literary theory prized imagination. Samuel Taylor Coleridge's *The Rime of the Ancient Mariner* (1798) and *Christabel* (1816) reveal his fascination with the inexplicable, and in chapter 13 of his *Biographia Literaria* (1817) he exalts imagination as "a repetition in the finite mind of the eternal act of creation in the infinite I AM." Plato's concept of the ideal is evident here: the artist's task is to lift the mask that the senses and reason impose.

Emotion, as well as imagination, was celebrated. A comparison of Pope's *Windsor Forest* (1713) and William Wordsworth's "Tintern Abbey" (1798) reveals that whereas early eighteenth-century literary theory and practice stressed a realistic portrayal of a scene, the Romantics sought to convey the emotional state of the observer. In the preface to the 1800 edition of *Lyrical Ballads*, Wordsworth stressed that "all good poetry is the sponta-neous overflow of powerful feelings." Coleridge condemned metaphysical poets like John Donne because they abandoned "the passion and passionate flow of poetry, to the subtleties of intellect, and to the starts of wit." For William Hazlitt, *King Lear* is Shakespeare's greatest play because it presents the most powerful emotions.

Though it was in poetry that the Romantic sensibility found its finest literary expression, other arts and genres were important for promulgating the new aesthetic, especially journals. While politics were a major motive for the creation of such periodicals as the *Edinburgh Review* (1802), the *Quarterly Review* (1809), *Blackwood's Edinburgh Magazine* (1817), the *London Magazine* (1820), and the *Westminster Review* (1824), they all carried literary criticism by the leading authors of the day, including Lord Byron, Coleridge, Hazlitt, Leigh Hunt, Charles Lamb, Thomas De Quincey, and Walter Scott. Moreover, daily newspapers such as the *Times* and *Morning Chronicle* printed reviews and critical essays. Romantic literary criticism thus reached even those who could not afford books, which remained expensive. The growth of the British press also fostered the rise of the professional critic.

Exalting powerful emotions over restrained comment or narrative explains why so much Romantic literary criticism is impressionistic; the critic reveals his feelings, and he hopes to reproduce them in his audience. Charles Lamb remarks of Cyril Tourneur's *The Revenger's Tragedy* (1606–7), "I have never read it but my ears tingle, and I feel a hot blush overspread my cheeks." His annotations in *Specimens of English Dramatic Poets* consist largely of remarks on the beauties of particular passages, and his praise of actors and writers elsewhere are similarly subjective. Thus he comments on his beloved Izaac Walton's *The Compleat Angler* (1653), "Don't you already feel your spirit filled with the scenes?—the banks of rivers—the cowslip beds—the pastoral scenes—the neat alehouses—and hostesses and milkmaids."

No other response was possible for Romantic critics because they rejected rules. Whereas Pope's *Essay on Criticism* (1711) provided universal guidelines, Edward Young's *Conjectures on Original Composition* (1759) maintained that only lesser artists need such instruction. Hazlitt claimed that genius and taste were not "reducible to rules," and in 1817 Coleridge praised *Lyrical Ballads* for breaking new poetical ground. William Blake's idiosyncratic mythology rests on his belief that the poet who fails to create his or her own system will become the slave of another's.

If these ideas strike the modern reader as commonplace, they do so because no aesthetic has replaced the one created by the critics of the Romantic era. Just as no one today would question the greatness of the poetry of John Keats or Percy Bysshe Shelley, so no one would dispute the principles that underlie their work. They and their fellow artist-critics wrought a revolution in sensibility that changed the way people write and read.

JOSEPH ROSENBLUM

Bibliography

Abrams, M. H. *The Mirror and the Lamp: Romantic Theory and the Critical Tradition.* New York: Oxford University Press, 1953.

Bate, Walter Jackson. *From Classic to Romantic: Premises of Taste in Eighteenth Century England.* Cambridge, Mass.: Harvard University Press, 1946.

Brown, Marshall, ed. *Romanticism. The Cambridge History of Literary Criticism*, vol. 5. Cambridge: Cambridge University Press, 1989.

Engell, James. *The Creative Imagination: Enlightenment to Romanticism*. Cambridge, Mass.: Harvard University Press, 1981.

Furst, Lilian R. *Romanticism*. 2nd ed. London: Methuen, 1976.

———. *Romanticism in Perspective*. London: Macmillan, 1969.

Mahoney, John J. *The Whole Internal Universe: Imitation and the New Defense of Poetry in British Criticism, 1660–1830*. New York: Fordham University Press, 1985.

McGann, Jerome J. *The Romantic Ideology: A Critical Investigation*. Chicago: University of Chicago Press, 1983.

Parrinder, Patrick. *Authors and Authority: A Study of English Literary Criticism and Its Relation to Culture, 1750–1900*. London: Routledge, 1977.

Peyre, Henri. *What Is Romanticism?* Tuscaloosa: University of Alabama Press, 1977.

Praz, Mario. *The Romantic Agony*. Translated by Angus Davidson. 2d ed. London: Oxford University Press, 1951.

Prickett, Stephen, ed. *The Romantics*. New York: Holmes, 1981.

Thompson, Gary Richard. *The Gothic Imagination: Essays in Dark Romanticism*. Pullman: Washington State University Press, 1974.

Wellek, René. *The Later Eighteenth Century. A History of Modern Criticism: 1750–1950*, vol. 5. New Haven, Conn.: Yale University Press, 1955.

———. *The Romantic Age. A History of Modern Criticism: 1750–1950*, vol. 2. New Haven, Conn.: Yale University Press, 1955.

LITERARY CRITICISM: FRANCE

At the beginning of the Romantic era, literary criticism continued to be dominated by the classical aesthetic. Literary texts were seen as the expression of a universal human nature characterized by reason, order, and harmony. Whereas the task of the writer was to communicate eternal truth and beauty through an adherence to a prescribed set of rules, that of the critic was to preside as judge, the ultimate aim being to strengthen the prevailing moral and political order.

This classical aesthetic continued to hold sway throughout the era. Fueled by the bourgeois desire for order, it reasserted itself with renewed vigor at the beginning of the nineteenth century, acquiring a new lease of life after the political events of 1830, 1848, and 1871. Notable defenders of the tradition included Jules Barbey D'Aurevilly, Jean-François de La Harpe, D. Nisard, and Gustave Planche.

By the mid-eighteenth century, however, significant opposition to the official classical doctrine was already beginning to make itself felt. Many Enlightenment thinkers—Voltaire and Denis Diderot included—rejected the notions of universal beauty and good taste (*le bon goût*), preferring to develop their own criteria of judgment. An increasing interest in literature from abroad—William Shakespeare in particular—coupled with the prevailing climate of philosophical relativism, contributed to undermining the belief in a single beauty and single truth. In his articles in *Encyclopédie* (*Encyclopedia*, 1751–72) Diderot challenged the hegemony of reason and order, declaring the emotions to be the source of literary and artistic beauty. He also developed the concept of the writer as genius, unfettered by adherence to convention.

At the beginning of the nineteenth century, this weakening of the classical doctrine by the *philosophes* and by novelists such as Jean-Jacques Rousseau and Bernardin de Saint Pierre led to the growth of a Romantic aesthetic or *critique de la diversité*. Exponents of this new approach rejected the Aristotelian concept of an unchanging model, emphasizing instead the role of historical context in the creation of artistic beauty. The critic's task was now to focus on the relationship of a text to a particular person (the author), place and time, the overriding concern being with originality rather than conformity to prescribed rules. The critic sought to explain a text and to communicate enthusiasm and admiration instead of sitting in judgment.

A central role in the establishment of this new aesthetic was played by the writer and critic Madame Anne-Louise-Germaine de Staël. In her *De la littérature considérée dans ses rapports avec les institutions sociales* (*A Treatise on Ancient and Modern Literature*, 1800)—one of the first examples of literary history in its more modern form—she examined the influence of religion, customs, and climate on the literary text. Developing the notion of a comparative literature, she urged writers to draw their themes from other countries as well as from France's past. Madame de Staël compared the literature of Christian northern countries, characterized by passion and spontaneity, with that of southern pagan countries with their stress on form and clarity. She displayed a marked preference for the literature of the north and considered emotion to be a privileged source of truth and beauty. It was the critic's task, therefore, to understand and to identify with these emotions. Staël's work laid particular stress on the feeling of melancholy—envisaged as the font of all human endeavor—and also gave powerful support to what came to be known as the *mal du siècle* (end-of-the-century world-weariness). Later in *De L'Allemagne* (*Germany*, 1813) she introduced German Romanticism and Idealism to French readers, popularizing the term *Romantic*. She also emphasized the values of introspection, spontaneity, dreams, and the imagination.

Many of these preoccupations were echoed in François-Auguste-René, Vicomte de Chateaubriand's *Le Génie du christianisme* (*The Genius of Christianity*, 1802), which explained aesthetic value by the religious qualities of a civilization. The historical approach was later developed by the influential critic Abel-François Villemain in his celebrated *Tableau de la littérature française au XVIIIe siècle* (*Survey of French Literature in the Eighteenth Century*, 1828–29).

A central role in both the elaboration and propagation of this new aesthetic was played by the writer and critic Charles-Augustin Sainte-Beuve. He emphasized the critical faculty of sympathy and called for a complete identification of the critic with the writer, an approach that gave rise to a form of biographical criticism valorizing the concept of sincerity. At the same time, his concerns became increasingly scientific; for example, he sought to classify writers by different psychological types that determined the nature of their work.

From 1827 to 1830, Sainte-Beuve became the main spokesperson of the burgeoning Romantic movement. In his *Tableau historique et critique de la poésie française and du théâtre français au XVIe siècle (An Historical and Critical Survey of French Poetry and French Theatre in the sixteenth Century,* 1828) as well as in articles in the influential journal *Le Globe,* he championed the cause of poets and writers, giving particular support to Victor Hugo; he also brought Etienne Pivert de Senancour's *Oberman* (1804) to the attention of French readers.

Although it did not produce a formal critical approach, the Romantic school of writers published a number of articles and manifestos clearly bearing the influence of Madame de Staël. In his *Shakespeare et Racine* (1823) Stendhal rejected the traditional unities of time and place as being unrealistic and false, and advocated the use of prose instead of verse in the theater; he felt that above all literary work should possess contemporary relevance and address a contemporary audience both in terms of mind and feeling. In his preface to *Cromwell* (1829), Victor Hugo attacked notions of good taste, replacing them with the concept of originality. He stressed the relativity of beauty and extolled in the critic the values of admiration and enthusiasm, views that were subsequently echoed by Honoré de Balzac, Charles Baudelaire, Théophile Gautier, and Gérard de Nerval.

At the same time, while rejecting the growing influence of scientific determinism, writers called for critics to devote more attention to the aesthetic qualities of a text. This was an approach successfully illustrated in Gautier's own appreciation of Balzac in the periodical *L'Artiste* (1858), and supported by Baudelaire who, in an article in the same journal on Gustav Flaubert's *Madame Bovary* (1857), declared the autonomy of art independent of morality or of social function. This article was reproduced in his book *L'Art romantique* (1868). For Baudelaire, then, poetry should have no other goal than itself. Gautier, too, insisted that the sole purpose of art should be the pursuit of beauty, and he attached great important to formal craftsmanship, which he saw as the outer expression of inner vision and spirituality. At the same time, he advocated a poetic theater animated by a pursuit of the ideal; like Baudelaire, he felt that art should not be an imitation but a performance of the real.

After writing numerous articles for *La Presse* and *Le Moniteur universel,* in 1856 Gautier became editor of *L'Artiste.* This enabled him to disseminate the doctrine of "art for art's sake" with which his name became increasingly associated. Gautier's critical writings exerted an immense influence on the thought of his age. Their importance was recognized by Baudelaire, who dedicated *Les Fleurs du mal (Flowers of Evil,* 1857) to him and later by Stephane Mallarmé and the symbolists. His aesthetic principles also had a strong impact abroad, notably on the works of T. S. Eliot, Henry James, and Algernon Charles Swinburne.

An aesthetic that began as a critical approach based on intuition and sympathy with Madame de Staël became, under the threat of Positivism, increasingly dogmatic. In the early 1830s, a rift opened up between the position of the Romantic poets and that of Sainte-Beuve, and this gap between creative writer and critic became ever wider as the century progressed. One of the most influential exponents of the positivist approach was the writer and critic Hippolyte-Adolphe Taine. Taine's method was essentially to explain an author by three factors: race, milieu, and historical moment. Anticipating both psychological and

Marxist sociological criticism, his method involved an examination of the "center moral" of a text, which was then studied in the light of a collective moral state and of prevailing social conditions.

This positivist approach was later developed by the critic Ferdinand Brunetière, who, influenced by Charles Darwin, introduced genre and its evolution as an important factor in the explanation of literature. Although perhaps of less abiding interest than the work of Taine, his writings do have the merit of focusing attention on the literary text.

The increasing trend toward dogmatism, as illustrated by Brunetière, provoked a reaction in the late nineteenth century, and impressionistic criticism flourished. In spite of this, positivistic literary history—revitalized in the 1880s by Gustave Lanson—continued to thrive and established itself as the official doctrine from the 1890s onward. Although condemned by Marcel Proust in his *Contre Saine-Beuve (By Way of Sainte-Beuve,* 1954) and others, it was not until the 1960s that this approach was to come under serious threat.

BRONWEN MARTIN

Selected Works

Brunetière, Ferdinand. *Etudes critiques sur l'histoire de la littérature française.* 6 vols. 1880–92.
———. *L'Evolution des genres.* 1890–1900.
Chateaubriand, François-René. *Le Génie du christianisme,* 1802.
Hugo, Victor. *La Préface de Cromwell.* 1827.
Nisard, D. *Histoire de la littérature française, 1841–1861.* 1844–61.
Sainte Beuve, Charles-Augustin de. *Literary Criticism of Sainte-Beuve.* Edited and translated by Emerson Marks. 1971.
———. *Tableau historique et critique de la poésie française et du théâtre français au XVIe siècle.* 1828.
Staël, Madame de. *De L'Allemagne.* 1813.
———. *De la critique considérée dans ses rapports avec les institutions sociales.* 1800.
Taine, Hippolyte-Adolphe. *Histoire de la littérature anglaise,* 1863–64.
———. *Origines de la France contemporaine.* 1876–96.
Villemain, Abel-François. *Discours sur les avantages et inconvénients de la critique.* 1814.

Bibliography

Abraham, Pierre, and Roland Desne. *Manuel d'histoire littéraire de la France, Tome IV, 1789–1848.* Paris: Editions sociales, 1972.
Didier, Beatrice. *Le XVIIIe siècle, III, 1778–1820.* Paris: Artaud, 1976.
Fayolle, Roger. *La critique.* Paris: Armand Colin, 1978.
France, Peter, ed. *The New Oxford Companion to Literature in French.* Oxford: Oxford University Press, 1995.
Hollier, D., ed. *De la littérature française.* Bordas, 1993.
Molho, Raphael. *La critique littéraire en France au XIXe siècle,* Paris: Buchet/Chastel, 1963.
Moreau, Pierre. *La critique littéraire en France.* Paris: Librairie Armand Colin, 1960.
Murray, Chris, ed. *Encyclopedia of Literary Critics and Criticism.* Vols. 1–2. London: Fitzroy Dearborn, 1999.
Raveau Rollo, Elizabeth. *Méthodes de critique littéraire.* Paris: Armand Colin, 1993.
Thumerel, Fabrice. *La critique littéraire.* Paris: Armand Colin, 1998.

LITERARY CRITICISM: GERMANY

That in the mid-eighteenth century there was no body of German literature that had been accorded canonical status was reflected in the lack of a native Germanic tradition of literary criticism and theory, which was dominated instead by French neo-Classicism. However, as the century wore on, the reaction against the hegemony of French culture within Germany, which can be understood as a product of German thinkers' desire to foster a sense of national identity, resulted in the emergence of a distinctive tradition of German literary criticism that blossomed in the Sturm und Drang movement of the 1770s, in the Romantic literary movement of the turn of the nineteenth century, and in the *Junges Deutschland* (Young Germany) movement of the 1830s.

As the author of *Gedanken über die Nachahmung der griechischen Werke in der Malerei und Bildhauerkunst* (*Thoughts on the Imitation of the Painting and Sculpture of the Greeks*, 1755), Johann Joachim Winckelmann was a pivotal figure in the evolution of German literary criticism. The neoclassical aesthetic he adumbrated in this text, as his most significant publication, was, like that of many of his French counterparts, premised on a Neoplatonic conception of the representation of nature in an idealized form as beautiful and therefore of universal and timeless aesthetic value. It was in response to Winckelmann's eulogy of the "noble simplicity and tranquil grandeur" of the *Laocoön*, as an exemplary work of Greek sculpture expressive of the moral virtue of the ancient Greeks, that Gotthold Ephraim Lessing formulated an aesthetic in which he sought to reconcile neoclassicism and naturalism. Winckelmann also inspired the so-called Weimar classicism of Johann Wolfgang von Goethe and Johann Christoph Friedrich von Schiller, an episode in the history of ideas of approximately twenty years duration which effectively concluded with Goethe's tributary article "Winckelmann" in 1805.

However, Winckelmann's importance in the history of German literary criticism stems not only from the distinctively Germanic neoclassicism he inaugurated, but from the historical awareness and direct sensory experience of art that informed his aesthetic thought. While for Winckelmann the beauty of classical art represented an ideal that was essentially ahistorical, he acknowledged that it was a product of the *milieu* of ancient Greece. Moreover while he equated the beautiful with the morally edifying, thus invoking the faculty of reason as essential to aesthetic experience, he was, as the modern critic René Wellek remarks, "deeply influenced by sensualism," his aesthetic experience being "concrete, vital, [and] organic." It was his historicism and sensualism that became of fundamental importance in the thought of Johann Gottfried von Herder, who formulated a coherent literary theory in the wake of the reaction against French Rationalism and neo-Classicism expressed by thinkers of the Sturm und Drang movement such as Gottfried August Bürger, Johann Georg Hamann, Friedrich Maximilian von Klinger, and Jakob Michael Reinhold Lenz.

Underpinning Herder's insight that "man has been the same in all ages; but he expressed himself in each case according to the circumstances in which he lived" was his conception of poetry and art as an expression of man's vital experience of his natural environment, with which the recipient of the work must empathize. This basic tenet of Herder's aesthetic and literary theory represented a significant departure from the neoclassical view of the literature and art of classical antiquity as a benchmark against which to evaluate that of all ages and as an ideal to be imitated in accordance with pre-established rules. Herder's conception of poetry and art was premised on the view he shared with other thinkers of the Sturm und Drang movement, of art as the counterpart of nature created by men of genius, whom nature has endowed with "divine inspiration" or "enthusiasm." His conception of art and poetry as expressive media, and his view of the creative process as at least partially spontaneous rather than merely rational, underpinned his preference for the language and literature of early societies and inspired his collection of *Volkspoesie* (*Popular Poetry*, 1778–79). It also informed his reevaluation of literature previously excluded from the neoclassical literary canon, such as the dramas of William Shakespeare, which both Herder and Goethe heralded as masterpieces before Shakespeare was widely feted as the quintessential Romantic inspiration.

The influence of Herder's historical relativism on subsequent German literary theory is illustrated by Schiller's preoccupation with the relationship between ancient and modern literature. This was the subject of Schiller's treatise *Über naive und sentimentalische Dichtung* (*On Naive and Sentimental Poetry*, 1794–95) in which he discussed the relationship between ancient, or "naive", poetry, and modern, or "sentimental," poetry. He conceived the former as "natural" poetry created by poets living in harmony with their natural surroundings, and the latter as "reflective" poetry that is the product of modern man's alienation from nature and of the divorce of his feeling from his intellect. While Schiller expressed a desire for the revival of naive poetry—a possibility he found realized in the work of Goethe—he ultimately called on contemporary poets to synthesize the naive and sentimental as a means of achieving the reconciliation of reason and emotion which was a primary concern of the Romantics.

That the relationship between ancient and modern poetry was a central *topos* of the literary theory of the *Frühromantiker* (early Romantics) is illustrated by the importance it assumed in the writings of thinkers such as Jean Paul, August Wilhelm von Schlegel, and Friedrich von Schlegel, all of whom distinguished between ancient and modern poetry as "classical" and "romantic," respectively, and yet endorsed Friedrich Schlegel's view that, as an expression of spirituality in various forms, "all poetry is or should be romantic."

The view articulated by such *Frühromantiker* of poetry, along with the other arts, as a metaphysical medium through which the author expresses his spirituality or "longing" (*Sehnsucht*) for a higher realm, was premised on their conception of the semantic ambiguity and musicality of verbal language as a means of evoking ineffable emotions. Accordingly their recognition of the multiple meanings of words, voiced by Friedrich Schlegel, who suggested that "words often understand themselves better than do those who use them," was expressed through the florid metaphorical prose style in which they couched their creative and critical writings. It also underpinned their view of texts as necessarily incomplete, a view that was given tangible embodiment in the collections of aphorisms or fragments in which thinkers such as E. T. A. Hoffmann, Novalis, the Schlegel brothers, and Friedrich Ernst Daniel Schleiermacher expressed their ideas.

The importance the *Frühromantiker* accorded to Romantic irony, as another means of creating "the romantic kind of poetry" that "should forever be becoming and never be perfected," was intrinsically linked to the interpretative role they assigned to the reader. The notion of Romantic irony was influentially defined by Friedrich von Schlegel as creative self-consciousness which entails the critical detachment of the author from his work, detachment most clearly expressed through the punctuation of a narrative with authorial interpolations. For the *Frühromantiker*, the corollary of this aspect of creativity was the necessity for the reader of a text to take an active interpretative role in order to recreate the self-transcendence of the author and thereby to empathize with his sense of spirituality. This view of aesthetic appreciation as an art in itself was reflected in the Romantics' concern with the aesthetic education of man, which found expression not only in didactic aesthetic treatises, but in the *Bildungsroman* genre.

The new interest of German literary critics of the 1820s, such as Ludwig Börne and Wolfgang Menzel, in the sociopolitical dimension of literature was accompanied by a increasingly widespread reaction against Romanticism. This culminated in the emergence of the literary movement known as *Junges Deutschland*, the most influential thinkers of which were Karl Gutzhow, Heinrich Heine, and Theodore Mundt. In their rejection of Romantic idealism and the concept of aesthetic autonomy, and in their interest in the relationship between literature and society, they anticipated the direction literary criticism was to take in the twentieth century.

ABIGAIL CHANTLER

Bibliography

Abrams, M. H. *The Mirror and the Lamp: Romantic Theory and the Critical Tradition.* Oxford: Oxford University Press, 1953.

Beddow, Michael. *The Fiction of Humanity: Studies in the Bildungsroman from Wieland to Thomas Mann.* Cambridge: Cambridge University Press, 1982.

Behler, Ernst. *German Romantic Literary Theory.* Cambridge: Cambridge University Press, 1993.

Bowie, Andrew. *From Romanticism to Critical Theory: The Philosophy of German Literary Theory.* London: Routledge, 1997.

Chamberlain, Timothy J., ed. *Eighteenth-Century German Criticism.* New York: Continuum, 1992.

Garber, Frederick, ed. *Romantic Irony.* Budapest: Akadémiai Kiadó, 1988.

Hardin, James, ed. *German Writers from the Enlightenment to Sturm und Drang, 1720–1764.* New York: Gale, 1990.

Hoffmeister, Gerhart, ed. *European Romanticism: Literary Cross-Currents, Modes, and Models.* Detroit, Mich.: Wayne State University Press, 1990.

Hohendahl, Peter Uwe, ed. *A History of German Literary Criticism, 1730–1980.* Lincoln: University of Nebraska Press, 1988.

Kohlschmidt, Werner. *Dichter, Tradition, und Zeitgeist: Gesammelte Studien zur Literaturgeschichte.* Bern: Franke Verlag, 1965.

Kontje, Todd. *The German Bildungsroman: History of a National Genre.* Columbia, S.C.: Camden House, 1993.

Kubiak, Christopher. "Sowing Chaos: Discontinuity and the Form of Autonomy in the Fragment Collections of the Early German Romantics," *Studies in Romanticism* 33 (1994): 411–49.

Lamport, Francis John. *German Classical Drama: Theatre, Humanity, and Nation, 1750–1870.* Cambridge: Cambridge University Press, 1990.

Muecke, D. C. *The Compass of Irony.* London: Methuen, 1969.

Mueller-Vollmer, Kurt, ed. *The Hermeneutics Reader: Texts of the German Tradition from the Enlightenment to the Present.* Oxford: Blackwell, 1986.

Nisbet, H. B., ed. *German Aesthetic and Literary Criticism: Winckelmann, Lessing, Hamann, Herder, Schiller, Goethe.* Cambridge: Cambridge University Press, 1985.

Pascal, Roy. *The German Sturm und Drang.* Manchester: Manchester University Press, 1953.

Polheim, Karl Konrad. *Die Arabeske: Ansichten und Ideen aus Friedrich Schlegels Poetik.* Paderborn: Verlag Ferdinand Schöningh, 1966.

Rajan, Tilottama. *The Supplement of Reading: Figures of Understanding in Romantic Theory and Practice.* Ithaca, N.Y.: Cornell University Press, 1990.

Reed, Terence James. *The Classical Centre: Goethe and Weimar, 1775–1832.* London: Crook Helm, 1980.

Scher, Steven Paul. "Hoffmann and Sterne: Unmediated Parallels in Narrative Method," *Comparative Literature* 28 (1976): 309–25.

Schlegel, Friedrich. *Dialogue on Poetry and Literary Aphorisms.* Edited and translated by Ernst Behler and Roman Struc. University Park: Pennsylvania State University Press, 1968.

———. *Philosophical Fragments.* Translated by Peter Firchow. Minneapolis: University of Minnesota Press, 1991.

Simpson, David, ed. *German Aesthetic and Literary Criticism: Kant, Fichte, Schelling, Schopenhauer, Hegel.* Cambridge: Cambridge University Press, 1984.

Wellek, René. *A History of Modern Criticism 1750–1950, Volume One: The Later Eighteenth Century.* Cambridge: Cambridge University Press, 1981.

———. *A History of Modern Criticism 1750–1950.* Vol. 2, *The Romantic Age.* Cambridge: Cambridge University Press, 1981.

Wheeler, Kathleen M., ed. *German Aesthetic and Literary Criticism: The Romantic Ironists and Goethe.* Cambridge: Cambridge University Press, 1984.

LITERATURE

In modern terms, the literature of the Romantic period (1760–1850), considered as written texts, encompasses an almost limitless range of genres and forms: revolutionary and nationalistic pamphlets, political treatises, scientific works, philosophical tracts, critical fragments, essays, journals, the novel, drama, the short story, poetry, folk literature, and newspapers. There is also a vast array of (often improvised) texts whose essence lies in their performance, including the stage versions of the commedia dell'arte, the burlesque, the concerto, the symphony, lieder, and opera. And one may speak of the genres of art—drawing, illustration, painting, sculpture, and architecture—as forms of literature as well. This early-twenty-first-century perspective on "literature"(an acknowledgment that the term encompasses not simply that which presents itself as literature, but anything that is capable of being interpreted and therefore constitutes a "text") is largely derived from the writers and critics of the Romantic period, for many of the approaches to reading that prevail today are arguably extensions of the theories of literature that were developed by the Romantics themselves.

One might single out, as initial points of reference, the French Revolution (1789–99) and the American Revolution (1775–83). These political events, in which democratic systems replaced divine-right monarchies and placed power in the hands of the people, have counterparts in the development of literature: the interrogation of social and class hierarchies and systems of government by the masses (Mikhail Bakunin, William Godwin, Thomas Paine, Alexis de Tocqueville); the move in the United States to abolish slavery (Frederick Douglass); and the questioning of patriarchal authority by advocates of women's rights (Mary Wollstonecraft). The Romantic period thus sees (at least in Europe and the United States) the beginning of a democratization of literature, and initial steps taken toward the collapsing of distinctions between high and low literature.

The resulting tension in literature between social hierarchies and their dissolution is revealed most clearly in Britain, in the dispute between William Wordsworth—who claimed, in the preface to *Lyrical Ballads* (1802) to speak "in the language of the common man" and to find no qualitative difference between poetry and prose—and Samuel Taylor Coleridge, who coauthored this text, but argued, in his *Biographia Literaria* (1817) that the former claim was merely an affectation, and the latter merely a misconception. This tension may be reconfigured in terms of a debate between the notion of aristocratic "taste" and the idea that literature should reflect the social realities of the masses. Thus the literature of the aristocracy gradually gives way to the literature of the middle classes, and a variety of popular literary genres; at the same time, there is a nostalgic grasping for the stability of the past, which manifests itself in the production of neoclassical literature (Vittorio Alfieri, André Chénier, Johann Christian Hölderlin, Walter Savage Landor) and fantasies inspired by medieval legends and fantasies.

In parallel with these social changes during the period, one finds an increasing shift, fueled by the philosophical forces of Enlightenment rationality (Denis Diderot, Georg William Friedrich Hegel, Immanuel Kant, Jean-Jacques Rousseau) away from a spiritual ethos toward the material. The crisis of reconciling the spiritual and the material is played out in the works of the Danish philosopher Søren Kierkegaard, concluding on the impasse of an either/or philosophy of the absurd, which can only be overcome through a leap of faith.

Reaction to this existential crisis and the new materialistic ethos reveals itself in the notion of inspired "creative genius" (William Wordsworth, John Keats, and Percy Bysshe Shelley in England; Novalis and August Wilhelm von Schlegel and Friedrich von Schlegel in Germany); thus Shelley is able to declare, in his *Defence of Poetry* (1821) that "Poets are the hierophants of an unapprehended inspiration . . . Poets are the unacknowledged legislators of the world." In Germany, the eighteenth-century Sturm und Drang movement led by Johann Wolfgang Goethe and Johann von Schiller under the influence of Jean-Jacques Rousseau, Johann Herder, and Gotthold Ephraim Lessing, provided similar impetus to the focus on subjectivity and the revolt of creative genius against the mores of the age.

Various attempts to revive the spiritual aspects of life also take the form of calls for a return to nature (Ralph Waldo Emerson, Henry David Thoreau, William Wordsworth), and the crisis gives rise to a new interest in madness and the irrational or supernatural, as revealed in the new literary, artistic and architectural genre of the Gothic (E. T. A. Hoffmann, Heinrich von Kleist, Matthew Lewis, Edgar Allan Poe, Marquis de Sade, and Mary Shelley) as well as in a fascination with folk tales (Jacob and Wilhelm Grimm) and medieval fantasies (Victor Hugo, Walter Scott).

The historians of the age (G. W. F. Hegel, Jules Michelet, Claude-Henri de Saint-Simon, Hippolyte-Adolphe Taine) see these social, cultural, and literary developments as both a continuation of the past and its constant reinterpretation; the literary critics (Samuel Taylor Coleridge, William Hazlitt, John Keats, Charles Lamb, and William Wordsworth, in Britain; François-Auguste-René, Vicomte de Chateaubriand, Madame Anne-Louise-Germaine de Staël, Stendhal, and Victor Hugo in France; Achim von Arnim, Adam Müller, and Jean Paul in Germany) attempt to theorize these changes by various means in spiritual, religious, social, or aesthetic terms.

But the clearest formulation of romantic "literature" as such appears in Germany, in Friedrich von Schlegel's "Athenaeum Fragment 116" (1798)—the word *poiesy* (poesy) comes from the Greek *poiesis*, meaning "making" or "creating," and is used synonymously with *literature*:

> Romantic Poiesy is a progressive, universal Poiesy. Its vocation is not merely to unify again all separated genres of poetry, and to put poetry in touch with philosophy and rhetoric. It wants to and also should, now mix, now melt together, poetry and prose, genius and criticism, art-poetry and nature-poetry; make poetry lively and sociable, and life and society poetic. . . . It alone can, like the epic, become a mirror of the whole surrounding world, an image of the age. . . . The romantic poietic genre is still in a state of becoming; indeed that is its proper essence, that it should only become, and never be fulfilled. It can become exhausted by no theory. . . . The Romantic poietic genre is the only one which is more than a genre, and is, as it were, the poietic art itself: for in a certain sense, all Poiesy is or should be, Romantic.

The cross-cultural internationalization of literature during this period, the questioning of social hierarchies, the interrogations of the fundamental principles of language and interpretation (Johann Herder, Alexander von Humboldt, Jean-Jacques Rousseau, Friedrich Schleiermacher)—all these have reappeared in the present age of globalization and critical theory in varying guises—as feminist or postcolonial theory, Marxist or psychoanalytic interpretation, genre or translation theory, reader-response criticism, deconstruction or postmodernism—and today it is unclear how, if at all, "romantic" literature can bve distinguished from the literature of our own era.

JOHANN PILLAI

Bibliography

Artz, Frederick B. *From the Renaissance to Romanticism: Trends in Style in Art, Literature, and Music, 1300–1830.* Chicago: University of Chicago Press, 1965.

Bate, Walter Jackson, ed. *Criticism: The Major Texts.* Enlarged ed. New York: Harcourt Brace Jovanovich, 1970.

Cassirer, Ernst. *The Philosophy of the Enlightenment.* Translated by Fritz C. A. Koelln and James P. Pettegrove. Boston: Beacon Press, 1955.

Gay, Peter. *The Enlightenment: An Interpretation. The Rise of Modern Paganism*. New York: Random House, 1968.

Lacoue-Labarthe, Philippe, and Jean-Luc Nancy. *The Literary Absolute: The Theory of Literature in German Romanticism*. Translated by Philip Barnard and Cheryl Lester. Albany: State University of New York Press, 1988.

Seyhan, Azade. *Representation and Its Discontents: The Critical Legacy of German Romanticism*. Berkeley and Los Angeles: University of California Press, 1992.

Smith, Preserved. *The Enlightenment 1687–1776. A History of Modern Culture*, vol. 2. New York: Collier, 1962.

Weiskel, Thomas. *The Romantic Sublime: Studies in the Structure and Psychology of Transcendence*. Baltimore, Md.: Johns Hopkins University Press, 1976.

Wellek, René *A History of Modern Criticism: 1750–1950. The Later Eighteenth Century*. New Haven, Conn.: Yale University Press, 1955.

———. *A History of Modern Criticism: 1750–1950. The Romantic Age*. New Haven, Conn.: Yale University Press, 1955.

White, Hayden. *Metahistory: The Historical Imagination in Nineteenth-Century Europe*. Baltimore, Md.: Johns Hopkins University Press, 1973.

LONGFELLOW, HENRY WADSWORTH 1807–1882

American poet

The most popular American writer during his lifetime and for a generation after his death, Longfellow's reputation subsequently waned. The sentimentality, simplicity of thought and diction, and optimistic didacticism that endeared him to nineteenth-century audiences rendered him uninteresting to a later age seeking ambiguity, tension, and irony. Yet precisely because Longfellow is so much a product of his time, his works illuminate the spirit of the age that so adored him.

Among the characteristics of Longfellow's poetry is a love of the medieval, which he shared with so many other Romantic writers. Longfellow gained his teaching post at Bowdoin College largely through a translation of Horace that he wrote as an undergraduate there. Repeatedly, though, he turned to the Middle Ages rather than the classics for inspiration. While still a student at Bowdoin, Longfellow began a series of essays in the *United States Literary Gazette* (March–October 1825), which appeared under the general title "The Lay Monastery" and which he signed "The Lay Monk." He described his novel *Hyperion* (1839) as resembling a Romanesque church. His *Hiawatha* (1855) he called "this Indian Edda," the *edda* being a thirteenth-century collection of Finnish folktales. Hiawatha partakes of the Arthurian: he civilizes his world, then leaves as the order he has established is about to change, but he promises to return in the unspecified future. *Tales of a Wayside Inn* (1863) is modeled on Giovanni Boccaccio's *Decameron* (1349–51) and Geoffrey Chaucer's *Canterbury Tales* (1386–1400). Several of the poems in Longfellow's *Tales* are set in the Middle Ages; among these are "The Saga of King Olaf," "Charlemagne," and "Emma and Eginhard." The most successful part of Longfellow's vast dramatic *Christus: A Mystery* (1872) is *The Golden Legend* (1851), based on the thirteenth-century Hartmann von Aue's *Der arme Heinrich* (*Poor Heinrich*). The first section of *Christus*, dealing with the life of Jesus, recalls the medieval passion play. Longfellow was the first American poet to translate any portion of Dante Alighieri's *Commedia* (1307–21; *Divine Comedy*) and served as the first president of the Dante Society of Cambridge, Massachusetts.

Although Longfellow was a professor at Bowdoin College and then at Harvard University, and although books heavily influenced him, he nonetheless shared with his fellow Romantics a love of simple language and commonplace subjects. Like William Wordsworth he believed that the poet is a man speaking to other men and therefore should write in a manner that all could understand. He praised the author of *Lyrical Ballads* (1798) for "the republican simplicity of his poetry." In Longfellow's translation of Esaias Tegnér's *The Children of the Lord's Supper* (1845), Jesus addresses the children in plain language because "sublimity is always simple." Conversely, Longfellow objected to writers who were not readily accessible. In an 1833 review of Richard Henry Dana's *Poems and Prose Writings*, Longfellow criticized Dana for "sometimes follow[ing] out a brilliant train of thought farther than minds less metaphysical than his own are capable of accompanying him or willing to do." Longfellow condemned Robert Browning's obscurity and Samuel Taylor Coleridge's use of what Longfellow termed "cumbersome phraseology."

"Gaspar Becerra" (1850) illustrates Longfellow's admiration for the simple and the commonplace. Longfellow's poem is based on a story in William Stirling-Maxwell's *Annals of the Artists of Spain* (1848) and recounts the inability of a sculptor to create a Virgin from precious wood imported from the Orient. The artist succeeds when he uses an oak plank that he has taken from his own hearth. The poem concludes, "That is best which lieth nearest; / Shape from that thy work of art." Many of Longfellow's poems celebrate handicrafts and people in humble walks of life. "Kéramos" (1878) treats the making of pottery; "The Building of the Ship" (1849) and "The Ropewalk" (1858) similarly deal with common labor. "Twilight" (1849) is set in the cottage of a fisherman whose family awaits his return. The title of the volume in which "The Building of the Ship" and "Twilight" appear, *The Seaside and the Fireside* (1849), attests to this fondness for the quotidian. *Evangeline* (1847) is a poem about simple people: the heroine is a farmer's daughter, her lover the son of a blacksmith.

Longfellow's appreciation for the simple and the close at hand is of a piece with his literary nationalism. In "The Literary Spirit of Our Country," which appeared in the *United States Literary Gazette* for April 1825, Longfellow urged writers to use American themes and American history. His first poem, "The Battle of Lovell's Pond" (1820), published when he was thirteen years of age, conforms to this belief, treating an American Indian battle. Other early examples of Longfellow's reliance on native materials are "The Indian Hunter," "Lover's Rock," and "Jeckoyva," all published before he graduated from Bowdoin. In his commencement address, "Our Native Writers" (1825), Longfellow again advocated a literature that was truly American.

While traveling in Europe in the late 1820s (1826–29), Longfellow wrote to Philadelphia publishers Cary and Lea proposing a collection of papers on New England, to be modeled on Washington Irving's *Sketch-Book* (1819–20), a work that Longfellow much admired. Longfellow praised his Bowdoin classmate Nathaniel Hawthorne for using American subjects in *Twice-Told Tales* (1837). *Evangeline* and *Hiawatha* are American epics; the final section of *Christus* consists of two dramatic poems recounting events in seventeenth-century New England. *The Courtship of Miles Standish* (1868) might be subtitled "A Romance of Pilgrim Massachusetts." In *Tales of a Wayside Inn* the Poet rejects European for homegrown subjects, and the Theologian maintains, "What is native still is best."

However, Longfellow's literary nationalism was hardly extreme. While *Tales of a Wayside Inn* includes the famous "Paul Revere's Ride," only six of the twenty-two tales have American settings, and three of the seven narrators are European. At the end of *Hyperion* the hero, Paul Flemming, leaves Europe for America, but the novel's chief interest for even contemporary readers was its descriptions of foreign places. The novel, a bildungsroman patterned after Johann Wolfgang von Goethe's *Wilhelm Meisters Lehrjahre* (*Wilhelm Meister's Apprenticeship*, 1795–96), reveals the influence of Heinrich Heine, Novalis, and Jean Paul Richter, as well as Goethe; it cites twenty-five German authors, and it contains Longfellow's translations of German ballads and folksongs. The earlier *Outre-Mer* (1833), envisioned as a collection of New England sketches, became instead a book about the Old World. As Henry James observed, "Mr. Longfellow . . . was perhaps interesting for nothing so much as for the secret of his harmony . . . and for the way in which his 'European' culture and his native kept house together."

Nowhere is this unity more evident than in what is arguably Longfellow's most important contribution to American letters, his introduction of European literature to his countrymen. He was one of the first professors of modern languages in the country and the first to offer an entire course on Goethe's *Faust*. Articles in the *North American Review* and "Ancient French Romances," a translation of Paulin Paris's French essay that Longfellow published in *Select Journal of Foreign Periodical Literature* (1833), exposed Anglophones to unfamiliar European authors. *Hyperion* offered literary criticism of such leading German writers as E. T. A. Hoffmann and Jean Paul Richter. Longfellow's first book was a translation of Spanish poet Jorge Manrique's *Coplas* (1833). In 1845, Longfellow edited and provided translations for *The Poets and Poetry of Europe*, with selections ranging from the early Middle Ages to the nineteenth century. In addition to his still readable translation of Dante's *Commedia* (1865–67), Longfellow produced English versions of some hundred foreign-language poems, thereby broadening the literary horizons of his countrymen. Though Longfellow is no longer the grand old man of American letters, no study of nineteenth-century American literature can ignore his contributions.

JOSEPH ROSENBLUM

Biography

Born in Portland, Maine, February 27, 1807. Attended Bowdoin College, Brunswick, Maine, 1822–25. Professor of Modern Languages at Bowdoin (1829–35) and Harvard University (1836–54). LL.D. from Cambridge University (1868) and D.C.L. from Oxford University (1869). Married Mary Storer Porter (1812–35) in Portland, Maine, September 14, 1831; married Frances Appleton (1817–61) in Boston, July 13, 1843. Died in Cambridge, Massachusetts, March 24, 1882.

Selected Works

Collections

Prose Works of Henry Wadsworth Longfellow. 2 vols. 1857.
The Complete Poetical Works. Edited by Ernest W. Longfellow. 1882.
The Writings of Henry Wadsworth Longfellow, with Bibliographical and Critical Notes. 11 vols. 1886.
The Letters of Henry Wadsworth Longfellow. 6 vols., Edited by Andrew Hilen. 1966–82.

Poetry

Voices of the Night. 1839.
Poems on Slavery. 1842.
Ballads and Other Poems. 1842.
The Belfry of Bruges and Other Poems. 1846.
Evangeline, A Tale of Acadie. 1847.
The Seaside and the Fireside. 1849.
The Song of Hiawatha. 1855.
The Courtship of Miles Standish and Other Poems. 1858.
Tales of a Wayside Inn. 1863.
Kéramos and Other Poems. 1878.
Ultima Thule. 1880.
In the Harbor, Ultima Thule, Part 2. 1882.
Michael Angelo. 1883.

Other

Outre-Mer: A Pilgrimage beyond the Sea, 1833–34. Enlarged ed., 1835.
Hyperion, A Romance, 1839. Revised ed., 1869.
The Poets and Poetry of Europe (editor), 1845. Expanded ed. 1871.
Kavanagh, A Tale. 1849.
The Golden Legend, 1851. Republished as part of *Christus*, 1872.
The Divine Comedy of Dante Alighieri. (translator). 3 vols., 1865–67.
The New England Tragedies, 1868. Republished in *Christus*, 1872.

Bibliography

Arvin, Newton. *Longfellow: His Life and Work.* Boston: Little, Brown, 1963.
Burwick, Frederick. "Longfellow and German Romanticism," *Comparative Literature Studies* 7 (1970).
DeArmond, Anna J. "Longfellow and Germany," *Delaware Notes* 25 (1952).
Henry Wadsworth Longfellow: His Poetry and Prose. New York: Ungar, 1986.
Mathews, Joseph Chesley, ed. *Longfellow Reconsidered: A Symposium.* Hartford, Conn.: Transcendental Books, 1970.
Thompson, Lawrence. *Young Longfellow, 1807–1843.* New York: Macmillan, 1938.
Viglione, Francesco. *La critica literaria di Henry Wadsworth Longfellow.* 2 vols. Florence: Vallecchi, 1934.
Wagenknecht, Edward. *Longfellow: A Full-Length Portrait.* New York: Longman, Green, 1955.
Williams, Cecil Brown. *Henry Wadsworth Longfellow,* New York: Twayne, 1964.

LOUTHERBOURG, PHILIPPE JACQUES 1740–1812

French painter, stage and costume designer, inventor, occultist, and faith healer

Philippe Jacques de Loutherbourg's father, a painter for the Court of Darmstadt, hoped his son would become an engineer. His mother advised him to train as a Lutheran minister. Loutherbourg decided on a career as a painter and, after his family moved to Paris to foster his talent, he was taught by François Joseph Casanova, Carle van Loo, and Jean-Georges Wille, In 1763 he exhibited his first painting, *Landscape with Figures and Animals*. Denis Diderot's enthusiasm for this work helped launch his career. Over the next eight years, Loutherbourg was celebrated as a painter of romantic and picturesque landscapes, and of biblical subjects. He was the youngest person ever to be elected to the Académie Royale in Paris and was nominated as a *peintre du roi* (royal painter).

Despite these successes, in November 1771 Loutherbourg moved to London, leaving his wife and children in Paris. He was to return to the continent only once, and never to France. On a number of occasions he denied his nationality, claiming to have been born in Switzerland and that his parents were of Lithuanian stock.

In England, Loutherbourg was introduced to David Garrick by a letter from Jean Monnet, director of the Opéra Comique, describing Loutherbourg as "un de nos plus grand peintres" ["one of our greatest painters"]. Garrick employed him as his chief stage designer at Drury Lane Theatre, for the sum of £500 per annum. From 1773 to 1789, he worked on at least thirty dramatic productions, first under Garrick and then, from 1776, under Garrick's successor Richard Brinsley Sheridan.

Loutherbourg played a key role in the transformation of stage scenery from an architectural to a pictorial aesthetic, setting a new standard for theatrical illusion. Rather than relying on a stationary, scenic backdrop, he extended the use of movable painted flats and drop scenes. He integrated scenery, costume, movement, and music to create a harmony of effects. Loutherbourg created an unprecedented sense of realism through the innovative use of lighting, sound, puppets, models, perspective and special effects. His widely praised productions included *A Christmas Tale* (1773), *The Maid of the Oaks* (1774), *Selimor and Asor* (1776), *The Camp* (1778), *The Critic* (1779), and *Robinson Crusoe* (1781).

Audiences often encountered scenery at Drury Lane that recalled the sublime landscapes to be found in Loutherbourg's work as a painter. While at Drury Lane, Loutherbourg's experiments with the theatrical representation of landscape culminated in the pantomime, *The Wonders of Derbyshire* (1779), which drew on sketches he had made during a visit the previous year to Derbyshire.

In 1781, after quarreling with Sheridan over his salary, Loutherbourg left Drury Lane. He returned to the theater only once, in 1785, as chief designer of John O'Keeffe's *Omai, Or, A Trip Round The World* (1785). This remarkable spectacle functioned both as pantomime and travelogue, as well as exhibition. Its extensive scenery and costumes—including a procession of about eighty people, representing thirteen ethnic groups—were based on drawings by John Webber, the official draftsman and landscape painter on Captain James Cook's third voyage to the Pacific. *Omai* became the most popular theatrical production of the decade, helping to establish popular interest in exotic peoples and landscapes, while celebrating England's role in the European exploration of the Pacific.

On February 26, 1781, soon after leaving Drury Lane, Loutherbourg opened the *Eidophusikon; or, Various Imitations of Natural Phenomena, represented by Moving Pictures*, first in London's Leicester Square and then, from 1786, in the Strand. On a small stage, approximately six feet wide and eight feet deep, Loutherbourg created landscapes, accompanied by realistic sounds and lighting effects, that seemed to be in motion. The spectator watched, for example, dawn break over a view from Greenwich Park up the river Thames. Clouds, painted on linen attached to large frames moved diagonally by a winding machine, passed naturally across the sky. In another scene, Satan and his troops were depicted on the banks of the "Fiery Lake," as Pandemonium rose from the deeps, gradually changing color from sulphurous blue to a lurid red, then a pale light, and finally to shades suggestive of "a bright furnace." The Eidophusikon quickly became one of the most popular entertainments in London, numbering among its patrons both Joshua Reynolds and Thomas Gainsborough. It has been claimed as a precursor of the panorama, the diorama, and the cinema.

After moving to London, Loutherbourg had extended his interest in alchemy to mesmerism and the mystical doctrines of Emanuel Swedenborg. In 1786 he met the magician and freemason "Count" Cagliostro, who instructed Loutherbourg in the occult sciences. When in June 1787 Cagliostro returned to the continent, Loutherbourg followed him. Six months later, they quarreled and Loutherbourg challenged Cagliostro to a duel. Early in 1788, Loutherbourg returned to London, where he and his wife set up as faith healers, working from their house at Hammersmith Terrace, Chiswick, apparently attracting thousands of patients. They claimed to deploy for therapeutic purposes the influxes that, according to Swedenborg, flow from heaven to earth. A list of their cures was published by a believer, Mary Pratt, in 1789. In the same year, a mob attacked their house and their public practice was abandoned, although Loutherbourg used his healing powers in private until at least 1804.

Loutherbourg's interest in the occult influenced some of the twenty-two pictures and approximately seventy-one vignettes that he produced over the next ten years for the publisher Thomas Macklin's six-volume edition of the Bible. During this time, Loutherbourg became a scholarly recluse, extending his knowledge of the Kabbalah and studying his library of rare religious books. Loutherbourg's designs for Macklin include studies in the apocalyptic sublime, such as *The Vision of the White Horse* (1798) and *The Angel Binding Satan* (1792). Loutherbourg's work as an illustrator also included plates for John Bell's edition of Shakespeare (1786–88) and the publisher Robert Bowyer's edition of *The History of England* by David Hume (1806). In the early nineteenth century, he published two collections of engravings, *The Picturesque Scenery of Great Britain* (1801) and *The Picturesque and Romantic Scenery of England and Wales* (1805).

Throughout the various phases of his career, with a brief lull in the late 1780s, Loutherbourg continued to paint in a variety of genres, producing pastoral scenes, topographical studies, portraits, landscapes, shipwrecks and battle scenes. His battle pictures, including scenes from contemporary history such as the *Battle of Camperdown* (1799) and the *Battle of the Nile* (1800) led to his appointment in 1807 as historical painter to the Duke of Gloucester. His representations of the natural sublime, such as *An Avalanche, or Ice-Fall, in the Alps* (1803) exerted a strong influence on J. M. W. Turner and, more broadly, on Romanticism. In paintings such as *Coalbrookdale by Night* (1801), the landscape of the industrial revolution is portrayed as a sublime of terror.

Modern studies have tended to foreground one aspect of Loutherbourg's career at the expense of the others. There is little doubt, however, that it is the cross-fertilization of entertainment, commerce, painting, theater, and the occult that was the catalyst for Loutherbourg's prolific genius.

PETER OTTO

Biography

Born in Strasbourg, October 31, 1740. Family moved to Paris, 1755. Married Barbe Burlât, January 10, 1764; elected to the Académie Royale and nominated as *paintre de roi*, 1766. Moved to London, leaving his wife and children in France, November 1771; became stage designer for David Garrick's Drury Lane Theatre, 1773. Married Lucy Paget, May 1774. Became full member of Royal Academy 1781; *Eidophusikon* opens in Leicester Square, February 26, 1781. Met Alessandro Cagliostro, 1786, whom he followed to Europe, 1787. Opened a practice as a faith healer, 1788; appointed historical painter to the Duke of Gloucester, 1807. Died March 11, 1812.

Bibliography

Allen, R. G. *The Stage Spectacles of Philip James de Loutherbourg.* Ph.D. diss., Yale University, 1960.

Joppien, Rüdiger. *Philippe Jacques De Loutherbourg, RA, 1740–1812.* Exhibition catalog. London: Greater London Council, 1973.

———. "Phillipe Jacques De Loutherbourg's Pantomime *Omai, or, a Trip Round the World* and the Artists of Captain Cook's Voyages," in *Captain Cook and the South Pacific.* Edited by T. C. Mitchell. Canberra: Australian National University Press, 1979. 81–136.

Paley, Morton. *The Apocalyptic Sublime.* New Haven, Conn.: Yale University Press, 1986.

LOVE, ROMANTIC

Love, one of the most basic tenets of the Romantic movement, given its emphasis on individuality and freedom of imagination, defies homogeneity. Literature, as its formative agent, celebrated it as the historically changing core of bourgeois intimacy. Love, intricately linked to creativity, represents a prefiguration of utopian possibilities for the individual defying all limiting norms. Romantic love reached its highest form in German literature at the turn of the nineteenth century. With this construct, the Romantics attempted to solve one of the pressing issues of Western thought since René Descartes: the integration or fusion of the sensual and spiritual forces of life. The strict separation of reason and the material world, of reason and the senses, had relegated feelings and passions as merely material functions of the body, resulting in the divorce of love from desire. Madeleine de Scudéry's *Clélie* (1660) exemplified the celebration of the purely spiritual aspects of love in a union of souls. Novels such as Pierre Carlet de Chamblain de Marivaux's *La Vie de Marianne ou les aventures de madame la comtesse de ****, (*Marianne*, 1731–42) and Pierre Ambroise François Choderlos de Laclos, *Les Liaisons dangereuses* (*Dangerous Liaisons*, 1782) resist the metaphysical dimension of love and focus instead on the refined art of seduction. After the conquest, women lose their appeal. Women like the Marquise de Merteuil in *Liaisons dangereuses* repay the callousness of men by becoming just like them. Here, passionate love and marriage are seen as mutually exclusive.

While the English courtly culture remained influenced by the French model well into the eighteenth century, the middle class formulated a domestic moralizing model of love. Under the influence of Puritanism and moral sense philosophy (Anthony Ashley Cooper, third Earl of Shaftesbury, and especially Francis Hutcheson), love, friendship, and enthusiasm, as the noble traits of man, form the basis of the companionate marriage, which is based on love as a unique form of friendship. Moral sense theories (that is, the faculty of perceiving moral excellence, considered to be inborn and natural) devalued passion, especially the sensual/sexual side of love, as animalistic and selfish. The new concept of chaste love became the dominant concept in George Lillo's *Merchant of London* (1731), Samuel Richardson's *Pamela* (1740–41), and Oliver Goldsmith's *Vicar of Wakefield* (1766). Richardson warned of passion, of seduction, of a marriage based on passion, and of parents' undue influence over their children's choices. He celebrated female virtue, domesticity, and marriage based on respect and friendship.

Over the course of the eighteenth century, the English influence made itself felt in France. In Antoine-François Prévost d'Exiles's *Manon Lescaut* (1728), Manon transforms her strong passions into a more complex kind of love, and in Françoise de Graffigny's "Lettres péruviennes" (1747), in which the pain caused by unrequited love makes women more aware of the strength of their love and that their capacity to love is greater than that of men. Jean-Jacques Rousseau's *Julie, ou La Nouvelle Héloïse* (*Julie, or the New Heloise*, 1761) is the most prominent novel exemplifying passion tempered by sensibility.

In Germany, the sentimentalism of Richardson and Rousseau's wavering between friendship and love, mysticism and enlightenment, come together. In novels such as Christian Fürchtegott Gellert's *Leben der schwedischen Gräfin von G.* (*The Life of the Swedish Countess of G.*, 1747) with its striving for virtue and perfection, as in Sophie LaRoche's *Fräulein von Sternheim* (*The History of the Lady of Sternheim*, 1771) the goal of marriage based on friendship was not passion but common organization of a household and its domestic duties. The cult of sensibility (*Empfindsamkeit*), dominating German literature and culture in the middle of the century, created a new interpersonal value system for dealing with the immediate circle of friends, lovers, and family. Empfindsamkeit with its specific concept of love based on personal emotive attraction, can be seen as both a contribution and reaction to the transformation of the cooperative estate society into a more functionally differentiated society. Heightened sensibilities led to the complexity and individualism of the highly self-reflexive subject. This highly individualized self required equally intense relationships, which not only threatened a loss of boundaries with the other and stood in opposition to social integration, but were, above all, necessarily exclusive. This decreased the likelihood of finding a suitable soul mate and increased the possibility that the subject desiring the most intimate communication remained without response. The stakes in interpersonal relationships became extremely high. Where romantic idealism remained unfulfilled, the self-transcendence perverted into an urge to self-destruct, as Johann Wolfgang Goethe's *Die Leiden des jungen Werthers* (*The Sorrows of Young Werther*, 1774), François-Auguste-René, Vicomte de Chateaubriand's *René* (1805), and Lord Byron's *Don Juan* (1819–24) document.

Friedrich Klopstock's odes intensified the enthusiasm for intense friendships, which were at the core of love as a fusion of love and virtue; the souls of the lovers are made for each other. An early example of the motif of *Liebestod*, the lovers wish to die with each other in order to be resurrected together. Goethe's groundbreaking *Werther* bridged Empfindsamkeit and Sturm und Drang (storm and stress) by fusing the sentimental traits with a qualitatively different and new intensity in the all-encompassing power of love as the force of creation and life. It was accompanied by a belief in love at first sight as a symbol of a predetermined divine destiny.

Sturm und Drang literature began to acknowledge the power of sensuality as natural, while at the same time critiquing the seduction of innocence. It was critical of the overly sentimental tendencies of Empfindsamkeit. Jakob Michael Reinhold Lenz's *Der Hofmeister* (*The Tutor*, 1774) points to the dangers of seductive literary fantasies, as Gustchen's innocence is destroyed by Romeo and Juliet fantasies and an imitation of a Héloïse and Abélard plot with her tutor.

Sturm und Drang, the form of pre-Romanticism in Germany, celebrated two types of women: the simple, naive, sentimental, virtuous woman, and the *Machtweib* (the strong woman), often an exquisite beauty with masculine traits, such as Adelheid in Goethe's *Götz von Berlichingen* (1773). It accepted love that cannot be willed or coerced as a natural force, and consequently attacked marriages of convenience and introduced the experiment of the love triangle. Goethe's *Stella* (1776), Karoline Lucius Schlegel's *Duval und Charmille* (*Duval and Charmille*, 1778), and Friedrich Jacobi's *Woldemar* (1779) paved the way for the experimentation with new models of love.

The Romantics affirmed that marriage lost its meaning once love ended and consequently experimented with various forms of romantic social arrangements. Sophie Mereau's *Amanda und Eduard* (*Amanda and Eduard*, 1803) portrayed a self-determined heroine in search of an equal partnership. The romantic love paradigm, not restricted to marriage, celebrated the fusion of emotion, sensuality, and sexuality. Friedrich von Schlegel's novel *Lucinde* (1799), which because of its celebration of extramarital eroticism and its double entendres caused a scandal when it was first published, became the romantic novel *par excellence*. It gave expression to the elements of romantic love: the desire for a

union of the delights of the sensual and the physical aspects of love with a deep spirituality. This fusion was to return men and women to their natural divine core, and love is consequently portrayed as a means to find one's own self. Despite the fact that the romantic love paradigm suggests a fusion of masculine and feminine traits in love (and marriage) as a higher form of human existence, the construct celebrates "the feminine" as the less alienated, more natural state of being, which can offer salvation to the modern schizophrenic male torn between the value systems of the public and the private spheres. For the Romantics, women were considered to be closer to nature and thus to possess easier access to their own core. Love became the center of life and its deepest meaning. It was more than a fleeting passion, more than sentimental feeling for which feeling is more important than the object itself.

Religious overtones in an intermingling of love for a woman and the universe were especially pronounced in Novalis. For him, the death of the beloved created a mystical religious intensification of love, in which love becomes the key to understanding nature. In love, the meaning of life reveals itself. Love enables the comprehension of nature and the universe (*Die Lehrlinge zu Sais*, 1798). In his *Hymnen an die Nacht* (*Hymns to the Night*, 1800), the darkness of night opens the poet's eyes to the deeper connections of life that the light of reason obscures.

Novalis's *Hymnen an die Nacht* and Gérard de Nerval's *Aurelia* (1855) are similar in their fervid visions of the poet's response to the central event of life, the death of the beloved. For Nerval, the dream is a second life that is more exciting than reality. The beloved is seen as an interceding angel between these areas. In their constructions of love, both works capture an elusive fleeting atmosphere of a union of the sensual and the rational.

The synthesis of physical and spiritual love that transcended the old duality between body and soul, that Friedrich Schlegel and Friedrich Daniel Ernst Schleiermacher postulated and that represented the innovative aspect of Romantic literature in Germany, soon lost its conviction. In the works of Clemens Brentano and Ludwig Tieck the struggle for unity of spiritual and physical experience in love failed.

Many writers of English Romanticism justified love that defied either marital or blood ties because its intensity diminished all other considerations. Picking up on older traditions, they considered marriage and passion to be incompatible. Marital ties required constancy, while, as Lord Byron noted, there is no "such thing as a life of passion any more than a continuous earthquake, or an eternal fever" ("Letter to Thomas Moore July 5, 1821"). In his play *Manfred* (1817) he portrayed the suffering that a socially alienated individual endures when he denies morality to follow his Faustian heart and imagination. Seeking the perfect woman, the mental prefiguration of a beloved as the female projection of himself, led him to an incestuous devotion. Percy Bysshe Shelley, in his concluding remarks to *Laon and Cythna* (published as *The Revolt of Islam*, 1817), justified sibling love because he regarded love as "the sole law which should govern the temporal world." Byron stresses the dynamic quality of passion as is evident in metaphors such as torrents, tempests, earthquake, fire, and lightning. Elemental love parallels the energies of nature. Yet for him the spiritual and physical union required innocence, youth, self-sacrifice, intense passion, and independence from social obligations. Due to its unique nature it could not be sustained for long even if achieved. With less inebriation of the senses, Samuel Taylor Coleridge, in a March 12, 1811 letter to Henry Crabb Robinson, also emphasizes the dynamic aspect of love. He characterizes reciprocal love as "like two correspondent concave mirrors, having a common focus," each reflecting and magnifying the other in "endless reduplication."

The lasting impact of the Romantics on the concept of love is their belief in the overwhelming power of love, which led them to explore all its potentialities. In their search of the true nature of love, they often defied traditional religious beliefs, laws, and social customs. Their belief in the essential goodness of love allowed them to postulate the important role of love in salvation on earth rather than merely in a spiritual afterworld. The Romantic concept of love is an attempt at an ideal fusion of the sexual body and the philosophical mind. As Jean Hagstrum argued, for the Romantics "natural love borders closely upon the higher realm of imaginative creation, but it is distinct and separate, although not entirely independent." It was no longer reason, as during the Enlightenment, not *Bildung* as during the classical period, that aided in the development of the individual subjectivity, but love. Love allowed glimpses at one's own core and at the same time allowed access to the universe. The painting *Wir Drei* (1805–7) by Philipp Otto Runge (depicting the artist and his wife with his brother) could be seen to exemplify the symbiotic romantic love relationship that is at the same time open to others. The trees in the background leaning into one another are a symbol for the lovers. The strong oak on the side mirrors the friend reclining away from the couple yet linked to the lovers with his hand. While this painting suggests a fusion of erotic love, which remains open to intimate friendships with others, the painting by Georg Friedrich Kersting, *Couple at the Window* (1817) depicts the relationship of the couple, the fusion of male and female, as opened to nature. Underscored by the large mirror next to them, both halves of the couple (we see the woman from the back and the man from the front) gaze through the open window onto nature. Nature dissolves into the nebulous dreamscape of their souls. Amplified by their postures, their glances at, or just past, each other through the opened window hint at the endless desire of the Romantics despite the idyllic confinement of the Biedermeier setting. The idolization of love

can be read as a search for alternatives to the increasing materialism of modern society. Romantic love as a counterpoint to an increasingly specialized and fragmented society has not lost its hold over the Western cultural imagination.

KARIN A. WURST

Bibliography

Beaty, Fredrick L. *Love in British Romantic Literature.* DeKalb: Norhern Illinois University Press, 1971.

Beer, John. *Providence and Love: Studies in Wordsworth, Channing, Myers, George Eliot, and Ruskin.* Oxford: Clarendon Press, 1998.

Daniels, Charlotte. *Subverting the Family Romance: Women Writers, Kinship Structures, and the Early French Novel.* Lewisburg, Penn.: Bucknell University Press, 2000.

Enscoe, Gerald. *Eros and the Romantics: Sexual Love as a Theme in Coleridge, Shelley and Keats.* The Hague: Mouton, 1967.

Foucault, Michel. *The Hisory of Sexuality.* Vol. 1. New York: Pantheon Books, 1978.

Furst, Lilian. "Novalis' *Hymnen and die Nacht* and Nerval's Aurelia," in *The Contures of European Romanticism.* London: Macmillan Press, 1979. 109–26.

Gay, Peter. *Erziehung der Sinne: Sexualität im bürgerlichen Zeitalter.* Munich: Beck, 1986.

Hagstum, Jean. *The Romantic Body: Love and Sexuality in Keat's Wordsworth, and Blake.* Knoxville: University of Tennessee Press, 1985.

———. *Sex and Sensibility: Ideal and Erotic Love from Milton to Mozart.* Chicago: University of Chicago Press, 1980.

Hunt, Lynn. *The Family Romance of the French Revolution.* Berkeley and Los Angeles: University of California Press, 1992.

Kluckhohn, Paul. *Die Auffassung der Liebe in der Literatur des 18. Jahrhunderts und in der deutschen Romantik* (1921). Tübingen: Niemeyer, 1966.

Luhmann, Niklas. *Liebe als Passion: Zur Codierung von Intimität.* Frankfurt: Suhrkamp, 1982.

Sasse, Günter. *Die Ordnung der Gefühle: Das Drama der Liebesheirat im 18. Jahrhundert.* Darmstadt: Wissenschaftliche Buchgesellschaft, 1996.

Shorter, Edward. *The Making of the Modern Family.* New York: Basic Books, 1975.

Singer, Irving. *The Nature of Love, Vol. 2, Courtly and Romantic.* Chicago: University of Chicago Press, 1984.

Stone, Lawrence. *The Family, Sex and Marriage in England 1500–1800.* London: Weidenfeld and Nicolson, 1977.

LUCINDE 1799

Novel by Friedrich von Schlegel

In 1799, at the height of Jena Romanticism, Friedrich von Schlegel published *Lucinde* as the first part of a longer novel. Apart from several prose fragments and some sixty poems intended for inclusion, the writing of subsequent parts did not advance, and Schlegel abandoned the project for good in 1812. The publication in 1799 caused a scandal and led to the widespread condemnation of the book. Both its radical formal innovations and its open advocacy of sensual love contributed to the fiasco. Decisive, however, seems to have been the reception as a *roman à clef*, which saw in the hero Julius the author, and in Lucinde the author's lover and later wife Dorothea Veit (née Mendelssohn), who had only recently been divorced. Schlegel's

use of autobiographical material, which encouraged this reductionist interpretation, met with criticism from his closest friends, while Dorothea's own reaction was a mixture of resignation, sacrifice, and compensation. Among both the contemporary and many of the later responses, Friedrich Ernst Daniel Schleiermacher's *Vertraute Briefe über Friedrich Schlegels Lucinde* (*Confidential Letters on Schlegel's* Lucinde, 1800) stand out as a critical achievement, doing justice to the intentions behind, and to the merits of, Schlegel's work. In line with many others, G. W. F. Hegel and Søren Kierkegaard considered the book immoral. The work met a more positive reception in 1835, when Karl Gutzkow celebrated *Lucinde* as a manifesto of sensual freedom. Today, it is widely recognized as one of the most important writings of Jena Romanticism, which links Schlegel's poetological, in many regards protomodernist, program to the broader philosophical and moral concerns of that movement.

The poetological significance of *Lucinde* lies in those of its features by which Schlegel tries to realize his ideal of romantic *Poesie* (literature, the poetic). According to his "Athenäum Fragment 116," romantic *Poesie* aims at the unification of the different literary genres with both criticism, or theory, and life itself. In "Brief über den Roman" ("Letter on the Novel," 1800), Schlegel defines the novel as a romantic book in this sense. For Schlegel, that is to say, *novel* does not designate a particular literary genre but a work that in the creation of a *gebildetes künstliches Chaos* (organized, artificial chaos) tries to imitate, and partake of, both the harmonious organism and the chaotic plenitude of life. The Schlegelian novel, moreover, strives to fulfill the task of theory by providing the *geistige Anschanung* (spiritual intuition) of its subject matter, that is, ideally, of both life and the novel itself. *Lucinde* is intended to realize this probably paradoxical program by its form as well as its allegorical and symbolic meaning. Schlegel replaces the traditional plot and the development of characters with a relatively loose arrangement of a great variety of literary genres. *Lucinde* represents a composition of letters, anthropological and moral reflections, characterizations, dialogues, "fantasias," allegories, and short narrative texts. It may find an organic center in the middle section, a condensed bildungsroman entitled "Lehrjahre der Männlichkeit" ("Apprenticeship of Manhood"), which, with its account of Julius's earlier life and his sexual and erotic experiences, illustrates the notion that in love alone a both harmonious and full personality can be formed. The structure of such a personality, Schlegel suggests in a number of ways, is identical with that of romantic *Poesie*, or of both the novel in general and *Lucinde* in particular. In Julius's first letter to Lucinde, for example, the author includes his hero's reflections upon the "confusing" form of his writing and its relation to love and life. The depiction of four youths in "Allegorie der Frechheit" ("Allegory of Insolence") illustrates Schlegel's ideas and plans as a novelist. The first youth—sensual, fanciful, witty, playing with a mask, and resembling a strong-willed and wanton (*mutwillig*) girl—was meant to represent *Lucinde*.

Schlegel's formal and self-referential experiments in *Lucinde* are closely related to his ambition, acknowledged in a letter to Schleiermacher, to found a new morality. Essential in this respect is the conception of the relation between the sexes which Schlegel developed not only in *Lucinde* but also in his articles on the culture of classical Greece, as well as in his criticisms of Friedrich Heinrich Jacobi's novel *Woldemar* and Johann Christoph Friedrich von Schiller's poem "Würde der Frauen" ("The Dignity of Women"). Schlegel's attack on contemporary views of love and women focused on the traditional opposition between the physical and the spiritual, between sex on the one hand and love as an erotic friendship of souls on the other. While this opposition frequently implied that the value of women was perceived as incompatible with their sexuality, *Lucinde*, in accordance with bourgeois intentions, conceives marriage as a relationship of love, but differs from bourgeois evaluations by its insistence on sexual fulfilment as an essential part of love. For Schlegel, moreover, the conventional views of women as passive, dependent, and weak, and of men as active, independent, and strong, fall short of the truly human realization of freedom.

"Only independent femininity, only gentle masculinity is good and beautiful," he maintained in "Über die Diotima" ("On Diotima," 1795). And in *Lucinde* each lover's playful adoption of those attitudes stereotypically reserved for the opposite sex counts as the symbol of the perfection of both the male and the female in a full and whole humanity. Schlegel's attribution, also, and even especially, to women, of the neoclassical ideal of the harmonious integration of sensual and intellectual faculties is remarkable for its time, but it hardly represents an unequivocal demand for women's emancipation or freedom. The distinction between the private female sphere and the public male one largely remains intact in the novel. And the character Lucinde represents less an independent person with her own voice than the expression of both Julius's and his author's ideals. In allegedly transcending all separations between the rational and the natural, after all, Lucinde is made to conform to Schlegel's ideal of *Poesie*. Precisely as the symbol of a culture, morality, or humanity in which the alienation of modern civilization would be overcome, she has no life of her own.

MARGARETE KOHLENBACH

Text

Lucinde, 1799. Translated as *Lucinda* by Paul Bernard Thomas, 1913. Also published in *Friedrich Schlegel's "Lucinde" and the "Fragments."* Translated and introduced by Peter Firchow, 1971.

Bibliography

Bauer, Mark. "Der verborgene Mittelpunkt: Issues of Death and Awareness in Friedrich Schlegel's 'Lucinde,'" *Monatshefte für deutschsprachige Literatur und Kultur* 82, no. 2 (2000): 139–63.

Behler, Diana. *The Theory of the Novel in Early German Romanticism.* Bern: Lang, 1978.

Blackall, Eric A. *The Novels of the German Romantics.* Ithaca, N.Y.: Cornell University Press, 1983.

Eichner, Hans. *Friedrich Schlegel.* New York: Twayne, 1970.

Finlay, Marike. *The Romantic Irony of Semiotics: Friedrich Schlegel and the Crisis of Representation.* Berlin: Mouton de Gruyter, 1988.

Friedrichsmeyer, Sara. "Romanticism and the Dream of Androgynous Perfection," in *Deutsche Romantik and English Romanticism.* Edited by Theodore G. Gish and Sandra G. Frieden. Munich: Wilhelm Fink, 1984.

Kluckhohn, Paul. *Die Auffassung der Liebe in der Literatur des 18. Jahrhunderts und der Romantik.* 3d ed. Tübingen: Max Niemeyer, 1966.

Lacoue-Labarthe, Philippe, and Jean-Luc Nancy. *The Literary Absolute: The Theory of Literature in German Romanticism.* Translated by Philip Barnard and Cheryl Lester. Albany: State University of New York Press, 1988.

Lovejoy, Arthur O. "The Meaning of 'Romantic' in Early German Romanticism," in *Essays in the History of Ideas* by Arthur O. Lovejoy. Baltimore: Johns Hopkins University Press, 1970.

Mattenklott, Gert. "Der Sehnsucht eine Form: Zum Ursprung des modernen Romans bei Friedrich Schlegel; erläutert an der *Lucinde*," in *Zur Modernität der Romantik.* Edited by Dieter Bänsch. Stuttgart: J. B. Metzler, 1977.

Peer, Larry H. "Friedrich Schlegel's Theory of the Novel Revisited," *Colloquia Germanica* 10 (1976–77): 25–40.

Schmidt, Thomas E. *Die Geschichtlichkeit des frühromantischen Romans: Literarische Reaktionan auf Erfahrungen eines kulturellen Wandels.* Tübingen: Max Niemeyer, 1989.

LYRIC

Two things can be taken as characteristic of the lyric, as distinct from the narrative or dramatic poem: the first is elements of elaborate and repetitive metrical patterning that betray its origins in song, and the second is its use of a personal voice. The lyric is a (usually short) poem mimetic both of musical structure and of an experience undergone by a distinctive sensibility.

By the early nineteenth century, England and much of the rest of Europe had channeled most of its literary energy and aspiration into lyric poetry. For English society during the Elizabethan and Jacobean periods and for seventeenth-century France, it was dramatic poetry that had most profoundly incorporated and interrogated human meaning and social value. The Enlightenment, on the other hand, is best represented either by prose or by a poetry that was satirical, expository or didactic (Alexander Pope in England, for example, and Voltaire in France). Epic poetry continued to be written throughout the modern period, but the most successful of the modern epics—John Milton's *Paradise Lost* (1667), Friedrich Gottlieb Klopstock's *Der Messias* (*The Messiah*, 1748–73), Lord Byron's *Don Juan* (1819–24), and Aleksandr Pushkin's *Evgeny Onegin* (*Eugene Onegin*, 1833)—struggle to establish themselves as (often ironic) alternatives to the heroic poetry of classical Greece and Rome. The lyric, however, affecting the "spontaneous overflow of powerful feelings" (according to William Wordsworth) and recording "the impression which the object under the influence of passion makes on the mind" (according to William Hazlitt), is the characteristic achievement of the Romantic period.

The rise of the lyric throughout the eighteenth century was encouraged by a number of related ideas and phenomena. There was, for example, certainly after Jean-Jacques Rousseau's *Essai sur l'origine des langues* (*Essay on the Origin of Languages*, c. 1750) the growing conviction that language itself originated in passion and that the lyrical was a direct expression of the core experience of a people, equating per (Johann Gottfried von Herder,) lyricism with nationalism. Primitivism and antiquarianism sought to recuperate "uncivilized" poetry from the past, or from cultures that were geographically and socially remote, as "spontaneous" and more "sincere" a fascination that led to James Macpherson's faked translations of the third-century Scottish bard Ossian (1760–63), to Thomas Percy's *Reliques of Ancient English Poetry* (1765), to Herder's collection of *Volksleider* (1774 and later), and to Clemens Brentano and Achim von Arnim's *Des Knaben Wunderhorn* (1805–08). Then there was the evolving idealist belief that perception was imaginative and that the individual consciousness was the foundation of human knowledge (Johann Gottlieb Fichte, G. W. F. Hegel, Immanuel Kant, Friedrich Wilhelm Joseph von Schelling). Poetry became identified as a mode of apprehension rather than as an artistic construction. " 'What is poetry?' is nearly the same question as, 'What is a poet?' " argued Samuel Taylor Coleridge, and Friedrich von Schlegel insisted that, like consciousness itself, "romantic poetry" was "in a state of becoming." Not only was the hierarchy of genres dismantled that in classical and neoclassical theory had only reluctantly accommodated certain kinds of lyric, but these intellectual and cultural developments conspired to make the lyric—defined as a passionate and imaginative utterance bringing head and heart into collaborative and creative activity—at once the originary and the quintessential expressive form.

The return to the lyric is manifest in many ways. On the one hand, we find examples of traditional forms like the sonnet, which experienced a renaissance in Britain during the period (Wordsworth, for example, wrote more sonnets than any other British poet); on the other hand, we find the more innovative form of the "greater Romantic lyric" identified by M. H. Abrams, a blend of the traditional hymn, poetry of meditation, the Pindarick ode of the seventeenth and eighteenth centuries, and the more recent loco-descriptive poem. The typical Romantic lyric is a private occasion. Addressing an image or idea in an inartificial (conversational) language that is nonetheless richly musical, even to the point of enchantment, it often identifies with the landscape and varies its mood with the season or time of day. As its heredity suggests, it is a blend of description, expression, song, and meditation, modulating from one to the other. The *experience* it re-presents and meditates—"emotion recollected in tranquillity" (according to Wordsworth)—demands attention to itself *as* an experience and to the experiencing self of the poet, at the same time as it demands attention to the poem's nominal object: a bird, a time of day, a vista, a state of mind, a loved one, and so on. Under the heading of the greater Romantic lyric we can include Wordsworth's "Tintern Abbey" (1798) and "Immortality Ode" (1802–4), Coleridge's "Frost at Midnight" (1798) and "Ode on Dejection" (1802), John Keats's *Odes* (1819), and Percy Bysshe Shelley's "Stanzas Written in Dejection" (1818) along with other major lyrics like the *Hymnen an die Nacht* (*Hymns to the Night*, 1799–1800) of Novalis; Friedrich Hölderlin's "Patmos" (1802–6); Brentano's "Schwanenlied" ("Swansong," 1840), Joseph von Eichendorff's "Mondnacht" ("Moonlit Night," 1849), "Zwielicht" ("Twilight," 1850), and "Sehnsucht" ("Longing," 1850); Alphonse de Lamartine's) "Le Lac" ("The Lake," 1817), of Alfred-Victor de Vigny's "Le Cor" ("The Horn," 1822); and Alfred de Musset's "La nuit de mai" ("A Night in May," 1835).

Insofar as the lyric also came to be seen as synonymous with poetry itself or as its most quintessential form, then along with the practice and promotion of lyric forms a distinct "lyricization" occurs. In the German poetry of the 1770s, such as in Gottfried Bürger's "Lenore" (1773) and Johann Wolfgang von Goethe's "Der König von Thule" ("The King of Thule," 1774) and "Erlkönig" ("King of the Elves," 1774), for example, the boundary between the objective, third person narrative and the subjective lyric is blurred, as it is in Klopstock's epic *Der Messias*. Wordsworth announces a conflation of the two forms in the title of his *Lyrical Ballads* (1798); in his *The Prelude* (1805) we get an epic poem in the first person on the growth of his own mind. With this, and in keeping with the Romantic tendency to construct large-scale narratives of spiritual and cultural evolution, an allegorization of a "lyric spirit" or of "lyricism" can be identified. Frequently characterized as feminine, it is envisioned as supervening upon the genres of epic and tragedy (masculinist, agonistic, complicit with authoritarianism) in a (prophetic) celebration of the fulfillment of the human spirit. The fourth act that Shelley added to his *Prometheus Unbound* (1821) involves a version of this myth of poetic genre, as does the final movement of Ludwig van Beethoven's Ninth Symphony, in which Johann Christoph Friedrich von Schiller's "An die Freude" ("Ode to Joy," 1787) is chosen as the archetypal lyric and reintegrated into the musical form from which the lyric evolved, as if brought home. So, later in the nineteenth century, while Edgar Allan Poe exalted the brief lyric beyond other art forms, the French *symbolistes* would insist that all art aspired to the condition of music.

WILLIAM CHRISTIE

Bibliography

Abrams, M. H. "Strcture and Style in the Greater Romantic Lyric." In *The Correspondent Breeze: Essays on English Romanticism.* New York: W. W. Norton, 1984.

Curran, Stuart. *Poetic Form and British Romanticism.* Oxford: Oxford University Press, 1986.

Hosek, Chaviva, and Patricia Parker, eds. *Lyric Poetry: Beyond New Criticism.* Ithaca, N.Y.: Cornell University Press, 1985.

Johnson, W. R. *The Idea of Lyric: Lyric Modes in Ancient and Modern Poetry,* Berkeley and Los Angeles: University of California Press, 1982.

Kaiser, Gerhard. *Geschichte der deutschen Lyrik von Goethe bis Heine: ein Grundriss in Interpretationen.* Frankfurt: Suhrkamp, 1988.

Lindley, David. *Lyric.* Critical Idiom Series. London: Methuen, 1985.

MacLean, Norman. "From Action to Image: Theories of the Lyric in the Eighteenth Century." In *Critics and Criticism.* Edited by R. S. Crane. Chicago: University of Chicago Press, 1952.

Preminger, Alex, and T. V. F. Brogan, eds. *The New Princeton Encyclopedia of Poetry and Poetics.* Princeton, N.J.: Princeton University Press, 1993.

Rogers, William Elford. *The Three Genres and the Interpretation of Lyric.* Princeton, N.J.: Princeton University Press, 1983.

LYRICAL BALLADS, WITH A FEW OTHER POEMS 1798

Poetry collection by Samuel Taylor Coleridge and William Wordsworth

What is a "lyrical ballad"? The hybrid points in two contradictory directions. The ballad implies narrative, however cryptic or truncated; the lyric promises an inward turn, subjectivity and feeling, reaction rather than action. Focusing on the emotions, often in extremes of passion, devotion, distress, or confusion, *Lyrical Ballads* drew on some familiar genres and subjects, but flaunted a break with eighteenth-century standards of poetic craft and verbal polish. The publication also refused (as William Wordsworth explained in the Preface to the next edition of 1800) to cater to the tastes cultivated by "the popular Poetry of the day," which featured servings of sensational incident. What distinguished the poems of *Lyrical Ballads* was that "the feeling therein developed gives importance to the action and the situation, and not the action and situation to the poetry."

Lyrical Ballads was no mere anthology of such instances, however, but a sustained, coherently conceived project. It was "to a certain degree *one work,* in *kind tho' not in degree,* as an Ode is one work," as Coleridge wrote in June 1798 (with Wordsworth looking over his shoulder) to their publisher, Bristol bookseller Joseph Cottle, adding, "our different poems are as stanzas, good relatively rather than absolutely." In *Biographia Literaria* (1817), Coleridge elaborated their different, but complementary ventures of imagination:

> My endeavours should be directed to persons and characters supernatural, or at least romantic; yet so as to transfer from our inward nature a human interest and semblance of truth sufficient to procure for these shadows of imagination that willing suspension of disbelief for the moment, which constitutes poetic faith. Mr Wordsworth, on the other hand, was to propose to himself as his object to give the charm of novelty to things of every day, and to excite a feeling analogous to the supernatural, by awakening the mind's attention from the lethargy of custom and directing it to the loveliness and the wonders of the world before us.

Coleridge's magnificently haunting work in his genre was the volume's longest work, "The Rime of the Ancyent Marinere, in seven parts." With "The Nightingale, a Conversational Poem"; "The Foster Mother's Tale"; and "The Dungeon," his poetry comprised about a third of the volume's pages. The other nineteen poems by Wordsworth presented a variety of genres: lyric, anecdote, quasi-dramatic monologue, conversation, and a blank-verse, first-person meditation, "Lines Written a few Miles above Tintern Abbey, on Revisiting the Banks of the Wye during a Tour, July 13, 1798."

A short prefacing "Advertisement" introduced the poets as innovators, sponsors of "experiments" to "ascertain how far the language of conversation in the middle and lower classes of society is adapted to the purposes of poetic pleasure." Toward this end, the poetry privileged rural society in close proximity to nature and an array of "low" forms, such as ballad and anecdote, in disdain of the polished forms and artificial diction of "high" eighteenth-century poetry. Readers "accustomed to . . . gaudiness and inane phraseology" were warned of having "to struggle with feelings of strangeness and awkwardness"; even those not bound by "pre-established codes of decision" and capable of "superior judgment" might find the language "too low," "too familiar, not of sufficient dignity."

The opening poem, Coleridge's "Rime," forced the question. The diction was strange, the spelling archaic, the idiom idiosyncratic, and the tale itself mysterious, unaided even by that (albeit problematic) marginal gloss Coleridge added, satirically, when he published the poem under his own name in 1817. Not just this possessed mariner, but a world of strange, heterodox figures—old men, vagrants, outcasts, convicts, spooked dalesmen, superstitious sea captains, obstinate children, a mad mother, a frantic mother, and an idiot boy—populated the pages, all soliciting sympathy, sometimes forcing social reflection.

The closing poem was Wordsworth's great, quasi-ode of troubled memory, inquiry and reflection, *Lines Written a few Miles above Tintern Abbey, on Revisiting the Banks of the Wye during a Tour, July 13, 1798.* The date so marked, one day before Bastille Day, and the opening words, "Five years have passed," were politically fraught. July 13 summons the revolutionary hopes of July 14, 1789, by which Wordsworth and his generation were inspired; the lapse of "five years" evokes 1793, the year that England and France went to war and the Reign of Terror sent Louis XVI, Marie Antoinette, and thousands more to the guillotine. By 1798, Napoleon had inherited the Revolution and was exporting a war of aggression against European monarchies and republics alike. In the inward turn of Wordsworth's "*Lines*", however, these horrific consequences are distanced and abstracted as the "still, sad music of humanity." Transforming a familiar genre of loco-description, Wordsworth proposed a new sense of self, vexed by the turmoils of recent history and life in the world, seeking solace in a myth of unchanging "Nature," its power impressed (however uncertainly) upon the senses, on the feelings, on memory, on the soul, as a source of perpetual, renewable "joy." Yet for all this seeming retreat into memory and spiritual solace, the poem is haunted by what John Keats called, "dark Passages," letter to John Hamilton Reynolds, (May 3, 1818), and for many it proves most compelling, as T. S. Eliot wrote of Alfred, Lord Tennyson's *In Memoriam* (1850), not "because of the quality of its faith, but because of the quality of its doubt."

Priced at five shillings (the poets were paid thirty pounds for the copyright), *Lyrical Ballads, With a Few Other Poems* was published in October 1798, anonymously because Coleridge worried that his reputation in controversial political journalism would contaminate the volume's reception. Its ten reviews were mixed, with only three really negative. There was praise for *Tintern Abbey*, displeasure at some of the socially polemical pieces, and disgust at some of the socially marginal or more eccentric characters. In addition to this cast of characters, the simplicity of poetic style, and the idealism of rural life and common language ruffled conventional literary tastes, with the most extravagant ridicule falling to Coleridge's *Rime*. Even so, this venture in "strange power of speech" weathered the reception to become, with *Tintern Abbey*, the best-known of the 1798 poems today, and the project as a whole survived its first wave of reviews to spawn a miniseries. *Lyrical Ballads, With Other Poems by W. Wordsworth* (still with Coleridge's "Rime" and a few other of his poems) appeared in two volumes early in 1801 (dated "1800"), with an ambitiously polemical "Preface" replacing the original "Advertisement." Volume 1 had mostly the 1798 poems, with some textual changes, a few altered titles, and reordering (Wordsworth's "debate" pair, "Expostulation and Reply" and "The Tables Turned," now commenced the volume instead of Coleridge's "Rime"). Volume 2, with a wealth of new poems by Wordsworth (over forty) could be purchased separately, and was, by those who already had the 1798 *Ballads*. *Lyrical Ballads, With Pastoral and Other Poems by W. Wordsworth* appeared in 1802 (also two volumes) with corrections, revisions, and an expanded Preface, including an Appendix on poetic diction. There was another edition in 1805, after which the contents were redistributed, with further revisions (Coleridge's in "Sibylline Leaves" [1817] and Wordsworth's in his 1815 *Poems*, under new subheads), and then into the collections of the 1820s, 1830s, and 1840s, right up to the final lifetime collection of 1849–50.

Lyrical Ballads, which many regard as the most important volume of English poetry since the Renaissance, can claim credit for inaugurating the "Romantic Revolution in poetry." Its strategically "simple" poems draw their power from a network of refusals: a refusal to emphasize action, to provide clear or consolidated conclusions, facile consolations, or tidy morals. The gaps, silences, and understatements call the reader's imagination into play. In despair of systemic political reform, the poets thus set out to reform poetry and its readers, challenging entrenched habits and preconceived notions of value, both literary and social, and encouraging the formation of individual, private powers of meditation as a means to communal sympathy. To learn to read this new poetic world, Coleridge and Wordsworth imply, and even insist, is to join a new, potentially democratic community of morally enlivened imagination.

SUSAN J. WOLFSON

See also **Coleridge, Samuel Taylor; Poetry: Britain; Wordsworth, William**

Text

Lyrical Ballads. Edited by Michael Mason. Longman, 1972.
Wordsworth and Coleridge: Lyrical Ballads. Edited by R. L. Brett and A. R. Jones, 2d ed. London: Routledge, 1991.
Lyrical Ballads and Other Poems, 1797–1800. Edited by James Butler and Karen Green. Ithaca, N.Y.: Cornell University Press, 1992.

First Reviews

Frances Wrangham, in the *British Critic* 14 (October 1799): 364–69.
Robert Southey, in the *Critical Review*. 2nd ser. 24 (October 1798): 197–204.
Anonymous, in the *Analytical Review* 28 (December 1798): 583–87.
Charles Burney, in the *Monthly Review*, 2nd ser. 29 (June 1799): 202–10.

Bibliography

Eilenberg, Susan. *Strange Power of Speech: Wordsworth, Coleridge & Literary Possession*. Oxford: Oxford University Press, 1992.
Glen, Heather. *Vision and Disenchantment: Blake's "Songs" and Wordsworth's "Lyrical Ballads."* Cambridge: Cambridge University Press, 1983.
Griffin, Andrew L. "Wordsworth and the Problem of Imaginative Story: The Case of Simon Lee," *Publications of the Modern Language Association* 92 (1977): 392–409.
Heffernan, James A. W. "Wordsworth's 'Leveling' Muse in 1798." In *1798: The Year of the "Lyrical Ballads."* Edited by Richard Cronin. London: Macmillan, 1998.
Jacobus, Mary. *Tradition and Experiment in Wordsworth's "Lyrical Ballads" (1798)*. Oxford: Oxford University Press, 1976.
Jordan, John E. *Why the "Lyrical Ballads"? The Background, Writing and Character of Wordsworth's 1798 "Lyrical Ballads."* Berkeley and Los Angeles: University of California Press, 1976.
Parrish, Stephen M. *The Art of the "Lyrical Ballads"*. Cambridge, Mass.: Harvard University Press, 1973.
Roe, Nicholas. *Wordsworth and Coleridge: The Radical Years*. Oxford: Clarendon Press, 1988.
Sheats, Paul D. *The Making of Wordsworth's Poetry, 1785–1798*. Cambridge, Mass.: Harvard University Press, 1973.
Wolfson, Susan J. "Speaker as Questioner in *Lyrical Ballads* 1798." In *The Questioning Presence*. Ithaca, N.Y.: Cornell University Press, 1987.

M

LORD MACAULAY, THOMAS BABBINGTON 1800–1859

English historian

Born in Leicestershire in 1800, Thomas Babbington, Lord Macaulay distinguished himself as a politician and as one of England's greatest historians. Success as a historian, however, came late in life; he devoted much of his youth to what would become a distinguished political career both as a member of Parliament and as a cabinet minister. Elected to Parliament in 1830, he played an important role as an advocate for the Parliamentary Reform Bill two years later. In 1834, he traveled to India to make his fortune, and he served there for four years. During that time he established a system of Indian education based on Western principles and drafted a penal code for the colony. He returned to England and to Parliament, serving from 1839 to 1847 and from 1852 to 1856. He also served as secretary of war from 1839 to 1841 and as paymaster of the forces from 1846 to 1847. Elevated to the peerage in 1857, he died two years later.

He first achieved success in his writing career in 1825 with an essay on the poet John Milton written for the Edinburgh *Review*. He followed up that essay with other essays written about Robert Clive, Warren Hastings, and other historical figures. In 1842, he published a collection of poems, *The Lays of Ancient Rome*. There he converted to verse stories from Roman history, using them to extol patriotism and sacrifice, virtues valued in nineteenth century England as in Classical Rome. An extract from "Horatius" provides an example:

> To every man upon this earth
> Death cometh soon or late.
> And how can men die better
> Than facing fearful odds,
> For the ashes of his fathers,
> And the temples of his gods.

While his work extols Roman themes, it differs from other British poets enamored of Rome in that Macaulay sought to imitate the songs that might have been written in Ancient Rome rather than seeking to imitate the poetic forms of Horace or Juvenal.

Macaulay's enduring fame, however, rests on his engaging and readable *History of England from the Accession of James II*. Macaulay eschewed scientific history in favor of the literary approach and Whig principles, a historical philosophy that stressed ideals of progress and liberty, expressed in elegant and accessible prose. Characterized by a devout belief in progress, the Whig interpretation of history, in its English incarnation, stressed themes such as the triumph of Protestantism in England and the rise of Parliament as a bulwark against encroachments on the rights of ordinary citizens. Through the works of Macaulay, the Glorious Revolution of 1688 came to be seen as a central event in English history by removing the Roman Catholic and tyrannical James II in favor of William III and Mary, Parliament, Protestantism, and liberty. The revolution, Macaulay believed, protected England from arbitrary government in part by requiring Parliamentary approval of any legislation, taxation, or standing armies.

While extremely popular history in the Victorian era and retaining momentum well into the early twentieth century, the Whig view was not without critics. Herbert Butterfield criticized the Whig interpretation for oversimplifying the past and labeling historical figures either friends or foes of progress. These are the tendencies that, when combined with features such as Macaulay's absolute certainty in his own, often shaky judgments, leave Whig history open to criticism. In addition, Macaulay viewed history as literature and did not employ the "scientific" approach to sources that would come to dominate the historical profession in the late nineteenth and twentieth centuries. While Macaulay's words remain vastly more readable than academic histories, his work lacks an academic attention to detail. "Scientific" history, the forerunner of the discipline as it is practiced today, would be born later in the century, in the works of the German historian Leopold von Ranke.

In other ways, Macaulay's history points the way forward to later nineteenth- and twentieth-century history in its third chapter. There Macaulay presents an early form of the social history that has risen to prominence in recent years. Macaulay examines the different orders of society and the military, and also focuses on various cities around England, examining London in detail; literature, the arts, and sciences do not escape his attention, either. Unfortunately, his discussion is also highly partisan; as his Whig sympathies leak through, Macaulay paints a damning portrait of country squires as overfed, oafish, drunken louts—more boorish but less entertaining than Henry Fielding's Squire Western. Biased as Macaulay's account is in some places, it marks a departure from earlier histories that focused heavily on political or military events—as does the rest of his *History*.

Macaulay draws a particularly injudicious portrait of John Churchill, First Duke of Marlborough. Marlborough's descendant, Winston Churchill, would later correct that assessment in his biography *Marlborough: His Life and Times*, based in part on Henry Paget's *New Examen*. In essence, Macaulay depicts Marlborough as one who used the fortunes of a rich, older woman to feed his monumental greed and who used the favor of King James II for advancement only to sell James out on the eve of the Revolution of 1688. William III, by contrast, is the hero of the *History*. To Macaulay, William combined right belief in Protestantism and a free England with courage: "He was proved by every test: by war, by wounds, by painful and depressing maladies, by imminent and constant risk of assassination—a risk which has shaken very strong nerves, a risk which severely tried even the adamantine fortitude of Cromwell. Yet none could ever discover what that thing was that the Prince of Orange feared."

MITCHELL McNAYLOR

Selected Works

Lays of Ancient Rome. London: Longman, Brown, Green, and Longmans, 1842.
The History of England from the Accession of James II. 5 vols. 1849–61.
Critical and Miscellaneous Essays. 5 vols. Carey & Hart, 1854.
The Selected Letters of Thomas Babington Macaulay. Cambridge: Cambridge University Press, 1982.

Bibliography

Butterfield, Herbert. *The Whig Interpretation of History*. London: G. Bell and Sons, 1950.
Clive, John. *Macaulay: The Shaping of the Historian*. New York: Alfred A. Knopf, 1974.
Firth, C. H. *A Commentary on Macaulay's History of England*. London: Macmillan, 1938.
Hamburger, Joseph. *Macaulay and the Whig Tradition*. Chicago: University of Chicago Press, 1976.
Millgate, Jane. *Macaulay*. London: Routledge and Kegan Paul, 1973.
Munby, A. N. L. *Macaulay's Library*. Glasgow: Jackson, 1966.
Trevelyan, George Otto. *Leipsic Edition of the Life and Letters of Lord Macaulay*. 1876.

MADEMOISELLE DE MAUPIN. DOUBLE AMOUR 1835

Novel by Théophile Gautier

Théophile Gautier's first novel is famous on two counts: for its spirited preface and for its subject matter, considered by most critics of the day to be highly immoral, although neither author nor publisher faced prosecution under the July Monarchy and editions published during the Second Empire escaped censorship. D'Albert's preference for pagan over Christian art and the erotic denouement were thought particularly shocking. While the work—which owes something to the libertine novels of the previous century—was admired by Honoré de Balzac, Charles Baudelaire, and Victor Hugo, it was not a commercial success until after 1850, at which point it was frequently reprinted and assumed cult status for the aesthetic movement in England and for continental writers of fin-de-siècle decadence.

A few details in the preface, dated May 1834 but probably not completed until the autumn of that year, were toned down when a new edition of the novel, shorn of its subtitle *Double Amour*, was published in 1845, but it remained a provocative attack on moralizing journalism, of which Gautier had been a victim in *Le Constitutionnel* of May 31, 1834 (following his article on François Villon in *La France littéraire* in January), on critical utilitarianism and the notion of human perfectibility. It is also an expression of the young writer's artistic credo, according to which art concerns beauty and pleasure and not morality, an idea that separates Gautier from the humanitarian vision of many of his Romantic contemporaries. The preface is now recognized as a key document in the development of the doctrine of art for art's sake (although Gautier does not use the formula *l'art pour l'art* until later), and asserts: "The only things that are truly beautiful are those which have no practical utility; everything that is useful is ugly."

The preface makes only passing, humorous, reference to the novel that follows, but the novel's hedonism and aestheticism nonetheless reflect the radical stance of the preface. The novel is set in an aristocratic milieu at an indeterminate time—apparently the late seventeenth century, when its eponymous prototype Madeleine d'Aubigny-Maupin was alive—but anachronisms, no doubt deliberate, abound. It owes little, apart from the names of some of its characters, to the life of the historical Maupin, an opera singer, accomplished swordswoman, occasional transvestite, and bisexual, who led a scandalous and adventurous life, and not much to Henri de Latouche's *Fragoletta* (1829), but is rather, with Alfred de Musset's *La Confession d'un enfant du siècle* (*The Confession of a Child of the Century*, 1836) the culmination of a tradition of Romantic introspection that goes back to the late eighteenth century. The twenty-two-year-old d'Albert (his age is that of Gautier in 1833, when he agreed with his publisher to write the novel) is a Romantic hero in the tradition of Johann Wolfgang von Goethe's *Die Leiden des jungen Werther* (*The Sorrows of Young Werther*, 1774), Étienne Pivert de Senancour's *Obermann* (1804), François-Auguste-

René de Chateaubriand's *René* (1805), and Benjamin Constant de Rabecque's *Adolphe* (1816), and like them he suffers from the *mal du siècle*. A narcissistic idealist, at times prey to a morbid solipsism that leads him to doubt the existence of others, he is tormented by self-doubt and by sexual desires which lead him to create an unrealizable ideal of perfect womanhood. Although he finds erotic fulfillment with the sensual Rosette, his metaphysical anguish remains and he appreciates her only as an emblem of the absolute feminine beauty he perceives in painting and mythology. At this point, he is attracted to Théodore de Sérannes, a young man of effeminate appearance, but is frightened by the prospect of homosexual love. Théodore, with whom Rosette is also in love, is in reality Madelaine de Maupin, who has disguised herself as a man in order to understand the workings of the male psyche and who harbors an idealistic conception of love similar to d'Albert's. The insight into men that her disguise affords her leaves her disillusioned but she has sympathy for d'Albert and Rosette. Ready to lose her virginity, Madelaine de Maupin spends a night of erotic passion with d'Albert. Although the narrator is coy on the matter, it also appears that Madelaine and Rosette have an erotic encounter. Madelaine then departs, explaining in her letter of farewell to d'Albert that she fears the ephemerality of relationships but will remember him. She may renounce sexual activity but hopes that he and Rosette will continue to be lovers and remember her as a beautiful dream; the latter detail is similar to the departing hero/heroine's exhortation to Wilfrid and Minna in Balzac's *Séraphîta* (1835).

The subtitle of the first edition, *Double Amour*, reflects the ambiguity of the sexual desires of the principal characters, and references to the Platonic myth of the androgyne and to the legendary figures of Salmacis and Hermaphroditus, who combined perfect male and female beauty in one body, suggest that total harmony of the sexes is restricted to the sphere of art. In a subtle *mise en abyme*, d'Albert comes fully to understand the nature of his passion while playing the part of Orlando to Théodore's Rosalind and Rosette's Phoebe in William Shakespeare's *As You Like It*, one of numerous works of art referred to in the novel and used here to illustrate Gautier's favored notion that the mask reveals truth. It is clear that Madelaine, who feels she represents a third sex that transcends male and female, represents not only eroticism but the elusive essence of ideal beauty. D'Albert, a poet who no longer writes, is thus the Romantic artist whose earthly desires have a metaphysical dimension. His brief involvement with Madelaine allows him to glimpse the Platonic absolute of beauty that is at the heart of Gautier's aesthetic, and of which the novel is a manifesto, but the reader is not told what the impact of this experience will be on d'Albert's subsequent life.

Often said to be poorly structured, the work is nevertheless technically sophisticated, mingling letters from D'Albert and Madelaine to third parties with third-person narration. Dramatic intensity and focus on the two main characters are maintained by excluding the replies from their correspondents. There are fine passages of psychological analysis, but the narrator is also self-consciously and playfully ironic at the expense of d'Albert, of the novel's polyphonic structure, and of literary convention in general.

PETER WHYTE

Work

Mademoiselle de Maupin. Double Amour. 2 vols. 1835–36. Revised edition: *Mademoiselle de Maupin.* Modern editions: *Mademoiselle de Maupin.* Edited by Jacques Robichez. Paris: Imprimerie Nationale, 1979. *Mademoiselle de Maupin*, edited by Claudine Lacoste-Veysseyre in Théophile Gautier, *Romans, contes et nouvelles*, vol. I, Paris: Gallimard, 2002. Translation: *Mademoiselle de Maupin.* Translated by Joanna Richardson. Harmondsworth, England: Penguin, 1981.

Bibliography

Albouy, Pierre. "Le mythe de l'androgyne dans *Mademoiselle de Maupin*," *Revue d'Histoire Littéraire de la France* 72 (1972): 600–608.

Avignon-Leroux, Véronique, "Romantisme et préciosité dans *Mademoiselle de Maupin*," *Bulletin de la Société Théophile Gautier* 17 (1995): 7–32.

Bouchard, Anne. "Le masque et le miroir dans *Mademoiselle de Maupin*," *Revue d'Histoire Littéraire de la France* 72 (1972): 583–99.

Brami, Joseph. *Mademoiselle de Maupin. Théophile Gautier.* Paris: Nathan, 1993.

Crouzet, Michel. "Gautier et le problème de 'créer'," *Revue d'Histoire littéraire de la France* 72 (1972): 659–87.

Fernández Sanchez, Carmen. "*Mademoiselle de Maupin* et le récit poétique," *Bulletin de la Société Théophile Gautier* 3 (1981): 1–10.

Jasinski, René. *Les Années romantiques de Théophile Gautier.* Paris: Vuibert, 1929.

Laforgue, Pierre. *L'Éros romantique. Représentations de l'amour en 1830.* Paris: Presses Universitaires de France, 1998.

Monneyron, Frédéric, *L'Androgyne romantique. Du mythe au mythe littéraire.* Grenoble: ELLUG, 1994.

Savalle, Joseph. *Travestis, métamorphoses, dédoublements. Essai sur l'œuvre romanesque de Théophile Gautier.* Paris: Minard, 1981.

Schapira, Marie-Claude. *Le Regard de Narcisse. Romans et nouvelles de Théophile Gautier.* Lyon: Presses Universitaires de Lyon, 1984.

Tortonese, Paolo. *La Vie extérieure. Essai sur l'œuvre narrative de Théophile Gautier.* Paris: Lettres Modernes, 1992.

Zenkine, Serge. "*Mademoiselle de Maupin*, éducation et histoire," *Bulletin de la Société Théophile Gautier* 16 (1994): 81–97.

MADNESS

Madness was a highly topical subject in Britain during the earlier years of the Romantic era. This was partly because King George III began to show signs of mental instability in 1788 and 1789, and was eventually replaced by his eldest son in 1810 and 1811. Newspapers continued to report regularly on his condition until his death in 1820. *King Lear* was tactfully dropped from the theatrical repertoire. Two attempts to assassinate the king by alleged lunatics only served to give madness more prominence. These attempts led to changes in the law on criminal insanity.

Madness was not only visible on the public stage, but also could be found in the domestic sphere. Jane Austen's brother George, Lady Caroline Lamb's son Augustus, and Augusta

Leigh's daughter Augusta Charlotte are just three of the upper-class children who were thought to be suffering from it. Many working-class families had the experience of members being taken away to workhouses, never to be seen again.

Although workhouses and private madhouses continued to be used to house the insane, the Romantic era was also notable for the growth of asylum culture and for the development of a form of treatment known as moral management. The Tuke family in York, who founded an asylum called The Retreat in 1796, was seen as pioneering more humane methods. The example was copied not just in Britain, but also in Europe and America. According to the advertisement of the time, management was preferred to medicine and physical restraint was only considered a last resort. The mad were to be cared for as human beings, rather than caged as wild and dangerous animals. Phillipe Pinel in France is also credited with changing perceptions of madness.

Although the number of asylums grew, particularly after the Lunatics' Act of 1845, many allegedly mad people were still confined at home. The most famous fictional example remains Bertha Rochester in Charlotte Bronte's *Jane Eyre* (1847). Yet it is also possible to see a wide range of other characters such as Miss Bates in Austen's *Emma* (1816) and Mr. Dick in Charles Dickens's *David Copperfield* (1849–50) as being cared for by the community rather than being placed in asylums. There was also a pattern in which regular visits to asylums could be interspersed with periods at home. This is how Mary Lamb lived her life after she killed her mother in a fit of insanity in 1796, being cared for whenever possible by her brother Charles.

Writers have always been fascinated by madness, as well as afraid of it. Lord Byron claimed that all poets were close to insanity, as a particularly impassioned bout of writing could produce forms of, or even be interpreted as a form of, madness. Lady Byron sought to prove that her husband was indeed mad when they separated in 1816. Writers who were viewed by their contemporaries as being mad include John Clare, William Cowper, Friedrich Hölderlin, Gerard de Nerval, and Christopher Smart. Clare spent a long period at the end of his life, from 1837 to 1864 with just one short break, confined in asylums. His doctors declared that his addiction to poetry was partly responsible for his madness.

Book 1 of Cowper's *The Task* (1785) contains the figure of Crazy Kate, who has been driven mad by the death of her lover. The madwoman also fascinated writers such as William Wordsworth in "The Female Vagrant" and elsewhere, as well as a number of painters. The madness of Ophelia became iconic by the middle of the century as a result of the work of the Pre-Raphaelites. Some forms of insanity, such as erotomania, were seen as being specifically female maladies and, more generally, women were claimed to be at greater risk of madness by male doctors, as their biology, as well as their nature, were held to render them particularly vulnerable.

ROGER SALES

Bibliography

Bynum, W. F. eds. *The Anatomy of Madness: Essays in the History of Psychiatry.* London: Tavistock, 1985.

Colley, Ann C. *Tennyson and Madness.* Athens; Ga.: University of Georgia Press, 1983.

Digby, Anne. *Madness, Morality and Medicine: A Study of the York Retreat.* Cambridge: Cambridge University Press, 1985.

Eigen, Joel Peter. *Witnessing Insanity: Madness and Mad-Doctors in the English Court.* New Haven, Conn.: Yale University Press, 1995.

Foucault, Michel. *Madness and Civilization: A History of Insanity in the Age of Reason.* Translated by Richard Howard. London: Tavistock, 1971.

Goldstein, Jan. *Console and Classify: The French Psychiatric Profession in the Nineteenth Century.* Cambridge: Cambridge University Press, 1987.

MacLennan, George. *Lucid Interval: Subjective Writing and Madness in History.* Leicester: Leicester University Press, 1992.

Martin, Philip W. *Mad Women in Romantic Writing.* Brighton: Harvester Press, 1987.

Parry-Jones, William. *The Trade in Lunacy: A Study in Private Madhouses in England in the Eighteenth and Nineteenth Centuries.* London: Routledge and Kegan Paul, 1970.

———. *Mind-Forg'd Manacles: A History of Madness in England from the Restoration to the Regency.* London: Penguin, 1988.

———. *A Social History of Madness: Stories of the Insane.* London: Weidenfeld and Nicolson, 1987.

Sales, Roger. *Jane Austen and Representations of Regency England.* London: Routledge, 1996.

Scull, Andrew. *The Most Solitary of Afflictions: Madness and Society in Britain 1700–1900.* New Haven, Conn.: Yale University Press, 1993.

Showalter, Elaine. *The Female Malady: Women, Madness, and English Culture 1830–1980.* London: Virago, 1987.

Shuttleworth, Sally. *Charlotte Bronte and Victorian Psychology.* Cambridge: Cambridge University Press, 1996.

Small, Helen. *Love's Madness: Medicine, the Novel and Female Insanity 1800–1865.* Oxford: Clarendon Press, 1996.

Skultans, Vieda, ed. *Madness and Morals: Ideas of Insanity in the Nineteenth Century.* London: Routledge and Kegan Paul, 1975.

MAIMON, SOLOMON 1754–1800

Solomon Maimon's career was a striking illustration of the ambivalence with which the Maskilim—that is, the followers of the Jewish Enlightenment, or Haskalah—lived and worked. This illustration had two aspects. First, there was the life he lived as the poor but brilliant Talmudist who was born Solomon ben Joshua in Nieswicz in the Lithuanian section of prepartition Poland, became a rabbi before he married at age twelve, taught himself to read German, went down the Niemen River to study medicine, became a friend of Moses Mendelssohn, both challenged and received praise from Immanuel Kant and Johann Gottlieb Fichte, and was denied burial within the Jewish cemetery at Glogau, where he died. Second, there is the portrait of that life that Maimon offered in his highly readable *Autobiography* (1792–93), published by Karl Philip Moritz and loosely inspired by Jean-Jacques Rousseau's *Confessions*.

Like Rousseau, Maimon celebrates his originality while showing himself to be a flawed but brilliant individual in continual struggle with society. His autobiography is brief and humorous. In portraying himself as highly intelligent, often put upon, and mischievous, Maimon uses his own life to show that Haskalah was a good thing, a necessary progress of intelligent Jews away from ignorance and superstition. (He records his attempt to abandon traditional Judaism for Hasidism, an experiment that confirmed him in his rationalism.) It was, by contrast, also a painful, tragic affair that alienated the Maskil from fellow Jews without achieving acceptance by the ambient Christian culture.

It is unwise, however, to think of Maimon only as an example of a type. He was too singular, too profoundly iconoclastic, to fit into any category easily. Though Mendelssohn warmly admired the autodidact, Maimon had never been his student and was influenced more by Mendelssohn's example than by his actual writings. That is, Maimon sought out Mendelssohn when Jews in Königsberg turned the would-be physician toward Berlin, from which—unlike Mendelssohn years earlier—he was turned away by a Jewish community fearful of adding a heterodox pauper to its rolls. Even after they became friends, Mendelssohn helped Maimon by conferring intellectual respectability on him, rather than by acting as an intellectual mentor; he mattered to Maimon by suggesting that, in enlightened Europe, a Jew could be intellectually eminent without being a Talmudist. Maimon, in turn, showed himself to be far brighter and more adventurous than Mendelssohn's followers, such as Naphtali Hirz Wessely, who edited and wrote for the Hebrew journal *ha-Meassef* (*Collector*). In his style and in his final failure to secure a place in society, Maimon anticipated the troubled career of Heinrich Heine.

This is not to deny that Maimon—after divorce, wandering across Germany and the Netherlands, and an unsuccessful attempt at conversion to Christianity—achieved no eminence in his own lifetime. In 1790 he published his dense, demanding *Versuch über Transcendentalphilosophie* (*Essay on Transcendental Philosophy*) in which he combined idealism and rationalism by introducing mathematics into the study of Kant. Maimon's essay has drawn attention to the present day, and Kant, whose work it criticized, praised Maimon in a letter to Marcus Herz for understanding him as no other had. Characteristically, however, most of Maimon's baffled contemporaries ignored the work, and the influential *Allgemeine Literatur Zeitung* slighted it. An undeterred Maimon kept writing. His *Autobiography* followed in 1793, and in 1794 he published his *Versuch einer neuen Logik oder Theorie des Denkens* (*Attempt at a New Logic or a Theory of Thought*). In his autobiography, Maimon also evinces an interest in experimental psychology, and he contributed to the *Magazin für Erfahrungsseelenkunde*. Although Maimon had ceased to be observant, he remained a philosophical Jew, and his continued critical interest in Judaism was apparent in his *Commentary on the "More Nevukhim" of Moses Maimonides*.

ROBERT SOUTHARD

Selected Works

Gesammelte Schriften. 7 vols. Hildesheim: 1965. Translated as *Autobiography* by Moses Hadas. New York: 1967.

Bibliography

Bergman, S. H. *The Philosophy of Solomon Maimon.* Jeruselem: 1967.
Buzaglo, Meir. *Solomon Maimon: Monism, Skepticism, and Mathematics.* Pittsburgh, 2002.
Kuntze, F. *Die Philosophie Solomon Maimons.* Heidelberg, 1912.
Sachar, Howard M. *The Course of Modern Jewish History.* Rev. ed. New York, 1990.

MAISTRE, JOSEPH-MARIE DE 1753-1821

French writer

When the nineteenth-century French critic Charles-Augustin Sainte-Beuve lists the name of Joseph-Marie de Maistre along with those of François-Auguste-René de Chateaubriand and Madame Anne-Louise-Germaine de Staël in referring to the seminal writers emerging in the aftermath of the French Revolution, he appears, to the modern critical eye, to be guilty of a misstatement. Maistre's writings might have seemed incredibly prophetic in 1814, at the time of the Restoration. But today, a cursory review of his works suggests that this unrepentant apologist for the monarchical regime, staunch defender of the Catholic Church, ardent denouncer of the evil of the French Revolution, and firm believer in the eventual resurgence and triumph of a kind of medieval Christian hegemony is blind to the permanent significance of the great political upheaval of the eighteenth century and unable to appreciate the relentless realities of historical evolution.

Yet a more searching look at Maistre's works proposes a far more nuanced assessment of his contribution. To a generation largely seduced by Jean-Jacques Rousseau's idea of the natural goodness of man, and radiantly confident in the upward progress of the species, Maistre responds by pointing to the constant, irrepressible reemergence, throughout human history, of original sin, most dramatically and most destructively reflected in recurring wars: an observation not lost on Charles Baudelaire, who recognized in Maistre a persuasive voice against both the simplistic notion of human perfectibility rampant in the eighteenth century and the commercialization of modern life. Moreover, while apparently at odds with the type of sentimental Christianity advocated by another apologist of the period, Chateaubriand, in *Le Génie du christianisme* (*The Genius of Christianity*, 1802), Maistre shares some of the preoccupations and propensities of the Romantics. Alphonse Marie-Louis de Lamartine, like Maistre a traditionalist and theocrat, though not so rigid as the latter, commends his spiritual integrity. More eclectically religious than Maistre, Victor Hugo is nevertheless like him in his interest, beyond the confines of traditional doctrine, in illuminism and in theosophical thinkers such as Emanuel Swedenborg and Louis-Claude de Saint-Martin. Perhaps just as important, Maistre signals, in his style, the oncoming, irresistible inroads of Romantic convention: his mythical description of the French Revolution and his overall historical writing that features a dramatic, colorful approach in the evocation of key figures, would later be typical of Romantic historians.

Considérations sur la France (*Considerations on France*, 1796), Maistre's first major work, was written in Switzerland, where he sought refuge after leaving the French province of Savoy to escape the invading revolutionary troops. Not surprisingly, this royalist, who had admired Edmund Burke's *Reflections on the Revolution in France* (1790), condemns the French Revolution, consistent with ideas expressed in his earlier *Etude sur la souveraineté* (*A Study of Sovereignty*, 1884), written between 1794 and 1796 but published only posthumously, in which he writes that God was the creator of society and the giver of laws and that kings ruled by divine right. What is surprising, however, is the radical nature of the condemnation: it is not merely that the French Revolution, unlike the British revolt against Charles I, did not take place within an acceptable framework of legitimacy; rather, the revolution is pure corruption, a unique occurrence in human history in that it has absolutely no saving grace. For Maistre, the carnage of the revolution is sobering testimony both to the rampant nature of evil in the world, of which war is a striking manifestation, and to the necessary sacrifice of innocent blood, a sacrifice sanctioned by God as atonement for the horrors consequent upon the sinful violation of His laws. Needless to say, there is nothing enlightening, in Maistre's view, about the Enlightenment, nor any credence to be attached to the theory of human perfectibility so optimistically advanced by the rationalist thought of the eighteenth century.

Two later works help to further explain both Maistre's disregard for the French Revolution and the hope, embodied in the *Considérations*, for an eventual reascendancy of Catholicism. In "Essai sur le principe générateur des constitutions politiques et des autres institutions humaines" ("Essay on the Generative Principle of Political Constitutions and Other Human Institutions, 1814), Maistre, persisting in his attack on the eighteenth-century philosophers, maintains that constitutions are not human creations, not consequences of a Lockean expression of the general will, but emanate directly from God. In *Du Pape* (*The Pope*, 1819), beyond the anticipated claim of papal infallibility, the declared superiority of Catholics over Protestants, and the unquestioned prominence of Latin, there is a vision of the future leadership of France in a Catholic revival that reestablishes that kind of religious unity characteristic of an earlier period of history, the Middle Ages. What also emerges clearly from these two works, beyond further confirmation of the doctrinal distance separating Maistre from Chateaubriand, is the ironic discord between Maistre's thought and that of the Restoration monarchy: in 1814, Louis XVIII approved a charter modeled on the English constitution, putting him at odds with the impassioned defender of the principle of the divine right of kings.

It was in the *Soirées de Saint-Pétersbourg* (*Saint-Petersburg Dialogues*, 1821), a work published after his death, that Maistre offered the most comprehensive elaboration of his ideas. In this series of eleven conversations involving a count (Maistre himself), a Russian senator, and a young French aristocrat, the dialectical process allows for a more refined and nuanced presentation of the main aspects of Maistre's thought. If Maistre continues predictably to exalt the Throne and the Altar, he develops in arresting fashion the roles of the soldier and the executioner in the historical preservation of order, and emphasizes the ennobling, if destructive, effect of warfare. The ongoing assault on eighteenth-century rationalism (predicated again on illuminist argument and the theosophic thinking of Saint-Martin) if not made more persuasive by Maistre's claim that he is not opposed to more legitimate forms of scientific enquiry, is nevertheless balanced with an analysis of, or an appeal to, those forms of human need, aspiration, and activity that, transcending logic, are not necessarily to be despised—such as religious conviction,

prayer, and even instinct and superstition. Remarkable in all of this is the heightened disclosure of a Maistre more impregnated with Romanticism than he himself realizes. This is a Maistre who openly manifests emotion at the contemplation of natural beauty, who not only finds descriptive language to render that emotion but also acknowledges the charm of those instances of literary creation when writing is the fruit of a sudden illumination rather than the result of a deliberate process.

Whatever the dogmatism and lack of realism of Maistre's views about the monarchy and the church, it is undeniable that his reservations about the panaceas of Enlightenment thought regarding humankind's nature and capacity for progress have in part been justified by the horrific lessons of modern history. In *L'Homme révolté* (*The Rebel*, 1951), Albert Camus does not hesitate to compare the thinking of Maistre and Karl Marx on the role of discipline and violence in the evolution of human history. As to Maistre's reflections on the widespread and resilient presence of evil in the world, and that theory of sacrifice and redemption that he calls the principle of reversibility, the Holocaust stands as a singularly frightful reminder of the demoralizing persistence of human depravity and the continual role of the innocent victim in the unfolding of human destiny. In the latter connection, one wonders how Maistre would have fared in a more modern series of discussions with the likes of Michel Foucault and René Girard on the implications of social suffering and the figure of the scapegoat, against the backdrop of a world order that, for all three, resists the human desire to explain and to comprehend.

NORMAN ARAJUO

Biography

Born in Chambéry, April 1, 1753. Studied law at the University of Turin, 1769. Completed law studies and was appointed magistrate in Sardinia, 1772. Married Françoise-Marguerite de Moraud; 1786; birth of first child, Adele, 1787. Became a senator in the Savoy Parliament, 1788. Birth of second child, Rodolphe, 1789. Fled French revolutionary troops invading Savoy and settled in Lausanne, 1792. Birth of third child, Constance, 1793. Went to Saint Petersburg as the Sardinian ambassador to Russia, 1803. Died February 26, 1821 at Chambéry.

Selected Works

Collections

Oeuvres du cte J. de Maistre. Edited by l'abbé Jacques-Paul Migne. 1841.
The Works of Joseph de Maistre. Translated and edited by Jack Lively. New York: Macmillan, 1965.

Fiction

Soirées de Saint-Pétersbourg, ou entretiens sur le gouvernement temporel de la providence, 1821. Translated *Saint-Petersburg Dialogues, or, Conversations on the Temporal Government of Providence* by Richard A. Lebrun. Montreal: McGill-Queen's University Press, 1993.

Other

Considérations sur la France, 1796. Translation: *Considerations on France*. Translated by Richard A. Lebrun. Montreal: McGill-Queen's University Press, 1974.
Essai sur le principe générateur des constitutions politiques et des autres institutions humaines," 1814. Translated as *Essay on the Generative Principle of Political Constitutions* by Elisha Greifer and Laurence M. Porter. Chicago: H. Regnety, 1959.

Du Pape, 1819. Translated as *The Pope* by Aeneas McD. Dawson. New York: H. Fertig, 1850.
Étude sur la souveraineté, 1884.

Bibliography

Bayle, Francis. *Les Idées politiques de Joseph de Maistre*. Paris: Éditions Domat Monchrétien, 1945.

Bradley, Owen. *A Modern Maistre: The Social and Political Thought of Joseph de Maistre*. Lincoln: University of Nebraska Press, 1999.

Descostes, François. *Joseph de Maistre avant la Révolution: Souvenirs de la société d'autrefois, 1753–1793*. 2 vols. 1893.

———. *Joseph de Maistre pendant la Révolution: Ses débuts diplomatiques, le marquis de Sales et les émigrés, 1789–97*. 1895.

Latreille, Camille. *Joseph de Maistre et la papauté*. Paris: Hachette, 1906.

Lombard, Charles M. *Joseph de Maistre*. Boston: Twayne, 1976.

Lebrun, Richard A. *Throne and Altar: The Political and Religious Thought of Joseph de Maistre*. Ottawa: University of Ottawa Press, 1965.

———. *Joseph de Maistre: An Intellectual Militant*. Montreal: McGill-Queens University Press, 1988.

Triomphc, Robert. *Joseph de Maistre: Étude sur la vie et sur la doctrine d'un matérialiste mystique*. Geneva: Droz, 1968.

MALCZEWSKI, ANTONI 1793–1826

Polish poet

The first important Polish Romantic is a man who died young and who owes his fame to a single publication. Malczewski is sometimes described as a representative of the so-called Ukranian school in Polish poetry, but in truth he is a lonely and unique author whose poetic tale *Maria. Powieść ukraińska* (*Maria: A Ukranian Tale*, 1825) created a new world for the Romantic imagination. Although this work is dedicated to Julian Ursyn Niemcewicz, a poet and playwright who had started his career in the eighteenth century, the greatest single influence on Malczewski was certainly Lord Byron, whose acquaintance he had made in Venice. This does not refer only to the genre of the work, but to some of the characters and their conduct as well.

Maria is a young woman of noble birth who marries higher than her class and suffers retribution for her temerity. It is based on a true story that originates from the late eighteenth century, based on Count Potocki's revenge on his unfortunate daughter-in-law, but Malczewski has moved the plot back to the sixteenth century, when incursions of Tartars and Turks often forced the nobility to take up arms against the invaders. By this token, the class conflict between the Wojewoda and the Miecznik and his family is turned into a betrayal of a different kind; Maria's assassination takes place while the menfolk of the family are away on patriotic duty. The plot is played out against the backdrop of the vast Ukranian steppe, portrayed as gloomy and mysterious, and the narrative opens with a Cossack riding a horse at great speed (Byron's *Giaour* also opens with an image of a galloping horseman). The characters of the tale are "traditional" in many respects, or at least they appear as such in the first canto: we see a valiant young Wacław and his loving wife Maria, a good-humored Miecznik and an evil, scheming Wojewoda. The highpoint of this sequence of the poem is Maria's passionate monologue "*Czy Maria ciebie kocha?*" ("Does Maria love you?"), which is a fine example of the "confessional" type of Romantic poetry.

In the second canto, when Wacław returns from the victorious battle, he cannot find Maria; there is only a mysterious young man, the page, who relates the events that took place in Wacław's absence. A horde of masked characters invaded the manor house singing songs about Venetian carnivals and celebrating Shrovetide, and it was they who drowned Maria in the lake. Before the murder (which is clearly carried out on the Wojewoda's orders), the masked men sing a gloomy tune, the refrain of which is "Ah! in this world everything withers / Even the lush flower is infested by a worm." The insertion of songs in the narrative is also a trait of Byron's poetic tales; there is also a certain similarity between the corsair's return to the island to find Medora dead and, of course, between the reaction of the Corsair and Wacław to the loss of their beloveds. The Corsair disappears with a broken heart; but Malczewski intimates that Wacław (who takes the page with him) is bent on revenge, which will only add to the gloom of the story. As for the old Miecznik, he cannot survive the pain of his daughter's untimely death; he also dies and is buried next to his wife and daughter. So *Maria*

Antoni Malczewski

ends with the image of three graves and with a triple lament: "And this lush Ukraine is empty, mournful, and full of nostalgia."

Malczewski's great achievement is the flexible way in which he uses the traditional thirteen-syllable line with rhyming couplets. His lines often include short questions or exclamations, the insertion of songs and monologues breaking up the relative monotony of the narration. The mood of the poem is truly Gothic, translated into the landscape of Polish-inhabited Ukraine, and this is a factor that makes it sharply different from similar "oriental" tales of Byron. It was read by and made an impact upon both Adam Mickiewicz and Joseph Conrad and found a number of imitators among lesser Polish poets. Fate, however, was not kind to Malczewski himself, who died in mysterious circumstances soon after the publication of *Maria*.

GEORGE GÖMÖRI

Biography

Born in 1793 in a wealthy family either in Warsaw or in Volhynia. Attended the famous school of Krzemieniec but failed to complete studies. In 1811, joined the Napoleonic Army of the Duchy of Warsaw; left it in 1816 to embark on extensive travels in western Europe. Climbed Mont Blanc in the summer of 1818. Returned to Poland around 1821 where he became involved with a married woman who suffered from a nervous ailment. Began writing while on his estate in Volhynia, but in 1824 moved to Warsaw. Published *Maria* at his own expense. Soon afterward, died in great poverty.

Text

Maria Powieść ukraińska, 1825. Translated as *Marya: A Tale of Ukraine* by Arthur Prudden Coleman and Marion Moore Coleman, 1935.

Bibliography

Dernalowicz M. *Antoni Malczewski*. Warsaw, 1967.
Gacowa, H. ed. *"Maria" i Antoni Malczewski. Kompendium zródlowe.* Warsaw: PWN, 1974.
Miłosz, Czesław. *The History of Polish Literature.* London: Collier-Macmillan, 1969.
Ujejski, Józef. *Antoni Malczewski. (Poeta i poemat).* Warsaw, 1921.

MAPU, ABRAHAM 1808–1867

Hebrew novelist

Although throughout the greater part of the nineteenth century, modern Hebrew literature was composed and largely read by Jews in the Pale of Settlement (the area between the Baltic and the Black Sea to which the Jews in Czarist Russia were confined), the Jewish population comprised in many respects an Oriental community. Their literature was the product of a deeply rooted society in transition, and pride of place in education was given to the study of the Hebrew bible and to the Hebrew and Aramaic of the Talmud and commentaries.

For all the poverty, hardship, and oppression that formed a constant accompaniment to life, Jewish tradition still provided a warm and comforting spiritual environment for large sections of the community. Families were large, and relatives richly abundant. The colorful ceremonies of Sabbath and festivals, which were geared to climatic conditions prevailing not in Russia but in Palestine, and the comforting rhythms of regular communal worship, with its rich symbolism, reflected a legacy of generations, fortifying the spirit against the increasingly savage buffetings of the outside world. Protected by close ties of a stable family structure and nourished almost exclusively on traditional Jewish texts that frequently made the contemporary scene less real than the world of the Bible and the Talmud, the Jewish child lived in a harsh and cruel environment suffused with the glow of a Romantic image. Indeed, the tendency to make dream and reality coalesce comprises an important element in Abraham Mapu's writings.

Born in Slobodka, a suburb of Kovno, Mapu was an impoverished elementary school teacher all his life, but he combined profound Talmudic learning with knowledge of several self-taught languages and considerable secular learning. An exponent of the Hebrew movement of enlightenment, known as Haskalah, Mapu endeavored to combine traditional Jewish values with the wider horizons of European culture. Consequently, his novels portray the glories of ancient Israel (freedom, heroism, and love) contrasted with the narrow confines of contemporary reality. With a consummate mastery of the neobiblical style favored by the exponents of Haskalah, Mapu accomplished the astonishing feat of composing three complete novels, confining himself to the vocabulary of the Hebrew Bible, which contains a mere five thousand words. The fact that his first novel, incidentally the first biblical novel in any language, entitled *Ahavat Ziyyon* (*The Love of Zion*, 1853) took twenty years to compose though it comprises only 150 pages, is an indication of the difficulty arising from such a limitation. Set in ancient Israel in the eighth century B.C.E., the novel comprises a strange mixture of heroism and romance with didactic moralizing. It proved to be an immediate success, and has been published in at least sixteen editions and translated into at least nine languages. It represents a turning point in modern Hebrew literature and it exerted a profound influence on many contemporary and later Hebrew writers. Of the many literary strands it reflects, the influence of the French romantic writers Alexandré Dumas *pére* and Eugène Sue is clearly discernible in the mingling of historical and fictional personages, the fusion of exciting adventures, heroic deeds, passionate loves and state intrigues as well as the idealization of the young heroines.

Mapu's real strength lies in his power of description, particularly the description of nature. His portraits of the scenes and landscapes of the land of Israel are outstanding. Living in the totally different surroundings of Lithuania, Mapu accomplished the remarkable feat of conjuring up a vivid and convincing picture of a country he had never seen. Relying on his deep knowledge of the Hebrew bible, which he exploited to the utmost with perhaps the additional aid of the geographical work on Palestine by Jacob Kaplan, he visualized the hills and valleys, the towns and villages with an uncanny accuracy.

The second novel, extending over five complete parts and titled *Ayit Tzavu'a* (*The Hypocrite*, 1858–69) was set in contemporary Lithuania and, in spite of its deficiencies, (it is long, involved, and rambling) became a model for most Hebrew novels over the next twenty years and ran into some ten editions. The influence of Sue's *Les Mystères de Paris*, translated into Hebrew by Kalman Shulman in 1857, is clear. But while the violence and intrigue encountered in the French novel are perfectly in keeping with the Paris underworld the story depicts, the attempt to superimpose such elements upon the background of Jewish society in Eastern Europe, which was characterized by sobriety, timidity, and a rigid control of the passionate emotions, is primarily responsible for the incongruity of the setting and the plot.

Of a third novel, *Hozei Hezyonot* (*The Visionaries*), which was sent to the Russian censor in 1858, only a fragment of seven chapters remains due to the violent opposition on the part of the fanatical Jewish pietists and Hasidim. The novel is concerned with events at the time of the notorious pseudo-Messiah Shabbetai Zevi in the seventeenth century. To the end of his days Mapu's grief over the loss of this book was inconsolable.

Sickened by the persecution engendered by these controversial novels, Mapu reverted to the Bible for the background of his fourth and last novel, *Ashmat Shomoron* (*The Guilt of Sama-*

ria, 1865–66), which appeared in ten editions. Set in ancient Israel in the same period as *Ahavat Ziyyon* and with some of the characters reappearing in the story, the novel again illustrates the extraordinary linguistic and descriptive skills of the author and reflects a considerable improvement in characterization.

Whereas in *Ahavat Ziyyon* the historical background serves only as a framework for the loves and intrigues of the individual characters, however, in *Ashmat Shomoron* it assumes much greater significance, emphasizing the national rivalries of the kingdoms of Samaria and Judea on the one hand, and the bitter struggle between the worship of Baal and the belief in God on the other.

For all their many weaknesses, Mapu's novels bear the stamp of greatness, for not only did they indicate the possibilities of a Hebrew novel, but in addition they gave expression to the mute longings and half-sensed gropings of a whole people toward a fuller and richer life.

DAVID PATTERSON

Biography

Born in Slobodka, a suburb of Kovno, 1808. *Ahavat Ziyyon* published, 1853. *Ayit Tzavu'a* published in five parts, 1858–69. *Hozei Hezyonot* sent to the Russian censor, 1858. *Ashmat Shomoron*, part 1, published 1865. *Ashmat Shomoron*, part 2, published 1866. Died 1867.

Selected Works

Ahavat Ziyyon. 1853.
Ayit Tzavu'a. 1858–69.
Ashmat Shomoron. Part 1, 1865.
Ashmat Shomoron. Part 2, 1866.

DIE MARQUISE VON O . . . 1808

Story by Bernd Heinrich Wilhelm von Kleist

First published in 1808 by Heinrich von Kleist in his own literary magazine, *Phöbus*, this story aroused the ire of a moralistic public; the author did himself no favors as he struggled to win himself a readership. Though there were, of course, some who did not take offence, it is no wonder many did: *Die Marquise von O . . .* touches on some very sensitive topics in what might be considered an irreverent and lighthearted fashion, and yet Kleist presented it to the public as high literature of the type he claimed to be disseminating in his journal.

The story begins with a seemingly inexplicable, and certainly highly unusual, circumstance: a widow of good reputation has advertised in order to find out who might be the father of her as yet unborn child. The remainder of the story is the unraveling of the mystery, a sophisticated tour de force of dramatic irony; it gradually dawns on the reader that he or she, like the characters in the novella, has really known all along that the conception must have occurred when the marquise was rescued from rape by a Russian count whose army has invaded her father's castle. Only when the reader looks at the episode again does it become

apparent that something (namely, the rape of the marquise by her erstwhile rescuer) has been omitted—elided, in fact, by a simple hyphen in the text. When the count appears and wards off the soldiers who threatened her, the marquise faints: "The count—arranged, as her frightened servants appeared shortly afterwards, for a doctor to be called." In the elision—the hyphen (interestingly called a *Gedankenstrich* or "elision of thought" in German)—the count has impregnated the marquise while she was in a state of unconsciousness. The only signal to the reader, apart from the hyphen, is that he sets his hat back on his head; in retrospect only does one realize that no reason has been given for the hat to have fallen off.

In Kleist's stories and plays there is always at least one character who is confronted with an *Umwälzung der Ordnung* (radical revolution of the order of things), who confronts an aporia of knowledge—the knowledge of the self, of the other, or of the world. Here it is the marquise: she thinks of the count, her rescuer, yet events reveal him to be her violator. She knows herself to be innocent of sexual misbehavior, and yet she needs to see the midwife. ("A clear conscience [*Bewußtsein*]—and yet a midwife!" her mother cries in astonishment and disbelief.) Only when the marquise can acknowledge the count to be both angel and devil—or neither—can the story resolve, which it does, at least ostensibly happily: they marry, still unreconciled. But within a year there *is* a reconciliation, and "a long series of little Russians" results from the union.

With its origins in a kind of *Schwank* or humorous (and naughty) story (with sources in Miguel de Cervantes Saavedra and Michel de Montaigne) it not surprising that some of his contemporaries took offense at its inclusion in a literary journal, nor that some modern critics have read the story primarily as a joke. Yet another tradition, likewise apparent from the start, sees the story in a much more serious light. For these readers the marquise is a sign of purity, of moral integrity maintained despite her sullying by an imperfect world. Like the swan that the count tells her he threw mud at when he was a boy so that he could watch it dive underwater and come up clean again, the marquise remains untouched by both human desire and human sin.

Some critics, however, have chosen not to gloss over the shocking events—the elided rape and a later scene with strongly incestuous overtones— but instead have shifted attention away from what the count did to the desires of the marquise. If we, the readers, know who the rapist is from the start, runs the argument, so does the marquise. Indicative of her suppression of the knowledge of her own desire is her use of the term *Bewußtsein* in the passage quoted above: literally, the marquise doesn't say she has a clear conscience, but a clear consciousness. She is in love with the count at first sight and cannot admit it because of a childish attachment to her father; hence she faints in order to avoid conscious thought. Upon the death of her first husband, we are told, she readily returned to live "in her father's house"; her father exhibits extreme signs of jealousy when the contrite count comes to court the marquise (before she realizes she is pregnant) and becomes dramatically violent when the pregnancy is revealed, shooting off a pistol and banishing his daughter from his house. What for the marquise's mother was a matter of untruth and deception becomes for the father a matter of jealous rage. A reconciliation is effected with the father some time later, in a graphically sexual scene that critics had up to then somehow managed to ignore: the marquise sits on her father's lap, her eyes shut, as he gives her "long, hot, and thirsty kisses" ("lange, heisse und lechzende Küsse") and fiddles with her lips. The mother observes through a keyhole, laughing joyously, as unable to see the incestuous connotations as had the previous critics.

More recent criticism following this train of thought has focused less on the marquise's putative guilt—for Kleist's stories are not so much about individual desire and character development—and instead stressed the creation and function of desire as shown here. Instead of psychoanalyzing a character, psychological insights have been brought to bear on the nature of the narrative.

Kleist's stories visit and revisit scenarios that quickly become familiar; often even the same language is used in similar situations. A character claims that his or her *Gefühl* or feeling is not in accordance with what *Verstand* (reason) would indicate must be the truth; a character loses consciousness or becomes dreamy and distracted, blushes or turns pale when confronted with an aporia, something that shakes his or her understanding of the world. Violence, natural or human, is usually the cause of the crisis. When the violence is perpetrated by humans, it is most frequently men who do violence to women, as if the author divided the active and passive principles along strict gender lines. Kleist's heros generally act without thinking, and then must live with the consequences; his heroines deal with aspersions cast upon their reputation and the usually violent consequences of the accusations (the marquise is not the only Kleistian character to be thrown out of her house by angry male relatives).

Active men and passive women all must come to terms with the shaken order of things and with the miscommunications thus engendered. Seen in this way, it is much less enlightening to see the marquise as an inhibited female unaware of her own sexuality, but instead to see her as one of many Kleistian characters confronted with a radical shake-up of her conception of self, other, and world. The scenes of illicit sexuality need not be elided or ignored by the reader, but neither should they be taken as a justification of the violence that has been done.

LAURA MARTIN

See also **Irony, Romantic; Kleist, Bernd Heinrich Wilhelm von;** *Über das Marionettentheater*

Work

Die Marquise von O . . . 1808. Translated in *The Marquise of O and Other Stories* by David Luke and Nigel Reeves. New York: Penguin, 1978.

Bibliography

Allan, Seán, " '. . . Auf einen Lasterhaften was ich gefaßt, aber keinen—Teufel': Heinrich von Kleist's *Die Marquise von O . . . ,*" *German Life and Letters* 50, no. 3 (1997): 307–22.

Bentzel, Curtis C. "Knowledge in Narrative: The Significance of the Swan in Kleist's 'Die Marquise von O . . .'," *German Quarterly* 64, no. 3 (1991): 296–303.

Blankenagel, John C. "Heinrich von Kleist's *Marquise von O . . . ,*" *Germanic Review* 6 (1931): 363–72.

Cohn, Dorrit. "Kleist's *Marquise von O . . .* : The Problem of Knowledge," *Monatshefte* 67 (1975): 129–44.

Dietrick, Linda. "Immaculate Conceptions: The Marquise von O . . . and the Swan," *Seminar* 27, no. 4 (1991): 316–29.

Dünnhaupt, Gerhard. "Kleists *Marquise von O . . .* and its Literary Debt to Cervantes," *Arcadia* 10 (1975): 147–57.

Esch, Deborah. "Toward a Midwifery of Thought: Reading Kleist's *Die Marquise von O. . . .*" In *Textual Analysis: Some Readers Reading.* Edited by Mary Ann Caws. New York: Modern Language Association, 1986.

Fischer, Bernd. *Ironische Metaphysik: Die Erzählungen Heinrich von Kleists.* Munich: Fink, 1988.

Gelus, Marjorie. "Patriarchy's Fragile Boundaries under Siege: Three Stories of Heinrich von Kleist," *Women in German Yearbook* 10 (1995): 59–82.

Krüger-Fürhoff, Irmela Marei. "Epistemological Asymmetries and Erotic Stagings: Father-Daughter Incest in Heinrich von Kleist's *The Marquise of O . . . ,*" *Women in German Yearbook* 12 (1996): 71–86.

Laurs, Axel. "Towards Idylls of Domesticity in Kleist's *Die Marquise von O . . . ,*" *Journal of the Australasian Universities Modern Language and Literature Association* 64 (1985): 175–89.

McGlathery, James. *Desire's Sway: The Plays and Stories of Heinrich von Kleist.* Detroit: Wayne State University Press, 1983.

Moering, Michael. *Witz und Ironie in der Prosa Heinrich von Kleists.* Munich: Fink, 1972.

Mortimer, Armine Kotin. "The Devious Second Story in Kleist's *Die Marquise von O . . .*," *German Quarterly* 67 (1994): 293–303.

Müller-Seidel, Walter. "Die Struktur des Widerspruchs in Kleists *Marquise von O . . .*," *Deutsche Vierteljahrsschrift für Literaturwissenschaft und Geistesgeschichte* 28 (1954): 497–515.

Murphy, Harriet. "Theatres of Emptiness: The Case of Kleist's *Marquise von O . . .*," *Oxford German Studies* (24): 80–111.

Pfeiffer, Joachim. "Die Wiedergefundene Ordnung. Literatur-psychologische Anmerkungen zu Kleists *Die Marquise von O . . .*," *Jahrbuch für Internationale Germanistik* 19, no. 1 (1987): 36–53.

Politzer, Heinz. "Der Fall der Frau Marquise: Beobachtungen zu Kleists *Die Marquise von O . . .*," *Deutsche Vierteljahrsschrift für Literaturwissenschaft und Geistesgeschichte* 51 (1977): 98–128.

Sembdner, Helmut, ed. *Heinrich von Kleists Lebensspuren: Dokumente und Berichte der Zeitgenossen*. Frankfurt am Main: Insel, 1977.

Smith, John H. "Dialogic Midwifery in Kleist's *Marquise von O . . .* and the Hermeneutics of Telling the Untold in Kant and Plato," *PMLA* 100, no. 2 (1985): 203–19.

Stephens, Anthony. *Heinrich von Kleist, The Dramas and Stories*. Oxford: Berg, 1994.

Swales, Erika. " 'The Beleaguered Citadel' ": A Study of Kleist's "*Die Marquise von O . . .*," *Deutsche Vierteljahrsschrift für Literaturwissenschaft und Geistesgeschichte* 51 (1977): 129–47.

Winnett, Susan. "The Marquise's 'O' and the Mad Dash of Narrative." In *Rape and Representation*. Edited by Carolyn G. Heilbrun and Nancy K. Miller. New York: Columbia University Press, 1991. 67–86.

THE MARRIAGE OF HEAVEN AND HELL 1790

Illuminated book by William Blake

The Marriage of Heaven and Hell is the most important of William Blake's early works in illuminated printing and arguably the first truly Romantic work in English literature. Written and printed in the year following the fall of the Bastille, it conveys an extraordinary sense of excitement and rebellious independence, evidently generated by what Blake took to be signs of an imminent apocalypse. The book satirizes conventional moralities, demythologizes religious dogma, and announces the beginning of an era of libidinal freedom.

The Marriage is notoriously difficult to categorize: in its pages, satire rubs shoulders with formal reasoned argument, proverbs are followed by visionary travelogues, and prophecy exists in tension with comedy. Although some critics align the poem with Menipean satire, others argue that it belongs to a genre of which it is the only member. Critics also disagree about the poem's structure. It has been described as a "scrapbook"; divided into three, six, and even seven parts; and organized according to both formal and thematic criteria. Although some are helpful, none of these descriptions does full justice to the text.

The most important influence on *The Marriage* is the thought of the Swedish mystic Emanuel Swedenborg—in particular, his *A Treatise concerning Heaven and Hell* (1784). It has been suggested that plates 21 through 24, which appear to have been the portion of the poem first printed by Blake, may initially have been conceived as an anti-Swedenborgian pamphlet. In the 1780s, Blake considered Swedenborg a fellow visionary. In 1790, however he radically revised his views, accusing Swedenborg of "Lies & Priestcraft." *The Marriage* was born of this reversal.

According to Swedenborg, earthly life unfolds between heaven (a realm of rational, spiritual order) and hell (a world of selfish, natural desires). As humankind is no more than an organ of life, and God alone is life, we must choose whether to be formed by influx from heaven or hell. If we choose the former, we assume angelic form. If the latter, we are shaped by the selfish desires of the body.

Blake radicalizes these ideas in *The Marriage* and inverts the hierarchies that structure Swedenborg's thought. Heaven and hell are troped as psychological states, the first associated with reason, the second with energy and imagination. In opposition to Swedenborg, the poem affirms that "Energy is the only life and is from the Body" and, far from creating a world of torment, "Energy is Eternal Delight." According to Blake, then, Swedenborg gets things exactly backward. He repeats "all the old falsehoods" because he neglects the devils, the active source of life and creation. For this very different knowledge, the poem turns to Isaiah and Ezekiel, Paracelsus and Jacob Behmen, Dante and William Shakespeare, and, most important, to Jesus.

If energy is the source of all things, then the terms of traditional morality must be reversed. What the religious call *good* is "the passive that obeys Reason," and evil "is the active springing from Energy." This suggests that evil is in fact good and good is evil. By the same token, the real Messiah is a figure much closer to Satan than to the Jesus of traditional piety. As Blake provocatively argues, Jesus broke every one of the commandments, yet was "all virtue" because he "acted from impulse: not from rules."

The title page maps this revisionist, mental geography, while suggesting how the static opposition between heaven and hell (mind and body) will be overcome. In the upper two-thirds of the page, a scene representing earth, along with the words HEAVEN and HELL, are all contained by a roughly outlined human head. In conformity with Swedenborgian doctrine, HEAVEN supports the sedate, compartmentalized life of earth, while at the same time dividing it from the word HELL beneath. In the bottom third of the page, however, a naked devil and angel—lying on couches of fire and cloud, respectively—are locked in erotic embrace. This is the "marriage" of contraries, the "improvement of sensual enjoyment" that the poem claims will "cleanse the doors of perception." From their embrace flames, clouds, and numerous naked couples are already rising toward Earth. Their arrival will turn winter into spring, precipitating the Last Judgment.

Not content with inverting the conventional, hierarchical opposition between reason and bodily energy, the poem recasts them as contraries, the struggle between them helping to shape human life. In Blake's words, "Without Contraries is no progression. Attraction and Repulsion, Reason and Energy, Love and

Hate, are necessary to Human existence." This effectively dissolves all firm foundations. Even the views of the devils, which are overtly celebrated in this poem, can be qualified by their contraries. Readers of this poem consequently find themselves active participants in an unending struggle between the claims of heaven and hell.

The desire to foster contrariness lies behind the poem's innovative attempts to uncover the voices hidden by dominant cultural forms. In what is perhaps the first symptomatic reading of a text, the poem argues that, despite his conscious intentions, *Paradise Lost* reveals John Milton's deep identification with Satan's rebellious spirit and creative energy. The myth of Satan's expulsion from heaven is read "against the grain" to reveal a primordial repression of energy. And the paradigmatic form of angelic wisdom, the proverb, becomes the natural vehicle for hellish insight.

Early accounts of Blake almost ignored *The Marriage.* By the end of the nineteenth century, however, its reputation was firmly established, with Algernon Charles Swinburne describing it as the "greatest of all [Blake's] books." In the twentieth century, *The Marriage of Heaven and Hell* has remained at the center of critical appraisals of Blake's work, even though some of its views are revised in Blake's later poetry.

PETER OTTO

See also **Blake, William;** *Songs of Innocence and Experience*

Work

The Marriage of Heaven and Hell, 1790. Facsimile reproduction of copy F (Pierpont Morgan Library, New York) in *The Early Illuminated Books.* vol. 3 of *Blake's Illuminated Books.* Edited by Morris Eaves, Robert N. Essick, and Joseph Viscomi, Princeton, N.J.: William Blake Trust and Princeton University Press, 1991–95.

Bibliography

Mee, Jon. "The Radical Enthusiasm of Blake's *The Marriage of Heaven and Hell,*" *British Journal for Eighteenth Century Studies* 14 (1991): 51–60.

Miller, Dan. "Contrary Revelation: *The Marriage of Heaven and Hell*: A Critical Study," *Studies in Romanticism* 24 (1985): 491–509.

Nurmi, Martin K. *Blake's "Marriage of Heaven and Hell": A Critical Study.* New York: Haskell House, 1972.

Viscomi, Joseph. "The Lessons of Swedenborg; or, the Origin of William Blake's *The Marriage of Heaven and Hell.*" In *Lessons of Romanticism: A Critical Companion.* Edited by Thomas Pfau and Robert F. Gleckner. Durham, N.C.: Duke University Press, 1998.

MARTIN, JOHN 1789–1854

English painter

Arguably one of the most striking artists of the early nineteenth century and certainly one of the most popular, John Martin developed a style of visionary landscape painting that gave vital expression to the dreams and nightmares of the first industrial age. Something of a misfit and a rebel in his own time, carving out a career for himself as an artist-entrepreneur in defiance of the Royal Academy, Martin has never been a favorite of the artistic establishment. This has to do partly with the way in which he broke down the barriers between fine art and other forms of visual spectacle, combining the high aims of conventional history painting with the protocinematic appeal of the panorama. His reputation, or lack thereof, can also be attributed to his distinctive style, which eschewed traditional humanist qualities in favor of a pictorial rhetoric that owed more to topographical drawing and architecture. Critics and connoisseurs have tended to be rather skeptical about Martin, wincing at his technical deficiencies (he is no master of the human figure), at his tiresome repetitions, and at the literalism of his "material sublime." But he has always been popular with the gallery-going public. This was especially true during the 1820s and '30s, when even his fiercest detractors were forced to acknowledge his work as a powerful expression of the spirit of the age.

Born in Hebden Bridge in Northumbria, he worked as a china and glass painter in London before exhibiting his first landscapes at the Royal Academy in 1811. His career progressed slowly at first, and he was forced to undertake much poorly paid hack work, which included topographical sketching for Ackermann. By the 1820s, however, he had found his niche, producing a series of biblical landscape paintings that took the public by storm. Of these, perhaps the best and most notable is his *Belshazzar's Feast* of 1820 and 1821, a great critical and commercial success, and entirely typical of his mature style (the same mood and message was repeated a number of times, in pieces such as *The Fall of Babylon* [1819], *The Fall of Nineveh, The Seventh Plague of Egypt* [both 1823], and the illustrations to *Paradise Lost* [1824]). *Belshazzar's Feast* depicts the celebrated moment from the Old Testament in which the writing on the wall appears to the Babylonian king Belshazzar in the middle of a grand banquet, and he summons the Hebrew prophet-in-exile Daniel to interpret its message. The prophecy is apocalyptic in the extreme: it foretells both the death of Belshazzar and the total destruction of Babylon, a punishment for the vanity and worthlessness of the king and for the general depravity of his people. In Martin's hands, the scene is more of a sublime cityscape than a human drama: Babylon is depicted in all its hubristic grandeur, with vast colonnades reaching back from the main banqueting square to the Hanging Gardens and Tower of Babel in the background. Daniel stands calmly by the main banqueting table, delivering his interpretation, while behind him a huge crowd, thrown into panic by the spectacle, runs hither and thither in the central square.

In 1821 it would have been easy to see *Belshazzar's Feast* as an allegorical satire on George IV and his much-vaunted program of "metropolitan improvements." Some recent critics have invoked Martin's millenarian background in an attempt to give weight to this reading. The problem is that, as a work of political prophecy or a piece of religious art, *Belshazzar's Feast* is a remarkably ambivalent performance. There is too much investment in the reconstruction and celebration of ancient Babylon for the painting to function as a straightforward satire. Martin takes an architect's pleasure in the city he has rebuilt. The complex relationship in him between futuristic daydreams and apocalyptic imaginings only intensified in the ensuing years. In the late 1820s, he submitted a proposal to the government for constructing a vast embankment running along both sides of the Thames, the interior of which would containing an elaborate aqueduct system bringing fresh water to London from the provinces. In the plans Martin submitted, the design is deeply reminiscent of the riverscape in *The Fall of Nineveh*, inviting interpretation of his paintings as a series of sketches depicting cities of the future, not lost empires of the past. But it is the doubleness of these images that constitutes their real meaning and signals them out as expressive of a particular historical moment. Martin painstakingly resurrects and reconstructs ancient cities to display them in all their immensity and apparent solidity at the very moment of their destruction. His vision is one in which the dazzling potential of material technology and its imminent historical ruin are simultaneously invoked.

That Martin was always trying to turn painting into something else is evident from the projects he took up in his later years. In the late 1820s he began to make and sell copies of his paintings in the form of highly detailed mezzotint engravings, the force and quality of which was often an improvement upon the original canvases. The project was hugely successful, and highly lucrative; so much so indeed that Martin began to gain an international reputation, developing a following in France, Australia, and the United States. His subjects were perfectly suited to mezzotint: in the "darkness visible" of the new form, his cityscapes took on a new kind of lurid intensity. With the passing of the vogue for apocalyptic subjects in the 1830s, Martin's career as an artist went into a gradual decline. But he continued to exhibit his work, and to illustrate the work of others. He also kept up his ambition to be an architect-engineer, endlessly resubmitting his water-system proposals to the Royal Commission. As an architect in his own right, John Martin was a failure, but as Francis Klingender points out, his influence on the first generation of industrial engineers and designers was not inconsiderable. Many of the first locomotive bridges and railway stations were modeled on designs from Martin's paintings, so that by a rather indirect route he became not merely the ambivalent prophet of industrial modernity but also its vicarious architect.

GREGORY DART

Biography

Born 1789, in Hebden Bridge, Northumbria. Apprenticed to a coachbuilder in Newcastle, 1803, where he learned to paint family crests and other decorative designs. Became pupil of Piedmontese painter Boniface Musso, 1804. Left for London to join Musso's son, Charles Muss, in his business as a china painter, 1806. Submitted first painting (*Clytie*) to Royal Academy, 1810; it was rejected. Exhibited *Sadak* at the Royal Academy, 1812. Achieved first major success with *Joshua*, 1816. *Belshazzar's Feast* brought greatest critical and financial success, 1821. Began to devote most of his time to engraving and producing mezzotints of his works, 1822. Devoted increasing amounts of time to schemes for improving London's water supply and other engineering and architectural projects, late 1820s. Continued to work periodically on large projects such as *The Coronation of Queen Victoria* and *The Last Judgement*, 1830s and '40s. Died on the Isle of Man, February 17, 1854; subsequently buried in Kirk Braddon Cemetery, Douglas.

Bibliography

Balston, Thomas. *John Martin 1789–1854, His Life and Works*. London, 1947.

———. *John Martin and Metropolitan Improvements*. Architectural Review 102, no. 612 (1947).

Feaver, William. *The Art of John Martin*. Oxford: Clarendon Press, 1975.

———, ed. *John Martin 1789–1854: Artist, Reformer, Engineer*. Newcastle: Laing Art Gallery, 1970.

"The Genius of John Martin," *Arnold's Magazine for the Fine Arts* 3, no. 2 (1833): 98.

Johnstone, Christopher. *John Martin*. London: Academy Editions, 1974.

Klingender, Francis D. *Art and the Industrial Revolution*. London: Evelyn, Adams and Mackay, 1968.

Monckton, Norah. *The Architectural Backgrounds in the Pictures of John Martin*. Architectural Review 104, no. 620 (1948).

Paley, Morton D. *The Apocalyptic Sublime*. New Haven, Conn.: Yale University Press, 1986.

Pendered, Mary L. *John Martin, Painter: His Life and Times*. London: Hurst and Blackett, 1923.

Seznec, Jean. *John Martin en France*. London, 1964.

Todd, Ruthven. *Tracks in the Snow*. London, 1946.

MARY, COUNTESS OF RICHMOND 1785–1788

Painting by Thomas Gainsborough

Thomas Gainsborough, like the other British painters of his time, worked in a context characterized by little or no state or church patronage of artists. Dependence on the upper-middle-class and aristocratic domestic market for paintings produced a concentration on a limited range of genres. Animal portraits and landscape provided Gainsborough with his earliest successes, but portraits of people became his major focus and talent. In this genre both the handling of the paint and the attitude toward the sitter differentiates him sharply from his contemporaries. While one cannot perhaps go as far as Ellis Waterhouse, who

remarked that "considering these pictures as works of art we must abandon all preconceptions about portraiture and judge them as if they were *Nympheas* by Monet," it is true that Gainsborough developed a technique characterized by an evanescence and a lightness of touch that emphasized both the momentary intensity of an encounter with another human being and the passing of that moment in time. His palette of color is remarkably unstereotyped, seemingly rethought from picture to picture, and the effect of movement and shimmering light is achieved by his characteristic method of drawing delicate veils of a thinned white paint over looser fields of thicker, darker pigment.

Gainsborough's aesthetic is similar to that of his era. Across all media, an interest had emerged in conversation and improvisation, and in the concepts of fancy and melancholy. When a musician friend, William Jackson, said that "the swallow in her airy course, never skimmed a surface so light as Gainsborough touched all subjects—that bird could not fear drawing more, than he dreaded deep inquisitions," he referred to the artist's conversation, but could equally well have been referring to his painting. Gainsborough named his favorite dog (his painting of him is in the Tate Britain Museum, London) Tristram, after *Tristram Shandy* by Laurence Sterne, to whose free, often whimsical writing style the painter's brushwork was often, in his time, compared.

An element of the conversational is evident in all the portraits; there is a strong sense of the artist's presence, as if his voice might suddenly wake the subject(s) of the portrait out of their pose (as indeed it did in the sittings—Gainsborough suddenly remarked to the actress Sarah Siddons, for example, "Your nose madam; is there no end to it?"). One sitter, surprised but impressed by the lack of obsequiousness on Gainsborough's part (in a context where painters were still largely seen as a kind of highly skilled servant), remarked that the artist "*knew his own value*; was reserved; and maintained an importance with his sitters."

All these elements come together in the portrait of Mary, Countess of Richmond. Born Lady Mary Bruce, she and her husband, Charles Lennox, Third Duke of Richmond, were friends of the antiquarian and Gothic novelist Horace Walpole, who described them as "the prettiest couple in England." They were both actively engaged in liberal causes of the time, including support for the American cause in the War of Independence, for universal male suffrage, and for Catholic emancipation. Gainsborough particularly responded to unconventional and intelligent female sitters, and tended to take them out of a domestic, neoclassical or allegorical setting and place them in a solitary or natural scene. While Joshua Reynolds portrayed Sarah Siddons in Classical dress as the "muse of tragedy," Gainsborough's

picture has her, in profile, dressed fashionably in furs, feathers, and silks, which the artist renders virtuosically to create a vividly sensuous and charismatic aura. Where Reynolds has the Countess of Richmond in a plain brown riding habit, engaged in needlework (encased in the proper uniform of her class and gender), Gainsborough shows her dressed in the "Van Dyck" costume, an free imitation of the fashions of the court of Charles I and Henrietta Maria, as recorded by their court painter. Gainsborough's first motive in this is undoubtedly a painterly wish to make larger statements of color than would be ordinarily afforded by the costume of his own time, and to evoke a subtle play of light and texture (his secondary purpose is most likely that of homage to a great painter of the previous century, Van Dyck). However, here is an odd resonance, on the eve of the French Revolution, in painting a liberal aristocrat in the costume of a class and a generation who fell victim to revolution in England. The countess' enigmatic Mona Lisa smile, and thoughtful far-seeing eyes, work with the autumnal coloring, and the disturbance of the woods and of her tawny hair, to suggest not only her personal passage from youthful beauty into middle age (she was in her forties at the time of the portrait), but also a proto-Romantic sense of coming change and a darkening sensibility.

EDWARD BURNS

Work

Mary, Countess of Richmond, 1785–88. Rothschild Collection, Ascott. England.

Bibliography

Cormack, Malcolm. *The Paintings of Thomas Gainsborough.* Cambridge: Cambridge University Press, 1991.
Hayes, John. *Thomas Gainsborough.* London: Tate Gallery, 1980.
Rosenthal, Micheal. *The Art of Thomas Gainsborough: "A Little Business for the Eye."* New Haven, Conn.: Yale University Press, 1999.
Waterhouse, Ellis. *Gainsborough.* London: Spring Books, 1966.
Williamson, Geoffrey. *The Ingenious Mr. Gainsborough.* London: Robert Hale, 1972.
Worman, Isabelle. *Thomas Gainsborough: A Biography 1727–1788.* Lavenham, England: Terence Dalton, 1976.

MATURIN, CHARLES ROBERT 1782–1824

Irish novelist and dramatist

Charles Robert Maturin is best remembered as the author of the remarkable and idiosyncratic Gothic novel *Melmoth the Wanderer* (1820). It is the tale of an immortal who plays both Faust and Mephistopheles at once, roaming through time and space in search of a human being wretched enough to assume his burden so that he might break his Satanic pact. The author of this fragmented masterpiece of Gothic excess and Christian allegory was an Anglican clergyman who wrote under the pseudonym Dennis Jasper Murphy to protect his ecclesiastic reputation.

Maturin was born in Dublin on September 25, 1780, the only surviving child of William Maturin and Fidelia Watson. He was raised as a strict Calvinist, his family being descended

from a Huguenot minister who had left France as a refugee after Louis XIV revoked the Edict of Nantes in 1685 (a law granting Protestants the freedom to worship, in a historical period that preoccupies *Melmoth the Wanderer*). Maturin studied at Trinity College, Dublin, graduating in 1800; in 1803 he was ordained and appointed to the curacy of Loughrea in Galway, and married Henrietta Kingsbury. Maturin became the curate of St. Peter's in Dublin in 1806, a position he held until his death eighteen years later, despite his desire for advancement in the church. Maturin's first novel was an ambitious Gothic work entitled *Fatal Revenge; or, The Family of Montorio* (1807), which draws upon the codes of the eighteenth-century Gothic while also reflecting more contemporary English Romanticism, and which attracted the favorable critical attention of Walter Scott (the two authors began a correspondence that lasted until Maturin's death, although they never met in person). This was succeeded by some more restrained romances, exhibiting the author's Irish nationalism in the manner of Maria Edgeworth and his friend and fellow Dublin novelist, Lady Morgan (Sydney Owenson). After the success of Lady Morgan's romance *The Wild Irish Girl* (1806), Maturin produced *The Wild Irish Boy* in 1807, which was followed by *The Milesian Chief* (1812) and the pseudo-satire *Women; or Pour et Contre* (1818); taken together, these works offer an often insightful social critique of Ireland after the 1801 Act of Union.

During this period, and indeed his whole life, Maturin's only major literary success was his tragedy *Bertram, or the Castle of St. Aldobrand* (1816), which was produced by Edmund Kean, who took the title role at Drury Lane Theatre on the recommendation of Scott and Lord Byron. Unfortunately, Maturin did not keep most of the thousand pounds he earned from this production, because he was already supporting his extended family after his father had been unfairly dismissed from a comfortable position in the post office in 1809; he had also stood surety for another relative in 1810 who had gone bankrupt, leaving Maturin liable for the sum guaranteed ("The Tale of Guzman's Family" in *Melmoth* may in part ironically allude to Maturin's own). In addition, he was forced to abandon his anonymity in order to capitalize on his success, which irrevocably damaged his theological career. Samuel Taylor Coleridge, whose own work had been passed over in favor of Maturin's at the Drury Lane, launched a sustained attack on *Bertram* for its allegedly atheist sentiments, and Maturin's next plays, *Manuel* (1817) and *Fredolfo* (1819), were humiliating failures. Unable to support his growing family on a modest curate's salary, Maturin was forced to write to survive, a condition he laments in the preface to *Melmoth*.

Melmoth the Wanderer is Maturin's return to the Gothic genre, which his letters to Scott show that he loved, though his stated desire to "out-Herod all the Herods of the German school" and the Satanic excesses of the novel indicate more of an allegiance to Matthew Lewis than to Ann Radcliffe. It is a Faustian tale, a variation on the myth of the "wandering Jew" with which William Godwin had also engaged in *St. Leon* (1799), and its fragmented, polyphonic narrative has much in common with Mary Shelley's equally metaphysical *Frankenstein* (1818). Through a series of interrelated tales, comprised of witness testimonies, travelers' tales, and ancient manuscripts, the contemporary "hero," John Melmoth, learns of the exploits of his damned ancestor, the narrative ranging from the seventeenth century to 1816, eventually allowed to collapse under its own weight when the wanderer appears in the present day—only to die due to his failure to find a single person willing to change places. The narrative is deeply anti-Catholic, reflecting the author's religious views, which he later published in *Five Sermons on the Errors of the Roman Catholic Church* (1824). The most notable story is the "Tale of the Indians," set on an exotic island between 1680 and 1684, and where the wanderer has his most visible role, attempting to seduce the innocent castaway Immalee, as did the serpent in the Garden of Eden. This novel, and Maturin's last, *The Albigenses* (1824), made little critical or commercial impact, and the author died in poverty on October 30, 1824. However, *Melmoth* was adored in France (Honoré de Balzac even wrote a sequel, *Melmoth Reconcilié* in 1835, suggest-

ing that if only Melmoth had looked in Paris, he would have been overwhelmed by takers), and Maturin was there accorded similar literary status to Edgar Allan Poe. When Oscar Wilde (a descendent of Maturin), traveled to France on his release from prison he called himself Sebastian Melmoth, as the name was still loaded with meaning there.

Melmoth is often cited as the last of the "original" eighteenth-century Gothic novels, yet it, and its author, elude easy categorization. Like *Frankenstein*, we might instead argue that *Melmoth* is a significant marker in the developing Protestant, Romantic, and Gothic trend toward the psychological, the turning inward of narrative in nineteenth-century literature; a process expanded by later Gothic writers, most notably James Hogg, Edgar Allan Poe, and Robert Louis Stevenson. Maturin's noisy, Shandyesque combination of comedy, tragedy, the grotesque, and the sublime also remains unique; his "moral" more fluid than he perhaps intended. Almost in anticipation of the condition of postmodern humanity, what stays with us is Melmoth's maniacal but ambivalent laughter.

STEPHEN CARVER

Selected Works

Melmoth the Wanderer, 1820. Edited by Victor Sage. London: Penguin, 2000.

Bibliography

Bayer-Berenbaum, L. *The Gothic Imagination*. London, 1982.
Butler, Elizabeth M. *The Fortunes of Faust*. Stroud: Sutton, 1998.
Fairclough, Peter, ed. *Three Gothic Novels*. London: Penguin, 1968.
Fierrobe, Claude. *Charles Robert Maturin (1780–1824): L'Homme et L'Oeuvre*. Paris, 1974.
Godwin, William. *St. Leon*. Edited by Pamela Clemit. Oxford: Oxford University Press, 1994.
Idman, Niilo. *Charles Robert Maturin: His Life and Works*. London, 1923.
Jackson, Rosemary. *Fantasy: The Literature of Subversion*. London: Routledge, 1981.
Lewis, Matthew. *The Monk*. Edited by Howard Anderson. Oxford: Oxford University Press, 1973.
Lloyd Smith, Allan, and Victor Sage, eds. *Gothick Origins and Innovations*. Amsterdam: Rodopi, 1994.
Marlowe, Christopher. *Doctor Faustus*. Edited John D. Jump. Manchester: Manchester University Press, 1988.
Morrison, Robert and Chris Baldick, eds. *Tales of Terror from Blackwood's Magazine*. Oxford: Oxford University Press, 1995.
Morrison, Robert. *The Vampyre and Other Tales of the Macabre*. Oxford: Oxford University Press, 1997.
Punter, David. *The Literature of Terror: A History of Gothic Fictions from 1765 to the Present Day*. 2d ed. 2 vols. London: Longman, 1996.
Radcliffe, Ann. *The Italian*. Edited by Frederick Garber. Oxford: Oxford University Press, 1968.
———. *The Mysteries of Udolpho*. Edited by Bonamy Dobrée. Oxford: Oxford University Press, 1966.
Ratchford, E. and William McCarthy, Jr., eds. *The Correspondence of Sir Walter Scott and Charles Robert Maturin*, 1937; Reprint New York: Garland, 1980.
Roberts, Marie. *Gothic Immortals: The Fiction of the Brotherhood of the Rosy Cross*. London: Routledge, 1990.
Sage, Victor. *Horror Fiction in the Protestant Tradition*. London: Macmillan, 1988.
Scholten, Willem. *Charles Robert Maturin, the Terror-Novelist*. Amsterdam, 1933.

MEDICINE

At the end of the eighteenth century, mainly under the influence of Immanuel Kant and Friedrich Wilhelm Joseph von Schelling, but also of other philosophical and theological thinkers of the past (Paracelsus, Plato, and Benedict de Spinoza), a transcendental and metaphysical form of medical theory and practice, later named Romantic medicine or, better, the medicine of Romanticism, was developed. Proponents of the Romantic tendency in medicine included the physicians Carl Gustav Carus, Adolph Carl August Eschenmayer, Johann Christian August Heinroth, Carl Wilhelm Ideler, Justinus Kerner, Dietrich Georg Kieser, Johann Christian Reil, Johann Nepomuk Ringseis, Andreas Röschlaub, Gotthilf Heinrich von Schubert, Philipp Franz von Walther, Carl Joseph Hieronymus Windischmann, and many others.

Anatomy, physiology, therapy, and surgery were interpreted and analyzed from a philosophical or metaphysical perspective by these physicians. Their philosophical orientation did not hinder them from making special observations and concrete inventions in all fields of medicine. Romantic medicine was neither scientific theory of this discipline, nor methodology of research in medicine. The physicians of the Romantic school formulated their critique of positivistic science, of Kant's transcendental philosophy of nature, and of the speculative method of Schelling and G. W. F. Hegel, despite the unquestionable influence, especially of Schelling, for their metaphysical understanding of nature, body and soul, and diagnostic and therapeutical practice.

Romantic medicine was not a single entity; various concepts were developed, differing conceptual and biographical answers given to the triumph of empiricism and positivism in medicine during the nineteenth century. Romantic medicine has no equivalent in other countries outside Germany; echoes or parallel tendencies can be observed only occasionally and randomly.

Romantic physicians believed strongly in the union between nature and mind, between natural history and cultural evolution, the belief in the historicity and metaphysical or religious meaning of disease and pain, the emphasis placed on the subjectivity or personality of the patient and the physician, on the physician-patient relationship as a dialectic bond of symmetry and asymmetry. Disease, like health, could only be understood in the framework of a mephysical cosmology and anthropology beyond the normal medical viewpoint, which was lost in senseless details, crude empiricism, and vain theories. Disease belonged to life and consisted in a disproportion of the vital forces or principles (sensibility, irritability, reproduction); health was the equilibrium of these forces or principles, but disease and death were the destiny of all. Health was not only or always positive—disease and pain could also have high human value.

The Romantic perspective was valid for physical as well as psychical diseases. The term *Psychiat(e)rie* was coined in 1808 by Reil, the term *Psychosomatic* by Heinroth, who believed guilt to be one cause of mental illness. The difference between the so-called *Somatiker* (somaticists) and *Psychiker* (psychicists) is best considered as an accentuation in regard to etiology rather than a total opposition. The "animal magnetism" of Franz Anton Mesmer was not approved unconditionally. Schubert developed a specific interpretation of dreams (*Symbolik des Traumes*, 1814), while Carus underlined the importance of the subconscious (*Psyche*, 1846).

The metaphysically influenced physicians of Romantism published general historical overviews as well as specific historical analyses, often from the perspective of the Hegelian philosophy of history. The historical development of medicine was a return to the origin, but on a new stage; the history of medicine became a "progressive regression." The development was genetic or organic, possessed an inner necessity and could not be regarded as accidental, or as dependent only on social or economic factors. The history of medicine, which comprises also the history of diseases, is the realization of an ideal system, a systematization of stages of knowledge and practice. Interruptions and retardations can happen, but only temporally, not principally. History is not only a museum of the past but a guide to the future.

Medicine in the nineteenth century followed the model of natural science as oppposed to that of the natural philosophy and philosophical anthropology of the Romantic era. Medicine concentrated on curing disease and neglected the contributions of the arts, literature, philosophy, and theology. The patient became more and more an object, his subjectivity or personality was disregarded, and the history of the patient was reduced to the history of the disease. Experimentation, statistics, and causal thinking became the main basis for medical theory and practice with many positive results in the field of diagnosis and therapy, but also fundamental losses from the anthropological perspective.

The historical scheme, by which all medical disciplines around 1800 passed through a phase of Romanticism and idealism, did not correspond to historical reality. According to Christoph Wilhelm Hufeland, medicine had to follow "the middle road between fruitless speculation and blind empiricism." Around 1820, the preceding decades were condemned by the anatomist Philipp Carl Hartmann, because during these times philosophy of nature "subjugated medicine and transformed it to accord with its basic views."

The controversy over the different positions of natural philosophies and medical disciplines around 1800 was not solved by argument or debate; rather, it was decided by the facts of scientific advancement. The advances in knowledge in the natural and medical sciences, with an abundance of technical-industrial results and diagnostic-therapeutical advances, the radiation of the scientific worldview into all areas of life and culture, and the specialization and the institutionalization of medicine, with an emphasis on research, sealed the fate of natural philosophy and Romantic medicine. Even so, a few lingering effects of its modes of thought and practice can be observed in developments of the nineteenth and twentieth centuries, including anthropological medicine, psychiatry, and psychoanalysis.

Romantic medicine was an important phase in the historical development of this discipline and its relationship with philosophy, and can correspond to central points in the critique of medicine in the present. The concept of the patient as person, the ethical dimensions of diagnosis and treatment, the social and cultural aspects of medicine have not lost their significance today. Despite their scientific shortcomings, the medical practices of Romanticism still provide valuable theoretical insights and perspectives.

DIETRICH VON ENGELHARDT

Bibliography

Benzenhöfer, U. *Psychiatrie und Anthropologie in der ersten Hälfte des 19. Jahrhunderts*, Hürtgenwald, 1993.

Engelhardt, Dietrich von "Romantische Naturforschung." In *Historisches Bewusstsein in der Naturwissenschaft. Von der Aufklärung bis zum Positivismus.* Edited by Dietrich von Engelhardt. Freiburg, 1979. 103–57.

Leibbrand, W. *Die spekulative Medizin der Romantik.* Hamburg, 1956.

Risse, G. B. " 'Philosophical' Medicine in Nineteenth-Century Germany: An Episode in the Relations Between Philosophy and Medicine," *Journal of Medicine and Philosophy* 1 (1976): 72–91.

Rosen, G. "Romantic Medicine: A Problem in Historical Periodization," *Bulletin of the History of Medicine* 25 (1951): 149–58.

Rothschuh, K.-E. "Naturphilosophische Konzepte der Medizin aus der Zeit der deutschen Romantik." In *Romantik in Deutschland.* Edited by Richard Brinkmann. Stuttgart, 1978. 243–66.

Wiesing, U. *Kunst oder Wissenschaft? Konzeptionen der Medizin in der deutschen Romantik.* Stuttgart, 1995.

LES MÉDITATIONS POÉTIQUES 1820

Verse collection by Alphonse Marie-Louis de Lamartine

Alphonse Marie-Louis de Lamartine's *Les Méditations poétiques* (*Poetic Meditations*), one of the half-dozen best-known collections of French verse, marked the emergence of a new sensibility in French life. Culturally, the Revolutionary and Napoleonic eras can be seen as representing an interruption rather than a real discontinuity. With the restoration in 1814 and 1815 of what looked like a modified ancien régime and the resumption of a continuous cultural evolution, a new sensibility had emerged that turned away from vast projects of social engineering, the Industrial Revolution (which came a little later in France than it did in England), and the coarser pursuit of material advantage. Encouraging ill-defined yearnings and a self-absorbed melancholy (the mal du siècle, or world-weariness, that would haunt French Romanticism), this sensibility was nurtured on nature's boundlessness and benignity, the lurking menace of its lakes, and the majesty and stillness of its mountains. A vaguely grandiose Christianity, reconciled with the rationalist religion of at least some of the eighteenth-century philosophers, was expanded beyond a religious cult to feelings of goodwill toward a humanity whose instincts were themselves essentially virtuous.

Born of Jean-Jacques Rousseau, heralded by Benjamin Constant de Rebecque, Etienne Pivert de Senancour, and Madame Anne-Louise-Germaine de Staël, and nurtured by Lord Byron, François-August-René de Chateaubriand, and Johann Wolfgang von Goethe, a generation reached maturity just as French society was settling back into normality after the profound and bloody upheavals of the Revolution and Napoleon Bonaparte's dramatic rise and fall. It needed to examine the implications of its newly regained security, and could now afford to explore the vulnerabilities, sensitivity, and higher aspirations of the individual. It wanted to feel that nature had a design and the individual a purpose, and to cultivate its most tender longings in forms that appealed directly to the feelings and did not require too demanding an intellectual effort.

Lamartine catered exactly to the emotional needs of this—his own—generation. What is powerful and original in his *Méditations* could have only been conceived and expressed as it was, with the collection's concentration on effect, in France, and only within a few years of 1820. The lyricism of the twenty-nine-year-old Lamartine could scarcely have been better tailored to fit the imaginative and emotional requirements of the 25 percent of twenty-year-olds who were literate, and therefore capable of absorbing an imaginative experience that could not be mediated by stage drama (the only form of literary experience, apart from recitations, that did not depend on literacy).

The first edition of the *Méditations*, containing twenty-four lyric odes and elegies, appeared anonymously on March 11, 1820; a second edition, with two additional poems but now no longer anonymous, was published in April of the same year. By January 1822 the collection was in its eighth edition. Four new poems were added in December 1822 and eleven more for the *Premières méditations* of 1831. By that date sales are estimated to have reached over 35,000 copies.

The expression of a cultivated melancholy required not only musical fluidity, but also, if it were not to degenerate into formless outpourings, strict formal restraints. Lamartine wrote mostly in Classical twelve-syllable alexandrines, lines that are too long to constantly ensure poetic density, and could without much poetic flair be extemporized as doggerel. He is as rigorous in splitting his alexandrines into component halves as he is in his use of meters, rhyme schemes, and syntax. He allows himself only an occasional inversion, and is adept at manipulating such simple rhetorical devices as apostrophe, repetition, antithesis, direct speech, exclamations, and rhetorical questions. The fluidity and music comes from an astonishingly skillful exploitation of sound patterns, mixing with calculated effect long and short vowels with labial, dental, and sibilant consonants. He inherited from an earlier generation the strict avoidance of concrete, down-to-earth, everyday language, and it is this attempt at an elevated style, intentionally vague, that, more than anything else, dates his poetry. It explains why, after its initial phenomenal success, it went out of fashion so quickly as the more full-blooded, passionate, and dramatic verse of his younger contemporaries such as Victor Hugo became popular. They caricatured Lamartine as *le pleurard* (the cry-baby).

A good example of his typical themes and their treatment is "Le Lac," one of the best-known poems in the collection. It was written in late August 1817 while Lamartine was waiting for Julie Charles to rejoin him. She was married, but there had been a passionate affair in Paris during the winter, a tearful parting in May, and there was now to be a reunion. Julie, however, was now too ill to travel; she was to die in December without seeing Lamartine again. His notebooks tell us that the poem was inspired by a visit to the lakeside seat where their first declaration of love and the first kiss had taken place; nonetheless, it relies heavily on passages from Rousseau's *Julie, ou la nouvelle Héloïse* (*Julie, or the New Heloise*, 1761).

Comprising sixteen four-line stanzas, the poem opens with a sighing rhetorical question, which translates as: "always moved on to new shores and unable to return from the everlasting night to which we are carried, can we never for a single day drop anchor in the ocean of time?" The second, third, and fourth stanzas address the lake, invited by the poet to remember the occasion when it first saw "her." There are no identifications, no concrete details, no description, merely an indication that two lovers once rowed on the lake's "harmonious waters."

The fifth stanza is narrative; the lake listened and "the voice dear to me" spoke. The next four stanzas give the woman's words in direct speech: "O time, halt your flight. . . ." She ends with Horace's celebrated carpe diem theme—let us rejoice while we can. There follow three stanzas of the poet's own reflections,

three more in which he addresses the lake again, and a final stanza expressing his desire that the couple's love should be remembered by wind, reed, scent, and all of the lake that can be heard, seen, or breathed. The poem's strength comes from a plaintive contrast that characterizes a great deal of Lamartine and his era: a contrast between the poet's passionate desire and the impossibility of its satisfaction.

ANTHONY LEVI

Bibliography

Birkett, Mary Ellen. *Lamartine and the Poetics of Landscape*. Lexington, 1982.
Denommé, Robert T. *Nineteenth-Century French Romantic Poets*. Carbondale and Edwardsville: Southern Illinois University Press, 1969.
Fréjaville, G. *Les Méditations de Lamartine*. Paris, 1931.
Lombard, Charles M. *Lamartine*. New York, 1973.

MÉHUL, ÉTIENNE-NICOLAS 1763–1817

French composer

Étienne-Nicolas Méhul was one of the leading composers of opera during the French Revolution and Napoleonic era. He was also the foremost symphonist of early nineteenth-century France. Although he died in 1817, his music continued to be published and performed well into the nineteenth century, influencing composers such as Hector Berlioz, Carl Maria von Weber, and even Richard Wagner. Although he lacked the technical expertise of his friend and colleague Luigi Cherubini, Méhul was unsurpassed in his ability to convey a sense of drama through inventive harmonic, motivic, and orchestral means. A prolific composer of operas, his innovations helped to redefine that genre for later generations.

All of Méhul's operas reflect his conviction that musical sense must grow out of the words being sung. As a result, his operas exhibit great stylistic variety. Each stagework possesses a distinct musical ambience, a feature of his music that Berlioz noted with approval. Building on the tradition of Christoph Willibald von Gluck's reform operas, Méhul strove to integrate his musical forms and processes more closely within the drama. Changes in the tone and structure of the librettos themselves prompted this response. Beginning in the 1780s and accelerating during the French Revolution, librettists introduced greater sentiment and seriousness of purpose into the genre we refer to as *opéra-comique*. Méhul reacted by introducing new and more complex forms within his operas, giving the orchestra a larger and more independent role, and writing unmelodic, declamatory vocal lines when the text required. In so doing he established a new and vital form of opera in France that influenced his colleagues and paved the way for the Romantic composers who followed him.

Méhul's reputation as a composer of originality was established with his first performed opera, *Euphrosine, ou le tyran corrigé* (*Euphrosine, or The Reformed Tyrant*, 1790), a work that would be performed regularly for the next forty years. The duet "Gardez-vous de la jalousie" ("Beware of Jealousy") from act 2

has received a great deal of critical attention since its premiere. In it, the composer developed a distinctive melodic motive in a new and original manner, as one singer warns another to beware of jealousy and its potential for destruction. The motive's association with jealousy is evident from its handling. Consisting of a simple, slow oscillation between two pitches a third apart, it saturates the accompaniment. In the duet's opening measures, the texture comprises only a vocal line and this motive, presented in octaves in the strings. Nothing else intrudes on this sinister musical surface. Over the course of the duet, Méhul develops this brief idea, inverting it, changing its rhythmic profile, and stating it simultaneously in different parts of the orchestra. The significance of this motive cannot be overestimated. Méhul not only relates it to the theme of jealousy found in the text, but also generates dramatic tension through the manipulation of it for expressive purposes. The motivic development within the duet parallels the growth of obsessive jealousy, which is at the heart of the opera's plot. Adding to the motive's impact, Méhul brings it back later in the opera whenever jealousy, or its effects, are felt by any of the opera's characters. The realization of the motive's potential in connection with the text anticipates Romantic opera, in which this nearly organic union of music and words was deemed an aesthetic ideal. A similar process can be found in *Mélidore et Phrosine* (1794). Several recurring motives, each associated with a different person or concept, are found in this overwrought tale of incestuous desire and romantic love. In *Ariodant* (1799), perhaps Méhul's best opera, motivic development becomes an integral part of the entire work. These three operas were not isolated experiments; Méhul explored similar possibilities in all his compositions.

Other aspects of Méhul's compositions that herald Romantic usage include his harmony and orchestration. He enjoyed experimenting with surprising modulations and was not afraid to use loud and arresting dissonances. Nonetheless, abrupt shifts of key and detours to remote tonal regions are never employed unless the dramatic action calls for them. In conjunction with the expansion of his harmonic palette, he also practiced a novel and imaginative approach to orchestration. In part this reflects his desire to create a musical world that would be unique to each opera. At times this meant using instruments that were not customarily a part of the theater orchestra, such as tam-tams or serpents. Conversely, in *Uthal* (1806), an opera based on James Macpherson's Ossian poems, Méhul did not use any violins. The emphasis on lower strings (violas, cellos, and double basses) in various combinations with wind instruments produced a thick, dark sound that suggested the untamed solemnity of the Scottish Highlands. In general, he explored the expressive capacity of lower instruments, like cello and horn, giving them a degree of independence within the orchestra that was unprecedented among French composers.

In his symphonic works, Méhul exhibited the same independent spirit that we see in his operas. Indeed, his opera overtures provide a clear stylistic connection with the large-scale orchestral works that he composed in the brief span between 1808 and 1810. Formally, his symphonies bear a strong resemblance to those of Franz Joseph Haydn, which were popular in France. The outward shape of the music, however, conceals a rhythmic drive and occasional harmonic departures that are more forward looking. Although he was familiar with the late symphonies of Wolfgang Amadeus Mozart as well as the first two symphonies of Ludwig van Beethoven, Méhul created a personal style that reflected his own musical background and interests. For example, recurring motives, an important feature of his operas, become a significant unifying element of Symphony No. 4 in E Major (1810), whereas the third and fourth movements of Symphony No. 1 in G Minor (1808–1909) explore new orchestral textures and combinations.

Méhul's influence was widely felt in France. The next generation of composers looked to him as a source of specifically French musical models. However, composers outside France found inspiration in his music, too. Felix Mendelssohn's enthusiasm for Méhul's Symphony No. 1, which he conducted in performance, finds echoes in his own orchestral writing. The trumpet calls from Beethoven's *Fidelio* (1805; first revision 1806; second revision, 1814) were based upon those in Méhul's *Héléna* (1803). Wagner led a performance of *Joseph* (1807) in 1838 while he was director of the opera house in Riga. In short, Méhul's legacy was surprisingly far reaching. Although others extended and refined his innovations, his originality remains as fresh today as it was in his lifetime.

MICHAEL E. McCLELLAN

Biography

Born in Givet, June 22, 1763. First studied music under a local organist in Givet. Moved to Paris around 1778. Studied there with Jean-Frédéric Edelmann. First successful opera, *Euphrosine*, performed at the Comédie-Italienne (later renamed Théâtre de l'Opéra-Comique), 1790. Founding member of the Institut National de Musique, 1793–95. Named inspector of the Conservatoire National de Musique, a title he retained for two decades, 1795–1814. Died in Paris, October 18, 1817.

Selected Works

Modern Editions

Stratonice. 1792. Facsimile edition, with an introduction by M. Elizabeth C. Bartlet. Stuyvesant, N.Y.: Pendragon Press, 1997.
Mélidore et Phrosine. 1794. Facsimile edition with an introduction by M. Elizabeth C. Bartlet. Stuyvesant, N.Y.: Pendragon Press, 1989.
Symphony No. 1 in G Minor. 1808–9. Edited by David Charlton. Madison, Wis.: A-R Editions, 1985.
Three symphonies. 1809–10. Edited by David Charlton; no. 3 coedited by Anthony Caston. New York: Garland, 1982.

Operas

Euphrosine, ou le tyran corrigé. Libretto by François-Benoît Hoffman. 1790.
Stratonice. Libretto by François-Beneît. Hoffman. 1792.
Mélidore et Phrosine. Libretto by Antoine-Vincent Arnault. 1794.
La Caverne. Libretto by Nicolas-Julien Forgeot. 1795.
Le Jeune Henri. Libretto by Jean-Nicolas. Bouilly. 1797.
Adrien. Libretto by François-Benoît Hoffman. 1799.
Ariodant. Libretto by François-Benoît Hoffman. 1799.
Héléna. Libretto by Jean-Nicolas Bouilly. 1803.
Utahl. Libretto by Jacques-Maximilien-Benjamin Bins de Saint Victor. 1806.
Joseph. Libretto by Alexandre Duval. 1807.
L'Oriflamme. Libretto by Charles-Guillaume Etienne and Louis-Pierre-Marie-François Baour-Lormian First performed 1814.

Other

Symphony No. 1 in G Minor. 1808–9.
Symphony No. 2 in D Major. 1808–9.
Symphony No. 3 in C Major. 1809.
Symphony No 4 in E Major. 1810.

Bibliography

———. "Bonaparte et Méhul," *Ardenne Wallone* 37–38 (1989): 57–77, 43–58.
———. *Etienne-Nicolas Méhul and Opera: Source and Archival Studies of Lyric Theatre during the French Revolution, Consulate and Empire*. Heilbronn: Galland, 1999.
———. "Méhul, Etienne-Nicolas." In *The New Grove Dictionary of Opera*. vol. 3. Edited by Stanley Sadie. London: Macmillan, 1997.
———. "A Newly Discovered Opera for Napoleon," *Acta Musicologica* 56 (1984); 266–96.
Boyd, Malcolm, ed. *Music and the French Revolution*. Cambridge: Cambridge University Press, 1992.
Charlton, David. *French Opera 1730–1830: Meaning and Media*. Aldershot: Ashgate, 2000.
———. "Méhul, Etienne-Nicolas." In *The New Grove Dictionary of Music and Musicians*. vol. 12. edited by Stanley Sadie. London: Macmillan, 1980.
Dent, Edward J. *The Rise of Romantic Opera*. Edited by Winton Dean. Cambridge: Cambridge University Press, 1976.
Grace, Michael D. "Méhul's *Ariodant* and the Early Leitmotif." In *Festschrift for Albert Seay: Essays by His Friends and Colleagues* edited by Michael D. Grace. Colorado Springs: Colorado College, 1982.
Laudon, Robert T. *Sources of the Wagnerian Synthesis: A Study of the Franco-German Tradition in Nineteenth-Century Opera*. Salzburg: Katzbichler, 1979.
Masson, Paul-Marie. "L'Oeuvre dramatique de Méhul," *Annales de l'Université de Paris* 12 (1937); 524–48.
Mongrédien, Jean. *La Musique en France des lumières au romantisme, 1789–1830*. Paris: Flammarion, 1986.

MELANCHOLY

Until the eighteenth century, the term *melancholy* almost invariably denoted a disease, felt to be caused by too much "black bile" and characterized by a variety of symptoms, but especially by unmotivated negative emotions (for example, fear or sorrow without any obvious cause). By the eighteenth century, however, the term had been expanded to the extent that it could also denote simply a negative mood itself—often a literarily productive mood, at that—without any necessary reference to an underlying physiological problem. Melancholy, understood as a mood, became a dominant literary theme for the eighteenth-century "graveyard poets" such as Thomas Gray and Edward Young, as well as authors of sensibility, such as Johann Wolfgang von Goethe. For many of these authors, melancholy also could be applied to nonhuman entities such as landscapes. Romantic era authors extended, developed, and secularized this literary understanding of melancholy, linking it firmly to notions of artistic genius and landscape while at the same time divorcing it from the traditional religious interpretation of the sorrows of melancholy that still characterized most eighteenth-century treatments of the term.

For most of its history, the causes and effects of melancholy were understood within the medical "humoral" theory established by Aristotle, Galen, and Hippocrates. Within this theory, the body was understood as composed of four elements, or "humors," (blood, phlegm, black bile, and yellow bile) that had to be kept in balance. Melancholy referred to those physical and mental problems caused by too much "black bile" (in Greek, *melas*, "black," and *khole*, "bile"). The range of symptoms attributed by such authors as Galen and Hippocrates to this surplus of black bile was extensive, and included *phrenzy*, the eruption of sores, and the sudden and unmotivated appearance of torpor and fear. The *Problems*, one of the most extensive ancient discussions of melancholy (written perhaps by Aristotle but more likely by one of his followers), also established a connection between the melancholy and "greatness," suggesting that all great men (for example, Hercules, Lysander, and Plato) suffered from too much black bile. (Perhaps because of the gendered nature of these ancient examples, medieval, Renaissance, and modern physicians generally claimed that melancholia struck men more frequently than women.) A number of important "humoral" treatises on melancholy were written in the medieval and Renaissance period—for example, Avicenna's *Black Bile and Melancholy* (c. 1170–87 A.D.) and Ficino's *Learned People of Melancholy* (1482)—and the basic tenets of ancient humoral theory guided understandings of melancholy even up until (and including) the publication of Robert Burton's massive *The Anatomy of Melancholy* (1621–51). Burton's enormous and popular text helped establish what would become an increasingly important connection between idleness, work, and melancholy, for he contended, "There is no greater cause of melancholy than idleness, no better cure than business."

The decline in popularity of humoral theory in seventeenth-century medical philosophy did not mean the end of melancholy as a disease (up until the twentieth century, *melancholy* still frequently denoted a physiological disturbance in both medical theory and popular opinion), but it did allow alternative understandings of the term to emerge. Raymond Klibansky, Erwin Panofsky, and Fritz Saxl argue that by the middle of the eighteenth century *melancholy* generally had ceased to refer primarily to a physical quality or state and instead denoted a mood or disposition. As such, the term could be applied even to nonhuman objects such as landscapes, and poets such as Thomas Gray, Edward Young, and James Thompson explored the "melancholy" nature of graveyards, night, and mountains and mist, while novelists such as Goethe explored the melancholy nature of acts such as suicide. Poets also began to explore possible connections between melancholy and creativity, and the middle of the eighteenth century witnessed an explosion of works explicitly concerned with melancholy, such as Thomas Warton's "The Pleasures of Melancholy" (1747) and James Beattie's "The Triumph of Melancholy" (1760). While earlier physicians had generally sought to eradicate, or at least control, melancholy, many of these eighteenth-century poets were interested in encouraging, or at least exploiting, melancholy moods (a position that received support from John Milton's "Il Penseroso" [1645], which had described the virtues of suffering and solitude). Yet Rickels notes that while this eighteenth-century valorization of melancholy was certainly new, the stress on the virtues of "melancholic" suffering and solitude had much in common with Classical and neo-Classical themes of world-weariness and the need to retreat to secluded places. Rickels also notes that many eighteenth-century authors interpreted melancholy within a traditional Christian framework, suggesting that the unhappiness attendant upon this mood prepared one for death and Christian salvation.

Romantic-era treatments extended and refined the eighteenth-century understanding of melancholy as a productive mood while at the same time minimizing the role of traditional religion. Yet this continuity between eighteenth-century and Romantic-era literary discussions of melancholy means that many Romantic treatments of melancholy are difficult, if not impossible, to distinguish from their eighteenth-century predecessors. So, for example, the song "To Melancholy," included in the penultimate chapter of Anne Radcliffe's *The Mysteries of Udolpho* (1794); Mary Robinson's "Ode to Melancholy" (1806) and "The Progress of Melancholy" (1806); and Thomas Love Peacock's "Philosophy of Melancholy" (1812) are only arguably "Romantic" in nature, and seem very close to eighteenth-century treatments of the term. Yet one can also observe an increasing secularization of the sublimity associated with melancholic experience. While many eighteenth-century authors sought compensation for melancholic suffering through traditional religious justifications, Romantic authors tended to suggest that melancholy had the capacity to reveal the infinite powers of the individual self or imagination. The ennui of the title character in Lord Byron's *Childe Harold's Pilgrimage* (1812–18), for example, is easily recognizable as a melancholic element, but it is dispelled (though only intermittently) by the poet narrator's reflections on the power of imaginative creation. The "grief without a pang, void, dark, and drear" that strikes the speaker of Samuel Taylor Coleridge's "Dejection: An Ode" (1802) "finds no nat'ral outlet" but presumably is productively transformed in the writing of the poem itself. In the most famous, and explicit, Romantic treatment of melancholy—John Keats's "Ode on Melancholy"

(1819)—the speaker advises the auditor how to respond to fits of melancholy in such a way that exalted pleasures will result.

The emphasis on nontraditional spirituality is also reflected in other artistic media, such as the work of German painter Caspar David Friedrich, who painted a number of "melancholy" landscapes—for example, *Two Men Contemplating the Moon* (1819) and *Chalk Cliffs on Rügen* (1819)—in which individuals confront scenes of infinitude (ranges of mountains, vast seas) without any supporting religious symbolism. Even when Friedrich included religious elements in his melancholic landscapes—for example in *Cross by the Baltic* (1815)—he insisted that the religious symbolism was not necessary to appreciate the melancholic mood of the painting.

ROBERT MITCHELL

Bibliography

Aristotle. *Aristotle: Problems*. volume 16. Translated by W. S. Hett, Cambridge, Mass.: Harvard University Press, 1957.

Batten, Guinn. *The Orphaned Imagination: Melancholy and Commodity Culture in English Romanticism*. Durham, N.C.: Duke University Press, 1998.

Beattie, James. *Poetical Works of Beattie, Blair, and Falconer*. Edited by George Gilfillan. 1854.

Burton, Robert. *The Anatomy of Melancholy*. Edited by Thomas C. Faulkner, Nicolas K. Kiessling, and Rhonda L. Blair. Oxford: Clarendon Press, 1989–95.

Keats, John. *Complete Poems*. Edited by Jack Stillinger. Cambridge, Mass.: Harvard University Press, 1982.

Klibansky, Raymond, Erwin Panofsky, and Fritz Saxl. *Saturn and Melancholy: Studies in the History of Natural Philosophy, History, and Art*. New York: Basic Books, 1964.

Lepennies, Wolf. *Melancholy and Society*. Translated by Jeremy Gaines and Doris Jones. Cambridge, Mass.: Harvard University Press, 1992.

Milton, John. *Complete Poems and Major Prose*. Edited by Merritt Y. Hughes. New York: Odyssey Press, 1957.

Peacock, Thomas Love. *The Works of Thomas Love Peacock*. volume 6. London: Constable, 1927.

Radden, Jennifer, ed. *The Nature of Melancholy from Aristotle to Kristeva*. New York: Oxford University Press, 2000.

Radcliffe, Ann. *The Mysteries of Udolpho: A Romance*. London: Oxford University Press, 1970.

Robinson, Mary. *Poetical Works, Including Many Pieces Never Before Published*. volume 1. London, 1806.

———. *Poems: 1791*. Edited by Jonathan Wordsworth. New York: Woodstock Books, 1994.

Sickels, Eleanor M. *The Gloomy Egoist: Moods and Themes of Melancholy from Gray to Keats*. New York: Columbia University Press, 1932.

Vaughn, William. *German Romantic Painting*. 2nd ed. New Haven, Conn.: Yale University Press, 1994.

Warton, Thomas. *The Pleasures of Melancholy; A Poem*. 1747.

Wu, Duncan. *Romanticism: An Anthology*. Oxford: Basil Blackwell, 1994.

MELVILLE, HERMAN 1819–1891

American novelist and poet

Now regarded as a key figure in American literary history, for most of his life Herman Melville struggled to make a living as a writer. Although his first book *Typee: A Peep at Polynesian Life* (1847) sold well on both sides of the Atlantic, the perceived obscurity of *Moby-Dick, or, The Whale* (1851), and the "ambiguous" sexuality of *Pierre: or, The Ambiguities* (1852) did serious damage to his literary reputation. The long poem *Clarel: A Poem and Pilgrimage in the Holy Hand* (1876) did nothing to revive his career; by the time it was published, Melville was working as an outdoor customs inspector on the New York docks, a job he took in desperation after a series of literary failures. It was not until the 1920s that scholars began to reconsider Melville's work, elevating him to his current place alongside Walt Whitman as one of America's most important nineteenth-century writers. As D. H. Lawrence, one of his early twentieth-century admirers, put it, Melville is perhaps "the greatest seer and poet of the sea."

Melville's father and mother both came from distinguished families, their fathers being senior officers in the Revolutionary Army, and key figures in the Revolutionary War. Such auspicious ancestry should have ensured a comfortable life for the Melvills (the "e" was added after the death of Herman's father), but a series of business failures in the early 1830s, and Allan Melvill's death in 1832, left the family with little money with which to support itself. For this reason, Herman's education was patchy, and he effectively finished his general schooling at the

age of twelve. In 1839, after working as a clerk and as a teacher, he embarked as a cabin boy on a voyage to Liverpool.

In 1841 Melville sailed for the south seas on the whaler *Acushnet*. Unhappy with life on the ship, he and Richard Tobias deserted on the island of Nukuheva and spent several weeks living with the Typees. These and subsequent experiences were to be replayed in three South Sea books, *Typee* (1846), *Omoo: A Narrative of Adventures in the South Seas* (1847), and *Mardi: and a voyage Thither* (1849), which gained him a following in America and Europe though some critics doubted that their author actually had any experience of the places and events that the books describe. Together with *Redburn: His First Voyage* (1847) and *White-Jacket; or, The World in a Man-of-War* (1850) these books mark the peak of Melville's fame. However, his tales of cannibalism and polygamy among the South Sea islanders also brought him notoriety.

The year 1850 marks a turning point in Melville's literary career. After writing an anonymous essay praising the work of Nathaniel Hawthorne, the pair became neighbors and good friends; indeed, there has been much speculation about the exact nature of this relationship. Melville was working on his masterpiece, *Moby-Dick* (then known as *The Whale*), but he had borrowed heavily to pay for the restoration of his Berkshires house "Arrowhead." With its extended factual chapters blended with the famous tale of obsession and madness, *Moby-Dick* was difficult, unpopular, and did not sell well. Yet Melville's work as a whole describes an emergent postrevolutionary American identity, struggling between propriety and the need to innovate and challenge orthodoxy.

As the example of *Moby-Dick* shows, Melville had always struggled to reconcile writing commercially with his desire to write as he pleased. *Pierre* tells the story of Pierre Glendinning, who tries to protect his prominent New York family from finding out about his half sister. The hints at incest contained in the narrative made the book difficult to publish, and in desperation Melville was forced to accept less than half the going rate for the manuscript. With his reputation in ruins, *The Confidence Man* (1857) was the last novel published in Melville's lifetime, and was also a financial failure. The satirical view of charity as proof of lunacy was not calculated to find sympathy with middle-class readers, and Melville's earlier work had in any case shown him to be a writer of dubious morals. *The Confidence Man* can be read as an expression of Melville's view of the new country, in which scams and confidence tricks are the driving force of the culture and economy. Yet there is a wry optimism in Melville's novel, which finds hope in the idea that people still exist who are innocent enough to be swindled.

Unable to make a living as a writer or public speaker, Melville became disillusioned. The poetry that he had been writing in secret since 1858 failed to find a publisher, and he was seriously injured when falling from a wagon in 1862. After he was appointed customs inspector in 1866, he and his family became increasingly reclusive, to the extent that when the English poet Robert Buchanan visited New York in the 1880s he was unable to find anyone among the New York literati who knew where Melville lived.

It was only on his resignation from the customs service that Melville resumed writing prose; *Billy Budd, Foretopman* (1888–91, published 1924), unfinished at his death, emerged from a poem of 1885 entitled "Billy in the Darbies." *Billy Budd* returns to one of Melville's key themes—namely, the apparent human impulse to destroy innocence. Falsely accused of encouraging mutiny on board ship, and with nobody prepared to defend him, the innocent Billy Budd is hanged. As with much of Melville's later output, including *The Piazza Tales* (1856), *Billy Budd* is a tale of despair, disillusionment, and the failure to communicate. As such, it combines Romantic ideas about the dichotomies of innocence and experience, good and evil, with a more modernistic approach to language and truth.

The revival of interest in Melville that began in the 1920s was part of a wider revival of interest in American literature that reached its peak after the Second World War. The nine books and sixteen tales published between 1845 and 1855 all contribute to the development of a distinctively American literary sensibility; that embattled optimism about human innocence which underpins Whitman's oeuvre, and which appears in the work of later writers such as F. Scott Fitzgerald and Ernest Hemingway.

CHRISTOPHER ROUTLEDGE

See also **Moby-Dick; or, The Whale**

Biography

Born in New York City, August 1, 1819; father was Allan Melvill, mother was Maria Gansevoort. Attended New York Male High School and Grammar School of Columbia College, for one year. Moved to Albany in 1830. When Allan Melvill died in 1832, family name changed to Melville. Took job as a bank clerk at age twelve, then worked in his brother's cap and fur store; attended Lansingburgh Academy and studied surveying and engineering. Published first work, "Fragments from a Writing Desk" in a Lansingburgh newspaper, 1839. Signed on to a ship to Liverpool, 1839. On his return, taught in a school in Brunswick on the Hudson, then sought work in Illinois and Manhattan. Signed on to whaling ship *Acushnet*, 1841. Jumped ship at the island of Nukuheva, 1842. Enlisted in U.S. Navy, 1843–44. Published *Typee*, 1846, based on his experiences at sea. Married Elizabeth Shaw, 1847. Popularity declined after *Moby-Dick*, 1851, but continued to write prose until *The Confidence Man*, 1857. Moved back to New York City, 1863. Began a nineteen-year career as customs inspector, 1866. *Clarel*, a long poem, published 1876. Final prose work was *Billy Budd*, published 1924. Died September 28, 1891.

Selected Works

Collection
The Writings of Herman Melville. Edited by Harrison Hayford, Hershel Parker, and G. Thomas Tanselle. Evanston: Northwestern University Press and Newberry Library, 1968– .

Novels
Typee: A Peep at Polynesian Life. 1846.
Omoo: A Narrative of Adventures in the South Seas. 1847.
Mardi: and a Voyage Thither. 1849.
Redburn: His First Voyage. 1849.
White Jacket; or The World in a Man-of-War. 1850.
Moby-Dick; or, The Whale. 1851.
Pierre; or, the Ambiguities. 1852.
Israel Potter: His Fifty Years of Exile. 1855.
The Confidence Man: His Masquerade. 1857.

Short Stories and Other Short Prose Works
The Piazza Tales. 1856.
John Marr and Other Sailors. 1888.
Billy Budd, Foretopman. Edited by Raymond Weaver. In *Billy Budd and Other Prose Pieces*. London: Constable, 1924.

Poetry
Battle-Pieces, and Aspects of the War. 1866.
Clarel: A Poem and Pilgimage in the Holy Land. 1876.
Timoleon. 1891.

Letters
Leyda, J., ed. *The Melville Log*. New York: Harcourt Brace, 1951.
Minnigerode, Meade. *Some Personal Letters of Herman Melville and a Bibliography*, New York: Brick Row Book Shop, 1922.

Bibliography

Allan, Gay Wilson. *Melville and His World*. London: Thames and Hudson, 1971.
Bloom, Harold, ed. *Herman Melville*. New York: Chelsea House, 1986.
Gale, Robert L. *A Herman Melville Encyclopedia*. Westport, Conn.: Greenwood Press, 1996.
Garner, Stanton. *The Civil War World of Herman Melville*. Lawrence: University Press of Kansas, 1993.
Higgins, Brian. *Herman Melville: An Annotated Bibliography, 1846–1930*. Boston: G. K. Hall, 1979.
———. *Herman Melville: A Reference Guide, 1831–1960*. Boston: G. K. Hall, 1987.
Higgins, Brian and Hershel Parker, eds. *Herman Melville: The Contemporary Reviews*. Cambridge, U.K.: Cambridge University Press, 1995.
Hillway, Tyrus. *Herman Melville*. Boston: Twayne, 1979.

Lawrence, D. H. "Herman Melville's *Typee* and *Omoo*" and "Herman Melville's *Moby Dick*." In *Studies in Classic American Literature*. London: M. Secker, 1924.

Lee, A. Robert, ed. *Herman Melville: Reassessments*. London: Vision, 1984.

Miller, James E. *A Reader's Guide to Herman Melville*. London: Thames and Hudson, 1962.

Robertson-Lorant, Laurie. *Melville: A Biography*. New York: Clarkson Potter, 1996.

MÉMOIRES D'OUTRE-TOMBE (MEMOIRS FROM BEYOND THE GRAVE) 1848–1850

Memoirs by François-Auguste-René, Vicomte de Chateaubriand

François-Auguste-René, Vicomte de Chateaubriand's memoirs are as self-revelatory, paradoxical, and rhetorically hyperbolic as one would expect from the so-called father of French Romanticism. In 1809, he described the introspective, confessional aim of what he then called the *Mémoires de ma vie* (*Memoires of my Life*) when he wrote "I am undertaking the history of my ideas and feelings, not of my life." But by 1832, his vision of both himself and of his place in French political and literary history had become more Romantically self-oriented, melancholic, and nostalgic, as evidenced when he wrote, "I am writing principally to give an account of myself to myself. I have never been happy. . . . Today . . . having attained life's highest point, I have already begun my descent to the grave; before my death, I want above all to recall my good years, and to explain my unexplainable heart." For more than forty years, from 1803 to 1847, Chateaubriand wrote and rewrote his narrative, seeing himself as a Byronic hero whose four careers—author, traveler, diplomat-politician, diarist-historian—would serve to recount, in epic style, the age of Revolution, of Napoleonic Empire, and of post-Restoration France. To do so, he divided his memoirs into four parts.

Part 1, comprised of books 1 through 5, was written primarily between 1811 and 1822, and recounts Chateaubriand's childhood in Brittany, his unhappy family life at Combourg, his love for his sister Lucile, his schooling, and the beginnings of his military career during which, in Paris in 1789, he witnessed the fall of the Bastille. In Part 2, books 6 through 12 he recounts his voyage to America and its literary influence on his worldview, his return to France on hearing of the arrest of Louis XVI, his enlistment in the royalist army, defeat and exile in England, and his love affair with Charlotte Ives. In this section, Chateaubriand also draws comparisons between himself and Lord Byron, the archetypal Romantic hero-figure. Like René, the hero of Chateaubriand's most successful novel of the same name, Childe Harold, hero of Byron's *Childe Harold's Pilgrimage*, rejected his wealthy, feudal background and upbringing. René came to serve as an iconic Romantic model, as did Childe Harold. Chateaubriand, mimicking Byron, had made his own pilgrimage to the East. However, in an imaginary dialogue with Byron, Chateaubriand rejects the notion of literary influence, insisting rather that he is an equal of Byron, as they are both contemporary creators of mythic heroes.

In Part 2, books 6 through 12, dated 1836, Chateaubriand recounts his life after his return to France in 1800, noting his first literary successes—*Atala, René, le Génie du christianisme* (*The Genius of Christianity*), and his resultant fame in France.

Appointed first secretary to the French embassy in Rome by Napoleon Bonaparte in 1803, Chateaubriand resigned his post a year later on receiving word of the execution of the Duke d'Enghien, one of the last Bourbon heirs. The event caused a break with Napoleon that lasted the rest of Chateaubriand's life. His travels in the Middle East in 1806–7 also figure in the *Mémoires*; he compares extracts from his diary with the *Itinéraire à Jérusalem*, which he had published in 1811.

Part 3, books 13 through 24, is divided into two chronological periods, marked by the fall of Napoleon and the Restoration. Books 13–18 present his political and diplomatic career while the remaining five (19–24) analyze his complex attitude toward Napoleon. Perhaps nothing shows more clearly Chateaubriand's Romantic nature than the ease with which he is able to maintain mutually contradictory sentiments over such a long period. For example, he writes about Napoleon, "I always felt great and sincere admiration for Bonaparte, even at the height of my attacks against Napoleon." Chateaubriand's paradoxical opinions may be explained by his politics. An aristocratic royalist, he abhorred democracy, although he felt obliged to achieve some sort of balance between his views and those of the majority of his peers. As a result, he secretly approved the emperor's absolutism. Chateaubriand, an aristocrat who would abandon politics in 1830 after the fall of Charles X—that least democratic of monarchs—confessed he was bewildered by the Emperor's popular success: "One wonders by what magic Bonaparte, who is so aristocratic, so much the enemy of the people, managed to achieve the popularity he enjoys."

Summarizing his political career after 1815, Chateaubriand recalls his position as French ambassador to Rome (in 1821 and again in 1828–29) and England (in 1822), his forced resignation from the position of minister of foreign affairs in 1824, and his abandonment of politics after the 1830 revolution and fall of Charles X, in Chateaubriand's estimation the last legitimate king of France. Also included in this section is Chateaubriand's portrait of the love of his life, Mme. Récamier, whose portrait by François Gérard remains an iconic artistic portrayal of the Romantic woman.

Part 4, the final twelve books, recounts his travels in the Alps, including a pilgrimage to Coppet to visit Madame Anne-Louise-Germaine de Staël's grave, and his visit to Charles X, exiled in Prague. He travels to Venice, which sets him meditating on Jean-Jacques Rousseau and once again on Byron, while its cemetery suggests to him Napoleon in Sainte Helena. In the final sentence of his autobiography, Chateaubriand even manages to go "beyond the tomb": "It only remains for me to sit on the edge of my grave, after which I will descend boldly, Crucifix in hand into Eternity."

A. W. HALSALL

Bibliography

Barbéris, Pierre. *Chateaubriand, une réaction au monde moderne.* Paris: Larousse, 1976.

Gautier, Jean-Marc. *Le Style des "Mémoires d'outre-tombe."* Geneva: Droz, 1964.
Guillemin, Henri. *L'Homme des "Mémoires d'outre-tombe."* Paris: Gallimard, 1964.
Painter, George D. *Chateaubriand: A Biography. Volume 1, 1768–93.* London: Chatto and Windus, 1977.

MENDELSSOHN, MOSES 1729–1786

German Jewish philosopher

A major figure in pre-Kantian German philosophy, Moses Mendelssohn spent his entire career managing a silk factory. He became fluent in German and Hebrew and competent in Latin, Greek, English, French, and Italian, though as the son of a Torah scribe, he was educated by the local rabbi, David Fränkel. An ardent rationalist, he spent the better part of his philosophical career analyzing the sense of beauty and our capacity for religious faith and observance. Most significantly, he moved fluidly, though not without controversy, between the Jewish community of Berlin and the world of German letters, philosophy, and, eventually, politics. Mendelssohn is widely regarded as the father of the Haskalah, or Jewish Enlightenment, movement. But to place Mendelssohn's writings on aesthetics and religion alongside his views on human freedom, prejudice, the natural and civil rights of minorities, and the collision of cultures is to find him anticipating major intellectual currents of the Romantic era.

Arriving in Berlin in the early 1740s, Mendelssohn was befriended by two men who widened his intellectual horizons considerably, Abraham Kisch and Aaron Solomon Gumperz. It was Gumperz who introduced Mendelssohn in 1754 to Gotthold Ephraim Lessing, with whom Mendelssohn maintained a vibrant correspondence until Lessing's death. As is well known, Mendelssohn was the model for Lessing's *Natan der Weise* (*Nathan the Wise*, 1779) and their shared interest in both metaphysics and tragedy shaped their literary and philosophical productions. Mendelssohn was a leading critic of then contemporary German writers, reviewing both philosophy and literature for the journals of Friedrich Nicolai. Shortly before Lessing's death, when Lessing argued that human reason evolves through history, Mendelssohn strongly, though tacitly, dissented. After Lessing's death, Mendelssohn took on the task of denying Friedrich Heinrich Jacobi's charge that Lessing had died a committed Spinozist. In *An die Freunde Lessings* (*To the Friends of Lessing*, 1786), he refuted Jacobi's charge, but the debate tapped painful, unresolved questions about Mendelssohn's own complex relation to Benedict de Spinoza, and Mendelssohn died of a heart attack within days of completing the manuscript.

Mendelssohn's early philosophical writings advance the notion of autonomous, subjective aesthetic judgment. Like Alexander Gottlieb Baumgarten, Johann Christoph Gottsched, and others, he elaborated the aesthetic and psychological ramifications of a metaphysics in the tradition of Gottfried Wilhelm Leibnitz and Christian Wolff. In *Briefe über die Empfindungen* (*Letters on the Sentiments*, 1755), he distinguished between metaphysical perfection and its imperfect, sublunar mode, the beautiful. When Mendelssohn expanded this aesthetics in his *Philosophische Schriften* (Philosophical Writings, 1761), he evoked a faculty theory of mind that was to be important to Immanuel Kant; perhaps in his writing on genius, which Mendelssohn takes to be productive of the beautiful, he comes closest to Kant's understanding of the mind's shaping powers. In 1763, he was awarded a first prize by the Prussian Royal Academy of Sciences, but even so, King Frederick II refused to ratify his 1771 election to the academy.

In his philosophical writings on religion, Mendelssohn explores the existence of God, the immortality of the soul, and the notion of human freedom, all within a rationalist framework. His theistic sympathy for revealed religion places him firmly within the Leibnitzian tradition of the German Enlightenment. In *Morgenstunden* (*Morning Hours*, 1785), he revives the ontological argument for the existence of God: to conceive of a perfect, divine God necessarily entails God's existence. Unlike the French deists, Mendelssohn conceived of God in moral terms as a being whose very existence promotes the moral perfection of humanity and the cosmos. In his *Phaedon* (1767), a reworking of Plato's *Phaedo*, Mendelssohn follows Leibnitz in arguing that the soul is an imperishable substance, not a compound, and that it outlasts the body; on the question of the soul's retention of consciousness, Mendelssohn appeals to the goodness of God, which impels souls toward moral perfection. Along these lines, he embraces divine retribution as but another way in which God secures goodness for humanity.

The tenor of Mendelssohn's approach to religion changed markedly in his public dispute with the Swiss clergyman Johann Kasper Lavater. In 1769, Lavater challenged Mendelssohn in print to convert to Christianity in light of the "irrefutable" arguments of the Calvinist theologian Charles Bonnet. Mendelssohn responded in 1770 by undermining the question, but this encounter launched a decade in which he came to terms philosophically, politically, and emotionally with his own Jewish faith and observance. Though Lavater himself apologized in 1771 (in part under pressure from fellow churchmen), Mendelssohn continued to be an object of attack in pamphlets, booklets, and sermons. Galvanized, Mendelssohn played a crucial role in obtaining civil rights and protections for Jews in Switzerland, Dresden, Saxony, Königsberg, and Prussia. When Alsatian Jews appealed to him to plead their case to the French government, Mendelssohn strategically asked a gentile jurist, Christian Wilhelm von Dohm, to write on their behalf. Dohm's essay *Über die buergerliche Verbesserung der Juden* (*On the Civil Improvement of the Jews,*

1781) (which some believe Mendelssohn to have coauthored), opened a crucial phase for Jewish emancipation in Europe, though Mendelssohn would take later issue with Dohm's characterization of Jewish "depravity."

Yet it was in Mendelssohn's magisterial *Jerusalem, oder Über religiöse Macht und Judentum* (*Jerusalem, or On Religious Power and Judaism*, 1783), that he finally synthesized his rationalist views on religion with his evolving thinking about Judaism. For Mendelssohn, religion is axiomatically a matter of conscience; therefore no religious institution has the right of coercion, including the right to excommunicate. Only the state has the right to use force on its citizens, though it must not infringe on the right to peaceful religious observances or limit a citizen's status or rights by virtue of his or her beliefs. Furthermore, Mendelssohn maintains that Judaism, unlike Christianity, is antidogmatic, and that Judaism lays no special claim to doctrines available to all human beings through reason. What distinguishes Judaism is Mosaic law, which Mendelssohn construes as an historical artifact, the particular way in which God ordained the Jewish people to approach moral perfection. Finally, Mendelssohn's rhetoric of tolerance and emancipation flatly rejects the notion that all religions can or should merge into one creed. Perhaps his final answer to Lavater lies in his conviction that "Reverence for God must draw a line between speculation and observance, beyond which no conscientious person may go." After Mendelssohn's death, several of his children would draw their lines elsewhere, converting to Christianity; most notable of these was Abraham, the father of the composer Felix Mendelssohn.

ESTHER SCHOR

Anonymous, *Moses Mendelssohn*. Reprinted courtesy of AKG.

Biography

Born in Dessau, September 6, 1729. Followed Rabbi David Fränkel to Berlin, 1743. Became tutor in household of Isaak Bernhard, 1750. Met Gotthold Ephraim Lessing, became accountant for Bernhard, 1754. "Letters on the Sentiments," 1755. Hebrew commentary on Maimonides's *Logical Terms*, 1760. Published *Philosophical Writings*; became a manager at Bernhard, 1761. Marriage to Fromet Gugenheim, 1762. Awarded first prize by the Prussian Royal Academy of Sciences for *Abhandlung über die Evidenz in den metaphysischen Wissenschaften* (*Essay on Evidence in Metaphysical Science*); birth of daughter, Sara, 1763. Death of Sara and birth of daughter, Brendel, 1764. Birth of son, Hayyim, 1766. Publication of *Phaedon* and birth of daughter, Reikel, 1767. Became comanager of firm with Isaak Bernhard's widow; birth of son Mendel Abraham, "Letter to Lavater," 1769. Lavater's reply, Mendelssohn's "Epilogue" and birth of son, Joseph, 1770. *Philosophical Writings* (second edition); denied membership in Royal Academy, 1771. Translated Torah into German, birth of daughter Yente; death of son Mendel, 1775. Birth of son Abraham, who became father of the composer Felix Mendelssohn, 1776. Visit to Kant and Hamann and intervention on behalf of Dresden Jewish community, 1777. Birth and death of daughter Sisa, 1778. Became sole manager of Bernhard firm, 1781. Birth of son, Nathan, 1782. Publication of Torah and Psalms translation and of *Jerusalem*, 1783. Died on January 4, 1786; posthumous publication of "To the Friends of Lessing," 1786.

Selected Works

Philosophische Gespräche. 1755.
Briefe über die Empfindungen. 1755.
Moses Mendelssohn an die Freunde Lessings. 1786.
Memoirs of Moses Mendelssohn. Translated by M. Samuels. 1825.
Gesammelte Schriften. 1843–45.
Gesammelte Schriften Jubiläumsausgabe, 1929–1984.
Jerusalem and Other Jewish Writings. Translated and edited by Alfred Jospe. 1969.
Jerusalem, or, on Religious Power and Judaism. Translated by Allan Arkush, Hanover: University Press of New England, 1983.
Philosophical Writings. Translated and edited by Daniel O. Dahlstrom. 1997.

Bibliography

Altmann, Alexander. *Moses Mendelssohn: A Biographical Study*, Tuscaloosa: University of Alabama Press, 1973.
Arkush, Allan. *Moses Mendelssohn and the Enlightenment*. Albany: State University of New York Press, 1994.
Beck, Lewis White. *Early German Philosophy: Kant and his Predecessors*. Cambridge, Mass.: Harvard University Press, 1969.
Beiser, Frederick C. *The Fate of Reason: German Philosophy from Kant to Fichte*. Cambridge, Mass.: Harvard University Press, 1987.
Dahlstrom, Daniel O. Introduction to Moses Mendelssohn, *Philosophical Writings*. Cambridge: Cambridge University Press, 1997.
Jospe, Eva, ed. and trans. *Moses Mendelssohn: Selections from his Writings*. New York: Viking, 1975.
Jospe, Raphael, ed. *Paradigms in Jewish Philosophy*. Madison: Fairleigh Dickinson University Press, 1997.
"Mendelssohn, Moses." In *Encyclopaedia Judaica*, CD-ROM ed. Judaica Multimedia (Israel) Ltd.

Rotenstreich, Nathan. *Jewish Philosophy in Modern Times: From Mendelssohn to Rosenzweig.* New York: Henry Holt, 1968.

———. *Jews and German Philosophy.* New York: Schocken, 1984.

MENDELSSOHN-BARTHOLDY, JAKOB LUDWIG FELIX 1809-1847

German composer

Jakob Ludwig Felix Mendelssohn-Bartholdy (known commonly as Felix Mendelssohn) was atypical of the early nineteenth-century generation of German Romantic composers in terms of ethnicity, musical education, and stylistic preferences. Born into a family of Jewish Protestant converts of financial wealth and cultural prominence, Mendelssohn was perceived during his lifetime as a musician catering to the conservative tastes of bourgeois and aristocratic audiences. Queen Victoria, one of his professed admirers, sang his songs with a delight documented in the composer's letters. The educated bourgeoisie, appreciative of art that stayed within the boundaries of received values, saw in Mendelssohn the exponent of a tradition of serenity and composure that was being vehemently challenged in the 1830s by rebellious figures such as Hector Berlioz (with whom Mendelssohn was on friendly terms in Rome in 1830) and the mesmerizing virtuosi Niccolò Paganini (Mendelssohn's companion at various private gatherings in London in 1833) and Franz Liszt (whom Mendelssohn had met in Paris when Liszt was a brilliant young pianist).

While Mendelssohn's facility in composing and the abundant variety of his melodic ideas have been frequently compared to those of Wolfgang Amadeus Mozart, and the size of the orchestral ensemble for which he wrote compared to that of Franz Joseph Haydn, the artful orchestration is indisputably his own. His early training, unlike that of many representative composers of the earlier part of the century, consisted of serious study of baroque counterpoint and fugue, chorale-tune harmonization, and classical orchestration under the rigorous guidance of Karl Friedrich Zelter, the director of the Berlin Singakademie and the last in a line of composers and teachers that had begun with Johann Sebastian Bach. The constant practice of eighteenth-century compositional techniques and genres was largely responsible for the impeccable technical skill and formal clarity manifested in Mendelssohn's works. His style is perhaps best characterized as "classicizing Romanticism" or "Romanticized baroque," both terms evoking the dexterous orchestral experiments and Romantic pictorial effects superimposed on forms of classical sobriety and distinction.

Critics generally agree in seeing Mendelssohn as a composer of vivid melodic imagination, respectfully bowing to the masters of the past. Mendelssohn held in special esteem the music of Bach and George Frideric Handel, both German Baroque composers of considerable stature among their own contemporaries. After Bach's death in 1750, the majority of his works were no longer performed and had been nearly forgotten, so Mendelssohn undertook to restore the composer's prestige among his German fellows. The 1829 Berlin performance of Bach's Passion According to St. Matthew at the Singakademie, with Mendelssohn conducting from the piano, was met with unprecedented enthusiasm and ultimately led to a considerable Bach revival in the nineteenth century. The culmination of this trend was the founding, in 1850, of the Bach Gesellschaft (the Bach Society) and the beginning of the publication of the first complete edition of Bach's works.

Mendelssohn's thirteen symphonies for strings, composed between 1821 and 1823, are the work of his youth; manifestly Classical in concept and style, they emphasize regularity of form and sparse instrumentation. His five mature symphonies make consistent use of the sonata-allegro form; this structure, comprised of three distinct sections of which the second is a development and the third a recapitulation of the first, responds to perfection and the expressed need of classicism for balance and symmetry. Baroque-like contrapuntal and fugal passages appear in the fourth movement of his Symphony No. 1 in C Minor (op. 11, 1824), a work that is also reminiscent of Mozart's Symphony No. 40 in G Minor and Beethoven's Fifth Symphony in C Minor in its shifting from a minor to a major key in the course of the last movement. The "Lobgesang" Symphony of 1840 (Symphony No. 2 in B-flat Major, op. 52), composed to celebrate the four hundredth anniversary of the invention of movable printing, uses soloists, choir, and organ in the manner of the Baroque cantata, on which its last movement is modeled. In this same movement, an even more distant past is evoked by the Renaissance-like a cappella singing of the chorale *Nun danket wir Gott.* Both the first and the last movement of the "Reformation" Symphony of 1832 (Symphony No. 5 in D Major, op. 107), a monument to the Romanticized Baroque originally composed for the 1830 anniversary of the Augsburg Confession, include Lutheran chorale tunes—*Ein feste Burg is unser Gott* (*A Mighty Fortress is Our God*) among them—and copious fugal writing of the kind Mendelssohn must have learned while apprenticing under Zelter, studying the scores of Bach's Passion According to St. Matthew and other eighteenth-century works.

Mendelssohn's two oratorios based on biblical texts, the St. Paul Oratorio (op. 36, 1836) and the Elijah Oratorio (op. 70, 1846), composed in the best Handelian tradition of oratorio writing, were and still are immensely successful, especially with English-speaking audiences. While Mendelssohn was careful to follow the models set forth by his illustrious predecessor and thus wrote arias, recitatives, and choruses, in the St. Paul Oratorio he refrained from composing a separate part for the narrator (*testo*)—a part that, consisting in the declamation of the story in recitative-like fashion, had been one of the main ingredients of the late-Baroque oratorio. Instead, the task of storytelling is divided among soloists and choir, with St. Paul being, as Leon Plantinga has noted, the only character "consistently subject to dramatic impersonation."

In an age when the composition of new religious music was nearly abandoned, its chief instrument of expression—the organ—was neglected and the relatively newly invented piano reigned supreme. Despite this, Mendelssohn—an experienced organist—wrote organ preludes, fugues, and sonatas exhibiting rigorous contrapuntal technique and employing hymn tunes taken from the Lutheran choral repertory.

While many Romantic composers of his generation were overt and impassioned supporters of program music, Mendelssohn's programmaticism was a subtle one; the composer (himself an admirable painter) excelled in converting visual or literary images into musical sounds, yet he did so discreetly and gracefully. His programmatic concert overtures were composed as one-movement pieces; four of them—*Ein Sommernachtstraum* (*A Midsummer Night's Dream*, op. 21, 1826), *Meeresstille und glückliche Fahrt* (*Calm Sea and Happy Voyage*, op. 27, 1832), *Die schöne Melusine* (*The Beautiful Melusine*, op. 32, 1833), and *Ruy Blas* (1839, op. 95)—were based on literary works by William Shakespeare, Johann Wolfgang von Goethe, Franz Grillparzer, and Victor Hugo, respectively. Their regular, classical sonata-allegro structures were instilled with a Romantic feel, a variety of instrumental color, and subtle shadings intended to suggest rather than state. In this respect, the use of pizzicato in the strings to depict an elflike, dreamy atmosphere in the overture to *A Midsummer Night's Dream*, a play for which, at some later point, Mendelssohn wrote complete incidental music, is rightly famous. The *"Italian" Symphony* (Symphony No. 4 in A Major, op. 90, 1833) and the *"Scotch" Symphony* (Symphony No. 3 in A Minor, op. 56, subsequently dedicated to Queen Victoria, 1842) were conceived in the same vein and are usually regarded as a pair of which the first depicts the classical landscapes, congenial people, and vivacious dances of the south: Mendelssohn, like Goethe (his Weimar host, friend, and mentor, to whom the composer was first introduced in 1821), had visited Italy as part of the customary "grand tour." The second work brings to the fore the sunless, enigmatic north, and evokes the tragic figure of Mary, Queen of Scots. The Scottish countryside, whose landscapes Mendelssohn sketched during an 1829 visit, is the protagonist of the concert overture *Die Hebriden* (*The Hebrides*, op. 26, 1830–32; also known as *Fingal's Cave*).

Mendelssohn had absolute mastery of all compositional tools then at the disposal of a gifted artist, and was not opposed by any means to innovation, albeit always mediated by impeccably proportioned formal contours. His contributions to the field of orchestration are distinguished, and his use of wind instruments to produce an astounding variety of orchestral color is brilliant and unprecedented. His occasional departure from classical rigor in musical forms is also notable, particularly with regard to the use of transitions to connect the traditionally discrete movements of the symphony: the four sections of the *"Scotch" Symphony* are united through passages reminiscent of motives found in the Introduction, as are the first and second movements of the *"Lobgesang" Symphony*. Such procedures aligned themselves with the iconoclastic treatment that composers more radically Romantic than Mendelssohn applied to forms inherited from a previous epoch. As with Beethoven's Ninth Symphony, in the *"Reformation" Symphony* Mendelssohn reversed the position of the slow and scherzo movements (normally the second and the third, respectively). By the turn of the century the minuet and trio forming the third movement of the classical symphony were replaced with the scherzo, a vigorous, bouncy section in triple meter followed by a contrasting trio and the return of the scherzo; although this provided dramatic contrast between the scherzo and the moderately paced second movement, and the scherzo and the fourth movement were distinct from each other in terms of character, texture, and meter, there was no great difference between the latter two in terms of tempo. Moving the scherzo into second position made a greater impact on the architecture of the symphony as a whole, as now the contrast between the third (slow) and fourth (fast) movements was clearly sharper. Mendelssohn's scherzos are not as wild and stormy—or as heavy—as Beethoven's; instead, they are almost ethereal, full of grace, and a preferred place for experiments with instrumental color, most notably strings and winds. In fact, even among his chamber works, those that include scherzos infused with his characteristic tone colors are more prominent: the Octet of 1825, the Piano Trio in C Minor (op. 66), and the String Quartet in A Minor.

As a youth Mendelssohn took violin lessons with Eduard Rietz and piano lessons with Ludwig Berger, and later became a virtuoso pianist in much demand on the continent and in England. His Violin Concerto in E Minor (op. 64, 1844) has survived in today's repertory due to the expert manipulation of the instrument's technical and expressive capabilities, sheer delightfulness of melodic lines, and innovative formal treatment of the first movement. Normally a sonata form with double exposition, this movement called for a first orchestral statement of two contrasting themes, both in the tonic key (the first exposition) followed by a second statement of the themes by the featured instrument with a modified key relationship (the second exposition). In this case, the orchestral exposition is dispensed with, and the violin makes its entrance from the onset of the movement after a few measures of orchestral introduction establishing the key. As with the violin concerto, the two piano concertos of 1831 (op. 25) and 1837 (op. 40) achieve a remarkable balance between Romantic bravura passages and Classical clarity of form. Mendelssohn popularized and promoted these works alongside the piano concertos of Mozart and Beethoven throughout his extremely active career as a pianist.

Of his works for piano, *Lieder ohne Wörte* (*Songs without Words*, opp. 19b, 30, 38, 53, 62, 67, 85, and 102), a collection of miniature pieces, were composed and published at intervals in six volumes—(two more volumes appeared posthumously)—and remain some of the most popular pieces in any pianist's repertory. The title of the collection is, in a way, a proclamation against programmaticism, that music can stand alone without the help of words. These miniatures were part of a trend that sought to encapsulate singular moods, thoughts, or scenes in musical aphorisms written for the most Romantic of instruments, the piano, and they were very much at home in the atmosphere of both bourgeois and aristocratic soirées and public concert halls. For piano solo Mendelssohn wrote innumerable fantasias, caprices, studies, scherzos, variations, sonatas, and much more. In all of them the hand is confident, the technique irreproachable; the harmony wisely traditional; and the melody of a lyrical, sometimes dreamy quality, with occasional vigorous strokes and bravura passages for good measure. Particularly representative of this style are the *Rondo Capriccioso* (op. 14, known in two versions: the early one, a study, dated 1828; the definitive version composed in 1830), and the *Capriccio* in F-sharp Minor (1825). Mendelssohn's lifelong fascination with baroque counterpoint and Bach's works, notably *The Well-Tempered Clavier*, is again apparent in the six preludes and fugues for piano composed at various times and collected in 1837.

Like most composers of the nineteenth century, Mendelssohn produced a plethora of literature for the voice: solo songs with piano accompaniment (some on poems by Johann Wolfgang von Goethe, Heinrich Heine, and Johann Christoph Friedrich von Schiller, some inspired by lesser poets), concert arias, choral songs, and sacred music. His music for the stage, including the youthful *Singspiele* (composed between 1820 and 1825) and the incidental music for *Ruy Blas*; Sophocles' *Antigone* (op. 55, 1841) and *Oedipus at Colonnus* (1845, op. 93), and Jean Racine's *Athalie* (op. 74, 1845) enjoyed some amount of success at the time but are no longer part of the modern standard repertory.

Mendelssohn's name has endured thanks to his gift of maintaining a singular balance between Classical and Romantic elements, his tuneful themes and rich orchestration, and his complete mastery of compositional techniques. As a conductor, pianist, and music director he expended an immense amount of energy in furthering the best interest of German music and musicians, and was rewarded by receiving an honorary doctorate from the University of Leipzig and an honorary citizenship from the City of Leipzig.

LUMINITA FLOREA

See also **Mendelssohn-Hensel, Fanny**

Biography

Born in Hamburg, February 3, 1809. Early musical studies in composition, piano, and violin; composed *Singspiele* (operas with German text), sacred choral works, symphonies for strings, chamber music, violin and piano concertos which he performed with his sister Fanny, 1821–29. Visited Goethe at Weimar (the first of many future meetings), 1821. Began study of drawing, parents converted to the Protestant faith, 1822. Confirmed in the Protestant faith, met G. W. F. Hegel and Heinrich Heine at the family residence in Berlin; with Fanny, read the novels of Jean Paul and the plays of Shakespeare, 1825. Matriculated at the University of Berlin, 1827. Attended Hegel's lectures on aesthetics, 1828–29. Conducted performance of J. S. Bach's *Passion According to St. Matthew*, 1829. Music director at Düsseldorf, excelled as a choral conductor, revived the oratorios of Handel and Haydn, 1833. Began activities as conductor of the Gewandhaus Orchestra in Leipzig, father died, 1835. Honorary doctorate from the University of Leipzig, meets Cécile Jeanrenaud in Frankfurt, 1836; married her in 1837. Conducted the first performance of Schubert's Symphony No. 9 in C Major, which had been rediscovered by Robert Schumann in Vienna, 1839. Conducted series of music festivals in Germany and England, 1838–40. Appointed Kapellmeister in Berlin; traveled constantly between Berlin and Leipzig; received at Buckingham Palace by Queen Victoria and Prince Albert, 1840. Mother died, 1842. City of Leipzig conferred honorary citizenship, became one of the founders of the Leipzig Conservatory, 1843. Sister Fanny died, 1847. Died in Leipzig, November 4, 1847, as a result of a series of strokes.

Bibliography

Citron, Marcia J. *The Letters of Fanny Hensel to Felix Mendelssohn.* Stuyvesant, N.Y.: Pendragon Press, 1987.

Cooper, John Michael. "Felix Mendelssohn-Bartholdy, Ferdinand David, und Johann Sebastian Bach: Mendelssohns Bach-Anffassung im Spiegel der Wiederentdecken der 'Chaconne,' " *Mendelssohn-Studien* 10 (1997): 157–79.

Deutsch, Otto Erich. "The Discovery of Schubert's Great C-Major Symphony: A Story in Fifteen Letters," *Musical Quarterly* 38 (1952): 528–32.

Elvers, Rudolf, ed. *Felix Mendelssohn: A Life in Letters.* Translated by Craig Tomlinson. New York: Fromm, 1986.

Jenkins, David and Mark Visocchi. *Mendelssohn in Scotland.* London: Chappell, 1978.

Jones, Peter Ward. "The Library of Felix Mendelssohn-Bartholdy." In *Festschrift Rudolf Elvers zum 60. Geburtstag.* Edited by Ernst Herttrich and Hans Schneider. Tutzing: H. Schneider, 1985.

Jones, Peter Ward. *The Mendelssohns on Honeymoon: The 1837 Diary of Felix and Cécile Mendelssohn-Bartholdy Together with Letters to their Families.* Translated by Peter Ward Jones. Oxford, U.K.: Clarendon Press, 1997.

Konold, Wulf. *Felix Mendelssohn-Bartholdy und seine Zeit.* Laaber: Laaber Verlag, 1984.

Richter, Arnd. *Mendelssohn: Leben, Werke, Dokumente.* Zurich: Altantis Musikbuch, 2000.

Todd, Larry R. "Piano Music Reformed: the Case of Felix Mendelssohn-Bartholdy." In *nineteenth-Century Piano Music.* Edited by Larry R. Todd, New York: Schirmer, 1990.

———, ed. *Mendelssohn and his World.* Princeton, N.J.: Princeton University Press, 1991.

Werner, Ralf. ". . . Ich sehe sie nun zugleich alle durch und lerne sie kennen . . .": Felix Mendelssohn-Bartholdy und die wirklich Alte Musik," *Basler Jahrbuch für historische Musikpraxis* 21 (1997): 101–28.

MENDELSSOHN-HENSEL, FANNY 1805–1847

German composer

Born in Hamburg to a musical family of Jewish converts, Fanny, the elder sister of Felix Mendelssohn, was a composer and performer in her own right who during the siblings' adolescent years was seen as more naturally gifted and technically accomplished than her brother. During this early period in her relationship with Felix, Fanny assumed the role of a mentor to her younger brother. The siblings' musical training followed an identical path: both studied composition with Carl Friedrich Zelter, both took piano lessons with Ignaz Moscheles, and both were thoroughly conversant with the music of Johann Sebastian Bach, Ludwig van Beethoven, George Frideric Handel, and Wolfgang Amadeus Mozart, the music of the "old masters," for whom both maintained a lifelong admiration and reverence. These, alongside Franz Joseph Haydn and Luigi Cherubini, were the composers Fanny included in her 1825 proposal to establish a society for instrumental music lovers. Brother and sister critiqued, and even completed, each other's works, and the correspondence between them during Felix's years at Düsseldorf (from 1833) and Leipzig (from 1835) includes ample discussions of compositions by both siblings. Their common interests were not limited to music; when in 1827 Felix was admitted to the University of Berlin, brother and sister frequented the course in physical geography taught by the illustrious naturalist, geographer, and explorer Alexander von Humboldt.

Fanny's and Felix's lives were so intimately connected that entire chapters in biographies of Felix have been devoted to Fanny and her relationship with her brother; yet for nearly a century and a half music history studies have seldom discussed Fanny Mendelssohn-Hensel's individual voice and contributions as a composer. That her works have been ignored for a long time is largely due to the fact that many of the relevant documents were, and still are, in private hands, and thus cannot be freely examined or published. The largest publicly-held collection, including letters, notebooks, and compositions by Fanny, is now in the Mendelssohn Archive at the Staatsbibliothek Preussischer Kulturbesitz in Berlin. The Bodleian Library is the keeper of a large number of her autograph letters to her brother—a lifelong correspondence, comprised of 279 letters, that began during Felix's visit of November 1821 to Weimar, where he was introduced to Johann Wolfgang von Goethe. The letters have been published only recently, and form an important source for scholarly investigation into Fanny's artistic biography.

On the other hand, the little attention Fanny's compositions have received derives from the general nineteenth-century expectations that a woman should devote her time to her family and direct her efforts toward becoming a good wife and mother. Unlike her brother Felix, whose efforts toward building a career as a professional musician were encouraged and applauded, Fanny's studying, composing, and performing of music were expected to merely enhance her femininity, not to provide her with a career. Writing to Fanny in 1828, her father Abraham Mendelssohn made it clear that from his perspective a woman's only profession was to be mistress of the house.

The young woman was not only a skilled composer, but a prolific one as well; information about her works, however, comes mainly from other people's references—for instance, a letter by Zelter informing Goethe that Fanny Mendelssohn had just finished composing her thirty-second fugue (a work whose whereabouts are unknown). Further references are found in her letters, such as the one she wrote to Felix in London announcing that she had completed a prelude for organ intended for her wedding.

In 1823, Abraham Mendelssohn, assisted by his wife Lea, initiated a series of musical gatherings after the fashion of the day; since these musical encounters took place in the family salon on Sundays, they were called *Sonntagsmusik*. A place for the family and friends to come together and make music once a week, the *Sonntagsmusik* provided the opportunity for Fanny's and Felix's compositions to be performed. The salons were discontinued for a few years, and when, after marrying court painter Wilhelm Hensel, Fanny reinstated them, they attracted the finest society of music lovers, and a local and international performing crowd that included several well-known virtuosi of the highest caliber alongside local amateur singers. In their company Mendelssohn-Hensel excelled not only as the mistress of the house and organizer of the musicales, but also as a solo pianist, accompanist, composer, and a choral and orchestral conductor. Her diaries, begun in 1829, are filled with detailed descriptions of performances and performers, and it is from these entries that one becomes aware of the ambitiousness of the enterprise: in

addition to solo, chamber music, and small-scale choral pieces, she put on scenes from Mozart's *Don Giovanni* and *La clemenza di Tito* with the participation of singer Clara Novello, Felix Mendelssohn's Saint Paul Oratorio, featuring the English contralto Mary Shaw, and Beethoven's *Fidelio*, performed by a choir of amateurs. Her own compositions were performed on occasion, and those by her brother occupied a place of honor. The musicales continued throughout Mendelssohn-Hensel's life, with two notable interruptions. The first was the interval between August 1839 and August 1840, when, accompanied by her husband and son Sebastian, she spent one full year in Italy.

Paralleling Felix Mendelssohn's earlier journey to that country, Fanny Mendelssohn-Hensel's travels, minutely recorded in her diary, took her to Milan, Verona, Padua, Venice, Florence, and Rome—where she befriended French painters Jean-Auguste-Dominique Ingres and Horace Vernet and the French composer Charles Gounod, whose acquaintance she later renewed at her *Sonntagsmusik* in Berlin. The Italian experience inspired Fanny to compose *Das Jahr* (*The year*, 1840 or 1841), a cycle of twelve character pieces for piano, each named after a month of the year; and *Einleitung zu lebenden Bildern* (1841) for narrator and choir. The musical encounters were discontinued again, for about a year and a half, after Lea Mendelssohn's death in 1842.

The "garden house" at 3 Leipziger Strasse in Berlin provided the perfect setting first for Abraham's and then for Fanny's *Sonntagsmusik*: when she married Wilhelm Hensel, the young couple moved to the garden-facing wing of the Mendelssohns' palatial home, where one of the rooms was used as a small concert hall. Wilhelm Hensel, a friend of Achim von Arnim, Clemens Brentano, and Adalbert von Chamisso, was to become one of Fanny's fiercest supporters where her music-making activities were concerned.

Mendelssohn-Hensel was a pianist of brilliant technique and exquisite musical taste, but, unlike Clara Schumann, who made a living by performing as a soloist, she limited her public playing to one appearance: in February 1838 she performed Felix Mendelssohn's Concerto in G Minor for piano in a benefit concert for the poor. With this one exception, her playing was meant solely for the ears of those attending her musical matinees, which were becoming more and more prestigious and were attended toward the end of her life by Franz Liszt and Clara Schumann. Several portraits of the illustrious personages participating in the Sunday musicales were drawn by her husband.

Mendelssohn-Hensel's more than four hundred compositions—lieder, piano sonatas, organ preludes, choral pieces, chamber music works, cantatas—remain mostly unpublished. As a composer she had a marked preference for solo piano pieces and for *lieder* (songs) with piano accompaniment, one of the favorite genres of the Romantic era. Her first lieder were published as Felix's works in 1827 and 1830, respectively; the first composition to appear under her name was *Die Schiffende*, a lied published in 1837 as part of an album including works by several other composers. Fanny tended to group her pieces into cycles of four or six; this is the arrangement of the six lieder on poems by Droysen, begun in 1829 when Felix Mendelssohn left for England.

Unlike her husband, who was very supportive in the matter of Mendelssohn-Hensel seeking publication of her works, Felix Mendelssohn openly discouraged her from doing so: it was mainly his opposition that caused nine years to elapse between *Die Schiffende*—a composition much admired by Robert Schumann, who at the time was the editor of *Die Neue Zeitschrift für Musik*—and the next group of works, which Mendelssohn-Hensel decided to publish at the exhortations of councilor Robert von Kendell, who was also an excellent pianist. In addition to the six lieder published under Felix Mendelssohn's name, only the pieces grouped under opus numbers one through five appeared in print during her lifetime.

Fanny Mendelssohn-Hensel died of a stroke on May 14, 1847, while rehearsing for one of her Sunday musicales. The day before she had completed her last work, the lied *Bergeslust*. Her brother Felix died six months later.

LUMINITA FLOREA

See also **Mendelssohn-Bartholdy, Jakob Ludwig Felix**

Biography

Born in Hamburg, November 14, 1805. Family moved to Berlin in 1809. Early musical studies with mother, Lea; studied music theory and composition with Zelter; studied piano with Ludwig Berger; chamber music, violin and piano concertos performed with her brother Felix Mendelssohn, with whom she read the novels of Jean Paul and the plays of William Shakespeare, studied piano with Marie Bigot in Paris, 1816. Composed her first work, a lied for her father's birthday, 1819. First three lieder published as Felix's works, 1827. Married Wilhelm Hensel, 1829. Son Sebastian born, 1829; organized the musical gatherings at 3 Leipziger Strasse, known as *Sonntagsmusik*, where she performed as a pianist and conductor. In the early 1830s, composed large-scale dramatic works (cantatas, oratorios). 1835, father died, 1839–40; traveled to Italy. Mother died, 1842. Another visit to Italy, 1845. Died in Berlin, May 14, 1847.

Selected Works

Piano Sonata in F. c. 1821.
Lieder von Fanny für Felix. 1829.
Prelude in F for Organ. 1829.
Prelude in G for Organ. 1829–33.
Lobgesang, cantata. 1831.
Hiob, cantata. 1831.
Oratorium nach Bildern der Bibel. 1831.
Zum Fest der heiligen Cäcilia. 1833.
String Quartet in E-flat. 1834.
Das Jahr: twelve Characterstücke. 1841.
Sechs Lieder, op. 1.
Vier Lieder für das Pianoforte, op. 2. 1846.
Gartenlieder: Sechs Gesänge für Sopran, Alto, Tenor und Bass, op. 3. 1847.
6 Mélodies pour le piano, opp. 4 and 5. 1847.
Piano Trio, op. 11. 1850.

Bibliography

Briscoe, James, ed. *Historical Anthology of Music by Women*. Bloomington: Indiana University Press, 1987.

Cooper, John Michael. *Felix Mendelssohn Bartholdy: A Guide to Research, with an Introduction to Research Concerning Fanny Hensel*. Composer Resource Manuals 54. New York: Routledge, 2001.

Gorrell, Lorraine. *The Nineteenth-Century German Lied*. Portland, Or.: Amadeus Press, 1993.

Helmig, Martina. *Fanny Hensel, geb. Mendelssohn Bartholdy: Das Werk*. Munich, n.p., 1997.

Hensel, Fanny. *The Letters of Fanny Hensel to Felix Mendelssohn*. Collected, edited, and translated by Marcia J. Citron. Stuyvesant, N.Y. Pendragon Press, 1987.

Hensel, Sebastian. *The Mendelssohn Family (1729–1847) From Letters and Journals*. 2nd rev. ed. Translated by Carl Klingeman and an American collaborator. 1882.

Jezic, Diane, and Elizabeth Wood, eds. *Women Composers: The Lost Tradition Found*. 2nd ed. New York: Feminist Press at the City University of New York, 1994.

Tillard, Françoise. *Fanny Mendelssohn*. Translated by Camille Naish. Portland, Or.: Amadeus Press, 1996.

MÉRIMÉE, PROSPER 1803–1870

French short story writer

Prosper Mérimée, perhaps best known as the author of "Carmen," which first appeared in the *Revue des Deux Mondes* (October 1, 1845), is somewhat of an anomaly among the Romantics of his generation; he is a writer whose literary production is not autobiographical in the sentimental sense attaching to many of the works of, say, Victor Hugo, Alfred de Musset, or George Sand. He frequented the salons of the Romantics, establishing friendships with Hugo as well as Stendhal, appreciating the paintings of Eugène Delacroix; yet the portrait of the man that emerges is one of an erudite, witty, prankish, but self-contained person disdaining overt displays of emotion and accepting only conditionally the Romantic program of literary reform. Like the Romantics, Mérimée loved to travel and was sensitive to the appeal of the exotic, but his notion of *la couleur locale* was more intellectual and rooted in a scholarly curiosity about history, custom, and language. Like Hugo and Stendhal, Mérimée champions the liberation of the French theater from the shackles of Classical conventions, but his advocacy of this change is not doctrinal but whimsical and humoristic, partly conveyed through the elaboration of a literary hoax. In the final analysis, what characterizes Mérimée's major contribution to the literature of his time is his capacity to filter the Romantic emotions, the Romantic glorification of love and fascination with violence, through an ironic temperament perfectly suited to the crafting of short stories notable for their brevity, compact organization, seemingly impersonal detachment, and incorporation of shocking details and cruel outcomes.

Mérimée as literary prankster is evident in his collection of plays *Le Théâtre de Clara Gazul, comédienne espagnole* (*The Plays of Clara Gazul, a Spanish Comedian*, 1825), presented as having been authored by a Spanish actress. But the plays, possibly inspired by his friend Stendhal's project for dramatic reform, *Racine et Shakespeare* (1823–25), advocate the abolition of the rule of the three unities and praise the freedom of the Spanish theater.

As if one literary hoax were not enough, Mérimée followed up *Le Théâtre de Clara Gazul* with *La Guzla* (1827), offered as a translation of the poems of an Illyrian bard. More than one "specialist" was fooled, and the Russian poet Aleksandr Pushkin was moved to translate *La Guzla* into Russian, much to Mérimée's simultaneous amusement and embarrassment.

Such prankishness, however brilliant, was only a prelude to a period in Mérimée's life—starting in 1829 and extending through 1845—that witnessed the flowering of his talent as exhibited particularly in that type of French short story known as *la nouvelle* and masterfully illustrated, among his initial endeavors in the genre, by "Mateo Falcone," which appeared first in the *Revue de Paris*, May 3, 1829, before being published in the collection *Mosaïque* (*Mosaic*, 1833). "Mateo Falcone" is a taut, tense tale in which a Corsican father, his actions dictated by the code of honor of his island, executes his only son for betraying the local rule of hospitality and turning in a criminal to the police. In this story, Mérimée's extraordinary and unique skills as a storyteller—his ability to condense the action in just a few pages; his unemotional evocation of shocking violence; his sparse depiction of characters in terms of their essential traits—are already manifest. The only element lacking is personal experience of Corsican culture. But in 1834, Mérimée was named inspector-general of historical monuments and began to travel widely, not only throughout France, but abroad, visiting England, Germany, Italy, Greece, Asia Minor, Spain, and Corsica.

"Colomba," which first appeared in the *Revue des Deux Mondes* on July 1, 1840, was testimony not only to Mérimée's general maturation as a writer but also to his extraordinary ability to blend in a most effective manner the fruits of his direct contact with the Corsican people, the literature he had read about the island, and the stylistic conventions of the short story. The resulting narrative, while appreciably longer than the typical Mérimée tale, abounds in authentic detail about Corsican dress, music, literature, and language as it weaves a story centered on the theme of violent revenge. The portrait of Colomba is typical of Mérimée's characterizations of strong women (as later to be encountered in "Carmen") who dominate, and often manipulate, the men in their lives.

If Mérimée's personal experience of Corsican culture enriched the fabric of "Colomba," the latter work was not to be the only one of this fruitful phase to benefit from the author's direct contact with land and the people evoked in his fiction. As much as Mérimée was taken with Corsica, he was even more enthralled with Spain, which he visited not only in 1830 but four times from 1840 to 1863. (It should be mentioned in passing that from 1826 to 1868 Mérimée made eighteen trips to England, as if to epitomize the vaunted love of travel associated with the Romantics.) The prime literary beneficiary of this enhanced familiarity with the Spanish scene was the short story destined to become forever linked with the writer's name, "Carmen." Not an instant success in 1847 when it appeared in book form (the work was fully appreciated only in later editions and mostly after 1875, the date of Georges Bizet's opera), "Carmen" features a narrator-archaeologist whose involvement in the story (he comes to know both Carmen and Don José) lends authenticity to the tale, even as it resurrects, in the reader's mind, recollections of the literary pranks of the younger Mérimée: for what is one to deem significant in this story, the violently Romantic, inevitably tragic account of Don José's impossible love for Carmen, the learned disquisitions of our narrator on the site of the battle of Munda, the physical characteristics and intriguing customs of the gypsies?

Yet lest one be tempted to represent Mérimée too narrowly as a striking ironic counterpoise to the extravagant sentimentalism of most of the chief Romantic writers of his time, it should be remembered that this learned, detached rationalist did not disdain the attractions of the *conte fantastique* (fantastic tale) cultivated also by the likes of Charles Nodier, among others. "La Venus d'Ille" (1837), which appeared first in the *Revue des Deux Mondes* on May 15, 1837, and "Lokis," written in 1869 but published only in 1873 in the collection *Dernières nouvelles* (*Last Tales*), were arresting examples of Mérimée's use of this genre. In "La Venus d'Ille," Mérimée again introduces a character of impressive erudition, the first-person narrator, and incorporates a plethora of realistic detail to counterbalance the inexplicable, fantastic circumstance of a statue that apparently comes to life with fatal consequences. In "Lokis," however, the element of enigma that both established and delimited the fantastic in "La Venus d'Ille" is missing: the story, possibly inspired by E. T. A. Hoffmann and a Danish short story appearing in the *Revue de Paris* in 1833, is that of a Lithuanian count who is at once a man and a bear (the word *lokis* means "bear" in Lithuanian).

Yet if Mérimée's literary range was perhaps wider than might initially be suggested by his unwillingness to embrace some of the tendencies of his Romantic comrades in arms, including the notion of the writer's political mission, it was nevertheless fairly limited. Mérimée's celebrity rests still on his reputation as the incisive and erudite, but dispassionate and unlyrical, master of the short story form. Indeed, so specifically focused was Mérimée in terms of his aesthetic or stylistic credo that even his literary criticism testified to his limitations in this regard: this sophisticated, cosmopolitan writer—who spoke English and Spanish and had a high regard for Russian literature (Aleksandr Pushkin, Nikolai Gogol, Ivan Turgenev) to the extent that it appeared to mirror his own tastes—was unimpressed with the French Parnassian poets, or with Hugo's epic sweep in *Les Misérables* (1862), Eugène Fromentin's idyllic reverie in *Dominique* (1862), Charles Baudelaire's *Les Fleurs du mal* (*Flowers of Evil*, 1857), or, of course, with George Sand's idealistically sentimental novels.

Finally, a friend, Stendhal, and an outstanding critic of the period, Charles-Augustin Sainte-Beuve, seemed to agree that, while Mérimée was a masterful practitioner of his art, that art was extremely circumscribed and did not rise to the level of great art in the comprehensive sense of the word, which in no way diminishes the uniqueness and the value of his position in the development of nineteenth-century French Romantic literature.

NORMAN ARAUJO

Biography

Born in Paris, September 28, 1803. Received law degree from the University of Paris, 1823. Appointed inspector-general of historical monuments, cataloging monuments in the south of France, 1834. Elected to the Académie Française, 1844. Was nominated to the Senate under Napoleon III, 1853. Died September 23, 1870 in Cannes.

Selected Works

Collections

Mosaïque, 1833. Translated as *The Mosaic* by Emily Waller and Mary Dey. In *The Novels, Tales, and Letters of Prospére Mérimée*, Boston: Jefferson Press, 1905.

Théâtre de Clara Gazul, Romans, Nouvelles. Edited by Jean Maillon and Pierre Salomon, Paris: Gallimard, Bibliothèque de la Pléiade, 1978.

The Novels, Tales, and Letters of Prosper Mérimée. Translated by Emily Waller, William Arnold, Mary Dey, Mary Lolyd, Olive Palmer, Louise Paul, Emily Weller, Boston: Jefferson Press, 1905.

Poetry

La Guzla, ou choix de poésies illyriques recueillies dans la Dalmatie, la Bosnie, la Croatie et l'Herzégovine. 1827.

Fiction

1572. Chronique du temps de Charles IX, 1829. Translated as *Chronicle of the Reign of Charles IX*, by George Saintsbury. London: J. C. Nimmo, 1890.

Colomba, 1841. Translation: *Colomba.* Translated by Edward Marielle. Harmondsworth: Penguin Books, 1965.

Carmen, 1847. Translated by Nicholas Jotcham. Oxford: Oxford University Press, 1998.

Dernières nouvelles, 1873. Translated by Emily Waller and Louise Paul in *The Novels, Tales, and Letters of Prosper Mérimée.* Boston: Jefferson Press, 1905.

Drama

Théâtre de Clara Gazul, comédienne espagnole, 1827; enlarged ed., 1830. translated as *The Plays of Clara Gazul, a Spanish Comedian* anonymously. London: G.B. Whittaker, 1825.

Other

Notes d'un voyage en Corse, 1840.
Études sur l'histoire romaine. 2 vols. 1844.
Monuments historiques. 1846.

Bibliography

Bowman, Frank and Paul Bowman. *Prosper Mérimée; Heroism, Pessimism, and Irony.* Berkeley and Los Angeles: University of California Press, 1962.

Chabot, Jacques. *L'Autre Moi.* Aix-en-Provence: Edisud, 1983.

Darcos, Xavier. *Mérimée.* Paris: Flammarion, 1998.

Raitt, Alan William. *Prosper Mérimée.* New York: Scribner's, 1970.

Tolo, Khama-Bassili, *L'Intertextualité chez Mérimée: L'Étude des sauvages.* Birmingham, Ala.: Summa, 1998.

Trahard, Pierre. *La Jeunesse de Prosper Mérimée (1803–1834).* 2 vols. Paris: Champion, 1925.

———. *Prosper Mérimée de 1834 à 1853.* Paris: Champion, 1928.

———. *Prosper Mérimée et l'art de la nouvelle.* Paris: Nizet, 1952.

———. *La Vieillesse de Prosper Mérimée.* Paris: Champion, 1930.

MESMERISM

The physician Franz Anton Mesmer developed his theory of animal magnetism to account for his therapeutic successes in Wolfgang Amadeus Mozart's Vienna and the agitated culture of prerevolutionary Paris (1778–84). As a theory, mesmerism tries to explain phenomena similar to certain features in the magicoreligious practice of exorcism as well as to those hypnotic or hypnosis-related elements in the interaction between doctor and patient that modern psychosomatic medicine discusses under the heading *suggestion.* Practical mesmerism, accordingly, is situated between exorcism and *magica naturalis* on the one hand and modern forms of psychotherapy, including psychoanalysis on the other. Although clearly influenced by the tradition of Paracelsian medicine, Mesmer relied for his explanation mainly on the materialism of the Enlightenment and its physiological adoption of Newtonian and Cartesian theorems. He argued that the manipulation, in the patient's muscles and nerves, of an invisible and utterly subtle "magnetic" fluid permitted the healing of all illnesses. This fluid pervaded not only the human body but also nature as a whole, and health was restored when the disturbed harmony between the patient's body and the cosmos was reestablished. Mesmer believed that his therapeutic manipulations were physical, yet conceded that they could be achieved, without observable physical contact, by the doctor's intention and thought. This lack of clarity in his position reflected his failure to verify the existence of the alleged magnetic substance, or force.

Not meeting the increasingly scientific standards of the academic and medical establishments, Mesmer was rejected as a charlatan in both Vienna and Paris, a rejection that had a rational basis neither in his failure as a scientist nor, indeed, in his lower-middle-class origins. In France, political and spiritual reinterpretations of mesmerism emerged from the very Sociétés de l'Har-monie through which Mesmer had hoped to gain recognition. Among the political adoptions of animal magnetism, that of the lawyer Nicolas Bergasse was perhaps the most influential; a member of the radical Kornmann group, which played a key role in prerevolutionary activities, Bergasse developed an egalitarian interpretation of Mesmer's concept of harmony. As regards spiritualistic reinterpretations, the Chevalier de Barbarin's influence on the Sociétés of Lyon and Ostende proved to be especially important. Some of Barbarin's followers believed that God, the supreme mesmerist, brought health exclusively through the human mesmerist's willpower and the patient's faith. The mesmerist's spiritual power increased further with the brothers' Puységur discovery or rediscovery of induced hypnosis, called "somnambulism" at the time. Mesmerism was of some importance in Germany and Britain from the 1780s onward, but received broader attention only after the Romantics' rehabilitation of Mesmer around 1814. Taking root in America during the 1830s, it became a widespread and controversial concern in Western societies, which linked medical and religious subcultures to the dominant philosophical and literary preoccupations of the Romantic era.

Already in Mesmer's own "enlightened" version, animal magnetism shares essential features of Romantic thought. The assumption of one substance or force that pervaded both inanimate and animate nature was apt to accommodate the Romantics' wish to replace that "mechanistic" fragmentation of nature, which they ascribed to the Enlightenment, with the belief in nature's dynamic wholeness. The connectedness of life and matter in Mesmer's theory, moreover, provided a promising starting point for their project of establishing the identity of spirit and nature. Along with galvanism and other related theories, animal magnetism thus represented a realm in which natural philosophers could search for an empirical confirmation of their speculative notion that the world was a spiritual being or, in Friedrich Wilhelm Joseph von Schelling's formulation, *Weltseele* (world soul). Attention accordingly focused on the rapport, or sympathy, between the mesmerist and his patient, which tangibly seemed to contradict both Cartesian dualism and the principle of individuation. Yet it was not exclusively due to their pantheistic tendencies that animal magnetism appealed to the Romantics. Mesmerism also permitted the reformulation of more orthodox religious beliefs. After his initial condemnation of mesmerism, Samuel Taylor Coleridge in 1818 planned to write on its relation to the divine character of Gospel history. For Gotthilf Heinrich von Schubert, somnambulism contained the promise of a supernatural, "higher" existence precisely because it activated the "lower," nonrational faculties of the human organism. Frequently, mesmeric rapport and somnambulism were metaphorically extended to characterize man's relation to nature or human relations outside the therapeutic realm, for example the erotic attraction and "unification" between equals, or the psychic domination of one person by another. Love, Johann Wilhelm Ritter maintained, is a reciprocal "magnetizing" in which each partner is both the mesmerist and the somnambulist. This notwithstanding, Ritter discovered in somnambulism the physicist's vocation to become the master over life, his female "beloved."

Descriptions of mesmeric operations and rapports figure in the literary works of many writers of the period, notably Honoré de Balzac, Charles Dickens, Novalis, and Friedrich von Schlegel, some of whom also engaged in experiments of practical mesmerism. More important, the literary representation of mesmerism provided a focus for religious, sociopsychological, and aesthetic reflection. Due in part to the relatedness of these different dimensions, mesmerism developed into a complex topic and metaphorical model which permitted writers to express and criticize the characteristic tensions, anxieties, and hopes of their time. In a great number of literary facets, the interest in, and ignorance about, the relation between mind and matter, which lie at the heart of mesmerism, were reinforced by the Romantics' hovering between monism and dualism, immanence and transcendence. This process contributed to the wealth, but also to the ambiguities and ambivalences, of what has been called the literarization of mesmerism.

Jean Paul used mesmerism as a vehicle to criticize the scientific disenchantment of human experience and to express his hope for the oneness of man and nature in a meaningful world. In E. T. A. Hoffmann's "Der Magnetiseur" ("The Magnetizer," 1814), by contrast, animal magnetism represents less the Romantic alternative to, than a radical and "diabolic" variety of, the destructive domination of (human) nature. Ludwig Achim von Arnim combines the representation of mesmerism as a mode of religious revelation with both the rejection of human sensuality as evil and an anti-Semitic construction of Jewish characters. Many authors represent the psychic or sexual suppression of the (mostly female) somnambulist; even those who do so critically, however, at times also celebrate in mesmerism erotic "oneness" or (male) willpower, or reject (female) emancipation. Especially in the works of Achim von Arnim, Nathaniel Hawthorne, and Hoffmann, the criticism of "magnetic" domination coexists with a positive adoption of mesmeric motifs and metaphors for the implicit poetology of the text, for its Romantic conception, that is, of imagination and literary communication. Thus, the Romantic literarization of mesmerism can also provide a starting point for the critical reflection of the very ethos of Romantic writing.

MARGARETE KOHLENBACH

See also **Arnim, Achim von; Balzac, Honoré de; Coleridge, Samuel Taylor; Dickens, Charles; Electricity and Magnetism; Gender; Goethe, Johann Wolfgang von; Hawthorne, Nathaniel; Hoffmann, Ernst Theodor (Wilhelm) Amadeus; Imagination; Kerner, Justinus Andreas Christian; Kleist, Bernd Heinrich Wilhelm von; Medicine; Melville, Herman; Mozart, Wolfgang Amadeus; Nachtstücke; Naturphilosophie (Nature Philosophy); Novalis (pseudonym of Friedrich von Hardenberg); Paul, Jean (Johann Paul Friedrich Richter); Poe, Edgar Allan; Schiller, Johann Christoph Friedrich von; Schlegel, Friedrich von; Schopenhauer, Arthur; Science and the Arts; Science in Germany; Shelley, Percy Bysshe; Sickness; The Supernatural; Theology and Religious Thought; The Unconscious; Women**

Bibliography

Barkhoff, Jürgen. *Magnetische Fiktionen: Literarisierung des Mesmerismus in der Romantik.* Stuttgart and Weimar: Metzler, 1995.

Burwick, Frederick. "Coleridge, Schlegel and Animal Magnetism." In *English and German Romanticism: Cross-Currents and Controversies.* Edited by James Pipkin. Heidelberen: Literarisierung des Mesmerismus in der Romantik. Stuttgart: Metzler, 1995.

———. "Coleridge, Schlegel and the Animal Magnetism of Enlightenment." In *Transformation and Tradition in the Sciences: Essays in Honor of I. Bernard Cohen.* Edited by Everett Mendelsohn. Cambridge: Cambridge University Press, 1984.

Ellenberger, Henry F. *The Discovery of the Unconscious: The History and Evolution of Dynamic Psychiatry.* New York: Basic Books, 1961.

Gode-von Aesch, Alexander. *Natural Science in German Romanticism.* New York: AMS Press, 1966.

Kaplan, Fred. *Dickens and Mesmerism: The Hidden Springs of Fiction.* Princeton, N.J.: Princeton University Press, 1975.

Leask, Nigel. "Shelley's 'Magnetic Ladies': Romantic Mesmerism and the Politics of the Body." In *Beyond Romanticism: New Approaches to Texts and Contexts 1780–1832.* Edited by Stephen Copley and John Whale. London: Routledge, 1992.

Marcus, Melissa K. *The Representation of Mesmerism in Honoré de Balzac's "La Comédie Humaine."* New York: Peter Lang, 1995.

Müller, Gerhard H. "*Wechselwirkung* in the Life and Other Sciences: A Word, New Claims and a Concept Around 1800 . . . and Much Later." In *Romanticism in Science: Science in Europe 1790–1840.* Edited by Stefano Poggi. Dordrecht: Kluwer Academic, 1994.

Schott, Heinz, ed. *Franz Anton Mesmer und die Geschichte des Mesmerismus.* Stuttgart: Franz Steiner, 1985.

Tatar, Maria M. *Spellbound: Studies on Mesmerism and Literature.* Princeton, N.J.: Princeton University Press, 1978.

MEYERBEER, GIACOMO (JAKOB LIEBMANN MEYER BEER) 1791–1864

German composer

Giacomo Meyerbeer spent most of his career in Paris, where he consolidated the genre of French grand opera. He grew up in a stimulating cultural environment: his family were wealthy Jewish bankers in Berlin, and his mother hosted a salon which attracted the city's leading intellectuals and artists. He had piano lessons from an early age, and made his debut as a performer at the age of eleven. In 1805 he began to compose in earnest, and five years later moved to Darmstadt to study with the renowned Abbé Vogler, although he was still known primarily as a virtuoso pianist rather than a composer at this time. In 1814 he made his first trip to Paris, which made a strong impact on him, and the following year he went to London, another city to which he was to return.

Meyerbeer visited Italy for the first time in 1816, and remained there for nine years. He was particularly impressed with Gioacchino Antonio Rossini's operas in Venice; his own early operas show this influence and were received with increasing enthusiasm. *Margherita d'Anjou* (1820) was based on a French melodrama, in which Meyerbeer established distinct musical personalities for the French and English, and for which La Scala's celebrated Alessandro Sanquirico designed the scenery. The opera that established him as an international composer was *Il crociato in Egitto* (*The Crusader in Egypt*, 1824), one of the last operas written for a castrato. The work is notable for combining elements of Italian and German style, and for foreshadowing his French works in terms of scale, innovative orchestration, and the depiction of conflicting groups of people.

The success of *Margherita* and *Il crociato* in Paris encouraged Meyerbeer to plan new operas for performance there, but difficult personal circumstances following the death of his father, his own marriage, and the death of two of his children delayed matters. In 1826 he had been commissioned to write a three-act *opéra comique* that he began in collaboration with the librettist Eugène Scribe, but *Robert le diable* (*Robert the Devil*) was completed only in 1831, now a five-act grand opera for the Paris Opéra itself. *Robert* established Meyerbeer at the head of the new school of grand opera, building on Auber's *La Muette de Portici* (*The Mute-Girl of Parties*, 1828) and Rossini's *Guillaume Tell* (*William Tell*, 1829), earlier essays in the genre. *Robert* depicted the legendary Robert being tempted into a Faustian pact with his devil father Bertram in thirteenth-century Normandy. Lavish scenery and spectacular supernatural effects were an integral part of the work, and bold and powerful effects were created with rich orchestration. The most celebrated—and controversial—scene involved a ballet of debauched nuns rising from their graves in the third act at Bertram's behest, to tempt Robert into pursuing immortality.

The extraordinary success of *Robert* was followed five years later by *Les Huguenots* (1836), widely regarded as Meyerbeer's finest opera. It depicts the unleashing of the notorious St. Bartholomew's Day Massacre of Protestants by the Catholic majority in sixteenth-century France. Inventive orchestration, juxtaposition of contrasting characters and moods, and ingenious use of offstage music combined to create the suspense, shock and horror of the massacre in an almost cinematic manner, notably in

Giacomo Meyerbeer—with Hand in Pocket. Reprinted courtesy of Lebrecht Music Collection.

the eruption of the massacre at the conclusion of the celebrated Blessing of the Swords scene in act 4, and in the penultimate scene of the opera when the lovers face the marauding Catholics.

Meyerbeer was appointed *Generalmusikdirektor* in Berlin, following the departure of Gaspare Spontini in 1842, but constant disputes led him to take permanent leave of absence in 1846, and two years later he resigned the post, though remaining director of royal court music. During this period he wrote a number of occasional pieces, including the festival Singspiel *Ein Feldlager in Schlesien* (1844), which depicts an incident from the life of Frederick the Great; he later reused some of the music in his opéra comique about Peter the Great, *L'Etoile du nord* (*The Star of the North*, 1854).

In 1847 Meyerbeer returned to Paris, where Giuseppe Verdi was beginning to make an impact, but *Le Prophète* (*The Prophet*, 1849) confirmed his continuing preeminence. This opera, like *Les Huguenots*, dealt with religious fanaticism, this time the Anabaptist uprising in Holland in 1532, concluding with the destruction of most of the characters in an explosion of the palace at Münster. The opera's public and critical success derived from

Meyerbeer's now trademark orchestral ingenuity and juxtapositions, the characterization of the mezzo role of Fidès (written for Pauline Viardot), and the impressive special effects. These included the use of electric lighting at the Paris Opéra for the first time, notably in act 3, where the sun breaks through the mists; the use of roller skates to create the effect of ice skating on the frozen lake; and the extraordinary coronation scene, with its twenty-two-piece stage band.

The idea for Meyerbeer's final grand opera, *L'Africaine* (1865) had been conceived in 1837, but the work was still incomplete at the composer's death, although rehearsals had already begun. Meyerbeer's health had begun to fail in 1850, and his output had slowed. *L'Africaine* was repeatedly shelved owing to Meyerbeer's anxieties about finding a suitable soprano for the central role, and the first phase of completion was achieved only in 1860. Following the death of the librettist Scribe in 1861, Meyerbeer became anxious about who would make alterations to the text during rehearsals. The opera was brought to the stage under the aegis of the composer and critic François-Joseph Fétis, and achieved moderate success. It depicts the love triangle of the adventurer Vasco da Gama, his beloved Inès in Lisbon and the Indian queen Sélica, set against the imperial aspirations of the Portuguese. The opera employs a fluid combination of recitative, arioso and aria, and illustrates Meyerbeer's continuing interest in striking orchestral effects and color.

Although remembered primarily for his operas, Meyerbeer also wrote a large number of songs and sacred musical pieces. He was regarded as uniting the national schools of Europe, and his operas synthesize not only musical styles, but also different art forms and point ahead to Wagner's achievement of the *Gesamtkunstwerk* (the complete artwork). Although popular with audiences, Meyerbeer was not always warmly received by critics. Envy of his success and wealth combined with the increasingly anti-Semitic atmosphere of the second half of the nineteenth century; Robert Schumann, Richard Wagner, and others wrote famously vitriolic attacks. His works continued to be performed internationally until World War I, but were banned in Germany by the National Socialists from the 1920s. His reputation is only just beginning to recover, and the significance of his influence on other composers is finally being recognized.

SARAH HIBBERD

See also **Les Huguenots; (Robert the Devil) Robert le diable**

Biography

Born Yaakov Liebmann Beer, Vogelsdorf, Germany, September 5, 1791. Moved to Italy and changed name to Giacomo Meyerbeer, 1810. Began writing vocal music in Italian, 1815. Moved to Paris and married, 1826. Appointed *Generalmusikdirektor* in Berlin, 1842. Died in Paris, May 2, 1864; buried in Berlin.

Selected Works

Margherita d'Anjou. Libretto by Felice Romani. 1820.
Il crociato in Egitto. Libretto by Gaetano Rossi. 1824.
Robert le diable. Libretto by Eugène Scribe. 1831.
Les Huguenots. Libretto by Eugène Scribe, Emile Deschamps, and Gaetano Rossi. 1836.
Le Prophète. Libretto by Eugène Scribe. 1849.
L'Etoile du nord. Libretto by Eugène Scribe. 1854.
L'Africaine. Libretto by Eugène Scribe, completed by François-Joseph Fétis. 1865.

Bibliography

Brzoska, Matthias. "Giacomo Meyerbeer." In *The New Grove Dictionary of Music and Musicians*. 2d ed., vol. 16. Edited by Stanley Sadie and John Tyrrell. London: Macmillan, 2001.
Coudroy, Marie-Hélène. *La Critique parisienne des "grands opéras" de Meyerbeer*. Saarbrücken: Galland, 1988.
Everist, Mark. "The Name of the Rose: Meyerbeer's *opéra comique, Robert le diable*," *Revue de musicologie* 80 (1994): 211–50.
Gerhard, Anselm. *The Urbanization of Opera: Music Theater in Paris in the Nineteenth Century*. Chicago: University of Chicago Press, 1998.

MICHELET, JULES 1798-1874

French historian

Jules Michelet's reputation as France's greatest historian is secure; his *Histoire de France* (*History of France*, 1833–67) and his *Histoire de la Révolution française* (*History of the French Revolution*, 1847–53) are landmarks in the national literary-historical culture. It is no exaggeration to say that, since his death, most major French historians have felt the need in some way to measure their work against his. Michelet accomplished pioneering work in fields that would subsequently be given specific designations: social history, oral history, women's history, art history, economic history, and the history of sexuality. Michelet infused his writing with the power of his imagination. He was a master of style and rhetoric and drew on the resources of image and metaphor to write a self-consciously literary form of history, one that fell out of favor with the succeeding positivist, post-Romantic generation of French historians. Michelet's vision of French history was grounded in his commitment to the French Revolution and to the values of liberty, equality, and fraternity.

He rejected the goal of impartiality, if that impartiality meant the wish to maintain a "discreet and prudent equilibrium between good and evil"; instead, he advocated a form of history written in the service of right and justice. He helped formulate ideas and disseminate values that still underpin French republican notions of citizenship and national identity. Throughout his life the abuse of power aroused Michelet's indignation. He inherited from Jean-Jacques Rousseau the conviction that as humans we possess an innate disposition for pity that counterbalances self-interest and self-love: we desire to help others because we share in their pain. Pity and compassion transcend social determinants, testify to the goodness of human nature and give hope that, despite the imperfections of individual character, a better society can be built. Michelet was moved by the suffering of the poor, and as an historian he considered it his duty to lend his voice to those who had been forgotten, to reinstate to historical record those whose contribution had not been recognized. The French people became the hero of French history: they had built France and made the revolution, and yet, they were still oppressed. No longer exploited by the aristocracy they had become the victims of the bourgeoisie and of industrialism. Nevertheless, Michelet still placed his faith in the people since, in his eyes, they were not exclusively identified with a specific social group, but embodied the core values on which a future national revival could be based.

Michelet himself came from humble origins. His father was a printer and as a child he helped out in the workshop, setting type. In 1808 he had the traumatic and humiliating experience of visiting his father in prison, where he was serving a sentence for debt. In his childhood Michelet benefited from the opportunities that the educational reforms of the revolutionary period had opened up. He worked hard and was outstandingly successful. In 1827 he was appointed to the École Normale, where he taught both history and philosophy. In 1830 he was made keeper of the historical section at the French National Archives, and in 1838 he was elected to a chair at the Collège de France. As a young man Michelet was a liberal in terms of his politics, although, as someone who relied exclusively on what he earned from his teaching, he steered a prudent course and avoided controversy. However, he enthusiastically endorsed the revolution of 1830 that overthrew the reactionary Bourbon monarchy. As time passed Michelet grew increasingly hostile toward the July Monarchy. During the 1840s he took on the mantle of opposition intellectual as he and his friend Edgar Quinet became high-profile figures opposing clerical influence in the battle over the role of the church in education. He was suspended from his lectures in January 1848, then reinstated by the Second Republic, but was deprived of all his teaching posts with the arrival of the Second Empire.

Michelet's output was enormous and his work rate phenomenal. He was also a conscientious letter writer with a network of correspondents. In addition, he somehow found the time to record not just the events of his daily life, but also his thoughts and dreams, in the pages of his voluminous *Journal* (published posthumously in 1959 and 1962). He was driven by an iron self-discipline; his overworking created periods of ill health, but Michelet continued tirelessly to research and publish, because by writing he was serving the cause of his nation. The act of writing history lay at the heart of his existence; it was a project imbued with a salvatory, redemptive dimension. However, he never played a genuinely political, public role. Indeed, there were moments when he wondered whether writing history was not a substitute for living, a retreat from engagement with the asperities of existence.

In the 1820s Michelet produced educational textbooks that established his reputation. These were followed by an abridged translation of Giambattista Vico's *Scienza nuova* (*The New Science*, 1827) and in the 1830s by books on Roman history, Martin Luther, and the origin of law in France. In 1831 he published his *Introduction à l'histoire universelle* (*Introduction to Universal History*); here he took world history as his province, describing in typically Romantic fashion how the general progressive movement of world history from east to west led ultimately to France and the French Revolution. For Michelet, the true France was that of the revolution. He later noted that only at the close of 1830, in the wake of the July Revolution, did he really begin to exist, to be, to write. In Michelet's case, patriotism amounted

to much more than feelings of national allegiance. France became a substitute religion. He embraced the collective world of social life as a new source of religious truth. He wrote in his diary, "It is to you I turn for aid, my noble country. You must take the place of the God who is escaping us and fill in us the incommensurable void which Christianity left when it died." History was more than a series of events, it was a narrative of fulfilment. History told of the never-ending struggle between freedom and necessity, spirit and matter; and for Michelet, this corresponded to the presence of the divine. History-as-progress explained France's position in the world and justified the revolution. In his *Histoire de France* Michelet described the influence of geography and race on the French people but he defined Frenchness as an ideal, an invention which transcended such determinants. History described the progressive actualization of justice, freedom, and right.

By the 1840s Michelet's position on religious matters was forthright. He judged that Christianity had failed, that the church was obsolete and a hindrance to progress. The real "second coming" had taken place in 1789, and thanks to France's leadership the world had entered into the third age, the age of spirit, as prophesied by Joachim of Fiore. In the wake of 1789, humans could dispense with the anthropomorphic trappings of traditional Christianity. Henceforth the kingdom was sacramentally present within the life of the nation. Michelet famously declared that France was a person. However, while Michelet proclaimed the redemptive role of the French people, he was saddened by the condition of his nation under the July Monarchy. In a memorable chapter of his *Histoire de la Révolution* (1847), he looked back longingly to the festival of the federations in 1790, to the moment when the nation had been as one, unified in its commitment to the ideals of 1789. This had been a brief, privileged moment of communion after which the Revolution rapidly descended into violence and oppression. In 1846 Michelet published *Le Peuple* (*The People*), in which he provided his diagnosis of the crisis facing France at that moment. Here he denounced class divisions, industrialism, mechanization, selfishness, and alienation. He castigated all in France who copied England, which he branded "the anti-France," the land of capitalism and rootless, domineering egoism. Michelet preached the gospel of revolutionary nationalism as an alternative, urged respect for the values of the peasantry, and advocated greater association, cooperation, friendship, and love. However, the subsequent failure of the Second Republic showed Michelet that his prescription for healing the nation had been inadequate. During the dark days of the Second Empire he set about educating and moralizing the nation. In addition to conventional works of history he wrote books that addressed moral and social issues and were aimed at a broad audience. In *L'Amour* (1858) and *La Femme* (1859) he focused on the role of women in society. His intention was to protect women from the abuse of male power, but to this end he adopted an antifeminist stance which valorized an ideal of domesticity, denying women a public role and asserting feminine weakness and inferiority.

During the Second Empire, Michelet also published a series of texts on natural history: *L'Oiseau* (*The Bird*, 1856), *L'Insecte* (*The Insect*, 1857), *La Mer* (*The Sea*, 1861), and *La Montagne* (*The Mountain*, 1868). These books struck a chord with the reading public. This new focus on nature has sometimes been represented as a turning away from history. It has been suggested that Michelet was seeking consolation in the natural world because he was disillusioned with the society and politics of the Second Empire. His embrace of nature has also been attributed to the influence of his youthful second wife, Athénaïs Mialaret. Neither explanation is adequate. Michelet's interest in history had always been accompanied by a desire to understand the workings of nature (in the 1830s he had attended the salon of the great naturalist Etienne Geoffroy Saint-Hilaire), but his views had continually evolved since that time. In his early writings he viewed nature as a power that threatened the achievements of humankind; it erased meaning and dissolved value. History was meaning, purpose, and direction, whereas nature was the proliferation of life without purpose. Michelet, however, grew unhappy with this negative construction of nature, and from the 1840s he embraced theories that positively valorized the transformative power that renewed and regenerated life in the natural universe. His exploration of natural history, as in his study of human history, involved a meditation on the meaning of life and death. His historical project was no arid work of disinterested scholarship: the historian embraced death, loved death in order to restore the dead to life. History was "a violent mental chemistry" and in the act of writing there took place a complex form of fusion between the historian and the energies and contradictory desires that animated the collective body of history. As a historian of nature he described the processes of creation and destruction, the profligacy and excess of life. And yet, in nature as in history, Michelet discerned an underlying purpose: change was metamorphosis; new life emerged from waste; and decay, death, and value emerged from the development of life on earth.

CERI CROSSLEY

Selected Works

Oeuvres complètes. Edited by Paul Viallaneix. Paris: Flammarion, 1971– .
The People. Translated by John P. McKay. Urbana and Chicago: University of Illinois Press, 1973.
Le Peuple. Edited by P. Viallaneix. Paris: Flammarion, 1974.
Mother Death: The Journal of Jules Michelet 1815–1850. Edited by E. Kaplan. Amherst: University of Massachusetts Press, 1984.
Correspondance Générale. Edited by L. Le Guillou. Paris: Champion, 1994– .

Bibliography

Barthes, Roland. *Michelet*. Translated by Ronald Howard. Oxford: Blackwell, 1987.
Crossley, Ceri. *French Historians and Romanticism: Thierry, Guizot, the Saint-Simonians, Quinet, Michelet*. London: Routledge, 1993.
Fauquet, Eric. *Michelet ou la gloire du professeur d'histoire*. Paris: Cerf, 1990.
Gossman, Lionel. *Between History and Literature*, Cambridge, Mass.: Harvard University Press, 1990.
Haac, Oscar. *Jules Michelet*. Boston: Twayne, 1982.
Kaplan, Edward. *Michelet's Poetic Vision*. Amherst: University of Massachusetts Press, 1977.
Mitzman, Arthur. *Michelet, Historian: Rebirth and Romanticism in Nineteenth-Century France*. New Haven, Conn.: Yale University Press, 1990.
———. *Michelet ou la subversion du passé*. Paris: La Boutique de l'Histoire, 1999.
Monod, Gabriel. *La Vie et la pensée de Jules Michelet*. Geneva: Slatkine, 1975.
Orr, Linda. *Jules Michelet: Nature, History and Language*. Ithaca; N.Y.: Cornell University Press, 1976.
Petitier, Paule. *La Géographie de Michelet*. Paris: L'Harmattan, 1997.
Viallaneix, Paul. *La Voie royale: Essai sur l'idée de peuple dans l'œuvre de Michelet*. Paris: Flammarion, 1971.
———. *Michelet, Les Travaux et les jours*. Paris: Gallimard, 1998.

MICKIEWICZ, ADAM BERNARD 1798–1855

Polish poet

A Lithuanian Pole born in (or near) the town of Nowogródek, Adam Bernard Mickiewicz comes closest to what is known as a national bard in some countries. His poetry was shaped by both Classical and Romantic models, yet it became the most poignant expression of Polish Romanticism, also serving as a powerful weapon in the hands of Polish patriots striving for independence. Political circumstances forced him into emigration, so his best writing was done outside Poland, in Germany and later in Paris, where he lived for over two decades. As a poet he achieved fame not only for pure lyrical poetry but also for the epic *Pan Tadeusz* (*Master Thaddeus*, 1834), a novel in verse form which painted a vast panorama of old Poland. He also left behind a Romantic image of the poet as leader of his community and this image of the bard, or *wieszcz*, made a lasting (and not wholly beneficial) impact on the Polish national psyche.

The young Mickiewicz, who studied at the Bathory University of Wilno, was preoccupied with his personal feelings and the aspirations of his own generation. According to Czesław Miłosz, he and his friends were "direct descendants of the eighteenth century" and it was the spirit of the Enlightenment (or quasi-Masonic solidarity) that informed such poems as his famous "Ode to Youth" (1820). Nonetheless, his first book of poetry, *Ballady i romanse* (*Ballads and Romances*, 1822), ushered in the epoch of Romanticism in Polish literature. This change was due to two factors: Mickiewicz's discovery of foreign models, notably those provided by Johann Christoph Friedrich von Schiller, German folk ballads, and Lord Byron; and his personal experiences as a struggling schoolteacher at Kowno. The latter meant contact not only with local Polish landowners but with Lithuanian and Byelorussian peasantry and a new interest in the folklore of the region. Add to this an unhappy love affair with Maryla, the daughter of a landowner (she was eventually married off to a baron), and you have poetic material for both ballads and romances. The centerpiece of Mickiewicz's first collection is a poem entitled "Romantycznosc" ("Romanticism"), which, discussing a daylight apparition and the reaction of simple folk to this totally "irrational" phenomenon, contains lines uncannily similar to the early William Wordsworth: "Faith and love are more discerning / Than lenses or learning." Mickiewicz here asserts the primacy of the "heart" to the "mind": only in your heart can you grasp "living truths."

Some of Mickiewicz's ballads are about historical myths or legends well known in the region, but soon afterward he tried his hand at a poetic tale that delved into medieval history. The chief heroine of *Grażyna* (*The Graceful One*, 1823) is a Lithuanian princess whose personal sacrifice leads to victory over Teutonic knights, a very Romantic story with complex political undertones. At about the same time that he wrote *Grażyna*, Mickiewicz started to translate Byron's *Giaour*. It is clear that the themes of treason and sacrifice exerted much influence on his imagination. As for his political loyalties, at the time he was still sympathizing with the pro-Russian policies of Prince Adam Czartoryski, a powerful adviser of Tsar Aleksander I. (The Congress of Vienna had created a semiautonomous Polish entity, the so-called Congress Kingdom, which existed until 1830.) Mickiewicz's other work printed in his 1823 collection included a verse drama, entitled *Dziady* (*Forefathers' Eve, part 2*), which was called by Miłosz "the most typical theatrical work of Polish Romanticism." It certainly displays all the favorite requisites of the Romantic spirit: it leans heavily on the supernatural, as it depicts the somber folk ceremony of the summoning up of spirits of the dead on All Souls' Day, but it also includes a personal note by meting out supernatural punishment for cold-hearted women who do not respond to their lovers' entreaties. This note is continued in *Dziady* (*Forefathers' Eve, part 4*), a pseudodrama that contains the Romantic ravings of the ghostly Gustaw in the house of a Greek Catholic priest.

The age of youthful dreams comes to an abrupt end in Mickiewicz's life with the Wilno arrests of 1823. On suspicion of plotting, tsarist authorities arrested and consequently exiled many students of Wilno University and also pupils of secondary schools. The fate of these young Poles made a huge impact on Mickiewicz. He himself received a mild sentence; he was exiled to Russia where he would eventually get a teaching position in Odessa. From 1824 to 1829, he was a Romantic exile whose poetry (and especially his improvisations in fluent French) were admired by Saint Petersburg society; in fact, he was not treated too harshly even after the failure of the Decembrist plot in 1825, though he had known and befriended Konrad Rylejev, one of the chief plotters. While in Russia, Mickiewicz wrote two very different longer works: *Sonety krymskie* (*Sonnets from the Crimea*, 1826), a masterful cycle of sonnets based on his visit to the Crimean Peninsula, and *Konrad Wallenrod* (1828), a wildly Romantic poetic tale with a camouflaged message. The Crimean sonnets followed a cycle of love sonnets written in Odessa and, while they also contained allusions to the poet's longing for his native country and to the changing nature of historical fortunes, their lush imagery and exotic background appealed to Mickiewicz's Russian friends and Polish readers alike. This was not the case for *Konrad Wallenrod*, the plot of which was taken from old Lithuanian chronicles but substantially changed to agree with Mickiewicz's intentions: his Wallenrod is a Lithuanian hero who only impersonates a Teutonic knight in order to become grand master of the Teutonic Order and defeat it through betrayal. It is this Byronic but at the same time intensely nationalistic tale that first establishes the poetic model cherished by Mickiewicz in later years—that of the bard, who in this story is Halban, Wallenrod's alter ego. Halban's "Piesn Wajdeloty"

("Tale of the Wajdelota") is a typical Romantic comparison of the greatness of valiant ancestors with the servile mediocrity of the present generation, written in flowing hexameters. It is also Halban who at the end of *Konrad Wallenrod*, while mourning his disciple, announces why he himself has to go on living, "to preserve [Wallenrod's] deed for the world," so that it should be handed down from generation to generation. The bard can also see into the future, where "There will rise up from that song an avenger of our bones," a reference to Dido's prophecy in the *Aeneid*.

This work's political implications were clear to everyone save the Russian censor. Mickiewicz takes his motto from Niccolò Macchiavelli and extols "patriotic treason" in this tale, also making a claim (through the figure of Halban) to national leadership. As the publication of this work preceded the 1830 uprising in Poland only by a few months, the young officer cadets who started the uprising drew encouragement from its message, which legitimized treason if committed out of patriotic motives. In later years Mickiewicz himself was startled by the unintended consequences of his poetic tale and would happily have retracted it if he could have done so. His younger rival Juliusz Slowacki wrote scathingly about *Konrad Wallenrod*, "Wallenrodism did indeed much good . . . / It introduced a certain method into treason / Out of one it made a hundred thousand traitors."

Leaving Russia in the early summer of 1829 opened up completely new vistas for Mickiewicz. He traveled through Germany, visited Johann Wolfgang von Goethe in Weimar, and through Switzerland made his way to Rome where he stayed for several months. In Rome he underwent a kind of religious conversion, manifesting itself in poems such as "Reason and Faith" and "Evening Discourse"; the earlier Romantic opposition now deepened into a mystical introspection and communication between God and humankind. It was also in Rome that he wrote the gloomiest poem of his life, "Do Matki Polki" ("To a Polish Mother"), which laid down the foundations of a Polish martyrology. While Mickiewicz did not believe that armed insurrection would liberate Poland, he could clearly see the necessity of confronting the oppressor. So his advice to Polish mothers is to prepare their children for future "martyrdom . . . without resurrection." Wiktor Weintraub sees "the Wallenrod complex" still at work in this poem, which, however, prepares the ground for the future glorification of the Polish nation as the "Christ of the nations."

The Polish uprising of 1830–31 was a turning point in Mickiewicz's life. On the one hand, he knew that he should have joined the insurrectionists; on the other hand, he did not believe in the success of the uprising, so instead of going to Warsaw he left for Paris. Later he stayed in Prussian-held Polish territory for several months, only to emerge in Dresden at a time when part of the Polish army had already fled the country. It was in Dresden that he wrote his greatest dramatic work, *Dziady, III* (*Forefathers' Eve, part 3*), also known as the "Dresden *Dziady*." This was partly self-therapy for his feeling of guilt for not joining the uprising, and partly an attempt to situate the fate of Poland in a mystical-Promethean context where the ambitions of the individual should be subordinated to the needs and future happiness of the nation. This play, a grand poetic enterprise, shows Mickiewicz at the height of his poetic powers.

The plot, at least in the first few scenes, is taken from Mickiewicz's own biography—that is, the period of detention in an old monastery in Vilno after the arrest of the students back in 1823. In the prologue to the drama, a guardian angel makes its appearance and, indeed, the whole play is full of good and evil spirits who fight for the soul of the prisoner first named Gustaw, then Konrad. In fact, the change of names is highly symbolic: Gustav, the unrequited, maudlin lover, turns into Konrad, the resolute fighter for the national cause. Konrad's problem, however, is his immense ambition. He is a poet, an extremely talented creative person who in the very lengthy "Grand Improvisation" actually challenges God to give him "power over the souls," for he can identify with and "speak for millions" of his compatriots. This plea is met with a stony silence from God, which reduces Konrad to near-blasphemy, and only the eagerness of an attendant devil spoils the victory of evil—Konrad faints and has to be exorcized. After the exorcism (which is carried out by a saintly Polish priest, Father Piotr), Konrad is ready to become a "pilgrim" and serve his people in this capacity. This part of *Dziady* has a dreamlike quality, including visions and mysterious prophecies about the future of the Polish nation, as well as realistic scenes (such as the one in a Warsaw salon where visiting Russian democrats denounce tsarist "colonial" policies in no-nonsense terms), a fact that resulted in a ban by the Communist authorities on the new staging of the play (directed by Kazimierz Dejmek) as late as 1968. It is hard to imagine another European country where the verse play of a national poet from the first half of the nineteenth century could have such incendiary effects as in Poland.

The printed version of *Dziady, III* was followed by a cycle of long poems entitled "Ustęp" ("Digression") which more or less summed up Mickiewicz's Russian experiences. It follows the young exile's itinerary from Vilno to Saint Petersburg and Milosz rightly characterizes it as a surprising switch of styles: from an ultra-Romantic drama Mickiewicz moves to "sharp, biting classical verse" in order to denounce Russia as the evil empire and its elegant capital as a monument to slave labor and horrible suffering. The imagery is wintry throughout the cycle and, characteristically, Mickiewicz puts the following question into the mouth of a Russian friend (the poet could have been Pushkin, whom he befriended): "But when the sun of freedom will throw its rays / And the western wind will warm these states . . . / What will happen to the cascade of tyranny?" These lines are a presentiment of the inevitable revolution that will sweep away old Russia. Mickiewicz, though he hates autocracy, is not an enemy of all the Russians; in the much-quoted poem "Do Pryjaciół Moskali" ("To My Muscovite Friends") he has words of praise for the Decembrists but only contempt for those who "dishonor" themselves by accepting high positions from the tsar. He sees the Russian people as a long-suffering, passive, "half-dormant" community that will, however, eventually "join hands" with freedom-loving Poles and shake off its shackles. It is in this context that one can speak about Mickiewicz's Pan-Slavism, which manifested itself more in his lectures at the Collège de France and his activities in the 1840s than in the first years of his exile in Paris.

It was during these first years that Mickiewicz once again wrote, almost simultaneously, a thoroughly Romantic pamphlet and also a very different epic work. *Księgi narodu polskiego i pielgrzymstwa polskiego* (*Book of the Polish Nation and its Pilgrimage*, 1832) was published anonymously; it is a "lay gospel" for the Polish refugees who, according to the author, have a mission:

they have to work for Poland's liberation, which can be achieved only by denying the materialistic values of the West and embracing genuine Christian values of humility and self-sacrifice. In this work the fate of Poland is likened to that of Christ; as He, the Polish nation was crucified but will be resurrected on "the third day" when "it shall rise and free all the peoples of Europe from slavery." The *Books of the Polish Nation* are written in rhythmical prose, in a language full of biblical undertones. It impressed some of Mickiewicz's contemporaries, especially his French friend Felicité de Lamennais, author of the religicorevolutionary *Paroles d'un croyant*.

If the *Books of the Polish Nation* addressed contemporary problems in a prophetic, utopian context, *Pan Tadeusz* is the product of poetic escapism. In this verse novel, told in twelve books using the thirteen-syllable line, Mickiewicz re-created the world of his childhood in Lithuania, describing the everyday life and festivities of the Polish gentry. This serene world no longer existed in the 1830s and that is why Stanisław Worcell, another eminent emigré, called *Pan Tadeusz* "a tombstone laid by the hand of a genius upon our Old Poland." Idyllic parts alternate with humorous events where the colorful characters seem to have stepped out of a mock-heroic epic; but the poem also has Romantic features. These are connected with young Tadeusz's love for Zosia (their marriage resolves the long-standing feud of two families) and even more so with the character of Father Robak, which is Jacek Soplica, a past murderer now atoning for his sins in disguise. History changes this traditional society in the last two books of *Pan Tadeusz*, where the Polish Army allied with Napoleon enters the region (before the disastrous campaign on Russia), all the young men join the army, and Tadeusz, in a gesture of goodwill, liberates his serfs. The poem ends on a note of general reconciliation and optimism; in the last lines Mickiewicz uses a formula that could be employed by a popular storyteller: "I was also there among the guests, drank mead and wine, / And what I saw and heard I put into these books of mine."

According to Wiktor Weintraub, Mickiewicz "overcame Romanticism" in *Pan Tadeusz*. This is true only in the sense that he overcame the extremes of his own "national Romanticism" or Messianism in a beautiful and nostalgic epic poem, but he never lost his zeal to act as a wieszcz, a poet turned into self-appointed national leader. *Pan Tadeusz* is now seen by many as the greatest achievement in nineteenth-century Polish literature. Having completed this work, Mickiewicz did not write any more poetry with the exception of a few lyrical poems of Classic poise and perfection (the so-called Lausanne lyrics). He might have lacked inspiration, but there was another factor that impeded his creative work: his involvement with Andrzej Towianski.

Towianski, a Lithuanian mystic, appeared in Paris in the early 1840s and soon formed his own "circle" consisting of Polish emigrés disillusioned with politics. Mickiewicz, already influenced by the writings of Saint-Martin and other mystics, was drawn into the circle fairly soon after Towianski's appearance: the latter used hypnotherapy to cure (temporarily) the mental illness of Mickiewicz's wife, Celina. After Towianski's expulsion from France in 1842, Mickiewicz himself acted as the spiritual leader of the circle for a while. Unfortunately, his involvement with this strange sect of Christian utopians also affected his lectures at the Collège de France. These "Paris lectures" were given in French on the subject of Slavic literatures between 1840 and 1844 and among them one finds acute critical observations and interesting theories (for example, those concerning the specific features of the Slavic theater) alongside Towianist ravings and Napoleonic propaganda. It was due to the latter that the French government finally banned the lecture course.

In 1848, Mickiewicz the political activist appeared once again. He traveled to Rome hoping for a revolution supported by the pope, but had to be content with the formation of a Polish Legion that was ready to fight for Italian independence. His political program at the time could be defined as "radical Pan-Slavism" with a strong democratic flavor. The legion was not much of a success, so a year later in Paris Mickiewicz took to the editing of a French-language paper of international revolutionaries, *La Tribune des Peuples* (supported financially by the eccentric Count Ksavery Branicki, Mickiewicz's compatriot). Though he no longer wrote Romantic verse, from time to time Mickiewicz continued to behave as a Romantic bard whose guidance was essential for his nation. After *La Tribune* was banned, he still believed in Napoleon III's statesmanship, and his last surviving poem is an Alcaic ode in Latin to the new emperor, glorifying the capture of Bommersund. The Crimean War gave Mickiewicz the last opportunity to "turn words into deeds" and he left Paris for the Near East to organize yet another legion, this time mostly consisting of Jewish Cossacks. It was in Constantinople that he contracted cholera, and he died in 1855. He was first buried in Paris, but in 1890 his remains were reburied in the Wawel Castle's crypt in Cracow, the Polish national Pantheon.

Mickiewicz's legacy was huge and not without contradictions. His lyrical and epic poetry, along with some of his poetic dramas, are the center of Polish Romanticism, and though posterity usually refers to the three great poets of the period (the others being Juliusz Słowacki and Zygmunt Krasiński), most critics see him towering above his contemporaries. He used the Polish language as no poet or writer before him and for moments managed to bring Poland into the focus of European interest. His poetic model of a "national bard," on the other hand, became a hindrance and eventually a dead weight on Polish poets and playwrights, who tried to shake themselves free from Mickiewicz's spirit. Not only Stanisław Wyspiański at the turn of the nineteenth century, but even emigré writer Witold Gombrowicz in the mid-twentieth century had to struggle with the legacy of Polish Romanticism and with the awesome power of the word as shaped by Adam Mickiewicz.

GEORGE GÖMÖRI

Biography

Born in Nowogródek or Zaosie, Lithuania, December 24, 1798. Attended the Dominican school at Nowogródek and in 1815 matriculated at the University of Vilno. Involvement there with the Society of Philomaths. First poem was published in 1818. A year later, having finished his studies in Vilno, became schoolteacher at Kowno, a post he held until 1823. The first volume of his *Poems* was published in 1822. In November 1824 the tsarist authorities arrested Mickiewicz, and he and his friends were interned in the Basilian Monastery in Vilno. Exiled to Russia in 1824, he spent the first months in Saint Petersburg and then left for Odessa. A visit to the Crimean Peninsula in the summer of 1825 resulted in the *Sonety Krymskie*, published in 1826. Between 1827 and 1829,

lived mostly in Saint Petersburg and in Moscow; *Konrad Wallenrod* was published in 1828. In 1829, obtained permission to leave Russia; traveled in Germany, Switzerland, and Italy. After a sojourn in Rome, in the spring of 1831 visited Paris. He did not join the uprising, but waited in the Poznan region until its collapse; in 1832 in Dresden he wrote *Dziady, III*. In the same year, established in Paris as an important figure of the new Polish emigration; published and edited the journal *The Polish Pilgrim*. In 1833, nursed Stefan Garczyński, a sick friend, who died in Avignon; after his death Mickiewicz returned to Paris. In 1834, married Celina Szymanowska and finished *Pan Tadeusz*. In 1839–40 taught Latin at the University of Lausanne; in 1840, received a professorship of Slavic languages and literature at the College de France; lectures there continued until 1844. Involvement with Andrzej Towianski's mystical sect lasted until 1846. In 1848, traveled to Rome and there formed the Polish Legion, drawing up its "List of Principles." In 1849 in Paris edited *La Tribune des Peuples*. In 1852, obtained a new post as librarian to the Arsenal. In March 1855 Celina Mickiewicz died; in September of the same year Mickiewicz left for Constantinople to help the Polish cause in the Crimean War. He died on November 26, 1855, presumably of cholera.

Selected Works

Collections

Dzieła. Wydanie narodowe. Edited by Leon Płoszewski et al. 16 vols. 1949–55.
Adama Mickiewicza wspomnienia i myśli. Edited by Stanisław Pigoń. 1958.
Dziełła. Wydanie rocznicowe 1798–1998. Edited by Zbigniew Jerzy Nowak et al. 1993– .

Collections in Translation

Konrad Wallenrod and Other Writings. Translated by Dorothea Prall Radin and George Rapall Noyes. 1925.
Selected Poems. Edited by Clark Mills. 1956.
New Selected Poems. Edited by Clark Mills. 1957.

Epic Poem

Pan Tadeusz, czyli Ostatni zajazd na Litwie, 1834. Translated as *Pan Tadeusz, or The Last Foray in Lithuania* by Watson Kirkconnell. 1962.

Verse Drama

Dziady, parts 2 and 4, 1823; parts 3, 1832; part 1, 1860. Translated as *Dziady (Forefathers' Eve, Dresden Text)* by Charles S. Kraszewski. 2000.

Bibliography

Kleiner, Juliusz. *Mickiewicz*. 2 vols. 2d ed. Lublin: KUL, 1948.
Kridl, Manfred, ed. *Adam Mickiewicz, Poet of Poland: A Symposiùm*. New York: Columbia University Press, 1951.
Lednicki, Waclaw, ed. *Adam Mickiewicz in World Literature*. Berkeley and Los Angeles: University of California Press, 1956.
Mills, Clark, ed. *Adam Mickiewicz: Selected Poems*. New York: Noonday Press, 1956.
Milosz, Czeslaw. *The History of Polish Literature*. London: Collier-Macmillan, 1969.
Sudolski, Zygmunt. *Mickiewicz. Opowiesc biograficzna*. Warsaw: PWN, 1995.
Weintraub, Wiktor. *The Poetry of Adam Mickiewicz*. The Hague: Mouton, 1954.
Welsh, David. *Adam Mickiewicz*. New York: Twayne, 1966.
Wyka, Kazimierz. *Pan Tadeusz*. vols 1–2. Warsaw: PIW, 1963.

MIDDLE AGES

The Romantic evocation of the Middle Ages performed different functions in different countries. For Joseph-Marie de Maistre and François-Auguste-René, Vicomte de Chateaubriand it was an antidote to restless Enlightenment questioning and Romantic yearning. For Victor Hugo it was aligned with Romanticism in its questioning of neoclassical aesthetic canons. In Germany, Friedrich von Schlegel and Wilhem Heinrich Wackenroder responded to its religious inspiration, Johann Gottfried Herder looked to it for folk traditions and origins, and Johann Wolfgang Goethe and Johann Christoph Friedrich Schiller saw it as an era of natural genius and of violence. Britain shared—indeed, originated—many of these concerns, and its contending national traditions and political tensions made Edmund Burke's "age of chivalry" the site of ideological struggles.

Richard Hurd's *Letters on Chivalry and Romance* (1762) had rehabilitated the romances disparaged as Gothic by the Augustans, examining the concentric and excursive structural principles of Edmund Spenser's *Faerie Queene* (1590) as an alternative to Classical linear progression. Hurd was particularly drawn to the poetic qualities of chivalric life and manners, a topic enthusiastically expanded by Jean Baptise de la Curne de Sainte-Palaye in a work of three volumes (*Mémoires de l'ancienne chevalerie*, 1759–81). Gothic architecture was patronized by George III at Windsor and in Horace Walpole's eclectic, theatrical Strawberry Hill. Collections of armor were popular enough to be satirized in the 1790s, and armor and castle architecture were major components of Walpole's *The Castle of Otranto* (1765), setting a trend for the Gothic genre. The publication of chivalric romances and chronicles increased at the turn of the century, British and French examples being joined by works on medieval Islam and Robert Southey's versions of Portuguese and Spanish poems. Thomas Percy's *Reliques of Ancient Poetry* (1765) advertised its antiquarian aspect in its title. His "corrected" versions of old ballads followed the habit of the earlier century in modernizing ancient authors to align them with cultivated contemporary tastes. Joseph Ritson's relish for a more authentic rudeness of expression marked the emergence of a more relativistic spirit, valuing past cultures and their forms, or, like Herder in Germany, sought expression of a folk identity.

Ritson's conception of the ballads as the product of the people rather than courtly poets was associated with his republicanism, a politicization of medievalist themes that became prominent in the 1790s. William Wordsworth claimed that his ballads belonged to a communal tradition as old as Geoffrey Chaucer, from which modern developments had been aberrations. His departures from decorum in style and subject drew politically motivated criticism from Jeffrey, and praise for his "levelling muse" from William Hazlitt. The Spenserians of the eighteenth century, such as James Beattie and James Thomson, took up the theme of individualistic encounters with indolence, pleasure, beauty, and despair without the clear-cut morality of Spenser's allegorical framework. Spenserian forms became oppositional, even radical, in William Wordsworth's "Salisbury Plain" (1794), Percy Bysshe Shelley's "Laon and Cythna" (1817), and Lord Byron's *Childe Harold's Pilgrimage* (1812–18). Burke's picture of the continuity of medieval tradition in British society was called into question by works that perceived the Middle Ages as replete with conflicts, echoing the struggles of the present. William Godwin, while complaining that the age of chivalry survived in oppressive state institutions and the caste system of aristocracy, nevertheless appealed to chivalric ideals of generous endeavor for the public good. His *Life of Chaucer* (1804) located the beginnings of independence, individuality, and the commercial spirit in the medieval age; and Shelley saw progressive developments in the treatment of women, the ideal of love, and the equality of Christian doctrines. Such notions colored the medievalism of Leigh Hunt and Keats. William Wordsworth's *Borderers* (1842) adapted aspects of Johann Wolfang von Goethe and Johann Christoph Friedrich von Schiller's *Sturm und Drang* (storm and stress) movement to a medieval time of insecure central authority, testing the personal and emotional loyalties of its subjects. Walter Scott's translation of *Wallenstein* (1800) primed him with the theme of the limits of personal freedom in the movements of history. Sympathetic to Ritson, Scott was also receptive to the idea of the "Norman Yoke" popularized by Catharine Macaulay as the eclipse of an original, more democratic Anglo-Saxon constitution. The conflicts between Saxons and Normans played out in Scott's *Ivanhoe* (1819) foreshadow nineteenth-century efforts to trace a mixed inheritance of Norman sophistication and Saxon hardiness and pragmatism in the British character and political constitution.

The union of classes in shared national and religious ideals and traditions of communal life, guarded by local magnates and headed by a charismatic monarch, became an ideal attributed to "organic" feudal society in Wordsworth's reinterpretations of national traditions and in Coleridge's political theory. Cobbett hoped to unite democratic independence with old ideas of the interdependence of the classes and the true role of a native aristocracy. Alfred Lord Tennyson's uncle Charles, a Whig supporter of reform and companion of Edward Bulwer-Lytton, remodeled Bayons, his Lincolnshire manor, to feature the baronial hall with its associations of communal feasts. Kenelm Digby's *The Broad Stone of Honour* (1822) did much to effect the transformation of the knight into the Victorian gentleman with high moral and domestic ideals and a paternalistic role in the community, but at the expense of divorcing him from the vulgarity of business. The medievalism of Young England, which inspired the Eglinton Tournament of 1839, was associated with a "one nation" Toryism claimed by Benjamin Disraeli, particularly devoted to shielding dependants from the logic of Malthusian liberal economics. Thomas Carlyle looked to a different type of aristocracy arising among industrialists in order to confront the realities of a new age. His exercise in medievalism, *Past and Present* (1843), denounces the mechanisms of democracy and characterizes the natural leader in the person of lowborn Abbot Samson, a man of mysteriously personal religious faith, but a faith that prompts action, producing economic and social order in the lax monastic community and dealing stern justice to the corrupt and insubordinate.

The contrast of medieval and modern, used by Southey in his *Colloquies* (1829) to regret the passing of unifying ideals, was similarly employed in Augustus Welby Pugin's *Contrasts* (1839) to popularize medieval architecture as a civic style, later to be adopted in Charles Barry's new Gothic Parliament buildings.

However, the Catholic associations of medievalism were a point of controversy. Coleridge's call for a national church on medieval lines inspired Thomas Arnold and the Anglican Broad Church movement, but John Henry Newman was also influenced by Romantic medievalism to emphasize the continuities of Anglicanism with Catholic doctrine. John Ruskin interpreted theGothic in a manner more satisfying to Protestants, insisting on the individuality and relative independence of the Gothic craftsman. Deriving the Gothic style from natural forms, he integrated medieval architecture with native English crafts, which were declining fast in an age of machine production and mechanical perfection.

CHRIS JONES

Bibliography

Bronson, Bertrand H. *Joseph Ritson, Scholar-at-Arms.* Berkeley and Los Angeles: University of California Press, 1938.

Butler, Marilyn. *Romantics, Rebels and Reactionaries.* Oxford: Oxford University Press, 1981.

Chandler, Alice. *A Dream of Order: the Medieval Ideal in Nineteenth-Century English Literature.* London: Routledge, 1971.

Duff, David. *Romance and Revolution: Shelley and the Politics of a Genre.* Cambridge: Cambridge University Press, 1994.

Francis, Mark and John Morrow. *A History of English Political Thought in the nineteenth Century.* London: Duckworth, 1994.

Girouard, Mark. *The Return to Camelot.* New Haven, Conn.: Yale University Press, 1981.

Hobsbawm, Eric and Terence Ranger, eds. *The Invention of Tradition.* Cambridge: Cambridge University Press, 1983.

Kucich, Greg. *Keats, Shelley, and Romantic Spenserianism.* University Park: Pennsylvania State University Press, 1991.

Macaulay, James. *The Gothic Revival 1745–1845.* Glasgow: Blackie, 1975.

Morse, David. *High Victorian Culture.* New York: New York University Press, 1993.

Wellek, René. *A History of Modern Criticism 1750–1950.* London: Jonathan Cape, 1955.

MIDDLE CLASS

The Romantic period has traditionally been seen as the moment in European history, and perhaps in British history especially, when the middle class not only grew in size but also became the dominant social and political force in society. The allure of the middle class is evident well before the Romantic period—consider Daniel Defoe's *Robinson Crusoe* (1717), which asserts that "the middle state" is "the best state in the world, the most suited to human happiness." Still, it is during the period between 1760 and 1850 that the middle class became dominant both as a concept and as a group. While the definition of the middle class varied significantly throughout the period, and the borders of the group remained somewhat unstable and amorphous, there is nonetheless little question that the middle class became vitally important in the cultural and political life of the Romantic era.

Several different disciplines offer compelling reasons why the Romantic period saw the middle class move toward cultural and political dominance. Economic historians explain the growth of the middle class in terms of increasing industrialization. Across Europe in the eighteenth century, this industrialization created a new commercial economy defined by wider global trading networks and increased domestic consumption. This commercial economy in turn created thousands of new jobs. However, these new jobs—which included work for laborers who produced and transported consumer goods and for those with expertise in banking and financial speculation—were not entirely stable. The South Sea Bubble, an early eighteenth-century investment scheme that led to feverish speculation about the wealth to be had from controlling trading privileges and which ended in the financial ruin of thousands, provides one dramatic example of the risks and failures that this new world order entailed. Still, economic historians identify those who worked to develop and maintain the new commercial economy as part of a new middle class: a group of people with no hereditary claim to wealth or landed property, but with more education and higher levels of disposable income than wage earners of earlier generations.

This new and relatively wealthy group developed new habits for leisure time. The home became a crucial site of middle-class identity, and new styles in furniture and decorating (notably the German and Austrian Biedermeier style, which focused on simplicity and comfort), helped to establish the middle class ideal of home as a haven from the pressures of the outside world. Within these homes, much emphasis was placed on domestic entertainments (music, portraiture, readings) and considerable attention was paid to literacy as well, at least in part because these middle classes often attained their new status by dint of education. Conduct books were part of the middle-class library (Daniel Defoe's *Complete English Tradesman* [1726] is one important example) but the novel was arguably a still more important genre for these literate professionals. Often framed as stories of upward mobility, novels presented middle-class readers with characters much like themselves; in fact, Ian Watt's 1957 groundbreaking study of the English novel linked the rise of the novel with the rise of the middle class, arguing that the novel's focus on individual consciousness and decision-making fit perfectly with the ways in which this new professional class understood themselves and their place in the social order. Watt's thesis has been challenged and revised considerably since his study first appeared, but there remains little doubt that the novel provided the emerging middle class with a key means of self-representation and self-understanding in the early part of the Romantic period.

The novel's influence continued throughout the Romantic period, and several important studies have suggested that this genre did much to secure middle-class hegemony by the 1830s. By focusing on individual subjectivities and characters' inner, usually domestic, lives—whether in the context of historical political events, as in the novels of Walter Scott, or in the context of very local concerns, as in the novels of Jane Austen—the novel essentially redefined individual worth. Protagonists emerged from novels as worthy, sympathetic characters not because of any predetermined status or power, but because of the way they interpreted and managed the personal and social challenges with which they had been presented. Some critics, perhaps most notably Nancy Armstrong, have argued that this way of defining individual worth meant that the novel celebrated not just the middle classes, but the middle-class *woman* in particular. Because the qualities of mind privileged by the novel were the typically female ones of sympathy and emotional response, the individuals represented in (and produced by) the novel bore the stamp of middle-class feminine domesticity.

While the novel gave society one important way to understand and imagine what the middle classes looked like, political discourse provided the means to understand the kinds of practical power and influence this group could have. Notably, political historians suggest that during the Romantic period, the middle classes were defined less as members of a new commercial order than as the new face of political moderation. Prior to the middle of the eighteenth century, political moderation had been linked to aristocratic landholders; their literal stake in the nation was thought to mean that they would not support reactionary political upheaval. But those who identified themselves as members of the emergent middle class rejected the idea that landed property was a prerequisite for engaging in civic life, and in fact suggested that landed property holders had a stake in perpetuating the status quo and its attendant corruptions. Consequently, political discourse from the 1790s onward increasingly identified these new middle classes with political moderation. Political historians such as J. G. A. Pocock, Edward Thompson, and Dror Wahrman persuasively show that in both Britain and France, the middle classes became the group to which national political stability was most closely tied during the Romantic period.

"The rise of the middle class" is a familiar phrase to those who study the Romantic period. While students of the period are right to be skeptical about accounts that describe a straightforward and linear middle-class march to cultural and political hegemony, there can be little doubt that the educational, political, economic, and cultural practices we now know as "middle class" do in many ways have their roots in the Romantic period.

BONNIE J. GUNZENHAUSER

Bibliography

Armstrong, Nancy. *Desire and Domestic Fiction: A Political History of the Novel.* New York: Oxford University Press, 1987.

Crossick, Geoffrey and Heinz Gerhard-Haupf. *The Petite Bourgeoisie in Europe, 1780–1914.* London: Routledge, 1995.

Cruz, Jesus. *Gentlemen, Bourgois, and Revolutionaries: Political Change and Cultural Persistence among the Spanish Dominant Groups, 1750–1850.* New York: Oxford University Press, 1996.

Hall, Catherine. *White, Male, and Middle-Class: Explorations in Feminism and History.* New York: Routledge, 1992.

Harrison, Carol E. *The Bourgeois Citizen in Nineteenth-Century France: Gender, Sociability, and the Uses of Emulation.* New York: Oxford University Press, 1999.

Kidd, Alan and David Nicholls, eds. *Gender, Civic Culture, and Consumerism: Middle-Class Identity in Britain, 1800–1940.* New York: St. Martin's Press, 1999.

Pocock, J. G. A. *Virtue, Commerce, and History: Essays on Political Thought and History, Chiefly in the Eighteenth Century.* Cambridge: Cambridge University Press, 1985.

Thompson, E. P. *The Making of the English Working Class.* New York: Random House, 1966.

Wahrman, Dror. *Imagining the Middle Class: The Political Representation of Class in Britain, c. 1780–1840.* Cambridge: Cambridge University Press, 1995.

Watt, Ian. *The Rise of the Novel: Studies in Defoe, Richardson, and Fielding.* Berkeley and Los Angeles: University of California Press, 1957.

MILL, JOHN STUART 1806–1873

English utilitarian philosopher

John Stuart Mill was the best known and most influential of the utilitarians, and utilitarianism is well known to be anathema to Romantics. Utilitarians hold that the human good is utility understood as pleasure or happiness, and that the right course of action, in both individual ethics and political policy, is whatever produces the most utility possible, or "the greatest good for the greatest number." This reduction of the good to a single standard, the calculative mentality that adds together interchangeable units of utility to arrive at the correct course, the resulting moderation and rationalization of life: all these stand, or seem to stand, in stark opposition to those concepts held dear by Romanticism, such as passion, extremism of emotion and commitment, an attraction to the incalculable, and diversity. And indeed, from the time of utilitarianism's founding by Jeremy Bentham, often portrayed as that quintessentially rational, cold, one-sided thinker, the two schools had leered disdainfully at each other across an apparently unbridgeable chasm. John Stuart Mill's influence has been profound in several areas of thought, but in none more than in his attempt to bridge that chasm, to fuse a broadened, more flexible utilitarianism with a suitably muted, tamed Romanticism. The resulting liberalism is with us still, in various forms; the question of its coherence is with us too.

The connections between Mill's life and his thought are especially clear and instructive. His childhood, as described in his *Autobiography* (1873), has evoked endless commentary as one of the most unusual in history. His father, James Mill, was a follower of Bentham and a considerable scholar in his own right. He taught John himself, with a rigor and irascible intensity that were to leave the child with lasting mental scars and a prodigious body of learning. He began Greek at the age of three, and by eight he had read widely in Xenophon, Herodotus, Plato, Hume, Gibbon, and many others. Then he started Latin and expanded his reading further. At twelve he began logic and political economy. By early adolescence, Mill had received an education worthy of an especially erudite adult. Throughout, the father instilled Benthamite doctrines in the child. It is perhaps not surprising that a mental crisis came. At twenty, in a dull mood, Mill chanced to ask himself whether the complete success of the Benthamite social and political project would bring him happiness. He was crushed to realize that it would not. A period of serious depression followed; he became convinced that he was a being without feeling, a disembodied intellect, only half human. The depression began to lift when he read a tragic passage in a novel and found that he *could* feel. (The passage involved the death of a father and his son's vow to take his place; the oedipal theme has not been lost on commentators.) Significantly, reading the Romantic William Wordsworth also helped in his recovery. Thereafter, Mill ambivalently drifted away from utilitarianism, never formally repudiating it but grafting Romantic elements onto it. He became the philosopher of individuality, of diversity, of liberty.

On Liberty (1859) and *Utilitarianism* (1861) best display Mill's blend of utilitarianism and Romanticism. In the former, Mill uses the image of the pollard to sum up his view of the human good and society's influence on individual well-being. An outside hand trims the pollard to a predetermined shape, but the real tree grows by an inner dynamic to its own natural shape. The central idea here is the importance of individual choice. Those who live by convention grow listless and mechanical; even when they believe the truth, the belief is lifeless and little affects their conduct. Those who live by an inner principle develop strong and vibrant personalities. The vision of this energetic character is central for Mill, and the condition for the development of this character is freedom. Mill's emphasis on this character type and the social condition of its development helps to illuminate diverse strands of his thought. The thesis of *On Liberty* is Mill's "harm principle," which states that society may interfere with individual conduct only to avoid harm to others: clearly an attempt to provide the precondition for strong character. Of the same stamp is Mill's dislike of governmental intervention to help those who can help themselves. His movement away from a Benthamite account of utility makes sense in this light as well. Mill included in utility the possession of strong and energetic character, not merely the experience of pleasure. And this, in turn, makes sense of the connection he saw between utility and liberty: denial of liberty stunted and weakened the character, and so decreased utility.

This import to utilitarianism is of Romantic origin, as can be seen by what this account implicitly rejects. Mill's notion of character, of its free, energetic development according to the individual's own tendencies, in effect denies that there is some fixed human nature which one must nurture and develop to find happiness. This denial that there is a nature of things that constrains us, in favor of individuality and diversity, is distinctively Romantic. The idea had to undergo some pruning, though, to fit into Mill's thought. The individual had to act according to the harm principle, and more generally to promote overall utility. Whether the true Romantic spirit can accept such constraints, or whether it would see them as an attempt to shape it to fit a preexisting mold, is an open question.

Mill sought to extend the ideas of liberty and energetic character in addressing the question of the status of women. In a time of general decline in the influence of ancient prejudices, Mill saw as especially anomalous the continued denial of freedom to women. In his prescient *The Subjection of Women* (1869) he called for the extension to women of the blessings to be derived from the free development of character. Doubtless the development of his thought in this, as in other areas, was influenced by his long-term friendship with Harriet Taylor, and his marriage to her in 1851, after the death of her first husband.

Mill's grafting of Romantic elements onto utilitarianism is only one example of a larger syncretistic tendency in his thought. In general he saw the truth, especially truth about complex human and social reality, as many-sided, with contending intellectual factions often each representing some part of a larger truth. His companion essays on Bentham and Samuel Taylor Coleridge represent a striking example of this tendency. Surprisingly, the essay on Bentham is quite critical, the one on Coleridge relatively laudatory. Bentham, Mill believed, had discovered the truth that lay outside received opinion, but the conservative Coleridge treated received opinion sympathetically, from the inside as it were, and articulated the truth it contained. Because Mill wrote the essays for an audience sympathetic to Bentham, he emphasized Bentham's shortcomings and Coleridge's strengths. As if to confirm Mill's point about the one-sidedness of intellectual factions, the Benthamites received what they saw as an attack on their hero coldly.

Sometimes Mill's complex relationship with his father had repercussions in his philosophical work. James Mill had written an *Essay on Government*, which came under withering attack from the historian Thomas Babington Macaulay. James Mill had based his argument for democratic government on certain rather abstract axioms about human psychology and the workings of the political order. Macaulay was dismissive of what he saw as *a priori* reasoning divorced from empirical reality. In his *A System of Logic* (1843) John Stuart Mill was concerned in part to provide the method for a science of society that would be empirically testable but that also could make use of higher-level, more abstract principles. A basic problem he saw with any science of society was that social phenomena are often embedded in such a welter of conflicting, causal crosscurrents that determining the principles governing them is extraordinarily difficult. To resolve this difficulty, Mill proposed three levels of assertions about the workings of the social order. At the lowest level were to be empirical generalizations that the scientist could observe. To explain these generalizations, however, two additional levels were needed. At the highest level was a set of basic psychological laws of the individual. Connecting these laws to the empirical generalizations was to be a middle level of "ethology" that laid out the laws governing the interactions of humans in groups, and which might vary from one culture to another.

Still other work was more immediately practical, and here his common sense was nurtured by his real-world political experience as an administrator of the East India Company (1823–57) and a member of Parliament (1865–68). In his *Principles of Political Economy* (1848) Mill laid out his economic theory. He distinguished between the production of goods, which is governed by fixed laws, and their distribution, over which humans can exercise control. Though here and elsewhere he flirted with socialism (less so later, in his *Chapters on Socialism* [1879]), another of his prescient attitudes was his dismissal of untried experiments in political and economic revolution. He saw the more radical socialists as motivated more by hatred than by a genuine desire to improve the lot of workers.

TIM HURLEY

Biography

Born in London, May 20, 1806, son of James Mill. Educated at home by his father, 1809–20. Further education, conversion to Benthamism, beginning of career with East India Company, 1821–30. Severe depression and departure from strict Benthamism, 1826–27. Met Harriet Taylor, 1830. Taylor's husband died, 1849; Mill and Taylor married, 1851. Retirement from East India Company, Harriet Taylor Mill died, 1858. Member of Parliament for Westminster, 1865–68. Died at Avignon, May 7, 1873.

Selected Works

The Collected Works of John Stuart Mill. 33 vols. Edited by J. M. Robson. Toronto, 1965–91.
On Liberty and Utilitarianism. New York: Alfred A. Knopf, 1969.
On Socialism. Buffalo, N.Y.: Prometheus Books, 1987.
The Subjection of Women. Arlington Heights, Ill.: Harlan Davidson, 1980.
Mill's Essays on Literature and Society. New York: Macmillan, 1965.
Principles of Political Economy and Chapters on Socialism. Oxford: Oxford University Press, 1994.

Bibliography

Anschutz, R. P. *The Philosophy of John Stuart Mill.* Oxford: Oxford University Press, 1953.
Berlin, Isaiah. "John Stuart Mill and the Ends of Life." In *J. S. Mill On Liberty in Focus.* London: Routledge, 1991. 131–61.
Courtney, W. L. *Life of John Stuart Mill.* 1889.
Cowling, Maurice. *Mill and Liberalism.* Cambridge: Cambridge University Press, 1963.
Donner, Wendy. *The Liberal Self: John Stuart Mill's Moral and Political Philosophy.* Ithaca, N.Y.: Cornell University Press, 1991.
Himmelfarb, Gertrude. *On Liberty and Liberalism: The Case of John Stuart Mill.* San Francisco: Institute for Contemporary Studies Press, 1990.
McCloskey, H. J. *John Stuart Mill: A Critical Study.* London: Macmillan, 1971.
Ryan, Alan. *J. S. Mill.* London: Routledge and Kegan Paul, 1974.
Skorupski, John, ed. *The Cambridge Companion to Mill.* Cambridge: Cambridge University Press, 1998.
Woods, Thomas. *Poetry and Philosophy: A Study in the Thought of John Stuart Mill.* London: Hutchinson, 1961.

MILTON, JOHN/PARADISE LOST 1667

For most English writers of the late eighteenth and early nineteenth centuries, John Milton was one of two supreme heroes in the national literary tradition (along with William Shakespeare), and *Paradise Lost* (1667) was his preeminent achievement. Even for Samuel Johnson, whose *Life of Milton* conveyed an antipathy for the man and delivered some famously cutting opinions about his epic ("No one ever wished it longer"), *Paradise Lost* has a "greatness" unlike any other poem. Prominent English poets and essayists admired it extravagantly; they exulted over Milton's superiority to continental rivals like Friedrich Gottlieb Klopstock. *Paradise Lost* became the one inescapable example of sublimity in English poetry.

Milton's literary magnitude has been alternately construed as inspirational and stifling to the Romantic poets who shared his epic ambitions. In *The Anxiety of Influence*, Harold Bloom argues that all Romantics wrote in the shadow of Milton and struggled by various conscious or unconscious means to "misread" *Paradise Lost* and thereby make room for their own creative efforts. Although Bloom's theory is hyperbolic and deliberately provocative, most contemporary scholars would concede that *Paradise Lost* vexed Romantic poets to some degree even as it nourished their work. Different critics have chosen to emphasize either the nourishment or the anxiety, but it makes sense to treat them as complementary elements of a single experience: Milton's epic produces anxiety precisely because it offers such attractive inspirational material.

The most conspicuous feature of Romantic readings and misreadings of *Paradise Lost* is the so-called satanic school of interpretation. A number of English Romantics, including William Blake, Lord Byron, and Percy Bysshe Shelley, despised Milton's God and admired Satan as the real hero of the poem. Blake put the case most strikingly in *The Marriage of Heaven and Hell*: "The reason Milton wrote in fetters when he wrote of Angels & God, and at liberty when of Devils & Hell, is because he was

a true poet and of the Devil's party without knowing it." Shelley spells out more plainly what he likes about Satan in the preface to *Prometheus Unbound*—his "courage, and majesty, and firm and patient opposition to omnipotent force"—and suggests in his *Defence of Poetry* that Milton knew well enough what he was doing: "Nothing can exceed the energy and magnificence of the character of Satan as expressed in *Paradise Lost*. It is a mistake to suppose that he could ever have been intended for the popular personification of evil." Although several twentieth-century Miltonists have deplored these satanic alliances, Romantic readings of Satan are not as simple as they have been portrayed. Shelley, for example, preferred Prometheus to Satan because of Satan's unattractive "desire of personal aggrandisement." Samuel Taylor Coleridge makes a similar point in his "Lecture on Milton and *Paradise Lost*": despite his "singularity of daring" and "grandeur of sufferance," the character of Satan is "pride and sensual indulgence."

Beyond the interesting but partially misleading headline of Satanism, Romantic reception of *Paradise Lost* had political, religious, and literary implications. Politically, a number of Romantic readers found support for republican causes (especially given the context of Milton's life). But Satan is as much a tyrant as a rebel, and Romantics whose enthusiasm for revolution waned could also quote the poem to support more traditional political positions. In matters of religion, the Romantic response was similarly complicated. William Cowper was compelled but alarmed by some of the harsher Calvinist features of the poem's theology. Blake worked to remold Milton's theology into a visionary Christianity based on "the poetic genius" that underlies every true religion. For Blake, Milton was an inspired but flawed poet-prophet. John Keats's more secular imagination suggested that the religious and philosophical premises of *Paradise Lost* were outdated, which gave modern poets like William Wordsworth the edge over Milton in "the grand march of human

Henry Fuseli, *Der triumphierende Messias* (Milton, Paradise Lost Vi, 824 ff.). Reprinted courtesy of AKG London.

intellect." Several Romantics saw *Paradise Lost* as a model of literary originality, most strikingly because of the way Milton rewrote scripture as literature. The Romantic construction of imagination also owes a debt to *Paradise Lost*, not only in connection with Satan, for whom "The mind is its own place, and in itself / Can make a Heav'n of Hell, a Hell of Heav'n," but with the epic narrator, whose invocations become increasingly personal. For Milton, if imagination was not in any simple way a virtue (as it was so often construed in Romantic ideology), it was potentially divine as well as satanic.

The most ambitious Romantics undertook epic projects that would answer, adapt, or reimagine *Paradise Lost* for a new age. Sometimes the attempt was simply too close to the original and failed as a result. Keats's *Hyperion*, for example, closely resembles *Paradise Lost* in the nature of its topic (fallen titans in battle with gods), the architecture of its narrative, and some Miltonic

tricks of versification; Keats eventually abandoned it ("I have given up *Hyperion*—there were too many Miltonic inversions in it"). Blake similarly risked proximity to the original, but his vigorous engagement with *Paradise Lost* saved him from the discouragement of imitation. His first epic draft, *Vala* (later *The Four Zoas*), delivers a complex rewriting of Milton's narrative of the fall. His first engraved epic makes Milton himself the hero: Milton, "unhappy tho' in Heav'n," returns to the world to address certain flaws in his original vision and to correct misinterpretations of his work that have aggravated conditions he intended to improve. An example of a more oblique response to *Paradise Lost* is Mary Shelley's *Frankenstein* (1818). Beyond several obvious echoes and allusions, the patterns of intertextuality are complicated: Victor Frankenstein becomes not only God but Satan, and his creature, an Adam who more subtly resembles Eve, also identifies heavily with Satan. Even a work like Wordsworth's *The Prelude* (1850), on the surface a very different sort of epic, responds to *Paradise Lost* in key moments. Wordsworth's epiphany on Mount Snowdon, for example, offers a telling revision of Milton's invocation. In place of the Holy Spirit "brooding on the vast Abyss," Wordsworth substitutes "a mind, / That feeds upon infinity, that broods / Over the vast abyss," and characteristically appropriates the Miltonic in the name of the Romantic.

WAYNE GLAUSSER

Works

Paradise Lost, 1667; 2nd ed., 1674.

Bibliography

Bloom, Harold. *The Anxiety of Influence*. Oxford: Oxford University Press, 1973.

Brisman, Leslie. *Milton's Poetry of Choice and Its Romantic Heirs*. Ithaca, N.Y.: Cornell University Press, 1973.

DiSalvo, Jackie. *War of Titans: Blake's Critique of Milton and the Politics of Religion*. Pittsburgh: University of Pittsburgh Press, 1983.

Griffin, Dustin. *Regaining Paradise: Milton and the Eighteenth Century*. Cambridge: Cambridge University Press, 1986.

Low, Lisa and Anthony John Harding, eds. *Milton, the Metaphysicals, and Romanticism*. Cambridge: Cambridge University Press, 1994.

Newlyn, Lucy. *"Paradise Lost" and the Romantic Reader*. Oxford: Clarendon Press, 1993.

Wittreich, Joseph Anthony, Jr. *The Romantics on Milton: Formal Essays and Critical Asides*. Cleveland: The Press of Case Western Reserve University, 1970.

———, ed. *Milton and the Line of Vision*. Madison: University of Wisconsin Press, 1975.

MINARDI, TOMMASO 1787–1871

Italian painter

Tommaso Minardi was a pupil of Vincenzo Camuccini, but he disagreed with his teacher's cool scholastic style, which adhered to the Classicism of the Napoleonic age as a model. Minardi broke away from Camuccini's influence due to his natural tendency toward detailed observation and exquisite taste for compo-

sition. Although influenced by the mode of statuary drawing (which had classical sculptures as models), he eventually dissociated himself from its formalism, preferring a clear drawing style marked by few shadings and some *highlights of white*, according to the theatrical style of his contemporary artists. Minardi was a great master of drawing and painting in the ancient sense of the word; in fact, many generations of painters and drawers were trained at his school. He was teacher and headmaster at the Academy of Fine Arts in Perugia; Annibale Angelini and Vincenzo Barboni were among his students. He also influenced the artistic Umbrian formation for several decades. In Rome in 1827, an unprecedented opportunity to observe fifteenth-century Italian art became available to him when Prince Tommaso Corsini entrusted him with the restoration of some paintings and the organization of the prince's gallery.

Minardi's natural inclinations aligned him with the Nordic purist taste, above all with the German Nazarenes, but his spontaneous and personal style remained distinctly his own. When in 1843 the writer and painter Antonio Bianchini published his paper *On Purism in Arts* (which is considered the Roman purism manifesto), Minardi signed it with enthusiasm, as did the other artists and writers of his circle, such as the sculptor Pietro Tenerani and Friedrich Overbeck, the leader of the Nazarene school.

Minardi was a great drawer, able to improvise compositions quickly and expertly; he was often inspired by Romantic poems and ancient history. He did not like painting on the canvas, but assigned this task, which he considered secondary, to his assistants. In addition to drawing, Minardi wrote on artistic issues and concerns. Some of his essays, which were initially only distributed among a narrow circle of readers, were gathered and edited by Ernesto Ovidi in 1864.

Minardi was very active throughout Rome and several Italian towns. His travels and familiarity with Italy allowed him to develop an understanding of his artistic heritage. He realized some of his paintings were inspired by the refined linear style of the fifteenth century Umbrian masters, as well as Beato Angelico, Giotto, Melozzo, and Raphael.

His best work is considered the *Autoritratto nella soffitta* (*Self-Portrait in the Garret*, 1813). It deals with a moving and Romantic subject: the painter is presented as a young man, sitting on a pallet, with the tools of his art near him. It is set in a garret, and the furniture is extremely simple: a bed and a bookshelf, a chair and a washbasin, a skull of a man and one of an animal. Everything is in deliberate disorder. The small and simple garret room is well-suited to a student's poor and irregular existence. Yet essential philosophical concerns are also suggested, as by the two skulls and their suggestions of mortality and the passing of time. The picture is emblematic of a Romantic sensibility. The young man in the garret might be considered the embodiment of a Romantic vision of life; he appears engrossed in existential meditation, perhaps in anticipation of the artist's turbulent life, which aligns him with the main character of *Ultime Lettere di Jacopo Ortis* (*Jacopo Ortis's Last Letters*) by Ugo Foscolo.

Many of Minardi's works illustrate the typically Romantic attraction to medievalism, both in style and subject matter; they also display a deep piety pervaded by mysticism. *la Madonna del Rosario* (*Our Lady of the Rosary, 1840*), is a fine oil on canvas, where the poses and gestures of the subjects suggest a subtly idyllic atmosphere; the Holy Virgin, holding a book, shares a knowing glance with the Holy Child, who is placing the Rosary Crown around the neck of a lamb. Purity and innocence are further evoked by the lily, placed in a vase behind the figures. This painting expresses another Romantic theme, whereby religiosity becomes devotion and sentiment. The theme is much more evident in *La visione di San Stanislao Kostka* (*Saint Stanislaus Kostka's Vision*, 1840). This work illustrates the painter's mystic and devotional intentions especially well: the Virgin Mary, surrounded by angels and saints, appears in front of Stanislaus, prepared to receive him into paradise. Another work with a religious subject is *La missione degli Apostoli* (*The Mission of the Apostoles*, 1848) which was commissioned by Pius IX. Among his drawings, *Paliano de' Colonnesi* (1815–19), in which the palace of Paliano is seen from west, its crenellated walls prominently visible, is especially notable. Here the Romantic appreciation of the medieval is predominant. The set of drawings on the *Challenge of Barletta* is another exceptional example of Romantic medievalism.

Minardi composed several drawings of masterpieces of figurative art. Among these drawings, destined to be engraved and then printed, there is the portrait of *Galileo* with his telescope and ring, from a painting of Passignano, engraved by Pietro Bettinelli and printed by Luigi Fabbri in Rome, and *Michelangelo's Doomsday*, printed in 1869.

ELVIO CIFERRI

See also **Art and Medievalism; Foscolo, Ugo; Overbeck, Johann Friedrich;** *Ultime lettere di Iacopo Ortis*

Biography

Born at Faenza on December 4, 1784; received initial education in his town at the school of Giuseppe Zauli. In 1803 traveled to Rome to study drawing and painting. Here he was helped by Prince Agostino Chigi and Duke Francesco Caetani, and thanks to them he met the painter Felice Giani, who permitted him to use his study room, including books and plaster casts. Attended Camuccini's school until he was considered a skilled drawer. Taught drawing at Perugia from 1819 to 1821. From 1822 to 1858, held the chair of drawing and painting at the Academy of Saint Luca, Rome. Associate in The Virtuosi of Pantheon Society (1830), the Academy of Fine Arts (1832), Arcadia (1836), and the British Academy (1845). Headmaster of the Vatican Study of Mosaics, inspector of public paintings, member of the Consultative Committee for Antiquities and Fine Arts of the Archeological Roman Academy, and of the Commission of Sacred Archeology. Affected by paralysis in 1868. Died on January 13, 1871 in Rome, where a monument was erected in his honor at the Cemetery of Verano on June 15, 1876.

Collected Works

Ragionamento detto alle Pontificie Accademie Romane di Archeologia e di San Luca in solenne adunanza, 1835.
Disegni di Tommaso Minardi (1787–1871), Roma, Galleria Nazionale d'Arte Moderna, 21 ottobre 1982–9 gennaio 1983. Rome: De Luca, 1982.
Tommaso Minardi: disegni, taccuini, lettere nelle collezioni pubbliche di Forlì e Faenza. Edited by Monica Manfrini Orlandi and Attilia Scarlini. Bologna: CLUEB, 1982.
Scritti del cavaliere Tommaso Minardi sulle qualità essenziali della pittura italiana dal suo risorgimento alla sua decadenza. Edited by Eruesto Ovidi. 1864. Translated as *On the Essential Quality of Italian Painting from its Renaissance to the Period of its Prescription* by Joshua Charles in *Nineteenth-century Theories of Art*. Edited by J. C. Taylor. Berkeley and Los Angeles: University of California Press, 1987.

Bibliography

Bernardi, Flora. *Tommaso Minardi*. Faenza: Dal Pozzo, 1935.
De Sanctis, Guglielmo. *Tommaso Minardi e il suo tempo*. Rome: Forzani, 1900.

Montanari, Antonio. *Cenni biografici del disegnatore e pittore Tommaso Minardi di Faenza*. Faenza: Stamperia Novelli, 1871.

Ovidi, Ennesto. *Tommaso Minardi e la sua scuola*. Rome: Pietro Rebecca, 1902.

Rossi Scotti, Giovanni Battista. *Il professor Tommaso Minardi e l'Accademia di Belle Arti di Perugia: ricordi storici*. Perugia: Vincenzo Bartelli, 1874.

MOBY-DICK; OR, THE WHALE 1851

Novel by Herman Melville

Written and published in under two years, *Moby-Dick* was a departure from Herman Melville's earlier work, and is now regarded as one of the key literary works of the late Romantic period. Originally conceived as a straightforward tale of a cantankerous captain and a disastrous voyage, the novel not only provides an encyclopedic commentary on the whaling industry, but is also a metaphoric treatment of the great myth of postrevolutionary America. In Ahab, Melville created a complex tragic hero whose mesmeric power over the crew of his doomed ship is every bit as mystical and fearsome as the Great White Whale himself, while the *Pequod* and her crew of wanderers and misfits form a metaphor for the American republic.

Melville began contemplating the novel that would become *Moby-Dick* in January 1850 on a voyage back from Europe, after arranging the British publication of two other novels, *Redburn: His First Voyage* and *White Jacket; or, the World in a Man-of-War*. Sometimes referred to as a handbook of whaling, *Moby-Dick* begins with a collection of extracts providing the literary context for the tale that follows. The story itself, however, was inspired by tales among the whaling communities of the New England coast and elsewhere, of an albino whale, known variously as "Old Tom" and "Mocha Dick" who terrorized the boats that pursued him. Aboard the whaler *Acushnet* in 1841, Melville had been told the story of the whaler *Essex*, rammed and sunk by a whale on November 20, 1820. Owen Chase, one of the sailors aboard the *Essex*, published his account of the disaster in 1821, and Melville is known to have referred to this work while writing his novel.

Melville produced much of *Moby-Dick* at his lodgings in New York, but substantially rewrote and completed the novel at Arrowhead, his house in rural Massachusetts, during the summer of 1851. It was published in London as *The Whale* in October of that year and appeared in New York in its complete form as *Moby-Dick* in November. In many ways, *Moby-Dick* is similar in approach and subject matter to Melville's earlier output in that it draws on his experiences as a sailor. Yet he was also fascinated by the superstitions and tall tales that proliferated among whaling communities, and it is in its treatment of the mythology of whaling as a means to explore grand metaphysical themes that *Moby-Dick* differs from the essentially straightforward adventure stories that had been Melville's stock in trade.

Moby-Dick has three principal characters: Ishmael, the narrator; Ahab, the monomaniac captain; and Moby-Dick, his quarry. Ishmael is an enigmatic figure, an innocent in whaling, like most of his audience, who has gone to sea, as he says in his opening monologue, because "meditation and water are wedded together." His narrative, therefore, is both informative and speculative, explaining the events of the voyage and detailing what he learns of whaling, but also pondering human existence and the final indifference of the natural world to the paltry efforts of humankind. Ahab, his alter-ego, dominates the central part of the novel almost to the exclusion of Ishmael. Driven only by his desire to destroy Moby Dick, Ahab is a Nietzshean superman who has looked into the abyss. Yet the abyss not only looks back into him but finally claims him as its own. Ahab's fate is the ultimate fate of all Romantic heroes; only Ishmael, bobbing on the swell and clinging to his life-raft coffin, reaches an existential acceptance of his own insignificance.

If Ishmael and Ahab form two uncertain and possibly contradictory halves of the novel's visualizing consciousness, the symbolism of the whale itself is no more straightforward. In its many abridged editions, *Moby-Dick* is usually reduced to the chase plot, in which Ahab drives his ship and crew to destruction in pursuit of the creature that robbed him of one of his legs. Ahab declares the white whale to be the embodiment of evil, and famously nails a gold doubloon to the mast for the first man to spot the creature. But critics have seen the whole Moby-Dick as a representative of all creation against which humankind is pitted, or as innocence, or even God. Those who have read the novel as an allegory about America have viewed the white whale as an idealistic vision of the continent and the new republic, pursued relentlessly until it and the civilization founded in its honor are destroyed.

Yet there is more to *Moby-Dick* as a literary masterpiece than the chase plot and the symbolic complexity of its central characters. Anticipating the nonlinear episodic structures of the Modernist novel, *Moby-Dick* begins with an etymology "supplied by a late consumptive usher to a grammar school," and a list of literary extracts selected by a mysterious sub-sublibrarian. Sections of plot are interspersed with detailed factual passages on such topics as cetology (the zoology of the whale), "The Whale as a Dish," and "Measurement of the Whale's Skeleton." There are also chapters in which dialogue is presented in the form of a script, as if reported in the transcript of a trial. The purpose of these sections may be to underline the truthfulness of the narrator's account of the voyage of the *Pequod*, but they have also been read as illuminating the relationship between the practical, industrial process of whaling and the epic heroic nature of the undertaking. Ahab is serving the financial interests of the owners of his ship, yet he is also engaged on a personal quest, a contradiction that has also been noted as a feature of the American project by writers as diverse as Norman Mailer and Ralph Waldo Emerson.

Moby-Dick was a financial failure in Melville's lifetime, marking the beginning of his decline as a well-known and popular literary figure. It is possible that readers were discouraged by the sheer bulk of the book or by the obscurity of its documentary passages. Nevertheless, since its revival in the 1920s *Moby-Dick* has been acknowledged as Melville's most impressive work. As an enigmatic critique of Romantic heroism, a tragic story of obsession, demonic possession, and what Harold Beaver calls "the drama of an individual soul," Ahab's battle with Moby-Dick rivals the ordeals of Faust and Sisyphus among the great literary explorations of the meaning of human existence.

CHRISTOPHER ROUTLEDGE

See also **Melville, Herman**

Work

The Whale. London, 1851. Republished, unexpurgated, as *Moby-Dick; or, The Whale*. 1851. Subsequently published as *Moby-Dick; or, The Whale*. Edited and with an introduction by Harold Beaver. Harmondsworth: Penguin, 1972; *The Writings of Herman Melville*, vol. 6. Evanston: Northwestern University Press and Newberry Library. Edited by Harrison Hayford, Hershel Parker, and G. Thomas Tanselle. 1988.

Bibliography

Allan, Gay Wilson. *Melville and His World*. London: Thames and Hudson, 1971.
Bloom, Harold, ed. *Herman Melville*. New York: Chelsea House, 1986.
Gale, Robert L. *A Herman Melville Encyclopedia*. Westport Conn.: Greenwood Press, 1996.
Higgins, B. and Parker, H. eds. *Herman Melville: The Contemporary Reviews*. Cambridge: Cambridge University Press, 1995.
Hillway, Tyrus. *Herman Melville*. Boston: Twayne, 1979.
Lawrence, D. H. "Herman Melville's *Moby Dick*." In *Studies in Classic American Literature*. London: M. Secker, 1924.
Lee, A. Robert, ed. *Herman Melville: Reassessments*. London: Vision, 1984.
Miller, James E. *A Reader's Guide to Herman Melville*. London: Thames and Hudson, 1962.
Robertson-Lorant, Laurie. *Melville: A Biography*. New York: Clarkson Potter, 1996.

MOCHNACKI, MAURYCY 1804–1834

Polish literary critic, publicist

Maurycy Mochnacki was the leading literary critic of the Polish Romantic movement. He was also engaged in political activities in Warsaw that resulted in his arrest in 1823. He was charged with organizing a conspiracy, but was freed after declaring his loyalty to the existing political order. In the second half of the 1820s Mochnacki worked as an editor of various journals. His writings significantly contributed to the breakthrough of the Romantic generation. Mochnacki's article "O duchu i źródłach poezji w Polszcze" ("On the Spirit and Sources of Poetry in Poland," 1825) relies on the principles of contemporary German aesthetics that define the sources of Romantic poetry in inspiration and creative power. This argument is repeated in his "Myśli o literaturze polskiej" ("Thoughts on Polish Literature," 1828), which is heavily influenced by Friedrich Wilhelm Joseph von Schelling's aesthetics and philosophy of nature. Mochnacki stresses the importance of creativity over experience, reason, and science. Mochnacki's study "O sonetach Adama Mickiewicza" ("On the Sonnets of Adam Mickiewicz," 1827) played a crucial role in the breakthrough of the Romantic generation in Poland. With this analysis Mochnacki became the first critic to give due importance to the sonnets of Mickiewicz, who had previously been acclaimed only for his epic poetry. Nevertheless, even Mochnacki identified Mickiewicz's epic poems as his most significant works.

Mochnacki's critical activities were not confined to literature; he was also an enthusiastic commentator on theater and musical performances. He showed special interest in William Shakespeare's plays. As a commentator of concerts, he wrote a review on a performance of Gioacchino Antonio Rossini's *Othello*. In his critique Mochnacki claimed that Shakespeare's spirit was not to be traced in the lyrics of the opera, but in its melody. Mochnacki also commented on Frédéric François Chopin's and Niccolò Paganini's musical performances. Mochnacki was himself a pianist and often played together with Chopin, whose lively and intuitive technique he highly appreciated.

A synthesis of Mochnacki's thoughts on literature appears in his *O literaturze polskiej w wieku XIX* (*On Polish Literature of the Nineteenth Century*, 1831) which was completed in the last months of the uprising of 1830 and 1831. This work consists of three parts. The first lays the philosophical framework for his investigation and calls for the creation of a Polish national philosophy; the second discusses the achievements of Polish literature in general terms; and the final part is dedicated to the analysis of the individual work of Polish artists and establishes comparisons with Roman literature. Mochnacki's aim with this work is to study the spirit and nature of Polish people because he understands literature as the reflection of the spirit of the people. Mochnacki's aesthetic principles are heavily influenced by Schelling's philosophy and he is familiar with the system of transcendental idealism. Following Schelling, he distinguishes between *imaginacija* (imagination) and *fantazja* (fantasy): he sees imagination as an unoriginal mirror image; on the other hand he associates fantasy with creative power. Applying the universal law of polarity, which Schelling saw in the whole nature, Mochnacki claims that classicist and Romantic literature were not only two different poetical forms, but two different systems. The first is based itself on antique, Greek culture, the second on the heritage of Christian Europe and the Middle Ages. He also distinguishes between what he calls the realist and subjective forms of art and identifies Shakespeare and Johann Wolfgang von Goethe as realist, Lord Byron, Jean-Jacques Rousseau, Mickiewicz, and Schiller as subjective artists.

Applying the rule of polarity for Polish literature, Mochnacki was unappreciative of the old school of Polish literature that followed the exquisite taste of French Classicism. He thought that Polish poetry in the second half of the eighteenth century was no more than the imitation of an imitation. In contrast, he believed that poets adhering to the principles of Romanticism represented a national poetry that formed links "with the old Poland and ancient wisdom." He identified northern mythology in the early Slavic period and the Middle Ages as the indigenous sources of Polish literature. His views on Slavonic antiquity and northern mythology were influenced by Joachim Lelewel's early writings. Mochnacki proudly claimed that contemporary Romantic poetry was "so national and primeval," as Roman poetry had never been. He defended Romanticism against the attacks of the traditionalists who were scandalized by the danger of elevating unrefined peasant culture to the rank of official culture. When analyzing the achievements of Polish literature of the nineteenth century, Mochnacki praised Mickiewicz's epic poem, the *Dziady* (*Forefathers Eve*) and claimed that no one since Shakespeare's time had painted such a beautiful picture of an adventurous love as did Mickiewicz. He also wrote highly of Mickiewicz's other epic poem, *Konrad Wallenrod*, which showed an example of sacrifice for the fatherland.

Together with Lelewel, Mochnacki actively participated in the organization of the uprising of 1830 and 1831 and took part in the armed resistance. After the failure of the uprising he emigrated to France and settled in Metz. Mochnacki was engaged in the political activities of the Polish emigres until his early death. He also wrote his memoirs on the uprising, *Powstanie narodu polskiego w roku 1830–31* (*The Uprising of the Polish Nation in 1830 and 1831*, 1834) which provide a valuable documentation of the antecedents as well as the actual events of the revolt.

Mochnacki took it for granted that in the future the freedom and prosperity of the Slavs and European civilization rested upon a strong and independent Poland. In the act of founding the Polish Democratic Society he proclaimed that for nearly one hundred years European nations had been recognizing the fact that "the Polish cause was the cause of civilization." In 1831 he chose the opening of Hamlet's soliloquy, "To be or not to be," to become the motto of the Patriotic Society. His writing of the same title warned that the Poles should not trust in diplomacy. Instead, he called for the moral uplifting of the Polish nation and claimed that "the strength with which a nation meets an external enemy is in direct proportion to its internal, material and moral strength and in order to increase the former it is necessary to multiply and intensify the latter." Mochnacki held that in Poland a privileged minority constituted the nation, while the majority was excluded from it and thought that all evil sprang from this disproportion. Consequently, he demanded that this injustice should be corrected through a social revolution.

MONIKA BAÁR

See also **Chopin, Frédéric François; German Idealism: Its Philosophical Legacy; German Romanticism: Its Literary Legacy; Liberty; Mickiewicz, Adam Bernard; Pan-Slavism;** **Poland: Cultural Survey; Poland: Historical Survey; Political Thought; Schelling, Friedrich Wilhelm Joseph von; Shakespeare: Europe**

Biography

Born in Lvóv, probably September 13, 1804. Studied law at Warsaw University, 1820–23; was expelled and arrested for conspiratorial activity. After release worked as a journalist and art critic. Editor of several journals, including *Dziennik Warszawski*, 1825; *Gazeta Polska*, 1827–29; and *Kurier Polski*, 1829–30. Actively participated in the uprising of 1830–31. After its suppression, emigrated to France and settled in Metz. Became involved in emigré political activities. Died December 20, 1834 of meningitis in Auxerre.

Selected Works

Collections
Dzieła. 3 vols, 1863.
Pisma krytyczne i politiczne. 2 vols. Edited by Jacek Kubiak, Elżbieta Nowicka and Zbiegniew Przychodniak. 1996.

Books
O literaturze polskiej w wieku XIX, 1831.
Powstanie narodu polskiego w roku 1830 i 1831, 1834.

Articles on Literature and Criticism
"O duchu i źródłach poezji w Polszcze." 1825.
"O Sonetach Adama Mickiewicza." 1827.
"Myśli o literaturze polskiej." 1828.
"Szekspir." 1830.

Articles on Politics
"Być albo nie być." 1831.
"O rewolucji społecznej w Polszcze." 1833.

Bibliography

Eile, Stanislaw. *Literature and Nationalism in Partitioned Poland, 1795–1918*. Basingstoke: Macmillan, in association with the School of Slavonic and East European Studies, University of London.
Kowalska, Aniela. *Mochnacki i Lelewel współtwórcy życia umysłowego warszawy i kraju 1825–30*. Warsaw: Państwowy Instytut Wydawniczy, 1971.
Krzemień-Ojak, Krystyna. *Maurycy Mochnacki program kulturalny i myśl krytycznoliteracka*. Warsaw: Państwowy Institut Wydawniczy, 1975.
Krystyna, Olszer, ed. *For Your Freedom and Ours: Polish Progressive Spirit from the 14th Century to the Present*. New York: F. Ungar, 1981.
Schroeder, Hildegard. *Studien über Maurycy Mochnacki mit besonderer Berücksichtigung des deutschen Einflusses*. Berlin: In Komission bei Otto Harrassowitz, 1953.
Śliwiński, Artur. *Maurycy Mochnacki. Żywot i dzieła*. Warsaw: Wydawnictwo M. Arcta, 1921.
Witkowska, Alina, and Ryszard Przybylski. *Romantyzm*. Warsaw: Wydawnictwo Naukowe PWN, 1997.

MODERNITY

The word *modern* and its cognates, ironically, date back to the sixth century, to late Latin *modernus*, from *modo*, meaning "just now." Its usage as a historical term seems to begin near the end of the Renaissance, when it appears in contradistinction to the words *ancient* and *medieval*, and it enters the vocabulary of aesthetic and literary criticism around the end of the seventeenth century in France, at the beginning of what came to be known as the "quarrel between the ancients and the moderns." The quarrel continued during the Romantic period, where at various moments it was reconfigured in terms of a distinction between the terms *Classical*, *Romantic*, and *modern*. At the end of the nineteenth century the word was used in theology to describe a movement within the Catholic Church to modify doctrines and beliefs in accordance with new scholarly findings; by the 1930s it had come to characterize the period, ethos, and styles of art of the late nineteenth and early twentieth centuries. The related compound term *postmodern* was already in use in the 1920s in theology; by the 1950s it appeared in architecture, history, and literature, where it began to accumulate a complex, and often contradictory congeries of meanings, in a development that has its origins in the Romantic period.

The "quarrel between the ancients and the moderns" essentially refers to a debate on the relative merits of Classical (ancient Greek and Roman) art and literature and the literature being produced during the contemporary period in which it is used (the seventeenth, eighteenth, and nineteenth centuries). The "ancients" are thus, at first glance, those who espouse the virtues of the ancient Greeks and Romans, and who therefore tend to be associated with neoclassicism; the "moderns" are those who claim that the art and literature produced by their (non-neoclassical) contemporaries and themselves is "new" and therefore on a par with, if not better than, the art and literature of antiquity.

This distinction, however, is an oversimplification of an extraordinarily complex debate, for several reasons: many of those involved who favor the "modern" are neo-Classical in their own writings, and their opponents may well be considered moderns in their own right; there is often confusion between the terms *Romantic* and *modern*; the arguments may be framed in terms of different aesthetic philosophies; in some cases the debate is couched in terms of a distinction between paganism (antiquity) and Christianity (modernity), the atheism of the Enlightenment notwithstanding; the word *modern* may be used disparagingly by one or other party in the debate to refer to works that are contemporaneous to yet different from their own; and occasionally, *classical* and *modern* are taken to refer to specific moments within a particular national literature.

Thus in France, for example, some writers fall clearly on one side, such as Bernard le Fontenelle (who wrote that "nothing restricts the mind so effectively as an excessive admiration for the Ancients") and Stendhal, who defines Romantic works as those that give pleasure to the people "in the present state of their customs and beliefs" and classical works as those that "yielded the most pleasure possible to their great-grandparents." On the other hand, there are examples such as Voltaire, who would seem to be a modern, but at the same time defends poetry against rationalists such as Friedrich de La Motte Fouqué; Denis Diderot can

disapprove of adulation of the ancients, but can declare that modern poets, "because of their lack of knowledge, sing nothing but melodious insipidities"; François-Auguste-René, Vicomte de de Chateaubriand tends to favor the Christian moderns over the ancients and against the skepticism and atheism of the eighteenth century; and Victor Hugo is able to dispense with the idea of distinct historical styles and genres altogether.

In Germany, Johann Wolfgang Goethe rejected Aristotle's theory of catharsis because it is affective rather than structural, but defined the "ancient" as the "strong, fresh, joyous, and healthy," and the "modern" or "Romantic" as "weak, morbid, or sickly"; Johann Christoph Friedrich von Schiller sees antiquity as "naive"—that is, natural and imitative of nature, while modernity is "sentimental"—reflective and self-conscious. For Adam Müller, the preeminence of modern over ancient reflects the superiority of Christianity over paganism; similarly, for August Wilhelm von Schlegel, classical Greek literature is a poetry of joy that has finite limits in natural forms, while the advent of Christianity introduced a poetry of the infinite, of desire and the limitless. The young Romantic Joseph Görres distinguishes the Greek worldview, based on Euclidean geometry, from the modern worldview based on differential and infinitesimal calculus; Friedrich von Schlegel moves from a conception of modern poetry as impure, artificial, mannered, and interested (as against ideal, pure, formally perfect, disinterested Greek poetry) to the notion of a Romantic "poiesy" that is "infinitely progressive" and mythopoietic, creating its own myth to replace the myths that grounded Classical literature.

In England, the quarrel takes the form of the "Battle of the Books" in Jonathan Swift; Percy Bysshe Shelley combines the Classical and the modern in the "chaos of a cyclic poem" in which all poets participate, from Homer, Dante, and John Milton to himself. Samuel Taylor Coleridge, heavily influenced by the German Romantics, reiterates the distinction between the Classical and the modern as being between finite and infinite; William Hazlitt echoes Schlegel's categories, but asserts that the genius of the poet must participate in the spirit of his age or country.

The range of perspectives that emerge in this debate reveals a fundamental problem—the crux of the paradox of "Romantic irony"—in the very notion of *modernity*: on the one hand it is represented as a sense of existential presentness, a contemporaneity or spontaneity, which is essentially *atemporal*; while on the other it tends to be characterized critically in temporal, or *historical*, terms. A direct consequence of the ironic incompatibility of these two modes of representation is that it throws into question the temporality of anything which might be called postmodern, for arguably, one can never be anything other than "modern." And it suggests, as Paul de Man remarks in his essay on "Literary History and Literary Modernity" (1969), that: "The spontaneity of being modern conflicts with the claim to think and write about modernity; it is not at all certain that literature and modernity are in any way compatible concepts . . . history and modernity may well be even more incompatible than literature and modernity." The paradox of modernity (and hence also, by extension, the fundamental crisis of postmodernity), as revealed in the Romantic period in the debate between the ancients and the moderns, is, in de Man's terms, that "the critical method which denies literary modernity would appear—and even in certain respects would be—the most modern of critical movements."

JOHANN PILLAI

Bibliography

Artz, Frederick B. *From the Renaissance to Romanticism: Trends in Style in Art, Literature, and Music, 1300–1830*. Chicago: University of Chicago Press, 1965.

Barzun, Jacques. *Classic, Romantic, and Modern*. New York: Anchor Books, 1961.

De Man, Paul. "Literary History and Literary Modernity." In *Blindness and Insight: Essays in the Rhetoric of Contemporary Criticism*. Minneapolis: University of Minnesota Press, 1983. 142–65.

———. *The Rhetoric of Romanticism*. New York: Columbia University Press, 1984.

Fry, Paul H. "Shelley's 'Defence of Poetry' in Our Time." In *The Reach of Criticism: Method and Perception in Literary Theory*. New Haven, Conn.: Yale University Press, 1983. 125–67.

Gay, Peter. *The Enlightenment: An Interpretation. The Rise of Modern Paganism*. New York: Vintage, 1968.

Livingston, Ira. *Arrow of Chaos: Romanticism and Postmodernity*. Theory Out of Bounds, vol. 9. Minneapolis: University of Minnesota Press, 1997.

Rosen, Stanley. *The Ancients and the Moderns: Rethinking Modernity*. New Haven, Conn. Yale University Press, 1991.

Wallis, Brian, ed. *Art After Modernism: Rethinking Representation*. New York: New Museum of Contemporary Art/Boston: David R. Godine, 1984.

Wellek, René. *A History of Modern Criticism: 1750–1950. The Later Eighteenth Century*. New Haven, Conn.: Yale University Press, 1955.

———. *A History of Modern Criticism: 1750–1950. The Romantic Age*. New Haven, Conn.: Yale University Press, 1955.

MOMENTS MUSICAUX, OP. 94 1828

Six individual works for the piano by Franz Peter Schubert

The six works comprising the *Moments musicaux* were published in July 1828 in Vienna with the title *Momens musicals*. The origin of this title is unknown; the received title of the works eventually became *Moments musicaux*. All of the autographs have been lost. The *Moments musicaux* are relatively short pieces, running between approximately fifty and one hundred and seventy measures, or roughly between three and eight minutes. They vary considerably in style, character, and complexity, and often manifest improvisatory qualities. Two of the works, nos. 3 and 6, held programmatic titles when first published. The titles were eventually dropped, but nonetheless encouraged a general acceptance of the entire group as lyrical character pieces. Franz Peter Schubert wrote them over an extended period of time (especially in view of his short life), during the period between 1823 and 1828, and is unlikely therefore to have conceived of them as a cycle—lyrical, programmatic, or otherwise. However, in subsequent performances, that is how they have been generally presented.

The provenance of small-scale keyboard works in the 1820s extended far back, certainly to Elizabethan music for virginals (William Byrd, John Bull, Thomas Tomkins) and French programmatic works for the harpsichord of the seventeenth and eighteenth centuries (François Couperin and Jean-Philippe Rameau). But Schubert's models were most likely short, characteristic works by more recent composers such as Vaclav Tomasek, written primarily for the emerging domestic instruments of the time. A certain economic urgency underpinned such writing in the early nineteenth century, for increasingly large numbers of younger musicians and amateurs of the expanding middle classes were purchasing the latest instruments and patronizing the most recent repertories, especially at home. Much of this music was specifically programmatic, but much was also of a highly generalized nature, and the latter characterization would seem to be more accurate concerning the *Moments musicaux*, especially in view of the fact that the titles supplied for nos. 3 and 6 were

tenuous at best—that is, "Air russe" ("Russian Air," vaguely exotic) and "Plainte d'un Troubador" ("Troubadour's Lament," exotically archaic). In addition to the early programmatic associations, a felicitous tonal arrangement encouraged the grouping of the pieces as well, and evidence indicates that Schubert did not discourage the notion. Robert Alexander Schumann, in praising some of the eight *Impromptus*, (opp. 90 and 142; it is reasonable to suggest that most were written and published at the same time as the *Moments musicaux)*, welcomed them as a potential cycle, perhaps even a sonata, rather than as individual works. Again, Schubert seems not to have discouraged the view, hoping to encourage greater sales.

The enduring presence, indeed prominence, of the *Moments musicaux* in public and private performance venues for the better part of two centuries derives chiefly from their individually distinctive and unexpected, even improvisatory nature. The music's rhythmic, harmonic, and formal surprises delight and startle to the present day. Consider, for example, the juxtaposition of phrasing, articulation and harmonic rhythm within (only) the first eight bars of no. 1; the surprising outburst of secondary material in dramatically new guise in the middle of the second work (confounding prior expectations of a more cordial and gentle ternary form); the tiny five-measure coda of the third, which expires bizarrely in brief gasps of conflicting style (graceful dance versus *toccata/étude*); or Schubert's use of blank measures in several of the works, as if to emphasize his prerogative of stopping musical time, enforcing "musical moments" of unanticipated silence.

However, the question of where the *Moments musicaux* fit within the larger body of Schubert's piano music is not entirely clear. A sufficiently broad interpretation of the diversity and import of his keyboard style in general, certainly in the decade before his death, has yet to be agreed upon. Working in the shadows of Ludwig van Beethoven (whom he venerated), and Italian opera (capturing and shaping public expectations to his detriment), Schubert for the most part eschewed the newer trends of nineteenth-century keyboard virtuosity. With few exceptions he moved away from the sparks, intensity, and formal innovations of his *Wanderer Fantasy* (1821–22), cultivating through melody and harmonic exploration a unique gift of "tone painting," as a notice in the Dresden press of 1828 put it (though in reference to the songs). It has most often been suggested that the *Moments musicaux* compare with the enormous number of Schubert's smaller works for piano, that they are best considered along with the *Impromptus*. But this is somewhat unsatisfactory in that one rarely finds in the *Impromptus* the kinds of "disjunctive" surprises populating the *Moments musicaux*, nor does one find in the *Moments musicaux* very much at all resembling the frankly virtuosic writing in several of the *Impromptus*. Rather, opus 94 falls somewhere between the hundreds of truly small-scale, often dance-inspired works, and the larger-scale *Impromptus*. Despite the delayed recovery of popularity accorded to Schubert's music in the nineteenth century, his *Moments musicaux* had splendid echoes, among them the truly novel *Lieder ohne Worte* (1832–45) of Felix Mendelssohn, the characteristic music of Schumann, the programmatic works of Edvard Grieg, and some of Johannes Brahms's later piano music (even if drawn on a larger canvas). Also, much European and American piano music of the fin-de-siècle and the early twentieth century mirrored the sociomusical exigencies engendering Schubert's *Moments musicaux* of the 1820s (that is, a few early pieces by Claude Debussy, and Sergei Rachmaninov's pieces by the same name—both from the 1890s, and many similar works found in the early twentieth-century American piano anthologies).

The *Moments musicaux* continue to fascinate, as they are puzzles within the larger puzzle of Schubert's musical thought expressed pianistically at a time when the modern instrument and the concert life within which they would soon flourish had not yet fully arrived. In the twentieth century the conceit of what might or might not constitute a "musical moment" inspired considerable critical attention, the perceived "disjunctiveness" of Schubert's opus 94 receiving theoretical, even hermeneutic attention, and the title migrating to a collection of Theodor Adorno's prose writings in 1964.

STEPHEN ZANK

See also **Music, Romantic; Schubert, Franz**

Work

Moments musicaux op. 94, 1828. In *Franz Schubert, Neue Ausgabe sämtlicher Werke*, Serie VII, Werke für Klavier zu zwei Händen, Band 5: Klavierstücke II. Edited by Christa Landon and Walther Dürr. Kassel: Bärenreiter, 1984.

Bibliography

Brown, Maurice. *The New Grove Schubert*. London: Macmillan, 1982.
———. *Schubert: A Critical Biography*. New York: Macmillan, 1982.
Chestnut, John. "Affective Design in Schubert's Moment Musical Op. 94, No. 6." In *Explorations in Music, the Arts, and Ideas: Essays in Honor of Leonard B. Meyer*. New York: Pendragon, 1988.
Cone, Edward T. "Schubert's Promissory Note: An Exercise in Musical Hermeneutics," *Nineteenth-Century Music* 5, no. 3 (1982): 233–41.
Dale, Kathleen. *Nineteenth-Century Piano Music*. London: Oxford University Press, 1954.
Deutsch, Otto E. *The Schubert Reader: A Life of Franz Schubert in Letters and Documents*. New York: W. W. Norton, 1947.
———. *Schubert: Thematic Catalogue of All His Works in Chronological Order*. London, 1951.
Escal, Françoise. "Moments musicaux: sur la forme brève chez Schumann," *Il Saggiatore Musicale: Rivista Semestrale di Musicologia* 4, no. 1 (1997): 113–55.
Fischer, Kurt von. "Von einigen Merkwurdigkeiten in Schuberts Metrik: eine Interpretationsstudie zum Moment Musical C-Dur D. 780/1." In *Franz Schubert: Der Fortschrittliche?* Tutzing: Schneider, 1989.
Fisk, Charles. "Rehearing the Moment and Hearing in-the-Moment: Schubert's First Two *Moments Musicaux*," *College Music Symposium* 30, no. 2 (1990).
Gauldin, Robert. "Schubert's Moment Musical No. 6," *In Theory Only* 5, no. 8 (1981): 17–30.
Kinderman, William. "Schubert's Piano Music: Probing the Human Condition." In *The Cambridge Companion to Schubert*. Edited by Christopher H. Gibbs, Cambridge: Cambridge University Press, 1997. 155–73.
McCreless, Patrick. "Schubert's *Moment-Musical* No. 2: The Interaction of Rhythmic and Tonal Structures," *In Theory Only* 3, no. 4 (1977): 3–11.
Rothgeb, John. "Another View of Schubert's Moments Musical, Op. 94/1," *Journal of Music Theory* 13, no. 1 (1969): 128–39.

MONDAUFGANG AM MEER (MOONRISE OVER THE SEA) 1822

Painting by Caspar David Friedrich

In keeping with German Romantic doctrine, the landscape art of Caspar David Friedrich frequently addresses the transition from day to night, offering vistas of mingled luminosity and darkness as visual equivalents for states of meditation or metaphysical insight. The hypnotic qualities of silvery moonlight particularly attracted him, and prompted his late experiments with the so-called *Transparentbild* (transparency picture), in which a lunar circle is literally cut from the canvas, and the whole image lit from behind by a candle.

Commissioned by the banker Consul Wagener as one of a pair of paintings—the companion piece is a daytime scene entitled *Der einsame Baum* (*The Lonely Tree*, 1822)—*Mondaufgang am Meer* (*Moonlight over the Sea*) epitomizes Friedrich's visionary mode. A nocturnal marine painting, it shows two ships on a calm sea, with three people witnessing the startling spectacle of a sweep of moonlit cloud. Huddled upon a bare rock, the figures turn away from the viewer, immersed in what the critic Franz Nemitz identifies as "cosmic silence." Their gaze is directed to the enigmatic horizon, where the earthbound yields to the otherworldly in a resolution made all the more poignant for being indistinct and perhaps precarious. Friedrich seems to suggest that the transitory phenomenon of moonrise can open up a perspective onto the eternal and the infinite, and his nuanced rendering of luminescence qualified by opacity endows his picture with connotations of the magical, the sacred, or the uncanny.

Like Friedrich's other works, this was painted inside his Dresden studio in 1822, though it implemented sketchbook details collected in the open air. Now entering upon the last decade of his career, the artist must have recalled the walking tour he had made around the Island of Ruegen four years before, during a summer holiday spent in his Baltic homeland with his brother Christian and their wives. The figures in the painting almost certainly allude to this intimate group, although identification is not enforced; an earlier work, *Kreidefelsen auf Rügen* (*The Chalk Cliffs at Ruegen*, 1818–19), had similarly cited three figures, but this time two men and only one woman. In both *Kreidefelsen* and *Mondaufgang* there appears the same brooding male in an old-fashioned beret and a thick coat; no doubt this is a self-conscious portrait of the artist as Germanic visionary. Another seascape of very similar design (now in the Hermitage) was produced a year earlier than *Mondaufgang* and bears the same title: it shows two yachts advancing toward a pair of men standing bolt upright on a low rock licked by waves, while a pair of women cuddle on a larger rock in the foreground. This anecdotal literalness—the symmetrical inclusion of two husbands and two wives—appears clumsy by comparison, as though the asymmetry of the 1822 trio were somehow more natural or more poetic.

While many of Friedrich's titles mention place names, the Baltic views tend to be nonspecific, their generalized Nordic features acting as a springboard for wider associations. One of Friedrich's early mentors was the poet Gotthard Ludwig Kosegarten, whose practice of delivering sermons on the Ruegen beach could have imprinted an indelible association between metaphysical feeling and that marginal locale. The critic Helmut Börsch-Supan insists that the picture is purely a Christian allegory, the rocks representing the solidity of faith, while the moonlight symbolizes Christ. Other commentators have been reluc-

tant to pin the image down, sensing eddies of elegiac or nostalgic sentiment, and perhaps even a hint of underlying angst. What can be said with assurance is that *Mondaufgang* exudes significantly more warmth than Friedrich's earlier masterpiece, *Der Mönch am Meer* (*Monk by the Sea*, 1809), where he deliberately painted out two ships in order to dramatize the utter solitariness of a tiny figure pinned against sand and sea and pressed below a very low horizon line. In *Mondaufgang*, the horizon-line rises halfway up the frame, and yet all three figures manage to rise higher still, to achieve the distinction of being silhouetted against the lambent sky. This silhouetting is a typical device of the artist, used to establish a link between near and far, between the world of immediacy and the realm of hope and desire. (It may be noted that the vertical emphasis of the mighty oak in *Der einsane Baum* functions in just this way.) Here, the two lofty ships, rendered in spectral blue and advancing in full canvas under what appear to be windless conditions, are like mirages skimming shorewards. (Close inspection reveals that the near ship has begun to furl its sails.) On the whole, their preternatural magnificence seems more reassuring than fearsome, as if shore, sea, and sky were being drawn into a sublime moment of plenitude and serenity. This impression of harmony is endorsed by the critic Willi Wolfradt, who points out the picture's satisfying compositional symmetry, whereby the parabolas formed by the curvature of the rocks in the foreground and by the illuminated zone of cloud meet at the central axis of the skyline, each curve mirroring the other.

The mystic Franz von Baader was one of many Romantic thinkers who thought it vital to absorb external facts through the medium of introspection, declaring that "it is the internal sense, and not the mere transcription of the external, which illuminates the progress of genius; and every authentic artist, every authentic poet, is a seer or a visionary." Likewise, Friedrich contended that what matters is not the world of mundane perception but the world reconstituted by intuition and imagination. His creative watchword is quintessentially Romantic: "Close your physical eye so that you may first see your picture with the spiritual eye. Then bring to the light of day that which you have seen in the darkness." A work such as *Mondaufgang am Meer* testifies to the absolute priority of subjective truth and reminds us that Romantic landscape art is above all else an invocation of spiritual values.

ROGER CARDINAL

Work

Mondaufgang am Meer, 1822. Oil on canvas, 55 cm x 71 cm. Nationalgalerie, Berlin.

Bibliography

Börsch-Supan, Helmut. *Caspar David Friedrich*. London: Thames and Hudson, 1974; 4th rev. ed., 1987.
Hofmann, Werner, ed. *Caspar David Friedrich 1774–1840*. Munich: Prestel, 1974.
Jankélévitch, Vladimir. "Le Nocturne." In *Le Romantisme allemand*. Edited by Albert Béguin. Paris: Bibliothèque 10–18. 94–109.
Koerner, Joseph Leo. *Caspar David Friedrich and the Subject of Landscape*. London: Reaktion/New Haven, Conn.: Yale University Press, 1990.

Caspar David Friedrich, *Mondaufgang am Meer*, 1822. Reprinted courtesy of AKG Photo.

Krieger, Peter, ed. *Caspar David Friedrich. Die Werke aus der Nationalgalerie Berlin Staatliche Museen Preussischer Kulturbesitz.* Berlin: Nationalgalerie, 1985.

Nemitz, Fritz. *Caspar David Friedrich. Die unendliche Landschaft.* Munich: F. Bruckmann, 1938.

Rautmann, Peter. *Caspar David Friedrich. Landschaft als Sinnbild entfalteter bürgerlicher Wirklichkeitsaneignung.* Frankfurt: Peter Lang, 1979.

Wolfradt, Willi. *Caspar David Friedrich und die Landschaft der Romantik.* Berlin: Mauritius-Verlag 1924.

MOORE, THOMAS 1779–1852

Irish poet, songwriter, playwright, journalist, historian, and biographer

Thomas Moore was arguably the most successful writer of the Romantic period. Edgar Allan Poe proclaimed in 1840 that Moore was "the most popular poet now living—if not the most popular that ever lived." In Britain, his only rivals in terms global renown were Walter Scott and Lord Byron.

By 1811, the publishing house Longmans had enough faith in Moore's popularity to advance him three-thousand guineas for an Oriental verse romance. *Lalla Rookh* (1817) handsomely repaid the investment: it garnered impressive reviews, passed through seven editions within a year and was even adapted for a stage performance featuring Grand Duke Nicholas of Russia. Its reputation was such that it was said to be the most translated poem of all time: by 1878, there were editions in French, German, Polish, Danish, Spanish and Italian. The rumor of versions in Sanskrit and Persian inspired Moore's friend Henry Luttrell to inquire wryly if *Lallah Rookh* "was sung, / (Can it be true you lucky man?) / By moonlight in the Persian tongue?"

It is in keeping with the awkward and contrary nature of Moore's life that, despite this immense global fame, he should be almost forgotten today. Not a single poetic *Works* was published in the twentieth century, and his prose has not been issued since the middle of the nineteenth century. There is a tiny critical heritage, and almost thirty years have elapsed since the last biography, by Terence de Vere White.

Instead, like Leigh Hunt and Thomas Love Peacock, Moore's standing depends largely upon his acquaintances with other writers: Moore's diaries, detailing his relationships with Samuel Taylor Coleridge, Walter Savage Landor, Scott, Mary Shelley, Percy Bysshe Shelley, Stendhal, and William Wordsworth, have been published regularly. In particular, Moore's friendship with Byron and his part in publishing *The Letters and Journals of Lord Byron, with Notices of his Life* (1830), has guaranteed his place in the canon.

In his day, Moore enjoyed constant success throughout his fifty-year career. His eclecticism as a writer was matched only by the variety of his pseudonyms, including Thomas Brown the Younger, Tom Crib, and Thomas Little. With the *Odes of Anacreon* (1800), Moore was a translator of erotic verse, said to have inspired Byron. *The Irish Melodies* (1807–34), *Sacred Songs* (1816, 1824), and *National Airs* (1818–27) established Moore as a songwriter, performer, and (to English high society) the palatable face of Irish nationalism.

Moore added light verse and satire to his repertoire. Although his comic opera *M.P., or The Blue Stocking* (1811) failed, his published works proved enormously successful: *The Sceptic: a Philosophical Satire* (1809), *Intercepted Letters; or the Two-Penny Post-Bag* (1813), *The Fudge Family in Paris* (1818), *Tom Cribb's Memorial to Congress* (1819), and *The Fudges in England* (1835). *Lalla Rookh* (1817) ushered in an era dominated by prose: besides his journalism for the *Edinburgh Review* (1814–34), there was *The Epicurean* (1827), biographies lives of R. B. Sheridan (1825) and Edward Fitzgerald (1831), Byron's *Works, with Letters and Journals, and his Life* (1835), and finally *The History of Ireland* (four volumes, 1835–46).

This versatility disturbed Moore's contemporaries: was he a natural-born populist or an opportunistic exploiter of literary fads? Moore was certainly sensitive to the poetic zeitgeist, being quick to anticipate, or at least closely follow, the tastes of his reading public: he cashed in on his triumphs, as the *Fudge Family* sequel suggests, and rarely repeated his failures, as signaled by the singularity of his failed dramatic effort. However, while *Lalla Rookh* appears to exploit the popular taste for Orientalism, Byron clearly advertizes Moore's poem in the preface to *The Corsair* (1814). Indeed, by the time *The Corsair* sold ten thousand copies in a day, Moore had been writing for almost three years.

Moore certainly won Byron's respect, although not without some reservations: "Moore," he noted, "has a peculiarity of talent . . . which never was, nor will be, possessed by another. But he is capable of still higher flights in poetry. By the by, what humour, what—every thing in the 'Post-Bag'! There is nothing Moore may not do, if he will but seriously set about it." The Shelleys were similarly positive: Moore is called by Percy Bysshe Shelley "The Sweetest lyrist of [Ireland's] saddest wrong," and Mary Shelley helped prepare Moore's biography of Byron. Friedrich Flotow showed his appreciation by incorporating a number of the Irish Melodies in his light opera *Martha*.

William Hazlitt, in contrast, believed that Moore "[pandered] to the artificial taste of the age" and that his poetry resembled "an exhibition of fireworks . . . that surprise for the moment, and leave no trace of light or warmth behind them. . . . His is the poetry of . . . the fashionable world: not the poetry of nature, of the heart, or of human life."

Leigh Hunt praised Moore in the verse epistle "To Thomas Moore" and *The Feast of the Poets* (1811), then fell out with his "dear coz" during the preparation of the *Liberal* periodical. John Keats was initially enthusiastic (*The Wreath and the Chain* inspired Keats's early poem, "*On Receiving a Curious Shell, and a Copy of Verses, from the Same Ladies*). Yet, his approval faded: Keats judged that *Tom Cribb's Memorial to Congress* had "nothing in it." Even Poe qualified his praise by declaring, "The popular voice, and the popular heart, have denied him that happiest quality, imagination."

For many, Moore's writing was inextricably linked to his unclear social and political affiliations. Radicals like Hazlitt enjoyed his satirical squibs, but distrusted a poet who had been patronized by the Prince Regent. Even Byron was not immune to Moore's social climbing: "Do but give Tom a good dinner," he once wrote, "and a lord . . . and he is at the top of his happiness. . . . TOMMY *loves* a Lord!"

Nor was his reputation clearer in Ireland. Born a Catholic, Moore sympathized with the armed struggle of the United Irishman against English rule: in 1803, Moore memorialized Robert Emmet's execution for treason in "Oh, Breathe Not his Name." Yet, he lived most of adult life in England and was content to court their ruling elite. This was the contradictory image inherited by writers of the Irish Literary Revival. Most would have agreed with Hazlitt's assessment that *The Irish Melodies* "[convert] the wild harp of Erin into a musical snuff-box!" Moore's influence on William Butler Yeats and James Joyce was small compared with James Mangan or Samuel Ferguson: in *The Portrait of an Artist as a Young Man*, the character Stephen Daedalus calls him "servile." Seamus Heaney concurs, suggesting he was "too light, too conciliatory, to colonise." Dominic Behan, in "Thank God We're Surrounded by Water," writes: "Tom Moore made his waters meet fame and renown / A lover of anything dressed in a crown."

Moore is perhaps a jack-of-all-trades who paid the price of trying to please all the people most of the time. Whether this adds up to Hazlitt's "fatal compromise" or was a sincere expression of Moore's own liberal and populist imagination is debatable. What is without doubt is that Moore is an underrated writer whose multifarious legacy should be remembered as much as his role in other writers' lives.

JAMES KIDD

See also **Coleridge, Samuel Taylor; Hazlitt, William; Hunt, Leigh; Landor, Walter Savage; Shelley, Mary Wollstonecroft; Shelley, Percy Bysshe; Stendhal; Wordsworth, William**

Biography

Born Dublin, May 28, 1779, the son of John Moore, a successful grocer and wine merchant, and Anastasia Codd. In 1793, first published verses, "To Zelia," in Dublin periodical *Anthologia Hibernica*. Entered Trinity College, 1794 (registered as a Protestant). Began friendship with Robert Emmet, who is later executed in 1803 for activities with the United Irishmen. Graduates, 1798. Leaves for England to study law at the Middle Temple, 1799. Appointed registrar of the admiralty prize-court at Bermuda, 1803. Returned to England, 1804, via United States and Canada, having left a deputy to perform his duties. August 1806, challenged Francis Jeffrey, editor of the Edinburgh Review, to a duel. Spent 1806–9 mainly in Ireland. March 1811, marries the actress Elizabeth Dyke, settling in Kegworth, then Derbyshire. November 4, 1811, meets Byron at Samuel Rogers's house. Death of daughter Olivia Byron, 1815. Death of daughter Barbara, 1817. The deputy in Bermuda embezzled around £6,000, for which Moore is liable, 1818. Left for the Continent to avoid debtors' prison, visiting Byron in Italy, October 1819, received first part of Byron's *Memoirs*. In 1822, after Longmans paid £1,000, breaks exile and returns to England. Byron's death begins long wrangle for the publication of his *Memoirs*, 1824. Moore buys back the manuscript of *Memoirs* and burns it, 1825. Deaths of father and daughter Anastasia, 1829. Final visit to Dublin after death of his mother, 1835. Death of son Russell, 1842. Death of Moore's last child, Tom, in Africa, 1845. Awarded Civil List pension, 1850. Died, February 26, 1852.

Selected Works

The Memoirs of Captain Rock: The Celebrated Irish Chieftain, with some Account of his Ancestors. 1824.
Memoirs of the Life of The Right Honourable Richard Brinsley Sheridan. 2 vols. 1825.
The Life and Death of Lord Edward Fitzgerald. 2 vols. 1831.
The Works of Lord Byron, with his Letters and Journals, and his Life. 17 vols., 1832–33.
Travels of an Irish Gentleman in Search of a Religion. 2 vols.
The History of Ireland. 4 vols. 1835–46.
The Epicurean: A Tale. 1862.
The Veto Controversy; Including Thomas Moore's Letter to the Roman Catholics of Dublin. Compiled by Brendan Clifford. Belfast: Athol Books, 1985.

Collections

The Poetical Works of Thomas Moore: Including His Melodies, Ballads, etc. 1827.
The Poetical Works of Thomas Moore. 10 vols. Edited by Thomas Moore. 1841.
Memoirs, Journal, and Correspondence. 8 vols. Edited by Lord John Russell. 1853–56.
Tom Moore's Diary. Edited by J. B. Priestly. Cambridge: Cambridge University Press, 1925.
The Letters of Thomas Moore. 2 vols. Edited by Wilfred S. Dowden. Oxford: Clarendon Press, 1964.
The Journal of Thomas Moore. 6 vols. Edited by Wilfred S. Dowden. Newark: University of Delaware Press, 1983–91.
The Life and Poems of Thomas Moore (Ireland's National Poet). Edited by Brendan Clifford, London: Athol Books, 1984.

Bibliography

Burke, James. *The Life of Thomas Moore.* Dublin: James Duffy and Sons, 1879.
Gwynn, Stephen. *Thomas Moore.* London: Macmillan, 1905.
Hall, S. C. *A Memory of Thomas Moore.* London: Virtue, 1879.
Jones, Howard Mumford. *The Harp that Once—: A Chronicle of the Life of Thomas Moore.* New York: Henry Holt, 1937.
Jordan, Hoover H. *Bolt Upright: The Life of Thomas Moore.* 2 vols. Salzburg: Salzburg Studies in English Literature, 1975.
MacColl, Seamus. *Thomas Moore.* London: Gerald Duckworth, 1935.
Majeed, Javed. *Ungoverned Imaginings: James Mill's The History of British India and Orientalism.* Oxford: Clarendon Press, 1992.
Sharafuddin, Mohammed. *Islam and Romantic Orientalism: Literary Encounters with the Orient.* London: Tauris, 1994.
Strong, L. A. G. *The Minstrel Boy: A Portrait of Tom Moore.* London: Hodder and Stoughton, 1937.
Vail, Jeffrey W. *The Literary Relationship of Lord Byron and Thomas Moore.* Baltimore: Johns Hopkins University Press, 2001.
White, Terence de Vere. *Tom Moore: The Irish Poet.* London: Hamish Hamilton, 1977.

MORE, HANNAH 1745–1833

English poet, playwright, essayist, and novelist

Hannah More was already in her fifties by the time of the publication of William Wordsworth and Samuel Taylor Coleridge's *Lyrical Ballads* in 1798, and she is, in many ways, most easily characterized as an eighteenth-century, rather than a Romantic, writer. As her poem "Sensibility" (1782) demonstrates, however, she saw herself in a position of transition, as she insists of the eighteenth-century luminaries whom she invokes (David Garrick, Soame Jenyns, Samuel Johnson, Joshua Reynolds), that "these are no more." An age has ended, and a new one, heralded by, for her, much-feared revolution, was emerging. For an evangelical reactionary such as More this held particular literary and political challenges. From the 1780s onward after the death of Garrick—her sponsor—More turned away from writing for the stage to writing a series of essays, conduct manuals, and poems, often of a religious nature. What is interesting is the way in which her nexus of concerns and her literary approaches overlapped with those of major English Romantic figures, while their reasons for such approaches were often profoundly at odds. More's writing on the role of women in society, based on her part in the "bluestocking" circle of predominantly female intellectuals (see her humorous poem "*Bas-Bleu*"), insistently called for rationality in women, for sense rather than just sensibility. Her *Strictures on the Modern System of Female Education* (1799), following hard on the heels of Mary Wollstonecraft's own demand for the education of women, *A Vindication of the Rights of Woman* (1792), is a curious mixture of conservatism and progressiveness. More, in a very Wollstonecraftian fashion, sharply points out the injustice that girls are given "a most defective education," that cannot fit them for their adult life, and are then sneered at for failing to fulfill unrealistic expectations. She insists that girls be taught to be rational, rather than simply to paint and to simper. While Wollstonecraft demanded "a revolution in female manners," More, who refused to read Wollstonecraft's book, was much more bound up in the maintenance of the status quo. Women, in her vision, were to recognize their subservient place in society, and to accept it: their education was to make them useful helpmeets in the domestic sphere, and women who moved beyond what was acceptable were to be ostracized by society. There is no doubt that, in this essay and in her hugely popular novel *Coelebs in Search of a Wife* (1809), a story that demonstrates the values of modesty and chastity, More is entering into an important contemporary debate about women and their place in society. It was a debate that was to be explored over the next few decades by a new generation of female writers, including Jane Austen, Maria Edgeworth, Susan Ferrier, Mary Hays, and Helen Maria Williams. It is here that the aims of male and female writers during the Romantic period can be seen to differ, for while the male tradition explores the overpowering force of the imagination, contemporary female writers insisted on the need for rationality—a revolutionary idea when that rationality was to be part of the female mind—and, as such, imagination was to be kept within strict limits.

A similar collision between Romantic theories and More's own conservative agenda can be seen in the series of *Cheap Repository Tracts* over which she presided, a collection of nearly two hundred poems and prose pieces written between 1795 and 1798, fifty of which were written by More herself. More vigorously opposed the French Revolution and these tracts were aimed at the working poor and designed to teach them to accept their position in society. They were hugely successful in terms of numbers sold: two million in the year following publication, mainly bought by charitable institutions who distributed them among the working classes. More's own involvement with Sunday schools that taught the laboring classes to read had brought into existence a potentially dangerous group of readers who could imbibe the spirit of Tom Paine by reading his books. In *Tom White, the Post-Boy*, the revolutionary potential is quashed, as the reader is told that "it was edifying to see how patiently Fanner White bore that long and severe frost" of 1795, while the title of "Patient Joe, or the Newcastle Collier," who "praised his Creator whatever befell" (whether the death of a child, or the loss of his lunch) makes plain More's evangelical and reactionary agenda. Again, it is very clear that More's thought and technique interlock with those of her contemporaries. More, writing before *Lyrical Ballads*, the culmination of a literary trend that used the so-called language of ordinary men in serious poetry, deliberately adopted the popular broadsheet ballad form, with its incremental repetition and simplicity of language, and used it to her own ends. "The Story of Sinful Sally" (1796), accompanied by woodcuts each showing a scene from Sally's life, deliberately imitated its popular counterpart, but did so in an attempt to make its reader moral, Christian, and subservient. Wordsworth, in "The Idiot Boy" (1798) employed a very similar technique, but to very different ends. Where Wordsworth aimed to explore the psychology of a frightened mother and, through her, human psychology in its elemental form, More mimicked the ballad as a way of cajoling her readers into agreeing with her. Despite the ostensible success of the *Cheap Repository Tracts* their intended readers were never really taken in. This clash between More's aims and the working-class response to them is embodied in her relationship with Ann Yearsley, "the poetical milkwoman," whose patron More became in 1784. Things fell apart when Yearsley demanded the profit from her writing and More refused to hand it over, basing her refusal on the belief that the working classes should accept their traditional position within society rather than try to escape from it. The deep conservatism of her views, however, did not prevent her from determinedly advocating the abolition of the slave trade (expressed in "Slavery" and "The Sorrows of Yamba", 1788), thus allying her with many of her Romantic contemporaries, including Anna Barbauld, William Blake, Robert Southey, and Ann Yearsley.

Lucy Bending

Biography

Born in Stapleton, near Bristol, February 2, 1745. Studied at her sisters' school in Bristol, where she later taught. A meeting with poet John Langhorne in 1773 prompted her to publish her first play. Moved in prestigious literary circles, including those of Edmund Burke, the Burneys, Samuel Johnson, and Horace

Walpole. There are few major events in her life apart from the writing of her literary works. Died in 1833, aged eighty-eight.

Selected Works

Plays

The Search after Happiness. 1773.
The Inflexible Captive. 1774.
Percy. 1777.
The Fatal Falsehood. 1779.

Poetry

Sir Eldred of the Blower and The Bleeding Rock. 1776.
Sacred Dramas, Chiefly Intended for Young Ladies, to which is added, Sensibility, A Poem. 1782.
Florio: A Tale for Fine Gentlemen and Fine Ladies: and The Bas Bleu; or, Conversation: Two Poems. 1786.
Slavery, A Poem. 1788.

Didactic and Educational Works

Essays on Various Subjects. Principally Designed for Young Ladies. 1777.
Thoughts on the Importance of Manners of the Great to General Society. 1788.
An Estimate of the Religion of the Fashionable World. 1791.
Cheap Repository Tracts. 1795–98.
Strictures on the Modern System of Female Education. 1799.

Novels

Coelebs in Search of a Wife. 1809.

Modern Edition

Selected Writings of Hannah More. Edited by Robert Hole. London, 1996.

Bibliography

Cole, Lucinda. "(Anti)Feminist Sympathies: The Politics of Relationship in Smith, Wollstonecraft, and More," *ELH 58* (1991): 107–40.
Collingwood, Jeremy and Margaret. *Hannah More*. Oxford, 1990.
Ellison, Julie. "The Politics of Fancy in the Age of Sensibility." In *Revisioning Romanticism: British Women Writers, 1776–1837*. Edited by Carol Shiner Wilson and Joel Haefner. Philadelphia, 1994. 228–55.
Hopkins, Mary Alden. *Hannah More and Her Circle*. New York, 1947.
Kelly, Gary. "Revolution, Reaction, and the Expropriation of Popular Culture: Hannah More's Cheap Repository." In *Man and Nature/L'homme et la nature*. Vol. 1 of *Proceedings from the Canadian Society for Eighteenth-Century Studies*. Edited by Kenneth W. Graham and Neal Johnson. 1987.
Kowaleski-Wallace, Elizabeth. *Their Father's Daughters: Hannah More, Maria Edgeworth, and Patriarchal Complicity*. New York, 1991.
Morris, R. J. *Class and Class Consciousness in the Industrial Revolution, 1780–1850*. London, 1979.
Myers, Mitzi. "Hannah More's Tracts for the Times: Social Fiction and Female Ideology." In *Fetter'd or Free?: British Women Novelists 1670–1815*. Edited by Mary Anne Schofield and Cecilia Macheski. Athens, Ohio, 1989.
Pedersen, Susan. "Hannah More Meets Simple Simon: Tracts, Chapbooks, and Popular Culture in Late Eighteenth-Century England," *Journal of British Studies* 25 (1986): 84–113.
Saunders, Julia. "Putting the Reader Right: Reassessing Hannah More's *Cheap Repository Tracts*," *Romanticism On the Net*. November 16, 1999.

MÖRIKE, EDUARD 1804–1875

German poet and fiction writer

Eduard Mörike is known for both his poetry and his short prose fiction. He is generally considered to be one of the most talented lyric poets of the post-Romantic and post-Goethe eras, associated by virtue of his overly sensitive and introspective nature with the turn toward inwardness and the withdrawal from society of the Biedermeier sensibility. His mature poetry is, in many respects, a precursor to Modernism in terms of its use of language and symbol.

Mörike's early poetry clearly shows the influence of both Johann Wolfgang von Goethe and the later German Romantics. His cycle of poems entitled *Peregrina*, for example, was written around 1823 after he had met a wayward young barmaid with whom he had had a brief relationship; they deal with the theme of demonic Romantic love, passions that threaten to destroy the individual. The poems suggest a talented young writer possessed of a unique lyric sensibility. Other early poems deal with the Romantic notion of the healing power of nature to regenerate the self that has been corrupted by society. They also point to a severely introverted personality that seeks to withdraw from all contact with the outside world (including nature) and to retreat into inner contemplation. There is the sense in these poems that consciousness and nature are fundamentally alienated from each other, and that this gap cannot be transcended,

as was suggested in earlier Romantic literature. This tendency toward withdrawal in Mörike's poetry has caused some critics to speak convincingly of his work in terms of existentialism; that is in terms of the concept of the alienation of consciousness from the objective world. Indeed, the Romantic theme of subjectivity is the precursor to modern existential thought. Mörike's nature poetry from around 1830 continues this questioning of the Romantic sensibility. Friedrich Wilhelm Joseph von Schelling's notion that consciousness and nature are identical is questioned in a number of Mörike's poems. The vision of nature for which the poet longs becomes increasingly aesthetized.

Mörike's 1832 novella, *Maler Nolten* (*Nolten the Painter*), is an "artist's novel," (*Künstlerroman*)—that is, a work of fiction that treats the development of the creative self. This complex and experimental text is a vehicle for both the poet's aesthetic views and a working out of psychological problems within his own personality. It deals with the story of the artist Nolten and his mentor, the actor Larkin, both representing aspects of Mörike's psyche. Nolten is a shy, overly sensitive artist who believes that he can transcend the world through aesthetic experience. He shows the influence of Romantic art on the young Mörike. Nolten's tendency to withdraw from the world into aesthetic contemplations cripples him emotionally, and his relationships with others suffer greatly. Larkin appears as the more extroverted side of Mörike's self, but he too suffers psychological problems: he is obsessed with overcoming a dark and mysterious past and so hides his true self from others through the masks of the actor. He helps Nolten to come out of himself but also manipulates the artist's relationships with the story's female figures, and thus precipitates the tragic ending. Mörike's novella has generally received positive responses from readers and critics despite its pathological characters.

After this rather gloomy story, he restricted himself to writing folk ballads and fairy tales, showing here the influence of the work of Jakob and Wilhelm Grimm. Yet even in these writings—such as the 1837 poem "Wald-Idylle" ("Forest Idyll")—Mörike still exhibits his tendency to withdraw from social contact (and his pastoral duties as well) and to indulge in the aesthetic contemplation of nature. He also began to write a number of occasional poems that echoed Greek and Roman models. In 1840 he visited Lake Constance in Switzerland and then produced a long epic poem written in Classical hexameter entitled *Idylle vom Bodensee* (*Idyll of Lake Constance*) that was published in 1846. The poem is one of Mörike's most famous and presents a humorous view of country people and their lives, written very much in the spirit of the Biedermeier idyll. The story concerns a fisherman named Martin and the tricks he plays on his greedy neighbors. In this lighthearted critique of middle-class rural values, Mörike exposes the smallminded materialism of the country people he describes so well. Another well-received poem, "Der alte Turmhahn" ("The Old Weathervane," 1852) presents an idealized version of Mörike's own domestic life as a village parson and is again an example of the Biedermeier sensibility with which his poetry has been associated.

Because of poor health, Mörike retired from his clerical duties in 1843. He continued to write occasional poetry, including a poem to his good friend Wilhelm Hartlaub and one devoted to his new hobby of fossil collecting. In the latter text, he mocks the grand Romantic vision of nature that had characterized his youthful work. His writing now turned toward the disciplined lyric of a mature neo-Classicism. One well-known poem, "Die schöne Buche" ("The Beautiful Beech Tree," 1842) presents a highly visual picture of this majestic tree and the creative solitude and peace that surrounds it. Mörike's most famous poem, "Auf eine Lampe" ("Concerning a Lamp," 1846), pictures, in highly sensuous language, a beautiful porcelain lamp that is transformed into an aesthetic object that evokes the beauty of a long-past Classical age. The language in both these poems points to the development of symbolist imagery in later nineteenth-century poetry and looks forward to the tradition of *Dinggedicht* (poetry about an object or thing) that was later cultivated by the nineteenth-century Swiss poet C. F. Meyer as well as Rainer Maria Rilke. This period in Mörike's poetic career is considered by most scholars to be his most creative. In 1853 he published a collection of his own original fairy tales entitled *Das Stuttgarter Hutzelmännlein* (*The Goblin of Stuttgart*). The 1856 novella *Mozart auf der Reise nach Prag* (*Mozart on the Way to Prague*) is considered to be his greatest prose work, a sometimes melancholic look at the artist's mortality. The text presents, in other respects, somewhat of a self-portrait of Mörike as a mature artist, a master of the imagery and musicality of lyric poetry. Despite a measure of international recognition in his last years, Mörike sought to carry on a secluded life of introspection and meditation.

THOMAS F. BARRY

Biography

Born in Ludwigsburg September 8, 1804. Studied theology at the Protestant Tübingen Seminary, 1822–26. Ordained as Lutheran minister, 1826. Parish vicar at various small churches and repeated efforts to leave the clergy due to emotional problems, 1826–34. Parish minister in Cleversulzbach, 1834–43. Marriage to Magarete von Speeth, 1851. Residence in Stuttgart and retirement from the clergy, 1851–67. Died in Stuttgart, June 6, 1875.

Selected Works

Poetry
Gedichte, 1838; expanded 1848, 1856, and 1867. Translated as *Poems* by Norah K. Cruikshank and Gilbert F. Cunningham. 1959.

Fiction
Maler Nolten: Novelle in zwei Theilen. 1832.
Das Stuttgarter Hutzelmännlein: Märchen. 1853.
Mozart auf der Reise nach Prag: Novelle. 1856. Translated as *Mozart on the Way to Prague* by Walter and Catherine Alison Phillips. Oxford: Blackwell. 1934.
Vier Erzählungen. 1856.

Bibliography

Adams, Jeffrey, ed. *Mörike's Muses: Critical Essays on Eduard Mörike.* Columbia, S.C.: Camden House, 1990.
———. "Eduard Mörike." In *Dictionary of Literary Biography.* vol. 133: *Nineteenth-Century German Writers to 1840.* Edited by James Hardin and Siegfried Mews. Detroit: Gale Research, 1993.
Mare, Margaret. *Eduard Mörike: The Man and the Poet.* London: Methuen, 1957.
Slessarev, Helga. *Eduard Mörike.* New York: Twayne, 1970.
Stern, J. P. "Eduard Mörike: Recollections and Inwardness." In his *Idylls and Realities,* New York: Ungar, 1971.
Ulrich, Martin Karl. *Eduard Morike Among Friends and "False Prophets": The Synthesia of Literature, Music and Art.* New York: Peter Lang, 1996.

MOZART, WOLFGANG AMADEUS 1756–1791

Austrian composer

Even at the time of his premature death in 1791, Wolfgang Amadeus Mozart's life and works lay at the heart of emerging conflicts between conservatives and moderns, between Classicists and Romanticists, and within a critical community as yet only incipiently concerned with music history and historical taxonomies. By and large the obituaries describe him as an exemplary composer: a notice in the Prague *Oberpostamts-Zeitung* stated that "Everything [Mozart] wrote bears the clear stamp of classical beauty," while Heinrich Christoph Koch, in 1802, described his quartets as the finest examples of the genre, the better-known quartets of Franz Joseph Haydn notwithstanding. Yet such praise was not universal, either during his lifetime or in the decade following his death. Conservative critics (among them writers who nevertheless considered Mozart a classic) dismissed many of his works, including all of the mature operas as well as some of the keyboard and chamber music, as bizarre, contrived, overly chromatic, overwhelmed by a multiplicity of ideas, decadently elaborate, too difficult, and lacking a sense of unity. Johann Friedrich Reichardt claimed that the instrumental music was "highly unnatural," while Triest described a "frequent transgression of the seemly . . . with an extremely frequent contrast between the comical and the tragic and with bizarre sequences of notes." At the same time, however, modern critics (who also saw Mozart as a Classicist) regarded these same characteristics as virtues, aspects of Mozart's music that not only set him apart from his contemporaries, but manifested a Romantic ethos. Ignaz Arnold described the "Prague" Symphony, K504, as "a true masterpiece of instrumental music, full of suprising modulations." C. A. Siebigke marveled in 1801 that Mozart's style, taken as a whole, "strictly follows the rules of modulation but via sudden transitions [away from] and then quickly back to the main key so surprise the listener that the artist [seems to have] dispensed with all previously-known rules of composition." In this respect, Mozart was seen to be a Romantic composer, if still a precursor to the arch-Romantic Ludwig van Beethoven; E. T. A. Hoffmann wrote that "Mozart leads us into the depths of the spirit world, but without torment; it is more of a premonition of the infinite."

These two images of Mozart persisted throughout the early decades of the nineteenth century and his works, together with those of Beethoven, were a focal point of burgeoning music-historical taxonomies. In 1805, a critic in the *Berlinische musikalische Zeitung* wrote that "The instrumental works of the Bachs, Grauns and Bendas changed little by little and finally entirely in the genial, Romantic works of Haydn, Mozart and their successors." Even as late as 1840, Gustav Schilling saw current music history as ending with the works of Haydn and Mozart, the initiators of the modern style, a view similar to that of Franz Stoepl, who similarly posited a new musical-historical period beginning with Mozart and continuing to the present day. A new historical paradigm began to emerge in the 1830s, first mooted in the writings of Augustus Wendt and Georg Kiesewetter, who at least implicitly recognized the notion of a Viennese classical period. And by 1848, when Karl August Kahlert described Mozart as "the most truly classical of all composers," with

Beethoven as the initiator of the "Romantic era," the historical transformation was complete: Mozart, together with Haydn, now marked the end of an historical line, the finest composer of a "Classical" period. In line with recently developed theories and models of musical form, chiefly sonata form, Kahlert also characterized the stylistic difference between classical and Romantic: "Classical composers [are] more interested in the formal structure of music, Romantic composers in free, untrammelled expression." This formulation made explicit an historical-aesthetic conjunction that dominated musical thinking, and reception of Mozart, throughout the nineteenth century and well into the twentieth, and led to the suppression for many years of most of Mozart's works except those of an obviously "Romantic" cast: the D Minor and C Minor concertos (K466 and K491), *Don Giovanni*, the G Minor Symphony (K550), and the Requiem. At the same time, even these "Romantic" works were understood to be "Classical" in style. Writing to Heinrich von Herzogenberg in October 1866, Johannes Brahms said of the G Minor symphony, "Everything is so absolutely natural that you cannot imagine it different; there are no harsh colors, no forced effects."

No doubt biographical considerations (his apparent mistreatment at the hands of the Archbishop of Salzburg, his difficult relationship with his father, the professional cabals against him, the brilliant successes of the early Vienna period, followed by a fickle public's rejection of his music, poverty, and premature death) played a role in fixing Mozart's historical importance as both classic and Romantic: although his works were ultimately seen stylistically as archclassical, here, apparently, was the first independent, Romantic artist, one whose music approached the spirituality, self-awareness, and ineffability of the Romantic. Given this biographical trope, it is not surprising that his canonization, even as a composer of "absolute" music, was achieved in no small part by his last vocal composition, the Requiem. More than any other work, the Requiem symbolized the privilege attached to the individual creative genius: it represented not only Mozart's death and his fear of the unknown, but could also, as a work of referentially independent absolute music divorced from its liturgical origin, be thought of as a universal sign of romantic longing and the inexpressible, an empty vessel into which society could pour its secret longings, desires, and fears. The reception of the work shows just this kind of development, from the private, self-reflexive work of a dying master to a representation of everyman's death. Restricted at first to performances given in memory of the composer, it came later to be used at the funerals of significant artists, writers, and composers as well as on state occasions: it was performed at obsequies for Beethoven, Napoleon Bonaparte, Frédéric François Chopin, Heinrich von Collin, and Friedrich Gottlieb Klopstock.

The escapism represented by the Requiem was not new to the mid-nineteenth century. As early as 1808, in the second edition of his biography of Mozart, Franz Niemetschek wrote, "After the turmoil of the newest composers how gladly we listen to the sublime, clear, so simple melodies of our favorite! How pleasing they are to our soul—it seems as if we had been transported from a chaotic confusion, out of dense darkness, into light and serenity." Mozart was perceived early on as pivotal to both the conduct and the meaning of musical history and musical style, straddling the line of Classicism and Romanticism, incorporating both in his life and works.

CLIFF EISEN

Biography

Born in Salzburg, January 27, 1756. Showed first signs of musical precocity about 1760. Extensive Europe-wide travels, including Austria, Germany, France, England, and Italy, 1762–73. Important later trip to Mannheim and Paris, 1777–78. Disagreements with Archbishop of Salzburg resulted in permanent removal to Vienna, 1781. Married Constanze Weber, 1782. Achieved universal success as composer of concertos and operas, as well as chamber and keyboard music. Died on December 5, 1791.

Selected Works

Masses
Missa solemnis in C Minor, K139, 1768.
Mass in C Major, "Dominicus," K66, 1769.
Missa Longa in C Major, K263, 1775.
Mass in C Major, "Credo," K257, 1776.
Missa brevis in C Major, K258, 1775–76.
Missa brevis in C Major, "Organ Solo," K259, 1775–76.
Mass in C Minor, unfinished, K427, 1782.
Kyrie in D Minor, K341, 1781 or ca. 1790.
Requiem in D Minor, unfinished, K626, 1791.

Miscellaneous Church Works
Motet "Exsultate, jubilate," K165, 1773.
Dixit Dominus and Magnificat, K193, 1774.
Offertory "Misericordia Domini," K222, 1775.
Litaniae de venerabili altaris sacramento, K243, 1776.
Vesperae solennes de confesore, K339, 1780.
Motet "Ave verum corpus," K618, 1791.

Oratorios, Sacred Dramas, and Cantatas
Die Schuldigkeit des ersten Gebots, K35, 1767.
La Betulia liberata, K118, 1771.
Davidde penitente, K469, 1785.
Laut verkünde unsre Freude, K623, 1791.

Operas and Church Dramas
Apollo et Hyacinthus, 1767.
La finta semplice, 1768.
Bastien und Bastienne, 1769.
Mitridate rè di Ponto, 1770.
Ascanio in Alba, 1771.
Il sogno di Scipione, 1772.
Lucio Silla, 1772.
La finta giardiniera, 1775.
Il rè pastore, 1775.
Idomeneo, 1780; rev. 1786.
Die Entführung aus dem Serail, 1782.
Der Schauspieldirektor, 1786.
Le nozze di Figaro, 1786; rev. 1789.
Don Giovanni, 1787; rev. 1788.
Così fan tutte, 1790.
La clemenza di Tito, 1791.
Die Zauberflöte, 1791.

Arias and Scenas for Voice and Orchestra
"Va, dal furor portata," K21, 1765.
"Alcandro, lo confesso . . . Non sò d'onde viene," K294, 1778.
"Misera dove son! . . . Ah! Non son io," K369, 1781.
"Vorrei spiegarvi, oh Dio," K418, 1783.
"Per pietà, non ricercate," K420, 1783.
"Non più tutto ascoltai . . . Non temer, amato bene," K490, 1786.
"Ch'io mi scordi di te . . . Non temer, amato bene," K505, 1786.
"Bella mi fiamma . . . Resta, o cara," K528, 1787.
"Ich möchte wohl der Kaiser sein," K539, 1788.
"Per questa bella mano," K612, 1791.

Songs
Das Veilchen (text by *Johann Wolfgang von* Goethe), K476, 1785.
Abendempfindung an Laura (text by Campe ?), K523, 1787.
An Chloe (text by Jacobi), K524, 1787.
Das Traumbild (text by Hölty), K530, 1787.

Symphonies
No. 25 in G Minor, K183, 1773.
No. 29 in A Major, K201, 1774.
No. 31 in D Major, "Paris," K297, 1778.
No. 35 in D Major, "Haffner," K385, 1782.
No. 36 in C Major, "Linz," K425, 1783.
No. 38 in D Major, "Prague," K504, 1786.
No. 39 in E-flat Major, K543, 1788.
No. 40 in G Minor, K550, 1788.
No. 41 in C Major, "Jupiter," K551, 1788.

Other Orchestral Work
Serenade in D-Major, "Haffner," K250, 1776.
Maurerische Trauermusik, K477, 1785.
Eine kleine Nachtmusik, K525, 1787.

Concertos
For violin: K207, K211, K216, K218, and K219, 1773–75.
For clarinet: K622, 1791.
For horn: K417 in E-flat major, 1783; K447 in E-flat Major, 1787; K495 in E-flat Major, 1786.
For piano: no. 9 in E-flat Major, "Jeunehomme," K271, 1777; no. 17 in G Major, K453, 1784; no. 20 in D Minor, K466, 1785; no. 21 in C Major, K467, 1785; no. 22 in E-flat Major, K482, 1785; no. 23 in A Major, K488, 1786; no. 24 in C Minor, K491, 1786; no. 25 in C Major, K503, 1786; no. 27 in B-flat Major, 1791.

Works for Wind Ensemble
Serenade in B-flat Major, K361, 1781–84.
Serenade in E-flat Major, K375, 1781.
Serenade in C Minor, K388, 1782.

Chamber Music for Strings and Winds or Strings and Keyboard
Quintet for Winds and Piano, K452, 1784.
Quartet for Piano and Strings in G Minor, K478, 1785.
Quartet for Piano and Strings in E-flat Major, K493, 1786.
Trio in G Major for Violin, Violoncello, and Keyboard, K496, 1786.
Trio in B-flat Major for Violin, Violoncello, and Keyboard, K502, 1786.
Quartet for Flute and Strings, K298, 1786–87.
Trio for Clarinet, Viola, and Keyboard, K498, 1786.
Trio in E Major for Violin, Violoncello, and Keyboard, K542, 1788.
Trio in G Major for Violin, Violoncello, and Keyboard, K564, 1788.
Quintet for Clarinet and Strings, K581, 1789.

Chamber Music for Strings
Six quartets dedicated to J. Haydn: K387, K421, K428, K458, "Hunt," K464, K465, "Dissonant," 1782–85.
Quartet in D Major, "Hoffmeister," K499, 1786.

Quintets in G Minor and C Major, K515 and 516, 1787.
Divertimento for Violin, Viola, and Violoncello in E-flat Major, K563, 1788.
Three "Prussian" Quartets, K575, K589, K590, 1789–90.
Quintets in D Major and E-flat Major, K593 and K614, 1790–91.

Violin and Keyboard Sonatas and Variations
K304 in E Minor, 1778.
K454 in B-flat Major, 1784.
K481 in E-flat Major, 1785.
K526 in A Major, 1787.

Sonatas, Variations, and Miscellaneous Works for Keyboard Solo
Sonatas in A Minor, K310, 1778; A Major, K331, 1783?; B-flat Major, K333, 1783?; C Minor, K457, 1784.
Fantasies in C Minor, K475, 1784.
C Major, "For Beginners," K545, 1788.
Variation in C Major on "Ah vous dirai-je Maman," K265, 1781–82.
Variations in G Major on "Unser dummer Pöbel meint," K455, 1784.
Variation in F Major on "EinWeib ist das herrlichste Ding," K613, 1791.
Rondo in D Major, K485, 1786.
Rondo in A Minor, K511, 1787.
Adagio in B Minor, K540, 1788.

Bibliography

Bauer, Wilhelm A., Otto Erich Deutsch, and Joseph Heinz Eibl, eds. *Mozart. Briefe und Aufzeichnungen*. Kassel. 1962–75.

Deutsch, Otto Erich. *Mozart: die Dokumente seines Lebens*. Kassel: 1961.

Einstein, Alfred. *Mozart: His Character, His Work*. New York: 1945.

Eisen, Cliff. *The New Grove Mozart*. London: 2001.

Gruber, Gernot. *Mozart and Posterity*. London: 1991.

Halliwell, Ruth. *The Mozart Family*. Oxford: 1997.

Jahn, Otto. *W. A. Mozart*. Leipzig: 1856.

Köchel, Ludwig Ritter von. *Chronologisch-thematisches Verzeichnis sämtlicher Tonwerke Wolfgang Amade Mozarts*. Leipzig, 1862; 6th ed. Edited by Franz Giegling, Alexander Weinmann, and Gerd Sievers. Wiesbaden: 1964.

Konrad, Ulrich. *Mozarts Schaffensweise. Studien zu den Werkautographen, Skizzen und Entwürfen*. Göttingen: 1992.

Landon, H. C. Robbins, ed. *The Mozart Compendium*. London, 1990.

Niemetschek, Franz. *Leben des k.k. Kapellmeisters Wolfgang Gottlieb Mozart nach Originalquellen beschrieben*. Prague, 1798.

Nissen, Georg. *Biographie W. A. Mozarts nach Originalbriefen*. Leipzig: 1828.

Schlichtegroll, Friedrich. *Mozarts Leben*. Graz, 1794.

Wyzewa, Théodore de, and Georges de St. Foix. *Wolfgang Amedée Mozart: sa vie musicale et son oeuvre*. Paris: 1912–46.

MÜLLER, ADAM HEINRICH 1779–1829

German economist, linguist, and philosopher

Adam Heinrich Müller is not well known outside the discipline of economic history. Perhaps this is because Müller's "Romantic" economics embodies many of the values of the post-Napoleonic conservative vanguard. His archaic, patriarchal, and nationalistic political beliefs reveal an unpleasant side of Romantic thought that scholars tend to avoid. But Müller's thought also demonstrates the extent to which Romanticism engages with crucial economic questions of agency, distribution, and value that scholars of literature and philosophy have only begun to appreciate.

At the heart of Müller's economics is the idealist concept of contrariety, which Müller adapted from the philosophy of Johann Gottlieb Fichte. Fichte claimed that Kantian transcendentalism should be reoriented around self-evident facts rather than philosophical categories. The principles of philosophy are constituted by a tension between the universal ideas and our experience of them in the world. Müller was also a close friend of Novalis, whose comprehension of the extreme tension between spirit and physicality is notably Fichtean. The politics of contrariety emerges in the political writings of Edmund Burke, whom Müller also admired. For Burke, our comprehension of political agency was to be learned through experience, otherwise we cannot be said to be genuinely free. But Burke also believed that this comprehension resulted in an appreciation of the order and stability of the nation; agency was a contrary experience of personal freedom and political responsibility.

The best way to appreciate how Müller brought this contrariety to economics is to compare his economic views to classical political economy, the dominant mode of economic thinking during the Romantic period. In very general terms, classical political economy is governed by four principles: 1) human beings are motivated to participate in the economy by the desire for property; 2) the value of all commodities, including labor and land, is determined by the competitive ebb and flow of supply and demand in the market; 3) the social inequality between those who work for wages and those who control production and profits is an inevitable and necessary result of this competition; 4) the capital necessary to improve these conditions must be unrestricted by state laws or national interests. Müller opposed these principles, and particularly the classical theory of capital, with the idea of "spiritual capital." In his first book, *Die Elemente des Staatskunst* (*Elements of Statecraft*, 1809), Müller argues that the health of the economy should not be estimated in terms of production or exchange, but rather in terms of land—specifically, how much land is required to satisfy the needs of the community and the nation. Economic agents learn to understand this limit through the experience of working the land and by recognizing the relation of that work to the needs and standards of the community. In contrast to the classical economists, who believe that economic agents are motivated by self-interest, Müller argued that agents are motivated by a sense of national well-being and historical pride. This understanding, he held, can then be used by the state as a guide for economic policy.

Müller's other important contribution to economic theory is in the field of monetary economics. Like his theory of capital, Müller's ideas about money emerged as a response to classical doctrine. His *Versuche einer neuen Theorie des Geldes* (*Essays on a New Theory of Money*, 1816) was inspired by ensuing debates in Britain over the power of banks and the relative value of paper money and precious metals. The bullionists, including Thomas Malthus and David Ricardo, claimed that the total value of the supply of precious metals held by a bank determined the amount of credit the bank could distribute. Müller argued with the anti-bullionists against this view. Only the extent of commercial activity, they claimed, determines the amount of credit required to sustain it. However, Müller also took this argument one step further. Since only the balance between the individual imagination and the knowledge of national interests could determine the extent of commerce, then logically and practically, money is a manifestation of that balance. Thus, the value of money has nothing to do with the medium by which it is circulated. Once the object chosen to be money is no longer used as money, it ceases to be money. In the *Versuche*, Müller usefully clarifies this definition of money by comparing it to language. Like a word, an individual unit of money means whatever we want it to mean, as long as there is consensus over its definition. Yet, economic exchange requires a means of determining the relative value of commodities in the same way that successful communication requires a universal grammar.

To be sure, Müller's economics is transcendental. This has made him unpopular and unappreciated. Alexander Gray, one of the few English-speaking economic historians to write about Müller, describes his economic theories as "the mystical, the nebulous, the symbolic, and, it is to be feared for most, the entirely incomprehensible." Holistic and transcendental as it may be, Müller's economics is not purely metaphysical. Müller was horrified by the consequences of industrial capitalism—poverty, destitution, factories, slums—consequences that he believed the classical economists ignored. If an economics could be developed that would prove that the limitation on capital expenditure was not only morally necessary but also logically inevitable, then surely it could provide a strong incentive against the proliferation of liberal capitalism. Müller's theories also help to justify the emphasis on state control in the conservative regimes of post-Waterloo Europe. Money, he argued, is a symbolic instrument for recognizing the eternal spiritual bonds between individual, land, and state. Money therefore also vindicates the state as the essential force behind economic activity and social consciousness.

Similar qualities are apparent in Müller's theories of language and art. Like many of his contemporaries, Müller sought in Sanskrit and Greek the roots of the Aryan ur-language that, once understood, would vindicate the metaphysical principles of German thought and the political supremacy of the German race. He believed art to be both the culmination of the psychic drive of self-expression and a moral sense of national and religious pride. For Gray, this combination of social benevolence and imaginative impulsiveness has all the earmarks of "national socialism," though it is unlikely that Müller himself would have thought of it in those terms. Nevertheless, Müller's thought suggests important affinities to later holistic theories of culture and economy, including those of Friedrich Nietzsche, Walter Pater, and John Ruskin.

ALEX DICK

Biography

Born in Berlin, 1779 and educated at the Universities of Berlin and Gottingen, where he was a good friend of Novalis. In 1805, converted to Catholicism, which accounts in part for his antipathy to the protestant dictates of classical economics as well as for his neofeudalism. Such commitments, in fact, got him into political trouble. Served for a time as economic advisor to the Prussian Court, but was forced to resign because he opposed the emperor's initiatives in favor of industrialization. Subsequently moved to Vienna and became an economic attaché to the Culture Ministry of Klemens Wenzel Nepomuk Luther Metternich. For his services to Austria he was made Ritter Von Nittendorf in 1826. In spite of these aristocratic pretensions, however, he continued to foster friendships among the German literati, notably with Otto Von Kleist. Died in Berlin in 1829.

Selected Works

Die Elemente der Staatskunst. 1809.
Schften zur Staatsphilosophie. Edited by R. Kohler. Munich: Theatiner, 1809.
Versuche einer neuen Theorie des Geldes mit besonderer Rückstick auf Grossbritannien, 1816. Edited by H. Liesser. Jena: Gustav Fischer, 1922.

Bibliography

Gray, Sir Alexander. *The Development of Economic Doctrine*. London: Longman, 1963.
Gray, Richard T. "Hypersign, Hypermoney, Hypermarket: Adam Müller's Theory of Money and Romantic Semiotics," *New Literary History* 31 (2000): 295–314.

MURGER, HENRY 1822–1862

French writer

The "Latin Quarter" of Paris on the Left Bank, where students traditionally eked out their impoverished lives with irrepressible good humor and either gained fame or disappeared without leaving a trace, became known in the first half of the nineteenth century as Bohemia ("la Bohème," with a grave accent, to distinguish it from "la Bohême," with a circumflex, which is a Czech province). It was, by repute and to some extent in fact, the favored haunt of penniless artists who sought to contradict their lack of material success by loudly proclaiming their genius and consoling their penury in love affairs with the even poorer working-class girls of the district. Freedom from the restraints of bourgeois respectability was, in the eyes of its denizens, ample recompense for privations and the dangers of disease and even early death in appallingly unsanitary conditions. Honoré de Balzac naturally touched on Bohemia in his accounts of Paris, but it was Henry Murger who conveyed the most beguiling image of Bohemia, peopling it with characters that speedily acquired an almost mythic status that they have retained for more than a century and a half.

Murger knew bohemian life from the inside; in fact, he knew little else until he became prosperous enough to leave it. He was born in Paris on March 27, 1822. He was a delicate child and his education was skimpy, but he apparently gained some glimpse of a superior lifestyle from tenants in the apartment block where his father had found work as a concierge. His first job was as a messenger boy for a lawyer, and additional cash came from the mysterious Count Jacques Tolstoy, who originally employed him as his secretary and then paid him to provide the Russian authorities what does not appear to have been very secret or particularly important information about French public opinion. The meager wages he paid were, however, enough for Murger to starve on, and for some fifteen years Murger's life was to follow what, thanks to him, appears to be the typical bohemian pattern. He took wretched lodgings on the Left Bank, and ate and drank as best he could, pawning his possessions when funds ran out. A succession of mistresses shared his bed, alternately gladdening and breaking his heart, and their illnesses and his led to stays in institutions that were called "hospitals," but were more in the nature of Dickensian workhouses.

Though the bohemian world was much with him, Murger maintained an ambition to write. From his teens he was swept away with a great enthusiasm for Victor Hugo, then in his pre-exile prime. This naturally led to extravagantly ambitious endeavors in the field of poetic drama. Realizing that he might do better on a smaller scale, Murger published a few poems and soon turned to journalism, trying his hand, for instance, at theater criticism and even comment on contemporary fashions. Success did not come at once when in 1845 he started writing short stories based on his experiences in Bohemia for *Le Corsaire*. For part of its existence published under the title *Le Corsaire-Satan*, this journal catered for an audience with a taste for something spicy. Murger was able to provide just what was wanted in a series of contributions under the title *Scènes de la Bohème* (*Scenes of Bohemia*). They combined the relatively undemanding narrative interest of short stories about a nucleus of recurring characters with the vividness of sketches of contemporary life in what was, for many readers, a forbidden quarter of Paris. Realism jostled with Romanticism, cynicism with sentimentality, ugliness with charm, and the language was no less varied. Murger had found the form that suited him. He also refashioned his name: adding an umlaut to "Murger," it turned out, was going too far for the sake of exoticism, but English "Henry" for French "Henri" became the norm.

Murger, as the title of his stories suggests, was not entirely unaware of dramatic potentialities in his work, but did nothing about it until Théodore Barrière, a War Office clerk with a good deal of experience of writing for the stage, intervened. The result was *La Vie de Bohème* (*The Life of Bohemia*) a drama constructed out of just a few of Murger's stories. Murger and his collaborator could not agree whether to make the ending tragic, but finally were wise enough to agree to do so. With Marguerite Thuillier as Mimi and Adèle Page as Musette, the play was a runaway success at the Théâtre des Variétés in 1849.

Murger sold the copyright of the narrative version of the collected *Scènes de la Bohème* to Michel Lévy for a price that appeared low only in hindsight, after its first publication as a book in 1851. The author promptly removed to a more respectable address on the Right Bank of the Seine, a little later acquiring property in the Forest of Fontainebleau. *Les Buveurs d'eau* (*The Water Drinkers*), the title referring to Bohemians who drink water not out of teetotal principles but because they cannot afford more stimulating beverages, represents an attempt to tap the same vein as the *Scènes*. A more interesting, if not entirely successful, departure was the writing of *Le Sabot rouge* (*The Red Clog*, 1860), which presents a series of hard-bitten tableaux of peasant life. Murger's health had, however, been undermined by his years on the Left Bank, and he was only forty when he died in 1862.

Murger shot to fame for a second time when on February 1, 1896, Giacomo Puccini's opera *La Bohème* had its premiere, with Arturo Toscanini conducting, at the Teatro Reggio in Turin; the libretto was the work of Giuseppe Giacosa and Luigi Illica. The composer had completed his *Manon Lescaut* three years before, and the librettists provided him with yet another tale from French literature with a heroine who stirred his sympathies. The first act, set in the garret, has the show-stopping moment when Rodolfo touches Mimi's "gelida manina" ("cold little hand"). This intimate moment, in near darkness, contrasts with the brilliance of the Café Momus in act 2. Next comes the chilly outdoor scene in winter in which Mimi appears abandoned, and act 4, her death scene, rivals the ending of Verdi's *La traviata*. Few composers have done justice to a literary source more successfully than does Puccini in his operatic version of Murger's tales.

CHRISTOPHER SMITH

Biography

Born Paris, March 24, 1822, son of a janitor in apartment block. Scanty education. About 1837, became secretary to Count Tolstoy, for whom he later undertook intelligence work. About 1839, started living "Bohemian life" in the Paris "Latin Quarter." In 1843, published some verse, without success; turned to journalism for *Le Castor* and *Le Corsaire*. Publication of *Scènes de la vie de Bohème*, a collection of the stories that had appeared earlier in *Le Corsaire*, 1848. Success of stage version of the *Scènes*, written with help from Théodore Barrière, 1849. Adopts bourgeois lifestyle, supporting himself with journalism, 1850. *Les Buveurs d'eau*, 1855. *Le Sabot rouge*, 1860. Died on January 28, 1861, in a *maison de santé* near Paris.

Selected Works

Nuits d'hiver: Poésies complètes. 1881. Translated as *Winter Nights*. By Arthur C. Kennedy. London: Gowan and Gray, 1923.
Vie de Bohème. Translated by Norman Cameron. London: Folio, 1968.
Scènes de la vie de Bohème. Edited by Loïc Chotard. Folio. Paris: Gallimard, 1988.

Bibliography

Baldick, Robert. *The First Bohemian: The Life of Henry Murger*. London: Hamish Hamilton, 1961.
Boisson, Marius. *Les Compagnons de la vie de Bohème*. Paris: Tallandier, 1929.
Groos, Arthur, and R. Parker. *Giacomo Puccini: "La Bohème."* Cambridge Opera Handbooks. Cambridge: Cambridge University Press, 1986.

John, Nicholas ed. *"La Bohème": Giacomo Puccini*. Opera Guides, no. 14. London: Calder, 1982.

Maillard, Frédéric *Les Derniers Bohémiens: Henri Murger et son temps*. Paris: Sartorius, 1874.

Montorgueil, Georges *Henry Murger*. Paris: Grasset, 1928.

Moss, Arthur, and E. Marve. *The Legend of the Latin Quarter: Henry Mürger and the Birth of Bohemia*. London: Allan, 1947.

MUSIC AND LITERATURE

Throughout the Romantic era, a powerful desire for fusion of the arts was evidenced perhaps most strikingly in the relations between music and literature. An aesthetic ideal of musical-poetic union was discussed by E. T. A. Hoffmann, who wrote, "[H]ow often in the soul of the musician does the music sound at the same moment as the words of the poet, and, above all, the poet's language in the general language of music?" Numerous Romantic critics elaborated upon the relationships between music and other arts, attempting to draw both concrete and abstract parallels between various forms. Hegel stated, "music is most closely related to poetry, since both arts affect the senses through the use of the same medium—sound." Johann Wolfgang von Goethe, whose work provided the most lavish and fertile literary field for musicians of the period to explore, felt that music and words found their most complete fulfillment only in one another; as he wrote to August Wilhelm von Schlegel in 1798, "the link between the two arts [poetry and music] is so crucial, and I already have so much in mind in relation to both."

Many artists came to perceive music, with its ability to evoke intangible effects beyond the reach of words alone, as a superior means of expression. Thus, even in pieces of music that did not actually set words, the use of poetic or literary titles served as a symbol of music's expressive force and potential. Franz Liszt, a leading composer of music with allusive content, noted that "it is in sounds that nature clothes her most intense expressions of the romantic spirit, and it is through the ear that ideas of extraordinary places and things can most readily be conveyed." The project of conflating music and literature was carried out in three main areas: opera, the Lied (or, in France, *mélodie*), and programmatic musical genres such as the symphonic poem. Opera had always been to some extent a literary endeavor, in its reliance on an original written text, or libretto. However, in the early nineteenth century preexisting literary forms such as novels and plays increasingly provided the basis for operatic works; in this regard the Romantic William Shakespeare revival and the rage for Walter Scott's historical novels, for example, proved to be potent influences on opera. The art song, or *Lied*, developed in tandem with the tremendous outpouring of emotion in poetry that occurred during this era. Musical settings of poems by Robert Burns, Lord Byron, Johann Wolfgang von Goethe, Heinrich Heine, Thomas Moore, and many other contemporary poets, along with such rediscovered masters as Petrarch and William Shakespeare, established a new genre that came to be regarded as quintessentially Romantic in its intimacy, introspection, and nuanced expression. Even purely instrumental music, particularly that for piano or orchestra, increasingly evoked literary themes or characters; by applying descriptive titles or epigraphs to musical works, composers could allude to well-known fictional or legendary topics in which they found inspiration, as well as enhancing the imaginative response of their listeners.

Among the many composers who contributed to this project, special mention must be made of Hector Berlioz, Liszt, Felix Mendelssohn, Franz Schubert, and Robert Schumann, all of whom possessed special affinities for literature that constantly fueled their musical creativity. Schubert, for example, is certainly the acknowledged master of the Lied, producing over six-hundred songs on texts by an eclectic assortment of poets (though eighty texts were by Goethe alone). His intense engagement with songwriting spilled over into his instrumental composition, for while he tended not to give allusive titles to his works, he frequently added poetic resonance by embedding within them themes from his own songs: thus his "Die Forelle" ("Trout," 1819) piano quintet, "Der Tod und das Mädchen" ("Death and the Maiden," 1824) string quartet, and "Wanderer" piano fantasy (1822). Berlioz's literary enthusiasms merged so completely with his composition that one searches in vain for any work by him published simply as "symphony" or "sonata." Most of his music demonstrates his devotion to literature, as in his

LA DAMNATION DE FAUST
Lithographie de Sorrieu pour la partition d'orchestre (1854)

Berlioz—*The Damnation of Faust*. Orchestra score cover by Sorrieu (1854). Reprinted courtesy of Lebrecht Collection.

passionate attachment to Shakespeare (with major works based on *Hamlet, Much Ado About Nothing,* and *Romeo and Juliet*). From Berlioz we also apprehend that literary stimulation could in itself prove more important to the composer than any precise depiction or narrative; for example, in the solitary viola solo with harp accompaniment in *Harold en Italie* (1834) a listener seems to hear Byron's Childe Harold as he plays his melancholy harp in canto 1 of *Childe Harold's Pilgrimage.* However, Berlioz had previously used this theme in his *Rob Roy* overture (1831), based on a Walter Scott tale quite different from the Byron work.

If any one literary masterpiece could be said to have dominated musical thinking in the nineteenth century, it would surely be Goethe's *Faust* (1808). This drama, about a human being whose ceaseless striving after knowledge and fulfillment knows no conventional boundaries, exerted a powerful fascination for artists. Moreover, Goethe himself constantly thought of his words in terms of their sound and rhythm, and much of *Faust* is inherently "musical," lending itself readily to interpretation by composers. Schubert, characteristically, concentrated on *Faust's* lyric possibilities, bringing to life the character Gretchen's internal musings in songs like "Gretchen am Spinnrade" ("Gretchen at the Spinning Wheel", 1814), "Der König in Thule" ("The King of Thule," 1816), and "Gretchen im Zwinger" ("Gretchen's Prayer," 1817). Berlioz remained obsessed with *Faust* throughout his career, first setting Gérard de Nerval's translation of it in *Huit scènes de Faust* (1828–29) and later producing his monumental "légende dramatique" for voices and orchestra, *La Damnation de Faust* (1845–46). Liszt explored the psychological worlds of Faust, Gretchen, and Mephistopheles in the three "character sketches" of his *Faust-Symphonie* (1854–57). Schumann devoted years to a large-scale cantata, *Szenen aus Goethes Faust* (1844–53), while Mendelssohn showed a preoccupation with the witches' scene, writing a cantata called *Die erste Walpurgisnacht* (*The First Walpurgis Night,* 1832), as well as evoking Goethe's final, musical lines from the Walpurgis Night's dream sequence in the sparkling scherzo of his Octet, Opus 20 (1825).

At least twenty-five scenes in Goethe's *Faust* invite or even require musical accompaniment. Moreover, Goethe wrote explicitly musical scenes in *Egmont* (1788), as well as *Wilhelm Meisters Lehrjahre* (*Wilhelm Meister's Apprenticeship,* 1795–96), in which the character Mignon represents music itself. Other writers also wove musical threads into their works; for example, Nikolaus Lenau's *Faust* depicts Mephisto as a virtuoso violinist, and E. T. A. Hoffmann's character Kreisler is a composer. Honoré de Balzac was smitten with Beethoven's work, and incorporated his ecstatic responses to Beethoven's music, especially the fifth Symphony, into the narrative structures of his works *César Birotteau* (1837) and *Gambara* (1837), a novel about a composer. Thus, writers as well as musicians played significant roles in fostering a Romantic symbiosis of music and literature.

KATHRYN L. SHANKS LIBIN

Bibliography

Barricelli, Jean-Pierre. *Melopoiesis: Approaches to the Study of Literature and Music.* New York: New York University Press, 1988.

Berlioz, Hector. *Memoirs of Hector Berlioz.* Translated by Rachel Holmes and Eleanor Holmes. Annotated by Ernest Newman 1932. Reprint, New York: Dover, 1966.

Grim, William E. *The Faust Legend in Music and Literature.* Lewiston, New York: Edwin Mellen Press, 1988.

Kramer, Lawrence. *Music and Poetry: The Nineteenth Century and After.* Berkeley and Los Angeles: University of California Press, 1984.

Le Huray, Peter and James Day, ed. *Music and Aesthetics in the Eighteenth and Early-Nineteenth Centuries.* Cambridge: Cambridge University Press, 1981.

Plantinga, Leon. *Romantic Music: A History of Musical Style in Nineteenth-Century Europe.* New York: W. W. Norton, 1984.

Rosen, Charles. *The Romantic Generation.* Cambridge, Mass: Harvard University Press, 1995.

Spaethling, Robert. *Music and Mozart in the Life of Goethe.* Columbia, S.C.: Camden House, 1987.

Whitton, Kenneth S. *Goethe and Schubert: The Unseen Bond.* Portland, Or.: Amadeus Press, 1999.

MUSIC: PERFORMANCE AND PATRONAGE

Economic upheaval and the new zeitgeist of the Romantic era had a profound impact upon the place of the composer within society. Musicians had traditionally found employment in the courts of the nobility, but by the early nineteenth century few aristocrats enjoyed sufficient means to keep composers and orchestras as permanent members of their households. However, they continued to commission new works and provided an important forum for the arts through salons. Material and social power passed into the hands of the increasingly prosperous middle classes, with wealthy businessmen and bankers organizing commercial concerts as well as musical gatherings in their homes.

The rise of public patronage led to more diverse opportunities for musicians, although the pace of change varied according to location, and certain remnants of older systems lingered on. The church continued to commission works and provide training for many musicians, but due to its declining social influence it now rarely acted as a direct patron. Only in the opera house did little alter in terms of patronage, opera having been a commercial venture from as early as the seventeenth century.

Romantic philosophy, which substituted the primacy of the individual for subservience to institutions, also had consequences for musical life. Where composers had previously been little more than servants beholden to the whims of their employers, they now emerged as autonomous artists. The careers of a selection of composers illustrate this shift. Franz Joseph Haydn may be viewed as a transitional figure, working as *Kapellmeister* to the Esterházy family for almost thirty years but later enjoying greater creative freedom when he was enticed to conduct his works in London by the impresario Johann Peter Salomon. Wolfgang Amadeus Mozart, meanwhile, attempted to break free from the constraints of traditional court patronage but his career ended in abject poverty, in stark contrast with the success enjoyed by Ludwig van Beethoven in Vienna only a few years later. Enjoying the patronage of princes, Beethoven obtained access to the highest aristocratic circles, but swiftly gained wider acclaim and was able to make a substantial living from public concerts. Furthermore, he demonstrated himself to be an astute businessman, playing one publisher off another, and securing publication rights for his works abroad.

After the time of Beethoven employment with a single patron was extremely rare, and composers were obliged to seek out alternative sources of income, as is illustrated by the career of Frédéric François Chopin, who lived by composition, teaching, and virtuoso performance. Receiving private patronage from the Rothschilds, among others, he attended fashionable salons and mixed with the most influential Parisian artists and writers of his time. Many musicians made a great success of their unpredictable freelance existence, profiting from advances in transport and communications to embark upon lucrative concert tours. Others, more idealistic or simply less fortunate, self-consciously cultivated the life of the starving Bohemian.

Changes in patronage led to new performance opportunities and a shifting performance culture. While the public concert as an institution had first developed in the eighteenth century, the early nineteenth century witnessed an unprecedented explosion in the number of concerts given across Europe. The first fully professional symphony orchestras (such as the Leipzig Gewandhaus Orchestra, 1781) date from this period, and the contemporaneous foundation of establishments providing musicians with high-quality training (such as the Paris Conservatoire, 1795) resulted in a dramatic improvement in standards of performance. Concert societies were established to promote the music of "serious" composers such as Beethoven, Haydn, and Mozart, and the performance of symphonies in their entirety, hitherto a rarity. Although the typical concert program of the turn of the century—a potpourri of overtures, movements from concertos, popular arias, and arrangements of vocal music for piano—coexisted alongside the symphony concert, the latter gradually came to predominate.

Under the new system of public patronage, composers were required to tailor their music to the demands of a wider audience. Commercial considerations led composers such as Giacomo Meyerbeer to write spectacular operas on a grand scale designed to appeal to popular taste. Many composers were keen to exploit the sensational possibilities offered by the massively expanded orchestra, while at the opposite end of the sound spectrum the Romantic era was also the age of the dazzlingly virtuosic solo instrumentalist. However, such music was not necessarily divest of artistic worth, and many musicians were able to straddle the divide between "popular" and "serious" music. The pianist Franz Liszt and violinist Niccolò Paganini reached such heights of success that they were able to appeal to both camps. Likewise, Beethoven was able to compose works of the utmost artistic originality yet was not averse to turning his hand to writing popular songs when required, while Chopin saw no contradiction in producing waltzes for domestic consumption alongside more technically demanding works.

More radical composers, however, disdained the public's demands for novelty and excess and preferred to compose exclusively for a close coterie of like-minded friends and for posterity. It was in the Romantic era that conditions were first ripe for the development of a musical avant-garde. Robert Alexander Schumann, for example, devoted himself to raising the intellectual profile of music, both through his compositions and through the burgeoning field of music journalism. Such figures cultivated the Romantic idea of the isolated composer as misunderstood genius expressing his inner soul, marking a new departure in the relationship between audience and musician.

Public concerts came to be dominated increasingly by professional performers, to the detriment of the skilled amateurs who had dominated the eighteenth-century subscription concerts. However, rising incomes and increased leisure time meant that music in the home became more widespread, with the ability to sing or play an instrument being viewed as a necessary accomplishment for a young lady in need of a husband. The fashion for domestic musicmaking also gave rise to a range of peripheral activities by which musicians might support themselves. A growing need for tuition and for sheet music catering for the needs of amateur players allowed many musicians to supplement their income with funds from teaching and publishing, while composers such as Muzio Clementi found an avenue for employment in instrument manufacture and retail.

As compositions increasingly came to be regarded as commodities, composers were forced to assume responsibility for marketing their works to the public. The decline of private patronage, while in many senses artistically liberating, also imposed upon composers the need to develop a sense of flexibility and a sound business acumen in order to survive.

ALEXANDRA WILSON

Bibliography

Biba, Otto. "Schubert's Position in Viennese Musical Life," *Nineteenth Century Music* 3, no. 2 (1979): 106–13.
Burchell, Jenny. *Polite or Commercial Concerts? Concert Management and Orchestral Repertoire in Edinburgh, Bath, Oxford, Manchester, and Newcastle, 1730–1799.* New York: Garland, 1996.
Denora, Tia. "Musical Patronage and Social Change in Beethoven's Vienna," *American Journal of Sociology* 97, no. 2 (1991): 310–346.
Hanson, Alice M. *Musical Life in Biedermeier Vienna.* Cambridge: Cambridge University Press, 1985.
Morrow, Mary Sue. *Concert Life in Haydn's Vienna: Aspects of a Developing Musical and Social Institution.* Stuyvesant, N.Y.: Pendragon Press, 1989.
Weber, William, *Music and the Middle Class: The Social Structure of Concert Life in London, Paris and Vienna.* New York: Holmes and Meier, 1975.
Young, Percy M. *The Concert Tradition: From the Middle Ages to the Twentieth Century.* London: Routledge and Kegan Paul, 1965.

MUSIC, ROMANTIC

The Romantic style in music is frequently described as radically opposed to its predecessor, the classical style. This is a somewhat simplistic view, for Romanticism in music, at least initially, was not a deliberate attempt to overthrow the principles of classicism. Early nineteenth-century Romanticism was far from being a conscious, concerted, homogeneous movement directed against classicism. By no means did all early Romantic composers (some trained in the classical and even Baroque traditions) disdain or discard the forms, genres, and techniques of their forefathers; conversely, traces of proto-Romanticism were apparent in the instrumental works of many composers active during the second half of the eighteenth century, the decades that were chiefly marked by the classical aesthetics of Franz Joseph Haydn, Wolfgang Amadeus Mozart, as well as Ludwig van Beethoven, in works prior to his Third Symphony the "Eroica" (1803).

Classicism in music emphasized objectivity, clarity, equilibrium, serenity, grace, elegance, and wit; classical forms were rational and restrained. The primary goal was the cultivation of symmetry and proportion as illustrated in the sonata form with its three sections: exposition (of two contrasting musical themes), development (of the two themes), and recapitulation (a reconciliation of the themes). This was the musical outline of the first movement of the classical keyboard sonata, symphony, string quartet, trio, and so on. The building blocks of the sonata form were four-measure phrases and clear-cut harmonic patterns endowed with specific formal functions. Throughout the last decades of the eighteenth century sonata form was one of the primary means of musical architecture, the very embodiment of classical conciseness, order, and logic.

Yet even during that time, Haydn (in his symphonies of the so-called Sturm und Drang, or storm and stress, period in the late 1760s and early 1770s) and Carl Philipp Emmanuel Bach (in most of his symphonies and clavier sonatas) insisted on the subjective and the emotional, expressed in dramatic dynamic contrasts; striking pictorial effects; a preference for abrupt pauses, daring chord structures, unexpected harmonic progressions, and modulations to remote keys; and sudden shifts of mood and formal distortions that clearly foreshadowed, albeit on a small scale, the musical aesthetics of the following century.

Within the historical and cultural context of the nineteenth century, Romanticism in music took two distinct paths: on the one hand, the progressive trend found its ideological sources in the French Revolution of 1789 through 1793 and the revolutionary movements of the following century: the July Revolution of 1830 in France and the 1848 European revolutions; on the wings of this social upheaval, composers cultivated innovation and sought to represent in their music the ardor, struggle, and heroism of the period. Beethoven originally dedicated his the *Eroica* to Napoleon Bonaparte, whom the composer saw at the time as the exponent of freedom, equality, and universal brotherhood; when, in 1804, Napoleon crowned himself as emperor of the French, Beethoven erased the dedication in angry disappointment.

On the other hand, the bleak political outlook resulting from the series of events beginning with Napoleon's storming of Europe and ending with his defeat and abdication followed by the Congress of Vienna (1814) triggered feelings of hopelessness and a vague, nostalgic longing for a lost Eden; like their literary counterpart, composers sought refuge in the recreation of history. The attempt to find comfort and solace in an idealized past, together with the increased awareness of an earlier musical tradition, until then largely ignored, were at the root of the preoccupation with Baroque and even Renaissance forms and techniques. Composers such as Felix Mendelssohn had a keen interest in reviving the almost forgotten works of Johann Sebastian Bach, whose *Passion according to St. Matthew* Mendelssohn conducted in Berlin in 1829. Mendelssohn took up the music of an even more distant period, using Lutheran chorale tunes such as "A Mighty Fortress" in his Fifth Symphony, the "Reformation" (1832). Both his oratorios, *St. Paul* (1836) and *Elijah*

(1846), were reminiscent of the Baroque magnificence associated with similar works by Bach and George Frideric Handel. Frédéric François Chopin composed his twenty-four preludes for piano (1836–39) as a deliberate attempt to emulate both the concept and structure of Bach's *Das Wohltemperierte Klavier (The Well-Tempered Clavier*, 1722 and 1744)—a two-volume work comprised of forty-eight preludes and forty-eight fugues in all major and minor keys. Later in the century, Johannes Brahms built the entire fourth movement of his Fourth Symphony (1885) as a *passacaglia* or *chaconne*, both variational forms typical of Baroque instrumental music.

The musical forms of the earlier part of the nineteenth century remained, generally speaking, those of the classical period. But the Romantic composer had an inclination for exaggeration and lack of balance that resulted in the reforging of the size of musical works: thus the abundance, in the first three or four decades of the century, of miniature forms—both vocal and instrumental—often arranged in sets or cycles and sometimes related either through a musical or a literary or autobiographical theme. The taste for miniatures was also prompted by the fashion of soirées (evening literary and musical gatherings of the aristocracy and bourgeoisie, of which of most enduring fame were the Schubertiads, associated with the composer Franz Schubert. Most Romantic composers were adept at penning small-scale piano pieces such as impromptus, waltzes, nocturnes, barcarolles, arabesques, and the like to be played in salons. Chopin, the composer of the Polish-inspired mazurkas and polonaises, also wrote waltzes and nocturnes—all of relatively diminutive size and imparting a sense of intimacy. In addition, the first part of the century witnessed a growing interest in the lied, a relatively short, simple solo song with piano accompaniment. *Die schöne Müllerin (The Pretty Millmaid*, 1823) and *Winterreise (Winter Journey*, 1827) were both composed by Schubert as lied cycles set to poems by Wilhelm Müller. In 1840 Robert Schumann wrote his two cycles of lieder on poems by Heinrich Heine (*Dichterliebe [Poet's Love]*) and Adelbert von Chamisso (*Frauenliebe und Leben [A Woman's Love and Life]*) as a love offering to his new bride, Clara Wieck. Still by Schumann, *Papillons (Butterflies*, 1832) is a series of small-sized, dancelike solo piano pieces of contrasting character, loosely related to the central idea of a swirling ball—like the ones described in the sentimental novels of Jean Paul, whose characters come to life in several of Schumann's compositions. Similarly, the various pieces comprising Schumann's *Carnaval: Scènes mignonnes sur quatre notes (Carnival: Small Scenes on Four Notes*, 1835) for piano are musical characterizations of several members of an imaginary Davidsbund (David's League) of the composer's own invention, whose mission was to fight the Philistines of contemporary culture; Clara Wieck and Ernestine (Schumann's former fiancée) each are represented with a miniature.

At the other end of the compositional spectrum there was the fascination with the sublime and colossal, which in turn brought about the swelling of the symphony to previously unheard-of dimensions. The sheer number of measures of the usual four movements was increased to sometimes almost unbearable lengths: a first step in this direction was taken by Beethoven in his Third Symphony, of which the first movement was double the size of corresponding movements in his first two symphonies of Classical extraction; the first public performance of the work was greeted by some contemporary critics with grunting disbelief: the symphony was seen as being of "inordinate length" and its effect on the audience was perceived as one that "wearies even the cognoscenti." Furthermore, the number of movements was sometimes increased from four to five, as in Beethoven's *Sixth Symphony*, the *Pastoral* (1808) and in the *Symphonie fantastique* composed in 1830 by Hector Berlioz. Individual movements were connected through passages reminiscent of the principal themes of the introduction (if there was one) or of the first movement; this technique, in addition to providing a sense of thematic unity throughout the work, was also aimed at creating the perception of the symphony as a gigantic one-movement piece comprised of contrasting sections: such is the case with Mendelssohn's Third Symphony, the "Scotch" (1842), and Schumann's Fourth Symphony (the 1851 version).

Further changes took place in terms of emotional content and individual character of movements themselves: thus the restrained, gracious, balanced classical minuet used in the third movement of Haydn's and Mozart's symphonies was replaced with a more vigorous, heavier, and faster Scherzo. Beethoven had already used a scherzo-like sound and tempo for the third movement of his First Symphony (1799–1800), although he labeled the movement a minuet; his Second Symphony (1801–2) made the change explicit. Sometimes the traditional order of the four movements itself was inverted, as the scherzo took the position of the slow, second movement, while the slow section was allotted to the third movement, as in Beethoven's *Ninth Symphony* (1822–24) or in Mendelssohn's Fifth Symphony.

The belief that music should seek to suggest or overtly express extramusical ideas taken from literature or painting—a concept known as programmaticism—was very close to the heart of the Romantic composer. Descriptive trends had been present in music long before the age of Romanticism: the Italian *caccia*, for instance—a fourteenth-century vocal genre, often performed with instrumental accompaniment—sought to express the tumult and excitement involved in hunting through the use of interjections on reiterated pitches; the vocal *chansons* (songs) of Clément Janequin were descriptive of battles ("Bataille de Marignan"), birdsongs ("Chant des oiseaux"), and street cries ("Cris de Paris"); in terms of eighteenth-century orchestral music, the four *concerti grossi* known as *I quattro stagioni* (*The Four Seasons*) by Antonio Vivaldi contained convincing musical depictions of seasonal changes, complete with musical replicas of birdcalls (*Spring*) and spirited dance rhythms (*Autumn*).

But in the early nineteenth century the concept of program permeated all levels of instrumental music, both solo and orchestral, and was a topic of discussion and spirited debate among supporters and detractors. Those who promoted programmaticism provided either descriptive titles or elaborate explanations of the meaning of their works—as seen in the solo piano pieces of Schumann, many of which express Romantic contradiction and tension through musically depicted characters of the composer's own invention: Florestan, the impulsive hero; Eusebius, the dreamer; Raro, the wise master. Schumann used these characters to voice his own opinions on the musical aesthetics of the time. Thus Florestan states, in one of the many aphorisms published by Schumann throughout his life, that "the painter sees a poem as a picture, the musician transforms paintings into tone." Mendelssohn, at one time not one of the outspoken supporters of program music, composed his *Lieder ohne Wörte* (*Songs without Words*), a cycle comprised of forty-eight miniature pieces

arranged in six books, to illustrate the idea that music can express states of the soul without the help of literature, whether lyrical, descriptive, or narrative (ironically, when the work was printed the publishers headed most of the pieces with descriptive titles such as "The Gondola Song," "The Spinning Song," and so on).

Orchestral music in the nineteenth century owes a large debt to Beethoven's symphonies: of these, the first two, the Fourth (1806–8), the Seventh (1811–12), and the Eighth (1812) are examples of pure or absolute music—in other words, music without program. On the other hand, the Third, Fifth, Sixth, and Ninth Symphonies are all programmatic, introducing extramusical images of various levels of explicitness. Thus the Third Symphony depicts the idea of the Romantic hero (Napoleon, but also the composer himself) and the Fifth Symphony (1807–8) was interpreted as a musical metaphor for man's titanic struggle with destiny; in the latter, the key of C minor in the first movement represents apprehension and gloom, while the last movement's C major expresses triumph and brightness: the forces of darkness have been overthrown. Beethoven provided descriptive titles ("Scene by the Brook," "Merrymaking of the Peasants," "Storm," and the like) for each of the five movements of his Sixth Symphony, the "Pastoral" (1808) whose music dwells on the Romantic theme of man's communion with nature and offers glimpses of idyllic country life. Finally, in the Ninth Symphony's fourth movement, the composer included soloists and a choir, and set to music fragments from Johann Christoph Friedrich von Schiller's *Ode to Joy* to express more convincingly with the help of words his belief in universal brotherhood.

The program, then, could be overtly stated as in Beethoven's "Pastoral" or Schumann's First Symphony, the "Spring" (1841), where the composer provided subtitles for each movement; it could also be more of a suggestion relying on a particular atmosphere, instrumental color, and rhythmic pattern, as in Mendelssohn's Fourth Symphony, the "Italian" (1833)—a work evocative of the sunny, vibrant landscapes and bouncy dances of the South.

The uncontested champion of program music in the earlier part of the nineteenth century was Berlioz. His *Symphonie fantastique-Scenes from the Life of an Artist*, composed in 1830 as an autobiographical piece, has since been alternatively interpreted as a narrative of his passionate love for the Irish actress Harriet Smithson—or a five-act drama stemming from drug-induced hallucination. The symphony's five movements are developed from the transformation and elaboration of a single, obsessive theme—the idée fixe, a soaring melody symbolizing the beloved woman. For the first performance of the symphony Berlioz provided an ample program of his own making, offering descriptive titles and a synopsis for each movement: the first three ("Daydreams-Passions" "A Ball," and "Country Scene") show the artist (the composer himself) haunted by the image of the woman with whom he "falls hopelessly in love," who "brings trouble to his spirit," and whose memory generates "a mixture of hope and fear . . . visions of happiness troubled by dark forebodings." The fourth and the fifth movements ("March to the Scaffold" and "Dream of a Sabbath Night") allude to material that Berlioz might have found in Thomas de Quincey's *Confessions of an English Opium Eater*: the hero has poisoned himself with opium and is experiencing a drug-induced nightmare; having—in his dream—murdered his mistress, he is taken to the scaffold and witnesses his own execution; then he "sees himself at a sabbath, surrounded by a hideous crowd of spirits . . ." while his mistress, stripped of her noble qualities, "joins the diabolic orgy" on a hideously distorted version of the idée fixe; a grotesque parody on the *Dies irae* (*Day of Wrath*), a sequence used in the Catholic funeral mass, concludes the symphony.

While Berlioz's best known programmatic work is a symphony—albeit of nontraditional structure and dimensions—the paragon of Romantic program music is found in the twelve tone poems of Franz Liszt published between 1856 and 1861 (*Symphonische Dichtung* ["symphonic poem"] is a term apparently coined by Liszt around 1853). These are one-movement compositions of various sizes, intense emotion, and striking pictorial effects, each bearing—upon publication—a preface that discloses its source of inspiration: *Les Préludes* (1856) is based on one of Alphonse Marie-Louis de Lamartine's poetic meditations; *Mazeppa* (1856) on a poem of the same title by Victor Hugo; *Hamlet* (1861) on William Shakespeare's play; *Hunnenschlacht* (*Battle of the Huns*, 1861) on a painting by Friedrich-August Kaulbach.

Throughout the eighteenth century European opera houses and their audiences had been under the spell of Italian opera; this state of affairs was perpetuated well into the nineteenth century, as in addition to the musical centers of Italy, both Vienna and Paris as well as the German cities produced time and again the operas—comic or serious—of Gioacchino Antonio Rossini, Gaetano Donizetti, Vincenzo Bellini, and Giuseppe Verdi. Italian composers and librettists concerned themselves with plausible, yet conventional, stage re-creations of the human comedy (or drama); history (whether Italian or otherwise), social context, or nature were seen as a mere background against which conflicts between individuals or groups arose, evolved and were resolved. Italian opera, rooted in two centuries of tradition, focused on true or plausible stories and beautifully carved, melodious arias of classical shape involving a high level of vocal virtuosity. The Italian aria, generally conceived as a showcase for the *prima donna* or the *primo uomo*, was the preferred vehicle for expressing emotions of every sort.

It did not, however, play a major role in French opera. Early in the nineteenth century Paris made a successful attempt to promote its own brand of operatic work, the *grand opéra*. A sumptuous affair involving large crowd scenes, grandiose ballets, lavish settings, and stage props built in the best tradition of the seventeenth-century "flying machines," the French opera was often composed on subjects adapted from medieval legends, classical mythology, or French history. These aspects are represented in *Les Huguenots* (1836), the work of Giacomo Meyerbeer, which is a kaleidoscope of rapidly shifting audio-visual *tableaux* depicting the conflicts between religious and political factions in France on the eve of the Night of St. Bartholomew. Richard Wagner—who later in the century became the loudest detractor of the traditional operatic conventions in general and, because of his Jewishness, of Meyerbeer in particular—had earlier succumbed to the charms of grand opera when he composed and revised *Tannhäuser* (first performed in 1845).

Neither the Italian nor the French approach, both believed to be too conventional, were satisfactory for the more meditative and philosophically-inclined German, who was looking for tales of trial and redemption involving supernatural forces—of which Mozart's *Die Zauberflöte* (*The Magic Flute*, 1791) was one illustrious example. The first lasting nineteenth-century operatic at-tempt to fulfill the German taste for stories incorporating fantastic elements and a wild, ominous nature was *Undine* (1813–14) by E. T. A. Hoffmann—who, like Schumann, was a composer, writer, and literary critic. *Der Freischütz* (*The Freeshooter*, 1821) by Carl Maria von Weber was the glorious heir to this tradition. Composed on the Faustian theme of man selling his soul to the devil in exchange for earthly favors (in this case, some magic bullets that would enable him to win a shooting contest and the hand of his beloved), the opera basks in the dark mystery of the Northern forest populated with fantastic characters. A battle between angelic and demonic forces ensues, at the end of which the hero redeems himself, emerging triumphant. Medieval legends of salvation and redemption also formed the basis for Richard Wagner's *Der fliegende Holländer* (*The Flying Dutchman*, 1843), *Tannhäuser* (1845), and *Lohengrin* (1850)—the latter considered the last important German Romantic opera. With *Tristan und Isolde* (1857–59), Wagner transcended the limits of the traditional concept of "number opera" consisting of well-delineated arias, recitatives, and chorus scenes, and plunged into the hitherto unexplored territory of continuous, unbroken melodic lines and intensely chromatic harmonies. Previously used in *Lohengrin*, the *leitmotif*—a reoccuring musical theme associated with particular personages, objects, or situations—became all-pervasive in *Tristan*, where the orchestra, often the carrier of such themes, was given a prominence that elevated its status to that of a prima donna.

As the nineteenth century wore on, Romantic ideology and aesthetics, together with the view of the musician's role in society, grew more radical. The rise of the composer and interpreter to the status of a superhuman hero, already visible in Beethoven's somewhat eccentric mannerisms, was accentuated towards the middle of the century and found its climax in the musical philosophy and practice of Liszt and Wagner, both narcissistic personalities who took immense pleasure in subjugating the crowds, and professed music as a quasi-religious ritual of which they viewed themselves the semiofficial priests.

With all this came a marked change in the concept of sound and, consequently, of harmony and instrumental color. The expansive use of chromaticism sought to infuse music with a profusion of harmonic nuances—thus with greater expressive potential; this, together with the widespread use of unexpected chord progressions and sudden modulations to distant keys, gradually "liberated" music from the conventions of the earlier part of the century. The harmonic language of the later nineteenth century saw the introduction of bold, complex chords and a nontraditional, shocking treatment of dissonances that stretched postclassical harmony to its utmost limits and, in works of Liszt (the "Faust" Symphony [1854]; *Nuages gris* [*Gray Clouds*, 1881] for piano) and Wagner (*Tristan and Isolde*, [1857–59, the trilogy *Das Ring des Nibeliungen* [*The Ring of the Nibelung*, completed in 1874], and *Parsifal* [1882]), challenged—and ultimately overthrew—the very concepts of traditional tonality, form, function, and structure.

LUMINITA FLOREA

Bibliography

Allanbrook, Wye J, Janet M. Levy, and William P. Mahrt, eds. *Conventions in Eighteenth and Nineteenth-Century Music.* Stuyvesant, N.Y.: Pendragon Press, 1992.

Barbier, Patrick. *Opera in Paris, 1800–1850: A Lively History.* Translated by Robert Luoma. Portland, Or.: Amadeus Press, 1995.

Bent, Ian, ed. *Music Theory in the Age of Romanticism.* Cambridge: Cambridge University Press, 1996.

Blume, Friedrich. *Classic and Romantic Music: A Comprehensive Survey.* Translated by M. D. Herter. New York: W. W. Norton, 1970.

Chapple, Gerald, Frederick Hall, and Hans Schulte, eds. *The Romantic Tradition: German Literature and Music in the Nineteenth Century.* Lanham, Md.: University Press of America, 1992.

Dahlhaus, Carl. *Between Romanticism and Modernism: Four Studies in the Music of the Later Nineteenth Century.* Translated by Mary Whitall. California Studies in Nineteenth-century Music 1. Berkeley and Los Angeles: University of California Press, 1980.

Daverio, John. *Nineteenth-Century Music and the German Romantic Ideology.* New York: Maxwell Macmillan International, 1993.

Deutsch, Otto Erich. *Schubert: Memoirs by His Friends.* Translated by Rosamond Ley and John Nowell. New York: Macmillan, 1958.

Einstein, Alfred. *Music in the Romantic Era.* New York: W. W. Norton, 1975.

Longyear, Rey Morgan. *Nineteenth-Century Romanticism in Music.* 3d ed. Prentice Hall History of Music Series. Englewood Cliffs, N.J.: Prentice Hall, 1988.

Minahan, John A. *Word like a Bell: John Keats, Music, and the Romantic Poet.* Kent, Ohio: Kent State University Press, 1992.

Mongredien, Jean. *French Music from the Enlightenment to Romanticism, 1789–1830.* Translated by Sylvain Fremaux. Edited by Reinhard G. Pauly. Portland, Or.: Amadeus Press, 1996.

Plantinga, Leon. *Beethoven's Concertos: History, Style, Performance.* New York: W. W. Norton, 1999.

——. *Romantic Music: A History of Musical Style in Nineteenth-Century Europe.* New York: W. W. Norton, 1984.

——. *Schumann as a Critic.* Yale Studies in the History of Music 4. New Haven, Conn.: Yale University Press, 1967.

Ratner, Leonard G. *Romantic Music: Sound and Syntax.* New York: Maxwell Macmillan International, 1992.

Siegel, Linda, ed. and trans. *Music in German Romantic Literature: A Collection of Essays, Reviews, and Stories.* Novato, Calif.: Elra, 1983.

Strunk, William Oliver, ed. *Source Readings in Music History from Classical Antiquity through the Romantic Era.* New York: W. W. Norton, 1950.

Weber, William. *Music and the Middle Class: The Social Structure of Concert Life in London, Paris, and Vienna.* London: Croom Helm, 1975.

Whittall, Arnold. *Romantic Music: A Concise History from Schubert to Sibelius.* London: Thames and Hudson, 1987.

MUSIC, ROMANTIC: AFTER 1850

In the second half of the nineteenth century, composers confronted a number of contradictory ideas about the arts and music. The failure of the 1848 revolutions in France, Italy, and a number of German states symbolized to many people the failure of the Romantic ideals of the late eighteenth and early nineteenth centuries. Literature and the arts were shifting to realism in style and subject matter, and the era of industrialization and modernization was quickly becoming a reality. As a result, composers of the mid-1800s were left with the task of creating a musical language and style befitting the new cultural climate. During this time of uncertainty and change, composers often felt torn between two conflicting emotions. They were inclined to idealize the past and yearn for a simpler time, yet they also felt excitement for the burgeoning era of progress and industrialization. Most composers of this era preferred to follow their own aesthetic inclinations rather than to strictly ascribe with any one stylistic pathway, and because of this music composed in the mid-to-late 1800s exhibits more diversity than music produced by previous generations of composers. In addition, a number of notable composers, such as Felix Mendelssohn, Frédéric François Chopin, and Robert Schumann, died in the mid-1800s, which greatly impacted the musical landscape of the second half of the century.

One of the most visible debates in Romantic musical aesthetics regarded the type of music to possess the highest music artistry and expressiveness. There were those who favored purely instrumental music such as symphonies or concertos, while others believed that music was enhanced when fused with literary elements. In light of this debate, Hungarian-born composer and piano virtuoso Franz Liszt, along with German composer Richard Wagner and French composer Hector Berlioz, created in the 1850s a progressive faction of composers known as the New German school that championed music's association with literary elements and opposed the Classicism of most Viennese composers. The New German school created three new musical genres: a multimovement composition associated with a story or poem called the *program symphony* (Berlioz), a one-movement, programmatic orchestral genre composed in free musical form called the *symphonic poem* (Liszt); and the *music drama* (Wagner), an idiom in which music, poetry, drama, and stagecraft all serve to enhance the dramatic work as a whole. In each of these genres the New German school created new approaches to composing large musical forms that involved thematic transformation, nontraditional modulation, and principles of cyclic unity. Late nineteenth-century works that typify these principles include Liszt's programmatic "Faust" Symphony and his twelve symphonic poems such as *Les préludes, Prometheus, Héroïde funèbre,* and *Hamlet*; Wagner's music dramas *Tristan and Isolde* and *Der Ring des Nibelungen* (*The Ring of the Nibelung*), a four-opera cycle based on Norse mythology comprised of *Das Rheingold* (*The Rhine Gold*), *Die Walküre* (*The Valkyrie*), *Siegfried,* and *Gotterdamerung* (*The Twilight of the Gods*).

German composer Johannes Brahms differed from many of the composers of the late nineteenth century with his outspoken opposition to the New German school. Brahms had a high regard for the forms and materials seen in the works of great classical composers such as Ludwig von Beethoven, Franz Joseph Haydn, and Wolfgang Amadeus Mozart, and his traditional yet innovative string quartets, symphonies, and concertos enjoyed great success. Brahms left a massive impact upon composers of the early twentieth century with his most famous works, including his *German Requiem* and Symphonies 1–4.

Austrian composer Anton Bruckner was much less of a neo-traditionalist than Brahms, as he agreed with some of the ideals of the New German school, but he too looked to the works of classical and Romantic composers for inspiration. Considered one of the most innovative composers of the second half of the nineteenth century, Bruckner is remembered primarily for his symphonies, vocal works, and sacred compositions.

Later German and Austrian composers Gustav Mahler, Richard Strauss, and Hugo Wolf struggled with the conflict and uncertainty that existed in music at the end of the nineteenth century. Strauss wrote symphonic poems such as *Don Juan* as well as conservative instrumental works, while Wolf and Mahler are remembered primarily for their songs, but Mahler also earned great acclaim for his orchestral works. Although Mahler, Strauss, and Wolf each exhibited some element of traditionalism in their work, their compositions were also quite innovative, and further challenged the boundaries of tone, harmony, and orchestration in late nineteenth century music.

In opera, Italian composer Guiseppe Verdi was the dominant figure in Italy after 1850, writing such as *La Traviata, Un ballo in maschera*, and *Don Carlos*, all of which became highly successful operas and gave him international success. In his later operas, such as *Aïda* and *Otello*, Verdi treated tonality and chromaticism much more freely than in his previous works. Verdi was succeeded by Giacomo Puccini, an Italian composer who produced two operas at the end of the nineteenth century: *La Bohème* (1896) and *Tosca* (1900), works that successfully fused lyric opera with elements from the emerging Italian operatic idiom called *verismo*. In late-nineteenth-century France opera was shifting from the spectacle and pomp of grand opera to *opéra lyrique*, a genre that focused on love stories drawn from literature. Works in this vein include *Carmen* by Georges Bizet, *Roméo et Juliet* by Charles Gounod, and *Manon* by Jules Massenet.

During the last two decades of the nineteenth century nationalism was a prominent element in many musical works produced by European composers. Nationalism was incorporated into music primarily through the use of national and folk music elements, as heard in Liszt's Hungarian-tinged *Missa Solemnis*, or through the use of national elements for the subject of a composition, such as in the opera *The Bartered Bride* by Czech composer Bedřich Smetana, a work based on a folk story of peasant life in Bohemia. Other notable Czech composers who wrote nationalistic music include Antonín Dvořák and Leoš Janáček. Nationalism was a prevalent feature in works of many late nineteenth-century Russian composers, including Mily Balakirev, Alexander Borodin, César Cui, Modest Musorgsky, and Nikolai Rimsky-Korsakov, a group who banded together as the "mighty handful"

in an effort to create a distinctly Russian school of music. Not all Russian composers chose to incorporate nationalistic elements into their music, but instead composed programmatic or absolute Romantic music, a faction that included Anton Rubinstein, Alexander Scriabin, and Pyotr Ilich Tchaikovsky, who composed highly acclaimed symphonies, ballets, and orchestral fantasias.

Music composition at the end of the nineteenth century was dramatically different in harmonic organization, tonal conceptualization, and musical form than works composed at the beginning of the century. During the Romantic era, composers had experimented with every facet of musical composition, and by the end of the nineteenth century it seemed that composers had pushed the limits of musical form to the extent that the ideals and aesthetics created at the beginning of the Romantic era were no longer appropriate for applications in new compositions. The modern era emerged in the early twentieth century, and in this age, composers such as Claude Debussy, Gustav Mahler, Aleksandr Nicolayevich Scriabin, and Richard Strauss seeking to compose works of distinction were forced to develop a new musical language that befit the changing times.

ERIN STAPLETON-CORCORAN

See also **Berlioz, Hector; Gounod, Charles; Liszt, Franz; Verdi, Giuseppe; Wagner, Richard**

Bibliography

Blaukopf, Kurt, and Herta Blaukopf, eds. *Gustav Mahler: His Life, Work and World.* London: Thames and Hudson, 2000.

Comberiati, Carmelo Peter, and Sidney Walter Finkelstein. *Composer and Nation: The Folk Heritage in Music.* New York: International, 1989.

Dahlhaus, Carl. *Nineteenth-Century Music.* Berkeley and Los Angeles: University of California Press, 1989.

Daverio, John. *Nineteenth-Century Music and the German Romantic Ideology.* New York: Schirmer, 1993.

Einstein, Alfred. *Music in the Romantic Era.* New York: W. W. Norton, 1947.

Plantinga, Leon. *Romantic Music: A History of Musical Style in Nineteenth-Century Europe.* New York: W. W. Norton, 1984.

Raeburn, Michael, and Alan Kendall, eds. *Heritage of Music: The Romantic Era.* Oxford: Oxford University Press: 1992.

Rosen, Charles. *The Romantic Generation.* Cambridge, Mass.: Harvard University Press, 1995.

Swafford, Jan. *Johannes Brahms: A Biography.* New York: Vintage Books, 1999.

Whittall, Arnold. *Romantic Music: A Concise History from Schubert to Sibelius.* London: Thames and Hudson, 1987.

MUSSET, (LOUIS-CHARLES-) ALFRED DE 1810–1857

French playwright and poet

Time and changing literary fashions have not dealt kindly with Alfred de Musset, and, paradoxically, one of the most striking figures in French Romanticism is now valued mainly for a dramatic work that was not highly appreciated in his own days. Belonging, like Alphonse Marie-Louis de Lamartine and Alfred Victor de Vigny, to an aristocratic family, Musset was born in 1810; when he made his appearance in Parisian literary circles he was welcomed by writers who were conscious that they had

been the pioneers of French Romanticism. Though a little apprehensive of a potential rival, Victor Hugo, for instance, invited him to his receptions in his house in the rue Notre-Dame-des-Champs, and the strikingly handsome young man made a great impression. He appeared to possess the Romantic temperament to the full. As early as 1828 he brought out a free translation of Thomas De Quincey's *Confessions of an Opium Eater*. It was followed just two years later by his *Contes d'Espagne et d'Italie*

(*Tales from Spain and Italy*). His subject matter and style, in verse no less than in prose, proclaimed adherence to Hugolian Romantic ideals with a whole-heartedness which some hailed with enthusiasm while others smiled at the only too obvious immaturity of the youthful author.

In 1831, again following where Hugo and other Romantic authors had for a few years already been showing the way ahead, Musset turned to the theater. The experience was bruising. Though drama was a medium that suited his temperament and facilitated its expression, the resounding failure of *La Nuit vénitienne (The Venetian Night)* to please the notoriously difficult audience of the Odéon in Paris persuaded Musset never again to run the risk of public performance on the professional stage. Between 1832 and 1836 Musset did write more plays, but published them in a volume with the tell-tale title of *Théâtre dans un fauteuil* (usually translated as *Armchair Theatre*). One facet of Musset's dramatic style is revealed in *On ne badine pas avec l'amour* (*Love's No Laughing Matter*) of 1834. Taking up the French fondness for little dramatic entertainments in prose that illustrate proverbs and sayings, Musset mingles comedy and tragedy in the approved Romantic manner in scenes of patent fragile contrivance that surprise the audience as a passionate love affair builds to it climax. In other *proverbes* Musset shows similar deftness in dialogue, without, however, reaching the same emotional intensity.

Lorenzaccio, also of 1834, appeared to be not only a tragedy that could never be staged; it was also a rejection both of Classical dramatic norms and of the new principles introduced by Alexandre Dumas *père* and Hugo. Transforming Lorenzo de Medici into a deeply flawed Hamletican hero whose status is undermined from the outset by the use of his diminutive nickname, Musset follows the Romantic convention of finding inspiration in the Renaissance, and is by no means alone in turning to Italy too. But he abandons the alexandrine, the reform of which figured large in Hugo's program, and substitutes prose. Far from being concentrated at least into five coherent acts, the action sprawls in scenes in different places and at different times in a manner that owes more to William Shakespeare than to even the Romantic tradition in French drama. Though admired for the depth of characterization of its hero, *Lorenzaccio* was considered unplayable until 1896 when Sarah Bernhardt gave a notable interpretation of the title role in an adaptation of the original text. Since then *Lorenzaccio* has played regularly and is now often regarded as the finest achievement in French Romantic drama.

In June 1833 Musset first made the acquaintance of George Sand, and a tempestuous, much-talked-about love affair soon developed; next, after a stay of some months in Venice, came the inevitable breakup, which was followed by various attempts at reconciliation. Musset, whose temperament was already unstable, was left stunned. With a title echoing the *Confessions* of Jean-Jacques Rousseau while highlighting what was then its actuality, his *Confession d'un enfant du siècle (The Confession of a Child of This Century)*, first published in its entirety in 1836, was notable as a Romantic autobiography, though writing it did not bring the solace its author was seeking.

Musset wrote a large amount of verse. In its day it was highly regarded, but modern critics find that it lacks the vigor and range of Hugo and judge Musset's work generally inferior in intensity and insight to the poetry written in French in the following generation. Sheer mellifluousness no longer seems to suffice, rhetoric undermines sincerity, and length challenges lyric integrity. Like many of his contemporaries, Musset often found inspiration in darkness, rather than the full light of day. Even some of his nocturnes, such as his "Ballade à la lune" ("Ballad to the Moon," 1832) seem to be exercises in sprightly versification rather than an adequate response to his theme. In the famous "La Nuit de Mai" ("The Night of May," 1835) it is hard to escape the sense that the poet doth protest too much—and also posture too much—in his dialogue with a muse who figures in classical guise complete with lute. Less heated in expression, "La Nuit de décembre" ("The December Night," 1833) has something of William Wordsworth's autobiographical tone until Musset introduces a stanza of resonant place-names in imitation of Hugo and concludes with a grandiloquent "vision." Nowadays many readers find more interest in Musset's journalism. He is at his best in *Les Lettres de Dupuis et Cotonet*. Written between 1836 and 1838, they provide a lively commentary on literary fashions. In "De la tragédie" ("On Tragedy"), his 1838 article on the début of the young actress Rachel (i.e. Elisabeth Félex) who was breathing new life into the Classical repertory, Musset comments perceptively on developments in theatrical art.

The final decades of Musset's life were a time of ill health and low spirits as his creativity gradually dried up. Though he was no longer among the leaders in literary developments, he was made a chevalier of the Légion d'Honneur in 1845 and was elected to the Académie Française in 1852, five years before his death.

CHRISTOPHER SMITH

Biography

Born Paris on December 11, 1810. Educated at the Collège Henri IV, Paris, winning prizes. Briefly followed law courses, 1828, but was more attracted to literature; first contacts with Hugo and other Romantic authors. In 1829, on publication of *Premières Poésies*, abandoned ideas of career and devoted himself to literature. Disastrous première of his play *La Nuit vénitienne*, 1830. Publication of *Un Spectacle dans un fauteuil*, 1832. Start of liaison with George Sand, 1833. Publication of *On ne badine pas avec l'amour* and *Lorenzaccio*, 1834. Start of publication of *Confession d'un enfant du siècle*, 1835. The actress Rachel becomes his mistress, 1839. Made chevalier de la Légion d'Honneur, 1845. Elected member of the Académie Française, 1852. After much illness, died in 1857. Buried in Père-Lachaise Cemetry, Paris.

Selected Works

Oevres complètes. Edited by Philippe Van Tieghem. Paris: Seuil, 1963.
Poésies complètes. Edited by Maurice Allem. Paris: Gallimard, 1957.
Théâtre complet. Edited by Maurice Allem. Paris: Gallimard, 1958.
Œuvres complètes en prose. Edited by Maurice Allem and Paul-Courant. Paris: Gallimard, 1960.
Confession d'un enfant du siècle. Rev. ed. Edited by Maurice Allem. Paris: Garnier, 1968.
Correspondance. Edited by Marie Cardroc'h. Paris: PUF, 1985.
Five Plays. Edited by Claude Schumacher. London: Methuen, 1985.

Bibliography

Castex, Pierre-Georges. *Études sur le théâtre d'Alfred de Musset.* 2 vols. Paris: SEES, 1978–79.

Crossley, Ceri. *Musset: "Lorenzaccio."* Critical Guides to French Texts, no. 25. London: Grant and Cutler, 1983.

Heyvaert Alain. *L'Esthétique de Musset*, Collection Esthétique. Paris: SEES, 1996.

Jeune, Simon. *Musset et sa fortune littéraire.* Tels qu'en eux-mêmes. Bordeaux: Ducros, 1970.

Lainey, Yves. *Musset, ou La Difficulté d'aimer.* Paris: SEES, 1978.

Levin, Susan. *The Romantic Art of Confession: De Quincey, Musset Sand, Lamb, Hogg, Frémy, Soulié, Janin.* Columbia, S.C.: Camden House, 1998.

Sices, David. *Theater of Solitude: The Drama of Alfred de Musset.* Hanover, N.H.: University of New England, 1974.

Whitaker, Marie-Joséphine. *Lorenzo ou Lorenzaccio? Misères et splendeurs d'un héros romantique.* Archives des Lettres modernes, no. 240. Paris: Lettres modernes, 1989.

MYTHOLOGY, CLASSICAL

The common view that the Romantic movement defined itself by rejecting all things Classical is an oversimplification, especially where Greek poetry and its mythological background are concerned. Between 1760 and 1850, Classical mythology was not an arcane field of interest only to scholars, but had direct relevance to contemporary culture. Not only Johann Christoph Friedrich von Schiller and Johann Wolfgang Goethe (who dissociated themselves from Romanticism), but also Samuel Taylor Coleridge, Percy Bysshe and Mary Shelley, Maurice de Guérin, Felicia Hemans, Friedrich Hölderlin, Alphonse Marie-Louise de Lamartine, August Wilhelm and Friedrich von Schlegel, and Alfred de Vigny all wrote on mythology and knew something of then current Classical scholarship. Artists such as John Flaxman, Anne-Louis Girodet, and Francisco de Goya y Lucientes depicted mythological subjects. Despite Schiller's view in *Über naïve und sentimentalische Dichtung* (1794–95) that the freshness and immediacy of the Classical poets was irretrievably lost in this more introspective age, he and his contemporaries eagerly explored mythological themes and looked to Greek culture for answers to contemporary dilemmas. Goethe and Schiller championed a Hellenistic liberal humanism, founded on Greek ideals of heroism and physical beauty. For the more pietistic Hölderlin, a revival of the spirit of Greek poetry seemed to offer a way back to authentic spiritual experience.

At least two factors contributed to the revival of interest in mythology: poets and artists sensed that the myths still offered rich symbols and narratives for reinterpretation, while historians believed that Greek cultural history raised important questions for contemporary art and aesthetics. Among the most frequently reinterpreted myths were those of Prometheus, champion and liberator of humanity, subject of poems by (most notably) Goethe, William Blake—whose Orc is both a Prometheus figure and a Christ figure—Lord Byron, and Percy Bysshe Shelley, as well as providing the mythological basis for Mary Shelley's *Frankenstein; Or, the Modern Prometheus* (1818); Apollo, healer, prophet, musician, and paragon of male beauty, often taken as the apotheosis of the classical aesthetic, celebrated by William Wordsworth (in *Excursion,* book 4), Keats, Lamartine, Gérard de Nerval, and Shelley; Bacchus, subject of an acclaimed prose poem "La bacchante" by Maurice de Guérin, and the presiding male deity of Alfred de Vigny's Theocritan idyll "La Dryade"; and the Cupid and Psyche story (retold by the Irish poet Mary Tighe in the epic *Psyche* [1805], which influenced Keats, and by Lamartine in *La mort de Socrate* [1823]).

In the 1770s, writers whose resistance to an oppressive social order associated them with Friedrich Maximilian Klinger's *Sturm und Drang* (Storm and Stress, 1776) took Prometheus,

defender of men against the tyranny of Zeus, as their mythic patron. Goethe's "Prometheus" describes the human race itself as resembling the Titan: suffering, weeping, yet taking delight in life, and defying Zeus. In both Germany and England in the 1780s and 1790s, interest in mythology drew additional energy from the belief that ancient sources might hold the key to a religion of "nature," which, once revived, would prove less oppressive than Christianity had become (identified as it was in many people's minds with the established order).

The greatest advances in the interpretation of mythology were made in Germany, where the existence of numerous universities and of liberal-minded aristocratic patrons supported a tradition of relatively free historical and philological enquiry. It was not without justification that Schlegel claimed, in *Über das Studium der griechischen Poesie* (1795–97), "In Germany, and only in Germany, has Greek aesthetics and the study of the Greeks reached a point that must necessarily entail a complete transformation of poetic art and taste." Enthusiasm for Classical art, expressed by critics as varied as Goethe, Schiller, Friedrich von Schlegel, Wilhelm Heinrich Wackenroder, and Johann Joachim Winckelmann, led many of the more probing minds to ask fundamental questions about the culture that could produce such art.

One obstacle to hopes for a new philosophical paganism was the fear that the mighty forms of Classical art made all modern productions seem puny, a fear given literal-minded expression in Henry Fuseli's drawing *The Artist Moved by the Grandeur of Antique Fragments* (1778–79). In 1755 Winckelmann had contrasted the diminished state of modern man with the simple grandeur of Greek statuary. Flaxman's line drawings of Homeric subjects (c. 1783) remain appealingly simple and uncluttered, but much Romantic representation of Greek subjects strove to convey the artist's sheer awe at the titanic dimensions of classical art. Benjamin Robert Haydon's "Torso of Dionysus" (1809) and J. M. W. Turner's "The Temple of Minerva at Sunim" (1832) are representative examples. The fact that Greece itself was under Turkish rule until 1830 added pathos to these representations, a pathos most strikingly expressed in Eugène Delacroix's *Greece Expiring on the Ruins of Missolonghi* (1827). But some artists went beyond such gloomily introspective responses. Girodet's *Sleep of Endymion* (1792) humanizes and naturalizes the scene, turning the goddess Selene into the gentle glow of a moonbeam illuminating her lover's bared breast. In a very different emotional register, Goya's *Saturn Devouring One of his Children* (1820–23) evokes atavistic violence, but also comments on a bloodthirsty age that seemed determined to cannibalize its own children.

It was in France that interest in mythology was most directly related to revolutionary politics. Charles François Dupuis's mammoth compilation *Origine de tous les cultes ou religion universelle* (1795) surveyed a range of myth traditions from Egypt, Asia Minor, and Greece to prove that astronomy and meteorology were the basis of all myth and religion. Before the gods were invented, our ancestors, impelled by sheer wonder at the powers of earth and sky, worshipped these powers themselves. Later they bestowed on them names such as Osiris, Apollo, and Mithras. Dupuis's work drew on the materialist philosophy of Paul Henri Thiry, Baron d'Holbach, and had a clear political motive. He wanted to show that Christianity was just one version of the *religion universelle* of humankind, inspired by awe at the wonders of the universe. Dupuis favored abolishing Christianity, which was corrupted by the mystifications of priests, and replacing it with the pure religion of nature, an aim he shared with the revolutionary government, at least until the fall of Maximilien de Robespierre. It was not, however, Dupuis's huge seven-volume work, but the more accessible *Les Ruines, ou méditation sur les révolutions des empires* (1791), by Constantin François Chasseboeuf, Comte de Volney, that made the "religion of nature" a matter of public debate throughout Europe. Volney, who had access to Dupuis's work well in advance of its publication, turned Dupuis's theory into a call to all the peoples of the world to follow the lead of France and accept that a just and free society could be founded only on the study of the wonders of Nature. It quickly became a classic of radical thought.

The deistic, prorevolution views of Dupuis and Volney attracted criticism from (among others) the Anglican orientalist and mythographer Thomas Maurice, the philosopher and scientist Joseph Priestley, and Coleridge's friend John Prior Estlin (a Unitarian minister). Coleridge attacked Volney in a public lecture he gave in 1795, and probably read at least part of Dupuis's work in 1796. English translations of Volney appeared in 1795 and 1802. Byron and Shelley knew Volney's book, and it features in Mary Shelley's *Frankenstein* as one of the works from which the creature learns humankind's history.

Blake and Coleridge, on the other hand, depended for at least some of their early understanding of myth on Jacob Bryant's *A New System, or, an Analysis of Ancient Mythology* (1774). Bryant took the Genesis account of ancient history (still customarily ascribed to Moses himself) as literal truth, and focused on the story of the Flood. His stated purpose in collecting the myths of the Greeks and others was "to bring evidence from every age, and from every nation . . . in support of the history, as it has been delivered by Moses." Blake (in *A Descriptive Catalogue*, 1809) mentions Bryant, with other "antiquaries," as having shown that all myths derive from a common source, while Bryant provided Coleridge with some of the mythological material that found its way into *Kubla Khan*.

Like Blake (and Shelley, another radical visionary), Coleridge was also familiar with the work of Thomas Taylor (known as "the English pagan"), especially Taylor's translation of Porphyry's *The Cave of the Nymphs* (1788–89) and his dissertations on the Orphic hymns (1787), on the Eleusinian and Bacchic mysteries (1791), and on the fable of Cupid and Psyche (1795). Taylor believed that Platonic philosophy was deeply informed by Orphic, Eleusinian, and other Greek mystery religions. He wanted to heal the unnecessary and harmful division between *myth* and *reason*, or *intellect*, as those terms were generally understood.

Among German writers in the late 1700s, the turn toward paganism (sometimes resembling a kind of pantheism) was often more openly sensual and hedonistic, rather than highminded and philosophical. Schiller's poem "Die Götter Griechenlandes" (1788) celebrates an erotically-charged vision of a sunlit Greece animated by gods and nymphs. The Arcadian landscape was peopled by Oreads, Dryads, and Naiads; gods, heroes, and men, brought together in bonds of love, worshipped Venus together. Now, however, the gods have departed and nature is "ungodded" ("entgötterte"). What remains to us is merely the unsouled word ("Und uns blieb nur das entseelte Wort"). Several more explicitly antichristian stanzas, which risked charges of blasphemy, were suppressed when the poem first appeared, but were published in *the Teutsche Merkur*, the magazine edited by Christoph Martin Wieland.

Goethe's enthusiasm for Greek culture similarly opposed its more frank sensuousness to Christianity's distrust of pleasure, most openly in *Die Braut von Corinth* (1797). Throughout the 1770s, Goethe had been a keen student of the classical dramatists and poets. At Weimar from 1775 to 1786, Goethe commissioned the court sculptor, Klauer, to make copies of Greek sculptures. His *Iphigenie* (begun 1778) is partly an attempt to find in a Greek source a pattern of human goodness and self-sacrifice that would bear comparison with the Christian one. But in February 1787, in a letter to Johann Gottfried Herder, Goethe took a decisive turn away from Christianity and toward an understanding of ethics that was humanistic in a "Greek" sense. During his second sojourn in Rome in 1787 and 1788, Goethe came to believe that humanistic values for the modern era could be rediscovered in Classical art and mythology. On June 6, 1787, Goethe returned to his apartment in Rome and, with Karl Philipp Moritz, studied Classical statuary, making his own sketches. He saw drawings of the Parthenon frieze (fragments of which were later to inspire John Keats's "Elgin Marbles" sonnet). His conversations with Moritz led to the publication of Moritz's *Die Götterlehre, oder mythologische Dichtungen der Alten* (1791).

In this work, referring to myths about how heroes were born from the unions of the gods with the daughters of men, and how those heroes won immortality, Moritz pointed out the fusion of mythological with historical explanation, so baffling to a modern mind. But Moritz was also excited by the way the myths exhibit the dawning of speculative thought, and noted how the "realm of Imagination" was a close neighbor of the real. For Moritz, as later for Keats in Hyperion (1820), the defeat of the Titans by the gods represented the victory of well-proportioned beauty over what was as yet crude and unformed. Though Moritz did not place as much emphasis on the ascendancy of priestly religions as Dupuis and Volney, he asserted, like them, that Greek myths reveal what natural forces create and sustain the world.

Two other influential studies to appear in the 1790s in Germany were Gottfried Hermann's *Handbuch der Mythologie* (1790) and Friedrich August Wolf's *Prolegomena ad Homerum* (1795). Hermann's *Handbuch* summarized the mythological system of the Orphic hymns, sometimes claimed to be very ancient and traditionally ascribed to the pre-Homeric poet Musaeus. It carried an introduction by the noted classical scholar Christian Gottlob Heyne, making the argument that the hymns, though not themselves particularly ancient, contained a distillation of the mysteries of the Orphic cult. Wolf's book stirred up greater controversy, however, for he claimed that the epic poems ascribed to Homer were not actually the work of a single author, but were assembled in the sixth century B.C.E. out of miscellaneous "lays." This was in a sense an extension of Johann Gottfried Herder's argument in *Stimmen der Völker* (1778) that ancient literatures should be viewed primarily as embodiments of the distinctive culture of ancient people.

Like Moritz's *Götterlehre*, Friedrich Schlegel's *Über das Studium der griechischen Poesie* emphasized how the early didactic poetry of the Greeks—the "Theogonies" and works of the physiologists and gnomic writers—properly belonged to the "mythic era" of poetry ("Das *ältere didaktische Gedicht* der Griechen, wie die Theogonien, der Werke der Physiologen und Gnomiker, findet nur im mythischen Zeitalter der Poesie seine eigentliche Stelle"). Poetry and myth were the germ and source of ancient culture, but what philosophy owed to myth, from which it originally sprang, had yet to be disentangled. Schlegel stressed the great divide between Classical and modern poetry, but called on modern poets to dedicate themselves to achieving the qualities he associated with Greek poetry.

Schlegel's literary notebooks testify to a continued sense of the vital role of mythology in ancient and modern poetry. In 1800, he remarked, "Homer is essentially not epic but mythic." Even the new Romantic poetry must then be "mythological" if it was to be equally creative and a vehicle of genius. By this time, however, Schlegel—like Goethe—had begun to doubt whether the total transformation of modern culture by an infusion of the "Greek spirit" was actually possible. A sense of the unbridgeable gap between ancient Greece and the modern era replaced earlier hopes for a pagan revival. In number forty-six of his *Critical Fragments*, Schlegel admitted the modern age was closer to that of the Romans, and could understand them better than the Greeks. And as early as 1797, Friedrich Hölderlin, in his prose romance *Hyperion; oder Der Eremit aus Griechenland*, questioned whether the idyllic Greece imagined by the romantic Hellenists could really be revived in the modern world. Hölderlin also accepted Herder's view that religion and poetry originated in Asia, not in Greece, but it was Friedrich von Schlegel who (in 1802) was first among the German Romantics to pursue this eastward quest by taking up the study of Sanskrit. His *Über die Sprache und Weisheit der Indier* (1808) thus combined philological and philosophical investigation.

Much of what Romantic writers like Schlegel found intriguing in Greek mythology—most particularly the possibility that it was the public or exoteric form of ancient esoteric teachings derived from the Orphic, Eleusinian and Samothracian Mysteries, and originating in Asia—was set out in sober prose by the Heidelberg classical scholar Georg Friedrich Creuzer. His *Symbolik und Mythologie der alten Völker* (1810–12) was both influential and controversial. Creuzer assembled evidence that priests from India were the first to bring metaphysical and spiritual doctrines to Greece; that the Pelasgians ("sea-people") who occupied Greece and much of the eastern Mediterranean and Aegean before the Hellenes had absorbed a mixture of Asian, Egyptian, and Phoenician religion and mythology; and that these religious ideas, expressed in mythic form, contributed to the earliest poetry and polytheistic religions of the Greeks. On this historical foundation, Creuzer was able to claim that Greek myths enshrined in symbol form philosophical doctrines or prin-

ciples based on teachings that predated the Hebrew Scriptures. Creuzer argued (as had his colleague at Heidelberg, Joseph Görres) that these teachings ultimately derived not from Greece or Asia Minor, but from India.

The controversy that followed publication of Creuzer's work attracted the attention of Coleridge, Gottfried Hermann, Goethe, and Friedrich Wilhelm Joseph von Schelling, among others. Schelling had argued that the earliest religion was polytheistic, and monotheism arose later; Creuzer at first seemed to agree, but later, in volume 1, of *Symbolik*, suggested that monotheism might have precedence after all. Coleridge took up the issue in his notebooks, affirming the priority of monotheism, a view that found public expression in his 1825 lecture "On the Prometheus of Aeschylus" (which also drew on the scholarship of Heyne, whose lectures he had heard at Göttingen, and Schelling's 1815 treatise *Über die Gottheiten von Samothrace*). Goethe strenuously objected to Creuzer's attempt to connect Zeus, Aphrodite, and Apollo with Asiatic deities. The exchanges between Creuzer and his chief critic, Hermann, appeared in print as *Briefe über Homer und Hesiodus* (1818). Hermann questioned the way Creuzer had too readily ascribed philosophical insight and intention to Homer and Hesiod. For Hermann, the issue was whether the poets *meant* to speak symbolically or (as he preferred to say) symbolic meaning was implicit in the matter narrated. In response Creuzer objected to Hermann's patronizing view of Homer as a naïve believer in the gods of mythology, citing evidence in the Iliad that Homer was well acquainted with priestly teachings and the mystery religions.

After 1820, mythological figures continued to appear in poems of the Romantics and their successors, sometimes simply as material for easy "Classicizing" allusions, sometimes prompting a more critical, historically-situated evaluation of myth, as in Lamartine's *La mort de Socrate*, which deploys mythological allusions to suggest a pantheistic vision of immortality ("Tout est intelligent, tout vit, tout est un dieu"); Alfred, Lord Tennyson's "Tithonus" and "The Lotus-Eaters" (1832); Alfred de Musset's *Rolla* (1833); or Elizabeth Barrett Browning's Pan poem "A Musical Instrument" (1860). The English antiquary and collector Richard Payne Knight published toned-down versions of his view (first expressed in *On the Worship of Priapus*, 1786) that all mythology derives from primitive fertility cults. Romanian scholar and writer Mihai Eminescu and others continued to enquire into the thought content and symbolic value of myth. But in general there was a movement away from attempts to universalize mythology. Although Jakob and Wilhelm Grimm followed Creuzer and Görres in believing that all myths could be traced back to an originary homeland, their work in Teutonic folklore studies treated myths and folk tales as local creations, rooted in a particular geography and the customs of particular communities. In the British Isles, the work of the Irish scholar Thomas Keightley reinforced this localizing of traditional narratives. The era of the "key to all mythologies"—the futile ambition of the unfortunate Casaubon in George Eliot's *Middlemarch*—appeared to be over.

ANTHONY JOHN HARDING

Bibliography

Aske, Martin. *Keats and Hellenism*. Cambridge: Cambridge University Press, 1985.

Behrendt, Stephen, ed. *History and Myth: Essays on English Romantic Literature*. Detroit: Wayne State University Press, 1990.

Blumenberg, Hans. *Work on Myth*. Translated by Robert M. Wallace. Cambridge, Mass.: MIT Press, 1985.

Boyle, Nicholas. *Goethe: The Poet and the Age*. vol. 1: *The Poetry of Desire (1749–1790)*. Oxford: Clarendon Press, 1991. vol. 2: *Revolution and Renunciation (1790–1803)*. Oxford: Clarendon Press, 2000.

Brion, Marcel. *Art of the Romantic Era: Romanticism, Classicism, Realism*. New York: Praeger, 1966.

Bryant, Jacob. *A New System, or, An Analysis of Ancient Mythology*. 2 vols. 1774.

Bush, Douglas. *Mythology and the Romantic Tradition in English Poetry*. Cambridge, Mass.: Harvard University Press, 1937.

Butler, Marilyn. "Myth and Mythmaking in the Shelley Circle," *English Literary History* 49 (1982): 50–72.

Cantor, Paul. *Creature and Creator: Myth-making and English Romanticism*. Cambridge: Cambridge University Press, 1984.

Coleridge, Samuel Taylor. "On the Prometheus of Aeschylus." In *Shorter Works and Fragments*. Edited by H. J. Jackson and J. R. de J. Jackson. 2 vols. *Collected Works*. Bollingen Series 75. London: Routledge/Princeton, N. J.: Princeton University Press, 1995. 1251–1301.

Creuzer, Georg Friedrich. *Symbolik und Mythologie der alten Völker*. 4 vols. Leipzig and Darmstadt, 1810–12, 2d ed. 6 vols. 1819–23.

Curran, Stuart. "The Political Prometheus," *Studies in Romanticism* 25 (1986): 429–55.

Dupuis, Charles François. *Origine de tous les cultes ou religion universelle*. 7 vols. 1795.

Estlin, John Prior. *The Nature and the Causes of Atheism . . . To which are added, Remarks on a Work, entitled Origine de tous les cultes, ou Religion universelle*. 1797.

Feldman, Burton, and Robert D. Richardson, eds. *The Rise of Modern Mythology 1680–1860*. Bloomington: Indiana University Press, 1972.

Furst, Lilian R. *Counterparts: The Dynamics of Franco-German Literary Relationships 1770–1895*. London: Methuen, 1977.

Gross, George C. "*Lamia* and the Cupid-Psyche Myth," *Keats-Shelley Journal* 39 (1990): 151–65.

Gruppe, Otto. *Geschichte der klassischen Mythologie und Religionsgeschichte während des Mittelalters im Abendland und während der Neuzeit*. Leipzig: B. G. Teubner, 1921.

Harding, Anthony John. *The Reception of Myth in English Romanticism*. Columbia: University of Missouri Press, 1995.

Hermann, Johann Gottfried Jacob and Georg Friedrich Creuzer. *Briefe über Homer und Hesiodus, vorzüglich über die Theogonie*. 1818.

Kramer, Lawrence. "The Return of the Gods: Keats to Rilke." *Studies in Romanticism* 17 (1978): 483–500.

Kuhn, Albert J. "English Deism and the Return of Mythological Syncretism," *Publications of the Modern Language Association of America* 71 (1956): 1094–1116.

Lewis, Linda M. *The Promethean Politics of Milton, Blake, and Shelley*. Columbia: University of Missouri Press, 1992.

Manuel, Frank. *The Eighteenth Century Confronts the Gods*. Cambridge, Mass.: Harvard University Press, 1959.

Mettler, Werner. *Die junge Friedrich Schlegel und die griechische Literatur. Ein Beitrag zum Problem der Historie*. Züricher Beiträge zur deutsche Literatur- und Geistesgeschichte, no. 11. Zürich: Atlantis Verlag, 1955.

Moritz, Karl Philipp. *Götterlehre oder mythologische Dichtungen der Alten*. 2d ed. 1795.

Phinney, A. W. "Keats in the Museum: Between Aesthetics and History," *Journal of English and Germanic Philology* 90 (1991): 208–29.

Priestley, Joseph. *A Comparison of the Institutions of Moses with those of the Hindoos and Other Ancient Nations; with Remarks on Mr. Dupuis' Origin of all Religions*. 1799.

Raine, Kathleen, and George Mills Harper, eds. *Thomas Taylor the Platonist: Selected Writings*. Bollingen Series 88. Princeton, N.J.: Princeton University Press, 1969.

Schelling, Friedrich. *Über die Gottheiten von Samothrace*. 1815.

Schlegel, Friedrich von. *Literary Notebooks, 1797–1801*. Edited with introduction and commentary by Hans Eichner. London: Athlone Press, 1957.

———. *Über das Studium der griechischen Poesie*. Edited with commentary by Paul Hankamer. Godesberg: Verlag Helmut Küpper, 1947.

Scott, Grant F. "Beautiful Ruins: The Elgin Marbles Sonnet in its Historical and Generic Contexts," *Keats-Shelley Journal* 39 (1990): 123–50.

Trevelyan, Humphry. *Goethe and the Greeks*. 2d ed. Cambridge: Cambridge University Press, 1981.

Tsigakou, Fani-Maria. *The Rediscovery of Greece: Travellers and Painters of the Romantic Era*. London: Thames and Hudson, 1981.

Vaughan, William. *Romantic Art*. London: Thames and Hudson, 1978.

Vries, Jan de. *Forschungsgeschichte der Mythologie*. Freiburg and Munich: Verlag Karl Alber, 1961.

Webb, Timothy. "Romantic Hellenism." In *The Cambridge Companion to British Romanticism*, Edited by Stuart Curran. Cambridge: Cambridge University Press, 1993. 148–76.

Weisinger, Kenneth D. *The Classical Façade: A Nonclassical Reading of Goethe's Classicism*. University Park: Pennsylvania State University Press, 1988.

N

NABUCCO 1842

Opera by Giuseppe Verdi

Nabucco is the third of Giuscppe Verdi's twenty-eight operas. Mostly composed in 1841, it premiered at La Scala, Milan, on March 9, 1842. The triumph of his first opera *Oberto* (1839) and the fiasco of his second opera *Un giorno di regno* (1840) preceded *Nabucco*. Verdi himself believed that his career as an important opera composer actually began with *Nabucco*, and most authorities agree with that assessment. Originally entitled *Nabucodonosor*, it was permanently abbreviated to the present name in 1844. Closely associated with the *risorgimento* movement, *Nabucco* eventually emerged as a symbol of Italian nationalism.

Babylonian forces defeated the Hebrews in 586 B.C.E. As the opera opens, the people of Jerusalem lament their tragic loss while Zaccaria, the high priest, attempts to inspire them with hope. Fenena, daughter of the Babylonian king, Nabucco, is held hostage under the protection of Ismaele, the king's nephew. During her captivity, Ismaele and Fenena have fallen in love, further complicating the scenario. Abigaille, supposed sister of Fenena, also loves Ismaele. She attempts to strike a political bargain with him in exchange for his love. Shortly after refusing her offer, Nabucco arrives at the temple as conqueror. Zaccaria threatens to kill Fenena, but Ismaele intercedes.

Nabucco elevates Fenena to the position of regent. Abigaille discovers that she is really a daughter of a slave and, consequently, plots to undermine Nabucco and Fenena before her true identity is revealed. Her supporters circulate rumors that Nabucco has died in battle, thus clearing the way for her assumption of the crown. The drama is further complicated when Nabucco appears, places the crown on his own head, and declares that he is God. The Hebrews are shocked by the blasphemous act, and a lightning bolt drives Nabucco insane. Abigaille resumes her position as ruler. She plans to exterminate the Hebrew people and cruelly taunts Nabucco. It is at this point in the drama that the Hebrew people sing nostalgically of their homeland in "Va pensiero" ("Go, Thought"), a chorus that became the unofficial Italian national anthem. Nabucco miraculously recovers from insanity. He embraces the Hebrew God as his own and prevents the execution of Fenena and her people. Abigaille dies of self-inflicted poison while the Hebrews celebrate Jehovah.

The libretto for *Nabucco* was written by Temistocle Solera, a free-spirited young man who remained Verdi's principal librettist for three years. Considering *Nabucco*'s association with nationalism, it is interesting to note that Solera was incarcerated by Austrian authorities for his involvement in the resistance movement. He based the text on an 1836 play by Anicet Bourgeois and Francis Cornue, as well as an 1838 ballet by Antonio Cortesi. Both of these works were entitled *Nabucodonosor*. The ballet was presented at La Scala in 1838, and Solera used its performance to fashion much of his libretto.

The chorus constitutes a vitally important element of the work; in fact, it sings the opera's first lines. The chorus represents the people and eventually symbolized oppressed masses. The extensive choral music in *Nabucco* and its successor, *I Lombardi* (1843), earned Verdi the title *il padre del core* (father of the chorus). Previous Italian composers had used choruses, but none had used them to such dramatic effect as Verdi. The chorus is used in all of Zaccaria's arias, reinforcing his leadership role of the Hebrews. The chorus "Va pensiero" does not exist in either the play or ballet versions of the story but is an addition by Solera. During rehearsal, the stage crew of La Scala stopped work to listen enthralled as the chorus sang it. They applauded and cheered the chorus when it ended, giving Verdi a boost of confidence in the potential success of the new opera. "Va pensiero" was rapturously received at the opera's premiere, prompting an encore of the chorus.

Like many of Verdi's later operas, *Nabucco* seems to have been modeled after French grand opera, particularly Gioacchino

Antonio Rossini's *Moise* (1827); therefore, it lacks some of the theatrical drive that characterizes most of Verdi's works. More emphasis is placed on static, oratorio-like tableau than on developing drama. This is true in spite of youthful energy and brashness in the score. Massive effects tend to be more important than character development or dramatic propulsion, though in many ways it is clearly an antecedent of *Aida* (1871).

While character development is somewhat limited and even awkward, it must be observed that even at this stage Verdi was a master at creating strong characters capable of expressing a wide range of emotions. In the title character, we see the prototype of the Verdi baritone, one of his most noteworthy contributions to art form. His leading baritone characters, including Nabucco, often exhibit extreme contrasts, ranging from villainy to nobility. Though lacking the finesse of later baritone roles like Rigoletto and Simon Boccanegra, Nabucco laid the groundwork for a new vocal category.

Verdi did not explore new vocal territory for the leading soprano role of Abigaille, but he did manage to compose a treacherous role that few sopranos can successfully tackle. It requires a wide range, dramatic power, and technical virtuosity. The first Abigaille was Giuseppina Strepponi, who became Verdi's second wife seventeen years later. Her performance of the role was imperfect, and some accounts suggest that it magnified her growing vocal problems of that period in her career. Many sopranos since have publicly failed to master this taxing role. As Verdi matured, he simplified his vocal writing, often avoiding fioritura in favor of more expressive vocal lines.

Though vocal writing was of paramount importance to Verdi, he did tend to avoid lengthy recitatives, even as early as *Nabucco*. This trait distanced Verdi from many of his predecessors. He seemed to be impatient with recitative, often employing it as rudimentary transition between arias. He also departed from tradition in *Nabucco* in making the love interest a subsidiary element. The romance between Fenena and Ismaele probably would have played a much greater, if not dominant, role later in Verdi's career. Obviously, the composer and librettist were much more interested in the villainous aspects of the plot.

The triumph of *Nabucco*'s première assured Verdi a secure place in Italian opera. It received sixty-five performances in its first year at La Scala. Productions were quickly mounted all over Italy and in many other nations. In Victorian Britain it ran into censorship problems because of the depiction of biblical characters on stage. For the 1846 London premiere, the title role was changed to Nino, king of Assyria, a bizarre absurdity given the work's text. This incident was relatively trivial compared to other political events that exposed Verdi to numerous more serious altercations regarding later operatic productions in Italy. Verdi became a national figure through *Nabucco*. "Va pensiero" was sung throughout Italy in political demonstrations for Italian unification and independence. Verdi died on January 27, 1901. When his body was interred at the Casa di Riposo on February 27, Arturo Toscanini conducted an 820-voice chorus in a performance of "Va pensiero" rather than a selection from one of his greater works. On that day, a crowd of 300,000 paid tribute not just to a great composer, but to a national hero.

THEODORE L. GENTRY

Bibliography

Budden, Julian. *The Operas of Verdi*. Rev. ed. Vol. 1. Oxford: Oxford University Press, 1992.

Lawton, David. "Analytical Observations on the *Nabucco* Revisions." In *III congresso internazaionale di studi verdianai* Milan (1972): 208–20.

Parker, Roger. "The Critical Edition of *Nabucco*," *Opera Quarterly* (1987): 91–98.

NACHMAN OF BRATSLAV 1772–1810

Hasidic rabbi and storyteller

A time of revolutionary upheaval in Western Europe, the late eighteenth century was also a time of contestation and controversy among the Jews of Eastern Europe. The brief life of Nachman of Bratslav gives ample evidence of these tensions. Mystic, spiritual leader, pilgrim, teller of tales, and founder of the Bratslaver (or Breslover) sect of Hasidim, Nachman of Bratslav was a great-grandson of Israel Baal Shem Tov, or "Besht," the founder of Hasidism. The Hasidim ("pious ones"), a movement originating in the Ukraine that stressed the paramount importance of joyous faith in God, were vehemently opposed by the *mitnagdim*, a Vilnius-based rabbinate loath to undermine the dialogical rigors of Talmudic study. Nachman's charismatic career is bracketed by two events that demonstrate the persistence of rationalism among European Jews: two years before his birth, the Hasidim were excommunicated by the *mitnagdim*; and within a decade of his death, the *Wissenschaft des Judentums* movement, a modernizing movement devoted to the scientific study of Judaism, would emerge in Germany. The vehemence with which Nachman lived out his messianic, kabbalistic creed attests to his familiarity with both rationalism and modernization. He played chess with the worldly and read the very philosophers whom he would proscribe to his followers. Even as his life and work revolved around the timeless realms of the divine, he was unmistakably a man of his age, in revolt against reason yet living always in relation to it.

By the time he turned twenty, Nachman already regarded himself as a *tzaddik*—a "righteous one"—and his teachings began to attract followers in Medvedevka in southwest Ukraine. Little is known about his early career, but clearly he did not shirk controversy; calling himself a *tzaddik hador* (the preeminent *tzaddik* of his generation) he challenged the authority of the eminent Dov Ber, Magid of Bezherich, and Aryeh Leib of Shpole, also known as the *Zeide* (old man) of Shpole. In 1798, he embarked on a pilgrimage to Palestine by way of Istanbul (ostensibly at the request of the spirit of the Besht), where he assumed a series of grotesque disguises, even play-fighting as a Napoleonic soldier with urchins. Like many features of his journey, these poses are enigmatic: perhaps they were a ritual of abjection, perhaps a variant of Romantic irony regarding the prideful persona of the *tzaddik hador* (which Elie Wiesel called his "falsest and most successful mask"); most likely, the arduous journey was itself a respite from the stress of continual controversy. Nachman's journey to Palestine took him to Jaffa, Haifa, Safed, and Tiberias; he apparently did not visit Jerusalem and left hurriedly through the port of Acco one step ahead of Napoleon's invading army.

Since the sole source for Nachman's journey is his hagiographer, Nathan ben Naphtali Hertz Sternhartz—better known as Nathan of Nemirov—it is hard to say which details are factual and which are designed by Nathan to enhance a spiritual allegory of death and rebirth. When the two first met after Nachman appeared to Nathan in a dream, Nathan was told, "We know each other a long time, but this is the first time we see each other." From then on, Nathan's work was to collect the Rebbe's teachings, casual sayings, *drashot* (readings of scripture), table talk, dreams, homilies, and ultimately the thirteen tales that are widely considered to be the beginning of the Yiddish art of storytelling.

Nachman of Bratslav began telling tales in 1806, in a period of crisis; he felt that his followers had failed to grasp his own messianic role, derived from a kabbalistic theology. At the center of kabbalistic theology, which originated in Provence in the late thirteenth century, is an elaborate myth of divine involvement in the world. As elaborated by Isaac Luria, Kabbalah presupposes a catastrophe-creation (*zimzum*), in which the vessels containing various divine emanations (*sfirot*) are shattered (*shvirat hakelim*); the vast labor of repairing the world (*tikkun olam*) is undertaken jointly by the human and the divine. At precisely the same time as Jakob and Wilhelm Grimm were collecting folktales redolent of an earlier, simpler age, Nachman begin telling tales expressly to bring a future, messianic age into being. In a sermon called "Patah Rabbi Simeon" (collected in *Likkutei Moharan*), he represented these tales as a jumble in need of holy repair, stressing their extrinsic origin as "tales that other people tell." Indeed, the tales are notable for lacking biblical personages and for their generalized settings and typical characters, including princesses, beggars, foundlings, though many contain grotesque, even scatological imagery. Second, he called them a "garb" for theology, one designed to protect the listener from the effulgence of the divine. Third, he located the space of narration as a kabbalistic emptiness from which the divine has withdrawn; the act of listening or interpreting must bring the divine back into this space. Announcing that these tales were designed to awaken souls "who sleep away their days," he divided them into three classes: those "in the midst of days," which pertain to the lower, mundane world; those "of the years of antiquity," which pertain to the higher, divine world; and a third class not limited to either one.

The tales appeared posthumously in 1812, published in a bilingual edition. A deeply Yiddishized Hebrew appears at the top of each page, and beneath it, a decidedly unliterary Yiddish. A critical debate over whether to read these as ethical tracts, kabbalistic homilies, or spiritual autobiography may partly be resolved by David Roskies's view that they were written for multiple audiences, for lettered initiates of kabbalah and those barely literate, probably for male and female readers alike. Several, particularly the lengthy final story, "The Seven Beggars," feature multiply impacted tales and structural asymmetries. But more salient than the structures themselves is the inexhaustible impetus to repair the world through narration, which exceeds these structures at every turn. Similarly, Nachman's life and work exceed the strict confines of his Hasidic world; his use of demotic diction and forms recalls Samuel Taylor Coleridge and William Wordsworth's *Lyrical Ballads*; his mysticism, William Blake's notion of "the infinite in all things"; he journeyed to the Levant in Napoleon Bonaparte's shadow; and his messianism recalls contemporary millenarian movements, many of which sought the conversion of Jews to belief in a Christian messiah. Above all, his magnified, brooding subjectivity and the tales that emerged from (and perhaps remedied) a spiritual crisis, mark him as a man of the Romantic era.

ESTHER SCHOR

Biography

Born, Medzibezh, Podolia, Ukraine, April 4, 1772. Married Sosia 1785, with whom he had three daughters and one son. Moved to Medvedevka, 1790. Traveled to Eretz Yisrael in 1798; left via Acco during Napoleon's siege, 1799; settled in Zlatopol, Kiev, 1800. Moved to Bratslav, 1802. Death of infant son, Shloime Ephraim, 1806; began tales that same year. Death of Sosia, June 1807; second marriage, September 1807. Onset of tuberculosis, 1807; journeyed to Lemberg (Lvov) for medical treatment, 1807–8; relocated to Uman, Ukraine, 1810. Died, October 16, 1810 in Uman.

Selected Works

Note: Nachman's tales and teachings were rendered by his disciple, Nathan ben Naphtali Hertz Sternhartz.
Likkutei Moharan. 1806.
Likkutei Moaharan Tinyana. 1811.
Sippurei Hama'asiyyot. Hebrew/Yiddish bilingual version, 1815, Translated as *Nachman of Bratslav: The Tales* by Arnold J. Band. New York: Paulist Press, 1978.
Likkutei Tefillot. 1821–27.

Bibliography

Band, Arnold, ed. *Nahman of Bratslav: The Tales*. New York: Paulist Press, 1978.
Buber, Martin. *The Tales of Rabbi Nachman*. Translated by Maurice Friedman. New York: Horizon, 1966.
Green, Arthur. *Tormented Master: The Life and Spiritual Quest of Rabbi Nahman of Bratslav*. Woodstock, Vt.: Jewish Lights, 1992.
Piekarz, Mendl. *Hasidut Braslav*. Jerusalem: Bialik Institute, 1972.
Roskies, David G. "Master of Prayer: Nahman of Bratslav." Chapter 2 in *A Bridge of Longing: The Lost Art of Yiddish Storytelling*. Cambridge, Mass.: Harvard University Press, 1995.
Scholem, Gershom G. "Hasidim: The Latest Phase." Ninth Lecture. In *Major Trends in Jewish Mysticism*. New York: Schocken, 1961.
Steinsaltz, Adin. *Beggars and Prayers: Adin Steinsaltz Retells the Tales of Rabbi Nachman of Bratslav*. Translated by Yehuda Hanegbi, Herzlia Dobkin, Deborah Frenh, and Freema Gottlieb. New York: Basic Books, 1979.
Weiss, Joseph G., and Moshe Hallamish, "Nahman of Bratslav" In *Encylopaedia Judaica*. Geoffrey Wigoder, Fern Sectbach, and Cecil Roth, eds. CD-ROM edition. Jerusalem: Judaica Multimedia, 1997.
Wiesel, Elie. *Souls on Fire: Portraits and Legends of Hasidic Masters*. New York: Simon and Schuster, 1972.

NACHTSTÜCKE

Collection of stories by E. T. A. Hoffmann

E. T. A. Hoffmann's second collection of stories, *Nachtstücke*, was originally published in two volumes, in 1816 and 1817. The first volume included two stories that had already been published separately—"Ignaz Denner" (1814) and "Der Sandmann" (1815)—together with "Die Jesuiterkirche in G." and "Das Sanctus." The second volume contained "Das öde Haus," "Das Majorat," "Das Gelübde," and "Das steinerne Herz." However, the *Nachtstücke* were not as popular with the reading public as the earlier *Fantasiestücke in Callots Manier* (1814), and no subsequent edition appeared during Hoffmann's lifetime.

The eight stories that make up the *Nachtstücke* are linked thematically by the motif of the night. The title of the collection alludes to the representation of objects illuminated either by moonlight or by artificial sources of light in painting. This technique produces extreme contrasts of darkness and light, such as are often to be found in the works of Correggio and Rembrandt. The deliberate rejection of an harmonizing aesthetic in favor of one placing more emphasis on extreme contrasts and distortion fascinated Hoffmann to such an extent that he attempted to make use of a similar aesthetic in his own fiction.

Like many of his contemporaries, Hoffman was greatly influenced by the intellectual climate of an age in which fundamental changes were taking place across the whole of Europe following a revival of political conservatism. As a result of such developments, many writers and intellectuals felt unable to endorse the optimistic revolutionary fervor of the early German Romantics, and began to turn their attention instead to the "darker side" (or *Nachtseiten*) of the human psyche. Among the most important works on this theme were Novalis's *Hymnen an die Nacht* (1800), Ernst August Friedrich Klingemann's *Die Nachtwachen des Bonaventura* (published anonymously in 1804), and Gotthilf Heinrich von Schubert's *Ansichten von der Nachtseite der Naturwissenschaft* (1808). In common with these and other authors, Hoffmann treats the motifs of night and darkness as the locus of pathological and demonic tendencies in human behavior, tendencies that, all too often, lead to criminal activities and even madness. Accordingly, his works focus on the instinctual and irrational aspects of human behavior and at the same time stand in stark contrast to the optimistic rationalism of the Enlightenment.

Hoffmann's stories are, however, not merely concerned with the threat posed to mainstream society by pathologically insane individuals. More often than not, the refusal of an individual to conform to the expectations of society is presented as an understandable rejection of a world in which only the most obtuse philistine can be truly at home and in which there is no genuine appreciation of such nonutilitarian activities as art, music and poetry. Caught up within the confines of an essentially materialistic society and trapped by the contingencies of human existence itself, the Romantic individual seeks to escape from both by exploring *das Nächtliche* and the deeper recesses of the human psyche.

The term *das Nächtliche* is to be understood in at least three senses. First, it refers to those hours during which dubious characters go about their shady business while "respectable" citizens are asleep in their beds; second, it alludes to the irrational component of the human psyche; and third, it evokes a state of social alienation which can, in extremes, cases result in a distorted sense of reality (and a corresponding loss of identity). Thus in *Die Jesuiterkirche in G.*, it is during the night that the artist, Berthold, works on the pictures in the church whilst struggling with the demons of his past; in *Der Sandmann*, it is under the cover of darkness that Nathanael spies on Coppelius and succumbs to the illusion that he and the mysterious Sandman are one and the same; and in *Das Majorat*, not only do almost all of the criminal activities perpetrated by the members of Freiherr Roderich von R.'s family circle take place at night, but, in addition, the crucial insights that are instrumental in shedding some light on the family secret have their origins in the realm of the irrational.

As a result, it is perhaps hardly surprising that Hoffmann's stories should have attracted the attention of literary critics with psychoanalytic leanings. Indeed, the sheer volume of critical scholarship on *Der Sandmann* is no doubt due, at least in part, to Sigmund Freud's seminal essay *Das Unheimliche* (1919), in that he interprets the recurrent motif of the physical threat to the human eye in terms of the male fear of castration. Nonetheless, Freud's rather idiosyncratic interpretation of this story should not be allowed to obscure the fact that Hoffmann offers other explanations that are couched in a more straightforward critique of society for the protagonist's disturbed state of mind. Nathanael is presented as a young man who, as a result of a traumatic childhood experience, is inwardly torn and suffers from a persecution complex. At the end of the story he loses sight of reality altogether and commits suicide. His fate contrasts with that of his prosaic, rationalistic fiancée, Clara, who, we are told, eventually finds happiness in a bourgeois marriage. But while Nathanael's increasing sense of social isolation is undoubtedly tragic, there is also something grotesque about his development. For the "woman" to whom Nathanael turns in his desperation—and who succeeds in replacing Clara in his affections—turns out to be an automaton, an artificial construction reflecting the needs and fantasies of "her" male admirers. In the figure of Olimpia, Hoffmann offers a sharp critique of relations between the sexes and exposes the bourgeois ideal of marriage as little more than an arrangement in which the male quest for identity leads to an idealization of woman (and a subsequent loss of identity for the woman in question).

Although almost all of the "Nachtstücke" end on a tragic note, Hoffmann also includes elements of humor in many of his fictional works. As a result, the reader often experiences a seamless transition from the grotesque to the overtly comic. Moreover, the inclusion of such humorous elements—at times ironic, at times carnavelesque—stands in stark contrast to the Early German Romantics' vision of unity, harmony, and redemption.

BIRGIT ROEDER

Bibliography

Cadot, Michel. "Art et artifice dans les *Nachtstücke*," in *E. T. A. Hoffmann et le Fantastique*. Vol. 2 of Bibliothèque le Texte et l'Idée. Edited by Jean-Marie Paul. Nancy: Centre de Recherches Germaniques et Scandinaves de l'Université de Nancy, 1992.

Drux, Rudolf, ed. *E. T. A. Hoffmann. Der Sandmann*. Erläuterungen und Dokumente, Reclam Universalbibliothek No. 8199. Stuttgart: Reclam, 1994.

Ellis, John M. "Clara, Nathanael and the Narrator. Interpreting Hoffmann's *Der Sandmann*," *German Quarterly* 54 (1981): 1–18.

Feldges, Brigitte, and Ulrich Stadler, eds. *E. T. A. Hoffmann. Epoche—Werk—Wirkung*. Munich: Beck, 1986.

Kremer, Detlef. *Romantische Metamorphosen. E. T. A. Hoffmanns Erzählungen*. Stuttgart, Weimar: Metzler, 1993.

McGlathery, James M. *Mysticism and Sexuality: E. T. A. Hoffmann*. New York: Lang, 1985.

Schönherr, Ulrich. "Social Differentiation and Romantic Art: E. T. A. Hoffmann's 'The Sanctus' and the Problem of Aesthetic Positioning in Modernity," *NGC* 66 (1995): 3–16.

Steinecke, Hartmut. *E. T. A. Hoffmann*. Stuttgart: Reclam, 1997.

NAPOLEON CROSSING THE ALPS AT THE GREAT SAINT BERNARD PASS
1801

Painting by Jacques-Louis David

Jacques-Louis David first met Napoleon Bonaparte in Paris on December 10, 1797, at a public reception given to honor the general after the victorious Italian campaigns of 1796–97. David asked to paint Napoleon's portrait, a request that was soon granted. Napoleon came to David's studio in the Louvre and gave him a single sitting of three hours, from which emerged the painted fragment of head and collar now in the Louvre. David's idea was to paint the general full-length on the plain of Rivoli holding the Treaty of Campo Formio. But no more sittings followed, and the picture remained unfinished. Yet this brief meeting had a profound effect on David, who announced, "Oh my friends, what a fine head he has! It's pure, it's great, it's as beautiful as the Antique! Here is a man to whom altars would have been erected in Ancient times; yes my friends, . . . Bonaparte is my hero!"

David's *Napoleon Crossing the Alps* was the first painting of Napoleon completed after he became first consul following the coup of Brumaire—though it was not actually commissioned by Napoleon himself but by King Charles IV of Spain in recognition of the young commander's notable victories and rise to power, and as homage to a powerful ally. It provided the definitive image of the warrior ruler that the publicity-conscious Bonaparte was then eager to promote. Fresh from his second conquest of Italy, David asked Napoleon to pose, but he refused, saying that the most important feature of a portrait was character not likeness, and added that Alexander the Great had certainly not posed for the ancient Greek artist Apelles. Napoleon also observed that: "No one knows if portraits of great men are likenesses: it suffices that genius lives." David was forced to agree and so had to make do with dressing up a mannequin, and occasionally his son and his student François Gérard, in the uniform Napoleon had worn at Marengo, with the added accessories of his coat, riding boots, bicorn hat, and an ornate mameluke sword. Having the uniform of the famous general in the studio led to some horseplay, and David was surprised and amused to find that Napoleon's head was much larger than his own; the borrowed hat fell over his eyes when he tried it on. David's idea was to show Napoleon sword in hand in the midst of battle, but Napoleon replied that battles were no longer fought in that way and announced that he wanted to be shown "calm on a fiery horse." David duly obliged, setting the portrait at the crossing of the Saint Bernard Pass. The long-established tradition of the equestrian portrait was used to glorify the victorious first consul, and on the rocks below the horse the name *Bonaparte* is inscribed with those of two previous transalpine conquerors, Hannibal and Charlemagne. But like many images of power, *Napoleon Crossing the Alps* is economical with the truth. Napoleon did not lead his army over the Alps riding on "a fiery horse"—he actually crossed a few days after the main advance and was led along a narrow track seated on a mule, a much less heroic scene that was depicted later in 1848 by Paul Delaroche.

Jacques-Louis David, *Napoleon Crossing the Alps (Saint Bernard's Pass, 20 May 1800)*. Reprinted courtesy of AKG.

David was painting a living hero for the first time; his previous subjects had been those from ancient history, or revolutionary martyrs like Jean-Paul Marat. But because Napoleon refused to pose, the end result was somewhat remote and impersonal, and it lacked the immediacy and vitality of direct contact seen in the earlier unfinished portrait. However, Napoleon was so taken by the final work that he ordered a replica, and David painted this and two other versions for him with the assistance of his pupils. When completed in 1801, the King of Spain's work and Napoleon's first copy were added to David's private paying exhibition of *Les sabines* (*The Intervention of the Sabine Women*, 1799) in the Louvre, so that the public would have the opportunity to see them.

Five major versions of *Napoleon Crossing the Alps* are extant. The original, now in the Château de Malmaison, Paris, shows Napoleon wearing a yellow cloak and seats him on a piebald horse. Napoleon's first version, with red cloak and bay-brown horse, is at Charlottenburg Castle in Berlin. Two further versions are at Versailles; the other is in the Kunsthistorisches Museum in Vienna.

David charged a little less for the replicas than for the original, and his wife was very active and persistent in pursuing Napoleon's ministers for employment and fees. Madame David played an increasingly assertive role in her husband's business affairs and was eager for him to cash in on his fame and talent. However, such tactics appeared undiplomatic and clumsy, and made David seem greedy and money hungry. In effect, he priced himself out of work and many commissions were given to cheaper artists who had formerly been his pupils, such as François Gerard, Anne-Louis Girodet, de Roussy-Trioson, and Antoine-Jean Gros.

Napoleon Crossing the Alps embodied the first consul's own definition of what made a good painting. Napoleon's artistic taste and understanding were very limited, and his minister of the interior, Jean-Antoine Chaptal, later wrote, "Napoleon did not care for the arts probably because nature had denied him the sensibility to appreciate their merit . . . Nevertheless . . . he always appeared to interest himself in the arts . . . He did this for political reasons in order to demonstrate his broadmindedness." More than anything else, Napoleon liked paintings in which he was the main character, and his brother Lucien later told David: "You must understand my dear David that my brother Napoleon takes an interest only in pictures in which he counts for something. It is his weakness and he has no objections at all to being in the limelight."

SIMON LEE

See also **David, Jacques-Louis**

Work

Bonaparte Crossing the Alps at the St. Bernard Passant, 1801. Oil on canvas, 260 cm × 221 cm. Château de Malmaison, Paris.

Bibliography

Lee, S. *David*. Phaidon, 1990.
Schnapper, A. *David: Témoin de son temps*. Freibourg: *Office du Live*, 1980.
Schnapper, A., and A. Sérullaz. *David*. Exhibition catalog. Paris: Editions de la Réunion des Musées Nationaux, 1989.

NAPOLEON IN THE PEST HOUSE AT JAFFA, 1804

Painting by Antoine-Jean Gros

On March 11, 1799, Napoleon Bonaparte visited the plague-stricken victims of his Middle Eastern campaign following the French conquest of Jaffa. The bubonic plague was spreading rapidly through the French army, which was living in cramped quarters, making for a tense situation. In the months and years following this campaign, Napoleon's reputation was also being challenged by the fact that he had massacred thousands of Turkish prisoners, and had planned to poison his own soldiers who had been struck by the plague. Napoleon had hoped such a visit could reduce the sense of fear regarding the situation by showing not only his concern and sympathy for the sick, but also that if he could walk through the plague house, unafraid of contracting illness himself, it would imply that the situation was not as dangerous as had been feared.

Antoine-Jean Gros's primary duty in painting a representation of this situation was to conceal and downplay its negative and less flattering aspects. While the work is categorized as a history painting, it is also a work of political propaganda. This point is further evidenced by the fact that, although according to written accounts Napoleon made a quick visit to the plague-stricken, Gros depicted the event in a manner that exaggerated its scale.

Gros came to paint this work under somewhat unusual circumstances. In 1801 he had won a commission to paint a scene celebrating the victory of General Andoche Junot at the Battle of Nazareth. Ultimately Napoleon, deciding that he did not want a massive work of art celebrating the accomplishments of another leader, halted Gros's work on that project, and awarded him the opportunity to paint the Jaffa episode in its place.

Gros produced a massive oil on canvas, measuring over five meters tall by seven meters wide, which was exhibited in the 1804 French Salon. The painting depicts Napoleon visiting the sick in a Near Eastern setting; he is both the physical and symbolic focus of the work. Napoleon's demeanor and attire reflect his relative calm in comparison with the other French officers who accompany him. While Napoleon touches a plague victim's bubo (inflamed, swollen lymph node) with his bare hand, the man in the French army uniform standing to his left covers his mouth with a handkerchief so as to protect himself from the surrounding germs. The man standing to his left fearfully watches as Napoleon approaches the victim. The plague victims seem to gravitate towards Napoleon, as if he is a source of miraculous salvation. In the foreground, a number of nude and semi-nude figures lie on the ground, appearing to be on the verge of death. By arranging the figures in such a manner and dressing

Antoine-Jean Gros, *Napoleon in the Pest House at Jaffa.* Reprinted courtesy of AKG.

Napoleon in his military uniform, Gros portrayed Napoleon as being immune not only to forces of man, but also to those of nature.

From an oil sketch now located in the New Orleans Museum of Art, one can see that Gros had originally planned to paint Napoleon's visit in a bare nineteenth-century hospital room without emphasizing the Oriental setting, as he did in the final composition. In the final painting Gros alluded to the fact that this makeshift hospital had once been a mosque through various Islamic architectural details. In the background, smoke rises from a distant battlefield and a disproportionately large French flag billows in the wind atop a Franciscan monastery, proclaiming a French victory. A viewer ignorant of the many casualties of the battle and Napoleon's mishandling of the situation would probably believe that the campaign was a French success, due in no small part to Napoleon's heroics.

The setting of the painting in Jaffa, located in what was then Palestine, adds to the image's sense of intrigue and allure. The theme of the Near East or the "exotic" would appear a number of times in French Romantic painting, in such famous works as Jean-Auguste-Dominique Ingres's *Odalisque* (1814) and Ferdinand-Victor-Eugène Delacroix's *The Massacre at Chios* (1822–24). The fact the event took place in the Holy Land, and the birthplace of Jesus, encouraged consideration of Napoleon as a miracle worker and implied his status as a Messiah-like figure.

This painting reflects an increasing trend in history painting at the time toward depicting events from recent history, populated by figures dressed in contemporary clothing. Benjamin West, the American painter who was active in London, played an important role in this development with his watershed painting *The Death of General Wolfe* (1770), that depicted an event from the French and Indian war. Jacques-Louis David (in whose studio Gros trained) had painted a number of scenes from ancient history, but later painted scenes of more recent history as in *The Death of Marat* (1793) and *Napoleon Crossing the Alps* (1800).

The theme of "healing" was not unknown to French art of the time. David had depicted an allegory of miraculous healing in his painting *St. Roch Interceding for the Plague Stricken* (1781), commemorating a plague which had struck the city of Marseilles in 1720. While David used figures from Christian history to project his message, Gros, in line with the goal of glorifying Napoleon, used a contemporary military hero. A few years later, Gros would paint another propagandistic history painting, *Napoleon on the Battlefield at Eylau on 9 February 1807* (1808), that also depicts Napoleon as a benevolent military leader.

In *Napoleon in the Pest House in Jaffa*, Gros depicts a contemporary figure and transformed him into a timeless hero. Regardless of how one feels about Napoleon, his actions in this situation, or his regime in general, the painting is so impressive for its brilliant composition, size, and powerful message, that it is recognized as one of the great masterpieces of French Romanticism. Gros not only immortalized Napoleon as a heroic and benevolent leader, but also immortalized himself as a premier history painter of the French Romantic era.

ALEXANDRA SCHEIN

See also **Gros, Antoine-Jean**

Work

Napoleon in the Pest House at Jaffa, 1804. Oil on canvas, 523 cm × 715 cm. Louvre, Paris.

Bibliography

Crow, Thomas. *Emulation: Making Artists for Revolutionary France.* New Haven, Conn.: Yale University Press, 1994.

Friedlaender, Walter. "Napoleon as Roi Thaumaturge," *Journal of the Warburg and the Courtauld Institues* 4 (1941): 139–41.

———. *David to Delacroix.* Translated by Robert Goldwater. Cambridge, Mass.: Harvard University Press, 1952.

O'Brien, David. "Antoine-Jean Gros in Italy," *Burlington Magazine* 137 (1995): 651–660.

Porterfield, Todd. *Art in the Service of French Imperialism, 1798–1836.* Princeton, N.J.: Princeton University Press, 1998.

Prendergast, Christopher. *Napoleon and History Painting: Antoine-Jean Gross La Bataille d'Eylau.* Oxford, U.K.: Claredon Press, 1997.

Rosenblum, Robert. *Nineteenth-Century Art.* Upper Saddle River, N.J.: Prentice Hall, 1984.

Wilson-Smith, Timothy. *Napoleon and His Artists.* London: Constable, 1996.

DIE NACHTWACHEN DES BONAVENTURA

Novel by unknown author

Although recently attributed to Ernst August Friedrich Klingemann (1777–1831), the authorship of *Die Nactwachen des Bonaventura* (which was first published anonymously in a minor periodical, *Journal von neuen deutschen Originalromanen*, in 1804) has long been the subject of considerable controversy.

The name Bonaventura in the novel's title is a reference to the adopted name of the medieval theologian Giovanni di Fidanza (1221–74). Like his real-life medieval counterpart, the hero of Klingemann's novel struggles with what he sees as the vanity of rational thought. The novel itself demonstrates affinities with a number of contemporary works in which the motifs of darkness and night play an important role, including Novalis' *Hymnen an die Nacht* (1800), Gotthilf Heinrich Schubert's *Ansichten von der Nachtseite der Naturwissenschaft* (1808), and E. T. A. Hoffmann's *Nachtstücke* (1816–17). In the light of the reactionary political changes taking place across Europe, many intellectuals found it increasingly hard to endorse the optimistic revolutionary fervor of the early German Romantics and turned instead to the study of the "darker" side of human nature. In these works, the night alludes to a condition of nihilism, fragmentation and a loss of identity bordering on insanity. The nature of the divided self and the inability to come to terms with the prosaic character of an essentially philistine and materialistic world is often explored through the figure of the artist, above all in the works of E. T. A. Hoffmann, Jean Paul, Ludwig Tieck, or Wilhelm Heinrich Wackenroder.

The protagonist of *Die Nachtwachen des Bonaventura* is Kreuzgang, a foundling named after the spot where he was first discovered. Despite harboring youthful desires to become an artist, he is a night watchman as an adult. During his nocturnal tours of the city he becomes caught up in a wide range of bizarre adventures. In Kreuzgang we are presented with a variant of a well-known literary character, the wise fool who through his naive and harmless questioning, exposes the absurd contradictions that lie thinly concealed behind the façade of bourgeois society. His nocturnal occupation provides him with the perfect opportunity to observe the foibles of his fellow men, for it is at night that the latter are most off their guard. Increasingly he leaves the mundane aspects of everyday reality behind him and gains an insight into some of the more inscrutable aspects of human behavior.

As the novel unfolds, the curious figure of Kreuzgang (who in the depths of his heart has never quite abandoned his dream of leading the life of an artist) comes to seem less like a whimsical fool, and more like a sharp-witted critic of the vanity and corruption of bourgeois society. The novel mercilessly makes fun of civil servants, lawyers, clerics, and the Church. Even the bourgeois ideals of love and marriage are exposed to ridicule. However, such criticism as there is, rarely comes directly from the mouth of Kreuzgang himself, but is teased out of the reader through the bald reporting of the night watchman's experiences.

Kreuzgang himself, however, is hardly a stable character within the madhouse that is the world of everyday reality. His mysterious origins (his mother, addressing him in the persona of a gypsy fortune teller, tells him that the devil himself was present at his conception) suggest that he too has a divided personality. Furthermore, he does not simply confront society as a detached, cynical observer, but is repeatedly forced to recognize the fact of his own helplessness. In this way the conventional image of the wise fool is developed into that of an individual who is constantly under threat from a society that cannot really offer any of its members a secure existence and that views him, in particular, with a degree of hostility. Indeed it is hardly coincidental that when the municipal authorities force him to spend a month in the local lunatic asylum he feels quite at home there, for the asylum is the one place where no attempt is made to impose any kind of order on a chaotic world in which the individual is alienated even from himself. Released from the asylum and back among the "sane" once more, he lends his services to a puppet theater whose puppets reflect the foibles of the watching public in grotesque fashion. Here the symbolism of the lifeless puppet whose limbs are manipulated by forces beyond its control, together with the motif of the mask, play a crucial role in underlining the falseness of a world in which the concept of individual authenticity has been rendered meaningless.

Alongside the often humorous and ironic observations on the conventional character of human behavior, there is also a tragic dimension culminating in the nihilistic exclamation with which the novel ends: "Und der Widerhall im Gebeinhaus ruft zum letzten Mal—Nichts!" The pessimistic character of the ending is quite out of keeping with conventional Romantic aesthetics. It may well be that in *Die Nachtwachen des Bonaventura* the reader encounters traditional Romantic images such as nymphs, shepherds, moonlit ruins, misunderstood poets, as well as references to the Kabbalah and the mysticism of Jacob Böhme; but here the conventional trappings of Romanticism are called into question and subverted through the inclusion of satirical observations, the juxtaposition of multiple levels of reality and the depiction of the protagonist's confusion. In *Die Nachtwachen des Bonaventura* the Romantic illusion gives way to an altogether different kind of reality. However, this reality is not that of the rational Enlightenment, but one rooted in the mysterious realm of the night, a realm in which paradox, contradiction, and the irrational hold sway with the result that all individual and social values are rendered meaningless.

This journey to a position of extreme nihilism is underscored by the novel's form. Although the reader is presented with sixteen chronologically-ordered accounts of Kreuzgang's experiences during his nocturnal rounds, these accounts are continually disrupted through the inclusion of the watchman's own literary and philosophical vignettes. At times these are incorporated into the surface level of narration with the result that the reader is left in a state of uncertainty as to the precise level of narration at which the story is being told. In this way, the novel's central theme is itself amplified by a fragmentary aesthetic that serves to enhance the reader's sense of disorientation.

BIRGIT RÖEDER

Bibliography

Hoffmeister, Gerhard. "Nachtwachen." In *Interpretationen. Erzählungen und Novellen des 19. Jahrhunderts*. Stuttgart: Reclam, 1988.

Katritzky, Linde. "Defining the genre of Bonaventura's 'Nachtwachen,'" *German Life and Letters* 52 (1999): 13–27.
———. *A Guide to Bonaventura's Nightwatches*. New York: Lang, 1999.

Sammons, Jeffrey L. *The "Nachtwachen von Bonaventura": A Structural Interpretation*. The Hague: Mouton, 1965.
Schillemeit, Jost, ed. *August Klingemann: Nachtwachen von Bonaventura*. Frankfurt: Insel, 1974.

NATIONALISM

The roots of the cultural and political nationalisms that are central to our modern sense of identity, and fundamental to the global system of states (even today, the discourses of postmodernism and globalization react to the Western nation-state as a cultural and political norm) are to be found in the interplay of Romantic thought and the Enlightenment ideas it railed against. Recent scholarship has focused on the means by which cultural nationalism, as fostered and disseminated by the intellectual elite, was translated into popular conviction and action, roughly between 1789 and 1848. Put differently, the Romantic era is a period notable for the transformation of "nationness" into "nationalism," and the transformation of the individual into not only a "citizen" but also a member of a "national" group. In this connection, it is crucial to distinguish between, on the one hand, Romantic ideas of the nation and, on the other, their geopolitical legacy. Wherever cultural-nationalist movements intersected with demands for liberal reforms, new nations tended to form, many of which (though by no means all) gained statehood by the end of the nineteenth century, or during the twentieth. The astonishingly potent brew of political and cultural nationalism had effects that were centripetal (events in Italy; and pan-Germanism, pan-Slavism, and even pan-Scandinavianism) as well as centrifugal (events in Poland, Iceland, and Ireland). However, scarcely had political nationalism become a concern of the masses than the Romantic era was over.

The idea of patriotism can be traced back to Greco-Roman times, but was usually associated with loyalty to a person rather than a territory. Until the mid-eighteenth century, the French terms *patrie* and *nation*, like the Italian *nazione*, had shifting geographical referents; but by the time the entry for *patrie* in Denis Diderot's *Encyclopédie* was written, the term was associated with patriotic self-sacrifice and the love of freedom. For Voltaire, national belonging was a voluntary act, whereas for Rousseau, generally regarded as the godfather of political nationalism, the territorially-bound *patrie* or *nation* was intrinsically connected to the state. Indeed, his ideal state was based on the nation, a collective act of the general will; in drawing up the system of law and government for the state, the national character should be given paramount consideration.

A nascent political nationalism crystallized in the wake of the French Revolution of 1789. One legacy of Napoleon's military adventures and geopolitical innovations was a much more widespread awareness of national "belonging." In postrevolution France, the nation-building process involved the consolidation of French language and culture throughout the multiethnic, multilingual territory. In Klemens Wenzel Nepomuk Lothar Metternich's Europe, we see the other side of the same coin: the desire of the nationally aware educated classes for a liberal polity and freedom from foreign rule, the same classes who were the producers and consumers of romantic, national culture in an era of print capitalism. The basis of their national conceptions was often peasant culture and the local vernacular, but the growth of the newspaper and the novel were also important in the construction of the national community.

In eighteenth-century Germany, the intellectual preference for French language and culture was one of the factors that led the young Johann Gottfried von Herder to expound the importance of a sense of the German *volk* (people) and of the use of the vernacular in the creation and dissemination of national culture. Herder considered the great empires of history to be abominations whose attempts to level out cultural difference were just as injurious as the creeping cosmopolitanism that had beset the Francophile urbanites of late-seventeenth century Germany. His nonaggressive brand of nationalism reacted against the universalism of the Enlightenment, seeking the particular and the unique in every national culture; by this same token, no culture should exalt itself over any other, a tenet that was forsaken by the nation builders of the late eighteenth century.

Central to Herder's conception of the *volk* was language; in particular, that the German language should be used in education and in worship, and should be used to rediscover the literary heritage of the *volk*. The latter task was performed by the celebrated folklorists Jakob and Wilhelm Grimm, whose pursuit and collection of "authentic" folklore and legend was paralleled, for example, in Finland by Elias Lönrott, and in Norway by Peter Christen Asbjørnsen and Jørgen Moe from the 1840s on. The folk song and story traditions of Scandinavia, Italy, Russia, Hungary, and most other European regions and nations were collated and transcribed by the intellectual elite and given back to the masses as national literature. Elsewhere, patriotic songs and anthems, vernacular translations of the Bible, as well as dictionaries and grammars of hitherto unstandardized tongues (thus meshing Enlightenment/scientific means with Romantic ends), ensured the vitality of "national" languages.

Historiography also reacted against the Enlightenment in the service of cultural and political nationalism. Herder's rejection of—and indebtedness to—the rationality and universalism of Enlightenment historians is apparent in his philosophy of history, which insists on the importance of the natural environment and the peculiarity of the inborn national character. The teleology of G. W. F. Hegel's purposive history was also predicated on the innate individuality of the nation, a concept whose lineage from David Hume and Charles-Louis de Secondat Montesquieu is clear. The Romantic trope of awakening dormant nations from their centuries of slumber has its echoes here, but the understanding of national history as a purposeful or necessary dynamic was later to find its fullest expression when romantic nationalism had done its work; for example, in the postunification German nationalist historiography of Heinrich von Treitschke (1834–96). The tendency of Romantic historiography was first and foremost to identify a past golden age of the nation, an age of heroism and virtue, and, often, to seek substantiation for Christian ethics in the pre-Christian past. This is especially the case in the Nordic romantic literature and translations of Nikolai Frederik Severin Grundtvig and Esaias Tegnér for example; in the German fascination with folk poetry such as the *Niebelungenlied*; in the obsession with national landscape and historical events in the visual arts (Francisco José de Goya y Lucientes and Christen Schiellerup Købke), and in the new genre of the historical novel, launched by Walter Scott with *Waverley* (1814) and imitated throughout Europe, notably by Manzoni, whose *I Promessi Sposi* (*The Betrothed*) was a key text in the Italian *risorgimento*. Archaeological finds, too, often inspired Romantic works of art (such as those of Adam Gottlob Oehlenschläger).

The cult of the Romantic genius as hero, as personified by Napoleon Bonaparte, was also essential for the development of popular nationalism. The successful nationalist movements were typically led by a charismatic figurehead. The unification process in Italy had its soldier in Garibaldi, its statesman in Cavour and its political idealist in Mazzini; Greece had its poet-soldier Lord Byron; and, later, Germany had its iron chancellor in Otto von Bismarck. Bismarck's *realpolitik*, and the failure of Cavour's orig-

inal policy of "Italia fara da se," however, showed that the Rousseauan act of collective will is insufficient to make a state of a nation; in the nineteenth century, as today, that is generally an international affair.

CATHERINE CLAIRE THOMSON

Bibliography

Anderson, Benedict. *Imagined Communities. Reflections on the Origins and Spread of Nationalism.* London: Verso, 1991.

Dann, Otto, and John Dinwiddy, eds. *Nationalism in the Age of the French Revolution.* London: Hambledon, 1988.

Gellner, Ernest. *Nations and Nationalism.* Oxford: Blackwell, 1983.

Hobsbawm, Eric, and Terence Ranger, eds. *The Invention of Tradition.* Cambridge: Cambridge University Press, 1992.

Llobera, Josep R. *The God of Modernity: The Development of Nationalism in Western Europe.* Oxford: Berg, 1994.

McCrone, David. *The Sociology of Nationalism.* London: Routledge, 1998.

Pearson, Raymond. *The Longman Companion to European Nationalism 1789–1920.* London: Longman, 1994.

Tägil, Sven, ed. *Ethnicity and Nation-Building in the Nordic World.* London: Hurst, 1995.

Woolf, Stuart, ed. *Nationalism in Europe 1815 to the Present: A Reader.* London: Routledge, 1996.

NATURAL SCIENCES

The epoch of Romanticism saw an engaged and substantial reaction of several naturalists, physicians, and philosophers against the general development of science and philosophy of the eighteenth century: a reaction defined as correction and complement, not as contrast or total alternative. The philosophical interpretation of nature of that epoch exercised a deep influence on the natural sciences, especially in regard to biology, but also to mathematics, physics, and chemistry.

Romantic natural scientists and speculative philosophers criticized the natural science of their time, but they in no way completely rejected the value and justification of an empirical, experimental, and mathematized approach to nature, although they disapproved of the separation of natural science from philosophy and the absolutizing of its positivistic perspective. Empiricism, the believed, should be combined with theory, physics with metaphysics Essential observations and inventions, as well as institutional innovations and foundations of scientific journals, derived from Romantic naturalists, but they did not form the central point of this movement; more important were the arguments for the unity of natural phenomena and natural sciences, the responsibility of man for nature, and the unity of nature and culture.

Above all Immanuel Kant and Friedrich Wilhelm Joseph von Schelling influenced the Romantic movement of the natural sciences, but other philosophers and earlier positions also proved to be significant. Exponents of this movement include the naturalists Karl Friedrich Burdach, Carl Gustav Carus, Joseph Görres, Hans Christian Oersted, Lorenz Oken, Johann Wilhelm Ritter, Gotthilf Heinrich von Schubert, Henrik Steffens, Gottfried Reinhold Treviranus, Ignaz Paul Vitalis Troxler, and many others. The now established distinction and separation of inor-

ganic and organic sciences had no value for these scientists; they took active interest in all branches of nature and often combined natural science and medicine.

As a very important contribution to the history of scientific institutions, the Gesellschaft Deutscher Naturforscher und Ärzte was founded in the Romantic spirit by Oken and several other naturalists and physicians in 1822. This scientific society of the Romantic era was the model for many other nineteenth-century scientific societies, such as the British Association for the Advancement of Science (1831), the Congrès Scientifiques (1833), the Riunione degli Scienziati Italiani (1839), and the Skandinavska Naturforskare och Läkare (1839). Oken also founded the interdisciplinary journal *Isis* in 1817, and it became a key periodical for delineating the history and culture of Romanticism.

The interpretations of inorganic and organic nature were guided by metaphysical and mathematical principles; by formal categories like difference and indifference, analogy, polarity, potency, and metamorphosis; but also by specific phenomena and processes of particular spheres of nature. A "speculative" or philosophical deduction in the form of the philosophy of nature of Schelling and G. W. F. Hegel should exceed the capacities of man. According to Troxler, the absolute that underlies nature and spirit cannot be grasped—neither by "intellectual contemplation" (*intellektuelle Anschauung*) nor by "reasonable faith" (Vernunftglaube)—any word for the absolute is only a "sign" of it. Ritter also confirmed: "The highest a priori deduction is a misunderstanding, and human beings are not its master." Faith, revelation, intuition, and presentiment are opposed to the idealistic concept of notion and philosophy; but all findings have to be confirmed by experience; the romantic naturalists did not glorify the irrational.

The conceptions of the Romantic naturalists of nature and science were based on the identity of nature and spirit; the laws of nature are supposed to correspond to spiritual laws. In this perspective Steffens declared, "Do you want to know nature? Take a look inside yourself, and in the stages of your spiritual development, you may have the chance of looking on nature's stages of development. Do you want to know yourself? Observe nature, and her works are of the same essence as your mind."

Nature must be conceived as a union and interrelationship of all phenomena and processes, dependent on metaphysical principles and immanently combined with the world of man. Schubert was guided above all by the principle of an internal or spiritual link among all natural phenomena, noting, "The history of nature has to do not just with individual, finite, immanently perishable being, but with an imperishable basis of all that can be seen, which unites it all and gives it soul. It teaches a love which loves in all things, a universal soul which sets everything, even that which is most remote and apart, is a living interplay that gives to all that can be seen, from the firmament of heaven to the ephemeral insect, one rythm of time and law of life."

In physics as well as in chemistry, Romantic naturalists made new observations and developed new interpretations and theories: famous examples are Johann Wilhelm Ritter (electrochemistry, ultroviolet radiation) and Hans Christian Oersted (electromagnetism). Of high importance were the empirical and theoretical contributions to biology.

In the organic disciplines of natural history, newly discovered living phenomena demonstrated the limits of the Cartesian mechanism and the chemical approach. Albrecht v. Haller (in the attention he paid to sensibility and irritability), Caspar Friedrich Wolff (in his theory of epigenesis), Georges Louis Leclerc de Buffon (in his temporalizing of nature), and Johann Friedrich Blumenbach (in his work on the process of reproduction) all stimulated new approaches in theory and research.

"Vitalism" appeared at the end of the eighteenth century; the term *biology* was first put into use around 1800 several times with varying meanings. Carl Friedrich Kielmeyer's famous lecture *On the Relations of the Organic Forces* (*Über die Verhältnisse der organischen Kräfte*) of 1793 on the gradation of organic forces was characterized by Schelling as the beginning of the "epoch of a totally new science of nature." Kielmeyer was regarded in France as "père de la philosophie de la nature," although his own orientation was explicitly a Kantian one.

The correspondence between nature and spirit follows, according to Troxler, from the fundamental "animation" of nature. The whole of nature is conceived as an organism. The *Deduction of the Living Organism* (*Dedukzion des lebenden Organism*, 1799) by Adam Carl August von Eschenmayer depends on the presupposition "that precisely this object comes under the necessary conditions of self-consciousness." Oken developed the concept of elementary units of living organisms (infusoria) and the vertebra as a general type, which caused a bitter priority quarrel with Goethe.

To understand nature as a total organism is to conceive its genesis, its genetic development. All natural phenomena change and adapt with the passage of time. These changes must be understood always in combination with the ideal systematic of nature and its forms and processes, furthermore they should correspond with the systematic of the psychical faculties of man and at the same time with the historical phases of the development of science and culture. The historization of nature was connected with the historization of the knowledge of nature, or the objective and the subjective dimensions of the historical conscience were brought into a union.

The development of nature was conceived as an ideal evolution, as metamorphosis of ideas, as *Idealgenese* and not as evolution in the Darwinian sense, as *Realdeszendenz*. Steffens developped in 1801 a "theory of evolution" (*Evolutions-Theoriep*), where he deduced the multiplicity of plants and animals from a dynamism of expansive and contractive forces; by this dynamism the "Totalorganisation" of nature is realized. Oken, too, rejected the conception of a real change: "To say that the earth and metal have been elevated to coral conveys as little as to say that the earth as such has really changed into coral, when he asserts above that it has become metal, or air has become sulphur." According to Oken, changes, death, and new formations are only the surface of the phenomena, the manifest and external side of nature, in the essential, substantial sphere of the phenomena no real beginning and no real ending are possible: "all is to be taken in a philosophical sense."

Nature has a history, and history has a nature. The history of mankind, of races and peoples, is combined with nature by the metaphysical identity of nature and spirit as well as by real phenomena and concrete processes. The history of man depends, in the eyes of the Romantic naturalists, on the history of nature, and vice versa. The mediated history of man and nature should lead to a new history of man and nature. History had its beginning with the first period of an identity of nature and spirit, the second period was the separated development of natural history and history of mankind, and this two-fold development should now pass in the third period to an epoch of union and freedom.

Scientific criticism in the nineteenth century took hardly any notice of the distinctions among Romantic, speculative, transcendental, scientific, and methodological directions in science and philosophy. Yet the decades around 1800 represent a singular phase in the history of science and of the philosophy of nature. This epoch greatly influenced contemporary perspectives on the relationships between science and society, natural and human sciences, and humankind and nature.

DIETRICH von ENGELHARDT

Bibliography

Ayrault, Roger. "En vue d'une philosophie de la nature." In *Ayrault: La genèse du romantisme allemand 1794–1804*. Vol. 1. Paris: Aŭbier, 1976.

Cunningham, Andrew, and Nicholas Jardine, eds. *Romanticism and the Sciences.* Cambridge: Cambridge University Press, 1990.

Engelhardt, Dietrich. "Romantische Naturforschung." In *Historisches Bewusstsein in der Naturwissenschaft. Von der Aufklärung bis zum Positivismus.* Freiburg: Karl Alber, 1979.

Gode-von Aesch, Alexander. *Natural Science in German Romanticism.* New York: Columbia University Press, 1941.

Poggi Stefano, and Mauridio Bossi, eds. *Romanticism in Science: Science in Europe, 1790–1840.* Dordrecht: Kluwer, 1993.

Porter Roy, and Mikŭlăš Teich, Eds.: *Romanticism in National context,* Cambridge: Cambridge University Press, 1988.

Snelders, Henricŭs Adrianŭs Marie. "Romanticism and Naturphilosophie and the Inorganic Natural Sciences 1797–1840: An Introductory Survey," Studies in Romanticism 9 (1970): 193–215.

NATURE

The concept of *nature* is one of the most central and most diverse concepts of the Enlightenment and Romantic eras. According to Isaiah Berlin, "when seventeenth- and eighteenth-century authors say 'nature,' we can translate that into 'life' perfectly easily," and some scholars have registered "no fewer than two hundred meanings which are attached to the word 'nature' in the eighteenth century alone" (75). The term is, indeed, best defined as one of the nodal points in the discourses of the time; in many respects it replaces God.

One of the most eloquent expressions of this universality of meaning is the so-called *Tobler Fragment* (1783) by the Swiss theologian Johann Georg Christoph Tobler (1757–1812), that was erroneously ascribed to Goethe for a long time. Written in the style of a prayer, this is a poetic anticipation of the paradoxes that characterize both idealist and Romantic thought from the 1790s onward. Personified nature is seen as the sum total of every conceivable property; in which any number of contradictory predicates can be ascribed: "even what is most unnatural is nature," "the present is eternity for her," "she is whole and yet always unfinished." The narrative voice, however, while formally including itself in this description ("It is not I who has spoken of her. No, what is true and what is false, all this she has spoken."), does not give up its authority over its object, nature. The real dilemma of nature as the all-encompassing "absolute" can only be seen in Novalis's *Monologue* of 1800, where human language is a self-referential system that is analogous to nature as language, and where the author has lost his authority. Only to the extent that he is inspired by language can the text be poesy and expressive of a truth about language and nature. Before Novalis, Johann Georg Hamann (1730–88) had already radically questioned the authority of the rational language of Enlightenment and of the Kantian project. His insistence on poesy (*Dichtung*) as the mother tongue of humankind, on aesthetic perception as the source of life and truth, set the tone for Romantic nature as a text to be read and to be written.

The pantheism of Spinoza (1632–77) distinguished between *natura naturata* (created natural objects) and *natura naturans* (nature in the process of creation), and it was the latter the Romantic imagination tried to follow. Nature, as the absolute, is living spirit, and only the imagination, being situated between the actual and the possible, the conscious and the unconscious, is able to follow it.

The period between 1770 and 1850 saw the transformation from natural history to the history of nature. Static and classificatory systems gave way to developmental models in geology, palaeontology, zoology, and botany, culminating in the works of Charles Darwin and Charles Lyell. "Natural philosophy," too, changed its meaning. In the Enlightenment it roughly meant Newtonian physics; now it became reflection on nature as the absolute, while science proper emerges as separate from it. In fact, the period sees the birth of practically all the academic and scientific disciplines to which we are accustomed. In this major reorganization of the production of knowledge the Romantics played a full part as scientists (or at least scientifically educated individuals), philosophers, and poets (and, characteristically, often all of these). Samuel Taylor Coleridge studied with the chemist Humphry Davy (Newtonian and Romantic in one);

Novalis with the geologist Gottlieb Werner at the Freiberg mining academy; Lorenz Oersted and Hermann Helmholtz, while not *Naturphilosophen* as such, created the foundations of electromagnetism and thermodynamics on the basis of a speculative and normative reasoning that owed a lot to the Romantic unity of nature. The complexity of the changes during this era is sometimes interpreted as a phase of historical trial and error at the end of which the correct methodologies of science and the humanities had established themselves (this is the image the nineteenth century liked to present), but increasingly, scholarship stresses the continuities and overlaps between Romanticism and both earlier Enlightenment and later positivist and empiricist science. In the course of the nineteenth century, scientific disciplines, in their self-understanding and in their understanding of the empirical world tend to follow the lead of physics, excluding the hermeneutic side of natural sciences from their considerations. Approaches that lie outside these parameters, such as those of Johann Wolfgang von Goethe and Lorenz Oken in biology or that of Jacob Friedrich Fries (1773–1843), who developed a theory of the organism straddling physics and biology, are no longer admissible. The observer and investigator is no longer seen as part of nature; the true scientist is a disembodied observer. This separation is the issue at the heart of, for example, Goethe's polemic against Newton's *Opticks* (1704) in his work on chromatics, *Zur Farbenlehre* (*Theory of Colors*, 1810).

The wider significance of separating nature from observer becomes clear when looking at natural philosophy and poetics. In Friedrich Wilhelm Joseph von Schelling's *Identitätsphilosophie*, for instance, the absolute is divided into nature and spirit (*Geist*). Hence, nature is in the process of regaining absolute self-consciousness and self-identity, an image with strong overtones of organic evolution; but still the speculative "absolute" is the beginning and end of it. Speculative idealism moves from abstract, often antagonistic concepts (such as Fichte's *Ich* and *Nicht-Ich*, Schelling's real and ideal with their "resolving" notions of the absolute and identity) to concrete phenomena, and the final result is predictable: the need for art as the redemption of nature, the resolution of all antagonism by synthetic imagination, Schelling's nature as visible spirit and spirit as invisible nature, his intellectual intuition as the "final stage of a reconciliation between the external and the internal" (Schneider, 104), Fichte's "hovering imagination."

While Romantic natural philosophy was looking for the identity of microcosm and macrocosm, individual and universe, and tried to reflect upon this identity in abstract terms, Goethe was looking for a dialogue with nature that would lead to an increasing amalgamation of experience (the phenomena as they appear), and theory (the phenomena as comprehended). Goethe describes our productive synthetic imagination in analytic and objective terms, claiming that we only know ourselves in so far as we know the world, and vice versa; each object contemplated in the right way (*wohl beschaut*) develops a new organ of perception in us. This reciprocal formation of subject and object he considers to be identical with the formation of knowledge, and he views it as a perennial process that can never end in a metaphysical totality. Coleridge, on the other hand, following Fichte and Schelling, assumes that the self (or mind) and nature (the physical world) can, as two interpenetrating forces, be fully reconciled by the power of what he calls primary imagination. What remain two autonomous spheres in "Goethean" Romanticism melt into one "living principle" that is given "in the process of our own self-consciousness" in Coleridge's version. Put this way, external nature loses the power to correct speculative imagination, and, in Percy Bysshe Shelley's *Defence of Poetry* (1821), the images used to express the aesthetics of human perception (such as Shelley's elaboration of Coleridge's eolian harp) become metaphysical models in which thought and physical nature are always already reciprocally implicated (cf. Black, 116f.). Paradoxically, then, Romantic reflection on poetics finally cuts itself off from the natural world that it wanted to "re-enchant."

Just one step before this, Romantic nature is at its most valuable in mediating between the aesthetic and scientific use of language and imagination. In William Wordsworth's 1802 preface to his *Lyrical Ballads*, nature is the concept that makes it possible to construct a relationship between science and poetry, insofar as nature is the touchstone of truth in both. The difference between the two is one of method, not of subject matter. Neither poetry nor science can reach the immediacy of expression created by the pressure of the passions in real life, but both aim to follow the movements of nature, or life, as closely as possible. Just like science, poetic sensibility is empirical and tries to convey "the image of man and nature" (258). Unlike science, it does not restrict itself to "external testimony" (258). Novalis is more cautious when discussing the relationships among science, poetry, and perception. In *The Apprentices at Sais*, the adaptation of human nature and nature as such is not taken for granted; it depends first on the nature of human perception, and second on the powers of human imagination that may either teach us about nature or separate us from it. This is where *Bildung*, the educational formation of the mental, spiritual, and physical person, becomes all-important.

John Keats wrote, in 1819, "As various as the lives of men are, so various become their souls, and thus does God make individual beings, souls, identical souls of the sparks of his own essence". These words express impartiality in the face of human diversity: there is but one human nature, and circumstance alters it into variously shaped individual souls, none of which is closer or further from God. What Keats postulates for psychic formation, Georg Büchner (1813–37) in 1835 and 1836 formulates as a universal law of beauty. The art of observation, at the same time compassionate and empirical, may disclose to us "an infinite beauty that passes from form to form, eternally changed and revealed afresh . . ." And the same law is operative in the organic world: For the philosophical school (which Büchner favored), "everything, form and matter alike, is bound by this law. All functions are its effects; they are not determined by purposes beyond themselves, and their so-called purposive interaction is none other than the manifestations of a single law, the effects of which naturally cannot be mutually destructive." Teleology is rejected and the emphasis is on the self-referential totality which constitutes organic beings. Büchner adds, though, that no method exists so far to make out the underlying single law. His position thus shows the Enlightenment side of Romantic thought on nature: it remains conscious of qualitative differences in nature's objects, and is cautious about the chances of adequately formulating the laws according to which nature develops. His use of authentic sources for his fictional writing aimed simul-

taneously to remain truthful to the facts of nature, and to Romanticize, or poeticize, nature, thereby replacing a simplistic conception of reality with truth.

The motif of the reenchantment of the world, the need to do so in order to save a disenchanted world, was not just the result of a private discontent, but a reaction to the political situation. The paradox of political and social alienation is turned into a paradox of nature: present nature is alienated, yet nature remains the touchstone for the absolute. The need to transcend present nature can then be translated into the need for revolution. (The examples of not only Büchner, but also of Lorenz Oken, show that not only the early Romantics were sympathetic toward revolution.)

The so-called state of nature plays an important role in political theory. For Jean-Jacques Rousseau (1712–78) alienation begins with society, and what Hobbes described as a state of nature, the war of all against all, is the first stage of such social existence. The romantic construction follows, according to which a lost paradise of a time before time has to be regained, giving the movement its double perspective of looking both nostalgically back and, in a utopian spirit, forward.

Whereas the doctrine of natural law in the seventeenth century had been based on the authority of reason and rationality, Rousseau's "nature" is not a text that allows a clear-cut interpretation from which a natural morality, or even political rules, could be deduced. Rather, it is that which lies outside our jurisdiction, and as such it calls for only one thing: freedom. Romanticism thus challenged the metaphysical foundation of natural law, replacing analogies between the physical and the moral world with, notes Helmut Schneider, "the new principle of a human creativity which was grounded in the trans-subjective and dynamic agency represented equally by the mind or *Geist* and by 'Nature.' " And creativity, by definition, defies formalization.

Perhaps the replacement of a metaphysical God with Nature, with "*imagination*," even, simply meant that the irresolvable difficulty of transcendence was displaced onto our own world-creating and world-disclosing powers. This remains the modern condition. And nature still possesses the double meaning of a present, and in some respects worrying, state of affairs, and a utopian ideal that rests on the implicit assumption that nature once was flawless.

At its best, the nature of Romanticism is neither purely sentimental nor purely naive; it is both at the same time. Edgar Allan Poe's (1844) *A Morning on the Wissahicoon (The Elk)*, sums it up: Poe is floating down a remote river in a boat in half-slumber, remembering the times when there were no water privileges and when "the red man trod alone, with the elk" (31): "I saw, or dreamed that I saw . . . one of the oldest and boldest of those identical elks which had been coupled with the red men of my vision." Poe kneels in his boat which is gently approaching the animal, when suddenly a negro advances and captures the animal: "Thus ended my romance of the elk. It was a pet of great age and very domestic habits, and belonged to an English family occupying a villa in the vicinity." The blending of reality and dream in this scene is not purely revenge on the scientific spirit of his time that has taken from Poe in his "Sonnet to Science," the "summer dream beneath the tamarind tree?"—a theft to which, interestingly enough, he adds a question mark. It is also a testimony to the indestructably auratic nature of experience.

"The naked senses," he wrote in *The Veil of the Soul*, "sometimes see too little, but then they always see too much." Hence Poe's definition of art as "the reproduction of what the senses perceive in Nature through the veil of the soul" (498). There is a continuous line of Romantic "nature" from writers such as Ralph Waldo Emerson, Friedrich Nietzsche and Henry David Thoreau, to Walter Benjamin, Bernhard, and Musil, yet the sensibility necessary for it seems an endangered species.

DANIEL STEUER

Bibliography

Bate, Jonathan. *Romantic Ecology*. London: Routledge, 1991.

Berlin, Isaiah. *The Roots of Romanticism*. London: Chatto and Windus, 1999.

Brinkmann, Richard, ed. *Romantik in Deutschland*. Stuttgart: Metzler, 1978.

Büchner, Georg. *Complete Plays, Lenz and Other Writings*. Translated by John Reddick. London: Penguin, 1993.

Coleridge, Samuel Taylor. *Biographia Literaria 1*. Vol. 7 of *Collected Works*. London: Routledge and Keegan Paul, 1983.

Cunningham, Andrew, and Nicholas Jardine, eds. *Romanticism and the Sciences*. Cambridge: Cambridge University Press, 1990.

Engelhardt, Dietrich von. "Romanticism in Germany." In *Romanticism in National Context*. Edited by Roy Porter and Mikuláš Teich. Cambridge, U.K.: Cambridge University Press, 1988.

Gode von Aesch, Alexander. *Natural Science in German Romanticism*. New York: Columbia University Press, 1941.

Goethe, Johann Wolfgang. *Scientific Studies*. Vol. 12 of *Collected Works*. Edited and translated by Douglas Miller. Princeton, N.J.: Princeton University Press, 1995.

Keats, John. Letter from John Keats to George and Georgiana Keats, 21 April 1819. In *Romanticism. An Anthology*. Edited by Duncan Wu. Oxford, U.K.: Blackwell, 1994.

Poe, Edgar Allan. "Morning on the Wissahicoon." In *The Short Fiction of Edgar Allan Poe*. Edited by Stuart and Susan Levine. Indianapolis: Bobbs-Merrill, 1976.

———. "Sonnet to Science" and "The Veil of the Soul." In *Selected Writings*. London: Penguin, 1967.

Poggi, Stefano, and Maurizio Bossi, eds. *Romanticism in Science: Science in Europe 1790–1840* (Boston Studies in the Philosophy of Science, vol. 152). Dordrecht, Boston, and London: Kluwer, 1994.

Schneider, Helmut J. "Nature," in *Romanticism*. Cambridge History of Literary Criticism. Vol. 5. Edited by Marshall Brown. Cambridge: Cambridge University Press, 92–114.

Shelley, Percy Bysshe. "A Defence of Poetry," in *Romanticism: An Anthology*. Edited by Duncan Wu. Oxford: Blackwell, 1994.

Steuer, Daniel. *Die stillen Grenzen der Theorie. Übergänge zwischen Sprache und Erfahrung bei Goethe und Wittgenstein*. Köln: Böhedü, 1999.

Wordsworth, William. "Preface to 'Lyrical Ballads'" (1802). In *Romanticism: An Anthology*. Edited by Duncan Wu. Oxford: Blackwell, 1994.

NATURPHILOSOPHIE (NATURE PHILOSOPHY)

Naturphilosophie was a theory of knowledge in which speculative thought and intuition were elevated above observation and experiment as reliable means to an understanding of the physical world (although observation and experiment were not excluded or rejected outright). The term *Naturphilosophie* became familiar through the titles of several books, for example *Ideen zu einer Philosophie der Natur* (1797), written by the German philosopher Friedrich Wilhelm Joseph von Schelling. Other influential philosophers associated with the nature-philosophical movement in science were Johann Gottlieb Fichte and G. W. F. Hegel, each of whom, like Schelling, advocated a type of philosophical Idealism.

Nature philosophy was an integral part of the wider cultural fashion of Romanticism that flourished during the period 1780–1830, especially in Germany, and to a significant extent also in such Nordic regions as Scotland and Scandinavia. During this period, a new perception of the world developed in reaction to the rationalist *Weltbild* (world concept) of the Enlightenment. The *Encyclopédie* lost its attractiveness, and fashion moved in the opposite direction, namely that of an interest in metaphysical and religious matters, of feeling and intuition, of the mystery of unseen forces, and of what was old, simple, and indigenous.

In the course of the second quarter of the nineteenth century, nature philosophy wilted under the onslaught of materialism, positivism, and scientific naturalism. Ever since, it has had a poor reputation. In recent years, however, the possibility that the nature-philosophy approach had a certain scientific validity has been seriously and sympathetically considered. Historians are divided over the scientific success of Naturphilosophie, but

some believe that the theory of electromagnetism owes much to its teachings. The Danish physicist Hans Christian Oersted and the English chemist Humphry Davy were influenced by nature philosophy. Moreover, it has been argued that the nature-philosophical program constituted a viable research tradition, especially in comparative anatomy and physiology; for example, the cell theory has been regarded as one of its fruits.

The impact of Naturphilosophie on the scientific study of nature was greatest in biology and medicine. Whereas the generation of the French naturalist Georg-Louis Leclerc, Comte de Buffon, and the Swedish botanist Carolus Linnaeus had been primarily concerned with the description and classification of individual species, Romantic naturalists were interested in establishing the relatedness of organic forms. In doing so, they argued for the importance of mind and mental ideas that transcend empirical reality and (they believed) constitute the unifying logic behind nature's phenomena. The merger of Romantic, idealist thought with the study of early-nineteenth-century biology produced what has been called "transcendental morphology." Simply put, this was the notion that organic diversity, as present in the myriad of different species, can be subsumed under one or a few ideal types. Characteristic of this was an interest in prototypes or archetypes, exemplified by Johann Wolfgang von Goethe's "Urpflanze" (an idealized or archetypal flower showing all major plant parts) and Carl Gustav Carus' generalized vertebrate skeleton. Carus's *Von den Ur-Theilen des Knochen und Schalengerüstes* (*On the Primal Components of Endo- and Exoskeletons*, 1828) was a classic instance of osteology in the nature-philosophical tradition.

The notion of recapitulation was one of the most pervasive of the holistic concepts popular with the nature-philosophical Romantics. It was put forward in embryology by the Halle anatomist Johann Friedrich Meckel, among others, who argued, as had the Tübingen physiologist Carl Friedrich Kielmeyer, that the successive stages of embryonal development in the higher animals are a recapitulation of the adult forms of the lower animals.

The German lands formed the heartland of *Naturphilosophie*, and the Thüringen town of Jena became its center. Here, Schelling's philosophy was applied to the study of nature by the idiosyncratic Lorenz Oken, for example in his *Lehrbuch der Naturphilosophie* (*Elements of Physiophilosophy*, 1809–11). In France, where Georges Cuvier was one of Naturphilosophie's powerful detractors, it never gained much ground, even though some of its notions were propagated in Paris by Cuvier's rival at the Muséum d'histoire naturelle, the zoologist Étienne Geoffroy Saint-Hilaire.

In Britain, too, the nature-philosophy movement never acquired a major following. However, it did have a number of influential representatives, both in Edinburgh and in London; the poet Samuel Taylor Coleridge was an early adherent. London's Royal Institution in particular, where Humphry Davy worked, and later Michael Faraday, provided a platform for German idealist thought. Naturphilosophie was also introduced into the Royal College of Surgeons, where Joseph Henry Green propagated Coleridgean ideas. The most accomplished English proponent of Naturphilosophie was Richard Owen, who instigated a translation into English of Oken's third edition of *Lehrbuch* (1843) under the title *Elements of Physiophilosophy* (1847). Owen's own major contribution was his *On the Archetype and Homologies of the Vertebrate Skeleton* (1848) in which he perfected the concept of a vertebrate archetype.

NICOLAAS A. RUPKE

Bibliography

Cunningham, Andrew, and Nicholas Jardine, eds. *Romanticism and the Sciences*. Cambridge: Cambridge University Press, 1990.

Gode von Aesch, Alexander. *Natural Science in German Romanticism*. New York: Columbia University Press, 1941.

Jacyna, L. S. "Romantic Thought and the Origins of Cell Theory." In *Romanticism and the Sciences*. Edited by Andrew Cunningham and Nicholas Jardine. Cambridge Cambridge University Press, 1990.

Knight, David. "Romanticism and the Sciences." In *Romanticism and the Sciences*. Edited by Andrew Cunningham and Nicholas Jardine. Cambridge: Cambridge University Press, 1990, 13–24.

Levere, Trevor H. *Poetry Realized in Nature: Samuel Taylor Coleridge and Early nineteenth-Century Science*. Cambridge: Cambridge University Press, 1981.

Poggi, Stefano, and Maurizio Bossi, eds. *Romanticism in Science: Science in Europe, 1790–1840*. Dordrecht: Kluwer, 1994.

Rehbock, Philip F. "Transcendental Anatomy." In *Romanticism and the Sciences*. Edited by Andrew Cunningham and Nicholas Jardine. Cambridge: Cambridge University Press, 1990, 130–43.

Rupke, Nicolaas A. "The Study of Fossils in the Romantic Philosophy of History and Nature," *History of Science* 21 (1983): 389–413.

———. *Richard Owen: Victorian Naturalist*. New Haven, Conn.: Yale University Press, 1994.

———. "Richard Owen's Vertebrate Archetype," *Isis* 84 (1993): 231–51.

Snelders, H. A. M. "Oersted's discovery of electromagnetism," in *Romanticism and the Sciences*. Edited by Andrew Cunningham and Nicholas Jardine. Cambridge: Cambridge University Press, 1990, 228–40.

NAZARENE ART

Nazarene art is a term used to designate a movement within Romantic Art that shaped public monumental and religious painting in Germany for a half-century after 1810. Its key proponents included Peter Cornelius, Ferdinand Olivier, Johann Friedrich Overbeck, Franz Pforr, Wilhelm Schadow, Julius Schnorr von Carolsfeld, and Philipp Veit. The Nazarenes stressed the primacy of the "idea" in art, considered religious and national historical subjects as preferable to the classical subject championed by the rationalist academies, felt truth to be linked to the "characteristic" in nature and art, and leaned toward medieval and early Renaissance models of art in the wake of the Napoleonic debacle. The Nazarenes evolved from a small secessionist group in Vienna, the *Lukasbund*, to a continental movement influencing religious and monumental art from London to Rome. Piety marked all the artists, although only a few devoted themselves exclusively, or even preponderantly, to religious subjects. A carefully observed linearism characterized Nazarene art, as well as an avoidance of fleeting light or color effects. The artists invested their monumental figurative compositions with a spiritually energized atemporality, which eventually lost its appeal to a public attracted by the quotidian leanings of the Biedermeier and realist eras.

Nazarene art began with the formation of the *Lukasbund* in Vienna. Johann Friedrich Overbeck, Franz Pforr, and Ludwig Vogel, joined with Konrad Hottinger, Joseph Sutter, and Joseph Wintergerst, as Lukasbrüder in July 1809. Uniting them was a distrust of the mechanistic qualities of academic training, an attraction to early Renaissance art found in the Belvedere, and a belief that engagement with nature through an uncorrupted heart yielded "truth" in art. Subjects drawn from the Bible and from national histories inspired them, yielding Overbeck's *Entry of Christ into Jerusalem* (1809–24), Pforr's *Entry of Rudolf into Basel* (1808–10), and Vogel's *Return of the Soldier from Morgarten* (1809–15).

In July 1810, the three leaders of the group traveled to Rome, where they resided for almost two years in the secularized monastery of San Isidoro. The communal life and study confirmed their interest in the ideas of Wilhelm Wackenroder and focused their attention on the power of friendship as expressed allegorically by Pforr in *Sulamith und Maria* (1811). However, in 1812, the death of Pforr, as well as the return of Vogel to Zurich, brought closure to the first phase of the Lukasbund. Thereafter its shape changed as new members such as Peter Cornelius and Wilhelm von Schadow were introduced and as the group was more richly integrated into the artistic life of the Rome's sizable

German community. Cornelius proved a decisive influence, intensifying the group's concern for the public impact of art through print cycles, such as his *Faust* (1810–15), and fresco projects.

The year 1816 witnessed the crystalization of Nazarene style in Overbeck's *Christ in the House of Mary and Martha* with its spiritual interaction of monumental figures. The opportunity to introduce the style in a fresco cycle devoted to the Old Testament story of Joseph for J. S. Bartholdy proved decisive to the artists' reputation and promoted Philipp Veit, who had recently come from Vienna, to a position of prominence within the Roman group.

A second strand of Nazarene art had been evolving in Vienna, where the influence of August Wilhelm von Schlegel and Friedrich von Schlegel was particularly strong. The Olivier Brothers—Friedrich and Ferdinand—had been inspired by *alt-deutsch* painting from their early years in Dessau and, after 1811, attracted a circle in Vienna in which a taut linearism comparable to that of the Lukasbund was used to reveal the presence of the divine in nature. In addition to the Oliviers, the circle embraced Julius Schnorr von Carolsfeld, Theodor Rehbenitz, and Veit. By 1818, most of the artists had traveled to Rome and, formally or informally, swelled the ranks of the Lukasbrüder.

In the fall of 1817, the "Weimar Friends of Art" (Johann Wolfgang von Goethe and Meyer) published "Neudeutsche religios-patriotische Kunst," criticizing Nazarene work as an irrational violation of classical taste and polarizing considerations of that work in the press. The following spring, Prince Ludwig of Bavaria made a much-celebrated trip to Rome in which he embraced the Nazarenes and set the groundwork for the move of Cornelius, Schnorr von Carolsfeld, and others to Munich in the following decades. In the wake of the Casa Bartholdy frescoes, commissions for the Museo Chiaramonti and the Casino Massimo reinforced Nazarene association with monumental decorative painting in that medium. Finally, the Nazarenes were given their first opportunity to exhibit their work collectively in a major exhibition at the Palazzo Caffarelli in April 1819. That event prompted two statements of Nazarene theory: Friedrich von Schlegel's "Über die deutsche Kunstausstellung zu Rom" (1819) and J. D. Passavant's *Ansichten der bildenden Künste* (1820).

In the 1820s and 1830s, the final stage of the Nazarene movement saw most of the artists (Overbeck being a notable exception) return north and assume positions of influence in cities throughout Germany. Cornelius and Wilhelm von Schadow provided leadership to the Düsseldorf Academy, where important history painters such as Wilhelm von Kaulbach and C. F. Lessing infused Nazarene monumentality with an enriched colorism and historicizing detail. Veit and Passavant became leading figures in the Städelsches Kunstinstitut in Frankfurt, where Veit's *Introduction of the Arts to Germany by Religion* (1832–34) and Overbeck's *Triumph of Religion in the Arts* (1829–41) gave rich, programmatic expression of the Nazarenes' devout tendencies. Nazarene art was championed in Dresden by J. G. von Quandt, who succeeding in bringing Schnorr von Carolsfeld to head the Academy in 1846. Prior to that Schnorr had worked for Prince Ludwig in Munich, where he produced cycles devoted to the *Nibelungenlied* and imperial histories in the Residenz. His work joined that of Cornelius and his students in linking Nazarene monumentality with Ludwig's dreams of Germanic glory. Cornelius had begun work in the Bavarian capital with mythological frescoes in the Glyptothek. He then went on to oversee the decoration of the Alte Pinakothek as well as the Ludwigskirche before moving in 1841 to Berlin, where he devoted much of the remainder of his life to a cycle for the Campo Santo.

Nazarene portraiture embraced historicist fantasies such as Overbeck's *Franz Pforr* (1810) and Schnorr's *Bianca von Quandt* (c. 1820), as well as delicate explorations of character such as Schadow's *Portrait of a Roman Woman* (1818). Landscape was an adjunct to figurative composition for Nazarene artists except for Ferdinand Oliver, whose print series, *Seven Views of Berechtesgaden* (1823), revealed a spiritualized vision of nature commensurate in richness to that of Caspar David Friedrich and Philipp Otto Runge. Finally, Rudolp Schadow evolved a sculptural style with Nazarene leanings by means of his chastely linear treatment of figures in reflective poses.

Nazarene influence stretched from Spain to Russia by mid-century. In Italy, their religious idealism was reflected in the work of T. Minardi and the Puristi. J. L. Lund brought their work to Copenhagen, while J. Scheffer von Leonardshoff and J. Führich maintained the tradition in Vienna. English enthusiasm for the intellectual side of Nazarene art crested at mid-century, when its impact could be felt on both the monumental decoration of the Houses of Parliament and the experimental painting of the young Pre-Raphaelite Brotherhood.

ROBERT MCVAUGH

Selected Works

Pforr, Franz. *Entry of Rudolf into Basel*, 1808–10.
Overbeck, Johann Friedrich. *Entry of Christ into Jerusalem*, 1809–24.
Vogel, Ludwig. *Return of the Soldiers from Morgarten*, 1809–15.
Overbeck, Johann Friedrich. *Franz Pforr*, 1810.
Pforr, Franz. *Sulamith and Maria*, 1811.
Cornelius, Peter. *Illustrations to Goethe's Faust*, 1810–11. Published 1815.
Schadow, Rudlop. *The Spinner*, 1816–17.
Overbeck, Johann Friedrich. *Christ in the House of Mary and Martha*, 1816.
Cornelius, Peter, Johann Friedrich Overbeck, Wilhelm von Schadow, and Philipp Veit. *Casa Bartholdy Frescoes*, 1816–17.
Schnorr von Carolsfeld, Julius. *Wedding at Cana*, 1818–19.
Schadow, Wilhelm von. *Portrait of a Roman Woman*, 1818.
Overbeck, Johann Friedrich, Julius Schnorr von Carolsfeld, Philipp Veit, Joseph Anton Koch, and J. Führich. *Casino Massimo Frescoes*, 1818–29.
Cornelius, Peter. *Glyptothek Frescoes*, 1819–25.
Schnorr von Carolsfeld, Julius. *Bianca von Quandt*, 1820.
Olivier, Ferdinand. *Seven Views of Berechtesgaden*, 1823.
Overbeck, Johann Friedrich. *Triumph of Religion in the Arts*, 1829–41.
Schnorr von Carolsfeld, Julius. *Nibelungenlied Frescoes*, 1831–67.
Veit, Philipp. *Introduction of the Arts to Germany by Religion*, 1834–36.

Bibliography

Andrews, K. *The Nazarenes: A Brotherhood of German Painters in Rome*. Oxford, 1964.
Bachleitner, R. *Die Nazarener*. Munich, 1976.

Büttner, F. "Der Streit um die "Neudeutsche religios-patriotische Kunst," *Aurora: Jahrbuch der Eichendorff-Gesellschaft* 43 (1983): 55–76.

Einem, H. von. *Deutsche Malerei des Klassizismus und der Romantik, 1760–1840*. Munich, 1978.

Fastert, S. *Die Entdeckung des Mittelalters. Geschichtsrezeption in der nazarenischen Malerei des 19. Jahrhunderts*. Berlin, 2000.

Gallwitz, K. et al. *Die Nazarener*. Frankfurt, 1977.

Gallwitz, K. et al. *Die Nazarener in Rom. Ein deutscher Künstlerbund der Romantik*. Munich, 1981.

Geismeier, Willi. *Die Malerei der deutschen Romantik*. Dresden, 1984.

Gerstenberg, K., and P. O. Rave. *Die Wandgemälde der Deutschen Romantiker im Casino Massimo zu Rom*. Berlin, 1934.

Jensen, J. C. "I Nazareni: Das Wort, der Stil," in *Klassizismus und Romantik in Deutschland*. Nuremberg, 1966.

Passavant, J. D. *Ansichten über die bildenden Künste und Darstellung des Ganges derselben in Toscana, zur Bestimmung des Gesichtspunktes, aus welchem die neudeutsche Malerschule zu betrachten ist*. 1820.

Riegel, H. *Geschichte des Wiederauflebens der deutschen Kunst zu Ende des 18. Jahrhunderts*. 1876.

Schlegel, Friedrich von. " 'Über die deutsche Kunstausstellung zu Rom,' im Frühjahr 1819, und über den gegenwärtigen Stand der deutschen Kunst in Rom," *Wiener Jahrbücher der Literatur* 7 (1819): 1–16.

Vaughan, W. *German Romantic Painting*. New Haven, Conn.: Yale University Press, 1980.

NERVAL, GÉRARD DE 1808–1855

French writer

Gérard de Nerval is often remembered for his provocative eccentricities (most famously, for walking a lobster on a blue silk lead in the gardens of the Palais Royal), his bouts of madness, and his suicide. Indeed, many of Nerval's contemporaries thought of him as merely *un fol délicieux* (a delightful madman). Nerval is of course partly responsible for his image as a charming bohemian, since no one worked harder than he did at the development of his own legend. But in contrast with what was sometimes a dismissive view of him as merely eccentric, posterity has judged him to be one of the major figures of French Romanticism, and at the same time a great and highly original poet who stands apart within the French tradition. Gérard Labrunie (he was later to adopt the pseudonym "de Nerval" after some land once belonging to his family) was born in Paris in 1808. He lost his mother at an early age and was raised by his grandfather until his father's return from the Napoleonic wars when he was six years old. These early events are of vital importance. The loss of his mother is often put forward as the source of much of Gérard's personal mythology. Even though his father evinced a lack of sympathy for his writing and lifestyle, Nerval maintained a close relationship with the rather severe Docteur Labrunie throughout his life.

Nerval published poetry while he was still a schoolboy, but he really entered the literary scene with his translation of Johann Wolfgang von Goethe's *Faust* at the age of nineteen. This translation impressed Goethe so much that he wrote to the young Gérard, "I have never understood myself so well as in reading you." The influence of Goethe was a major Romantic inspiration for his translator, who was soon to live among the group of Parisian poets and artists for whom the expression "la vie de Bohême" was originally coined. His friends included all the great names of French Romanticism, among them the leader of the movement, Victor Hugo, Nerval's school friend Théophile Gautier, and Alexandre Dumas, with whom he went to Germany. Gérard traveled widely at different periods in his life, most famously in the east in 1843–44 (particularly Egypt, Syria, and Constantinople), which he wrote about in his *Voyage en Orient* (*Journey to the Orient*, 1851), but also to Italy, England, Holland,

and Belgium, as well as Germany, where he felt particularly at home. He published other translations from the German, among them the poems of his friend Heinrich Heine, and wrote various dramatic pieces, which were produced with varying degrees of success. Yet he was dogged by recurring mental crises, in February and March 1841 and several times from 1849 onward. Released from his clinic against the advice of his doctor, who appears to have cared for him in a most humane and intelligent way, he was found hanged in a Parisian street on the morning of January 26, 1855.

Although he spent years writing for the theater, Nerval is above all remembered for the poetry and poetic prose written toward the end of his life. This was inspired by an intensely personal mythology informed by mysticism and magic. He was particularly fascinated by the theme of the *doppelgänger* (double); mirrored figures of himself or of the woman he loved inspire a sensation of vertigo in several of his works. Another preoccupation appears in his quest for the defeat of time through ritual or circular movement (combined, for example, in the image of dancers in a ring), the renewed contact with tradition (embodied, for instance, in folksongs), and timeless ideals. Marcel Proust, one of his great admirers, was among the first to recognize the originality of Nerval's writings on memory and the dreamlike evocation of a lost childhood world.

Several female characters play a significant part in this mystical vision. Among them is the figure of the actress, no doubt originally inspired by Nerval's unhappy love for a real actress, Jenny Colon. Female figures often appear linked to the theme of loss, which reflects his mother's death when he was a small child, the loss of a childhood friend, Adrienne, and perhaps also, as some argue, the loss of an older woman loved during his early life. Beyond personal experience, however, these different female figures coalesce into the one figure of the Mother, at the meeting of two mystical traditions: that of the Virgin Mary, inspired by Catholicism, and that of Isis, springing from occult and orientalist traditions. Nerval was fascinated by mysticism and sought salvation through his own personal form of worship, in which the actress appeared as a new Isis and the theater was a place of inner regeneration. In this Romantic vision the ideal woman, necessarily unattainable, was the only escape from the pettiness of the times. Yet Nerval, in his own mythology of self, is guilty of some nameless fault whose pretext shifts from one banal act to another, but which is to blame for his rejection and exclusion from the perfect community and harmony of a prelapsarian state. This is most explicit in the mystical vision of *Aurélia*, Nerval's last work, which was published posthumously in 1855.

It is of course tempting to trace links between Nerval's madness and the themes recurrent in his writing, yet the latter were very much the product of his times. His Romantic disappointment with reality, for example, reflects the alienation of a whole generation of young intellectuals under the July Monarchy. Nor is it surprising that his quest for selfhood and personal identity should have fallen under the shadow of Napoleon, that great Romantic example of self-fulfillment, from whom he claimed descent during some of his bouts of madness. And his dreams and anguish epitomize the spiritual quests of a period when many sought answers to the doubts raised by the double heritage of enlightenment and revolution by turning to Catholic or oriental mysticism.

The intensity and, sometimes, grandeur of Nerval's personal world have led critics such as Albert Béguin to call *Aurélia* a "metaphysical epic" or "a vast myth of human destiny." Yet the visionary nature of Nerval's writing is in constant tension with the rational, often ironic voice of his narrative texts and particularly with his elegant and lucid prose style, most notable in "Sylvie" (1853), published as part of *Les Filles du feu* (*Daughters of Fire*) in 1854. This tension can be seen as reflecting the contradictions inherent in Nerval's avowed project: "diriger mon rêve éternel au lieu de le subir" ("to direct my eternal dream rather than submit to it").

Nerval's best-known poems are the twelve sonnets published in 1854 under the title *Les Chimères* (*The Chimeras*). They can be seen as prefiguring the symbolist movement of the end of the century, and the poems of Stéphane Mallarmé. They pose an enduring problem for criticism, since Nerval himself declared of them that they "would lose their charm by being explained, were such a thing possible." This poetry seems to refer to a mystical reality whose only tangible trace is in the beauty of words, but in which their author appears to believe fervently. And although Nerval's writing is obviously tempting ground for a psychoanalytical reading, his greatest prose, like his poetry, resists exegesis.

JENNIFER YEE

Biography

Gérard Labrunie born in Paris, May 22, 1808. Finished his schooling in 1826; 1826–27 translated Gœthe's *Faust*; In 1831, adopted the name Gérard de Nerval and began career as playwright; 1832–34 studied medicine; 1835 founded the journal *Monde dramatique*, which left him bankrupt in 1836; he then worked as a journalist. From 1834 to 1854, frequent trips within Europe; in 1843, traveled in the "Orient." First crisis and stay in clinic, 1841; from 1849 to 1854 recurrent mental crises and periods of internment; found hanged in Paris January 26, 1855.

Selected Works

Prose

Le Voyage en Orient, 1851. Translated as *The Woman of Cairo* by Conrad Elphinstone. 2 vol., 1929. Translated as *Journey to the Orient* by Norman Glass. New York: New York University Press, 1972.
Les Filles du feu, 1853. Translated as *Daughters of Fire.* by James Whitall, 1922. Translated by Richard Sieburth, 1995.
Aurélia, 1855. Translated by Richard Aldington, 1930. Translated by Geoffrey Wagner, 1957. Edited in *Aurelia and Other Writings*, 1996. Translated by Richard Sieburth. In *Selected Writings*, 1999.

Poetry

Les Chimères. Translated as *Chimeras: Transformations of "les Chimères" by Gérard de Neval* by Andrew Hoyem, 1966. Translated as *Les Chimères* (bilingual edition), by William Stone. London: Menard Press, 1999.

Bibliography

Béguin, Albert. *Gérard de Nerval*. Paris: José Corti, 1946.
Bénichou, Paul. "Gérard de Nerval," in *L'École du désenchantement*. Paris: Gallimard, 1992.
———. *Nerval et la chanson folklorique*. Paris: José Corti, 1971.
Jones, Robert Emmet. *Gérard de Nerval*. New York: Twayne, 1974.
Kofman, Sarah. *Nerval: le charme de la répétition*. Lausanne: L'âge d'homme, 1979.
Richard, Jean-Pierre. "Géographie magique de Nerval." In *Poésie et profondeur*. Paris: Editions du Seuil, 1955.
Sowerby, Benn. *The Disinherited: the Life of Gérard de Nerval, 1808–1855*. London: Peter Owen, 1973.

NETHERLANDS: CULTURAL SURVEY

In the cultural history of the Netherlands (present-day Holland and Belgium), the decades around 1800 are not typically Romantic. Until well into the nineteenth century, culture was dominated by neo-classical and late-Enlightenment tendencies, which manifested themselves, for example, in classic design and attempts to achieve harmony between reason and sentiment. Although it was recognized that artists should have genius, their imaginations had to be controlled by common sense, knowledge and good taste. Romanticism, insofar as it occurred in the Netherlands, was usually more moderate and utilitarian than elsewhere. Artists were seen as the spiritual leaders of the nation. One of their roles in society was to provide patriotic comment

on political events. Art was supposed to have a civilizing effect on the public and to inspire it with the ideas of the middle class elite. In this sense the Netherlands was sometimes out of step with its neighbors.

Around 1780, however, the strict Classicist approach to literature had eroded to such an extent that it left space for the expression of individual experiences, as in *Julia* (1783) by Rhijnvis Feith (1753–1824), a fashionable epistolary in the Sentimentalist tradition. As a didactic, Feith also played a key role in the cultural scene of the early nineteenth century, along with Willem Bilderdijk (1756–1831). An opponent of Enlightenment philosophy, Bilderdijk had become one of the most individual Romantic thinkers in the Netherlands by about 1800. He inspired the Réveil, a pietistic Protestant movement, and his ideas were disseminated by a small circle of like-minded thinkers.

Meanwhile, most Dutch intellectuals held onto Enlightenment ideals. The Kantian Johannes Kinker (1764–1845), for example, formulated an all-embracing ideal in *Het Alleven of de Wereldziel* (*Universal Life or the Soul of the World*, 1812). Much more accessible was the poetry of Hendrik Tollens (1780–1856), which was related to the *Biedermeier* tradition. For generations, his *Gedichten* (*Poems*, 1808–15) won him a sizeable school of followers whose "homely" poetry had its counterpart in idealistic genre painting, offering instruction and enjoyment to a broad public. They used scenes from daily life to promote enlightened Christian ideals and middle class values such as brotherly love, devoutness, simplicity, homeliness, and patriotism. This *poésie du foyer* gave expression to personal and noble feelings with which everyone could identify, such as contentment with a humble existence. It used standard means of expression and did not allow itself to experiment with prosody. The preference was for simple and conventional forms of verse such as idylls and folk songs.

From about 1835 onward, landscape and historical painting became more colorful, and artists used stronger contrast effects to evoke emotional responses. However, painters held on to the classical genre hierarchy. In terms of theory, the French Classicist tradition in poetry and drama was still considered superior as well. The genre theory of drama was undermined in the theaters, however, which tried to attract large audiences with bourgeois dramas, spectacles, melodramas, lyrical drama, and enchanting ballets that were almost exclusively imported from abroad. This was one of the ways in which Romantic influences from abroad reached the Netherlands in the first decades of the nineteenth century. Composers such as Carl von Weber and Felix Mendelssohn were popular, and the work of certain Romantic poets and prose writers also had a receptive audience, whether or not in translation. However, the Dutch cultural elite largely disapproved of the modern tendency to undermine the artistic establishment. French Romanticism was regarded as revolutionary and immoral; German Romanticism as too fantastic. The works of Walter Scott met with more appreciation. In the 1830s this even led to "Scottomania," which was fueled by the nationalist sentiment of the time.

Linked to the nationalism of Johann Gottfried Herder and Jean-Jacques Rousseau, this sentiment had been growing in the Netherlands since the end of the eighteenth century. The Dutch were becoming uncomfortably aware of their nation's economic and cultural decline and that it was trailing behind other countries. They looked back nostalgically on their splendid past. Moreover, Dutch-speaking Flanders was increasingly dissatisfied with the social and cultural hegemony of the French-speaking elite. After the Southern Netherlands had become part of the kingdom of the Netherlands in 1815, that dissatisfaction resulted in the Flemish movement's struggle for emancipation. Within the context of the Great Netherlands ideal, the movement sought cultural unity with the north but was above all committed to establishing a Flemish-Belgian identity. Hendrik Conscience (1812–83) was a key figure in this. The nationalism of the northern Netherlands, rekindled during the period of French rule (1795–1813) and again during and after the Belgian

revolution (1830), was generally much less dogged and more complacent than that of the *Flamingants*.

Although the character of nationalism in the northern and southern Netherlands differed, in both cases it was more backward-looking than in other countries. It inspired historical and philological studies, national commemorations and historical parades, poignant depictions of a glorious past in romances, historical novels and novellas, historical plays and paintings. In the Catholic south this historicism was almost entirely oriented towards the Middle Ages. In the mainly Protestant north, it also focused on the Golden Age of the sixteenth and seventeenth centuries, when the Dutch Republic, it was presumed, still had enough fortitude to display the strength of a world power.

These patriotic fixations may partly explain the modest influence of international Romanticism in the Netherlands. Here, only a brief period of "black Romanticism" was experienced with the "Romantic Club." During the period 1833–37, this group of young writers, including Nicolaas Beets (1814–1903), recited the works of Lord Byron, Victor Hugo, and other Romantics, and adopted their style. Outside their own circle, the members of the Romantic Club were criticized for being merely epigones, and by around 1840 they had already moved on from their "black period." In the decades that followed, Tollens remained as the guiding light in Dutch literature, although, during the 1850s and 1860s, other writers such as Guido Gezelle (1830–90) and Multatuli (Eduard Douwes Dekker, 1820–87) made their debuts and took Dutch Romanticism to a new level. The literary beacon of Tollens was finally extinguished in around 1880, with the advent of a new generation of writers who were now influenced by early English and German Romantics such as Johann Wolfgang von Goethe, John Keats, John Milton, von Platen, Percy Bysshe Shelley, and Algernon Charles Swinburne. Likewise, Dutch culture would continue to be influenced by the Romantic tradition during the century that followed.

TON VAN KALMTHOUT

Bibliography

Anbeek, Ton. *Het donkere hart: Romantische obsessies in de moderne Nederlandstalige literatuur*. Amsterdam: Amsterdam University Press, 1996.

Berg, Willem van den. *De ontwikkeling van de term "romantisch" en zijn varianten in Nederland tot 1840*. Assen: Van Gorcum, 1973.

Bork, G. J. van, and N. Laan, eds. *Twee eeuwen literatuurgeschiedenis, 1800–2000: Poëticale opvattingen in de Nederlandse literatuur*. 2d ed. Amsterdam: Aarts, 1997.

Eijssens, Henk, et al., eds. *De Negentiende Eeuw* 8, no. 2 (1984). Special issue, "Romantiek in Nederland (1800–1850)."

Erenstein, R. L., et al., eds. *Een theatergeschiedenis der Nederlanden: Tien eeuwen drama en theater in Nederland en Vlaanderen*. Amsterdam: Amsterdam University Press, 1996.

Grijp, Louis Peter, et al., eds. *Een muziekgeschiedenis der Nederlanden*. Amsterdam: Amsterdam University Press, 2001.

Kloek, Joost, and Wijnand Mijnhardt. *1800: Blauwdrukken voor een samenleving*. The Hague: Sdu, 2001.

Schenkeveld-van der Dussen, M. A., et al., eds. *Nederlandse literatuur, een geschiedenis*. Groningen: Nijhoff, 1993.

Tilborgh, Louis van, and Guido Jansen, eds. *Op zoek naar de Gouden Eeuw: Nederlandse schilderkunst 1800–1850*. Zwolle: Waanders, 1986.

Zonneveld, P. A. W. van. *De Romantische Club: Leidse student-auteurs 1830–1840*. Leiden: Athenae Batavae, 1993.

NETHERLANDS: HISTORICAL SURVEY

The United Provinces of the Netherlands, today commonly know as Holland, had been the greatest shipping and trading nation in the world in the seventeenth century, a time that the Dutch quite aptly named their golden age. That age came to an abrupt end—politically, at least—with the conclusion of the Spanish War of Succession (1713), which left the United Provinces both financially exhausted and politically leaderless, with the death of William III in 1701. The Netherlands was by then a nation in economic decline, beset by domestic social disruption. Prussia's growing military posed a potential threat to the Netherlands' vulnerable eastern border, while Britain's threatening sea power and economic supremacy threatened the Netherlands economic prosperity built on overseas trade and her East Indian empire. Unlike the much-lauded values and praised cultural dynamism of the golden age the eighteenth century was therefore denigrated as an era of cultural, political, and economic decline.

Domestic Dutch politics were split between those (the Orangist royalists) who wanted greater power for the Stadthouder (the lord protector, or de-facto king) and those (the "Patriots") who wanted to restore the political "freedoms" of the old (*stadtholderless*) republic. The patriots had the support of Europe's freest and most outspoken press: of which *De post van den Neder-Rhijn* (*Lower Rhine Post*), was the first revolutionary and openly anti-Stadhouder paper in contrast to the tamer *Gazette de Leyden* (*Leyden Gazette*). While the Orangists were mildly Anglophile in their attitudes, the Patriots leaned toward France to provide support against what they perceived was an Anglo-Prussian protectorate over the Netherlands. Their mutually vicious political struggle came to a head during the Fourth Anglo-Dutch War (1780–84) which ended with a dismal defeat. This triggered the patriot uprising in 1787 that became a full-scale revolution a year later, but was crushed by a Prussian invasion and occupation. Patriot refugees sought sanctuary in France, which itself was by now on the verge of a revolution of its own.

In 1795 the patriots had their revenge. The French made a surprise winter offensive across the Rhine and occupied the country with hardly any resistance from the Dutch. The old United Provinces were abolished and William IV fled into exile and political oblivion. He lived until 1806 at Kew Palace outside London. The Patriots set up a new Batavian Republic built on the principles of the golden age: frugality, hard work, and trade. Reality was a lot different since the Batavian Republic was crippled by war indemnities and French interference. The Dutch were heavily defeated at Camperdown (Kamperduin) in 1797, which proved beyond doubt that the Batavian regime had not revitalized the armed forces although two years later an Anglo-Russian landing in northern Holland was defeated with French assistance. That "assistance" came in the shape of overbearing arrogance, heavy indemnities and changes in regime: in 1798 a regime far too radical for Paris' taste was overthrown by the French. The radical editor of the *Hollandische Historiche Courant* (*Dutch Historical Courier*), Wybo Fijnje, was the real power behind that throne (January-June 1798) but his immoderate radicalism (coupled with elitist revolutionary snobbery) proved together with impulsiveness not only the political undoing of himself but also of the semiindependent republic.

His direct opposite both politically and emotionally, Izaak Gogel (1756–1812), reformed the antiquated tax system and introduced valuable educational reforms. He could do so under the patronage of Rutger Schimmelpennick (who lasted in power until 1801) and then Napoleon Bonaparte's phlegmatic younger brother Louis who became King Lodewijk I of the Netherlands (1806–10). Louis quickly identified with his newfound subjects, defended their interests with such enthusiasm and energy that Napoleon decided to invade and annex the Netherlands in June 1810. He was most concerned that the Dutch were collaborating in the smuggling of British goods into the continent behind the backs of the French and that only a direct imperial presence could put a stop to these nefarious activities.

He was sorely disappointed, since the Dutch continued to smuggle British goods into the continent. Napoleon was never able to snuff out the stubborn Dutch sense of nationalism or make them more French in their opinions and acts. His only political ally, General Herman Daendels, was removed from power as viceroy of Java, where until his removal from the post in 1810 he did valuable work in building up its economy and defense. A year later (1811) Lord Minto, accompanied by a young Thomas Raffles, occupied Java, and the island (the pearl of the Dutch East Indies) was handed back five years later.

By that time the Netherlands had already been liberated by the allied armies spearheaded by the Russians. The old Orangist demagogue, intellectual, and later Romantic Gijsbert van Hogendorp, had already worked out a compromise between royal and parliamentary powers. He wrote a well balanced new constitution for a brand new monarchy the Kingdom of the Netherlands ruled by William I (1772–1843). Except for a much underappreciated participation in the battle of Waterloo the Dutch kept out of the European wars. Britain and Prussia, as a barrier to renewed French "adventures," had given the former Imperial (Austrian) Netherlands (Belgium) to the Kingdom.

Guizot's ideas about representative government (1820–22) inspired Belgian romantics such as Jan Willems (1793–1846) to write national romantic poems praising national independence from the Dutch. A revolt broke out in 1830 but the Dutch were unable (without British support) to prevent Belgian independence (recognized in 1829). The union had never been a happy one and had only short period of prosperity (1825–28) until the political contradictions broke it apart. One reason for the Dutch failure was that they were distracted by the largest native uprising on Java (1825–30) since the Dutch had established control there in 1609. The Javanese uprising was crushed; the Belgian was not. The end result was the establishment of an indigenous Dutch romantic movement led by newspaper editors E. J. Potgeiter and J. R. Thorbecke (1798–1872). Thorbecke had studied in Germany (1820–24) and came back a full-fledged Romantic in 1825.

But he was never attracted to radical or republican Romanticism and was made a professor of history by grateful William I. That conservative king did not live to see royal powers curtailed and revised by new constitution in 1848.

CHRISTER JÖRGENSEN

Bibliography

Baxter, Stephen B. *William III*. London: Longmans, 1966.
Blok, Petrus J. *History of the People of the Netherlands*. New York: AMS Press, 1970.
Boxer, C. R. *The Dutch Seaborne Empire 1600–1800*. London: Penguin, 1990.
Bromley, J. S., and E. H. Kossman. *Britain and the Netherlands*. The Hague: Martinus Nijhoff, 1975.
———. *Britain and the Netherlands in Europe and Asia*. London: Macmillan, 1968.
Carter, Alice C. *Neutrality and Commitment: The Evolution of Dutch Foreign Policy, 1667–1795*. London: Edward Arnold, 1975.
Duke, Alastair. *Reformation and Revolt in the Low Countries*. London: Hambledon Press, 1990.
Geyl, Peter. *The Netherlands Divided (1609–1648)*. London: William and Norgate, 1936.
Israel, Jonathan I. *Spain, the Low Countries and the Struggle for World Supremacy 1585–1713*. London: Hambledon Press, 1997.
———. *The Dutch Republic: Its Rise, Greatness and Decline 1477–1806*. Oxford: Clarendon Press, 1998.
Schama, Simon. *Patriots and Liberators: Revolution in the Netherlands 1780–1813*. New York: Vintage Books, 1992.

NEW WORLD

From its alleged first discovery by Christopher Columbus in 1492, the New World of the Americas led a dual existence in the minds of European intellectuals and artists. On the one hand, it was a real, geographical place, to be explored, mapped, settled and exploited; but on the other, it existed as an imaginative projection of European preconceptions and concerns, a blank space onto which utopian fantasies could be imposed, whether material (Christopher Columbus's conviction that he had found India, or the Spanish legend of El Dorado) or spiritual (the Puritan "City on the Hill"). In the Romantic era, the New World continued to exert this fascination. During the Enlightenment, the traditional structures of European society, which concentrated power and wealth in the hands of elite aristocracies and monarchies, came under insistent scrutiny. This social and intellectual climate led to a geopolitical idealization of the New World as a place of Edenic purity in which utopian ideals of social reform could be realized. The sublime landscapes and enormous spaces of America provided an aesthetic model of nature in its unspoiled state, and this, in turn, contributed to a vision of political reinvention which ultimately generated the impetus for the American Revolution.

This geopolitical vision mirrored a similar anthropological and social preoccupation with primitivism, the conviction that morality and integrity are fostered by a "natural" and simple mode of education and existence. Traces of this primitivist agenda can be seen as early as Aphra Behn's *Oroonoko* (1688), and certainly in Daniel Defoe's *Robinson Crusoe* (1719), and the whole subgenre of "Robinsonnades" that Defoe's novel inspired; it gained an increasing currency as the eighteenth century progressed, partly as a reaction to the strictures of Augustan neoClassicism. The New World was broadly conceived to be the locus for this idealized primitivism, and, as the map of the world was again redefined by the voyages of explorers such as Captain James Cook, the imaginative trope of the New World was broadened to embrace diverse geographical regions: the Americas, parts of Africa, and the South Seas.

Central to this view of the New World was the figure of the *savage*, a term that encompassed the American Indian and the South Sea Islander, and revived most notably in the miscellaneous crew of the Pequod in Herman Melville's *Moby-Dick* (1851). For the purposes of primitivism, the savage was cast as an innocent child of nature, a classification for which there was a long tradition, dating back at least to Michel Eyquem de Montaigne's essay *De Cannibales* (1580).

Jean-Jacques Rousseau crystallized this position by radically reworking the bleak Hobbesian conception of the "state of nature" as "solitary, poore, nasty, brutish, and short" (*Leviathan*, 1651). In a variety of works, including his *Discours sur l'origine de l'inégalité* (*Discourse on the Origin of Inequality*, 1755), Rousseau advanced the theory that civilization had produced nothing but enervating luxury and social inequality. Although the state of nature for Rousseau was still far from perfect, it nevertheless had the advantage of liberty, and was dictated only by genuine needs. The implication of Rousseau's theories—that "primitive" man contains mankind's virtues in their purest form—was immensely influential on subsequent Romantic thought, both in literary and political terms.

There was, of course, a contrary argument—that the indigenous populations of "uncivilized" countries were inferior to civilized man in almost every way—exemplified by the Puritan response to the heathen savages of North America. But this procivilization stance had a scientific as well as religious voice. The *Histoire naturelle* (1749), by the French naturalist le Comte de Buffon, one of the preeminent figures of the French Enlightenment, argued that all natural productions, animal and vegetable, including man himself, were subject to degeneration when transplanted from the old world to the new. This theory was adapted from the biological sphere to the political by the Abbé Raynal in his *Histoire Philosophique et Politique des Établissement et du Commerce des Européens dans les deux Indes* (1770), in which he suggested that the Americas would never produce a system of government, commerce, and law to rival that of Europe, and that distance from the mother countries of the old world would diminish the efficacy even of their inherited systems. Both works, it should be noted, were written and circulated in the period when France was losing its grip on its dominions in North America.

The European idealization of America as a refuge from moral and political corruption and intellectual tyranny persevered among the radical thinkers at the forefront of European Romanticism. Strongly influenced by books of description and travel in America, such as J. Hector St. John de Crèvecoeur's *Letters from an American Farmer* (1782), William Bartram's *Travels* (1791), and Gilbert Imlay's *A Topographical Description of the*

Western Territory of the United States (1792), and fired by the radical political theory of William Godwin's *An Enquiry Concerning Political Justice* (1793), the young Samuel Taylor Coleridge and Robert Southey conceived of a plan, in 1794–95, to establish a "pantisocracy" (a utopian farming community consisting of six families) on the banks of the Susquehanna river. Although this scheme never reached fruition, the radical Unitarian minister Joseph Priestley, greatly admired by Coleridge and his circle, actually emigrated to the United States in 1794. The wilderness of America was consistently used to signify a region of moral purity by radical writers of the 1790s; the eponymous hero of Robert Bage's *Hermsprong* (1796), for instance, owes his extraordinary integrity to his upbringing with a tribe of North American Indians, and the young brave at the center of William Wordsworth's poem "Ruth" demonstrates a similar natural vigor and love of liberty.

Some of the most influential texts of early French Romanticism equally owe their origin to this highly artificial conception of the Edenic new world. François-Auguste-René de Chateaubriand, having traveled extensively in the western regions of the United States in 1791, and having been inspired by his reading of Rousseau and of Johann Wolfgang von Goethe's *Die Leiden des Jungen Werther* (*The Sorrows of Young Werther*) used the experience to create *Atala* (1801), *René* (1802), and also *Les Natchez*, which was conceived in this period but remained unpublished until 1826. All three feature instinctively virtuous, eloquent noble savages and selfless, pious Christian missionaries, designed, in Chateaubriand's words, to illustrate "the harmonies of the Christian religion with the scenes of nature and the passions of the human heart."

Atala and *René*, upon their initial publication, were enormously popular and much imitated, and established the Romantic fascination with the interaction of Christian law and natural law, as well as the archetype of the melancholy, egocentric young man (*René*), searching for meaning and direction in a modern world where old moral and social certainties have been shattered by revolution, who yearns for the simplicity lost to civilized man: "O happy Savages! Why can I not enjoy the same peace that always goes with you? While I wander so fruitlessly through so many lands, you, seated quietly under your elms, let the days pass by without counting them."

Even Lord Byron, who was far from the piety of Chateaubriand and had no liking for earlier Romantics such as Coleridge, Southey, and Wordsworth, adopted the American wilderness as a symbol of vigorous natural virtue. In canto 8 of *Don Juan* (1819–24), he cites "The General Boon, backwoodsman of Kentucky," as an example of the benefits of life among the forests of the new world; and he laments that "The inconvenience of civilization / Is that you neither can be pleased nor please."

Frequently, however, the reality of emigration to America failed to meet European expectations. Frances Trollope and her family lived in the States from 1827–30, unsuccessfully trying to establish a shop in Cincinatti; after the failure of the business, she turned her experience of American life to good effect with the publication of *Domestic Manners of the Americans* (1832), a scathing, satirical description of what she felt to be the evils of American society, which earned her some notoriety in the United States. The pattern repeated itself for Charles Dickens, who arrived in America in 1842 hoping and expecting to like it, but found the sublimity of the American landscape marred by the ugliness of the cities, the coarseness of American manners, and the horrific fact of slavery: *American Notes* and *Martin Chuzzlewit* were the results. As the nineteenth century progressed, the interior of the continent was explored and mapped, native populations were removed or exterminated, political divisions over slavery demonstrated the failings of the idealistic American political system, and American citizens became more prominent and recognizable on the world stage. "America" lost the imaginative resonance of the unknown, and could no longer support utopian notions of moral purity or social reinvention. The New World had lost its mystique.

ROWLAND HUGHES

Bibliography

Blow, Robert, ed. *Abroad in America: Literary Discoverers of the New World from the Last 500 Years*. Oxford: Lennard, 1989.

Brandon, William. *New Worlds for Old: Reports from the New World and their Effect on the Development of Social Thought in Europe, 1500–1800*. Athens, Ohio: University of Ohio Press, 1986.

Chew, William L., ed. *Images of America: Through the European Looking Glass*. Brussels: VUBUP, 1997.

Connelly, Frances S. *The Sleep of Reason: Primitivism in European Art and Aesthetics, 1725–1907*. University Park: Pennsylvania State University Press, 1995.

Dame, William Frederick. *Jean-Jacques Rousseau and Political Literature in Colonial America*. Lewiston, N.Y.: Edwin Mellen, 1996.

MacGillivray, James Robertson. *The Pantisocracy Scheme and its Immediate Background*. Toronto: University of Toronto, University College Studies in English, 1931.

Marx, Leo. *The American Revolution and the American Landscape*. Washington, D.C.: Oxford University Press, 1975.

Moss, Sidney P. *Charles Dickens' Quarrel with America*. Troy, N.Y.: Whitson, 1984.

Mulvey, Christopher. "Ecriture and Landscape: British Writing on Post-Revolutionary America," in *Views of American Landscapes*. Edited by Mick Gidley and Robert Lawson-Peebles. Cambridge, U.K.: Cambridge University Press, 1989.

Rennie, Neil. *Far-Fetched Facts: The Literature of Travel and the Idea of the South Seas*. Oxford: Clarendon Press, 1995.

NEWMAN, JOHN HENRY 1801-1890

Religious commentator and poet

In the twentieth century, John Henry Newman was recognized as both a precursor to Vatican II and a profound psychological and philosophical thinker, while to the nineteenth century, he was a brilliant but controversial religious commentator and poet. The trajectory of his life is interwoven with his theology; the moment that marks Newman most significantly is his conversion to Roman Catholicism in 1845 and those events, before and after, connected to this episode.

Newman was born on February 21, 1801 at 80 Old Broad Street, London, to John Newman, a banker, and Jemima Fourdrinier, both practicing members of the Church of England and averse to evangelicalism. In May 1808, Newman boarded at the private school Ealing, and found himself more interested in David Hume and Voltaire than the church fathers, developing an interest in religion years later through the evangelical clergyman Walter Mayers. Experiencing a spiritual change under Mayers in 1816, Newman went on to reject evangelicalism for a Catholic and apostolic reading of the church, one that stressed the role of antiquity as exponent of Christian doctrine and basis of the Church of England. He developed these views further at Oxford University, where he won a college scholarship in 1818 and fellowship in 1822, despite performing poorly in examinations after a minor breakdown caused by overwork.

Having resolved to lead a single life at Ealing, Newman decided to seek Anglican orders and was made deacon in 1824 at Oriel College, accepting the curacy of St. Clement's, Oxford. Resigning the curacy in 1826 for a tutorship at Oriel, Newman met Richard Hurrell Froude, who, along with Edward Bouverie Pusey and John Keble, encouraged his high church beliefs, Froude in particular endorsing the doctrine of the real presence and devotion to the Virgin Mary. Newman, however, was unpopular with the Oriel authorities, treating his tutorship as a chance to spread the gospel and so denied further pupils by the provost, Edward Hawkins. Released from his teaching duties, Newman published *The Arians of the Fourth Century* (1833) for Charles Rivington's Theological Library, focusing on how to define the truths of holy scripture, understand the Holy Trinity, and communicate the importance of revealed religion. Newman preached on these themes regularly at St. Mary's and gained authority through his own example, practicing a disciplined regime of prayer and fasting and writing intensely. His official university sermons also defined Newman's beliefs, addressing the lack of reverence society expressed towards antiquity, ecclesiastical unity, the Catholic creed, and theological education.

In 1832, Newman toured the Mediterranean with Froude, visiting Malta, Corfu, Greece, Rome, and Naples, and returned alone to Sicily in 1833. Inspiring much of Newman's poetry, including "Lead kindly Light" (1833), the Mediterranean affected the preacher intensely and caused him to see Rome, not as the antichrist as the Church of England held, but as an authority of the true patristic church. Newman's understanding of religion deepened, and he began to welcome states of sickness and delirium, provoked by his ascetic lifestyle, as conduits for visions through which to embrace the supernatural aspect of Christianity. His God became a Romantic construction, transcendent, spiritual, and sublime, notions that he later Catholicized to describe a Roman divinity, but initially learned from Samuel Taylor Coleridge, Walter Scott, Robert Southey, and William Wordsworth. As Newman claimed in his autobiography, the writings of these Romantic figures, along with John Keble's 1833 Assize sermon "National Apostasy," grounded the Oxford movement, and those who joined were often literary, as well as religious, men. Uniting such figures as Richard Hurrell Froude, Edward Bouverie Pusey, and Isaac Williams, the movement sought to spread Catholic principles through the publication of ninety *Tracts for the Times* written between 1833–41. Newman wrote more than a quarter of the *Tracts*, and dedicated several to defining the English church as a *via media* between evangelicalism and popery, an idea he underlined as editor of the *British Critic* from 1838 to 1841. This work was undone, however, by Newman's *Tract 90* which argued that the Thirty-Nine Articles was compatible with the Council of Trent and Catholic doctrine. The pamphlet provoked the Bishop of Oxford to insist on an end to the *Tracts* series and forced Newman to retire to Littlemore, where he initiated a semimonastic retreat for visitors and scholars.

Resigning his Anglican orders in 1843, Newman was finally received into the Church of Rome in 1845 by Father Dominic Barberi and enrolled at the College of Propaganda in Rome the following year with his friend, Ambrose St. John. Impressed by the Oratory of St. Philip Neri, a community of secular priests dedicated to prayer, teaching and study, Newman determined to replicate the institution in Birmingham, England in 1848–49. Preaching his first Catholic sermons here, Newman also completed *Loss and Gain* (1848), a novel describing the turmoil of an Oxford convert caught in the controversy produced by the Oxford movement. His second novel, *Callista* (1856), explores the anguish of a third-century Christian convert, persecuted and martyred for his faith. Both narratives reflect Newman's own suffering as a believer, underlined at this time by the public disgrace and libel he suffered from the ex-Dominican Giacinto Achilli, whom he had denounced for his scandalous anti-Catholic performances. Retreating to Dublin, Newman was invited by the Irish bishops to found a Catholic university, a project on which he commented in *The Idea of a University* (1852–59). The school was hindered, however, by the refusal of the bishops to allow the university autonomy; Newman resigned his rectorship in 1858 and returned to the Birmingham Oratory.

Still committed to the diffusion of religious education, in 1859 Newman accepted the editorship of the Catholic literary magazine, *The Rambler*; its incumbent editor, Richard Simpson, having resigned for publishing an article deemed disloyal to the bishops. The article, addressing the government's royal commission on elementary education, suggested that the bishops' refusal to cooperate with the enquiry would isolate Catholic education, a sentiment Newman supported in his first editorial. In doing so, Newman suggested that the laity be consulted on the question of education, a proposition that the theologian John Gillow proclaimed as heresy and communicated via a mistranslation of

Newman's text to the Congregation of Propaganda in Rome. Compelled to resign from *The Rambler* within a month of assuming his position there, Newman returned humiliated to the diminished community of the Oratory, frowned upon by Rome and rendered a popish traitor by the Church of England.

However, in 1864 Charles Kingsley made a minor attack on Newman in a review for *Macmillan's magazine*, provoking the preacher to write his respected autobiography, *Apologia Pro Vita Sua* (*A Defense of His Life*, 1864). The *Apologia* enabled Newman to defend his conversion and faith and thus restore his reputation, one accentuated further by the publication of *The Dream of Gerontius* in 1865, published in the *Month* and set to music by Edward Elgar. Inspired in part by the death of Ambrose St. John, the poem describes the moment of death, judgement, and entry into purgatory and once again exhibits Newman's interest in revealed religion. His final attempt to explain how one can believe in that which cannot be evidentially proven appeared in *An Essay in Aid of a Grammar of Assent* (1870), celebrated for its psychological elaboration of Newman's "illative sense." The illative sense described that faculty of judgement which leads one to a reasoning grounded in a personal conviction of what seems right and certain, rather than what appears logical, the latter suited to history and science rather than religion. Such thought secured Newman's status as a profound psychological and philosophical thinker in the twentieth century for critics and believers alike, and his theories are collectively acknowledged as an important precursor to Vatican II. In 1878, Newman became the first Honorary Fellow of Trinity College, Oxford, and was made cardinal in 1879 by Pope Leo XIII with the special privilege that he could remain in Birmingham rather than join the curia in Rome. Continuing to write on the subject of revealed religion while working at the Oratory for the next eleven years, Newman died on August 11, 1890, and was venerated by the Catholic Church a century later on January 22, 1991.

EMMA MASON

Biography

Born in London, February 21, 1801. Educated at Ealing School, 1808, and Trinity College, Oxford, 1817. Fellow of Oriel College, Oxford, 1822–45. Ordained deacon and made curate at St. Clement's, Oxford, 1824. Ordained Anglican priest, 1825. Tutor at Oriel, 1826. Vicar at St. Mary's, Oxford, 1828–43. Traveled to Mediterranean, 1832. Editor of the *British Critic*, 1838–41. Moved to Littlemore, 1842. Received into the Roman Catholic Church, 1845. Moved to Maryvale, Birmingham, 1846. Ordained as a Catholic priest, 1847. Founded Oratory of St. Philip Neri at Birmingham, 1848. Rector of the Catholic University of Ireland, 1851–58. Elected honorary fellow of Trinity College, 1877. Uniform edition of Anglican writings published, 1877. Made a cardinal, 1879. Died August 11, 1890.

Selected Works

The Arians of the Fourth Century. 1833.
Tracts for the Times by Members of the University of Oxford, nos. 1–3, 6–8, 10–11, 15, 19–21, 31, 33–34, 38, 41, 45, 47, 71, 73–76, 79, 82–83, 85, 88, and 90. 1833–41.
Parochial and Plain Sermons. 8 vols. 1834–43.
Lectures on the Prophetical Office of the Church. 1837.
Lectures on the Doctrine of Justification. 1838.
Oxford University Sermons. 1843.
Sermons on Subjects of the Day. 1843.

An Essay on the Development of Christian Doctrine. 1845.
Discourses Addressed to Mixed Congregations. 1849.
Certain Difficulties felt by Anglicans in submitting to the Catholic Church. 2 vols. 1850–75.
Lectures on the Present Position of Catholics in England. 1851.
Discourses on the Scope and Nature of University Education. 1852.
The Idea of a University. 2 vols. 1852–58.
Sermons Preached on Various Occasions. 1857.
Lectures and Essays on University Subjects. 1859.
On Consulting the Faithful in Matters of Doctrine. 1859.
Apologia Pro Vita Sua. 1864.
A Letter to the Reverend E. B. Pusey on his Recent "Eirenicon." 1866.
An Essay in Aid of a Grammar of Assent. 1870.
Two Essays on Scripture Miracles and on Ecclesiastical. 2nd ed. 1870.
Essays Critical and Historical. 2 vols. 1871.
Discussions and Arguments on Various Subjects. 1872.
Fifteen Sermons Preached before the University of Oxford. 1872.
Historical Sketches. 3 vols. 1872.
The Present Position of Catholics in England. 1872.
Tracts Theological and Ecclesiastical. 1874.
A Letter to the Duke of Norfolk. 1875.
The Via Media of the Anglican Church. 2 vols. 1877 and 1883.
Select Treatises of St. Athanasius. 2 vols. 1881.
On the Inspiration of Scripture. 1884.
Meditations and Devotions. 1893.

Poetry and Fiction
Lyra Apostolica. 1836.
Loss and Gain: The Story of a Convert. 1848.
Callista: A Sketch of the Third Century. 1856.
The Dream of Gerontius. 1865.
Verses on Various Occasions. 1868.

Bibliography

Abbot, Edwin A. *The Anglican Career of Cardinal Newman*. 2 vols. London: Macmillan, 1892.
Chadwick, Owen. *Newman*. Oxford: Oxford University Press, 1983.
Dessain, Charles Stephen. *John Henry Newman*. London: Thomas Nelson and Sons, 1966.
Gilley, Sheridan. *Newman and His Age*. London: Darton, Longman, and Todd, 1990.
Goslee, David. *Romanticism and the Anglican Newman*. Athens: Ohio University Press, 1996.
Ker, Ian. *John Henry Newman: A Biography*. Oxford: Clarendon Press, 1988.
Ker, Ian, ed. *The Achievement of John Henry Newman*. London: Collins, 1990.
Mozley, Dorothea, ed. *Newman Family Letters*. London: SPCK, 1962.
Newsome, David. *The Convert Cardinals: John Henry Newman and Henry Edward Manning*. London: John Murray, 1993.
Nicholls, David and Fergus Kerr, eds. *John Henry Newman: Reason, Rhetoric, Romanticism*. Bristol: Bristol Press, 1991.
Trevor, Meriol. *Newman: Light in Winter*. London: Macmillan, 1962.
Turner, Frank. *John Henry Newman: The Challenge to Evangelical Religion*. New Haven: Yale University Press, 2002.
Vaiss, Paul. *From Oxford to the People: Reconsidering Newman and the Oxford Movement*. Herefordshire: Gracewing, 1996.
Ward, Maisie. *Young Mr. Newman*. New York: Sheed and Ward, 1948.
Ward, Wilfrid. *The Life of John Henry Cardinal Newman: Based on his Private Journals and Correspondence*. 2 vols. London: Longmans, Green, 1912.
Withey, Donald A. *John Henry Newman: The Liturgy and the Breviary*. New York: Sheed and Ward, 1996.

NICOLAI, FRIEDRICH 1733–1811

German publisher, editor, critic, and writer

Friedrich Nicolai holds the dubious honor of having antagonized the most famous names in German Sturm und Drang (storm and stress), classicism, and Romanticism. He pursued individual feuds with Johann Wolfgang von Goethe, Johann Christoph Friedrich von Schiller, August Wilhelm and Friedrich von Schlegel, Ludwig Tieck, and the philosophers Johann Gottlieb Fichte, Immanuel Kant, and Friedrich Wilhelm Joseph von Schelling. They in turn were united in their opinion of him as the personification of vacuous, soulless rationalism in literature and literary criticism. Although his position in German literary history has subsequently been determined by the insults of his canonical adversaries, Nicolai was one of the main representatives of the German Enlightenment and, due to his public position as critic, editor, and publisher, one of the most influential men of letters of his time. He was also a popular author of satirical fiction, and a scrupulously exact cultural historian and topographer.

Throughout Nicolai's long life he held firm to his belief in progress through the power of reason. He evaluated literature on the basis of its direct practical, social, and moral usefulness for the individual and for society. The act of artistic creation had to be subordinated to reason, and clarity was essential in the end result. In promoting these aesthetic tenets, Nicolai tried to stem the tide of the new developments in art and literature that were sweeping through Europe at the end of the eighteenth century.

Nicolai was, however, on his own terms an innovator. His *Briefe über den itzigen Zustand der schönen Wissenschaften in Deutschland* (*Letters concerning the Present State of the Arts in Germany*, 1755) earned him the attention and friendship of Gotthold Ephraim Lessing and Moses Mendelssohn. His most significant editorial venture continued over a forty-year period. The *Allgemeine Deutsche Bibliothek* (*ADB*) (*Universal German Library*, 1765–1806) reviewed all new German publications, creating a unified national forum for literary criticism within the disunited German territories. The importance of this venture cannot be overestimated for the writers of this period. At the same time, Nicolai's *ADB* both contributed to and reflected the development (that is, both the popularization and the degeneration) of the Enlightenment in the pre-Romantic and Romantic eras.

Debate and criticism were for Nicolai the guarantors of progress. He was a member in the 1780s and 1790s of the most prestigious debating circles of the Enlightenment, precursors of the Romantic salons, the Monday Club and the Wednesday Society, and hosted regular musical and literary gatherings in his home in Berlin. He used these and any other means at his disposal (such as organizing literary competitions to encourage new talent) to educate the public of the middle classes, by whom he was considered an authority. What separates Nicolai from the true representatives of the Enlightenment, however, is his unwillingness, which became more pronounced with age, to direct the concept of criticism toward himself. Instead of initiating debate as a fruitful exchange of often contradictory ideas, Nicolai exploited it to persuade others of the reasonableness of his own opinions. It is on this basis that Nicolai clashed with everything that was young, new, and revolutionary in German literature in one of its most productive periods.

Nicolai's first novel, *Das Leben und die Meinungen des Herrn Magister Sebaldus Nothanker* (*The Life and Opinions of Master Sebaldus Nothanker*, 1773–76), is his most successful social satire. This is almost certainly due to the fact that at this stage in his intellectual development all aspects of society, including the Enlightenment, are examined critically, and this work is perhaps the only example of self-critical analysis we have from Nicolai. Written in the tradition of Laurence Sterne, it was immensely popular. In subsequent works, Nicolai directed his satirical skills against aspects of modern literature and thought of which he disapproved. In *Vertraute Briefe von Adelheid B. an ihre Freundin Julie S.* (*Intimate Letters from Adelheid B. to her Friend Julie S.*, 1799) he presents Friedrich Schlegel as a dangerous influence on society and promotes the virtues of social responsibility and moderation. From a modern perspective, however, the story highlights the limitations and even inhumanity of these abstractions. Nicolai criticized the emotionalism and concomitant lack of clarity of the *Sturm und Drang* movement, claiming that these authors had no real knowledge of folk art (his satirical collection of 1777–78 was directed against Johann Gottfried von Herder). In 1775 he published a *Werther* parody, and although the satire was directed against the reception of the novel and not against Goethe as a poet, Nicolai made an enemy of the latter for many years. Nicolai rejected Kant's revolutionary philosophy and feared its effect on society. He campaigned against speculative philosophy in *Geschichte eines dicken Mannes* (*Story of a Fat Man*, 1794), and *Leben und Meinungen Sempronius Grundiberts, eines deutschen Philosophen* (*Life and Opinions of Sempronius Grundibert, a German Philosopher*, 1798). Kant and Fichte retaliated, the latter in a pamphlet *Friedrich Nicolai's Leben und sonderbare Meinungen* (*Friedrich Nicolai's Life and Strange Opinions*, 1801), criticizing Nicolai as the prototype of banal reason, even calling him a *literarisches Stinktier* (literary skunk). Nicolai's comeback was to prevent Fichte's admission to the Berlin academy of Science in 1805. In a lecture to this academy in 1799, Nicolai had attempted to crush all belief in speculative thought by narrating his own experience of what seemed to be supernatural apparitions, which appeared to him in 1791 after a period of illness and nervous exhaustion. He was cured, he explains, from these products of his confused imagination by leeches applied to his backside. With this serious public statement Nicolai the satirist played into his enemies' gleeful hands. As well as responding to Nicolai's attacks in essays and journal articles (as did Goethe and Schiller in *Xenien* and the Schlegels in *Athenäum*), Goethe, E. T. A. Hoffmann, and Tieck could now immortalize this advice in their works and successfully perpetuate the view of Nicolai as a contemptible and laughable fool.

Nicolai was not always unjust in his evaluations, and the biographical portraits he made of his friends are sensitive and intelligent. To achieve a rounded picture of Nicolai's abilities and his contemporary importance, one must also review his historical and topographical works. In 1781 he undertook a grand tour with his eldest son. This journey was meticulously planned and gave rise to a twelve-volume *Beschreibung einer Reise durch Deutschland und die Schweiz* (*Description of a Journey through Germany and Switzerland*, 1783–96), offering detailed statistical and factual information rather than subjective impressions and experiences. The same careful source work underpins Nicolai's *Beschreibung der Königlichen Residenzstädte Berlin und Potsdam* (*Description of the Royal Residencies Berlin and Potsdam*, 1769) now an invaluable reference guide to the period, and his *Anekdoten von König Friedrich dem Zweyten* (*Anecdotes of King Friedrich II*, 1788–92). Nicolai also wrote surveys on hairpieces and wigs, on the church, and on freemasonry. Each shows evidence of an innovative and very modern understanding of historical source evaluation.

In all of his ventures Nicolai was a representative of the Enlightenment. He did not lack perspicacity as a critic of the new literature and philosophy of his day, and it can be salutary for modern readers to view the latter through his jaundiced eyes.

SHEILA DICKSON

Biography

Born in Berlin, March 18, 1733. Apprenticed as bookseller, Frankfurt an der Oder, 1749–51; on death of his father in 1752, entered family bookselling business, run by his elder brother; took over business in 1758, after his brother's death. In 1760, married Elisabeth Macaria Schaarschmidt (died 1793); of eight children none outlived their father. Member of the Munich Academy of Science, 1781. Member of the Berlin Academy of Science, 1798. Died January 6, 1811.

Selected Works

Collections

Vertraute Briefe von Adelheid B. an ihre Freundin Julie S.: Ein Roman. Werther-Parodien, zeitgenössische Rezensionen und Schmähungen. Edited by Günter de Bruyn. Frankfurt: Fischer-Taschenbuch-Verlag, 1983.
Gesammelte Werke. Edited by Bernhard Fabian and Marie-Luise Spieckermann. Hildesheim: Olms, 1985–.

Novels

Das Leben und die Meinungen des Herrn Magisters Sebaldus Nothanker. 3 vols. Berlin and Stettin: Nicolai, 1773–76; Translated as *The Life and Opinions of Master Sebaldus Nothanker*, by John R. Russell. Columbia, S.C.: Camden House, 1998.
Freuden des jungen Werthers. Leiden und Freuden Werthers des Mannes. Berlin: Nicolai, 1775.
Geschichte eines dicken Mannes, worin drey Heurathen und drey Körbe nebst viel Liebe. 2 vols. Berlin and Stettin: Nicolai, 1794.
Leben und Meinungen Sempronius Gundiberts, eines deutschen Philosophen. Nebst zwey Urkunden der neusten deutschen Philosophie. Berlin and Stettin: Nicolai, 1798.
Vertraute Briefe von Adelheid B. an ihre Freundin Julie S. Berlin and Stettin: Nicolai, 1799.

Edited Journals

Bibliothek der schönen Wissenschaften und der freyen Künste. Leyzy: Dyck, 1757–59.

Briefe, die neueste Literatur betreffend. Berlin and Stetin: Nicolai, 1759–65.
Allgemeine Deutsche Bibliothek. Berlin and Stettin: Nicolai, 1765–92; *Neue Allgemeine Deutsche Bibliothek*, ed. by Carl Ernst Bohn. Berlin and Stettin: Nicolai, 1793–1800. *Neue Allgemeine Deutsche Bibliothek.* 1800–1806.

Criticism

Briefe über den itzigen Zustand der schönen Wissenschaften in Deutschland. Berlin: Nicolai, 1755.
Beschreibung der königlichen Residenzstädte Berlin und Potsdam, aller daselbst befindlicher Merkwürdigkeiten in der umliegenden Gegend. Berlin: Nicolai, 1769; 2nd rev. ed., 2 vols. Berlin: Nicolai, 1779; 3rd rev. ed., 3 vols. Berlin: Nicolai, 1786.
Ein feyner kleyner Almanach. Vol schoenerr echterr liblicherr Volckslieder, lustigerr Reyen, vnndt kleglicherr Mordgeschichte. 2 vols. Berlin and Stettin: Nicolai, 1777–78. Published as *Friedrich Nicolai's Kleyner feyner Almanach.* Edited by Georg Ellinger. Berlin: Paetel, 1888.
Beschreibung einer Reise durch Deutschland und die Schweiz im Jahre 1781. Nebst Bemerkungen über Gelehrsamkeit, Industrie, Religion und Sitten. 12 vols. Berlin and Stellin: Nicolai, 1783–96.
Anekdoten von König Friedrich dem Zweyten von Preussen und einigen Personen, die um ihn waren. Nebst einigen Zweifeln und Berichtigungen über schon gedruckte Anekdoten. 6 vols. Berlin and Stettin: Nicolai, 1788–92.
Ueber den Gebrauch der falschen Haare und Perrucken in alten und neuern Zeiten. Eine historische Untersuchung. Berlin and Stettin: Nicolai, 1801.
Einige Bemerkungen über den Ursprung und die Geschichte der Rosenkreuzer und Freymaurer. Berlin and Stettin: Nicolai, 1806.
Philosophische Abhandlungen. Grösstentheils vorgelesen in der Königlichen Akademie der Wissenschaften zu Berlin. 2 vols. Berlin and Stettin: Nicolai, 1808.

Biographical Essays

Ehrengedächtniss Herrn Ewald Christian von Kleist. Berlin: Nicolai, 1760.
Leben Justus Mösers. Berlin and Stettin: Nicolai, 1797.
Gedächtnissschrift auf Johann Jakob Engel. Berlin and Stettin: Nicolai, 1806.
Gedächtnissschrift auf Dr Wilhelm Abraham Teller. Berlin and Stettin: Nicolai, 1807.
Gedächtnissschrift auf Johann August Eberhard. Berlin and Stettin: Nicolai, 1810.

Bibliography

Albrecht, Wolfgang, ed. *Friedrich Nicolai: "Kritik ist überall, zumal in Deutschland nötig." Satiren und Schriften zur Literatur.* Munich: Beck, 1987.
Fabian, Bernhard, ed. *Friedrich Nicolai 1733–1811: Essays zum 250. Geburtstag.* Berlin: Nicolai, 1983.
Jacob-Friesen, Holger. *Profile der Aufklärung: Friedrich Nicolai— Isaak Iselin. Briefwechsel (1767–1782). Edition, Analyse, Kommentar.* Berne: Haupt, 1997.
Möller, Horst. *Aufklärung in Preußen. Der Verleger, Publizist und Geschichtsschreiber Friedrich Nicolai.* Berlin: Colloquium, 1974.
Mollenhauer, Peter. *Friedrich Nicolais Satiren. Ein Beitrag zur Kulturgeschichte des 18. Jahrhunderts.* Amsterdam: Benjamins, 1977.

NIEBUHR, BARTHOLD GEORG 1776–1831

German historian

Widely recognized as Germany's first great scholar of antiquity, Barthold Georg Niebuhr initiated the search for the origins and development of early Roman history through a critical treatment of its long-hallowed tradition. No longer content with mere erudition, Niebuhr's "critical history" attempted to use a combination of intuition and interrogation of sources to ascertain the significance and continuity of early Roman events. Though he is best remembered as the historian of the early Roman republic, Niebuhr was not exclusively an historian, and actively served as a statesman both in his native Denmark and in his adopted fatherland, Prussia. Karl Wilhem von Humboldt characterized Niebuhr as the scholar among statesmen and the statesman among scholars. The relation is not accidental, and Niebuhr himself claimed that "no one can write a history of this great people without being a statesman, and a practical one too." Indeed, Niebuhr's experiences in the more tumultuous events of his time underwrote most of his analogies between ancient Rome and contemporary Germany.

Niebuhr's most famous work is his *Römische Geschichte* (*Roman History*, 2 vols., 1811–12). Thomas Babington Macaulay declared that the "appearance of the book is really an era in the intellectual history of Europe." Based on his lectures at the University of Berlin from 1810 to 1812, the work is more a history of the development of Roman institutions than a history of famous Romans. In contrast to the annalistic history of Rome that originates with Livy, Niebuhr implied that the early history of every nation can only be understood through institutions rather than events, through classes rather than individuals. Accordingly, Niebuhr's history focuses on the development of Roman agrarian law, which, he asserts, was built around a struggle between the patricians and the plebians; each order sought to dominate the other, and every constitutional solution designed to regulate relations between classes was temporary. New laws were periodically needed to reassert the spirit of old laws and to redress the imbalance between classes. In keeping with the Romantic conception of culture as an organic national product, Niebuhr was interested, above all, in the organic development of Rome as a great state, and he attempted to trace Rome's political, legal, and economic institutions to their origins so that he could better understand their growth. In tracing the organic development of the Roman state, Niebuhr made his most significant contribution to historical method, for which he continues to receive recognition today: the critical interrogation of early Roman sources, and the use of philologic analysis to enlighten historical inquiry.

The *Römische Geschichte* was startling for its critical methodology, but perhaps its most contentious claim was what we might call the "ballad theory" of Roman history: Niebuhr's confident speculation that early Roman history had been transmitted through songs, certain features of which could still be discerned in later historians. His search for early Roman poetry was certainly influenced by the Ossianic fervor that swept Germany at the turn of the nineteenth century that, even after the exposure of the poems as an imaginative construct by James Macpherson, formed a cornerstone of Nordic Romanticism. Niebuhr's evidence for the ballad theory was slight. For example, he looked at the internal structure of the Romulus legend and noted that much in the spirit of an old legend, key episodes were given largely without reference to time. Such an insight was then confirmed by Cicero's mention of Cato's reference to ancient *carmina* (songs). The ballad theory allowed Niebuhr to assert that Roman civilization developed through three stages: a completely poetic period, a mythicohistorical period, and a historical period. Faced with a paucity of evidence for the early period of Rome, Niebuhr defended his thesis by analogy. He suggested that all nations go through a similar process of development and, noting the existence of heroic poetry in Scandinavia, Greece, Serbia, and Scotland, he claimed that such heroic poems must be a universal phenomenon. Niebuhr's development process is not the same as the stages of society posited by such Scottish Enlightenment historians as Adam Ferguson and John Millar, however, because for Niebuhr development was determined by the inner dynamic of a nation's life. But because history, like nature, is governed by laws, the history of one nation can illuminate the history of another. Indeed, the *Römische Geschichte* continually refers to Ireland, England, India, and, especially, Niebuhr's native Denmark to clarify unrecorded features of early Roman society. Niebuhr saw such analogical reasoning as inherent in the historian's craft and wrote to a friend that "I am an historian, for I can make a complete picture from separate fragments, and I know where the parts are missing and how to fill them up. No one believes how much of what seems to be lost can be restored."

Niebuhr's claims provoked passionate responses. Many philologists found Niebuhr too willing to assume the existence of a primitive historical tradition, while educated Germans trained in the classics were outraged at the dismissal of Livy as mere fable. Goethe was said to have asked incredulously, "What do we want with such an impoverished truth? If the Romans were great enough to fabricate it, we should at least be great enough to believe it." Two great representatives of German Romanticism, August Wilhelm and Friedrich von Schlegel, disagreed in their assessment of Niebuhr's work. Friedrich accepted the hypothesis that ballads had existed and he credited Roman patriotism with sponsoring such truly creative poetry. In contrast, August thought it inconceivable that a people ruled by priests with a harsh language could produce an indigenous poetic tradition. Niebuhr's ballads, rather, showed the projection of Greek influence back into early Roman history. The most influential figure in discrediting the ballad theory, however, was Theodor Mommsen, who scorned Niebuhr's philological method and argued instead that the most reliable historical data derived from nonliterary sources such as inscriptions, coins, and buildings.

Outside Germany, Niebuhr's work had a particular influence in England, where, after its translation in 1828, the *Roman History* sold more copies than in Germany. Niebuhr's ideas were debated for years in the *Quarterly Review*. Matthew Arnold's father, the historian Thomas Arnold, learned German in order to read Niebuhr and became a key exponent of his method. On their European tour of 1828, Samuel Taylor Coleridge and William Wordsworth are known to have met Niebuhr at

Godesberg. Wordsworth, who owned a copy of the *Roman History*, included three sonnets alluding to Niebuhr in his sequence "Memorials of a Tour in Italy, 1837." The poet was disturbed by Niebuhr's arguments and asked (in a vein similar to Goethe, above), "These old credulities, to nature dear / Shall they no longer bloom upon the stock / Of History, stript naked as a rock / 'Mid a dry desert?" The same year that Wordsworth's sequence was published (1842), Macaulay's "Lays of Ancient Rome" attempted to re-create the lost original ballads that Niebuhr had hypothesized.

In addition to his work as a critical historian of Rome, Niebuhr also made contributions to philology and archaeology through translations, the issue of new editions, and the restoration of palimpsests. When he returned to Bonn in 1823, he initiated the publication of Byzantine historians, the *Corpus Scriptorum Historiae Byzantina* (*Collection of Byzantine Histories*), and he founded the *Rheinsches Museum*, a journal of classical studies and archaeology. Today, however, Niebuhr is best remembered for his innovations in critical methodology. While some claim that Niebuhr's philological methods and synthetic logic represent the culmination of an Enlightenment historical tradition, most scholars agree that Niebuhr's work makes a fundamental contribution to the Romantic conception of culture as an organic national product.

JONATHAN SACHS

Biography

Born Copenhagen, August 27, 1776, the son of Carsten Niebuhr, the noted Danish traveler. Raised in the province of Dithmarsh, Holstein. Studied history and law at the University of Kiel, 1794–96. Private secretary to Danish Minister of Finance, 1796–98. Stayed in Britain, where he finished his studies at the University of Edinburgh, 1798–99. Entered the Danish Civil Service, 1800; became director of the National Bank, 1804. Answered call of Baron von Stein to help reorganize Prussia, 1806; became privy state councilor and head of the section for state debts and banking, soon resigned, 1810. Elected member of the Academy and joined faculty of the new University of Berlin as a specialist in Roman jurisprudence, 1810. Prussian ambassador to the Vatican, 1816–23. Appointed member of the Prussian State Council, 1823. Taught at the University of Bonn, 1823–31. Married Amélie Behrens, 1800. Died Bonn, January 2, 1831.

Selected Works

Zur Geschichte der Römischen Staatsländereien. 1803–6.
Römische Geschichte. 3 vols., 1811–32. Translated as *History of Rome*, by J. C. Hare and C. Thirwall. 1828–42.
Kleine historische und philologische Schriften. 2 vols. 1828–43.
Nachgelassene Schriften nichtphilologischen Inhalts. Edited by Marcus Niebuhr, 1842.
Geschichte des Zeitalters der Revolution. Edited by Marcus Niebuhr. 2 vols. 1845.
Vorträge über römische Geschichte. Edited by Meyer Isler. 3 vols. 1846–48.
Vorträge über alte Geschichte, an der Universität zu Bonn gehalten. Edited by Marcus Niebuhr. 3 vols. 1847–51.
Vorträge über alte Länder- und Völkerkunde. Edited by Meyer Isler, 1851.
Vorträge über römische Alterhümer. Edited by Meyer Isler, 1858.

Bibliography

Bernal, Martin. *Black Athena: The Afroasiatic Roots of Classical Civilization.* New Brunswick, N.J.: Rutgers University Press, 1987–91.
Bridenthal, Renate. "Was there a Roman Homer? Niebuhr's Thesis and Its Critics," *History and Theory* 11 (1972): 193–213.
Christ, Karl. *Von Gibbon zu Rostovtzeff: Leben und Werk führender Althistoriker der Neuzeit.* Darmstadt: Wissenschaftliche Buchgesellschaft, 1972.
Forbes, Duncan. *The Liberal Anglican Idea of History.* Cambridge, U.K.: Cambridge University Press, 1952.
Gooch, George Peabody. *History and Historians in the Nineteenth Century.* London: Longman, 1913.
Manning, Peter J. "Cleansing the Images: Wordsworth, Rome, and the Rise of Historicism," *Texas Studies in Literature and Language* 33 (1991): 271–326.
Momigliano, Arnoldo. "Perizonius, Niebuhr, and the Character of Early Roman Tradition," *Secondo Contributo alla storia degli studi classici.* Rome: Edizioni di Storia e letteratura, 1960.
Reill, Peter Hanns. "Barthold Georg Niebuhr and the Enlightenment Tradition," *German Studies Review* 3 (1980): 9–26.
Rytkönen, Seppo. *Barthold Georg Niebuhr als Politiker und Historiker.* Helsinki: Suomalainen Tiedeakatemia, 1968.
Walther, Gerrit, ed. *Barthold Georg Niebuhr: Historiker und Staatsmann.* Bonn: Röhrscheid Verlag, 1984.
Witte, Barthold C. *Der preussische Tacitus: Aufstieg, Ruhm und Ende des Historikers Barthold Georg Niebuhr, 1776–1831.* Dusseldorf: Droste, 1979.

NIGHT

Night is an indispensable term in Romantic discourse: far from an abstract concept, it hastens Romantic thinking as the source of a myriad of associations. As a daily occurrence, nightfall brings shadows, silence, and stillness, perhaps even solitariness, which can seem constraining to the average person. Yet for the Romantic sensibility, night's poetic and spiritual resources appear boundlessly liberating: the annulment of sunlight and the shift to a profound darkness relieved only by moon and stars are the prelude to metaphysical rapture and sublime illumination. Novalis recognizes this when, in *Hymnen an die Nacht* (*Hymns to the Night*, 1800), he marvels at "those infinite eyes which Night has opened up within us."

Attributes of mystery, fearfulness and mesmerizing power have been ascribed to night at least since antiquity (as illustrated by certain lines in Virgil's *Aeneid* describing Aeneas's jittery descent into Hades). The specifically funereal note in Romantic art may be traced to Edward Young's *The Complaint, or Night Thoughts on Life, Death and Immortality* (1742–44), which ushered in a vogue of morbid poetic rumination and foreshadowed the paradigm-shift from Enlightenment lucidity to the darker modes of Romantic reverie and introspection.

Frequently linked to notions of death and oblivion, night was an intimate familiar to most Romantic poets. Percy Bysshe Shelley imagines unlit spaces that harbor resonances of death, now envisaged as "mild / And terrorless as this serenest night" ("A Summer Evening"). The eponymous hero of Keats's allegorical *Endymion* is in love with the lunar goddess Diana; elsewhere, the nightingale (that quintessentially nocturnal bird) becomes the addressee of an impassioned ode invoking night in terms of blissful expiry: "Now more than ever seems it rich to die, / To cease upon the midnight with no pain. . . ." As for Lord Byron, he could find no more telling comparison for his beloved than to say, "She walks in beauty, like the night. . . ."

The same nocturnal fixation inspired such music as Fréderic Chopin's *Nocturnes* for piano, influenced by Vincenzo Bellini's opera *La Sonnambula* (*The Sleepwalker*, 1831), and Robert Schumann's *Nachtstücke* (*Night Pieces*, op. 23, 1839), keyboard modulations designed to fade into a silence suggestive of the wordlessness of nocturnal reverie. Himself the author of *Songs without Words* for the piano, Felix Mendelssohn-Bartholdy included a pensive *Nocturne* for horns in his incidental music to William Shakespeare's *A Midsummer Night's Dream*.

Painters such as Washington Allston, Caspar David Friedrich, and Joseph Wright regularly exploited the striking contrast of moonlight and impenetrable shadow. Late in his career Friedrich perfected the two-sided transparency picture, in which a diurnal scene is converted into a nocturnal one by a candle set behind it. Some of Samuel Palmer's most entrancing landscapes are premised upon the numinous aspect of twilight, while John Martin's apocalyptic canvases conjure up gulfs of black immensity split by zigzags of lightning. Artists like Francisco José de Goya y Lucientes or Henry Fuseli (author of *The Nightmare* [1781]) favor nocturnal settings for their macabre tableaux, much in the way that the Gothic novelist Maturin thrills his reader in *Melmoth the Wanderer* (1820) by having his malefic hero repeatedly loom forth out of an opaque darkness. Night is an unmistakable marker of the antastic in the tales of E. T. A. Hoffmann (author of the collection *Nachtstücke* [*Night Pieces*, 1817], which inspired Schumann) and of Théophile Gautier, in whose *Arria Marcella* (1852) the long-dead town of Pompeii is reanimated by the silvery moonlight.

Romantic ideology equates night with the sleep of reason and the awakening of man's latent faculties. Reverie, dreams, and trance states offer privileged access to nature's secrets. Schubert's lectures, *Ansichten von der Nachtseite der Naturwissenschaft* (*Aspects of the Night-Side of Natural Science*, 1808), established a program of scientific observation modified by subjectivity; while the Swiss mystic Ignaz Paul Vitalis Troxler (1780–1866) pictured the deeper unity attainable through an imaginative plunge into the depths of dream, a return to origins wherein spirit and matter are ecstatically fused. The parapsychologist and therapist Kerner emphasized the positive aspects of such phenomena as somnambulism and clairvoyance. Another doctor, Carl Gustav Carus, produced the treatise *Psyche* (1836), which points to the remarkable activity taking place below the surface of waking consciousness, and anticipates the model of the Unconscious elaborated decades later by psychoanalysis. (Carus was also a competent painter of nocturnal landscapes.)

In the 1850s, Victor Hugo undertook nocturnal experiments in table-turning and pioneered a form of automatic ink-drawing allegedly shaped by otherworldly stimuli. His verse collection *Les Contemplations* (1856) revolves obsessively around night as a metaphysical absolute. The lengthy "Pleurs dans la nuit" ("Sobbings in the night") bristles with images of a nocturnal realm at once terrifying and revelatory. Hugo's somber novel *Les Travailleurs de la mer* (*The Toilers of the Sea*, 1866) comprises spellbinding interludes in which night is figured as the crucible of multiple visions: "the disorder of the whirlpool and the fixity of the sepulchre, the enigma which both shows and hides its face, the infinite masked by blackness, such is the night."

In similarly extravagant vein, Alphonse Marie Louis de Lamartine's poem "Hymne de la nuit" ("Hymn of the Night") interprets the nameless abyss of the night sky as a glorious cosmic architecture fashioned by an ubiquitous deity. Thomas de Quincey's rhapsodic prose, exemplified in *The English Mail-Coach* (1849), elaborates upon giddy, nightmarish visions stimulated by dreaming or laudanum; these are in part indebted to long insomniac journeys made by night in his youth. A rather less alarming nocturnalism is manifested in Samuel Taylor Coleridge's serene and humane meditation "Frost at Midnight," while Giacomo Leopardi's poem "La Sera del d di festa" ("The Evening of the Fiesta") describes a realm of innocent wonder: "tender and clear is the night, and windless." In a decisive reminiscence in *The Prelude* (1805; revised 1850), William Wordsworth records an illicit boat trip he made as a child by night on Ullswater, which imparted "a dim and undetermined sense / Of unknown modes of being."

For their part, poets such as Friedrich Hölderlin, Nikolaus Lenau, and Gérard de Nerval nurtured an affinity for the nocturnal to the point of entirely losing their grasp on lucidity and lapsing into psychosis. (In Germany, a contemporary euphemism for madness was *Umnachtung*—as it were, "the embrace of night.") Nerval composed his poetic memoir *Aurélia* (1855) as a lament for lost love and a demonstration of the efficacy of dreams; with its motto "Je suis le ténébreux . . ." ("I am the man of shadows . . ."), his oracular sonnet "El Desdichado" invokes an orphic journey to the Underworld and portends his literal suicide.

If the Romantic project consisted, in large measure, in reconciling interiority with the outer forms of nature, thereby opening windows onto fresh spaces and liberating potentialities hitherto repressed, then night was the objective condition for the subjective transmutation of reality: its "Romanticization," in Novalis's phrase. As a property of the phenomenal world, night simultaneously flowed through the creative mind. As fertile as it was imponderable and indefinable, it was the perfect correlative to the totalizing vision of a universe redeemed by the imagination, and in this respect functioned as perhaps the most versatile topos in Romantic expression.

ROGER CARDINAL

See also **Allston, Washington; Bellini, Vincenzo; Byron, Lord George Noel Gordon; Carus, Carl Gustav; Chopin, Fréderic; Coleridge, Samuel Taylor; De Quincey, Thomas; Dreams and Dreaming; Drugs and Addiction; Friedrich, Caspar David; Fuseli, Henry; Gautier, Théophile; Hoffman, Ernst Theodor Amadeus; Hugo, Victor-Marie;** *Hymmen an die Nacht;* **Keats, John; Kerner, Justinus Andreas Christian; Lamartine, Alphonse Marie Louis Prat de; Leopardi, Giacomo; Madness; Martin, John; Mendelssohn-Bartholdy, Felix; Mesmerism;** *Moonrise over the Sea;* **Nachttücke; Nerval, Gérard de;** *Nightmare, The;* **Novalis; Palmer, Samuel; Schumann,**

Robert; Shelley, Percy Bysshe; Wordsworth, William; Wright, Joseph

Bibliography

Barrère, Jean-Bertrand. *La Fantaisie de Victor Hugo*. 3 vols. Paris: Klincksieck, 1972–73.
Bays, Gwendolyn. *The Orphic Vision: Seer Poets from Novalis to Rimbaud*. Lincoln: University of Nebraska Press, 1984.
Béguin, Albert. *L'Ame romantique et le rêve*. Paris: Corti, 1939.
Cardinal, Roger. "Night and Dreams." In *The Romantic Spirit in German Art 1790–1990*. Edited by Keith Hartley, Henry Meyric Hughes, Peter-Klaus Schuster, and William Vaughan. Edinburgh: National Galleries of Scotland, 1994, 191–96.
Huch, Ricarda. *Die Romantik. Ausbreitung, Blütezeit und Verfall* Tubingen: Rainer Wunderlich Verlag Hermann Leins, 1951.
James, Tony. *Dream, Creativity, and Madness in Nineteenth-Century France*. Oxford: Clarendon Press, 1995.
Jankélévitch, Vladimir. "Le Nocturne," in *Le Romantisme allemand*. Edited by Albert Béguin. Paris: Bibliothque 10–18, 1966.
Perella, Nicolas James. *Night and the Sublime in Giacomo Leopardi*. Berkeley and Los Angeles: University of California Press, 1970.
Privateer, Paul Michael. *Romantic Voices. Identity and Ideology in British Poetry, 1789–1850*. Athens, Ga.: University of Georgia Press, 1991.
Raymond, Marcel. *Romantisme et rêverie*. Paris: Corti, 1978.
Rosenblum, Robert. *Modern Painting and the Northern Romantic Tradition: Friedrich to Rothko*. London: Thames and Hudson, 1975.
Prawer, S. S., ed. *The Romantic Period in Germany*. London: Weidenfeld and Nicolson, 1970.

THE NIGHTMARE 1781

Painting by Henry Fuseli

Henry Fuseli's painting *The Nightmare* was one of the most familiar images of its time. It was not only widely plagiarized, but parodies of it were used by George Cruikshank and others for political caricature, with the goblin-like creature of the night afflicting, among others, Napoleon Bonaparte, Charles James Fox, Louis XVIII, and William Pitt. Lord Nelson, in one cartoon, *is* the goblin, eager to explore under Emma Hamilton's dress. There was an engraving of it on the wall of Sigmund Freud's studio, and his disciple Ernest Jones used it as the frontispiece for his book *On the Nightmare* (1931). In Ken Russell's film *Gothic* (1986), the goblin is a mischievous presence at the Villa Diodati house party of Lord Byron, Claire Clairmont, Mary Shelley, and Percy Bysshe Shelley. The image is inescapably sexual, and the presence, on the back of Fuseli's first version, of an unfinished portrait of a confidently smiling but aloof young woman, suggests a context personal to Fuseli. She has been identified as Anna Landolt, a niece of the Swiss physiognomist Johann Caspar Lavater, Fuseli was passionately in love with her, and though he felt unable to tell her this, he recorded passionate erotic dreams of possessing her while she slept. This is the only real evidence for the identification, but in any case the contrast of the commanding female figure on one side of the canvas, and the oppressed sleeper on the other is suggestive; this is a drama of erotic subjection, with a crucial ambiguity as to who—the female sleeper or the male, grotesquely dwarfish and generically ambiguous demon—is dreaming the dream.

The four surviving versions of the picture are markedly different. The first, in the Detroit Institute of Arts, is the one that Fuseli exhibited in London's Royal Academy in 1782. It made his name in London, and secured his reputaion as a painter of dreams and nightmares. Although many of his subsequent works were illustrations of, among others, John Milton and William Shakespeare, his influence in treating the supernatural in these writers as a kind of hallucinatory sublime is in continuity with *The Nightmare*, as is his more private oeuvre of semipornographic drawing, often featuring dominant women and sadomasochistic scenarios. In this version, the woman seems completely lifeless, a white, golden-haired figure in a painting largely composed of reds, yellows, and ochres. She lies with her head to the viewer's right, and the squat, round-eyed figure sits comfortably on her stomach, staring out of the picture at the viewer, his hand on his knee, his mouth downturned, and stroking his chin as if in a complicit moment of puzzlement.

In the second, smaller, and possibly better known version now in Frankfurt, the woman is bent more extravagantly backward on the couch, her head this time towards the left, and one knee bent upward. She has a bolster comfortably supporting her shoulders, and seems to have fallen back from a mirror, which occupies the right of the picture. Even more striking than the suggestions in the ecstatic but comfortable pose, and the facing mirror, that the figure is conscious of the creatures visitation, has indeed willed or conjured it, is the form of the creature itself. This time he is looking down, with shaded eyes and an ambiguous smile, into the woman's face, and unlike the almost

Henry Fuseli, *The Nightmare*. Reprinted courtesy of AKG.

comically priapic gnome of the first version, he has pointed, catlike ears.

The only significant difference in either of the other two versions is the addition, in the painting now in a private collection in Basle, of a statuette on the dressing table of a man and woman in an erotic pose, a detail which suggests Fuseli interpreting his own image as the woman's fantasy, or, conversely, adding an acknowledgement of the image's source in his own thwarted feelings. The horse, common to all these, seems not to have been present in the original drawing, which Fuseli's contemporary biographer, Knowles, says he saw in the painter's studio in St. Martin's Lane. At least one contemporary engraving does not include it. Highlighted in quickly applied white paint, and with sightless blank eyes, it may have been an after thought, but it is crucial to the success of the painting in its suggestion of violent movement, which is then suppressed in the stillness of the two main figures. The source seems to have been classical statuary; in that context it would represent passion or animal energy under control. Here the horse is riderless, unrestrained and blind. The word *nightmare* has nothing, etymologically, to do with horses, but that the spectral horse gets into the picture as wordplay, a linguistic mistake, is itself a token of the picture's dreamlike, proto-Freudian logic.

EDWARD BURNS

Bibliography

Antal, Frederick. *Fuseli Studies*. London: Routledge and Kegan Paul, 1956.

Keay, Carolyn. *Henry Fuseli*. London: Academy Editions, 1974.

Knowles, John. *The Life and Writings of Henry Fuseli M.A., R.A.* 1831.

Powell, Nicholas. *Art in Context, Fuseli: The Nightmare*. London: Penguin, 1973.

Schiff, Georg. *Johann Heinrich Fussli (1741–1825)*. Zurich: Prestel, 1972.

NOBLE SAVAGE

Along with the legend of the scholar Faust and the story of the great lover Don Juan, the myth of the noble savage is a major theme of the Romantic era. The origins of the nineteenth-century concept of the noble savage are to be found in the pre-Romantic era of the European Enlightenment, in discussions of the idealized notions of nature and the "natural" man (the savage of primitive cultures who followed natural impulse) versus culture and the "civilized" man (the European who followed social custom and opinion). The Romantic era placed a high value on nature as a spiritual entity, a kind of secularized religious sensibility. Communion with nature represented a kind of ecstatic mystical union with the divine and the uncivilized "savage" stood in closer proximity to the divine than did the individual of modern society. The belief was that more primitive peoples of the past, the ancient Greeks for example, existed in a "golden age" in harmony with nature, and were therefore more simple, childlike, and blessed, whereas civilized people of the modern era lived at odds with nature and were thus more alienated and unhappy. The noble savage is an expression of the greater notion of primitivism in Western culture, chronological primitivism being the belief that the earliest stages of human history are the best, and cultural primitivism being the belief that the achievements of "civilization" have been largely negative, that is, they have led mankind astray. The mythical archetype of this idea of a previously existing age of harmony of man and nature is to be found in almost every world culture, and in Western religious thought it goes back to the chronological primitivism of the Judeo-Christian vision of Adam and Eve in the Garden of Eden.

The Romantic myth of the noble savage is most closely associated with the writings of Jean-Jacques Rousseau. Although Rousseau had a somewhat unstable personality and harbored great resentments against the Parisian society that spurned him, his radical criticisms of European culture had important and wide-ranging social and political implications. His diatribes against modern civilization and its corrupt governments, economies, and educational systems argued for a culture that would be more in harmony with natural processes and therefore produce a more equitable and harmonious society. Wealth, luxury, the pursuit of private property, and the overly acute intellect has brought about the decline of all advanced civilizations, and Rousseau argued for a "return to nature" in order to restore mankind's more pristine state. Human beings, according to his reasoning, had fallen from their primeval spiritual harmony with nature as a result of greed and had fallen into a depraved state of materialism, thereby producing the corrupt modern state. In part as a result of Rousseau's writings and his antipathy toward urban dwellers, the Romantic era turned to an idealized vision of the peasant-pastoral lifestyle as one of simplicity, innate wisdom, and even (in William Wordsworth's time) poetic insight. In the later nineteenth and twentieth centuries, the Romantic vision of the peasant turned towards the idealization of the poor masses of the metropolitan centers. In more recently articulated feminist positions, there has been a revalorization of the "feminine" perspective as one close to that of the noble savage that also features more intuitive insight into human behavior, and a more "natural" and holistic relationship to the life force, than is to be found in the analytical and scientific views of the traditional "masculine" perspective.

A corollary to this discussion is the chronological primitivism in the important Romantic notion that the child is somehow more natural and free of sin and the adult is more devious and constrained. Rousseau argued that the child was naturally spontaneous and pure of "heart" and that the educational system corrupted its innate innocence. He called for a progressive pedagogical practice that would allow children to be treated as children and not as potential adults.

To be sure, there is in Rousseau and in the Romantic era's idealization of the noble savage-peasant-child (as being pure and closer to nature) a "darker" side, that is, an element of anti-intellectualism that privileges feeling and intuition as the sole mode of knowing reality. This antirational stance that is implicit in the Romantic posture later had dire political and social consequences in the development of twentieth-century fascism in Germany and Italy and the ultimate savagery of the world war that followed in its wake.

One interesting example of the widespread public interest in the noble savage of the Romantic era was the case of the so-called "wild boy of Aveyron." In 1799, a boy about twelve years old was found wandering alone in the forest near Aveyron, France. The boy had been abused and deprived of all contact with other humans, thus stunting any normal socialization process. Huge crowds came to Paris to see the child who had grown up free of the influence of culture and was therefore thought to be in a pristine "savage" state. Another famous case was that of the mysterious German Kaspar Hauser, found standing in the center of Nuremberg in 1828, another abused boy who had grown up in total isolation from society.

The notion of the noble savage underwent somewhat of a neo-Romantic rebirth, reinvigorated during the hippie movement of the later 1960s. Middle-class youth in a number of postindustrial Western nations rejected the postwar materialism and status consciousness of their elders and embraced a childlike innocence as well as a kind of Rousseau-like "return to nature." They abandoned bourgeois lifestyles and lived in communal settings, growing their own "natural" foods and raising children according to nontraditional educational principles. The sixties generation harbored many Romantic elements, including the interest in drugs and visionary states of consciousness and a turn toward the inwardness of Eastern mysticism, most especially in the renewed interest in the works of the German neo-Romantic author Hermann Hesse.

THOMAS F. BARRY

Bibliography

Ashcraft, Kent. *The Noble Savage: A Sixties Fantasy.* Native Son, 1999.
Cranston, Maurice William. *The Noble Savage: Jean-Jacques Rousseau, 1754–1762.* Chicago: University of Chicago Press, 1991.
Ellingson, Terry Jay. *The Myth of the Noble Savage.* Berkeley and Los Angeles: University of California Press, 2001.
McGregor, Gaile. *The Nobel Savage in the New World Garden: Towards a Syntactics of Place.* Bowling Green, Tenn.: Bowling Green State University Press, 1988.
Stelio, Cro. *The Noble Savage: Allegory of Freedom.* Wilfrid Laurier University Press, 1990.
Whelan, Robert. *Wild in Woods: The Myth of the Noble Eco-Savage.* IEA Studies on the Environment 14. Coronet, 1999.

NODIER, CHARLES 1780–1844

French short story writer

Charles Nodier was a part of the Romantic generation, but he was a writer whose importance and influence has been partially obscured by major figures such as Victor Hugo and Alphonse Marie-Louis Prat de Lamartine. Yet this son of a magistrate who presided at court trials during the Reign of Terror, and early admirer of Johann Wolfgang von Goethe's hero Werther, was the worthy representative of an aspect of the Romantic movement, illustrated also by authors such as Gérard de Nerval, who, even as they shared the general disillusionment and dissatisfaction of their contemporaries, known as the *mal du siècle*, displayed an even more pronounced and intense interest in the imagination and the world of dreams, both as an escape from the boredom or horror of everyday life, and as a means of gaining access to a higher reality. In his *contes fantastiques* (fantastic tales), Nodier sought to demonstrate that sleep was not only the most fecund state of the mind but also the most lucid; dreams, revealing to us the subconscious, allowed us better to grasp the intricacies of self, and, at the same time, penetrate mysteries of the universe not penetrable in the everyday world of appearances. Given his cultivation of the imagination, and his fascination with dreams, it is not surprising that Nodier should call to mind the Nerval of *Aurélia* (1855), and appear, in retrospect, as a precursor of the symbolists and the surrealists, not to mention Sigmund Freud and Carl Gustav Jung.

But Nodier's importance is not exhausted by reference to his passionate concern with the world of dreams. Before Hugo (born like Nodier in Besançon) began drawing the young writers of his time to his Parisian literary salon known as Le Cénacle in 1827, the learned Nodier was already promoting the Romantic ideal in literature, entertaining authors in his own salon at the Bibliothèque de l'Arsenal, where he had been named librarian in 1824, and writing literary criticism favorable to the new movement, as well as dictionaries and works on entomology and linguistics. Of the Romantic writers, none more than Hugo himself benefited from the mentoring and support of Nodier, before becoming the acknowledged leader of the Romantic legions. But Hugo would soon eclipse Nodier, and the latter would progressively retreat into the more alluring recesses of the dream, his full significance as writer and literary critic only to be recognized decades later.

While Nodier gained some notoriety with the publication in 1803 of a satire directed against Napoleon Bonaparte for which he was imprisoned, and expressed his melancholic view of life in novels like *Les Proscrits* (*The Outcasts*, 1802) and *Le Peintre de Saltzbourg* (*The Painter of Saltzburg*, 1803), it was rather with the publication of "Smarra ou les démons de la nuit" ("Smarra or The Demons of the Night," 1821) that he offered his first truly significant contribution to French literature. Influenced by the *genre frénétique* (featuring the fantastic, iconoclasm, satanism, and the macabre), that grew out of the Gothic novels and the vampirism of the early part of the century (Nodier himself collaborated in the composition of a play called *Le Vampire*, presented in Paris's Théâtre de la Porte Saint-Martin in 1820), "Smarra" is noteworthy because in it Nodier presents a nightmarish dream experience that, for all its horror, seems personal and rings true. Moreover, in the very narrative technique of the tale, Nodier seeks to create that impression of confusion, incoherence, and inconsistency that one would imagine in the case of the dreamer as narrator, the narrator recounting the circumstances of his frightening adventure not in lucid or logical terms but according to the illogic of dream sequences. Nodier's very departure from the usual pattern of vampire literature, his absorption in the dream to the detriment of "external" action, left critics and readers alike confounded.

Nodier's fascination with the genre frénétique was short-lived. After a trip to Scotland in 1821, in the course of which he met Walter Scott, Nodier wrote a short story set in that country called "Trilby ou le lutin d'Argail" ("Trilby, the Fairy of Argyle," 1822). In one sense, "Trilby" is quite different from "Smarra": the nightmarish atmosphere has disappeared, and the reader is charmed by the endearing activities of a well-meaning sprite whose pleasure it is to assist with household chores. But, in a deeper sense, Nodier's tale is a significant variation on the dream theme: Trilby incarnates the amorous fantasies of an unhappily married woman, Jeannie, as Nodier further takes the fantastic tale into the realm of the *fantastique intérieur* (internal fantastic), where the dream is explored both as a revelation of the complexities of the human psyche and as a compensatory device for contending with the sentimental disappointments of daily life.

Between "Trilby" and the next significant work to flow from Nodier's pen, there occurred in the author's life a period of considerable professional success and personal satisfaction, and then one of almost equally considerable professional frustration and personal regret. The first related to Nodier's activity as both librarian and salon host at the Arsenal, when, not yet challenged by Hugo, he could command the respect and admiration of the literati of Paris, and indulge at the same time his bibliophile's passion for books. The second, starting around 1830, was characterized by Nodier's increasing sense of loneliness and emptiness, as the literary confreres who once gravitated around him—the likes of Alfred de Musset and Alfred de Vigny—turned to Hugo, and as Nodier struggled to accept the marriage, and departure, of his beloved daughter Marie, whose presence at the Arsenal's literary gatherings had been a delight to his guests. Under these circumstances, it was not at all unexpected that Nodier's literary production should reflect his heightened desire to turn away from reality and to lose himself in that ideal existence accessible only through dream and imagination, and that the very protagonists of this literary production should be people like himself, desperate to escape from this world and favorably looked upon by the author not as madmen and madwomen but as, in his terminology, *lunatiques*, or wise people. Indeed, some of Nodier's works published just in the year 1832, like "Jean-François les Bas-bleus," "Le Songe d'or" ("The Dream of Gold"), and "La Fée aux miettes" ("The Crumb Fairy"), featured such "innocent" heroes.

The last work in this enumeration, "La Fée aux miettes," is at once Nodier's longest, most involved work and one of his finest. Here, perhaps more so than in any other of his stories, the distinction between reality and the dream, between consciousness and the subconscious, is lost: when Michel goes to the inn at Greenock and finds himself in a room with a bailiff from the Isle of Man whose outstanding characteristic is that he has the head of a Great Dane, we do not know if what is being related to us is the content of a remarkable dream or the actual stuff of reality. Whatever the case, despite the indeterminate atmosphere of the story, the blurring of the line of demarcation between what is directly experienced and what is dreamed, Nodier's tale does appear to have a specific point. Michel's eventual happy acceptance of the world of illusion, his quest for the magic mandrake, or the ideal, at the benevolent urging of the Fée aux miettes, and his eventual discovery of the mandrake in a lunatic asylum, are consistent with Nodier's conviction that wisdom is not to be found in the conventional pursuit of rationalistic and positivistic verities. Moreover, beyond the confusing shifts between what is "real" and what is "dreamed" there is, for Michel, a kind of pilgrim's progress, in that he must endure multiple trials before acceding to the wisdom of "lunacy." Viewed from this detached perspective, "La Fée aux miettes" appears to promote specific values: love, justice, and a simple openness to the pursuit of the ideal.

Nodier's effective use of the conte fantastique, which remains as one of his most enduring contributions to French literature, was not the consequence of creative fancy but rather a deliberate choice, especially after 1830. In that very year, Nodier published an article in the *Revue de Paris* entitled "Du fantastique dans la littérature" ("On the Fantastic in Literature"). In this piece, he traced the development of the fantastic in literature from the time of the Greeks up to contemporary German literature and E. T. A. Hoffmann. To the degree that this article argues for the value of the imagination in the area of literary creation, it reinforces once again the vital link between Nodier and the broad outreach of Romantic literature toward the realm of the oneiric, a link whose ramifications were unrecognized or inadequately appreciated for so long due to a superficial understanding of French Romanticism.

NORMAN ARAUJO

Biography

Born in Besançon, April 29, 1780. Enrolled in the École Centrale, 1796. Imprisoned for authorship of the satirical poem, *La Napoléone*, 1803. Married Désirée-Liberté Charve, 1808, birth of daughter Marie, 1811. Became librarian and director of *Le Télegraphe Illyrien* at Laybach, 1812. Wrote for Hugo's newspaper, *La Muse française*, 1823. Was made librarian of the Bibliothèque de l'Arsenal, 1824. Lost his post as librarian, 1830. Elected to the Académie Française, 1833. Founded the *Bulletin du bibliophile*, 1834. Died January 27, 1844.

Selected Works

Collections
Oeuvres complètes. 12 vols., 1832–1837.
Romans. 1850.
Contes. Edited, with an introduction, by Pierre-Georges Castex. Paris: Darnier, 1961.
"*La Fièvre*" *et autres contes.* Edited by Jacques-Remi Dahan, postface by Jean-Luc Steinmetz, Langres and Lille: L'Homme au Sable/ Thierry Bouchard, 1986.

Poetry
"La Napoléone." 1802.

Fiction
Les Proscrits, 1802. Revised and enlarged as *Stella, ou les Proscrits*, 1820.
Le Peintre de Saltzbourg, journal d'un cœur souffrant, 1803. Revised and enlarged, 1820.
"Smarra," 1821. Translated by Judith Landry. Sawtry: ledalis, 1993.
"Trilby, ou le lutin d'Argail. Nouvelle écossaise," 1822. Translated as *Trilby, the Fairy of Argyle* and with an introduction by Nathan Haskell Dole. Boston: Estes and Lauriat, 1895. Translated by Judith Landry. Sawtry: ledalus, 1993.

"Franciscus Columna," 1844. Translated as *Francesco Colonna: A Fanciful Tale of the Writing of the Hypnerotomachia* by Theodore Wesley Koch. Chicago: R.R. Donnelly, 1929.

Drama

Le Vampire, mélodrame en trois actes, 1820. Written with Pierre-Frédéric-Adolphe Carmouche, and Achille de Jouffroy.

Other

Dissertation sur l'usage des antennes dans les insectes, et sur l'organe de l'ouïe dans les mêmes animaux. 1798.
Mélanges de littérature et de critique. 2 vols., 1820.
Promenade de Dieppe aux montagnes d'Écosse, 1821. Translated as *Promenade from Dieppe to the Mountains of Scotland*, 1822.
Dictionnaire raisonné des onomatopées françaises, 1808. Revised and enlarged, 1828.
Vocabulaire de la langue française, extrait de la dernière édition du Dictionnaire de l'Académie, publié en 1835, 1836. Written with Paul Ackermann.

Bibliography

Castex, Pierre-Georges, ed. "Nodier et ses rêves." in *Le Conte fantastique en France de Nodier à Maupassant.* Paris: Corti, 1951.
Charles Nodier. Colloque du deuxième centenaire. Besançon, mai 1980. Paris: Les Belles Lettres, 1981.
Hamenachem, Miriam S. *Charles Nodier: Essai sur l'imagination mythique.* Paris: Nizet, 1972.
Larat, Jean. *La Tradition et l'exotisme dans l'œuvre de Charles Nodier (1780–1844). Étude sur les origines du romantisme français.* Paris: Champion, 1923.
Nelson, Hilda. *Charles Nodier.* New York: Twayne, 1972.
Nodier, sous la direction de Georges Zaragoza. Dijon: Éditions Universitaires de Dijon, 1998.
Olivier, Alfred Richard. *Charles Nodier: Pilot of Romanticism.* Syracuse, N.Y.: Syracuse University Press, 1964.
Sangsue, Daniel. *Le Récit excentrique: Gautier, de Maistre, Nerval, Nodier.* Paris: Corti, 1987.

NORWID, CYPRIAN KAMIL 1821–1883

Polish poet

The perception of Cyprian Kamil Norwid's place in Polish literature has been changing ever since the poet's death in 1883 and his "rediscovery" at the turn of the twentieth century. While his reputation has been growing steadily throughout the century, culminating in the publication of his collected works (*Pisma wszystkie*) in eleven volumes in the 1970s, literary historians are still debating particular aspects of his work, some assigning him to late Romanticism, others arguing for a more contradictory and nuanced view of his achievement.

One thing is certain: the roots of Norwid's poetry lie in Romanticism, though it is not the national or Messianistic kind of Romanticism characteristic of Adam Mickiewicz. His first poems, written in his Warsaw period (he left Poland in 1842, never to return to his native country) are on stock Romantic themes such as loneliness, deprivation, and death, but they already contain subtle psychological observations (for example the many forms of silence, varying from situation to situation) and a style replete with symbols. In the later Italian and Paris periods of his creative development, Norwid uses historical and cultural symbols with great frequency, thereby situating his poetry in a "European Greco-Christian," rather than a purely Polish, context. Since throughout his life he worked as an artist producing many drawings and paintings, and his interest in philosophy was considerable, it may be best to consider his work under the triple moniken: poet-thinker-craftsman.

The first important piece of Norwid's writing was in fact a long treatise on aesthetics in verse, *Promethidion* (1850). This poem, a result of discussions between Polish artists and art lovers, reproduces conversations in a salon about the nature of art and defines the artist's task in quasi-religious terms. Norwid sees art as "a banner of the tower of human work," assigning to creativity a very high role in society. He does not, however, wish art (or poetry) to serve any specific ideology or social movement and vehemently opposes the messianic message (the individual's duty is to sacrifice himself for the nation) with its moral ambiguity.

Work should be infused with a "spiritual content," a somewhat utopian suggestion in the mid-nineteenth century, the callous materialism of which is rejected by this indigenous but proud Polish exile.

As for his shorter poems, Norwid very rarely touches upon love. While he has a Romantic admiration for heroes, for great individuals whose sacrifice will shape history (as in "Funeral Rhapsody to Bem's Memory" and "To Citizen John Brown"), as well an ambiguous relationship with the great Polish Romantics (of whom he had full admiration only for Juliusz Słowacki), his main concern seems to be the state and future of Christian civilization. In this respect one finds in his writing "new and original motifs which transcend the horizon of Romantic thought" (according to Maria Zmigrodzka), especially in his stress on the importance of labor. His thinking on contemporary society is best reflected in the collection *Vade-mecum* (*Come With Me*), a carefully composed collection of mostly short poems which was ready by 1865 but printed in its entirety only after the poet's death. As Virgil leads Dante Alighieri through hell, so Norwid extends a hand to the reader to lead him through contemporary society, and in the best pieces of the cycle he manages to combine subtle irony with striking imagery, foreshadowing the technique of modern Symbolism. As Norwid (after a two-year episode in America) returned to Paris and lived there from 1854 to his death, he must have read Charles Baudelaire's *Les Fleurs du Mal*, though his reaction to this work was rather negative: he saw the French poet as someone who "washes his muddy boots in a clean spring." Had *Vade-mecum* been published soon after its completion, it could have changed (as Norwid expected) the course of Polish poetry; but he had a presentiment of non-recognition expressed in these lines: "the sons pass by this writing, but you, my distant grandchild, will read it . . . when I'll be no more" ("The Hands Were Swollen By Clapping . . .").

Of Norwid's longer poems, *Quidam* (1857) is a poetic tale emphasizing Christian self-sacrifice. It takes place in the Rome of the Emperor Hadrian and has some perceptive descriptions of the ancient city. *Rzecz o wolności słowa* (*A Poem About the Freedom of the Word*, 1869) is a long treatise in verse that discusses the progress of the word through the centuries from "the word of the race" to the "word of the nation" and that of "civilization." Although it was an instant success when Norwid recited this poem in a Polish scholarly society in Paris, today it reads more as versified philosophy than intellectual poetry. The most successful of Norwid's narrative poems is probably "Assunta" ("The Ascended One," finished around 1879), the tale of the poet's love for a mute woman who is much idealized and yet real, but who suddenly dies. The background to this poem written in *ottava rima* is Norwid's short love affair with Zofia Węgierska, whose premature death plunged him into deep depression. "Assunta" reflects Norwid's ideal of Christian love, which was so rarely embodied in his lifetime.

Cyprian Norwid also tried his hand as a playwright, though his very first attempt in this field, *Zwolon* (1848), was a failure. It was followed by two mystery plays, *Krakus* and *Wanda* (about two figures of Polish mythology), which are interesting from a technical point of view, Norwid attempting in one of them the Polish hexameter. It was, however, with three social comedies, plays in verse, that the poet found his real genre within the theater: *Aktor* (*Actor*), *Za kulisami* (*Behind the Scenes*), and *Pierścień Wielkiej Damy* (*The Ring of a Grand Lady*) are about different aspects of Polish society in the middle of the nineteenth century. The first of these is the story of the transformation of Count Jerzy, who had lost his fortune in a financial crash, from art-loving aristocrat into an actor playing William Shakespeare; the second, which takes place in the vestibule of a Warsaw theater, is about both real and social playacting. *Pierścień Wielkiej Damy* is, in a theatrical sense, the most accomplished of all Norwid's plays, with an interesting plot and characters from different social milieus—it is an ironical commentary on the impossibility of bridging social distance even through the hallowed Romantic device of "unselfish love." It remains to this day Norwid's most frequently performed play.

Norwid wrote both narrative and discursive prose, that is, short stories and essays. He was suspicious about the novel, a relatively new genre in Polish literature, and even his narrative prose has strong autobiographical connections. The best of these are *Czarne kwiaty* (*Black Flowers*, 1856) and *Białe kwiaty* (*White Flowers*, 1857). *Czarne kwiaty* is a collection of impressionistic sketches about the death or impending death of artists and poets close to Norwid, such as Chopin, Mickiewicz, and Słowacki. It is written in a somewhat melancholic, poetic style, focusing on certain expressions or gestures of people who are to depart from this world. *Białe kwiaty* is more essayistic, though it is also based on memories: here Norwid illustrates the different kinds of silence experienced during his travels, including the deep silence of the ocean during a wintry passage to America. Many years later, in the essay "Milczenie" ("Silence"), Norwid expounded his rather modern theory of "meaningful silence" as an important part of the literary work, but *Białe kwiaty* is also interesting for the subtlety of its psychological observations.

Toward the end of his life Norwid wrote several short stories that, for all their symbolism, show his skill in this increasingly popular genre. "Stygmat" ("Stigma"), "Tajemnica Lorda Singelworth" ("Lord Singelworth's Secret"), and "Ad leones!" ("To the Lions!"), all written in 1882 and 1883, reflect his distaste for a society in which money rules supreme and where the artist has to prostitute himself if he wants to escape starvation. This is particularly true of "Ad leones!" which takes place in Rome, where a sculptor is at work on a group of Christians thrown to the lions at the time of the Emperor Domitian. He is eventually persuaded by an American journalist to alter his work according to the taste of the consumer, so that it should represent an apotheosis of Free Enterprise, that is, capitalism. This sadly ironical story ranks equal to Norwid's best poems.

Norwid also wrote a number of perceptive essays on art, among them "O sztuce: dla Polaków" ("About Art: For Poles") but his aesthetic views were best encapsulated in a series of lectures on Juliusz Słowacki given in 1860, as well as in his long poem about Frédéric Chopin, "Fortepian Szopena" ("Chopin's Piano"). In the former he defined the poet's task as "to bear witness to truth" and in this context he extolled the achievement of Lord Byron, a great role model for many European Romantics. Norwid believes that "Byron was more religious than his Church and his age . . ." and that by his death at Missolonghi Byron ended the epoch of Romanticism. Słowacki is rated highly among the Polish Romantics, though mostly for his unparalleled mastery of the language. Norwid, in these lectures, makes it clear that the post-Romantic age calls for a different kind of poetry: it should not so much delight the reader as make them think about the most important national and individual issues. The new role for the poet is not that of a *wieszcz*, but of an apostle.

For the most admired Polish artist of his age, Norwid names Chopin, but even Chopin has imperfections, for no human being can create anything truly perfect. Chopin's piano was destroyed by the Cossacks in 1863 when they ransacked the Zamoyski Palace in Warsaw. This act is interpreted symbolically in "Chopin's Piano" which ends with the enigmatic lines: "Distant grandson, rejoice! / The dumb stones—groaned aloud: / The ideal has reached the pavement—." This poem, which is number ninety-nine in the *Vade-mecum* cycle, also shows Norwid's technical virtuosity; the poem is written in rhyming free verse with frequent changes of rhythm and it includes, apart from numerous cultural allusions, impressionistic reflections on Chopin's music. It is not a poem to be learned by heart, but its complex use of images and metaphors heralded symbolism, which in the second half of the nineteenth century became the leading trend in European poetry.

GEORGE GÖMÖRI

Biography

Born September 24, 1821 in Laskowo-Gluchy near Warsaw, Poland. Went to school in Warsaw, then studied art in a private art school for a year (1837–38). His first poem, "My Last Sonnet," was printed in a Warsaw journal in 1840. In 1841 and 1842 he published more poetry and visited Warsaw salons where he made the acquaintance of the philosopher August Cieszkowski. In September 1842, left Poland for studies abroad. Between 1843 and 1845 he lived in Florence and Rome, also visiting Naples. In 1845, met Maria Kalergis, the great unrequited love of his life. In the same year Norwid visited a friend in Silesia and there he gave away his passport to a Polish deserter from the Russian Army. When the deserter turned up in Paris, a warrant was issued to arrest Norwid and in 1846 he was arrested in Berlin. Spent only a few weeks in jail, but that was enough to undermine his health. After his release he went to Brussels, where he established contact with emigré circles. In 1847–48 lived in Rome, earning a living as an artist. He met Zygmunt Krasinski and in the spring of 1848 clashed with Adam Mickiewicz in Rome, objecting to the older poet's "Towianism." His move from Rome to Paris in 1849 was followed by the publication of some of his longer poems (such as *Pieśń społeczna* in Poznan). In Paris he moved both in Polish and cosmopolitan circles (such as Emma Herwegh's salon) and met Jules Michelet. Published *Promethidion* in 1850; it was received with hostility. His worsening financial situation and final break with Maria Kalergis forced him to emigrate via England to the United States, where he lived for a year and a half (1853–54), working—among other things—as an artist for the memorial album of the Universal Exhibition. In June 1854 he returned on a boat to France, again via London. In Paris he wrote and published the two prose pieces, *Czarne kwiaty* and *Białe kwiaty*, and also started working on *Quidam*. In 1860 he gave a successful series of six lectures on Juliusz Słowacki in Polish, it was published in Paris in 1861. In the next year Brockhaus in Leipzig published a collection of his poetry entitled *Poezje* (*Poems*), but the publication of *Vade-mecum* was indefinitely postponed on account of the Prussian-Austrian War of 1866–67. He fell in love with Zofia Węgierska in 1869, but she died soon afterward; he wrote *Assunta*. During the Franco-Prussian war he was starving and his health deteriorated. As his efforts to raise funds for a move to Italy failed, in 1877 he was forced to move to the Saint Casimir Asylum for Polish veterans in Ivry. It is there that he wrote his last stories which remained unpublished. Norwid died on May 23, 1883, was first buried in Ivry, but in 1888 his remains were transferred to the Polish cemetery in Montmorency.

Selected Works

Collections

Pisma zebrane. Vols. A (Parts 1–2), C, E, 1911–13. Vol. F, edited by Zenon Przesmycki, 1946. (Vols. B, D, G and H were never published).

Wszystkie pisma Cypriana Norwida po dziś w całości lub fragmentach odszukane. Vols 3–9. Edited by Zenon Przesmycki, 1937–39.

Pisma polityczne i filozoficzne. Edited by Zbigniew Zaniewicki, 1957.

Vade-mecum. 2d, corrected, ed. Edited by Juliusz W. Gomulicki, 1969.

Dzieła zebrane. 2 vols. Edited by Juliusz W. Gomulicki, 1966.

Pisma wszystkie. 11 vols. Edited by Juliusz W. Gomulicki, 1971–76.

"Chopin's Piano," translated by Keith Bosley, *Comparative Criticism* 6 (1984): 308–12.

Poezje/Poems. Edited and translated by Adam Czerniawski, 1986.

Poems, Letters, Drawings. Edited and translated by Jerzy Peterkiewicz, 2000.

Bibliography

Borowy, Waclaw. *O Norwidzie*. Warsaw: PIW, 1960.

Czerniawski, Adam. *Cyprian Kamil Norwid: Poezje-Poems*. Bilingual ed. Cracow: Wydawnictwo Literackie, 1984.

Gomulicki, Juliusz W., and Jan Zygmunt Jakubowski, eds. *Nowe studia o Norwidzie*. Warsaw: PWN, 1961.

Gömöri, George. *Cyprian Norwid*. New York: Twayne, 1974.

Gömöri, George, and Boleslaw Mazur, eds. *Cyprian Norwid (1821–1883): Poet-Thinker-Craftsman. A Centennial Conference*. London: Orbis, 1988.

Lapinski, Zdzislaw. *Norwid*. Cracow: Znak, 1971.

Miłosz, Czeslaw. *The History of Polish Literature*. London: Collier-Macmillan, 1969.

Trojanowicz, Zofia. *Rzecz o mlodosci Norwida*. Poznan: Wyd Poznanskie, 1968.

Trybus, Krzysztof. *Epopeja w tworczosci Cypriana Norwida*. Wroclaw: Ossolineum, 1993.

Wyka, Kazimierz. *Cyprian Norwid, poeta i sztukmistrz*. Cracaw: Polska Akademia Umiejetnosci, 1948.

NOTRE-DAME DE PARIS (THE HUNCHBACK OF NOTRE DAME) 1831

Novel by Victor Hugo

After writing a gothic novel (or *roman noir*), *Han d'Islande* (*Hans of Iceland*, 1823), and an adventure novel set in exotic Saint Domingo, *Bug Jargal* (*The Slave King*, 1826), Victor Hugo next exploited the then-current renewal of enthusiasm among young Romantic writers for the Middle Ages by writing his popular historical novel *Notre-Dame de Paris*. In 1828, he visited Notre Dame many times, along with Sculptor David d'Angers, painter Eugène Delacroix, and writer Charles Nodier, in whose apartment at the Bibliothèque de l'Arsenal young writers, artists, and musicians formed the Cénacle to develop the doctrines of the new movement. Hugo also became friendly with an eccentric priest, l'Abbé Oegger, who encouraged his interest in the symbolism of the cathedral's many architectural features and hagiographic figures.

But Hugo's principal influence in his new novel was literary: Walter Scott's historical novels were as popular in translation in France as in England and Hugo, who in 1823 had complimented Scott on his representation, in *Quentin Durward*, of Louis XI

(the "Spider King," notorious in the popular imagination for his cruelty and cunning), was to make the same monarch responsible for the execution of Esmeralda in his own first historical novel. After reading Scott, Hugo also conceived the idea of using the historical novel to re-create a whole medieval world, thus transposing from the spatial to the temporal dimension the Romantic notion of *couleur locale* (local color). To do so required an imaginative reconstruction of medieval Paris, both topographical and psychological. It involved creating character types to personify beggars, bourgeoisie, nobles, and clergy, giving them motivations that would contribute to Quasimodo's tragedy, played out in Notre Dame. But, as in Scott's novels also, historical reconstruction must not reduce the excitement engendered by a dramatic plot, engineered out of a series of confrontations between warring opposites: the mob against the hunchback, the king against the poet Gringoire, Esmeralda at the mercy of her torturers, and the public executioner, her lover Phoebus, knifed by Claude Frollo, and so on.

The novel's dramatic structure may be seen from the plot. In 1482, on the Feast of Fools, Gringoire's mystery play is performed in Paris's Palais de Justice. Claude Frollo, an archdeacon at Notre Dame who is obsessed with Esmeralda, a gypsy dancing girl, orders Quasimodo, the cathedral's bell ringer, to kidnap her. Captain Phoebus de Chateaupers saves her from the ambush. Gringoire, who has accidentally wandered into the Court of Miracles, domain of the thieves of Paris, is saved from hanging by Esmeralda, who agrees to marry him. She also brings water to Quasimodo, parched after his flogging at the public pillory. Jealous of Phoebus, Frollo stabs him and allows Esmeralda to be accused of the crime. She is then condemned to death for witchcraft and murder and forced to make public repentance at Notre Dame, where a grateful Quasimodo saves her by carrying her to sanctuary in the cathedral. The Parisian mob tries to free her by attacking Notre Dame, but Quasimodo thwarts them. Frollo, to spite her for her rejection of him, hands her over to a madwoman for punishment. She, however, recognizes Esmeralda as her lost daughter, kidnapped as a child by gypsies, and unsuccessfully tries to save her from execution by the king's soldiers. From the turrets of Notre Dame, Frollo watches her death and laughs. Quasimodo throws him off the turret and then dies in his turn, starving to death by the side of Esmeralda's corpse in the charnel-house at Montfaucon.

Hugo's emotionally charged retelling for a popular audience of the fairy tale "Beauty and the Beast" added to it descriptive and discursive elements that make of his novel one of the primary influences on France's gothic revival. *Notre-Dame de Paris* contains, as well as an exciting plot, a number of chapters urging Hugo's fellow citizens to undertake the defense and protection of the French medieval monuments that, in 1830, stood in danger of ruin through official neglect over centuries. The long chapter "A Bird's-Eye View of Paris" reconstructs the medieval city by presenting detailed descriptions of its Gothic monuments and topography, as seen from the towers of Notre Dame. Medieval Paris in the novel thus becomes the *chronique de pierre* (chronicle in stone), consisting of the city on its island in the Seine with the Sorbonne on the left bank and, on the right, the royal palace and dungeons of the Louvre, as well as the place of execution, the "place de Grève," where Esmeralda will be hanged. Its streets are frequented by the mendicants from the Court of Miracles, ironically so called because there, at the end of their day's begging, cripples, the blind, and the maimed miraculously transform themselves into healthy drinkers and lusty lovers. All combine in Hugo's descriptions to present an imaginative, albeit romantically distorted, view of medieval Paris.

Equally detailed, the many long passages devoted to the cathedral's architecture insist upon the religious symbolism of its iconography as a *bible de pierre* (bible in stone). In the chapter entitled "This will kill That," Hugo's narrator suspends the action to speak at length about the future of the church and mon-

archy in France, alluding indirectly to the execution of Louis XVI in 1793. Having set the hunchback's story in 1482, just ten years before Columbus's discovery of the New World, which may be said to have brought the Middle Ages to an end, Hugo also predicts that the invention of printing would bring to an end the church's virtual monopoly on popular education through its sermons, both verbal and as expressed in the stones of its cathedrals. In celebrating this new freedom of expression, Hugo probably has in mind his own problems with the censorship and public condemnation of his works in his own time. (The Catholic Church placed *Notre-Dame de Paris* on its index of condemned books in 1834 and, when the libretto of the opera that Hugo drew from the novel (with music by Louise Bertin), went to the French censor in January 1836, a change of title, *La Esmeralda*, was imposed, as was, throughout, the removal of the word "priest".)

Always didactic, Hugo's novels survive nowadays only in truncated form in their various abridgments and adaptations: films, plays, musicals, and cartoons by Disney and others reduce to a minimum their historical and philosophical underpinnings to concentrate on the pathetic hunchback's hopeless love for the heroine, thus returning them to their source in popular folklore.

ALBERT W. HALSALL

See also **Fiction: France; Hugo, Victor-Marie**

Text

Notre-Dame de Paris—1482, 1831; 8th edition, 1832. Including three extra chapters said to have been "lost" in 1831. Translated as *The Hunchback of Notre-Dame* by Frederic Shoberl, 1833. Translated as *Notre Dame: A Tale of the Ancient Regime*, by William Hazlitt the Younger, 1833. Translated as *Notre-Dame de Paris* by Alban Krailsheimer. Oxford: Oxford University Press, 1993.

Bibliography
Brombert, Victor. *Victor Hugo and the Visionary Novel.* Cambridge, Mass.: Harvard University Press, 1984.

Grant, Richard. B. *The Perilous Quest: Image, Myth and Prophecy in the Narratives of Victor Hugo.* Durham, N.C.: Duke University Press, 1968.

Halsall, Albert, W. *Victor Hugo et l'art de convaincre. Le récit hugolien: rhétorique, argumentation, persuasion.* Montréal: Éditions Balzac, 1995.

Leuilliot, Bernard. "Ceci tuera cela: le roman et le paradoxe littéraire," *Littérature* 36 (1979): 3–18.

Lukacs, Gyoergy. *The Historical Novel.* Translated from the German by Hannah and Stanley Mitchell. Harmondsworth, England: Penguin, 1969.

Robb, Graham. *Victor Hugo.* London: Picador, 1997.

Zumthor, Paul. "Le Moyen âge de Victor Hugo." In *Victor Hugo. Oeuvres complètes.* vol. 4. General editor, Jean Massin. Paris: Le Club français du livre, 1966–71.

NOVALIS (FRIEDRICH VON HARDENBERG) 1772–1801

German poet

Georg Philipp Friedrich von Hardenberg, the most famous and influential poet-philosopher of the early Romantic era, was born into a family of noble lineage, which in the seventeenth century had moved from Lower Saxony to settle in Thuringia. He was related to the famous Prussian reformer Karl August von Hardenberg. In 1798 the poet adopted the nom de plume Novalis, meaning "virgin land," a name partly referring to his family background, and partly as a symbol of his novel approach to poetry. Novalis's childhood was profoundly marked by the family's pietist background and his father's association with the Herrenhut brotherhood, a pietistic movement founded by Count Zinzendorf. His language of pietism, in particular the water metaphors and an often mystical vocabulary, are indebted to this family influence. His early writings were influenced by key thinkers of the late Enlightenment (Johann Gottfried von Herder, Christoph Martin Wieland) and of the sentimental period (Johann Georg Jacobi, Friedrich Gottlieb Klopstock, and the Hainbund, a loosely associated circle of Göttingen writers formed in 1772 and opposed to French neo-Classicism). From 1790 to 1792 Novalis studied law at the university at Jena, where he met Johann Christoph Friedrich von Schiller and was introduced to Kantian philosophy. During subsequent studies in Leipzig and Wittenberg, he formed a friendship with Friedrich von Schlegel, who became crucial to his later work. He embarked on a career as an administrator and, at this time, met thirteen-year-old Sophie von Kühn, to whom he became engaged. He was profoundly moved by her death in 1797 and this experience was the key to his interest in transcendental philosophy. Scholarship in the nineteenth century tended to sentimentalize this loss, often failing to recognize that Novalis transformed personal tragedy into philosophy and poetry. In 1798 he studied geology under Abraham Gottlob Werner, a leading representative of Neptunism (the theory that all elements have originated from a liquid state). Novalis had a profound impact on the early Romantic school, which in turn interpreted his work in a sentimentalized manner, extolling the blue flower as his symbol of otherworldliness. French symbolists and twentieth-century writers such as Hermann Hesse, Hugo von Hofmannsthal, Thomas Mann, and Robert von Musil, were also deeply indebted to his work.

The philosopher Novalis was not fully appreciated until the 1960s, when for the first time a critical edition of his works assembled his fragments in strictly chronological order. The main influence on Novalis was Johann Gottlieb Fichte's transcendental philosophy, later complemented by Friedrich Wilhelm Joseph von Schelling's philosophy of nature and by Frans Hemsterhuis's neo-Platonic philosophy of dematerialization, which particularly influenced his concept of an *organ moral*, reflecting the universe within man. During his later friendship with Ludwig Tieck (1799), Novalis was introduced to the cosmogony of the seventeenth-century mystic Jakob Böhme. The foundation of Novalis' philosophy is indebted to Fichte's epistemology, especially to the reflective interrelationship of ego and nonego, whereby the former determines the latter, ultimately transforming it into perpetual action. Novalis's own concept of the imagination is also based on Fichte, leading to the "romanti-

cizing of the world," a process wherein all aspects of the universe become identified with the subject, and are thereby refined and ennobled *ad infinitum*. Novalis's understanding of "encyclopedistics" is a variation on this attempt to romanticize the world, embracing ideas from Werner's mineralogy as well as Johann Wilhelm Ritter's galvanic electricity. Prompted by Jean Le Rond d'Alembert's rationalist classification, *encyclopedistics* rather seeks to overcome all opposites and divisions, uniting all elements and perceptions into a cosmic totality, to create a mystical union or *Totalwissenschaft*. The essentially infinite openness of this operation is reflected in Novalis's use of the fragment, or aphoristic "seedcorn," yet to reach its full potential. Related both to his "encyclopedistics" and his philosophy of the imagination is his concept of death. Through death, man overcomes the "egoism" of individual existence, philosophically conceived as transcendence of the *principium individuationis* to seek the "universality of the subject." In this respect love and poetry achieve similar results; they also dissolve individuality and become "magic events." Even illness comes within this sphere, where the influence of John Brown and his theory of increased sensitivity is of importance. It also influenced Novalis's concept of the poet as a mediator who, through sympathetic imagination, can redeem nature and elevate it to a higher power.

References here will be confined to Novalis's lesser works, not mentioned elsewhere in this volume. The fragmentary novel *Lehrlinge zu Sais* (*The Apprentices at Sais*, 1798) is essentially a dialogue between the master and his apprentices, on nature and man's relationship to the organic and inorganic world. Novalis employs here the "magic wand of allegory": man and nature

Eduard Eichens, *Novalis.* Reprinted courtesy of Bildarchev.

become interwoven, man is perceived as the "Messiah of nature" who also gains absolute knowledge from a total understanding of himself. Next to the "Hyazinth and Rosenblüth" fairytale, the myth of the goddess of Sais is of central importance. Novalis responds here to Schiller's poem "Das verschleier Bild zu Sais" ("The Goddess of Sais," 1788) by transforming its Kantian message that man cannot attain absolute knowledge. Schiller's hero is destroyed by this experience, whereas Novalis presents a different solution in the distich: "One person succeeded, he lifted the veil of the goddess of Sais. But what did he see? . . . wonder of wonders—he saw himself." Most controversial among Novalis's works was his essay on "Christianity or Europe." Written in the autumn of 1799 under the influence of Friedrich Daniel Ernst Schleiermacher's *Über die Religion, Reden an die Gebildeten unter ihren Verächtern* (*Speeches on Religion*, 1799), it sought to give a chiliastic (that is, referring to the doctrine that states Jesus Christ will reign on earth for a period of a thousand years) quality to the Romantic formula of the golden age, in which the Middle Ages as well as other mythological utopias could find their expression. Originally conceived as a speech rather than an essay, its first reading to the Jena circle resulted in an overwhelmingly negative response and it was rejected for publication in the *Athenäum*. Read as a political statement, it repelled his contemporaries with its exceeding Catholicism, its conservative antirationalism, and its unhistorical nature. Modern critics have interpreted it in a different light, recognizing its dialogical nature, its poetological attempt to unite all aspects of life: in short, that it was conceived as an essay on "romanticization." Chronologically, this essay should be considered alongside a cycle of fifteen religious poems, *Geistliche Lieder* (*Spiritual Songs*, 1799). Although not conceived by Novalis in their present cyclical form, they express his very personal understanding of Christianity as the antecedent to a more cosmopolitan world religion. They celebrate the poetic penetration and ennoblement of religion in a highly individualistic and nonconformist nature, falling, like the totality of his work, outside a clearly defined Christian worldview. Some of the poems have been set to music by Frederick Loewe, Franz Peter Schubert, and others.

HANS-JOACHIM HAHN

Biography

Born May 2, 1772 at Oberwiederstedt, Thuringia. First poems, University of Jena, 1788. University of Leipzig, friendship with Friedrich von Schlegel, 1791–92. Administrator at Tennstedt, 1793, friendship with Sophie von Kühn, followed by engagement, 1795, acquaintance that year with Fichte, followed by extensive studies of Fichte's philosophy. Death of Sophie and of his brother Erasmus, 1797, began training in mineralogy at Freiberg, met A. G. Werner. In 1798, publication of *Blütenstaub* fragments and of *Glauben und Liebe*; undertook scientific studies; engagement to Julie von Charpentier. Friendship with Tieck and studies of Schleiermacher, 1799, wrote "Die Christenheit oder Europa," appointed assessor at salt mines at Weißenfels that same year. Completion and publication of *Hymnen an die Nacht* and ends work on the fragmentary manuscript of *Heinrich von Ofterdingen*, 1800. March 25, 1801; died of tuberculosis.

Selected Works

Critical edition

Novalis Schriften: Die Werke Friedrich von Hardenbergs. Edited by Paul Kluckhohn and Richard Samuel, in cooperation with Hans-Joachim Mähl and Gerhard Schulz. 5 vols. 3rd ed. Stuttgart: Kohlhammer, 1977ff.

Translations

Sacred Songs and other Publications. Translated by Eileen Hutchins. Aberdeen: Selma, 1956.
Henry von Ofterdingen. Translated by Palmer Hilty. New York: F. Ungar, 1990.
Hymns to the Night; Spiritual Songs. Translated by George MacDonald. London: Temple Lodge, 1992.

Bibliography

Hiebel, Friedrich. *Novalis: German Poet, European Thinker, Christian Mystic*. 2d ed. Chapel Hill: University of North Carolina Press, 1959.
Neubauer, John. *Novalis*. Boston: Twayne, 1980.
O'Brien, William Arctander. *Novalis: Signs of Revolution*. Durham, N.C.: Duke University Press, 1995.
Saul, Nicholas. *History and Poetry in Novalis and in the Tradition of the German Enlightenment*. London: Institute of Germanic Studies, University of London, and Atlantic Highlands: N.J.: Humanities Press, 1991.
Uerlings, Herbert. *Friedrich von Hardenberg, genannt Novalis, Werk und Forschung*. Stuttgart: Metzler, 1991.

O

OEHLENSCHLÄGER, ADAM GOTTLOB 1779–1850

Danish writer

In 1829, in Lund Cathedral, the Swedish bard Esaias Tegnér bestowed the title of "King of Nordic Poetry" upon Adam Gottlob Oehlenschläger, an epithet that reflects the Dane's undisputed status as Denmark's greatest Romantic poet. With the seminal poem *Guldhornene* (*The Golden Horns*, 1803), the comedy *Aladdin* (1805), the tragedy *Hakon Jarl* (*Hakon Jarl, A Tragedy*, 1808), and a handful of other outstanding works, Oehlenschläger imbued the Danish language with a new lyrical sensuousness and the Danish nation with a new sense of its history.

Oehlenschläger's career spanned, almost exactly, the first half of the nineteenth century, and scarcely a year of this tumultuous period of Danish history passed without some new piece of work from his pen. From the military and financial *Ragnarok* (Norse apocalypse) of the Napoleonic Wars came a new "golden age" of Danish art and literature, which Oehlenschläger, aptly, inaugurated with his *Guldhornene*, in his first published collection *Digte* (*Poems*, 1803).

The legend attached to this poem attributes its inspiration to a sixteen-hour conversation with the Norwegian scientist and natural philosopher Henrik Steffens one summer evening in 1802, in the course of which Oehlenschläger was converted to the ideas of the German new (that is, Romantic) school. *Guldhornene* is the lyrical interpretation of an actual historical event: the finding and mysterious disappearance of a pair of ancient golden artefacts, gifted to modern Danes by some universal spirit as a symbol of the unity of the Nordic past with the national present, but stolen away again when men failed to appreciate the horns for more than their material worth.

The influence of German Romanticism can be traced in other aspects of the young Oehlenschläger's work. He was preeminent among Danish poets as an exponent of the *Romanze*, a popular genre that owes much to the German *kunstballade*. Moreover, his first collections display an astonishing talent for that alchemic juxtaposition of metric forms, genres, and themes recommended by Friedrich von Schlegel, perhaps most notably in the dialogic play of *Sanct Hansaften-Spil* (*Midsummer's Night Play*, 1803, in *Digte*) and in *Aladdin*.

The latter drama is generally lauded as the greatest achievement of Danish universal Romanticism. It is a joyous adaptation of the well-known story from *The 1001 Nights*, innovative in terms of language and verse forms, switching between the exotic and the everyday. This Aladdin, like Oehlenschläger, is a *lykkebarn* (fortune's child), privy to the mysteries of nature.

Oehlenschläger found the writings of Immanuel Kant, Johann Gottlieb Fichte, and Friedrich Wilhelm Joseph von Schelling, which he had tackled while a student, emotionally rather than intellectually stimulating. By the end of his *dannelsesrejse* (formative tour) of Europe between 1805 and 1809—during which he met Johann Wolfgang von Goethe, the brothers August Wilhelm and Friedrich von Schlegel, Madame Anne-Louise-Germaine de Staël, and Ludwig Tieck—a new orientation toward a more bourgeois idealism is in evidence in his writings: essentially, the shift was from universal to national Romanticism, as is apparent in the collection *Nordiske Digte* (*Nordic Poems*, 1807).

The very title of this collection of 1807 makes plain the significance Oehlenschläger attached to the Nordic mythological legacy. This was not a new obsession. As early as 1800, as a young law student, Oehlenschläger wrote the prize-winning essay in a competition organized by the University of Copenhagen, on the subject "Would it be advantageous for the literature of the North, if the ancient Nordic mythology were introduced and widely employed, instead of the Greek?" Oehlenschläger's tightly argued answer is a resounding yes: to his Nordic ancestors he attributes nobility, strength, and an intimate relationship to nature, qualities that imbue the myths of this neglected period, which could be tapped and used as fresh material to awaken the national spirit. Although his grasp of the Old Norse language seems not to have been especially sound, Oehlenschläger drew directly from Old Norse poetry in a few of his early works, while *Nordens Guder* (*The Gods of the North*, 1819) effectively constitutes his own version of the *Elder Edda*.

Oehlenschläger strove to interpret Nordic history in the light of his "romantic awareness" of a universal order, of which the old Nordic culture had been a valid expression. The story of the struggle between the heathen Earl Hakon and the Christian Olaf Tryggvason for dominion over Norway forms the basis of Oehlenschläger's first great "national" tragedy, *Hakon Jarl*. The eponymous tragic hero, as corrupt as his belief system, is vanquished as history dictates, but Hakon's complex character elicits the sympathy of the audience. This characterological complexity has been criticized as inimical to the success of Oehlenschläger's dramas as tragedies in the classical sense. His tragedies also demanded dramatic techniques that were beyond most Danish actors, and provincial audiences, of the time. However, *Hakon Jarl* was roundly praised by none other than Goethe.

Of Oehlenschläger's later dramas, mention should be made of the one-act tragedy *Yrsa* (in *Helge*, 1814). In the best tradition of "universal poetry," *Yrsa* forms a trilogy, together with the prose text *Hroars Saga* (*The Saga of Hroar*, 1817) and the epic poem *Hrolf Krake* (*Hrolf Krake*, 1828).

Nevertheless, Oehlenschläger's contemporaries and modern scholars are united in their assessment that his dramatic output deteriorated markedly in quality from the early 1810s onward. The poet Jens Baggesen's declarations on this issue ignited a literary feud that smoldered for most of the decade (Johan Ludvig Heiberg eventually took over the torch of opposition) and opened a rift between two schools of thought in Danish literature for the next thirty years.

Oehlenschläger's popular and critical breakthrough in Germany came with *Corregio* (1811), a tragedy written in German and recounting the life and unrecognized genius of an Italian artist. He also corresponded, at length, with Sir Walter Scott in 1823 regarding his own attempt at the fashionable genre of the decade, the novel *Øen i Sydhavet* (*The South-Sea Island*, 1824–25).

Adam Oehlenschläger's acknowledged ability to move in the vanguard of literary fashion did not blind his younger critics to the patchy quality of his later works, his increasing recourse to sentimentality, and his lack of irony; but his youthful works of genius continue to enjoy canonical status in Denmark. Aside from these, his most enduring legacy is, arguably, the national anthem he wrote in 1819, "Der er et yndigt land" ("There is a Charming Land"), a song that has firmly established the national Romantic vision of the topography and history of Denmark in the imagination of generations of Danes.

CATHERINE CLAIRE THOMSON

Biography

Born Adam Øhlenslaeger, Vesterbro, Copenhagen, in 1779. Had a short and unsuccessful acting career 1797–99, then took his graduation exam in 1800, financed by H. C. Ørsted, followed by studies in law at the University of Copenhagen. Changed name to Oehlenschläger in 1805. Traveled in Europe 1805–9: in Halle (1805), Paris (1806–8), Switzerland and Italy (1808–9). Appointed professor of aesthetics at University of Copenhagen 1809, and married Christiane Heger the next year. Died 1850 from a liver abscess.

Selected Works

Digte. 1803.
Poetiske Skrifter. 1805.
Nordiske Digte. 1807.
Aladdin, eller Den Forunderlige Lampe, 1808. Translated as *Aladdin, or the Wonderful Lamp, a Play* by Henry Meyer. 1968.
Hakon Jarl. Et Sørgespil. 1808–9.
Palnatoke. Et Sørgespil. 1809.
Axel og Valborg: Et Sørgespil. 1810.
Corregio: Tragedie i Fem Akter. 1811.
Helge: Et Digt. 1814.
Hroars Saga. 1817.
Nordens Guder: Et episk Digt. 1819.
Samlede Digte. 3 vols. 1823.
Øen i Sydhavet. 4 vols. 1824–25.
Hrolf Krake. Et Heltedigt. 1828.
Selections in *A Book of Danish Ballads*. Selected and annotated by Axel Olrik, *The Golden Horns* (from *Digte*, 1803), and "There is a Charming Land" (from *Samlede Digte*, 1823), translated by Robert Silliman Hillyer. 1939.

Bibliography

Andersen, Vilhelm. *Adam Oehlenschläger*, 3 vols. Copenhagen: Det Nordiske Forlag, 1899–1900.
Ingwersen, Niels. "The Tragic Moment in Adam Oehlenschläger's 'Hakon Jarl hin Rige,'" *Scandinavica* 9, no. 1 (1970): 34–44.
Mitchell, P. M. *A History of Danish Literature*. Copenhagen: Gyldendal, 1957.
Rossel, Sven, ed. *A History of Danish Literature*. Lincoln: University of Nebraska Press, 1992.
Steffens, Henrich. *Indledning til filosofiske Forelæsninger*. Det danske sprog- og litteraturselskab. Copenhagen: C. A. Reitzel, 1996.

OERSTED, HANS CHRISTIAN 1777–1851

Danish scientist

Hans Christian Oersted was born August 14, 1777, in Langeland, Denmark; he died March 9, 1851, in Copenhagen. His father, Soeren Christian Oersted, was a pharmacist and could only offer him and his younger brother Anders Sandoe Oersted (who eventually would become president of Denmark), a modest education. In 1794 Oersted, who had served since age eleven as an assistant in his father's pharmacy, began studying astronomy, physics, chemistry, mathematics, and pharmacy. In 1797 he received a degree in pharmacy; he also won a golden medal for his response to the exam topic on the difference between poetry and prose. Based on his dissertation *Dissertatio de forma metaphysices elementaris naturae externae*, he received his doctorate in 1799. In the same year he published a book on metaphysics, which was clearly influenced by the philosophy of Immanuel Kant.

For a short period of time, Oersted ran a pharmacy while also delivering lectures on topics in chemistry and natural philosophy. During this period he made the acquaintance of the physicist and natural philosopher Henrik Steffens, who would prove to be both an admirer and an influence. In 1801, while traveling, he also made the acquaintance of the philosophers Johann Gottlieb Fichte and Friedrich Wilhelm Joseph von Schelling, the physicist Johann Wilhelm Ritter, and the scholars and critics August Wilhelm von Schlegel and Friedrich von Schlegel.

Oersted returned to Copenhagen in 1804, where he continued to deliver lectures on physics, at this point receiving payment for them. Eventually, these lectures earned him a professorship in physics. Oersted continued his travels, visiting Germany, England, and France in 1812–13, 1822–23, and 1849.

His private and public lectures, delivered over the course of the next four decades, were greatly admired and well received. In an 1820 lecture, he famously announced his discovery of the influence of electricity on magnetism. Oersted founded the Danish Society for the Diffusion of Scientific Knowledge in 1824 and assisted in the founding of the Magnetic Observatory and the Polytechnic Institute in Copenhagen; he was named the first director of the Institute in 1829. He also served as rector of the University of Copenhagen (in 1825 and again in 1850).

Throughout his career, Oersted was honored with memberships in various scientific academies in recognition of his achievements. For his discovery of electromagnetism, the Royal Society of London awarded him the Copley Medal. The discovery of electromagnetism (published in Latin in 1820 as *Experimenta circa effectum conflictus electrici in acum magneticam* and eventually translated into many languages) was the result of his theory that magnetic effects are produced by the same forces that create electricity. This theory was rooted in Oersted's adherence to the philosophical principle that all phenomena, regardless of external differences, are ultimately derived from the same original source. This belief is already evident in the French title of *Recherches sur l'identité des forces chimiques et électriques* (*Searches for the Identity of Chemical and Electrical Forces*, 1813). Oersted observed that the electric current affects or moves a magnetic needle, and that the magnitude of the force is dependent upon the placement and distance of the magnet, the power of the operating battery, and the quality of the connecting conductor. His discovery of the relationship between electricity and magnet-

ism produced high interest within the scientific community; although his ideas were initially controversial, they eventually gained wide acceptance. André-Marie Ampère and Michael Faraday would further prove him right in the years to follow, with their own experiments.

Oersted also devised (again on the basis of his philosophical convictions and his empirical research) the so-called piezometer, which measures the compressibility of fluids. In 1824 he isolated aluminum; prior to Oersted's work, aluminum ore was available, but it had not been further separated into aluminum.

His contributions to the natural sciences were collected and published as *Scientific Papers* and *Correspondences with Various Scientists*, both in 1920. In addition to his scientific discoveries, Oersted was active in the development of the Danish educational system. In his later years, he propagated the view that science and religion or aesthetics need not be diametrically opposed. As he wrote, "Spirit and nature are one, viewed under two different aspects. Thus we cease to wonder at their harmony."

DIETRICH VON ENGELHARDT

Bibliography

Danish Ministry of Foreign Affairs, ed. *Hans Christian Oersted, 1777–1977.* Copenhagen: Danish Ministry of Foreign Affairs, 1977.

Dibner, Bern. *Oersted and the Discovery of Electromagnetism.* Norwalk, Conn.: Burndy, 1961.

Hennemann, Gerhard. "Der Dänische Physiker Hans Christian Oersted und die Naturphilosophie der Romantik." in *Philosophia Naturalis* 10 (1967): 112–22.

Meyer, Kirstine. "The Scientific Life and Works of H. C. Oersted." In *Oersted: Scientific Papers.* Vol. 1. Copenhagen: Høst in Komm., 1920.

Shanahan, Timothy. "Kant, Naturphilosophie and Oersted's discovery of Electromagnetism: A Reassessment," in *Studies in History and Philosophy of Science* 20 (1989): 287–305.

Snelders, Henricus Adrianus Marie. "Oersted's discovery of electromagnetism." In *Romanticism and the Sciences*, edited by Andrew Cunningham and Nicholas Jardine. Cambridge: Cambridge University Press, 1990.

Stauffer, Robert C. "Speculation and Experiment in the Background of Oersted's Discovery of Electromagnetism," *Isis* 48 (1957): 33–50.

Wiederkehr, Karl Heinrich. "Oersteds *Ansicht der chemischen Naturgesetze* (1812) und seine naturphilosophischen Betrachtungen über Elektrizität und Magnetismus." *Gesnerus* 47 (1990): 161–83.

Williams, L. Pearce. "Oersted, Hans Christian." In *Dictionary of Scientific Biography.* Vol. 9. Edited by Charles Coulston Gillispie. New York: Scribner, 1970.

OKEN (OR OKENFUSS), LORENZ 1779–1851

German natural scientist

Lorenz Oken was the most outspoken of a generation of Romantics to apply the idealist philosophy of Johann Gottlieb Fichte and Friedrich Wilhelm Joseph von Schelling to the study of nature. They subscribed to a theory of knowledge called *Naturphilosophie* in which speculative thought and in particular intuition, more than observation and experiment (but not to their

exclusion), were put forward as a reliable means of understanding the physical world.

As a precocious student in his early twenties, Oken wrote a *Grundriss der Naturphilosophie* (*Outlines of Nature Philosophy*, 1804), in which he maintained that the classes of animals are to be understood as representations of the organs of sense and must be classified accordingly. His *Lehrbuch der Naturphilosophie* (*Elements of Nature-philosophy*, 1809–11) offered a compendious system of classification in which Oken interpreted higher taxonomic categories as repetitions of lower levels, thus construing nature as an integrated totality of "all in everything." From this holistic notion, Oken developed his mineral, plant, and animal systems, each higher one recapitulating the one below. According to his theories, humankind, the highest form of organization, summarizes the entire animal kingdom. Conversely, the animal kingdom can be understood as the dissected exposition of a human being or, to put it differently, the animal kingdom is humankind exhibited in its component parts. The history of life therefore represents, in essence, the becoming of *Homo sapiens*.

Oken elaborated on his early taxonomic ideas and argued that there must be as many cardinal groups of animals as humans have cardinal organs or sense organs. These are five in number, corresponding to feeling, taste, smell, hearing, and sight. He rejected the idea of a single, linear chain of being and believed that the interrelation of minerals, plants, and animals can be indicated by a three-dimensional network. Later historians have interpreted the organicist, developmental language of Oken in terms of organic evolution. However, his language is ambiguous with respect to the origin of species. On the one hand it can indeed be understood to express a Darwinian descent; on the other, it can be interpreted equally well in terms of an ideal progression. It is certain that the origin of species was not a central issue on the research agenda of the nature philosophers.

One of the better known examples of Oken's *Naturphilosophie* was the vertebral theory of the skull. In his inaugural lecture at Jena, "Über die Bedeutung der Schädelknochen" ("On the Meaning of Skull Bones," 1807), Oken maintained that the cranium must be understood as a repetition of the vertebral column. He recounted that during the summer of 1806, while traveling through the Harz Mountains, he had come upon the bleached skull of a deer and, looking intently at it, the idea had flashed through his mind that the cranium represents a vertebral column. Later, during the period 1830–60, a priority dispute over this discovery took place that pitched Oken and his followers against the admirers of Johann Wolfgang von Goethe. It was instigated by G. W. F. Hegel, who in 1830 accused Oken of plagiarism. Apparently, Goethe, too, had experienced a flash of insight when in 1790, during a visit to Venice, he had chanced upon the bleached skull of a ram, and the idea had occurred to him then that its face was composed of vertebrae.

Naturphilosophie found its most fruitful area of scientific application in comparative anatomy and physiology. Yet any lasting contributions to these fields of scientific study by Oken were few in number and relatively minor in significance. He did, however, exert a considerable beneficial influence as an organizer of the German biomedical sciences. In 1816 he founded the periodical *Isis oder Encyclopaedische Zeitschrift*, which promoted the sciences, especially physiology. In the 1821 issue he suggested that German naturalists should come together annually, and the following year the first assembly of the Gesellschaft Deutscher Naturforscher und Ärzte (Association of German Scientists and Doctors) took place in Leipzig. It formed the prototype of other such organizations, in particular the British Association for the Advancement of Science.

Oken also promoted the teaching of natural history to the public, and he wrote many books for schools and laypeople, among these the *Allgemeine Naturgeschichte für alle Stände* (*German Natural History for All Classes*, 1833–41). His style was characterized by a gushy enthusiasm. Oken mixed his scientific writings with outspoken and often radical political views, and his drive for the organizational integration of German science went together with an advocacy of a politically unified Germany under an Austrian emperor.

NICOLAAS A. RUPKE

Biography

A farmer's son from the Black Forest, Oken studied medicine and natural history at the University of Freiburg from 1800. In 1804 he left for the University of Würzburg, where he completed his medical training. The following year he went to Göttingen, and after his habilitation Oken set up as a *privatdozent* (nonsalaried university lecturer). In 1806 he was elected to the exclusive Königliche Akademie der Wissenschaften in Göttingen. A year later, in 1807, on the recommendation of Goethe (1749–1832), he was appointed extraordinary professor of medicine at the University of Jena, and in 1812 was promoted to full professor. A decade on, amid political controversy, Oken resigned his chair and returned to private teaching (1822–27). In 1828 he resumed his university career in Munich, but left in 1833, again for political reasons. He found a lasting position at the newly founded university of Zurich where he taught until his death in 1851 at the age of seventy-two.

Selected Works

Grundriss der Naturphilosophie, der Theorie der Sinne und der darauf gegründeten Classifikation der Thiere. 1804.
Über die Bedeutung der Schädelknochen. 1807.
Lehrbuch der Naturphilosophie. 3 vols. 1809–11. Translated as *Elements of Physiophilosophy* by Alfred Tulk, 1847.

Bibliography

Ecker, Alexander. *Lorenz Oken: eine biographische Skizze.* Stuttgart: Schweizerbart, 1880. Translated as *Lorenz Oken: A Biographical Sketch* by Alfred Tulk, 1880.
Hübner, Georg Wilhelm. *Okens Naturphilosophie prinzipiell und kritisch bearbeitet.* Borna-Leipzig: Noske, 1909.
Kuhn-Schnyder, Emil. *Lorenz Oken 1779–1851: Erster Rektor der Universität Zürich.* Zurich: Rohr Verlag, 1980.
Mischer, Sibille. *Der verschlungene Zug der Seele: Natur, Organismus und Entwicklung bei Schelling, Steffens und Oken.* Würzburg: Königshausen und Neumann, 1997.
Pfannenstiel, Max. *Lorenz Oken. Sein Leben und Wirken.* Freiburg: Schulz, 1953.
Strohl, Jean. *Lorenz Oken und Georg Büchner: Zwei Gestalten aus der Übergangszeit von Naturphilosophie zu Naturwissenschaft.* Zurich: Corona, 1936.

OLIVIER, JUSTE 1807–1876

Swiss writer

Juste Olivier's work is probably the most representative of the impact French Romanticism had on the Swiss intellectual scene. Although Olivier was celebrated as the "national poet" of French-speaking Switzerland soon after he died, his artistic practices were strongly influenced by foreign literary figures. Contrary to Rodolphe Töpffer, who radically fought for cultural autarchy, Olivier constantly strove to build bridges between the French literary world and Switzerland. In particular, he had a long friendship with the French critic Charles-Augustin de Sainte-Beuve, who would often visit the Oliviers in Lausanne and, more importantly, taught his famous course on Port-Royal at the Academy of Lausanne in 1837. Sainte-Beuve's contribution to the *Revue Suisse*, a literary journal edited by Olivier from 1843 to 1846, was another important step toward the assimilation of French-speaking Switzerland to the French literary field. Sainte-Beuve, then Paris's most influential literary critic, would write a regular chronicle destined to the Swiss readership, in which he crudely criticized works that he strategically did not strongly disparage in French newspapers. Swiss readers would thus take part in Paris's literary debates from a remote but particularly well-informed standpoint.

While Olivier considered France as the leading country in matters of literature and culture, he was highly sensitive to the differences existing between Paris and Lausanne. Above all, he was well aware that the French capital was the only linguistic center of the French-speaking world, and that this cultural subjection prevented the literature of marginal regions from spreading. Puzzlingly enough, he thus acknowledged the French linguistic norm on the one hand and rejected it on the other. This stance is very emblematic of the condition of many Swiss writers in the nineteenth and twentieth centuries, but Olivier is unquestionably the first to express it with such intelligibility, as in his *Le Canton de Vaud: sa vie et son histoire* (*The Canton of Vaud: Its Life and History*, 1837): "Language of avant-garde and domination, French has a very bright, very clear, very unique and very complete history. . . . Accordingly, this language gives the peoples who speak it not only a splendid treasure, but also a right. No doubt that even we, who are but a small tribe lost on its borders, are very indebted to it. It is for us . . . the language of civilization; it is the field of our thought, it breathes life in and out of us, it follows our moves, and collects our progresses." This celebration of French as a language of cultural development is accompanied with remarks on the sluggishness and lack of grace characterizing the French spoken in Switzerland: "It is generally a little heavy, slow, lazy. It never passes lightly over anything." This strong interiorization of norms and the feeling that a Swiss writer will always remain dominated in the French literary field is central in Olivier's poetry.

However, Olivier is confident that "our Swiss French is susceptible to be successfully promoted. It still possesses great resources, it has words and idioms of great energy, the artlessness of old languages, ease in what is peculiar to itself, . . . and it has harmony and color in its sounds. Its rudeness and vulgarity will disappear by itself. . . ." This ambivalence regarding his own use of the French language culminates in the imprecise assumption

that the French spoken in Switzerland should become "the language of our most intimate nationality, our little voice, beside the big one, where our whispers are hardly heard." In short, Olivier wishes to enable this "little voice" to be heard on an international plane, thanks to an unmitigated approval of romantic style and forms imported from France. The distinctiveness of Swiss writers, then, must be to depict typically Swiss scenes, most of them taking the Alps as their setting. "Many French poets have turned their eyes to our Alps," he writes, "but they can never love them and understand them as well as we, who are their sons." Hence his famous mottos, both taken from his poem "Le Canton de Vaud" (1831): "Un génie est caché dans tous ces lieux que j'aime" ("a genius lies hidden in all those places I love") and "Vivons de notre vie" ("Let us live our own life").

But these axioms are ambiguously applied in Olivier's practice itself. Characteristically, his poems illustrate the beauties of Switzerland, but are addressed to the French readership (his *Poèmes suisses* [*Swiss Poems*, 1830] and his novels [*Donald*, 1865; *Héléna*, 1861] were published in Paris). The article that the critic Daniel Maggetti singles out as being the most representative of Olivier's literary opinions, "Mouvement intellectuel de la Suisse" ("The Intellectual Movement of Switzerland," 1844), in which Olivier underlines the attachment of French-speaking Switzerland to its Romance origins, comes out in the distinctively Parisian *Revue des Deux Mondes*. Likewise, his literary apprenticeship took place in Paris, where he met, besides Sainte-Beuve, such key figures as Victor Hugo, Alfred de Musset, and Alfred-Victor de Vigny (Olivier's diary, published under the title *Paris en 1830*, is a fascinating account of the life of the young Romantics during this decisive year). Olivier's work bears the mark of their formal and intellectual influence, even in its most "national" aspects. This can be explained by the fact that, to a certain extent, the defense of Swiss particularisms was felt by Olivier as a corollary of the rediscovery of national history. Halfway between a strong attraction toward a prestigious literary community and the affirmation of an autonomous culture, his situation prefigures that of Charles-Ferdinand Ramuz, the most celebrated French-speaking Swiss writer of the twentieth century.

Olivier's works are highly neglected nowadays, even in his own country. In a way, Olivier predicted this neglect: he saw it as the fate of every writer confined to the limited sphere of French-speaking Switzerland. As he puts it in his poem "Le Poète suisse",

Swiss poet! Here is your destiny
You would like to seize and follow the dreams of your
   heart . . .
But the too-heavy belt of these rocks
As a black camp of immoveable giants
With hearts of ice, with eyes sunken and dry
Holds you, and stifles your whisper . . .
There, in the fertile plains . . .
Poetry rises, at the heart of cities
Switzerland is poor, and has no city
No poet and no immortality.

Nevertheless, Olivier deserves to be rediscovered for his poetry, which is stylistically innovative for its place and time, and for his historical narratives, whose vivid depictions sometimes remind one of Vigny's *Cinq-Mars*. If he hadn't been confined—and, in a way, hadn't confined himself—to being a symbol of national culture, Olivier would probably have been considered as a very valuable *petit romantique*. But, above all, it is Olivier's lucid point of view on the French literary field that strikes the modern reader.

MAXIME GOERGEN

See also **French Romanticism: Its Literary Legacy; Sainte-Beuve, Charles Augustin de; Switzerland: Cultural Survey; Switzerland: Historical Survey; Töpffer, Rodolphe**

Biography

Born October 10, 1807, in Eysins, canton of Vaud. Brought up as a peasant. In 1815 his family moved to Bois-Bugny, near the town of Nyon. Undertook studies of theology at the academy of Lausanne, but interest for poetry discouraged him from becoming a minister. First poems ("Marco Botzaris," 1825, and "Julia Alpinuna," 1829) distinguished by local literary prizes. In 1830, named teacher of literature at the Gymnase de Neuchâtel, but was required to spend six months in Paris in order to perfect his knowledge of French culture and literature. During his stay, kept a diary providing a firsthand insight into the literary world and political conflicts of the French capital. Returned to Switzer-land in August and started teaching at Neuchâtel. His first collection of poems, *Poèmes helvétiques*, published in Paris. In 1833, returned to Lausanne to teach history at the Academy of Lausanne. In 1837, invited Sainte-Beuve to give a series of talks. Compelled to resign in 1846 because of political troubles. Back in Paris, continued to contribute to the *Revue suisse*, which he had edited from 1843 onward. Published poems (*Chansons lointaines*, 1847) and a novel (*Le Batelier de Clarens*, 1861). Worked in several schools, including his own boarding house, as a teacher of rhetoric and language. Returned to Switzerland in 1870, where he spent the rest of his life. Died January 7, 1876.

Selected Works

Les Deux Voix. 1835.
Le Canton de Vaud: sa vie et son histoire. 1837. Reprint, 1978.
Le Batelier de Clarens. 1861.
Les Chansons lointaines. 1869.
Oeuvres choises. 1879.
Paris en 1830, Journal. Paris: Payot, 1951.

Bibliography

Maggetti, Daniel. "Les écrivains romantiques." In *Histoire de la littérature en Suisse romande*, vol. 2, edited by Roger Francillon. Lausanne: Payot, 1997.
———. *L'Invention de la littérature romande: 1830–1910.* Lausanne: Payot, 1995.
Godet, Antoinette. *Bibliographie des oeuvres de Juste Olivier.* Lausanne, 1943.
Delhorbe, Cécile. *Juste et Caroline Olivier.* Neuchâtel: Attinger, 1935.

ON NAIVE AND SENTIMENTAL POETRY 1795–1796

Philosophical treatise by Johann Christoph Friedrich von Schiller

Johann Christoph Friedrich von Schiller's antithetical distinction between the naive and the sentimental refers to a classification of literature based on the author's relationship to the world. This new criterion draws on and overcomes several dichotomies in eighteenth-century thought. The controversies about the ancient and the modern, and nature and culture, yield to an ahistorical distinction that centers on literature rather than writers' cultural environments. The new approach breaks down barriers between periods and schools and shows modern, sentimental writing to be more than simply a failure to be ancient. On a personal level, Schiller's argument distinguishes his artistic toil from Johann Wolfgang von Goethe's magisterial ease, seemingly at odds with the agony of modernity, without showing one to be inferior to the other. Theoretical reflections are backed up by a vast range of references, and the essay offers a wealth of incidental insights into, for example, pornography and the dangers of abstraction in art.

Schiller begins by introducing the naive as a distinct category of experience that reveals the superior harmony and order of nature and, in so doing, puts to shame the artifice and corruption of culture. Loss of proximity to nature amounts to an expulsion from Eden, but a return is neither possible nor desirable: like sin, civilization is a product of freedom, but Schiller affirms freedom as a precious feature of humanity and sees the ultimate goal as restoring the balance of the natural world by human—and humane—means.

The naive writer need not rise to that challenge; he already feels that he is a part of the natural order; this sense of belonging enables him to effortlessly turn his experience into poetry. The sentimental writer, by contrast, feels banished from paradise. He is driven by an idea of nature that he must reconcile to his own experience if he is to find peace in the world. In different ways, each writer is (according to Schiller) a custodian of nature. This typological distinction yields new classifications for literature, based not on genre or style, but on different ways of seeing the world. The naive writer's relationship to the world appears straightforward, but the sentimental writer has two distinct ways of articulating his alienation: satire and elegy. In satire, the author contrasts the ideal with reality so as to show up the deficiencies of the world. Satire can be either mocking or punitive. For it to be art, mockery must be carried over into beauty, and punitiveness into the sublime, which, in Schiller's usage, denotes the impotence of the rational will in the light of overwhelming adverse conditions. His commitment to reconciliation to the world leads Schiller to the view that comedy pursues a higher goal than tragedy. While he sees tragedy as showing the individual's moral aims frustrated, true comedy reduces the iniquities of life to gentle entertainment and thus demonstrates an intact view of the world. Schiller's own strengths lay in tragedy.

Like satire, elegy can be subdivided into two categories. Elegy expresses the writer's distance from nature and the impossibility of regaining that level of harmony through progress. Caught between two models of perfection he finds himself frustrated by the inadequacies around him. Alternatively, in the guise of the idyll, elegy offers a vision of the end of the struggle between the individual and the world, the coming together of the aspirational ideal and reality: the idyll is filled with tranquil fulfillment and quasi-divine stasis that is attained through total harmony and perfection. Such stasis represents the end of the sentimental project and is at odds with the development essential to poetry. Unsurprisingly, therefore, Schiller quickly abandoned a plan to write a sentimental idyll based on the apotheosis of Hercules.

Having moved from the experience of nature to art, Schiller moves back from art to the world (the dualism of mind and body, as well as understanding and reason, pervades his aesthetic writings). He next construes the naive and sentimental as being, when deprived of their poetic elements, realism and idealism. The realist is committed to the world of sensory experience and bases his understanding of the world on individual cases. The idealist is driven by abstract reason and judges moral issues by appeal to the moral law alone. While the former runs the risk of being confined to immediate experience and lacking a wider understanding, the latter risks becoming too concerned with the universal to be sensitive to the individual. The two positions are shown to be complementary; realist and idealist can learn from one another.

The startling feature of *On Naive and Sentimental Poetry* is the exhaustive nature of the basic distinction: a writer either is or is not at one with the world. The distinction does not allow for exceptions and can be applied to all literature regardless of national origin or style. The underlying programmatic assumption is that art must not deal with itself or the poet, but, ultimately, lead an estranged humanity back to the world. That essential concern gives the essay its central place in Weimar Classicism, while the endless striving of the sentimental writer, who is forever traveling through modernity in search of nature, looks ahead to Romanticism.

DANIEL GREINEDER

See also **Art; Classical Antiquity; Germany: Cultural Survey; Goethe, Johann Wolfgang von; Literary Criticism: Germany; Literature; Modernity; Nature; Progress; Rousseau, Jean-Jacques; Schiller, Johann Christoph Friedrich von; The Sublime**

Text

Über naive und sentimentalische Dichtung. First published in three installments from 1795 to 1796 in the journal *Die Horen* and, in its entirety, in 1800 in *Kleinere prosaische Schriften von Schiller*, part 2. Translated as *Naive and Sentimental Poetry* by Julius A. Elias. New York: Ungar, 1966. Translated as *On the Naive and Sentimental in Literature* by Helen Watanbe-O'Kelly. Manchester: Carcanet New Press, 1981.

Bibliography

Koopmann, Helmut, ed. *Schiller-Handbuch*. Stuttgart: Alfred Kröner Verlag, 1998.

Reed, T. J. *Schiller*. Oxford: Oxford University Press, 1991.

Sharpe, Lesley. *Friedrich Schiller: Drama, Thought and Politics*. Cambridge: Cambridge University Press, 1991.

Szondi, Peter. "Das Naive ist das Sentimentalische. Zur Begriffsdialektik in Schillers Abhandlung." In Peter Szondi, *Schriften*, edited by Jean Bollack, Henriette Beese, Wolfgang Fietke, Wolfgang Fietkan. Frankfurt: Suhrkamp, 1978.

ONSLOW, ANDRÉ GEORGES LOUIS 1784–1853

French composer

In the Romantic era, when composers began to aspire to cultural and economic independence, André Georges Louis Onslow was especially interesting. A scion of an aristocratic English family, he had the independent means that enabled him to choose his style and genres of composition (rather than satisfy the marketplace or the whims of patrons). It also enabled him to subsidize the performance of his works. This exceptional situation offers an interesting (if tangential) insight into the conservative musical culture of England, France, Germany, and Austria during the first half of the nineteenth century.

In 1781 his father, Edward Onslow, a member of Parliament, the younger son of the First Earl of Onslow, was involved in a homosexual scandal and was compelled to leave England until the focus on the affair diminished. He traveled in France where, in 1783, he fell in love with and married Rosalie Marie de Bourdeilles de Brantôme, became a Roman Catholic and founded the French branch of the family. Two of his sons were painters; his eldest, Georges, became a musician.

Georges Onslow received a nobleman's education (which included the "civilized" activities of music, travel, horsemanship, and hunting). He spent most of his school years in London, where his studies included the piano. He acquired competence at the keyboard but did not show any marked predilection for music; it was aroused later by a group of musical amateurs when he returned to the family's Auvergne estates. He became interested in string chamber music and studied the violoncello in order to perform with this group of friends. Later, during a two-year sojourn in Germany and Austria, he extended his musical experience and began to compose.

His first work, a set of three string quintets, was written in 1806. A year later, he published these in Paris (at his own expense). He was now so interested and involved in music that he decided that he had to study it more closely. He began studies in theory and composition with the Bohemian composer Antonin Reicha, when he settled in Paris in 1808. Reicha was a very competent composer of traditional tendencies and this shows clearly in Onslow's works, which betray very little evidence of Romantic harmony, structure, or ethos. The programmatic fifteenth Quartet attempts to portray the various phases of an illness brought on by Onslow's deafness in one ear (the result of a stray bullet during a boar hunt). However, this is not a Romantically subjective work, but rather more a pictorialization of events in the baroque manner.

Onslow's status and contacts resulted in many honors. In 1830 he followed Felix Mendelssohn as the second honorary member of the Philharmonic Society of London, and in 1842 he was elected to a vacant chair of the Institute de France (his rivals for the position included Daniel-François-Esprit Auber and Hector Berlioz).

Onslow was a competent composer. His songs and piano variations satisfied the current taste for somewhat saccharine sentiment and piety. His three operas are very conservative for their time, reflecting the influence of Maria Luigi Carlo Cherubini and Etienne-Nicolas Méhul. His characterization is weak because his vocal lines lack individuality and he shows little capacity to distinguish individual characters within ensembles. His orchestration is competent, but conventional. The same features characterize his symphonies. These works had minimal success and no longevity.

Onslow's piano works show greater merit and display considerable idiomatic finesse. At their best (as in the Piano Duet, op. 22) they show freshness of ideas and a fine formal feeling. This practitioner's sense of idiom also characterizes his largest body of compositions: his chamber works. Remarkably, he was the only French composer of the time to create a substantial body of chamber music. He usually tried out new compositions with his friends, revised them in the light of this practical experience and then had them performed in Paris during the winter season. Then, after further revision, he published them. His early works were published at his own expense, but his elevated social position, as well as the proficiency of his works, led to international recognition and publication. By the 1830s the prestigious firm of Breitkopf und Härtel had published his complete chamber works as instrumental parts and as miniature scores. This brought his compositions to the attention of a wide and appreciative audience, especially musical amateurs.

Onslow's merits as a composer are limited, his greater interest to the period and musical history being sociological: it lies in his ability to choose his own medium and style without having to pay heed to the commercial or cultural demands of others. In this he offers an important insight into current taste, albeit within a very restricted realm.

BENEDICT SARNAKER

Biography

Born in Clermont-Ferrand, in the Auvergne, July 27, 1784. His aristocratic background gave him a gentleman's education. In 1808 married Charlotte Françoise Delphine de Fontagnes, the only daughter of a rich Aurillac landowner. After a few years of astringency, a major inheritance made Onslow a wealthy man. This independence enabled him to add musical composition and performance to his other activities as a gentleman. He had considerable success among amateurs and represents an important, if narrow, aspect of nineteenth-century musical life. Died in Clermont-Ferrand, October 3, 1853.

Selected Works

Opera	*Le Coloporteur, ou l'Enfant du Bucheron*	(1827)
Piano	Second Grand Duet for two performers on the pianoforte	(1825)
Chamber Music	Quartets Nos. 19–21 op. 46	
	Quartet No. 36 op. 69	
	Quintet Nos. 1–3 op. 1	
	Quintet No. 15 op. 38	
	Quintet No. 21 op. 51	
	Quintet No. 32 op. 78	
	Quintet No. 33 op. 80	
	Quintet No. 34 op. 82	
	Sextet op. 30 (Piano, Flute, Clarinet, Horn, Bassoon, Double Bass)	
	Nonet op. 77 (Violin, Viola, 'Cello, Double Bass, Flute, Oboe, Clarinet, Horn, Bassoon)	
	Septet op. 79 (Piano, Flute, Oboe, Clarinet, Horn, Bassoon, Double Bass)	

Bibliography

Darlhaus, Carl, ed. *Studien zur Trivialmusik des 19. Jahrhunderts.* Regensburg: Gustav Bosse Verlag 1967. Ortigue, J. d' "Une visite à Georges Onslow en 1832," *Le Ménestrel* 31 (1864): 113.

Eckart-Bäcker, Ursula. *Frankreichs Musik zwischen Romantik und Moderne.* Regensburg: Gustav Bosse Verlag, 1965.

Foster, Myles Birket. *History of the Philharmonic Society of London 1813–1912.* London: John Lane, 1912.

Halévy, Jacques-François Fromental. *Notice sur Onslow*, 1835. Reprinted in J. F. Halévy. *Souvenirs et portraits.* 1861.

Marmontel, Antoine. *Symphonistes et Virtuoses—Silhouettes et Médaillons.* Paris: A. Chaix et Cie, 1881.

Newman, William S. *The Sonata since Beethoven.* Chapel Hill: University of North Corolina Press, 1969.

Sirker, Udo. *Die Entwicklung des Bläserquintetts in der ersten Halfte des 19.Jahrhunderts.* Regensburg: Gustav Bosse Verlag, 1968.

Vulliamy, Colwyn Edward. *The Onslow Family 1528–1874.* London: Chapman & Hall 1953.

OPHELIA 1851–1852

Painting by John Everett Millais

Painted by the Pre-Raphaelite artist John Everett Millais for the British Royal Academy exhibition of 1852, *Ophelia* remains one of the most famous and enduring images of the nineteenth century. It draws on Gertrude's description of Ophelia's death from act 4, scene 7 of William Shakespeare's *Hamlet*, in which the heroine, driven mad by her lover's rejection and the death of her father, is drowned in a stream. Although the painting established the artist's reputation, it was not altogether well received by contemporary critics. A reviewer in the *Athenaeum* argued that it showed "no pathos, no melancholy, no brightening up, no last lucid interval," while the *Art-Journal* described the rendering of Ophelia's death as the "least practicable subject in the entire play." It is true that in depicting this particular scene from *Hamlet*, Millais demonstrated some originality (although this is often forgotten in the plethora of images that followed) but the painting of subjects from William Shakespeare had become increasingly popular since the eighteenth century. Shakespeare was listed by the Pre-Raphaelites as an "Immortal," a figure of outstanding brilliance and genius, and Millais had already painted a scene from *The Tempest, Ferdinand Lured by Ariel*, in 1849. The cross-referencing between painting and literature was familiar in the artistic climate of mid-nineteenth-century Britain, where narrative paintings reigned supreme and where pictures were intended to be "read" as well as seen.

While Millais was influenced in his picturing of Ophelia's death by the general trend toward literary paintings, it was also the rich description evoked by Gertrude's words that made this "least practicable" of subjects the most appealing. With its account of the "weeping brook" and the different types of plants that surround it, the speech sets up a verbal scene that Millais painstakingly attempts to reproduce in paint. His focus on nature, which he shares with fellow members of the Pre-Raphaelite brotherhood, situates Millais as an inheritor of Romantic ideals and this is beautifully rendered in *Ophelia*. The Romantic tradition that this image participates in, however, comes in a sense indirectly: through the teachings of John Ruskin, the most influential British art critic of the mid-nineteenth century. Millais followed Ruskin's advice to artists to be original in their thinking and to "go to Nature in all singleness of heart." In this picture, nature has the dreamlike and mystical qualities that characterize earlier Romantic paintings, but it is juxtaposed with a photographic realism that makes its attention to detail almost scientific, as if the artist were looking through a microscope. According to the French critic Théophile Gautier, who viewed the painting in the Exposition Universelle in Paris in 1855, it was this meticulousness that prevented the picture from being properly categorized as Romantic. As well as their botanical fidelity, the natural elements here assume a symbolic status that furthers the narrative: the poppy at Ophelia's right hand signifies death, the daisies are symbolic of innocence, roses of youth, pansies of unrequited love, the fritillary floating in the stream at the bottom right of the painting symbolizes sorrow, and the violets that hang around Ophelia's neck represent faithfulness.

In terms of the date of its exhibition and the techniques that it employs, *Ophelia* marks the climax of Romanticism, with a curious blending of early and mid-nineteenth-century ideologies, competing discourses and values, that render its fixed definition as either a Romantic or a Victorian painting highly problematic. The emotional intensity of the image, captured in the haunting stare and parted lips of the heroine, seems at odds with the stillness of the scene and the glossy finish of the painting (an effect that was achieved by the Pre-Raphaelite device of painting on a wet white canvas). The subject matter itself marks a jarring opposition, of the death of Ophelia with the fecundity of nature, and of the madness of the female figure with the controlled brushstrokes of the artist. Ophelia, as she is depicted here, is the Romantic figure par excellence: torn apart by the force of her passion, she lies engulfed by the murky waters of the stream and at one with nature. But even this might owe more to the specific cultural context of the painting than to

John Everett Millais, *Ophelia*. Reprinted courtesy of AKG London/ Erich Lessing.

Romantic ideals. The focus on female sexuality and madness in the Victorian period made Ophelia the prototype for many a mad woman in scientific tracts as well as in fiction. The figure of the female driven to despair and death by the rejection of a lover was also familiar in contemporary literature and art and aptly suggested the stereotypical frailty and passivity of the Victorian woman.

Adopting the Romantic ideal of truth to nature, Millais went to some extraordinary lengths in painting the image, setting up his canvas in a field on the River Hogsmill at Ewell in Surrey, where he was frequently troubled by the wind, swarms of flies, and swans who insisted on floating on the exact stretch of water that he wished to paint. For the figure of Ophelia, Millais used Elizabeth Siddal, Dante Gabriel Rossetti's future wife, as a model, lying her in a bath full of water that was kept warm by lamps underneath. When she caught a severe cold, her father threatened to sue the artist for damages until he agreed to pay the doctor's bills. Despite these practical difficulties, however, *Ophelia* placed Millais in the role of a Romantic artist, with a poetic insight and powerful imagination that Ruskin was quick to recognize. When he saw the painting in the Royal Academy, the critic wrote to Millais that "there is a refinement in the whole figure—in the floating and sustaining dress—such as I never saw before expressed on canvas. In her most lovely countenance there is an Innocence disturbed by Insanity and a sort of Enjoyment strangely blended with lineament of woe."

JULIA THOMAS

Work

Ophelia. John Everett Millais. Oil on canvas, 76.2 cm. × 111.8 cm. Tate Gallery, London.

Bibliography

Altick, Richard D. *Paintings from Books: Art and Literature in Britain, 1760–1900*. Columbus: Ohio State University Press, 1985.
Des Cars, Laurence. *The Pre-Raphaelites: Romance and Realism*. London: Thames and Hudson, 2000.
Fleming, Gordon Howard. *John Everett Millais: A Biography*, London: Constable, 1998.

Marsh, Jan. *Pre-Raphaelite Women: Images of Femininity in Pre-Raphaelite Art*. London: Weidenfeld and Nicolson, 1987.

Parris, Leslie, ed. *The Pre-Raphaelites*. London: Tate Gallery, 1984.

Showalter, Elaine, "Representing Ophelia: Women, Madness, and the Responsibilities of Feminist Criticism." In *Shakespeare and the Question of Theory*. Edited by Patricia Parker and Geoffrey Hartman. New York and London: Methuen, 1985.

OPIE, AMELIA 1769-1853

English novelist and poet

Amelia Opie was born just one year before William Wordsworth and three years before Samuel Taylor Coleridge, and as such she can be viewed as a first-generation Romantic whose main literary interests and political agendas were informed by the revolutionary climate of her early twenties. She later described the 1790s, and in particular 1794, the date of the infamous treason trials (alarmed by the French Revolution, the British government charged several leading reformers with treason, but the men were quickly acquitted), as "the most interesting period of my long life." Like Coleridge and Wordsworth, Opie addressed the political climate in her writings and wrote about many of the contemporary issues of the period, in particular the debate on the abolition of the slave trade, gender politics, and the socially outcast. Although usually remembered now as a novelist, Opie was an extremely versatile writer, publishing between 1790 and her death in 1853 seven novels, seven collections of tales, one play, and three volumes of poetry. Several of her novels and two of her poetry collections were very successful and appeared in numerous editions. Most recent critical attention, however, has continued to focus on her novels and on her involvement with the radical dissenting circles based in Norwich.

Opie's literary output can be divided into two periods, defined by her changing religious beliefs. Her parents were Unitarian dissenters and as such belonged to one of the most liberal and progressive groups in society. Opie's father seems to have actively encouraged his daughter's literary talents and introduced her to radical figures of the day. This upbringing clearly affected her literary interests and, like other women writers of the period born to dissenting parents, including most notably Anna Letitia Barbauld, Opie was drawn to social and political issues in her work. In 1814, however, Opie left the Unitarian Church and began to attend Quaker services, and from around this time the tone and content of her writing changed. Her story *Temper*, published in 1812, is the first real evidence of a shift, and from this date onward her literary output took on an increasingly moralistic stance, culminating in her last major publication, a collection of devotional poems titled *Lays for the Dead* in 1834. In relation to Romanticism, it is therefore the novels and poems published before her conversion to Quakerism that are of greatest interest.

Although Opie's novels are little read now, at the turn of the nineteenth century they were very popular, and recent critics have argued that they played an important role in the development of the novel as a genre. Her novels are perhaps best compared to those by Mary Wollstonecraft in terms of their political subtext, and to those by Jane Austen in terms of their often ironic representation of middle-class society. Most critical attention has been given to Opie's 1805 novel *Adeline Mowbray*, which is

certainly her most politicized work and is most obviously the product of her involvement in radical intellectual circles. It was in this Norwich-based dissenting community that Opie met William Godwin in 1794. Godwin had recently published *Political Justice*, his treaty arguing for the abolishment of all institutions such as the legal system and marriage, and his radical opinions were well known. Opie and Godwin struck up a friendship that seems to have been founded primarily on shared political beliefs and intellectual interests, although there is some evidence that on Godwin's side this friendship developed into romance. Certainly there were rumors to this effect within the social circle in which they both moved. However, in 1796 Opie met and struck up a friendship with Wollstonecraft, a figure she had long admired, and in this same year Godwin and Wollstonecraft became lovers. In March of the following year they married, to the contradiction of both of their professed antimarriage principles. Opie seemed disappointed with the disjunction between principles and practice this event highlighted, and the relationship between her fictional characters, Frederic Glenmurray and her eponymous heroine, Adeline Mowbray, has been read by most critics as a commentary on the controversial real-life relationship between Godwin and Wollstonecraft. Although there is a general critical consensus that the novel addresses the political, social, and philosophical issues thrown up by this liaison, there is some debate as to whether or not it expresses support or criticism of their radical ideas. Contemporary readers of *Adeline Mowbray* read it as a critique of Wollstonecraft's and Godwin's radicalism. However, more critics have suggested that the novel engages with the debates about marriage and society in more complex ways than this, and that Opie condemns not radical theory itself but the *consequences* of radical theory, in particular the consequences for women. In its depiction of society's cruel treatment of the unmarried heroine, Opie seems to offer a revealing critique of both conservative social mores and the idealistic philosophical theories of Godwin.

Opie's most important literary involvement in contemporary politics is her work addressing the slave trade, in particular her two poems "The Negro Boy's Tale," published in 1802, and "The Black Man's Lament," published as an illustrated pamphlet in 1826. Both of these texts demonstrate Opie's lifelong commitment to the slaves' cause, even after she had abandoned other political interests. She contributed to abolitionist literature in important ways, in particular in her experimentation with Jamaican Creole dialect to express the slaves' plight.

Opie's other poems have tended to be dismissed as sentimental effusions. However, of her three collections of poetry—*Poems* (1802), *The Warrior's Return, and Other Poems* (1808), and *Lays for the Dead* (1834)—the earlier two collections offer a number of interesting intersections with other key Romantic poetic publications. Several of the poems from both her 1802 and 1808 collections, can, like Mary Robinson's *Lyrical Tales*, be read alongside *Lyrical Ballads*. In poems like "The Despairing Wanderer" (1802) and "The Mad Wanderer, A Ballad" (1808), a Wollstonecraftian critique of society's expectations about feminine behavior intersects with the contemporary fascination with society's outcasts that we find in Wordsworth, providing an alternative-gendered sociopolitical poetic vision.

PENNY BRADSHAW

Biography

Born Amelia Anderson in Norwich, England, on November 12, 1769. Had little formal education but was taught French through private tuition. Began publishing poetry in Dissenting journals in the early 1790s and first novel, *The Dangers of Coquetry*, published anonymously in 1790. Married the society portrait painter John Opie in May 1798 and moved to London. Published further poems in the *Annual Anthology* in 1799 at the request of Robert Southey. Her two major novels, *The Father and Daughter: A Tale, in Prose* and *Adeline Mowbray*, published in 1801 and 1805, respectively. Husband died in 1807. Left Unitarian Church in 1814 and converted to Quakerism. Her last work, *Lays for the Dead*, published 1834. Died at the age of eighty-four, on December 2, 1853.

Selected Works

Prose

The Father and Daughter: A Tale in Prose, 1801. Subsequent edition, with introduction by Peter Garside, 1995.
Adeline Mowbray. 1805.
The Works of Mrs. Amelia Opie. 1974.

Poetry

Poems. 1802.
The Warrior's Return, and Other Poems. 1808.
Lays for the Dead. 1834.

Bibliography

Brightwell, Cecilia Lucy. *Memorials of the Life of Amelia Opie, Selected and Arranged from her Letters, Diaries and Other Manuscripts*. 1854.
Eberle, Roxanne. "Amelia Opie's *Adeline Mowbray*: Diverting the Libertine Gaze; or, The Vindication of a Fallen Woman," *Studies in the Novel* 26 (1994): 121–52.
———. " 'Tales of Truth?' Amelia Opie's Antislavery Poetics." In *Romanticism and Women Poets: Opening the Doors of Reception*. Edited by Harriet Kramer Linkin and Stephen C. Behrendt. Lexington: University of Kentucky Press, 1999.
Howard, Carol. " 'The Story of the Pineapple': Sentimental Abolitionism and Moral Motherhood in Amelia Opie's *Adeline Mowbray*," *Studies in the Novel* 30 (1998): 355–76.
Kelly, Gary. "Discharging Debts: The Moral Economy of Amelia Opie's Fiction," *The Wordsworth Circle* 11 (1980): 198–203.
Ty, Eleanor. *Empowering the Feminine: The Narratives of Mary Robinson, Jane West, and Amelia Opie, 1796–1812*. Toronto: University of Toronto Press, 1998.

ORCHESTRA

The eighteenth-century orchestra looked much the same as it does today, though smaller in size. During the Romantic period, the orchestra would more than double in size, encouraged by the emergence of public concerts. The Romantic view that the prime function of music was the expression of emotion resulted in a new awareness that different instruments could evoke disparate passions. As the Romantic composer sought unconventional sonorities in his quest for evocative orchestral coloration and emotional expressiveness, the craftsman modified and improved the instruments, while the performer mastered the new techniques demanded by the refined instruments.

The late eighteenth-century Viennese ensembles incorporated approximately thirty-five participants. The core of this ensemble, the string section, boasted between six and eight first violins with the same number of seconds, four each of violas and cellos, and two string bases. The woodwind section included pairs of flutes, oboes, clarinets, and bassoons. The brass consisted of pairs of trumpets and horns. A timpanist completed the group, while the harpsichord, acting as basso continuo, supplied the foundation. The score gave most of the work to the strings, sometimes doubled by the winds.

String instruments already possessed the necessary range and agility for symphonic music. Their construction has essentially remained unchanged since the seventeenth century. The nineteenth century witnessed only slight development and elaboration in fingering and bowing techniques as composers called for a higher level of virtuosity.

Woodwinds endured basic limitations as a result of the nature of their construction. A woodwind instrument is essentially a length of pipe having variously spaced holes that the player covers with his fingers depending on the desired notes. There are three problems inherent in this construction. First, if the instrument has enough holes for the entire chromatic scale, the number of holes will exceed the number of fingers. Second, the proper acoustic locations for precise pitches are often not within reach of one another. Third, the holes need to be large enough for the optimal sound quality yet small enough to be covered by a finger. The nineteenth century witnessed the invention of a system of keys and levers that solved these problems and brought the woodwinds to the level of the strings in range and agility.

The brass instruments, as well, were limited by their essential nature. A brass instrument is a cone or cylinder. Longer and narrower than a woodwind, and without holes to alter its length, the instrument is able to produce only a single fundamental pitch and the restricted number of tones in the harmonic series above. This limitation in the range of notes available always relegated the brass to a supporting role. The invention of valves (c. 1815) provided an easy mechanical way to achieve all the notes of the chromatic scale on a single instrument. As the various brass instrument families gradually acquired valves, the nineteenth century saw the section achieve a more equal footing with the strings and woodwinds. The invention of valves also facilitated the creation of entirely new brass instruments, such as the tuba. Curiously, the slide trombone, which had solved the problem two hundred years earlier by using a sliding section of tubing, did not even begin to enter the orchestra until the late eighteenth century.

The percussion section increased from one to as many as five performers. At the end of the eighteenth century, the percussion section saw the addition of drums adopted from military bands. The late eighteenth-century craze for an exotic Turkish sound (witness the many Turkish marches, and pieces labeled *alla turca*) led to the addition of triangle, glockenspiel, and cymbals.

The relatively small eighteenth-century orchestra had little difficulty keeping time and staying together. The first violinist started and stopped the ensemble with a mere flick of his bow or his head. The continuo player provided the harmonic framework, and the music rarely required a change in tempo. With dynamic markings clearly notated in each performer's music, eye contact was all that was necessary to keep them together. However, as the size of the orchestra increased, two things happened. First, the continuo became superfluous as the modernized winds and brass provided the resources to fill out the harmonies. Second, eye contact among the increased number of ensemble members became impossible. Thus composers began standing before the rehearsing ensemble, keeping time with a rolled-up sheaf of music papers. As musical demands began to include tempo changes and interpretation, the conductor with his baton became an indispensable part of the ensemble. More than a mere timekeeper, the conductor eventually developed into the principal performer, with the orchestra as his instrument.

Hector Berlioz, one of the most innovative of the Romantic orchestrators, was among the first who considered instrumental timbre to be primary to symphonic composition. His *Symphonie Fantastique* introduced the use of many new instruments, such as cymbals, harps, and bass drum, and employed instruments in innovative combinations (e.g., English horn with timpani in the slow movement). Berlioz authored the first treatise on orchestration, *Traité de L'instrumentation et d'Orchestration Modernes* (1844), in which he described each instrument, evaluated its strengths and weaknesses, and recommended its most effective use.

By the end of the nineteenth century, the symphony orchestra had ballooned from the thirty-five of a century earlier to sometimes as many as hundred performers. The string section alone might number as many as sixty players: from twenty-four to thirty-two violins (first and second), as many as eight to twelve each of violas and cellos, and six to eight string basses. While the woodwind section maintained its original core of flutes, oboes, clarinets, and bassoons, now the pairs might be trios of each; the further addition of piccolo, English horn, bass clarinet, and double bassoon augmented the standard woodwind forces. The brass section expanded to between four and eight French horns, two to five trumpets, three trombones, tuba, and bass tuba. Percussion was now a section in its own right, with as many as four or five players. Besides the timpani and other assorted drums, one might find tambourine, triangle, cymbals, gong, castanets, celesta, glockenspiel, xylophone, and other "special effects" instruments. One or two harps completed the ensemble. The level of virtuosity had enormously increased and Romantic expressiveness demanded a conductor to hold the group together and interpret the composer's intentions.

NANCY F. GARF

Bibliography

Chappell, Herbert. *Sounds Magnificent: The Story of the Symphony.* London: British Broadcasting Corporation, 1984.

Hurd, Michael. *The Orchestra.* New York: Facts on File, 1980.

Peyser, Joan, ed. *The Orchestra: Origins and Transformations.* New York: Scribner's, 1986.

Ulrich, Homer. *Symphonic Music.* New York: Columbia University Press, 1952.

Younghusband, Jan. *Orchestra!* London: Chatto and Windus, 1991.

ORIENTALISM: LITERATURE AND SCHOLARSHIP

The symbiosis between academic and popular Orientalism is perfectly illustrated in the career of Antoine Galland. A talented French Arabist, Galland had completed and published his teacher Barthélemy d'Herbelot's *Bibliothèque Orientale* (1697), but his name and fortune were made by his leisure time recreation of translating popular tales from a diverse collection of manuscripts. The runaway success of *Les Mille et une nuits* (*1001 Nights*, 1704–17) revealed how skillfully he had judged his readers' tastes, rendering the products of Oriental oral tradition accessible and acceptable to a metropolitan audience. The craze for sensual and sensational escapism involved invasion of the forbidden space of the seraglio. Amid scented sexuality, at once infinitely varied and continually available, the inexhaustible potency of the sultan was disturbingly juxtaposed to the castrated eunuch, whose incompleteness figured the voyeurism of the reader.

One celebrated reader, Lady Mary Wortley Montagu, having gained access to a Turkish harem, assured her sister that "those very tales were writ by an Author of this Country and (excepting the Enchantments) are a real representation of the manners here." Her letters, published in 1763, revealed a similar mixture of popular and scholarly Orientalism; they include the famous description of two hundred naked women in the hot baths at Sofia that she addressed to a female friend, and the verses by Ibrahim Pasha, "wonderfully ressembling the Song of Solomon," that she sent to Alexander Pope in both literal and poetical translations. She asserted, "I am pritty far gone in Oriental Learning," and she found her Turkish experience illuminated passages from both the Bible and the *Iliad*.

Pope had translated Homer's epic two years earlier, detecting in its "unequalled fire and rapture" both the sublimity of the Scriptures and "the Spirit of the Orientals." Eastern languages had been valued predominantly as ancillary to Old Testament exegesis, but the influential *De Sacra Poesi Hebraeorum* (1753) by Bishop Robert Lowth considered the Bible as oriental literature. Lowth's insights influenced German biblical criticism and later in the century J. G. Eichhorn's reading of the book of Revelation as an Oriental poem based upon the fall of Jerusalem encouraged Samuel Taylor Coleridge to contemplate a sublime and "anti-classical" epic.

Orientalism, inevitably wedded to the colonial enterprise and prone to political and commercial rivalries, produced a diverse and mind-expanding body of information that was frequently difficult to classify and assimilate. The intrepid young French linguist, Abraham Hyacinthe Anquetil-Duperron, fresh from communicating with Parsees in Pondicherry, published his pioneering translation of *Zend-Avesta, ouvrage de Zoroastre* (*The Work of Zoroaster*, 1771), whose preface included criticism of Oxford University scholarship. Rising to the defense of his alma mater in a published reply, an equally youthful William Jones dismissed this French research, revealing his own ignorance of ancient Persian while effectively demolishing Anquetil-Duperron's reputation. Despite the chauvinistic aspects of this unfortunate incident, Jones had earlier retranslated *Les Mille et une nuits* into the original Arabic with the aid of a native of Aleppo, and that very year he earned the soubriquet of "Persian" Jones, with the publication of his *Grammar of the Persian Language* (1771). A useful work for the East India Company in training their writers in the Moghul court's official language, it was also a poet's grammar featuring verse translations of elegant and exotic Persian poems, including "A Persian Song of Hafiz," and its appearance marked the beginnings of Romantic orientalism.

One of Jones's longest-held ambitions was to initiate the West into the vast literary treasures of the East: he thought that a Europe poetically saturated with Greco-Roman culture should look eastward for inspiration. Appreciating that the sybaritic luxury and erotic power-fantasy of the oriental(ized) tale could pall, Jones traced the sources of classical Arabic literature in the dynamic authenticity of the pre-Islamic *Moallakát* (1782) rather than *Les Mille et une nuits*. His concerns for accuracy of translation and comparative linguistic method created a demand for genuine Eastern products while significantly adjusting racial and political stereotypes.

It was India that was to provide the greatest challenge to Western notions of cultural hegemony. Under the encouragement and patronage of Warren Hastings, Governor-General of Bengal, Charles Wilkins and Sir William Jones revealed through their mastery of Sanskrit a classical culture independent of Greece, Rome, or the Levant. Hastings saw his orientalist regime as mediating between the worlds of politics and scholarship, and described Wilkins's translation of *The Bhăg văt-Gēētā* (1785) as "a work of wonderful fancy, almost unequalled in its sublimity of conception, reasoning, and diction," declaring that Indian writings "will survive when the British dominion in India shall have long ceased to exist, and when the sources which it once yielded both of wealth and power are lost to remembrance." In London's Soho, William Blake depicted the Brahmans, guardians of hermetic wisdom, as role models to compete with the bards and druids of emergent Romanticism in number 10 of *A Descriptive Catalogue*.

Jones founded the groundbreaking Asiatick Society in January 1784, and in 1786 his "Third Anniversary Discourse" disturbed the West with its thesis of an Indo-European family of languages, radically adjusting preconceptions of European cultural superiority, and introducing disconcerting notions of relationship between the rulers and their black subjects. His *Hymns to Hindu Deities* (1748–88) explored Indian concepts of creativity and the nature of perception, helping to make them Romantic preoccupations. Jones's prefatory argument to "A Hymn to

Náráyena" (1785) with its valuable insights into the substantial overlap of the artistic and the religious, the philosophic and the literary, is in itself a seminal document in the history of Romanticism.

A further and revolutionary contribution to orientalism was Jones's translation of Kālidāsa's *Sacontalá* (1789), which initiated an "oriental renaissance." The play concerns the aesthetic and erotic entrancement of King Dushmanta by the beauty of Sacontalá, the daughter of a Brahman sage and a heavenly courtesan, and the level of European audience identification was quite remarkable. The blend of the divine and the erotic in a story that Kālidāsa had adapted from the *Mahābhārata* was at once delightfully pagan and profoundly religious; it appealed to the vogue for "sensibility." British reviewers such as Mary Wollstonecraft fell under its spell, but in Germany it caused a sensation. The play was for Johann Gottfried Herder his "indische Blume"; (Indian flower); Johann Christoph Friedrich von Schiller rhapsodized about Sacontalá as the ideal of feminine beauty; Novalis addressed his fiancée as "Sakontala"; Friedrich von Schlegel announced, "Im Orient müssen wir das höchste Romantische suchen" ("In the Orient we must seek the supreme Romanticism"); and Johann Wolfgang Goethe captured the essence of *Sacontalá* fever in the line: "Nenn ich, Sakontala, dich, und so ist Alles gesagt" ("When I name you, Sakontala, everything is said").

Jones's translations and original poetry established the genre of the Romantic verse tale for the orientalizing of Lord Byron, Walter Savage Landor, Thomas Moore, Percy Bysshe Shelley, and Robert Southey. His research facilitated the Romantic orientalism of novels as different as William Beckford's *Vathek* (1786) and Sydney Owenson's *The Missionary: An Indian Tale* (1811), The Indian novel was developed by women writers and Phebe Gibbes's *Hartly House, Calcutta* (1789) represents the initiating text of this fascinating subgenre; it was arguably the first novel about India written from firsthand experience (Frances Sheridan's *The History of Nourjahad* [1767] belongs to the genre of the oriental tale; *The Indian Adventurer* [1780] and *Rajah Kisna* [1786] remain anonymous).

Romantic-period writers produced characteristically individual responses to the East; the earlier verse narratives such as Landor's *Gebir* (1798) and Southey's *Thalaba the Destroyer* (1801) largely established the parameters of the genre, gothicizing the decadent decay of expired civilizations in response to the radical historical analysis of Constantin Volney's *The Ruins: or a Survey of the Revolutions of Empires* (1791), and the Napoleonic invasion of Egypt in 1798. Partly as an overcompensation for his "flattering misrepresentation" of Islam, Southey's next Eastern epic, *The Curse of Kehama* (1810), develops the use of the oriental to encode the alien and the other in terms of both external threat and internal corruption by characterizing Hinduism as "the most monstrous" of all "false religions." Southey displayed his fierce animus against Hinduism by opening his poem with the widow-burning ritual of *satī*, providing powerful propaganda for the Evangelicals who were lobbying Parliament to secure missionary activity in British India.

Its delightful horror impressed the young Shelley; ultimately, however, it was not a poem designed to gothicize, but a novel that romanticized India, opposing interventionist cultural and religious policies, that reignited Shelley's poetic imagination. Shelley reacts to Luxima, the Kashmiri Brahman priestess heroine of Owenson's *The Missionary*, with the same rapture as the German Romantics had idolized Śakuntalā. His desire to bring Luxima to life is never totally achieved, but etherealized versions of this Indian Maid reappear in his poetry from *Alastor* (1816) onward.

"Stick to the East;—the oracle, [Madame de] Staël told me it was the only poetical policy," wrote Byron to Moore in May 1813. It proved sound advice; the public was indeed orientalizing, and the publisher Longman's advance for Moore's *Lalla Rookh* (1817) brought the poet three thousand guineas. Meanwhile Byron was instrumental in the publication of another celebrated poem of the Orient, Coleridge's "Kubla Khan" (1816). As the only Romantic to reach Asia, Byron transformed his exotic reading into sensual reality and back again into literature; the book of the tour was *Childe Harold's Pilgrimage* (I and II) (1812). His version of orientalizing involved the simultaneous construction of both the East and the myth of himself, blurring the Eurocentric binary of self and other. But the enabling imaginary spaces of the East jostled against the political realities of empire and empire building. The footnotes to Byron's oriental tales compare Muslim and Christian rites and practices in an apparently syncretic fashion that might be seen as implicitly supporting a policy of religious toleration, but in June 1813 the *Morning Chronicle* announced that "several Petitions for facilitating the introduction of Christian Knowledge into India, were presented by Viscount Lord Sidmouth and Lord Byron." Furthermore, the radical atheistical Shelley wrote in his "Philosophical View of Reform" (1819) that "the zeal of the missionaries . . . will produce beneficial innovation" in India.

In Calcutta, Henry Thomas Colebrooke had further adjusted the metropolitan construction of India. His mathematical bent freed him of the Romantic imperative of seeing India as spiritual, mysterious, exotic, or other. Thus his pioneering analysis of classical Indian philosophy, which included his "discovery" of the Hindu syllogism, and a rationalist tradition, European logicians and historians of philosophy were prepared to take Indian thought seriously. Colebrooke's departure from India in 1814 coincided with Horace Hayman Wilson's elevation to the ranks of the foremost Sanskritists in Bengal. His scholarly annotated translation of Kālidāsa's elegant *Meghadūta* (1813) was the first in an impressive series of publications that made him the leading orientalist of his generation.

With James Mill's hegemonic *History of British India* (1817), Anglicism came to dominate policy-making in India, modernization became synonymous with Westernization, and oriental learning was seriously devalued. Wilson fought stubbornly against the combined forces of Anglicism, utilitarianism, and evangelicalism, but his departure from India in 1833 marked the prelude to their victory.

As Wilson left India, Thomas Babington Macaulay arrived, and two years later Lord William Bentinck's English Education Act (1835), making English the language of instruction in Indian education, followed closely on the heels of Macaulay's Minute of 1835, that declared, "A single shelf of a good European library is worth the whole native literature of India and Arabia." The oriental renaissance had seen India educating the West, now that process was reversed; English literature would provide the authoritative texts and the Subcontinent would be reeducated. Calcutta was soon reproducing Byronic clones such as Henry Derozio and the heads of young Bengali writers were full of Thomas Moore and Walter Scott.

At the same time among British writers in India the adaptation of metropolitan conventions of sensibility to the melancholy of colonial exile in poets such as Bishop Reginald Heber, John Leyden, and Thomas Medwin, was being replaced by a distinct vein of antiorientalist burlesque in works such as Charles D'Oyly's "Tom Raw the Griffin" (1828), inspired by Byron's *Don Juan* (1819–24). The Anglo-Indian novel was also emerging as a distinct genre and its first best-seller, Philip Meadows Taylor's *Confessions of a Thug* (1839), demonstrated more Hindu horrors against the reassuring background of British rule. While the British reading public was enthralled with this tale of ritual mass murder, Edward Fitzgerald and Alfred, Lord Tennyson were translating the scented love-lyrics of Hafiz. The Orient continued to offer terror and desire.

The growth of Romanticism and orientalism was synchronous in the West, and the European Romantic imagination was saturated with orientalism, but it reflected European ambivalence concerning the East, complicated in Britain by colonial anxiety and imperial guilt. The participation of German Romanticism in Indology was innocent of involvement in external colonialism and German oriental scholarship became preeminent in the 1830s. Intercultural translation proceeding from Calcutta problematized absorption of Romanticism with mythic and idealistic revaluation of human potential and complicated its construction and deconstruction of planes of consciousness, meaning, and identity.

MICHAEL J. FRANKLIN

Selected Works

Beckford, William. *Vathek*. 1786.

Beddoes, Thomas. *Alexander's Expedition down the Hydaspes and the Indus to the Indian Ocean*. 1792.

Blake, William. *The First Book of Urizen*. 1794; *Europe*. 1794; *The Book of Los*. 1795.

Byron, George Noel Gordon, Lord. *Childe Harold's Pilgrimage I* and *II*. 1812; *The Giaour*. 1813; *The Bride of Abydos*. 1813; *The Corsair*. 1814; *Lara*. 1814; *The Siege of Corinth*. 1815; *Hebrew Melodies*. 1815; *Manfred*. 1817; *Beppo*. 1818; *Don Juan*. 1819–23; *Sardanapalus*. 1821; *Cain*. 1821; *The Island*. 1823; *Heaven and Earth*. 1823.

Coleridge, Samuel Taylor. "Kubla Khan." 1797–99.

Galland, Antoine. *Les Mille et une nuits*. 1704–17.

Gibbes, Phebe. *Hartly House, Calcutta*. 1789.

Goethe, Johann Wolfgang von. *Werke*, edited by W. A. Weimar. 1887–1912.

Hamilton, Eliza. *Letters of a Hindoo Rajah, to which is Prefixed a Preliminary Dissertation on the History, Religion and Manners of the Hindoos*. 1796.

Jones, Sir William. *Collected Works*, edited by Anna Maria Jones. 6 vols., 1799; 13 vols., 1807.

Keats, John, *Endymion*. 1818; *Hyperion*. 1820.

Landor, Walter Savage. *Gebir*. 1798.

Lawrence, James. *The Empire of the Nairs, or The Rights of Women, an Utopian Romance*. 1811.

Mill, James. *History of British India*. 1817.

Montagu, Lady Mary Wortley. *The Complete Letters*, edited by Robert Halsband. 3 vols. Oxford: Clarendon Press, 1965.

Moore, Thomas. *Lalla Rookh*. 1817; *The Epicurean*. 1827; *Poetical Works*. 1840–41.

Owenson, Sydney (Lady Morgan). *Woman: or, Ida of Athens.* 1809; *The Missionary: An Indian Tale.* 1811.

Reeve, Clara. *The Progress of Romance.* 1787.

Schlegel, Friedrich. *Über die Sprache und Weisheit der Indier.* 1808.

Shelley, Percy Bysshe. "Zeinab and Kathema." 1811–12; *Queen Mab.* 1813; *Alastor.* 1816; *The Revolt of Islam.* 1818; *Prometheus Unbound.* 1820.

Southey, Robert. *Thalaba the Destroyer.* 1801; *The Curse of Kehama.* 1810.

Taylor, Philip Meadows. *Confessions of a Thug.* 1839.

Volney, Constantin. *Les Ruines.* 1791.

Wilkins, Sir Charles. *The Bhăgvăt-Gēētā.* 1785.

Wilson, Horace Hayman. *Meghaduta.* 1813.

Bibliography

Barrell, John. *The Infection of Thomas de Quincey: A Psychopathology of Imperialism.* New Haven, Conn.: Yale University Press, 1990.

Brantlinger, Patrick. *Rule of Darkness: British Literature and Imperialism, 1830–1914.* Ithaca, N.Y.: Cornell University Press, 1988.

Butler, Marilyn. "Orientalism." In *The Penguin History of Literature: The Romantic Period.* Edited by David B. Pirie. London: Penguin, 1994.

Drew, John. *India and the Romantic Imagination.* Delhi: Oxford University Press, 1987.

Figueira, Dorothy. *Translating the Orient: The Reception of Śakuntalā in Nineteenth-Century Europe.* Albany: State University of New York Press, 1991.

Franklin, Caroline. *Byron's Heroines.* Oxford: Clarendon Press, 1992.

Franklin, Michael J., ed. *Sir William Jones: Selected Poetical and Prose Works.* Cardiff: University of Wales Press, 1995.

Franklin, Michael J., ed. *Representing India: Indian Culture and Imperial Control in Eighteenth-Century British Orientalist Discourse.* 9 vols. London: Routledge, 2000.

———, ed., *Europe Discovers India: Key Indological Sources of European Romanticism.* London: Ganesha Press, 2001.

Halbfass, Wilhelm. *India and Europe: An Essay in Understanding.* New York: State University of New York Press, 1988.

Inden, Ronald. *Imagining India.* Oxford, Blackwell: 1, 1990.

Kejariwal, O. P. *The Asiatic Society of Bengal and the Discovery of India's Past 1784–1838.* Delhi: Oxford University Press, 1988.

Kopf, David. *British Orientalism and the Bengal Renaissance: The Dynamics of Indian Modernization 1773–1835.* Berkeley and Los Angeles: University of California Press, 1969.

Leask, Nigel. *British Romantic Writers and the East: Anxieties of Empire.* Cambridge: Cambridge University Press, 1993.

———. "Towards an Anglo-Indian Poetry? The Colonial Muse in the Writings of John Leyden, Thomas Medwin and Charles D'Oyly". In *Writing India 1757–1990*, edited by Bart Moore-Gilbert. Manchester: Manchester University Press, 1996.

MacKenzie, John M. *Orientalism: History, Theory and the Arts.* Manchester: Manchester University Press, 1995.

McGann, Jerome J. *New Oxford Book of Romantic Period Verse.* Oxford: Oxford University Press, 1993.

Mukherjee, S. N. *Sir William Jones: A Study in Eighteenth-Century British Attitudes to India.* Cambridge: Cambridge University Press, 1968.

Raine, Kathleen. *Blake and Tradition.* 2 vols. Princeton, N.J.: Princeton University Press, 1968.

Raychaudhuri, Tapan. *Europe Reconsidered: Perceptions of the West in Nineteenth Century Bengal.* Delhi: Oxford University Press, 1988.

Richardson, Alan and Sonia Hofkosh, eds. *Romanticism, Race, and Imperial Culture, 1780–1834.* Bloomington: Indiana University Press, 1996.

Said, Edward. *Orientalism.* London: Routledge, 1978.

Schwab, Raymond. *The Oriental Renaissance: Europe's Rediscovery of India and the East.* Translated by Gene Patterson-Black and Victor Reinking. New York: Columbia University Press, 1984.

Shaw, Graham. *Printing in Calcutta to 1800.* London: Bibliographical Society, 1981.

Viswanathan, Gauri. *Masks of Conquest: Literary Study and British Rule in India.* London: Faber, 1990.

Willson, Leslie A. *A Mythical Image: The Ideal of India in German Romanticism.* Durham, N.C.: Duke University Press, 1964.

OSSIAN

Ancient Celtic poet (inauthentic)

The name Ossian is surrounded by controversy and national prejudice. In 1759 the Scottish playwright John Home met a young man named James Macpherson, whom he persuaded to help him find out more about Scottish Gaelic poetry. Home knew no Gaelic and was delighted when Macpherson, who had been brought up in the Highlands, offered to show him English translations of some traditional poetry. Encouraged by Home, in 1760 Macpherson published at Edinburgh fifteen *Fragments of Ancient Poetry, Collected in the Highlands of Scotland, and Translated from the Galic or Erse Language.* These fragments of prose poetry, none more than a couple of pages long and many in dialogue form, were written in a rhythmic, repetitive language full of stark natural imagery and Celtic names. For the most part they purported to be based on the lives, and often the deaths, of ancient Caledonian heroes and their loved ones in the dark ages of early British history. In the unsigned preface, Hugh Blair of Edinburgh University attempted to show that the poems were "coeval with the very infancy of Christianity in Scotland," handed down through the centuries, "some in manuscript, but more by oral tradition," and ascribed them to Scottish bards, beginning with Fingal's son Ossian.

Prompted by Macpherson, Blair suggested that the fragments were in fact parts of an epic poem about Fingal, and the preface ended with the stated hope that the whole work might be recovered. Macpherson accordingly traveled through the north of Scotland in search of more poems by Ossian, and at the end of 1761 there duly appeared *Fingal, An Ancient Epic Poem, in Six Books Translated from the Galic Language by James Macpherson.* This was accompanied by several other poems "composed by Ossian, the son of Fingal," and followed in 1763 by another epic, *Temora.*

The excitement caused by these discoveries was immediate and intense. In Scotland and Britain they satisfied the need for a national literary tradition, especially one not indebted to classical models, though Blair and others, including Macpherson, pointed out choice parallels among Ossian, Homer, and Virgil. Just as telling for eighteenth-century readers, however, was the extravagant nobility of the supposedly primitive warriors in the poems and the deep cast of melancholy thrown over their mighty speech and actions. Here seemed to be firm evidence of the natural moral superiority of a people unaffected by the sophistication of modern civilization.

Unfortunately for Macpherson, not everyone was content merely to indulge in the emotional effect of Ossian. The poems were presented as translations, and there was talk of manuscripts. Those of a scholarly bent (notably, Samuel Johnson) asked to see the manuscripts and test the accuracy of the translations. When Macpherson proved unable or unwilling to satisfy these demands, the claim that the poems had been handed down by oral tradition became the target of growing skepticism. Johnson himself, accompanied by his future biographer, James Boswell, journeyed through the Highlands and islands of Scotland in 1773 to assure himself that nothing like Macpherson's Gaelic epics existed, and thereafter did not hesitate to call Macpherson a liar and a cheat. The controversy soon became political, with the Scots mostly defending Ossian as a matter of national pride, and the English accusing Macpherson of forgery. Macpherson's actual use of Gaelic material was ignored.

In the rest of Europe and in North America, this British quarrel was hardly heard. Macpherson's depiction of the ancient Celts maintained its power, as it also did for many British readers. The Scottish Highlanders, who had been bloodily defeated in the Jacobite Rebellion of 1745 and their culture destroyed by political repression, became heroic figures of a spirit-laden past, set against a background of mountains and lakes. Macpherson's outline had to be colored in by Sir Walter Scott for its full effect, but he had begun the transformation of the Highlands and its people into the mythic race that is the foundation of much modern romance and tourism.

In addition, Ossian's works encouraged the thought that if the bleak mountains of Scotland could contain such literary gems perhaps there was similar treasure to be had among marginal peoples in other lands. However unfortunate Macpherson's methods (and their consequences), he did at least introduce something of Gaelic culture into mainstream modern European culture, and in turn inspired other, more careful researchers in Wales, Ireland, and other countries.

Macpherson's Gaelic "translations" were in turn translated into many languages, and his work found its way into surprising hands: in America, Thomas Jefferson declared that Ossian was a "source of daily and exalted pleasure"; the protagonist reads Ossian in Johann Wolfgang Goethe's *Die Leiden des jungen Werthers* (*The Sorrows of Young Werther*); and Napoleon Bonaparte took an Italian version of Ossian to Moscow. The emperor's enthusiasm for Ossian inspired several works by his favored painters, notably, *Ossian évoque les fantômes an son de la harpe* (*Ossian Evoking the Spirits*) by François Gérard and the remarkable *L'Apothéose des héros français morts pour la patrie pendant la guerre de la Liberté* (*Ossian Receiving Napoleon's Generals*) by Anne-Louis Girodet de Roucy-Trioson (both c. 1810), and *Le Songe D'Ossian* (*The Dream of Ossian*, 1813) by Jean-Auguste-Dominique Ingres.

It is not surprising that the major English Romantic poets were cautious in alluding to Ossian's works, given their notoriety. The exception was William Blake, who enthusiastically enrolled Ossian in the line of prophets to which he thought he himself belonged (Macpherson's quasi-biblical prose is surely

Jean-Auguste-Dominique Ingres, Le Songe D'Ossian. Reprinted courtesy of AKG London.

one influence on the style of Blake's prophetic verse). The other English Romantics are more reticent about Ossianic influences, though one might suspect their interest in things Scottish has one of its roots in the Ossian controversy. William Wordsworth, for example, sought out the so-called grave of Ossian on his tour of Scotland in 1803 and wrote a poem about it. The most famous response to Ossian, though, comes later, and in another art form. Joseph Banks (1743–1820), the secretary of the Royal Society in London, made famous the remarkable geological structures on the Hebridean island of Staffa under the name *Fingal's Cave*. This title was attached to Felix Mendelssohn's overture *The Hebrides* (1832). Though the composer had been too seasick on his visit to the island to have direct experience of things Ossianic, his music introduced a lasting evocation of Macpherson's world into the concert hall.

CHRISTOPHER MACLACHLAN

Selected Works

Fragments of Ancient Poetry. 1760.
The Poems of Ossian. 1773.

Bibliography

Baines, Paul. "Ossianic Geographies," *Scotlands* 4, no. 1. (1997): 44–61.
Gaskill, Howard, ed. *Ossian Revisited.* Edinburgh: Edinburgh University Press, 1991.
Johnson, Samuel, and James Boswell. *Journey to the Western Islands*

of Scotland and Journal of a Tour to the Hebrides, Edited by R. W. Chapman. Oxford: Oxford University Press, 1924.

Stafford, Fiona J. *The Sublime Savage: James Macpherson and the Poems of Ossian*. Edinburgh: Edinburgh University Press, 1988.

Thomson, D. S. *The Gaelic Sources of Macpherson's "Ossian."* Edinburgh: Oliver and Boyd, 1952.

Womack, Peter. *Improvement and Romance: Constructing the Myth of the Highlands*. London: Macmillan, 1989.

OVERBECK, FRIEDRICH 1789–1869

German painter

Friedrich Overbeck helped lay the foundations for Pre-Raphaelitism and set the parameters for modern popular religious imagery. His work gave visual expression to the conviction that art and religion are interdependent. He challenged the value of academic training in the visual arts while insisting that art should address a broad public rather than an elite minority, and extolling the art of Raphael and his predecessors as the optimal model for nineteenth century artists.

Overbeck expressed his artistic philosophy in *Triumph of Religion in the Arts*, a painting unveiled, with the artist's own commentary, in 1841. Divided into heavenly and earthly registers reminiscent of Raphael's frescoes at the Stanza della Segnatura, the *Triumph* presents an earthly zone populated by approximately seventy figures, most of whom represent historical artists of the thirteenth through sixteenth centuries. They gather around a central fountain of art, which surges upward toward the heavenly realm. There, Solomon, David, St. Luke and St. John present sculpture, song, painting, and architecture to the Virgin and Child, who, as the font of poetry, sits amid supporting New and Old Testament hosts.

The conceptual framework of Overbeck's artistic credo had been set during his experience at the Academy in Vienna, where he studied under H. Füger in 1805. He was dissatisfied with the mechanical nature of the instruction, which he found to be devoid of "Heart, Soul, and Feeling." Like Asmus Jakob Carstens a decade earlier, Overbeck was convinced that truth in art was dependent on ideas given form through artistic individuality, rather than on the mastery of academic conventions. Overbeck was supported in his rejection of academic practice by other students in Vienna, most notably Franz Pforr and Ludwig Vogel. In 1809 they joined three others to become the Lukasbund, a secessionist group that became the heart of the Nazarene movement.

In 1810 Overbeck traveled with Pforr, Vogel, and Franz Hottinger to Rome, where he was to remain for the rest of his career. The group enjoyed a kind of monastic seclusion reflective of their enthusiasm for Wilhelm Heinrich Wackenroder's *Herzensergiessungen* during a two-year residence in the secularized monastery of San Isidoro. Collective life drawing as well as compositional studies continued (although Overbeck refused to draw from the female nude for fear of corrupting his sensibilities). He began (*Portrait of Franz Pforr*, 1810–65), a fanciful celebration of the artists' profound friendship. Pforr is seated at a symbolically laden window frame, through which is seen a Gothic interior with pious helpmate as well as a view in a medieval northern town. The linear clarity of the painting is rooted in the tradition of Carstens and John Flaxman, while the medieval exuberance of the details may be paralleled to the work of Caspar David Friedrich and Karl Friedrich Schinkel. The resounding calm of the painting is distinctive to Overbeck, however, and reveals his preoccupation with spiritual piety.

Pforr's death in 1812 marked a turning point within the Lukasbund and prompted Overbeck's conversion to Roman Catholicism the following year. Peter Cornelius joined the group in 1812, served as a powerful complement to Overbeck, and helped focus the Lukasbund's attention on public art within Germany's post-Napoleonic culture. As early as 1810, Overbeck had been drawn to the ideas of Johann Heinrich Pestalozzi concerning the potential of art to teach the common people. Cornelius believed this philosophy would be well-served by the genre of the fresco, which he considered an appropriately monumental and public medium, and in 1816–17 the two artists joined Franz Catel, Wilhelm Schadow, and Philipp Veit to produce the Casa Bartholdy frescoes. Overbeck's panels, *Seven Lean Years* and *The Sale of Joseph*, reflect his exploration of primitive prototypes, such as the Aegina Temple sculptures and the work of Perugino (Pietro di Cristoforo Vannucci). When, in the wake of the Bartholdy commission, Overbeck agreed to execute frescoes on themes from Tasso's *Jerusalem Liberata* for the Casino Massimo (1818–27), his mature style coalesced around the early Roman work of Raphael.

Overbeck's active role in the Roman artistic community waned following his marriage in 1818 and the return of many of his contemporaries to Germany by 1820. His work coalesced stylistically, however, and in his *Vittoria Caldoni* (1821) and *Italia und Germania* (1810–28) he gave form to a female ideal that transcended sensuality. With his execution of *The Vision of St. Francis of Assisi*, he committed himself completely to religious art. Major compositions of his mature years appeared in Lübeck (*The Entry of Christ into Jerusalem*, 1809–24, and *Lamentation*, 1839–45), Poznan (*Spozalizio*, 1828–36) and Cologne (*The Assumption of the Virgin*, 1829–54) in Germany; in Leeds, England (*The Incredulity of St. Thomas*, 1847–51); and in other cities. Pope Pius IX commissioned *Christ Evading His Pursuers* 1848–57) for the Palazzo Quirnal. Finally, two late programs capture the breadth and monumentality of Overbeck's vision: the unexecuted Sieben Sacramente (*Seven Sacraments*) for the Orvieto Cathedral (tapestry version, 1861) and the fresco cycle for the cathedral in Djakovo (1865–67). Reproductive prints of all his major compositions were widely distributed, and they, along with his engraved *Forty Scenes from the Gospels* (1844), helped imprint his vision on the religious imagination of the century.

Criticisms of Overbeck's ideals were raised by the 1840s, when it became apparent that his work went against the grain of the materialism informing Biedermeier and realist painting.

Yet throughout the century, Overbeck's position in German art history was secure. He and Cornelius were identified as the heirs to Carstens and as fathers of the "new German art" that dominated public and religious painting throughout Overbeck's lifetime.

ROBERT MCVAUGH

Biography

Born on July 3, 1789, to Christian Adolf and Elisabeth Overbeck in Lübeck. Drawing instruction under N. Peroux in 1804. Following year Overbeck came to know A. Kestner and his collection of drawings after Italian masters. In January 1806 traveled to Hamburg, where he met J. H. W. Tischbein and Philipp Otto Runge, and then later in the year traveled to Vienna, where he enrolled at the Academy under F. H. Füger. He formed the antiacademic Lukasbund with Franz Hottinger, Franz Pforr, J. Sutter, Ludwig Vogel, and J. Wintergerst in 1809. With Hottinger, Pforr, and Vogel, departed the following year for Rome, residing briefly in the secularized monastery of San Isidoro. Converted to Roman Catholicism in 1813. Occupied a leading place within the Catholic faction of the Germanartists in Rome thereafter. In 1818 married AnnaSchiffenhuber-Hartl; their son Alfons was born the following year. Traveled briefly in Germany in 1831, 1855, and 1865. Otherwise remained in Rome, where his son died in 1840, and his wife in 1853. Awarded honorary membership in academies in Munich (1829), Rome (1831), Vienna (1836), Florence (1844), Berlin (1845), and Antwerp (1863). Died November 12, 1869, and was buried in San Bernardo alle Terme in Rome.

Selected Works

Portrait der Franz Pforr. 1810–65. Nationalgalerie, Berlin.
Seven Lean Years and *Sale of Joseph* from the Casa Bartholdy Frescoes. 1816–17. Nationalgalerie, Berlin.
Scenes from Tasso's Jerusalem Liberated. 1818–27. Casino Massimo, Rome.
Vittorio Caldoni. 1821. Neue Pinakothek, Munich.
Italia und Germania. 1811–28. Neue Pinakothek, Munich.
Triumph of Religion in the Art. 1829–41. Städel, Frankfurt.
Lamentation. 1839–45. St. Marien, Lübeck. Germany.

Bibliography

Blühm, Andreas, and Gerhard Gerkens, eds. *Johann Friedrich Overbeck.* Lübeck: Museum für Kunst und Kulturgeschichte der Hansestadt Lübeck, 1989.

Heise, Brigitte. *Johann Friedrich Overbeck. Das künstlerische Werk und seine literarische und autobiographischen Quellen.* Cologne, 1999.

Hinz, Berhard. "*Der Triumph der Religion in den Künsten:* Overbecks 'Werk und Wort' im Widerspruch seiner Zeit," *Städel Jahrbuch,* n.s. 7 (1979): 149–70.

Jensen, Jens Christian. *Zeichnungen von Friedrich Overbeck in der Lübecker Graphiksammlung.* Lübeck, 1969.

Lindtke, Gustav. "Overbecks *Einzug in Jerusalem,* Zur Geschichte eines Bildes," *Sankt Marien Jahrbuch* (1961): 48–61.

Seeliger, Stephan. "Overbecks Sieben Sacramente," *Jahrbuch der Berliner Museen* 6 (1964): 151–72.

THE OVERCOAT, (SHINEL) 1842

Work of fiction by Nikolai Gogol

Nikolai Gogol, according to Donald Fanger, is a major representative of so-called Romantic realism, whose aesthetic views developed under the direct or indirect influence of Honoré de Balzac, Charles Dickens, Jean Paul, Friedrich von Schlegel, and especially E. T. A. Hoffmann, with his trademark blend of the fantastic and the banal. Charles E. Passage has referred to Gogol as a "Russian Hoffmannist." *Shinel* (*The Overcoat*) might arguably be named among those works of Gogol on which Hoffmann had an (perhaps subconscious) effect.

Written in the popular Russian genre of *povest'* (a cross between the short story and the novel), *Shinel* has succeeded in making many generations of readers ignore the rather obvious fact that its plot is completely implausible and its central character's main distinguishing feature seems to be the absence of any such features. An aging Saint Petersburg copyist in the rank of a titular councilor (the ninth in the table of fourteen ranks for civil and military service, introduced by Peter the Great) works for a pittance of a salary at an unspecified (for fear of possible complaints on the part of real-life prototypes) state department. When he decides to devote a significant amount of time to saving up for a much-needed new overcoat, he suddenly discovers a whole new world outside his miserable routine (which he otherwise thoroughly enjoys). After months of self-imposed deprivation, the copyist finally has his overcoat made, only to be robbed of it on the first day he wears it in public. In his bid to recover the stolen property, he pleads his case with a general who, instead of helping the copyist, takes him to task for no other reason than to demonstrate his own superiority. Devastated by this unprovoked display of disrespect, the copyist dies, only to return as a Hoffmannesque ghost from beyond the grave and relieve other people of their overcoats. He inflicts considerable damage on the inhabitants of Saint Petersburg and only stops when he takes revenge on the general who had humiliated him.

For more than half a century after its publication, *Shinel* was being misread as a work that champions the cause of Russia's so-called little men in their stand against the powers that be (the insensitive but influential critic Vissarion Belinsky should be granted priority in such an interpretation). For Gogol, however, the copyist himself is undoubtedly a subject of mockery, as his quite unusual first name and patronymic suggests (Akaky Akakievich, in the mind of the native Russian speaker is invariably associated with feces, *kaki*).

In fact, *Shinel* is an unobtrusively subversive and perhaps even revolutionary work of art that satirizes and questions many traditional values, from literary conventions to the very foundations of Russian society at that time. As for literary conventions, the narration is constantly interrupted and digresses at every possible opportunity, to the deliberate detriment of the development of the story line. The characters in the story are supposedly portrayed with a certain degree of depth, allegedly in accordance with generic requirements, but only the most insignificant information about them is divulged, such as a disfigured nail on a tailor's toe, or the fact that this tailor's wife wore a bonnet and not a shawl. Topically, *Shinel* should be examined against a fairly long, and by that time already cliché-ridden, tradition of depicting titular councilors as a laughing stock of Russian officialdom. The criticism of the table of ranks, which forced society to judge its members on the basis of their rank rather than their character (and, in general, those human qualities that the rank does not necessarily merit), is obvious in the story. Gogol finds it important to emphasize that Akaky Akakievich and the general have things in common. Thus, both are completely overwhelmed by the signs of power bestowed on them on behalf of the omnipotent bureaucracy (the former by his new overcoat, and the latter by a recent promotion); both feel relaxed after consuming, on entirely different occasions, two glasses of champagne and start going after women as a result.

Far less obvious is Gogol's skeptical attitude to the family. Akaky Akakievich's relationship with his new overcoat is grotesquely described in terms of marriage, the tailor's wife communicates with her husband mostly by calling him names, and the saccharine scenes of the general's family life are notably counterbalanced by his intended visit to his mistress, which leads him straight into the hands of Akaky Akakievich the ghost (this, some critics believe, could be explained by Gogol's repressed homosexuality). The Christian idea of human compassion comes under attack in the rhetorically overblown passages that summarize the feelings of Akaky Akakievich's younger colleague, who used to tease the copyist together with the rest of the clerks but suddenly saw the light and changed his ways. The ideas of afterlife and of posthumous reward are ridiculed in the rather preposterous denouement.

Following (and perhaps rivaling) the success of Aleksandr Pushkin's *Tales of Ivan Petrovich Belkin* (1831), a cycle of novellas with cardboard characters and far-fetched plots, which also emerged as a literary joke but later acquired a cult status through a relatively large number of interpretations and reinterpretations, *Shinel* influenced many Russian authors. Fyodor Dostoevsky reportedly said, referring to the writers of his generation, "We all came out from under Gogol's *Overcoat*." Quite characteristically for Gogol's surreal and elusive piece, Russianists are still struggling to locate the exact source of the Dostoevsky quotation.

ANDREI ROGACHEVSKII

Text

Shinel. First appeared as part of the four-volume *Sochineniia* (Collected Works), 1842; translated as *The Overcoat* by Constance Garnett. In *The Overcoat and Other Stories*. London: Chatto & Windus. 1923.

Bibliography

Fanger, Donald. *Dostoesky and Romantic Realism: A Study of Dostoevsky in Relation to Balzac, Dickens, and Gogol*. Cambridge, Mass.: Harvard University Press, 1965.

Graffy, Julian. *Gogol's Overcoat*. Bristol: Bristol Classical Press, 2000.

Jenness, Rosemarie Krais. *Gogol's Aesthetics Compared to Major Elements of German Romanticism*. New York: Peter Lang, 1995.

Karlinsky, Simon. *The Sexual Labyrinth of Nikolai Gogol*. Cambridge, Mass.: Harvard University Press, 1976.

Nabokov, Vladimir. *Lectures on Russian Literature*. London: Weidenfeld and Nicolson, 1981.

Passage, Charles E. *The Russian Hoffmannists*, The Hague: Mouton, 1963.

Rancour-Laferriere, Daniel. *Out from under Gogol's Overcoat: A Psychoanalytic Study*. Ann Arbor, Mich.: Ardis, 1982.

Trahan, Elizabeth, ed. *Gogol's "Overcoat": An Anthology of Critical Essays*. Ann Arbor, Mich: Ardis, 1982.

OWEN, ROBERT 1771–1858

British industrialist, philanthropist, and social theorist

As manager of one of the largest cotton mills in Europe at New Lanark, Scotland, from 1800 on, Robert Owen was impressed by the immense productive capacity of associated labor and modern science. It convinced him that Thomas Malthus had been wrong in opposing scarcity, and consequent vice and misery, as an insuperable barrier to improving the lot of the laboring classes. His own efforts to improve the conditions and moral character of his workforce led to equally unorthodox conclusions. In *A New View of Society* (1813–4) and *A Report to the County of Lanark* (1821), he argued that the current competitive, individualistic, profit-oriented, and market-dependent way of managing such potential abundance was contrary to the true interests of humanity. Proclaiming that only he possessed the true "science of society" and true principles of political economy, he developed the possibilities of "united labor, expenditure, and property" to deliver universal prosperity and happiness in place of postwar hardship and unemployment. His plan for "villages of cooperation" inspired many communitarian experiments and his championing of the power of association as a means of social

revolution put him at the head of the trade union movement in 1833–34. Friedrich Engels and Karl Marx were initially impressed with the critical power of Owen's ideas, which had become known as socialism, but later criticized as "utopian" his refusal to recognize the necessity of class conflict.

Owen presented himself as the prophet of a new moral world, led by the light of reason rather than by former thinkers, but many of his ideas seem to have been gathered from his early, unsystematic reading and his self-education in the artisan society of London in the 1780s and Manchester in the 1790s. His millennialism is reminiscent of that period, and his central principle, that the happiness of the individual is found in procuring the happiness of all, is one that William Godwin had divorced from religious sanctions. Like Godwin, Owen emphasized reason and the formation of character by circumstances in order to stress the reformative power of those who create propitious circumstances, especially in a Rousseauian infant-education program. It is from Thomas Paine that Owen might have derived the idea of "society" as a cooperative enterprise, operating mutually beneficial trade and providing social welfare in its organized capacity, as distinguished from a "government" concerned solely with law, coercion, and warfare. Owen was aware of similarities to Thomas Spence's plan for the common ownership of land.

Samuel Taylor Coleridge and Robert Southey planned pantisocracy under such influences, and Owen similarly thought his scheme capable of regenerating society by example. Owen's view was never less than imperial in its scope, and his ever more grandiose architectural plans for communal facilities supported his assertion that his associators would be envied even by those privileged in the old world. His fame as a successful industrialist and the established institutions of New Lanark, which became a showplace for continental visitors, seemed to guarantee the practicality of his plans, though several crucial elements were not fully worked out. Adopting David Ricardo's principle of labor as the measure of value, Owen planned to return to the laborer "a fair proportion" of the value of his labor despite his emphasis on united property. He established a network of exchanges to manage a new currency that would not fluctuate in value, based on the number of hours of labor used to make an article, but the value of labor notes was still calculated in terms of the "going rate" in the old world. The details of his economic theory he left to others, such as William Thompson, to develop. Politically his assumption of a natural harmony of interests proved utopian indeed as his plans to unify the trade unions and use the strike weapon foundered when employers used strike-breaking tactics and forced employees to renounce union membership. Leadership of working-class movements then passed to the chartists. Owen also failed in efforts to unite followers of Charles Fourier and Claude Henri de Saint-Simon under his association. For many socialist thinkers Owenism was just one stage in their development, despite their reverence for his idealism. None of the communities he inspired in Britain or America had a long life, but their breakdown could be blamed on factors other than their ideology. In one case, an Irish patron lost the land he lent to the Ralahine community at the gambling table.

Owen cooperated with the first Sir Robert Peel in preparing a Factory Act endeavoring to limit the hours worked by children, the first of a line of such acts challenging the powers of owners, but from 1817 on he had little influence on official policy. In that year he publically attacked religion, characterizing it as a force that perverts the rational mind, though he increasingly used apocalyptic biblical language to announce his secular millennium. His radical views on marriage and the family as restrictive and socially divisive further outraged conventional morality. Owenism as a counterculture attracted former followers of millennialist sects and communicated its spirit of cooperative experiment in all aspects of life to trade unionists and chartists. It used its communal buildings for educational purposes, published numerous periodicals, established a secular form of "naming" and of marriage, and held feast days in competition with the Christian calendar, including rambunctious Sunday celebrations.

Opinion has been divided as to whether Owen belongs to the tradition of Tory paternalistic philanthropy developed to oppose a liberal political economy. Owen certainly recommended his plan to the dominant groups in society since they had the resources to establish them, and his regulations can often sound totalitarian. But he envisaged communities moving toward self-government. In *A New View of Society* his system of universal education is launched into incalculable futurity, and "it will never more return even into the control of its projectors." In his spiritualist phase Owen recorded a visit from the spirit of Percy Bysshe Shelley, and his project does seem to have more in common with Shelley's radical vision of society, the vision renounced by the first Romantics.

CHRIS JONES

Biography

Born in Newtown, Wales, in 1771 and by his own account largely self-educated. At the age of ten left home and found work as a draper's assistant in Stamford, Lincolnshire, moving in 1784 to a London firm and in the next year to Manchester; formed a partnership to manufacture spinning machinery and then became manager of Drinkwater's factory. In 1800 formed a partnership to take over the New Lanark mill, but it was not until 1813 that a third partnership, involving William Allen and Jeremy Bentham, gave Owen latitude to develop his ideas and his educational institution. Plan for cooperative villages was first proposed as a remedy for postwar unemployment in 1817 but grew into a blueprint for a new society, for which Owen campaigned. In 1825, inaugurated the community of New Harmony, Indiana, in which he invested his own fortune. The only other community in which he was substantially involved was Queenwood, Hampshire, England, from 1839 to 1845. Through publications, lectures, and correspondence maintained his titular leadership of Owenite Cooperative Societies throughout the country, though they tended to develop his ideas in their own ways, and proselytized prominent continental figures. Continued to found grandly titled associations up to his death in 1858 at age eighty-seven.

Selected Writings

A New View of Society; or, Essays on the Principle of the Formation of Human Character. 4 vols. 1813–4.
Observations on the Effect of the Manufacturing System. 1815.
Report to the Committee of the Association for the Relief of the Manufacturing and Laboring Poor. 1817.
Report to the County of Lanark. 1821.

Two Upper Cotton Works, New Lanark Textile Mills, 1796. (engraving). Reprinted courtesy of The Bridgeman Art Library.

Outline of the Rational System of Society. 1830.
The Book of the New Moral World. 7 vols. 1836–44.
Ten Lectures on the Evils of Indissoluble Marriage. 1840.
Socialism Misrepresented and Truly Represented. 1848.
Selected Works of Robert Owen. 4 vols. Edited by Gregory Claeys. London: Pickering 1993.

Bibliography

Armytage, W. H. G. *Heavens Below: Utopian Experiments in England, 1560–1960*. London: Routledge, 1961.
Cole, G. D. H. *The Life of Robert Owen*. London: Macmillan, 1930.
Frow, Edmund, and Ruth Frow. *The New Moral World: Robert Owen and Owenism in Manchester and Salford*. Manchester: Manchester Working Class Movement Library, 1986.

Harrison, J. F. C. *Robert Owen and the Owenites in Britain and America*. London: Routledge, 1969.
Morton, A. L. *The Life and Ideas of Robert Owen*. London: Lawrence and Wishart, 1962.
Podmore, Frank. *Robert Owen, a Biography*. London: Hutchinson, 1906.
Pollard, Sidney, ed. *Robert Owen, Prophet of the Poor*. London: Macmillan, 1971.
Royle, Edward. *Robert Owen and the Commencement of the Millennium: A Study of the Harmony Community*. Manchester: Manchester University Press, 1998.
Silver, Harold. *The Concept of Popular Education: A Study of Ideas and Social Movements in the Early Nineteenth Century*. London: Methuen, 1977.

P

PAGANINI, NICCOLÒ 1782–1840

Violin virtuoso and composer

The career and the physical and mental suffering of the exceptional artist in whatever domain was a favorite theme in the Romantic drama and fiction. Niccolò Paganini, like Franz Liszt, who was his equal as an instrumental virtuoso and his superior as a composer, was to live it out in reality, strikingly embodying the contradictory traits that were supposed the warrant of true genius.

Born in 1782 into a Genoese family that was not rich, Paganini started his education at the age of five when he took up the mandolin. He turned to the violin two years later. His father was his first violin teacher. Whether he appreciated in those early days what exceptional talents were possessed by his son is uncertain, but he spared no effort to make him practice long and hard. After a short time he arranged for the boy not only to continue his instrumental training with Antonio Cervetto, a violinist in the local theater orchestra, but also to begin lessons in harmony with a young opera composer, Francesco Gnecco. Such was the young Paganini's progress that he was next accepted as a pupil by Giacomo Costa, a prominent Genoese musician, who arranged for him to give his first public performance, during mass in the church of San Filippo Neri in 1794. It was probably a year later that the Polish virtuoso A. F. Duranowksi made a deep impression on Niccolò, his playing revealing to him both technical tricks and a style of musical showmanship that he emulated in later life. In his early teens Paganini went to Rome, studying composition, most significantly with Fernando Paër, and on his return to Genoa in 1796 he took up the guitar.

Paganini's career as a full-fledged public performer began under the inauspicious circumstances of the French campaigns in Italy. He succeeded in establishing himself in Lucca, where, in addition to teaching and giving recitals, he composed a set of sonatas for violin. He also found fulfillment in Princess Baciocchi's orchestra, but only for a while. Feeling his abilities were not properly appreciated, he embarked on the career of an independent recitalist. He was by no means the only musician to do so at this period, but it was a sign of the times that performers like him were no longer content to accept the relative constrictions of a court appointment for the sake of financial security. A dozen recitals in Milan, with some of his own compositions in the programs, made Paganini famous in Italy, and he performed in all the major cities, despite the setback of a serious illness that left him with a disturbingly haggard appearance. Successful performances in Vienna in 1828 inaugurated a concert tour across Europe, to Prague (where he had to have all his teeth removed), across Germany to Paris and then Britain. His schedule was punishing: in autumn of 1833, for instance, he made more than forty appearances in more than thirty different British cities in a period of less than three months. The financial rewards were great, but Paganini had wrecked his already precarious health and spoiled his reputation by overexposure. Returning to Italy, he entered the service of the Grand Duchess Marie-Louise at Parma, but soon tired of it, briefly tried to restart his career as a virtuoso, and then became involved in unsuccessful entertainment ventures in Paris. While there, he attended a concert of music by Hector Berlioz. He was sufficiently impressed to make a generous gift to the composer, and he responded by dedicating to him his *Harold in Italy*, which prominently features the viola, the instrument that Paganini took an interest in during his later years. After prolonged suffering, Paganini died in 1840.

The Bishop of Nice denied Christian burial to a man who had declined the last sacraments, inadvertently helping perpetuate the myth of a demonic fiddler possessed by Satan that had a place in folklore and was developed by Giuseppe Tartini with his so-called Devil's Trill Sonata. Cadaverous in appearance and possessing names that invited naive interpretations, Paganini played like a man possessed. It was only too tempting to see in him a character analogous to some of the otherworldly figures peopling the Gothic novel and the melodramatic stage in the Romantic era.

Wolfgang Amadeus Mozart's *Figaro*) to "God Save the King," were the mainstay of the concerts designed to show off his skills. The set of twenty-four *Caprices*, dating from about 1805 but published only a decade and a half later, remain among the most challenging works for solo violin. Themes from it have also inspired a remarkably large number of composers, particularly Sergei Rachmaninov, whose 1934 *Rhapsody on a Theme of Paganini* still propagates a vivid impression of the Romantic violinist. Paganini also wrote three violin concertos. They too are technically demanding, and their construction reflects both the training in composition that Paganini had received and the seriousness with which he approached his task. They do not, however, rank among the leading Romantic works in the form. Though attractive, they were surpassed by those of Ludwig Spohr, who challenged Paganini as a virtuoso and was highly rated as a composer in the first half of the nineteenth century, and by the *Violin Concerto in E Minor* by Felix Mendelssohn.

CHRISTOPHER SMITH

Jean-Auguste-Dominique Ingres, *Niccolò Paganini*. Reprinted courtesy of AKG.

Paganini's violin technique was dazzling, doubtless making an even deeper impression on the audiences of the time because they did not hear virtuoso performances on radio or recordings. With his upper arm held close to his body, he controlled his bow exclusively with his forearm and wrist, producing a wide range of dynamics, amazing agility, and absolute control of double-stopping and harmonics. His extraordinary left-hand pizzicato, which related to his interest in the guitar, added another dimension. For special effects he had recourse to scordatura, altering the normal tuning of his violin, and sometimes startled audiences by performing works on just one string.

Like other virtuosos of the time, Paganini was also a composer. His own works, especially the numerous sets of variations on well-known tunes ranging from "Non più andrai" (from

Biography

Born Genoa, October 27, 1782. First lessons on mandolin, 1787. Violin lessons, first with father, then with Antonio Cervetto, 1789. First concert in Genoese church, 1794. Impressed by Duranowski; to Parma to study composition with Paër, 1795. To Livorno, to escape dangers of French occupation of Genoa; embarked on career as recitalist, 1800. To Lucca, where he obtained court appointment, 1801. Many recitals in Italy, 1810–28. Traveled across Europe—to Vienna, Prague, Germany, France, and Britain—giving recitals, 1828–34. Returned to Italy, in poor health, 1834; court appointment in Parma, but could not settle in. Commercial ventures in Paris, 1837. Dies in Nice after long illness, May 27, 1840; denied Christian burial.

Bibliography

Barri, P. *Paganini: La vita e le opere*. Edited by M. Monti. Milan: Bompiani, 1982.

G. I. C. de Courcy. *Chronology of Nicolò Paganini*. Wiesbaden: Erdmann, 1962.

———. *Paganini the Genoese*. 2 vols. Norman: Oklahoma University Press, 1957.

Moretti, M. R., and A. Sorrento, eds. *Catalogo tematico delle musiche di Nicolò Paganini*. Genova: Commune di Genova, 1982.

Neill, E., ed. *Nicolò Paganini Epistolario*. Genova: Siag, 1982.

Stowell, Robin. "The Nineteenth-Century Bravura Tradition." In *The Cambridge Companion to the Violin*. Edited by Robin Stowell. Cambridge, U.K.: Cambridge University Press, 1992. 61–78.

Sugden, J. *Nicolo Paganini: Supreme Virtuoso or Devil's Fiddler?* Tonbridge Wells: Midas, 1980.

PAINE, THOMAS 1737–1809

English political writer

Thomas Paine was a radical thinker and polemicist. While steeped in the political discourses of eighteenth-century Britain, his writings helped to transform the language and style in which political issues could be addressed. He involved himself as an author and an activist in the turbulent events of his times—the French and American Revolutions—and the explosion of British radical dissent in the 1790s. He is best known for *Common Sense* (1776), *Rights of Man* (part 1, 1791; part 2, 1792), and *Age of Reason* (part 1, 1794; part 2, 1796). He wrote many other pamphlets, including indictments of slavery, the most important being a work of political economy, *Agrarian Justice* (1797).

Paine's first major work, *Common Sense*, was written in the context of the American struggle with British colonial rule in the 1770s with the aim of galvanizing support for a rebellion against English taxation. However, it also marked a dramatic departure in political writing in two senses: in its substance and in its style. First, previous complaints against colonial rule had been couched in terms of a restoration of traditional British rights to American citizens in the face of unreasonable demands from England; Paine, in contrast, argued strenuously for the self-determination of the American states and the institution of an American government based on natural rights. Further, he attacked the very elements of the British government, a system that was often held up as a political ideal. Paine espoused a vision of society based on the defense of property. The hereditary principle, he argued, was merely justification of a government based on state-sanctioned theft, disguised by an absurd and falsely rhetorical defense of historical right. The resulting aristocratic and monarchical forms of government were unjust and subject to a self-perpetuating, degenerative corruption. From this, he felt, America should free itself.

These arguments were not all new to political discourse. What made them so was the form in which Paine presented them. In *Common Sense* he developed a unique style of political writing that he maintained across his works, and that was as much a part of his message as what he wrote. His style must be seen against thinking about the status of written language at the time. Education was limited to the moneyed classes, and such works on language as Samuel Johnson's *Dictionary*, with their emphasis on rule, models, and classical learning, demonstrated an ideological investment in maintaining writing as the preserve of this elite. Paine refused to abide by the rules of this discourse. His appeals were based not on precedent, history, and antique models but on the forthright exposition of a self-consciously logical argument. He drew the allusions from which he structured his rhetoric from common experience and popular works of literature such as the myths of John Bunyan and Don Quixote, as well as the Bible. This approach evinces a conception of politics that is not the concern of other people, but something present to and pressing upon each individual. Many writings by nineteenth-century radicals inspired by Paine bear witness to the power and originality of Paine's approach.

This style found its ideal target in the emotional rhetoric of Edmund Burke's *Reflections on the Revolution in France*, to which Paine responded in *Rights of Man*. In the *Reflections*, Burke had attacked any theorization of rights and vindicated the virtues of the seemingly unsystematized traditions of the British government. Paine attacked Burke's argument that these institutions possessed an organic and venerable character. Instead, Paine contended, British history was marked by the violent usurpation of natural right from the Norman conquest onward. This past was its disability, he felt, and not its pride.

In part 1 of *Rights of Man*, Paine refutes the naturalness of primogeniture, identifying in the idea that the living should be tied to the demands of the dead and the unborn an unhealthy morbidity. Society, he writes, is a natural development from basic human association, and as such is open to revision by each

generation for the mutual good. Government is purely a negative check upon the destructive impulses of mankind. The domination of society by government, through taxation and through the corrupting influences of luxury made possible by that taxation, is a dominance by potentially the worst, not the best, elements of society. Paine refutes Edmund Burke's sentimental defense of monarchy and reinterprets it as collusive in a theatrical show, or what he calls a "pantomimical contrivance," of government used cynically to disguise its corruption and disregard of the distresses of the majority. Paine counters this with a self-conscious plainness and self-evidence of style that complements his ideas of what is natural to society. Part 2 of *Rights of Man* extends this attack by providing a countertheory of how government should operate in society. Paine's proposed scheme is remarkably modern, suggesting a plan of social welfare that would ameliorate the hardships endemic in a market society, including pensions and other benefits for the poorest in society, funded through redistributive taxation. In *Age of Reason*, Paine extends his critique of society to religion, arguing that established religion was used as a tool of social injustice, drawing arguments from the philosopher David Hume and the French historian Constantine Volney. While Paine explicitly states his belief in God in *Age of Reason*, its deism, and its analysis of religion as a political tool, was felt to be extreme and invited refutations even from prominent radicals, such as Joseph Priestley. This dismayed Paine; indeed, in 1796 he founded a group of "theophilanthropists" in order to counter atheism.

One of the distinctive features of Paine's career was the mass availability of his writings. The estimated figures for his sales, although uncertain, are staggering. *Common Sense* sold an estimated 100,000 copies in its first year; *Rights of Man* parts 1 and 2 sold perhaps 200,000. The low selling price of his works was seen in itself as indicative of seditious intent, and led to his indictment on treason charges in 1792. This was a direct response to Paine's impact: *Rights of Man* prompted some four hundred or five hundred responses, many recording its empowering influence for would-be radicals. Indeed, this is Paine's legacy in the nineteenth century and beyond: his rhetoric is visible in the works of William Blake, William Cobbett, Francis Place, and William Wordsworth. A reprint of *Rights of Man* in 1816–1817 led to the arrest of its publisher, Richard Carlisle, but eventually also influenced the repeal of the laws under which he was imprisoned.

SUZIE JORDAN

Biography

Born in Thetford, Suffolk, on January 29, 1737 to a Quaker family; apprenticed to his father's trade of staymaking; married Mary Lambert, 1759. From 1764 to 1774 employed variously as an excise man, shopkeeper, and teacher, and was active in scientific researches, debating societies, charitable work and campaigns for higher wages for excisemen; Married Elizabeth Ollive, 1771. Published *The Case of the Officers of Excise*, 1772. Met Benjamin Franklin, and emigrated to America, 1774. Edited the *Pennsylvania Magazine*, 1775, published *Common Sense*, enlisted in the American army, and wrote pamphlets for the American cause, including *The Crisis* series, 1776. From 1777 to 1787, held various junior offices in the American government and traveled to France. Returned to France and England in 1787, promoting a new design of bridge. From 1789 to 1790, lived in France. In 1791, returned to England and published *Rights of Man* (part 1). In February, 1792, published *Rights of Man* (part 2), was charged with sedition, and fled to France where he was elected to the French Convention. In 1793, wrote *Age of Reason*, partly in the Luxemborg prison. Published part 1 of *Age of Reason*, 1794. Readmitted to the French Convention, 1795. Published part 2 of *Age of Reason*, 1796. Wrote *Agrarian Justice* in 1797. Returned to America, 1802. Dies June 8, 1809.

Selected Works

Collections

The Writings of Thomas Paine. Edited by Moncure D. Conway, 4 vols., 1894–96.
The Complete Writings of Thomas Paine. Edited by Philip S. Foner. 2 vols., 1945.
Political Writings. Rev. ed. Edited by Bruce Kuklich. 2000.

Political Writing

Common Sense, 1776. Edited by Isaac Kramnick. 1976.
Rights of Man. 1791–92. Edited by Eric Foner. 1984.

Bibliography

Boulton, James T. *The Language of Politics in the Age of Wilkes and Burke*. London: Routledge and Kegan Paul, 1963.
Butler, Marilyn. *Burke, Paine, Godwin, and the Revolution Controversy*. Cambridge: Cambridge University Press, 1984.
———. *Romantics, Rebels, and Reactionaries: English Literature and its Background 1760–1830*. Oxford: Oxford University Press, 1981.
Claeys, Gregory. *Thomas Paine, Social and Political Thought*. Boston: Unwin Hyman, 1989.
Dyck, Ian, ed. *Citizen of the World: Essays on Thomas Paine*. London: Christopher Helm, 1987.
Smith, Olivia. *The Politics of Language 1791–1819*. Oxford: Clarendon Press, 1984.
Thompson, E. P. *The Making of the English Working Class*. Harmondsworth, England: Penguin, 1968.

PALMER, SAMUEL 1805–1881

English artist

With virtually no schooling and little artistic tuition, Samuel Palmer exhibited a precocious talent; his first exhibited picture was sold when he was just fourteen years old, and during the next six years he was well represented at both the British Institution and the Royal Academy. During this period, Palmer's work was similar to that of John Constable, and he was also impressed by J. M. W. Turner (in 1819 he saw Turner's *Orange Merchantman* at the Academy). Turner's influence is not only discernible in early works by Palmer, such as *Hailsham, Sussex: Storm Effect* (1821), but also in later works, like *Landscape with Rain-cloud* (c. 1848–50) and *Tintagel Castle: Approaching Rain* (c. 1848–50). Other influential events in Palmer's early career included hearing John Flaxman lecture on sculpture. In addition, John Linnell, an established artist, sympathized with the young artist's perception of the divine in exactly realized scenes of nature and, most significantly, introduced Palmer to William Blake. Already familiar with Blake's work, and what Palmer referred to as his "primitive grandeur," the young artist seems to have undergone a spiritual awakening in the presence of this aging visionary. Palmer, too, saw religious apparitions, and the "sweet encouragement" Blake offered gave Palmer the confidence to express his individual talents.

Palmer's sketchbook of 1824 reveals the extent to which he rejected the traditions of landscape painting. However, although Blake's influence can be seen in sketches of this period, including *God Creating the Firmament* (1824) and *Ruth Returned from the Gleaning* (c. 1826–27), they remain isolated (and not very successful) attempts at this style. Where Palmer significantly departs from Blake is in his perception of nature. For Blake, the material world is regarded as mere vegetation, which is subordinate to the imagination. For Palmer, by contrast, nature is a veil through which we can glimpse heaven. Location also heightened the spiritual qualities of nature, and from 1826, Shoreham in Kent (south of London) replaced Dulwich as his inspirational base. This artist, however, was not concerned with the specific; he viewed the landscape as a "gate into the world of vision" that would reveal paradise to all "true poets."

At this point, Palmer was not concerned with naturalism, but a highly stylized response to the landscape. His subjects were earthy, including trees, ears of corn, hills, and the moon, yet they appear mystical. In the drawing *The Valley Thick with Corn* (1825), a resting laborer is encircled by almost uniform sheaves of corn and harvested bundles that strike the viewer as childlike in their simplicity, while the background consists of rounded hills and globular trees. The even distribution of detail and the rhythmic symmetry of shapes are suggestive of fairytales (exemplified in *The Skirts of a Wood*, 1825 and *Early Morning*, 1825). Furthermore, the modernity of such works as *The Magic Apple Tree* (1830), in which a farm laborer and his surroundings are characterized by bold forms and firm lines, prefigures Jean-François Millet's work, and the gaudy use of primary colors combined with a striking originality of vision suggests parallels with Vincent van Gogh. The Shoreham period is best remembered for these sepia sketches, but a small number of oils and watercolors with tempera were also produced during this time. *A Hilly Scene* (c. 1826) represents one of the triumphs of European Romanticism. It is an extremely compact painting of a church visible above a field of golden corn situated at the base of hills. The whole scene is framed by two trees whose branches create a Gothic arch above a crescent moon which mirrors the circular shape of the hills beneath. The viewer is invited into the painting by an open gate which leads to a path between the corn where one can worship (thus the inclusion of the church spire) the spiritual power and luminosity of Nature at twilight. Palmer was particularly interested in liminal times of the day, such as dawn and dusk, and autumnal scenes.

The house where Palmer lived with his father and nurse from 1827, Waterhouse, was the setting for the meetings of a group of friends who called themselves "The Ancients." A precursor of the Pre-Raphaelite Brotherhood, these artists were similarly inclined towards medievalism (although Palmer greatly admired Raphael). Edward Calvert, whose drawings of this period are decidedly Palmeresque, despite the artist's maturity and formal training, wrote of the Ancients, "We were brothers in art, brothers in love, and brothers in that for which love and art subsist— the Ideal—the Kingdom within." The atmosphere was one of social and artistic freedom, but what Calvert described as the "Kentish embodiment of an Arcadian dream" soon ended. Even though Palmer wrote to one of the Ancients, George Richmond, that "By God's help I will not sell away his gift of art for money," the necessity of earning a living became pressing and Linnell, who Palmer had previously hailed as a savior for "pluck[ing] him from the pit of modern art," suggested that he could earn money as an engraver. Palmer left Shoreham for what he referred to as a "pigsty neighbourhood" in London.

A few years later, Palmer married Linnell's eldest daughter, Hannah. She was a talented artist with whom Palmer could share his visionary ideas, and the newlyweds subsequently embarked on a two-year tour of Italy. Palmer's drawings of this time display a technical mastery, but in comparison with his Shoreham work they are disappointingly conventional. For much of the remainder of his career, Palmer struggled with his style, turning increasingly to what he referred to as a direct "imitation" of nature (producing some Ruskinian studies of nature) in a bid to enhance the fluidity and salability of his landscapes and, thus, ease the demands of private teaching that kept him in the city. Hannah and their children spent long periods at her parent's home, which increased Palmer's frustration at not having access to the country for inspiration. Writing in 1859, Palmer concedes, "I seem doomed never to see again that first flush of summer splendour which entranced me at Shoreham." Palmer's self-confessed tendency to "haunt the caves of melancholy" was aggravated by the death of two of his children, and after living in many unsuitable properties the artist agreed to live in the neighborhood of his father-in-law. The house where

Palmer would remain for the rest of his life represented a pretentious gentility that both the artist and his father had so vehemently opposed. The only compensations were the views of Surrey and the Sussex downs and a token rebellion in the cultivation of weeds. Palmer complained of stagnation, but during this period he executed several remarkable series of etchings based on the work of John Milton and Virgil. Much of his later work also draws thematically on the Romantic poets; in addition to the obvious parallels with John Clare in his view of the pastoral, Palmer derived inspiration from the burial place of John Keats and *The Sleeping Shepherd* (1857) illustrates the cover of John Barnard's edition of Keats's poems, alluding to the languorous figure of Endymion, who sees mystical visions within the natural landscape.

SARAH WOOTTON

Biography

Born in Walworth, January 27, 1805. Attended the Merchant Taylor's School for a few months in the summer of 1817; after the death of his mother, studied art under William Wate, 1818, and sold his first exhibited painting, *Landscape Composition*, at the British Institution. Met John Linnell, September 1822; met William Blake, October 9, 1824, first visit to Shoreham, and commenced sketchbook; took up permanent residence in Shoreham, 1827. Lived in London from 1832 on. Married Hannah Linnell on September 30, 1837; journey to Italy. Returned from Italy, November 1839; elected an Associate of the Royal Society of Painters in Watercolours, 1848; death of his father, December 17, 1848. Elected member of the Etching Club, February 19, 1850. Elected full member of the Society of Painters in Watercolours, 1854; moved to "Furze Hill House," Surrey, May 1862. Died May 24, 1881.

Bibliography

Abley, Mark, ed. *The Parting Light: Selected Writings of Samuel Palmer.* Manchester: Carcanet with MidNAG, 1985.

Grigson, Geoffrey. *Samuel Palmer's Valley of Vision.* London: Phoenix House, 1960.

Harrison, Colin. *Samuel Palmer.* Oxford: Ashmolean Museum, 1997.

Lister, Raymond. *Catalogue Raisonné of the Works of Samuel Palmer.* Cambridge: Cambridge University Press, 1988.

———. *The Letters of Samuel Palmer.* 2 vols. Oxford: Clarendon Press, 1974.

———. *The Paintings of Samuel Palmer.* Cambridge: Cambridge University Press, 1985.

———. *Samuel Palmer: A Biography.* London: Faber and Faber, 1974.

———. *Samuel Palmer and "The Ancients."* Cambridge: Cambridge University Press, 1984.

———. *Samuel Palmer: His Life and Art.* Cambridge: Cambridge University Press, 1987.

Paley, Morton D. "The Art of 'The Ancients,' " *Huntington Library Quarterly* 52 (1989): 97–124.

Palmer, A. H. *The Life and Letters of Samuel Palmer.* London: Seeley, 1892.

Payne, Christiana. "John Linnell and Samuel Palmer in the 1820s," *Burlington Magazine* 124 (1982): 131–36.

Peacock, Carlos. *Samuel Palmer: Shoreham and After.* London: John Baker, 1968.

Samuel Palmer, *Hilly Landscape with Farmers Ploughing.* Reprinted courtesy of the Bridgeman Art Library.

PALUDAN-MÜLLER, FREDERIK 1809–1876

Danish writer

If Frederik Paludan-Müller's overriding concern, like most Danish writers of the nineteenth century, was the conflict between the desires of the individual and the mores of society, he, more than anyone, wrote about this dichotomy from excruciating personal experience. Although Paludan-Müller is seldom read today, his contributions to the "golden age" of Danish literature were hailed as worthy of Lord Byron by his contemporaries. However, Paludan-Müller is associated more with the later Danish manifestation of Romanticism known as *romantisme*; he rejects the metaphysical presuppositions of universal Romanticism, and his later work takes on marked melancholic and religious overtones, leading some critics to draw parallels with Søren Kierkegaard's brand of existentialism.

As a student in 1830s Copenhagen, Paludan-Müller's entry into the most fashionable social circles was assured by his family name, but an excess of high living was brought sharply to a halt by disease (typhoid fever) and self-disgust. He was nursed back to health by the loyal but stern Charite Borch, whom he later married, and he withdrew from the decadence of the social whirl, observing and exposing what he saw as the deterioration of national life from the sidelines. However, Paludan-Müller was already something of a cause célèbre thanks to his lengthy verse-novel *Danserinden* (*The Dancer*, 1833). The touchstone for *Danserinden* was Lord Byron's *Don Juan* (1819–24); both texts were composed in the reader-friendly *ottava rima*. From his moral standpoint outside the story, the narrator relates an illicit and doomed love affair between a dancer and a count, offering an ironic critique of Biedermeier bourgeois society. However, the narrator's philosophical asides in *Danserinden* offer no alternative philosophy, other than total despair at the inconstancy of love and of men. The work is particularly notable, though, for its beautiful erotic scenes.

The lyrical drama *Amor og Psyche* (*Amor and Psyche*, 1834) reiterates the theme of earthly love as the cause of all suffering, but suggests that this can bring spiritual compensations. Indeed, the late 1830s was a time of tribulation for Paludan-Müller; wracked by typhoid, and in personal crisis over the conflict of his decadent lifestyle with his religious faith, his two-volume collection of poetry, *Poesier* (*Verses*, 1836–38) betrays a movement toward more religious and psychological contemplation, and was badly received. His next published work, a dramatic poem, *Venus* (1841), makes explicit his new concern: the distinction between erotic obsession, personified here by the goatish Actaeon, and the spiritual love of Hermione, who chooses death before sexual dishonor and is reunited with her betrothed in the afterlife.

The call to renunciation of life's pleasures, from a writer who himself struggled with his erotic impulses, is repeated in *Tithon* (1844) and *Dryadens Bryllup* (*The Marriage of the Dryad*, 1844) two dramatic poems that appeared within a month of each other. In the former, Prince Tithon is seduced by Aurora and granted eternal life, but not eternal youth. When he tires of immortality and returns to earth, he finds that he is also tired of worldly existence; the figure of the prince symbolizes the pointlessness of the escapism and aesthetic preoccupations of romantic poetry.

Meanwhile, Paludan-Müller had been working on what was to become his masterpiece: *Adam Homo* (1841–48), a two-volume novel in ottava rima, a generic hybrid, successfully splicing comedy and lyricism, earthly satire and spiritual idealism, and pleasing both the traditionalists and the avant-garde in Danish literary circles. The eponymous main character turns from a life of debauchery to one of quiet contemplation with the simple gardener's daughter Alma, but his essential moral weakness leads him to marry into high society, achieving professional success, but at the expense of his spiritual well-being. At the end of his life, he is saved from damnation only by the prayers and intercessions of the godly Alma. At the heart of the work is the necessity of reflection, evaluation of one's conduct, and recognition of one's mortality. Childhood is a lost paradise; the adult must strive for salvation in the knowledge of approaching death.

On the one hand, *Adam Homo* is an exposition of mid-nineteenth-century bourgeois society and its moral failings. Adam's name suggests "everyman," but Paludan-Müller was anxious that the setting should be strictly contemporary, and a delay of a year in publication of the second volume led him to worry that it might have lost its freshness. A generation later, Georg Brandes, the great Danish man of letters, praised Paludan-Müller's satirical epic as the first work of realism in Danish literature. On the other hand, the novel looks unflinchingly to Heaven as the fount of all salvation, which is earned through earthly suffering; this is the path of martyrdom chosen by Alma, the idealized female figure. *Adam Homo*'s idealism and didacticism, then, stand in contrast to the moral resignation of *Danserinden*.

Paludan-Müller looked on in horror as Danish society absorbed the new political ideals of liberalism and democracy in the 1840s. The poem *Luftskipperen og Atheisten* (*The Airship Pilot and the Atheist*, 1853) is a gleefully vindictive attack on those who believe in the supremacy of man and of nature. The poet's moral code is an absolute one: atonement can only come when society, like the unfortunate atheist in the poem, is stripped bare of its fripperies and facing its doom.

National-liberal Denmark did indeed experience a kind of doomsday a decade later—a humiliating defeat at the battle of Dybbøl of 1864. Paludan-Müller's response was to write *Ivar Lykkes Historie* (*The Story of Ivar Lykke*, 1866–73), at two thousand pages in length the weightiest novel of the decade and one that looks back to 1848 and the previous war against Prussia. Paludan-Müller still stresses the necessity of suffering on the road to redemption, but in this case the hero is permitted to retire quietly to his farm and his sweetheart when he has run the gauntlet of life. This is perhaps an allegory for the rebirth of the nation, as well as the soul, after a cathartic struggle.

That this reclusive "poet of the soul," as Paludan-Müller has been called, wrote for and of his own times perhaps accounts for the lack of attention paid to his work during the twentieth century. The "soul" of *Adam Homo*, however, lives on in another Scandinavian classic, for which it provided at least part of the inspiration: the rather better-known figure of Henrik Ibsen's *Peer Gynt*.

CATHERINE CLAIRE THOMSON

Biography

Born in Kerteminde, Denmark, 1809, son of Bishop Jens Paludan-Müller. In 1828 he passed with distinction the school-leaving examination, then studied law at the University of Copenhagen, graduating in 1835, although he never practiced law. Became seriously ill with typhoid fever in 1838, and married Charite Borch the same year (they had no children). Died 1876.

Selected Works

Danserinden, et Digt. 1833.
Amor og Psyche. Lyrisk Drama. 1834.
Poesier. 2 vols., 1836–38.
Venus. Et Dramatisk Digt. 1841.
Adam Homo. Et Digt. 3 vols., 1842–49. Translated by Stephen I. Klass. 1981.

Dryadens Bryllup. Et Dramatisk Digt. 1844.
Tithon. Et Dramatisk Digt. 1844.
Ungdoms Arbeider. Rev. ed. 2 vols., 1847–59.
Luftskipperen og Atheisten. Et Digt. 1853.
Tre Digte. 1854.
Nye Digte. 1861.
Paradiset. Bibelsk Drama. 1862.
Ivar Lykkes Historie. 3 vols., 1866–73.
Adonis. Et Mythisk Digt. 1874.
Tiderne Skifte. Skuespil i Tre Akter. 1874.

Bibliography

Andersen, Vilhelm. *Paludan-Müller.* Copenhagen: Gyldendal, 1910.
Haugsted, Mogens. *Frederik Paludan-Müllers Prosaiske Arbejder.* Copenhagen: Branner, 1940.
Rossel, Sven H., ed. *A History of Danish Literature.* Lincoln: University of Nebraska Press, 1992.

PAN-SLAVISM

While today generally associated with Russian aspirations for hegemony, the Pan-Slavism that emerged during the Romantic period denotes the movement of the disparate Slav people of Europe toward the recognition of their common ethnic background, and their various attempts to achieve a unified front against the dominant nations of Europe through the awakening of their national consciousness. Inspired by Johann Gottfried von Herder's idea of *Volksgeist*, the distinctive spirit entailed in every nation, as well as his celebration of the Slavs as a peace-loving, humanitarian, and democratic people destined to lead other nations toward a better future, the emergence of Pan-Slavism in the early nineteenth century was both an emulation of German Romantic trends calling for a unification of all Germans under one state, as well as a reaction to the threat posed by this "Pan-Germanism." Essentially, however, Pan-Slavism constituted a response to the suppression of the various Slav tribes by Austrian, Russian, and Magyar rule and expressed their desire for cultural and political autonomy.

Although the first initiatives for Slav unity date back as far as the seventeenth century, it was not until the libertarian ideals of the French Revolution and the nationalistic tendencies sparked by the Napoleonic Wars and suppressed by the European Restoration that the first two major advocators of Pan-Slavism, both Slovaks, appeared: the poet Jan Kollár and the literary scholar and linguist Pavel Josef Šafařik. Both their careers serve to illustrate the strong literary stance of Pan-Slavism.

Šafařik spent the first part of his life in southern Hungary before moving to Prague, the center of Slav scholarship, in 1833, where he followed in the footsteps of the Catholic Abbé Josef Dobrowsky, an enlightened thinker and author of books on Czech grammar and the history of the Czech language and literature, and thus a forefather of Pan-Slavism, by publishing his works *Geschichte der Slawischen Sprache und Literatur* (*History of the Slav Language and Literature*, 1826) and *Starožitnosti slovanské* (*Slav Antiquities*, 1837).

Kollár studied in Bratislava, Slovakia, under the Czech historian František Palacký, who would later head the Czech delegation to the "Ethnographical Congress" of the Slavs in Moscow in 1863 before spending two years at the German University of Jena (1817–19), which was then the focal point of German Romanticism and nationalism. There, he came in contact with the patriotic German fraternities, whom he joined in the Wartburg Festival of 1817 meant to commemorate three centuries of Luther's reformation and the fourth anniversary of the *Völkerschlacht* (Battle of the Nations) of Leipzig against Napoleon. He also retraced the past of the Elbe Slavs in Thuringia, who had been annihilated by the Germans in the ninth century in sectarian disputes and to whose existence many town names still bear witness. Inspired by the troubled history of the Slav people, and by Lord Byron's mourning of the decline of Greece in *Childe Harold's Pilgrimage*, Kollár wrote his epic poem *Slávy Dcera* (*The Daughter of Slava*, 1824), in which he describes the past triumphs and defeats of the Slav people along with prophesies of a glorious global future under Slav supremacy. The book soon became the bible of Pan-Slavism and a major source of its lyrical and sentimental overtones.

Kollár, like Šafařik and most other popular advocates of Pan-Slavism, adopted Herder's view of the Slavs as the archetype of humanity and Christianity, although his romantic belief in the superiority of the Slav people violated the German scholar's egalitarian and humanitarian views. Pan-Slavism also espoused Herder's emphasis on language, national history, tradition, culture, and education as the means of national unity and liberation, which is aptly reflected in the word "Slav" itself with its twofold allusion to the Slavonic words *slava* (glory) and *slovo* (the word). As a result, while failing to draw up any realistic political goals, Pan-Slavists encouraged their fellow Slavs to learn the four principal Slavonic languages (Czech, Illyrian, Polish, and Russian), which they regarded as dialects of the same original mother tongue spoken by the various tribes of the Slav nation, a relationship celebrated by Kollár in his pamphlet on the literary reciprocity between the diverse tribes and dialects of the Slav nation, published in 1837.

Pan-Slavism, and the plight of the Slav people, first entered the consciousness of Western European liberals with the violent suppression of the Polish uprising of 1830–31 against Russian occupation and the fate of famous political exiles such as Frédéric Chopin and Adam Mickiewicz (who became the first professor of Slavonic literature at the Collège de France in Paris in 1840 and whose works *Dziady* (*Forefather's Eve*, 1823–33) and *Pan Tadeusz* (*Master Thaddeus*, 1834) represent two of the most patriotic texts of Slav Romanticism. To Mickiewicz, Poland's destiny rendered it "the Christ of the nations," a martyr for humanism and Christianity, and his moral messianism was echoed by other Polish Pan-Slavists, such as the poet and professor of Polish literature Kazimierz Brodzinski, whose essay *On the Spirit of Polish Poetry* (1818) aimed to reinforce Herder's link between national literature and the national spirit, and Andrzej Towianski, who embraced Catholic mysticism and Napoleonic revolutionism and whose religious fervor had an enormous impact on Mickiewicz's own piety.

Mickiewicz's epic poem *Konrad Wallenrod* (1828) portrayed one of the most crucial problems faced by Pan-Slavism: the age-old antagonism between Poland and Russia, which was furthermore worsened by hostile relations between Roman and Orthodox Catholics. Although calls for a union of all Slavs under the political protection of the mighty Russian Empire and the religious guidance of the Catholic Church can be traced back to the writings of the seventeenth-century Croat priest Juraj Krizanic, nineteenth-century Russia's commitment to the other members of the Holy Alliance (Austria and Prussia) forbade active approval of Pan-Slavism, which Tsar Nicholas I hence persecuted as a manifestation of anarchic liberalism. Russian tendencies towards Slav unification where thus reduced to "Pan-russianism" and the oppression and "russification" of Poles, Ukrainians, and White Russians living in Russian territories, while Poland oppressed its own Ukrainian and White Russian minorities. Poland's pride and domineering disposition were attacked by the Czech satirical writer and journalist Karel Havlicek Borovský, whose sober style contrasted with the overly romantic and idealistic inclinations of popular Pan-Slavism.

Such friction among the Slav nations made a harmonious Pan-Slavic enterprise unrealizable from the outset. Unsurprisingly, therefore, the first Slav Congress, held in Prague in the spring of 1848 in direct response to the first German parliament of the *Frankfurter Volksversammlung*, failed to unify Pan-Slavic viewpoints and soon turned into a conference of Slavs of the Habsburg monarchy, who aimed to counteract Austro-Magyar suppression by seeking integration in the empire, a movement that has come to be known as "Austroslavism." The various Slav nations of the nineteenth century thus failed to live out their Pan-Slavic ideals, and it is with Russian ascendancy rather than cultural and political autonomy that one usually associates twentieth-century Pan-Slavism.

KATHARINA KROSNY

See also **Bonaparte, Napoleon; Chopin. Frédéric;** *Dziady*; **Herder, Johann Gottfried; Jews; Mickiewicz, Adam Bernard; Nationalism;** *Pan Tadeusz*; **Poland: Cultural Survey; Poland: Historical Survey, Russia: Cultural Survey; Russia: Historical Survey; Volksgeist**

Bibliography

Clementis, Vladimir. *Panslavism: Past and Present*. London: Williams, Lea, 1943.
Erickson, John. *Panslavism*. London: Historical Association, 1964.
Kohn, Hans. *Pan-Slavism: Its History and Ideology*. Notre Dame, Ind.: University of Notre Dame Press, 1953.
Orton, Lawrence D. *The Prague Conference of 1848*. Boulder, Co.: East European Quarterly, 1978.

PAN TADEUSZ (MASTER THADDEUS, OR THE LAST FORAY IN LITHUANIA) 1834

Epic poem by Adam Mickiewicz

Whether *Pan Tadeusz* is Adam Mickiewicz's greatest work is debatable. What cannot be doubted is the grip it has had on the Polish psyche from its very first publication. *Pan Tadeusz* has been called the last European epic; it is generally acknowledged to be the national epic of Poland, and for generations of Poles since the mid-nineteenth century it has embodied the very essence of Polishness. As such, it has been honored with mass reverence and rejected, as an accursed straitjacket, by authors such as Witold Gombrowicz, who parodies the work in his great novel *Trans-Atlantyk* (1953).

The story is simple enough. Young Tadeusz Soplica, who has just finished his education in the city, has returned to the ancestral home of his family in the Lithuanian provinces. He is to be groomed to take possession of the family seat, which will pass into his hands from his uncle and guardian, the judge. Furthermore, plans are afoot to betroth him to the lovely Zosia. This girl, also under the protection of the Soplica family, is the scion of a local aristocratic family, the Horeszkowie. This marriage is to bring an end to a long-standing feud between the two families, which has been brewing for some time around the possession of a certain castle, once the seat of the family Horeszko, now in the possession of the Soplicas. Although the matter seems about to be settled amicably enough between the judge and the count (a distant relative of the Horeszkos), an untoward quarrel erupts at a banquet given in the presence of both families at the somewhat dilapidated castle. Gerwazy Rebajlo, self-styled keeper of the castle and ardent supporter of the Horeszkos, has been filling the young count's overly romantic head with the Gothic beauty of the site, and, at the outbreak of the quarrel, convinces him to assuage his ravaged honor not in the courtroom, but in the old style, via an armed attack on the Soplicas. Hence the title of the work: *Pan Tadeusz, czyli ostatni zajazd na Litwie* (*Master Thaddeus, or the Last Foray in Lithuania*). The raid is a success, at first. Then, the minor nobles who make up the body of the count's forces set to eating and drinking, and in a short period of time, all of the victors pass out, inebriated. In the meantime, the Russian authorities have been notified of the "rebellion," and the count's men awaken to find themselves firmly bound by Russian gendarmes. Despite the attempts at peaceful intervention by the Bernardin priest Father Robak, a quarrel erupts at breakfast between the Soplicas and the Russian officers, and the feuding nobles forget their quarrels now that a real enemy has shown up. Soplicas, Horeszkos, and their allies fight as one man to overcome the Russians, and the feud is patched up once and for all. Those Poles who were most remarkable in the fight are urged to escape across the Niemen to Poland proper, so as to avoid prosecution. This includes Tadeusz, who leaves with a heavy heart, having won that of Zosia. He returns, however, along with the Polish Legions of Napoleon Bonaparte's Grande Armée on the march to Moscow in 1812, and the epic ends with a festive celebration of Polishness, with great hopes (to be dashed, alas) for the freedom of Poland from the empires who subject it.

Much of this seems firmly ensconced in the bucolic idyll tradition, and indeed one of Mickiewicz's models for the work was *Wiesław* (1820), an idyll by the pre-Romantic Kazimierz Brodziński. Yet what separates *Pan Tadeusz* from the pastoral tradition of Brodziński, or the "novel-in-verse" genre of Aleksandr Pushkin's *Evgeny Onegin* (1833), is the solidly patriotic, nationalistic motif that runs through the work. While *Pan Tadeusz* shares many superficial characteristics common to epics (the high style, Vergilian division into twelve books, invocations, epic digressions, longing for a golden age, and feats of heroism), true epics speak of the fate of an entire nation, and in this *Pan Tadeusz* excels.

The epic is set in the years 1811–12. Poland had been under complete subjugation to Austria, Prussia, and Russia since 1795, but with the rise of Napoleon, who embraced the cause of a free Polish ally, it seemed that the restoration of independence was not far off. Indeed, the whole rationale for Father Robak's presence in the novel (besides the fact that he turns out to be Tadeusz's father, long thought dead) is as an emissary between the Poles of the "Congress Kingdom" across the river to prepare the Poles of Lithuania for an uprising: thus the logic of the family feud. Only the Russians benefit from petty quarrels between Poles; could the Poles but unite their strengths, based on a shared love for Poland, the Poles could, as Tadeusz's namesake Kościuszko put it, chase the oppressors from their land. Even the frequent sarcastic comedy and mock-epic elements to be found in *Pan Tadeusz* serve this serious idea. Early in the work, the Poles are satisfied with the frivolous pleasures of hare or fox hunting, when they ought to seek glory on the field of battle.

In this connection, it is interesting to see how Mickiewicz elevates love for country to a level that mixes patriotism inextricably with love for God. This tendency is especially evident in the person of Father Robak. He is a good priest, with a true vocation, yet he is also a militant priest "who knows politics better than the *Lives of the Saints.*" However he tries to repair matters with the Russians once the feud breaks out into the open, the fact remains that he is the one who transported weapons to the Poles in his wagon, and, with his military expertise, he directs a good part of the successful operations against the "Moskale." Wounded in the battle, he dies, rejoicing at the word that Napoleon has indeed declared war on Russia. In the same context, Mickiewicz goes out of his way to describe the Jew Jankiel, tavern owner and musician, as a "good Pole," once again placing devotion to Poland above, or at least at the same level as, devotion to one's religion. In one of the most striking images of the epic, the consecration of the Polish people is effected by the breeze that lifts the garlands of flowers adorning the altar at an outdoor Mass and wafts them onto the brows of the worshippers.

Thus, the castle, once contended over in a petty way by the families, and then successfully defended by their united strength against the Russian oppressors, becomes a symbol of Poland, and Mickiewicz's hope for the future. It is not coincidental that the twelfth and final book of the epic, with its joyous celebration of Polishness, is entitled "Let us love one another!" And even though the epic was written with the hindsight of the military failures of 1812 and 1830 (the November Uprising), the main thrust of the epic is toward hope and confidence. Book 11, "The Battle," is perhaps the most stirring of the entire work, and best exemplifies this idea. For the Homerics here are not sarcastic at all: the heroes are real heroes, and the poet transforms these very prosaic, often laughable, nobles into the peers of Achilles and Menelaus. The message is clear: if such as *these* can win glory for the fatherland, why can't *we*?

CHARLES S. KRASZEWSKI

Text

Pan Tadeusz, 1834. Translated as *Master Thaddeus, or The Last Foray in Lithuania* by Maude Ashurst Biggs. 2 vols., 1885. Translated as *Pan Tadeusz, or The Last Foray in Lithuania* with an introduction, by Kenneth Mackenzie. 1966.

Bibliography

Gille-Maisani, Jean-Charles. *Adam Mickiewicz. Poète national de la Pologne. Étude psychanalytique et caractérologique.* Montréal: Bellarmin/Paris: Les Belles Lettres, 1988.

Gross, I. G. "Adam Mickiewicz, a European from Nowogrodek," *East European Politics And Societies* 9, no. 2 (1995): 295.

Jastrun, Mieczyslaw. *Adam Mickiewicz.* Warsaw: Polonia, 1955.

Kołodziej, Léon. *Adam Mickiewicz au carrefour des romantismes européens, essai sur la pensée du poète.* Aix-en-Provence: Éditions Ophrys, 1966.

Koropeckyj, Roman. "Narrative and Social Drama in Adam Mickiewicz's *Pan Tadeusz.*" *Slavonic and East European Review* 76, no. 3 (July 1998): 467–84.

Krajski, Stanisław. *Pan Tadeusz na nowo odczytany.* Warsaw: Agencja SGK, 1999.

Kridl, Manfred, ed. *Adam Mickiewicz, Poet of Poland: a Symposium.* New York: Greenwood Press, 1951.

Lednicki, Wacław, ed. *Adam Mickiewicz in World Literature: a Symposium.* Berkeley and Los Angeles: University of California Press, 1956.

McQuillan, Colleen. "Private pleasures made public: Voyeurism in *Pan Tadeusz,*" *Polish Review* 43, no. 4 (1998): 419–28.

Miłosz, Czesław. *A History of Polish Literature.* Berkeley and Los Angeles: University of California Press, 1983.

Mitosek, Zofia, ed. *Adam Mickiewicz aux yeux des Français / textes réunis, établis et présentés avec l'introduction, commentaires, et notes.* Warsaw: PWN, 1992.

Szweykowski, Zygmunt Marian. *Pan Tadeusz, poemat humorystyczny.* Poznań: Nakl. Poznańskiego Tow. Przyjaciól Nauk, 1949.

UNESCO. *Adam Mickiewicz, 1798–1855; in Commemoration of the Centenary of his Death.* Paris: UNESCO, 1955.

Walc, Jan. *Architekt arki.* Chotomów: Verba, 1991.

Welsh, David J. *Adam Mickiewicz.* New York: Twayne, 1966.

Wojciechowski, Konstanty. *Pan Tadeusz Mickiewicza a romans Waltera Scotta.* Kraków: Nakl. Akademji Umiejetności, 1919.

PARKER, THEODORE 1810–1860

American theologian and social reformer

A Unitarian minister and Boston intellectual, Theodore Parker, like Ralph Waldo Emerson, formulated a philosophy based on individualistic intuition and self-development, cast in religious terms (most famously in his *Discourse of the Transient and Permanent in Christianity* [1841]). The conservative wing of the Unitarian establishment branded him a follower of Thomas Carlyle, Victor Cousin, Friedrich Ernst Daniel Schleiermacher, and Perry Bysshe Shelley; he did indeed spend much of his career articulating and defending "heretical" and reformist points of view. Like other transcendentalists, Parker believed that nature was a source of truth, but unlike Henry David Thoreau, he seldom wrote about landscape and concentrated instead on human nature, specifically on its relation to divinity and society. In his work as a theologian and a social reformer, Parker still more profoundly betrayed his debt to the philosophical and political theories of the Romantic era. To a large extent, Parker's achievements were the translation and popularization of the theological and sociopolitical ideas of others.

In Boston transcendentalist circles, Parker was closer to one-time Unitarian minister George Ripley, the founder of Brook Farm, than to Emerson or Margaret Fuller. Yet Parker avoided joining the Brook Farm social utopia, and he enthusiastically contributed to Emerson's and Fuller's transcendentalist journal, the *Dial* (1839–44), and later edited the *Massachusetts Quarterly* from 1848 to 1850. Most of Parker's contributions to the *Dial* were theological in nature, just as many of his later pieces in the *Quarterly* were on political or economic topics. Always, though, he maintained a strong allegiance to transcendentalist principles, his scholarly fondness for German idealists aligning him with transcendentalist anti-Lockean views.

Parker's most common platform for his transcendental ideas was his theological writing. Parker's radical religious views found early expression in his editorship of the *Scriptural Interpreter* (1835–36) when he was a student at the Harvard Divinity School. Soon after he was ordained a minister in 1837, he found himself in conflict with conservative Unitarians in Boston. A characteristic and famous dispute Parker had with this establishment was the so-called miracles controversy. While conservatives maintained that Biblical miracles served as a proof of the truth of Christianity, Parker, along with other liberal theologians, argued that personal intuition was the basis of the "permanent" in Christian truth. Parker developed a theology inspired by the so-called German Higher Critics, who emphasized the personal, the human, and the historical in Christianity. He was especially inspired by Wilhelm M. L. De Wette's *Einleitung in Das Alte Testament* (*Introduction to the Old Testament*) which he translated, expanded, and published as *A Critical and Historical Introduction to the Canonical Scriptures of the Old Testament* (1843). Such "heretical" studies brought Parker official censure and ministerial isolation, and it was not until 1845 that he achieved his ambition of a Boston pulpit in the form of a "free church," the Twenty-Eighth Congregational Society. Although originally inclined to be a scholar, Parker increasingly entered the realm of public controversy and defined himself as a conscientious and embattled activist.

Parker's passion for social action grew out of both his pastoral experience and his association with prominent Bostonian reformers. His concerns encompassed women's rights, education, prostitution, temperance, and poverty, but by the 1850s his main cause was the abolition of slavery. He condemned the Fugitive Slave Law of 1850 (notably in *Theodore Parker's Review of Webster*, 1850) and gained additional notoriety in 1854 when his impassioned incitement against the rendition of a captured slave, Anthony Burns, resulted in a charge of treason. *The Trial of Theodore Parker for the Misdemeanor of Speech in Faneuil Hall against Kidnapping; with a Defense* (1855) probably exaggerated Parker's legal battle (the case was dismissed) but extensively and persuasively cataloged the wrongs of slavery. Like earlier Parker antislavery tracts, it is detailed and thorough if at times rhetorically weak. Such writings reflect Parker's personal Christian viewpoint as well as his belief in "industrial democracy" as a social model; Parker hoped that democracy would redress the wrongs of industrial capitalism. Like other abolitionists, Parker focused on white morality more than black suffering.

In his antislavery works, Parker displays the contradictions that characterize his career in general and that define the question of his historical and literary importance. Much of Parker's writing is expansive and repetitive (Parker wanted his sermons and lectures to be clear to his audiences); many of his ideas, as he himself admitted, were not original to him. And yet Parker's radicalism and social conscience in many ways now seem modern, and his best writing (for example his autobiographical *Theodore Parker's Experience as a Minister*, 1859) reflects the warmth and personal commitment that attracted large numbers of his contemporaries to his causes.

PAUL FISHER

Biography

Born in Lexington, Massachusetts, August 24, 1810; taught school in various Massachusetts towns, 1827–30; enrolled at Harvard College, 1830–34; studied at Harvard Divinity School, 1834–37, editing the *Scriptural Interpreter* there, 1835–36. Married Lydia Cabot, 1837; ordained a Unitarian minister, 1837; served as minister of the Spring Street Church, West Roxbury, 1837–47. Traveled in Europe, 1843–44. Worked in Boston as minister and lecturer, 1847–59; edited *Massachusetts Quarterly Review*, 1848–50. Traveled to Europe for his health, 1859; died of tuberculosis in Rome, May 10, 1860.

Selected Works

The Collected Works of Theodore Parker. Edited by Frances P. Cobbe. 14 vols., London: Trübner, 1863–74.
Centenary Edition of the Works of Theodore Parker. Edited by Charles W. Wendte. 15 vols., Boston: American Unitarian Association, 1907–1912.
Theodore Parker, An Anthology. Edited by Henry Steele Commager: Boston: Beacon Press, 1960.

Bibliography

Albrecht, Robert C. *Theodore Parker*. New York: Twayne, 1971.

Brown, Jerry Wayne. *The Rise of Biblical Criticism in America, 1800–1870: The New England Scholars*. Middletown, Conn.: Wesleyan University Press, 1969.

Chadwick, John White. *Theodore Parker: Preacher and Reformer*. Boston: Houghton Mifflin, 1901.

Commager, Henry Steele. *Theodore Parker*. Boston: Little Brown, 1936.

Dirks, John Edward. *The Critical Theology of Theodore Parker*. Westport, Conn.: Greenwood Press, 1948.

Grodzins, Dean. *American Heretic: Theodore Parker and Transcendentalism*. Chapel Hill, N.C.: University of North Carolina Press, 2002.

Meyerson, Joel. *The New England Transcendentalists and the Dial: A History of the Magazine and Its Contributors*. Rutherford, N.J.: Fairleigh Dickinson University Press, 1980.

———. *Transcendentalism: A Reader*. Oxford: Oxford University Press, 2000.

Rose, Anne C. *Transcendntalism as a Social Movement, 1830–1850*. New Haven, Conn.: Yale University Press, 1981.

PAUL, JEAN (JOHANN PAUL FRIEDRICH RICHTER) 1763–1825

German novelist and humorist

In both his philosophical outlook and the mode of expression through which this was voiced in his creative and critical writings, Johann Paul Friedrich Richter (usually known simply as Jean Paul) was influenced by a number of key eighteenth-century thinkers. In particular he endorsed the views of his close friend Johann Gottfried von Herder, whose conception of religious experience as individual intuition of the infinite and whose rejection of the orthodoxy of the Lutheran church he shared. In postulating an affinity between aesthetics and ethics, Jean Paul betrayed his indebtedness to Immanuel Kant, whose understanding of the sublime was reflected in Jean Paul's seminal definition of humor. His literary style was influenced by that of eighteenth-century English novelists, such as Laurence Sterne and Henry Fielding, whose sense of irony was examined in Jean Paul's *Vorlesungen über die Aesthetik* (*School for Aesthetics*, 1804). The *Vorlesungen über die Aesthetik* is arguably Jean Paul's most significant contribution to the history of thought, and is best understood as an example of Romantic literary theory in so far as "it is not an aesthetics but rather a poetics" within which Jean Paul developed ideas that were central to the poetics of other *Frühromantiker* (early Romantics) such as Novalis, Friedrich and August Wilhelm von Schlegel, and Ludwig Tieck.

Through the florid, metaphorical prose style in which Jean Paul, like many of his contemporaries, couched both his creative and critical writings, he expressed the view he shared with them of criticism as an author's poetic or creative response to a work—a view encapsulated in Novalis's statement that "[Friedrich] Schlegel's writings are philosophy as lyric," and in Jean Paul's comment that there is "no simple reception without production or creation." This view was premised on the recognition of the semantic indeterminacy of verbal language voiced by Friedrich von Schlegel, who suggested "that words often understand themselves better than do those who use them." The corollary of this insight was the conception of texts as necessarily incomplete and fragmentary expressions of authors' ideas, a conception that found embodiment in the collections of aphorisms or fragments published anonymously in the *Athenaeum* (1798–1800) and in the ideas and quotations Jean Paul recorded in copybooks throughout his life. Jean Paul's engagement with the early Romantic view that texts assume an autonomous existence over which the author has no control was reflected in his creative writings in so far as, through the frequent authorial interpolations which punctuate his narratives, he emulated the self-parodying, ironic literary style of Sterne.

Jean Paul's engagement with the aesthetics of the *Frühromantiker* is further illustrated by his conception of the author as a "genius" who expresses a personal, subjective view of the world in his works. He conceived the "poetic genius" as one in possession of both "reproductive imagination" or "memory" (*Einbildungskraft*) and "creative imagination" (*Phantasie*) that "writes all parts into wholes and transforms all parts of the world into worlds." He conceived the creative process as that which draws on the unconscious, as akin to dreaming, but emphasized the necessity for "poetic reflectiveness" as the essential condition for the "high separation of the self from its own inner world" that enables the author to view his work with critical detachment. Thus central to Jean Paul's understanding of the creative process was the dialectical relationship between reason and emotion as complementary opposites that are synthesized in the work of genius. This was a central *topos* of Romantic aesthetics and philosophy which found expression not only in Jean Paul's poetics, but in his fantastic fiction. The notion of the *Doppelgänger* (double), pervasive in his creative writings, was given tangible representation in *Das Flegeljahre* (*Years of Indiscretion*) in the twin brothers Walt, the dreamy introvert, and Vult, the rationalistic extrovert.

For Jean Paul it was the ability to reconcile reproductive imagination and "instinct," as "the sense of the future," with creative imagination and poetic reflectiveness which distinguished the genius from the man of "talent." He conceived the man of talent as one who "has instinct or the one-sided direction of all the faculties," that embraces "acumen, wit, understanding, and the mathematical or historical reproductive imagination," but who is deficient in creative imagination and poetic reflectiveness. Accordingly, Jean Paul maintained that "men of talent, differentiated by degree, can destroy and replace one another," their works displaying "no excellence that cannot be imitated."

It was in accordance with Jean Paul's conception of texts as autonomous entities which require active interpretation that he created a "third class" of genius: the "feminine, receptive, or passive geniuses." He conceived the passive genius as an individual in possession of the creative imagination and poetic reflec-

Heinrich Pfenninger, *Jean Paul*. Reprinted courtesy of AKG.

tiveness necessary for the appreciation of works of genius, but lacking the ability to express their individual worldview in an original work. He stated that passive geniuses "comprehend the world and beauty with philosophical and poetical freedom. But when they themselves want to create, an invisible chain binds half their limbs and they create something other or smaller than they wanted." The notion that the recipient of a work must be gifted with the sensibility to appreciate poetic art was a central tenet of Romantic aesthetics that had its origins in eighteenth-century thought. In the article on "Genius" in Jean-Jacques Rousseau's *Dictionnaire de musique* Rousseau stated that genius "communicates to those who possess responsive hearts," but "knows of nothing to say to those in whom his seed is not planted." That Jean Paul conceived artistic sensibility as an attribute that could be acquired is suggested by the coexistence in his thought of the notion of a passive genius and that of the cultivation of the human being (*Bildung des Menschen*) as an ideal.

That in articulating his poetics Jean Paul was not merely concerned with the aesthetic education of man, but with poetry as a vehicle for morality, is suggested by his definitions of wit, the ridiculous, and humour. He equated a sense of wit, as the discovery of "similarities between incommensurable magnitudes, between physical and spiritual worlds," with a sense of freedom and equality. Accordingly, he stated that "one finds [the comic spirit] wherever there is either inner freedom, among the young at universities . . . for example, or outer freedom, as in the very

largest cities," and condemned "the poverty and slavery of the true comic poetic spirit" in Germany.

Jean Paul conceived both the ridiculous and humour as akin to the sublime. He defined the ridiculous as the subject's perception of incongruity between two ideas, such as "a healthy man who considers himself to be sick," the ridiculousness of which is wholly dependent on the subject's recognition of the absurdity of the man's concerns, and thus "like the sublime never resides in the object but in the subject." Jean Paul conceived humour as "inverse sublimity" which "measures out the small world . . . against the infinite world and sees them together," resulting in "a kind of laughter . . . which contains pain and greatness," and simultaneously fostering an awareness of the triviality of earthly life and a spiritual sense of the infinite.

In discussing the relationship between ancient and modern poetry—a central preoccupation of the *Frühromantiker*—Jean Paul rejected the distinction Johann Christoph Friedrich von Schiller drew between "naive" and "sentimental" poetry as "atomistic sterility." However, he nevertheless endorsed "the great distinction between Greek and romantic poetry" expressed by Friedrich von Schlegel in *Über das Studium der griechischen Poesie* (*On the Study of Greek Poetry*, 1795), as that between "objective" poetry and "romantic" poetry that is "derived from Christianity." It was the view Jean Paul inherited from Johann Gottfried von Herder, of poetry as an expression of the spirituality of the era in which it is conceived, that led him to espouse Schlegel's later view "that all poetry should be romantic," and to conceive of Homer, Petrarch, and William Shakespeare as representations of "various romanticisms."

The influence of the aesthetic ideas presented in Jean Paul's *Vorlesungen* on the literary theory of his contemporaries is reflected in the writings of Thomas Carlyle, Samuel Taylor Coleridge, Karl Solger, and Friedrich Theodor von Vischer, among others. That his fantastic imagination also inspired his contemporaries is illustrated by the fantastic tales of E. T. A. Hoffmann, whose *Fantasiestücke in Callot's Manier* (*Fantasy Pictures in the Style of Callot*, 1814–15) was first published with a preface by Jean Paul; and by the fantastic compositions of Robert Schumann, whose *Abegg Variations* (1830) op. 1, *Papillons* (1829–31) op. 2, and *Carnaval* (1834–5) op. 9 were all inspired, wholly or in part, by *Das Flegeljahre*. As an exponent of Romantic literary theory, Jean Paul also numbered among those who articulated the basic tenets of poststructuralism over a hundred years before critical theory came into being.

ABIGAIL CHANTLER

Biography

Born Johann Paul Friedrich Richter in Wundsiedel, Bavaria, March 21, 1763. Studied theology at Leipzig University, 1781–84; engaged as private tutor, 1787–90; established and managed primary school in Schwarzenbach, 1790–94; married Karoline Meyer, 1801. Died in Bayreuth, November 14, 1825.

Selected Works

Die Briefe Jean Pauls. 4 vols. Edited by Eduard Berend. Munich: Georg Müller, 1922–26.
Sämtliche Werke. 3 vols. Edited by Eduard Berend. (Weimar: Herman Bohlans and Beelin: Akademie-Verlag), 1927–96.
Jean Paul und Frau von Krudener im Spiegel ihres Briefwechsels. Edited by Dorothea Berger. 1957.

Jean Paul und Herder: der Briefwechsel Jean Pauls und Karoline Richters mit Herder und der Herderschen Familie in den Jahren 1785 bis 1804. Edited by Paul Stapf. 1959.

Vorlesungen über Aesthetik, 1804. Revised 1813 and 1825. Translated as *Horn of Oberon: Jean Paul Richter's School for Aesthetics* by Margaret R. Hale. 1973.

Jean Paul: A Reader. Edited by Timothy J. Casey. Translated by Erika Casey. 1992.

Bibliography

Behler, Ernst. *German Romantic Literary Theory.* Cambridge: Cambridge University Press, 1993.

Birzniks, Paul. "Jean Paul's Early Theory of Poetic Communication," *Germanic Review* 41 (1966): 186–201.

Bruyn, Gunter de. *Das Leben des Jean Paul Friedrich Richter: eine Biographie.* Frankfurt: Fischer Taschenbuch Verlag, 1991.

Debold, Annette. *Reisen bei Jean Paul: Studien zu einer real-gattungshistorisch inspirierten Thematik in Theorie und Praxis des Dichters.* Saint Ingbert: Röhrig Universitätsverlag, 1998.

Frauke, Otto. *Robert Schumann als Jean Paul-Leser.* Frankfurt: Haag and Herchen, 1984.

Hammer, Stephanie Barbé. *Satirizing the Satirist: Critical Dynamics in Swift, Diderot, and Jean Paul.* New York: Garland, 1990.

Hoffmann, E. T. A. *E. T. A. Hoffmann's Musical Writings: Kreisleriana, The Poet and the Composer, Music Criticism.* Edited by David Charlton. Translated by Martyn Clarke. Cambridge: Cambridge University Press, 1989.

Jensen, Eric Frederick. "Explicating Jean Paul: Robert Schumann's Program for *Papillons*, Op. 2," *Nineteenth-Century Music* 22, no. 3 (1998): 127–43.

Koepke, Wulf. "Jean Paul Richter's School for Aesthetics: Humor and the Sublime," in *Eighteenth-Century German Authors and Their Aesthetic Theories: Literature and the Other Arts.* Edited by Richard Critchfield and Wulf Koepke, Columbia, S.C.: Camden House, 1988.

Le Huray, Peter, and James Day, eds. *Music and Aesthetics in the Eighteenth and Early-Nineteenth Centuries.* Cambridge: Cambridge University Press, 1981.

Modiano, Raimonda. "Humanism and the Comic Sublime: From Kant to Friedrich Theodore Vischer," *Studies in Romanticism* 26 (1987): 231–44.

Muller, Gotz. *Jean Pauls Asthetik und Naturphilosophie.* Tubingen: Niemeyer, 1983.

Plantinga, Leon. *Schumann as Critic.* New Haven, Conn.: Yale University Press, 1967.

Schweikert, Uwe. *Jean Paul.* Stuttgart: Metzler, 1970.

Ueding, Gert. *Jean Paul.* Munich: Beck, 1993.

Unger, Christoph. *Die ästhetische Phantasie Begriffsgeschichte, Diskurs, Funktion, Transformation: Studien zur Poetologie Jean Pauls und Johann Wolfgang Goethes.* Frankfurt: Peter Lang, 1996.

Weigl, Engelhard. *Aufklarung und Skeptizismus: Untersuchungen zu Jean Pauls Fruhwerk.* Hildesheim: Gerstenberg, 1980.

Wellek, René. *A History of Modern Criticism 1750–1950.* Vol. 2, *The Romantic Age.* Cambridge: Cambridge University Press, 1981.

Wheeler, Kathleen M., ed. *German Aesthetic and Literary Criticism: The Romantic Ironists and Goethe.* Cambridge: Cambridge University Press, 1984.

Wölfel, Kurt. *Jean Paul Studien.* Edited by Bernhard Buschendorf, Frankfurt: Suhrkamp, 1989.

PEACEABLE KINGDOM 1816–1849

Paintings by Edward Hicks

The best-known and a much-beloved image in nineteenth-century American folk art, *Peaceable Kingdom* by Edward Hicks, is not one oil painting but sixty-two surviving versions (of the perhaps 100 he completed) illustrating Isaiah 11:6–9, in which one reads "The wolf also shall dwell with the lamb, and the leopard shall lie down with the kid; and the calf and the young lion and the fatling together; and a little child shall lead them. And the cow and the bear shall feed; their young ones shall lie down together: and the lion shall eat straw like the ox." Fixated on this biblical passage, Hicks, an unpaid Quaker minister who supported his family mainly by his trade of painting trade signs and ornamenting coaches, painted variations on his *Peaceable Kingdom* for his last three decades, right up to the evening before his death. Hicks, like so many of his literary and artistic contemporaries, stresses in these paintings the value of the simple life, the need for spiritual and political freedom, and the necessity of living in harmony with nature. The plain, ordered world of Hicks may at first seem alien to nineteenth-century American painters such as Thomas Cole, who depicts grand allegorical scenes and Hudson River school landscapes. Both painters, however, articulate a Romantic vision of peaceful coexistence with a natural world pervaded by the divine.

Edward Hicks was born north of Philadelphia in rural Bucks County, Pennsylvania, where he lived all his life. The flat, well-defined, clear-colored images of his sign-painting career merged with his deeply-felt Quaker convictions to produce the animals and human figures of his *Peaceable Kingdom*, a subject that even Quakers who had criticized Hicks for his worldly artistry could approve. Hicks found some aspects of his design in the engraving, published in several Bibles, of Richard Westall's *The Peaceable Kingdom of the Branch* (1800–15). In Westall and elsewhere Hicks observed the exuberant vegetation, hollow stumps, and blasted trees so characteristic of eighteenth- and nineteenth-century landscape painting: these Romantic features form the background in the *Peaceable Kingdom* paintings.

The strong graphic design in the *Peaceable Kingdom*, as well as Hicks's emphasis on such balanced contrasts as the wolf and the lamb, the leopard and the kid, the lion and the ox, the bear and the cow, suggest works by his contemporary William Blake, then unknown to Hicks but like him laboring well outside the mainstream. In 1837, Hicks preached at the Goose Creek meeting house in Loudon County, Virginia, using Isaiah 11:6–7 as one of his texts; that sermon provides a key to what the painter intended by his pairs of contrasting animals in the *Peaceable Kingdom*. Using the categories of "humors" dating back to the medieval period, Hicks divides humanity into four temperaments, each compounded of the traditional elements (earth, air, water, and fire) and symbolized by a wild animal (melancholy: the wolf; sanguine: the leopard; phlegmatic: the bear; choleric: the lion). Those who give up their self-will and are redeemed

Edward Hicks, *The Peaceable Kingdom*. Reprinted courtesy of the Bridgeman Art Library.

by the "Inward Light" of God's voice can be signified by those wild animals' domestic counterparts: the lamb, the kid, the ox, and the cow.

In his Goose Creek sermon, Hicks praises the Society of Friends (the Quakers), but not for what he considered to be its weak and fragmented state in 1837. He instead favored the group as it was, both in doctrine and discipline, in the days of such founders of the society as Richard Barclay, George Fox, and William Penn. The split of American Quakerism into "Orthodox" and "Hicksite" (named for Edward Hicks's New York cousin Elias) had been growing in the early years of the nineteenth century and peaked in 1827 with the withdrawal of the Hicksites from the Philadelphia Yearly Meeting. The conflict was complex, but it set rural Quakers emphasizing loose structures and direct communication with God through each member's "Inward Light" against urban Quakers who preferred written doctrines and more organized worship. As the religious division grew, a prominent cleft appeared in the tree in the background of the *Peaceable Kingdom* paintings. Furthermore, the Goose Creek sermon identifies the "orthodox" Quakers with various unpleasant tendencies associated with the wild animals. In addition to these paintings' other meanings, Hicks's wild and domestic animals came more and more to portray this separation

in the Society of Friends and a hope that the harmony promised in Isaiah could be restored to the Quakers.

Art historian Carolyn Weekley has grouped the *Peaceable Kingdom* paintings into early, middle, and late periods. In the first thirteen paintings (through the early 1820s), the animals are pleasant and calm. All these works but one have borders lettered with the biblical quotation. Early on, Hicks introduced at the painting's left-hand side a scene of Penn, the founder of Pennsylvania, signing his famous "Great Treaty" with the native Lenni Lenape (or Delaware) tribe; thus the human and the animal kingdoms both show how to live in peaceful unity. Paintings of the middle period, the later 1820s into the late 1830s, reflect the dissension in American Quakerism; a distinct unease can be seen in some of the animals' faces, and more of them energetically crowd the picture. At this stage, the *Peaceable Kingdom* seems more like a hope than a reality. In the late period, the last ten years of Hicks's life, he seems to have become increasingly aware that he would not live to see the religious split healed (in fact, it was not resolved until 1955). Some of the animals, especially the lion and sometimes the leopard, stare back at the viewer with haggard faces and sunken eyes; there is occasional bickering among the creatures. A vignette of Penn's treaty still survives on the left-hand side, but nevertheless the title *Peaceable Kingdom* strikes many viewers with at least a tinge of irony.

Although he did complete some other easel paintings, Hicks's artistic energy was consumed by the many permutations of the *Peaceable Kingdom*. For religious reasons, Hicks painted fewer portraits, landscapes, and history paintings than did his contemporaries; but he left posterity one of the most recognizable images by any American painter. "If the Divine law had not prohibited," noted Hicksite leader John Comley, Hicks "might have rivaled [Charles Willson] Peale or [Benjamin] West."

JAMES A. BUTLER

Bibliography

Ford, Alice. *Edward Hicks: His Life And Art*. New York: Abbeville Press, 1985.

———. *Edward Hicks: Painter of the Peaceable Kingdom*. Philadelphia: University of Pennsylvania Press, 1998.

Mather, Eleanore Price, and Dorothy Canning Miller. *Edward Hicks: His Peaceable Kingdoms And Other Paintings*. Newark: University of Delaware Press, 1983.

Tatham, David. "Edward Hicks, Elias Hicks, and John Comley: Perspectives on the Peaceable Kingdom Theme," *American Art Journal* 13 (1981): 5–20.

Weekley, Carolyn J. *The Kingdoms of Edward Hicks*. New York: Abrams, 1999.

PEACOCK, THOMAS LOVE 1785–1866

English novelist and poet

Thomas Love Peacock is often regarded as a somewhat eccentric figure, a lesser member of the "second generation" of English Romantics who was then marginalized even further by the self-appointed guardians of Percy Bysshe Shelley's posthumous reputation. It is unlikely, however, that Peacock found this situation particularly burdensome. Indeed, it may even have reinforced the detached, skeptical perspective that made

him such an acute observer of English culture in the post-Napoleonic era. Moreover, despite Peacock's comparatively limited talents, he did exert an important influence on Shelley's intellectual development. Peacock was a minor versifier of little distinction or originality when he first met Shelley in 1812, but over the next few years he became one of the younger poet's closest confidants (an intimacy that he rewarded in his old age with a scrupulously evenhanded memoir, published in *Fraser's* magazine, June 1858–March 1862). Peacock's liberal, freethinking classicism and precocious, autodidactic absorption in European literary tradition proved extremely congenial to Shelley, who also gradually warmed to his probing skepticism and learned wit.

These qualities found their first true literary expression in *Headlong Hall* (1814), which established the formula that would shape Peacock's most successful "novels of opinion": an eclectic group of sages, cranks, and controversialists (often based loosely on leading figures of the day) dispute, digress, eat and drink, typically in the setting of a country residence, their intellectual misunderstandings countered with a lightly sketched plot of romantic entanglement. The narratives of the Peacockian novel are continually interrupted as the characters engage in parodic versions of philosophical dialogue: a debased form of Socratic disputation, filtered through eighteenth-century liberal ideals of rational enquiry and infused with an idiosyncratic blend of irony, satire, and genial wit. While his technique and tone were in many respects unique among contemporary novelists, Peacock himself seems to have identified his literary practice with a long-standing European comic tradition, originating in Aristophanes and in Menippean satire, and running through François Rabelais and Voltaire to Henry Fielding and Jonathan Swift.

The overarching intellectual focus of *Headlong Hall* is the conflict between progress and primitivism, a theme with far-reaching implications for both politics and the arts, and which remained a central preoccupation of Peacock's writings. But *Headlong Hall* is also quite typical of his subsequent works in its concern with more localized, ephemeral controversies such as phrenology and landscape gardening, the topicality of which can sometimes be lost on the modern reader, but which perform the essential function of anchoring Peacock's more abstract satirical themes at an appropriate level of intellectual bathos. *Melincourt* followed in 1817, a slightly less successful work combining elements of romance pastiche with a further satire on the liberal cult of progress. Peacock's ongoing critique of contemporary morals and manners was now effected principally through the delightful character of Sir Oran Hout-ton, an ape educated as a gentleman and intended by the novel's hero, Sylvan Forester, for a seat in parliament. *Melincourt* is also notable for its unsympathetic caricatures of the English "lake poets" Samuel Taylor Coleridge, Robert Southey, and William Wordsworth, whose turn to political conservatism was a growing source of disappointment and anger within the Shelley circle in the years after Waterloo.

While the lake poets embraced the established Anglican religion, Peacock's idealized pagan ethics found expression in *Rhododaphne* (1818), a poetic reworking of classical myth and an implicit attack on the repressive nature of modern sexual morality. But Peacock was also increasingly disturbed by certain unhealthy tendencies among the literary representatives of liberal opinion. In *Nightmare Abbey* (1818), he satirized not just the "transcendental" Germanic obscurity of Coleridge, but also the misanthropic, melodramatic excesses of Lord Byron and Shelley. While prescriptive readings of Peacock's novels as straightforward *romans à clef* often prove misleading, his good-humored impatience with Shelley's self-indulgent, Gothic fixations is clear enough in the character of Mr. Scythrop, and was recognized as such by its victim. Nevertheless, Peacock and Shelley remained friends and continued to correspond after the latter left England for Italy in 1818.

The following year, Peacock embarked on a career in the East India Company, which was rapidly becoming an outpost of Benthamite, utilitarian politics under the influence of the company's chief examiner, James Mill. Peacock's Enlightenment liberalism, his religious skepticism, and his sensitivity to the dangers of an ineffectual poetic idealism were all shared in some measure by Jeremy Bentham and his circle, with whom Peacock consequently enjoyed largely cordial relations. He was therefore particularly well placed to discern a potential rift within English liberal culture between the rival adherents of "utility" and "imagination." His concerns on this score were crystallized in "The Four Ages of Poetry" (1820), a witty and provocative essay that presented a forceful, and somewhat exaggerated, version of the utilitarian case against imaginative fiction. By celebrating the decline of poetry before the truly progressive historical forces of "useful" knowledge, "The Four Ages of Poetry" constituted a thoroughgoing denial of the politically and socially transformative power of poetry. Rising to this challenge, Shelley was provoked to answer Peacock with his "Defence of Poetry," a work that has often been considered one of the most important aesthetic manifestos of English Romanticism.

Peacock's next two novels took on a more antiquarian flavor, but without completely forsaking their author's contemporary preoccupations. *Maid Marian* (1822) used an irreverent treatment of the Robin Hood legend to debunk neofeudal conservative nostalgia; while in *The Misfortunes of Elphin* (1829), Peacock indulged his longstanding interest in Welsh literature and history, while once again sustaining a palpable undercurrent of political satire. By this time, however, the literary reformism of the Shelley circle was in retreat, while utilitarianism had become the dominant ideology of middle-class radicalism. Unable to reconcile himself to the more "philistine" and narrow-minded tendencies within the Benthamite party, Peacock vented his distaste for the new school of reform in *Crotchet Castle* (1831). A satirical treatment of the "march of intellect," the novel ridicules the naive faith in progress exhibited by liberal economists and social reformers. Peacock's satire is never entirely partisan, and *Crotchet Castle* also includes a motley collection of antiquaries, cranks, and obscurantists (including, once again, a character modeled on Coleridge). Nevertheless, Peacock's principal target was now the reductive identification of "progress" with material wealth, a theme that he had previously explored in the *Paper Money Lyrics* (1825–26), and that resurfaces amid the elegiac conviviality of *Gryll Grange* (1860), his final novel.

PHILIP CONNELL

Biography

Born in Weymouth, Dorset, on October 18, 1785. Educated at Engelfield Green, Surrey, until the age of twelve; thereafter, self-taught. Briefly engaged in trade; secretary to Sir Home Riggs Popham, 1808–9; traveled in Wales, 1810–11, before settling in Marlow, Buckinghamshire. Employee of the East India Company, 1819–56 (chief examiner from 1836); married Jane Gryffydh, 1820, with whom he had four children. Died January 23, 1866.

Selected Works

Collections

Works. Edited by H. F. B. Brett-Smith and C. E. Jones. 8 vols. London: Constable, 1924–34.

Novels

Headlong Hall. 1815.
Melincourt. 1817.
Nightmare Abbey. 1818.
Maid Marian. 1822.
The Misfortunes of Elphin. 1829.
Crotchet Castle. 1831.
Gryll Grange. 1861.

Poetry

Rhododaphne, or the Thessalian Spell. 1818.
Paper Money Lyrics, and other Poems. 1837.

Bibliography

Butler, Marilyn. *Peacock Displayed: A Satirist in his Context.* London: Routledge, 1979.
Dawson, Carl. *His Fine Wit: A Study of Thomas Love Peacock.* Berkeley and Los Angeles: University of California Press, 1970.
Madden, Lionel. *Thomas Love Peacock.* London: Evans Bros., 1967.
Mayoux, Jean Jacques. *Un Epicurien anglais: Thomas Love Peacock.* Paris, 1933.
Mills, Howard. *Peacock: His Circle and his Age.* Cambridge: Cambridge University Press, 1968.
Prance, Claude A. *The Characters in the Novels of Thomas Love Peacock, 1785–1866, with Biographical Lists.* New York: Mellen, 1992.
Van Doren, Carl. *The Life of Thomas Love Peacock.* London: J. M. Dent, 1911.

PEALE, CHARLES WILLSON 1741-1827

American painter

Charles Willson Peale was responsible for the production of over one thousand portraits of individuals who, by their political, military, scientific, or cultural achievements, created the United States and sustained it in its early decades. When Peale moved his family from Maryland to Philadelphia in the auspicious year of 1776, he landed in the thick of the American Revolution, and his acquaintances and portrait sitters included Benjamin Franklin, Thomas Jefferson, the Marquis de Lafayette, and George Washington. Contemporary received visual images of the heroes of the early republic are in large part Peale's creation; and yet even without his portraits, history paintings, and landscapes, Peale would command attention. Founder of one of the nation's first natural history museums, organizer of the country's first art school, inventor and holder of patents in bridge design, vapor baths, and fireplaces, excavator of a mastodon skeleton, and creator of a famous landscape garden: these varied accomplishments have earned Peale characterization as an American Leonardo da Vinci. An emphasis on "American" is crucial: in all his endeavors, Peale demonstrated how the achieved ideals of the Revolution—justice, equality, and freedom—made his country a model for a world in search of a rational, harmonious, and benevolent society.

As a young man Peale was trained as a saddlemaker, but in his early twenties he became more interested in painting. He studied briefly with the American painters John Singleton Copley and John Hesselius, but a group of wealthy Maryland landowners organized a fund to send Peale to London from 1767 to 1769, where he studied with his countryman Benjamin West. In London, Peale exhibited two portraits and three miniatures at the Society of the British Artists; when not yet thirty, Peale saw his work shown with such British masters as Thomas Gainsborough and Richard Wilson. When he returned to Maryland, Peale worked in what was a new style in American portrait painting, producing portraits of his subjects (and sometimes their families) set intimately within their individual landscapes or homes.

Among the portraits Peale chose to paint in this style, those of his own family are particularly fine. *The Peale Family,* begun around 1770 but not completed until 1809, is an early example. Here all family members, including relatives, companions, a much-loved family nurse, and even the family dog Argus, gather in affection and harmony around the dining room table in Peale's Annapolis, Maryland, home. Few of the sitters look at the viewer, instead engaging in cheerful and animated conversation as Charles teaches his brother St. George to draw their mother. Perhaps the most well-known of the family portraits is Peale's lifesize *trompe l'oeil* painting of his sons: *"The Staircase Group": Raphaelle and Titian Ramsay Peale* (1793). The boys, one carrying painting supplies, turn from ascending a stair to look at the viewer; Peale's displaying of the artwork in a doorway and with an actual wooden step built in at the painting's base heightened the illusion of reality. According to another son, Rembrandt, when George Washington visited Peale's museum he bowed politely to the boys in the painting, thinking them to be alive.

In spring 1776, a few months after Peale moved to Philadelphia, he heard the Declaration of Independence proclaimed at the State House and then enlisted in the city militia, seeing action at the battles of Trenton and Princeton. He was also active in various roles in Philadelphia politics. In 1779 the Supreme Executive Council of Pennsylvania commissioned Peale to paint George Washington, victorious at Princeton, for their council chambers. This formal life-size painting, the first "official portrait" of Washington, became tremendously popular and helped to establish Peale's prominence as a portraitist. Over the next half century, he gained commissions to paint many, perhaps most, of the principal figures of note in colonial America. He portrayed these people objectively and rationally, sometimes surrounding them with symbols of the new country's republican spirit.

In 1786, Peale opened his natural history museum in Philadelphia, displaying mounted specimens in their natural habitats. Over the years, William Clark, Thomas Jefferson, Meriwether Lewis, George Washington, and many others added to the collection, which in 1799 had 100 quadrupeds, 700 birds, 150 amphibians, and thousands of other exhibits. In this first natural history museum in America, Peale aimed to celebrate and to educate his fellow citizens in the glories of nature, and specifically of an American physical world. Like Benjamin Franklin, Peale was a Deist, and he placed these words on a placard above the entrance to his museum:

The book of Nature open—
—Explore the wond'rous work.
A solemn Institute of laws eternal
Whose unaltered page no time can change
No copier can corrupt.

As Peale wrote in his "Discourses Introductory to a Course of Lectures" (1800), he believed in a "chain of creation" wherein one could trace each species' beauty "in its relative situation to other beings." He argued that God formed a universe in which artist and naturalist make manifest the creator's supreme designs. Peale's worldview is thus that of Alexander Pope in his *Essay on Man* (1733–34) rather than that of Romantic artists and writers of later generations who frequently celebrated an untamed, sublime, and visionary natural world.

Ironically, the highlight of Peale's scientific career—his unearthing of a mastodon fossil near Newburgh, New York—presaged the chaotic world of evolutionary change rather than reinforcing the fixed, eternal "chain of creation." Those skeletal mastodon remains were accepted by French scientist Georges Cuvier as an example of an extinct species. Thus Peale's work contributed to the nineteenth-century debate over geologic time and the possibility of extinction. Characteristically, Peale merged science, art, and autobiography, using his paleontologic work as the basis for *The Exhumation of the Mastodon* (1806–08), placing seventy-five figures, including living and dead family members, in the painting.

As he approached his eighth decade, Peale retired to a country estate that he called Belfield, six miles north of Philadelphia. There he farmed, painted, and corresponded extensively with his friend Thomas Jefferson, similarly retired at Monticello in Virginia. At Belfield, now a national historic landmark on the campus of La Salle University, Peale created a notable landscape garden, with an obelisk, a pedestal of memorable events, a summer house designed "in the Chinese taste, dedicated to meditation," another summer house topped with a bust of George Washington, a fountain, and a cave. As with his museum, the garden's purpose was educational, aimed at increasing the visitor's appreciation of the natural world.

Near the end of his life, Peale completed two autobiographies, one in prose and the other in paint. His *The Artist in His Museum* (1822) contains a full-length self-portrait of Peale lifting a curtain to reveal his portraits, his stuffed natural history specimens, and the mounted skeleton of his mastodon. On a table nearby are his palette and his brushes. In this painting, Peale (as he wrote to his son Rembrandt) wanted not only "a lasting ornament to my art as a painter" but something "expressive that I bring forth into public view the beauties of nature and art."

JAMES A. BUTLER

Biography

Born in Queen Anne's County, Maryland, April 15, 1741. Apprenticed as a saddlemaker, 1754; freed from apprenticeship and set up a shop in Annapolis, Maryland, 1761; married Rachel Brewer, 1762; studied painting in London, 1767–69; Raphaelle Peale, first surviving child, born, 1774. (There were seventeen children in all, eleven of whom survived into adulthood.) Moved family to Philadelphia, 1776; opened Philadelphia Museum (Peale's Museum), 1786; married Elizabeth DePeyster, 1791; undertook expedition to exhume mastodon, displayed its skeleton, 1801; assisted in establishing the Pennsylvania Academy of Fine Arts, 1805; married Hannah Moore, 1805; retired to country estate Belfield, gave ownership of museum to son Rubens, 1810; again took over management of museum, 1822. Died in Philadelphia, February 22, 1827.

Bibliography

Alderson, William T., ed. *Mermaids, Mummies, and Mastodons: The Emergence of the American Museum.* Washington, D.C.: American Association of Museums for the Baltimore City Life Museums, 1992.

Brigham, David R. *Public Culture in the Early Republic: Peale's Museum and Its Audience.* Washington, D.C.: Smithsonian Institution Press, 1995.

Miller, Lillian B., ed. *The Peale Family: Creation of a Legacy, 1770–1870.* New York: Abbeville Press, 1996.

Miller, Lillian B., Sidney Hart, and Toby A. Appel. *The Selected Papers of Charles Willson Peale and His Family.* 7 vols. New Haven, Conn.: Yale University Press, 1983– .

Miller, Lillian B., and David Ward. *New Perspectives on Charles Willson Peale, A Two Hundred Fiftieth Anniversary Celebration.* Pittsburgh: University of Pittsburgh Press, 1991.

Richardson, Edgar P., Brooke Hindle, and Lillian B. Miller. *Charles Willson Peale and His World.* New York: Abrams, 1983.

Sellers, Charles Coleman. *Charles Willson Peale.* New York: Scribner, 1969.

PELLICO, SILVIO 1789–1854

Italian writer and patriot

Silvio Pellico was one of the greatest Italian patriots and a representative intellectual of the Romantic era. Writer, dramatist, and poet, his works were inspired by the typically Romantic feelings of patriotism and love, a desire to return to the ideals of the middle age, and a belief in the necessity of God's presence in the life of human beings. He wrote in the literary journal *Il Conciliatore* on Romanticism and his desire for Italy's freedom.

Sentenced to imprisonment for his patriotic ideas, he contemplated the meaning of life, and those reflections influenced his conversion to Catholicism.

Le mie prigioni (*My Prisons*, 1832), an autobiographical work written during Pellico's time in Spielberg prison, is regarded as his masterpiece. It rapidly became popular and was translated into many different languages. In this work he relates, in simple and unaffected prose, his experiences and emotions during his imprisonment. There is no tone of bitterness in his approach; during his entire stay in prison he displays the attitude of a Catholic resigned to his fate and willing to place his fate in God's hands. He relates in great detail, often in a rueful tone, about his everyday experiences in prison. His short story on the spider which he trained to eat from his hand is one of the best known passages of modern Italian prose. The gentleness and simplicity of its narrative made Pellico's *Prigioni* a favorite story of the time. It has also been said that the book did more harm to Austria than any defeat on the battlefield. He wrote this work, persuaded by his confessor, in order to show how religion may help in human misadventures. When *Le mie prigioni* was published, some Catholics questioned the sincerity of his conversion (including Monaldo, father of Giacomo Leopardi). Patriots had accused Pellico of betraying of his liberal principles. Nevertheless, the success of the work was indisputable. The key to its success was its subject: spirituality and patriotic love captured the hearts of the people. Another key theme is the sublimation of suffering; the writer demonstrates that misery, supported by faith, may help us to become better human beings.

The main characters of Pellico's works are people of the lower stratum of society and people he met in prison, both jailers and other prisoners. Descriptions of the female characters of the book, Maddalena and Zanze, are very touching. In *Le mie prigioni* we can read an interesting psychological analysis of human personality in the example of the old prison guard Schiller: a good person with a great name and a modest origin. He is a Swiss farmer who, after completing military service, spends a great part of his life as "a prisoner of his own job" in the Spielberg prison.

Through his writing we also witness Pellico's internal battles, including his desperate struggle with depression and suicidal thoughts. The detailed descriptions of prison cells, and extreme situations a human being may find himself in, made this book a credible study of the pressures the individual must face in such difficult, unfavorable conditions.

Pellico also wrote a great number of tragedies, several on medieval subject matter. *Laudamia* (1812), his first tragedy, received the praise of Ugo Foscolo. The next tragedies—*Turno, Nerone, Calpurnio Pisone,* and *Dante* (unfinished)—were written from 1814. His most successful tragedy, *Francesca da Rimini* (1815), describes a pathos-riddled tale of passionate love as embodied by Paolo and Francesca, the condemned couple made famous by Dante Alighieri in his *Inferno*. Pellico's work is primarily focused on the description of temptation and the couple's strenuous battles with it. The work immediately captured the attention of Lord Byron, who translated it into English. At the same time, Pellico started writing *Beatrice d'Este, Pia dei Tolomei, Matilde, Attilio Regolo Lombardo, Guido da Crema,* and *Eufemio da Messina* (1820). While he was in prison in Venice he wrote *Ester d'Engaddi* (1830) and *Iginia d'Asti* (1830), and in prison at Spielberg he wrote *Leoniero da Dertona* (1832). Other tragedies written by Pellico are *Gismonda da Mendrisio* (1832), *Erodiade* (1832), *Boezio, Tommaso Moro* (1834), *Corradino* (1834), *I Francesi in Agrigento* (1834), and *Raffaella da Siena* (1834).

Pellico was also a poet. He published *Poesie* (1838), poems full of religious devotion and patriotic fervor, and *Cantiche* or *Novelle poetiche* (1831), inspired by the Romanticism and concerning medieval life and manners. The most important of these were *Tancreda, Rosilde, Eligi e Valafrido, Adello, Adelaide,* and *La morte di Dante.* He wrote also a prose version of Byron's *Manfred* (1842).

His historical work *Notizie intorno alla Beata Panasia,* published in 1862, is the true story of a young girl who lived in the Middle Ages, was killed by her stepmother due to her devotion to Christ, and is venerated by the people of Novara. In *La Marchesa Di Barolo* (*Life of the Marchesa Giulia Falletti di Barolo, Reformer of the Turin Prisons,* published in 1864), he narrates the life of Marquise de Barolo, a very religious person, great benefactress, and a personal friend.

I doveri degli uomini (*The Duties of Men,* 1834) is a compilation of precepts and examples, intended to teach the young how to lead a decent life. Inspired by Catholic morality, it was frequently used as a reading book in schools. This work was scorned by many patriots, while it simultaneously gained Pellico a devoted Catholic audience, thus dissolving any suspicions regarding the sincerity of his conversion.

ELVIO CIFERRI

See also **Catholicism; Foscolo, Ugo; Byron, Lord George Noel Gordon.**

Biography

Born at Saluzzo, in Piedmont, on June 25, 1788 to Onorato Pellico and Margherita Tournier. Spent his youth moving from place to place, making a four-year stay in Lyons. At the age of twenty he went to Milan, where he met several of the best Italian writers, among them Ugo Foscolo, Alessandro Manzoni, and Vincenzo Monti. Here he held a position of a French teacher in a school run by the government for orphans of the military. When Austrian officials dismissed him from his post, he started giving private tuitions in various families. He played a significant role in the editing of the journal *Il Conciliatore.* In 1820 he was, along with his coworker Pietro Maroncelli, arrested by the Austrians, who suspected him to be a member of the Carboneria Society. He was jailed first in the Piombi at Venice, and next in the prison of San Michele di Murano. After a fast trial he and Maroncelli were sentenced to death, but this punishment was soon changed to one of imprisonment with hard labor. They were placed in the fortress of Spielberg in Moravia. After eight years of imprisonment, Pellico was set free in 1830. For the rest of his life, impaired by the difficulties of imprisonment, he kept entirely away from politics, and preferred a solitary life. He died in Turin on January 31, 1854.

Selected Works

My Ten Years' Imprisonment. Translated by Thomas Roscoe. 1833.
The Duties of Men. Translated by Thomas Roscoe. 1834.
Euphemio of Messina. Translated by Elizabeth Fries Ellett. 1834.
Epistolario. Edited by Guglielmo Stefani. 1856.
Opere. Collected works. 1857.
Notizie intorno alla Beata Panasia. 1862.
Life of the Marchesa Giulia Falletti di Barolo, Reformer of the Turin Prisons. Translated by Georgiana Fullerton. 1866.
On the Duties of Young Men. Translated by R. A. Vain. 1872.
Francesca da Rimini. Translated by Joel Foote Bingham. 1897.
Le mie prigioni (selections) and Francesca da Rimini. Edited by Kenneth McKenzie. Chicago: University of Chicago Press, 1924.
Opere. Selected works. Torino: UTET, 1954.
Lettere milanesi (1815–1821). Edited by Mario Scotti. Turin: Loescher, 1963.

My Prisons. Le mie prigioni. Translated by Isaias Gerard Capaldi. London: Oxford University Press, 1963.

Bibliography

Allason, Barbara. *La vita di Silvio Pellico.* Milan: Mondadori, 1933.

Ballabio, Eugenio. *Silvio Pellico, un pentito illustre.* Massarosa: Del Bucchia, 2000.

Barbiera, Raffaello. *Silvio Pellico.* Milan: Alpes, 1926.

Bellorini, Egidio. "Le idee letterarie di Silvio Pellico." in *Giornale Storico Letterario Italiano* 48 (1905).

———. *Silvio Pellico.* Messina: Principato, 1916.

Briano, Giorgio. *Silvio Pellico.* Turin: Unione Tipografico-Editrice, 1861.

Gontier, Mario. *Silvio Pellico ospite comunque: appunti sulla vita di un piemontese d'Europa.* Pinerolo: Società Storica Pinerolese, 1990.

Gustarelli, Andrea. *La vita, "Le mie prigioni" e "I doveri degli uomini" di Silvio Pellico.* Florence: Sansoni, 1917.

Kauchtschischwili, Nina. *Silvio Pellico e la Russia.* Milan: Vita e Pensiero, 1963.

Luzio, Alessandro. *Il processo Pellico-Maroncelli.* Milan: Tipografia Vescovile San Vincenzo, 1903.

Morigo, A. *Il romanticismo di Silvio Pellico e la Francesca da Rimini.* Como: Unione Tipografica, 1905.

Parenti, Marino. *Bibliografia delle opere di Silvio Pellico.* Florence: Sansoni, 1952.

Pedraglio, Clelia Luisa. *Silvio Pellico.* Como: Omarini, 1904.

Rinieri, Ilario. *Della vita e delle opere di Silvio Pellico.* Turin: Libreria Roux, 1898–1901.

Romano, Angelo. *Silvio Pellico.* Brescia: Morcelliana, 1948.

Savio, Carlo Fedele. *Silvio Pellico liberale e credente.* Bologna: Forni, 1972.

LE PÈRE GORIOT, 1834–1835

Novel by Honoré de Balzac

Le Père Goriot by French novelist Honoré de Balzac was published in four installments in the *Revue de Paris* and in revised book form in 1835. There would in fact be additional revisions to the text in subsequent editions before it was included in what would eventually be the collection *La Comédie humaine* (*The Human Comedy*).

Despite the title, the hero is not Goriot but Eugène de Rastignac, a handsome, naive young man from a poor aristocratic family who has gone to Paris to study law. The novel, set in 1819, is the drama of his temptation and initiation, as he is taught the useful, but hard, lessons about the workings of the world. From Vautrin, a fellow boarder at the Pension Vauquer, he learns that one must struggle against society, but by its own rules: a legal career, therefore, is a slow and arduous climb to financial success. An easier, quicker way is to marry a woman with great expectations, who happens to live in the same boardinghouse and to like Eugène already. For a commission, Vautrin is willing to cause the death of Victorine Taillefer's brother, thereby making her the sole heir to her father's fortune.

Less crudely but in the same vein, the high-born Claire de Beauséant, Eugène's wealthy cousin, tells him to use women as one does relay horses, abandoning them at each successive rung up the ladder. She further advises him to choose Delphine de Nucingen over Anastasie de Restaud (both *nées* Goriot) for his mistress because, as a noodlemaker's daughter, she desperately wants to enter high society. After Delphine receives an invitation to Mme. de Beauséant's, she rewards Eugène with an elegant apartment paid for by her father.

Old Goriot also teaches him a valuable lesson. Through statements and actions, he asserts that fatherhood equals sacrifice ("Always giving, that's what being a father means"), although a deeper, more unsettling conclusion is made obvious to Rastignac. After he observes Goriot's complete self-annihilation for his demanding daughters, leading to a wretched existence and death, he realizes that, as in King Lear, filial love and gratitude are just empty notions.

By revealing to Eugène the mysteries of aristocratic and bourgeois society as microcosms of the world, the three mentors show that only those who are strong succeed by accepting society for what it is and that, behind the façade (luxury mansions or dilapidated tenements), the same meanness and ugliness of spirit prevail. As he vacillates between these contrary options and his own sense of moral conduct (supported by his affection for his family and his friend, Horace Bianchon), he changes from an inchoately ambitious young man into an opportunist, with a desire to "succeed! . . . succeed at all costs!" To survive in such a calculating world, he must strike a compromise with evil that necessarily subordinates his own passionate nature to the exigencies of the quest for wealth and status.

This explains why, for Eugène, love has none of its Romantic connotations. Since ambition is his motivating force, he will choose the woman who will help him achieve the most. He can, therefore, consider Anastasie first and then "settle" for the sexually frustrated Delphine who, ignored by her husband and abused by her lover, should be very willing to accept him as her lover in a new form of contract in which love is seen not as passion, but as barter by which both participants profit. In fact, in other novels, we will see Rastignac, thanks to his enrichment through Baron de Nucingen's financial manipulations, married to the Nucingen daughter after a twenty-year liaison with Delphine.

Eugène's education is complete when he watches a delirious "Christ of Paternity" (in Balzac's phrase) die in squalor, abandoned by his egotistical daughters. From the heights of the Père-Lachaise cemetery, in a grand challenge at society, the disillusioned former law student declares, "It's between us now!" as he goes off to dine with Delphine. Earlier, he saw the three ways of dealing with the world ("Obedience, Struggle, Revolt"). Now, he chooses struggle, not in reaction to a cosmic injustice but in acknowledgment of Vautrin's world view that there are no principles, only opportunities, and no laws, only circumstances.

Moreover, such a gesture is also an embrace of all that Paris, lying at his feet, has to offer him. That Paris is often compared to a new Babylon, an ocean, a cavern, a jungle, a prostitute, a battlefield, a mudhole, "a forest in the New World [with] twenty

Honoré Daumier, *Vautrin*. Reprinted courtesy of AKG.

kinds of savage tribes" reinforces the victorious survivor's need for strength, cunning, and determination, unfettered by meaningless moral doubts.

Besides depicting the mostly corrupting importance of money in private lives and presenting a well-evidenced historical context (a concept borrowed from Walter Scott) and claiming that "[a]ll is true," Balzac is the first novelist to point out the revelatory nature of objects and faces and to analyze a milieu's influence on the characters' personality. This is particularly so in his detailed descriptions of Parisian neighborhoods and the Pension Vauquer. His readers, then, could no longer skip page-long descriptions, as had been their custom, because these were now full of clues that one could read and decipher, the better to understand the world and the people in it.

Like many Romantics, Balzac liked to portray larger-than-life protagonists. For example, Vautrin is a "horrible and majestic spectacle," a "fallen archangel," a "human volcano" endowed with such elemental qualities as "infernal fires" and "lava and fire," while Goriot is "sublime . . . illuminated by the fires of his paternal passion," and Mme. de Beauséant has "the stature of goddesses in the *Iliad*."

Finally, it is in this work that Balzac had the brilliant idea of having characters (fictional and real) cross from one novel to another (including those published before 1835) so that Eugène de Massiac, the hero of the serialized *Père Goriot*, is in a later printing reborn as *La Peau de chagrin*'s Rastignac (*The Wild Ass's Skin*, 1831). This reappearing cast, which eventually comprises some two thousand characters, helps in creating the illusion of life itself, so dear to Balzac.

PIERRE L. HORN

See also **Balzac, Honoré de; Fiction: France**

Text

Le Père Goriot, 1834–35. Translated as *Daddy Goriot*, 1860. *Père Goriot*, translated by Burton Raffel. New York: Norton, 1998; also translated by A. J. Krailsheimer. New York: Oxford University Press, 1999.

Bibliography

Barbéris, Pierre. *"Le Père Goriot" de Balzac: Ecriture, structures, significations*. Paris: Larousse, 1972.
Beizer, Janet. *Family Plots: Balzac's Narrative Generations*. New Haven, Conn.: Yale University Press, 1986.
Bellos, David. *Honoré de Balzac: "Old Goriot."* Cambridge: Cambridge University Press, 1987.
Kanes, Martin. *"Père Goriot": Anatomy of a Troubled World*. Boston: Twayne, 1993.
Lock, Peter W. *Balzac: "Le Père Goriot."* London: Arnold, 1967.
Riegert, Guy. *"Le Père Goriot" de Balzac*. Paris: Hatier, 1973.

PESTALOZZI, JOHANN HEINRICH 1746–1827

Swiss educator and philanthropist

Johann Heinrich Pestalozzi was an idealist of extraordinary stature who championed the cause of the dispossessed and repeatedly offered refuge and education to destitute children. To this day charitable institutions known as Pestalozzi Villages provide shelter and schooling for disadvantaged young people from all over the world. Pestalozzi is considered to be the founder of modern pedagogy, and was one of the first advocates of a holistic education for all. His belief in a child's potential for "organic" development, his notion of educating the "head, heart and hand," and his innovative teaching practices contributed to reforms in elementary schools everywhere, from nineteenth-century Prussia to modern Japan, and underlie the educational theories of Friedrich Fröbel, Maria Montessori, and Rudolf Steiner, and even those of the American behaviorist B. F. Skinner.

Pestalozzi was born in Zürich, Switzerland. His ancestors, originally from Chiavenna in northern Italy, settled in protestant Zürich in the sixteenth century. His grandfather had been a pastor and his father worked as a clerk and a surgeon until his death in 1751, when his son was only five years old. Henceforth Pestalozzi, together with his elder brother and younger sister, were brought up in poverty, but with utter devotion, by their mother and a faithful female servant. Later in life Pestalozzi would come to identify the lack of a paternal presence at a crucial stage in his development as the source of his own difficult character. At the same time he never abandoned his almost mystical belief in the importance of the mother in the upbringing of a child.

From his earliest years it was obvious that Johann Heinrich Pestalozzi was an unusual person. He was small, slight, and unusual-looking, but of exceptional physical resilience. As a schoolboy he was hyperactive, clumsy, and inattentive, and yet he learned quickly and easily. As an adult he alienated many of his contemporaries with his bizarrely effusive manner, his grubby attire, and his pockmarked face. Yet his selfless concern for the welfare of children, as well as his progressive views regarding social justice and the education of the young of all classes and creeds, earned him much attention and respect. These same qualities also caused him to embark on a series of worthy but doomed projects that tended to expose him to ridicule and derision.

His interest in the liberalizing ideas that had begun to sweep Europe and, above all, his admiration for Jean-Jacques Rousseau prompted him to abandon his early ambition of becoming a pastor. In 1769 he borrowed money, bought some land, built a large farmhouse and, together with his new wife Anna Schulthess, tried to build a model farm. The couple had a son, Jean-Jacques, named after Rousseau. Within three years Pestalozzi's general lack of aptitude for the task, as well as some misfortunes, forced him to abandon the venture. He then turned the family house into a home for the children of the poor. He planned to teach them the basic skills of spinning and weaving, so that ultimately they might become self-supporting; but by 1780 this project too had collapsed.

A modest reversal in fortune occurred when Pestalozzi, in desperation, began to publish his writings. A compilation of poignant musings and aphorisms was published as *Die Abendstunde eines Einsiedlers* (*The Evening Hour of a Hermit*) in 1780. It was followed in 1781 by a simple village tale, *Lienhard und Gertrud. Ein Buch für das Volk.* (*Leonard and Gertrude: A Book for the People*). A lengthy and more reflective sequel argued the essential goodness of man and the potential of education to achieve moral and social reform. An essay of 1783, entitled *Über die Gesezgebung* [sic] *und Kindermord* (*On the Law and Infanticide*), deals with the problem of unwed mothers who murder their newborn babies, and places much of the blame upon society at large. Further writings include *Ja oder Nein* (*Yes or No*) of 1793, in which Pestalozzi condemns both the abuse of power of monarchs and the foolishness and violence of revolutionaries. These writings brought income and recognition even from beyond the Swiss border, and in 1792 Pestalozzi was declared an honorary French citizen by the revolutionary government in Paris. With the initial encouragement of Johann Gottlieb Fichte, who stayed near Zürich in 1793, he now embarked on *Meine Nachforschungen* (*My Research*, 1797), an ambitious treatise in which he develops, with impulsive ardor rather than measured reasoning, his theories on the innate spirituality of all men and the crucial role of education in developing true religious feeling and a sense of social responsibility.

Following the French invasion of Switzerland in 1798, scores of orphaned or abandoned children began to roam the countryside, and Pestalozzi was approached by the Swiss authorities to find a solution. He took to the task with alacrity and opened an orphanage in an old convent in Stans, near Lucerne, where he dedicated himself virtually single-handedly to becoming "father, mother, teacher and servant" to approximately eighty destitute children. The establishment lasted exactly six months, until the French turned the house into a military hospital in July 1799.

After this disappointment, Pestalozzi, now fifty-three years old, decided to become an apprentice teacher in Burgdorf, near Berne. Here he set up rigid timetables for different types of lessons, devised visual aids to teach the alphabet, chanted questions and answers from the Catechism in unison with the children, made them learn and recite by heart, and provided them with slates and chalk to practice their writing. He took them on outings to nearby mountains and rivers and encouraged them to march in step while singing songs. His teaching methods were so successful that he became known as the "miracle teacher," and claims were made that his pupils learned in half a year as much as others learned in three. He consolidated his international fame with an exposition on his teaching practices in *Wie Gertrud ihre Kinder lehrt* (*How Gertrude Teaches her Children*, 1801).

In 1802, Napoleon invited him to a consultative conference to help draw up a new Swiss Constitution. Pestalozzi traveled to Paris expecting to contribute to progressive legislation on education. However, this issue was summarily dismissed as unimportant, and he left the conference early, disappointed once more. Moreover, with the recent withdrawal of French troops from the Canton of Berne, the Bernese patricians reasserted their power, and Pestalozzi was removed from the school in Burgdorf. In 1806 he finally succeeded in establishing his own school at Yverdon, near Lake Neuchâtel. It soon flourished and by 1809 housed approximately 150 boys from all social classes and several nations. However, quarrels with benefactors, disagreements and problems among the teachers, and, above all, the repressive political climate that followed the Vienna Congress caused the school to go into decline, and by 1825 Pestalozzi was forced to dissolve it. He spent the last two years of his life working on his memoirs, *Schwanengesang* (*Swan Song*, 1826), while accepting honors and fending off attacks in equal measure. He died of old age in 1827.

AGNÈS CARDINAL

Biography

Born in Zürich, Switzerland, January 12, 1746. Studies in philology and philosophy at the Collegium Carolinum in Zürich, 1763–65. Farmer's apprentice, 1767–68. Marriage to Anna Schulthess, 1769. Moved to Neuhof farm in Birrfeld near Brugg, 1771. Three years of mismanagement and ultimate failure of farm. Opened a home for the children of the poor on Neuhof, 1774. Gradual failure of children's home and financial difficulties. Publication of *Abendstunde eïnes Einsiedlers* (*Evening Hour of a Hermit*), 1780. *Lienhard und Gertrud, 1. Teil* (*Leonard and Gertrude, Part 1*) published 1781. *Lienhard und Gertrud, 2–4. Teil* (*Leonard and Gertrude, Parts 2–4*) published 1783–87. Honorary citizenship of France, 1792. Head of orphanage in Stans, 1798–99. Teacher in Burgdorf, near Berne, 1799. 1801 publication of *Wie Gertrud ihre Kinder lehrt* (*How Gertrud teaches her Children*). 1802 attends Napoleon's "Consulta" in Paris. 1806 founding of school in Yverdon. 1806–1809 success of school, followed by its gradual decline and closure in 1825.

1826 publication of *Schwanengesang* (*Swansong*). Death on February 17, 1827 in Brugg, Canton Aargau, Switzerland.

Selected Works

Sämtliche Schriften. 15 vols. 1819–26.
Leonard and Gertrude. A Book for the Poor. Vol. 1. Translated by Eliza Shepherd. 1824.
Leonard and Gertrude. A Book for the People. Vol. 1. Translator anonymous. 1824.
Letters on Early Education. Addressed to J. P. Greaves. 1827.
How Gertrude Teaches her Children. Translated by Lucy E. Holland and Francis C. Turner. Edited by Ebenezer Cooke. 1894.
Pestalozzi's Educational Writings. Edited by J. A. Green with F. A. Collie. London: Edward Arnold, 1912.
Gesammelte Werke. 10 vols. Edited by Emilie Bosshart, Emanuel Dejung, Lothar Kempter, and Hans Steitbacher. Zürich: Rascher, 1944.
The Education of Man: Aphorisms. Translated by H. Norden and R. Norden. London: Greenwood Press, 1951.
Ausgewählte Schriften. Edited by Wilhelm Flitner. Düsseldorf: Küppner, 1954.

Bibliography

Anderson, Louis Flint. *Pestalozzi.* London: Greenwood Press, 1931.
Green, John Alfred. *The Educational Ideas of Pestalozzi.* London: Greenwood Press, 1914.
Hayward, Frank H. *The Educational Ideas of Pestalozzi and Fröbel.* London: Greenwood Press, 1979.
Heafford, M. *Pestalozzi. His Thought and its Relevance Today.* London: Methuen, 1967.
Liedtke, Max. *Johann Heinrich Pestalozzi mit Selbstzeugnissen und Bilddokumenten.* Hamburg: Rowohlt, 1968.
Schifferli, Dagmar. *Anna Pestalozzi-Schulthess. Ihr Leben mit Heinrich Pestalozzi.* Zürich Pendo, 1998.
Silber, Käte. *Pestalozzi: The Man and his Work.* London: Routledge and Kegan Paul, 1973.
Wild, Rebecca. *Raising Curious, Creative, Confident Kids: the Pestalozzi Experiment in Childbased Education.* Los Angeles: Shambhala, 2000.

PETER SCHLEMIHLS WUNDERSAME GESCHICHTE (THE STRANGE STORY OF PETER SCHLEMIHL) 1814

Novella by Adelbert von Chamisso

Adelbert von Chamisso's best-known literary work is paradoxically both his most Romantic creation and the one whose Romantic credentials have been most frequently contested. This first-person tale, addressed by the protagonist to "his friend" Chamisso, tells the story of a man who sells his shadow to the devil (referred to as the Grey Man) for a bottomless purse and is subsequently brought to the brink of relinquishing his soul to regain the forfeited shadow. The work clearly owes much to folklore, fairytale, and legend, yet the first edition's fictive claim that *Peter Schlemihl* had been "edited by [Friedrich de la Motte-] Fouqué," whose *Undine* (1811) the author particularly admired, already gives some indication of the way Chamisso had recast his fable of temptation, resistance, and partial reconciliation to accommodate his religious source material to Romantic tastes. When tempting the impoverished Schlemihl, who has just arrived at a north German commercial seaport in search of employment and an *entrée* into society, the Devil offers him a series of inducements that are the stuff of well-known Romantic fairytales and German folklore: a root capable of unlocking all doors, a mandrake able to divine the location of buried treasure (familiar from Achim von Arnim's *Isabella von Ägypten* [*Isabella of Egypt*, 1812]), a magic coin guaranteed always to return to its owner, a magic tablecloth, a lucky purse, and a diminutive devil in a bottle (derived from Friedrich Heinrich Karl Fouqué's *Das Galgenmännlein* [1810]). Schlemihl is in essence being asked of which Romantic plot he would like to become the hero. Later, having resisted temptation, the protagonist is rewarded with another stock Romantic possession: a pair of seven-league boots, familiar to both Schlemihl and his creator from *Leben und Taten des kleinen Thomas, genannt Düaumchen*, Ludwig Tieck's version of *Tom Thumb* (in *Phantasus* [*Tales from the Phantus*, 1812]). As such pronounced intertextuality indicates, the author of *Peter Schlemihl* knowingly incorporates material from a variety of contemporary Romantic sources, ingeniously amalgamating it with motifs from chapbook versions of earlier German legends and from Hans Jacob Christoph von Grimmelshausen's fiction, as well as with echoes of the *Nibelungenlied*, Dante Alighieri's *Inferno*, and the biblical account of Jesus' temptation in the wilderness.

The manner in which these motifs are employed in the new context is by no means always of a Romantic nature. After initially reveling in the power of his seven-league boots to take him around the world, Schlemihl soon chooses to abandon modish "wanderlust" and put them to the distinctly un-Romantic use of facilitating global field trips for the purpose of collecting and studying the flora and fauna that are the subject of his scholarly treatises for the University of Berlin. While still bereft of his shadow and forced to shun society (the stigma of having had dealings with the devil marks him for life), Schlemihl has by the end of the story developed from a stereotypical suffering Romantic outsider into someone committed to pragmatic scholarship and various acts of altruism. After he has resolutely dismissed the devil, the remaining proceeds from the bottomless purse are put to philanthropic purposes (the hospital founded in his name, the Schlemihlium, is the first positive use of his fortune for the public good); in the same spirit, even his "wondrous story" has been written in the hope of offering moral edification. The hero's development thus supplies a didactic contrast to the superficial values of the *nouveau riche* society encountered at the beginning of the work, consisting of people who have, by implication, already sold their souls to the devil and whom Schlemihl had been on the verge of joining.

This pronounced progression from Romanticism to philanthropic and scholarly activities has led to Chamisso's work being seen as "a Romantic story with a Biedermeier ending" or a parody either of unworldly Romantic aspirations or of the *larmoyance* of the sentimental fiction of the period. Within such an *Entwicklungsnovelle* (novella of development) framework, *Peter Schlemihl* displays the juxtaposition of fantastic and realistic elements already a central feature of Tieck's *Der blonde Eckbert* (*Fair-Haired Eckbert*, 1812) and E. T. A. Hoffmann's *Fanatasiestücke in Callots Manier* (*Fantasy Pieces in the Style of Callot*, 1813). In 1815 the author of the latter paid tribute to the "Hoffmannesque" quality of *Peter Schlemihl* with the double compliment of introducing Chamisso's character into *Die Abenteuer der Silvester-Nacht* (*The Adventures of the Night of New Year's Eve*) and echoing his fabulous adventures in the same collection's *Erzählung vom verlornen Spiegelbilde* (*Story of the Lost Reflection*). Chamisso's highly developed combination of fantasy and closely observed contemporary detail has given rise to much debate about whether *Peter Schlemihl* should be classified as a novella, a fairytale, a *Kunstmärchen*, a hybrid *Märchennovelle*, or a didactic fable. What particularly distinguishes the work from other German fiction of the Romantic period is the degree of realistic specificity in Chamisso's handling of the temptation scene at a garden party and the imaginative depiction of the predicament of shadowlessness, as well as Schlemihl's own urbane humor. In contrast, the eerie interplay between the fantastic and the real has a more destabilizing effect in Tieck's *Der blonde Eckbert* and was to be harnessed to an ironic depiction of the conflict between the artist and society in the works of Hoffmann.

Bertha's words in *Der blonde Eckbert* that her strange story should not be confused with a fairytale could stand as Chamisso's motto. Prefatory material, including a letter from Chamisso to Hitzig telling how Schlemihl even delivered his manuscript incognito the previous day, is intended to authenticate the hero's existence. Further spoof correspondence, revolving around the question of whether it would be indiscreet to publish such a private document, also helps substantiate the fiction that Schlemihl is a real person. The protagonist's narrative displays a parallel vested interest in assuring his readers that what has befallen him is a matter of fact, not fantasy.

Peter Schlemihl tends to be remembered above all for its first half: the unforgettable story of a man who loses his shadow in a moment of naiveté and learns the social price of dealing with the devil. In the English-speaking world, the tale enjoyed an even greater success than in nineteenth-century Germany, not least on account of George Cruikshank's series of illustrations, which captured the wit and humor of *Peter Schlemihl*'s unique narrative tone.

I. A. AND J. J. WHITE

Text

Peter Schlemihls wundersame Geschichte, 1814. Second, revised edition, 1827. Translated as *Peter Schlemihl* by Sir John Bowring, 1823. Translated as *The Strange Story of Peter Schlemihl* by Harry Steinhauer. Berkeley: University of California Press, 1977.

Bibliography

Atkins, Stuart. "Peter Schlemihl in Relation to the Popular Novel of the Romantic Period," *Germanic Review* 21 (1946): 191–208.

Danès, Jean-Pierre. "Peter Schlemihl et la signification de l'ombre," *Etudes Germaniques* 35 (1980): 444–48.

Fink, Gonthier-Louis. "Peter Schlemihl et la tradition du conte romantique," *Recherches Germaniques* 12 (1982): 24–54.

Flores, Ralph. "The Lost Shadow of Peter Schlemihl," *German Quarterly* 47 (1974): 467–84.

Freund, Winfried. *Chamisso: "Peter Schlemihl": Ein bürgerlicher Bewußtseinsspiegel. Entstehung—Struktur—Didaktik.* Paderborn: Schöningh, 1980.

Koepke, Wulf. "Introduction" to Adelbert von Chamisso, *Peter Schlemihl. Reprint of the Original Translation by Sir John Bowring.* Columbia, S.C.: Camden House, 1993. v-xxxi.

Kuzniar, Alice A. " 'Spurlos . . . verschwunden': Peter Schlemihl und sein Schatten als der verschobene Signifikant," *Aurora* 45 (1985): 189–204.

Schulz, Franz. "Die erzählerische Funktion des Motivs vom verlorenen Schatten in Chamissos *Peter Schlemihl*," *German Quarterly* 45 (1972): 429–42.

Swales, Martin. *The German "Novelle."* Princeton, N.J.: Princeton University Press, 1977.

Walach, Dagmar. "Adelbert von Chamisso: *Peter Schlemihls wundersame Geschichte* (1814)." In *Romane und Erzählungen der deutschen Romantik: Neue Interpretationen.* Edited by Paul Michael Lützeler. Stuttgart: Reclam, 1981.

White, John and Arnn. "The Devil's Devices in Chamisso's *Peter Schlemihl*," *German Life and Letters* 45 (1992): 220–25.

Wiese, Benno von. *Die deutsche Novelle von Goethe bis Kafka: Interpretationen.* Düsseldorf: Bagel, 1956.

PETÖFI, SÁNDOR 1823–1849

Hungarian poet

The first generation of Hungarian Romantics, using the achievements of the language reform, created a new literary language with all the institutions necessary for a dynamic cultural life. It was on this new cultural scene in the Hungarian capital city of Pest-Buda, with its Hungarian-language theater and numerous journals, that a youthful Sándor Petöfi appeared in 1842 with a drinking song. At the time few noticed, but two years later when his first book of poetry, *Versek* (*Poems*), was published thanks to the poet Mihály Vörösmarty, it became clear that Petöfi represented a "popular" tone that challenged the previously accepted premises of Romanticism. Petöfi lowered the lofty tone of the Romantics, shifting their traditionally patriotic rhetoric brooding on past exploits toward a simpler, more democratic style which often mimicked the folk song. He discovered the beauty of the Hungarian *Alfold* (lowland), his native region, and wrote elegiac poems about his family and childhood, which quickly became popular.

The young Petöfi made two excursions into the field of epic poetry. *A helység kalapácsa* (*The Hammer of the Village*, 1844) is a mock-heroic epic in four cantos. It is a parody of the Romantic tendency to glorify the nation or the race, and it shows Petöfi's sense of humor and dislike of bombastic phrases. *János vitéz*

(*John the Hero*, 1845), on the other hand, is a fairy tale centered around a foundling shepherd boy who evolves, during the twenty-seven cantos of the narrative, from Johnny Maize into John the Hero, saving (among other things) the King of France from a Turkish invasion. Although he is knighted and offered the hand of the king's daughter in marriage, he politely refuses and continues his wanderings to Fairyland, where he can finally find happiness with his first sweetheart, Iluska. The message is simple: only true love makes you happy. For all the simplicity of the language, the story is still Romantic in a way that touches a chord in the imagination of the "common people." Of all contemporary poets, perhaps only Aleksandr Pushkin created something that could be compared with this tale of "popular Romanticism."

The period between 1844 and 1846 is usually described as the "Clouds" years, after the work *Felhök* (*Clouds*), which was published in 1846. Although established at Pest as the subeditor of a magazine, he left his job in the spring of 1845 in order to travel in Upper Hungary, an experience he related in the brisk, humorous *Úti jegyzetek* (*Notes on a Journey*, 1845). His poetry from this period shows signs of an internal crisis; the world is gloomy, full of contradictions that mankind is unable to solve or overcome. Some critics see Lord Byron's and Percy Bysshe Shelley's influence on these short poems oozing Romantic pessimism. Athough Petöfi read English, he was possibly even more influenced by the French Romantics; this is at least what his (not particularly successful) play *Tigris és hiéna* (*Tiger and Hyena*, 1845) suggests. By early 1846, Petöfi overcame the crisis of this play's reception, and assumed a new role: that of a revolutionary Romantic.

This new commitment to radical change and the awakening of the Hungarian nation from its state of inertia found expression in a number of poems, influenced by the French poet Pierre Béranger and the Irish writer Thomas Moore. His *ars poetica* was now summed up in the evocative statement: "Liberty, love! These two I need. / For love I'll sacrifice my life, / For liberty I'll sacrifice my love." From 1846, Petöfi was dreaming of a democratic revolution which would transform Hungary; he saw himself (prophetically) as a possible leader of the revolution and even wished to die on the battlefield for the final victory of "World Freedom" (as expressed in the poem "I'm Troubled by One Thought"). The radicalization of his worldview ran parallel with a great change in his private life: in 1846 he fell in love with Julia Szendrey, whom he married the following year against the wishes of the Szendrey family, who looked down on the poet. Petöfi wrote his most beautiful love poems to Julia (she was an emancipated woman of her age who smoked and read George Sand), among them the haunting "At the End of September," a poem in anapestic lines expressing the promise of supernatural loyalty and eternal love.

In March 1848, his group of young writers and intellectuals, congregating in the Café Pilvax of Pest, led the revolution that forced the Hungarian Diet in Pozsony (now Bratislava in Slovakia) to pass radical reforms, including the liberation of serfs. The ensuing freedom of the press was greeted with enthusiasm by Petöfi, whose "Nemzeti Dal" ("National Song") played an important part in the March revolution. Nevertheless, when he stood for a seat in the Diet in his native constituency a few months later, he was defeated by an unscrupulous rival. It was this event that provoked the narrative poem *Az apostol* (*The Apostle*, 1848). The hero, Szilveszter, is a social outcast who rebels against an unjust system of government and suffers persecution and rejection. While partly autobiographical, it is primarily a portrait of a solitary rebel who appears prematurely, when social conditions are not prepared for him. According to Lorant Czigány, "*The Apostle* shows signs of acute Romantic idolization" of the main protagonist.

Petöfi's last poems show complete identification with the cause of the Hungarian nation. He joined the Transylvanian Army and became aide-de-camp to the Polish General József Bem. During these months, he wrote fiery poems about the campaign against the Austrians and then the invading Russians, including a piece in which he blamed "the stillness in Europe," the calm after suppressed revolutions, for the isolation of the Hungarians in their struggle against overwhelming odds. Petöfi died in battle at Segesvár (now Şigishoara in Romania) in July 1849. His death confirmed that, for all the realism of his shorter epic work, he was perhaps the most consistent Romantic European poet since Byron.

GEORGE GÖMÖRI

Biography

Born Sándor Petrovics of Slovak parents in Kiskörös, January 1, 1823. Secondary education at Pest and Aszód and Selmecbánya (now Banska Štavnica in Slovakia), from which he ran away in 1839. Between 1839 and 1843 he was a traveling actor and a soldier in the Austrian Army—mainly in Graz—with a short interlude at the grammar school of Pápa where he met Mór Jókai. First collection of poetry published at Pest in 1844. Assistant editor of *Pesti Divatlap* (*Pest Fashion*) 1844–45. Tour of Upper Hungary in 1845. Met Julia Szendrey in Nagykároly, married her in September 1847. Founding member of the Society of the Ten (later, Young Hungary), a radical democrat whose "National Song" calls for action and becomes emblematic poem of the March Revolution of 1848. Ran for seat in the Diet and was defeated at Szabadszállás, summer of 1848. During the War of Independence followed the Hungarian Government to Debrecen, joining the Transylvanian Army in the rank of a captain in January 1848. Having clashed with Hungarian military authorities, he returned to General Bem in Transylvania, and was promoted to major. Moved his family (with baby son, Zoltán) from Debrecen and returned to Transylvania to join Bem. Died on the battlefield of Segesvár (now Şigishoara in Romania) on July 31, 1849. Rumors about his capture by the Russians and possible exile to Siberia are totally unfounded.

Selected Writings

Összes m vei. 6 vols. Edited by Adolf Havas. 1892–96.
Összes m vei. 7 vols. Academy edition. 1951–64.
Összes költeményei. 2 vols. 1959.
Összes prózai m vei és levelezése. 1960.

Bibliography

Basa Molnar, Enikö. *Sándor Petöfi*. Boston: Twayne, 1980.
Czigány, Lóránt. *The Oxford History of Hungarian Literature*. Oxford: Clarendon Press, 1984.

Fekete, Sándor. *Petöfi romantikájának forrásai*. Budapest: Gondolat, 1972.

Gömöri, George. "Petöfi—The Irish Connection." In *A Journey into History, Essays on Hungarian Literature*. American University Studies, Series 19, vol. 25. Edited by M. Moses Nagy. New York: Peter Lang.

Hatvany, Lajos. *Igy élt Petöfi, I-II*. Budapest: Akadmémiai, 1967.

Horváth, János. *Petöfi Sándor*. Pallas: Budapest.

Illyés, Gyula. *Petöfi*. Budapest, 1936. Translated by G. F. Cushing as *Petöfi*. Budapest: Corvina, 1974.

Jones, Mervyn, D. *Five Hungarian Writers*. Oxford: Clarendon Press, 1966.

Köpeczi, Béla, ed. *Rebel or Revolutionary? Sándor Petöfi as Revealed by his Diary, Letters, Notes, Pamphlets and Poems*. Translated by Edwin Morgan and G. F. Cushing. Budapest: Corvina Press, 1974.

PETROVIC, PETAR II NJEGOS 1813–1851

Prince-Bishop and national poet of Montenegro

Few men are blessed with great artistic skills or those of a wise, talented ruler. Even fewer have ever combined the two. Usually, as in the case of Roman Emperor Nero, a ruler may believe himself, falsely, to be talented in both areas. Rarest of all is when these talents are real and combined in one man. Prince Petar II Petrovich Njegos is an example of that rare combination.

Since the Ottoman invasion and occupation of the Balkans, Montenegro had maintained a unique independence. The clan-oriented and fiercely independent Orthodox Serb Montenegrins had, with slight reluctance, accepted the rule of their bishop and his assumption of princely, secular powers. This was the only alternative to Turk rule, which was vehemently opposed. Initially, the prince-bishops were elected (during the years 1516–1697), but after 1697 the title became hereditary within the Petrovich family. Since the bishops had to be celibate (as they belonged to the higher clergy of the Holy Orthodox Church) the title was passed to the nephew of the ruling prince.

Peter's uncle was the formidable Saint Peter I, who managed to force the Turks to accept Montenegro's independence (1799) and defied Napoleon (1806–13), who had threatened to invade. His uncle left a strong mark on both Njegos and Montenegro; nevertheless, he also left much undone. As the Turks continued to view Montenegro as an annoyance, Peter II's first act upon taking power was to create a standing army. Although ostensibly meant to provide protection against an outside threat, this army was also to be used against unruly clans and their chiefs, or *knezes*, who threatened internal law and order. To curb their power, Njegos abolished the office of civil governor, exiled governor Radovitch, brought the senate under his personal control, drew up Montenegro's first budget, and secularized the trappings of his office. He viewed himself as a secular prince and saw secularization as a necessary step toward the creation of a modern Montenegro. A sign of this was the abolition of the red fez in 1846, in order to remove a highly visible vestige of Oriental-Turkish cultural influence. Two years earlier, Njegos had shown his willingness to pay any price to keep Montenegro united and safe when he condoned the assassination of his rival, Knez Nikola "Konsul" Vasojevici, at Zagarac. His excuse (and that of his supporters) for this act was the threat Knez Nikola posed to the unity of Montenegro. Unity had to be maintained at all costs, against the ever-present Turkish threat.

Montenegro had no secure borders, and Montenegrin men were armed and always ready to raid into Turkish territory. In 1832, Namik Halil Pasha invaded Montenegro with seven thousand troops, but the new Montenegrin army defeated them after fierce fighting for the town of Zabliak. Six years later Montenegro was fighting both the Austrians (to reach the sea) and the Turks (to conquer more fertile land). While Metternich forced Njegos to accept an unfavorable settlement, the dispute with the Turks ended with a treaty signed September 1842 in the city of Dubrovnik (Ragusa), where he met the Vizier of Mostar, Ali Pasha Rizvanbegovic. Njegos, like all Montenegrins, distrusted all Turks as a threat to their national, even physical, survival, but he realized that their Moslem Slav brethren in Bosnia had their uses.

It is quite amazing that Njegos found time and peace to write poetry in the midst of this constant political turmoil. What makes it even more remarkable is the quality of his writing. He had written and published "The Hermit of Cetinje" in 1834, but it was not until a decade later (1845) that Njegos wrote the *Loutcha Mikrokozma* (*The Ray of the Microcosm*). Although an original work, it is based upon John Milton's *Paradise Lost* and has much in common with Dante Alighieri's *Divine Comedy*. Njegos's language is inspired by Church Slavonic and Russian, but did not contribute to Vuk Karadzic's victory in favor of modernization of the Serb language. The poem itself is the story of light (the cosmic light being identified with God) versus cosmic darkness (Satan). Njegos believed that humans were intrinsically evil and had to be diverted from their natural path toward evil. The poem is a strange mixture of deep theological thought, portrayals of local life, and the fate of the Serbs after the Battle of Kosovo (1389).

Two years later, Njegos wrote his greatest and best known poem, *Gorski vijenac* (*The Mountain Wreath*, 1847). It is a great historical drama set during the reign of Prince Danilo I (1697–1735), when a supposed massacre of Turks took place. Njegos, who identifies himself with Danilo, excused the massacre as necessary to protect Montenegro. The hero, Vuk Micunovic, hates the Turks, yet Njegos portrays his protagonist, Mustaj Kadi, as heroic and fanatical in the defence of his faith. This is an ode, above all, to heroism on all sides. It also shows that Njegos was a poet of the great historical events and not everyday life. He was a child of his time and a son of the Balkans, evidenced by his belief that even tragedy has its place in the great scheme of thing. Renegades to Islam had to be eliminated if they were not to subvert the nation from the inside, and the Turks had to be fought from the outside.

Gorski vijenac is divided into three parts. A long monologue by Danilo at Mount Lovcen to encourage his men to resist the Turks comprises the first part. The second, and longest, part of the poem concentrates on the events and disputes around the Feast of Nativity at Cetinje, and the justifications for massacring the Muslims. The third and shortest section details the massacre, district by district, across Montenegro. In a poem inspired by Greek drama, Njegos states:

> The Crescent and the Cross, great Symbols twain,
> Do not advantage gain save in a world of slain!
> It is our lot to sail this crimson stream. (339)

Njegos had given Montenegro its national poem that explains the country's national and personal dilemmas (until, that is, the Ottomans were expelled from the Balkans a century later).

Unfortunately Njegos, who was a tall and powerful-looking man, proved less robust in reality. He had been prone to tuberculosis much of his life, and in 1851 the last prince-bishop of Montenegro died prematurely. He left behind a stronger, better organized, and centralized state that would, under his successors Prince Danilo II and King Nicholas I, achieve true independence.

CHRISTER JÖRGENSEN

Biography

Njegos was born in Njegusi (Montenegro), 1813. His tutor Simo Milutinovic (Serbia's most romantic poet) had a lasting influence during Njegos's years in Cetinje, 1827–31. It was Milutinovic's own work and encouragement that inspired the prince to begin writing. Njegos became a monk in 1831, and he was ordained by the Russian Orthodox Church as bishop a few years later. He was made Vladivka of Montenegro in 1830, and in 1838 Njegos received the Saxon king on a royal visit, establishing contact with the West. *The Ray of the Microcosm* (1845) was followed by the publication two years later of the "*Mountain Wreath.*" He became very ill in 1850 and died of consumption in 1851.

Selected Works

Loutcha Mikrokozma, 1845. Translated as *The Ray of the Microscosm* by Clarence A. Manning, 1953. Translated and with a foreword by Anica Savic-Rebac and edited by Darinka Zlicic. Belgrade: Vajat, 1989.
Gorski vijenac, 1847. Translated as *The Mountain Wreath* by James Wiles, 1930. Translated and edited by Vasa D. Mihailovich. Belgrade: Vajat, 1989.

Bibliography

Works about Njegos

Andric, Ivo. *Njegos ako tragicni junak kosovske misli*. Belgrade: Biblioteka Kolarcevog narodnog univerziteta, 1935.

Aubin, Michel. *Visiones Historique et Politiques dans l'oeuvre poétique de P. P. Njegos*. Paris: Sorbonne Press, 1972.
Djilas, Milovan. *Njegos: Poet, Prince, Bishop*. Introduction and translation by Michael B. Petrovich. New York: Harcourt, Brace and World, 1966.
Durkowicz-Jakszicz, Lubomir. *Petar II Perovic Njegos (1813–1851)*. Warszawa: Rozpranoy historyczne Towarz. nauk. Warszawskiego, 1938.
Spasic, J. Krunoslav. *Pierre II Petrovic-Njegos et les Francais*. Paris: Sorbonne Press, 1972.

Travel Accounts and Histories of Montenegro

Coquelle, P. *Histoire de Monténégro et de la Bosnie depuis les origines*. Paris: Ernst Leroux, 1895.
Creagh, James. *Over the Borders of Christendom and Eslamiah: A Journey through Hungary, Slavonia, Serbia, Bosnia, Hercegovina, Dalmatia and Montenegro, to the North of Albania in the summer of 1875*. London: Samuel Tinsley, 1876.
Cvijic, Jovan. *La Peninsule balcanique, geographie humaine*. Paris: A. Colin, 1918.
Devine. *Montenegro in History, Politics and War*. London: Fischer Unwin, 1918.
Djurdjev, Branislav. *Turska vlast u Crnoj Bori u XVI i XVII veku*. Sarajevo: Svjetlost, 1953.
Jackson, T. G. *Dalmatia, the Quernero and Istria with Cettinge in Montenegro and the Island of Grado*. 3 vols. Oxford, U.K.: Clarendon Press, 1887.
Karadzic, Vuk S. *Crna Gora i Boka Kotorska*. Belgrade: Srpska Knjizevna Zadruga, 1922.
Kohl, J. G. *Reisen nach Istrien, Dalmatien und Montenegro*. 2 vols. Dresden: Arnold, 1851 and 1856.
Lamb, Charles. "A Ramble in Montenegro," *Blackwood's Magazine* (1845): 33–51.
Layard, Henry A. *Autobiography and Letters*. New York: Scribner, 1903.
Lenorman, Francois. *Description et histoire du Monténégro*. Revue Orientale et Américaine, 1849.
Lindau, Wilhelm. *Dalmatien und Montenegro mit einem Ausfluge nach der Hercegowiana und einer geschichlicthen Uebesicht der Schidsale Dalmatiens und Ragusas*. 2 vols. Leipzig: Verlag von Gustav Maner, 1849.
Paton, A. A. *Highlands and Islands of the Adriatic*. 2 vols. London: Chapman and Hall, 1848.
Vialla de Sommières, L. O. *Travels in Montenegro, Containing a Topographical, Picturesque and Statistical Account of that Hitherto Undescribed Country*. London: R. Phillips, 1820.
Wilkinson, J. Gardner. *Dalmatia and Montenegro, with a Journey to Mostar in Hercegovina and Remarks on the Slavonic Nations*. 2 vols. London: J. Murray, 1848, 1863.

PFORR, FRANZ 1788–1812

German painter

Franz Pforr was one of the two founding members of the German artistic community of the Romantic period that called itself the Brotherhood of Saint Luke (Lucas Brotherhood) and was later termed the Nazarenes. Although he died at an early age, his aspiration for an art born of a meditative and reflective life certainly contributed significantly to the Brotherhood's first exercises in artistic craft for young men of enterprise and vocation.

Pforr, a native of Frankfurt, initially studied art with his father Georg, a famous and highly capable horse painter, in Vienna from 1805 to 1810. Not unexpectedly for the time, some of the younger Pforr's early works manifest traces of genre painting. But from his childhood, he had also been fascinated by the image of of an idealized, highly imaginative Middle Ages and began sketching knights and ladies in Gothic settings.

At the Vienna Academy of Art he became acquainted with another young painter, Johann Friedrich Overbeck, who shared many of his philosophical, aesthetic, and technical interests. Technically, both young men preferred a decisive and final, hard, and sharply pointed pencil—or at least a pen or thin brush—over the soft and, in effect, correctable chalk employed at the academy. This linear approach reflected their penchant for the defined edges of wood engravings such as those by Albrecht Durer (which Pforr had collected from earliest youth) as well as by Lucas Cranach and Hans Holbein, whose work they imitated, and to which they added clear and bright coloration. Furthermore, they increasingly distinguished themselves in opposition to neoclassical academic practices, beliefs, and even subjects by their admiration of late medieval and early Italian Renaissance painting, such as the works of Perugino and the young Raphael, that defied the academy's partiality for artwork of the High Renaissance and beyond. In their idiosyncrasy, Overbeck and Pforr, therefore, were following the admonitions of Wilhelm Heinrich Wackenroder, whose *Effusions on an Art-Loving Monk*, (1797) was an important and powerful statement of Romantic principles in its identification of the Christian artist as the medium for his own divinely inspired emotions. While these concepts led some German Romantic artists such as Caspar David Friedrich and Phillip Otto Runge toward highly individualized artistry, Overbeck and Pforr sought to revive the intimate medieval workshop community as the conditions under which to create didactic and symbolic narrative art and to restore innocence to their discipline and its topics. Obviously, though, to the degree that they energetically rejected academic standards, they were themselves ostracized. Still, there were enough likeminded souls at the academy for a small community to develop. With two Swiss, two Swabians, and an Austrian, most of whom were of apparently rather indifferent talent but great enthusiasm, they united in 1808 and a year later celebrated their academic secession and union as a brotherhood, named after the Evangelist legend declared to be an artist, St. Luke. Other groups would renounce academic rigidity as well, but this assembly was the first to attempt to live what they pronounced. They sought to invigorate art, to regain the virtues of primitive representation, and to achieve spiritual grace by seeking what at times sounds like a platonic ideal of nature by paradoxically adopting highly naturalistic, though often also excessively detailed, crowded, and mechanical (even to the point of sterility in the minds of some later critics) representation, which they felt would encourage morality, in counterpoise to the effects of what they perceived to be academic fraudulence. And Pforr, in particular, embraced Wackenroder's view that the contemplation of art ought to be a devotional exercise, a pietistic practice. At the same time as all of this, Pforr wrote and illustrated an allegory in tribute to his new allegiances, called *Friendship*.

Yet however heady their iconoclasm, the youths found that the academy performed one notable and indisputable function; it enabled its artists to secure commissions. Thus, when the French occupation of Vienna severely curtailed the academy's operations, it seemed all doors had slammed shut, so that May 1810 became a propitious moment for Overbeck, Pforr, and their two Swiss comrades-in-arms to relocate to the town of Raphael and the shrine of Christian art—Rome—to begin anew.

In Rome, they located a mostly abandoned Irish convent, St. Isidoro, in which they could enact the clerical aesthetic Wackenroder had described. They implemented a daily monastic routine of household and artistic tasks, with each brother having his own cell as a studio/bedroom, following the model of their beloved Fra Angelico, with evenings in the refectory for quiet work. But they also managed to visit the art collections of the Vatican and travel through the Italian landscape, the influence of both of which is clearly present in their art, and they were known as well for boisterous evenings of highly intoxicated revelry.

They continued working on projects they had started in Germany, Pforr with his ambitious processional painting *Entry of Rudolf of Habsburg into Basle* (1808–10), which reflects his medieval and symbolic as opposed to expressly religious and allegorical predilections. What Pforr sought to depict, rather than historical authenticity, was the ambience of the medieval period, cast in a spirit of patriotism, though some critics today see the work as self-consciously primitive, perhaps recalling some of his early training in genre depiction. The group collectively, having always favored frescoes as a matter of principle, received two major wall-painting commissions in Rome, as well as encouragement and support from leading expatriates in Roman society. And they were joined professionally by others, too, including Joseph Wintergerst, who had been one of their Swabian confreres back in Vienna, and, most notably, Peter von Cornelius in 1811, who retrospectively came to outshine those who had

Johann Friedrich Overbeck, *Portrait des Malers Franz Pforr*. Reprinted courtesy of Bildarchiv.

laid the Lucan groundwork and to replace Pforr at the side of Overbeck.

However, Pforr was not destined to survive to see the developments of his movement, when the group came to be, somewhat derisively, known as the Nazarenes. Most of the adherents became Roman Catholics and its most lasting legacy, symbolic landscape and enduring, disaffected Gothicism, came to be realized. Besides traveling to Naples in the penultimate year of his life, Pforr began increasingly to suffer from tuberculosis and would die of it, like John Keats, in his mid-twenties, away from his native land, in Rome. Pforr's last work, *Shulamit and Maria* (1811), is an allegorical diptych dedicated to Overbeck and celebrating their friendship; today it is viewed as one of the splendors of German Christian Romanticism, realizing the grace of brightly-colored and basic, uncomplicated shapes. Nursed by Wintergerst, Pforr succumbed to his disease in July 1812 in Albano. His death devastated Overbeck and the others, in effect, ended the monasticism of the alliance, freeing it, whether he would have approved or not, to move in more worldly directions, including those that would bring international acclaim.

LAURA DABUNDO

Bibliography

Andrews, Keith. *The Nazarenes.* Oxford, U.K.: Clarendon Press, 1964.

———. "Nazarenes and Pre-Raphaelites." *Bulletin of John Ryland's Library* 71 (1989): 31–46.

Bailey, Colin. "The Nazarenes in Rome," in *Burlington Magazine* 125 (1983): 701–702.

Canaday, John. *Mainstreams of Modern Art.* New York: Holt, Rinehart and Winston, 1959.

"Cornelius, Peter von." In *Encyclopedia Britannica Online.* Last accessed August 3, 2000, at http://search.eb.com/bol/topic?idxref=183763.

Frank, Mitchell Benjamin. *German Romantic Painting Redefined: Nazarene Tradition and the Narratives of Romanticism.* Burlington, Vt.: Ashgate, 2001.

Lucie-Smith, Edward. *Art and Civilization.* New York: Harry N. Abrams, 1993.

"Overbeck," *Encyclopedia Britannica Online.* Last accessed August 3, 2000, at http://search.eb.com/bol/topic?idxref=183759.

Vaughan, William. *Romantic Art.* New York: Thames and Hudson, 1985.

THE PHENOMENOLOGY OF SPIRIT 1807

Philosophical work by G. W. F. Hegel

Die Phänomenologie des Geistes (*The Phenomenology of Spirit*) by the German philosopher G. W. F. Hegel is one of the greatest books of modern philosophy and an important work in the history of German Romanticism. While Hegel did not think of himself as one of the Romantics, his book is one of the most imaginative and bold works in philosophy. He wrote it in 1806, while he was teaching at the Prussian city of Jena, just at the time that Napoleon's troops were on the march, and it was published the following year. Hegel intended his *Phenomenology* as the introduction to a "system" of philosophy. It was supposed to establish the standpoint of absolute knowledge from which a philosophical system could be formulated. This task occupied Hegel for his entire career.

The *Phenomenology* is both a philosophical marvel and a dialectical mess. Kantian themes and post-Kantian ambitions are still in evidence (the book concludes with a modest chapter immodestly titled "Absolute Knowing"). But between the introduction and opening chapters, in which skepticism and Immanuel Kant's theory of knowledge are quickly dispatched, and the brief conclusion, in which the post-Kantian ambitions are summarily concluded, the book is an unwieldy monster. There are chapters on various Greek philosophies, on various eccentric movements in ethics as well as an open attack on Kant's "categorical imperative" on contemporary history including the Enlightenment and the French Revolution, bits of literary criticism, philosophical investigations of weird science, and an oddly shaped survey of the world's religions, all put forward in an almost unreadable, abstract Kantian jargon that makes the Kantian *Critiques* seem easy reading by comparison. The *Phenomenology* did not turn out to be, as originally intended, merely a demonstration of "the absolute." It became a magnificent conceptual odyssey that carries us from the most elementary conceptions of human consciousness to the all-encompassing notion of *Geist* (Spirit). It also, in its obscure forms and transitions, summed up the aspirations and confusions of a frenzied age.

Its three uneven parts represent the three "levels" of consciousness in ascending order: consciousness (sense certainty), self-consciousness, and reason (the full realization of *Geist*). The introduction to the *Phenomenology* begins where Kant's first *Critique* ends, with the rejection of skepticism and a declaration of transcendental idealism. At the beginning of the *Phenomenology* is the common-sense notion that Hegel calls "sense certainty," the idea that we simply know, prior to any description or understanding, what it is that we experience. Hegel demonstrates that such a conception of knowledge is woefully inadequate and needs to be supplemented by a more comprehensive and sophisticated conception or "form of consciousness." In a few quick steps, he brings us from naive realism through a number of theoretical variations in which can be recognized the major insights of Gottfried Wilhelm Leibniz and some of the British empiricists and the philosophy of Kant's first *Critique*, in which knowledge is demonstrated to be a form of self-understanding. Hegel then tackles the Kantian notion of the *Ding an sich* (thing-in-itself) by way of an extended *reductio ad absurdum*. Suppose, he says, that the real world, the world in itself, consists of properties exactly opposed to the properties of the world of our experience, so that black is white, good is evil, and so forth. The very idea is thus reduced to nonsense.

Throughout the *Phenomenology*, Hegel displays the inadequacies of one form of consciousness after another, and so we are guided from one form to another in an ongoing dialectic, eventually to reach "absolute knowledge," which includes an all-encompassing overview of all that has preceded it. The dialectic often proceeds by way of conflict and confrontation, when one form of consciousness contradicts another. But it is a misunderstanding of Hegel to think of the dialectic as a mechanical meeting of "thesis" and "antithesis," resolved by a "synthesis." That formulation, which comes from Kant, Hegel explicitly criticizes as "formulaic." The dialectic is rather a complex interplay of conceptions, some of which are simply improvements on others, some of which are indeed opposites demanding synthetic resolution; but others simply represent conceptual dead ends that indicate a need to start over. Indeed, it is not at all clear that Hegel's dialectic is a linear progression from simplicity to the absolute but rather a phenomenological tapestry in which the forms of human experience and philosophy jostle against one another and compete for adequacy. Within that tapestry, however, can be found much of the history of Western epistemology and metaphysics, a great deal of ethics and social history, and the history of religion. Whether or not Hegel reaches the "absolute," as he states so proudly in his preface, he gives us an eclectic but systematic philosophy that boldly demonstrates both the complex inner life of ideas and the role of those ideas in defining human history and consciousness.

Once the *Phenomenology* has made the turn to "self-consciousness," it begins with "self-certainty," a common-sense conception of the self, reminiscent of René Descartes's "I think, therefore I am." Hegel goes on to show that the self is not certain at all. In the confusion of desire and the urges of what he calls "life" (a central element in Johann Gottlieb Fichte and Friedrich Wilhelm Joseph von Schelling's philosophy), the self is itself confused. The argument here serves two important purposes: as in the more epistemological chapters that precede it, Hegel brings us from a naive view to a more complex and sophisticated philosophical standpoint, eventually leading up to *Geist* (the cosmic super-self), and, in contrast to the preceding chapters, Hegel now insists that there is what we would call an essential "practical" dimension to knowledge.

What follows then is the best-known and most dramatic single chapter in the *Phenomenology*, the parable of the "master and slave." The point there is to show that, first, selfhood develops not through introspection but rather through mutual recognition. The self is essentially social, not merely psychological or epistemological. But Hegel is also concerned with showing the nature of a certain kind of interpersonal relationship, presupposed by many philosophers (such as Thomas Hobbes and Jean-Jacques Rousseau) in their hypotheses about the "state of nature." The common assumption is that human beings are first of all individuals and only later, by mutual agreement, members of society. Hegel thinks that this assumption is nonsense, for individuality begins to appear only within an interpersonal context.

Later in the *Phenomenology*, Hegel takes up some central themes in the philosophy of nature, which was an obsession for Schelling, Arthur Schopenhauer, and the Romantics, and various themes in ethics, including various attitudes and means for dealing with sin and evil in the world. He reformulates a particularly telling critique of Kant's ethics and gives us an early formulation of his later analysis (in *Grundlinien der Philosophie des Rechts oder Naturrecht und Staatswissenschaft im Grundrisse* [*The Philosophy of Right and Law*, 1820–21]) of the individual as the product of "civil society." It is not that the individual doesn't count, but rather that the meaning of the individual is dependent on the social context in which he or she lives. In civil society, that context is the context of the law. Hegel uses this notion of social embeddedness to discuss Sophocles's tragedy *Antigone*. Antigone was simultaneously embedded in two societies: the "divine" tribal society of her family, in which family duty and honor were all, and civil society ruled by Creon, in which law and obedience were essential. Her individual case was tragic and irresolvable, but the movement of history and the dialectic provided a resolution to the conflict that was not available for the tragic heroine. The development of modern civil society promised the flourishing of individuality, plurality, and the public good simultaneously.

In the expansive final chapters of the book, Hegel gives us a glimpse of an all-encompassing religious attitude (the attitude called *Geist*) in which the world's peoples, and the world itself, could be finally comprehended as one. It was a fitting statement of the new internationalism of the Romantic age, and it is relevant, too, to the new globalism of our own new century.

ROBERT C. SOLOMON

Text

System der Wissenschaft: Erster Theil: Die Phänomenologie des Geistes, 1807. Translated as *The Phenomenology of Mind* by J. B. Baillie, 1910. Translated as *The Phenomenology of Spirit* by A. V. Miller, 1977.

Bibliography

Harris, H. S. *Hegel: Phenomenology and System*. Indianapolis: Hackett, 1995.

———. *Hegel's Ladder*. Indianapolis: Hackett, 1995.

Rauch, Leo, and David Sherman. *Hegel's Phenomenology of Self-Recognition*. Albany: State University of New York Press, 1999.

Rockmore, Tom. *Cognition: An Introduction to Hegel's Phenomenology of Spirit*. Berkeley and Los Angeles: University of California Press, 1997.

Shklar, Judith. *Freedom and Independence: A Study of Hegel's "Phenomenology of Mind."* Cambridge, U.K.: Cambridge University Press, 1976.

Solomon, Robert C. *In the Spirit of Hegel: A Study of G. W. F. Hegel's Phenomenology of Spirit*. New York: Oxford University Press, 1985.

PHILHELLENISM

Within the context of Romanticism, the term *philhellenism* refers generally to a love of Greece, foundational to which were the beliefs that Greece had a direct cultural link to Western civilization as a whole, and that, concomitantly, the "modern Greeks" (that is, the Greeks of the Ottoman and modern periods) were the direct descendants, biologically and culturally, of the ancient Greeks. In its most specific sense, philhellenism refers to the nineteenth-century historical phenomenon of western Europeans (largely British, French, and German) rallying behind the Greek struggle for independence from Ottoman rule (1821–30). The link between philhellenic sentiment and the Greek War of Independence was evident in the numerous cases of western Europeans contributing money, materiel, and in some cases manpower to the Greek war effort. In the specifically Romantic context, it was evident in the turn-of-the century efflorescence of paintings, works of literature, and musical compositions with a central Hellenic theme.

A famous visual instance of this Romanticist artistic fascination with Greece is the frontispiece to Marie Gabriel, Comte de Choiseul-Gouffier's 1782 *Voyage Pittoresque de la Grece*, an engraving entitled "Greece in Chains," in which Greece, allegorized as a beautiful but manacled woman, reclines upon a tomb in a cemetery dotted with monuments to such great men of antiquity as Lycurgus, Miltiades, and Themistocles. The image captures perfectly the Romantic vision of Greece as noble but faded, glorious yet much reduced, enslaved but poised to be free once more. Also quintessential of Romantic philhellenism is the explicit link the image draws between the modern Greeks of the late Ottoman period and the Hellenic greats of antiquity.

In the years just prior to and during the Greek War of Independence, countless such images were in wide circulation in Western Europe—the most famous, perhaps, being those of Eugène Delacroix (1798–1863), the consummate representative of French Romantic philhellenism. Delacroix's *Le Massacre de Chios* depicted the 1821 devastation of Chios, where 98,000 Greeks were killed or sold into slavery, while his *Greece on the Ruins of Missolonghi* commemorated the brave Greek defense of Nissolonghi from 1825 to 1826, when it was besieged by the Egyptian armies of Ibrahim Pasha. These twin themes of tragic defeat and inestimable bravery, pathos and stoicism, typify philhellenic sentiment of the period, as does Delacroix's personal dedication to the Greek cause.

The antecedents to the development of philhellenic sentiment were, in addition to classicism, Romanticism, and western liberalism, the centuries-long period during which the "grand tour" was a virtually institutionalized component of the elite western European gentleman's education. While in the seventeenth and eighteenth centuries such "tourists" favored Switzerland as a destination, after the Napoleonic Wars Italy, and, increasingly, Greece, became the key destinations. Through their travels, Western visitors believed that they had the opportunity to witness firsthand the vestiges of classical tradition; in their encounters with the current residents, they believed that they came as close as possible to interacting with the classical figures they knew so well from their study of Latin and Greek.

This cultural trend worked hand in hand with political developments in the Ottoman Empire to fuel growing interest within Europe for Greece and the modern Greeks. While the travel accounts penned by "grand tourists" were hugely popular, the apparent military and economic decline of the Ottoman Empire commanded huge attention, particularly in Britain, which felt that British imperial fortunes were tied to the political status quo. While the Congress of Vienna (1814–15), which concluded the Napoleonic Wars, emphasized the need to keep the Ottoman Empire intact, growing numbers of philhellenes felt that the special cultural link between Greece and the West demanded intervention on behalf of the Greeks under Ottoman rule. In this debate, the philhellenic position would ultimately dominate, with Britain ending up a major backer of the Greek struggle and the subsequently formed new Greek state.

The wide circulation of a number of Western works which had as their central theme the exoticisms and depravities of the Ottomans (and the plight of the noble Greeks who suffered beneath their rule) furthered the scope of philhellenism, to the extent that general sentiment in Europe gradually overcame the initial political position of European governments regarding the Greek War of Independence. Lord Byron, François-August-René de Chataubriand, and Johann Wolfgang von Goethe are the best known creators of such works, but a veritable plethora of lesser-known literary, musical, and artistic figures followed the themes popularized by them.

Philhellenism is properly understood as a reflection not of any reality concerning Greece and the Greeks, but rather as the manifestation of a purely European, and not entirely magnanimous, impulse. That is to say, the passionate response with which the Greek War of Independence was met in the West was less a reflection of European love of the modern Greeks than of European love of the idea that Western civilization as a whole could be traced back to Pericles-era Athens. Europe's fascination with the classical Greek past was thus, at heart, a fascination with its own past, and, in many instances, it did not naturally lead to a love of the modern Greeks. Indeed, many philhellenes who traveled to Greece with high hopes became rapidly disgusted by the locals, whom they regarded as poor and degraded shadow versions of the noble Greeks of yore. Implicit in such views, of course, was the condescending presumption that western European philhellenes knew better than the Greeks themselves what form "true Greekness" was meant to take.

Since the Romantic period, philhellenism has retained its double edge: on the one hand, Greece's very livelihood has long been sustained by the western European love of Greece and its infatuation with the classical past. The Greek economy, first in the form of Western loans and now in tourist dollars, has been kept afloat by the material benefits of philhellenism. On the other hand, however, Greece has long chafed at the ways in which philhellenism has been used as a pretext for Western intervention in Greek affairs.

K. E. FLEMING

Bibliography

Dakin, Douglas. *British and American Philhellenes during the War of Greek Independence, 1821–1833.* Thessaloniki: Hidryma Meleton Chersonesou tou Haimou, 1955.

Howarth, David. *The Greek Adventure: Lord Byron and Other Eccentrics in the War of Independence.* New York: Athenaeum, 1976.

St. Clair, William. *That Greece Might Still be Free: The Philhellenes in the War of Independence.* London: Oxford University Press, 1972.

Spencer, Terence. *Fair Greece Sad Relic. Literary Philhellenism from Shakespeare to Byron.* London: Weidenfeld and Nicolson, 1954.

Woodhouse, C. M. *The Philhellenes.* London: Hodder and Stoughton, 1969.

PIANO

In the nineteenth century, the piano achieved a technological maturity essentially unchanged to the present day, winning in the process an unprecedented significance to the public, private, and commercial spheres of everyday life. Its development ran parallel to, and most often in tandem with, the growing dominance of cultural life by the middle class, newly discovered systems of manufacturing and merchandising, and with the phenomenon of nineteenth-century instrumental virtuosity in major centers of Western musical activity such as London, Paris, Vienna, and New York. Its unique capabilities as both a solo and a collaborative instrument had been exploited in the eighteenth century, but the innovations of the British were quickly appropriated and reconceived, first by the French in the decades following the Revolution, then by the Americans. Upright, vertically-strung instruments replaced horizontally strung square pianos and the larger grand pianos, already prominent in eighteenth-century public venues, acquired prestige. A number of other changes, such as the color reversal of white and black keys, and the reduction of pedals and devices to alter sound, unfolded as well.

England's Industrial Revolution had spawned a rich urban musical culture in London. A native entrepreneur, John Broadwood, and a transplanted genius, Muzio Clementi, best divined the dimensions of change afoot. Clementi, keenly aware of new parameters of public consumption before the turn of the century, lent his name to the building and merchandise of new pianos and wrote challenging and idiomatic works for them.

Since publishing titles often indicated one or another instrument (probably for sales purposes) between the time of Johann Christian Bach's London sonatas and concertos (c. 1770) and Clementi's works written exclusively for the new instrument (closer to the turn of the new century), a certain interchangeability in much of the active repertory may be presumed between the early nineteenth-century piano and its predecessors (the clavichord and the harpsichord). By the turn of the century there were some forty piano manufacturers in London, and Broadwood alone had brought to market at least a thousand grands and probably five or six times as many square instruments. Broadwood quickly gained the lead worldwide in manufacturing and held it well into the nineteenth century.

Sebastien Érard, having started to build square pianos in Paris just as Clementi glimpsed the future in London, fled the revolution for England. When the political situation in France had calmed, he returned to resume production there with the very best of British models and practice in mind. Érard discovered a performing-practice loophole untended to by the British: by the 1820s, Broadwood had patents on iron sheeting and braces to reinforce his increasingly powerful instruments, but their ability to sustain better, thicker strings and greater tensions required heavier hammers and coverings, making their key actions more difficult, in effect, "slower" to negotiate. Érard refined a "double-escapement" action that allowed for the more rapid and efficient repetition of individual keystrokes, thereby making his instruments easier to play.

The Viennese builders competed too, but their instruments were far different, manifesting a warmer, crisper sound, their builders having eschewed iron braces and case reinforcements. The Viennese continued building along these lines until roughly midcentury, producing lighter instruments with actions that were fleet, if not especially fast. The future of piano manufacture, however, was dictated in an important sense: the inevitable drift toward larger volumes of sound demanded by the public both in concert halls and in larger salons at home, which could not be satisfied by designing ever-stronger wooden frames and casings. The expanding lyric homophony and the increasingly complex, virtuosic, even orchestral textures and passage work of nineteenth-century music were better served, and to some extent inspired by, the evolving dynamic capabilities of competing instruments.

Heftier, more powerful pianos meant heavier actions, and with time virtuosos everywhere came to prefer some kind of "escapement" in their instrument actions. Érard's great contribution, then, had been to mark a compromise of sorts between the graceful speed of Viennese actions and the unavoidable weight engendered by the more powerful English Broadwoods.

By 1830 the center of virtuoso piano playing had shifted from London to Paris, and by the 1840s the market everywhere for smaller domestic instruments began to increase exponentially. Until this time upright pianos tended to be essentially rearranged grand or square models, suspended or tipped upright with different keyboard mechanisms to adjust for gravity. Early in the century Robert Wornum in London invented a reliable action for upright instruments, and Henri Pape in Paris patented a system of cross-stringing to enhance the resonance of smaller instruments for the home, and more reliable and resonant models began to appear on the market. In the wake of Niccolò Paganini's spectacular successes (programmatic as much as musical), Franz Liszt and other pianist/composers began to furnish similar repertories for a public increasingly captivated by individual displays of virtuosity. Moreover, the reification and retransmission of contemporary operatic spectacle outside of large concert halls could proceed more fully by way of newer instruments in greater numbers, whether modestly vertical in bourgeois households, or grandly horizontal in the salons and concert halls of the nouveau-riche and influential.

The Europeans made the great piano advances up until mid-century, at which point they were overtaken by the Americans. The American manufacturers moved quickly; Broadwood had experimented with a single-piece iron frame for his instruments, but it was Alpheus Babcock in the United States who, in 1825, took out a patent and tinkered long enough to transfer the appropriate technology from square instruments (longer preferred in America than elsewhere) to the newer grands. By 1843, Jonas Chickering of Boston was producing grands with Babcock's powerful iron frame, which (especially important in the severe climates of the United States) was far less prone to warp and wreak havoc with tuning.

Heinrich Steinweg (who called his company Steinway) emigrated to New York around 1850 and set up a company that grew rapidly over the course of a few years. Steinway's genius lay in incorporating the European innovations (such as cross-stringing, conceived by Pape in Paris), with those of the United States (single-piece iron frames, greater power, expanded ranges)—all while adapting to the new paradigms of mass production, which meant that his factories, from 1860 on, could simultaneously produce large powerful grands and solid, reliable upright instruments in consistently large quantities. The piano's role in the second half of the nineteenth century was transformed: it became ubiquitous in public and private life, a vital part of the economic landscape.

Only the Germans were able to keep pace, though on a smaller scale. French manufacturers, Érard and (chiefly) Pleyel (Chopin's preferred instrument), were wary of the new technologies of mass production and of selling abroad; they retreated, their sales stagnating considerably as a result. The English, too, found it difficult to compete after midcentury. By the 1860s, then, the American instrument and its system of production dominated, but the foundations for its phenomenal success, both sociomusical and socioeconomic, had long been prepared in Europe. Again, Clementi, very early on, had foreseen the dense social and economic matrix of the instrument's future, its unique ability to express a single player's (Romantic) sensibilities, to accompany or to share in those of others, to transmit myriad musics. The nineteenth-century piano became a glorious, indispensable machine, mass-produced, desired in one form or another virtually everywhere.

STEPHEN ZANK

Bibliography

Ehrlich, Cyril. *The Piano: A History*. London: Dent, 1976.

Good, Edwin M. *Giraffes, Black Dragons, and Other Pianos: A Technological History from Cristofori to the Modern Concert Grand*. Stanford, Calif.: Stanford University Press, 1982.

Hanson, Alice M. *Musical Life in Biedermeyer Vienna*. Cambridge: Cambridge University Press, 1985.

Loesser, Arthur. *Men, Women, and Pianos*. New York: Simon and Schuster, 1954.

The New Grove Piano. New York: W. W. Norton, 1988.

Parakilis, James, ed. *Piano Roles*. New Haven, Conn.: Yale University Press, 2000.

Ritterman, Jane. "Piano Music and the Public Concert, 1800–1850," in *The Cambridge Companion to Chopin*. Edited by Jim Samson. Cambridge: Cambridge University Press, 1992. 11–31.

Roell, Craig H. *The Piano in America, 1980–1940*. Chapel Hill: University of North Carolina Press, 1989.

Rowland, David, ed. *The Cambridge Companion to the Piano*. Cambridge: Cambridge University Press, 1998.

Temperley, Nicholas. *The Romantic Age, 1800–1914*. London: Athlone Press, 1981.

Weber, William. *Music and the Middle Class: The Social Structure of Concert Life in London, Paris, and Vienna*. New York, 1975.

PICTURESQUE

The term *picturesque* (perhaps since John Ruskin's definition of it as "parasitical sublimity") tends often to be used in derogatory fashion. Even for some students of the late eighteenth century it signifies that which is pre-Romantic, mannered, and concerned with landscape rather than nature. According to a popular teleology, the picturesque is the necessary precursor of Romanticism, superficial in relation to the sublime transcendence of the latter. However, original usage of the word does not place it in opposition to the sublime. Indeed, much of the psychological language of the picturesque is also that of the Burkean sublime. If anything, the picturesque is pitched against neoclassical concepts of beauty, and what Richard Payne Knight called the "dull, vapid, smooth and tranquil scene."

Theorists of the eighteenth century introduced the picturesque as an extra aesthetic category to those of the sublime and the beautiful (although some twentieth-century commentators see the picturesque as a *synthesis* of the sublime and the beautiful). It is a new experiment in taste that for Christopher Hussey (1927) was the first step toward a pure aesthetic. Certainly it has a defiantly antifunctional dimension, and radically distances itself from the pleasing pastoral and the association of beauty with usefulness. As the Reverend William Gilpin, the picturesque's first theoretician, observed, "the picturesque eye looks at scenes of cultivation with disgust" and "[m]oral, and picturesque ideas do not always coincide."

From about the 1770s onward, the picturesque eye learns to appreciate that which is "shaggy," "irregular," "tufted," "rugged," "interesting," "fring'd," "rough," "varied." For many, the seventeenth-century Salvator Rosa was the picturesque artist par excellence. The picturesque eye is not interested in the generalities of ideal nature, noted Gilpin, but relishes "endless varieties" and "elegant particularities," and "ever delights in the bold, free, negligent strokes, and roughnesses of nature." In terms of available technology, watercolor pigment was now to be had in portable ready-made cakes, making the moment right for the capturing of the irregular landscape in all its moods, and topographical prints and reproductions of landscape art in guidebooks were becoming available to a wider public with the invention of aquatint. There was, according to Gilpin, growing interest in the effects of perspective and of light on perception: "Nay we sometimes see (in a mountainous country especially) a variation of light alter the whole disposition of a landscape." Gilpin particularly favored "haziness"; in British mist the picturesque artist could celebrate obscurity, lack of clarity, indistinctness—that which is veiled.

The picturesque is self-consciously (though not exclusively) native, and determinedly focuses on the wilder parts of the British landscape: the Lakes, the Wye Valley, Snowdonia, the Scottish Highlands. Hussey calls it the "art of landscape" and it can be found in poetry, painting (exemplified by artists such as Thomas Gainsborough, Thomas Girtin, Paul Sandby, and J. M. W. Turner), landscape gardening, novels, and even in architecture, for there is a strong interest in ruins. The picturesque meets the Gothic, and there are innumerable prints of ruined abbeys and Gothic cathedrals. Ann Bermingham has argued that the fondness for the neglected landscape, the overgrown and ruinous, and the value accorded the past can be viewed in terms of a specific class ideology, all these features being associated with old wealth rather than with the estates of the *nouveaux riches*. The Herefordshire landowners, landscape gardeners, and theoreticians of the picturesque Richard Payne Knight and Uvedale Price (both, incidentally, friends of Gainsborough), who, in the 1790s, were engaged in controversy about whether the picturesque was to be found in external features or was a product of a mode of vision, despised the gardens of Capability Brown and Humphrey Repton.

The picturesque artist is often caught in a compromise as regards his or her own attitude toward nature. On the one hand, Gilpin noted, "the picturesque eye . . . ranges after nature, untamed by art, and bursting wildly into all its irregular forms"; on the other, "Nature is always great in design; but unequal in composition." Although wild nature becomes a fit subject for art, it is somewhat of a corrected nature. For Alan Liu, picturesque terminology is a Foucauldian language of the correction and discipline of nature, obsessed with definitions, classification, and measuring. Certainly the picturesque is intent on screens and framing, and the internal frame (in the form of an overhanging rock or branch, for example) is one of its characteristics.

The sexual dynamic of the picturesque was commented on early in its career. The pedantic hero of William Combe's satiric poem "Doctor Syntax's Tour in search of The Picturesque" (1812) exclaims, with clumsy lechery,

> Nature, dear Nature, is my goddess,
> Whether arrayed in rustic bodice,
> Or when the nicest touch of Art
> Doth to her charms new charms impart . . .

The idea of nature's wanton femininity is continued in the works of Knight and Price. For Price, the picturesque is "the coquetry of nature," an art based on teasing "partial concealments" and sudden variation. Knight (also, curiously, an early historical anthropologist, writing an interesting essay on ancient priapic worship) wrote in *The Landscape* of "the cunning nymph, with giddy care / and wanton wiles." The picturesque is nature *deshabillée*, whose "greatest art is aptly to conceal; / To lead, with secret guile the prying sight" and "To charm the eye and capivate the soul."

Picturesque tourism boomed from the 1770s to the late 1790s. Malcolm Andrews's *The Search for the Picturesque* gives the best account of the phenomenon. For Andrews, the picturesque tourist "is typically a gentleman or gentlewoman engaged in an experiment in controlled aesthetic response to a range of new and often intimidating visual experiences." A whole range of inventions came to provide some of this control: special tinted Claude glasses for viewing and "fixing" the scene. Popular tourist destinations, such as the Wye Valley, doing duty as an Alpine substitute during the war with France in the 1790s, were dotted with "stations" that provided viewpoints over the best prospects, and also provided other features (such as giants' caves) to stimulate the tourist's imagination.

However, picturesque tourism should not be written off as mere commodification of landscape. Reading the travelers' journals it is evident that for many a whole new feeling for nature was coming into being. The picturesque tourist was willing to spend days in fog and mist, and could be found moving through (rather than merely surveying) nature, overwhelmed by the cascading torrents and overhanging cliffs, in situations that are illustrated by the low viewpoint employed by landscape painters. As for what has been described as picturesque writing, though for some writers it is a case of, as Andrews noted, "If you found the right scenery, then your tour journal would logically proclaim the discovery in the appropriate current vocabulary," others—both published and unpublished—were engaged in massive experimentation with a new and stimulating language of nature. Writers of thrilling and thrilled sensibilities were attempting to express their sense of the autonomy of the scene, the temporality of the landscape, and to find a new language of perspectives and of the overwhelming or sudden discovery of subjectivity.

EMMA MCEVOY

Selected Works

Gilpin, William. *Observations, Relative Chiefly to Picturesque Beauty, Made in the Year 1772, On Several Parts of England; Particularly; the Mountains and Lakes of Cumberland, and Westmoreland.* 1786.
Knight, Richard Payne. *The Landscape: A Didactic Poem in Three Books.* 1794.
Price, Uvedale. *Essay on the Picturesque.* 1794.

Bibliography

Andrews, Malcolm. *The Search for the Picturesque: Landscape, Aesthetics and Tourism in Britain, 1760–1800.* Aldershot, England: Scolar Press, 1989.
Bermingham, Ann. *Landscape and Ideology: The English Rustic Tradition 1740–1860.* London: Thames and Hudson, 1987.
Hussey, Christopher. *The Picturesque: Studies in a Point of View.* London: G. P. Putnam's Sons, 1987.
Liu, Alan. *Wordsworth: The Sense of History.* Stanford, Calif.: Stanford University Press, 1989.
Michasiw, Kim Ian. "Nine Revisionist Theses on the Picturesque," *Representations* 38 (1992): 76–100.

PIRANESI, GIOVANNI BATTISTA 1720–1778

Italian architect and engraver

Giovanni Battista Piranesi is one of the most representative figures of the shift from neoclassicism to Romanticism, not only for his works but also for his stature as an artist. Destined for an architectural career, he began a traditional apprenticeship with his uncle, Matteo Lucchesi, the architect in charge of constructing the *Murazzi* (the walls that separate the Venetian lagoon from the sea), and with Giovanni Scalfarotto, who introduced him to the Palladian style, exemplified by his church of St. Simeone Piccolo (completed in 1738).

In 1740, Piranesi went to Rome as a draughtsman in the Venetian ambassador's retinue at the papal court, but once he arrived he started building his artistic career in the social system of the court, eventually entering the studio of the most important engraver of *vedute* (views), Giuseppe Vasi. Piranesi realized that the richest clients were more frequently not sitting in aristocratic courts, but in the coaches along the route of the Grand Tour. The French Revolution was still far off, but the public was already changing, with the middle class taking on the role of art patron privileged client. Therefore Piranesi, who was also working for Pope Clement XIII (in San Giovanni in Laterano), devoted himself to the potentially most profitable art, both for the scale of demand and for its reproducibility.

Some of his artistic choices (for example, the unconventional width of his *vedute*) seem to be due to a desire to distinguish himself in a competitive market. Although he was one of the most eminent archeologists and antiquarians of his time (he was among the first scholars to ascertain that Roman architecture derived from the Etruscans and not from the Greeks), he did not hesitate in speculating on excavations (as a dealer as well as a forger).

Piranesi's awareness of the current transformation of the role that the artist played in society was clearly reflected in his works. In his first etchings, the *Prima Parte di Architetture e Prospettive* (1743), and in the plates for the *Varie Vedute di Roma Antica e Moderna* (1745), he had already placed several etchings of ruins (such as the *Tempio di Venere, e Cupido* [1745?]) next to conventional *vedute* (such as the *Prospetto d'un Regio Cortile* [1743]), in which he began to represent his new idea of time and history, supported by the pictorial nature of his etching technique.

The *vedutisti* (painters of views) traditionally placed ruins in the background of their works as an elegant and languorous, but ultimately static, element. Piranesi, however, according to the predominant Arcadian sensibility, brought them to the foreground. In fact, sometimes he chose such a close viewpoint that his plates could not include the entire buildings depicted but had to focus on details, such as in *Tempio di Giunone Regina* (c. 1745). If ruins embodied the dynamic nature of time, and, consequently, the relativity of every authority and the precariousness of every human work, they also allowed Piranesi to strip buildings of their surface and bring their "bones," their hidden structure, to light.

Therefore, while the awareness of the transience of experience enabled him to replace the principle of *auctoritas* with the principle of *authorship* (that is, the poetics of *imitatio* with the poetics of originality), a focus on details of ruins allowed him to undertake the didactic task of the late eighteenth-century intellectual. Temples, arches, and villas choked with brambles and plants were not perceived as symbols of death, but as signs of the life that proceeded from one form to another. The memory of the past, and its strength, went on living in the overgrown vegetation. The vestiges of the highest achievements of mankind turned into nature, outlining a new relationship between them. The possibility of connection with nature was no longer reserved for only the ancients. Modern humankind could identify with essential reality, not by ancient models. It had to find its own methods.

Piranesi achieved his originality primarily with two main artistic techniques: angular perspective and shading effects. By privileging the angular over the frontal perspective, Piranesi replaced the central vanishing point with various crossing diagonals, and this lent the plates a new sense of depth and a more dramatic character (see, for example, *Idea d'un atrio reale* in *Opere varie*, 1750). Piranesi's plates did not simply depict a scene. The powerful dynamism of the multiplicity of the vanishing points, combined with received associations and characterizations of antiquity, communicated to the audience a sense of motion and development.

The dramatic nature of this device was further strengthened by the contrast between light and darkness. The main innovation Piranesi brought to the art of etching was attention to color and to the structuring power of light. Despite the remarks of his masters, Piranesi exploited the chromatic sensitivity peculiar to the Venetian school to express (and to awaken) the dismay of contemporary man in facing the decay of the past's highest achievements. It is from this point of view that the *Carceri d'Invenzione* (*Fanciful Prisons*, 1760), his most successful collection (but only after his death, following the Romantic rereading), has been interpreted as a bewildering portrait of the recesses of consciousness.

The didactic value of ruins is equally worthy of notice. The late eighteenth century was still dominated by the classical poetics of *utile dulci*; therefore Piranesi, who was first of all an architect, did not renounce the opportunity to use ruins in order to highlight ancient (as well as modern) building techniques. The fanciful *Vedu Carceri d'Invenzione ta di una Parte de' Fondamenti del Teatro di Marcello* (in *Le antichità romane* [*The Antiquities of Rome*, 1756]) and *Blackfriars Bridge* are exemplary in this sense.

PAOLO RAMBELLI

Biography

Born in Venice, October 4, 1720. Trained as an architect (under Matteo Lucchesi and Giovanni Scalfarotto) and as an etcher (under Carlo Zucchi), 1735–40. Lived in Rome, where he entered the studio of the etcher Giuseppe Vasi, 1740–42; published *Prima parte di Architetture, e Prospettive*, 1743. Back in Rome, after a short period in Venice, he published his *Varie vedute di Roma antica e moderna*, 1744–45; started the lifetime work *Vedute di Roma*, 1747; took part in the edition of the *Nuova pianta* di Roma, 1748; published *Opere varie di architettura, prospettive, grotteschi*, 1750; published the first part of *Antichità romane* (which eventually came to four volumes), 1756; completed and published the *Carceri*, begun fifteen years earlier during a stay in Venice, 1761; published *Blackfriars Bridge in London*, 1764; completed the restoration of the church Sta. Maria del Priorato, 1766; published *Diverse maniere d'adornare i camini*, 1769; published *Trofeo o sia Magnifica colonna coclide di marmo* (devoted to *Trajan* and *Antonino's Columns*), 1773–75. Died of an illness probably due to acids used in etching, November 9, 1778.

Selected Works

Lettere di Giustificazione Scritte a Milord Charlemont. 1757.
Osservazioni sopra la Lettre de M. Mariette, accompanied by *Parere su l'Architettura* and by *Della Introduzione e del Progresso delle Belle Arti in Europa de' Tempi Antichi*. 1765.

Bibliography

Bianconi, Gian Lodovico. "Elogio Storico del Cavaliere Giambattista Piranesi celebre antiquario ed incisore di Roma." 1779.
Duchesne, Jean. *Quelques Idées sur l'Établissement des Frères Piranesi.* 1802.
Eisenstein, Sergei. "Piranèse ou la Fluidité des Formes," in *La Non-indifferente Nature* 1 (1976): 211–35. Translated as "Piranesi or the Fluidity of Forms" by R. Reeder, in *Oppositions* 2 (1971).
Ficacci, Luigi. *Piranesi: The Complete Etchings.* Köln: Taschen, 2000.
Fleming, John. *Robert Adam and His Circle in Edinburgh and Rome.* London, 1962.
Focillon, Henri. *Giovanni-Battista Piranesi (1720–1778).* Paris: H. Laurens, 1918.
Gavuzzo-Stewart, Silvia. *Nelle "Carceri" di G. B. Piranesi.* Leeds: North Universities Press, 1999.
Legrand, Jacques Guillaume. *Notice sur la Vie et les Ouvrages de J. B. Piranesi.* Paris, 1799. Manuscript is in the Bibliothèque Nationale in Paris.
Negri, Renzo. *Gusto e Poesia delle Rovine in Italia fra il Sette e l'Ottocento.* Milan: Ceschina Casa Editrice, 1965.
Nicholas, Penny. *Giovanni Battista Piranesi.* London: Orësko, 1978.
Roach, Joseph R., Jr. "From Baroque to Romantic: Piranesi's Contribution to Stage Design," *Theatre Survey* 19, no. 2 (1978): 91–118.
Rosemblum, Robert. *Transformation in Late Eighteenth Century Art.* Princeton, N.J.: Princeton University Press, 1967.
Scott, Jonathan. *Piranesi.* London and New York: Academy Editions, 1975.
Szondi, Peter. *Antico e Moderno nell'Arte dell'Età di Goethe.* Milan: Guerini, 1995.
Tafuri, Manfredo. *La Sfera e il Labirinto: Avanguardie e l'Architettura da Piranesi agli Anni '70.* Torino: Einaudi, 1980. Translated as *The Sphere and the Labyrinth: Avant-gardes and Architecture from Piranesi to the 1970s* by P. D'Acierno and R. Connolly. Cambridge, Mass., 1992.
Wilton-Ely, John, ed. *G. B. Piranesi: the Polemical Work.* New York, 1972.
———. *Giovanni Battista Piranesi: The Complete Etchings.* San Francisco: Alan Wofsy, 1994.
———. *The Mind and Art of Giovanni Battista Piranesi.* London: Thames and Hudson, 1978.

PIXÉRÉCOURT, RENÉ CHARLES GUILBERT DE 1773–1844

French writer of melodrama

Born in Nancy into an aristocratic Lorraine family, René Charles Guilbert de Pixérécourt was forced, by the French Revolution, into a life of adventure; he was eventually recognized as the most popular French author of melodramas, with the success of *Coelina ou l'enfant du mystère* (*Coelina, or the Mysterious Child*, 1800). During his tumultuous life, he abandoned his law studies in order to emigrate, enlisted in the Army of the Princes against the Revolutionary forces, lived as a fugitive, escaped arrest, faced poverty, and experienced a passionate love affair. Then, suddenly, he achieved wealth and great success as the most prolific writer of the melodrama, the most popular Parisian dramatic genre of the day. His ninety-four plays have been performed approximately thirty thousand times in Paris and the provinces, and have been constantly translated and retranslated into all the European languages; it is little wonder that France christened him *le Père du mélodrame*.

If that title is hyperbolic, Pixérécourt nonetheless wrote the plays that enjoyed the greatest popular success on the Parisian Boulevard du Temple, also called the *Boulevard du crime*, between 1797 and 1830. His first play, the comedy *Les Petits Auvergnats* (*The Children from Auvergne*, 1797), brought fame, and Pixérécourt's reputation grew with each succeeding triumph: *Victor ou l'enfant de la forêt* (*Victor, or the Forest Child*, 1798), *Coelina* (1800), *les Ruines de Babylone* (*The Ruins of Babylon*, 1810), *Christophe Colombe* (1815), and *La Fille de l'exilé*

(*The Exile's Daughter*, 1819). So great was his popular success that, after 1830, he hired collaborators to share in the labor of producing his melodramas (much as Alexandre Dumas *père* was doing in the same period). In his *Histoire de la littérature dramatique* (1853–58), the drama critic Jules Janin imparted some idea of Pixérécourt's celebrity during the Romantic period, noting,

> Men, young and old, children and young girls, their hands joined, followed him from afar when, wearing his Legion of Honour, he deigned to stroll on the Boulevard du Temple. They followed him in silence, pointing him passionately out to one another: "That's him! There he is! He who punishes all crimes, the lover of justice who can read the corrupt human heart!"

Sentimentality and sensational spectacle principally characterized Pixérécourt's plays and popular melodrama between 1800 and 1830. In *Valentine, ou le Séducteur* (*Valentine, or the Seducer*), generally considered to be Pixérécourt's least crudely melodramatic play, the virtuous heroine addresses the following to the audience, "Oh! I am betrayed, dishonoured, abandoned! . . . Seduced, the victim of a skillful impostor, Nothing, nothing remains! . . . Oh father! Your terrible prediction has come to pass: poverty, shame, disgrace alone are left to unhappy Valentine." Soliloquy in popular melodrama serves both to heighten the emotional experience of the audience and, clearly, to remind slower-witted spectators exactly what has occurred thus far in the narrative. Popular melodrama is also marked by a notable moralistic strain; generally, poetic justice is meted out, innocence is protected, vice punished, and the state remains unthreatened. As such, popular melodrama offered the opposite worldview to that presented in the Romantic dramas of Victor Hugo, Alexandre Dumas père, Alfred de Musset, and Alfred de Vigny.

Pixérécourt himself provided a striking example of the importance of sensational spectacle in his plays when he described a scene in *The Exile's Daughter*, imparting much more than setting and stage directions. He wrote technical explanations of how some of the most spectacular of the special effects necessary to the action were to be achieved. For the 1819 production of the play, for example, he describes how the set designer and stagehands had managed the chief attraction, forming his play's climax: an onstage flood. They used their entire resources of understage frames and supports equipped with rollers, which passed through slots in the scenery, as well as strategically positioned strips of cloth simulating water, mounted on a chassis stretching all the way across the stage. Trolleys were employed to move scenery back and forth. The final maneuver involved raising the "water," with every element on the set playing its part in achieving the effect. Thanks to such special effects, Marvin Carlson notes that audiences at *The Exile's Daughter* could expect to see the heroine "floating offstage on a plank."

In his *Réflexions sur le mélodrame*, which prefaced the 1832 edition of his *Oeuvres choisies*, Pixérécourt contended, with a condescension born presumably of experience, that "the Melodrama will always offer a means of instructing the people, because the genre is, at least, within the people's grasp." And in his *Dernières réflexions sur le mélodrame* (*Final Thoughts on Melodrama*), published posthumously in 1847, Pixérécourt declared that he had always based his melodramas on "religious ideas of Providence and moral sentiments."

A. W. HALSALL

Biography

Born January 22, 1773 in Nancy into the noble Guilbert family, with distinguished French and Polish connections. From 1778 to 1788 he was a pious Catholic student at the Collège de Nancy; his law studies were interrupted later by the revolution. Emigrated to Germany, 1789, enlisting in a regiment made up of sons of French noble families. Fell in love with "la belle Clothide" (daughter of the Abbess of Engleporte). Clothilde died

of tuberculosis, 1790. Became a fugitive in France, 1790–93; in 1793, as "Citoyen Guilbert," he escaped being arrested for a one-act play satirizing Marat-Mauger, the Nancy representative to the National Convention. Marries Marie-Jeanne-Françoise Quinette de la Hogue, 1795; the union produced one daughter, Anne-Françoise, but did not succeed as a marriage. In 1797, his one-act comedy, *les Petits Auvergnats*, opened at Paris's Théâtre de l'Ambigu-Comique and enjoyed a run of seventy-three performances. In 1797, *Victor ou l'enfant de la forêt*, his first melodrama, ran at the same venue for more than 1,400 performances. *Coelina* repeated this success (1800) as did his next melodramas; between 1800 and 1830 he was the leading playwright of Paris's Boulevard theaters: in 1801, *le Pèlerin blanc*; in 1805, *la Forteresse du Danube, Robinson Crusoé*; in 1809, *la Citerne* (*The Cistern*). In 1810, *Marguerite d'Anjou* combined melodrama and historical personages and events and gave Pixérécourt a success he would repeat both in the plays he wrote alone and with collaborators; *les Ruines de Babylone* triumphed the same year. In 1814, *le Chien de Montargis ou la Forêt de Bondy* has a dog as one of its stars. In 1821, *Valentine ou la séduction* confirmed his title as "le Corneille des Boulevards." In 1822–27 he successfully directed Paris's Opéra-Comique. From 1830 to 1847 his health increasingly betrayed him and, after 1835, the Parisian public turned against his melodramas; he took to editing his plays and attacked the "immorality" of Romantic dramatists like Hugo and Dumas. After a series of strokes, Pixérécourt died in Nancy, largely forgotten, in 1844.

Selected Works

Théâtre choisi. 4 vols. Geneva: Slatkine Reprints, 1971.
Coelina ou l'enfant du mystère. Edited by Norma Perry. Exeter: University of Exeter Press, 1972.

Bibliography

Allévy, Marie-Antoinette. *La Mise en scène en France dans la première moitié du dix-neuvième siècle.* Paris: E. Droz, 1938.
Carlson, Marvin. "French Stage Composition from Hugo to Zola," *Educational Stage Journal*, December 1971, 363–78.
Halsall, Albert W. *Victor Hugo and the Romantic Drama.* Toronto: University of Toronto Press, 1998.
Howarth, W. D. *Sublime and Grotesque: A Study of French Romantic Drama.* London: Harrap, 1975.
Janin, Jules. *Histoire de la littérature dramatique.* 6 vols. Paris: Michel Lévy, 1853–58.
Jomaron, Jacqueline de, ed. *Le Théâtre en France.* Paris: Armand Colin, 1992.
Marcoux, J. Paul. *Guilbert de Pixérécourt.* New York: Peter Lang, 1992.
Ubersfeld, Anne. *Le Drame romantique.* Paris: Éditions Belin, 1993.

POE, EDGAR ALLAN 1809–1849

American writer

Best known as a writer of Gothic horror stories and as the inventor of modern detective fiction, Edgar A. Poe, as he preferred to sign himself, was also an accomplished poet, essayist, and magazine editor. A prolific writer, most of his literary output was carefully judged to meet a specific demand for mystery and romance. As such, Poe's writing is more often than not driven by a fierce commercialism, yet in his lyric poetry and tales, Poe

speaks both to his own time and anticipates the literary developments of the late nineteenth and early twentieth centuries. At his best, Poe the critic is capable of powerful insights on the nature of art and the role of the artist.

Poe began his literary career as a poet, and his underlying belief in the work of art as the product of the interplay of emotion and reason through intuition has been used to place him firmly in a Romantic tradition. Certainly his fascination with travel and orientalism which emerges in poems such as "Al Aaraaf" (1829) supports the comparison with John Keats and Percy Bysshe Shelley, while the collection *Tamerlane, and Other Poems* (1827) borrows heavily from the language and posturing of Lord Byron. Yet overall, Poe's work and career defy such categorization. He was far from consistent in his theoretical pronouncements, and poems such as "The Raven" (1845) and "Ulalume" (1847) are concerned with self-revelation and isolation, themes associated more with American than European Romantic traditions.

Born in Boston, Massachusetts, to actor parents, by the age of three young Edgar Poe had been abandoned by his father and had witnessed the death of his mother from tuberculosis. With little extended family, Poe went to live with John Allan, a Scottish tobacco importer in Richmond, Virginia. When the Allans moved temporarily to England, Poe attended schools in Chelsea and Stoke Newington, London, an experience that provided material for the story "William Wilson" (1839). Returning to the United States, he was later expelled from the University of Virginia when he failed to repay gambling debts. John Allan is reputed to have turned away creditors for a full year after Poe left the university.

After his discharge from West Point Military Academy for neglect of military duty, and estranged from John Allan, Poe began to make his way in the literary world. As an editor and critic his skills were considerable: in just two years he raised the circulation of the *Southern Literary Messenger* from 500 to 3,500 copies. Yet his literary significance was recognized in Europe much earlier than in his native country. The reason for this is unclear, but it may be that his interest in the philosophy of Samuel Taylor Coleridge, Blaise Pascal, Friedrich von Schlegel, and Percy Bysshe Shelley made his work more accessible to European sensibilities. This is especially true of France, where his stories and poems were translated by Charles Baudelaire.

Nevertheless, the strong American flavor of his Romanticism is evident in many of his works, in particular those tales dealing with psychological motives and nervous disturbances. The writings of Charles Brockden Brown and Washington Irving provide early examples of the fascination in American literature with links between the psyche and the uncanny. Brown's moral tales contain many of the tropes of Poe's fiction: lookalikes, unreliable narrators, and unlikely coincidences. His psychological studies had a strong influence on Poe and others such as Herman Melville and Nathaniel Hawthorne. Indeed, all three of the later writers went on to create characters who fail to recognize their own self-destructive motives.

But where stories such as Irving's "The Legend of Sleepy Hollow" (1819–20) treat tales of strange events as provincial legends underpinned with a rational explanation and Brown's novels are essentially moral melodramas, Poe's approach is unsurprisingly more open-minded. While there may indeed be a rational explanation for the collapse of the House of Usher, for example, Poe is interested in more mysterious, less comforting causes.

As a young poet Poe declared that poetry is opposed to science in that its object is pleasure. Later, in his treatise "The Poetic Principle" (1850), he would temper this with the statement that beauty, rather than truth, is the poem's primary aim. Diverging from the Romantic ideals of his youth, he suggested that the poet and the man should remain separate: while the man may be passionate, the poet must be a craftsman. His own difficult personal life may have led Poe to this conclusion, but nevertheless it marks a significant shift away from the interaction of these two in more conventional Romantic thinking.

While he has become famous for his *Tales*, Poe's first published book of prose was *The Narrative of Arthur Gordon Pym of Nantucket* (1838). Written in response to the publisher's refusal to publish a collection of stories, this adventure narrative is driven by illusion, psychological uncertainty, and the breakdown of order; all staples of Gothic tales such as "The Fall of the House of Usher" (1839), "The Black Cat" (1843), and "The Pit and the Pendulum" (1843). Poe's other tales, the "tales of ratiocination" mark the invention of the modern detective story. "The Murders in the Rue Morgue" (1841), "The Mystery of Marie Rogêt" (1842), and "The Purloined Letter" (1845) all feature the amateur detective C. August Dupin, whose rational method in combination with his poetic tendencies demonstrate Poe's ideas on rationalism and science, outlined theoretically in *Eureka* (1848).

Ever the fabulist, as his fame as a critic and writer spread, Poe reinvented himself as a model university student, an outstanding athlete and the writer of many works under assumed names. The biographical facts, which include his marriage to his thirteen-year-old cousin, Virginia Clemm, a succession of underpaid jobs on various magazines, and a history of mental instability and susceptibility to the effects of alcohol and drugs, are lurid enough. Combined with the invented biography, they have turned Poe into a curiosity of literary Americana. More realistically, however, the mythological quality of such stories conceals a life of poverty, tragedy, and illness.

In the twenty-first century, Poe's influence on contemporary American culture should not be underestimated: "The Raven" is a common requirement in high school literature classes, while many of the tales have been dramatized on film. Recent critical approaches to Poe have focused on his destabilization of the relationship between reader and text, and the uncertainties of his narrators. The growth of interest in the areas of Gothic literature, sexual identity, and detective fiction in the 1990s has also triggered a resurgence of interest in the *Tales*. But it is as a writer who worried at the fraying edges of Romanticism that Poe made his greatest contribution. While he was certainly capable of striking Romantic poses in print and in life, his efforts to express deep psychological disturbance through language, and his philosophical objections to the common Romantic view of the poet as prophet or moral arbiter, mean that his work can also be seen to anticipate impressionism and symbolism. As Kenneth Silverman reminds us, one of the foundations of literary modernism is Poe's "determined separation of the man who suffers and the artist who creates."

CHRISTOPHER ROUTLEDGE

Biography

Born Edgar Poe in Boston, Massachusetts, January 19, 1809. From 1811 (after the death of his mother), lived with the family of John Allan, tobacco merchant, in Richmond, Virginia; attended schools in England and the United States; left University of Virginia after ten months in December 1826. Enlisted in U.S. Army, May 26, 1827; published "Tamerlane and Other Poems," Boston, 1827; estranged from the Allan family; dismissed from West Point Academy in 1831. Lived in poverty in Baltimore, 1831–35; published prize-winning story "MS. Found in a Bottle"; employed by *Southern Literary Messenger*, Richmond, 1835–37; married Virginia Clemm (1823–47), May 6, 1837. Employed as coeditor of *Burton's Gentleman's Magazine*, 1839–40; employed as literary editor of *Graham's Magazine*, 1841–1842; contributed a tale a month to *Graham's*, including "The Murders in the Rue Morgue," April 1841; literary critic for the *New York Mirror*, 1844–45. Died destitute in Baltimore, possibly from a brain lesion, October 7, 1849.

Selected Works

Collections

The Poetical Works of Edgar Allan Poe. Edited by James Hannay, with illustrations by E. H. Wehnert. 1865.
The Works of Edgar Allan Poe. With "Preface" to the 1849 edition by Maria Clemm; "Edgar Allan Poe," by James Russell Lowell; "Death of Edgar Allan Poe," by Nathaniel Parker Willis; "Memoir of the author," by Rufus Wilmot Griswold. Boston: Jefferson Press, c. 1900.
The Complete Works of Edgar Allan Poe. Edited by James A. Harrison. 17 vols. New York: G. D. Sproul, 1902.
The Letters of Edgar Allan Poe. Edited by John Ward Ostrom. Cambridge, Mass.: Harvard University Press, 1948.
The Centenary Poe: Tales, Poems, Criticism, Marginalia and Eureka. Edited and with an introduction by M. Slater. London: Bodley Head, 1949.
The Complete Works of Edgar Allan Poe. New York: AMS Press, 1979.
Marginalia. With an introduction by John Carl Miller. Charlottesville: University Press of Virginia, 1981.
Edgar Allan Poe: Essays and Reviews. Library of America Series. New York: Viking, 1984.
Essays and Reviews of Edgar Allan Poe. Selected and with notes by Gary Richard Thompson. Cambridge: Cambridge University Press, 1984.
The Fall of the House of Usher and Other Writings. Edited by David Galloway. Harmondsworth, England: Penguin, 1986.
Literary Theory and Criticism. Edited by Leonard Cassuto, New York: Dover, 1999.

Poetry

Tamerlane and Other Poems, 1827. Facsimile edition with an introduction by Thomas Ollive Mabbott. New York: Columbia University Press, 1941.
Al Aaraaf, Tamerlane and Other Poems, 1829. Facsimile edition with a bibliographical note by Thomas Ollive Mabbott. New York: Facsimile Text Society, 1933.
Poems, 1831. Facsimile edition with a bibliographical note by Killis Campbell. New York: Facsimile Text Society, 1936.
The Raven and Other Poems. 1845.
Eureka, 1848. Reprinted. New York: Sun and Moon Press, 1997.

Tales

The Narrative of Arthur Gordon Pym of Nantucket. 1838.
Tales of the Grotesque and the Arabesque. 1839.
Tales. 1845.

Other

"The Philosophy of Composition," *Graham's Magazine*. 1846.
"The Rationale of Verse," *Southern Literary Messenger*. 1848.
"The Poetic Principle." Lecture, December 20, 1848. Published in *Union Magazine*. 1850.

Bibliography

Baudelaire, Charles. *Baudelaire on Poe: Critical Papers*. Translated and edited by Lois and Francis E. Hyslop Jr. Philadelphia: Bald Eagle, 1952.
Bellas, Patricia H. *Poe, Master of Macabre*. Baltimore: Xavier, 1995.
Buranelli, Vincent. *Edgar Allan Poe*. Boston: Twayne, 1977.
Carlson, Eric W., ed. *A Companion to Poe Studies*. Westport, Conn.: Greenwood, 1996.
Chase, Lewis Nathaniel. *Poe and His Poetry*. Norwood, Penn.: Norwood Editions, 1977.
Eliot, T. S. *From Poe to Valery*. New York: Harcourt, Brace, 1948.
Frank, Frederick S. and Anthony Magistrale. *The Poe Encyclopedia*. Westport, Conn.: Greenwood, 1997.
Meyers, Jeffrey. *Edgar Allan Poe: His Life and Legacy*. New York: Cooper Square, 2000.
Moss, Sidney P. *Poe's Literary Battles: The Critic in the Context of his Literary Milieu*. Durham, N.C.: Duke University Press, 1963.
Quinn, Arthur Hobson. *Edgar Allan Poe: A Critical Biography*. Baltimore: Johns Hopkins University Press, 1997.
Rosenheim, Shawn, and Stephen Rachman, eds. *The American Face of Edgar Allan Poe*. Baltimore: Johns Hopkins University Press, 1995.
Silverman, Kenneth. *Edgar A. Poe: Mournful and Never-Ending Remembrance*. London: Wiedenfeld and Nicholson, 1992.

POETRY: BRITAIN

British poetry during the Romantic era has long been defined in terms of six male poets whose writing reached its peak between 1798, the year in which Samuel Taylor Coleridge and William Wordsworth's *Lyrical Ballads* first appeared, and 1824, the year of Lord Byron's death. These six poets—William Blake, Byron, Coleridge, John Keats, Percy Bysshe Shelley, and Wordsworth—tend to be lumped together as "Romantics," but stylistically, thematically, and politically they are quite disparate, and the attempt to define what they have in common has often become an elusive attempt to define Romanticism itself. Generally, these poets share an emphasis on the individual self and mind, a focus on the figure of the poet (often but not always identified with the author himself), a concern for the shaping power of imagina-tion, an interest in altered states of consciousness (such as sleep, visions, and spiritual possession), an emphasis on landscape and the natural world, and an interest in the exotic, whether in time (medievalism, primitivism, Hellenism) or place (Greece, the "Orient," the Americas). Often divided into two generations, the "first generation" of Blake, Coleridge, and Wordsworth were immediately shaped by the events of the French Revolution and its aftermath, while the "second generation"—Byron, Keats, and Shelley—began writing during the Napoleonic era and were crucially shaped by the social and political unrest in England following the end of the war in 1815. These poets wrote in many genres, especially the lyric and the romance verse tale, using a variety of forms such as the sonnet (newly popular in the 1780s in the poetry of William Lisle Bowles and Charlotte Smith), the ballad (influenced by Thomas Percy's 1765 *Reliques of English Poetry* and the German ballads of Gottfried August Bürger), the Spenserian stanza, blank verse, and the ode (following the example of mid-eighteenth-century poets such as Mark Akenside, William Collins, and Thomas Gray).

Byron achieved a high level of fame and notoriety during this time, but several writers and poets beyond this group of six were writing at the time. Walter Scott achieved great success with his collection of Scottish border ballads and the series of Scottish historical verse romances which appeared in the first decade of the 1800s, paving the way for his even greater fame as a historical novelist. Thomas Moore became prominent through his *Irish Melodies* (1808–34), collections of lyrics in the Irish folk tradition, and through his best-selling oriental tale *Lalla Rookh* (1817). Robert Southey, often associated with Coleridge and Wordsworth as a member of the "lake school" of poetry, achieved notoriety and eventually the laureateship with a series of lengthy verse epics. Writing in heroic couplets more typical of the eighteenth century, George Crabbe produced his stark narratives of the rural English poor during the period, while other poets such as Thomas Campbell and Samuel Rogers combined poetic innovation with adherence to characteristic eighteenth-century forms and themes.

The latter half of the eighteenth century in poetry has often been described as a turning away from the neoclassical or Augustan verse modes, especially public satire, toward the lyric, with its emphasis on individual feeling, inspiration, and genius. Themes of melancholy, solitude, sublimity, and the wild natural landscape which would become so significant to the Romantic era found early expression in the work of the "Graveyard Poets," especially Thomas Gray, the poetry of Joseph and Thomas Warton, Oliver Goldsmith's nostalgic *Deserted Village* (1770), and later the sonnets of William Bowles and Charlotte Smith. Thomas Chatterton's "Rowley" poems and James Mcpherson's "Ossian" poems in the 1760s and 1770s touched off major critical controversies by purporting to offer discoveries of medieval English and ancient Scottish poetry, respectively, stimulating the general interest in medievalism, primitivism, the sublimity of the natural landscape, and an original folk poetry. Robert Burns' Scottish dialect poems, many of them rewritten from songs gathered in his trips through the Scottish countryside, also contributed to these vogues for Scotland, folk poetry, and the charismatic central figure of the poet, as did the Scottish poet James Beattie's *The Minstrel* (1771–74). William Cowper's rambling blank-verse narrative *The Task* (1784) called attention to the poet figure in a different way, mixing a conversational account of the poet's own experience with wide-ranging social and religious commentary, making Cowper one of the most popular English poets throughout the Romantic period.

The literary movement of sensibility, calling attention to personal feeling and the connection between body and mind, also became prominent during the final decades of the eighteenth century, especially among female poets such as Ann Batten Cristall, Charlotte Dacre, Mary Robinson, Charlotte Smith, and Helen Maria Williams. Other female poets of the period wrote explicitly on public events or debates, including Hannah Moore, Helen Maria Williams, and Ann Yearsley in (1788) poems against slavery, Charlotte Smith's *The Emigrants* (1793) on the effects of the French Revolution and its aftermath, and Anna Laetitia Barbauld's *Eighteen Hundred and Eleven* (1812). Attacks by reviewers eventually discouraged most women from writing political poetry. Female poets, however, continued to be equally—and often more—prominent than their male counterparts throughout the Romantic period. In the 1820s and 1830s Felicia Hemans, for example, achieved a poetic celebrity second only to Byron's. Hemans and Elizabeth Laetitia Landon, another female poet who achieved widespread recognition at this time, typically focused their poetry on the domestic sphere and romantic love, writing in a tone of pervasive elegiac melancholy. Hemans's poetry is often set in foreign or exotic locations, both celebrating domestic attachments and lamenting their inevitable destruction; Landon typically writes of beautiful, melancholy women whose lovers have died, disappeared, or rejected them.

This elegiac tone, with its emphasis on death, nostalgia, and the isolation of the individual speaker, would become predominant at the end of the Romantic and beginning of the Victorian periods: in Alfred, Lord Tennyson's poems of abandoned women, such as "Mariana" and *The Lady of Shalott* (1832), and in his long elegy for his friend Arthur Hallam, *In Memoriam* (1850); in Matthew Arnold's "Dover Beach," Marguerite poems, and his elegy *Thrysis* (all 1867); in the poetry of Anne, Charlotte, and Emily Brontë; and later in the work of Christina Rossetti and the pre-Raphaelites. Other mid-century poets, such as Matthew Arnold and Arthur Clough, proclaimed a sense of cultural fragmentation and paralysis together with the felt imperative of social duty. Toward the end of the Romantic period, Robert Browning began to explore individual subjectivity in relation to philosophical, religious, and aesthetic issues in his dramatic monologues, while his wife Elizabeth Barrett Browning explored social and religious issues in relation to her position as a woman, as in her bildungsroman verse novel, *Aurora Leigh* (1856).

SCOTT HESS

Bibliography

Abrams, M. H., ed. *English Romantic Poetry: Modern Essays in Criticism.* 2d ed. London: Oxford University Press, 1975.

Armstrong, Isabella. *Victorian Poetry: Poetry, Poetics, and Politics.* London: Routledge, 1993.

Curran, Stuart. *Poetic Form and British Romanticism.* Oxford, U.K.: Oxford University Press, 1986.

Feldman, Paula, and Theresa Kelley, eds. *Romantic Women Writers: Voices and Countervoices.* Hanover, N.H.: University Press of New England, 1995.

Jackson, J. R. de J. *Poetry of the Romantic Period.* Boston: Routledge and Kegan Paul, 1980.

Kroeber, Karl, and Gene Ruoff, eds. *Romantic Poetry: Recent Revisionary Criticism.* New Brunswick, N.J.: Rutgers University Press, 1993.

McGann, Jerome. *The Poetics of Sensibility.* Oxford, U.K.: Clarendon Press, 1996.

Woodman, Thomas, ed. *Early Romantics: Pespectives in British Poetry from Pope to Wordsworth.* New York: St. Martin's Press, 1998.

POETRY: FRANCE

For those who have been schooled in the Romantic poetry of England or Germany, their first encounter with the corresponding poetry of France can come as a surprise, if not a disappointment. To read a celebrated example of the genre—be it "Le Lac" of Alphonse Louis-Marie de Lamartine or "Tristesse d'Olympio" of Victor Hugo is to discover that, in traversing the relevant national boundaries, the term *Romantic* seems to have been purged of its connotations of spontaneity, unalloyed emotion, and formal innovation, and that, in the hands of the very society that led the Western world in political revolution, contemporary poetry retains much of the character that is more readily associated with its prerevolutionary classical past.

A comparison between the meditations on the loneliness of leadership contained in Alfred de Vigny's "Moïse" (1822) and in the soliloquy of the Emperor Augustus from act 2 of Pierre Corneille's *Cinna* (1640) would serve to confirm how little French poetry appears to have evolved in conception and expression over the intervening two centuries. Both writers employ a systematically analytical approach to a moment of crisis, which befits an age of order and clarity, but has little in common with the tumbling emotions displayed by Lord Byron's Manfred or Johann Wolfgang von Goethe's Egmont. In much the same way, a study of the representation of nature in Lamartine's *Méditations poétiques* (1820) is likely to reveal a closer affinity with the cultured landscapes of Claude or Watteau than with the leafy wildernesses of Fichendorf or William Wordsworth. In search of a poetic seachange in France of the kind we associate with a Novalis or even the "lake poets," it is more customary to turn to Charles Baudelaire, to the symbolists of the final decades of the nineteenth century and, beyond them, to the surrealists of the early twentieth century. Even here, tradition is never very far from the surface.

This is not to say that France experienced no authentically Romantic age or that it can boast no authentically Romantic poetry. A culture steeped in the method of René Descartes, the poetics of Boileau and the grammatics of the French Academy would, however, not only be slow to espouse the Romantic revolution as it swept through European literature, but would never be entirely at ease with a movement which implied abandoning reason and dispensing with the belief that art involved the application of established rules and conventions. Though he is, in many respects, one of the least conventionally-minded of the poets under consideration, Victor Hugo exemplifies the point when, in the same sequence of poems from his collection *Les Contemplations* (1856), he can claim to have mimicked through his poetry the events of 1789 by capping the hallowed French dictionary with the red Phrygian bonnet of revolution, only to translate this proclamation of lexical emancipation into the formal symmetries and sequential logic of the concluding line, "Car le mot, c'est le Verbe, et le Verbe, c'est Dieu."

Even the poem that is often singled out from the French Romantic canon for its Rimbaldian self-abandon, "El Desdichado" by the Germanophile Gérard de Nerval, reveals itself, on closer inspection, as a studied piece of Cartesian reasoning. When an English or a German poet writes, suggests one observer of this contrast, his primary purpose is to convey feeling; when his French counterpart writes, his first concern is to be understood. In one

we are dealing with raw experience, conveyed in its disorientating and hallucinating effect upon the mind, as instanced by Samuel Taylor Coleridge's *Rime of the Ancient Mariner*; in the other with the idea behind that experience, with its intellectual identification rather than with its direct and intimate transmission. Nordic Romantic poetry is generated from within from where it reaches toward the exterior; the French is generated from without and, in so being, remains conscious of itself as an argument and as an artifact. It is Hugo again who reminds us, in this case in the document that came to be regarded as the manifesto of the new dramatics and poetics in France, his *Préface de Cromwell* (1827), that nature will, for the French mind, always be the servant of art and not art that of nature.

Far removed from the rustic simplicity of Grasmere or the meandering folk poetry so admired by Johann Gottfried von Herder, the supreme characteristic of this poetic style is noble and rhetorical and, as implied by the overlay of the two genres in Hugo's *Préface*, its rhetoric is never far from that of his nation's most enduring contribution to European literature, epic drama. When Lamartine employs the periphrasis of "le char vaporeux de la reine des ombres" to describe the moon rising over the Lac du Bourget, or begins a stanza from his poetic dialogue "La Vigne et la maison" with the series of apostrophes "0 famille! 6 mystère! 6 coeur de la nature!" he is resorting to a poetic language still ringing with the public elegances of the court of Versailles. When Alfred de Musset, in his celebrated *Nuits* of 1829, confides to his muse his torment at the hands of his unfaithful mistress, the account smacks of the agonized self-analysis of Racine's jealous Hermione. Vigny's somber "La Mort du loup" is composed with the structural rigor of a tragedy in three acts. Hugo's "A Villequier" is an embittered exchange with God over the cruel death of his daughter. There are always beginnings, middles, and ends to this style of poetry and, in the case of the Olympian Hugo himself, the end is, as often as not, a clarion chord: "C'est toi qui dors dans l'ombre, ô sacré souvenir!"

Not only does the poet's language also share with its classical past the prosodic form that first made its appearance in the middle ages, the twelve-syllable Alexandrine, but its lexical currency remains that of the idealized and the general. Where the isometric "foot" of English verse is the fundamental source of its rhythm, the Alexandrine, with its traditional division into two hemistiches derives its music from its syllabic and rhythmic regularity, and the infringement of the rules that govern it is still a shock to French sensibilities. Concessions to the spirit of a liberated Romantic age were consequently cautious—an infrequently exploited "ternary" or "Romantic" version of the Classical *hemistiche*, the occasional neglect of the prized "rime riche"—or, as in the case of the famous enjambement employed by Hugo in the first act of his *Hernani* of 1830, could become in themselves the calculated essence of novelty. Something like the same effect is achieved when, in his exquisite "Booz endormi" from *La Légende des siècles* of 1859, there should appear a bodily word like *ventre*. As with Corneille or Racine in the seventeenth century, Hugo's is a poetic environment in which the physical still startles by its presence and of which Musset is the more typical in couching his outburst of jealousy in the vocabulary of pure abstraction.

Within such cultural constraints, however, we must recognize that we are still dealing here with attitudes and values which are the unique heritage of the Romantic experience. When his first volume of *Méditations poétiques* appeared in the early years of the French Restoration, Lamartine's responsive countrymen found themselves confronting a vision of the world in which the testimony of the personal and the immediate had been substituted for the timeless and universal truths espoused by the Enlightenment. Whatever the artificiality of the language employed, the grief or ecstasy particular to a moment in the life of an individual had entered the domain of poetry in a manner which had not been witnessed since the Renaissance and would have proved abhorrent to the seventeenth-century classical mind. The themes of the collection entertained the ideas of change, existential disquiet, the melancholy twilight of time, in a way unheard of in a previous era of unquestioning optimism. If Musset's later *Nuits* offer little to compare with the journeys into the unconscious represented by Novalis's *Hymnen an die Nacht*, the private anguish and self-doubt of which they treat spoke similarly to an age which had come to appreciate and to share the experience of consciousness turned inward on itself, of quasi-adolescent longings and unabsolved guilt. In spite of his Cornelian grandiloquence, Vigny's sense of pessimism and of the fatality of the flesh, so painfully laid bare in the poems of the posthumous collection of *Les Destinées*, is more evidently the product of the century of Arthur Schopenhauer than of Voltaire. His excesses of bravado aside, we cannot read the works of Hugo without recognizing in his message of historical progress and social redemption the truly revolutionary language of G. W. F. Hegel and Claude Henri de Rouvroy, Comte de Saint-Simon.

It is certainly not without significance that a majority of these writers—Lamartine, Musset, Vigny—shared a common heritage as minor aristocrats whose families had been threatened under the Revolution and, in a bourgeois postrevolutionary world, were sensitive to their situation of political and social marginalization. What is powerfully Romantic here and as special to the French Romantic experience as the form in which it is couched, is the music of insecurity, of finding oneself in an unfamiliar world and seeking to come to terms with it. That most aristocratic of Romantic poets, Vigny, typifies the point when he identifies himself with the cornered wolf, impassively confronting the advancing hounds and huntsmen. Like that of Honoré de Balzac or perhaps Alexis de Tocqueville, his is a Romanticism born of nostalgia and of protest at the very conditions which brought Romanticism into being.

As in many other things, Hugo is the exception to this political stereotyping—his father had emerged from obscurity to become a general in Napoleon's army—but he is no less conscious of living through the aftershock of dramatic political change, and his poetry, like his prose fiction, is imbued with its dynamics. If it is as easy to read a poem such as the apocalyptic "Mors" from *Les Contemplations* of 1856 as a political allegory as much as a religious allegory, it is inescapably because political revolution is an abiding influence on French Romantic thought and art, shaping its preoccupations and clouding its conservative outward face.

It is when, indeed, the two contrary tendencies that can be identified here, the one Apollonian and formal, the other Dionysian and existential, that the true coherence of French Romantic poetry and the true source of its special beauty begin to come to light. At many different levels, the poetry of the period mirrors the tensions that are found in contemporary politics in that the forces of order and disorder appear to be struggling for mastery over the French soul. If a sense of dissolution, of the inrush of night, emptiness, chaos, could be said to constitute the dominant theme of Lamartine's poetry, it acquires its melancholy music from the contrast with the disciplined precision of his poetic voice. If Musset, in his personal anguish, constantly invokes the reassurance of his guardian muse, it is as though words, like an echo from a more stable past, remain his ultimate ally against despair. Where the id of nature or emotion beckons, the ego of linguistic reason struggles to prevail. Olympio, in despair at the eclipse of youth and love by the shadow of time, discovers a verbal signpost—"le souvenir"—to lead him out of his emotional labyrinth. Vigny's Samson reveals his inner self to Dalilah only to reclaim it at the last in an angry reaffirmation of the power of mind and will over body and heart. Whether inspired by woman, death, or political chaos, the demon of confusion is the ever-present threat and poetic harmony the angel of salvation: "Que tout ce qu'on entend, l'on voit ou l'on respire / Tout dise: 'Ils ont aimé.' "

There is thus an instructive distinction to be drawn between the French and other national versions of that supreme principle of Romantic art in general, the belief, namely, in the superiority of the artistic "genius" over the common and uncomprehending run of men. Goethe expresses this view, as, of course, does Byron, and it is implicit in the parallels that we find constantly in the French poetry of the period between the poet and Moses, the poet and Samson, the poet and the brooding occupant of Mount Olympus. Where Goethe is, however, disposed to identify creative hypersensitivity with communion with the earth spirit, and Byron to equate it with the release of the demonic within him, Vigny and his contemporaries find genius in a Gallic aristocracy of mind and pen. In one case, the poet is the intoxicated adventurer into realms unknown; in the other, the magus, the fathering leader of an errant society or the alchemical translator of its anguish into hope and reason.

It was thus entirely consistent with this notion of the artist that Lamartine should become a key political player during the short-lived Second Republic of 1848 or that Hugo, even more dramatically, should assume for himself the role of mentor to his nation with his exile to the Channel Islands in 1852. Like the prophet on the mountain, the poet feels an obligation to share his insights with the waiting world in the belief that the commandments of his craft, its order and its harmonies, are potentially those of society at large. As Vigny puts it, writing in "La Maison du berger," poetry is like a pure crystal formed from the travail of eons of human reflection and continuing to guide it.

The aesthetic merges here with the moral and ultimately the philosophical and religious in the sense that the poetic art has assumed the nature of a hieratical or messianic calling and its language that of an incantatory medium linking fallen man with the unseen realm of the Absolute. In Hugo's terms in the punning line from the sequel to his "Réponse a un acte d'accusation" quoted earlier, the word of poetry is to be equated with the Verb of the New Testament and hence directly with God.

If Victor Hugo is, even in the eyes of his detractors, by far the most imposing performer on this stage, it is perhaps because of his unparalleled ability to explore and exploit its possibilities. Where others of his day tended to be poets of a single voice—a tremulous lyre in the case of Lamartine, a plaintive oboe in the case of Musset, a mournful cello in the case of Vigny—Hugo appears to have an entire poetic orchestra at his finger tips. The dark for him is that much darker, the light that much brighter, while his poetry is born out of the resolution of these titanic contrasts—"les rayons et les ombres" of existence—into harmony and unity. And this, of course, is his fundamental and representative message. In Hugo's hands, poetry becomes a confrontation between language and the chaotic or rebarbative surface of life in a demonstration of its underlying beauty and meaning. The aspect of the humblest flower is replicated in the rays of the glorious sun; death in the persona of the scything reaper of revelation is belied by the appearance of the angel-harvester of souls; the drowning of a beloved child is open to reinterpretation as a message of salvation: "Tout se tient." The thread linking all creation may be contorted or invisible, but it is unbroken. The wheel turns and yet is forever still. A poet who could turn his daughter and son-in-law's death on their honeymoon into a message of hope for all mankind has a belief in the regenerative and conciliatory power of poetic language akin to that of prayer.

When Pierre Albouy, in a reflection of the poet's own words from the collection, describes the poet of *Les Contemplations* as a "new Orpheus, taming beasts by means of language," he is pointing also to the essential myth governing French Romantic poetry at large. For Hugo and his contemporaries, the underworld is the fertile location of inspiration, but return to the light through the authority of their music is the goal. In this regard, their relationship with the forces shaping Romantic thought and art would always involve a degree of irony or of disbelief in the reality or permanence of the new literary role in which they were cast. Lamartine would, after all, privately dismiss as "de la *graine de niais*" his highly acclaimed collections of lyrical verses, and Hugo, as though dissatisfied with the fragmented conception of experience conveyed by a passing poem, would prefer to bind these individual poetic building blocks into a more enduring and purposeful architectural whole. Significantly perhaps, what the German Romantic mind construed as the condition of *Weltschmerz*—that is, a universal, indeterminate state of modern malaise, the French would characterize as "la maladie du siècle," a disease belonging to a precise era in human history, to be surpassed, corrected, some day cured.

The end of this style of poetry making in France is signaled by the breakdown of the comfortably allegorical view of the world on which it depends. Hugo, its timeless genius, would soldier on, refusing to look back, but, even as he published *Les Contemplations*, a new generation of poets was emerging who would accept reality as dense with uncertainty where he and his fellow Romantics had seen it as redolent with hidden meaning. If Paul Valéry can invite us to acknowledge a crucial division between the first generation of nineteenth-century French poets and the second, which included the names of Gautier, Leconte de Lisle and, most important, Baudelaire, it is because the poetry with which we associate the terms "l'art pour l'art" and subsequently, symbolism, and which has its beginnings in the early and disillusioning years of the Second Empire, is distinguished by the renunciation of the imperatives of narrative and significance, and the cultivation of a poetic discourse that separated the ideal of artistic beauty from the idealization of reality. The poet of *Les Fleurs du mal* occupies, as Charles Augustin de Sainte-Beuve argued, a place at the extreme limit of Romantic art in France; he acknowledges the same dialectical confrontation between art and life as his predecessors, but he refuses to collude in their belief in its transience.

Symbolism is the language of poetry that has broken free of its Cartesian anchors and launched its own imaginative ark onto the troubled waters of modern experience and, to this degree, Baudelaire and his later nineteenth-century successors might be held to represent the authentic realization of a process which Hugo and his poetic generation had merely begun. Where the work of the latter could be summed up as an endeavor to maintain a poetic bridge over the oceanic abyss of time and change, it would fall to Arthur Rimbaud at last to echo the chant of the sailors in the new world's drunken boat.

DAVID LEE

Bibliography

Bénichou, Paul. *Les Mages romantiques*. Paris: Gallimard, 1988.
Bishop, Michael. *Nineteenth-Century French Poetry*. New York: Twayne, 1993.
Brereton, Geoffrey. *An Introduction to the French Poets, Villon to the Present Day*. London: Methuen, 1956.
Hazard, Paul. "Les caractéres nationaux du lyrisme romantique français." In *Quatre études*. New York: Oxford University Press, 1940.
Moreau, Pierre. *Le Classicisme des romantiques*. Paris: Plon, 1932.
Schenk, H. D. *The Mind of the European Romantics: An Essay in Cultural History*. London: Constable, 1966.
Shroder, Maurice Z. *Icarus: The Image of the Artist in French Romanticism*. Cambridge, Mass.: Harvard University Press, 1961.
Valéry, Paul. "Avant-propos à la connaissance de la Déesse," 1920. In *Variété Oeuvres*. Bibliothèque de la Pléiade, vol. 1. Paris: Gallimard, 1957.

POETRY: GERMANY

The Romantic period in Germany comprises the generations that reached maturity and began to write between the outbreak of the French Revolution in 1789 and the fall of Napoleon in 1815. The major figures include Achim von Arnim, Clemens Brentano, Joseph von Eichendorff, Karoline von Günderode, Sophie Mereau, Novalis, brothers August Wilhelm and Friedrich von Schlegel, Dorothea Schlegel, and Ludwig Tieck. Even this chronology omits one writer whose entire career engages with German Romanticism and whose earliest poems appeared just after 1815: Heinrich Heine.

The early Romantics, associated with the university town of Jena, consciously developed a radical new aesthetic in response to the idealist philosophy of Immanual Kant and Johann Gottlieb Fichte. In keeping with the Schlegels' scholarly training in classics, their manifesto journal *Athenäum* included translations from Greek as well as *Die Gemälde* (*the Paintings*) that mixed dialogue, essay, and verse "transpositions d'art." Novalis experimented with quantitative meters (alcaic, third asclepiadic) and translated one of Horace's *Odes*. His poetry reflects discursively as well as lyrically on central subjects such as love or the isolation of the poet. Only

Friedrich Hölderlin, in this generation, made the classical meters a vehicle for complex states of mind and feeling. The currency of quantitative meters made stressed Germanic measures, often based on the four-line stanza of folksong, an expression of different values. Yet however much Romantic poetry may seem naïve and spontaneous, in reality it is the result of calculation, framing the poem in self-conscious irony. In the mixed form of Romantic prose fiction, where poems are introduced as song or ballad narrative, the poem is again self-consciously a glimpse of that *Poesie* which becomes the absolute project of the Romantics, without being completely realized anywhere. Both Kant's empty subject, left only as a space connecting concepts and intuitions, and the expanded self of the later idealists Fichte and Friedrich Wilhelm Joseph von Schelling, encouraged belief in the limitless powers of the imagination. Its intimations might restore a sense of the deep unity of the human mind with nature in a process of constant interaction. This philosophical commitment is matched by a concentration on poetry reflecting mood, rather than narrating experience. Tieck is the earliest exponent of mood. In his fairytale *Blonde Eckbert* (1797) recurrent verses evoke the solitude of the forest as "Waldeinsamkeit": the new style is notoriously represented by his poem *Miracle of Love* (1804) with its atmospheric "moonlit magic nights" ("Mondbeglänzte Zaubernächte"). The underlying tone is pastoral and its major historical resource is the folksong.

Based in Heidelberg and Berlin, the second generation of Romantic poets promoted and exploited the folksong as the appropriate form for German poetry. Arnim and Brentano made a momentous breakthrough with their anthology *Des Knaben Wunderhorn* (*The Boy's Magical Horn*, 1805), which gathered genuine folk material and printed works from the sixteenth and seventeenth centuries, alongside subtle pastiches, to create a bygone age of the imagination. The collection provided a repertoire of forms and licensed a new flexibility in poetic diction and syntax that exercised immense influence. The folksong strain provides a repertoire of imagery that could be used repeatedly. Eichendorff is one of the great exponents of this narrow expressive compass. The central themes of nostalgia, homesickness, and memory open his poems onto the landscapes of his youth in Silesia, with a profound religious sense of exile from a paradise, return to which may only be possible through death. "Abschied" ("Departure: Ye Woods and Vales of Pleasure," 1815) in its setting by Felix Mendelssohn is one of his best known poems and captures the simple faith evoked by the forest landscape; Richard Strauss's setting of "Im Abendrot" ("At Sunset") perfectly illustrates the understated transparency of nature and transcendence when two weary "wanderers" ask, in the twilight solitude of woods and hills, "Could this perhaps be death?"

In Hardenberg's doctrine of magical idealism, the book of poesy and the book of nature are distinct. The *Wunderhorn* (like its prose successor, Joseph von Görres's collection of German chapbooks, *Die teutschen Volksbücher*, 1807) creates a fantasy of continuity between poetic diction, the language of the "Volk" (understood simultaneously as the simple, such as peasants, soldiers, children, and as the Nation) and the sounds of nature itself. This trumps the idealism of Jena: what art had negotiated as the commerce of spirit and the material world, aided by metaphor (in Friedrich von Schlegel's "Im Walde" ["In the Forest"], for instance) can become a seamless continuum. A poetry that sees itself as an expression of folk-spirit desires poetry as spontaneous as birdsong. The limited diction and narrow thematic range of folksong and its imitations yielded a poetry based on variation. Versifying games were devised in which the elements of a short motto-poem had to be worked into larger, more sophisticated stanzas, but finally it is the acoustic qualities of language that come to dominate.

Clemens Brentano, certainly the most prolific poet of the Romantic period, drives poetic musicality to astonishing extremes, drawing on all the powers of rhyme, assonance, and alliteration, and using medieval sources such as Walther von Klingen for the repetitive acoustic form of "Wie sich auch die Zeit will wenden, enden" ("However Much the Times May Bend, End," 1802). Surprisingly, he also admired Hölderlin in the bowdlerized and simplified versions he knew. In his later work, however, Brentano also begins to recognize that a gap has opened up between self-absorbed poetry and the real world. In highly erotic antilove poems (*Dirnenpoesie*) he faces his own abandonment. He realized that poems that take their life from close relationships among friends and lovers were too frail for the sheer popularity they had gained in print, through almanacs and anthologies. What is still delicately alive in oral performance cannot survive in black and white print. Brentano's response is to conceal personal reflection and meaning in a poetry of pure sound which, in its proverb-like riddling, seems to anticipate the hermetic writing of modernism.

The exhaustion of the whole Romantic repertoire of themes and images is apparent to the last of the Romantic poets in the early years of Klemens Wenzel Nepomuk Lothar Metternich's Restoration. Heine's poetic career struggles to be done with the limited diction and metaphors of the Romantic poem, but he is constantly drawn back to its moonlight world. For many subsequent generations Romantic poetry comes to be the measure of all poetry, by its sense of musicality and sensuous evocation, and its influence is still felt by the great neo-Romantic and modernist poets, such as Hugo von Hofmannsthal and Rainer Maria Rilke, and even Ingeborg Bachmann and Paul Célan.

ANTHONY PHELAN

Selected Works

Anthologies

Gedichte der Romantik. Edited by Wolfgang Frühwald. Stuttgart: Philipp Reclam, 1984.
German Poetry of the Romantic Era. Edited by Osman Durrani. Leamington Spa, England: Oswald Wolf and Berg, 1986.

Translation

German Poetry from 1750 to 1900. The German Library, vol. 39. New York: Continuum, 1984.

Bibliography

Fetzer, John. "Die romantische Lyrik," in *Romantik-Handbuch.* Edited by Helmut Schanze. Stuttgart: Kröner, 1994.
Frühwald, Wolfgang. Einleitung to *Gedichte der Romantik.* Edited by Wolfgang Frühwald. Stuttgart: Philipp Reclam, 1984.
Prawer, S. S., ed. *The Romantic Period in Germany.* London: Weidenfeld and Nicholson, 1970.

POLAND: CULTURAL SURVEY

The majority, if not the entirety, of Polish art and literature produced during the Romantic age must be seen through the prism of the Partitions. Beginning in the early eighteenth century, Poland's three powerful neighbors, Austria, Prussia, and especially Russia, began to chip away at the nation's autonomy. The country was partitioned three times, eventually to disappear in 1795. The loss of independence was a galling trial for a proud nation of strong democratic traditions, and the cultural life of the nation during the nineteenth century is most accurately measured by political upheavals. These include the Napoleonic struggles (from the turn of the century until 1815), the November Uprising (1830–31), less widespread revolts in 1846 and 1848, and the January Uprising of 1863, the year generally accepted as the closing date of the Polish Romantic era.

The lack of a Polish head of state to unify the Poles, now recognized as either Prussian, Austrian, or Russian subjects, led to the development of a curious cult of poets. Logically enough, the great writers of the nineteenth century, the preservers of the Polish cultural tradition, were considered objects of national pride around which to rally politically. In partitioned Poland, Shelley's dictum of the poet as the legislator of mankind was especially apposite, all the more so because they were acknowledged as such.

Three names have dominated the pantheon of Polish letters since the Romantic era. Zygmunt Krasiński, Adam Mickiewicz, and Juliusz Słowacki were, during their lifetimes or shortly thereafter, lauded as national bards, and have been so considered ever since. Mickiewicz is the author of the most influential Central European drama outside of Johann Wolfgang von Goethe's *Faust*. His *Dziady* (*Forefathers' Eve*, 1823–32) played a great role in the development of Polish messianism, the main theme of which was "Poland is the Christ of the nations." He also wrote *Pan Tadeusz* (*Master Thaddeus, or The Last Foray in Lithuania*, 1834), the Polish national epic. Słowacki, his rival, developed a vibrant theatrical tradition heavily influenced by William Shakespeare. Krasiński, the highest-born of the three, was the most socially conservative. His most notable work, *Nieboska komedia* (*Undivine Comedy*, 1835), foresees the class struggles that were to erupt shortly in Europe, and posits that only Christ can bring peace to the insoluble difficulties of modern man. His defence of the social status quo in the *Psalmy przyszlosci* (*Psalms of the Future*, 1845, 1848), greatly angered Słowacki, who was much more democratic in his views, and whose *Król-Duch* (*King Spirit*, 1847), an unfinished epic poem meditating on Polish history, betrays a much more "progressive" take on historical and social issues.

Since the beginning of the twentieth century, Cyprian Kamil Norwid has received much of the same adulation traditionally reserved for the above three poets. His experimental, intellectual lyrics were ahead of their time. Misunderstood by his contemporaries, his elevation in our day and age is not unlike that enjoyed by Gerard Manley Hopkins in English letters.

All four of these writers spent most of their creative years in exile. Other Polish romantics who remained for the most part on Polish territory include Aleksander Fredro, writer of comedies and known as the "Polish Molière," and Józef Ignacy Kraszewski,

a prolific novelist, poet, critic, and publicist whose gigantic cycle of historical novels played a central role in maintaining the cultural and historical memory of the nation.

In music, the name Frédéric Chopin comes immediately to mind. He is to Polish music what Mickiewicz is to Polish poetry, and more, for his compositions, drawing heavily on Polish folk music and traditions, effectively popularized Poland and Poland's cause beyond the country's borders. Henryk Wieniawski was a virtuoso violinist who, during his lifetime, rivaled Niccolò Paganini in popularity. Stanislaw Moniuszko was a talented operatic composer with an uncanny ear for melody. Both his great operas, *Straszny dwor* (*The Haunted Manor*, 1861–64) and *Halka* (1846), have nationalistic and patriotic subtexts. Besides this, his twelve-volume collection of Polish songs, the *Spiewnik domowy* (*Home Songbooks*, 1837–72), popularized both the works of Polish lyricists and indigenous melodic forms, such as the mazurka and the polonaise.

Polish painting of this time was just as eager to represent military themes or political aspirations as was literature and music. January Suchodolski, one of the most popular artists of the period, enjoyed representing battle scenes, especially those of the Napoleonic troops. The same is true of Piotr Michałowski, a former Napoleonic soldier. His canvasses, such as *Somosierra* (1837), are full of the stirring movement of a brave attack. He painted many portraits of all social types and was a famous equestrian painter. His style of quick, urgent strokes looks forward somewhat to the Impressionists. Wojciech Korneli Stattler was a talented academician, whose historical canvasses are similar to those of Nicolas Poussin and Jacques-Louis David. Stattler's *Maccabees* has a political resonance: in it, he boldly draws associations between the ancient Jewish uprising and Polish hopes of independence. The second generation of Polish Romantic painters, including Artur Grottger and Jan Matejko, was also nationally conscious. But while Matejko chose to paint vast murals depicting important scenes from Polish history, such as *King Stefan Batory's Victory Over the Russians at Pskov* (1872), Grottger painted scenes, sometimes in series, describing contemporary events, like the January Uprising and Suvarov's butchery of Praga. Of course, nonpatriotic themes were not neglected. French-born Jean-Pierre Norblin popularized the *fête galante* in Poland; Jan Nepomucen Głowacki created awesome views of the Tatra mountains, some in the style of Caspar David Friedrich; and Józef Szermentowski was Poland's first and most successful painter of landscapes which, until his advent, had been used only as backgrounds and never as subjects in themselves.

Polish sculptors of the Romantic age achieved fame both at home and abroad. Kazimierz Jelski, a pupil of Le Brun, carved portraits. Ludwik Kaufman and Jakub Tartarkiewicz worked with allegorical figures in such works as Kaufman's *Rivers Vistula and Bug* and Tartarkiewicz's *Caritas Romana* and *Motherhood*. Oskar Sosnowski's statue of the Jesuit preacher Piotr Skarga is one of the most famous religious sculptures in Poland. Władyslaw Oleszczyński, who, like Jelski, studied abroad (under David d'Angers), was commissioned to sculpt figures for the tomb of Napoleon, among them the allegorical *Reception of the Polish Emigrants by France*.

The Romantic movement in architecture, and especially the English neo-Gothic style, had an effect on Polish construction. Adam Idźkowski rebuilt the cathedral in Warsaw according to the perpendicular style. In Kraków, the Collegium Maius, the oldest building of the university where both Nicholaus Copernicus and Johann Heinrich Faust studied, was covered over with a neo-Gothic exterior by the Austrians; only in the twentieth century was it stripped away to reveal the original medieval walls. Christian Piotr Aigner favored a more neo-classical style (as in his St. Aleksander's Church in Warsaw, modeled on the Pantheon in Paris). Henryk Marconi adapted the styles of his native Italy (Palazzo Pitti, for example) for his structures in Poland, whereas Franciszek Maria Lanci was the first to introduce iron and more modern forms into his designs.

With the failure of the January Uprising, revolutionism—and Romanticism—come to an end in Poland. The rest of the nineteenth century was given over to building a stable industrial and economic infrastructure for the day when independence should return to the banks of the Vistula River. In terms of culture, this meant a turning away from idealism and passion, patriotic or otherwise, and an emphasis on the practical. From Romanticism, we enter into the periods of positivism and realism, the battle cries of which were patience, steadfastness, and "organic work."

CHARLES S. KRASZEWSKI

Bibliography

Coleman, Marion Moore. *Polish Literature in English Translations: A Bibliography*. Cheshire, Conn.: Cherry Hill Books, 1963.
Davies, Norman. *God's Playground: a History of Poland*. New York: Columbia University Press, 1982.
Faczyński, Jerzy. *Studies in Polish Architecture*. Liverpool: Liverpool University Press, 1946.
Jarociński, Stefan. *Polish Music*. Warsaw: PWN, 1965.
Klimaszewski, Bolesław, ed. *An Outline History of Polish Culture*. Warsaw: Interpress/Jagiellonian University, 1984.
Kraszewski, Charles S. *The Romantic Hero and Contemporary Anti-Hero in Polish and Czech Literature: Great Souls and Grey Men*. Lewiston: Edwin Mellen Press, 1997.
Kridl, Manfred. *A Survey of Polish Literature and Culture*. The Hague: Mouton, 1956.
Krzyżanowski, Julian. *Polish Romantic Literature*. London: Allen and Unwin, 1930.
Miłosz, Czesław. *A History of Polish Literature*. Berkeley and Los Angeles: University of California Press, 1983.
Morawińska, Agnieszka. *Polish Painting: Fifteenth to Twentieth Century*. Warsaw: Auriga, 1984.
Peterkiewicz, Jerzy. *Five Centuries of Polish Poetry, 1450–1950*. Oxford: Oxford University Press, 1970.
Reiss, J. W. *Mała historia muzyki*. Kraków: PWM, 1987.
Śmiałek, William. *Polish Music: A Research and Information Guide*. New York: Garland Press, 1989.
Zarnecki, Jerzy. *Polish Art*. Birkenhead: Polish Publications Committee, 1945.

POLAND: HISTORICAL SURVEY

By 1795, the three major partitions of Poland (among Russia, Austria, and Prussia) had erased the country from the map of Europe. So it is no surprise that the Romantic era in Poland was dominated by an armed, and simultaneously cultural, struggle for national reestablishment. Polish artists, musicians, writers, and intellectuals were overwhelmingly committed to sustaining a national sense of identity and history.

Poland entered the span of European history in 965, when Mieszko I married the Czech princess Dubrava, with the approbation of Emperor Otto I. One year later, the entry of Poland into the Latin-rite church took place. From that time on, Poland was never absent from the European stage. In 1014, Canute, son of Swein Forkbeard, king of Denmark, and his Polish queen, Świętosława (Mieszko's daughter), conquered England with a force that included three hundred Polish lancers. The early pietist dynasty made Poland a force to be reckoned with east of the Oder, while during the Renaissance, the Jagiellonians turned the eyes of Poland eastward toward Lithuania. Eventually, with the political union of Poland and Lithuania in the sixteenth century, the commonwealth became the largest state, territorially, in Europe. Trade with the west flourished: the English word *spruce* is of Polish derivation: it is a corruption of the Polish *z Prus*, or "from Prussia," a tag attached to the timber sent out of the Baltic ports of northern Poland for cities along the southern English shoreline. Poland long defended the bulwark of Christianity against the expansion efforts of the Ottoman Turks. It was a Polish king, Jan III Sobieski, who lifted the Turkish siege of Vienna in 1683, turning back the last great wave of Muslim expansion in Europe.

Despite the strength of Polish arms and trade, the widespread aristocratodemocratic traditions of the commonwealth inhibited the strong, centralized type of monarchy necessary for the creation of a modern state. Most destructive was the practice of *liberum veto*, whereby any noble might rise in the parliament and, with a single "I disagree," shelve the most important and necessary legislation proposed by that body. Although it would be overly simplistic to attribute the fall of Poland to this alone, this weakness was exploited by Poland's neighbors, and as early as 1717 Poland found its sovereignty greatly diminished by legislative dependence on Russia. From then on, Poland's status as a distinct national entity was continually weakened and threatened. The Confederation of Bar, an armed rebellion of 1771–72 against Russian influence, led by Kazimierz Pułaski, among others, resulted in the First Partition of Poland among Prussia, Austria, and Russia. Poland was further reduced, by over 50 percent, in 1793 after a war with Russia in defense of the Constitution of May 3. Three years later, after an heroic but desperate insurrection led by American Revolutionary War hero Tadeusz Kościuszko, the Polish state was partitioned one more time between the three empires, and disappeared entirely from the map of Europe.

Very few Poles were willing to accept their new status as Austrian, Prussian, or Russian subjects. The Romantic era in Poland was to be a struggle for national survival, and much of the country was to become a battlefield. Polish soldiers and officers swelled the ranks of foreign armies: sometimes, as in the case of the troops of Colonel Denisko, for the simple reason of wanting to fight against the partitioning government of Austria on the side of the Turks. Others, like the Polish legions of Jan Henryk Dąbrowski, battled alongside French troops in the hope of eventually marching into Poland with Napoleon Bonaparte.

Most Poles clung to Napoleon as a last hope. But, despite their fierce devotion and superb battle record, Napoleon's interest in the Polish cause was to prove equivocal, to say the least. Indeed, he allowed the formation of the Grand Duchy of Warsaw in 1807 to placate the Poles, who had fought and died at his side on all the battlefields of Europe, yet he exploited this fief mercilessly to forward his own war effort. Also, when to his advantage, he made treaties with his (and Poland's) enemies prejudicial to the Poles. Such treaties included those of Campo Formio (1797) and Lunéville (1801); at both, Napoleon agreed to terms favorable to Austria.

Although they never refused their aid to Napoleon's France—indeed, half of the military guard allowed him in his exile on Elba was made up of Polish lancers—the Poles learned by bitter experience that independence for their homeland could only arise from their own efforts. This was made evident by the failure of the so-called Congress Kingdom, set up by the European heads of state following Napoleon's defeat in 1815. A semiautonomous "kingdom" under the scepter of Russian tsar Alexander I, it was formally dissolved by this "liberal" ruler in 1820 when he found that he could not stomach the democratic traditions of a country he had sworn to uphold. Ten years of legislative oppression and attempts at the Russification of the country boiled over in the November Uprising of 1830. Successful raids on the Belvedere Palace (seat of the tsarist viceroy) and the Russian cavalry barracks in Warsaw led to a general insurrection that drove the Russians out of Poland for over a year. Successful military campaigns by ex-Napoleonic officers and troops, strengthened by whole regiments of volunteers from all over Europe as well as Poland itself, increased hopes for a successful revolution. However, missed opportunities and poor tactics by the somewhat defeatist General Jan Skrzynecki allowed the Russians to recoup their strengths. Eventually, the Uprising came to an end in the autumn of 1831. Nicholas I, the new tsar, began a brutal campaign of Russification at the conclusion of hostilities, abolishing the Polish parliament (Sejm), closing Polish institutions of higher education, empowering a new cadre of Russian administrators, and distributing the confiscated estates of Polish families among Russian officers and bureaucrats. The impact of the failed uprising on Polish cultural life was enormous, with many Polish artists and intellectuals (among them Adam Mickiewicz and Frédéric Chopin) emigrating, particularly to Paris, which became the main center of Polish émigré culture and nationalism.

Poland lay exhausted and dormant for the next fifteen years. A failed uprising in Galicia, the Austrian partition of Poland, in 1846 led to a massacre of the Polish nobility in the eastern marches by the Ukrainian peasantry, abetted by the government itself. Then, two years later, the Spring of the Peoples (the revolutions of 1848), which shook all Europe, affected Poland as well. Initial revolutionary successes were noted in the Prussian-held Grand Duchy of Poznań and the Republic of Kraków in the Austrian sphere of influence. However, the stronger empires again prevailed. Kraków and Lwów were bombarded into sub-

mission in November 1848, and the last vestiges of even nominal autonomy in these two regions were summarily erased.

Polish political life, which for most of the nineteenth century had been centered in émigré groupings in Paris and various British cities, flourished again toward midcentury in the so-called *Koło rolnicze*, or Agricultural Society. Originally concerned with the reformation of matters affecting the peasantry and landed aristocracy in a country which had traditionally been agricultural, the movement began to assume, in the words of historian Adam Zamoyski, the stature of a de facto Polish Sejm. This, of course, was not a development that an autocratic tsar might sanction. In the winter of 1861, fearing another uprising, the government of the Russian sector began a policy of arresting suspects. Patriotic meetings were dispersed, a religious procession was attacked (leaving five dead), and martial law was established in the entire territory held by the Russians. Another precautionary measure, the selective conscription of "troublemakers" into the Russian army, was to set off the last major insurrection of the Romantic era, the January Uprising.

Even before the conscription, in the spring and summer of 1862, a Polish underground state had been established by a revolutionary group known as the "Reds," who were planning a nationwide insurrection. When the Russians got wind of this and quelled it before it could get off the ground, other, more prudent patriots, known as the "Whites," took over the task of preparing the insurrection they were earlier opposed to, and on January 22, 1863, at a signal from the National Committee, the nation rose again. However, despite the best of wills and further help from volunteers from Italy, Ireland, England, France, and Germany, the January Uprising died on the vine. Help from abroad, except for these volunteers and a joint protest signed by the governments of Britain, France, and Austria, was not forthcoming. In March of 1864 the tsar deprived the Poles of the support of the peasantry by beating them to the emancipation of the serfs and dispensing generous land grants. Faced with little hope of success, the Poles surrendered. The kingdom of Poland became the Russian Province of the Vistula, and the Romantic age in Poland came to an end. Further attempts by the Russians to stamp out the Polish national character were to be met with quiet educational initiatives and efforts toward preparing a strong economic infrastructure against the day when the country should be reunited and free. This is the program of "organic work," and it belongs not to Romanticism, but to the positivist period.

CHARLES S. KRASZEWSKI

Bibliography

Cegielski, Tadeusz, and Łukasz, Kądziela. *Rozbiory Polski: 1772, 1793, 1795*. Warsaw: WSP, 1990.

Davies, Norman. *God's Playground: A History of Poland*. New York: Columbia University Press, 1982.

Goddeeris, Idesbald. "The First Years of Belgian Alien Policy: Decentralization Measures and Government Relief for Polish Refugees in the 1830's," *Polish Review* 45, no. 1 (2000): 65–96.

Kalembka, Sławomir. *Powstanie styczniowe 1863–1864*. Warsaw: PWN, 1990.

Kallas, Marian. "Le système administratif du Duché de Varsovie," *Canadian Slavonic Papers* 19, no. 3 (1975): 259 ff.

Kowalski, Józef. *Die russische revolutionäre und der Warschauer Aufstand 1863*. Berlin: Rütten u. Loening, 1954.

Kutolowski, John F. "Polish Exiles and British Public Opinion: a Case Study of 1861–62." *Canadian Slavonic Papers* 21, no. 1 (1977).

Szczaniecki, Kazimierz. *Pamiętnik: Wielkopolska i powstanie styczniowe we wspomnieniach galicyjskiego ziemianina.* Poznań: Poznańskiego Towarzystwa Przyjaciół Nauk, 1995.

Serejski, Marian Henryk. *Europa a rozbiory Polski.* Warsaw: PWN, 1970.

Stanley, John. "The French Residents in the Duchy of Warsaw," *Canadian Slavonic Papers* 21, no. 1 (1983).

Stone, Daniel. "The End of Medieval Particularism: Polish Cities and the Diet, 1764–1789," *Canadian Slavonic Papers* 25, no. 4 (1986).

———. "The First (and Only) Year of the May 3 Constitution," *Canadian Slavonic Papers* 35, nos. 1–2 (1993): 69–86.

Zajewski, Władysław. *Powstanie listopadowe: 1830–1831.* Warsaw: PWN, 1980.

Zamoyski, Jan. *The Polish Way: A Thousand-Year History of the Poles and Their Culture.* London: John Murray, 1987.

POLIDORI, JOHN WILLIAM 1795–1821

English fiction writer, poet, and physician

The years of John William Polidori's life exactly coincide with John Keats's. He was Catholic, handsome, and hot-tempered, given to fits of vanity and anger, and ruinously attracted to gambling: his short life ended when he committed suicide in his father's house. He tried different professions and wrote in several different areas, but is best known for his tumultuous relationship with Lord Byron, and his tale of terror, "The Vampyre."

Polidori's diverse interests are evident from the start of his career. His first sustained work was a poetic tragedy, *Count Orlando; or, The Modern Abraham*, which he wrote at seventeen years of age and published as *Ximenes* (1819). The play featured an oriental setting, a gloomy and fated hero, and several overheated scenes of violence, seduction, and remorse. It exploited the contemporary vogue for exotic verse tales, and drew most clearly on Lord Byron's *Giaour* (1813). Polidori's 1815 Edinburgh doctoral thesis on somnambulism concerned itself primarily with questions of memory and perception in sleepwalkers, and earned him his medical degree at the unusually early age of nineteen. While looking for the opportunity to pursue his medical career, however, he turned his thoughts to the law, and wrote an essay, "On the Punishment of Death" (1816), in which he argued that capital punishment was unfair and ineffective.

In the spring of 1816, Polidori's life changed irrevocably when he became personal physician to Byron, who was leaving England for the Continent after the disastrous collapse of his marriage. Byron's publisher John Murray offered Polidori £500 to write an account of the tour. Byron and Polidori left England in late April and settled at the Villa Diodati on Lake Geneva, where they were daily in the company of Claire Clairmont, Mary Godwin (later Shelley), and Percy Bysshe Shelley. Polidori's *Diary* provides perhaps the most vivid account of the life of this remarkable group. On June 18 he recorded that "Mrs. S[helley] called me her brother," and later that same day Byron "repeated some verses of Coleridge's *Christabel*" which caused Percy to run "shrieking . . . out of the room" because he had suddenly recalled "a woman he had heard of who had eyes instead of nipples." Polidori threw water in his face "and after gave him ether." Yet Polidori never became an intimate member of the Byron/Shelley circle. He alienated Mary, was the butt of Byron's jokes, and soon became jealous of Percy. His arrogance and quick temper only exacerbated the situation. When Percy beat him in a sailing race he "threatened to shoot" him. By the middle of September Byron had had enough, and Polidori was dismissed.

Sometime during the course of the summer, though, Polidori fictionalized the complicated and unsatisfactory nature of his relationship with Byron in one of the most famous tales of terror of all time. "The Vampyre" was a product of the same ghost story competition at the Villa Diodati that produced Mary Shelley's *Frankenstein*, and Polidori acknowledged that it was based in part on an unfinished prose fragment by Byron entitled "Augustus Darvell." There had been earlier appearances of vampires in English literature, but Polidori was the first to recognize the much greater potential of the myth. He reworked the conventional figure of the upper-class rake, giving him new resources for seduction and making him even more fatally attractive. More crucially, he transformed the foul-smelling ghoul of earlier vampiric mythology into the wealthy and mobile aristocrat whose violence and sexual allure made him, literally, a lady-killer. The result was a tale of guilt, paralysis, wish fulfilment, and entrapment in which the worshipful Aubrey's enthrallment to Lord Ruthven has often been read as Polidori's projection of his own passive submission to the dominating presence of Lord Byron. Yet in true vampiric fashion, Polidori also resisted Byron, borrowing the name Ruthven from Caroline Lamb's recent unflattering portrait of him in her novel *Glenarvon* (1816), and adopting a detached attitude toward his villain that was sometimes condemnatory and sometimes ironic. "The Vampyre" did not appear until 1819, when an unscrupulous publisher issued it under Byron's name as yet another installment in a long line of lurid self-dramatizations that had included, most recently, *Manfred* (1817). Polidori's authorship, however, was soon established. His tale touched off a vampire craze that even today shows no signs of diminishing.

"The Vampyre" was not Polidori's only response to the 1816 ghost story competition. His only full-length novel, *Ernestus Berchtold; or The Modern Oedipus*, was begun that same summer and, as its subtitle suggested, explicitly concerned incest. Ernestus is a Swiss soldier and a veteran of the Napoleonic Wars who ends up marrying his own sister. Byron again featured as a sophisticated rake, this time an Italian name Olivieri, who is saved by Ernestus but ends up corrupting him in a relationship that strongly parallels Aubrey's with Ruthven (and, Polidori felt, his own with Byron). There are supernatural spirits and a Faustian pact, and Polidori modified several episodes from his own past, including his travels through Switzerland and Italy and those scenes which detailed Ernestus's devastating gambling habit. The novel has much in common with other work produced at this time by the ghost story competitors, from Shelley's *The Revolt of Islam* to Byron's *Manfred* and Mary Shelley's *Frankenstein*, but it has never achieved anything like their popularity.

Polidori concluded his career with three very different works. In 1817 he again drew on his experiences as a traveler to write the text for R. Bridgens's *Sketches Illustrative of the Manners and Costumes of France, Switzerland, and Italy* (1821). In *An Essay upon the Source of Positive Pleasure* (1818) he incorporated various elements of his Edinburgh education to distinguish between positive and absolute pleasure, and to argue that, strictly defined, positive pleasure was always unattainable. Finally, in *The Fall of the Angels: A Sacred Poem* (1821), Polidori inevitably borrowed from John Milton's handling of the same theme, though he introduced a variety of twists, including the reason the angels rebelled, and who defeated them when they fell. Polidori's forte, however, was terror fiction, and his fame rests on having introduced Romanticism's most glamorous and successful monster.

ROBERT MORRISON

Biography

Born in London on September 7, 1795, the eldest son of a distinguished Italian scholar. Educated at Ampleforth, a Catholic college near York, 1804–11; attended medical school at the University of Edinburgh, 1811–15; became Lord Byron's personal physician and travelling companion; present at the famous ghost story competition at the Villa Diodati on Lake Geneva, 1816; traveled in Italy; established medical practice in Norwich, 1817. "The Vampyre" and *Ernestus Berchtold* both published 1819. Admitted to Lincoln's Inn to study law, 1820; *The Fall of the Angels: A Sacred Poem* published 1821. Committed suicide on August 24, 1821.

Selected Works

Collection

The Vampyre and Ernestus Berchtold; or The Modern Oedipus: Collected Fiction of John William Polidori. Edited by D. L. Macdonald and Kathleen Scherf. Toronto: University of Toronto Press, 1994.

Nonfiction

"On the Punishment of Death." 1818.
An Essay upon the Source of Positive Pleasure. 1818.

Fiction

Ernestus Berchtold; or The Modern Oedipus. 1819.
The Vampyre: A Tale. 1819.
Ximenes, The Wreath, and Other Poems. 1819.
The Fall of the Angels: A Sacred Poem. 1821.
Sketches Illustrative of the Manners and Costumes of France, Switzerland, and Italy (with Richard Bridgens). 1821.
The Diary of Dr. John William Polidori, 1816, Relating to Byron, Shelley, etc. Edited and elucidated by William Michael Rossetti. London: Elkin Mathews, 1911.

Bibliography

Astle, Richard Sharp. "Ontological Ambiguity and Historical Pessimism in Polidori's *The Vampyre*," *Sphinx* 2 (1977), 8–16.
Auerbach, Nina. *Our Vampires, Ourselves.* Chicago: University of Chicago Press, 1995.
Barbour, Judith. "Dr. John William Polidori, Author of *The Vampyre*," in *Imagining Romanticism: Essays on English and Australian Romanticism.* Edited by Deidre Coleman and Peter Otto. West Cornwall, Conn.: Locust Hill Press, 1992.
Frayling, Christopher, ed. *Vamyres: Lord Byron to Count Dracula.* London: Faber, 1991.
Gelder, Ken. *Reading the Vampire.* London: Routledge, 1994.
Grudin, Peter D. *The Demon Lover.* New York: Garland, 1987.
Macdonald, D. L. *Poor Polidori: A Critical Biography of the Author of The Vampyre.* Toronto: University of Toronto Press, 1991.
Rieger, James. "Dr. Polidori and the Genesis of *Frankenstein*," in *Studies in English Literature* 3 (1963): 461–72.
Senf, Carol. *The Vampire in Nineteenth-Century English Literature.* Bowling Green, Ohio: Bowling Green State University Press, 1988.
Stuart, Roxana. *Stage Blood: Vampires of the 19th-Century Stage.* Bowling Green, Ohio: Bowling Green State University Press, 1994.
Switzer, Richard. "Lord Ruthven and the Vampires," in *The French Review* pp. 107–112 29 (1955).
Twitchell, James. *The Living Dead: A Study of the Vampire in Romantic Literature.* Durham, N.C.: Duke University Press, 1981.

POLITICAL THOUGHT

Romanticism was necessarily political, for its ideas on the absolute and subjectivity naturally produce certain consistent ideas about the principles of ideal societies. Important aspects of Romantic political ideology include: liberty and liberation; revolution and resistance against oppression; the sanctity of selfhood and identity; national identity; and the aspiration for universal harmony achieved through the collective transcendent experiences of individuals. However, Romantic political thought eludes clear definition because Romanticism does not beget clear political systems or clearly identifiable political thinkers (most would call themselves poets first). To complicate matters, Romantic ideological drives often manifest themselves in ironically competing and conflicting ways. Finally, the encounter of Romantic ideology with the realities of political events would ultimately lead to bitterness, disillusionment, and alienation from politics.

Political events are often used to establish the timeframe of Romanticism. Romanticism could not have been what it was without the French Revolution, and thus Romantic political thought begins in the wake of the revolutionary hopes of 1789. The largely failed Revolutions of 1848 effectively mark the end of anything that might be called "political Romanticism," and even before this time many of the revolutionaries had become the reactionaries of this later age. Between these two points we find the rise and fall of Napoleon (the dominant political persona of the Romantic era), the Russian Decembrist uprising of 1825, the French revolution of 1830, and the struggles for liberation in Spain, Greece, and Poland.

The Romantics embraced calls for liberty and brotherhood, and their reaction to the ideology of the French Revolution was generally favorable. The Romantics had been adolescents at the time of the Revolution, and the zeal of youth carried over into their early mature attitudes. In *Athenaeum Fragment* 216, Friedrich Schlegel writes, "The French Revolution, Fichte's philosophy, and Goethe's *Meister* are the greatest tendencies of the age." However, one cannot isolate a simplistic association of the spirit of the French Revolution with the spirit of Romanticism. A number of Romantics, notably Schlegel and William Wordsworth, turned away from the Revolution and were disillusioned by the excesses of the 1790s. In many respects the "political" thought of Romanticism reacted against the idea of politics itself. Despite the fact that Romanticism had more continuity with the Enlightenment than the Romantics themselves would admit, the notion of politics was associated with rationalism and self-interest, and by extension with such figures as Jeremy Bentham and Adam Smith. The Romantic idea of a universal society implied the need to progress beyond politics and into new condition, a transcendent state often characterized in aesthetic terms. In one of the most comprehensive statements of early German Romanticism, Novalis's "Christendom or Europe" (1799) argues that accepting the political idea of "Europe" impedes progress into a harmonious universal society, and for Novalis the French Revolution is an adolescent stage in the world's maturing. Instead of accepting the idea of Europe, humanity should strive to (re)establish the idea of Christendom, a universal world unified by its heeding of the subjective internal "organic spark" and its collective pursuit of the absolute.

In numerous cases Romantics poeticized the political, a statement made by themselves and their detractors. Schlegel wrote in *Ideas* (1800) that one should not "waste your faith and love on the political world" and should instead "offer up your inmost being in a fiery stream of eternal creation," and he asserted that the greatest need of the age was "a spiritual counterweight" to the Revolution and to its despotism rooted in self-interest. For Schlegel, as for Novalis and Friedrich Schleiermacher, the new world culture was to be founded on religion, and by extension poetry and philosophy. In England, William Blake and Wordsworth composed long poetic works in which liberty is a dominant theme. Both also engaged in a poeticization of politics in their treatment of marginalized and oppressed figures, and an implicitly political statement appears in Wordsworth's poeticization of the rustics who populate his works and their speech. His "Simon Lee, the Old Huntsman" (1798), for example, describes the plight of a man stooped by a life of excessive labor and burdened by inescapable poverty: "And now he's forced to work, though weak—The weakest in the village." Blake composed some of the earliest portraits of an oppressed urban underclass in lyrics such as "Holy Thursday," "The Chimney Sweeper," and "London" from the *Songs of Experience* (1794). In "London" we read,

> I wander thro' each charter'd street.
> Near where the charter'd Thames does flow
> And mark in every face I meet
> Marks of weakness, marks of woe.

An indictment of dreadful economic exploitation also appeared in the visual arts, perhaps most famously in J. M. W. Turner's *The Slave Ship* (1840) in which slaves are being tossed overboard in a storm, their blood mingling with the turbulent waves.

In subsequent years, more expansive and grandiose statements on liberty and brotherhood were expressed. In a gesture metaphorically capturing the Romantic ambivalence to the French Revolution and to Napoleon—the larger-than-life hero of a world liberated from monarchy—Ludwig van Beethoven dedicated his Third Symphony to Napoleon Bonaparte and then furiously recanted after Napoleon invaded Austria. Later, as his Ninth Symphony culminates in majestic triumph, an added prefatory line to Friedrich Schiller's "Ode to Joy" calls for universal brotherhood to replace discord: "O friends, not these sounds! Rather let us tune our voices more pleasantly and more joyously." Romanticism also produced the most recognizable rendering of liberty in the visual arts, Eugène Delacroix's *Liberty Leading the People* (1830). The allegorical rendering of Liberty summons the street urchin, the bourgeois, and the proletarian as she strides boldly into the revolutionary struggle. The canvas also depicts the violence and loss associated with Romantic revolution, and Delacroix extends the allegory as Liberty steps over the bodies of the fallen and into the foreground.

In the 1820s Romantic thought often focused on liberation, and the spirit of liberation was simultaneously bound to evolving Romantic ideas of the nation. By this later period Romantics no longer expressed the politics of a unified world, but rather emphasized the need for national self-determination. Thus Romanticism, which had earlier spawned the universality of Novalis, now generated various forms of nationalism. A number of figures projected the Romantic emphasis on identity and selfhood to national identity, and in Greece and Poland, which had fallen prey to imperialist expansion, the quest for selfhood commingled with the Romantic spirit of the people to generate a culture of rebellion and independence. In Poland this atmosphere was further combined with the Romantic poet-messiah to produce the cultural phenomenon of poets seen as those who would deliver the oppressed nation into a new, free era. Adam Mickiewicz's *Forefathers' Eve*, (1823) exemplifies this trend as it emphasizes the collective memory of the nation's history and prophesies a restored and free Poland. The Greek struggle for liberation attracted attention throughout Europe, and it inspired two especially famous statements of poeticized politics: Delacroix's *Greece on the Ruins of Missolonghi*, (1826), an allegory and a tragic obverse to his *Liberty*; and Byron's "On This Day I Complete My Thirty-sixth Year" (1824), written in the fields of Missolonghi. Making his life from the art of poeticized politics, Byron traveled to Missolonghi in order to participate in the cause of liberation, and he would soon meet his death there. In "On This Day" he writes,

> The sword, the banner, and the field,
> Glory and Greece, around me see!
> The Spartan, borne upon his shield,
> Was not more free.

One also finds similar sentiments in Francisco José de Goya's politically charged *The Third of May 1808* (1814), painted in honor of the Spanish War of Liberation. The canvas depicts the horrific scene of a French firing squad executing a group of men before a grieving crowd.

In the established and independent nations of Russia and France, the politics of Romanticism played significant roles in uprisings against governments seen as authoritarian and oppressive: the Decembrist rebellion of 1825 and France's July Revolution of 1830. The Russian rebellion had modest goals, the most important being a call for a constitution. The poets Vilgelm Kyukhelbeker and Kondratii Ryleev, and Alexandr Bestuzhev-Marlinskii, one of Russia's first successful prose authors, were among the rebellion's collaborators and suffered execution or exile when Tsar Nicholas I quashed the rebellion.

One should also realize that the spirit of Romanticism conversely begat strong political support for established nations and even for reactionary nationalism. During the Napoleonic campaigns, poets and artists celebrated the heroism of their own nation. In the French visual arts, war and paintings of Napoleon himself were a standard of the age. In appropriate contrast, the defeat of Napoleon and France aroused artistic and poetic sentiment in Russia and England.

Any sense of Romantic political sentiment waned in the 1830s and 1840s. Heinrich Heine's writings during his Parisian exile comprised a valediction for mystical Romanticism and anticipated the emergence of the next trend in revolutionary politics, the most certainly post-Romantic trends of Friedrich Engels, Karl Marx, and the "Left Hegelians." More centrist political attitudes would soon be dominated by more traditionally "politi-cal" thinkers such as John Stuart Mill. In literature, the age of the poet would yield to the age of the novelist, and the literary portraiture of the underclass evolved from the lyrics of Blake to the novels of Charles Dickens.

ANDREW SWENSEN

Bibliography

Baker, Keith, Colin Lucas, and François Furet, eds. *The French Revolution and the Creation of Modern Political Culture.* Vols. 1–4. Oxford: Oxford University Press, 1987–1994.

Beiser, Frederick C., ed. *The Early Political Writings of the German Romantics.* Cambridge: Cambridge University Press, 1996.

Blake, William. *America: A Prophecy* and *Europe: A Prophecy.* In *The Lambeth Prophecies.* Princeton, N.J.: Princeton University Press, 1994.

Dann, O., and J. Dinwiddy, eds. *Nationalism in the Age of the French Revolution.* Ronceverte: Hambledon, 1988.

Dickinson, H. T., ed. *Britain and the French Revolution.* London: 1989.

Heine, Heinrich. *Selected Prose.* Translated by Ritchie Robertson. New York: Penguin, 1993.

Izenberg, Gerald. *Impossible Individuality: Romanticism, Revolution, and the Origins of Modern Selfhood, 1787–1802.* Princeton, N.J.: Princeton University Press, 1992.

Wordsworth, William. *The Prelude,* books 9 and 10. In *Poetical Works.* Oxford: Oxford University Press, 1961.

PORTRAITURE: BRITAIN

In a society that was experiencing rapid commercial growth and an expanding middle class with money to spend on luxury goods, portraits provided sitters with a means of asserting social status. In late eighteenth-century Britain, portraiture predominated over other genres, subverting the academic hierarchy which placed history painting higher than portraiture, landscape, and still-life. Portraits gained new audiences and outnumbered other genres at the exhibiting societies founded in the 1760s, including the Society of Artists and the Royal Academy. For artists, portraiture was an economic necessity; there was simply more demand for portraits than for history painting. Beyond the capturing of physiognomic likeness, eighteenth-century portraiture is understood to have constituted a system whereby the social status of the sitter was rendered visible through pose, setting, costume, scale, and the treatment, or "style," of a given artist. During this period, portraits increasingly demonstrated an interest in manifesting the psychological character, thoughts, and feelings of the sitter, following the Romantic cults of emotionality and the individual. William Hazlitt registered this view of portraiture in asserting for it the status of "a *bonafide* art" and adding that "that is the best portrait which contains the fullest representation of human nature."

As well as oil on canvas, portraits took the form of miniatures, pastels, and prints. The latter were particularly vital to the portrait business. The publication of James Granger's *Biographical History of England, from Egbert the Great to the Revolution* in 1769 initiated a craze for portrait collecting. Many artists recognized the importance of prints for disseminating their work and commissioned engravings or mezzotints after their own paintings. Joshua Reynolds kept a portfolio of prints after his own portraits in his studio for his sitters to peruse. Most portrait painters, with the exception of Thomas Gainsborough, operated studios with assistants. Sitters came to have their faces painted by the artist, and their bodies and costume were completed later by the artist and his assistants. As well as assistants, artists were dependent on a network of other trades, including color men (who made the paints), frame makers, and engravers. Because they purchased their canvases ready-stretched and primed, the sizes of portraits were standardized: for a single sitter, the choice of canvas consisted of the "kit-cat" (usually used for life-sized portraits showing the sitter's head and shoulders), the half-length, the three-quarter length, and the full-length. Portraits could depict single or multiple sitters. The price of a portrait was based on its size and the number of figures depicted, as well as on the skill and reputation of the painter.

Portraits tended to be composed as types, wherein certain themes pertaining to Romantic thought can be discerned, particularly in the three-quarter and full-length portraits, that offered a greater range of possibilities for pose and settings. Historical portraits were particularly significant during the earlier part of this period, when the artist's status was uncertain and the portrait painter was particularly concerned to claim portraiture's intellectual qualities. The artist primarily responsible for elevating the status of both portraits and portraitists was Joshua Reynolds. Attempting to elevate portraiture to the level of history painting, he appropriated poses and themes from antiquity, often dressing his female sitters in pseudoclassical robes, as in his *Three Ladies Adorning a Term of Hymen (The Montgomery Sisters)* (1765). Although capable of intimate characterizations, Reynolds's portraiture is generally deemed too intellectual to be termed Romantic. The exception, *Sarah Siddons as the Tragic Muse* (1784), combines references to classical figures and Michelangelo's Sistine ceiling with a representation of genius and melancholy. The portrait was recognized by its contemporaries to be a sublime representation of the sensibility of the tragic actress, capturing the character as well as the features of the sitter.

The placement of subjects in a landscape setting was another type that served to amplify the sensibility of the sitter. Thomas Gainsborough's approach, particularly in the late 1770s and 1780s, captured the mood and personality of his subject, often fusing the figure with its landscape background by employing the same fluid, flickering brushstrokes to denote hair, lace, leaves, and sky. A subgenre of this type portrayed men engaged in intellectual pursuits in open landscape, such as Joseph Wright of Derby's portrait of Sir Brooke Boothby, the English editor of Jean-Jacques Rousseau's *Dialogues*, deep in contemplation in a forest setting (1781). The use of the landscape setting to dramatize the sitter reached its apogee in the portraits of Thomas Lawrence, who often employed a low viewpoint to bring the viewer into close contact with the sitter, setting his subject against turbulent skies. Lawrence was the ultimate Romantic portraitist, possessed with the ability to render the sensitivity of his own response to the sitter through his skill in the manipulation of paint. Portraits like his *Elizabeth Farren, Later Countess of Derby* (1790) capture character while adding glamour to the subject with glittering and bravura renderings of the details and textures of costume. Children were also often portrayed in landscape settings, the depiction of nature referencing the cult of innocence which characterized the period's "rediscovery" of childhood.

Military portraiture appealed both to the heroic imagination and the interest in contemporary events which has also been seen as one of the strains of the Romantic movement. Portraits of men in military attire, such as the Scottish painter Henry Raeburn's portrait *Captain Patrick Miller* (1788), tend to show their subjects sternly posed against somber skies, marking the gravity and the grandeur of their roles. John Singleton Copley's modern history paintings, such as the *Siege of Gibraltar* (1783–91) were based on extensive portrait studies of their participants, and appealed to the Romantic sensibility for both the historical accuracy sought after and the intense interest in the emotional responses of the paintings' subjects.

With the passing of the "golden age" of Gainsborough, Reynolds, and George Romney, portrait painting entered something of a decline, particularly after the death in 1830 of Lawrence, the preeminent portraitist of the Regency period. Society portraiture in the 1830s and 1840s was dominated by George Hayter, the official painter to Queen Victoria, who produced a number of large group portraits depicting the monarch's coronation, marriage, and the christening of her first son. Edwin Landseer, known for his painting of animals and genre scenes, also painted an intimate portrait of the royal family, *Windsor Castle in Modern Times* (1841–45), which harked back to the eighteenth-century tradition of conversation pieces. Beginning in the 1850s, portraiture would be revitalized by the pre-Raphaelite painters.

ELEANOR SIAN HUGHES

Bibliography

Asleson, Robin, ed. *A Passion for Performance: Sarah Siddons and Her Portraitists.* Los Angeles: J. Paul Getty Museum, 1999.

Pointon, Marcia. *Hanging the Head: Portraiture and Social Formation in Eighteenth-Century England.* New Haven, Conn.: Yale University Press, 1993.

Reynolds, Joshua. *Discourses on Art.* Edited by Robert R. Wark. New Haven, Conn.: Yale University Press, 1997.

Romantic Art in Britain, Paintings and Drawings 1760–1860. Philadelphia: Philadelphia Museum of Art, 1968.

Treherz, Julian. *Victorian Painting.* London: Thames and Hudson, 1993.

Tscherny, Nadia. "Likeness in Early Romantic Portraiture," *Art Journal* 46, no. 3 (1987): 193–99.

Vaughan, William. *British Painting: The Golden Age.* London: Thames and Hudson, 1999.

PORTRAITURE: GERMANY

The Swiss teacher and writer on aesthetics, Johann Georg Sulzer, in his *Allgemeinen Theorie der schönen Künste* (*A General Theory of the Fine Arts*, 1771–74), defined a good portraitist as a painter of the soul, one who allowed the viewer to recognize an individual human spirit in the person portrayed. This subjective concept of portraiture became the genre's most significant feature during the Romantic period in Germany. Portrait painting had flourished in the eighteenth century, as preeminent neoclassical artists such as Anton Graff and Johann Heinrich Tischbein established their reputations by portraying different sectors of society. These subjects included members of the growing bourgeoisie, who desired increasingly to have their likenesses captured for posterity (a trend that continued throughout the Romantic era, even when the Napoleonic Wars wrought economic chaos). The neoclassical period set in motion many other tendencies in portraiture that were taken up and developed further by Romantic artists, whose impassioned search for the subject's inner being, for example, along with their purposeful and sensitive emphasis on facial features, were inflected by Johann Caspar Lavater's popular theorization (in *Physi-ognomical Fragments*, 1775–78) that physical traits could express a person's character. The German Romantic portrait carefully balanced a realistic impulse toward truth in physical resemblance with an idealistic impulse toward inner correspondence.

A new bourgeois intimacy followed in the late eighteenth-century shift away from large-formatted aristocratic portraits of the Baroque tradition. Portraits from the Romantic era often strove for a casual effect, with sitters posed in a relaxed fashion, surrounded by minimal finery. Rather than present an imposing image, there was a decided attempt to create a sense of engagement between viewer and subject. This was the case even in depictions of the aristocracy, such as Joseph Karl Stieler's *König von Bayern, an seinem Schreibtisch sitzend.* (*Maximilian I, King of Bavaria, Sitting at His Desk*, 1814), in which the monarch, looking rather like a banker at his desk, turns toward the viewer as though he has just been interrupted in his work (the very antithesis of Jean-Auguste-Dominique Ingres's regal *Napoléon Ier Sur le trône impérial* [*Napoleon Sitting on His Imperial Throne*, 1806]). Bust-length figures set against a flat, dark background, and a style that emphasized

Philipp Otto Runge. *Wir Drei*. Reprinted courtesy of AKG.

the face, were among the most prevalent formats for portraits throughout the era, and recall the earnest bourgeois portrait tradition of the seventeenth century. But under the influence of the English school, and in response to the Romantic cult of nature, outdoor settings also became quite popular, as exemplified by Wilhelm von Schadow's portrait *Agnes D'Alton-Rauch* (1825), whose subject is placed in front of an overgrown, forested landscape that becomes almost as much the focus of the painting as the subject herself.

Since many German Romantic artists heavily invested in their ambitious goals of developing a new type of landscape painting or renewing the practice of history painting, they disdained the idea of earning their living through commissioned portraits. Some executed portraits only of family, friends, or themselves, and these were often small, private works. Among the most prominent northern artists, Carl Blechen, Ernst Ferdinand Oehme, and Ludwig Richter rarely devoted themselves to portraiture, while the few portraits by Caspar David Friedrich, almost all graphic works, were produced early in his career. His depictions of family members follow in the tradition of the bourgeois portrait bust, but his self-portraits, typically of the period, betoken a new, subjective understanding of the artist. Of the northern artists, it was Philipp Otto Runge who made the most significant contribution to the genre of portraiture, especially in his startling portrayals of dynamic children. His monumental depictions of family and friends are a potent mix of the heightened realism resulting from his clear, classicizing style and the intensely personal symbolic language involving a spiritualized nature that ultimately lends the pictures a significance well beyond a simple portrait.

Other than Runge, German artists of the south, especially the so-called Nazarenes, produced some of the most striking developments in Romantic portraiture. Looking to fifteenth- and sixteenth-century painting as the epitome of artistic tradition, these retrospective portraits work at a deliberately archaizing effect through the naive manner of composition and the historical attire and settings. Half-figured models wearing tunics and other old-fashioned garments were portrayed sitting thoughtfully (and often stiffly) inside Gothic or Renaissance structures, with back-

ground landscapes revealed through arches, windows, arcades, or curtains pulled to one side in the manner of Italian Renaissance portraits (such as Julius Schnorr von Carolsfeld's *Mathilde Winz*, [1827–29] and *Frau Bianca von Quandt* [c.1820], and Friedrich Overbeck's portrait of *Franz Pforr* [1810]). Nazarene portrait paintings are idealized images that capture the essence of the sitter through complicated, programmatic symbolism, often employing a formality that had been discarded in portraits by other artists of the period. By contrast, their penetrating portrait drawings use precisely-drawn line and meticulous detail to concentrate solely on the sitter's facial features and head, leaving out all indications of any spatial dimension, resulting in a powerful display of technical bravura and keen perception that compares to Ingres's own graphic portrait work.

Portraits of fellow artists were especially popular, suggestive of the cult of friendship that characterized German Romantic culture. While the German Romantic self-portrait had a tendency to depict the artist without his tools of the trade, portrayals of colleagues often showed the artist engrossed in his work. These illustrated the intentness of the artist's pursuits and offered clues to his personality through the depiction of his working methods. Georg Friedrich Kersting's paintings of Friedrich in his studio, with its barricaded windows and dearth of objects, are incisive demonstrations of the painter realizing his dictum to use inner vision when portraying the outer world. Mementos of joint outings into the countryside (such as Schnorr von Carolsfeld's *Friedrich Olivier am Königssee* [*Friedrich Olivier Sketching*, 1817]) also testify to the close-knit nature of artist communities, as do the *Freundschaftsbilder* or friendship portraits that were a staple of the era, which depicted the artist together with like-minded companions.

In the later phase of the Romantic era, with the arrival of the *Biedermeier* aesthetic, there came an increase in portraits depicting the sitter absorbed in activities such as reading (for example, Friedrich Wassman's *Die Schwester des Künstlers* [*Minna Wasman, Sister of the Artist*, 1822] and Johann August Krafft's *Der Richter Jacob Wilder* [*Judge Jacob Wilder*, 1819]). These paintings removed the pictorial emphasis from the face and cast the sitter as unaware of being observed, thus achieving a genre-like effect. Happy groupings of loving family members, surrounded by the accessories of the home, also became a staple of portraiture in the 1820s and 1830s. The introspective, subjective nature that epitomized the most innovative German Romantic portraiture, while not entirely disappearing, eventually gave way to the more prosaic concerns of realism.

MARGARET DOYLE

Bibliography

Börsch-Supan, Helmut. *Die Deutsche Malerei von Anton Graff bis Hans von Marées 1760–1870*. Munich: Beck and Deutscher Kunstverlag, 1988.

Jensen, Jens Christian. "Die Bildniskunst der Nazarener," in *Die Nazarener in Rom. Ein deutscher Künstlerbund der Romantik*. Munich: Prestel, 1981. 38–43.

Lankheit, Klaus. *Das Freundschaftsbild der Romantik*. Heidelberg: Carl Winter Universitätsverlag, 1952.

Neidhardt, Hans Joachim. "Solitude and Community." In *The Romantic Spirit in German Art 1790–1990*. Edited by Keith Hartley. London: Thames and Hudson, 1994.

Vaughan, William. *German Romantic Painting*. 2d ed. New Haven, Conn.: Yale University Press, 1994.

PORTRAITURE AND SELF-PORTRAITURE: UNITED STATES

As virtually the only artistic vehicle for painters in colonial America, portraiture remained the most popular—and profitable—type of art throughout the Romantic era, practiced by almost every American artist until well into the nineteenth century. A crucial question of how best to represent the new nation and its people followed the Revolution, and American portraitists, folk artists, and miniaturists played a significant part in the shaping and the strengthening of national, regional, and individual identities.

Almost all of the early republic's successful portraitists studied overseas at the celebrated London studio of expatriated American painter Benjamin West, represented in Michael Pratt's group portrait *The American School* (1765). Although West was primarily a landscape artist, portrait paintings such as *Robert Fulton* (1806) also ushered in an age of Romantic portraiture, positioning the distant gaze, moody features, and tousled locks of the sitter before the brooding vision of a burning boat and a stormy sky. But while West was painting a full-length portrait of George III in the revolutionary year of 1776, other American portraitists were eager to capture George Washington on canvas. Building a national identity called for the construction of national heroes, and the virtuous, victorious general was considered to be the ideal face of the new republic. Washington was painted by many well-respected artists, Charles Willson Peale included, but it was Gilbert Stuart's *George Washington* (*The Athenaeum Portrait*) of 1796, the timeless and monumental image of Washington's face that was used as the model for the dollar bill, that defined a national icon for generations to come.

Rembrandt Peale's *George Washington* (*The Porthole Portrait*) of 1823, depicting a noble and uniformed Washington, also gained a place in the canon of Washington iconography, and embodied the wider resurgence of national pride and historical portraiture that followed the War of 1812. In 1814, New York City commissioned a series of full-length portraits of military heroes from the current war. The visit of the Marquis Marie-Joseph-Paul de Lafayette in 1824 and the fiftieth anniversary of the signing of the Declaration of Independence in 1826 inspired a number of portraits of older, Revolutionary heroes. Samuel Waldo (in 1817) and Thomas Sully (in 1845) both painted Romantic portraits of an idealized Andrew Jackson, and in John Vanderlyn's full-length portrait of *James Monroe* (1822), the President's proprietary hand, resting upon a map of newly acquired territory, suggests that the United States no longer perceived itself as a fledgling republic, but as an established nation, ready to embark upon the course of empire.

As one would expect in a nation that proclaimed equality and extolled the individual, public heroes were far from being the only subjects of portraiture. The faces of private citizens proliferated as folk art became a burgeoning industry, and artists such as Ammi Phillips offered affordable flat portraits to ordinary Americans. The wealthier citizens commissioned full-length portraits and intricate miniatures of themselves and their families, while artists such as Washington Allston and Peale also drew primarily upon their families for their inspiration and the subjects of their art. Often perceived as the founder of American Romanticism, Allston painted dreamlike and mysterious portraits, applying many layers of paint and varnish in order to achieve a luminous transparency and sonorous harmony of light and color. His own *Self-Portrait* (1796–1800) depicts a serious, sensitive youth with haunting eyes, half in shadow, anticipating the moody and Romantic artist of Edward Malbone's miniature, *Washington Allston* (c. 1800–1801). For Peale, self-portraits such as *The Artist in his Museum* (1822) and family paintings such as *The Staircase Group* (1795) articulated his wider search for artistic identity and intellectual community in the new republic, representing the pragmatic relevance of the artist in the everyday world of American life. The popularity of double portraits, such as John Singleton Copley's *Mr. and Mrs. Thomas Mifflin* (1773), echoed Enlightenment ideals of equality in marital relationships, while portraits of women and children were inspired by the influential Jean-Jacques Rousseau, his avocation of proactive parenting, and the natural maternal bond. Sully's *Mother and Son* (1840) and Copley's *Sir William Pepperrell and His Family* (1778), for example, both emphasize the physical closeness and emotional bond between mother and child. Reflecting the Romantic interest in childhood, both paintings also represent natural, squirming children who undermine the order of the adult world through their irrepressible energy and sheer force of personality.

While other major portraitists followed Congress to Washington in the 1790s or positioned themselves along the wealthy seaboard towns, Ralph Earl adopted a simple, unpretentious style and became an itinerant portraitist in rural New England. He eschewed the studio and instead painted his Connecticut subjects in their own homes and fields, representing his patrons' growing sense of regional identity, their appreciation of American landscape, and their dislike of pretentious shows of wealth and gentility. Earl's full-length portrait of the young merchant Elijah Boardman (1789), displaying his wares in his shop, celebrates the entrepreneurial spirit of the young republic and exhibits a democratic directness that anticipates John Neagle's most powerful portrait, *Pat Lyon at the Forge* (1826). A self-made working man, Pat Lyon represents the energy and optimism of an increasingly industrialized United States, and Neagle's portraits can be viewed as visual counterparts to the self-confident, celebratory poetry of Walt Whitman.

Portraits of the Indians, meanwhile, sought to obscure the darker face of a rising America. Declaring that the Indians were "doomed and must perish," George Catlin hoped that through his portraits, they would "live again upon canvas, and stand forth for centuries to come, the living monuments of a noble race." The romanticized, nostalgic image of the "noble savage" dominated Indian portraits of the Romantic era, finding its apotheosis in a group portrait by Charles Bird King, called *Young Omahaw, War Eagle, Little Missouri, and Pawnees* (1821). Composed of five remarkably similar Indian torsos and modeled on the busts of the Roman republic, the portrait erases individual characteristics in order to emphasize the generic nobility of the Indian race.

Unlike the ubiquitous Indian brave, the black man was rarely celebrated. Black individuals were rarely painted at all in fact, and when they did appear on canvas, it was usually as a dutiful servant, relegated to the sidelines, as in Edward Savage's portrait of *The Washington Family* (1798). There were notable exceptions though, such as Copley's expressive and unstereotyped *Head of a Negro* (1777–78) and Nathaniel Jocelyn's ennobling portrait of *Cinqué* (1839), commemorating the chief mutineer aboard the slaving ship *La Amistad*. Practicing in the 1820s and 1830s, itinerant portraitist and fervent abolitionist William Matthew Prior painted portraits of prominent African Americans such as William Lawson and William Whipper. Prior's intelligent and highly-individuated portraits argued the abolitionist cause, asserted a black identity, and countered both the cartoon images of the genre painters and the widespread black stereotypes developing in popular culture.

By the 1840s, the newly discovered daguerreotype was proving particularly popular in America. It displaced the miniature almost entirely and contributed to the more detailed, realistic style of portraiture that was emerging in the mid-nineteenth century, as practiced by portraitists such as Charles Loring Elliot, George Peter Alexander Healy, and Daniel Huntington. Yet Romantic portraiture in the United States, at its height in the 1820s and 1830s, had never really lacked or abandoned reality; its mysterious hues, dramatic gestures, and emotional depth could not conceal its underlying fascination with material reality as well as the inner personality of each individual subject.

SARAH WOOD

Bibliography

Dunlap, William. *History of the Rise and Progress of the Arts of Design in the United States*. 2 vols. New York: Dover, 1969.

Eisenman, Stephen F., et al. *Nineteenth-Century Art: A Critical History*. London: Thames and Hudson, 2nd ed., 2002.

Encyclopedia of World Art. Vol. 1. New York: McGraw-Hill, 1959.

Fabian, Monroe H. *Mr. Sully, Portrait Painter: The Works of Thomas Sully*. Washington, D.C.: Smithsonian Institution, 1983.

Hughes, Robert. *American Visions: The Epic History of Art in America*. London: Harvill Press, 1997.

Johnson, Dale T. *American Portrait Miniatures in the Manney Collection*. New York: Metropolitan Museum of Art, 1990.

Kornhauser, Elizabeth Mankin, with Richard L. Bushman, Stephen H. Kornhauser, and Aileen Ribeiro. *Ralph Earl: The Face of the Young Republic*. New Haven, Conn.: Yale University Press, 1991.

McCoubrey, John W. *American Art, 1700–1960: Sources and Documents*. Englewood Cliffs, N.J.: Prentice-Hall, 1965.

McElroy, Guy C. *Facing History: The Black Image in American Art 1710–1940*. San Fransisco: Bedford Arts, 1990.

Mendelowitz, Daniel M. *A History of American Art*. New York: Holt, Rinehart and Winston, 1970.

Miles, Ellen. *Portrait Painting in America: The 19th Century*. New York: Main Street, 1977.

Miles, Ellen G., and Richard H. Saunders. *American Colonial Portraits 1700–1776*. Washington, D.C.: Smithsonian Institution, 1987.

Novak, Barbara. *American Painting of the Nineteenth Century: Realism, Idealism, and the American Experience*. New York: Pall Mall, 1969.

Parry, Ellwood. *The Image of the Indian and the Black Man in American Art, 1590–1900*. New York: George Braziller, 1974.

Quick, Michael. *American Portraiture in the Grand Manner: 1720–1920*. Los Angeles: Los Angeles County Museum of Art, 1981.

Richardson, Edgar P. *American Romantic Painting*. New York: Weyhe, 1944.

Simon, Robin. *The Portrait in Britain and America*. Oxford: Phaidon, 1987.

Wilmerding, John. *American Art*. Harmondsworth, England: Penguin, 1976.

PORTUGAL: CULTURAL SURVEY

During the second half of the eighteenth century, an antibaroque movement initiated in the universities instituted neoclassicism as the driving force in Portuguese culture, controlling artistic production. The first signs of a Romantic sensibility in Portuguese art and culture are therefore difficult to find until near the year 1800. Italy was the prime destination for musicians, painters, sculptors, and architects, who generally obtained scholarships to travel to that country and acquire knowledge and practice in their respective fields. Theater was dominated by the Spanish repertoire, which was far more popular than neoclassical tragedy, with a few exceptions, such as João Baptista Gomes' *Nova Castro* (1788). When it came to opera, the Italians had no rivals. Cimarosa, Paisiello, and Salieri shared the earlier programs of the opera house (founded in Lisbon in 1793) with national composers using mostly Italian language and models, such as Leal Moreira and Marcos Portugal. The mezzo-soprano Luisa Todi obtained international recognition in this period. Instrumental music was widespread in both public and private performances, as William Beckford testified during his stay in Lisbon from 1787 to 1788. Musical magazines such as the *Jornal de Modinhas* (1792–96) were very popular, providing pieces (including *modas*, *lunduns*, and *canzonets*) for one or two voices, pianoforte and sometimes other instruments also, with lyrics generally in Portuguese. Remaining in fashion for decades, they would become a vehicle that would help popularize Romantic poetry.

Domingos Bomtempo, the most representative composer in early-nineteenth-century Portugal, undertook as his task the renewal of Portuguese music. Living in Paris and London until 1820 (where he gained considerable recognition as a pianist), he became the first director of the Music Conservatoire created after the liberal revolution, in 1835. His *Requiem à Memória de Camões* (1816?) played a significant role in nationalist Romanticism.

In late eighteenth century painting, neoclassical allegories replaced religious themes, without any meaningful technical changes taking place. Two painters escaped the dominating Roman influence while introducing Romantic aspects: Vieira Portuense and Domingos Sequeira. Vieira, in his constant traveling, absorbed the Venetian atmosphere and German pre-Romantic taste in Dresden. He tried to combine classical structure and drawing with "a picture of souls" in his dramatic historical scenes (*Filipa de Vilhena armando seus filhos cavaleiros*, 1801). His rival Sequeira survived him and became the official painter of the liberal revolution (*Alegoria à Constituição de 1822*, 1822), after a period of imprisonment for cooperating with the French invaders (*Junot protegendo Lisboa*, 1808). Exiled in Paris, he presented, in the Salon of 1824, a mythical icon of Portuguese Romanticism (*A morte de Camões*), which later disappeared. His portraits suggested new possibilities for Portuguese painting (see *Retrato dos filhos do pintor*, 1816). The emphasis at this time was on portraiture; landscape and genre painting would have to wait for the next generation of artists, such as Anunciação and Cristino.

By the end of the eighteenth century, literature was severely regulated by neoclassical principles, as prescribed by the *Arcadia Lusitana* (1757–74), the best known of the literary academies. Horace's *On the Art of Poetry* and Boileau's *Art Poétique* were unquestioned bibles for poets. Nevertheless, some poets displayed pre-Romantic characteristics in their works. Tomás António Gonzaga, for instance, found in Brazil a sense of nature that invaded his sentimental and nostalgic poetry (*Marília de Dirceu*, 1792). José Anastácio da Cunha, a mathematician dismissed from the university and imprisoned during the inquisition, translated William Shakespeare and wrote of passionate, tormented love haunted by death in poems only published in 1839. Leonor de Almeida, later Marquise of Alorna, imprisoned in a convent until the age of twenty seven and exiled in London for conspiracy from 1804 to 1814, blended in her poetry the praise of enlightened reason, science, and freedom of thought with a preference for nightly sceneries, ruins, melancholic loneliness, and an acute sense of fate. She returned to Portugal shortly before the liberal revolution of 1820. Although her views in politics became increasingly conservative, she kept a literary circle that played a decisive role in influencing the younger literary generation. Herculano was her most brilliant disciple. Her complete works were only published in 1844, when a second Romantic generation was emerging.

The first generation, headed by Castilho, Garrett, and Herculano, was intensely active during the 1820s and 1830s, establishing and consolidating Romanticism as a cultural movement in Portugal. Working in a variety of genres and media, they published their own poetry, novels, and plays, and wrote critical analyses in their self-produced journals. In so doing, they changed the public's taste, imposing a Romantic culture focused, as Garrett put it, on "modern, national and popular" values. They aimed for a literature able to consolidate national identity, independent from classical principles and models. Garrett was the first to notice how the old traditional ballads known as *romances* fit this purpose, populated as they were by medieval reminiscences and structured in a simple, short verse form known as *redondilha*. His *Adozinda*, published in London in 1828, presents a theoretical defence and a practical approach to this kind of narrative poetry that found numerous followers. He conceived and imposed a complete program for the renewal of drama and the novel as well, based on the same principles: to depict national characters in an accessible language, although in his lyrical poetry he would take longer to achieve that simplicity.

A medieval revival dominated the 1830s and early 1840s. Romantic taste was mainly spread by the numerous journals that emerged then. A special role was performed by the so-called encyclopedic journals (*O Panorama*, 1837–68; *Revista Universal Lisbonense*, 1841–57; *Archivo Popular*, 1837–43). They combined information of all sorts with literary production and criticism, providing a complement to education not to be neglected in a period so concerned about the democratization of culture. The diffusion of historical knowledge, for instance, was one of their main purposes, along with the printing of historical novels by Herculano, Rebelo da Silva (1822–71), and others. These periodicals also show how literature became gradually more interested in contemporary life by the end of the 1840s. Novels and drama started to depict matters and characters of the present, as António Pedro Lopes de Mendonça did in *Memórias de um Doido* (1849).

A particular kind of journal comprised of only poetry gained special favor with the public, surviving until the late 1860s and publishing together successive groups of poets responsible for many examples of Romantic lyric poetry. The first of these, *O Trovador* (1844–48), was shortly followed by *O Novo Trovador* (1851–56), and they defined a second Romantic generation: João de Lemos, Palmeirim, and Soares de Passos are some representative names. The tremendous success enjoyed by the gothic ballad *O noivado do sepulcro* published by Passos in a verse magazine (*O Bardo*, 1852) shows the existence of a sizable audience for Romantic-themed works. In the 1870s, the preferences of this audience would be ferociously criticized by realist writers. However, a poet belonging to the realist generation is considered by many as the major Romantic poet of Portugal: Antero de Quental, whose earlier poems were printed under the title of *Primaveras Românticas* (1872). Despite the absence of most of the more obvious motifs of Romanticism, he nevertheless achieved an almost philosophical idealism in his *Sonetos* (1886).

A similar case of chronological displacement is exemplified by Camilo Castelo Branco (1825–90), a prolific novelist, poet and playwright, who began his career with an almost gothic novel, *Anátema* (1851) and published a key Portuguese Romantic novel, *Amor de Perdição* (1862). These examples illustrate that, until the relatively late date of 1865, Romanticism can still be considered aesthetically dominant in Portugal.

FÁTIMA FREITAS MORNA

Bibliography

AAVV. *Estética do Romantismo em Portugal*. Lisbon: Grémio Literário, 1974.

Alexander, Boyd, ed. *The Journal of William Beckford in Portugal and Spain 1787–1788*. London: Ruppert Hart-Davis, 1954.

Brito, Manuel Carlos. *Estudos de História da Música em Portugal*. Lisbon: Estampa, 1989.

Brito, Manuel Carlos, and David Cranmer. *Crónicas da Vida Musical Portuguesa na Primeira Metade de Oitocentos*. Lisbon: INCM, 1990.

Buescu, Helena Carvalhão, ed. *Dicionário do Romantismo Literário Português*. Lisbon: Caminho, 1997.

Cruz, Duarte Ivo. *História do Teatro Português. O Ciclo do Romantismo*. Lisbon: Guimarães, 1988.

França, José-Augusto. *A Arte em Portugal no Século XIX*. 3d ed. 2 vols. Lisbon: Bertrand, 1990.

———. *Le Romantisme au Portugal. Étude de Faits Socio-Culturels*. Paris: Klincksieck, 1974. Translated as *O Romantismo em Portugal* by the author. 3d ed. Lisbon: Livros Horizonte, 1997.

Machado, Álvaro Manuel. *Les Romantismes au Portugal*. Paris: Fondation Calouste Gulbenkian-Centre Culturel Portugais, 1986.

Rebello, Luiz Francisco. *O Teatro Romântico*. Lisbon: ICALP, 1980.

Reis, Carlos, and Maria da Natividade Pires. *História Crítica da Literatura Portuguesa*, 5 *O Romantismo*. Lisbon: Verbo, 1993.

Santos, Maria de Lourdes Lima dos. *Para uma Sociologia da Cultura Burguesa em Portugal no Século XIX*. Lisbon: Presença/Instituto de Ciências Sociais, 1983.

———. *Intelectuais Portugueses na Primeira Metade de Oitocentos*. Lisbon: Presença, 1988.

PORTUGAL: HISTORICAL SURVEY

In the last decades of the eighteenth century, Portugal was attempting to recover from the crisis generated by a 1755 earthquake that had destroyed its capital, Lisbon, and damaged other parts of the country. The Marquis of Pombal, prime minister of King Joseph I, took this opportunity to expand his power and rebuild most of the city according to his enlightened views. The development of industries (such as wine, fishing, cotton, and silk) was an important accomplishment of his government, as was the increased colonial development of Brazil. He initiated a general reform of the university in 1772, and created several institutions to promote scientific knowledge, after expelling the Jesuits from the country. (Until that time, they had been the primary teaching force in the nation.) The death of King Joseph in 1777 put his daughter Mary I in the throne. She banished the Marquis (who was convicted in trial in 1781) and canceled most of his reforms. Nevertheless, the first schools for girls were created by her, as were the Royal Academy of Sciences (1779) and the opera house (Royal Theater of São Carlos, 1793). She also ordered the acquisition from England of the first steam engine, in 1778. From 1789 on, rebellions for independence started succeeding in Brazil. In 1792, her son John assumed the role of regent, as she was considered unfit due to madness. He only became King John VI after her death in 1816.

A brief war with Spain known as the Oranges War (1801) anticipated the Iberian Peninsular War, during which Napoleon Bonaparte's armies invaded the country three times (in 1807, 1809, and 1810) as a result of Portugal's refusal to close its harbors to British ships. The royal family left Lisbon in 1807 and established a court in Rio de Janeiro, Brazil until 1821. The British troops, commanded by Wellesley, honored an old alliance by entering the country in 1808 to support the resistance against the French. An English general, William Beresford, was even given command of the Portuguese army in 1809. He remained in Portugal long after the French withdrawal of 1811, and gained increasing despotic power from 1815, when Brazil was declared a kingdom (although still tied to Portugal). A climate of conspiracy took over the country, strongly supported by freemasonry, culminating in a liberal revolution burst in Oporto in 1820. At this time, the first free elections took place. The parliament conceived a liberal constitution (approved in 1822) and forced the king to return and swear to uphold it. Brazil immediately proclaimed its independence (acknowledged by Portugal in 1825), choosing the king's elder son, Peter, as its first emperor. Some important measures had meanwhile been taken, such as the closing of Santo Ofício (the Court of Inquisition), the regulation of freedom of the press, the creation of the first Portuguese bank, and a National Society to promote the development of industry, in addition to a regular connection between the two major cities (Lisbon and Oporto) by steamboat.

In 1823 a revolt known as Vilafrancada, led by the king's second son, Michael, brought the conservative forces back to power. They were defeated a year later after another military revolution known as Abrilada, forcing the prince to seek exile in Austria. This was the beginning of a very complex period, with almost constant changes of power between liberals and conservatives, aggravated by King John's death in 1826. The crown was inherited by his elder son, Peter IV, by then emperor of Brazil, and so the Regency was committed to his sister Isabel Maria. He approved a moderate version of the constitution, known as *Carta Constitucional* (1826) and abdicated in favor of his daughter Mary (aged seven by then), confirming his sister as regent. Conservatives, however, tried to react in favor of Prince Michael, causing military confrontations.

In an attempt to pacify the country, young Queen Mary II, still in Brazil, was married by power of attorney to her uncle Michael, still in exile, who swore loyalty to his brother and to the liberal Constitution. Once in Portugal, he proclaimed himself king with total power, dismissing the parliament and revoking the constitution in 1828. Years of terror followed. Liberals were persecuted, forced into exile, or massively imprisoned and executed. The civil war began as the resistance started organizing itself abroad and achieved military victories. After winning an important battle in the Atlantic islands of Azores, a liberal council under the Duke of Palmela (former ambassador in London) established a parallel government in Terceira (Azores) in 1830. Peter IV renounced the throne of Brazil and joined the rebels, taking the regency on behalf of his daughter. After several failed attempts, the liberal army reached Oporto (1832) and finally Lisbon (1833). Peace was declared in 1834, the liberal regime restored and self-proclaimed King Michael banished. Peter IV died that same year and Mary II at last took her throne in a kingdom devastated and impoverished by the war.

In the following years Portuguese society saw several decisive changes. Freedom of the press was restored. Religious orders were shut down and their property confiscated and sold in auction to support the development of the country. Commercial and industrial associations were created, and education became obligatory. Legal measures were taken to fight poverty, and the traffic in slaves was abolished in the African colonies, which were increasingly explored. Nevertheless, the political situation was far from d stable. In 1836, another revolution, the Setembrista, restored the first liberal constitution of 1822, almost immediately followed by a coup d'état and several rebellions. A reformed constitution, approved in 1838, was revoked four years later. Costa Cabral, a minister who came to prominence in the late 1830s, became dictator in 1842, promoting reforms on legal codes, public health, education, and communications. Attacked by both sides—both the remaining ultraconservative forces and the radical liberals—he fell under a severe financial crisis (1846) but returned to power after three years of civil war, and was finally dismissed in 1851. By then, however, the country showed some signs of modernization such as public gas lighting in the capital (1848) and macadam roads (1849). Modernization and industrialization would be the priority of the regeneration period after 1851, when political stability was finally achieved.

FÁTIMA FREITAS MORNA

Bibliography

Marques, A. H. de Oliveira. *História de Portugal*. Vol. 2. Lisbon: Ágora, 1972. Translated as *History of Portugal*. Vol. 2: *From*

Empire to Corporate State by the author. New York: Columbia University Press, 1972.
Mattoso, José, ed. *História de Portugal*. Vols. 4 and 5. Lisbon: Círculo de Leitores, 1999.

Saraiva, José Hermano, ed. *História de Portugal*. Vols. 5 and 6. Lisbon: Alfa, 1983.
Serrão, Joel, ed. *Dicionário de História de Portugal*. 6 vols. Lisbon: Iniciativas Editoriais, 1975–78.

POTGIETER, EVERHARDUS JOHANNES 1808–1875

Dutch essayist, poet, and critic

Everhardus Johannes Potgieter's Romanticism is located in his rejection of his own time and culture in favor of the passed Dutch golden age, which he believed could be revived in the Netherlands of the early nineteenth century. The Romantic movement took on national proportions in the 1830s in that country. The liberal journal *De Gids* (*The Guide*) was its primary voice, and Potgieter was the journal's editor for almost twenty years. However, Potgieter has also been termed an anti-Romantic, due to the shift in his later writing away from the idealization of the concept of Romantic individualism and toward the glorification of a model national citizenship. It was his conviction that the bourgeoisie were predestined to restore the Netherlands to its former glory. Potgieter's biographer, the poet Albert Verwey, characterized his work in terms of "droom en tucht" ("dream and discipline")—"dream" for the Romantic that Potgieter essentially was, but "discipline" for his unique brand of Romanticism, reined in as it was by the dictates of reason.

Although Amsterdam was Potgieter's home for most of his life, the three extended periods he spent abroad had a decisive influence on his work. As a child he lived in Zwolle until 1821, when he moved with an aunt to Amsterdam because of financial and domestic difficulties. At thirteen he was already employed in the leather trade. Five years later, his place of work was temporarily closed, only to reopen as a sugar company. Potgieter was transferred to Antwerp to work in the new business as a clerk. Arriving in Belgium in 1827, he observed how resistance by the Southern Netherlands to the administration of the United Kingdom of the Netherlands was gathering momentum. The most valuable acquaintance he made in Belgium was Jan Frans Willems, the founding father of the Flemish movement, which called for the revival of Dutch as a literary language. While Willems felt that literature from the Middle Ages embodied those characteristics essential to this revival, Potgieter displayed admiration for seventeenth-century writers such as P. C. Hooft and Joost van den Vondel throughout his writing. During his time in Antwerp, he also came to admire Romantics such as Lord Byron, Alphonse Louis-Marie Lamartine, and Victor Hugo. Their work encouraged him to regard his anguish at the financial and moral shortcomings of his family as a topic suitable for poetry.

In 1830, the Belgian Revolution forced Potgieter to return to Amsterdam. He read widely and deepened his understanding of the English Romantics, particularly John Keats and Percy Bysshe Shelley. A business trip to Sweden the following year also proved crucial to his development as a writer; his extended stay inspired *Het Noorden, in omtrekken en tafereelen* (*The North, in Sketches and Scenes*), essentially his literary debut, which was published in two volumes between 1836 and 1840. While in Sweden he moved in highly educated circles, and followed with great interest developments in Swedish literature, meeting eminent Romantic writers such as Frederike Bremer and Esaias Tegnér. His later study *Frederike Bremer* (1842) demonstrates his admiration for this Swedish author; Potgieter saw in her work the embodiment of Tegnér's ideal, in which truth, virtue, and beauty are united.

Back in Amsterdam, he began work on a magazine, *De Muzen* (*The Muses*), with his friends Aarnout Drost and R. C. Bakhuizen van den Brink. Launched in 1834, it soon ceased publication. It was superseded in 1837 by *De Gids*, which was to become the leading literary magazine of the Netherlands. It was characterized by a progressive rejection of traditional literature and a politically liberal position. *De Gids* owed its immediate success to Potgieter, the initially anonymous editor, who contributed critical articles on contemporary literature as well as his own prose and poetry. His trenchant criticism earned the journal the nickname "de blauwe beul" ("the blue executioner," so called due to its blue cover). By the late 1830s, Potgieter had turned away from the melancholy poetry of his youth toward a new focus on the essential and the pragmatic. He exchanged notions of paradise for an acceptance of reality, believing that disillusionment and disappointment also needed to be artistically expressed.

Potgieter's unceasing condemnation of his own time is worked into the allegorical satire *Jan, Jannetje en hun jongste kind* (*Jan, Jannetje and Their Youngest Child*, 1841), in which the unmotivated child Jan Salie symbolizes contemporary moral and cultural decline. Potgieter's glorification of the golden age is perhaps best expressed in the essay "Het Rijksmuseum te Amsterdam" ("The Rijksmuseum at Amsterdam"), which appeared three years later. The art collection in the Rijksmuseum is promoted as a source of inspiration for a revival of the golden age. This preference for the art of a passed age also influenced the *Liedekens van Bontekoe* (*Songs from Bontekoe*, 1840), a volume of poems set to seventeenth-century tunes.

The late 1850s were a productive period for Potgieter, who was inspired by his friendship with the liberal clergyman Conrad Busken Huet, who later joined the editorial board of *De Gids* in 1863. Potgieter's interest in foreign literature was rekindled at this time, expressed in wide-ranging studies on figures such as Pierre-Jean de Béranger (1858) and George Crabbe (1858–59). In 1865, a conflict among the editors of *De Gids* led to Huet's resignation. In an expression of support for his friend, Potgieter also resigned. To console himself, he traveled to Florence with Huet. At this time, the six hundredth anniversary of Dante Alighieri's birth was being celebrated. This inspired Potgieter's ambitious poem "Florence," in the first collection simply titled *Poëzy* (1868). Both in form and content it pays homage to Dante. Written in tercets (the same verse form used in the *Divine Comedy*), its theme is that of the ideal citizen sent into exile.

Near the end of his life, Potgieter focused his energies on a new cycle of poems, which appeared as the second *Poëzy* in 1875 and included "De nalatenschap van den landjonker" ("The Country Squire's Legacy"). Published shortly before his death, its beauty and conscious use of artifice made it, even at that time, appear dated. With this final work, Potgieter returned to, and once again gave expression to, his early Romantic ideals, rather than those more rational ambitions he had prized in the 1830s.

ALISON E. MARTIN

Biography

Born in Zwolle, June 27, 1808. Apprenticed in the leather trade, Amsterdam, 1821–27. Entered the sugar trade as a representative and clerk, Antwerp, 1827. Visited Sweden, 1831–1832. Editor of *De Gids*, 1837. Resigned coeditorship of *De Gids*, 1865. Died in Amsterdam, February 3, 1875.

Selected Works

Fiction
Proza 1837–1845. 1864.
Het Noorden, in omtrekken en tafereelen. 1875.
Schetsen en verhalen. 1875.
Kritische studieën. 1875. With Jon. C. Zimmerman.
Jan, jannetje en hun jongste kind. Zutphen: Thieme, 1969. With Jacob Smit.
Florence den XIVden mei 1265–1865 aan Cd. Busken Huet. Rwolle: Tjeenk Willink, 1960. With Jacob Smit.
Afrid ter valkenjacht. Het Rijksmuseum te Amsterdam. Rotterdam: Backhuys, 1981. With Geertruda. M. J. Duyfhuizen.

Poetry
Poëzy. 1877.
Verspreide en nagelaten poëzy 1828–1874. 1886.

Correspondence
Potgieter, E. J., Conrad Busken Huet, and Jacob Smit. *De volledige briefwisseling van E. J. Potgieter en Cd. Busken Huet*. Groningen: Tjeenk Willink, 1972.
Verwey, Albert, and Conrad Busken Huet. *Brieven aan E. J. Potgieter*. Haarlem: Tjeenk Willink, 1925.

Biography
Leven van R. C. Bakhuizen van den Brink. Haarlem: Tjeenk Willink, 1885.

Bibliography
Busken Huet, C. *Potgieter (1860–1875) persoonlijke herinneringen*. Haarlem: Tjeenk Willink, 1901.
Smit, J. *Leven en werken van E. J. Potgieter 1808–1875*. Leiden: Nijhoff, 1983.
Verwey, A. *Het leven van Potgieter*. Haarlem: Tjeenk Willink, 1903.

THE PRELUDE 1850

Epic poem by William Wordsworth

The Prelude exists in three, or possibly four, versions: a two-book version completed in 1799; a five-book version that dates from 1804 (though whether this is a complete version is controversial); a text of 1805 in thirteen books; and the text of 1850 in fourteen books, which was published posthumously. William Wordsworth worked on the poem at various periods throughout his life but chose not to publish it. The 1805 text was eventually published in 1926, the two-book version in 1973, and the five-book version in 1997. The title (in its full form *The Prelude; or Growth of a Poet's Mind: An Autobiographical Poem*) was not Wordsworth's own but was supplied by his wife for the publication of the work in 1850. It had been originally intended as the introduction to a much larger poem, *The Recluse*, only one additional part of which, *The Excursion*, was completed.

The Prelude is a poem on an epic scale and this may partly explain why Wordsworth did not publish the 1805 version. Epic poems normally require elevated subjects of a heroic or mythological nature. But *The Prelude* is an autobiographical poem about episodes in Wordsworth's life. It is probable that Wordsworth had doubts about whether a poem about his own life could aspire to the status of an epic poem, thus his continual revision of it. The fact that the language of the 1850 version is more Miltonic than the 1805 version perhaps indicates some anxiety about whether the subject of the poem was worthy of its epic scale.

Traditional epics are well known for beginning in medias res. *The Prelude* departs from this convention by having a beginning, middle, and end in the normal temporal order since it begins by describing scenes from Wordsworth's childhood. This part of the poem is the most obviously appealing to readers but it can be argued that the childhood scenes are misunderstood if read on their own without taking into account the later books of the poem. The childhood scenes take on their full significance only in the context of what comes later. Wordsworth's description or, more accurately, interpretation of these scenes from his childhood is only possible because he has gone through certain experiences that have led him to see his childhood in a new light.

Fundamental to an understanding of *The Prelude* is that it is a poem written out of spiritual and psychological crisis. But this crisis is not merely a personal one; it reflects a wider cultural crisis. Wordsworth's personal crisis and his attempt to recover from it are representative of his era, and this is what gives the poem its claim to epic status. To understand the basis of such a crisis one has to go beyond the early books of the poem to Wordsworth's experience of the French Revolution. Perhaps the best-known lines of the poem occur in book 11 of the 1850 version, describing Wordsworth's idealistic hopes for the Revolution: "Bliss was it in that dawn to be alive, / But to be young was very heaven."

When Wordsworth went to France to participate in the French Revolution, he was an extreme Enlightenment idealist: that is, he believed that the world could be transformed by the force of reason. Following on the lines above, he spells out this idealism:

When reason seemed the most to assert her rights,
When most intent on making of herself
A prime enchantress—to assist the work,
Which then was going forward in her name!
Not favoured spots alone, but the whole Earth,
The beauty wore of promise.

Wordworth's psychological crisis occurs when this idealism is shattered by such events in France as the September massacres, the regime of Maximilien de Robespierre, and the Terror. Instead of the Revolution leading to the triumph of reason, it seemed to have brought into being moral anarchy, so that Wordsworth lost:

All feeling of conviction, and, in fine,
Sick, wearied out with contrarieties,
Yielded up moral questions in despair.

The Prelude is a crucial Romantic text, as it records an extreme sense of disillusionment with the ideology of the Enlightenment through its depiction of Wordsworth's experience of the French Revolution. The poem then faces the consequences of this personal crisis—which is representative of a wider cultural crisis—and goes on to seek an alternative to Enlightenment rationalism, with the last three books giving an account of his recovery from his mental crisis. The previous books, however, have anticipated this recovery by showing how his earlier life and experience formed the basis for the philosophy of life that is spelled out in the last three books. Enlightenment rationalism had cut him off from crucial experiences of his early years, the significance of which he had not realized at the time, but in recovering connection with these experiences he finds the basis of an alternative philosophy to that which had failed him during his period of commitment to Enlightenment ideals. The last three books attempt to give a more philosophical account of the meaning of certain experiences in his early life.

For example, in book 12 Wordsworth discusses "spots of time" in which "our minds / Are nourished and invisibly repaired," and "Such moments / Are scattered everywhere, taking their date / From our first childhood." This helps one to understand the significance of the apparently trivial experiences

Wordsworth recounts in the opening books of the poem, such as when he steals a boat or the effect of the presence of nature while he is ice skating. The ordinariness of these experiences is part of the point, for they are the kind of experiences anyone could have and thus can form the basis of the renewal of life not only for Wordsworth but for others also. It is out of such concrete experiences that one can forge a nature philosophy that can be an alternative to Enlightenment rationalism.

The Prelude is arguably the most ambitious poem written in English between John Milton's *Paradise Lost* and twentieth-century poems such as T. S. Eliot's *The Waste Land* and Ezra Pound's *Cantos*. It can also be argued, however, that it was something of a tragedy for English literature that Wordsworth did not publish it in 1805 and that it was unread by his Romantic successors.

K. M. Newton

Text

The Prelude 1799, 1805, 1850: Authoritative Texts, Contexts, and Recent Critical Essays. Edited by Jonathan Wordsworth, M. H. Abrams, and Stephen Gill. New York: W. W. Norton, 1979.
The Fourteen-Book "Prelude." Edited by W. J. B. Owen. Ithaca, N.Y.: Cornell University Press, 1985.
The Prelude, 1798–1799. Edited by Stephen Parish. Ithaca, N.Y.: Cornell University Press, 1988.
The Thirteen-Book "Prelude." Edited by Mark L. Reed. 2 vols. Ithaca, N.Y.: Cornell University Press, 1991.
The Five-Book "Prelude." Edited by Duncan Woo. Oxford: Blackwell, 1997.

Bibliography

Abrams, M. H. *Natural Supernaturalism: Tradition and Revolution in Romantic Literature.* New York: W. W. Norton, 1971.
Bloom, Harold, ed. *William Wordsworth's "The Prelude."* New York: Chelsea House, 1986.
Hartman, Geoffrey. *Wordsworth's Poetry 1787–1814.* Cambridge, Mass: Harvard University Press, 1964.
Johnson, Kenneth R. *Wordsworth and "The Recluse."* New Haven, Conn.: Yale University Press, 1984.
Lindenberger, Herbert. *On Wordsworth's "Prelude."* Princeton, N.J.: Princeton University Press, 1963.
McConnel, Frank D. *The Confessional Imagination: A Reading of Wordsworth's "Prelude."* Baltimore: Johns Hopkins University Press, 1974.
Onorato, Richard J. *The Character of the Poet: Wordsworth in "The Prelude."* Princeton, N.J.: Princeton University Press, 1971.
Wood, Nigel, ed. *The Prelude.* Buckingham: Open University Press, 1993.

PRE-RAPHAELITE BROTHERHOOD 1848–1853

Group of British artists

The distinguishing characteristics of the Pre-Raphaelite Brotherhood are essentially Romantic: rebellion, idealism, naïveté, a concern with nature, and the quest for an elusive "truth." The Brotherhood was founded by young, enthusiastic, and inexperienced students who were dissatisfied with the Royal Academy and the state of British painting in general; therefore, they precipitated a revolution in art. The original Brotherhood only lasted approximately four years, but pre-Raphaelitism influenced

generations of artists; a second movement flowered in the late 1850s, giving rise to Aestheticism, while late Romantic painters such as Cadogan Cowper, Frank Dicksee, Byam Shaw, and John William Waterhouse took "post-Pre-Raphaelitism" into a new century.

The Brotherhood was formed in 1848 by William Holman Hunt, John Everett Millais, and Dante Gabriel Rossetti. The first Pre-Raphaelite paintings were exhibited at the Royal Academy in 1849, signed with the initials "PRB." Hunt and Millais were already close friends, bonded through their experience of studying at the Academy, when Rossetti saw Hunt's *The Eve of St. Agnes* (1848) hanging in the Summer Exhibition and expressed his admiration to the painter. Rossetti ceased taking still-life classes from Ford Madox Brown and adopted Hunt as his new tutor. However, Rossetti soon emerged as the leader of the group, and his desire to create an artistic fraternity attracted new members. Of the four "artists" who joined the Brotherhood, only one, James Collinson, was actually a painter: both William Michael Rossetti (Dante's brother) and F. G. Stephens became art critics, while Thomas Woolner was a sculptor who had not produced anything remotely Pre-Raphaelite.

With such inauspicious beginnings, what did the Brotherhood hope to achieve? As with all Romantic art movements, the Pre-Raphaelites intended to regenerate art, primarily by detaching themselves from the rules that governed painting (for example, chiaroscuro and the application of bitumen). The Brotherhood identified a past president of the Royal Academy, Joshua Reynolds, as the main exponent of "sloshy" work. Reynolds was also guilty of suggesting that the defects of nature should be perfected for the glory of God (Rossetti had recently purchased William Blake's critique of this aesthetic, "Annotations to Sir Joshua Reynolds' Discourses"). For the Pre-Raphaelite Brotherhood, idealization denoted falsehood, and they denounced what they saw as the mediocrity of art from the time of Raphael, thus the title *Pre-Raphaelite*. However, apart from Lasinio's engravings of the Campo Santo frescos in Pisa, a subject on which Leigh Hunt had been effusive, very few examples of art before Raphael would have been available to these painters. (Moreover, as John Ruskin observed, they were attempting to imitate "not Pre-Raphaelite art, but Pre-Raphaelite honesty.") Certainly, the Brotherhood was impressed by the sincerity of art in the Middle Ages, and a consciously archaistic style and setting is evident in Millais's first Pre-Raphaelite painting, *Isabella and Lorenzo* (1849), yet, as the title suggests, this work is based on John Keats's poem "Isabella; or, the Pot of Basil." The vivid, fresh colors, highly stylized details, and finely wrought portraiture display the influence of pre-Renaissance art, but thematically Millais is commenting on a Keatsian discourse of romantic love, social aspirations, and greed. In the early days of the Brotherhood, a "List of Immortals" was drawn up that consisted primarily of immediate precursors and contemporaries: Elizabeth Barrett Browning, Robert Browning, Lord Byron, John Flaxman, Thomas Hood, John Keats, Percy Bysshe Shelley, Alfred Tennyson, David Wilkie, and William Wordsworth.

Alongside Millais's depiction of violence and rebellion in *Isabella and Lorenzo*, Hunt exhibited *Rienzi* (1848), a work inspired by Edward Bulwer-Lytton's novel of that name, on the theme of liberty. Both works were well received, with the *Art Journal* acclaiming the artists as future masters. However, when Rossetti exhibited *Ecce Ancilla Domini* (*The Annunciation*, in which a youthful virgin Mary is shown receiving the news of her pregnancy from the Archangel Gabriel) alongside Walter Deverell's *Twelfth Night* at the Free Exhibition of 1850, the response was hostile. Millais's *Christ in the House of His Parents* (1850), a realistic depiction of Christ as a child among his laboring family, was singled out by the *Times* as particularly offensive, while Charles Dickens similarly criticized the work in *Household*

Words. The *Athenaeum* also joined the assault on this secret society that was almost universally regarded as both presumptuous and, in the light of political instability across Europe, a threat to artistic orthodoxy.

However, even though the critics opposed the Pre-Raphaelite Brotherhood, a number of academicians and patrons, such as Thomas Combe, supported their work. Although Rossetti vowed never to publicly exhibit his paintings again, both Hunt and Millais entered a productive period in which they worked on some of their most memorable pieces. Hunt painted *Claudio and Isabella* and exhibited *Valentine Rescuing Sylvia from Proteus* at the Royal Academy in 1851, where Millais was represented by three paintings, including *Marianna* (a richly symbolic work that capitalized on the popularity of the new poet laureate, Alfred, Lord Tennyson). The critical reception was negative, but crucially Ruskin took up the cause of the Brotherhood at this juncture. As the author of *Modern Painters*, in which he directs all artists to the meticulous study of nature, Ruskin was impressed by the Pre-Raphaelites' "finish of drawing and splendour of colour." Most significantly [in his letters to the *Times*] Ruskin expressed a hope that the Pre-Raphaelites would "lay in our England the foundation of a school of art nobler than the world has seen for three hundred years." Ruskin adopted Millais as his new protégé, seeing in him a natural successor to J. M. W. Turner. Ruskin's influence can be seen in the accomplished *Ophelia* (1852) and a celebrated portrait of himself (painted during the ill-fated holiday in Glenfinlas when Millais fell in love with Ruskin's wife). Although the events that followed—including a scandalous divorce and Effie's remarriage to Millais—eventually soured the friendship between the two men, Ruskin was responsible for altering the tide of opinion in favor of the Pre-Raphaelites.

By 1856, Ruskin proclaimed that the battle for Pre-Raphaelitism was won, yet the Brotherhood had disbanded many years earlier. Rossetti, whose aims and ideals had always been widely different from those of Hunt and Millais, drifted away from the Brotherhood after their early, Gothic stage, and around 1851 began producing small, intense sketches and watercolors with literary and medieval themes. During this year, Ros-

William Holman Hunt, *The Eve of St. Agnes, or the Flight of Madelaine and Porphyro during the Drunkeness Attending the Revelry.* Reprinted courtesy of the Bridgeman Art Library.

setti also began his love affair with Elizabeth Siddal; as a model and a painter, she made her own contribution to the Pre-Raphaelite movement (as did many of the women associated with or influenced by the Brotherhood). Rossetti's work of this period attracted others to the fold, including Arthur Hughes, Edward Burne-Jones, and William Morris, whose careers introduced this phase of Pre-Raphaelitism to an international audience and laid the foundations for the European Symbolist Movement. The later careers of both Millais and Hunt also contributed to the phenomenon of Pre-Raphaelitism. The latter remained loyal to the original precepts of the Brotherhood, producing widely disseminated works with a religious or social theme, while Millais abandoned the precision and depth of his earlier work to become the most influential and successful painter of the age. Yet Pre-Raphaelitism retained a controversial edge; the literary periodical *The Yellow Book*, for example, shows Rossetti's work alongside Aubrey Beardsley's distorted brand of Pre-Raphaelitism. The Pre-Raphaelite Brotherhood was the Victorian heir of the British Romantics, and, in turn, those artists looked forward to the modernity of the twentieth century.

SARAH WOOTTON

Biography

Hunt and Millais meet, c. 1844; Rossetti introduces himself to Hunt, May 1848; Pre-Raphaelite Brotherhood founded in Millais's house at 83 Gower Street, September 1848; first Pre-Raphaelite paintings exhibited at the Royal Academy and Free Exhibition, 1849; Collinson leaves Pre-Raphaelite Brotherhood, and Millais exhibits *Christ in the House of His Parents* at the Royal Academy, 1850; Ruskin writes two letters to the *Times* and publishes a pamphlet entitled *Pre-Raphaelitism*, 1851; Woolner emigrates to Australia, and Millais holidays with Ruskin and his wife, 1852; Millais becomes an Associate Academician, November 1853; Hunt leaves England for Egypt and the Holy Land, January 13, 1854.

Bibliography

Bell, Quentin. *A New and Noble School: The Pre-Raphaelites.* London: Macdonald, 1982.

Cherry, Deborah, and Griselda Pollock. "Patriarchal Power and the Pre-Raphaelites," *Art History* 7 (1984): 480–95.

———. "Woman as Sign in Pre-Raphaelite Literature: A Study of the Representation of Elizabeth Siddall," *Art History* 7 (1984): 206–27.

Harding, Ellen, ed. *Re-framing the Pre-Raphaelites: Historical and Theoretical Essays.* Bournemouth: Scolar Press, 1996.

Hewison, Robert, Ian Warrell, and Stephen Wildman. *Ruskin, Turner and the Pre-Raphaelite Brotherhood.* London: Tate Gallery, 2000.

Hilton, Timothy. *The Pre-Raphaelites.* London: Thames and Hudson, 1970.

Holman Hunt, William. *Pre-Raphaelitism and the Pre-Raphaelite Brotherhood.* 2 vols. New York: AMS Press, 1967.

Marsh, Jan. *Pre-Raphaelite Women: Images of Femininity in Pre-Raphaelite Art.* London: Weidenfeld and Nicolson, 1987.

Marsh, Jan, and Pamela Gerrish Nunn. *Pre-Raphaelite Women Artists.* London: Manchester City Art Galleries, 1997.

Parris, Leslie, ed. *The Pre-Raphaelites.* London: Tate Gallery, 1984.

Pointon, Marcia. *Pre-Raphaelites Re-Viewed.* Manchester: Manchester University Press, 1989.

Watson, Margaretta Frederick, ed. *Collecting the Pre-Raphaelites: The Anglo-American Enchantment.* Guilford: Ashgate, 1997.

Wood, Christopher. *The Pre-Raphaelites.* London: Weidenfield and Nicolson, 1981.

PRE-ROMANTICISM IN MUSIC

Pre-Romanticism in music denotes not a single artistic movement striving toward a unified set of aesthetic aims, but a loose collection of regionally and chronologically distinct groups of composers. Their work may be seen, retrospectively, as prefiguring in certain respects those Romantic qualities subsequently expressed in the writings of E. T. A. Hoffmann, Jean Paul, August Wilhelm and Friedrich von Schlegel, Ludwig Tieck, and Wilhelm Heinrich Wackenroder. The so-called *empfindsamer Stil* (tender style) and works exhibiting Sturm und Drang (storm and stress) may be included under the "pre-Romantic" heading, principally because they tend to emphasize features that were typically peripheral within musical classicism as practiced in the second half of the eighteenth century. Such features include extreme expressive contrasts, incursion of disruptive recitative-like passages within the musical "prose" (giving the impression of an abrupt turn toward a "narrative" mode of discourse, as if switching to the first person), instability of key, sudden opposition of register, dynamic contrast, and exciting orchestral effect (or quasi-orchestral effect upon a solo keyboard). All of these features were applied for dramatic purpose, rather than forming any part of the underlying thematic or tonal procedures that governed the structure. Some of the keyboard sonatas of Carl Philipp Emmanuel Bach, for many years keyboard player to Frederick the Great of Prussia and profoundly affected by the cultural ambience of that court, reflect the hypersensitive spirit of *Empfindsamkeit* (sensibility), and may be linked to the composer's well-documented gift for fascinating improvisations at the keyboard, during which he appeared to enter a trance-like state, abandoning himself and his playing to the moment. In symphonic music of the Sturm und Drang type (the title follows that of a 1776 play by Sebastian Klinger), the emphasis is often on the portrayal of darker emotional concepts and especially of the wild and sublime realm of nature—for example, storm scenes such as that depicted in the finale of the Mannheim composer Ignaz Holzbauer's symphony *Fuor del Mare* (1769). Such works accord unusual prominence to minor keys; examples include Franz Joseph Haydn's Symphony no. 49 in F Minor, "La Passione" [1770–71] and Wolfgang Amadeus Mozart's Symphony in G Minor, K183 [1773].

Generically, such compositions as these embrace the fantasia, a free form normally understood by contemporary theory as a temporary departure from conventional procedures, in which rules regulating thematic and tonal composition are suspended. Attempts by eighteenth-century theorists to articulate the character of the fantasia rely on a structural opposition of "normalcy" and "deviance," defining it by contrast and positioning it at the periphery of genre as an alternative mode of discourse. Incorporated into the heart of works written according to mainstream classical practice, however, the fantasia had the potential to unsettle the intellectual purity and predictable, reassuring symmetry symbolized by classical music in a manner that parallels contemporary philosophical and sociological debates. It is this fascination with the realms of feeling (and perhaps, too, the revelation of individuality) opened up by such suspension of normality that arguably dominates those strands of later eighteenth-century music that we term *pre-Romantic*. This made itself felt especially strongly in instrumental, rather than vocal, music. Early nineteenth-century critical accounts of the type inspired by Hoffmann's article "Beethoven's Instrumental Music" (1813) strongly privileged instrumental rather than vocal repertories. The notion of "absolute music," in which, freed from the associations or dictates of a text, music might speak "purely," entirely within the terms of its own metaphorical "language" (that is, its internal structural inter-relations), became powerfully evocative of the highest achievements of Viennese classicism.

Adjacent to the preoccupation with the fantasia's ability to reveal new and untamed worlds of personal expression was a theoretical dimension. Empowered by an emergent neoplatonic aesthetic in the late eighteenth century, according to which genius became a privileged term pointing the way beyond mere reason to a world of feeling (in opposition to the former Aristotelian, rule-based approach to art philosophy), the irrational gained an important foothold in conceptions of artistic value. In contrast to the Aristotelian stance, critical thinking through the second half of the eighteenth century developed a renewed interest in the treatises of Plato, which accorded the highest place to "inspiration," a quality that could not be taught in treatises, and, for that very reason, symbolic for those of a pre-Romantic disposition of an escape from the structured paths of classicism in art. For instance, in Plato's *Phaedrus*, Socrates' second speech deals with types of "divine madness" by which man is, from time to time, possessed. He believed that such madness was of great benefit to the true poet, declaring

The third type of possession and madness is possession by the Muses. When this seizes upon a gentle and virgin soul it rouses it to inspired expression . . . But if a man comes to the door of poetry untouched by the madness of the Muses, believing that technique alone will make

him a good poet, he and his sane compositions never reach perfection, but are utterly eclipsed by the performances of the inspired madman.

This element of wonderful irrationality underlies Hoffmann's description of the pre-Romantic harbingers of Ludwig van Beethoven's instrumental works; for him, Franz Joseph Haydn and Wolfgang Amadeus Mozart had pointed the way toward what Beethoven ultimately achieved independently of a text. Hoffmann notes that

Mozart and Haydn, the creators of our present instrumental music, were the first to show us the art in its full glory; the man who then looked on it with all his love and penetrated its innermost being is—Beethoven! The instrumental compositions of these three masters breathe a similar romantic spirit. . . . In Haydn's writing there prevails the expression of a serene and childlike personality. . . . Mozart leads us into the heart of the spirit realm. . . . Beethoven's instrumental music opens up to us also the realm of the monstrous and the immeasurable.

JOHN IRVING

Bibliography

Batteux, C. *Les Beaux-Arts réduits à une Même Principe.* 1746.

Downs, P. G. *Classical Music: the Era of Haydn, Mozart, and Beethoven.* New York: W. W. Norton, 1992.

Einstein, A. *Music in the Romantic Era.* New York: W. W. Norton, 1947.

Fubini, E. *Music and Culture in Eighteenth-Century Europe.* Translated and edited by B. J. Blackburn. Chicago: University of Chicago Press, 1994.

Hoffmann, E. T. A. "Beethoven's Instrumental Music," in *Strunk's Source Readings in Music History.* Rev. ed. Vol. 6. *The Nineteenth Century.* Edited by R. A. Solie. New York: W. W. Norton, 1998.

Hosler, B. *Changing Aesthetic Views of Instrumental Music in Eighteenth-Century Germany.* Ann Arbor: University of Michigan Press, 1981.

Longyear, R. *Nineteenth-Century Romanticism in Music.* 2d ed. Englewood Cliffs, N.J.: Prentice-Hall, 1973.

Nahm, M. C. *Readings in Philosophy of Art and Aesthetics.* Englewood Cliffs, N.J.: Prentice-Hall, 1975.

Neubauer, J. *The Emancipation of Music from Language: Departure from Mimesis in Eighteenth-Century Aesthetics.* New Haven, Conn.: Yale University Press, 1986.

Plato. *Phaedrus and Letters VII and VIII.* Translated by W. Hamilton. Harmondsworth, England: Penguin, 1973.

PRE-ROMANTICISM: BRITAIN

Pre-Romantic is a term devised in the late 1930s to designate certain common traits of European music and literature of the middle and late eighteenth century that preceded and anticipated Romanticism. In the eighteenth century the term often used for these traits was *sentimental*, because they emphasized the individual's affective and intellectual sentiments, or "sensibility," and a corresponding expressiveness in art. By the Romantic period there was some reaction against overly expressive art and hackneyed emotionalism, however, and *sentimental*, along with *sentimentality* and *sentimentalism*, was usually pejorative there-

after. With the rise of the modernist movement in the early twentieth century, sentimental literature, music, and art again lost favor. *Pre-Romantic* and pre-Romanticism could be used interchangeably with *sentimental* and *sentimentalism*, with the same implicitly pejorative sense. In addition, the nature of the word "*pre-Romantic*" could suggest that it was merely a forerunner of Romanticism and artistically inferior to it. Some cultural historians now see the movement as the specifically cultural aspect or expression of a broad, late-eighteenth-century movement for social, economic, and political reform, linked to both the

Enlightenment and Romanticism but distinct from them, and accordingly they prefer *sentimental* (or *sensibility*) to *pre-Romanticism*, without negative connotations.

The characteristics of pre-Romanticism began to circulate widely in European upper- and middle-class society and culture from about the mid-eighteenth century, beginning in France, and inspired especially by Jean-Jacques Rousseau. Sensibility was circulated in Britain, throughout Europe, and beyond, especially by translations and imitations of such novels as Rousseau's *Julie, ou la nouvelle Héloïse* (*Julie, or the New Eloise*, 1761), the Abbé Prévost's *Manon Lescaut* (1731), Jean-Francois Marmontel's *Contes moraux* (1761 and 1798–92), Jacques-Henri Bernardin de Saint-Pierre's *Paul et Virginie* (1787), and Johann Wolfgang von Goethe's *The Sorrows of Young Werther* (1774). These reinforced the popularity of British novels such as Frances Sheridan's *Sydney Biddulph* (1761), Oliver Goldsmith's *The Vicar of Wakefield* (1766), and Henry Mackenzie's *The Man of Feeling* (1777). There was also a Europe-wide enthusiasm for sentimental drama, lasting from at least the mid-eighteenth century well in the nineteenth. In England the sentimental drama field was led by Richard Cumberland, John Home, and Edward Moore.

In many ways, sensibility was an idealized form of middle-class and gentry culture, designed to distinguish those who adopted it from the decadent and courtly upper class, the merely commercial lower middle class, and the uncultured lower classes. The philosophical foundations of the movement are indicated by two distinct but linked meanings of *sensibility* at that time: physical sensitivity and affective, aesthetic, and moral susceptibility. The link was provided by Enlightenment materialist epistemology: the idea that the individual's knowledge, feelings, and identity are built from physical sensations received through the bodily senses. This link was argued by philosophers such as Claude-Adrien Helvétius in France and Joseph Priestley in England, and was widely pursued by writers on physiognomy and medicine. Enlightenment materialist philosophers also argued that different individuals and different social classes had varying degrees of physical and subjective sensitivity, and inhabited diverse material and social worlds; these differences were used to explain the diversity of individuals, social groups, and races, present and past. In fact, however, as developed in the literature and culture of sensibility these ideas promoted an idealized image of certain elements of the European upper and middle classes, and thus served their struggle for cultural, social, economic, and political power against the old order of aristocratic and monarchic hegemony.

This oppositional, reformist impulse of sensibility is indicated by its major themes. Individual sensibility, or distinctive and meritorious subjective identity, implicitly opposed forms of ascribed, social identity on which the old order was based. Disciplined and educated selfhood was promoted against what was seen as a lottery mentality, or upper- and lower-class cultures of improvidence, immediate gratification, opportunism, and fatalism. The ideology of the sovereign subject also validated both economic individualism and individual political rights against historical systems of aristocratic patronage and plebeian customary culture thought to obstruct economic, social, and cultural modernization, as argued by the Scottish philosopher Adam Smith in two connected works, *Theory of Moral Sentiments* (1759) and *Wealth of Nations* (1776). Nature, naturalness, simplicity, and even the primitive were celebrated against the supposed overrefinement, decadence, and corruption of the old order and a system of fashionable consumption dominated by the upper class. Local, everyday, and rustic life were celebrated against metropolitan life dominated by upper and lower classes and cosmopolitan culture dominated by the aristocracy. Social sympathy and philanthropy were promoted against rigid and harmful social distinctions reflected in great differences of wealth and exploitation of the weak, including women, children, the poor, and slaves. Kindness to animals was promoted against a historical aristocratic and plebeian culture of bloodsports and cruel exploitation of animal labor, and aimed to disrupt a long-standing cultural bond between upper and lower classes. In Britain, these values were promoted in the work of some widely read and imitated poets, including William Cowper (*The Task*, 1785), Thomas Gray, William Mason, Charlotte Smith (*Elegiac Sonnets*, 1784), and James Thomson (*The Seasons*, 1726–30).

At the same time that sensibility aimed to displace historic upper and lower class cultures, it also aggressively appropriated elements of them. For example, "philosophical historians" such as Edward Gibbon and Charles Robertson exposed the pretensions of medieval upper-class feudal and chivalric culture to heroism and nobility. Meanwhile, poets, dramatists, and novelists, led by Ann Radcliffe and followed by many others, represented a glamorized version of this culture as a historical anticipation of that of the eighteenth-century British middle classes. There was such a vogue for things feudal, chivalric, and "Gothic" (meaning medieval)—a term that was pejorative at the century's beginning and positive by its end—that art patrons such as William Beckford and Horace Walpole hired builders and artisans to fake ruins and artifacts, novelists and playwrights took up medieval themes and settings, and the poet Thomas Chatterton created a literary sensation by forging "medieval" manuscripts.

Lower-class culture and literature were treated similarly. On the one hand, plebeian customary or "traditional" knowledges, values, and social and economic practices were disparaged by writers such as John Brand, in *Observations on Popular Antiquities* (1775), as "superstitions" that obstructed modernization. Social reformers such as Jonas Hanway and Hannah More waged local and national campaigns to extirpate popular culture and replace it with a version of middle-class culture. Others, however, such as Henry Ellis in his expansion and adaptation (1813) of Brand's work, and Walter Scott in *Minstrelsy of the Scottish Border* (1802–3), appropriated forms of lower-class culture for emergent institutions of a supposedly historic national culture transcending differences of class and region. This was the beginning of what became known as the folklore movement, in which middle-class writers and researchers collected elements of folktale, folk songs, and proverbial wisdom. Thomas Percy initiated a European vogue for such literature with his collection *Reliques of Ancient English Poetry* (1765). Where such materials could not be found they were faked, as in James Macpherson's "Ossian poems" (1760–63), supposedly translated from fragments of ancient Gaelic epic; Ossian would be the favorite poet of Napoleon Bonaparte, and during the Romantic period such forms of plebeian literature—actual, adapted, or faked—would become major elements in the invention of national literatures in Britain and elsewhere.

As this instance suggests, pre-Romanticism, or sensibility, formed the generation in Britain, Europe, and beyond who founded modern states much as we still know them. In the process, however, sensibility also became associated with revolutionary excess and thus was discredited in the eyes of many, leaving Romantic generations to reconstruct sensibility for their own, postrevolutionary age.

GARY KELLY

See also **Aesthetics and Art Criticism; Autobiographical Writing: Britain; Beckford, William Thomas; Bentham, Jeremy; Bernardin de Saint-Pierre, Jacques-Henri; Burke, Edmund; Burns, Robert; Chatterton, Thomas; Cowper, William; Day, Thomas; Education; Folk Literature: Britain; Fuseli, Henry; Genius; Goethe, Johann Wolfgang von; Graveyard Poets; Lavater, Johann Caspar; Love, Romantic; Madness; Middle Ages; Noble Savage; Ossian; Paine, Thomas; Rousseau, Jean-Jacques; Self and Subjectivity; Sensibility; Siddons, Sarah; Sincerity; Sturm und Drang; Walpole, Horace; Williams, Helen Maria; Wollstonecraft, Mary; Women**

Bibliography

Benedict, Barbara M. *Framing Feeling: Sentiment and Style in English Prose Fiction, 1745–1800.* New York: AMS Press, 1994.
Brissenden, R. F. *Virtue in Distress: Studies in the Novel of Sentiment from Richardson to Sade.* London: Macmillan, 1974.
Johnson, Claudia L. *Equivocal Beings: Politics, Gender, and Sentimentality in the 1790s: Wollstonecraft, Radcliffe, Burney.* Chicago: University of Chicago Press, 1995.
McGann, Jerome J. *The Poetics of Sensibility: A Revolution in Literary Style.* Oxford: Clarendon Press, 1996.
Mullan, John. *Sentiment and Sociability: The Language of Feeling in the Eighteenth Century.* Oxford: Clarendon Press, 1988.
Todd, Janet M. *Sensibility: An Introduction.* London: Methuen, 1986.
Van Sant, Ann Jessie. *Eighteenth-century Sensibility and the Novel: The Senses in Social Context.* Cambridge: Cambridge University Press, 1993.

PRE-ROMANTICISM: FRANCE

While the development of French Romanticism does not form an easily traceable pattern, there remains a satisfactory sequence of common denominators to explore. Most observers, when looking back to the origins of French Romanticism in the mid-eighteenth century, emphasize key concepts such as a break from classicism, a reliance on self-taught knowledge, indulgence in sentimentality, and a willingness to examine the dark side of human nature. However, a wide variety of opinions has produced a number of contradictory definitions, such as Romanticism liberates while it destroys, and it separates itself from historical reality; imagination triumphs over reason; the Romantic artist is a humanitarian egotist, tormented and proud, unable to accept normative values.

While these notions oversimplify a complex phenomenon, they reinforce the timeless qualities and modern importance of debates associated with Romantic ideals. Irving Babbitt saw in Jean-Jacques Rousseau's ideas the dissolution of social order, and other polemical views associate Romanticism with postmodern thinking centered on a philosophy of existence in which inventiveness and engineering skill can somehow immortalize human life.

For most pre-Romantic authors, "le moi romantique" was a personality trait without the mystic moodiness of nineteenth-century protagonists suffering from *le mal du siècle.* The eighteenth-century hero or heroine was generally someone free from religious and social constraints, and the chief concern of the pre-Romantic artist was to articulate this doctrine of moral relativism. However, as philosophical novels mixed with sentimental fiction, the characters seemed to move closer to the edge of fatalistic behavior by demanding a right to indulge in Dionysian acts. Thus the French novel, drama, and painting became increasingly receptive to pathos, which appealed to the more reserved culture of the aristocracy, and to the bourgeois tendency to emphasize compassion and self-pity.

Pre-Romantic sensibility can be found in French literature as far back as the seventeenth century in authors such as Comtesse Marie-Madeleine de LaFayette, Jean Racine, and Madeleine de Scudéry. By the middle of the eighteenth century, English authors such as Daniel Defoe, James Thomson, Edward Young, and especially Samuel Richardson influenced French writers, who carved plots from domestic life and travel accounts. The most distinguishing characteristic was a deeper psychological edge that called for first-person narrations, usually in the form of letters or memoirs. Madame Françoise de Graffigny, Pierre Marivaux, the Abbé Prévost, and Madame Claudine-Alexandrine Guérin de Tencin set the stage for the explosion of interest in sentimental fiction after 1750. Although Rousseau and Denis Diderot (*La Religieuse* [*The Nun*, 1760] and *Le Neveu de Rameau* [*Rameau's Nephew*, 1761–64]) are the better known names, several significant authors such as Bacalard d'Arnaud, Madame Elie de Beaumont, Jean-François Marmontel, and Marie-Jeanne Riccoboni contributed to this vogue from the 1750s to the 1770s, when a prerevolutionary band of authors intensified the idea of writing pseudohistories in order to promote political ideologies. Chief among the authors of this later period are Pierre-Augustin de Beaumarchais (*Le Mariage de Figaro* [*The Marriage of Figaro*, 1784] and *Le Barbier de Séville* [*The Barber of Seville*, 1775]); (Nicolas-Edme) Restif de la Bretonne (*La Paysanne Pervertie* [*The Corrupted (Female) Peasant*, 1774], *Le Paysan Perverti* [*The Corrupted (Male) Peasant*, 1776], and *Les Contemporaines* [*Modern Women*, 1780–85]); Isabel de Charrière (*Lettres de Mistress Henley publiées par son amie* [*Mistress Henley's Letters*, 1784]; Jean-Pierre Claris de Florian (*Estelle et Nemorin* [1787]); and Bernardin de Saint-Pierre (*Paul et Virginie* [1788]). The circulation of these novels was promoted by a group of influential women following the pattern of strong female reader response to Samuel Richardson's *Clarissa* and to Rousseau's *Julie, ou la nouvelle Héloïse* (1761), among them Madame Marie-Jeanne Roland, Madame Stéphanie-Félicité de Genlis, Olympe de Gouges, and ultimately, Madame Anne-Louis-Germaine de Staël, who represents the final phase of transition toward fully developed nineteenth-century Romanticism.

Another cultural development that must be taken into account was the increasing demand after 1750 for frivolous English memoir-novels in French translation. Traffic in the production and sale of these "Frenchified" English novels (known as *le genre triste*) was largely carried out by Dutch publishing houses. Many factors contributed to this phenomenon, including: secular clergy who contributed to Diderot's 1751–72 *Encyclopédie* were eager to work for the Dutch publishers; copyright law reform in England and France; the universality of the French language in Europe; the continental communication network established by Huguenot refugees in Holland and England; and Samuel Johnson's "Rambler No. 4" (1750) examining the "new fiction." French Anglomania intensified after 1750 to the point where hundreds of novels appeared in incrementally-increasing fashion, especially after 1777 when the French police directed most of their efforts toward the surveillance of politically subversive texts and authors. Thus, the spread of silly, euphemistic fiction was largely unchecked; French taste was forever transformed, as was the *Ancien Régime*.

Perhaps the most controversial issues to emerge from French society before the Revolution were those associated with Rousseau's *Le Contrat social* (*The Social Contract*, 1761) and *Émile* (1762). Rousseau contended that humans had deviated from nature by the desire to own property, to acquire more than basic needs, and to form communities ruled by tyrants. In doing so, they forfeited their natural rights and lost the innocence and equality of the natural order. Rousseau echoed Edward Young's credo ("Born Originals how does it come to pass that we die Copies!") and conceived of a pastoral age in which human fulfilment could be achieved without competition. As with other utopian thinkers, Rousseau was convinced that noble savages living in new world societies were happier and more virtuous than their European counterparts. No matter how naive this view seems, one of the great achievements of the age was to raise questions of fundamental importance regarding cultural superiority. Rousseau's theories of education also transformed society; an entire generation of children was raised in the 1770s based on the idea that they should reject traditional values, think for themselves, and grow up freely in an atmosphere of benevolent love and trust. Idealistic reformers such as Johann Heinrich Pestalozzi and many others after him reshaped the standard curriculum, and Rousseau's ideas continue to bear fruit.

In the early nineteenth century, in addition to Madame de Staël, two other writers contributed to the final phase of pre-Romanticism in France: François-Auguste-René, Vicomte de Chateaubriand and Henri-Benjamin Constant de Rebecque. From 1800 until her death in 1817, Madame de Staël wrote a series of books that challenged the nationalism of the Napoleonic era by questioning the relationship between literature and social institutions, examining the results of the French Revolution, and exploring French culture in relation to other countries such as Russia, Italy, and Germany. Constant's *Adolphe* (1816) depicts the life of a lonely wanderer who clings to certain memories, perceptions, and places that stimulate his imagination in order to ward off melancholy. This intensely psychological novel promotes Madame de Staël's cultural relativism. Chateaubriand's incomplete novel *René* (1805) and its companion piece *Atala* (1801) combine elements already noticeable in Rousseau and in Johann Wolfgang Goethe's *Die Leiden des jungen Werthers* (*The Sorrows of Young Werther*, 1774)—a lyrical and rhetorical style free of self-consciousness, and a stubborn determination to expose the inner life at all costs. In addition, Chateaubriand drew upon a visit to America to present the peaceful abundance of Indian village life as an alternative to the agitated aimlessness of the European soul.

The pre-Romantic imagination was essentially directed toward the transformation of values, as if some profound change in the psyche called for the creation of a new personality. Diderot's *Neveu de Rameau* might serve as the archetype of this new worldview; in it we read, "Self-disciplined and aware of his superior intelligence, Rameau's nephew is a compound of elevation and abjection, of good sense and lunacy . . . he has no greater opposite than himself . . . what a novelty, what a monster, what a prodigy!"

Robert J. Frail

Bibliography

Babbitt, Irving. *Rousseau and Romanticism*. New York: AMS Press, 1976.

Brissenden, R. F. *Virtue in Distress: Studies in the Novel of Sentiment from Richardson to Sade*. New York: Harper and Row, 1974.

Green, Frederick C. *French Novelists: Manners and Ideas from the Renaissance to the Revolution*. New York: D. Appleton, 1930.

Hilles, F. and H. Bloom, eds. *From Sensibility to Romanticism*. New York: Oxford University Press, 1965.

L'Aminot, Tanguy, ed. *Politique et Revolution chez Jean-Jacques Rousseau*. Studies in Voltaire and Eighteenth-Century Culture. 324. Oxford: The Voltaire Foundation, 1994.

May, Gita. *De Jean-Jacques Rousseau à Madame Roland: Essai sur la sensibilité préromantique et révolutionnaire*. Geneva: Droz, 1964.

McFarland, Thomas. *Romanticism and the Heritage of Rousseau*. New York: Oxford University Press, 1995.

Starobinski, Jean. *Transparency and Obstruction*. Translated by Arthur Goldhammer. Chicago and London: University of Chicago Press, 1988.

Trilling, Lionel. *Sincerity and Authenticity*. Cambridge, Mass.: Harvard University Press, 1974.

PRE-ROMANTICISM: GERMANY

In his celebrated Mellon Lectures on Romanticism in 1965, Isaiah Berlin asked rhetorically, "Where did the romantic movement take its rise?"; and, although he acknowledged the importance of Jean-Jacques Rousseau in pre-Romanticism, his equally rhetorical answer was unequivocal: "It occurred not in England, not in France, but for the most part in Germany." Two visionary anthropological and cultural theorists were, he argued, particularly responsible for what he characterized as the spread of antirationalism in the late eighteenth century: Johann Georg Hamann, the so-called Magus of the North, with his creed of vitalism and individualism; and Johann Gottfried Herder, who advocated historical relativism and pluralism of standards in the study of human culture.

Certainly Herder was the key figure in the Sturm und Drang (storm and stress) movement, the most conspicuous manifestation of pre-Romanticism in Germany. In 1773 he edited *Von deutscher Art und Kunst* (*On German Character and Art*), a collection of short essays amounting to a kind of manifesto of pre-Romanticism, or at least of opposition to neoclassicism. He himself contributed "Über Ossian und die Lieder alter Völker" ("On Ossian and the Lays of Ancient Peoples"), in which he praised the spontaneity and artlessness of primitive folksong (of which he supposed the fake Celtic works of Ossian to be part), defending its lack of logical structures, what he called its "leaps and bounds." A second essay by Herder was devoted to Shakespeare, whose disregard of the classical unities, especially unity of time, he not only condoned but extolled. Perhaps the most significant essay in the volume, however, is a polemical and ebullient piece by the young Johann Wolfgang von Goethe in praise of Gothic architecture, "Von deutscher Baukunst" ("On German Architecture"). Taking Strasburg Cathedral as his model, he mistakenly views the Gothic as a specifically German style and identifies its essence as "the significantly rough-hewn." Gothic vaulting, he asserts, is no less aesthetically valid than the flat roofs and colonnades of antiquity. Neoclassical architecture, in emulating the archaic conventions of a past culture, is contrived, "inappropriate and unnecessary." The Gothic cathedral, by contrast, results from the spontaneous, independent impulse of a "strong, rough, German soul" and is indigenously authentic. As such it possesses intrinsic coherence and "necessity": it is not constructed according to the rules and principles of classicism but grows organically like one of "god's trees." Prescription is inimical to genius; the creative artist is a second or greater Prometheus conveying "the bliss of the gods" to mortals.

Goethe was already putting these aesthetic convictions into literary practice, in particular in the first draft of *Faust*, the so-called *Urfaust*, composed between 1769 and 1775. It is a play about a turbulent and wayward genius, itself written in turbulent and wayward form, modeled according to Herder's program on Shakespeare and the folk song violent in its language and passionate in its themes, alternating ("leaps and bounds") between farce and melodrama, obscenity and pathos. Goethe makes his Faust denounce learned eloquence in favor of the outpourings of the heart and plead for a personal religion based on intuition rather than theological doctrine: "feeling is everything," Faust tells Gretchen. In Goethe's poems of the same period, emphasis is again placed on naturalness, passion, and defiance of authority; *Prometheus*, for example, glorifies human genius and derides the impotence of the gods. Schiller, ten years Goethe's junior, soon began to write plays in a similarly iconoclastic Sturm und Drang vein. In *Die Räuber* (*The Robbers*, 1781), *Kabale und Liebe* (*Intrigue and Love*, 1784), and *Don Carlos* (1784), defiant sons rebel against tyrannical fathers and corrupt social hierarchies, ending in martyrdom or self-destruction. Yet the most revolutionary writer of this generation was Jakob Michael Reinhold Lenz, whose play *Der Hofmeister* (*The Private Tutor*, 1774) portrays the symbolic self-castration of a bourgeois intellectual emasculated by the lack of a fulfilling role in a class-ridden society. The subversive and melodramatic visions of the Sturm und Drang playwrights find their pictorial correlative in the disturbed images of a painter who moved in their circle, the Swiss-born Henry Fuseli, later active among the English Romantics, whose powerful figures and grotesque fantasies betray his unease with the placid stability of Enlightenment society.

Another aspect of pre-Romanticism in Germany in the 1770s was the cult of *Empfindsamkeit* (Sensibility). Deriving in no small measure from Rousseau's critique of reason, it elevated feeling and sensitivity to the status of supreme human faculties. Effusive emotionalism, an emphasis on self-sacrificing and intense friendship as well as on ardent romantic love, and lachrymose outbursts of gratuitous sentiment are its hallmarks. In Germany it was reinforced by the popularity among the educated bourgeoisie of pietism, a species of protestantism that emphasized spiritual intensity and direct communion with a personal deity in preference to the mediation of the priesthood and an institutionalized church. Friedrich Gottlieb Klopstock produced religious and nature poetry of a hymnic kind, but the most notable exponents of Empfindsamkeit were the so-called Göttinger Hain (Grove of Göttingen) writers, who published elegiac poetry and idylls. It was Goethe again who provided, in one and the same novel, the most poignant celebration of Empfindsamkeit ideals and the most uncompromising exposure of its fallacies. In *Die Leiden des jungen Werthers* (*The Sorrows of Young Werther*), first published in 1774, he created a character whose obsessive cultivation of his feelings, sincerely noble and liberal though they are, leads inexorably to suicide and violation of the rights and sensitivities of others. Yet Werther was to become, ironically and to Goethe's annoyance, an iconic figure among the Romantic generation throughout Europe.

By the mid-1780s the Sturm und Drang had passed despite its popularity with the adolescent Romantics; but in other ways the Enlightenment was being increasingly undermined in Germany. Karl Philipp Moritz tried to show in his "psychological novel" *Anton Reiser* (1785–90) that the imaginative and intellectual energies of a repressed younger generation could find no outlet in the ordered provincial world of the particularist German states. In his aesthetic writings, Moritz began to preach the Romantic doctrine that truth was to be found less through reason than through art. Wilhelm Heinse published the first of the genre of artist novels that were to dominate German Romantic fiction from Ludwig Tieck's *Franz Sternbalds Wanderungen* (*The Travels of Franz Sternbald*, 1798) to Eduard Friedrich Mörike's *Maler Nolten* (*Nolten the Painter*, 1832). Heinse's *Ardinghello und die glückseligen Inseln* (*Ardinghello and the Blessed Islands*, 1787) evokes an exotic, sensual lifestyle offering alternative values to those of rationalist utilitarianism. These developments remained undercurrents; it took the phenomenalism of Immanuel Kant and the subjectivist epistemology of Johann Gottlieb Fichte on the one hand, and the ideological provocation of the French Revolution on the other, to turn the instinctive pre-Romanticism of Germany under the ancien régime into the conviction Romanticism which was flourishing in Berlin and Jena by 1797.

RICHARD LITTLEJOHNS

Bibliography

Berlin, Isaiah. *The Roots of Romanticism.* Edited by Henry Hardy. Princeton, N.J.: Princeton University Press/London: Chatto and Windus, 1999.

Lange, Victor. *The Classical Age of German Literature 1740–1815.* London: Arnold, 1982.

Pascal, Roy. *The German Sturm und Drang.* Manchester: Manchester University Press, 1953.

Swales, Martin. *Goethe: The Sorrows of Young Werther.* Cambridge and New York: Cambridge University Press, 1987.

PRIESTLEY, JOSEPH 1733–1804

Philosopher and scientist

A list of Joseph Priestley's achievements seems to defy any single professional categorization: in ethics and political philosophy he was the author of the utilitarian principle (the greatest good for the greatest number); his histories of religion include a masterpiece of syncretism in the history of ideas (*Doctrines of Heathen Philosophy Compared with Those of Revelation*, 1804); he was the first scientist to isolate oxygen (though he persisted in explaining the gas as ordinary air from which "phlogiston" had been removed), and he discovered and isolated ammonia, sulphur dioxide, nitrous oxide, and nitrogen dioxide. It was Priestley who performed the initial work on the discovery and analysis of photosynthesis. He discovered the function of the blood in respiration, and he was one of the clearest and most forceful proponents of philosophical materialism (in opposition to doctrines of a soul distinct from the physical body). In his study of electricity he produced a scale of conductivity as a common property of different substances, and he discovered the unified inverse square form of the law of force obtaining between electrical charges. In contrast to earlier doctrines of ether and particles, he articulated a unified theory of the relation of substance and light, matter and motion. He was the most prolific defender of English religious dissent in the eighteenth century; and so influential was his support of the democratic revolution in France that his house, laboratory, and library in Birmingham were destroyed by a church-and-king mob in an attack that was artificially incited by a hostile government, according to Samuel Taylor Coleridge. A bibliography of Priestley's works is difficult to enumerate because he was prolific in the publication of expanded editions of his works, editions accompanied by published objections, then his replies to the objections, and then further objections and further replies, and so on, indefatigably; but at the least one can count many dozens of voluminous works by Priestley in science, political philosophy, history, metaphysics, rhetoric, theology, and ethics.

This array of subject matter on which he lavished his intellectual gifts and his inexhaustible energies (he died within an hour of completing corrections on a last book that he had been determined to finish), together with the lucidity and matter-of-factness of his style of writing in the Enlightenment mode of plain speaking, would seem to foreclose an effort to place his work coherently in a context of Romantic period thought and literature, or in any coherent theoretical context. However, thanks largely to the work of Jack Lindsay, the theoretical coherence of these disparate endeavors emerges in a precisely Romantic context. In his writings on science, political philosophy, metaphysics, and the history of religion, Priestley constructs a theory of apparently discrete and often binary terms in the form of a unified-field theory. The project of a higher-order conceptual unification makes Priestley's science intelligible (including the overcoming of the ether-particle binary, or the principle of common conductivity). The same project of intellectual unification is carried on in the metaphysical terms of Priestley's radical materialism, in which, following David Hartley but going much further, Priestley denied all dualism in the articulation of his more totally explanatory and monistic materialism. In ways characteristic of Romantic-period writers, Priestley drew upon a syncretic

method of cultural and intellectual history to unfold the shared structure of mythological formations. And just as the apparent dichotomy of body and soul, or wave and particle, or energy and matter is overcome in the conception of a materialistic monism that resolves surface oppositions in a structural unity, so too the apparently disparate forms of disciplinary endeavor in which Priestley was almost equally preeminent are taken into a higher unity within the corpus of his prolific and comprehensive range of intellectual work.

Priestley's influence was even greater than his massive list of published works (a sample of which appears in the bibliography below) can indicate. Thomas Jefferson, who wrote to Priestley to encourage his writings on comparative religion, also advised James Madison to study Priestley's political philosophy books. Priestley's *Letters to the Right Honourable Edmund Burke* (published by Joseph Johnson in 1791) was already in a third edition in its first year. Priestley was widely recognized as "the most dangerous enemy of the established religion, in its connection with the state" while the intellectuals in the Johnson circle and the French revolutionaries themselves were celebrating his writings for their power to help in the "liberating of all the powers of man." Earlier, Benjamin Franklin had consulted with Priestley when he was in London seeking to negotiate peace for the American colonies. Threatened with persecution in England, Priestley fled to America in 1794, and there civic associations and learned societies alike welcomed him as one of the world's most effective fighters against tyranny and bigotry and as one of the leading proponents of liberty in political, philosophical, and religious life.

Controversy and persecution followed him in America, too, however, even amid simultaneous fame and admiration: President John Adams's secretary of state, Timothy Pickering, attempted to deport Priestley under the Alien and Sedition Act, though ultimately Adams relented. However, Thomas Cooper, who helped Priestley with the revision of some of his last writings, was imprisoned. In 1804, happy at last and for the first time in a country whose leadership (under Jefferson) was friendly to him, and as he was dying, Priestley finished *Doctrines of Heathen Philosophy Compared with Those of Revelation*, in which he analyzes the ethical systems of Aristotle, Arrian, Epictetus, Epicurus, Jesus Christ, Marcus Aurelius, Plato, Pythagoras, Seneca, and Socrates. As with William Blake (in "All Religions Are One" [1788], for example), and Percy Bysshe Shelley, who wrote of "harmonizing the contending creeds" (*Letters*), Priestley formulated large conceptual unifications that are distinctive for their extensiveness, complexity, trenchancy, and historical effects.

TERENCE HOAGWOOD

Biography

Born 1733 in Birstal Fieldhead (near Leeds). In schools and at home, learned many ancient and modern languages, mathematics, religious history, biological and chemical experimentation. To dissenting academy at Daventry in 1752. Dissenting minister, 1755. Tutor at Warrington Academy, 1761. Doctor of laws, University of Edinburgh, 1764. To London for scientific work for Royal Society, 1765. Received patronage of William Perry,

Earl of Shelburne, in 1773. To Birmingham as minister of the New Meeting-House in 1780, associating with Erasmus Darwin and Lunar Society. House, laboratory, and library destroyed by church-and-king mob, 1791. To America, 1794. Died in Northumberland, Pennsylvania, in 1804.

Selected Works

Theory of Language. 1762.
The History and Present State of Electricity. 1767.
An Essay on the First Principles of Government; and on the Nature of Political, Civil, and Religious Liberty. 1768.
The History and Present State of Discoveries Relating to Vision, Light, and Colours. 1772.
Institutes of Natural and Revealed Religion. 1772.
Experiments and Observations on Different Kinds of Air. 1774–77.
Philosophical Empiricism. 1775.
Disquisitions Relating to Matter and Spirit. 1777.
Letters to a Philosophical Unbeliever. 1780.
An History of the Corruptions of Christianity. 1782.
An History of the Early Opinions Concerning Jesus Christ . . . Proving that the Christian Religion Was at First Unitarian. 1786.
Lectures on History and General Policy. 1788.
An Appeal to the Public, on the Subject of the Riots in Birmingham. 1791.
Letters to the Right Honourable Edmund Burke. 1791.
A Political Dialogue on the General Principles of Government. 1791.
A Comparison of the Institutions of Moses with Those of the Hindoos and Other Ancient Nations. 1797?
Notes on All the Books of Scripture. 1803.
Doctrines of Heathen Philosophy, Compared with Those of Revelation. 1804.

Memoirs of Joseph Priestley, to the Year 1795, Written by Himself; with a Continuation, to the Time of His Decease, by His Son, Joseph Priestley, and Observations on His Writings, by Thomas Cooper . . . and the Rev. William Christie. 1806.

Bibliography

Blake, William. *All Religions Are One.* In *The Complete Poetry and Prose of William Blake.* Edited by David V. Erdman. Garden City, N.Y.: Doubleday, 1982.
Bowen, Catherine Drinker. *John Adams and the American Revolution.* Boston: Little, Brown, 1950.
Curran, Stuart. *Shelley's Annus Mirabilis.* San Marino, Calif.: Huntington Library, 1975.
Hoagwood, Terence Allan. Introduction to *Doctrines of Heathen Philosophy, Compared with Those of Revelation.* Delmar, N.Y.: Scholars' Facsimiles, 1987.
————. *Prophecy and the Philosophy of Mind: Traditions of Blake and Shelley.* Tuscaloosa: University of Alabama Press, 1985.
Kuhn, Albert J. "English Deism and the Development of Romantic Mythological Syncretism," *PMLA* 71 (1956): 1094–1116.
Lindsay, Jack. Introduction to *Autobiography of Joseph Priestley.* Bath: Adams and Dart, 1970.
Parton, James. *Life of Thomas Jefferson,* 1874. Reprint New York: Da Capo Press, 1971.
"Priestley." In *General Biographical Dictionary,* Rev. ed. Edited by Alexander Chalmers. London: J. Nichols, 1812.
Seznec, Jean. *The Survival of the Pagan Gods.* New York: Bollingen, 1953.
Shelley, Percy Bysshe. *Letters.* Edited by Frederick L. Jones. Oxford: Oxford University Press, 1964.
Smith, Edgar F. *Priestley in America, 1794–1804,* 1920. Reprint New York: Arno Press, 1980.

PROGRAM MUSIC AND TONE PAINTING

The question of whether instrumental music can or should depict nonmusical images and ideas was central to Romantic discussions of the art. The classic ideal of pure music, as reflected in the eighteenth-century propensity for generic titles (such as sonata, symphony), contrasts with the Romantic ideal of program music, as reflected in a much higher percentage of nineteenth-century works with descriptive titles. Both E. T. A. Hoffmann and Wilhelm Heinrich Wackenroder argued that abstract instrumental music, because of its lack of external associations, was purer than vocal music or music with descriptive titles, while Romantic composers from Hector Berlioz onward preferred to give their listeners tangible evidence of their intentions. Ludwig van Beethoven stood on the cusp of these two practices, giving most of his works generic titles but occasionally adding extramusical connotations through descriptive subtitles for individual movements (as in the Pastoral Symphony or the Lebewohl [Farewell] Sonata) or texts (as in Symphony No. 9). As the nineteenth century progressed, the practice became so popular that publishers and critics added programmatic titles to works that had not been so designated by their composers (for example, Beethoven's "Moonlight Sonata" and Frédéric Chopin's "Revolutionary Etude").

For those composers who chose to attach extramusical meanings to their works, the range of possibilities was extensive. Beethoven's isolated uses of descriptive attributions tended to be general rather than specific, as did several of the symphonic poems of Franz Liszt based on metaphysical ideas or feelings. Berlioz's *Symphonie fantastique* (1830) and Bedřich Smetana's *Vltava* (1874–79), by contrast, are works with very specific imagery contained in a detailed verbal description and reflected closely in the musical score. The short character pieces for piano that were so ubiquitous during the nineteenth century show a similar range of specificity, as illustrated by Robert Schumann's *Papillons* (*Butterflies*), op. 2, with no descriptive titles for individual pieces, and *Carnaval*, op. 9, with descriptive titles for each piece.

Program music sometimes—though by no means always—made use of tone painting as well. This technique involves the practice of making audible reference to familiar sounds, such as thunder or bird song, in a musical context. The synesthetic experience of depicting visual or verbal stimuli through instrumental music was particularly appealing to nineteenth-century composers and their audiences, though it predates the Romantic era by several centuries. From Beethoven's Pastoral Symphony No. 6 (1808), with its evocation of bird songs, peasant folk music, a brook, and a thunderstorm, through Berlioz's *Symphonie fantastique*, with its evocation of the guillotine and a witches' sabbath, and culminating in Richard Strauss's graphic orchestral depictions of a myriad of sounds, from the bleating of sheep to a domestic squabble, the ever-increasing resources of the orchestra allowed composers to expand the realm of possibility for tone painting.

The term *Programmusik* was coined by Liszt in 1855 to denote music that depends for its meaning on an external, written program. The context of his designation was a review of Berlioz's symphony with viola solo written for Niccolò Paganini and inspired by Lord Byron's *Childe Harold*. In this influential review, Liszt not only introduced a new term to the discussion of musical depiction, but he provided a rationale for the descriptive nature of his own symphonic poems and by extension to the entire aesthetic direction of the "New German" school of composers. He argued in favor of works like his own that were not structured on the basis of traditional forms, but rather used a program as the basis of organization. In order to strengthen his case, he suggested hearing programmatic meanings in certain works of Beethoven, thereby linking his own innovations to a distinguished forebear. As Vera Micznik has pointed out, however, attaching programmatic connotations to past works blurs the distinction between program and absolute music, thus creating difficulties of categorization that continue to plague discussions of this issue today.

The terminological imprecision associated with Liszt's use of the term has led to widely divergent views on the subject. During the polemical debates between the New German school of Liszt and the defenders of tradition led by Eduard Hanslick in the late nineteenth century, absolute music and program music were seen as two sides of an irreconcilable dichotomy. For critics like Hanslick and composers like Johannes Brahms, program music represented formlessness and debasement of the purity of instrumental music; for the followers of Liszt and Richard Wagner, absolute music was an archaic, formalistic leftover from a past age. Other analysts have downplayed the differences by arguing radically inclusive views: Friedrich Niecks suggested that all music from 1600 to 1900 was programmatic, whether or not its composer intended it to be, while Carl Dahlhaus suggested that the two are not polar opposites but rather part of a continuum, with each individual work falling at some point in between.

The reason for such contentious debate is that program music strikes at some of the fundamental issues of musical expression.

The notion that music's expressiveness is most powerful at exactly the point that it transcends verbal description is undermined by linking music with specific verbal imagery. Additionally, the act of assigning a program to a musical work prejudices the listener towards the composer's interpretation rather than allowing free association to suggest alternate meanings. Finally, composing according to a story or other external stimulus leads to unconventional formal structures, seen by some as innovative and by others as rambling. The most important new form to emerge from program music was the symphonic poem, pioneered by Liszt around 1850 and practiced by every major European composer with the exception of Brahms between 1850 and 1920. In rebutting the charge that symphonic poems lacked formal structure, Wagner argued that formal structure can be equated with the hilt of a sword: when it is in use it is hidden in the hand, while the blade does the work. For these reasons, the debate over program music assumed vital importance to late nineteenth-century critics, especially as the practice of adding descriptive titles and verbal programs became increasingly widespread.

E. DOUGLAS BOMBERGER

Bibliography

Altenburg, Detlef. "Programmusik." In *Die Musik in Geschichte und Gegenwart*. 2nd ed. Edited by Ludwig Finscher. Kassel: Bärenreiter, 1997.

Dahlhaus, Carl. "Thesen über Programmusik." In *Beiträge zur musikalischen Hermeneutik*. Edited by Carl Dahlhaus. Regensburg: Bosse, 1975.

Liszt, Franz. "Berlioz und seine Haroldsymphonie," *Neue Zeitschrift für Musik* 43 (1855): 25–32 ff.

Micznik, Vera. "The Absolute Limitations of Program Music: The Case of Liszt's 'Die Ideale'," *Music and Letters* 80 (1999): 207–40.

Newman, William S. "Programmists vs. Absolutists: Further Thoughts about an Overworked Dichotomy." In *Convention in Eighteenth- and Nineteenth-Century Music: Essays in Honor of Leonard G. Ratner*. Edited by Wye J. Allanbrook, Janet Levy, and William P. Mahrt. Stuyvesant, N.Y.: Pendragon Press, 1992.

Niecks, Friedrich. *Program Music in the Last Four Centuries*. London: Novello, 1906.

PROGRESS

The idea of human perfectibility—of progress in virtue, knowledge, happiness, and power over nature—can be found in most cultures to apply to certain privileged individuals. When, on the other hand, it is applied to whole peoples or (more universally) to humankind, as it has been sporadically in the West since the time of ancient Greece and Rome, then we identify a form of historical and political thinking that is *progressive*. In progressive thinking, humankind is envisaged as having had its origins in savagery, ignorance, and physical discomfort and as having then developed socially and intellectually toward an improved present, after which it will continue to develop toward some more or less hypothetical, more or less attainable utopian moment: According to Anne-Robert-Jaques Turgot

> manners are softened, the human mind enlightened, isolated nations brought together; commercial and political ties finally unite all parts of the globe; and the total mass of human kind, through alternations of calm and upheaval, good fortune and bad, advances ever, though slowly, toward greater perfection.

Though this progress might be driven and informed by divine teleology, as in the case of St. Augustine's *De civitate Dei* (*The City of God*, 412–27), the idea of inexorable progress has been most prevalent as a secular theory of history in which society is seen as evolving through a series of usually specified stages. (Strictly speaking, the Judeo-Christian doctrine of original sin made the idea of human advancement heretical.) So that, while the idea of progress could hardly be said to have begun with the Enlightenment, because of the secularization of human history that came with the Scottish and French *philosophes*, progress of one kind or another became a commonplace during the eighteenth century. Major writers—from Jacques Bénigne Bossuet's *Discours sur l'histoire universelle* (*Discourse on Universal History*, 1681) through Turgot's *Tableau philosophique des progrès successifs de l'esprit humain* (*Philosophical Review of the Successive Advances of the Human Mind*, 1750) and the *Encyclopédie* (1751–72), to the Marquis de Condorcet's *Esquisse d'un tableau historique des progrès de l'esprit humain* (*Sketch for a Historical Review of the Progress of the Human Mind*, 1795), Adam Smith's *The Wealth of Nations* (1776), and the various histories of David Hume and William Robertson—all expound or assume a version of human progress. In Adam Smith's typically Scottish construction of history as a "natural progress of opulence," from a primitive through a feudal to a "commercial society" of the kind he believed Europe enjoyed at the time, this last stage was held to preserve not just economic, but also political and civil liberty. Indeed, for the eighteenth century, freedom was more often than not at once the goal and the condition of progress.

That the idea of progress was not universal during the eighteenth century is evident from the fact that one of its major thinkers, Jean-Jacques Rousseau, wrote eloquently of civilization not as progress (restlessly self-improving though he believed mankind to be), but as a regression or decadence from a state of primitive equality. It is for this reason, however, that Rousseau was once looked upon as the father of European Romanticism, many of whose major writers were less than sanguine about the progress celebrated by their Enlightenment forebears. Indeed, much of Romanticism can be seen as a retreat from the kind of historical optimism that identified the present as the most morally, scientifically, and economically advanced epoch of human history. Those late-eighteenth-century movements often identified as pre-Romantic (for example, primitivism, Hellenism, the valorization of Celtic and Norse mythology and society, and other forms of antiquarianism) are all predicated on theories of historical regression that saw contemporary society as decadent: sophisticated, corrupt, effeminate. Progress became associated with the incursions of agnosticism or deism in religion, with philosophical scepticism and materialism, and with the commercial spirit of the liberal economists. Leading Romantics like Friedrich von Schlegel and Friedrich Wilhelm Joseph von Schelling in Germany, and Samuel Taylor Coleridge and Thomas Carlyle in Britain, spoke out against the encroachment upon individual liberty and social order entailed by the progress of a commercial and a mass society.

One form of resistance to the idea of progress among Romantic thinkers derived from their exalted attitude to the arts, which far from following the pattern of linear progression characteristic of, say, scientific knowledge was seen either to go in cycles or (in extreme versions of primitivism) to manifest an unremitting decadence. Here "progress" must be recognized as various and relative: social progress and advances in knowledge and power might be endorsed in the same breath in which they are charac-terized as inimical to creative endeavor. Even at the height of Enlightenment optimism about its own civilized achievements, it is not unusual to find a residual nostalgia and an insecurity about the cost of those achievements: As Christopher Lasch notes, "The convergence of technological optimism with cultural despair, of the worship of progress with nostalgia, has been a persistent current in modern thought ever since the Enlightenment." The idea of progress necessarily invokes its contrary, the idea of decadence, and the two often pivot on the distinction between the individual and the species, for the world cannot get any better than it has always been for certain select individuals.

Not all thinkers of the Romantic era renounced the faith in progress of the *philosophes*, however. Immanuel Kant, for example, in his *Idee zu einer allegemeinen Geschichte in weltbürgerlicher Absicht* (*Idea for a Universal History with a Cosmopolitan Intent*, 1784), insisted that for the species at least history should be read as a comedy. But for no thinker of the period was the idea of human history as a gradual and progressive unfolding of civilization through successive stages more important than it was for G. W. F. Hegel. Hegel's *Die Phänomenologie des Geistes* (*The Phenomenology of Spirit*, 1807) is a treatment of what he calls progressive "formations of consciousness," in which the *Geist* (mind, or spirit) is a self-conscious, self-reflective, and self-skeptical form of social life that advances historically by persistently undermining the terms it evolves to define itself and its own aspirations, as each new form that social life takes is legitimated by the failures and insufficiencies of the previous form of social life. For Hegel, as for the Enlightenment, the development of world history is also a story of the progressive realization of the social conditions necessary for the full equality of freedom, but Hegel's idea of freedom was markedly ethnocentric and, in its emphasis on the cohesion and power of the state, a long way from the liberal individualism of Smith and Turgot—part of a teleology that influenced Karl Marx, for whom universal progressive history as the rise of freedom could not stop at bourgeois constitutionalism.

WILLIAM CHRISTIE

Bibliography

Lasch, Christopher. *The True and Only Heaven: Progress and Its Critics.* New York: W. W. Norton, 1991.

Melzer, Arthur M., Jerry Weinberger, and M. Richard Zinman, eds. *History and the Idea of Progress.* Ithaca, N.Y.: Cornell University Press, 1995.

Nisbet, Robert. *History of the Idea of Progress.* London: Heinemann, 1980.

Pollard, Sidney. *The Idea of Progress: History and Society.* London: Watts, 1968.

Sasso, Gennaro. *Tramonto di un mito: l'idea di "progresso" fra Ottocento e Novecento.* Bologna: Il Mulino, 1984.

Spadafora, David. *The Idea of Progress in Eighteenth-Century Britain.* New Haven, Conn.: Yale University Press, 1990.

PROMETHEUS UNBOUND 1820

Poem by Percy Bysshe Shelley

Prometheus Unbound is one of the greatest long Romantic poems. As with William Blake's *Jerusalem* (1804), it concerns itself with nothing less than the redemption of human beings and the world in which they live. Just as Blake protests against the false ideologies that would enslave him and others, Percy Bysshe Shelley articulates a vision of resistance to spiritual and political tyranny that avoids the desire for revenge. It was this desire that, in his view, had disfigured the French Revolution, and in one aspect *Prometheus Unbound* represents a corrective reimagining of the Revolution: in Shelley's work love, not revenge, dominates. Although it avoids the merely specific and contingent, and can be seen as "embodying the discoveries of all ages," as Shelley noted in a letter to Thomas Love Peacock in 1819, the poem is rooted in the historical turmoil of the postrevolutionary decades. More particularly, the work represents a powerful response to, and reaction against, the reactionary political arrangements following Napoleon Bonaparte's defeat at Waterloo: arrangements that saw the restoration of monarchies in France and Spain, and the erosion of political freedom throughout England and Europe.

Attempting to imagine the worst and the best in the human condition, *Prometheus Unbound* represents the nearest approximation in English literature to Dante Alighieri's vision in *La divina commedia* (*The Divine Comedy*, 1321), a work of great importance for Shelley. Written at intervals between 1818 and 1820 (the year in which it was published as the title poem of the volume *Prometheus Unbound, with Other Poems*), Shelley's poem also resembles Dante's masterpiece in focusing on the act of choice, on the right and wrong ways of using the human will. For both authors, human will needs to be brought into conformity with a larger design. For Dante, the imperative is that it should subordinate itself to God's providential design; for Shelley, the requirement is that it should not yield to despair or to tyrannical or dogmatic systems of power or belief, but should learn self-government and, submitting itself to the "going out of our own nature" that *A Defence of Poetry* calls "Love," should be able to take advantage of opportunities of improving the human condition. The enigmatic Demogorgon presides over such opportunities, and stands for Shelley's grasp of an extrahuman dimension (not identifiable with the Christian God) that catalyzes, rather than brings about, change. Demogorgon brings into play Shelley's idea of Necessity, the idea that certain events will follow from certain causes: in this case, that tyranny is doomed to implode upon itself.

The poem originates as an answer to Aeschylus's vision in *Prometheus Bound*. But Shelley's first act harnesses Aeschylean sublimity to a vision at odds with that supposedly contained in a lost sequel to *Prometheus Bound* in which the Greek dramatist, in Shelley's terms, set about "reconciling the Champion with the Oppressor of mankind." Another work called to mind only for its ideological implications to be reversed is *Paradise Lost* (1665) by John Milton; Prometheus is Satan-as-hero, except that he is exempt from those "taints," in Shelley's words from the preface, "which in the Hero of Paradise Lost, interfere with the interest." Shelley's work also enters into corrective dialogue with the pessimistic vision put forward by Byron in his lyrical drama

Manfred (1817). To all his predecessors, Shelley addresses the work's epigraph, a quotation extant in Cicero from a lost play of Aeschylus, which translates as: "Do you hear these things, Amphiaraus, hidden under the earth?"

The initial stage direction reads, "Morning slowly breaks," and throughout act 1 Shelley's hero waits for the coming of a renovated universe, refusing to yield to Jupiter's persuasions or the tortures carried out by Mercury and the Furies. The latter taunt Prometheus with images that suggest the futility of idealism: Christ's teaching gave rise, against the spirit of his gospel, to religious warfare, and the French Revolution, meant to promote fraternity and equality, turned to bloody slaughter. These taunts reach their climax in a speech in which a Fury represents human impulses as locked in contradiction: "The good want power, but to weep barren tears. / The powerful goodness want: worse need for them." Act 1, characterized by agony and struggle, is among the quintessential scenes of embattled, triumphant Romantic rebellion, comparable with Ludwig van Beethoven's *Fidelio* (1805) in its representation of the capacity to endure and sustain hope. In it, Prometheus strives to embody a humanist ethos as "The saviour and the strength of suffering man."

In act 2, a series of scenes centers on Asia (Prometheus' beloved, from whom he is separated), and her growing awareness of the coming of "spring," a season laden with symbolic overtones in the poem. Asia, accompanied by Ione and Panthea, experiences the dawn (and the melting into it of an ideal-sustaining morning star), the interchange of hope-awakening dreams, and the descent—prompted both by her own wishes and the forces of Necessity—into Demogorgon's cave. Here occurs an encounter with Demogorgon, in which some of the play's most searching metaphysical questioning takes place, concluding with the view, at once skeptical and idealist, that "the deep truth is imageless." Finally, in a scene of great lyrical beauty, she undergoes a transfiguration into something like an embodiment of intellectual beauty, at once dazzling and indefinable.

Act 3 focuses initially on the overthrow of Jupiter, ironically at the very moment when he proclaims his imminent triumph over Prometheus. It is Demogorgon who drags Jupiter from his throne, leaving some readers uncomfortable about Shelley's apparent readiness to disengage his hero from covering his hands in the blood of revolution. But Shelley's emphasis is on an alteration in the human spirit, which, in turn, brings about a corresponding change in the natural world. This alteration is stressed by the Spirit of the Hour at the end of act 3, in a speech combining intricacy of redefinition (often managed through negative formulations) with a questing, Utopian desire to enter "unascended heaven." Act 4 is the antithesis of act 1. Where the first act is full of near-tragic stasis and pain, the last offers, in verbal terms, a multigeneric celebration, full of song, dance, and harmonious interchange as Shelley replaces the heavens of Dante and Milton with his own paradise of transformed mind and matter. In the third act, Prometheus (now liberated from his chains) and Asia retire to a cave, passing on to others (including the reader) the duty of bearing the torch of hope, but Demogorgon reappears at the end, emphasizing the possibility that tyranny may return and enjoining the *dramatis personae*, should that return occur, "to hope, till Hope creates / From its own wreck the thing it contemplates": an injunction at the heart of this radiant and subtle Romantic masterpiece.

What makes *Prometheus Unbound* "radiant and subtle" is the way in which, subtitled as it is, "*A Lyrical Drama*," it remodels genres and cultural traditions in a literary venture of great daring and complexity. Lyrical in its metrically diverse evocations of mental functions and of the material world gifted with a voice, the work is lyrical more generally in its impulse to transform reality into its own poetic image and likeness. Through its recurring and reworked metaphors and symbols, the poem becomes the "perpetual Orphic song" of which the fourth act speaks. It is dramatic in its division into acts and scenes, its deployment of a theater of the mind, and its readiness to stage conflict. Conflict in the poem pivots on potentiality, the presence within any situation of opposing possibilities. The drama centers on the hero's attempt to actualize the potential for good and for change in his predicament; thus, for all its opposition to tyrannical systems of thought and political rule, its deepest conflict in act 1 is internalized. The work also centers on the capacity for love, embodied in Asia, and thus avoids the merely defiant, opening up in acts 2, 3, and 4 into visions of a transformed existence.

MICHAEL O'NEILL

See also **Mythology, Classical; Poetry: Britain; Shelley, Percy Bysshe**

Text

Prometheus Unbound, first published in *Prometheus Unbound, with Other Poems*, 1820. This edition was full of errors. The best modern editions are *Shelley's Prose and Poetry*, edited by Donald H. Reiman and Neil Fraistat (New York: Norton, 2002); *The Poems of Shelley*, edited by Geoffrey Matthews and Kelvin Everest, vol. 2, 1817–1819 (London: Longman, 2000); and *Shelley: The Major Work*, edited by Zachary Leader and Michael O'Neill (Oxford: Oxford University Press, 2003). See also the well-edited and helpfully annotated selections in *Percy Bysshe Shelley: Poetry and Prose*, edited by Timothy Webb (London: Dent, 1995). Important textual evidence is contained in *The "Prometheus Unbound" Notebooks*, edited by Neil Fraistat. Volume 9 of *The Bodleian Shelley Manuscripts*. General editor Donald H. Reiman (New York: Garland, 1991).

Bibliography

Abrams, M. H. *Natural Supernaturalism: Tradition and Revolution in Romantic Literature*. New York: W. W. Norton, 1971.

Armstrong, Isobel. *Language as Living Form in Nineteenth-Century Poetry*. Brighton: Harvester, 1982.

Bloom, Harold. *Shelley's Mythmaking*. New Haven, Conn.: Yale University Press, 1959.

Cameron, Kenneth Neill. *Shelley: The Golden Years*. Cambridge, Mass.: Harvard University Press, 1974.

Clark, Timothy. *Embodying Revolution: The Figure of the Poet in Shelley*. Oxford: Oxford University Press, 1989.

Cronin, Richard. *Shelley's Poetic Thoughts*. Basingstoke, England: Macmillan, 1981.

Dawson, P. M. S. *The Unacknowledged Legislator: Shelley and Politics*. Oxford: Oxford University Press, 1980.

Gelpi, Barbara Charlesworth. *Shelley's Goddess: Maternity, Language, Subjectivity*. Oxford: Oxford University Press, 1992.

Hogle, Jerrold E. *Shelley's Process: Radical Transference and the Development of his Major Works*. New York: Oxford University Press, 1988.

Keach, William. *Shelley's Style*. London: Methuen, 1984.

Leighton, Angela. *Shelley and the Sublime: An Interpretation of the Major Poems*. Cambridge: Cambridge University Press, 1984.

O'Neill, Michael. *The Human Mind's Imaginings: Conflict and Achievement in Shelley's Poetry*. Oxford: Oxford University Press, 1989.

Reiman, Donald H. *Percy Bysshe Shelley*. Rev. ed. Boston: G. K. Hall, 1988.

Sperry, Stuart M. *Shelley's Major Verse: The Narrative and Dramatic Poetry*. Cambridge, Mass.: Harvard University Press, 1988.

Webb, Timothy. *Shelley: A Voice Not Understood*. Manchester: Manchester University Press, 1977.

Weinberg, Alan. *Shelley's Italian Experience*. Basingstoke, England: Macmillan, 1991.

PROUDHON, PIERRE-JOSEPH 1809–1865

French social theorist

Pierre-Joseph Proudhon can fairly be described as an anti-Romantic who clung to peasant-artisan attitudes that he believed were practical and realistic. He spent a fair amount of ink insulting other socialists for the impracticality of their visions. He was remembered as the most famous and influential advocate of autonomous producer cooperatives, although his advocacy of a people's bank might reasonably be considered a dream far removed from economic reality. His views were sometimes conflicting, ambivalent, or unpopular. He had little faith in the embryonic democratic system introduced in France in 1848 and from time to time declared support for Louis-Napoleon, who reestablished an empire in 1852. Unlike a number of other early socialists he had no time for women's rights and earned the hostility of feminists for his comment that woman's role was in the home and outside it she could aspire to be no more than a courtesan. Yet his own solution to the social question of his day was, like that of many of his contemporaries, a fundamentally Romantic association, a utopian construct in which money would disappear, a dream not unlike that of Étienne Cabet.

Proudhon was one of few socialists who had direct knowledge of the social problems of his day. His father was a cooper and, although he attended the local high school in Besançon and his uncle was a professor of law in Dijon, his family could never afford to buy him basic school books. The best known of his own books was his first, a prize-winning scholarship essay for the Academy of Besançon, *Qu'est-ce que la propriété? (What is Property?* 1840). Proudhon could have been a star in advertising copywriting; his first unforgettable slogans were "property is theft" and "the right of property is the origin of all the evil in the world." In the rest of the book Proudhon made it clear that he was no enemy of private possession, but condemned those who owned more property than they needed. Social harmony and equality would never be achieved while gross inequalities of property-holding persisted. On the other hand, he fervently believed that private ownership should continue. In *Système des contradictions économiques ou philosophie de la misère* (*System of Economic Contradictions: or, The Philosophy of Poverty*, 1846) he criticized communists, like Cabet, who sought its abolition. His ideal was a community in which as many people as possible owned modest quantities of land, enough to sustain a family and in which industry was small-scale and based around artisans.

Proudhon wanted equality and liberty. Equality, independence, the rule of law and proportionality: this for him constituted liberty. Proportionality was a way of equalizing without the egalitarianism of communism. Proudhon distinguished between property and possession—the former brought unreasonable profit, the latter merely the opportunity to earn a decent living: "Suppress property, while maintaining possession, you will revolutionize law, government, the economy and institutions." Also: "Profit," he wrote, "is impossible and unjust."

The appalled Besançon Academy retaliated with an unsuccessful prosecution. Proudhon moved to Paris, where he met Mikhail Bakunin, Aleksandr Herzen, and Karl Marx, and established permanent friendships with Bakunin and Herzen. (Marx dismissed Proudhon as a "petit bourgeois" thinker.) Proudhon did not become a full-time writer. When his scholarship ended, he went to work for a shipping company in Lyon; his employers were friends and left him time to write. Proudhon was convinced that neither revolution nor the centralized state would solve the social problems of the day. He opposed Louis Blanc's socialism from above; socialism had to come from the people. Whereas other socialists proposed innovative economic systems to replace capitalism, Proudhon offered mutualism, which he defined as a harmonizing equilibrium. The term must have been suggested to him by the name of the Lyon silk workers' association, the mutualists. His mutualism was a sophisticated form of barter. It involved the free association of producers engaged in the equal exchange of goods. Capitalism would be replaced by contracts negotiated between free individuals and expressed in letters of credit.

During the Second Republic (1848–52) Proudhon promoted this idea in the form of a people's bank as a solution to constant economic crises and unemployment. The bank would offer cheap or even interest-free credit. He planned to set up warehouses in which finished goods could be stored prior to being traded for goods of equal value or in exchange for notes issued by the bank. The scheme attracted 27,000 subscribers, but never materialized. Proudhon was a vigorous publicist, running a series of newspapers, notably *Le Peuple*. He was elected to the National Assembly in June 1848, but his fellow deputies were appalled when he proposed a temporary reduction of 33 percent on all debt to enable businesses to pull out of the recession. He was regarded as an inspiration for the numerous producer and retail cooperatives and mutual-aid societies that were set up during the Republic. When he wrote *Idée générale de la Révolution* (*The General Idea of the Revolution*, 1851), which sold three-thousand copies and was instantly reprinted, he hoped that a democratic, self-governing bank of exchange could be created to replace the Bank of France: "In place of laws, we will put contracts . . . in place of political powers, we will put economic forces . . . In place of standing armies, we will put industrial associations."

Proudhon wanted an economic, not a political, revolution, which he explained in one of his typically cryptic aphorisms in *Confessions d'un révolutionnaire pour servir à l'histoire de la révolution de février* (1849): "I wage war against old ideas, not old men." His was no class war to bring the proletariat to political power, but a new equilibrium, a just society, in which no one would suffer from extremes of deprivation and no one indulge in excess wealth. He assumed that the basis of this change would be moral and that man, a fairly rational being, would see its benefits. The state had no role to play. When Prince Napoleon, son of Jérôme Bonaparte, asked Proudhon what would be his ideal society, he answered, "I dream of a society in which I would be guillotined as a conservative."

PAMELA PILBEAM

Selected Works

Two editions of Proudhon's prolific complete works were published in France, the first in 26 volumes (1867–70) and the second between 1923 and 1959 (reprinted 1982). *Qu'est-ce-que la propriété?* (1840) is his best known and most translated work, the most recent edition being that of the Cambridge Texts in the History of Political Thought Series, edited by Donald R. Kelley and Bonnie G. Smith (Cambridge: Cambridge University Press, 1994). The first English edition of Proudhon's *Idée générale de la révolution* (1851) was published by Freedom Press in 1923; the most recent (1989) is the work of Robert Graham. *Selected Writings*, edited by Stewart Edwards and translated by Elizabeth Fraser, appeared in 1969.

Bibliography

Copley A. "Pierre-Joseph Proudhon: A Reassessment of His Role as a Moralist," *French History* 3, no. 2 (1989): 194–221.
Dagognet F. *Trois philosophies revisitées: Saint-Simon, Proudhon, Fourier*. Paris, 1997.
Fitzpatrick, M. "Proudhon and the French Labour Movement," *European History Quarterly* 15 (1985): 407–30.
Hoffman, R. L. *Revolutionary Justice: The Social and Political Theory of P. J. Proudhon*. Chicago, 1972.
Pilbeam, P. *French Socialists before Marx. Workers, Women and the Social Question in France*. Teddington: Acumen, 2000.
Vincent, K. S. *Pierre-Joseph Proudhon and the Rise of French Republican Socialism*. Oxford, 1984.
Woodcock, G. *P. J. Proudhon: A Biography*. 3rd ed. 1987.

PUGIN, AUGUSTUS WELBY NORTHMORE 1812–1852

English architect and propagandist

The Gothic revival began before Augustus Welby Northmore Pugin, but no single person did more than he did in accelerating its influence, progress, and ascendancy as the national style of Romantic and Victorian Britain. His father, Augustus Charles, was a refugee from France who came to London in 1792, becoming a draughtsman for the architect John Nash, one of London's great town planners and a leading light in the picturesque movement. Augustus senior married the beautiful but austere Presbyterian Catherine Welby, "the Belle of Islington," in 1802, and their only child was born on March 1, 1812. A delicate child, Pugin attended the "Bluecoat School" (Christ's Hospital, Newgate Street), as a day-boy, where he demonstrated an intellectual capacity that was matched only by his energy, one master remarking that "he would learn in twenty-four hours what it took other boys weeks to acquire," a resource that would soon allow him to pack a vast amount of work into a tragically short life. He also exhibited a natural talent for drawing, and he assisted his father in the books on Gothic architecture that he edited for Nash, such as *Specimens of Gothic Architecture* (1821). Nash disliked the style, but was obliged to supply the demand. Before the age of twenty, Pugin was designing furniture for Windsor Castle, and for a while he was interested in theatrical set design, notably working on a production of Walter Scott's historical romance *Kenilworth* in 1831. Son succeeded father in 1835 by completing *Examples of Gothic Architecture* (1835), a work in progress at the time of his father's death in 1832. Pugin had a passion for the sea (at one time even owning and commanding a merchant ship that traded with Holland), and preferred to wear the casual dress of a sailor. After losing his first (of three) wives after only two years of marriage, he converted to Catholicism in 1834, perhaps due more to architectural than theological reasons, his other passion being Christian (that is, Roman Catholic) architecture, specifically the opulent "second pointed" style of the late thirteenth and early fourteenth centuries.

After his conversion, Pugin built himself a house near Salisbury, Saint Marie's Grange, where in 1836 he wrote and self-published his radical book on national morality and religious architecture, *Contrasts; or, a Parallel between the Noble Edifices of the Fourteenth and Fifteenth Centuries, and Similar Buildings of the Present Day: Showing the Present Decay of Taste* (1836). The title says it all; while Cardinal Newman still favored a utilitarian approach to church building, Pugin fervently argued that such "an absence of Catholic feeling among its professors" was an outward sign of the spiritual decay of the nation, illustrating his point by juxtaposing engravings of an ancient building or town scene with a modern one (hence the title *Contrasts*). The book appeared as the Gothic revival was steadily gaining credibility, while scholars and politicians fretted in public about how to express this new age. Its publication coincided with a growing interest in the preservation of ancient monuments (soon to reach its peak with the publication of William Harrison Ainsworth's immensely popular romance, *The Tower of London*, in 1840); the public seemed generally ready to accept that pointed arches were suddenly "holier" than round ones. The *British Critic* of 1841, however, responded that *Contrasts* "betrays an utter want of either soundness or fairness in its pretence at argument," which was largely true,

while an Irish wag, one "Mr. M'Cann," penned an explanatory poem from which the following is extracted:

> The Catholic Church, she never knew—
> Till Mr. Pugin taught her,
> That orthodoxy had to do
> At all with bricks and mortar.

Pugin would later publish more balanced pieces on the subject, such as *True Principles of Pointed or Christian Architecture* (1841; written after he was appointed professor of ecclesiastical antiquities at St. Mary's College, Oscott, in 1837), *An Apology for the Revival of Christian Architecture in England*, and *The Present State of Ecclesiastical Architecture in England* (both 1843), as well as numerous lesser books and pamphlets.

From 1836 onward, Pugin worked with Sir Charles Barry on the Houses of Parliament; Barry was no expert on Gothic detail, and Pugin therefore designed almost all of it, from the facades down to the inkstands, while also simultaneously working on numerous designs for new churches, houses, ironwork, tiles, and all kinds of furniture. He always worked alone, once claiming that if he employed a clerk, "I should kill him in a week." In addition to the parliament building, his finest work is generally agreed to be the church at Cheadle in Staffordshire (1841–46), Nottingham Cathedral (1842–44), and St. Augustine's Church, Ramsgate (begun in 1846, left incomplete when he died), which he funded himself and which stands by his own house; it is here that his ideals are perhaps most perfectly expressed.

Pugin was never either physically or emotionally strong; he was often plagued by depression, self-doubt, and despair, and he became increasingly violent and irrational toward the end of his life. He was particularly undermined by a destructive attack in the *Ecclesiologist* in 1846, leading him to doubt, if not disown, much of his work, which he would measure against his ideal and always find wanting. As he wrote in *Some Remarks* (1850), "I have never had the chance of producing a single fine ecclesiastical building, except my own church, where I am both paymaster and architect; but everything else, either for want of adequate funds or injudicious interference or control, or some other contingency, is more or less a failure."

From 1851 Pugin was effectively insane; he died of a stroke on September 14, 1852 and was buried in his church of St. Augustine. We might almost view Pugin as a prophet, a Blakean figure with some unusual ideas about the relationship between moral and aesthetic value that he believed in with a passion. His designs became the basis for the generation of ecclesiastical buildings that would follow his own, and his tragedy is that he never recognized his own seismic impact on British architecture and national identity.

STEPHEN CARVER

Selected Works

Contrasts; or, A Parallel Between the Noble Edifices of the Fourteenth and Fifteenth Centuries, and Similar Buildings of the Present Day; shewing the Present Decay of Taste: Accompanied by appropriate Text. 1836.

The True Principles of Pointed or Christian Architecture: set forth in two Lectures delivered at St Marie's, Oscott, by A. Welby Pugin, Architect, and Professor of Ecclesiastical Antiquities in that College. 1841.

The Present State of Ecclesiastical Architecture in England. 1843.

Some Remarks on the Articles Which Have Recently Appeared in the "Rambler," Relative to Ecclesiastical Architecture and Decoration. 1851.

Bibliography

Belcher, Margaret. *A. W. N. Pugin: An Annotated Critical Biography.* London: Mansell, 1967.

Clark, Kenneth. *The Gothic Revival: An Essay in the History of Taste.* London: Constable and Co., 1928.

Clarke, Basil F. L. *Church Builders of the Nineteenth Century.* London: SPCK, 1938.

Eastlake, C. L. *A History of the Gothic Revival in England.* 1872.

Ferrey, Benjamin. *Recollections of A. N. Welby Pugin and his Father Augustus Pugin.* 1861.

Ferriday, P., ed. *Victorian Architecture.* London, 1963.

Gwynn, Denis. *Lord Shrewsbury, Pugin and the Catholic Revival.* London: Hollis and Carter, 1946.

Harris, John. *Pugin: An Illustrated Life of Augustus Welby Northmore Pugin, 1812–1852.* Aylesbury, England: Shire, 1973.

Hitchcock, H. R. *Early Victorian Architecture in Britain.* 2 vols. New Haven, Conn.: Yale University Press, 1954.

Houghton, Walter E. *The Victorian Frame of Mind 1830–1870.* New Haven, Conn.: Yale University Press, 1957.

Macaulay, James. *The Gothic Revival 1745–1845.* London: Blackie, 1975.

Muthesius, S. *The High Victorian Movement in Architecture.* London, 1972.

Pevsner, Nikolaus. *Some Architectural Writers of the Nineteenth Century.* Oxford, 1972.

Scott, George Gilbert. *Remarks on Secular and Domestic Architecture, Present and Future.* 1857.

Stanton, Phoebe. *Pugin.* London: Thames and Hudson, 1971.

Summerson, J. *Nash.* London, 1952.

Trappes-Lomax, Michael. *Pugin: A Medieval Victorian.* London: Sheed and Ward, 1932.

Watkin, David. *English Architecture.* London: Thames and Hudson, 1978.

PUSHKIN, ALEKSANDR 1799–1837

Russian poet

Aleksandr Pushkin's relationship with Romanticism is best understood as a dynamic series of artistic affiliations and repudiations in which a key Romantic figure, genre, or topic becomes an object of Pushkin's critical experimentation. In attempting to define Romanticism in the article "On Classical and Romantic Poetry" (1825), Pushkin balked at a comprehensive prescription of genres and themes; instead he construed Romantic literature broadly in terms of its formal and thematic departures from classical and neoclassical models. In a playful evasion of philosophical or philological precision, he propounded the simple view that works that were new in substance or form were modern and could therefore be considered Romantic. But Pushkin's own oeuvre is a sensitive template of contemporary literary and intellectual trends, and his response to Romanticism can be traced through a number of key texts that demarcate shifting modes of thought and representation.

The foundation of Pushkin's poetic sensibility can be traced to his thorough knowledge of European neo-Classicism, with a marked preference for the erotic themes and small forms of *poésie légère*, and Horatian-style satire. When the popular success of his mock epic *Ruslan and Lyudmila* (1820) coincided with his exile from Russia on political grounds, it was only natural that comparisons were drawn with Lord Byron's career and life after the publication of *Childe Harold's Pilgrimage* (1812). From 1821 to 1823 Pushkin cultivated the comparison, writing poems in which Byronic self-fashioning is the dominant motif. His apostrophe "To the Sea" (1820) is suffused with echoes of *Don Juan* (1819–24), while poems such as "The Black Shawl" (1820) and "The Dagger" (1821) replicate the dark and dangerous persona of Byron's Romantic exile. In "To the Greek Woman" (1821) Pushkin pays tribute to the English poet's legendary erotic success by recording a visit he paid to his Greek mistress, Calypso Polichronia. In musing on the way in which she captivated Byron's imagination, Pushkin fantasizes about how she might have similarly inspired

him, but then retreats by pleading the weariness of the Byronic outcast and wanderer. Byron influenced Pushkin's life as well as his art, and numerous anecdotes survive of escapades during his southern exile in which he flaunted the authorities and sported exotic costumes. Perhaps the most obvious visual evidence of his Byronic infatuation is Orest Kiprenskii's famous portrait; with curly hair and sideburns in the Byronic manner, his open shirt, and a defiant stare, Pushkin embodies the Romantic image. It did not take long before Pushkin became disillusioned due to what he viewed as Byron's self-infatuation. In the 1827 essay "On Byron's Drama," Pushkin wrote that Byron "presented us with a ghost of himself. He reproduced himself, under the head-dress of the renegade, now in the cloak of the Corsair, now as the Giaour. . . . In the final analysis he achieved, created and described a single character (his own, that is)."

Rejection of the Byronic model (and a congruent rejection of Napoleon) was a productive step, and it initiated a new direction in Pushkin's assimilation of Romantic themes and techniques. The poem "Demon" (1823), an ambivalent tribute to a Byron-crazed friend, marked a turning away from the cynical and world-weary hero. "The Captive of the Caucasus" (1822) and "The Fountain of Bakhchisarai" (1824), two of the narrative poems written between 1821 and 1824, display the hallmarks of Byronic description: lush picturesque landscape, orientalism, an alienated hero, a mysterious *femme fatale*, and narrative pathos. "The Gypsies" (1824), the third and most important of his southern narratives, reveals a far more dynamic approach to key principles of Romantic theory and to Byron's influence. Set on the banks of the Black Sea, the story follows the fortunes of the outcast Russian soldier Aleko, who has fled society in pursuit of an ideal of freedom that he hopes to realize by joining a band of gypsies. He falls in love with the beautiful Zemphira, who in keeping with the Romantic ethos of freedom refuses to grant him an exclusive claim on her affections. In a jealous rage, Aleko murders Zemphira. He is rejected by the gypsies, who then depart. In terms of the Byronic model, the work offers a striking formal revision: stark and elliptical description, rapid dialogue, abrupt scene changes, abstract characterization, and highly psychological monologues condense the verse-narrative into a taut drama. In terms of reader-response criticism, the work is innovative because, in dispensing with the usual cues and props of Romantic action and landscape, it assumes that a reader steeped in the conventions of the period will provide these details imaginatively and automatically. Here the focus is on the drama and the philosophical conclusion reached by Aleko, namely, that freedom is an illusion. By implication, "The Gypsies" attacks the Rousseauian myth of the noble savage as well as the Romantic idealization of nature as the place where the subjective consciousness can be harmoniously dissolved.

The most continuous literary reflection of Pushkin's complex and fluid relation to the literary and intellectual trends of Romanticism is his novel-in-verse, *Eugene Onegin*, which was composed over seven years starting in 1823. Imbued with the spirit of Romantic irony, the work refuses to offer an authoritative viewpoint on its plot and to draw moral conclusions, instead manipulating contrasting perspectives and inviting the reader to see events and ponder questions from multiple, subjective viewpoints. For example, the first chapter features a narrator who, despite his nostalgia for youthful pleasures, has overcome his Byronic phase and ironically reviews his earlier infatuation with the Romantic type. In addition, despite numerous deliberate hints that point to shared biographies, and in an ironical swipe at Byron, the narrator explicitly warns the reader not to confuse him with Pushkin. By contrast, his characterization of the hero, who is a self-made outcast from society lacking political commitment, a fixed moral compass, and emotional vitality, strips away any heroic or glamorous element from the Romantic hero, now exposed as superfluous and marginal. And yet, while these portraits throw a critical light on the Romantic view of literary character, the third figure in the novel, the poet Lensky, offers a more ambivalent response. Fresh from Göttingen, imbued with the spirit of German Romanticism, and overflowing with a derivative literary love of nature and friendship, Lensky provokes the affectionate mockery of the narrator, who exposes the artificiality of his poetry and the naiveté of his values. When Lensky dies in a duel with Onegin, however, the narrator pays tribute, mourning his lost promise and talent. Despite his initial silliness, and whatever the immaturity of his talent, Lensky occupies a special place because he is a poet. In this respect, Pushkin follows the lead of Lensky's own Romantic masters, Johann Wolfgang von Goethe and Friedrich Wilhelm Joseph von Schelling, in regarding the poet as a privileged source of knowledge and wisdom.

Until the 1830s, writers cultivated the role of amateur, but this position was increasingly untenable as soon as the writer's social position and function became part of the definition of the writer; in other words, as soon as his ability to write became contingent on external factors such as income. The theme of the poet is rooted in Pushkin's Romantic self-perception as well as in the psychological dictates of autobiography. A number of poems are written in defense of the creative liberty and imaginative freedom of the poet, from "The Prophet" (1828) to the defiant self-justification of the poems known as the *Easter Cycle* (1836). Their forlorn defiance parallels the views of William Wordsworth, who in 1815 claimed that, for the poet, the consequence of originality was disappointed commercial expectations. In Pushkin's case, the assertion of an imaginative autonomy, free from commercial pressure, and the claim of authority over a readership by virtue of literary merit, is in a tense relationship with his concurrent attempts to turn a vocation into a profession.

It is in the treatment of the theme of the poet, more than in his approach to landscape, nature, or love, that Pushkin's portrayal to a Romantic ideal is most conspicuous. From the late 1820s a number of poems accord prominence and superior talent to the poet. In part, the new note of assertiveness and defiance is a response to dramatic changes in Russian print culture and the development of a new commercial readership, which led to a coarsening of literary taste and a decreasing commercial viability of the poet. Despite censorship, declining financial affairs and an uncertainty about his own artistic success (all of which cumulatively amounted to a type of, in Lucy Newlyn's term, anxiety of reception) Pushkin was still able to display varying modes of self-assertion in his poetry. Certain poems, such as "The Prophet," which assert divine authority for poetry as public service, and other poems, which re-establish the primacy of the private imagination and reject the public, are both assertions about who controls the imagination and who has authority over the poet's words. In "The Prophet," Pushkin is a poet of the revelatory and illuminating moment; it is not Wordsworth's "gentle shock of mild surprise," but a violent start and wished-for epiphany. Pushkin gave programmatic importance to the poem in his 1829 collection by placing it first in the section of poems written in 1827. In "The Prophet," divine elevation is not sought but imposed on the poet, so that poetry as public service is not

Vasili Andreevich Tropinin, *Portrait of Alexander Pushkin*. Reprinted courtesy of the Bridgeman Art Library.

the result of private volition; whereas in "From Pindemont" (1836) and "The Poet" (1828) the refusal to market ideas, to compromise independence by allowing a dependency on readers who were seen as hostile, and the conservation of integrity, is an act of self-control. "The Prophet" describes the revival of the poet who begins as a moribund mortal, the moment of inspiration and the power of his poetic gift; the chief feature about this model of creativity is the unexpected elevation of the subject who is able to cast off petty cares and to extract himself from the "vain world." Some critics argue that in Pushkin's view, inspiration is not the product of unconscious powers. Rather, the poet's tremendous powers of insight and overview are the result of a visionary wisdom that allows him to penetrate to the very essence of things. However, the poem seems to suggest that the source of wisdom and prophetic ability is suffering. The poet does not begin as a divine creature, but as a human who acquires momentary divinity. In "The Poet" the same division is drawn between the poet-as-mortal, subject to human caprice and failing, and the poet as an elevated figure, with a direct connection to a higher inspiration. "The Prophet" has been read as a civic poem, and in part the source of its confidence in the poet as a visionary and teacher lies in the tradition of political verse fostered among the contemporary political group known as the Decembrists.

Although Pushkin is not a notable landscape poet, two of his greatest lyrics explore the psychology of poetic creation and memory in relation to nature. As with Wordsworth, whose "Tintern Abbey" (1798) has been suggested as a subtext, "Once again I revisit . . ." (1835) follows the consolation of memory and imaginative projection onto the landscape as it compensates for nature's silence and alienation from man. In "Autumn" (1833), which has a Keatsian richness of sensuous detail, decay and wintry stillness paradoxically stimulate the imagination to create a series of fantasies that eventually go beyond language and lead to fragmentation. In the final lines, elision replaces words, and the nonverbal representation of poetic creation implicitly enacts a theory of the imagination that bears comparison with John Keats's theory of "negative capability." Although his poetics remain rooted in neoclassical ideas of clarity, signification, and restraint, in the variety and generic innovation of his oeuvre Pushkin unquestionably affirmed the spirit of innovation as the definitive quality of the Romantic. It is perhaps in his biography, with his exotic Byronic period of exile and tragic death in a duel fought for the sake of honor, that Pushkin has been unproblematically viewed as the embodiment of the Romantic poet.

ANDREW KAHN

See also **Eugene Onegin**

Biography

Born in Moscow May 26, 1799 to an old but declining gentry family; educated at the élite Lyceum at Tsarskoe Selo as a member of its first class, 1811–1817. Made his debut in print with the publication of poems in a literary journal, gaining the attention of a number of established poets and joining their Petersburg circles, 1816. After graduating from the Lyceum, briefly held an appointment in the civil service while pursuing his literary activities; investigated and arrested for subversive behavior linked to the poem "Liberty" (1820), leading to exile in southern Russia from 1820 to 1824; first major public success with *Ruslan and Lyudmila* (1820), followed by the composition of major narrative poems and the first chapter of the novel *Eugene Onegin* (1824). End of exile in the south, followed by two years on the family estate at Mikhailovskoe until he was recalled and pardoned by Nicholas I, who became his official censor. Resumed active career as critic and poet, and saw first collection of poems into print (1826), but in 1828 was put under permanent surveillance by the security services for possible authorship of the blasphemous mock-epic *The Gabriliad* and a poetic tribute to André Chenier. Traveled to Caucasus, recorded in his *A Journey to Erzurum*—the farthest extent of his travels from Russia. Engagement in 1831 and marriage to Natalya Goncharova, a famous beauty and favorite at court from a distinguished but impoverished family. Began writing and publishing prose fiction to little critical or commercial success, 1830–1831; elected to membership of the Russian Academy, 1832; with the agreement of the tsar, in 1833 traveled to the Urals in connection with research that led to the composition of his only novel, *The Captain's Daughter*, and substantial historical work on the Russian eighteenth century. Under continued financial pressure, Pushkin published last comprehensive collection of verse in 1835 and in 1836 founded the journal *The Contemporary* as a showcase for literary talent; January 26, 1837, goaded into a duel with the French officer George d'Anthès due to scandalous rumors about his liason with Pushkin's wife; died of his wounds January 29, and by order of the tsar was buried outside the capital for fear of popular demonstrations.

Selected Works

Polnoe sobranie sochinenii. 17 vols. Moscow and Leningrad, 1937–49.
Polnoe sobranie sochinenii. 10 vols. Moscow and Leningrad, 1949.
The Letters of Alexander Pushkin. 3 vols. Edited and translated by J. Thomas Shaw. Bloomington: Indiana State University Press, 1963.
Selected Verse with Introduction and Prose Translations. Translated by John Fennell, 1964. Reprinted Bristol: Bristol Classical Press, 1991.
Pushkin Threefold: Narrative, Lyric, Polemic and Ribald Verse. Translated by Walter Arndt. New York: Dutton 1972.
Complete Prose Fiction. Edited and translated by Paul Debreczeny. Stanford, Calif.: Stanford University Press, 1983.
Pushkin on Literature. Edited and translated by Tatiana Wolff. Stanford, Calif.: Stanford University Press, 1986.
The Queen of Spades and Other Stories. Edited by Andrew Kahn and translated by Alan Myers. Oxford: Oxford University Press, 1997.

Bibliography

Bayley, John. *Pushkin: A Comparative Commentary*. Cambridge: Cambridge University Press, 1971.
Clayton, Douglas. *Ice and Flame: Alexander Pushkin's "Eugene Onegin."* Toronto: University of Toronto Press, 1985.
Greenleaf, Monika. *Pushkin and Romantic Fashion: Fragment, Elegy, Orient*. Stanford, Calif.: Stanford University Press, 1994.
Kahn, Andrew. *Pushkin's The Bronze Horseman*. Bristol: Dackworth, 1998.
Sandler, S. *Distant Pleasures: Aleksandr Pushkin and the Writing of Exile*. Stanford, Calif.: Stanford University Press, 1989.
Terts, A. *Strolls with Pushkin*. Translated by C. T. Nepomnyashchy and S. I. Yastremski. New Haven, Conn.: Yale University Press, 1993.
Todd, William Mills. *Fiction and Society in the Age of Pushkin*. Cambridge, Mass.: Harvard University Press, 1986.

R

RADCLIFFE, ANN 1764-1823

British novelist

Ann Radcliffe was one of the most popular authors of her day. Not only did she command large audiences, receiving what are now almost legendary sums for her works (£500 for *The Mysteries of Udolpho*, and £800 for *The Italian*), but she also gained enthusiastic critical esteem. Criticism of her work takes the cue from her novels; for Nathan Drake she was the "Shakspeare [*sic*] of Romance writers," and for Sir Walter Scott she was "the mighty magician of *The Mysteries of Udolpho*" (1821–24). With surprising regularity, critics of her novels refer to the chasteness and propriety of her style. This chasteness was evidently felt to be remarkable considering the potentially inflammatory nature of the material: young girls in the hands of middle-aged villains in corrupt Catholic countries, being pursued through the disturbingly labyrinthine architecture of the remains of the feudal world.

Between the years 1789 and 1797, Radcliffe published five novels in the genre we now know as Gothic. The first, *The Castles of Athlin and Dunbayne* (1789) is very much an apprentice piece, with too much breathless plot and too little variety; it is the only one of her novels that locates the terror of the Gothic in the British Isles (amid the barbaric sublime of Scotland). *A Sicilian Romance* (1790) made the transition to the more exotic Catholic continent. The three most celebrated works are *A Romance of the Forest* (1791), *The Mysteries of Udolpho* (1794), and *The Italian* (1797).

These three novels have a certain formulaic quality, partly as a result of the genre (though it must be remembered that Radcliffe is to an extent responsible for what we consider to be Gothic features), but mostly because, by this time, the author had discovered her peculiar strengths. The novels are experienced through the central consciousness of what is, by today's standards, a perversely passive heroine, possessed of exquisite taste, exemplary moral and aesthetic sensibilities, and strengthened by "conscious innocence"—she is also, as E. J. Clery has noted, a woman of "genius." Both novel and heroine journey away from home and into terror, relying on the dictates of a providence that causes the meek to triumph over the strong. Even Radcliffe's heroes are passive: the hero of *The Italian*, Vivaldi, finds himself in the hands of the Inquisition—betrayed, imprisoned, and incapacitated in what has been described as a very feminized subject position. Her heroines tend to be orphans who encounter a range of nightmarish father figures, a fact that Rictor Norton in a recent biography attributes to Radcliffe's estranged relations with her own parents.

Radcliffe's final work, *Gaston de Blondeville*, published posthumously in 1826, is the only one to contain the real rather than explained supernatural. Its introductory section reveals Radcliffe as an able theoretician, and her investigation of the terror/horror distinction has been much quoted: "Terror and horror are so far opposite, that the first expands the soul and awakens the faculties to a high degree of life; the other contracts, freezes, and nearly annihilates them." She continues in Burkean fashion to discuss "uncertainty and obscurity" as the necessary conditions for terror. Radcliffe herself is a terror writer (and her reaction to the horror of Matthew Gregory Lewis's *The Monk* [1796] can be felt in the revised, somewhat sanitized aesthetic of *The Italian*). She works by suggestion, stimulating the nerves of her readers with mystery upon mystery, the explanations of which are sometimes delayed several hundred pages until the mysteries themselves are almost forgotten. The rational element of her work (the error/explanation format of her famous "explained supernatural") is out of synchrony with its emotional structure.

Radcliffe's novels are not merely tales of terror. She provides her readers with a multigeneric aesthetic experience treating them to verbal descriptions of the landscapes of Claude Lorrain, Nicholas Poussin, and Salvator Rosa, epigrams from the poetry of John Milton, James Thomson and others, fantastic poetry supposedly composed by her heroines, and "Shakespearean" scenes. Her work encompasses not only what we now think of as Gothic, but the realms of the sublime, the beautiful and the picturesque, the fantastic, low comedy, and even neoclassical satire.

Her numinous landscape descriptions, though praised, were also castigated for undue length and inappropriate positioning, and it was with joy that the critics hailed her volume of travel writing that appeared in 1794. As one wrote, "It is partly the language of poetry and partly of painting; but the feeling mind acquiesces in its propriety. . . . Language cannot do much more in a supposed state of perfection."

Though the canonized Romantic poets often commented on her work with familiarity that bordered on contempt, Radcliffe was an influential literary figure. In some respects her contribution to the novel (and through the Gothic mode to many other novelized genres, including film) is difficult to estimate because so much of what she initiated has become habitual. William Hazlitt declared that though "her characters are insipid, the shadows of a shade," her "great power lies in describing the indefinable, and embodying a phantom." Perhaps this "power" is related to a quality that more recent critics such as Marilyn Butler and Robert Kiely have recognized when they hail Radcliffe as one of the first creators of a plausible interiority. Radcliffe's heroines, it is true, do not have the subjectivity or the character of later heroines (there is a sense in which being so marked by characteristics would be too unladylike, and Racliffe's is a very feminine Gothic) but what they do not have in the way of character they abundantly compensate for in their ability to feel. Their experience is overwhelming, and it also overwhelms the reader. Radcliffe's reader-response aesthetic is one of the first and most convincing essays of its kind. And it contributed to a new way of creating an affective art. Grounded in the novel of sensibility it branched out to suggest a wider, more sublime, interiority, and endowed this capacity to the terror aesthetic of the Gothic novel, and to the experiential capacities, the conjuring-up of feeling, of the novel in general.

EMMA MCEVOY

Biography

Born Ann Ward in 1764. Married William Radcliffe, 1787. Published her first five novels 1789–1797. Inheritances from parents, 1798 and 1800. Died of asthma, 1823.

Selected Works

The Castles of Athlin and Dunbayne. 1789.
A Sicilian Romance. 1790.
The Romance of the Forest. 1791.
The Mysteries of Udolpho. 1794.
A Journey Made in the Summer of 1794 through Holland and the Western Frontier of Germany with a Return down the Rhine: To Which Are Added Observations during a Tour to the Lakes of Lancashire, Westmoreland, and Cumberland. 1795.
The Italian. 1797.
Gaston de Blondeville or The Court of Henry III Keeping Festival in Ardenne. 1826.

Bibliography

Butler, Marilyn. "The Woman at the Window: Ann Radcliffe in the Novels of Mary Wollstonecraft and Jane Austen," *Women and Literature* 1 (1980): 28–48.
Castle, Terry. "The Spectralization of the Other in The Mysteries of Udolpho." In *The New Eighteenth Century: Theory, Politics, English Literature.* Edited by Felicity Nussbaum and Laura Brown. London: Methuen, 1987.
Clery, Emma. *Women's Gothic—from Clara Reeve to Mary Shelley.* Plymouth, England: Northcote House, 2000.
Drake, Nathan. *Literary Hours.* 1800.
Hazlitt, William. *Lectures on the English Comic Writers.* 1819.
Kiely, Robert. *The Romantic Novel in England.* Cambridge, Mass.: Harvard University Press, 1972.
Miles, Robert. *Ann Radcliffe: The Great Enchantress.* Manchester: Manchester University Press, 1995.
Norton, Rictor. *Mistress of Udolpho: The Life of Ann Radcliffe.* Leicester: Leicester University Press, 1999.
Poovey, Mary. "Ideology and The Mysteries of Udolpho," *Criticism* 21 (1979): 307–30.
Scott, Walter. *Lives of the Novelists.* 1821–4.

RĂDULESCU, ION HELIADE 1802–1872

Romanian poet, philologist, literary critic, and cultural entrepreneur

Born near Târgovişte in Wallachia, Romania, in 1802, the son of a regional constable, Rădulescu studied first with a Greek monk (as was standard in the early nineteenth century), and then with the Transylvanian George Lazar (1779–1824), who founded the first modern Romanian high school in Wallachia. In 1825 Rădulescu replaced Lazar, and two years later was involved in establishing a literary society that recruited widely among the Wallachian nobility and promoted the foundation of progressive cultural institutions. In 1828 he published the first Romanian grammar guide based on modern principles, a work that was largely copied from a French boarding-school manual and followed the linguistic ideas of Etienne de Condillac. He also edited the first newspaper in Bucharest (*Curierul rumânesc*, 1829–48), and ran the most active publishing house in all Romanian lands (1830–48). He was a leading figure in the *Philharmonic Society*, a musical and theatrical association with masonic undertones established in 1833, and influential in developing a tradition of public theatre in Wallachia. After 1840 he began experimenting with the writing of Romanian in Latin script, devising a variety of "transition alphabets" (half-Latin, half-Cyrillic), and formulating increasingly bizarre grammatical and orthographic systems for the Latinization of the language.

More than anyone else, Rădulescu was responsible for the establishment of the rules of the literary game in Romanian culture, not only in terms of the aforementioned cultural institutions, but also as regards poetic genres—he practiced virtually all the major forms of poetic composition—and the professional and social role of poets, "men with lively imaginations and generous hearts . . . patriarchs of the intellect," as he defined them in 1832. He initiated grandiose utopian schemes for a *Universal library* (1843) to translate European classic and Romantic literature into Romanian, and equally utopian ideas of reforming the language on the model of Italian. He himself translated the New Testament as well as the work of Lord Byron, Miguel de Cervantes Saavedra, Alexandre Dumas, Hesiod, Alphonse Louis-Marie de Lamartine, Jean-Jacques Rousseau, William Shakespeare, Torquato Tasso, Voltaire, Edward Young, and others into Romanian, working from the French in most cases. His famous exhortation to fellow Romanian authors and would-be authors to "Write, boys, just write!," although probably apocryphal, is indicative of the enthusiasm he exuded in attempting to promote the production of Romanian literature at double speed in order to catch up with Western norms.

Rădulescu's talent for demagogy and theatrical gestures pushed him into the forefront of the 1848 revolution in Wallachia, although in practical terms he occupied rather conservative ground, opposing for instance the distribution of land to the peasantry. He spent the years from 1849 to 1859 in exile in France and Turkey. Rădulescu's later writings descend into a rather schematic and overblown philosophical systematizing, influenced by both Charles Fourier and G. W. F. Hegel, and not uncharacteristic of some general trends in East European Romanticism. His megalomaniac personality (he saw himself not so much as a Romanian Byron as a Romanian Moses) and his undoubtedly ludicrous political and literary schemes attracted the derision of the following generation, who criticized him and his peers for having introduced "forms without foundation" in both the literary and political spheres.

The vividness of Rădulescu's imagination, his stylistic brilliance, and his entrepreneurial talent remain indisputable. His poetic masterpiece is the ballad "Sburătorul" ("The Incubus," 1844), which brilliantly integrated Romanian folk beliefs of erotic possession into a setting reminiscent of that in François-Auguste-René, Vicomte de Châteaubriand's *Tombeaux champêtres*.

ALEXANDER DRACE-FRANCIS

Biography

Born 1802 near Târgovişte in Wallachia. Accepted position as principal of first Romanian high school, 1825. Established literary society, 1827. Published the first Romanian grammar guide, 1828. Edited the first newspaper in Bucharest, *Curierul rumânesc*, 1829–48. Director of publishing house, 1830–48. Began devising his "transition alphabets," 1840. In exile in France and Turkey, 1849–59. Died in debt, 1872.

Selected Works

Souvenirs et impressions d'un proscrit. 1850.
Opere. 2 vols. Edited by D. Popovici. Bucharest: Fundaţia pentru Literatură şi Artă "Regele Carol II," 1939–43.
Gramatica românească, 1828. Critical edition by Valeria Guţu Romalo. Bucharest: Eminescu, 1980.

Bibliography

Anothi, Sorin. *Imaginaire culturel et réalité politique dans la Roumanie moderne*. Paris: L'Harmattan, 1999.
Close, Elizabeth. *The Development of Modern Rumanian. Linguistic Theory and Practice in Muntenia, 1821–1838*. Oxford: Oxford University Press, 1974.

RAFT OF THE MEDUSA 1819

Painting by Jean Louis André Théodore Géricault

In July 1816 the French frigate *Medusa* sank off the coast of Senegal. When the news finally broke it caused a political scandal in France, where critics of the Bourbon Restoration (established 1814/15) saw the loss of the ship as a symbol of the new regime's weakness, incompetence, and corruption. The captain, a recently returned émigré, had been appointed because of his political loyalties rather than his ability; the ship was ill-equipped; and some officers, in order to save their own lives, had abandoned 150 people on a large raft. When the raft was found two weeks later, only fifteen people were still alive; their survival had entailed murder and cannibalism.

Though a headstrong royalist only a few years earlier (he had been one of the cavalry officers who escorted Louis XVIII into exile when Napoleon Bonaparte returned from Elba), Jean Louis André Théodore Géricault, quickly becoming disillusioned with the Restoration, had begun a number of (unsuccessful) works openly critical of the new regime. With the loss of the *Medusa* he found a theme that allowed him to focus all his creative and political energies in a single monumental work. The result was the first masterpiece of emergent French Romanticism. A transitional work linking the stern neoclassicism of Jacques-Louis David and the full-blown Romanticism of Eugène Delacroix, it

illustrates how difficult it is to characterize early French Romanticism, for Géricault—like many of his contemporaries, notably François Gérard, Antoine-Jean Gros, Anne-Louis Girodet de Roussy-Trioson, and Jean-Auguste-Dominique Ingres—was steeped in Davidian classicism. His Romanticism was not a conscious and strident rebellion against the past, and he would certainly have accepted Delacroix's claim that David was *le père de toute l'école moderne* (the father of the entire modern school).

For eighteen months Géricault worked with a passion and obsession that became part of the Romantic mythology of genius. He interviewed survivors and studied firsthand accounts. A debonair man-about-town, he shaved his head so that he wouldn't be able to go to the races or the theater, had the *Medusa*'s own carpenter build a model of the raft, and used survivors and his own friends (including the young Delacroix) as models. In a hospital near his studio he made studies of the dead and the dying in order to capture as accurately as possible the expressions of those in extremis, and even acquired body parts to study the various stages in the decomposition of flesh; his studio was filled with their stench.

These strange, carefully composed studies—of the heads of guillotined criminals and severed limbs from an operating theater—offer a fascinating insight into the conflicting tendencies not only in Géricault but also in Romanticism: some have brutal realism that suggests a desire to achieve an intense immediacy of vision and emotion; others, a macabre and melancholy sensuality that hints at decadence. (John Ruskin observed that such a pursuit of "sensual pleasure" would lead inevitably to an "insane . . . gloating over the garbage of death.") They illustrate a key form of Romanticism, the fragment, and (as Delacroix later noted in his *Journal*) their finish and self-sufficiency hint at a new conception of subject that challenged traditional conceptions of genre.

His numerous preparatory sketches show that he explored all the major episodes of the disaster, including scenes of mutiny, cannibalism, and rescue. He finally chose the moment the survivors saw a distant rescue ship that had not yet seen them. Though less melodramatic, this scene allowed him to focus on a theme that dominated France after the fall of Napoleon—the uncertain balance between fatalistic tragedy and revolutionary hope.

This theme is implicit in the composition, with a strong diagonal, largely formed by the figures themselves, sweeping up from the bottom left of the picture, where the dead are lying, to a young man on the top right who, supported by others, is waving to the distant ship. At the bottom end of the diagonal, as an emotional and thematic counterbalance, is a father with his dead son on his knees, a figure with all the tragic dignity of a protagonist in a Greek drama. He is the only one who looks out of the picture toward the viewer. (This image, whose source is Gros, may be intended to bring to mind Count Ugolino in Dante's *Divine Comedy*, and so may be an allusion to the cannibalism he chose not to depict.)

It is clear that Géricault wanted to create a monumental history painting (*grande machine*) in the manner of David. The picture is vast—nearly five meters (sixteen feet) high and over seven meters (twenty-three feet) long—and is largely painted in the "grand manner" of high art: the survivors are not emaciated and brutalized wrecks, but athletic figures modeled on classical sculptures, on Michelangelo (Géricault had recently returned from Rome), and on the heroic nudes of David. The body, tense, powerful, and tragic, plays a central role in Géricault's imaginative world, which is one of heroic (though constantly threatened) masculinity.

Jean Louis André Théodore Gericault, *Raft of the Medusa*, 1818/19. Reprinted courtesy of AKG Photo.

As the work progressed, a specific political message was transformed into a universal statement about the human condition. Géricault was determined to create "great art," and was indignant when critical response to the *Raft* seemed to divide along largely political lines.

But it is also clear that in style, subject, and theme *The Raft of the Medusa* completely subverts the genre to which it aspires. History painting was considered the most important genre of painting as it dealt explicitly with society's central moral, political, and spiritual values. It required not only a lofty subject but also, according to the aesthetic principle of *decorum*, an appropriately elevated (i.e., neoclassical) style.

But Géricault's monumental style is Baroque in inspiration rather than neoclassical. The scene is lit by a lurid contrast of light and shadow derived from the tenebrism of Michelangelo da Caravaggio, and the dynamic diagonal of the composition (recalling Peter Paul Rubens) sweeps not only across the scene, but into it (neoclassicism favored a stage-like composition, the dramatis personae arranged parallel to the picture plane). Moreover, some elements (as Gustave Courbet was to observe approvingly during the 1840s) are depicted with a striking (and incongruous) realism.

There is also a new attitude to subject matter. A history painting was expected to be an *exemplum virtutis*, and classical subjects were the usual choice; David's ardent republicanism drew him to Livy and Plutarch. Increasingly, contemporary events were accepted (they were in fact encouraged as part of the glorification of Napoleon's achievements), but they had to be suitably heroic. Gros's innovative *Napoleon in the Pest House at Jaffa* (1804), a painting that strongly influenced Géricault, is important in this respect because it does not depict a battle—the commonest contemporary subject in history painting—but a makeshift hospital in Jaffa during Napoleon's unsuccessful campaign in the Middle East. But standing amid the vividly painted bodies of the dead and dying is a Christ-like Napoleon, his hand raised as if in healing. His presence transforms the scene. Géricault's *The Raft of the Medusa* also depicts the suffering of a group of ordinary, nameless individuals—but it has no hero or classical context to provide a clear moral theme. These castaways are not the victims of the tragic failure of a grand ambition, or of a patriotic struggle against tyranny. They are the chance victims of nature and human weakness who, in order to survive, had to kill the weak and infirm, and (in some cases) to resort to cannibalism.

As Géricault's letters make clear, the *Raft of the* Medusa was intended as an affirmation of human values, and it is probably no coincidence that the young man waving at the distant ship is African—Géricault planned a series on slavery. This was certainly how it was understood by contemporaries, notably the historian Jules Michelet, who later referred to the raft as an image of "France herself" abandoned by incompetent leaders. But this affirmation is set against an increasingly complex and problematic vision of the human condition. The Enlightenment belief in the rationality of both man and nature has been replaced by a tragic (and here literal) vision of the individual adrift in a cruel and uncertain world (compare Casper David Friedrich's *Arctic Shipwreck* and J. M. W. Turner's *Slavers Throwing Overboard the Dead and the Dying*). From the first, the political ambitions of French Romanticism were often threatened by a retreat into melancholy and a deepening sense of impotence. In post-Napoleonic France—the France of Stendhal and Alfred-Victor de Vigny—the longing for heroism was necessarily a nostalgic longing.

The Raft of the Medusa transforms the neoclassical exemplum virtutis, an art of public values, into a Romantic study in the dynamic sublime. In its political modernism—a commitment to the contemporary maxim *il faut être de son temps* (one must be of one's own time)—there is an explicit concern with human tragedy and grandeur, seen largely in terms of the heroic male body. But there is also a deepening sense of the threat of the overwhelming and the irrational.

C. J. MURRAY

See also Géricault, Jean Louis André Théodore

Work

Raft of the Medusa (*Le Radeau de la Méduse*), 1818–19. Oil on canvas, 491 cm × 716.6 cm. Louvre, Paris.

Bibliography

Antal, Frederick. "Reflections on Classicism and Romanticism III–V," *Burlington Magazine* 77 (1940): 72–80, 188–92; and 78 (1941): 14–22.

Athanassoglou-Kallmyer, Nina. "Géricault's Severed Heads and Limbs: The Politics and Aesthetics of the Scaffold," *Art Bulletin* 74 (1992): 614.

Bryson, Norman. "Géricault and 'Masculinity'," in *Visual Culture: Images and Interpretations.* Edited by Norman Bryson, Michel Ann Holly, and Keith Moxey. Hanover, N.H.: Wesleyan University Press, 1994.

Eitner, Lorenz. *Géricault's "Raft of the Medusa."* London: Phaidon, 1972.

Friedlaender, Walter. *David to Delacroix.* Cambridge, Mass.: Harvard College, 1952.

Klingender, F. D. "Géricault as Seen in 1848," *Burlington Magazine* 91 (1942): 254–56.

Nochlin, Linda. *The Body in Pieces: The Fragment as a Metaphor of Modernity.* London: Thames and Hudson, 1994.

Pelles, Geraldine. *Art, Artists and Society: Origins of a Modern Dilemma: Painting in England and France, 1750–1850.* Englewood Cliffs, N.J.: Prentice-Hall, 1963.

Rosen, Charles, and Henri Zerner. *Romanticism and Realism: The Mythology of Nineteenth-Century Art.* New York: W. W. Norton, 1984.

Rosenblum, Robert. *Transformations in Late Eighteenth Century Art.* Princeton, N.J.: Princeton University Press, 1967.

RANKE, LEOPOLD VON 1795–1886

German historian

Few German historians had such an outstanding impact on the intellectual, conceptual, and methodological development of German and non-German historical writing as Leopold Ranke, who was ennobled as von Ranke in 1865. While already considered a classic historian in the nineteenth century, he is still widely read today. He remains the subject of debates about the role of the individual in history, about the moral implications of the historicism, and about the distinctions between political, social, and cultural history and their evaluation. Many of Ranke's books have been translated, including his famous *History of the Popes* (1834–36), *History of the Reformation* (1839–47), and *Histories of the Latin and Germanic Peoples* (1824). His collected works run to fifty-four volumes, not including the nine books of his *Universal History* (1885). Thus Ranke's enormous productivity, together with his oft-quoted plea for objectivity in history (that is, for historians to write history as it actually was ["wie es eigentlich gewesen"]), guaranteed his position as the "father" of modern historiography, and indeed, with Barthold Georg Niebuhr, as the founder of historicism, which introduced critical methods into historical research.

Ranke was born into a Lutheran family, and always had a strong interest in theological questions. In his French, English, and German national histories he concentrated principally on the sixteenth and seventeenth centuries, the age of the great religious conflicts. However, he remained a secular historian insofar as he believed in forces in history that were either inherent in the national tradition of the countries he studied, or part of universal trends, major tendencies, or principles reflecting the Enlightenment traditions of historiography. Religious and political history are closely connected in Ranke's work. While acknowledging the significance of nineteenth-century nationalism for the political and ethnic aspects of history, he also believed in the European values of the pre-1789 era. Ranke thus sought to combine some remnants of the German and European tradition of the Romantic era with the rising role of nationality in the post-Napoleonic period. For both strands he thought that the ancient institutions of the church, the monarchy, and Roman law were the pillars on which modern world history was based. Against the background of his studies on the papacy and European monarchies, Ranke therefore began his *Universal History* toward the end of his career, but he did not complete it. The form and method of his work mirrored its theoretical basis, namely that we understand history only by proceeding from the individual to the general. This puts him into contrast with his contemporary, the French historian Jules Michelet, who also wrote a national and a universal history, but who followed the more Romantic idea that the historian should reflect on the past in its totality. The discovery of historical thinking in the nineteenth century had its roots in the French Romantic era, according to Michelet, while Ranke tended to distinguish more clearly between the different historical ages.

The tension between universal history and national history plays a central role in Ranke's historical thinking. In his pioneering book on the Latin and Germanic peoples, Ranke described the two major powers, the state and Protestantism, as preconditions for the emergence of the modern world. This idea was systematically thought through in most of his other books, showing Ranke's close proximity to G. W. F. Hegel and German idealistic philosophy on the one hand and to Lutheran pietism on the other. Yet in contrast to both Hegel's philosophy and Thomas Babington Macaulay's Whiggism, Ranke did not believe in a grand scheme of history or in the project of progress.

Here again he differs from Michelet, as the great French historian thought of the history of man as the history of humanity toward the values of the French Revolution. Ranke believed that history possessed the means of opening our eyes to moral forces inherent in the past and present, but it also needed to be studied objectively and impartially—as he famously demanded; the study of primary sources made it more scholarly and, ultimately, professionalized it. History was part art, part science. In Ranke's view, instead of making judgments, the historians' task was to detect and understand the inner coherence of history by devoting themselves to archival studies. This is the real message of his famous plea for "wie es eigentlich gewesen," not, as is often suggested, a limitation to established facts. Accordingly he regarded each epoch and each nation and its people as unique entities being "immediate to God," as he termed it. This also means that Ranke saw states as embodying positive values, and acting positively, so long as they followed their own interests. In this way, history makes sense, but as a result, historiography acquires an ethical relativism if all historical phenomena possess their own value. No other nineteenth-century historian subsequently trained so many influential intellectuals as Ranke, although not all of them, of course, followed his methodological paths; whether Jacob Burckhardt, Theodor Mommsen, Heinrich von Sybel, or Georg Waitz: Ranke's mark shines through in the works of this first genuinely professional generation of German historians.

BENEDIKT STUCHTEY

Selected Works

Geschichten der romanischen und germanischen Völker. 1824–25.
Fürsten und Völker von Südeuropa im sechzehnten und siebzehnten Jahrhundert. 4 vols., 1827–36.
Die römischen Päpste, ihre Kirche und ihr Staat. 3 vols., 1834–36; 10th edn. published as *Die römischen Päpste in den letzten vier Jahrhunderten,* 1900.
Deutsche Geschichte im Zeitalter der Reformation. 6 vols., 1839–47 (*History of the Reformation in Germany.* 3 vols., 1845–47).
Neun Bücher preußischer Geschichte. 3 vols., 1847–48, revised 1874.
Französische Geschichte, vornehmlich im sechzehnten und siebzehnten Jahrhundert. 5 vols., 1852–61.
Englische Geschichte, vornehmlich im sechzehnten und siebzehnten Jahrhundert. 7 vols., 1859–67.
Sämtliche Werke. [*Collected Works*], 54 vols., 1867–90.
Geschichte Wallensteins. 1869.

Die deutschen Mächte und der Fürstenbund. Deutsche Geschichte von 1780 bis 1790 [*The German Powers and the Princes' League 1780 to 1790*], 2 vols., 1871.
Denkwürdigkeiten des Staatskanzlers Fürsten von Hardenberg. 5 vols., 1877.
Weltgeschichte. 9 vols., 1881–88 (*Universal History.* 1885).
Das Briefwerk. Edited by Walther Peter Fuchs. 1949.
Neue Briefe. Edited by Hans Herzfeld. 1949.
Aus Werk und Nachlaß. 4 vols. Edited by Walther Peter Fuchs and Theodor Schieder. 1964–75.
The Theory and Practice of History. Edited by Georg G. Iggers and Konrad von Moltke. 1973.
The Secret of World History. Selected Writings on the Art and Science of History. Edited by Roger Wines. 1981.
Die großen Mächte. Politisches Gespräch. Edited by Ulrich Muhlack. 1995.

Bibliography

Bahners, Patrick. "Die göttliche Komödie. Leopold von Ranke und Hayden White," *Storia della Storiografia* 24 (1993): 71–108.
———. " 'A Place among the English Classics': Ranke's *History of the Popes* and Its British Readers." In: *British and German Historiography, 1750–1950: Traditions, Perceptions, and Transfers.* Edited by Benedikt Stuchtey and Peter Wende. Oxford: Oxford University Press, 2000.
Berding, Helmut. "Leopold von Ranke." In: *Deutsche Historiker* [*German historians*]. Edited by Hans-Ulrich Wehler, Vol. 1. Göttingen: Vandenhoeck and Ruprecht, 1971.
Buck, Thomas Martin. "Zu Rankes Diktum von 1824. Eine vornehmlich textkritische Studie." *Historisches Jahrbuch* 119 (1999): 159–85.
Gilbert, Felix. *History: Politics or Culture? Ranke and Burckhardt.* Princeton, N.J.: Princeton University Press, 1990.
Krieger, Leonard. *Ranke: The Meaning of History.* Chicago: University of Chicago Press, 1977.
Mommsen, Wolfgang J., ed. *Leopold von Ranke und die moderne Geschichtswissenschaft.* Stuttgart: Klett-Cotta, 1988.
Muhlack, Ulrich. "Leopold von Ranke." In *Deutsche Geschichtswissenschaft um 1900.* Edited by Notker Hammerstein. Stuttgart: Steiner, 1988.
Powell, James M., and Georg G. Iggers. *Leopold von Ranke and the Shaping of the Historical Discipline.* Syracuse, N.Y.: Syracuse University Press, 1990.
Schulin, Ernst. *Die weltgeschichtliche Erfassung des Orients bei Hegel und Ranke.* Göttingen: Vandenhoeck and Ruprecht, 1958.
Syracuse University. *The Leopold von Ranke Manuscript Collection of Syracuse University.* Rev. ed. Syracuse, N.Y.: Syracuse University Press, 1983.

RATIONALISM AND IRRATIONALISM

In the context of the Romantic period, it is important to distinguish, in philosophical terms, between rationality and rationalism on the one hand, and irrationality and irrationalism on the other. The term *rationality* refers to the cognitive logic of reasoned assessment, and therefore engages the "rational" (the adoption of beliefs on the basis of reason), and its counterparts the "nonrational" (agents incapable of rational thought, or beliefs that require no reasoned basis, as in matters of taste) and the "irrational" (the beliefs or actions of rational agents in violation of principles of reason). However, because irrationality has come to signify simply a lack of reason, illogicality or absurdity, it is of limited use as a critical term. It is therefore more productive to speak of rationalism, which refers to systems of belief based on the primacy of reason, including intellectual intuition and reflection but excluding sensory, emotional, or social authority (it is hence also opposed to "empiricism," or the doctrine that all knowledge derives from and must be tested against sense experience); and of its counterpart irrationalism, which describes a principled opposition to and transgression of the boundaries created and demarcated by reason.

The establishment of the rationalist tradition in the Romantic period is easy to document, because it is both the motivating force and the pedagogical intention of Enlightenment propaganda. The period sees several shifts in perspective: from a philosophy of the absolute to a scientific ethos; from neoclassicism to modernity; from a theological history based on eschatological revelation to skepticism and the secular logic of deism, which led to a reconsideration of history and morality in terms of human reason. These shifts are documented in the huge encyclopedic projects of Jean Le Rond d'Alembert and Denis Diderot in France and Christoph Friedrich Nicolai in Germany; in the taxonomies and natural histories of Georges-Louis Buffon and Carolus Linnaeus; in developments of Newtonian science and chemistry (Robert Boyle, Benjamin Franklin, Luigi Galvani, Antoine-Laurent Lavoisier, Joseph Priestley); in the extreme materialism of Paul-Henri Dietrich d'Holbach and Julien Offroy de La Mettrie. They appear in the liberal economic theories of the physiocrats (Charles-Louis Montesquieu, François Quesnay, Anne-Robert Jacques Turgot), in the political writings of the *philosophes* Jean-Jacques Rousseau and Voltaire, and in the critical philosophy of Immanuel Kant. In historiography the new ethos appears in the writings of Etienne Bonnot de Condillac, David Hume, William Robertson and Voltaire; in political philosophy the social implications of deism spread to the New World, where they are developed in the works of Ethan Allen, Benjamin Franklin, Thomas Jefferson, and Thomas Paine.

It is less easy to document the tradition of irrationalism in this period, because it has been eclipsed by the propaganda of the Enlightenment, and tends to be dismissed as "popular belief." Under this category would be included not simply the concurrent and widespread tendencies throughout the period to believe in the "supernatural" (revealed religion, mysticism, witchcraft, cosmology, magic, the tarot), but also the resurrection and publication of Rosicrucian writings, the Kabbalah, Gnostic and Neoplatonic works, and the dissemination of Paracelsian alchemical and iatrochemical texts, all of which have their own rationality, but which stand in ambivalent relation to the texts of the rationalists.

Philosophically speaking, four fundamental moments can be singled out in this tradition: the interrogation of the limits of the prevalent Rousseauian representation of man and morality by the "desire" of the Marquis de Sade; the either/or philosophy of the absurd developed by Søren Kierkegaard culminating in a "leap of faith"; the mathematical development of "irrational numbers" and the calculus in the wake of Gottfried Wilhelm Leibniz and Isaac Newton, and the analogous development in literary theory of "Romantic irony" as an infinite interrogation of the limits of systemic thought by Friedrich von Schlegel.

These moments themselves have to be understood as taking the form of critical question marks in the context of broader epistemological shifts which the "archeological" work of Michel Foucault has brought to light, In particular, the development during this period of new, universally applied disciplinary power structures—medicine, the establishment of hospitals, psychology, the establishment of asylums; penality, rehabilitation, and the embodiment of the law in the shape of the police force and new juridical structures—that attempted to demarcate societal limits of rational human behavior and thought from what was considered the "irrational" ("unreason" or "madness," sickness, criminality, immorality, social inutility). These shifts accompany a gradual change in the understanding of language, from its treatment as a tool of individual expression to its consideration as the fundamental ground of the self-conscious mode of rational thought, from its perception as "literature" to its analysis as "criticism."

Ironically, it is the Romantic legacy of criticism itself that is, at the beginning of the twenty-first century, recovering the "irrational," by revealing that what has been considered outside the limits and excluded by reason is better understood as a movement *within* reason itself, a mirror held up to reason by its own demarcation of limits. Thus the irrational appears in our own age as both the founding ground of reason and that on which it founders; and it becomes the mode of interrogation of systemic thought in poststructuralist theory (as practiced by Roland Barthes, Jacques Derrida, Michel Foucault and Jacques Lacan) as well as, with its foregrounding of nonclosure, the nonplace of desire, the "arbitrary nature of the signifier," marginality, hybridity, and particularism, the shifting ground of what has come to be called postmodernism.

JOHANN PILLAI

Bibliography

Cassirer, Ernst. *The Philosophy of the Enlightenment.* Translated by Fritz C. A. Koelln and James P. Pettegrove. Boston: Beacon Press, 1951.

Clive, Geoffrey. *The Romantic Enlightenment. Ambiguity and Paradox in the Western Mind (1750–1920).* New York: Meridian Books, 1960.

Derrida, Jacques. "Cogito and the History of Madness." In *Writing and Difference.* Translated by Alan Bass. Chicago: University of Chicago Press, 1978.

Feyerabend, Paul. *Against Method: Outline of an Anarchistic Theory of Knowledge.* London: Verso, 1978.

Foucault, Michel. *The Birth of the Clinic: An Archaeology of Medical Perception.* Translated by A. M. Sheridan Smith. New York: Random House, 1973.

———. *Discipline and Punish: The Birth of the Prison.* Translated by Alan Sheridan, N.Y.: Vintage Books, 1979.

———. *Madness and Civilization: A History of Insanity in the Age of Reason.* Translated by Richard Howard. New York: Vintage Books, 1988.

———. *The Order of Things: An Archaeology of the Human Sciences.* London: Routledge, 1970.

Herrick Jim. *Against the Faith: Essays on Deists, Skeptics and Atheists.* Amherst, N.Y.: Prometheus Books, 1985.

McCrone, John. *The Myth of Irrationality: The Science of the Mind from Plato to Star Trek.* London: Macmillan, 1993.

Stafford, Barbara Maria. *Body Criticism. Imaging the Unseen in Enlightenment Art and Medicine.* Cambridge, Mass.: MIT Press, 1991.

Wallis, Brian, ed. *Art After Modernism: Rethinking Representation.* New York: New Museum of Contemporary Art/Boston: David R. Godine, 1984.

DIE RÄUBER (THE ROBBERS) 1781

Play by Johann Christoph Friedrich von Schiller

Johann Christoph Friedrich von Schiller's first play was conceived and written during the last two years of his stay at the Hohe Karlsschule in Stuttgart, where he qualified as a military doctor in 1780. This was an ambivalent institution: utterly repressive on the one hand, yet contributing in some important ways to Schiller's education on the other.

Die Räuber is not a revolutionary play in the sense that it proposes a new order of society, or "Romantic" in the sense that it vindicates a return to nature or glorifies the outsider, for its hero, Karl Moor, reforms and eventually gives himself up to justice. But it bristles with radical ideas and expresses, as few other works do, the spirit of its age. It was born, in Schiller's phrase, of the "unnatural copulation of subordination and genius." He published it himself, anonymously, in 1781.

We can best understand this remarkably bold and influential work in terms of a number of key motifs and ideas which are linked together, if not in a thoroughly unified or logically consistent manner in dramatic terms, then at least a totally invigorating one. First, there is the "lost son" motif: Karl Moor has abandoned his former style of life and seeks adventure, glory, autonomy, and freedom by becoming the leader of a group of robbers. When plans go awry and crimes are committed in the name of freedom, he returns to his childhood home and seeks forgiveness from his father. Karl's father dies and Karl himself only obtains satisfaction by cutting his ties with his robber-friends, and surrendering. The biblical story is thus radically transformed.

Second, there is fraternal enmity: Karl's younger brother Franz, egotistical and jealous of his privileged position, sows seeds of hatred in his father's mind, seeking to eradicate both of them. But again the biblical story (here of Cain and Abel) is a mere pretext for Schiller's exploration of deeper matters. Through his characters he encodes his reckoning with currents of thought in his own time: Enlightenment thought (natural law, French materialism), medical and anthropological thought, (the latter just in its infancy), as well as educational and religious thought. Franz's attempt to justify evil in intellectual terms is mercilessly exposed. But in his attempt to achieve autonomy and freedom from restrictions, he is similar to his brother Karl.

Third, there is opposition to the establishment: if youth (Karl) is set against patriarchy and old age (old Moor), the opposition is not absolute, for Karl returns to his father to seek forgiveness. Weak as old Moor is, he is yet the victim of the evil designs of his younger son. Moor's youthful rebellion is against institutionalized learning, tyranny, and organized religion, yet it oversteps the bounds of reason, even for himself, and another paradox, divine justice (albeit it in the form of contemporary eschatological thinking) is invoked as Nemesis in the case of Franz Moor.

Schiller also built ideas into the play that he had absorbed as a student of medicine at the Hohe Karlsschule, such as those relating to the health and sickness of the body from a physiological angle (the surging of feeling and the need for recuperation).

Schiller's play was a stimulus to Romanticism in its depiction of an apparently carefree style of life, the theme of rebellion and the seemingly uncompromising way it is presented, the legend which grew up around its author, its refusal to be pigeonholed with forms of established drama and its vibrant style. In Germany it was important for early Romanticism, particularly for Ludwig Tieck; in England it was championed by Thomas Carlyle and Samuel Taylor Coleridge. But the idea of seeing the play (or even the Sturm und Drang) as Romantic, is a fallacy that goes back to Madame Anne-Louise-Germaine de Staël.

Echoes of John Milton and William Shakespeare abound. Schiller took much from the Sturm und Drang in terms of both verbal and nonverbal style, and at the same time demonstrated the limits to which this style could be taken, running the risk of descending into melodrama and being parodied. The original version was subtitled a *Schauspiel* (play); it avoids the formula for tragedy found in popular domestic tragedies and aims at stark effects. In order to have his play staged, Schiller made several changes at the suggestion of the director of the Mannheim Theater, Baron Heribert von Dalberg, giving it a late medieval setting and toning down the social criticism. He then published it in a *Trauerspiel* (tragedy) version, which included these concessions to popular taste and showed a meeting of the two brothers, but it is less true to his intentions.

An eyewitness account indicates the effect of the play at its first performance on January 13, 1782; we read,

> The theatre resembled a madhouse: rolling eyes, clenched fists, stamping feet, hoarse screams in the auditorium! People unknown to each other fell sobbing into each others' arms, women reeled, almost fainting, to the door. It was a general release as in chaos, out of whose mists a new creation arises.

Other contemporaries found the play crude, shocking, and *monstrous* (a word even Schiller himself used to describe it). It could not be ignored. Like most of Schiller's other plays, it continues to be performed on the German stage today.

JOHN GUTHRIE

Text

Die Räuber. In *Schillers Werke. Nationalausgabe. Dritter Band.* Edited by Herbert Stubenrauch. Weimar: Böhlau, 1953.
Die Räuber. Edited with introduction and notes by F. J. Lamport. London: Bristol Classical Press, 1993.

Bibliography

Alt, Peter-André. *Schiller. Leben—Werk—Zeit.* Hamburg: Beck, 2000.
Dewhurst, Kenneth, and Nigel Reeves. *Friedrich Schiller: Medicine, Psychology, Literature.* Oxford: Sandford Publications, 1978.
Pugh, David. *Schiller's Early Dramas: A Critical History.* Columbia S.C.: Camden House, 2000.
Sharpe, Lesley. *Friedrich Schiller. Drama, Thought and Politics.* Cambridge: Cambridge University Press, 1991.

RELIGION: BRITAIN

Religion in the Romantic period was predominantly protestant, the Anglican Church of England having merged with the Church of Wales in 1536, and the Church of Ireland from 1801, though most Irish citizens were Roman Catholic and the Welsh were primarily nonconformist. Anglicanism's monopoly was undermined, however, by the 1689 Act of Toleration, which legalized dissenting congregations, and an increasingly influential anticlericalism, which drew attention to the corruptions of the church, most serious in rural areas. While Anglicanism and rational dissent alike remained under threat from Enlightenment reason and developing scientific discourses, Britain remained a chiefly Christian country throughout the nineteenth century, and was thus wholly caught in the religious debates that structured the changing status of the church.

The early eighteenth century witnessed the beginnings of a Protestant revival, which sought to reawaken believers from the inertia and corrupt hierarchy of the established church. Both Evangelicals (adherents of the Reformation) and Methodists (proponents of personal conversion of the Atonement of Christ) privileged a resolute commitment to the reality of faith over simply the performance of good works. The revival was thus marked by a message of justification by faith, one tirelessly promoted by John Wesley, leader of the influential Methodists who emerged from the student-based Holy Club at Oxford in the 1720s. Where the university-educated Wesley represented the disciplined and devotional aspect of the movement, George Whitefield, an Anglican deacon from rural Gloucester, voiced its pioneering fervor as the originator of field preaching. Offering believers an at once ecclesiastically traditional and enthusiastic belief system, Methodism embraced almost half a million converts in Britain between 1740 and 1840.

Wesley's "religion of the people" sustained itself throughout the Romantic period due to several factors. First, its simple and direct mode of worship made religion an accessible and attractive prospect for believers from every social stratum, molded by the sincerity and ardor of its preachers. Second, it created a sense of society and community through an emphasis upon prayer, which it stressed should be practiced daily in services, four times a year at "love-feasts," and on the last night of each year in "watch-night" events. Moreover, the importance attributed to prayer in the home spurred a publishing industry, of which Henry Thornton's 1834 Evangelical manual, *Family Prayers*, was perhaps the most popular. A third related factor was Methodist hymnody, a pedagogical tool for communicating doctrine as well as invoking moods of repentance, religious joy, and social responsibility. Wesley's *A Collection of Hymns for the Use of the People called Methodists* (1780) was as much a commentary on scripture as a song book, and inspired Evangelicals like John Berridge and Martin Madan to produce similar anthologies while forwarding a hymnal meter deeply influential on Romantic poetics. Preaching was also enhanced by the intercession of sung praise, which served to underline the preacher's main three tasks: to convert, to edify, and to sanctify. The latter was achieved partly through communion, which Methodism highlighted as a path to spiritual life, a mark of continuity with the traditional Christian Church, and a signifier of its investment in sacramentalism. Wesley's high sacramentalism rendered him a forerunner of the Oxford Movement of John Keble and John Henry New-

man, and, like Tractarianism, Methodism sought to spread the Word to both the middle and laboring classes in the city and countryside alike.

Other religious groups notable in this period for refusing to conform to the doctrines and practices of the Church of England were labeled as dissenters or nonconformists, a group comprising Presbyterians, Congregationalists, Baptists, and the Society of Friends (Quakers). Presbyterianism later splintered into Congregationalism and Unitarianism, the latter aiding the repeal of the Test and Corporation Acts in 1828 and the passage of the Dissenting Chapels Act in 1844. As the name implies, Unitarianism rejected the Trinity and thus the divinity of God, a position notably forwarded by the Enlightenment philosopher Joseph Priestley in his *History of the Corruptions of Christianity* (1782). Priestley's tutorial role at the celebrated Warrington Academy also encouraged religious free thought as represented by figures such as the medical innovator John Aikin; Reverend William Turner, founder of the Newcastle Literary and Philosophical Society; and, indirectly, the eminent poet and religiopolitical commentator, Anna Laetitia Barbauld. Priestley's influence, and the status of Unitarianism in general, declined in the wake of the French Revolution, dissent negatively associated with violent war. Dissent thus lost its impetus and religious debate turned to the historicist arguments exemplified by William Paley's *A View of the Evidences of Christianity* (1792), the debate over deism and atheism and the "new" orthodox dissent of which Jabez Bunting's Methodism and Anglican Evangelicalism were part.

Anglican Evangelicalism paralleled Methodism in its stress on the emotional experience of conversion, belief in original sin, and focus on prayer and communion, although it doubted the orthodoxy of lay preaching. Both movements also voiced a loyalty to the "invisible" rather than "visible" church, centralizing Christian conversion over denominational allegiance and so opening a space for interdenominational bodies such as the British and Foreign Bible Society of 1804. Where Wesleyan Methodism had touched the working class, Evangelicalism profoundly influenced the middle class, emphasizing the salvation of individuals in return for their contribution to promoting equality in society. Thus the philanthropic practices of voluntary charity and moral reform became central to an Evangelical message that promoted abolitionism, poor law and welfare amendment, education for all through the formation of Sunday Schools, and, to some extent, rights for women. Many of the "bluestocking" women, for example, derived their education in part from attendance at chapel or church, and the prominent thinker Mary Wollstonecraft rejected the orthodox beliefs of her youth for a personal vision of God that grounded her feminist writing.

The more general reformation of Christian society was forwarded through literature published by the Society for Promoting Christian Knowledge, founded in 1698 but highly active in this period, reissuing the work of writers such as William Wordsworth to provide a model of Anglican piety and virtue. Indeed the pantheistic deism usually associated with the Romantics is not entirely different from Anglicanism's emphasis on religious pathos, such as Samuel Taylor Coleridge's writing in 1802 that he believed, "not because I understand," but "because I feel." As the genre most associated with the overflow of this kind of feeling, poetry was deemed the most ideal expression of religious sentiment, often creating a Christianized sense of the sublime in the reader. Romantic poetry is thus marked by its religious foundations, whether it be nonconformism (Barbauld) Unitarianism (Coleridge), Anglicanism (Felicia Hemans and William Wordsworth), Evangelicalism (Hannah More), Calvinism (Lord Byron), or millenarianism (William Blake and Percy Bysshe Shelley). Although not a believer, John Keats, too, was concerned with the spiritual aesthetic associated with Catholicism, a religion revived on the continent in the 1820s and legalized in Britain after the Catholic Emancipation Act of 1829.

If the main religious questions debated in Britain in this period were of a Christian nature, other less dominant belief systems underlined these debates. Judaism, for example, expanded rapidly from 1750, achieving an emancipated status in 1833 through the efforts of Isaac Lyon Goldsmid and Nathan Rothschild, and the impact of Eastern spirituality on the Romantic imagination (the classics of Tao, Vedanta, Buddhism, and Sufism were gradually being made available through the systematic development of comparative linguistics) remains fundamental to an understanding of nineteenth-century subjectivity.

EMMA MASON

Bibliography

Davies, Horton. *Worship and Theology in England: From Watts and Wesley to Maurice 1690–1850*. Princeton, N.J.: Princeton University Press, 1961.

Fairchild, Hoxie Neale. *Religious Trends in English Poetry*. Vol. 4, 1830–1880: *Christianity and Romanticism in the Victorian Era*. New York: Columbia University Press, 1957.

Gill, Frederick C. *The Romantic Movement and Methodism: A Study of English Romanticism and the Evangelical Revival*. New York: Haskell House, 1966.

Hempton, David. *Methodism and Politics in British Society 1750–1850*. London: Hutchinson, 1984.

Jasper, David. *The Sacred and Secular Canon in Romanticism: Preserving the Sacred Truths*. London: Macmillan, 1999.

Jay, Elisabeth. *The Evangelical and Oxford Movements*. Cambridge: Cambridge University Press, 1983.

———. *The Religion of the Heart: Anglican Evangelicalism and the Nineteenth Century*. Oxford: Clarendon Press, 1979.

Prickett, Stephen. *Romanticism and Religion: The Tradition of Coleridge and Wordsworth in the Victorian Church*. Cambridge: Cambridge University Press, 1976.

———. *Words and the Word: Language, Poetics and Biblical Interpretation*. Cambridge: Cambridge University Press, 1986.

Ryan, Robert M. *The Romantic Reformation: Religious Politics in English Literature 1789–1824*. Cambridge: Cambridge University Press, 1997.

Shaffer, E. S. "Religion and Literature." In *The Cambridge History of Literary Criticism*. Vol. 5, *Romanticism*. Edited by Marshall Brown. Cambridge: Cambridge University Press, 2000.

Webb, R. K. "Religion." In *An Oxford Companion to the Romantic Age: British Culture 1776–1832*. Edited by Iain McCalman. Oxford: Oxford University Press, 1999.

Weiskel, Thomas. *The Romantic Sublime: Studies in the Structure and Psychology of Transcendence*. Baltimore: Johns Hopkins University Press, 1976.

RELIGION: CHRISTIANITY

As T. E. Hulme's famous remark that Romanticism is "spilt religion" suggests, religion in this age was one of the foremost tides in the course of human events. And as critics such as Robert Ryan have recently argued, "religion became the primary arena in which the Romantics [that is to say, the highly politicized, canonized male poets] engaged the power structure of their society. . . ." Thus, at the outset of a consideration of the issue of religion in this period, a dichotomy emerges, with one pole for the established church(es) of Christianity and its mostly Protestant variants, significantly yoked to the general power establishment of the nation, contrasted with the individual and lasting reaction and opposing commentary, which is reflected in the art of the age. For as William Blake declared, one must either devise one's own religious system or adhere (to be "enslaved" as Blake saw it) to that of another. And therefore European Romantic writers were essentially practicing, lapsed, or heterodox Christians, mirroring the preponderant distribution of population in western Europe at that time. And they were also largely Protestant, though the often Gothic and medieval interests of the period were certainly congruent with medieval and Roman Catholic sacerdotalism (the belief that priests act as mediators between God and the people).

In Britain, the Church of England was politically and legally part of the power structure of the nation in the nineteenth century, subject to the monarchy and Parliament, of which its bishops were a part. As the established church, therefore, its lords were patrons of the status quo at all levels of society, and, as is evident from Jane Austen's novels alone, rural livings, which at this time were the majority of the parishes, were not staffed on the basis of merit but rather through patronage and in effect a spoils system, resulting in great absenteeism, poor training, and negligent stewardship among the clergy who served the multitude of villages. Consequently, the church, though its membership was the vast majority of the population, was ripe for attack and correction during this period. Men who were not baptized in the Church of England were disenfranchised and ineligible for matriculation at Oxford and Cambridge universities and for government employment. (Such opportunities were not available to women at all.)

The situation was comparable throughout the British Isles, although of course in Ireland the Roman Catholic Church claimed an overwhelming majority of the populace as its adherents (but still the Anglican-associated Church of Ireland reigned politically supreme through its ties to England), and in Scotland the Presbyterian Kirk served the mass of the people. In 1828 and 1829, Parliament passed acts that opened up Parliament and government service to Protestants outside the established church (known as nonconformists or dissenters, primarily Presbyterian, Baptist, Congregationalist, newly emergent Unitarian, and Quaker, altogether somewhat less than a tenth of the population) and to Roman Catholics, whose less than 1 percent of the nation came largely from many ancient, landed families dating back to the Tudors and from growing numbers of Irish immigrants.

Much of the theological energy of the Romantic period derived from the highly nostalgic German philosophy of the age. Isaiah Berlin discerned the taproots of Romanticism in German Pietism, a highly individualistic, spiritual, and biblically based variant of Lutheranism. From this foundation sprang Kantian Idealism, leading to Johann Christoph Friedrich von Schiller's overpowering sense of personal will and freedom, and culminating in the notions of the infinite and the inexhaustible in Friedrich Wilhelm Joseph von Schelling, which are both within and beyond humanity and to which only artistic representation, symbolism, can aspire. These ideas spread, finding fertile ground in England via primarily Samuel Taylor Coleridge, who transmitted them to William Wordsworth, articulating notions of creativity that also had theological implications and Germanic predecessors, and thence to the spirit of the age and to later Romantic writers. Parallel developments in France were characterized by the writings of Chateaubriand, Jean-Jacques Rousseau, Stendhal, François-Auguste-René and ultimately Victor Hugo and other French Romantic writers. The French example is conflicted because its Christian heritage is Roman Catholic and not Protestant; yet, France contributed the preeminent political revolution to the age, one linked to atheism, which may perhaps therefore have sufficiently loosened the bonds to Roman Catholicism to find congenial these other influences, especially, via Immanuel Kant, platonic idealism (the origins of which Thomas Aquinas had first reconciled theologically with the holy Catholic ecclesia so many ages past). A third national version is Italian Romanticism, in which Antonio Rosmini, as Bernard Reardon has argued, brought Romantic thought into his church, thereby preparing the way for modern Roman Catholicism by locating the creative and the ideal in the divine, which humans may apprehend but which are ultimately beyond "man's grasp, or what's a heaven for," as Robert Browning said. Nonetheless, in all of these ideas one can recognize the familiar ideation of Romanticism writ large, such as nostalgia, Gothicism, medievalism, individualism, idealism, revolution, and concepts of creativity, free will, the infinite, and the symbolic.

As the influence of Lutheran Pietism makes evident, notwithstanding the religious orientation of Romantic writers, they were certainly biblically well read, and their texts are frequently interwoven with scriptural allusion. To take as the most extreme example, even Percy Bysshe Shelley, expelled from Oxford for propagating his tract *The Necessity of Atheism,* laced his prose and poetry, as critic Bryan Shelley has painstakingly established, with textual echoes of and traces from biblical quotations, themes, plots, and antitypes for artistic purposes other than piety or faith. In fact, Stephen Prickett has argued that French, German, and English Romantic thought in general was "steeped through and through in biblical references." In the nineteenth century, German hermeneutical critics began finding disparate authors responsible for portions of Genesis previously unquestionably and entirely ascribed to Moses and then proceeded relentlessly, and some clearly thought heretically, toward similar scrutiny of all the texts through the Revelation of St. John the Divine. This advance, coupled with the publication of *The Origin of the Species* and other works of evolutionary science, led some interpreters of the Bible to move increasingly away from literalism and its attendant strictures to reveal a set of documents

paradoxical, contradictory, and often fluid and unfinished, in harmony with the notion of the Romantic text, as Prickett has shown.

Two religious movements of this time were of signal importance to Romanticism. First was the development and spread of what became known as Methodism and Evangelicalism within and without the protestant church, and in particular the Anglican Communion in which most of the British Romantic writers were nurtured.

Initiated by John Wesley and his brothers, who were deeply influenced by German Pietists, a highly individualistic, socially aware, and activist practice, committed to "good works," arose in the late eighteenth and early nineteenth centuries to reform the corruptions in the established church. The core of this interest was termed "enthusiasm"—that is, a highly charged, personal, and emotional conversion experience, comparable to what Wordsworth later described in terms of poetic inspiration as "the spontaneous overflow of powerful feeling," and therefore much unlike the tight-laced, pew-bound, and increasingly remote local parishes. This spiritual awakening became a very popular missionary movement, and recent scholars have begun to explore its tangency with Romantic expression.

Whereas this was a division that spread rapidly among the newly franchised and the working classes, in the 1830s and 1840s a theological awakening among the intellectual elite at Oxford led to what has been called the Oxford movement to purify, refine, and render the church even less progressive and more Catholic. Eventually, many of these exponents, most notably John Henry (later Cardinal) Newman, renounced their Anglicanism in favor of the church at Rome, at the same time modeling a kind of nostalgic retrograde turn emblematic of one strand of Romanticism and sharing its sense of commitment and dedication, as Wordsworth wrote in *The Prelude* in very religious terms concerning his awakening and rebirth as a poet:

> My heart was full; I made no vows, but vows
> Were then made for me; bond unknown to me
> Was given, that I should be, else sinning greatly
> A dedicated Spirit. On I walk'd
> In blessedness

Romanticism, in short, developed in a highly religious era and entered into frequent dialogue with the leading voice of the day, Protestant Christianity, even as it struggled against it.

LAURA DABUNDO

Bibliography

Berlin, Isaiah. *The Roots of Romanticism.* Edited by Henry Hardy. Princeton, N.J.: Princeton University Press, 1999.

Collins, Irene. *Jane Austen and the Clergy.* London: Hambledon Press, 1994.

Ford, Boris (ed.). *The Romantic Age in Britain: The Cambridge Cultural History.* Cambridge: Cambridge University Press, 1992.

Litvack, Leon B. "Religion." In *Encyclopedia of Romanticism: Culture in Britain, 1780s–1830s.* New York: Garland, 1992.

Marks, Clifford J. "George Eliot's Pictured Bible: *Adam Bede's* Redeeming Methodism." *Christianity and Literature* 49 (2000): 311–30.

Prickett, Stephen. *Origins of Narrative: The Romantic Appropriation of the Bible.* Cambridge: Cambridge University Press, 1996.

Reardon, Bernard M. G. *Religion in the Age of Romanticism: Studies in Early Nineteenth Century Thought.* Cambridge: Cambridge University Press, 1999.

Ryan, Robert. *The Romantic Reformation: Religious Politics in English Literature, 1789–1824.* Cambridge: Cambridge University Press, 1997.

Shelley, Bryan. *Shelley and Scripture: The Interpreting Angel.* Oxford: Clarendon Press, 1994.

Webb, R. K. "Religion." In *An Oxford Companion to the Romantic Age, British Culture, 1776–1832.* Edited by Iain McCalman. Oxford: Oxford University Press, 1999.

RELIGION: FRANCE

For A. N. Whitehead, the revolution in favor of what he terms "value" distinguishes the Romantic era in Europe from the preceding Age of Enlightenment; he argues, however, that value is no better exemplified than by the restoration of religious sensibility to a place of prominence in early nineteenth-century Western experience. The previous three centuries, beginning with the Renaissance, had come to view the universe as a self-sufficient system, subject merely to natural laws and explicable exclusively through the instrument of science. The holistic embrace of Romantic consciousness, however, reaches out to the broadly mysterious and rationally unaccountable beyond its own cognitive boundaries, and entertains the reentry into its worldview of the numinous of the prescientific past. "Whereas the last century," wrote the French Catholic spokesman Genoude, reflecting on this cultural shift from the vantage point of the early years of the French Restoration, "produced an alarming consensus of able minds against religion, the nineteenth century is beginning in a totally opposite way." This bald truth is, however, apt to conceal the historical, sociological, and psychological processes governing a phenomenon of undeniable significance for the modern era, whose advent it arguably marks. If the Romantic revolution was also a religious revolution, it was so in a way that redefined the scope and nature of religion itself, its role in political life, its relations with society, with culture, and with its erstwhile antagonist, scientific reason.

In the specific context of Romantic religious awareness in France, an initial distinction needs to be drawn between the French Catholic Church as an established institution and the beliefs, moral or spiritual, represented by Christianity at large, or indeed by other forms of faith. Though the religious revival of the first decades of the nineteenth century is in part commensurate with the renaissance of an ailing church temporal, it is far more profoundly characterized by the emergence of types of religious belief that exposed the shortcomings of France's narrowly national faith and would contribute, in the course of a hundred years, to its disestablishment. As regime displaces regime in the period under review, the political ties binding French Catholicism prove a constant source of vulnerability, while other factors, philosophical, sociological or psychological, separately determine the impact of religion upon men's and women's minds.

Two logically opposed impulses are always at work in this process, and their coexistence does much to explain the discernible ambivalence attending the nineteenth-century religious revival. The cult of the individual and the rejection of authority, which are equally familiar features of the Romantic *Weltanschauung*, stand here in fine balance with the anxiety that this spirit of independence simultaneously breeds. As Jean-Paul Sartre would later argue, the more intense and immediate the individual's awareness of selfhood and personal liberty, the stronger his craving for instruments of hierarchy and guidance. If the Romantic generation inclines toward religious belief, it is for the very reason that it has abandoned religion's official sanctuary only to find itself confronting the abyss of existential isolation. The undertow beneath all aspects of the Romantic religious renaissance, and that which shapes its ultimate nature, lies thus, ironically, in the debt which it owes to the corresponding advance of the sceptical and secular.

An assessment of the status of religion in France during the final years of the ancien régime already reveals such a dichotomy, albeit an inverse one, between the formal status of the Catholic Church and its popularity and psychological health. While state law still sanctioned compulsory confession well into the middle years of the eighteenth century, the intrinsic appeal of what was taught from the pulpit had withered to a point where a whole generation knew no other than the scornful view of it adopted by Denis Diderot, Voltaire, and their fellow "philosophes." The very identification of the church with the centralized regime of Louis XVI exposed it to the seismic events of 1789 and, when the guillotine began falling four years later, it found itself the object of comparable persecution and violence. Thousands of priests and nuns were executed or exiled against a background in which, inspired by the doctrines of the heroes of the Enlightenment, the Paris Commune chose to celebrate an alternative "Festival of Reason." The centuries-old church bells around the country fell silent and it was left to a handful of courageous "refractory" priests to recite the mass or hear the confessions of the devout in secret.

These were, however, the unpromising circumstances in which the religious revival identified with the new century properly begins. With persecution and inevitable instances of martyrdom came a sympathy for the church that it had not encountered for decades. Out of the unrelenting disquiet and insecurity induced by civil instability was born a nostalgia for the consolation and reassurance afforded by religious conviction. The French revolution, that had drawn its inspiration from the Age of Reason, had rekindled a preoccupation with the darker recesses of experience, and would provide the instigation for a new national mood whereby these counted for more than the exhilaratingly destructive but superficial and unsupportive doctrines of the preceding era. There was thus a shrewd political logic behind Napoleon Bonaparte's decision, following his appointment as first consul in 1799, to set in train negotiations with Pope Leo XII that would eventually lead to the signing of the Concordat with Rome of 1802. The future emperor was no devout Christian, but he was quick to recognize that his divided and war-torn country was thirsting for the kind of security that only the banished church could provide. "France," he conceded, "having learned from her misfortune, has brought back the Catholic religion into her midst."

The impact of the Revolutionary years would not, however, be so abruptly erased; nor, indeed, was this Bonaparte's intention. His ultramontane overtures were primarily aimed at ensuring that a restored Church remained under Imperial control, and the schism thus engendered between the religion of Rome and the religion of France remains an abiding feature of the period. Under the succeeding Bourbon Restoration, it is true, the Catholic Church witnessed a brief return, in material and political terms, to something approaching its old ways and standing. The reactionary regimes of Louis XVIII and, more particularly, of his successor, Charles X, favored clerical influence in the affairs of the state and over the behavior of its citizens, to the point where, writing in *Le Rouge et le noir* of 1830, the novelist Stendhal could depict the priesthood as the most promising career for a young man with sociopolitical ambitions. Once again, however, it was the Church's establishment which would prove to be its undoing. Though never on the scale of 1793, the last years of the Restoration witnessed renewed acts of anticlerical vandalism and, with the fall of the Bourbons following the July Revolution, the briefly resurgent alliance between political regime and national religion was abruptly halted. It is estimated, in fact, that, by the end of the Restoration period, the orthodox Catholic Church had ceased to represent the beliefs of the majority of Frenchmen.

In reality, however, the significant religious debate was already being conducted on the margins of the official Church and at a different level from its conventional teachings. Like Judaism in the sixth century before Christ, French Catholicism in the wake of the Revolution had experienced a diaspora that left it chastened and tempered. Those of its adherents who had evaded the guillotine had been scattered to the far corners of Europe and the seminaries that trained its officiants disbanded or neglected.

No longer united in a community of doctrine or by a supporting bureaucracy, the new generation of religious thinkers who emerged into the light of Napoleon's initial gesture of reconciliation is characterized by the diversity of its constituent personalities and corresponding religious opinions. What its members nonetheless shared was a sensitivity to the arguments and methods of religion's enemies and an awareness that religious belief must henceforth acknowledge the vicissitudes of historical change to which it had been subject, and the secularizing and liberalizing tendencies that the upheavals of 1789 had irreversibly unleashed. Like society as a whole, French Christianity in the first decade of the nineteenth century stood at a new and challenging crossroads where ancient, absolutist standards and those of modern historical relativism confronted one another. Seen through the eyes of one of the new century's most unrepentent religious reactionaries, Joseph de Maistre, the encounter imposes a radical choice. A new religion, he declared, in his *Considérations sur la France* of 1796, needs to be created, or else Christianity must be revitalized in an unprecedented way.

The outcome of this theological ground clearing was a panoply of religious ideas and systems, some of which, in strictly orthodox terms, would barely qualify as religions at all. The sustained onslaught on Christian dogma on the part of the Enlightenment rationalists and empiricists had left its mark, and its effects, in combination with those of the Revolution, are felt in the inclination, so characteristic of the period, toward religions based on the experience of conscience, the heart, or the imagination, rather than on threadbare notions of revelation. Jean-Jacques Rousseau, in political terms perhaps the most powerful source of revolutionary inspiration, is here, in another guise, the guiding light, together with the late-eighteenth-century Scots philosophers Thomas Reid and Dugald Stewart, the inclusion of whose epistemology of "common sense" on the syllabus of Catholic seminaries by the mid 1830s is an indication of how far the church itself had been obliged to acknowledge the post-Enlightenment democratic sea change.

Even for ardent revivalists such as Maistre, Louis de Bonald, and their energetic disciple Félicité de Lamennais, religion's task is henceforth to take account of history and political upheaval in a way that made of them less genuine theologians or advocates of the spiritual than theocrats who saw a legitimate manifestation of the power of God in ecclesiastical sovereignty. Bonald's intriguing theory of language, which holds that verbal function is a precondition of thought, provides him with evidence of the necessary dependence of social man on the authority of the divinely given word. Maistre most resembles an Old Testament patriarch and his God a vengeful Yahweh exacting retribution on an errant Revolutionary France. The fact, indeed, that the author of the *Considérations* was a practicing freemason says much about the true nature of his particular brand of fundamentalism. Rather than those of the Christian church, the values of the Society of Freemasons speak of the pursuit of a secret hierarchy beneath the surrounding chaos, of an alternative, magical transcendentalism located in the cabalistic mysteries of sign or number.

When Lamennais, in his *Réflexions sur l'état de l'Eglise en France pendant le XVIIIe siècle* of 1808, took up the the challenge of Napoleon's papal posturing and called for a restoration of the authority of Rome, he, too, was clutching at a symbol of the church's waning power. A populist rather than a patrician, however, he found it in the basic religious instincts he believed to be present in all mankind and, when he began publishing his *Essai sur l'indifférence* nine years later, his own brand of zealotry was already in germ. As revealed by his subsequent *Paroles d'un croyant*, what Lamennais shares with Maistre is apocalyptic anger at defeat and marginalization and the search for redress through tribalism or totemism. Maistre's thought, suggests one of his commentators, contained the ingredients that would later reemerge as Nazi totalitarianism, and Lamennais' contained those of Marxist socialism. Ironically, the very city, Saint Petersburg, where the former found asylum from one form of ideological confrontation would one day serve as the arena for another to which he had, unwittingly, contributed.

The broadly spiritualist but heterodox teachings of Victor Cousin, who enchanted a war-exhausted public with the academic lectures he began delivering soon after the fall of Napoleon in 1815, offer a more conciliatory example of the incorporation of historical consciousness into the new religious teachings. By background and education, Cousin was a thoroughgoing child of the new, postrevolutionary generation, sensitive to its disorientation and able, through his subtle blend of theism and rationalism, to offer it an identity and a soul. A distinctive feature of Cousin's doctrine is a form of religious sensibility which was already enjoying a vogue in English intellectual circles and would find as many if not more adherents in France with its longstanding neoclassical traditions. When in 1820 the poet Alphonse Mavie Louis de Lamartine published his seminal *Méditations poétiques*, his readers found themselves soothed by a religious voice that, when faced by those classic sources of human anxiety—change, bereavement, and death—no longer turned to an anthropomorphic creator for explanation and understanding but to the reassuring stability of creation as a whole. The recognition of the religious in the totality of things, and specifically in the permanence of the natural world, so characteristic also of the Wordsworth of *The Prelude*, is perhaps the clearest example of the way in which, in the early Romantic years, the doctrinally Christian river of the pre-Enlightenment ages becomes engulfed by a broader emotional tide demanding unmediated contact with the transcendental. Enlightenment rationalism, which had first revealed the natural world to be one of perfection and harmony, is inescapably part of this confluence. The leap is not a vast one between devotion to the secular goddess, reason, and worship of the nature deity, Pan.

The classic instance of the meeting of the existential and the spiritual is, however, afforded by the writer who, for the majority of Lamartine's French contemporaries, was the very embodiment of the new religious awareness, François-Auguste-René de Chateaubriand. Himself an exiled aristocrat like Maistre, Chateaubriand had, in the course of his lonely sojourn in England between 1793 and 1800, personally made the psychological journey of his entire nation from prerevolutionary religious scepticism to postrevolutionary religious sympathy, via the medium of emotional trauma: "I wept," he summarized in a much-quoted formula from the Preface to his *Génie du Christianisme* (1802), "and I believed." As its title already implies, this highly influential volume, the draft of which the young Breton brought with him on his return to Napoleonic France, is, rather than a work of apologetics, a celebration of the Christian religion as the cultural muse of civilized Europe. Chateaubriand declares his aim as "deriving the cause from its effects," and in so doing signals his awareness that the starting point for any new debate about religion must be the condition of man himself. By initially incorporating into his book the fictional narratives *Atala* and *René*, the author of *Le Génie* isolates, furthermore, a latent aspect of the Catholic religion that would profoundly influence the following decades. The identification of the religious with the aesthetic and the literary—of religion with art and art with religion—has ramifications that lie beyond the scope of this study to discuss. From Alfred de Custave Musset to Flaubert and beyond, however, it is clear that the new century would incline to the world of books for its confessional, its prayers, and its martyrs. In the guise of prose fiction, an immanentist yet spiritually hungry nineteenth century would fashion its alternative Bible, telling of human fall and human redemption. Through the language of its poetry, as Victor Hugo most immediately demonstrates, it would re-create that of the psalmist and the prophet.

Where the liberalized and secularized and the new religious consciousness ultimately have their meeting, however, is in those forms of "religion" that seek an alliance between revived religious aspirations and those of the revolution itself: humanity, egalitarian socialism, and even the Enlightenment's own counterculture, science. The founder of the positivist movement, Auguste Comte, offers, perhaps, the clearest example of this oxymoronic tendency, but it is shared by his mentor Claude Henri de Saint-Simon and by Chateaubriand's fellow Breton of the following

generation, Ernest Renan. Renan's demythologizing *Vie de Jésus* of 1863 will always constitute his most celebrated contribution to the balancing act performed by his century between intellectual doubt and emotional allegiance to the Christian story, but the proclamation of a religion of science with which he opens his earlier *L'Avenir de la science* (1848) is more conspicuously the product of a Romantic age disposed to annex the religious to every aspect of its own experience. When the clumsily enthusiastic Comte almost simultaneously instituted the Universal Church of the Religion of Humanity, devoted to the dissemination of his positivist doctrines, and declared himself its high priest, he was thus completing the circle travelled by the Romantic religious mind. What had begun as a search by society for the value that lay hidden in the sacred seemed to be culminating in the sacralization of social mankind itself.

The psychological phenomenon represented here might, in all its aspects, most readily be encapsulated in the term "religiosity," a sentimental form of the properly speaking religious where this latter is understood to mean the unquestioning acceptance of words and events held to be of uniquely divine origin or inspiration. Where true religiousness of mind, as instanced perhaps by Blaise Pascal in the seventeenth century, can always distinguish between the yearnings of the human heart and the distance which separates it from a supernatural God, religiosity of mind arrogates the sacred to its own experiences and aspirations. No longer clearly divorced from the transcendental, the immanent becomes identified with it, whether in the form of nature, of society, or of human activity in general. Indelibly marked by religious doubt while charmed by religious feeling, the Romantics had divested faith of the very aspect that gave it meaning by conceiving it as no more than a pervasive condition of being human. While formulating on the one hand his own version of a religion of history, G. W. F. Hegel was thus consistent in proclaiming on the other that God had died, and Karl Marx, following Hegel, saw religion as a mere social placebo. The romanticization of religion, as of other aspects of human experience, entails its cultivation as nourishment for the subjective imagination, irrespective of the truth or relevance of its objective content. "What matters the name, the form or the belief?," asked Musset in 1836, "Isn't there holiness in everything good?"

The optimism of a Comte, a Cousin, or a youthful Renan notwithstanding, there is in fine, and as the language of the poet perhaps begins to suggest, a degree of malaise beneath the religious experimenting of the Romantics to the point where it begins to reveal itself as the manifestation of a spiritual crisis. The pan-European nature of this unease is, of course, testified to by Johann Wolfgang von Goethe, when he has his dissatisfied Enlightenment hero, Faust, turn enviously and destructively to the simple religious trust represented by Gretchen. In a different form it is conveyed in the most famous of the "dream poems" of the highly influential Jean Paul when he invokes, as would Alfred-Victor de Vigny later, a dying Christ denied the receiving embrace of a Heavenly Father. For Lord Byron, writing in his *Ravenna Journal* of 1821, it is a matter of an impossible call for the anaesthetization of the skeptical mind: "It is useless to tell one *not* to reason but to *believe*. You might as well tell a man not to wake but to sleep." For Chateaubriand, the career of the unhappy René epitomizes the modern neurosis of "le vague des passions," a state of psychic rudderlessness born of unrequited spiritual longings that are the remnants of once vigorous certainties: "Our hearts may be full, but we inhabit an empty world."

If the impact of this decadence can most readily be detected in Catholic France rather than in Protestant England or Lutheran Germany, however, the explanation may lie with the nature of Catholicism itself. Protestantism had, of course, its own advocates in Romantic France (a distinguished example being the novelist and author of his own study of contemporary religion, Benjamin Constant de Rebecque), but the true source of the dilemma resides in the nation's collective memory of its ancestral creed. In its authoritarian character, Catholicism afforded a less flexible model in postrevolutionary times than the personally reflective style of worship with which the Reformers of the sixteenth century had sought to replace it. In its appeal to the aesthetic and sensual as an avenue to the sacred, rather than to individual moral conscience, it was, on the other hand, already a religion of romance and the imagination. An English or even a German Chateaubriand is inconceivable in that the author of *Le Génie du Christianisme* depicts Christianity as a venerable cultural talisman inspiring visceral feelings of loyalty and devotion. The transpositions effected by Maistre or even Comte are thus understandable, but so too are the frustrations and contradictions that accompany them.

Chateaubriand, the perceptive author of *René*, is the source of a final and relevant insight when, pursuing his meditation on "le vague des passions," he suggests that the revolution being undergone by his society has altered the prevailing balance in the sociopolitics of gender. The old religion, more especially in its Catholic form, is patriarchal: its language speaks of a Father, of His authority and the protection He offers a world prepared to renounce itself for Him. The new, even when it still called itself Christianity, would speak of nature, of the mobility of ideas, of the sacred located in creation rather than in creation's author. Half a century after Pope Leo was offered the hand of reconciliation by Napoleon Bonaparte, his successor on the Throne of St Peter, Pius IX, thus took a symptomatic step when, in his bull *Ineffabilis Deus* of December 1854, he pronounced the Virgin Mary the Immaculate Conception—a divinity in her own right and not merely the human bearer of a divine son. In the age of a second Napoleon, the French Romantics' search for a religion of their own sensibilities had led them to this appropriate conclusion: not only had they democratized and de-Judaized the old faith; they had, by the same token, also feminized it.

DAVID LEE

Bibliography

Charlton, D. G. *Secular Religions in France, 1815–1870*. London: Oxford University Press, 1963.
Dansette, Adrien. *Histoire religieuse de la France contemporaine. Vol. 1, De la Révolution à la Troisième République*. 2d ed. Paris: Flammarion, 1952.
Dawson, Christopher. *The Gods of Revolution*. London: Sidgwick and Jackson, 1972.
Derré, Jean-René. *Lamennais, ses amis et le mouvement des idées à l'époque romantique*. Paris: Klincksieck, 1962.
Menczer, Béla, ed. *Catholic Political Thought, 1789–1848*. London: Burns Oates, 1952.
Reardon, Bernard. *Liberalism and Tradition: Aspects of Catholic Thought in Nineteenth-Century France*. Cambridge: Cambridge University Press, 1975.
Viatte, A. *Le Catholicisme des romantiques*. Paris: Boccard, 1922.
Whitehead, Alfred North. *Science and the Modern World*. Cambridge: Cambridge University Press, 1930.

RELIGION: GERMANY

Although there had been discontent with the Roman Church in many quarters during the Middle Ages, the Protestant Reformation, when it happened, was essentially the work of a lone German monk. The consequences for the German nation as a whole were severe. In contrast to northern and southern Europe, which opted for the new doctrine and the old respectively, Germany was split into a patchwork of small principalities by the provisions of the Augsburg Accord of 1555, which gave local princes the right to determine the spiritual allegiance of their subjects. This agreement covered only Roman and Lutheran creeds; all others were proscribed, and dissenters were nominally free to move to neighboring states. By the beginning of the Romantic period, some of the tensions had been defused by the wars that ensued, notably the devastating Thirty Years War of 1618–48, which confirmed the Augsburg provisions. Accordingly, there were overwhelmingly Protestant areas (Prussia, Württemberg) and staunchly Catholic regions (Bavaria, Austria, parts of the Rhineland) that coexisted somewhat uneasily, with the often despotic nobility using the ideal of religious autonomy to justify the continuation of their miniature empires.

The late eighteenth century saw several attempts to overcome this centuries-old legacy. The Deist Reimarus and his defender, Gotthold Ephraim Lessing, as well as numerous freethinkers, including Johann Wolfgang von Goethe, Immanuel Kant, and Friedrich von Schiller, tried to open their readers' eyes to the value of reason. In his famous "Parable of the Rings" (1779), Gotthold Ephraim Lessing implied that all religions might be equally true or equally false. Kant's "categorical imperative" suggested that moral laws are to be found within ourselves rather than in supernatural revelations. Goethe saw less difference between good and evil than between action and passivity. The neoclassicists, especially Goethe, Schiller and Friedrich Hölderlin, were united in their conviction that Greek antiquity was morally as well as artistically superior to modernity.

With the coming of Romanticism a change set in. In contrast to the British Romantics, the German poets tended to hold strong religious convictions. Novalis was influenced by Nitolaus Ludwig Zinzendorf, the architect of Protestant pietism along Moravian lines. Clemens Brentano returned to his Catholic faith and devoted several years to transcribing the visions of a stigmatized nun. A substantial number of the artists styled themselves Lukasbrüder and migrated to the monastery of San Isidoro in Rome, where their old-fashioned, iconic tableaux earned them the sobriquet "Nazarenes." In 1813, their leader, Friedrich Overbeck, encouraged several Jewish and Protestant members to join the Roman Church.

The reasons why Christianity played such a significant role in German Romanticism are complex. Popular reaction against

Enlightenment teachings was one factor. This was related to anti-French sentiment occasioned by the Napoleonic incursions into German territory. For many Germans, the Enlightenment itself was an alien construct from across the Rhine, treacherously imported into their midst by Francophile potentates such as Frederick the Great. Encouraged by the sentimentalizing approach of Claudius and Friedrich Gottlieb Klopstock no less than by the treatises of Novalis, August Wilhelm and Friedrich von Schlegel, and Wilhelm Heinrich Wackenroder, they tended to see the medieval world as one of political harmony and cultural unity.

In northern Germany, the Protestant painters Caspar David Friedrich and Phillip Otto Runge experimented with fusions of secular and religious strands, as Runge did in *Der Morgen* (*Morning*, 1808), where Venus and Mary appear to coalesce. Friedrich's *Kreuz im Gebirge* (*The Cross in the Mountains*, also known as the *Tetschen Altarpiece*) was the subject of intense animosity when exhibited in Dresden in 1808; there were those who claimed that, since it did not depict the crucifixion but merely a crucifix among fir trees atop a Nordic mountain, it had no theological content and could not serve as the focus of devotion. Others saw it as a subversive attempt to equate religion with nature worship. The underlying paradox that the Dresden public perceived when viewing Friedrich's altarpiece was that in a secular age, even ostensibly "religious" art could not be stripped of its secular touches. And indeed, while appearing to observe the customary conventions, Romantic Christianity has an artificial quality. The paintings of the Nazarenes may superficially recall Botticelli and Raphael, yet most of them lack specific religious content and reference. Julius Schnorr von Carolsfeld's *Madonna mit kind* (*Mary and Her Child*, 1820) could be taken as representing any mother and child; the painting avoids specific Christian symbols (cross or tree, chalice, sacrificial lamb) that would have accompanied the infant savior in the early Renaissance works he sought to emulate. Nor does Schnorr's Christ Child look toward us with the stern gaze of an adult, to admonish or forewarn, but backward, at his mother, as any normal toddler would. The same goes for many works by Peter Cornelius and Wilhelm von Schadow.

It eventually transpired that the Romantics had done little to halt the process of secularization that had begun one century earlier. Jewish painters and writers (Eduard Bendemann, Heinrich Heine) may have converted to Christianity, but they did so under pressure and in order to obtain, as Heine put it, an "entry ticket to European culture" rather than from passionate conviction. It may have been an overstatement to blame medievalism for an increase in anti-Semitism, as Heine did. There were many who shared "Turnvater" F. L. Jahn's hopes for a return to a Holy Roman Empire under the Habsburg monarchy, perhaps because, like Joseph von Eichendorff, they held that religion and culture could unite only within a Catholic context; but Germans were beginning to look farther afield and take an interest in oriental beliefs and practices. Moses Mendelssohn had paved the way for greater understanding between Christians and Jews, though it was many years before Jewish people enjoyed adequate rights as citizens. Enlightened monarchs such as Joseph II of Austria, whose *Toleranzpatente* of 1781–89 improved the Jews' conditions, were more interested in conversions and assimilation than acceptance. Prussia conceded limited rights to Jews in 1812 (*Emanzipationsedikt*), on condition that they demonstrate loyalty to the state. Ironically, this involved supporting the war against their erstwhile liberator, Napoleon Bonaparte.

Yet at the same time, the frontiers of belief were being extended. Goethe may have been attracted to Islam as a counterpoint to the Nazarene fervor, and he was not alone: Friedrich Creutzer, Friedrich Rückert, and the Schlegel brothers were all prominent Romantics for whom the Christian mythology was too limited and who also sought inspiration in the religious writings of the Orient and made strenuous, often unpopular attempts to communicate this enthusiasm to their readers. The Romantic experiment, which had been based on the oxymoron of a medieval futurism, was unable to sustain its focus on a religion that many perceived to be inappropriate to the modern age. By the time attempts were made to revive it, by the Pre-Raphaelites in Britain and by neo-Romantics in Germany (Hugo von Hofmannsthal and Rainer Maria Rilke), the Christian component had become little more than an incidental ornament.

OSMAN DURRANI

Bibliography

Berghahn, Klaus L. *Grenzen der Toleranz: Juden und Christen im Zeitalter der Aufklärung.* Köln: Böhlau, 2000.

Callmann, Erna. *Der religiöse Gehalt der Romantik.* Düsseldorf: Schwann, 1927.

Dru, Alexander. *The Church in the Nineteenth Century: Germany 1800–1918.* London: Burns and Oates, 1963.

Goldberg, Ann. *Sex, Religion, and the Making of Modern Madness in Germany, 1815–1849.* New York: Oxford University Press, 1998.

Jansen, Gudrun. *Die Nazarenerbewegung im Kontext der katholischen Restauration. Die Beziehung Clemens Brentano-Edward von Steinle als Grundlage einer religionspädagogischen Kunstkonzeption.* Essen: Die Blaue Eule, 1992.

Jasper, David. *The Sacred and Secular Canon in Romanticism: Preserving the Sacred Truths.* Basingstoke, England: Macmillan, 1999.

Julius Schnorr von Carolsfeld, Die Bibel in Bildern und andere biblische Bilderfolgen der Nazarener. Exhibition catalogue. Neuss: Clemens-Sels-Museum, 1982.

Och, Gunnar. *Imago Judaica. Juden und Judentum im Spiegel der deutschen Literatur 1750–1812.* Würzburg: Königshausen and Neumann, 1995.

Robertson, Ritchie, ed. *The German-Jewish Dialogue: An Anthology of Literary Texts, 1749–1993.* Oxford: Oxford University Press, 1999.

Rose, Paul Lawrence, ed. *History of Religion and Philosophy in Germany by Heinrich Heine.* Townsville, Australia: James Cook University of North Queensland, 1982.

Schieder, Wolfgang, ed. *Religion und Gesellschaft im 19. Jahrhundert.* Stuttgart: Klett-Cotta, 1993.

Scribner, Robert W., and Trevor Johnson, eds. *Popular Religion in Germany and Central Europe, 1400–1800.* Basingstoke, England: Macmillan, 1996.

Sheppard, John. *Letters Descriptive of a Tour through some Parts of France, Italy, Switzerland, and Germany in 1816, with Incidental Reflections on Some Topics Connected with Religion.* 1817.

Sorkin, David. *The Transformation of German Jewry, 1780–1840.* New York: Oxford University Press, 1987.

RENÉ 1802

Novel by François-Auguste-René, Vicomte de Chateaubriand

Despite its brevity, *René* is one of the key novels in the development of French Romanticism. It belongs to what is sometimes described as the period of pre-Romanticism in France, but it already reflects several Romantic themes. The first-person narrator, as the brief framing story tells us, is a young Frenchman who has left Europe for mysterious reasons to settle in the wilds of Louisiana, where he now lives among the tribe of the Natchez. He tells his story to his blind adoptive father, Chactas, one of the Natchez, and Father Souël, a missionary.

After a melancholy childhood warmed only by the love of his sister Amélie, René's travels and meditations on ancient ruins and nature alike serve only to reconfirm his disillusionment with life, whether in society or in solitude. Amélie saves him from suicide and makes him promise to live, before herself withdrawing to a convent. During the ceremony of initiation, as Amélie symbolically enters the tomb, she murmurs some words that reveal to her brother the criminal nature of her love for him. Having thus lost his sister, and understanding the reason for his loss, René leaves for America. He lives for some years among the Natchez before a letter informs him of Amélie's death, and his ensuing grief provokes his friends to insist on hearing his story.

René, written during Chateaubriand's exile in England after his travels in America, was originally intended to be an episode of what the author planned as an "epic of wild man" set in the New World, much of which would eventually be published under the title *Les Natchez* in 1826. Nevertheless, after his return to religion from 1798 onwards, Chateaubriand decided to incorporate it into his great apologia for Catholicism, *Le Génie du Christianisme* (*The Genius of Christianity*), published in 1802. *René*, and its companion piece *Atala*, were extremely successful, particularly when published together in a single volume, detached from the *Génie*, in 1805. It was in this form—as a separate publication alongside *Atala*—that *René* was to have its widest distribution.

René appears to have struck a chord with contemporary readers through its portrayal of an individual, introspective sensibility, one of its characteristically Romantic traits. It thus marked the arrival in France of what came to be called the *mal du siècle*, that Romantic malady which was, in varying forms, to haunt the century. René suffers from an ill-defined condition that can roughly be described as dissatisfaction with the limitations of modern society, a sense of alienation and an inability to turn toward the traditional solution of faith. Although the text does not make this explicit, this condition is clearly rooted in a precise historical moment, reflecting Chateaubriand's own alienation as an aristocrat in postrevolutionary France, and the doubts of a generation that inherited the Enlightenment's questioning of religion without its optimism. René's melancholy state reflects the influence of Johann Wolfgang von Goethe's *Die Leiden des jungen Werthers* (*The Sorrows of Young Werther*, 1774) and Jean-Jacques Rousseau's autobiographical writings; it also marks the introduction into France of a long tradition that would lead, through Gustave Flaubert's disaffection with society and Charles Baudelaire's spleen, to the alienated heroes of existentialism.

René is also, it must be remembered, a companion piece to *Atala*: whereas the latter is the story of a native American confronted with European culture, *René* is the story of a European who seeks a new life in the wilds of America. As such, both belong to a literary tradition that criticized Western society, reaching back at least to the *Lettres persanes* and, more immediately, reflecting the influence of Jean-Jacques Rousseau. Chateaubriand was at first a great admirer of Rousseau's philosophy of the noble savage and the nefarious effects of the civilized state. Chateaubriand belonged to a generation of avid readers of *Paul et Virginie* (1788), the novel in which Rousseau's disciple, Bernardin de Saint-Pierre, sought to portray the felicitous harmonies of nature, and he is justly famous for his own descriptions of the exotic natural environment. Nevertheless, partly as a result of his conversion to Catholicism, he came to question Rousseau's philosophy, and one of his aims in incorporating *René* and *Atala* into *Le Génie du Christianisme* was to highlight the necessity of society and of the Church.

This shift in Chateaubriand's own attitudes helps to explain the ideological ambiguity of the text. He was to claim, later in life, that if *René* did not exist he would no longer write it and, were it now possible, he would destroy it. For although his avowed intention in publishing *René* was to present the necessity of Christianity and the dangers of social disaffection, the story owed its success among its contemporaries and the next generation of Romantics to its portrayal of a melancholy, alienated hero. Is it to be read as a radical rejection of society, or as a conservative condemnation of the ills of a generation of dreamers, as its closing pages would seem to imply? A moral judgment of René's romantic disaffection is expressed by Father Souël in the closure of the framing story, but the reader's sympathies are almost inevitably with René himself. The figure of René is close to that of the author in his autobiographical writings (let us not forget that Chateaubriand's first name was François-Auguste-René and that even his more political writings take the form of a highly personal, introspective meditation), which adds a certain ambivalence to the condemnation of the young Romantic hero's excessive introspection.

JENNIFER YEE

Text

René. Published as part of *Le Génie du Christianisme*, 1802. Revised version, as *René*, published in a separate volume with *Atala*, 1805. Translated in *The Beauties of Christianity* by Frederic Shoberl, 3 vols., 1813; and in *Atala/René*, trans. Irving Putter, 1952. Reprint, Berkeley: University of California Press, 1980.

Bibliography

Barbéris, Pierre. *René de Chateaubriand, un nouveau roman*. Paris: Larousse, 1973.

Charlton, D. G. "The Ambiguity of Chateaubriand's *René*," *French Studies* 23 (1969): 229–43.

Guggenheim, Michel. "Deux formes d'individualisme romantique: René et Julien Sorel," *Symposium* 26, no. 1 (1972): 24–38.

Smethurst, Colin. *Atala and René*. London: Grant and Cutler, 1995.

REPTON, HUMPHRY 1752–1818

English landscape gardener

From a rather modest background, Humphry Repton became one of the most important arbiters of taste in matters concerning landscape gardening in late Georgian and Regency Britain. His early interest in landscape design was exercised at Sustead, the small estate in Norfolk that he bought when an inheritance allowed him to leave the textile firm where he was employed. At Sustead he devoted himself to all the practical aspects of cultivation and husbandry. After he was obliged to sell the estate in 1783, Repton began to devote himself to art criticism, publishing a companion to the collection of paintings at Somerset House (1788) and a descriptive catalog for Josiah Boydell's *Shakespeare Gallery* (1789). Soon he started to receive landscape commissions and gradually established himself as one of the most sought-after gardeners and the acknowledged heir to Launcelot "Capability" Brown, preparing himself by visiting and studying various sites developed by Brown and William Kent. His first important commission was at Cobham in Kent (about 1790), and by 1794 he had renovated over fifty country-house parks belonging to both Whig and Tory aristocratic patrons.

Still quite conservative, Repton's early work respected the fundamentals of Capability Brown's style, maintaining, for instance, the latter's principle of the serpentine layout. In *Sketches and Hints on Landscape Gardening* (1795), Repton listed those qualities that afford pleasure in gardens: picturesqueness, intricacy, simplicity, variety, novelty, contrast, association, grandeur, appropriation, animation, and the seasons. Particularly, he put much stress on "appropriation," that is, the incorporation of the area around the estate into the space of the house and park. His aim was to harmonize both spaces by making important buildings in the estate villages mirror the style of the house and, more symbolically, by making sure that the family's coat of arms appeared everywhere on the estate. He also revalued the approach and entrance to the park, usually matching the style of the lodge to that of the main house. Finally, from the early 1790s, he gradually returned to formal gardening based on patterned planting inspired by the geometric shapes that had been popular in the seventeenth and eighteenth centuries.

His success and the numerous commissions from the aristocracy attracted the criticism of the connoisseur and art critic Richard Payne Knight who, in his poem "The Landscape" (1794), attacked Repton and accused him of pandering to the taste of a decadent ruling class. Similarly, Uvedale Price denounced Repton's landscape interventions in the first volume of his "Essay on the Picturesque" (1794), to which Repton answered with a polite and conciliating "Letter to Uvedale Price, Esq." (1794). These attacks were part of a wider polemic, raging in the 1790s, on the idea of the picturesque and aimed at Capability Brown's and his followers' renovations, generally accused of producing unnatural landscapes as opposed to those generated by centuries of agricultural activities.

In *Mansfield Park* (1814), Jane Austen briefly discusses Repton's work, associating his name and style with forms of relentless improvement and the transformation of country estates as a sign of economic wealth and social standing. For Austen, Repton's renovations stand in stark contrast with more tra-ditional ways of managing aristocratic estates and, indeed, Repton's later interventions changed according to the socio-economic shifts in early-nineteenth-century Britain, especially with the rise of a new group of landowners from the merchant classes. Unlike Austen's characterization, however, Repton always revered the idea of an immutable English social order, and his hierarchic principles were parodied by Thomas Love Peacock in the character of the "renovator" Mr. Milestone in *Headlong Hall* (1816). In the same period Repton started introducing gardens and terraces near the main house, the former usually laid out in formal patterns rather than the open parkland favored in the eighteenth century. He also added a certain historical flavor to his designs, creating "Gothic" gardens in keeping with residences built in this style (as at Ashridge, Hertfordshire). Such interventions proved very popular with his new patrons, the rich middle-class owners of small "villa estates," rather than with the aristocratic owners of large country estates. Designing for the smaller scale and concentrating on highly patterned planting schemes, Repton anticipated later practitioners such as John Claudius Loudon, author of *The Encyclopedia of Gardening* (1822) and *The Suburban Gardener and Villa Companion* (1838).

Characteristically, Repton's early-nineteenth-century activities tended toward a synthesis of different styles that mirrored the eclecticism of regency design. He introduced the use of trellis ("treillage"), soon to become one of his hallmarks, which was generally identified with French gardens and images of classical gardens from the frescoes discovered at Pompeii. Moreover, Repton produced designs for the gardens of two of the most outstanding orientalist buildings in regency England, Sezincote in Gloucestershire, for which he prepared a few sketches overlaid with his characteristic fly-leaves, and the Brighton Pavilion, for which he wrote *Designs for the Pavillon at Brighton* (1808).

By 1803, Repton had carried out nearly two hundred renovations, and more than four hundred by 1816. The reasons for this success lay also in his marketing abilities, and especially in his invention of the *Red Books*, bound volumes describing his ideas for each of his commissions. These books contained "before" and "after" images, made with overlays and transparencies, so that the potential patron could see at a glance the transformations and improvements of his estate. The books also contained watercolors and a text detailing all the proposed changes. Finally, Repton's renown as the most influential garden designer of his generation came through his publications on the theoretical aspects of landscape gardening. Always deeply aware that the gardener needs a thorough knowledge of architecture, he regularly collaborated with and sought the assistance of architects. In particular, in the last part of his life he was introduced to John Nash, their close collaboration giving rise to revolutionary ideas such as those of the irregular house and the garden city.

DIEGO SAGLIA

See also **Aesthetics and Art Criticism; Art and Medievalism; Classical Antiquity; Landscape and Garden Design; Nature; Picturesque; Shakespeare: Britain**

Biography

Born near Bury Saint Edmunds, Suffolk, May 2, 1752. Training for business, studied Dutch, and lived in Holland, 1764–68; worked in a textile company in Norwich; inherited a small income and bought a small estate in Sustead, Norfolk, 1778; forced to sell it and move to a cottage in Romford, Essex, 1783; turned to art criticism and started receiving his first landscape and garden design commissions, 1788; attacked by Richard Payne Knight in the poem "The Landscape," 1794, and by Uvedale Price in "Essay on the Picturesque," 1794–98; replied with a conciliatory "Letter to Uvedale Price, Esq.," 1794; suffered an accident in London that injured his spine, 1811. Died March 24, 1818.

Selected Works

The Bee; A Critique on Paintings at Somerset House. 1788.
The Bee; or a Companion to the Shakespeare Gallery. 1789.
"Letter to Uvedale Price, Esq." 1794.
Sketches and Hints on Landscape Gardening. 1795.
Observations on the Theory and Practice of Landscape Gardening. 1803; facsimile ed., 1980.
An Inquiry into the Changes of Taste in Landscape Gardening, with some Observations on Its Theory and Practice. 1806.
Designs for the Brighton Pavillon. 1808.
On the Introduction of Indian Architecture and Gardening. 1808.
Fragments on Landscape Gardening. 1816.
The Landscape Gardening and Landscape Architecture of the Late Humphrey Repton, esq. Being His Entire Works on These Subjects. Edited by John Claudius Loudon, 1840.

Bibliography

Daniels, Stephen. *Humphry Repton: Landscape Gardening and the Geography of Georgian England.* New Haven, Conn.: Yale University Press, 1999.

Hunt, John Dixon. *The Figure in the Landscape: Poetry, Painting, and Gardening during the Eighteenth Century.* Baltimore: Johns Hopkins University Press, 1976.

Malins, Edward Greenway, ed. *The Red Books of Humphry Repton.* 4 vols., London: Basilisk Press, 1970.

Morley, John. *Regency Design: Gardens, Buildings, Interiors, Furniture.* New York: Harry N. Abrams, 1993.

Stroud, Dorothy. *Humphry Repton.* London: Country Life, 1962.

RESTIF DE LA BRETONNE (RESTIF, NICOLAS-EDME) 1734–1806

French writer

Born into a modest farming family in the small village of Sacy near Auxerre in Burgundy, Nicolas-Edme Restif (later known as Restif de la Bretonne) took a long time to turn his hand to writing, publishing his first work in 1767. From these humble origins and being essentially self-taught, he developed into one of the most prolific writers in eighteenth-century France. From then up to the time of his death in 1806 he published an astonishing fifty thousand pages in around two hundred volumes of work ranging in form and content from novels, short stories, drama, philosophical treatises, and projects of reform, along with a number of works that defy traditional classification. Often decried as a poor man's philosopher, his reputation has struggled to shrug off disparaging monikers such as the "Jean-Jacques des Halles" ("The Rousseau of the Marketplace") and, worst of all, the "Rousseau du Ruisseau" ("The Rousseau of the Gutter"). While it is true that many of his works are plagued by repetition, digressions, a sensibility that frequently descends into sentimentality and declamation into platitude, Restif nonetheless, beyond the sheer volume of his work, demands attention for his singular imagination and talent for innovation. He was also the first writer to depict in detail the lower classes of late eighteenth-century and revolutionary France.

After having been sent to Auxerre as an apprentice to a printer, he moved to Paris to ply his trade as a typesetter in 1755. It would appear that the printing of others inspired him and his first considerable success came with the publication of *Le Paysan perverti* (*The Corrupted Country-Boy*) in 1775. This semiautobiographical epistolary novel recounts the adventures of Edmond, an apprentice painter who moves from the country to Paris along with his sister Ursule. They both fall under the influence of a sinister cleric named Gaudet d'Arras, whom many critics see as a prefiguration of Honoré de Balzac's Vautrin (the archcriminal who appears in several of Balzac's works, notably *Le Père Goriot*, 1835). Edmond and Ursule fall victim to the all-pervasive debauchery in the capital, where violent abductions, degradation, rape, and even incest abound. Edmond is condemned to the galleys, news that provokes the death of his parents. The hapless Edmond finds his way back to Paris and murders his sister Ursule who, unknown to him, has repented for her sins and is leading a good life. Significant for its concentration on lower-class characters, this novel is also important for its depiction of the apparent opposition between the city and the countryside, although it should be noted that the latter is not necessarily depicted as a pastoral idyll. By the same token, Restif's relationship with Paris is significant because, while often seen as overwhelmingly negative, it is, in fact, quite ambivalent and complex. The presence of an elder brother Pierre, who serves as the narrator of the story, provides the moralizing commentary on the fall from grace of the ingenuous hero and heroine. Yet, the fascination with their degradation suggests an attraction which would bring Restif closer to the Marquis de Sade who, in reality, was his sworn enemy. Indeed, Restif published his *Anti-Justine* (*Pleasures and Follies of a Good-natured Libertine*, 1798) as a critique of Sade's libertine narrative. *Le Paysan* proved to be such a success that Restif later returned to the same story for Ursule's predominantly female version entitled *La Paysanne pervertie* (*The Corrupted Country-Girl*, 1784) and even considered the works profitable enough to combine them into one work, *Le Paysan et la paysanne pervertis* (*The Corrupted Ones*, 1787).

Restif was also notorious for always having an opinion on a wide variety of social issues. His assorted treatises calling for reform included *La Mimographe* (1770) on the theater, *Le Pornographe* (1769) on the regulation of prostitution (apparently much appreciated by Joseph II of Austria), *Les Gynographes* (1777) and *L'Andrographe* (1782) on the status of the sexes, and *Le Thesmographe* (1790) on legislation. His commentaries on language are found scattered through many texts. This point is especially significant because Restif often ignored conventional spelling (his name is also alternatively spelled Rétif) and grammar; his use of ellipsis, especially in *Les Nuits de Paris* (*Paris Nights*, 1788–94), prefigures the stream of consciousness narrative of Louis-Ferdinand Céline.

Another successful work, *La Vie de mon père* (*My Father's Life*, 1779) depicts the countryside and family life in decline. Despite the pastoral tone, Restif almost prefigures Marcel Proust in an effort to retrieve time and identity from the past. Paris once again serves as the focus of one of Restif's most original works, *Les Nuits de Paris*. Seemingly the collected musings and adventures of Le Hibou ("The Owl"), *Les Nuits* constitutes a series of disparate anecdotes, held together by the narrator but not presented in any logical sequence. Restif attempts to excite the reader with an insistence on "scènes extraordinaires" and his selflessness in exposing himself to the danger of the streets in order to serve as a chronicler of Paris's secrets that are only revealed under the cover of darkness. This creative commentary on Paris after dark represents a side of the city later rediscovered by Charles Baudelaire, Joris-Karl Huysmans, the surrealists, and, most especially, Gérard de Nerval, who acknowledged a considerable debt to Restif.

One of Restif's later achievements was the monumental *Monsieur Nicolas, ou le coeur humain dévoilé* (*Monsieur Nicolas, or the Human Heart Unveiled*, 1794–97), an ambitious project of autobiography where Restif once again represents his life as a strange hybrid of reality, wish fulfillment, and fiction. This work was much appreciated by Johann Wolfgang von Goethe and Johann Christoph Friedrich von Schiller, who both admired Restif's talent while bemoaning the lack of appreciation of his works in his homeland. Restif never became wealthy through his writing. Indeed, his obsession to publish his voluminous outpourings was often the reason behind his poverty. Partially because of his poor rural roots and also due to personal battles (Restif's tendency to break with friends and family was notorious) he never truly established himself in circles of wealth and influence. Obsessed with procreation, an avowed foot fetishist, and with an extreme paternal instinct that led eventually to incest, Restif's personal life was fraught with trauma, and this saw him attempt to justify himself in his works. His wife, son-in-law, assorted former friends, book counterfeiters, and many others all face Restif's wrath in the pages of his oeuvre. Although he had friends and could count on the protection of luminaries such as Madame de Beauharnais, Pierre-Augustin Beaumarchais, and Louis-Sébastien Mercier, he struggled against poverty, especially in his final years. He gained a modest income working at the Ministry of Police (some say as a spy) from 1798 until 1802, but Restif died in poverty four years later, at age seventy two.

JOHN PATRICK GREENE

Biography

Born in Sacy, France, October 23, 1734. In 1740, his father (Edme Rétif) bought the house and land at La Bretonne in the eastern side of the village of Sacy. Sent to school in Joux-la-Ville for a limited education, 1745. Became an apprentice typesetter to the printer François Fournier in Auxerre, 1751. Moved to Paris and worked as a typesetter, 1751. Married Agnès Lebègue, 1760. Birth of four daughters, 1761–64 (only two of which, Agnès and Marion, reach adulthood). Separated from Agnès Lebègue, 1785. Incest with eldest daughter Agnès, 1788. Moved to final domicile (Rue de la Bûcherie), bought a small press and began printing at home, 1788–90. Divorced Agnès Lebègue, 1794. Restif awarded financial help from the convention for writers in need. Appointed history teacher at the École Centrale de Moulins, 1798 but failed to take up this post due to an appointment at Ministry of Police. Death due to an unspecified illness that had rendered him bedridden, February 3, 1806.

Selected Works

Collection

Oeuvres complètes. 207 vols. Edited by Henri Bachelin. Geneva: Slatkine, 1988–89.

Novels and Other Fiction

Le Paysan perverti. 1775.
La Vie de mon père. 1779. Translated as *My Father's Life* by Richard Veasey. Gloucester: Alan Sutton, 1986.
La Paysanne pervertie. 1784.
Le Paysan et la paysanne pervertis. 1787. Translated as *The Corrupted Ones* by Allan Hull Walton. London: Neville Spearman, 1967.
Les Nuits de Paris. 1788–94. Translated as *Les Nuits de Paris or the Nocturnal Spectator* by Linda Asher and Ellen Fertig. New York: Random House, 1964.
Monsieur Nicolas, ou le coeur humain dévoilé, 8 vols. 1794–97. Translated as *Monsieur Nicolas, or the Human Heart Unveiled* by Robert Baldick. London: Barrie & Rockliff, 1966.
L'Anti-Justine, 1798. Translated as *Pleasures and Follies of a Good-natured Libertine, Being an English Rendering of "L'Anti-Justine"* by Pieralessandro Casavini (pseud. of Austryn Wainhouse). Paris: Olympia Press, 1955.

Bibliography

Baruch, Daniel. *Nicolas-Edme Restif de la Bretonne*. Paris: Fayard, 1996.
Cellard, Jacques. *Un génie dévergondé: Nicolas-Edme Rétif, dit "de la Bretonne" (1734–1806)*. Paris: Plon, 2000.
Coward, David. *The Philosophy of Restif de la Bretonne*, Vol. 283 of Studies on Voltaire and the Eighteenth Century Series. Oxford: Voltaire Foundation, 1991.
Europe 732 (1990). Special edition on Restif de la Bretonne.
Porter, Charles. *Restif's Novels, or an Autobiography in Search of an Author*. New Haven, Conn.: Yale University Press. 1967.
Rétif de la Bretonne et la ville: Journées d'étude organisées par le Groupe d'Etude du XVIIIe siècle. Strasbourg: Presses Universitaires de Strasbourg, 1993.
Revue des Sciences Humaines 212 (1988). Special edition on Restif de la Bretonne.
Testud, Pierre. *Rétif de la Bretonne et la création littéraire*. Geneva: Droz, 1977.
Wagstaff, Peter. *Memory and Desire: Rétif de la Bretonne, Autobiography and Utopia*. Amsterdam: Rodopi, 1996.

RETHEL, ALFRED 1816–1859

German painter and woodcut artist

Alfred Rethel's varied talents bridge the divides between brilliant idealism and reflective Romanticism, Italian clarity, and German sentiment, the consummate draughtsmanship of Albrecht Dürer and the psychological subtlety of Caspar David Friedrich. Were it not for his ill heath and premature demise, Rethel might have become the foremost German artist of the period. His early works are done in a realistic style reminiscent both of the Nazarenes and of French classicist artists such as Jacques-Louis David. The influence of the early nineteenth-century illustrators, especially Peter Cornelius and Wilhelm Kaulbach, both of whom maintained a lifelong interest in depicting scenes from the work of Johann Wolfgang von Goethe and from German fables, is not insignificant. Rethel's art has both a religious and a historical dimension, studies of St. Boniface being a personal favorite from the age of fifteen onward. It is a motif in which important events from national and ecclesiastic history can be brought together in a seamless composition (*Bonifaz predigt den Heiden* [*St. Boniface Preaching to the Heathens*], 1835; *Bonifaz lässt eine Kapelle bauen* [*St. Boniface as a Church Builder*], 1836). It was his skill in producing large group portraits according to the Düsseldorf method that qualified him for the complex murals that he was to execute in Frankfurt and Aachen. The method he used involved a close study of each model on its own, and, notably, a tendency not to overpaint, but to select only those portions of individuals that would actually be visible in the completed work.

By the mid-1830s, Rethel's sense of color and preference for monumental, dramatic subjects had begun to mark him out sufficiently from the Nazarenes, making him the ideal choice for the embellishment of the Kaisersaal (Imperial Hall) in Frankfurt. *Versöhuung Kaiser Ottos mit selnem Bruder Heinrich* (*The Reconciliation of Emperor Otto I with His Brother Henry*) and *Der Monch am Sarg Heinrichs IV* (*The Monk at the Coffin of Henry IV*) are significant works from this period, in which the influence of Italian masters, primarily Titian, is increasingly evident.

Yet in contrast to Rethel's vibrant tableaux depicting carefully staged scenes from history and myth, there are more somber allegories, such as *Nemesis Pursuing a Murderer*, which are characteristic of his later output and foreshadow the woodcuts of the 1840s. How far Rethel had moved on from the somewhat anemic world of the Nazarenes is evident in both subject and execution of his later works. It is not widely known that he produced one of the first canvases depicting an industrial plant several years before Adolf Menzel began to concentrate on such scenes. This is *Fabrik Harkort bei Burg Wetter* (*Harkort Factory at Burg Wetter* c., 1834), in which a ruined castle sets off the grim contours of a modern workplace, showing the erosion of the feudal world by the relentless process of industrialization. The factory seems to encroach on the viewer, obliterating much of the castle and most of the church in whose foreground it has established itself. The building had a private significance, as it was where his father worked after his own chemical works burned down.

Rethel was not a radical in the mold of Carl Friedrich Lessing and the many broadsheet illustrators of his time. While moving on from the Nazarenes' techniques, he shared their vision of a return to harmony under a powerful and unified state in which the secular and religious elements would be properly integrated. But he did not eschew modern topics, as his illustrations for Karl von Rotteck's *Allgemeine Geschichte* (*General History of the World*, 1830–34) demonstrate, for which he supplied illustrations ranging from those of antique heroes to George Washington.

The major cycles of his maturity include six watercolors depicting stages from Hannibal's march across the Alps and the frescoes of the life of Charlemagne that adorned the town hall at Aachen prior to the severe damage they sustained during the war. Although the latter commission was a major success (not least financially, as the reward was 25,000 thalers), it was far from uncontroversial. Johann Gottfried Schadow opposed his appointment, and while the town council would have preferred the pictures to celebrate the glorious past of their own city, Rethel used most of the paintings to put across a personal view of the inseparable unity of church and state. There was some resentment of the lurid and gloomy symbolism of his designs in the local press, and he only managed to retain his right to proceed with the project after securing backing from the King of Prussia. The artist did not survive to complete the series. There has been speculation that Rethel's interest both in the regeneration of empire and in the cause of German unity waned after the failed revolution of 1848. The work was finally halted by the onset of a serious nervous illness from which he never recovered.

Among his woodcuts, the most striking is the *Dance of Death* cycle, a personal response to the bloody events of 1848 that were taking place all around him as Rethel labored reluctantly, it would seem, on the lofty images of Charlemagne. He had produced illustrations for a lavish edition of the medieval epic *The Lay of the Nibelungs* in 1840–41, perfecting the art of integrating the restrictive techniques of woodcut with the capabilities of the modern printing press. The macabre *Dance of Death* woodcuts, accompanied by sarcastically instructive texts by Robert Reinick, are a direct attack on the would-be revolutionaries who fail to realize that they are playing into the hands of the grim reaper. Conceived in the style of popular broadsheet cartoons, with numerous reminiscences of Dürer and deliberate echoes of the Peasants' War of 1525, they concentrate on the horrors of internecine strife, and were a considerable financial success, especially for their publisher, Georg Wigand; four separate editions running to 14,500 copies were sold out in the first few months after release. They were distributed to civil servants and even employed as schoolbook illustrations warning against the dire consequences of popular uprisings. This is unlikely to have been the artist's main aim; it was the wider theme of human blindness that preoccupied him, as is obvious from his last two woodcuts, *Death as an Avenger* and *Death as a Friend*: powerful evocations, in William Vaughan's words, of "instinctive states of being." The former concentrates on the consequences of a cholera epidemic while the latter shows death as benign, almost sorrowful, as he announces the passing away of the old watchman with his keys dangling uselessly at his side, a dignified, solitary figure who had seen many others come and go before he, too, was summoned to the grave. It should be remembered that nearly all Rethel's masterpieces were produced as cycles, and part of their fascination is to observe the developments that take place from one closely related image to the next.

OSMAN DURRANI

Biography

Born at Diepenbend near Aachen, May 15, 1816, the son of a chemical manufacturer. Taught initially by Johann Baptiste Bastiné, a follower of Jacques-Louis David. At the early age of thirteen he entered the Düsseldorf Academy in 1829, where he was taught by Wilhelm von Schadow. Moved to Frankfurt in 1836, where he worked with Philip Veit at the Städelsches Kulturinstitut, developing an increasing sense of color and a pronounced feeling for dramatic situations. His first major commission was the interior of the Frankfurt Old Town Hall, for which he supplied four full-length portraits of emperors: Philip of Swabia, the two Maximilians, and Charles V (1839–40). His next major success was to win the closed competition for a grandiose project in Aachen, where illustrations of the life of Charlemagne were required for the town hall. Visited Rome 1844–45. Completed a *Resurrection* as an altarpiece for St. Nikolaus Church in Frankfurt, 1845. Continued to produce large-scale historical frescoes, as well as numerous woodcuts, including scenes from the *Nibelungenlied* (1841) and a *Dance of Death* sequence that coincided with the revolution of 1848. Married Marie Grahl, daughter of the miniaturist August Grahl, in 1850. Shortly after his second visit to Italy (1852–53), at the age of only thirty-six, Rethel lapsed into insanity and spent the last six years of his life in the care of his mother and sister. He died in an institution in Düsseldorf, December 1, 1859.

Bibliography

Einem, Herbert von. "Die Tragödie der Karlsfresken Alfred Rethel's." In *Karl der Grosse. Lebenswerk und Nachleben.* Vol. 4. Edited by Wolfgang, Braunfels and Percy Ernst Schramm. Düsseldorf, *Das Nachleben*, 1967.

Frank, Hans. *Alfred Rethel.* Berlin: Lautenbach, 1937.

Groll, Karin. *Alfred Rethel: "Auch ein Totentanz aus dem Jahre 1848."* Messkirch: Gmeiner, 1989.

Koetschau, Karl. *Alfred Rethels Kunst vor dem Hintergrund der Historienmalerei seiner Zeit.* Düsseldorf: Verlag des Kunstvereins für die Rheinlande und Westfalen, 1929.

Oellers, Adam C. *Alfred Rethel: die Karlsfresken im Aachener Rathaus und die Ölstudien im Museum Burg, Aachen.* Suermondt-Ludwig-Museum, 1987.

Preising, Dagmar, ed. *Alfred Rethel (1816–1859), Zeichnungen und Ölstudien, Suermondt-Ludwig-Museum, 2. August bis 15. September 1991.* Aachen: Museen der Stadt Aachen, 1991.

Rethel, Alfred. *Auch ein Totentanz. Todesdarstellungen von 1828 bis 1852.* Düsseldorf: Städtisches Kunstmuseum, 1956.

———. *Eine Ausstellung im Krönungssaal d. Aachener Rathauses zur Erinnerung an sein Todesjahr.* Aachen: Suermondt-Museum, 1959.

———. *Nachgelassene Zeichnungen von Alfred Rethel: 1816–1859.* Düsseldorf: Boerner, 1968.

Ponten, Josef, *Studien über Alfred Rethel.* Stuttgart: Deutsche Verlags-Anstalt, 1922.

———, ed. *Alfred Rethel. Des Meisters Werke in 300 Abbildungen.* Klassiker der Kunst in Gesamtausgaben, no. 17. Stuttgart: Deutsche Verlags-Anstalt, 1911.

REVOLUTION

The use of the word *revolution* in the modern sense can be traced to the late eighteenth century in Europe, and especially to debate on the French Revolution. The word's meaning in English went through significant changes during the seventeenth and eighteenth centuries: from denoting a cyclical, repetitive action (as in astronomical movements), through signifying a gradual, often providential mutation; and finally meaning a great, powerful event, and, specifically in its political sense, one resulting in a discontinuity from past social organization. It was not only the word, but the concept itself, that was invented in the years following the French Revolution. Before then there had been no event in European history that corresponded very closely to the modern idea of revolution as a society changing its mode of government by the manifestation of its *internal* contradictions, giving rise to a distinct rupture from past social organization; this as opposed to a change of monarchical dynasty or a shifting of influence from one aristocratic group to another. Instead of a society renewing itself from within, it was often assumed in eighteenth-century political theory that it would take an intervention from outside, which, because it came from outside, would be disinterested and equitable; in eighteenth-century political thought, the world could be moved, as it were, but an external fulcrum must first be found. The model here was most often that of the law-giving of Lycurgus in the setting up of the Spartan republic, of which Jean-Jacques Rousseau made especially important use.

The first event we may think of in our contemporary sense of revolution is the American struggle for independence, although this was also the throwing off of a colonial power by inhabitants who still required the help of rival colonial powers to succeed. Before that, there had been some examples of historical events that approached this modern sense. The Lutheran Reformation had parallels ecclesiologically, but was not followed through in the temporal world. From British history, there was the English civil war, the Stuart Restoration, the events of 1688, and the Jacobite rebellions of 1715 and 1745, all of which had been referred to occasionally as "revolutions." The most important was the Glorious Revolution, and interpretation of this event was informing the concept of revolution by 1789. In one interpretation, it was a natural, providential progression of royalist traditions, but in another it had affirmed certain rights, most importantly the rights of the people to superintend their rulers, and as such represented a significant break from tradition, although the project had yet to be completed. These two interpretations may be found, respectively, in Edmund Burke's *Reflections on the Revolution in France* (1791) and Richard Price's *Discourse on the Love of One's Country* (1789).

The progression of the French Revolution from 1789 until 1795 was radically new because it continually surpassed expectations of what its outcome would be. As Karl Marx was to argue in "Der Achtzehnte Brumaire des Louis Napoleon" ("The Eighteenth Brumaire of Louis Bonaparte," 1852) a revolution is very difficult to conceptualize precisely because it is new and breaks from the past, and has necessarily to fall back on past models. Contemporary writing about the French Revolution was often characterized by imperfect parallels with past events (the Glorious Revolution, the English civil war, the Fronde, and the French Wars of Religion, among others), which gave rise to expectations about the pattern of events to come; these expectations were uniformly disappointed or surpassed, largely because of the interventions of the Paris mob, which pushed the revolution forward from bourgeois adjustment, through radical republicanism, to the Terror, and then to bourgeois reaction. When events surpassed all precedent and expectation, those writing about the French Revolution could see it as a magical event (as did Thomas Paine), a sublime happening that kept on transcending itself so could not properly be grasped (as did William Wordsworth), or as absurd and grotesque because consisting of illegitimate political action (as did Edmund Burke).

The idea of revolution gave rise, so Georg Lukács has argued, to a new historical consciousness in European thought from the beginning of the nineteenth century; the discontinuity the French Revolution had represented, together with the pace of changes to which the Republican and Napoleonic victories gave rise, made people aware of historical process and encouraged them to seek further emancipation in Germany, the Habsburg lands, Poland, Italy, Greece and the rest of the Ottoman empire, and Ireland. Yet there was, of course, a pronounced split in the cultural sphere in attitudes towards such developments. Much Romantic culture reacted against this process; this was pronounced in English Romanticism, with the later writings of former revolutionaries Samuel Taylor Coleridge and Wordsworth, who lamented the ever more powerful role of capital and commodification of the elements of traditional community, while sublimating the revolutionary impulse into a personal and aesthetic narrative. There was a conservative tendency across Europe to react against the idea of historical development by looking to earlier times, especially to the Middle Ages, as representative of a unified, organic society, from which revolutionary crisis and the competing claims of individualism, nationalism, and capitalism were excluded. On a political level, this was reflected in the followers of Klemens Wenzel Nepomek Lothar Metternich, who used all means possible to preserve the largely legitimist principles of the Treaty of Vienna. At the other extreme, most revolutionary theories of this period were, as Marx lamented, of a primarily utopian nature, as in French socialism, or, as in Italy and Germany, heavily reliant on ahistorical myths of nationalism and heroism. Or, in a twist, the revolutionary impulse would become ironized in an attempt to cope with the impossibility of its position, as in the writings of Lord Byron, who died while fighting for Greek independence in their revolt against Ottoman rule. Byron's Don Juan is created as the revolutionary but ironic hero in default of a satisfactory figure, radical Europe having been consistently disappointed by the likes of Napoleon Bonaparte, Marie Joseph Lafayette, and Maximilien de Robespierre.

By far the most pervasive response in Romantic culture was, however, one that held a progressivist discourse and that saw the French Revolution and those in Poland and Greece especially as necessary and worthy, but was nevertheless mindful of the violence that revolution had produced. G. W. F. Hegel may be seen as the archetype of this response—as a young man he had been excited by the Napoleonic reorganization of the German states from 1806, and in 1816 claimed that the French Revolution had shown that a casting aside of tradition was possible, not to proclaim completely new principles, but to make men aware of rational principles they had not fully appreciated before. But the problem becomes one of how to progress toward rationality without instability; humanity had learned from the French experience not to fall for demagogy again, and the German states became, for Hegel, the home of ongoing reform. This became theorized more systematically in *Grundlinien der Philosophie des Rechts oder Naturrecht und Staatswissenschaft im Grundrisse* (*Philosophy of Right and Law*, 1821), in which Hegel, beyond the dialectical movements between individual consciousness and society, between the ethical and civil lives, dreams of the state as an organic totality, the concrete form of the progress of mind. However, it can be argued that it was the idea of revolution, and the pace of change in postrevolutionary Europe, that allowed Hegel to interpret history in this way. An apparently very different but actually quite similar treatment of the role of revolution in history is to be found in Sir Walter Scott's historical novels; they represent British history as a series of crises between competing interests that are as necessary as they are destructive, but these crises are resolved by personable heroes from Middle England, giving the impression of an organic progression without, in the end, serious rupture.

This kind of consciousness had its effect time and time again in periods of unrest, in 1830 France, for example, where bourgeois liberals, having necessarily co-opted insurgents on the streets of Paris to oust Charles X's illiberal government, decided on a moderate compromise in the Orléanist Louis-Philippe. The aristocracy, the church, and the republicans lost out equally. A similar story can be told of the widespread revolutions of 1848, in which popular insurgence in France, Germany, Italy, and the Habsburg lands seemed to be about to precipitate the start of revolutionary republics before the fear of rupture and the unknown brought back the establishment of similar regimes, altered for the most part in so far as middle classes no longer suffered from exclusion from aristocratic privilege. The failure of these revolutions was to leave the idea of revolution as a noble, sublime endeavor that was doomed to failure. As Karl Marx commented in 1851, the revolutionaries were unable to break free from their history, and in a significant Utopian moment that is indicative of the problems of conceptualizing revolution in this period, desired that, in a modern revolution, "the content would go beyond the phrase," rather than the other way round. Meanwhile, the two more machiavellian statesmen who were to mastermind European history for the next half century, Otto von Bismarck in German Prussia and Camillo Benso di Cavour in Italian Piedmont, foresaw that, if the nationalist aspirations of radicals in those countries were to be realized, it would take the interposition of a great power rather than internal insurgence and renewal. The yearning for a Lycurgus had not departed European political consciousness.

PETER HOWELL

Bibliography

Furet, François. *Interpreting the French Revolution*. Translated by Elborg Forster. Cambridge: Cambridge University Press, 1981.
Hobsbawn, Eric. *The Age of Revolution*. London: Wedenfield and Nicolson, 1995.

Lukács, Georg. *The Historical Novel*, 1937. Trans. Hannah and Stanley Mitchell. Harmondsworth, England: Penguin, 1981.

Marx, Karl. "The Eighteenth Brumaire of Louis Bonaparte" (1851). In *Karl Marx—Selected Writings*. Edited by David McLellan. Oxford: Oxford University Press, 1977.

Paulson, Ronald. *Representations of Revolution 1789–1828*. New Haven, Conn.: Yale University Press, 1983.

Williams, Raymond. "Revolution." In *Keywords: A Vocabulary of Culture and Society*. London: Croom Helm, 1976.

REYNOLDS, JOSHUA 1723–1792

English painter, theorist, and president of the Royal Academy

Perhaps best known for his formally posed, classically inspired portraits and his *Discourses*, a series of lectures on art delivered as part of his presidency of the Royal Academy between 1769 and 1790, Joshua Reynolds greatly expanded the definition of art and the status of artists in eighteenth-century England. Reynolds's *Discourses* established a philosophical basis for the ideal in art while providing practical advice to young artists on achieving this. Though Reynolds exhorted young artists to paint "some eminent instance of heroick action, or heroick [*sic*] suffering" he was best known as a portraitist. Reynolds's wistful portraits of Georgian women and fancy pictures of rustic or mythological subjects, with their broad brushwork and rich color, inspired artists from Henry Fuseli to John Singer Sargent. While Reynolds's name has become synonymous with the Grand Manner, his oeuvre speaks of a more complex artist and, while it would be going too far to declare Reynolds a Romantic, his works, both written and painted, demonstrate his sensitivity to the age.

Reynolds's early career began at age seventeen with his apprenticeship to the portrait painter Thomas Hudson. Hudson was the son-in-law of Jonathan Richardson, a portraitist whose writings on art Reynolds credited with inspiring his own art and theory, including the eminence of history painting. Reynolds exhibited his combination of history painting and portraiture in his *Portrait of Commodore Augustus Keppel* (1753–54). In 1749, Reynolds had accompanied Keppel to the Mediterranean, spending two years in Rome. In the painting, Keppel stands on the rocky shore of a storm-tossed sea with the wreckage of a ship behind him. The shipwreck probably refers to the loss of Keppel's ship the *Maidstone* in a skirmish in 1747, just before he met Reynolds. Though the painting was not intended as a historical representation of the wreck, this detail does imbue the painting with a heightened sense of drama, a technique Reynolds would employ frequently thereafter. The portrait combines many other characteristics often associated with Reynolds's portraiture: rich color, broad brushwork, and dramatic lighting. Indeed, because of such techniques, Reynolds's style has been seen as representative of the sublime, as elucidated in Edmund Burke's *Philosophical Enquiry into the Origin of Our Ideas of the Sublime and Beautiful* (1757).

Though Reynolds would later repeatedly promote history paintings as the top of the hierarchy of genres in his *Discourses*, he owed his career and eventual presidency of the Academy to his abilities as a portraitist. After the Keppel portrait had established his name, Reynolds painted many of the elite of London society, including King George III and Queen Charlotte. In such neoclassical paintings as *Lady Sarah Bunbury Sacrificing to the Graces* (1763), Reynolds imbues his images with classical details, as here Lady Sarah dressed in vaguely classical garb makes an offering in a temple setting. In other portraits, such as *Garrick between Tragedy and Comedy* (1762) and *Mrs. Siddons as the Tragic Muse* (1784), Reynolds combined allusions to classical literature and mythology with references to the contemporary London stage, as both David Garrick and Sarah Siddons were famous performers. In addition to their importance as theatrical images, these portraits also attest to Reynolds's involvement with the print industry. Both paintings, in addition to numerous others, were engraved and distributed throughout England and Europe, gaining fame not just for Reynolds but also for the subjects he depicted.

While best known now for his portraits, Reynolds devoted much time and attention to his subject or "fancy" pictures, particularly in the 1760s and 1770s when more portrait commissions went to competitors such as Thomas Gainsborough and George Romney. His images of children, such as *Cupid as a Link Boy* (c. 1773) and its pendant *Mercury as a Cutpurse* (c. 1773), demonstrate a new emotional (and sometimes sexualized) understanding of children, in the vein of Jean-Baptiste Greuze. *Count Ugolino and His Children* (1775), one of Reynolds's most famous and admired historical paintings, demonstrates the artist's studies of old masters such as Michelangelo and Annibale Carracci, familiarity with the study of expressions by Charles Le Brun, and his use of sources beyond classical literature, such as Dante Alighieri's *Divine Comedy*.

The 1760s in England witnessed increasing agitation for an improvement of the status of artists in society, with the foundation of such groups as the Free Society of Artists and the Incorporated Society of Artists. Established in 1768 by members of the Incorporated Society, the Royal Academy received royal support and elected Reynolds the first president. The Academy not only helped to differentiate artists from craftsmen such as printmakers and sign painters, but also created a school for the proper education of young artists and provided a venue for artists to exhibit their works.

As president of the Royal Academy, Reynolds regularly delivered lectures to the students, outlining his theories of art. These *Discourses* were widely published in both pamphlet and book form and were highly influential on taste and aesthetics in the late eighteenth century. *Discourse* 1 (1769) introduces the benefits of an academy and the proper education of young artists. Continuing this topic in *Discourse* 2 (1769), Reynolds notes three stages in the education of an artist: learning the correct language of art; learning all that has gone before; and learning to identify and create perfection. In several discourses, Reynolds explains the "grand style," instructing artists in *Discourse* 3

(1770) that "it is not the eye, it is the mind which the painter of genius desires to address." Poetry and imagination, which are explored at length in *Discourse* 13 (1786), are the keys to the creation of an art not enslaved to imitation, which Reynolds abhorred, particularly in the realism of the Dutch school. In *Discourse* 15 (1786), Reynolds recommends Michelangelo as the best example for artists to follow:

Michael Angelo [*sic*] possessed the poetical part of our art in a most eminent degree: and the same daring spirit, which urged him first to explore the unknown regions of the imagination, delighted with the novelty, and animated with the success of his discoveries, could not have failed to stimulate and impel him forward (1790)

Praising the poetry and imagination of one of the heroes of the Romantic era, Reynolds declares, "I should desire that the last words which I should pronounce in this Academy, and from this place, might be the name of—Michael Angelo."

Indeed, this was his last discourse to the Academy. Having lost sight in one of his eyes in 1789, and quickly losing sight in the other, Reynolds stopped painting in 1790 and died two years later.

JAMIE W. JOHNSON

Biography

Born in Plympton, England, July 16, 1723. Apprenticed to Thomas Hudson, painter, in 1740; left apprenticeship early, in 1743. Worked in London and Devon, 1743–50; in Italy, 1750–52. Returned to England and painted in London, 1752–68; elected President of Royal Academy in 1768; delivered the first *Discourse* and was thereupon knighted in 1769. James Northcote became Reynolds's student in 1771. First seven *Discourses* published as a book in 1779; named painter in ordinary to the King in 1784. Lost vision in left eye in 1789; delivered final *Discourse* in 1790; Last public appearance at Royal Academy dinner in 1791. Died of a tumor in his liver on February 23, 1792.

Bibliography

Barrell, John. *The Political Theory of Painting from Reynolds to Hazlitt.* New Haven, Conn.: Yale University Press, 1986.
Hutchinson, Sidney C. *The History of the Royal Academy, 1768–1986.* London: Robert Royce, 1986.
Mannings, David, and Martin Postle. *Sir Joshua Reynolds: A Complete Catalogue of His Paintings.* 2 vols. New Haven Conn.: Yale University Press, 2000.
Penny, Nicholas, ed. *Reynolds.* New York: Harry N. Abrams, Publishers, 1986.
Postle, Martin. *Sir Joshua Reynolds: The Subject Pictures.* Cambridge: Cambridge University Press, 1995.

RICHTER, ADRIAN LUDWIG 1803–1884

German painter and illustrator

Often viewed as the last of the great German Romantic artists, Richter remained true to the principle of depicting scenes from nature and folklore with a childlike simplicity in his many paintings, engravings, and woodcuts. He consistently set his face against the enigmatic and somber symbolism of predecessors such as Caspar David Friedrich, concentrating on clear outlines in combination with a recognizable narrative and topographical content. Instead of Friedrich's mythically interpreted Baltic Sea and Riesengebirge Mountains or the fantasy castles of Schwind, Richter often locates his subjects in familiar places, such as Berchtesgaden (*Watzmann*, 1824) or the River Elbe (*Die Überfahrt über die Elbe am Schreckenstein* [*Crossing the Elbe near Schreckenstein near Aussig*], 1837). *Watzmann* is not without patriotic connotations (the mountain marks the border with Austria), yet Richter painted it in Rome and filled it with a wealth of imaginative detail, with the result that the finished canvas with its secluded woodland chapel, thundering waterfalls, and imperiled human dwelling places can be read as a narrative.

In most of Richter's work, man appears to live in harmony even with the most alarming-looking landscapes. The farmhouse in *Watzmann* shows all the signs of having survived tempests and floods, but it is only the outbuildings that display visible evidence of damage. The Schreckenstein cliff and castle loom threateningly over the little ferryboat, crossing the treacherous river belatedly and precariously over-laden, yet all is serene on board the little vessel: the musician strums his harp, the lovers gaze into each other's eyes, a tourist stands up as if to catch a better view, and a little boy, oblivious to the breathtaking surroundings, dangles a stick in the benign-looking waters. The observer recognizes that each character has a story to tell, even if the whole may only be glimpsed: the lovelorn youth, the maiden standing guard over her bundle of hay, and the ferryman contentedly puffing on his clay pipe. Yet there is, even in this innocuous scene, a dim allusion to a grander tradition: the doom-laden Lorelei or the legend of Charon transporting the dead across the River Styx. The mood is melancholy, the image of the little group suspended in a self-contained world of their own looks back to countless disasters at sea, but also forward to modern visions of suffocating isolation, such as Arnold Böcklin's *Island of the Dead* (1880) and Georg Kolbe's *The Golden Isle* (1898).

The majority of Richter's compositions are overtly euphoric in their presentation of man and his environment. Richter remained a fundamentally pious artist who never abandoned his veneration for fresh natural scenery. For this reason the British Pre-Raphaelites, notably Edward Burne-Jones, held him in high esteem. While a fairytale sense of innocence surrounds many of his idylls, such as *Spring Has Arrived* (1870) and *Peace in the Evening* (1871), it is not hard to detect an awareness of social injustice in his scenes from everyday life in town and country. Child labor and urban poverty feature repeatedly in the illustrations he drew for Leipzig publisher Georg Wigand's *Deutscher Volkskalender* and many other similar publications. *Knabe und Hund ziehen einen Karren* (*A Young Boy and Dog Pulling a Wheelbarrow*, in *Die Spinnstube*, 1850), depicts a father importuning his famished son and miserable-looking dog as they attempt to drag a wheelbarrow out of the mire. Christmas scenes often concentrate on the difference between dreams and reality, as in the bitterly ironic *Weihnachts-Markt* (*Christmas Market*, 1853), a woodcut depicting two children selling Christmas trinkets beside a notice announcing that their shop is to be dispossessed. But such Dickensian moments are rare, as are examples of overt humor, such as the snuff-taking schoolmaster who claims to "see" a few nonattenders among his pupils (in *Sächsischer Volkskalender*, 1845). An illustration of 1853 depicts two corpulent *bon-viveurs* confronted by a beggar; they promise to assist their "brother" by drinking a toast to him.

Richter's acquaintance with Wigand proved decisive. Wigand accepted Richter's proposals for a comprehensive record of Germany's most picturesque and romantic spots, concentrating on the three rivers Danube, Elbe, and Rhine. What is noteworthy about this project, which led to a ten-volume edition of sketches appearing between 1837 and 1841, is that Richter depicted typical local characters against the striking backdrops he had chosen as his primary motifs. Scenery and human figures coalesce in one work, which helps to explain why this series established Richter's popularity throughout Germany at a time when the process of integrating the many independent principalities was gaining momentum.

While the harsher realities of nineteenth-century life are not entirely ignored, it is not for these that Richter is remembered. The one hundredth anniversary of his death was celebrated simultaneously in East and West Germany at commemorative events in Dresden and Essen, after plans for a joint exhibition had to be abandoned. In Essen, the focus was on Richter's sketches, and the case was made that coloring was merely incidental to his work. Richter's subjects, far from being Romantic in the sense of idyllic and grandiose, emerge as intimate and everyday. His love of detail and his fidelity to nature are stressed, and his fame is attributed not least to an increasing market for lavishly illustrated editions of the evergreen classics. The Dresden exhibition was a more lavish affair, in which Richter was presented neither as an icon of German *Gemüt* (sentiment) nor as a general-purpose purveyor of neat insights into a sanitized past; the emphasis was on viewing the artist as the sympathetic champion of the small man, whose work was to be commended not merely because it registered the vicissitudes of provincial life, but because it addressed itself primarily to the untutored layman. In both interpretations of his work, there is a common theme: Richter did not paint, as Alfred Rethel and others had done, for wealthy patrons, civic institutions, or churches, but for the bourgeois or peasant subscriber to calendars, broadsheets, and anthologies of fairytales. In this respect he was the product of commercial forces that marked the threshold of a new age of consumerism in which mass production was to take the place of the unique artefact. His preferred topoi may have been Romantic, but the market for which he worked had patently become a modern one.

OSMAN DURRANI

Biography

Born in Dresden, September 28, 1803, the son of a copperplate engraver. Traveled extensively in his youth (Strasbourg and southern France 1820–21, Italy 1823–26). In Rome, he made contact with the extensive Nazarene circle, which at that time numbered around twelve hundred artists, and was taught by the landscape painter Joseph Anton Koch as well as by Julius Schnorr von Carolsfeld. In 1828, Richter began to work as an instructor at the porcelain works in Meissen. This provided financial stability, and here, while perfecting the art of the miniature, Richter also painted numerous Italianate and Bohemian landscapes which he sold mainly to the Saxon Art Association ("Kunstverein"). In 1836, he became professor of landscape painting at the Dresden Academy, and received a commission to produce drawings for a survey of Germany's most picturesque and romantic locations, for which he traveled extensively. Book illustrations from the same period include the folk tales and chapbooks of the fifteenth and sixteenth centuries, as well as Oliver Goldsmith's *The Vicar of Wakefield*. In 1848, the publisher Wigand produced an enormously successful *Richter-Album* comprising the artist's most popular woodcuts. From 1850 onward, Richter concentrated almost entirely on engravings and woodcuts as illustrations for around 150 volumes and pamphlets. Became an honorary member of the Dresden and Munich Academies in 1853, and of the Berlin Academy in 1874. After retirement from teaching in 1876, he compiled a lively though fragmentary account of his career (*Lebenserinnerungen eines deutschen Malers*), which focused on his spiritual awakening as well as on his travels and on the practical difficulties he faced in establishing himself as an artist in Germany. Died Dresden, June 19, 1884; the autobiography was finished by his son Heinrich.

Bibliography

Friedrich, Karl Joseph. *Die Gemälde Ludwig Richters*. Berlin: Deutscher Verein für Kunstwissenschaft, 1937.

Golz, Bruno. *Ludwig Richter, der Mann und sein Werk*. Leipzig: Voigtländer, 1920.

Hoff, Johann Friedrich. *Adrian Ludwig Richter, Maler und Radierer. Verzeichnis seines gesamten graphischen Werkes mit Bildnis und Handschriftprobe Ludwig Richters*. Rev. ed. edited by Karl Budde. Freiburg: Ragoczy, 1922.

Kalkschmidt, Eugen. *Ludwig Richter: Sein Leben und sein Schaffen*. Berlin: Grote, Rev. ed. Munich: Münchner-Verlag, 1948.

Müller-Bohn, Jost. *Ludwig Richter. Das geistliche Leben eines deutschen Malers*. Lahr-Dinglingen: Schweickhardt, 1983.

Neidhart, Hans Joachim. *Ludwig Richter*. Leipzig: Seemann and Vienna: Schroll, 1969.

Stubbe, Wolf, ed. *Das Adrian Ludwig Richter Album: Sämtliche Holzschnitte*. 2d ed. Munich: Rogner and Bernhard, 1971.

THE RIME OF THE ANCIENT MARINER 1798

Poem by Samuel Taylor Coleridge

Samuel Taylor Coleridge's ballad was first published in 1798, in his collaborative venture with William Wordsworth, the anonymously published *Lyrical Ballads*, under the original title *The Rime of the Ancyent Marinere*. This heterogeneous collection of verse contained four poems by Coleridge, and nineteen by Wordsworth, and was written at a time when the two poets enjoyed what Wordsworth later described as their "most unreserved intercourse" together. Coleridge explained in his *Biographia Literaria* (1817) that the joint work was intended to be composed of two sorts of poems. The first, written by Coleridge, were aimed at "persons and characters supernatural, or at least romantic." They were endowed with "a semblance of truth sufficient to procure . . . that willing suspension of disbelief for the moment, which constitutes poetic faith." Wordsworth's poems were, by contrast, to direct the reader's mind "to the loveliness and the wonders of the world before us."

Rime, which is the opening poem of *Lyrical Ballads*, tells the story of a ship that having crossed the equator, is in Coleridge's words, "driven by storms to the cold Country towards the South Pole" and how the mariner "cruelly and in contempt of the laws of hospitality killed a Seabird and how he was followed by many and strange Judgements." The poem was conceived on a wintry afternoon walk over Quantoxhead with Dorothy and William Wordsworth in November 1797. It was originally intended to be a collaboration, but Wordsworth later recalled that "the greatest part of the story was Mr Coleridge's invention; but certain parts I myself suggested." These included the key moment of the killing of the albatross and "the navigation of the ship by the dead men, but [I] do not recall that I had anything more to do with the scheme of the poem." Written in self-consciously old-fashioned English, Coleridge devised a complex rhythm for the poem. This transcended the four-line, four-stress style traditional for the ballad stanza, and included a great deal of internal rhyme. (Tellingly, it was also at this time that Coleridge started work on the unfinished poem "Christabel.") Some five months were spent on the writing and redrafting of *Rime*, which incorporated many of the philosophical concerns that interested him at that time. These included such themes as exile and homecoming, dreams and madness, humankind and nature. Coleridge clearly brought strong personal emotions to the work, merging the natural with the supernatural into a powerful and dramatic motif of human suffering. *Rime* has been variously interpreted as an exposition of original sin, guilt, and humanity's desecration of the natural world. Other more immediate influences included the then fashionable Gothic style of Matthew Gregory Lewis, whose play *The Castle Spectre* had appeared in 1797. Coleridge had quickly read this work, though he found it "flat" and "unimaginative." Another influence was Gottfried August Bürger, translations of whose *Lenore* were then appearing in the *Monthly Magazine*. The poetry of both the German Sturm und Drang movement and the English Gothic revival were clearly at work on Coleridge's imagination at that moment. But there were older influences, too. One of Coleridge's older brothers had been an officer in India. He had sent home letters of the "romantic East" that helped fire Coleridge's love of travel books. As a child he had also read *The Arabian Nights*. He particularly recalled the tale "of a man who was compelled to seek for a pure virgin" that made "so deep an impression on me . . . that I was haunted by spectres, whenever I was in the dark—and I distinctly remember the anxious & fearful eagerness, with which I used to watch the window, in which the books lay." Notably, Coleridge had never been at sea when he first wrote *Rime*, but still he succeeds in creating a profound nautical effect, and the strong impression of a tale told by the mariner himself—a character with which Coleridge would come closely to identify himself. Only later sea-borne journeys would bring amendments to the poem based on actual experience.

Coleridge was an active abolitionist in Bristol from at least 1795, writing in his newspaper the *Watchman* that the slave trade had turned British mariners into "rather shadows in their appearance than men." The poem has thus been interpreted as a metaphor for the slave trade. The sources of many of its images have been traced to contemporary debates on abolition and emancipation, with the central albatross motif standing as a symbol of the colonial enslavement of native populations. However, the poem, which Coleridge described as a work of "pure imagination," has been endlessly analyzed, with new interpretations constantly emerging.

In an anonymous article published in the *Critical Review* in October 1798 Coleridge's friend Robert Southey declared of

"Beyond the shadow of the ship, / I watched the water-snakes." Illustration by Gustave Doré. Reprinted courtesy of the Mary Evans Picture Library.

Rime that though many of its stanzas were laboriously beautiful . . . in connection they are absurd or unintelligible." He claimed not to understand the story, describing it as "a Dutch attempt at German sublimity. Genius has here been employed in producing a poem of little merit." Charles Lamb, by contrast, told Southey that the poem was "a right English attempt, and a successful one, to dethrone German sublimity." Wordsworth believed that the inclusion of the poem in *Lyrical Ballads* had "upon the whole been an injury to the volume, I mean that the old words and the strangeness of it have deterred readers from going on." He suggested in 1799 that if a second edition were to be published, "I would put in its place some little things which would be more likely to suit the common taste." The poem was not removed from the 1800 edition, though many of its archaisms were removed. Wordsworth explained in a note to the poem that he had encouraged Coleridge to publish it, but also that "many persons have been much displeased with it." Wordsworth's notes to the *Lyrical Ballads* led to some division between the two poets, and Coleridge later explored some of these issues in his *Biographia Literaria* (1817). Nevertheless, *Rime* has gone on to enjoy an excellent reputation, and remains one of Coleridge's best-known and best-loved works.

DAVID HAYCOCK

Bibliography

Ebbotson, J. R. "Coleridge's Mariner and the Rights of Man," *Studies in Romanticism* 11 (1972).

Holmes, Richard. *Coleridge: Early Visions*. London: Hodder and Stoughton, 1989.

Jones, Alun R., and William Tydeman, eds. *Coleridge: The Ancient Mariner and Other Poems: A Casebook*. London: Macmillan, 1973.

Keane, Patrick. *Coleridge's Submerged Politics: "The Ancient Mariner" and "Robinson Crusoe."* Columbia: University of Missouri Press, 1994.

Lamb, Jonathan. " 'The Rime of the Ancient Mariner': A Ballad of the Scurvy." In *Pathologies of Travel*. Edited by Richard Wrigley and George Revill. Amsterdam: Rodopi, 2000.

Bloom, Harold, ed. *Samuel Taylor Coleridge's "The Rime of the Ancient Mariner."* New York: Chelsea House, 1986.

Lee, Debbie. "Yellow Fever and the Slave Trade: Coleridge's 'Rime of the Ancient Mariner,' " *English Literary History* 65 (1998): 675–700.

Wallen, Martin, ed. *Coleridge's Ancient Mariner: An Experimental Edition of Texts and Revisions, 1798–1828*. Barrytown, N.Y.: Station Hill Press, 1993.

Stevenson, Warren. *A Study of Coleridge's Three Great Poems—Christabel, Kubla Khan, and The Rime of the Ancient Mariner*. Lewiston, N.Y.: Edwin Mellen Press, 2001.

ROBERT THE DEVIL (ROBERT LE DIABLE) 1831

Score by Giacomo Meyerbeer, libretto by Augustin-Eugène Scribe and Germain Delavigne

"The score of *Robert le diable* is not only Meyerbeer's masterpiece, but it is also a milestone in the history of music": thus wrote critic François Joseph Fétis after the opera's premiere at the Paris Opéra on November 21, 1831. Its composer, Giacomo Meyerbeer, had arrived in Paris from Italy some six years earlier to oversee the French premiere of *Il crociato in Egitto* (*The Crusader in Egypt*, 1824), the work which had grounded his reputation in opera. After *Robert*'s resounding success, not only did it quickly become a mainstay in the repertoire of the Paris Opéra, but it ensured an auspicious future for Meyerbeer in Paris, then the most important operatic center in Europe. After equally successful productions outside of France, *Robert* also garnered international fame for Meyerbeer, placing him, as Fétis would note, at the forefront of the German school, ahead of his friend and colleague Carl Maria von Weber.

Set in medieval Sicily, *Robert* is the tale of a knight born of the demonic seduction of a beautiful princess. Unbeknown to Robert, his fiendish sire is none other than his comrade, Bertram. Much of the plot's conflict revolves around Bertram's attempts to gain Robert's immortal soul. However, the efforts of Alice, Robert's foster sister, save him, and as the defeated Bertram is swallowed up into the earth at the end of the opera, Robert is led off to a happy life with his bride-to-be, the Princess Isabelle. *Robert*'s Gothic overtones place it firmly in an already popular operatic tradition established with works such as François-Adrien Boieldieu's *La Dame blanche* (*The White Lady*, 1825) and Weber's *Der Freischütz* (*The Freeshooter*, 1821, which had been produced on the French stage under the title *Robin des bois*). Notwithstanding these forerunners, it was *Robert* that unleashed a surge of "fantastic" operas all across Europe.

In addition to being one of the nineteenth century's most significant "*diableries*" (plots in the vein of Johann Wolfgang von Goethe's *Faust*, which center on a protagonist whose soul balances uncertainly and precariously between eternal salvation and damnation), *Robert* is considered an important example of French grand opera. During the Empire, Napoleon had insisted upon spectacle in productions at the Opéra, but later technical developments, including the introduction of gas lighting in 1822, allowed artists such as Louis-Jacques-Mande Daguerre to utilize exciting new technical strategies for set designs. Yet display was not the only determinant in *grand opéra*. Much depended on a new direction in drama. A major innovator in this area was *Robert*'s librettist, Augustin-Eugène Scribe, whose *La muette de Portici* (*The Mute Girl of Portici*, 1828, with score by Daniel-François-Esprit Auber) fixed the standard characteristics of the new style: historical drama, local color, and large-scale spectacle highlighted by rich scores (with many possibilities for large choral ensembles), sets, and dance. After *Robert*, their first joint project, Scribe and Meyerbeer became one of the most successful teams in the Parisian operatic arena; their later grand opera collaborations included *Les Huguenots* (1836), *Le prophéte* (1849), and *L'Africaine* (posthumously produced in 1865). Scribe also worked with Meyerbeer on *Ein Feldlager in Schlesien* (*A Camp in Silesia*, 1844), the music of which later was used as the basis for their opéra-comique *L'étoile du nord* (*The North Star*, 1854).

Given the features of grand opera, *Robert* offered an almost textbook example of the genre. Lavish set designs from the atelier of Pierre-Luc-Charles Ciceri cost even more than the costumes. Scribe further crafted stage spectacle by furnishing the libretto with not only the traditional operatic set pieces such as strophic arias, cavatines, and cabalettes, but also with large choral numbers featuring knights, villagers, courtiers, and demons. Dance, always a requisite in French opera, also added to *Robert*'s pageantry; the most famous ballet, immortalized in contemporary engravings, is performed by a group of dead nuns who have been summoned by Bertram from their graves to dance in a moonlit cloister, demonstrating the pleasures of sin to Robert. Although Scribe had supposedly long awaited an opportunity to implement this scene, some surmise that the display entitled "Holyrood Chapel by Moonlight" in Daguerre's diorama exhibit may well have provided the inspiration to insert it into *Robert*. Meyerbeer's score, especially his ability to use the orchestra to highlight drama and evoke a sense of the plot's local color and mystery, assured a box office success as well as a profitable future for the opera.

After citing *Robert* as an example of grand opera, it may seem ironic that the work was originally conceived in 1825 for the Opéra-Comique, only to be revised between 1829–30 for the Paris Opéra. A theater that catered to the middle-class paying public (although members of the Paris Opéra's upper-class audiences often frequented its productions, which by and large were more experimental and less restrictive), the Opéra-Comique strove to appeal to contemporary bourgeois tastes. At the center of its artistic activity were Auber and Scribe, as much theatrical promoters as creators. Together with Scribe and Delavigne, Meyerbeer began *Robert* in 1825. However, plans to produce the work at the Opéra-Comique were halted after the theater's director resigned. In 1829, a contract was signed with the Paris Opéra, and the work underwent the necessary revisions for that theater: in addition to changes in the plot, spoken dialogue (the norm at the Opéra-Comique) had to be set as recitative, and the composition was reorganized and expanded from three to five acts. Surviving sketches from *Robert*'s days as an *opéra comique* not only help to date the beginnings of the Meyerbeer–Scribe partnership, but, as Mark Everist has demonstrated, serve to document the changes in Parisian music drama during the 1820s. Thus, to study *Robert*, now considered one of the most successful operas of the early Romantic era, solely as grand opera is to ignore its full cultural and historical importance.

DENISE P. GALLO

Score

Robert le diable. Facsimile edition of orchestral score. Vol. 19, *Early Romantic Opera*. New York: Garland, 1980.

Bibliography

Cohen, H. Robert, ed. *The Original Staging Manuals for Twelve Parisian Operatic Premieres*. Vol. 3 of *Musical Life in 19th-Century France*. Stuyvesant, N.Y.: Pendragon Press, 1991.

Döhring, Sieghart, and Arnold Jacobshagen, eds. *Meyerbeer und das europäische Musiktheater*. Laaber: Laaber-Verlag, 1998.

Edgecombe, Rodney Stenning. "Meyerbeer and Ballet Music in the Nineteenth Century: Some Influences with Reference to *Robert le Diable*," *Dance Chronicle* 21 (1998): 389–410.

Everist, Mark. "Giacomo Meyerbeer, the Théâtre Royal de l'Odéon and Music Drama in Restoration Paris," *19th-Century Music* 17 (1993): 124–48.

———. "The Name of the Rose: Meyerbeer's Opéra Comique, *Robert le diable*," *Revue de musicologie* 80 (1994): 211–50.

Frese, Christhard. *Dramaturgie der grossen Opern Giacomo Meyerbeers*. Berlin: Lienau, 1970.

Gier, Albert. " 'Et quoi! Ton coeur hésite entre nous deux?' *Robert le diable* und das Melodram." In *Giacomo Meyerbeer, Musik als Welterfahrung: Heinz Becker zum 70. Geburtstag*. Edited by Sieghart Döhring and Jürgen Schläder. Munich: Ricordi, 1995.

Walsh, T. J. *Second Empire Opera: The Théâtre Lyrique, Paris 1851–1870*. London: J. Calder/New York: Riverrun Press, 1981.

ROBINSON, HENRY CRABB 1775–1867

English diarist

One of the best assessments of Henry Crabb Robinson's place in literary history is the one he provided himself, in which he wrote, "I found early on that I had not the literary ability to give me such a place among English authors as I should have wished; but I thought that I had an opportunity of gaining a knowledge of many of the most distinguished men of the age, and that I might do some good by keeping a record of my interviews with them." It was perhaps his very lack of literary ambition, combined with his gregariousness and knowledge of German and French, that enabled Robinson to meet and befriend many of the leading English and German writers of the first half of the nineteenth century, and to serve as a conduit of information about, and among, those writers. His diary, begun in 1811 and maintained for the remaining fifty-six years of his life, offers the most continuous and detailed contemporary record of London intellectual life in the first half of the nineteenth century.

By his own account, Robinson's upbringing as a religious Dissenter predisposed him to sympathize with the French Revolution and with English radicals such as Thomas Hardy and John Thelwall, both of whom he met shortly after their acquittal of treason charges in 1794. As a Dissenter he was barred from taking a university degree, so he reluctantly settled on law as a career, becoming a clerk in a London law office with the intention of eventually qualifying as a solicitor. But a £100 legacy from an uncle permitted him to give up his clerkship in 1798 and devote himself fully to reading, theatergoing, and frequenting radical and Unitarian circles (where he met William Hazlitt, probably in 1799). During his first visit to Germany in 1800–05, he traveled widely within the German states, learned the language fluently, and attended lectures at the University of Jena. Robinson's most important intellectual encounter in these years was with Immanuel Kant's philosophy, which he credited with enabling him "to detect so many false reasonings in our [empiricist] school." But his effort to interest the English public in Kant in a series of articles on German literature and intellectual life published in the *Monthly Register* between August 1802 and May 1803 was unsuccessful. His summary of Friedrich Wilhelm Joseph von Schelling's lectures on esthetics remained unpublished till 1976, but was shown to Anne-Louise-Germaine de Staël in 1804.

In letters written from Germany to his brother in London, Robinson began to display the powers of minute observation and independent judgment that were to characterize his later diary of London life. Under the tutelage of Christian Brentano, younger brother of poet Clemens Brentano, Robinson immersed himself in contemporary German literature, and this knowledge, combined with his extensive knowledge of English literature, clearly endeared him to the numerous German writers he met from 1801 on, including Jakob Grimm, Johann Gottfried von Herder (to whom he lent a copy of William Wordsworth and Samuel Taylor Coleridge's *Lyrical Ballads* [1798]), Karl Ludwig von Knebel, Johann Christoph Friedrich von Schiller, Friedrich von Schlegel, Ludwig Tieck, and Christoph Martin Wieland. In January 1804, on account of his fluency in English and French, he was enlisted to provide Madame de Staël, then visiting Weimar, with information about German philosophy. Though Robinson claimed to his brother to have written "4 dissertations on the new Philosophy" for her use, the actual extent of his contribution to the book subsequently published as *De l'Allemagne* (*On Germany*, 1813) remains uncertain. His own assessment, offered decades later, was characteristically modest: "The knowledge she obtained from [August Wilhelm von Schlegel] was in every respect so superior to anything I could communicate that I take very little credit for anything I found in her book." For her part Staël introduced Robinson to Johann Wolfgang von Goethe, Henri-Benjamin Constant de Rebecque, and August Wilhelm von Schlegel. On a return visit to Weimar in 1829, he became better acquainted with Goethe and tried to persuade him of Wordsworth's greatness as a poet.

Robinson's journalistic career, as a war correspondent for *The Times*, lasted from 1807–9 and cost him some of his radical friends. (His Jacobin sympathies had long since faded, and the long stay in Germany had hardened his antipathy to Napoleon.) Between assignments in Denmark and Spain, he met Robert Southey and Wordsworth and attended the first of Samuel Taylor Coleridge's literary lectures. By 1810, the year in which Coleridge and Wordsworth had a serious falling out, Robinson was sufficiently close to both poets to act as a mediator, effecting a partial reconciliation between them in 1812. He remained a friend of both, as well as of Anna Laetitia Barbauld and Charles Lamb, for the rest of their lives, and was a tireless proselytizer on behalf of Wordsworth's poetry. Though he considered William Blake insane, Robinson visited him frequently from 1810 to 1827, wrote an article on him for a German periodical in 1810, and gave valuable information to Blake's first biographer, Alexander Gilchrist.

After his retirement from the bar, Robinson began to play a more active role in public affairs by supporting the new University of London financially and administratively, agitating for the abolition of slavery (in *Strictures on a Life of Wilberforce* [1838] and *Exposure of Misrepresentations . . . in the Preface to the Correspondence of William Wilberforce* [1840], the former being ghost-written for Thomas Clarkson), lobbying politicians and bishops to pass the Dissenters' Chapels Act of 1844 (which gave Nonconformists legal title to their churches), and establishing a gallery at University College London (the name of the University of London after 1836) to display the works of his late friend, the sculptor John Flaxman.

Though extracts from Robinson's diary, reminiscences, and correspondence have been published since his death, his newspaper articles have never been collected and much manuscript material (the bulk of it, including the diary, at Dr. Williams's Library, London) remains unpublished.

NICHOLAS HALMI

See also **Blake, William; Coleridge, Samuel Taylor; *De l'Allemagne* (*On Germany*); Staël, Anne-Louise-Germaine (Madame) de; Wordsworth, William**

Biography

Born in Bury St Edmunds, May 13, 1775. Articled with an attorney in Colchester, 1790–95; employed as a clerk in London, 1796–98; travelled in Germany, 1800–1801; studied at Jena, 1802–5; wrote articles on German subjects for *The Monthly Register*, 1802–3; met Madame de Staël, 1804; returned to England, 1805; served as foreign correspondent for *The Times* in Denmark, 1807, and Spain, 1808. Began his diary, 1811, and studied for the bar, 1812; practiced as a barrister on the Norwich circuit, 1813–28; joined the Athenaeum Club, 1824. Helped found the University of London, 1828, and served as vice president of its senate, 1847–66. In Germany and Italy, 1829–31; with Wordsworth in Italy, 1837. Supported the Dissenters' Chapels Bill, 1844. Died in London, February 5, 1867.

Selected Works

Diary, Reminiscences and Correspondence. 3 vols. Edited by Thomas Sadler. 1869; revised eds., 3 vols., 1869, and 2 vols., 1872.
Blake, Coleridge, Wordsworth, Lamb, &c.: Being Selections from the Remains of Henry Crabb Robinson. Edited by Edith J. Morley. Manchester: Manchester University Press, 1922.
The Correspondence of Henry Crabb Robinson with the Wordsworth Circle (1808–1866). 2 vols. Edited by Edith J. Morley. Oxford: Clarendon, 1927.
Henry Crabb Robinson in Germany, 1800–1805: Extracts from His Correspondence. Edited by Edith J. Morley. London: Oxford University Press, 1929.
Henry Crabb Robinson on Books and Their Writers. 3 vols. Edited by Edith J. Morley. London: Dent, 1938.
The Diary of Henry Crabb Robinson: An Abridgement. Edited by Derek Hudson. London: Oxford University Press, 1966.
The London Theatre, 1811–1866: Selections from the Diary of Henry Crabb Robinson. Edited by Eluned Brown. London: Society for Theatre Research, 1966.
"William Blake, Künstler, Dichter, und religiöser Schwärmer." *Vaterländisches Museum*, 1811. Reprinted and translated in G. E. Bentley Jr., *Blake Records*. Oxford: Clarendon Press, 1969.
Penelope J. Corfield and Chris Evans, eds. *Youth and Revolution in the 1790s: Letters of William Pattisson, Thomas Amyot and Henry Crabb Robinson.* Stroud: Sutton, 1996.

Bibliography

Ashton, Rosemary. *The German Idea: Four English Writers and the Reception of German Thought, 1800–1860.* Cambridge: Cambridge University Press, 1980.

Baker, John Milton. *Henry Crabb Robinson of Bury, Jena, The Times, and Russell Square.* London: Allen and Unwin, 1937.

Behler, Diana. "Henry Crabb Robinson and Weimar." In *A Reassessment of Weimar Classicism.* Edited by Gerhart Hoffmeister. Lewiston, N.Y.: Mellen, 1996.

———. "Henry Crabb Robinson as a Mediator of Early German Romanticism to England," *Arcadia: Zeitschrift für vergleichende Literaturwissenschaft* 12 (1977): 117–55.

———. "Henry Crabb Robinson as a Mediator of Lessing and Herder to England," *Lessing Yearbook* 7 (1975): 105–26.

Behler, Ernst, "Schellings Ästhetik in der Überlieferung von Henry Crabb Robinson," *Philosophisches Jahrbuch* 83 (1976): 133–38.

Benson, A. B. "Fourteen Unpublished Letters by Henry Crabb Robinson," *PMLA* 31 (1916): 395–420.

Maertz, Gregory. "Henry Crabb Robinson's 1802–1803 Translations of Goethe's Lyric Poems and Epigrams," *Jahrbuch des Wiener Goethe-Vereins* 100, no. 1 (1996–97): 69–92.

———. "Reviewing Kant's Early Reception in Britain: The Leading Role of Henry Crabb Robinson." In *Cultural Interactions in the Romantic Age: Critical Essays in Comparative Literature.* Edited by Gregory Maertz. Albany: State University of New York Press, 1998.

Marquardt, Hertha. *Henry Crabb Robinson und seine deutschen Freunde: Brücke zwischen England und Deutschland im Zeitalter der Romantik.* 2 vols. Göttingen: Vandenhoek and Ruprecht, 1964–67.

Morley, Edith J. *The Life and Times of Henry Crabb Robinson.* London: Dent, 1935.

Singh, G. "Henry Crabb Robinson on Italian Literature," *Italica* 43 (1966): 404–28.

Wellens, Oskar. "Henry Crabb Robinson, Reviewer of Wordsworth, Coleridge, and Byron in the Critical Review: Some New Attributions," *Bulletin of Research in the Humanities* 84 (1981): 98–120.

ROBINSON, MARY DARBY 1758–1800

British poet, novelist, playwright

The work of Mary Robinson is remarkable for its artistic excellence as well as its principled and vigorous feminism. Her repudiations of the sentimental conventions of sexual love are explicit: in her characterization, Sappho enjoins British women to "aspire / above the treach'rous spells of low desire." The example of Sappho's self-destructive behavior, enslaved to an illusion, is used by Robinson to teach women to "disdain love's dread control."

Nonetheless, as her contemporary, Jane Porter, remarked, Robinson was herself "usually styled the British Sappho," and the poet was frequently mistaken for the characters whose folly she exposes. (For an example of a hostile writing that imputes to Robinson the vices of her counterexemplary characters, see the review of her *Poetical Works* that appeared in *The Annual Review and History of Literature for 1806.*) In keeping with her commitment to Enlightenment principles, Robinson writes, in her *Sonnet 43* "Welcome returning Reason's placid beam"; but as she points out in her posthumously published *Memoirs*, she and her work were attacked in the press in terms of her love life, in both harsh reviews and in what Judith Pascoe has called "fictional accounts of her love affairs" that were "cast in pornographic terms."

As her *Memoirs* clearly state, Robinson was a child (born Mary Darby) when she learned to distrust and to resist the sentimental illusions with which sexual relationships were advertised in her culture. Her father abandoned her mother and herself, preferring a mistress and promising to pay for boarding school for Mary and for rented rooms for her mother, but he subsequently failed to make the promised payments. According to various sources, she entered a loveless marriage to Thomas Robinson at the age of fourteen, fifteen, or sixteen; her husband had deceived her mother about his financial situation. After their marriage, Mary found that he kept a mistress, and later she was imprisoned for her husband's debts. On her release, she acted at the Drury Lane Theatre as a protege of David Garrick (1777–80), during which time she suffered the unwanted attentions of lords, the unwanted courtship of a captain (who proved to be married), exploitation by royalty, public defamation, slander, and humiliation. The Duke of Portland offered £600 to estrange her from her husband. In the year in which the Prince of Wales (later George IV) seduced her with false promises, her second child died in infancy. While the prince never paid the £20,000 that he had promised (to compensate for the damage he brought to her professional life), Charles James Fox was able to arrange for her an annuity of £500 in 1783, after receipt of which she suffered abandonment by others, insulting offers from powerful men to alleviate her financial troubles in exchange for sexual favors, crippling disease, and death at the age of forty-two.

Robinson developed great skill in literary forms, including monologues and soliloquies, such as most of the sonnets in *Sappho and Phaon*, in which she criticizes the conventional forms of sexual relations and their literary propaganda. She wrote political epistles including "Ainsi Va le Monde" (1790), a poem in praise of the democratic revolution in France, verse tales in the manner of folk literature (notably the poems gathered in her last book, *Lyrical Tales* [1800]), and polemical prose including the essays prefixed to *Sappho and Phaon* and, if conventional attributions are correct, *Thoughts on the Condition of Women* (n.d.) and *Letter to the Women of England on the Injustice of Mental Subordination* (1799).

Often Robinson's work was appropriated by precisely those interests whose falsity she spent her adult life exposing. A book of her feminist poetry (*Sappho and Phaon*) was reprinted after her death by the Minerva Press and offered for sale among novels and romances such as *Female Sensibility* (1783), *A Tale for Misses and Their Mammas* by "Prudentia Homespun," *Woman As She Should Be* by Mrs. Parsons, and *A Dictionary of Love.* Robinson repudiated the illusory comforts of romance fictions; as Jacqueline Labbe has shown, Robinson goes as far as "infesting the romance with violence." In contrast, the Enlightenment notions of social determinism foster both a critique of existing society and a progressive optimism. She notes that "when only monks could write, and nobles read, authority rose triumphant over right; and the slave, spell-bound in ignorance, hugged his fetters without repining"; but "that era is rapidly advancing, when talents will tower like an unperishable column, while the globe will be strewed with the wrecks of superstition"; and, in an anticipation of Percy Bysshe Shelley's rhetoric in *A Defence of Poetry*, "there are both POETS and PHILOSOPHERS, now living in Britain, who, had they been born in any *other* clime, would have been honoured with the proudest distinctions."

Apart from the deliberately trivial playfulness of her participation in "Della Cruscan games" in periodicals (what her *Memoirs* call "glitter and false taste"—see, for example, her "Ode to Della Crusca"), Robinson's enduringly important poetry falls into three groups: the poetry of revolution and reaction in the period of the French Revolution, the poetry of sexual politics, written in the years immediately after Mary Wollstonecraft's *Vindication of the Rights of Woman* and at the time she befriended William Godwin (to whom she was introduced by Robert Merry, who had been in Paris in 1792 helping to plan a revolutionary invasion of England); and the contentious poetry of social-class conflict (antislavery, antiwar, antiracism, antiimperialism) that she gathered into *Lyrical Tales*.

Though Robinson was the author of a volume of poems that appeared in 1775 and *Captivity, A Poem; and Celadon, A Tale* in 1777 (she wrote *Captivity* in prison), it was the publication of "Ainsi Va le Monde" in 1790 and of the collected volume *Poems* in 1791 (including "Ainsi Va le Monde") that brought her poetry to national attention and prominence. (A second collected volume followed in 1793.) Strangely, the 1791 *Poems* was published with the encouragement of Edmund Burke, who was more eloquently opposed than any other writer to the revolution that Robinson celebrated in her poetry. Reportedly, Burke's son Richard was an admirer of at least one short, occasional, and impromptu poem by Robinson, and perhaps Burke's sponsorship of her entire collected works was owing to that slight fancy. Other writings by Robinson are more clearly in accord with Burke's own opinions, including a pamphlet entitled *Impartial Reflections on the Present Situation of the Queen of France, by a Friend of Humanity* (1791) and poems including "Marie Antoinette's Lamentation, in Her Prison of the Temple" and "A Fragment. Supposed to be written near the Temple, at Paris, on the Night Before the Execution of Louis XVI" (both 1793). Other circumstances surrounding the publication of the 1791 *Poems* are similarly surprising; for example, the first name in the volume's list of subscribers is that of the Prince of Wales, who had been estranged and hostile for ten years. Further, this volume of poetry that praises the French Revolution was published by John Bell, who, when war erupted, became a correspondent with the British Army in war-torn Flanders.

Robinson herself set out for Flanders in 1792 (having previously visited and even resided there, supposedly for the sake of healthful baths at Spa). Though Judith Pascoe reports that Robinson somehow managed to escape safely on July 2, 1792 when British citizens were detained in France, according to Robinson's *Memoirs* it was September 2, 1792—the day on which the September Massacres began—when that inexplicable escape occurred. What Robinson's actual business in France might have been in 1792 is as obscure as her means of successful flight while the British around her were detained. Her cottage in France was subsequently used as headquarters for a French general.

Most of the passages in "Ainsi Va le Monde" are about poetry and art; only the last six of the poem's fourteen pages discuss the French Revolution directly. The argument of the pages on art is that freedom fosters and improves art, government, science, and philosophy. This is also the argument of *The Progress of Liberty*, a long poem in two books that was first published in the posthumous *Memoirs*. In "Ainsi Va le Monde," the pages on the revolution suggest that "dazzling splendours" were vain in France, where "luxury" sought "To hide pale Slavery in a mask of smiles," and (in a metaphor that Charlotte Smith was later to develop in her own poem on the French Revolution, *The Emigrants* [1793]), to "lead the victim in a flow'ry chain." The poem accuses the French monarchy (and especially Louis XIV) of "pious fraud" and alleges that, historically, "avarice" wrought destruction in France, while "power was law." The poem welcomes the daybreak of freedom in 1789, and it specifically praises the French National Assembly and more loftily "the natural Rights of Man"; finally the poem foretells the spread of liberty from France to other nations.

In addition to the sonnets of *Sappho and Phaon*, Robinson's critique of the amatory tradition in poetry is expressed in her sonnet "Laura to Petrarch" (*The Morning Post*, April 3, 1800) where she reverses the conventionally gendered roles of speaker and addressed, and where Laura advises the poet of love to stop advertising (and promoting) sexual obsession—"find in friendship's balm sick passion's cure."

Like "Laura to Petrarch" and *Sappho and Phaon*, many of the poems in *Lyrical Tales* take the form of dramatic monologues; Robinson was an experienced playwright as well as a poet, and her play *The Sicilian Lover* appeared in the same year as *Sappho and Phaon*. The first eighty-four lines of "The Lascar," in *Lyrical Tales*, are one speech spoken by a starving Indian sailor surrounded by the pointless but lavish luxuries enjoyed by the ruling class in "the City." A speech of eighty lines in "The Negro Girl" (also in *Lyrical Tales*) complains of "Oppression . . . Slavery and woe" and narrates an episode in which shackled slaves die and even drown themselves in desperation.

Some poems combine the position on sexual politics with her opinion on class politics: in "The Maniac" (1793), feelings of sexual love can deceive many, leaving "only keen regret behind, / To tear with poison'd fangs thy mind," and sexual charms "beguile" people "Till the blithe harbinger of day / Awakes thee from thy dream." The poem proceeds from the ideology of love to the evil of the war against revolutionary France that began in January 1793 ("The victor's savage joy") and injustices arising from class conflict ("cold Poverty's abyss"). In "The Murdered Maid," a hermit monk in the Alps hears screams, investigates, and finds the body of a murdered woman; immediately the "Hermit hears the clang of arms. . . . Thund'ring peals / From warfare's brazen throat, proclaim'd the approach / Of conquering legions."

Throughout her work, the falsity of ideological representations is an important theme: the ideology of sexual obsession imputed to women (an ideology whose genre is "romance"), the ideology of war, and the ideology of a class-stratified society of opulence and starvation. In "January, 1795" (1795) her satirical sketch of London includes "Candour spurn'd, and art [i.e., artificial semblances] rewarded." Her father was not only guilty of the moral and pecuniary failing in abandoning his family to poverty in lustful preference for a mistress, but also folly—he was, according to her *Memoir*, the "dupe of his passions." Her autobiographical volume condemns the conventional elements of the genre of romance as "delusive visions." Like her friend Godwin, and like Mary Hays, Mary Wollstonecraft, Thomas Paine, Joseph Priestley, and other progressive intellectuals in the revolutionary decades at the end of the eighteenth century, Robinson voiced often and brilliantly the hope that enlightenment by intellect could liberate humanity from the enslavements of political oppression, economic inequality, and conventionally gendered passions.

TERENCE A. HOAGWOOD

Selected Works

Poems. 1775.
Captivity, A Poem; and Celadon, A Tale. 1777.
Poems. Vol. 1, 1791.
Vancenza, or, The Dangers of Credulity. 1792.
Poems. Vol. 2, 1793.
A Monody to the memory of the Late Queen of France. 1793.
"*Sight.*" "*The Cavern of Woe.*" "*Solitude.*" 1793.
The Widow. 2 vols. 1794.
Sappho and Phaon. In a Series of Legitimate Sonnets, with Thoughts on Poetical Subjects, and Anecdotes of the Grecian Poetess. 1796. Reprinted with an introduction by Rebecca Jackson and Terence Hoagwood. Delmar, NY: Scholar's Facsimiles, 1996.
The Sicilian Lover. 1796.
Angelina. 3 vols. 1796.
Hubert de Sevrac. 1796.
Walsingham, Or, The Pupil of Nature. 4 vols. 1797.
The False Friend. 4 vols. 1799.
The Natural Daughter. 1799.
Lyrical Tales. 1800.
Memoirs of the Late Mrs. Robinson, Written by Herself. With Some Posthumous Pieces [by Maria Elizabeth Robinson]. 4 vols. 1801.
Poetical Works of the Late Mrs. Mary Robinson. 3 vols. 1806.

Bibliography

Anonymous review of *The Poetical Works of the Late Mrs. Mary Robinson.* In *The Annual Review and History of Literature for 1806.* 1807.
Curran, Stuart. "Mary Robinson's *Lyrical Tales* in Context." In *Re-Visioning Romanticism: British Women Writers, 1776–1837.* Edited by Carol Shiner Wilson and Joel Haefner. Philadelphia: University of Pennsylvania Press, 1994.
Labbe, Jacqueline M. "Selling One's Sorrows: Charlotte Smith, Mary Robinson, and the Marketing of Poetry." *Wordsworth Circle* 25, no. 2 (1994): 68–71.
Lee, Debbie. "*The Wild Wreath*: Cultivating a Poetic Circle for Mary Robinson," *Studies in the Literary Imagination* 30, no. 1 (1997): 23–34.
Luther, Susan. "A Stranger Minstrel: Coleridge's Mrs. Robinson," *Studies in Romanticism* 33, no. 3 (1994): 391–409.
McGann, Jerome. "Mary Robinson and the Myth of Sappho," *Modern Language Quarterly* 56, no. 1 (1995): 55–76.
———. *The Poetics of Sensibility.* Oxford: Oxford University Press, 1996.
Miskolcze, Robin L. "Snapshots of Contradiction in Mary Robinson's *Poetical Works*," *Papers in Language and Literature* 31, no. 2 (1995): 206–19.
Pascoe, Judith. "The Spectacular *Flaneuse*: Mary Robinson and the City of London." *Wordsworth Circle* 23, no. 2 (1992): 165–71.
Pascoe, Judith. "Mary Robinson and the Literary Marketplace." In *Romantic Women Writers.* Edited by Paula Feldman and Theresa M. Kelly. Hanover, N.H.: University Press of New England, 1995.
Mary Robinson: Selected Poems. Edited and with an introduction by Judith Pascoe. Peterborough, Ontario: Broadview, 2000.
Peterson, Linda H. "Becoming an Author: Mary Robinson's *Memoirs* and the Origins of the Woman Artist's Autobiography." In *Re-Visioning Romanticism: British Women Writers, 1776–1837.* Edited by Carol Shiner Wilson and Joel Haefner. Philadelphia: University of Pennsylvania Press, 1994. 36–56.
Shteir, Ann B. "Mary Robinson." In *A Dictionary of British and American Women Writers 1660–1800.* Edited by Janet Todd. Totowa, N.J.: Rowman and Littlefield, 1987.

ROGER AND ANGELICA

Painting by Jean-Auguste-Dominique Ingres

Roger et Angelica (*Roger and Angelica* [or *Roger Delivering Angelica,* or *Roger Freeing Angelica*]) represents a moment taken from Canto 10 of Ludovico Ariosto's epic poem *Orlando Furioso.* The unfortunate Angelica has been left naked and chained to a rock on the Isle of Tears, to be sacrificed to the orc, a sea monster. Ingres pictures the moment when Ruggiero, seated on his hippogriff (a mythical creature that is half eagle, half-horse), enters into combat with the orc.

In its theme, Ingres's subject is closely related to others—such as that of St. George and the Dragon and Hercules and Hersione—that appealed to the imaginations of his generation and formed part of a wider penchant for the literature, drama, music, and poetry of mythic and chivalric rescue that characterized the Romantic generation. Indeed, the composition of *Roger and Angelica* evolved from an idea for a subject based on the myth of Perseus and Andromeda.

In the narrative of Roger and Angelica, as Ariosto tells it, Roger is unable to pierce the monster's flesh with his lance, and eventually has to temporarily stun the orc with his magic shield, so he can free Angelica and get her to safety. In a version of the painting dated much later, but which Wildenstein believed to be anterior to the 1819 Louvre version, Ingres depicts the magic shield in action. However, in all the later versions, it is the ultimately futile, first combat that Ingres chooses to depict. This allows him to construct a pictorial dynamic of some virtuosity, in which the contrasting diagonals of the rearing hippogriff and downward-thrusting lance play against the dynamism of the sea and its monster, and contrast, too, with the limp and static Angelica. The composition also allows for a play of textures (the slimy skin of the orc, the glint of the metallic armor and the point of the lance, the feathers of the hippogriff, the billowing silk cloak) that illustrate Ingres's considerable abilities in the representation of fabric and surface. But it also allows for the heroic depiction of Roger, firmly in control of his rearing hippogriff and lance, eyes downcast in studied concentration but also in chivalrous deference to the nudity of Angelica. In the essential heroism of the depiction, and in the rearing posture and wild eyes of the animal and the billowing cloak, there may even be a faint, conscious echo of Jacques-Louis David's canonical (but by this time problematic) *Napoleon Crossing the Alps at the Great Saint Bernard Pass*, by which the generation of David's pupils had come to understand masculine military heroism.

The depiction of Angelica, with her swollen, impossibly strained neck, her eyes whose pupils have almost entirely disappeared, leaving only an expanse of white, and her arms draped with limp, almost resigned elasticity through her chains, has engaged commentators repeatedly. Early critics of the painting, reacting to its exhibition at the Salon of 1819, were shocked by what they saw as its jarring archaism. Modern commentators, on the other hand, have tended to find in its oddness rich material for post-Freudian or poststructural analysis. Compositionally, Angelica's neck is an extreme variant of those extended and smoothly straining necks that are featured in earlier compositions such as *Venus Wounded by Diomedes* (c. 1803) and *Jupiter and Thetis* (1811). This particular feature can trace its lineage back to Ingres's fascination with antique vase painters (for example, the Kleophrades painter) and in the influence of those artists (Jean Broc, John Flaxman, Benigne Gagnereux, and Maurice Quai) who had looked to antique vase painting for inspiration for a purification and stylization of neoclassicism in the early 1800s. Angelica's odd breasts and unformed pudenda, while partially explicable as the result of Ingres's deep knowledge of the conventions of antique statuary, might also be seen as a conscious or unconscious infantilization of Angelica (who, in the original narrative, is a complex heroine and at this point in the poem orders Roger to free her and cease the useless attempts to kill the orc in combat). Ingres's representation of Angelica succeeds in accentuating and dramatizing a polarization between the active, free, and liberating male, and the enclosed, captive, passive female. This opposition was central to this painting's dynamic, and (as feminist scholars have shown) was a key trope of the wider Romantic imagination. The particular characterization of man, woman, and monster in Ingres's composition may also point to a profound fear of the female, which in a bizarre way makes the feminine itself monstrous.

More concretely, there is no doubt that the contradictory combination of open voyeuristic delight in the play of curves of the chained, naked victim (from the fleshy back to the delicate, balletic poise of the feet), and the simultaneous courtly prudishness of deflected glances and smoothed anatomies, a marked departure from the rugged sensuality of the characters in the original narrative, creates a peculiar and disturbing tension palpable to viewers of any of the major versions of this picture. It is perhaps these and other disjunctions as much as the extraordinary draftsmanship and animation that lend Ingres's large scale historical canvases their peculiar fascination. Certainly, something of the peculiar tensions and undercurrents of Ingres's *Roger and Angelica* would be reflected in the work of later historicizing and consciously revivalist artists such as the Pre-Raphaelites in England, on whom Ingres clearly exercised an important influence.

While the figures of Roger and Angelica, and the dynamic of their encounter, are at the central interest of the painting, there is much that is remarkable in its other elements. The pecul-

Jean-Auguste-Dominique Ingres, *Ruggero Freeing Angelica*. 1841. Reprinted courtesy of AKG.

iar murky quality of the light and the predominantly dark palette of the background lend the setting the atmosphere of a cave (particularly in the 1839 National Gallery version, which compresses the picture space). Here Ingres seems to draw his vocabulary not from the ancients, but from other—perhaps less often acknowledged—sources of inspiration, including Anne-Louis Girodet de Roussy-Trioson's experiments in *Endymion* and other canvases, and the rocks and seas of such key French Romantic paintings as Antoine-Jean Gros's *Sappho* (1801).

Like many of Ingres's other subjects, this one was repeated, with variants, throughout his career. Often the variations were minor, but the repeated refinements are a sign of a profound and contradictory urge that drove Ingres to endlessly refine his work and thereby create an ultimately "open" and unfinished oeuvre. We cannot say which of the versions currently extant is to be considered the final or definitive one. The paintings of Roger and Angelica are ultimately a set of variations on a theme, whose modularities, one might argue, indicate not a pedantic and austere imagination, but a complex and restless one.

MARK LEDBURY

Work

Roger et Angelica, 1819. Oil on canvas, 57.9 in. × 74.75 in. Louvre, Paris.
Ruggero Freeing Angelica. 1841. Oil on canvas, oval, 21.25 in. × 18.25 in. Musée Ingres, Montauban.

Bibliography

Condon, P., ed. *In Pursuit of Perfection: The Art of J-A-D Ingres*. Exhibition catalog. Louisville, 1984.
Filho, J. "Ingres: Rogério libertando Angélica," *Revista de história da arte e arqueologia* 1 (1994): 99–107, 305–8.

Fingering Ingres. Art History 1 (2000). Special volume edited by Susan Siegfried.

Johns, D. "Une decouverte recente," *Bulletin du Musée Ingres* 51–52 (1983): 3–10.

Lapauze, H. *Ingres: Sa vie, son oeuvre*. 1911.

Ockman, C. *Ingres Eroticised Bodies. Rethinking the Serpentine Line*. New Haven, Conn.: Yale University Press, 1995.

Rifkin, A. *Ingres Then, and Now*. London, 2000.

Rosenblum, R. *Jean-Auguste Dominique Ingres*. 1967.

Siegfried, S. "Ingres and His Critics 1806–1824." Ph.D. diss., Harvard University, 1980.

Ternois, D. *Ingres*. Paris, 1980.

Wildenstein, D. *The Paintings of J-A-D Ingres*. Rev. ed. London, 1956.

ROMANCE

Musical and literary genre

As with so many genres with a long history of usage, musical works with the title *Romance* have been characterized by changes of type and function, not only over time, but in different countries and areas, and according to whether they were free-standing pieces or components of larger groupings. The term is often interchangeable with *ballad*, a designation more common in British usage.

Originally a literary term, it was used in the Middle Ages to describe courtly verse—stories based on honor and chivalry and dealing with three main groups of legends: the Arthurian and Carolingian cycles, and classical mythology, together with well-known incidents in European history, using a vernacular language rather than Latin. It was the late eighteenth- and early nineteenth-century rediscovery and re-creation of these tales—particularly in the works of Sir Walter Scott and John Keats—that formed an important element in the subject matter of Romanticism and, indeed, from which the very name was coined. As well as chivalry, there is a strong evocation of place and landscape—usually exotic in terms of topography or location—together with a sense of the magical and/or supernatural in these tales.

The overall history of the romance as a musical genre charts a movement from courtly realms through those of the folk singer—occasionally via the church—and then to art music. Love became paramount, the active, heroism becoming more central to the ballad. In eighteenth-century Spain, the romance became a kind of "mini-cantata," complete with recitatives, arias, and choruses, whereas, by the end of the twentieth century, it became almost indistinguishable from the Iberian folk song. Its most noticeable development was in France and the Germanic countries.

The simplicity and sentimentalism that imbued the French romance in the eighteenth century was perfect for inclusion in *opéra comique* by such writers as Grétry, Monsigny, Philidor, and Jean-Jacques Rousseau, and was characterized by strophic form, simple melody—unaffected and unembellished—and an unobtrusive accompaniment. In this form romances were published in collections for domestic performance, with scaled-down accompaniments, one such being *Consolations des misères de ma vie ou Recueil d'airs, romances et duos de J-J. Rousseau* (*Consolations for My Life's Miseries, or, Collection of Airs, Romances, and Duos, by J-J. Rousseau*, 1781), and became very much in vogue, even in the French court. A romance entitled *Ah s'il est dans mon village* is attributed to Marie Antoinette, but the prime example remains J. P. A. Martini's *Plaisir d'amour* (*Pleasure of Love*). Romances quickly took on a more republican, patriotic tone after the French Revolution, often commenting on contemporary events; Devienne's *Romance patriotique sur la mort du jeune Bara* (*Patriotic Romance on the Death of the Young Bara*) and the *Ode sur l'enfance* (*Ode to Childhood*) by François Joseph Gossec are instances among other works by Boieldieu, Rodolphe Kreutzer, Méhul, and Plantade. As the nineteenth century wore on, the solo vocal romance became indistinguishable from the *mélodie* and the *chanson* and appears as such among the works of Georges Bizet, Henry Duparc, Gabriel-Urbain Fauré, Charles-François Gounod, and Camille Saint-Saëns. The great French influence in Russia resulted in many *romances* being written, and later composers, Sergey Vasilycvich Rachmaninoff and Pyotr Ilich Tchaikovsky among them, continued the tradition.

In the German-speaking countries, the composer's *romanze*, like most cultural products in the eighteenth century, was heavily influenced by the French *romance*—especially the more urban, Parisian version. Soon, however, a characteristically Teutonic flavor emerged, due to a number of factors. In a period in which German nationalism was very much in the air, folk music had a palpable influence, and composers of the second generation of the Berlin lieder school in the late eighteenth century were already writing songs that had parallel traits to those of the romances, and publishing collections, among them J. A. P. Schulz's *Lieder im Volkston* (*Songs in the Folk Style*, 1782) and C. F. Zelter's *Lieder, Balladen und Romanzen* (1810). The appearance of the *Lieder, Balladen und Romanzen von Göthe* (1817) by Peter Grønland [Grönland] reminds us of another of these factors, that some of the great poets of the period wrote *romanze*, texts that were eagerly set to music by composers; Johann Wolfgang von Goethe, Johann Gottfried von Herder, Johann Christoph Friedrich von Schiller, and Ludwig Tieck were among those who provided *romanze* texts. Paralleling the popularity of the French romance within opéra comique, the Teutonic romanze was a welcome component of its German-language equivalent, the *singspiel*. One of Wolfgang Amadeus Mozart's works of this kind, *Die Entführung aus dem Serail* (*The Escape from the Harem*, 1782; also known as *Il seraglio* [*The Harem*]) has a romanze that harks back to the earlier connotations of the name in its exotic, Eastern location and its plucked-string accompaniment, imitating the guitar. In later works, the form took on some of the gruesomeness and supernatural/magical qualities of many of the librettos' subjects, as in Carl Maria von Weber's *Der Freischütz* (*The Freeshooter*, 1821) and Lindpainter's *Die Vampyr* (*The Vampire*, 1828). There are occasional singspiels with the title *Romanze* by some of the great German composers: Ludwig van Beethoven's *Que le temps me dure* (with words by Rousseau) and Frauz Schubert's *Sah' ein Knab* are examples.

The romance as a purely instrumental form had already appeared in the eighteenth century, and the term was applied to slow movements of simple structure or to sets of variations and had been used by François-Joseph Gossec, by Franz Joseph Haydn and by Mozart in his Piano Concerto in D Minor and his *Eine kleine Nachtmusik*. The characteristic traits of the vocal form made it particularly attractive to the Romantics. Frédéric Chopin used it for the slow movement of his E-Minor

Piano Concerto (dedicated to a youthful love of his) and Clara Wieck Schumann wrote a set of *Romances variées*, while the two *romanzen* for solo violin with orchestra of Beethoven provide the ideal instrumental choice for the lyrical beauty of the music.

DEREK CAREW

ROMANIANS

In the eighteenth century, the Romanians inhabited various provinces of the Ottoman and Habsburg Empires. Wallachia and Moldavia, tributary principalities under Ottoman rule, were governed by Greek princes who held native nobilities and established Orthodox ecclesiastical and intellectual traditions. Transylvania was under Habsburg sovereignty, but with its own Diet, where the dominant nations were the Hungarians, Szeklers (related to the Hungarians), and the Saxons. The Romanians—they called themselves *rumâni* or *români*, but were generally known as Wallachians—were a merely tolerated nation, with little social or cultural standing. *Romania* as a name referring to all the territory inhabited by Romanians did not occur in the language until the 1840s.

Romantic Europe knew little about them. Johann Gottfried von Herder called them "a confused jumble of the remains of various people and languages." Jean Charles Léonard Simonde de Sismondi thought they spoke Bulgarian; other scholars speculated on the language's potential resemblance to Gaelic. Although William Wordsworth praised the Wallachian nightingales, John Keats did not, and Percy Bysshe Shelley, while exalting the Greek spirit in *Hellas* (1821), contrasted it with that of the "false Moldavian serf." Meanwhile in 1833, Senancour added to his melancholic novel *Obermann* an equally melancholic (and bogus) "Chant funèbre d'un Moldave," which he claimed to have had translated from the Sclavonian.

The political decline of the Ottoman Empire, and the corresponding territorial ambitions of Russia and Austria, wrought paradoxical effects on Romanian culture. The political status quo was threatened, and parts of Moldavia and Wallachia were annexed by the European empires; autonomies were weakened, and the traditional, basically neo-Byzantine culture of the Romanians challenged. On the other hand, the number of books being published in Romanian increased, from under a hundred in the 1760s to over a thousand in the 1840s. Secular ideas were being introduced, through Greek and Austrian channels in particular. From 1760 to 1850 we can follow several stages in the formulation of Romantic ideology among the Romanians and identify features such as the prolonged effects of programmatic Enlightenment; a focus on national history and philology; a tension between the discovery of traditions and their abandonment. Key metaphors (childhood, suffering, death and awakening, landscape, genius) were seized upon and elaborated to characterize not just the Romantic disposition but the whole nation.

A fully worked out Romantic ideology did not develop until after 1830, and was mainly present in Wallachia and Moldavia. But the efforts of Transylvanian Romanian writers in developing literary culture in the preceding period should not be ignored. From the 1770s the Austrians were interested in educational and economic cultivation of their subjects, and Romanians were encouraged to produce works of history, philology, and pedagogy. It was here that the key tenets of national history were developed, at first with official encouragement, but after 1790 in much more difficult circumstances. The purely Roman origin of the Romanians was asserted; attempts were made at using the Latin alphabet for the first time; a historiography asserting continuity of settlement in Transylvania (Roman Dacia) was elaborated. The efforts of these intellectuals, of modest origin and known collectively as the Transylvanian school, culminated in the *Lexicon Valacho-Latino-Hungarico-Germanum* (1825) and Petru Maior's *Istoria pentru începutul romanilor din Dacia Traiană* (*The History of the Origin of the Romanians in Trajan's Dacia*, 1812). The only major literary work of the Transylvanian Romanians is the *Tiganiada* (*Gypsiad*) of the administrator Ion Budai-Deleanu, this remarkable mock epic poem, set in Vlad the Impaler's fifteenth-century Wallachia, owes something to the model of Metastasio's *Temistocle*, and was not published until 1876. The political changes that these cultural endeavors envisaged did not, however, materialize, and Transylvanian Romanian culture did not undergo a serious Romantic revolution until 1848.

In Moldavia and Wallachia, Greek princes and successive Russian invasions against the Turks (1768–74; 1788–92; 1806–12; 1822; 1828–34; 1848–49) brought not only destruction and famine, but also new ideas, utopian projects, European fashions, and the attention of diplomats and political philosophers. Grigory Aleksandrovich Potemkin published the first newspaper in Iaşi in French, the *Courier de Moldavie* (1790); local boyars subscribed to Western gazettes; women came to the table, learned to waltz, and were seen reading French novels. Italian, German, and Greek theater companies toured the capitals.

After the Greek revolt of 1821, the Ottomans replaced the Greek princes with native Romanians, but the key phase came after 1829, when a Russian protectorate was formally established: this meant not only a modern constitution, but a public school system, official newspapers, secular printing houses, societies, *cabinets de lecture*, and so on, not to mention censorship. Romanian publications in Wallachia and Moldavia began to outnumber those in more Western Transylvania, and secular works to outnumber religious ones, although literacy remained confined to a tiny elite. Modernization was conceived in terms of establishing structures of order and good behavior: a conservative, official Romanticism was condoned by the authorities. We now see not only translations (which continue in the 1830s: Lord Byron, Alphonse Marie Louis de Lamartine, Aleksandr Pushkin, Johann Christoph Friedrich von Schiller), but original poetical production in book form. In Wallachia, poets like Vasile Cârlova, Ion

Heliade Rădulescu, and others apostrophized the landscape in stereotypical Romantic terms (ancient ruins, yearning for the historic and personal past, idealization of rural folk such as shepherds), while others like Grigore Alexandrescu imitated older models, particularly Jeau Lafontaine's fables, to disguise a more modern, politically critical message. The historian and revolutionary Nicolae Bălcescu published sources and documents in the *Magazin istoric pentru Dacia* (1845–48) and left unfinished his epic study of the reign of the medieval prince Michael the Brave. In Moldavia, the schools inspector Gheorghe Asachi churned out neo-Petrarchan verses of some interest, as well as the country's first lithographs; while his younger rival Mihai Kogălniceanu modernized Romanian literature in all fields. His review *Dacia litterară* (1840), though closed by the authorities after a year, established a critical basis for Romanian literature, and published the first successful historical novella in Romanian, his friend Constantin Negruzzi's (c. 1812–68) *Alexandru Lăpuşneanu*. Kogălniceanu also collaborated with Vasile Alecsandri in running Moldavia's state theater from 1840 to 1843, where a "national" repertoire was built up out of comedies adapted from the French and often satirizing the social changes of which they were part.

The assumption of Romanticism thus both prepared Romanians for national development and the revolutionary messianism of 1848; and constructed a teleology of expectations and repertoire of postures for the recovery of cultural legibility. A Romantic paradigm was prolonged to the end of the nineteenth century: Romania's national poet Mihai Eminescu, whose work belongs to a later period and will not be discussed here, has been described as "Europe's last Romantic," while many standard Romantic stereotypes have endured up to today. However superficial the immediate effects of Romantic ideology on society as a whole, the resulting intellectual schism was profound.

ALEXANDER DRACE-FRANCIS

Bibliography

Beiu-Paladi, Luminita. "Bibliographie du romantisme roumain (contributions)," *Cahiers roumains d'études littéraires* 2 (1978): 82–100.

Bochmann, Klaus. *Der Politisch-soziale Wortschatz des Rumänischen von 1821 bis 1850*. Berlin: Akademie, 1979.

Călinescu, G. *History of Romanian Literature from Its Origins to the Present Day* [1941]. 4th edn. Translated by Leon Levitchi. Milan: Nagard/UNESCO 1988.

Cornea, Paul. *Originile romantismului românesc*. Bucharest: Minerva, 1972.

Durandin, Catherine. *Révolution à la française ou à la russe. Polonais, Roumains et Russes au XIXe siècle*. Paris: Presses Universitaires de France, 1989.

Duţu, Alexandru. *European Intellectual Movements and Modernization of Romanian Culture*. Bucharest: Academy of the Romanian Socialist Republic, 1981.

Eliade, P. *La Roumanie au XIXe siècle*. 2 vols. Paris: E. Leroux, 1914.

Georgescu, Vlad. *Political Ideas and the Enlightenment in the Romanian Principalities 1750–1831*. Translated by Mary Lăzărescu. Boulder, Colo.: East European Monographs, 1971.

Hitchins, Keith. *The Romanians 1774–1866*. Oxford: Clarendon Press, 1996.

Marino, Adrian. *Littérature roumaine—littératures occidentales. Rencontres*. Translated by Annie Bentoiu. Bucarest: Enciclopedică, 1981.

Michelet, Jules. "Légendes démocratiques du Nord," 1853. In *Oeuvres completes*. Vol 16. Paris: Flammarion, 1980.

Pippidi, Andrei. *Hommes et idées du sud-est européen à l'aube de l'âge moderne*. Paris and Bucarest: CNRS—Académie Roumaine, 1980.

Popovici, D. *La littérature roumaine à l'époque des lumières*. Sibiu: Centru de Studii şi Cercetări privitoare la Transilvania, 1945.

Quinet, Edgar. *Les Roumains*. In *Oeuvres*. Vol. 6. Paris: Pagnerre, 1856.

Zub, Al, ed. *La révolution française et les Roumains. Études à l'occasion du bicentenaire*. Iaşi: Université "Al. I. Cuza," 1989.

DIE ROMANTISCHE SCHULE (THE ROMANTIC SCHOOL) 1832–1835

Collection of literary essays by Heinrich Heine

These literary and philosophical essays were first published in France in 1832 under the title *État actuel de la littérature en Allemagne*. They appeared the following year in German, as excerpts entitled *Zur Geschichte der neueren schönen Literatur in Deutschland* and were later published in an extended and somewhat modified form in 1835 as *Die Romantische Schule*. The work, divided into three parts, comprises a series of essays that herald Heinrich Heine's move away from the idealism of the age of Johann Wolfgang von Goethe and the Romantics toward his adoption of the political agenda of the literary *Vormärz*, a period that lasted from the French July Revolution to the German revolutions of 1848–49. He wrote the book as a response to Madame Anne-Louise-Germaine de Staël, partly as a continuation of her work beyond 1810, partly to counter her somewhat idealistic and openly pro-German version of the cultural and literary scene in Germany during the Napoleonic age. Heine, who in his younger years had been part of Germany's Romantic movement, displays in these essays an element of self-hatred,

reinforced by his experience as a Jew as an exile in Paris. The most significant aspect of his witty, unashamedly subjective style is the sardonic irony that he employs to ridicule even the most esteemed figures of German literature and dislodge them from their Olympian heights. The book should also be read as Heine's attempt to vindicate "the natural rights of matter against the usurpation of the spirit," expressing his own belief in humanist sensualism as opposed to Romantic spiritualism. For Heine, this work represents both an attack on spiritualism and a defense of Hellenic sensualism, the emancipation of the flesh. By concentrating on the later Romantic movement, he neglects the philosophical dimension, particularly with regard to Friedrich von Schlegel. Viewing the present in almost exclusively materialistic terms and reflecting popular Saint-Simonism, Heine fails to appreciate Schlegel's idealistic and utopian concerns with his own age. The death of Goethe (1832), associated with the end of the *Kunstperiode*, an age defined by culture and art rather than politics, proved a turning point in Heine's understanding of literary history. The outdated aristocratic order was to be overthrown by a revolution, albeit within the confines of philosophy and literature.

Heine defines Romanticism primarily in a typological sense, unrelated to any specific period. The term *school*, however, signifies a particular era; it was deployed to castigate those followers of some spiritualized Christendom, which itself provided "proven support for despotism" and measured "the present time by the norms of the past." Heine's venom is directed primarily against August Wilhelm and Friedrich von Schlegel and Ludwig Tieck, while Goethe is portrayed as the pagan Jupiter who elevated himself on a pedestal above the contemporary scene. Heine relates Goethe's criticism of the Romantics, while remaining silent about the many testimonies of support the younger representatives had received from him in earlier years. Acutely aware of the period's major tendencies, Heine is often wrong when it comes to detail and is chiefly responsible for stereotyping Romanticism as an age of sickness, in contrast to the healthy well-being of pagan and rationalist ages.

Book 1 describes how the Christian Middle Ages took over from antiquity. In Heine's words, "Rome, the Hercules among nations, was consumed by the Judaic poison, to the extent that his helmet and armor slid off his limp body and his imperious battlecry degenerated into the whimpering of priestly prayer and the trilling of castrati." Romanticism, in aspiring toward infinity and spiritualism, had to rely on the parabolic and the symbolic, expressing human suffering and pain as tortured ugliness and sublime renunciation. Marlin Luther's Protestantism represented the first revolt against this spiritualist subversion, although Renaissance art had afforded a more genuine emancipation of the flesh: "the loins of [Titian's] Venus are far more effective as theses than those which the German monk stuck on the church door at Wittenberg." Heine accuses the Romantic generation of a patriotism, based not on humanism and love of freedom, but on a fawning devotion to their princes. Goethe's position is ambivalent; praised as a great free thinker and sensualist, he is also criticized for proclaiming art to be the greatest good, an attitude which induced indifference and callousness. His works are compared to barren statues, which in their sterility cannot contribute toward "a regeneration of the fatherland."

Book 2 focuses on the first generation of German Romantics. Heine's attack on August Wilhelm Schlegel is merciless and deeply personal, descending into a mischievous description of his physical appearance. In Schlegel's younger years "on top of his thin head gleamed just a few silvery locks and his body was so lean, so emaciated, so transparent, that it seemed all spirit. . . ." In later years, he became all body with no spirit: "his thin spiritualist legs had acquired some flesh, one could even see a belly and above it a multitude of ribbons with decorations. A yellow wig adorned his otherwise ancient little head. He was dressed in the height of fashion of the year in which Mme de Staël had died." Both Schlegel brothers are accorded some merit for their literary style and their translations, but are otherwise dismissed as void of talent. Ludwig Tieck fares slightly better. Heine praises his early literary work and his translations of Miguel de Cervantes Saavedra and William Shakespeare, but his quixotic Catholicism and inept imitation of Goethe are ridi-

culed. Friedrich Wilhelm Joseph von Schelling, too, is derided for having betrayed his philosophy of identity in favor of "catholic propaganda." E. T. A. Hoffmann and Novalis are both assessed in pathological terms, one in the grip of some grotesque fever, the other subject to a debilitating consumptive spiritualism.

Book 3 deals with the Heidelberg circle, representatives of the *Schwäbische Schule*, together with Jean Paul and the new literature of the Young Germany school. Although Achim von Arnim and Clemens Brentano are attacked for a catholic agenda, their collection of folk songs, *Des Knaben Wunderhorn* (*The Boy's Magic Horn*, 1805–08) is applauded for presenting the common folk in a realistic manner, free of all sentimentality. Heine is also appreciative of their modern fantastic style, aesthetic rather than pathological in tone, which is also evident in Tieck's plays and in Paul's narrative (although compared to Laurence Sterne, Jean Paul's ironic style falls all too easily into sentimental emotion). Karl Gutzkow, Heinrich Laube, and other representatives of the Young Germany school are compared to Jean Paul, dedicating their writing to the present with a passionate belief in progress. Friedrich Heinrich Karl de Fouqué, Ludwig Uhland, and Zacharias Werner gain some respect for reaching out to the people and for their more realistic presentation of the Middle Ages, but are ultimately regarded as irrelevant, belonging to a past generation and lacking in originality. Joseph von Eichendorff is mentioned only in passing. Heine ends with a return to the Middle Ages and a comparison of its reception in France and Germany. While the French evince only a superficial, artistic interest in this period, the Germans are deemed to "have dragged the Middle Ages from the grave" in order to undermine the freedom and the good of the fatherland.

While Heine's discussion of the Romantic period has lost nothing of its pertinence and still serves as an interesting introduction, it should be read with caution. In order to accommodate his sometime expressed belief in progressive sensualism, Heine perpetuates such stereotypes as that of the "blue flower" and reactionary religiosity.

HANS-JOACHIM HAHN

Text

Heinrich Heine. *Die Romantische Schule*. Critical edition edited by Helga Weidmann. Stuttgart: Reclam, 1976. Translated as *The Romantic School* by C. G. Leland in *The Works of Heinrich Heine*. 1891–1905. Also translated in *Travel-pictures, including the Tour in the Harz, Norderney and Book of Ideas, together with The Romantic School*, by F. Storr. 1887.

Bibliography

Bohrer, Karl Heinz. "Heinrich Heine: *Die romantische Schule*." In *Die Kritik der Romantik*. Edited by Karl Heinz Bohrer. Frankfurt: Suhrkamp, 1989.

Clasen, Herbert. *Heinrich Heines Romantikkritik. Tradition-Produktion-Rezeption*. Hamburg: Hoffman und Campe, 1979.

Hohendahl, Peter-Uwe. "Geschichte und Modernität. Heines Kritik an der Romantik," *Jahrbuch der deutschen Schillergesellschaft* 17 (1973): pp 318–61.

Iggers, Georg G. "Heine and the Saint-Simonians: A Re-examination." *Comparative Literature* 10 (1958): pp 289–308.

ROMANZERO (ROMANCERO) 1851

Collection of poems by Heinrich Heine

Romanzero is the third of the four collections of poems that Heinrich Heine prepared in his lifetime. Having regained the favor of his Hamburg publisher Campe, Heine promised that the book would constitute "the third pillar of my poetic fame," alongside the early *Buch der Lieder* (*Book of Songs*) of 1827 and the *Neue Gedichte* (*New Poems*) of 1844. In important ways, the third collection is a marked departure from the earlier work: its title, a Germanicized spelling of the Spanish *romancero* (a collection of romances), was Campe's suggestion, though Heine claimed it reflected the dominant lyric tone of the volume. The first section, "Historien" ("Tales") draws on the traditions of ballad and romance, and broadly Spanish local color appears in a number of poems, notably "The Moorish King," "Spanish Atrides," "Vitzliputzli" on Cortez and the Aztecs, and the poem of the Jewish poets of medieval Spain, "Jehuda ben Halevy." In reality, however, the title was designed to cash in on the success of similar publications across Europe. Campe marketed *Romanzero* vigorously, and until political proscription and uncomprehending reviews ("repellent frivolities," "bestialities") intervened, it met with tremendous success, going into a second print run only weeks after its appearance. Heine seems to anticipate this very modern approach to the book market in poems that reflect on the fate of poetry in the cash nexus ("The Poet Firdausi") and the survival of the poetic tradition in the world of commodities ("Jehuda ben Halevy").

The poems included in *Romanzero* were written, with very few exceptions, between 1844 and 1851, and the majority of these, as Heine states in his postscript, were composed between 1848 and 1849. This historical genesis means that in many poems Heine engages with the very process of modernity as it had been experienced through the revolutions of 1848 and their aftermath. Heine tells Campe he is a maestro of organization ("Meister der Anordnung"). The systematic disposition of poems in lyric sequences and within a larger architecture, which had made *Buch der Lieder* a cryptic autobiography, is deployed in the later collection to develop an historical argument: the Tales present universal decline from the comic *lèse majesté* experienced by King "Rhampsinitus" of Egypt and the *noblesse oblige* enforced on his betters by the "Knave of Bergen," through the certainty of the "Valkyries" or on "The Battlefield at Hastings" that "the worst will win the day." Beyond simply chronicling this story of moral and physical defeat, Heine's poems capture the very moment of historical change.

While "Karl I" appears to *rehearse* the popular form of the ballad, with the reminiscences of a feudal-aristocratic society appropriate to its genre, Heine's poem opens up the generic text to contemporary reference. Its first publication, in 1847, meditated on a moment before the decisive act of regicide. As Charles I sings to the child who could prove to be his executioner, the ballad projects both the anxieties of a feudal order, aware of the growth of forces which will ultimately overthrow it, and the ideological lullaby that is designed to prevent those forces from recognizing their own strength. Reprinted in *Romanzero* after 1848, however, the ballad evokes a recognition that democratic aspirations have come to nothing. The simple chronological parallel between 1649 and 1847–49 provides the groundwork for a complex argument about literature (the ballad as a popular form), ideology (the maintenance of feudal order in Germany), and revolutionary change. This is a pessimism of the intellect without much optimism of the will, and it finally resolves into postrevolutionary disappointment. The argument of the poem hence remains historical; it can at most take the measure of a *deferred* modernity, which modern readers sense as an element of pastiche in "Karl I." The great poems at the center of the Tales ("Pomare" on the fate of a Parisian grisette; "The God Apollo," reimagining the god as a shabby street performer) express this sense of disappointment as a secular experience of disenchantment.

Under the biblical title "Lamentations," the second book of *Romanzero* articulates the encounter with modernity as a farewell to the diction and sylvan imagery of German Romanticism, before settling accounts with old friends and enemies (Franz Dingelstedt, Georg Herwegh, August Graf von Platen and his followers). Then an extraordinary cycle of twenty poems under the general title "Lazarus" introduces the pain and illness of Heine's last years. The ironic disillusionment of Heine's earlier verse undergoes here, according to David Constantine, a "mortal intensification." The political defeats of 1848–49 still resonate ("The Dying," "In October 1849"), but they are registered through and even *as* Heine's own physical debility after 1848: increasing paralysis leaves him marking time in both senses, immobilized but also providing a measure of the times. Everything from the memory of a friend's death in childhood ("Memory") to the prospect of anniversaries of his own death (in "Commemoration Service"), and the persistent anger caused by arguments with his cousins over his inheritance, provides a correlative for the dereliction of the liberal cause after the revolutions. In this Lazarus cycle (and later there were to be more poems associated with the same persona), Heine devises a poetry of great simplicity and directness, couched in a plain style that can still cling to the modest pleasures of the everyday while facing disease and death.

There is no sign here of the return to religious belief that had been rumored before *Romanzero* appeared. The first two poems of the three making up the last book, "Hebrew Melodies," variously recall the traditions of Judaism and Jewish culture. "Princess Sabbath" evokes the splendor of the Sabbath feast, but finally dwells on the disenchantment and poverty of the diaspora: the last of the Sabbath lights to be extinguished repeats the dying of the light at the end of Lazarus 18: "It goes out." "Jehuda ben Halevy" sees the very idea of Jewish tradition threatened with extinction, and the whole collection ends on a dissonance when the argument between the Rabbinical and Franciscan theologians of "Disputation" is simply abandoned.

ANTHONY PHELAN

Text

Romanzero. 1851. Published in the critical edition *Historisch-kritische Gesamtausgabe*. Vol. 3.1 edited by Frauke Bartelt and Alberto Destro. 1992. Vol. 3.2 edited by Bernd Kortländer.

1997. Translated as *Romancero* by Margaret Armour, 1905. Also translated as *Romancero* by Hal Draper in *The Complete Poems of Heinrich Heine*. Oxford: Oxford University Press, 1982.

Bibliography

Bayerdörfer, Hans-Peter. "Politische Ballade: Zu den 'Historien' in Heines Romanzero," *Deutsche Vierteljahrsschrift* 46 (1972): 435–68.

Constantine, David. "Heine's Lazarus Poems." in *Heine und die Weltliteratur*. Edited by T. J. Reed and Alexander Stillmark. Oxford: Legenda, 2000.

Cook, Roger, F. *By the Rivers of Babylon: Heinrich Heine's Late Songs and Reflections*. Detroit: Wayne State University Press, 1998.

Höhn, Gerhard. *Heine-Handbuch: Zeit, Person, Werk*. 2d ed. Stuttgart: Metzler, 1997.

Prawer, S. S. *Heine, The Tragic Satirist*. Cambridge: Cambridge University Press, 1961.

ROSMINI SERBATI, ANTONIO 1797–1855

Italian philosopher

Antonio Rosmini Serbati, along with Pasquale Galluppi (1770–1846) and Vincenzo Gioberti (1801–1852), was one of the most significant representatives of spiritualism, a characteristically Romantic movement in nineteenth-century Italian philosophy.

Rosmini wished to lay the foundation for an objective philosophy which would act as a counterpoint to the skepticism that had emerged during the Enlightenment. He strongly believed that philosophy, science, and religion were different means working toward the same end, and should thus be regarded as cooperative, not oppositional. Rosmini considered faith and reason to be "the two wings on which the human spirit rises to the contemplation of truth." Regardless of those adversaries, both secular and clerical, who disagreed, Rosmini trusted that an objective truth could be attained. However, his ideas were met with little enthusiasm outside Italy (with the exception, to some degree, of England).

Rosmini believed that salvation and the perfection of the soul were essential for all humankind. Based on this conviction, he founded the Institute of Charity. Rosmini's spiritual pupil and closest friend was Alessandro Manzoni, the great Italian Romantic writer.

Rosmini himself wrote more than one hundred works, most of them published during his life. *Nuovo saggio sull'origine delle idee* (1830) is considered his most important writing, and his philosophical masterpiece. Rosmini addresses and questions fundamental assumptions concerning the development and lineage of philosophical ideas. In his opinion, the connections traced by his predecessors between various theories and schools and thought were inadequate.

He goes on to offer his opinions and thoughts on a variety of major philosophical thinkers. The introduction to *Nuovo saggio sull'origine delle idee* is a meditation on the achievements of Condillac, John Locke, and the Scottish school of philosophers. He considers Immanuel Kant's theories and assails David Hume forcefully. Rosmini also writes on the Scottish thinkers Thomas Reid and Dugald Stewart, and on transcendental idealism. He emphasizes the great strides made by these thinkers in their attempts to unlock philosophical truths.

Rosmini places an especially high value on innatism, drawn from the Platonic tradition and reconsidered by Christian philosophers including St. Augustine, Thomas Aquinas, Bonaventure, and others. Referring to reason metaphorically as "light," the essential component of human consciousness that cannot be modified, he concludes by stating that the intellect simply cannot exist without this so-called light, for in the light of reason, all things are seen for what they truly are. Reason is received by humankind as the basis of their sacred dignity and rights as conscious beings (thus the term *light* highlights associations with divinity as well as knowledge). Errors in judgment may dim the light of reason, but it is never put out. Its continual presence within the individual's soul allows retained connection with God, justifies the human yearning for immortality and guides the individual, as long as he or she recognizes that its source is essential and beyond the self. Morality, justice, and human dignity and rights appear to be embedded in the objective state being, not in limited subjectivity.

However, the existence and role of subjectivity is not disregarded. Rosmini argues that the fundamental functioning of human thought is a result of continual improvements to, and refinement of, the senses and emotions. He individually lays out the facets of the individual soul that, when taken together, deliver a useful and simple method of accurately assessing his theory on reason. Rosmini acknowledges that the light of being, the objective part of the human intellect, results in the concept of measure of certitude, the power of a priori reasoning and the first division of the sciences. Certainty, while solid and rational, must adapt to truth. The strength and proportion of a priori reasoning is rated to demonstrate where it may carry the intellect without the help of sensory and emotional knowledge, how it can emphasize the importance of rational rules of thought, and how the philosopher may ultimately propose those corollaries that prove the existence of a supreme being.

Delle cinque piaghe della Santa Chiesa (1848) is the best-known of Rosmini's works. In this political and religious writing he condemns the subjugation of the Catholic Church to temporal power. The work was condemned by the church and led to Rosmini's repeated persecution, particularly by the Jesuits. Eventually he was rehabilitated, and his canonization has been in process since 1994.

Other important works are: *Dell'educazione cristiana* (1823), *Saggio sull'unità dell'educazione* (1826), *Costituzioni dell'Istituto della Carità* (1828), *Massime di perfezione cristiana* (1830), *Panegirico di Pio VII* (1831), *Principi della scienza morale* (1831), *Storia dell'Amore cavata dalle Divine Scritture* (1834), *Frammenti di una storia della empietà* (1834), *Il rinnovamento della filosofia in Italia* (1836), *Principio della scienza morale e storia comparativa e critica dei sistemi intorno al principio della morale* (1837), *Catechetica* (1838), *Antropologia in servizio della scienza morale* (1838), *Prose ecclesiastiche* (1838–50), *Trattato della coscienza morale* (1839–40), *Manuale dell'esercitatore* (1841), *Filosofia del diritto* (1841–45), *Teodicea* (1845), *Psicologia* (*Psychology*, 1846–50), *La costituzione secondo la giustizia sociale: con un'appendice sull'unità d'Italia ed una lettera sull'elezione dei vescovi a clero e popolo* (1848), *Lettere sulle elezioni vescovili* (1849), *Il comunismo ed il socialismo* (*Communism and Socialism*, 1849), *Introduzione alla filosofia* (*Introduction to Philosophy*, 1850), *Risposta ad Agostino Theiner* (1850), *Logica* (*Logic*, 1854), *Catechismo disposto secondo l'ordine delle idee* (1854) and the posthumously published: *Del principio supremo, della metodica e di alcune sue applicazioni al servizio dell'umana educazione* (1857), *Aristotele esposto ed esaminato* (1857), *Teosofia* (1859–74), *Della missione a Roma di Antonio Rosmini negli anni 1848–49* (1881), *L'introduzione del Vangelo secondo San Giovanni* (1882), *Saggio storico critico sulle categorie e la dialettica* (1882), *Antropologia soprannaturale* (1884), and *Epistolario completo* (*Complete Letters*, 1887–94).

ELVIO CIFERRI

See also **Catholicism**

Biography

Born in Rovereto, Italy, on March 24, 1797, the second child of the noble Pier Modesto and Giovanna countess Formenti di Biascesa. Studied theology at Padova University and on April 21, 1821 was ordained a priest. In 1828, founded the religious order Institute of Charity (Rosminians) and in 1830 the Sisters of Providence. In 1838, with the consent of the Pope Gregory XVI, became Father Superior of the order he had founded. In the years 1848–49 was the ambassador of King Charles Albert of Piedmont in Rome and Gaeta, where the pontifical court was based. Died on July 1, 1855, at Stresa, of liver disease.

Works

Psichology. 1884–88.
The Ruling Principle of Method Applied to Education. Trans. W. Grey. 1887.
Epistolario completo. 1887–94.
Opere. Edited by E. Castelli. 46 vols.; incomplete. Roma: Fratelli Bocca, 1934–75.
Opere edite ed inedite. Edited by International Center of Rosminian Studies of Stresa. Roma: Città Nuova Editrice. 1977– .
Anthropology as an Aid to Moral Science. Trans. D. Cleary and T. Watson. Durham: Rosmini House, 1991.
The Philosophy of Politics. Trans. D. Cleary and T. Watson. Durham: Rosmini House, 1994.
Carteggio Alessandro Manzoni-Antonio Rosmini. Edited by G. Bonola. Stresa: Edizioni Rosminiane, 1996.

Bibliography

Bessero Belti, R. "Rosmini Serbati Antonio." In *Bibliotheca Sanctorum*. Rome: Città Nuova Editrice, 2000.
Bergamaschi, C. *Bibliografia degli scritti editi di Rosmini*. Milan: Marzorati, 1970–99.
———. *Bibliografia rosminiana.* Milan: Marzorati, 1967–99.
———. *Grande dizionario antologico del pensiero di Antonio Rosmini.* Rome: Città Nuova Editrice, 1997.
Cleary, D. *Antonio Rosmini, Introduction to His Life and Teaching.* Durham: Rosmini House, 1992.
De Paoli, N. *Antonio Rosmini: una lunga storia d'amore.* Cinisello Balsamo: San Paolo, 1997.
Lockhart, W. *Life of the Rev. Antonio Rosmini, Founder of the Institute of Charity.* 1883.
Pagani, G. B. *Il Rosmini e gli uomini del suo tempo.* Florence: Giannini, 1918.
———. *Vita di Antonio Rosmini.* 1897. Translated as *The Life of Antonio Rosmini.* London: George Routledge and Sons, 1907.
Paoli, F. *Della vita di Antonio Rosmini.* 1880.
Tommaseo, N. *Antonio Rosmini.* Turin. 1855.
Valle, A. *Antonio Rosmini, il carisma del fondatore.* Rovereto: Longo, 1991.

ROSSINI, GIOACCHINO ANTONIO 1792–1868

Italian composer

Gioacchino Antonio Rossini's life—though not his work—spans a period of fundamental change in opera. His crucial part in that transformation is beyond question, but there is some dispute about the nature and extent of his influence and there is continuing puzzlement regarding his early retirement from the operatic stage: his last opera *Guillauame Tell* (*William Tell*, 1829) appeared when he was thirty-seven. He then retired, a *bon viveur* in Paris, and died at the age of seventy-six. In the later period of his life he wrote no operas, but (apart from a series of exquisite trifles) he composed a *Stabat Mater* (1833) and the distinctive *Petite messe solennelle* (1864).

Rossini refurbished the forms, vocal style, size and treatment of the chorus, and the orchestral writing of a medium that had become stale and stultified. He transformed the function of the orchestra and curtailed the worst excesses of singers. While he changed some aspects of the content of Italian opera, his drama-turgy, characterization and psychological values remained mostly within eighteenth-century bounds and, as with many Italians, he remained suspicious of trans-Alpine Romantic values and subjective expressiveness. This lack of sympathy with Romantic ideals offers one rationale for his reluctance to write new stage works after 1829, when such values (most clearly typified by Giacomo Meyerbeer) became dominant. Other reasons involved extensive litigation after a change of regime in France, which deprived Rossini of his contractual income. By the time the litigation was settled (in Rossini's favor) he had long been retired.

From his earliest opera, Rossini's works display vitality of rhythm, sensuality, and brilliance. These characteristics are most directly evident in his comic works, while his equally remarkable *opere serie* and mixed-genre works faded from the stage after Rossini's retirement. The finesse and quality of such serious works as *Semiramide* (1823) were not fully appreciated until the second half of the twentieth century. This was partly because the agile, mellifluous bel canto singing required by these works was displaced in favor of the greater power and weight required by larger Romantic works, and partly because the characterization, dramaturgy, and ethos of his serious works belong to the stratified social structures of a pre-Romantic age.

His influence and power during his own lifetime rested not only on his undoubted abilities, but also on a transformation of the status of the operatic composer. Until Rossini's time, the operatic composer stood below singers and librettists, both in stature and in material remuneration. Rossini achieved a remarkable financial independence that augmented his growing artistic stature and that enabled him to make demands on singers and theatrical management beyond any envisioned by his predecessors. This elevation of the individual composer (as well as the material success that Rossini earned) made him both a model and the envy of Romantic composers, especially those (such as Hector Berlioz) who faced a constant struggle for recognition.

Rossini's great successes in Milan and Venice in 1812 and 1813 caused Domenico Barbaia, the shrewd gaming magnate and powerful impresario of the Neapolitan Teatro di San Carlo, to invite Rossini to Naples. Although very conservative, the Teatro di San Carlo at that time was the most lavishly financed and equipped opera house in Europe. Barbaia had also gathered a splendid roster of singers whom Rossini deployed to superb effect. Particularly in the nine works written for the San Carlo Company (and the nine works written for other cities during his six-year tenure in the Neapolitan position) Rossini developed his most radical technique and wide-ranging subject matter. During this period he also, however subtly, absorbed some of the technical advances of Germanic music.

For too long Rossini was considered to be casual in his attitude toward dramatic texts. This view coincides with the fiction about his laziness, the notion of which was assiduously cultivated by Rossini himself. Both characterizations probably mask a hardworking, obsessive personality with tendencies toward depression and anxiety. These myths must be dismissed as a studied pretense on Rossini's part that numerous documents belie. If one considers his background, Rossini was unusually well-read and devoted great care to the choice and treatment of his texts. Even a superficial examination of his work shows a remarkable range. He selected originals by Voltaire (*Tancredi*, 1813; *Semiramide*, 1823), William Shakespeare (*Otello*, 1816), Pierre-Augustin Caron de Beaumarchais (*Il Barbiere di Siviglia*, 1816), Torquato Tasso (*Armida*, 1817) Sir Walter Scott (*La donna del lago*, 1819), Jean Racine (*Ermione*, 1819), and Johann Christoph Friedrich von Schiller (*Guillaume Tell*, 1929).

The contract that Barbaia offered Rossini was worth between 8,000 and 120,000 francs. It required Rossini to compose, administrate, and supervise the musical preparation of his own operas as well as those of other composers. However, the contract also included shares in Barbaia's gambling syndicate and this formed the basis of an independent fortune that enabled Rossini to become more selective in the projects that he accepted. This in turn allowed Rossini to devote greater care and time to the execution of each work, and to make heavier demands on his performers, despite his pretense of indolence.

Rossini's success and his operatic treatment reestablished Italian opera as a leader on the international scene and profoundly affected all his Italian successors. It also exposed them to a range of Romantic subjects and to some of the technical transformations of French and Austro-German music. Even in retirement, Rossini kept a close watch on current affairs and supported younger singers and composers. Every composer of note visited him in Paris (most famously a long visit by Richard Wagner) and paid close attention to Rossini's works and techniques. He not only transformed Italian opera (in all its genres), but also blended the French and Italian traditions in such works as the epic political drama of *Guilllaume Tell* and the comic *Le Conte Ory* (*Count Ory*, 1828). These (as well as his Italian compositions) greatly influenced such diverse and important Romantic composers as Hector Berlioz, Giacomo Meyerbeer, Jacques Offenbach, and Richard Wagner. This influence was primarily technical, in that they admired his operatic stagecraft and vocal finesse. They also, inevitably, envied his enormous material success.

In his own time, Rossini was admired as *the* supreme master of the operatic stage. He enabled those who followed to create a modern dramatic medium that could articulate newer dramatic subjects. He radically influenced the structure and scale of French grand opera and set the example, which Meyerbeer extended to a new magnitude. Conversely, he was not sympathetic to the ethos of personal subjectivity nor to the harmonically intensified musical manner of the Romantics, and this probably contributed to his withdrawal from the operatic stage. Consequently, his reputation diminished during the second half of the nineteenth century, resting on a few comic operas and the continued popularity of his overtures. During the latter part of the twentieth century, when Romanticism had run its course, he was rediscovered and shown to be a remarkable composer not only of comic, but also mixed genre and serious opera. The appearance of a new breed of singers (such as Montserrat Caballe, Maria Callas, Marilyn Horne, and Conchita Supervia), and a postmodernist revisionism have made possible a vivid revival of Rossini's reputation and work. A new, critical edition of his complete works is in progress and this should lead to further clarification and deeper evaluation of his output.

BENEDICT SARNAKER

Biography

Born 1792 in Pesaro, Italy, of musical parents. His father was a famous horn player (and public *trombetta* of Pesaro), his mother an able singer. Rossini appeared on stage as a boy soprano and entered Bologna's prestigious Accademia Filharmonica at the precocious age of fourteen. He was greatly influenced in his vocal style by the Spanish soprano Isabella Colbran (whom he later married) and the castrato Velluti (whose purity of tone, flexibility, and penetrating accent formed the model for Rossini's vocal writing). He left the academy prematurely and wrote a number of successful one-act *farse* for the Teatro S. Moisè in Venice. In these works he established a very useful structural plan that later became the template for the first act of his larger comic operas. At this time he also formulated and refined the operatic overture whose vitality, formal control, and orchestral brilliance continue to delight concert audiences.

Huge successes in Milan with *La pietra del paragone* (*The Touchstone*, 1812) and in Venice with *Tancredi* (1813) spread his fame nationally and led to a contract in Naples that transformed his career. He remained in Naples for six years. Major seasons of his works (in Vienna in 1822 and London in 1824) and his increasing dissatisfaction with the Italian operatic process caused him to settle in Paris in 1824 and he became the *éminance grise* of Franco-Italian opera. He died in Passy, France in 1868.

Selected Works

Tancredi. 1813.
Il barbiere di Siviglia. 1816.
La Cenerentola. 1817.
La gazza ladra. 1817.
Armida. 1817.
Mosé in Egitto. 1818.
Ermione. 1819.
La donna del lago. 1819.
Semiramide. 1823.
Guillaume Tell. 1829.

Bibliography

Cagli, Bruno, Philip Gossett, and Alberto Zedda. "Criteri per l'edizione critica delle opre di Gioachino Rossini," *Bolletino del Centro rossiniano di studi, 1.* (1974): Fondazione Rossini Pesaro.

Emanuele, Marco. *L'ultima stagione italiana: le forme dell'opera seria di Rossini da Napoli a Venezia*. Florence: Passigli 1997.

Gossett, Philip. "Le fonti autografe delle opere teatrali di Rossini," *Nuova rivista musicale italiana 2* (1968): 936.

———. "Gioachino Rossini and the Conventions of Composition," *Acta musicolsogica 42* (1970): 48–58.

Mount Edgcumbe, R. *Musical Reminiscences of an Old Amateur*. 1824.

Radiciotti, Giuseppe. *Gioacchino Rossini: vita documentata, opere ed influenza su l'arte*. 3 Vols. Tivoli: Arti grafiche Majella di A. Chicca, 1927–29.

Righetti-Giorgi, Geltrude. *Cenni di una donna già cantante sopra il maestro Rossini*. 1823.

Rognoni, Luigi Gioacchino. *Rossini*. Turin: ERI, 1968.

Stendhal. *Rome, Naples, et Florence en 1817*. 1817.

———. *Vie de Rossini*. 1824.

Toye, Francis. *Rossini: a Study in Tragi-Comedy*. London: A. Barker, 1954.

Viviani, Vittorio, ed. *I libretti di Rossini*. Milan, 1965.

Weinstock, Herbert. *Rossini: A Biography*. New York: A. A. Knopf, 1968.

LE ROUGE ET LE NOIR (THE RED AND THE BLACK) 1830

Novel by Stendhal

Le Rouge et le Noir was conceived toward the end of the Restoration regime. It tells of the difficulties facing a young man attempting to make his way through post-Napoleonic French society. The choices that the character Julien Sorel faces are symbolized in the title: *le rouge* refers to the scarlet of military uniforms, *le noir* to the clergyman's attire. In this world where self-affirmation on the battlefield is no longer possible (the Battle of Waterloo is long since past), success seems merely to be a function of hypocrisy. Julien trains with local clergy, where his phenomenal memory of the Bible is developed, so as to impress his future employers, the Rênals of Verrières. The focus on the progression of Julien through French society (starting in provincial Verrières and reaching the salon culture of Paris), only to be catapulted back to the church at Verrières in the final part of the novel, offers a particular twist to that novelistic tradition often referred to as the bildungsroman, or novel of education. Such tales of parvenus who move up the social ladder were in keeping with the fantasy of social aspiration very much alive in the free-for-all that was capitalist bourgeois France.

In spite of his awareness of the political events of 1830 as he corrected the proofs for the novel, Stendhal did not choose to let such events change his text, as if he suspected that even such a radical rupture would not alter the fundamental dynamics of a society dominated by the greed of those on the make. Instead, he added a fictitious "publisher's note" that makes the false claim that the writing of the novel dates back to 1827. The events of the 1830 revolution are, he suggests, "peu favorable aux jeux de l'imagination" (unfavorable to the games of the imagination). For Stendhal, the democratizing process of 1830 may help the political modernization of France, but it is only under tyranny that the genius of the imagination is truly exercised. The playfulness of this reference is typical of the way in which Stendhal seems to authenticate his narrative only to pull the rug from under his reader's feet. If this is a *chronique de 1830*, as Stendhal claims, then it is one of a very peculiar kind, not least because during the representation of 1830 in this "contemporary" novel, when Louis-Philippe should replace the reactionary Charles X, nothing of the sort actually occurs.

Stendhal shows the conflict between amorous and social aspiration, as Julien is forced to choose between private and public versions of self-fulfillment. Is he to be the authentic lover? Or is love merely a script that he internalizes so as to make his way on the public stage? The binary choice in the title is itself thus subject to a further level of choice, between love and ambition, for Julien's bildungsroman consists in no small degree of learning how to use desired women in the service of professional or social self-advancement. The structure of the novel is itself a binary affair. Shortly after the encounter between Julien and his all-male family, he is sent to the Rênals, where he will serve as a tutor. Madame de Rênal is relieved to learn that he has no intention of beating her children. At one remove from the violence of his own family and the military ideal of masculinity, Julien succeeds in seducing the beautiful Madame de Rênal precisely because of the sensitivity that he thinks he must hide. The only thing she cannot resist are Julien's tears. Feminized and infantilized, it is in his relationship with Madame de Rênal that he finds the maternal figure missing from his own family.

This pattern of regression runs counter to the progressive structure of social aspiration as Julien is introduced to the salon culture of Paris, where he meets Mathilde de la Môle, the daughter of a powerful aristocrat. Madame de Rênal represents the *amour de coeur* of naive provincial love; Mathilde represents the glamour and intellectual sophistication of aristocratic society, and thus a means to his ultimate social goals. Theirs is an *amour de tête* and it is fitting that after Julien's execution Mathilde is offered merely his head. Their passion is presented by Stendhal as a threat not merely to the society depicted in the novel, but also as a provocative challenge to the novel as a genre. Just as we are invited to ask whether and how Julien might remain authentic in the face of the demands of ambition, so too we must ask whether the novel itself can maintain its authenticity while depicting a relationship that appeared to contemporary critics to be both immoral and implausible.

Once Mathilde has became pregnant by Julien, her father fulfills Julien's social ambition by bestowing on him a noble title. Julien's fantasy of being an aristocratic foundling has come to an end, and he can now proclaim that "mon roman est fini" (my novel is over). As with many of the nods and winks by which the narrator leads and misleads the reader, this observation is truer than Julien realizes. Madame de Rênal writes to Mathilde's father to embarrass Julien. In the most enigmatic moment of the novel, Julien returns to the church in Verrières and shoots her. Julien has in effect committed suicide and thrown away any chance of completing the bildungsroman of social success. It is as if we have entered another novel. Julien has torn up his script and returned to that maternal icon with whom he cannot stay and from whom he cannot quite escape. For all his ascents, displacements, and progressions, in psychosexual terms it seems that Julien is merely transposed between different versions of the same topographical enclosure, be it the walled town of Verrières, the garden at Vergy, the cells of the seminary, or the "happy prison" where our Romantic antihero finally finds peace.

NICHOLAS WHITE

Text

Le Rouge et le Noir. Paris, 1830. Translated as *The Red and the Black* by Catherine Slater. Oxford: Oxford University Press, 1991.

Bibliography

Auerbach, Erich. "In the Hôtel de la Mole." In *Mimesis.* Princeton, N.J.: Princeton University Press, 1953.

Bloom, Harold, ed. *Stendhal's "The Red and the Black."* New York: Chelsea House, 1988.

Brooks, Peter. "The novel and the Guillotine, or Fathers and Sons in *Le Rouge et le Noir.*" In *Reading for the Plot: Design and Intention in the Narrative.* New York: Knopf, 1984.

Haig, Stirling, *Stendhal: The Red and the Black.* Cambridge: Cambridge University Press, 1989.

Mitchell, John. *Stendhal, "Le Rouge et le Noir."* 1973.

Mossman, Carol A. *The Narrative Matrix: Stendhal's "Le Rouge et le Noir."* Lexington, Ky.: French Forum, 1984.

Mouillaud, Geneviève. *"Le Rouge et le Noir" de Stendhal: le roman possible.* Paris: Larousse, 1973.

Pearson, Roger, *Stendhal: "The Red and the Black" and "The Charterhouse of Parma."* London: Longman, 1994.

Prendergast, Christopher. "Stendhal: The Ethics of Verisimilitude." In *The Order of Mimesis.* Cambridge: Cambridge University Press, 1986.

ROUSSEAU, JEAN-JACQUES 1712–1778

Swiss philosopher

One of the most important philosophers of the post-Renaissance period and certainly one of the most controversial, Jean-Jacques Rousseau made original contributions in almost every field of the humanities—most notably, philosophy, political theory, autobiography, and sentimental fiction. Every genre he touched was transformed. Even today, his thought continues to provoke heated debate, a powerful testament to its dramatic—some would say devastating—influence on the course of modern history. The explosiveness of his work lies in its profound skepticism about the project of liberal enlightenment, a skepticism that manifests itself not in a series of open-ended inquiries (as in the work of his close contemporary Denis Diderot), but in a fervent and sustained critique. Rousseau is a perfect embodiment of the paradox at the heart of Romanticism in this respect: his thought exemplifies that profound ambivalence about progress that is the defining characteristic of modernity.

He was born in 1712, into a family of poor but respectable Genevan Protestants. After a disrupted early life (his mother died in childbirth, and his father left him in the care of relatives at the age of ten) he set out at sixteen on a life of wandering that took him all over Switzerland, southeastern France, and northern Italy. He converted to Catholicism during this period, and spent the years between 1733 and 1741 in the company of the Savoyard gentlewoman Louise de Warens, who was at first a kind of adopted mother to him and then his lover. During this time he worked hard to educate himself in philosophy and literature. With the awakening of ambition, he moved to Paris, intending to make his name as a dramatist and composer. There he made the acquaintance of D'Alembert, Diderot, Grimm, and Holbach, the leading lights of the French *éclaircissement*. It was during this time that he began his lifelong association with the serving girl Therese Le Vasseur, who bore him five children, all of whom were sent to the state orphanage in Paris as soon as they were born.

At the age of thirty-eight he burst upon the literary scene with his controversial *Discours sur les Arts et les Sciences*, which won the gold medal of the academy of Dijon in 1750. Another polemical essay, the *Discours sur l'Inégalité*, followed shortly afterward. Taken together, these works launch a daring critique of the Enlightenment concept of history-as-progress, comparing the enslavement and alienation of man in civilized society to the liberty and self-possession once enjoyed in "the state of nature." There was an eloquence and urgency about Rousseau's writing that contemporaries found impossible to ignore; but they were troubled from the beginning by its ambiguous rendering of the relationship between history and theory. What was the state of nature? Had it ever really existed, or was it merely a regulative idea? Would it be possible, or ever desirable, for modern man to stage a return? Rousseau's famously paradoxical style both encouraged and frustrated such inquiries, goading his readers to divest themselves of their civilized prejudices, and to think the unthinkable.

In the late 1750s Rousseau consolidated his position as the philosophical gadfly of the eighteenth century. His *Lettre à D'Alembert* (1758) offered an eloquent critique of the theater, reading it as a corrupt institution reflecting the iniquitous divisions of aristocratic society, most notably in the distinction it made between those who were privileged to act, and those condemned to merely observe. In place of the theater, Rousseau recommended the popular festivals of ancient Greece and modern Switzerland, utopian spaces of social unity and transparency in which every individual was both actor and spectator, spectacle, and audience. In this way the *Lettre* served to flesh out Rousseau's political critique of modernity while also elaborating his enthusiastic admiration of ancient republican forms. A couple of years later he produced his spectacularly popular epistolary novel, *Julie, ou la Nouvelle Heloise* (1761). In this book Rousseau explored every aspect of the new language of feeling, speculating freely on its utopian possibilities, but also hinting at its nightmarish implications. What began life as a series of meditations on the modern religion of sensibility soon developed into its unofficial bible. In the same year he also published *Du Contrat Social*, a highly abstract (and therefore highly tantalizing) work of political theory in which the principles of civic republicanism were reinvented and re-presented to a contemporary audience. In the *Contrat* Rousseau tried to imagine ways in which a modern nation like France might transform itself into a direct democracy, in the likeness of an ancient city-state. Impatient with contemporary theories of representation and delegation, he proposed a legislative system based upon a powerful identification of the will of the individual citizen with the "general will" of the nation. Highly theoretical, not to say metaphysical, in nature, the *Contrat Social* encouraged the French to hanker after a form of republican government so democratic as to be decidedly antiinstitutional, while giving them little or no indication how such a utopian situation might be brought about. Powerful and progressive in its insistence upon the inalienable sovereignty of the people, the treatise was far less strong on the practical details of executive government. It firmly upheld the right of the people to overthrow all laws or corporate bodies perceived to be in conflict with the "general will" but gave little indication of how any institution might accrue to itself the minimum degree of authority necessary to rule. This had profound consequences for political life during the French Revolution, which was thickly populated with republicans deeply wedded to a notion of political virtue as something not only independent of property, but also above and beyond the control of political institutions. In the eyes of many commentators, it was as a direct result of this metaphysic of virtue that the Terror was born.

It was during the 1760s that "the citizen of Geneva," as Rousseau had begun to style himself, finally fell out with his philosopher friends. In 1762 he published the last of his major theoretical works, *Emile, ou l'Education*, in which he laid down the fundamental principles of a natural (i.e., simple and virtuous) education. In the fourth part of this work, *La profession de foi du vicaire Savoyard* (*Profession of Faith of a Savoyard Vicar*), he embarked upon an extended treatment of religion and its relation to morality. Primarily, this section was intended as a refutation of contemporary philosophers: Rousseau's vicar began with an explicit attack on the utilitarianism of Helvetius, which he

countered by arguing for the existence of an innate moral sense or conscience (a formulation that had a considerable influence upon Immanuel Kant). But in placing such emphasis upon the divine principle of morality residing within the heart of the individual, *Profession de foi* ended up striking a remarkably deist (not to say atheist) note, offending both Catholics and Protestants in equal measure. *Emile* was condemned, and Rousseau was forced to flee to avoid arrest, first to Switzerland, then to England. All in all, he spent many years being hounded by the authorities. By the time the furor died down in the 1770s, the damage had already been done: the tendency toward paranoia at the base of Rousseau's character had been given full vent, and he developed a firm conviction that the entire world was against him. His last years were spent composing autobiographical works designed to vindicate his life and conduct. He died in 1778, at Ermonville, but he was never far from public consciousness during the 1780s, for it was during this decade that the two volumes of his *Confessions* were first published, to sensational effect. In 1794 his remains were transferred to the Pantheon in Paris: a potent symbol of the extent to which he had been adopted as the patron saint of the Jacobin regime.

Rousseau's legacy to the Romantic generation was twofold. It was at once philosophical and stylistic: he bequeathed a formidable array of rhetorical techniques as well as a heady mix of ideas. Broadly speaking, his reception had two phases. Before 1789 it was as a novelist and a moral philosopher that he was best known; after the outbreak of the French Revolution other aspects of his work gained greater prominence, most notably his autobiography and his political theory. His status as a radical commentator on culture and society was well established before 1789; but the outbreak of the French Revolution transformed his reputation forever. Before that time it had been relatively easy for commentators to incorporate him within the broad church of liberal enlightenment; for all his eccentricities, the "citizen of Geneva" was never quite beyond the pale. With the development of the Revolution, however, Rousseau's work took on a different character. His work was increasingly seen by counterrevolutionaries as the Revolution's "canon of holy writ" (the phrase is from Edmund Burke), and was subjected to a series of vehement attacks.

During the Terror, Rousseau's ideas passed through the fire: hence for aftercomers many aspects of his thought were forever fraught with dangerous implications. But the new fundamentalism he had brought to the world of politics and to the leading questions of social life still found some surreptitious adherents. Writers in England and Germany continued to be inspired by his example: Schiller's *Letters on the Aesthetic Education of Man* (1794) took a line from *La Nouvelle Heloise* as its epigraph, and can be read as an extended philosophical meditation on the central issues raised in that novel. In a series of poems and prose works written during the 1810s Percy Bysshe Shelley engaged with many aspects of Rousseau's literary and philosophical legacy, regarding him as central to an understanding of the age. And indeed Rousseau's influence permeates Romantic literature, despite or even because of the fact that it is so often suppressed or denied. The *Confessions* offers perhaps the best example of this. In this work autobiography became the means of consolidating Rousseau's critique of modern society: by supplying a full list of his sufferings he attempted to refute the various charges laid against him, by giving a transparent account of the history of his feelings he strove to oppose the dissimulation and hypocrisy that characterized contemporary life. This passion for candor was transformed into a cult during the revolutionary period; Jacobin statesmen drew heavily on the autobiographical rhetoric of the *Confessions* when they presented themselves to their public. And it proved a double-edged legacy to the Romantics: at once a powerful mode of literary communication (nobody could deny the force of his confessional manner) and a medium fraught with unfortunate connotations, most notably the self-regarding rhetoric of Maximilien Robespierre and the notorious impulse to transparency at the heart of the Terror. Because of this, Romantic autobiography is always haunted by Rousseau's *Confessions*, forced to situate itself in relation to that precedent. In the case of Chateaubriand's *Mémoires d'Outre-Tombe* the aim is clearly to Christianize Jacobin confession, in the case of William Wordsworth's *Prelude* of 1805 to redeem it. In both projects Rousseau is at once everywhere and nowhere, so much so, indeed, that it is tempting to think of their stylistic deviousness and emotional ambivalence—in short, their Romanticism—directly in terms of their agonized response to Rousseau, and to the dangerously intoxicating ideas he set forth.

GREGORY DART

Biography

Born June 12, 1712, in Geneva to a watchmaker and the daughter of a minister, his mother died after giving birth. Father was exiled from Geneva after a fight and moved to Lyons, 1722; Rousseau stayed in Geneva in the charge of his mother's relations. Ran away from his apprenticeship and wandered about Italy, France, and Switzerland, 1728, met Louise de Warens, a young widow and philanthropist, after converting to Catholicism in Turin. Lived in Chambery protected by Madame de Warens, who eventually became his mistress, 1731–40. Moved to Paris, 1741. Unsuccessfully presented a new system of music to the Academy of Sciences, 1742; became secretary to the ambassador to Venice, M. de Montaigu. In 1743, met Therese le Vasseur, who would become his mistress, bearing him five children, and whom he married near the end of his life. Returned to Paris, 1745. Collaborated on the *Encyclopedia* with Denis Diderot. Published *Discours sur les Arts et les Sciences*, 1751. Production of his opera the *Village Soothsayer*, 1752. Returned to Geneva and abjured his previous abjuration of the Protestant religion, 1754. Published *Discours sur l'Inégalite*, 1755. Moved back to Paris in a cottage at Montmorency, wrote *Julie, ou la Nouvelle Heloise*, 1756. Left Montmorency for nearby Montlouis after a quarrel with Diderot, 1757. Publication of *Lettre à D'Alembert* and final rupture in his relations with Diderot, 1758.

Publication of *Julie*, 1761. Publication of *Emile, ou l'Education* and *Du Contrat Social*, which forced him to leave France to avoid arrest, 1762. Lived briefly in Neuchatel, and in 1763 renounced citizenship of Geneva. Driven from Motiers to the Island of Saint-Pierre, 1765. David Hume offered him asylum in England, 1766. Began work on *Confessions*. In 1767, returned to live in various provinces of France; in 1770 returned to Paris. Wrote many of his most important works while in Paris over the next eight years, including his *Dialogues* and *Reveries*. In 1778, moved to Ermenonville, where he died suddenly on July 2 of that year.

Selected Works

English Translations

The Confessions. Translated by J. M. Cohen. London: Penguin, 1953.

Politics and the Arts: Letter to D'Alembert. Translated by Allan Bloom. Ithaca, N.Y.: Cornell University Press, 1968.

The Social Contract. Translated by Maurice Cranston. Harmondsworth: Penguin, 1968.

Reveries of the Solitary Walker. Translated by Peter France. Harmondsworth: Penguin, 1979.

A Discourse on Inequality. Translated by Maurice Cranston. Harmondsworth: Penguin, 1984.

Political Writings. Edited by Alan Ritter and Julia Conaway Bondanella. Translated by Julia Conaway Bondanella. New York: W. W. Norton, 1988.

Emile. Edited by P. D. Jimack. London: Dent, 1989.

Julie, or the New Heloise: Letters of Two Lovers Who Live in a Small Town at the Foot of the Alps. Edited by Philip Stewart and John Vache. Hanover, N.H.: Dartmouth University Press, 1997.

French Edition

Oeuvres Complètes. Edited by Bernard Gagnebin and Marcel Raymond. 4 vols. Paris: Gallimard/Bibliotheque de la Pleiade, 1959–69.

Bibliography

Blum, Carol. *Rousseau and the Republic of Virtue.* Ithaca, N.Y.: Cornell University Press, 1986.

Dart, Gregory. *Rousseau, Robespierre and English Romanticism.* Cambridge: Cambridge University Press, 1999.

Deane, Seamus. *The French Revolution and Enlightenment in England 1789–1832.* Cambridge, Mass.: Harvard University Press, 1988.

Duffy, Edward. *Rousseau in England.* Berkeley and Los Angeles: University of California, 1979.

Roussel, Jean. *Jean-Jacques Rousseau en France après la Révolution 1795–1830.* Paris, 1972.

Starobinski, Jean. *Jean-Jacques Rousseau: La transparence et l'obstacle.* Paris: Gallimard, 1971.

RÜCKERT, FRIEDRICH 1788–1866

German poet, translator, and orientalist

To many it will come as a surprise to learn that several of his contemporaries regarded Friedrich Rückert as the major lyric poet of his day. In the last twenty years of his life alone, he produced nearly ten thousand poems, exceeding by far the total output of Johann Wolfgang von Goethe and Johann Christoph Friedrich von Schiller. Rückert himself viewed his literary oeuvre as a massive *Liedertagebuch* ("diary in verse"). Felix Dahn, one of the few people who had access to the full range of Rückert's posthumous writings, once stated, "If it were up to me, [Rückert's] literary legacy would be published in its entirety, for there is nothing trivial in it." But as it happened, it took much longer than expected for publication to take place. One hundred thirty-five years after his death, the first volumes of a critical edition began to appear.

Today, Rückert is remembered for a few poems that are still anthologized ("Chidher," "Barbarossa") and for his *Kindertotenlieder*, a posthumous cycle that was reclaimed from oblivion when it was set to music by Gustav Mahler in the early twentieth century. Relatively few modern authors (one being Hermann Hesse) claim to have learned from, or been inspired by, Rückert. His accomplishments as a translator and interpreter of oriental poetry are still appreciated by a small number of academics and specialists. His most ambitious work, a didactic cycle of 2,788 gnomic poems, *Die Weisheit des Brahmanen* (*The Brahmin's Lore*, 1836–39) was not so much an exploration of Hindu mythology as a grandiose, though inevitably fragmentary, synthesis of eastern philosophy and Christian, Hindu, and Islamic scriptures that also incorporates thought from many medieval and modern Western sources. Its sheer size means that the identification of a central core of ethical ideas has rarely been undertaken and is unlikely to be.

Rückert's fascination with the "exotic" non-Christian world may seem incompatible with the pietist roots of Romanticism, yet his views were perhaps truer to the original Romantic credo than those of many others who are today more closely associated with the movement. Following Friedrich von Schlegel, he believed that poetry was "progressive and universal"; hence his attempts to embrace Eastern culture in its many individual manifestations. Like Novalis, he felt it incumbent on the artist to poeticize life, to abstract and synthesize what is best in art, and to mediate between those outstanding works and the lay reader. His interests were both Germanic and international, his poetic strategies simultaneously didactic and naive. In its essence, poetry was song, as Johann Gottfried von Herder and the collectors of folk verse had always sought to demonstrate. But Rückert followed his scholarly aspirations and intuition, and his poems frequently betray both erudition and patriotism, the latter especially as the tide turned against Napoleon and "poetry of liberation" became the order of the day, as an accompaniment to the Wars of Liberation that were sweeping Europe. Rückert's "Deutsche Gedichte," and particularly the seventy-two "geharnischte Sonette" ("sonnets in armour," 1814) brought him popular recognition on account of their declamatory style and solidly German, bitterly anti-French focus. For several years he edited one of Germany's most respected newspapers, Cotta's *Morgenblatt für gebildete Stände*.

It was perhaps inevitable that the man who followed so closely in the footsteps of the earliest German Romantics and defended their principles against an allegedly unpatriotic and agnostic Goethe should in the end have taken up the challenge of embracing and interpreting cultures which in the early nineteenth century were much more alien to Germans than they are today. His translations from the many languages of the East (which he taught himself) were numerous, though commercially less successful than his lyric poetry, which ran to an edition of six volumes (1834–38) and commanded admiration not least on account of its combination of homeliness and sagacity.

The enormous acclaim that Rückert enjoyed during the second half of the nineteenth century has disappeared so completely that an explanation is necessary. The sheer volume of his published poetry and unpublished papers is daunting, but more than that, his literary stature is affected by doubts as to where to place him. Is he best viewed as a poet or as a scholar? A Romantic or a neoclassicist? A German provincial or a figure on the world stage? And in regard to his technique, was he a mechanical verse generator, who in the course of his life expressed himself on all subjects on which an educated man of his time could express himself? Or was he, despite his apparently methodical approach, fundamentally undisciplined and unable to curtail the sheer volume of his output, much as the early Romantics were unable to curb their flights of fancy? These are some of the questions addressed by Helmut Prang and other recent scholars. Their provisional conclusions point to the inseparable coexistence of a poetic and a scholarly strand in his life, in which a gradual shift of emphasis takes place, as the poet-scholar becomes, in Prang's words, a scholar-poet.

Rückert demonstrates the difficulties that the truly committed Romantic poet had to face in an increasingly mechanized epoch. His dogged insistence on maintaining a poetic journal throughout his life earned him criticism from Jost Hermand, on the grounds that only someone lacking critical self-awareness would have yielded so completely to the unbridled urge to create. His proclaimed commitment to bourgeois virtues was in sharp contrast to the "immoderate" excesses of those who, like Clemens Brentano, Nickolaus Lenau, and Novalis poured passion into their lives as well as into their writings. The rabid nationalism of his early years has also tarnished his image, and for all his commitment to tolerance and internationalism, his references to certain ethnic and religious groups are repugnant by today's standards. What is most overlooked, however, is the relaxed and often playful ease with which he manipulates language, turning from the homely folksong to constructive, perceptive, and utopian modes of expression. Both naive and worldly wise, Rückert could evoke a sunset as ably as any disciple of Romanticism, but no other Romantic could interpret Rumi or quote from the Vedas. He introduced several oriental meters, including the ghazel, to German prosody. This master craftsmen may ultimately have earned his place in history as an intercultural mediator. In this respect, too, his labors fall within the Romantic canon.

OSMAN DURRANI

Biography

Born May 16, 1788 in Schweinfurt, Franconia, Germany, to a father who was a successful lawyer and local administrator. He grew up in an idyllic setting in the village of Oberlauringen. After attending school in Schweinfurt, he entered college in 1805 to study law and classical philology in Würzburg, Heidelberg, and finally Jena, where he lectured on Greek and oriental mythology from 1811 onward. Encouraged by the Swabian minister Carl August von Wangenheim, he became involved in controversial plans to draw up a constitution for the newly created Kingdom of Württemberg. In this he was guided by hopes that a modern national identity could be founded on the basis of medieval concepts of heroism. A journey to Italy in 1817–18 was undertaken with other like-minded spirits, partly in the hope of reexperiencing the Germanic roots of the long-defunct Holy Roman Empire. The stages of this tour are described in a diary in verse that reveals Rückert's unquenchable thirst for creative insights and impressions. These were ultimately to lead him away from his early, Romantic fixation on Germany and toward a more cosmopolitan outlook, initially as a result of firsthand observations of Italy's increasingly vociferous claims to political independence. From the early 1820s onward he immersed himself in the study of oriental languages—initially Persian and Arabic, later Sanskrit and Chinese. It is at this juncture that the erstwhile poet discovered his vocation as a scholar. In 1826 he was called to the chair of oriental languages in Erlangen, and moved to Berlin in 1841 at the invitation of the King of Prussia in the hope of assisting in the regeneration of a newly consolidated German state. His program was, however, completely out of keeping with the new wave of liberalism that inspired the young revolutionaries of the Junges Deutschland movement. Rückert backed the Prussian monarchy, and envisaged a return to an almost medieval order based on religious values and a hierarchical class system. The frustrations of the confused political arena and of a narrowly academic career eventually got the better of him, and Rückert sought permission to retire from public life, where his position had remained marginal at best. After the failed attempt to unify the nation in 1848 he withdrew to an extended active retirement, viewed by many as a solitary patriarch who still remained unflinchingly faithful to ideas that were Romantic in essence. He died on January 31, 1866 in Neuses, near Coburg.

Selected Works

Single Works

Reimar, Freimund (pseudonym). *Deutsche Gedichte.* Heidelberg, 1814.
Östliche Rosen. Drei Lesen. 1822.

Gesammelte Gedichte. 6 vols. 1834–38.
Die Weisheit des Brahmanen. Ein Lehrgedicht in Bruchstücken. 6 vols. 1836–39.
Liebesfrühling. 1844.
Kindertotenlieder. 1872.

Collected Editions

Rückerts gesammelte poetische Werke in 12 Bänden. 1868.
Rückerts Werke in 6 Bänden. Edited by Conrad Beyer. Leipzig: Hesse, 1900.
Rückerts Werke. Auswahl in 8 Teilen. Edited by Edgar Gross and Elsa Hertzer. Berlin: Bong, 1910.
Rückert-Nachlese: Sammlung der zerstreuten Gedichte und Übersetzungen Friedrich Rückerts. 2 vols. Edited by Leopold Hirschberg. Weimar: Selbstverlag, 1910–11.
Ausgewählte Werke, 2 vols. Edited by Annemarie Schimmel, Frankfurt: Insel, 1988.
Jetzt am Ende der Zeiten. Unveröffentliche Gedichte. Edited by Richard Dove. Frankfurt: Athenäum, 1988.
Friedrich Rückerts Werke. Historisch-kritische Ausgabe. 3 vols. to date. Edited by Hans Wollschläger and Rudolf Kreutner. Göttingen: Wallstein, 1998– .

Bibliography

Fischer, Wolfdietrich, ed. *Friedrich Rückert im Spiegel seiner Zeitgenossen und der Nachwelt. Aufsäize aus der Zeit zwischen 1827 und 1986.* Würzburg: Ergon, 1988.
Friedrich Rückert. Dichter und Sprachgelehrter in Erlangen. Referate des 9. interdisziplinären Colloquiums. Neustadt (Aisch): Degener, 1990.
Golffing, Franz Carl. *Friedrich Rückert als Lyriker. Ein Beitrag zu seiner Würdigung.* Dissertation, Vienna, 1935.
Kranz, Christa. *Friedrich Rückert und die Antike. Bild und Wirkung.* Schweinfurt: Fördererkreis der Rückert-Forschung, 1965.
Majut, Rudolf. *Ein englishcer Besucher Rückerts. Mit einem Ausblick auf die Aufnahme Rückerts in England und Amerika* (reprint). Schweinfurt: Rückert-Gesellschaft, 1973.
Prang, Helmut. *Friedrich Rückert als Diener und Deuter des Wortes.* Schweinfurt: Festvortrag, 1963.
———. *Friedrich Rückert. Geist und Form der Sprache,* Schweinfurt: Stadt Schweinfurt, 1963.
Schimmel, Annemarie. *Friedrich Rückert. Lebensbild und Einführung in sein Werk.* Freiburg: Herder, 1987.
———. *Weltpoesie ist Weltversöhnung.* Schweinfurt: Rückert-Buchhandlung, 1967.
Schmitz, Walter. "Friedrich Rückert." In *Deutsche Dichter.* Edited by Gunter E. Grimm and Frank Rainer Max. Stuttgart: Reclam, 1993.
Wiese, Benno von. *Friedrich Rückert. Erlanger Universitäts-Reden.* No. 23. Erlangen: Universitàts-Verlag, 1938.

Website

http://gutenberg.aol.de/autoren/rueckert.htm

RUNGE, PHILIPP OTTO 1777–1810

German artist

Born into a pious north German Lutheran family, the son of a shipowner in the small port of Wolgast and initially employed in his brother's business in Hamburg, Philipp Otto Runge was, by the age of thirty, a successful artist who had entered into a dialogue with Johann Wolfgang von Goethe on the theory of art, and had developed a network of contacts among German Romantic writers. Artistically productive for barely a decade, he was nevertheless innovative and influential in his work in three ways that are identifiably Romantic: in his intimate and searching portraiture, in his symbolic idealizations of children, and in the programmatic visual representation of Romantic anthropology and cosmology that he achieved in his *Tageszeiten* (*Times of Day*) cycle of drawings (1803).

Among Runge's first works as an aspiring professional artist were chalk drawings of his mother and of himself. Both are essentially personal studies: resigned or wistful individuals in everyday dress stare alone into vacant space. Thus, from the outset, Runge broke with the eighteenth-century tradition of portrait painting, particularly as practiced in Britain, with its celebration of public figures exhibiting their social status and success. He painted and drew uneasy Romantic introverts, not stolid bourgeois or complacent grandees. From 1801 on he was befriended by the painter Anton Graff, who had portrayed Johann Christoph Friedrich von Schiller and other prominent personalities in German cultural life, but despite Graff's technical influence, Runge confined himself largely to candid self-portraits or studies of his relatives and friends. The *Wir Drei* (*We Three*, 1805), showing Runge with his wife and his brother, is perhaps most typical of these works: a vulnerable and pensive family clings together, an intellectually uncertain generation living through the economic and political turmoil of the Napoleonic era. The same melancholy intensity is apparent in *Die Eltern des Künstlers* (*The Artist's Parents*, 1806), in three severe portraits of his wife (1804–10), in all his self-portraits, particularly *Selbstbildnis mit braunem Kragen* (*Self-Portrait with Brown Collar*, 1802) with its angular and soulful facial features, and even in his affectionate portrait of the four-year-old Luise Perthes (1805).

In this last portrait, however, as in general in his representations of children, Runge also has another agenda. The Romantic writer Novalis, whose work he admired, had written "Wo Kinder sind, da ist ein goldenes Zeitalter" ("Where there are children, there is a golden age"). In Runge's work, also, children serve as symbols of uncorrupted spontaneity, in contrast with an adult society fallen from grace and oppressed by utilitarianism. In *Die Eltern des Künstlers* the frail elderly couple stand with furrowed brows against a somber background, but at their feet the artist's infant son and nephew move in sunlight among flowers with expressions of innocent composure. In *Bildnis Otto Sigismund im Klappstuhl* (*Portrait of Otto Sigismund in his High Chair*, 1805), Runge's chubby son sits at ease and reaches out across his table top expectantly and without inhibition, while *Die Hülsenbeckschen Kinder* (*The Hülsenbeck Children*, 1805–6) shows three siblings serenely engrossed in their play in an idyllic garden landscape from which adult reality is banished to more or less distant buildings.

Angelic children again function as symbols of pristine innocence, although in the form of stylized and androgynous *putti*, in Runge's most symbolically charged work, the *Tageszeiten* drawings. Here too human society, as manifested in *Mittag* (*Midday*), is presented as an alienation from paradise. Yet the themes of the *Tageszeiten* extend well beyond social criticism. In Hamburg, Runge had enthusiastically read the work of August Wilhelm and Friedrich Schlegel, Ludwig Tieck, and Wilhelm Heinrich Wackenroder, with its emphasis on transcendent spirituality. Later, studying art in Dresden, he struck up a friendship with Tieck, who introduced him to the writings of the speculative mystic Jakob Böhme and to Romantic *Naturphilosophie* (nature philosophy). From these sources Runge derived the concept of nature animated by divine energies that he sought to express in the *Tageszeiten*. The four drawings, first made in 1803, represent not only morning, midday, evening, and night, but also the four seasons (their alternative title), and more generally four stages in an everlasting cycle of birth, maturity, decline, and death. They thus imply that divine creation of the earth occurs afresh each morning regardless of human transgression. In what Runge saw as a new allegorical form of landscape painting he uses plants to embody these processes, in particular the lily of innocence and purity rising at dawn and sinking at night after the degeneration of daytime. The pantheistic implications of these scenes are mitigated by orthodox Christian iconography in the framework panels of the drawings. Issued as engravings in a limited edition in 1805 and made generally available in 1807, the *Tageszeiten* attracted the admiration of Goethe and especially of the maverick Romantic philosopher Joseph von Görres in Heidelberg, who published a rhapsodic interpretation of them. Runge was now attempting to create color reworkings of the cycle, but by 1810 he had produced only provisional painted versions of *Morgen* (*Morning*).

These attempts led Runge to write a treatise on the theory of color, entitled *Farbenkugel* (*Color Sphere*, 1810), again earning the approval of Goethe, who was then working on his own *Farbenlehre* (*Doctrine of Color*). As a result of Görres's article on the *Tageszeiten*, Runge also came into contact with the other Heidelberg Romantics Achim von Arnim and Clemens Brentano. In 1808, Arnim's *Zeitung für Einsiedler* (*Hermits' Journal*) carried Runge's version of a Low German fairy tale, "Von den Machandel Bohm" ("The Juniper Tree"). This and another such dialect tale recorded by Runge, "Von den Fischer un syne Fru" ("The Fisherman and his Wife"), were later incorporated by Jakob and Wilhelm Grimm into the *Kinder- und Hausmärchen* (1812–22), their anthology of fairy stories. Such conservation and collection of exemplars of German popular culture was prompted by the wave of nationalistic fervor aroused in Germany after 1806 by the French occupation, and Runge now played his part in this Romantic crusade. In Hamburg in 1809 he joined a patriotic society and also drew a set of illustrations for the periodical *Vaterländisches Museum* (*Museum of the Fatherland*) showing allegorically the fall of Germany and its imminent resurrection. At the time of his premature death Runge was thus fully involved in the ideological and cultural program of the Late Romantics in Germany.

RICHARD LITTLEJOHNS

Biography

Born July 23, 1777 in Wolgast, (Swedish) Pomerania, Germany. Apprenticed in his brother Daniel's trading company in Hamburg, 1795–99. Studied at the Academy of Art in Copenhagen, 1799–1801, and at the Academy of Art in Dresden, 1801–3. From 1801 on, had recurrent contact with the painter Caspar David Friedrich, a fellow Pomeranian. Visited Tieck in Ziebingen and Goethe in Weimar, 1803. Professional artist in Hamburg, 1803–6. Married Pauline Bassenge, 1804; they later had three sons and a daughter. In Wolgast, 1806–07. In Hamburg as Daniel Runge's business partner from 1807 until his death from tubercolosis on December 2, 1810.

Bibliography

Bisanz, Rudolph M. *German Romanticism and Philipp Otto Runge*. DeKalb: Northern Illinois University Press, 1970.

Hartley, Keith, *et al.,* eds. *The Romantic Spirit in German Art 1790–1990*. London: Thames and Hudson.

Hofmann, Werner, ed. *Runge. Fragen und Antworten*. Munich: Prestel, 1979.

———. *Runge in seiner Zeit*. Munich: Prestel, 1977.

Rosenblum, Robert. *The Romantic Child. From Runge to Sendak*. London: Thames and Hudson, 1988.

Simson, Otto Georg von. "Philipp Otto Runge and the Mythology of Landscape," *Art Bulletin* 24 (1942): 335–50.

Traeger, Jörg. *Philipp Otto Runge und sein Werk: Monographie und kritischer Katalog*. Munich: Prestel, 1975.

Vaughan, William. *German Romantic Painting*. New Haven, Conn.: Yale University Press, 1980.

RUSSIA: CULTURAL SURVEY

Secular art and music entered Russia in the middle of the eighteenth century. Until Russia's empresses imported baroque and neoclassical architecture into the new capital, Saint Petersburg, church and folk traditions provided the only models for artists and musicians. Under Catherine the Great neoclassical tastes led to a revival of Greek and Roman architecture and sculpture, the dominant art forms of the end of the eighteenth and first half of the nineteenth centuries. However, artists from France and Italy had carried out the great building projects of Saint Petersburg. To remedy this situation, Empress Elizabeth founded the Imperial Academy of Fine Arts in 1757. In 1763, Catherine made it a teaching establishment for Russian artists, who hitherto had studied in Europe. By the first decades of the nineteenth century, Russian artists could master basic techniques at home; they now went to Europe only to hone their skills.

At the beginning of the nineteenth century, painters began to express Romantic sentiments in their works. Orest Kiprenskii admired French and German Romantic painters and had studied Friedrich Wilhelm Joseph von Schelling, Friedrich von Schlegel, and Novalis. Though he never fully rejected the academy's neo-classicist canon, his portraits derive much of their power from his ability to depict the inner nature of his subjects. Karl Briullov also painted Romantic portraits, some even darkly Byronic in tone. He earned his reputation in Russia and the West primarily with his historical paintings, the most famous of which is *Poslednii den' Pompei* (*The Last Day of Pompeii*, 1833). Aleksandr Ivanov focused his art on profoundly religious and moral ideas; he may be the most "Russian" of his contemporaries because of the messianic philosophy of his art, as the didactic *Iavlenie Khrista narodu* (*The Appearance of Christ to the People*, 1837–57) demonstrates.

Pavel Fedotov, Vasilii Tropinin, and Aleksei Venetsianov exemplify a new native, realistic trend in Russian art of the first half of the nineteenth century. Fedotov's paintings comment on the dreary aspects of reality and are often satirical in tone. Tropinin painted sincere and charming portraits that transform everyday Russian life and individuals into subjects worthy of artistic representation. Venetsianov took art to the countryside by insist-

ing that one must paint from nature. *Gumno* (*Threshing Floor*, c. 1821), which depicts a typical peasant interior in natural light, was a successful experiment that made the *intérieur* an acceptable genre. His lyrical country scenes established a school of landscape painting that found its full expression in the next generations of Russian painters.

The history of Russian music follows patterns of development similar to those of Russian art. Unlike artists, however, musicians had no academy until the mid-1860s. By the second half of the eighteenth century, musicians could find patrons in wealthy nobles, who set up orchestras, choirs, and opera houses on their estates. Most of the performers were serfs trained by foreign professionals. Because Italian opera dominated eighteenth-century Russia, two native composers, Evstignei Fomin and Vasilii Pashkevich, followed Italian models in writing their own operas. By the end of the century, Russia had produced several gifted native composers, among them Maksim Berezovskii and Dmitrii Bortnyanskii. Both composed vocal and instrumental pieces, but are best known as masters of sacred choral music. Bortnyanskii introduced harmony and polyphony to Russian sacred chant, which led to his being known as the Russian Palestrina.

Under the influence of the French Enlightenment, Catherine the Great became interested in the "simple folk," whose spirit, music, and art enchanted her. Aristocrats followed suit and began collecting folk music. Soon folk epics, fairy tales, stories of the supernatural, and (after the War of 1812) patriotic themes engaged the composers of the first part of the nineteenth century. They mainly composed for the theater: vaudeville, opera, melodramas, and "dramatic cantatas." The first Russian composer of note before Mikhail Glinka was Aleksei Verstovskii, who earned distinction primarily from two of his six operas, *Vadim ili dvenadtsat' spiashikh dev* (*Vadim, or the Awakening of Twelve Sleeping Maidens*, 1832) and *Askol'dova mogila* (*Askold's Tomb*, 1835), which reflect the Russian people's emerging national consciousness. Both works are set in the time of the ancient Slavs, with their seasonal rites, folk music, and arcane customs; *Askol'dova mogila* additionally catered to the popular demand for historical themes. Verstovskii and Glinka, along with Aleksandr Aliab'ev, also popularized "Russian romances" or Russian art songs. They composed melodies to the words of Russia's leading contemporary poets. The main subject matter of these songs is generally sentimental or romantic: love, nature, friendship, beauty, patriotism, isolation, separation, exile, and melancholy.

Glinka eclipsed his contemporaries to become the founder of the Russian national school and one of its greatest composers. He understood which qualities, when imparted to music, made it Russian. Glinka did not simply incorporate folk music as a convention; he elevated it as a form worthy of artistic respect. His orchestral masterwork, *Kamarinskaia* (1848), best exemplifies this particular talent. The opera *Zhizn' za tsaria* (*A Life for the Tsar*, 1836), which depicts a historical event from Russia's "Time of Troubles" (1598–1613), became the benchmark for all subsequent Russian operas. Another opera, *Ruslan and Liudmila* (1842), is based on a narrative poem with fairy tale elements by Aleksandr Pushkin.

Drama of the period did not fare as well. Productions of unimaginative imitations of neoclassical tragedies flooded the stage. The theater began to come to life with the introduction of vaudevilles and comic plays, mainly by Prince Aleksandr Shakhovskoi. Then Aleksandr Griboedov brought true comic genius to the theater with his comedy *Gore ot uma* (*Woe from Wit*, 1825). Written as rhymed verse of variable iambic lines, the dialogue sounds like natural speech and lines from the play have entered Russian lore. The characters have become national archetypes despite the fact that Griboedov used French classical comedy as his model. Pushkin tried writing a Romantic historical drama set in the Time of Troubles, *Boris Godunov* (1825; published 1831). Though not a complete success, the play lives on in Modest Mussorgsky's opera of the same name. Pushkin's four closet dramas, *Malen'kie tragedii* (*The Little Tragedies*, 1830), on the other hand, are true gems of the theater. Mikhail Lermontov attempted a Romantic melodrama, *Maskarad* (1835–36), that examines the dark side of man's soul through the plot of a gambler who, suspecting his innocent wife of infidelity, kills her.

Russian drama of the first half of the century reached its peak in Nikolai Gogol's hilarious comedy, *Revizor* (*The Inspector General*, 1836), with its plot based on mistaken identity. Wrongly perceived as a criticism of Russia's social problems, *Revizor* satirizes the moral failures of all humanity. Russian drama hit a nadir when the literary plebeians took control of the theater with contrived historical dramas that catered to Tsar Nicholas I's conservative doctrine of "Official Nationality." The title of one play by the most popular (but not the best) playwright of the day, Nestor Kukol'nik, tells the whole story: *Ruka Veevyshniago otechestvo spasla* (*The Hand of the Almighty Has Saved the Fatherland*, 1834). The Russian stage had to wait many years for a successor to Gogol.

CHRISTINE A. RYDEL

Bibliography

Goldovskij, Grigorij, Eugenija Petrova, and Claudio Poppi, eds. *La Pittura Russa Nell'età Romantica*. Bologna: Nuova Alfa Editoriale, 1990.

Greenleaf, Monika, and Stephen Moeller-Sally, eds. *Russian Subjects. Empire, Nation, and the Culture of the Golden Age*. Evanston, Ill.: Northwestern University Press, 1998.

Hodge, Thomas P. *A Double Garland. Poetry and Art-Song in Early Nineteenth Century Russia*. Evanston, Ill.: Northwestern University Press, 2000.

Karlinsky, Simon. *Russian Drama from Its Beginnings to the Age of Pushkin*. Berkeley and Los Angeles: University of California Press, 1985.

Leach, Robert, and Victor Borovsky, eds. *A History of Russian Theatre*. Cambridge: Cambridge University Press, 1999.

Leonard, Richard Anthony. *A History of Russian Music*. New York: Macmillan, 1968.

Massie, Suzanne. *Land of the Firebird: The Beauty of Old Russia*. New York: Simon and Schuster, 1980.

Rice, Tamara Talbot. *A Concise History of Russian Art*. New York: Frederick A. Praeger, 1967.

Rzhevsky, Nicholas, ed. *The Cambridge Companion to Modern Russian Culture*. Cambridge: Cambridge University Press, 1998.

Stavrou, Theofanis George. *Art and Culture in Nineteenth-Century Russia*. Bloomington: Indiana University Press, 1983.

Taruskin, Richard. *Defining Russia Musically: Historical and Hermeneutical Essays*. Princeton, NJ.: Princeton University Press, 1997.

Varneke, B. V. *History of the Russian Theatre: Seventeenth through Nineteenth Century*. Translated by Boris Brasol. Revised and edited by Belle Martin. New York: Macmillan, 1951.

Wachtel, Andrew Baruch. *Intersections and Transpositions: Russian Music, Literature, and Society*. Evanston, Ill.: Northwestern University Press, 1998.

RUSSIA: HISTORICAL SURVEY

When European Romanticism blossomed in the late eighteenth century, Russia was ruled by Catherine II, the epitome of an enlightened despot. Her all-important patronage worked against the first stirrings of the movement, which were few and obscure. In 1790, frightened by the implications of the French Revolution, she suppressed all independent thought. Paul I, her son and heir, continued this policy until his assassination. Thus, the true beginning of Romanticism in Russia coincides with the accession of Alexander I.

One of the most popular acts of the new tsar was to lift restrictions on intellectual life. Much was expected of him, and in addition to founding three new universities, Alexander began moving towards the abolition of serfdom and the rule of law. However, the implications of these reforms for the institution of absolute monarchy were frightening, and in 1804 the sovereign abandoned domestic reform for foreign affairs. Russia, for the second time since 1798, was at war with Napoleon Bonaparte.

The War of the Third Coalition (1805–7) went badly for Russia, and the 1807 Treaty of Tilsit pledged the country to recognize Napoleon's gains in Europe, and to join the Continental System, a French blockade of British trade. On the other hand, Russia was one of the only three remaining great powers, and the empire continued to grow. Alexander defeated Sweden and annexed Finland in 1809; and in the Caucasus, where the rulers of Georgia requested a protectorate in order to save them from the Turks and the Persians, Russia had to fight Turkey and Persia. Napoleon had promised to use his influence with the Turks, but in fact he urged them to maintain hostilities. For their part, the Russians ceased enforcing the terms of the Continental System.

To regain some of his lost prestige at home, Alexander returned to his program of incipient reform, even allowing an adviser, Michael Speranskii, to draw up a proposal that included a national legislative assembly. But the project fell prey to growing conservative sentiment among the gentry and the state bureaucracy. With international tensions increasing, the tsar dismissed Speranskii and once again turned to war.

In June 1812, Napoleon invaded with an army eventually numbering over 500,000 men. He was opposed by forces one-quarter as large, and divided into two armies. The events of this campaign, in particular the destruction of Smolensk, the Battle of Borodino, and the Great Moscow Fire, constituted modern Russia's first national experience. Stymied by the Russian Army and weakened by the early onset of winter, Napoleon's army staggered back into Poland less than one-tenth of its original size. But Alexander followed, rallying country after country to desert the French and to drive Napoleon out. Russian forces held their 1814 Easter celebrations in Paris.

Alexander's participation in the reconstruction of post-Napoleonic Europe once again encouraged those who championed reforms at home. But the tsar, who insisted on constitutions for France, Finland, and even Poland, never went further than consideration of a few tentative proposals for Russia. Increasingly he turned to conservative mystics in his appointments while frustrated young army officers, recently returned from France, formed secret societies dedicated to drastic means and idealistic constitutional schemes. Alexander died unexpectedly at Taganrog, and in December 1825, the authorities fell into confusion over his successor. Seeing an opportunity, the secret societies struck in what came to be known as the Decembrist Revolt.

On the first day of his reign, Nicholas I, the second-youngest brother of Alexander, was faced with a revolutionary demonstration. Guards' regiments, which were occupying Saint Petersburg's

Christian Johann Oldendorp, *The Fire of Moscow*. Reprinted courtesy of AKG.

Senate Square, demanded a constitution. When negotiations failed, the tsar reluctantly ordered his cannons to open fire. In the aftermath, the ever-loyal gentry class expected mercy for the well-meaning conspirators. Instead, most were exiled to Siberia, and five, rather arbitrarily chosen, died in a botched execution. The tragedy of December 14 marked the beginning of an ever-widening split that divided the state from its educated subjects.

Nicholas I was well-informed about the problems of his realm, and while he had no enthusiasm for constitutions, he disapproved of serfdom. However, even more than his brother, Nicholas feared the consequences of action. A soldier by choice and training, his vision of Russia was that of a vast parade ground of obedience and order. To that end he adopted a policy formally known as "official nationalism" whose principles were "orthodoxy, autocracy, and nationality." Nicholas also established the Third Section, a political police organization that symbolized his reign. Censorship, arrest, and exile escalated with every sign of trouble in Europe, and after the 1848 revolutions, the general suppression of all intellectual life was unusually severe. This inflexible dedication to order earned him the sobriquet Gendarme of Europe.

The tsar's principal foreign policy task was to maintain the political map of Europe drawn up by the victorious powers at Vienna in 1815. However, for decades, Russian statesmen had harbored a policy of expansion and hegemony reaching towards the Turkish Straits at Constantinople. In the Balkans, the two policies met and intertwined. In 1827, Russia went to war with Turkey in a successful effort to liberate Greece, an orthodox country with which the Russian elite had many connections. In 1832, the tsar's forces intervened to protect the sultan from a revolutionary force issuing from Egypt. Each of the treaties concluding these actions, the Treaty of Adrianople in 1829 and the Treaty of Unkiar Skelessi in 1833, wrested more concessions from Turkey. In 1841, the British government was alarmed by Russian imperialism and insisted on a general Straits Convention that cancelled out all unilateral agreements.

Not only Russia's Balkan interventions but also Nicholas's dedication to the 1815 settlement tended to alienate Western powers. In 1830, revolutions in France and Belgium nearly provoked him to war, but the Polish uprising in the same year distracted his forces. European sympathy was with the Poles. In 1848, the tsar nearly despaired that he was not called in to help, but finally the Austrians called for Russian aid in their struggle against Hungarian separatists. Again, Russia was perceived as opposed to the spirit of the age.

At length, in 1853, when Russia once more went to war with Turkey, this time over a trivial diplomatic issue, Britain and France entered the conflict on the side of the Turks. Even Austria adopted a malevolent neutrality. The Crimean War (1854–56) exposed Russia as a corrupt and backward country barely deserving of the respect due a major power. Nicholas died in 1855, dismayed by the disaster. With him also died his policy of intellectual repression. However, for Russian Romantics, it was too late. Their age was coming to a close all over Europe.

EDWARD ALAN COLE

Bibliography

Almedingen, Edith M. *The Emperor Alexander I.* New York: Vanguard Press, 1964.

De Madariaga, Isabel. *Russia in the Age of Catherine the Great.* New Haven, Conn.: Yale University Press, 1981.

Lincoln, W. Bruce. *Nicholas I: Emperor and Autocrat of All the Russias*. Bloomington: Indiana University Press, 1978.

Malia, Martin. *Alexander Herzen and the Birth of Russian Socialism, 1812–1855*. Cambridge, Mass.: Harvard University Press, 1961.

Martin, Alexander. *Romantics, Reformers, Reactionaries: Russian Conservative Thought and Politics in the Reign of Alexander I*. DeKalb: Northern Illinois University Press, 1997.

Raeff, Marc. *The Origins of the Russian Intelligentsia*. New York: Harcourt and Brace, 1966.

Riasanovsky, Nicholas V. *A Parting of Ways: Government and the Educated Public in Russia, 1801–1855*. Oxford: Clarendon Press, 1976.

Wortman, Richard S. *Scenarios of Power: Myth and Ceremony in Russian Monarchy*. Vol. 1. Princeton, N.J.: Princeton University Press, 1995.

S

SAAVEDRA, ANGEL PÉREZ DE, DUKE OF RIVAS 1791–1865

Spanish poet, dramatist, and politician

Much has been written about Romanticism and its meaning and special characteristics in Spain. While absolute agreement has been elusive with regard to a number of important matters, such as dating the movement, identifying its precedents, and distinguishing its salient qualities, most historians of literature agree that Angel Pérez de Saavedra is one of Spanish Romanticism's most illustrious figures. Saavedra inherited the title of Duke of Rivas in 1834 following the death of his elder brother and is generally known by that title rather than the patronym. He owes this reputation to two principal works: his play *Don Alvaro o la fuerza del sino* (*Don Alvaro or the Power of Destiny*, 1835) and *Romances históricos* (1841), a collection of poems inspired by both factual and legendary episodes of the history of Spain.

A student of art and letters from an early age, the Duke of Rivas began his writing career under the influence of neoclassical models, publishing a collection of poetry and a play, *Ataúlfo*, in 1814, followed by a second enlarged poetry edition (1820–21) and a political play, *Lanuza* (1822). Saavedra's identification with liberal causes led to a period of exile abroad; beginning in 1823, he spent a few months in Gibraltar, lived in London, and finally settled in Malta, where he and his family remained until 1830. In Malta the duke met John Frere, former English ambassador to Madrid and an ardent admirer of Spanish literature. Frere is thought to have introduced him to the works of English and continental writers and to have encouraged his friend to become familiar with literary practices outside of Spain. Frere also prompted the Duke of Rivas to appreciate Spanish classics from the Golden Age and to consider Spanish history a worthy inspiration for literature. Last but not least, Frere is credited with leading Saavedra to abandon neoclassical forms in favor of a more subjective and suggestive approach to literature. Saavedra, in turn, acknowledged Frere's influence in *El moro expósito* (*The Foundling Moor*, 1834), to whom the work is dedicated. Pub-

lished in France in 1834, where the duke was then residing, *El moro* is a long narrative poem (over fourteen thousand lines) that relates a famous, albeit fictional, episode from the Castilian Middle Ages, the fate of the legendary Infantes de Lara, seven brothers of a noble family who, following a betrayal, meet a cruel death. Their death is eventually avenged by their half-brother Mudarra, the hero of the story.

El moro, while not a pristine example of Romanticism, displays several features associated with the movement. For example, the work revolves around the role of destiny in determining the fate of its characters; it mixes tragic and comic elements, expresses in colorful language the local landscape, and makes frequent use of the mysterious and the grotesque, of blood, ghosts, and tombs.

The Duke of Rivas's definitive move in the direction of Romanticism is evident in his *Don Alvaro o la fuerza del sino*, a play in five acts that premiered in Madrid in the early part of 1835. It tells the story of Don Alvaro, the son of a Spanish nobleman and an Inca princess, who falls in love with Leonor against the wishes of her aristocratic family. Don Alvaro accidentally kills Leonor's father, and in the confusion that ensues believes his beloved to have died as well. Instead, unbeknownst to him, she has become a hermit. As the plot develops, Don Alvaro kills Leonor's brother (who had become Alvaro's friend, unaware of his true identity) and mortally wounds a second brother who, before his own death, stabs Leonor to death in front of Don Alvaro. Don Alvaro and the wounded brother had gone to the hermitage looking for help; instead, they found Leonor. Upon her death, Don Alvaro, disconsolate, kills himself.

The play was performed nine times in a two-week period between March and April 1835, causing an uproar. Critical opinion was sharply divided, with more than one critic expressing bewilderment. Many judged *Don Alvaro* immoral and its hero unworthy. The manner of his death by suicide, as well as features of his mixed blood, character, and speech, were deemed outrageous. That fate should be fulfilled and honor satisfied through such bloody means was a further affront to the public's sensibilities.

Others, however, found *Don Alvaro* a moral play in that the protagonist suffered a fate deserved. To its defenders the work was a new way of writing for the stage, an excellent example of Romanticism, a faithful reflection of reality, and a harbinger of the future glory of the theatre in Spain.

In conjunction with what historians of literature consider the apogee of Spanish romantic poetry (1840–41), the Duke of Rivas published *Romances históricos*, a collection of eighteen *romances*, considered by many to be Saavedra's most valuable contribution to Spanish letters. Echoing brothers August Wilhelm and Friedrich von Schlegel, a portion of whose writing had been translated into Spanish by Johann Böhl von Faber, a German-born resident of Cádiz, Saavedra writes in his prologue that ballads are the true national poetry and particularly well suited to Romantic expression. The collection is made up of anecdotes from Spanish history and lore from the fourteenth to the nineteenth centuries, including the war against Napoleon. In 1844 the duke published *El desengaño en un sueño* (*Disillusionment in a Dream*), which, next to *Don Alvaro*, is his best dramatic work. It has been labeled a "romantically romantic" play; in it the author abandons any effort at dramatic convention, mixes verse and prose, and makes frequent and elaborate use of sound effects, lighting, and a large cast of fifty-six.

The Duke of Rivas wrote little prose fiction, but continued his career as a writer in spite of involvement in public life and a series of increasingly prestigious official posts. In 1854 he published his collected works in five volumes; much of his later lyrical and dramatic writing displays a more profound religiosity and a more conservative nationalistic tone than his earlier and more renowned works.

CLARA ESTOW

Biography

Born in Cordova, Spain, March 10, 1791. Entered Royal Seminary for the Nobility in Madrid, 1803. Joined Royal Guards, 1806. Fought against the French, 1809–10. Elected to represent Cordova to the cortes (parliament) in Madrid, 1821. Exiled, 1823–34. Married María de la Encarnación de Cueto y Ortega, 1825. Inherited noble title in 1834 and returned to Spain; took family seat in upper house of parliament, appointed secretary of that body and then vice president. Exiled a second time, 1836–37. Appointed ambassador at the court of Naples, 1844–50; ambassador to France, 1857–58. Elected director of Royal Spanish Academy, 1862. Died June 22, 1865, in Madrid.

Selected Writings

Poetry
Poesías de Don Angel de Saavedra Remírez de Baquedano. 2 vols. 1820–21.
Romances históricos. Edited by Salvador García Castañeda. Madrid: Cátedra, 1987.

Drama
Don Alvaro o la fuerza del sino. Edited by Donald L. Shaw. Madrid: Castalia, 1986.

Collection
Obras completas. 3 vols. Edited by Jorge Campos. Biblioteca de autores españoles. Madrid: Ediciones Atlas, 1957.

Bibliography

Adams, Nicholson B. "The Extent of the Duke of Rivas' Romanticism." In *Homenaje a Rodríguez-Moñino*. Madrid: Castalia, 1966.
Crespo, Angel. *El Duque de Rivas.* Gijón: Júcar, 1985.
Homenaje a Angel de Saavedra, Duque de Rivas en el bicentenario de su nacimiento 1791–1991. Córdoba: Instituto de Bachillerato "Angel Saavedra," 1991.
Kirkpatrick, Susan. "Spanish Romanticism." In *Romanticism in National Context*, edited by Royel Poster and Mikules Teich. Cambridge: Cambridge University Press, 1988.
Lovett, Gabriel. *The Duke of Rivas.* Boston: Twayne, 1977.
Navas-Ruiz, Ricardo. *Imágenes liberales: Rivas, Larra, Galdós.* Salamanca: Ediciones Almar, 1979.
Romero Tobar, Leonardo. *Panorama crítico del romanticismo español.* Madrid: Editorial Castalia, 1994.
Schurlnight, Donald E. *Spanish Romanticism in Context: Espronceda, Larra, Rivas, Zorrilla.* Lanham, Md.: University Press of America, 1998.

SADAK IN SEARCH OF THE WATERS OF OBLIVION 1812

Painting by John Martin

John Martin was born in 1789, the thirteenth child of an unemployed tanner, in Haydon Bridge, Northumberland. When in 1803 the family moved to Newcastle, he was apprenticed to a coach builder in order to learn decorative painting and heraldry. Martin eventually showed larger talents and began taking weekend lessons in oil painting. He moved to London in 1805 to pursue his studies, and to work as a painter on china and glass. After an initial unsuccessful attempt to exhibit there, his *Landscape Composition* was exhibited at the Royal Academy in 1812, an event that prompted the hostility of his fellow employees, and thus his resignation. The following year he exhibited *Sadak in Search of the Waters of Oblivion*, which he claimed to have painted, out of financial desperation, in a month. It was bought for fifty guineas by a governor of the bank of England, whose dying son had been moved by its depiction of the slight solitary figure clinging perilously to a ledge.

The success of the painting was crucial in moving Martin from the subject matter of decorative art to the apocalyptic imaginary landscapes and cityscapes that, with their puny but heroically defiant human figures, struck a chord in post-Romantic England and France. Though his financial status was always precarious, and he remained aesthetically and socially something of an outsider, his mastery of the medium of the mezzotint brought his work to a wide audience, and influenced the ways in which the nineteenth century imagined the biblical and pre-biblical past in a way that, it has been argued, lingers on into early cinema.

It is significant that Martin found his vision in glass painting, or transparencies to be displayed in a window. Martin sought to create in his oils a glow, or an effect of light, that illuminates the landscape from behind, and to obtain the maximum effect from a limited range of color, most particularly from those blues, greens, and reds that share hues with the pigments that commonly stain glass. A major influence on this, and a major spectacle in London at the time that Martin first arrived there, was the work of Philip de Loutherbourg and his various successors. Loutherbourg had painted sublime landscapes; designed and painted stage sets for David Garrick, among others; and above all created, in 1781, the *Eidophusikon*, a miniature theater that combined painting, moving scenery, transparencies, and various lighting effects in a spectacle of the civilizations of the past. The success of *Sadak* confirmed Martin's pursuing of a theatrical grandeur, and a sense of event that still imposes itself when we see his paintings in a gallery—the paintings that both made and eventually undid his career.

The subject of *Sadak in Search of the Waters of Oblivion* is a tale by James Ridley, a chaplain of the East India Company, of what (typically for an age that delighted in literary fakes) purports to be an English diplomat's translation of a Persian manuscript. It was published in his *Tales of the Genii* in 1764. In it, Sadak has been tricked by an evil sultan into seeking the waters of oblivion, little suspecting that the sultan wishes to give them to Sadak's wife, and so to seduce her. In the end, the sultan himself is engulfed by the waters. The story was dramatized for the London stage by Charles Dibdin in 1797, and again in 1814. Martin's version focuses, with brilliant economy, on Sadak on the brink of an abyss, as Lord Byron's heroes are so often on a brink, the difference being that Sadak, like the always aspirant outsider Martin, is clinging on and struggling to go forward, untouched by melancholic fantasies of the fall.

When an engraving was published in the *Keepsake* of 1828, it was accompanied by a poem, *Sadak the Wanderer*, which has been argued to be the work of Percy Bysshe Shelley:

Like a dying star the sun
Struggles on through cloud-wreaths dun;
From yon mountains shelter'd brow
Bursts the lava's burning flow:
Warrior! Wilt thou dare the tomb
In the red volcano's womb!

As a response to the picture, this registers, in the apostrophe to the "warrior," its immediacy and sense of drama but also the almost anatomical sense of the landscape; the blood reds and the visceral juxtaposition of fire and water, heat and cold, heighten a sense that a minaturized Sadak is exploring his own interior. It is not clear whether the version now in the Southampton Art Gallery is the original, as bought by the banker in memory of his son. But its dimensions (30 × 20 inches) seem roughly similar to those recorded at the time. In any case, the relatively small scale of the picture might come as a surprise to us when we see it in reproduction. Skills acquired in observing the illusions, panoramas, and commercial spectacles of his time, and in devel-

John Martin, *Sadak in Search of the Waters of Oblivion*. Reprinted courtesy of The Bridgeman Art Library.

oping his technique in commercial, artisanal techniques rather than through the academies, left Martin with both a shrewd sense of how to communicate with his public, and how to create a version of the sublime subtly minaturized, and apt for mass production. His canvases became grand advertisements for the mezzotints that he hoped to sell due to the ensuing publicity.

He remained a regular exhibitor at the Royal Academy, and by the time he died in 1854, still working on his monumental series on the Last Judgment, he had made a lasting impact on the Anglo-American visual imagination, producing memorable images from the Bible, William Shakespeare, Thomas Gray, and John Milton. He had also forwarded plans to remake the architecture on the banks of the Thames in a style of preclassical grandeur, while at the same time putting himself, perhaps irrevocably, outside the bounds of aesthetic respectability. A critic in 1831, perhaps imagining a last judgment on Martin himself, said he had "much to answer for at the bar of Taste." Samuel Taylor Coleridge, with a more intuitive sense of the artist's interests, said that "it seemed to me that Martin never looked at Nature except through bits of stained glass." "Nature" was hardly Martin's aim; his lack of training became the source of, rather than a hindrance for, a popular visionary style.

EDWARD BURNS

Work
Sadak in Search of the Waters of Oblivion, 1812. Oil on glass, 30in. × 20in. Southampton, England.

Bibliography

Feaver, William. *The Art of John Martin*. Oxford: Clarendon Press, 1975.

Johnstone, Christopher. *John Martin*. London: Academy Editions, 1974.

Maas, Jeremy. *Victorian Painters*. London: Barrie and Rockliff, 1969.

Ridley, James. *HORAM, the son of Asmar: The Tales of the Genii; or the delightful lessons of Horam, the son of Asmar*. Translated from the Persian manuscripts by Sir C. Morell. 1764.

Seznec, Jean. *John Martin en France*. London: Faber and Faber, 1964.

Todd, Ruthven. *Tracks in the Snow: Studies in English Science and Art*. London: Grey Walls Press, 1946.

SADE, MARQUIS DONATIEN-ALPHONSE-FRANÇOIS DE 1740–1814

French writer

The name *Sade* has been immortalized in the word *sadism*, which refers broadly to taking pleasure in, and specifically to deriving sexual satisfaction from, cruelty or the infliction of pain on others. It has also come to be associated with the name of Leopold von Sacher-Masoch, from which the word *masochism* is derived, meaning the derivation of sexual pleasure from submitting oneself to cruelty or inflicted pain.

Marquis Donatien-Alphonse-François de Sade's life and works have typically been read in this narrow context of sexual violence, and there has been a tendency among critics to read his life—a series of arrests for sexual excesses and debauchery, escapes, banishments, and incarcerations in various prisons and asylums, as well as a Jesuit education, marriage into royal blood, a distinguished military career, and an appointment as a magistrate—into his works. This type of reading is attractive because it allows for an easy and formulaic psychoanalytic approach. There is also a lingering traditional view in criticism that the text of an author's personal life can be privileged as a normative reference point in relation to which the texts of his fictional creations can be situated, and from which they acquire their "intention" or meaning. In the contexts of modern literary theory, however, both simplistic psychoanalysis and unqualified appeal to authorial intention have been thrown into question. More productively, there is a case to be made for understanding Sade's numerous works, some of which he refused to acknowledge publicly as his own, as seminal literary and philosophical experiments in the context of the Enlightenment.

Thus, for example, in the short *Dialogue between a Priest and a Dying Man* (1782), written during Sade's incarceration at Vincennes, the dying man argues, on the basis of reason, against the "vain sophistries of superstition" on which religions are constructed. The dialogue ends with both himself and the priest enjoying carnal pleasures with six women. "[A]fter he had been a little while in their arms the preacher became one whom Nature has corrupted, all because he had not succeeded in explaining what a corrupt nature is." *Les 120 Journées de Sodome, ou l'école du libertinage* (*The 120 Days of Sodom, on the School for Libertines*, 1785) is a vast, repetitive, and graphically detailed catalog of imagined violent and sexual crimes, categorized as "simple," "complex," "criminal," and "murderous" passions; this work constitutes an "encyclopaedia" in the style of Denis Diderot and Jean Le Rond d'Alembert, but it is an inverted encyclopedia of the desires and instincts of irrationalism repressed or excluded by the tradition of rationalism that dominated the era. Two other well known texts, *Eugenie de Franval* (1788), and

Justine, ou les malheurs de la virtue (*Justine; or, The Misfortunes of Virtue*, 1791), were also written by Sade while he was imprisoned in the Bastille: They are generally considered to be masterpieces in the genre of the eighteenth-century novel. In both cases, the narrative follows the tribulations of the female character, who is forcibly introduced to her own sexuality through a series of confinements, rapes, and other violent crimes; both texts are presented as "moral tales," and in a letter to his lover Marie-Constance Renelle, Sade describes *Justine* as "one of the sublimest parables ever penned for human edification."

But perhaps the clearest statement of Sade's philosophy appears in *La Philosophie dans le Boudoir* (*Philosophy in the Bedroom*), written during a brief period of freedom in 1795. This work takes the form of six dialogues, where the various (male and female) participants engage in graphically described sexual acts across gender lines (including incest, oral sex, and sodomy) for the purpose of "educating" a fifteen-year-old girl, Eugénie de Mistival. At the same time, or when recovering from their exertions, they engage in philosophical arguments on the nature of truth, desire, the family, manners, social law, gender roles in society, republicanism, religion, and Nature. In the fifth dialogue one character, the Chevalier de Mirvel, is invited to read from a treatise on these issues ("Chevalier, you possess a fine organ, read it to us"): "Yet Another Effort, Frenchmen, If You Would Become Republicans." The work as a whole is dedicated "To Libertines," and the dedication opens with a statement of its main theme: "Voluptuaries of all ages, of every sex, it is to you only that I offer this work; nourish yourselves upon its principles: they favor your passions, and these passions, whereof coldly insipid moralists put you in fear, are naught but the means Nature employs to bring man to the ends she prescribes for him; hearken only to these delicious promptings, for no voice save that of the passions can conduct you to happiness."

Yet beyond its graphic revelation of desire and the passions, of what is *unthought* in the rational tradition, the achievement of Sade's work, and this text in particular, lies in its form, whereby it uses reason to interrogate reason itself; and demonstrates—against the rational arguments of Jean-Jacques Rousseau and others for the "noble savage" and the "general will" as founding principles of civil society—that the "social contract" and civil reason are constructed not on the basis, but on the repression, of human nature. It illustrates that philosophical reason and language in general are predicated on desire, which is nevertheless precisely what escapes both reason and the order of language; and which must therefore appear within them as that which they exclude and cannot think—as rupture, as violence, as crime, as madness, as sexuality; in short, as transgression.

It is for this reason that the secret locked rooms, castles, and chateaus, by which confinement is thematized within Sade's texts, have reappeared in the transmission and reception of these texts: written in, and emerging from, his confinement in prisons and asylums as the criminal unthought or the irrational, they have been contained protectively within the rational discourse of psychoanalysis; excluded from philosophy, they have reappeared as "literature"; and even as literature, and even during most of the twentieth century they circulated underground or, falling prey to the panoptic gaze of censorship, appeared only in excerpted form.

Yet Sade's works anticipated Richard Krafft-Ebing and Sigmund Freud, and influenced writers from Fyodor Dostoyevsky, the Comete de, Lautréamont, and Algernon Charles Swinburne, to Charles Baudelaire, André Breton, Georges Bataille, Franz Kafka, and Lawrence Durrell, among many others. A distinguished critical tradition in the twentieth century (that of Guillaume Apollinaire, Roland Barthes, Simone de Beauvoir, Maurice Blanchot, Gilles Deleuze, Michel Foucault, Maurice Heine, Pierre Klossowski, Jacques Lacan, Maurice Nadeau, Jean Paulhan, Octavio Paz, and Mario Praz) attempted to restore Sade to his place in the history of reason and language.

Even though the name of Sade is well known and often cited today, few if any of his works are read, even in literature courses at universities. This suggests that this oeuvre, even in our own age of critical "enlightenment," has not emerged from the exclusionary web of unease woven around it by the paradigms of "reason" during the Romantic era. As Maurice Blanchot remarks, "In a sense, this was one of Sade's ambitions: to be innocent by dint of culpability; to smash what is normal, once and for all, and smash the laws by which he could have been judged." The academic disciplines of literary criticism and theory that circumscribe "literature," secure within their own self-imposed and self-censoring limits, have yet to face pedagogically the graphic tableaux and dark reflections of the man whom Charles Swinburne described as "the martyred Marquis," Beauvoir as "a great moralist," Apollinaire as "the freest spirit that ever lived," and Blanchot as "the master of the great themes of modern thought and sensibility," and whose work was perhaps ahead not only of its own time but of ours as well.

JOHANN PILLAI

Biography

Born rue de Condé, Paris, June 2, 1740. Education entrusted to his uncle, the abbé of the Benedictine monastery of Saint-Léger d'Ebreuil, 1745; entered Jesuit College d'Harcourt, 1750. With genealogical proof of nobility, admitted to the Light Cavalry of the King's Guard, 1754; served in the war with Prussia in 1757; retired from the army in 1763 with rank of captain in the Cavalry Regiment de Bourgogne. Married to a woman of royal blood, Renee-Pelagie de Montreuil in 1763; committed that year to the fortress of Vincennes and to house arrest for a year for excesses committed in a brothel. Took an actress-prostitute, Beauvoisin, as a mistress, 1765; birth of his first son, Louis-Marie, in 1767; arrested in 1768 for taking a woman home, threatening her with a knife, and flogging her. Birth of his second son, Donatien-

Claude-Armand, 1769; reinstated in his military duties, 1770. Imprisoned for a week for debts in 1771. Charged with "poisoning," "homosexual sodomy," and "unnatural advances" in 1773 after an orgy with his valet Latour and five prostitutes, some of whom ate sweets laced with "Spanish fly" extract; fled but recaptured after some months, later escaped. Charged with kidnapping and sexual abuse by parents of his wife's domestics at Lyons in 1775; reports emerged that the marquis was kidnapping and abusing young girls and boys at La Coste. In 1777 accused by three domestics of soliciting sex for money; caught and imprisoned again at Vincennes. Tried in 1778, found guilty of debauchery and excessive libertinage, fined, and banished from Marseilles for three years, but still kept prisoner; escaped, was recaptured, and returned to Vincennes. In 1784 transferred to the Bastille; in 1789 transferred to the asylum at Charenton; released in 1790 and formed lifelong liaison with widowed actress Marie-Constance Renelle. Became an "active citizen" and secretary of the Paris Section des Piques; in 1792 organized the cavalry of the eighth Company of the Section; in 1793 appointed magistrate, delegate to the National Convention, and chair of the Section. Arrested and imprisoned in 1794 for "moderantism" and later released. Arrested in 1801 with his publisher, and copies of *Justine* and *Juliette* were confiscated; imprisoned at Sainte-Pélagie. Transferred to Charenton in 1803, and determined to be "incorrigible" and in a state of "constant licentious insanity"; made his will in 1806. Died in 1814, either of "pulmonary congestion" or "adynamic and gangrenous fever" and was buried in Charenton Cemetery; inventory of Sade's effects and manuscripts at Charenton completed in 1815. When the cemetery was redesigned in 1830, Sade's body was exhumed and the cranium removed, later to be misplaced and lost by a phrenologist.

Selected Works

Dialogue entre un prête et un moribund. 1782.
Les 120 Journées de Sodome, ou l'école du libertinage. 1785.
Eugénie de Franval. 1788.
Oxtiern, ou les malheurs du libertinage. 1791.
Justine, on les malheurs de la virtue. 1791.
La Nouvelle Justine . . . suivi de l'histoire de Juliette sa soeur. 1797.
Aline et Valcour, ou le roman philosophique . . . 1793.
La Philosophie dans le boudoir. 1795.
Justine, Philosophy in the Bedroom, and Other Writings. Translated by Richard Seaver and Austryn Wainhouse. New York: Grove Press, 1965.
The 120 Days of Sodom and Other Writings. Edited by Richard Seaver. New York: Grove Press, 1987.

Bibliography

Barthes, Roland. *Sade/Fourier/Loyola.* Translated by Richard Miller. New York: Hill and Wang/Farrar, Straus and Giroux, 1976.
Beauvoir, Simone de. "Must We Burn Sade?" In *Marquis De Sade. An Essay by Simone de Beauvoir With Selections from his Writings Chosen by Paul Dinnage.* Translated by Annethe Michalson. New York: Grove Press, 1953.
Deleuze, Gilles. "Coldness and Cruelty". In *Masochism.* Translated by Jean McNeil. New York: Zone Books, 1991.
Foucault, Michel. *Madness and Civilization: A History of Insanity in the Age of Reason.* Translated by Richard Howard. New York: Vintage Books/Random House, 1988.

Gray, Francine du Plessix. *At Home With the Marquis de Sade: A Life.* New York: Penguin, 1999.

Klossowski, Pierre. *Sade My Neighbor.* Translated by Alphonso Lingis. Evanston, Ill.; Northwestern University Press, 1991.

Praz, Mario. *The Romantic Agony.* New York: Meridian Books, 1967.

Rousseau, Jean-Jacques. *The Social Contract and Discourses.* Translated by G. D. H. Cole. Revised by J. H. Brumfitt and John C. Hall. Updated by P. D. Jimack. London: Everyman/J. M. Dent, 1993.

Weiss, Peter. *The Persecution and Assassination of Jean-Paul Marat as Performed by the Inmates of the Asylum of Charenton under the Direction of the Marquis de Sade: A Play.* Translated by Geoffrey Skelton. Verse adaptation by Adrian Mitchell. New York: Atheneum, 1966.

SAINTE-BEUVE, CHARLES-AUGUSTIN DE 1804–1869

French critic, poet, novelist, and historian

Charles-Augustin de Sainte-Beuve achieved lasting renown mainly as a critic, even as the "prince of critics" as he was dubbed in his own time, then as the object of Marcel Proust's famous attack on biographical criticism in *Contre Sainte-Beuve* (*Against Sainte-Beuve*, posthumously published in 1954). His most direct links with the French Romantic movement, however, are through his lesser-known works as a poet and novelist. Inspired as a sixteen-year-old boy by Alphonse Marie-Louis de Lamartine's *Méditations*, he made his first impact on the developing movement with a critical study on Victor Hugo, when one of his former teachers, Paul-François Dubois, a founder of *Le Globe*, asked him to review the *Odes et ballades*. This was the first of a series of studies in defense of the young poet's talent in several reviews during the hard-fought campaign of the French Romantics and the start of a close association between the two writers (though, as his admiration for Hugo waned, Sainte-Beuve developed an even closer relationship with Hugo's wife, Adèle, who became his mistress in 1832).

Sainte-Beuve frequented Hugo's group, and associated with other Romantic luminaries such as Honoré de Balzac, Jacques-Louis David, Eugène Delacroix, Alexandre Dumas, Lamartine, Franz Liszt, and Alfred-Victor de Vigny. The early development of Sainte-Beuve's tastes and convictions can be traced in his revised *Globe* articles published as the volume *Tableau historique et critique de la poésie française et du théâtre français au XVIe siècle* (*Historical and Critical Survey of French Poetry and Theater in the Sixteenth Century*, 1828), where the empiricism and scientific convictions recently derived from the "Idéologues" and the classical tastes inherited from his education yield to his advocacy of Romantic principles and praise for the new wave of poets.

In 1827 Sainte-Beuve gave up his medical studies and turned to writing poetry himself. His natural bent was for barely veiled autobiographical and lyrical verse, notably in the first and the most significant of his four collections, the *Vie, poésies et pensées de Joseph Delorme* (*The Life, Poetry, and Thoughts of Joseph Delorme*, 1829). The others were: *Les Consolations* (*Consolations*, 1830), dedicated to Hugo, where the poet exalts friendship as a consolation for the irretrievable loss of religious faith; *Pensées d'août* (*August Thoughts*, 1837), where he develops a poetics of intimate reverie and commonplace reality, which contrasts with the heroics of much French Romantic writing of the time and was inspired to some degree by the English "lake poets"; and the privately printed *Livre d'amour* (*Book of Love*, 1843), the fruit of his affair with Adèle Hugo. The autobiographical aspect of *Joseph Delorme* is disguised by the device of presenting the work with its tripartite division (life, poetry, and thoughts) as an edition of the manuscripts of a fictitious but supposedly real poet doomed by tuberculosis to waste away and die young. In general terms, the work is very much in the Romantic tradition of Johann Wolfgang von Goethe's *Die Leiden des jungen Werthers* (*The Sorrows of Young Werther*, 1774), François-Auguste-René de Chateaubriand's *René* (1805), and Etienne Pivert de Senancour's *Obermann* (1804) but contains more specific echoes of the fate of Thomas Chatterton and Henry Kirke White, and, more precisely still, of Robert Southey's edition of *The Poetical Works and Remains of Henry Kirke White* (1806). Sainte-Beuve's poetry is little known and read today, but his *intimiste* manner influenced the Hugo of *Feuilles d'automne* (*Autumn Leaves*, 1831) the Chateaubriand of *Jocelyn* (1836), and later poets, notably Théodore de Banville, Charles Baudelaire, and Paul-Marie Verlaine, expressed their admiration and debt to "uncle Beuve's" lyric poetry.

Much the same could be said of Sainte-Beuve the novelist. *Volupté* (*The Sensual Man*, 1834), his only completed venture in the form, which he began to write in 1831, is another veiled autobiographical work, presented as an edition of a supposedly authentic manuscript: the confessions of a Breton priest, Amaury, who, as he sails to America to pursue his missionary vocation, recounts for the edification of a young friend his past life and loves, his wasted existence (in the pursuit of *volupté*), and his salutary conversion and entry into a seminary. Apart from its background representation of political activities during Napoleon Bonaparte's reign and the transposition that it contains of the author's relations with the Hugos, the novel is significant as a moral and spiritual allegory—*une vie morale*, as its original title suggests—and has been compared to Madame Barbara Juliane de Vietinghoff, (usually known as Madame de Krüdener) baronne de Krüdener's *Valérie* (1803) and Benjamin Constant de Rebecque's *Adolphe* (1816). Despite its stylistic diffuseness, Sainte-Beuve's reputedly "failed masterpiece" inspired Balzac in *Le Lys dans la vallée* (*The Lily of the Valley*, 1835) and Gustave Flaubert in *L'Education sentimentale* (*Sentimental Education*, 1869).

Even though for a brief spell in 1830–31, enthused by Claude-Henri Saint-Simon and other utopian reformers, Sainte-Beuve was caught up in the humanitarian socialism of the French Romantics and even though, during the 1830s, his Romantic credentials and wit earned him entry into the fashionable salons of Marie de Flavigny, Comtesse d'Agoult, Marie de Castries, and Madame Jeanne-Françoise Récamier, he progressively asserted his independence from the Romantics during this period and by 1840, disappointed at the lack of critical success of his own creative works and despairing of ever achieving the eminence to which he had aspired as a writer, he decided to devote his efforts fully to his work as a historian and critic. In his 1848–49 lectures in Liège, published in 1860 as *Chateaubriand et son groupe littéraire sous l'Empire* (*Chateaubriand and his Literary Group under the Empire*), a thoroughly documented historical and critical study of the very origins of the French Romantic movement, he exorcized the Romantic demons that still held sway over him.

By the middle of the century, Sainte-Beuve had developed and refined the art of the biographical "portrait" in some 150 articles on literary and historical figures, periods and works, past and present, and had expanded his lectures into what he called his "most enormous Portrait," the monumental history of Port-Royal (1840–59). Yet, even more monumentally, he produced over the next twenty years some six hundred weekly (or fortnightly) *causeries* on almost four hundred different topics, dealing mainly with French history and literature from the Middle Ages to the nineteenth century. Initially, these *Causeries du Lundi* (1851–62) and *Nouveaux Lundis* (1863–70) had regularly appeared, by dint of a rigorously disciplined routine, on a Monday in *Le Constitutionnel, Le Moniteur*, and *Le Temps* before being collected into twenty-eight volumes.

As a critic, Sainte-Beuve developed a distinctive method of literary portraiture that involved steeping himself fully in the life and works of writers or historical figures, starting from a total familiarity with their texts and drawing upon all available documentary evidence. The purpose of this process, which combined erudite and recondite research with an intuitive sympathy with his subject's character and circumstances, was to construct a living portrait of a (usually dead) author and discern the characteristic traits that would provide the key to the writer's talent or genius. As Sainte-Beuve's description of the ultimate stage of the process reveals—"the portrait speaks and lives, the man has been discovered"—the interpretation of literary works was not his primary preoccupation but would become the main precursor and model of biographical and historical criticism. Though he is often given credit for turning his attention to secondary figures and to neglected women writers, he is frequently blamed for underestimating the achievements of such major contemporary writers as Balzac, Baudelaire, Flaubert, and Stendhal, a failing that has been attributed by his detractors to a bias and resentment born of his own inability to match them or, more charitably, to an inherent conservatism and to a critical practice more appropriate to the study of writers of the past. Nevertheless, his portraits, written with subtlety, artistry, and wit, along with the more objective and, as he claimed, more scientific causeries, would be Sainte-Beuve's major legacy; and though he had long renounced his earlier convictions, their vast scope and their attempt to raise criticism to the level of a creative art owe much to the spirit and the aspirations of the Romantic era.

DAVID BAGULEY

Biography

Born in Boulogne, December 23, 1804. Attended lectures at the Athénée, 1821; studied at the Ecole de Médecine in Paris, 1823–27; famous liaison with Adèle Hugo, 1832–37; gave a course (the future *Port-Royal*) at the Académie de Lausanne, 1837–38; *conservateur* at the Bibliothèque Mazarine, 1840–48; elected to the French Academy, 1844; gave courses on French literature and Chateaubriand at the University of Liège, 1848–49; named professor of Latin poetry at the Collège de France from 1854; lectured at the École Normale Supérieure, 1857–61; senator during the Second Empire. Died October 13, 1869.

Selected Writings

Collections
Oeuvres. 2 vols. Edited by Maxime Leroy. 1956–60.
Sainte-Beuve, Selected Essays. Translated and edited by Francis Steegmuller and Norbert Guterman. 1963.
Literary Criticism of Sainte Beuve. Translated and edited by Emerson R. Marks. 1971.

Poetry and Other Fiction
Vie, poésies et pensées de Joseph Delorme. 1829.
Les Consolations. 1830.
Volupté 1834; as Volupté, the Sensual Man, translated by Marilyn Gaddis Rose. 1995.
Pensées d'août. 1837.
Livre d'amour. 1843.

Criticism
Tableau historique et critique de la poésie française et du théâtre français au XVIe siècle. 1828.
Critiques et portraits littéraires. 5 vols. 1836–39.
Port-Royal. 5 vols. 1840–59.
Portraits de femmes. 1844.
Portraits contemporains. 3 vols, 1846; enlarged editions, 1869–71, 1889.
Causeries du lundi. 15 vols. 1851–62; 3rd edition, 15 vols. 1857–72.
Derniers Portraits littéraires. 1852.
Chateaubriand et son groupe littéraire. 1861.
Nouveaux Lundis. 13 vols. 1863–70.

Bibliography

Billy, André. *Sainte-Beuve, sa vie et son temps*. 2 vols. Paris: Flammarion, 1952.
Bonnerot, Jean. *Bibliographie de l'oeuvre de Sainte-Beuve*. 4 vols. Paris: Giraud-Badin, 1937–52.
———. *Un Demi-siècle d'études sur Sainte-Beuve*. 3 vols. Paris: Les Belles Lettres, 1957.
Chadbourne, Richard M. *Charles-Augustin Sainte-Beuve*. Boston: Twayne, 1977.
Lehmann, A. G. *Sainte-Beuve: A Portrait of the Critic, 1804–1842*. Oxford: Clarendon Press, 1962.
Madelénat, Daniel. "Quelques échos du romantisme européen dans Port-Royal." In *Pour ou contre Sainte-Beuve, le "Port-Royal" Actes du colloque de Lausanne, septembre 1992*. Geneva: Labor/Paris: Société des Amis de Port-Royal, 1993.
Moreau, Pierre. *La Critique selon Sainte-Beuve*. Paris: SEDES, 1964.
Regard, Maurice. *Sainte-Beuve, l'homme et l'oeuvre*. Paris: Hatier, 1959.

SAINT-PIERRE, JACQUES-HENRI BERNARDIN DE 1737–1814

French writer

Jacques-Henri Bernardin de Saint-Pierre was born in Le Havre in 1737 and died in Eragny in 1814. His life was long and exciting, taking him to Russia, eastern Europe and Mauritius (then called the Ile de France) before he finally settled in Paris, made the acquaintance of Jean-Jacques Rousseau, and became a major literary and cultural figure of the period 1780–1800.

His first published work is the account of his journey to the Ile de France and a description of his life on the island (*Voyage à l'Ile de France*, 1773). The work was not a success but it is considered today in the context of its relationship with the author's best-selling novel, *Paul et Virginie* (1788). This novel was first published in the third edition of *Les Études de la Nature*, the first edition of which appeared in 1784. Bernardin had compiled this major philosophical study of nature while living on the breadline in Paris and surviving through the generosity of a few friends and various charitable sources. The *Études* were a major literary success and brought about a change in his fortune; he became a figure of note and received many letters from readers and admirers, most of which have survived in the library at Le Havre.

The *Études* represent, according to the author, an attempt to write the history of nature and to seek in nature the basis of morality and political and religious systems. Bernardin was greatly affected by the death of Rousseau in 1778, and his influence is felt throughout Bernardin's writing. Bernardin was not a professional scientist and he knew the botanical sciences only as an amateur observer. Nevertheless, he sought in the *Études* to demonstrate the harmony of nature and man's close relationship with the world in which he lived.

When *Paul et Virginie* first appeared it received immediate critical acclaim and encouraged many new readers to write to Bernardin. The novel, published independently in 1789 and available in print ever since, is a striking and beautiful love story set in an exotic paradise. Two young children are brought up close to nature, raised by their respective mothers and taught the virtues of frugal living and adoration of the divinity. Bernardin produced lavish poetic descriptions in this short novel, based on his firsthand knowledge of life on Mauritius. The idyllic love story has a tragic ending as the young heroine, Virginie, who is sent to France to see a rich aunt and thus separated from her beloved Paul, returns to seek continued happiness on the island but is caught in a hurricane and drowned in the sea within reach of safety because she is unwilling to remove her clothes to allow a sailor to carry her to the beach. Critics have disagreed about the ending; some believe that Virginie dies to preserve her modesty, others that she has been corrupted by her stay in Europe and cannot return, pure, to the island. Yet others believe that the conclusion is a religious one in which Virginie chooses to die to depart this world and live in a heavenly paradise. Whatever the interpretation of the conclusion, few critics would disagree that Bernardin has found the perfect recipe for a successful novel: a tragic love story, an exotic landscape, a serious political and religious message (there is a short episode on the fate of a female slave and a lengthy dialogue that involves serious criticism of contemporary France), and the finest example of poetic prose to be found in France in the eighteenth century. Bernardin is an evident precursor of François-Auguste-René de Chateaubriand, who was a great admirer of *Paul et Virginie*.

Such was the success of Bernardin's novel that a young writer, Etienne Pivert de Senancour, future author of *Obermann* (1804), wrote to him for advice about leaving civilization and settling on a tropical island that would offer him the benefits he read about in the novel. The letter survives in Le Havre but we have no record of Bernardin's reply if, indeed, there was one. In 1790 Bernardin wrote and published a short novel, *La Chaumière Indienne* (*The Indian Cottage*). The text is the account of a philosopher's journey in India, seeking happiness and the foundations for it. It is an overtly deistic account in which the author withdraws his support for organized religion and shows that the key to happiness is a simple life shared with a good companion and spent trusting in God's generosity. The influence of Rousseau is clearly visible here.

The French Revolution found Bernardin working on other projects, in particular the *Harmonies de la Nature* and a play involving a white slave, *Empsaël et Zoraïde*; neither was published in Bernardin's lifetime. Many projects remained unfinished but survive in the vast archives in Le Havre. Bernardin's widow became the wife of his secretary, Louis Aimé-Martin; they initiated a vast publishing operation in the 1820s and Aimé-Martin set about producing an edition of the complete works of Bernardin. It is apparent to us now that many of the posthumously published works were not edited according to today's standards and norms; it is hoped that a reliable edition will soon be planned.

Bernardin's influence was enormous. It is safe to say that no writer of the Romantic era was unaware of the novel *Paul et Virginie*, and references to his text are to be found in authors as diverse as Albert Camus and Gustave Flaubert.

MALCOLM COOK

Biography

Born Jacques-Henri Bernardin de Saint-Pierre in Le Havre, January 19, 1737, to a bourgeois family. Sailed on an uncle's ship to Martinique, 1749. Returned to Normandy; studied at a Jesuit school in Caen and the Jesuit Collège de Rouen until 1757; awarded a prize in mathematics. Attended the École des Ponts et Chaussées, 1757–58. After the school closed, transferred to the military school at Versailles; obtained a commission as a military engineer. Joined the Rhine army under the Comte de Saint-Germain, 1760. Returned to France; appointed to Malta as engineer-geographer, 1761. Returned home destitute after commission was refused recognition. Traveled to Holland and on to Russia, 1762; served as sublieutenant in the engineering corps at Moscow; obtained the protection of the French ambassador, the Baron de Breteuil. Traveled to Finland on a captain's commission from Catherine II. Returned to France via Poland, Austria, and Berlin, 1765–67. Left penniless after inheritance from his father went in its entirety to his stepmother. Lived in

Paris, virtually destitute, 1767. Commissioned as engineer captain to sail to Madagascar, 1767; after a quarrel with the head of the mission, refused to disembark and continued to Mauritius; stayed as a builder until 1770. Returned to Paris, 1771. Published *Voyages à l'Île-de-France*, 1773. Stayed with Breteuil in the Tuileries; began associating with philosophers in Paris, including Jean-Jacques Rousseau. Volumes 1–3 of *Études de la Nature* published, 1783. Third edition, including *Paul et Virginie*, published 1787. *Intendant* (head) of the Jardin du Roi, later the Jardin des Plantes, 1792; installed the zoo at the Jardin that same year. The post of *intendant* was suppressed; granted compensation by the Convention 1793. Married Félicité Didot (died 1799), daughter of the publisher of *Études*, 1793; they had one daughter, Virginie, and two sons, both called Paul, one of whom died in infancy. Appointed *professeur de philosophie morale* at the École Normale Supérieure, 1794 (school was closed, 1795). Member of the Institut de France, 1795; Académie Française,

1803. Married Desirée de Pelleporc, 1800; one son (born 1802; died 1804). Chevalier, Légion d'Honneur, 1806. President of the Académie Française, 1807. Awarded pension from Napoleon in acknowledgment of his support. Completed *Harmonies de la nature*, 1812. Died in Eragny-sur-Oise, January 21, 1814.

Selected Works

Les Etudes de la Nature. 1784.
Paul et Virginie. Published as part of the *Etudes*, 1784. Published independently, in 1789. Subsequent edition, edited by Racault, Jean-Michel. Paris: Livre de Poche, 1999.
La Chaumière indienne. 1790.

Bibliography

Maury, F. *Etude sur la vie et les oeuvres de Bernardin de Saint-Pierre.* 1892. Reprinted Geneva: Slatkine Reprints 1971.
Souriau, M. *Bernardin de Saint-Pierre d'après ses manuscrits.* Paris: Société Française d'Imprimerie et de Librairie, 1905.

SAINT-SIMON, CLAUDE-HENRI DE ROUVROY, COMTE DE 1760–1825

French social theorist

No study of Romanticism would be complete without a consideration of Claude-Henri de Rouvroy, Comte de Saint-Simon and Saint-Simonianism. Saint-Simon's solution to the dominant social question of his time was far from utopian, resting as it did upon the development of representative government involving not members of old noble families, like himself, but those who made an active contribution to national prosperity. In direct contrast, the Saint-Simonians became parodies of Romanticism and turned their initial practical plans for reform into religious mysticism.

Saint-Simon initially stated his belief that the state was controlled by an anachronistic elite, indifferent to the real needs of the nation, in 1802 in an anonymous *Lettre d'un habitant de Genève à ses concitoyens* (*Letters of an Inhabitant of Geneva to His Contemporaries*). In 1816 Saint-Simon published four issues of a journal, *L'Industrie*, which was financed by industrialists and scientists. He attacked the thieves and parasites who made no productive contribution to society, contrasting them with the industrious Americans. In 1819, in his new periodical, *Le Politique*, he pursued his claim that contemporary ills were the result of the dominance of the "idlers," those who lived on investments and made no positive contribution to society.

People began to pay attention to Saint-Simon when chance made a dramatic parallel between his claims and reality. In the newpaper *L'Organisateur*, he asserted that the loss of the French royal family and senior clerics would barely be noticed, whereas the loss of France's major businessmen and industrialists would be very damaging. He was charged with insulting the royals and his jury trial coincided with the actual, rather than the literary, assassination of the heir to the throne, the Duc de Berri, in February 1820. Saint-Simon was acquitted and his name was made famous.

In 1822 he issued a two-volume collection of his pamphlets, titled *Système industriel*, followed a year later by a further collection of pamphlets, *Catéchisme des Industriels*. Like many contemporary theorists, Saint-Simon addressed the combined problems of the repercussions of the French Revolution and the impact of economic change in the context of social evolution over a long time span. Since the revolution, class conflict had become a major issue, and he argued that a complete rethinking of the basis of government and society was needed to take account of the increasing variety of sources of wealth. The contribution of industry and commerce could not be ignored. A radical reworking of the social framework was vital to address the urgent problems of poverty and social inequality.

The language and arguments Saint-Simon used about class were adopted by the early socialists in their analyses of class conflict, although the rivalries that most concerned him were not between rich and poor but those within the elite, between those he dismissed as idlers and those he thought added value to society. For him *oisifs* (idlers) were parasites who lived on the efforts of others, especially wealthy landowners and investors. The *industriels* were the productive sector and embraced everyone who had to do some work to survive, as farmer, artisan, doctor, journalist, and so on. In some ways, the industriels, as described in his *Catéchisme des industriels*, corresponded to the *pays légal* of 1814, the elite that qualified for a vote on the basis of their tax payment, although he may have planned to include a wider cross-section of income in his politically active group. His analysis of what was wrong with society appealed to the opposition liberals during the Restoration. Saint-Simon wrote fast and frequently changed his mind; it is easy to distinguish contradictions in his thought. Although his account of social problems was simple enough, his solutions were more vague. He did not develop a single, coherent blueprint for the future. In his last months he came to the view that the fundamental issue was less the nature of the ruling elite than the loss of religious faith and his last book was titled *Nouveau Christianisme* (*New Christianity*, 1825). Shortly before his death, therefore, Saint-Simon had accomplished the transition from enlightened rationalist to Romantic.

His followers completed the metamorphosis into mysticism. Toward the end of his life, Saint-Simon acquired a band of disciples, many of whom were engineers trained at the École Polytechnique, who, after his death tried to develop a program of practical social reform based on the same assumptions as Charles Fourier, that the worst faults of their own society were the repression of women and workers. They embarked on small-scale individual reform projects to promote initiatives by the workers themselves. Saint-Simon, on the other hand, had looked to a more cosmic statement of the problem, to be addressed by changing the state. The affinity of Saint-Simonians to Saint-Simon was closest in the increasing importance they placed in a revivalist "new" Christianity. Saint-Simonians addressed the social question from a spiritual base, turning their organization into a sect. One of their members, Prosper Enfantin, asserted his right to be their pope and rallied them to search for a female pope. He pushed the case for the liberation of women into sexual license, which led to misery and tragedy for some of the young female workers who had been recruited and who apparently found their "pope" irresistible. In 1832 Enfantin was convicted on a charge of corrupting public morals and the movement collapsed, but a substantial number of former Saint-Simonians became socialists, while others took a lead in developing the role of the state during the Second Empire.

PAMELA PILBEAM

Selected Writings

Oeuvres de Claude-Henri de Saint Simon. 6 vols. 1966.
Henri Saint-Simon (1760–1825): Selected Writings. Edited and translated by Keith Taylor. 1975.

Bibliography

Carlisle, R. B. *The Proffered Crown: Saint-Simonianism and the Doctrine of Hope.* Baltimore, 1987.

Manuel, F. E. *The New World of Henri Saint-Simon.* Cambridge, Mass: Harvard University Press, 1956.

Moses, C. G. "Saint-Simonian Men/Saint-Simonian Women: The Transformation of Feminist Thought in 1830s France," *Journal of Modern History* 54 (1982): 240–67.

Pilbeam, Pamela. "Un aristocrate précurseur des socialistes: Henri de Saint-Simon." In *Le second ordre: L'idéal nobiliare*, edited by C. Grell and A. Ramières. Paris, 1999.

SALIERI, ANTONIO 1750–1825

Italian-born Viennese composer

Antonio Salieri, although an Italian-born musician, lived most of his life in Vienna. He was active as a composer (primarily of operas) during the Enlightenment of the late eighteenth century. Salieri's operas, which reflect the influence of Christoph Willibald Gluck's reform opera movement, belong solidly in the classical period of music history. However, two factors extend Salieri's influence into the Romantic era. Since his life continued almost a quarter of a century beyond his professional career, he was able to remain active as a teacher well into the core years of the Romantic age. He took a great interest in his pupils since he, as a young orphan, had been befriended by composer Florian Leopold Gassmann, who gave him a thorough musical education and introduced him to the imperial court of Vienna. In turn, Salieri instructed and inspired many members of the succeeding generation of Romantic composers, including Ludwig van Beethoven, Carl Czerny, Johann Nepomuk Hummel, Franz Liszt, Franz Peter Schubert, and others. Perhaps more relevantly, Salieri's proximity to Wolfgang Amadeus Mozart at the time of Mozart's premature death in 1791 at age thirty-five, and the burgeoning web of rumors surrounding that tragic event, turned Salieri into a quintessential tragic Romantic figure: ostensibly, as the legendary murderer of Mozart, driven by artistic jealousy. This reputation was revived in the late twentieth century by Peter Shaffer's 1979 play *Amadeus* and the 1984 film adaptation of the play directed by Milos Forman.

Indeed, Mozart and Salieri were colleagues, perhaps even rivals, during the brief period Mozart spent in Vienna, which would be the last decade of his life. By the time Mozart arrived on the scene in 1781, Salieri had already spent fifteenth years in Vienna and was a member of the emperor's chamber ensemble for most of that time, enjoying professional acclaim as an opera composer. Mozart, the brilliant young upstart only six years Salieri's junior, had come to Vienna seeking to ingratiate himself with the imperial court and make his name.

Although there is no corroborating evidence, Salieri would certainly have recognized and admired Mozart's genius. Any possible pangs of jealousy would surely have been mitigated by Salieri's lofty position in the court hierarchy and by his own many successful operas. Mozart, for his part, probably coveted Salieri's position with the emperor, perhaps even considering himself better suited to Salieri's duties. Although cognizant of the fact that Salieri never had anything but praise for his works, Mozart tended to be temperamental and paranoid, imagining enemies everywhere. In his frequent letters to his father, Mozart complained that the emperor cared for no composer other than the court composer Salieri. Mozart and his father feared an "Italian cabal," led by Salieri, that would endeavor to sabotage any opera by Mozart. Both father and son expected Mozart's *The Marriage of Figaro* to fall victim to this cabal, but were proved wrong when *Figaro* enjoyed enormous success.

Mozart, a frail, sickly man, always lived beyond his physical and monetary means. He died late in 1791, during the depths of the harsh Viennese winter, the culmination of a year of particularly ill health. The official cause of death was "rheumatic inflammatory fever," a set of symptoms consistent with his medical history. This diagnosis, however, did not prevent the circulation of rumors of his having been poisoned. Adding to the mystery, Mozart had recently received a secret commission for a requiem from an anonymous stranger, a count who wished to pass off the composition as his own. Mozart was said to have feverishly toiled over this requiem, with premonitions of his own death hanging over his head. However, at this time, Salieri's name did not come up in connection with Mozart's demise, even though Salieri had visited Mozart on the day preceding his death.

Toward the end of the century, Salieri gradually began to withdraw from composition, writing smaller-scale, more conservative music. By 1804 he had given up composition entirely. Retaining his position as *Hofkapellmeister*, he continued to fulfill his administrative duties at the court, but no longer provided his own compositions for performance. Considered the leading Viennese authority on composition and voice, he concentrated on his teaching. He remained highly active in the musical society of Vienna, especially as conductor for the Tonkünstler-Sozietät, a charity for widows and orphans of musicians and as member of the governing board of the Gesellschaft der Musikfreunde (Society of Friends of Music). A self-effacing man, and an honest critic of his own abilities, he devoted much of his later years to going back over his own compositions, revising, adapting, and adding marginal commentary. With an eventual biographer in mind, he prepared a catalog of his works and began an outline of his life that included many anecdotes and reminiscences.

Once Salieri stopped producing new operas, however, his fame was eclipsed by the new composers of the moment, the fate then shared by all musicians. Mozart was the first exception to this rule. By 1820, when Salieri had been all but forgotten, Mozart's posthumous reputation was in full flower. The aging Salieri had outlived himself, the only public interest in him now being confined to the fact that he had actually been acquainted with the great Mozart. Salieri spent his last years hospitalized, suffering from ill health, confusion, and depression. Reports of Salieri's confession of having poisoned Mozart survive alongside accounts of his denial. These accounts, in tandem with the original suspicions surrounding Mozart's demise, swept Vienna and caught the imagination of Russian poet and dramatist Aleksandr Pushkin.

Pushkin's 1830 play, *Motsart i Salyeri* (*Mozart and Salieri*), purports neither to be a historically accurate account nor an attempt to solve the mystery. Rather, Pushkin intended to depict the conflict between two contrasting artistic personalities using Salieri and Mozart as his archetypes. The Salieri character is the devoted lover of his art who hopes, through self-sacrifice, diligence, and prayer, to elevate himself and his craftsmanship above the mundane. By contrast, the Mozart character is the madman and idler who, without effort, is blessed with the gift of immortal genius. In the play, Salieri is angry with God for the unfairness of Mozart's possessing the genius Salieri so earnestly desires, and of which he feels himself to be more deserving. The play ends with Mozart's death at Salieri's hand. In some circles, Pushkin received criticism for defaming the memory of Salieri without a shred of proof.

Ironically, Salieri, one of many late eighteenth-century *Kleinmeisters* (the large body of talented but forgotten musicians eking out their living at the time when Vienna was the city of Mozart and Beethoven), would be no more than a footnote in music history today, if not for the legend, and both Pushkin's and more contemporary dramatizations of it.

NANCY MOSES

Biography

Born Legnago, near Verona, August 18, 1750. Studied music there until his father died, 1765; moved to Venice with a wealthy patron to study harmony and singing, discovered there by composer F. L. Gassmann, who took him to Vienna and provided for his education, 1766. Appointed court composer and began studies with Gluck, 1774. Married Theresia Helferstorfer 1775; they had eight children. Court *Kapellmeister* at Vienna, 1788–1824; did not conduct operas after 1790; duties largely administrative after 1800. Conductor of Tonkünstler-Sozietät until 1818. Died of senility and old age, Vienna, May 7, 1825.

Bibliography

Angermüller, Rudolph. *Antonio Salieri, Sein Leben und seine weltlichen Werke unter besonderer Berücksichtigung seiner "großen" Opern*. 3 vols. Munich: Emil Katzbichler, 1971.

Braunbehrens, Volkmar. *Salieri: Ein Musiker im Schatten Mozarts*. Germany: R. Piper GmbH, 1989. Translated as *Maligned Master: the Real Story of Antonio Salieri* by Eveline L. Kanes. New York: Fromm, 1992.

Della Corte, Andrea. *Un Italiano All'Estero: Antonio Salieri*. Turin: Paravia, 1936.

Rice, John A. *Antonio Salieri and Viennese Opera*. Chicago: University of Chicago Press, 1989.

Thayer, Alexander Wheelock. *Salieri: Rival of Mozart*. Edited by Theodore Albrecht. Kansas City: Philharmonia of Greater Kansas City, 1989.

LE SALON DE 1846

Essay by Charles-Pierre Baudelaire

As a critic, Charles-Pierre Baudelaire wrote on art more than anything else, and this essay, *Le Salon de 1846*, is a significant contribution to nineteenth-century art criticism. Baudelaire wrote a number of *Salon* pieces including *Le Salon de 1845, Le Salon caricatural de 1846*, and *Le Salon de 1859*, but *Le Salon de 1846* is a key work because it brings together discussion of various exhibited French artists with his ideas about Romanticism, modernity, the role of the imagination, color, and line. In this essay, Baudelaire boldly and directly challenges the bourgeois reader to acknowledge the relationship between art and politics: "Car se laiser devancer en art et en politique, c'est se suicider." ("To allow oneself to be forestalled in art and politics is to commit suicide.") It was first published as a pamphlet in May 1846 and signed Baudelaire Dufaÿs, Dufaÿs being his mother's maiden name. Salon reviews in mid-nineteenth-century France tended to subscribe to a formula of general exposition followed by individual sections describing artists and their work in terms of subject matter and technique.

Baudelaire adapted this format, structuring his essay around a series of contemporary issues and provocative questions. *Le*

Salon de 1846 is subdivided into nineteen sections arranged under the following headings: "Aux Bourgeois" ("To the Bourgeois"); "À Quoi Bon La Critique?" ("What is the Good of Criticism?"); "Qu'est-ce Que Le Romantisme?" ("What is Romanticism?"); "De la Couleur" ("Of Color"); "Eugène Delacroix"; "Des Sujets Amoureux et de M. Tassaert" ("Of Amorous Subjects and Tassaert"); "De Quelques Coloristes" ("Of Some Colorists"); "De L'Idéal et Du Modèle" ("Of the Ideal and the Model"); "De Quelques Dessinateurs" ("Of Some Draughtsmen"); "Du Portrait" ("Of the Portrait"); "Du Chic et Du Poncif" ("Of Chic and Poncif"); "De M. Horace Vernet" ("Of Horace Vernet"); "De L'Éclecticisme et Du Doute" ("Of Eclecticism and Doubt"); "De M. Ary Scheffer et Des Singes du Sentiment" ("Of Ary Scheffer and of the Apes of Sentiment"); "De Quelques Douteurs" ("Of Some Doubters"); "Du Paysage" ("Of Landscape"); "Pourquoi La Sculpture est Ennuyeuse" ("Why Sculpture Is a Bore"); "Des Écoles et Des Ouvriers" ("Of Schools and Journeymen"); and "De L'Héroïsme et de La Vie Moderne" ("Of Heroism and Modern Life"). From this list, it is possible to appreciate the wide range of issues that preoccupied Baudelaire at this time. The essay opens with thoughts on Romanticism and closes with reflections on modernity, yet for Baudelaire these are not separate states, but part of an integrated reality whereby Romantic *is* modern and vice versa. The largest section by far in the essay concerns Delacroix, who, for Baudelaire, was the Romantic painter par excellence, whose use of the "dictionary" of nature and color was supreme. Delacroix is described as a poet in painting, who is able to portray the extremes of human suffering and invest his works with sublime imaginative power. Comparing him with Jacques-Louis David and Jean-Auguste-Dominique Ingres, the masters of drawing, Baudelaire finds in Delacroix's work the epitome of the Romantic spirit, which he defines as inwardness, spirituality, color, and a yearning for the infinite.

An important theme in *Le Salon de 1846* is the use and function of color in painting. Baudelaire rhapsodizes on the "hymne compliqué" (complex hymn) of color in nature, distinguishing between the rational pursuits of draughtsmen who are like philosophers and dialecticians, and the more instinctual practices of colorists, like Delacroix, who are like epic poets. The power of color, Baudelaire claims, comes from the way one color relates to and harmonizes with another—"la rouge chante la gloire du vert; le noir . . . intercède le secours du bleu ou du rouge" ("red sings the glory of green; black . . . intercedes on behalf of blue or red")—and he describes the "concessions réciproques" (reciprocal concessions) made by tones. His emphasis

on synesthesia, on the musical notions of harmony, melody, and counterpoint to describe color relationships, was taken up by symbolist poets later in the century and was closely related to his notion of "correspondances" whereby images, sounds, scents, and memories interact and reveal worlds of experience beyond the material one. Sensitivity to the ephemeral nature of human life was, Baudelaire believed, a vital feature of great artists' work. Those who were not attuned in this way became "apes of sentiment," like the painter Ary Scheffer, who toyed with the "double piété de l'art et de la religion" (twin pieties of art and religion). Great art was achieved by close observation of changes in the natural world, which are then distilled and crafted. Invoking the Aristotelian notion of *ut pictura poesis*, Baudelaire describes the artist as translator, and the correspondence between the different art forms, poetry, painting, music, underlies all his writing. In *Le Salon de 1846*, Baudelaire asserts the importance of art criticism as an art form in itself and claims that it should be partial, entertaining, and poetic, and take the form, if necessary, of a sonnet or elegy. He writes, "La critique touche à chaque instant à la métaphysique" ("criticism verges constantly on metaphysics").

The essay closes with a theme to which he returns in "The Painter of Modern Life" (1857). This theme—the heroism of modern life—underpinned much of Baudelaire's work as a poet and critic. He argues, for example, that painters should paint figures in contemporary dress, rather than in archaic costumes from the past (like the historical paintings of Horace Vernet), and that the contemporary, in all its diverse and fleeting guises, has a heroic or epic dimension. His idea of modernity was not merely a question of being up-to-date or subject to swiftly changing fashions, although these were symptomatic of modern experience. Rather, he claims that in the pursuit of beauty, the Romantic and modern are conjoined.

JANE DESMARAIS

Text

Le Salon de 1846, 1846. Reissued posthumously in 1868 in *Curiosités esthétiques*. Translated by P. E. Charvet in *Charles Baudelaire: Selected Writings on Art and Literature*. 1972.

Bibliography

Benjamin, Walter. *Charles Baudelaire: A Lyric Poet in the Age of High Capitalism.* 1983.
Carrier, David. *Charles Baudelaire and the Origins of Modernist Painting.* 1996.
Howells, Bernard. *Baudelaire: Individualism, Dandyism, and the Philosophy of History.* 1996.
Moss, A. *Baudelaire and Delacroix.* 1973.

SALONS AND LITERARY SOCIETIES: GERMANY

The history of German salons and literary societies is associated both with the Enlightenment concern for the rehabilitation of the German language after the depredations of the Thirty Years' War, and with the need for a semipublic space where ideas could be exchanged and new social relations developed without regard to the constraints of court etiquette. The former led to the formation of the so-called *Sprachgesellschaften* (language societies) and *Dichterorden* (poets' guilds) during the later seventeenth and

early eighteenth centuries, while the latter sought its models in the European tradition, most notably in the salons of late seventeenth-century France, and developed in Germany in the second half of the eighteenth century. Thus, the history of German salons is coextensive with the history of the German bourgeoisie.

While sociability in Germany as a whole took a wide variety of forms, the most prominent examples flourished in Berlin around 1800, among assimilated Jews, specifically Jewish intellectual women. In the 1780s and 1790s, the Jewish doctor and philosopher Samuel Herz hosted discussions of academic questions, while his wife Henriette gathered around her a kind of literary *jeunesse dorée* (golden youth). One can therefore speak of a "double salon" in the Herz household. Dorothea Veit, the daughter of the Jewish philosopher Moses Mendelsohn who was married to the banker Simon Veit, opened up her husband's mansion to a salon similar to that of Henriette Herz, devoted to the appreciation of literature and its role in the development of human sensibility. Having met the young Friedrich von Schlegel in 1797, Dorothea eloped with him to Jena, where she became involved in the Jenaer Frühromantik (early romantic movement in the town of Jena). Rahel Levin, the daughter of a Jewish jeweler, invited people from almost all walks of life—penniless poets and the son of the Prussian King, distinguished male members of the German intelligentsia, as well as aristocratic or bourgeois women who had almost no access to academic education—into her garret, to take part in exceptionally witty, intelligent and independent-minded conversations. This combination of participants, brought and held together by an intellectually and socially distinguished hostess, gave the salon its quality. Conversations focused mainly on literature, art, and the latest developments in thought and philosophy, but the salon was also a place for acting, storytelling, and musical performance. Napoleon Bonaparte's occupation of Prussia and financial problems led to the closure of Rahel Levin's garret salon in 1806. Although she later married the Prussian diplomat Varnhagen von Ense and went on hosting salons throughout her life, she never repeated her first success. It was on such Berlin salons that Friedrich Daniel Ernst Schleiermacher based his *Versuch einer Theorie des geselligen Betragens* (*Essay on the Theory of Sociable Behavior*, 1799).

At the same time as the Berlin salons were flourishing, Duchess Anna Amalia of Saxe-Weimar and the first lady of her court, Luise von Göchhausen, also founded important social circles. The small town of Weimar was dominated by its ducal court and an educated class which, in terms of sheer numbers, was unusually prominent. The circle convened by the duchess consisted exclusively of aristocrats and some specially invited artists; the guests of her first lady came from a slightly broader social spectrum. The sociable activities of both circles were comparable to those in Berlin and elsewhere, but they crucially enjoyed the active participation of Johann Wolfgang von Goethe. This is particularly important because he was the absent idol of so many other salons such as that of Rahel Levin. During the summer months, meetings moved to Amalia's country estate in Tiefurt, which gave its name to the participants' privately published *Journal von Tiefurth*. Amalia's so-called *Musenhof* was succeeded in 1806 by the less formal literary salon hosted by Johanna Schopenhauer, widow of a Hamburg merchant (and mother of the philosopher Arthur). It was precisely her ability to create a culturally, socially, and even politically liberal space during the French occupation that enabled her to begin a salon when others were giving up. Some of Amalia's former guests, including Goethe, were "inherited," but the range was extended to include educated middle-class people from a wide variety of professions. Again, Goethe's presence gave the meetings their special reputation and was most probably responsible for the high numbers of visitors from all over Germany. However, this Goethe cult also threatened the free and democratic character of the salon by introduc-

ing an inhibiting hierarchical tendency. This led indirectly to Schopenhauer's concentration on her own writing and hence to her development as an independent authoress.

A mere fifteen miles away, in the same duke's university town of Jena, a group of young poets and philosophers gathered around the brothers Friedrich and August Wilhelm von Schlegel and their wives Dorothea and Caroline. They set up house together in 1799. The aim was to create a communal space where aesthetic production was not strictly separated from the rest of social life. Their *Sympoesie* (Sympoetry) and *Symphilosophie* (Symphilosophy) found expression above all in the form of the fragment and the notion of Romantic irony. The latter refers to the self-conscious nature of their gatherings and the works they produced, while the fragment has associations of exchange and fluidity, ferment and catching at transience. Poets and scholars such as Clemens Brentano, Johann Gottlieb Fichte, Sophie Mereau, Novalis, Friedrich Wilhelm Joseph von Schelling, Friedrich Daniel Ernst Schleiermacher, Henrik Steffens, Ludwig Tieck, and Wilhelm Heinrich Wackenroder were frequent participants in these meetings. The public organ of this movement, in which traditional notions of genre and authorship were overturned, was the journal *Athenaeum*, which had been founded by the Schlegels in Berlin in 1798. The actual Jenaer Frühromantiker group only stayed together for two years, but in many respects it formed the kernel of German Romanticism.

Subsequent Romantic groupings can be found, for example in Heidelberg, Dresden, and Göttingen. The female influence gradually waned and political, particularly national, and even occasionally anti-Semitic tendencies came to the fore, as the name of Achim von Arnim's Christlich-Deutsche Tischgesellschaft (Christian-German Dining Society), held in Berlin from 1811, suggests.

Indeed, the general decline of salons and literary societies toward the middle of the nineteenth century was bound up with a process of increasing institutionalization and formalization. The characteristics of a semipublic space were replaced by a demonstrative public function serving either the display of art as cultural capital, or the pursuit by a body with fixed statutes and a regulated membership of particular sociocultural agendas.

ASTRID KÖHLER

See also **Arnim, Achim von; Brentano, Clemens; Fichte, Johann Gottlieb; Fragment; Goethe, Johann Wolfgang von; Irony, Romantic; Novalis (pseudonym of Friedrich von Hardenberg); Schlegel, August Wilhelm von; Schlegel, Dorothea; Schlegel, (Karl Wilhelm) Friedrich von; Schleiermacher, Friedrich Ernst Daniel; Staël, Madame Anne-Louise-Germaine de; Tieck, Ludwig; Varnhagen von Ense, Rahel; Women**

Bibliography

Blackall, Eric. *The Emergence of German as a Literary Language 1700–1775.* Cambridge: Cambridge University Press, 1959.

Bruford, Walter Horace. *Culture and Society in Classical Weimar 1775–1806.* London: Cambridge University Press, 1962.

Gleichen-Rußwurm, Alexander von. *Geselligkeit, Sitten und Gebräuche der europäischen Welt 1789–1900.* Stuttgart: J. Hofmann, 1910.

Habermas, Jürgen. *Strukturwandel der Öffentlichkeit.* Luchterhand: Neuwied, 1962. Translated as *The Structural Transformation of the Public Sphere: An Inquiry into a Category of Bourgeois Society* by Thomas Burger with the assistance of Frederick Lawrence. Cambridge, Mass.: MIT Press, 1989.

Hertz, Deborah. *The Literary Salon in Berlin 1780–1806. The Social History of an Intellectual Institution.* Minneapolis: University of Minnesota Press, 1979.

———. *Jewish High Society in Old Regime Berlin.* New Haven, Conn.: Yale University Press, 1988.

Hof, Ulrich im. *Das gesellige Jahrhundert. Gesellschaft und Gesellschaften im Zeitalter der Aufklärung.* Munich: Beck, 1982.

Hoffmann-Axthelm, Inge. *Geisterfamilie: Studien zur Geselligkeit der Frühromantik.* Frankfurt: Peter Lang, 1973.

Köhler, Astrid. *Salonkultur im klassischen Weimar. Geselligkeit als Lebensform und literarisches Konzept.* Stuttgart: Metzler and Poeschel, 1996.

Meyer, Bertha. *Salon Sketches. Biographical Studies of Berlin Salons of the Emancipation.* New York: Bloch, 1938.

Meyer, Michael A. *The Origins of the Modern Jew. Jewish Identity and European Culture in Germany, 1749–1824.* Detroit: Wayne State University Press, 1967.

Peter, Emanuel. *Literatur, Gruppenbildung und kultureller Wandel im 18. Jahrhundert.* Tübingen: Niemeyer, 1999.

Schultz, Hartwig, ed. *Salons der Romantik. Beiträge eines Wiepersdorfer Kollquiums zu Theorie und Geschichte des Salons.* Berlin: Mouton de Gruyter, 1997.

Seibert, Peter. *Der literarische Salon—ein Forschungsüberblick.* In *Internationales Archiv für Sozialgeschichte der Deutschen Literatur (IASL).* Vol. 3. Sonderheft Tübingen: Niemeyer, 1993.

———. *Der lit erarische Salon. Literatur und Geselligkeit zwischen Aufklärung und Vormärz.* Stuttgart: Metzler, 1993.

Tornius, Valerian. *Salons: Bilder gesellschaftlicher Kultur aus fünf Jahrhunderten.* Leipzig: Klinkhrdt & Biermann, 1913. Translated as *The Salon: Its rise and Fall: Pictures of Society through Five Centuries* by Agnes Platt. London: Butterworth, 1929.

Wilhelmy, Petra. *Der Berliner Salon im 19. Jahrhundert (1780–1914).* (Veröffentlichung der Berliner Historischen Kommision. Vol. 73) Berlin: Mouton de Gruyter, 1989.

SAND, GEORGE (ARMANDINE-AURORE-LUCIE DUDEVANT, NÉE DUPIN) 1804–1876

French writer

Once remembered merely as a lover of great men (including other great Romantic artists such as Frédéric François Chopin and Alfred de Musset), as the friend of Gustave Flaubert (who wrote "Un coeur simple" for her), and the author of rustic novels, George Sand has since benefited from growing critical interest in French women's writing in the nineteenth century. Though she would return in person and in writing to her beloved home town Nohant, her personal and literary affiliations reflect her important position on the broader canvas of French cultural life (witnessed not least by her correspondence), and of the July Monarchy in particular. Just as Sidonie-Gabrielle Colette would do at the turn of the century, Sand began her career by coauthoring with a male partner, producing *Rose et Blanche* (1831) with her lover Jules Sandeau. Like Colette, she would outgrow her sponsor (from whom she did, however, forge her masculine nom de plume). Her range is considerable, including travel writing, long and short fiction, drama (such as *Cosima*, performed in 1840), autobiography, and social and political commentary. Though contemporaries, most notably Charles Baudelaire, decried her writing (and her person), she was the dominant female voice of French Romanticism. Her audience was both popular and intellectual, and though Émile Zola was to be a harsh critic, subsequent research has shown how she fused the utopian and pastoral inclinations of Romanticism with a painstaking evocation of contemporary reality.

Though her sexual politics did not sit unambiguously with the nascent radical feminism of the age, her writing continually returns to the issue of women's liberty and its limits. In particular, she attacked the unfair treatment of women under the marriage laws of the Napoleonic Code and the paltry education offered to them. *Indiana* (1832), her first individual effort at fiction and an immediate success, explored the effect of marriage on women. *Valentine* (1832) introduced the theme of relation-ships between characters not only of different genders but of different classes. In *Lélia* (1833; the ending was changed in 1839) Sand overcame the habitual association of women's writing with the love theme. In spite of its melodramatic evocation of the *mal du siècle* (the spiritual sickness of Romantic melancholy diagnosed by François-Auguste-René Chateaubriand in *Le Génie du christianisme*) *Lélia* also conveys philosophical, political, and religious reflections. Sand's relationship with Musset, tempestuous like so many of her others, informs *Jacques* (1834), which treats suicide and a love triangle around a May-to-September marriage. In *Mauprat* (1837) she locates the love plot back in her native Berry.

Her left-wing political tendencies came to the fore during the late 1830s and 1840s under the influence of Félicité de Lammenais and Pierre Leroux. *Spiridon* (1838–39) charts the link between political and religious progress in its account of the spiritual quest for a new religion. *Le Compagnon du tour de France* (*The Companion of the Tour of France*, 1840) represents the perspective of politically aware workers on such problems. Her most important text of the period, the novel *Consuelo* (1842), and its sequel *La Comtesse de Rudolstadt* (*The Countess of Rudolstadt*, 1843), tells of a music tutor's marriage to the revolutionary Albert, her subsequent love for him and their journey through eastern Europe where they preach socialism and universal charity. *Le Meunier d'Angibault* (*The Miller of Angibault*, 1845) takes us from peasant life to the proposal of a utopian community. These works express Sand's hopes for spiritual and political regeneration, characteristic of the Romantic yearning for utopia.

During the 1840s, Sand started to publish those rustic novels on which much of her subsequent popularity lay. *Jeanne* (1843) recounts the tale of Jeanne d'Arc in the form of an idealized peasant girl who is the object of men's desire. In *La Mare au diable* (*The Devil's Pool*, 1846) the widower Germain falls in

Eugène Delacroix, *George Sand*. Reprinted courtesy Topham Picturepoint, © 1991.

love with the poor girl Marie when they both lose their way to the village where he is supposed to marry an eligible widow. After disappointing encounters with the widow and Marie's new employer, both return to their village, where initially Marie resists Germain's passion. In Sand's next work, *François le Champi* (*The Country Waif*, 1847–48), the hero is a foundling brought up first by a goodhearted but illiterate mother and then by Madeleine Blanchet. Madeleine's husband and mother-in-law are opposed to this arrangement and François is forced to leave to seek work elsewhere. He returns to help the now-widowed Madeleine (with money from his unknown mother) and finally they marry, overcoming the age gap to find conjugal happiness. Sand uses patois in literary form to evoke provincial life, a method theorized in her introduction.

These portraits of rustic life also convey much authentic detail on folk tradition and folklore (such as the appendix in *La Mare au diable* on marriage customs in provincial France before the Industrial Revolution), but are characterized by Sand's passion for social justice. She was active in the revolution of 1848; however, she chose neither to run for election in 1848 nor to pursue lionization amid the Académie Française, and after Napoleon III's coup d'état in 1851 she largely turned away from the political arena. Her rustic fiction continued with *Les Maîtres sonneurs* (*The Master Pipers*, 1853) which also reflects on the nature of music. A year later, her autobiographical *Histoire de ma vie* (1854–55) appeared. Sand fictionalized her relationship with Musset (he had died the previous year) in *Elle et lui* (*He and*

She, 1859). Before her own death she wrote *Contes d'une grandmère* (*Tales of a Grandmother*, 1872–76) which recapitulate her interest in the formation of relationships and character in spite of the brutalizing forces of dogma and social order.

NICHOLAS WHITE

Biography

Born Aurore Dupin in 1804. Her grandmother became her legal guardian in 1809 and raised her at Nohant in Berry; sent to a convent in Paris to complete her education, 1818–20; in 1822 she married Casimir Dudevant by whom she had her son Maurice the next year; gave birth to Solange in 1828, probably fathered by one of her lovers; problems with Casimir culminated in 1830 when it was decided that she would spend half the year in Paris; had a string of lovers including Sandeau (1830–33), Musset (1833–34), and from 1838 on, Chopin (liaison ended in 1847 when he sided with Solange, who disobeyed Sand in marrying Auguste Clésinger); legally separated from Casimir in 1836; drawn to left-wing politics, particularly in the late 1830s and 1840s; active in the revolution of 1848, collaborated on the *Bulletin de La République* and helped to found *La Cause du Peuple* but refused to stand for election to parliament; from 1865 on her friendship with Flaubert blossomed; death of Casimir in 1871. Died at Nohant in 1876.

Selected Writings

Indiana. 1832. Translated as *Indiana* by Sylvia Raphael. Oxford: Oxford University Press, 1994.

Valentine. 1832. Translated as *Valentine* by George B. Ives. Chicago: Academy Chicago, 1996.

Lettres d'un voyageur. 1837. Translated as *Lettres d'un voyageur* by Sacha Rabinovitch and Patricia Thompson. Harmondsworth: Penguin, 1987.

Mauprat. 1837. Translated as *Mauprat* by Sylvia Raphael. Oxford: Oxford University Press, 1997.

Un hiver à Majorque. 1842. Translated as *A Winter in Majorca* by Robert Graves. London: Cassell, 1956.

Le Meunier d'Angibault. 1845. Translated as *The Miller of Angibault* by Donna Dickenson. Oxford: Oxford University Press, 1995.

François le champi. 1847. Translated as *The Country Waif* by Eirene Collis. Lincoln: University of Nebraska Press, 1977.

Les Maîtres Sonneurs. 1853. Translated as *The Master Pipers* by Rosemary Lloyd. Oxford: Oxford University Press, 1994.

Histoire de ma vie. 1854. Translated as *Story of My Life* by Thelma Jurgràu. Albany: SUNY Press, 1991.

Bibliography

Brée, Germaine. "Le mythe des origines et l'autoportrait chez George Sand et Colette." In *Symbolism and Modern Literature*. Edited by Marcel Tetel. Durham, N.C.: Duke University Press, 1978.

Crecelius, Katherine. *Family Romances*. Bloomington: Indiana University Press, 1987.

Dickenson, Donna. *George Sand: A Biography*. Oxford: Berg, 1988.

Didier, Béatrice. "George Sand ou l'éros romantique." In *L'écriture-femme*. Paris: PUF, 1981.

Mallet, Francine. *George Sand*. Paris: Grasset, 1976.

Miller, Nancy K. "Writing (from) the Feminine." In *The Representation of Women in Fiction*. Edited by Carolyn Heilbrun and Margaret Higonnet. Baltimore: Johns Hopkins University Press, 1981.

Mozet, Nicole. "Signé le voyageur: George Sand et l'invention de l'artiste," *Romantisme* 55 (1987): 23–32.

Naginski, Isabelle. *George Sand: Writing for Her Life.* New Brunswick, N.J.: Rutgers University Press, 1991.

Powell, David. *George Sand.* Boston: Twayne, 1990.

Schor, Naomi. *George Sand and Idealism.* New York: Columbia University Press, 1993.

SARMIENTO, DOMINGO FAUSTINO 1811–1888

Argentine writer and statesman

The life and works of Domingo Faustino Sarmiento testify to the energy, intelligence, and, some might say, genius of their protagonist. Sarmiento is a towering figure in nineteenth-century Argentine and Latin American letters and public life, and no analysis of Romanticism in the Americas would be complete without his *Vida de Juan Facundo Quiroga o civilización y barbarie* (*Facundo; or, Civilization and Barbarism*, 1845). Though this book is arguably his most enduring literary work, it is by no means his only accomplishment of note. Born to a family of modest means in the province of San Juan, Sarmiento in time became minister of education (1856), foreign minister (1860), and president of Argentina 1868–74. His formidable political trajectory was only matched by his voluminous output, collected posthumously in fifty-two volumes.

Sarmiento's life, like that of his contemporary Esteban Echeverría, is marked by two major events: the May Revolution in 1810 and the dictatorship of Juan Manuel de Rosas, who ruled Argentina from 1830 to 1852. As such, most of Sarmiento's writing revolves around the reorganization of Argentina after independence and after Rosas, against whom he employed both pen and sword. As a result of being in the *unitario* army, which opposed Rosas's *federales*, Sarmiento went into exile in 1829. He remained in Chile until 1836, when he returned to San Juan. During this time, he started a chapter of Echeverría's Asociación de la Joven Argentina (Association of Argentine Youth) but was politically persecuted and eventually imprisoned in 1840. Sarmiento fled to Chile once more, where he continued as a journalist and published his first major work, *Mi defensa* (*My Defense*, 1843).

The *Vida del General Fray Félix Aldao* (*Life of General Fray Félix Aldao*, 1845) came before the publication of *Facundo*. Infused with the pervasive sense that the best hopes of the *libertadores* had become lost illusions, the *Facundo* is a call against the tyranny of Rosas. Sarmiento suggests that economic inequality, a lack of civic spirit in the ruling class, and a weak government led to civil wars that give rise to a "third element" in Argentine culture beyond the control of the two parties, whether unitario or federal. The "third element" of Facundo and Rosas, *caudillismo*, is born to measure itself against "las ciudades y la civilización europea" ("cities and European civilization").

Yet the dialectic between European civilization and American barbarity that Sarmiento establishes in the first chapters of *Facundo* becomes complicated once he enters into history proper. *Facundo* develops three separate understandings of civilization and barbarity: Europe versus America; America versus Europe; and the third, which he defines in *Facundo*; America against itself. Readers of *Facundo* have remarked on the comparisons that Sarmiento makes between gauchos and the "nomad tribes" of Asia, a comparison that arises from the European interpretation of Eastern culture. "Esta extensión de llanuras imprime por otra parte a la vida del interior cierta tintura asiática. . . . Es el capataz un caudillo, como en Asia es el jefe de la caravana." ("This extension of lands imposes a certain Asiatic tincture on life in the interior. . . . The *capataz* is a caudillo, as in Asia he is the leader of a caravan.") Sarmiento appeals to European sympathies by presenting the gaucho in orientalist typology. He nonetheless resists Walter Scott's pronouncement on the gaucho. He quotes Scott, who writes, "Las vastas llanuras de Buenos Aires, no están pobladas sino por cristianos salvajes, conocidos bajo el nombre de Guachos (por decir Gauchos)" ("The great plains of Buenos Aires are populated by savage Christians known as Guachos [meaning Gauchos]"). In an unexpected outburst of patriotism, Sarmiento adds "¡Sería bueno proponerle a la Inglaterra por ver no más, cuántas varas de lienzo y cuántas piezas de muselina daría por poseer estas llanuras de Buenos Aires!" ("It would be good to propose to England, just to see, how many pieces of muslin and cotton it would give to own these great plains of Buenos Aires!") Sarmiento corrects Scott and exposes the imperialist motives behind the gaucho's characterization. It is one thing for an American to speak about civilization and barbarity; it is a very different one for a European to characterize Americans as savages.

When it is his turn to speak about civilization and barbarity in the Americas, Sarmiento paints a chilling portrait of the caudillo Facundo Quiroga, to whom he assigns the epithet of *salvaje* (savage). Facundo's portrait holds up a mirror to Rosas's dictatorship, which "destroys the works of centuries, civilization, and liberty" because it follows Facundo's system, "el terror sobre el ciudadano . . . el terror sobre el gaucho . . . el terror suple al entusiasmo, suple a la estrategia, suple a todo" ("terror to command the citizen . . . terror to command the gaucho . . . terror is behind enthusiasm, terror is behind strategy, it is behind everything"). In Sarmiento's eyes, Rosas's barbarism is more dangerous because it comes dressed in the trappings of civilization, and it is supported by mass propaganda. Sarmiento shows how Rosas permeates all aspects of Argentine daily life, from forcing people to wear a red ribbon that declared their allegiance to the Rosista party, to the constant display of Rosas's portrait in homes and at public celebrations. Sarmiento's *Facundo* insists on the barbarity of terror and ideological compulsion, though this insistence is complicated by Sarmiento's racist idiosyncrasies.

Later in 1845, the Chilean government sent Sarmiento to compare school systems and study methods of colonialism in various countries. Upon his return he published *De la educación popular* (*On Popular Education*, 1849) and *Viajes en Europa, África y Estados Unidos* (*Voyages in Europe, Africa, and the United*

States, 1849). *Viajes* records Sarmiento's experiences during the two-year voyage. In Paris he met the aging José de San Martín, whose silence during his exile of thirty years in France profoundly impressed Sarmiento. His U.S. itinerary included Washington, D.C., Philadelphia, New York, and Boston, where he met and befriended educator Horace Mann, who became a lifelong friend.

Argirópolis and *Recuerdos de Provincia* (*Provincial Rememberances*), both published in 1850, followed. In 1851 he fought alongside General Urquiza to overturn Rosas but became disenchanted with Urquiza and returned to two brief periods of exile in Chile (1852 and 1854), where he continued to publish. He returned to Buenos Aires in 1855, and his political career began in earnest. Political office, however, did not impede Sarmiento's writing, which became concerned with the state of the school system in Argentina. He found time to start two magazines, *Ambas Américas* (*Two Americas*, 1867) and *Educación común* (*Public Education*, 1876).

While serving as foreign minister for Urquiza in 1868, Sarmiento traveled to Washington, D.C., and there received the news he had been named president. His presidency bore the stamp of the nineteenth-century ideology of progress. He continued the task of unifying Argentina, even if it was by exterminating the gauchos and indigenous peoples in the provinces; a census was done of the population and eight hundred new schools were created. Communications were improved through railways, the telegraph, and the transoceanic cable. After his term in office, Sarmiento held a number of government posts, first as superintendent of education, then as a general. In the last decade of his life, he published *Conflicto y armonía de las razas en América* (*Conflict and Harmony of Races in America*, 1883) where he elaborates the idea of progress in terms of social Darwinism via Herbert Spencer, identifying progress as a Euro-American phenomenon, and *Vida de Dominguito* (*Life of Dominguito*, 1886), a memorial to his only son, who had died in the war against Paraguay.

If San Martín's silence affected Sarmiento, the contemporary scholar will find himself strangely perplexed by the strains that run throughout Sarmiento's oeuvre. The same man who masterfully denounced the terror of Rosas's regime and who believed in the education of all citizens as the only way to secure the stability of a democratic republic also suggested that Latin Americans had to purify "la barbarie insumida en las venas" ("barbarism flowing through their veins"). Sarmiento's monumental but conflicted life and works finally do not define civilization and savagery, but suggest the beginning of a more complex idea, that civilization is not always the measure of savagery.

JOSELYN M. ALMEIDA

Biography

Born January 15, 1811 in San Juan. Taught in San Juan 1826; joined the *unitario* army 1829. First exiled to Chile, 1831. Returned to San Juan, 1836; suffered prison for political reasons, 1840; second exile to Chile. In 1842 became director of the Escuela Normal, and professor at the University of Chile. Traveled to Europe, Africa, and the Americas, 1845–47. Married Benita Martínez upon his return. Fought against dictator Juan Manuel Rosas in 1851. Returned to Chile in 1853; returned to Argentina in 1855. Became senator, 1860; governor of San Juan, 1862, and foreign minister, 1864. Son Domingo dies, 1866. Became president of Argentina, 1868–74. Continued in various government offices until he left for Paraguay in 1887. Died in Asunción, September 11, 1888.

Selected Writings

Collection
Obras completas. Edited by Luis Montt and Augusto Belín Sarmiento. 52 vols. 1948–56.

Prose
Educación común. Edited by Gregorio Weinberg. 1987.
Facundo. Edited by Carlos Altamirano. 1994. Translated as *Facundo; or, Civilization and Barbarism* by Mary Mann. 1998.
La correspondencia de Sarmiento. 3 vols. Edited by Carlos Segreti. 1991.
Viajes por Europa, África y América 1845–1847. Edited by Javier Fernández. 1993.

Bibliography

Anderson Imbert, Enrique. *Sarmiento.* Buenos Aires: Editorial Universitaria, 1967.
Botana, Natalio R. *La tradicion republicana: Alberdi, Sarmiento y las ideas de su tiempo.* Buenos Aires: Sudamericana, 1984.
Martínez Estrada, Ezequiel. *Meditaciones sarmientinas.* Santiago de Chile: Editorial Universitaria, 1968.
Halperin, Tulio, Ivan Jaksic, and Gwen Kirkpatrick. *Sarmiento, Author of a Nation.* Berkeley and Los Angeles: University of California Press, 1994.
Goodrich, Diana Sorensen. *Facundo and the Construction of Argentine Culture*, Austin: University of Texas Press, 1996.
Katra, William H. *The Argentine Generation of 1837.* Madison, N.J.: Farleigh Dickinson University Press, 1996.
Pérez Guilhou, Dardo. *Sarmiento y la constitución.* Mendoza: 1989.
Salomon, Noël. *Realidad, ideología y literatura en el Facundo de D. F. Sarmiento.* Amsterdam: Rodopi, 1984.
Vardevoye, Paul. *Sarmiento, éducateur et publiciste, entre 1839 et 1852.* Paris: Institute de Hautes Etudes de l'Amerique Latine, 1963.
Weinberg, Gregorio. *Modelos educativos en la historia de América Latina.* Buenos Aires: Kapelusz, 1984.

SARTOR RESARTUS (THE TAILOR RETAILORED) 1833

Novel by Thomas Carlyle

In a letter to Thomas Carlyle written in 1835, John Sterling praises the deep wisdom of Carlyle's novel *Sartor Resartus* and then asks, "How then comes it, we cannot but ask, that these ideas, displayed assuredly with no want of eloquence, vivacity or earnestness, have found, unless I am much mistaken, so little acceptance among the best and most energetic minds in this country?" Sterling then answers his rhetorical question by pointing to the "positively barbarous" language in a "Rhapsodico-Reflective" style marked by ugly German compound constructions and a "plethoric fullness" that often takes "the shape of sarcasm or broad jest, but never subsiding into calm."

Sterling's remarks are perceptive and have suffered little dissent over the years, for *Sartor Resartus* is a literary sport, a novel only in "a very special sense," as George Levine notes. Gerry H. Brookes rejects any classification of *Sartor Resartus* as a novel "because its narrative is not consistent, because its characters and other fictions do not have the intricate and sustained interest that fictions have in a novel but serve the persuasive purpose of the whole work." Nor, posits Brookes, is *Sartor Resartus* a "work of 'expression' in the sense that M. H. Abrams defined such works in *The Mirror and the Lamp*." It is instead, a "persuasive essay," a work "designed to move the reader to believe in and to act by a view of the universe that will bring him hope now and bring his society in time a new and brighter form."

Yet whatever complaints about its style and questions about its genre have been registered, *Sartor Resartus* has been broadly acknowledged as an imaginative creation of great power, an act of genius struggling upstream against the intellectual currents of its time. G. B. Tennyson will not label Carlyle an enemy of progress, allowing only that "[t]he machine becomes to him the great enemy, because it dehumanizes; it severs the organic relation of man to nature and God." As for the grotesque prose, Kerry McSweeney and Peter Sabor quote Carlyle's admission to John Stuart Mill of the dangers of his ironic style and of his "singularly unreasonable temper," emphasizing Carlyle's lament that he "could have been the merriest of men, *had I not* been the sickest & saddest." In Carlyle's defense, McSweeney and Sabor insist that the 1820s and 1830s were difficult times for writers who wished to combat the increasing dominance of the rational scientific intellect and of utilitarian modes of thought and feeling with the great Romantic positives of fantasy and intuition.

A lengthy harangue in three books, couched in a fantastic style, *Sartor Resartus* rails against the materialism and philosophical rationalism of Carlyle's age. The metaphor of the title comes from Jonathan Swift's *Tale of a Tub* (1704) and expresses Carlyle's conviction that civilization needs new institutional garments. Clothes are also a figure for the shroud of matter in which all spirit presents itself in this world of sense experience. Carlyle's eccentric hero, Diogenes Teufelsdröckh (the name means "born-of-God devil's dung"), becomes professor of Allerley-Wissenschaft at the University of Weissnichtwo (or professor of things in general at the University of Know-Not-Where). Teufelsdröckh's nationality and the blizzard of German phrases and capitalized nouns reinforce Carlyle's admiration for "deep-thinking Germany" and its idealist tradition in philosophy.

In book 1 the narrator is preoccupied with Teufelsdröckh's new book, *Die Kleider ihr Werden und Wirken* (*Clothes: Their Origin and Influence*). The narrator applauds Teufelsdröckh's assault on Enlightenment rationalism, with its tedious "Cause-and-Effect Philosophers," and he dwells approvingly on Teufelsdröckh's stress on the inadequacy of rational systems. Intuition, Teufelsdröckh preaches, convinces us of the spiritual basis of nature and the certainty of a plan that governs it. Teufelsdröckh denigrates "Vulgar Logic," praising instead "Pure Reason," a direct intuition that perceives in humans "A Soul, a Spirit, and divine Apparition." Matter remains good because it is the manifestation of Spirit, but the absorption of Science in matter weakens the force of the mystery of existence. Book 1 ends with the narrator receiving six large paper bags full of Teufelsdröckh's manuscripts from Teufelsdröckh's assistant, Herr Hofrath Heuschrecke (Mr. Councillor Grasshopper), long quotations from which form the substance of book 2.

The papers reveal that the infant Teufelsdröckh was dropped off in a basket at the home of the aging couple Andreas and Gretchen Futteral in the village of Entepfuhl (Duck Pond). He enjoys an idyllic childhood, but Teufelsdröckh's disillusionment at his university education prompts from Carlyle a withering attack on the barrenness of rationalism. After leaving the university, Teufelsdröckh fails at a legal career, endures a terrible disappointment in love, and goes off to enjoy his Byronic self-pity as a wanderer in the mountains.

Teufelsdröckh conquers his religious despair in chapter 7, "The Everlasting No," by clinging to his belief in a transcendent Truth and the demands of Duty. Looking outward at the world, the "*Not-me,*" he enjoys the bliss of escape from his solipsism, or absorption in self. In chapter 8, "Centre of Indifference," the rejuvenated hero revels in the spectacle of the world and asserts the importance of the great man in history. Cured of his mewling Byronism, Teufelsdröckh asks, "Pshaw! What is this paltry little dog-cage of an Earth; what art thou that sittest whining there?" Finally, his mystical breakthrough in chapter 10, "The Everlasting Yea," frees Teufelsdröckh from Calvinist worrying about original sin and inspires a vision of a living universe full of the immanent God and a nature he calls "the living garment of God." These three chapters form the centerpiece of *Sartor Resartus* and conclude, "Work while it is called To-day, for the Night cometh wherein no man can work."

Book 3 exploits the same ideas in a variety of conceits. "Church Clothes" figures government as the outer skin of a society in which religion becomes "the inmost Pericardial and Nervous Tissue, which ministers Life and warm Circulation to the whole." The utilitarians are "Motive-Millwrights," the artist is a prophet (Johann Wolfgang Goethe is Carlyle's model), and Jesus is "our divinest Symbol." "The Phoenix" envisions a saving remnant revitalizing a church suffering from rationalist contempt, and "Natural Supernaturalism" sneers at the pettiness of science compared with the miracles we witness daily. God's presence shines throughout the universe, and each of us lives as a ghost, "a shadow-system gathered round our Me." We come into this world and take a bodily shape before disappearing again, "through Mystery to Mystery, from God and to God."

The American transcendentalist Ralph Waldo Emerson, Carlyle's transatlantic counterpart in many ways, published his famous meditation *Nature* in 1836, announcing his own version of Carlyle's idealism; and Emerson's essay "Self-Reliance" (1841) testified in support of Carlyle's hero worship. In their fierce defense of a supersensible realm of spirit, their condemnation of the positivism of the age, and their proclamation of the individual's freedom to achieve greatness through efforts of the will, Carlyle and Emerson contributed greatly to the history of their times.

FRANK DAY

Text

Sartor Resartus. Published anonymously in monthly issues of *Fraser's Magazine* in 1833–34, with fifty-eight copies bound in book form for private issue in 1834. Published as a book in Boston in 1836, with an unsigned preface by Ralph Waldo Emerson. Published under Carlyle's name in England in 1838 with minor revisions and the added subtitle: *Sartor Resartus: "the Life and Opinions of Herr Teufelsdröckh."* The second volume of the projected eight-volume edition of Carlyle's works is the 774-page scholarly, annotated edition *Sartor Resartus: The Life and Opinions of Herr Teufelsdröckh in Three Books*. Edited by Rodger L. Tarr and Mark Engel. Berkeley and Los Angeles: University of California Press, 1999.

Bibliography

Baker, L. C. R. "The Open Secret of *Sartor Resartus*: Carlyle's Method of Converting His Reader," *Studies in Philology* 83 (1986): 218–35.

Brookes, Gerry H. *The Rhetorical Form of Carlyle's "Sartor Resartus,"* Berkeley and Los Angeles: University of California Press, 1972.

Dale, P. A. "*Sartor Resartus* and the Inverse Sublime: The Art of Humorous Deconstruction." In *Allegory, Myth and Symbol*, edited by Morton W. Bloomfield. Cambridge, Mass.: Harvard University Press, 1981.

Kaplan, Fred. *Thomas Carlyle: A Biography*. Ithaca, N.Y.: Cornell University Press, 1983.

Levine, George. *The Boundaries of Fiction: Carlyle, Macauley, Newman*. Princeton, N.J.: Princeton University Press, 1968.

McSweeney, Kerry, and Peter Sabor. "Introduction." *Sartor Resartus*. Oxford and New York: Oxford University Press, 1987.

Mellor, Anne K. "Carlyle's *Sartor Resartus*: A Self-Consuming Artifact." In her *English Romantic Irony*. Cambridge Mass.: Harvard University Press, 1980.

Sterling, John. "Letter to Carlyle." In *Thomas Carlyle: The Critical Heritage*. Edited by Jules Paul Siegel. London: Routledge and Kegan Paul, 1971.

Tennyson, G. B. *Sartor Called Resartus*. Princeton N.J.: Princeton University Press, 1965.

SATAN AND SATANISM

The frequency with which the devil—Satan, or Lucifer—appeared in the work of the Romantic era owed less to a literal belief in his existence than it did to the desire for a symbol that was capable of expressing a range of contemporary ideas. Earlier in the eighteenth century, the philosophers of the Enlightenment had prompted many theologians to reconsider the role of the supernatural. A corollary of this was that the Protestant emphasis on the role of Satan, which could be largely attributed to Martin Luther, had to be rethought. The new wave of theological reflection found expression in the writings of Friedrich Daniel Ernst Schleiermacher, who is often described as the father of modern theology. Schleiermacher objected to a belief in the metaphysical existence of Satan on several grounds; nevertheless, he recognized its poetic value, claiming that it would "be inexpedient and in many ways unjustifiable to wish to banish the conception of the devil from the treasury of song." This metaphorical view of Satan allowed greater freedom for others to use and revise the symbol outside of an overtly theological context.

As a result, it is no surprise that the best known references to Satan in this period come from the arts—particularly literature—rather than theology, although the new interpretations drew on older stories and myths, notably the legend of Faust and John Milton's *Paradise Lost* (1665). Johann Wolfgang von Goethe's *Faust* (1808) is a text that consciously replaces an explicitly Christian understanding of Satan with one that is multifaceted. Its influence was enormous. Ferdinand-Victor-Eugène Delacroix published seventeen vivid and grotesque lithographs to illustrate a new French translation of *Faust* in 1828, while the majority of Faust operas written after 1808, including those by Hector Berlioz and Charles-François Gounod, owed a similar debt to Goethe. Milton's *Paradise Lost* provided another vision of Satan of which Romantics made use, recasting Satan as a hero. Mario Praz has suggested that the "characteristic quality" of the many forms in which the Romantic hero appeared, from the sublime criminal to the fatal hero of Lord Byron, was Satanism. This reading is supported by Percy Bysshe Shelley's observation in the preface to "Prometheus Unbound" (1820) that, in spite of certain poetical limitations, "the only imaginary being resembling in any degree Prometheus, is Satan."

In his preface to "Prometheus Unbound," Shelley acknowledged that the rehabilitation of Satan from the prince of darkness to an advocate of freedom was beset with difficulties. The tension is obvious in the work of a number of other poets. God and Satan are paralleled in William Blake's verse through the figures of Urizen and Orc. While Orc's struggle against the tyranny of Urizen induces sympathy, his excessive violence also provokes loathing. In Byron's *Cain: A Mystery* (1821), the depiction of Lucifer as the champion of humanity is compromised by his malevolence. As Martin Priestman reminds us, "Byron seems to have it several ways at once: this Lucifer is at once right and bad for you."

The mixed characteristics that Satan possesses in the work of many Romantic poets is not an accident. In part this is because he is used as a device for exploring the dark and unexplored recesses of the human mind, an area neglected by Enlightenment rationality but of central concern in works such as Johann Heinrich Fuseli's *The Nightmare* (1781). Another reason for the ambiguity of Satan is that while the dualism of Manichaeism is often entertained, it is also resisted. This is particularly evident in Blake's "The Marriage of Heaven and Hell" (1793). The claim that "without contraries there is no progression" is not meant to suggest that good and evil are in permanent opposition, but rather that they are intrinsically linked. A similar idea lies behind the deployment of the doppelganger device in E. T. A. Hoffmann's *Satan's Elixirs* (1816) and James Hogg's *The Private Memoirs and Confessions of a Justified Sinner* (1824). In the latter, the use of the double calls local theological beliefs about the nature of the diabolic into question and makes it more difficult to see Satan as a discrete embodiment of evil.

Nevertheless, the darker side of Romanticism continues to associate Satan and his followers with a vision of evil. This is hauntingly depicted in the illustrations that Gustave Boulanger did for some of Victor Hugo's works, and in the fourteen *Black Paintings* produced by Francisco José de Goya Lucientes (which include the disturbing picture, *Witches' Sabbath*, 1821–23). It is also visible in the literary tales of vampires that emerged in the aftermath of the famous discussions among Byron, Matthew Lewis, Gaetano Polidori, and Shelley. Further incarnations of the diabolic occur in the Gothic fiction of the period. On the surface, these stories appear to return to a medieval conception of Satan. A powerful example of this can be found in Matthew Gregory Lewis's *The Monk* (1796). Ambrosio rapes Antonia after murdering her mother, an event that takes on a more disturbing twist when Satan reveals that Antonia is his sister. And yet the horror of this final revelation is undermined when the reader reflects on the fact that the source of this disclosure is a liar. Satan may symbolize evil, but he does so in a highly unstable manner.

Peter Schock has argued that the increasingly negative depictions of Satan during this period suggest "an abortive mode in Romantic mythmaking" that is the consequence of the Romantic attempt to appropriate a traditional mythological figure "for the project of fashioning new protagonists as the vehicles of new values, energies and ideas." One might go further than this by focusing less on the Romantic inability to find a symbol that is really radical, and more on the degree to which the concept of Satan involves certain inescapable yet problematic properties. The symbol of Satan is useful in so far as it has the ability to concretize and personify evil. This is why the attempt by some Romantics to reconstruct Satan in the terms already outlined was doomed to failure. At the same time, there is a range of theological difficulties involved in trying to equate Satan with absolute evil. This accounts for the difficulties that writers frequently encountered when using Satan as a symbol of evil and goes some way toward explaining the declining interest in Satan as the nineteenth century unfolded.

This was particularly marked in the American context. Although writers such as Nathaniel Hawthorne, Herman Melville, and Edgar Allan Poe made evil a central theme of their writings, they had little use for the symbol of Satan. Hawthorne's well-known tale "Young Goodman Brown" (1835) may be centered around the diabolic, but the range of possible readings that it offers all point toward the humanness of evil. Poe is similarly disparaging in his use of Satan, choosing to employ him as a comic device rather than as a serious tool for exploring evil. In the European context, Jeffrey Burton Russell reminds us that "[a]part from the solemnity of Hugo and the pompous Satanism of Lévi, irony, parody, and whimsy were the dominant features

Eugene Delacroix, *De temps en temps j'aime a (. . .) (Mephistopheles Flies over a City).*—Lithograph from a series of seventeen Faust illustrations. Reprinted courtesy of AKG London.

of Satan throughout the 19th century." Those writers who did devote their attention to diabolism, such as the decadents that followed in the footsteps of the Marquis de Sade, were far from convincing in their descriptions of Satan. As Brian Horne concludes in relation to Charles Baudelaire, "It is as though he wants with all his heart to believe in Satan, but cannot."

MARK KNIGHT

See also **Blake, William; Byron, Lord George Noel Gordon; *Faust*; Gothic Fiction; Hoffmann, Ernst Theodor (Wilhelm) Amadeus; Hogg, James; *The Marriage of Heaven and Hell; Paradise Lost,* Poe, Edgar; Prometheus Unbound; Sade, Allan Marquis Donatien-Alphonse-François de; Schleiermacher, Friedrich Ernst Daniel; Shelley, Percy Bysshe; The Supernatural**

Bibliography

Horne, Brian. *Imagining Evil.* London: Darton, Longman and Todd, 1996.

Praz, Mario. *The Romantic Agony.* 2nd ed. London: Oxford University Press, 1970.

Priestman, Martin. *Romantic Atheism: Poetry and Freethought; 1780–1830.* Cambridge: Cambridge University Press, 1999.

Russell, Jeffrey Burton. *Mephistopheles: Satan in the Modern World.* Ithaca, N.Y.: Cornell University Press, 1986.

Schleiermacher, Frederick. *The Christian Faith*, 1830, translated by H. R. Mackintosh and J. S. Stewart. Edinburgh: T. and T. Clark, 1968.

Schock, Peter. "Satanism." In *Encyclopedia of Romanticism: Culture in Britain, 1780s–1830s*, edited by Laura Dabundo. London: Routledge, 1992.

SAVIGNY, FRIEDRICH KARL VON 1779–1861

German legal historian

The implications of Friedrich Karl von Savigny's historiography had profound implications for European Romanticism, but he was a legal historian and theorist rather than a literary figure. His legal education began early because of a personal tragedy. He was orphaned at age thirteen, but his aristocratic parents' friend von Neurath, the assessor to the *Reichskammergericht* at Wetzlar, acted as Savigny's guardian and personally taught the child Roman law through rote memorization and questioning. Savigny then formally studied legal history in 1795 at the University of Marburg and, in the next year, at the University of Göttingen, where Gustav Hugo taught. There von Savigny acquired a worldview as well as a legal education. Hugo made him see law as organic growth rather than human creation. This notion was fundamental to what is called the "historical school of law," which Savigny would continue and develop in the next generation. After receiving his doctorate in 1800, Savigny taught briefly at Marburg and then declined professorships from Greifswald and Heidelberg Universities. Savigny took vigorous part in the appreciation of the Middle Ages, a key aspect of Romanticism. He was financially comfortable enough to travel widely in western Germany and France, where he researched the medieval history of Roman law.

The results of this research appeared in his magisterial *Geschichte des römischen Rechts im Mittelalter* (*History of Roman Law in the Middle Ages*), which appeared in six volumes between 1815 and 1831. Then and now, this work was essential to an understanding of the postimperial history of Roman law which, Savigny showed, remained in force in the barbarian Germanic kingdoms and, from the time of the legal scholar Irnerius (d. 1125), became the object of systematic study. In the first two volumes, Savigny gave a very positive view of the Germanic invaders of Rome. Far from destroying cities and rooting out Roman institutions, the German kings allowed urban Romans, who now enjoyed greater freedom than under emperors, to retain and use their own institutions. Thus, von Savigny's book became a history of medieval institutional and legal life throughout the reaches of the former Roman Empire, as well as an account of scholarly exposition of Roman law between the twelfth and fifteenth centuries. By clear implication, the Middle Ages were a time of legal vitality and learnedness, rather than of indolence and ignorance.

Earlier, in 1803 Savigny published his *Recht des Besitzes* (*Property Law*), which demonstrated that ancient Romans saw property more in terms of effective occupancy than absolute possession, and on its strength was appointed in 1808 to a professorship at the University of Landshut. His talent as a lecturer and his known German patriotism in a time of French invasion led Wilhelm von Humboldt to effect his appointment to the new faculty at the University of Berlin in 1810, which was charged with rebuilding Prussia through education in the wake of the calamitous defeat of the older absolutist Hohenzollern monarchy. The high value that he placed on the past, of course, undergirded this patriotism. Savigny would teach there until 1842, when he left academia for a cabinet-level appointment in Prussia as "great chancellor" (a revived title given a century before by Frederick the Great to a legal codifier). He was charged with codifying and revising certain areas of Prussian law, notably the laws of divorce. The actual results that Savigny achieved were fairly modest, but there is some irony in his undertaking the work in the first place. This irony stems from his famous controversy with the great legal scholar Anton Friedrich Justus Thibaut at Heidelberg, in which Savigny published an essay that was, in effect, the charter of the "historical school."

In 1814 Thibaut called for the codification of German law on the pattern of Napoleon Bonaparte's *Code civile*. This meant the rationalization of German laws and, in the process, their selective revision in accordance with reason and natural law. Savigny's instantly famous rebuttal, *Vom Beruf unserer Zeit für Gesetzgebung und Rechtswissenschaft* (*On the Vocation of our Age for Legislation and Jurisprudence*), would go through several revisions but always maintained its basic argument, that laws should not be made, except in small and inevitable increments because, properly, they evolve organically in accordance with the *Volksgeist* (the spirit of the people or nation).

As was to be expected, Savigny argued this case with support from the history of medieval Roman law that he knew so well. This argument, which gathered force from German national resentment at the reforms of the French occupiers, also supported conservative resistance to middle class demands for structural reforms and a sharing of power. Savigny's essay became a classic in political and historical theory and had a major future career in German political debate. In the shorter term, it led to his collaboration with Karl Friedrich Eichhorn (another pivotal figure in the school) and Johann Friedrich Ludwig Göschen in the founding of their journal *Zeitschrift für geschichtliche Rechtswissenschaft*, whose opening statement drew on arguments from *On the Vocation of our Age*.

Savigny did not reject all legal innovation. No historian could deny or delegitimate all change in history. In his correspondence, the politically active historian Johann Gustav Droysen noted this fatal weakness in Savigny's argument, since supposed "historical rights" and the "right of history" to effect radical change were reciprocal functions. All laws had been made some time, and later ages had the same right to create as had earlier ages. As if to illustrate this point, one of Savigny's most successful students—Heinrich von Sybel—based his own politically charged theory of progressive change on the notion of an evolving *Volksgeist* that Savigny taught him. These inconsistencies point up the theoretical weakness of Savigny's outlook, but, if noticed, they probably did not bother him. He was alarmed at the prospect of sweeping change rather than at change as such and disputed the sovereignty of reason in law rather than the use of any rational standards in legislation. He was a conservative pragmatist with deep learning and great respect for the past, which is what recommended him to the conservative Romanticist Friedrich Wilhelm IV of Prussia in the first place.

This pragmatism was of a piece with his scholarship. There had never been anything merely antiquarian about Savigny's vast erudition in Roman law. His 1803 book on property law was, in part, an attempt to demonstrate the use of Roman procedure. His history of Roman law in medieval times was a demonstration in six volumes of how later ages could appropriate and adapt, in keeping with their later needs and abilities, the laws of past

times. His last major work, published between 1840 and 1849 in eight volumes, was *System des heutigen römischen Rechts* (*System of Contemporary Roman Law*), an approving demonstration of the continuing coherence and applicability of Roman law. His work as Prussian great chancellor in and after 1842 was a further demonstration of the continued vitality of Roman law and, so, of the ongoing relevance of its history.

ROBERT SOUTHARD

Bibliography

Horst Schroder. *Friedrich Karl von Savigny—Geschichte und Rechtsdenkern beim Übergang vom Feudalismus zum Kapitalismus in Deutschland.* Frankfurt, 1984.

Adolf Stoll, *Friedrich Karl von Savigny.* 2 vols. Berlin, 1929–39.

SCANDINAVIA AND FINLAND: HISTORICAL SURVEY

Northern Europe on the eve of the French Revolution was divided between two long-established kingdoms. In the east, Sweden was no longer the great power that had dominated much of the Baltic region throughout the seventeenth century, but it still retained a foothold in northern Germany and its eastern frontier encompassed most the territory of the present-day republic of Finland. For much of the eighteenth century, the affairs of the country were managed by the nobility, which dominated the state council and the Swedish parliament (Riksdag). In 1772 the young king Gustav III (1772–92) staged a bloodless coup that restored royal power. Gustav III's Form of Government (1772) and Act of Union and Security (1789) preserved far more of the aristocratic constitutional structure and institutions of the realm than the settlement imposed by Frederik III of Denmark in 1660, which created an absolutist, unitary state (*helstat*) embracing Norway, Greenland, Iceland, the Faero Islands and sundry small colonial possessions in the West Indies and Asia, as well as Denmark.

Royal absolutism in the helstat was, however, tempered by the reformist policies of the king's ministers, particularly during the long reign of the mentally incapable Christian VII (1766–1808). The Danish peasantry was freed from repressive bondage, the children of the peasantry were provided with a sound elementary education, and by the 1830s the new generation of freehold farmers were beginning to articulate their own demands. Peaceful reform, not violent revolution, distinguished both northern kingdoms. Although the French Revolution had its admirers, especially among the nobility, it had no imitators. The assassination of Gustav III by a small group of discontented nobles in 1792 did not change the existing order. Sweden and Denmark managed to keep out of the wars raging on the Continent in the 1790s. These were lucrative years for Danish and Swedish traders, but the tightening of British controls on neutral shipping brought Denmark into the firing line in 1801, when Admirals Sir Hyde Parker and Horatio Nelson attached the fleet off Copenhagen, and 1807, when the fleet was once more attacked and the island of Zealand invaded by the British. This last attack drove Denmark into the French camp. Gustav IV Adolf remained bitterly opposed to Napoleon Bonaparte, whose

campaigning in central Europe culminated in the Treaty of Tilsit (1807), which bound Russia to eliminate Sweden from the list of France's enemies.

In the spring of 1808, Russian troops occupied southern Finland, and in spite of a brief counterattack by Swedish-Finnish forces in the summer, the Finnish half of the kingdom was effectively under Russian control for the third time in less than a century. This time, however, the Russian emperor Alexander I determined to incorporate Finland into his realm, a position he subsequently modified after discussions with a delegation of Finnish notables in December 1808. A meeting of the Finnish estates was convened in the town of Porvoo (Swedish: Borgå) to swear fealty to the new ruler; Alexander for his part promised to uphold Finland's inherited laws, liberties, and religion. The Finnish lands were formally transferred from Sweden to Russia at the Treaty of Hamina (Swedish: Fredrikshamn) in September 1809.

A fortnight before the Porvoo assembly, the Swedish army had been instrumental in forcing Gustav IV Adolf to abdicate. The Riksdag enacted a new constitution and provided for the succession. After the premature death of the first choice, the Danish Prince Christian August, the Swedes plumped for one of Napoleon's marshals, Jean-Baptiste Bernadotte (King Carl XIV Johan, 1818–1844). Bernadotte succeeded in reorienting Swedish foreign policy, allying himself with Alexander I in 1812 and securing Norway from Denmark in 1814. Sweden accepted the Norwegian constitution drafted on May 17, 1814, at Eidsvoll as the price of union between the two countries.

Neither in Norway nor in Finland was there much hankering after the restoration of old ties. Both acquired a new, distinctive political identity, though the precise contours of a national identity remained to be established. The creation of a national culture and language to replace that of the former dominant power began to gain momentum by the 1850s. Danish was gradually modified into an acceptable language of the realm (*riksmål*), but a more radical language of the land (*landsmål*), based on a synthesis of Norway's rural dialects, was developed by Ivar Aasen in the 1840s. Patriotic writers such as the poet Johan Ludvig Runeberg continued to write in Swedish, the language of the nobility and the educated classes in Finland, but there was also a movement to provide Finnish with its own epic literature (the *Kalevala*, first published in 1835) and eventually to replace Swedish with Finnish as the dominant national language.

That movement suffered a temporary setback in 1848–50, as a result of a Russian clampdown on all activity deemed the slightest bit radical, but began to blossom from the 1860s, a period of general reform that extended Finland's self-government and established Finnish as an official language alongside Swedish. Elsewhere, the impact of the 1848 revolutions was most dramatic in Denmark, which was peacefully transformed into a constitutional monarchy with a two-chamber parliament (Rigsdag). The king of Denmark was also drawn into a series of short wars against his fractious subjects (and their German allies) in Schleswig-Holstein. The Scandinavianist movement, which had developed in student circles in the 1830s, eagerly championed the Danish cause, and was to urge Swedish intervention to free Finland from Russia during the Crimean War (1853–56). Finnish opinion was, however, firmly against such an idea; self-rule and the prospect of career advancement in Imperial Russian service seemed a better alternative to provincial status in Sweden.

The territorial and constitutional changes at the beginning of the nineteenth century set both Norway and Finland on the road to nationhood. Liberal currents proved stronger in Denmark than in Sweden, where Crown Prince Oscar abandoned his enlightened reformism in his early years as king. Issues of national identity grew in importance in all four countries, driven by social and economic change and the increasing participation in public life of the people (*folket*).

DAVID KIRBY

Bibliography

Barton, Arnold. *Scandinavia in the Revolutionary Era 1760–1815*. Minneapolis: University of Minnesota Press, 1986.

Derry, Thomas. *A History of Scandinavia*. London: George Allen and Unwin, 1979.

Kirby, David. *The Baltic World, 1772–1993. Europe's Northern Periphery in an Age of Change*. London and New York: Longman, 1995.

THE SCARLET LETTER, 1850

Novel by Nathaniel Hawthorne

Along with the short story "Young Goodman Brown," *The Scarlet Letter* is the best known of Nathaniel Hawthorne's writings. The fact that there have been eleven filmed interpretations of the novel from a silent 1908 black-and-white version to the 1995 color version starring Demi Moore, attests to the popularity of this somber tale. *The Scarlet Letter* is generally considered to be the author's masterpiece and is representative of the major themes and style of his writing. Set in the seventeenth-century Puritan town of Salem, Massachusetts, it is the tragic tale of Hester Prynne, who has committed adultery and is forced to wear an embroidered letter *A* on her dress because she refuses to reveal the name of the father of her illegitimate child. Arthur Dimmesdale, the town's minister and the father of the child, lacks the moral courage to reveal his identity and is mercilessly tormented by Roger Chillingworth, Hester's real husband who has been away but who knows the truth of his wife's affair. It is a story of paradox and ambiguity, of the dark psychological complexity of the individual and the sometimes violent and cruel nature of the social and moral codes that bind human communities together.

Chillingworth is, as his name suggests, a stern figure who places the law of Puritan principle above any sense of compassion and forgiveness. The novel indicates that he is a scholarly person who places the intellect above feeling as a mode of knowing reality. He represents Hawthorne's typically Romantic critique of the scientist who eschews emotions and intuitions in favor of cold facts and figures. The scholar-scientist figure suffers from an imbalance of the head over the heart and may thus fall victim to what for Hawthorne is a cruel perversion of a true humanistic morality. That Chillingworth places an abstract and absolute law of morality above the very human actions of his wife, who wrongly but understandably sought comfort for her loneliness in the arms of a man not her husband, condemns him in Hawthorne's view. For the author, the universe remains an often morally ambiguous place of individual human interactions to which absolute conceptual rules cannot be applied and for which the quality of merciful understanding is sometimes necessary. That Chillingworth unconsciously uses an abstract principle of moral behavior in order to repress his own hurt and shame over his wife's deed also suggests Hawthorne's highly acute sense of the workings of human psychology.

Dimmesdale also stands as a figure of ambiguous moral certainty. He is morally "dim" in that he is unable to take the moral stand that his conscience tells him he should and he suffers as a result of his inaction. He is a perfect example of the theme of secret guilt and its psychological consequences that so fascinated Hawthorne. Dimmesdale endures great inner torment but this suffering also serves to clarify his spirit, transforming him into a better individual in the process. The claim to genuine virtue remains hollow unless it has been truly tested by its opposite. His inability to integrate his guilt, however, finally drives him to an obsessed and narcissistic religiosity and a final public confession that frees him from Chillingworth's persecution but also tragically from the natural humanity of Hester.

Hester Prynne is the novel's central character. Like Dimmesdale, her secret sin paradoxically serves to transform her into a more vibrant and beautiful woman, a better and more caring person. Her power and vitality—as well as that of her illegitimate child, Pearl—make her an expression of natural passion and the exact counterpart to the cold calculations of Chillingworth. Yet her position as sinful outsider hardens her soul, and in this lies her personal tragedy. Hester in the end is not a victim of sinful passion but of a social order that is inimical to true humanity. In Hawthorne's Romantic individualism, culture and society, perhaps inevitably and sometimes tragically, pervert the true pattern of nature.

Although Hawthorne's descriptions are realistic and rich in visual detail, they are often highly symbolic and allegorical, and, in this sense, they present a Romanticized vision of objective reality. Realistic literature seeks to describe reality as it is in the manner of verisimilitude, whereas Romantic texts tend to imbue the objects of the world symbolically with the inner qualities of human feeling. An example can be found in the introductory chapter of this framed narrative, "The Custom House," in the detailed description of the American eagle emblem that is attached to the front of the building. Its fierce and stern countenance that shows "no great tenderness," with thunderbolts and arrows clutched in its claws, seems to "threaten mischief to the inoffensive community" around it. The eagle becomes more than simply a carved object; it becomes symbolic of Hawthorne's distrust of all governments and laws that claim absolute authority over the sanctity of the individual, which he holds to be supreme. In this description of the wooden eagle in Salem, Hawthorne encapsulates the central message of the novel: that the strict and unyielding moral code of the Puritans has fundamentally violated the freedom and the existence of the citizens in its community, the privacy of their inner emotional lives, and is therefore morally wrong.

Hawthorne's symbolic text is also one of the most architecturally crafted of nineteenth-century American literature. This can be seen in the image of the scaffold that signifies Puritan punishment and that gives the narrative a tripartite structure: Hester's emergence from prison to the scaffold at the beginning; Dimmesdale's suffering on the scaffold at midnight in the middle of the text; and the public confession with Hester and Pearl on the scaffold at its end. Hawthorne's carefully wrought aestheticism—that is, his concern with artistic form as well as content—also links him to the main tenets of Romantic literature.

The Scarlet Letter illustrates Hawthorne's greatest gift as a Romantic writer and his significance for early American literature: his ability to create fictional characters of psychological complexity, with well-defined and compelling personalities, who are caught up in ambiguous situations that mirror, in a sense, the typically American theme of the conflict of the individual versus society.

THOMAS F. BARRY

Text

The Scarlet Letter: A Romance. 1850.

Bibliography

Andrews, Elmer Kennedy, ed. *Nathaniel Hawthorne: The Scarlet Letter.* Columbia Critical Guides. New York: Columbia University Press, 2000.

Baym, Nina. *The Scarlet Letter: A Reading.* Twayne Masterwork Studies, no. 1. New York: Twayne, 1986.

Bloom, Harold, ed. *Hester Prynne.* Major Literary Characters. Philadelphia: Chelsea House, 1990.

———. *Nathaniel Hawthorne's The Scarlet Letter.* Bloom's Reviews: Comprehensive Research and Study Guides. Philadelphia: Chelsea House, 1998.

Golding, William. *Nathaniel Hawthorne's: The Scarlet Letter.* Modern Critical Interpretations. Philadelphia: Chelsea House, 1988.

Kesterson, David B. *Critical Essays on Hawthorne's The Scarlet Letter,* Boston: G. K. Hall, 1988.

Morey, Eileen, ed. *Readings on the Scarlet Letter.* Greenhaven Press Literary Companion to American Literature. Greenhaven Press, 1998.

Murfin, Ross C., ed. *Scarlet Letter: A Case Study in Contemporary Criticism.* Case Studies in Contemporary Criticism. Boston: Bedford Books, 1991.

SCHADOW, JOHANN GOTTFRIED 1764–1850

German sculptor and illustrator

Johann Gottfried Schadow's elegant yet simple sculptures recall the neoclassicism of Antonio Canova rather than a Romanticism that allowed free reign to the imagination. He helped to create a monumental capital for the Prussian kings with the aid of statues that can appear hard as steel and glisten coldly as if frozen in time. Yet Schadow's productive life spanned the period from the French Revolution to the upheavals of 1848, and for all his commitment to the principles of classical harmony, he could not remain unaffected by the new artistic approaches that came and went while he practiced his art.

Schadow was born into the world of the late rococo in Berlin, where the Prussian king Frederick the Great was firmly committed to the doctrine of the Enlightenment. At the Prussian court, the young Schadow was instructed by the French sculptor Jean-Pierre-Antoine Tessaert between 1778 and 1783 before moving briefly to Rome, where he continued his studies at Alexander Trippel's academy. It was soon obvious that he was unwilling to commit himself wholly to the aesthetic principles of antique art. Despite the monumental effects and the overall impression of restraint, his works are characterized by a lightness of touch that is modern in origin. His heroic figures always seem to go beyond the superficial display of virtue and valor by managing to appear thoughtful and fundamentally human at the same time.

Following the death of Frederick, Berlin experienced a flowering of the arts that provided Schadow with excellent opportunities to perfect his technique. The city was expanding rapidly, and if it was to catch up and vie with other European capitals, its many open spaces, conceived as parade grounds for Frederick's extensive army, would need to be embellished. Much of his early work remained hidden from the public, being concentrated in the palaces of Berlin, Potsdam, and Lichtenau. It was not until the 1790s that his input became highly visible, when he was invited by King Frederick Wilhelm II to collaborate with the architect Carl Gotthard Langhans on the Brandenburg Gate. The ornate group of four horses plus chariot (Quadriga) is his most distinctive work. In designing the horses, Schadow was initially intent on copying Marcus Aurelius's stallion from the Roman Capitol, but, characteristically, abandoned this plan in favor of a natural model. Both the Iron Cross and the Prussian

Eagle were later additions (by Karl Friedrich Schinkel) that do not accord with Schadow's original design and help to explain why the monument became less a symbol of peace and more of an icon of Prussian nationalism. Sensitive to such matters, the government of the German Democratic Republic removed Schinkel's additions in 1958.

What places Schadow in the proximity of Romanticism is the manner in which he succeeded in the portrayal of the great and famous as private, unpretentious people. Thus the Prussian princesses Luise and Friederike (in the statue of 1795–97) are stripped of their regalia and dignified surroundings to become simple, graceful girls such as one might imagine encountering in any German family. Although contemporary observers stressed the "genuine Greek style" and even obliged Schadow to remove a flower basket that seemed "un-Greek" to them, the informality of the group and especially the delicate balance struck between innocence and erotic effect may be read as outward signs of a romanticizing approach.

Schadow produced well over one hundred busts of famous individuals. Most of his subjects are treated from the same sympathetic and easygoing perspective, in which nature repeatedly wins out over idealistic posturing and pathos. For many years, Schadow hoped to receive a request for a statue of Frederick the Great, whom he much admired. Finally, Crown Prince Ludwig of Bavaria approached Schadow, but rejected the artist's proposal when it was presented to him in 1821. A bronze statue was completed in the following year, showing the elderly king supporting himself on a stick in the company of his favorite hounds. The king's uniform had been preserved and was therefore copied faithfully, but the type of greyhound favored by him had died out and proved to be the greatest challenge. Yet the dogs were essential: the homely quality they help to impart is typical of Schadow's refusal to monumentalize even the most lofty of his subjects.

Following the restoration of Prussia after 1815, Schadow's works found less favor with royalty, and his position was overshadowed by that of Christian Daniel Rauch. Schadow's controversial statue of Leopold I of Anhalt-Dessau (*Der alte Dessauer,* 1798) showed the warrior prince, who had died in 1747, in what had become extremely unfashionable clothes: knee breeches, tricorn, and a tight-fitting jacket. When placed in Berlin's Lustgarten in 1800, it was promptly vandalized, presumably by members of the old guard offended by its embarrassing naturalism. The public would have preferred flowing robes of faintly Grecian appearance to the studied historicity of authentic garments. Here, too, the effects of a progressive, "warts and all" approach to history can be discerned.

His work received much criticism around this time on account of his "old-fashioned" approach, and Johann Wolfgang von Goethe objected to the way art was being politicized in Berlin. To answer these challenges, Schadow published a defense of his work in *Eunomia* (1802). In 1805 he became deputy director of the Berlin Academy of Arts, advancing to its director in January 1816. During the French occupation of Berlin, he played a major role in (unsuccessfully) attempting to halt the theft of artistic monuments by Napoleon Bonaparte's agent Dominique-Vivant Denon, who even managed to remove the Quadriga from the Brandenburg Gate to Paris. In this context, Schadow also produced a number of anti-Napoleonic cartoons.

Johann Gottfried Schadow, *Selbstbildnis (Self-portrait)*, 1838. Reprinted courtesy of AKG London.

In the end, Schadow proved to be a more adaptable artist than his grandiose sculptures of the Prussian nobility would make him seem. Their carefully observed poses conceal an informality that contemporaries deprecated and that lost him some important commissions in later life, notably the tomb of Queen Luise, which was executed by Rauch. Schadow merely commented that his fame had gone up in *Rauch* (smoke). But unlike his predecessors, Schadow received many commissions from private individuals. These were indicative of the changing patterns of patronage in the nineteenth century. Some clients now requested informal family portraits, others asked for busts of famous artists, musicians, or actresses. Some were commissioned by amateur groups and financed by public subscription. However, some of Schadow's greatest works, such as *Reclining Maiden* (1826), were created for his own pleasure rather than for specific clients.

Another type of statue for which demand was increasing was the allegory. *Friederike Unger als Hoffnung (Friederike Unger portrayed as Hope,* 1802; no longer extant), was an outstanding example of this transitional art that bridges the divide between classical formality and Romantic eccentricity with an ease characteristic of Schadow's talent. In his patriotic works, including monuments to Gebhard Leberrecht von Blücher (1818), Martin Luther (1821), and Goethe (1823), he never lost sight of the all-too-human factors, and when creating allegories, his aim was not to capture the timeless essence of the ideal but to show the well-proportioned image of a normal human being in a new context. The unadulterated truth was always more important to him than powerful but contrived effects. In this respect, too, Schadow was closer to modernity than might be assumed.

Several of Schadow's sons went on to play an important role in the Romantic movement. The eldest, Ridolfo, began working in his father's studio before moving to Rome where he became a disciple of Bertel Thorvaldsen. His second son, Friedrich Wilhelm, is a major representative of Romantic art in Germany.

OSMAN DURRANI

Biography

Born the son of a tailor in Berlin, May 20, 1764, and brought up in relatively impoverished circumstances. Entered the Prussian Royal Academy at the age of fourteen as a sculptor trainee. There he received instruction from the chief sculptor to the Prussian Court, the Frenchman Jean Pierre Antoine Tessaert, between 1778 and 1783. Supported by his father-in-law, he was able to continue his studies in Rome for two years at Trippel's academy. Shortly after Tessaert's death, Schadow was appointed court sculptor and became a full member of the Berlin Academy of Arts. The first major sculpture was the completion of the tomb of Count Alexander von der Mark (begun by Tessaert); soon after that, Schadow received the commission to work on the Brandenburg Gate. His best-known sculptures are monuments to Blücher (1818), Luther (1821), and Goethe (1823). He received an honorary doctorate from the University of Berlin in 1830. Between 1830 and 1842, he supplied fourteen heroic busts for the grandiose Walhalla near Regensburg, the pet project of the Bavarian monarch Ludwig I. One year before his death he published a survey of his life's work, *Kunst-Werke und Kunst-Ansichten*. After many honors in Germany and abroad, including the title *von* Schadow (1839), he died in Berlin on January 27, 1850.

Bibliography

Albrecht, Petra, et al. *Schadows Berlin. Zeichnungen von Johann Gottfried Schadow: Katalog zur Ausstellung 2.–26.11.1999.* Exhibition catalog. Berlin: Akademie der Künste, 1999.

Börsch-Supan, Helmut. *Abbilder-Leitbilder: Berliner Skulpturen von Schadow bis heute.* Exhibition catalog. Berlin: Neuer Berliner Kunstverein, 1987.

Eckardt, Götz. *Johann Gottfried Schadow 1764–1850—Der Bildhauer.* Leipzig: Seemann, 1990.

Kaiser, Konrad. *Gottfried Schadow als Karikaturist.* Dresden: Verlag der Kunst, 1955.

Krenzlin Ulrike. *Johann Gottfried Schadow—Ein Künstlerleben in Berlin.* Berlin: Verlag für Bauwesen, 1990.

———. *Johann Gottfried Schadow, die Quadriga. Vom preussischen Symbol zum Denkmal der Nation.* Frankfurt: Fischer, 1991.

Mackowsky, Hans. *Johann Gottfried Schadow: Jugend und Aufstieg 1764 bis 1797.* Berlin: Grote, 1927.

———. *Schadows Graphik.* Berlin: Deutscher Verein für Kunstwissenschaft, 1936.

———. *Die Bildwerke Gottfried Schadows.* Introduction by Paul Ortwin Rave. Berlin: Deutscher Verein für Kunstwissenschaft, 1951.

Schmidt, Martin H. *"Ich machte mir: eine Büste von Goethe"—Schadows Widerstreit mit Goethe.* Frankfurt: Peter Lang, 1995.

Tucholski, Barbara Camilla. "Friedrich Wilhelm von Schadow 1789–1862: Künstlerische Konzeption und poetische Malerei." Ph.D. diss., University of Bonn, 1984.

SCHELLING, FRIEDRICH WILHELM JOSEPH VON 1775-1854

German philosopher

Friedrich Wilhelm Joseph von Schelling's intellectual life has been variously divided by critics into four parts according to the centrality of Jakob Böhme, Johann Gottlieb Fichte, Plato, and Benedict de Spinoza, and into three phases characterized by his philosophies of nature, identity, and the ages of the world. He himself chose to divide it into two parts: negative and positive philosophy. Biographical details—such as his public break with Fichte and then Georg Wilhelm Friedrich Hegel, his discovery of Böhme through Franz von Baader, and his royal appointment to the University of Berlin to battle the "dragon's seed of Hegelianism"—make it possible to talk about this German idealist in terms of abrupt discontinuities.

His real development, however, is far less tidy, and his constant renewal of philosophical form and terminology was, in fact, a process both gradual and logical, with each work challenging and correcting the last. Novalis famously described to Caroline Michaelis, the Romantic intellectual who would later leave August Wilhelm von Schlegel for Schelling, how he "grasps well, retains more poorly and is least able to reproduce." By this, the poet meant that Schelling moved perhaps too quickly from his empirical data to a speculative universal whole, itself never fully or unproblematically articulated or, in Hegel's prophetic words, "still not a scientific whole organized in all its branches."

Yet, to be fair, had Schelling been in this sense more gifted at "reproducing" or representing phenomenal forms, defined in contrast to Immanuel Kant's unknowable things-in-themselves, he would never have been able to continue from where Fichte leaves off. Fichte has observed how Kant's delimiting of knowledge to only the realm of appearances prevents him from satisfactorily explaining the involuntary nature of the cognitive act itself. His interpretation inversely sees this unconditional status of the self-reflecting self as distinct from immanent reality and thus spiritual. The intellectual intuition, so understood, opens up the possibility for an idealist study of the spiritual, which Fichte also initiates by seeing all nature as the self's endless construction of an opposite necessary for self-definition.

Shortly after his first work of strong Fichtean content, the four-page "*Über die Möglichkeit einer Form der Philosophie überhaupt* (*On the Possibility of a Form of Philosophy in General*, 1795), written as a student, Schelling came to recognize what was eventually debatable in Fichte. His next work, *Vom Ich als Prinzip der Philosophie Absolute* (*Of the I as Principle of Philosophy*, 1795), qualifies the Fichtean principle by differentiating the "I" that posits its own being from its less conscious act of positing itself. Because Fichte fails to take into proper account why the "I" must still go out of itself and oppose itself, to speak of it as "the unconditional thing is a contradiction." His one-sided relationship cannot, therefore, be used to harmonize mind and nature, and this understanding enables Schelling to invert Fichte as Fichte has inverted Kant: by seeing self-consciousness as not an original act but, in fact, a creative outcome.

With such a suggestion of something less than conscious or unconscious, a few strands became progressively detectable in Schellingian thought. The most prominent and immediate were his experiments from 1797, in Jena, with a two-sided philosophy, or a philosophy of nature, which could clarify an identity uniting the thinking of the subject and the processes of nature; its goal, he declares, is to reach a point where "nature is to become invisible mind and mind invisible nature." Mere matter, or nature's unconscious product, is spoken of as issuing from nature's abortive attempts to reflect itself and is thus "fossilized" intelligence, intelligence inferred only by means of its externality or phenomenon. In this philosophical system, the perfect scientific "theory of everything" is one where nature can be resolved entirely into a unified intelligence by submerging all matter in form, that is to say, where the phenomenal disappears completely and all that remains are the laws of intuitive perception alone.

Schelling's idea of the whole therefore resembles the universal identity of Spinoza but differs from it in that his is neither static nor resolved. He has internalized the lesson of Friedrich Heinrich Jacobi's assault on Spinozism which shows how a total philosophy can only either be complete but ungrounded, doomed to seek endlessly for the conditions of what is unconditional, or incomplete but grounded, by opening into the realm of faith. This, as Schelling's second strand, anticipates his later turn to philosophical theology and, as early as 1804, its development was already postulated as an inevitability. In *Philosophie und Religion* (1804), he remarks how a negative philosophy that reflects in formal terms on the ascension of the real to the ideal must be complemented by a positive philosophy that can record a corresponding descending of the ideal and its dispersion among the real. *Über das Wesen der menschlichen Freiheit* (*On the Nature of Human Freedom*, 1809), which discusses human evil and sickness in the light of divine freedom, and the Böhmean *Die Weltalter* (The *Ages of the World*, 1811–15) must accordingly be read as preparatory writings for such a positive philosophy.

A further third strand sees Schelling merging the formal content of philosophy and aesthetics: relying on the thoughts of Novalis and Friedrich von Schlegel, he finds himself capable of positing art as that event that proves the possibility of a thing not to appear as mere object. Like the absolute whole uniting the conscious and the unconscious, the creative work joins its aesthetic production with an ability to reflect on this production; it emerges from both a productive imagination that gracefully offers its freedom to necessity, its ideal to the real, and its own capacity to reveal itself as a site of freedom, its real unveiling the ideal. A curious convergence therefore takes place: Schelling can bring together the often incompatible fields of natural science and pure art by seeing how each may bear its distinct methodological relation to and within the absolute but, in an opposition, fulfills both halves of an object-subject orientation by which nature should be observed. In short, Schelling has arrived at a very stable metaphysics that can simultaneously achieve a deduction of science as well as effect a grounding for the aesthetic.

Its complexity, however, made the formulation a recurring subject of misunderstanding, and Schelling's own clarification was soon drowned out by the explosive criticism of his one-time roommate and colleague Hegel. Earlier, Novalis had also grown increasingly hostile to his ideas and especially to *Von der Weltseele* (*Of the World-Soul*, 1798), the same work that had led Friedrich Hölderlin, another good friend, to praise him for penetrating human nature "with rare integrity and adroitness." Criticizing what seems to be a problematic recourse to Platonic idealism, Hegel caricatures Schelling's absolute as "an oracle" emanating "blindly from itself" as if "shot out of a pistol." What is not "utterly senseless drivel" Hegel develops as part of his own fully rational universal dialectics, but what he rejects he regards as "thoughts so trivial that we might well doubt our having correctly understood their meaning." His most famous ridicule of Schelling's absolute as the "night when all cows are black" was mostly a calculated misreading against which Schelling had warned years before: his opponent had described how most would see "in the being of the absolute nothing but a pure night" where, "unable to know anything . . . it dwindles away for them into a mere negation of multiplicity."

Even more noteworthy, as early as 1801 and particularly with his philosophy of identity, Schelling was already imagining what would thereafter evolve into the most sustained critique of Hegelianism, our fourth strand. Rational thinking since René Descartes has assumed consistently that the "I" that thinks or the "I" that is owns that which it thinks and is; the belief has been that the self and its thoughts and essence are mutually constitutive and the same. What falls short of proper recognition here, however, is the fact that the I's thinking and being are not fundamentally its own: the I may predicate existence but it does not precede it and cannot be itself without it. Yet, for the self to recognize itself in the reflection of I = I, it must nonetheless have known itself before the reflection so that it can know what is reflected as the object of itself, in other words, it must have known itself by what does not appear in the reflection. Seeing that this groundlessness which, as the ground before self-grounding, cannot be distinct from the self, Schelling reconceives of it as the freedom that precedes the I's self-necessitation. If the absolute identity is in this sense always an identity of two, it follows that any total and rational system of reflection like Hegel's is inherently unrealizable because it is nonrational existence that is inevitably "the link of a being as One, with itself as a multiplicity."

With the rise of Hegelianism and his wife Caroline's death in 1809, Schelling withdrew from public life and became so removed that when he assumed Hegel's chair in Berlin a decade after his rival's death in 1831, Friedrich Engels hailed him as a specter "intellectually dead for three decades" but now claiming "the full power and authority of life." In reality, the unpublished period of Schelling's life is immensely significant and among its crucial works is *Die Weltalter*, which seeks to expound no less than the history of God. Building on the premise that philosophy cannot ultimately explain existence, he merges the earlier philosophies of Nature and identity with his newfound belief in a fundamental conflict between a dark unconscious principle and a conscious principle in God. God makes the universe intelligible by relating to the ground of the real but, insofar as nature is not complete intelligence, the real exists as a lack within the ideal and not as reflective of the ideal itself. The three universal ages—distinct only to us but not in the eternal God—therefore comprise a beginning where the principle of God before God is divine will striving for being, the present age, which is still part of this growth and hence a mediated fulfillment, and a finality where God is consciously and consummately Himself to Himself.

The understanding allows Schelling to properly confront issues about the source and nature of human evil and, contrary to popular belief, questions like these did not begin with his *Über das Wesen der menschlichen Freiheit*. They took root as early as his master's dissertation, written at seventeen, on human evil and the origin of philosophy. His unfinished *Philosophie der Offenbarung* (*Philosophy of Revelation*, 1841–42) and *Philosophie der Mythologie* (*Philosophy of Mythology*, 1842) trace more specifically the nature of the dissemination of the ideal through both Christian revelation and classical mythology: The process is differently studied here as the relation of God's dark power in the age of myth to Christ's manifestation in the modern age, as the tension between sinful man and divine nature, and as the procedure whereby God raised Himself up as the principle of religion through Christ's incarnation. Yet, in a twist to such an astonishing comeback, Schelling's lectures on revelation were promptly plagiarized by the theologian Heinrich Eberhard Gottlob Paulus. Upon failing repeatedly to win a legal case against him, the disillusioned philosopher at last gave up his post and ceased lecturing altogether.

His crucial Berlin lectures were to have nonetheless an unexpected effect on the rest of the nineteenth century for among his listeners were Mikhail Bakunin, Jakob Burckhardt, Engels, Ludwig Feuerbach, and Søren Kierkegaard, all of whom would later develop ideas that could in part relate back to Schellingianism. Kierkegaard notably recounts how the "embryonic child of thought" leapt within him when this speaker mentioned the word *actuality* in connection to philosophy. Schelling had admitted that the science of reason could not engage existence and that "if the positive does not come quickly, the negative easily becomes obscured, and the logical is taken away for actual." A major influence on the German Romantics during his lifetime, with his death Schelling's influence extended through Nietzsche, the rise of psychoanalysis, and even more recent theorists such as Jacques Derrida, Martin Heidegger, Jacques Lacan, and Emmanuel Levinas. Both Samuel Taylor Coleridge's system of life and Arthur Schopenhauer's will are famous products of his philosophy, as are the approaches of the American thinkers Ralph Waldo Emerson and Charles Sanders Peirce; it has also been claimed that his idea of a ground uniting all phenomena contributed to the discovery of electromagnetism by Hans Christian Oested in 1820.

LI SUI GWEE

Biography

Born in Leonberg, Württemberg, on January 27, 1775; attended school at Nürtingen, 1784; entered the Tübingen seminary, where he befriended Hegel and Hölderlin, 1790–95; tutor for a noble family, 1795–97. Moved to Leipzig, 1796; appointed as extraordinary professor at the University of Jena, 1798–1803. Coedited *Kritisches Journal der Philosophie* (*Critical Journal of Philosophy*) with Hegel, 1802. Moved to a chair at University at Würzburg and married Caroline Michaelis, 1803. Public break with Fichte, 1805. General secretary of the Munich Academy of Plastic Arts, 1806–20; Caroline's death, 1809; private lectures at Stuttgart, 1810; married Pauline Gotter, 1812. Lectured at University of Erlangen, 1820–27; appointed to University of Munich, 1827. Hegel's death, 1831. Taught the Bavarian prince and later king Maximilian II, 1835. Appointed to University of Berlin by Frederick William IV, 1841. Made member of the Prussian Academy of Sciences, 1842; Paulus published his plagiarized *Die endlich offenbar gewordene Philosophie der Offenbarung* (*The Philosophy of Revelation Finally Clarified*), 1843; died in Bad Ragaz, Switzerland, on August 20, 1854.

Selected Works

Über die Möglichkeit einer Form der Philosophie überhaupt. 1795. Translated as *On the Possibility of an Absolute Form of Philosophy* by Fritz Marti. In *The Unconditional in Human Knowledge: Four Early Essays*. Lewisburg Pennsylvania: Bucknell University Press, 1980.

Vom Ich als Prinzip der Philosophie Absolute oder über das Unbedingte im menschlichen Wissen, 1795. Translated as *Of the I as Principle of Philosophy or on the Unconditional in Human Knowledge* by Fritz Marti. In *The Unconditional in Human Knowledge: Four Early Essays*. Lewisburg Pennsylvania: Bucknell University Press, 1980.

Ideen zu einer Philosophie der Natur als Einleitung in das Studium dieser Wissenschaft, 1797. Translated as *Ideas for a Philosophy of Nature* by Errol E. Harris and Peter Heath. Cambridge: Cambridge University Press, 1988.

Von der Weltseele, eine Hypothese der höheren Physik zur Erklärung des allgemeinen Organismus. 1798.

System des transzendentalen Idealismus, 1800. Translated as *System of Transcendental Idealism* by Peter Heath. Charlottesville, Virginia: University Press of Virginia, 1978.

Bruno, oder über das göttliche und natürliche Prinzip der Dinge, 1802. Translated as *Bruno, or On the Natural and the Divine Principle of Things* by Michael G. Vater. Albany: State University of New York Press, 1984.

Philosophie der Kunst. 1802–3.

Philosophie und Religion. 1804.

Philosophische Untersuchungen über das Wesen der menschlichen Freiheit und die damit zusammenhängenden Gegenstände, 1809. Translated as *Of Human Freedom* by James Gutmann. Chicago: Open Court, 1936.

Clara, oder Zusammenhang der Naturmit der Geisterwett, 1810? Translated as *Clara, or On Nature's Connection to the Spirit World* by Fiona Steinkamp. Albany: State University of New York Press, 2002.

Die Weltalter, 1811–15. Translated as *The Ages of the World* by Frederick de Wolfe Bolman, Jr. New York: Columbia University Press, 1942.

Über die Gottheiten von Samothrake, 1815. Translated as *Treatise on "The Deities of Samothrace,"* by Robert F. Brown. Missoula, Montana: Scholars Press for American Academy of Religion, 1977.

Zur Geschichte der neueren Philosophie, 1833–34. Translated as *On the History of Modern Philosophy* by Andrew Bowie. Cambridge: Cambridge University Press, 1994.

Philosophie der Offenbarung. 1841–42.

Philosophie der Mythologie. 1842.

Bibliography

Bowie, Andrew. *Schelling and Modern European Philosophy: An Introduction*. London: Routledge, 1993.

Esposito, Joseph L. *Schelling's Idealism and Philosophy of Nature*. London: Associated University Presses, 1977.

Frank, Manfred. *Der unendliche Mangel an Sein. Schellings Hegelkritik und die Anfänge der Marxschen Dialektik.* Frankfurt: Suhrkamp, 1975.

Hegel, Georg Wilhelm Friedrich. *Lectures on the History of Philosophy: The Lectures of 1825–1826.* Vol. 3. Translated by Robert F. Brown, J. Michael Stewart, and Henry Silton Harris. Berkeley and Los Angeles: University of California Press, 1990.

Heidegger, Martin, *Schelling's Treatise on the Essence of Human Freedom.* Translated by Joan Stambaugh. Athens, Ohio: Ohio University Press, 1985.

Henrich, Dieter. *Selbstverhältnisse: Gedanken und Auslegungen zu den grundlagen der klassischen deutschen Philosophie.* Stuttgart: Philipp Reclam, 1982.

Hogrebe, Wolfram. *Prädikation und Genesis. Metaphysik als Fundamentalheuristik im Ausgang von Schellings "Die Weltalter."* Frankfurt: Suhrkamp, 1989.

Jaspers, Karl. *Schelling: Größe und Verhängnis.* Munich: Piper, 1955.

Sandkühler, Hans Jörg. *Friedrich Wilhelm Joseph Schelling.* Stuttgart: J. B. Metzler, 1970.

Schneeberger, Guido Federico. *Friedrich Wilhelm Joseph von Schelling.* Bern: Franke Verlag. 1954.

Schulz, Walter. *Die Vollendung des deutschen Idealismus in der Spätphilosophie Schellings.* 2nd ed. Pfullingen: Günther Neske, 1975.

Tilliette, Xavier. *Schelling une philosophie en devenir.* 2 vols. Paris: J. Vrin, 1970.

White, Alan. *Schelling: Introduction to the System of Freedom.* New Haven, Conn.: Yale University Press, 1983.

Žižek, Slavoj. *The Invisible Remainder: An Essay on Schelling and Related Matters*, London: Verso, 1996.

SCHILLER, JOHANN CHRISTOPH FRIEDRICH VON 1759–1805

German dramatist, poet, and literary theorist

The plays Friedrich Schiller wrote in the 1780s help define pre-Romanticism in Germany. Rebellious and impassioned, they denounce social injustice and reject authority and order in favor of the feelings and beliefs of the individual. In *Die Räuber* (*The Robbers*, 1781), two sons react to an authoritarian father by resorting to violence and tragically stepping outside the rule of law. *Kabale und Liebe* (*The Minister*, 1784) exposes the inhumanity of a corrupt aristocratic regime that seeks to destroy the love between the son of its ruler and the daughter of a miller. In *Don Karlos* (1787), at the court of the autocratic Philip II of Spain, the ideal of individual freedom is asserted by the liberal Marquis Posa, a fictional character created by Schiller. Even in these early plays, however, romantic revolt is tempered by an awareness that rebels themselves can be seduced into tyranny by belief in the absolute rectitude of their principles.

In fact, Schiller's commitment to personal freedom never did derive from Romantic subjectivism and sentiment but emanated instead from his own persecution under eighteenth-century absolutism and from the libertarian rationalism of the Enlightenment. The experiences of his middle years confirmed these influences and took him in different directions from the rising Romantic generation. Work on *Don Karlos* aroused his interest in history and led him to write his *Geschichte des Abfalls der vereinigten Niederlande von der spanischen Regierung* (*History of the Rise and Progress of the Belgian Republic*, 1788), followed by the *Geschichte des 30 jährigen Krieges* (*History of the Thirty Years War*, 1790). These historical studies developed his grasp of the exigencies of power and of the difficulty of maintaining morality in the face of political necessity. His study of the works of Immanuel Kant in 1791 induced in him the conviction that personal inclination should be subordinated to ethically governed self-direction. Finally, the course of the French Revolution, to which he had initially lent instinctive support, convinced him that democratic freedoms produced only anarchy and violence if not rooted in altruism.

From 1794 to 1805, Schiller collaborated intensively, though not without tension, with Johann Wolfgang von Goethe, helping him shape Weimar classicism. During these years Schiller recruited Romantic writers, especially August Wilhelm and Friedrich Schlegel and the philosopher Johann Gottlieb Fichte, for editorial projects such as his journal *Die Horen* (*The Horae*) but eventually quarreled with them on both ideological and personal grounds. His relationship with Goethe, an alliance of opposites, was the basis for his influential treatise on cultural history *Über naive und sentimentalische Dichtung* (*On the Naive and Sentimental in Literature*, 1795), in which he distinguished two fundamental types of writer: those who write intuitively, like the Greeks (and, by implication, Goethe), and those internally divided or reflective, in general modern writers, including himself. Sharing Goethe's disdain for standards of education and taste in Germany, he wrote a series of essays, most notably *Über die ästhetische Erziehung des Menschen in einer Reihe von Briefen* (*On Aesthetic Education in a Series of Letters*, 1793), in which he expounded a new purpose for the arts and for the theater in particular. He agreed with the German Romantics, particularly Novalis (Friedrich von Hardenberg), in arguing that events in France showed that lasting political reform could not come about without a prior regeneration of the human spirit. However, while the Romantics envisaged this change coming about through a revival of religion or the advent of some mythological golden age, for Schiller the route to human ennoblement lay pragmatically through cultural activity, in a process of "aesthetic education."

Schiller's plays in this classicist phase therefore show a series of characters acting as exemplars of what he termed, in Kantian fashion, "moral dignity" or "the sublime," the capacity to sacrifice their personal desires or disregard extreme suffering in the interest of altruistic causes. Thus Max Piccolomini in the *Wallenstein* trilogy (1799), acting as a moral counterfoil to the opportunistic and presumptuous Wallenstein, sacrifices his love for Wallenstein's daughter and rides to death in battle in order to maintain his loyalty to the emperor. Similarly, in *Maria Stuart* (1800) the lifelong sensualist Mary accepts her unjust death sentence willingly in atonement for a previous but unpunished crime; while in *Die Jungfrau von Orleans* (*The Maid of Orleans*, 1801) Joan overcomes her love for an English knight and dies on the battlefield in obedience to her patriotic mission. In both cases an apparently religious transfiguration of the heroine symbolically celebrates the triumph of the human will. Although *Die Jungfrau von Orleans* is subtitled "a romantic tragedy" and makes use of supernatural motifs akin to those in contemporary Romantic drama, Schiller's insistence in all these plays on a human rather than transcendent salvation separates him from his Romantic contemporaries. He takes a similar position in his philosophical and didactic poetry in this classicist period; a vision of the ideal is proclaimed as an alternative to imperfect social reality, but the vision is potentially realizable within human nature: "Nehmt die Gottheit auf in euren Willen" ("absorb divinity into your will"). Schiller's determination to present poetic rather than naturalistic truth led him not only to rewrite history for his own thematic and theatrical ends but also to imitate Greek tragedy in *Die Braut von Messina* (*The Bride of Messina*, 1803), in the preface to which he declares his radical opposition to surface realism in the drama. The plays of his youth had been written in an often colloquial prose, but beginning with *Don Karlos* he employs verse and an elevated rhetorical style.

Schiller's development from iconoclastic Sturm und Drang rebellion to classicist insistence on moral order is only apparently inconsistent. He was motivated throughout by an austere dedication to philanthropic idealism and an indignant contempt for all forms of injustice or venality. Goethe later summed up the unity of Schiller's work neatly when he said that Schiller had been concerned throughout with freedom, but that in his youth the emphasis had been on physical freedom (the absence of externally imposed restraint) while later it had been on moral freedom (the retention of freedom of choice by means of self-imposed restraint). Such a resolute humanist and moralist, fascinated in both his academic and dramatic work with the use and abuse of political power, could never accommodate himself more than tenuously to the Romanticism that prevailed in his lifetime.

RICHARD LITTLEJOHNS

Biography

Born in Marbach, Germany, November 10, 1759. Required by the duke of Württemberg to attend the Military Academy in Stuttgart 1773–80, concentrated on the study of medicine. From 1780 on, was regimental surgeon in the Württemberg army. Deserted in 1782 and fled to Bauerbach in Thuringia. Official dramatist at the theater in Mannheim, 1783–84. In Leipzig and Dresden 1785–87 in the circle surrounding Christian Gottfried Körner. In Weimar, 1787–88. Appointed professor of history at the University of Jena and settled in Jena in 1789. Married Charlotte von Lengefeld in 1790; they had two sons and two daughters. In 1794 had first exchange of views with Goethe, extensive correspondence with him until 1805. In 1799 moved back to Weimar. A succession of illnesses from 1794 ended with his death from an intestinal disorder May 9, 1805.

Selected Writings

Collections
Schillers Werke: Nationalausgabe. Edited by Julius Petersen et al. Weimar: Böhlau, 1943–.

Sämtliche Werke. 5 vols. Edited by Gerhard Fricke et al. Munich: Hanser, 1958–59.

Poetry
Anthologie auf das Jahr 1782. 1782.
Gedichte. 2 vols. 1800–03.
The Poems of Schiller, Complete. Translated by Edgar Alfred Bowring, 1856.

Fiction
Der Verbrecher aus verlorener Ehre. 1786. Translated as *The Dishonoured Irreclaimable* by R. Holcroft, in *Tales from the German,* 1826.
Der Geisterseher (uncompleted). 1787. Translated as *The Armenian; or, the Ghost-Seer* by W. Render, 1800. Translated as *The Ghost-Seer* by Henry G. Bohn, 1992.

Drama
Die Räuber. 1781. Translated as *The Robbers* by A. F. Tytler, 1792. Translated as *The Robbers* by Francis J. Lamport, London: Penguin Books, 1979.
Die Verschwörung des Fiesko zu Genua. 1783. Translated as *Fiesco: or, the Genoese Conspiracy* by G. H. Noehden and J. Stoddart, 1796.
Kabale und Liebe (originally titled *Luise Millerin*). 1784. Translated as *The Minister* by Matthew Gregory Lewis, 1798. Translated as *Intrigue and Love* by Charles E. Passage, 1971.
Don Karlos. Infant von Spanien, 1787. Translated as *Don Carlos* by G. H. Noehden and J. Stoddart, 1798. Translated by Hilary Collier Sy-Quia, Oxford University Press, 1996.
Wallenstein, 1799. Translated as *Wallenstein: a Drama in two Parts* by Samuel Taylor Coleridge, 1800. Translated by Francis J. Lamport, London: Penguin Books, 1979.
Maria Stuart. 1800. Translated by Joseph C. Mellish, 1801. Translated by Hilary Collier Sy-Quia, 1996.
Die Jungfrau von Orleans. 1801. Translated as *The Maid of Orleans,* by John Elliott Drinkwater, 1835. Translated as *Joan of Arc* by Robert David Macdonald, 1987.
Die Braut von Messina. 1803. Translated as *The Bride of Messina* by George Irvine, 1837. Translated by Charles E. Passage, 1962.
Wilhelm Tell, 1804. Translated by R. L. Pearsall, 1825. Translated by John Prudhoe, Manchester University Press, 1970.

Aesthetic Writings
Über Anmut und Würde. 1793.
Vom Erhabenen. 1793.
Über das Pathetische. 1793.
Über die ästhetische Erziehung des Menschen in einer Reihe von Briefen, 1793; Translated as *On Aesthetic Education in a Series of Letters* by Elizabeth M. Wilkinson and L. A. Willoughby, Oxford: Clarendon Press, 1967.
Über naive und sentimentalische Dichtung, 1795. Translated as *On the Naive and Sentimental in Literature* by Helen Watanabe-O'Kelly, Manchester: Carcanet Press, 1981.

Historical Works
Geschichte des Abfalls der vereinigten Niederlande von der spanischen Regierung, 1788. Translated as *History of the Rise and Progress of the Belgian Republic* by Thomas Horne, 1807.
Was heißt und zu welchem Ende studiert man Universalgeschichte? 1789.
Geschichte des 30jährigen Krieges, 1790. Translated as *The History of the Thirty Years War* by A. J. W. Morrison, 1899.

Correspondence
Der Briefwechsel zwischen Schiller und Goethe, 1829. Translated as *Correspondence between Goethe and Schiller 1794–1805* by George H. Calvert, 1845. Translated as *Correspondence between*

Goethe and Schiller 1794–1805 by Lieselotte Dieckmann, Bern: Peter Lang, 1994.
Der Briefwechsel zwischen Schiller und Körner, 1847. Translated as *Correspondence of Schiller and Körner* by Leonard Simpson, 1849. Subsequent German edition, edited by Klaus L. Berghan. Munich: Winkler, 1973.

Bibliography

Borcherdt, Hans Heinrich. *Schiller und die Romantiker. Briefe und Dokumente*. Stuttgart: Cotta, 1948.
Carlyle, Thomas. *Life of Schiller*. 1823.
Graham, Ilse. *Schiller's Drama: Talent and Integrity*. New York: Barnes and Noble/London: Methuen, 1974.
Mainland, William F. *Schiller and the Changing Past*. London: Heinemann, 1957.
Miller, R. D. *The Drama of Schiller*. Harrogate: Duchy Press, 1963.
Sharpe, Lesley. *Schiller and the Historical Character*. Oxford: Oxford University Press, 1982.
———. *Friedrich Schiller: Drama, Thought and Politics*. Cambridge: Cambridge University Press, 1991.
Stahl, Ernst Ludwig. *Schiller's Drama: Theory and Practice*. Oxford: Clarendon Press, 1954.
Ungar, Frederick. *Friedrich Schiller: An Anthology for our Time*. New York: Ungar, 1959.
Witte, William. *Schiller*. Oxford: Blackwell, 1949.

SCHINKEL, KARL FRIEDRICH 1781–1841

German architect, painter, and designer

In 1816, just as Karl Friedrich Schinkel's career as an architect was beginning in earnest, Johann Wolfgang von Goethe expressed the hope that "such a rich talent may be granted an equally broad sphere of action." This hope was to be amply fulfilled, for Schinkel, who in the preceding eleven years had already distinguished himself as a painter and interior designer, soon afterward became the most prominent and influential architect in Prussia, responsible both for overseeing official building programs and for designing numerous public and private buildings himself. Supported by the Prussian king and crown prince, Schinkel succeeded, within the economic constraints of the post-Napoleonic period, in conveying architecturally (with a handful of neoclassical buildings) Berlin's status as the capital of a reemergent European power. As Nikolaus Pevsner has argued, "If he was not a man of genius [as Soane was], he was a man of the highest professional achievement, the best architect of his generation in Europe" and widely acclaimed by succeeding generations of architects for his combination of stylistic restraint and technological innovation.

Like Leo von Klenze, his schoolmate at the Berliner Bauakademie, Schinkel was influenced by Friedrich Gilly, whose proposed monument to Frederick the Great (1797) is said to have inspired Schinkel to become an architect, and to a lesser extent by Jean-Nicolas-Louis Durand, whose utilitarian principles he assimilated but qualified in his architectural practice and writings (particularly the unfinished theoretical work, *Das architektonische Lehrbuch*) with a close attention to what he called "the historic and the poetic." His affinity with German Romantic thought is evident not only in his ideal of the organic unity of function, construction, and style in architectural design but also in his insistence on its expression of a "freedom" defined as "submitting oneself freely to a higher law on the basis of reason or poetic feeling." But the freedom expressed most clearly in his early career, when he was immersed in Fichte's subjective idealist philosophy and compelled by the lack of architectural commissions to work primarily as a painter of dioramas and landscapes, was a freedom from Prussian political reality during and immediately after the Napoleonic wars. In accordance with the Romantic conception of the Gothic as a distinctively German style, Schinkel promoted the fantasy of German nationhood in symbolic paintings of imaginary Gothic cathedrals, such as *Mittelalt-*

erliche Stadt an einem Fluss (*Medieval City by a River*, 1815), in which the rainbow arching over castle, cathedral, and town suggests the unity of society under the authority of the king shown returning triumphantly from battle) and in the unbuilt 1815 design for a Gothic Revival cathedral commemorating the Wars of Liberation. In 1813 he designed the Iron Cross, Prussia's best-known military decoration, which remained in use until 1945. Although his ardor for the Gothic eventually cooled, Schinkel did build some notable Gothic Revival structures, such as the cast-iron pinnacle at Kreuzberg (1821), a vestige of his earlier cathedral project, and the brick Friedrich Werder Church (built 1824–30), the final design of which was chosen by the crown prince from the architect's four alternative proposals.

Having been appointed to the Prussian public works authority in 1810, on the recommendation of Wilhelm von Humbolt (whose villa, Schloss Tegel, he remodeled in 1824), Schinkel was put in charge of its Berlin bureau in 1815. His first major commission was the New Guard House (1816–18) on Unter den Linden, Berlin, which he designed with a Greek Doric portico and massive corner pylons reminiscent of a Roman castrum. This was followed by the Schauspielhaus (1818–21), the scale, severe elegance, and location of which between two eighteenth-century churches on the Gendarmenmarkt established that square as Berlin's symbolic center. Behind an Ionic entrance portico that relates the theater to the neighboring churches, Schinkel built a pedimented central block incorporating the auditorium and stage house, and two smaller pedimented side wings, encasing both in a highly original trabeated grid of mullions, architraves, and large windows. The architect himself, exploiting his experience as a diorama painter, designed sets for the inaugural performance, as well as for numerous other theatrical productions from 1815 to 1828, most notably for Wolfgang Amadeus Mozart's *Die Zauberflöte*.

Schinkel's third major public building in Berlin was his masterpiece, the Altes Museum (1823–30). Symbolically facing the royal palace across the Lustgarten (which Schinkel transformed into a public park), the museum was intended to display ancient sculptures on one floor and Renaissance paintings on the other. The rectangular galleries are arranged around two internal courtyards, while the central block (between the courtyards and behind the entrance hall) is occupied by a Pantheon-like rotunda

Karl Friedrich Schinkel, *Gotischer Dom am Wasser* (*Gothic Cathedral by the Water*). Reprinted courtesy of AKG London.

whose dome is hidden on the exterior by a raised square attic. The building is fronted by an Ionic portico extending its entire length (83.7 m.) and height (19.4 m.), and its columned entrance hall, dominated by a double staircase, is open to the outside, as if to abolish the distinction between inside and outside. Out of financial necessity the sides and back were built in local brick, a material that Schinkel later used unabashedly and even decoratively in his own favorite of his buildings, the School of Architecture, built 1832–35 within view of the Altes Museum and significant in legitimizing naked brick exteriors in Prussia. Schinkel's increasing acceptance of vernacular materials such as brick and terracotta was encouraged in part by the technical achievement of English industrial architecture, which he observed on a visit to England in 1826. He was particularly interested in cast iron, which he used both architecturally (e.g., for the staircase of the Palais Prinz Albrecht) and in furniture, the latter with the purpose of making classical design more accessible to the public through mass production.

In his domestic architecture, particularly the summer villas he designed for members of the Prussian royal family (e.g., the Neue Pavillon, Schloss Glienicke, and Charlottenhof), Schinkel drew not only on classical and Italian Renaissance sources but on English conceptions of the picturesque, adopting asymmetrical floorplans and carefully integrating the design of the buildings with that of the gardens. But he was also capable of astonishing originality, as in the Antonin hunting lodge of 1822–24, a three-story wooden octagon enclosing a galleried atrium and central chimney stack. His most fantastic late projects, vast royal palaces in Athens and the Crimea, remained on paper. At his death, Schinkel's service to Prussia was acknowledged with a state funeral and the acquisition of his papers by the government.

NICHOLAS HALMI

Biography

Born in Neuruppin, Mark Brandenburg, March 13, 1781. Studied at a *Gymnasium* in Berlin, 1794–98; left the *Gymnasium* to study architecture with David and Friedrich Gilly, 1798. Studied at the Bauakademie, Berlin, 1799–1800; traveled through Sax-

ony, Austria, Italy, Sicily, and France, 1803–5. Made his livelihood chiefly by painting, 1807–15; married Susanne Berger, 1809. Appointed senior assessor of public works by Friedrich Wilhelm III, 1810; appointed to the Academy of Fine Arts, Berlin, 1811. Appointed superintendent of the Berlin bureau of the Prussian building authority, 1815. Appointed professor of architecture, Academy of Fine Arts, Berlin, 1820. Traveled to Italy, 1824; traveled to France and England, 1826; traveled to Switzerland and Italy, 1830. Appointed privy councillor in charge of the Prussian building authority, 1830. Suffered a stroke and fell into a coma, September 1840; died in Berlin, October 9, 1841.

Selected Works

Collected Works
Karl Friedrich Schinkel Lebenswerk. 17 vols to date. General editors Paul Ortwin, Rave and Margarete Kühn. Berlin: Deutscher Kunstverlag, 1939.

Buildings (with dates of completion)
Neue Wache. Berlin. 1818.
Kreuzberg monument. Berlin. 1821.
Schauspielhaus. Berlin. 1821 (exterior restored to original appearance after World War II).
Reconstruction of Schloss Tegel. Near Berlin. 1824.
Schlossbrücke. Berlin. 1824.
Jagdschloss Antonin. Near Poznan, Poland. 1824.
Neue Pavillon (now called the Schinkel Pavilion). Charlottenburg. Potsdam. 1825.
Schloss and Casino Glienicke. Potsdam. 1827.
Charlottenhof, Schloss Sansoucci. Potsdam. 1828.
(Altes) Museum. Berlin. 1830 (restored after World War II).
Friedrich-Werdersche-Kirche (now the Schinkel Museum), Berlin. 1830 (restored after World War II).
Neue Packhof. Berlin. 1832 (demolished).
Palais Prinz Albrecht. Berlin. 1833 (destroyed).
Bauakademie. Berlin. 1836 (demolished).
Reconstruction of Schloss Stolzenfels am Rhein. Near Koblenz. 1847.
Nikolaikirche. Potsdam. 1849 (restored after World War II).

Paintings
Panorama von Palermo, 1808. Oil on canvas, 500 cm. × 4500 cm. Now lost.
Der Morgan, 1813. Oil on canvas, 76 cm. × 102 cm. Nationalgalerie, Berlin.
Die Schlacht bei Leipzig, 1814. Panorama, oil on canvas, now lost; preliminary ink sketch at the Kupferstichkabinett (Sammlung der Zeichnungen), Berlin.
Gotischer Dom am Wasser. 1814. Oil on canvas, 80 cm. × 106.5 cm. Original destroyed, copy by Wilhelm Ahlborn (1823) at the Nationalgalerie, Berlin.
Mittelalterliche Stadt an einem Fluss. 1815. Oil on canvas, 94 cm. × 140 cm. Nationalgalerie, Berlin.
Stage designs for *Die Zauberflöte*, 1815. Gouache. Twelve sketches of scenes; sets and two sketches lost, remaining sketches now at the Kupferstichkabinett (Sammlung der Zeichnungen), Berlin; eight hand-colored aquatint etchings printed in *Decorationen auf den beiden königlichen Theatern in Berlin*, (1819–24).

Writings
Sammlung architektonischer Entwürfe, 28 fascicles, 1819–40. Translated by Karin Cramer as *Collection of Architectural Designs*, Chicago: Exedra Books, 1981 (reprinted New York: Princeton Architectural Press, 1989).

Vorbilder für Fabrikanten und Handwerker, (with Peter Beuth). 3 vols. 1821–37.
Werke der höheren Baukunst. 2 vols. 1840–48. Rev. ed., 1878.
Aus Schinkels Nachlass. 4 vols. Edited by Alfred von Wolzogen. 1862–64.
Reise nach England, Schottland und Paris im Jahre 1826. Edited by Gottfried Riemann and David Bindman. 1986. Translated as *The English Journey: Journal of a Visit to France and Britain in 1826* by F. G. Walls. New Haven: Yale University Press, 1993.
Das architektonische Lehrbuch, edited by Goerd Peschken. Munich: Deutscher Kunstverlag, 1979 (second edition, 2001).

Bibliography

Bergdoll, Barry. *Karl Friedrich Schinkel: An Architecture for Prussia*. New York: Rizzoli, 1994.
Forssman, Erik. *Karl Friedrich Schinkel: Bauwerke und Baugedanken*. Munich: Schnell, 1981.
Grisebach, August. *Carl Friedrich Schinkel: Architekt, Städtebauer, Maler*. 2d ed., Munich: Piper, 1981.
Pevsner, Nikolaus. "Karl Friedrich Schinkel." In *Studies in Art, Architecture, and Design*. Vol. 1. London: Thames and Hudson, 1968.
Pundt, Hermann. *Schinkel's Berlin: A Study in Environmental Planning*, Cambridge: Harvard University Press, 1972.
Riemann, Gottfried, and Christa Heese. *Karl Friedrich Schinkel: Architekturzeichnungen*. Berlin: Henschel, 1991.
Snodin, Michael, ed. *Karl Friedrich Schinkel: A Universal Man*. New Haven, Cann.: Yale University Press, 1991.
Szambien, Werner. *Schinkel*. Paris: Hazan, 1989.
Watkin, David, and Tilman Mellinghof. *German Architecture and the Classical Ideal*. London: Thames and Hudson, 1987.
Zadow, Mario. *Karl Friedrich Schinkel*. Berlin: Rembrandt, 1980.
Zukowsky, John, ed. *Karl Friedrich Schinkel, 1781–1841: The Drama of Architecture*. Chicago: Art Institute of Chicago, 1994.

SCHLEGEL, AUGUST WILHELM VON 1767-1845

German critic, philologist, poet, dramatist and translator

August Wilhelm von Schlegel, with his younger brother Friedrich, defined the philosophical basis of the modern movement of his time, identified its literary-historical origins, and negotiated the transition from neoclassicism to the new weltanschauung they called Romanticism. His main contributions are the Berlin and Vienna lectures that defined a modern view of literature: *Vorlesungen über schöne Literatur und Kunst* (*Course of Lectures on Art and Literature*, 1884) and *Vorlesungen über dramatische Kunst und Literatur* (*Course of Lectures on Dramatic Art and Literature*, 1809–11). He clarified differences between ancient and modern perceptions of the world and identified the medieval romance as the genesis of modern Romanticism. He questioned neoclassicism by exposing false assumptions about antiquity, and announced the advent of a German national literature. In his lectures and *Kritische Schriften* (*Critical Writings*, 1828) Schlegel established modern principles of literary criticism. His advocacy of William Shakespeare and Pedro Calderón de la Barca shaped his definition of the Romantic drama, and his translations of Shakespeare are still canonical, as are those of *Spanisches Theater* (*Spanish Theater*, 1803–9) and southern European poetry, *Blumensträuße italiänischer, spanischer und portuguesischer Poesie* (*Bouquets of Italian, Spanish, and Portuguese Poetry*, 1804). His reputation as a poet began with *Gedichte* (*Poems*, 1800) and *Poetische Werke* (*Verse Works*, 1811); and as a dramatist with a tragedy, *Ion* (1803), modeled on Euripides.

Schlegel endorsed his brother's division of history into ancient and modern on the basis of a static ideal of "perfection" versus a "perpetually becoming" creativity. Schlegelian Romanticism was a new manifestation of a universal historical process, and, simultaneously, a continuation of the spontaneous, imaginative literature of the age of chivalry. Art, he felt, must be new and dynamic, free and original. There is no place in a progressive, infinite world for static, finite neoclassical dictates like prescribed forms and styles, dramatic unities, "taste," and imitation. Schlegel took the battle against neoclassicism to Paris with a bold attack titled *Comparaison entre la Phèdre de Racine et celle d'Euripede* (*A Comparison of Racine's and Euripides' Versions of Phèdre*, 1807). Euripides was great because his dramas are free and original. Neoclassicism is deemed false because its basis is imitation of the forms of classical works without comprehension of the spirit that shapes content.

Schlegel's *Lectures on Dramatic Art and Literature* is a systematic study of world literature from the ancient Greeks to the German Romantics. He eloquently isolated neoclassicism, noting, "Those very ages, nations, and ranks who felt least the want of a poetry of their own, were the most assiduous in imitation of the ancients; accordingly, its results are but dull school exercises, which at best excite a frigid imagination."

He honed this strategy by giving the great French dramatists their due and ascribing their failures to the curtailment of genius by false principles. The true heirs of antiquity, he felt, were not the neoclassicists but the Romantics, because ancient and Romantic literature are both original. "Vital motion," derived from a play of harmony with contrast, defined the true course of history, not perfection. He wrote, "In this idea we have perhaps discovered the true key to the ancient and modern history. . . . Those who adopted it, gave to the peculiar spirit of *modern* art, as contrasted with the *antique* or *classical*, the name of *romantic*."

Antique art is pagan, modern art is Christian. The poetry of the Greeks was based on a consciousness of harmony. The "fancy" of the Christian moderns is incorporeal; everything finite and mortal is lost in contemplation of infinity. The Greeks invented the poetry of joy, while modern poetry expresses desire. From this Schlegel arrived at an original definition of the ancient-modern division: "The spirit of ancient art is *plastic* (*plastische*), but that of the moderns is *picturesque* (*pittoresk*)." The ancients' perception of the world was corporeal (*körperlich, die Körperlichkeit*) because the man of antiquity was at one with nature and therefore his poetry appealed to the physical senses in the same way that sculpture appeals to touch. The poetry of modern man gives rise to ideas; it appeals to the imagination like pictorial art. Ancient poetry was corporeally conceived and received because language itself was corporeal—it acted directly upon the senses, and could thereby express all that ancient man perceived in his finite world. Modern poetry appeals to the imagination, which can intuit more than is said.

Schlegel asserted the specific origins of Romanticism: "Chivalry, love, and honor, together with religion itself, are the subjects of that poetry of nature which poured itself out in the Middle Ages . . . and preceded the more artistic cultivation of the [modern] romantic spirit." The term *Romantic* is appropriate because "the word is derived from romance—the name originally given to the languages which were formed from the mixture of the Latin and Old Teutonic dialects." The origins of Romanticism were Germanic—an assertion that justified claims to a German national literature: "After Christianity, the character of Europe has, since the commencement of the Middle Ages, been chiefly influenced by the Germanic race of Northern conquerors, who infused new life and vigor into a degenerated people." The modernization that led to Romanticism began in the sixteenth century with a new kind of drama: the Romantic drama. The Romantic drama—another original discovery—arose spontaneously in sixteenth-century Spain (Calderón) and England (Shakespeare). Modern dramas should be neither tragedies nor comedies, but they should be Romantic. Dramas must comprehend "the whole of life" and cannot be confined to time and place.

Controversy marked Schlegel's life and work. His collaboration with Johann Christoph Friedrich von Schiller ended in enmity. With his wife Caroline he attracted his brother, Friedrich Wilhelm Joseph von Schelling, Ludwig Tieck, Novalis, and Clemens Brentano to the evenings that brought about the Jena school, but he broke with most of these, arguing even with Friedrich and losing Caroline to Schelling. His chauvinistic assertion of a Germanic Romanticism was not appreciated. The result was the so-called north-south debate. In the view of Jean-Charles-Léonard Sismonde de Sismondi (*De la littérature du midi de l'Europe*, 1813), we attempt in vain "to discover in the manners or the traditions of the Germans the birth of chivalry." Instead, "the poetry of romance" was introduced into Europe by the Provençals, and the age of chivalry can be traced to contact in the south with the Arabians of the East. Madame Anne-Louise-Germaine de Staël, on the other hand, became Schlegel's advocate and took the battle once again to Paris by propagating and elucidating his ideas in her widely influential *De l'Allemagne* (1813). It is to her that we owe continued interest in his modernizing ideas.

LAUREN G. LEIGHTON

See also ***De l'Allemagne* (on Germany)**; **Irony, Romantic; Schlegel, (Karl Wilhelm) Friedrich von; Schlegel-Schelling, Caroline; Sismondi, Jean-Charles-Léonard Simonde de; Staël, Madame Anne-Louise-Germaine de**

Biography

Born in Hanover, September 8, 1767. Studied philology, Göttingen University, 1787–91; at Jena, studied Schiller's journals, married Caroline Michaelis Schirmer, began Shakespeare translations, 1796–97. Appointed extraordinary professor at University of Jena, 1798; coeditor with brother Friedrich of *Athenäum*, 1798–1800. At University of Berlin, lectured on art and literature, began translations of Italian, Spanish, and Portuguese literature, 1802–4; divorced from Caroline, liaison with Madame de Staël, 1804. At University of Vienna, lectured on dramatic art and literature, 1808. Secretary to crown prince of Sweden, Bernadotte, 1813–14. At University of Bonn, became authority on oriental studies, founded Sanskrit scholarship in Germany, 1818–45. Published journal *Indische Bibliothek*, 1823–30; edited the *Bhagavad-Gita* with a Latin translation, 1823; edited the *Ramayana*, 1829. Died in Bonn, May 12, 1845.

Selected Works

Vorlesungen über dramatische Kunst und Literatur, 1813, 1817. Translated by John Black, revised by Rev. A. J. W. Morrison as *Course of Lectures on Dramatic Art and Literature*, 1846. Reprint New York: AMS Press, 1965.

Sämmtliche Werke. 12 vols. 1846–47. Reprint New York: Olms, 1971.

Shakespeares dramatische Werke. 10 vols. Translated by August Schlegel and Ludwig Tieck, 1897.

Geschichte der deutschen Sprache und Poesie. Berlin: Behr (Feddersen), 1913.

Vorlesungen über dramatische Kunst und Literatur. 2 vols. Bonn: Schroeder, 1923.

A. W. Schlegel's Lectures on German Literature from Gottsched to Goethe. Oxford: Blackwell, 1944.

Athenäum [*Atheneum*], 1798–1800. Reprint Darmstadt: Wissenschaftliche Buchgesellschaft, 1960.

Ausgewählte Briefe [*Selected Letters*]. Stuttgart: Kohlhammer, 1974.

August Wilhelm von Schlegel. Reprinted courtesy of Bildarchiv Preussischer Kulturbesitz.

Bibliography

Atkinson, Margaret E. *August Wilhelm Schlegel as a Translator of Shakespeare; A Comparison of Three Plays with the Original.* Oxford: B. Blackwell, 1958.

Ewton, Ralph W. *The Literary Theories of August Wilhelm Schlegel.* The Hague: Mouton, 1972.

Schirmer, Ruth. *August Wilthelm Schlegel und seine Zeit: ein Bonner Leben.* Bonn: Bouvier Verlag/Herbert Grundmann, 1986.

SCHLEGEL, DOROTHEA 1764–1839

German translator, critic, novelist, and poet

Born Brendel Mendelssohn, the oldest child of six of Moses Mendelssohn, the philosopher and theologian of Judaism, Dorothea Schlegel was raised in the cultivated milieu of Berlin's intellectual society. By the time of her marriage in 1784 to a banker, Simon Veit, she was participating in literary salons organized by elite Jewish women such as Henriette Herz, who attracted a wide following of authors, painters, musicians, and philosophers. In the 1790s she and her lifelong friend, Rahel Varnhagen von Ense, led vibrant discussions about the key elements of German Romanticism, drawing upon ideas associated with the philosophers Johann Gottlieb Fichte, Immanuel Kant, Johann Christoph Friedrich von Schiller, and Friedrich Daniel Ernst Schleiermacher.

Brendel bore four children, two of whom died in infancy. The surviving brothers, Philipp and Johannes Veit, became prominent painters, well-known in European artistic circles. Her life changed forever in 1797 when the author Friedrich von Schlegel attended one of the Berlin literary salons. Within a year, her marriage was dissolved and in 1799 she went to Jena where Friedrich's brother August Wilhelm had recently taken up a university position. Her former husband generously provided for her and the children; this was fortunate given that Friedrich von Schlegel struggled throughout his life to earn a living from his writings. In an effort to bring in a greater income, she began a literary career by copying and editing many of Schlegel's essays and by contributing poems and critical reviews to *Das Athenäum*, a journal edited by the Schlegel brothers and Ludwig Tieck.

The Jena circle was comprised of some of the most dynamic thinkers in Europe: Clemens Brentano and Johann Christoph Friedrich von Schiller were there; Johann Wolfgang von Goethe had come over from Weimar; Novalis lived nearby; and Friedrich Wilhelm Joseph von Schelling and Caroline von Schlegel (who later married Schelling) were also there. The presence of all these artists and intellectuals contributed to an atmosphere of constant stimulation. Brendel, Schelling, and Caroline von Schlegel studied Italian under Friedrich von Schlegel's mentorship. The group was at the height of its productivity. In one of her letters, she wrote, "Such an eternal concert of wit, poetry, art, and science surrounds me here; this can easily make one forget the rest of the world."

Brendel Veit began to call herself Dorothea after the publication in the second volume of *Das Athenäum* of an essay by Friedrich von Schlegel "Über die Philosophie: An Dorothea" ("An Essay on Philosophy: To Dorothea"), in which he advocates higher education for women and their inclusion in public affairs. He took the name Dorothea from the heroine of Goethe's narrative poem "Hermann und Dorothea" (1797). In the spring of 1799, Schlegel wrote *Lucinde*, based on his love affair with Dorothea and his previous encounters with women. Because of the scandal surrounding this unfinished novel, it was not reissued until 1835, six years after his death. The protagonists, Julius and Lucinde, share an idealistic, sensual attachment centred on a mutual faithfulness, which alone constitutes a full relationship; thus, legal and religious sanctions are superfluous.

The libertine lifestyle that Dorothea Veit and von Schlegel espoused was hardly unique, but the Schlegel brothers had many literary rivals who exploited this opportunity. *Lucinde* is an imaginative but ambiguous novel and readers in subsequent generations used it to promote the doctrine of free love, which actually contradicts Schlegel's intentions. Dorothea's family was offended by the negative attention brought to the Mendelssohn name, and only when Dorothea lived a respectable life in the Viennese café society of 1815 did she resume regular correspondence with all her brothers and sisters. Another reason for Dorothea's alienation from her family was her willingness to break away from the Judaic traditions of her formative years. The members of the Jena circle were especially intrigued by Roman Catholicism and the mysticism of the Middle Ages, not only as an alternative to the secularization endorsed by Enlightenment thinkers but as a force of unification that would support the creation and propagation of a single, worldwide mythology and literature, as Novalis declared, "Christianity is thus raised to the dignity of being the base . . . of a new world edifice and a new humanity." Novalis's study *Die Christenheit oder Europa* (*Christianity or Europe*, 1799) established the Romantic conception of the Middle Ages and lent its name to the periodical *Europa* (1802–4), edited by Friedrich von Schlegel in Paris and published in Leipzig, to which Dorothea von Schlegel contributed poems and critical reviews.

In 1801, *Florentin* was published. This unfinished novel compares favorably with Tieck's *Franz Sternbalds Wanderungen* (1798), Schlegel's *Lucinde*, and Goethe's *Wilhelm Meisters Lehrjahre* (1795–96). Love, friendship, and self-indulgence are the chief catalysts in the hero's development. Dorothea von Schlegel possessed a natural gift for storytelling and this compelling tale of a foster child in search of his true parents offers a litany of Romantic conceptions of self-discovery and fulfillment, and anticipates Goethe's *Wilhelm Meisters Wanderjahre* (1821). In 1804 she produced the *Sammlung Romantischer Dichtungen des Mittelalters* (*An Anthology of Romances from the Middle Ages*), a two-volume collection of French and Latin medieval romances in German translation. The most well-known stories are *Die Geschichte des Zauberers Merlin* (Merlin the Magician), *Die*

Geschichte der Jungfrau von Orleans (The Maid of Orleans), and *Die Geschichte der Margaretha von Valois* (A History of Marguerite de Valois). This work, as with much of her writing during the Paris years (1802–8), was attributed to Friedrich von Schlegel. From this period, *Lother und Maller* (1805), translated from a Cologne dialect of the fifteenth century, and a four-volume translation of Madame Anne-Louise-Germaine de Staël's *Corinne, ou l'Italie* (*Corinne, or the Italien*, 1807–8) are significant. After moving to Vienna in 1808, she collaborated with Karoline Pichler and Josef von Eichendorff on a journal, *Kreises*, devoted to art and culture. Perhaps her greatest contribution to the Romantic era is the correspondence between herself and Friedrich and the letters to her sons, family members, and friends. They represent the chronicle of an entire age, and all the doctrines and theories of German Romanticism are vigorously articulated in an unpretentious, anecdotal, and sprightly style.

In 1808, when Dorothea and Friedrich von Schlegel were accepted into the Roman Catholic church at Cologne, skeptics accused them of posturing (she had converted to Protestantism in 1804 in order to marry Friedrich in Paris), but as a couple they had perhaps entered their finest hour. Their severest critics contended that it was never clear whether the couple represented "Catholic Romanticism or Romantic Catholicism." Nevertheless, despite declining health, Friedrich von Schlegel maintained a dignity of bearing that was rewarded by rank and title in 1815 after several years of diplomatic service to Austria–Hungary during the Napoleonic Wars. Dorothea von Schlegel was content to work with a close-knit circle of Catholic friends in Vienna and acted as a mentor for her sons, visiting them in Rome (1818–20). This balance between art and religion and a renewed sense of purpose in their lives was underestimated by a younger generation of Romantics who extolled artistic expression as an agent of social and political change. After her husband's death, Dorothea von Schlegel lived in Frankfurt with her son Philipp, where she helped her nephew, the composer Felix Mendelssohn, establish his career. At his wedding to Cecile Jeanrenaud in March 1837, this grande dame of European letters was the only witness for the Mendelssohn clan. She bore herself regally and was well received.

ROBERT J. FRAIL

Selected Works

Fiction
Florentin: Roman, Fragmente Variaten, 1801, edited by L. Weissberg. 1987.

Translations
Sammlung Romantischer Dichtungen des Mittelalters. 1804.
Corinne oder Italien. by Anne-Louise-Germane de Staël. 1807–8.
Lother und Maller. 1805.

Letters
Dorothea von Schlegel geboren Mendelssohn und deren Söhne Johannes und Philipp Veit, Briefwechsel edited by J. M. Raich. Mainz: Franz Kirchheim, 1881.
Briefe von Dorothea und Friedrich Schlegel an die Familie Paulus, edited by Rudolf Unger. Berlin: B. Behr, 1913.
Briefe von und an Friedrich und Dorothea Schlegel, edited by Josef Körner. Berlin: As Kanischer, 1926.

Bibliography

Eichner, Hans. *Friedrich Schlegel*. New York: Twayne, 1970.
Hughes, Glyn Tegai. *Romantic German Literature*. New York: Holmes and Meier, 1979.
Prawer, Siegbert Salomon, ed. *The Romantic Period in Germany: Essays by Members of the London University Institute of Germanic Studies*. London: Weidenfeld & Nicolson, 1970.
Stern, Carl. *Das Leben der Dorothea Schlegel*. Göttingen: H. J. Bernert, 1990.
Walzel, Oskar Franz. *German Romanticism*. New York: Frederick Ungar, 1965.

SCHLEGEL, (KARL WILHELM) FRIEDRICH VON 1772–1829

German philologist and philosopher

Karl Wilhelm Friedrich von Schlegel was a philosopher who elaborated in original ways the ideas developed before him by Johann Gottlieb Fichte and Immanuel Kant and after him by his older brother August Wilhelm and others. His work is considered a philosophical conception of life and an artistic program. In the early 1790s he began his study of philosophy and philology with an examination of antiquity, and in 1795 published "Über das Studium der griechischen Poesie" ("On the Study of Greek Poetry") in which he delineated a modern period of European literary history. He included the essay in his first book *Die Griechen und Römer* (*Greeks and Romans*, 1797), which together with *Geschichte der Poesie der Griechen und Römer* (*History of the Poetry of the Greeks and Romans*, 1798) expressed his admiration for classical antiquity. Schlegel did not fully commit himself in these works to modern literature, but his superior knowledge of antiquity enabled him to expose what he saw as the falsity of neoclassical views.

During the 1790s, in reviews and essays on contemporary German writers, Schlegel defined the modern period as heir to the spontaneous, imaginative literature of the age of chivalry and evaluated modern literature in terms of its originality, departures from prescribed styles and forms, and continuous development. He consolidated his position in a collection titled *Gespräch über die Poesie* (*Dialogue on Poetry*, 1800). According to Schlegel, modern literature is universal and free. It originates in the Middle Ages, particularly the age of chivalry and the medieval romance from which the modern novel (*roman*) developed. The *roman* is understood as a concept encompassing the entire tradition of medieval culture and a modern genre that expresses "the whole of life."

Schlegel's concept of "modern" was asserted most vigorously in two sets of "incomprehensible" *Kritische Fragmente* (*Critical Fragments*) written to establish the legitimacy of a new manifestation of a continuing literary-historical process he termed "Romantic." In the *Lyceums-Fragmente* (*Lyceum Fragments*, 1797) he delineated ancient from modern by noting the "classical" appreciation of the "perfected letter" and a modern preference for the "spirit [in process of] becoming." In other words, the Greeks perfected their genres (drama, epic, lyric) but modern forms will constantly and continually develop. In the *Athenäums-Fragmente* (*Athenaeum Fragments*, 1798) Schlegel offered his most compact and contradictory definition of Romanticism. Modern Romanticism continues a literary-historical process that is "progressive and universal." It is literature and life in a state of becoming, never perfected. Its creative forces were freedom and inspiration. Schlegel emphasized plurality, variegation, change, contradictions, and infinity as Romantic tenets. He recommended mixing genres as a means of generating new forms.

The *Critical Fragments* and the *Ideen* (*Ideas*, 1798) included with them are open-ended, chaotic, contradictory, changeable—in short, Romantic. For Schlegel, contemporary Romantic humankind and its art are eternally striving, never "being." Schlegel saw in this dialectic a perpetual struggle between chaos and order, variety and unity, change and stagnation, "self-creation" and "self-destruction." Central to this view is his most far-reaching idea, that irony is a form of paradox. In the *Athenaeum Fragments* he wrote that Romantic irony is the continual self-creating interchange of two conflicting thoughts. Romantic irony is motivated by wit (*der Witz*); and wit is not a mere rhetoric device, but "the highest principle of knowledge" and a "prophetic power." Wit, not logic, is the basis of philosophy. Wit is dialectical: it synthesizes contradictory ideas into new, original relationships and nullifies old ideas.

Language is central to Schlegel's concept of Romantic irony. Throughout his 1812 Vienna lectures, published as *Geschichte der alten und neuen Literatur* (*History of Ancient and Modern Literature*, 1815), he refers to language, defined as "thought in words." Spirit and language, thought and word are one. The man of antiquity lived at one with nature in a world perceived as finite, and this world ended when he lost contact with nature. The language of the man of antiquity was, like his world, finite, and therefore directly received. Modern man, Schlegel said, has became accustomed to thought and imagination. His dilemma—his irony—is that his infinite imagination can intuit more than language can express. Language is structured, and in a perpetually changing world structure limits communication.

In his *History* Schlegel completed his delineation of world history into ancient and modern. His is an erudite, theoretical interpretation of the history of literature understood also as thought, religion, and philosophy. His commitment to the modern period was now strong, as was his antagonism regarding neoclassicism. Romanticism as he saw it is not opposed to "the true antique." Homer and the legends of Troy are original and dynamic, therefore Romantic. Classical antiquity is contradicted not by the Romantics, but by those false erudites, the neoclassicists, "who strive to imitate the form without being gifted with any portion of the enthusiasm of the ancients." In modern history Schlegel preferred Dante Alighieri, Johann Wolfgang von Goethe, Friedrich Gottlieb Klopstock, Gotthold Ephraim Lessing, John Milton, and Johann Christoph Friedrich von Schiller. His praise of Pedro Calderón de la Barca and William Shakespeare ratifies his brother's definition of the Romantic drama.

A historical play in the style of Calderón, *Alarcos* dates from 1802, and a first collection *Gedichte* (*Poetry*) dates from 1809. Schlegel's novel *Lucinde* (1799) is his attempt to write the novel

Delphine de Custine, *Friedrich von Schlegel*, 1816. Reprinted courtesy of AKG London.

he advocated in theory. Like his definition of Romanticism, it is composed of fragments—contradictory, disjointed, without plot order. It realizes his advice to mix genres by combining epistolary prose with dialogue, exposition, and meditations. *Lucinde* is an idealized autobiographical love novel and roman à clef based on his courtship and marriage to Dorothea Veit. It is also a product of his early revolutionary convictions, an attack on a social order based on a dual public–private morality, an advocacy of a "religion of love" that celebrates both the sensual and the spiritual, and a protest against inequality of the sexes and suppression of sensuality. In its time it was denounced as pornography.

Schlegel's early political views were informed by admiration of Napoleon Bonaparte as a liberator. After his conversion to Roman Catholicism in 1808 he became an apologist for the Austrian Empire. Some of his most brilliant ideas date from this time, but his conservatism led to attempts to create an antiempirical theosophy of the soul, as evident in *Philosophie des Lebens* (*Philosophy of Life*, 1828), *Philosophie der Geschichte* (*Philosophy of History*, 1829), and *Philosophie der Sprache und des Wortes* (*Philosophy of Language and the Word*, 1830). These sometimes mystical works diminished his reputation, but he is recognized today as the precursor of Russian formalism and Bakhtinism, new criticism, structuralism and semiotics, and poststructuralism, including deconstruction and new historicism.

LAUREN G. LEIGHTON

See also **Fichte, Johann Gottlieb; Goethe, Johann Wolfgang von; Irony, Romantic; Kant, Immanuel; Romance; Schiller,**

Johann Christoph Friedrich von; Schlegel, August Wilhelm von; Schlegel, Dorothea

Biography

Born in Hanover, March 10, 1772. Studied law, University of Göttingen, 1790–91, University of Leipzig, 1791–94; devoted to philology and philosophy from 1794. University of Dresden, 1795–96; University of Jena, 1796–97; University of Berlin, 1798–99; University of Jena, 1799–1801. Co-editor of *Athenäum* with brother August, 1798–1800. To Paris, lectured on philosophy, began study of Sanskrit, liaison with Dorothea Mendelssohn Veit, advocate of French Revolution and Napoleon, 1802–4. Editor of review *Europa*, 1803–5; University of Cologne, 1804–7. To Vienna, marriage to Dorothea, conversion to Roman Catholicism, 1808. Appointed imperial court secretary at the headquarters of Archduke Charles, became conservative apologist for Klemens Metternich's Holy Alliance, lectured on ancient and modern literature, 1812. Frankfurt, appointed to Austrian Legation at the Diet, 1815; Vienna, editor of *Concordia*, 1820–23. Lectured on philosophy of life and history, 1827–28; University of Dresden, lecture on philosophy of language, 1828. Died in Dresden, January 11, 1829.

Selected Works

Sämtliche Werke. 10 vols. 1822–25; 2nd ed., 15 vols. 1846.
Die Philosophie des Lebens, 1827. Translated by A. J. W. Morrison as *The Philosophy of Life* in *The Philosophy of Life and Philosophy of Language*, 1847, 1866. Reprint New York: AMS Press, 1973.
Philosophische Vorlesungen, insbesondere über Philosophie der Sprache und des Wortes, 1830. Translated by A. J. W. Morrison as *Philosophy of Language* in *The Philosophy of Life and Philosophy of Language*, 1847, 1866. Reprint New York: AMS Press, 1973.
Philosophie der Geschichte, 1829. Translated by James Burton Robinson as *The Philosophy of History in a Course of Lectures Delivered at Vienna*, 1849. Reprint New York: AMS Press, 1976.
Geschichte der alten und neuen Literature, 1815. Translated as *Lectures on the History of Literature, Ancient and Modern*, 1896.
Fragmente zur Poesie und Literatur, 1797–1800. Translated by Ernst Behler and Roman Struc as *Literary Aphorisms* in *Dialogue on Poetry and Literary Aphorisms*. University Park, Pennsylvania: Penn State Press, 1968.
Gespräch über die Poesie, 1800. Translated by Ernst Behler and Roman Struc as *Dialogue on Poetry* in *Dialogue on Poetry and Literary Aphorisms*. University Park, Pennsylvania: Penn State Press, 1968.
Fragmente, 1797–1801. Translated by Peter Firchow as *Fragments* in *Friedrich Schlegel's Lucinde and the Fragments*. Minneapolis, Minnesota: University of Minnersota Press, 1971.
Lucinde, 1799. Translated by Peter Firchow in *Friedrich Schlegel's Lucinde and the Fragments*. Minneapolis, Minnesota: University of Minnesota Press, 1971.

Bibliography

Alford, Steven E. *Irony and the Logic of the Romantic Imagination.* New York: Peter Lang, 1984.
Behler, Ernest. *Friedrich Schlegel in Selbstzeugnissen und Bilddokumenten.* Reinbek: Rowohlt, 1966.
Eichner, Hans. *Friedrich Schlegel.* New York: Twayne, 1979.
Finlay, Marike. *The Romantic Irony of Semiotics: Friedrich Schlegel and the Crisis of Representation.* Berlin and New York: Mouton de Gruyter, 1988.
Huge, Eberhard. *Poesie und Reflexion in der Ästhetik des frühen Friedrich Schlegel.* Stuttgart: J. B. Metzler, 1971.
Mellor, Ann K. *English Romantic Irony.* Cambridge, Massachusetts: Harvard University Press, 1980.
Nüsse, Heinrich. *Die Sprachtheorie Friedrich Schlegels.* Heidelberg: C. Winter, 1962.

SCHLEGEL-SCHELLING, CAROLINE 1763–1809

German salon hostess and letter writer

Known as "Dame Luzifer" ("Lady Lucifer") and "das Übel" ("the Evil One") by Johann Christoph Friedrich von Schiller and his circle, admired and adored by others, Caroline Michaelis-Böhmer-Schlegel-Schelling was a woman who created extreme reactions in her contemporaries. This was due, at least in part, to the dramatic path her life took. She was married three times and divorced once, gave birth to four children (one illegitimate), all of whom died before reaching adulthood, was imprisoned for three months for her suspected involvement in the revolutionary Mainz republic of 1792–93 and subsequently banned from entering her home town of Göttingen, and played a leading role in the early German Romantic circle at Jena. Though she published no work under her own name, she wrote and contributed to reviews for several different journals and was a prolific writer of letters, the first collection of which was published posthumously in 1871.

If opinions about Schlegel-Schelling were divided during her lifetime, critics have since held varying views about her role in German literary history. For many, her importance lies predominantly in her connections with famous men, particularly her second husband August Wilhelm von Schlegel, his brother Friedrich, and her third husband Friedrich Wilhelm Joseph von Schelling. Others have focused on her personality, writing about her sometimes in condemnatory, but more often in idealizing terms, and her life has been the subject of several novels, from Heinrich König's *Die Clubisten in Mainz* (*The Club Members in Mainz*, 1847) to Brigitte Struzyk's *Caroline unterm Freiheitsbaum* (*Caroline Beneath the Freedom Tree*, 1988). Late twentieth-century critics, particularly those influenced by feminist thinking, considered her as a literary figure in her own right, reading her letters not as sources of literary historical or purely biographical information, but as works of imaginative literature.

Schlegel-Schelling's contribution to the Jena circle was, first, a practical one. The house she shared with August Wilhelm von Schlegel was the circle's primary meeting place, and as well as entertaining its various different members (she was a talented conversationalist), she fed and looked after them. She worked as secretary, researcher, and editor for the circle's journal *Athe-*

naeum, read and commented on Friedrich von Schlegel's work and helped August Wilhelm von Schlegel with his translations of William Shakespeare. She also influenced the thinking of members of the early Romantics in important ways. When he first met her in 1793, Friedrich von Schlegel was struck (as was Schelling some years later) by what he saw as her harmonious combination of male and female qualities. Her example helped him arrive at the concept of androgynous perfection discussed in his essay *Über die Diotima* (*On Diotima*, 1795), and she is considered to have inspired much of his later novel fragment *Lucinde* (1799). According to critic Sara Friedrichsmeyer, it was also through Schlegel-Schelling that the Jena Romantics first became acquainted with the ideals of the French Revolution. "The revolutionary consciousness on which the circle's aspirations were based," writes Friedrichsmeyer, "is impossible to imagine without Schlegel-Schelling."

Both Friedrich von Schlegel and Novalis suggested that Schlegel-Schelling write a novel, but she never completed more than a two-page sketch. Critics such as Sigrid Damm have argued that she chose life above art, that her real achievement lay "in ihrem einfachen Dasein" ("in her simple existence"). The work she did leave behind should not be underestimated, however. The numerous reviews on art and literature that critics have identified as hers, or as containing passages by her, in the *Athenaeum*, Schiller's journal *Die Horen*, the *Allgemeine Literatur Zeitung*, and, later, the *Neue Jenaische Literatur Zeitung* are insightful, lively pieces of writing. In some she dismisses works she finds wanting with a few witty, well-chosen words; in others, such as "Ueber Shakespeares Romeo und Julia" ("On Shakespeare's Romeo and Juliet," 1797) she displays a gift for imaginative, sympathetic character analysis. It is her letters, however, of which over four hundred have survived, that most clearly demonstrate her talent as a writer. They span an impressive range of subjects and styles: Schlegel-Schelling writes about her everyday life, both its domestic details and its tragedies; analyzes her feelings and her decisions; comments on the literature she has read and the plays she has seen; draws humorous, merciless portraits of people she meets; gives advice to her correspondents; and makes passing reference to political and social events of the day. She also offers interesting insights into the cultural life of her circle, describing, for example, the opening night of the theater in Weimar after its renovation by Johann Wolfgang von Goethe (letter to Friedrich Schlegel, October 14, 1798), or the mirth of the Jena Romantics on reading Schiller's poem "Das Lied von der Glocke" ("The Song of the Bell,") letter to Auguste Böhmer, October 21, 1799). The fluent, often colloquial tone of the letters has meant that critics have frequently considered them as *schriftliche Gespräche*—that is, as the written continuation of her conversations. But a lengthy letter of 1784, at the end of which Schlegel-Schelling expresses surprise at her addressee Luise Gotter's sustained silence, before "realizing" that she has fallen asleep—"Kein Wörtchen Gegenrede? Ach Du schläfst!" ("Not a single word in reply? Oh, you've fallen asleep!" April 3, 1784)—both testifies to the conversational style of the letters and exposes it as a rhetorical device. The letters, as critics have established, tend to be highly crafted. Despite Schlegel-Schelling's connection with the Jena circle, however, they are not typically Romantic pieces of writing. In them, she shies away from expressions of extreme emotion and displays little interest in nature, religion, or the transcendental realm, preferring to concentrate in a rational and often ironic vein on the concrete details of this world. She also manifests few signs of internal conflict or torment: in fact, her letters record an unquestioning confidence in herself, or, in her words, in her "heart" (letter to Schelling, Braunschweig, March? 1801) and a determined refusal to be unhappy—"Göttern und Menschen zum Troz will ich glücklich seyn," she writes ("I would defy gods and human beings to be happy," letter to Friedrich Ludwig Wilhelm Meyer, July 11, 1791). This healthy insistence on her right to earthly joy makes her letters unconventional, both for her gender and her period.

ANNA RICHARDS

Biography

Born in Göttingen, Germany, September 2, 1763, daughter of the well-known university professor Johann David Michaelis. Educated at a boarding school in Gotha for two years, otherwise at home. Married Johann Franz Wilhelm Böhmer, a physician, and moved to Clausthal, 1784; first child, Auguste, born 1785; second child, Therese, born 1787 (died 1789). Returned to Göttingen on the death of Böhmer, 1788; third child, Wilhelm, born 1788 (died a few weeks later). Ran her brother's household in Marburg, 1789–91. Moved to Mainz, 1792, where she had an affair with a French revolutionary officer, Jean-Baptiste Dubois-Crancé; imprisoned for three months in Königstein im Taunus, April–July 1793; gave birth to Crancé's son, Julius, 1793 (died 1795). Married August Wilhelm von Schlegel and moved to Jena, 1796; hostess of the early Romantic salon in Jena 1796–1800. Death of her only surviving daughter, Auguste, 1801. Divorced Schlegel, May 1803. Married Friedrich Wilhelm Joseph von Schelling, June 1803; lived in Würzburg, 1803–6, and Munich, 1806–9. Died of dysentery, September 7, 1809, in Maulbronn.

Selected Writings

Caroline: Briefe an ihre Geschwister, ihre Tochter Auguste, die Familie Gotter, F. L. W. Meyer, A. W. und Fr. Schlegel, J. Schelling u. a. nebst Briefen von A. W. und Fr. Schlegel. 2 vols. Edited by Georg Waitz. 1871.
Novalis: Briefwechsel mit Friedrich und August Wilhelm, Charlotte und Caroline Schlegel. Edited by J. M. Raich. 1880.
Rezensionen über schöne Literatur von Schelling und Caroline in der Neuen Jenaischen Literatur-Zeitung. Edited by Erich Frank, 1912.
Caroline: Briefe aus der Frühromantik. Nach Georg Waitz vermehrt 2 vols. Edited by Erich Schmidt. 1913. Reprint, 1970.
Caroline und Dorothea Schlegel in Briefen (Caroline and Dorothea Schlegel in their Letters). Edited by Ernst Wieneke. 1914.
"Caroline Schlegel-Schelling: Selected Letters," Translated by Janice Murray, in *Bitter Healing: German Women Writers from 1700 to 1830.* Edited by Jeannine Blackwell and Susanne Zantop. 1990.
"Caroline Schlegel-Schelling: Selected Letters/Reviews/Parody." In *Theory as Practice: A Critical Anthology of Early German Romantic Writings.* Edited by Jochen Schulte-Sasse et al. 1997.

Bibliography

Bürger, Christa. "Luziferische Rhapsodien. Carolines Briefwerk." In *Leben Schreiben: Die Klassik, die Romantik und der Ort der Frauen.* Stuttgart: Metzler, 1990.
Daley, Marymargaret. *Women of Letters: A Study of Self and Genre in the Personal Writing of Caroline Schlegel-Schelling, Rahel Levin*

Varnhagen, and Bettina von Arnim. Columbia, S.C.: Camden House, 1998.

Damm, Sigrid. Introduction in *Caroline Schlegel-Schelling. Die Kunst zu leben*, Frankfurt: Insel Taschenbuch, 1997.

Dischner, Gisela. *Caroline und der Jenaer Kreis: Ein Leben zwischen bürgerlicher Vereinzelung und romantischer Geselligkeit.* Berlin: Wagenbach, 1979.

Frederiksen, Elke. "Die Frau als Autorin zur Zeit der Romantik: Anfänge einer weiblichen literarischen Tradition." In *Gestaltet und Gestaltend: Frauen in der deutschen Literatur.* Edited by Marianne Burkhard. Amsterdam: Rodopi, 1980.

Friedrichsmeyer, Sara. "Caroline Schlegel-Schelling: 'A Good Woman, and No Heroine'." In *In the Shadow of Olympus:*

German Women Writers around 1800. Edited by Katherine Goodman and Edith Waldstein. Albany: State University of New York Press, 1992.

Mangold, Elisabeth. *Caroline: Ihr Leben, Ihre Zeit, Ihre Briefe.* Kassel: Wanderoth, 1973.

Nickisch, Reinhard M.G. "Briefkultur: Entwicklung und sozialgeschichtliche Bedeutung des Frauenbriefs im 18. Jahrhundert." In *Deutsche Literatur von Frauen.* vol. 1. Edited by Gisela Brinker-Gabler. Munich: Beck, 1988.

Struzyk, Brigitte. *Caroline unterm Freiheitsbaum.* Darmstadt: Luchterhand, 1988.

SCHLEIERMACHER, FRIEDRICH ERNST DANIEL 1768–1834

German theologian, philosopher, and pedagogue

Friedrich Ernst Daniel Schleiermacher, who was acquainted with Johann Wolfgang von Goethe and Johann Christoph Friedrich von Schiller and enjoyed the friendship of Wilhelm von Humboldt, played a critical role within the circles of the early Romantic movement. His importance falls into three broad categories: (1) his contribution to a new theology generated a Romantic interest in religion and later influenced the existentialist theology of Karl Barth and Richard Niebuhr; (2) his approach to philosophy, first applied to his Plato translation and continued in his biblical exegesis, made him an early advocate of hermeneutics, a discipline that later became crucial for the definition of *Geisteswissenschaften*; and (3) his contribution to the Prussian reform movement, especially to university education, was vital for the rejuvenation of German intellectual life.

Schleiermacher's new emphasis on religion is here confined to his first work, *Über die Religion* (*On Religion*, 1799), with later works, such as *Monologe* (1806) and *Der christliche Glaube nach den Grundsätzen der evangelischen Kirche* (*Christian Faith in Accordance with the Principles of the Evangelical Church*, 1821), presenting no fundamental difference and being less important for the Romantics. Schleiermacher's understanding of religion can be seen as a renewal of Johann Gottfried von Herder's concept of humanity, which was itself based on the definition of man as a profoundly religious entity who was subsequently secularized by neoclassical humanism. Schleiermacher's *On Religion* was received enthusiastically by the early Romantics, including most notably Novalis and Friedrich von Schlegel, but it also influenced Johann Gottlieb Fichte's *Reden an die deutsche Nation*. Schleiermacher's pietistic background, in particular the Herrenhut Brotherhood, had a profound impact on his religious outlook, but the influence of Kant and Fichte was equally formative. Both philosophers had formulated a new concept of freedom, based on human self-determination. Influenced by Fichte's dialogic polarity between Ego and NonEgo, Schleiermacher focused initially on the self, the subject, as determined by its universal origins. While advocating the strongest development of the "I," he suspended it in a further operation to perceive "the universe in all its clarity . . . and to gain the feeling of infinity in you." Schleiermacher's work is therefore not primarily theological or dogmatic, but claims to be "psychological" in the wider

Romantic sense, attempting to define man in relation to his environment. His new concept of Christianity criticized deism as well as natural religion, in the last resort opposing a definition of religion as either metaphysics or a reduction to Christian ethics.

On Religion bears the subtitle "Reden an die Gebildeten unter ihren Verächtern" ("Addresses to the Educated among Those Who Despise It"). The audience addressed here is not the rationalists or skeptics of the Enlightenment, but those educated in the new tradition of German humanism, able to respond to the changed intellectual atmosphere and feeling, as Schleiermacher did, the need for an attitude of awe-inspired reverence to the sacredness of the universe. Schleiermacher approached religion from different angles, its essence being neither thought nor action, but contemplation and empathy. As such it is a natural feeling present in all; it must be trained and expanded, for its capacity determines the clarity and scope of man's sensitivity. The quintessential nature of religion is described in the fifth address as "that feeling of an unsatisfied longing which addresses a great object of whose infinite nature we are aware." This "longing" is synonymous with an existential "mixture of the holy with the profane, of the sublime with the humble, resulting in a sensation of *heilige Wehmut*," a poignant awareness of the immense gulf between our present life and our recognition of an original form of existence which can only be achieved in infinity. Schleiermacher's definition not only reinforced the Romantics' perception of history as *Heilsgeschichte* (yearning for a golden age) but also closely resembled their desire to reconcile opposites, as expressed in Schlegel's *Lyceumsfragment* 116 and in Novalis's fragment on the nature of Romanticism. Religion is ultimately defined as *Heimweh*, man's awareness of his imperfection. Schleiermacher wished to demonstrate that truthfulness is an inalienable part of our human disposition, evident in religious "mediators," predominantly in the life of Christ, it has to be experienced rather than taught.

As in religion, where objective dogmas, moral codes, and metaphysical systems pale behind our subjective interaction with the universe, Schleiermacher's hermeneutics is also concerned with understanding, in Romantic terminology, an interaction between Ego and NonEgo. Such interaction occurs first in "translation," a discipline of the greatest importance at the time and used by Schleiermacher in his Plato translation (1804). Schleiermacher understood translation to be the means not merely of converting a text into another language but also of bringing the text to life, thus facilitating its optimal understanding. This process of understanding was, for Schleiermacher, the gradual elimination of misunderstanding, an endless process, consisting of the language-related element, defined as "grammatical interpretation," and the psychological translation. While the former is a boundary-setting exercise, "understanding as something drawn out of language," the latter focuses on allusion and nuance and contributes to the understanding of an author's individuality, also described as *subtilitas intelligendi*. Both aspects must interact with each other, and this interaction of the part with the whole, of the individual with the generic, effectively anticipates the "hermeneutic circle," a method fully developed by Wilhelm Dilthey (1833–1911). In his *Kompendienartige Darstellung* (*Brief Outline of the Study of Theology*, 1819), Schleiermacher described hermeneutics in an accessible manner by resolving the problem "how do we initially learn to understand?" By learning this most difficult operation in childhood, through a comparison that "leads us to an inner unity," understanding becomes a referential operation: to understand something outside ourselves, we must compare it with something familiar to us. The specific becomes part of ourselves and vice versa. This interaction between individual and universe falls outside logic, it is based on "divinatory" or prophetic intuition, a "transformation of oneself into the other," so as to conceive the other in its most immediate form. Other Romantics, notably Novalis and Schlegel, also adopt this term and, in effect, Schleiermacher's concept of hermeneutics, as in Novalis's statement "poetry dissolves an alien existence in our own."

Schleiermacher's religion and philosophy contain the profoundly pedagogical concept of "understanding," which is remote from rational training or skills acquisition. If religious feeling is necessary for the development of "clear judgement, the gift of empathy with the arts and a universal morality" and if the cultivation of an innate urge for the miraculous and mysterious alone will achieve the fullest awareness of profundity and imagination necessary for the experience of the totality of life, then students will have to acquire an academic freedom that will liberate them from specific skills and a narrow curriculum. As cofounder of Berlin University and director of the Prussian ministry of culture and education, Schleiermacher played a leading part in the reform of the German education system at the beginning of the nineteenth century.

HANS-JOACHIM HAHN

Biography

Born in Breslau, Silesia, on November 21, 1768. Studied theology, philosophy, and languages at Halle University, and was a private tutor for several years after graduation and an occasional preacher. Professor of Theology at Halle, after 1805, preacher at the Berlin *Charité*, appointed by Humboldt as director of the Prussian Ministry of Culture and Education, Dean of Theology at Berlin University, 1813–26. Died 1834 in Berlin.

Selected Writings

Über die Religion: Reden an die Gebildeten unter ihren Verächtern, 1799. Translated as *On Religion: Speeches to its Cultured Despisers* by Richard Crouter, 1988. Cambridge University Press.
Hermeneutik, nach den Handschriften, Heidelberg: Winter. Translated as *Hermeneutics: The Handwritten Manuscripts* by James Duke and Jack Forstman, 1977.

Bibliography

Redeker, Martin. *Schleiermacher: Life and Thought*. Philadelphia: Fortress Press, 1973.
Forstman, Jack. *A Romantic Triangle: Schleiermacher and Early German Romanticism*, 1977.
Palmer, Richard. *Hermeneutics: Interpretation Theory in Schleiermacher, Dilthey, Heidegger and Gadamer*. Evanston, Ill.: Northwestern University Press, 1969.

SCHOPENHAUER, ARTHUR 1788-1860

German philosopher

Coming at the end of the post-Kantian tradition of German Idealist thought, Arthur Schopenhauer represents one conclusion of the tradition emerging through Johann Gottlieb Fichte and Friedrich Wilhelm Joseph von Schelling; G. W. F. Hegel, about whom Schopenhauer was bitterly and polemically critical, represents its polar opposite. Whereas, for Hegel, the *Idee* (idea) was a concept that came to actuality in the concrete world, for Schopenhauer it remained resolutely Platonic—that is, ideal. And, again in opposition to Hegel's belief in historical progress, Schopenhauer's outlook famously contained a strong element of pessimism. While this pessimistic attitude stands in contrast to the perfectionist and optimistic aspects of Romanticism, it displays, in an extreme form, the nihilism that results when the mission to "romanticize" the world is seen to fail. Johann

Wolfgang von Goethe pointed to the shortcomings of Schopenhauer's outlook when he wrote in his autograph-book in 1814, "Willst du dich deines Wertes freuen, / So musst der Welt du Wert verleihen" ("If you want to enjoy your full value, / You must lend value to the world").

In fact, Schopenhauer worked with Goethe on the theory of color in 1813 and 1814, publishing in the treatise *Über das Sehn und die Farben* (*On Vision and Colors*, 1816), before moving to Dresden and, within five years, producing his major work *Die Welt als Wille und Vorstellung* (*The World as Will and Representation*, 1819). As Schopenhauer pointed out in the preface to the first edition, his philosophy starts from Immanuel Kant's, presupposing a detailed knowledge of it; but it goes far beyond Kant, as his appendix to the first volume, "Criticism of the

Kantian Philosophy," shows, and as his own claims suggest: "Subject to the limitation of human knowledge, my philosophy is the real solution of the enigma of the world. In this sense it may be called a revelation." In his *Nachlass*, Schopenhauer wrote that he also considered his philosophy to be "an art," and his system goes further than any other, until the emergence of twentieth-century process-philosophy, in the importance it attaches to the aesthetic, which acquires a salvific function. Whereas, for Kant, aesthetic judgment was a means of traversing the "great gulf" fixed between "the realm of the natural concept, as the sensible, and the realm of the concept of freedom" (see his introduction to the *Critique of Judgment*); and, for Schelling, "infinity represented in a finite manner is beauty" (see his *System of Transcendental Idealism*); then, for Schopenhauer, "art, the work of genius ... repeats the eternal Ideas apprehended through pure contemplation, the essential and abiding element in all the phenomena of the world." Hence his admiration for Dutch still-life and landscape painters (especially Jacob van Ruysdael); because art "achieves just the same thing as is achieved by the visible world itself, only with greater concentration, perfection, intention, and intelligence," it may be called "the flower of life." In the case of music, he went one further, describing it as "a copy of the will itself." The view of art expressed by the musician Joseph Berglinger in Ludwig Tieck and Wilhelm Heinrich Wackenroder's *Herzensergiessungen eines kunstliebenden Klosterbruders* (*Outpourings of an Art-Loving Monk*, 1797), recapitulated and ironized by E. T. A. Hoffmann's mad musician Johannes Kreisler, is taken here to an extreme conclusion. In such works of art as the Apollo Belvedere and the sufferings of Gretchen in Goethe's *Faust*, Schopenhauer saw an anticipation of his own doctrine of the denial of the will to live, programmatically summarized in the formula: "No will: no representation, no world."

Having reached this conclusion and established the complete theoretical account of his philosophical outlook by the time of his late twenties, Schopenhauer's subsequent writings (*Der Wille in der Natur* [*On the Will in Nature*, 1836/1854], *Die beiden Grundprobleme der Ethik* (*The Two Fundamental Problems of Ethics*, 1841/1860, the second volume of *Die Welt als Wille und Vorstellung* [1844]) developed, but did not add anything substantially new, to that outlook. In his *Parerga and Paralipomena* (*Essays and Aphorisms*, 1851), he offered a collection of essays on various subjects, all treated from the same perspective as *Die Welt als Wille und Vorstellung* including the lively and entertaining "Aphorisms for the Wise Conduct of Life." The latter in particular gives the lie to the view that because, as Schopenhauer told Christoph Martin Wieland, he regarded life as "an unpleasant business" and had resolved to spend his own reflecting upon it, he had no appreciation of the world as a locus for practical activity (see, for example, his comments on polite behavior).

Given the significance Schopenhauer attached to music, it is perhaps not surprising that Richard Wagner alighted upon *Die Welt als Wille und Vorstellung* for support for his own aesthetics in the 1850s, although, as Friedrich Nietzsche pointed out, nothing could be "more contrary to the spirit of Schopenhauer" than the spirit of Siegfried. And just as Decadence represents the last outpost of French Romanticism, so Des Esseintes, the aesthete hero of J. K. Huysmans's novel *A rebours* (*Against Nature*, 1884), finds that only the aphorisms of this *grand Allemand* can calm his thoughts. Meanwhile, in the twentieth century, one of Schopenhauer's most sensitive readers was Thomas Mann who, in 1938, described Schopenhauer's philosophy as "an artist-philosophy *par excellence*." However, Mann detected in Schopenhauer an "extremist position, a grotesque and dualistic antithesis in his nature, a *romanticism* (in the most colorful sense of the word) which removed him further from the Goethean sphere than he would ever have let himself even dream of," pointing out that "ascetism belongs to a world of romantic contrasts." Ultimately, Mann concluded that Schopenhauer was "modern," even *zukünftig* (of the future); yet Schopenhauer remains also very much a thinker of the nineteenth century. His Kantian assumptions (given a Platonic twist), and his elaborate, albeit elegant prose, have tended to inhibit access to his work, while twentieth-century theorists, from the Frankfurt School to the postmodernists, have tended to orient themselves around Hegel and Friedrich Nietzsche. A "return to Schopenhauer" thus seems unlikely, although anyone reading his philosophy will be rewarded by an insight into the more profound implications of the world-denying tendencies of Romanticism.

PAUL BISHOP

Biography

Born in Danzig, February 22, 1788. Death of father from suicide, 1805; beginning of study at *Gymnasium* in Gotha, 1807. Study of medicine, science, and philosophy at university of Göttingen, 1808–11, and Berlin, 1811–13. Awarded doctorate from university of Jena, 1813. Move to Dresden to write *Die Welt als Wille und Vorstellung*, 1814–18. First visit to Italy, 1818–19. Qualified to lecture at University of Berlin, 1820. Second visit to Italy, 1822–23. Move to Frankfurt, 1833. Died in Frankfurt, September 21, 1860.

Selected Writings

Collections
Sämtliche Werke. 5 vols. Edited by Wolfgang Freiherr von Löhneysen. Frankfurt am Main: Suhrkamp, 1986.
Der Briefwechsel Arthur Schopenhauers. 3 vols. Edited by Carl Gebhardt and Arthur Hübscher, Munich: R. Piper, 1929–42.
Gesammelte Briefe. Edited by Arthur Hübscher. Bonn: Bouvier, 1978.
Die Schopenhauers: Der Familien-Briefwechsel von Adele, Arthur, Heinrich Floris und Johanna Schopenhauer. Edited by Ludger Lütkehaus. Zurich: Haffmans, 1991.

Essays
Ueber die vierfache Wurzel des Satzes vom zureichenden Grunde: Eine philosophische Abhandlung, 1813. Translated as *On the Fourfold Root of the Principle of Sufficient Reason* by E. F. J. Payne. La Salle, IL: Open Court, 1974.
Über das Sehen und die Farben, 1816. Translated as *On Vision and Colors* by E. F. J. Payne. Oxford and Providence, RI: Berg, 1994.
Die Welt als Wille und Vorstellung, 1819. Translated as *The World as Will and Representation* by E. F. J. Payne. New York: Dover, 1969.
Der Wille in der Natur, 1836. Translated as *On the Will in Nature* by E. F. J. Payne. New York and Oxford: Berg, 1992.
Die beiden Grundprobleme der Ethiki, 1841. 2 vols. vol. 1 translated as *Prize Essay on the Freedom of the Will* by E. F. J. Payne. Edited by Gunter Zöller, Cambridge and New York: Cambridge

University Press, 1999. Vol. 2 translated as *On the Basis of Morality* by E. F. J. Payne. Rev. ed., Providence: Berghahn Books, 1995.

Parerga und Paralipomena: Kleine Philosophische Schriften, 1851. Translated as *Parerga and Paralipomena: Short Philosophical Essays* by E. F. J. Payne. 2 vols. Rev. ed., Oxford and New York: Clarendon Press and Oxford University Press, 2000.

Bibliography

Abendroth, Walter. *Arthur Schopenhauer mit Selbstzeugnissen und Bilddokumenten dargestellt.* Reinbek: Rowohlt, 1967.

Fox, Michael, ed. *Schopenhauer: His Philosophical Achievement.* Brighton: Harvester Press/Totowa, N.J.: Barnes and Noble, 1980.

Gardiner, Patrick. *Schopenhauer.* Harmondsworth, England: Penguin, 1963.

Gwinner, Wilhelm. *Arthur Schopenhauer aus persönlichem Umgang dargestellt*, 1922. Reprinted Frankfurt: W. Krammer, 1963.

Janaway, Christopher. *Self and World in Schopenhauer's Philosophy*, Oxford: Clarendon Press, 1989.

Janaway, Christopher. *Schopenhauer.* Oxford: Oxford University Press, 1994.

Janaway, Christopher, ed. *The Cambridge Companion to Schopenhauer.* Cambridge: Cambridge University Press, 1999.

Magee, Bryan. *The Philosophy of Schopenhauer.* Oxford: Clarendon Press, 1983.

Mann, Thomas. "Schopenhauer" [1938]. In *Essays of Three Decades.* Translated by H. T. Lowe-Porter. London: Secker and Warburg, 1947.

Robert, Julian. "Schopenhauer," In *German Philosophy: An Introduction.* Cambridge and Oxford: Polity Press, 1988.

Safranksi, Rüdiger. *Schopenhauer und die Wilden Jahre der Philosophie.* Munich: Carl Hanser Verlag, 1987. Translated as *Schopenhauer and the Wild Years of Philosophy* by Ewald Osers. Cambridge, Mass.: Harvard University Press, 1989.

Spierling, Volker, ed. *Schopenhauer im Denken der Gegenwart: 23 Beiträge zu seiner Aktualität.* Munich: Piper, 1987.

SCHUBERT, FRANZ PETER 1797–1828

Austrian composer

Franz Peter Schubert is, along with Ludwig van Beethoven, an essential composer to consider when defining Romantic music. His innovations in terms of musical structure and expressivity are arguably even more far-reaching than those of the elder composer. This influence, however, was almost entirely posthumous. In his lifetime, Schubert was principally known as a composer in what were considered lightweight genres (short piano pieces for two or four hands, dances, and songs). He was responsible, however, for the establishment of solo songs and piano duets as works that could potentially carry the emotional power and aesthetic worth of large-scale public genres. Schubert's attempts to forge a reputation beyond his native Vienna, and in the more significant genres of piano sonatas, large chamber works, and symphonies, led him to create works that are among the most experimental of their time. His early death, at a time when his music was beginning to receive much more serious critical attention, was followed by the gradual public discovery over the following fifty years of the majority of his musical oeuvre.

Schubert showed musical ability early in life and was commended as a boy treble by Antonio Salieri, the imperial court *kapellmeister*. When, at the age of eleven, he passed the intensely competitive audition to become a chorister at the Hofkapelle, he was enrolled at the Kaiserlich-königlich Stadtkonvikt, where he received an education normally reserved for sons of wealthy families (Schubert's father was a schoolmaster). Some of his fellow pupils became lifelong friends and promoters of his music—in particular, Joseph von Spaun, a law student and founding member of the school's orchestra. It was the Stadtkonvikt that provided Schubert with his musical education, introducing him not only to the liturgical works he sang daily but also to chamber and orchestral music. He was particularly impressed by Wolfgang Amadeus Mozart's Symphony No. 40 and Ludwig van Beethoven's Symphony No. 2, both among the works performed by the school's orchestra. Spaun enabled Schubert to hear performances of Italian opera, promoted also by Salieri, with whom Schubert studied composition.

When Schubert's voice broke in 1812, he decided not to accept a scholarship to continue at the Stadtkonvikt, training instead as a teacher in order to support his by now prodigious compositional activity. On qualifying in 1814, he began working as an assistant in the German-language school run by his father, and simultaneously produced his first acknowledged masterpiece, the song "Gretchen am Spinnrade" ("Gretchen Spinning"), written on October 19, 1814. During the next few years, Schubert was a member of two student circles: a *Bildungskreis* (self-improvement circle) and the *Unsinnsgesellschaft* (Nonsense Club). The self-improvement circle was dominated by young men from Linz, friends of Spaun, who had returned from a post in the civil service there; their beliefs in the inherent value of aesthetic experience and their dedicated work ethic were of great influence on Schubert. In the Nonsense Club, he made the acquaintance of young artists (particularly writers). In contrast to the somewhat puritan devotion to classicism of the self-improvement circle, the Nonsense Club was an arena for the emerging German Romanticism of Schubert's generation. This immersion in the ideas circulating among young German-speaking artists was a formative experience. Schubert had already proved himself a prolific composer, but the torrent that now flowed from his pen is unparalleled in music history. In a single year, 1815, he wrote nearly 150 songs alone. These circulated widely in manuscript form among school and student acquaintances and were performed privately at musical soirées that soon became known as "Schubertiades." At a time of much greater conservatism than the closing decades of the eighteenth century, Schubert made his reputation with a genre identified with gatherings of friends, part of the social and political nexus of Biedermeier Vienna.

Schubert's songs, while influenced by his older contemporaries Johann Zumsteg and Carl Reichardt, represented an entirely new development in Austro-German music. While earlier writers on the nature of Romanticism—particularly August Wilhelm von Schlegel—often represented it as a translation of musical qualities into literary or visual form, Schubert's song settings are perhaps the first thoroughgoing project successfully to produce in music the effects of Romantic poetry. This is true both of his choice of texts and of his stylistic development of the music. Although the most famous poets of the preceding decades, such as Johann Wolfgang von Goethe and Johann Christoph Friedrich von Schiller, were frequently set to music by Schubert, he was from the beginning drawn to poets of his own generation, including personal friends Eduard von Bauernfeld, Johann Mayrhofer, Franz von Schober, and Spaun, among many others. This concentration on the New German school of poetry became more pronounced as time went on. The poetry set by Schubert frequently shows the delight in nature, the prominence of folk narrative, and the celebration of the individual characteristic of his contemporaries in German-speaking countries (Heinrich Heine, Friedrich Rückert) and abroad (Théophile Gautier, William Wordsworth). The most significant aspect of Schubert's musical style is his ability to combine simple, ravishing lyricism with a sense of drama. In "Gretchen am Spinnrade," the music is adapted in each strophe according to the text, and the representation of the spinning wheel in the piano accompaniment makes it genuinely one of the protagonists of the poem. This, typically for Schubert, enlarges the scope of the poetic imagery while exploiting the powers of the piano, which was undergoing rapid technical development at the time.

While Schubert wrote many songs in which the music is simply repeated in each strophe, he also developed much more complex dramatic structures. Indeed, his earliest surviving songs include lengthy, involved narratives, beginning with "Hagars Klang," written in 1811. In 1815 this search for dramatic articulation produced "Erlkönig" ("Erl King"), the most popular of his songs published in his lifetime. Goethe's poem was set by several other composers, including Reichardt, but Schubert's most effectively combines the drama of the folk-tale narrative with a Romantic's depiction of the psychological subtext. The music is "through-composed" rather than following the strophic patterning of the poem, and the vivid portrayal of the galloping horse's hooves in the piano part is the unifying feature of the setting. Here, a *moto perpetuo* accompaniment uses rapidly repeating chords in the right hand, with a recurrent melodic figure in octaves exploiting the resonance of the bass register. The technique used in these pieces goes beyond simple word painting in the manner of earlier music; rather, the most central of the poetic images in the text is converted into the constant accompaniment of the sung text, in a quintessentially Romantic concern to penetrate the essence both of the poetry and of the experience depicted.

The possibility of investing song form with greater aesthetic significance was further advanced by the invention of the song cycle as a genre. Here, the emotional force of individual songs was harnessed to the larger-scale narrative of a linked series of poems, creating a work of roughly the same overall dimensions as a sonata, string quartet, or symphony. Beethoven's *An die ferne Geliebte* (*To the Distant Beloved*) of 1816 was the first work to be published under the title *Liederkreis* (*Song Cycle*), and Schubert's two cycles, *Die Schöne Müllerin* (*The Beautiful Miller Maid*, 1823–24) and *Winterreise* (*Winter Journey*, 1827–

Franz Schubert, Title page of *Winterreise*, 1827. Reprinted courtesy of the Lebrecht Collection.

28), defined the form for the remainder of the Romantic era. Both cycles are to poetry by Wilhelm Müller, and in both cases the poems form linked series treating the theme of erotic adventure leading to despair. *Die Schöne Müllerin* has the more straightforward narrative, where disappointment in love leads the protagonist, a young miller, to contemplate suicide. The most significant dramatis persona of the song cycle in Schubert's hands is the brook, which is the miller's companion on his wandering journey, his confidante when he falls in love, and his eventual consoler in despair. The character of the brook is constantly depicted by the piano, giving psychological depth to what is a Romantic personification of the miller's alter ego.

This concern with psychological complexity finds even greater realization in *Winterreise*, published in two parts, part 1 in early 1828, and part 2 posthumously (he was correcting its proofs on his deathbed).

The winter journey of the title is a voyage through a mental as well as a physical landscape. Its starting point is romantic disappointment; part 1 ends with the poem "Solitude," and the whole cycle concludes with one of Schubert's most profound achievements, "Der Leiermann" ("The Hurdy-Gurdy Player"), in which the recurrent, haunting tune of the hurdy-gurdy is constantly repeated and varied in alternation between the piano accompaniment and the voice. Here Schubert's depiction of psychological trauma, romantic disillusionment, and the transcendent potential of music collude in one of the greatest musical texts of Romanticism. In the last months of his life, Schubert appears possibly to have been planning one, or maybe two, further song cycles. He left a collection of thirteen songs in a single manuscript, seven of them settings of poems by Ludwig Rellstab (a friend of Müller), and the remaining six of them settings of Heine, from *Heimkehr* (*Homecoming*, 1823–24). All thirteen, along with another song, were published together another with the sentimental title *Schwanengesang* (*Swan Song*, 1828), an invention of the publisher. But it has recently been suggested that the Heine settings in particular were selected and arranged in order by Schubert as an embryonic further song cycle. Certainly these settings of Schubert's exact contemporary were directly influential on the later history of the form, especially Robert Alexander Schumann's own Heine song cycle, *Dichterliebe* (*Poet's Love*, 1840).

The desire to bring music to the state of articulate speech is reflected by the many instrumental works that base a musical structure on self-quotation from one of Schubert's songs. Examples are the piano quintet *Die Forelle* (*The Trout*, 1819), the *Wanderer-fantasie* (*Wanderer Fantasy*, 1822), and the string quartet *Der Tod und das Mädchen* (*Death and the Maiden*, 1824), all of which exhibit experiment with form. The desire to achieve a "speaking" articulateness is also a desire to transcend the constraints of words condemned to denotative meaning. Beethoven's resort to voices in the last movement of his Symphony No. 9 in fact demonstrates a divergence between his aesthetic and Schubert's. The confident assertions of Schiller's poetry are unthinkable as the grounds of artistic statement in Schubert, a gap perhaps best demonstrated by the work that was a conscious memorial to Beethoven, the String Trio in E flat of 1828.

Schubert's lyrical gifts, which have never been doubted, were employed to expand the dimensions of musical form, whose outlines nearly always remained discernibly related to eighteenth-century practice. The resulting transformation gave rise to what Schumann dubbed "himmlische Länge" ("heavenly length") in relation to Schubert's Symphony No. 9. This process was at once a matter of musical style and aesthetic intent. Schubert's summer job as a teenager, coaching the daughters of Count Johann Esterházy, was the occasion for the composition of many pieces for piano duet; that genre reaches its acme, in terms of the combination of extended formal design and melodic expressiveness, with the work of his final year dedicated to his erstwhile pupil Caroline, the Piano Fantasy in F minor.

While Schubert remains to this day best remembered as a composer of songs, in the fifty years following his death, his stature as a composer of instrumental music steadily increased with the gradual discovery and publication of his other works. His earliest works unsurprisingly show the influence principally of Mozart and Franz Joseph Haydn, but his experimentation with musical language and form in his maturity was no less innovative (and eventually influential) than Beethoven's. The balance of musical keys in the eighteenth-century style, preserved there within expressively dramatic structures, is adapted by Schubert through a fondness for abrupt changes of key, often between keys very distant from each other. In Beethoven this sort of experiment is always ultimately in the service of triumphant and affirmative integration of keys into an unified structure. In Schubert, however, the music often gives a much more insecure impression. The ability of music to transcend earthly experience, so important to philosophers such as August Wilhelm von Schlegel, is certainly central to these effects; but this utopian world, opened up by music, is always fragile or evanescent. In Schubert's late works, in particular, the most serene slow movements are frequently interrupted by unforeseen outbursts of tremendous violence: examples are the String Quintet, the Octet, Symphony No. 9, and the Piano Sonata in A. This duality has frequently been connected to speculation concerning Schubert's biography, especially whether his death was caused by syphilis and whether he was an active homosexual (both contentions are heatedly debated). These musical effects are crucial to the development of the art form's expressive powers in the early nineteenth century.

ROBERT SAMUELS

Biography

Born in Vienna, January 31, 1797. Admitted as chorister in the Hofkapelle, 1808, and educated at the Kaiserlich-Königlich Stadtkonvikt, 1808–13. Studied at St. Anna Normalhauptschule (for teaching qualification), 1813–14. Teaching assistant in his father's German-language school 1814–18. Music tutor to daughters of Count Johann Karl Esterházy in Zseliz, summer 1818 and summer 1819. Professional composer in Vienna from 1819 on. One "academy" devoted to his compositions, March 26, 1828. Died Vienna, November 19, 1828.

Selected Works

Schubert's oeuvre numbers more than 1,000 pieces, including more than 630 songs. The following lists predominantly those works significant to the development of musical Romanticism. They are identified by the numbers established by Otto Erich Deutsch's catalog of Schubert's works.

Hagars Klang, song, D5. 1811.
Gretchen am Spinnrade, song, D118. 1814.
Erlkönig, song, D328. 1815.
Symphony No. 5 in B-flat, D485. 1816.
Der Wanderer, song, D489. 1816.
Der Tod und das Mädchen, song, D531. 1817.
An die Musik, song, D547. 1817.
Die Forelle, song, D550. 1817.
Piano Quintet in A, *Die Forelle*. D667. 1819.
Symphony No. 8 in B minor. D759. 1822.
Piano Fantasy in C, *Wanderer-fantasie*. D760. 1822.
Die Schöne Müllerin, song cycle, D795. 1823–24.
Octet in F. D803. 1824.
Quartet in D minor, *Der Tod und das Mädchen*. D870. 1824.
Symphony No. 9 in C. D944. 1825.
Winterreise, song cycle. D911. 1827–28.
Piano Trio in E-flat, D929. 1827–28.
Fantasy in F minor, piano duet. D940. 1828.
Quintet in C. D956. 1828.
Schwanengesang, collection of songs. D957. 1828.
Piano Sonata in C minor, D958. 1828.
Piano Sonata in A. D959. 1828.
Piano Sonata in B-flat, D960. 1828.

Bibliography

Deutsch, Otto Erich. *Franz Schubert: Thematische Verzeichnis seiner Werke in chronologische Folge*. Rev. ed. Kassel: Bärenreiter, 1978.
———. *Schubert: A Documentary Biography*. Translated by Eric Blom. London: Dent, 1946.
———. *Schubert: Memoirs by his Friends*. Translated by Rosamond Ley and John Nowell. London: A & C Black, 1958.
Dürr, Walther, and Andreas Krauser, eds. *Schubert Handbuch*. Kassel: Bärenreiter, 1997.
Erickson, Raymond, ed. *Schubert's Vienna*. New Haven, Conn.: Yale University Press, 1997.

Gibbs, Christopher. *The Life of Schubert*. Cambridge: Cambridge University Press, 2000.

———, ed. *The Cambridge Companion to Schubert*. Cambridge: Cambridge University Press, 1997.

Hanson, Alice M. *Musical Life in Biedermeier Vienna*. Cambridge: Cambridge University Press, 1985.

Hilmar, Ernst. *Franz Schubert in his Time*. Portland: Amadeus, 1988.

Kramer, Richard. *Distant Cycles: Schubert and the Conceiving of Song*. Chicago: University of Chicago Press, 1994.

———. "Schubert's Heine," *19th-Century Music* (1984–5). 8:213–25. Berkeley: University of California.

Newbould, Brian. *Schubert: The Music and the Man*. London: Gollancz, 1997.

Norman Mckay, Elizabeth. *Franz Schubert: A Biography*. Oxford: Oxford University Press, 1996.

"Schubert: Music, Sexuality, Culture," *19th-Century Music* 17 (1993), special issue.

Steblin, Rita. *Die Unsinnsgesellschaft: Franz Schubert, Leopold Kuppelweiser, und ihr Freundeskreis*. Vienna: Bohlau, 1998.

Winter, Robert. "Schubert." In *New Grove Encyclopedia of Music and Musicians*. 2d ed. Edited by Stanley Sadie and John Tyrell. London: Macmillan, 2001.

Youens, Susan, "Song Cycle." In *New Grove Encyclopedia of Music and Musicians*. 2d ed. Edited by Stanley Sadie and John Tyrell. London: Macmillan, 2001.

SCHUMANN, ROBERT ALEXANDER 1810–1856

German composer, critic, and writer

There is much about Robert Alexander Schumann that is typical of the creative Romantic: his love of codes, hidden references, and secret societies; his extreme sensitivity; his unrequited loves and long-thwarted pursuit of his wife-to-be Clara Wieck; his attempted suicide and descent into insanity; his insistence on self-expression; his love of improvisation and distaste for theoretical rules; his penchant for the more modern, Romantic forms such as the characteristic piece and the lied; and his passion for literature. (His father, August, was a publisher with a fine library, and encouraged his son's literary ambitions.)

By the time he left school, with a distinguished record, many of Schumann's chief influences were operative: in music these were Ludwig van Beethoven, Johann Nepomuk Hummel, Ignaz Moscheles, and Franz Peter Schubert, and in literature, principally Jean Paul, from whom, he said, he learned more about counterpoint than any musician. Of his early musical compositions, only a dozen or so songs survive, and these show not only his sensitivity to the texts but an already well-developed musical technique.

Following the wishes of his guardian and his mother, he matriculated at Leipzig University in March 1828 to study law. In Munich they visited Heinrich Heine. Heine would provide the texts for two of Schumann's greatest song cycles, *Dichterliebe* (*Poet's Love*, 1840) and *Liederkreis* (*Song Cycle*, 1840), as well as other separate songs.

Once settled in Leipzig, Schumann never attended lectures at the university, according to a friend, but spent his days in pianistic improvisation and literary effusions à la Jean Paul. Although Schumann was now becoming aware of his need for theoretical musical study, it was as a piano pupil that he enrolled with the well-respected teacher Friedrich Wieck, at whose house he met many of the local musicians and took part in chamber music. This resulted in his Eight Polonaises for Piano Duet, inspired by Schubert.

Stimulated partly by a school friend's letters, with their sparkling descriptions of life at Heidelberg University, and partly by the reputation of Justus Thibaut, a professor there whose recent book on musical aesthetics *Über die reinheit der Tonkunst* (*On Purity in Musical Art*, 1825) had impressed Schumann, he gained his mother's permission to spend a year there. He turned his thoughts toward living composers at this time and began to study the works of Carl Czerny, Henri Herz, Hummel, and Moscheles.

He was finally allowed to change to music. His first published opus, the *Thême sur le nom "Abegg" varié pour le pianoforte* (*Abegg Variations*, 1831), encapsulates several of the preoccupations that were to characterize his music from then on. The name in the title, Abegg, was attached to a girl, Meta, whom he romantically called "Countess Pauline d'Abegg."

An important event was his discovery of Frédéric François Chopin's music. This, in turn, gave rise to Schumann's career as a music critic, inspiring his first review (December 1831) for the influential periodical *Allgemeine Musikalische Zeitung*, which contained the daring and prophetic words, "Hats off, gentlemen, a genius!" More daring, however, was the style in which the review was written: that of a contemporary novel, a mixture of Jean Paul and E. T. A. Hoffmann and more of a general commentary on the style and effect of the music than a critique in the accepted manner. As he had done for some time, Schumann now introduced two characters representing contrasting facets in Schumann's own personality: "Eusebius," the dreamy, and "Florestan," the fiery aspect. These unmistakably echo the brothers Walt in Jean Paul's unfinished novel *Die Flegeljahre* (*The Awkward Age*, 1804–5), a favorite of Schumann's. At this time also, he and some like-minded friends, calling themselves the *Davidsbündler* (the League of [the biblical] David against the Philistines) decided to found their own journal, the *Neue Zeitschrift für Musik*, whose editorial responsibilities he soon assumed.

Schumann's career was affected by the crippling of his right hand, possibly due to mercury poisoning from treatment for syphilis, a consequence of his promiscuity. In an age when the virtuoso performer-composer was the norm, this put a performing career out of the question, and, in an ironic echo of Beethoven's fate through deafness, concentrated the younger man's mind on the inner, creative strain of his musical personality.

Schumann was also thwarted in his romantic ventures. He wished to marry Clara Wieck, daughter of his piano teacher (and former landlord, Schumann having lived with the Wiecks for some time), but her father disapproved. Schumann and Clara took legal action against Wieck, and finally the lovers won the right to marry. The year in which this happened, 1840, is also remembered as the *Liederjahr* (the year of song), one of tremendous creativity in which Schumann produced 138 songs, sometimes at the rate of several a day.

Schumann's miniaturist penchant, however much in tune with the times, was expected to be a relatively small part of a composer's output; larger-scale public works were required. Even Schubert, known almost exclusively at this time for his smaller works, had written symphonies, so Schumann focused some of his attention on grander works. In 1841 he composed the First Symphony in B-flat ("Spring") completed in just over a month.

Schumann began to feel very much in the background. In early 1842, frustrated by his wife's much more esteemed public reputation (she was on tour at this time, having forged for herself a career as a composer and virtuoso pianist), he produced, in rapid succession, three string quartets, a piano quintet, quartet, and trio, and other works, revised later.

The following year the Schumanns reconciled with Wieck. That same year Schumann had several meetings with Hector Berlioz and composed *Das Paradies und die Peri* (*Paradise and the Peri*), the text translated from Thomas Moore's *Lalla Rookh*, which represented a new operatic departure, although he described the work as "an oratorio—but for cheerful people." Its performance marked Schumann's debut as a conductor.

A concert tour of Russia claimed the first half of 1844. The Schumanns were welcomed by musicians and aristocracy alike, Schumann receiving private performances of some of his works. He also suffered illness and several fits of depression and, on their return, after exhausting himself setting part of Johann Wolfgang von Goethe's *Faust* to music, had a nervous breakdown.

This prompted a move to slower-paced, more provincial Dresden. Schumann's health began to improve although his compositional output was sporadic. By the end of 1847 and into the next year, Schumann was again in full compositional flow with the *Adventlied* (*Advent Song*) for chorus and orchestra; *Bilder aus Osten* (*Oriental Pictures*) for piano duet; *Waldscenen* (*Forest Scenes*), op. 82, for piano; and the *Phantasiestücke*, op. 73, for clarinet and piano.

The period from 1848 to 1851 was productive and works included a new symphony (No. 3 in E-flat, "Rhenish"); concert overtures; pieces for chorus and orchestra; songs; two violin sonatas (A Minor, op. 105, and D Minor op. 121), and the G minor Piano Trio. He also collected his critical and other writings, which were published in four volumes as *Gesammelte Schriften über Musik und Musiker* (*Collected Writings on Music and Musicians*, 1854).

However, his health was again suffering, and this manifested itself, in mid-1852, in slurred speech and difficulty of movement. Composition continued, including a fantasy and a concerto written for the young violinist Joseph Joachim. A great comfort, in these last years (and to Clara, for many years to come) was the appearance of the twenty-two-year-old Johannes Brahms, who impressed them greatly as a pianist and composer and gave rise to Schumann's first critical article in ten years, titled "Neue Bahnen" ("New Paths"), in which he extolled the young composer as a genius. He was also directly responsible for Brahms's first publications.

In February 1854 Schumann's mental state deteriorated dramatically, with aural and visual hallucinations. After a failed suicide attempt, he was committed to a comfortable private asylum in 1854, where he was not allowed to see Clara for two and a half years, until two days before his death on July 29, 1856. He died alone.

It is surprising that, in spite of his adulation for Beethoven and Chopin, there is little trace of their direct influence on his music apart from quotation, which is evident especially with Johann Sebastian Bach and Beethoven. Rather, it is the less-than-first-rank composers—Hummel, Moscheles, Schubert, and Ludwig Spohr the miniaturist—who are mirrored in Schumann's earliest works, mostly in the textures and pianism. His improvisational, aphoristic character pieces were very much in tune with the period and, although there were models available in Beethoven's bagatelles and Schubert's impromptus and *moments musicaux*, the same characteristics are widely seen in the writings, well known to Schumann, of the *Frühromantiker* (early Romantics) and in his contemporaries, such as the Novalis of the *Blütenstaub* (*Pollen*, 1798), Friedrich von Schlegel of the *Athenäum Fragmente* (*Athenaeum Fragments*, 1799–1800), and E. T. A. Hoffmann, Jean Paul, Tieck, and Wilhelm Heinrich Wackenroder. He also shared, in his literary as well as his musical creations, their common interest in the fantastic and outlandish, and several of the characters in their novels and stories took hold of his imagination: Walt and Vult have been mentioned, but Hoffmann's alter ego Kapellmeister Johannes Kreisler, and his astounding pianistic improvisations gave rise to Schumann's *Kreisleriana*, op. 16. Indeed, improvisation was, and remained, the well-spring of Schumann's creativity; all his piano works bear the stamp of it, and it gives rise to many of his flights of chromatic fancy and much of his lyric strain. The very form of his piano cycles, involving a group of pieces of variegated moods that appear structurally loose but are nonetheless interconnected suggests the butterfly-like flights of fantasy that produced them.

Schumann's interest in childhood gave rise to one of his greatest pieces, the *Kinderszenen*, op. 15, and to the *Album für die Jugend*, op. 68 (*Album for the Young*, 1848). Being virtually self-taught, Schumann was aware of the difficulties in musically structuring larger-scale works, which is why many of these, though containing much beautiful music, fail to sustain interest in the way that his great models do. This also explains his need for extramusical props—poetic text in songs and choral works, literary quotations, program, explanatory titles—and his relatively small output in that most musically taxing of genres, instrumental chamber music.

DEREK CAREW

Biography

Born in Zwickau, Saxony, June 8, 1810. Intended for legal profession at the University of Leipzig, 1828–29, and the University of Heidelberg, 1829–30. Studied piano with Friedrich Wieck, and theory with Heinrich Dorn, Leipzig, 1830–32. In 1839 discovered Schubert's C-Major Symphony and prepared it for performance. Honorary Ph. D. conferred by university of Jena, and marriage to Clara Wieck, 1840. Lived in Dresden, 1844–50. Municipal music director at Düsseldorf, 1850. Committed to private lunatic asylum, at Endenich, near Bonn. Died there July 29, 1856.

Selected Works

Choral Work
Das Paradies und die Peri.

Opera
Genoveva.

Piano Works
"Abegg" Variations, op. 1. 1831.
Papillons, op. 2. 1831.
Davidsbündlertänze, op. 6. 1837.
Carnaval, op. 9. 1837.
Phantasiestücke, op. 12. 1838.
Symphonische Etüden, op. 13. 1837.
Kinderszenen, op. 15. 1839.
Kreisleriana, op. 16. 1838.
Phantasie in C, op. 17. 1839.
Arabeske in C, op. 18. 1839.
Humoreske in B-flat, 1839.

Song Cycles
Liederkreis (Heine), op. 24. 1840.
Myrthen (various), op. 25. 1840.
Zwölfe Gedichte (Kerner), op. 35. 1841.
Liedrekreis (Eichendorff), op. 39. 1842.
Frauenliebe und Fraunleben (Chamisso) op. 42. 1843.

Collected Writings
Gessamelte Schriften über Musik and Musiker. 1854.

Bibliography

Brion, Marcel. *Schumann et l'âme romantique.* Translated as *Schumann and the Romantic Age* by G. Sainsbury. London, 1956.
Brown, T. A. *The Aesthetics of Robert Schumann.* New York, 1968.
Chissell, J., *Schumann.* 4th rev. ed. 1977.
Litzmann, B. *Clara Schumann: Ein Künstlerleben.* 3 vols. tr. 1913.
Plantinga, L. *Schumann as Critic.* New Haven, Conn.: Yale University Press, 1967.
Taylor, R. *Robert Schumann: His Life and Work.* London, 1982.
Todd, R. L., ed. *Schumann and his World.* Princeton, N.J.: Princeton University Press, 1994.

SCHWIND, MORITZ VON 1804–1871

German painter

Moritz von Schwind's artistic genius is most evident in a tumultuous wealth of ideas that range, sometimes within the same work, from the lofty and monumental to the mundane and scurrilous. He commands an astonishing ability to depict, with subtlety and precision, a huge range of expressions, attitudes, costumes and poses against backgrounds that may be contemporary, natural, or mythological.

Schwind was competent in nearly all branches of the figurative arts and spent much effort on perfecting his abilities in such diverse areas as the commanding frescoes he designed for castles and public buildings (most notably the Wartburg in Thuringia, the Munich Residenz, and the Karlsruhe Museum), and book illustrations in miniature format. Although he is thought of primarily as a draftsman with an expert eye for small details, his extensive productions include landscapes, portraits, and cartoons as well as allegorical, religious, and historical subjects. True to Friedrich von Schlegel's definition of the Romantic genius, Schwind could be poetic and prosaic at the same time, and lofty subjects are often found, on close inspection, to incorporate cryptic details that are the visual derivatives of a waggish sense of humor.

It is difficult to define the true epicenter of his oeuvre. Schwind is remembered for his fanciful evocations of imaginary episodes that have a strong narrative quality within a fairytale setting. The most famous of these is probably *Kuno von Falkenstein's Ride*, completed in 1843, a complex oil painting that merges elements from various sagas and depicts two separate planes of imagined "reality." The top half concentrates on the realm of light, in which a baron keeps protective watch over his daughter, while the lower half discloses a different but complementary sphere: the underworld, the province of anguished and ungainly gnomes. Poised exactly halfway between the two,

Kuno, the knight, elegantly rides his white horse up a flight of steps that the gnomes have built overnight, in response to the baron's promise to give his daughter to the first man who can ride up the rock face to his inaccessible abode. What rescues this carefully executed painting from slipping into bizarre, Teutonic kitsch is the astonishing modernity of its psychological subtext. For all his apparent valor, the resplendent horseman patently owes his victory to dark, subterranean forces. Without the gnomes (amazing creatures combining the sinewy muscles of Arnold Schwarzenegger with the dynamism of Michelangelo's torsos), the sublime knight would have lost his wager and his bride. In a supremely ironic touch, Kuno is depicted rewarding the king of the gnomes with the very hand that is about to salute his beloved. A single subject is read from conflicting points of view: as a wondrous evocation of chivalry and, simultaneously, as a grotesque acknowledgment of the darker forces of Nature that make possible acts of human bravado.

Yet Schwind was too great an experimenter to adopt a single style as his hallmark. It seems incongruous that realistic studio portraits in the style of Jean-Auguste-Dominique Ingres (for example, his portrait of Karoline von Hetzenecker, 1848) were executed side-by-side with bizarre fairytale scenes, stained glass windows for churches, and designs for richly ornamented tobacco pipes. Schwind may have remained a Romantic at heart, but his natural curiosity led him to explore ephemera and to accept commissions for a variety of wealthy patrons. The commemorative exhibition in Karlsruhe (1996–97) represented the first attempt to bring together works that had been painted in many parts of Germany and abroad. The result was an amazingly vibrant collection of some five hundred originals of the most varied types. The early criticisms of Schwind's works, such as the charge that he used oils as though they were watercolors, are long forgotten. Nor can he be dismissed as a provider of lavish though insubstantial feasts for the eyes. There is nothing automatic, repetitive, or predictable about his art.

Those who regard the underlying ethos of his work as bland would do well to consider *Die Heimkehr des Grafen Ernst von Gleichen* (*The Return of Count Ernst von Gleichen*, 1864). This is another deeply and overtly Romantic subject in which the errant crusader returns to his loving wife and family, but on close inspection, he proves to be in the company of a second wife whom he acquired on his travels, giving the facial expression of the welcoming party a deeper and far more ambiguous meaning. The complex story of how Gleichen was rescued by the Saracen princess whom he subsequently married with the aid of a special dispensation from Pope Gregory IX was controversial, to say the least. Schwind's canvas needs to be read in the light of such audacious pleas for reform as Johann Wolfgang von Goethe's drama *Stella*, with its support for greater openness in regard to bigamous liaisons. The context becomes even more involved when one considers that the story had been written by Edward von Bauernfeld as a libretto for an opera to be composed by none other than Franz Schubert, until the Viennese government censor got wind of the project in 1826 and declared the subject taboo. Schwind's continuing interest in the theme can be taken as evidence of his unwillingness to conform to the restrictive morality of the time.

Schwind's artistic precision places him at the very forefront of nineteenth-century art. In some of his works he shows himself to be a precursor of the Pre-Raphaelite movement in Britain. His cartoons and genre paintings recall-Carl Spitzweg, whom he surpasses in terms of technical skill, although his meticulous work lacks the latter's impressionistic informality. Ancient legends are given a new lease of life: among them, his famous *Rübezahl* (1851), the cycle of the Seven Ravens, and the legend of Melusine. His *Cats' Symphony* (1866) is a delightful cartoon sketch in which the black silhouettes of the lively animals cavort among the staves of a musical score. Some of his most original works look forward to art nouveau and to twentieth-century fantasy art. The glassy, smooth surfaces of his canvases, no less than the timeless allegories that they depict, are first and foremost intended as vivid suggestions of a harmonious past. Yet Schwind never tires of exposing the questionable aspects of the pictured harmony, and even the seemingly effortless execution of many of his masterpieces is deceptive. Some of these took years to complete, proving that even the most Romantic artifacts are grounded in untiring labor.

OSMAN DURRANI

Biography

Born in Vienna, January 21, 1804, the son of a diplomat. Brought up in Vienna and Bohemia, attended the same school as Nikolaus Lenau, whose close friend he remained. Entered Vienna University at the age of fifteen to study philosophy, mathematics, and aesthetics, leaving without a degree in 1821, when he began to take classes at the Viennese Academy of Art. Schwind was predisposed toward the Romantic ideology and was strengthened in his commitment to it when he began to work with Ludwig Ferdinand Schnorr von Carolsfeld. Albrecht Dürer was another important influence. From 1823, Schwind parted company with the academy and continued to perfect his style independently. Friends included Eduard von Bauernfeld, Grillparzer, Franz Schubert, and other prominent Viennese artists, many of whom were enthusiastic admirers of the German Romantics of the period: Achim von Arnim, E. T. A. Hoffmann, and Ludwig Tieck. Schwind's early works included illustrations of literary works, including Daniel Defoe's *Robinson Crusoe* and Hoffmann's *Meister Martin*. He moved to Munich in the late 1820s, and started work on a series of commissions, including frescoes and ceiling paintings in the library of the royal palace. After a journey to Rome in 1835, he worked on large-scale frescoes in the stairway and ground-floor exhibition rooms of the Karlsruhe Museum of Fine Art. After extensive periods of travel in Karlsruhe and Frankfurt, he returned to Munich in 1847 to take up a lecturing post, adding to his income by drawing illustrations for the satirical magazine *Fliegende Blätter*. The major works of his maturity were the frescoes painted in the Wartburg Castle, a location redolent with historical associations. (It was here that medieval song contests between the minstrels of the *Minnesang* were said to have taken place, as well as where Martin Luther translated the Bible.) These magnificent paintings, which include geometric designs as well as religious and historical subjects, kept him busy for several years (1853–56). Schwind visited Britain in 1857 and designed stained glass windows for Glasgow Cathedral and St. Michael's Church in London. He accepted the most varied commissions until late in life; these included scenery for a production of the *Magic Flute* at the Vienna opera, and a series of watercolors for the notoriously extravagant King Ludwig II of Bavaria. Died February 8, 1871.

Bibliography

Annan, Thomas. *The Painted Windows of Glasgow Cathedral: A Series of Forty-Three Photographs.* 1867.

Bowron, Edgar Peters. *Romantics, Realists, Revolutionaries.* Munich: Prestel, 2000.

Elster, Hans Martin. *Moritz von Schwind. Sein Leben und Schaffen.* Berlin: Horen, 1924.

German Masters of the Nineteenth Century: Paintings and Drawings from the Federal Republic of Germany. Exhibition catalog. New York: Metropolitan Museum of Art, 1981.

Göltl, Rainhard. *Franz Schubert und Moritz von Schwind: Freundschaft im Biedermeier.* Munich: Nymphenburger, 1992.

Hofmann, Werner. *Das irdische Paradies: Motive und Ideen des 19. Jahrhunderts.* 3rd ed. Munich: Prestel, 1991.

Jensen, Jens Christian. *Malerei der Romantik in Deutschland.* Cologne: DuMont, 1985.

Moritz von Schwind—Meister der Spätromantik. Exhibition catalog. Ostfildern: Gerd Hatje, 1996.

Schall, Petra, et al. *Die Schwind-Fresken auf der Wartburg.* Bad Homburg: Ausbildung und Wissen, 1998.

SCIENCE AND THE ARTS

In the late eighteenth century, the gap separating the "two cultures" of science and art, as identified by C. P. Snow, was yet to materialize. Poets such as Alexander Pope praised Isaac Newton, while popular digests would set his discoveries to verse. Within a few decades, however, accelerating advances in knowledge and the increasing specialization of scientific activity were to place intolerable strains upon what had hitherto been the unitary pursuit of "natural philosophy." By the 1830s the emergence of increasingly separate and autonomous disciplines such as biology, chemistry, and geology had divided the arts and sciences forever, with William Whewell coining the term *scientist* and John Stuart Mill later declaring that poetry was the "logical opposite" of science.

Romanticism is generally associated with hostility toward the mechanistic natural philosophy and empirical, reductive world view of Newtonian science. Something of a sea change in sensibility brought about a reaction of the natural, organic, human spirit against the cold rationality of the Enlightenment. Several famous examples highlight this antipathy, most notably Johann Wolfgang von Goethe's attack on Newton's theories of light and color, Charles Lamb's toast "confusion to mathematics," and John Keats's lines from "Lamia" (1819): "Do not all charms fly / At the mere touch of cold philosophy?"

However, the Romantic view of science was not necessarily one of outright rejection, with many artists—most notably poets—embracing and adopting the metaphoric imagery offered by the scientific perception of the natural world. Where William Blake railed against Newton and all his works, Samuel Taylor Coleridge took great delight in "the beauty and neatness" of his experiments, and regularly incorporated scientific and philosophical thought into his poetry.

Scientific allusion is perhaps used most consistently in the poetry of Percy Bysshe Shelley. His lengthy 1813 work, *Queen Mab*, made extensive use of scientific imagery in both the verse and in the poet's own extensive notation, which exhibited his familiarity with the very latest theory and knowledge, including the work of Paul-Henri Dietrich Holbach and Pierre-Simon Laplace. His verse drama *Prometheus Unbound* (1819), though ostensibly set in the Aristotelian universe of classical mythology, nevertheless makes much use of contemporary Newtonian cosmology, and crackles with electrical imagery from the world of Sir Humphrey Davy. Several passages clearly echo the lectures of his childhood astronomy tutor Adam Walker, and the poem also owes much to the botanical poetry of Erasmus Darwin. Throughout the Shelley canon can be found imagery borrowed from the emerging earth sciences of geology and meteorology, vividly illustrating the poet's fascination with volcanoes, storms, and earthquakes, with descriptions of violent seismic upheaval often used allegorically to represent radical political opinion and revolutionary change.

Lord Byron, though himself somewhat aloof from the world of science, fathered Ada Lovelace, a prodigiously talented mathematician, whom he disdainfully labeled "the princess of parallelograms." In later life she would assist Charles Babbage, creator of the mechanical ancestor of the computer, and she has been credited with writing the world's first computer program.

The impact of Mary Shelley's gothic novel *Frankenstein: or, the Modern Prometheus* (1818) still resonates as one of the great literary metaphors for public perception of the role played by scientists in modern society, and fear of uncontrolled experimentation. Though often cited as a precursor of the science-fiction genre, her narrative makes only sparing use of scientific detail and method, and concentrates more upon the moral consequences of the creation of the creature.

Occasionally, practicing scientists themselves could be moved to verse. The physician Erasmus Darwin was renowned for producing lengthy biological verse-treatises such as *The Botanic Garden* (1791) and *Zoonomia* (1794–96), both of which contain protoevolutionary passages anticipating the work of his grandson, Charles Darwin. Humphry Davy, who had helped edit William Wordsworth's *Lyrical Ballads*, and whose public lectures vividly introduced such Romantic concepts as the sublime into popular perceptions of science, committed to poetry in his notebook how he had searched into nature's hidden and mysterious ways: "as poet, as philosopher, as sage."

The world of the visual arts was also transformed by the advent of industrial technology. The arrival of the argand lamp in 1780 gave a new dimension to the term *enlightenment*, providing cheap and effective artificial illumination for public places such as theaters and galleries. The French artist Anne-Louis Girodet de Roussy-Frioson's *Pygmalion* was both painted and exhibited by lamplight in 1819, while Wilhelm Bendz's depiction of a life class at the Charlottenburg Academy of Fine Arts in 1826 shows an assistant focusing a bank of argand lamps on the model. The iron foundries of the Industrial Revolution provided artists such as Jacques-Philippe de Loutherbourg with spectacularly volcanic explosions of color and light, such as that depicted in *Coalbrookdale by Night* (1801). More generally, J. M. W. Turner made some use of Goethe's theories of light and color, while William Blake famously depicted the figure of Newton vainly attempting to measure the poet's mystical cosmos with geometric calipers.

Although the Romantic reaction to the Enlightenment and the new worldview it presented to humanity was by no means a consistent or uniform one, Romantic artists could hardly disregard the immense effect that the Age of Reason had upon human consciousness of our place within the universe. To Romantic observers, the upheavals in humankind's perception of nature and the cosmos were every bit as significant in their seemingly endless implications for humanity as the political upheavals that had taken place in France and America. The pathway opened by the new advances in knowlege had, Coleridge noted, "been pursued with an eagerness and almost epidemic enthusiasm which, scarcely less than its political revolutions, characterize the spirit of the age." From the most practical advantages gained as aids in daily life to the highest levels of philosophical thought, humankind now lived, he said, in "an era of enlighteners, from the Gas Light Company to the dazzling Illuminati in the Temples of Reason."

CHRISTOPHER GOULDING

Bibliography

Abrams, M. H. *The Mirror and the Lamp.* New York: Oxford University Press, 1953.

Cunningham, Andrew, and Nicholas Jardine, (eds.) *Romanticism and the Sciences.* Cambridge: Cambridge University Press, 1990.

Levere, Trevor H. *Poetry Realised in Nature: Coleridge and Early Nineteenth Century Science.* Cambridge: Cambridge University Press, 1981.

McCalman, Iain, ed. *The Oxford Companion to the Romantic Age.* Oxford: Oxford University Press, 1999.

Piper, H. W. *The Active Universe.* London: University of London/Athlone Press, 1962.

SCIENCE IN GERMANY

Although Germany in the Romantic era was not yet the scientific leader it would later become, it did have a very active scientific culture, and one particularly strongly influenced by Romanticism. This influence was manifested in both directions; German Romantics were nearly all interested in natural science, and only a few articulated the distrust of it expressed by some French and British Romantics.

As was the case elsewhere, interest in science was rising in late eighteenth-century Germany. The reorganization of the Berlin Academy in 1744 boosted German science, which was also strong in the universities, particularly the medical faculties. There was a significant eighteenth-century rise in the publication of German scientific periodicals in astronomy, botany, physics, physiology and chemistry by the end of the century. In medicine alone, nearly 200 new medical periodicals were launched in the last third of the century.

Although Germans were part of the international scientific community, German science also had a distinct national character and context. German scientists emphasized the relation of scientific knowledge to wealth and power, and sometimes asserted the superiority of German science over other national sciences—a particularly important source of pride, given Germany's political fragmentation. This sometimes had deleterious effects on German science. For example, acceptance of the French noble Antoine-Laurent Lavoisier's anti-phogistonic chemistry was delayed in Germany for several years because of pride in the German tradition of chemistry and distrust of French innovation.

The influence of Romanticism on German science in notable in many ways. Although some early German Romantics, such as J. G. Hamann, distrusted the materialism of science, other German writers took an interest in it, the most notable being Johann Wolfgang von Goethe. Goethe's anti-Newtonian stance, shared by other German scientists, was in part motivated by Romantic distrust of the mechanical and reductionist "Newtonian" universe. Germans, like other Romantics, tended to think in terms of historical development. German science was also historical, and the universe was considered to be in a state of development (one frequently-invoked metaphor was the idea of the universe as a pregnant woman). German biologists devoted a great deal of effort to embryology, tracing the stages of development of the embryo before birth. Geology, particularly as practiced by the great "Neptunist" school founded by Abraham Gottlob Werner, did not simply describe the current state of the earth, but endeavored to discover its past history and development. German geologists and other Romantic scientists were particularly fascinated with caves, which they believed offered direct access to the Earth's past. German Romantics were interested in archetypes, an interest which extended to scientists.

Different botanical forms, for example, were understood as variants on an archetypal leaf. Applied to zoology, this led to an emphasis on the similarities of different living things. Goethe's discovery of the intramaxillary bone in human beings was prompted by his Romantic (but not evolutionary) belief that human beings were on a continuum with other creatures, notably monkeys and apes, who also possessed intramaxillary bones.

One of the most influential syntheses of German Romanticism and German science was known as Naturphilosophie. Its primary founder was Friedrich W. J. Schelling, who published the central document of the movement, *Ideas for a Philosophy of Nature,* in 1797. Another influential champion of the movement was the biologist Lorenz Oken (1779–1851). For *Naturphilosophen* (nature-philosophers), the investigation of nature was a spiritual quest with an ultimately spiritual goal. Nature itself was not a material phenomenon which existed outside humans, but ultimately a product of the human spirit. *Naturphilosophie* was not primarily oriented toward technological progress. The mission of *Naturphilosophie* was ultimately to restore, on a higher level, the original unity of man and nature believed to have existed in the Golden Age (i.e., before the Fall of man), when the products of the human spirit became separated from the human spirit itself. Nature itself was moved by spiritual forces, such as a drive to organization manifesting itself in the crystallization of minerals or the growth of living things. What the scientist should study was not phenomena taken in isolation, but systems. Only the *Naturphilosoph* (nature-philosopher), with his spiritual awareness, was able to truly understand nature. *Naturphilosophen* criticized traditional scientific methods and objectives as mere fact-gathering. *Naturphilosophen* and other German Romantic scientists were holists, emphasizing entities as wholes that worked in a certain, specific way, rather than collections of parts. Their holism was combined with dualism; *Naturphilosophen* saw the world as governed by pairs of opposed forces, and placed great emphasis on symmetry.

Naturphilosophen, despite their penchant for mystical language, were not outsiders in the scientific community. When they practiced science, they followed the classic experimental methods of early modern and Enlightenment science. *Naturphilosophie*'s mysticism and transcendental orientation led to its (partially deserved) poor reputation as an impediment to the development of science; nevertheless, it could also be scientifically productive on occasion. One example is the German Romantic physicist and *Naturphilosoph* Johann Wilhelm Ritter's (1776–1810) discovery of ultraviolet light. When Ritter learned of William Herschel's discovery of infrared light, he quickly theorized that, because the universe operated on a principle of duality, there must be something at the opposite end of the spectrum from infrared. He devised an ingenious series of tests which demonstrated the existence of ultraviolet light. Like many Romantic scientists, Ritter was particularly interested in phenomena that fell beyond the scope of classical Newtonian physics, such as electricity.

The area on which German Romanticism and *naturphilosophie* had the most impact in the early nineteenth century was the biological sciences; indeed, the word "biology" was coined by a German scientist of the period, Gottfried Reinhold Treviranus, in 1802. Like many German Romantic biologists, Treviranus was not a *Naturphilosoph*. He drew on Immanuel Kant rather than Schelling and favored a less transcendental approach to scientific practice. But the vitalism of early nineteenth-century German biologists, with its refusal to reduce living beings to a series of mechanical interactions at the expense of a spiritual component, was deeply Romantic.

After approximately 1830, a reaction against Romantic science set in. New leaders of German science, such as the organic chemist Justus von Liebig (who famously referred to *Naturphilosophie* as the "Black Death"), and the physiologist and physicist Hermann Helmholtz, asserted the primacy of mechanical and reductionist science over Romantic vitalism.

WILLIAM BURNS

Bibliography

Brock, William H., *Justus von Leibig: The Chemical Gatekeeper*. Cambridge: Cambridge University Press, 1997.

Broman, Thomas H. "J. C. Reil and the 'Journalization' of Physiology" in *The Literary Structure of Scientific Argument*, edited by Peter Dear. Philadelphia: University of Pennsylvania Press, 1991.

Cunningham, Andrew, and Nicholas Jardine (editors). *Romanticism and the Sciences.* Cambridge: Cambridge University Press, 1990.

Hufbauer, Karl, *The Formation of the German Chemical Community 1720–1795*. Berkeley, Los Angeles and London: University of California Press, 1982.

Jardine, Nicholas. "*Naturphilosophie* and the Kingdoms of Nature" in Cultures of Natural History, edited by N. Jardine, J. A. Secord, and E. C. Spary. Cambridge: Cambridge University Press, 1996.

Lenoir, Timothy, *The Strategy of Life: Teleology and Mechanics in Nineteenth Century German Biology*, Dordrecht: D. Reidel, 1982.

Low, Reinhard. "The Progress of Organic Chemistry during the Period of German Romantic Naturphilosophie (1795–1825)," *Ambix* 27 (1980), 1–11.

SCIENCE OF THE PAST

The natural philosophy of classical antiquity still loomed very large during the Romantic Era, in Britain at least, largely due to the continuing predominance of the classical system of education in schools and universities. Indeed, for many young men, a reading of Pliny's *Historia Naturalis*, or Lucretius's *De Rerum Natura* might well have been their only exposure to natural philosophy during their formal education.

The theories relating to matter and its nature in *De Rerum Natura* were to exert a lasting influence on the physical sciences that would last well into the eighteenth century. Erasmus Darwin's verse epic *The Botanic Garden* drew upon Lucretius's influence in using poetry as a medium for the expression of scientific ideas, and became an inspiring text for many Romantic poets. In his preamble to the poem, Darwin notes that much of the "heathen mythology" of ancient Egypt, Greece, and Rome, along with more recent alchemic and Rosicrucian lore, was an early precursor to science, and thus he does not hesitate to make use of such imagery in his work. The influence of both Lucretius and Darwin is apparent throughout the poetry of Percy Bysshe Shelley, whose early exposure to classical science at Eton College had also included Pliny.

The eternal verities of mathematics held as true as they had two millennia earlier, but no less influential was the imagery of the geocentric cosmos of Aristotle and Ptolemy. Notwithstanding Galileo Galilei and Issac Newton, the harmony of the Aristotelian universe still held as much fascination for the Romantic poets as it had for John Milton and William Shakespeare. When William Herschel identified a new planet in our solar system—the first discovered in recorded history—the contemporary nomenclature of "the Herschel planet" or "Georgium Sidus" quickly gave way to that of Uranus, one of the earliest senior deities of classical Greek tradition. This reflected a lingering tendency among astronomers still to nod unconsciously toward a mythologically based cosmology, also evident in their frequent referral to heavenly objects such as the sun, moon, and planets in terms of "he" and "she."

In the realm of ontological philosophy, the phantom cosmos of Plato still cast its metaphoric shadow over Romantic metaphysical notions of the nature of existence and of human perception of the external world. Elements of Platonism lingered within contemporary theories of philosophical idealism and influenced the formation of concepts such as that of the Hegelian "world soul."

Alchemic terminology remained in use among some chemists well into the nineteenth century, with more traditional names such as "brimstone" still preferred by some to the modern nomenclature of sulphur. In literature, alchemic imagery that would have been recognizable to Geoffrey Chaucer persisted, whereby the archaic elements such as gold, silver, and iron were perceived as retaining certain supernatural characteristics, and were each related to a planet and its corresponding god from classical mythology. Attempting in 1812 to impress his future father-in-law with details of his philosophical interests, Shelley told William Godwin that he had "pored over the reveries of Albertus Magnus and Paracelsus" alongside his reading of David Hume and John Locke. Even recently discredited scientific concepts such as the Phlogiston theory (propounded in the seventeenth century and consigned to history by Antoine-Laurent Lavoisier in the late eighteenth century) lived on in popular scientific digests long after their time.

Medicine had only begun to release itself from the grip of Hippocrites and Galen during the seventeenth century. Advances in medical knowledge during the eighteenth century had given rise to quasi-Newtonian concepts of the human body as a machine in Paul-Henns-Dietrich d'Holbach's *Systeme de la*

Nature (1770). The rejection of such mechanistic views found a voice in Mary Shelley's *Frankenstein: or, The Modern Prometheus* (1818), while for the reemergence of a holistic view of the human mind and body at one with an organic universe, Romanticism called upon aspects of the herbalism of Paracelsus and the alchemic search for an elixir of life, in which doctors were viewed more as Promethean healers. Upon the death of the idealistic young poet in his poem "Alastor," Percy Shelley yearned "O, for Medea's wondrous alchemy."

Johann Wolfgang von Goethe sought to reunite metaphorically the arts and sciences in his novel *Die Wahlverwandtschaften* (*Elective Affinities*, 1809). This novel attempted to explore emerging scientific theories of chemical action, affinity, and reaction as influences upon human behavior, and at the same time placed them within the context of the pre-Renaissance concept of sympathia, whereby the universal order, from human thoughts and actions to the movements of the stars, operated by means of a unifying alchemic force pervading the cosmos.

The Bible remained a staunch opponent of modern science, most notably with reference to the creation of the universe, the formation of the earth, and the origins of life. However, biblical orthodoxy was occasionally able to lend support to contemporary scientific debate. One such case was the support lent by the legend of Noah's flood to the "Neptunist" faction in the fledgling science of geology, who held that the earth's features owed their formation to the actions of a great ocean that had once covered the planet (as opposed to the "Plutonist" theory, which ascribed the shaping of land masses to volcanic and seismic activity).

There was, nevertheless, a rejection of many of the proto-scientific values of the past, particularly those that had been precursors of empiricism and the Enlightenment. By and large, Romanticism sought to reject the desire for sovereignty over nature implicit in the writings of Francis Bacon and René Descartes, preferring a holistic approach more attuned to transcendental unity with the natural world.

CHRISTOPHER GOULDING

Bibliography

Gottlieb, Anthony. *The Dream of Reason: A History of Western Philosophy from the Greeks to the Renaissance.* London: Penguin, 2000.

Grant, Edward. *Foundations of Modern Science in the Middle Ages.* Cambridge: Cambridge University Press, 1996.

Koestler, Arthur. *The Sleepwalkers.* London: Hutchinson, 1968.

Lloyd, G. E. R. *Early Greek Science: Thales to Aristotle.* London: Chatto and Windus, 1970.

Mathias, Peter, ed. *Science and Society 1600–1900.* Cambridge: Cambridge University Press, 1972.

Silver, Brian L. *The Ascent of Science.* Oxford: Oxford University Press, 1998.

Taylor, F. Sherwood. *The Alchemists: Founders of Modern Chemistry.* London: Heinemann, 1951.

SCOTT, SIR WALTER 1771–1832

English novelist

Sir Walter Scott is little read today, but he was one of the few Romantic writers to achieve world historical importance in his time. Scott gave the world a literary form—the sociohistorical novel—used by generations of imitators and readers around the world to enable their formation of liberal constitutional states. Such states are based on an ideology of sovereign subjects expressing their interests through representative democratic institutions, usually prescribed in a written constitution. In different discourses, the liberal constitution and the historical romance embody social, cultural, and economic interests of the middle-class reading publics, who enthusiastically consumed the novels of Scott and his numerous imitators, from Honoré de Balzac and Alessandro Manzoni through James Fenimore Cooper and George Eliot to Lev Tolstoy and beyond, while engaged in liberal state formation.

Scott's world-historical fictions appeared during the revolutionary and Napoleonic cataclysm that produced the first liberal constitution (at Cádiz, Spain, in 1812), a model invoked repeatedly through the nineteenth century. Politically Scott was a Tory, or conservative; nevertheless, his novels, like the Cádiz constitution, were designed to address a series of critical contemporary challenges while advancing the interests of those who both read novels and wrote new constitutions. These issues were both particular and general. The most immediate challenges were particular ones: plebeian revolutionary mobilization and Napoleonic imperialism. Yet the liberals, and Scott to a lesser extent, adopted key elements of the French revolutionary and Napoleonic systems while resisting revolutionary and Napoleonic imperialism. They did so mainly because old forms of court monarchy and aristocratic government were clearly unable to manage the forces unleashed by the broader challenge of modernization, which the revolution and Napoleon Bonaparte claimed to embody. In his novels, Scott provided, in comprehensible yet authoritative narrative form, a forceful vision of mediation between unmodernized past, modernizing present, and modernized future, without the necessity of revolutionary cataclysm or Napoleonic totalitarian empire.

Modernization is historians' term for transformation of customary and feudal social structures, economic relations, modes of production, cultural practices, and political institutions into "modern" ones: open and egalitarian social structures, "civil society," capitalist modes of production, "rational" and "enlightened" cultural forms, and more broadly representative state institutions. Modernization challenged the ancien régime, and itself produced further challenges. As the French Revolution demonstrated, modernization provoked both lower-class resistance and middle-class claims to share in modernization's benefits. In re-sponse, the defensive ancien régime relied more than ever on state churches to meet opposition from both dissident religious groups and Enlightenment religious skeptics. Partly entangled in these religious differences were historic regional, national, and imperial differences now exacerbated by the French

Revolution and Napoleonic imperialism. Modernization placed new stresses on social relations of all kinds, including gender, as middle-class women were increasingly called on to eschew their supposed "natural" weaknesses and to spearhead moral, social, and cultural reform and national and imperial defense within, and from, the home.

In his novels and other writings Scott addressed all of these challenges. His social, professional, intellectual, and literary background equipped him admirably to do so. Throughout Europe, the professional middle classes played a large role in the Enlightenment and modernization, and even more so in Scotland. Scott was educated at Edinburgh, a major center of the European Enlightenment, and, while not an outstanding student, he absorbed Enlightenment ideas and assumptions, particularly "philosophical" or critical history. As a youth, Scott also spent much time in the countryside around Edinburgh, where he delighted in cultural forms that would inform his verse and prose fictions—especially the rich repertories of historic Scottish street literature, or cheap print, and of Scottish folk song and tale. Scott participated briefly in the German Sturm und Drang movement's imitation of folk literature but returned to indigenous material with his collection *Minstrelsy of the Scottish Border* (1802). He embraced the new interest in feudalism, chivalry, medieval romance, and local antiquarianism, and published editions of several romances. He was skeptical, however, toward such sentimental literary fads as the supposedly rediscovered poems of the medieval Gaelic bard Ossian (which were in fact fabrications by the Scottish clergyman James Macpherson). "Ossian" became a European best-seller and, incidentally, the favorite poet of a young Corsican-French officer named Napoleon Bonaparte.

Disdaining forgery, Scott undertook fiction, first fusing folk song, romance, and history into best-selling poems such as *The Lay of the Last Minstrel* (1805), *Marmion* (1808), and *The Lady of the Lake* (1810). When sales of such wares (he repeatedly referred to his writings as commodities) began to slacken, and Lord Byron's best-selling narrative poems began to appear, Scott turned to the novel. Using his vast knowledge of antiquarianism, folklore, and Enlightenment "philosophical history," Scott adapted the work of women contemporaries such as Jane Porter's Ossianic historical romance *The Scottish Chiefs* (1810) to produce best-selling novels from *Waverley* (1814) through two dozen works known collectively as the *Waverley* novels. Scott's poems and novels financed his rise from Edinburgh lawyer to "laird" (lord) of Abbotsford, his imitation Gothic mansion and estate on the River Tweed. Scott seemed the model of successful modernization that his novels quietly promoted: he managed to combine the intellectual professional man, the (secret) middle-class capitalist, and the newly made landed gentleman. Eventually, however, his relentless acquisition of land for Abbotsford and secret partnership with his publisher, Ballantyne, precipitated his ruin during the financial crisis of 1826. He extricated Abbotsford and thus his family's acquired social status from this ruin, but at the cost of writing himself to death over the next six years.

Scott left Abbotsford to his descendants, but the *Waverley* novels to generations of readers and imitators who used them to build modern liberal states. The novels are varied in subject matter but similar in form, and the ideology implicit in this form—especially setting, characterization, plot, and narration—

made them useful for that purpose, and thus of world-historical importance.

Scott chooses settings in some place and time like his own, of history-changing collision among classes, societies, cultures, regions, nations, or empires. In *Waverley*, for example, Highland Scotland collides with Lowland Scotland, Scotland with England, Stuart dynasty with Hanoverian, feudal order with modernization, Roman Catholic with Protestant, Britain with France, one kind of masculinity with another, one kind of femininity with another, aristocrat with plebeian—all during the Jacobite rebellion of 1745. In the late novel *Count Robert of Paris* (1831), Christendom collides with Islam, Western with Eastern Christianity, barbaric yet vigorous feudal western Europe with the civilized but decadent eastern Roman Empire at the time of the First Crusade.

The revolutionary and Napoleonic cataclysm drew forth extraordinary characters. Scott depicts similar historical and fictional figures, but his protagonists are "waver-ly." Torn between contending forces, they usually find the "right" side—morally "right" as well as victorious—thanks to innate goodness, virtuous helpers, luck, and historical movements beyond their ken and control, and embodied in characters good or bad, major and minor. Only the narrator, and thus the reader, fully understands these movements, however. Edward Waverley in *Waverley*, Ivanhoe in *Ivanhoe* (1819), Jeannie Deans in *The Heart of Midlothian* (1818), and many like them end up, though unwittingly, on the side of what narrator and reader know to be "progress." The protagonist's plot and the plot of history eventually coincide, and only rarely does a protagonist disappear into history's abyss of superseded ideologies, values, cultures, and institutions, as with Ravenswood in *The Bride of Lammermoor* (1819), who is symbolically swallowed by quicksand.

Scott's main characters interact against three kinds of intertwined background—topographical, social, and historical. Scott adapted gothic novelists' landscape description to both Enlightenment ideas of topography's influence on national and individual character and Romantic nationalist ideas of national character rooted in national territory. Scott adapted techniques of predecessors from Miguel de Cervantes Saavedra to Tobias Smollett to create social backgrounds with characters from all classes, often as a chorus commenting on the main action, but also ignorant of larger historical forces. This knowledge is provided by the omniscient narrator alone, though a few characters, such as the Duke of Argyll in *The Heart of Midlothian*, understand the historical plot of modernization and "progress," avoiding and reconciling extremes of religious, social, or political fanaticism—the bane of Scott's own day. The novels' readers are called on to do the same, and since the implied outcome of this plot is the formation of some kind of modern constitutional state comprehending diverse identities and interests, the novels could assure those busy forming such states that such work is part of and sanctioned by history.

Certainly there were other writers who performed similar tasks for their own and succeeding generations, and there are elements of liberal ideology not fully developed in the *Waverley* novels, such as the complex representation of subjectivity, but these were well supplied by other Romantic writers, from Johann Wolfgang von Goethe through François-Auguste-Renée de Chateaubriand to Byron. The *Waverley* novels led the literary creation of what Benedict Anderson calls the "imagined community" of the nation-state, and these novels and their imitators continued to be widely read by those classes forming modern liberal states around the globe, for better and for worse. By so powerfully enabling this process Scott became one of the few Romantic writers of world-historical importance.

GARY KELLY

See also **Balzac, Honoré de; Byron, Lord George Noel Gordon; Chateaubriand, François-Auguste-René, Vicomte de; Goethe, Johann Wolfgang von; Nationalism; Ossian;** *Waverley, Or, 'Tis Sixty Years Since*

Bibliography

Anderson, Benedict. *Imagined Communities: Reflections on the Origin and Spread of Nationalism.* Rev. edit. London: Verso, 1991.

Brown, David. *Walter Scott and the Historical Imagination.* London: Routledge and Kegan Paul, 1979.

Johnson, Edgar. *Sir Walter Scott: The Great Unknown.* 2 vols. New York: Macmillan, 1970.

Jones, Howard Mumford. *Revolution and Romanticism,* Cambridge, Mass.: Harvard University Press, 1974.

Kelly, Gary. *English Fiction of the Romantic Period.* London: Longman, 1989.

Lukács, Georg. *The Historical Novel.* Translated by Hannah and Stanley Mitchell. Harmondsworth, England: Penguin, 1969.

Sanderson, Stephen K. *Social Transformations: A General Theory of Historical Development.* Oxford: Blackwell, 1995.

Schulze, Hagen. *States, Nations and Nationalism: From the Middle Ages to the Present.* Translated by William E. Yuill. Oxford: Blackwell, 1996.

SCULPTURE

In 1866 the French critic and novelist Theophile Gautier published his obituary for the Romantic movement, and in it he examined what he saw as the failure of sculpture to participate in this movement: "One can say that this art, so noble and so pure, thrives even today on the antique tradition, and that it has degenerated every time it has moved away from it." His view of the essentially classical character of sculpture was shared by the influential scholar Johann Joachim Winkelmann who, in his *Thoughts on the Imitation of Greek Works of Art* (1755) discussed the eternal relevance of ancient Greek statues as the embodiment of all that was virtuous. He advocated the emulation of their essential aesthetic and moral qualities, which he described as being "noble simplicity and calm grandeur in Gesture and Expression." Sir Joshua Reynolds reinforced this view in his discourse on sculpture that he delivered to the members of the Royal Academy in London in 1780. Reynolds insisted that the "grave and austere character of Sculpture" meant that it was suited to only one style—the classical tradition—and he also dismissed the attempts of modern sculptors to deny the qualities of the materials with which they worked by attempting to make it imitate picturesque or ornamental effects.

However, Romanticism is a complex phenomenon, and although the essential form of sculpture meant that it was less likely to be classified as Romantic on the grounds that the Romantic attitude opposed materialism in favor of the spiritual, there were aspects of Romanticism that inspired many sculptural works of the era such as: the free expression of passion and the appeal to the senses rather than the intellect, the exploration of extreme mental conditions such as madness, the admiration of the hero, the martyr or the genius, and the sublimity of the unknown, the grotesque, and death.

Although Antonio Canova is regarded as the quintessential neoclassical sculptor of the period, his emotive interpretations, such as in *Orpheus and Eurydice,* can be read as Romantic and many of his works, though neoclassical in treatment and form, often inspired truly Romantic reactions in the viewer. Like Canova, the Danish sculptor Bertel Thorwaldsen was inspired by antique sculpture in form as well as in subject matter; however his long devotion to the creation of a religious cycle for the Church of Our Lady in Copenhagen is expressive of the sculptor's deep religiosity in that it was inspired by passion as opposed to being an intellectual exercise. This passion was reflected in much of the work of Romantic artists, and was also apparent in some of the church monuments of the English sculptor John Flaxman.

While Flaxman's full-size figures of British heroes reflect his personal admiration for Canova as well as the classical training that gave preference to the stoic hero rather than the Romantic genius, his belief that the artist possessed a special gift which should be used to inspire morality and "a noble way of thinking" betrays Flaxman's Romantic tendencies as well as his nostalgia for the past, and also his friendship with the artist and poet William Blake.

Thomas Banks is believed to have produced the first truly Romantic work in England. This was a monument that, when shown at the Royal Academy in 1793 before its erection in Ashbourne, Derbyshire, caused visitors to the exhibition, notably Queen Charlotte and her daughters, to weep. The monument was in commemoration of a young girl, Penelope Boothby, whose father was an ardent devotee of Jean-Jacques Rousseau. It depicted his daughter on her bed, asleep rather than dead. Although the treatment of the monument is classical, it was in the strength of the emotions it aroused in the viewer and the originality of the conception that caused it to be regarded as Romantic.

Death, commemoration, and the graveyard were themes that also excited responses from those associated with the Romantic movement, whether writers, philosophers, or artists. The great cemetery of Père Lachaise in Paris became a popular place for sight-seers because it was the resting place of renowned men and women, such as Abelard and Heloise, Jacques-Louis David, and Moliere. When the young Romantic artist Théodore Gericault was buried in Père Lachaise in 1824 his grave remained unmarked for seventeen years. This was rectified when the sculptor Antoine Etex created a splendid monument that not only included an effigy of the artist "lying on his sickbed, palette in hand, painting up until his final hour" but also a bas-relief of the artist's most renowned work, *The Raft of the Medusa.*

Francois Rude, *Arc de Triomphe: La Marseillaise*. Reprinted courtesy of Bildarchiv Preussischer Kulturbesitz.

One of the greatest French sculptors of this period, François Rude, received a rigorous classical training, but as a fervent Bonapartist he went into exile in 1814. On his return to France in 1828 he began to work on themes which romanticized events from his country's past, such as the highly charged group, *The Departure of the Volunteers of 1792* for the Arc de Triomphe. Other French sculptors who have been described as Romantic preferred to work in bronze, because this was a medium that was regarded as being more faithful to modelling than marble. Antoine-Louis Barye took for his inspiration themes of violence and conflict in the animal world. His work was seen as particularly subversive because in it the intellect, represented by man, was displaced by the purely sensory in the form of the beast.

Thore praised Auguste Preault's *The Slaughter* (1834–50) as possessing "an agitation of the soul" that expressed inner tension and dramatic brutality through screaming mouths and clenched fists. Another work by this sculptor was a bronze bas-relief inspired by the Shakespearean story of Ophelia, who Preault depicted at the moment of her death by drowning, tortured and twisted in her despair and madness. Just as the Romantic painters had turned to new sources from literature for creative motivation, so too did sculptors. Other than the tragedies of Shakespeare, the most popular works were John Milton's *Paradise Lost*, Aristo's *Orlando Furioso*, and, most important, Dante Alighieri's *Divine Comedy*, which was also later to provide the inspiration for Auguste Rodin's *Gates of Hell*. Before this, however, Preault depicted *Virgil and Dante in Hell* while Jean-Baptiste Carpeaux chose to illustrate the tortured despair of *Comte Ugolino* (1863) who had been imprisoned in a tower, with his sons and grandsons, by Archbishop Ruggieri because he had betrayed his country. Ugolino, consigned to hell by Dante for his sin, says that during his imprisonment he was powerless to prevent his beloved family from starving to death in front of him, and when finally left alone with their bodies he himself went blind. He says that at the end "hunger proved more powerful than grief." Many have read this to mean that in his madness Ugolino resorted to cannibalism. Carpeaux chose to portray Ugolino chewing on his own hands and isolated in both his madness and blindness, as his children lay dying, still vainly pleading for help, at his feet. The count is a powerful figure, a tragic and Romantic reminder of the frailty of man.

CHERRY SANDOVER

See also **Aesthetics and Art Criticism; Blake, William; Canova, Antonio; Flaxman, John; Gautier, Théophile; Genius; Gericault, Jean Louis André Théodore; Hero; Madness;** *Raft of the Medusa***; Rousseau, Jean-Jacques; Shakespeare, William: Britain; Shakespeare, William: Continental Europe; Thoraldsen, Bertel**

Bibliography

Dante. *The Divine Comedy*. Vol. 1, *Inferno*. Translated by Mark Musa. London: Penguin, 1984.

Flynn, Tom. *The Body in Sculpture*. London: George Weidenfeld and Nicholson, 1998.

Gunnis, Rupert. *Dictionary of British Sculptors 1660–1851*. London: Abbey Library, 1951.

Normand-Romain, Antoinette Le. "Sculpture under Louis-Philippe." In *Sculpture: From the Renaissance to the Present Day*. Koln: Taschen, 1999.

Reynolds, Sir Joshua. *Discourses*. London: Penguin, 1992.

Vaughan, William. *Romantic Art*. London: Thames and Hudson, 1978.

Whinney, Margaret. *Sculpture in Britain 1530–1830*. Revised by John Physick. Harmondsworth, England: Penguin, 1988.

SELF AND SUBJECTIVITY

The self and its historic transformations as a concept are notoriously difficult to define, as the origins of the modern self have been claimed for almost every period dating back to classical antiquity. The Romantic era, however, is generally identified as a watershed for the full emergence of the modern, autonomous self, with the sense that each individual possesses a uniquely personal "inner" identity, that society exists as a collection of essentially separate individuals, and that self-expression or self-realization provides a fundamental meaning and value. In literature as well as in philosophy, the self was generally equated with consciousness, especially with an acute self-consciousness and emphasis on memory that allowed the individual to construct his or her own identity as if independent from others but that also, for this same reason, threatened solipsism and alienation.

The self during this period provided the premise for a major shift in aesthetic and philosophical theories while at the same time becoming the foundation of liberal possessive individualism, with its assertion of the individual's inalienable rights and inherent dignity, and the related new science of political economy or economics, which reinterpreted human society in terms of individual motivations and economic activity.

The final half of the eighteenth century, sometimes called the "age of sensibility," witnessed an increased emphasis on personal sentiment in the arts and religion that focused attention on the individual self. Intensely personal religious pietism swept Britain and Germany especially, in such religions as Methodism and the Moravian Church. In the arts the novel of sensibility emerged as a major new form, as Samuel Richardson's *Clarissa* (1748–59), Jean-Jacques Rousseau's *Julie: ou, la nouvelle Héloïse* (*Julie: Or, The New Eloise*, 1761), and Johann Wolfgang von Goethe's *Die Leiden des jungen Werthers* (*The Sorrows of Young Werther*, 1774) successively swept Europe, investing personal sentiment with a quasi-religious moral significance. During this same period, personal expression began to emerge as central to the lyric, which would become the dominant genre of Romantic poetry in the hands of poets such as Goethe, Heinrich Heine, Johann Christian Friedrich Hölderlin, Victor Hugo, John Keats, Alphonse Marie-Louis de Lamartine, Aleksandr Pushkin, Percy Bysshe Shelley, and William Wordsworth. The idea of poetry as the sincere personal expression of the individual author emerged as central to the Romantic lyric and to aesthetics and hermeneutics more generally, connected to the increasingly important idea of genius as a uniquely personal power of creative imagination and expression. Individual self-assertion, often directly in opposition to society and at once both heroic and destructive, emerged as a related theme in figures such as Goethe's Faust, the veiled autobiographical heroes of Lord Byron's poetry, the protagonist of Mikhail Lermontov's *A Hero of Our Time* (1840), and Captain Ahab of Herman Melville's *Moby-Dick* (1851). Ralph Waldo Emerson's essays, Henry David Thoreau's *Walden* (1854), and Walt Whitman's *Song of Myself* (1855) provided more positive, American variations on this theme of self-reliance and individuality.

Personal expression also became crucial to Romantic movements in other arts, such as painting and music. In music as in literature, the artist and his genius became a center of attention in its own right, with the emergence of Romanticism in the later works of Ludwig van Beethoven, the defining musical genius of his time. The virtuoso performer emerged as a central figure of music during this period, as embodied by the tempestuous, Byronic violinist Niccolò Paganini and the pianists Franz Liszt and Frédéric François Chopin, as music was reinterpreted as an expression of the composer's and performer's individual personality and emotion. The subjective emotional expression of the lied, or song, also emerged as an important musical form at this time, as in the songs of Franz Peter Schubert and Robert Alexander Schumann, matching the general turn to the lyric in poetry as a vehicle of individual subjective expression. This new emphasis on personal expression in the arts influenced painting as well, as evident in J. M. W. Turner's fascination with the transient effects of light, Eugène Delacroix's exploration of color and emotional expressivity, and in the unique personal visions of artists such as William Blake, Henry Fuseli, and Francisco José de Goya y Lucientes (in his later works). Ideas of genius

and personal artistic expression led to major shifts in aesthetic theory throughout the arts, recentering meaning around the self of the individual artist in relation to the individual listener, viewer, or reader.

The Romantic period also produced a sudden efflorescence of autobiographical writing that concentrated—unlike earlier examples of the genre—on the uniquely personal character, life history, and development of its subject. Rousseau's *Confessions* (1765–70) offered an intimate history of the author's most personal feelings and imaginative development from earliest childhood onwards, opening with an unprecedented claim of personal uniqueness. Later autobiographies by François-Auguste-René de Chateaubriand, Goethe, and Wordsworth continued to call attention to their authors' personal development as the product of a unique life history and character; the related genre of the bildungsroman, with an important precedent in Rousseau's *Émile* (1762) and a paradigmatic example in Goethe's *Wilhelm Meisters Lehrjahre* (*Wilhelm Meister's Apprenticeship*, 1795–96), traced the education and development of the individual into adulthood as a central novelistic theme.

Together with these aesthetic developments, a major shift in philosophy took place during the period, positing the unified self as an epistemological and ontological foundation in response to Enlightenment empiricism and its tendency to break down the coherence of the individual self, as in David Hume's theory of the self as an unstable bundle of perceptions. Immanuel Kant's three critiques initiated this Copernican shift in philosophy by claiming each individual's self-sufficient reason as the fundamental basis of knowledge, perception, and ethical value. Later philosophers in the German idealist tradition, such as Johann Gottlieb Fichte and Friedrich Wilhelm Joseph von Schelling, posited the individual ego as the foundation of all reality. G. W. F. Hegel took up this idea and transformed it into an all-embracing theory of history through his model of the developing *Weltgeist* (world spirit). The self also became fundamental to the idea of the individual self-affirming will, expressed in Arthur Schopenhauer's philosophy and later in that of Friedrich Nietzsche, in the related emphasis on individual affirmation and the leap of faith in the religious writings of Søren Kierkegaard and Friedrich Daniel Ernst Schleiermacher; and in the American transcendental movement of Emerson and Thoreau, for whom it served as a vehicle of direct religious intuition and truth.

Overall, the Romantic period witnessed the transformation of the religious idea of the soul into the secular idea of the self. The idea of the unique and autonomous personal self became fundamental not only to aesthetics but to religion, philosophy, and the social sciences, and to the general construction of identity. The modern disciplines of psychology and economics and the world views they support can be understood as a direct legacy of this emergence of the Romantic inner personal self.

SCOTT HESS

Bibliography

Bloom, Harold, ed. *Romanticism and Consciousness: Essays in Criticism*. New York: W. W. Norton, 1970.

Campbell, Colin. *Romantic Ethic and the Spirit of Modern Consumerism*. Oxford: Blackwell, 1987.

Cox, Stephen. *"The Stranger Within Thee": Concepts of the Self in Late Eighteenth-Century British Literature*. Pittsburgh: University of Pittsburgh Press, 1981.

Foucault, Michel. *The Order of Things*. New York: Random House, 1970.

Garber, Frederick. *The Autonomy of the Self from Richardson to Huysmans*. Princeton, N.J.: Princeton University Press, 1982.

Rzepka, Charles. *The Self as Mind*. Cambridge, Mass.: Harvard University Press, 1986.

Sennett, Richard. *The Fall of Public Man*. New York: Alfred A. Knopf, 1977.

Taylor, Charles. *Sources of the Self: The Making of the Modern Identity*. Cambridge, Mass.: Harvard University Press, 1989.

Williams, Raymond. *The Long Revolution*. New York: Harper and Row, 1966.

SELF-PORTRAIT AT AN EASEL 1789–1790

Painting by Elisabeth-Louise Vigée Le Brun

In the autumn of 1789, Elisabeth-Louise Vigée Le Brun left Paris and headed for Italy on the pretext that she wished to further her artistic education. In truth, her departure was also expedient, given the political upheaval in France, for she was an ardent monarchist and had enjoyed royal patronage for more than a decade. En route to Rome, the artist stopped her journey in Florence. It was there that she was commissioned to paint her self-portrait for the illustrious grand ducal collection of artists' self-portraits in the Uffizi Gallery. She probably began the painting when she was still in Florence, but she finished it in Rome in 1790. Roman society flocked to see the portrait when she unveiled it, but she kept her promise to return the work to the Uffizi, where it hangs to this day.

In her *Souvenirs* (published 1835–36), Vigée Le Brun tells of her excitement at this great honor. Above all, she was proud that her self-portrait would hang alongside that of Angelica Kauffman, "one of the glories of our sex," as she called her. Implicitly she suggests that women are finally acceding to the pantheon of great artists, which has hitherto been inhabited only by men.

She would certainly not have forgotten her treatment by the Paris Academy of Painting and Sculpture a few years ealier. For a long time this body refused her membership, despite her growing reputation as an artist; it was only after the queen's intervention that she was grudgingly accepted. It must have been both refreshing and flattering to receive very different treatment in Italy. Before she reached Florence, she was invited to become a member of the celebrated academy in Bologna; she was subsequently given membership to the academies in both Rome and Parma.

The Uffizi self-portrait is one of Vigée Le Brun's finest works, and it exudes happiness and self-confidence. The artist depicts herself at work on a portrait of Marie-Antoinette, a palette and brush in her hand. She looks several years younger than her actual age (thirty-five) and she wears a dark velvet dress with a sash and an elaborate lace collar. But the picture should not be read simply as flattering and decorative; rather, it embodies many of the complexities of female self-portraiture. It challenges the prevailing opinion that it was impossible to be a both a talented artist and an attractive woman. Here Vigée Le Brun portrays herself as fully in command of both spheres, turning momentarily away from her canvas to acknowledge her beholders with a steady gaze. Artistic production is presented as easy and graceful, not fraught with difficulty.

Paradoxically, her pose also illustrates the constraints on women's self-representation. So fragile was the position of female artists at this time that Vigée Le Brun could not afford to present herself as a marginal figure: she had to show herself in a way that was acceptable to polite society, notably to her patrons and clients. Reducing her years gives her the status of a child prodigy, which is perhaps a more palatable image than that of an ambitious and experienced woman. Her need for professional legitimacy is evident from the fact that she portrays herself at work, alert and active. For all its prettiness, the Uffizi self-portrait demonstrates a certain practicality. The notion of genius, potentially threatening in a woman, is absent. Hence it contrasts with her portraits of the painter Hubert Robert (1788) and the composer Giovanni Paisiello (1791), which, with their rapt expressions, draw on the well-honed iconography of male genius.

Within the constraints of female self-portraiture, however, Vigée Le Brun adopted various innovative and playful strategies. The mob-cap that she wears in this portrait is a deft allusion to Rembrandt van Rijn's berets; moreover, her costume owes something to portraits by Anthony Van Dyck. (The artist's iden-

Elisabeth-Louise Vigée Le Brun, *Self-portrait at an Easel*. Reprinted courtesy of AKG London.

tification with the old masters is something of a pattern in her self-portraits.) Her famous "chapeau de paille" of 1782 consciously models itself on Peter Paul Rubens's portrait of Suzanna Lunden wearing a straw hat, and her 1786 portrait with her daughter evokes Raphael's *Madonna della sedia*. The artist experimented with her own image throughout her career, subtly altering her features and coloring in order to create an attractive, interesting composition. But she was not afraid to depict herself in a much plainer mode than in the Uffizi portrait: her self-portrait, done a year later for the Academy of Saint Luke in Rome, is a sober head study, its features visibly older.

The traits of Marie-Antoinette are clearly distinguishable on the canvas upon which the artist worked, an obvious allusion to her prestigious royal connections. In portraits of the queen, Vigée Le Brun actively conspired to present her as a sensitive woman and a loving mother. In her *Souvenirs*, she stresses their close personal relationship: reworking a common topos of artists' biographies, she relates how the queen stooped to pick up the paintbrushes that the artist had dropped on the floor, knowing that she is heavily pregnant. The reference to the queen in the Uffizi self-portrait is also politically charged, since Marie-Antoinette's brother was ruling in Italy at the time, and she undoubtedly would have had her supporters there (at this point, she had not yet fallen victim to the guillotine).

The Uffizi self-portrait was universally admired. The artist's old friend François-Guillaume Ménageot, who had become director of the French Academy in Rome, wrote to Comte de la Billarderie D'Angiviller, Charles-Claude de Flahaut, in March 1790, stating that the work was one of her most beautiful compositions, and that she had made great progress since he had left France. Chevalier Pelli, the director of the Uffizi, called the work a masterpiece, and claimed that it was admired by professionals and connoisseurs alike.

At least one replica of the portrait exists, as well as several copies. The replica, slightly larger than the original, was done in Rome in 1791 for Frederick Hervey, Earl of Bristol and Bishop of Derry. In this version, the head of Marie-Antoinette has been replaced by an unidentified head. It now hangs at Hervey's former residence, Ickworth House in Suffolk.

MELISSA PERCIVAL

Work

Self-Portrait at an Easel, 1789–90. Oil on canvas, 100 cm. × 81 cm. Uffizi Gallery, Florence.

Bibliography

Baillio, Joseph. *Elisabeth Louise Vigée-Lebrun (1755–1842)*. Seattle and London: University of Washington Press, 1982.
De David à Delacroix, La Peinture française de 1760 à 1830. Paris: Galeries Nationales du Grand Palais, 1973.
Goodden, Angelica. *The Sweetness of Life: A Biography of Elisabeth Vigée-Lebrun*. London: André Deutsch, 1997.
The Memoirs of Elisabeth Vigée-Le Brun. Translated by Siân Evans. London: Camden Press, 1989.
Radisich, Paula Rea, " 'Que peut définir les femmes?' Vigée-Lebrun's Portraits of an Artist," *Eighteenth-Century Studies* 25 (1992): 441–67.
Sheriff, Mary. *The Exceptional Woman: Elisabeth Vigée-Lebrun and the Cultural Politics of Art*. Chicago: University of Chicago Press, 1996.
Vigée-Lebrun, Elisabeth. *Souvenirs*. 2 vols. Edited by Claudine Herrmann. Paris: Des Femmes, 1984.

Website

http://www.batguano.com/vigee.html

SELF-PORTRAITURE: BRITAIN

British artists' self-portraits during the Romantic era are a scattered and inconsistent category. Oscillating between exterior projections of a public self and more private investigations of interior psychological and emotional states, some self-portraits were painted as gifts to friends or on commission, while others remained in the collections of the artists until after their death. While certain artists made a number of self-portraits throughout their careers, others, like the portrait painter Thomas Lawrence, were uninterested in portraying themselves. It can be said, however, that the artist's self-portrait in this period underwent a general transition, from works in which painters asserted their own status in a manner akin to the way that portraitists marked that of their sitters, to works that played on the connections between exterior appearance and interior state.

Joshua Reynolds employed the self-portrait to assert the image of the artist that he sought throughout his career to promote. In his self-portrait of around 1773 he is seen as an intellectual, wearing the robes of his honorary doctorate from the University of Oxford and posing beside a bust of Michelangelo. Referencing Rembrandt van Rijn's painting *Aristotle Contemplating the Bust of Homer* in pose, composition, and dress, the painting invokes multiple artistic traditions while effacing any evidence of the manual elements of his craft. Artists did not always shy away from displaying themselves at work. Johann Zoffany's self-portrait of 1761, for example, shows him in a reflective, three-quarter view, holding a pen in one hand. In his shirt-sleeves, with collar and waistcoat unbuttoned, the painting gives the impression of a private view of the artist in his studio.

Other artists made more implicit claims about their status by depicting themselves in relation to the continuum of contemporary portraiture. In the case of a portrait painter such as Thomas Gainsborough, this could mean making a picture in the same style and format used for his sitters. Gainsborough consistently portrayed himself as a gentleman. His early self-portraits, like his group portraits of the same period, show him seated with family members in an outdoor setting. His last self-portrait, from 1787, suggests conversational ease, conveying both directness and humor in the slight lift of an eyebrow. Similarly, George Stubbs, the period's supreme painter of horses and sometimes also their aristocratic owners, painted himself in a full-length portrait of 1782 seated on horseback, much as he would have portrayed a patron. The medium used could also make claims concerning an artist's skill; Stubbs's *Self-Portrait on a White Hunter* is painted in enamel on earthenware, a process

J. M. W. Turner, *Self-Portrait*, c. 1798. Reprinted courtesy of AKG London/Erich Lessing.

with which he experimented in the 1780s with the help of Josiah Wedgwood. Similarly, John Flaxman, who exhibited a number of portrait reliefs at the Royal Academy in London in the 1770s, made his own 1779 self-portrait in the form of a wax relief.

Later self-portraits demonstrate more penetrating psychological explorations. Samuel Palmer's glassy-eyed self-portrait of 1827 has aptly been described by William Vaughan as registering artistic sensibility in "that receptiveness to every fleeting nuance: overflowing with excitement in the moment, but passive and visionless when it has passed." Henry Fuseli's 1779 self-portrait in black chalk expresses a similar level of intensity. The style of Romantic portraiture could also be employed in a self-portrait to place the painter within an artistic context, but without engaging in the kind of psychological exploration demonstrated in Palmer's self-portrait. In William Etty's self-portrait of 1825, for example, the artist displays none of that interest in interiority but employs a dashing profile view with a high contrast between light and shadow, dramatizing himself in much the same manner

that Thomas Lawrence dramatized his sitters. By using a profile view and an oval format, Etty both referenced a mode of portraiture with classical antecedents and at the same time denied the oscillating subjectivity provoked by head-on self-portraits.

The Irish-born artist James Barry painted the most vehement and complex portraits of the period, combining the assertion of his status as an artist with the revelation of his emotional self-involvement. In life Barry was uncompromising about what he perceived to be his own heroic role as a history painter and obsessively chose subjects for his history paintings that reflected his own self-image as a persecuted genius. His self-portraits dramatize his sense of struggle against the lack of recognition of his abilities. They incorporate both private works, including drawings and mezzotints in which the artist records his likeness and emotional state with unrelenting directness, and paintings that present his artistic self-image to a wider public and that consistently place the artist in relation to the classical artistic tradition he sought to emulate. The first of these "public" self-portraits, dating from Barry's period of study in Rome, depicts Barry as an idealized youthful genius with two fellow artists observing and sketching the Belvedere Torso (c. 1767), which Barry considered to be a work of unique perfection. A later painting cast Barry and Edmund Burke as characters in an episode of Homer's *Odyssey* (1776). Although cast as a historical subject, the painting's composition and focus insist on its status as a portrait, albeit one imbued with complex layers of meaning and overtones of danger and terror. As such, it has been recognized as an early example of the interior exploration characteristic of Romantic artists. In a third self-portrait, begun around 1780 and completed in 1803, Barry appears as the Greek artist Timanthes, seated before a statue of Hercules trampling the serpent of Envy (an image with biblical connotations) and holding a painting of the cyclops, based on the Belvedere Torso. In his re-creation of such works, Barry asserted his artistic stature, defining himself in relation to the authority of an antiquity imbued with Christian symbolism while foregrounding his individuality through the expression of his emotional state.

ELEANOR SIAN HUGHES

Bibliography

Hoffman, Katherine. *Concepts of Identity: Historical and Contemporary Images and Portraits of Self and Family*. New York: Harper Collins, 1996.

Mannings, David. *Sir Joshua Reynolds: A Complete Catalogue of His Paintings*. New Haven, Conn.: Yale University Press, 2000.

Pressly, William L. *James Barry: The Artist as Hero*. London: Tate Gallery, 1983.

Vaughan, William. *Romanticism and Art*. London: Thames and Hudson, 1994.

Walker, Richard. *Regency Portraits*. London: National Portrait Gallery, 1985.

SELF-PORTRAITURE: GERMANY

The German Romantic self-portrait, with its new emphasis on inwardness, reflects a changing understanding of the artist and his place in society that arose in the late eighteenth century across Europe. A younger generation, many of whom viewed their chosen vocation as a spiritual calling, rejected traditional definitions of the artist as craftsman or court painter whose work was subject to the dictates of aristocratic and churchly patrons and circumscribed by rigid rules about art formulated in the academies. Rather than rely upon income from commissioned works or from steady jobs as instructors to noble families, many

German artists, like their European counterparts, began instead to paint primarily for the market place, seeking an independent creative life. While this was a liberating gesture, it also led to a more precarious economic situation for those who produced works without prospective buyers. Amid such circumstances, an image of the artist sprang up that reverberated throughout the nineteenth and twentieth centuries: that of a lonely, struggling genius who was misunderstood, ignored, or rejected by society, but who nevertheless chose a life of poverty rather than surrender his personal vision. Accordingly, a self-portrait by a German Romantic artist is less likely to be a picture, in the baroque tradition, of a confident and successful professional at work, sitting next to a canvas with paint brush and palette in hand and surrounded by a rich assortment of studio accessories (such as Adélaïde Labille-Guiard, *Auto-portrait avec deux élèves* (*Self-Portrait with Two Pupils*, 1785). Instead, the Romantic self-portrait typically conveys an introspective image, that of a sensitive and serious soul who stares out hauntingly at the viewer with piercing eyes. This mindset of self-understanding and its correlating concept of "genius" were limited primarily to male artists, for women were confined by established formulas regarding the depiction of their sex. Although they readily portrayed themselves as serious artists, women were less likely to adopt this more visibly "masculine" image of unfettered genius for their self-portrait.

Although the Romantics were not the first to strip their self-portraits of all artist's accouterments, there was a surge of such portrayals in the early nineteenth century that paralleled the demise of the courtly self-portrait. Many Romantic self-portraits depict only the head or half figure set against a flat, neutral background, thus underscoring the prominence of the face as a mirror of the artist's essence rather than any accompanying paraphernalia. Unlike their French and English counterparts, German Romantic artists tended to work in a meticulous linear fashion, which lent itself well to the intense scrutiny of the face, especially in drawings. The fixation on the countenance, with particular emphasis given to eyes, is indicative of the keen interest in physiognomy sparked by Johann Caspar Lavater's book on the subject, *Physiognomical Fragments* (1775–78), and also of the Romantic obsession with inwardness.

A belief that alienation was the primary condition of the artist's life strongly affected northern German artists' perceptions of themselves, with Caspar David Friedrich and Philipp Otto Runge especially inclined toward expressing their sense of solitude. Friedrich's self-portrait drawing from 1810, which portrays him with overgrown hair and sideburns, wearing a monklike tunic and gazing warily from beneath bushy eyebrows, exudes a heavy solemnity that embodies the Romantic notion of the disquieted genius isolated from society. A Runge chalk drawing from 1802 shows a more self-assured twenty-five-year-old gazing with feeling at the viewer, his open collar, wrinkled overcoat, and tousled hair producing an entirely disheveled appearance. This is hardly a model of bourgeois decorum, but rather an unmistakable representation of the outsider status of visionary genius that remained characteristic of portraits of artists, writers, composers, and other creative types throughout the Romantic era. The ill health that plagued a number of artists became another recognizable feature in Romantic self-portraits, as illustrated vividly in Victor Emil Janssen's tuberculous *Selbstbildnis Vor der Staffelei* (*Self-Portrait in front of Easel*, 1829).

In the south, it was the idealization of the Middle Ages and early Renaissance that inspired German artists. The Nazarene identification with the artists of the past led to a deliberate archaizing effect in their self-portraits, many of which clearly hark back to the portraits of Hans Holbein and Albrecht Dürer and to Italian proto-Renaissance portraiture. This is evident not only in the *altdeutsch* or old German clothing and hairstyles they wear (e.g., dark berets, tunics, cloaks, long hair), but also in the flat rendering of space, the stiff, serious poses, and the settings such as columned windows looking out onto landscapes that evoke fifteenth- and sixteenth-century portraiture. Other retrospective tactics include Wilhelm von Schadow's Latin inscription at the bottom edge of his *Self-Portrait* (c. 1811–19), and the triangular composition of Johann Friedrich Overbeck's *Family Portrait* (1820–22), which evokes the theme of the Holy Family, lending a kind of reverent dimension to the picture that accentuates its own sense of gravitas. After the Napoleonic Wars, altdeutsch clothing, which was worn by many as a symbol of Germany's golden age, was banned in some districts for its supposed demagogic connotations; thus the purposive evocation of great German artists that such clothing aroused in Nazarene self-portraits also carried with it political implications.

Rather than acting as a formal public statement of the artist's achievement, the German Romantic self-portrait was often an intimate picture created as a private memento for family or friends. The strong bond of family was a repeated theme, as indicated by Runge's intense portrayal of himself with his wife and brother, *Wir Drei* (*We Three*, 1804), or Wilhelm Ahlborn's *Selbstbildnis mit Bruder* (*Self-Portrait with Brother*, 1827), in

Casper David Friedrich, *Selbstbildnis* (*Self-portrait*), c. 1818–20. Reprinted courtesy of AKG London.

which the two siblings are pressed closely together, crowding the boundaries of the picture frame. The veneration of friendship that led German artists to form their own communities, such as the Brotherhood of St. Luke (also known as the Nazarenes) also resulted in the frequent exchange of self-portraits, most often drawings. This ritual was especially common among the Nazarenes, whose painstakingly precise drawings count among their greatest achievements, but was practiced by northern artists such as Friedrich as well. The *Freundschaftsbild* (friendship picture)—for example, Carl Julius Milde's painting *Self-Portrait between Julius Oldach and Erwin Speckter* (1826) or Schadow's *Die Brüder Schadow mit dem Bildhauer Thorvaldsen* (*Triple Portrait of the Artist, His Brother Rudolf, and Bertel Thorvaldsen*, 1814)—portrayed the artist and close friends whose spiritual solidarity with him was indicated by physical proximity as well as similar earnest demeanor and attire. Such representations of collegiality acted as declarations of artistic conviction by depicting an artist among like-minded colleagues whose presence reinforced and sanctioned his own inclinations.

The Romantic cult of the artist, which exalted him as a kind of priestly leader, was ignited in part by idealized characterizations of the creative life prominent in German literature. *Von Deutscher Baukunst* (*On German Architecture*, 1772), for example, Goethe's panegyric to the supposed architect of Strasbourg Cathedral, Erwin von Steinbach, celebrated the notion of the genius whose vision alone was responsible for the making of a masterpiece. Another significant work was Wilhelm Heinrich Wackenroder's *Herzensergiessungen eines kunstliebenden Klosterbruders Confessions from the Heart of an Art-Loving Friar*, 1797), which associated artists of the fifteenth and sixteenth century with a spiritually inspired art, arousing an intense interest in the artistic culture of that period. And Ludwig Tieck's *Franz Sternbalds Wangerungen* (*Franz Sternbald's Journeys*, 1798), a Bildungsroman about a pupil of Albrceht Dürer, glorified the person of the artist and his heightened sensitivity to the beauty of nature. Such writings reinforced the artist's belief in the importance of his mission.

In many ways the practice of self-portraiture in Germany corresponds to similar trends in other countries, especially France, where painters such as Théodore Géricault contributed greatly to the Romantic definition of the artist. But the Romantic self-portrait in Germany was distinguished by the intensity with which a spiritualized aspect permeated the artist's self-image, and by the nostalgic and patriotic attachment to artists of the past. Its legacy has been influential well beyond the Romantic era, especially in the angst-ridden portraits of the German expressionists.

MARGARET DOYLE

Bibliography

Heraeus, Stefanie. "Zum Bildnis des Kunstlers." In *Künstlerbildnisse: Porträts von Tischbein bis Beuys*. Kassel: Staatliche Museen Kassel, 1996.

Hofmann, Werner. "Das neue Selbstbewußtsein der Künstler." In *Europa 1789: Aufklärung, Verklärung, Verfall*. Cologne: DuMont, 1989.

Honour, Hugh. *Romanticism*. New York: Harper and Row, 1979.

Jensen, Jens Christian. "Die Bildniskunst der Nazarener." In *Die Nazarener in Rom. Ein deutscher Künstlerbund der Romantik*. Munich: Prestel, 1981.

———. *Malerei der Romantik in Deutschland*. Cologne: DuMont, 1985.

Klaus, Lankheit. *Das Freundschaftsbild der Romantik*. Heidelberg: Carl Winter Universitätsverlag, 1952.

Neidhardt, Hans Joachim. "Solitude and Community." In *The Romantic Spirit in German Art 1790–1990*, edited by Keith Hartley. London: Thames and Hudson, 1994.

SENANCOUR, ETIENNE PIVERT DE 1770–1846

French novelist and philosopher

Etienne Pivert de Senancour, whose work spans the period from 1792 to 1834, was discovered by the Romantics in the 1830s, who saw him as a forerunner of their movement, after living in relative obscurity. Although he considered himself a philosopher, Senancour owes his reputation primarily to his semiautobiographical novel *Oberman* (1804), viewed as the quintessential expression of the mal du siècle.

Born in Paris to a devout Christian family, Senancour encountered as a student the culture of the Enlightenment together with a philosophical tradition rooted in antiquity. Inspired in particular by the teachings of the Stoics and Epicurians, as well as by those of Benedict de Spinoza, Senancour's subsequent work—both fictional and nonfictional—would engage with central philosophical concerns such as happiness, free will, determinism, and the role of the senses. Senancour was a copious reader sensitive to the intellectual currents of his time, and was particularly influenced by the writings of Jean-Jacques Rousseau. Of special interest to him were three aspects of Rousseau's thought: (1) the valorization of dream-like states and of the imagination; (2) a concern with the relationship of humankind to nature viewed as the locus of truth and harmony between the self and world; and (3) the quest for a social Utopia.

In 1792 Senancour published his first text, *Les Premiers Ages* (*The Early Ages*). This focused on "the primitive state" of humankind and expressed a nostalgia for a lost happiness and for a golden age associated with rural life. The book was followed by *Les Générations Actuelles* (*The Generations of Today*, 1793), a virulent attack on religious dogma and on all forms of prejudice in which Senancour deplored the blind worship of the intellect, a symptom of the separation of the human from the natural. In 1795 the short epistolary novel *Aldomen* was published, being concerned primarily with the self and with a personal quest for happiness. A number of recurring themes in Senancour's work were developed: a love of nature and of a simple country life, a sense of alienation from the natural, a love of beauty, and a fondness for travel.

In 1799 Senancour published his *Rêveries sue la nature primitive de l'homme* (*Reveries on the Primitive Nature of Man*). Drawing inspiration from the occult theories of Louis Claude de

Saint-Martin and Jakob Böhme, he developed the concept of resemblance between the structure of the self and the structure of the external world. This analogical mode of thinking was later to become an important feature of French Romanticism.

It was with the publication in 1804 of *Oberman* that Senancour's thought achieved its most powerful and lyrical expression. Based on his own experiences of "errance" in Switzerland and France after a conflict with his parents in 1789, the novel portrays the quintessentially Romantic themes of spiritual longing, the inner void, solitude, restlessness, uncertainty, and melancholia. Its central concern is the quest for identity and an unchanging self, which is here inseparable from a quest for the absolute.

In his travels Oberman experiences moments of revelation and of ecstasy, in which he gains access to a spiritual world through a fusion with the elemental. These experiences can be triggered by contemplation of the night sky (the famous *nuit de Thiel*) or, as in William Wordsworth's poems, by climbing mountains. They are characterized by a transgression of barriers and by the fusion of self and object, time and space, and consciousness and matter, a state that would come to embody a central Romantic ideal. These descriptions were rendered all the more evocative through Senancour's embrace of Emanuel Swedenborg's notion of "correspondances" and of synesthesia.

In *Oberman* the Utopian theme is also developed and given a strong concrete representation in the description of Imenstrom, a place associated with austere, almost monastic living, and with the Masonic and Pythagorean ideals of peace, order, union, and justice.

The composition of *Oberman* was followed by a period of sterility in which only two texts of interest were published: *De L'Amour* (*On Love*, 1806), a philosophical treatise in which Senancour advocated divorce and which caused a minor public scandal; and *Observations sur le Génie du christianisme* (*Observations on the Genius of Christianity*, 1816), a virulent attack on the brand of Roman Catholicism represented by François-Auguste-René de Chateaubriand. This attack—renewed with vigor in the 1820s—was fuelled by opposing political beliefs; Senancour associated himself with more liberal tendencies, in contrast to the conservative royalism of Félicité de Lamennais and Chateaubriand.

Les Libres Méditations (*The Free Meditations*, 1819) was a turning point in Senancour's intellectual development. Abandoning the antireligious stance of his earlier works, he expounded a spiritualism that owed much to the New Testament as well as to the thought of Saint-Martin.

In the 1820s Senancour developed an interest in the concept of a universal religion and in a synthesis of philosophy and religion. He adopted an essentially deistic theosophical position in *Traditions morales et religieuses* (*Moral and Religious Traditions*, 1825), declaring that Christ was not the Son of God, but a wise man. For this he was condemned in 1827 but acquitted on appeal in 1830.

Senancour's brief fame after his discovery by Charles-Augustin Sainte-Beuve and by George Sand enabled him to produce newer editions of his earlier work, the most beautiful being that of the *Rêveries* (1833). He also wrote a third novel, *Isabelle* (1833), which owed much to Madame Anne-Louise-Germaine de Staël's *Delphine* (1802).

There has been a revival of interest in the work of Senancour in recent years. Critics have stressed the modernity of his writing, seeing him as a predecessor not only of James Joyce and Marcel Proust but also—in the weight attached to description—of the *nouveau roman*. His preoccupation with the question of identity, in particular, the relationship of the self to the nonhuman and elemental, and with the state of reverie or ecstasy, has also taken on a contemporary resonance in the works of, for example, Lorand Gaspar and J. M. G. Le Clézio.

BRONWEN MARTIN

Biography

Born in Paris, November 16, 1770; strict religious upbringing. Entered the Collège de la Marche, 1795; encounters with culture of Enlightenment and of antiquity contributed to loss of religious faith; refused to follow parents' wishes and embark on a religious life at Saint-Sulpice; conflict led to secret departure from France in August 1789. Lived intermittently in Switzerland and France, 1789–1802; married Marie Daguet in Freiburg, 1790. Serious depression precipitated by failure of the French Revolution to fulfill its ideals and by the failure of his marriage and death of both parents, 1795. Interest in mysticism and pantheism triggered by Swiss landscape; became tutor to children of Cesar d'Houdetot; returned to settle in France permanently, 1802; further depression and inability to write, 1810–12; lived hermit's life in Paris from 1818 onward; discovered by Sainte-Beuve and George Sand, 1833. Last years of life characterized by intense suffering and physical paralysis; died Saint-Cloud, 1846.

SENSE AND SENSIBILITY 1811

Novel by Jane Austen

Jane Austen might have started her career as author with a version of *Pride and Prejudice* in 1798 or of *Northanger Abbey* in 1805, if publishers had been more enthusiastic. Instead of being associated with witty, satirical comedy or scintillating technical virtuosity, however, she established her credentials with a novel befitting its anonymous authoring "by a Lady." The device of two contrasting sisters, and the paradigmatic opposition of respectable sense with suspect sensibility, harked back to feminine

fictions of the 1790s and thereafter, by authors such as Maria Edgeworth and Amelia Opic. The first version, "Elinor and Marianne," belongs to that time, and critics have seen vestiges of a cruder work of conservative satire beneath revisions undertaken in 1797 and before publication in 1811.

The novel does not, however, fit neatly into the mold of these fictions, nor into that of later versions influenced by Evangelicalism and middle-class reformism. The female characters of sensibility in anti-Jacobin fictions usually rebel through passion against the authority of the patriarchal family, become prey to Jacobinical revolutionary notions which alienate them from a predominantly healthy society, and meet miserable ends. The Evangelical reformer and novelist Hannah More had a greater value for sensibility that, for her, should animate domestic and religious life, though it must be a chastened or "chastised" sensibility. Novels inspired by this view maintain an opposition to "society," which is presented in terms of the dissipation and irregular passions of a town-based aristocracy unmindful of its religious and social duties. They validate the domestic affections of a true patriarchal family, responsibly managing a rural estate. Society in *Sense and Sensibility* is dominated by fashion, worship of rank and wealth, and the materialistic values that flow from these. Colonel Brandon's estate, in which the "chastised" Marianne finds fulfillment in ministering to his happiness and performing her duties to family and village, is a poor representative of Evangelical virtues. Brandon, a duelist, chooses his clergyman not for the soundness of his doctrines but for the resemblance of Edward Ferrars's situation to his own history of thwarted passion.

The novel explores the wide range of ideas associated with the concepts announced in its title and does not confine them to purely female applications. Marianne is neither irrational nor sensual and, despite the fall that allows Willoughby to act the male rescuer, she is not weak. Edward Ferrars has more of the dependence and indecisiveness associated with the female. Marianne does not oppose the social world so much as neglect it in her enthusiastic self-cultivation and integrity. Her subjective idealism and elitism is similar to that criticized in William Godwin's *Fleetwood* (1805) as the tendency of William Wordsworth's move away from social engagement. Marianne believes, with theorists like Robert Blair and Wordsworth, that the artist experiences the elevated feelings he describes and communicates them to the sensitive reader. Edward Ferrars's uninspired reading of William Cowper diminishes him in her eyes. The suspicion of affectation in taking elevation of feeling as a measure of worth is rebutted (she is not acting up to a stereotype in her grief) but this attitude is held responsible for the unresisted intensity of her suffering on Willoughby's desertion. Elinor's creed of general civility and outward conformity requires her occasionally to tell lies, but it also enables her to appreciate compensating qualities in those whom Marianne dismisses. Her restraint in expressing her feelings conforms to female propriety, saves her the embarrassment of gossip, and is held, somewhat unconvincingly, to diminish the sufferings of loss. The parallel situations in this highly structured novel, however, tend to break down the distinctions between the sisters.

Elinor's confined expression of "esteem" for Edward conforms to conduct-book injunctions but fools no one. Her conviction of their mutual affection survives on far less than Marianne's love for Willoughby. It even survives Lucy Steele's objective evidence of his engagement. Her promise of silence to Lucy spares her the pain of criticism of Edward by her family. Her

love does not allow her to blame him, though she might project her frustration in her condemnation of Willoughby's parallel conduct. Elinor's "sense" is an essentially self-protective quality that hides a most romantic sensibility.

"Sense" in the novel comes close to being identified with the hypocrisy and self-seeking of Lucy Steele, sensibility with a reverence for authentic feelings and cultivated minds, the sensibility championed by Mary Wollstonecraft. The narrator echoes Wollstonecraft's distinction between the debased social meaning of a term like *respectable* (for which John Dashwood qualifies) and a more individual sense including warmth and humanity (for which he does not). The question the book seems to pose is the possibility of living an authentic life of human relationships in a materialistic society, the theme of many earlier novels of sensibility inspired by Jean-Jacques Rousseau and Johann Wolfgang von Goethe. The Dashwoods' cottage, with its genuine cultural activities, is superior to the empty magnificence of Barton Park. It has the same appeal for men entangled in worldly affairs as Charlotte's female household in Goethe's *Die Leiden de Jungen Werthers*. Austen also poses some stark alternatives. If Elinor, reprimanding Marianne, maintains that one's happiness should not depend on one man, she not only attacks monogamy but joins the likes of Lucy Steele and Miss Morton, whose desires run in the grooves of self-interest or parental control. Marianne, seeking an authentic relationship, has to undergo the pain of loss, something that Wollstonecraft theorized as personal growth but practically succumbed to as a "female Werther" in her notorious suicide attempts. While evoking the tragedies of sensibility, Austen gives her novel ironic resolutions. Many characters display real, though not particularly elevated, qualities of benevolence, and even John Dashwood's conscience occasionally pricks him. The world might have corrupted Willoughby but resistance and even triumph is possible on the personal and local level. Elinor marries her first love and Marianne marries a man with whom, despite the narrator's satirical remarks, she experiences the same emotional closeness and happiness as with Willoughby, something she had feared was only possible in her exorbitant imagination.

CHRIS JONES

Text

Sense and Sensibility, 1811. Edited by James Kinsley with introduction by Margaret Anne Doody. Oxford: Oxford University Press, 1990.

Bibliography

Butler, Marilyn. *Jane Austen and the War of Ideas*. Rev. ed. Oxford: Clarendon Press, 1987.
Clark, Robert, ed. *Sense and Sensibility and Pride and Prejudice*. Basingstoke, England: Macmillan, 1994.
Moler, Kenneth L. *Jane Austen's Art of Allusion*. Lincoln: University of Nebraska Press, 1968.
Ruoff, Gene W. *Jane Austen's Sense and Sensibility*. London: Harvester Wheatsheaf, 1992.
Tanner, Tony. *Jane Austen*. London: Macmillan, 1986.

SENSIBILITY

Often conflated or confused with "sentiment" and "sentimentality," sensibility is an idea that is of central importance to the eighteenth century. It describes fundamental assumptions about the attributes of human beings' nervous organization and moral character and an aspect of an influential literary tradition.

Sensibility as a psychological concept has its origins in John Locke's *Essay Concerning Human Understanding* (1690), which postulates that ideas originate in sensation. Anthony Ashley Cooper, Third Earl of Shaftesbury, popularized Locke's associational theories, emphasizing the importance of emotion as a path to knowledge. When emotion is coupled with a moral sense allied with reason and intuition, an individual's susceptibility to the experience and expression of sincere and spontaneous emotion are a measure of the delicacy of the nervous system, and a means by which individuals can move from self-interest to benevolence. The moral philosophers of the mid-eighteenth century continued the shift from materialism to morality: David Hume, Francis Hutcheson, Adam Smith, and others reject the efficacy of reason as a guide to moral action, elevating sympathy as the operative emotional agent guiding human beings toward moral behavior and social harmony. Smith's *Theory of Moral Sentiments* (1759), widely regarded as the culmination of the theoretical elaboration of sensibility, argues that moral judgments are based on a sympathetic response to the sight of suffering or distress; Smith thereby links sight, sensation, emotion and morality as the constituent elements of sensibility.

The literature of sensibility was part of the larger tradition of sentimental literature that dominated the eighteenth and nineteenth centuries, and it diverged in the 1750s from its origins, remaining prominent through the 1790s. Its practitioners, novelists, dramatists, and poets were concerned with ways to address and educate the "faculty of feeling," a shorthand description of the refined and sophisticated ability to experience and display emotion that underpinned the moral theory of sensibility. Its later critics suggest that this education began with literary efforts to teach readers how to respond decently (in moral, ethical, and emotional terms) to life's experiences and wound up with efforts to teach readers when and how to weep.

On a formulaic level, the essential aims of narrative and descriptive technique for works of sensibility rely upon depictions of scenes of pathos and unqualified virtue and the promotion of subjective responses in the reader to events and sights in the external world. In formal terms, they share a reliance upon generalized statements of moral principle to reinforce narrative effects: frequent pathetic, relatively static tableaux depicting emotionally laden situations. Finally, as Janet Todd writes, all forms of sentimental literature, including the literature of sensibility, are based on the conviction that "life and literature are directly linked, not through any notion of a mimetic description of reality but through the belief that the literary experience can intimately affect the living one." Linkage between word and life depends both upon the power of the text and the reader's ability to respond to that power. The sentimental reader acted on the assumption that the affective text had the power to educate its readers; through the experience of the text, the reader was trained in appropriate emotions *and* appropriate action. The effects of these lessons in proper feeling could be taken from the pages of a book into the activities of daily life. Thus, for example, a proper response to the fictional depictions of suffering and pathos contained in Henry Mackenzie's *The Man of Feeling* (1771) would translate into spontaneous sympathy for, and charity toward widows, orphans, and other worthy victims.

Early practitioners of the literatures of sentiment and sensibility invoked images that would inspire meaningful engagement with the sublime, from Edward Young's preoccupation with life, death, and immortality to Edmund Burke's promotion of the overwhelming poetic power of terror. As the eighteenth century came to an end, the primary locus for the evocation of sentimental effect moved to the domestic realm, where it remained for much of the nineteenth century. Appealing to readers through the representation of familiar, domestic objects and situations, sentimental literature, particularly in England, offered a place of honor to the talent of provincial writers; many, including Bernard Barton, Robert Burns, and Walter Scott profited by the shift from universalized to localized depiction. At the same time, however, the primary audience for sentimental works became increasingly female, as did the sentimental protagonist-victim, and the texts themselves were implicated in the perceived limitations of women's place in society. The result was that the emphasis of sentimental literature on sympathetic emotional response to the suffering of virtuous domestic victims was increasingly derided as a passive and dangerous emotional indulgence for emotion's sake. Coupled with increasing sensationalism in the depiction of ever-more pathetic victimization (Samuel Johnson wondered if Frances Sheridan, author of *Memoirs of Miss Sidney Bidulph* [1761], had the right to make her readers suffer so much), and ultimately associated with the excesses of the French Revolution, sentiment became a synonym for emotional excess, sensibility for self-indulgence, and sentimentality for hypocrisy.

However, the literature of sensibility (as exemplified by the novels of Charlotte Brooke, Henry Brooke, Oliver Goldsmith, Henry Mackenzie, Samuel Richardson, Frances Sheridan, Charlotte Smith, Laurence Sterne, and Mary Wollstonecraft and the poetry of James Beattie, Edward Collins, Thomas Gray, James Macpherson, Helen Maria Williams, and others) made an enduring impact upon cultural assumptions about the transformative powers of literature: productive moral change and positive ethical action based on readers' responses to emotionally evocative literary representations were real and hopeful possibilities as the eighteenth century ended.

ALISON SCOTT

Bibliography

Harold Bloom, ed. *Poets of Sensibility and the Sublime*. New York: Chelsea House, 1986.

Brown, Herbert Ross. *The Sentimental Novel in America, 1789–1860*. New York: Pageant Books, 1959.

Conger, Syndy McMillen, ed. *Sensibility in Transformation: Creative Resistance to Sentiment from the Augustans to the Romantics: Essays in Honor of Jean H. Hagstrum*. Rutherford, N.J.: Fairleigh Dickinson University Press, 1990.

Dwyer, John. *Virtuous Discourse: Sensibility and Community in Late Eighteenth-Century Scotland.* Edinburgh: John Donald, 1987.

Jones, Chris. *Radical Sensibility: Literature and Ideas in the 1790s.* London: Routledge, 1993.

Mullan, John. *Sentiment and Sociability: The Language of Feeling in the Eighteenth Century.* Oxford: Clarendon Press, 1988.

Todd, Janet. *Sensibility: An Introduction.* London: Methuen, 1986.

SHAKESPEARE, WILLIAM: BRITAIN

The Romantic period is often credited with a rediscovery of William Shakespeare, evidenced by powerful performances of his plays, and the influence he exerted in both theatrical and nontheatrical contexts. The critical rationale for this is what was—and often has been claimed since as—Shakespeare's infinite capacity to imaginatively inhabit, and so to empathetically dramatize, various individuals. The few details known of Shakespeare's biography—which suggest a quiet, unadventurous external life contrasted with an adventurous and active imagination—fit the Romantic stereotype of the poet, opposite but equal in currency to the Byronic idea of the artist as hero. As John Keats put it in a famous letter of 1817, aligning himself to Shakespeare and distinguishing both of them from what he refers to as "the Wordsworthian, or egotistical sublime," writing, "As to the poetical character itself . . . it is not itself—it has no self—it has every thing and nothing—it has no character—it enjoys light and shade—it lives in gusto, be it foul or fair, high or low, rich or poor, means or elevated,—it has as much delight in conceiving an Iago as an Imogen; what shocks the virtuous philosopher delights the chameleon poet." The source of the idea that Shakespeare's preeminence lies in his ability to empathize with and project a seemingly infinite range of human emotions stems from the late seventeenth-century poet, critic and dramatist John Dryden. However, in the Romantic period, this notion acquired a renewed and greater value, stemming from both a new nationalism, and from an increasing interest in subjectivity and character. This new emphasis was first articulated on the stage at a time when the stage was very much at the center of British urban culture. It can be traced back to a revolution in acting styles earlier in the century, when first Charles Macklin as Shylock in *The Merchant of Venice*, and then David Garrick, in a variety of roles (especially as Romeo, Lear, Hamlet and Macbeth), used a more realist vocabulary of movement and speech, and the visual impact of costume and set design, to emphasize the power and emotional immediacy of individual character. Paradoxically, given that, initially at least, theater was the starting point of this reconsideration of Shakespeare's importance, a Romantic sense of the genius of Shakespeare—a sense of an ineffable, infinite capacity of the kind indicated, and hoped for, by Keats—brings with it a decline in the reputation of the theater, now considered inadequate, by virtue of its very nature, to the realization of the plays' true potential. Charles Lamb put it this way:

> I cannot help being of the opinion that the plays of Shakspere [sic] are less calculated for performance on a stage, than those of almost any dramatist whatever. Their distinguishing excellence is a reason that they should be so. There is so much in them, which comes not under the province of acting, with which eye, and tone, and gesture, have nothing to do . . . I remember the last time I saw Macbeth played, the discrepancy I felt at the changes of garment which he varied . . . if things must be represented, I see not what to find fault with in this. But in reading, what robe are we conscious of? Some dim images of royalty—a crown and sceptre, may float before our eyes, but who shall describe the fashion of it? . . . the reading of a tragedy is a fine abstraction.

The problem lies in the materiality of the stage, its insistence on physicality, and the limitations of the actual. Lamb values "dim images . . . fine abstraction" as he values reading above theatrical spectatorship for its very freedom from the specific and the material. There is an additional problem in the theater's perceived lack of social respectability. Garrick had done much to reinstate theater to an aesthetic and cultural centrality in England, and Sarah Siddons set a rare example of the actress as respectable married woman, but the move toward social acceptance was not fully realized until Sir Henry Irving was knighted, toward the end of her reign, by Queen Victoria. Even the most prestigious theaters were associated with prostitution and aristocratic license, and, as the following report of a lecture by Samuel Taylor Coleridge indicates, were generally regarded as too large and financially powerful to stay faithful to Shakespeare's vision: "the Macbeth's of the Kembles . . . were not the Macbeth's of Shakespear; he was therefore not grieved at the enormous size and monopoly of the theatres, which naturally produced many bad and but few good actors; and which drove Shakespear [sic] from the stage, to find his proper place, in the heart and in the closet"

Thus, for many writers and artists of this era, the true value of Shakespeare was found only in private reading, as William Wordsworth described it in his 1850 revision of *The Prelude*: "When, having closed the mighty Shakespeare's page, / I mused, and thought, and felt, in solitude." Alternatively, Shakespeare was best appreciated in family readings conducted out loud, such as those of William and Dorothy Wordsworth in Grasmere, or of the Bertram and Crawford families of Jane Austen's *Mansfield Park*. The very ambiguity of Shakespeare's place between the communal and the private increased an imaginative power reflected in the verbal textures of every ambitious English writer of the age. But the great actors of the age—Edmund Kean, the Kembles, William Charles Macready, Eliza O'Neill, Sarah Siddons—were amply recognized not only by the public of the massive patent (in other words, government-licensed) theaters of Covent Garden and Drury Lane, but by enthusiastic cultural journalists like Thomas De Quincey, William Hazlitt, and Keats. Hazlitt's response to Kean's performance of Coriolanus illustrates that the play was regarded as immediately topical: "*Coriolanus* is a store-house of political common-places. Any one who studies it may save himself the trouble of reading Burke's

Reflections, or Paine's *Rights of Man*, or the debates in both Houses of Parliament since the French Revolution or our own."

The debate as to the place of Shakespeare in British culture developed alongside a proto-Romantic conception of "genius," and, in relation to the French Revolution and the Napoleonic Wars, of national rivalry. Shakespeare is "discovered" (or perhaps, more strictly speaking, *remade*) as the great English genius, and the English genius is supreme, a universal genius, in world historical terms. This would be Coleridge's position; Hazlitt's is that Shakespeare belongs in the public arena of the stage, and in a context of national and international debate. One way or another, Shakespeare acquires, in the Britain of the Romantic era, the status of being both intensely English and distinctly universal.

The impact of Shakespeare on the other British arts in this period is less powerful than it was in Europe; an attempt, led by the entrepreneur Josiah Boydell, to establish Shakespeare's plays as source material for a British school of "history painting" was unsuccessful commercially and, largely speaking, artistically. With the exception of the work of the Swiss artist Henry Fuseli, and those native painters who followed him in exploring Shakespeare's creation of a fairy world of "fancy," Shakespeare painting remained at the level of illustration, just as (with the partial exception of a cantata on supernatural characters by Thomas Linley, and a London-commissioned setting by Franz Josef Haydn of words from *Twelfth Night*) musical settings were whimsical and decorative. Shakespeare's

value for Britain in this period was much as it has remained; as an assertion of cultural eminence, but within a context where the political meaning of such an assertion, and of the implications of the material on which it is based, are open to lively debate.

EDWARD BURNS

Bibliography

Bate, Jonathan. *Shakespeare and the English Romantic Imagination*. Oxford: Clarendon Press, 1986.

Bate, Jonathan, ed. *The Romantics on Shakespeare*. London: Penguin, 1992.

Burns, Edward. " 'The Babel Din': Theatre and Romanticism." In *A Guide to Romantic Literature: 1780–1830*. Edited by Geoff Ward. London: Bloomsbury, 1993.

Dobson, Micheal. *The Making of the National Poet: Shakespeare, Adaptation and Authorship, 1660–1769*. Oxford: Clarendon Press, 1992.

Donohue, J. W., Jr. *Dramatic Character in the English Romantic Age*. Princeton, N.J.: Princeton University Press, 1970.

Foakes, R. A., ed. *Coleridge's Criticism of Shakespeare: A Selection*. London: Athlone Press, 1989.

Friedman, Winifred H. *Boydell's Shakespeare Gallery*. New York: Garland, 1976.

Taylor, Gary. *Reinventing Shakespeare: A Cultural History from the Restoration to the Present*. New York: Weidenfeld and Nicholson, 1989.

Vickers, Brian, ed. *Shakespeare: The Critical Heritage 1623–1801*. 6 vols. London: Routledge and Kegan Paul, 1974–81.

SHAKESPEARE, WILLIAM: CONTINENTAL EUROPE

While there is evidence that at least some of William Shakespeare's plays had been performed in northern Europe by touring theater groups when the plays were relatively new, the influence of Shakespeare as an aesthetic force across the continent, not only in the theater but in practically every art form, was a product of Romanticism and revolution. To understand why, we might turn to the essayist and *salonniere* Madame Anne-Louise-Germaine de Staël, who in her *Germania* (1810) argued that Shakespeare now provided a more apt model for the development of drama than the classical playwrights, belonging as he did to the northern European world and reflecting an age of political violence that ended with the same revolutionary act that marked Staël's own context, the murder of a king. Shakespeare's lack of observance of neoclassical rules (in showing violent acts on stage, in mixing comedy and tragedy, in depicting a wide range of different social classes in his characters, in a wide-ranging sense of time and space, and in an investment in the depiction of late medieval and Renaissance, rather than Greek or Roman history) offered a way out of neoclassicism into a new Romantic drama. This, in the work of Victor Hugo, Aleksandr Pushkin, Johann Christoph Friedrich von Schiller (the riot at the first performance of whose *Ernani* is often seen as marking the watershed of a transition from neoclassicism) and many others, was a pan-European phenomenon, with only the Italian states, dominated as they were by the influence of Vittorio Alfieri, and the continuing currency of Carlo Goldoni and Pietro Metastasio, failing to follow suit. But even here,

Shakespeare, and Romantic Shakespeareans, provided much of the material for the consolidation of opera into a popular political art form analogous with Elizabethan theater. Gioacchino Autonio Rossini's *Otello* and Vincenzo Bellini's *I Capuleti e I Montecchi* bring Shakespeare's stories back to their Italian contexts and sources, and Giuseppe Verdi's *Macbetto* contextualizes his subtly psychological exploration of the central couple's marriage with an implied parallel to the politics of the *risorgimento*. Verdi closed his career with the two greatest of all Shakespearean operas, *Otello* and *Falstaff*.

Other Shakespeare operas still (occasionally) performed today include Hector Berlioz's *Beatrice et Benedict* (based on *Much Ado about Nothing*), Charles Gounod's *Romeo et Juliette*, Friedrich Nicolai's *Lustige Weibe von Windsor* (*The Merry Wires of Windsor*), Ambroise Thomas's *Hamlet*, and Richard Wagner's *Das Liebersverbot* (*Measure for Measure*). But perhaps more important for musicians was the association of Shakespeare with "fancy," and an unequalled imaginative freedom, particularly when it came to imagining the supernatural. This association goes back in English writing at least as far as John Milton (who refers to "sweetest Shakespeare, Fancy's child / Warbling thy native wood-notes wild," in *L'Allegro and Il Penseroso*), but it gave a further liberation to the European Romantic imagination, particularly for the Frenchman Berlioz, whose passionate love for (and less happy marriage to) the actress Harriet Smithson, whose performances as Ophelia and Juliet he saw in Paris, consolidated his identification with the dramatist, and was dramatized in *La*

Symphonie Fantastique, an instance of Shakespeare offering a liberation within an entirely different medium than his own. The symphony-oratorio *Romeo et Juliette* followed; perhaps the most significant movement there is the "Queen Mab" scherzo, particularly when taken with the great masterpiece of illustrative Shakespearean Romantic music, Felix Mendelssohn-Bartholdy's *A Midsummer Night's Dream* music, written first as an overture when the composer was a teenager, then expanded into a full score for a production. "Fairy" music offered the same freedom to play with new sonorities and rhythms as the fairy picture did, in Britain at least, to explore a dangerous sexuality in an increasingly respectable world. It was the plays that touch upon the supernatural—*Hamlet, Macbeth, A Midsummer Night's Dream, The Tempest*—that, along with the archetypically Romantic *Romeo and Juliet*, allowed Shakespeare's influence to be more than simply literary. Ludwig van Beethoven may not have gotten very far with his *Macbeth* opera, but it is supposed to lie behind passages in his "Ghost" trio, and although debatable, it has often been claimed that the piano sonata "The Tempest" is a reflection on the play. Shakespeare provided not only the plot lines, but the aesthetic license that facilitated a growing interest in illustrative, narrative music, displayed in the development of the genres of the concert overture and the tone poem, for composers as widespread as Antonin Dvorak (*Othello*) Bedrich Smetana (*Richard III*), Richard Strauss (*Macbeth*) and Pyotr Ilich Tchaikovsky (*Romeo and Juliet, The Tempest*, and *Hamlet*).

European painting drew far less inspiration from Shakespeare than music. Eugene Delacroix was as impressed as Berlioz by the British actors who visited Paris, and produced a series of powerful works based on *Hamlet*. The British investment in Shakespeare as a source of material for history painting, and for painting on a grand scale, stemmed from the lack of either a classical or, in the aftermath of Protestant iconoclasm, a religious artistic tradition. Without this need, the verbal as opposed to the pictorial focus of Shakespeare's art, its fascinating ambiguity as to visual specifics, tended to push painters elsewhere.

The most influential critic of Shakespeare (with an influence on Samuel Taylor Coleridge that often, at the time, led to accusations of plagiarism) was August Wilhelm von Schlegel, whose *Lectures on Dramatic Art and Literature* (1808–11) consolidated Shakespeare's reputation by countering the cliché of his rough and untutored genius in an emphasis on the "organic unity" of true works of art, and on Shakespeare's miraculous ability to achieve this. But perhaps the true value of Shakespeare for European Romanticism was in an opening up of aesthetic experiment, and in the idea that continues until Friedrich and Karl Marx Engels propose, in their *Letters to Friedrich Lasalle*, that Shakespeare in the histories still provides the best model for a dramatization of historical change, and that the aim of such experiment should be an acknowledgment of the variety and danger of human experience, both private and communal.

EDWARD BURNS

Bibliography

Bate, Jonathan, ed. *The Romantics on Shakespeare*. London: Penguin Books, 1992.

Berwick, Frederick. *Illusion and the Drama: Critical Theory of the Enlightenment and Romantic Era*. Pennsylvania: Penn State University Press, 1991.

Daniels, Barry V. *Revolution in the Theatre: French Romantic Theories of Drama*, Westport, Conn.: Greenwood Press, 1983.

LeWinter, Oswald, ed. *Shakespeare in Europe*. New York: World Publishing, 1963.

Pascal, Roy. *Shakespeare in Germany 1740–1815*. Cambridge: Cambridge University Press, 1937.

Raby, Peter. *"Fair Ophelia": A Life of Harriet Smithson Berlioz*. Cambridge: Cambridge University Press, 1982.

Sauer, Thomas G. *A. W. Schlegel's Shakespearean Criticism in England, 1811–1846*. Bonn: Bouvier Verlag Herbert Grundmann, 1981.

Williams, Simon. *Shakespeare on the German Stage I: 1586–1914*. Cambridge: Cambridge University Press, 1990.

SHELLEY, MARY WOLLSTONECRAFT 1797–1851

British novelist

Mary Wollstonecraft Shelley always referred to herself as Mary Wollstonecraft Godwin until she became Mary Wollstonecraft Shelley through marriage. Born in London in 1797, she was the daughter of William Godwin, the radical philosopher and writer, and of Mary Wollstonecraft, the protofeminist author of *A Vindication of the Rights of Woman* (1792) who died two weeks after Mary's birth. In 1814 she moved to Europe with Percy Bysshe Shelley, and they married in 1816.

Very few people in literary history have had to live up to such a pedigree, and Shelley's creative work is heavily influenced by her biological inheritance. In the 1831 Introduction to *Frankenstein: or, The Modern Prometheus* (1818), she describes herself as the guardian and inheritor of her relatives' thoughts and ideology, and she emphasizes the mimetic relation between her writing and the knowable reality of her background. This idea of an unbroken continuity between life and text, between the life of a daughter, wife, and mother (her numerous and unhappy pregnancies are always considered as major interpretative clues) and the genesis of her creative work, is the source of an enduring critical assumption that has conditioned the reception of Shelley's work. The other critical preconception surrounding Shelley is that she is a one-book author. She is too often known as only the author of *Frankenstein*. Although Shelley's first novel stands out as a major achievement and one of the key nineteenth-century texts (not simply because it is the work of a nineteen-year-old), she is the author of another six novels, numerous short stories, literary biographies, criticism and travel writing.

The sum total of her work secures her status as a major player of the Romantic era on several grounds. As a mythmaker she captured modern consciousness and helped delineate its contours. As the editor of her husband's Romantic poetry and prose she shaped a certain lasting image of Romanticism. As a novelist she paved the way for a generic revolution and opened up traditional gothic fiction to new territories (in particular with *The*

Last Man (1824), a science-fiction novel). Deeply inscribed with Romantic ideology, her work nonetheless offers a new perspective, a female standpoint on traditional views.

The story of the conception of *Frankenstein* is now legendary, and the plot itself, endlessly rewritten and adapted on stage and screen, is well known. During the wet summer of 1816 on the shores of Lake Geneva, a young girl in search of inspiration for a playful ghost-story competition dreamed the story of a young scientist who created a monster out of corpses. Rejected by its creator, the creature wreaks havoc in his life and, to revenge himself, destroys the entire family. The myth of Frankenstein captures the spirit of Romantic Prometheanism and turns it into a horror story. It embodies the deepest beliefs of the Enlightenment in human progress and perfectibility, only to turn them into a nightmarish vision of destruction. Born in the age of revolutions, *Frankenstein* challenges the idea that reason will necessarily triumph over obscurantism. Man is not omnipotent and his expanding intellectual and scientific abilities are not the guarantee of a better future. Having unleashed the dark forces that inhabit the human mind and overcast the power of reason, *Frankenstein* offers a corrective to the excesses it describes from within the Enlightened tradition. *Frankenstein* is a myth, and as such it presents a compromise, an answer to the contradictions of an age. As a political, a scientific, a social, or a psychological metaphor it clearly demonstrates that inclusion and integration of opposites is the way to avoid inhumanity. Promoting an egalitarian vision of society, it suggests that the separation of spheres, class division, and sexual difference, together with exclusively intellectual pursuits, are the source of chaos.

In Shelley's work, the family organized around equal female and male forces is seen as the model for all organisational structure. And the quest for this nuclear harmony as the source of coherence in all human interactions, whether intra- or interpersonal relations, informs all her writing after *Frankenstein*.

Mathilda (1819), a novel about the incestuous relationship of a motherless daughter and her father, remained unpublished during Shelley's life and was the cause of much grief between the author and her own father. There again, the lack of balance between the daughter and the dominant male figure is the source of Gothic distortion. In *Valperga: or, The Life and Adventures of Castruccio, Prince of Lucca* (1823), a novel on which Shelley worked before the death of her husband, she tries to demonstrate this principle of inclusion in the political sphere. Euthanasia dei Admirari dreams of a new Roman republic from her Castle of Valperga, whereas the man she loves, the powerful Castruccio, strives towards an oligarchy. Euthanasia becomes Castruccio's prisoner as she refuses to acquiesce to his conquest and drowns on her way to prison in Sicily. Her death signifies the impossibility of a republican, egalitarian state in which men and women have equal access to education and decision making. After 1822 Shelley made it her life's goal to ensure her husband's reputation for posterity. As his editor, she endeavored to rewrite his extreme positions and in so doing, she contributed to misperceptions regarding what his Romantic thought and ideology truly implied. Shelley becomes an angelic nature poet under her revisionary annotations, and their turbulent marriage is conveniently transformed into a period of harmony and intense communion. But the truth behind the Romantic myth is suggested in *The Last Man* (1826), a futurist fantasy that replays the convictions of *Frankenstein* to show the destructive powers of self-centeredness and the limits of egalitarianism. Taking place in the last decades of the twenty-first century, this end of the world novel envisions a country devastated by plague. Adrian, the Duke of Windsor and a clear fictional double of Percy Bysshe Shelley, finally decides to sacrifice himself for the public good and become lord protector, ensuring peace and comfort among the shrinking number of his countrymen. Ultimately, only three people survive the epidemic and its consequences. But Adrian ultimately fails to save the human race (through union with Clara) as he decides to sail to Greece with Clara and her uncle Lionel, the narrator, against the latter's injunctions. Clara and Adrian drown, leaving no hope for the future. Idealism and egalitarianism seem unable to survive egotism in Shelley's world.

The Fortunes of Perkin Warbeck (1830) was written in the tradition of the Jacobin novels of the 1790s, and explores in turn the theme of inclusion of opposites through the issue of how to introduce reforms in a society where many remain alienated by ruling-class corruption. *Lodore* (1835) and *Falkner* (1837) reiterate Shelley's quest for equality and mutual respect in the domestic circle. Her two heroines learn happiness beyond the father-daughter relationship through unions with unambitious, generous men. Both novels present ideal visions of a domestic sphere constructed around mutual respect.

Like her monster with his creator, Shelley struggled all her life to receive the equality and recognition she needed from her husband, her father, and her father-in-law. It is in her relation with her only surviving child, Percy Florence, that she finally embodied her ideal. In this mother-son relationship she nurtured but was also nurtured. It is with her son and his devoted wife that she lived the last years of her life on the family estate, appeased and fulfilled after years of insecurity and depression.

CHRISTINE BERTHIN

Biography

Born in London, August 30, 1797. Mother died September 10, 1797. In 1801, her father remarried. In 1812, Mary visited the Baxters in Scotland where she was happy and spent most of her time until 1814, when she began a friendship with Percy Bysshe Shelley. In July 1814 they fled to the Continent with Claire Clairemont, Mary's stepsister. In November 1814, Shelley's wife Harriet gave birth to his second child. In 1815, Mary gave birth to a premature baby girl who died within days. In 1816 Mary gave birth to a son, traveled to Geneva to live close to Lord Byron; started *Frankenstein* in June; went to Chamonix in July; half-sister Fanny Himlay committed suicide in October. In December, Shelley's wife Harriet drowned herself in Hyde Park; Mary and Percy married at the end of that month. In 1817 Mary gave birth to a girl, who died the following year. In 1819, death of Mary's son. That same year Mary's fourth child, Percy Florence was born. In 1822, Mary had a miscarriage, nearly causing her death, and Percy Bysshe Shelley drowned. In 1836, Godwin died. In 1841, Percy Florence Shelley finished his studies in Cambridge and traveled with Mary in Germany and Italy. In 1844 they moved to Field Place, the Shelley property that

Percy Florence inherited. Mary Shelley died there on February, 1, 1851.

Selected Works

A History of a Six Weeks' Tour. 1817.
Frankenstein. 1818. Rev. 1831.
Mathilda. 1819.
Valperga. 1823.
The Last Man. 1824.
The Fortunes of Perkin Warbeck. 1830.
Lodore. 1835.
Lives of the Most Eminent Literary and Scientific Men of Italy, Spain and Portugal. 3 vols. 1835–1837.
Falkner. 1837.
Rambles in Germany and Italy. 1844.
Collected tales and Stories. Edited by Charles Robinson. Baltimore: Johns Hopkins University Press, 1976.

Bibliography

Bennett, Betty T., ed. *The Letters of Mary Wollstonecraft Shelley.* 3 vols. Baltimore: Johns Hopkins University Press, 1980–83.
Fish, Audrey, Anne Mellor, and Esther Schor. *The Other Mary Shelley.* New York: Oxford University Press, 1993.
Marshall Florence A. *The Life and Letters of Mary Wollstonecraft Shelley.* 1889.
Mellor, Anne K. *Mary Shelley: Her Life, Her Fiction, Her Monsters.* London: Routledge, 1988.
Nitchie, Elizabeth. *Mary Shelley—Author of Frankenstein.* New Brunswick, N.J.: Rutgers University Press, 1953.
Spark, Muriel. *Mary Shelley—A Biography.* New York: E. P. Dutton, 1987.
Smith, Johanna. *Mary Shelley.* Evanston, Ill.: Northwestern University Press, 1996.
Williams, John. *Mary Shelley, A Literary Life.* London: Macmillan, 2000.

SHELLEY, PERCY BYSSHE 1792–1822

English poet

Along with Lord Byron and John Keats, Percy Bysshe Shelley belongs to the second generation of English Romantic poets. Shelley's literary reputation has undergone significant fluctuations: he was considered a major poet in the nineteenth century, but in the early twentieth century his reputation was seriously attacked, most notably by T. S. Eliot. In an essay in his collection *The Use of Poetry and the Use of Criticism* (1933), in which he refers to Shelley's "abuse of poetry," Eliot claimed that Shelley was a poet for whom ideas came first and that these ideas were adolescent. According to Eliot, this made it difficult to take Shelley seriously as a poet: "is it possible to ignore the 'ideas' in Shelley's poems, so as to be able to enjoy the poetry?"

Eliot's critical judgements were very influential both on F. R. Leavis, probably the most significant twentieth-century British critic, and on "New Criticism," which became the dominant critical approach in America between the 1940s and the 1960s. Shelley's reputation consequently suffered. Leavis, for example, demanded that poetic language should achieve "a sensuous realization" that enables it apparently to "enact its meaning," so that ideas or emotions for their own sake, or mere beauty of sound, were held in check. Shelley's poetry was found wanting when evaluated by such criteria. However, it could be argued that Shelley was being judged in accordance with a poetic and critical ideology based to a considerable degree on an admiration for poetry that employed wit in the manner of the metaphysical poets. The elaborate conceits and complex metaphors that one finds in John Donne are not to be found in a poem such as "Ode to the West Wind" (1819) which works rather in terms of the association of ideas. The connections Shelley makes in the "Ode" to which Leavis objects ("In what respects are the 'loose clouds' like 'decaying leaves'?") work through association and can be easily justified in terms of the poetic logic that Shelley employs in the poem. Shelley was one of the most intellectual of English poets and was extremely knowledgeable about philosophy and science. His associationism was almost certainly influenced by David Hume's philosophy, which claimed that the "association of ideas" was the basis of our understanding of the world.

Both Leavisism and New Criticism declined in influence after the 1960s and alternative critical approaches influenced by structuralism and poststructuralism emerged in the 1970s. Deconstructive criticism, in particular, was especially interested in Shelley. For example, in a volume designed to exemplify deconstructive criticism in action, titled *Deconstruction and Criticism* (1979), Shelley was discussed by several significant critics. It seems safe to assume that Shelley's reputation has recovered from the attacks by Eliot, Leavis, and their supporters.

If one looks at Shelley in the context of Romantic writing, which critics such as Leavis and the early New Critics had little interest in doing, his status as a major Romantic poet is difficult to deny. What is striking about Shelley is that he is both the most subjective and political of the Romantic poets. Romantic poetry in general is characterized by a tension between the subjectivity or imagination of the poet and the material world which is a resistant force. In Shelley subjectivity or imagination makes its strongest effort to overcome the recalcitrance of the material world and impose its vision on it. As he puts it in his *Defence of Poetry* (1821), the poet "not only beholds intensely the present as it is, and discovers those laws according to which present things are ordered, but he beholds the future in the present, and his thoughts are the germs of the flower and the fruit of latest time."

Shelley reacted strongly against the earlier Romantic poets, particularly William Wordsworth, both in poetic and in political terms. In Wordsworth one gains a strong sense of the otherness of the world, of nature. The mind and the imagination have to work hard to find or impose any meaning on something so vast and powerful as nature. Wordsworth and the other Romantics, apart from Shelley, tended to take a pessimistic view of the power of the imagination, believing that it inevitably diminished in power over time. Related to this was the political disillusionment of the first generation of Romantics with the idealism that fueled the French Revolution. In terms of the visionary and the political, it seemed necessary to settle for less. Shelley, however, rejected such pessimism, in regard both to the imagination and to politics. Though clearly an idealist, he believed politics could not, and should not, be separated from the visionary power of the imagination, and if both imagination and political idealism were strong enough there could be a total transformation of reality.

Shelley's idealism, however, did not entail a lack of interest in or a rejection of material reality. Ideals provided the mental power to fight against a corrupt and unjust society, and Shelley's political ideals were strongly influenced by such works as Thomas Paine's *Rights of Man* (1791) and William Godwin's *Enquiry Concerning Political Justice* (1793). Shelley was also a political activist. He wrote poems that directly engaged with political and social issues, notably *The Mask of Anarchy* (1819), provoked by the Peterloo massacre. He also wrote several political pamphlets and actively took part in political protest. He can be compared with William Blake in that they both refused to accept existing reality, seeing it as embodying previously created mental constructs that had become hardened and reified. For both Blake and Shelley, the chains of reality were "mind-forged," as Blake put it in his poem "London." The political implications of this are clear in the declaration by Shelley that "[t]he system of society as it exists must be overthrown from the foundations with all its superstructures of maxims and of forms before we shall find anything but disappointments in our intercourse with any but a few select spirits."

Though Shelley was strongly influenced by Plato, in his *Defence of Poetry* he rejects Plato's view that poetry is dangerous because there is no necessary connection between the aesthetic and the moral: "Poetry strengthens the faculty which is the organ of the moral nature of man, in the same manner as exercise strengthens a limb." He goes on to write, "the functions of the poetical faculty are two-fold: by one it creates new materials of knowledge, and power, and pleasure; by the other it engenders in the mind a desire to reproduce and arrange them according to a certain rhythm and order which may be called the beautiful

Joseph Severn, *Percy Bysshe Shelley (1792–1822)*. 1845. Reprinted courtesy of the Bridgeman Art Library.

and the good." A significant difference between Shelley and his Romantic predecessors is that he proclaimed himself an atheist, whereas Wordsworth, for example, returned to established Christian forms of belief. This suggests that for Shelley the imagination must function with even greater power to overcome the negative forces of the material world. He could not rely on God to help; this must be a purely human undertaking.

Some of Shelley's major poems can be seen as implicitly in dialogue with the work of his Romantic predecessors. In "Hymn to Intellectual Beauty" (1816), Shelley is concerned with why the visionary power visits us only inconstantly: "It visits with inconstant glance / Each human heart and countenance." This power, which he addresses as the "Spirit of BEAUTY," cannot be easily sustained and its loss is a human tragedy: "Why dost thou pass away and leave our state, / This dim vast veil of tears, vacant and desolate?" Only it can give life meaning and value, which makes it all the more inexplicable why it is so fleeting.

Shelley is implicitly alluding to the work of other Romantic poets who were also disturbed by the difficulty of retaining contact with a vision of meaning and value, one which can create beauty even in the midst of a reality of pain, ugliness and death. Wordsworth, in his "Ode: Intimations of Immortality" (1802–4) writes,

> Shades of the prison-house begin to close
> Upon the growing boy,
> But he beholds the light and whence it flows,
> He sees it in his joy . . .
> At length the Man perceives it die away
> And fade into the light of common day.

Samuel Taylor Coleridge expresses similar sentiments in "Dejection: An Ode" (1802): "My genial spirits fail, / And what can these avail / To lift the smoth'ring weight from off my breast?" And Shelley's contemporary, Keats, cannot sustain his vision of the Nightingale:

> Forlorn! The very word is like a bell
> To toll me back from thee to my sole self!
> Adieu! The fancy cannot cheat so well
> As she is famed to do, deceiving elf.

Though "Hymn to Intellectual Beauty" begins apparently in the same despairing vein, the poem refuses to accept such pessimism. The poem goes on to explore the nature of the vision and why it fades. Shelley recounts his first experience of it as a boy and how he vowed to dedicate his powers to serving it. Unlike Wordsworth, he is not willing to accept as consolation for its loss a more philosophical perspective on reality. For Wordsworth, "Though nothing can bring back the hour / Of splendour in the grass, of glory in the flower; / We will grieve not," but find solace "In the faith that looks through death, / In years that bring the philosophic mind." Shelley, however, is determined to preserve the visionary gleam, despite its inconstancy and the difficulty of maintaining contact with it in maturity. For him it is associated with a political force that can transform the world: "never joy illumed my brow / Unlinked with hope that thou wouldst free / This world from its dark slavery." As in "Ode to the West Wind," "Hymn to Intellectual Beauty" has a powerful democratic undercurrent. Shelley is not interested in the visionary for its own sake or in elevating the poet above people in general. The role of poetry is to strive to liberate humanity so that everyone is potentially able to experience the "Spirit of BEAUTY."

Romantic poetry is associated with a preoccupation with nature, and if one considers Shelley's work in relation to this theme it can seem intangible and lacking in concreteness if one compares his poetry with that of Coleridge and Wordsworth. Shelley's treatment of nature, however, has to be seen in relation to his idealism and his political perspective. In "To a Sky-lark" (1820) Shelley can again be seen as going beyond his Romantic predecessors in that he remains committed to the belief that the subjective vision can triumph over a resistant reality. When Wordsworth writes about nature one usually has a strong sense of something objectively present even if that is transformed through interaction with the poet's imagination. The first thing Shelley does in "To the Sky-lark" is to deny the objectivity of the bird: "Hail to thee, blithe spirit! / Bird thou never wert." What appeals to Shelley about the skylark as an image of nature is that it cannot be seen. It is so high in the sky that its song seems to be coming from a world beyond the natural one. This allows an imaginative engagement with its song greater than that which would take place if one could see the bird that is producing the sound.

Shelley goes on to create a series of images and associations that translate the bird's song into something transcendental: "Though dost float and run; / Like an unbodied joy whose race is just begun." Again its materiality is denied, with its being compared to an "unbodied joy." An association is suggested between the bird's song and poetry, since both can bring joy and vision into the world without bird or poet needing to be visible: "Like a Poet hidden / In the light of thought, / Singing hymns unbidden." Poetry, like the song of the unseen bird, transcends the poet's life and personality. The poem goes on to create a number of comparisons in which the connection between the object and what the object produces is broken. The effect is to release one from the constraints of time and change, and to liberate the imagination from dependence on the material world. Again poetry emerges not as a means of reflecting or commenting on the world but as a transformative force.

If Shelley is open to criticism, it is that his language is sometimes overblown and self-indulgent, as in this line from "Hymn to Intellectual Beauty": "I shrieked, and clasped my hands in ecstasy!" Often, however, what appears to be emotional self-indulgence can be justified in dramatic terms, as for example with the fourth stanza of "Ode to the West Wind" that contains the line "I fall upon the thorns of life! I bleed!" At this point Shelley is at his lowest ebb after having previously elevated himself to identification with the wind. This mental and emotional effort cannot be sustained and he entreats the wind to support him. In the final stanza his mental strength returns and he overcomes this temporary crisis, again identifying with the wind. It can be argued not only that it is this psychologically convincing, but that it is also structurally justified, as it prevents the poem being one-dimensional and creates an interesting dramatic interplay.

Perhaps one of the main reasons why Shelley is again considered a major poet also relates to his use of language. His poetry suggests that language is itself material and, when harnessed by the imagination, has the performative power to change our conception of reality.

K. M. NEWTON

Biography

Born Sussex 1792. Educated at Eton College and University College, Oxford; sent down after two terms in 1811 after publishing, with his friend James Hogg, *The Necessity of Atheism.* Married Harriet Westbrook, 1811. First important published poem, *Queen Mab*, 1813. Corresponded with William Godwin; left Harriet for Godwin's daughter Mary Wollstonecraft Godwin, 1814; married her in 1816 after wife Harriet's suicide; met Byron in Switzerland 1816; left England in 1818 and lived in various parts of Italy; drowned July 8, 1822.

Selected Works

The Letters of Percy Bysshe Shelley. 2 vols. Edited by Frederick L. Jones. Oxford: Clarendon Press, 1964.

The Complete Works of Percy Bysshe Shelley. 10 vols. Edited by Roger Ingpen and Walter E. Peck. London: Ernest Benn, 1965.

Shelley's Poetry and Prose: Authoritative Texts, Criticism. Edited by Donald H. Reiman and Sharon B. Power. New York: W. W. Norton, 1977.

Poems of Shelley Volume One 1804–1817. Edited by Geoffrey Matthews and Kelvin Everest. London: Longman, 1989.

Poems of Shelley Volume Two 1817–1819. Edited by Kelvin Everest and Geoffrey Matthews. Harlow, England: Longman, 2000.

Bibliography

Baker, Carlos. *Shelley's Major Poetry.* Princeton, N.J.: Princeton University Press, 1948.

Bloom, Harold, ed. *Deconstruction and Criticism.* London: Routledge and Kegan Paul, 1979.

Bennett, Betty T., and Stuart Curran eds. *Shelley: Poet and Legislator of the World.* Baltimore: Johns Hopkins University Press, 1996.

Cameron, Kenneth Neill. *The Young Shelley: Genesis of a Radical.* New York: Octagon, 1973.

Cameron, Kenneth Neill. *Shelley: The Golden Years.* Cambridge, Mass.: Harvard University Press, 1974.

Chernaik, Judith. *Lyrics of Shelley.* Cleveland, Ohio: Western Reserve University Press, 1972.

Dawson, P. M. S. *The Unacknowledged Legislator: Shelley and Politics.* Oxford: Clarendon Press, 1980.

Eliot, T. S. *The Use of Poetry and the Use of Criticism: Studies in the Relation of Criticism to Poetry in England.* London: Faber, 1968.

Leavis, F. R. *Revaluation: Tradition and Development in English Poetry.* London: Chatto and Windus, 1936.

Leighton, Angela. *Shelley and the Sublime: An Interpretation of the Major Poems.* Cambridge: Cambridge University Press, 1984.

O'Neill, Michael, ed. *Shelley.* London: Longman, 1993.

Swinden, Patrick, ed. *Shelley: Shorter Poems and Lyrics: A Casebook.* London: Macmillan, 1976.

Wasserman, Earl. *Shelley: A Critical Reading.* Baltimore: Johns Hopkins University Press, 1971.

Webb, Timothy. *Shelley: A Voice Not Understood.* Manchester: Manchester University Press, 1977.

SHERIDAN, RICHARD BRINSLEY 1751–1816

Irish playwright

Richard Brinsley Sheridan's theatrical works fill a gap between the more traditional strains of comedy and the fresh stimuli of the cult of sentiment introduced by Jean-Jacques Rousseau and Laurence Sterne. Sheridan had the great merit of restoring the most purely comical nature of comedy by infusing it with fresh vitality and humor.

Sheridan's career as a playwright was unusually short, and his most important works were written during a brief burst of creativity between 1775 and 1779. His early life offered a vital source of inspiration. His romantic entanglement with Elizabeth Linley originated a series of adventurous circumstances, including the opposition to their union by his and Elizabeth's families, an elopement, an illegal wedding in a French convent, and two duels with a rival.

Sheridan's first work, *The Rivals* (1775), met with considerable success although the first version, unrehearsed, too long, and even risqué in places, was harshly criticized. Plot and theme were to a great extent traditional (Captain Jack Absolute's passion for Lydia, opposed by their elders, Sir Anthony and Mrs. Malaprop, a romantic subplot with Julia and Faulkland, plus the usual machinery of comic side characters and unwilling duellers), but the strength of the piece lies in Sheridan's depiction of the absurdities and foibles of individual characters. Sheridan shows his linguistic ability in the brilliant verbosity of Mrs. Malaprop, to the point that the term "malapropism" in its current use denotes the pretentious and comical misuse of words.

The School for Scandal (1777), Sheridan's best-known work, is a classic of English comic theater. The plot is again based on a romantic intrigue and deception that is finally revealed, but the characterization of the two Surface brothers indicates that Sheridan could enrich a traditional comic framework with all the nuances of human nature. Joseph appears to be virtuous, but his virtue is deceiving and false, while Charles seems to be light-hearted but finally reveals himself as generous and loyal. Charles and Joseph were, in many respects, two sides of the same personality, two conflicting but indivisible and necessary aspects of Sheridan's own character, ever torn between generosity and perfidy, honesty and intrigue. The famous "screen scene" is the most celebrated display of Sheridan's skills in maneuvering and manipulating characters and settings in order to reveal the characters' real nature and motivations.

The Critic (1779) closed the happiest season of Sheridan's dramatic career. Inspired by George Villiers, second Duke of Buckingham's *The Rehearsal* (1671) and centering on the rehearsal of a tragedy, *The Spanish Armada*, the work was a satire on theater itself, and its environment and critics. Prime targets were the exhausted mode of heroic tragedy and in particular the playwright Richard Cumberland, who appears in the play as Sir Fretful Plagiary. As the late eighteenth-century drama was soon to decline into melodrama, Sheridan's attack on the excessively spectacular character and bombastic tone of the rehearsed tragedy was in many ways prophetic.

Besides his three major comedies, Sheridan wrote the farce *St. Patrick's Day* (1775), perhaps the fullest expression of Sheridan's own uneasy sense of Irishness. The Irish soldier O'Connor manages to marry the daughter of the old Justice Credulous and, with the aid of his skills in disguise, to persuade his father-in-law to accept him as a member of the family despite his nationality. *The Duenna* (1775), a comic opera, had a number of fine songs written by Sheridan's father-in-law Thomas Linley. *A Trip to Scarborough* (1777), an adaptation of John Vanbrugh's *The Relapse*, was written as soon as he took charge of the management of the Drury Lane Theatre.

From 1779 onward, politics attracted the greatest share of Sheridan's time and attention. A prominent member of the Whig circle of Holland House, he constantly refused to be labeled as a man of theater and struggled for recognition and success in politics rather than on the stage. However, the two aspects of Sheridan's life cannot be separated: while the rhetorical force of his speeches in Parliament derived from his own dramatic instinct (an example of this was his speeches about the impeachment of the governor of India, Warren Hastings, in 1787–88), his dramatic works, although mostly devoid of any explicit reference to contemporary events, presented characters and situations that were often imbued with his libertarian and typically Whig ideology (an instance is the criticism of parental tyranny in *The Rivals*). Sheridan's political radicalism came to the fore in his last work, the declamatory and spectacular tragedy *Pizarro* (1799), an adaptation of August von Kotzebue's *The Spaniards in Peru*, in which Sheridan drew on the same conventions he had satirized in *The Critic*.

Criticism has often paired Sheridan with Oliver Goldsmith on the basis of their alleged common hostility for the mode of the "comedy of sentiment" and their promotion of the "comedy of laughter." According to this view, Goldsmith and Sheridan advocated the restoration of the primary target of comedy as the vices of mankind and attacked the new generation of playwrights who had adulterated the original essence of comedy by introducing into it the cult of sentiment and feeling and the fundamentally benign vision of human nature popularized by the novels of Henry Mackenzie, Rousseau, and Sterne. However, Sheridan had an ambivalent attitude to sentimentalism; he mocked many of the conventions of sentimentalism but at the same time found in them necessary dramatic materials (this is evident from the presentation of Charles Surface's charity).

Sheridan infused the ruling sensibility of the age with the comical masquerades of the Italian *commedia dell'arte* and the whimsical humor of Restoration comedy, free of its attendant vulgarity. These were the qualities that were most appreciated by the Romantics. William Hazlitt and Charles Lamb thought highly of *The School for Scandal*, while Lord Byron, who shared with Sheridan the devotion to Whig ideals and wrote a "Monody on the Death of Richard Brinsley Sheridan," learned more than one lesson on the satire of human hypocrisy from the playwright, as is brilliantly evident in *Don Juan*.

MASSIMILIANO DEMATA

Biography

Born in Dublin, October 30, 1751. Son of Thomas, an actor and theater manager and Frances, a respected playwright and novelist. Attended school at Harrow and in 1770 joined his family in Bath. Moved to London in 1773 after marrying Elizabeth Linley, an accomplished singer, despite the opposition of his father and her family. His first son, Thomas, born in November 1775. Successful career as a playwright: *The Rivals* (premiered at Covent Garden on January 17, 1775; revised version on January 28); *St Patrick's Day* (Covent Garden, May 2, 1775); *The Duenna* (Covent Garden, November 21, 1775). In 1776 bought a large share of the Drury Lane Theatre and acted as business and artistic manager. More works followed: *A Trip to Scarborough* (Drury Lane, February 24, 1777); *The School for Scandal* (Drury Lane, May 8, 1777); *The Critic* (October 7, 1779); and, much later, *Pizarro* (Drury Lane, May 24, 1799). Elected member of Parliament for Stafford in 1780, became an intimate friend of Whig leader Charles James Fox and, like Fox himself, strenuously supported the French Revolution but later condemned Napoleon Bonaparte. Held ministerial posts in 1782, 1783, and 1806. In 1792 wife Elizabeth died, and in April 1795 married Hester Jane Ogle, by whom he had a second son, Charles Brinsley, in January 1796. Patronized the reconstruction of the Drury Lane Theatre in 1791, but the new building burned down in 1809. Failed reelection in October 1812. Plagued by debts and drunkenness, died on July 7, 1816, and was buried in Westminster Abbey.

Selected Works

The Rivals. 1775.
The School for Scandal. 1777.
The Critic. 1779.
Pizarro. 1799.

Bibliography

Auburn, Mark S. *Sheridan's Comedies: Their Contexts and Achievements.* Lincoln: University of Nebraska Press, 1977.
Davison, Peter, ed. *Sheridan: Comedies.* Basingstoke, England: Macmillan, 1986.
Kelly, Linda. *Richard Brinsley Sheridan: A Life*, London: Sinclair-Stevenson, 1997.
Loftis, John. *Sheridan and the Drama of Georgian England.* Oxford: Basil Blackwell, 1976.
Morwood, James. *The Life and Works of Richard Brinsley Sheridan.* Edinburgh: Scottish Academic Press, 1985.
Morwood, James, and David Crane, eds. *Sheridan Studies.* Cambridge: Cambridge University Press, 1995.
Rhodes, R. Crompton. *Harlequin Sheridan.* Oxford: Basil Blackwell, 1933.
Worth, Katharine. *Sheridan and Goldsmith.* Basingstoke, England: Macmillan, 1992.
Wills, Jack C. "Lord Byron and 'Poor Old Sherry,' Richard Brinsley Sheridan." In *Lord Byron and His Contemporaries; Essays from the Sixth International Byron Seminar.* Edited by Charles E. Robinson. Newark, Del.: University of Delaware Press, 1982.

SICKNESS

"I call the classic healthy, the romantic sickly." Johann Wolfgang von Goethe's statement points to a Romantic fascination with suffering, decay, and death. To some extent this interest derives from Edmund Burke's theory of the sublime, which finds aesthetic value in pain and terror, relocating the aesthetic within the body of the viewing subject. Whereas Burke emphasizes pain's appeal to the mind, the Marquis de Sade finds that it stimulates the "nether regions." Both, however, find pain to be the source of the most intense passions. Paradoxically, Romantic thought is drawn both to the aspirations of the spirit and the sensations of the mortal body. At times, this amounts to an unequal dualism in which immaterial things take precedence over material ones: "Heard melodies are sweet, but those unheard/Are sweeter" (John Keats, "Ode on a Grecian Urn"). More often, however—and especially in the work of Keats and Percy Bysshe Shelley—beauty and pleasure come to depend on mortality and to be intensified by it. Both Shelley's "Ode to the West Wind" and Keats's "To Autumn" address a season "sweet though in sadness" (Shelley), understanding, as Wallace Stevens would put it, that "Death is the mother of beauty." Mario Praz has aptly named this aesthetic "the Romantic agony."

To a large extent, this aestheticization of suffering grows out of an eighteenth-century interest in the interrelation of mind and body. At the same time that science was making the body more visible, bodily urges and sensations posed a challenge to the Enlightenment dominance of reason. While the enlightened mind was often portrayed as trapped in a limited and decaying body, neoclassicism simultaneously maintained an emphasis on the body's aesthetic form. Thus Jean-Louis David's *Death of Socrates* portrays the philosopher's reason triumphing over both the pleasures and pains of the body, and yet the body is depicted in its ideal, muscular form. Increasingly, however, the mind's ability to escape the body's limitations came into question. Eighteenth-century writers seem both plagued and fascinated by melancholy, or "the spleen," and James Boswell published a series of essays called The *Hypochondriack* for the *London Magazine* (1777–83).

Disease could still be used as a metaphor for moral corruption, but increasingly this infection was seen as the product of desire, whether possessive or repressed, as in William Blake's poem "The Sick Rose." Love itself becomes an infection in such works as Matthew Lewis's *The Monk*, Keats's "La Belle Dame Sans Merci," and Charles Baudelaire's *Les Fleurs du Mal.* (The last title is generally translated as *The Flowers of Evil*, but *mal* connotes sickness as well.) The German idealists Novalis and Friedrich Wilhelm Joseph von Schelling develop a "poetics of the baneful" in which moral and physical evil are one; and yet ironically, to try to separate good from evil, health from sickness, is itself wicked. Illness and sexuality thus become two sides of the same process through the imagery of touching and contagion.

Illness also occurs in Romantic writing as a consequence of violating natural law in its various senses. Samuel Taylor Coleridge's protagonist in *The Rime of the Ancient Mariner* suffers bodily and mental illness after slaying the albatross, and some recent studies have connected his journey with colonial expansion and the slave trade. In Mary Shelley's *Frankenstein: or, The Modern Prometheus*, Victor falls ill immediately after bringing the creature to life and several times subsequently in the narrative, as though replicating and suffering in his own body the violation of nature he has perpetrated. In other Gothic novels, the body and its suffering are presented as a means of encountering the "uncanny," the repressed bodily fears that challenge the delineation of self and other. Even in the apparently less embodied novels of Jane Austen, discussions of health and illness both disguise and expose the operation of social and gender politics.

The paintings of Eugène Delacroix, Theodore Géricault, Francisco Jose de Goya y Lucientes, and Antoine-Jean Gros all emphasize the suffering body, even when their themes are public and historical. The shipwrecked survivors in Géricault's *Le radeau de la Méduse* (*Raft of the Medusa*), for example, may be seen as representing what Hugh Honour calls a "cult of failure" among the Romantics, in which the artist becomes a victim of his own unfulfilled genius. Disease, by extension, became less a mark of shame than of honor. The very sensitivity and imagination that marked the artist also endangered him and, it was thought, rendered him susceptible not only to madness and melancholy but also to physical illness.

Literary and artistic representations of bodily illness were increasingly influenced by philosophical medicine and the cult of sensibility. With the shift from reason to feeling, the body became identified as the seat of emotion and sympathy. It is not surprising, therefore, that actual physical illness came to be seen as either a sign or a cause of increased emotional sensitivity. Tuberculosis became the incarnation of the "melancholy character": as Shelley wrote to Keats, "this consumption is a disease particularly fond of people who write such good verses as you have done." To list all the Romantic figures who were actually ill would be impossible, but Jane Austen, Emily Brontë, Frédéric François Chopin, Samuel Taylor Coleridge, Thomas De Quincey, Novalis, Jean-Jacques Rousseau, as well as Keats all had illnesses that both shaped and hindered their work. Dorothy Wordsworth's journals attest to frequent ill health on the part of herself and her brother William, despite their robust walking habits. In the case of Coleridge and De Quincey, chronic physical pain led to dependence on opium, an addiction that was not yet recognized as a disease in itself but that further shaped their understanding of imagination and the mind. Biography slips into symbolism, so that the writer's illness, whether physical or mental, becomes a sign of his marked condition as *poète maudit*. Insofar as the writer or artist is different from others, he suffers; his suffering in turn increases the sensitivity that made him different in the first place. The question remains, however, whether that suffering increases his empathy for others, as in Shelley's *Prometheus Unbound*, or his solipsism, as in Shelley's *Alastor*. Sickness thus represents one way in which Romanticism grapples with the relation between internal and external realities, self and other, subjectivity and objectivity.

JENNIFER DAVIS MICHAEL

Bibliography

Bewell, Alan. *Romanticism and Colonial Disease*. Baltimore: Johns Hopkins University Press, 1999.

Bruhm, Steven. *Gothic Bodies: The Politics of Pain in Romantic Fiction*. Philadelphia: University of Pennsylvania Press, 1994.

Crook, Nora, and Derek Guiton. *Shelley's Venomed Melody*. Cambridge: Cambridge University Press, 1986.

de Almeida, Hermione. *Romantic Medicine and John Keats*. New York: Oxford University Press, 1991.

Goellnicht, Donald C. *The Poet-Physician: Keats and Medical Science*. Pittsburgh: University of Pittsburgh Press, 1984.

Honour, Hugh. *Romanticism*. London: Penguin, 1979.

Krell, David Farrell. *Contagion: Sexuality, Disease, and Death in German Idealism and Romanticism*. Bloomington: Indiana University Press, 1998.

Praz, Mario. *The Romantic Agony*. 2d ed. New York: Oxford University Press, 1970.

Sontag, Susan. *Illness as Metaphor*. New York: Farrar, Straus and Giroux, 1978.

Stafford, Barbara Maria. *Body Criticism: Imaging the Unseen in Enlightenment Art and Medicine*. Cambridge, Mass.: MIT Press, 1991.

SIDDONS, SARAH 1755–1831

English actress

Sarah Siddons was a member of a theatrical dynasty, the Kembles, which was both to dominate the London theater scene and—in the enthusiastic reception of audiences, critics and artists in various media—to establish on a much wider scale a powerful new convention for the physical and vocal expression of passion and pathos. She performed in Shakespeare, in the later seventeenth-century tragedies of Thomas Otway and Nicholas Rowe, and in a few, always classical and historical, plays by contemporary writers. She played the role of Jane in Joanna Baillie's *De Monfort*, where she developed a heightened but emotionally intimate style of acting that audiences felt embodied familiar characters with a new immediacy. Siddons surpassed her actor brothers Charles and James in fame, to become a cultural icon whose allure and complexity depended on her ability to project irresistibly powerful emotions, notably of despair and grief, but also, as in her performance of Volumnia in William Shakespeare's *Coriolanus*, of a triumphalist sense of grandeur and self-worth. Her most powerful roles were those that presented her as mother and wife; in this, and in its continuity with the image she built up of her private life, she redefined for her period the actress in a way that countered the association of the profession with the transgressive and the unrespectable.

She was by no means an immediate success. Discovered in the provinces by an agent of David Garrick, she was unable to cope with the demands of the Drury Lane Theatre, with its huge and often noisy audience, and her early performances as Shakespeare's Portia in *The Merchant of Venice* and as Lady Anne in *Richard III* were unsuccessful. But she soon found a style of acting that projected vividly into those cavernous, gas-lit spaces, learning to use her powerfully expressive, very dark eyes, and exploiting her height and her classical profile in a language of gesture that was often taken to be "timeless," certainly not of the mundane world. She pioneered a freer style of costuming, abandoning the still current hoop skirts and wigs for flowing hair and loose drapery (playing the sleepwalking scene in *Macbeth*, for example, in simple white satin). This allows a language of movement both spontaneously expressive and "universal," and a tragic transcendence of time and place. It was central to her concept of this particular character, as outlined in her published "Remarks on the Character of Lady Macbeth," that an essential femininity was the source of her power over her husband, and that it was the tension between her personal vulnerability and a willed ruthlessness which gave her force but eventually destroyed her. Perhaps most important, she found a voice of a plaintive singing quality, often described by her contemporaries as "melodious," but capable also of causing some amusement, as she tended to drop into it, often inappropriately, in daily life.

The hard work and intelligence that lay behind the intensive preparation for her great roles were highly unusual at a time when actors and actresses often knew little, apart from their own roles, of the play they were in, let alone its context. Siddons would, for example, leave her dressing room door open when she was playing Constance in Shakespeare's *King John* so that she could hear the characters on stage laying the plots to deprive her and her son of the throne, and so build the emotions for her entrance accordingly. She was famed also for remaining entirely in character even when not speaking, or when her presence in a scene was secondary. More recent critics have often seized on this as evidence that other actors of this period lapsed out of role entirely, but it seems more like a token of an intense emotional concentration on her part, still rare and very difficult to achieve, as a glance away from the speaking characters to the silent in almost any modern Shakespeare production is just as likely to reveal.

The result of this was an adulation, a reputation for absolute preeminence, to be only matched by the effect made in the mid-twentieth century by the opera singer Maria Callas. William Hazlitt (a political skeptic, but always a passionate appreciator of performance), in a retrospect of 1818, wrote about Siddons that she "raised Tragedy to the skies, or brought it down from thence. . . . Power was seated on her brow, passion emanated from her breast as from a shrine. She was tragedy personified. . . . She was not only the idol of the people, she not only hushed the tumultuous shouts of the pit in breathless expectation, and quenched the blaze of surrounding beauty in silent tears, but to the retired and lonely student, through long years of solitude, her face has shone as if an eye had appeared from heaven; her name has been as if a voice has opened the chambers of the human heart, or as if a trumpet had awakened the sleeping and the dead. To have seen Mrs Siddons, was an event in every one's life." Other writers (such as Samuel Taylor Coleridge and Charles Lamb) who deny her value do so reductively, and without detail, putting her success down to a trick of voice or gesture. They seem to resist the force of theater in embodying the power of an abstract idea, and in uniting the crowd and the solitary imagination, which Hazlitt celebrates through Siddons. Her rep-

utation survived a gradual estrangement from her husband, who managed her business affairs with some inefficiency, and seems to have resented her success, and survived her scandalous involvement with a younger couple attached to the theater, the Galindos, who seem to have exploited her financially while involving themselves in her emotional needs, to the point where Mrs. Galindo published a defamatory pamphlet, accusing Siddons of emotional cruelty in hyperbolic but unspecific terms.

Wisely, Siddons retired from the stage while still greatly in demand, to give the occasional highly esteemed solo show, most notably a one-woman reading of *Macbeth*. Her funeral was very much a public, almost regal, occasion, emphasizing that the stage had not simply achieved a central cultural status but had, in a period when the monarchy was plagued by scandal and a marked failure of charisma, come close to replacing it as an imaginative focus for at least the metropolitan public.

EDWARD BURNS

Biography

Born, 1755, while her parents were on tour, in Brecon; Debut, 1767, in her parents' company, in Worcester; discovered, 1775, by an agent of David Garrick's, playing Shakespeare's Rosalind in Cheltenham; made an unsuccessful debut at the Drury Lane Theatre as Portia (*Merchant of Venice*); returned, 1782, to Drury Lane, to triumph in the title role of Thomas Southerne's *Isabella*; first performances as Shakespeare's Lady Macbeth, 1784. Drury Lane pulled down, 1791, to be rebuilt and reopened in 1794; in the interim, the Kembles played at the Haymarket. Created the role of Jane in Joanna Baillie's *De Montfort*, 1800. Took on her last new role, Hermione in Shakespeare's *The Winter's Tale*, 1802. Siddons, the Kembles, and Elizabeth Inchbald moved their operation from Drury Lane to Covent Garden. In 1812 gave farewell performance at Covent Garden, as Lady Macbeth. Gave public readings from Shakespeare and Milton, 1812–13; Charles Kemble retired, 1821; Siddons died in 1831 and was given a public funeral.

Bibliography

Boaden, James. *Memoirs of Mrs. Siddons.* 1827.

Booth, Micheal R., John Stokes, and Susan Basnett. *Three Tragic Actresses: Siddons, Rachel, Ristori.* Cambridge: Cambridge University Press, 1996.

Manvell, Roger. *Sarah Siddons.* London: G. P. Putnam's Sons.

Richards, Sandra. *The Rise of the English Actress.* London: Macmillan, 1993.

Schofield, Mary Anne, and Celia Macheski. *Curtain Calls: British and American Women and the Theater 1660–1820.* Athens, Ohio: University of Ohio Press, 1991.

Straub, Kristina. *Sexual Suspects: Eighteenth Century Players and Sexual Ideology.* Princeton, N.J.: Princeton University Press, 1992.

West, Shearer. *The Image of the Actor.* New York: St. Martin's Press, 1991.

SIMMS, WILLIAM GILMORE 1806–1870

American novelist, poet, playwright, biographer, and literary editor

William Gilmore Simms was a preeminent literary figure of the antebellum American South. He is best remembered today as the author of historical romances set in South Carolina during the colonial and revolutionary periods, but he was a prolific and energetic practitioner of nearly every literary form. Through his numerous editorships of literary magazines and newspapers, he was able to encourage and assist fellow Southern writers, including Edgar Allan Poe, and generally advance the cause of American literature, Southern literature in particular.

Simms was the only surviving child of reasonably prosperous parents in Charleston, South Carolina. After the death of his mother in 1808, his father, a merchant, moved first to Mississippi, then Tennessee, and he remained in the care of his maternal grandmother. Throughout a lonely childhood, he spent his time reading avidly and began publishing poetry (heavily influenced by Lord Byron, in particular) in local papers when only sixteen. His first book, a long poem called *Monody* (1825), was published when he was nineteen. In 1824 he visited his father in the Southwest and traveled extensively in Indian country, experiences that he would later put to profitable use in his fiction.

After practicing law for a couple of years, Simms gave up the relative security of that profession to pursue his literary career, becoming editor of the Charleston *City Gazette* in 1829. The failure of that venture in 1832, coupled with his first wife's death, left him despondent. Seeking a new direction, Simms traveled to the north, to New York, Philadelphia, and Massachusetts, to cultivate literary friendships and professional contacts. A series of minor successes eventually led to Simms's attempting a long work of fiction, and in 1834 he produced *Guy Rivers*, the first of what would come to be known as his "border romances." A novel of high adventure and romance, set on the frontier of Georgia during the American Revolution, *Guy Rivers* proved to be enormously popular in both the north and south and firmly established his literary reputation.

Simms has often been dismissed by critics as a writer whose explicit bias for the south rendered his works unpalatable for any audience outside his native region, even at the time they were published. However, in the mid–1830s, at the height of his popularity, if not his creative power, this does not seem to have been the case; during this period Simms was one of the most successful authors in America, in financial and critical terms. In novels such as *The Yemassee* (1835) and *The Partisan* (1835), Simms satisfied the public's appetite for straightforward tales of heroism, with a strongly nationalistic flavor and distinctively American settings. In this, he was clearly working in the tradition of James Fenimore Cooper and Walter Scott; but his works also show the Gothic influence of Charles Brockden Brown and William Godwin, or a psychological fascination with crime borrowed from Edward Bulwer-Lytton, as in *Martin Faber* (1834) or *Confession* (1841). Simms always argued that he wrote "romances" rather than novels; this form freed him from certain constraints, and aligned him with an epic, poetic tradition: "They involve sundry of the elements of heroic poetry. They

are imaginative, passionate, metaphysical; they deal chiefly in trying situation, bold characterization, & elevating moral. . . ."

Although he acknowledged his debt to Cooper, Simms is a better writer than his more famous contemporary in many ways. His plots are more streamlined and plausible (if equally clichéd), his dialogue more fluent, and his depiction of Indians, in particular, indicates a degree of firsthand knowledge that Cooper lacked, evident in his greater interest in tribal ritual and cultural tradition. Perhaps most strikingly, the lush, romantic style of Simms's writing imbues the landscape itself with an animating sexual potency. A famous instance of this occurs in *The Yemassee*, in which Simms describes, using highly eroticized language, how his heroine, a Puritan minister's daughter, is transfixed by a snake. The implication here is typical of Simms: that the Southern environment engenders different moral, physical, and emotional responses that that of the North.

In the early part of his career, Simms's political opinions, despite his Southern pride, were firmly Unionist; it was his refusal to compromise his editorial stand against nullification in 1831–32 that led to the decline of the *City Gazette*. His main concern, in common with his literary contemporaries Robert Montgomery Bird, James Fenimore Cooper, and James Kirke Paulding, was the promotion of a national literature. As he wrote in an advertisement for *Magnolia* magazine in 1842, "The creation of a national literature is, next to the actual defence of a country, by arms, against the invader, one of the first duties of patriotism." But national literature and sectional literature were not mutually exclusive; by celebrating the history of a part, Simms maintained, he was giving strength to the whole.

In the 1840s, while continuing to produce novels, Simms branched out into biography, history, and political writing, resumed his career as an editor, and even served in the South Carolina legislature. As his career progressed, he made several ill-advised attempts to shift the scene of his novels to exploit his long-term interest in Spanish colonialism, but this caused commercial and critical failures. However, each new instalment of his border romances—which he conceived, collectively, to be an "epic of the South"—demonstrated his burgeoning confidence and ability as a writer, making it ironic that *Guy Rivers*, the first of the series, should remain the best known.

However, Simms gradually began to resent what he perceived to be the oppression of the South by the industrial North. This sentiment took an increasingly strong hold of him, and by the late 1840s he was actively secessionist in his political views. Unfortunately for Simms's reputation, then and now, the period of his greatest literary maturity coincided with the emergence of this political stance. In the four novels published between 1851–56—*Katharine Walton, The Sword and the Distaff* (later renamed *Woodcraft*), *The Forayers*, and *Eutaw*—Simms uses the Revolutionary War as an analogy and justification for the Southern desire for independence, and this led him to be ostracized by his publishers, and by Northern literary magazines. As a result, these works, which show a command of structure, characterization, and dialogue far superior to his earlier books, were largely neglected.

Simms's world was torn apart by the Civil War he had been anticipating for the previous decade. His second wife died in 1863; and Woodlands, his plantation home, was burned down by Union soldiers, resulting in the loss of his enormous library. Disillusioned by the defeat of his beloved South, Simms nevertheless endeavored to support his large family with his pen in the last five years of his life, while maintaining his plantation (now bereft of slaves), and editing three different newspapers. His final collapse in 1870 was inevitable.

Simms suffered the fate of all the historical romancers of the early nineteenth century, and was dismissed by the literary realists who flourished after the war, although his works remained in print until about 1900. To the case against Simms could be added his entrenched support for the defeated South, which remains an obstacle to his reintroduction to the canon of American literature. However, in the last thirty years, some critical attention has been refocused on Simms, rightly conceiving him to be of enormous cultural importance, because of the evolution of his political beliefs. However, despite his talent, his popularity, his prolific output, and the breadth of his influence on American life and letters, Simms will always be inextricably linked with the slave-owning culture of which he was a chronicler, apologist, and representative product.

ROWLAND HUGHES

Biography

Born in Charleston, South Carolina, April 17, 1806. Entered College of Charleston in 1816, for two years; apprenticed to pharmacist, 1818–24; visited father in Southwest, 1824. Published first book, the poem *Monody*, 1825. Began to study law, and was admitted to the South Carolina Bar in 1827. Married Anna Malcolm Giles in 1826; they had one daughter in 1827. Gave up law to edit *City Gazette*, 1829–32. Father died, 1830; wife died, February 1832. Published dramatic poem *Atalantis* in 1832, with reasonable success; began writing fiction with *Martin Faber* in 1833, and started career as professional writer. Married Chevillette Eliza Roach in 1836—they eventually had twelve children. Moved to wife's family home, a plantation called Woodlands. Edited *Magnolia* magazine, 1842–43; *Southern and Western Magazine and Review*, 1845; and the *Southern Quarterly Review*, 1849–54. After the Civil War, edited the *Columbia Phoenix*, 1865; the *Daily South Carolinian*, 1865–66; and the *Courier*, 1870. Died June 11, 1870.

Selected Works

Fiction
Martin Faber. 1833.
Guy Rivers. 1834.
The Yemassee: A Romance of Carolina. 1835. Edited by Joseph V. Ridgely. New Haven, Conn.: College and University Press Twayne, 1964.
The Partisan. 1835.
Mellichampe. 1835.
Richard Hurdis. 1838.
Border Beagles. 1840.
Beauchampe. 1842.
The Wigwam and the Cabin. 1845.
Katharine Walton. 1851.
The Sword and the Distaff. 1852. Later retitled *Woodcraft*.
The Forayers. 1855.
Eutaw. 1856.
The Cassique of Kiawah. 1859.
The Cub of the Panther. 1869.
Voltmeier. 1869.

Poetry
Poems Descriptive, Dramatic, Legendary and Contemplative. 1853.

Nonfiction
The History of South Carolina. 1840.
The Life of Francis Marion. 1844.
Views and Reviews (first and second series). 1846.
The Letters of William Gilmore Simms. Collected and edited by Mary C. Simms Oliphant, Alfred Taylor Odell, and T. C. Duncan Eaves; introduction by Donald Davidson; biographical sketch by Alexander S. Salley. Columbia: University of South Carolina Press, 1952–1982.

Bibliography

Guilds, John Caldwell, ed. *Long Years of Neglect: The Work and Reputation of William Gilmore Simms.* Fayetteville: University of Arkansas Press, 1988.
Guilds, John Caldwell, and Caroline Collins, eds. *William Gilmore Simms and the American Frontier.* 1997.
Parks, Edd Winfield. *William Gilmore Simms as Literary Critic.* Athens, Ga.: University of Georgia Press, 1961.
Ridgely, J. V. *William Gilmore Simms.* New York: Twayne, 1962.
Wakelyn, Jon L. *The Politics of a Literary Man: William Gilmore Simms.* Westport, Conn.: Greenwood Press, 1973.
Watson, Charles S. *From Nationalism to Secessionism: The Changing Fiction of William Gilmore Simms.* Westport, Conn.: Greenwood Press, 1993.
Wimsatt, Mary Ann. *The Major Fiction of William Gilmore Simms: Cultural Traditions and Literary Form.* Baton Rouge: Louisiana State University Press, 1989.

SINCERITY

Sincerity, in simplest terms the correspondence between an actual feeling or belief and its expression, gained new importance as a value and ideal during the Romantic period. The word *sincerity*, from the Latin *sincerus* (pure, unadulterated), is present in French (*sincérité*) as early as the thirteenth century and in English in the sixteenth century; early usage generally referred to the genuineness of a Christian doctrine or belief. In the Romantic period, the emphasis that writers put on personal experience and feeling amounted to an unprecedented commitment to sincerity. This commitment reflected the changing status of the self and of poetry during that period. The dissolution of the authority of political and religious tradition resulted in a new focus on the personal experience of the individual as a repository of truth. Meanwhile, the Enlightenment emphasis on reason and the advances of science were seen to threaten poetry's claims to truth. As M. H. Abrams explains in *The Mirror and the Lamp*, poets defended themselves against the rationalists by implicitly claiming that their writings were true because they were sincere. For Romantic writers, sincerity was no longer an attractive but dispensable social trait (as it appears to have been in the writings of the earlier eighteenth century); it had become an indispensable foundation of truth itself.

The Romantic commitment to sincerity is widely recognizable (almost any poem from the period might serve as an example) but difficult to define consistently because Romantic writers did not explicitly theorize it. The term seldom appears within their works, and it is not discussed by the theorists of Romanticism in Germany or by England's major theorist, Samuel Taylor Coleridge. Nonetheless, two writers from the period might be named the founders of Romantic sincerity: Jean-Jacques Rousseau and William Wordsworth. Their disparate works demonstrate some of the concerns and problems characteristic of the Romantic emphasis on this quality.

In the French tradition, Romantic sincerity is exemplified by Rousseau's *Confessions* (1781), in which the writer declares: "I have resolved on an enterprise which has no precedent, and which, once complete, will have no imitator. My purpose is to display to my kind a portrait in every way true to nature, and the man I shall portray will be myself."

Rousseau's personal honesty in this document is indeed unprecedented, including detailed accounts of his sexual development and difficulties, disclosures of wrongdoing, and evidence of his growing mental instability. Rousseau's claim to sincerity is based not on the universal applicability of his experience but on his originality: "I am made unlike any one I have ever met; I will even venture to say that I am like no one in the whole world." A different version of Romantic sincerity can be identified in Rousseau's political philosophy. His *Discours sur les sciences et les arts* (*A Discourse on the Sciences and the Arts*, 1750) argues that, rather than purifying morals, the sciences and arts corrupt humankind's original, essential nature. Implicit in this argument is the suggestion that sincerity requires clinging to this essential nature and resisting the corruptions of literary artifice. This version of sincerity, instead of depending upon personal originality, depends upon a belief in a universal human nature as the foundation of truth.

It is this latter version of sincerity that is recognizable in Wordsworth's writings, in particular his preface to the *Lyrical Ballads* (1802). Here Wordsworth commits himself to sincerity by claiming that "all good poetry is the spontaneous overflow of powerful feelings" and suggests that these feelings should be conveyed in the tone of "a man speaking to men." He argues that poetry should avoid the elaborate neoclassical style of his predecessors and sets forth what might be called an aesthetics of sincerity to counter this style, an aesthetics of spontaneity and simplicity based on a "humble and rustic life . . . because, in that condition, the essential passions of the heart find a better soil in which they can attain their maturity, are less under restraint, and speak a plainer and more emphatic language." (The idea of spontaneous, natural poetry is also explored under the label of "naïve" poetry in Johann Christoph Friedrich von Schiller's *Uber naïve und sentimentalische Dichtung* [*On Naive and Sentimental Poetry*, 1795–96], perhaps the closest thing in German Romantic writing to a theory of poetic sincerity). In the "Essay upon Epitaphs" (1810), an essay much less influential than the well-known Preface, Wordsworth attempts to establish "a criterion of sincerity," but, perhaps symptomatically, finds it easier to describe sincerity's absence than its presence. His strongest statements about the importance of sincerity, however, can be found in this work: "Literature is here so far identified with morals, the quality of the act so far determined by our notion of the aim and purpose of the agent, that nothing can please us, however well executed in its kind, if we are persuaded that the primary virtues of sincerity, earnestness and a moral interest in the main object are wanting."

The examples of Rousseau and Wordsworth demonstrate some of the possible contradictions of a commitment to sincerity. Sincerity might entail a commitment to personal originality or it might entail a search for an essential and universal human nature. The association of sincerity with feeling marks a new trust in feeling as a morally positive and socially beneficial faculty, instead of an anarchic force that must be controlled by reason. But it will be clear that the simultaneous demand for natural simplicity and emotional intensity that Romantic sincerity makes has the potential to create conflict. In the English tradition, for example, the rural tales found in Wordsworth's *Lyrical Ballads* differ greatly from the interest in extreme states of emotion exhibited by Lord Byron and Percy Bysshe Shelley. Romantic sincerity is perhaps best understood as a cluster of newly urgent questions—Is it possible to be true to myself? If so, to which self am I to be true? What kinds of aesthetic projects are most conducive to honest self-expression?—rather than a quality that can be dependably located or defined.

DEBORAH FORBES

Bibliography

Ball, Patricia M. "Sincerity: The Rise and Fall of a Critical Term," *Modern Language Review* 59, no. 1 (1964): 1–11.

Forbes, Deborah. *Sincerity's Shadow: Self-Consciousness in British Romantic and Mid-Twentieth-Century American Poetry.* Cambridge, Mass.: Harvard University Press, 2004.

Guilhamet, Leon. *The Sincere Ideal: Studies on Sincerity in Eighteenth-Century English Literature.* Montreal: McGill-Queen's University Press, 1974.

Perkins, David. *Wordsworth and the Poetry of Sincerity.* Cambridge, Mass.: Harvard University Press, 1964.

Peyre, Henri. *Literature and Sincerity.* New Haven, Conn.: Yale University Press, 1963.

Trilling, Lionel. *Sincerity and Authenticity.* Cambridge, Mass.: Harvard University Press, 1971.

SISMONDI, JEAN-CHARLES-LÉONARD SIMONDE DE 1773–1842

Swiss historian and economist

Jean-Charles Léonard Simonde de Sismondi was nothing if not prolific. He established his reputation with a sixteen-volume history of the Italian republics (which was the first work to treat Italy as a nation and survey its post-Roman history) and concluded his career with a thirty-one volume history of France, left unfinished at his death. In between, Sismondi published, among other works, a historical novel set in the year 492 C.E., a history of the fall of Rome, and an array of pamphlets on such topics as paper money, the slave trade, the French constitution of 1815, prejudice, the future, America, and the progress of religion in the nineteenth century. Though in his own lifetime Sismondi was known primarily as an historian, he has since received attention for his writings on economics. He began as an advocate of classical laissez-faire principles in a French-language popularization of Adam Smith, but Sismondi later became one of the earliest critics of classical political economy and engaged in disputes with Thomas Malthus, David Ricardo, and Léon Say.

Histoire des républiques italiennes du moyen âge (*A History of the Italian Republics*, 1807–18), for which Sismondi received notice throughout Europe, surveys the history of Italy from the fall of the Western empire to Sismondi's own time, though it focuses most closely on the history of the republics from the twelfth to the sixteenth centuries. After an introductory volume that moves quickly from the fall of the Western empire in 476 C.E. through the centuries that followed, Sismondi settles into his detailed narrative with the struggle of Barbarosa (Frederich I) and the Lombard cities in the twelfth century. No friend to political despots or the Roman Catholic Church, Sismondi suggests that after the dominance of feudalism, kings, and priests, the Italian republics, especially Florence, emerged from the Dark Ages and, through strength of civic devotion and love of freedom, recaptured and transmitted to the rest of Europe the liberty lost with the demise of the Greco-Roman world. The Italian Renaissance is explained as an outgrowth of this individual and civic freedom. The work as a whole underscores Sismondi's lifelong commitment to the view that it is not race or climate, but rather the social order, that forms the character of society and determines its wellbeing. As Sismondi states, his concern is with the influence of "l'ordre social sur le charactère du citoyen" ("the social order on the character of the citizen") and that "pour comprendre l'organisation des peuples libres, il fallait les voir agir plutot qu'étudier leur legislation" ("to understand the organization of free people, one needs to see them act rather than study their law"). We know from Mary Shelley's journal that Percy Bysshe Shelley read Sismondi in 1819, and it seems likely that Sismondi's account of the Italian republics influenced Shelley's emphasis on Italy in the descriptions of the trajectory of liberty found in the "Ode to Liberty," *Hellas*, and the *Defence of Poetry*. Lord Byron, too, was an admirer, and, in 1821, used the Italian history as source material for *The Two Foscari*.

The publication of the initial volumes of his Italian history earned Sismondi a considerable reputation, and in 1810 he was asked by his native Geneva to deliver a series of public lectures on European literature. These were later developed into *De la littérature du Midi de l'Europe* (*Historical View of the Literature of the South of Europe*, 1813), a survey of Italian, Provençal, Spanish, and Portugese literature notable for its turn away from the orthodoxy of French classicism. Sismondi sought to judge literature not based on preestablished principles but rather on an author's intentions, and he placed great value on imaginative vigor. For this reason, many critics include Sismondi among the initiators of French Romanticism. The volume is marked by a concern with the relation between social conditions and literature, and Sismondi repeatedly asks about the effects on literature of political and religious changes. This, of course, had been the earlier topic of Madame Anne-Louise-Germaine de Staël's *De la littérature considerée dans ses rapports avec les institutions sociales* (*A Treatise of Ancient and Modern Literature* and *The Influence of Literature upon Society*, 1800). Where, however, Madame de Staël saw the literature of northern Europe as Romantic and the south as classical, Sismondi suggested that only French literature was truly classical, and where Staël insisted on the importance of climate in shaping culture, Sismondi stressed the importance of institutions and, as he was articulating in the Italian history, firmly believed that free institutions produced better literature. Despite his move away from classicism, Sismondi remained too classical for William Hazlitt, who reviewed *De la littérature* in the *Edinburgh Review* in 1815, eight years before the publication of its English translation. While Hazlitt found some passages "highly interesting," Sismondi's characterizations of Dante Alighieri, Giovanni Bocaccio, and Petrarch drew fire. Sismondi's bias for external image, Hazlitt asserted, prevented him from appreciating the internal power of the three Tuscans, whom Hazlitt claimed as contemporaries to be judged by their quality of passion and imagination.

Though he was known as an unwavering opponent of Napoleon Bonaparte, Sismondi, who was in Paris overseeing the eighth through tenth volumes of his Italian history through the press, witnessed the emperor's return in 1815 and supported Napoleon during his brief second reign, the Hundred Days. The reversal is difficult to explain but was likely motivated both by Sismondi's disgust at the strength of European reactionary forces and by his belief that the seemingly chastened emperor offered the best prospects for European liberalism. Sismondi published four articles in the *Moniteur universal*, France's official government newspaper, in support of Napoleon's proposed constitution, which was written by his friend and fellow Staël protégé, Benjamin Constant de Rebrecque. Sismondi's support of the emperor was, however, likely due to more than cool reason. Napoleon's return captured Sismondi's imagination and he later described his private audience with Napoleon as one of the greatest moments of his life. With the restoration of the monarchy in July, Sismondi promptly returned to Geneva.

Sismondi's belief in political liberty and his insistence on the power that institutions have to shape individual lives and the national character, evident in his historical writings, also shaped his economic thought, which, after his 1803 volume *De la richesse commerciale* (*On Commercial Wealth*) was increasingly opposed to laissez-faire policies and in favor of state intervention. Indeed, Sismondi was one of the pioneering advocates of unemployment insurance, sickness benefits, and pension schemes. Because Sismondi's economic writings emphasized the interests of the working classes and attacked more popular economists who favored landlords and fundholders, his work was largely ignored. Among economists, he has been remembered as an early opponent of Say's Law in the so-called general glut controversy, which reached its peak during the 1820s. Say's Law basically asserted the unlimited growth potential of the economy and was used to imply that equilibrium was possible at any level of aggregate production; that, in other words, supply always equals demand and a general glut is a logical impossibility. Sismondi, along with Malthus, however, recognized that because investment increased output capacity it is possible, in the short run, to have a supply of consumer goods in excess of the demand for consumption. Though Sismondi's arguments were largely ignored by Ricardo and his supporters, he did develop a prolonged friendship and correspondence with Say. Later, Karl Marx went so far as to characterize Thomas Malthus's *Principles of Political Economy* (1820) as merely the "English translation" of Sismondi.

John Stuart Mill called Sismondi's work "sprightly, and frequently eloquent," and Thomas Babbington Macaulay referred to him as "a favourite writer." Sismondi has, however, earned few laurels as a prose stylist. His writing is long-winded, and full of countless anecdotes and an overabundance of details. "Sismondi interests me," the French historian Louis Clair de Beaupoil, Comte de Saint-Aulaire declared, "as much as it is possible to be interested when one is bored." Still, what he lacks in narrative skill, Sismondi makes up for in force of expression, insight, and principle, and his writings all share an interest in widening and preserving liberty while amending its abuses.

JONATHAN SACHS

Biography

Born in Geneva, May 9, 1773. Apprenticed in the Lyon office of the Swiss commercial house Eynard et Cie, 1792; moved with his family to England, 1793–94. Returned to Geneva, where he was briefly incarcerated, 1794. Ran family farm in Pescia Tuscany, 1794–1800; returned to Geneva, 1800. Secretary of the Council of Commerce, Arts, and Agriculture in Geneva (which had been annexed to France) and then secretary of Chamber of Commerce of Leman, 1801. Associated with Mme. de Staël's Coppet circle, 1804–17. Began lecturing at Geneva Academy on history and economics, 1809. Visited Paris for the first time, staying five months, 1813. Elected to the Representative Council, Geneva, 1814. Married Jessie Allen, 1819. Elected to French Légion d'Honneur, 1841. Died June 25, 1842.

Selected Works

Tableau de l'agriculture Toscane. 1801.
De la richesse commerciale, ou prinicipes d'économie politique appliqués à la législation du commerce. 2 vols. 1803.
Histoire des républiques italiennes du moyen âge. 16 vols. 1807–18.
De la littérature du Midi de l'Europe. 4 vols. 1813.
Nouveaux principes d'économie politique, ou de la richesse dans ses rapports avec la population. 2 vols. 1819.
Histoire des Français. 31 vols. 1821–44.
Julia Sévéra, ou l'an quatre cent quatre-vingt-douze. 3 vols. 1822.
Histoire de la renaissance de la libértie en Italie, de ses progrès, de sa décadence et de sa chute. 2 vols. 1832. (Condensed version of *Histoire des républiques italiennes du moyen âge.*)
Histoire de la chute de l'Empire romain et du déclin de la civilisation. 2 vols. 1836. (Appeared first in English as *A History of the Fall of the Roman Empire.* 2 vols. 1834).
Études sur les sciences sociales. 3 vols. 1836–38.
Précis de l'Histoire des Français. 2 vols. 1838.
Epistolario. 4 vols. Edited by Carlo Pellegrini. Florence: La Nuova Italia. 1933–54.

Bibliography

Coleman, William. *Death Is a Social Disease: Public Health and Political Economy in Early Industrial France.* Madison: University of Wisconsin Press, 1982.
Corrigan, Beatrice, ed. Introduction to *Italian Poets and English Critics, 1755–1859.* Chicago: University of Chicago Press, 1969.
Gooch, George Peabody. *History and Historians in the Nineteenth Century.* London: Longman, 1913.
Pappé, H. O. "Sismondi's System of Liberty," *Journal of the History of Ideas* 40 (1979): 251–66.
"Sismondi," *Blackwood's Edinburgh Magazine* 57 (1845): 529–48.
Sowell, Thomas. "Sismondi: A Neglected Pioneer," *History of Political Economy* 4 (1972): 62–88.
Vandewalle, G. "Romanticism and Neo-romanticism in Political Economy," *History of Political Economy* 18 (1986): 33–47.
Waeber, Paul. *Sismondi: Une biographie.* Geneva: Slatkine, 1991.

THE SKETCH BOOK OF GEOFFREY CRAYON, GENT 1819–1820

Collection of sketches by Washington Irving

The Sketch Book of Geoffrey Crayon, Gent is Washington Irving's most important contribution to nineteenth-century American Romantic writing. Comprising a series of thirty-three sketches and an introductory piece, "The Author's Account of Himself," *The Sketch Book* was published briefly in America in 1819–20 and then in two volumes by the London publisher John Murray in 1820. Irving had traveled to England in 1815, where he befriended the Scottish novelist Walter Scott; Scott helped publicize the book and encouraged favorable reviews. The sketches are briefer than short stories, offering vignettes and glimpses of Irving's travels, ranging from essays to travelogues to a series of Christmas pieces focusing on English life, to folk tales set in America, with the most famous pair of tales "Rip van Winkle" and "The Legend of Sleepy Hollow" displaying Central European influences. Some American critics complained that Irving celebrated English culture as a point of cultural reference too soon after the American War of Independence. Nevertheless, Irving received favorable critical and popular reviews on both sides of the Atlantic.

The Irving persona Geoffrey Crayon, who introduces the sketches, is a complex character, prefiguring the Romantic artist who valorizes imagination over intellect and echoing the "oldstyle" literary gentleman, distant from the commercial affairs and in love with antiquity. Crayon is a traveler and amateur artist who expresses his desire to observe "strange characters and manners," from the "foreign parts and unknown regions" of New York State to "the shifting scenes" of European life. In "The Author's Account of Himself," Crayon expresses his delight in surprise discoveries; he is "caught sometimes by the delineations of beauty, sometimes by the distortions of caricature, and sometimes by the loveliness of landscape." Although his primary intention is to delight the reader (rather than to didactically instruct), he warns that disappointment lies in store for those who anticipate a grand European tour with "great objects studied by every regular traveller." Instead, his sketches focus on "nooks, and corners, and by-places," reflecting the weird sensations he feels as a stranger "in the land of my forefathers." This emphasis on obscure ephemera and overlooked experiences is a strong Romantic focus of Irving's work, giving *The Sketch Book* an emotional immediacy and balancing the grander historical and biographical accounts of Christopher Columbus and George Washington.

"Rip van Winkle," in which an old Dutch settler falls asleep for twenty years, not only is the most famous and well-crafted of Irving's folk tales but a story that has become part of American mythology. It is framed by a preface, stating that the tale was discovered among the papers of the late Diedrich Knickerbocker (another of Irving's recurring characters) and represents "a history of the province during the reign of the Dutch governors." Set in New York State in the Kaatskill (Catskill) Mountains, which are reputedly "haunted by strange beings," the story opens during British rule over the America with a plaque of the head of George III swinging over the local inn. One of the chief pleasures of the tale is the manner in which the landscape, hills, and village are evocatively sketched, and the way in which the reader experiences the everyday but magical world of Rip van Winkle. Winkle is portrayed as a kind and goodly man with a "well-oiled disposition, who takes the world easy," but he prefers telling and listening to stories to working and his wife rails at him for being lazy. While wandering in the woods with his dog, Winkle encounters a dwarf who leads him to a mountain, where he drinks deeply and falls asleep. When he awakes it is unclear how long he has slept. The reader realizes the lapse in time only slightly more quickly than Winkle does, as he finds his old rusted gun and meets strangers on his return to the now expanded village. The most notable change is that the plaque of the king's head has been replaced by that of George Washington, signaling that Winkle has slept through the War of Independence. At first he is unsure of his identity and is treated suspiciously, but he is slowly accepted as a wise man who conveys valuable cultural lore through his tales. The question of why Irving chose this particular historical period is not answered by the tale, but the suggestion is that questions of personal identity and imaginative existence are closely bound to the forging of a national sensibility as America enters the postrevolutionary period. In order to encourage the reader to question the tale's meaning, the postscript emphasizes its strangeness (rather than concluding with an edifying homily), while also confirming its historical validity to guard against it being read purely as an imaginative work lacking social significance.

"The Legend of Sleepy Hollow" is also presented as a "found" tale, but it is longer than "Rip van Winkle," adding psychological complexities that make it more of a short story than a sketch. Like "The Spectre Bridegroom" (also in *The Sketch Book*), in its manner of telling and ghostly mise-en-scène the tale foreshadows Edgar Allan Poe's 1840 *Tales of the Grotesque and Arabesque*. But, whereas Poe's stories dwell on irrationality, perversity, and supernatural phenomena to explore the human condition, "The Legend of Sleepy Hollow" exposes the way in which myths and superstition distort truths by creating their own reality. The tale involves a "native of Connecticut," Ichabod Crane, who instructs the children of Sleepy Hollow, a dreamy and haunted village in New York State. Crane is described as a "man of great erudition," but he is also a pedant and overblown with his own importance. Despite his learning, he has an "appetite for the marvellous," with no tale being "too gross or monstrous for his capacious swallow." The narrative describes his attempts to court Katrina van Tassel, the daughter of a prosperous Dutch farmer, but her other suitor Brom Bones scares him off with the tale of the headless horseman that had been popular in Sleepy Hollow since the Revolutionary War. In a descriptive and highly dramatic scene in which Crane is on his way home from the van Tassels' house, he is pursued and attacked by the horseman and then mysteriously disappears. Whether this is a supernatural happening or an assault perpetrated by Brom Bones is open to question (although Bones "always burst into a hearty laugh at the mention of the pumpkin" that was found where Crane was attacked), but this incident is subsequently added to the store of stories that the "old country wives" enjoyed telling. As in "Rip van Winkle," the postscript is balanced between the suggestion that "The Legend of Sleepy Hollow" contains an identifiable moral and the implication that it is an "extravagant" fabrication designed to question the status and provenance of legends. Either way, it is the ambiguity at the heart of these tales, together with the imaginative currents that run throughout *The Sketch Book*, that mark Irving as an important early American Romantic writer.

MARTIN HALLIWELL

Text

The Sketch Book of Geoffrey Crayon, Gent. was first published as seven paperbound issues in the United States (from the firm of C. S. van Winkle) between 1819 and 1820. The British version was published in two volumes by the London publisher John Murray in 1820. A revised edition of *The Sketch Book* appeared as part of the *Works of Washington Irving*, edited by G. P. Putnam, 1848.

Bibliography

Adermann, Ralph M., ed. *Critical Essays on Washington Irving*. Boston, G. K. Hall, 1990.

Bradbury, Malcolm. *Dangerous Pilgrimages: Trans-Atlantic Mythologies and the Novel*. London: Penguin, 1996.

Clendenning, John. "Irving and the Gothic Tradition," *The Bucknell Review* 12 (1964): 90–98.

Hoffman, Daniel. "Irving's Use of American Folklore in the Legend of Sleepy Hollow," *PMLA*, 68 (1953): 425–35.

Kasson, Joy S. *Artistic Voyagers*. Westport: Greenwood Press, 1982.

Myers, Andrew B. *A Centenary of Commentary on the Works of Washington Irving, 1860–1974*. Tarrytown, N.Y.: Sleepy Hollow Restorations, 1976.

Seed, David. "The Art of Literary Tourism: An Approach to Washington Irving's Sketch Book," *Ariel* 14, no. 2 (1983): 67–82.

SLAVERY AND EMANCIPATION

Slavery was one of the most significant social, political, and cultural issues of the Romantic era. The brutality of chattel slavery in the colonies and former colonies of European nations appalled many and, though defended by some, led to widespread popular movements for abolition and emancipation. These movements influenced, and were influenced by, wider political considerations, and the question of whether any person could have absolute sovereignty over another was central not only to the existence of plantation slavery but also to ideas about the political organization of the state. In turn, both the theory and practice of slavery, abolition, and emancipation gave rise to many cultural productions. Writers, artists, and musicians responded to the question in their work, and in many cases were at the forefront of campaigns to bring about an end to slavery.

Mid-eighteenth-century slavery was a highly organized industry, with thousands of African and European slave traders ultimately transporting millions of Africans across the Atlantic Ocean, in crowded and disease-ridden ships, to work in New World plantations. Most were put to work growing such crops as sugar, tobacco, and cotton—crops that demanded back-breaking labor. Plantation discipline was harsh, and slaves faced floggings, mutilations, and summary execution for trivial offenses. In the mid-eighteenth century, a number of people, initially prompted by Quakers in the British American colonies, began tentatively to call for an end to slavery and the slave trade. By the 1780s a substantial antislavery movement had come into existence, organized by European groups such as the Society for Effecting the Abolition of the African Slave Trade in England and Les Amis Des Noirs in France. These were among the first political pressure groups in modern history, and their then-new techniques of lobbying, petitioning, and organizing consumer boycotts remain central to activist groups to this day. Despite a sophisticated countercampaign from slave owners and their supporters, the campaign received widespread support across Europe, particularly in Britain. The French Revolution disrupted the campaign, however. In Britain a new conservatism, and an unwillingness to tamper with colonial and maritime policy during wartime, stalled abolition. French colonists were divided between supporters and opponents of the Revolution, and in the French colony of Santo Domingo civil war and widespread slave uprisings erupted. In 1794 the Convention abolished slavery in French colonies, and in 1797 Toussaint L'Ouverture, a former slave, became commander-in-chief of the colony. Napoleon Bonaparte reintroduced slavery in 1802. Toussaint was captured and later died in a French prison, but French forces were defeated on the island, leading to the formation in 1804 of the republic of Haiti, the first black republic.

In 1792 Denmark became the first nation to outlaw its slave trade. Britain, the foremost slave-trading nation, did not follow it for another fifteen years, when the Whig government of 1806–7, taking advantage of British naval supremacy after Horatio Nelson's victory at Trafalgar in 1805, fulfilled a long-standing promise. The United States passed a similar law in 1808. Britain henceforth took upon itself to extend this law to other European nations, and by a long process of treaty and coercion the other main slave-trading states (France, The Netherlands, Spain, and Portugal) were forced to abandon their trade. However, despite the short French experiment, slavery remained legal in European colonies and the United States long after the trade had been abolished. New campaigns were initiated to secure emancipation. The British "Reformed Parliament" voted in 1833 to end slavery by 1838. In the United States, slavery proved to be a far more divisive issue, and the abolition campaign of the 1840s and 1850s culminated in civil war. Slavery, one of the causes of that war, was formally abolished with the passing of the Thirteenth Amendment in 1865. Although some countries, Brazil for example, maintained slavery until late in the nineteenth century, slavery was henceforth a marginal economic and social phenomenon, at least in the Western world.

Slavery, and the political struggle to abolish it, had profound consequences for political thought. In Britain the eighteenth-century Whig ascendancy celebrated the post-1688 constitution as one that enshrined the liberty of the individual and prevented Britons from becoming slaves to Roman Catholicism, foreign powers, or Stuart tyrants. Colonial slavery sat uncomfortably alongside Whig notions of liberty. In France the question of individual liberty became a highly charged one with the Revolution, and the slavery question became the occasion of actual conflict in Santo Domingo. In the United States, where slavery was also a cause of conflict, much political discussion centered on the question of why the inalienable rights enshrined in the constitution were not extended to a significant part of the population. Defenders of slavery attempted to answer these questions by developing theories that posited European races as innately superior to non-European races. Racism in the eighteenth century was not highly theorized to start with, and those who held that Africans were inferior did so from simple prejudice. Many in the eighteenth century subscribed to the notion of the "noble savage," which, though it relegated Africans to savagery, asserted their humanity and nobility. However, in the late century, and more particularly in the next, a pseudoscientific approach emerged in which elaborate theories of racial difference were articulated. According to these, Africans had less well-developed intellectual and moral faculties than Europeans, little capacity for abstract thought, and a natural aversion to doing productive work. For these early theorists of racism, slavery could be justified as a positive benefit to Africans, as it took them away from the unproductive and unfulfilling lives they supposedly led in Africa. In the end, the antislavery campaigners won the argument, but the racist theories developed by proslavery campaigners were later adopted on a grand scale by European imperialists.

Historians have long debated the causes of abolition and emancipation, asking why nations—particularly Britain, which appeared to be profiting greatly from slavery—should have abandoned the practice. Self-congratulating Victorians tended to put it down to national virtue, but in 1944 Eric Williams challenged this view, arguing that the plantations were abandoned only because they were no longer profitable. Williams's thesis is now seen as unsophisticated, but the debate he initiated is still unresolved. While economic factors are acknowledged to be significant, a shift in popular sensibility is now thought to be far more central than he suggested. Moreover, some historians have stressed the part played by the slaves themselves, through acts of individual and group resistance, and through participation in political and cultural arenas.

Discussion of slavery infused the literature, art, and music of the Romantic era. From the 1760s, writers of the "age of sensibility" introduce slaves (or Africans, more generally) to demonstrate the universality of human suffering, and to call for sympathy for their condition. In 1766 Laurence Sterne recounted the tale of a "poor Negro girl" in the last book of *Tristram Shandy*, while in the same year Sarah Scott published a plan for a humane slave plantation in *The History of Sir George Ellison*. Seven years later, "*The Dying Negro*" by Thomas Day became the first major poem to attack slavery. However, it was not until the 1780s that slavery entered the literary mainstream. Between 1785 and 1795, dozens of poems, plays, and novels considering slavery were published annually. Most of these portrayed free or enslaved Africans either as noble savages or as suffering men and women of sensibility. William Roscoe's *The Wrongs of Africa* (1787–88) is an excellent example of the former, while William Cowper's poems, including "The Negro's Complaint" and "Pity for Poor Africans," exemplify the latter. Hannah More's *Slavery: A Poem* and Ann Yearsley's *Poem on the Inhumanity of the Slave Trade* (both 1788) combine these approaches, while William Blake's poems, including "The Little Black Boy" (1789), are characteristically divergent from the mainstream. Novels and plays opposing slavery are in general less convincing, although Day's *History of Sandford and Merton* (1782–89) introduced a generation of children to antislavery sentiment. Significant, too, was the development of the slave narrative, a form that appeared fully developed with the publication of *The Interesting Narrative of the Life of Olaudah Equiano, or, Gustavus Vassa, the African* in 1789. Literary representations of slavery were not confined to the English-speaking world. Bernadin de St. Pierre's *Paul et Virginie* (1787) was a best-seller in France and was widely translated, while even Germany, little involved in the trade, produced antislavery texts such as August von Kotzebue's *Die Negersklaven* (*The Negro Slaves*, 1796). French antislavery literature, however, tended more toward the philosophical, and celebrated attacks on slavery appeared in the works of Marie-Jean-Antoine-Nicholas Condorcet, Charles-Louis de Montesquieu, and Jean-Jacques Rousseau.

With the collapse of the abolition movement after 1792, writing on slavery declined but did not disappear. A new generation of writers approached the topic in a way that was more sophisticated but arguably more ambivalent. Samuel Taylor Coleridge wrote in 1792 an "Ode on the Slave Trade" and lectured on the subject in Bristol in 1795, but his enthusiasm for the cause waned along with his support for the French Revolution. Although William Wordsworth called the slave trade the "most rotten branch of human shame," he admitted that the campaign to end it "had ne'er / Fastened on my affections" (*The Prelude*, 1805). Wordsworth, at least at this time, saw the success or failure of abolition as bound up with wider questions of liberty and humanity. Maria Edgeworth's tale "The Grateful Negro" (1804) is equally complicated, seemingly confusing the politics of a plantation with those of Ireland under the English ascendancy. As the nineteenth century progressed, British writers routinely incorporated discussion of slavery into longer works, but, other than those political writings directly associated with the emancipation campaign of the 1820s and 1830s, it was rarely addressed as a single topic.

The same was not true of the United States. While slave owners and their supporters were vociferous in defense of their rights, as they saw them, antislavery writing took on a vigor rarely encountered in Europe. Central to this was the rapid development of the slave narrative. Several hundred of these autobiographies of slaves or former slaves appeared during the nineteenth century, the most celebrated of which is the *Narrative of the Life of Frederick Douglass* (1845). These narratives promoted African American solidarity, and brought the lived experiences of slaves directly to the educated, urban middle class of the northeast, the group who became the most committed white supporters of emancipation in the years before the civil war. Among these were John Greenleaf Whittier, a New England Quaker, whose poetry between 1831 and 1865 is almost entirely devoted to abolition, and Harriet Beecher Stowe, the author of *Uncle Tom's Cabin* (1851–52). This novel, now considered deeply problematic, was in its time a key contribution to the abolition debate, credited by some as the work that set the United States on the road to civil war.

Slavery also figures in music and the visual arts. Africans and slaves made an impact on music, both as performers and composers. In England, Ignatius Sancho composed music, and George Polgreen Bridgtower was known as a virtuoso violinist and a friend of Ludwig van Beethoven. African musicians often performed in Turkish clothes, and the so-called Turkish music in Beethoven's Ninth Symphony might more accurately be described as African music. Its position next to the "Ode to Joy," which calls for a universal brotherhood of man, can be interpreted as an antiracist statement.

Slaves appear regularly in the visual arts of the period, particularly in portraiture. In the mid-eighteenth century it was fashionable for the wealthy to be depicted with their slaves. Toward the end of the century this practice declined, although slaves still appear in colonial and plantation landscapes. Most antislavery works take the form of prints to accompany abolitionist literature, but a notable exception is J. M. W. Turner's *The Slave Ship* (1840). Painted after emancipation in British colonies, this painting recalled the worst of British slave-trading history and served as a reminder that slavery was still a reality in many parts of the world.

BRYCCHAN CAREY

Bibliography

Baum, Joan. *Mind-Forg'd Manacles: Slavery and the English Romantic Poets.* Hamden, Conn.: Archon, 1994.

Blackburn, Robin. *The Overthrow of Colonial Slavery 1776–1848.* London: Verso, 1988.

Davis, David Brion. *The Problem of Slavery in the Age of Revolution: 1770–1823.* Ithaca, N. Y.: Cornell University Press, 1975.

Drescher, Seymour. *Econocide: British Slavery in the Era of Abolition.* Pittsburgh: University of Pittsburgh Press, 1977.

Ferguson, Moira. *Subject to Others: British Women Writers and Colonial Slavery. 1670–1834.* London: Routledge, 1992.

Fryer, Peter. *Staying Power: The History of Black People in Britain.* London: Pluto Press, 1984.

Fulford, Tim, and Peter J. Kitson, eds. *Romanticism and Colonialism: Writing and Empire, 1780–1830.* Cambridge: Cambridge University Press, 1998.

James, C. L. R., *The Black Jacobins: Toussaint L'Ouverture and the San Domingo Revolution*. 3d ed. London: Allison and Busby, 1980.

Kolchin, Peter. *American Slavery: 1619–1877*. New York: Penguin, 1995.

Sypher, Wylie. *Guinea's Captive Kings: British Anti-Slavery Literature of the Eighteenth Century*. Chapel Hill: University of North Carolina Press, 1942.

Thomas, Hugh. *The Slave Trade: The History of the Atlantic Slave Trade 1440–1870*. London: Picador, 1997.

Williams, Eric. *Capitalism and Slavery*. London: André Deutsch, 1964.

SŁOWACKI, JULIUSZ 1809–1849

Polish poet and dramatist

Perhaps the most versatile Polish Romantic, Juliusz Słowacki shared the fate of his older fellow poet and rival, Adam Mickiewicz: both of them spent the larger part of their life in emigration. Słowacki wrote poetry and plays and had philosophical ambitions that were only partly fulfilled. His imagination may not have been as powerful as that of Mickiewicz, but he had a wider range, and his language often dazzles with its sheer virtuosity. Having left Poland during the Polish–Russian War of 1830–31, Słowacki lived the life of a cosmopolitan traveler, often expressing longing for his homeland in sad, wistful poems.

Although Słowacki became first known in Warsaw through his lyrical poems hailing the uprising, the first two volumes published in Paris in 1832 consisted mostly of poetic tales and two tragedies (*Mindowe and Maria Stuart*). Among his early poems there were few outstanding ones, except for "Godzina mysli" ("An Hour of Thought"), which Czesław Miłosz has called "the purest example of a melancholy, meditative trend in early Polish Romanticism." It was inspired by the memory of a dead friend; indeed, an intimation of early death colors the work of the mature Słowacki, including the majestic poem "Testament mój" ("My Will and Testament") in which he foretells his fame for posterity. Lyrical poetry, though, has a secondary importance for Słowacki; what fascinates him in the 1830s is writing for the stage, following in the footsteps of William Shakespeare and Mickiewicz.

His play *Kordian* (1834) is probably the best among the "historical" plays, devoted to conflicts in Polish history or prehistory. What makes it particularly interesting is that, like Mickiewicz's *Dziady III*, this play is a reckoning with the near past and the forces that shaped the outcome of the November Uprising of 1830. Kordian is a Hamletesque figure, in that he could influence history but lacks the deliberation and the unscrupulousness required for political murder. In fact, his reluctance to embrace violent methods is clear from the end of act 1 where he pleads "Winkielriedism" against "Wallenrodism." (Winkelried is a Swiss hero who sacrifices his own life for the nation while staying on moral high ground). Kordian's tragedy is that toward the end he begins to doubt his own mission; he is an idealistic soldier affected by inertia. Although there are women in acts 1 and 2, *Kordian* is basically a play focused on themes traditionally associated with men, such as courage, hypocrisy, decision making, and Romantic individualism.

Another play, *Balladyna* (1839), brings the viewer back into Slavonic prehistory via Shakespeare. While the plot to some extent resembles *Macbeth* (the young peasant heroine kills her sister and eventually rises to the throne through a series of murders), in other respects it is clearly inspired by *A Midsummer Night's Dream*, with its mischievous spirits and fairies. *Balladyna* remains one of Słowacki's most popular plays, and it is certainly a better drama than the gruesome *Lilla Weneda* (1840), which attempts to fill a gap in Slavonic prehistory with a bloody conflict between two tribes, the peaceful "Wenedes" and the aggressive "Lechs." The latter play is a typically Romantic melodrama with, according to Milosz, "rather gratuitous horrors." The unfinished *Horsztynski* (1835; published posthumously) is Słowacki's first play after *Kordian* grounded in recent history. The hero is the son of an eighteenth-century Polish magnate who is a traitor to his country, and the main conflict appears to be a clash between the hero's patriotism and family loyalties.

Among Słowacki's historical plays, *Mazepa* (1840) also enjoyed some popularity, being one of the rare plays that was staged in the author's lifetime. It does not deal with the later career of the famous Hetman of the Cossacks but invents a plot based on love and intrigue in the court of King Jan Casimir to which the young Mazepa falls victim. Modern critics prefer to *Mazepa* a tragicomedy left untitled in manuscript, given the title *Fantazy*, which was written around 1841, but published only in the twentieth century. The eponymous hero, Count Fantazy (Słowacki apparently took the hero's name from a play by Alfred de Musset) is but one of the characters in this interesting play that shows how the poet applied his imagination to current social problems. Fantazy (and his counterpart Idalia) are "posturing" Romantics and stand in contrast to the real Romantic pair of lovers, Jan (a Polish insurgent, exiled to Siberia and returning from there in disguise) and Diana. The so-called realists in the play, Count Respekt and his wife, are quite prepared to sell their daughter's hand in marriage to Fantazy in order to pay their debts. The supreme Romantic, however, is the "Russian" (in reality Cherkes) major whose sacrifice of life at the end of the play resolves the situation and allows Jan and Diana to get married. The construction of the play shows how much Słowacki learned from the contemporary French theater. As for the Respekts, their attitude pinpoints the dilemma arising from what Juliusz Kleiner calls "the economic ruin of the nobility and the moral decay that follows from the fact."

Yet it was in epic poetry that Juliusz Słowacki managed to get close to his archrival Mickiewicz, whose opinion about the younger man's first poetic efforts was rather condescending. He first wrote the enchanting poetic tale "W Szwajcarii" ("In Switzerland," 1839), a story of love awakening and blossoming against the blue, white, and gold of the Swiss landscape, a sentimental poem idealizing the narrator's partner. The idyll of love is spoiled here by the mysterious death of the young woman, which is not explained, although the reasons for it are deeply imbedded in the poet's psyche. In fact, Słowacki never had a satisfactory romantic relationship and preferred to live the life of the lonely cosmopolitan traveler. A product of his travels (taking a cue from Lord Byron's *Childe Harold's Pilgrimage*), "Podróz do Ziemi Święetej z Neapolu" ("Journey to the Holy Land from Naples," 1836–39; published posthumously), was a poem in sestinas characterized by linguistic inventiveness, wit, and ingenuity. Canto 8 of this poem, known as "Grób Agamemnona," is often quoted for its biting social criticism. In this sequence Słowacki compares the heroism of the ancient Greeks (symbolized by Thermopylae) with the less heroic conduct of Poles in the 1830–31 war with Russia and declares, "O Poland! As long as you confine your angel's soul / in the skull of drunken nobleman / so long will the executioner hack your inert body." He does not give up hopes for Poland's resurrection but suggests this will happen only as the result of a great spiritual effort uplifting the nation.

Competing with Byron did not lessen Słowacki's wish to compete with Mickiewicz, and his *Anhelli* (1838) can be read as a counterpart to the Mickiewicz's *Books of the Polish Nation*. It is a symbolic prose poem written in a biblical tone, and its narrative is sketched against a Siberian landscape where three groups of Polish exiles vie for political influence. The hero, Anhelli, does not belong to any of these groups but is chosen by a shaman to accept suffering and death and in consequence becomes, according to Milosz, a kind of "passive redeemer." The conclusion of *Anhelli* points to the future: a knight appears on horseback to announce the hour of universal revolution—but Anhelli will die before this much-expected event. Słowacki's symbolic message to the Polish exiles in one respect is clear—namely, that no one should expect major political changes in the near future, for Poland will not regain its independence in the lifetime of his generation.

Many critics regard *Beniowski* (the first five cantos published in 1841) as Słowacki's best work. This is an epic poem written in *ottava rima* about the exploits of an eighteenth-century Polish hero born in Hungary, Count Maurycy Beniowski. While the hero himself published his memoirs back in 1790, Słowacki did not use the most colorful material for his poem: the historical Beniowski fought in the Confederacy of Bar and having fallen into Russian captivity was deported to Kamchatka. He managed to escape with some fellow rebels and sailed back to France but not before establishing a colony in Madagascar where he was elected honorary chieftain by one of the tribes. Słowacki's narrative, however, ends during the war with the Russians, and his Beniowski is a typical Polish nobleman rather than an exotic adventurer. His lack of historical veracity is not really important, for *Beniowski* is a typical "poem of digression" not unlike Byron's *Don Juan*. It provides an opportunity for Słowacki to display once again his considerable language skills as well as his irony, settling accounts with his rivals and enemies. It attacks, among other things, all Polish political parties in emigration as well as the pope who, during the Polish struggle for independence, sided with the tsar ("Poland—your fall is in Rome!") and makes fun of Mickiewicz, whose claims for leadership Słowacki finds unacceptable. He himself comes across as an "aristocratic revolutionary" who appeals to the future when his truth will at last become victorious: "Though today you should resist me—the future is mine, / And mine will be the victory beyond the grave!" While

it certainly increased his number of political and literary enemies, after *Beniowski* Słowacki was also recognized as a major literary figure.

Słowacki's last creative years are characterized by a growing mysticism and an effort to create great historical systems of thought in writing. *Genesis z Ducha* (*Genesis from the Spirit*) certainly points in this direction. The main thesis of this work, written in free-flowing, solemn prose, is the complete supremacy of the spirit over everything and its leading role in history. The spirit is the motor of all revolutions that, notes Milosz, are "spasms of birth, until humanity, transformed, approaches Christ." Słowacki also spells out his theory of metempsychosis (the transmigration of souls) that is instrumental in the appearance of outstanding individuals carrying on "historical missions," often against enormous odds. *Genesis z Ducha* is nowadays more often quoted than read for the simple reason that, as Juliusz Kleiner puts it, here "Romantic individualism reached its most extreme expression."

The last enterprise of this poet and keen letter writer (the letters to his mother, Salomea, provide an important aid to his biography) is once again an epic poem but it is, in a sense, the very opposite of *Beniowski*. It is a grand survey of human history with the appropriate title *Król-Duch* (*King-Spirit*), of which only the first part was published in 1847. It presents the wanderings of the spirit throughout the centuries of European civilization, of which Poland is an integral part. The spirit of Her Armeńczyk, a heroic soldier mentioned by Platon, comes to new life in Popiel, a mythical king of prehistoric Poland, and continues to be embodied in Polish kings and saints of the Middle Ages. *Król-Duch* is written in eleven-syllable verse in six-line stanzas with an A-B-A-B-C-C rhyme scheme, and while parts of it are taught in Polish schools, it remains more of a literary oddity than a real achievement, not mentioning its rather dubious ethical message, that great individuals have a license from God (the spirit) to perpetrate cruel and inhuman deeds.

There is much irony in the fact that while *Król-Duch* holds today mainly the interest of literary historians, some of Słowacki's small visionary lyrics from the last period enchant with their translucent beauty and effortless sonority. While his views on progress in history and Poland's best traditions are controversial, his mastery of the language continues to impress and much of his work remains alive even in times that cease to be influenced by the "prophetic" or "bardic" tradition of the great Polish Romantics and their social or national message.

GEORGE GÖMÖRI

Biography

Born in Krzemieniec (today in the Ukraine), September 4, 1809. After the death of his father in 1814 was brought up by his widowed mother Salomea Januszewska, who in 1818 married Dr. A. Bécu, a university professor in Vilno. Between 1825 and 1828 Słowacki studied law at Vilno University. It was here that he befriended Ludwik Szpitznagel, a friend who committed suicide, and fell in love (unrequited) with Ludwika Śniadecka. (Unrequited love was a sentiment expressed more than once in his literary works). In February 1829 he left for Warsaw, where he worked for the Ministry of Finance; his first poems were published soon after the outbreak of the 1830 uprising against Russia. Having left Warsaw in March 1831, he traveled as diplomatic courier for the Polish government to Paris and London. After Poland's defeat in the war with Russia he settled down in Paris, publishing several books of poetry in 1832 and 1833. Lack of recognition from fellow emigrés (which included a scathing remark by Mickiewicz) spurred him to leave Paris. From December 1832 to February 1836 Słowacki lived in Switzerland, mostly in Geneva and for a short time in Vevey. This was a very productive creative period in his life; he wrote several plays and the poem "In Switzerland," which demonstrates the high ideal of Romantic love that foiled any long-lasting relationship he might have had with women. In 1836 he visited Rome, and from there made a tour of the Middle East and Greece. The literary harvest of his exotic travels was the poetic itinerary *Podróz z Ziemi Świetej do Neapolu* as well as the prose poem *Anhelli*. Upon his return to Italy in 1837 he spent a year and a half in Florence studying art and writing up his travel experiences. From Christmas 1838 to the end of his life Słowacki lived in Paris, save a short trip to the Prussian-held part of Poland in 1848 where he met his mother in Wroclaw. During these years he reached the apogee of his artistic possibilities with *Beniowski*, and wrote a number of plays, of which *Fantazy* has won most critical recognition. In 1842–43 he was briefly associated with Towiański's mystical circle, an episode that helped him in formulating his own philosophy, a kind of "dialectical idealism" based on belief in the transmigration of souls. His ideas were encapsulated in works such as *Genesis z Ducha* and *Król-Duch*, fully published only after his death. He died of tuberculosis on April 3, 1849, and was buried in Montmorency. In 1927 his remains were brought to Poland and interred in Kraków in the Royal Crypt of Wawel Castle.

Selected Works

Dzieła wszystkie. 17 vols. Vols. 1–11 edited by J. Kleiner. Vols. 12–17 edited by W. Floryan. 1952–1976.
Dzieła. Vols. 1–14. 3rd ed. Edited by J. Krzyżanowski. 1959.
Korespondencja. Vols. 1–2. Edited by E. Sawrymowicz. 1962–63.

Bibliography

Filip, T. M., ed. *A Polish Anthology*. Duckworth: London, 1944.
Folkierski, W., M. Giergelewicz, and St. Stroiński, eds. *Juliusz Słowacki, 1809–1849, Księga zbiorowa w stulecie zgonu*. London: Polish Research Centre, 1951.
Kleiner, Juliusz. *Słowacki*. 5th ed. Wroclaw: Ossolineum, 1972.
Kridl, Manfred. *The Lyric Poems of Juliusz Slowacki*. The Hague: Mouton, 1958.
Makowski, S. *Juliusz Słowacki*. Warsaw: Biblioteka Polonistyki, 1980.
Milosz, Czeslaw. *The History of Polish Literature*. London: Collier-Macmillan, 1969.
Norwid, Cyprian. "Czarne kwiaty." In *Pisma wybrane*. Vol. (4), *Proza*. Warsaw: PIW, 1968.
Treugutt, Stefan. *"Beniowski."* In *Kryzys indiwidualizmu romantycznego*. Warsaw: PIW, 1964.
Ciemnoczolowski, A., K. Pecold, and B. Zakrewski, eds. *Sądy współczesnych o twórczości Slowackiego*. Wroclaw: Ossolineum, 1963.

SNELLMAN, JOHAN VILHELM 1806–1881

Finnish philosopher and statesman

Johan Vilhelm Snellman has been called Finland's national philosopher. Correctly understood, it is a fair accolade, but as an introduction it hardly does justice to the enormous contribution Snellman made to the stability and independence of Finland at a time of political uncertainty and anxiety. Philosopher he certainly was, but it was rather the application of his philosophical ideas in preparing Finland to become a nation in its own right that has earned him his reputation as one of the greatest figures in Finnish history.

Until 1809 Finland had been part of Sweden, and the main language of administration and education was still Swedish. Snellman himself, though born in Stockholm, was a Swedish-speaking Finn. In the aftermath of the Napoleonic Wars Finland had become a grand duchy within the Russian Empire, and while it retained its Swedish law and a degree of autonomy in its administration, the way in which this new relationship with its mighty neighbor might develop was far from clear. Turku (Åbo to the Swedish-speaking Finns) was the cultural center of Finland at this time, and the political future was debated there with an eagerness that occasionally exceeded the tolerance of the Russian authorities.

As a student at Turku, Snellman took a leading role in this exchange of ideas. His studies led to dissertations on George Wilhelm Friedrich Hegel and Gottfried Wilhelm Leibnitz, and teaching books on philosophy, logic and Latin etymology. In 1835 he was appointed senior lecturer (*docent*) in philosophy at Turku, and from there took study leave to travel to Germany to pursue his study of Hegel. During his time abroad, he was able to compare the rich cultural life of the continent, which he partly recorded in his travelogue *Tyskland, Skildringar och omdömen från en resa 1840–1841* (*Germany, Descriptions and Opinions from a Journey*, 1892), with the backwardness of his own country, and, absorbing German ideas of National Romanticism, began to formulate his own program for a national awakening in Finland. Important publications followed on free will (*Versuch einer speculativen Entwicklung der Idée der Persönlichkeit*) and on the theory of the state (*Läran om staten*). In this latter work, Snellman laid out the core of his beliefs in the importance of nationhood for civilization. Education, he argued, should be the strength of a nation—particularly a small nation—and the education of all its citizens was essential to the integrity of the state.

Snellman also spent some time in Stockholm, where he tried his hand at literary ventures. One of these was a supposed continuation of the Swedish poet and writer Carl Jonas Love Almqvist's novel *Det går an*, in which Snellman ridiculed the defense of free love in the original, by bringing all the protagonists to a bad end. More importantly, he also honed his skills in journalism by contributing many polemical articles to various publications.

On returning to Finland, he became headmaster of a school in Kuopio in the remote but beautiful area of lakes in southeastern Finland. Here he began to realize his program for a national awakening through education and debate. The cornerstone of his campaign was the Finnish language—a radical solution considering his own language was Swedish. For Finland to be able to take its place among the nations of Europe, he argued, it must have its own literature in its own language, and that language had to be Finnish. Three further points were central to his thinking. First, education must be made available to all Finnish citizens, and the language of education should be in the students' own language. Second, the Swedish-speaking elite must be persuaded to promote the Finnish language and assist in the education of the masses. And third, this must be carried out with the acceptance of the Russian authorities.

To promote his ideas he founded a series of newspapers. With the backing of the great folklorist Elias Lönnrot he began a Finnish language paper *Maamiehen ystävä*. The seminal Swedish language paper *Saima* was more successful until the local censor closed it down in 1847. Almost immediately Snellman started a new paper, *Litteraturblad för allmän medborgerlig bildning*, which was nominally edited by Lönnrot since Snellman was then banned from editing a paper. In these organs, Snellman carried out his crusade with great enterprise and energy, debating every conceivable topical issue, bringing foreign writers to the notice of his devoted readership, and promoting his own ideas with tireless enthusiasm, if also sometimes with a degree of ill-temper.

In 1855, Nicholas I died. His successor, Alexander II, was an educated and a liberal man. One of his first initiatives in Finland was to prepare the ground with a preliminary committee to reconvene the senate, which had last met in 1809 when Finland first came under Russian dominion. While Snellman was certainly considered dangerous in some respects, the Czar acknowledged his conciliatory arguments concerning Russian authority by appointing him professor of philosophy at Helsinki University, and then, in 1863, senator. Snellman was immediately able to make significant progress in the language question by persuading Alexander to support legislation giving official status to Finnish in education and in administration.

In 1865 Snellman was made head of the exchequer (*finansexpedition*), where he was able to complete the currency reform begun by his predecessor, which resulted in Finland having the mark (*markka*) instead of the rouble. In 1866 he was ennobled. This latter stage of Snellman's career as politician and statesman enabled him in a remarkable way, with significant practical measures, to round off his life's task of guiding the Finnish people toward their own politically and culturally sustainable nation. He began as a thinker, working out according to sound Hegelian principles a system of ideas for promoting his vision of a Finnish state: the Finnish people had to be awakened to the concept of their own individuality as a nation, and they must develop their own culture and literature as a prerequisite for political nationhood. That he was able to combine such single-minded energy in the dissemination of this vision with a politically astute pragmatism enabled Finland to move a long way to making it a reality, without the confrontation and unrest that was very much evident elsewhere in Europe at that time.

THOMAS LAWRANCE

See also **Almqvist, Carl Jonas Love**

Biography

Born May 12, 1806. Studied philosophy and theology at Turku University, acquiring master's degree, 1832. Senior lecturer in philosophy at the university in Helsinki, 1835. Travels in Sweden, Germany, Austria, and Switzerland, 1839–42. On return to Finland, became headmaster of school in Kuopio, 1843, where he produced various literary and topical papers. Appointed professor in Helsinki, 1856. Senator, 1863, becoming chief of finance, 1865. Ennobled 1866. Chairman of *Finska Litteratursällskapet* (Finnish Literary Society), 1870. Died July, 4, 1881.

Selected works

Philosophisk elementarcurs. 1837–40.
Det går an. En tafla ur lifvet. Fortsättning. 1841.
Om det akademiska studium. 1840.
Versuch einer Spekulativen Entwicklung der Idée der Persönlichkeit. 1841.
Fyra giftermål. Taflor i Terburgs manér. 3 vols. 1842.
Läran om staten. 1842.
Tyskland Skildringar och omdömen från en resa 1840–1841. 1842.
Samlade arbeten. Vols. 1–12. 1992–1999.

Bibliography

Havu, Ilmari. *Snellmaniana.* Helsinki: Otava, 1970.
Knapas, Rainer. "J. V. Snellman och nationallitteraturen." In *Finlands svenska litteratur-historia.* Vol. 1, edited by Johan Wrede. Helsinki: Atlantis, 1999.
Numminen, Jaakko, et al. *J. V. Snellman och hans gärning. Ett finskt-svenskt symposium hållet på Hässelby slott 1981 till 100-årsminnet av Snellmans död.* Kungl. Vitterhets Historie och Antikvitets Akademiens serie (Konferenser 10). Stockholm: 1984.
Rein, Thiodolf. *Johan Vilhelm Snellman.* (4th edition). Helsinki: Otava, 1981.
Snellman, K., ed. *Johan Vilhelm Snellmans och hans hustrus brevväxling jämte orienterande översikter och hågkomster från hemmet.* 1928.
Wilenius, Reijo. *Snellmaninlinja: henkisan, kasvun filosofia.* Jyväskylä: Gummerus, 1978.
Wrede, Johan, ed. *Finlands svenska litteratur-historia.* Vol. 1. Helsinki: Atlantis, 1999.

SNOW STORM—STEAM-BOAT OFF A HARBOUR'S MOUTH 1842

Painting by J. M. W. Turner

Snow Storm—Steam-Boat off a Harbour's Mouth making Signals in Shallow Water, and going by the Lead. The Author was in this Storm on the Night the "Ariel" left Harwich is the full title of this masterly oil painting by the English artist J. M. W. Turner. This work expresses Turner's lifelong interest in the power of nature—in this case its threatening and destructive quality—that he had displayed effectively two years earlier in the tempestuous ocean that amplified the drama of his *Slavers Throwing Overboard the Dead and the Dying—Typhon Coming On (The Slave Ship).* It also underscored his enthusiastic engagement with nineteenth-century steam technology. Throughout his career, Turner led the way among Romantic painters in illustrating industrial urbanism, railway technology, and steam navigation, most famously in *The Fighting "Temeraire"* of 1839.

Snow Storm depicts the envelopment of a steamboat in a cyclonic pattern of water and atmosphere. The elaborate title points to several perils, making it necessary to go "by the lead" and to "make signals" so as not to run aground or collide with other shipping. The vessel, tilted on a wave, is clearly articulated, unusually for a painting from this late in Turner's career, with wooden superstructure and black iron stack easily discernible. Its semicircular paddle wheel is central and, judging by the touches of white paint at its base, relentlessly turning to retain stability and to push safely out of the storm. The surrounding natural elements are rendered with startling expressive and technical freedom, which results in a high level of emotional involvement. Central to the composition is a vortex arrangement that acts as a focus while heightening the drama through the fusion of diverse elements (wind, snow, wave) to unite new forces of unprecedented power and terror while pulling fire and smoke from the stack of this frantically overtaxed machine. While Turner's claim to have been on this particular vessel during the storm in question has been discounted, his experience as a traveler could have provided him with knowledge of such an event. Equally suspect is his highly Romantic memory of seeking to sample the full effect of nature's power while on this steamboat: "I wished to show what such a scene was like; I got the sailors to lash me to the mast to observe it; I was lashed for four hours, and I did not expect to escape, but I felt bound to record it if I did." Yet his autobiographical reference, combined with the viewer's detached perspective, produces a painting that links internal and external viewpoints simultaneously.

Snow Storm culminated Turner's decade-long investigation of the clash of the steamboat with the powers of nature, the key theme in his earlier paintings *Staffa, Fingal's Cave* (1832) and *Rockets and Blue Light (Close at Hand) to Warn Steam-Boats of Shoal-Water* (1840). Several watercolors likewise anticipate the 1842 canvas, including *Steamboat in a Storm* (1841?), *Steamer at Sea* (1840), and *Yarmouth Roads* (1840). In *Snow Storm*, the steamboat is closely observed, revealing an engine-driven mechanism competing desperately with the vastly superior might of nature. Here, optimism in the technological and scientific advances of the modern age are checked and momentarily held in contempt by forces beyond human control.

Most of the contemporary critical response to *Snow Storm* was negative. The *Athenaeum* found it baffling: "Where the steam-boat is—where the harbour begins, or where it ends—which are the signals, . . . are matters past our finding out." The most famous jibe was expressed by a writer who called the painting "soapsuds and whitewash," words that provoked from the artist, "What would they have? I wonder what they think the sea's like? I wish they'd been in it." However, John Ruskin, rising to Turner's defense in the first volume of *Modern Painters* (1843), considered the work "one of the very grandest statements of sea-motion, mist, and light, that has ever been put on canvas." The commentator for the *Morning Post*, while unhappy with the painting, at least acknowledged Turner's effort: "Some new touch of nature has occurred to him which he has introduced with all the freshness of studentship. It may be a failure, but still he looked for it in nature."

It has been observed that Turner may have alluded to scientific developments in the painting—especially the work of his friends Mary Somerville and Michael Faraday on magnetic fields of energy and the arched patterns they were capable of producing. He may also have been aware of advances in meteorology through his acquaintance with David Brewster who, in 1839, published an extended article on the nature of vortex storms in the *Edinburgh Review.*

Turner exhibited *Snow Storm* along with several other paintings, including a magnificent study of an oceangoing steamer at rest, *Peace—Burial at Sea.* While this is usually considered with its companion *War: The Exile and the Rock Limpet,* Turner might have intended this painting to be compared with *Snow Storm,* to contrast the great, dark, stationary machine it depicts with another, smaller vessel battling against the forces of nature.

WILLIAM RODNER

J. M. W. Turner, *Snowstorm at Sea,* 1842. Reprinted courtesy of AKG London/Erich Lessing.

Work

Snow Storm—Steam-Boat off a Harbour's Mouth, 1842. Oil on canvas, 91.5 cm. × 122 cm. Clore Gallery for the Turner Collection, Tate Britain, London.

Bibliography

Butlin, Martin, and Joll, Evelyn. *The Paintings of J. M. W. Turner.* 2 vols. Rev. ed. New Haven, Conn.: Yale University Press, 1984.

Hamilton, James. *Turner and the Scientists.* London: Tate Gallery, 1998.

Hewison, Robert, Ian Warrell and Stephen Wildman. *Ruskin, Turner and the Pre-Raphaelites.* London: Tate Gallery, 2000.

Rodner, William S. *J. M. W. Turner: Romantic Painter of the Industrial Revolution.* Berkeley and Los Angeles: University of California Press, 1997.

SOANE, SIR JOHN 1753–1837

English architect

John Soane was born in 1753, the son of a bricklayer, at Goring-on-Thames, England, and rose to become the dominant architect of the period 1790–1830. He was, in effect, the state architect, virtually rebuilding the Bank of England and designing several parliamentary buildings and courts. But his personal vision of the dominant neoclassical idiom was eclectic, risky, and strange, often suffused with a baroque extravagance; megalomaniac exteriors were belied by delicately decorated interiors, unexpected spatial arrangements, and introspective and sometimes sinister lighting effects.

Soane learned his craft as a draughtsman in the offices of George Dance and Henry Holland, but also attended courses at the Royal Academy in London, where he was a regular exhibitor. In 1776 he won the Royal Academy's gold medal with a design for a colossal *Triumphal Bridge*, which also led to a traveling scholarship, enabling him to study in Italy between 1778 and 1780. Influenced by the architecture he saw in Italy, he produced a number of fantastic, monumental designs for palaces, prisons, and mausoleums; it was the architecture of a mind that continued to be obsessed with power and death to the end. He developed a small practice, designing country houses and estate buildings, and published volumes of designs in 1788 and 1793, the latter displaying his interest in primitivist and picturesque effects. In 1788 he was appointed architect to the Bank of England, a position that, with financial independence from an inheritance in 1790, gave him the chance to explore some of his more magnificent ideas. For the next forty-five years he redeveloped the bank, producing a complex honeycomb of offices within a windowless curtain wall. Most of the rooms had no external walls, leading Soane to provide for lighting through high lanterns and other top-lit structures over low-curved vaults, a remarkable feature of his architecture generally and one that gave the rooms of the bank a sense of atmosphere, a kind of Gothic effect produced from the extreme distortion of classical modes.

In 1806 Soane was appointed professor of architecture at the Royal Academy, a position for which he assiduously prepared an extravagantly illustrated series of lectures. From 1812 onward, Soane developed a collection of art and antiquities at his house in Lincoln's Inn Fields, London. Using (by 1824) three adjacent buildings, he created an architectural office, art museum, and private house. The collection numbers about three thousand objects, crammed together rather haphazardly as a personal anthology of world art: Greek, Roman, and Egyptian antiquities, bronzes, instruments, ceramics, vases, architectural models, mummies, and medals, together with a library, paintings, and thousands of architectural drawings. Soane created a "Monk's Parlour" and "Monk's Cell" in his basement in which to house some of his Gothic pieces. The "Crypt" itself housed an extraordinary Egyptian sarcophagus; when Soane acquired this in 1825 he held a series of evening parties, subtly lit by candles and oil lamps, to show it off.

Soane was closely associated with the painter J. M. W. Turner, who shared Soane's interest in unusual lighting effects. In his house Soane used stained glass, clerestories, hidden lamps, apertures, convex mirrors, arches, and niches to create mysterious and unexpected glimpses of the objects in the collection. The first guidebook, by John Britton, was called *The Union of Architecture, Sculpture and Painting* (1827), to illustrate Soane's belief in the emotive alliances between art forms. Soane's own *Description* (from 1830) indicated how the effects of the arrangement were to be perceived, both as records of his own mental study and as guides for his draughtsmen and future artists. By a private act of Parliament in 1833 the museum was bequeathed to the nation, to be kept just as it was at his death: a complete architectural record, including his personal archive, contained in an oddly lit, atmospheric interior. The Sir John Soane Museum truly displays the "poetry of architecture" in quintessence.

Soane had already built the first public art gallery in England, the Dulwich Picture Gallery of 1812–15. The incorporation of a picture gallery, almshouses, and a mausoleum for the donor, his friend Sir Peter Bourgeois, was a particular challenge, producing a result that was regarded by some as an affront to classical dignity in its eclectic style and detail, but that has always seemed Soane's most personal work after his house. The combination of the intimate, somber mausoleum, lit through amber glass, with the more lively picture gallery, affirms an emotional interpenetration of life and death; Soane designed the combined building so that visitors should come full circle through the two zones.

Soane's ardent association with pictorial art found a worthy exponent in the artist Joseph Michael Gandy, who worked for Soane from 1798. Gandy's paintings bring out the strange romanticism of Soane's style. He provided glorious watercolor visions of the *Triumphal Bridge* design, set in an imaginary Eastern landscape; Soane's early *Triangular Royal Palace Design* is similarly realized by Gandy in a way that it could never be in stone. His stormy view of the Dulwich gallery emphasizes its picturesque skyline. The *Bank Stock Office* shows how Soane's top-lit structure was meant to work, but also gives it an eerie, tomb-like stillness. His birds-eye perspective of the Bank of England shows the complex in cutaway, so that Soane's ground plan can be appreciated; but Gandy also bathes the structure in an apocalyptic light, cutting the ground from beneath the edifice and rendering the powerhouse of England a deserted, picturesque ruin. A further illustration considered the rotunda of the bank explicitly as such a ruin. Gandy also executed brilliant watercolors of the house in Lincoln's Inn Fields, producing ideal, if exaggerated, views of the perspectival design and pervading *lumière mystérieuse* that Soane adored. He painted vast conglomerated paintings of Soane's buildings, in a Soanian interior, or set in imaginary landscapes: records of achievement, or melancholy testimonies to what might have been.

Soane claimed that architecture was "an Art purely of Invention, and Invention is the most painful and the most difficult exercise of the human mind." Despite his dominant position, in his difficult imaginative zone, Soane found himself at odds with the world. Attracted to powerful figures such as Napoleon Bonaparte and William Pitt, and determined to prove himself, Soane was a man of prodigious energy and rigorous, perfectionist work habits, a "dear old tyrant" as one of his assistants termed him. He could inspire devotion and awe, but both his sons rebelled against him. According to A. J. Bolton, he embroiled himself in controversies about the eclectic style of his public buildings, which in all their monumentality nonetheless reveal traces of his personality as seen, sympathetically, by his assistant, George Wightwick, as "an acute sensitiveness, and a fearful irritability, dangerous to himself if not to others; an embittered heart, prompting a cutting and sarcastic mind; uncompromising pride, neither respecting nor desiring respect; a contemptuous regard for the feelings of his dependants; and yet himself the very victim of irrational impulse; with no pity for the trials of his neighbour, and nothing but frantic despair under his own."

PAUL BAINES

Biography

Born at Goring-on-Thames, September 10, 1753. Gold medal from the Royal Academy, 1776; toured Italy 1776–78. Married Eliza Smith, 1784. Architect to the Bank of England, 1788. Fellow of the Royal Academy, 1802. Professor of architecture at the Royal Academy, 1806. Knighted, 1831. Retired from practice, 1833. Died January 20, 1837.

Selected Works

Description of the House and Museum on the North Side of Lincoln's Inn Fields. 1830–35.
Memoirs of the Professional Life of an Architect between the Years 1768 and 1835. 1835.
Lectures on Architecture. Edited by Arthur T. Bolton. London: Sir John Soane's Museum, 1929.

Bibliography

Bolton, A. T. *The Portrait of Sir John Soane, R. A. (1753–1837) Set Forth in Letters from His Friends (1775–1837).* London: Art and Technics, 1927.
Ptolemy, Dean. *Sir John Soane and the Country Estate.* Aldershot: Ashgate, 1999.
Ruffinière du Prey, Pierre de la. *John Soane: The Making of an Architect.* Chicago: University of Chicago Press, 1982.
———. *Sir John Soane.* London: Victoria and Albert Museum, 1985.
Schumann-Bacia, Eva-Maria. *John Soane and the Bank of England.* London: Architecture Design and Technology Press, 1991.
Summerson, Sir John. *Sir John Soane.* London: Art and Technics, 1952.
———. *John Soane (Architectural Monograph).* London: Academy Editions, New York: St. Martin's Press, 1983.
Stroud, Dorothy. *The Architecture of Sir John Soane.* London: Studio, 1961.
Thornton, Peter, and Helen Dorey. *A Miscellany of Objects from Sir John Soane's Museum.* London: Lawrence King, 1992.

SOLGER, KARL WILHELM FERDINAND 1780-1819

German philosopher

The German philosopher Karl Solger, who taught in Frankfurt and Berlin, was a key figure in the development of German Romantic aesthetics, his works linking the ideas of the brothers August Wilhelm and Friedrich von Schlegel (under whom he studied in Jena), Johann Gottlieb Fichte, and G. W. F. Hegel. He is best known for his theory of irony, a central concept in Romanticism, yet his particular notion of irony differed considerably from that underlying the concept of Romantic irony, as espoused by Friedrich von Schlegel from 1798 on. Solger's major work, *Erwin: Vier Gespräche über das Schöne und die Kunst* (*Erwin: Four Conversations about Beauty and Art,* 1804), was widely read in literary circles of the time, but his death at the age of thirty-nine came at a time when the momentum of Romanticism in Germany had begun to wane. Hegel acknowledged his debt to Solger, and the "preexistentialist" theologian Søren Kierkergaard, for whom the concept of irony had particular significance, considered his ideas worthy of challenge as late as the 1840s. Heinrich Heine reserved considerable praise for Solger in *Die Romantische Schule* (*The Romantic School,* 1836), calling him superior to the more famous Schlegel brothers in critical acumen.

Like so many of the Romantics, Solger thought in terms of the polarity of infinity and finitude, and much of his theorizing is predicated on this polarity. Writing in clearly Platonic terms, Solger depicts a higher reality of spirit and idea above and beyond the lowly horizons of the material, immediate, imperfect present. (Ultimately, these two realms are relations of one and the same reality, or ground of being, for appearance in itself is revelation and points to the divine.) To Solger, art represents an attempt to reconcile the two realms through the creation of the beautiful and the sublime. But art itself is subject to a platonic hierarchy; the highest, most universal form of literature, for instance, is drama, because it represents not a relationship of subject matter (*Stoff*) and idea, but infinite idea itself, realized in pure action. Drama is revelation, and revelation is divine. In the experience of revelation, mere existence is transcended, or as Solger puts it, *aufgehoben* (abolished, canceled out). Moreover, tragedy completes this process of revelation in a purer fashion than comedy (which is always at base more or less parodistic) because it has a dual directionality, so to speak, leading to the destruction of the hero, which occurs simultaneously with the rising moment of truth. In dying, the hero momentarily experiences transcendent idea, and the divine is thus revealed as existing in the world, as immanent. This concept anticipates Hegel's *Weltgeist* (world spirit) acting in history, though Solger's intention is to synthesize the pheonomenal and the absolute, not to locate the absolute in the phenomenal world.

In any case, the descent of the hero converges with the ascent of perfection in the form of the beautiful, the true. In tragedy, death is transfiguration. Solger criticized the Schlegels for failing to recognize this essentially ironic feature of tragedy. Clearly irony is also present in the relationship of the audience and the actors in comedy—it is often essential that the audience knows or thinks it knows more than the characters do. But this light irony of "mood" is not what Solger intends. Solger's irony exists on an ontological level before the mere technicalities of dramatic humor or even, as with Ludwig Tieck and other Romantics, the destruction of the illusion of art through the interruption of action on the stage. An example is Tieck's play *Der gestiefelte Kater* (*Puss in Boots*, 1797), in which the author demonstrates, through a series of authorial interventions, his ironic detachment from his creation.

Solger endowed irony with a profundity previously unassociated with it. In particular, he emphasized its affirmative power, especially, as we have seen, in the aesthetic experience of tragedy, where the mood created by the action on stage reveals in the vanity and limitations of human life not senselessness but the presence of the transcendent. Nor is this mood *necessarily* absent in comedy; it is to be found, for example, in the work of Aristophanes as well as in William Shakespeare. Solger rejected August Wilhelm von Schlegel's belief that the ancients celebrated the senses more openly and were less melancholy, less conscious of human inadequacy, than more modern writers. Just as he identified a mood of irony in both tragedy and comedy, Solger also found a "certain sadness" as well as cheerfulness (*Heiterkeit*) in all forms of art. Drama in particular, he argued, exhibits art's capacity for allowing one to experience the pain and sadness of mortal existence but also the transcendence of the immediate world.

Like Friedrich Wilhelm Joseph von Schelling, Solger made a distinction between two kinds of imagination, *Phantasie* and *Einbildungskraft*. The former can be interpreted as something like "ideational imagination" (the associative, combinatory realm of notions and ideas) whereas the latter is the active, conceptualizing function that manifests itself in artistic creation. (Compare Samuel Taylor Coleridge's distinction between "fancy" and "imagination" in his *Biographia Literaria*.) Another of Solger's basic distinctions was between *Witz* and *Verstand*, between wit and the analytic power of reasoning, the antithesis of spontaneous association and combination in *Phantasie*. Art emerges when these distinctively different features of consciousness—*Phantasie* and *Einbildungskraft, Witz* and *Verstand*—are united in what has been called Solger's "dialectical unity." Solger was the first to systematize the aesthetic ideas of Schelling's philosophy.

Solger's synthesis of the transcendental and the immanent realms is also reflected in his concept of the symbol, which he sees as the physical manifestation of the idea. In the symbol, the physical and the spiritual cannot be separated; the symbol is what it signifies. Solger, in other words, posits a vital symbolism always in the process of becoming, in which art is, in its essence, action represented in the form of "individualized idea." (This emphasis on "activity" reflects the influence of the philosophy of Fichte, who applied the concept in a primarily moral sense.)

Aesthetics was at the time focused almost exclusively on the nature of beauty; art did not yet, with a few notable exceptions (e.g., the exchange of sexual roles in Friedrich von Schlegel's novel *Lucinde*, 1799), play the modern role of provocation and social criticism nor was the field as a whole fully sympathetic to the grotesque or uncanny. Thus, much of Solger's theoretical work centers on beauty as the prime question of aesthetics. He always looks to antiquity in his eminently philological approach; his first published work was in fact a translation of Sophocles' *Oedipus* in 1804. Solger's philosophy should not be seen as free of social consciousness, however, for his idea of beauty emphasizes its unifying *Geselligkeit* or "companionableness." Elaborating on ideas he traces to Edmund Burke, Solger distinguishes between the sublime—a quality of art that appeals to the urge for individual self-realization, self-sufficiency, and self-preservation—and the beautiful, which appeals to the urge for the bond of common experience. As is so often the case, Solger deals in dualities; there is for him no truly great art without both the sublime and the beautiful. The sublime can also possess the negativity of emptiness, threatening the beholder's individuality. This tension then fuels the progressive movement of the work of art, its action, leading toward a positive denouement in which the beautiful breaks down that tension. These and other ideas, as well as Solger's criticisms of the aesthetics of Johann Gottfried Herder, Gotthold Ephraim Lessing, and the influential eighteenth-century classical scholar Johann Joachim Winckelmann, can be found in the posthumously published *Vorlesungen über Ästhetik* (*Lectures on Aesthetics*, 1829).

Solger's star soon faded. But while he lived he was a persuasive lecturer and eloquent partner in conversation with many major literary figures of the age, including, while a student at Jena in the early 1800s, Johann Wolfgang von Goethe and Johann Christoph Friedrich von Schiller. His circle of friends in Berlin included the philologist Friedrich von der Hagen, the theologian Friedrich Daniel Ernst Schleiermacher, and Tieck, among others. Tieck and Friedrich von Raumer edited his posthumous papers.

MARK R. MCCULLOH

Biography

Born in Schwedt in northern Brandenburg, November 28, 1780. Studied law at the University of Halle beginning in 1799. Moved to Jena in 1801 to study under Schelling. Military, 1805–6. Doctoral degree, University of Berlin, 1809. Lecturer at the University of Frankfurt; full professor in Berlin in 1811; became rector of the University of Berlin and married Hernriette von Groeber in 1813. Died October 25, 1819.

Selected Writings

Translations
Sophocles, *Oedipus*. 1804.

Theory and Criticism
Erwin: Vier Gespräche über das Schöne und die Kunst. 1815.
  Reprinted 1907.
Philosophische Gespräche. 1817.
Vorlesungen über die Ästhetik. 1829.

Letters
Nachgelassene Schriften und Briefwechsel. 2 vols. 1826.
Tieck and Solger: The Complete Correspondence. 1933.

Bibliography

Dechem, Friedheim. *Die Ästhetik K.W.F. Solgers*. Heidelberg: Carl Winter, 1994.
Heller, Josef Elias. *Solgers Philosophie der ironischen Dialektik*. Berlin: Reuther und Reichard, 1928.
McCulloh, Mark R. "Karl Wilhelm Ferdinand Solger." In *Encyclopedia of Literary Critics and Criticism*, Vol. 2. Edited by Chris Murray. London: Fitzroy Dearborn, 1999.
Müller, Gustav. "Solger's Aesthetics—A Key to Hegel." In *Corona: Studies in Celebration of the eightieth Birthday of Samuel Singer*. Durham, N.C.: Duke University Press, 1941.

SOLITUDE AND COMMUNITY

Of the many stereotypical images of Romanticism, none has proved more lasting than that of the autonomous self often regarded as an invention of this period: the solitary, contemplative, typically male hero celebrated in such texts as William Wordsworth's great autobiographical poem *The Prelude*, or—very differently—in Lord Byron's *Childe Harold's Pilgrimage* and *Manfred*. This image of selfhood is epitomized by the figure represented in Caspar David Friedrich's painting *The Wanderer*: a single man, his back to the viewer, left alone to commune with the sublimity of nature and his own thoughts. Despite the seeming ubiquity of such images of autonomous selfhood, however, many literary and philosophical texts of the Romantic period reflect a keen understanding of the reciprocal and mutually determining relationship between self and society, and show an acute sensitivity to the relations between public and private affairs. Far from opposing solitude and community, then, most Romantic authors explicitly defined these terms in relation to each other.

In the emergence of solitude and community as interrelated themes, the importance of the so-called culture of sensibility is profound. In Britain, eighteenth-century moral philosophers such as David Hume and Adam Smith argued that emotion and sensibility—and not, as was traditionally asserted, reason and understanding—were the hallmarks of civilized, polite humanity. Much of the impetus for such theories was provided by a rapidly growing commercial and consumer society that was increasingly dependent upon trade for its prosperity. Within such a society, it was not merely expedient but necessary to cultivate virtues that would unite individuals as well as larger communities in networks of mutual interest. In novels such as Oliver Goldsmith's *The Vicar of Wakefield*, Henry Mackenzie's *The Man of Feeling*, and Laurence Sterne's *Sentimental Journey*, authors thus promoted a vision of a society held together by bonds of sympathy and affection.

Though the culture of sensibility is justly remembered for having fostered new models of social attachment, the fiction and philosophy of this period was just as significantly a source for conceptions of psychological interiority that were equally important to the subsequent development of Romantic thought and literature. If the phenomenal success of Johann Wolfgang von Goethe's sentimental novel, *Die Leiden des Jungen Werthers* (*The Sorrows of Young Werther*), could be taken as evidence of a network of sensibility that extended to and connected distant parts of the world, the novel itself was often seen as promoting a condition of morbid self-enclosure in its readers, some of whom reportedly went so far as to follow Goethe's protagonist in committing suicide. Moreover, though an acute sensibility was typically regarded as an indicator of social refinement, such conditions uneasily straddled the line that separated privilege from pathology. Though sensibility was closely tied to the social virtues, it was also responsible for countless hysteric ladies and hypochondriacal gentlemen, whose excesses were later parodied in texts such as Jane Austen's *Sense and Sensibility*, Maria Edgeworth's *Belinda*, and Thomas Love Peacock's *Nightmare Abbey*. Such novels revealed how an excess of physical and emotional sensibility might lead as much to solipsism as to the love of community. These and other Romantic texts criticize not only the morbid interiority of ladies and gentlemen of the "polite" ranks but also the sublime inwardness of figures who, such as Wordsworth, were led to prefer the countryside and mountain top to the coffeehouse or salon.

If one consequence of the culture of sensibility was to foreground tension between solitude and community, the cataclysmic events of the French Revolution had the effect of throwing such tensions into even greater relief. Not only was it possible, among opponents of the revolution, to describe mob activity in France or England as a kind of mass contagion and therefore a pathological expression of sensibility; from an opposite direction, one might accuse the revolutionaries—and the discourse of the "rights of man" generally—of having irreparably damaged traditional social bonds that once obtained between members of society. In the *Reflections on the Revolution in France*, Edmund Burke excoriated the revolutionaries and their British sympathizers whose politics, based on principles of rationalism and self-interest, would reduce the commonwealth to "the dust and powder of individuality." Burke's basis for making such claims clearly lay within the culture of sensibility, whose rhetoric he modified for a vastly transformed political reality.

Burke's characterization of an age in which individualist beliefs vitiated social bonds would prove deeply influential for the subsequent development of Romanticism, even among writers who did not share Burke's conservative values. In novels such as William Godwin's *Caleb Williams* and Mary Shelley's *Frankenstein*, readers were introduced to characters whose solitude was not conceived as a blessing—a privilege or prerogative of the individual rights-bearer—but rather as a curse imposed upon them through their own limitations and by a society that refused them sympathy. What is often described as the sympathetic imagination of Romantic literature thus clearly emerges against fears of entrapment, as John Keats puts it in the "Ode to a Nightingale," within the confines of the "sole self." In such Romantic works, individuality is not conceived as a privilege so much as a prison from which it is necessary to escape.

If Romanticism was a period that promoted the image of the solitary individual, then, it is the same period that saw an explosion in communal ideas and ideals as well: of social philosophies dedicated to the cause of universal suffrage, for instance, and the popularization of literary genres (such as the ballad) intended for wide popular audiences. Just as significantly, the assertion of autonomy in this period is often conceived as a means of realizing a new basis for community in the first place. Immanuel Kant's critical philosophy provided the conceptual foundations for such an approach, while G. W. F. Hegel elaborated the mutually-constitutive relationship between the subject and society. Within British Romanticism, a similar understanding informs lyric poems such as Wordsworth's "Lines, Written a Few Miles above Tintern Abbey" and Samuel Taylor Coleridge's "Frost at Midnight," which explore the private habits of mind required for realizing a sense of community through the activity of self-reflection. Such poems exemplify the effort on the part of many Romantic writers to reconcile the individual and the community without effacing the differences between these.

NOEL JACKSON

Bibliography

Barker-Benfield, G. J. *The Culture of Sensibility: Sex and Sociability in Eighteenth-Century England*. Chicago: University of Chicago Press, 1993.

Ferguson, Frances. *Solitude and the Sublime: Romanticism and the Poetics of Individuation*. New York: Routledge, 1992.

Garber, Frederick. *The Autonomy of the Self from Richardson to Huysmans*. Princeton, N.J.: Princeton University Press, 1982.

Janowitz, Anne. *Lyric and Labour in the Romantic Tradition*. Cambridge: Cambridge University Press, 1998.

Mullan, John. *Sentiment and Sociability: The Language of Feeling in Eighteenth-Century England*. Oxford: Oxford University Press, 1988.

Pinch, Adela. *Strange Fits of Passion: Epistemologies of Emotion, Hume to Austen*. Stanford, Calif.: Stanford University Press, 1995.

SOLOMOS, DIONYSIOS 1798–1857

Greek poet

Dionysios Solomos, like his near contemporary Andreas Kalvos, has enjoyed since the end of the nineteenth century the reputation of "national" poet. This is not only because the opening stanzas of his Ymnos eis tin Eleftherian (*Hymn to Liberty*, 1823) celebrating the Greek war of independence against the Ottoman Empire, became in 1865 the Greek national anthem, but also because his strong defense of the spoken form of Greek (in his *Dialogos* [*Dialogue*] of 1824) as the natural language of poetry endeared him to poets and readers, especially during the twentieth century. Solomos is credited with establishing, in his poetry, an authoritative literary form of the modern Greek language, comparable to the achievement of Dante Alighieri, Geoffrey Chaucer, Johann Wolfgang von Goethe, or Aleksandr Pushkin.

Like Kalvos, Solomos is not traditionally seen by Greek criticism as a Romantic writer. Partly this is due to a famous working note, one of a series associated with his ambitious, unfinished poem Oi eleftheroi poliorkemenoi (The Free Besieged), in which Solomos proposes to himself a kind of "third way" between Classicism and Romanticism. Partly, too, it is due to the strong influences of Italian neoclassicism in his early work. There has also been a reluctance to attach the term *Romantic* to a major Greek writer in Greek criticism since the turn of the twentieth century; it is generally restricted to minor writers of the period 1830–80, and Solomos is excluded from this group on grounds of his undisputed preeminence as well as of chronology.

Despite this, from today's perspective Solomos emerges as the most profound and sophisticated Greek writer to engage creatively with the ideas and poetic practice of the Romantic age. To some extent this is already visible in his early work.

He was a student at Pavia when the three manifestos of Italian Romanticism (by Giovanni Berchet, Pietro Borsieri, and Ludovico di Breme) appeared in 1816. In addition to the nationalism and patriotism of some of his early poetry, Solomos shared with these early Italian Romantics an admiration for Lord Byron, on whose death in 1824 he composed an impassioned poem. The unfinished long poem "Lambros," on which Solomos worked in the late 1820s, and whose vestigial plot revolves around a transgressor-hero, has generally been seen as conceived in the Byronic mold.

Despite his enthusiasm for the Greek national struggle, Solomos never set foot in independent Greece. In 1828 he moved from Zakynthos to Corfu, where he remained for the rest of his life. It was during his first years in Corfu that he became acquainted with the work of (among others) Gottfried Bürger, Johann Gottlieb Fichte, Goethe, G. W. F. Hegel, Friedrich Gottlieb Klopstock, Novalis, Johann Christoph Friedrich von Schiller, and Friedrich von Schlegel. Of these, the most important for Solomos's work was probably Schiller. Solomos read the Germans, whom he so much admired, not in the original language, but through translations into Italian provided for him by friends, often in response to very specific requests. Particularly during the years 1830–36, Solomos was avidly immersed in reading selections from German Romantic thinkers and poets.

This most productive period of his life was brought to a close by a bitter and protracted lawsuit, which began in 1836, when his half-brother challenged his claim to the title and property he had inherited from his aristocrat father (Dionysios had been born illegitimate).

In the poems of his Corfu period, once the war of independence on the Greek mainland was over, Solomos moved beyond the vibrant patriotism of his earlier work. Several of these works were conceived on a grand, "epicolyrical" scale; none was finished to the poet's satisfaction, and none was published during his lifetime. Ironically, therefore, the poems that should have determined the future course of a distinctively Greek branch of Romantic poetics and aesthetics were unknown to all but a handful of Solomos's contemporaries and became available only after his death. (Indeed the prose satire, H Gynaika tes Zakythos ("The Woman of Zakynthos"), which depicts the evil inverse of the ideal pursued in the poems, was suppressed by Solomos's first editor and first saw print in 1927, a century after it had been started.)

"The Free Besieged" was first conceived as the epic of the resistance by the Greek defenders of Mesolonghi against superior Ottoman forces, which had ended in a doomed attempt by the survivors to break out, in April 1826. By 1833 the raw event had been subsumed, in a very different second draft of the poem, into a lyrical exploration of the paradox of its title. In an evident echo of Schiller, the besieged citizens of Mesolonghi are subjected to a final temptation by the beauties of nature that surround them in spring, in order for their souls to achieve true freedom in the renunciation of all earthly things. But Solomos, like many other Greek writers after him, resists the abstract separation between soul and body that he found in Schiller and the German Romantics. In "The Free Besieged" the ideal of absolute freedom is attained only in this world, in the decision of the defenders, suspended between the beauty and vitality of spring time nature on the one hand and the destructive power of the enemy, to lay down their lives in an act of heroic defiance on the other.

A similar nexus of themes can be observed in "O Kretihos, ("The Cretan," 1833) and "O Porfyras" ("The Shark," 1849). In the first, the hero of the title is depicted swimming away from a shipwreck on a stormy night, with his fiancée in his arms. While in the sea, he experiences a transcendent vision and sound, and the storm is miraculously calmed. He brings the girl to shore, only to discover, in the poem's very last word, that she is dead. In "The Shark," about the violent death of a British soldier while bathing off Corfu, the lightning-flash that brings wholeness and self-knowledge comes on the very cusp between life and death.

Throughout his life, Solomos was evidently more at ease writing in Italian, the language of his formal education, than in Greek. Many of his poems were drafted first in Italian prose, and only then put into Greek verse. In his later years, he wrote only in Italian.

RODERICK BEATON

Biography

Born in Zakynthos (Zante) April 8, 1798, the illegitimate son of Count Nikolaos Solomos and a servant girl whom the count later married. Studied at Cremona, 1808–15, then at the law school of the University of Pavia, 1815–17. Returned to Zakynthos, 1818. Published his first poems (in Italian), 1822. Left Zakynthos definitively for Corfu, 1828. Poems published in the *Ionian Anthology*, 1834; lawsuit brought by his half-brother over right to the title of count and to property (won by Solomos), 1836–38. Title of count confirmed by the Ionian Islands parliament, 1840. Musical setting of his *Hymn to Liberty* as a cantata by Nikolaos Mantzaros, 1844. Awarded Gold Cross of the Order of the Saviour by King Otto of Greece, 1849. Died of a stroke, Corfu, February 9, 1857.

Selected Writings

Collections

Apanta. 3 vols. Edited by Linos Politis. Athens: Ikaros, 1948–91.
Poiemata kai peza. Edited by Stylianos Alexiou. Athens: Stigme, 1994.
The Free Besieged and Other Poems. Edited and translated by Peter Mackridge. Nottingham, England: Shoestring Press 2000.

Poetry

Rime improvvisate. Corfu: privately published, 1822.
Ymnos eis tin Eleftherian, 1825. Mesoloughi: D. Mesthenis. Published in Italian as *Inno alla Libertà*, 1825. Translated as *Hymn to Liberty* by Charles Brinsley Sheridan, 1825.
Ta Evriskomena. Corfu: privately published, 1859.

Fiction

O Dialogos. In *Ta Evriskomena.* 1859.
E Gynaika tis Zakythos. Athens: Stochastis, 1927.

Bibliography

Beaton, Roderick. "Dionysios Solomos: The Tree of Poetry," *Byzantine and Modern Greek Studies* 2 (1976): 161–82.
Coutelle, Louis. *Formation poétique de Solomos.* Athens: Ermis, 1977.
Jenkins, Romilly. *Dionysius Solomòs.* 1940. Reprint, Athens: Denise Harvey, 1981.
Mackridge, Peter. *Dionysios Solomos.* Studies in Modern Greek. Bristol, Eng.: Bristol Classical Press/New Rochelle, N.Y.: Aristide Caratzas, 1989.
Raizis, Marios Byron. *Dionysios Solomos.* World Authors Series. New York: Twayne, 1972.
Sherrard, Philip. *The Marble Threshing Floor: Studies in Modern Greek Poetry.* 1956. Reprint Athens: Denise Harvey, 1981.

SONATA

The period 1760 to 1850 was the golden age of the sonata. Before the mid-eighteenth century—that is, during the Baroque and early classical era—the genre had not yet reached maturity. Thus the early trio sonata, *sonata da chiesa* (church sonata), and *sonata da camera* (chamber or court sonata) represent concepts to a greater or lesser degree foreign to the genre as we understand it today. From the mid-nineteenth century, however, a variety of factors led to the sonata's decline, the most important of which concern first the incompatibility of Romantic philosophy with a genre which had traditionally placed a strong emphasis on formal elements, and second, compositional problems in reconciling the era's complex harmonic palette with sonata form's dependence on readily discernible harmonic movement.

Reflecting the prestige of the sonata, a truly remarkable diversity of forms and styles emerged during this period. Broadly speaking, these follow an evolutionary development parallel with the musical periods (classical, then Romantic) in which they were written. Consequently, eighteenth-century sonatas tend to feature a relatively transparent and concise formal plan as well as clear harmonic structures, while nineteenth-century sonatas involve increasingly lengthy and complicated designs, and often include so-called "cyclic" elements (which serve to tighten the links between the separate movements, thus heightening a sense of the work as a whole).

Common to all sonatas is the presence of sonata form in at least one of the movements. This form is constituted most fundamentally by:

1. An exposition section, in which the most important themes are presented and in which the harmonic structure is relatively stable;
2. A development section, in which these themes are reworked and/or new themes are introduced and in which the harmonic structure is more exploratory;
3. A recapitulation section, in which all or most of the exposition's themes return and any harmonic "loose ends" are tied up.

In its textbook manifestation, the music follows a path to its climax in the development, with a sense of closure provided by the recapitulation.

Although the individual treatment of sonata form by great eighteenth-century composers such as Franz Joseph Haydn, Wolfgang Amadeus Mozart, and the early Ludwig van Beethoven naturally varied, virtually all their works share one common trait: a compositional style that thrived on a well-balanced, almost crystalline sectionalization, a trait which in fact typifies the classical period as a whole. Most obviously, this is illustrated both visually and aurally by the frequent presence of repeat signs between the exposition and development. By the beginning of the nineteenth century, however, a trend toward continuity had begun to impact upon sonata form. More than anything else, it was Beethoven's sense of drama that demanded an end to overt sectionalization, since junctures create the effect of stopping and starting, thus undermining the kind of gathering momentum required in order to evoke successfully a powerful emotional journey. (Indeed, the increasingly compelling emotional content of sonatas written by turn-of-the-century composers such as Beethoven, Jan Ladislav Dussek, and later Franz Peter Schubert is representative of Romantic music in general.) The emphasis on drama also impinged on the relative weight of component parts within sonata form. Starting with Beethoven, development sections became increasingly lengthy and, likewise serving to maximize dramatic tension, the overall climax of movements tended to occur as late as possible, in order to avoid an anti-climactic recapitulation. Related to this, coda sections, which during the eighteenth century usually consisted of just a few closing bars tagged on to the end of the recapitulation, gained an increasingly important function. In works such as Beethoven's "Waldstein" Sonata, op. 53, and the "Appassionata," op. 57, the coda actually contains the harmonic apotheosis and dramatic climax, respectively, of the movement.

This same principle was applied also to the work as a whole: that is, the tension arched over and through the individual movements, continuing until it was resolved in the finale. As such, the constituent movements of a sonata could often no longer be regarded as truly separate entities; they formed parts of a greater whole. This revolutionized the entire concept of the sonata. Before Beethoven, the greatest weight tended to be apportioned to the first movement, something quite natural given the serious nature of a typical sonata-form movement. If, however, the sonata is treated as a whole—that is, as a "cycle" of linked movements—and tension sustained from beginning to end of the work, then the overall climax must occur in the final movement. Although the most famous examples of this occur in Beethoven's Fifth and Ninth Symphonies, his late piano sonatas (from op. 101 to op. 111) also feature a similar strategy, in which the greatest weight is clearly allotted to the finale. Later composers, particularly Schubert and Franz Liszt, involved cyclic elements in their sonatas. The most extreme application of this principle involves the fusing together of different movements, so that the music flows uninterrupted and without a resting point from one movement into another. The most magnificent example of this occurs in Liszt's B minor Sonata, in which the boundaries between all the movements are dissolved to produce a single monumental gesture.

Correlated with the aforementioned sense of drama and need to express a wider range of emotions, the first two decades of the nineteenth century also witnessed an exploration of increasingly intricate and exotic harmonies—indeed, this is one of the hallmarks of Romantic music. In this respect, Beethoven and especially Schubert were instrumental in forging a path for later composers. Particularly noteworthy is Schubert's lifelong reliance on harmonic areas other than the traditional dominant (such as the mediant and sub-mediant) at key points within sonata form. Given that the next generation of composers, including Robert Alexander Schumann, Frédéric Chopin, and Liszt were born too late to experience the classical age first-hand, it should come as no surprise that the application of increasingly intricate and exotic harmonic structures further accelerated. To an extent, the growing harmonic complexities of the Romantic age actually began to obfuscate and undermine the long-term harmonic strategy upon which the form had always been based. Romantic composers tended to compensate for this by tightening the melodic threads (motives) woven through the music's fabric.

Following the deaths of Beethoven and Schubert (and with them the classical period as a whole), the golden age of the sonata began to approach its end, though this is not to deny that some of the greatest works in the genre were written only later in the nineteenth century. The reason why the keyboard sonatas of Schumann, Chopin, and Liszt can each be numbered on the fingers of only one hand (in contrast to the combined total of 120 such works by Haydn, Mozart, Beethoven, and Schubert) seems to lie at the very heart of the Romantic spirit: one which thrived on spontaneity and freedom, and even reveled in throwing off the careful, calculated elements of balance so characteristic of classical-period music. Although sonata form was without doubt extremely malleable in the hands of individual composers, it nevertheless remained an inherently complex form. It should therefore come as no surprise that many nineteenth-century composers sought liberation from it; indeed, a proliferation of small, simple forms characterizes Romantic music, especially that stemming from the first half of the nineteenth century. (And in the case of those composers for whom abstract form in general had lost its attraction, an extra-musical program often served as a viable alternative to hold the music together.) Thus Schumann is not famous for his sonatas but rather his cycles of intimate piano pieces. Chopin is likewise famous for his nocturnes, polonaises, and mazurkas and not his sonatas, which like Schumann's have sometimes been criticized for sounding overly academic and self-conscious. Only Liszt succeeded in truly reconciling the sonata and sonata form with Romantic philosophy, for the formal structure underlying works like the Dante Sonata (1839) and the mighty B minor Sonata (1853) so perfectly resonates with the musical content that it remains virtually invisible.

TALLIS BARKER

Bibliography

Griffiths, Paul, William, Newman Michael. Tilmouth and "Sonata." In *New Grove Dictionary of Music and Musicians*. In London, 1980.

Newman, William. *The Sonata in the Baroque Era*. New York, 1983.

———. *The Sonata in the Classic Era*. New York, 1983.

———. *The Sonata after Beethoven*. New York, 1983.

Rosen, Charles. *The Classical Style*. New York, 1972.

———. *Sonata Forms*. New York, 1988.

Stein, Leon. *Structure and Style*. Princeton, 1979.

Webster, James. 'Sonata Form.' In *New Grove Dictionary of Music and Musicians*. London, 1980.

SONGS OF INNOCENCE AND OF EXPERIENCE

Collection of poetry by William Blake, 1794

With the possible exception of "Jerusalem," which was set to music by Sir Hubert Parry, *Songs of Innocence and of Experience* (1794) is by far William Blake's best-known work. The poems in this collection are also among his most anthologized, and so they have reached a far greater readership than he had in his own lifetime. By his own standards, however, the *Songs* were very popular. Blake himself printed twenty-six copies of the *Songs of Innocence* and twenty-four copies of the combined *Songs of Innocence and of Experience*. His later poetry was never published in this many copies; they had no immediate market and Blake's laborious printing technique was hardly conducive to mass publication.

Although Blake's illuminated printing technique prevented him from mass production, it gave him the freedom to publish his own poetry. It also allowed him to combine color illustrations on a page with the printed text. This technique is described on plate 15 of "The Marriage of Heaven and Hell" (1790), where "flaming fires" melting "metals into living fluids" evoke an infernal atmosphere. If these details are interpreted literally as well as metaphorically, the infernal production can be seen as a reference to the eating away of acids on the copper plates that Blake used to print his illuminated poetry, thus acknowledging that his achievement is a combination of metaphorical poetics and literal, visual craftsmanship.

In "The Marriage," the conventional meaning of good and evil is explicitly turned upside down; it is therefore likely that the concepts of innocence and experience in *Songs*, which were begun around 1789, are more complex than the title would seem to imply. On the surface, the state of innocence seems to be an idyllic, pastoral world where children are free from hardship and abuse, but beneath the surface, and especially when read in light of "The Book of Thel," this same childish freedom and naïveté is boxed in by its dependence on the adult world because permanent childhood implies stagnation. Likewise, the state of experience is superficially a harsh world of suffering and cynical abuse of authority, but although it represents a dystopian view of Blake's contemporary society, the ironic tone of the poetry indicates that there is another and better way of living life. According to M. H. Abrams this dialectic understanding of innocence and experience is similar to William Wordsworth's notion of a fortunate fall into the world of experience where the pain of experience is outweighed by the knowledge gained.

Part of the explanation for the popularity of the *Songs* is that they have an easily accessible surface: they are pretty to look at, the texts are easy to understand, and many of the poems seem to have a moral that even a child can extract. Indeed, the *Songs of Innocence* (1789) in particular appear ideally suited for children, because superficially they seem to illustrate Jean-Jacques Rousseau's focus on children's natural innocence and purity (in contrast to the corruption of adulthood). Notably, Blake continued to print *Songs of Innocence* alone even after he had written *Songs of Experience*, but *Songs of Experience* was always published in combination with *Songs of Innocence*. This indicates that it is possible to read the idyllic and pastoral *Songs of Innocence* alone, whereas the harsher aspects of *Songs of Experience* need to be balanced with the state of innocence.

Unlike G. W. F. Hegel's philosophy of dialectics, Blake's concepts of innocence and experience do not transcend their differences by merging into a synthesis; their true value lies in the energy that is produced when they collide, for "Without Contraries is no progression" (plate 3, "The Marriage"). This fruitful conflict is not just one of innocence and experience. It is also the collision of child and adult, Christianity and Platonism, wealth and poverty, and sincerity and hypocrisy. This underlying state of tension is directly built into the dialectic structure of the *Songs*, and represented thematically inside each poem and poem pair. The tension spans the issues of religion ("The Garden of Love"), race ("The Little Black Boy"), interpersonal relations ("My Pretty Rose Tree" and "The Angel"), contemporary social criticism ("The Chimney Sweeper" and "London"), and ethics ("A Poison Tree" and "The Human Abstract") while never overshadowing the beauty of the poetry. The power of this poetry lies in its ability to encompass all of these conflicting tendencies, and subsequently, in its ability to harness the energy that they engender.

The most famous pair of poems in the collection is "The Lamb" and "The Tyger." The persona in both poems addresses an animal, and the nature of the address is dependent on the nature of the animal. "The Lamb" is written in soft, undulating tetrameters that underline the meekness of both the little boy

William Blake, *The Fly*; plate 41 from *Songs of Innocence and of Experience*, c. 1802–8. Reprinted courtesy of The Bridgeman Art Library.

and the lamb he is addressing. In contrast, although written in the same four-footed line, "The Tyger" is written in hard, direct thrusts of syllables, befitting both the violence of the tiger and the persona's state of experience.

The difference between the two poems is also reflected in their imagery: The lamb is an animal associated with the pastoral tradition, and in the Christian tradition it is a symbol for Jesus Christ. This religious symbolism is made quite clear in the second stanza when the persona says that "He is called by thy name / For he calls himself a Lamb / He is meek and he is mild / He became a little child." The Christian imagery is, however, not purely reassuring, because behind the idea of Jesus as a lamb— *Agnus Dei*—lies the violence of the sacrifice on the cross, and so the apparent idyll of the world of innocence carries within itself the seeds of the imagery of experience. In "The Tyger" the imagery is no longer organic and brightly colored; it is now dark, metallic, and threatening. The tiger is fabricated symmetrically in a forge and its creation out of blacksmith's tools dominates

the imagery with infernal connotations, thus adding an ironic dimension to the poem. Indeed, if "The Tyger" is read in the light of "The Marriage," such devilry is no longer unequivocally negative. The irony that is so obvious in "The Marriage" is arguably also present in the *Songs of Innocence and of Experience*, because there is latent violence in the imagery of "The Lamb" and potentially positive energy in the power of "The Tyger." So, the conflict between the states of innocence and experience can be seen to exist within each single poem as well as in each diametrically opposed pair.

Of all the connections between the two poems, and perhaps between all of the poems in *Songs of Innocence and of Experience*, the most obvious and powerful link is line 20 of "The Tyger," which asks, "Did he who made the Lamb make thee?" Superficially, the question may seem rhetorical and therefore unanswerable, but beneath the surface it is nothing less than the question of theodicy.

HENRIETTE B. STAVIS

Selected Works

Songs Of Innocence and Songs Of Experience: Shewing the Two Contrary States of the Human Soul. c. 1789.
Songs of Innocence and of Experience. Introduction and commentary by Geoffrey Keynes. Oxford: Oxford University Press, 1967.
The Complete Poetry and Prose of William Blake. Edited by David V. Erdman. Commentary by Harold Bloom. New York: Doubleday, 1988.
Songs of Innocence and of Experience. Edited by Andrew Lincoln. London: William Blake Trust, 1991.

Bibliography

Abrams, M. H. *Natural Supernaturalism: Tradition and Revolution in Romantic Literature.* New York: W. W. Norton, 1971.
Bloom, Harold. *The Pastoral Image in Blake's Apocalypse.* London: Victor Gollancz, 1963.
Bottrall, Margaret, ed. *Songs of Innocence and Experience: A Selection of Critical Essays.* London: Macmillan, 1974.
Frye, Northrop. "The Refiner in Fire." In *Fearful Symmetry: A Study of William Blake.* Princeton, N.J.: Princeton University Press, 1947.
Fuller, David. "Before 'The Four Zoas'." In *Blake's Heroic Argument.* London: Croom Helm, 1988.
Gardner, Stanley. *Blake's Innocence and Experience Retraced.* London: Athlone Press, 1986.
———. *The Tyger, the Lamb and the Terrible Desart: "Songs of Innocence and of Experience" in its Times and Circumstances.* London: Cygnus Arts, 1998.
Johnson, Mary Lynn, and John E. Grant, eds. *Blake's Poetry and Designs.* New York: W. W. Norton, 1979.
Paley, Morton D. "Tyger of Wrath." In *Energy and the Imagination: A Study of the Development of Blake's Thought.* Oxford: Clarendon Press, 1970.

Website

The William Blake Archive. Edited by Morris Eaves, Robert Essick, and Joseph Viscomi. <http://jefferson.village.virginia.edu/blake/>

THE SORROWS OF YOUNG WERTHER (DIE LEIDEN DES JUNGEN WERTHERS) 1774

Novel by Johann Wolfgang von Goethe

The Sorrows of Young Werther is the story, told in epistolary form, of a young man who falls hopelessly in love with a woman betrothed to another man. Unable either to win her over or to subdue his feelings, Werther eventually commits suicide with pistols borrowed from his beloved's husband. While Johann Wolfgang von Goethe's novel may seem to be related more closely to the eighteenth-century cult of sentiment than to Romanticism, it was nonetheless a radical text that helped to make possible the sorts of cultural change that Romanticism represented. It is because of *Werther*, for instance, that the calm introspectiveness of Jean-Jacques Rousseau's *Reveries of a Solitary Walker* (1782) was able to be transformed into the brooding and volatile interiority of Lord Byron's *Childe Harold's Pilgrimage* (1812–18). The German Romantics much preferred those other writings by Goethe, such as *Wilhelm Meister's Lehrjahre* (1821–29) and *Faust* (1808, 1832), that emphasized an ongoing and restless process of self-development. Indeed, Friedrich von Schlegel proclaimed *Wilhelm Meister* one of the great accomplishments of the age.

It is worth noting that *Werther* was based to a certain extent upon Goethe's own experiences. While staying in Wetzlar in 1772, Goethe formed a great passion for Charlotte Buff, who was betrothed to the remarkably understanding Johann Christian Kestner. The story, recounted to Goethe by Kestner, of a young man in a similar situation who committed suicide in despair provided the inspiration for the transformation of this experience into a novel. Ironically, after the publication of *Werther*, Goethe moved to Weimar, where he fell in love with a married woman named Charlotte von Stein. The relationship proved to be as intense and frustrating as the one depicted in *Werther*. It took a long vacation in Italy to cure Goethe of this passion.

In terms of Goethe's own literary development, *Werther* seems to have functioned as a transitional work. Falling between the exuberance of his Sturm und Drang works and the austere restraint of Weimar classicism, *Werther* seems to be a culminating point of emotional excess in Goethe's work. Subsequently, Goethe successfully sublimated such excess. Thus, despite the fact that the novel was his most successful and famous work, Goethe maintained a cautious and circumspect relationship to it.

One of the most noted facts about *Werther* is the fantastic success it enjoyed in Europe. The reception accorded to the novel was so ardent that in Germany it was termed *Wertherfieber* ("Werther fever"). Not only was the novel retold, continued, and parodied in novels, poems, and plays, but it inspired fashions (the signature blue jacket and yellow vest worn by *Werther*), prints, porcelain designs, and a rash of imitative suicides. It even boasted among its fans Napoleon Bonaparte, who claimed he carried it in his pocket during his expedition to Egypt.

However, *Werther* was much more than a broad popular success. It was one of the key indices of a sea change in European culture, helping to make clear that the shift from the Enlightenment to Romanticism was not simply a shift in cultural fashion but a transformation of sensibility. It contributed to this change on both formal and conceptual levels.

On the formal level, the language in the novel was characterized by clarity and immediacy of emotional expression. The epistolary format of the novel helped Goethe to achieve this effect. Moving away from the use of letters (as in Tobias Smollett's *Humphry Clinker*, 1771) to underscore the picaresque, episodic nature of narrative, Goethe pursued a path forged by Samuel Richardson, employing letters to delve ever more deeply into the interiority of the protagonist. Moreover, the language of the letters, while dealing with emotions in extremis, is characterized by a transparent directness. It is this aspect that rooted the novel in the larger articulation of a form of subjectivity specific to a middle class that was gradually emancipating itself. As Jürgen Habermas has argued with regard to sociopolitical formations, and as Ian Watt has argued more specifically with regard to the genre of the novel, the emergent middle class required discursive forms that were characterized by their communicability. These discursive forms facilitated a mastery of the physical and social environment as well as oneself. Indeed, in a world characterized less and less by the preestablished strictures

Illustration for Johann Wolfgang von Goethe's *Die Leiden des Jungen Werthers* (*the Sorrows of Young Werther*). Reprinted courtesy of AKG London.

of feudalism, self-direction, self-awareness, and self-management became essential. Thus, for example, the linkage of novels such as Richardson's *Pamela* (1740) to conduct manuals is not as coincidental as it may at first seem. However, Goethe's novel ultimately exceeds the bounds of these discursive forms, in that it is the story of the ultimate failure of self-management.

On the conceptual level, *Werther* helped to introduce the notion of an expansive interiority that the subject itself did not fully understand or control. This uncontrollability was crystallized in the form of passion. Passion—true to its etymology—was a force at the innermost core of interiority that the subject had no choice but to suffer. In its milder forms it helped to make possible the transition from the meticulous cataloging of interiority to be found in Rousseau's *Confessions* (1782–89) to the frustratingly ex post facto understanding of the self to be found in William Wordsworth's *Prelude* (1850). In its more exaggerated forms, it helped to give license to the demonic passion of Wolfgang Amadeus Mozart's *Don Giovanni* (1787) to become the frank *Liebestod* of Richard Wagner's *Tristan and Isolde* (1865). Werther's passion, accordingly, assumed the form of a spectacle, with its own attendant and inexorable stations of the cross, revealing that the minute inspection of the self could turn into an abyss from which no form of management or regulation might be salvaged.

Goethe's novel thus contributed to the articulation of a middle-class subjectivity, but in a way that pinpointed the fissures that threatened to sunder that very subjectivity. The government of the self—which is the essence of the subjective and social revolution of the middle class—was shown to be a dangerous illusion. Indeed, in Goethe's novel, the eroticized relation to one's own subjection that self-government (in all its senses) necessitated is exposed as leading to the dissolution of the self. Hence, while *Werther* still serves as a document of a profound change in sensibility in the eighteenth century, there remains something dangerous and subversive about it. For if it is an index of the articulation of a new discourse of passion, as well as middle-class subjectivity, the novel makes clear how unstable, excessive, and destructive these new formations could be. It is ultimately a document not of the articulation but of the disarticulation of a discourse. This aspect of *Werther* was brilliantly captured by Roland Barthes, who made the novel a touchstone for his own 1977 *Lover's Discourse*.

STUART BARNETT

Text

Die Leiden des Jungen Werthers, 1774. Translated as *The Sorrows of Young Werther* by Catherine Hutter in *The Sorrows of Young Werther and Selected Writings* (New York: New American Library, 1962); by Elizabeth Mayer and Louise Brogan in *The Sorrows of Young Werther and Novella* (New York: Modern Library, 1971); by Victor Lange and Judith Ryan in *The Sorrows of Young Werther, Elective Affinities, and Novella* (New York: Surkhamp, 1988); and as *The Sorrows of Young Werther* by Michael Hulse (New York: Viking, 1989).

Bibliography

Atkins, Stuart. *The Testament of Werther in Poetry and Drama.* Cambridge, Mass.: Harvard University Press, 1949.
Blackall, Eric. *Goethe and the Novel.* Ithaca, New York: Cornell University Press, 1976.
Friedenthal, Richard. *Goethe: His Life and Times.* New York: World Publishing, 1963.
Hatfield, Henry. *Aesthetic Paganism in German Literature: From Winckelmann to the Death of Goethe.* Cambridge, Mass.: Harvard University Press, 1964.
Lukács, Georg. *Goethe and His Age.* London: Merlin Press, 1968.
Vincent, Dierde. *Werther's Goethe and the Game of Literary Creativity.* Toronto: University of Toronto Press, 1992.

SOUTHEY, ROBERT 1774–1843

English poet

Robert Southey was one of the "lake poets," Lord Byron's trio of William Wordsworth, Samuel Taylor Coleridge, and Southey, whom he dismissed in *Don Juan* (1819–24) as being respectively "crazed beyond all hope . . . drunk . . . and all quaint and mouthey." The association links Southey with two leading Romantics, while the dismissal demonstrates that another, Byron, distanced himself from them. The term "lake poets," however, implies a coherent vision that was in fact lacking. Although he thought that Wordsworth was the greatest of English poets, Southey did not use him as a model for his own poetry, his principal poems being long verse epics. As for Coleridge, Southey distrusted his metaphysical and philosophical continental influences, being much more the typical Englishman in his empiricism. He was very distrustful even of English utilitarianism. Indeed, in many respects Southey was distinctly un-Romantic, even anti-Romantic, in his attitudes. Thus, though he flirted briefly with Unitarianism in his youth, he never rejected orthodox religion for atheism or pantheism, and became a firm Anglican in his later years.

Southey was educated at Westminster School, from which he was expelled for his contribution to the *Flagellant* of an article that was highly critical of corporal punishment. His expulsion cost him a place at Christ Church, Oxford. The sheer injustice of the experience seems to have converted the naturally conservative Southey into a radical critic of the establishment. Thus, in 1795, he delivered a series of twelve public lectures in Bristol on European history from classical Greece to the American Revolution in which he boasted that he had proclaimed the truth and divinity of the doctrines of Tom Paine. His political stance at the age of twenty-one was that of a republican and a leveler. With Coleridge he wrote a verse drama, *The Fall of Robespierre* (1794); the two poets shared the enthusiasm of the first generation of English Romantics for the French Revolution. They also devised schemes to settle a colony on the banks of the Susquehanna River in America on principles they termed "pantisocracy," or the rule of all. Although this Romantic scheme collapsed through its sheer impracticality, echoes of it can be discerned in Southey's epic *Madoc* (1805). The hero of this poem is a Welsh warrior who decides to leave Wales after its conquest by the Saxons to take refuge in the wilds of America. Southey had toyed with the idea of settling his utopian community in Wales after deciding that he could not afford to go to Pennsylvania. Southey in fact spent the years 1795–96 in Portugal. While most Romantics were exposed to northern European and especially Germanic influences, Southey was influenced by Portuguese and Spanish culture.

Southey's first major poem, *Joan of Arc*, was published in 1796. It sold well, meriting a second edition in 1798. Southey later attributed its success to the fact that it was written in a republican spirit "such as may easily be accounted for in a youth whose notions of liberty were taken from the Greek and Roman writers, and who was ignorant of history and of human nature to believe that a happier order of things had commenced with the independence of the United States, and would be accelerated by the French Revolution."

On his return from Portugal, Southey contributed poems to the *Morning Post* and reviews to the *Critical Review*, including one on lyrical ballads in which he dismissed Coleridge's *Rime of the Ancient Mariner* "as a poem of little merit." In 1800 he completed another epic, *Thalaba the Destroyer*. This was an Arabian tale, Southey's contribution to the orientalism that was a significant feature of Romanticism.

The aspects of English life that the youthful Southey disliked so much that they led him to contemplate immigration, even to Portugal, were the subject of his first major prose work, *Letters from England by Don Manuel Alvarez Espriella*, which appeared in 1807. He began in 1808 to contribute essays and reviews to the newly launched *Quarterly Review*, for which he wrote regularly until 1839. This marked the turning point in his political views from radicalism to conservatism. He had found a cause in Spain's resistance to Napoleon Bonaparte that was to absorb his political energies. His acceptance into the establishment was regarded as the ultimate political betrayal by those who recalled his radical youth. He himself was given an embarrassing reminder of his earlier republicanism by the pirate publication in 1817 of *Wat Tyler*, which he had written in 1797. Southey tried to dismiss his defense of the rebel as being "among the follies of my youth," but much damage was done to his reputation.

Further damage was inflicted on Southey by his long-standing opponent, Byron. On the death of George III in 1821, Southey continued the quarrel by publishing a eulogy *A Vision of Judgement*, in the preface of which he attacked what he termed the "Satanic school" of poets; although he did not name individuals it was obvious that his main target was Byron. Byron could not resist the challenge and riposted with a parody of Southey's poem, *The Vision of Judgment* (1822), which mocked not only the conceit of the original poem but also the poet himself.

Southey had dubbed the younger Romantics the "Satanic school" because of their atheism. He himself became increasingly

religious as he grew older, and saw the Church of England as a bulwark against papism on the one hand and anarchy on the other. This philosophy inspired him to write *The Book of the Church* (1824). It also informed his *Sir Thomas More, or Colloquies on Society*, which he published in 1829 after reflecting upon its subject matter for a decade or more. Southey's last major work was *The Doctor* (1834–47), a rambling fiction inspired by Laurence Sterne's *Tristram Shandy* (1759–67). It is chiefly remembered now for containing one of the earliest versions of "The Story of the Three Bears."

W. A. SPECK

Biography

Born in Bristol August 12, 1774. Educated at Westminster School and Balliol College, Oxford. Married Edith Fricker, 1795. In Portugal and Spain, 1795–96 and 1800. Settled in Keswick, 1803. Poet Laureate, 1813. Married Caroline Bowles in 1839 after the death of his first wife. Died in 21 March 1843 after a decline of his mental powers.

Selected Works

Poetry
Joan of Arc. 1796.
Thalaba the Destroyer. 1801.
Madoc. 1805.
The Curse of Kehama. 1810.
Roderick the Last of the Goths. 1814.
Wat Tyler. 1817.
A Vision of Judgement. 1821.

Fiction
Letters from England by Don Manuel Alvarez Espriella. 1807.
Sir Thomas More, or Colloquies on Society. 1831.
The Doctor. 7 vols. 1835–47.

Nonfiction
The History of Brazil. 3 vols. 1810–19.
The Life of Nelson. 1813.
The Life of Wesley and the Rise and Progress of Methodism. 1820.
A History of the Peninsular War. 3 vols. 1823–32.
The Book of the Church. 1824.
Vindiciae Ecclesiae Anglicanae. 1826.

Bibliography

Carnall, Geoffrey. *Robert Southey and His Age: The Development of a Conservative Mind*. Oxford: Oxford University Press, 1960.
Curry, Kenneth. *Southey*. London: Routledge and Kegan Paul, 1975.
Madden, Lionel, ed. *Robert Southey: The Critical Heritage*. London: Routledge and Kegan Paul, 1972.
Smith, Christopher. *A Quest for Home: Reading Robert Southey*. Liverpool: Liverpool University Press, 1997.
Storey, Mark. *Robert Southey: A Life*. Oxford: Oxford University Press, 1997.

SPAIN: CULTURAL SURVEY

The Spanish Romantic period is often portrayed as backward, and lacking in sustained radicalism. However, the cultural development of Spain between 1760 and 1850 is a complex matter not so easily explained by simple narratives. It was a time that saw debates and changes that have been of continued relevance throughout the modern period.

Despite significant obstacles (notably high illiteracy rates and the liberal exile of 1814–20 and 1823–33), Spanish culture and institutions sought to adapt to wider European—especially French—models. Foreign books (and translations of them) circulated, sometimes secretly under the ancien régime, more freely under liberal rule. Such awareness of European culture and ideas was reinforced by exile in Britain and France.

Important developments can be traced back to the second half of the eighteenth century, sometimes referred to by Russell Sebold's term "first Romanticism," with works such as the formally and intellectually provocative tale of necrophilia, *Noches lúgubres* (*Mournful Nights*, early 1770s) by José Cadalso y Váquez.

At the same time, in the visual arts, the arrival, presence, and influence of the neoclassical painter Anton Raffael Mengs and the Rococo painter Giambattista Tiepolo at the "Enlightened Despotic Court" were not the sole highlights of the period. Attention should be drawn to the achievements of native artists: outstanding among them is Francisco José de Goya y Lucientes, but other important artists include Goya's one-time mentor and brother-in-law Francisco Bayeu, the vivid still-life painter Luis Meléndez, the more extravagant Luis Paret, and Mariano Salvador Maella. The difficulty in tracing a simple, single path may be seen not simply in the complexities of Goya's own trajectory as court artist and dark visionary, but by comparing his works to those of his younger contemporaries, influenced by Jacques-Louis David, José Aparicio Inglada, José de Madrazo, Juan Antonio de Ribera, or in the detailed approach of Vicente López, a favored court painter after 1814.

Late Enlightenment or pre-Romantic Spain saw debates about natural law and revolution. Early forms of historicism arose, including a Liberal Nationalist tradition dedicated to reviving in modern form a supposed medieval parliamentary past. Thinkers discussed the balance between neoclassical form and the marked divergences from it attributed to traditional Spanish literature, embodied in particular in the drama and poetry of Spain's golden age (c. 1500–c. 1680).

Though there had been earlier efforts (notably by the absolutist Johann Niklaus von Böhl von Faber in the 1810s), Agustín Durán was the key figure within Spain to make a Schlegelian defense of Spanish literature's heterogeneity, flexibility, and rich images, reconciling it with Liberal Nationalism from 1828 onward. In the mid-1830s, liberalization and the return of exiles brought a further influx of Romantic ideas, especially from France, though also from England, where the historical novel had developed. Like Victor Hugo, Spanish Liberals saw the new literature as a key component of the new society. And like many French critics, they were concerned with integrating its freer subjectivism, its exploration of ethical boundaries, and sublime and grotesque with the Liberal order. They sought to consider how the new literature might relate to Spanish Liberal National-

ist views. In this, they echoed political theorists on left and right who, troubled over the destiny of Liberal Nationalist aspirations and influenced by French writers (Victor Cousin, François Guizot, Jean Louis Eugène Lerminier), sought to reintegrate the energy of revolution into a philosophical theory of historical development that would explain a new era.

The theater of the mid-1830s (that of Antonio García Gutiérrez, Juan Eugenio Hartzenbusch, and Angel de Saavedra, Duque de Rivas)—dynamic and free in its use of the stage, verse form, and structure—was resonant with unsettled issues. Poets like Salvador Bermúdez de Castro, José de Espronceda y Delgado, and Jacinto Salas y Quiroga employed dramatic transitions in image, meter, or tone in an organic fashion, perhaps to emulate the "traditional" Spanish style. They often thereby dramatized the psychological and philosophical uncertainties of the unsettling new age and its mal du siècle. Their innovations have their roots in the turbulent confessional mode, as famously practiced by Juan Meléndez Valdés at the end of the eighteenth century. In the wake of Hugo's poetry collection *Orientales* and the works of the earlier writer Gaspar María de Nava Álvarez, conde de Noroña, an interest in sensual and exotic depiction of the Orient spread.

In the periodical press, and influenced by Joseph Addison and Victor-Joseph Étienne (Jouy) observers of everyday life (*costumbristas*), like Mariano José de Larra, Modesto Lafuente, Antonió Neira de Mosquera, or Ramón de Mesonero Romanos, chose to deal in the ephemeral, depicting in a deliberately unsystematic, even sketchy fashion, the changes in Spanish life. In the visual arts these were echoed, not just by prints, but in the painting and drawings of street scenes by Leonardo Alenza y Nieto.

As literature developed in tandem with critical and political concerns, it changed but did not lose the ability to surprise. Efforts to transcend the more open dynamism of the initial Romantic theater, for all their shortcomings, are nonetheless suggestive. Alongside later works by García Gutiérrez, Saavedra, and José Zorrilla y Moral, the Republican brothers Eusebio and Eduardo Asquerino introduced into their political dramas apparent happy endings that were in fact deeply ambiguous, thus echoing the Golden Age dramatist Pedro Calderón de la Barca. The ever-popular comedy of mores developed, from Manuel Bretón de los Herreros through to the high comedy of the 1840s.

Reflections on national identity led in several different directions. There was the treatment of local customs almost primarily for their aesthetic value among the commercial Andalusian painters and the costumbrista serafín Estébanez Calderón. But there was a long tradition of more probing approaches: in Gaspar Melchor de Jovellanos, in the violently twisting imagery of rebirth in the revolutionary poet Manuel José Quintana, and among exiles in the exploration of the national psyche. That lineage continued with Saavedra's *Romances históricos* (1840), the propagandistic fragment of contemporary revolution *El Romancero del Conde-Duque* (*Ballad Cycle of the Count-Duke*, 1842) by Antonio Ribot y Fontseré, and in the imaginative and searching responses of the *Leyendas españolas* (*Spanish Legends*, 1840) by José Joaquín de Mora and *Historias caballerescas españolas* (*Spanish Chivalric Histories*, 1843) by Gregorio Romero Larrañaga. The painter Jenaro Pérez Villaamil, meanwhile, followed the Scottish artist David Roberts (who visited Spain in the 1830s) in depicting half-fantastically the Spanish landscape; in contrast, José Elbo painted sober images of imposing bulls.

Literature that was more gentle in tone is not necessarily less important. The diaphanous imagery and subjective lyric verse of Enrique Gil y Carrasco is today attracting increasing admiration, alongside his poeticized chivalric novel *El señor de Bembibre* (*The Lord of Bembibre*, 1844), and there is a resonance to the simplicity Pablo Piferrer preferred in his folkloric verse. The realistic folkloric myth for a modern world, *Pedro Saputo* (1844) by Braulio Foz, is also rising in critical esteem. The simple depiction of national customs in *La Gaviota* (*The Seagull*, 1849) by Fernán Caballero is not without its provocative ironies.

At all events, more frenetic tendencies did not disappear. Influenced by Eugéne Sue, Wenceslao Ayguals de Izco and others provided their own *mystères* in an effort to represent contemporary Spain. *Doce españoles de brocha gorda* (*Twelve Spaniards Poorly Done*, 1846) by Antonio Flores delves into the more sordid underbelly of national life.

The rich developments in Spain helped to nurture one of its most impressive cultural achievements: a radically experimental literature. Espronceda's striking innovations must be placed alongside those of his friends Antonio Ros de Olano and Miguel de los Santos Álvarez. The latter developed dreamy short stories with hardly any story line; the former provoked readers by rising in cool laughter over the absurdity and triviality of life. Ildefonso

Ovejas argued that there was no need for a surface unity between images in literature, and produced poetry to match his theory.

ANDREW GINGER

Bibliography

Abellán, José Luis. *Historia crítica del pensamiento español*. vol. 4, *Liberalismo y romanticismo (1807–1874)*. Madrid: Espasa Calpe, 1984.
Carnero, Guillermo, ed. *Historia de la literatura española: Siglo XIX*. Vol. 1. Madrid: Espasa Calpe, 1997.
Flitter, Derek. *Spanish Romantic Literary Theory and Criticism*. Cambridge: Cambridge University Press, 1992.
Fontanella, Lee. *La imprenta y las letras en la España romántica*. Berne: Peter Lang, 1982.
Ginger, Andrew. *Political Revolution and Literary Experiment in the Spanish Romantic Period (1830–1850)*. Lampeter, Wales: Edwin Mellen Press, 1999.
Glendinning, Nigel. *A Literary History of Spain: The Eighteenth Century*. London: Ernest Benn, 1972.
Lloréns, Vicente. *Liberales y románticos: Una emigración española en Inglaterra (1823–34)*. Madrid: Castalia, 1979.
Peers, Allison. *A History of the Romantic Movement in Spain*. 2 vols. Cambridge: Cambridge University Press, 1940.
Reyero, Carlos, and Meira Freixa. *Pintura y escultura en España: 1800–1910*. Madrid: Cátedra, 1995.
Romero Tobar, Leonardo. *Panorama crítico del romanticismo español*. Madrid: Castalia, 1994.
Sebold, Russell. *Trayectoria del romanticismo español*. Barcelona: Crítica, 1983.
Shaw, D. L. "Towards the Understanding of Spanish Romanticism," *Modern Language Review* 48 (1963): 190–95.

SPAIN: HISTORICAL SURVEY 1760–1850

By the mid-18th century, the Bourbon dynasty was entrenched in Spain. Its entry into Spanish affairs, however, began inauspiciously. The first of the line, Felipe V (1700–1746) was the grandson of Louis XI of France. Felipe came to the throne upon the death of the last Spanish Hapsburg, Carlos II, who left no heirs. The War of the Spanish Succession broke out shortly thereafter (1701), following Louis's designation of Felipe as heir to the French throne as well. Suspicious and fearful of the French boast that the "Pyrenees had disappeared" and its effect on the European balance of power, Austria, England, Holland, and Portugal, among others, declared war on Spain and France. When the war ended thirteen years later, Spain paid a heavy price. The Treaties of Utrecht (1713) and Rastadt (1714) forced Felipe to relinquish his claim to the French crown and to make important territorial and trade concessions to the victors, chiefly Austria and England.

Carlos III (1759–78) is arguably the most notable of the Spanish Bourbons. A learned and energetic ruler, he is credited with institutionalizing important ideas and practices of the Enlightenment and attempting to reverse the long period of economic decline, poverty, and backwardness into which Spain had fallen since the seventeenth century. Because Carlos III pursued his policies autocratically, he is frequently singled out as one of the best examples of the enlightened despot. He sought to curtail the influence of the Roman Catholic Church, along with his economic and administrative reforms, and open support for im-

provements in the kingdom's infrastructure and intellectual endeavors. In 1767, citing their vow of obedience to the papacy, Carlos ordered the expulsion of the Jesuits from Spain and its overseas possessions. This anticlerical stand earned Carlos the opprobrium of many of his deeply religious Spanish subjects and introduced into political discourse in Spain a vision of the church at odds with her image as the traditional helpful partner; instead, the church began to be portrayed as a threat to royal authority and an obstacle to progress. The conflict between the fervent Catholicism of the Spanish people and the reformist aims of Carlos III and future like-minded leaders would periodically emerge as a serious and divisive issue, eventually becoming a contributing factor to the Spanish Civil War (1936–39).

Spain continued to pay a heavy toll because of its relationship with France. When the French Revolution began, Carlos IV (1778–1808), sympathetic to his Bourbon relations and wishing to stem the revolutionary tide in Spain, pursued a contradictory and ineffective policy that ultimately allowed Napoleonic troops into Spain (ostensibly to subdue Portugal) and led to Carlos's abdication in favor of his son Fernando. And while the king was heavily influenced by his minister Manuel Godoy (who was also his wife's lover), Carlos was held responsible for the failure of his policies as both father and son became exiles in France while Napoleon Bonaparte's brother Joseph became king of Spain (1808). Spontaneous popular uprisings against the French invaders erupted in Madrid and elsewhere; thus began the so-called war of independence, which would last until 1813.

The war ended with the return of Fernando VII to the throne, in the midst of general jubilation. However, this optimism proved short-lived. Immediately after Fernando's restoration, Spain entered into a period of great political turmoil and instability, conditions that strengthened independence movements throughout the Spanish Empire in America. By the mid-1820s, Spanish armies had been defeated and expelled from their colonial headquarters in the American mainland; all that remained of the once-glorious Spanish Empire in the New World were the islands of Cuba and Puerto Rico.

The Napoleonic occupation of the Iberian Peninsula exacerbated existing tensions within Spain, and Fernando VII proved unequal to the task of governing a divided kingdom. During the French occupation, groups of citizens convened as a *cortes* (parliament) in Cádiz and redacted Spain's first constitution in 1812. Notwithstanding the presence in the cortes of people of various political persuasions, from popular anticlerical liberals to staunch supporters of royal absolutism brought together by their common goal of expelling the French, the new constitution enjoyed little popular support; Fernando quickly disavowed it (1814) yet was ineffectual in promoting political stability and consensus among the various factions. Conditions worsened when the king died in 1833 leaving as heir his three-year-old daughter, Isabel II (1833–68).

Isabel's long rule was politically disastrous, and the circumstances of her succession to the throne exposed the profound weaknesses of the Spanish state. When Fernando chose Isabel as his heir, he was in violation of Salic law (brought to Spain from France at the end of the War of Succession), which barred female succession. Opponents of Isabel supported the king's brother Carlos, along with a political platform that favored strong ties with the church and the rejection of a single constitution in favor of traditional regional customs and privileges in existence since the Middle Ages. Known as the *Carlistas*, supporters of these views declared open war on the monarchy shortly after Fernando's death. Thus began the first of several Carlists Wars, which would recur periodically throughout the second half of the nineteenth century, notwithstanding Prince Carlos's renunciation in 1860 of his rights to the throne.

In spite of frequent changes in leadership and constant political instability, Isabel II was able to remain queen until 1868 when, devoid of political and military support, she went into exile. A series of political experiments followed, including the brief establishment of a Spanish republic (1873–74), before the restoration of the Bourbon dynasty in 1875 upon the return of Isabel's son; he ruled as Alfonso XII until 1885, when he died prematurely at age twenty-eight.

One of the most destructive legacies of the history of Spain in this period was the strategic involvement of the armed forces in civic life. Used as a means of maintaining order and protecting the crown, this practice exposed the weakness of the political system and made the state dependent on the authority of the army for its own survival. It was only a matter of time before the generals believed themselves better equipped than their monarchs and other political authorities to run the country. Equally evident during this period was the failure of civil institutions to promote agreement and compromise among the various factions with regard to such fundamental issues as the legitimate role of the church in political and economic life; the role of centralization versus regional autonomy; the challenges and opportunities offered by liberalism in the face of entrenched conservative values; an agricultural economy under which wealth was unevenly distributed in the face of emerging industrial models, among other issues.

CLARA ESTOW

Bibliography

Artola, Miguel, ed. *Las Cortes de Cádiz*. Madrid: Marcial Pons, 1991.

Encuentro de la Ilustración al Romanticismo: La identidad masculina en los siglos XVIII y XIX: de la Ilustración al Romanticismo, 1750–1850. Cádiz: Servicio de Publicaciones, Universidad de Cádiz, 1997.

Fernández García, Antonio, et al. *Los fundamentos de la España liberal (1834–1000): La sociedad, la economía y las formas de vida*. Madrid: Espasa-Calpe, 1997.

Marichal, Carlos. *La revolución liberal y los primeros partidos polílitocs en España, 1834–1844*. Madrid: Cátedra, 1980.

Martínez Shaw, Carlos. *El siglo de las luces: las bases intelectuales del reformismo*. Madrid: Historia 16, 1996.

Morales Moya, Antonio, M. E. Vega, et al. *Las bases políticas, económicas y sociales de un regimen en transformación (1759–1834)*. Madrid: Espasa-Calpe, 1998.

Moreno Alonso, Manuel. *Los españoles durante la ocupación napoleónica: la vida cotidiana en la vorágine*. Málaga: Editorial Algazara, 1997.

Perez, Joseph, and Armando Alberola, eds. *España y América entre la Ilustración y el liberalismo*. Alicante: Instituto de Cultura Juan Gil-Albert, 1993.

Las revoluciones hispánicas: independencias americanas y liberalismo español. Edited by Francois-Xavier Guerra. Madrid: Editorial Complutense, 1995.

Rueda Hernanz, Germán. *El reinado de Isabel II: La España liberal*, Madrid: Historia 16, 1996.

Sánchez-Blanco, Francisco. *La Ilustración en España*. Madrid: Akal Ediciones, 1997.

Shubert, Adrian. *A Social History of Modern Spain*. London and Boston: Unwin Hyman, 1990.

SPANISH AMERICA AND BRAZIL: CULTURAL SURVEY

The period of 1760 to 1850 is generally regarded as a transitional moment in Spanish America and Brazil due to the development of independence movements that occurred at this time. It is commonly accepted that Romanticism as a cultural movement was active in Spanish America and Brazil from 1840 to 1890. Given that its influence dominated longer in Spanish America and Brazil than in European nations, it sometimes overlapped with realism and even modernism. Romanticism influenced the subsequent development of Spanish and Brazilian literature to the point of manifesting itself in some features of early-twentieth-century writing. In the eighteenth century, dependence on Spanish and Portuguese models had been severe. As the century progressed, Spanish Americans would seek and find a cultural voice of their own, led by intellectuals such as Francisco Miranda, José Antonio Rojas, and Simón Rodríguez.

José Joaquín Fernández de Lizardi is a key poetic figure. He published *Noches tristes* (*Sad Nights*) in 1818, and *El día alegre* (*The Happy Day*) a year later, in which a Romantic sensibility is clearly evident for the first time. In the late eighteenth and early nineteenth centuries, José Joaquín de Olmedo wrote on Simón Bolívar's political activity. Olmedo was primarily a patriotic, neoclassical poet who regarded the fight for political independence as the final and necessary step in the progress of Western civilization; his main work is *Oda a la Victoira de Junín: canto a Bolívar* (*Ode to Victory of Junín: A Song to Bolívar*, 1825). Another important author is Andrés Bello, poet, philologist, scholar, and author of *Gramática de la lengua castellana* (*Grammar of the Spanish Language*, 1847), a work that reflected his concern with America. He felt that there was an affinity between Spain and America and that language helped to make the cultural bonds stronger. Culturally influenced by Britain and France, he translated Victor Hugo and Lord Byron. His was a reflexive Romanticism, in which serious consideration was given to the topic of mortality, reflected in the landscapes described in his poems. He was the first poet to make America a poetical theme; his depictions of nature, along with his praise of virtue and freedom, show a literary personality in which neoclassical and Romantic elements coexist.

In the early years of the nineteenth century, a new poetic mode made its debut. *Poesía gauchesca* (gauchesque poetry) has its roots in the southern part of the continent. It has been considered as the first genuine, native, literary output of America, primarily because of the local color and aesthetics it displays. This type of poetry arose when the gaucho did not exist any longer and consequently might have become a sort of culturally mythical figure. Critics are not in unanimous agreement about the creator of this form. Some argue that it was Juan Gualberto Godoy, others claim that Bartolomé Hidalgo developed it; Hilario Ascasubi, whose greatest work was *Santos Vega o Los mellizos de la flor* (*Santos Vega or the Twins of Flower*, 1872) should receive the honor, however. And whatever the origins of the genre, it is clear that its great masterwork is José Hernández's *Martín Fierro* (1876).

The early years of the nineteenth century saw the dissemination of foreign influences. The work of British authors such as Thomas Gray, the mythical Ossian (generally understood to be the creation of James Macpherson), and Edward Young, along with that of French writers including François-Auguste-René de Chateaubriand, Ugo Foseolo, and Victor Hugo were translated into Spanish and reached a broad readership. José María Heredia displayed early on in his poetry a fusion of Romantic ideals with neoclassical rhetoric. All the major Romantic topics are evident in his poetry: death, melancholy, and the subjective depiction of landscape.

Simón Bolívar is regarded as the first writer of Spanish American Romantic narrative; however, he is a political writer whose work was focused on gaining independence for Latin American countries. The rise of the novel was delayed in these countries, as nation building took precedence over artistic innovation. The assimilation of foreign trends also helped delay the emergence of a literary genre. As well, in the early years of the nineteenth century, the picaresque novel was still a dominant popular form, although writers felt it no longer afforded creative opportunities, having grown stale.

José Joaquín Fernández Lizardi is one of the main authors of the period, *El Periquillo Sarniento* (1816) being his most significant achievement. Didacticism was still one of the major concerns of narrative fiction at the end of the eighteenth century, and novelists (if these writers can be considered such) rejected fancy as a source for literature. The novel of the Romantic age in Spanish America and Brazil, because of its dependence on outdated models, placed itself in an anachronistic cultural space. It was some time before it developed into a modern narrative fiction. Later in the century, Jorge Isaacs published one of the Latin American masterworks, *María* (1867). As in poetry, topics of the novels of this time did not differ essentially from those of European works; the only primary exception was a literary moment called *indigenismo* (nativism), which focused on native and local sources, and was particularly influential in the nineteenth and twentieth centuries. Juan León Mera's *Cumandá* (1869) and Clorinda Matto de Turner's *Aves sin nido* (*Birds without a Nest*, 1889) are key works of late Romanticism.

Other cultural and social genres and modes of thought were overwhelmingly dominated by European influence. Philosophy was heavily shaped by French sources, such as Etienne Bonnot de Condillao, Denis Diderot, Jean-Jacques Rousseau, and Voltaire (although in the Caribbean, Thomas Jefferson and Thomas Paine were quite influential). The most important philosophical writer of the period was Andrtés Bello, whose range extended well beyond traditional philosophy. He was a humanist whose influence on literature, philosophy, and linguistics can be felt even today.

Painting was especially influenced by Spain. The Spanish Academis de San Fernando was the model on which Latin American academies were founded. They established a neoclassical pattern and despised baroque and popular arts, although in Mexico the latter did develop significantly.

Music, too, was deeply influenced by European standards. This impeded the development of a rich popular musical tradition, as Latin Americans of the period preferred to create operas in the European style.

SANTIAGO RODRÍGUEZ GUERRERO-STRACHAN

Bibliography

Bellini, Giuseppe. *Historia de la literatura hispanoamericana*. Barcelona: Crítica, 1985.

Brushwood, John S. *Genteel Barbarism: Experiments in the Analysis of Nineteenth-Century Spanish-American Novels*. Lincoln: University of Nebraska Press, 1981.

Carilla, Enrique. *El Romanticismo en la América Hispánica*. 3rd ed. Madrid: Gredos, 1975.

Castagnaro, R. Anthony. *The Early Spanish American Novel*. New York: Las Américas, 1971.

Franco, Jean. *Historia de la literatura hispanoamericana*. Barcelona: Ariel, 1981.

Goic, Cedomil. *Historia y crítica de la literatura hispanoamericana*. Vol. 2, *Del romanticismo al modernismo*. Barcelona: Editorial Crítica, 1990.

Grossmann, Rudolf. *Historia y problemas de la literatura latinoamericana*. Madrid: Ediciones de la Revista de Occidente, 1972.

Historia de la Humanidad. Desarrollo cultural y científico: El siglo XIX. Vol. 2. Barcelona: Planeta, 1980.

Jozef, Bella. *Historia de la literatura hispanoamericana*. 2d ed. Rio de Janeiro: Francisco Alves, 1982.

Madrigal, Luis Íñigo. *Historia de la literatura hispanoamericana.* Madrid: Cátedra, 1987.

Nikolayevna Kuteischikova, Vera. "El Romanticismo y el problema de la conciencia nacional en la literatura latinoamericana en el siglo XIX." In *Literatura y sociedad latinoamericanas del siglo XIX.* Edited by Evelyn Picon Garfield and Ivan Schulman. Urbana: University of Illinois Press, 1991.

Paz, Octavio. *Los hijos del limo: del romanticismo a la vanguardia,* Barcelona: Seix Barral, 1974. Translated as *Children of the Mire:*

Modern Poetry from Romanticism to the Avant Garde by Rachel Phillips. Cambridge, Mass.: Harvard University Press, 1974.

Picón Salas, M. *De la conquista a la Independencia.* Mexico City: Fondo de Cultura Económica, 1944.

Sommer, Doris. *Foundational Fictions: the National Romances of Latin America.* Berkeley and Los Angeles: University of California Press, 1991.

Yáñez, Mirta. *La narrativa del romanticismo en Latinoamérica.* Havana: Letras Cubanas, 1989.

THE SPIRIT OF THE AGE OR, CONTEMPORARY PORTRAITS, 1825

Collection of essays by William Hazlitt

The Spirit of the Age or, Contemporary Portraits is the English essayist William Hazlitt's most famous book, and still one of the most penetrating assessments of the Romantic era. It is comprised of twenty-six character sketches and includes extended discussions of key philosophers, poets, politicians, economists, jurists, journalists, and men of letters. Hazlitt sees the "spirit of the age" as originating in the French Revolution and as constituted by a series of dramatic paradoxes that created deep divisions between (and within) individual writers, and within himself. But whereas in earlier work he placed himself at the center of such conflicting tensions, in *The Spirit of the Age* he is more resigned, detached, and wittily ironic. The book is his summing-up of a lifetime of radical dissent, and his *Prelude* in its exploration of the forces that shaped his mind.

The Spirit of the Age draws from several sources. Hazlitt adapted or reprinted three essays from earlier publications: "Character of Cobbett" ("Essay VI" in *Table Talk*, 1821), "Mr. Crabbe" (May 1821, *London Magazine*) and "Mr. Canning" (July 1824, *Examiner*). He took an additional five essays from his 1824 *New Monthly Magazine* series on the (plural) "spirits of the Age": "Jeremy Bentham," "Rev. Mr. Irving," "The late Mr. Horne Tooke," "Sir Walter Scott," and "Lord Eldon." He then wrote the remaining eighteen portraits specifically for the book: "Mr. Godwin," "Mr. Coleridge," "Lord Byron," "Mr. Southey," "Mr. Wordsworth," "Sir James Mackintosh," "Mr. Malthus," "Mr. Gifford," "Mr. Jeffrey," "Mr. Brougham," "Sir F. Burdett," "Mr. Wilberforce," "Mr. Campbell," "Mr. T. Moore," "Mr. Leigh Hunt," Charles Lamb ("Elia"), Washington Irving ("Geoffrey Crayon"), and "Mr. Knowles." There are some striking omissions, such as profiles of Edmund Burke and the Duke of Wellington, and Hazlitt included some figures who have now largely faded from view, most notably Francis Burdett, Lord Eldon, and Sheridan Knowles. But incisive essays on Lord Byron, Samuel Taylor Coleridge, William Godwin, Charles Lamb, Walter Scott, Robert Southey, and William Wordsworth are at the center of the volume, presenting a view of the age that was unrivaled at the time for its complexity and range, a view that is still influential.

For Hazlitt, "the spirit of the age" denotes a faith in the genius, liberty, innovation, and individualism born of the French Revolution, and more broadly invokes the reactionary forces of legitimacy, custom, abstraction, and egotism bent on destroying or ignoring that faith. In a number of instances he uses the phrase to make black-and-white distinctions: The *Edinburgh Review*

is "eminently characteristic" of the spirit of the age, while the *Quarterly Review* seeks to "discountenance and extinguish" it. Lord Byron "panders" to it, while Edward Irving and Lamb oppose it. Wordsworth's genius is "a pure emanation" of it, while "the spirit of the monarchy" is at "variance" with it. More characteristically, however, Hazlitt sees the spirit as a complicated interplay of opposing forces, so that it was "never more fully shown than in its treatment" of William Godwin, whose philosophical radicalism Hazlitt continued to embrace, long after others who had initially shared his enthusiasm had forgotten or renounced it. "Is truth then so variable?" he asks. "Is it one thing at twenty and another at forty?" For Hazlitt, the age's "love of paradox and change" and "its dastard submission to prejudice and to the fashion of the day" are writ large in its celebration and subsequent abandonment of Godwinian ideals.

Perhaps the most revealing moments in the book, however, are those in which Hazlitt's own radical commitments are undermined by his admiration of the powers of the individual imagination. How could Scott, for example, be the most brilliant novelist of the day *and* a truculent Tory blackguard? Hazlitt's summary of the most prominent scenes and characters in the *Waverley* novels leads him to exclaim, "What a thing is human life! What a power is that of genius! . . . [Scott's] works . . . are almost like a new edition of human nature." But at the same time, in the "political bearing" of the novels, Scott "administers charms and philtres to our love of Legitimacy, makes us conceive a horror of all reform, civil, political, or religious, and would fain put down the Spirit of the Age." Scott is then introduced in the next essay on Lord Byron, where he is described as "aristocratic in principle," but where the disinterested powers of his imagination are contrasted with the omnipresent egotism of Byron, "who in his politics is a *liberal*" but "in his genius is haughty and aristocratic." Hazlitt's recognition of the conflicting political and imaginative impulses within these writers, and his betrayal of his own paradoxical reaction to these impulses, most fully reveal the warring dialectics at the conceptual center of the spirit of the age.

Hazlitt's involvement in the conflict was less impassioned than it had been on several previous occasions, however. He was still capable of invective, and William Gifford, the editor of the Tory *Quarterly Review*, came in for particular abuse as a man and writer "altogether petty, captious, and literal." But Hazlitt is notably more charitable in this book. He discusses the arch utilitarian Jeremy Bentham with wry wit rather than anger. He is willing to concede that, "where humanity has not become obnoxious, where liberty has not passed into a by-word, Mr. Southey is still liberal and humane." He had often attacked Coleridge, but now he is simply disappointed. "What is become of all this mighty heap of hope, of thought, of learning and humanity?" he asks after a breathtaking summary of Coleridge's intellectual career. "It has ended in swallowing doses of oblivion and in writing paragraphs in the *Courier*." The French Revolution had promised so much, but its legacy had pitted intellectual progress against stagnation and suppression. From a perspective largely above the fray, Hazlitt in *The Spirit of the Age* explores the diverse and often contradictory forces that shaped the Romantic era and his perceptions of it.

ROBERT MORRISON

See also **Bentham, Jeremy; Byron, Lord George Noel Gordon; Cobbett, William; Coleridge, Samuel Taylor; Crabbe, George; Godwin, William; Irving, Washington; Lamb, Charles; Moore, Thomas; Sir Walter, Scott; Southey, Robert; Wordsworth, William**

Text

The Spirit of the Age, or Contemporary Portraits, 1825. In *The Complete Works of William Hazlitt*, vol. 11. Edited by P. P. Howe. London: Dent, 1930–34. Also in *The Selected Writings of William Hazlitt*, vol. 7. Edited by Duncan Wu. London: Pickering and Chatto, 1998.

The Spirit of the Age, Edited by E. D. Mackerness. London: Collins, 1969.

Bibliography

Baker, Herschel. "*The Spirit of the Age*." In *William Hazlitt*. Cambridge, Mass.: Harvard University Press, 1962.

Chandler, James K. "Representative Men, Spirits of the Age, and other Romantic Types." In *Romantic Revolutions: Criticism and Theory*. Edited by K. R. Johnston et al. Bloomington: Indiana University Press, 1990.

Kinnaird, John. "Portraits of an Age." In *William Hazlitt: Critic of Power*. New York: Columbia University Press, 1978.

Paulin, Tom. "Hazlitt *faciebat: The Spirit of the Age*." In *The Day-Star of Liberty: William Hazlitt's Radical Style*. London: Faber, 1998.

———. "Hazlitt's Definition of the Spirit of the Age," *Wordsworth Circle* 6 (1975): 97–108.

———. "Emblems of Infirmity: Contemporary Portraits in Hazlitt's *The Spirit of the Age*." *Wordsworth Circle* 10 (1979): 81–90.

Uphaus, Robert. "*The Spirit of the Age*." In *William Hazlitt*. Boston: Twayne, 1985.

SPITZWEG, CARL 1808–1885

German painter

Although his often diminutive canvases lack the grandeur of Caspar David Friedrich's, the meticulous execution of Moritz von Schwind's, the religious sentiment of Ludwig Ferdinand Schnorr von Carolsfeld's, and the keen social and historical perceptions of Adolf Menzel's and Franz von Lenbach's, Carl Spitzweg's reputation has increased to the point that he is now probably the most popular German artist of the nineteenth century. Many would agree that his strength is in his meticulous chronicling of a longed-for past, albeit from a somewhat idiosyncratic and voyeuristic perspective. The success of the exhibitions devoted to his work in Munich (1967) and Kiel (1972) surprised even their organizers, and today no review of nineteenth-century German painting would be complete without a few examples of Spitzweg's genre scenes. A prolific painter of sharply observed small-town characters and of landscapes in oil and watercolors, Spitzweg also accepted commissions for book illustrations and contributed cartoons to the burgeoning satirical press, especially to the magazine *Fliegende Blätter*. For many, he is quintessentially German: his alpine landscapes, village priests, stuffy schoolmasters, bashful maidens, and pedantic officials sum up the atmosphere of rural southern Germany in a manner that is quaint if not exactly appealing. While his contemporaries may have seen themselves mirrored in overwhelmingly harmless contexts, the effect of his art is, on closer inspection, rendered unsettling by an uneasy balance between realism and caricature.

Although many of his scenes are outwardly idyllic, and the natural elements are rarely perceived as threatening in the manner of Friedrich or Spitzweg's French contemporaries such as Pierre-Etienne-Théodore Rousseau, the human world as revealed in his work is deeply flawed. Romantic themes, love, religious sentiment, mythology and harmonious empathy with natural forces are more often travestied than celebrated. The unadulterated sentiment that appears to have inspired works like *Abschied* (*Farewell*, 1848–52), with its tender evocation of a lovers' embrace, is something of a rarity. More often, the lovers are unequal: an old dandy presents flowers to a blushing girl, a monk eyes a woman standing in a doorway. Sometimes, these rituals are set against a surprisingly public background: a roué serenades a lady at the village fountain in full view of the bemused passers-by (*Der ewige Hochzeiter* [*The Eternal Suitor*] 1855–58). Sometimes, the would-be lover is overshadowed by threatening mountains or gloomy, crumbling edifices, and often a chaperone is present, only to be confused or outwitted by some upstart paramour. The recurring figure of the lonely male appears as a pathetic, dismal or sinister reminder that love may just as easily bypass as inspire one. The somber hat and cloak of the haughty, solitary walker in *Der Hagestolz* (*The Confirmed Bachelor*, 1847–49) is one of many striking examples of this subject, in which critics have tended to see self-portraits of an artist who never married.

But the suggestion that Spitzweg was an embittered loner who poured out his scorn in misanthropic imagery has found little favor. His humor is evident in countless vignettes, nowhere more so than in those innocent scenes of rural life in which a naturalist is surprised by a pair of exotic butterflies far too large to fit into his net, or a huntsman receives a visit from an inquisitive-looking deer at the precise moment that he has hung his rifle on an inaccessible branch and is getting ready to unpack his lunch. Each of these paintings tells its own ironic story, and the whimsical quality that underlies them is sometimes likened to the work of the novelist Jean Paul, author of numerous literary sketches of outsiders, cranks, and other marginal figures. Spitzweg's myopic cactus growers, manic alchemists, and obsessive bibliophiles are products of the same mold.

Yet the artist was not content to merely chronicle the petty foibles of his contemporaries. True to his background, which is closer to Biedermeier than to Romanticism or realism, he avoids political subjects and portrayals of outright corruption. But in many subtle ways, he finds the means to expose the glaring hypocrisies and injustices of an environment he had obviously studied with critical detachment.

Spitzweg's Roman Catholic figures are invariably corpulent and jolly; as such, they are in keeping with tradition. But he goes to some lengths to convey their hypocrisy. A young lady may be glimpsed approaching a hermit, while the latter quickly stuffs some tasty-looking delicacy into a pouch. Is he hiding it from her innocent glance? Or is it perhaps intended as a gift for the lady, as payment for some unspecified service? The titles speak volumes. *Hermit, Roasting a Chicken* (1841) may seem contradictory, but when one examines the scene, one finds the hermit turning the spit on which his dinner is cooking with his hands clasped together as if in prayer. There can be no more cruel indictment of religious bigotry. Other pictures show monks who squabble like schoolboys and accompany their disputations with rude gesticulations.

Other favorite denizens of Spitzweg's world are soldiers, guardsmen, and customs officials. Tollhouses, a familiar sight in a Germany then composed of several hundred petty principalities, often stand out against vistas of natural grandeur. Invariably, the miserable officials are shown receiving bribes while rifling through trunks that have been dragged from the citizens' carriages. Soldiers, by contrast, are rarely observed at work. Instead, Spitzweg portrays them asleep, darning their socks or sewing patches on their trousers. True, *Der strickende Wachtposten* (*The Knitting Sentryman*, 1855–60), painted in warm, vibrant colors, has a cannon at his side, pointing directly at the viewer,

but the guard himself is harmless enough as he manipulates his knitting needles. It is in such incongruous scenes that Spitzweg's talent for combining the quaint and the unsettling achieves a distinctively powerful effect.

No account of this artist's work would be complete without a reference to his most celebrated canvas, *Der arme Poet* (*The Impoverished Poet*), which was received with dismay when first exhibited in Munich in 1839. Here, a lonely figure in a garret, under a leaking roof, surrounded by yellowing tomes, purses his spidery fingers in an ambiguous gesture. Opinions vary as to whether he is expressing pleasure at some clever literary image, or mechanically counting out the syllables of a line of verse, or, more probably, squashing a bug that has invaded his hideout. The great poet is unrecognized and alone, with only vermin for company. It seems odd that this quirky satirist, who received little acclaim during his lifetime, should have been elevated to an icon of the German soul within a few years of his death. Stranger still, the painter of lackadaisical officers and lazy grenadiers was a personal favorite of Adolf Hitler, who is reported to have amassed at least fifty of his paintings for the Museum of German Art that he hoped to build at Linz.

OSMAN DURRANI

Biography

Born February 5, 1808 into a well-to-do merchant family in Munich. Trained as a chemist and worked both in his native city and in the provincial town of Straubing, where he began sketching humorous scenes of everyday life. After suffering a serious illness, possibly typhus or cholera, in 1832, devoted himself entirely to his art, in which he was largely self-taught. Financial independence enabled him to travel widely across Europe, visiting Austria, Bohemia, Dalmatia, England, France, and Italy. The World Exhibition of 1851 in London enabled him to acquaint himself with leading French artists as well as with John Constable and J. M. W. Turner in Britain. Now regarded as quintessentially German, he had relatively little success during his lifetime and was embroiled in various disagreements with the Munich Academy (Kunstverein), which he accused of placing his pictures in unfavorable locations. His landscapes show the influence of Narcisse Diaz de la Peña and the tradition of *paysages intimes* that was evolving in France. His interest in the exotic is considerable, and Eastern themes painted after travels in Bosnia include *In der Synagoge* (*Inside the Synagogue*, 1850), *Türkisches Kaffeehaus* (*A Turkish Coffee Shop, 1855–60*), and *Gähnender Türke* (*The Yawning Turk*, c. 1865). After 1863 Spitzweg's journeys become infrequent, and he spent the last twenty-two years of his life painting in his Munich studio. He died of a stroke on September 23, 1885.

Bibliography

Betz, Gerd. *Carl Spitzweg. der Künstler und seine Zeit.* Stuttgart: Belser, 1981.

Jensen, Jens Christian. *Malerei der Romantik in Deutschland.* Cologne: DuMont, 1985.

Jensen, Jens Christian. *Carl Spitzweg—Zwischen Resignation und Zeitkritik.* 5th ed. Cologne: DuMont, 1986.

Müller, Kristiane, and Urban, Eberhard. *Carl Spitzweg.* Stuttgart: Unipart-Verlag, 1995.

Carl Spitzweg, *Der arme Poet* (*The Impoverished Poet*), 1839. Reprinted courtesy of AKG London.

Niess, Ulrich. *Die trügerische Idylle: Carl Spitzweg und der Mannheimer Kunstverein*. Mannheim: Brandt, 1997.

Roennefahrt, Günther. *Carl Spitzweg: Beschreibendes Verzeichnis seiner Gemälde und Aquarelle*. Munich: Bruckmann, 1960.

Schirmer, Lisa. *Carl Spitzweg*. 2d ed. Leipzig: Seemann, 1998.

Spitzweg, Wilhelm. *Der unbekannte Spitzweg: Ein Bild aus der Welt des Biedermeier. Dokumente, Briefe, Aufzeichnungen*. Munich, 1958.

Wichmann, Siegfried. *Carl Spitzweg: Zeichnungen und Skizzen*. Munich: Bruckmann, 1990.

———. *Das grosse Spitzweg Album*. Herrsching: Schuler, 1984.

Winkler, Arnim. *Carl Spitzweg: Maler, Bild-Erzähler und Poet*. 2d ed. Munich: Südwest Verlag, 1977.

Website

http://www.spitzweg.de/galerie.htm

SPOHR, LOUIS 1784–1859

German composer

Louis Spohr was one of the most accomplished and acclaimed musical artists of the early Romantic period, occupying a stylistic position between the classicism of Joseph Haydn and Wolfgang Amadeus Mozart on one hand and the modernism of Richard Wagner on the other. At the apex of his career he was widely regarded as a proponent of all that was fresh and innovative in composition; in 1843 J. W. Davison described Spohr as "founder of a new feeling, if not of a new school in music." Moreover, his music inspired the kind of rapturous response required by Romantic imaginations, with audiences and even performers, such as the soprano Maria Malibran, reduced to tears upon listening. Only toward the end of his career, with the rise of musical nationalism and establishment of the Wagner cult, did Spohr's reputation decline.

Spohr's early musical tastes were shaped by performances of Carl Ditters von Dittersdorf, Johann Adam Hiller, Mozart, and other composers of German origin, along with the Giovanni Battista Viotti school of violin playing and French opera, which he heard in his native Brunswick. Trained as a violinist, Spohr founded his reputation through tours as a virtuoso soloist in which he presented his own works. Particularly noteworthy both in stylistic terms and as a significant contribution to the genre are his fifteen concertos for violin and orchestra. Characterized by rhapsodic melodies, an assimilation of operatic idioms such as the use of recitative, and an increasingly symphonic orchestral style, Spohr's concertos outstrip those of his virtuoso contemporaries in both substance and seriousness. Like Mozart, Spohr was also drawn to the clarinet and produced works for it that greatly extended its repertory and stimulated further technical developments on the instrument. His four clarinet concertos, written between 1808 and 1828 for Simon Hermstedt, offer a formidable challenge even to the seasoned clarinetist.

As a natural outgrowth of his violin playing Spohr turned to directing ensembles and was pivotal in defining the new role of conductor, a position necessitated by expansions in orchestral size and increasingly complex orchestral music. During his years as *konzertmeister* in Gotha and at music festivals in Frankenhausen and Erfurt (1810–12), Spohr made innovative use of a baton to conduct, lending extra control and precision to his performances.

His first symphony was written for the Frankenhausen Festival in 1811. A critic of the *Allgemeine musikalische Zeitung* commented, "we have not heard a new work of this kind for many years which possesses so much novelty and originality without singularity or affectation, so much richness and skill without bombast or artifice." Over the coming years Spohr would compose nine more symphonies (the tenth went unpublished) that reflect his increasing mastery of form and orchestral color, as well as his preoccupation with realizing extramusical ideas. Along with Hector Berlioz, Spohr was one of the earliest exponents of instrumental music that required audiences to read a program in order to fully grasp the music's meaning. His fourth symphony, titled *Die Weihe der Töne: Charakteristisches Tongemälde in Form einer Sinfonie* (*The Consecration of Sound: Characteristic Sound Painting in the Form of a Symphony*, 1832), musically represented a poem by Spohr's recently deceased friend Carl Pfeiffer. The popular success of this work encouraged Spohr to experiment further with programmatic works, including a novel pastiche called *Historische symphonie im Styl und Geschmack vier verschiedener Zeitabschnitte* (*Historical Symphony in the Style and Taste of Four Different Periods*, 1839). His seventh symphony, *Irdisches und Göttliches im Menschenleben* (*The Earthly and Divine in Human Life*, 1841), depicted the progression of humankind from childish innocence through adult passion to divine revelation, using an ensemble of solo instruments to represent spirituality and the full orchestra to evoke earthly humanity. Schumann reacted enthusiastically to these works, writing "an intention develops itself in music as in poetry; in these compositions of Spohr it dictates itself in the noblest and most emphatic way; therefore honour to the great German master."

From his earliest years as a composer Spohr devoted himself to drama, and over the course of his career completed ten operas. In these works lie some of his most striking and influential innovations, including a use of leitmotif and through-composed structures that foreshadowed Wagnerian techniques. Three of Spohr's operas, *Faust*, *Zemire und Azore*, and *Jessonda* are especially important in his career and in the history of the genre. *Faust*, composed in 1813, was the first to devise a system of leitmotifs, including not only simple reminiscences of previous themes but also symbolically charged musical references to specific persons and ideas. Weber, who conducted *Faust* at its Prague premiere, recognized Spohr's technique, describing "a few melodies, carefully and felicitously devised, which weave through the whole work like delicate threads, holding it together intellectually." Although Spohr's work is based on an original libretto by Joseph Carl Bernard, rather than on part 1 of Johann Wolfgang von Goethe's *Faust*, it is one of the first major musical works to engage the Faust legend in what would practically become a Faust industry among Romantic composers. Unlike Goethe's *Faust*, which proposes redemption for the protagonist, Bernard's drama ends in damnation for Faust and catastrophe for all those around him. *Zemire und Azor* (1818) belongs more to the Romantic fairy tale operatic genre, though Spohr continued here as well to evolve a structure of leitmotifs. Spohr's greatest operatic success was achieved with *Jessonda* (1823), which offered not only the exotic locale of India to intrigued audiences, but also some of Spohr's most affecting lyrical passages and most colorful harmonies.

In certain respects, Spohr embodied the Romantic artist: his years as a dashing touring performer who charmed audiences with his virtuosity contributed to this image, along with his liberal political sympathies, his progressive tendencies toward programmatic instrumental music, and his embedding of dramatic meanings in musical gestures. However, in other ways he was a throwback to an earlier era, especially in his preservation of classical formal structures and his attention to the broadest range of compositional endeavor (he wrote numerous string quartets as well as other chamber music, sacred choral music, and songs). When he accepted a lifetime appointment in Kassel, he allied himself with an older generation of officially employed middle-class musicians and thus forfeited some of the lustre attached to a cosmopolitan, freelance virtuoso. Ultimately Spohr came to be seen as representative of an older tradition; areas in which he had produced innovations were brought to a more modern fruition by others.

KATHRYN L. SHANKS LIBIN

Biography

Born in Brunswick, April 5, 1784. Studied violin with French émigré Lieutenant Dufour, 1791–96; entered Collegium Carolinum in Brunswick, 1797. Official solo debut in Brunswick, 1803. Konzertmeister in Gotha, 1805–12. Married virtuoso harpist Dorette Scheidler, 1806. Years of joint concert tours with wife, 1807–21. Conducted at music festivals in Frankenhausen and Erfurt, 1810–12. Directed orchestra of Theater an der Wien in Vienna, 1813–15. Directed opera in Frankfurt, 1817–19. Engagement with London Philharmonic Society, 1820. Correspondent for *Allgemeine musikalische Zeitung*, 1821. Life appointment as Kapellmeister in Kassel, 1822. Published violin method, 1832. Death of wife, 1834. Married pianist Marianne Pfeiffer, 1836. Appointed Generalmusikdirektor at Kassel, 1847; retired with pension, 1857. Died October 22, 1859.

Selected Works

Written Works
Violinschule, 1832. Translated as *Louis Spohr's Celebrated Violin School* by John Bishop. London: Royal College Editions, [1843].
Selbstbiographie. 2 vols., 1860–61. Translated as Louis Spohr's Autobiography by unknown, 1865. Partially translated as *The Musical Journey of Louis Spohr* by Henry Pleasants. Norman: University of Oklahoma Press, 1961.
Ludwig Spohr: Neue Auswahl der Werke. 10 vols to date. Edited by Folker Göthel and Herfried Homburg. Tutzing: Hans Schneider, 1963– .
Lebenserrinerungen, Edited by Folker Göthel. Tutzing: Hans Schneider, 1968.

Selected Works of Louis Spohr. 10 vols. Edited by Clive Brown. New York: Garland, 1987–90.

Chamber Music
Sonata for harp and violin in D major, op. 113. 1806.
Sonata for harp and violin in D major, op. 114. 1811.
Quintet for piano, flute, clarinet, bassoon, and horn in C minor, op. 52. 1820.
Trio for piano, violin, and cello in E minor, op. 119. 1841.
Trio for piano, violin, and cello in F major, op. 123. 1842.
Septet for piano, flute, clarinet, bassoon, horn, violin, and cello in A minor, op. 147. 1853.

Concertos
Concerto for violin in E minor, op. 38. 1814.
Concerto for violin in A minor, op. 47. 1816 ("Gesangsszene").
Concerto for violin in D minor, op. 55. 1820.
Concerto for violin in G major, op. 70. 1825.
Concerto for clarinet in C minor, op. 26. 1808.
Concerto for clarinet in F minor, Wo O 19. 1821.
Concerto for clarinet in E minor, Wo O 20. 1828.

Opera
Faust. Libretto by Joseph Karl Bernard. 1813.
Zemire und Azor. Libretto by Johann Jakob Ihlée after Jean François Marmontel. 1818–19.
Jessonda. Libretto by Edward Gehe after Jean Frédéric-Auguste Lemierre. 1822.
Der Berggeist. Libretto by Georg Döring. 1824.
Pietro von Abano. Libretto by Karl Pfeiffer after Ludwig Tieck. 1827.
Der Alchymist. Libretto by Karl Pfeiffer after Washington Irving. 1829–30.
Die Kreuzfahrer (grosse Oper, 3 acts). Libretto by Louis and Marianne Spohr after August Friedrich Ferdinand von Kotzebue. 1843–44.

Oratorios
Das jüngste Gericht. 1812.
Die letzten Dinge. 1827.
Des Heilands letzte Stunden. 1834–35.
Der Fall Babylons. 1839–40.

Orchestral Works
Symphony no. 1 in E-flat, op. 20. 1811.
Symphony no. 2 in D minor, op. 49. 1820.
Symphony no. 3 in C minor, op. 78. 1828.
Symphony no. 4 ("Die Weihe der Töne") in F major, op. 86. 1832.
Symphony no. 5 in C minor op. 102. 1837.
Symphony no. 6 ("Historische Symphonie im Styl und Geschmack vier verschiedener Zeitabschnitte") in G major, op. 116. 1839.
Symphony no. 7 ("Irdisches und Göttliches im Menschenleben") in C major, op. 121. 1841.
Symphony no. 8 in G major, op. 137. 1847.
Symphony no. 9 ("Die Jahreszeiten") in B minor, op. 143. 1849–50.

Sacred Choral Music
Mass in C minor op. 54. 1821.
Requiem in C minor, 1857–58.

String Quartets
Quartet in E-flat major, op. 58 no. 1. 1821.
Quartet in B-flat major, op. 74 no. 2. 1826.
Quartet in D minor, op. 74 no. 3. 1826.

Bibliography

Becker, Heinz, and Rainer Krempien, eds. *Louis Spohr: Festschrift und Ausstellungskatalog zum 200. Geburtstag*. Kassel: Bärenreiter, 1984.

Brown, Clive. *Louis Spohr: A Critical Biography*. Cambridge: Cambridge University Press, 1984.

———. "Spohr, *Faust*, and Leitmotif," *Musical Times* 125 (1984).

Göthel, Folker, ed. *Louis Spohr: Briefwechsel mit seiner Frau Dorette*. Kassel: Bärenreiter, 1957.

Homburg, Herfried. *Louis Spohr: Bilder und Dokumente seiner Zeit*. Kassel: Bärenreiter, 1968.

SPONTINI, GASPARE 1774–1851

Composer

After training in Italy and attracting some attention there with his operas, Gaspare Spontini settled for nearly two decades in Paris, where he became one of the most successful opera composers of his time. His most outstanding work was *La Vestale*, which received its premiere at the Paris Opera on December 15, 1807. François-Adrien Boieldieu, Luigi Carlo Cherubini, and Etienne-Nicolas Méhul had been offered it previously, but they failed to see the strengths that Spontini revealed in a work that was to bring him great acclaim. Like many works that are immediately popular, *La Vestale* was by no means thoroughgoing in its innovations; it stood, instead, at the confluence of more than one tradition, combining new with old. Set in Rome in the third century B.C., the opera has a classical aspect that many in France found attractive a decade and a half before the advent of Romantic drama, when Napoleon Bonaparte was promoting a revival in French seventeenth century drama as cultural propaganda. Archaeological interests, prompted especially by discoveries at Pompeii and the French expedition to the Near East at the turn of the century, found their reflection in the settings and costumes. *La Vestale* presented an image of ancient Rome that was, however, markedly different from the traditional one. Changes of attitude may be seen in a detail that, though apparently small, was significant for a public so conservative in linguistic matters as the French. It has long been accepted practice to give French forms to classical names, but here the heroine was called Julia (not Julie), and the hero Licinius (not Licinie). What is more striking still is the fact that these two characters do not behave with the regard for duty and decorum that Pierre Corneille, in the classical period, had presented as typical of the admirable ways of ancient Rome.

Five years before the action of the opera begins, Julia had fallen in love with Licinius, but her parents had disapproved of the unpromising young man and consigned her to the Temple of Vesta. Her duty there now is to tend the sacred flame, and her fate (somewhat unhistorically, it appears) is perpetual virginity. Ceremonies are performed by a chorus of votaries before a crowd of Romans; the high priestess is alternately sacerdotal in her insistence on total obedience and sympathetic in her attitude toward the unfortunate Julia. The return of Licinius in triumph stirs Julia's latent passions and, after a highly dramatic episode in which she is threatened with a dire fate and saved only by what appears to be divine intervention, a happy ending is achieved.

The plot came, according to Jouy, from the German historian Johann Joachin Winckelmann and had been used for earlier French dramatic works. It takes up and places in the classical era the sexually charged theme of forced religious vocations that had been treated in several anti-Catholic plays at the time of the French Revolution. There was too a certain topicality in making the lover a soldier who had made his name and was now returning in triumph to claim his due reward. The refusal to envisage a tragic conclusion, as in other "rescue operas" such as Ludwig van Beethoven's *Fidelio*, accorded with the general climate of optimism that was inherited from the eighteenth century and would soon be displaced by Romantic convictions that humanity's position was irredeemably tragic. The ready response to the emotional forces of religion that was coupled with a distrust for religious institutions and codes was likewise testimony to attitudes common at the time. The extinguishing of the sacred flame can be seen as a powerful symbol, even more so since its counterpart is the triumph of human passions that were initially seen as sinful and misplaced.

Musically, *La Vestale*, with its ceremonies and public celebrations, reflects not only religious rites but also the great festivals of the revolution and of the empire. For the most part Spontini works with relatively brief solos, in a manner derived from Christoph Willibald Gluck, and creates his greatest effects by building up extended scenes from a number of related elements. In the role of Julia the soprano has great opportunities, especially when she joins in duet with the high priestess, whose part calls for a mezzo. *La Vestale* was revived in the twentieth century for Rosa Ponselle and for Maria Callas. The opera has, however, been overshadowed since 1831 by Vincenzo Bellini's *Norma*, which takes up many of its themes, adds a French nationalist element, and gives the soprano a genuine wide-ranging chromatic coloratura role.

With a libretto by Jouy, once again, and Jean A. d'Esmenard, Spontini's *Fernand Cortez* depicts the conquest of Mexico in 1520. Written at Napoleon's express desire as a form of propaganda for the campaign that he planned in Spain, it received its premiere, with only limited success, in Paris in 1809. Though ostensibly based on history, the three-act plot, which is packed with farfetched incidents, many of them heightened by religion and extravagant spectacle, ends with reconciliation and general rejoicing.

Agnes von Hohenstaufen, which premiered in Berlin's Königliches Opernhaus on June 12, 1829, is a three-act historico-Romantic opera. The libretto was by Ernst Raupach, who set the action in 1194 and created a series of grandiose scenes involving major historical characters that led up, once more, to the concluding triumph of love. Though Spontini labored over what was to be his last opera, *Agnes* has never found many admirers, though a shortened version was well received in Florence in 1954.

CHRISTOPHER SMITH

Biography

Born November 14, 1774 in Maiolati (west of Ancona), Italy; son of artisan; originally intended for the church, but musically gifted. In 1793, entered Conservatorio della Pietà. In 1796, first of his *opere buffe* performed in Rome. Around 1797, with Bourbon court at Palermo. In 1800, went to Paris, where he composed operas and gave singing lessons. First success at Théâtre Italien, Paris, in 1804; Empress Josephine became his patron. In 1807, long delayed première of *La Vestale*. In 1809, premiere of *Fernand Cortez*. Made director of *opéra buffa* at the Théâtre, de l'Impératrice; married Marie Erard, daughter of the great piano maker, 1810. With some difficulty, retained his post, upon the restoration of Louis XVIII to the throne, 1814. Obtained French naturalization, 1817. Obtained royal pension, 1818. Traveled to Berlin at invitation of King of Prussia, 1820. Premiere of *Agnes von Hohenstaufen*, 1827. In 1842, returned to Italy. In 1845, made a count by Pope Grogory XVI. Died January 24, 1851.

Bibliography

Galatopoulos, Stelios. *Callas*. London: Allen, 1976.

Abraham, Gerald. "The Best of Spontini." *Music and Letters*, xxiii (1942), pp. 163–71.

Dent, Edward J., ed. Winton Dean, 2nd ed. *The Rise of Romantic Opera*. Cambridge: Cambridge University Press, 1976 (see pp. 95–109).

Fragapane, Paolo. *Spontini*. Bologna: Sansoni, 1954.

Ghislanzoni, Alberto. *Gaspare Spontini: Studio storico-critico*. Roma: Ateneo, 1951.

Grout, Donald J. *A Short History of Opera*, 2nd ed. New York: Columbia University Press, 1965 (see pp. 306–308).

STAËL, MADAME ANNE-LOUISE-GERMAINE DE 1766-1817

French novelist and political and literary essayist

As the devoted daughter of the Swiss-born financier and statesman Jacques Necker, Anne-Louise-Germaine de Staël was destined for a life of active participation in intellectual and political debate. Her Calvinist background not only encouraged a moral seriousness and the deployment of a critical and independent mind, but also instilled in her a particular sensitivity to persecution.

Madame de Staël's intellectual coming of age coincided with the outbreak of the French Revolution. If all her subsequent work constitutes a reflection on liberty, she adopted a characteristically independent stance politically, supporting the movement toward reform but also making efforts to save the lives of the monarch and his supporters. Her virulent opposition to Napoleon Bonaparte is manifest in all her writing after his assumption of power. This caused her to be in almost permanent exile from 1802 until his abdication in 1814. The emperor's implacable persecution of Staël sharpened her resolve and, together with Benjamin Constant de Rebecque, with whom she enjoyed a complex relationship based on a mutual emotional and intellectual dependence, she became a leading figure in the liberal opposition.

Staël's fictional counterpart in Constant's autobiographical novel, *Cécile* (1810–11) is appropriately described as being, through her writings and her conversation, the most famous person of her age. On her extensive European travels, Staël sought out the foremost writers and intellectuals of the age, on whom she invariably left her mark. Her salon in the family home at Coppet, near Geneva, attracted leading intellectuals sympathetic to the liberal cause. The "Groupe de Coppet" thus included the historians Prosper Brugière, baron de Barante and Jean Charles Leonard Simonde de Sismondi, and the critic August Wilhelm von Schlegel, as well as Constant, always Staël's most stimulating interlocutor.

The scandalous neglect of Staël's importance in the history of European Romanticism, which has only recently begun to be redressed, may partly be considered an overreaction to the eminence and notoriety she enjoyed in her lifetime. It is almost certainly also explained by her willingness to allow a male-dominated world to make her an object of gentle mockery, so that it could protect itself from her threat to its exclusivity. She continued to be the victim of history long after her death, her opposition to Napoleon being at odds with the nineteenth-century's gradual mythification of the emperor, and her pro-German stance as anathema in the period from 1870 to 1918.

Staël's Romantic sensibility was first and foremost visible in her (rather public) private life. Indelibly marked by her reading of Jean-Jacques Rousseau, she pursued an ideal of romantic love that was to remain unfulfilled at least until, in late middle age, she married a younger man. Under Rousseau's influence, her ideal was pursued with scant respect for convention and with a deep mistrust of the tyrannical institution of marriage. As such, her private life was enmeshed with her intellectual and political thinking. Her lovers included fellow members of the Coppet group and a number of other men of outstanding intellect and force of character, to whom she considered herself an equal. In particular, her long and embattled relationship with Constant (in which neither was faithful and from which Constant failed to extricate himself, even after his marriage to Charlotte von Hardenberg) had a beneficial effect on their respective intellectual enterprises and the literary works that derived from the tensions in their emotional lives.

Staël's failure to achieve her ideal, together with her enforced role as outsider as a result of her persecution, served to heighten her exemplary status as a Romantic at odds with herself and with society. However, the popular, rather more ambivalent, image of her may be seen in the response of the young Honoré de Balzac, who maintained in a letter to the Duchesse d'Abrantès in 1825 that women were to be divided into two broad categories: the "Isidora type" (Isidora was a character in Charles Robert Maturin's widely admired Gothic novel, *Melmoth the Wanderer*, 1820), the "touching emblem of gracefulness and submission"; and the "Staël type," in whom "masculine ideas, bold conceptions, and sheer forcefulness coexist strangely with all the weaknesses of the fair sex."

The precocious Staël began to write as a child. By the time she was twenty-one, she had composed three plays and a number

F. P. Gérard, *Anne Louise Germaine de Stael-Holstein.* Reprinted courtesy of Bildarchiv Preussischer Kulturbesitz.

of stories. From 1788 onward, her scope extended to embrace essays on Rousseau, the influence of the passions on the happiness of individuals and of nations, and the trial of Marie Antoinette, together with three other political pamphlets. The first of these, on the subject of peace, was published in 1794 and addressed jointly to William Pitt the Younger and the French. It was followed the next year by a pamphlet on internal peace, in which Staël reaffirmed her belief in the republic but pleaded for a middle way that avoided the destructive war between opposing forms of extremism. In 1798 she turned her attention to ways of ending the revolution, but thought better of publishing the pamphlet in question.

*Essai sur les fiction*s was published in 1795 and subsequently translated into German by Johann Wolfgang von Goethe. From a perspective that is today more commonly associated with reactions to world war or the Holocaust, Staël addresses the question of how the novel should develop in the light of the atrocities committed during the Terror. The middle path she characteristically identified was one that eschewed the extremes of history and romance and advocated a form of fiction that sought to give a likeness of truth. *De la littérature considérée dans ses rapports avec les institutions sociales* (*A Treatise of Ancient and Modern Literature and the Influence of Literature upon Society,* 1800) was, as the title suggests, an ambitious attempt to consider the relationship between literature and social institutions. Be that as it may, the remarkable historical and geographical range deployed in *De la littérature* makes it a canonical text in the history of comparative literature. More important still, it was a progressive manifesto that looked forward to both a new literature and a new society mutually sustained by a common respect for the genuine forces of civilization, forces that had nothing to do with tyranny, whether ancient or modern. Reflecting her liberal stance, the underlying principle consisted of a respect for the personal values of the individual human being.

Staël's two novels duly represent an attempt to create modern fictions out of authentic personal experience. As such, they were also the product of her relationship with Constant, both in terms of the insight this gave her into the difficult fusion of self and other, and as a result of the way in which each partner's theory and practice were likely refined in the course of their shared political and philosophical reflections. An epistolary novel, *Delphine* (1802), presents the reader with an idealized self-portrait of the author. Like her creator, the heroine is a superior and highly independent being who is denied happiness in her love for an attractive—and altogether less remarkable—nobleman, both as a result of their incompatibility and of the way society's values and the ungenerous behavior of others work against them. Set in the early years of the revolution, it is an opportunity for Staël to indicate her standpoint with regard to the questions that had occupied her in her political pamphlets, and, more pertinently, to protest against the fundamental inequality present in society's treatment of the two sexes. Her heroine ends up committing suicide.

In her second novel, *Corinne, ou l'Italie* (*Corinne, or Italy,* 1807), Staël wisely abandoned the epistolary form and, to Napoleon's considerable displeasure, was rewarded with even greater public success. Growing out of her recent travels in Italy, *Corinne* presents the inevitable failure and unhappiness of the half-English, half-Italian heroine who in addition to being a striking beauty is a creative genius whose celebrated poetic improvisations allow Staël to indulge her scholarly interest in Italian literature and art and Roman history. The object of Corinne's love is a melancholic Scottish nobleman who inevitably ends up taking the safer option of obeying his dead father's wishes and marrying her more conventional half-sister. *Corinne* is thus an opportunity for Staël not only to continue the fundamental theme of *Delphine* but also to map out a Romantic geography, the coordinates of which are provided by the contrasting climes of north and south. The novel ends, predictably, with the heroine's premature death. Although it is difficult for the modern reader to respond with enthusiasm to Staël's emotional rhetoric, or to her rather stilted incorporation of cultural erudition, *Corinne* remains a remarkable novel as a result of the vehemence of its author's convictions. After her death, Staël was immortalized as Corinne in a painting by Baron François-Pascale-Simon Gérard (*Corinne at Capo Miseno,* 1819; Musée des Beaux-Arts, Lyon). Through its emphasis on the decline of Italian culture and society, *Corinne* also exerted a significant influence in favor of the Italian *Risorgimento.*

Madame Staël's masterpiece is, arguably, *De l'Allemagne* (*On Germany*), published in London in 1813, after Napoleon had ordered the destruction of the manuscript and proofs in 1810. It is divided into four parts, which consider in turn Germany and its manners and customs, its literature and (minimally) its art, its philosophy and its ethics, and its religion and its "enthusiasm" (one of the author's favorite concepts, as may be seen from chapter 10, in part 4). Part 2 opens with a discussion of why

Frenchmen have never been able to appreciate German literature for its true worth. After reading the work, Johann Wolfgang von Goethe observed that the wall of French national prejudice with regard to German culture had now been thoroughly breached. Yet *De l'Allemagne* was far from being an academic study; nor was it narrowly concerned with Germany. Instead, this attempt to identify an organic national identity through an ambitious engagement with the totality of one nation's imaginative and intellectual activity sought also to lay the cultural and political foundations for a new European Romanticism. This new Romantically envisioned state would be rooted in the souls of individuals and nations alike, and would triumph over the flimsy, military "union" imposed by Napoleon. A work of barely disguised propaganda, *De l'Allemagne* is, as John Isbell has remarked, "full of deliberate lies, and dangerously Revolutionary." Much admired by Fanny Burney, *De l'Allemagne* also wielded an enormous (and acknowledged) influence outside France, most crucially on Ralph Waldo Emerson, Giacomo Leopardi, and Alexandr Pushkin.

MICHAEL TILBY

Biography

Born in Paris, April 22, 1776, daughter of Louis XVI's future finance minister, Jacques Necker, a Swiss-born Protestant. Visited England with parents, 1776. Married Eric Magnus Staël von Holstein, Swedish attaché in Paris, 1786; they separated in 1800. Affairs with Charles Maurice de Talleyrand and Louis de Narbonne, 1788. Birth of son Auguste (by Narbonne), 1790. New constitution largely drawn up in her Paris salon, 1791. Devised escape plan for Louis XVI, which was rejected by Marie Antoinette; birth of Albert, her second son by Narbonne, 1792. Allowed by Maximilian de Robespierre to leave for her family's residence at Coppet, near Geneva, 1792. Spent first six months of 1793 in England before returning to Coppet. Began her long and fraught relationship with Benjamin Constant, 1794. Reopened her salon in Paris, 1795. Uneasy relationship with the various revolutionary governments, 1795–99. Birth of her daughter Albertine, 1797. Became friends with Juliette de Récamier, 1798. Friendship with Swiss historian and economist Sismondi, 1801. Exiled from Paris by Napoleon, 1802. In Germany with Constant, 1803–4; decided against marriage to him in 1804. In Italy, initially with August Wilhelm von Schlegel (tutor to her children) and Sismondi, 1804–5. Liaison with future Portuguese prime minister Pedro de Sousza, and beginning of five-year affair with the historian Prosper de Barante, 1805. In Vienna, 1807–8. The newly married Constant followed her to Coppet, 1809. Returned to France but again exiled, with Napoleon also ordering the seizure of the manuscripts and proofs of her *De l'Allemagne*, 1810. In Switzerland, 1810–12. Journeyed to Russia and Sweden; supporter of Bernadotte's claim to the throne, 1812. Spent a year in London, 1813–14. Returned to Paris on Napoleon's abdication, and reestablished her salon, 1814; reluctantly supported Bourbons after failure of Bernadotte's candidacy. Left Paris for Coppet ten days before Napoleon's reentry, to return after his second abdication, 1815. Second period in Italy, 1815–16. Secretly married her younger lover John Rocca in 1816 (to whom she had been betrothed since 1811 and with whom she had had a son, Louis-

Alphonse, in 1812). Died in Paris, July 14, 1817; Constant's articles of posthumous homage published in *Le Mercure de France* and *Le Journal général de France*.

Selected Works

Essai sur les fictions. 1795.
De la littérature considérée dans ses rapports avec les institutions sociales, 1798. Edited by Axel Blaeschke. Paris: Garnier, 1998.
Delphine, 1802. Edited by Simone Balayé and Lucia Omacini. 2 vols. Geneva: Droz, 1987. Translated by Avriel H. Goldberger. DeKalb, Ill.: Northern Illinois University Press, 1995.
Corinne ou l'Italie, 1807. Edited by Simone Balayé. Collection Folio, Paris: Gallimard, 1983. Translated as *Corinne, or Italy* by Sylvia Raphael. Oxford: Oxford University Press, 1998.
De l'Allemagne, 1813. Edited by Simone Balayé. Paris: Garnier-Flammarion, 1966.
Considérations sur la Révolution française, 1818. Edited by Jacques Godechot. Paris: Tallandier, 1983.
Dix années d'exil, 1820. Edited by Simone Balayé and Mariella Vianello Bonifacio. Paris: Fayard, 1996.
Correspondance générale. Edited by Beatrice W. Jasinski. 6 vols. to date. Paris: Jean-Jacques Pauvert, vols. 1–4; Hachette, vol. 5; Klincksieck, vol. 6. 1962– .
An Extraordinary Woman: Major Writings of Germaine de Staël. Translated and edited by Vivian Folkenflik. New York: Columbia University Press, 1992.
Oeuvres de jeunesse. Edited by Simone Balayé and John Isbell. Paris: Desjonquères, 1997.

Bibliography

Balayé, Simone, *Madame de Staël. Ecrire, lutter, vivre*. Geneva: Droz, 1994.
——— *Madame de Staël: lumières et liberté*. Paris: Klincksieck, 1979.
Balayé, Simone, ed. *L'Eclat et le silence. "Corinne ou l'Italie" de Madame de Staël*. Paris: Champion, 1999.
Barbéris, Pierre. "Mme de Staël: du romantisme, de la littérature et de la France nouvelle." *Europe* 693–94 (1987): 6–22.
Bredin, Jean-Denis. *Une singulière famille: Jacques Necker, Suzanne Necker, et Germaine de Staël*. Paris: Fayard, 1999.
Brookner, Anita. "Corinne and Her *Coups de foudre*," In *Soundings*. London: Harvill Press, 1997.
Cahiers staëliens. Ongoing journal. 1960– .
Constant, Benjamin. "De Madame de Stael et de ses ouvrages." In *Mélanges de littérature et de politique*. 1829. Reprint, *Portraits, mémoires, souvenirs*. Edited by Ephraïm Harpaz. Paris: Champion, 1992.
Delon, Michel, and Françoise Mélonio. *Mme de Staël*. Actes du colloque de la Sorbonne du 20 novembre 1999. Paris: Presses de l'Université de Paris-Sorbonne, 2000.
Diaz, José Luiz. *Madame de Staël, "Corinne ou l'Italie". L'âme se mêle à tout*, Paris: SEDES, 1999.
Didier, Béatrice. *"Corinne ou l'Italie" de Madame de Staël*. Collection Foliothèque. Paris: Gallimard, 1999.
Dubé, Pierre H. *Bibliographie de la critique sur Madame de Staël 1789–1994*. Geneva: Droz, 1998.
Gutwirth, Madelyn. *Madame de Staël, Novelist*. Urbana: University of Illinois Press, 1978.
Isbell, John Claiborne. *The Birth of European Romanticism: Truth and Propaganda in Staël's "De l'Allemagne," 1810–1813*. Cambridge: Cambridge University Press, 1994.
Macherey, Pierre. "Corinne philosophe," *Europe* 693–94 (1987): 22–37.

Miller, Nancy K. *Subject to Change: Reading Feminist Writing.* New York: Columbia University Press, 1988.

Perchellet, Jean-Pierre, ed. *Madame de Staël, "Corinne ou l'Italie."* Paris: Klincksieck, 1999.

———. *Un deuil éclatant du bonheur. Madame de Staël, "Corinne ou l'Italie."* Orléans: Paradigme, 1999.

Winegarten, Renée. *Mme de Staël.* Leamington Spa, England: Germany Berg, 1985.

Website

www.stael.org

STAGNELIUS, ERIK JOHAN 1793–1823

Swedish poet

The short life of Erik Johan Stagnelius, spanning only twenty-nine years, was marred by ill health and loneliness. Perhaps as a result of this, his poetic genius was able to come to fruition early. He published only four books of poetry during his lifetime, but the remaining manuscripts, published posthumously, revealed to the Swedish public, despite the incomplete nature of the collection, some of the scope of his creative talent. He did not enjoy particular recognition during his life, but after his death his work quickly grew in popularity.

Except for the barest of biographical details, little else is known about Stagnelius. He was a loner from childhood, preferring to climb trees by himself rather than play with his siblings. His greatest joy was reading, a passion he was able to freely indulge in his father's extensive library. The young Stagnelius was given a classical education at home, and his early poetry (the earliest remaining dates from 1812–14) shows clear influences from the Roman authors. He learned the art of the pre-Romantic ballad from the works of Johann Wolfgang von Goethe, Adam Gottlob Oehlenschläger, and Johann Christoph Friedrich von Schiller, and was further influenced by the Swedish poets of the 1700s, Bengt Lidner and Johann Gabriel Oxenstierna. The classical influence was part of his poetry for a long time; Stagnelius was one of the few Swedish Romantic authors successful in uniting the classical with the Romantic.

During his university years in Uppsala, Stagnelius further consolidated his knowledge of the classical authors and learned about the young Romantic movement. He had no direct contact, however, with the main protagonists of the Swedish Romantic movement, such as Per Daniel Amadeus Atterbom, who also walked the streets of Uppsala. He never contributed to the literary magazines instrumental to the development of Romanticism in Sweden and met only a few of his contemporaries: Carl Jonas Love Almqvist, Erik Gustaf Geijer, and Lorenzo Hammarsköld, and possibly Johan Olof Wallin. He corresponded only with his family, and even Almqvist, who worked with him as a clerical assistant, was later only able to contribute a few anecdotes to Stagnelius's biography. It is important to note that these two colleagues, Almqvist and Stagnelius, are generally considered to be the two great geniuses of Swedish Romantic literature.

Stagnelius is described as the most Romantic of all the Swedish poets writing at the time. His isolation and the lack of extensive biographical detail highlight the sense of mystery surrounding him. The reader is forced to try and glean his character from his poems, though that is difficult. His childhood reminiscences, "Afsked till lifvet" ("Farewell to Life") and "Mig fostrade, i nardusrika ängar," ("I Was Brought Up in Spikenard Filled Fields") are hardly autobiographical in the concrete sense, but rather take childhood as a symbol of innocence and reject the harshness of the adult world in favor of a pilgrimage in search of a lost Eden.

It is perhaps unsurprising that as the son of a bishop Stagnelius chose to base his first mature poems around the theme of religion. The first religious poems are dated 1813 and 1814, coinciding with the spate of psalmlike poems inspired by the ongoing production of a new psalm book (published in 1819, the team of authors was led by the Romantic poet Wallin). Stagnelius's discussion of religious problems was deeply personal, and he suffered a religious crisis. His first published work was the poem "Wladimir den store" ("Vladimir the Great," 1817). The subject matter is taken from ancient Russian history and is also linked to the Russian policy of Sweden's king, Karl XIV Johan. The main purpose of the material was, however, to describe a soul's conversion to Christianity. The Russian king fears the mystery of life and the only way to suppress this is through heroic deeds in battle. Upon meeting the Christian prisoner Anna, however, he realizes where redemption is to be found. The religious motive in Stagnelius's poetry is often depicted as a pilgrimage from antiquity to Christianity. The peak of his religious poetry came in 1821 with the publication of "Liljor i Saron" ("Lilies in Sharon"), when his conversion to a committed if unorthodox Christianity was confirmed.

In the year 1815, the name Amanda first appeared in Stagnelius's poetry. Amanda represents the strong erotic theme running through his work. There has been much speculation as to her true identity, and two possible women are suggested: Fredrique Almgren, the very beautiful daughter of a woman with whom Stagnelius's mother stayed for a time, and Constance Magnét, a childhood sweetheart. It is, however, more rewarding to see Amanda as the personification of the poet's longing for love.

Stagnelius reportedly possessed a strong erotic longing but was unable for various personal and social reasons, as yet unexplained, to find release for these longings in a meaningful relationship. In his poetry, however, he was able to compensate for this deficiency and his youthful poems are filled with wishful sexual dreams. The feeling of exclusion and loneliness increased throughout his life and although he may have experienced bought or easily gained sexual pleasures, they did not satisfy him. The romantic triumphs are restricted to his poetry and even these were not sufficient. No one would give him real, true love and he was therefore forced to invent Amanda, the ultimate in desirable women.

Stagnelius owned feelings of love that poured forth feverishly hot as never before in Swedish literature. His unhappiness provided him with a source of inspiration and was perhaps therefore not the heaviest of burdens. In the poem "Amanda," he writes of his longing for her; he sees her everywhere but is condemned in the last verse to search for this elusive, scorning woman forever, never to reach her. In "Näktergalen och rosen" ("The Nightingale and the Rose," 1818), Amanda is a rose enclosed by thorns, and the nightingale that watches over her is condemned to sing forever in the hope that he might eventually win her love. Stagnelius's longing for love produces a poetry that gives the poet a softer and more human appearance.

Stagnelius, more than any other Swedish Romantic author, dared to explore the theoretical and artistic extremes of Romanticism. In his case one is convinced of a strong inner need behind the ultra-Romantic thought development. The despairing dualism between the earthbound and the eternal, sensuality and reason, darkness and light, and material and spiritual in his poetry indicate a deeper psychological trauma. The last years of stagnelius's life were tortured by ill health and increasing isolation. He took comfort in alcohol and probably also opium, and the death he had written about for so long in poems such as "Till Förruttnelsen" ("To Putrefaction," 1818; in it he writes of a longing for freedom from pain and the peacefulness of sleeping, while storms and catastrophes threaten the earth) came in 1823.

Stagnelius stands out from other Swedish Romantic poets as a tortured genius, his great poetical talent appearing as compensation for his unsightly features and ill health. These "gifts" led him to isolate himself and also perhaps provoked his early death. He tackled those questions that mankind will never tire of asking in highly accomplished poetical form. The uncertainty over what he could have achieved had he lived a longer life continues to add to the mystery surrounding him

CAMILLA FRASER

Biography

Born in Öland, October 14, 1793. Educated at home, Gärdlösa on Öland (island off Sweden) and Kalmar from 1810 where his father was bishop. To university of Lund for a term from October 1811, and then to Uppsala from 1812 on. Moved to Stockholm, 1815, and worked as a copier and clerical assistant until his death. Published four books of poetry 1817–22, *Wladimir den store* (*Vladimir the Great*) in 1817, *Liljor i Saron* (*Lilies in Sharon*) and *Martyrerna* (*The Martyrs*) in 1821 and *Backanterna* (*The Bacchantes*) in 1822. Remaining manuscripts published posthumously 1824–26. Died April 3, 1823 from a stroke, in a rented room in the south of Stockholm, aged twenty-nine.

Selected Works

Erik Johan Stagnelius Dikter. Edited by Hans Levander. 1954.
Erik Johan Stagnelius Samlade Skrifter. Vols 1–4. Edited by Fredrik Böök. 1911.

Bibliography

Andrae, Daniel. *Erik Johan Stagnelius.* Stockholm: Natur och Kultur, 1955.
Bergsten, Staffan. *Erotikern Stagnelius.* Stockholm: Bonniers, 1966.
Böök, Fredrik. *Stagnelius än en gång.* Stockholm: Bonniers, 1942.
———. *Stagnelius: Liv och dikt.* Stockholm: Bonniers, 1954.
Gustafson, Alrik. *A History of Swedish Literature.* Minneapolis: University of Minnesota Press, 1961.
Lönnroth, Lars, and Sven Delblanc. *Den Svenska Litteraturen: Upplysning och Romantik 1718–1830.* Stockholm: Bonniers, 1988.
Malmström, Sten. *Studier Över Stilen i Stagnelius Lyrik.* Stockholm: Bonniers, 1961.
Simonsson, Johan Bernhard. *Erik Johan Stagnelius: Lif och dikt.* Lund: Gleerup, 1909.
Tigerstedt, E. N. *Svensk Litteraturhistoria,* Stockholm, Natur och Kultur, 1953.
Tigerstedt, E. N., ed. *Ny Illustrerad Svensk Litteraturhistoria.* Stockholm, Natur och Kultur, 1956.

STEFFENS, HENRIK 1773–1845

Danish philosopher and physicist

Henrik Steffens was born on May 2, 1773, to the surgeon Hinrich Steffens and his wife, the deeply religious Susanne Christine Bang, in Stavanger, which belonged at that time to Denmark. At a young age Steffens became acquainted with scientific works in his father's library. His education took place in Latin schools in Helsingör and Roskilde, thereafter continuing privately in Copenhagen, where he attended Georges-Louis Leclec Buffon's lecture on his work *Histoire Naturelle, générale et particulière* (begun in 1749).

Steffens began studying natural sciences at the University of Copenhagen in the autumn of 1790, where he was greatly influenced by the lectures and experiments of the naturalist Christian Gottlieb Kratzenstein. During the period 1792–94, medical and scientific studies by Matthias Claudius, Johann Gottfried von Herder, Friedrich Gottlieb Klopstock, Johann Caspar Lavater, Gotthold Ephraim Lessing, and Karl Philipp Moritz influenced intellectual developments. In the sessions of the Naturhistoriske Selskab (Natural History Society) founded by Ole Hieronymus Mynster, Steffens gave several lectures; he also edited the *Physikalsk, Oeconomisk och Medico-Chirurgisk Bibliothek for Denmark og Norge* (1794) for the first few years of publication. His specialist interest was mineralogy; he also constructed a herbarium and studied Antoine-Laurent Lavoisier's modern oxygen chemistry.

In 1793 Steffens participated in an expedition to the west coast of Norway. After a short stay in Hamburg, Steffens lived for a year with his father in Rendsburg, worked on a mineralogical handbook and translated Karl Ludwig Willdenow's *Grundriss der Kräuterkunde* (*Outlines of Botany,* 1794) into Danish. His studies continued in Kiel, where in 1796 he received the *venia legendi* (right to give lectures) for natural history on the basis of a thesis on the theory of generation; a promotion in philosophy followed in 1798.

Steffens obtained a traveling scholarship from the Danish government to go from Hamburg, via the mountains of Harz and Erfurt, to Jena; the scholarship also allowed him to make trips to the forest of Thuringia in order to conduct geological studies. Steffens read Johann Gottlieb Fichte's *Das System der Sittenlehre nach den Prinzipien der Wissenschaftslehre* (*The System of Morality as Based on the Science of Knowledge*, 1798) at this time. In the winter of 1798–99 he attended lectures at the university of Jena on natural philosophy and became acquainted with Johann Gottlieb Fichte, Johann Wolfgang von Goethe, Novalis, Johann Wilhelm Ritter, August Wilhelm von Schlegel and Friedrich von Schlegel, as well as with the natural scientists A. J. G. K. Batsch, Christian Wilhelm Büttner, and Johann Georg Lenz. Geological studies conducted in Freiberg in 1801, with Abraham Gottlob Werner, helped him to formulate his own viewpoint in the quarrel between the Neptunians and Vulcanists. In his *Beyträgen zur innern Naturgeschichte der Erde* (*Contributions to the Internal Natural History of the Earth*, 1801), Steffens touched on the *Grundthema* (fundamental theme) of his whole life. In the winter of 1802–3, Steffens lectured on nature, history, philosophy, and art in Copenhagen (published as *Indledning til philosophiske Forelaesningar* [*Introduction to the Philosophical Lectures*], 1803). In 1803 he also married Johanna Reichardt, daughter of the composer Johann Friedrich Reichardt.

In 1804 Steffens took up a full professorial chair at the University of Halle in the philosophy of nature, physiology, and mineralogy. His friendships with the physician Johann Christian Reil, the theologian Friedrich Daniel Ernst Schleiermacher, and the philologist Friedrich August Wolf were initiated through the university. He found that positions on the philosophy of nature varied highly among his professorial colleagues; the physicist Ludwig Wilhelm Gilbert, for example, was strongly opposed to Steffens' stance.

In 1809 Steffens published *Über die Idee der Universitäten* (*About the Idea of Universities*, 1809). In this work Steffens put forth his ideas on education; specifically, he argued for a reorganization of German high schools and a rejection of the heavy influence French modes of thought had on the German school system.

During his time in Breslau (1811–32) as professor of physics, Steffens lectured not only on physics but also on philosophy, and founded the Institute of Physics. The fall of the French army in Russia led to his engagement in battle against France, an unusual role for a German professor. At Paris he met the famous natural scientist Georges Léopold-Chrêtien Cuvier.

Steffens then published the *Vollständiges Handbuch der Oryktognosie* (*Complete Handbook of Oryktognosy*, 1811–24), an obituary for Reil (who died of typhoid in 1813), several books and articles on natural history and chemistry, and *Anthropologie* (2 vols., 1824), all of which were well received. In 1821 he was appointed associate member of the Kongelige Danske Videnskabers Selskab (Royal Danish Society of Natural Sciences) and in 1824 foreign member of the Medicinsk Selskab in Copenhagen. In 1815 the degree of *doctor honoris causa* (honorary) in medicine was conferred on Steffens by the University of Kiel.

In 1832, with his appointment as professor of physics at the University of Berlin, his connection with former acquaintances and friends was revived and intensified. Natural philosophy, anthropology, philosophy of religion, and psychology were the main staple of his lectures, for he had gradually lost interest in the fields of experimental physics and mineralogy. Steffens considered both philosophers and natural scientists his intellectual opponents. Despite any differences of opinion, Steffens retained the respect and admiration of his colleagues. In the autumn of 1834, he was elected rector of the University of Berlin.

Steffens died on February 2, 1845. According to the naturalist Gotthilf Heinrich von Schubert, as he explained in his *Ehrengedächtniss* at the Bayerische Akademie der Wissenschaften, Steffens created, with Schelling, a "union of spirits which forms in the history of the deeper understanding of nature the starting point of a new significant period." In a memorial speech, Schelling emphasized Steffens's spiritual attachment to his work, and how he considered his study of the relationship between science as of fundamental importance.

Steffens was read and discussed by his contemporaries with both appreciation and criticism. Goethe met *Grundzüge der philosophischen Naturwissenschaft* (*Outlines of the Philosophy of Natural Sciences*, 1806), with a lack of understanding and disapproval. Novalis was stimulated by Steffens's zoological ideas. Reading *Beyträge (Contributions)* Schubert was pushed "away from the clear path of the empirical sciences" and brought to the "cognition of the forces of an inner and higher knowledge."

Steffens's Romantic work varies widely in form and subject; in addition to scientific and philosophical treatises, his oeuvre includes political, historical, theological, and fictional works. His ten-volume autobiography, *Was ich erlebte. Aus der Erinnerung niedergeschrieben* (*What I Experienced. Written by Memory*, 1840–44) is a valuable cultural and historical document of his era. Steffens, like other Romantic naturalists, considered the delineation of the essential identity of nature and spirit to be of utmost importance. The unity of all natural processes, and the corresponding accord between the various sciences, was incontrovertible, he felt, as was the assumed compatibility of philosophy and science. Nature and culture could and should coexist. Science should serve the real needs of humankind, so as to improve the conditions of life on a practical level, while also concerning itself with the development and refinement of intellectual assumptions and beliefs.

DIETRICH VON ENGELHARDT

Bibliography

Engelhardt, Dietrich von: *Einleitung*, In: *Henrich Steffens: Was ich erlebte: Aus der Erinnerung niedergeschrieben*. Vol. 1. Stuttgart: Frommann-Holzboog, 1995, p. 9–79.

Hultberg, Helge: *Den unge Henrich Seffens, 1773–1811*. Copenhagen: Reitzel, 1973.

Hultberg, Helge: *Den aeldre Henrich Steffens, 1811–1845*. Copenhagen: Reitzel, 1981.

Lorenz, Otto, and Bernd Henningsen, eds. *Henrik Steffens— Vermittler zwischen Natur und Geist*, Berlin: Berlin-Verl. Spitz, 1999.

Paul, Fritz. *Henrich Steffens: Naturphilosophie und Universalromantik*. München: Fink, 1973.

Waschnitius, Viktor *Henrich Steffens: Ein Beitrag zur nordischen und deutschen Geistesgeschichte*. Neumünster: Wachholz, 1939.

STENDHAL (MARIE-HENRI BEYLE) 1783-1842

French novelist

The pseudonym Stendhal conceals the identity of a writer caught between the need for sincerity in literary self-expression and the desire for the privacy that would save him from the embarrassment of self-revelation. The meaning of such a confected name has itself resisted the hypotheses of generations of critics. Born Henri Marle-Beyle, he spent his early years in the provincial town of Grenoble, which he found stultifying. This is depicted in his disjointed yet evocative autobiographical work of 1835, *Vie de Henry Brulard*, where his initials, H. B., are reconfigured. In a text that traces the meandering of memory between a detested childhood and the present moment of writing, he recounts the loss of his beloved mother and his tense relationship with his father, then two escapes, first to Paris in 1799 to study at the École Polytechnique, and then to Italy in May 1800 as a second lieutenant in Napoleon Bonaparte's army. Henceforth, France and Italy represented opposing poles in the life and writing of Stendhal. By profession he followed a diplomatic career that was to take him back to Italy on numerous occasions. An amateur of Italian opera, Stendhal drew a distinction between, on the one hand, the Cartesian rationality of French *esprit*, and on the other, the emotional range of Italian sentiment and culture.

In 1802 he returned to France where his father's financial support allowed him to pursue his literary ambitions, in particular his abortive attempt to become a comic playwright, the Molière of his age. His private writings reveal not only the inner turmoil of the frustrated young writer, but the desire to create and guard a gap between that inner core and projected public personae that came to be the mark of Stendhal's novelistic heroes. His complex accounts of Napoleon (1817, 1836) owed much to his period in the emperor's service from 1806 until Napoleon's first exile in 1814 to Elba. Stendhal's own exile during the early years of the Restoration period shaped the ambivalence of the political positions that underpin his satirical depiction of modern society. Though motivated by liberal sentiments and perturbed by the reactionary regimes of Europe after 1815, he could not resist an aestheticism that might appear aristocratic. For all its political virtue, modern democracy threatened to suffocate the feeling and imagination of those *âmes supérieures* (superior souls) in whom Stendhal believed. Indeed, he doubted the capacity of all but the "Happy Few," a phrase borrowed from Oliver Goldsmith for the dedication of *La Chartreuse de Parme* (*The Charter house Parma*, 1839) to appreciate his writing. He would project his fantasies of an empathetic (and largely female) readership into the future, 50 or 150 years, and indeed it was during the twentieth century that the cult of Stendhal genuinely took root. It was during exile in Milan that he began to write for a public audience. He cobbled together accounts of the lives of Franz Joseph Haydn, Pietro Metastasio, and Wolfgang Amadeus Mozart (1817), produced his *Histoire de la peinture en Italie* (*History of Painting in Italy*, 1817), and his travel study *Rome, Naples et Florence en 1817* (1817, augmented 1826). The latter marks the first use of the pseudonym Stendhal.

The geographical schematism that contrasts France and Italy owes something to the relativism of Enlightenment thinkers such as Charles-Louis de Secondat Montesquieu, whose influence can also be found in *De l'amour* (*Love*, 1822), in which Stendhal defines the geographical and historical diversity of love. He draws distinctions between different forms of love: *amour-passion*, *amour de tête*, *amour de vanité*, and *amour physique*. In particular he develops his theory of *cristallisation* in which he suggests that the experience of love characterizes merely that moment in which we feel that our pre-conceived ideals have been fulfilled by the arrival of the desired other. The tension between duty and love that Stendhal experienced is reflected in the dilemmas of his heroes. In his early twenties he pursued an actress to Marseilles, where he served behind the counter of a grocer's shop. In Milan his fiery encounters with Angela Pietragrua (1811–15) were to be overshadowed by his unrequited passion for Matilde (Métilde) Dembowski, to whom there are many coded references in *De l'amour*: "Je tremble de n'avoir écrit qu'un soupir, quand je crois avoir noté une vérité." ("I tremble at having merely written a sigh when I think I have noted a truth.") Afterward his most significant adventures involved the countess Clémentine Curial (1824–26) and Giulia Rinieri (1830–33).

Between 1821 and 1830, Stendhal spent most of his time in Paris, though he visited England and Italy. During this period he led a busy social life, had his first encounter with the young Romantic movement, and published his first novel, *Armance* (1827). Like Honoré de Balzac, Stendhal does not fit easily into the narrow definitions of French Romanticism offered by earlier critics. Their useful inclusion in a less monochromatic depiction of Romanticism is one of the advantages of a wider critical definition of the term. Stendhal's pamphlet *Racine et Shakespeare* (published in two installments, 1823 and 1825) at first proposes a manifesto for a national prose tragedy, unfettered by the constraining unities of time and place so dear to neoclassical theater. This is amplified in his personal definition of Romanticism. He mocks the cultural conservatism of the Académie Française and the traditionalism of the liberal press, and encourages writing on contemporary society that will attract modern audiences, rather than mere imitations of Racine and Shakespeare. This increased concern for politics and society is also visible in his second Italian travel book, *Promenades dans Rome* (1829), and his fictitious travel journal *Mémoires d'un touriste* (*Memoirs of a Tourist*, 1838) on France.

Armance set Stendhal on his path as a novelist. It depicts the tragic love of the noble Octave de Malivert and his cousin Armance de Zohiloff. The enigma around his melancholia is concealed from the reader but revealed in Stendhal's correspondence: Octave is impotent. Their "mariage blanc" ends with his suicide and her retreat to a convent. The year 1829 saw the publication of a contemporary tale of passion, *Vanina Vanini*, the first of the *Chroniques italiennes* (1829–36), published anonymously in journals and collected posthumously in 1855. (The other tales take place either in the eighteenth century or a rather mythical sixteenth century.) They contrast grand Italianate passions (for justice, power, honor, and love) with Stendhal's diagnosis of petty France. *Les Cenci* (a subject also adopted by Percy

Bysshe Shelley) tells of oppression and retribution; *L'Abbesse de Castro* depicts the efforts of an impassioned bandit to attack the convent where his beloved is confined. Meanwhile Stendhal had published his first masterpiece, *Le Rouge et le Noir* (*The Red and the Black*, 1830), the tale of the rise and fall of Julien Sorel.

The Revolution of 1830 that felled the restoration and installed the July Monarchy would last almost until Stendhal's death (it was replaced by the Second Republic one year before, in 1848). In *Le Rouge et le Noir* and the novels he wrote after the July days, Stendhal displays apparently contrary but ultimately complementary impulses toward social observation and intimate self-exploration. His social observation has led critics to return to the realistic aspects of his writing. Indeed, Stendhal is often cherished by critics of literary realism for the way in which he undermines the assumptions of such mimetic writing. Rather than merely offering us a banal copy of the everyday, he teases his readers, luring them into a reconstruction of the social universe only to undermine the very mimetic model on which he seems to rely. In this, as in his aestheticism, Stendhal reaches back to the eighteenth century, the France that preceded the cataclysm of 1789. Indeed, French Romanticism voices the uncertainties of postrevolutionary France, and for Stendhal these include an incoherence in the author-reader relationship that reflects the maelstrom of the new social order. Before staging the agonies and ecstasies of the inner self, Stendhal always stops to consider his audience—hypocritical, vain, avaricious, violent—and dons a mask before he goes on.

In 1832 his first attempt at autobiographical self-revelation appeared, *Souvenirs d'égotisme*, which depicts his life in Paris during the 1820s. The unfinished *Lucien Leuwen* (1834–36) tells of the heartbreak of a junior officer in Nancy, tricked into believing that the beloved widow, Madame de Chasteller, has had an illegitimate child. He returns to Paris where he succeeds in the amoral universe of politics, saturated with financial greed in the bourgeois age of Louis-Philippe, that Stendhal satirizes. The final part, in which Lucien was to be reunited with his love, was never written. In 1839 Stendhal began another novel, *Lamiel*, which would not be finished either. The Normandy heroine emerges from her adoptive bourgeois family and the protection of a duchess to embrace the breadth of life's experiences. The amoral doctor, Sansfin, encourages her to elope to Rouen with the son of the duchess, from where she follows that well-worn path to Paris and the domain of kept women. The authenticity and energy of her engagement with life and its passions leave her disgusted with the hypocrisy already described in *Lucien Leuwen*.

In that same year, 1839, his second, and final, masterpiece, *La Chartreuse de Parme* was published, having been dictated to a secretary in under two months. Set in modern Italy, it recounts the tale of Fabrice del Dongo, apparently the illegitimate son of the Marquise del Dongo and a French officer. Indeed, the novel opens with a depiction of the energizing effect on Milan of the arrival of Napoleon's armies. The hero is raised by his mother and his aunt, Gina Pietranera, who is married off by arrangement once her husband has died, becoming the duchesse de Sanseverina. Like Julien Sorel, Fabrice is in conflict with the men around him, in this case his legal (if not biological) father and elder brother, who support the Austrian forces who have succeeded Napoleon. In a notorious instance of what Balzac called *illusions perdues* (lost illusions), Fabrice goes to fight for his hero, Napoleon, at Waterloo, only to see war in all its inglorious chaos. He rides about the battlefield with no clear idea of what is going on, as Stendhal's corrosive irony reveals the absurd comedy—as well as the violent tragedy—of postrevolutionary history. This description of the paltriness of war inspired Leo Tolstoy's *War and Peace*.

Afterward, Fabrice pursues a successful career in the church in Parma, where his aunt now resides with her lover, Count Mosca, a man of both cunning and passion. Gina's tacit desire for Fabrice unsettles her nephew, who starts an affair with an actress, kills her lover, and is incarcerated in the citadel of Parma. As at the end of *Le Rouge et le Noir*, it is only when the state imposes isolation on the Romantic hero that solitude brings emotional clarity. In prison he finds his true love, Clélia Conti. After an unwilling escape from prison, to which he soon returns, he only avoids poisoning because Gina agrees to sleep with the young prince (who has succeeded the tyrant of Parma whom she has already had assassinated in revenge for the treatment meted out to her beloved Fabrice). Toward the end of the novel Fabrice returns to Clélia, who has married and vowed never to cast eyes on him again. They meet in secret and are happy for three years, until Fabrice's wish to see their son leads to the death of Clélia and their child. By wanting more than is permitted by the rules of the game (in this case, by transgressing the ethical law of the vow), he loses everything and retires to a monastery, to die a year later. Gina then passes away too. Though the publisher forced Stendhal to cut later parts of the novel, these chapters still have the compelling strategic complexity of a chess game.

NICHOLAS WHITE

Biography

Born Henri Beyle in 1783; grew up in Grenoble. Went to Paris in 1799 to study at the École Polytechnique; in May 1800 headed for Milan, where he joined Napoleon's army. In 1802–6, mainly in Paris, receiving a pension from his father. In 1806–14 served Napoleon all over Europe. Angela Pietragua becames his mistress in 1811. Upon Napoleon's fall, went into exile in Milan; in 1818 his passion for Métilde Dembowski began. Expelled by the Austrian government in 1821. Mainly back in Paris 1821–30. After the July Days of 1830 until his death, French consul at Civitavecchia in the Papal States, but given leave in France, 1836–39. Made a chevalier de la Légion d'honneur in 1835. Died in Paris in 1842.

Selected Works

Vies de Haydn, de Mozart et de Métastase. 1817. Translated as *Lives of Haydn, Mozart and Metastasio* by Richard N. Coe. 1972. London: Calder and Boyars.

De l'amour. 1822. Translated as *Love*, by Gilbert and Suzanne Sale. Harmondsworth: Penguin, 1975.

Racine et Shakespeare. 2 vols. 1823–25. Translated as *Racine and Shakespeare* by Guy Daniels. 1962. New York: Crowell-Collier, 1962.

Armance. 1827. Translated by C. K. Scott Moncrieff. 1928. Reprinted London: Soho Book Co., 1986.

Le Rouge et le Noir. 1830. Translated as *The Red and the Black*. by Catherine Slater. Oxford: Oxford University Press, 1991.

La Chartreuse de Parme. 1839. Translated as *The Charterhouse of Parma* by Margaret Mauldon. Oxford: Oxford University Press, 1997.

Vie de Henry Brulard. Edited by Casimir Stryienski. 1890. Translated as *The Life of Henry Brulard*, by John Sturrock. London: Penguin, 1995.
Lucien Leuwen. 1894. Translated as *Lucien Leuwen* by H. L. R. Edwards. Revised by Robin Buss Harmondworth: Penguin, 1991.

Bibliography

Beauvoir, Simone de. "Stendhal ou le romanesque du vrai." In *Le deuxième sex*. Vol. 1. Paris: Gallimard, 1949.
Brombert, Victor. *Stendhal: Fiction and the Themes of Freedom*. New York: Random House, 1968.

Crouzet, Michel. *Stendhal et le langage*. Paris: Gallimard, 1981.
Felman, Shoshana. *La "folie" dans l'oeuvre romanesque de Stendhal*. Paris: Corti, 1971.
Genette, Gérard. "Stendhal." In *Figures*, Vol. 2. Paris: Seuil, 1969.
Jefferson, Ann. *Reading Realism in Stendhal*. Cambridge: Cambridge University Press, 1988.
Keates, Jonathan. *Stendhal*. New York: Carroll and Graf, 1994.
Pearson, Roger. *Stendhal's Violin. A Novelist and his Reader*. Oxford: Clarendon Press, 1988.
Starobinski, Jean. "Stendhal pseudonyme." In *L'Oeil vivant*. Paris: Gallimard, 1961.
Wood, Michael. *Stendhal*. London: Elek, 1971.

STIRNER, MAX (JOHANN CASPAR SCHMIDT) 1806–1856

German philosopher

One of the more enigmatic figures of the late Romantic period, Max Stirner (born Johann Caspar Schmidt) had few supporters during his life, and despite attracting interest around 1900 and again in 1968, he remains an oddity on the fringes of mainstream thought. Given the extreme individualism that he advocated, his role as an outsider was probably inevitable. Yet even among leading anarchists, notably Mikhail Bakunin and Pierre-Joseph Proudhon in the nineteenth, and Pyotr Alekseyevich Kropotkin and Mühsam in the twentieth century, what little commentary there has been has tended to be dismissive. Not much is known about his private life, and his successive apologists, from the Caledonian-German revolutionary poet John Henry Mackay to his postwar editors Hans Georg Helms and Ahlrich Meyer, have provided at times idiosyncratic and unreliable assessments of his achievements. Mackay sees him as an ultraliberal champion of universal equality, while Helms and Meyer, despite much praiseworthy work of the editorial variety, were tempted to suggest unwarranted parallels with twentieth-century fascism.

Stirner's reputation rests very largely on a single controversial publication, *Der Einzige und sein Eigentum*, a unique and sustained attempt to present a philosophy of total nihilism. Leftist circles have taken their cue from Karl Marx's suppressed refutation (the inordinately long and impassioned attack on "Saint Max," first published in its entirety in 1932) and tend to dismiss him, in their leader's words, as "a petit-bourgeois who went wild." There have also been conspiracy theories, initially voiced by Eduard von Hartmann in 1888, to the effect that Marx and/ or Nietzsche were encouraged in their own positions by his trenchant dismissal of conventional morality, and this supposedly led them to conceal all traces of the debt they owed him.

Stirner's thought proceeds linearly from that of Enlightenment thinkers and their successors: Johann Gottlieb Fichte, Johann Georg Hamann, C. W. F. Hegel, Johann Gottfried von Herder, and Immanuel Kant. Other major influences include Bruno Bauer, one of Stirner's few close and enduring personal friends, Ludwig Andreas Feuerbach, and David Friedrich Strauss. He shared with Kant the view that humankind must free itself from self-inflicted servitude, and with the Sturm und Drang (storm and stress) movement the belief that self-fulfillment was preferable to enslavement to general moral principles; and he believed that Hegel's zeitgeist (world spirit) was

subverted into a radically unique self. Taking Fichte's concept of the absolute ego one step further, Stirner stripped it of its absolute quality and acknowledged only the primacy of a unique, personal ego. After a Hegelian typology of history in which commitment to possessions (classical antiquity) was succeeded by commitment to thoughts (Christianity), Stirner envisaged an epoch of true freedom in which humankind lives for itself alone ("Nothing is worth more to me then myself"). In human development terms, the child was the realist, the adolescent became an idealist, and the mature adult was the egoist whose ultimate objective was an anarchic shaking off of all "tyrannies," be they God, the state, specific laws, or general morality.

The inevitable consequence of his radical solipsism was that Stirner mounted attacks on anyone who might have been a potential ally. Feuerbach and the materialists were summarily rejected on the grounds that they had elevated the abstract concept of humanity above the immediate reality of the self. He was less concerned with dismissing religious thinkers than with attacking those who substituted new gods for old, foremost of whom were the communists. By dignifying labor they did not free man from his chains, but rather the opposite: they chained the laborer and peasant all the more firmly to the workplace, adding insult to injury by suggesting that our value as human beings lies in the services we render to a society that greedily consumes the output of our labor.

Atheists and free-thinkers were dismissed for similar reasons: they claimed to free man from the tyranny of a prescriptive agency, and then prescribed a moralistic humanism on those they liberated from dependency on religions and revelations. Stirner did not see humankind moving from immaturity toward a goal, but rather as starting out from the goal it has already reached, merely by being itself. "Bring out from yourselves what is in you" is the central dictum of his philosophy, which in some respects anticipates the radical reversal of values that Nietzsche would soon undertake with greater public success.

Where Stirner parted company with Fichte, Marx, and Nietzsche was in his uncompromising nihilism. For him, there was no antiego that had substance or meaning. There was also no repetition. The essence of the ego or self was that it was unrepeatable. Anything that could be expressed or have meaning was repeatable, but the ego in its uniqueness could not be replicated, and therefore could not be expressed and thus had no meaning. Nietzsche may have followed Stirner in exposing the unacknowledged teleology of much supposedly "free" thought, but he ended up substituting a teleology of his own in the form of the superhuman being (*Übermensch*) and in his doctrine of eternal recurrence. He remained a discursive thinker, while Stirner pursued a characteristically Romantic solipsism to its logical conclusion without seeking a way out of the prison house of the self that he had so clearly defined. The most productive, though not unproblematic, approach to Stirner might be to see him as a precursor of existentialism, where the figure of the radical loner surfaces in literary portraits by Albert Camus, André Gide, and Jean-Paul Sartre.

Few still remember Stirner's many other occasional publications, but it is important to point out that he was also an educationalist who played a lively part in the debate about whether humanism or realism should be at the heart of the school syllabus. Stirner remained skeptical of both positions, deriding both the "empty elegance" of the humanist and the "useful citizenship" of the realist approach to education. The former would produce papery aesthetes, the latter gun-bearing taxpayers. Both roads would lead to the same end: a submissive bourgeoisie in which all forms of conventional knowledge imposed burdens on the learner. Stirner, far ahead of his time, equated education with liberation and proposed debate in place of instruction, in the interests of awakening the idea of freedom in those we hitherto sought merely to indoctrinate. Here, too, he envisaged a battle between individualism and collectivity, the fundamental polarity at the heart of his philosophy.

OSMAN DURRANI

Biography

Born Johann Caspar Schmidt on October 25, 1806, in Bayreuth. After the premature death of his father, a manufacturer of musical instruments, he moved briefly to Prussia with his mother before returning to his home town to be raised by his godfather. Entered Berlin University in 1826, where he studied under G. W. F. Hegel and Friedrich Daniel Ernst Schleiermacher for several years. His studies were interrupted by travels through Germany and it was not until 1839 that he found employment as a schoolteacher, initially of Latin, later of history and literature. Between 1839 and 1844, he frequented Hippel's Weinstube in Berlin's Friedrichstrasse, the haunt of a disorderly association of freethinkers (including Karl Marx and Friedrich Engels) known simply as "die Freien." He used the pseudonym Stirner, apparently a childhood nickname derived from his broad forehead, in connection with articles written for newspapers and periodicals. His most important work, *Der Einzige und sein Eigentum*, (*The Ego and His Own*), appeared in 1844 (but was dated 1845). *The publication of this philosophic tour de force led to a succession of scandals, the result of which was that its author was treated as a pariah, ostracized by liberals and socialists alike. There were numerous attempts to ban the work, though in Saxony it was freely sold as being "too absurd to be dangerous." Several prominent au-*

thors produced devastating responses, the most significant of which was by Marx, although Marx withheld publication, perhaps out of a deep-seated sympathy for some of Stirner's arguments.

Stirner's first wife died in childbirth; his second marriage, to the billiard-playing, cigar-smoking heiress Marie Dähnhardt, allowed him to relinquish his teaching post in 1845, after which he attempted to support himself by working as a journalist and critic, and eventually—bizarrely—as a milk merchant. His wife's fortune was squandered and she left him in 1847. He played no further part in public life and died, impoverished and largely forgotten, on June 25, 1856, possibly as the result of an insect bite. It was not until many years after his demise that the general public began to recognize the importance of this solitary and discordant figure in nineteenth-century German thought, and his theories were much debated at the turn of the twentieth century, when his affinities with Nietzsche, not least as a master of the playful use of the German language, became apparent. His work has been reevaluated by Bernd Laska, who portrays him as an Enlightenment figure who saw himself forced to break with Enlightenment values in a radical manner.

Work

Der Einzige und sein Eigentum und andere Schriften, 1845. Edited by Hans Georg Helms. Munich: Hanser, 1969. Translated as *The Ego and His Own* by Steven Tracy Byington, 1907. Reprinted London: Rebel Press, 1982.

"Stirner's Critics," translated by Frederick M. Gordon, *Philosophical Forum* 8, no. 2 (1978): 66–80.

Bibliography

Carlson, Andrew. *Anarchism In Germany: The Early Movement*, Metuchen, N.J.: Scarecrow Press, 1972.

Carroll, John. *Break-out from the Crystal Palace: The Anarcho-Psychological Critique: Stirner, Nietzsche, Dostoevsky*. London: Routledge and Kegan Paul, 1974.

Clark, John P. *Max Stirner's Egoism*. London: Freedom Press, 1976.

Helms, Hans Georg. *Die Ideologie der anonymen Gesellschaft: Max Stirners "Einziger" und der Fortschritt des demokratischen Selbstbewusstseins vom Vormärz bis zur Bundesrepublik*. Cologne: M. DuMont Schauberg, 1966.

Krimermann, Leonard I., and Perry Lewis, eds. Patterns of Anarchy: A Collection of Writings on the Anarchist Tradition. New York: Doubleday, 1966.

Laska, Bernd A. *Ein dauerhafter Dissident. 150 Jahre Stirners "Einziger." Eine kurze Wirkungsgeschichte*. Nüremberg: LSR, 1996.

Mackay, John Henry. *Max Stirner: sein Leben und sein Werk. Mit drei Abbildungen, mehreren Facsimilen und einem Anhang*. 1898. Reprint, Freiburg: Mackay-Gesellschaft, 1977.

Marx, Karl. "Saint Max." In Karl Marx and Friedrich Engels, *Collected Works*, vol. 5. Based on Progress publishers, Moscow, edition. Editorial Commissions: Jack Cohen, Maurice Cornforth, E. J. Hobsbawm, et al. London: Lawrence and Wishart, 1976.

Paterson, R. W. K. *The Nihilistic Egoist Max Stirner*. Oxford: Oxford University Press, 1971.

Website

http://www.df.lth.se/~triad/stirner/

STOWE, HARRIET BEECHER 1811–1896

American writer

According to legend, when Harriet Beecher Stowe met Abraham Lincoln in 1862, the tall, lanky president turned to the petite writer and exclaimed, "So you're the little woman who wrote the book that started this great war!" The president may have been overestimating the influence of Stowe's *Uncle Tom's Cabin* (1852), but not by much. When it appeared in book form, abolitionists celebrated its ability to transform the hearts and minds of the American people. Slaveholders, by contrast, excoriated it, believing that it misrepresented slavery and a slaveholding population that actually embodied a civilized and decent culture. It electrified the nation, fueling the passions that would culminate in the ferocity of the Civil War. In its first year 300,000 copies were sold, and in its day, it ultimately sold more copies than any book in the world except for the Bible.

Stowe was the wife of a theology professor and a mother. She was also born into one of nineteenth century America's most remarkable families, the Beechers. Her mother, Roxana Foote Beecher, died when Harriet was four years old, and she felt the loss deeply. In 1832, when her father became president of Lane Theological Seminary in Cincinnati, Ohio, Harriet and her sister Catharine accompanied him. Harriet took an active part in literary and school life and in 1836 married Calvin Ellis Stowe, a clergyman and seminary professor. Calvin was himself an eminent biblical scholar, he encouraged her literary activity and urged her to retain her maiden name. She wrote continually, even while raising her children, and in 1843 she published *The Mayflower; or, Sketches of Scenes and Characters among the Descendants of the Pilgrims.*

Life brought slavery to the forefront of her consciousness during Stowe's eighteen years in Cincinnati. She and her family were strong abolitionist sympathizers, and their antislavery sentiments intensified when, in 1850, the Fugitive Slave law forced the slavery issue upon the consciences of the entire Northern population. Stowe was roused to indignation. In response to her sister-in-law's urging that she write something "to make this whole nation *feel* what an accursed thing slavery is," she is reported to have risen to her feet and vowed passionately, "I *will* write something . . . I will if I live." She was settled in Brunswick, Maine, at the time, where her husband Calvin had become a professor at Bowdoin College, and she began writing *Uncle Tom's Cabin* in 1851, basing her tale on her reading of abolitionist literature and on her personal observations in Ohio and Kentucky. The specific idea of the book came to her one February day while taking communion in church. A vision arose before her of a saintly black man being whipped to death and praying for his torturers as he died. She rushed home and wrote out the scene that would become the climax of her famous novel, and then read it to her children, who allegedly wept and expressed their hatred of slavery. But although a scene of violence sparked the writing, in fact the central evil of slavery in her imagination was its destruction of family bonds and its consequent threat to the souls of slaves.

Her tale was published serially from 1851 to 1852 in the *National Era*, an antislavery paper published in Washington, D.C., and then published in novel form by John P. Jewett in Boston. It was an immediate best-seller, translated into many languages, and counted among its European fans George Sand, Lev Tolstoy, who called it one of the greatest productions of the human mind; Henry James, who called it a "wonderful 'leaping' fish," and Heinrich Heine, who found deep spiritual inspiration in the figure of Uncle Tom. Stowe traveled to England in 1853, where she was received enthusiastically and formed friendships with many leading literary figures. In the same year that the novel came out in book form, in response to Southern dismissals of its veracity Stowe published *A Key to Uncle Tom's Cabin*, a compilation of documents and testimonies in support of disputed details in the novel. After *A Key*, Stowe wrote a second antislavery novel, *Dred: A Tale of the Great Dismal Swamp* (1856). Stowe thereafter turned her attention to regionalist depictions of New England life, writing eight more novels over the course of her career. Among these are *The Minister's Wooing* (1859), a critique of the Calvinism under which her father raised her; *The Pearl of Orr's Island* (1862); and *Oldtown Folks* (1869).

In many ways, *Uncle Tom's Cabin* is a recognizable product of the Romantic movement in art and literature that had been sweeping through America and Europe for almost a century. It exhibits many of the most characteristic Romantic themes. Above all, it shares with Romanticism a critique of the dehumanizing aspects of capitalism and industrialism, such as materialism and utilitarianism. As with typical Romantic works, it optimistically emphasizes the capacities for spiritual growth embedded in human nature. Likewise, its critique of slavery is part of a broad Romantic critique of all social organizations that decrease the capacity of each individual for self-realization and that degrade the potentially limitless capacities of the human being. More specifically, with Romanticism it shares feelings of horror toward all forms of cruelty inflicted upon powerless people, and it uses Gothic imagery in its effort to communicate that horror. Perhaps one of the most important ways that Stowe marks herself as a Romantic author is in her privilege of intuition and feeling, and her gut sense that logic and reason are insufficient epistemologies for true moral knowledge.

However, Stowe can hardly be seen as a typical Romanticist. She shared none of the Romantics' championing of sexual liberation. In 1869 she published a piece titled *Lady Byron Vindicated* in the *Atlantic Monthly*, a scathing exposé of Lord Byron's incestuous affair with his half-sister, and a defense of his wife (and her own friend) Lady Byron. The article created an uproar in England and cost her much of her popularity there, but she remained a leading author and lecturer in the United States. Stowe also marked her difference from Romantics through a Calvinist outlook that outlasted her midlife conversion to Episcopalianism.

Furthermore, Stowe's aesthetic form of choice—sentimentalism—differed from a Romantic aesthetic as much as it resembled it. Whereas Romanticism is frequently antisocial in that it privileges the encounter of an individual with the vast cosmos, Stowe's literature is above all else social, affirming social harmony, domestic comforts, and the loving bonds of family and friends. Heaven for her can best be understood as a family gathered around a bountiful table with a loving mother presiding. Her outlook solidly affirms the fellowship of the Christian church rather than expressing hostility toward conventional, organized religion, as a more purely Romantic artist might be expected to do. Her understanding of the self also differs from the self typical of Romantic imagining. Selves in Stowe's sentimental imagination are defined through affectional bonds, inclined to cherish ties with others rather than curse them or seek to negate them, as a Ralph Waldo Emerson or Henry David Thoreau might be tempted to do. And rather than strive to foster feelings of grandeur, effusive despair, or pride, as a Romantic artist might be expected to do, Stowe's sentimental art strives for tears and warmth. Stowe, in other words, is one of the most important American authors of the Romantic era, though she is not as typical a representative of that movement as were the transcendentalists, her New England neighbors.

MARIANNE NOBLE

Biography

Born June 14, 1811 in Litchfield, Connecticut. In 1824, attended the Hartford Female Seminary. In 1832, moved to Cincinnati, Ohio. In 1836 married Calvin Stowe. In 1850, moved to Brunswick, Maine, and soon began writing *Uncle Tom's Cabin*. In 1851, *Uncle Tom's Cabin* is serialized in the antislavery paper the *National Era*. In 1852 *Uncle Tom's Cabin* published as a book. In 1853, published *A Key to Uncle Tom's Cabin* and took a triumphant trip to Europe. In 1856, published *Dred, A Tale of the Great Dismal Swamp*. In 1859, published *The Minister's Wooing*. In 1869, published *Oldtown Folks*. Died at home in Hartford, Connecticut, July 1, 1896.

Selected Works

Uncle Tom's Cabin; or Life among the Lowly. 1852.
A Key to Uncle Tom's Cabin. 1853.
Dred, A Tale of the Great Dismal Swamp. 1856.
The Minister's Wooing. 1859.
The Pearl of Orr's Island. 1862.
Oldtown Folks. 1869.
Poganuc People. 1878.

Bibliography

Ammons, Elizabeth, ed. *Critical Essays on Harriet Beecher Stowe*. Boston: G. K. Hall, 1980.
Brodhead, Richard. "Sparing the Rod: Discipline and Fiction in Antebellum America," *Representations* 21 (1988): 67–95.
Brown, Gillian. *Domestic Individualism: Imagining Self in Nineteenth-Century America*. Berkeley and Los Angeles: University of California Press, 1990.
Donovan, Josephine. *Uncle Tom's Cabin: Evil, Affliction, and Redemptive Love*. Boston: Twayne, 1991.
Douglas, Ann. *The Feminization of American Culture*. New York: Alfred A. Knopf, 1977.
Fisher, Philip. *Hard Facts: Form and Setting in American Fiction*. New York: Oxford, 1985.
Gossett, Thomas F. *Uncle Tom's Cabin and American Culture*. Dallas, Tex.: Southern Methodist University Press, 1985.
Hedrick, Joan. *Harriet Beecher Stowe: A Life*. New York: Oxford University Press, 1994.
Noble, Marianne. *The Masochistic Pleasures of Sentimental Literature*. Princeton, N.J.: Princeton University Press, 2000.
Samuels, Shirley, ed. *The Culture of Sentiment: Race, Gender and Sentimentality in Nineteenth-Century America*. New York: Oxford University Press, 1992.
Sundquist, Eric. *New Essays on Uncle Tom's Cabin*. Cambridge: Cambridge University Press, 1986.
Tompkins, Jane. *Sensational Designs: The Cultural Work of American Fiction 1790–1860*. New York: Oxford University Press, 1985.

STRAUSS, DAVID FRIEDRICH 1808–1874

German theologian and biographer

Friedrich Wilhelm Nietzsche remarks, with David Friedrich Strauss in mind, "He who has once contracted Hegelism and Schleiermacherism is never quite cured of them." Before Georg Wilhelm Friedrich Hegel and Friedrich Ernst Daniel Schleiermacher, Strauss was drawn to Jakob Böhme, Friedrich Heinrich Jacobi, Friedrich Wilhelm Joseph von Schelling, and Johann Tauler, and had, as guides, the writer-spiritualist Justinus Kerner as well as the theologians Ferdinard Christian Baur and Heinrich Kern. A bizarre mix of influences therefore formed the background to *Das Leben Jesu kritisch bearbeitet* (*The Life of Jesus Critically Examined*, 1835–36); it was, in fact, this early work from which Strauss never fully recovered.

To say so is not only to have observed how *Das Leben Jesu* repeatedly affected the course of Strauss's life, ending his academic career at Tübingen in 1836 and Zurich in 1839, but later paving his way into politics through a misplaced public belief in his radicalism. Strauss's own thoughts also never strayed too far away: his study of the Christian system of religion, *Die christliche Glaubenslehre* (*The Doctrine of the Christian Faith*, 1840–41), reapplied its method, while *Das Leben Jesu für das deutsche Volk bearbeitet* (*The Life of Jesus Adapted for the German People*, 1864) addressed Ernest Renan's *La Vie de Jésus* (*The Life of Jesus*, 1863), a popular but more conservative reworking of its ideas. When Strauss clashed with Daniel Schenkel, author of *Das Charakterbild Jesu* (*The Character Study of Jesus*, 1864), he wrote *Die Halben und die Ganzen* (*The Halves and the Wholes*, 1865), which curiously attacked liberalism by first distinguishing his account of Jesus from that of Schenkel.

A Straussian legacy may thus be spoken of in terms of the twofold proposal already laid out in *Das Leben Jesu*. On one level, the Gospels are doggedly shown to embody the popular hopes of early Christians, an understanding Strauss founds on the inadequacies of two common approaches: the supernatural interpretation, which believes in the New Testament miracles, and a purely rational explanation for these events. His own mythological alternative begins and ends with the Gospels as historical narratives bent around the goal of proving Jesus' Messiahship; in this light, miracles and fulfilled prophecies were but belated inclusions to match, if not surpass, the myths of the Old Testament.

If such an argument directly undermines the basis of orthodox Christianity, on another level, Strauss also recognizes the demythologizing of Christianity as what fulfills the promise of Christianity itself. A knowledge of Jesus as all too human should not just dismantle the personality cult of Christianity but must go on to establish the idea that had initially made Jesus special as its true religious meaning. The ecclesiastical Jesus is the mystification of this fact that it has always been humanity, born of both nature and spirit, "who dies, rises and ascends to heaven since, from the negation of its finite natural life, there always proceeds a higher spiritual life."

Strauss's grafting of Hegelianism onto Christianity subsequently demands a different moral framework, one which, by the time of *Der alte und der neue Glaube* (*The Old Faith and the New*, 1872), he was already calling the "new Christianity." This involves a direct personal seeking after the spirit defined as the "dry" spirit of scientific progress revitalized by a crucial Romantic supplement. Strauss's interest in the Romantic genius here is not surprising if we consider the kind of poetry he habitually imitated and his excessive reading of Eduard Friedrich Mörike, Novalis, and Ludwig Tieck. The power of subjectivity to invent the real is itself a theme of *Das Leben Jesu* so contagious that nearly every notable Christological study written in its wake responded to it. Bruno Bauer, for example, concluded that Christianity was wholly the work of one poet, the writer of Mark, while Theodor Keim was led to observe how Jesus' Messianic consciousness developed.

From hindsight, Strauss's revisionist focus on experience in religion therefore only continued the Romantic incursion into theology begun by Schleiermacher, though, historically, this was far from how the general public received it. Christoph von Eschenmayer's satiric use of Strauss to prove demonic existence, having even Satan fictiously award him hell's most prestigious prize, was representative of a wide social reaction that saw Strauss as the biblical Antichrist. Arguments ranged from the numerical equivalence of his name to 666 to the calculations of the highly esteemed Johann Albrecht Bengel, who had predicted that the world would end in 1836. All these were, of course, ironic in view of the support they actually lent to Strauss's theory of a social projection resolving the arena of inner conflicts; the argument itself was to prefigure Sigmund Freud by more than half a century.

Perhaps Strauss's best intentions may be observed in the biographies he wrote when he increasingly saw this form of writing as a counterpart to his theological project. Strauss chose individuals he believed were intellectuals facing "light and freedom" and opposed to tyranny and priesthood; he also regarded these as dream images of what gave rise to his antidogmaticism and, as such, took extreme liberties in interpreting their lives. Subjects included the Renaissance poet and philologist Nikodemus Frischlin; the Reformation radical Ulrich von Hutten; the proto-Romantic Friedrich Gottlieb Klopstock; the Enlightenment philosopher Hermann Samuel Reimarus, who dismissed the Gospels as lies and frauds; and Christian Friedrich Daniel Schubart, a Sturm und Drang (storm and stress) poet spurned by both church and royalty. Strauss wrote on Ludwig van Bee-

thoven and Gotthold Ephraim Lessing as well and prepared a series of lectures on Voltaire for the Princess of Hesse-Darmstadt, daughter of Queen Victoria.

Nietzsche was so critical of Strauss's speculative biographies that he dismissed his praise of Lessing via Beethoven and Franz Joseph Haydn, writing, "*His* Beethoven-confectionary is not *our* Beethoven and *his* Haydn-soup is not *our* Haydn." To Strauss's endless bewilderment, Nietzsche openly called Strauss "a true philistine with a narrow, dried-up soul" and mocked his method by beating him at his game; he analyzed Strauss as an embodiment of the cultural philistinism of the German bourgeoisie after the Franco–Prussian War. Nietzsche's own distance from Strauss is, in fact, a step away, the missing link here being Ludwig Andreas Feuerbach's *Wesen des Christentums* (*Essence of Christianity*, 1841); Feuerbach applied Strauss's mythological approach to the concept of God itself and, in doing so, laid the foundation for all of Nietzsche's anti-Christian pronouncements.

LI SUI GWEE

Biography

Born in Ludwigsburg, Württemberg, on January 27, 1808; attended a junior seminary at Blaubeuren, 1821–25. Studied at the Evangelical Theological College, Tübingen, 1825–30. Curate at Klein-Ingersheim, 1830–31; tutor at the Maulbronn seminary, 1831; befriended Hegel and Schleiermacher during a crucial visit to Berlin in October of that year. Tutor at the Tübingen seminary, 1832. Published Volume 1 of *Das Leben Jesu*, 1835. Transferred from Tübingen to a Ludwigsburg lyceum before release of Volume 2 and his resignation, 1836. Professorship appointment at Zurich university canceled due to popular outcry, 1839. Published *Die christliche Glaubenslehre*, 1840–41. Marriage to Agnese Schebest, a famous actress, 1842–47. Elected representative to the Württemberg Diet, 1848–49. Wandered around Cologne, Munich, and Weimar 1849–55. Stayed in Heidelberg, 1855–61. Published *Das Leben Jesu für das deutsche Volk bearbeitet*, 1864. Settled in Darmstadt, 1865–71. Published *Der alte und der neue Glaube*, 1872. Returned to Ludwigsburg in 1872, where he died on February 8, 1874.

Selected Works

Das Leben Jesu kritisch bearbeitet. 2 vols. 1835–36. Translated as *The Life of Jesus Critically Examined* by George Eliot, 3 vols. 1846.

Über Vergängliches und Bleibendes im Christentum, 1838. Translated as *Soliloquies on the Christian Religion*, 1845.

Die christliche Glaubenslehre in ihrer geschichtlichen Entwicklung und im Kampfe mit der modernen Wissenschaft dargestellt. 2 vols. 1840–41.

Christian Daniel Friedrich Schubarts Leben in seinen Briefen. 2 vols. 1849.

Leben und Schriften des Dichters und Philologen Nikodemus Frischlin. Ein Beitrag zur deutschen Kulturgeschichte in der 2. Hälfte des 16. Jahrhunderts. 1855.

Ulrich von Hutten. 2 vols. 1857. Translated as *Ulrich von Hutten: His Life and Times* by Jane Sturge. 1874.

Hermann Samuel Reimarus und seine Schutzschrift für die vernünftigen Verehrer Gottes. 1861.

Das Leben Jesu für das deutsche Volk bearbeitet. 1864. Translated as *A New Life of Jesus.* 2 vols. 1865.

Der Christus des Glaubens und der Jesu der Geschichte: Eine Kritik des Schleiermacher'schen Lebens Jesu. 1865.

Die Halben und die Ganzen: Eine Streitschrift gegen Schenkel und Hengstenberg. 1865.

Voltaire: Sechs Vorträge. 1870.

Der alte und der neue Glaube: Ein Bekenntnis. 1872. Translated as *The Old Faith and the New* by Mathilde Blind. 1873.

Poetisches Gedenkbuch. Gedichte aus dem Nachlasse von D. F. S. Edited by Eduard Zeller. 1878.

Bibliography

Barth, Karl. *From Rousseau to Ritschl: Being the Translation of Eleven Chapters of Die protestantische Theologie im 19. Jahrhundert.* Translated by Brian Cozens. London: SCM Press, 1959.

Eck, Samuel. *David Friedrich Strauss.* Stuttgart: J. G. Cotta'sche Buchhandlung Nachfolger, 1899.

Harris, Horton. *David Friedrich Strauss and His Theology.* Cambridge: Cambridge University Press, 1973.

Lawler, Edwina G. *David Friedrich Strauss and His Critics: The Life of Jesus Debate in Early Nineteenth-Century German Journals.* Frankfurt: Peter Lang, 1986.

Müller, Gotthold. *Identität und Immanenz: Zur Genese der Theologie von David Friedrich Strauss.* Zurich: EVZ-Verlag, 1968.

Nietzsche, Friedrich. *Untimely Meditations.* Edited by Daniel Breazeale. Translated by Reginald John Hollingdale. Cambridge: Cambridge University Press, 1997.

Schweitzer, Albert. *The Quest of the Historical Jesus: A Critical Study of its Progress from Reimarus to Wrede.* Translated by William Montgomery. Preface by Francis Crawford Burkitt, London: Adams and Charles Black, 1910.

Sandberger, Jörg F. *David Friedrich Strauss als theologischer Hegelianer: Mit unveröffentlichten Briefen.* Göttingen: Vanderhoeck und Ruprecht, 1972.

Welch, Claude. *Protestant Thought in the Nineteenth Century.* 2 vols. New Haven, Conn.: Yale University Press, 1974.

Zeller, Eduard. *David Friedrich Strauss in His Life and Writings, Authorized Translation.* 1874.

Ziegler, Theobald. *David Friedrich Strauss.* 2 vols. Strassburg: Karl J. Trübner, 1908.

STUBBS, GEORGE 1724–1806

English painter and anatomist

George Stubbs was born in 1724 in Liverpool, then a newly prosperous port and manufacturing town. His father curried (dressed and colored) and dealt leather. Stubbs was supposed to have begun his anatomical studies at the age of eight. If there seems to have been a contradiction between his upbringing and the rural and/or upper-class settings of his later work (including the studies of exotic animals, which tended to be the inmates of aristocratic menageries), then it serves as a reminder that his interest in animals, especially horses, of which he became the preeminent European painter, was primarily practical; that is, as an anatomist, Stubbs was primarily interested in how they worked as objects in motion. Indeed, this point could be extended to inanimate objects in his work; carriages, and even clothes, are depicted with a careful sense of their use. There is none of the Romantic or impressionistic drapery that animates the work of Thomas Gainsborough or Joshua Reynolds, for example, in Stubbs's portraits of ladies and gentlemen. Stubbs's subjects are taking exercise or leisure as part of their daily routine and are sensibly dressed for the outdoors. This objectivity is never impersonal, however, and the depiction of servants, especially grooms, jockeys, and stable boys, are all portraits as carefully observed and executed as those of their masters. Stubbs is also observant of how social groupings worked, and how rank is maintained (for example, as in a display in which the horse is a central status symbol). The coincidence of his arrival in London with the peak of an aristocratic investment, both financial and emotional, in hunting and horseracing, was the foundation of the prosperity of his middle years.

After his father's death, Stubbs was employed to copy the pictures of the most powerful local lord, the earl of Derby, and though it is not clear where he went from there, he was in York in 1745 studying anatomy with Charles Atkinson. He supported himself by painting portraits of minor gentry and prosperous local bourgeois (few of which have survived); he seems to have been self-taught. His first publication was a set of eighteen engraved plates for John Burton's "Essay towards a Complete New System of Midwifry," in 1751. When in 1754 he traveled to Italy he was, he later claimed, testing the powers of art against those of nature. It would seem that nature (in the sense of empirical investigation of the real), won out. Stubbs spent the next four years dissecting and drawing for what he planned as his major work, *The Anatomy of the Horse.*

Although he was unsuccessful on a visit to London in 1758 to find an engraver for the *Anatomy*, he seems to have made contacts that allowed him to return, probably in 1760, and to begin a series of commissioned pieces that included, in 1762 alone, portraits of the horses *Whistlejacket* and *Molly Longlegs.* The first was depicted riderless and rearing, and painted life-sized, with illusionistic solidity from a blank background. The second was portrayed as febrile but demurely held in check by an attentive and sensitively individualized groom. Stubbs was invited by the wealthy landowner Sir Richard Grosvenor to paint *The Grosvenor Hunt* (1762); the composition is marked by a meticulous and uncannily accurate observation of movement (of water, as well as of animals and men) that helps to recreate the event as drama, without resort to any conventionally theatrical devices of the Old Masters (of whom Stubbs's trip to Italy seems to have been a kind of exorcism). In 1765 his *Cheetah with Indian Servants* was again composed to suggest movement and drama in a situation in which the carefully observed and dignified presences of animal and human figures are necessarily still. The Romantic themes of exile, and the tension between wildness and containment implied in the ambiguous locale, and in the resignation and beauty of the blinkered animal, arise accidentally, but Stubbs's subdued objectivity makes them more, rather than less, present to the viewer, an effect paralleled in other works of the series of exotic animal portraits, which stand alongside the equine studies at the core of his career.

The Anatomy of the Horse was finally published in 1766 and gained Stubbs a European reputation. He described himself on the title page as a "painter," and in correspondence with admirers of the work put his aesthetic "curiosity" above scientific ambition. Knowledge and the pursuit of beauty went together for Stubbs, as the plates and drawings for *Anatomy* vividly, and sometimes eerily, testify. In 1777 he began a less successful set of experiments, working with the ceramicist Josiah Wedgwood on a new technique of painting in enamels on biscuit earthenware. He seems to have been disappointed in his lack of control over oils, particularly in matters of permanence and exactness of color. The pictures were not popular, and as the technique did not catch on with other artists, Wedgwood found it to be financially unviable, and withdrew. The most successful of these are probably the portrait of a woman friend, *Isabella Saltonshall as Una from Spenser's Faerie Queene*, where the heroine's animal companions include a more amiable reprise of the lion from the horse series, looking distinctly more comfortable now he is no longer required to seem fierce (one of four such enamels exhibited at the Royal Academy in 1782) and the *Haymakers* and *Reapers* of 1783. But while the translucent colors and fanciful miniaturization seem to suit these subjects, the larger scale versions, in oils, of the last two subjects, serve to emphasize that Stubbs's gift for composition needed a larger canvas as an outlet, and that his choice of subject matter paradoxically benefited from the connotations of grandeur that come from the more traditional medium.

The major project of Stubbs's last years was the *Comparative Anatomical Exposition of the Structure of the Human Body with That of a Tiger and a Common Fowl*, published in parts between 1804 and 1806, the year of his death. After he died, the contents of his studio were sold, and the proceeds split between Mary Spenser, his companion and assistant, whom he never married, and Isabella Saltonshall, who had supported the couple with loans, and who had bought many works herself. Stubbs's reputation, outside the specialized genre of field or hunting pictures, is a late-twentieth-century phenomenon.

That he is difficult to place in art historical terms is a coincidence of his autodidacticism; he can be linked to no predecessor, and seems to have consciously sought to work from nature rather than tradition. Despite the admiration of Eugène Delacroix and Theodore Géricault, Stubbs may seem more of an Enlightenment than a Romantic figure. But he only seems to resist inclusion if Romanticism is linked exclusively to subjectivity and fancy. There is a Romantic objectivity too; the writer William Hazlitt praises the Elgin Marbles for the exactness of their observation of muscle and movement, and the distinctness of their figures against empty backgrounds. The rearing *Whistlejacket* (1762), when seen at the end of a neoclassical vista in England's National Gallery, escapes from and challenges its surrounding; the popularity of this image connects Stubbs to trends in contemporary art, in which the objective gaze creates mystery and resonance in its very refusal of fiction or commentary.

EDWARD BURNS

Biography

Born in Liverpool, England, 1724. Studying painting and anatomy in York, 1745. Traveled to Italy, 1754. Worked in Horkstow, Lincolnshire, on dissections and drawings for "The Anatomy of the Horse," 1756–58. Established himself in London as a painter of horses, with commissions from the duke of Richmond, 1760. *Whistlejacket and The Grosvenor Hunt*, 1762. *Cheetah with Indian Servants*, 1763. *The Anatomy of the Horse* published in 1766 to great acclaim in Britain and Europe. *Horse Frightened by a Lion*, 1770. Elected president of the Society of Artists, 1772. *Lion and Dead Tiger*, 1779. Elected to the Royal Academy, 1781. Published *Comparative Anatomical Exposition of the Structure of the Human Body with That of a Tiger and a Common Fowl* (unfinished), 1804–6. Died, financially unsuccessful, in London, 1806.

Selected Works

The Grosvenor Hunt. 1762.
Molly Longlegs. 1762.
Whistlejacket. 1762.
Cheetah with Indian Servants. 1765.
The Anatomy of the Horse. 1766.
Haymakers. 1783.
Reapers. 1783.
Comparative Anatomical Exposition of the Structure of the Human Body with That of a Tiger and a Common Fowl. 1804–06.

Bibliography

Egerton, Judy. *George Stubbs, Anatomist and Animal Painter*. London: Tate Gallery, 1976.
———. *George Stubbs 1724–1806*. London: Tate Gallery, 1984.
Mayer, Joseph. *Early Exhibitions of Art in Liverpool with Some Notes for a Memoir of George Stubbs, R.A.* Liverpool: privately printed.
Milner, Frank. *George Stubbs: Paintings, Ceramics, Prints and Documents in Merseyside Collections*. Liverpool: National Museums and Galleries on Merseyside, 1987.

STURM UND DRANG

The Sturm und Drang (storm and stress) was a literary movement that flourished in Germany in the 1770s and 1780s and represented the protest of a group of young university-educated men against the norms of polite society. Instead of the ideals of reason and balance, which seemed to them unnatural and oppressive, they insisted on the primacy of authenticity and the intensity of experience. For this reason, the Sturm und Drang movement has often been interpreted as an anti-Enlightenment movement, a particularly intense strand within German pre-Romanticism that was historically important both for its irrationalism and for the emancipation of a German national culture from French models. More recent studies have emphasized the way in which the Sturm und Drang movement radicalized themes already present in the Enlightenment.

The term *Sturm und Drang* is sometimes used today to refer in general to the exuberant wildness of youth, and sometimes to parallel developments in the other arts, notably music, but its precise meaning is a literary-historical one that goes back to a play by Friedrich Maximilian Klinger. The title of his play, *Sturm und Drang* (1777), which was suggested by Christoph

Kaufmann, was soon adopted to refer to the unconventional and deliberately disordered style of writing and manner of living championed by the two of them, and by Johann Wolfgang Goethe, Jacob Michael Reinhold Lenz, and others with whom they were loosely affiliated.

The central figure of the Sturm und Drang movement was Goethe, not only through his own writing but also through his personal friendships with other young men who, like himself, reveled in new forms of expression, and also rediscovered older ones. The intellectual father of the Sturm und Drang movement was Johann Gottfried Herder, himself strongly affected by the visionary writings of Johann Georg Hamann; Goethe's meeting with Herder in Strasbourg in 1770 was the catalyst that allowed Goethe to discover his own potential as an original writer. Herder argued, like Jean-Jacques Rousseau, that the advance of civilization had alienated humankind from nature—that is, from humankind's own inherent nature and from the natural environment. Book learning was for Herder an obstruction to true understanding and was symptomatic of a society in which artistic creativity was no longer organically one with the core activities of the members of society, the *Volk*. From this followed Herder's enthusiastic advocacy of forms of art that drew their energy from the directness of lived experience rather than superimposed norms of correctness. He was conscious of the cultural relativity of art forms and rejected the supposedly universal models of the French neoclassical tradition, seeking inspiration instead in the folk songs he and his friends collected, in the work of Homer, in the Old Testament and Ossian, but most significantly in William Shakespeare. In the modern world, he argued, art could only be created by the force of individual genius, not by adherence to rules, and indeed early histories of literature used the term *Geniezeit* (age of genius) to refer to the movement now known as the Sturm und Drang. Although by conventional standards Herder's argument lacked logical rigor, it was historically decisive because it provided a more thorough and more radical formulation of ideas that had begun to emerge, for example, in the writing of Gotthold Ephraim Lessing and Heinrich Wilhelm Gerstenberg, especially in their defense of Shakespeare. More fundamentally, the Sturm und Drang reflected the growth of modern individualism and the challenge that middle-class ideas of selfhood presented to so-called enlightened absolutism, that is to say, to political and cultural structures that sought legitimacy by assimilating elements of bureaucratic rationalism.

Lenz and Goethe made decisive contributions to the regeneration of lyric poetry and prose narrative in the late eighteenth century. In particular, Goethe's *Die Leiden des jungen Werthers* (*The Sorrows of Young Werther*, 1774), with its sensitive portrait of unrequited love, led a whole generation in the exploration of an inner emotional self exposed by its exclusion from a social world that offered no means of self-realization. But it was in drama that the Sturm und Drang made its most distinctive mark on German literature. Their wilful and extravagant disregard for the unities of time, place, and action allowed the writers of the Sturm und Drang to use drama for portraying historical processes (for example, in Goethe's *Götz von Berlichingen Ironhand*, 1771, 1773) or for analyzing complex social relations (as seen in Lenz's *Die Soldaten* [*The Soldiers*, 1776]), and, in both cases, by giving drama the capacity for presenting and criticizing the real historical world they made a significant shift toward the realism of the nineteenth and even the twentieth century. Other plays, such as Goethe's *Clavigo* (1774 and Klinger's *Die Zwillinge* (*The Twins*, 1776) were by contrast more conventional in their form, but what links all these texts is the idea of the individual striving for self-realization. Many of Goethe's poems express this as a longing for oneness with nature, especially through love, but the dramas of the Sturm und Drang movement more commonly show how the will to self-realization is thwarted, sometimes by the social environment but most fundamentally by internal contradictions which reveal that for psychological, social, or existential reasons the will to self-realization is incompatible with the actuality of self-realization. Similarly, the private realm, and specifically the family, came to be presented as a place of conflict, and there was a new focus on irrational behavior and on the unconscious processes of the individual psyche.

As a literary movement, the Sturm und Drang was short-lived. Many writers, including writers one might describe as pre-Romantic, remained outside the group, which in any case began to fall apart in the late 1770s as Goethe became established at Weimar. It is debatable whether or not the young Johann Christoph Friedrich Schiller should be included: his writing from the 1780s has many stylistic and thematic similarities to the writing of the Sturm und Drang group, but he had no personal links with them and even his early plays show a stronger sense of formal balance and of moral judgment. By the time of the Romantic generation, both Goethe and Schiller had left the Sturm und Drang movement far behind them, and its direct influence on German Romanticism was limited, not least because of the complicated relationship of the Romantic writers to Goethe and Goethe's complicated relationship to his own earlier writing. The Sturm und Drang was nevertheless an important forerunner of Romanticism in its formal experimentalism, its enthusiasm for popular culture and the primitive, its acceptance of the power of unconscious, irrational forces, and above all its concern with individual experience. On the other hand, the realism of the Sturm und Drang movement distinguishes it from the transcendental idealism of early German Romanticism and looks forward to the 1830s when Georg Büchner rediscovered Lenz, and beyond, to the experimental realism of the later nineteenth century.

DAVID HILL

Bibliography

Boyle, Nicholas. *Goethe: The Poet and the Age*. Vol. 1, *The Poetry of Desire*. Oxford: Oxford University Press, 1992.

Duncan, Bruce. *Lovers, Parricides, and Highwaymen. Aspects of Sturm und Drang Drama*. Rochester, N.Y.: Camden House, 1999.

Huyssen, Andreas. *Drama des Sturm und Drang: Kommentar zu einer Epoche*. Munich: Winkler, 1980.

Karthaus, Ulrich. *Sturm und Drang: Epoche—Werke—Wirkung*. Munich: Beck, 2000.

Luserke, Matthias. *Sturm und Drang: Autoren-Texte-Themen*. Stuttgart: Reclam, 1997.

McInnes, Edward. *"Ein ungeheures Theater": The Drama of the Sturm und Drang*. Studien zur deutschen Literatur des 19. und 20. Jahrhunderts. 3 Frankfurt: Lang, 1987.

Pascal, Roy. *The German Sturm und Drang*. Manchester: Manchester University Press, 1953.

Plachta, Bodo, and Winfried, Woesler eds. *Sturm und Drang: Geistiger Aufbruch 1770–1790 im Spiegel der Literatur*. Tübingen: Niemeyer, 1997.

THE SUBLIME

Abducted by ruffians and imprisoned within a convent, Ellena Rosalba, the Gothic heroine of Ann Radcliffe's *The Italian, or the Confessional of the Black Penitents* (1797), discovers a window at the end of a corridor adjacent to her room that opens onto the outside world. The "vast precipices of granite," "lines of gigantic pine bending along the rocky ledges," and "accumulation of overtopping points" of the mountains seen through this window mimic the powerful human forces ranged against her. Measured against this scenery and the natural powers that have shaped it, she is as nothing; yet she does not despair. Instead, this wild landscape arouses a sense of "dreadful pleasure." As her eyes range "over the wide and freely-sublime scene without," "consciousness of her prison" is lost and she briefly sees "beyond the awful veil which obscures the features of the Deity, and conceals Him from the eyes of his creatures." This in turn transports her above the natural world, making the forces that once dwarfed her seem small. Even "man, the giant who now held her in captivity," is diminished. In a converse movement, Ellena feels that she has gained in stature: with "a mind thus elevated," she enthuses, the "utmost force" exerted by her captor will be unable "to enchain her soul, or compel her to fear him."

The tripartite narrative illustrated by this episode appears repeatedly in eighteenth-century accounts of the sublime. First, an overwhelming power (or sublime object) stops the spectator in his tracks, destroying his equanimity. Next, as this power takes hold of the spectator's mind, standstill is replaced by transport and, frequently, rapture. Finally, as the experience subsides, the spectator emerges with a heightened sense of her own significance and a newfound reverence for the sublime power. As James Usher writes in *Clio; or a Discourse on Taste* (1769), for example, "The sublime, by an authority which the soul is utterly unable to resist, takes possession of our attention, and of all our faculties, and absorbs them in astonishment. . . . In all other terrors the soul loses its dignity, and as it were shrinks below its usual size: but at the presence of the sublime, although it be always awful, the soul of man seems to be raised out of a trance; it assumes an unknown grandeur . . . it is rapt out of the sight and consideration of this diminutive world, into a kind of gigantic creation, where it finds room to dilate itself to a size agreeable to its present nature and grandeur."

Although this primary narrative remains reasonably constant throughout the eighteenth century, it appears in a surprising number of guises, and critics offer significantly divergent accounts of its operation. Joseph Priestley's observation in *A Course of Lectures on Oratory and Criticism* (1777) that "Sublimity hath been used in a more vague sense than almost any other term in criticism" is owing at least in part to this diversity. Although the sublime is arguably the most important term in the aesthetic discourse of the second half of the eighteenth century and of Romanticism, disagreements over how to explain the passage from standstill to transport and then elevation, and debates about the sublime's collocation of violence and pleasure (described by John Dennis as "pleasing rape upon the very soul of the reader"), continue to the present day.

The eighteenth-century vogue of the sublime takes as its point of departure the first-century Greek treatise titled *Peri Hupsous* (On the Sublime), usually attributed to Longinus. According to

Longinus, as translated by William Smith (1743), "the sublime is a certain eminence or perfection of language" that, "when seasonably addressed, with the rapid force of lightning has borne down all before it," showing "at one stroke the compacted might of genius." In contrast to the art of persuasion, which aims at voluntary acquiescence, the "surprising force" of the sublime "triumphs over every hearer" and "throws an audience into transport." The plot of the sublime reaches its conclusion when "the mind . . . sensibly affected with its lively strokes . . . swells in transport and an inward pride, as if what was only heard had been the product of its own invention."

In the work of Joseph Addison, John Baillie, Edmund Burke, Alexander Gerard, and David Hume, among others, Longinus's rhetorical sublime is reframed as a natural sublime, and interest shifts from the elevated language requisite for sublimity, to the effects on the spectator of the sublime objects found in nature. In his influential *A Philosophical Enquiry into the Origin of our Ideas of the Sublime and Beautiful* (1757), for example, Burke describes the objects that prompt, and the emotions that are the psychological foundation of, the sublime. Terror, he claims, is the sublime's "ruling principle," and "the common stock of every thing that is sublime." Indeed, he continues, "Whatever is fitted in any sort to excite the ideas of pain, and danger . . . is a source of the sublime." Obscurity, power, privation, vastness and infinity can therefore all be productive of sublimity. They rouse "the passions which belong to self-preservation" and, so long as they do not "press too nearly . . . are delightful." The elation (in Burke's words, the "swelling and triumph") with which an experience of sublimity concludes is a result of the proclivity of the human mind to claim "to itself some part of the dignity and importance of the things which it contemplates."

In the religious sublime, interest is shifted to the supramundane reality or faculty glimpsed in the moment of transport. John Dennis contends, for example, that "where Terror is mov'd to a Height . . . that Place requires the belief of a God, and particular Providence." Two of the most popular poems of the eighteenth century, James Thomson's *The Seasons* (1726–30) and Edward Young's *The Complaint, or Night Thoughts on Life, Death and Immortality* (1742–45) exemplify these ideas. In the former, terror at the destructive power of nature modulates into devotion and a sense of awe at God's much greater power. In the latter, the "thought of death" brings our life to a standstill, revealing that what previously had seemed the limitless expanse of the temporal world is a narrow dungeon. This loss throws into relief a faculty (reason/the soul) purportedly not subject to time, which in turn provides strong proof of our kinship with the divine. Rather than being subject to nature, we are elevated above it, assured of our "supersensible destiny."

Until the last decade of the eighteenth century, theorists of the sublime assumed that its ultimate source lay outside the reader or spectator. In contrast, Immanuel Kant argued in *Critique of Judgment* (1790) that "the sublime, in the strict sense of the word, cannot be contained in any sensuous form" because the ground of sublimity is "in ourselves and the attitude of mind that introduces sublimity into the representation of nature." Kant achieved this Copernican turn by framing sublimity as a conflict between faculties: imagination and reason in the mathematical sublime; imagination and desire (the will) in the dynamical sublime.

In the mathematical sublime one encounters an object (or a number) of a magnitude that can be thought by reason but cannot adequately be represented by the imagination. Nature, for example, is considered sublime when "its phenomena . . . convey the idea of their infinity." In attempting to represent such phenomena, the imagination is pushed to the limits of its powers and then breaks down, unable to comprehend the whole in a single, sensuous intuition. This failure provides the backdrop against which the much greater power of reason can be seen, a faculty able effortlessly to think infinity and totality without contradiction. Where the imagination cannot pass beyond the sensuous world, in the sublime we glimpse the dimensions of a power at home with ideas far in excess of that world (freedom, immortality, God).

In Kant's metaphysics, the imagination is described as the "greatest faculty of sense" because, working in harmony with the understanding, it gives shape to the phenomenal world. The emergence of a power greater than imagination is therefore not an insignificant development. It brings into focus a "supersensible side of our being," which empowers us "to pass beyond the confines of sensibility." It offers evidence that we should "esteem as small in comparison with ideas of reason everything which for us is great in nature as an object of sense." In other words, what is *absolutely great* (the sublime) is to be found within us rather than in nature.

In an experience of the dynamic sublime, nature is represented as a limitless power against which we can mount no effective resistance. In comparison with "[v]olcanoes in all their violence of destruction, hurricanes leaving desolation in their track, the boundless ocean rising with rebellious force," our own powers of resistance are insignificant. With regard to our physical existence, nature will continue to threaten our "worldly goods, health, and life." In Kant's view, however, the dynamic sublime challenges us to find in our moral being a power able to regard the loss of such things as insignificant. Our freedom to refuse nature's "rude dominion" over us brings into the foreground a human power (desire or the will) much greater than merely physical might. The true source of sublime is once again within us rather than in natural objects. As Kant writes, "nature is here called sublime merely because it raises the imagination to a presentation of those cases in which the mind can make itself sensible of the sublimity of the sphere of its own being, even above nature."

The Romantic sublime repeats Kant's subjective turn, while reversing the relation between its key actors. Reason (the understanding) is now the lesser power, unable to proceed beyond the confines of the natural world. The imagination, as the creator of the (phenomenal) world within which reason is enclosed, is the greater power, able to move beyond the limits imposed by nature. In an experience of the Romantic sublime it is, therefore, the failure of the understanding that throws into relief the much greater power of the imagination.

William Wordsworth's account, in book 6 of the *Prelude* (1805) of his journey in 1790 across the Alps, through the Simplon Pass, offers a paradigmatic instance of the Romantic sublime. If this episode had been structured in accord with earlier versions of the sublime, one would expect an encounter with natural phenomena that conveyed "the idea of their infinity."

In fact, Wordsworth's crossing of the Alps proves an anticlimax. Rather than being stopped in his tracks, he passes the highest point in his journey without realizing it, leaving him with a baffled sense of frustration and of the mismatch between expectation and reality. In Wordsworth's Romantic sublime, however, this rather ordinary event provides the moment of blockage that is resolved by the revelation that this disjunction between what the mind can imagine and nature can present offers an indirect presentation of the power of the imagination. This revelation turns disappointment into transport:

> Imagination!—lifting up itself
> Before the eye and progress of my song
> Like an unfathered vapour, here that power,
> In all the might of its endowments, came
> Athwart me. I was lost as in a cloud,
>   Halted without a struggle to break through,
>   And now, recovering, to my soul I say
>   "I recognise thy glory".

As this example suggests, the Romantic sublime radically revises the way in which the sublime is understood. If the ultimate source of the sublime is the imagination's ability to produce "impressive effects out of simple elements" or, more dramatically, to reshape the phenomenal world, then even quite ordinary things can be sublime. William Blake writes in "Auguries of Innocence" (c. 1801–5), for example, that it is possible to "To see a World in a Grain of Sand / And a Heaven in a Wild Flower." William Wordsworth observes in "Ode: Intimations of Immortality from Recollections of Early Childhood" (1807), that even "the meanest flower that blows can give / Thoughts that do often lie too deep for tears." Such experiences offer a moment of insight into the ground of both nature and the self. In the aftermath of perhaps the most famous of sublime encounters, the ascent of Mt. Snowdon described in the last book of the *Prelude*, Wordsworth recognizes a shaping force in nature that is "a genuine counterpart / And brother of the glorious faculty [the imagination] / Which higher minds bear within them as their own."

The Wordsworthian sublime is, of course, not the only type of Romantic sublimity. In a letter to Richard Woodhouse dated October 27, 1818, John Keats famously distinguished his own poetry from what he called Wordsworth's "egotistical sublime." Where the latter confirms the poet's identity and power, Keats declares that "the poetical Character . . . has no self—it is every thing and nothing—It has no character . . . it lives in gusto, be it foul or fair, high or low, rich or poor, mean or elevated." One might say that where Wordsworth's sublime takes as its locus the third stage of the sublime (elevation), Keats emphasizes the second, when the poet is rapt from his own identity. Or to take another example, in his "On Murder Considered as One of the Fine Arts" (1827–54), Thomas DeQuincey questions the assumption that sublimity can be interpreted as an indirect presentation of a power (whether God, reason or the imagination) that is fundamentally benign. All the effects of sublimity, he provocatively argues, can be produced by an act of overwhelming violence such as murder, a theme explored in the twentieth century by writers such as Jean Genet.

The passage from the rhetorical to the Romantic sublime is not quite as ordered as this analysis suggests. Rather than being superseded, the natural, rhetorical, and religious sublimes in particular helped prepare an audience for, as well as exerting a strong influence on, the literature of Romanticism. Gothic fiction, the most popular genre of Romantic prose, draws heavily on the tropes of the natural sublime, developing them into a language for talking about the psyche. The natural and rhetorical sublime, in particular, played a key role in preparing public taste for works such as *Fingal* (1762) and *Temora* (1763), supposedly by the ancient bard Ossian, which in turn exerted a strong influence on both German and English Romanticism. The view that the Bible is the most sublime of works, fostered by the religious sublime and exemplified by Robert Lowth's *Lectures on the Sacred Poetry of the Hebrews* (published in Latin in 1753; an English translation appeared in 1787), helped shape the poetics of key Romantic writers such as William Blake. More broadly, early versions of the sublime, by offering an alternative to a neoclassical aesthetics of taste and decorum, prepared the ground for a Romantic aesthetic that valorises emotion, spontaneity, genius, imagination and the individual.

Recent critics of the sublime have argued that it offers an exemplary instance of the modern struggle to reconcile private and public values, and of the transition from theological to humanist understandings of the self. There is an extensive debate as to whether the sublime offers a way for opening us to, or merely a mechanism for mastering, excess. Critics have mapped the remarkable extent to which gender inflects the discourse of the sublime. Rather than being a universal category, it is in the eighteenth century commonly associated with the masculine and defined in opposition to the supposedly feminine category of beauty. This has led some contemporary critics to wonder whether there could be a feminine sublime. Owing to the influence of postmodernism, the sublime has over the last three decades become once again a key notion of literary and philosophical discourse.

PETER OTTO

Bibliography

Ashfield, Andrew, and Peter De Bolla. *The Sublime: A Reader in British Eighteenth-century Aesthetic Theory.* Cambridge: Cambridge University Press, 1996.

De Bolla, Peter. *The Discourse of the Sublime: Readings in History, Aesthetics, and the Subject.* Oxford: Basil Blackwell, 1989.

Burke, Edmund. *A Philosophical Enquiry into the Origin of our Ideas of the Sublime and the Beautiful.* 1757. Reprint, Oxford: Oxford University Press, 1990.

Ferguson, Frances. *Solitude and the Sublime: Romanticism and the Aesthetics of Individuation.* New York: Routledge, 1992.

Freeman, Barbara Claire. *The Feminine Sublime: Gender and Excess in Women's Fiction.* Berkeley and Los Angeles: University of California Press, 1995.

Hertz, Neil. *The End of the Line: Essays on Psychoanalysis and the Sublime.* New York: Columbia University Press, 1985.

Kant, Immanuel. *The Critique of Judgement.* 1790. Translated by James Creed Meredith, 1952. Reprint, Oxford: Clarendon Press, 1982.

Longinus. *On the Sublime.* Translated with a commentary by James A. Arieti and John M. Crossett. Texts and Studies in Religion. vol. 21. New York: Edwin Mellon Press, 1985.

Monk, Samuel. *The Sublime: A Study of Critical Theories in Eighteenth Century England.* Ann Arbor: University of Michigan, 1935.

Pease, Donald E. "Sublime Politics," *boundary 2*, 12, no. 3–13, no. 1 (1984): 259–79.

Weiskel, Thomas. *The Romantic Sublime: Studies in the Structure and Psychology of Transcendence.* 1976. Reprint, Baltimore: Johns Hopkins University Press, 1986.

Wlecke, Albert O. *Wordsworth and the Sublime.* Berkeley and Los Angeles: University of California Press, 1973.

SUE, MARIE-JOSEPH EUGÈNE 1804–1857

French novelist

Marie-Joseph Eugène Sue is best remembered for his monumental best-seller *Les Mystères de Paris* (*The Mysteries of Paris*, 1842–43), which in its sentiment, championship of the poor, socialist calls to action, and envisioning of subsequent social harmony embodies many of the features of social Romanticism. Sue's career, however, spanned the duration of the July Monarchy and the first few years of the Second Empire, encompassing three distinct phases in his life and his literary style.

In an essay on Sue for *La Revue des Deux Mondes* in 1840, Charles Augustin Sainte-Beuve wrote that Sue's novels drew skillfully from each of the literary trends of the day without letting any particular tone predominate. This observation highlights the difficulty of assigning Sue's early work to any one movement. Until his bankruptcy in 1837, brought about by his legendary extravagance and financial mismanagement, it seems that Sue's main motivation for writing was to maintain favor in the society and literary salons of Paris. His novels ranged from maritime adventures to narratives of Gothic horror and historical tales, and displayed variously the influence of Lord Byron, James

Fenimore Cooper, Jean-Jacques Rousseau, and Walter Scott. Equally diverse, Sue's professions of political affiliation fluctuated. He took little interest in the July Revolution of 1830, preferring to cultivate his reputation as a dandy, and although his works often lampooned Louis-Philippe he nonetheless frequented royalist salons and dedicated novels to the king. His hauteur and lack of commitment prevented him from forming any real alliance with the Romantics.

Despite this, Sue's early work demonstrates his awareness of Romantic trends. *Plik et Plok* (1831), *Atar-Gull* (1831), and *La Salamandre* (*The Salamander, a Naval Romance*, 1832), all maritime novels in which Sue drew on his experiences of travel in the West Indies and Guadeloupe, featured the violent and "monstrous" prototypes of the pirate, the smuggler, and the slave trader, in addition to the valiant sea captain. Sue prefaced *Atar-Gull* with a letter to James Fenimore Cooper, explaining how he had broken with the unities of time, place, and action in favor of a more fragmentary form of representation, and paid homage in its pages to Napoleon Bonaparte, Byron, François-

Auguste-René de Chateaubriand, Johann Wolfgang von Goethe, Scott, and William Shakespeare. Like Théodore Géricault, who took pains to accurately reproduce the colors and tones of amputation and death in *Le Radeem de la Méduse* (*The Raft of the Medusa*, 1819), Sue consulted medical reports on the effects of hunger and thirst on the Medusa's survivors for his depiction of a shipwreck in *La Salamandre*. The latter novel was admired in the salons, and Franz Liszt even considered taking the final chapter, which relates the protracted death of the victims, as the basis for a composition. With these and his historical novel, *La Vigie de Koat-Ven* (*The Temptation, or the Watch Tower of Koat-Ven*, 1833), Sue gained the sobriquet of "the French Walter Scott."

In the wake of his financial ruin and the critical failure of *Latréaumont* (*Latréaumont, or The Conspiracy*, 1837) and *Histoire de la marine française* (*History of the French Navy*, 1835–37), Sue lost confidence and was counseled by his friend Ernest Legouvé to model himself on Goethe by depicting his own disillusionment. The result was *Arthur* (1838–39), a confessional novel in which the eponymous hero narrates his perpetual inability to trust the kindness of those around him. In Arthur's self-criticism and self-doubt, Sue offers an extended analysis of the relationship between self and society. The central theme is that of inner conflict, "une lutte perpétuelle entre mon coeur qui me disait: *crois, . . . aime, . . . espère, . . .* et mon esprit qui me disait: *doute, . . . méprise, . . .* et *crains!*" ("a perpetual struggle between my heart, which told me: *believe, . . . love, . . . hope, . . .* and my spirit, which said: *doubt, . . . despise, . . . and be fearful!*"). Sainte-Beuve was to write that Sue had encapsulated perfectly the disaffection and pessimism of a whole generation during the July Monarchy; their aristocratic pretensions, and their use of socialist, religious, or libertine jargon; their craze for regency fashions, and the fine line drawn between brutality one moment and sentiment the next.

Arthur stands alone in Sue's work for its depth of psychological analysis and attentive observation of human behavior. It also, however, marks the new engagement with contemporary reality and social evils that characterizes Sue's subsequent works. *Mathilde* (1840–41), for example, took as its subject the plight of women trapped by convention and by property laws into abusive and loveless marriages. *Mathilde* and *Les Mystères de Paris* were both affected by Sue's fabled conversion to socialism after a meeting with Fugères, a politicized artisan who astounded Sue with his explanation of the theories of Auguste Comte, Charles Fourier, and Claude Henri de Saint-Simon, and who was later to die on the barricades in the fight against the Second Empire. "Notre unique espoir," claimed Sue, in *Les Mystères*, "est d'appeler l'attention des penseurs et des gens de bien sur de grandes misères sociales, dont on peut déplorer, mais non contester la réalité" ("Our only hope is to draw the attention of thinkers, and of philanthropists to those great social distresses, whose reality one can deplore, but not contest"). The impact of *Les Mystères de Paris* was immediate and wide-ranging, confronting readers with uncomfortable facts about poverty and crime in the city. It provoked copycat social "mysteries" in European capitals and provinces and in America, within the decade, and instigated many examples of practical social reform.

Sue's subsequent novels developed his political engagement, becoming increasingly doctrinaire while still retaining the vibrant contrasts characteristic of his style. *Le Juif errant* (*The Wandering Jew*, 1845), which attacked the Jesuits, was as successful as its predecessor, although its fierce anticlericalism led to condemnation of Sue by the Roman Catholic church. *Martin l'enfant trouvé* (*Martin the Foundling*, 1847) dealt with rural poverty and ended with a manifesto outlining social reforms. Sue's last serialized novel, the epic *Les Mystères du peuple* (*The Mysteries of the People*, 1849–57), gave a new twist to the Romantic obsession with the past in its aim to rewrite history in the light of the 1848 revolution, taking the disinherited Gauls as its collective hero and hailing insurrection as the only effective method of recreating the homeland.

Sue's social theories were sharply criticized by Vissarion Belinskii and Karl Marx, but through the medium of the *roman-feuilleton*, he both communicated the urgency of the need for social reform and encouraged a positive (self-) image of the industrious working classes. It was in this regard that he came closest to the ideals of the Romantics and was acclaimed, alongside Pierre-Jean de Béranger, Félicité de Lamennais, and George Sand, as one of the four social and philanthropic giants of the age.

SARA JAMES

Biography

Born in Paris, January 26, 1804. Educated at Lycée Bonaparte (now Lycée Condorcet), 1816–21. Surgical aide with French Navy at Toulon, 1821–25. In Paris, early 1826. medical auxiliary on the ship *Breslaw* in the East, 1826–27. Studies with maritime painter Théodore Gudin in Paris, 1828. In Paris, writing for pleasure, 1829–37; financial ruin, 1837. Success of *Les Mystères de Paris* and *Le Juif errant* led to publishing contract with *Le Constitutionnel*, 1845. Ran as Socialist candidate, April 1850. Self-imposed exile in Annecy following coup d'état of December 2, 1851. Died of a stroke in Annecy, August 3, 1857.

Selected Works

Plik et Plok. 1831.
Atar-Gull. 1831.
La Salamandre. 2 vols. 1832. Translated as *The Salamander, a Naval Romance*, by Henry William Herbert. 1845.
La Vigie de Koat-Ven. 4 vols. 1833. Translated as *The Temptation; or, The Watch Tower of Koat-Ven*. 1845.
Histoire de la marine française. 5 vols. 1835–37.
Latréaumont. 2 vols. 1837. Translated as *Latréaumont; or, The Conspiracy*, by U. P. James. 1840?
Arthur, journal d'un inconnu. 3 vols. 1838–39. Translated as *Arthur* by P. F. Christin, 1844.
Mathilde. 3 vols. 1841. Translated as *Mathilde; or, The Memoirs of a Young Woman*, by Henry William Herbert. 1843.
Les Mystères de Paris, 10 vols. 1842–43. Translated as *The Mysteries of Paris*, 1844. Edited by Francis Lacassin. Paris: Laffont, 1989.
Le Juif errant. 10 vols. 1844–45. Translated as *The Wandering Jew*, by H. D. Miles, 1846. Edited by Francis Lacassin. Paris: Laffont, 1983.
Martin l'enfant trouvé, 1847. Translated as *Martin the Foundling; or, The Adventures of a Valet-de-chambre*, 1847.
Les Mystères du peuple, ou, Histoire d'une famille de prolétaires à travers les âges, 8 vols. 1849–57. Translated as *The Mysteries of the People*, by Daniel and Solon Deleon, 1904–16. Edited by Régine Deforges. 2 vols. Paris: Régine Deforges, 1978.

Bibliography

Atkinson, Nora. *Eugène Sue et le roman-feuilleton*. Paris: Nizet et Bastard, 1929.

Bory, Jean-Louis. *Eugène Sue, le roi du roman populaire*. Paris: Hachette, 1962.

Evans, David-Owen. *Social Romanticism in France, 1830–1848*. Oxford: Clarendon Press, 1951.

"Eugène Sue," *Europe*, (1982).

Galvan, Jean-Pierre. *Les Mystères de Paris: Eugène Sue et ses lecteurs*. 2 vols. Paris: L'Harmattan, 1998.

Levi, Anthony. "Eugène Sue." In *Guide to French Literature, 1789 to the Present*. London: St. James Press, 1992.

Morrissey, Robert. "Whose House Is This? Feeling at Home with the Past." In *Home and Its Dislocations*. Edited by Suzanne Nash. Albany: State University of New York Press, 1993.

Pickup, Ian. "Eugène Sue." In *Nineteenth Century French Fiction Writers: Romanticism and Realism, 1800–1860*. Edited by Catherine Savage Brosnan. Detroit: Gale, 1992.

SULLY, THOMAS 1783–1872

American painter

When offered the choice of either following the Sully family vocation and becoming an actor, or apprenticing first to his brother-in-law and then his elder brother, Lawrence, in order to become a painter, Thomas Sully chose the latter. He began his long career as a painter of miniatures in Virginia, where he quickly surpassed his brother and teacher. This was fortunate since he would shortly be faced with supporting his brother's widow, whom he would later marry, and her children. Sully moved rapidly from painting miniatures to busts and full-length portraits both because his skill and ambition allowed him to do so and because they brought a higher price. Sully was a conscientious businessman and kept a register of the paintings he produced throughout his career. Whether or not he sold the work, he assigned a monetary value to each painting. The values reflected practical details such as the size of the portraits and whether or not the subject's hands were included, but also the artists's own estimation of the portrait's success.

Sully's American education followed a traditional early-nineteenth century pattern. After apprenticing with his brother he sought out America's major painters, including Gilbert Stuart, who recognized Sully's skill and encouraged him to pursue European training. Sully heeded this advice, and through subscriptions for copies of European paintings, he raised the necessary funds to go to London, where he stayed for nine months in 1809–10. Armed with letters of introduction, he immediately sought out the president of the Royal Academy, Benjamin West, an American who received Sully as warmly as he did many of Sully's American colleagues. West allowed Sully to borrow and copy works by himself and other artists in his collection, which served to both educate Sully and enable him to fulfill his subscriptions.

Sully's experience in London was central to his success in the United States. On the practical side there were not yet well-established American academies, and therefore formal training was difficult to obtain. Equally important was West himself, an astute judge of a student's gift and technical skill to render the figure, landscape, or history; he wisely counseled Sully to pursue a career as a portrait painter. He introduced Sully to Thomas Lawrence, the most prominent English portrait painter at that time. This introduction was vital to Sully's mature development as an artist. He adapted Lawrence's brushwork and color to his own style, and upon his return to the United States, became known as the "American Lawrence."

In the United States and England of the eighteenth and nineteenth centuries, the hierarchy within portrait painting differentiated between painters of the poetic or historic and the "common" portrait painters. Painters of poetic or historic portraits received greater recognition because they were not mere copyists, but rather interpreted their subject. This meant that artists such as Sully, who specialized in portraits, sought occasions upon which to paint historic or well-known figures "in character." According to his biographers, Sully established his career with his portrait *George Frederick Cooke as Richard III* (1811). Commissioned by the Pennsylvania Academy of Fine Arts in Philadelphia, Sully painted the famous English actor while he was touring the United States. The commission for a public collection, combined with the subject's fame, made it a rare opportunity. William Gerdts suggests that the theatrical portrait in the tradition of Sir Joshua Reynolds's *Mrs. Siddons as the Tragic Muse* allowed the artist to demonstrate his ability to paint the actor's likeness, to paint the character the actor portrayed, and to paint the actor's interpretation of the character, thus demonstrating the artist's virtuosity in depicting the many levels of his subject just as the actor portrays the complexities of his character.

Sully also pursued public commissions to paint important figures such as the Marquis de Lafayette (1825), whose portrait was commissioned for the city of Philadelphia; Thomas Jefferson (1822), and James Monroe (1832) whose portraits, among others, he painted for the United States Military Academy at West Point, New York. This association with such illustrious men, combined with his technical skill, greatly contributed to Sully's reputation. Possibly the most successful of Sully's portraits of public figures was his 1838 painting of the young Queen Victoria. This work was commissioned by the Society of the Sons of St. George in Philadelphia. Sully painted a full-length formal portrait, as well as several smaller portraits that remained in English collections. The success of the full-length portrait initiated the second major phase of his career.

Sully was a Romantic in style more than in temperament. Unlike many artists of his time, he was a good businessman and used his artistic talent to his economic advantage. The looser brushwork that characterized his mature style made his portraits appear less severe. Sully asked one young painter, C. R. Leslie, to describe Sully's "leading fault." Leslie replied that "your pictures look as if you could blow them away." A later author, Henry Tuckerman, noted that Sully's "fairy-like, unsubstantial manner" made it well suited to certain subject and sitter types. Sully's style was probably best suited to portraits of lovely women in willowy poses, such as *Lady with a Harp: Eliza Ridgely* (1818). In it, Eliza Ridgely is posed leaning against a harp that mimics her own curving form, while in the background are linear architectural details that serve as a contrast to her sinuous curve. The harp is both a pretty detail and a signifier of the sitter's refinement. Sully's approach in paintings such as *Lady with a Harp* is also found in his paintings of children and in what he called his "fancy" pictures. These were sweetly composed genre scenes that particularly suited his light approach.

Sully was enormously influential in the United States, and as his portrait of Queen Victoria indicates, his talent was also recognized abroad. However, as with many artists with long careers, his influence waned and his style became less fashionable toward the middle of the of the nineteenth century, when a more realistic approach became popular.

KATHLEEN L. BUTLER

Biography

Born June 19, 1783, Horncastle, Lincolnshire. To Charleston, South Carolina, in 1792. Studied with brother-in-law Jean Belzons and his elder brother, Lawrence Sully. Worked in Virginia with Lawrence Sully, 1801–3. In 1806, married his brother Lawrence's widow, Sarah Annis Sully; Thomas and Sarah had nine children. In Boston in 1807, and met Gilbert Stuart. In 1809 became an American citizen. To London, 1809–10 to study with Benjamin West; met Thomas Lawrence. In 1827 named an Honorable Member of the Scottish Academy. To England again in 1837; painted Queen Victoria's portrait. Died in Philadelphia, November 5, 1872, at the age of eighty-nine.

Bibliography

Biddle, Edward, and Mantle Fielding. *Life and Works of Thomas Sully*. Lancaster, Penn.: Wickersham Press, 1921.

Dunlap, William. "Thomas Sully." In *History of the Rise and Progress of Arts of Design in the United States*. 1834. Reprinted New York: Benjamin Blom, 1965.

Fabian, Monroe H. *Mr. Sully, Portrait Painter: The Works of Thomas Sully (1783–1872)*. Washington, D.C.: Smithsonian Institution Press, 1983.

Quick, Michael, ed., *American Portaiture in the Grand Manner: 1720–1920*, Los Angeles: Los Angeles County Museum of Art, 1981.

Simon, Robin. *The Portrait in Britain and America*, Boston: G. K. Hall, 1987.

Tuckerman, Henry T. "Sully." In *Artist-Life, or Sketches of American Painters*. New York: D. Appleton, 1847.

THE SUPERNATURAL

The term *supernatural* encompasses a broad range of beliefs, spanning the divide between rationalism and irrationalism, for it may be applied to anything believed to exist outside the natural world, including deities and spirits; however, it may also be used to characterize miraculous or inexplicable forces that intervene in or are coextensive with the natural world. The *supernatural* is thus contingent on a definition of the *natural*, which varies according to the paradigm of belief within which one is operating. Thus, for example, there is no clear distinction between belief in the supernatural and various kinds of experiential empiricism, because one may have an "experience" of the supernatural that defies explanation. Or again, a natural theology would try to explain or demonstrate the problem of evil or the existence of God using standard rationalist methods; whereas a supernatural theology would follow methods believed to be revealed by God, or beliefs that defied rational explanation. Similarly, while a writer such as Isidore-Auguste-Marie-François-Xavier Comte could see social development as progressing in stages—from the theological (believing in the supernatural) to the metaphysical (treating ideas as reality) to the positive (explaining the world through observation and experimentation)—and while deists such as Voltaire rejected belief in biblical revelation, the belief that a supernatural God created the universe, nevertheless, remained an assumption of such philosophies. Supernaturalism in general thus seems to cover belief systems ranging from mythology, religion, mysticism, alchemy, and astrology to pantheism, spiritualism, transcendentalism, and philosophical idealism.

During the medieval period, the classical Greek and Roman traditions joined with the Judaic and Christian by the assimilation of Plotinian Neoplatonism with the thought of Christian philosophers such as Boethius, Origen, Augustine, and Thomas Aquinas. During the Romantic period, these traditions (promoted in Germany by such writers as Gotthold Ephraim Lessing and Johann Joachim Winckelmann, and in England by Lord Byron, John Keats, and Percy Bysshe Shelley) emerge in the neoclassicism that becomes the central point of contention in the quarrel between the ancients and moderns; it is in this debate that the idea of "modernity" first becomes a critical issue. In classical Greek myths and popular mystery cults, the gods were believed to have supernatural power over the human realm, limited by the forces of Fate; these myths were tempered through later philosophical rationalizations. But in the Romantic period, as the "moderns" gradually prevailed over the "ancients," the classical mythological deities came to assume new forms as literary devices or conceits: they tended to appear as broader metaphors of psychological or spiritual states (for example, the Muses as inspiration, Pan as the spirit of nature), or of social or technological developments (for example, Pandora or Prometheus representing social ills or uncontained technology). An analogous development can be seen in the renewed interest in legends (appropriated in the service of the new myth of "the nation"); and fairy tales (generally functioning as moral parables), as evidenced by the popularity of the collections of Jakob and Wilhelm Grimm in Germany and Hans Christian Andersen in Denmark.

The period is also characterized by a growing popular interest in mysticism, alchemy, and the occult, and hundreds of texts were published on such topics as the kabbalah, gnosticism, and alchemical applications in medicine. Witchcraft, magic, and divination were practiced in various forms, and astrological theories were disseminated in almanacs and horoscopes. People of all social ranks participated in Satanic rituals and seances to communicate with or raise the spirits of the dead; there was widespread belief in supernatural entities such as ghosts, and omens such as comets; it was common practice, even among the most educated, to consult wizards or alchemists; and there were occasional outbursts of religious hysteria. Esoteric organizations sprang up, including those of the Rosicrucians and the Freemasons, the latter including Voltaire and Johann Wolfgang von Goethe. Elements of the Jewish kabbalistic tradition were introduced by the scholars Moses Hayyim Luzzatto in Italy, Jacob Frank in Poland, and Moses Mendelssohn in Germany. The theosophical writings of Paracelsus and Jakob Böhme influenced such writers as Gotthold Ephraim Lessing and Friedrich Wilhelm Joseph von Schelling; their mystical philosophies, and the quest of the esoteric alchemists for spiritual self-understanding, appeared in the texts of the German Romantics, where they became elements of the theory of Romantic irony. Böhme's writings, and those of the Swedish theologian Emanuel Swedenborg, inspired William Blake and other English Romantic poets.

Around the same time, the works of German idealism (Johann Gottlieb Fichte, Immanuel Kant, and Friedrich Wilhelm Joseph von Schelling) and Romanticism (Novalis, August Wilhelm and Friedrich von Schlegel, Karl Solger, and Ludwig Tieck) influenced the British writers Thomas Carlyle and Samuel Taylor Coleridge, and through their mediation, mystical and theosophical thought entered America, where it informed the views of Bronson Alcott, Ralph Waldo Emerson, Margaret Fuller, Henry David Thoreau, and others—the poets and essayists of New England associated with transcendentalism. The transcendentalists' philosophy of a self-evident and intuited life of the spirit stands against the "rational" theology of the Unitarian Church and the growing materialistic ethos of the age, creating a vision of the symbolic relation between God or spirit and the universe or matter, analogous to the pantheistic symbolism of William Wordsworth and the English Romantics. The Jena Romantics had a similar vision of the relation between truth and language, which can be traced back to classical, medieval, and Renaissance gnostic and alchemical theories of the relation between macrocosm and microcosm. This vision is taken up later by writers such as Emily Dickinson, Robert Frost, William James, Wallace Stevens, and Walt Whitman.

Other philosophical and literary manifestations of the supernatural during the period range from the instinctive "laws of nature" proposed by the Marquis de Sade against Jean-Jacques Rousseau's "social contract," to the opium-induced visions of Coleridge and Thomas De Quincey, the morbid obsessions of Percy Bysshe Shelley, and the medievalism of Thomas Chatterton. But it was with the emergence of the new Gothic genre of romance and tales that the supernatural captured the popular imagination in literature. Deriving its aesthetic framework from the superstition, scholasticism, mysticism, and tales of chivalry that manifested themselves in the awe-inspiring rib vaults, stained-glass windows, flying buttresses, and gargoyles of medieval cathedrals and castles, the Gothic supernatural appeared in Germany most famously in Goethe's *Faust* (1808, 1832) and the tales of E. T. A. Hoffman; in France in the Marquis de Sade's *Les 120 Journées de Sodome, ou l'école du libertinage* (*The 120 Days of Sodom*, 1785) and Victor Hugo's *Notre Dame de Paris* (*The Hunchback of Notre Dame*, 1831); and in the United States in the tales of Washington Irving and Edgar Allan Poe and the novels of Charles Brockden Brown and Nathaniel Haw-

thorne. In Britain the genre was established by Horace Walpole's *Castle of Otranto* (1765), and taken up in novels by Charlotte Brontë, Matthew Lewis, Ann Radcliffe, Walter Scott, and Mary Shelley, setting a precedent for the later work of Bram Stoker, Henry James, and Daphne du Maurier, and for the genres of the horror film and the psychological thriller in the twentieth century.

Although these modes of belief may be easy to dismiss as facile or intellectually untenable from a rationalist academic standpoint, from the perspective of the popular imagination the Romantic period sees a shift in ethos, from a sense of the supernatural as an exterior phenomenon, to its understanding as the projection and reflection of inner, psychological states of fear, madness, fantasy, and mythopoesis in the face of the unknown. Through this shift, the supernatural finds its figure in the title of Francisco José de Goya y Lucientes's etching from *Los Caprichos* (1796–98), *The Sleep of Reason Produces Monsters*. In art, literature, and philosophy, it appears as the demonic dream that emerges from the unconscious of the "natural" and of "reason," revealing the fragile, limiting, psychological boundaries on which all our rational concepts and systems are founded. From the standpoint of the popular imagination, the achievement of the art and literature of the period was to foreground the "supernatural"—what remained unthought in the context of Enlightenment rationality—as an aspect of the "natural" order, within consciousness. Yet the same period saw a transition from alchemy to modern inorganic chemistry, and the beginnings of modern physics, biology, and psychology. With these changes came new perspectives based on the glorification of materialism, science and technology, and a dismissal of manifestations of the supernatural as chimeras and superstitions of the popular imagination. Thus, writing near the middle of the nineteenth century and looking back on the close of the Romantic period, Jules Michelet could say of the latest developments in science and technology: "I see realized in practice [today] the dreams and longings of the Middle Ages, the most apparently chimerical fantasies of former days. . . . This is divine sorcery indeed! . . . If Satan does this, we are bound to pay him homage, to admit he may well be, after all, one of the aspects of God."

JOHAN PILLAI

Bibliography

Abrams, M. H. *The Mirror and the Lamp: Romantic Theory and the Critical Tradition.* Oxford: Oxford University Press, 1953.

Abrams, M. H. *Natural Supernaturalism: Tradition and Revolution in Romantic Literature.* New York: W. W. Norton, 1973.

Benz, Ernst. *Mystical Sources of German Romantic Philosophy.* San Jose, California: Pickwick, 1983.

Bloom, Harold. *Kabbalah and Criticism.* New York: Seabury Press, 1975.

Burwick, Frederick. *Poetic Madness and the Romantic Imagination.* University Park, Penn.: Pennsylvania State University Press, 1996.

Clemens, Valdine. *The Return of the Repressed: Gothic Horror from "The Castle of Otranto" to "Alien."* SUNY Series in Psychoanalysis and Culture. Albany: State University of New York Press, 1999.

Meyer, Paola. *Jena Romanticism and Its Appropriation of Jakob Böhme: Theosophy, Hagiography, Literature.* McGill-Queen's Studies in the History of Ideas. Vol. 27. Toronto: McGill-Queen's University Press, 1999.

Michelet, Jules. *Satanism and Witchcraft: The Classic Study of Medieval Superstition*. Translated by A. R. Allinson. Seacaucus, N.J.: Citadel Press, 1992.

Praz, Mario. *The Romantic Agony*. Translated by Angus Davidson. New York: Meridian Books/World Publishing Company, 1967.

Rudolph, Kurt, *Gnosis: The Nature and History of Gnosticism*. Translated by Robert McLachlan Wilson. San Francisco: Harper San Francisco, 1987.

Scholem, Gershom, *Major Trends in Jewish Mysticism*. New York: Schocken Books, 1995.

Seligmann, Kurt. *Magic, Supernaturalism, and Religion*. New York: Universal Library, 1968.

Smith, Preserved. *The Enlightenment 1687–1776*. Vol. 2 of *A History of Modern Culture*. New York: Collier Books, 1962.

Weiskel, Thomas. *The Romantic Sublime: Studies in the Structure and Psychology of Transcendence*. Baltimore: Johns Hopkins University Press, 1976.

SWITZERLAND: CULTURAL SURVEY

As a federation of twenty-three cantons practicing two main religions, Switzerland is difficult to survey culturally, although the four national languages of French, German, Italian, and Romansh have contributed to crystallizing a specific Swiss culture. In three of the four cases, the cultural and political events of the country's geographical neighbors have also influenced the development of said culture. In several cases, it is during the Romantic era that such literary and cultural traditions came into being.

The Swiss-German literary tradition, for example, depends on the intricate relationship of Swiss-German dialects to *Hochdeutsch*. This early literature came out of the abbey of Sankt Gallen in the Middle Ages, when monks secretly put together a glossary intended to help local students understand Latin texts. By the twelfth century, there existed a literature of knighthood poetry inspired from the French tradition, which stressed themes of fault and redemption. This was complemented by epics, such as Heinrich Wittenwiler's satirical *Der Ring*, and educational books like Konrad von Ammenhausen's *Schachzabelbuch*, a collection of popular tales.

The dual trend of satire and poetry carried on in the seventeenth century, as exemplified by Zurich poet Johann Wilhelm Simmler and satiricists Johannes Grob and Franz Veiras. Some of the works reflected the hardening of confessional conflict, which also limited the impact of baroque literature (which had a limited impact in Swiss German circles).

The recurring satirical dimensions of Swiss literary works also reflect the development of a politically critical tradition in the early modern period of Switzerland, just as the rise of an aristocratic cast slowed down political developments and clashed with the demands of intellectuals for greater political freedom. The eighteenth century in particular signaled the beginnings of new literary waves, associated with the Enlightenment, and, in turn, with Romanticism. However, there was no revolutionary atmosphere as such. The Swiss Enlightenment benefited from this state of relative unrest in that rational thought, and Christian belief came to be considered no longer as automatically contradictory. A clear example of this came in the sciences, where observation of nature was deemed to match biblical descriptions of the work of God. This appears clearly in the writings of Zurich natural scientist Johann Jakob Scheuchzer. Also, the Bernese Albrecht von Haller, while critically evaluating Swiss society, emphasized the idyllic dimension of simple life in his didactic poetry.

The intellectual elite of the confederation was generally comprised of the same members as the political one, and discussions about a renewal and improvement of the nation often came from it, or associations issued from it. For example, the Société Helvétique formed in 1761 in Schinznach contributed to spreading Swiss Enlightenment notions in both Catholic and Protestant cantons. This does not mean that they were successful. Often ignored, Swiss intellectuals found themselves criticizing the blissful ignorance of their compatriots but lacked the tools to effect change. Often, they had greater success with foreign intellectuals abroad or in the Helvetic region. The advent of the novel is a case in point.

The novel did not really arrive in Switzerland until the appearance of Jean-Jacques Rousseau's *Julie, ou La nouvelle Héloise* (*Julie or The New Heloise*), and Jacob Vernes's *Confidences philosophiques*. Once it did, however, the nation found itself flooded in countless novels, most of average quality written by women of the high bourgeoisie. Several writers, however, quickly distinguished themselves. Agnès-Isabelle de Charrière, a Dutch baron's daughter who married a Swiss preceptor, inspired a new romantic wave through the publication of her *Lettres neuchâteloises*. Others, like Isabelle de Montolieu (who authored over one hundred novels), spread romantic notions, but by inspiring themselves from clichéd love stories borrowed from the German tradition. Montolieu had been part of an early wave of women who, facing the troubles of the French Revolution, had come to Switzerland. To pass time, they thought of writing short stories based on sketches. Montolieu's more insightful work, *Châteaux suisses*, is a valuable essay of imaginary literature as applied to Swiss history. Together with Louis Bridel's *Etrennes helvétiennes* (*Swiss Castles* Bridel; also pioneered a national poetic tradition) and Mme. Françoise-Louise de Pont-Wullyamoz's *Anecdotes suisses*, it contributed to the beginnings of a national Swiss-French literature. More important, though, the practice of the essay, as reflected in the work of Benjamin Constant de Rebeque and Madame Anne-Louise-Germaine de Staël, took off and spread widely into French-speaking Switzerland.

Not all writers of that era focused on idyllic notions. Several, like Jeremias Gothelf or Johann Heinrich Pestalozzi, emphasized idealist notions without, however, forgetting to note harshly a certain decadence in their social portrayal, hoping to incite social change. Yet the Swiss cultural reform movement they were part of failed to sway antiquated political structures, and only movements from France and Germany, as well as political upheaval, would eventually cause a shift.

The French revolutionary wars and the resulting Helvetic Republic and Mediation Era in Switzerland (1798–1813) saw an early attempt at creating a common national culture through a formal office and a national university system despite the multiple languages. This centralization attempt, however, clashed with the Swiss federalist tradition and could only be carried out partially.

With the return to independence in 1815, Swiss restoration also saw the late appearance of a distinctly Romantic wave of literature. In poetry, in particular, Pestalozzi's work was in great vogue, as were the popular works of Carl Attenhofer, Richard Flury, Adolf Frey, Meinrad Lienert, Sophie Haemmerli-Marti, and Josef Reinhart, among others. Many of these were put into music, either in dialect, or by musicians influenced by the great composers who had spent time in Switzerland, like Carl Czerny and Franz Liszt.

Soon, however, the influence of liberal ideas also became clear in literary works, though it often took the form of a rejection of existing conditions. Carl Spitteler, in emphasizing individual choice, grudgingly accepted democratic notions, while Robert Walser closed the door to the outside world out of fear that the perceived Swiss idyll would be destroyed. Both writers, however, shared this angry intellectual outlook that would make its way into the twentieth century and influence the works of Friedrich Dürrenmatt and Max Frisch.

One should note in passing the appearance of a new form of satire, that of Genevan Rodolphe Toepffer and his *Histoires de Monsieur Jabot*, which is considered one of the first true attempts at developing a story through comic-strip drawing.

The influence of Switzerland's neighbors—especially France and Germany—remained key in the evolution of intellectual endeavors. In the nineteenth century it became fashionable for Swiss-French students to complete their education at a German university (Albert Béguin, for example, wrote a dissertation on German pre-Romanticism). Some Swiss writers were, in fact, noticed abroad more than at home. Frédéric Amiel, inspired by Rousseau's *Confessions*, wrote a 17,000-page journal and inspired Lev Tolstoy, but went unnoticed in his home town of Geneva. Yet despite the heavy foreign influence, Switzerland did not face internal dissension based on Romantic notions of national warfare or empire creation. This is in part due to its restricted size, which prompted such writers as Conrad Ferdinand Meyer to struggle to find important Swiss historical characters that could be rendered into novel form.

In the Italian-speaking canton of Ticino, the literary tradition remained limited until the land began to industrialize and became part of Switzerland in 1803. Then, Ticino actually became a haven for northern Italian writers. Indigenous publications did exist, however, especially the poetry and novels of Francesco Chiesa and Angelo Nessi.

Finally, Canton Graubünden, where a minority speaks Romansh (either the Ladin or Surselvan dialects), did not develop a literary tradition in this language until the nineteenth century, limiting itself till then to oral tradition, administrative and church pamphlets, and history manuals. The return to the Engadina region of émigrés infused a new Ladin poetry laden with nostalgic sentiment. Conradin de Flugi, but also Simeon Caratsch and Giovannes Mathis are part of such tradition. The latter two also chose regional folklore as themes of their writing.

Overall, Swiss culture in the Romantic era as exemplified by its literature was extremely rich, although subject to the influence of ideas from abroad. By the twentieth century, however, it would further develop into a separate body that would question, praise, and also attack Swiss identity in the manner of other national literary traditions.

GUILLAUME DE SYON

See also **Switzerland: Historical Survey**

Bibliography

Bächtold, J. *Geschichte der deutschen Literatur in der Schweiz*. Frauenfeld: Huber, 1919.

Baud-Bovy, Daniel. *La Vie romantique au pays romand*. Geneva: Jullien, 1930.

Biancamaria, Fontana. *Benjamin Constant and the Post-Revolutionary Mind*. New Haven, Conn.: Yale University Press, 1991.

Bochet, Henri. *Le romantisme à Genève*. Geneva: Jullien, 1930.

Campbell, Clarissa. "Romanticism in Switzerland." In *Romanticism in National Context*. Edited by Roy Porter and Mikulas Teich. Cambridge, 1988.

Dangerfield, Elma. *Byron and the Romantics in Switzerland, 1816*. London: Ascent Books, 1978.

Liebi, Alfred. *Das Bild der Schweiz in der deutschen Romantik*. Bern: Paul Haupt, 1946.

Rossel, Virgile. *Histoire littéraire de la Suisse romande des origines à nos jours*. Neuchâtel: F. Zahn, 1903.

Spevack, Edmund. "August Adolf Ludwig Follen (1794–1855): Political Radicalism and Literary Romanticism in Germany and Switzerland," *Germanic Review* 71, 1(1996): 3–22.

Taylor, Samuel S. B. "The Enlightenment in Switzerland." In *The Enlightenment in National Context*. Cambridge: Cambridge University Press, 1981.

SWITZERLAND: HISTORICAL SURVEY

Founded in 1291 as a defensive alliance between three mountain cantons, the Swiss confederation slowly grew to include some thirteen states by the beginning of the Romantic era. By 1848 the number had almost doubled, and the political structure had changed substantially.

In the 1760s the alliance that characterized the Swiss states was considered dated, and the ruling structures ossified. A parliamentary diet met occasionally to discuss the common administration of certain regions, or whether to deploy troops to a threatened member, or to smooth confessional differences between Catholic and Protestant cantons. However, the country had not undergone the process that made several of its neighbors nation-states with a centralized power system. Intellectuals within the dominant political class had become aware of a need for reform, as reflected in the anonymous 1758 pamphlet *Rêves patriotiques d'un confédéré sur un moyen de rajeunir la confédération vieillie* (*Patriotic Dreams of Confederate about a Means to Refresh an Aging Confederation*). The impulse for change, however, came through the French Revolution, and defined the period 1798–1848 as a kind of "Swiss revolution."

News of the events in France (which included the 1792 taking of Louis XVI's Tuileries palace, defended by Swiss troops), along with the immigration of French nobility abroad, prompted small groups of the Swiss bourgeoisie to plan spontaneous rebellions. One such movement began in Basel in January 1798 and led to some minor political concessions in Zurich and Schaffhausen, as well as a failed Lemanic republic in Canton Vaud. The Directory government in Paris used the pretense of supporting the movements to invade Switzerland. The subsequent capitulation of all Swiss troops in March 1798 signaled the death of the Confederation as a loose alliance of thirteen cantons.

French representatives then remodeled the confederation into a Helvetic Republic. The constitution of April 6, 1798, included a directory of five members (as in France), with a *Grosser rat* (great assembly) of 152 and a senate of 76. Central Switzerland, however, resisted the new constitution in 1798 but eventually capitulated. The following year saw the confrontation of French troops against the Russians and Austro-Hungarians on Swiss soil, but France retained control of Helvetian territory.

From then until 1802, the Helvetic Republic witnessed a struggle between two major Swiss parties: the Unitarier, who wanted to keep a centralized state, and the Federalists, who wished for a return to the old structure. As a result, five different governments were seated and removed, and violent clashes prompted Napoleon Bonaparte to bring in French troops. One of his advisers, Marshall Ney, acted as negotiator, and in February 1803 forced representatives of the thirteen cantons to accept his solution of reducing the number of states from thirteen to six. Currency and measure units were standardized along revolutionary lines, and censorship of the press was eased. This state of affairs lasted ten years and became known as the Mediation Period, an era of peace without independence.

Napoleon, for example, retained the right to raise Swiss soldiers for his campaigns, and did so, incorporating them into four Helvetic regiments. In all, some ninety-thousand Swiss served the French emperor, of which fifty thousand died in war. The last Swiss regiment was disbanded shortly after Switzerland had booted out French troops and regained its independence in late 1813. The confederation then agreed to send a representative, the Genevan Pictet de Rochemont, to the Congress of Vienna to defend Swiss interests in the redrawing of Europe.

The decision of the Congress of Vienna in 1815 to confirm the Swiss nation as a buffer state set the stage for a maturation process that, following two constitutional drafts, would redesign Switzerland into a neutral, federal democratic state by the end of the nineteenth century. At the congress, the permanent borders of Switzerland were also set, and Switzerland ended its mercenary practices, with the exception of the Swiss Guard contingent, still in the service of the Vatican today. The rebuilding of the confederation was internally guaranteed through a thirty-year pact and several cantons joined the confederation, bringing the total to twenty-two, a number unchanged until the addition of Jura in 1978. However, the pact lacked a clear federal structure, and political unrest would take advantage of such a weakness.

The three-decade period that followed was by turn reactionary until 1830, then liberal, reflecting similar waves in France.

During the restoration phase, progressives were forced into the underground but made a point of helping political refugees in Switzerland, in turn angering reactionary sovereigns. The fall of Charles X in France prompted new demonstrations that generally resulted in concessions to liberal movements, but attempts at designing a federal constitution to replace the weakening federal pact failed in 1833. This signaled a growing rift between liberals and conservatives in various cantons. Multiple provocations on both sides along with acts of violence eventually prompted the secret formation of the Sonderbund, an alliance of conservative-led cantons. The later discovery of this secret alliance prompted a majority federal vote ordering the dissolution of the secret alliance, then the outbreak of civil war in the fall of 1847, known as the Sonderbund War. The liberals, siding with the diet, chose Henri Dufour as general to command federal troops. The war was short and very limited in scope, and led to a liberal victory, while conservative leaders of the Sonderbund fled abroad.

The diet then appointed a commission to put together a new constitution. The commission offered a draft inspired from the United States Constitution the following year, and it was accepted by popular referendum. The diet was dissolved, to be replaced with a federal assembly. The legislative body in turn chose a federal council, an executive body of seven members. The federal government assumed most of the responsibilities relating to foreign and military policies, and increased its say in matters of education, social, and religious legislation. Ironically, the measure units and currency (*franc*) imposed by the French revolutionaries then rejected in 1815 were adopted anew as a unified national system. Finally, Bern became the federal city where the government carried out its functions.

Thus, in 1848, Switzerland formally became a nation-state. It had yet to experience industrialization, though the pauperization of the peasantry had begun to take place. It would also undergo several more constitutional changes over the following century and a half, but its fundamental federal system and its international status would remain unchanged.

GUILLAUME DE SYON

See also **Switzerland: Cultural Survey**

Bibliography

Craig, Gordon. *The Triumph of Liberalism: Zurich in the Golden Age, 1830–1869.* New York: Scribner's, 1988.

Guillon, Edouard. *Napoléon et la Suisse 1803–1815.* Plon/Lausanne: Paris; Payot, 1910.

Ozment, Steven. *The Reformation in the Cities: The Appeal of Protestantism to Sixteenth-Century Germany and Switzerland.* New Haven, Conn.: Yale University Press, 1975.

Remak, Joachim. *A Very Civil War: The Swiss Sonderbund War of 1847.* Boulder, Colo.: Westview, 1847.

Ruter, Alfred, and Jean-René Suratteau. *La Suisse et la Révolution française.* Paris: Société des Études Robespierristes, 1974.

Steinberg, Jonathan. *Why Switzerland?* 2d ed. New York: Cambridge University Press, 1996.

Thürer, Georg, and R. P. Heller. *Free and Swiss: The Story of Switzerland.* Coral Gables, Fla.: University of Miami Press, 1971.

LA SYLPHIDE 1832

Ballet by Filippo Taglioni

According to Ivor Guest, *La Sylphide* "sealed the triumph of Romanticism in the field of ballet." The days of the often rather soulless ballets of classical antiquity were over. As Théophile Gautier famously perceived: "after *La Sylphide, Les Filets de Vulcan* and *Flore et Zéphire* were no longer possible; the Opéra was given over to gnomes, undines, salamanders, elves, nixes, wilis, peris—to all that strange and mysterious folk who lend themselves so marvelously to the fantasies of the *maîtres de ballet*." *La Sylphide* brought together many relatively new elements in ballet (costumes, set, lighting, and the use of pointe work) and it was this symbiosis that resulted in so potent an evocation of a theme already familiar to Romantic art and literature; that of a supernatural being falling in love with a mortal, of a mortal's struggle between his own world and a spiritual one.

Set in Scotland, the story concerns James Reuben, a Scots peasant, and his fiancée Effie. At the beginning of act 1 James is asleep in his chair as the sylphide (a winged sprite) kneels at his feet. She rises gracefully, dances and gazes at him adoringly. She wakes him with a kiss, but as he reaches out to her she becomes afraid and vanishes up the chimney. Confused as to whether the sylphide was real or not, he questions his friend Gurn, but Gurn has been sound asleep and witnessed nothing. Wedding preparations continue, but James is clearly preoccupied and almost has to be reminded to greet Effie with a kiss. Even when the young couple kneel to receive Effie's mother's blessing and bridesmaids bring presents and good wishes, James remains distracted. As he stares into the fireplace searching for the sylphide, suddenly Madge, the village witch, appears. She reads the girls' palms and tells Effie that she will be happy in marriage, that James does not love her, but Gurn does. James angrily drives her from the house and his indignation reassures Effie that he loves her after all. She leaves to dress for the wedding and the sylphide reappears in the window and floats into the room. The sylphide admits to James that she has fallen in love with him and while they dance together he reveals she has been in his thoughts constantly. As the wedding guests approach, James hides her in his chair with his plaid. Gurn accuses James of disloyalty, but, when the plaid is removed, the chair is empty. Dancing at the wedding ceremony begins, but James and Effie's pas de deux is often a peculiar pas de trois with the sylphide, who is visible only to James: thus James's imaginary or spiritual love distracts him from his real love. James is about to place his ring on Effie's finger when the sylphide seizes it and darts out of the window, closely followed by James.

Act 2 opens in a misty forest with the focus on Madge and her coven dancing round a bubbling cauldron, out of which they produce a beautiful shimmering scarf. As the witches and the mist disperse, James enters, searching for the sylphide. She, however, continually eludes him and he is further confused by the presence of so many similar sister sylphides. He explains his plight to Madge, who offers him the scarf, instructing him to wrap it around the sylphide so that she will be unable to fly away. James does this, but the sylphide's wings fall to the ground and she dies. Her body is carried aloft and, while James lies forlorn, the wedding procession of Effie and Gurn passes in the distance.

It was, however, not only the theme that accounted for the success of this ballet: Filippo Taglioni's skill in choreographing a work to showcase his daughter Marie and her particular dancing style should not be overlooked. The effortlessness of her dancing allowed her to embody the otherworldliness of the sylphide with greater ease. Although this was not the first time pointe work had been seen in a ballet, it was the first time that it fully established itself and became a means to an end, the ballerina rising on to pointe to emphasize the ethereal, intangible nature of the sylphide.

Dance and choreography were not alone in their contribution to the success of *La Sylphide*: costumes, set, and lighting also played their role. The white diaphanous calf-length dresses with tight-fitting bodices, designed by Eugène Lami, became the uniform of the *ballet blanc* (the supernatural ballet) reflecting the lightness and fluidity in the fabric as well as the dance, and the ghostly gas lighting effectively mirrored the otherworldliness of the sylphides.

The Ballet of the Nuns in Giacomo Meyerbeer's opera *Robert le Diable* (1831) was *La Sylphide*'s immediate predecessor. It had also used spectral gas lighting and long white dresses, and inspired lead tenor Adolphe Nourrit to write the libretto for *La Sylphide*, basing it loosely on Charles Nodier's *Trilby, ou le Lutin D'Argaïl* (*Trilby, or the Imp of Argail*, 1822), a tale of a male sprite who falls in love with a Scottish fisherman's wife.

Although *La Sylphide* did much to promote the ascendancy of the ballerina, critics often consider James pivotal. As Susan Au observes, James is often perceived as representing "the Romantic artist, restless, discontent with the world as it is, and filled with inchoate longings." The sylphide could then be said to represent James's desire in feminine guise, his unattainable ideal.

La Sylphide was hugely successful and was produced throughout Europe, often with Marie Taglioni in the title role. Many choreographers staged their own versions, the most important being the 1836 production by August Bournonville in Copenhagen to a new score by Herman Løvenskjold. Bournonville's version, with himself and Lucile Grahn in the principal roles, is noted for its drama and also for the equality between the male and female dancer; an equality almost unheard of during the nineteenth-century reign of the ballerina. Most revivals have been based on this version, much of Taglioni's original choreography having been lost. It has been in the repertoire of the Royal Danish Ballet ever since and successful productions have been staged by Marius Petipa and Pierre Lacotte (after Taglioni), and Elsa Marianne von Rosen, Harald Lander, Erik Bruhn, Hans Brenaa, Peter Schaufuss, and Peter Martins (after Bournonville). Much has been changed, added, and removed over the years, but nothing can take away from the impact that *La Sylphide* had at that time, paving the way for the most famous Romantic ballet, *Giselle* (1841).

SHONA M. ALLAN

Work

La Sylphide, 1832. Ballet in two acts. Choreography by Filippo Taglioni. Music by Jean-Madeleine Schneitzhoeffer. Libretto by Adolphe Nourrit. Set by Pierre Ciceri and costumes by Eugène Lami. First production at the Théâtre de l'Academie Royale de Musique, Paris, on March 12, 1832, with Marie Taglioni (La Sylphide), Joseph Mazilier (James), Lise Noblet (Effie).

Bibliography

Adair, Christy. *Women and Dance: Sylphs and Sirens*. New York: New York University Press, 1992.

Au, Susan. *Ballet and Modern Dance*. New York: Thames and Hudson, 1988.

———. "*La Sylphide*." In *International Encyclopedia of Dance*, vol. 6, pp. 57–59. Edited by Selma Jeanne Cohen. Oxford: Oxford University Press, 1998.

Banes, Sally. *Dancing Women: Female Bodies on Stage*. London: Routledge, 1998.

Beaumont, Cyril W. *Complete Book of Ballets*. London: Putnam, 1937.

Bournonville, August. "*La Sylphide*." Translated by Patricia McAndrew. In *Dance as a Theatre Art*. 2d ed., pp. 77–85. Edited by Selma Jeanne Cohen. Princeton, N.J.: Princeton Book Company, 1992.

Foster, Susan Leigh. *Choreography and Narrative: Ballet's Staging of Story and Desire*. Bloomington: Indiana University Press, 1996.

Gautier, Théophile. "Farewell Performance of Marie Taglioni." In *The Romantic Ballet as Seen by Théophile Gautier*. Translated by Cyril W. Beaumont. New York: Dance Horizons, 1973.

Guest, Ivor. *The Ballet of the Second Empire*. London: Pitman, 1974.

———. *The Romantic Ballet in Paris*. 2d ed. London: Dance Books, 1980.

Mason, Francis, ed. *Balanchine's Complete Stories of the Great Ballets*. Garden City, N.Y.: Doubleday, 1954.

Moore, Lilian. "*La Sylphide*: Epitome of the Romantic Ballet." *Dance Magazine*, (March 1965), 42–47.

SYMBOL AND ALLEGORY

Allegory first began to be considered as a literary genre rather than as a rhetorical figure in Enlightenment aesthetics. With the notable exception of Johann Joachim Winckelmann, who labeled as allegorical the numinous ideality he discerned in ancient Greek art, Enlightenment critics conceived of allegory as a narrative that refers to a meaning outside itself, just as, according to Lockean psychology, the mind organizes within itself ideas derived from impressions of the external world. Because allegory communicates by what Jean-Baptiste Dubos, in his influential *Réflexions critiques sur la poésie et sur la peinture* (*Critical Reflections on Poetry and Painting*, 1719), invidiously designated "artificial signs," it risks confusing or deceiving the reader—that is, it risks mimicking madness—unless the narrative it presents to the eye is strictly and transparently separate from the meaning it presents to the intellect. Hence the widespread disapproval, among eighteenth-century critics, of John Milton's inclusion of the characters Sin and Death in the nonallegorical narrative of *Paradise Lost*, and the widespread confinement of allegory, among eighteenth-century poets, to didactic and satirical literature.

It was this Enlightenment conception of allegory from which Goethe and the painter Heinrich Meyer first distinguished the symbol in jointly planned but separately written essays of 1797–98, each titled "Über die Gegenstände der bildenden Kunst" ("On the Subjects of Figurative Art"). Unlike Goethe, Meyer published his essay in which, by identifying symbolic art as unifying expression and meaning, he implicitly claimed for the symbol the status of "natural signs." (Dubos, referring specifically to painting, had denied natural signs to be signs at all, in the strict sense of the word, because they place "nature itself before our eyes.") Goethe's later, better-known distinctions between symbol and allegory (e.g., in *Maxims and Reflections*) follow chronologically and conceptually the more theoretically significant elaborations by Friedrich Wilhelm Joseph von Schelling, Friedrich Ast, K. W. F. Solger, and the classicist Friedrich Creuzer. In England, perhaps influenced by a passing reference in August Wilhelm von Schlegel's *Vorlesungen über dramatische*

Kunst und Literatur (*Lectures on Dramatic Art and Literature*, 1811), Samuel Taylor Coleridge opposed symbol and allegory in terms similar to those used by his German contemporaries.

Though probably derived from Immanuel Kant's *Critique of Judgment* (in which "the symbolic" is distinguished from "the schematic") and unquestionably introduced in discussions of art, the Romantic symbol was neither exclusively, nor even primarily, an aesthetic concept. Its opposition to allegory, a concept that remained largely confined to aesthetics, is therefore misleading, fostering the impression that the Romantics sought either to describe a distinct form of figurative expression or to disguise authentically allegorical practice with self-mystified theory. In Schelling's lectures on art (delivered 1802–3 and 1804–5), we encounter a remarkable recursive taxonomy in which the genus *symbol* is opposed to the genus *allegory*, and yet subdivided into the species *symbol* and *allegory*. That Schelling conceived the genus to be capacious enough to include itself and its opposite suggests that he was concerned less with maintaining the opposition itself—and hence less with identifying separate instances of symbolism and allegory—than with promoting the concept of the symbol and extending its applicability to the whole of reality. Thus he designated nature and art, ancient myth and modern poetry alike as symbolic. Like Goethe, who in a letter of April 27, 1818, proclaimed that "everything that happens is a symbol," Schelling used the concept of the inherently and inexhaustibly meaningful symbol as the theoretical justification of a disposition to discover meaning precisely where it was not intuitively evident. Naturalizing the symbol as a mode of representation in which, so Schelling claimed, "meaning is simultaneously being itself," was the prerequisite to making nature symbolic—a goal that Coleridge and Novalis also affirmed. In *The Statesman's Manual* (1816) and *Aids to Reflection* (1825), Coleridge characteristically encapsulated this semiotics of identity in a neologism, defining the symbol as *tautegorical* ("i.e. expressing the *same* subject but with a *difference*"), in explicit contradistinction to *allegorical* ("i.e. expressing a *different* subject but with a resemblance"). Much later, Schelling himself adopted Coleridge's term, paying tribute to its creator in his lectures on mythology (1842).

In order to accomplish the intellectual sleight-of-hand of equating meaning with being, both Coleridge and Schelling resorted to a metaphysics of participation, according to which a whole can be fully represented in one of its parts, like the universe in Gottfried Wilhelm Leibniz's monads. That is, the symbol must be the same ontologically as its referent because it is a part of its referent, and—what is not an equivalent statement—the referent must be the same as its symbol because it is manifested wholly in the symbol. "True natural philosophy is comprized in the science and language of *symbols*," Coleridge explained in *The Statesman's Manual*, merging science with aesthetics: "The power delegated to nature is all in every part: and by a symbol I mean, not a metaphor or allegory or any other figure of speech or form of fancy, but an actual and essential part of that, the whole of which it represents. . . . The genuine naturalist is a dramatic poet in his own line." Schelling found it equally easy to dissolve the distinction between art and nature in his discussions of the symbol, for the principle of representation *pars pro toto* (the entire universe manifesting itself fully in each organism) had been fundamental to his *Naturphilosophie*, worked out in the late 1790s, even before he turned his attention to aesthetic matters. In Ast's case the concept of the synecdochical symbol served an important (if not fully acknowledged) hermeneutic function, allowing him to claim, in the *Grundlinien der Grammatik, Hermeneutik und Kritik* (*Fundamentals of Grammar, Hermeneutics, and Criticism*, 1810) that the "spirit of antiquity" (*Geist des Altertums*) could be deduced from an individual ancient text.

Creuzer, too, assimilated the concept of the symbol to the study of Greek antiquity, but more originally and controversially than his predecessors. The introduction to his *Symbolik und Mythologie der alten Völker* (*Symbolism and Mythology of Ancient Peoples*, 1810–12, rev. 1819–21) added temporality to the points of distinction between symbol and allegory: the symbol presents a "momentary totality" (*momentane Totalität*), allegory the "progress through a series of moments" (*Fortschritt in einer Reihe von Momenten*).

Important as the concept of the symbol itself was in Romantic thought, its opposition to allegory was not widely observed.

Thus, Friedrich Schlegel used the terms synonymously, Schopenhauer treated the symbol as a species of allegory, and G. W. F. Hegel categorized the symbolic and allegorical not as antithetical, but as geographically and historically distinct forms of art. In his dialogue *Erwin* (1815), Solger adopted the Romantic conception of the symbol as "the deep and inseparable fusion of the universal and the particular in one and the same reality," but he rejected the opposition of symbol and allegory in favor of a more nuanced (or at least less clear) distinction: appearance and idea are unified and at rest in the symbol, but in motion in allegory.

NICHOLAS HALMI

See also **Aesthetics and Art Criticism; Coleridge, Samuel Taylor; German Idealism: Its Philosophical Legacy; German Romanticism: Its Literary Legacy; Goethe, Johann Wolfgang von; Literary Criticism: Germany; Schelling, Friedrich Wilhelm Joseph von; Schlegel, August Wilhelm von; Solger, Karl Wilhelm Ferdinand**

Bibliography

Adams, Hazard. *Philosophy of the Literary Symbolic*. Tallahassee: Florida State University Press, 1983.

Benjamin, Walter. *Ursprung des deutschen Trauerspiels*. In *Gesammelte Schriften*, edited by Rolf Tiedemann and Hermann Schweppenhäuser, vol. 1. Frankfurt: Suhrkamp, 1972.

De Man, Paul. "The Rhetoric of Temporality." In *Blindness and Insight*. 2d ed. Minneapolis: University of Minnesota Press, 1983.

Gadamer, Hans-Georg. "Symbol und Allegorie." in *Umanesimo e simbolismo*. Edited by Enrico Castelli. Padua: Milani, 1958.

Halmi, Nicholas. "An Anthropological Approach to the Romantic Symbol," *European Romantic Review* 3 (1993): 13–33.

Sørensen, Bengt Algot, ed. *Allegorie und Symbol: Texte zur Theorie des dichterischen Bildes im 18. und frühen 19. Jahrhundert*. Frankfurt: Athenäum, 1972.

———. *Symbol und Symbolismus in den ästhetischen Theorien des 18. Jahrhunderts und der deutschen Romantik*. Copenhagen: Munksgaard, 1963.

Titzmann, Michael. "Allegorie und Symbol im Denksystem der Goethezeit." In *Formen und Funktionen der Allegorie*. Edited by Walter Haug. Stuttgart: Metzler, 1979.

Todorov, Tzvetan. *Théories du symbole*. Paris: Seuil, 1977.

SYMPHONIE FANTASTIQUE 1830

Symphony by Hector Berlioz

Since its premiere in December 1830, Hector Berlioz's program symphony has become an important landmark of musical Romanticism. Its music creates a stunning impact, utilizing an exceptionally large orchestra for both sonic power and a kaleidoscopic array of tone color. The *Symphonie fantastique* represents Berlioz's first attempt to infuse the genre of the symphony with increased dramatic power drawn from literature, in this case through an explanatory and narrative program to be read before hearing the piece. Programmatic instrumental music was not a new idea, but the length, detail, and drama of Berlioz's program and the complexity of its interconnection with the music makes

the *Symphonie fantastique* stand apart from both its immediate predecessors and most subsequent program symphonies.

In quintessential Romantic fashion, Berlioz placed himself as the subject of his composition, which he called *Épisode de la vie d'un artiste* (*Episode from the Life of an Artist*). In later life, however, he almost always referred to the symphony as *Symphonie fantastique*, and its original autobiographical title fell into disuse. In the first movement, "Reveries, Passions," a "young musician" is smitten with the *vague des passions* described in François-Auguste-René de Chateaubriand's autobiographical novel *René* (1805). This emotional turbulence centers around "the beloved," a reference to the composer's infatuation with Shakespearean actress Harriet Smithson. The program associates the beloved with a musical theme, the *idée fixe*. This is introduced near the beginning of the first movement and recurs in abbreviated form throughout the rest of the work. In the second movement, "A Ball," the artist sees the beloved amid the tumult of a grand waltz. The third movement, "Scene in the Country," portrays a mood of abject melancholy, representing the artist's frustration in failing to attract the beloved's attention. In a fit of despair, the artist poisons himself with opium, but miscalculates the dosage, plunging himself into a surrealistic nightmare for the final two movements. In the fourth, "March to the scaffold," he imagines that he has killed his beloved, and had been found, tried, and condemned to the guillotine. The final movement, "Dream of a Witches' Sabbath," represents an after-death experience in which ghouls and goblins are assembled for his funeral. Shockingly, the beloved arrives as a witch to lead the fiendish orgy. Here the composer distorts the *idée fixe* through rhythm, pitch, and timbre, a significant musical touchstone for later Romantic composers such as Franz Liszt, who adopted the technique of "thematic transformation."

Musically, the fifth is the most explicitly narrative movement. Its program, especially in its earliest versions, closely follows the sequence of events in Victor Hugo's 1825 ballad *La Ronde du sabbat* (*The Sabbath Round–Dance*), in which infernal demons, led by the devil, gather at an abandoned monastery to celebrate a witches' sabbath. Louis Boulanger's engraving of the scene, which Hugo published as the frontispiece for his *Odes et ballades* starting with the fourth edition (1828), provides a spectacular visual overview of the scene. Berlioz's music is equally astonishing. Beginning with the "weird noises" described at the outset of the ballad, it then conjures up Hugo's sacrilegious mockery of Roman Catholic ritual by quoting the traditional *Dies irae* sung at the Requiem Mass. To represent the circling movement of the witches' round dance, Hugo constantly returns to a two-line refrain, while Boulanger visually depicts a massive, swirling vortex of figures. For his part, Berlioz surprisingly turns to the highly academic form of the fugue and uses the constant entry and reentry of the fugal subject to suggest the circling motion of the witches. The real musical tour de force is a contrapuntal combination of the *Dies irae* melody with the tune of the witches' round dance at the end of the movement, a feat to which the program draws conspicuous attention.

Berlioz wrote that he initially conceived the *Symphonie* under the spell of having read Johann Wolfgang von Goethe's *Faust*, and scholars have identified several other literary works that may have shaped its creation. The term *fantastique*, however, links the symphony with the literary genre that was much in vogue at the time. E. T. A. Hoffmann's *Fantasiestücke* had just appeared in French translation as *Contes fantastiques*, and in November 1830, just one month before the symphony's première, Charles Nodier published his seminal essay "Du fantastique en littérature" in the *Revue de Paris*. The final movements of the *Symphonie* offer a superb musical realization of the darker, Gothic side of the fantastic, often called the *frénétique* (frenetic). The fourth movement, in fact, shows affinities to a signature literary work in this style, Charles Nodier's short novel *Smarra, ou, Les démons de la nuit* (1821). Like Berlioz's artist, Nodier's protagonist experiences a surrealistic nightmare, dreaming that he is accused of murder, condemned to death, and beheaded. Berlioz further

"La Ronde du Sabbat" ("The Sabbath Round–Dance") from Victor Hugo's *Odes et ballades*. Engraving by Louis Boulanger. Reprinted courtesy of AKG London.

explored the *frénétique* in pieces like the "Brigand's Scene" in *Lélio* and the "Orgy of the Brigands," the final movement in his next program symphony, *Harold en Italie*. Moving in tandem with writers from the period, however, he later turns to the *merveilleux* (marvelous) and the *féérique* (fairylike), gentler sides of the fantastic that can seen in pieces such as the "Queen Mab" scherzo from *Roméo et Juliette*.

After its premiere, Berlioz conducted the *Symphonie* at least annually in concerts at the Paris Conservatory and, beginning in 1842–43, often included it in his European concert tours. He continued to make a substantial number of revisions and did not allow the orchestral score and parts to be published until 1845, after he had settled on a definitive text and personally established an authoritative performance tradition. In 1831, Berlioz completed a second part to the *Épisode de la vie d'un artiste*, which he titled *Le retour de la vie* (*The Return Life*; later titled *Lélio*). He envisioned that the two compositions would be performed in tandem to make a "grand concert dramatique." For this special performance situation, Berlioz altered his original program for the *Symphonie* to make the entire work an opium dream, leading to physical and spiritual reawakening in *Lélio*. Over time, however, *Lélio* has been seldom performed, alone or with the *Symphonie*, partly due to its unusual mixture of monologue and melodrama.

The positive reception of the *Symphonie fantastique* in the years following its premiere was due, in part, to the efforts of

Franz Liszt and Robert Schumann. Liszt, who attended the premiere, published a piano transcription in 1834, long before the full score and parts were available. It was Liszt's piano transcription that caught the attention of Schumann, who used it as the basis for his extensive and enthusiastic review in the *Neue Zeitschrift für Musik*.

The engaging music of the *Symphonie fantastique* and its colorful, idiosyncratic program have made it a favorite for modern audiences; often, however, it is the only work by Berlioz with which they are familiar. History and music appreciation books continue to showcase the *Symphonie fantastique* as the prototype of the Romantic program symphony, even though its detailed and explicit written program makes it somewhat atypical.

GREGORY W. HARWOOD

Bibliography

Banks, Paul. "Coherence and Diversity in the *Symphonie fantastique*," *19th Century Music* 8 (1984): 37–43.

Berger, Christian. *Phantastik als Konstruktion: Hector Berlioz's "Symphonie fantastique."* Kassel: Bärenreiter, 1983.

Clavaud, Monique. *Hector Berlioz: Visages d'un masque. Littérature et musique dans la "Symphonie fantastique" et "Lélio."* Lyon: Jardin de Dolly, 1980.

Dömling, Wolfang. *Symphonie fantastique*. Munich: W. Fink, 1985.

Hugo, Victor. *Odes et ballades*. 4th ed. Paris: Hector Bossagne, 1828. Translated by A. Baillot as *Odes and Ballads Hugo's Works*, vol. 19. Edited by Alfred Barbou, 1892.

Nodier, Charles. "Du fantastique en littérature," *Revue de Paris* (November 1830). Reprinted in *Oeuvres de Charles Nodier*. Vol. 5. 1832.

———. *Smarra, ou, Les démons de la nuit: Songes romantiques traduits de l'esclavon du comte Maxime Odin*. Paris: chez Ponthieu, 1821. Reprinted in *Oeuvres de Charles Nodier*. vol. 3. 1832. Translated as *"Smarra" and "Trilby"* by Judith Landry, with an introduction by John Clute. Sawtry, England: Dedalus, 1993.

Schneider, Marcel. *La littérature fantastique en France*. Paris: Payard, 1985.

Temperley, Nicholas. "The *Symphony fantastique* and Its Program," *Musical Quarterly* 57 (1971): 593–608.

SYMPHONY

The prevailing attitude in late-eighteenth-century Vienna was that the symphonic genre had already realized its full potential. The great masterworks of Franz Joseph Haydn and Wolfgang Amadeus Mozart represented the classical symphonic ideal, and the accomplishments of the Viennese school were historical fact. Every European composer spoke and understood the common symphonic language of Vienna.

However, ongoing cultural changes had begun to alter the composer's position regarding his source of income, his craft, and himself. As the new century dawned, the symphony composer was gradually evolving from an eighteenth-century artisan crafting a product to the divinely inspired artist creating a masterpiece. With the demise of the earlier patronage system, a tradition of public concerts arose as composers scrambled for a new means of support. The symphonist no longer had an employer to honor and aggrandize; the new Romantic composer wrote for self-glorification. Thus, the symphony assumed added meaning and weight, becoming the most ambitious of the instrumental genres, while self-imposed demands and requirements constrained the symphonist's prospect of artistic freedom.

A new awareness of history, which began to flourish in the nineteenth century, exerted additional pressure on the aspiring Romantic symphonist. For the first time, music from earlier generations was receiving notice. Older composers and styles, lately rediscovered, were beginning to occupy a position in the mainstream. Music of past generations now routinely appeared on the concert program, in direct competition with freshly composed pieces. Whereas newly composed music had heretofore been presumed an improvement over the old-fashioned styles, the emerging view was that older music was at least as worthy and might even be superior. Along with the new respect for history came a propensity for introspection on the part of the composer. The Romantic composer came to view his own works as a legacy that future generations would evaluate in comparison with the music of other generations.

The Romantic symphonist's shining example and crushing nemesis was Ludwig van Beethoven. Beethoven's life span (1770–1827) bridged the late classical and early Romantic style periods. Beethoven took the classical symphony, already presumed developed to its greatest possibility, and reinvigorated it, bringing it into the new century and setting the standard for the Romantics. Beethoven enlarged and magnified the proportions of the symphonic form. His innovations included longer introductions and developments; his lengthened codas approached the weight of a second development section. He redefined the role of the last movement from a light, breezy finale to a new center of gravity, a culmination. He eliminated that courtly vestige, the minuet, and replaced it with the scherzo. His introduction of trombones, piccolo, contrabassoon, voices, and his increased use of dynamics added heft to the ensemble. Beethoven experimented with cyclical coherence between the movements in two ways, by blurring the boundaries between movements and by reintroducing thematic material in later movements.

The Romantics considered Beethoven's Ninth Symphony (1824), the only symphony written during his final stylistic period (1816–27), to be the absolute symphonic zenith. The perceived futility of writing in "Beethoven's genre" caused most of the nineteenth-century composers to shy away from the symphony for fear of Beethoven's lengthy shadow and in apprehension of the inevitable comparisons. Thus, with few exceptions, most of the Romantic composers delayed symphony composition until later in their respective careers. Hence, the Romantic era witnessed a decline in the total numbers of symphonies written by any given composer, while each symphony assumed a relatively greater significance.

The coherent thread of the symphony, a genre that had arisen uniformly across Europe during the eighteenth century, unraveled in the nineteenth century. The more conservative German Romantics adhered to the Viennese ideal, while the radical French moved in the direction of programmatic symphonies, based on literary sources. Moreover, nationalist composers, from the outlying regions of Europe, turned to their native musics for symphonic inspiration.

We begin to witness the combination of classical symphonic architecture with Romantic lyricism in Franz Schubert, Beethoven's first successor. Schubert's symphonies exhibit the innovations that would soon become predominant Romantic techniques, expressiveness in instrumental scoring, a penchant for setting secondary themes in unexpected keys, and the use of woodwinds for thematic presentation; motivic development, the hallmark of classical construction, transmutes into the lingering, eloquent theme. Felik Mendelssohn and Robert Schumann, a generation after Schubert, continue to infuse the classical four-movement structure with their own Romantic refinements. Mendelssohn, one of the few to attempt symphonic composition while still in his teenage years, adhered closely to the Beethovenian model. Schumann, a celebrated music critic as well as composer, wrote about the symphony for many years, decrying the problem of the Beethoven model versus the necessity for a new symphonic prototype, before finally writing a symphony of his own.

Hector Berlioz, in the vanguard of the radical Romantic symphonists, cultivated both the program symphony and his own reputation as a revolutionary composer with his *Symphonie fantastique* (1830). This work enlarged the orchestral ensemble and increased symphonic proportions to gigantic dimensions. Berlioz demonstrated unprecedented thematic unity through use of the idée fixe, an extended theme that appears in different guises in each of the five movements. A lengthy narrative or program, probably inspired by a tempestuous love affair, supplements the composition. Franz Liszt combined the concert symphonies of Beethoven and Mendelssohn with the programmatic symphonies of Berlioz and propelled the symphony in a new direction. His "symphonic poems," based on a literary or pictorial inspiration, were orchestral compositions not necessarily in the classical style. Liszt's innovations, encompassing harmonic experimentation and use of chromaticism, lyricism, and counterpoint, exerted influence on the balance of the nineteenth century and well into the twentieth.

The late nineteenth century saw Johannes Brahms return to the classical four-movement symphonic style, rescuing the genre from its anticipated natural decline and its being supplanted by the symphonic poem. Anton Bruckner and Gustav Mahler also embraced the genuine symphonic form while beginning the experimentation with atonality that would come to define twentieth-century music. The nationalist composers, including Mikhail Borodin, Antonin Dvořák, and Pyotr Tchaikovsky, helped convey the outlying regions into the mainstream of the European music tradition.

NANCY F. GARF

Bibliography

Bonds, Mark Evan. *After Beethoven: Imperatives of Originality in the Symphony.* Cambridge, Mass.: Harvard University Press, 1996.

Cuyler, Louise. *The Symphony.* New York: Harcourt Brace Jovanovich, 1973.

Holoman, D. Kern, ed. *The Nineteenth-Century Symphony.* New York: Schirmer, 1997.

Lang, Paul Henry, ed. *The Symphony 1800–1900.* New York: W. W. Norton, 1969.

Stedman, Preston. *The Symphony.* Englewood Cliffs, N.J.: Prentice-Hall, 1979.

SYMPHONY NO. 9, "ODE TO JOY"

Symphony by Ludwig van Beethoven

Doubtless one of the most influential and monumental works of Western music, Ludwig van Beethoven's Ninth Symphony (premiered Vienna, May 7, 1824) has become firmly associated with the supreme ideals of a universal humankind—due in no small measure to Johann Christoph Friedrich von Schiller's poem set to music in the final movement—and continues to be performed on ceremonial occasions and mass celebrations in various parts of the world. Japan and Germany have a tradition of grand performances of the work on New Year's Eve, the fall of the Berlin Wall in 1989 was sealed with an "Ode to Freedom" (Leonard Bernstein), and Beethoven's music of the "Ode" itself, taken out of its symphonic context, has been employed, quite diversely, as the international anthem of the League of Nations (1933), the NATO anthem (1967), the European anthem (Council of Europe, 1972), and the theme for the 1998 European Football Championship.

The sheer scale and complexity of the work was unprecedented in the symphonic repertoire, and it is understandable that legends surrounding the work arose almost immediately after the first performance, which was conducted by the deaf composer. While several features of the work are reminiscent of other works by Beethoven, notably the Choral Fantasy, the *Eroica* Symphony, or *Fidelio*, the musical structure of the work exhibits unusual—or, to perpetuate the mystique of the work, enigmatic—features at various levels, which became a veritable compendium of later nineteenth-century symphonic writing. The work opens, as though ex nihilo, with string tremolos and harmonically ambiguous open fifths. In the later nineteenth century, these effects became almost a cliché of Romantic music (found for instance in several of Anton Bruckner's symphonies and Richard Wagner's *Rheingold* prelude). The second subject areas of both outer movements are in the harmonically remote submediant, B-flat. The conventional sequence of symphonic movements is changed by placing the slow movement after the scherzo (as alluded to in Gustav Mahler's Sixth Symphony). The last movement includes such diverse and frequently imitated elements as recalls of the main themes of the previous three movements (Hector Berlioz's symphony *Harold en Italie*), the so-called *Schreckensfanfare* ("fanfare of terror," Wagner's term), followed by a recitative and the "Song of Joy" (Johannes Brahms's Symphony no. 1), and extended choral sections (Felix Mendelssohn's Symphony no. 2 [*Lobgesang*]). The form of the final movement is particularly resistant to conventional formal patterns and remains subject to some controversy up to this day.

However, by far the most far-reaching consequences, not only in terms of the exceptionally well-covered history of compositional influence but also in music aesthetics at large, arise from the addition of vocal parts to the orchestral texture. The two main camps of nineteenth-century music aesthetics—the formalist-classicist "Brahmins" versus the programmatic-progressive "Wagnerians," who both claimed Beethoven for their side—stood firmly opposed in their judgment of the Ninth Symphony and its significance with regard to the notion of absolute music. On the one hand, Wagner used the work in his evolutionary view of music history explored in the Zurich writings, above all *Opera and Drama* (1851). With Beethoven's Ninth, the symphony had exhausted itself as a purely instrumental genre. In introducing greater means—the human voice—to attain adequate expression of its melodic essence, Beethoven had, in Wagner's view, anticipated the music drama. Speaking for the "Brahmins," on the other hand, Eduard Hanslick was critical of the vocal finale. For him it represented no more than "a gigantic shadow . . . cast by a gigantic body." Since Hanslick regards instrumental music already as "heightened language," it compromises the status of music—rather than elevating it—to set words to it.

Much analytical attention has been given to the setting of Schiller's poem "An die Freude" (the term "Ode" appears to be Beethoven's own addition, and may reflect the new structure the poem receives in his rearrangement of the verses), not least because the apparently concrete significance of the words would seem to provide a reference point for any interpretation. The poem, first published in 1785, was one of Schiller's most popular works, and had been set to music on numerous occasions. Beethoven himself had planned to set the original, radically revolutionary version of "An die Freude" since 1792, but in the symphony Beethoven used Schiller's far more moderate revised version of 1803 as the basis of the last movement. The political use of the symphony—which has on occasion been turned against its overtly universal humanitarian character as an affirmation of German, and indeed French, nationalism—can be related to the political content of Schiller's poem. Soon after its premiere, the symphony was recognized as a covert symbol of freedom in the novella *Das Musikfest oder die Beethovener* (1838)

by Wolfgang Robert Griepenkerl. In this sense, modern versions that stress the political content of the work, such as Bernstein's 1989 adaptation or the controversial performance (Simon Rattle and the Vienna Philharmonic Orchestra, 2000) on the site of the former concentration camp Mauthausen, have early historical (if fictional) precedents.

The Ninth Symphony has long been recognized as an example—indeed, the paradigm—of the sublime in music, not least because of the monumental proportions, the ambiguous musical structure, and the utopian content of the work. However, critics have begun to view the problem of representation in the Ninth in a different light: the work does not resist interpretation so much as rather to invite and then overwhelm it with a welter of referents. No other musical work in the Western canon has been adapted, appropriated, and domesticated with greater ease for a multitude of different functions and meanings than has the Ninth. Yet its forever "unconsummated symbols," according to Nicholas Cook, ensure that the symphony, despite its affirmative character, continues to resist any full and definitive interpretation.

ALEXANDER REHDING

Bibliography

Buch, Esteban. *Beethoven's Ninth: A Political History.* Tr. Richard Miller. Chicago: University of Chicago Press, 2003.

Cook, Nicholas. *Beethoven: Symphony No. 9.* Cambridge: Cambridge University Press, 1993.

Eichhorn, Andreas. *Beethovens Neunte Symphonie: Die Geschichte ihrer Aufführung und Rezeption.* Kassel: Bärenreiter, 1993.

Levy, David Benjamin. *Beethoven: The Ninth Symphony.* New York: Schirmer, 1995.

Solie, Ruth. "Beethoven as a Secular Humanist: Ideology and the Ninth Symphony in Nineteenth-Century Criticism." In *Explorations in Music, the Arts and Ideas: Essays in Honor of Leonard B. Meyer.* Edited by Eugene Narmour and Ruth Solie. Stuyvesant, N.Y.: Pendragon Press, 1988.

Taruskin, Richard. "Resisting the Ninth." In *Text and Act: Essays on Music and Performance.* Oxford: Oxford University Press, 1995.

Treitler, Leo. "History, Criticism, and Beethoven's Ninth Symphony." In *Music and the Historical Imagination.* Cambridge, Mass.: Harvard University Press, 1989.

SZÉCHENYI, ISTVÁN 1791–1860

Hungarian statesman, political writer, and diarist

Count István Széchenyi was born into a wealthy family of pro-Hapsburg Hungarian aristocrats; his father Ferenc donated his art collection to the Hungarian nation, thereby creating the basis for the National Museum. As a young man Széchenyi fought in the Napoleonic Wars, traveled extensively in western Europe and, generally speaking, lived the carefree life of a young aristocrat with no great social obligations. He spoke several languages fluently, but in his early youth Hungarian was not one of these: even with his father he corresponded in German. The great

change in his reputation and lifestyle occurred in the autumn of 1825 when (partly to impress Crescence Zichy, with whom he had fallen in love and whom he married nine years later) he addressed the diet in Hungarian and offered the equivalent of a yearly income of his estates toward the founding of the Hungarian Academy of Sciences. This gesture turned him at once into a public figure and a hero of the reform movement. Until then mainly known as an admirer of English stables and a promoter of racehorses in Hungary, Széchenyi now harnessed his energy toward politicoeconomic treatises serving the cause of reform.

The first of these, *Hitel* (*Credit*, 1830) analyzed the legal and financial reasons why Hungary could not develop rapidly enough, bidding the ruling classes to follow the English example and make concessions to the less privileged strata of society, if for no other reason than to avoid revolution. *Hitel* was greeted with enthusiasm but it also provoked protests. Széchenyi's next work, *Világ* (*Light*, 1831) was a reply to criticism to his previous book, reiterating the view that only the abolition of serfdom could secure the future development of Hungary. Political developments in 1831 (the great cholera epidemic and the rebellion of Slovak peasants in northern Hungary) justified the urgency of reforms, and this moved Széchenyi to write *Stadium* (*The State of Affairs*), where, addressing the central government in Vienna, he summed up his plans of reform in twelve specific propositions. This was deemed too radical by Klemens Fürst von Metternich, so the book was printed only in Leipzig in 1833 and smuggled into Hungary.

Széchenyi had literary ambitions as a young man; in 1820 he planned to translate Lord Byron's *Childe Harold's Pilgrimage* (1812–18), although it is not quite clear whether he meant to do so into German or Hungarian. He felt a great affinity with Byron and admired William Shakespeare, and he met François-Auguste-René de Chateaubriand in London. His most personal—and, for the modern reader, most interesting—literary work is his *Napló* (*Diary*) kept from 1814 to his death in 1860, but published in its most complete selection in Hungarian only in 1978. Széchenyi's diary was written mostly in German but the text is interspersed with English, French, and, of course, Hungarian passages or quotes. Although the text was censored after his death by his secretary, Antal Tasner, ("compromising" sentences or passages were deleted from the manuscript), *Napló* shows us an enterprising young man who, after extensive traveling, settles down to serve the cause of reform in his native country with much enthusiasm and dynamism, only to yield to self-recrimination and despondency in later years. Self-directed irony is a salient feature of this diary and this led to the following remark by Mihály Szegedy-Maszák: "The general laws of the formation of a Romantic ironic consciousness make the world visions of Széchenyi and Kierkegaard comparable in a number of respects." As the political situation took a turn for the worse and the peaceful 1848 revolution and its results were threatened by a war between the emperor and Hungary, Széchenyi's mood darkened. "It is clear to me," he wrote in his diary in 1848, "that I bear the greatest responsibility for the general misery . . . that now afflicts Austria and even more so Hungary."

The above self-accusation is rather exaggerated. While it is true that Széchenyi began the reforms that in the end propelled Hungary toward a sharp confrontation with Vienna, responsibility for the final conflict has to be shared between Lajos Kossuth and Metternich, rather than Széchenyi. The latter carried out a number of practical reforms: introduction of steamships on the Danube, the regulation of the River Tisza, improving navigation on all waterways, and the construction of a permanent stone bridge between Buda and Pest. (The Chain Bridge was built by the Scottish engineer Adam Clark, whom Széchenyi invited to Hungary on Marc Isambard Brunel's advice). These exploits earned him the title of "the greatest of all Magyars" given by him by Kossuth, whom he attacked in a pamphlet *Kelet népe*

("People of the East," 1841) for inciting the peasantry to rebellion and paving the way for a clash with Vienna, which would not accept the demands of Hungarian nationalism. In any event, Kossuth's policies prevailed and though Széchenyi first accepted the post of minister of transport in the first independent Hungarian government appointed by the king of Hungary in April 1848, he resigned in September of the same year when a nervous breakdown forced him to withdraw from politics and leave for Vienna.

Széchenyi's following years were spent in the mental asylum of Döbling near Vienna, where he suffered from a severe depression. By 1857 his health improved to the point at which he was able to begin writing again. This resulted in the *Nagy Magyar Szatíra* ("*The Great Hungarian Satire*"), a grand pamphlet on the political situation of the Austrian Empire that remained, however, only in manuscript form. Two years later Széchenyi read Alexander Bach's (anonymously) published propaganda treatise *Rückblick*, an attempt to justify Austria's post-1849 policies of repression. He found Bach's claims fraudulent and answered them in *Ein Blick auf den anonymen "Rückblick"* (*A Glance at an anonymous "Glance Back"*), published in London in 1859. *Ein Blick* contains most of the arguments of *The Great Hungarian Satire* and is written in a vivid, sarcastic style; its publication provoked an official investigation into the authorship of the book and eventually led to Széchenyi's suicide. His works were published in nine volumes only after the 1867 compromise between Austria and Hungary. In the twentieth century he was seen as perhaps the greatest of the Hungarian reformers of his age, whose political objectives often clashed with his fiery temper to make him one of the great unfulfilled Romantic heroes of the Romantic era.

GEORGE GÖMÖRI

Biography

Born in Vienna, September 21, 1791, into an aristocratic family; was educated at Nagycenk and Sopron (Hungary). Joined the imperial army at the age of seventeen, took part in the war against Napoleon Bonaparte in 1813. Visited Italy in 1814, then Paris and London. From 1820 onward spent much time in Hungary. Resigned from the army and took his seat in the diet's upper house; his important initiative at the diet of 1825 marks the traditional beginning of the reform age. Published several books from 1830 to 1841; visited England once again and invited Adam Clark to build the Chain Bridge, which was finished in 1849. In 1836 he married Crescence Zichy, the great love of his life. Was minister of transport in the first independent Hungarian government in 1848, but fled to Vienna in September of same year after a nervous breakdown. From 1849 lived in the mental asylum of Döbling, Austria, first as a genuine patient, later as a political writer who found refuge there. Police investigation into the authorship of his book, published in 1859 in London, and the fear that other compromising material would be found, led to his suicide by shooting on April 8, 1860.

Selected works

Munkái. Vols. 1–9. Edited by Antal Zichy and Béla Majláth, 1884–1896.

Naplói. Vols. 1–6. Edited by Gyula Viszota. 1925–39.

Irói és hirlapírói vitái Kossuth Lajossal. Published by Gyula Viszota. 1927–30.

Napló. Edited by Ambrus Oltványi, Translated by Zoltán Jékely and Miklós Gyorffy. 1978.

Bibliography

Bárány, George. *Stephen Széchenyi and the Awakening of Hungarian Nationalism 1791–1841.* Princeton, N.J.: Princeton University Press, 1968.

Halász, Gábor. "A fiatal Széchenyi." In *Válogatott írásai.* Budapest; Szépirodalmi, 1959.

Czigány, Lóránt. *The Oxford History of Hungarian Literature.* Oxford: Clarendon Press, 1984.

Gergely, András. "Széchenyi István, mint író," *Irodalomtörténeti Közlemények* (1, no. 2 1986).

Horváth, Károly. "Széchenyi és a magyar romantika," *Irodalomtörténeti Közlemények* (1961).

Szegedy-Maszák, Mihály. "Romanticism in Hungary." *A Journey into History: Essays on Hungarian Literature.* Edited by Moses M. Nagy. New York: Peter Lang, 1990.

T

TAGLIONI, FILIPPO 1777–1871, AND MARIE 1804–1884

Italian dancer and choreographer; Italian dancer

The Taglioni family, and especially Filippo and his daughter Marie, exerted an enormous influence on ballet in the eighteenth and nineteenth centuries. Filippo Taglioni was himself an excellent dancer and ballet master, but it was as choreographer of many ballets for his more famous daughter and as her teacher that his real influence can be seen. Although Marie Taglioni was taught in Paris by Jean-François Coulon, as Filippo himself had been, when she arrived in Vienna in 1821 she had to be coached intensively by her father for her debut at the Hoftheater in June 1822, in his *La Réception d'une jeune nymphe à la cour de Terpsichore* (*The Reception of a Young Nymph at the Court of Terpsichore*). It was Filippo Taglioni who instilled in Marie a style that was to make her one of the most famous ballerinas of all time. Her lightness, almost veering on weightlessness, her grace, her fluidity and aerial quality, and her effortlessness allowed her to exude an impression of ethereality: a style which was ideally suited to the portrayal of the fairies, elves, and sylphs who populated ballet from the 1830s.

Filippo Taglioni failed to get Marie an engagement at the Paris Opera in 1824, and it was only after several years, during which both father and daughter danced in Stuttgart, that Marie returned to make her Paris debut on July 23, 1827. It was this performance and the sensation it created that Ivor Guest (1980) calls "the beginning of the golden age of Romantic ballet."

One of the conditions of her contract was that she should only dance to her father's choreography, but this turned out to be a mutually beneficial partnership. Although the success of Filippo Taglioni's ballets was often attributed to Marie, rather than to his extraordinary choreography, his resourcefulness and skill in creating ballets to showcase Marie's qualities is unmistakable. His ballet in Auber's opera *Le Dieu et la Bayadère* (*The God and the Bayadere*, 1830) gave Marie her next triumph, which was soon followed by the *Ballet of the Nuns* in Giacomo Meyerbeer's *Robert le Diable* (1831). There she danced the role of

the leader of the dead nuns, the abbess Helena, in ballet's initial foray into that supernaturalism which had already become so prevalent in Romantic art and literature.

This paved the way for *La Sylphide* (*The Sylphide*, 1832), which Ivor Guest (1980) considered "as momentous a landmark in the chronicles of Romantic art as *The Raft of the Medusa* and *Hernani*." This ballet was the zenith of Filippo Taglioni's career and is the only one which is still regularly performed today.

In the years that followed, Filippo continued to produce new ballets for his daughter, including *Nathalie; ou, La Laitière suisse* (*Nathalie; or the Swiss Milkmaid*, 1832), *La Révolte au Sérail* (*The Revolt in the Serail*, 1833), and *La Fille du Danube* (*The Daughter of the Danube*, 1836).

Success continued as both father and daughter left Paris for Saint Petersburg, where Filippo Taglioni created the ballet with which he had his greatest triumph in Russia, *La Gitana* (1838). This was doubtless because of its story: a young girl is stolen by gypsies in Spain and recovered ten years later in Russia. This ballet gave Marie the opportunity to reveal her proficiency in the fiery Spanish gypsy dances more often associated with Fanny Elssler. In 1839 Marie danced Angela in her father's ballet *L'Ombre* (*The Shadow*), the story of a ghost of a murdered woman who is reunited with her lover in death, and went on to dance in his other Russian ballets, including *Aglaë; ou L'Élève d'amour* (*Aglaia; or the Pupil of Love*, 1841), until Filippo took up a post in Warsaw in 1843 as ballet master and director of the company, and Marie toured Europe.

Marie Taglioni was what might be termed the supreme embodiment of the Romantic ballerina, and it was she who started the trend for ballerina worship as the male dancer was relegated to the ignoble task of supporting act. After her 1822 Viennese debut, where she revealed her ability in various styles of dance, she danced in Munich and Stuttgart, before making her Paris Opera debut in 1827, partnered by her brother Paul. Much of

Marie Taglioni (1804–84) in *La Sylphide*. Engraving by Richard James Lane (1800–72), 1836 (color lithograph). Reprinted courtesy of the Bridgeman Art Library.

this debut performance was on *pointe*, but her effortlessness, fluidity, and weightlessness were revolutionary in making pointe work no longer an end in itself, but an integral part of the beauty and poetry of the dance. Such was the success of this performance that a new verb was coined: *taglioniser*, meaning to dance like Taglioni. She had thus created a new style, characterized by graceful arabesques and floating leaps, giving the impression of flight and otherworldliness. This style, and Marie Taglioni, enjoyed their greatest triumph in *La Sylphide*, a ballet with which she has been associated ever since.

But it was not only in technique that Marie Taglioni broke new ground: the diaphanous dress she wore in *La Sylphide*, with a tight-fitting bodice and a bell-shaped skirt, was the prototype for the tutus still worn by classical ballerinas today. These white costumes of a light fabric, emphasizing the supernatural nature of the ballets' heroines, gave rise to the term for a new kind of ballet, the *ballet blanc*.

If Marie Taglioni represented the ethereal side of Romanticism with her elevation and lightness, her antithesis was to be found in the earthly Romanticism of her greatest rival Fanny Elssler; a contrast that Théophile Gautier famously described in terms of Taglioni as the "Christian" dancer and Elssler the "pagan." Marie's interpretation of the title role in *La Gitana* (1838), however, proved that she was also capable of successful character dancing, considered Elssler's trademark. The Taglioni-Elssler rivalry was not discouraged, for it made good financial sense.

In London in 1845, Jules Perrot choreographed a *Pas de quatre* for her and three other famous ballerinas, namely Fanny Cerrito, Lucile Grahn, and Carlotta Grisi. He succeeded in highlighting each ballerina's strengths without denting their respective egos, and Taglioni's grace, fluidity, and elevation were clear.

After her retirement in 1847, Marie returned to Paris in 1858 to coach Emma Livry and choreographed *Le Papillon* (*The Butterfly* 1860) for her. This ballet enjoyed some success, but Marie's second ballet was never realized because of Livry's untimely death.

Marie remained in Paris during the 1860s as *inspectrice de la danse* and then as *professeur de la classe de perfectionnement*, and just as she had broken new ground with her own technique and style, she instituted many changes at the Paris Opera. It is hardly surprising that, in her school of ballroom dancing and deportment in London, the "Queen of the Romantic ballet" placed great emphasis on gracefulness.

Whatever faults and limitations Filippo and Marie may have had, it is certain that together their impact on Romantic ballet was incisive.

SHONA M. ALLAN

Biography

Filippo Taglioni

Born in Milan, November 5, 1777. Studied in Italy; performed female roles throughout Italy, 1790s. Studied with Jean-François Coulon in Paris, 1799–1802. Debut at the Paris Opéra, 1799. Premier danseur and ballet master, Stockholm, 1802–5. Debut as choreographer in Vienna, 1805. Worked in theaters all over Europe including Berlin, Copenhagen, Kassel, Milan, Munich, and Turin, 1810–19; worked at the Hoftheater, Vienna, 1819 and became ballet master, 1821. Coached daughter Marie, 1821–22; choreographed the ballet in which she made her debut, 1822. Danced in Stuttgart, 1824–28. Moved to Paris, 1828; debut as choreographer in Paris, 1830. Worked in Saint Petersburg, 1837–42. Ballet master and director of ballet company and school in Warsaw, 1843–53. Married Edwige Sofia Karsten in Stockholm, 1803; father of Marie, 1804–1884 and Paul, 1808–1884. Died in Como, September 11, 1871.

Marie Taglioni

Born in Stockholm, April 23, 1804. Studied with Jean-François Coulon in Paris. Studied with her father, in Vienna from 1821 on. Debut at the Hoftheater, Vienna, 1822; danced in Vienna, Munich, and Stuttgart, 1820s. Debut at the Paris Opéra, 1827; danced at the Paris Opéra, 1827–37. Danced in Saint Petersburg, 1837–42. Danced in theaters throughout Europe, including Berlin, London, Milan, Stockholm, Vienna, 1830s and 1840s; returned to Paris, 1858. Debut as choreographer, Paris, 1860; inspectrice de la danse and later professeur de la classe de perfectionnement, Paris Opéra, 1859–70. Ran a school of ballroom dancing and deportment, London, 1870–80. Married Count Gilbert de Voisins, 1832; separated, 1835; two children, Georges Gilbert and Eugénie-Marie-Edwige. Died in Marseilles, April 22, 1884.

Selected Works

Filippo Taglioni

La Réception d'une jeune nymphe à la cour de Terpsichore. 1822.
Le Dieu et la Bayadère. 1830.
Ballet of the Nuns in Meyerbeer's opera *Robert le Diable.* 1831.

La Sylphide. 1832.
La Révolte au Sérail. 1833.
La Fille du Danube. 1836.
La Gitana. 1838.
L'Ombre. 1840.
Aglaë. 1841.

Marie Taglioni
Le Papillon. 1860.

Bibliography

Beaumont, Cyril W. *Complete Book of Ballets.* London: Putnam's, 1937.

Burian, K. V. *The Story of World Ballet.* London: Allan Wingate, 1963.

Gautier, Théophile. "Farewell Performance of Marie Taglioni." In *The Romantic Ballet as Seen by Théophile Gautier.* Translated by Cyril W. Beaumont. New York: Dance Horizons, 1973.

————. *The Ballet of the Second Empire.* London: Pitman, 1974.

————. *The Romantic Ballet in England.* London: Pitman, 1972.

————. *The Romantic Ballet in Paris.* 2nd ed. London: Dance Books, 1980.

Hill, Lorna. *La Sylphide: The Life of Marie Taglioni.* London: Evans Brothers, 1967.

Levinson, André. *Marie Taglioni.* Translated by Cyril W. Beaumont. London: Dance Books, 1977.

Testa, Alberto. "Taglini family" in *International Encyclopedia of Dance.* Edited by Selma Jeanne Cohen. vol. 6, pp. 69–77. Oxford: Oxford University Press, 1998.

Vaillat, Léandre. *La Taglioni, ou la vie d'une danseuse.* Paris: A. Michel, 1942.

Wiley, Roland John. "Images of *La Sylphide*: Two Accounts by a Contemporary Witness of Marie Taglioni's Appearances in St. Petersburg," *Dance Research* 13 (1995): 21–32.

TALES 1831–1849

Collection of short stories by Edgar Allan Poe

While he was also a poet, reviewer, and magazine editor, the collected *Tales* are Edgar Allan Poe's greatest literary achievement. An early American practitioner of the short story at a time when the three-volume novel was reaching the height of its popularity, Poe regarded long narratives as lacking in unity and what he called "totality of effect." The novel, he thought, presented too much material for the mind to comprehend at one time, a limitation that damaged its ability to convey truths. The short story, in contrast, entertained the reader "without excessive and fatiguing exertion" (review of *Night and Morning* [1841]). In less than twenty years, Poe produced a remarkable variety of stories. Some are tales of wild Gothic imagination such as "Berenice" (1835), "Morella" (1835), and "The Assignation" (1844). There are also comic pieces such as "Bon Bon" (1835) and "Loss of Breath" (1835), and adventures such as the prize-winning "MS. Found in Bottle" (1833) and "A Descent into the Maelstrom" (1841). He also established many of the central principles of classic detective fiction in "The Murders in the Rue Morgue" (1841).

Poe wrote the tales for publication in various literary magazines, including *Graham's* and the *Southern Literary Messenger,* and they were later collected as *Tales of the Grotesque and the Arabesque* (1839) and *Tales* (1845). Always a highly prescriptive and forthright critic, his approach to the composition of his stories was rigorous, beginning with the outcome or "solution" and working backward to the motivation. Yet unlike the poetry, the tales rarely show distracting signs of having been created to demonstrate some theoretical point, even though most of them are near-perfect examples of Poe's theories about unity in art. For example, one of the most chilling tales, "The Pit and the Pendulum" (1843), derives at least some of its atmosphere of claustrophobia from descriptive detail and repetition, a kind of linguistic enclosure. This is what Poe called the concentrated effect, in which every part of the story has some relation to the whole. With this in mind, it could be argued that the descriptive repetition and the emotional swings of the narrator are as one with the murderous arc described by the great pendulum of the story's title.

Despite their variety, the tales are usually divided into two categories: the Gothic tales and the "tales of ratiocination." Those in the Gothic category include stories of premature burial, nervous collapse, and medieval torture, and have clear links to the tradition of Matthew Lewis, Ann Radcliffe, and Horace Walpole, although their setting is often in Poe's own time. Their frequent focus on the psychology of the individual, rather than external horrors, takes the genre in a new direction. The Gothic tales abound with solitary individuals, who are set apart from society and looking on in a melancholy, disjointed way; horrors are as much imagined as real, and uncertainty and disillusion are their central moods. The restricted first person perspective of many of the tales, including "The Pit and the Pendulum," "The Black Cat" (1843), "A Cask of Amontillado" (1846), and "William Wilson" (1839), heightens the sense of real psychological disturbance.

Although Poe set many of his stories outside of America (in England, France, and Germany, for example), he was also aware of the Gothic possibilities of his own country. Anticipating the work of American painters such as Frederic Church and the illustrator Porte Crayon, tales such as "The Fall of the House of Usher" (1839) satisfy similarly an interest in impenetrable depths and uncertain footings. The theme of an old family collapsed into madness in a crumbling mansion fits well with the European Gothic tradition. But the landscape in which it takes place bears more than a passing resemblance to the "Great Dismal Swamp" of Virginia, where Poe grew up, and reflects the hesitancy of antebellum literature in choosing between nature as a source of moral insight, and as a symbol of chaos and disorder.

While the tales of horror and Gothic imagination remain some of the most accomplished in the genre, still more significant is Poe's contribution to the development of detective fiction. Poe's ideas about science are often badly informed, but they include the view that the universe is a perfect plot constructed through a combination of technical skill and imaginative vision. The appeal to ratiocination in the detective stories may be seen in the context of Poe's overall appeal to unity in the cosmos. In *Eureka* (1848), Poe challenges the idea that science is the province of rationality alone, so while his detective C. Auguste Dupin finds solutions through his apparently rigorous rational method, he is also capable of dramatic imaginative leaps and is well-versed in poetry, philosophy, and the arts. Dupin is the blueprint for poet–mathematician detectives such as Arthur Conan Doyle's Sherlock Holmes, whose rigorous deductive sense is balanced with more bohemian and mystical tendencies. Dupin first appeared in "The Murders in the Rue Morgue," and is featured twice more, in "The Mystery of Marie Rogêt" (1842) and "The Purloined Letter" (1845).

In their structure, too, the "tales of ratiocination" inaugurated the classic detective story. They feature incompetent, though methodical, police and a narrator-sidekick who is a precursor of Doyle's Dr. Watson, while the most fundamental trope of all, the principle of the locked room, is the key feature of "The Murders in the Rue Morgue." Poe believed that the rational principles of detection established in these stories could be applied in real life, and indeed "The Mystery of Marie Rogêt" was his attempt to "solve" the real mystery of the murder of Mary Rogers in New York. Besides the overt detective tales, other stories point toward the future of detective fiction. "The Gold Bug," for which Poe won a prize in the *Dollar Newspaper* competition, involves the deciphering of a code, while "The Man of the Crowd" describes a flâneur familiar to readers of Charles Baudelaire, and a loose prototype for American detectives such as Sam Spade and Philip Marlowe.

Although Poe's great talent was for the short story, his first published prose work was the novella *The Narrative of Arthur Gordon Pym of Nantucket* (1838). Many of the characteristics of the *Tales* can be found in this longer work—in particular, the feature Kenneth Silverman describes as "Getting his hero into trouble and keeping him there." The themes of deceit, illusion, and uncertainty run through *Pym* as they do through the shorter tales. Innovative, horrifying, and unsettling by turns, Poe's *Tales* helped establish a tradition of short story writing by American writers, a tradition to which they continue to provide some of the finest examples.

CHRISTOPHER ROUTLEDGE

Text

The Narrative of Arthur Gordon Pym of Nantucket first published by Harper's, New York, 1838.
Tales of the Grotesque and the Arabesque, 1839. Reprinted as *Tales* in 1845. Reprinted in many editions of collected and selected works including *Poetry and Tales* (New York City: Library of America), 1984.

Bibliography

Bellas, Patricia H. *Poe, Master of Macabre*. Baltimore: Xavier, 1995.
Carlson, Eric W., ed. *A Companion to Poe Studies*. Westport, Conn.: Greenwood, 1996.
Eliot, T. S. *From Poe to Valery*. New York: Harcourt, Brace, 1948.
Frank, Frederick S., and Anthony Magistrale. *The Poe Encyclopedia*. Westport, Conn.: Greenwood, 1997.
May, Charles E. *The New Short Story Theories*. Athens, Ohio: Ohio University Press, 1994.
Poe, Edgar Allan. "Review of *Night and Morning: A Novel by Edward Bulwer Lytton*," *Graham's Magazine*, April 1841.
Silverman, Kenneth. *Edgar A. Poe: Mournful and Never-Ending Remembrance*. London: Wiedenfeld and Nicholson, 1992.

TALES 1835–1872

Collection of stories by Hans Christian Andersen

There were both social and psychological reasons to explain why Hans Christian Andersen found the truest expression of his genius in the genre of fairy tales. Coming from the lower class, Andersen felt like an outsider throughout his life. His desperate, but often unsuccessful, attempts to adjust and accommodate himself to upper and middle class mores and values resulted in a nervous disposition characterized by oversensitivity, hypochondria, vanity, and a craving for recognition. He was emotionally volatile, overreacting to the smallest perceived slight, but also feeling exultation and delirious happiness at seemingly trivial occurrences. He would expose himself to countless dangers in traveling through Europe, while being in constant fear of having his passport and documents rejected and always carrying a rope with him so that he could escape in case of fire. His social insecurity, ambivalent sexuality, and fear of sex and death are all well documented.

These factors made Andersen a very neurotic and difficult person to associate with, and probably impossible to live with, but they also made him a superb observer. As an outsider, he noticed the behavior and habits of members of different social classes in minute detail, including people's foibles and idiosyncrasies, and their individual ways of speaking. It enabled him to comment on social norms and established customs from new and surprising angles—and at a certain distance—and he could do this simply by transforming his own raw emotions, experiences, triumphs, and defeats into the worlds of animals, objects, or human beings in fairytale settings. His descriptions of poverty, misery, rejection, vanity, haughtiness, and the like are often very physical and sensual (frozen feet, shabby clothes, ugly features, etc.), but they are, at their best, enchanting and at the same time full of biting irony and profound comments on the human condition.

Nevertheless, when he published his first four fairy tales in 1835, Andersen did not seem to realize the importance of this new departure for his subsequent career and fame. Admittedly, he did in passing say in a letter to the writer Bernhard Severin Ingemann early in that year that he had "begun some Fairy Tales Told for Children" and that he believed that he had succeeded, and in another letter he wrote jokingly that he was going to "win over future generations." But when he reported that his friend H. C. Ørsted, the famous physicist and discoverer of electromagnetism, had predicted that if *The Improvisatore* made him famous, those tales would make him immortal, he remarked tersely: "I myself do not think so."

Indeed, only one of the first four tales ("Little Ida's Flowers") was truly original; the three others were folk stories he had heard from his grandmother, but he wrote them "exactly the way I would tell them to a child." This is an all-important comment, which shows a crucial difference between Andersen's tales and previous types, such as Jean La Fontaine's fables, Charles Perrault's stories, and above all the fairy tales of the German Romantics (E. T. A. Hoffmann, Novalis, and Ludwig Tieck), culminating in Jakob and Wilhelm Grimm's collection. What distinguishes Andersen's tales from all of these, apart from the above, is his subtle and often assumed naïveté, the constant presence and commentary of the narrator, and above all the quirky, colloquial and intimate nature of the language, its special "tone." It is not always easy to know whether something is said or thought by one of the characters or by the narrator; their voices merge. His *Tales* are not allegories or abstract symbolic vehicles, though they certainly contain many symbolic features. Rather, they can be read on several different levels, which is why it is a fundamental mistake to see them as primarily children's literature. Andersen gradually realized that the "Told for Children" was potentially misleading and tried to rectify it by dropping the words from later collections and expanding the title to "Fairy Tales and Stories," but the damage had been done, and the misconception persists to this day.

The stories, 156 in all, appeared in several collections between 1835 and 1872, and they are extraordinarily diverse. They may be—and have been—divided into a number of different groups and types. Some tales have animals as their main characters (for example, "The Happy Family," "The High Jumpers," "It's Perfectly True," "The Ugly Duckling"); others have trees or plants (for instance, "The Fir Tree," "Little Ida's Flowers"); and in some of them inanimate objects become animated (for example, "The Collar," "The Daring Needle," "The Steadfast Tin Soldier"). These all talk and behave like humans—and may even mix with them—but in ways that are in tune with their various characteristics. The natural elements may play a decisive role in the greater social and moral order and as symbolic markers; thus, to give but a few examples, the sun in "There is a Difference," the sea in "The Little Mermaid," the wind in "Everything in its Right Place," the ice in "The Snow Queen," etc. Elements of magic are found in several tales, for instance, "The Flying Trunk" and "The Travelling Companion."

There is a fairly clear distinction between "borrowed" (or derived) and original tales. To the first category belong, for example, some of the early tales ("The Tinderbox" with its Aladdin theme, "Little Claus and Big Claus," "The Princess and the Pea," "The Traveling Companion," "The Wild Swans"). However, Andersen put his inimitable stamp on them all through often subtle structural changes and his own special language.

Social satire is found in many tales, such as the ridicule of vanity in "The Emperor's New Clothes" and of gossip in "It's Perfectly True," while social criticism is the theme of "The Little Matchgirl," "Everything in its Right Place," and "She Was No Good," the latter inspired by his own mother.

Some tales become symbols of life in general, such as "The Fir Tree," "The Story of a Mother," "The Bell," "The Shadow," and "The Ugly Duckling," "The Bell" and "The Shadow" belong to Andersen's more philosophical tales: the first ends in the image of reason and imagination—science and poetry—united in the great church of nature (cf. German *Universalpoesie*); the second is Andersen's most demonic and haunting tale, with its chilling reversal of established bourgeois norms and values.

Inevitably, there are many "self-portraits" in the tales, and this has proved a happy hunting ground for critics. Most famous is the portrayal of the ugly duckling that turns into a swan, but numerous others could be mentioned, such as the theme of rejected love in "The Swineherd" and "The Sweethearts," hypersensitivity in "The Princess and the Pea," restlessness and over-ambition in "The Fir Tree"; and, of course, the experience of the outsider in "The Little Mermaid" and "The Ugly Duckling," among others.

Although Andersen's fairy tales are among the most translated literary texts in world literature, they have often been distorted and misunderstood because of poor translations. It takes consummate skill, as well as an intimate knowledge of Danish, to render them into another language. This is mainly due to his very idiosyncratic and colloquial style, with frequent use of modal adverbs to add subtle nuances to descriptions, opinions, and commentary. Despite many references to now-dated details in the tales, these seem essentially as fresh and intriguing as when they were written. Andersen's tales deserve to be read carefully.

TOM LUNDSKÆR-NIELSEN

See also **Andersen, Hans Christian**

Texts

The Complete Andersen: all of the 168 stories by Hans Christian Andersen, I–VI, trans. Jean Hersholt, New York: The Limited Editions Club, 1949. (One-volume edition, New York: The Heritage Press, 1952).

H. C. Andersen's Eventyr, 1–7, Erik Dal, Erling Nielsen, and Flemming Hovmand (eds.), Copenhagen: Hans Reitzel, 1963–90.

The Complete Fairy Tales and Stories, trans. Erik C. Hauggaard, New York: Doubleday, 1974.

Hans Christian Andersen 80 Fairy Tales, trans. R. P. Keigwin, Odense: Hans Reitzel, 1976.

Tales and Stories by Hans Christian Andersen, trans. Patricia L. Conroy, and Sven H. Rossel (eds.), Seattle/London: University of Washington Press, 1980.

Hans Andersen's Fairy Tales: A Selection, trans. L. W. Kingsland, Oxford: Oxford World's Classics, 1984.

Hans Christian Andersen Fairy Tales, trans. Reginald Spink, London: Everyman, 1992.

Samlede Eventyr og Historier, Svend Larsen (Jubilæumsudgaven) (ed.), Odense, Hans Reitzel, 1995.

Further Reading

Mylius, Johan de, *The Voice of Nature in Hans Christian Andersen's Fairy Tales*, Odense: H. C. Andersen–Centret, Odense University, 1989.

Rossel, Sven H., *Hans Christian Andersen und das Märchen heute*, Vienna: Picus, 1996.

TANNHÄUSER UND DER SÄNGERKRIEG AUF WARTBURG 1845

Opera in three acts by Richard Wagner

Despite numerous revisions (chief among them the 1860 publication of the revised edition or "Dresden version," the 1861 revision and translation for Paris performance; 1867 and 1875 revisions for Munich and Vienna performances; and publication of a revised edition as the "Paris version"); and although he wrote it at an early stage in his career, Richard Wagner still considered *Tannhäuser und der Sängerkrieg auf Wartburg* unfinished in the year of his death. His wife Cosima noted in her diary Wagner's now famous remark that he "still owed the world *Tannhäuser*." Partly prompted by this comment, critics tend to express dissatisfaction with the work, although it contains some of Wagner's most popular music (such as the Pilgrims' Chorus, Venusberg Bacchanal, Wolfram's Cavatina, and Entry of the Guests at the Wartburg). More important than the first performances in Dresden and Weimar is the 1861 Paris production, which had to be cancelled after only three performances, largely due to sabotage of the production by the Paris Jockey Club. Yet the opera left a deep impression on Charles Baudelaire, whose recollection of the performance, "Richard Wagner et Tannhauser à Paris" (1861), is an important founding document of French *Wagnérisme*.

Tannhäuser is Wagner's first opera based on a German medieval subject, and it is an important document in the Romantic reception of the Middle Ages. The historical Tannhäuser (c. 1200–70) was a south German *Minnesänger* (minstrel-knight), whose poetry exhibited a marked preference for sexual fulfillment over courtly chastity. It is debatable, however, to what extent Tannhäuser's poetry contributed to subsequent popular myths that developed around him. These myths focus on the minstrel-knight's pilgrimage to seek forgiveness from the pope for his sexual intemperance in the Venusberg. The pope's verdict that Tannhäuser cannot be forgiven, just as his staff will not bear fresh leaves, drives the knight back into Venus's arms before the papal message reaches him that, miraculously, the dead staff has blossomed with green leaves. Not least because of its prominent use of some of the principal topics of the Romantic imagination, this legend was a popular source in Wagner's time, existing in versions by the Brothers Grimm, Heinrich Heine, Ludwig Tieck, and in *Des Knaben Wunderhorn* (an anthology of German folksongs compiled by Achim von Arnim and Clemens Brentano in 1806). Wagner combined this story, which forms the basis of acts 1 and 3 of the opera, with elements of the tale of Heinrich von Ofterdingen and the "singers' war," which apparently took place at the Wartburg in central Germany in 1206–7. In Ernst Theodor Amadeus Hoffmann's adaptation of the tale (which, besides *Tannhäuser*, provided Wagner with motifs for *Die Meistersinger von Nürnberg* [1868] and *Parsifal* [1882]), Ofterdingen offends the courtly society with his daring song at the singing contest and, ousted as a sinner who has succumbed to evil powers, is finally defeated by the pure art of the meek Wolfram von Eschenbach. In equating Ofterdingen with Tannhäuser, Wagner followed a dubious philological hypothesis advanced in the 1830s, notably propagated by Ludwig Bechstein and Christoph Theodor Leopold Lucas. In Wagner's opera the two story lines cohere further by the introduction of Elisabeth, the central female character and the Margrave of Thuringia's niece (prefigured in Bechstein's and Hoffmann's work). During the act 2 singing contest, she shields Tannhäuser from the knights who threaten to kill him when he admits to his sojourn in the Venusberg. Her pure love motivates Tannhäuser on his pilgrimage to Rome. Finally, in act 3, when Elisabeth realizes that Tannhäuser has not found forgiveness in Rome, as he does not return with the other pilgrims, she dies, selflessly sacrificing herself, and thus redeems the condemned Tannhäuser.

In this constellation, the two female characters, Venus and Elisabeth, come to epitomize lust and love, between which the searching character of Tannhäuser is torn. A traditional interpretation of this opera (prevalent particularly during Wagner's lifetime, though not supported by him) holds that Catholicism is triumphant with Elisabeth's virgin death and Tannhäuser's ensuing redemption. However, this interpretation is difficult to maintain with cynical elements pervading the representation of the church authority in the opera. In fact, the libretto suggests a more complex and nuanced opposition between Venus and Elisabeth. Thus, in act 2, during Tannhäuser's initial outbursts against his rival Wolfram's praise of chastity, the stage instructions direct Elisabeth to make "a movement to signal her approval but, seeing that everybody remains silent, she coyly resists." Even after her complete transformation from the passionate human of act 2 into the lofty saint figure of act 3 (Wagner's model for this character was St. Elisabeth of Hungary), allusions to her congruence with Venus are still present, most notably in Wolfram's Cavatina "to the Evening Star," which is ostensibly addressed to the departing Elisabeth but also refers to Venus (the evening star).

The majority of the revisions that Wagner made concerned the figure of Venus. Wagner conceded that in the Dresden version, the act 1 music of Venus's love grotto was tame and unconvincing. However, the luxurious post–*Tristan and Isolde* (1865) musical depiction of Venus's magic world, arguably the most outrageous music Wagner ever wrote (and added as a ballet for the notorious 1861 Paris performance), is actually in danger of overshadowing the more stolid act 2 Wartburg music by being too seductive. According to Hans Mayer, "musically, the Venusberg wins." Moreover, Wagner has repeatedly been criticized for the stylistic discrepancies that he introduced with these revisions. However, to a certain extent, this stylistic diversity serves to underline the opposition of the hedonistic disorderly world of Venus and the orderly feudal hierarchy of the Wartburg. That Tannhäuser belongs to neither is perhaps most clearly conveyed in "Tannhäuser's Song": sung in act 1 in the context of Venus's harmonically and metrically-slippery world, it sounds stable, four-square, almost march-like, while in act 2 the same song appears musically daring and impassioned.

For Wagner, this opera held a special significance (perhaps because he considered it unfinished), and in his writings and correspondence he habitually cited *Tannhäuser* as a crucial stepping stone. However, in the teleology commonly applied to Wagner's artistic development, the opera may be said to have contributed little to the advancement of the principles of Wagnerian music drama; somewhat inconclusively the critics Carolyn Abbate, Carl Dahlhaus and Barry Millington have each identified one leitmotif. Couched between the music-historically more significant Romantic operas *Der fliegende Holländer* (*The Flying Dutchman*, 1843) and *Lohengrin* (1850), *Tannhäuser* is usually considered as occupying a lesser position in Wagner's oeuvre. The operatic structure on the whole, with the notable exception of Tannhäuser's epic "Rome Narration" in act 3, remains largely indebted to French grand opera and Italianate traditions (especially the finales of acts 1 and 2). Nevertheless, its cultural impact on the whole should not be underestimated: the ever-yearning Tannhäuser is often considered along the lines of a Don Juan or Faust character, *Tannhäuser* is a prime document of the reception of the Middle Ages in the Romantic era, and as Baudelaire's fascination with the opera shows, it has left a lasting mark, particularly in France.

ALEXANDER REHDING

Bibliography

Abbate, Carolyn. "The Parisian Vénus and the 'Paris' *Tannhäuser*," *Journal of the American Musicological Society* 36 (1983): 73–123.

Cicora, Mary A. *From History to Myth: Wagner's* Tannhäuser *and its Literary Sources*. Bern: Peter Lang, 1992.

Csampai, Attila, and Dietmar Holland, eds. *Richard Wagner: Tannhäuser*. Reinbek bei Hamburg: Rowohlt, 1986.

Dahlhaus, Carl. *Richard Wagner's Music Dramas.* Translated by Mary Whittall. Cambridge: Cambridge University Press, 1979.

John, Nicholas, ed. *Tannhäuser*. Opera Guides Series. London: John Calder, 1988.

Müller, Ulrich, and Peter Wapnewski, eds. *Wagner Handbook.* English translation edited by John Deathridge. Cambridge, Mass.: Harvard University Press, 1992.

Skelton, Geoffrey. "I Still Owe the World *Tannhäuser*: The Dresden and Paris Versions." In *Richard Wagner in Thought and Practice*. London: Lime Tree, 1991. 143–81.

TENNYSON, ALFRED, LORD 1809-1892

English poet

Alfred, Lord Tennyson is typically regarded, with Robert Browning, as one of the two key Victorian poets, and insofar as Victorianism is seen as a reaction against the aesthetic tenets of Romanticism, he is often studied as a post-Romantic figure. But his first poems were published in 1827, ten years before Victoria came to the throne, and throughout his career his work manifests the abiding influence of British Romantic writing. His verse embodies a deeply Keatsian verbal lushness and beauty, matched with an often mournful apprehension of alienation and solitude (as in "The Lady of Shalott"); and his masterpiece *In Memoriam* (1850) is a powerfully interior exploration of a state of extreme consciousness, grieving, that can therefore be thought of as a deeply Romantic text. He praised John Keats's "high spiritual vision," and declared his love for the work of William Wordsworth and Lord Byron, writing, "You must love Wordsworth ere he will seem worthy of your love. As a boy I was an enormous admirer of Byron. . . . I was fourteen when I heard of his death. It seemed an awful calamity; I remember I rushed out of doors, sat down by myself, shouted aloud, and wrote on the sandstone *Byron is dead*."

Alfred Tennyson was the third surviving son of George Tennyson, a rector, and Elizabeth Tennyson. His father was an alcoholic, melancholic, and sometimes violent man, and Tennyson grew up an introspective and sometimes gloomy individual. In 1827 Tennyson published *Poems by Two Brothers*, a volume that actually contains poetry by *three* of the Tennyson brothers (Alfred, Charles, and Frederick). The volume was little noticed. In November he went to Trinity College, Cambridge University, where he met Arthur Hallam, who swiftly became his closest friend. His first sole-authored work, *Poems, Chiefly Lyrical* (1830), is a collection of lush, often mournful lyrics of varying beauty and sentimental morbidity. This volume was unfavorably reviewed by John Gibson Lockhart and John Wilson, although Arthur Henry Hallam managed to place a positive review in the *Englishman's Review* in 1831. After the death of his father that same year, Tennyson left Cambridge without taking a degree. His second collection, *Poems* (1832), contains some of Tennyson's most enduring works

(including "The Lady of Shalott" and "The Lotos Eaters"), although once again the bulk of reviews were negative.

In September 1833 the key event of Tennyson's life occurred. Hallam, traveling by himself in Europe, died unexpectedly of a brain hemorrhage. Tennyson was plunged into profound grief. He began composing poems to try to come to terms with his loss, writing several pieces that were to appear in his next collection, *Poems* (1842; "Ulysses," "Tithonus," "Break, Break, Break," "Morte D'Arthur"), as well as composing many of the lyrics that were eventually to constitute *In Memoriam*. While it may seem a little callous to say so given the intensity of Tennyson's emotional pain, Hallam's death gave his sometimes rather pasty and even formulaic Keatsian poetry of alienation and loss a powerful, concrete theme. From 1833 onward it can be argued that all of Tennyson's poetry in one shape or another encountered the fact of death through the actual experience of losing Hallam, giving it an emotional and poetic depth it lacked before. In his hands, the sometimes hackneyed pseudo-Gothic Romantic fascination with "the premature death of the beautiful young person" acquires a moving, personal resonance.

In 1836 Tennyson fell in love with Emily Sellwood (whom he had first met in 1830). They did not marry until 1850, and their engagement was broken off in 1840 for reasons that remain unclear but may have had to do with financial uncertainty about Tennyson's career. This fourteen-year courtship period was not unusual in early Victorian Britain, but doubtless reflects an emotional caution that certainly emerges in Tennyson's poetry. The publication of *Poems* (1842) in two volumes, the first containing a selection of his earlier work and the second with all new poems, helped cement his reputation. For the first time he experienced some more favorable critical attention, and the volume helped him obtain a Civil List pension of £200 a year in 1845. In 1847 he published *The Princess*, a lengthy blank-verse poem in seven books concerning the establishment of a women-only university.

In Memoriam, regarded by many as his masterpiece, was published anonymously in May 1850. In June of that year Tennyson finally married Emily. Following William Wordsworth's death in April, there was much speculation concerning who was best suited to becoming the next poet laureate; Tennyson was appointed to the post in November. The establishment sanction of Tennyson's work led to a number of "official" poems; for instance his 1852 *Ode on the Death of the Duke of Wellington* commemorating the recently dead military leader and politician. It also consolidated plans that Tennyson had harbored for many years to write an epic of English myth centered on the legends of King Arthur, a project that would enable him to explore and in part define "Englishness." This epic, which had been in his mind since the 1830s, did not finally emerge as twelve books of blank verse, *The Idylls of the King*, until 1885.

Other laureate work, although touching on official topics, was more personal. His experimental dramatic monologue *Maud, or the Madness* (1855) tells a morbidly Gothic tale in part derived from William Shakespeare's *Hamlet*: the narrator's love for the beautiful Maud is interdicted by her haughty brother; the two men fight and Maud's brother is killed. Maud herself dies of grief and the narrator goes mad, only to recover his senses in time to enlist in the Crimean War (1853–56). Despite a rousingly jingoistic conclusion, the impact of this formally bold, oblique, and often very beautiful poem has more to do with the delineation of a diseased consciousness.

The "official" status of Tennyson, with *In Memoriam* as his key work, was established by 1861, the year in which Prince Albert, the Queen's Consort, died. Victoria took great comfort from Tennyson's elegy, keeping a copy on her bedside table. Tennyson's later career falls increasingly outside the scope of a study such as this one. The twelve *Idylls of the King* appeared at interludes between 1859 and 1880. From 1875 onward he began writing for the stage, publishing eight plays, many of which were staged by Henry Irving. In 1883, as a mark of his establishment status, he was offered, and accepted, a barony. He died in 1892.

ADAM ROBERTS

Biography

Born in Lincolnshire, England, 1809; enrolled at Louth Grammar School 1816–20. Entered Trinity College, Cambridge, 1827. Death of his father; left university without a degree, 1831. Death of his closest friend, Arthur Henry Hallam, 1833. Became engaged to Emily Sellwood, 1837. Engagement broken off, 1840. Awarded a Civil List pension, 1845. Married Sellwood and was appointed poet laureate, 1850. Settled on the Isle of Wight, 1853. Made a baron, 1883. Died October 6, 1892.

Selected Work

The Letters of Alfred Lord Tennyson. 3 vols. Edited by Cecil Y. Lang and Edgar F. Shannon. Oxford: Clarendon, Press, 1982–90.
The Poems of Tennyson. 2nd ed. 3 vols. Edited by Christopher Ricks. London: Longman, 1987.
Tennyson. Edited by Adam Roberts. *Oxford Authors* series. Oxford: Oxford University Press, 2000.
In Memoriam. Edited by Susan Shatto, and Marion Shaw. Oxford: Clarendon Press, 1982.

Bibliography

Armstrong, Isobel. *Victorian Poetry: Poetry, Poetics and Politics*. London: Routledge, 1993.
Vanden Bossche, Chris R. "Realism versus Romance: The War of Cultural Codes in Tennyson's *Maud*," *Victorian Poetry* 24 (1986): 69–82.
Buckley, Jerome H. *Tennyson: the Growth of a Poet*. Cambridge, Mass.: Harvard University Press, 1960.
Griffiths, Eric. *The Printed Voice of Victorian Poetry*. Oxford: Clarendon Press, 1989.
Hair, Donald S. *Tennyson's Language*, Toronto: University of Toronto Press, 1991.
Jordan, Elaine. *Alfred Tennyson*. Cambridge: Cambridge University Press, 1988.
Joseph, Gerhard. *Tennysonian Love: the Strange Diagonal*. Minneapolis: University of Minnesota Press, 1969.
Jump, John D., ed. *Tennyson: the Critical Heritage*. London: Routledge, 1967.
Lourie, Margaret. "Below the Thunders of the Upper Deep: Tennyson as a Romantic Revisionist," *Studies in Romanticism* 18 (1979): 3–27.
Martin, Robert Bernard. *Tennyson: The Unquiet Heart*. Oxford: Oxford University Press, 1980.
Ormond, Leonée. *Alfred Tennyson: A Literary Life*. London: Macmillan, 1993.
Page, Norman, ed. *Tennyson: Interviews and Recollections*. London: Macmillan, 1983.
Ricks, Christopher. *Tennyson*. 2nd ed. London: Macmillan, 1989.
Shannon, Edgar F., Jr. *Tennyson and the Reviewers*. Cambridge, Mass.: Harvard University Press, 1952.
Shaw, W. David. *The Lucid Veil: Poetic Truth in the Victorian Age*. London: Athlone, 1987.
———. *Tennyson's Style*. Ithaca, N.Y.: Cornell University Press, 1976.
Sinfield, Alan. *Alfred Tennyson*. Rereading Literature Series. Oxford: Blackwell, 1986.
Stott, Rebecca, ed. *Tennyson*. Longman Critical Readers series. London: Longman, 1996.
Tennyson, Hallam. *Alfred, Lord Tennyson: A Memoir*. 2 vols. 1897.
Turner, Paul. *Tennyson*. London: Routledge, 1976.

THEOLOGY AND RELIGIOUS THOUGHT

While one cannot identify "Romantic theology" as a single, consistent theological system, the original foundation of Romanticism rests on certain theological assumptions, and we find in Romanticism a number of consistent patterns and tendencies. For many figures of the period, Romanticism indeed emanates from theological innovations, for Romanticism redefines the relationship between God and the self. Important theological principles appearing in Romanticism include the immanent presence of God in the self; Christian Neoplatonism; pantheism; the idea of the poet as the voice of God (the poet as *vates*, the poet-seer); art as the positing of God in the aesthetic object; and *poesy*, or artistic creation, as an emulation of God's divine creative work.

It is a convention to speak of Romanticism as a reaction against Enlightenment and neoclassical thought, and similarly one can contrast Romantic theological currents with the deism, and even theological indifference, that appear in the eighteenth century. Unlike the deistic God, the Romantic God is typically more dynamic and more immediately present, both in nature and in the self, and such ideas have significant consequences for the relationship between God and the individual. In these conceptions one can perhaps see a reaction against David Hume and Voltaire. However, as with any movement in intellectual and literary history, Romantic thought and theology depended on, and developed from, previous trends and movements. One could not have the French Revolution without the Enlightenment, and one could not have Romanticism without the French Revolution. And as we see in the work of Jean-Jacques Rousseau beforehand and William Blake and Friedrich Schlegel afterward, the French Revolution was very much an event in the history of religious thought.

The most important immediate predecessor to developments in Romantic theology was Immanuel Kant; without him, Romanticism generally and Romantic theology specifically would not have been what they were. Kant's three great critiques (of pure reason, practical reason, and judgment) exert a profound impact in their discussion of the individual's ability to perceive God, and in the ideas they present concerning the teleological progress of society and the individual toward the absolute. Kant also provides the Romantics with a language for the connection between the theological and the aesthetic. Rousseau informs Romanticism in many respects, and in the area of theology his *Confessions* (1782–89) and *Reveries of the Solitary Walker* (1782) anticipate Romantic ideas of the intimate relationship between the individual and God and also provide a theological foundation for the individual's isolation from society. The linkage of solitude and theology has a long tradition in Judeo-Christian thought (the prophet and the mystic), and Rousseau provides the Romantics with a paradigm in his solitary walker, a figure in dialogue with God but misunderstood by the world. Other influences include Gotthold Ephraim Lessing and his idea of progressive revelation; Emanuel Swedenborg (famously parodied in William Blake's *The Marriage of Heaven and Hell* [1793]); and Friedrich Schiller, whose *Aesthetic Education*, (1793–1801) first developed Kant's theological–aesthetic linkage; and the mystical and even pantheistic strains to come out of Freemasonry.

In order to understand any religious thought in Romanticism, one must first understand that Romanticism does not view art, philosophy, and religion as separate, discrete entities. William Blake, Samuel Taylor Coleridge, Novalis, Friedrich Schelling, Friedrich and August Schlegel, Friedrich Schleiermacher, and William Wordsworth all contribute to Romantic theology. However, of this group only Schleiermacher is remembered as a theologian per se, and even in his case we speak of him as an innovator in the area of literary criticism perhaps as much as in theology. Blake and Novalis are regarded as poets, but in both cases their poetry emerges from theological aesthetics: poetry as the expression of, and the merging with, the divine. Friedrich Schlegel, the first to use the term *Romantic*, predicated his aesthetics and his "divinatory criticism" on a theological idea; for him, subjectivity and the expression of the self brought one closer to and even, ideally, *into* the presence of God. Schelling, now treated as a philosopher, composed three prominent works during the early Romantic period; they examine the presence of God in nature, the presence of God in the self, and the presence of God in art. In Russia, the most active and innovative theological discussions of the day appear in the literary journals edited typically by prominent poets. Ralph Waldo Emerson, one of America's true Romantics, also belongs in this discussion, and while posterity remembers Emerson as a philosopher and poet, he began his adult life as a minister and never lost his sense of sacred mission.

Romantic theology rests on the Romantic idea of selfhood and the divine immanent in the self. Kant's arguments about the individual's ability to perceive God in *The Critique of Practical Reason* (1788) and *The Critique of Judgment* (1790) exert a profound impact on the Romantics. Schiller (not a Romantic himself) and Schelling work forward from Kant, and Kant's "invisible self possessing true infinitude" acquires a progressively more aesthetic character. In England, Romantic selfhood takes shape in the poetry and prose of Coleridge and Wordsworth, and Wordsworth's *The Prelude* (1850), in many respects the most comprehensive Romantic statement on selfhood, is rich in theological implications.

The absolute subjectivity of Romantic selfhood leads to several patterns regarding humanity and nature (the Creation). Some Romantics adapted the three-age view of history, especially prevalent in post-Kantian thought: a past in the immediate presence of God; the present defined by awareness of, but separation from, God; and a future reunification with God. The model follows the conventional Judeo-Christian pattern of Eden, the Fall, and the return to God's presence. Blake, Novalis, Schelling, and Friedrich Schlegel used some manifestation of this scheme in their various theological contemplations. More generally, it informed the Romantic inclination for Neoplatonism and Neoplatonic pantheism, which are founded on the principle that all creation originally existed in a harmonious unity (the One), then fragmented (the Many), and now longs to return to a state of unity. As we now dwell in the age of fragmentation, we all possess some kernel of the original "One" within ourselves—again, the divine immanent—we sense the presence of the divine in all other things, and also sense the cosmos within ourselves. Because of the divine impulse for reunification of the cosmos, we maintain "hopes for a universal personality" in Novalis's phrasing. The three-age view also underlies Romantic ideas of historical teleology, most notable in those dependent on Kant, and here the goal is the establishment of the Kingdom of God on earth. Friedrich Schlegel exemplified this tendency when he wrote, "The revolutionary desire to realize the kingdom of God on earth is the elastic point of progressive civilization and the beginning of modern history."

The most familiar aspects of Romantic religious thought appear in the treatment of art, and poetry in particular. As Schelling noted, "The immediate cause of all art is God." Yet Romantic theological aesthetics vary from characterizations on the nature of creative genius and imagination, to mystical visions of the poet-prophet, and even to a Romantic messianism, whereby the poet realizes the Kingdom of God on earth. For the Romantic, imagination, genius, and inspiration all proceed from God, and the poetic act comprises three theologically defined phenomena: God acting through the poet in poetic creation, the poetic object as the infinite posited in the finite, and the reading of poetry as the reception of the divine. In his *Biographia Literaria* (1817), Coleridge developed some of the most significant ideas on Romantic imagination and describes his "primary Imagination" as "the living Power and prime Agent of all human Perception, and as a repetition in the finite mind of the eternal act of creation in the infinite I AM." The privileged ability of the poet to hear the "voice of God" naturally inclined a number of Romantics to the idea of the poet-prophet. Different expressions of this idea appear in Blake's emulation of Isaiah, Jeremiah, and Ezekiel in his illuminated books of prophecy, and in Percy Bysshe Shelley's "Defence of Poetry" (1821). The idea was especially prevalent in Russia and Poland, most famously in the poetry of Alexandr Pushkin and Adami Mickiewicz, and these nations consistently ascribed to the poet a special "gift," a word with clear theological connotations.

Romantic poetry also acts as the force that reconciles the subject and the universe, the internal and the external, the ideal and the real. Schleiermacher termed the "intuition of the universe" as the "hinge" of his landmark theological tract, *On Religion* (1799), and Emerson noted, "It is dislocation and detachment from the life of God that makes things ugly, and the poet, who re-attaches things to nature and the Whole" ("The Poet," 1844). In Germany, the Schlegels and Novalis moved forward from Schiller's "On Naive and Sentimental Poetry" to a variety of expressions on the poet's role in positing the ideal. In a mystically inclined teleology, the reconciliation of the individual and the All becomes the realization of God, and poetry becomes God's self-knowledge and self-expression. Thus, Novalis wrote, "If our intelligence and our world harmonize—then we are like God"; and he encapsulates his Romantic teleology in the statement: "It is highly understandable why, in the end, all becomes poetry."

Romantic theology furthermore begets the great irony of Romanticism. The subject can perceive the divine and even momentarily posit the divine, but while the individual (and all history) strives to attain the ideal, the ideal necessarily defies realization. The implications of this irony appear with increasing frequency as Romanticism evolves. Many of the later theological statements by Romantics reflect anguish over alienation from God, and awareness of the separation from God begets Romantic

prometheanism and demonism. The self consequently is associated with spiritual exiles such as Cain, Lucifer, or unnamed fallen angels. Prominent examples include Lord Byron's "Cain" (1821), Alfred-Victor de Vigny's "Eloa" (1824), and Mikhail Lermontov's "The Demon" (1841); Mary Shelley's *Frankenstein* (1818) is often seen as a parable of the tragic hubris implicit in aspiring to be "like God." This tendency also appears in the Romantic reception of John Milton's *Paradise Lost* (1655–74) and Johann Wolfgang von Goethe's *Faust* (1808).

ANDREW SWENSEN

Bibliography

Abrams, M. H. *Natural Supernaturalism*. New York: W. W. Norton, 1971.

Blake, William. "All Religions Are One," "There Is No Natural Religion," and "The Marriage of Heaven and Hell." In *The Early Illuminated Books*. Princeton, N.J.: Princeton University Press, 1993.

Coleridge, Samuel Taylor. "Biographia Literaria." In *The Collected Works of Samuel Taylor Coleridge*. Vol. 7. Princeton, N.J.: Princeton University Press, 1987.

Emerson, Ralph Waldo. "Spiritual Laws," "The Over-Soul," and "The Poet." In *The Essays of Ralph Waldo Emerson*. Cambridge, Mass.: Belknap Press, 1987.

Novalis [Friedrich von Hardenburg]. "Encyclopedia." In *Pollen and Fragments*. Translated by Arthur Versluis. Grand Rapids, Mich.: Phanes, 1989.

Reardon, Bernard M. G. *Religion in the Age of Romanticism*. Cambridge: Cambridge University Press, 1985.

Schelling, Friedrich Wilhelm Joseph von. *The Philosophy of Art*. Translated by Douglas W. Stott. Minneapolis: University of Minnesota Press, 1989.

Schlegel, Friedrich. "Athenaeum Fragments" and "Ideas." In *Philosophical Fragments*. Translated by Peter Firchow. Minneapolis: University of Minnesota Press, 1991.

Schleiermacher, Friedrich. *On Religion*. Translated by Richard Crouter. Cambridge: Cambridge University Press, 1988.

Smart, Ninian, et al., eds. *Nineteenth Century Religious Thought in the West*. Cambridge: Cambridge University Press, 1985.

THIERRY, JACQUES-NICOLAS-AUGUSTIN 1795–1856

French historian

Jacques-Nicolas-Augustin Thierry was born and educated in Blois. He subsequently studied at the Ecole Normale in Paris between 1811 and 1813. Initially he seemed destined for a career in teaching, and was indeed appointed to a post at a school in Compiègne. However, in 1814 he was recommended by a fellow *normalien* to the post of secretary to the utopian socialist philosopher Claude-Henri de Saint-Simon. He occupied this position for three years, during which his role was to prepare and order the philosopher's thoughts for written publication. It is generally agreed that he made a substantive contribution to Saint-Simon's *De la réorganisation de la société européenne* (*On the Reorganization of European Society*, 1814). However, Thierry left Saint-Simon's employment in 1817 after a disagreement. During the Restoration he was allied to the liberal opposition, and contributed to some of the leading journals of the day, notably the *Censeur Européen* and the *Courrier Français* between 1817 and

1820. Like his fellow liberals François Charles Louis Comte and Barthélemy Charles Pierre Dunoyer, he recognized the importance of an economic liberalism based on the English model. This led him to explore the writings of English historians and to develop an interest in the Norman Conquest. As a consequence he became fascinated with history, and also became convinced of the need to provide a redefinition of historiography appropriate for the nineteenth century. He articulated his views in a series of articles, subsequently collected in book form: *Lettres sur l'histoire de France* (*Letters on the History of France*, 1827), and *Dix ans d'études historiques* (*Ten Years of Historical Studies*, 1835). In 1825 Thierry published the work on which his posthumous reputation largely rests: *Histoire de la conquête de l'Angleterre par les Normands* (*History of the Conquest of England by the Normans*). This was a considerable publishing success. Thierry believed that the original hostility between conquered Saxons and victorious Normans explained the pattern of class conflict in English history. (There was also an obvious parallel to be drawn with the controversial and politically charged Franks–Gauls theme within French historiography). The fact of conquest had produced enduring social tensions in England, and in Thierry's eyes these had been reinforced by biological and racial factors.

Thierry became the most celebrated and influential historian of his day. In France his work was read avidly throughout the nineteenth century, and historians such as Jules Michelet defined their own projects in relation to Thierry's achievement. However, while French Romantic historians and historically minded thinkers were often tempted to play an active role in politics (one thinks of Philippe-Joseph-Benjamin Buchez, François-Pierre-Guillaume Guizot, and Edgar Quinet), Thierry was constrained by illness to lead a retiring life. His health began to decline as early as 1822, deteriorating dramatically; his eyesight began to fail and in 1830 he was left totally blind. With remarkable fortitude, he bore a further thirty years of illness, receiving constant support from friends, his brother Amédée (also a historian) and his wife Julie de Querengal, whom he had married in 1831 and who died in 1844. Contemporaries usually attributed Thierry's illness to overwork, but Anne Denieul Cormier has shown that he was in fact displaying the symptoms of tabes, a form of syphilis, probably contracted during his adolescence. The true nature of this illness went unrecognized. What is remarkable is the extent to which, with the help of his wife, he continued to produce scholarly work. For much of the time he was only able to function for about two hours a day, organizing his research and giving dictation. After 1835 Guizot came to his aid with the appointment of a secretary. He also arranged for a team of students to be placed at Thierry's disposal. Under his direction, they produced four volumes of unpublished documents relating to the history of the Third Estate. During the July Monarchy, Thierry also published significant individual works, among them his well-received *Récits des temps mérovingiens* (*Narratives of the Merovingian Era*, 1840) and a highly interesting but sadly neglected work of historiography, *Considerations sur l'histoire de France* (*Considerations on French History*, 1840) in the course of which he indicated the distance that separated his view of his discipline from the more philosophical, symbolic history being written by, for example, Michelet. The year 1853 saw the publication of Thierry's final work, *Essai sur l'histoire de la formation et des progrès du tiers état* (*The Formation and Progress of the Third Estate*).

While Thierry recognized the need for the liberal left to ground its political opposition to the government of the Restora-

tion in a new account of history, he also found a principle of legitimation in history which endorsed his conception of the bourgeois nation-state. He articulated a strong sense of the nation as a collective being, of the masses as agents of change. He believed that old-fashioned royalist historiography needed to be discarded because it was inaccurate, unscholarly, and self-serving. He wanted it to be replaced by a new, reliable form of historical writing, one which effectively validated the political project of the liberal opposition. In Thierry's view, the historian aspired to scientific truth but he also remained an artist, a maker of meanings. The Romantic historian was more than an antiquarian, because in order to bring the past to life he performed an act of imaginative reconstruction.

Thierry was in sync with his times and in touch with the spirit of Romanticism. His historical writings included local color. He drew effective contrasts and maintained the reader's attention by focusing on narrative development. He imbued history with a progressive dimension. The content of history was the growth of political freedom, a process of emancipation that began with the rise of the Communes and which continued until the triumph of the Third Estate in 1789. In Thierry's eyes, the history of France was both a narrative of struggle and a grand movement toward national unity and cohesion, a movement which transcended human goals because it corresponded to the actualization of a greater providential design. Before 1830 Thierry's writing had a radical dimension, whereas his later work tended to emphasize the extent to which France had been built by the people and the monarch working together. After July 1830, Thierry confidently believed that, from then on, the middle classes would share power with a constitutional monarch. The future, however, contained an unpleasant surprise. The February Revolution of 1848 and the sudden overthrow of the July Monarchy threw Thierry into despair, and led him to briefly question the validity of liberal interpretation of history. Was bourgeois history itself perhaps provisional? Nevertheless, during his final years, Thierry remained an Orleanist, equally opposed to both the Second Republic and the Second Empire.

CERI CROSLEY

Bibliography

Crossley, Ceri. *French Historians and Romanticism: Thierry, Guizot, the Saint-Simonians, Quinet, Michelet.* London: Routledge, 1993.
Denieul Cormier, Anne. *Augustin Thierry: L'histoire autrement.* Paris: Publisud, 1996.
Gossman, Lionel. *Between History and Literature.* Cambridge, Mass.: Harvard University Press, 1990.
Smithson, Rulon Nephi. *Augustin Thierry: Social and Political Consciousness in the Evolution of a Historical Method.* Geneva: Droz, 1972.

THIERS, LOUIS-ADOLPHE 1797–1877

French politician

Louis-Adolphe Thiers was born in Marseille, rapidly abandoned by his father, and brought up by a devoted mother and grandmother. He was educated at the local *lycée* before studying law at Aix-en-Provence (1815–18). He was admitted to the bar in 1818, and followed his close friend François-August-Marie Mi-

gnet to Paris in September 1821. He cultivated relationships with the powerful and influential while working as a journalist. Thiers rapidly attracted attention as a contributor to the liberal newspaper *Le Constitutionnel*, earning the patronage of Charles-Maurice de Talleyrand and the German publisher Baron Johann

Friedrich Cotta. Recognized for his hard work, self-confidence, and ambition, Thiers was also a brilliant conversationalist welcome in salon society. However, he aroused mixed feelings due to his arrogance and cynicism.

Early in 1822, Thiers began work on an *Histoire de la Révolution française* (*History of the French Revolution*, 10 vols., 1823–27). Largely based on conversations and interviews with participants and witnesses, it contributed to the rehabilitation of the first stages of the Revolution through vigorous defense of the Constitution of 1791 and the principles of constitutional monarchy, together with condemnation of the excesses of the Jacobin Terror and popular involvement in politics. Thiers's political ideal would remain "liberty," combined with "order." His other major history, the *Histoire du Consulat et de l'Empire* (*History of the Consulate and Empire*, 20 vols., 1845–62), would make a major contribution to the glorification of Napoleon, chronicling his military exploits and role in the reestablishment of order in the aftermath of revolution. He would, as a minister, be instrumental in organizing the triumphant return of the Emperor's remains from Saint Helena. Subsequently he would maintain that the essential lesson he had derived from his studies was that "however great, however wise, however vast the genius of a man, never must the destinies of a country be delivered to him."

With his financial stability secured by the dowry acquired through marriage in 1833 to Elise Dosne, and having taken advantage of his father-in-law's connections to acquire the post of secretary with the Anzin mining company, Thiers was able to engage more fully in politics. In 1829, Thiers was dissatisfied with the excessively cautious position taken by *Le Constitutionnel* and founded with Mignet and Armand Carrel a new newspaper, *Le National*, which demanded constitutional monarchy on the British model, with governments responsible to parliament rather than to the monarch, insisting on principle that "Le roi regne et ne gouverne pas ('The king reigns and does not govern'). Although personally committed to legal opposition, the ambiguity of the document which Thiers helped to draft on July 26, 1830 to denounce the legality of Charles X's repressive ordinances helped to provoke revolutionary violence on the streets of Paris. Afraid that the Republic would be proclaimed by the crowds, Thiers helped to persuade fellow liberals to offer the crown to the Duc d'Orléans.

The 1830 Revolution inaugurated Thiers's rapid rise to ministerial office; his career was marked by the brutal repression of popular protest as interior minister, and a preference for an adventurous foreign policy which led twice to his removal from office by Louis-Philippe. In opposition from 1840, Thiers was critical of François-Pierre-Guillaume Guizot, the king's new chief minister, for his unwillingness to reward virtue by gradually extending the vote to the property-owning middle classes, and from the end of 1845 he allied himself with Camille-Hyacinthe-Odilon Barrot to demand a limited extension of the franchise and parliamentary reform. In February 1848, when another revolutionary situation unexpectedly developed, Thiers was asked by the king to form a ministry in a desperate attempt to save the regime, but it was too late. Paradoxically, Thiers's efforts had helped to bring down the regime to which he would remain most attached.

With 1848 and the establishment of the Second Republic, the prospect of social reform was a reality which terrified Thiers. He had risen from obscurity to affluence and was determined to defend the social system that had allowed and made possible his ascent. For a popular audience he quickly penned *De la propriété* (*On Property*, 1848), a defense of private property and an attack on proposals to recognize the right to work, establish cooperatives, and tax the wealthy. He would denounce suffrage for enfranchizing the "vile multitude." Thiers supported the candidacy of Louis Napoleon for the presidency of the republic as a means of restoring social order, and because he believed Bonaparte to be a clown he could dominate (despite Marshal Bugeaud's warning that the overwhelmingly rural electorate would be electing an emperor). Subsequently, as well as supporting restrictions on voting rights, this notoriously anticlerical man would press for an expansion of the Roman Catholic teaching orders and of religious instruction in the primary schools as a means of inculcating conservative principles in the young.

Thiers welcomed Bonaparte's *coup d'état* in December 1851, but never forgave its instigator for imprisoning him for a few days, along with other potential opponents. During the 1850s he concentrated on his writing while remaining influential within the political elite. He was elected to the *Corps législatif* in 1863, and would prove to be the foremost critic of the Second Empire, condemning the Emperor's personal power and demanding a return to parliamentary government and recognition of the "necessary liberties." He favored alliances with conservative powers, especially Austria and the Papacy, in defence of the balance of power and moral order, and his criticism of Napoleon III's support for "nationalities" attracted wide support. He attacked a free-trade policy that opened the economy to competition in order to accelerate modernization, and which threatened the Anzin company's massive profits. As both the internal and international political situations grew more difficult in the late 1860s, Thiers opposed the extension of conscription, preferring a smaller professional army better suited to the preservation of order. In 1870, quite courageously, he opposed a war with Prussia for which he believed the country was ill-prepared.

Following catastrophic defeat and the collapse of the Second Empire, Thiers played a major role in the negotiation of first an armistice and then peace, and then as head of government did much to provoke the Paris Commune and to smash it in an orgy of bloodshed involving the former imperial army, released from German prisoner-of-war camps for the purpose. He proved that a conservative republic might be as proficient in preserving order as a monarchical regime. This controversial figure, who played a central role in French politics for fifty years, was above all a pragmatist. An opponent of political reaction in 1830, he would become the leading liberal critic of the Second Empire. In 1848 and 1871, fearing a socialist revolution, he became a ferocious counter-revolutionary. While preferring a constitutional monarchy, he was prepared to accept a Third Republic as the regime that divided France and the French the least.

ROGER PRICE

Biography

Born in Marseille, 1797. Admitted to the bar. 1818. Began *Histoire de la Révolution française*. 1822. Founded *Le National*. 1829; played leading role in revolution, elected deputy, 1830. Interior Minister, 1832, 1834–36. Leading figure in liberal opposition. 1840–48. Began *Histoire du Consulat et de l'Empire*.

1845. Leading conservative deputy during Second Republic, 1848–51. Leading figure in liberal opposition to Second Empire, 1863–70. Major figure in peace negotiations and in suppression of Paris Commune, 1870–1871. President of the Republic, 1871–73. Died in 1877.

Selected Works

Histoire de la Révolution française. 10 vols. 1823–27.
De la propriété. 1848.
Histoire du Consulat et de l'Empire. 20 vols. 1845–62.
Discours parlementaires de M. Thiers. 16 vols. 1879–89.

Bibliography

Agulhon, M., et al. *Monsieur Thiers d'une République à l'autre.* Paris: Publisud, 1998.
Bury, J. P. T., and R. P. Tombs. *Thiers 1797–1877: A Political Life.* London: Allen and Unwin, 1986.
Collingham, H. *The July Monarchy.* London: Longman, 1988.
Girard, L. *Les Libéraux français.* Paris: Aubier, 1975.
Guiral, P. *Adolphe Thiers ou de la nécessité en politique.* Paris: Fayard, 1986.
Price, R. *The French Second Empire: an Anatomy of Political Power.* Cambridge: Cambridge University Press, 2001.

THE THIRD OF MAY 1808–1814

Painting by Francisco José de Goya y Lucientes

Francisco Goya's painting of the aftermath of a popular uprising in Madrid has become an iconic image of repression, popular martyrdom, and the horrors of civil strife. However, in more recent times, the liberal sentiments that have been understood to lie behind its creation have been called into question, just as the nature of the popular patriotic uprising that it depicts has been analyzed from fresh critical perspectives.

Mystery still surrounds many elements of the painting's conception. In modern times it has always been viewed as one of a pair (with *The Second of May*), but it is now believed that it may have been designed as one of a series of four paintings. These paintings were not commissioned, but proposed as a project by Goya, who was in a precarious financial situation, and who may have wished to gain favor with the regime of Fernando VII to avoid being accused of having collaborated with the Napoleonic occupation.

The events which Goya depicts took place against the background of the French invasion and the monarchic crisis it provoked. On March 17, Manuel de Godoy's residence in Aranjuez was stormed, and the influential minister was captured and beaten by a mob. Further riots forced the abdication of Carlos IV in favor of Fernando, in an attempt to save Godoy's life. During April, French troops entered Madrid and were at first welcomed by the new king. However, when Napoleon invited the royal household to Bayonne in late April, he persuaded Ferdinand to return power to Carlos, who promptly abdicated in favour of Joseph Bonaparte. On news of the final evacuation of members of the Royal family from Madrid on May 2, rioting began. The response to this rioting, summary executions by Napoleonic troops, is the subject of Goya's *Third of May*.

Recent archival research by Janis Tomlinson has shown that the rioters were a motley gang of ex-prisoners, vagabonds, and transients, but by the time of the commemoration of these events in 1814, after Ferdinand VII's return to Madrid, the rioters had become an heroic, patriotic representation of the common man. It has been suggested that Goya's paintings were designed as part of these celebrations. However, although they are in effect historical paintings commemorating recent events (a genre familiar to all those, including Goya, acquainted with contemporary painting in France, but almost unknown in Spain), they refuse to adopt in any simplistic way the then-fashionable neoclassical visual idiom or the easy rhetoric of popular heroism that had been the staple of, for example, images glorifying the *sans-culottes* storming of the Tuileries in France and engraved representations of the events of the second of May in Spain. Instead, Goya's work creates a more ambiguous, but therefore more deeply resonant, pathos.

There is no evidence to support the myth of Goya having witnessed the uprisings himself. It is now clear that *The Third of May* is a highly imagined and constructed painting. To help him construct his scene, Goya turned (as Jacques-Louis David had when he was called upon to portray popular Martyrdom in the *Marat*) to images of sacred martyrdom, and to engravings and popular prints representing scenes of execution by firing squad; these included an anonymous print of the *Assassination of Five Valencian Monks* (1813), which featured monks facing a firing squad in poses very similar to those of the dying protesters, and the print by Paul Revere of the *Boston Massacre*. Goya's resort to popular imagery should not surprise us, given his interest in and awareness of the vitality of popular culture, but in the context of this large-scale, historical painting, his obvious indebtedness to such nonelite forms is noteworthy, and anticipates the practice of painters such as Gustave Courbet and Édouard Manet.

However, in order to appreciate the image's complexity we must examine the picture in detail, and explore the way in which Goya transformed his sources. Janis Tomlinson has recently argued that Goya's portrayal of the populace in the image represents them as a threatening mob rather than a heroic band, but other commentators see hopelessness rather than threat as central to their depiction. Whichever interpretation one opts for, there is, undoubtedly, something disquieting (even ironic) in the transfer of the poses and gestures of hopeless and nonviolent monks in the Valencia print to the insurgents in Goya's painting. The stigmata marks and the pose of the victims of course recall religious scenes, but here they graft an unexpected air of quietism and passivity on to the supposedly heroic and muscular populace.

Despite its inclusion of familiar landmarks, Goya's setting is not a precisely recognizable or realist cityscape of Madrid, but rather a composite, imaginary landscape. It is a night scene, dramatically lit by the vivid lantern which casts light on the

Francisco José de Goya y Lucientes, *The Third of May, 1808*
(*Execution of the Rebels on the Montana del Principe Pio*). Reprinted
courtesy of AKG Photo.

victims while spreading an ominous shadow over the line of
Napoleonic troops, which is both faceless and seemingly endless
(stretching as it does into the far right distance). The sense of
perspective is confused by the way in which Goya groups the
figures representing the insurgents and the crowd, and by the
compression of the picture space, which places the bayonets of
the rifles so near to the victims. This structure, together with
the combination of extreme expressivity on certain faces and the
blank or hidden physiognomies of others, lends a hallucinatory,
dreamlike atmosphere to this ostensibly realist image.

It might also be remarked that, as an experiment in historical
painting, *The Third of May* subtly exploits two different languages to express tensions between France and Spain in terms
of the formal languages of painting. One side of this composition
(the "French side") contains more rigid geometries (the lineup
of soldiers with its faint and ironic reminder of David's *Horatii*,
the muskets, the lantern, even the architectural background) and
a smooth finish to the sword and helmets, which might remind
us of French neoclassicism; the other (the "Spanish side") is
more fluid, more energetic in its use of pose and gesture, and
freer in its use of paint and particularly impasto—this side is
much nearer to Goya's own habitual representation of artisan
and peasant classes. The split nature of the composition thus
embeds the Franco-Spanish conflict in the very fabric of the

picture, and at the same time represents a bold pictorial experiment in a hybrid kind of history painting.

What the picture tells us about Goya's liberal sympathies is
difficult to establish, both because of the utter lack of documentation surrounding the work and because of the context of the
notoriously illiberal regime of Ferdinand VII. The heroicization
of the rebels of May 2, a process in which Goya's canvas participates, might be seen as part of the policy of antiliberal populism
that defined an essentially repressive regime after 1814. There
is a frustrating lack of evidence concerning how the image was
viewed, however, and the only thing that does seem clear is that
the image disappeared into storage shortly after its completion
and remained there until at least 1835.

Like Goya's more personal depictions of civil war brutality,
the *Disasters of War* (which were not published until 1863), this
painting had only a delayed impact on the art world. Perhaps
the most famous appropriation of Goya's painting was that of
Manet, an enthusiast for Spanish art, who took essential elements of the composition as the basis of his *Execution of Maximilian* of 1867. Since then, The *3rd May* has continued to be seen
as testimony to the brutality of oppression and to the heroism
of popular resistance, and this reputation seems still to stubbornly resist the firing squad of art historical revisionism.

MARK LEDBURY

Work

Oil on canvas, 1814. 104¾ in. × 136 in. Museo del Prado,
Madrid.

Bibliography

Andioc, Rene. "Algo más—o menos?—sobre el Tres de Mayo de
Goya," *Goya* 265–66 (1998): 194–203.
Auge, Jean-Louis. "Précis de composition: le 2 mai 1808 et le 3 mai
1808 de Goya," *Connaissance des arts* 537 (1997): 84–89.
Baticle, Jeannine. "Lux et Tenebris. Goya entre la légende et la
réalité," *Colloquio artes* 48 (1981): 51–59.
Bialostocki, Jan. "The *Firing Squad* from Paul Revere to Goya: The
Formation of a New Theme in America, Russia and Spain." In
The Message of Images. Vienna: 1988.
Glendinning, Nigel. "Imaginación de Goya: Nuevas fuentes para
algunos de sus dibujos y pinturas," *Archivo Español de Arte* 49
(1976): 273–92.
Gully, Anthony Lacy. "The Unexpected Source of Goya's Painting,
May 3, 1808," *Studies in Iconography* 9 (1983): 99–106.
Krahl, Ilse. *Goyas Diptychon: Der 2. und 3. Mai*. Duisburg: 1997.
Tomlinson, Janis. *Goya in the Twilight of Enlightenment*. New
Haven and Conn.: Yale University Press, 1992.

THORARENSEN, BJARNI 1786–1841

Icelandic poet

Accepted by most as Iceland's "first Romantic," Bjarni Thorarensen has often been compared unfavorably with his great successor, Jónas Hallgrímsson. Indeed, in comparison with
Hallgrímsson's smooth and modern diction, Thorarensen's poetic language seems uneven and archaic. His ideas can also seem
old-fashioned and orthodox (for example, his adherence to the
traditional division of mind and body)—antihumanitarian,

even—whereas Hallgrímsson is egalitarian and sympathetic toward all things great and small. Although this may all be true,
there is much to be said about Thorarensen as a poet, and in
some respects his achievement outdoes that of Hallgrímsson.

Thorarensen is perhaps best understood as a poetic exponent
of the Nordic sublime. This kind of approach was suggested by
one of his contemporaries (Grímur Thomsen, 1845), but it has

not yet been taken into full account. Instead of being related to eighteenth- and nineteenth-century theories and discourse of the sublime, Thorarensen's poems and ideas have been subject to a narrower kind of reading, one based on the assumption that he was strongly influenced by Charles Montesquieu's ideas. In *De l'esprit des lois* (*Of the Spirit of the Laws*, 1748), Montesquieu argued that climate and natural conditions had a crucial effect on human character. Although Thorarensen did to a degree have similar views (there are, however, very few indications that he was familiar with Montesquieu's writings), they should rather be regarded as part and parcel of his interest in the Nordic sublime. By placing all the emphasis on the connection between climate and character, on the supposedly positive effects of harsh climate and conditions on people like the Icelanders (and correspondingly negative effects of mild climate and conditions), Thorarensen's readers have interpreted his poems on ethical, nationalistic, and pedagogical grounds. This is unfortunate, as the aesthetic factor tends to be overlooked.

While studying in Copenhagen, Thorarensen is reported to have heard some of Henrich Steffen's 1802–3 lectures inaugurating Romanticism in Denmark. Also inspired by his favorite poet, Adam Oehlenschläger, Thorarensen began reviving Old Norse meters and motives and putting them to new use in his poetry. Citing Oehlenschläger's *Axel og Valborg* he later wrote an otherwordly love poem, "Sigrúnarljóð" ("Lines to Sigrún," 1820), in which he fuses eddic elements with Romantic sentiments, producing an effect of Gothic sublimity. Arguing for the unconventional aesthetics of beauty in death, the speaker of the poem addresses his beloved and says that death could not undo but would only enhance her beauty. Were she to die before him, he would like her to return as a ghost and crush him in her arms, so that they could be joined together beyond the grave in a blissful flight across the night sky, their burning embrace blending with the northern lights. In comparison with Jónas Hallgrímsson's Platonic love poems, Thorarensen's poems of this kind are quite carnal.

The radical esthetics of the sublime are also manifest in his impressive poem "Veturinn" ("Winter," 1823). Personifying winter as a medieval knight of gigantic proportions, riding a huge horse across the universe, Thorarensen argues for its alternative beauty (on the grounds that it is sublime and not beautiful in a conventional way) and also for its essential part in the development of life through antithesis, based on seasonal changes between hot and cold. Thus subverting traditional views of winter as a barren and unfavorable season, Thorarensen again puts the poetic Edda to fruitful use, reviving its meters (*fornyrðoislag* and *ljóðoaháttur*) and inventing a diction that fuses the medieval and the modern in a highly original way.

Sublime images of nature are also prominent in the genre at which Thorarensen excelled: memorial poems. As an elegist, he is second to none in the history of Icelandic literature. In such poems as "Sæmundur Magnússon Hólm" (1821) and "Oddur Hjaltalín" (1840), Thorarensen uses violent images and metaphors, often drawn from nature, to describe physical and mental suffering, or the human condition at large. These elegies are written as a kind of apology for the deceased ones, who often were gifted but eccentric friends of the poet. Thorarensen brings out their character with great psychological insight, showing at the same time his Romantic and individualistic view of life, as in "Oddur Hjaltalín," where he strongly warns those who allow themselves to be carried downstream in life's current not to blame the salmon running upstream and jumping the cascades.

In this way, Thorarensen was writing against the grain. Unlike Hallgrímsson, he did not aim for smoothness and elegance. Far from being clumsily composed, as sometimes is assumed, Thorarensen's poems match form and subject matter perfectly. Written with unconventional esthetics in mind, they convey the poet's original and deep thoughts with discordant images, which are often excessively heaped together (excess being one of the main characteristics of the discourse of the sublime).

Thorarensen's poetic career was discontinuous. It can be divided into three periods with long intervals in between, during which he wrote few, if any, poems. The first period, 1808 to 1811, is characterized by poems on nature and nationality, along with translations of classical authors such as Ovid; the second, from 1815 to 1825, is characterized by love poems; and the third and final one, from 1835 to 1841, by elegies.

SVEINN YNGVI EGILSSON

See also **Hallgrímsson, Jónas; Oehlenschläger, Adam Gottlob**

Biography

Born December 30, 1786 in Brautarholt near Reykjavík, but grew up at Hlíðoarendi in Fljótshlíðo (a farm in south Iceland best known for being the home of a hero of the medieval *Saga of Burnt Njal*). Tutored mostly at home, showing exceptional gifts; entered the University in Copenhagen at fifteen and completed his law study at twenty. Served in government offices in Copenhagen. Became a deputy justice, 1811, and justice of the Supreme Court in Reykjavík, 1817. Made governor of north and east Iceland in 1833, residing in the north (Möðoruvellir in Hörgárdalur in the Eyjafjörðour region) until his death on August 24, 1841.

Selected Works

Ljóðomæli vols. 1 and 2. Edited by Jón Helgason. Copenhagen: Hiðo íslenzka fræðoafélag, 1935.

Bréf vols. 1 and 2. Edited by Jón Helgason. Copenhagen: Hiðo íslenzka fræðoafélag, 1943–86.

Benedikz, Eiríkur, (ed). *An Anthology of Icelandic Poetry*. Reykjavík: Ministry of Education, 1969.

Bibliography

Beck, Richard. "Bjarni Thorarensen: Iceland's Pioneer Romanticist," *Scandinavian Studies and Notes* 15 (1938–39): 71–80.

———, ed. *Icelandic Lyrics*. Reykjavík: Þórhallur Bjarnarson, 1930.

Bjarnason, Páll. *Ástakveðoskapur Bjarna Thorarensens og Jónasar Hallgrímssonar*. Studia Islandica 28. Reykjavík: Menningarsjóðour, 1969.

Einarsson, Stefán. *A History of Icelandic Literature*. New York: Johns Hopkins Press for the American-Scandinavian Foundation, 1957. 231–33.

Guðonason, Bjarni. "Bjarni Thorarensen og Montesquieu." In *Afmælisrit Jóns Helgasonar*. Reykjavík: Heimskringla, 1969.

Hauksson, Þorleifur. *Endurteknar myndir í kveðoskap Bjarna Thorarensens*. Studia Islandica 27. Reykjavík: Menningarsjóðour, 1968.

Hauksson, Þorleifur. "Inngangur." In Bjarni, Thorarensen. *Ljóðomæli: Úrval*. Reykjavík: Rannsóknastofnun í bókmenntafræðoi and Menningarsjóðour, 1976.

Helgason, Jón. "Æviágrip." In Bjarni, Thorarensen. *Ljóðomæli* vol. 1. Copenhagen: Hiðo íslenzka fræðoafélag, 1935.

Stefánsson Hjaltalín, Torfi K. *Eldur á Möðoruvöllum: Saga Möðoruvalla í Hörgárdal frá öndverðou til okkar tíma* I. Reykjavík: Flateyjarútgáfan, 2001.

Thomsen, Grímur. "Bjarni Thorarensen: En Skizze." In *Gæa: Æsthetisk Aarbog*. 1845.

Þorsteinsson, Steingrímur J. "Bjarni Thorarensen: Embættismaður og skáld." In *Afmælisrit Jóns Helgasonar*. Reykjavík: Heimskringla, 1969.

THOREAU, HENRY DAVID 1817–1867

American prose writer

In 1837, having recently graduated from Harvard College and embarked upon a career as a teacher, Henry David Thoreau joined the Hedge Club in Concord, Massachusetts, a transcendentalist group that met under the auspices of Ralph Waldo Emerson. Anglo-European Romanticism came to America in various formats, one of which was the transcendentalism centered around Emerson and his teachings. It was presented with particular force in his small book *Nature* (1836), which was eagerly read by young intellectuals seeking an antidote to the rationalism still lingering from the eighteenth century. *Nature* located spirit in nature, which in Emerson's reading took in everything not specifically included in the self (the "*me*"; all else is the "*not-me*"). He located the human as the center to which the natural world relates, and he found in figuration the tool and key with which to read that world. Most Anglo-European Romanticism would have understood (if not always agreed on) those radical elements, to which Emerson and his disciples added, firmly, the need to establish a distinctly American voice, one that would link Wordsworthian Romanticism with an unmistakably American perspective. In "A Natural History of Massachusetts" (1842), Thoreau laid out his earliest comprehensive reading of these issues. The essay begins with an echo of William Wordsworth's "Tintern Abbey" (1798)—along with the "Ode to Immortality" (1802), this was the most influential of Wordsworth's poems on the American Romantics—and continues with an occasional allusion to Jean-Jacques Rousseau ("society is always diseased, and the best is the most so"); but his primary concern in his comments on the American seasons is nature's organic circularity, which he read principally in a Goethean-Wordsworthian mode, dwelling on the idea of a spirit that runs through and beyond nature and links the whole in organic unity. It became Thoreau's main business to echo, but also to qualify and reject aspects of Romantic claims made by Anglo-European sources, and he did so in each of his major texts. His reading was deeply dialectical and ironic, built on elements of nature that he treated in such a way as to question those elements at the same time as he affirmed them.

Thoreau's first book shows him realizing how difficult his chosen project would be. On August 31, 1839, he and his brother John set out on a two week trip on New England waters. *A Week on the Concord and Merrimack Rivers* (1849) assembles much he had been thinking about in relation to literature and spirituality. The text is largely a series of meditations purportedly made as the boat traveled upstream, from Concord, Massachusetts, to Concord, New Hemisphire, and back. Between their arrival at and departure from New Hampshire, they spent a week walking to the source of the rivers, an event the text barely mentions. Thoreau sets up a series of such symmetries, sometimes intersecting: the circular travel narrative is also cyclical (it ends with their tying the boat to the same tree they had linked it to earlier in the season). A series of related shapes makes a series of related statements, yet not quite so: the pattern fails at a crucial point. What ought to have been a significant walk up to the source has at its center a silly, briefly drawn story about a young recruit going to join his regiment. For the grandeur that ought to be there Thoreau is compelled to substitute, elsewhere in the text, a brilliant set piece on a journey he took to the top of Mount Saddleback several years before, comparable in kind and quality to Wordsworth ascending Mount Snowdon. Whatever its extraordinary achievement, that patchwork cannot stand in for what *A Week* required. Thoreau could not bring off the ultimate symmetry, a failure he would not forget.

That he was working on the text of *A Week* during his sojourn at Walden Pond suggests that *Walden; Or Life in the Woods* (1854) might well have such issues in mind; in fact its handling of these issues adds another dimension to *Walden*'s masterliness. Thoreau treats the question as a matter of narratives in constant, unsettled interplay, as the first paragraph shows: his acts are ordered cyclically ("At present I am a sojourner in civilized life again"), implying a direct counterpart to the organic natural cycle, yet he also tells us that he lived at the pond "two years and two months," which means that the text is ordered in the form of an annual natural cycle (a typically Emersonian emblematic move). This is characteristic of Thoreau's art: he works the interplay of time and act by human invention/intervention, not passive reproduction. Nature, this implies, is not by itself enough, an idea already suggested in *A Week* and developed through the rest of his work. This is an especially telling version of Thoreau's dialectical mission to state in such a way that the statement may well be a questioning, may even be an undoing. He had, after all, argued that "yes and no are lies." What does this mean for the Goethean immanentism in the great scene of the melting of the sandbank, nature's sap flowing, figuring the activities of the leaf, and the hand? Thoreau was a skilled and often ironic manipulator of archetypes, playing with master narratives, each of which claims ascendance in the workings of the world. The Goethean narrative comes full circle in the "Spring" chapter, but the text as a whole (the transcendent narrative) does not. "Conclusion," in counterproposal, posits the ideal figure for our lives as the parabola, a nonreturning curve forever on a tangent to our sphere, our presence in this world. *A Week* had made the point differently: near the end Thoreau says that "here or nowhere is our heaven" (another quotation from Johann Wolfgang von Goethe), yet he follows it in a few pages with one of his few competent poems: "I am a parcel of vain strivings" suggests a higher nature than what we have access to now. This is another archetypal narrative. "Yes and no are lies"; radical contraries are simultaneously present; we seek, impossibly, to live by each at once. It is precisely Thoreau's awareness of this impossible possibility that establishes the ground of his work, figured most brilliantly in *Walden* and his journal.

The rest of Thoreau's books are largely collections of essays that came together in logical packages: the trips to Maine became *The Maine Woods* (1864), the trips to Cape Cod became *Cape Cod* (1868). An ironic symmetry links those two collections. *Walden*'s initial impetus came from a desire to test Emersonian self-reliance on local grounds. *The Maine Woods* tests it on the rawest primitive grounds, a project Thoreau admires, though he prefers more domestic locales. Maine's world is that of endless density and a distinctly unfriendly nature (its cold heart seen at the top of Mount Ktaadn). The nature of Cape Cod is equally inhospitable, but in an opposing way: it proffers barrenness rather than overwhelming density; it is as deadly in its spareness as Maine is in its profusion. Thoreau's passion for fearful symmetry is fully at play in the interrelations of these books. His testings lead toward grim qualifications that he did not live fully to explore.

Much of his exploration from the early 1850s went into the journal he began after college and kept at for most of his life with increasing concentration. At first it was largely a repository for ideas, drafts of material that went into his writing, records of reading and commentary, all interspersed with remarks on nature of varying generality. Gradually the journal dealt with more about natural cycles, still more about natural detail. By the early 1850s it had become a thing to itself, a self-defining, self-demarcating project that could never be concluded but only given up. His changing attitudes toward history and grand narratives in a world replete with things, his developing understanding of diurnal meaning, a curious, fertile mix of incompleteness and connectedness by which, somehow, we live: as more of Thoreau's journal becomes published and absorbed it looks increasingly like a project unique in its time, prefiguring our own. It compels another look at his remarkable canon, a reconsideration of what it was learning to see and say.

FREDERICK GARBER

Biography

Born July 12, 1817 in Concord, Massachusetts, and attended Harvard University from 1833 to 1837. After graduation began to teach, resigning from his first job because he was ordered to flog six students. Taught at Concord Academy from 1838 to 1841, at the same time assisting his father in the latter's pencil business. On July 4, 1845 (United States Independence Day), moved into a cabin he had built at Walden Pond on land owned by Ralph Waldo Emerson, and lived there until September 6, 1847. From 1849 on he practiced surveying in order to support himself. Died of tuberculosis on May 6, 1867.

Selected Works

"Natural History of Massachusetts." July 1842.
"Civil Disobedience." 1848.
A Week on the Concord and Merrimack Rivers. 1849.
Walden; or Life in the Woods. 1854.
Excursions. 1863.
The Maine Woods. 1864.
Cape Cod. 1868.
Journal. (Edited by various editors, 7 vols. to date. Princeton, N.J.: Princeton University Press, 1981– .)

Bibliography

Buell, Lawrence. *The Environmental Imagination: Thoreau, Nature Writing, and the Formation of American Culture.* Cambridge, Mass.: Belknap Press of Harvard University Press, 1995.
Burbick, Joan. *Thoreau's Alternative History: Changing Perspectives on Nature, Culture, and Language.* Philadelphia: University of Pennsylvania Press, 1987.
Cameron, Sharon. *Writing Nature: Henry Thoreau's* Journal. New York: Oxford University Press, 1985.
Garber, Frederick. *Thoreau's Fable of Inscribing.* Princeton, N.J.: Princeton University Press, 1991.
———. *Thoreau's Redemptive Imagination.* New York: New York University Press, 1977.
Krutch, Joseph Wood. *Henry David Thoreau.* New York: Sloane, 1948.
Paul, Sherman. *The Shores of America: Thoreau's Inward Exploration.* Urbana: University of Illinois Press, 1958.
Peck, H. Daniel. *Thoreau's Morning Work: Memory and Perception in* A Week on the Concord and Merrimack Rivers, *the Journal, and* Walden. New Haven, Conn.: Yale University Press, 1990.
Richardson, Robert D. *Henry David Thoreau: A Life of the Mind.* Berkeley and Los Angeles: University of California Press, 1986.

THORVALDSEN, BERTEL 1770–1844

Danish sculptor

Bertel Thorvaldsen's career spans more than half a century. At the beginning, his work consisted of mythological figures and reliefs in accordance with neoclassicist idealistic striving toward beauty, peace, and harmony; toward the end, it was of monumental portrait and equestrian statues, and sepulchral monuments in commemoration of, or representing, historic figures or contemporary persons, dressed in the costume of the respective periods. Also, Thorvaldsen produced biblical figures, executed as manifestations of political or national ideas, whether these were commissioned by the crown, the church, the aristocracy,

or for governments. Thorvaldsen further accomplished the modeling of approximately 170 portrait busts, which make up quite an international portrait gallery of his time. This sculptor's artistic development is demonstrated in a remarkable way in his self-portraits from 1810 and 1839, both of which were commissioned works. The strict form and stylized physiognomy of the early, larger-than-life-sized self-portrait conveys more than a depiction of Thorvaldsen the individual: in a wider sense, it is a tribute to the heroic genius of the artist, portrayed as a Greek god. The burning idealism in the facial expression caused his patron to exclaim, "You have never seen anything so impressive, so alike. It is Jupiter's gaze, it is flesh." With his later likewise larger-than-life-sized self-portrait statue, from 1839, the sculptor has created a naturalistic representation of himself—he is standing, wearing an artist's smock tied with a belt, reminiscent of Thor, the Norse god of war. This similarity is by no means unintended: Thorvaldsen holds in his hand a hammer and chisel, suggesting that the hammer, the mark and weapon of Thor, is also the tool of the sculptor.

At eleven years of age, Bertel Thorvaldsen was admitted to the Royal Academy in Copenhagen in 1781. During his early years, he was influenced by the Danish sculptor Johannes Wiedewelt, a friend of Joseph Winckelmann, and the painter Nicolai Abraham Abildgaard. Both artists were representative of the classicist form prevailing during the second half of the eighteenth century. Thorvaldsen's traveling scholarship led him to Rome, where he took up his permanent residence for the following forty years. He soon became a central figure in the artistic community within the city—next to the Italian Antonio Canova, Thorvaldsen was the most significant of neoclassicist sculptors on the continent, his circle of themes being the gods and heroes of classical literature. The turning point in Thorvaldsen's career was a tribute to the new man in the shape of a figure from Homer's *Iliad*. *Jason with the Golden Fleece* (1802–3) was a heroic male figure, a colossal statue captured in a moment between rest and forward movement. This statue created a sensation in Rome, where Canova described it as an expression of "a new and grandiose style." Thorvaldsen modeled the statue in clay, and it was some twenty years before it was carved in marble. In the relief *Briseis is Led Away*, 1803, from Homer's *Iliad*, Thorvaldsen shows the anger of Achilleus as expressed through a use of body language rarely found in the artist's oeuvre. In the same way that his mentor, Abildgaard, had described the pain of Philoctetes, Thorvaldsen demonstrated how feelings can be portrayed in posture, in flowing form and rhythm alone, without the help of facial expression and similar evocative, rigid effects. August Wilhelm von Schlegel, the German philosopher, described Achilleus as the only figure among Thorvaldsen's work to have a modern touch. The artist's subsequent works comprise a series of figures from Greco-Roman mythology, for example, *Bacchus* (1804), *Apollo* (1805), *Ganymede* (1805), *Hebe* (1806), and *Psyche* (1806). The pinnacle of his career was *The Entry of Alexander the Great into Babylon* (1812) for the Quirinale Palace in Rome, which had been commissioned by the French occupying forces in anticipation of Napoleon Bonaparte's entry into the city. This thirty-five-meter plaster frieze, depicting the peaceful triumphal entry by Alexander the Great into Babylon, alluded to Napoleon, its form inspired by the Parthenon frieze (the Elgin Marbles). During Thorvaldsen's visit to Copenhagen several years later, the principal writer of the Danish Romantic era, Adam Gottlob Oehlenschläger, suggested that Thorvaldsen should consider finding inspiration in Norse mythology and the history of the Danish people. Thorvaldsen himself never followed this advice; however, his assistant and pupil of many years, Danish sculptor Hermann Ernst Freund, was the first to create a new, original imagery for Norse mythology. As a parallel to his master's *Alexander* frieze, Freund's work includes the Ragnarok frieze depicting the downfall of the Gods, made for the Christiansborg Palace, Copenhagen.

In a series of pieces from the second decade of the nineteenth century, Thorvaldsen breaks away from the circle of themes inspired by classical antiquity to seek inspiration from actual life, although still maintaining a classicist appearance; see, for example, *Shepherd Boy* (1817). His statue *Hope* (1817) reflects a union between classical severity and Romantic aspiration, akin to German Romantic paintings in contemporary Rome. An outstanding example of Thorvaldsen's work is *The Swiss Lion* (1819–21) in Lucerne, probably the most Romantic of all his pieces. This monument, intended as a memorial to the Swiss guard killed during the 1792 storming of the Tuileries in Paris, plays on the contrast between art and nature—the figure of the wounded lion has been carved as a colossal relief directly into the rockface next to a lake in a scenic garden.

Although still living in Rome in the years 1820–38, Thorvaldsen received several commissions for monuments from Germany, Poland, and Denmark. One such project was for Copenhagen Cathedral, the 1821–24 statues of Christ and the Apostles. At a time when the Nazarenes were pressing for the revival of Christian art on a monumental scale in the form of fresco paintings, Thorvaldsen created twelve strictly classicist, larger-than-life-sized marble statues for the Cathedral. His figure of Christ, made for the altar of this Protestant church building, is unusual in its type: it shows a Christ who affectionately opens his embrace with the words "Come unto me," doubtless inspired by a painting by the Nazarene artist Peter von Cornelius from 1816. This white marble figure was placed in a tabernacle against a gilded recess, perhaps a reference to the polychromy debate raging at that time. Although a Protestant, in 1823 Thorvaldsen was commissioned to produce a sepulchral monument to Pope Pius VII, to be placed in the principal Catholic church, St. Peter's in Rome. A clay sketch model shows how Thorvaldsen went about this task without prejudice—he depicts the pope sitting on a sarcophagus, one hand resting on his tiara, which he has taken off and put down by his side. During the following years, Thorvaldsen received commissions for monuments, portrait statues, equestrian statues, and sepulchral monuments from all corners of Europe. In other commissions, scientists, such as the astronomer Copernicus (for the Polish Academy of Sciences, 1820), and Johan Gutenberg (for the city of Mainz), were depicted as seated, as was the poet, Lord Byron, whose statue was commissioned by a committee in 1829, five years after his death (Trinity College, Cambridge). Byron sits in a nonchalant manner with one foot resting on a truncated Doric column, dressed in modern attire and cloak, his pen resting on his chin as if in an inspired moment—all far removed from Thorvaldsen's early work, *Jason*, and its classical contrapposto. For the statue of another contemporary heroic figure, the Polish hero of the Napoleonic wars, Count Jozef Poniatowsky, Thorvaldsen went against his patrons' wishes for modern costume and imposed an antique garb, completely devoid of national characteristics. This piece (completed 1826–27, cast in bronze in 1832) was inspired by the Marcus Aurelius equestrian statue on the capitol in Rome. Furthermore, a statue of Johann Christoph Friedrich von Schiller was erected in Mainz in 1839.

METTE BLIGAARD

Biography

Born in Copenhagen November 19, 1770. Admitted to the Royal Academy, Copenhagen, 1781. Awarded traveling scholarship by the Academy, 1795. Arrived in Rome in 1797, to be his home for the next forty-one years. Member of the Florence Academy, 1804. Professor at the Royal Academy in Copenhagen, 1805. Member of the Accademia di San Luca in Rome, 1808. Member of the Academies in Berlin and Milan, 1811. Member of the Academy in Munich. Professor at the Accademia di San Luca in Rome, 1812. President of the Accademia di San Luca, 1827–28. Director of the Royal Academy in Copenhagen, 1833–44. Returned to Copenhagen to settle there in 1838. Honorary Citizen of Copenhagen, 1838. Bequeathed his collections to the city of Copenhagen, 1838. Died March 24, 1844. Buried in the courtyard of the Thorvaldsen Museum, the first museum in Denmark to be dedicated to the work of a single artist, erected by the city of Copenhagen to house the sculptor's collections in 1839–48.

Selected Works

Jason, 1802–03 (cast 1828). Marble statue. Thorvaldsens Museum, Copenhagen.
Briseus Is Led Away, 1803. Marble relief. Thorvaldsens Museum, Copenhagen.
The Entry by Alexander the Great into Babylon, 1812. Plaster relief. Palazzo del Quirinale, Rome.
Priam Pleads with Achilluse, 1815. Marble relief. Thorvaldsens Museum, Copenhagen.
The Swiss Lion, 1819. Lucerne.
Christ and the Apostles, 1821–24. Vor Frue Kirke, Copenhagen.
The Sarcophagus of Pius VII, 1824–25. Marble. St. Peter's Basilica, Rome.
Count Jozef Poniatowsky, 1826–27. Equestrian statue, bronze. Warsaw. Destroyed 1944; new version 1852).
Lord Byron, 1831–35. Marble statue. Trinity College, Cambridge.
Friedrich Schiller, 1836. Bronze statue. Mainz.
Self-portrait, 1839. Plaster statue. Nysø, Denmark.

Bibliography

Berter Thorvaldsen: Untersuchungen zu seinem Werk und zur Kunst seiner Zeit. Cologne: Museen der Stadt Köln, 1977.
Einem, Herbert von. *Thorvaldsens Kristus.* Berlin: Festschrift E. Trier, 1981.
Gravgaard, Anne-Mette, and Eva Henschen. *On the Statue of Christ by Thorvaldsen.* Copenhagen: Thorvaldsen Museum and the church of Our Lady, 1997.
Hartmann, J. B., and Klaus Parlasca. *Antike Motive bei Thorvaldsen.* Tübingen: 1979.
Helsted, Dyveke. *Thorvaldsen: Drawings and Bozzetti.* London: Heinz Gallery, 1973.
Künstlerleben in Rom: Bertel Thorvaldsen. Der Dänische Bildhauer und seine deutschen Freunde. Nuremberg: Germanisches Nationalmuseum, 1991.
Sass, Else Kai. *Thorvaldsens Portrætbuster I–III.* Copenhagen: 1963–65.
Spray, N. L. *Bertel Thorvaldsen's Revisions: The Evolution of the Artist's Style.* Berkeley and Los Angeles: University of California Press, 1983.
Wittstock, J. In *Ideal und Wirklichkeit der bildenden Kunst im späten 18. Jahrhundert.* Berlin: 1984.

TIECK, LUDWIG 1773–1853

German writer and editor

Ludwig Tieck's role in German Romanticism is paradoxical. Prolific writer though he was, he did not produce any of the era's most profound or innovative works. His significant contributions were confined to the *Herzensergiessungen eines kunstliebenden Klosterbuders* (*Outpourings of an Art-Loving Friar*, 1796), in which the crucial ideas came from Wilhelm Heinrich Wackenroder; the flawed novel *Franz Sternbalds Wanderungen* (*The Travels of Franz Sternbald*, 1798); and a memorable quatrain from the forgotten play *Kaiser Octavianius* (*Emperor Octavian*, 1804) which begins with an encapsulation of Romantic wonder, "mondbeglänzte Zaubernacht" (moonlit night of enchantment). Yet he was involved in the German Romantic movement in all its phases, he collaborated with almost all of its main protagonists, and he was influential as an editor of their works, as a mediator of ideas, and as a correspondent, critic, essayist, literary historian, and translator.

At university Tieck acquired a lifelong fascination with William Shakespeare, and in 1795 he published a German adaptation of *The Tempest* with an essay on Shakespeare's treatment of the miraculous. He began his own literary career by producing imitative potboilers for his mentors in Berlin and for the rationalist publisher Friedrich Nicolai, to whose periodical *Straussfedern* he contributed a number of short stories. Yet by the mid-1790s his sympathy with emergent Romanticism was demonstrated in a variety of genres. The epistolary novel *William Lovell* (1795–

96) built on pre-Romantic morbidity and melancholia to create a radical pessimism which anticipated nineteenth-century *ennui*. Editing a series entitled *Volksmärchen* (*Folk Tales*, 1797), Tieck published versions of German legends such as those of Bluebeard and the Fair Magelone. He added modern fairy tales such as *Der blonde Eckbert* (*Fair-Haired Eckbert*) and *Der Runenberg* (*The Mount of the Runes*), which portray an unstable world where human beings are threatened simultaneously by their own irrationality and the intrusion of supernatural powers. His satirical comedies *Der gestiefelte Kater* (*Puss in Boots*, 1797), *Die verkehrte Welt* (*The Topsy-Turvy World*, 1799), and *Prinz Zerbino* (1799) toy ingeniously with theatrical illusion and pillory the philistinism of contemporary German culture. In the trilogy of works arising from his collaboration with Wackenroder (the *Herzensergiessungen* and the *Phantasien über die Kunst* [*Fantasies on Art*, 1799], which he edited, and *Sternbald*, which he wrote up after Wackenroder's death) he helped disseminate the Romantic doctrine that art arises from irrational inspiration and conveys otherwise inaccessible spiritual truth.

Between 1798 and 1801, Tieck associated closely with the group of early Romantics based in Jena, particularly August Wilhelm and Friedrich Schlegel and Novalis, whose works he edited for posthumous publication. In his *Poetisches Journal* (1800), he included a number of pieces polemically attacking the opponents of the Jena circle, and also two lengthy *Briefe über W. Shakespeare*

(*Letters on W. Shakespeare*). The path into history, legend, and mystery marked by *Sternbald* and the fairy tales now led him to two verse dramas programmatically embodying Romantic convictions: *Leben und Tod der heiligen Genoveva* (*Life and Death of St. Geneviève*, 1800) and *Kaiser Octavianus*. Both draw on German chapbooks and nostalgically evoke the romance, wonder, and spiritual unity of the Catholic Middle Ages. They also evince the influence of Shakespeare and Pedro Calderón de la Barca. Tieck's interest in Spanish literature was further reflected in his translation of *Don Quixote* (1799–1800). At this time Tieck also became interested in the seventeenth-century mystic Jakob Böhme, whose speculative philosophy is reflected in *Der Runenberg* and was transmitted by Tieck to Novalis and to the painter Philipp Otto Runge. It was Runge who supplied illustrations for Tieck's anthology *Minnelieder aus dem schwäbischen Zeitalter* (*Courtly Love Songs of the Swabian Age*, 1803), the first example of his activity as an editor and popularizer of German medieval literature. *Genoveva* and *Der Runenberg* had appeared in an anthology of Tieck's works with a title proclaiming his literary allegiance: *Romantische Dichtungen* (*Romantic Fictions*, 1799–1800).

Soon, however, the Jena circle of Romantics broke up, and between 1803 and 1819 Tieck lived on a country estate in a seclusion interrupted intermittently by trips to Munich or abroad. It was a period of personal unease and minimal literary productivity. He did, however, continue researching on Shakespeare, and in 1811 published a collection of Elizabethan plays in translation: *Alt-Englisches Theater*. He also worked on medieval German literature, especially the *Nibelungenlied* and *Das Heldenbuch*. Yet in the fictional collection *Phantasus* (1812–16), he did little more than assemble his previously published fairy tales and augment them with comparable new texts. After this interval his creative work changed in character and is arguably no longer Romantic. Between 1822 and 1841 he published over thirty novellas; some of them are set in the Middle Ages or draw on legendary sources, and some are set outside Germany; others reflect the social reality of the Biedermeier age. All of them, however, are written in the urbanely realistic style of the post-Romantic epoch. This last phase of Tieck's output was to culminate in 1840 with the publication of the historical novel *Vittoria Accorombona* (*The Roman Matron*).

The shift to a socially oriented narrative style is connected with Tieck's return to Dresden in 1819, after which he resumed an active role in a literary community. He associated with the Dresden "Liederkreis," a group of minor late Romantic poets; he was acquainted with the composer Carl Maria von Weber, and the physician and painter Carl Gustav Carus; and he was a member of the group of Dante Alighieri enthusiasts surrounding Prince Johann of Saxony. His dramatic recitations became a tourist attraction. He edited and publicized the works of Heinrich von Kleist, of the Sturm und Drang (storm and stress) dramatist Jakob Michael Reinhold Lenz, and of the Romantic aesthetic theorist Karl Solger. He published numerous theater reviews and assumed a key role in the artistic management of the Dresden Court Theater. He was never to realize his ambition to publish a comprehensive study of Shakespeare, but in Dresden he was able to see to completion the standard Shakespeare translation begun by August Wilhelm Schlegel in the 1790s. It has become known as the Schlegel–Tieck translation, but Tieck's role was confined to that of coordinator and editor, for most

of the later translations were undertaken by Tieck's daughter Dorothea or by Count Wolf von Baudissin.

Critics—most famously Friedrich Gundolf, one of the circle surrounding the poet Stefan George—have persistently attacked Tieck's writing on the grounds of superficiality, condemning the lack of unity in his work and accusing him of accommodation to changing taste. It was his storyteller's attraction to the poetic and imaginative that allied him with Romanticism, not religious or philosophical conviction. Yet without him as facilitator, German Romanticism would neither have engaged so much with other European literatures nor have made the national impact that it did. His voluminous correspondence documents the entire German literary scene in the Romantic era. He was indeed, as the dramatist Friedrich Hebbel remarked in an obituary, "der König der Romantik" (the king of Romanticism).

RICHARD LITTLEJOHNS

Biography

Born in Berlin, May 31, 1773. His sister Sophie (1775–1833) became the author of numerous literary works; his brother Friedrich (1776–1851) achieved recognition as a sculptor. Tieck himself attended the Friedrichswerdersche Gymnasium, 1782–92; studied theology in Halle, Göttingen, and Erlangen, 1792–94. Returned to Berlin as a freelance professional writer. Married Amalie Alberti (1769–1837) in 1798; they had two daughters: Dorothea (1799–1841) and Agnes (1802–80). In Jena 1799–1800 and Dresden, 1801–3. Lived in Ziebingen near Frankfurt an der Oder, 1803–19. In Rome, 1805–06; in Munich, 1808–10. In London and Paris, 1817. Lived in Dresden from 1819, and acted as Saxon court dramaturgist from 1825. Took up a similar post in Berlin in 1841, and lived there under the patronage of Friedrich Wilhelm IV of Prussia until his death on April 28, 1853.

Selected Works

Collections

Schriften. 28 vols. Berlin: Reimer, 1828–54.
Gesammelte Novellen. 14 vols. Breslau: Max, 1835–42.
Kritische Schriften. 4 vols. Leipzig: Brockhaus, 1848–52.
Ludwig Tieck's Nachgelassene Schriften. 2 vols. Leipzig: Brockhaus, 1855.
Werke. Edited by Marianne Thalmann. 4 vols. Munich: Winkler, 1963–66.
Ausgewählte kritische Schriften. Edited by Ernst Ribbat. Tübingen: Niemeyer, 1975.
Schriften. 12 vols. Edited by Manfred Frank, Paul Gerhard Klussmann, Ernst Ribbat, Uwe Schweikert, and Wulf Segebrecht. Frankfurt: Bibliothek Deutscher Klassiker, 1985– .

Poetry

Gedichte. 3 vols. Dresden: Hilscher, 1821–23; 2d rev. ed. Berlin: Reimer, 1841.

Novels and Other Fiction

Abdallah. 1792.
William Lovell. 3 vols. 1795–96.
Peter Lebrecht. 2 vols. 1795–96.
Der blonde Eckbert. 1797. Translated as *Fair-haired Eckbert* in *German Literary Fairy Tales*. by Thomas Carlyle, 1983.
Franz Sternbalds Wanderungen. 1798.
Der Runenberg. 1804.
Der Aufruhr in den Cevennen. 1826. Translated as *The Rebellion in the Cervennes* by Madame Burette, 1845.

Der Alte vom Berge. 1828. Translated as *The Old Man of the Mountain* by J. C. Hare, 1831.
Der Hexen-Sabbath. 1831.
Der junge Tischlermeister. 1836.
Vittoria Accorombona. 1840. Translated as *The Roman Matron*, 1845.

Plays

Ritter Blaubart. 1797.
Der gestiefelte Kater. 1797. Translated as *Puss in Boots* by Lillie Winter. In *The German Classics of the Nineteenth and Twentieth Centuries*. 1914.
Die verkehrte Welt. 1799. Translated as *The Land of Upside Down* by Oscar Mandel. Rutherford: Fairleigh Dickinson University Press, 1978.
Prinz Zerbino. 1799.
Leben und Tod der heiligen Genoveva. 1800.
Kaiser Octavianus. 1804.

Criticism

Über Shakspeare's Behandlung des Wunderbaren, 1795.
Herzensergiessungen eines kunstliebenden Klosterbuders with Wilhelm Heinrich Wackenroder, 1796. Translated as Wackenroder, *Confessions and Fantasies* by Mary Hurst Schubert, University Park and London: Pennsylvania State University Press, 1971, and as *Outpourings of an Art-Loving Friar* by Edward Mornin, New York: Ungar, 1975.

Phantasien über die Kunst (with Wilhelm Heinrich Wackenroder), 1799.

Bibliography

Crisman, William. *The Crises of "Language and Dead Signs" in Ludwig Tieck's Prose Fiction*. Columbia, S.C.: Camden House, 1996.
Gundolf, Friedrich. "Ludwig Tieck" in *Romantiker*. 1931. (Reprinted in *Ludwig Tieck*. Edited by Wulf Segebrecht. Darmstadt: Wissenschaftliche Buchgesellschaft, 1976.)
Immerwahr, Raymond. *The Esthetic Intent of Tieck's Fantastic Comedy*. St. Louis: Washington University Press, 1953.
Lillyman, William J. *Reality's Dark Dream: The Narrative Fiction of Ludwig Tieck*. Berlin: de Gruyter, 1979.
Paulin, Roger. *Ludwig Tieck*. Stuttgart: Metzler, 1987.
———. *Ludwig Tieck: A Literary Biography*. Oxford: Clarendon Press, 1985.
Rath, Wolfgang. *Ludwig Tieck: Das vergessene Genie*. Paderborn: Schöningh, 1996.
Ribbat, Ernst. *Ludwig Tieck: Studien zur Konzeption und Praxis romantischer Poesie*. Kronberg/Taunus: Athenäum, 1977.
Trainer, James. "Ludwig Tieck." In *German Men of Letters*. Vol. 1. Edited by Alex Natan. London: Wolff, 1961.
Trainer, James. *Ludwig Tieck: From Gothic to Romantic*. The Hague: Mouton, 1964.
Zeydel, Edwin H. *Ludwig Tieck, the German Romanticist*, 1935. (Reprinted Hildesheim: Olms, 1971.)

TIGHE, MARY 1772–1810

Irish poet

Mary Tighe is most famous for her book-length poem *Psyche, or the Legend of Love* (1805). An allegorical retelling of Apuleius's story of Cupid and Psyche, *Psyche* consists of six cantos in the stanzaic style of Edmund Spenser's *Faerie Queene* (1590–95). In employing this form, Tighe represents (and largely anticipates) a more general Romantic Spenserianism, also practiced by poets such as Lord Byron and John Keats. The technical excellence and elegance of Tighe's prosody, maintained over so many lines, and the poem's less sustained but nevertheless sometimes brilliant psychological insight, make this a remarkable work. However, its adherence (some might say subservience) to a strict, conservative, male-dominated tradition, its affirmation of oppressive gender roles, and its setting in a world far removed from economic and political reality, combine to decrease its appeal for many readers today.

Tighe's early reception was similarly mixed, though for different reasons. John Keats made the most famous contemporary remark about her when he wrote "Mrs Tighe and Beattie once delighted me—now I see through them and can find nothing in them—or weakness—and yet," he adds, "how many they still delight." Felicia Hemans, whose poem "On the Grave of a Poetess" is dedicated to Tighe, remarked "her poetry has always touched me greatly from a similarity which I imagine I discover between her destiny and my own." In her own day, reviewers were often as concerned with her destiny as with her poetry. The *Quarterly* condemns many of the shorter poems published with *Psyche*, saying they "mostly bear marks of haste or carelessness." Yet it transcribes one of these, as it "was the last production of the author, penned only three months before her death . . . much of the interest, which it seems calculated to excite, must be ascribed to the circumstances amidst which it was composed." Another reader, Sir James Mackintosh, found the final three stanzas of *Psyche* "of such exquisite beauty that they quite silence me. They are beyond all doubt the most faultless series of verses ever produced by a woman." Yet he concluded that "I cannot consent to depose Madame de Staël, or even Joanna Baillie, to make room for your Irish queen. The masculine understanding of the one and the Shakespearian genius of the other, place them, in my opinion, above this most elegant poetess."

That Tighe's poetry exerted a major influence on that of John Keats was the thesis of Earle Vonard Weller's 1928 comparison of the two poets. Weller finds parallels to Tighe in virtually every one of Keats's poems. Such extended influence has never been asserted by more recent critics, but persuasive evidence has been offered that Keats had not entirely forgotten Tighe's poetry when he wrote his major works. Influencing the poetry of Keats is itself an important accomplishment in the Romantic period, but Tighe's critics are united in looking for something more.

Little consensus exists among critics today. Some scholars of women's poetry in the period are sharply critical. Marlon Ross has written of "the virtual absence of vision" in Tighe, "any attempt to construct a philosophical system, to transmit prophecy, to claim a hold on the wholeness of all experience." Others make a similar point tacitly, by omission: Tighe is not included among the many women poets represented in Anne K. Mellor and Richard E. Matlak's influential anthology *British Literature 1780–1830*.

Still other critics are enthusiastic in Tighe's support. Harriet Kramer Linkin, who calls *Psyche* "a crucial bridge between William Wordsworth and Percy Shelley," speaks of the "sophisticated critique" that *Psyche* "offers of masculinist Romanticism's objectification of the female." Linkin says Tighe "anticipates . . . feminist revisionists" like Angela Carter, Jean Rhys, and Anne Sexton, in their "reworkings of myths, fairy tales, and classic literary narratives" and notes her "effect on Felicia Hemans and Letitia Elizabeth Landon, who further her influential exploration of the Romantic aesthetic's objectification of the female." Jonathan Wordsworth says (in his introduction to the facsimile edition) that in *Psyche* Tighe "has the rare distinction of producing a memorable poem while writing in Spenser's own idiom."

JOHN M. ANDERSON

Biography

Born Mary Blachford in Ireland, October 9, 1772. Married her cousin, Henry Tighe, an Irish member of Parliament, 1793. Wrote *Psyche*, 1802–3; died of tuberculosis at Woodstock, County Wicklow, on March 24, 1810, at the age of 37.

Selected Works

Psyche, or The Legend of Love. 1805.
Psyche, with Other Poems. 1811.
"Anecdotes of Our Family Written for My Children." Edited by Patrick Henchy. *Journal of the Bibliographical Society of Ireland* 6, no. 6 (1957).
Selena. (Unpublished novel.)

Bibliography

Ashfield, Andrew, ed. *Romantic Women Poets. 1770–1838: An Anthology.* Manchester: Manchester University Press, 1995.
Henderson, Andrea. "Keats, Tighe and the Chastity of Allegory," *European Romantic Review* 10, no. 3 (1999): 279–306.
Kucich, Greg. *Keats, Shelley, & Romantic Spenserianism.* University Park: Pennsylvania State University Press, 1991.
Kucich, Greg. "Gender Crossings: Keats and Tighe," *Keats Shelley Journal* 44 (1995): 25–39.
Linkin, Harriet Kramer. "Romantic Aesthetics in Mary Tighe and Letitia Landon: How Women Recuperate the Gaze," *European Romantic Review* 7 (1997): 159–88.
———. "Romanticism and Mary Tighe's *Psyche*: Peering at the Hem of Her Blue Stockings," *Studies in Romanticism* 35 (1996): 55–72.
———. "Teaching the Poetry of Mary Tighe: *Psyche*, Beauty, and the Romantic Object." In *Approaches to Teaching British Women Poets of the Romantic Period.* Edited by Stephen C. Behrend and Harriet Kramer Linkin. New York: Modern Language Association, 1997.
———. "How It Is: Teaching Women's Poetry in British Romanticism Classes," *Pedagogy: Critical Approaches to Teaching Literature, Language, Composition and Culture* (2001): 91–115.
Mackintosh, James, *Memoirs of the Life of the Right Honourable Sir James Mackintosh.* Edited by Robert James Mackintosh. Boston: Little Brown, 1853. Volume II, 195–96.
Ross, Marlon. *The Countours of Masculine Desire: Romanticism and the Rise of Women's Poetry.* New York: Oxford University Press, 1989.
Weller, Earle Vonard. *Keats and Mary Tighe.* New York: Century, 1928.
Wilson, Carol Shiner, and Joel Haefner, eds. *Re-visioning Romanticism: British Women Writers, 1776–1837.* Philadelphia: University of Pennsylvania Press, 1994.

THE TITAN'S GOBLET, 1833

Painting by Thomas Cole

"The Titan's Goblet" (also known by the title *The Giant's Chalice*) is without doubt one of Thomas Cole's strangest paintings, and has always attracted considerable interest. Cole's friend and biographer, the Reverend Thomas Noble, published a pamphlet devoted to this single picture, and in the early twentieth century, with the emergence of Surrealism, the canvas enjoyed a resurgence of popularity as a protosurrealist work. The painting shows a landscape of lakes and mountain peaks, dotted with boats and cities, above which towers an enormous goblet, seemingly left there by some absentminded Titan. The rim of the goblet is covered with woods, fields, and buildings, and small boats sail across the lake that fills its bowl. Presumably the inhabitants of this place think of it as a secure world, and are unaware of how small they are in the greater scheme of things, or of how precariously they are placed; for surely, if the Titan returns to recover his goblet, their whole world will be casually overturned.

While fantastic in conception, the conceit of the painting is based on two concerns that were fundamental to Cole's work: a sense of the impermanence of empire, and a sense of man's smallness in relation to the larger universe. An awareness of the fragility of human civilization was a major preoccupation of late

eighteenth-and early nineteenth-century writers. It was explored in Romantic poems such as Lord Byron's *Childe Harold's Pilgrimage* (1811), as well as in historical studies such as Edward Gibbon's famous *Decline and Fall of the Roman Empire*, (1776–1778), or Comte de Voleny's book, *Les ruines, ou meditations surs les revolutions des empires* (1791). Throughout his career, Cole was fascinated by this theme, and it is striking that in the very year that he painted *The Titan's Goblet* he began work on his most ambitious treatment of the rise and fall of a civilization—his five-part series of paintings *The Course of Empire*, which he completed in 1836 for his New York patron Luman Reed.

The importance of contrasts of scale was also a theme that had come to the fore in this period, particularly in aesthetic theory. In his *Philosophical Inquiry into the Origin of our Ideas on the Sublime and the Beautiful* (1756), Edmund Burke had argued that objects that are sublime—that is, terrifying in their grandeur—are particularly suitable for painting, and Cole's earliest American landscapes often explore this concept, by dwarfing human activities with enormous mountains and natural forms. The notion of a complete civilization of miniature scale was one that Cole would have been familiar with from the description of Lilliput in Jonathan Swift's famous satire, *Gulliver's Travels* (1726).

In addition to these general intellectual influences, several specific sources may well have inspired the painting. Cole's interest in a race of giants had been expressed earlier in some sketches he made of Ulysses and the Cyclops, Polyphemus, although he never actually executed a painting on this subject. Moreover, when climbing Mount Holyoke in 1833, Cole probably admired rock formations known as the "Columns" and "Titan's Pier," which were described at length in a geological report prepared by Edward Hitchcock, a professor at Amherst College. Finally, perhaps the closest parallel to the imagery of the painting is a passage in the writings of the Roman architect Vitruvius; he reported that Dinocrates, the Macedonian architect, had suggested to Alexander the great that Mount Athos be formed into a colossal statue. The left hand of this statue would hold a spacious city, while the right would hold "huge cup, into which shall be collected all the streams of the mountains, which shall thence be poured into the sea."

Cole was also interested in geology, and in the relationship between natural processes and familiar man-made forms. His notebooks of this period contain several drawings of large vases and huge crater-like basins, ringed with vegetation. No doubt Cole's conception *of The Titan's Goblet* was ultimately based on such playful explorations of natural processes.

HENRY ADAMS

See also **Cole, Thomas**

Work

The Titan's Goblet, 1833. Oil on canvas, Metropolitan Museum of Art, New York.

TIUTCHEV, FEDOR IVANOVICH 1803–1873

Russian poet

Fedor Ivanovich Tiutchev may have written a comparatively small number of poems, but he is indisputably one of Russia's greatest poets. He is also one of Russia's most paradoxical writers. Though he almost exclusively spoke French, he wrote his poems in Russian. He spent almost one-third of his life in the West and preferred life abroad, but ardently defended the conservative policies of Tsar Nicholas I and Slavophile ideology. Acknowledged as Russia's foremost nature poet, Tiutchev's best nature poems invariably depict German scenes. He married two German women, yet arguably the love of his life was a Russian. He advocated Russian orthodoxy, but probably was a nonbeliever. Rigorously trained in the classics, Tiutchev is one of Russia's greatest Romantics. The historian Nicholas V. Riasanovsky even calls Tiutchev Russia's only genuine Romantic poet. Others rank him second after Aleksandr Pushkin.

While Tiutchev was in Germany, he became enamored of the Bavarian landscape that inspired some of his greatest lyrics. He also fell under the influence of the poets he translated, including Johann Wolfgang von Goethe, Heinrich Heine, Johann Gottfried von Herder, and Johann Christoph Friedrich von Schiller; he found themes that appealed to his tastes in Clemens Brentano, Joseph von Eichendorff, and Novalis. Tiutchev's first nature poems depict German mountains with their snowy peaks and freely running streams, either in the rosy lights of sunset or the golden glow of the daytime sun. Early poems such as "Vesennyaya groza" ("Spring Storm," 1828), "Letniy vecher" ("Summer Evening," 1828), "Utro v gorakh" ("Morning in the Mountains," 1829) and "Snezhnye gory" ("Snowy Mountains," 1829) display the full range and power of Tiutchev's descriptive powers.

If the scenes Tiutchev described were Romantic, so were the themes in most of his early poems. In them he contrasts day with night, the mysterious time when poets discern secrets of the universe: "Problesk" ("The Gleam," 1825), "Videnie" ("A Vision," 1829), "Bessonnitsa" ("Insomnia," 1829). He also describes the tension between the poet and the crowds who do not understand his exalted role as in "Ty zrel ego v krugu bol'-shogo sveta" ("You Saw Him in Society," 1829–30). He expresses the need of the poet to break free from earthly bonds in "Dusha khotela b byt' zvezdoy" ("The Soul Would Like to Be a Star," 1836).

While in Germany, Tiutchev fell under the spell of Schelling's *Naturphilosophie*; debate on the extent of Schelling's influence over Tiutchev still continues. The poems of this period investigate the parallels between human and natural spheres and become more speculative and philosophical in tone. For Tiutchev at this time, nature becomes a refuge and a place of renewal, and occasionally the poems almost border on the pantheistic. Tiutchev wrote some of his most celebrated lyrics during this period: "Mal'aria" ("Malaria," 1830), "Ya lyuteran lyublyu bogosluzhen'e" ("I Love the Service of the Lutherans," 1834), "Son na more" ("Dream at Sea," 1833–36); "Net, moego k tebe pristrat'ya" ("No, I Can't Hide My Fondness for You, Mother Earth," 1836); "O chem ty voesh', vetr nochnoy ("Why Do You Howl, Night Wind?," 1836); and "Den' i noch'" ("Day and Night," 1839). The poem, "Silentium!" ("Silence!" 1830) which contains the famous line, "The spoken thought is but a lie," describes the poet's spiritual isolation. In this almost existential lyric, the poet exhorts his reader to remain silent and bury his most secret feelings and dreams deep in his soul, for no one else can understand another's inner thoughts.

Tiutchev's early love poems fall into two phases of his German sojourn. The first group expresses lofty, almost ideal emotions, as in "Tvoy milyi vzor, nevinnoy strasti polnyi" ("Your Sweet Glance Full of Innocent Passion," 1824). But very soon appear hints of a less ideal, a more passionate, almost decadent view of love. In "K N.N." ("To N.N.," 1829), the lyrical narrator praises his mistress for perfecting the arts of deception and skills of adultery. The decadent strain evolves in lyrics where the narrator experiences a kind of sensual pleasure when the woman he loves is suffering or is carried away by passion: "Vostok belel" ("The East Grew White," 1836), "Lyublyu glaza tvoi, moy drug"

("I Love Your Eyes, My Friend," 1836), "Vchera, v mechtakh obvorozhennykh" ("Yesterday, in Charmed Dreams," 1836), "V dushnom vozdukha molchan'e" ("In the Stifling Silence of the Air," 1836), and "Ital'yanskaya villa" ("Italian Villa," 1837). However, a poem dedicated to one of Tiutchev's first loves, Baroness Barbara Juliane Krüdener, breaks the pattern. "Ya pomnyu vremya zolotoe" ("I Remember a Golden Time," 1834–36) describes the idyllic aura of their happy times together; he repeats the sentiments in a poem he wrote upon meeting the baroness again after almost forty years: "Ya vstretil vas" ("I Met You— and All of the Past Came to Life in My Withered Soul," 1870).

A few years after Tiutchev's return to Russia, he fell deeply in love with Elena Deniseva, a woman almost twenty-five years his junior. The intensity and vicissitudes of the affair produced an extraordinary group of poems known as the "Deniseva Cycle." Some dozen poems chronicle Tiutchev's changing moods and attitudes toward his beloved, from early joy to later despair. Several poems particularly stand out for their depth of feeling: "O, kak ubiistvenno my lyubim" ("O, How Murderously We Love," c. 1851), "Ne govori: menya on, kak prezhde, lyubit" ("Do Not Say: He Loves Me as Before," c. 1851–52), "Ya ochi znal—o, eti ochi!" ("I Knew Eyes—Oh, Those Eyes!," 1851–52), and especially "Poslednyaya liubov'" ("Last Love," 1853). The poems of this cycle are acknowledged as some of the greatest love poems in Russian.

Except for the love poems of this period, Tiutchev did not write much distinguished poetry in his later years. Many of the lyrics were occasional pieces or poems with a political or religious content, long acknowledged as his weakest format. However, one poem, "More i utes" ("Sea and Cliff," 1848–51) stands out for the power of its imagery, where Russia is a mighty cliff withstanding the surging seas of revolution. Two other poems, "Eti bednye selen'ya" ("These Poor Villages," 1855) and "Nad etoy temnoyu tolpoyu" ("Over This Dark Crowd," 1857) describe Russia's misery, but at the same time praise its people, whose long-suffering patience only Jesus Christ will reward. However, Tiutchev best expressed his conservative political and religious views in a series of articles that found favor with the tsar: "Lettre à M. le Docteur Gustave Kolb," published separately as "La Russie et l'Allemagne ("Russia and Germany," 1844); "La Russie et la Révolution" ("Russia and the Revolution," 1848); and "La Papauté et la Question Romaine" ("The Papacy and the Roman Question," 1849). One of Tiutchev's often quoted poems best summarizes his views of his native land, "Umom Rossiyu ne poniat'" (1866): "You cannot understand Russia with your mind, / You cannot measure her with a common yardstick: / She has a special character— / You can only believe in Russia."

Though Tiutchev was a popular guest in influential salons and social circles because of his celebrated wit and scintillating conversational skills, he was relatively unknown as a poet until his first collection appeared in the mid-1850s. By that time, unfortunately, people were more interested in reading prose. It was only with Russia's symbolist poets, at the end of the nineteenth century, that a sustained public interest in poetry returned. Since then, Tiutchev's popularity in Russia has never waned.

CHRISTINE A. RYDEL

Biography

Born November 23, 1803 in Ovstug. Educated at home; main tutor was poet S. E. Raich, who trained him in classics. In 1809, joined philological faculty of Moscow University, received *kandidat* degree 1821. January 1822, enrolled in Collegium of Foreign Affairs, in June of that year he left for Munich as member of Russian legation; spent most of next twenty-two years in diplomatic posts. In 1826, married Eleanor (Nelly) Peterson, née Bothmer, who died in 1838. Dismissed from service when abandoned post (Russian *chargé d'affaires* in Turin) to marry Baroness Ernestine Dornberg (née Pfeffel), 1839. Returned to Russia, 1844; engaged in many affairs, most important of which was with Elena Aleksandrovna Denis'eva (1850–64), with whom he had three children. Continued in government service (chairman of Committee on Foreign Censorship), December 1872, suffered stroke that led to paralysis; suffered other strokes until death, July 15, 1873.

Selected Works

Collections

Tiutcheviana: Epigrammy, aforizmy i ostroty F. I. Tiutcheva. With a preface by Georgiy Ivanovich Chulkov. 1922.
Polnoe sobranie Stikhotvoreniy. 2 vols Edited by Chulkov. 1926.
Polnoe sobranie stikhotvoreniy. 2 vols. Edited by V. V. Gippin's and K. V. Pigarev. 1939.
Lirika. 2 vols. Edited by Pigarev, 1963. Expanded edition, 1965.

Books

Stikhotvoreniya. 1854.
Stikhotvoreniya. 1868.
Versions from Fyodor Tiutchev, 1803–1873. Translated by Charles Tomlinson. 1960.
Poems & Political Letters of F. I. Tiutchev. Translated by Jesse Zeldin. 1973.
Poems of Night and Day. Translated by Eugene M. Kayden. 1974.
On the Heights of Creation: The Lyrics of Fedor Tiutchev. Translated by Anatoly Lieberman. 1993.

Other

Pis'ma F. I. Tiutcheva k ego vtoroi zhene, urozhd. Bar. Pfefel, 1840– 1867. 2 vols. 1914–16.
Fedor Ivanovich Tiutchev v pis'makh k E. K. Bogdanovoi i S. P. Frolovu (1866–1871 gg.). Edited by E. P. Kazanovich. 1926.

Bibliography

Aksakov, Ivan Sergeevich. *Fedor Ivanovich Tiutchev: Biograficheskiy ocherk.* 1874.
Bilokur, Borys. *A Concordance to the Russian Poetry of Fedor I. Tiutchev.* Providence, R.I.: Brown University Press, 1975.
Chulkov, Georgiy Ivanovich. *Letopis' zhizni i tvorchestva F. I. Tiutcheva.* Moscow-Leningrad: Academia, 1933.
Chulkov. *Poslednyaya lyubov' Tiutcheva (Elena Alkesandrovna Denis'eva).* Leningrad: M. and S. Shabashnikov, 1928.
Conant, Roger. *The Political Poetry and Ideology of F. I. Tiutchev.* Ann Arbor, Mich.: Ardis, 1983.
Darsky, D. S. *Chudesnye vymysli: O kosmicheskom soznanii v lirike Tiutcheva.* Moscow: Tovarichestvo skoropechati A. A. Levenson, 1913.
Gregg, Richard A. *Fedor Tiutchev: The Evolution of a Poet.* New York: Columbia University Press, 1965.
Koroleva, Inna Aleksandrovna, and Aleksandr Aronovich Nikolaev, eds. *F. I. Tiutchev. Bibliograficheskiy ukazatel' proizvedeniy i*

literatury o zhizni i deyatel'nosti 1818–1973. Moscow: Kniga, 1978.

Lane, Ronald C. *Bibliography of Works by and about F. I. Tiutchev to 1985.* Nottingham: Astra Press, 1987.

Lezhnev, Abram Zakharovich. *Dva poeta, Geine. Tiutchev.* Moscow: Khudozhestvenaya literatura, 1934.

Pigarev, Kirill Vasil'evich. *Zhizn' i tvorchestvo Tiutcheva.* 1962. Abridged and revised as *F. I. Tiutchev i ego vremya.* Moscow: Sovremennik, 1978.

Pratt, Sarh Claflin. *Russian Metaphysical Romanticism: The Poetry of Tiutchev and Boratynskii.* Stanford, Calif.: Stanford University Press, 1984.

Pratt. *Semantics of Chaos in Tiutchev.* Munich: Verlag Otto Sagner, 1983.

Schulze, Almut. *Tjut(evs Kurzlyrik. Traditionszusammenhänge und Interpretationen.* Munich: Vilhelm Fink Verlag, 1968.

Strémooukhoff, D. *La poésie et l'idéologie de Tioutchev.* Paris: Les Belles Lettres, 1937.

TOCQUEVILLE, ALEXIS CHARLES HENRI DE 1805–1859

French political philosopher and sociologist

Alexis Charles Henri de Tocqueville deserves his reputation as one of the most perspicacious and enduring thinkers of the nineteenth century, although his full significance for his own and subsequent ages can only be appreciated when his contributions to the fields of political science and political history are recognized as forms of profound and far-reaching cultural reevaluation. Like that of John Locke, Karl Marx, or Charles-Louis Montesquieu, his political thought constantly opens onto the sociological and thence to the philosophical and psychological. In this respect, his writing has the scope and economy of the classical age, where his social and temperamental roots properly lay, whereas its focus is the postrevolutionary Romantic period in which he lived and the tensions that he encountered within it. Tocqueville was an aristocrat by birth, blinking into the dawn of a bourgeois century, and was at once the embodiment and the supreme diagnostician of the unease felt by a number of major French Romantic figures toward the process of revolutionary emancipation which was implied by the Romantic age. What the poets of his day lamented as an unspecific malady assumed for him the character of a precise historicopolitical problem. While he championed social justice and personal liberty, he sensed that the postfeudal egalitarian state exposed these very values to threats from an unenvisaged quarter. "The political world," he would come to write, "Is metamorphosed: new remedies must henceforth be sought for new disorders."

A descendant on his father's side of a noble Norman family and, on his mother's, of Louis XVI's advocate before the Revolutionary tribunal, Chrétien Guillaume de Lamoig Malesherbes, Tocqueville was a man divided between his aristocratic heritage and his awareness that the days of the aristocracy were over. His marriage in 1835 to Mary Mottley, an Englishwoman from a middle-class background, might itself be seen as a manifestation of this tension, as was his political career, in the course of which as deputy minister and briefly as minister of state he hesitated between obedience to upstart governments and his instincts for tradition and constitutional legality. After training as a lawyer in Paris during the Restoration, he accepted an appointment in Versailles in 1828, where he met his future wife and began a lifelong friendship with fellow lawyer Gustave de Beaumont. Two years later, however, his caste and civic loyalties were tested by the overthrow of the last of the Bourbons and the proclamation of the "bourgeois" monarchy of Louis-Philippe. Persuaded that the constitution and manners of the "most peaceful and most complete" democratic state model might prove beneficial to a politically unstable France, Tocqueville used the pretext of undertaking a study of the American penal system to obtain leave to visit the United States of America, for which he set out in the company of Beaumont in April 1831. Returning home nine months later after a journey which took them from the Great Lakes to the mouth of the Mississippi River, the two Frenchmen published their findings on American penitentiaries, and Tocqueville began work on what would become the first part of *De la Démocratie en Amérique* (*Democracy in America*, 1835). The book's success encouraged its author to publish a further edition five years later, including a second part, and in 1841 his scholarship was rewarded by his election to the Académie française. Tocqueville was appointed deputy for Valognes in 1839, and meanwhile had begun a parliamentary career, in the course of which he championed the emancipation of slaves throughout French territory, but he also warned of the risk to his country of further destructive revolutionary activity. A member of the constituent and legislative assemblies during the short-lived Second Republic, Tocqueville was named minister of foreign affairs in 1849 after the election the previous year of Louis Napoleon as president, but he challenged the legitimacy of the Bonapartist coup d'état of December 1851 and withdrew thereafter to his Normandy domain. Though weakened by tuberculosis, he maintained his interest in political affairs and, in 1856, published *L'Ancien régime et la Révolution* (*The Old Regime and the Revolution*) intending to add a sequel which his death in 1859 prevented him from completing.

Tocqueville's insatiable mental curiosity led him to reach out, through a vast correspondence on subjects ranging from the social and economic future of Europe to the management of his own estate, to harvest the knowledge and ideas of contemporary diplomatic and political minds on both sides of the Atlantic. The kernel of his thinking is to be found in his two major works, composed in very different circumstances, but nevertheless to be seen as two sides of the same coin. What preoccupies the author of *De la Démocratie en Amérique* are the implications for society of the advent of what was then an entirely new form of government, liberal democracy. Of the two elements of this term, it is clear that Tocqueville's prime attachment is to the first; his achievement lay in recognizing that the transition that Western civilization was undergoing from a feudal-aristocratic to a democratic world order, however historically inevitable, entailed acquiescence to a sociopolitical mentality which, if abused, would threaten to separate the individual from the very state of

Charles Alexis Tocqueville. Reprinted courtesy of Bildarchiv Preussischer Kulturbesitz.

liberty it was intended to facilitate. Before Karl Marx, Tocqueville was the prophet of the modern malaise of alienation, identified in his case not as the condition of the industrialized proletariat, but of the courageous and independent-minded who find themselves in a society where equality is construed as sameness and individual difference is choked beneath grey uniformity. "Every citizen," he wrote of the American way of life, "being assimilated to all the rest, is lost *in the crowd*, and nothing stands conspicuous but the great and imposing image of the people at large." His much-quoted disquiet at the potential "tyranny of the majority," voiced toward the end of the first part of *De la Démocratie en Amérique*, derives from the awareness that democracies, for all their egalitarian virtues, tend to stifle dissent by the instrument of social and psychological ostracization as effectively as the rack or the executioner of former ages. The flaw in democracy lies in its appeal to the self-interested and conformist, and thereby in its ready collusion with despotism.

Writing in the early 1830s after his visit to the United States, Tocqueville was still prepared to acknowledge the possible benefits that the political system he found there could deliver to his own troubled nation. A quarter of a century later, with the experience of the Revolution of 1848 and the advent of the popularly mandated but despotic regime of Napoleon III behind him, he was far more inclined to emphasize his warning that the modern mass age was courting an ancient danger. Tocqueville's last book is a work of history and, in this respect, superficially distinct from his sociological and largely a priori analysis

of American politics and manners. Yet its anti-Napoleonic stance in a second period of Napoleonic imperialism betrays its underlying contemporary theme: while Anglo-American society appears to afford a haven for liberty, France has twice delivered the fruits of revolution into the hands of a demagogue. The difference can be explained by the centralizing and absolutist tendencies displayed in French institutions well before the Revolution, and still alive in its wake, if not in its very manifestation. For Tocqueville, liberty is a quasi-transcendental ideal, and its pursuit a vital passion all too easily contaminated by other, less noble drives. "The man who asks of freedom anything other than itself," he declares in *L'Ancien régime*, "is born to be a slave."

DAVID LEE

Biography

Born in Paris July 29, 1805 to Hervé-Bonaventure Clérel and Louise Le Peletier Rosanbo. Attended secondary school and Collège Royal in Metz before studying law in Paris, 1825–27. Appointed *juge auditeur* in Versailles, where he befriended Gustave de Beaumont and met his future wife Mary Mottley. Reluctantly swore oath of loyalty to Louis-Philippe after Revolution of 1830. Given leave to study American penal system, and embarked with Beaumont in April 1831. Returned to France in February 1832 and began first part of *De la démocratie en Amérique* (published in 1835). Married in 1835, and a year later inherited family estate near Valognes, for which he was elected deputy in 1839. Publication of second part of *De la démocratie en Amérique* in 1840 led to election to *Académie française*. Elected to Constituent Assembly after Revolution of 1848, which he had predicted. Appointed minister of foreign affairs by Louis Napoleon, but was replaced after three months. Briefly imprisoned in December 1851 for opposition to coup d'état. Retired to Chateau de Tocqueville where he completed *L'Ancien Régime et la Révolution* (pub. 1856). Died in Cannes from tuberculosis on April 16, 1859.

Selected Works

De la Démocratie en Amérique. 4 vols. part 1, 1835; part 2, 1840.
L'Ancien régime et la Révolution. 1856.
Souvenirs. 1893.
Oeuvres complètes. 9 vols. 1864–66.

Bibliography

Brogan, Hugh. *Tocqueville.* London: Collins/Fontana, 1973.
Drescher, Seymour. *Dilemmas of Democracy: Tocqueville and Modernization.* Pittsburgh: University of Pittsburgh Press, 1968.
Herr, Richard. *Tocqueville and the Old Regime.* Princeton, N.J.: Princeton University Press, 1962.
Jardin, André. *Alexis de Tocqueville.* Paris: Hachette littérature, 1984.
Lamberti, Jean Claude. *Tocqueville and the Two Democracies.* Cambridge, Mass.: Harvard University Press, 1989.
Lively, Jack. *The Social and Political Thought of Alexis de Tocqueville.* Oxford: Clarendon Press, 1965.
Mayer, J.-P. *Alexis de Tocqueville.* New York: Harper, 1960.
Pierson, George Wilson. *Tocqueville and Beaumont in America.* New York: Oxford University Press, 1938.
Reeves, Richard. *American Journey: Travelling with Tocqueville in Search of Democracy in America.* New York: Simon and Schuster, 1982.
Schleifer, James T. *The Making of Tocqueville's "Democracy in America."* Chapel Hill: University of North Carolina Press, 1980.

TÖPFFER, RODOLPHE 1799–1846

Swiss writer, artist, and art critic

Rodolphe Töpffer's work is protean. Although the late twentieth century chiefly saw him as the forerunner of the modern-day comic strip artist (see his 1845 *Essai de physiognomonie*), this Geneva-based professor of rhetoric was also a novelist (*Le Presbytère*, 1839; *Rosa et Gertrude*, 1847), a playwright (*L'Artiste*, 1828), and a travel writer (*Voyages en zigzag*, 1844). The many genres explored by Töpffer reveal a man keen to push the borders of genres, and with a particular gift for emphasizing interactions between different modes of artistic expression. Typically, his caricatures or collections of sketches (*Histoire de M. Jabot*, 1833; *Histoire de M. Crépin*, 1837), partly inspired by William Hogarth, illustrate the interdependence of texts and images. This "littérature en estampes" ("literature in engravings") actually shows the achievement of a perfect semiotic unity between words and drawings. His other enterprises display, to a lesser degree, a highly modern interest in the interplay between, and translatability of, artistic forms: *Voyages et aventures du docteur Festus* (1840) was conceived simultaneously as a novel and as an illustrated book, for example.

This groundbreaking inventiveness is partly restricted by Töpffer's declared conservatism and regionalism in both art and politics. The grandson of a German tailor, Töpffer was still a newcomer to the very static and monolithic elite of the town. However, his professional ambitions and his sentimental attachment to his hometown as a land of refuge convinced him to adopt without reservation the ideology of the local ruling classes, and to act as the spokesperson for its agenda of political, social, and cultural protectionism. In the realms of literature and painting, this moral commitment was displayed by a formal rejection of Romanticism, and in the promulgation of new criteria of aesthetic judgment. In opposition to the eccentricities of French Romanticism, Töpffer pleaded for a "national art" based on the refusal of grandiloquence and, as a corollary, on the promotion of the high mountains as the distinctive feature of Helvetic culture ("De l'artiste et de la Suisse alpestre," 1837).

In contrast to the Romantic myth of the artist as an inspired genius, Töpffer's writings constantly show a narrator conscious of his own limitations, and aware of a necessary critical distance between the text and himself; this disjunction is essential to his style, especially in some of his short stories ("La Bibliothèque de mon oncle" ["My Uncle's Library"], 1832), where a dense and sentimental autobiographical content is mitigated by the frequent interventions of a teasing and moralizing storyteller. This irrevocable separation between two visions of the self—the one instinctive and cheerful, the other nostalgic and critical—is at the very core of Töpffer's writing. Critics have pointed out that many of his works bear the trace of a psychomachia between these opposite principles (Bridel). It is arguable that this makes him all the more representative of his time and origin: writing in a Calvinist city, on the margins of the French literary market, during decades of political and cultural instability, Töpffer is torn between the Romantic temptation of unbridled, individual expression and the necessity to fight, in the wake of Rousseau, for the recognition of literary standards in conformity with the spirit of his nation.

Töpffer's defense of a distinct Swiss literary culture is especially obvious in the vision of the Alps conveyed by such short stories as "Le Grand Saint-Bernard," where he confronts the well-worn Romantic vision of the Alpine landscape (symbolized by a pedantic French writer) with the more straightforward and sensible perception of his fellow countrymen. His point is that Romantic imagery has changed our perception of nature and turned it into a series of clichés marked by exaggeration and artificiality. The task of the Swiss artist, in both painting and poetry, is to reconsider nature with fresh eyes, and to "remove the alpine Switzerland form the profanations of dabblers, in order to enable it to eventually enter the realm of art" (*Mélanges sur les beaux-arts*). Töpffer applies this recommendation to himself in his *Voyages en zigzag* by considerably modifying the commonplace description of the journey to the Alps. The representation of Alpine peaks becomes a pretext for a playful evocation of characters and an amused account of the vagaries of travel. As almost everywhere in Töpffer, this offhand evocation is interrupted by aesthetic considerations tracing the lineaments of an artistic program; He writes,

> [T]he more one thinks, the more one observes oneself, the more one is convinced that painting is not a representation but a language; that a landscape is not a translation but a poem; that a landscape artist is not a copyist but an interpret . . . . it's up to you, poets, to depict these things; to depict them, that is to say to recount their charms in some fresh, natural and simple verse . . . . not to describe them. To describe, for a poet, is to crawl; to depict is to soar into the skies. . . .

The posthumously published volume *Réflexions et menus propos d'un peintre genevois* (*Thoughts and Minor Comments of a Genevese Painter* (1848) constitutes Töpffer's most substantial contribution to the definition of an alternative to Romanticism. In this collection of essays, it becomes clear that, for Töpffer, the only function of the new French literary school is revolutionary, and accordingly negative. The Romantic doctrine has supplanted the classical orthodoxy without getting any closer to a true expression of nature or the self. Instead, it has introduced artificiality and affectation in the way the artist considers the world and expresses it. In this sense, he especially condemns and stigmatizes Théophile Gautier's ideal of "art for art's sake."

Moreover—and this is decisive for the conservative and patriotic Töpffer—Romanticism represents the joint invasion of the dangerous democratic spirit he tried to repel from Geneva, and of a foreign aesthetics diverging from his autarchic aspirations.

Töpffer tries to respond to this double invasion through the development of a complex aesthetic system, at the core of which lies the subjective notion of "aesthetic faculty," which

> develops itself through approach, through contact, through direct imitation (of the works of art), from the beautiful we feel to the beautiful we aim for (. . .) that is to say that the young artist, the young poet, are inclined to conceive and to realize the beautiful as far as they have

not learnt it, but felt it . . . the aesthetic faculty pursues the beautiful only, without any other object to interfere.

The quest for the beautiful is the only valid mission of art. But, contrary to formalism, this quest is characterized by its solidarity with the concepts of truth and morality. Töpffer appropriates Plato's idea that "the beautiful is the splendor of truth." However, the idea that the beautiful is a self-sufficient notion is crucial here, as art's dependence on doctrines, theories, and aesthetic systems is precisely what Töpffer found profoundly harmful in Romanticism. According to his conception then, the pursuit of the beautiful is necessarily deeply personal, and cannot obey predetermined schemes. It is the expression of the impact of beautiful things on the artist's individuality, through the mediation of beautiful works of art. If we are to believe this definition, real art is neither imitation (Töpffer was a strong opponent of the daguerreotype, which he did not consider art), nor abstract formalism (as Romanticism tends to be); rather, it is the syncretic product of an interaction between the poet's ability to perceive and translate essential beauty and the inspiration provided by nature. Fundamentally, Töpffer's vision of art is based on two pillars: idealism and freedom.

It is hard to tell exactly how far away from the Romantics Töpffer *really* was in his aesthetic conceptions. Though he strongly criticized Victor Hugo's plays, for instance, he did not hesitate to plead for the importance of the "local color" in dramas (which was also a key point of many Romantic manifestos). Many ideological positions defended by the French Romantics he despised (such as Honoré de Balzac) were quite similar to his. However, Töpffer must be understood in his specific context: behind his apparently unambiguous stand against Romanticism lies the private conflict of an author participating in the vast renewal of European culture from a peripheral point, attempting to defend an original artistic position by means of a specific Helvetic context. As Marie Alamir-Paillard convincingly argues, admiring the Alps, defending his local culture, fighting democracy, or freeing the notion of the beautiful from the straightjacket of doctrines was all one to Töpffer. His recurring concern is to preserve the principles of simplicity, freedom, and autonomy in art, politics, and writing. But it is worth noting that most of these issues, if not all, were directly inspired by Romantic ideals: many of Töpffer's battles were waged at the same time by the French authors he so strongly opposed. The principles exposed in his *Réflexions* are thus particularly ambiguous: Töpffer unceasingly strives to go beyond the opposition between Romanticism and classicism, but can only end up by resorting to the very imprecise and hardly convincing notion of "aesthetic faculty" (without ever formally defining such central concepts as the beautiful!) to escape the aporia of a "Romanticism in the margins." In this sense, obviously, Töpffer's dilemma is highly representative of the cultural issues raised by Romanticism in the French-speaking part of Switzerland.

MAXIME GOERGEN

See also **Aesthetics and Art Criticism; Book Illustration; Olivier, Juste; Switzerland: Cultural Survey; Switzerland: Historical Survey; Travel Writing: France**

Biography

Born in Geneva, January 31, 1799. His vocation as a painter was thwarted by the discovery of a visual impairment in 1818. Studied in Paris in 1819–20. Became a teacher in a private college in 1822. Married Anne-Françoise Moulinié in 1823, with whom he had four children. Created his own boarding school in 1824. Trips taken to the Alps with his pupils would be the inspiration to the *Voyages en zigzag* (1844). Started drawing sketches, writing comedies (*L'Artiste*, 1828) and critical essays. In 1830, became a regular contributor to *La Bibliothèque universelle de Genève*, a monthly paper in which he published the first of his many *Réflexions et menus propos d'un peintre genevois*, posthumously collected in two volumes in 1848. Publishing of his first short stories, *La Bibliothèque de mon oncle* and *Le Presbytère*, in 1832. Nominated professor of rhetoric at the Academy of Geneva the same year. The writing and publishing of short stories and essays was henceforth uninterrupted. In 1833 he published *Histoire de M. Jabot*, the first of his "stories in images." This would be followed by *Histoire de M. Crépin, Histoire de M. Vieux-Bois* (both in 1837), or *Voyages et aventures du Docteur Festus* (1840). In 1841, a collection of his short stories was published in Paris under the title *Nouvelles genevoises* and reviewed by the French critic Charles-Augustin Sainte-Beuve. After the radicals (leftist liberals) came to power in Geneva in 1841, he contributed to a conservative newspaper, *Le Courrier de Genève* (1842–43). Serious health problems forced him to take a "water cure" at Lavey and Vichy (1843–45), while his activity as a writer and a critic of aesthetics continued. Died June 8, 1846.

Selected works

Nouvelles. 1841.
Mélanges sur les beaux-arts. 2 vols. 1953–57.
Voyages en zigzag. 1844.
Nouveaux Voyages en zigzag. 1864.
Réflexions et menus propos d'un peintre genevois ou Essai sur le beau dans les arts. 1848.
Correspondance complète. Vol. 1. 1807–20.
L'Artiste. 1828.
M. Jabot; M. Crépin; M. Vieux-Bois; M. Pencil; Docteur Festus; Histoire d'Albert; M. Cryptogame. 1833–46.
Voyages et aventures du docteur Festus. 1840.

Bibliography

Alamir-Paillard, Marie. "Aux arts, citoyens! Rodolphe *Töpffer ou la critique militante (1826–1832).*" In *Critiques d'art de Suisse romande. M. Töpffer à Budry.* Edited by Philippe Junod and Philippe Kaenel. Lausanne: Payot, 1993.
Bridel, Yves. "Rodolphe Töpffer." In *Histoire de la littérature en Suisse romande.* Vol. 2. Edited by Roger Francillon. Lausanne: Payot, 1997. 61–78.
Groensteen, Thierry, and Benoît Peeters, eds. *Töpffer. L'Invention de la bande dessinée.* Paris: Hermann, 1994.
Junod, Philippe. "Actualité de Rodolphe Töpffer. Un précurseur de la sémiotique visuelle," *Etudes de lettres* 4 (1983): 75–84.
Maggetti, Daniel. *L'Invention de la littérature romande: 1830–1910.* Lausanne: Payot, 1995.
———, ed. *Rodolphe Töpffer.* Genève: Skira, 1996.
Töpffer, pratiques d'écriture et theories esthétiques. Cahiers Robinson 2 (1997).

TRANSCENDENTALISM

As an aesthetic and religious category, transcendentalism is most closely associated with the flowering of American Romanticism in New England in the 1830s and 1840s. Critical works tend to examine transcendentalism in three interrelated ways: first, as a theological, reformist, and literary movement among intellectuals in Boston and Concord, Massachusetts; second, as a matrix of philosophical and aesthetic ideas deriving from European Romanticism, but distinctly American in character; and third, as an idealistic current running through American culture, from the early Romantics Ralph Waldo Emerson and Henry David Thoreau, to late-nineteenth-century thinkers such as William James and George Santayana, to the work of recent literary critics and cultural theorists such as Stanley Cavell, Irving Howe, and Cornel West. While transcendentalism in America has taken on a number of historical guises, attempts to reconcile individualism with community, tradition with radicalism, and freedom with democracy distinguish the work of all these thinkers.

Transcendentalism was first used as a literary term in America in the early 1830s to describe writing that was "outlandish" or "vague," in contrast to strict interpretation of scripture or concrete empirical fact. When Emerson resigned as a Boston pastor in 1832, he rescued the term, employing it to describe to a form of inner spirituality that could only be expressed through imaginative or poetic language. In his 1838 "Divinity School Address," Emerson praised the "moral sentiment" of intuition against reason as the foundation of faith, opposing, with his belief in the powers of human creativity, the Calvinist conviction that humans are naturally depraved. These beliefs were embodied in the Transcendentalist Club, a select group of writers (including Bronson Alcott, Orestes Brownson, James Freeman Clarke, Margaret Fuller, and Theodore Parker), formed by Emerson in 1836 that met regularly until 1843. The club discussed religious and artistic ideas, focusing particularly on the themes of nature, inspiration, spiritual truth, and revelation. These ideas were developed in essays published in the quarterly magazine The *Dial* from 1840, which became the chief vehicle for promoting Transcendentalist values. The critic Paul Boller describes the collective work of the club as "a quest . . . to find meaning, pattern, and purpose in a universe no longer managed by an amiable and genteel Unitarian God." Although the transcendentalists remained religious, God was transformed into a metaphysical "Over-Soul" for Emerson (in his essay of 1841 of the same name) and an expression of a pantheistic and benevolent spirit for Thoreau in *Walden; Or Life in the Woods* (1854).

Important expressions of transcendentalist principles can be found in the writings of the pacifist and reformist William Ellery Channing, in Fuller's early feminist work *Woman in the Nineteenth Century* (1845), and in Alcott and Elizabeth Peabody's *Record of a School* (1835), in which they pioneered new educational methods by arguing that students should be inspired with the joy of learning and should be encouraged to unlock their potential to be uniquely creative. While there was a common currency in transcendentalist thought, differences in emphasis can be detected from thinker to thinker. For example, Alcott's Neoplatonist description in "Psyche" (1836) that "Man's force, his individual will, his free-agency, cometh by submission to the superior Force that ever presseth against him" contrasts with Emerson's

belief in the freedom of individuals to become creators rather than passive channels for spiritual forces. This emphasis on creativity and nonconformity found a later scientific manifestation in the psychological theories of William James. Developing Emerson's poetic descriptions in *Essays: First Series* (1841), and in *Varieties of Religious Experience* (1901), James argued that only the precarious blend of energetic action and a surrender to a "higher" self can position individuals at "the new centre of personal energy."

The critic Anne Rose views the reformist ethos of transcendentalism as a crucial "part of the social life of antebellum America." She argues that the late 1830s marked a period of transition for radical intellectuals who shifted their attention from religious issues to wider social reform. Two experimental communities were established in Massachusetts at this time that attempted to put transcendentalist principles into practice. Alcott's communitarian Fruitlands in Harvard (1843–44) avoided trade and civic activity in favor of subsistence level farming, and George Ripley's Brook Farm (1841–47) in West Roxbury simplified agricultural techniques to preserve time for spiritual and intellectual learning. The Brook Farmers adopted the ideas of the French social reformer Charles Fourier, particularly his theory that society would best function as a series of self-sufficient cooperatives. Although both communities had some success, the Fruitlands experiment reached a natural conclusion, while Brook Farm suffered fire damage and ended in bankruptcy.

Literary historians have retained their interest in the early manifestations of transcendentalism, but American cultural theorists have also begun to consider its impact on contemporary thought. For example, Peter Carafiol detects that the notions of exceptionalism and idealized national identity running throughout American cultural history have their roots in transcendentalism. He argues that critical works on American Romanticism tend to tell a "coherent story" of American culture's development, to the exclusion of "disorderly" ideas that might question or undermine its cohesion. As such, Carafiol suggests that critics should be wary of transcendentalism as a defining term and should reconsider texts that do not quite fit the label, such as Thoreau's *A Week on the Concord and Merrimack Rivers* (1849) and Nathaniel Hawthorne's description of his stay at Brook Farm in *The Blithedale Romance* (1852).

Whereas Carafiol is critical of transcendentalism as an elitist manifestation of Romantic ideas, Cavell and West see an emancipatory promise in transcendentalist writing still valid for contemporary American culture. Cavell claims that the "quest" of Romantic thought is "the recovery of the self," as a form of spiritual "rebirth" from the leveling forces in modern society. He argues that such recovery is not merely a moment of Romantic epiphany, but also a moral commitment to live with the threat of skepticism and self-doubt. In this way, Cavell suggests it is possible to retain the spirit of transcendentalism without swallowing "the discredited romantic picture of the author or artist as incomprehensibly original." Both Cavell and West link the moral thrust of American Romanticism with the pragmatism of John Dewey and James, demonstrating the ways in which "creative democracy" often runs contrary to custom and tradition. For West, Romanticism and pragmatism both counter the strict logic of "epistemology-centered philosophy," embodying instead "a conception of philosophy as a form of cultural criticism." Whether this cultural criticism is manifested in Emerson and Thoreau's creative writing or in the communities on Brook Farm and Fruitlands, Cavell and West argue that the experimental and interrogative mode of American Romanticism is self-renewing and keeps the spirit of transcendentalism very much alive.

MARTIN HALLIWELL

Bibliography

Boller, Paul F, Jr. *American Transcendentalism, 1830–1860: An Intellectual Inquiry.* New York: Putnam's, 1974.

Buell, Lawrence. *Literary Transcendentalism: Style and Vision in the American Renaissance.* Ithaca, N.Y.: Cornell University Press, 1973.

Carafiol, Peter. *The American Ideal: Literary History as a Worldly Activity.* New York: Oxford University Press, 1991.

Cavell, Stanley. *Conditions Handsome and Unhandsome: The Constitution of Emersonian Perfectionism.* Chicago: University of Chicago Press, 1990.

Howe, Irving. *The American Newness: Culture and Politics in the Age of Emerson.* Cambridge, Mass.: Harvard University Press, 1986.

Matthiessen, F. O. *American Renaissance: Art and Expression in the Age of Emerson and Whitman.* New York: Oxford University Press, 1941.

Newfield, Christopher. *The Emerson Effect: Individualism and Submission in America.* Chicago: University of Chicago Press, 1996.

Rose, Anne C. *Transcendentalism as a Social Movement, 1830–1850.* New Haven, Conn.: Yale University Press, 1981.

West, Cornel. *The American Evasion of Philosophy: A Genealogy of Pragmatism.* Madison: University of Wisconsin Press, 1989.

TRANSLATION

The English word *translation* (Latin *trans* + *latus*) and its German equivalents (*Übersetzung, Übertragung*) etymologically indicate something "carried across." The transformations involved in this movement may be physical, historical, social, psychological, spiritual, etc.; or of place, function, state, or form, so that *translation* echoes with a vast range of rhetorical and philosophical resonations, including metaphor, metonymy, simile, irony, analogy, allegory, paraphrase, metaphrase, gloss, amplification, explication, and indeed, interpretation. The indeterminacy of the concept is captured in the well-known Italian maxim, *traduttore, traditore* ("translator, traitor"): the play on pronunciation in the original cannot be "carried across" precisely as such into English, and when the maxim is translated, approximately, it suggests that the act of translation is itself an act of betrayal. But what is it precisely that is "carried over" or betrayed in this act; to where or whom; to what extent and to what ends; with what consequences is it revealed?

During the period 1750–1850 a few long essays and articles were published attempting to theorize the problems involved in this carrying over/betrayal, the most notable being, in Britain, Alexander Fraser Tytler's *Essay on the Principles of Translation* (1790); in France, the entry on "Translation" ("La traduction") by Jean le Rond Alembert and Denis Diderot in their *Encyclopedia* (1751–65); and in Germany, Friedrich Schleiermacher's *Über die verschiedenen Methoden des Übersetzens* (*On the Different Methods of Translation*, 1813).

For the most part, however, the texts of the Romantic Age dealing with translation are not essays or treatises as such: they are often brief references to translation in letters or sections of larger essays on literature or reviews; or they take the form of fragments; or appear as the caveats, prescriptions, and apologies of forewords or prefaces written by translators to the literary works they have translated. These include, in Britain, J. Nott's (1795) and George Lamb's (1821) prefaces to their respective translations of the poems of Catullus and John Hookham Frere's preface to his translation of Aristophanes (1840); in France, Alembert's preface to his translation of Tacitus (1758), Antoine Prévost's preface to his rendering of Richardson's *Pamela* (1760), and Jacques Delille's preface to his *Georgics* of Virgil (1769); and

in Germany, Johann Gottfried Herder's *Fragmente* (*Fragments*, 1766, 1767), passages in August Wilhelm Schlegel's essay "Etwas über Wilhelm Shakespeare bei Gelegenheit Wilhelm Meisters ("Something about William Shakespeare on the occasion of *Wilhelm Meister*," 1796) and his review "Homers Werke von Johann Heinrich Voss" ("The Works of Homer by Johann Heinrich Voss," 1796), various moments in Johann Wolfgang von Goethe's *Dichtung und Wahrheit* (*Poetry and Truth*, 1811–1814) and his essay "Übersetzungen" ("Translations," 1819), and Wilhelm von Humboldt's preface to his translation of Aeschylus's *Agamemnon* (1816).

In various ways, and with varying emphases, these texts—both explicitly, in their thematic arguments, and implicitly, in what are taken to be their assumptions, biases, omissions, and moments of blindness, as they are seen in retrospect from a range of different theoretical perspectives in our own historical moment—raise fundamental issues about the nature and function of translation which even today remain unresolved.

The question of what constitutes an original in a particular language is crucial: is there a "unity," "truth," "spirit" or "genius," an "essence" or "intention" that lies behind or within the material surface of the language of the original? If so, does this transcendental subject reflect an "author," "nature," "world spirit," or a "national character," or indeed the will, inspiration, or genius of language itself, understood as the founding ground of human activity (d'Alembert, Goethe, Herder, Schlegel)? The relation of such a transcendental subject to the material medium of communication—the phoneme, the letter, the word, the enunciation of an act of speech, language in general—and how it would be accessible to a reader who wished to translate it must also be addressed (Humboldt, Schleiermacher).

The nature of the material or spiritual relation between languages is another fundamental issue: whether "human nature" or human experience transcends the specific historical, sociocultural differences between languages (Frere, Tytler), or is coded in and constituted by language (Goethe, Nott); whether the interaction between languages contributes to the corruption, or to the growth and development of a language (Delille, Schleiermacher). To what extent does translation of a text from one language to another constitute an act of violence—to the text, by removing it from its moment in one particular history of social codes, mores, and tastes, and transplanting it into another with different criteria of class, nationhood and ethnicity, gender, creed, style, and aesthetic education; into a different audience milieu and context of reception (Frere, Goethe, Schleiermacher)?—to the source language, making it unnecessary, by replacing its linguistic and culturoideological codes with those of the target language, and by domesticating, using conscious or unconscious processes of censorship, euphemism, assimilation, acculturation, and recontextualization, all that informs its character, its "otherness" in the original text, through the idiom of the target language (d'Alembert, Frere, Herder, Lamb, Prévost)?—or to the target language, through the orientalist and protectionist strategy of producing a "natural"-sounding or fluent translation within its own cultural-ideological codes, thereby attenuating, deflecting, and closing off any interrogation, critique, or development of them that might be effected by the codes embedded in the source language (Delille, Frere, Lamb, Prévost)? Should not the goal of translation be rather to eschew fluency in favor of preserving some semblance of the foreignness, the cultural alterity of the "original" (Goethe, Nott, Schleiermacher)?

These issues reverberate in the politics and history of our own times as well as in the Romantic era: they arise in both epochs in response to the communicative needs of international diplomacy, law, science, and economics (where technical translation is understood to be simply mimetic, and language merely instrumental); and in the general sphere of globalized culture, as individual identities are fragmented and formed in the construction of authorship and copyright law, and as national, ethnic, gendered, and other types of group identities are both deracinated and constructed around imagined communities.

They are also inseparable from the general theories of hermeneutics and language, which emerge in the Romantic Era—in the works of Johann Martin Chladenius (1710–59), the linguistic and philological explorations of Schleiermacher (1768–1834), Humboldt (1767–1835), Friedrich Schlegel (1772–1829), and Friedrich von Hardenberg (1772–1801); and later, in the historiographical studies of Johann Gustav Droysen (1808–84) and the philological investigations of Philip August Boeckh (1785–1867)—theories that take on new dimensions in the twentieth century, in the writings of John Langshaw Austin, Mikhail Bakhtin, Walter Benjamin, Noam Chomsky, Jacques Derrida, Hans-Georg Gadamer, Martin Heidegger, Niklas Luhmann, Ferdinand de Saussure, John Searle, Benjamin Lee Whorf, and others.

And yet, as J. Hillis Miller suggests in an essay on "Translating Theory":

the theoretical formulation in its original language is already a translation or mistranslation of a lost original. This original can never be recovered because it never existed as anything articulated or able to be articulated in any language. Translations of theory are therefore mistranslations of mistranslations, not mistranslations of some authoritative and perspicuous original.

An attempt to address these issues, to interpret "translation" in the Romantic Age, must therefore be nothing more nor less than a *translation* of *translation*, across the social, political, cultural, and historical spaces that separate its horizons from our own—that is, a recontextualization or "betrayal" in its most dangerous, and most constructive sense.

JOHANN PILLAI

Bibliography

Anderson, Benedict. *Imagined Communities: Reflections on the Origin and Spread of Nationalism.* Rev. ed. New York: Verso, 1991.

Bassnett, Susan. *Translation Studies.* London: Methuen, 1980.

Bassnett, Susan, and André Lefevere, eds. *Translation, History and Culture.* London: Pinter, 1990.

Benjamin, Andrew. *Translation and the Nature of Philosophy: A New Theory of Words.* New York: Routledge, 1988.

Benjamin, Walter. "The Task of the Translator. An Introduction to the Translation of Baudelaire's "*Tableaux Parisiens.*" In *Illuminations.* Edited by Hannah Arendt, translated by Harry Zohn. New York: Schocken Books, 1985.

Berman, Antoine. *The Experience of the Foreign. Culture and Translation in Romantic Germany.* Translated by S. Heyvaert. Albany: State University of New York Press, 1992.

Derrida, Jacques. *The Ear of the Other: Otobiography, Transference, Translation.* Edited by Christie McDonald, translated by Peggy Kamuf. Lincoln: University of Nebraska Press, 1988.

Gadamer, Hans-Georg. *Truth and Method.* 2d rev. ed. Translation revised by Joel Weinsheimer and Donald G. Marshall. London: Sheed and Ward, 1989.

Gentzler, Edwin. *Contemporary Translation Theories.* London: Routledge, 1993.

Graham, Joseph F., ed. *Difference in Translation.* Ithaca, N.Y.: Cornell University Press, 1985.

Horguelin, Paul. *Anthologie de la manière de traduire.* Montreal: Linguatech, 1981.

Lefevere, André. *Translating Literature: The German Tradition.* Assen: Van Gorcum, 1977.

Lefevere, André. *Translation/History/Culture: A Sourcebook.* London: Routledge, 1992.

Miller, J. Hillis. "Border Crossings, Translating Theory: Ruth." In *The Translatability of Cultures: Figurations of the Space Between.* Edited by Sanford Budick and Wolfgang Iser. Stanford, Calif.: Stanford University Press, 1996.

Mueller-Vollmer, Kurt, ed. *The Hermeneutics Reader: Texts of the German Tradition from the Enlightenment to the Present.* New York: Continuum, 1989.

Palmer, Richard O. *Hermeneutics: Interpretation Theory in Schleiermacher, Dilthey, Heidegger, and Gadamer.* Evanston, Ill.: Northwestern University Press, 1969.

Rener, Frederick M. *Interpretatio: Language and Translation from Cicero to Tytler.* Amsterdam: Rodopi, 1989.

Robinson, Douglas. *The Translator's Turn.* Baltimore: Johns Hopkins University Press, 1991.

Schulte, Rainer, and John Biguenet, eds. *Theories of Translation: An Anthology of Essays from Dryden to Derrida.* Chicago: University of Chicago Press, 1992.

Venuti, Lawrence. *The Translation Studies Reader.* New York: Routledge, 2000.

———, ed. *Rethinking Translation: Discourse, Subjectivity, Ideology.* New York: Routledge, 1992.

———. *The Translator's Invisibility: A History of Translation.* New York: Routledge, 1995.

TRAVEL WRITING: BRITAIN

The eighteenth century inherited sixteenth- and seventeenth-century debates about the educational usefulness of European travel. (William Bennett's observation in 1785 that "Travellers always buy experience which no books can give" is typical of attempts to privilege the category of "travel" over "literature" as the most effective means of moral, intellectual, and social improvement.) Yet the century's increased emphasis on the social significance of leisure was accompanied by a growing acknowledgment and acceptance of the pleasurable—as opposed to specifically educational—resources of travel. The significant increase in the number of British travelers to Europe in the second half of the eighteenth century (a time that also witnessed the first use of the word *tourist* in our modern sense of "one who travels for pleasure or culture") included larger numbers of female and middle-class travelers, whose abbreviated tours are distinguishable from the classical, masculinist, and pedagogical underpinnings of the Grand Tour.

The "Grand Tour" refers to a conventional formularization of European travel pursued by young, aristocratic, and usually British males primarily as a means to acquire those polite attainments that formed a necessary criteria of social advancement; it is a practice usually thought to date from the beginning of the seventeenth century up to the first decades of the nineteenth century. Although itineraries varied according to such things as seasonal alterations, political events, and the wish to witness certain local events such as the Carnival at Venice, it normally included the Low Countries, Germany, Switzerland, and France, and held as its symbolic center a view of Italy—especially Rome. James Boswell recalls Samuel Johnson's view that "A man who has not been in Italy, is always conscious of an inferiority, from his not having seen what it is expected a man should see. The grand object of travelling is to see the shores of the Mediterranean." From Calais, the traveler could pursue a number of routes into Italy, the majority traveling through Paris and Lyons, followed either by the Alps (usually via the Mt. Cenis pass to Turin and then to either Lombardy or Genoa) or, less popularly, the sea route to Leghorn. Few traveled south of Naples, or to Iberia, Eastern Europe, and the Balkans, although travel to Southern Europe was promoted by and in publications such as Henry Swinburne's *Travels in the Two Sicilies, in the Years 1777, 1778, 1779, and 1780* (1783–85), and Richard Ford's *Hand-Book for Travellers in Spain* (1845). Itineraries were dictated in part by fashion, with Vienna, Dresden, and Berlin serving as popular locations toward the end of the eighteenth century, while the Low Countries, which were relatively well-frequented in the seventeenth century, decreased in estimation.

This period of travel coincided with a revolution in taste, particularly in relation to the aesthetics of the sublime and the picturesque. This is apparent in changing attitudes to mountainous landscapes. The Alps, for instance, came to be regarded less as a painful obstacle en route to Italy and more as an intrinsic source of aesthetic interest, and even as a symbol of Romantic self-transcendence. This changing evaluation is measurable by comparing Tobias Smollett's decision to travel from Nice to Rome in 1764 by sea rather than by "clamber[ing] along the mountains at the rate of two miles an hour, and at the risque of breaking your neck every minute" with Childe Harold in Lord Byron's *Childe Harold's Pilgrimage* (1812–18), who declares that "To me, high mountains are a feeling," a comment which points to a characteristic concern of Romantic poetry to collapse distinctions between man and nature. Indeed, toward the end of the eighteenth century, the pattern of European travel altered partly in response to this new, aesthetic appreciation of mountain scenery (which took as one of its principal texts Edmund Burke's *Philosophical Enquiry into the Origin of Our Ideas of the Sublime and Beautiful* [1757]), as fewer travelers proceeded beyond Switzerland to Italy. (William Wordsworth, in his European travels of 1790 and 1820, crossed the Alps without proceeding to Rome.)

Travel narratives are frequently concerned to maintain fidelity to those impressions or sensations received by the traveler. Laurence Sterne's *A Sentimental Journey through France and Italy* (1768) prefigures Romantic travel narratives by swapping objective testimony for subjective modes of expression. His concern to detect the "unifying presence" of nature behind national differences exposes the national prejudices of British travelers represented by the characters Mundungus and Smelfungus, the latter a reference to Tobias Smollett's splenetic narrative self-presentation in the *Travels through France and Italy* (1766), a work that casts aspersions on the politeness, cleanliness, hospitality, and convenience of France and Italy. *A Sentimental Journey* does, however, resemble Smollett's *Travels* in placing at the center of the narrative the character experiencing the scenes described, and in identifying travel as a genre spanning such subjects as aesthetics, politics, and economics, and incorporating epistolary forms of communication, autobiography, and elements of the picaresque: a generic mixture compounded by the lack of any firm distinction between travel and fiction.

The early decades of the nineteenth century witnessed the decline of the Grand Tour and the emergence of mass tourism, a sociological phenomenon facilitated by such things as the advent of steam travel. Tourism proved inimical to Romantic (vague, unprogrammed, idiosyncratic) itineraries, such as that described by William Wordsworth in *The Prelude* (1805, 1850). While a Romantic conception of the methods and purposes of travel may be said to include an association of literary creativity with travel-as-travail and a willingness to surrender the self to a potentially disorientating engagement with otherness, a touristic conception can in contrast be broadly characterized by a preference for relatively fast, efficient, and comfortable modes of travel, and by the requirement that the engagement with things foreign meet certain limiting criteria. Indeed, in its opposition to a Romantic view of travel, tourism recalls both the Grand Tour (which also pursued selective itineraries of designated sights), and eighteenth-century aestheticism (which also adopted a standard of objective contemplation)—parallels that suggest that attitudes towards travel are not neatly period-specific.

MELANIE ORD

See also **Travel Writing: France; Travel Writing: Germany; Travel Writing: United States**

Bibliography

Black, Jeremy. *The British and the Grand Tour*. London: Croom Helm, 1985.

Bohls, Elizabeth A. *Women Travel Writers and the Language of Aesthetics, 1716–1818*. Cambridge Studies in Romanticism. Cambridge: Cambridge University Press, 1995.

Boswell, James. *Boswell's Journal of a Tour to the Hebrides with Samuel Johnson, 1773*. Edited by Frederick A. Pottle and Charles H. Bennett. London: Heinemann, 1963.

Cardinal, Roger. "Romantic Travel." In *Rewriting the Self: Histories from the Renaissance to the Present*. Edited by Roy Porter. London: Routledge, 1997.

Chard, Chloe. *Pleasure and Guilt on the Grand Tour: Travel Writing and Imaginative Geography 1600–1830*. Manchester: Manchester University Press, 1999.

Cotsell, Michael. *English Literature and the Wider World. Vol. 1, 1660–1780: All Before Them*. Edited by John McVeagh. London: Ashfield Press, 1990.

Gilroy, Amanda, ed. *Romantic Geographies: Discourses of Travel, 1775–1844*. Manchester: Manchester University Press, 2000.

Hibbert, Christopher. *The Grand Tour*. London: Weidenfeld and Nicolson, 1969.

Smollett, Tobias George. *Travels through France and Italy*. Edited by Frank Felsenstein. Oxford: Oxford University Press, 1979.

Sterne, Laurence. *A Sentimental Journey through France and Italy, to Which Are Added the Journal to Eliza and A Political Romance*. Edited by Ian Jack. London: Oxford University Press, 1968.

Wollstonecraft, Mary. *Letters Written During a Short Residence in Sweden, Norway, and Denmark*. Edited by Carol H. Poston. Lincoln: University of Nebraska Press, 1976.

TRAVEL WRITING: FRANCE

The constellation of factors that would result in a Golden Age of travel writing during the first half of the nineteenth century, once French Romanticism had reached its full expression, was already forming during the second half of the eighteenth-century. While the cultural elite continued the Renaissance tradition of travel to Italy, the accounts they wrote revealed a new sensibility, especially evident in their meditations on the passing of time, inspired by contemplation of the ruins of Greco-Roman civilization. Voyages of discovery, including those described in Louis-Antoinede Bougainville's *Voyage autour du monde* (1772) and Jacques-Henri Bernardin de Saint-Pierre's *Voyage à l'île de France* (1773), revealed "primitive" cultures and lush landscapes hitherto ignored. Such travel accounts helped stimulate the period of intense philosophical reflection known as the Enlightenment. Diderot's *Supplément au Voyage de Bougainville* (c. 1772) illustrates the interest philosophers took in the unfamiliar lands described in such travel accounts, as does Jean-Jacques Rousseau's notion of the superiority of humanity in its uncivilized, "natural" state. In France, the publication of accounts of voyages to imaginary lands permitted writers to criticize the political and social status quo without fear of reprisals. The philosophical reflection stimulated by travel accounts both real and imaginary led to a new sense of historical and cultural relativism. Later in the century, a recognition of the dignity and equality of all, institutionalized by the French Revolution (1789), became a critical factor contributing to the flowering of travel writing during the first half of the nineteenth century.

The eighteenth-century consciousness of historical and cultural relativism was intensified by the wars following the French Revolution. As Alfred de Musset's narrator explains in *La Confession d'un enfant du siècle* (*Confession of a Child of the Century*, 1836), young Frenchmen were curious to see for themselves the lands described by those who had participated in the Napoleonic wars, whether they be Spain or Russia, Italy or Egypt. The French colonization of Algeria, begun in 1830, also contributed to a fascination with all things Oriental, a fascination which would deepen as France expanded its colonial empire. Finally, technological progress, which made travel less arduous and expensive, also played a significant role in the popularity of travel writing in early nineteenth-century France. Steam power, harnessed both by the newly invented train and by improved sea-going vessels, facilitated travel in France, throughout Europe and beyond.

Nineteenth-century French writers responded to the sharpened interest in unfamiliar places in many ways. Some contributed extensively to the ever-increasing number of newspapers and journals, later often compiling their articles into book form. Literary authors traveled more frequently than in the past, at times for the express purpose of enhancing their ability to accurately describe the foreign landscapes and societies they had chosen as a backdrop for their fictional works. François-Auguste-René de Chateaubriand's narratives *Atala* (1801) and *René* (1802) and Victor Hugo's collection of poetry *Les Orientales* (1829) or his play *Hernani* (1830) are but a few of the many examples of this interest in "local color," already evident in the descriptions of exotic nature in Bernardin de Saint-Pierre's *Paul et Virginie* (1787). However, if major eighteenth-century authors never chose to write narratives of their own travels (a fact that Rousseau would admit to regretting, in his *Confessions* [1782 and 1789]), in early nineteenth-century France literary authors joined journalistic travel writers in composing narratives based upon their own travel experiences.

The writing of travel accounts held special attraction for nineteenth-century authors because it was particularly well-suited to express the preoccupations central to French Romanticism. The first of these was the belief that truth is individual and not collective, particular and not general. This led to a perception that travel accounts, especially those written in the first person, provided a reliable source of knowledge about the world and the traveler alike. Moreover, the political, socioeconomic, and ideological dislocations that characterized not only the Revolutionary and Napoleonic periods, but also the aftermaths of the 1815 Restoration and 1830 July Revolution, frustrated the personal and collective hopes of many, and helped to foster a melancholy psychological state often called the *mal du siècle*. Travel to foreign lands—or reading about such travel—offered an avenue of escape, for there life was perceived to hold the promise of happiness or, at least, of distraction. In addition, the defense of national identity, notably by Madame Anne-Louise-Germaine de Staël in her *De l'Allemagne* (*On Germany*, 1810), created new interest in the pre-Renaissance history of France, including the architecture of the Middle Ages, which classical aesthetics had scorned. This stimulated travel to architectural sites thoughout the French provinces, which had been neglected for centuries. Finally, a curiosity about geographical areas which appeared untouched by modern life, including the physical and social changes that were being wrought by the Industrial Revolution, captured the French imagination. Mountains (the Alps, the Pyrenees, and the Scottish Highlands, among others) and the countries of the Mediterranean basin, participated in this nineteenth-century fascination with the "primitive."

It was the travel narrative's particular ability to express Romanticism's central preoccupation with the ideas and perceptions of the individual which explains its great popularity during this period. Developed commentary, which revealed the intimate life of the traveler, constitutes one of the discursive features characteristic of the French Romantic travel narrative. In addition, travel writing was transformed into a modality of autobiography by the fact that many authors adopted the diary or letter form in order to suggest both the authenticity of their account and their own sincerity. Long and detailed description, included to satisfy the public's thirst for images of the exotic and picturesque, is another important discursive characteristic of the French Romantic travel narrative. Moreover, through their use of formal and stylistic techniques typically associated with traditional literary genres, French authors writing during the first half of the nineteenth century helped raise the aesthetic status of the travel narrative to that of "literary" genre. It is the interest a traditionally minor genre held for major Romantic authors, including Chateaubriand, Alphonse-Marie-Louis de Lamartine, Hugo, and Stendhal, that led to this genre's change in literary status during this period.

While expressing the Romantic fascination with the exotic, the poems in Charles Baudelaire's *Les Fleurs du Mal* (1857) also attest to the midcentury perception, at least on the part of many literary authors, that the hopes pinned upon travel and the writing it inspired had been disappointed, and that other modalities of escape would need to be explored. Romantic subjectivity, which had found in travel writing a privileged avenue of expression, came to be criticized, as knowledge and truth were increasingly thought to be attained through scientific objectivity. Travel writing continued during the second half of the nineteenth century, as travel itself became possible for an ever-growing number of the bourgeoning middle class. However, the intrepid *voyageur* of earlier times increasingly gave way to the tourist, and, despite some notable exceptions such as Pierre Loti, the travel narrative failed to capture the interest of literary authors as it had done during the Romantic era.

WENDELIN GUENTNER

See also **Travel Writing: Britain; Travel Writing: Germany; Travel Writing: United States**

Selected Works

Ampère, Jean-Jacques. *Littérature, voyages et poésies*. 1850.

Bernardin de Saint-Pierre, Jacques-Henri. *Voyage à l'île de France*. 1773.

Bougainville. Louis-Antoine. de. *Voyage autour du monde par la frégate du Roi La Boudeure et la flute l'Etoile en 1766, 1767, 1768, et 1769 . . .* 2 vols. 1772.

Chateaubriand, François-Auguste-René de. *Itinéraire de Paris à Jérusalem et de Jérusalem à Paris en allant par la Grèce, et revenant par l'Egypte, la Barbarie et l'Espagne*. 1811.

———. *Voyage en Amérique, Voyage en Italie in Oeuvres complètes*. 31 vols. 1826–31.

Custine, Astolphe de. *L'Espagne sous Ferdinand VII*. 4 vols. 1838.

———. *La Russie en 1839*. 4 vols. 1843.

———. *Mémoires et voyages ou Lettres écrites à diverses époques pendant des courses en Suisse, en Calabre, en Angleterre et en Ecosse*. 2 vols. 1830.

Du Camp, Maxime. *Souvenirs et paysages d'Orient*. 1848.

Dumas, Alexandre. *Excursions sur les bords du Rhin*. 3 vols. 1841.

———. *Impressions de voyage (Suisse)*. 1834.

———. *Nouvelles impressions de voyage (Midi de la France)*. 2 vols. 1841.

Flaubert, Gustave. *Par les champs et par les grèves (1847–1848)*. Edited by A. Tooke. 1987.

Gautier, Théophile. *Voyage en Espagne (Tras las montes)*. 1843.

———. *Voyage en Italie*. Paris: Charpentier, 1852.

———. *Voyage pittoresque en Algérie (1845)*. Geneva: Droz, 1973.

Hugo, Victor. *Le Rhin, lettres à un ami*. 1842.

———. *Voyages, France, et Bélgique, 1834–1837*. Edited by Claude Gély. Grenoble: Presses Universitaires de Grenoble, 1974.

Lamartine, Alphonse Marie-Louis de. *Souvenirs, impressions, pensées et paysages pendant un Voyage en Orient 1832–1833 ou Notes d'un Voyageur*. 1835.

Marmier, Xavier. *Du Rhin au Nil: Tyrol, Hongrie, Provinces danubiennes, Syrie, Palestine, Égypte; souvenirs de voyages*. 2 vols. 1847.

———. *Lettres sur l'Algérie*. 1847.

———. *Lettres sur le nord. Danemark, Suède, Norvège. Laponie et Spitzberg*. 2 vols. 1840.

———. *Nouveaux souvenirs de voyage (Franche-Comté)*. 1845.

Nerval, Gérard de. *Voyage en Orient*. 1851.

Nodier, Charles. *Promenade de Dieppe aux Montagnes d'Ecosse*. 1821.

Nodier, Charles, with Auguste Regnier and Champin. *Paris historique. Promenade dans les rues de Paris*. 1838.

Nodier, Charles, with Baron Isodore-Justin-Séverin Taylor and Alphonse de Cailleux. *Voyages pittoresques et romantiques dans l'ancienne France*. 23 vols. 1820–63.

Quinet, Edgar. *Mes vacances en Espagne*. 1846.

Ramond de Carbonnières. *Observations faites dans les Pyrénées, pour servir de suite à des observations sur les Alpes insérées dans une traduction des Lettres de W. Coxe sur la Suisse*. 2 vols. 1789.

Sand, George. *Lettres d'un voyageur*. 1837.

———. *Un hiver à Majorque*. 2 vols. 1841.

Stendhal. *Mémoires d'un touriste*. 2 vols. 1838.

———. *Promenades dans Rome*. 2 vols. 1829.

———. *Rome, Naples et Florence en 1817*. 1817.

Tristan, Flora. *Les pérégrinations d'une paria*. 2 vols. 1838.

———. *Promenades dans Londres*. 1840.

Le Voyage en Orient: anthologie des voyageurs français dans le Levant au XIXe siècle. Edited by J.-C. Berchet. 1985.

Bibliography

Bain, Margaret I. *Les Voyageurs français en Ecosse 1770–1830 et leurs curiosités intellectuelles*. Paris: Librairie Anciennne Honoré Champion, 1931.

Bedner, Jules. *Le Rhin de Hugo: Commentaires sur un récit de voyage.* Gröningen: J. B. Wolters, 1965.

Berty, Valérie. *Littérature et voyage: un essai de typologie narrative des récits de voyage français au XIXe siècle.* Paris: L'Harmattan, 2001.

Carré, Jean-Marie. *Voyageurs et écrivains français en Egypte.* Cairo: Institut Français d'Archéologie Orientale, 1932.

Del Litto, V., and Emanuele Kanceff, eds. *Le journal de voyage et Stendhal.* Geneva: Slatkine, 1986.

Guentner, Wendelin. *Esquisses littéraires: Rhétorique du spontané et récit de voyage au XIXe siècle.* Saint-Genouph: Nizet, 1997.

———. *Stendhal et son lecteur. Essai sur les "Promenades dans Rome."* Tübingen: Gunter Narr, 1990.

Monicat, Bénédicte. *Itinéraires de l'écriture au féminin. Voyageuses du 19e siècle.* Amsterdam-Atlanta: Rodopi, 1996.

Moussa, Sarga. *La relation orientale: Enquête sur la communication dans les récits de voyage en Orient (1811–1861).* Paris: Klincksieck, 1995.

Rajotte, Pierre, with the collaboration of Anne-Marie Carle and François Couture. *Le récit de voyage au XIXe siècle: aux frontières du littéraire.* Montreal: Editions Triptique, 1997.

Schaeffer, Gerald. *Le Voyage en Orient de Nerval: Etudes de structures.* Neuchâtel: La Baconnière, 1967.

Wetzel, Andreas. *Partir sans partir: le récit de voyage littéraire au XIXe siècle.* Toronto: Paratexte, 1992.

Wiegand, Horst Jürgen. *Victor Hugo und der Rhein.* Bonn: Bouvier Verlag Herbert Grundmann, 1982.

Wolfzettel, Friedrich. *Ce désir de vagabondage cosmopolite. Wege und Entwicklung des französischen Reiseberichts im 19. Jahrhundert.* Tübingen: Max Niemeyer Verlag, 1986.

TRAVEL WRITING: GERMANY

Given that the public's passion for travel had reached epidemic proportions, according to *Der Teutsche Merkur* of November 1784, travel literature as such was slow to achieve recognition in Germany. Medieval quests, represented by Wolfram von Eschenbach's *Parzifal* and Hartmann von Aue's *Iwein*, are early examples of a related type of work, in which a pedagogic process unfolds as the traveling hero undergoes distinct stages of interaction with representative individuals. German Romantic narrators were fond of inventing a series of meaningful encounters with crusaders, hermits, and mysterious maidens in medieval or Italianate landscapes; the journey through time and space in pursuit of alterity is an important element even in those works not overtly constituting travel literature. One noteworthy Romantic travelogue was Justinus Kerner's *Reiseschatten* ("Shades of Travel," 1811), a subjective and satirical compilation interspersed with local legends. Johann Gottfried Seume's arduous walk to Syracuse and back, published as *Spaziergang nach Syrakus im Jahre 1802*, adopts a more critical stance that was unusual for its time.

It was Johann Wolfgang von Goethe who established the modern novel of "character development," the bildungsroman, with an account of the gradual maturing of a talented actor and would-be poet, Wilhelm Meister. Despite its sensitive depiction of an aspiring artist's career, *Wilhelm Meisters Lehrjahre* (*Wilhelm Meister's Apprenticeship*, 1795–96) ends in renunciation and thus failed to satisfy the younger generation. Novalis was so enraged by what he saw as Meister/Goethe's "peregrination in the direction of aristocratic privilege" that he penned an (unfinished) response, *Heinrich von Ofterdingen* (posthumous, 1802), in which the youthful poet of the same name undergoes a journey from Eisenach to Augsburg that is neither historic nor realistic; Ofterdingen was to find fulfillment in the realms of myth, suggesting that true poetic excellence is only attainable via an inner journey of the soul. "In ourselves or nowhere" is where Novalis would have us journey in pursuit of truth.

The Romantics tended to see themselves as aimless wanderers rather than as focused travelers, preferring imaginative improvisation to prearranged routes and schedules. They take liberties with time, place, and linearity. Ludwig Tieck's novel *Franz Sternbalds Wanderungen* (*Franz Sternbald's Travels*, 1798) is set in the time of Albrecht Dürer (late fifteenth and early sixteenth centuries) and recounts journeys to the Netherlands and Italy, though without permitting its hero much in the way of personal development. Its evocations of landscapes are full of the kind of pathos that was to become the hallmark of Romantic nature worship, and in his longing to depict "the infinite" in his paintings, Sternbald fully embodies the sweeping but ultimately unachievable artistic ambition of his time. Given the centrality of "yearning" (*Sehnsucht*) in the Romantic creed, and given the sustained efforts by Friedrich Schlegel and others to evolve a new mythology for the modern epoch, it was inevitable that the literary travelogs of the early nineteenth century should be fantastic pilgrimages rather than precise itineraries. This is true of the novels and short stories of Joseph von Eichendorff no less than of the complex narratives of Clemens Brentano (*Godwi*, 1801) and the many *Bildungsromane* that appeared between Friedrich Schlegel's *Lucinde* (1799) and Eduard Mörike's *Maler Nolten* (1832).

Actual travel texts, Heinrich von Kleist's *Reise nach Paris* (*Journey to Paris*) Brentano's *Reisebilder* (*Travel Sketches*) Mörike's *Der Bodensee* (*Lake Constance*) are of less interest than these authors' major creative works. The same goes for Goethe's belated record of his experiences in Italy (*Italienische Reise* [*Italian Journey*], 1817, completed 1829). The lifting of restrictions after the Napoleonic Wars persuaded many others to go and see the world for themselves, while within Germany, "Turnvater" Friedrich Ludwig Jahn recommended "patriotic wandering" as providing a cure for the ills of mind and body (*Deutsches Volkstum* [*German Nationalism*], 1810). A fresh note is struck in Heinrich Heine's *Harzreise* (*Journey through the Harz Mountains*, 1826). Although ostensibly a realistic account of the young poet's wanderings from Göttingen to Clausthal, Goslar, and Mount Brocken, the style is a complex amalgam of clear-sighted observation, sarcasm, and satire on the one hand, and Romantic sensitivity and lyricism on the other. As in Eichendorff, poetry is interpolated into the prose text; but essentially Heine is out of sympathy with many aspects of Romantic sentiment and distances himself not only from provincial philistinism, as others had done, but also from Christian morality. His contribution to the genre reaches its apex in *Reisebilder* (*Pictures from a Journey*, 1826–31), which continues to form a bridge between Romantic devices, the fragment and the intensely lyrical nature poem, and a modern, and an increasingly anti-German, passionately egalitarian, pro-Napoleonic ethos. His account "North Sea" is shot through with sarcastic portraits of privilege and arbitrary behavior; the section on Italy is used, among other things, to ridicule the neoclassical August von Platen; and in England, which the author explored in 1827, he finds little evidence of true democracy. Shortly after the completion of the *Reisebilder*, Heine moved permanently to France, preferring the life of an exiled political journalist to that of a Romantic dream weaver.

Like the novel itself, travel literature proved to be a rapidly evolving genre. The experience of travel is increasingly recorded with clarity and precision. Eichendorff's ideal topographies, seen in "Das Marmorbild" ("The Marble Statue," 1818) and "Aus dem Leben eines Taugenichts"("Memoirs of a Good-for-Nothing," 1826) give way to well-researched journeys of known people, such as Mörike's "Mozart auf der Reise nach Prag" ("Mozart on his Journey to Prague," 1855), which, despite its symbolism, maintains a focus on real events in the life of a known personality. In Eichendorff, cities like Rome are evoked with Romantic ambivalence, idealized and demonized at one and the same time. As literature became increasingly tied to reality, fantastic voyages were less in demand than factual travelogs.

One such was provided by the poet Aldelbert von Chamisso, who accomplished a journey of epic proportions when he sailed around the world in 1815–18. This was another instance in which the Romantic longing for exotic experiences was fulfilled, but in such a way as to shift attention from fanciful speculation toward the meticulous observation of reality. Chamisso's report (*Reise um die Welt* [*A Journey around the World*], 1836) was written from the point of view of a man who was not only a poet and thinker, but a botanist, geologist, and geographer as well. It records the places and people he visited side by side with botanical, anthropological, linguistic, and other data that struck the observer as significant.

The careers of second-generation Romantics like Chamisso, Heine, and Nickolaus Lenau show poet-travelers interacting with the real world in a way that was more clear-sighted and critical than the intuitive but simplistically speculative approach of Eichendorff, Novalis, and Tieck. The slow transition to realism is not infrequently accompanied by a measure of disillusionment. When he crossed the Atlantic, Lenau was to lament that the primeval forests of his dreams were not inhabited by grizzly bears and proud natives, but by shopkeepers and degenerate hangers-on. Heine began as a poet, but survived as a journalist.

In his narrative poem "Salas y Gomez" (1830), Chamisso describes a Robinson Crusoe figure in realistic rather than idealized terms, as a lonely outcast on a remote island, haunted by memories and fearful of contact with the new. Almost imperceptibly, the dream-landscapes of the 1790s had yielded to the world of the steamship and railway engine.

OSMAN DURRANI

See also **Travel Writing: Britain; Travel Writing: France; Travel Writing: United States**

Bibliography

Adams, Percy G. *Travel Literature and the Evolution of the Novel.* Lexington: University of Kentucky Press, 1983.

Blanton, Casey. *Travel Writing: the Self and the World.* (Studies in literary themes and genres 15) New York: Twayne, 1997.

Brenner, Peter J. *Der Reisebericht in der deutschen Literatur: ein Forschungsüberblick als Vorstudie zu einer Gattungsgeschichte.* Tübingen: Niemeyer, 1990.

Bürgi, Andreas. *Weltvermesser. Die Wandlung des Reiseberichts in der Spätaufklärung.* Bonn: Bouvier, 1989.

Buzard, James. *The Beaten Track: European Tourism, Literature, and the Ways to Culture, 1800–1918.* Oxford: Clarendon Press, 1993.

Chamisso, Adelbert von. *A Voyage Around the World with the Romanzov Exploring Expedition in the Years 1815–1818 in the Brig Rurik, Captain Otto von Kotzebue.* Honolulu: University of Hawaii Press, 1986.

Gilroy, Amanda, ed. *Romantic Geographies: Discourses of Travel, 1775–1844.* Manchester: Manchester University Press, 2000.

Heimrath, Ulrich, ed. *Deutsche Reiseliteratur: Texte von der Aufklärung bis zur Gegenwart.* Frankfurt/M: Diesterweg, 1985.

Hentschel, Uwe. *Studien zur Reiseliteratur am Ausgang des 18. Jahrhunderts: Autoren–Formen.* Frankfurt/M: Lang, 1999.

Hölz, Karl, ed. *Beschreiben und Erfinden: Figuren des Fremden vom 18. bis zum 20. Jahrhundert.* Frankfurt/M: Lang, 2000.

Komar, K. L. "The Structure of Heine's 'Harzreise': Should We Take the Narrator at His Word?" *Germanic Review* 56 (1981): 128–33.

Mayer Hammond, Theresa. *American Paradise: German Travel Literature from Duden to Kisch.* Heidelberg: Winter, 1980.

Schulz, A. R. "Goethe and the Literature of Travel," *Journal of English and Germanic Philology* 23 (1949): 445–68.

Schweizer, Niklaus Rudolf. *A Poet Among Explorers: Chamisso in the South Seas.* Berne: Herbert Lang, 1973.

Seixo, Maria Alziro. *Travel Writing and Cultural Memory.* Amsterdam: Rodopi, 2000.

TRAVEL WRITING: UNITED STATES

The earliest writing associated with the United States was by European explorers and travelers, such as Bernal Diaz del Castillo, describing the physical environment, its resources, and its inhabitants. Later authors such as Alexis de Tocqueville and Frances Trollope related their experiences and perceptions of America and Americans from a position of confidence in their own European citizenship.

In contrast, American authors such as James Fenimore Cooper and Washington Irving, who were proving themselves as literary symbols of American "civilization," wrote from a position of recent and tenuous citizenship that was, and would continue to be, achieved through violence. If ownership signified belonging, and the land had been taken either from oppressors

or the oppressed, the sense of belonging achieved through ownership remained insecure because surely the land could be lost in the same manner it had been gained.

The years between 1760 and 1850 were culturally and politically traumatic, and travel writing during these years reflects this in the recurring theme of the individual's desire to at once belong or possess and remain independent. Much of American travel writing, whether the protagonist traveled in the United States or abroad, focused on searching for a past to which one could lay claim while seeking out a present in which true citizenship was possible.

That exploration and ownership seem to be inextricably interwoven should come as no surprise in light of the American exploring expeditions initiated as early as 1804. Expeditions such those led by Meriwether Lewis and William Clark, Zebulon Pike, and Stephen Long between 1804 and 1820 had multiple purposes, including mapping the land, cataloging its resources, and assessing the nature of its indigenous inhabitants, laying claim to the land for the nation, and opening it up to new settlement. The knowledge gained from the geological and geographical expeditions that continued throughout the nineteenth century resulted in the alignment of the natural landscape and its plentiful resources with the presence of the divine. This presence however, led to a conflict between Americans' confidence in their apparently "God-given" right to exploit resources such as Niagara Falls and Yellowstone, and their responsibility to conserve a landscape so closely associated with creation. In addition to conflict, however, the expeditions generated popular accounts of the exploration and discovery of the still-expanding country. Book-length chronicles of the expeditions and newspaper and magazine articles were widely available to citizens hungry for information about and adventures in America's untamed wilderness.

In Cooper's novels such as *The Pioneers* (1823), the anxiety caused by ownership of disputed land either between Euro- and Native Americans or among Euro-Americans is ever present, making a sense of belonging difficult to achieve. In contrast to Cooper's American stories, in his European essays published between 1836 and 1838 the contention over ownership appears to have been settled long ago. Seeking a link to European history and culture as both Cooper and Irving did, yet being American, was uncomfortable and parallels the discomfort each felt in his own citizenship.

The voyages of discovery that Herman Melville participates in release him, and his characters, from American society's expectations. In *Omoo* (1846) and *Typee* (1847), rather than in the land of his patrimony, Melville's characters seek freedom in a tropical wilderness but ultimately return to a familiar society in the form of the ship. Similarly, the title character of *Redburn* (1849), who goes in search of his guidebook-based perception of his father's English heritage, finds only disappointment and states that guidebooks *are the least reliable books in all literature*. Unlike Irving's Geoffrey Crayon, who is able to turn the squalor and the guidebook disappointments of London into a unique experience, Redburn cannot, and it is his decision to return to the familiar that provides him with his sense of belonging, however short-lived.

Washington Irving expressed his anxiety differently through the persona of Geoffrey Crayon, "Gent." At home and abroad he sought out opportunities for discovery, for experiences that were his own as an individual yet could make him feel at home in the broader society. Irving envisioned himself as not just a narrator but as a guide for his readers, and is able to achieve intimacy with his reader by writing in the first person and directly addressing his reader as if he or she were at his side. In *The Sketch Book of Geoffrey Crayon, Gent.* (1819–20), Irving's tales are located in England and the United States. As a traveler, Irving/Crayon is a seeker of authentic experience. In the first essay of *The Sketch Book*, entitled "The Author's Account of Himself," Irving writes that it is "the fashion for modern tourists to travel pencil in hand and bring home their portfolios filled with sketches . . . [however] I fear I shall give equal disappointment with an unlucky landscape painter, who had traveled the continent, but, following the bent of his vagrant inclination, had sketched in nooks and corners and bypasses . . . [and] had neglected to paint St. Peter's, or the Coliseum. . . ." Thus, Irving frees himself and his readers from the grueling pilgrimage to every major European monument. Irving's essays provide models for the manner in which the process or work of travel leads to personal discoveries.

Essays such as Irving's "Boar's Head Tavern, Eastcheap," in which the narrator diligently sets out to find an undiscovered piece of Shakespearean history but instead experiences contemporary London, offered a model for authors such as Nathaniel Hawthorne on his visit to Niagara Falls. Hawthorne's essay "My Visit to Niagara" begins with bitter disappointment at his apparent inability to have his own authentic experience of the Falls, but ends with the joyous "but the spot, so famous through the world, was all my own!" Better known than his essay on his journey to Niagara Falls is Hawthorne's novel, *The Marble Faun; or the Romance of Monte Beni* (1859). Like Irving, Hawthorne opens his work with the preface in which he speaks directly to the reader, and he maintains the immediacy of his story by continuing to insert himself as the narrator/guide. *The Marble Faun* as Hawthorne describes it is a romance; in addition, for his readers, it became a guidebook for Americans' physical and spiritual experience of Rome.

Since the Eastern United States appeared to possess no picturesque ruins that might be likened to those in England or Italy, American visual artists were also compelled to search abroad for the subjects that would validate their skills and education for their American audiences. Even Thomas Cole, founder of the American school of landscape painting, traveled to England and Europe in search of instruction and experience. Together with Washington Allston and other artists, Cole returned to the United States with canvases such as *Aqueduct near Rome* (1832), and *Dream of Arcadia* (1838). Paralleling his literary counterparts, through his landscapes Cole at once demonstrated his knowledge of Virgil's poetry and Claude Lorrain's paintings, his ability to take on a venerated subject and make it his own, and finally his capacity to not only meet but to shape his viewers' expectations of his subject.

Traveling through the natural and cultural landscape, Hawthorne and Irving sought experiences that were at once individual and shared, making the author and reader part of a continuous tradition. Through their essays and novels, Hawthorne and Irving became guides for their readers' experiences of the European cultural landscape and part of the tradition of American travel writing to which Henry James, Mark Twain, and Edith Wharton would continue to contribute.

KATHLEEN L. BUTLER

See also **Travel Writing: Britain; Travel Writing: France; Travel Writing: Germany**

Bibliography

Greenfield, Bruce. *Narrating Discovery: The Romantic Explorer in American Literature, 1790–1855*. New York: Columbia University Press, 1992.

Marder, Daniel. *Exiles at Home: A Story of Literature in Nineteenth Century America*. New York: University Press of America, 1984.

Harris, Neil. *The Artist in American Society*. New York: George Braziller, 1966.

LES TROIS MOUSQUETAIRES (THE THREE MUSKETEERS) 1844

Novel by Alexandre Dumas *père*

Les Trois Mousquetaires has become the archetypal adventure story, as well as the best known and the most widely read (and adapted) of all French novels. In the historical context of its production it was also the prototype of the *roman-feuilleton* (serial novel), which enjoyed phenomenal success in France in the 1840s and was an enduring feature of the French newspaper until the end of the century. In its heyday, the roman-feuilleton, which was published in instalments in the bottom panel of a mass-circulation newspaper, was usually episodic, full of thrilling sequences and suspense, recounting tales of passion and vengeance, providing Gothic thrills, and preferably peopled with the blackguards, heroes, and heroines of melodrama, all the better to maintain the interest and the subscriptions of the paper's readers. It provided a natural outlet for Alexandre Dumas's talents and energies, as he combined elements of the historical romance of Sir Walter Scott with the formulas and themes of the roman-feuilleton as exemplified most famously by the narratives of Eugène Sue, whose *Mystères de Paris* had appeared in 1842–43 to widespread acclaim.

In 1844, along with *Le Comte de Monte-Cristo* (*The Count of Monte Cristo*), which began publication in the same year, *Les Trois Mousquetaires* immediately became a bestseller at a time when the phenomenon was still a novelty. This text and its sequels, *Vingt Ans après* (*Twenty Years After*, 1845) and *Le Vicomte de Bragelonne* (*The Viscount of Bragelonne*, 1850), were written in collaboration with Auguste Maquet, a history teacher and aspiring dramatist who produced under Dumas's direction first drafts of novels that Dumas then rewrote, modified, and amplified, and on which he imposed his characteristic manner and style. The original idea for the *Les Trois Mousquetaires* and for the events of the first few chapters derived from the first of the three volumes of the (pseudo) *Mémoires de M. d'Artagnan* (*Memoirs of Monsieur Artagnan*, 1700) by Gatien de Courtilz de Sandras, who claimed to have used authentic documents found among the papers of Charles de Baatz d'Artagnan as the source of his own narrative. Dumas complicates the question of the provenance of the novel by claiming in his preface to the work that he is merely reproducing another set of chronicles—which are entirely fictitious—the "Memoirs of M. le comte de La Fère." This authorial posture, of which the reader, along with the author, soon loses sight, serves, like the use of real historical figures such as Cardinal Richelieu, Anne of Austria, and the Duke of Buckingham, as an authenticating strategy. Indeed, as F. W. J. Hemmings writes, "History, in short, was used by Dumas in much the same way as science by Zola: to confer a semblance of veracity on his fiction." The chronology of the novel is vague, confused, and frequently anachronistic, but the events are set supposedly from April 1625 to August 1628, during the middle years of the reign of Louis XIII.

The unifying thread of the novel is the noble d'Artagnan's clash with the femme fatale, the wicked Milady, a Richelieu agent, which imparts on this somewhat rambling work not only a binding structure in its evolving phases but also a certain psychological and allegorical depth, most dramatically in the ending where the unfolding Gothic atmosphere of the novel culminates in the final scenes of bloody retribution. The stark opposition between upright and evil characters and the theme of an ultimately propitious Providence are further borrowings from the world of the melodrama and the serial novel. The characters are markedly stereotypical. The heroic male protagonists belong to a thoroughly masculine ethos that extols comradeship, bravery, youthful imprudence, and a taste for adventure, while the few women who appear in the work tend to the angelical or the diabolical. The novel is, however, remarkable for its generic complexity in an age which had still not entirely given up on classical strictures and demarcations. There are tragic, epic, picaresque strains, with comic interludes within the framework of the historical drama or romance, along with elements of the thriller or mystery tale. The beginning is Quixotic and reminiscent of the *roman d'initiation*, as the hero's confrontation with the tyrannical mother is counterbalanced by the quest for the noble father. But, above all, *Les Trois Mousquetaires*, in which narrating itself takes on a thematic importance equal to skirmishing with the enemy and to the values of chivalry, generosity, and panache as they are illustrated in the daring deeds of the archetypal Romantic hero and his comrades, is a supreme example of the narrative art. Anthony Burgess, among others, has heralded Dumas as "one of the great myth-makers" of his and of any age.

Not surprisingly, the novel was translated immediately into several languages and re-edited constantly throughout the century. Indeed, during the nineteenth century, several editions in English were issued almost every year. Already in 1844, six pirated Belgian editions were on the market. As usual, the measure of the success of the novel can be gauged by the huge number of vaudevilles, parodies, sequels, and theatrical adaptations that have been inspired by Dumas's novel. Inevitably, it has been adapted several times for the cinema, from 1908 onward, in versions starring such screen legends as Douglas Fairbanks, Gene Kelly, and even John Wayne as the hero and Lana Turner as a sultry Milady. There has also been a Walt Disney version with the usual Hollywood adjustments to the plot and a number of sequels, such as the recent French film *La Fille de d'Artagnan* (*D'Artagnan's Daughter*, 1998), have also appeared. Indeed, not only have the media of popular culture in their multiple manifestations appropriated Dumas's novel in this way, but it has even fallen prey to consumer commodity industries, lending its name, for example, to a chocolate bar in North America. At such developments, Dumas would, no doubt, have been delighted.

DAVID BAGULEY

Text

Les Trois Mousquetaires. Published as a serial in *Le Siècle* from March 14 to July 14, 1844, then in 8 volumes in the same year; 2d edition, 1846. Translated as *The Three Musketeers; or, the Feats and Fortunes of a Gascon Adventurer* by William Barrow, 1846.

Bibliography

Bassan, Fernande, and Claude Schopp, eds. *Les Trois Mousquetaires. Le Comte de Monte Cristo. Cent cinquante ans après*, Marly-le-Roi: Champflour, 1995.

Bem, Jeanne. "D'Artagnan, et après. Lecture symbolique et historique de la trilogie de Dumas," *Littérature* 22 (1976): 13–30.

Jan, Isabelle. *Alexandre Dumas romancier.* Paris: Editions ouvrières, 1973.

Molino, Jean. "Alexandre Dumas et le roman mythique," *Arc: cahiers méditerranéens* 71 (1978): 56–69.

Picard, Michel. "Pouvoirs des feuilletons, ou d'Artagnan anonyme," *Littérature* 50 (1983): 55–76.

Tranouez, Pierre. "*Cave filium*! Etude du cycle des Mousquetaires," *Poétique* 71 (1987): 321–31.

TRUMBULL, JOHN 1756–1843

American painter

As Jules Prown has observed, John Trumbull was deeply conflicted as an artist and an individual. Throughout his life he was deeply religious and patriotic, yet he fathered an illegitimate son who would later fight on the side of the British in the War of 1812. He began a series of American history paintings while in England—where, not surprisingly they were unpopular—but in the case of *The Death of General Warren at the Battle of Bunker's Hill* (1786) he chose to emphasize the magnanimity of the English officer, making the picture unpopular in America as well.

One of Trumbull's earliest conflicts arose in his youth when he announced to his father that he would become a history painter. His father disapproved, believing his son should become a lawyer or clergyman. In deference to his father's wishes, Trumbull agreed to attend Harvard College, from which he graduated at age seventeen, but he did not abandon his aspiration to become a painter. In 1780, after serving in the military during the Revolutionary War, Trumbull left for Paris to conduct family business. The arrangement fell through, leaving him free to pursue studies with Benjamin West in London; during his stay, Trumbull was arrested on suspicion of espionage and remained in prison for eight months. While in prison he continued his studies by copying works that West loaned him. Eventually when Trumbull was released, it was with John Singleton Copley and West acting as his "securities." Later works such as *The Death of General Warren at the Battle of Bunker's Hill* and *The Death of General Montgomery in the Attack on Quebec* (1786) demonstrate their influence.

As an ardent follower of West, Trumbull believed that paintings of historical or religious subjects represented the highest level of artistic achievement. Bad timing plagued Trumbull, who found that the American public was not yet ready for historical or religious works in the European tradition, no matter how morally uplifting. Portraiture was acceptable, but epic works were not. Partly in response to this view, in 1794 Trumbull accepted a position with the Jay Treaty Commission in London. The result was a ten-year hiatus in his painting career. Though it did not signal the end of his career, his departure for England did represent the end of his most accomplished period.

Upon returning from England, Trumbull painted a number of portraits of prominent figures, and eventually became *the* painter of New York. Many of his portraits of political figures, such as *John Jay* (1805), were hung in public buildings where Trumbull hoped they would garner attention for himself, and more altruistically, where they would instruct the public and encourage young American artists.

During his ten years abroad, Trumbull had acquired Old Master paintings, and when he returned, he held the first exhibition of these works in the United States. The exhibition was a failure with the public, but as with his public portraits, it represented Trumbull's desire to bring attention to himself and to educate the masses. To achieve these ends he became a founding member of the New York Academy of Fine Arts, whose stated goal was "educating public taste." This organization later became the American Academy of Fine Arts, and Trumbull served as its president for nineteen years. Trumbull did not share West's reputation for generosity toward the education of younger artists. However, Trumbull discovered Thomas Cole, spoke highly of his work to William Dunlap and Asher B. Durand, and introduced him to his first major patron, Robert Gilmor.

In addition to history and portraits, Trumbull painted the American landscape, and is considered one of the first professional American artists to adopt landscape as a subject, if only for a short time. The style of his intimate paintings is similar to Thomas Cole's early work, and has been described as proto-Romantic for its depiction of the untamed landscape. Trumbull took a different approach to Niagara Falls: it was a national symbol, and his paintings depict a civilized sublime peopled with serene figures. He intended to use his paintings of Niagara Falls as the basis of a panorama. Upon his return to London in 1808 he sought out Robert Barker, who had popularized the form, to create a panorama based upon those paintings. Barker refused, even after Trumbull imposed upon West to take up his request. Niagara Falls remained a subject of great interest in the United States, and in 1831 an English entrepreneur, Robert Burford, brought a panoramic spectacle to New York with great success.

In pursuit of his lifelong goal to represent the nation's history to the public, Trumbull went to Washington, D.C., where he lobbied Congress to award him the commission to paint four large panels to be installed in the rotunda of the Capitol Building. Trumbull's tenacity was rewarded, and together with President James Madison, he chose The Declaration of Independence, The Surrender of Lord Cornwallis, The Surrender of General Burgoyne, and The Resignation of General Washington as his subjects. The first two were based upon two of Trumbull's earlier successful paintings. By the time he received the commission, however, his eyesight had deteriorated and he had lost much of his skill. The paintings for the rotunda were completed, accepted, and installed in spite of criticism of the veracity and technical weaknesses of the works.

Toward the end of his life, Trumbull found himself in financial need, and arranged to give his paintings to Yale College in return for an annuity for the remainder of his life. At this time he moved to New Haven, Connecticut, to live with his nephew-in-law Benjamin Silliman, who convinced Trumbull to write his autobiography. This autobiography, written in part in response to the highly critical essay William Dunlap wrote on Trumbull in his *History of the Rise and Progress of Arts of Design in the United States* (1834), was the first by an American artist.

The private and public conflicts that resulted from Trumbull's deeply held personal vision for his art and for art in America, a vision that combined patriotism, spirituality, and commerce, was the source of many "firsts" in the history of American art.

KATHLEEN L. BUTLER

Biography

Born June 6, 1756, Lebanon, Connecticut. Graduated Harvard College, 1773. Served in the army, 1775–77. To London in 1780, imprisoned, returned to United States. London, 1784–89, studied with Benjamin West. To Paris in 1786, met Jacques-Louis David. To London, 1794–1804, on Jay Treaty Commission and as diplomat; and again in 1808–16. Married Sarah Hope Harvey, October 1, 1800. Founding member New York Academy of Fine Arts, 1805 (later called American Academy of Fine Arts), served as its president, 1817–36. Capitol Rotunda commission, 1817–26. Lived in New Haven, Connecticut, 1837 until his death, on November 10, 1843.

Bibliography

Cooper, Helen A. *John Trumbull: The Hand and Spirit of the Painter*. New Haven, Conn.: Yale University Press, 1982.

Dunlap, William. "John Trumbull." In *History of the Rise and Progress of Arts of Design in the United States*. 1834. Reprinted New York: Benjamin Blom, 1965.

Jaffe, Irma, B. *John Trumbull: Patriot-Artist of the American Revolution*. Boston: Little, Brown, 1975.

Morgan, John Hill. *Paintings by John Trumbull at Yale University Art Gallery*. New Haven, Conn.: Yale University Press, 1926.

Sizer, Thomas, with Caroline Rollins. *The Works of Colonel John Trumbull, Artist of the American Revolution*. New Haven, Conn.: Yale University Press, 1967.

Trumbull, John. *Autobiography, Reminiscences and Letters by John Trumbull from 1756 to 1841*. New Haven, Conn.: B. L. Hamlen, 1841.

TURNER, JOSEPH MALLORD WILLIAM 1775–1851

British artist

The leading landscape painter of the Romantic era, Joseph Mallord William Turner was born in London of humble origins, and rose by virtue of his talent to become the most respected—if controversial—artist of his age in Britain.

Turner's achievement indicates the position attained by landscape painting in the early nineteenth century. Along with such fellow British artists as John Constable and Samuel Palmer and the German Caspar David Friedrich, he demonstrated the potential of the art to exemplify the new veneration of nature and also (even more importantly) that interplay of outward observation with subjective inner feeling that was being manifested at the same time by writers such as Francois-Auguste-René de Chateaubriand, Novalis, and William Wordsworth. He also showed, as these other artists did, that such a development in painting was not simply a matter of illustrating literary texts or philosophical theories, but rather a means of exploring a parallel world of visual experience. While introducing new levels of reference and association into landscape painting, Turner was also one of the most experimental practitioners of the time, producing in his later years works of extraordinary boldness of effect that had no parallel in art prior to the twentieth century.

It may be argued whether Turner was matched by other major landscapists of the day in terms of scope and vision. What is certain is that he undoubtedly excelled among his peers in terms of the sheer range of his work. His art was truly protean. As the critic John Ruskin observed, it was an art of extremes in which the wildest storms and the quietest calms could be found. During the course of his long working career he covered every known genre of landscape, as well as attempting (not always happily) many forms of figure painting. Even when his art failed in the mastery of certain fields, it retained a unique sense of vigor and curiosity. As his rival John Constable remarked, Turner had a "wonderful range of mind." He was hampered in verbal expression by lack of formal education, but his understanding of and interest in intellectual matters was marked. He kept up with scientific advances, taking a particular interest in geology, meteorology, and optical matters. He had a deep love of poetry, and often exhibited works accompanied by verses. He favored in particular the subtle and detailed descriptions of natural phenomena by James Thomson. He turned less often to Samuel Taylor Coleridge, Wordsworth, or other leading poets of his own generation.

However, he developed a great liking for Lord Byron, whose work he frequently drew upon in later years. It would seem that he was attracted both that poet's topographical variety, and by the vein of irony that ran through his work. Turner himself attempted verse, working for decades on an unfinished epic entitled *The Fallacies of Hope*. While patchy in quality, the poem provides a critical key to the understanding of Turner's thought. He explored in it the irony of man's relation to nature, in particular the deep sense of empathy with natural forms which are, in themselves, indifferent to human fate.

Unlike Constable, Friedrich, and Palmer, Turner was not a religious man in any conventional sense. While thrilling to the power of nature, he appears to have had little faith in either divine benevolence or in personal immortality. His first great apologist, John Ruskin, attempted to read a religious intention into Turner's work, but the artist did not support him in this. It is typical of this situation that Ruskin should have confected from stray remarks of the artist in his last days some divinely orientated final utterance for him: "The Sun is God." Turner's actual last words, addressed to his doctor, were far more revealing of his fundamental pessimism: "So, I am soon to be a nonentity."

Turner's intellectual position makes him the most modern in outlook of the major landscape painters of the period. His

William Turner, *Rain, Steam and Speed—The Great Western Railway*, 1844. Reprinted courtesy of Bildarchiv Preussischer Kulturbesitz.

pictorial achievement—while staggering in its power and variety—can be said to focus upon a novel, vivid perception of light. This led not only to unprecedented boldness of atmospheric effects, but also to a new use of paint, in bold veils and slabs of color, that made them, as Lawrence Gowing observed, "colour equivalents" of the natural effects they were recording. While these might seem to be prophetic of the developments of abstraction in the twentieth century, they are perhaps better understood as means of recording the transient effects of nature. Like other Romantic landscape painters, Turner focused upon the changeable, upon growth and decay, and atmospherics. But above all it was the sun, the source of light and life, that captured his imagination. Ruskin may have been inaccurate when he had his hero proclaim the sun a deity, but he was correct in perceiving its centrality to Turner's art.

The son of a barber, Turner grew up in central London in modest circumstances. His mother had an "ungovernable nature" and was eventually to be confined in a lunatic asylum. Turner was, perhaps understandably, closer to his father, who remained a supporter and confidant in adult life. It may be that Turner's experience of his mother's violence caused him never to get married himself—although he had a series of mistresses and fathered several children. It was perhaps a combination of such irregularities and a shyness about his own humble background that caused him to live a highly secret "double life," his personal arrangements being kept strictly unknown to his professional acquaintances. He was also extremely careful with money—a characteristic inherited from his father—and amassed a considerable wealth by the end of his life.

Part of the reason for the sheer variety of Turner's art lies in the nature of his career. Coming from a poor background, he had to earn his way in life from a very early age. He started at the bottom of the landscape market, producing topographical views, and gradually worked his way up through the hierarchy to produce grand historical landscapes that gained the approval of academia. However, as he mastered new forms of landscape, he did not abandon old ones, but rather enlarged his repertoire.

Throughout his life he continued to produce topographical works alongside more ambitious pictures.

Turner's early watercolors were a response to the taste for relatively inexpensive views of buildings and scenery occasioned by the growth of the Picturesque movement in the later eighteenth century. Such work caused a pattern that was to remain throughout Turner's life—that of making tours (usually in the summer) to visit places famed for their natural beauty or remarkable features, followed by a period (usually winter) in which the sketches made on such journeys would be worked up into views for sale or exhibition. In 1789 Turner began to work with the topographical draughtsman Thomas Malton, gaining a firm grounding in architectural views. In the same year he enrolled as a student at the Royal Academy. The training he received there greatly enlarged his horizons and proved critical for his later success. In 1790 he exhibited for the first time at a Royal Academy exhibition, commencing a practice that he was to continue for the rest of his life.

During the 1790s Turner was in the forefront of a movement encouraging the development of watercolor as a major art form. Around 1794 he was employed by Dr. Thomas Monro, a noted physician and connoisseur, to copy watercolors of British masters, in particular the moody atmospheric views of John Robert Cozens. He worked with Thomas Girtin, who was almost exactly his age and the only watercolorist to match him in innovation and subtlety. Girtin died young, in 1802. Turner's later comment, "If Tom had lived, I would have starved," was a rhetorical tribute that showed how much he valued the quality of his rival.

Turner would not, however, have starved for the simple reason that, unlike Girtin, he had branched out from topographical watercolor painting into the production of more ambitious oil paintings. It was his skill in the latter that caused him to be elected a full academician at the early age of twenty seven in 1802. While his first oils, such as *Fishermen at Sea* (1796), related to his topographical practice, they also showed his interest in light effects. Soon Turner was constructing pictures that rivaled the classical scenes of the French seventeenth-century masters Claude and Poussin and their eighteenth-century British emulator Richard Wilson. During these years he took what opportunities he could to study the works of the old masters. In 1802 he also took advantage, like many other British artists, of the temporary cessation of hostilities during the Napoleonic Wars with France to travel to Paris, where he could study the fabulous collection in the Louvre. He also made a trip at that time to the Alps, gaining a knowledge of a kind of mountain scenery far more dramatic than any he had encountered in Britain.

Turner's rivalry with his predecessors was rooted in his training at the Royal Academy, where it was held—following the precepts of Sir Joshua Reynolds in his *Discourses*—that imitation was the means by which an artist attained mastery. Reynolds recommended the designing pendants to hang beside the paintings of the old master's as a means of absorbing the qualities of such artists. Turner's adherence to this notion can be seen in his stipulation, when he left his collection to the nation on his death, that two of his pictures should hang between two by Claude in the National Gallery in perpetuity. But, as that particular comparison makes clear, Turner's notion of imitation went beyond that of Reynolds to include an outdoing of the qualities of the master being emulated. Turner extended the effects achieved by those he copied. Indeed, one might say that this shift represents a critical distinction between imitation and invention that lay behind the Romantic revision of pictorial practice. Thus, in his *Shipwreck* (1805) he achieves a level of sensationalism that goes far beyond that of the Dutch seventeenth-century master of storms, Adrian van der Velde, whose manner he is supposedly imitating. While such a process was lamented by connoisseurs of the day—notably Sir George Beaumont—it did become the means whereby Turner established a manner truly his own, thereby according to prevalent notions of original genius.

Such originality can be seen fully developed in his large, dramatic painting *Snowstorm: Hannibal and his Army crossing the Alps* (1812). While showing the Carthaginian hero battling against the elements to reach Italy in his struggle with Ancient Rome, it has always been taken to incorporate a coded reference to Napoleon, then about to embark on his fatal invasion of Russia. The underlying theme of the picture is adumbrated in a quotation from Turner's *Fallacies of Hope*, in which the "promised land" seen glinting in the distance beyond the dramatic snowstorm gives a false promise; for Hannibal is to meet his defeat when he reaches Rome. Such a picture shows a patriotic sentiment, but there was nothing triumphalist about Turner's nationalism. A few years later he was to paint a picture mourning the fallen of the *Field of Waterloo* (1818), in which a quote from Byron's *Childe Harold's Pilgrimage* is used to stress his own distaste for war.

In the post-Napoleonic period, Turner developed with increasing independence, exploring effects of light and color in an unprecedented manner. A visit to Italy in 1819 introduced him to the luminosity of Mediterranean lands, demonstrating in his eyes how wider of the mark classical landscapists had been in showing such places as a verdant paradise. He saw a terrain scorched by a fierce and powerful sun. Turner was to make many other visits to Italy—where Venice was to become a favorite— as well as ranging widely throughout Northern Europe. To some extent he was encouraged to do so by his topographical interests. After Waterloo, the continent became easily accessible once again to the British. Improved means of travel encouraged a new kind of middle-class tourist, one who became a ready market for watercolor views and prints of celebrated sites in Europe.

Yet Turner's new sense of color was also encouraging him to rethink the nature of historical landscape. A key picture in this development was *Ulysses Deriding Polyphemus* (1829). Depicting the moment when the Homeric hero is taunting the Cyclops whom he and his sailors have recently blinded, and from whom they have escaped, the artist includes in the painting a sunrise of overwhelming power. This showed his new "prismatic" way of working, in which primary colors are used side by side to vivid effect. One critic complained that just because Ulysses had put out the eye of Polyphemus there was no need for the artist to put out our eyes with his violent colors. But it was probably the artist's intention to create a discordant effect. The harsh chromatic chord in the sky is a visual expression of the pain and loss of the Cyclops. In such pictures one sees what Charles Baudelaire was later to call *synesthesia*, in which color emulates the effects of sound. Turner's mastery of color puts him at the heart of Romantic aesthetics, which in contrast to classical art theory sees color as being as important as line in the construction of a picture. Interestingly, Eugène Delacroix, the leading French

artist associated with Romanticism, was undergoing a similar conversion to the primacy of color around this time.

The fruits of Turner's enhanced perception of color can be seen in many subsequent pictures. Spurred on by a new sense of atmospherics, he explored interior scenes, such as those based on Petworth House, the home of a major patron, the Third Earl of Egremont. Similarly he responded to the rich effects of Venetian scenes. Venice, then a city in decline, encouraged him to explore such effects in relationship to destruction and decay.

By this time, Turner's originality was causing increasing concern at the Royal Academy exhibitions. As an Academician, Turner was able to exhibit without having his work vetted by the exhibition jury. Yet there were fears that he had taken leave of his senses. The position was all the more paradoxical because he continued to enjoy a popular following for illustrations of his works in books. The engravers who copied his works for publication endowed them with a level of detail that the artist no longer included. By such means his pictures appeared more acceptable in reproduction than in their original state. One such publication, Turner's illustrations to Samuel Roger's topographical poem *Italy* (1830), was given to Ruskin as a child. It became the source of his admiration for the artist. In 1843, Ruskin's first volume of *Modern Painters* boldly defended Turner as the greatest of modern artists, and to some extent this helped stem the decline in the artist's reputation. Ruskin argued that the artist's troubling but powerful later works showed the fullest development of his genius. However, even he could not approve the most challenging of these.

It was in the period 1838–45 that Turner produced the works that have done most to secure his reputation as a modern master. The most celebrated of these dealt with contemporary themes. Many of these were tough works dealing with modern themes. *The Fighting Temeraire* (1839) shows an old Napoleonic battleship being towed by a tug toward the dock where it will be broken up—a poignant meditation on transience. *The Slave Ship* (1840) exposes the horror of that traffic at a time when there was renewed concern for the problem of slavery. *Rain Steam and Speed* (1844), one of the earliest paintings to treat the theme of the recently invented railway, uses bold atmospheric effects and dynamic forms to characterize modernity. Yet while innovative in appearance, these works remain history paintings in their use of narrative and moral purpose.

Original though such works are, they are not as radical visually as the large number of unexhibited works that were discovered in the artist's studio after his death. Some of these, notably *Norham Castle* (after 1844), appear to prefigure impressionism in their painterly evocation of light. Because of the terms of his will, such work was preserved as part of the artist's bequest to the British National Gallery, first in the vaults of the National Gallery and later at the Tate Gallery. Arguments have raged since Turner's lifetime about the status of such works, some regarding them as no more than preparatory studies, or even "studio scrapings." Others see them as the most profound side of his production; too advanced to be shown in public during the artist's lifetime but gradually appreciated as aesthetic taste has caught up with them. There is probably no way of resolving this dichotomy. Perhaps it is most revealing as showing the tension between the private and public sides of Turner's life and art. In this he can be seen perhaps as a typical product of the Romantic era, preserving a sense of originality and inner worth, while at the same time engaging in a form of showmanship, startling the public with staggering and sometimes puzzling displays.

ROBERT VAUGHAN

See also **Girtin, Thomas; *Snow Storm: Steam Boat off a Harbour's Mouth***

Biography

Born London, April 23, 1775. Enrolled in the Royal Academy Schools, 1789. One of his first oil paintings, *Fishermen at Sea*, displayed at the Royal Academy, 1796. Made his first tour of Wales, 1792. Elected an associate of the Royal Academy of Art, 1799. Granted full membership into the Royal Academy, 1802. Elected "professor of perspective" at the Royal Academy, 1807. Died in his home in London, December 19, 1851.

Bibliography

Butlin, Martin, and Evelyn Joll. *The Paintings of J. M. W. Turner.* 2nd ed. New Haven, Conn.: Yale University Press, 1984.

Gage, John. *J. M. W. Turner, "A Wonderful Range of Mind."* New Haven, Conn.: Yale University Press, 1987.

Gowing, Lawrence. *Turner: Imagination and Reality.* New York: Museum of Modern Art, 1966.

Herrmann, Luke. *Turner Prints: The Engraved Work of J. M. W. Turner.* New York: New York University Press, 1990.

Joll, Evelyn, ed. *The Oxford Companion to J. M. W. Turner.* Oxford: Oxford University Press, 2001.

Reynolds, Graham. *Turner.* London: Thames and Hudson, 1969.

Ruskin, John. *Modern Painters.* Vol. 1. 1843.

Lindsay, Jack. *The Sunset Ship: The Poems of J. M. W. Turner.* Scorpion Press, 1966.

———. *Turner: The Man and his Art.* Granite Impex, 1985.

Smiles, Sam. *J. M. W. Turner.* London: Tate, British Artists Series, 2000.

Wilton, Andrew. *The Life and Work of J. M. W. Turner.* Academy Editions, 1979.

TWENTY-FOUR PRÉLUDES, OP. 28 1839

Set of piano pieces by Frédéric Chopin (1810–1849)

As its name suggests, the prelude (*preludio* or *praeludium*) traces its origin to the warming-up exercises used by a player or singer to prepare before playing or performance, in order to get the feel of an instrument which may be unfamiliar, or is being played in unfamiliar acoustic surroundings. It is thus very much an improvisational mode, and was common in public recitals well into the twentieth century, where it also had the function of easing the audience gently in to the piece(s) which it preceded.

However, the technique also crystallized into a short, complete piece, which was used to introduce another piece or set of pieces and became particularly associated with the keyboard—harpsichord, clavichord, organ, and later, piano. The form came into its own in the baroque period, with the particularly German pairing of prelude and fugue and as the first movement in dance suites. The greatest examples of the former are to be found in the *fourty-eight Preludes and Fugues* (two books of twenty-four, one in each of the twelve major and twelve minor keys) of *Das wohltemperirte Clavier* (*The Well-Tempered Clavier*, 1722,—referring to the specialized method of tuning necessary to allow all the keys to be used) of Johann Sebastian Bach. The prelude preceding a set of pieces is also to be found in other works by Bach, particularly in the six *English Suites* of dances, and in George Frideric Handel, as well as in many of the suites of the French *Clavecinistes* (keyboard composers), such as Louis Couperin, D'Anglebert, and Jean-Philippe Rameau. François Couperin ("*Le grand*") (1668–1733), like Bach, also wrote free-standing preludes.

It was this form, after a comparative lapse during the classical period, which was seized upon by the early Romantic composers in their quest for the short, more-or-less independent, individual mood piece, the characteristic piano piece so typical of the period, the best examples of which are the *Nocturnes* of Frédéric François Chopin and John Field and Robert Schumann's piano cycles. Spurred on by the equally Romantic interest in all things past, the prelude became a piece to emulate, another formal old bottle into which to pour the heady new wine of Romanticism. Johann Nepomuk Hummel's set of twenty-four preludes (op. 67) "in all the major and minor keys," many, though by no means all, of which are clearly of the "introductory" kind, appeared around 1814–15.

Chopin's debt to Hummel is well known, and the older master's set may have been vaguely in his mind when he conceived the idea of his own set of twenty-four preludes in 1836. They were finished in the winter of 1839, when he and his mistress, the French novelist George Sand, vacationed with their two children on the island of Majorca. The preludes are traditionally performed as a complete set, since, like Hummel's, they follow the cycle-of-fifths key sequence, interspersed with the relative minors—that is, C major–A minor; G major–E minor; D major–B minor, and so on—though Chopin's are in every way more substantial.

Chopin's Prelude No. 1 in C Major, while presenting the fast arpeggiated texture associated with this key in keyboard—especially piano—works, manages to evoke the ultimately lute-inspired textures of Bach by prolonging certain notes to yield an inner melody that prevails throughout.

Prelude No. 2, with stretches of dissonant chords, gives little indication of its A-minor key until the last notes, and Prelude No. 3 in G has the character of a study for the left hand. The fourth prelude, in E minor, is an enigmatic piece, with wayward pulsating chords under a minimal melody, and the fifth prelude, like the first, relies on texture, with interwoven, rather than obvious, melody, in this case short two-note scraps.

The next pair of preludes is more normative, with melody and accompaniment clearly delineated—No. 6 (B Minor) with an arpeggiaic, wide-ranging melody underneath long stretches of repeated notes in the right hand, and No. 7, a delightful short waltz in A. With the eighth, a long *molto agitato* (*very agitated*) prelude in F-sharp minor, we are back to texture with inner melody, and the ninth, in E, is a cross between a hymn and a slow march, both interpretations compromised by the infill of chords in groups of three. The hymnlike quality remains in the short Prelude No. 10, in the relative minor (C-sharp), but interspersed with passages reminiscent of the style of Felix Mendelssohn's *Midsummer Night's Dream* "fairy music," and triplet groupings are the basis of the eleventh prelude, in B. The passionate G-sharp minor (twelfth prelude) feels like a cross between two of Chopin's favorite forms, a waltz—though a rather fierce one—and a mazurka, and this is followed by what is effectively a short, beautiful, nocturne, Prelude No. 13 in F-sharp Major.

Prelude No. 14, in the unusual key of E-flat minor, calls forth equally unusual music; in a kind of dry run for the very similar finale of his Sonata in B-flat Minor (a closely related key, especially in terms of keyboard technique), Chopin gives us a single, angular melody line in unbroken triplets doubled at the octave. The D-flat prelude, No. 15, popularly called because of its repeated A flat/G sharp quavers the "Raindrop," is possibly the one George Sand heard Chopin playing while raindrops fell monotonously from the eaves of the abandoned monastery in which they stayed on Majorca. Perhaps it was their surroundings that prompted her to conjure up a funeral march of dead monks' ghosts in the minor-key middle section of this miniature tone poem, the longest of the twenty-four preludes.

The turbulent Prelude No. 16 in B-flat Minor has the feeling of a piano study, and is followed by No. 17, another long prelude based on repeated triplets that tend to coagulate into stretches of waltz rhythm. These triplets again appear in Prelude No. 19 in E-flat, preceded by another blustery piece, Prelude No. 18 in F Minor. Prelude No. 20 is a short funeral march in C minor, and the *cantabile* (*songlike*) Prelude No. 21 is sung without words in its gentle musical dialogue between two hands. Prelude No. 22 in G Minor has a similar dialogue, but far more tempestuous—argumentative, even. And Prelude No. 23, like several others in the set, keeps the listener constantly alert by hinting at melodic lines and phrases at different levels of the music—now in the bass, now hidden in the righthand figuration. A brooding miniature masterpiece, Prelude No. 24 in D Minor concludes the set, with long stretches of the same harmony counterpoised with jagged scraps of melody, ending on three low-D hammer blows.

The E minor and B minor preludes, in an arrangement for organ, were played at Chopin's funeral service in the Madeleine, Paris.

DEREK CAREW

Work

Twenty-four Preludes, op. 28. 1839.

Bibliography

Kallberg, J., "Small 'forms': in defence of the prelude," in Samson, J. (ed.), *The Cambridge Companion to Chopin*, Cambridge, 1992.

U

ÜBER DAS MARIONETTENTHEATER (ON THE PUPPET THEATER) 1810

Essay by Heinrich von Kleist

The essay "Über das Marionettentheater" first appeared in Heinrich von Kleist's newspaper the *Berliner Abendblätter*, in four consecutive installments in December 1810. E. T. A. Hoffmann makes positive reference to the essay in 1812, but it is safe to say that the essay was forgotten by the next generation. Material from the *Berliner Abendblätter* was not taken up in Ludwig Tieck's editions of Kleist's work in 1821 and 1826, and the essay did not reappear in print until Eduard von Bülow included it in his publication of 1848. From its ignominious beginnings, however, "Über das Marionettentheater" soon found itself as a main focus of Kleist studies, and has even been taken as a key to all of Kleist's oeuvre.

Structurally, the essay is set up as the account of a dialogue between the narrator ("HvK": this essay is among the one-third of *Berliner Abendblätter* contributions Kleist signed with his initials) and a dancer acquaintance, Herr C. The latter defends himself from the sardonic attack of the narrator, who criticizes him for visiting a lowly puppet show, the entertainment of the masses. The dancer claims that contrary to all expectations, he finds in the little wooden figures an inspiration for his own work; puppets, he claims, possess a grace (*Grazie*) beyond the power of self-conscious human beings. When the narrator demurs, Herr C. adduces examples of graceless dancers among his own colleagues, and he illustrates his meaning with algebraic formulae. This inspires the narrator to tell his own account of a young man he saw lose his "grace" by catching sight of himself in a mirror in a pose resembling the famous statue of the youth pulling a thorn from his foot. Once he sees this image of himself, the young man can no longer act naturally, but becomes corrupted by his own constant posing and his knowledge of this posing. Herr C. then recounts his own anecdote: of a fencing bear able to distinguish a feint from a thrust that is really meant, and thus able to defeat his human opponents. Herr C. concludes by claiming that the puppets are imbued with the grace of the

unconscious, natural being (presumably as in the bear); humans, being self-conscious, have lost grace, which they will only be able to regain, paradoxically, by an increase in consciousness, in other words, by "eating again from the Tree of Knowledge" and thus becoming like a god. This, so claims Herr C., will be "the last chapter of the history of the world."

"Über das Marionettentheater" has been mined as a source of Romantic thinking on world history, namely for the tertiary structure of thesis-antithesis-synthesis which Herr C. uses in his argument. Man is in a fallen state caused by consciousness, as in the biblical story of Adam and Eve. However, redemption does not come about in this secularized, Romantic account from above, by God, nor does it come from a turning back to the original innocent state; rather it comes through moving ahead and becoming even more conscious, just as traveling along a cyclical path will lead one eventually to come full circle. For Novalis, this growth in consciousness involved an inward turning and what he termed a "romantization" of one's perception of the world. Kleist's Herr C. is not so specific in his instructions.

Yet a close reading of the text of "Marionettentheater" reveals many problems with any interpretation that takes the essay at face value. Firstly, it is highly unlikely that anyone could truly find mere puppets more graceful than real dancers, and it is hardly possible that they could be so superior to human dancers that they should be taken by the latter as a model. The puppets' movement is described as *Zappeln* (a twitching or wriggling)—hardly a dancer's goal. The narrator, in fact, expresses his doubts quite clearly; he looks, embarrassed, at the ground as Herr C. speaks, and twice he seems to agree, but only in an ironic way. Once he jokes to himself that the puppets cannot make intellectual or spiritual mistakes when they have no intellect/spirit: "Ich lachte.—Allerdings, dachte ich, kann der Geist nicht irren, da, wo keiner vorhanden ist." (I laughed.—True, I thought to myself, the spirit or intellect can't go wrong where there isn't any spirit or intellect to be found.) Earlier he has admitted that the puppets are as graceful, not as real dancers, but as the depiction in a painting of peasant dancers: surely this is damning with faint praise. Nor is he ever adequately answered by Herr C., who instead presents supposedly scientific evidence that is in itself highly dubious.

It is only with the narrator's story of the youth in front of the mirror that the conversation turns to matters concerning *human* grace, and only here is the relation of physical gracefulness and providential grace made in any way clear. Yet neither this story nor that of the fencing bear illustrates Herr C.'s claims for the puppets; Herr C. instead bowls the narrator (and perhaps the reader) over by the sheer force of his rhetorical prowess in the neatly wrapped-up conclusion to the essay. Furthermore, the relationship of any of the anecdotes or other evidence to the sweeping claims made about the "end of history" must take place in the reader's imagination, if anywhere; it certainly is never made clear in the essay. In fact, the narrator's "confusion" when confronted with this generalization, that he is "ein wenig zerstreut" (somewhat absentminded), should function as a check on all-too-ready acceptance of the conclusion as valid.

Not only has Herr C.'s evidence been called into question, but so has the entire narrative structure of Kleist's essay. A straight dialogue would give equal weight to both interlocutors; this, however, is a reported dialogue, and is necessarily skewed in favor of the narrator who reports it. Has Herr C.'s side of the story been fairly represented? If it is so strange for Herr C. to be seen watching the puppet show, then what is the narrator doing there? Is this narrator to be trusted? After all, in his anecdote about the boy and the mirror, he actually reveals himself to be less than kind. Posing as the mentor of the younger male, in actual fact, he abuses the power he has over him to destroy the boy's self-esteem. Could it be that the story is not so much one of the coming into consciousness (thought there *are* hints of sexual awakening, as the self-conscious youth becomes obsessed with his effect on women) as one of the abuse of power, in particular the power of knowledge, and even of the power of the esthetic discourse about reality? Paul de Man, for one, famously reads this "curiously unread and enigmatic text" as a commentary upon and answer to the politically compelling nature of Johann Christoph Friedrich von Schiller's *Aesthetic Letters*. It is just possible, too, that the narrator's scene of warped pedagogy is being replayed before us in the scene with Herr C., where the narrator plays the role of ephebe (youthful student) compelled and persuaded by discursive and rhetorical means utilized by the older dancer.

Thus, rather than an account illustrating any real conclusions as to the nature of world history, the essay is about the nature of discursive knowledge. It shows the narrator accepting an argument not on its logical merits, but because it reminds him of an emotion-filled incident of his past (the episode with the youth and the mirror) and even the respected Herr C. himself argues with more passion than logic. In this way, the essay can be said to be a key to Kleist's work not because of its putative adherence to Romantic notions of the growth of self-consciousness, but because, like Kleist's other work, (see, especially, "Über die allmähliche Verfertigung der Gedanken beim Reden" ["On the Gradual Perfection of Thought while Speaking"]) it shows meaning and knowledge to be constructed through discourse.

LAURA MARTIN

Text

"Über das Marionettentheater." In *Sämtliche Werke und Briefe*. Vol. 2. Edited by Helmut Sembdner. Munich: Deutsche Taschenbuchverlag, 1984. Translated as "On the Puppet Theater," by David Constantine. In *Selected Writings by Heinrich von Kleis*. Edited and translated by David Constantine. London: Dent, 1997.

Bibliography

Allemann, Beda. "Sinn und Unsinn von Kleists Gespräch 'Über das Marionettentheater,' " *Kleist-Jahrbuch* (1981/82): 50–65.

Brown, Hilda Meldrum. *Heinrich Von Kleist: The Ambiguity of Art and the Necessity of Form*. Oxford: Clarendon Press, 1998.

Cixous, Hélène. "Grace and Innocence: Heinrich von Kleist." In *Readings: The Poetics of Blanchot, Joyce, Kafka, Kleist, Lispector and Tsvetayeva*. Edited, translated, and with an introduction by Verena Andermatt Conley. New York: Harvester Wheatsheaf, 1992.

De Man, Paul. "Aesthetic Formalization: Kleist's 'Über das Marionettentheater.' " In *The Rhetoric of Romanticism*. New York: Columbia University Press, 1984, pp. 263–90.

Gram, Andrea. "Die Rede über den Körper. Zum Körperdiskurs in Kleists Texten 'Die Marquise von O . . .' und 'Über das Marionettentheater.' " In *Text and Kritik Sonderband Heinrich von Kleist*. Munich: Weber Offset GmbH, 1993.

Hart, Gail. "Anmut's Gender: The 'Marionettentheater' and Kleist's Revision of 'Anmut und Würde', " *Women in German Yearbook* 10 (1995); 83–95.

Janz, Rolf Peter. "Die Marionette als Zeugin der Anklage zu Kleists Abhandlung 'Über Das Marionettentheater.' " In *Kleists Dramen. Neue Interpretationen*. Edited by Walter Hinderer. Stuttgart: Reclam, 1981.

Kreutzer, Hans Joachim. "Kleists Aufsätze." In *Die dichterische Entwicklung Heinrich von Kleists. Untersuchungen zu seinen Briefen und zu Chronologie und Aufbau seiner Werke*. Berlin: Schmidt, 1968.

Schneider, Helmut J. "Deconstruction of the Hermeneutical Body: Kleist and the Discourse of Classical Aesthetics." In *Body and Text in the Eighteenth Century*. Edited by Veronica Kerlly and Dorothea E. von Mücke. Stanford, Calif.: Stanford University Press, 1994.

Sembdner, Helmut. "Kleists Aufsatz über das Marionettentheater. Nachwort zu einer Sammlung von Studien und Interpretationen." In *Sachen Kleist. Beiträge zur Forschung*. Munich: Hanser, 1974.

Sembdner, Helmut, ed. *Kleists Aufsatz über das Marionettentheater. Studien und Interpretationen*. Berlin: Schmidt, 1967.

UHLAND, LUDWIG 1787–1862

German poet, literary scholar, and political activist

Ludwig Uhland was very much a figure of the southern German Swabian school of Romantic writers based in Stuttgart and Tübingen. The son of a university administrator, Uhland was born and spent his formative years in the historic university town of Tübingen, from where he was able to explore the idyllic landscape of the Swabian Alps and the Black Forest. Various romantic settings, such as the small country church at Wurmlingen or the old Cistercian monastery at Bebenhausen, were to feature in his poems and dramatic romances. Attracted at an early age to Ossianic poetry and to the literary circle of Ludwig Christoph Heinrich Hölthy, he was also influenced by Johann Gottfried von Herder's collection of folk songs and Thomas Percy's *Reliques of Ancient English Poetry* (1765). Following his father's wishes, however, he studied law at Tübingen, earned a doctorate, and subsequently moved to Stuttgart, at first to work in the ministry of justice and later, after some disagreements with the minister, as an advocate. He remained in Stuttgart from 1812 until 1830; legal work was never his true vocation and provided him with only a meager living. This situation changed in 1820, when he married Emilie Vischer; she provided them with a secure income for the rest of their lives.

Uhland's significance for the Romantic movement is three-fold: as a poet and dramatist, as a scholar of medieval German and European literature, and as a politician, initially as a member of the Württemberg Landtag (parliament) and later of the first all-German national parliament in the Frankfurt Paulskirche. His literary work is often dismissed today as somewhat naive and lacking the intellectual buoyancy of other major representatives of the movement. Until the 1960s, however, it was widely read in schools and, with much of his poetry set to music by contemporaries such as Konradin Kreutzer, Felix Mendelssohn, and Friedrich Silcher, it was popular with many amateur choral societies. He began writing poetry while in his teens, mostly for family occasions; his major creative period occurred between 1805 and 1829, with his first collection of poems published by Cotta in 1815. Rich in local color, his poetry was strongly influenced by the collection of Achim von Arnim and Clemens Brentano, *Des Knaben Wunderhorn* (*The Boy's Magic Horn*, 1805–8). Uhland's lyrical poems tend to invoke a folkloric atmosphere, an affinity to landscape and the seasons (in particular the spring), while avoiding subjective introversion. Frequently introduced by a minstrel and with subjects drawn from medieval or ancient Germanic origin, his ballads are often narrative in style and have a strong moralistic message. Uhland's first drama, *Ernst Herzog von Schwaben*, completed in 1817, demonstrates his interest in the late Middle Ages, but also reveals an unease with the contemporary political scene and a perceived loss of early forms of constitutionalism. Uhland soon emerged as the central figure of the *Swabian school*, a literary circle of the later Romantic/early Biedermeier period (1810–50), which included other regional writers such as Wilhelm Hauff, Justinus A. Kerner, Herrmann Kurz, Karl Mayer, Gustav Schwab, and Friedrich Theodor Vischer.

After finishing his doctorate in 1812, Uhland traveled to Paris, where he spent a great deal of time in the Bibliotheque Nationale, studying its collection of French, German, and Spanish medieval documents. This inspired him to become not only an avid lifelong collector of medieval chivalric romance and of *Minnelieder* (medieval German lovesongs), but also an eminent editor of such manuscripts. On his return to Germany, he published an acclaimed essay on ancient French epic poetry. His 1822 edition of the thirteenth-century German minstrel Walther von der Vogelweide established his reputation as an acknowledged authority and expert on medieval European literature. In 1829 he was appointed the first professor of German at Tübingen University, where he lectured on the Nibelungenlied, medieval *Minnelieder*, and Germanic heroic poetry. His scholarly studies earned him the respect and friendship of other "Germanists," especially Jakob Grimm, Moritz Haupt, Karl Lachmann, and Freiherr Joseph von Lassberg, who gave him valuable bibliographic assistance and whose Meersburg library he visited several times. In contrast to most other scholars of German, Uhland avoided an exclusive involvement with national issues and demonstrated his appreciation of other medieval European literatures.

Uhland's political activities were informed by the long-established southern German liberal tradition, which was more influenced by the political legacy of the Enlightenment than was the case in Prussia or other northern German states. During the wars of liberation against Napoleon (1813) he supported the new patriotic German alliance, but never saw active service. A passionate believer in the old laws of Württemberg, Uhland felt unable to continue in the king's service when Frederick abandoned the constitution. On the accession of King William, a compromise solution allowed the *Landtag* to reassemble and the citizens of Tübingen elected Uhland as their representative. He worked arduously for constitutional reform and for the disenfranchised and remained a lifelong opponent of the concept of a two-chamber government, where the upper chamber represented the nobility. Indeed, Uhland was vehemently opposed to any distinction between the nobility and ordinary citizens, rejecting even his own ennoblement by the Prussian king. Uhland was an early activist in the German revolutions of 1848, addressing a large gathering at Tübingen University to demand an all-German parliament, the establishment of a German militia, full press freedom, trial by jury, and a system of local government. By this time he had been dismissed from his university post on the grounds that a civil servant should not be involved in political activities. Elected by a huge majority as a delegate of the Tübingen-Rottenburg district, he joined the first wave of parliamentarians to enter the Frankfurt parliament. His decision not to join a political faction limited his full participation in parliamentary affairs; nevertheless, he supported both the war against Denmark over the duchies of Schleswig and Holstein and Prussia's occupation of the province of Posen where, for once, nationalist sentiments got the better of him. His primary interest was as an advocate of the greater German solution, passionately supporting the inclusion of Austria into a German nation-state. He also fiercely opposed the monarchical model, maintaining that "no head should radiate over Germany that has not been anointed with a full measure of democratic oil." He remained faithful to the parliamentary cause throughout the existence of the National Assembly and moved with the rump parliament to Stuttgart in June 1849. When this body was finally disbanded, Uhland largely withdrew from public life, though he still championed the defeated Baden revolutionaries and actively campaigned against the death sentence. He spent the last phase of his life in Tübingen, still exploring the local countryside and assiduously expanding his significant collection of medieval and scholarly books, as well as continuing with academic work. Uhland died from pleurisy in February 1862.

HANS-JOACHIM HAHN

Biography

Born in Tübingen April 26, 1787. Entered Tübingen University, 1801, to study law and philology; graduated with a doctorate in law. Moved to Paris, 1810–11, to study medieval French and German manuscripts. Practiced as a lawyer in Tübingen and at the Württemberg Ministry of Justice, Stuttgart, 1812–14, followed by return to private practice. Member of Württemberg *Landtag*, 1819–26 and 1833–38; member of first all-German National Assembly in Frankfurt/Main, 1848–49; withdrew from public life in 1850. Literary reputation led to appointment as professor of German literature at Tübingen, 1830–33. Main publications: *Gedichte* (poetry, 1815; 42 reprints during his lifetime); *Ernst Herzog von Schwaben* (drama, 1817); *Ludwig der Baier* (drama, 1819). Scholarly works included *Walther von der Vogelweide, ein altdeutscher Dichter* (1822) and *Alte hoch- und niederdeutsche Volkslieder* (1844–45). Died November 13, 1862, in Tübingen.

Selected Works

Collections
Uhlands Briefwechsel. Edited by Julius Hartmann. 4 vols. Stuttgart: Cotta, 1911–16.
Ludwig Uhland. *Werke.* Edited by Hartmut Fröschle and Walter Scheffler. 4 vols. Munich: Winkler, 1984.

Translations
Specimens from Schiller and Uhland. Edited and translated by George C. Swayne. 1848.
Ballads of Uhland, Goethe, Schiller. Edited and translated by Charlee Bielefeld. 1863.
Poems of Uhland. Edited and translated by Max Friedlaender and W. T. Hewett, 1896.

Bibliography

Bausinger, Hermann ed. *Ludwig Uhland, Dichter—Politiker—Gelehrter.* Tübingen: Attempt., 1988.
Fröschle, Hartmut. *Ludwig Uhland und die Romantik.* Cologne: Böhlau, 1973.
Storch, Helmut, ed., *Ludwig Uhland: Werk und Wirkung. Festschrift des Uhland-Gymnasiums Tübingen zum 200. Geburtstag des Politikers, Gelehrten, Dichters.* Tübingen: Uhland Gymnasium, 1987.

UKRAINE: HISTORICAL AND CULTURAL SURVEY

The Romantic movement in Ukraine coincided with the emergence of a national Ukrainian self-consciousness; both contributed to a cultural renaissance. Ukraine entered the nineteenth century as a stagnant province of imperial Russia. The century-long emigration of local intellectuals, scholars, and scientists to the cities of Russia, and the denationalization of the nobility were devastating to Ukrainian culture. Western ideas of Romantic nationalism, especially those of Johann Gottfried von Herder, spurred attempts to rediscover Ukraine's historical past, which in turn instigated the efforts of the educated elites for national self-assertion. The cultural and historical legacy of Kievan Rus, and the glorious era of the Cossack Sich and the Hetmanate, were embraced by the Ukrainian intelligentsia. Historical scholarship comprised an integral part of the national movement, as did ethnographic studies. Numerous collections of historical and folk materials were published.

Before the emergence of Romanticism in Ukraine, Ukrainian historical, ethnographic, and folk materials were employed in the Romantic literatures of neighboring Russia and Poland. Adherents of "Ukrainian schools" in Russian and Polish literatures viewed Ukraine as a quintessentially exotic terrain. They admired the wild and freedom-loving Ukrainian Cossacks, drew on Ukraine's rich folklore, and admired the lush beauty of its countryside. Kondratii Ryleev was among the first of the Russian Romantics to extensively explore the Ukrainian Cossack past. His duma *Bohdan Khmelnitskii* (1822), numerous poems, and the verse tales *Voinarovsky* (1824) and *Nalivaiko* (1825) championed the Ukrainian cause, giving a Romantic interpretation to Ukraine's struggles for independence. Ukrainian thematic materials were employed in Faddei Bulgarin's novels *Dmitrii Samozvanets* (*Dmitrii the Pretender*, 1830) and *Mazepa* (1834), in Aleksandr Pushkin's historical epic *Poltava* (1828), and in Nikolai Gogol's cycles of stories *Evenings on a Farm near Dikanka* (1831–32) and *Mirgorod* (1835). Gogol was the most important Russian writer of Ukrainian descent. Of lesser significance were Evhen Hrebinka, Mykola Markevych, and Orest Somov. The Ukrainian school in Polish literature was represented by such Romantic poets as Seweryn Goszczynski, Antoni Malczewski, and Bohdan Zaleski. Many more Polish Romantics employed Ukrainian subject matter in their writings; some even tried to write in Ukrainian. Works by Polish, and especially Russian representatives of Ukrainian schools had a great impact on the Ukrainian intelligentsia, and played an important role in the development of the Ukrainian Romantic movement. Foreign language translations of these works were instrumental in popularizing Ukraine in the West.

Kharkiv University became the first ideological center of Ukrainian Romanticism. Among the most prominent members and ideologists of the Kharkiv group were Mykola Kostomarov, Amvrosii Metlyns'kyi, and Ismaiil Sreznevskyi. They were determined to facilitate Ukraine's national awakening by their scholarly, poetic, and linguistic efforts. In their philosophical debates on Ukraine's national development, they relied on the ideologies of German idealism and Romanticism, instigating the group's enthusiasm for ethnographic and historical research. Ukrainian folk poetry, which was deemed to reflect the essence of national spirit, was meticulously compiled and studied by Sreznevskyi and other members of the group. Kostomarov and Metlyns'kyi contemplated mythological and symbolic dimensions of folklore, which in their opinion reflected the very soul of the people. Another important venue of the group's interests was Ukraine's historical past and its expression in a Ukrainian folk genre, the duma. On par with historical and ethnographic scholarship, members of the group produced literary works in vernacular Ukrainian, which they published in separate collections as well as in Russian periodicals. Metlyns'kyi wrote somber philosophical poetry, Sreznevskyi published pseudo–folk verse. Kostomarov tried his hand at both poetry and in drama. In 1844 he presented his master's thesis, titled *Ob istoricheskom znachenii russkoi narodnoi poezii* (*On the Historical Importance of Russian Folk Poetry*). Oleksandr Korsun, Mykhailo Petrenko, Iakiv Shchoholiv, and Opanas Shpyhots'kyi were lesser poets of the Kharkiv group.

In Western Ukraine, the Romantic movement was represented by the Lviv group, the "Ruthenian Triad." Its members, the poets Yakiv Holovatskyi, Markiian Shashkevych, and Ivan Vahylevych, became the voice of the budding national awakening in Galicia. In 1836, the group published their almanac *Rusalka Dnistrovaia* (*The Dniester Nymph*).

For the Ukrainian Romantics, the linguistic issue was an urgent one. The educated classes in Eastern Ukraine were virtually bilingual. Yet while the Russian language was recognized as the empire's official language and was employed for official and artistic purposes, Ukrainian was regarded as the mundane language of the peasants. It was considered appropriate only for lower, comical genres. Not only was it important for Ukraine to develop a language of literary expression, it was also essential to prove its aesthetic value and applicability in a variety of genres. The first step in this direction was made by the classicist poet Ivan Kotliarevskyi, whose travesty *Eneida* (*Aeneid*, 1798) was a great success in pioneering vernacular Ukrainian as a literary language. This work had a great and long-lasting impact on the Ukrainian Romantics, who conscientiously directed their efforts on elevating the vernacular to the status of literary legitimacy. They also attempted to widen the genre horizons of the Ukrainian language. This objective, however, was not attained: the majority of the Ukrainian Romantics worked in the genre of lyrical poetry and, except for a few epic poems by Shevchenko, a few second-rate dramas by Kostomarov, and Kulish's historical novel *Chorna rada* (*The Black Council*, 1857), dramatic, epic, and prose genres remained virtually unexplored in the Romantic period.

In the mid-1840s, Kyiv University assumed the role of the second center of the Romantic movement. Its first rector, the eminent ethnographer Mykhailo Maksymovych, was instrumental in advancing research in the area of Ukrainian studies. He compiled several collections of Ukrainian songs, and published them in 1827, 1834, and 1849. These compilations not only had enduring scholarly value, but also a great impact on the Ukrainian Romantic movement.

The three founders of the Ukrainian national renaissance— Mykola Kostomarov, Panteleimon Kulish, and Taras Shevchenko—were the most important representatives of Kievan Romantics, and of Ukrainian Romanticism in general. In 1840, Shevchenko published his first collection of poetry, *Kobzar* (*The Minstrel*), which brought him immediate recognition as a great Ukrainian poet, and also marked the birth of modern Ukrainian literature. A poet of world stature, Shevchenko elevated vernacular Ukrainian to the level of a literary language and became an international representative of the Ukrainian nation. Shevchenko's friend, admirer, and critic, Panteleimon Kulish, was a tireless contributor to the Ukrainian cause, and Ukrainian literature. An eminent scholar of history, ethnography, and literature, he was also a translator, and above all a talented poet and writer. The third titan of Ukrainian Romanticism, Mykola Kostomarov, was a historian, a writer, and a literary critic. He moved from Kharkiv to Kyiv, where he continued his scholarly career as a faculty member at Kiev University. Kostomarov, Kulish, and Shevchenko belonged to a clandestine organization, The Brotherhood of Saints Cyril and Methodius, which championed the idea of liberation of Slavic nations and their ultimate union in a federation. The Romantic-Christian ideology of the Brotherhood found its expressions in Kostomarov's treatise *Knyhy bytiia ukrains'koho narodu* (*Books of the Genesis of the Ukrainian People*), which became the group's manifesto.

In 1847 the group was suppressed and its members exiled. The Ukrainian renaissance as well as the Romantic movement abated. The last surge of Ukrainian Romanticism was connected with the return from exile of the Brotherhood leaders and members, who in the late 1850s and the 1860s resumed their literary activities in St. Petersburg around the journal *Osnova* (*The Foundation*).

Despite the comparatively small literary output of Ukrainian Romantics, they accomplished several important goals. The Ukrainian national renaissance was launched. The country's rich historical and ethnographic heritage was discovered, explored, and popularized. The modern language of the educated classes and literary expression was developed, and a number of works were written in this language. All in all, for Ukraine the era of Romanticism was the time of its emergence as a nation aware of, and proud of, its own historical and cultural accomplishments.

SVITLANA KOBETS

Bibliography

Chyzhevskyi, Dmytro. *A History of Ukrainian Literature: From the Eleventh to the End of the Nineteenth Century*. Trans. Dolly Ferguson, Doreen Gorsline, and Ulana Petyk. With an overview by George S. N. Luckyj. New York: N.Y. Ukrainian Academy of Arts and Sciences/Englewood Colo.: Ukrainian Academic Press, 1997.

———. *On Romanticism in Slavic Literature*. Trans. D. S. Worth. The Hague: Mouton, 1957.

Genyk-Berezovska, Zinaida. *Hrani kul'tur: Baroko, Romantyzm, Modernism*. Kiev: "Helikon," 2000.

Grabowycz, George G. *Toward a History of Ukrainian Literature*. Cambridge, Mass.: Harvard University Press for the Harvard Ukrainian Research Institute, 1999.

Iefremov, Serhii. *Istoriia ukranns'koho pys'menstva*. Kiev: Ukrainian Nakladnia, 1919.

Kostomarov, Mykola. *Knyhy buttia ukranns'koho narodu*. Toronto: Vsesvitnia khrystyians'ka misiia, 1980.

Lindheim, Ralph, and Luckyj, George S. N., eds. *Towards an Intellectual History of Ukraine: An Anthology of Ukrainian Thought from 1710 to 1995*. Toronto, Buffalo, and London: University of Toronto Press and Shevchenko Scientific Society, 1996.

Luckyj, George S. N., ed. *Shevchenko and the Critics 1861–1980*. Toronto, Buffalo, and London: University of Toronto Press and the Canadian Institute of Ukrainian Studies, 1980.

———. *Young Ukraine: The Brotherhood of Saints Cyril and Methodius in Kiev, 1845–1847*. Ottawa: University of Ottawa Press, 1991.

ULTIME LETTERE DI IACOPO ORTIS
(LAST LETTERS OF JACOPO ORTIS) 1802

Novel by Ugo Foscolo

Ugo Foscolo's novel is now generally studied as a seedbed for the themes that would be more fully explored in his later poetical works. When it first appeared in 1802, however, it seemed to offer nothing particularly innovative in terms of genre. The epistolary novel had been successfully launched by Samuel Richardson in the 1740s, and exploited to great effect by Jean-Jacques Rousseau in his *Julie, ou La Nouvelle Héloise* (*Julie, or the New Eloise*, 1761) and Johann Wolfgang von Goethe in his *Die Leiden des Jungen Werthers* (*The Sorrows of Young Werther*, 1774). The storyline of *Ultime lettere di Iacopo Ortis* involves youthful idealism, star-crossed lovers, and a suicide, themes that have all been dealt with in countless other literary works. In fact, one of Foscolo's earliest and most severe critics, Scalvini, disputed the fact *Ultime lettere* was a novel at all, as the narrative arc was anything but clear, and that it was little more than "a muddle of gloomy emotions and pathetic reflections endlessly set down one after another. This work is not meant to relate a story to the reader, but rather to disturb and confuse him, and drive him to insanity."

In his own commentary, written in England in 1818, Foscolo made comparisons between his novel and Goethe's *Die Leiden des Jungen Werthers*. He argued that, despite superficial similarities, what differentiated his novel *Ultime lettere* from Goethe's is that politics play such a key thematic role. Certainly the contemporary history of Italy plays a role much more significant than that of Germany in *Werther*.

The origins of the novel can be traced back to a document of 1796, where the first mention of the project of an epistolary novel appears as *Laura-Lettere* (*Laura – letters*), which centers on a tragic love story, more than likely with its roots in Foscolo's own amorous adventures. The catalyst for the later version, which Foscolo began writing in 1798, was the Treaty of Campoformio (1797), by which Napoleon ceded Venice and the surrounding territories to Austria in exchange for Belgium. Those who had nurtured great hopes of some sort of Italian unity were bitterly disappointed, and further upheavals were to ensue in the Austrian and Russian invasions of Italy during Napoleon's Egypt campaign. Without the consent of the author, an unauthorized version of the unfinished novel appeared in Bologna in 1799, with an epilogue written at the publisher's request. A revised edition was printed in Milan in 1802, but Foscolo continued working on the novel, and a final version was printed as late as 1817.

The novel is in two parts, with the love interest featuring mainly in the first section, but there is a certain intertwining, if not blurring, of the romantic and political elements. The novel opens with a strong sense of political disillusionment felt by the protagonist after his flight from Venice in the wake of Campoformio. Ortis's spirits are lifted when he encounters Teresa, only to find that the object of his affections has been promised to another out of political expediency, as her father had compromised himself with the previous regime, and the proposed fiancé, Odoardo, would provide both finan-

cial and political protection. Ortis is passionately opposed to such an arrangement, but his friendship with Teresa's father and strong moral idealism make it impossible for him to intervene, and he pours his heart out to his confidant, Lorenzo, who publishes the letters.

While the atmosphere is one of almost unmitigated doom from the outset, there is nevertheless a broad shift in the novel from personal concerns to wider political and social issues, as Ortis becomes the champion of values which seem irrelevant to his materialistic contemporaries. He is very much the archetype of the Romantic hero, out of step with his own time, and the influence of Alfieri can be felt above all. Mario Fubini has dubbed Ortis "una tragedia alfieriana," and in many respects the protagonist resembles one of Alfieri's heroic figures, in the solitude that confirms his sense of his own dignity and nobility, his struggle for personal and political freedom, and, especially, in his recourse to suicide as an act of defiance and self-affirmation rather than despair. At a certain stage Ortis is overheard declaiming lines from Alfieri's *Saul*, but this is not the only point at which art intrudes upon life, as throughout the work reality is overlaid with literary echoes and illusions (the protagonist's forename is derived from that of Rousseau), as when the two young people read Petrarch and Sappho together. This in itself is a hint that the destiny of Ortis is one of renunciation, and he does indeed leave, rather than compromise Teresa.

In his subsequent travels through Italy, Ortis reflects on its history, and the divisions that continue to beset it. In an episode later to be incorporated into Foscolo's poem "Dei sepolcri," Ortis visits the tombs of great Italians such as Galileo and Michelangelo in Florence's Santa Croce. The question of the relation of the artist to society is also explored in a long interview between Ortis and the aging poet Parini in Milan, over the course of which Parini convinces Ortis that nothing can remedy the political situation. The novel ends with a return to the personal, as Ortis decides on suicide after learning of Theresa's marriage.

The novel presents the reader with a series of themes and hints, some of which remain incoherent and uncorrelated: these include the indifference of nature, man's need for illusions to survive the cruelty of life, the consolation of beauty and the very idea of literature itself. Foscolo himself termed it a "harmony of dissonances," but Glauco Cambon, a more modern critic, has seen in the "first-person narrative, vindication of subjective experience, open form, approximation of an oral style and testimonial stance . . . principles that define the new art of fiction." Foscolo's novel remains a monument to his tendency toward autobiography and literary studies, but above all to his sense of history and political commitment.

LYNNE PRESS

Text

An incomplete and unauthorized version was published in Bologna as *Vera storia di due amanti infelici* (*True story of two unhappy lovers*) in 1799. Foscolo then published a complete version in Milan in 1802 as *Ultime lettere di Iacopo Ortis*. A third version was published in Zurich in 1816, but with the false date and place of London, 1814; a final version was published in London in 1817. Translated as *The Last Letters of Jacopo Ortis*, by J. G. Nichols. London: Hesperus Press, 2002.

Bibliography

Binni, W. *Foscolo e la critica*. Florence: La nuova Italia, 1966.

Cambon, Glauco. *Ugo Foscolo, Poet of Exile*. Princeton, N.J.: Princeton University Press, 1980.

Fubini, Mario. *Ugo Foscolo*. Florence: La nuova Italia, 1962.

Kroeber, Karl. *The Artifice of Reality*, Madison: University of Wisconsin Press, 1964.

THE UNCONSCIOUS

The contemporary popularity and dominance of psychoanalytically derived understandings of the unconscious have tended to obscure the extent to which this concept was a Romantic-era invention. It was in this period that a significant number of authors began to use the term *unconscious* to denote a realm of the psyche that determined aspects of, but was not directly accessible to, consciousness itself. Versions of the unconscious were integral to a number of projects now understood as typically Romantic, such as the critique of the Enlightenment belief in the absolute power and validity of "reason" and self-consciousness, the attempt to determine the psychological sources of artistic creation, and an understanding of the mind as in essential conflict with itself. Interest in the unconscious in this period was especially intense in three interrelated fields:

1. psychoanalytical therapy and theory;
2. creative literature focused on nonconscious phenomena such as dreams, madness, and horror;
3. the mode of philosophical idealism initiated by Friedrich Wilhelm Joseph von Schelling.

Belief in external forces that control consciousness and human actions is ancient, but the unconscious almost invariably denotes a force that is *internal* to consciousness or the psyche. Several contemporary commentators have located the foundation for the emergence of notions of the unconscious in René Descartes's dualist philosophy, which divided being into the realms of matter (defined as extension) and mind (defined as self-aware consciousness). For one historian of ideas (L. L. Whyte), this dualism prepared the ground for the unconscious to the extent that it overly restricted the definition of mind to complete self-awareness, an error later commentators had to correct through the development of notions of unconscious mental processes. Yet however much Descartes may have provided the necessary groundwork for notions of the unconscious, all historians agree that explicit interest in the "unconscious" aspects of mental life remained subdued until the late eighteenth century. The realm of mental process that lay outside of self-consciousness was not completely ignored in the first two-thirds of the eighteenth century, of course—philosophers such as Christian August Crusius, Gottfried Wilhelm Leibniz, Jean-Jacques Rousseau, and Christian Wolff all expressed theoretical interest in nonconscious psychic phenomena—but the unconscious did not become an explicit theme of research until the end of the eighteenth century.

Much of the ground for the emergence of the unconscious as a discrete term was laid by the followers of therapist Anton von Mesmer. The mesmerists were primarily interested in curing what is now thought of as mental illnesses, but they and many others were fascinated by the fact that patients in the therapeutic "trance" exhibited behavior that seemed incompatible with their waking states. Some therapists interpreted this as a sign that the therapeutic trance allowed access to an otherwise hidden, or secret, realm of consciousness and personality. A number of late eighteenth- and early nineteenth-century philosophical and literary figures named this hidden mental realm "the unconscious." German novelist Jean Paul, for example, suggested in 1804 that the unconsciousness was like an "inner Africa," as yet unexplored: "[t]he unconscious is really the largest realm in our minds . . . whose unknown boundaries may extend far away."

The notion of a dynamic and turbulent realm of mental activity that only infrequently revealed itself appealed to many Romantic-era poets, playwrights, and novelists. A number of authors, including Samuel Taylor Coleridge, Johann Wolfgang von Goethe, and Johann Christoph Friedrich von Schiller, claimed that artistic creation itself originated in the unconscious, while William Wordsworth suggested, in his *Preludes*, that his abilities as a poet were partially dependent on the fact that as a child, he "held unconscious intercourse / With . . . eternal beauty." Many British and German authors wrote poetry and fiction that investigated (and frequently valorized) liminal phenomena such as dreams and madness. For example, the protagonist of E. T. A. Hoffmann's "Der goldene Topf" ("The Golden Pot," 1817) oscillated back and forth between the everyday world and the world of dreams, and neither he nor the reader is entirely clear where one realm begins and the other ends. Hoffmann was also fascinated by mesmerism, and in his story "Das Sanktus" the protagonist Bettina loses then regains her voice as a function of the actions of a mesmerist. Some critics have seen the more general Romantic-era fascination with sublime and awesome physical settings (for example, the frozen wastes and glaciers of Mary Shelley's *Frankenstein* [1818]) as significant of an urge to externalize the unconscious "realm" of the mind in the form of landscape.

The German idealist philosopher Schelling developed a much more explicit analysis of the connections between consciousness and the unconscious, linking that latter term with the notion of dynamic activity. Johann Gottlieb Fichte had suggested in his *Grundlage der gesammten Wissenschaftslehre* (*Foundations of the Entire Science of Knowledge*, 1794) that the ultimate basis of consciousness was a mode of *activity* that could itself never come into consciousness, a suggestion that Schelling developed at length in *System des transzendentalen Idealismus* (*System of Transcendental Idealism*, 1800). Schelling argued that the foundation of the ability of consciousness to present something to itself was a necessarily unconscious productive activity. For Schelling, too, this relationship between consciousness and unconsciousness was best exemplified by artistic creation. In *Die Welt als Wille und Vorstellung* (*The World as Will and Representation*, 1819), Arthur Schopenhauer adopted this framework of conflict between unconscious activity and consciousness, but connected unconscious activity, which he called "will," with sexuality, suggesting that consciousness was constantly manipulated by an "unconsciousness" that was constitutive of the world and of the representations of consciousness in general.

While philosophers such as Schelling and Schopenhauer understood the unconscious as a metaphysical principle, early- and mid-nineteenth-century psychologists often focused upon the relationship between the individual and unconscious mental activities. In *Psychologie als Wissenschaft, neugegründet auf Erfahrung, Metaphysik and Mathematik* (*Psychology as Science, Newly Founded on Experience, Metaphysics and Mathematics*, 1824), German psychologist Johann Friedrich Herbart argued that ideas often became inhibited, sinking below the level of consciousness, but nevertheless remaining active in the mind and exerting a pressure on consciousness. Following in this psychological tradition, physician and painter Carl Gustav Carus elevated the unconscious into an even more central part of the psychology developed in *Psyche: Zur Entwickelungsgeschichte der Seele* (*Psyche: History of the Development of the Soul*, 1846), arguing that several layers of the unconscious exist, some accessible and others not, and that through the unconscious we maintain an essential connection with other humans.

Interest in the unconscious became even more intense as the century progressed, culminating in Eduard von Hartmann's *Philosophie des Unbewussten* (*The Philosophy of the Unconscious*, 1879) and Sigmund Freud's psychoanalytic version of the term. Yet key elements of these post-Romantic philosophies of the unconscious had been established already in the Romantic era, including an emphasis on the conflicted relationship between the unconscious and consciousness, an understanding of artistic creation as dependent upon the unconscious, and a belief in the generative role of the unconscious in mental illness.

ROBERT MITCHELL

Bibliography

Carus, Carl Gustav. *Psyche: Zur Entwickelungsgeschichte der Seele.* 1846.

Ellenberger, Henri. *The Discovery of the Unconscious: The History and Evolution of Dynamic Psychiatry.* New York: Basic Books, 1970.

Fichte, Johann Gottlieb. *Grundlage der gesammten Wissenschaftslehre.* 1794.

Garnder, Sebastian. "Schopenhauer, Will, and the Unconscious," in *The Cambridge Companion to Schopenhauer.* Edited by Christopher Janaway. Cambridge: Cambridge University Press, 1999.

Hartmann, Eduard von. *Philosophie des Unbewussten.* 1869. Translated as *The Philosophy of the Unconscious* by William Chatterton Coupland, 1893.

Henry, Michel. *Génélogie de la psychanalyse.* Paris: Presses universitaires de France, 1985. Translated as *The Genealogy of Psychoanalysis* by Douglas Brick. Stanford, Calif.: Stanford University Press, 1993.

Herbart, Johann Friedrich. *Psychologie als Wissenschaft, neugegründet auf Erfahrung, Metaphysik und Mathematik* (1824). In *Sämtliche Werke.* 1850.

Klein, D. B. *The Unconscious: Invention or Discovery? A Historico-Critical Inquiry.* Santa Monica, Calif.: Goodyear, 1977.

Paul, Jean. *Jean Paul's sämtliche Werke.* 1840–42.

Schelling, Friedrich Wilhelm Joseph von. *System des transzendentalen Idealismus.* Hamburg: F. Meiner, 1992. Translated as *System of Transcendental Idealism* by Peter Heath. Charlottesville: University Press of Virginia, 1978.

Schopenhauer, Arthur. *Die Welt als Wille und Vorstellung.* 1819. Translated as *The World as Will and Representation* by E. F. J. Payne. New York: Dover, 1966.

Whyte, L. L. *The Unconscious before Freud.* London: Friedman, 1979.

UNITED STATES: CULTURAL SURVEY

The historical period from the end of the American Revolution to the Civil War (1776–1861) marked a profound intellectual shift from the eighteenth-century Enlightenment emphasis on reason and knowledge (in the thought of Benjamin Franklin and Thomas Jefferson) to the cultural flowering of Romanticism between the 1830s and 1850s. The prorevolutionary campaigner Thomas Paine brought from Europe to America the fusion of political and literary radicalism in his pamphlet *Common Sense* (1775), which sold very well, and in which he argued for America's independence from Britain and eschewed the propriety of Enlightenment writing for a plain, direct style that foreshadowed the British Romantic poet William Wordsworth's egalitarian emphasis of a "man talking to men." Although Paine was an important Romantic pioneer in Revolutionary America (until he returned to Europe in the early 1780s), Romanticism did not become fully manifest in American culture until the publication of the Gothic tales of Edgar Allen Poe and the nativist writing of Ralph Waldo Emerson and Walt Whitman in the 1830s and 1840s. The Romantic intellectual currents of this period not only created the conditions for a national culture, but also cemented many of the themes that continued to stimulate American thinkers and writers through the nineteenth and into the twentieth century.

The eighty years between the two wars can be divided into three cultural and social phases: the postrevolutionary period (1790s–1820s), the Romantic period (1830s–50s), and the pre–Civil War period (1840s–50s). The ideology of "exceptionalism" as an expression of America's spiritual destiny was a dominant current linking political, economic and cultural activity throughout these three phases, from westward expansion and the frontier sensibility to the literary flowering of New England. Here the focus will be on American literary culture as a barometer of cultural transition during these eighty years, but the shift from Enlightenment to Romantic thought can also be detected in, for example, the move from the commemorative civic paintings of John Trumbell in the 1780s to the Romantic landscape paintings of Albert Bierstadt in the 1860s, and in the emergence of Margaret Fuller's feminist writing and the educational reformist work of Bronson Alcott published in the mid-nineteenth century.

Literature in the years following the American Revolution reflected the political attempts to cement the new Republic by instructing the reader into being a good citizen. However, the neoclassical mode of Benjamin Franklin's writing was on the wane by the late 1790s with the general rise of literacy and the public appetite for fiction, stimulated by the European taste for Romantic tales of imagination. The idea of fiction was an anathema to eighteenth-century Puritans, for whom writing should provide a faithful interpretation of scriptures and not a means for self-expression. The two emerging fictional modes in America at the turn of the century—the picturesque and the Gothic—sought to delight the reader with intrigue and romance rather than providing serious lessons of good conduct; according to Washington Irving, fiction should attempt to delight and instruct at the same time. A major example of the tensions between Enlightenment and Romantic thought can be found in Charles Brockden Brown's romances *Wieland* (1798) and *Edgar Huntly* (1799). These two novels address the failings of a rational Jeffersonian worldview by using such sensational devices as spontaneous combustion, ventriloquism, hauntings and somnambulism. Although there is often a rational explanation for supernatural happenings in Brown's work, his fiction explores Enlightenment themes, such as the nature of evil, the reliability of the senses, and the assumed self-knowledge of rational individuals. The Gothic veneer of Brown's work was later developed into a distinct fictional mode in Irving's ghostly tales, "The Legend of Sleepy Hollow" and "The Spectre Bridegroom" (1819) and in Poe's Gothic collection of short stories *Tales of the Grotesque and Arabesque* (1840).

The full flowering of American Romanticism (described by F. O. Matthiessen as "the American Renaissance") was inaugurated by Emerson's "Divinity School Address" of 1838, in which Emerson distanced himself from orthodox religion by promoting imagination and human creativity, while reinforcing the need for an American cultural independence from Europe. This celebratory Romanticism is expressed most fully in Emerson's description of his walk on Boston Common in "Nature" (1836), the transcendental individualism of his essay "Self-Reliance" (1844), Henry David Thoreau's paean to Nature in *Walden* (1854), and Whitman's poetic volume *Leaves of Grass* (1855). Irving Howe compares the "newness" of this creative exuberance to Nathaniel Hawthorne's more skeptical response to Romantic optimism (as expressed in Hawthorne's short story, "The Celestial Railroad," 1843). This idea of "newness" epitomizes America in its cultural infancy before the toll of slavery, civil war, and industrialization had tempered idealistic yearnings, but Herman Melville and Orestes Brownson also counterbalanced the excitement of early Romanticism by "shadowing hopes with doubts, enthusiasms with quizzical silence" in their writing and rejecting Emerson's spiritual clarity by exploring the ambiguity of human existence. However, although Emerson may appear overly optimistic in the 1830s, mature essays such as "Fate" (1852) reveal a darker vision of a nation drawing closer to bloodshed. Emerson's anti-slavery essays in the 1840s and 1850s also represent efforts to ground the abstract musings of his earlier essays by dealing with the pressing realities of slavery and social inequality. But, even though Emerson responded directly to specific events, such as his two addresses

on the emancipation of the West Indies (1844 and 1845), Anne Rose has argued that there is a Romantic "abstraction in his approach to slavery which made his occasional musings on the agencies of abolition ... comparatively desultory." While Rose is severe in her criticism, Emerson's argument that widespread reform would result from depriving Southern slaveholders of "the Bowie-knife, the rum-bowl," and "the dice-box" is less tenable than the ways in which Frederick Douglass and Harriet Beecher Stowe sought institutional change.

As the most striking examples of pre-Civil War literature, Douglass's *Narrative of the Life of Frederick Douglass, an American Slave* (1845) and Stowe's *Uncle Tom's Cabin* (1852) are socially oriented texts halfway between realism and romance, linking social criticism with spiritual renewal. In Douglass's autobiographical account of his escape from slavery, the first-person narrative voice is neutral and hardheaded in describing the realities of bondage, from his birth in Maryland and his early life in captivity, to his intellectual development and his flight to New England. Despite his realistic approach, passages such as when Douglass watches ships in the harbor (as elusive symbols of freedom) and his firm conviction that emancipation must be psychological and spiritual (as well as economic) are clear expressions of his Romantic sensibility. The emotive tone and sentimental characterization of Stowe's *Uncle Tom's Cabin* are much closer to Romantic expression than Douglass's autobiographical voice, but a negative dimension also manifests itself in Stowe's novel. The term *Romantic racist* has been used to describe Stowe's portrayal of African Americans as innocent children unaware of social complexities. Stowe describes black Americans as an "exotic race" in her preface, and she envisages the "hand of white benevolence" reaching out to help "the lowly, the oppressed, and the forgotten."

Uncle Tom's Cabin can either be seen to encapsulate the author's belief in racial equality (with one race helping the other), or it can be argued that Stowe actually maintains white superiority despite her wish to abolish slavery on Christian and moral grounds. Whichever way it is interpreted, in its realistic dialogue and episodic plot *Uncle Tom's Cabin* is a prime example of the waning of Romanticism as a movement in the pre-Civil War period. Strains of Romantic thought did, however, continue into the 1870s and 1880s, in the writings of Mark Twain and Henry James and through to the naturalism of Frank Norris at the turn of the twentieth century.

MARTIN HALLIWELL

Bibliography

Bradfield, Scott. *Dreaming Revolution: Transgression in the Development of American Romance.* Iowa City: University of Iowa Press, 1993.

Brown, Gillian. *Domestic Individualism: Imagining the Self in Nineteenth-Century America.* Berkeley and Los Angeles: University of California Press, 1990.

Cogliano, Francis. *Revolutionary America: 1763–1815: A Political History.* London: Routledge, 2000.

Emerson, Ralph Waldo. *Emerson's Antislavery Writings.* Edited by Len Gougeon and Joel Myerson. New Haven, Conn.: Yale University Press, 1995.

Goodman, Russell. *American Philosophy and the Romantic Tradition.* Cambridge: Cambridge University Press, 1990.

Gross, Louis. *Redefining the American Gothic: From* Wieland *to* Day of the Dead. Ann Arbor, Mich.: UMI Research Press, 1989.

Howe, Irving. *The American Newness: Culture and Politics in the Age of Emerson.* Cambridge, Mass.: Harvard University Press, 1986.

Madsen, Deborah L. *American Exceptionalism.* Edinburgh: Edinburgh University Press, 1998.

Matthiessen, F. O. *American Renaissance: Art and Expression in the Age of Emerson and Whitman.* New York: Oxford University Press, 1981.

Rose, Anne C. *Transcendentalism as a Social Movement, 1830–1850.* New Haven, Conn.: Yale University Press, 1981.

Stowe, Harriet Beecher. *Uncle Tom's Cabin.* Edited by Elizabeth Ammons. New York: W. W. Norton, 1994.

UPJOHN, RICHARD 1802–1878

Anglo-American architect

Richard Upjohn was born in the market town of Shaftesbury, Dorset, England. During Upjohn's youth the town leaders denied the Great Western Railroad access to Shaftesbury, and as the Industrial Revolution hurried along to the north, Upjohn immersed himself in the traditional pursuits of religion and carpentry. Upjohn's family hoped he would enter the Church, but instead he apprenticed as a cabinetmaker, ultimately opening his own business. By 1829 he had made no financial headway and decided to emigrate with his wife and young son to America.

Upjohn landed in America during a time of great change. Andrew Jackson had just entered the White House, forever changing the country's cultural landscape. Before Jackson, American culture had been beholden to the ideas and expression of classicism. Faced with designing a modern republic, the classical tenets of enlightened democracy, rational order, and social unity seemed to complement the evolving national ethos. With this new style of leadership, Jackson—variously described as "nature's nobleman" and "educated in Nature's school"—seemed at one with a country rediscovering itself as "nature's nation." Opposed to the austerity of previous presidents, Jackson was more Romantic hero than classical statesman.

During Upjohn's early years in America, two important influences came to bear on the nation, complementing the country's cultural shift and facilitating many of Upjohn's achievements. Sir Walter Scott's popularity introduced America to medieval Romanticism, and Edmund Burke's *A Philosophical Enquiry into the Nature of the Sublime and the Beautiful* (1756) helped many to understand their increasing fascination with nature. In his thesis, Burke indelibly linked the natural sublime to the architectural Gothic. Previously, Americans had viewed the Gothic as contrary to national ideals, representing instead the superstition and social persecution of feudal Europe. After Jackson, however, the Gothic almost entirely replaced neoclassicism as the preferred eclectic style. And this was in no small measure attributable to the work of Upjohn.

Upjohn arrived in America a cabinetmaker and soon after reinvented himself as an architect. Coming upon plans for a courthouse in New Bedford, he announced that "if that's architecture, then I am an architect." After setting up an independent practice, Upjohn established a small yet loyal following. His early work is marked by a temperate application of eclectic forms.

His first known work is the Isaac Farrar House in Bangor, Maine (1833–36); shortly after its construction, he received a residential commission from Farrar's brother Samuel (1836). Both houses are solidly of the Greek revival, with the latter more

overtly so. Between the two Farrar houses came the design of the R. H. Gardiner residence "Oaklands." Although somewhat naive in application, the structure was praised by Nathaniel Hawthorne and marked Upjohn's first foray into the Gothic style.

As a High Church Episcopalian, Upjohn was often more concerned with ecclesiastical thought than architectural trends. Throughout the 1830s he followed the ecclesiological movement in England, and his identification with it was strong. Exemplified in the figure of Augustus Welby Northmore Pugin, this group felt the contemporary church to be debased and called for a return to the forms and rituals of the medieval church. Upjohn's first religious commission, St. John's Church, Bangor (1836–39), was a direct response to these ideas. Although not reaching the style's mature expression, St. John's marked an important advance in America's Gothic revival.

Upon completion of St. John's, Upjohn was charged with constructing lower Manhattan's prestigious new Trinity Church (1839–46). Seven years later, Upjohn's reputation would be sealed and the Gothic revival fully validated in America. It would be hard to overestimate the importance of Upjohn's Trinity Church. The diarist Philip Hone felt it was "the glory of the city," and Paul Goldberger has called it "the Empire State Building of the nineteenth century . . . the spire that symbolized the entire city." Certainly an architectural triumph, Trinity's main legacy is perhaps more ecclesiastic than aesthetic. With Trinity's consecration, the Gothic was legitimized as the only style fit for American church architecture.

Upjohn consequently found himself as America's preeminent religious architect at a time when church finances and congressional numbers were growing significantly. Work flooded into his office, and over the next twenty years he designed more than eighty religious buildings. Demonstrating his versatility, Upjohn applied the Gothic style with equal success to both urban and rural settings. With such works as St. Paul's, Baltimore (1854–56), he was able to incorporate an increased congregation within a tight urban grid system while retaining the architectural forms specific to Christian ritual. With Christ Church, Raleigh, North Carolina (1848–54), the Gothic revival was extended into the South.

Although most often identified with the Gothic revival, Upjohn's domestic and civic work encompassed many of the styles commensurate with the rise of Romanticism in American architecture. Mostly this took the form of Romanesque or Italianate forms, but he also worked within the Renaissance revival. In such works as New York's Trinity Building (1851–52) and Corn Exchange Bank (1854), Upjohn anticipated the Romantic Modernism of Henry Hobson Richardson and Louis Sullivan. For William Pierson, Upjohn's most enduring legacy can be found in his application of the *Rundbogenstil* ("round arch style") championed by the German Romantics Leo von Klenze and Karl Friedrich Schinkel, rather than his use of Gothic forms.

Undoubtedly a major figure in the rise of architectural Romanticism in America, Upjohn would not have appreciated the label. Had he lived into the twentieth-century, Upjohn would have strongly disapproved of the "Romanticism" of New York's Woolworth Building (1913). To use the Gothic style for a commercial building was anathema to the High Church architect. Wayne Andrews has characterized Upjohn as "not an architect who happened to be an Episcopalian, but an Episcopalian who happened to be an architect." Despite his Romantic credentials, Upjohn viewed the production of religious architecture as an act of devotion, not as an aesthetic problem. At least once per year he donated his talents to struggling parishes, and in 1846 he caused a controversy by refusing, on religious grounds, to design a Unitarian church. Unlike such key Romantic figures as Samuel Taylor Coleridge and August Wilhelm and Friedrich von Schlegel, Upjohn did not seek aesthetic transcendence in the Gothic style but in religious tradition. A key figure in nineteenth-century architecture, he was less a Romantic by design than by accident.

RICHARD HAW

Biography

Born in Shaftesbury, Dorset, England January 22, 1802. Married Elizabeth Parry in London, November 14, 1826; son Richard Mitchell born, March 7, 1828; emigrated to America, April 1829; worked for Samuel Leonard in New Bedford, 1830; began to solicit work as an architect, 1833; moved to Boston to work in the architectural offices of Alexander Parris, 1834; naturalized as American citizen, 1836; moved practice to Brooklyn and began affiliation with the General Theological Seminary, 1842; son Richard Mitchell joined practice, 1846; made honorary member of New York Ecclesiological Society, 1849; traveled to Europe, 1850; published *Upjohn's Rural Architecture*, 1852; founded the American Institute of Architects (AIA) and was elected its president, 1857; elected honorary member of the Royal Society of British Architects and the Royal Society of Portuguese Architects, 1867; retired from practice and moved to Garrison, New York, 1872; resigned as president of AIA, 1876; died of natural causes at home, August 17, 1878.

Bibliography

Andrews, Wayne. *American Gothic*. New York: Random House, 1975.

Cherol, John A. "Kingscote in Newport, Rhode Island," *Antiques* 118 (1980): 476–85.

Early, James. *Romanticism and American Architecture*. New York: A. S. Barnes, 1965.

Patrick, J. "Ecclesiological Gothic in the Antebellum South," *Winterthur Portfolio* 15, no. 2 (1980): 117–38.

Pierson, William H. *American Buildings and Their Architects: Technology and the Picturesque, the Corporate and the Early Gothic Styles*. Garden City, N.Y.: Doubleday, 1978.

———. "Richard Upjohn and the American *Rundbogenstil*," *Winterthur Portfolio* 21, no. 4 (1986): 223–42.

Stanton, Phoebe B. *The Gothic Revival in American Church Architecture: An Episode in Taste, 1840–1856*. Baltimore: Johns Hopkins University Press, 1968.

———. "Richard Upjohn." In *Macmillan Encyclopedia of Architects*, vol. 4. Edited by Adolf K. Placzek. New York: Free Press, 1982.

Upjohn, Everard M. *Richard Upjohn: Architect and Churchman*, 1939. Reprint, New York: Da Capo, 1968.

Upjohn, Richard. *Upjohn's Rural Architecture*, 1852. Reprint, New York: Da Capo, 1975.

V

VARNHAGEN VON ENSE, RAHEL 1771–1833

German salonnière and diarist

Rahel Levin was born in the early years of the Romantic era in Germany. She experienced the heyday of the Berlin school of Romantics, and knew many of the figures associated with *Junges Deutschland* (Young Germany)—notably, Heinrich Heine. As a woman and a Jew in an age in which emancipation was a topic of conversation but hardly a manifest reality, Rahel (scholars often refer to her by her first name) seems to have been destined to find no satisfactory measure of social, intellectual, or artistic fulfillment. Her struggles, dreams, disappointments, and joys are chronicled in her many letters, a selection of which was first published by her husband, the diplomat and publicist Karl August Varnhagen von Ense (1785–1858) in the year after her death. Rahel's character sketches provide compelling insights into the lives of her contemporaries.

Rahel's reputation rests for the most part on her husband's book *Rahel. Ein Buch des Andenkens für ihre Freunde* (*Rahel. A Book of Remembrance for Her Friends*, 1834), as well as other letters and diary entries published subsequently. Feminist scholarship on Rahel's writings has been ample in recent years, and with the rediscovery of the lost Varnhagen *Nachlass* in the late 1970s (it had been missing since the end of World War II), a complete edition of her collected writings in ten volumes was made possible; this was published in 1983.

Rahel's appeal, then as now, is attributable to her unconventionality, her sensitivity, her eloquence, and her stubborn egalitarianism. Her forceful and dazzling personality is in a sense her true oeuvre, since she left no single major literary accomplishment behind, only a record of her thoughts and sentiments in prodigious and prolific epistolary writing, and in the comments of others who knew her at one time or another. By the same token, she was conscious of crafting an identity and a legacy in her writing. She worked in collaboration with her husband, who made sure some of her essays appeared anonymously in respectable periodicals while she was alive, and whose plan was to edit and publish her work eventually, even posthumously (he was fourteen years her junior.)

Rahel grew up in the context of a progressive Berlin Jewry devoted to education, philanthropy, and the arts. The late eighteenth century was an age in which the philosopher Moses Mendelssohn and the scientist Marcus Herz could attain prominence though not total assimilation. (Jews were not even considered citizens in Prussia until 1812.) And though boys and girls were not given the same formal training by any means, Rahel's parents made sure she received an excellent education at home, and her precocious intellect thrived from an early age. In addition to conventional domestic skills, she learned several foreign languages, music composition, and was versed in several literatures.

The informal social gatherings known as salons permitted Jews to mingle not only with the gentile bourgeoisie, but with virtually anyone, from actors to aristocrats; these were generally the only occasions where any degree of close contact was possible for representatives of such disparate social strata. The salon, begun on the French model by Henriette Herz in 1784, was the perfect stage for Rahel to display her talents as a conversationalist and her insights into literature, aesthetic theory, philosophy, and politics. The majority of such weekly "open houses" in Berlin were held by Jewish women such as Rahel, beginning, in her case, in the late 1790s. Her brilliance quickly made the parlor in her parental home a popular meeting place for certain members of the nobility (Count Wilhelm von Burgdorf, Prince Louis Ferdinand, Friedrich von Gentz) and for writers and intellectuals such as Clemens Brentano, Alexander and Wilhelm von Humboldt, Jean Paul, Friedrich von Schlegel, Friedrich Schleiermacher, and Ludwig Tieck. Performers who frequented Rahel's salon included the opera singer Maria Marchetti, and the well-known contemporary actors Johann and Sophie Louise Fleck and Friedrike Unzelmann. The famous French commentator on

Michael Moritz Daffinger, *Portrait of Rahel Varnhagen von Ense.* Reprinted courtesy of AKG.

German literature, Madame Anne-Louise-Germaine de Staël, visited Rahel's salon in 1804.

Rahel was a utopian; her abiding dream was the cultivation of a humane society of enlightened persons striving for perfection of their talents and capabilities. The freer associations permitted by the salon were, she and others hoped, a prelude to a new age in which social distinctions would disappear and women and members of minorities would be taken on their own terms, as social and, ideally, intellectual equals. In this struggle for a better world she treasured the spiritual support provided by the works of Johann Wolfgang von Goethe, and she and her husband were among the first *Goetheaner*, unwavering admirers of the author in his later years, when his popularity had waned, and in the years after his death. She never lost hope for a renewal and emancipation of society, and in the last two years of her life was instrumental in introducing to educated Berlin the ideas of the early utopian socialist Claude-Henri Comte de Saint-Simon.

For all the praise lavished upon her during her lifetime by the guests she entertained, Rahel nonetheless frequently encountered discrimination and bias because of her gender and her Jewishness, as recorded throughout her epistolary work. The discrimination she encountered was perhaps all the more painful because it was inflicted in a gentile society that professed the ideals of rationality, *Bildung* (self-cultivation through education), tolerance, and Christian charity. Unbeknownst to her,

there was also subtle criticism by ostensible friends, such as Brentano and Humboldt's contention that she lacked powers of discrimination. Tieck bemoaned the "capriciousness" of her nature. History itself dealt Rahel a heavy blow: the defeat of Prussia by Napoleon in 1806 meant the demise of the Jewish salon as a meeting place. It would be 1819 before she and her husband could reestablish the institution in Berlin, where her cultural soirées thrived until shortly before her death in 1833.

MARK R. MCCULLOH

Biography

Born the first child of the well-to-do Jewish merchant, Markus Levin, and his wife Chaie on May 26, 1771 in Berlin; converted to Christianity and married Karl August Varnhagen in 1814; spent sojourns in Paris (1801), Prague (1814), Vienna (1815), and in Karlruhe during her husband's diplomatic assignment to the Grand Duchy of Baden (1816–9). Died in Berlin on March 7, 1833.

Selected Works

Galerie von Bildnissen aus Rahel's Umgang und Briefwechsel. 2 vols. Edited by Karl August Varnhagen von Ense. 1836.
Aus dem Nachlass Varnhagen's von Ense: Briefwechsel zwischen Rahel und David Veit. Edited by Ludmilla Assing. 1861.
Aus dem Nachlass Varnhagen's von Ense: Briefwechsel zwischen Varnhagen und Rahel. 6 vols. Edited by Ludmilla Assing. 1874–75.
Gesammelte Werke (Rahel-Bibliothek). 10 vols. Edited by Konrad Feilchenfeldt, Uwe Schweiker, and Rahel E. Steiner. 1983.
Jeder Wunsch wird Frivolität genannt: Briefe und Tagebücher. Edited by Marlis Gerhardt. 1983.
"Im Schlaf bin ich wacher": Die Träume der Rahel Levin Varnhagen. Edited by Barbara Hahn. 1990.

Bibliography

Arendt, Hannah. *Rahel Varnhagen: The Life of a Jewish Woman.* Translated by Richard and Clara Winston. San Diego: Harcourt Brace Jovanovich, 1974.
Goodman, Katherine. "The Impact of Rahel Varnhagen on Women in the Nineteenth Century." In *Gestaltet und gestaltend. Frauen in der deutschen Literatur.* Edited by Marianne Burkhard. Amsterdamer Beiträge zur neueren Germanistik 10. Amsterdam: Rodolpi, 1980.
Goodman, Katherine R. "Rahel Levin Varnhagen." In *Bitter Healing: German Women Writers 1700–1830.* Edited by Jeanine Blackwell and Susanne Zantop. European Women Writers series. Lincoln: University of Nebraska Press, 1990.
Guilloton, Doris Starr. "Rahel Varnhagen von Ense." In *German Writers in the Age of Goethe 1789–1832.* Vol. 90 of the *Dictionary of Literary Biography.* Edited by James Hardin and Christoph Schweitzer.
Hahn, Barbara, and Ursula Isselstein, eds. *Die Wiederentdeckung einer Schriftstellerin.* Göttingen: Vandenhoeck and Ruprecht, 1987.
Tewarson, Heidi Thomann. *Rahel Levin Varnhagen: The Life and Work of a German Jewish Intellectual.* Lincoln: University of Nebraska Press, 1998.
Weissberg, Liliane. " 'Turns of Emancipation' On Rahel Varnhagen's Letters." In *In the Shadow of Olympus: German Women Writers around 1800.* Edited by Katherine R. Goodman and Edith Waldstein. Albany: State University of New York Press, 1992.

VERDI, GIUSEPPE 1813-1901

Italian composer

A towering giant of opera, Giuseppe Verdi is one of a small handful of composers who dominate the repertory of opera houses throughout the world. For half a century he virtually defined Italian opera. He achieved a level of veneration and popularity that is unparalleled in the history of Italian music. An important figure in Italian nationalism, especially the *risorgimento* movement, he became one of the most revered men in Italy. From rather humble beginnings (his father was an innkeeper) he achieved greatness and accumulated substantial wealth while still in the prime of life, and set an artistic standard in Italian opera that remains unequaled.

Verdi inherited a notable tradition from predecessors in Italian Romanticism, especially Vincenzo Bellini, Domenico Gaetano Maria Donizetti, Saverio Mercadante, Stefano Pavesi, and Gioacchino Antonio Rossini. In developing his craft, Verdi built upon this heritage and renewed it with ingenious individuality. Unlike Richard Wagner, his German contemporary, Verdi did not attempt to revolutionize music in Italy. In fact, Verdi has been regarded as rather conservative since he continued to use the conventions and forms that characterized Italian opera of the eighteenth century. But even his earliest and most conservative works reveal a personal stamp. Though he used set forms, he was not enslaved by them; his genius enabled him to transcend the rules without relinquishing their use. He greatly expanded the traditional aria form that consisted of cavatina, tempo di mezzo, and cabaletta. Sometimes he would even eliminate the cabaletta, as in Lady Macbeth's sleepwalking scene (*Macbeth*, 1847), while creating effective drama through the cavatina alone. In duets, he sometimes eschewed traditional forms (especially cascades of parallel thirds and sixths) in favor of more dramatic declamation and conflict even while adhering to the general outlines of the operatic duet. The scene between Gilda and her father at the end of the second act of *Rigoletto* (1851) illustrates this tendency. Both characters have different material.

Drama drove Verdi's creative energy in redefining traditional forms. He compressed the libretto for dramatic effect. As a result, some plots of his early operas have gaps, but by midcentury he had thoroughly mastered the art. Throughout his career, he remained intimately involved in the libretto-writing process. He did not create his own texts but constantly revised the work of his librettists; Arrigo Boito, Salvatore Cammarano, Francesco Piave, and Temistocle Solera were his principal collaborators.

He prodded them to cut lengthy narrative in order to avoid long recitatives. His voluminous letters reveal his intense desire to search for the essential elements of the storylines. His plots, therefore, tended to be simpler and more self-propelling than those of earlier composers. For inspiration, Verdi drew from important and wide-ranging literary figures, including Lord Byron, Victor Hugo, Johann Christoph Friedrich von Schiller, Eugène Scribe, and William Shakespeare.

In searching for material, Verdi stressed the need for striking characters involved in tense conflict. He insisted on knowing the singers contracted for his new operas so that he could tailor the roles for specific voices. His contracts usually stipulated this requirement, following a similar custom practiced by most Italian opera composers. For subsequent revivals, he would often sanction and even compose revisions in order to suit different casts more effectively. Verdi markedly differed from Richard Wagner in that he gave the voice the primary consideration in opera. In Verdi operas, the voice always dominates the orchestra, which is never treated symphonically; though Verdi became increasingly skilled in orchestration, it always served in a subordinate position to the voice. Vocally, Verdi contributed two distinctive voice types. In his oeuvre the baritone and dramatic mezzo-soprano emerged as important and pivotal voices. A substantial number of title characters were composed for baritone, ranging from *Nabucco* (1842) to *Simon Boccanegra* (final version in 1881). Though Verdi wrote no title roles for mezzo-sopranos, they often steal scenes from the leading soprano in works such as *Il Trovatore* (1853) and *Aida* (1871). Verdi infused his major baritone and mezzo-soprano roles with multifaceted characterizations that reveal a mastery of character development; however, many of his most important tenor and soprano roles are surprisingly one-dimensional.

Since he deemed the voice and its role in the dramatic situation to be of primary importance, it is not surprising that Verdi's operas do not exhibit the harmonic and formal tendencies of German composers. Verdi never had a real tonal plan to unify acts or scenes. Closed forms often begin and end in different keys. He does occasionally associate some characters with certain keys; for example, flat keys represent the nobility in *Il Trovatore*, while sharp keys are used for the underclass, particularly the gypsies. In the Italian tradition, arias and even entire scenes were often transposed to accommodate individual singers. Therefore, the concept of a unifying tonal scheme was foreign to practical Italian composers. Furthermore, Verdi was not a motivic composer like Wagner. He did frequently use reminiscence motives, such as the pledge motive in *Ernani* (1844), the curse motive in *Rigoletto*, and the kiss motive in *Otello* (1887). But these motives never come close to the motivic development of northern Europeans, and certainly cannot be confused with Wagnerian *leitmotifs*.

Despite this distinction between Verdi and Wagner, one must observe the gradual but inexorable progression from number opera to continuous opera in Verdi's long career. Wagner's influence on this development is subject to debate. Evidence of this tendency can even be seen in early works from the 1840s. In his mature works, Verdi demonstrates a mastery of the Italian opera tradition while simultaneously exploring new territory through continuous drama. It must be pointed out, however, that even in *Otello*, he does not completely abandon the number opera format.

Verdi's early operas are often characterized by youthful energy and even brashness. Such traits complemented the political environment of the time. Verdi fervently believed in Italian nationalism and became one of the leaders of the risorgimento movement. Several operas composed in the 1840s became associated with this movement, including *Nabucco* (1842), *I Lombardi* (1843), *Ernani* (1844), *I due Foscari* (1844), *Giovanna d'Arco* (1845), *Attila* (1846), and *La Battaglia di Legnano* (1849).

Though current political events were never depicted in these works, the underlying message of patriotism was clearly understood by the public.

At the time of Verdi's birth, Napoleon Bonaparte still ruled Italy. After his defeat in 1815 most of the pre-Napoleonic ruling families were restored to power. The Congress of Vienna in 1815 resulted in Austrian dominance of Italy. Austria's influence produced police states and repressive regimes, causing many Italians to seethe with revolutionary resentment. "Carbonari" societies were established and dedicated to overthrowing non-Italian rule. Giuseppe Mazzini founded La Giovine Italia (Young Italy), an organization that engaged Italian youth in this effort. The resultant move toward independence became known as the risorgimento. Giuseppe Garibaldi brought the movement to culmination with the overthrow of Austrian control and subsequent installation of Vittorio Emanuele II as king of a unified Italian peninsula (excepting the papal state).

Verdi was keenly interested in these political developments and played a key role in the process. Choruses in some of his operas became rallying cries for revolutionary sentiment. "Va, pensiero" in *Nabucco* is sung by the Jewish people in exile as they yearn for their fatherland. In *Macbeth*, the chorus of exiled Scots sing similar sentiments. In *I Lombardi*, the chorus calls the Lombards to battle against the Saracens. During the upheavals of the late 1840s, Verdi left Paris for Rome, where he supervised the 1849 production of *La Battaglia di Legnano*. Audience passions peaked as the opera depicted Frederick Barbarossa's defeat by the Lombards in 1176. The historical nature of the dramatic material thinly veiled the patriotic sentiments of the opera.

By midcentury Verdi had become both a cultural and a political icon in Italy. His name was converted into an acronym, "Vittorio Emanuele Re D'Italia"; consequently, "Viva Verdi!" became a rallying cry for Italian nationalism. He was elected a member of the first Italian parliament, where he served from 1861 to 1865, and it was during this period that his early operas began to be identified with the risorgimento movement.

Italian censors were sensitive to the political overtones in his works, and Verdi was plagued with censorship problems throughout most of his career. Even after reaching the pinnacle of his career he endured interference from censors. For example, in 1859 he was forced to create a character change when King Gustavus III of Sweden became the fictitious Earl of Warwick in *Un ballo in maschera*. The censors objected to the depiction of a royal assassination on stage.

Considering Verdi's extramusical activities, it is hardly surprising that the pace of his compositional work slowed considerably after *La Traviata* (1853). By this time his position as a composer was secure, and financial success enabled him to limit his projects. During his "galley years" he produced more than one opera a year, an extraordinary output. Beginning in the early 1850s he explored other interests, both political and domestic. Furthermore, he was kept busy revising and adapting earlier works for revivals and premières. He lived in Paris for extended periods, where he produced longer and therefore more time-consuming operas like *Les vepres siciliennes* (1855) and *Don Carlos* (1867). The French influence on his work is noteworthy. The emphasis on spectacle and larger-than-life characterizations that typify French grand opera can be seen in many works, including those that do not have French texts, such as *Aida*.

In the latter decades of his career, new works became increasingly sporadic. He accepted a commission only if he was intrigued by its possibilities. After *Aida* (1871), a long interval separates that opera and the last two, *Otello* (1887) and *Falstaff* (1893), though he did produce the *Requiem* (1874) and major revisions of *Simon Boccanegra* and *Don Carlos* during this period. For his final two operas he collaborated with his finest librettist, Arrigo Boito, who captured the essence of Shakespeare's dramas in his adaptations for the opera stage. In crafting *Falstaff*, Verdi admitted that now he was composing more for himself than for the public. In so doing, he produced one of his greatest achievements.

In the latter years of his life, Verdi became increasingly concerned about the trend toward Wagnerism in Italian music. He emphatically desired that Italy retain its musical identity, revealing a strong nationalistic bent. It is rather ironic that Arrigo Boito, one of Verdi's closest collaborators, was one of Italy's most Wagnerian composers.

Throughout the last half of the nineteenth century, Verdi seemed to set his own individual path in Italian culture. His work is unique when compared with other Italian contemporaries. It is interesting to note that he did not exert the influence on successive composers that one would expect from a composer of his stature. In most respects he stands alone in Italian music history. He was followed by other popular opera composers, such as Ruggero Leoncavallo, Pietro Mascagni, and Giacomo Puccini, but no one has been able to duplicate his mastery of the craft.

THEODORE L. GENTRY

Biography

Born in Le Roncole, Parma, October 9 or 10, 1813; moved to Busseto in 1823; there he studied with Ferdinando Provesi in 1825; studied composition with Vincenzo Lavigna in Milan, 1832–35; married Margherita Barezzi May 4, 1836. First opera, *Oberto*, premiered at La Scala, November 17, 1839; wife died in June 1840, preceded in death by their two children. Third opera, *Nabucco*, 1842, firmly established Verdi's reputation as leading opera composer. Lived in Paris with Giuseppina Strepponi, 1847–9; married her in 1859; Member of Italian parliament, 1861–5. Final opera, *Falstaff*, opened at La Scala, February 9, 1893. Strepponi died in 1897; Verdi died on January 27, 1901.

Selected Works

Oberto. 1839. La Scala, Milan.
Un giorno di regno. 1840. La Scala, Milan.
Nabucco. 1842. La Scala, Milan.
I Lombardi. 1843. La Scala, Milan.
Ernani. 1844. La Fenice, Venice.
I due Foscari. 1844. Teatro Argentina, Rome.
Giovanna d'Arco. 1845. La Scala, Milan.
Alzira. 1845. Teatro San Carlo, Naples.
Attila. 1846. La Fenice, Venice.
Macbeth. 1847. Teatro della Pergola, Florence.
I Masnadiera. 1847. Her Majesty's Theatre, Haymarket, London.
Jerusalem. 1847. Opera, Paris.
Il Corsaro. 1848. Teatro Grande, Trieste.
La battaglia di Legnano. 1849. Teatro Argentina, Rome.
Luisa Miller. 1849. Teatro San Carlo, Naples.
Stiffelio. 1850. Teatro Grande, Trieste.

Rigoletto. 1851. La Fenice, Venice.
Il Trovatore. 1853. Teatro Apollo, Rome.
La Traviata. 1853. La Fenice, Venice.
Les vepres siciliennes. 1855. Opera, Paris.
Simon Boccanegra. 1857. La Fenice, Venice.
Aroldo. 1857. Teatro Nuovo, Rimini.
Un ballo in maschera. 1859. Teatro Apollo, Rome.
La forza del destino. 1862. Imperial Theatre, St. Petersburg.
Don Carlos. 1867. Opera, Paris.
Aida. 1871. Opera House, Cairo.
Otello. 1887. La Scala, Milan.
Falstaff. 1893. La Scala, Milan.

Bibliography

Budden, Julian. *The Operas of Verdi*. Rev. ed. Oxford: Oxford
   University Press, 1992.

————. *Verdi*. London: J. M. Dent, 1985.
Kimbell, David R. B. *Verdi in the Age of Italian Romanticism*. New
   York: Cambridge University Press, 1981.
Martin, George. *Aspects of Verdi*. New York: Dodd, Mead, 1988.
Noske, Frits. *The Signifier and the Signified: Studies in the Operas of
   Mozart and Verdi*. The Hague: Nijhoff, 1977.
Osborne, Charles. *The Complete Operas of Verdi*. New York: Alfred
   A. Knopf, 1970.
————. *Verdi: A Life in the Theatre*. New York, 1987.
Parker, Roger. *Studies in Early Verdi 1832–1844*. New York:
   Garland, 1989.
Phillips-Matz, Mary Jane. *Verdi: A Biography*. New York: Oxford
   University Press, 1993.
Walker, Frank. *The Man Verdi*. Chicago: University of Chicago
   Press, 1982.
Weaver, William, and Martin Chusid, eds. *The Verdi Campanion*.
   New York: W. W. Norton, 1979.

VERNET, (EMILE-JEAN-) HORACE 1789–1863

French painter

Emile-Jean-Horace Vernet (known as Horace Vernet) was third in a familial line of distinguished painters. His grandfather, Claude-Joseph, had been one of the leading landscape and marine painters of his time; his father, Antoine-Charles-Horace, was known for the large-scale battle scenes he painted for Napoleon, and for his position, after the Restoration, as official painter to Louis XVIII.

It was, first and foremost, as the nostalgic chronicler of battle scenes of the Napoleonic era that Vernet gained celebrity. Today he is the victim of relative neglect, but at the height of his fame, Vernet was commissioned (and generously rewarded) by both Louis-Philippe and Tsar Alexander II of Russia to depict the military glories of their nations. While representing, with epic passion and patriotism, the great events of French military history, Vernet's paintings of the 1814–30 period, such as *Bataille de Tolosa* (*The Battle of Tolosa*, 1817), and *Bataille de Jemappes* (*The Battle of Jemappes*, 1821), also reflect the Romantic mood in their traces of a shift from idealism to realism, even pessimism. The latter painting depicts the French victory over the Austrians on November 6, 1792, and the occupation of Flanders, with an almost photographic attention to detail, but the ordinary soldier's suffering is clearly portrayed and the natural environment seems to conspire to increase that suffering. Individual tragedy had already been given direct and poignant expression in Vernet's earlier celebrated work, *Le Cheval du trompette/Le Trompette blessé* (*The Wounded Trumpeter*, 1819); and here, following the example of Eúgene Delacroix, Jean Louis André Théodore Géricault and Antoine-Jean Gros, Vernet creates a Romantic empathy with an animal whose intensity of feeling is equal to that of the human actors in the drama presented. As Robart Rosenblum notes notes, it is the horse that expresses the horror and pain provoked by the sight of his dead master, just as in *Mazeppa aux loups* (*Mazeppa with Wolves*, 1826), it is the horse to which the hero is strapped that conveys Mazeppa's terror. Similarly, in *Bataille de Tolosa*, the horse carrying the King of Navarre expresses the nobility and triumph of his rider. These early paintings found an enthusiastic critic in Stendhal who saw

them as the embodiment of youth, vigor, and the Romantic spirit of rebellion, far removed from what he saw as the cold, static scenes of Jacques-Louis David. Indeed, at an early stage, Vernet had rejected what he saw as the constraints of the classical school, quickly eradicating any traces of David's influence from his own style.

While it was Vernet's military commissions that first took him to the Middle East, like so many painters of the day, he also at this time succumbed to the lure of the fantasized East, with reflections of the oriental stereotype of cruelty present in paintings such as *Massacre des Mamelucks* (*The Massacre of the Mamelukes in the Citadel of Cairo*, 1819). Dominating this painting, notes Auguste de Forbin, is the "fixed and terrible gaze" of the ruler who has ordered the massacre and who casually smokes his narguile as he watches the violent scenes unfold before him.

Critics persuasively argue that Vernet's mature (post-1830) style marks a departure from his earlier work, and that he begins around this time to reject the ardor and passion of the Romantic style. Vernet's style becomes markedly more naturalistic. Detached and unemotional, the painter approximates the photographer in his almost ethnographic desire to convey minute detail. Certainly, the military scenes of this later period, such as *Siège de Constantine (10 octobre 1837)* (*The Attack on Constantine in October 1837*, 1838), or *Prise de la Smalah d'Abd-el-Kader* (*The Taking of the Smalah of Abd el Kader*, c. 1843–44) are all but stripped of the heroic intensity of the earlier paintings. This new objectivity is only emphasized by the impression of arbitrariness in the structure of the paintings, and the apparent lack of hierarchy among the figures represented. This latter painting was roundly criticized, notably by both Baudelaire and Gautier. The primary criticism was that, in this work, Vernet lacks of a sense of, and appropriate respect for, the epic.

Between 1835 and 1854, Vernet also executed ten biblical paintings. These are controversial because they present biblical characters and scenes in modern Arab settings and dress. In a statement that he read before the Académie des Beaux-Arts and published in *L'Illustration* in February 1848, Vernet explained and justified his decision to "pursue as far as possible the comparisons that might be established between holy writ and contemporary practice." Critics, however, responded with bemusement and condemnation. Interestingly, however, in these paintings the desire for precision of documentation that characterizes his later military scenes seems to combine with a sensibility more reminiscent of his earlier style. The biblical paintings frequently depict seductions or other intimate scenes, and reveal a sensuality uncommon in biblical paintings that play on preconceptions of Oriental eroticism prevalent among nineteenth-century Romantic painters. His *Juda et Tamar* (Judah and Tamar) (1840) is one such example: Tamar, disguised as a prostitute to entice Judah, is provocatively presented in a seminude state.

Vernet, like Jean-Auguste-Dominique Ingres and Eugène Delacroix, was honored with a retrospective at the Universal Exhibition in 1855, and in his *Histoire des artistes vivants* (*History of Living Artists*, 1856), Théophile Sylvestre ranked Vernet, alongside Jean-Baptiste-Camille Corot, Gustave Courbet, Delacroix, and Ingres, among the eight leading artists of the time. His work, particularly his later work, prompted mixed responses from his contemporaries, however, and his reputation has not endured like that of those artists with whom he was once ranked. His paintings today are perhaps of greatest interest as historic and ethnographic witnesses to his time.

MARGARET TOPPING

Biography

Born in Paris, June 30, 1789. First military paintings date from 1807; in 1814, named chevalier de la Légion d'honneur. January to April 1820, visited Rome with Carle Vernet; *Joseph Vernet attaché au mât d'un navire pendant une tempête* (*Joseph Vernet, lashed to a mast, studies the effects of the storm*, 1822) was the only one of his paintings to be accepted at the Salon of 1822. Vernet's response was to organize an exhibition in his atelier of fifty of his own works including those that were rejected by the Salon. Named officer de la Légion d'honneur 1825; elected to the Académie des Beaux-Arts, 1826. Inauguration, attended by Carle and Horace, of the Vernet gallery at the Musée Calvet in Avignon, their ancestral home, 1826. Director of the Académie de France in Rome, 1829–34. Visit to Algeria, 1833 (also 1837, 1839, 1845, 1853). Professor at the École des Beaux-Arts, 1835–63. First trip to Russia, 1836. Trip to Middle East, 1839–40. Second trip to Russia, 1842. Returned to France to meet with Louis-Philippe after the death of the Duke of Orléans; August 1842, charged by Louis-Philippe to bring about a *rapprochement* between the tsar of Russia and France; returned to Russia, spent September and October traveling there with Alexander II and his generals. July 1843, returned to Paris; 1843–47, undertook decoration of the library of the Chambre des Députés. Traveled to Rome, 1850. Trip to Crimea, 1854–55. Twenty-four of Vernet's paintings exhibited at the Universal Exhibition of 1855. December 1862, seriously ill, named grand officier de la Légion d'honneur. Died January 17, 1863; Posthumous exhibition of his work in Paris in August of that year.

Selected Works

Bataille de Tolosa, 1817. Oil on canvas, 46 cm. × 55 cm. Private collection, Paris.

Massacre des Mamelucks, 1819. Oil on canvas, 386 cm. × 514 cm. Musée de Picardie, Amiens.

Le Cheval du trompette / Le Trompette blessé, 1819. Oil on canvas, 53.1 cm. × 64.4 cm. Wallace Collection, London.

Bataille de Jemappes, 1821. Oil on canvas, 177.2 cm. × 288.3 cm. National Gallery, London.

La Vague, 1825. Oil on canvas, 49.8 cm. × 62 cm. Private collection, Paris.

Mazeppa aux loups, 1826. Oil on canvas, 100 cm. × 130 cm. Préfecture. Avignon.

Pape Pie VIII porté dans la basilique de Saint-Pierre, 1829. Oil on canvas, 85 cm. × 65 cm. Musée de Picardie, Amiens.

Le duc d'Orléans se rendant à l'hôtel de ville, 1830, 1832. Oil on canvas, 228 cm. × 258 cm. Musée National du Château de Versailles. Versailles.

Arabes dans leur camp écoutant une histoire, 1833. Oil on canvas, 99 cm. × 136.5 cm. Wallace Collection, London.

Siège de Constantine (10 octobre 1837), 1838. Ink and graphite with white highlights on tinted paper, 52.5 cm. × 94.3 cm. Musée National du Château de Versailles, Versailles.

Agar renvoyée par Abraham, 1837. Oil on canvas, 82 cm. × 65 cm. Musée des Beaux Arts, Nantes.

Juda et Tamar, 1840. Oil on canvas, 129 cm. × 97.5 cm. Wallace Collection, London.

Prise de la Smalah d'Abd-el-Kader, c. 1843–44. Oil on canvas, 32 cm. × 41 cm. Musée des Arts Africains et Océaniens, Paris.

L'Enfant adopté, 1848. Oil on canvas, 54 cm. × 46.5 cm. Galleria Civica d'Arte Moderna. Milan.

Bibliography

Académie de France, Rome, and École nationale supérieure des Beaux-Arts, Paris. *Horace Vernet, 1789–1863*. Exhibition catalog. Introduction by Robert Rosenblum. Rome: De Luca, 1980.

Blanc, Charles. *Une famille d'artistes: Les trois Vernet, Joseph, Carle, Horace*. 1898.

Durande, Amédée. *Joseph, Carle et Horace Vernet. Correspondance et Biographies*. 1864.

Goupil-Fesquet, Frédéric. *Voyage d'Horace Vernet en* Orient. 1843.

Peltre, Christine. *Orientalism in Art*. Translated by John Goodman. New York: Abbeville, 1998.

Rees, Janet. *Horace Vernet*. Illustrated Biographies of the Great Artists. 1880.

Sylvestre, Théophile. *Histoire des artistes vivants*. 1856.

VIAGENS NA MINHA TERRA (TRAVELS IN MY HOMELAND) 1846

Novel by João Baptista da Silva Leitão de Almeida Garrett

Viagens na Minha Terra, which was published as a novel in 1846 (with its first chapters appearing in a periodical three years earlier), represents a landmark in the history of the novel in Portugal, not only because of what it manages to present in terms of tradition and heritage, but also by the future possibilities it suggests for the Portuguese novel. On one level of the plot, a narrator ostensibly recounts his journey from Lisbon to Santarém. On another level, a story unfolds that is centered on one

Joaninha and her romantic involvement with her cousin Carlos, a liberal soldier returning to the Santarém Valley, the place where he had spent his childhood, after a period of political exile due to his antiabsolutist beliefs. Both narratives overlap in a reflection about the hopes and despair that Garrett, barely disguised by an anonymous narrator, manifests as his own and as those of a generation whose commitment to ideals ultimately results in failure.

The title, in its plural and symbolic forms, suggests a journey tracing the obvious disenchantment of a man who deeply believes that the future only exists because "his homeland" will find a way to flourish, but simultaneously, this man sees his present occupied by figures such as the baron, who are "usuriously revolutionary and revolutionarily usurious." The travels are, as he puts it, both physical and symbolical: because they take him to Santarém, because they move through various periods of Portuguese history, from the Middle Ages to the present, and because they make it possible for the narrator to exhibit his expertise in several fields of knowledge. The reader is made aware of the narrator's wide-ranging opinions, his value judgments about the Portuguese political situation, his ideologies and their philosophical basis, as well as the ever-present possibility of their degeneration in social practice. The narrator educates the reader about literature, from the popular *romanceiro* to the Poet par excellence, Luis Vaz de Camões, and also about canonical works and authors from classical tradition and contemporary European literatures. The Romantic opposition between Don Quixote and Sancho Panza as emblems for the contradictions of modern man is discussed, as are love and friendship, liberty and democracy, psychology, architecture, and history. *Viagens na Minha Terra* is a rich and fascinating compilation of Garrett's concerns, both intellectual and personal, in all their diversity, including contradictions and paradoxes. Its style expresses the depth and heterogeneity of a subject who assumes a shifting perspective on the world he discovers to be constantly changing.

But the psychological, physical, historical, and cultural travels find yet another dimension, that could be termed, following the Garrettian metaphor, as a "discursive travel," prefigured by the importance and scope of the dialogue. In fact, the whole text simulates, in a consistent way, a dialogue with the potential reader (in particular women: the narrator addresses a "feminine reader" and by extension a feminine readership), through which the Portuguese novel incorporates, for the first time in a systematic way, a voluntary proximity to day-to-day language. *Viagens na Minha Terra* mimes a real conversation in which the narrator acknowledges his interaction with the reader and simulates a project of discursive spontaneity that is nevertheless obviously as constructed as any other. On the other hand, digression and dialogue overlap significantly, placing the narrator in the center of the novel, and making it possible to recognize the importance of yet another Garrett characteristic, irony (deeply indebted to Romantic irony in general). All these elements emphasize the primary aesthetic dimensions of Garrett's prose.

The secondary plot of the novel, centered around the relationship between Carlos and Joaninha in the Santarém Valley, structurally relates to the other narrative by the process of alternation, which implies that mutual connections have to be considered. This plot mimics a "family novel" (typical of a Romantic setting) founded upon three main issues, all of which are condensed around the protagonist Carlos: the mysterious past that acts as a source of guilt, sentimental complexity (resolved in a unilateral and thus reductive way), and historical and ideological treason that mirrors and enhances the previous resolution.

The (later confirmed) intuition that something exists in the family's past that establishes an unspoken yet striking guilt is at the root of retrospective analyses that through sustained interventions (such as the long letter from Carlos to Joaninha) or allusions and innuendos (mainly connected to figures as the blind grandmother or the mysterious friar Dinis), span the whole novel. One can also mention a consciousness of a familiar and historical weight that projects itself from the past into the present, covering it in shadow (this may be seen in other major works by Garrett, such as the drama *Frei Luís de Sousa* [1843]). Then there are those whose innocence implies death (Joaninha), and those, such as Carlos, who manage to survive through complex maneuvers transformed into morally dubious pacts, a choice that attests to a state of despondency and dejection that Garrett, as a Romantic writer, fully recognizes.

Viagens na Minha Terra is a pivotal text in the foundation of modern Portuguese literature due to its thematic, semantic, and structural density. It is notable for the primacy given to ideological values that would be central to several esthetic and literary movements throughout the nineteenth and twentieth centuries. Garrett's language in the novel vigorously combines ductility, irony, metaphoric creativity, rhetorical density, persuasiveness, and an apparent colloquial spontaneity.

HELENA CARVALHÃO BUESCU

Text

Viagens na Minha Terra. 1846. Translated as: *Travels in my Homeland*, by John M. Parker. London: Peter Owen/UNESCO, 1987.

Bibliography

Buescu, Helena Carvalhão. *Incidências do Olhar. Percepção e Representaç*. Lisbon: Caminho, 1991.

Coelho, Jacinto do Prado. *A Letra e o Leitor*. Lisbon: Portugália, 1969.

Mendes, Vítor J. *Almeida Garrett. Crise na Representação das "Viagens na Minha Terra."* Lisbon: Cosmos, 1999.

Monteiro, Ofélia Paiva. *A Formação de Almeida Garrett. Experiência e Criação*. 2 vols., Coimbra: Centro de Estudos Ronânicos, 1971.

———. "*Viagens na Minha Terra*, o nascer da modernidade literária portuguesa." In *Viagens na Minha Terra*. 3d facsimile ed. Lisbon: 1993.

VIGÉE LE BRUN, ELISABETH LOUISE 1755–1842

Artist

Elisabeth Louise Vigée Le Brun's life spanned the Romantic era, yet she has never been labeled a Romantic. She has tended to be classified as a brilliant but conservative artist who embodies the elegance and decadence of the ancien régime. But her cosmopolitan lifestyle made her sensitive to artistic trends and currents across Europe, and her innovative brand of sentimental portraiture can be associated with Romanticism in several respects.

Born in Paris in 1755, Vigée Le Brun was the daughter of an artist. Her talent for drawing was fostered from an early age through her close contacts with artists such as Gabriel-François Doyen, Hubert Robert, and Joseph Vernet. Moreover, her marriage to the influential picture dealer Jean-Baptiste-Pierre Le Brun in 1776 gave her access to the most sought-after art works of the day. She became adept at the classical practice of imitation, frequently incorporating references to Raphael, Peter Paul Rubens, and Anthony Van Dyck into her work. Her gender was an obstacle to her becoming a member of the Royal Academy of Painting and Sculpture, but after royal intercession she was eventually received in 1783. Her aspirations as a history painter were never fully realized, and instead she settled for a productive and lucrative career as a portrait painter. Her success was a consequence of her abundant talents and considerable energy, qualities that were undoubtedly aided by her attractive appearance and easy charm.

Vigée Le Brun played on the imaginary possibilities of portraiture by incorporating elements of mythological and religious painting. She commonly depicted her aristocratic female clients as bacchantes, sibyls, and Saint Cecilias. One of her finest portraits was of Emma Hamilton as a sibyl (1791–92), which was closely modeled on Domenichino's *Cumaean Sibyl*. Inspired by the cult of antiquity, she eschewed contemporary costumes and draped her sitters in timeless robes, shawls, and garlands of flowers. Behind this lay the artist's fondness for dressing up and play-acting, which most notoriously manifested itself in her elaborate Greek dinner party, her "souper grec" of 1788.

While her paintings have a theatrical quality to them, they also reveal a yearning for simplicity. When she did have recourse to contemporary dress, she promoted the fashion for light gauzy fabrics and straw hats that had begun in England. Vigée Le Brun's interest in the natural extended to dramatic open-air backdrops. Particularly stunning is her portrait of the Countess Potocka in a grotto next to a waterfall, probably based on the Tivoli gardens (1791).

The artist also experimented with facial expression. A common feature was her use of the upturned or distant gaze, which was derived from baroque poses of religious ecstasy. Influenced by Jean-Baptiste Greuze, her work sees a transposition from the "rhetorical" passions in the tradition of Charles Le Brun to sentimental poses of reverie or contemplation.

Mothers and children are common subjects in Vigée Le Brun's oeuvre, reflecting the contemporary cult of motherhood. Two touching self-portraits (1786 and 1789) depict the artist in a close embrace with her adored daughter, Julie. Her portrait of Marie-Antoinette with her children, exhibited at the Salon of 1787, was an attempt to rehabilitate the queen in the eyes of the public by showing her as a devoted mother.

The events of 1789 were traumatic for the artist. She left France in the autumn of that year, and spent much of the next two decades traveling, visiting Italy, Austria, and Russia. Her *Souvenirs* (first published 1835–36) are one of the most vivid travelogues of the period. Entranced by the artistic treasures she encountered, the artist also revealed her sensitivity to natural beauty and local color, such as the ruins of the Roman forum and the marvels of the Bay of Naples.

Returning to France in 1802, Vigée Le Brun soon became restless again and went to England, a country that little impressed her. In contrast, she was intoxicated by the beauty of Switzerland and visited twice, in 1807 and 1808. In the *Souvenirs*, she casts herself as a Rousseau pilgrim, and writes of her own enthusiasm with a fine comic touch. In Switzerland she also turned to landscape painting, the least known part of her oeuvre. She visited Madame Anne-Louise-Germaine de Staël at Coppet and painted the author's portrait as the eponymous heroine of her novel *Corinne* (1807). This was an original variation on the theme of inspired genius, which the artist had already tackled in her portraits of Hubert Robert (1788) and the composer Giovanni Paisiello (1791).

Back in France, Vigée Le Brun continued to paint, yet there was no radical evolution in her style. After the Restoration, she founded a salon in Paris, which was a gathering place for survivors from the ancien régime, but she also welcomed young talents such as Honoré de Balzac, Paul Gavarni, and Horace Vernet. Her friendship with Antoine-Jean Gros also flourished. The last years of her life were spent peacefully at Louveciennes in the company of her nieces.

Vigée Le Brun was aware of her own worth, and she was delighted to be honored by academies throughout Europe. Her numerous and varied self-portraits display her as both talented and attractive. Moreover, the *Souvenirs* consciously evoke the traditional topoi of artists' biographies. With shrewd pragmatism and more than a trace of self-mockery, Vigée Le Brun was aware that other writers might not be disposed to paint a female artist in a positive light. Her robust practicality could not be more at odds with the alienated Romantic conception of the artist. Yet the *Souvenirs* are also tinged with melancholy. The artist's personal life was marred by tragedy: an unhappy marriage (she divorced in 1794), and her daughter's own disastrous marriage and early death. In her writing, Vigée Le Brun often comes across as a solitary figure. She believed that, as an artist, she possessed a hypersensitive physiological makeup, and this is reflected in her acute sensitivity to noise and her craving for tranquility. To an extent, her travels are represented as a period of exile, strongly marked by nostalgia for a bygone era, and darkened by the shadow of Revolution.

MELISSA PERCIVAL

Bibliography

Baillio, Joseph. *Elisabeth Louise Vigée-Lebrun (1755–1842)*. Exhibition catalog. Seattle: University of Washington Press, 1982.

Goodden, Angelica. *The Sweetness of Life: A Biography of Elisabeth Vigée-Lebrun*. London: André Deutsch, 1997.

Percival, Melissa. "The Expressive Heads of Elisabeth Vigée Le Brun," *Gazette des Beaux-Arts*. Forthcoming.

Radisich, Paula Rea. " 'Que peut définir les femmes?' Vigée-Lebrun's Portraits of an Artist," *Eighteenth-Century Studies* 25 (1992): 441–67.

Shaefer, Jean Owens. "The 'Souvenirs' of Elisabeth Vigée-Lebrun: The Self-Imaging of the Artist and the Woman," *International Journal of Women's Studies* 4, no. 1 (1981): 35–49.

Sheriff, Mary. *The Exceptional Woman: Elisabeth Vigée-Lebrun and the Cultural Politics of Art*. Chicago: University of Chicago Press, 1996.

Vigée-Lebrun, Elisabeth. *The Memoirs of Elisabeth Vigée-Le Brun*. Translated by Siân Evans. London: Camden Press, 1989.

———. *Souvenirs*. 2 vols. Edited by Claudine Herrmann. Paris: Des Femmes, 1984.

Website

http://www.batguano.com/vigee.html

VIGNY, ALFRED VICTOR, COMTE DE 1797–1863

French writer

"The time is out of joint." Alfred Victor, Comte de Vigny, who knew his Shakespeare well, must have shared Hamlet's feelings. His parents both belonged to the nobility, but as the revolutionary period gave way to the Napoleonic epoch, aristocracy was, morally as well as materially, more a burden than an advantage. Vigny's elderly father, an ailing veteran of the Seven Years War, did little more than look on disapprovingly at events, and his mother, a woman of strict principle who was already aged forty when her gifted son was born, could do little but inculcate a sense of duty. For his secondary schooling he (rather surprisingly) attended the Lycée Bonaparte in Paris, where English was on the curriculum. The restoration of Louis XVIII in 1814 appeared to offer the opportunity of starting a military career under the Bourbons, and Vigny's parents promptly purchased a commission for him in the aristocratic Compagnies Rouges of the Garde Royale. The sensitive seventeen-year-old had scarcely discovered that army life did not suit him when the bewildering events of the Hundred Days sent Louis XVIII into exile again, with Vigny loyally following, until Waterloo sealed Napoleon's fate. All this made a disconcerting start to Vigny's military career, and he left the army in 1827 with a deep sense of being unfulfilled.

By then Vigny had made contact with Victor Hugo, who was already recognized as a leader of the progressive party in literature, and begun publishing some of his own works in periodicals. His *Poèmes antiques et modernes* (1826; revised in 1829 and 1837) signaled the new direction in his life. Like Hugo and Alfred de Musset, Vigny was not content with a single literary form for the expression of his sensibility, and in fiction, drama and verse, his ambition was to participate in the reform of French literature through the adoption of foreign models. In 1822, and again in 1827–28, performances by English companies excited great interest in Shakespeare. His work had been known in France for nearly a century, but only partially and in versions, for example, by Jean-François Ducis, that had been thoroughly refashioned to suit French tastes. Now came a wave of what were at least conceived as more faithful translations and adaptations. Vigny contributed *Le More de Venise* (i.e. *Othello*) in 1829 and *Le Marchand de Venise* ten years later. In *Racine et Shakespeare* (1823) Stendhal had called for counterparts to Shakespeare's histories, and Vigny took up the challenge in 1831 with *La Maréchale d'Ancre*, which is based on events from the reign of Louis XIII. Vigny was more successful with *Chatterton* (1835), which presents the English eighteenth-century poet Thomas Chatterton as an exemplary figure.

The influence of Sir Walter Scott is clear in *Cinq-Mars* (1826), a romance that is set in early seventeenth-century France and relates a conspiracy by Louis XIII's favorite, the eponymous hero, against the Duc de Richelieu. The choice of topic invites interpretation as an attack on events leading to triumph of classicism under Louis XIV. In *Stello* (1832) Vigny takes three stories to develop the theme of the poet's lot that he was later to explore in *Chatterton*.

Alfred de Vigny. Reprinted courtesy of Bildarchiv.

Comprising three stories with ample connecting discussions, *Servitude et grandeur militaires* (1835) constitutes Vigny's major effort to make sense of his army life and of the demands of loyalty in a time when one regime followed another that was in turn soon swept away. Starting with the spectacle of a young officer who, as Vingy had done, is following the fleeing Bourbons at the start of the Hundred Days War, *Laurette, ou Le Cachet rouge* goes back to 1793 to explore not only the fate of a young author condemned for his indiscretion, but also the burden of responsibility on the shoulders of the sea-captain who has orders to execute him at an opportune moment. *La Veillée de Vincennes* shows soldiers under pressure when fire imperils the powder magazines of the fortress. The July Revolution of 1830 provides an striking opening for *La Vie et la Mort du Capitaine Renaud, ou La Canne de Jonc*, which then goes back in contemporary history to create, in a handful of vignettes, an incomparable portrait of Napoleon as a charismatic leader with feet of clay. It is a powerful warning against "séidisme" or, as Carlyle would call it just six years later, hero-worship. Great panoramas, such as the spectacle of the French fleet off Malta as the standard of the military knights is lowered for the last time, and details like the description of a castrato singing—with "the voice of a seraph issuing from a shriveled countenance"—are both realistic and symbolic, like all the experiences related by eye-witnesses in the three stories.

As well as showing the strains of military life, particularly that of officers of modest rank, under changing regimes, Vigny also argues that regular soldiers, as opposed to feudal hosts and conscript armies, form a race apart in modern society. Confined in barracks and subject to the obligations of obedience, their life style resembles that of monks. Among their chief merits is uncomplaining self-abnegation. This stoic theme is developed by Vigny in other contexts in his verse, of which a major collection appeared as *Les Destinées* posthumously in 1864.

Vigny was a philosophical, rather than a lyric poet, often presenting his ideas in long poems that are enlivened only by some striking central image. In *La Mort du loup* (*The Death of the Wolf*, for instance, the animal world is held up as an example of heroism with such success that some would argue that Vigny's explicit pointing of the moral is otiose, not to say patronizing. *Moïse* (*Moses*) takes the prophet to embody the anguish inevitably besetting the exceptional figure who aspires to be a leader. Also inspired by the Old Testament and within a fashionable Oriental setting, *La Colère de Samson* captures the rage and frustration that built up in Vigny as his emotional reserve was shattered in the course of unsatisfactory relationships with women throughout his life. Generally sounding high-minded rather than ringing with prophetic fervor, Vigny's sober and traditional poetic style was to be outmoded well before the end of the nineteenth century

CHRISTOPHER SMITH

Biography

Born on March 27, 1863 at Loches (Indre-et-Loire), into a noble family disaffected by the French Revolution. At Restoration, commissioned in 1814 in the aristocratic compagnies-rouges; to Ghent as part of escort for Louis XVIII. Served as army officer, mainly in garrisons, 1816–25. First verse in *Le Conservateur littéraire*, evidence of adherence to the Romantic group around Hugo, 1820; *Poèmes antiques et modernes* and the historical novel *Cinq-Mars* published, 1826. Translation of Shakespeare's *Othello* well-received at Comédie-Française, 1829. *Chatterton* and *Servitude et Grandeurs militaires* published, 1835. Elected to Académie-Française, 1845. Died in Paris on September 17, 1863. Posthumous publication of *Les Destinées*, a collection of Vigny's philosophical poems, 1864.

Bibliography

Barsan, Fernande. *Alfred de Vigny et la Comédie-Française*. Tübingen: Narr, 1984.
Castex, P. G., ed. *Relire les "Destinées" d'Alfred de Vigny*. Paris: SEES, 1980.
Doolittle, James. *Alfred de Vigny*. New York: Twayne, 1967.

A VINDICATION OF THE RIGHTS OF WOMAN 1792

Polemic by Mary Wollstonecraft

A Vindication of the Rights of Woman by the English writer Mary Wollstonecraft is widely and deservedly regarded as a touchstone of feminism: its argument for the treatment of women as rational human beings, who deserve the right to exercise virtue, stands as a landmark of rationalist advocacy for the rejection of dead traditions well in keeping with the radical transformations of society in the revolutionary age in which it was written.

A Vindication of the Rights of Woman is dedicated to Charles-Maurice de Talleyrand-Périgord, the anticlerical bishop who had participated in the drafting of the French constitution of 1789, and in September 1791 published *Rapport sur L'Instruction Publique, fait au nom du Comité de Constitution*, calling for a national system of free education. In the dedication, Wollstonecraft asks for his consideration of the rights of women within such a system, urging that "if [woman] be not prepared by education to become the companion of man, she will stop the progress of knowledge and virtue; for truth must be common to all."

In the thirteen chapters that followed, Wollstonecraft's consistent theme is that conventional education, which enforces subordination upon women and misogyny upon all, is the primary source of women's and society's misery. When she refers to education, she is not simply referring to formal instruction, but is concerned with what may be more broadly identified as socialization. Wollstonecraft believes that human character is not sex-specific: men and women alike have immortal souls, which, as the source of reason and the site of virtue, are not gendered. Character, she believed, takes its shape from the conditions under which individuals are formed. While there may be biological imperatives embedded in our bodily structures that determine important, and in some instances, unchangeable, aspects of our lives, socialization makes us human and, more to the point, makes us particular kinds of human beings. It was therefore imperative that children's education be carefully considered and properly conducted.

In Wollstonecraft's analysis, it is by virtue of our possession of reason and capability for virtue and knowledge that human beings naturally occupy a position of "pre-eminence over the brute creation." However, prejudices, tradition, convention, and "various adventitious circumstances," including hereditary honors, the unequal distribution of wealth, the elevation of fashion over virtue and power over reason, all contribute to a situation in which

> [t]he civilization of the bulk of the people of Europe is very partial; nay, it may be made a question, whether they have acquired any virtues in exchange for innocence, equivalent to the misery produced by the vices that have been plastered over unsightly ignorance, and the freedom which has been bartered for splendid slavery.

Under these conditions, Wollstonecraft believes that human beings were trained in tyranny, either to exercise it or to accept it. The results are, inevitably, the oppression and misery of the many, the luxurious self-indulgence of the few, and the moral corruption of all. Further, she believes that neither political reform nor revolution can ultimately result in the most necessary reform of all: changes in education, in the day-to-day practices that form human character. Such changes are necessary to allow the exercise of genuine reason in all social relations to take its natural priority over ignorance and sensuality.

While mankind in general was educated for tyranny, Wollstonecraft saw that women in particular were educated for dependence: her overriding complaint against women's education was that female members of the human race were trained just to be women. She found this exemplified by contemporaries she had earlier admired: Dr. John Gregory, author of *A Father's Legacy to His Daughters* (1774), who advised women to conform if they wished to be happy; and Jean-Jacques Rousseau, whose novel *Émile, ou l'Education* (1762) exemplified the idea that "women should glory in a weakness that allowed them mastery and sexual submission."

Wollstonecraft argues that education was socially constructed to keep women in a state of ignorance and subservience, with the result that women become nothing more than "gentle, domestic brutes," unable to function as reasoning human beings, subject to their own whims and the caprices of their husbands, incapable of fulfilling their maternal duty to rear children to be virtuous citizens. The insult added to this injury is that men, who have constructed and profited from the circumstances that turned women into brutes, blame women for their "natural" deficiencies. She writes, "Men complain, and with reason, of the follies and caprices of our sex, when they do not keenly satirise our head-strong passions and grovelling vices. Behold, I should answer, the natural effect of ignorance!"

Despite the abundance of evidence that she adduces, Wollstonecraft does not believe that the situation is immutable: her proposed solution to this admittedly dismal state of affairs is the fundamental reform of female education, designed with the explicit intention of forming women into fully dimensional human beings and citizens, with a vitally important stake in public and political life. Institutionally, she believes this will be most feasible through a nationally funded system of day schools that will reduce the inequalities based on parents' wealth, allow children to remain with their families throughout the years of their education, and allow educators to perform their duties without being dependent upon parents' goodwill for their livelihood. She concludes her argument with a plea, "Let woman share the rights and she will emulate the virtues of man; for she must grow more perfect when emancipated, or justify the authority that chains such a weak being to her duty."

It is clear that Wollstonecraft's attention was primarily directed toward the middle classes—the upper classes were hopelessly corrupted by their status and wealth and the lower classes by their lack of both—which limits the radical thrust of her analysis, and her discussion is more concerned with morals than with politics per se. Nonetheless, her advocacy of the rights of women to full humanity, to participation in civil society, and to rational discourse sets her apart from most of her more politically radical contemporaries and justifies her designation as the foremother of modern women's liberation.

ALISON SCOTT

Text

A Vindication of the Rights of Woman with Strictures on Political and Moral Subjects, 1792. Another edition was published the same year, with minor revisions.

Modern Editions

A Vindication of the Rights of Woman: An Authoritative Text, Backgrounds, the Wollstonecraft Debate, Criticism. 2d ed. Edited by Carol H. Poston. 1988.
A Vindication of the Rights of Woman. Rev. ed. Edited and with an introduction by Miriam Brody. 1992.

Bibliography

Kelly, Gary. *Revolutionary Feminism: The Mind and Career of Mary Wollstonecraft.* New York: St. Martin's Press, 1992.
McCann, Andrew. *Cultural Politics in the 1790s: Literature, Radicalism and the Public Sphere.* New York: St. Martin's Press, 1999.
Shapiro, Virginia. *A Vindication of Political Virtue: The Political Theory of Mary Wollstonecraft.* Chicago: University of Chicago Press, 1992.
Todd, Janet. *Mary Wollstonecraft: A Revolutionary Life.* London: Weidenfeld and Nicolson, 2000.

VIOLIN

The violin is an ancient instrument, but it was adapted during the eighteenth century to give it more power and range than the Stradivarius had offered. By about 1800, the neck of the instrument had been lengthened and the angle from the plane of the violin increased; the fingerboard was lengthened, the bridge was made higher and more arched, and stronger strings were produced. The bow was redesigned to give a much stiffer surface to the hair, and make the sound of the string louder and potentially both more percussive and more lyrical; it was also held more firmly. The chin rest was added by Louis Spohr about 1820, and the violin was now meant to be held tightly between chin and shoulder, so that the left hand, which had previously supported the instrument, was left free for demanding technical shifts, a pronounced vibrato, and very high notes. The strengthening of the instrument was partly intended to allow it to be heard in the increasingly large concert halls of the 1790s, but it was also the result of new musical demands made by composers for a greater variety of expressive sound and nuance.

Chief among the influential composer-performers of the late eighteenth century was Giovanni Battista Viotti, a disciple of the Italian school who settled in Paris in 1782 and produced a new fusion of French (operatic) and Italian (virtuosic) styles, in all essentials the "modern" style of playing: sustained lyricism and cantabile, rapid passagework, sudden crescendo and diminuendo, deep sonorities produced by high positions on low strings, and a great variety of bowstrokes. Viotti's influence on a whole generation of European composers and violinists was transmitted mainly through the concerto, the archetypal form for the performer as "hero." The fashion for groups of soloists (the Baroque concerto grosso of Johann Sebastian Bach and George Frideric Handel) died out almost completely, though its place was partly taken by the newly invented string quartet, itself dominated by the violin. Viotti's concerti were written for a solo performer conspicuously foregrounded against a relatively full symphony orchestra. While the basic format of the three-movement concerto (fast–slow–fast) remained standard from the seventeenth century through to the twentieth, the tendency was for the concerto to become much longer, much more difficult technically, and much more like some form of emotionally expressive statement, the instrument often appearing as dramatically embattled in its symphonic environment before (usually) achieving a triumphant unity with it. Viotti's lead was supplemented by Wolfgang Amadeus Mozart, who was trained as a violinist, and whose five violin concerti show increasing mastery and experimentation. His fifth concerto has a slow lyric introduction, an unusual contrapuntal slow movement, and a "Turkish" episode in the finale (a reminder of the taste for exoticism occasionally present in Romantic music). Ludwig van Beethoven's one large-scale concerto of 1806 was slow to achieve its now dominant position in the repertory, partly because—as with Mozart's concerti—though it is difficult it is not showy: its purpose is fundamentally symphonic rather than virtuosic, with simple material developed through a great range of emotional states and harmonic and rhythmic contrasts.

In the nineteenth century, the development of the instrument and its technique led to something of a split between composer-performers such as Niccolò Paganini, whose astonishing technical facility produced pieces of flamboyant showmanship (such as the concerti and the twenty-four caprices of 1820), and "pure" composers who regarded such tricks as solos on the G string, double-stopping in tenths, or trilling in harmonics as trivial and who sought a more organic form of musical expression, in which the soloist, while highlighted, was not simply a dominant hero posturing above a quiescent orchestra. The virtuoso tradition did not die out: Paganini toured Europe in the 1830s and Henry Vieuxtemps, Henryk Wieniawski, and Eugène Ysaÿe likewise

continued to perform their own pyrotechnic showpieces. But the separation of the roles of composer and performer produced the more interesting work. Felix Mendelssohn's highly innovative concerto of 1844, with its abandonment of the traditional exposition and its bridges between movements, was written in consultation with a leading performer, Ferdinand David. It also had a written-out cadenza, placed centrally in the first movement, rather than offering the performer a space to show off technical skill. (Johannes Brahms wrote the last major concerto in which the cadenza was to be supplied by the performer.) Beethoven's concerto was revived by the violinist Joseph Joachim, with Mendelssohn conducting, and many of the major composers of the late nineteenth century wrote their concerti either for, or in consultation with, Joachim, indicating a careful consideration by the nonspecialist composer of the potentialities of the instrument. There were also signs of an intense condensation of effort in the period: while Viotti wrote twenty-nine concerti for the violin, Mozart produced only five authenticated examples, Franz Joseph Haydn four, and the majority of Romantic composers (Beethoven, Johannes Brahms, Antonìn Dvoràk, Edward Elgar, Mendelssohn, Robert Schumann, Jean Sibelius, and Pyotr Ilich Tchaikovsky) put all their energies into one (major) concerto apiece. The Romantic concerto lasts, on average, about three times as long as a concerto from a century earlier. A similar concentration is visible in the sonata for violin and piano, a more intimate form of the expressive range of the concerto: Mozart produced about thirty, Beethoven ten, Schumann two, Brahms three, and Elgar one. Composers also began to experiment with freer structures and combinations in which the development of material could take explicitly emotional forms: romances, fantasies, rhapsodies, and "poems."

The instrument that is most definitively Romantic is unquestionably the piano, with its huge power and range; it inspired music of intense individual exploration as no other instrument had done before. Nonetheless, the violin, with its agility, brilliance, and richness, had a special place in the hierarchy of instruments. In his *Méthode de Violon* (*Method of the Violin*, 1858), Charles Auguste de Bériot, one of the foremost composer-violinists of the French school, noted that "the fever of technique which, in the last years, has seized the violin, has often diverted it from its true mission, that of imitating the human voice, a noble mission which has earned for the violin the glory of being called the King of instruments."

PAUL BAINES

Bibliography

Einstein, A. *Music in the Romantic Era.* London: Dent, 1947.

Heron-Allen, E. *Violin-Making as It Was, and Is.* London: Lock & Co., 1884.

Longyear, R. M. *Nineteenth-Century Romanticism in Music.* Englewood Cliffs, N.J.: Prentice-Hall, 1969.

Stowell, Robin. *Beethoven: Violin Concerto.* Cambridge: Cambridge University Press, 1998.

Swalin, B. F. *The Violin Concerto: A Study in German Romanticism.* Chapel Hill: University of North Carolina Press, 1941.

Van der Straeten, E. *The History of the Violin.* London: Cassell & Co., 1933.

White, C. *From Vivaldi to Viotti: A History of the Early Classical Violin Concerto.* Philadelphia: Gordon and Brach, 1992.

VIOLIN CONCERTO, OP. 64

Concerto by Jakob Ludwig Felix Mendelssohn-Bartholdy

Felix Mendelssohn's final work for violin and orchestra, in a genre that he cultivated his entire life, is one of the most substantive and imaginative examples of its kind, retaining pride of place among a handful of others (those of Ludwig van Beethoven, Johannes Brahms, and Pyotr Ilich Tchaikovsky) as most loved and often performed in the active repertories of the past 150 years. Conceived as early as 1838, the concerto was intended for the composer's close friend Ferdinand David, concertmaster of the Gewandhaus Orchestra in Leipzig, where Mendelssohn exerted a profound and lasting influence. It was completed in 1844 and had its premiere in Leipzig on March 13, 1845. Orchestral parts and a violin and piano score were published in that year, but a complete edition appeared only posthumously, in 1862. The manuscript, long thought missing from the Deutsche Staatsbibliothek in Berlin, was rediscovered in 1988 in Kraków by Luigi Alberto Bianchi, where it remains today, along with a copy with corrections originally intended for the printers.

Mendelssohn began writing concertos early on, completing at least eight between 1822 and 1844 for combinations of the two instruments with which he was most familiar—violin and piano. Among them is an accomplished work for violin and string orchestra written at the age of fourteen, and it appears that near the end of his life, upon hearing the virtuoso Alfredo Piatti, he may also have sketched a concerto for violoncello and orchestra. Mendelssohn was wary of subjugating musical style to considerations of instrumental virtuosity and found concerto writing to be a challenge. However, it had become increasingly difficult to circumvent such considerations in the decades following Beethoven's superb concerto of 1806, written for the (somewhat lapsed) virtuoso Franz Clement. Although a virtuoso pianist and fine string player, Mendelssohn could not do for his violin concerto what Ferdinand David and others might. Hence the unfolding drama of nineteenth-century instrumental virtuosity played a part in his five-year struggle to complete the work (the outlines of which may be perceived in correspondence with David and others, and through subsequent source and sketch studies). The quandaries inherent in writing a concerto (as opposed to a symphony or a solo sonata form) were both abstract and socio-musical. The difficulty lay in the need to reconcile the formal requirements of the genre (double, divided, and/or novel expositions, different notions of development, recapitulation, transitions) with the proclivities of newly popular performers and concomitant public expectations. Mendelssohn had struck a typically elegant balance in his solo piano concertos, (op. 25, 1831; and op. 40, 1837), by making sophisticated concessions to contemporary keyboard virtuosity (thundering octaves in the first concerto, in the manner of Frédéric Kalkbrenner, of whom Mendelssohn was not terribly fond, and ingenious "three-hand" textures deriving from the style of Sigismund Fortuné François Thalberg in the second). However, in the violin concerto, and most especially in the wake of Niccolò Paganini, whose successes of the preceding decade had been as much programmatic as musical, Mendelssohn was deeply indebted to the advice gained over several years from Ferdinand David. Robert Alexander Schumann had been decrying for some time in the *Neue Zeitschrift* that the common currency of instrumental writing was being debased, and Mendelssohn's careful, balanced exploitation of the violin's expanded capabilities was a marvel of its time. More important, however, is that the idiomatic and grateful solo writing serve to illuminate the formal and stylistic genius of the concerto.

Cast in a traditional three-movement format, the work begins most unconventionally: soloist and orchestra concurrently usher in an uncommon, even foreboding, "shared" exposition of the minor modality. Indeed, the opening is an "antiexposition" of sorts, conveying to the listener the sensation of having entered into something already underway. Mendelssohn's placement of the solo cadenza before the recapitulation of the first movement is conspicuous as well—doubly so when one realizes that its conclusion mirrors the perceptual ambiguities of the concerto's opening. Once again, the listener is drawn into something already in progress: in this case, the recapitulation, as opposed to the exposition (as may be observed in the soloist's extended arpeggiation bridging the cadenza recapitulation). The oft-noted and imaginative elision of first and second movements had been anticipated in both of Mendelssohn's solo piano concertos (and also in the earlier works of Wolfgang Amadeus Mozart and Carl Maria von Weber): in this case a single note in the bassoon is held over in the final cadence, the first of several voices in a thin scaffolding framing the modulation from E minor to C major, the key of the second movement. In the "B" section of the second movement, essentially a *Lied ohne Worte*, Mendelssohn turned to Paganini for a textural rather than harmonic scaffolding. In order to elaborate contrasting material, the accompanimental tremolos divided between first and second strings of the orchestra migrate to the soloist, who spins them out simultaneously with the new theme in the manner of Paganini's G-Minor Caprice (1805). In lieu of connecting the second and third movements Mendelssohn pushed further, creating a reflective interlude for soloist and orchestra, recalling first- and second-movement materials and heightening curiosity about the work's conclusion. And perhaps with William Shakespeare's forest in mind, Mendelssohn experimented even further by writing eight measures of introduction to the joyous sonata-rondo finale, his mature and virtuosic exploration of the kinetic instrumental exuberance so clearly manifest twenty years earlier in the Octet and *Midsummer Night's Dream*.

This violin concerto was clearly the triumph of Mendelssohn's sustained effort in writing concertos. To solve the inherent formal problems, to reconcile his deeply classical training with the exigencies of a public clamoring for new kinds of musical spectacle, to write brilliantly and beautifully for an essentially one-voiced instrument whose sound was neither as piercing nor as powerful as the emerging piano: all this was to succeed in doing something requiring acute perception. Ferdinand David, having written five violin concertos himself and having advised Mendelssohn in detail about the work he premiered in 1845, was horrified to find himself carrying the composer's coffin only two years later.

STEPHEN ZANK

Work

Felix Mendelssohn Bartholdys Werke. Durchgesehene Ausgabe von Julius Rietz. Serie 4, no. 18. Concert, Op. 64. 1874–77. Reprinted London: Gregg International, 1968.

Bibliography

Bianchi, Luigi Alberto, and Franco Sciannameo, eds. *Mendelssohn's Violin Concerto in E Minor, Op. 64: A Facsimile*. New York: Garland, 1991.

Finson, John and R. Larry Todd, eds. *Mendelssohn and Schumann*. Durham, N.C.: Duke University Press, 1984.

Kerman, Joseph. *Concerto Conversations*. Cambridge, Mass.: Harvard University Press, 1999.

Köhler, Karl-Heinz, Eveline Bartlitz, and R. Larry Todd. "Felix Mendelssohn." In *The New Grove Early Romantic Masters*, vol. 2. London: W. W. Norton, 1985.

Krautwurst, Franz. "Felix Mendelssohn-Bartholdy als Bratschist." In *Gedenkschrift Hermann Beck*. Edited by Hermann Dechant and Wolfgang Sieber. Laaber: Laaber Verlag, 1982.

Krummacher, Friedhelm. "Virtuosität und Komposition im Violinkonzert: Problème der Gattung zwischen Beethoven und Brahms" *Neue Zeitschrift für Musik* 135, no. 10 (1974): 604–13.

Lang, Paul Henry, ed. *The Concerto, 1800–1900*. New York: W. W. Norton, 1969.

Schumacher, Gerhard. "Im Konzertsaal gehört: Felix Mendelssohn Bartholdy: Konzert für Violine und Streichorchester d-Moll," *Neue Zeitschrift für Musik* 145, no. 9 (1984): 25–28.

Swalin, Benjamin. *The Violin Concerto: A Study in German Romanticism*. Chapel Hill: University of North Carolina Press.

Todd, R. Larry. "An Unfinished Piano Concerto by Mendelssohn." *Musical Quarterly* 48, no. 1 (1982): 80–101.

———, ed. *Mendelssohn and His World*. Princeton, N.J.: Princeton University Press, 1991.

VIOLLET-LE-DUC, EUGÈNE EMMANUEL, 1814–1879

French architect

The principal architect of France's "Gothic Revival," Eugène Emmanuel Viollet-le-Duc, was the official restorer of France's medieval architectural splendors, as imagined and celebrated by Romantic authors including Victor Hugo and Prosper Mérimée. Although modern architectural critics such as Sir John Summerson see him, along with Leon Battista Alberti, as one of the "two supremely eminent theorists in the history of European architecture" he is more often (dis-)credited with representing, in iron and stone, French Romanticism's highly subjective view of the Middle Ages. His great successes, both as the protégé of Mérimée (inspector-general of ancient buildings and author of *Carmen*) and as the preferred architect of Napoleon III and the Empress Eugénie, suggest that he knew how to manipulate the architectural zeitgeist. Viollet-Le-Duc's talent for restoring medieval monuments (including cathedrals, castles, and fortified towns such as Carcassonne) brought him state and imperial sponsorships, medals and honors of all kinds, and commissions throughout France and beyond.

When Viollet-le-Duc was seventeen, Victor Hugo's *Notre-Dame de Paris* (*The Hunchback of Notre Dame*, 1831) appeared, which lamented the dilapidation that France's medieval monuments suffered due to neglect, revolutions, and incompetent "renovation" by French architects obeying the dictates of neoclassical "good taste." With his restoration of Notre Dame, and his design and reconstruction of the cathedral's spire (the absence of which had scandalized Hugo), Viollet-le-Duc helped reinstate the prestige of France's medieval architecture, in accordance with the tenets of Romanticism, a movement that extolled medievalism.

After conducting extensive research into the principles and forms of the French medieval Gothic style, Viollet-le-Duc chose as his ideal the middle-pointed style of the thirteenth century, the style of Reims, Amiens, Westminster Abbey. If the style was anachronistic in certain structures, or if (as in his restoration of the Chateau of Pierrefonds for Napoleon III) the style turned a medieval fortress into a Renaissance-style stately home, Viollet-le-Duc had an answer prepared for any critics. In the entry "Restoration" in his *Dictionnaire raisonné de l'architecture française du XIe au XVIe siècle*, he wrote, "To restore a building is not to preserve it, to repair or rebuild it, but to bring it back to a state of completion such as may never have existed at any given moment." This statement demonstrates Viollet-le-Duc's Romantic mindset; its mixture of hyperbole and oxymoron illustrates a commitment to architecture as a creative art, and an unwavering faith in the self and the self's artistic endeavors.

But the Romantic was only one aspect of Viollet-le-Duc, as Nikolaus Pevsner recognizes when he compares the Frenchman's vision of nineteenth-century Gothic to that offered by John Ruskin. For Pevsner, Viollet-le-Duc was "rational," whereas Ruskin was "emotional." His rationality may be seen in his theory of Gothic architecture. The *Dictionnaire raisonné* establishes clearly, for instance, the functionalism of medieval building techniques, showing that the arches and tracery of Gothic cathedrals were solutions to architectural problems, rather than mere decorative additions. Viollet-le-Duc was an active restorer, too busy to complete all the commissions he was offered. Ruskin was contemplative, a much more eloquent writer, and a literary critic of architecture, capable of saying that "Restoration . . . means the most total destruction which a building can suffer." For Viollet-le-Duc, however, restoration was a means of improving upon the past. Despite his familiarity with, and appreciation of, medieval architecture, Viollet-le-Duc did not hesitate to lengthen the nave of Clermont-Ferrand Cathedral nor construct for it an anachronistic thirteenth-century west front it had never possessed. His view of Gothic as offering a logic of rational construction thus overcame any desire for a pure and unified reconstruction of the past.

Viollet-le-Duc's updating of medieval structures is most striking in the "restored" chateau of Pierrefonds. After restoring the fourteenth-century castle's moat, drawbridge, towers, and double sentry walks, Viollet-le-Duc installed emplacements for cannons, and built a series of small defensive turrets outside the perimeter wall. Thus isolated, they could have served no practical function in medieval warfare. The castle's interior, with its Hall of the Valiant Knights (with statues of Charlemagne, Roland, and other legendary medieval figures); a spectacular staircase; and balustrades decorated with mythical beasts proclaims the influence of Romantic authors such as Alexandre Dumas père, Victer Hugo, and Sir Walter Scott.

A. W. Halsall

Biography

Born in Paris, January 14, 1814. Attended the Morin Institute, Fontenay-aux-Roses, and the Collège Bourbon, 1825–30. Served with architects Jean-Marie Huvé and Achille Leclère, 1830–31. Traveled throughout France: Normandy, Provence, the Loire Valley, and elsewhere, 1832–35. Spent sixteen months in Italy studying architecture, 1836–37. Placed, by his friend Prosper Mérimée, in charge of the restoration of the Abbey Church of Vézelay, 1839; restoration continued until 1859. Appointed second inspector of restorations at Paris's Sainte-Chapelle, 1840. Won a competition, with Jean-Baptiste Lassus, to restore Notre Dame in Paris, 1844. (Restoration stretched from 1845 to 1865.) Appointed head of the French Office of Historic Monuments, 1846. Member of the Commission for Religious Art and Buildings, the committee supervising the restoration of medieval buildings, 1848. Restorations included the Abbey of Saint Denis (1848–79); Amiens Cathedral (1850–75); the fortifications at Carcassonne (1852–79); the Synodal Palace, Sens (1855–65); the ramparts at Avignon (1859–68); the site of Reims Cathedral (1861–73), and others. Wrote and published his *Dictionnaire raisonné de l'architecture française du XIe au XVIe siècle*, 1854–68, and his *Dictionnaire raisonné du mobilier français de l'époque carolingienne à la Renaissance*, 1858–75. Reconstructed, for Louis Napoleon/Napoleon III, the chateau of Pierrefonds, 1858–70. Published *Entretiens sur l'architecture*, 1860–72. Published *L'Art russe*, 1877. Published *La Décoration appliquée aux édifices*, 1879. Died in Lausanne, Switzerland, September 17, 1879.

Bibliography

Cook, Edward Tyas, and Alexander Wedderburn, eds. *The Works of John Ruskin.* 39 vols. London: G. Allen; New York: Longmans, Green and co, 1903–12. (Library of Congress) Ruskin's *The Seven Lamps of Architecture* is volume 7 of this edition.

Farrant, Penelope, ed. *Eugène Emmanuel Viollet-Le-Duc 1814–1879.* London: Academy Editions, 1980.

Gout, Paul. *Viollet-Le-Duc, sa vie, son oeuvre, sa doctrine.* Paris: Champion, 1914.

Pevsner, Nikolaus. *Ruskin and Viollet-Le-Duc: Englishness and Frenchness in the Appreciation of Gothic Architecture.* London: Thames and Hudson, 1969.

Viollet-Le Duc, Eugène Emmanuel. *Dictionnaire raisonné du mobilier français de l'époque carolingienne à la Renaissance.* Paris: A. Morel, 1975.

———. *The Foundations of Architecture: Selections from the Dictionnaire raisonne.* Translated by Kenneth D. Whitehead, introduction by Barry Bergdoll. New York: George Braziller, 1990.

VIOTTI, GIOVANNI BATTISTA 1755–1824

Italian violinist and composer

Giovanni Battista Viotti stands at the end of the era of the classical style of violin playing, and at the beginning of the transition to the Romantic style. Inheriting a crisp Italian virtuoso technique, he was noted for introducing a powerful element of sensuous lyricism to violin performance. Charismatic both as performer and individual, admired for his personal idealism and sensitivity, his career was divided between patronage and independence; displaced by political events in both France and England, he died humbled and embittered by economic failure.

Viotti was born at Fontanetto da Po in Piedmont on May 12, 1755, the son of a blacksmith who played the horn. He was a child prodigy, and at the age of eleven he was taken to Turin by the Marchesa di Voghera, who housed and educated him. From 1770 he was taught by Gaetano Pugnani, himself the inheritor of the Italian virtuoso tradition of Arcangelo Corelli and Giuseppe Tartini. In 1775, Viotti began playing in the orchestra of the Royal Chapel at Turin, but in 1780 he and Pugnani set out on a concert tour around northern Europe; he then made his own way to Paris, making a public debut at the Concert Spirituel on March 17, 1782. He was an instant and sensational success. He displayed prodigious technical assurance and bravura: he held the violin firmly under the chin, giving greater freedom to the left hand for movement, high positions, double-stopping, and the like. He also produced remarkable strength and power of tone, and an emotive singing style; his sonorous adagio playing, especially on the low G string, coordinated perfectly with the extra power and resonance being given to the violin by makers of the period, though Viotti himself played a Stradivarius, perhaps adapted (as most such instruments were). He had a great variety of touch, especially on the bow; sudden, attacking bowstrokes were a notable feature of his performance style, as was the so-called Viotti-stroke, a form of slurred staccato. Francois Tourte, who created what is essentially the modern, powerful bow, is said to have taken advice from Viotti on its design.

After eighteen months of public performances, Viotti took a number of court appointments, working principally for Marie Antoinette at Versailles. In 1788 he began a second successful career as manager of a new theater. In 1792 Viotti decamped to London to avoid the repercussions of the French Revolution, and returned to the concert platform as soloist. He performed successfully for two seasons of the impresario Johann Peter Salo-

Portrait of Giovanni Battista Viotti. Reprinted courtesy of AKG.

mon's series of concerts and engaged in various theatrical ventures. In 1794 the London *Times* signaled Viotti's undiminished virtues, noting that he "astonishes the hearer; but he does something infinitely better—he awakens emotion, gives a soul to sound, and leads the passions captive." He often played privately for aristocrats and wealthy patrons, including the Prince of Wales. In 1798 he was expelled from Britain on suspicion of Jacobin activity, a charge he vigorously denied in a brief autobiographical memoir written that year. About two years later he returned to London as a wine dealer, though he continued to publish his compositions and to play in private for friends: as late as 1818 his talent appeared undiminished. His business, however, failed in that year, leaving him greatly in debt. After struggling to start a career as director of the Paris Opera, he returned to London and died there in March 1824 at the home of his friend George William Chinnery. Chinnery's wife had lent Viotti money he could not repay, and she was the main beneficiary of his somewhat bitter and regretful will.

Viotti wrote a number of chamber works, but his main efforts were always directed toward the violin as a concerto instrument. The twenty-nine violin concertos were mostly written before 1800, nineteen of them in Paris and the remainder in London

(Concerto No. 23 in G was given the subtitle "John Bull" to signal Viotti's sense of his new audience). They have certain characteristics in common, such as the traditional use of a three-movement, fast–slow–fast structure. The first movements generally open with a brisk, large-scale symphonic tutti, though the weighty adagio introduction to Concerto No. 16 in E Minor is a sign of Viotti's developing formal inventiveness. The rapid brilliance associated with Viotti's Italian inheritance is evident in fast runs, prominent trills, double stopping in octaves, leaps across strings, and use of very high notes; but such passage work is blended with a lyrical and melodic inventiveness. While orchestra and violin cooperate elegantly, the violin performing an agile dance above a placid and ordered accompaniment, there are often dark chromatic moments and unexpected changes of mood. The slow movements often exploit the violin's talent for imitation of the human voice, with light, susurrous accompaniments. The solo line that opens the adagio of Concerto No. 22 in A Minor sounds to begin with like an operatic aria, though it is soon varied beyond the scope of the voice. The corresponding movement in Concerto No. 23 in G Major stays even closer to an operatic model, the solo line consisting of a fragile, lyrical elegy of little technical difficulty over a hymn-like orchestral texture. The final movements are often dance-like, sometimes with exotic or folk elements, and sometimes driven by a jumpy, demonic anxiety (especially in the finales of Concertos 16 and 22). The flamboyant display power of the soloist as hero, a key element of much Romantic writing for the violin, is rendered emotionally poignant by a nervous, sometimes stormy, expressiveness. Viotti's orchestration in the London concerti is relatively full, often with prominent horns and woodwinds, and the symphonic scope of the orchestra as a whole was a notable and popular feature of his concerti. The later concertos are also more experimental and forward-looking in form, with more sense of organic connection between movements.

Viotti was not in the public eye as a performer for very long, nor did he teach many students directly. But the stylistic force and depth of his playing was much reported and quickly became a pervasive ideal for performers; it was embodied in several violin methods of the nineteenth century, and the concerti were widely published and arranged. Viotti's performance style outlived the greater technical showmanship of Niccolò Paganini's example in the 1820s. His influence on other composers was also strong: Wolfgang Amadeus Mozart added trumpet and timpani parts to Viotti's Concerto No. 16 in A Major, and Concerto No. 22, premièred in 1803, was one of Ludwig van Beethoven's models for his own single concerto of 1806. When Joseph Joachim, the dominant violinist of the later nineteenth century, revived the latter concerto, Johannes Brahms, who wrote one major concerto and a double concerto for violin and cello, told Clara Schumann that it was a *Prachtstuck*—that is, a masterpiece.

PAUL BAINES

Biography

Born in Fontanetto da Po, Piedmont, Italy, May 12, 1755. Taken to Turin, 1766, studied under Pugnani, 1770. Paris debut, 1782. Director of Theatre de Monsieur, 1788. Fled to London, 1792, expelled from there 1798, but returned in 1800 as a wine merchant. Failure of wine business, 1818. Director of Paris Opera, 1819. Returned to London, 1823. Died in London, March 1824.

Bibliography

Giazotto, Remo. *Giovan Battista Viotti*. Milan: Bocca, 1956.

Pougin, Arthur. *Viotti et l'ecole moderne de violon*. Paris, Bruxelles, 1888.

Schwarz, Boris. "Beethoven and the French Violin School," *Musical Quarterly* 44 (1958): 431.

White, Chappell. *From Vivaldi to Viotti: A History of the Early Classical Concerto*. Philadelphia: Gordon and Breach, 1992.

VIRTUOSO

Exceptional speed and agility have been desirable attributes for musicians throughout history; in the first half of the nineteenth century, these qualities were accorded central importance. Owing to a number of concurrent trends in society and the arts, virtuosity enjoyed a heyday, particularly between the July Revolution of 1830 in France and the Revolutions of 1848 throughout Europe.

Contributing to the development of virtuosity were at least four trends, the most important of which was the rise of public concerts. Concerts that were not restricted to the nobility but to which anyone could gain access by paying an admission fee were a rarity before 1700 and still a novelty before 1750. But as the power of the aristocracy weakened and a new moneyed bourgeoisie began to exert social influence, the institution became much more prevalent. By the early nineteenth century, public concerts had replaced aristocratic salons as the most important venues for new music. To support this new institution, municipal governments as well as instrument manufacturers built concert halls of varying sizes in the major cities. It was these halls that provided traveling virtuosos with places to perform before the increasingly numerous crowds of middle-class concertgoers.

Concurrent with the rise of public concerts were improvements in transportation that allowed virtuosos to travel from city to city in search of new audiences. When Wolfgang Amadeus Mozart toured Europe as a child in the 1760s, his family endured long and dangerous journeys by coach, staying at each destination for months at a time. By the 1840s, Franz Liszt and his contemporaries were able to travel by steamship and railway, allowing them to cover greater distances and move more frequently. By midcentury it even became practical (if not especially comfortable) for performers like soprano Jenny Lind and pianist Sigismund Thalberg to travel to the United States to take advantage of American wealth.

The third essential ingredient of the rise of virtuosity was brought about by the Industrial Revolution in the form of significant technological improvements to musical instruments. The piano in particular benefited from these innovations, as an increased compass, steel strings, felt hammers, the double-escapement action, and the cast-iron frame made it an instrument of unprecedented power and subtlety. The woodwind instruments were completely overhauled in the first half of the century, while the addition of valves turned the trumpet from a relatively limited military instrument to an instrument capable of playing with great agility in any key.

Finally, the Romantics glorified genius and personal expression, granting special status to artists such as Lord Byron and Ludwig van Beethoven, whose Promethean struggles epitomized the human grappling with personal weakness or insurmountable obstacles. The ability of the virtuoso to overcome technical difficulties in a superhuman manner made him a powerful symbol for the Romantic era.

The archetype of the Romantic virtuoso was the Italian violinist Niccolò Paganini. Though known at least locally as a consummate master of his instrument in his youth, it was not until the final decades of his life that he achieved international stardom. He cultivated a set of dazzling technical skills, including left-hand pizzicato, playing on one string, double stops, artificial harmonics, and extreme speed, that were simultaneously thrilling to audiences and suspect to musicians of the classical school. A life of debauchery and health problems left him pale and emaciated, while rumors abounded about a purported prison term for murder and a secret pact with the devil, combining to create a Romantic mystique that only enhanced his reputation for superhuman technical feats and inflated ticket prices wherever he played.

Paganini traveled extensively throughout Europe, but it was in Paris that he enjoyed his greatest triumphs. In a series of concerts in 1831 and 1832 he capitalized on an unparalleled public appetite for music and extensive press coverage to create a furor unmatched in that city. Most important, he made himself known to the large and thriving community of musicians there, touching off a revolution in musical taste and technique. Liszt was one of many musicians who set out to emulate him by transferring his technical innovations to the piano. The twenty-year-old Hungarian had been resident in Paris since the age of twelve and had enjoyed a reputation as one of the city's leading performers. The inspiration of Paganini, however, caused him to work feverishly to revamp his technique, and in short order Liszt became the outstanding pianist of his generation.

Like Paganini, Liszt traveled extensively throughout the continent, attracting attention through his brilliance as well as his scandalous romantic liaisons. When he visited Berlin in 1842, the hysteria was so intense that journalists coined the term *Lisztomania* to describe the phenomenon. He toured almost constantly from 1837 to 1847, at which point he left the concert stage, never to return to the virtuoso role in the remaining four decades of his life. So significant was this retirement that Carl Dahlhaus dates the end of the virtuoso era at September 1847, when Liszt played his last public concert.

Crucial to Romantic virtuosity, with its implications of both technique and style, is the aspect of competition. Paganini engaged in a famous musical duel with Charles Lafont in Milan in 1816, while Liszt took on Thalberg in an even more famous duel in 1837. Their rivalry, which was discussed in salons and newspapers throughout the winter, was a clash of two opposing styles of pianism. Both men played with breathtaking technical skill, but whereas Liszt thundered noisily (some said tastelessly) and gesticulated wildly, Thalberg exuded perfect repose and emphasized the melodic potential of the instrument. Contemporary reviews called the showdown in Princess Belgiojoso's salon a draw, but history has favored the rough vitality of Liszt over the elegant refinement of Thalberg.

If music provides the most obvious paradigm of Romantic virtuosity, it would be misleading to ignore the trend in other fields. Paul Metzner has argued that the drive to excel through public, self-aggrandizing displays of technical skill was manifested in a surprising array of professions during the Age of Revolution. He examines this phenomenon in the fields of chess, cooking, crime detection, music, and automaton-building, concluding that these diverse manifestations of virtuosity resulted from a proliferation of public spaces, an appreciation in the value of practical knowledge, and a dissemination of the self-centered worldview.

E. Douglas Bomberger

Bibliography

Bernstein, Susan. *Virtuosity of the Nineteenth Century: Performing Music and Language in Heine, Liszt, and Baudelaire.* Stanford, Calif.: Stanford University Press, 1998.

Bomberger, E. Douglas. "The Thalberg Effect: Playing the Violin on the Piano," *Musical Quarterly* 75 (1991): 198–208.

Dahlhaus, Carl. "Virtuosity and Interpretation," in *Nineteenth-Century Music.* Trans. J. Bradford Robinson. Berkeley and Los Angeles: University of California Press, 1989.

Metzner, Paul. *Crescendo of the Virtuoso: Spectacle, Skill, and Self-Promotion in Paris during the Age of Revolution.* Berkeley and Los Angeles: University of California Press, 1998.

Peckham, Morse. *The Romantic Virtuoso.* Hanover, N.H.: Wesleyan University Press, 1995.

Penesco, Anne, ed. *Défense et illustration de la virtuosité.* Lyon: Presses universitaires de Lyon, 1997.

Walker, Alan. *Franz Liszt.* Rev. edn, 3 vols. Ithaca, N.Y.: Cornell University Press, 1987–97.

VOLKSGEIST

The term *Volksgeist*, meaning "national spirit," was coined by Johann Gottfried von Herder, "the father of modern nationalism," who believed every nation (*Volk*) to be endowed with its own idiosyncratic spirit (*Geist*), an innate God-given character, which can be made to flourish through national culture and education. Herder viewed each nation as an organic whole bound together by a mother tongue and a community of blood ties (*Blutsgemeinschaft*), and depending on a sovereign nation-state for the realization of its potential. As a consequence, Herder rejected the German nation's political fragmentation at the end of the eighteenth century, when the German people were scattered across eighteen hundred disparate states, kingdoms, and municipalities—a situation that has come to be known as German Particularism (*deutscher Partikularismus*) and which was responsible for Germany's idiosyncratic process of unification (*deutscher Sonderweg*). He dismissed the cosmopolitan worldview advocated by the Enlightenment as unnatural, and condemned Frederick the Great's embrace of French influences on Prussia. At the same time, he celebrated the diversity of cultures and languages pervading the earth, convinced that cultural and political autonomy of nations would guarantee world peace. In his tripartite function as philosopher, anthropologist, and theologian, he viewed separate nations as the natural division of the human race and their languages as their distinctive and sacred possession, the vital medium of the nation's soul.

Despite this emphasis on the group, Herder pointed to individuation as the prerequisite of conscientious and critical citizenship and political autonomy. He maintained that the individual had to reach beyond the state of a mere thinking being (*Besonnenheit*) and achieve a position of conscious awareness (*Besinnung*) through socially orientated education, which would enable him to unfold his genetic makeup and appreciate his relation to society and the universe as a whole. To do so, Herder believed that the working people (*Volk der Bürger*) had to undergo an instructional phase at the hands of the intelligentsia (*Volk der Gelehrsamkeit*), through which they would become mindful of their national history and cultural heritage, thus reaching a level

of insight that would lead them to overcome their present state of degradation and guarantee self-determination and self-perfection. Once this process had been achieved, the intellectual elite would surrender their leadership and make way for the realization of the *Volksgeist* in democracy and the fulfillment of its own humanity (*Humanität*), which he considered to be the telos (ultimate goal) of every nation. This goal could only be reached by a combination of education and intuition as a means of cultivating national identity.

While the German Romantics embraced Herder's view of the German nation and its history, in particular his rehabilitation of the Middle Ages, and considered themselves fit to take on the mission of the intellectuals, they soon deviated from Herder's egalitarian perspective. Men like Adam Müller and Novalis elevated medieval society to the embodiment of an integral national character based on religious piety and reinforced by the *Ständeordnung* (system of estates) and feudal society. Rather than reject all leadership, they celebrated the aristocratic ruler as a benevolent patriarch and obedience as the single guarantor of social stability, thus discrediting Herder's positive notion of the family as a blueprint for social order. As Müller posited, "The secret government lies in obedience; the soul's craving for elevation in voluntary surrender; freedom in complete devotion to the fatherland."

German Romanticism's understanding of *Volksgeist* was furthermore marred by patriotic militarism based on the experience of French oppression and the Napoleonic Wars. The *Völkerschlacht* (Battle of Nations) of Leipzig in October 1813, in which volunteers from the minor German states, together with the Prussian, Austrian, and Russian armies, brought about a decisive victory over Napoleon, and became a symbol of the unified forces of German nationalism and the individual's sacrifice for the sake of the nation. It was later commemorated in the Wartburg Festival of 1817 near Jena, where student fraternities (*Burschenschaften*) also celebrated the fourth centenary of Martin Luther's Reformation and demonstrated their aversion to the European Restoration established at the Viennese Congress of 1815, which had failed to unite the German people under one nation-state. While the members of the fraternities were censored and persecuted by the administration of Klemens Wenzel Nepomuk Lothar Metternich because of their liberalism and revolutionary ideas, their outlook was tinged by xenophobia (in particular, toward the French), anti-Semitism, and aggression, which reached its climax with the murder of August Friedrich Ferdinand von Kotzebue, a German writer working for the Russian tsar, by the fraternity member Karl Ludwig Sand in 1819. The assassination led to the prohibition of the fraternities and the persecution of their members as demagogues by the *Karlsbader Beschlüsse*, while Sand's public execution rendered him a martyr for the national cause.

The German Romantics' notion of the German *Kulturstaat* was furthermore characterized by pious mysticism and a reactionary insistence on tradition as the panacea for national as well as international discord. While adopting Herder's view of folklore and folk tales as the most genuine expression of the (German) *Volksgeist*, thinkers such as Johann Gottlieb Fichte, in his *Reden an die deutsche Nation* (*Addresses to the German People*, 1807), glorified the German people as the bearers of a special world-historical and spiritual mission, with German acting as the purest original language of mankind, the *Ursprache*. In *Deutsches Volkstum* (*German Nationality*, 1810), Friedrich Ludwig Jahn admonished the German people to preserve their racial purity, while the poet Ernst Moritz Arndt, in his aptly entitled *Catechism* (1813), praised the love for the fatherland as the highest form of religion and postulated an innate superiority of the German nation.

While Herder saw an egalitarian national community as the natural prerequisite for the individual's personal fulfilment and freedom ("Der Naturstand des Menschen ist der Stand in der Gesellschaft"), German Romantics tended to uphold the Lutheran tradition of obedience and subordination to the ruling classes, that is, to the nobility, and oppose the democratic forces of industrialization. By glorifying war and aristocratic legitimacy as instruments of national unity, they, in fact, reinforced the reactionary powers of the European Restoration. Thus, while the notion of *Volksgeist* motivated the national liberation movements of the failed European revolutions of 1848–49 and had a major impact on Pan-Slavism, it was through Otto von Bismarck's aggressive foreign policy of war that the German people finally achieved unity in 1871.

KATHARINA KROSNY

See also **Fichte, Johann Gottlieb; Germany: Cultural Survey; Germany: Historical Survey; Hegel, Georg Wilhelm Friedrich; Herder, Johann Gottfried; Kleist, Heinrich Bernd von; Müller Wilhélm, Adam Heinrich; Nationalism; Novalis; Pan-Slavism; Schleiermacher, Friedrich Daniel Ernst**

Bibliography

Barnard, F. M. *Herder's Social and Political Thought: From Enlightenment to Nationalism.* Oxford: Oxford University Press, 1965.

Berlin, Isaiah. *Vico and Herder.* London: Hogarth, 1976.

Dann, Otto, and John Dinwiddy, eds. *Nationalism in the Age of the French Revolution.* London: Hambledon, 1988.

Ergang, R. R. *Herder and the Foundations of German Nationalism.* New York: Columbia University Press, 1931.

Giesen, Bernhard, and Kay Junge. "Vom Patriotismus zum Nationalismus. Zur Evolution der 'Deutschen Kulturnation.'" In *Nationale und kulturelle Identität. Studien zur Entwicklung des kollektiven Bewußtseins in der Neuzeit.* Frankfurt: Suhrkamp, 1991.

Hughes, Michael. *Nationalism and Society. Germany 1800–1945.* London: Arnold, 1988.

Reiss, H. S. *The Political Thought of the German Romantics.* Oxford: Blackwell, 1955.

VOLNEY, CONSTANTIN FRANÇOIS DE CHASSEBOEUF, COMTE DE
1751–1820

French philosopher and historian

An important political philosopher and intellectual of the Romantic period, Constantin François de Chasseboeuf, Comte de Volney was often a controversial figure. Best known for his radical work *Les Ruines, ou méditations sur les révolutions des empires* (*The Ruins, or Meditations on the Revolutions of Empires*, 1791) and its influence on the young Romantic poet Percy Bysshe Shelley, Volney was also an influential geographer, travel writer, historian, and statesman.

Although little is known of Volney's early life, his first published work reflects his interest in eighteenth-century rationalism and in philosophies of natural law. An account of an extensive tour of the Levant, the *Voyage en Syrie et en Égypte* (*Travels through Syria and Egypt*, 1787) offered his readers a description of the political situation in the Near East, emphasizing the perils of superstition, religion, and despotic government. During his travels in Asia and Africa, Volney seriously studied Arabic, and his proficiency in the language later contributed to his reputation as an Oriental scholar. Throughout the 1790s, he published several influential works on the study of Eastern languages, including an essay *Simplification des langues orientales* (*On the Simplification of Oriental Languages*, 1795). Meanwhile, this first travel volume was so popular and the account judged so insightful that, in addition to many favorable reviews, Volney was awarded a medal of gratitude from Empress Catherine the Great of Russia for the work within a year of its publication. Further testimony to the account's veracity was provided by Napoleon Bonaparte, who used Volney's *Travels* as a source of political and geographical information during the 1798 Egypto-Syrian campaign.

In *The Ruins*, Volney expanded upon themes of empire and religion. Fancifully staging for a time traveler a survey of world history, Volney's narrator demonstrates the slow degradation of human character and of civil society by pomp and superstition and offers the traveler a vision of the future redeemed by the corrective powers of reason and sympathy. In its emphasis on the transformative power of reason, *The Ruins* epitomizes the

Enlightenment philosophy that was popular in France and in other parts of Europe during the late eighteenth century. Nevertheless, *The Ruins* was a surprisingly controversial publication, in part because it was published in the early years of the French Revolution, when radicalism was viewed as particularly dangerous. One particularly controversial aspect of the work was the inclusion of a series of imagined debates between world leaders and theologians: the criticisms of Christianity articulated within the text provoked impassioned responses. Although numerous responses to Volney's work were published during the next decade, especially in the periodical press, Percy Bysshe Shelley's early poem "Queen Mab" (1813) has long been seen as one of the most important literary reactions to *The Ruins*.

In addition to the *Travels through Syria and Egypt*, Volney wrote two other travel narratives. In 1792, he visited a recently acquired estate in Corsica and published *Précis de l'état de la Corse* (*An Account of the Present State of Corsica*, 1793), in which Volney candidly assessed the contemporary political situation on the island. Due to the nature of his criticisms, the account was very unpopular with his Corsican neighbors. From 1795 to 1798 he traveled throughout North America and published *Tableau du climat et du sol des Etats-Unis d'Amérique* (*On the Climate and Soil of the United States*, 1803), which included the first geological map of the country. While neither narrative was particularly influential in Europe, the description of North America was immediately popular in the United States, although less for what Volney wrote than for who he was. While in America, Volney established several prominent relationships, including a correspondence with Thomas Jefferson, and his political perceptions are thought to have influenced early American statecraft. Meanwhile, the radical émigré Joseph Priestley mounted an attack on Volney and his work in the American press. Controversy ensued, and Volney's reply was published in 1797. Finally, Volney was something of a curiosity, having recently survived the Reign of Terror in revolutionary France—a period which, as an opponent of Maximilien de Robespierre, Volney had spent as a prisoner in the Bastille (1793–94).

Upon his return to France in 1798, Volney became actively involved in revolutionary politics. Indeed, although largely remembered today as a philosopher, he was also a prominent politician, having served the Republic since its inception, as deputy of the states-general in 1789 and as secretary to the National Assembly in 1790. In addition, several of his less significant early works directly engaged with contemporary political issues, including his *Considerations sur la guerre actuelle des Turcs* (*Con-*siderations on the War of the Turks*, 1788) and *La loi naturelle; ou, Catéchisme du citoyen français* (*The Law of Nature; or, The French Citizen's Catechism*, 1793). Now, Volney had returned in time to support Napoleon Bonaparte and Emmanuel-Joseph Sieyès in the coup of 18 Brumaire (1799), and in this respect he was responsible for helping to establish Napoleon as France's political leader at the beginning of the nineteenth century. In an apparent violation of his early republican principles, Volney was later to remain loyal to Bonaparte even after the transition to empire, serving as a member of Napoleon's imperial Senate and accepting an elevation to the title of *comte d'empire* (count) in 1808. This peerage was reconfirmed by Louis XVIII in 1814.

In 1794, Volney lectured as professor of history at the newly instituted state university in Paris (École Normale), and after 1800 he once again turned his attention to historical subjects. In 1800, Volney collected and published his popular university *Lecons d'histoire* (*Lectures on History*). However, his efforts as an academic historian culminated with the publication in 1814 of his voluminous *Recherches nouvelles sur l'histoire ancienne* (*New Research on Ancient History*). In recognition of his intellectual contributions—in history and in other subjects—Volney was nominated to several institutes of honor, including the prestigious Académie Française.

TILAR J. MAZZEO

Selected Works

Voyage en Syrie et en Égypte. 1787. Translated as *Travels through Syria and Egypt* by M. Volney. 1787.
Les Ruines, ou méditations sur les révolutions des empires. 1791. Translated as *The Ruins, or Meditations on the Revolutions of Empires* by M. Volney. 1795.
Précis de l'état de la Corse. 1793.
Simplification des langues orientales. 1795.
Tableau du climat et du sol des Etats-Unis d'Amérique. 1803. Translated as *On the Climate and Soil of the United States*. 1804.
Recherches nouvelles sur l'histoire ancienne. 1814. Translated as *New Researches on Ancient History* by Colonel Corbet. 1819.

Bibliography

Chinard, Gilbert. *Volney et l'Amérique . . . sa correspondance avec Jefferson*. 1923.
Daru, Count. "Life of Volney." In *The Ruins; or, Meditations on the Revolutions of Empire*. 1926.
Durozoir, Charles. *A Life of Volney: Translated and Abridged from the Article of Durozoir*. N.p., n.d.
LeCoats, Nanette. *Neither Fable nor Science: Volney's Writings on Travel and History*. 1985.
Oeuvres complètes de Volney. 1857.

VÖRÖSMARTY, MIHÁLY 1800–1855

Hungarian poet

There is a broad consensus in critical literature about the role of Mihály Vörösmarty: he is considered the greatest poet of Hungarian Romanticism. It was a movement with its roots in the 1810s, coinciding with the conclusion of the Napoleonic Wars, but its first work of real significance is Vörösmarty's heroic epic poem *Zalán futása* (*Zalan's Flight*, 1825). Written in flowing hexameters, this poem reached back for its theme into the legendary national past in order to strengthen the resolve of the Magyars to be worthy of their great forebears. Apart from masterful descriptions of nature, and battles fought between the opponents, Vörösmarty also weaves a love story into his narrative that is largely independent of the main plot of war.

Zalán Futása was followed by other, shorter epic poems of the Hungarian past such as *Cserhalom* (1825) and *Eger* (*Agria*, 1827). *Tündérvölgy* (*The Valley of the Fairies*, 1826) and the unfinished *Délsziget* (*Southern Island*, 1826) were both ventures in a purely imaginative Romantic direction. The latter, written in hexameters and rich in imagery, is a story of longing and separation. Occasionally the two threads (the patriotic/social and the personal/emotional) come together, as in the tale *A rom* (*Ruin*, 1830) in which a young man's search for happiness is almost successful, for his wishes are granted by the magic power of the ruin, but his last wish—freedom and independence for an enslaved people—cannot be fulfilled. Vörösmarty's last poetic tale, *A két szomszédvár* (*The Two Neighboring Castles*, 1831), is a knightly romance in four cantos; its subject is the blood feud between two noble families in the thirteenth century. This poem is again in hexameter and, for all its blood-curdling parts, is more loquacious and dated than some of the previous epic poems by the same author.

Transience, death, and the futility of human existence are constant themes of Vörösmarty's work. They also inform his plays, some of which also deal with the national past. His best play is *Csongor és Tünde* (*Csongor and Tünde*, 1831), which is based on the sixteenth-century Hungarian fairy story *Árgirus* (*Prince Argirus*). Its theme transcends national borders and has been, on occasion, compared to William Shakespeare's *Midsummer Night's Dream*. The lovers Csongor and Tünde are separated by the intrigues of the wicked witch Mirigy, who forces Csongor to wander the world in search of his lost happiness. It is a world full of fairies, goblins, and symbolism. After various adventures, Csongor and Tünde meet again, but must relinquish their immortality for a few "fleeting years of joy" on earth.

Between 1833 and 1841, Vörösmarty wrote a number of other plays centered on Romantic passion, but none equaled *Csongor és Tünde*. Some of these plays were written to satisfy the growing demand of the new Hungarian-language National Theater of Pest and entertain the theatergoing public, but neither *Vérnász* (*Blood Wedding*, 1833) nor *Marót bán* (*Ban Marót*, 1838) has a coherent plot or deeply perceived characters. As a translator of Shakespeare, Vörösmarty fared much better: his translations of *Julius Caesar* (1839) and *King Lear* (1854) were excellent, remaining in the repertory of the Hungarian theater well into the twentieth century.

Mihály Vörösmarty's greatest achievement lies in the field of lyrical poetry. While there was always a strong lyrical vein in most of his epic work, it was only from 1835 onward that this genre began to take precedence over other forms. While his early lyrics are either imitations of folksongs or neoclassical epigrams on diverse themes, from the early 1830s the main sources of his inspiration are either patriotic sentiment or private passion. The patriotic poems have a dramatic intensity rarely found in Hungarian poetry before Vörösmarty; only Dániel Berzsenyi and Ferenc Kölcsey had written poems comparable to Vörösmarty's. His "Szózat" ("Appeal," 1836) is often referred to as Hungary's second national anthem. Both poems invoke the struggles of the past in order to give hope for the future. The central theme of the poem is characteristically Romantic and considers the binary options of liberty or death as it applies not only to the individual, but to the entire nation. The possibility of the nation's demise

originates both from the "prophecy" of Johann Gottfried Herder (that the Magyars would die out in a sea of Slavs) and from the defeat of the Polish struggle for independence in 1830 and 1831. Nevertheless, "Szózat" ends with a truly Romantic appeal for loyalty to the homeland.

Patriotism, however, is only part of Vörösmarty's liberal, progressive program; some of his great poems written before 1848 show both his faith in the progress of mankind, and his doubts about the possibility of the moral improvement of human nature. While "A Guttenberg-albumb" ("For the Gutenberg Album," 1840), written in distichs, upholds the ideals of European humanism and lists the conditions for the happiness of mankind, the long, blank-verse meditation of "Gondolatok a könyvtárban" ("Thoughts in the Library," 1844) poses the question: Has the world advanced through books? The answer is a qualified *yes*, but Vörösmarty despairs at the enormous cost of progress in terms of individual lives and deplores the inequality and slavery that still exist in the world. Yet only two years later, after the suppression of the Galician uprising and the massacre of the Polish nobility that followed, Vörösmarty wrote "Az emberek" ("On Mankind," 1846), a poem in regular rhyming stanzas with the bitterly pessimistic refrain "Nincsen remény" (All hope is vain).

Notwithstanding a short period of renewed optimism following the March Revolution of 1848, which created the first independent government of Hungary, Vörösmarty once again fell into a state of deep depression after the defeat of the Hungarian bid for independence by the joint Austrian and Russian armed forces. Yet the crowning achievement of this period is the rhapsody "A vén cigány", ("The Ancient Gipsy," 1854), a visionary reflection of the poet's own state of mind against the background of contemporary events, specifically the Crimean War. The poem is written in a ten-line rhyming stanza, with the recurring refrain "Strike up, Gypsy, let our troubles go!" and with a wish for a cleansing cataclysm that will destroy the old world of "sins, squalor and delusions." For all the disappointments and lost illusions, the poem ends on a note of hope for the future.

Vörösmarty also wrote a number of love poems to his wife, Laura Csajághy, of which the best known is "A merengohoz" ("To the Daydreamer," 1843). Among his ballads "Szép Ilonka" ("The Fair Helen," 1833) is the most popular. Vörösmarty rarely wrote humorous poems, but of the few that he wrote, "Petike" ("Young Pete") stands out, with its bouncy rhymes and joking tone. It is both the power and breadth of his language, and his impressive achievement in several genres, that make Vörösmarty an outstanding figure of Hungarian Romanticism.

GEORGE GÖMÖRI

Biography

Born in 1800 at Pusztanyék, Hungary, in a family of the lower nobility (his father was employed on a large estate), Vörösmarty went to school first at Székesfehérvár and then at Pest. Studied philosophy from 1817 to 1820, law in 1824, and passed his qualifying examination in the same year. As his father had died in 1817, Vörösmarty had to support himself from teaching and for a number of years was tutor to the three sons of the landowning Perczel family, first at Pest and then at the Perczel's Transdanubian estate, and fell in love with Adél (Etelka) Perczel, who inspired many of his first poetic efforts. He began work on his epic poem *The Flight of Zalán* in 1823; its publication in 1825 brought immediate fame. He resigned as tutor in 1826, moved to Buda, and devoted himself to writing, but it was only in 1828 that he found a suitable job out of which he could make a living: he became editor of the magazine *Tudományos Gyüjtemény* (*Scholarly Miscellanea*), a post he held until 1832. In 1830 he became a member of the Hungarian Academy. He won literary prizes with his dramas in 1833 and again in 1834; he founded the *Kisfaludy Társaság* with József Bajza and others in 1836. He began the review *Athenaeum* with Bajza and Ferenc Toldy in 1837. In 1840 his new poems were published in four volumes; these won an award from the Hungarian Academy in 1842. In 1843 he married the much younger Laura Csajághy. Politically, he first supported István Széchenyi, then Lajos Kossuth; in 1842 he became president of the National Circle and in 1847 of the Circle of the Opposition. After the March Revolution of 1848 he was parliamentary deputy and, because of his moderate views, quarrelled with his earlier protegé Sándor Petofi. He followed the revolutionary government to Debrecen in January 1849, and having returned for a short period to Pest, he ended up at Arad in August 1849. After a period of hiding, he rejoined his family in 1850. From that year onward he lived in the country, renting land to support his family, but fell into a state of deep depression made worse by heavy drinking. His funeral in November 1855 turned into a national demonstration against Habsburg absolutism.

Selected Works

Minden munkái. 12 vols. 1861–64.
Összes munkái. 8 vols. 1884–85.
Összes müvei. 18 vols. to date. Budapest, 1960.
Válogatott müvei. 3 vols. Budapest, 1974.

Bibliography

Czigány, Lóránt. *The Oxford History of Hungarian Literature.* Oxford: Clarendon Press, 1984.

Gyulai, Pál. *Vörösmarty Mihály életrajza.* Budapest: Franklin, 1879.

Jones, Mervyn D. "Vörösmarty (1800–1855): From Classic to Romantic." In *Five Hungarian Writers.* Oxford: Clarendon Press, 1966.

Makkai Ádám. *In Quest of the "Miracle Stag": The Poetry of Hungary.* Atlantis-Centaur; M. Szivárvány; Corvina: Chicago-Budapest, 1996.

Reményi, Joseph. "Mihály Vörösmarty, Poet, Playwright and Critic, 1800–1855." In *Hungarian Writers and Literature.* New Brunswick, N.J.: Rutgers University Press, 1964.

Tóth, Dezsö. *Vörösmarty Mihály.* 2d rev. ed. Budapest: Akadémiai, 1974.

WACKENRODER, WILHELM HEINRICH 1773–1798

German writer

Despite his premature death at the age of twenty-four, generally attributed to his fragile constitution and remarkable sensibility (*Empfindsamkeit*), Wilhelm Heinrich Wackenroder left behind a carefully formulated aesthetic and philosophical worldview, which was to have a major impact on Arthur Schopenhauer's approach to music and anticipated the crisis of language experienced by late nineteenth-century writers such as Hugo von Hoffmannsthal. At the heart of Wackenroder's convictions lies the equation of all sentiment with religion, which gives rise to a secularized pietism and the celebration of art as the richest source of emotion, in particular music and the symphony. Wackenroder praised instrumental music as the highest art form because of its autonomy from empirical fact and its ability to reach the "dark" and "mysterious" corners of every individual's soul and act as a medium of spiritual communion between souls, thus highlighting the inadequacy of language as a communicator of truth.

Born the son of a privy councillor of war and later first mayor of justice in Berlin, he underwent a strict Prussian education meant to prepare him for a career in law, which resulted in his lifelong struggle between a dutiful and mundane existence on the one hand, and, on the other, the striving for an elevated mode of being, made possible through the study and creation of music and art in general and inspired by what he called *ätherischer Enthusiasmus* (ethereal enthusiasm). This conflict lies behind the conception of his alter ego, the musician Joseph Berglinger, whose biography *Das merkwürdige musikalische Leben des Tonkünstlers Joseph Berglinger* (*The Strange Musical Life of the Sound Artist Joseph Berglinger*, 1796) is a highly romantic and creative depiction of Wackenroder's own circumstances.

The fictitious Berglinger is the inherently talented and sensitive (two attributes that make him a specimen of the Romantic genius) son of an impoverished and disillusioned local surgeon in southern Germany, who spends his childhood in daydreams and fantasies triggered by the enjoyment of music, through which he escapes the reality of his wretched circumstances. Desperate to escape the sobering influence of prosaic life, he finally refuses to adopt his father's philanthropic profession and seeks his fortune in an Episcopal town where he had learned to love church music during his childhood visits and where he now hopes to train as a musician. Yet, having become a successful composer at court, Berglinger comes to doubt the value of art, which the aristocracy seems to regard as little more than a profane entertainment, and grows increasingly troubled that by dedicating his life to art he could be worshipping a vain and egotistical idol while at the same time cruelly ignoring the suffering of the common man. Furthermore, having acquired the techniques necessary for his creativity, he realizes that musical composition too is but an earthly construct and mourns the days of his youthful idealism, when music still appeared to him as a divine gift. Berglinger's predicament is finally resolved when the pain and regret he experiences at his father's death inspire him to compose a passion, thus translating his suffering into art. Having exhausted his potential in one masterpiece, Berglinger promptly succumbs to a nervous fever.

The story of Joseph Berglinger constitutes the artistic climax of a collection of stories and essays entitled *Herzensergiessungen eines kunstliebenden Klosterbruders* (*Outpourings of an Art-Loving Monk*, 1796), which was published on the initiative of Wackenroder's close friend Ludwig Tieck, who also contributed to the work. Their creative friendship represents the first in a line of fruitful collaborations in German Romanticism, with the ambitious and outgoing Tieck, who descended from a line of craftsmen, complementing Wackenroder's more reclusive and shy personality. It was also Tieck who published the remainder of Wackenroder's written work after the latter's death as *Phantasien über die Kunst* (*Fantasies on Art*, 1799), to which he made such a substantial contribution that the precise details of individual authorship remain uncertain.

In his writings, which form the first major body of text of early German Romanticism, Wackenroder insists on a holistic and harmonious worldview in which all is pervaded by God's spirit and in which artistic creation acts as the most divine of human endeavors by bringing out the godlike within man. As a consequence, his aesthetic criticism precludes any comparison between artists and their work, treating each as an intensely personal manifestation of the godly spirit instead. Thus Albrecht Dürer is praised for portraying the humanity within the soul of the ordinary man, while Raphael's ideal vision is hailed for emphasizing man's divine and ethereal aspect. Wackenroder thus effectively rejects the art critic in favor of the art lover, who regards the artist as saint and the life in art as a noble because godly alternative to earthly existence.

Wackenroder first came in contact with Dürer's work in his travels through Bavaria, undertaken during his year of law study at Erlangen University, when he visited Nuremberg, Bamberg, Bayreuth, and Schloss Pommersfelden. During this period he acquired a taste for the rituals of Catholicism and its use of Renaissance and Baroque architecture, the visual arts and music as media of religious faith and human spirituality. Wackenroder recognized Catholicism and the Holy Roman Empire as responsible for the flourishing of medieval and Renaissance art and became the first German Romantic writer to celebrate pre-Reformation Germany. His "art-loving monk" thus stands for a mystical life devoted to the aesthetics of religion and art, secluded from the demands and compromising conditions of external reality.

Despite his short life, Wackenroder came into contact with some of the most prolific artists of German Romanticism, such as Friedrich Gottlieb Klopstock, who played a vital role in establishing the literature of *Empfindsamkeit*, and the musician Johann Friedrich Reichardt, under whom he studied. Wackenroder's own relevance and impact tends to be neglected because, in order to give voice to his pious medievalism, which had a major influence on the Nazarene group of artists, he often reverts to a deliberately naive style of writing that tends to undermine the validity of his argument. However, his views on music and the visual arts, and his skeptical approach to language (which he regards as inferior to the expressive power of nature and the arts), combined with his ambivalent attitude toward art itself as either an instrument of the divine or a tool of human vanity and solipsism, reveal a more complex portrait of this first German Romantic.

KATHARINA KROSNY

See also **Aesthetics and Art Criticism; Art; Artist, Changing Conceptions of the; Catholicism; Genius; Nazarene Art; Reli-gion: Germany; Runge, Philipp Otto; Schopenhauer, Arthur; Sensibility; Tieck, Ludwig**

Biography

Born in Berlin, July 13, 1773. First meeting with Ludwig Tieck at the Friedrich-Wedersche Gymnasium; separation from Tieck during preparatory study year in Berlin, 1792; study of law in Erlangen, Bavaria, 1792–93; first trips to Bayreuth, Nuremberg, Bamberg, Schloss Pommersfelden, and various Bavarian monasteries, 1793; study of law in Göttingen, 1793–94; return to Berlin for training at the Supreme Court, 1794; second trip to Dresden with Tieck, 1796; *Herzensergießungen eines kunstliebenden Klosterbruders* published anonymously, autumn 1796, dated 1797. Died February 13, 1798 of "nervous fever" in Berlin.

Selected Works

Herzensergießungen eines kunstliebenden Klosterbruders. Edited by and in collaboration with Ludwig Tieck. 1797.
Phantasien über die Kunst. Edited by and in collaboration with Ludwig Tieck. 1799.
Phantasien über die Kunst, von einem kunstliebenden Klosterbruder. New revised edition by Ludwig Tieck. 1814.
Werke und Briefe. Edited by Friedrich von der Leyen. 2 vols. Jena: Diederichs, 1910.
Confessions and Fantasies. Translated and edited by Mary Hurst Schubert. University Park: Pennsylvania University Press, 1971.

Bibliography

Alewyn, Richard. "Wackenroders Anteil," *Germanic Review* 19 (1944): 48–58.
Francke, Christa. *Philipp Otto Runge und die Kunstansichten Wackenroders und Tiecks*. Marburg: Elwert, 1974.
Frey, Marianne. *Der Künstler und sein Werk bei Wilhelm Heinrich Wackenroder und E. T. A. Hoffmann. Vergleichende Studien zur romantischen Kunstanschauung*. Bern: Language, 1970.
Hubert, Ulrich. *Karl Philipp Moritz und die Anfänge der Romantik. Tieck, Wackenroder, Jean Paul und August Wilhelm Schlegel*. Frankfurt: Athenäum, 1971.
Jost, Walter. *Von Ludwig Tieck zu E. T. A. Hoffmann. Studien zur Entwicklungsgeschichte des romantischen Subjektivismus*. Frankfurt: Diesterweg, 1921.
Kahnt, Rose. *Die Bedeutung der bildenden Kunst und der Musik bei Wilhelm Heinrich Wackenroder*. Marburg: Elwert, 1969.
Robson-Scott, W. D. "Wackenroder and the Middle Ages," *Modern Language Review* 50 (1955): 156–67.
Stöcker, Helene. *Zur Kunstanschauung des 18. Jahrhunderts. Von Winckelmann bis zu Wackenroder*. Berlin: Mayer und Müller, 1904.
Zipes, Jack D. "Wilhelm Heinrich Wackenroder. In Defense of his Romanticism," *Germanic Review* 44 (1969): 247–58.

WAGNER, RICHARD 1813–1883

German composer, writer, and intellectual

Richard Wagner remains one of the most important cultural, creative, and intellectual figures of the Romantic era. His ideas and concepts have shaped music, theater, motion pictures, and politics for more than a century following his death. His prolific and grandiose musical compositions, and profuse number of written works, are a monumental legacy. Wagner, his ideas, and his works were controversial during his lifetime, and this controversy has continued up through recent debate about the appropriateness of performing his works in Israel. Both contemporaries and succeeding generations of artists (including visual artists and writers) tend to line up as being either Wagnerian or anti-Wagnerian in their approach to art.

While Wagner has significant abilities with orchestral and instrumental composition, the main focus of his work is vocal. In fact, the majority of his reputation rests on ten operas—or music dramas, as he preferred to call them. These ten works include *Die fliegender Hollander; Tannhäuser; Lohengrin; The Ring of the Nibelungs* series: *Das Rheingold, Die Walküre, Siegfried,* and *Götterdämmerung; Tristan und Isolde; Die Meistersinger von Nürnberg;* and *Parsifal.* His lengthy works were dramatically different from the other operatic work of his time and attracted a good deal of attention and critical commentary.

Stylistically, they show major innovations and developments in almost every aspect of music. In fundamental structure Wagner moves away from individually numbered movements in opera (recitatives, arias, choral movements) and creates continuous flowing textures that last for extended periods being broken up only with the conclusion of an act of the drama. This macro style of construction results in two specific techniques that are closely linked to the unbroken cascade of the music. One of these is the concept of "continuous melody" in which the melodic interest moves from one part of the texture to another, seemingly without interruption. This results in the vocal part not always being the primary melodic line. Rather, the vocal lines are treated as equivalent to individual instrumental lines. The listener follows the most prominent part of the melody wherever it may be found within the large textural context. The other concept resulting from the nonmovement based music is a highly fluid style of rhythmic writing. This highly flexible type of rhythmic composition can easily result in passages (sometimes extended) that seem to the listener to have little or no obvious metric organization. The primary focus of the rhythmic writing is based on speech patterns of spoken German. Harmonically, Wagner's music is adventurous within the context of the major-minor tonal system. Beginning with the composition of the "Ring" operas and *Tristan und Isolde,* the type of suppleness found in other musical components of his music dramas becomes more pronounced in his harmonic writing. In part, this is owing to the large expanse of time the acts encompass. It is difficult to remain restricted to a group of related keys in the kinds of extended idioms in which Wagner was working. Generally, chromaticism became a major harmonic factor in middle and later romantic music. With the exploration of distant and uncommon tonal relationship over an extended period, chromaticism tends to negate the sense of a tonal center. Wagner formalized this effect, in a more compact idiom, in the prelude to *Tristan und Isolde.* Here he composes a work that is major-minor tonal, but without a tonal center. The piece in effect begins in one key, progresses through numerous chromatic tonal relationships, and concludes in a tonality that is not the same as the beginning. This work is viewed by many music theorists and historians as a landmark in the history of harmonic writing.

One of his most important practices in his later musical compositions was the introduction of the leitmotiv. This is a melodic idea, motif, or fragment that is identified with a particular dramatic character, object, or situation. The leitmotiv recurs throughout the work (or, in the case of the Ring operas, throughout four works) to aid listener identification of the return of specific dramatic situations. Wagner preferred the terms *Grundthema* or *Hauptmotiv,* which have essentially the same meaning as the term *leitmotiv.* While the concept of recurring themes with prescribed associations existed prior to Wagner, it is in the works of Wagner that the technique gains widespread recognition. Additionally, it is used as a major part of the structural, thematic, and transformative nature of his large works. Wagner's concept of leitmotiv is prominent today in many film scores, especially those composed by John Williams for *Jaws* and for the *Star Wars* series.

While not known for his purely instrumental writing, Wagner was a master of instrumental music and orchestration. The musical interpretation and translation of the dramatic action is assigned primarily to the orchestral writing, where symbolism, beyond use of leitmotivs, is a foundation of his compositional idiom. Orchestras of substantial size are usually required for Wagnarian music dramas. His orchestrations often emphasize brass instruments in lower ranges. To this end some of the later music dramas utilize up to eight French horns as well as bass trumpet and bass trombones. Wagner developed an instrument called the "Wagner tuba" for the "Ring" cycle. It is an instrument that exists in both tenor and bass ranges and outwardly resembles a euphonium. When designing the *Festspielhaus* in Bayreuth, Wagner introduced an orchestra pit design that was terraced (in reverse) and where a considerable portion of the orchestra was housed beneath the stage; the strings were on the terraces closest to the audience while the louder brass instruments occupied the lowest part of the terraced pit. This resulted in highly specific orchestration for the "Ring" operas and for *Parsifal.* It also explains the large number of brass instruments that are required for these musical dramas.

Wagner was a self-made intellectual. He read widely and studied the works of German literary and intellectual giants. His ideas, whether developed independently or the espousal of more widely held romantic concepts, had a wide-ranging impact both during his lifetime and for seventy-five years or more following his death. In his literary works *Die Kunst der Zukunft (The Artwork of the Future)* and *Oper und Drama (Opera and Drama)* the composer proposed and later endeavored to realize a philosophical and artistic concept he called the *Gestamtkunstwerk* (the complete art work). It was Wagner's belief that all of the arts should be integrated into one large presentation. While these works were primarily grounded in music and dramatic enactment, the other forms he included in this "complete art work" were literature, poetry, myth and history, theatrical lighting, costume creation, painting and scenic design, acting, and dance.

Another idea that Wagner extended and popularized was gargantuanism. While there had been exceptionally large works prior to his operas and music dramas (Hector Berlioz's *Les Troyens,* for example), it was Wagner who popularized and promoted the gigantic musical and theatrical spectacle. This concept is realized via the techniques of tonal prolongation and the general increase in the size of operatic and orchestral works. In music, followers of Wagner who created exceptionally large works include Anton Bruckner, Gustav Mahler, Arnold Schoenberg, Richard Strauss, and Igor Stravinsky. Interestingly, this grandiosity becomes part of romantic culture and can be found in other artistic idioms such as literature, and architecture.

Art as a type of religion was another romantic concept associated with Wagner. He believed in a type of redemption through the knowledge about, participation in, or observance of great works of art. To this end the building of the *Festspielhaus* in

Bayreuth represents a "temple" to his art. In the nineteenth and early twentieth centuries, Wagner's followers made "pilgrimages" to Bayreuth to witness the creator's artistic visions. Among the diverse group of well-known figures who visited Bayreuth, or were influenced by his work, were Claude Debussy, T. S. Eliot, James Joyce, Thomas Mann, George Bernard Shaw, Igor Stravinsky, Virginia Woolf, and, most controversially, Adolf Hitler.

The controversies that surround Wagner are numerous and date to as early as the 1840s. During his life, his notoriety centered around the following issues: (1) his political and revolutionary tendencies, which were at odds with his solicitation of funds from establishment figures and institutions; (2) his personal morality, which for the time was considered highly disreputable; (3) his moralistic pronouncement about others and their behavior, religion, or beliefs, often in a disapproving manner; (4) his practice of using other people for self-centered purposes (this was especially directed toward patrons and other musicians); and (5) his egomania. Wagner believed in his own superiority and the natural superiority of the German-speaking people, their history, and their culture. Over the years, however, many of these controversies have faded.

The continuing debate rests primarily on his blatant anti-Semitism. His ideas are formally expressed in "Das Judentum in der Musik" (*Judaism in Music*, 1850, revised 1869), first written under the pseudonym of K. Freigedank. One cannot find overt anti-Semitism in his operas and music dramas, but the emphasis on German myth, history, and culture does provide a subtle method for excluding non-Germanic cultures. Pierre-Auguste Renoir wrote in a letter following a meeting with Wagner in Italy, "He detests German Jews, including Wolff" and in a postscript Renoir quotes Wagner as saying, " 'The German Jews! But, Monsieur Renoir, I know that there are decent people in France, whom I don't lump together with the German Jews.' " Unfortunately, Wagner's ideas had a great influence upon Hitler, who felt that the highest honor the German nation could award to patriotic Germans or wounded military personnel was admission to the summer festival in Bayreuth to see a performance of one of Wagner's musical dramas. This, in turn, has led to an unofficial boycott of Wagner's works by the state of Israel, in deference to survivors of the Holocaust and their families. As recently as the summer of 2001, Wagner was once again in the newspaper headlines, due to a breach of this boycott by an internationally known conductor.

JEFFREY WASSON

Biography

Born in Leipzig, Germany, May 22, 1813. He attended a school near Dresden, where he began his musical studies by taking piano lessons. In 1827, he moved back to Leipzig, where first he studied composition with Christian Müller. Later, he studied at the Thomasschüle (where Johann Sebastian Bach taught) with the music director, Christian Weinlig. Weinlig was instrumental in Wagner's first publication, a sonata issued by the prestigious firm of Breitkopf und Härtel. Beginning in 1832, his compositions began to receive important performances by such distinguished organizations as the Gewandhaus Orchestra of Leipzig. About this time, he formed an association with a group of intellectuals that included Heinrich Heine and Heinrich Laube.

These relationships expanded his literary and political horizons. His first published writing, " Die Deutsche Oper," appeared in June 1834, in Laube's *Zeitung für die elegant Welt.* His focus on opera began in 1833. Two years later, Wagner made his opera conducting debut, leading a performance of Wolfgang Amadeus Mozart's *Don Giovanni.* He met his first wife, Christine Wilhelmine (Minna) Planer, and they were married on November 24, 1836. The marriage was a tempestuous relationship.

In the summer of 1837, he was appointed music director of the theater in Riga, Latvia. During the two seasons he was in Riga, he finished the libretto and began to compose the music to *Rienzi.* The Wagners left Riga and moved to Paris in 1839. The two years in the French capital did not prove productive. Giacomo Meyerbeer tried to help him, but the political and monetary landscape of Paris prevented the German composer from flourishing. *Rienzi* was completed in November 1840, and during 1840 and 1841 the composer envisioned, wrote the libretto, and composed *Der fliegender Holländer* (*The Flying Dutchman*). With help from Meyerbeer, *Rienzi* received it first production in Dresden in October of 1840. Because of its success, Wagner was appointed music codirector of the Dresden Court. *Tannhäuser* was his next operatic project, with the writing of the libretto and composition spanning the years 1842 to 1845. During the second half of the 1840s, he was occupied with three projects: a verbal draft of *Die Meistersinger von Nürnberg* (*The Master Singer of Nuremberg*) literary sketches of *Parsifal*; and *Lohengrin.* However, it was *Lohengrin* that became the compositional focus of the later 1840s.

Wagner had shown revolutionary political tendencies for a good number of years and in 1849, when political unrest occurred in Dresden, Wagner became involved. After the Prussian military put down the revolution, the Wagners escaped to Paris and then moved to Zurich. It was here that he wrote *Die Kunst un die Revolution* (*Art and Revolution*). Following this, he wrote a group of literary-philosophical works that influenced his art and life, as well as influencing the broader artistic and political communities for many years. *Die Kunst der Zukunft* (*The Artwork of the Future*) and *Oper und Drama* provided the basis for aesthetics, artistic concepts, and the role of the author/composer in theatrical creation. His concept of the "complete art work" (*Gesamptkunstwerke*) is elucidated here. A group of shorter essays also was written in this period; the most controversial and therefore of greatest historical significance is "Das Judentum in der Musik" (*Judaism in Music*) which was issued under the pen name K. Freigedank. Beginning in October of 1848, and continuing almost three decades, Wagner began his work on the Nordic myth of the Niebelungs. The time and financial underpinnings that were necessary for a project of this scope came from the generosity of patrons, especially Otto Wesendonck. He worked on the project with intensity until August 1857. Fatigued with the project of the "Ring" operas, Wagner turned his attention to other projects, the most important of which was the composition of *Tristan und Isolde.* Another work, now known by the title *Wesendonck Lieder*, with texts by Wesendonck's wife, Mathilde, was in the process of composition when the relationship between the composer's wife Minna and Mathilde became so strained that it was crucial for the Wagners to again move, this time to Vienna.

A staging of *Tannhäuser* in Paris on March 13, 1861, turned into a debacle that sent Wagner's life into a downward spiral.

When King Ludwig II of Bavaria came to power, Wagner was fortunate to find him to be a generous new patron. About the same time, the composer's love interest was directed to Cosima von Bülow, the daughter of Franz Liszt, and the wife of Han von Bülow. She joined him in Munich about 1864 and in an unusual circumstance for the time, they lived together unmarried until 1870. Minna Wagner died in 1866, and in the summer of 1870 Cosima von Bülow's marriage was dissolved. Prior to their marriage in August 1870, they had three children: two daughters, Isolde (born in 1865) and Eva (born in 1867), and a son, Siegfried (born in 1869). During this period Wagner worked on the libretto of *Parsifal*, continued composition on *Die Meistersinger*, redirected his attention to the "Ring" cycle, and saw the first performance of *Tristan*. Against his better judgment and under pressure from King Ludwig, Wagner allowed performances of *Das Rheingold* in 1869 and *Die Walküre* in 1870. The "Ring" opera *Siegfried* was completed in 1871 and *Götterdämmerung* was finished in 1874. Both were first performed in 1876.

The composer's next major conceptual project was the design and projected building of a festival theater in Bayreuth. Funds were secured from the Bayreuth town council, King Ludwig II, and other contributors. The Wagners moved to Bayreuth in 1872, the construction of the theater was accomplished between 1872 and 1876, and it opened in the summer of 1876 with a performance of the "Ring" funded by King Ludwig II. While artistically successful, the festival was a major disappointment financially.

Following a hiatus, he again began to work on *Parsifal*. The composition of his final opera spanned the years 1877–82. Richard Wagner died on February 13, 1883, while in Venice. This occurred several hours after a quarrel with Cosima about a young cast member of *Parsifal*, Carrie Pringle, with whom he had become captivated.

Selected Works

Orchestral Works

Twenty-two complete orchestral works, mostly overtures or incidental music. The majority were written before 1840, and the most important of Wagner's orchestra work is *Siegfried Idyll* (1870). Also, there is a *Grosser Festmarsch* (*Centennial March*) written in 1876, for the centennial of the United States. There are about five projected, incomplete, or sketched works that survive.

Piano Works

There are thirteen works for piano dating from 1832–76. Three early sonatas are lost.

Choral Works

Thirteen or fourteen choral works of various kinds survive, dating from 1831 or 1832 to 1880. Several of the later works are for children's voices.

Songs and Solo Arias

Ten independent solo vocal works; seven pieces for Goethe's *Faust*; and the five *Wesendonck Lieder*, this last group being the most significant contribution to this category. There are eight works that are lost sketches or fragments.

Planned or Incomplete Dramatic Works

Fifteen including: *Jesus von Nazareth, Achilleus, Die Sieger*, and *Luthers Hochzeit*.

Operas and Music Dramas

There are thirteen if each of the four "Ring" music dramas is counted as an independent work: *Die Feen; Das Liebesverbot; Rienzi; Der fliegende Holländer; Tannhäuser;* and *Lohengrin. Der Ring des Nibelungen: Das Rheingold, Die Walküre, Siegfried,* and *Gotterdämmerung. Tristan und Isolde;* Die Meistersinger von Nürnberg; and *Parsifal*.

Books, articles, reviews, program notes, and public speeches

Extensive and numerous. Selected important ones include: "Die deutsche Oper" (1834); "Autobiographical Sketch" (1842–43); "Der Nibelungen-Mythus: als Entwurf zu einem Drama" (1848); "Theater-Reform" (1849); "Die Kunst und die Revolution" (1849); *Das Kunstwerk der Zukunft* (1850); "Das Judentum in der Musik" (1850, revised 1869); *Oper und Drama* (1850–1851); "Deutsche Kunst und deutsche Politik" (1867); "Vortwork zu Mein Leben" (1870); "Über die Aufführung des Bühnenfestspieles: *Der Ring des Nibelungen* und memorandum über Aufführung des *Ring* in markgräflichen Opernhaus Bayreuth" (1871); "An Friedrich Nietzsche" (1872); "Das Bühnenfestspielhaus zu Bayreuth: nebst einem Bericht über die Grundsteinlegung desselben" (1873); and "Religion und Kunst" (1880).

Writings by Richard Wagner in English translations and reference works

Wagner on Music and Drama: A Compendium of Richard Wagner's Prose Works. Edited by Albert Goldman and Evert Sprinnchorn and translated by William Ashton Ellis. New York: E. P. Dutton, 1964.

Richard Wagner's Prose Works. 8 vols. Edited and translated by William Ashton Ellis. 1892–99. Reprinted New York: Broude Brothers, 1966.

Richard Wagner: Sämtliche Werke, in Verbindung mit der Bayerischen Akademie der Schönen Künste München. Edited by Carl Dahlhaus, Egon Voss, and others. Mainz: B. Schott's Söhne, 1970.

Barth, Herbert, Dietrich Mack, and Egon Voss, eds. *Wagner: A Documentary Study*. New York: Oxford University Press, 1975.

Spencer, Stewart, ed. *Wagner*. Ongoing journal about Wagner and his works). 1980– present.

Deathridge, John, Martin Geck, and Egon Voss. *Wagner-Werk-Verzeichnis (WWV): Verzeichnis der musikalischen Werke Richard Wagners und ihrer Quellen.* Mainz: B. Schott's Söhne, 1986.

Selected Letters of Richard Wagner. Edited by Stewart Spencer and Barry Millington. New York: W. W. Norton, 1988.

Wagner, Richard. *My Life (Mein Leben).* Translated by Andrew Grey and edited by Mary Whittall. New York: DaCapo Press, 1992.

Bibliography

Adorno, Theodor W. "Wagner, Nietzsche, and Hitler," *Kenyon Review* 9 (1947): 155–62.

Aberbach, Alan David. *The Ideas of Richard Wagner: An Examination and Analysis of His Major Aesthetic, Political, Economic, Social, and Religious Thoughts.* Rev. ed. Lanham, Maryland: University Press of America, 1988.

Amerongen, Martin, van. *Wagner: A Case History.* Trans. Stewart Spencer and Dominic Cakebread. London: J. M. Dent and Sons, 1983.

Barzun, Jacques. *Darwin, Marx, Wagner: Critique of a Heritage.* 2d ed. Chicago: University of Chicago Press, 1981.

Burbidge, Peter, and Richard Sutton. *The Wagner Companion.* New York: Cambridge University Press, 1979.

Cooke, Deryck. *I Saw the World End: A Study of Wagner's "Ring."* London: Oxford University Press, 1979.

Dahlhaus, Carl. *Richard Wagner's Music Dramas.* Translated by Mary Whittall. Cambridge: Cambridge University Press, 1979.

Deathridge, John, and Carl Dahlhaus. *The New Grove Wagner.* New York: W. W. Norton, 1984.

Donington, Robert. *Wagner's "Ring" and Its Symbols: The Music and the Myth.* 3rd ed. London: Faber and Faber, 1974.

Furness, Raymond. *Wagner and Literature.* Manchester: Manchester University Press, 1982 (New York: St. Martin's Press, 1982).

Katz, Jacob. *The Darker Side of Genius: Richard Wagner's Anti-Semitism.* Hanover, N.H.: Brandeis University Press and University Press of New England, 1986.

Large, David, and William Weber, eds., in collaboration with Anne Dzamba Sessa. *Wagnerism in European Culture and Politics.* Ithaca, N.Y.: Cornell University Press, 1984.

Magee, Elizabeth. *Richard Wagner and the Niebelungs.* Oxford: Clarendon Press/New York: Oxford University Press, 1990.

Mann, Thomas. *Pro and Contra Wagner.* Translated by Allan Blunder, with an introduction by Erich Heller. Chicago: University of Chicago Press, 1985.

Mayer, Hans. *Richard Wagner in Bayreuth: 1876–1976.* Stuttgart: Besler, 1976.

Millington, Barry, ed. *The Wagner Compendium: A Guide to Wagner's Life and Music.* New York: Schirmer Books, 1992.

Müller, Ulrich, and Peter Wapnewski. *Wagner Handbook.* Edited and translated by John Deathridge. Cambridge, Mass.: Harvard University Press, 1992.

Nietzsche, Friedrich. *The Case of Wagner. The Twilight of the Idols. Nietzsche contra Wagner. Works of Friedrich Nietzsche,* vol. 11. Translated by Thomas Commoni. New York: Macmillan, 1924.

Newman, Ernest. *The Life of Richard Wagner.* 4 vols., 1933–47. Reprinted Cambridge: Cambridge University Press, 1976.

———. *The Wagner Operas,* 1963. Reprinted Princeton, N.J.: Princeton University Press, 1991.

Sadie, Stanley, ed. *Wagner and His Operas.* London: Macmillan/New York: St. Martin's Press, 2000.

Shaw, George Bernard. *The Perfect Wagnerite: A Commentary on the Nibelung's Ring,* 1898. Reprinted New York: Dover, 1967.

Voss, Egon. "Once Again: The Secret of Form in Wagner's Works," *Wagner* 4 (1983): 66–79.

Wagner, Cosima. *Cosima Wagner's Diaries.* Edited by Martin Gregor-Delin and Dietrich Mack. Translated and with an introductioin by Geoffrey Skelton. 2 vols. London: Collins, 1978.

Westernhagen, Curt von. *The Forging of the Ring: Richard Wagner's Composition Sketches for* Der Ring des Niebelungen. Translated by Arnold and Mary Whittall. Cambridge: Cambridge University Press, 1976.

WALDEN 1854

Prose nature study by Henry David Thoreau

Walden is Henry David Thoreau's best-known work. It is not only an American classic but an internationally recognized masterpiece; only "Civil Disobedience" comes close in popularity and influence. Most estimates also consider it his most important work, though some favor his remarkable, barely plumbed *Journal*. The text is usually described as promoting a way of living in nature, its counterparts found among such works as William Wordsworth's *Prelude*; yet *Walden* is that and much more, representing many moods and many dimensions whose relations Thoreau explores with concentrated precision. On the basis of his study of two years of living in the woods, he builds a dense, nuanced reading of the political, economic, and psychosocial ramifications implicit in any experience of "life in the woods." *Walden* suggests that no reading of such a life can be innocent of those aspects. Every reading must show that, outside of privileged moments like that at the beginning of "Sounds," our connectivity with nature takes in more than what we ordinarily speak of as "natural." Being in nature is a mode of being in the world, a mode so radical that it takes in most things to which we relate, not just the hugging of trees. Relation is, then, not only a persistent practice but an act fundamental to our being in the world. We perform it every day at a multiplicity of levels in a multitude of contexts.

That is why Thoreau begins *Walden* by locating the solitary "I" in the woods near a village for a precise length of time, linking the geography to the completion of a cycle: "At present I am a sojourner in civilized life again." To locate the "I" in this way is to establish the temporal and spatial parameters of relation, specifically his connection to a community. That connection is, at once, social, political, and economic, the latter affirmed by his emphasis on the fact that he lived alone and made his living "by the labor of [his] hands only." Taken in its broadest sense, economy is shown to be a category touching on the social, the political, and the personal. Economic ramifications extend to every aspect of Thoreau's experience as well as the text that describes them and the language that does the describing; yet what is true of the economic is true of other categories as well. In fact, we need them all: no single category fits every aspect of his world; no single mode of experience can adequately describe them all. Our world is best handled through multiplicity and manifold modes of relation.

What these varied modes pronounce are the discourses associated with the various categories (taking "discourse" to mean a speech that brings into play the values implicit in an ideology). After addressing the question of "I" at the beginning of *Walden*, Thoreau slips quickly through images of excursion and exotica to an extreme of the alien, the Brahman practice of "penance," the torturing of the body beyond its "natural" position. That language put into place, he turns its implications to Concord practices: Brahmanic discourse becomes the language of an allegory on what his neighbors do to themselves. Commenting ironically on the family of humankind, a set of foreign values comes to figure some of the drearier aspects of the domestic. As he puts the question of such figures in the chapter "The Bean-field," "some must work in fields if only for the sake of tropes and expression, to serve a parable-maker one day"; and in fact that analogy builds on the allegorical potential of two further discourses, the agricultural and the prophetic. Such interlocking becomes a major practice in *Walden*, as allegories multiply and combine to extend their force. A master rhetorician, fascinated by the promise of allegory in certain modes of discourse, Thoreau begins his book with an economic model and, typically tongue in cheek, gets quickly to the point of using the language of quest romance, itself the archetype of Western allegory, to figure the meaning of his sojourn in the woods: "I long ago lost a hound, a bay horse, and a turtledove, and am still on their trail." Discourses from various directions meet and mingle in *Walden*. The text is a shrewd and potent heteroglossia in which the familiar language of nature encounters, qualifies, and is qualified by a complex of other discourses at Thoreau's command. In fact, all the discourses interrogate each other, their meeting a matter of mutual illumination.

Of course, those meetings affect the text's tonality. Because *Walden* holds so many aspects and considerations in suspension, it owns a potential for paradox and self-contradiction, indeed has a penchant for them. The text is shot through with ambiguities and ambivalence, especially pertaining to the life in Nature, the Wordsworthian life of things, that is its guiding theme. To make the encounter of discourses plainly legible, Thoreau frames their meeting in terms of a master narrative, the passage of the seasons; indeed, he squeezes an experience of two years, two months, and two days into a single instance of the cycle. Just as the opening paragraph maps his relation to community, so does that master narrative, humankind's oldest and most inclusive allegory, map his relation to history and the termini of experience. In fact, a glance at the table of contents makes clear its organization in terms of the acts of organic nature, the ubiquitous, central, and centrifying trope of every nature-based Romanticism. Thus does *Walden* identify itself as Romantic text, placing itself in cultural history. Thus do the bundlings of discourse begin their interplay and lead the text through rich and ironic dialectics. In this dialogue one comes across, for example, Rousseauistic sympathy with nature (the beginning of "Solitude") and, several chapters later (in the study of "Higher Laws" and the body's materiality), a passionate insistence that "Nature is hard to be overcome, but she must be overcome." *Walden* spends most of its length undoing the implications of its table of contents, putting particular effort into the ending of the text. The cycle does not finish in the ultimate chapter, but in the penultimate; *Walden* ends with a "Conclusion" that exhorts us to start on a tangent to the cycle's sphere, avoiding engulfment until we are "sun down, moon down, and at last earth down too." But in this text so taut with ongoing dialectics such urgency cannot be more than one more voice in the plethora of voicings, the radical debate Thoreau reports on in his text. Whatever the title of its ultimate chapter, *Walden*, like its counterpart in *The Prelude*, like texts as different as *Don Juan* and the theories and fiction of Friedrich von Schlegel, never ends conclusively, never brings its Romantic dialectics to a rest.

FREDERICK GARBER

Text

Walden; or Life in the Woods. 1854.

Bibliography

Buell, Lawrence. *The Environmental Imagination: Thoreau, Nature Writing, and the Formation of American Culture.* Cambridge, Mass.: Belknap Press of Harvard University Press, 1995.

Cavell, Stanley. *The Senses of* Walden. San Francisco: North Point Press, 1981.

———. *Thoreau's Redemptive Imagination.* New York: New York University Press, 1977.

Garber, Frederick. *Thoreau's Fable of Inscribing.* Princeton, N.J.: Princeton University Press, 1991.

Paul, Sherman. *The Shores of America: Thoreau's Inward Exploration.* Urbana: University of Illinois Press, 1958.

Peck, H. Daniel. *Thoreau's Morning Work: Memory and Perception in* "A Week on the Concord and Merrimack Rivers," "the Journal," and "Walden." New Haven, Conn.: Yale University Press, 1990.

Stoller, Leo. *After* Walden: *Thoreau's Changing Views on Economic Man.* Stanford, Calif.: Stanford University Press, 1957.

WALPOLE, HORACE 1717–1797

English author and antiquarian

Horace (Horatio) Walpole was the fourth son of the English prime minister Sir Robert Walpole. He was educated first at Eton, where he formed intensely close friendships with three like-minded young men, Thomas Ashton, Richard West, and, most significantly, the future poet Thomas Gray; the coterie together dubbed themselves the Quadruple Alliance. While at Eton, Walpole also established friendships with Henry Fiennes Clinton (ninth Earl of Lincoln), Charles Lyttelton, Henry Fiennes Lyttelton (later Bishop of Carlisle), George Montagu, and his dearly beloved cousin, Henry Seymour Conway. In 1735 he moved to King's College, Cambridge, where he remained until 1739.

Walpole's mother, Lady Catherine Walpole, to whom he was deeply attached, died in 1737, and only six months later his father married his long-term mistress, Maria Skerret (who herself died in 1738). The suddenness of these events may have hastened Horace's decision to embark on a modified "grand tour," which he undertook with Thomas Gray in the spring of 1739. The two men made their way through France toward Italy, where Walpole first met an individual who was to be a lifelong friend and correspondent, Horace Mann, who was then the assistant or chargé d'affaires to the absentee British minister at the court of Tuscany. After over two years of traveling together, however, Walpole and Gray engaged in a quarrel, a dispute that resulted in Gray's swift and solitary return to England (the two men were to be reconciled some five years later through the efforts of a mutual unidentified friend).

Following his own return to England in 1741, Walpole commenced his duties, such as they were, as member of Parliament (MP) for Callington in Cornwall (he was elected to the family borough while still abroad; he was later MP for Castle Rising and Lynn). His father had also secured a place in the Exchequer worth several thousand pounds a year. He was deeply affected by the death of his father in 1745, although in the years following his return to England the two had been able to spend some productive time together at Sir Robert's spectacular estate at

Houghton in Norfolk. Shortly after his father's death Walpole purchased the property Chopp'd Straw Hill on the banks of the Thames across from Richmond Park. In the years to come, Walpole effected a miraculous metamorphosis in the undistinguished and largely unpromising three-story home, transforming its precincts in time into one of the greatest architectural follies ever to be constructed in England. In so doing, he almost single-handedly transformed cultural and aesthetic history, turning the epithet from a term of scorn and derision into a style of decoration characterized by a lighthearted and fanciful sense of nostalgia and English playfulness. Strawberry Hill, as it soon became known, was to be calculatedly turned into what could be taken for the set of a medieval play, from the ornate library and the medieval refectory or great parlor, to the little Venetian parlor, the China closet, and the so-called beauty room (a ground-floor bedroom decorated with portraits of English kings and queens). In 1757 Walpole started a printing press at Strawberry Hill. (His own early attempts at poetry had already appeared in Robert Dodsley's enormously popular *A Collection of Poems by Several Hands*, 1748.)

Walpole began writing his own *Memoirs* in 1741; he was to continue work on the project for forty years. The volumes readied for publication at Strawberry Hill included his *Catalogue of Royal and Noble Authors* (1758), a five-volume *Anecdotes of Painting in England* (1762–80), and his own tragedy, *The Mysterious Mother* (1768). His *Castle of Otranto* was printed in 1764, and his *Historic Doubts on the Life and Reign of King Richard the Third* appeared in 1768. Walpole was a prolific writer of letters; his correspondence is easily among the most formidable and engaging in the English language. Later in life, he often visited Paris and enjoyed a close friendship with Madame de Deffand (his letters to her were destroyed on his death). In December, he succeeded his nephew as the fourth Earl of Orford. He died

in 1797 at his London home in Berkeley Square. Walpole's correspondence and memoirs have in the twentieth century been collected into an edition of forty-eight volumes.

ROBERT L. MACK

Biography

Born 1717. 1735–39: attended King's College, Cambridge. Embarked on a European Grand Tour with Thomas Gray, 1739. Returned to England, taking up a position as member of Parliament for Callington in Cornwall, and began writing his *Memoirs*, 1741. *The Castle of Otranto* published, 1764. Died at home in Berkeley Square, London, 1797.

Selected Works

A Letter from Xo Ho, a Chinese Philosopher at London. 1757.
A Catalogue of Royal and Noble Authors. 1758.
Anecdotes of Painting in England. 1762–80.
A Catalogue of Engravers. 1764.
The Castle of Otranto. 1765.
Historic Doubts on the Life and Reign of Richard the Third. 1768.
The Mysterious Mother. 1768.
Hieroglyphic Tales. 1785.
Walpole's Correspondence. Edited by W. S. Lewis. 48 vols.

Bibliography

Fothergill, Brian. *The Strawberry Hill Set: Horace Walpole and His Circle.* London: Faber and Faber, 1983.
Haggerty, George E. "Walpoliana," *Eighteenth Century Studies* 34, no. 2 (2001): 227–50.
Ketton-Cremer, R. W. New York: Longmans Green, 1940.
Mowl, Timothy. *Horace Walpole: The Great Outsider.* London: John Murray, 1996.
Sabor, Peter. *Horace Walpole: The Critical Heritage.* New York: Routledge and Kegan Paul, 1987.

WAR

The Romantic era in warfare lasted from the Valmy Campaign of 1792, when a French people's army shocked Europe by deflecting a coalition of European powers, to the wave attacks on the Somme in 1916. The legacy of this revolutionary age exploded into the wars and liberation struggles of the twentieth century, and echoes still in the underdeveloped regions of the world.

The transformation of warfare during the Romantic Era was characterized by three related dynamics: the nationalization of identity, the Romantic idealization of the military experience, and the industrialization of society. Europe's epidemic of nationalism infected entire populations, as the industrialization of production and the rationalization of agriculture created rootless masses desperate to reestablish group identities (waves of vitriolic nationalism and religious revivals often occurred in tandem). Increasingly superseded by the professional classes, and jarred by their loss of authority over the common man, the gentry embraced political conservatism and an idealized, sanitized vision of their heritage. This infatuation with a mythologized past soon filtered down to the literate, emulative middle class. After the convalescent decades following the Napoleonic fracture of

Europe and the restorative surgery of the Congress of Vienna, the combination of a proletariat embracing a national identity and the disposition of the officer classes to romanticize war in chivalric terms combined to make warfare greater in scale, bloodier in practice, and more difficult to resolve on a durable basis than it ever had been before. When it came to peace treaties, kings relented, but the masses resented.

By the latter half of the nineteenth century, the limited war had been replaced definitively by limited peace (Alsace-Lorraine, the Balkans, imperial frontiers); while dynastic rationalism had been replaced by a heady popular sense of grievance, and the wars of the professional had been replaced by wars of the citizen-in-arms. The same dynamics reenergized the European colonial experience, in which heroism again excused inhumanity, the sense of national destiny justified the seizure of raw materials and the forcible opening of markets, and industrial power could not be resisted by agrarian societies.

To the extent that one can gloss the pattern of development in the Romantic era's transformation of war, it might go as follows: without the land clearances and the initial concentration of production in mill towns, there is no Sir Walter Scott; without

Scott and his imitators down to G. A. Henty, there is no ability to persuade the new professional classes to equip mass armies; without mass armies, there are no lightning wars of nation against nation; and without the aberration—and ultimate illusion—of lightning wars, there are no world wars. Meanwhile, each stage of development saw increased lethality, due to the acceleration of industrialization, then mechanization.

Despite revived, highly specific codes of chivalry between the officers of opposing armies, noncombatants again became fair game, though on modern terms: European armies raped and plundered less (except in colonial possessions), but rationalized the internment and execution of civilians, from the suppression of the bourgeois insurrections of 1848, through the slaughter of the Parisian *Communards*, to the British scorched-earth policy and establishment of concentration camps in the Boer War (one may argue whether the Romantic era in warfare truly ended on the Somme or only in Auschwitz).

Although the earlier sense of nationhood in Europe is often underappreciated, the French Revolution indisputably unleashed forces of collective identity that, exacerbated by the industrial revolution, transformed dynastic struggles into popular struggles. For the first time since Europe advanced beyond tribal organization, workers and peasants identified with war efforts and volunteered en masse for military service. This difference in perception is highlighted powerfully in literature, from Grimmelshausen's seventeenth century portrayal of warfare as an unmitigated curse, to Theodor Fontane's late-Romantic insistence that making war was ennobling, purifying, and a duty for each able-bodied citizen. One of the most profound changes in military history occurred between the days of peasants fleeing into the forest to escape impressment into royal or ducal service and the enthusiasm of young men by the millions to go "over the top" to near-certain death.

While some young males always have been drawn to the military (or warrior) experience in every recorded culture, the Romantic era ideal of the military hero popularized an image of the dashing young officer whose battlefield exploits would be rewarded—after a picturesque flesh wound, perhaps—by the accolades of an adoring nation and the favors of a virginal female from a social station higher than his own. The hero's selfless friend might die—nobly—but never the hero himself (see works such as Lev Tolstoy's *Voina i Mir* [*War and Peace*], Sienkiewicz's *Ognyom i Myechom* [*With Fire and Sword*], or Scott's Waverley novels). In the aspirant societies of nineteenth century Europe, these ideals filtered down from the officer classes to those from which the other ranks were drawn, in utter contradiction to the realities of military campaigns. Napoleon sacrificed entire armies to personal ambition; in the Crimean War, cholera and poor logistics killed more soldiers than did enemy action; and grotesque faux chivalry—inspired by the novels of Sir Walter Scott—prolonged the American Civil War past half a million deaths. Yet, the idealization of warfare only accelerated.

The decade between 1861 and 1871, particularly, marked a turning point in human history. Each of the Romantic era currents that would make modern war so deadly and destructive came into full flood. Dismissed by European staffs as the result of New World incompetence, the bloodbath of the American Civil War (1861–65) would be repeated on an unprecedented scale on the Western Front between 1914 and 1918. The Civil War saw the first effective integration of railways for strategic mobility, the telegraph for national command of armies, and the quantum leap in lethality wrought by mass-produced, rifled weapons in the hands of citizen armies. During General William T. Sherman's "March to the Sea," it also saw the inauguration of the "total war" against enemy property that Europeans of the next century would elaborate into wars of extermination against enemy populations and the state's minorities, continuing the tradition through the most recent Balkan conflicts. In mid-decade, the Austro-Prussian War (1866) excited a faith in lightning campaigns that the subsequent Franco-Prussian War (1870–71) appeared to confirm. Finally, the Paris Commune (1871) wed nationalism to ideology in a form that prefigured the great totalitarian movements of the twentieth century, just as the Commune's bloody suppression collapsed the line between combatants and noncombatants.

Another particularly lethal development was the Romantic era's perversion of the scientific method inherited from the Enlightenment (in the liberal arts as well as in the military sphere). Awed by the power of rational inquiry, clinical observation, and higher mathematics to advance the sciences, various military charlatans (especially Baron Henri de Jomini and his disciples) constructed pseudoscientific theories that purported to "solve" the problems of military operations. The narrow and deficient education of military officers made them particularly susceptible to half-baked theories adorned with the trappings of science. By the long twilight of the Romantic Era, attempts to find the philosopher's stone of warfare, to make science of what was, at best, an art, and to impose geometric order on mankind's most disorderly endeavor, led to the sacrifice of millions on the battlefields of the Great War. Only Carl von Clausewitz, the West's sole philosopher of war and a Romantic figure of promethean obsessions, rejected formulae and described, as no one else in any culture has done, the risks, confusion, and dynamism of warfare. It was his fate to be read superficially and selectively by lesser minds, who transmuted his investigative thinking and abstract examples into prescriptions for wars of annihilation.

Romantic Era warfare culminated in mass delusions, mass armies, mass production, mass slaughter, and the worst destruction in the history of humankind.

RALPH PETERS

See also **Clausewitz, Carl von**

Bibliography

Chandler, David. *The Campaigns of Napoleon*. New York: Macmillan, 1966.

Clausewitz, Carl von. *Vom Kriege*. Bonn, Germany: Jubilaeumsausgabe, Duemmler Verlag, 1980.

Fontane, Theodor. *Der Krieg Gegen Frankreich*. Berlin: 1870–1871, 1873–1876.

Hedin, Sven. *Nach Osten!* Leipzig: Brockhaus, 1916.

In herausgegeben vom Militaergeschichtlichen Forschungsamt. "*Deutsche Militaer Geschichte*." Vol. I–IX. Munich: Bernard and Graefe, 1983.

Jomini, Baron de. *The Art of War*. Trans. Mendell and Craighill. Westport; Conn.: Greenwood, 1971.

Weigley, Russell F. *The Age of Battles*. Bloomington: Indiana University Press, 1991.

WATSON AND THE SHARK 1778

Painting by John Singleton Copley

In 1749, Brook Watson was fourteen years old and employed on a trade ship. While the ship was at anchor in Havana Harbor, Watson went swimming and was attacked by a shark. On the first pass the shark stripped Watson's right calf to the bone, and on returning took the right foot. Before the shark could strike a third time, a launch reached the boy and the shark was driven off with a boat hook. Watson underwent amputation and recovered.

By the mid-1770s, Watson, who would later serve as a member of Parliament, as Lord Mayor of London, and as chairman of Lloyds of London, was a successful trans-Atlantic merchant. It was during these years that he decided to have his life's most dramatic and defining moment memorialized on canvas. In 1775 John Singleton Copley left Boston, Massachusetts to pursue an artistic career in London. He received Watson's commission shortly thereafter.

Copley's *Watson and the Shark* was first exhibited in April 1778 at the British Royal Academy. Shown under the title *A boy attacked by a shark, and rescued by some seamen in a boat, founded on a fact which happened in the harbour of the Havannah*, the canvas caused a minor sensation. One reviewer wrote that it "reflected the highest honour on the composer," and Copley was subsequently elected a full member of the Royal Academy of Arts. Yet the accolades afforded the work are puzzling. As an example of the historical genre, Copley's painting was as revolutionary as the Academy was conservative. Eight years earlier, Benjamin West had revolutionized the historical genre with *The Death of General Wolfe* (1770), in the process causing a scandal that roused even George III to comment. It was "very ridiculous," the king felt, "to exhibit heroes in coats, breeches and cock's hats"; the proper depiction of heroes required the trappings of antiquity.

Copley, however, went a step further than West had. Like *The Death of General Wolfe*, *Watson and the Shark* is large, painted in the "grand style," and in a setting that is wholly modern. Yet the subject matter is anonymous. Despite being advertised as "founded on a fact," the characters were not named nor was it a recognizable event. In contradistinction, Théodore Géricault's Romantic masterpiece *The Raft of the Medusa* (1819), despite its concern with the lower orders, was based on an event that had commanded national attention. Just as Arthur Miller would later elevate the mundane actions of an obscure American salesman into high tragedy (*Death of a Salesman*, 1949), so Copley raised a boy of no moment into an important historical subject. In doing so, Copley democratized the historical genre. By depicting the heroism and struggle of those who labor outside the national gaze, Copley took West's revolution and extended it toward Romanticism.

In common with Géricault's *Raft*, *Watson* highlights the power of emotional empathy. The shark (more a representation of the sublime than a realistic likeness) is placed in confrontation with both Watson and the audience. This nexus of unnamed subject, audience, and sublime terror introduced viewer identification into historical painting. As Thomas Flexner states, "we

are asked to sympathize with an unfortunate only because he is a human being like ourselves."

The painting's relation to the New World has often been debated. This is understandable given the date of composition, the trans-Atlantic concerns of Watson, and Copley's nationality. To some, Watson's missing leg is linked to the American secession, and to others the painting's "shark-infested waters" are a metaphor for the New World in general. Yet these interpretations are too schematic and fail to acknowledge the historical events.

As Roger Stein details, more important than political symbolism are the painting's contributions to Romanticism and the American landscape. Both Hector Saint-John de Crèvecoeur and Herman Melville drew strong analogies between the ocean and the American continent in their writing. For the new man in the New World, the natural sublime was to be confronted, not contemplated or extolled: the ocean had to be crossed and the wilderness settled. Faced with a potentially lethal environment, action, not worship, defined the American Romantic. In this regard, Watson anticipates Captain Ahab's "Thy right worship is defiance." At heart, the painting presents the boat community confronting the natural sublime and acting. As Stein writes, "the miracle is effected not by a transfigured Christ but by men in a boat."

In the painting, a black sailor occupies a strong central position. If viewed as a triangular composition, with the base formed by Watson and the shark and the pinnacle by the black sailor, the canvas lends itself to an antislavery reading. Certainly, by placing the black sailor in a position of compositional power, Copley was subverting the Classicism of Joshua Reynolds, yet there is little further evidence to support the racial motif. By 1778 Copley was avidly apolitical, feeling politics to be a distraction from art. Watson, on the contrary, made much of his fortune via the slave trade, and as a member of parliament argued strenuously for its retention. When the canvas is viewed as a whole, however, the black sailor occupies an ambiguous position. While he occupies the triangular apex, he does not hold a position of equality with the other—all Caucasian—sailors. In comparison, he is strangely immobile and, further, is directly juxtaposed with the one sailor in the picture who is engaged in attack rather than rescue. Reminiscent of images of St. George, this attacking sailor is dynamic heroism personified. He is the focal point of the boat crew's determination; in comparison, the black sailor's movements toward Watson seem ineffectual.

Morality is perhaps the painting's most prominent theme. When it was bequeathed to London's Christ's Hospital—an institution for the care of boys—Watson hoped it would provide a "most usefull Lesson to Youth," illustrating the presence in the universe of both good and evil and the possibility of salvation and redemption. Realized by Copley, this moral spectacle placed the modern and obscure on a par with the great heroes of antiquity. As such, the work deserves its place alongside the prime documents that helped define the new Romantic consciousness.

RICHARD HAW

Work

Watson and the Shark. Oil on canvas, 182.25 cm by 230 cm. First exhibited as *A boy attacked by a shark, and rescued by some seamen in a boat, founded on a fact which happened in the harbour of the Havannah*, London Royal Academy, April 1778; bequeathed to London's Christ's Hospital, 1803; acquired by the National Academy of Art, Washington, D.C., 1965.

Bibliography

Abrams, Ann Uhry. "Politics, Prints, and John Singleton Copley's *Watson and the Shark*," *Art Bulletin* 61, no. 2 (1976): 265–76.

Boime, Albert. "Blacks in Shark-Infested Waters: Visual Encodings of Racism in Copley and Homer." *Smithsonian Studies in American Art* 3 (1989): 19–47.

Dos Passos, John. "A Narrative Painting," *Art in America* 42, no. 2 (1959): 48.

Flexner, James Thomas. *John Singleton Copley*. Boston: Houghton Mifflin, 1948.

Honour, Hugh. *The Image of the Black in Western Art*. 4 vols. Cambridge, Mass.: Harvard University Press, 1989.

Jaffe, Irma B. "John Singleton Copley's *Watson and the Shark*," *American Art Journal* 9 (1977): 15–25.

Masur, Louis P. "Reading *Watson and the Shark*," *New England Quarterly* 67, no. 3 (1994): 427–54.

Mills, Ellen G. "Copley's *Watson and the Shark*," *Antiques* 143 (1993): 162–71.

Prown, Jules David. *John Singleton Copley*. 2 vols. Cambridge, Mass.: Harvard University Press, 1966.

Stein, Roger. "Copley's *Watson and the Shark* and Aesthetics in the 1770s." In *Discoveries & Considerations: Essays on Early American Literature and Aesthetics Presented to Harold Janta*. Edited by Calvin Israel. Albany, N.Y.: State University of New York Press, 1976.

Wallace, Michele. "Defacing History," *Art in America* 78 (1990): 120–29, 184–86.

WAVERLEY, OR, 'TIS SIXTY YEARS SINCE 1814

Novel by Sir Walter Scott

Waverley is set during the second Jacobite rebellion of 1745. Its hero, Edward Waverley, a young Englishman of Romantic sensibilities from an old Jacobite family, receives his commission and joins his regiment in Scotland. Waverley is encouraged by his uncle to visit an old family friend, the Baron of Bradwardine, at his mansion in Tully-Veolan, Perthshire. Bradwardine is also a Jacobite sympathizer, and Waverley is strongly attracted to his daughter, Rose. Waverley becomes fascinated by stories of Highland bandits, which he interprets as Romantic, and visits the Highlands at the invitation of Evan Dhu of the Clan Ivor; here he meets and befriends the clan chieftain, Fergus Mac-Ivor (or Vich Ian Vohr, "the Son of John the Great," to give him his full Gaelic name and title), a clever politician, and his beautiful and fanatical Jacobite sister, Flora, with whom Waverley promptly falls madly in love. Such fraternization with the enemy causes Waverley considerable trouble with his superior officers when he rejoins his regiment, and he is soon dismissed when an attempted mutiny in the ranks is erroneously attributed to him, with only the intervention of Rose Bradwardine saving him from prison. Outraged and confused by this injustice, and encouraged by Flora and Mac-Ivor, Waverley joins the cause of Charles Stuart. By saving the life of the English colonel, Talbot, during the Battle of Prestopans when the Jacobite forces are routed, Waverley secures a pardon for his treason. His friends, however, are not spared during the Highland clearances that follow the decisive victory of the English Hanovarians at Culloden, and Mac-Ivor and Evan Dhu are executed. At the conclusion of the narrative, Flora rejects Waverley and enters a convent in France, and he finally marries Rose.

Waverley was Walter Scott's first novel, begun as early as 1805, and finally published anonymously in 1814, the author later writing, "My original motive for publishing the work anonymously, was the consciousness that it was an experiment on the public taste which might very probably fail." *Waverley*, of course, did not fail, appearing in four editions in the first year of publication. Its success turned Scott, previously a rather outmoded Romantic poet, into what William Hazlitt later described as "undoubtedly the most popular writer of the age." Nonetheless, *Waverley* was indeed an experiment in the novel, something the author signals clearly by distancing himself from both the Gothic and the chivalric romance in his opening chapters. As Ian Duncan has written, the publication of *Waverley* "was a decisive event in the institutional formation of the modern narrative." Although writing in a narrative tradition that can easily be traced back to Thomas Deloney and Thomas Nashe in the sixteenth century and refined by Daniel Defoe in the eighteenth century, Scott's version of the historical narrative was decisive in its innovation and influence (the Victorian vogue for antiquity can be directly traced to *Waverley*). In *Waverley* and his subsequent novels, Scott offers a historical narrative that does not center around the politically powerful, but instead examines the subjective, personal, and social implications of living through seismic political events that one can neither control nor fully comprehend. As Georg Lukács has argued, Scott's work represents a post-Enlightenment and progressive historicism that breaks with the conception of the unalterable nature of humanity, exposing the contradictions endemic within the bourgeois Whig interpretation of history, with the prosaic replacing the poetic in terms of both "hero" and moral. Edward Waverley is therefore, in Lukácsian terms, "mediocre"; his role in the great Jacobite adventure summarized in volume 2 of the novel thus: "he contemplated the strangeness of his fortune, which seemed to delight in placing him at the disposal of others, without the power of directing his own motions." Waverley's experiences are always portrayed subjectively. In the manner of Lev Tolstoy, for example, both he and the reader miss the crucial battle of the rebellion (Culloden, the last battle to be fought on British soil); his experiences and perceptions come from traveling to Edinburgh in its aftermath. Such defamiliarization leads Lukács to argue that Scott's work is a "renunciation of Romanticism," but it can equally be argued that Scott's trick is to actually fuse his new, humanist historicism with the codes of Romanticism, and to leave both apparently contradictory positions to coexist.

Such a device may represent the author's own self-consciousness, yet the Romantic impulse is by no means dismissed; rather, it is merely pragmatically mediated. When Flora escorts Waverley into a secluded glen to recite some Gaelic poetry to him, she deliberately chooses a complementary setting notable for "the Romantic wildness of the scene." When Waverley encounters his first Highlander, the wild and woolly Evan Dhu, he is surprised by his perfect English and when Evan, eager to impress, takes a pot shot at an eagle with his pistol he misses. Similarly, clan chieftain Mac-Ivor has spent much of his life in the French Court and, we are told, "at the moment he should unsheathe his claymore, it might be difficult to say whether it would be most with the view of making James Stuart a king, or Fergus Mac-Ivor an earl." This is not to say that Scott's purpose is to deconstruct even Waverley's naive Romanticism (hence his disclaimer of Miguel de Cervantes Saavedra in volume 1), but to reconcile it with historical reality, much as Waverley does himself: "he felt himself entitled to say firmly, though perhaps with a sigh, that the romance of his life was ended, and that its real history had now commenced." Mac-Ivor, and especially Flora, cannot so easily adapt to expediency and therefore belong to a lost race that Scott has in part, through transcribing folk ballads and highland traditions, set out to commemorate, but not necessarily condone. They are the last of their line, ancestors, but not our ancestors; it is the children of the stable, if rather boring, Rose and Edward Waverley that shall inherit the earth, while probably still learning the same stories that so enchanted the author of *Waverley* in his youth.

STEPHEN CARVER

Bibliography

Anderson, W. E. K., ed. *The Journal of Sir Walter Scott*. Oxford: Clarendon Press, 1972.

Duncan, Ian. *Modern Romance and Transformations of the Novel: The Gothic, Scott, Dickens*. Cambridge: Cambridge University Press, 1992.

Ellis, S[tewart] M[arsh]. *The Solitary Horseman, or The Life and Adventures of G.P.R. James*. London: Cayme Press, 1927.

Gordon, Robert C. *Under Which King? A Study of the Scottish Waverley Novels*. Edinburgh, 1969.

Hart, Francis R. *Scott's Novels: The Plotting of Historic Survival*. Charlottesville: Virginia University Press, 1966.

Hayden, John O., ed. *Scott: The Critical Heritage*. London: Routledge and Kegan Paul, 1970.

Hazlitt, William. *The Spirit of the Age or Contemporary Portraits* (1825). Reprinted, London: Collins, 1969.

Hillhouse, James T. *The Waverley Novels and Their Critics*. New York, 1936.

Hobsbawm, Eric, and Terence Ranger, eds. *The Invention of Tradition*. Cambridge: Cambridge University Press, 1989.

Johnson, Edgar. *Sir Walter Scott The Great Unknown*. London, 1970.

Lukács, Georg. *The Historical Novel*. Trans. Hannah and Stanley Mitchell. London: Merlin Press, 1974.

Parsons, Coleman O. *Witchcraft and Demonology in Scott's Fiction*. Edinburgh: Oliver and Boyd, 1964.

Rance, Nicholas. *The Historical Novel and Popular Politics in 19th Century England*. London: Vision, 1975.

Robertson, Fiona. *Legitimate Histories: Scott, Gothic, and the Authorities of Fiction*. Oxford: Clarendon Press, 1994.

Sanders, Andrew. *The Victorian Historical Novel, 1840–1880*. London: Macmillan, 1978.

Welsh, Alexander. *The Hero of the Waverley Novels*. Princeton, N.J.: Princeton University Press, 1963.

Williams, Ioan, ed. *Sir Walter Scott on Novelists and Fiction*. London: Routledge and Kegan Paul, 1968.

WEBER, CARL MARIA (FRIEDRICH ERNST) VON 1786–1826

German composer

Carl Maria von Weber's life was curtailed by tuberculosis, but his contribution to German Romantic culture was of the greatest importance. This was so for instrumental music and, above all, for the development of music drama—the latter both for German culture in general and for opera as a Romantic medium.

An intensely peripatetic youth in his father's touring theater company resulted in a very patchy education. It also provided an exceptionally intimate contact with a wide range of theatrical repertory and a deep mastery of theatrical process and effect. It also resulted in a tendency towards stereotyped characterization and treatment of dramatic situation and (after his contact with foreign operas) to a facile combination of differing genres and musical treatment. At his best (as in the remarkable *Der Freischütz*) this eclecticism expanded the medium of German opera into a hybrid but intensely Romantic medium. At other times, it weakened potentially powerful works.

Weber's father was a town musician in Eutin who gave up his post and moved to Hamburg to start his own theater company in which all his family participated. Weber's education was very sporadic, since most of his childhood was spent touring in popular plays and singspielen. During a longer stay in Hildburghausen (necessitated by his mother's illness) Weber received more extended musical tuition from Johann Peter Heuschkel, a talented musician who provided him with a sound musical foundation and the basis for his pianistic virtuosity. Weber also studied with Michael Haydn in Salzburg (where he published his first compositions).

The family moved to Munich after his mother's death and there Weber composed his first opera, *Die Macht der Liebe und des Weins* (*The Power of Love and Wine*, 1798). More itinerant travels finally found Weber in Vienna in 1803. There he studied with the renowned Abbé Vogler—whose interest in folklore and the exotic deeply influenced Weber. Vogler also recommended Weber for the post of kappellmeister in Breslau, which Weber took up in June 1804 at the age of seventeen. His desire to reform the organization and repertory of a very conservative company met with strong resistance from the older musicians who resented the young upstart.

A period in Karlsruhe was unproductive and in July 1807 he moved to Stuttgart. Three further years of restless travel around Germany produced his first piano concerto (1810) and two clarinet concertos. Despite some structural weaknesses these works are major contributions to the Romantic concerto literature and the later *Koncertstück* for piano and orchestra also extends the form of the Romantic concerto.

During this period he completed an opera, *Silvana*, which was produced in Frankfurt on September 16, 1810. This is a curiously muddled mixture of expanding genius, containing many of the elements that would come to fruition in his later operas, and clichéd theatrical effects. It also evidences Weber's love of the picturesque and the bizarre, and of creating powerfully evocative emotions and portraying natural phenomena.

A one-act singspiel, *Abu Hassan*, is less ambitious, but more coherent. It received a successful production in Munich in 1811. Two years later Weber was persuaded to accept the directorship of the opera in Prague. He transformed the opera house in Prague: not only the music, but also the acting, staging, costumes, and scenery received his detailed attention. He was attempting to treat opera as a complete work of art and wanted the public to view it thus. He also emphasized German opera (introducing Prague to Ludwig van Beethoven's *Fidelio*, Giacomo Meyerbeer's *Wirth und Gast*, and Ludwig Spohr's *Faust*), but since there were too few high-quality German operas, he also produced French works by a wide range of composers. This growing familiarity with the French repertory considerably influenced Weber's own work. Weber also refined his concepts and ideals by extensive discussions with other composers and by writing on the subject of the future of German opera.

These ideals were most fully articulated in *Der Freischütz* (*The Freeshooter*, 1821). This is undoubtedly his finest achievement and remains a monument of German Romantic art. Its performance in Berlin on June 18, 1821 was a triumph that rapidly spread throughout Germany and abroad. This work combined folk elements (in characterization and plot as well as some of the musical numbers) with other sections of ornate vocal treatment (an influence of French opera). To this Weber added very powerful evocations of the natural and supernatural world (most notably in the "Wolf's Glen" scene). Tapping a strong vein of nationalism, this eclectic mixture made *Der Freischütz* the most popular German opera of its era. Beyond this popularity, *Der Freischütz* (with Spohr's *Faust*) took singspiel to the furthest extent it reached as a vehicle for German Romanticism. The influence of *Der Freischütz* was of the greatest import. It extended both the nationalist subject matter and motivic musical treatment beyond anything that had preceded it and formed the basis for later Romantic achievements by composers such as Marschner and Richard Wagner.

Weber completed two more operas. The first was *Euryanthe*, written for Vienna. In this work Weber, convinced that German opera must become completely through-composed, eliminated spoken dialogue and used orchestrally accompanied recitative. There are many passages of great dramatic power and the transitions between sections are very effective. However, overall, this work is crippled by a weak and amateurish libretto by Helmina von Chezy.

A further invitation came from Charles Kemble, the manager of the Royal Opera House, Covent Garden, to write a new opera for London. Weber accepted the invitation (mainly for mercenary reasons) and started work on an English libretto (by Planché) of *Oberon*. He traveled to London in February 1826. Although the opera was rapturously received and has much great music, the pantomimic libretto was, if anything, even poorer than that for *Euryanthe* and the opera is dramatically feeble. Weber intended to revise it, but, exhausted by effort and illness, he died on June 5, 1826, the day before he had planned to return to Germany.

BENEDICT SARNAKER

See also **Der Freischütz; Wagner, Richard**

Biography

Born in Eutin, Germany, probably November 18, 1786. Spent his youth as an itinerant theater performer. Later held various posts as director of music and opera. The major success of *Der Freischütz* (*The Freeshooter*, 1821) made him nationally and internationally famous. Two more major works had major problems and his early death from tuberculosis prevented Weber from creating further work or revising these flawed operas. He died in London on June 5, 1826.

Selected Works

Concerto for Clarinet and Orchestra No. 1. 1811.
Concerto for Clarinet and Orchestra No. 2. 1811.
Koncertstück for Piano and Orchestra. 1821.
Der Freischütz. 1821.
Euryanthe. 1823.
Oberon. 1826.

Bibliography

Becker, W. *Die deutsche Oper in Dresden unter der Leitung von Carl Maria von Weber, 1817–26*. Berlin, 1962.

Berlioz, Hector. "Le Freyschütz de Weber." In *Voyage musicale en Allemagne et en Italie*, vol. 1. 1842.

Dalhaus, Carl. "Webers 'Freischütz' und die Idee der romantischen Oper," Österreichische Musikzeitschrift 38 (1983): 381–88.

Finscher, Ludwig. "Weber's Freischütz: Conceptions and Misconceptions" Proceedings of the Royal Musical Association 110 (1983–84): 79–90.

Jones, G. "Backgrounds and Themes of the Operas of Carl Maria von Weber." Ph.D. diss., Cornell University, 1972.

Kind, F. *Freischütz-Buch*. 1874. Includes firsthand account of the opera's composition.

Kröplin, E. *Wagner und Weber: der Vorgang einer Theatralisi erung*. Dresden, 1987.

Tusa, Michael C. *Euryanthe and Cal Maria von Weber's Dramaturgy of German Opera*. Oxford, 1991.

Wagner, Richard. "Der Freischütz in Paris." In *Gesammelte Schriften und Dichtungen*. vol. I. Leipzig, 1871.

Warrack, John. *Carl Maria von Weber*. London, 1976.

———, ed. *Carl Maria von Weber: Writings on Music*. Cambridge, 1981.

Weber und der Gedanke der Nationaloper. Dresden, 1986. A collection of important essays.

WELHAVEN, JOHAN SEBASTIAN 1807–1873

Norwegian poet

Johan Sebastian Welhaven belongs to that group of poets who have a fairly limited range, but within that range produce some of the great poems of their language. It is as such a poet that Welhaven might have been remembered had his path in life not brought him into conflict with Norway's greatest poet, Henrik Wergeland, whom he accused of writing undisciplined verse. From that point on, his life and work became irrevocably linked with that of Wergeland and acquired historical significance.

Welhaven was born in Bergen in western Norway, an area that he loved and returned to often in his poetry. He was the son of the chaplain to the leper hospital and, by all accounts, a sensitive boy. At school he met a teacher who was to have a decisive influence on his literary taste and development. The teacher, Lyder Sagen, had spent his youth in Copenhagen during the golden age of Danish Romanticism, dominated by such names as Johan Ludvig Heiberg and Adam Gottlieb Oehlenschläger. He found in Welhaven a ready pupil when he taught that a work of art should have absolute harmony of form and content. This aesthetic principle, though developed and elaborated, was to remain the basis of Welhaven's life, literary practice, and criticism.

When Welhaven moved to Christiania (now Oslo) to study, he quickly became part of a circle of highly intelligent, cultured young men who reacted against what they saw as the wildness and uncouthness of Wergeland and his circle. Wergeland was democratic and forward-looking, Welhaven more elitist and nostalgic, and though both believed in Norway's independence and in a national literature and a richer cultural life, Welhaven did not see the point in Norway rejecting its Danish cultural heritage. Welhaven's first prose work, *Henrik Wergelands Digtekunst og Polemik ved Aktstykker oplyste* (*Henrik Wergeland's Poetry and Polemics Illustrated with Examples*, 1832) is not only a highly critical study of Wergeland's poetry, but also an impassioned attack on the whole cultural trend Wergeland represented. This attack in prose was soon followed by one in verse. *Norges Dæmring* (*The Dawn of Norway*, 1834) is a polemical poem made up of seventy-six sonnets in which Welhaven attacks not only Wergeland, but also what he sees as the materialist spirit of the age, the empty cultural snobbery of the educated classes, and the pretentiousness of the rich farmers. Very little escape Welhaven's criticism: even individual towns throughout Norway are named and then derided for their various foibles.

Welhaven's attack on Wergeland and his circle continued in *Digte* (*Poems*, 1838), but here it is clothed in allegorical garb from classical antiquity, in such poems as "Glaukos" and "Sisyphos," or from the Bible, in poems such as "Goliath" and "Nehemias." But the volume also contains impressions from a trip to France, and elegiac poems about Bergen and the surrounding area, that are full of the vocabulary of nostalgic Romanticism.

In 1837 Welhaven proposed to and was accepted by the twenty-year-old Ida Kjerulf, but her parents objected to the match. For three years the couple remained secretly loyal to each other, but three weeks after Welhaven gained a university lectureship in philosophy that might have made him a more eligible suitor in Ida's parents' eyes, she died. This event had a profound effect on Welhaven's poetry and his second collection of poems, *Nyere Digt* (*Recent Poems*, 1844) reflect his loss. But there are no uncontrolled outbursts of grief. Welhaven has followed his aesthetic principle, which in its mature form dictated that not only should there be unity of form and content in a poem, but that this should be a reflection of an achieved inner harmony in the emotional life of the poet. The result of this discipline and aesthetic is a number of poems of deep feeling expressed with classical simplicity, such as "Det omvendte Bæger" ("The Overturned Cup") in which a knight rejects a cup which would make him forget the anguish caused by the death of his wife. As he rejects the drink his pain turns to grief, but also releases a flood of memories that will be his comfort. The collection also contains perhaps his best and most famous poem "Digtets Aand" ("The Spirit of Poetry"), in which Welhaven manages to condense his aesthetic philosophy into a poem of great clarity and simplicity.

The 1840s were the high point of Norwegian national Romanticism, and Welhaven's contribution was a number of so-called national romances based on Norwegian legends. Poems such as "Asgaardsreien" ("The Ride of the Asgaard"), "En Vise om Hellig Olaf" ("A Ballad about Saint Olaf"), and "Harald fra Reine" ("Harald from Reine") all belong to this group and many express rebellious passions that seem at odds with Welhaven's aesthetic ideals. But it is precisely in the synthesis of powerful feelings and formal control that Welhaven shows his mastery.

Many of the national romances first appeared in *Halvhundrede Digte* (*Half a Hundred Poems*, 1847), the first of Welhaven's three late collections of poetry. The other two, which both contain examples of poems in all the styles and moods that Welhaven mastered, are: *Reisebilleder og Digte* (*Travel Pictures and Poems*, 1851) and *En Digtsamling* (*A Collection of Poems*, 1859).

In 1846 Welhaven, who had been a lecturer at the University of Christiania since 1840, was made a professor of philosophy, and among his later works are studies of the Dano-Norwegian writer Ludvig Holberg and the seventeenth-century Norwegian poet-clergyman Petter Dass. His last study was *Ewald og de norske Digtere* (*Ewald and the Norwegian Poets*, 1863).

In the cultural battle between Wergeland and Welhaven, Welhaven, as the lesser talent, suffered most. Whereas Wergeland's genius could shrug off involvement in literary skirmishes and polemics, Welhaven's talent probably suffered some distortion in the early years. Indeed, in the poem "Det tornede Træ" ("The Thorny Tree," 1838), he actually says that a thorn is a twig that was damaged in its development. That said, Welhaven's poems are still read and enjoyed, whether it be the national romances, the elegaic nature poems, or the deeply felt personal poems expressed in a clarity of form that gives them an enduring strength.

MARIE WELLS

Biography

Born in Bergen, Norway, December 22, 1807. Matriculated 1825 and started to study theology. Secretly engaged to Ida Kjerulf, 1837. Appointed lecturer at the University of Christiania, death of Ida Kjerulf, 1840. Married Josephine Bidoulac, named professor in philosophy, 1845. Josephine Welhaven died, 1866. Welhaven retired, in ill health, 1868. Died October 21, 1873.

Selected Work

Samlede verker. Edited and introduced by Ingard Hauge. 5 vols. Oslo: Universitetsforlaget, 1990–92.

Bibliography

Aarnes, Asbjørn, *J. S. Welhaven: kritikern og dikteren.* Oslo: Norske studentersamfunds kulturutvalg, 1955.
Andersen-Næss, Reidar. *J. S. Welhaven: mennesket og dikteren.* Oslo: Universitetsforlaget, 1959.

WELT ALS WILLE UND VORSTELLUNG, DIE (THE WORLD AS WILL AND REPRESENTATION) 1819–1844

Philosophical work by Arthur Schopenhauer

In his preface to the first edition of *Die Welt als Wille und Vorstellung* (*The World as Will and Representation*), Arthur Schopenhauer advises the reader "to read the book twice," but it in fact takes several readings to appreciate fully Schopenhauer's central philosophical text. For as well as using the traditional terminology of German metaphysics, Schopenhauer develops a style that is richly creative and explicitly "literary." In his preface, he also points out that the introduction to the work had appeared five years earlier as *Ueber die vierfache Wurzel des Satzes vom zureichenden Grunde: Eine philosophische Abhandlung* (*On the Fourfold Root of the Principle of Sufficient Reason*, 1813), his doctoral thesis. In that text, he had discussed the principle, as formulated by Gottfried Wilhelm Leibniz, that "nothing is without a reason for its being." Now, this principle becomes the basis for Schopenhauer's claim that there is no object without a subject (and vice versa), and hence the bold opening statement of *The World as Will and Representation*: " 'The world is my representation': this is a truth valid with reference to every living and knowing being." In other words, "[man] does not know a sun and an earth, but only an eye that sees the sun, a hand that feels the earth." To this extent, the world is what the Indians call "the veil of Maya." Yet his position is far from being a solipsistic one, for although we know the world as (in Immanuel Kant's terms) phenomenon or, as Schopenhauer put it, "representation," we can also know it as noumenon, (a major departure from Kant's position), as will: "This truth, which must be very serious and grave if not terrible to everyone, is that a man also can say and must say: 'The world is my will'." And we can know it as such, Schopenhauer argues, through the body, which exists for us as an object among other objects, but also as the object of immediate perception. In his doctoral thesis, Schopenauer had spoken of "the identity of the subject of willing with that of knowing" as "a miracle par excellence." By means of which "the word 'I' includes and indicates both, is the knot of the world, and hence inexplicable." In *The World as Will and Representation*, that identity is not only explained, but this metaphysical argument also provides the basis for his aesthetics and, in turn, his theory of salvation.

In the world of space and time that we inhabit, there exists a multiplicity of objects, yet these objects are, according to Schopenhauer, all manifestations of the same, one will. So this will, which is the will to live, is free from such plurality, which arises as the will manifests itself in the world (as representation) through *Ideas*. "With me," Schopenhauer wrote, "the word [*idea*] is always to be understood in its genuine and original meaning, given to it by Plato . . . by *Idea* I understand every definite and fixed grade of the will's objectification." On Schopenhauer's account, we have immediate knowledge of the will itself through the body, but we have knowledge of the Ideas only through aesthetic experience. Key to "aesthetic pleasure," be it called forth by the "contemplation" (*Anschauung*) of nature and life, or by "art, the work of genius," is "pure perception" (*reine Kontemplation*) of the Ideas. For Schopenhauer, the aesthetic experience involves two moments. On the side of the object, art (that is, the aesthetic attitude) "plucks the object of its contemplation [*Kontemplation*] from the stream of the world's course, and holds it isolated before it." And on the side of the subject, the "individual" subject becomes the "pure subject" of knowing: "[T]he person who is involved in this perception is no longer an individual, for in such perception the individual has lost himself; he is *pure* will-less, painless, timeless *subject of knowledge*," continuing to exist only as a "clear mirror of the object," "the clear eye of the world." This account of art, which places hardly any emphasis on the material, sensory component of aesthetic experience, sets Schopenhauer, for all his indebtedness to it for the notions of aesthetic distance and *Anschauung*, against the classical view of aesthetics propounded by Johann Wolfgang von Goethe and Johann Christoph Friedrich von Schiller, and marks him out as a Romantic, albeit of a more consequent and extreme kind than almost any other.

Through art "we can also reach that disposition of mind which alone leads to true holiness and to salvation from the world." Through art, Schopenhauer's argument runs, we obtain knowledge of Ideas; we become pure subject; and we cease to will. Cessation of willing alone puts an end to suffering, which is synonymous with existence, but this has important implications. "If I were to take away the thinking subject," Kant wrote in his *Critique of Pure Reason*, "the whole corporeal world would have to disappear." Schopenhauer draws the same conclusion, but more radically. If the subject ceases to will, it also ceases to know, and hence the world as "representation" is also no more: "To those in whom the will has turned and denied itself, this very real world of ours with all its suns and galaxies, is—nothing." For Schopenhauer, aesthetics leads to asceticism, and thence to nihilism. Anticipating existentialism, which might well be called the Romanticism of the twentieth century, Schopenhauer's creed is one of dark and almost unremitting pessimism. He posits, "If we were to conduct the most hardened and callous optimist through hospitals, infirmaries, operating theatres, through prisons, torture-chambers, and slave-hovels, over battlefields and to places of execution; . . . he too would certainly see in the end what kind of a world is this *meilleur des mondes possibles*. For whence did Dante get the material for his hell, if not from this actual world of ours?" Against this undoubtedly gloomy vision of the world, Schopenhauer nonetheless invests art, and aesthetic experience in general, with soteriological significance, promoting it to the position of the sole means of salvation. That salvation is at all possible means that, ultimately, Schopenhauer is less than the out-and-out pessimist he is often taken to be.

PAUL BISHOP

Text

Die Welt als Wille und Vorstellung. 1819; 2d ed., with expanded second part, 1844; 3rd ed., 1859. Translated as *The World as Will and Representation* by E. F. J. Payne. 1958. Reprinted New York: Dover Publications, 1969.

Bibliography

Copleston, Frederick. *Fichte to Nietzsche. History of Philosophy.* Vol. 7. London: Burns and Oates, 1963.

Hamlyn, D. W. *Schopenhauer. Arguments of the Philosophers series.* London: Routledge and Kegan Paul, 1999.

Mann, Thomas. "Schopenhauer." [1938] In *Schriften und Reden zur Literatur, Kunst und Philosophie.* Vol. 2. Frankfurt: Fischer, 1968. Translated as "Schopenhauer" by Helen T. Lowe-Porter. In *Essays of Three Decades.* London: Secker and Warburg, 1947.

Möbuss, Susanne. *Schopenhauer für Anfänger: Die Welt als Wille und Vorstellung: Eine Lese-Einführung.* Munich: Deutscher Taschenbuch Verlag, 1998.

Spierling, Volker, ed. *Materialien zu Schopenhauers "Die Welt als Wille und Vorstellung."* Frankfurt: Suhrkamp, 1984.

Tanner, Michael. *Schopenhauer: Metaphysics and Art.* London: Phoenix, 1998.

WERGELAND, HENRIK 1808-1845

Norwegian poet, dramatist, historian, educator, social, and political activist

Henrik Wergeland is considered by many to be Norway's greatest poet. The sheer volume of his output, the range of his subject matter, and his vivid imagination set him apart. His poetic works are in keeping with much of his educational and political activity. The inspiration for both derives from a passionate belief in freedom: political and religious freedom, freedom from oppression and injustice both at home and abroad, and freedom from ignorance and superstition. This belief derives partly from the Enlightenment and partly from a radical Romanticism with its roots in the French Revolution.

Wergeland's first collection of poetry, *Digte. Første Ring* (*Poems. First Cycle*, 1829) reflects the inseparability of his lyrical and political concerns. His heavenly muse Stella appears even in his "political" poems, such as the long poem *Napoleon*. This is because Wergeland's roots in Romantic philosophy enable him to see Napoleon as a spark of the divine genius that took up residence in a human soul, and then grew until it could overthrow the European absolute monarchs.

Both in his life and thereafter, Wergeland has been accused of writing chaotic, uncontrolled poetry, and the poem that first gave rise to this accusation was his vast dramatic poem, *Skabelsen, Mennesket og Messias* (*Creation, Man and Messiah*, 1830). The 720-page poem charts the history of the world from its creation to the nineteenth century, and is the history of the struggle between life and death, light and dark, and freedom and oppression as they are made manifest in history. It is no coincidence that this poem was published in the revolutionary year of 1830, (Wergeland called the poem a bible for republicans), and his revolutionary spirit inspired many poems in *Digte. Anden Ring* (*Poems. Second Cycle*, 1833) as well as two cycles of poems also from 1833: *Spaniolen* (*The Spaniard*) and *Caesaris* (*Caesar*). Wer-

geland's only trip abroad—to England and France—also took place during this period.

The person who first accused Wergeland's writing of lacking clarity was a contemporary of his, a student named Johan Sebastian Welhaven. The fact that their "debate" (although that is probably too polite a word for their exchanges) reverberated beyond the walls of the university can in part be explained by the fact that Christiania (now Oslo) was a small place at that time and its cultural life limited. More important, Wergeland championed a democratic trend of development for the new Norway, which had achieved a modicum of independence in 1814. Wergeland wanted the farmers, to whom had been allocated two-thirds of the parliamentary seats, to use the power that had been given to them. Many in Norway, including Welhaven, looked at such possible developments in alarm, believing that power should remain, at least for the time being, in the hands of the educated classes, and that culturally, Norway had little (as of yet) of which to be proud.

Wergeland, though he championed the farmers, was not unaware that many were trapped in ignorance, poverty and superstition, and that they lacked the education they needed if they were to use wisely the power that had been granted to them in the constitution. Therefore, between 1830 and his death in 1845 he wrote a great number of educational pamphlets under various headings such as *For Almuen* (*For the Peasantry*, 1830–34), *For Menigmand* (*For the Common Man*, 1836–38), and *Arbeidsklassen* (*The Working Class*, 1839–45).

There is a strong dramatic element in much of Wergeland's poetry, and this finds more direct expression in the many farces and plays he wrote during the 1830s. In the farces he mocks social pretensions and attitudes, such as the upper-class predilection for all things Danish in *Harlequin Virtuous* (1830), but his serious plays, such as *Den indiske Cholera* (*Indian Cholera*, 1835) and *Barnemordersken* (*The Child Murderess*, 1835), are also much concerned with the issues of social injustice. His best play from the period, *Campbellerne* (*The Campbells*, 1837), was a competition entry for a play to celebrate the reopening of the Christiania Theater.

The year 1838 was a watershed one in Wergeland's life. It was then that he met and courted Amalie Sophie Bekkevold, his future wife, but his rowdy behavior one evening caused him to lose the parish that was going to support the couple. As if this was not bad enough, he soon later accepted a stipend from King Karl Johan, and was derided as a court pensioner by his enemies; as a republican, his acceptance of royal money appeared hypocritical. After these setbacks, however, his life flowed more smoothly, and his work entered a new, more serene phase.

A major cycle of poems from this late phase is *Jan van Huysums Blomsterstykke* (*Jan van Huysums Flower Piece*, 1840), a Romantic piece that starts as a contemplation of a flower painting by the Dutch painter Jan van Huysum and develops into a mythical narrative and a philosophical discussion on the nature of art and the artist. Other major cycles of poems are *Den engelske Lods* (*The English Pilot*, 1844), a narrative poem with a melodramatic, sentimental plot but brilliant descriptive passages, and *Jøden* (*The Jew*, 1842) and *Jødinnen* (*The Jewess*, 1844), two cycles of poems that were part of Wergeland's campaign to repeal the clause in the constitution that forbade the entrance of Jews into Norway (his efforts eventually resulted in the lifting of the ban).

In 1844 Wergeland contracted tuberculosis, from which he was to die eighteen months later. But he kept writing till the end, and in fact produced some of his most memorable poems during this period. However much he loved every aspect of life on earth, he had an unshakeable belief in the reality of the world of the spirit, and he had the poetic genius that enabled him to express that reality in images of astounding beauty and variety.

Wergeland is a national figure, the person who instituted the celebration of May 17, Norway's Constitution Day, and who wrote poems of universal appeal. But the diversity and complexity of his talent has only been fully revealed as studies have been published on his world of ideas, his imagery and versification.

MARIE WELLS

Biography

Born in Christiansand, Norway, June 17, 1808. Moved to Eidsvoll, 1817; sent to the Cathedral School in Christiania, 1819–25. Matriculated in 1825 and in 1829 took his second-level and theological examinations. Lived mainly at home until his father's death in 1834, then started to study medicine. In 1836, was appointed Amanuensis at the University of Christiania Library. From 1838 to 1840 granted a royal stipend that he used in adult education work. Married Amalie Sophie Bekkevold, 1831. Appointed director of the State Archives, 1840. Died July 12, 1845.

Selected Works

Collections
Samlede Skrifter: trykt og utrkyt. Edited by Herman Jæger, Didrik Arup Seip, Halvdan Koht, and Einar Høigaard. 23 vols. Kristiania: Steen, 1918–40.
Henrik Wergelands skrifter. Edited by Leiv Amundsen and Didrik Arup Seip. 8 vols. Oslo: Cappelen, 1957–62.

Translation
Poems. Translated by G. M. Gathorne-Hardy, Jethro Bithell, and Illit Grøndahl, with an introduction by G. M. Gathorne-Hardy, and a preface by Francis Bull. 2d ed. Oslo: Gyldendal, 1960.

Bibliography

Beyer, Harald. *Henrik Wergeland*. Oslo: Aschehoug, 1946.
Heiberg, Hans. *Så stort et hjerte. Henrik Wergeland*. Oslo: Aschehog, 1972.
McFarlane, James Walter. "Henrik Wergeland." In *Ibsen and the Temper of Norwegian Literature*. Oxford: Oxford University Press, 1960.

WEST, BENJAMIN 1738–1820

American artist

Had Benjamin West painted nothing other than his acclaimed *Death of General Wolfe* (1771), his claim to fame would have been assured, for the work instantly acquired an iconic status. In reproductions from cheap engravings to transfer prints, and in political parodies by Boyne and James Gillray, visual allusions to West's canvas demonstrate a widespread recognition of this work in late-eighteenth-century Britain. Yet had West never imagined the death of General James Wolfe, his life and output are remarkable enough to justify his inclusion in any survey of the Romantic era.

West was born in Springfield, Pennsylvania, on October 10, 1738, a time and place in which white colonists and Native Americans were managing to live in relative harmony. (The detail immediately assumes relevance if one studies the Native American warrior seated in a stereotypical Greco-Roman con-

templative post at the dying Wolfe's feet on the 1771 canvas.) His Quaker community was supportive of his wish to become an artist and approved periods of study in Philadelphia and New York City. Having learned all that he felt he could in this context, West left America for Italy in 1760, demonstrating the continuing importance attached to an artistic apprenticeship in Rome. Just as British "grand tourists" gravitated toward the eternal city, so did aspiring artists hungry to study classical statuary and the Renaissance masters. West spent three years in Italy where an early friendship with Thomas Robinson, later the Second Baron Grantham, led to an introduction to the important art dealer and collector Cardinal Alessandro Albani. According to West's first biographer, John Galt (whose installments of West's life began appearing in 1816 with West's sanction), Albani was responsible for showing West the famous *Apollo Belvedere*.

Following three years in Italy during which he studied Classical sculpture and copied the old masters, but produced nothing original of note, West quit Italy for England. As West sought out patrons, a family connection brought General Robert Monckton to his studio. A survivor of Wolfe's Quebec campaign, Monckton was impressed by the evidence of West's classical apprenticeship and commissioned a full-length portrait. West executed this to his client's great satisfaction, figuring Monckton as a recognizably modern *Apollo Belvedere*. Flattered by this reflection of himself, Monckton secured West an introduction to Sir Joshua Reynolds and soon, according to William Carey, "artists and amateurs flocked to [West's] apartments to inspect the works of a painter from the New World." From this time (1764) the first preliminary sketches that would metamorphose into the *Death of General Wolfe* begin to appear. Before that canvas was complete, West had already realized visions of mourning, for example, *Venus Lamenting the Death of Adonis* (1768) and visions of honor in death—for example, the huge canvas *Agrippina Landing at Brundisium with the Ashes of Germanicus* (1768). He had also demonstrated that his fascination for orchestrating groups on canvas was informed by a keen interest in individuals within the group, and paintings such as the *Portrait of Diana Mary Baker* (1766) show him experimenting with the creation of a greater sense of intimacy than epic canvases would allow. The *Death of General Wolfe* (1771) is, however, the painting that has become synonymous with West's name, for both his contemporaries and subsequent generations.

When General Wolfe took the Heights of Abraham from the forces of the Marquis de Montcalm de Saint-Véran in September 1759 and effectively secured Quebec for the British crown, Wolfe reportedly lived long enough to be assured of his victory before succumbing to a fatal wound. Whether Wolfe did in fact die in the knowledge of a clear-cut British victory was, for the imperial propaganda machine, of less interest than the imagined patriotic scene: a young general with everything to live for dies at the height of his victory in a battle in which, in xenophobic retelling, a French tactical advantage proves no match for British ingenuity, determination, and love of country. (That Montcalm paid the same price was often overlooked.) Britons, apparently, were united in their clamor for a fitting monument to the general. With historical hindsight, the political will to continue celebrating Wolfe's victory in a decade when the unpopular Stamp Act (1765) led to a dramatic worsening of Britain's relations with its American colonies may be seen as a none-too-subtle reminder of British imperial might on the North American continent. But as an American, West had long been surrounded by writers and artists from both sides of the Atlantic trying to find a suitably fitting tribute to Wolfe that would cement his immortality and might guarantee their own.

Though West believed his most famous canvas drew admiring crowds because of the innovation of clothing the chief players in their own dress rather than in stylized classical costumes, the ma-

jority of contemporary commentators focus on the painting's representation of emotion. And while the actor David Garrick delighted one of the crowds viewing West's canvas by falling to the ground and demonstrating how he thought a dying general *ought* to have looked, one fact was indisputable: the painting was set to become *the* defining image of British victory in Canada. On the basis of its success, West received several royal commissions from George III and was appointed as historical painter to the king in 1772 with an annual allowance of one thousand pounds (although he would later lose the position after injudiciously voicing support for Napoleon Bonaparte). When Reynolds died in 1792, West became president of the British Royal Academy.

The titles of a mere handful of West's other works will serve to illustrate how influential the *Death of General Wolfe* was in suggesting to West the artistic possibilities of tragic deaths linked to the fate of empire, or historical turning points. Among many canvases, special mention should be made of *Penn's Treaty with the Indians* (1772), *Oliver Cromwell Dissolving the Long Parliament* (1782), *Pharaoh and His Host Lost in the Red Sea* (1792) and *The Fatal Wounding of Sir Philip Sidney* (1805). If West's skill seems to have suffered by an inability ever to capture the public imagination as it had been captured by the *Death of General Wolfe*, it would be a disservice to him to assume that he did not experiment with his art. Painted three years before his death, *Death on a Pale Horse* (1817) is in many ways a departure from his earlier work and anticipates developments in French Romantic painting. On his death in 1820, West was accorded an elaborate funeral in St. Paul's Cathedral, a measure of his significant contemporary influence.

GLYNIS RIDLEY

Biography

Born Springfield, Pennsylvania, October 10, 1738 in a Quaker community. Studied art in Philadelphia and New York City before spending 1760–63 in Rome. Key works include *Agrippina Landing at Brundisium with the Ashes of Germanicus* (1768) and the *Death of General Wolfe* (1771). West was appointed historical painter to the king in 1772 and president of the Royal Academy in 1792. Married Elizabeth Shewell of Philadelphia in London, and they subsequently had four children. Died March 11, 1820, of natural causes at the age of eighty-one.

Bibliography

Erffa, Helmut Von, and Allen Staley. *The Paintings of Benjamin West*. New Haven, Conn.: Yale University Press, 1986.

Galt, John. *The Life and Studies of Benjamin West, Esq., President of the Royal Academy of London, Prior to his Arrival in England: Compiled from Materials Furnished by Himself*. 1816.

McNairn, Alan. *Behold the Hero: General Wolfe and the Arts in the Eighteenth Century*. Liverpool: Liverpool University Press, 1997.

Solkin, David H. *The Visual Arts and the Public Sphere in Eighteenth-Century England*. New Haven, Conn.: Yale University Press, 1993.

WHITMAN, WALT 1819–1892

American poet

Walt Whitman's poetic works, beginning with his first edition of *Leaves of Grass* in 1855, appeared late in the Romantic era and in many ways prefigured modernity more than they referenced the past. Although he conceived of himself as an American poet, Whitman also showed connections to European Romanticism through his sympathy with the 1848 revolutions, his love for Italian opera, and his influence by and support from the English Pre-Raphaelites, with their interest in sensuality and "naturalistic" writing. Like William Wordsworth, Whitman strove to craft a new poetic idiom based on ordinary experience and common language, although in his inventive colloquial free verse and in his radical glorification of working-class democracy, he outstripped or abandoned earlier poetic models.

Whitman's strongest Romantic influence was probably New England transcendentalism. Whitman's early poems, in particular, build on a transcendentalist vision of nature as an emblem of divinity. The 1855 version of "Song of Myself," for example, enacts the mystical and ecstatic themes of Ralph Waldo Emerson's essays by creating a transcendent self through which Whitman reflects and encompasses all of nature and humanity. Initially, Emerson welcomed Whitman's work as a late revival of transcendentalism, out of fashion by the 1850s. Later however, Emerson and Whitman increasingly disagreed, especially on Whitman's inclusion of the sexualized body in his poetry. That Emerson described *Leaves of Grass* as a blend of the *Bhagavad Gita* and the *New York Herald* (a sensationalist newspaper of the time) shows both Emerson's appreciation of Whitman and his patrician New England uneasiness with Whitman as a New York journalist and exponent of popular causes.

As a newspaper editor and freelance writer in the 1840s, Whitman espoused social reforms that later informed his concept of democracy. He wrote editorials and tracts on behalf of temperance, women's rights, the abolition of capital punishment, and free-soil antislavery. Whitman's journalistic concerns were often local and changeable, and much has been written in recent decades about prejudices against African slaves that he evidently shared with many of his abolitionist contemporaries: Whitman's political focus remained on the white working class, whose virtues he saw as endangered by the moral evils of slavery. His idealization of expansive American democracy, as well, led him to support the manifest destiny of the Mexican-American War and to lionize General George Custer as a hero of westward expansion. Over time Whitman's passion for Jeffersonian and Jacksonian democracy grew more complicated, especially in reaction to the horrors of the American Civil War, which he witnessed firsthand as a volunteer nurse.

Whitman embodied Romantic rebelliousness in other important respects besides his political views. Though he could write inspiringly about nature (for example, the "Sea-Drift" poems on the shore of his native Long Island), he was primarily a poet of developing urban life, especially that of New York. The most controversial feature of his poetry in the nineteenth century, however, was his open exploration of sexuality. Significantly, Whitman's homoerotic "Calamus" poems (added to *Leaves of Grass* in 1860) hardly made a ripple in his time. His phrenologi-

cally derived "adhesiveness" (male companionship) seemed less pernicious to contemporaries than his "amativeness" (heterosexual love), expressed in his "Children of Adam" poems. Such daring portrayals of erotic experience alienated members of the genteel literary establishment and led to attempts to edit, censor, and ban Whitman's poems. Though Whitman often had defenders, his sexual frankness hurt his poetic reputation until the canons of literary taste began to change late in the nineteenth century.

Critical acclaim of Whitman, both during his lifetime and subsequently, has primarily focused on his revolutionary poetic originality. His free, speech-like rhythms, expansive vernacular lines, escalating oratory, and oracular mysticism are examples of his poetic innovations. Fueled by transcendentalism, Whitman created an imaginative and distinctive poetics that gave voice to the energy and optimism of working-class and middle-class America in the nineteenth century. He liked to see himself as a homegrown American genius, and his fresh and fearless poetry has more often been compared to that of Homer, Dante Alighieri, and William Shakespeare than to that of his contemporaries. A recent biographer, Jerome Loving, has called Whitman "the inventor of modern American poetry," and it is indeed Whitman's raw and sublime inventiveness that perhaps most persuasively echoes the spirit of the Romantic era and assures him of readers now and in the future.

PAUL FISHER

See also **American Romanticism: Its Literary Legacy; Art and Politics; Carlyle, Thomas; Emerson, Ralph Waldo;** *Essays: First Series*; **Gay Approaches to the Romantic Period;** *Leaves of Grass*; **Opera; Pre-Raphaelite Brotherhood; Sand, George; Slavery and Emancipation; Transcendentalism; United States: Cultural Survey**

Biography

Born in West Hills, New York, May 31, 1819; attended public school in Brooklyn, 1825–30. Taught school on Long Island, 1836–41. Published first poems and journalistic essays, 1838. Edited *New York Aurora* and heard Emerson lecture on "The Poet," 1842; edited *Brooklyn Daily Eagle*, 1846–48. Traveled to the South to work for the *New Orleans Crescent*, 1848; published first edition of *Leaves of Grass*, 1855. Nurse to wounded Union soldiers, 1862–64. Published *Democratic Vistas* and *Passage to India*, 1871. Suffered first paralytic stroke, 1873. Published final edition of *Leaves of Grass* 1891–92. Died of bronchial pneumonia, March 26, 1892.

Selected Works

Collections

The Complete Writings of Walt Whitman. 10 vols. New York: G. P. Putnam's Sons, 1902 (not complete).
The Collected Writings of Walt Whitman. Edited by Gay Wilson Allen. New York: New York University Press, 1963–84.
Whitman Poetry and Prose. Edited by Justin Kaplan. New York: Viking Press, 1982.

Poetry

Leaves of Grass: The First (1855) Edition. Edited by Malcolm Cowley. New York: Viking Press, 1959.

Drum-Taps and Sequel (1865–66): A Facsimile Reproduction. Edited by F. De Wolfe Miller. Gainesville, Fla.: Scholars' Facsimiles and Reprints, 1959.

Leaves of Grass: Facsimile of the 1860 Text. Edited by Roy Harvey Pierce. Ithaca, N.Y.: Great Seal Books, 1961.

Leaves of Grass: Comprehensive Reader's Edition. 2 vols. Edited by Harold Blodgett and Sculley Bradley. New York: New York University Press, 1965.

Leaves of Grass: A Norton Critical Edition. Edited by Sculley Bradley and Harold Blodgett. New York: Norton, 1973.

Correspondence and Prose

Walt Whitman: The Correspondence. 6 vols. Edited by Edwin Haviland Miller. New York: New York University Press, 1961–77.

Walt Whitman: Prose Works 1892. 2 vols. Edited by Floyd Stovall. New York: New York University Press, 1963–64.

Daybooks and Notebooks of Walt Whitman. 3 vols. Edited by William White. New York: New York University Press, 1978.

Bibliography

Erkkila, Betsy. *Whitman the Political Poet*. New York: Oxford University Press, 1989.

Fone, Byrne. *Masculine Landscapes: Walt Whitman and the Homoerotic Text*. Carbondale: Southern Illinois University Press, 1992.

Kaplan, Justin. *Walt Whitman: A Life*. New York: Simon and Schuster, 1980.

Loving, Jerome. *Emerson, Whitman, and the American Muse*. Chapel Hill: University of North Carolina Press, 1982.

———. *Walt Whitman: The Song of Himself*. Berkeley, Calif.: University of California Press, 1999.

Matthiessen, F. O. *American Renaissance: Art and Expression in the Age of Emerson and Whitman*. London: Oxford University Press, 1941.

Price, Kenneth M. *Whitman and Tradition: The Poet in His Century*. New Haven, Conn.: Yale University Press, 1990.

Reynolds, David S. *Walt Whitman's America: A Cultural Biography*. New York: Knopf, 1995.

Zweig, Paul. *Walt Whitman: The Making of a Poet*. New York: Basic Books, 1984.

WIELAND, CHRISTOPH MARTIN 1733–1813

German novelist, dramatist, poet, translator, and editor

Christoph Martin Wieland was without doubt one of the most multitalented and prolific writers of eighteenth-century German literature. For a period of some sixty years, he dominated the Rococo literary scene as one of its most popular authors, sometimes referred to as the German Voltaire for his universal learning, cosmopolitan spirit, and social criticism. His popularity was due in part to the often rather erotic nature of his writings; in this celebration of emotion and feeling, he is to be considered a precursor to the German Sturm und Drang (storm and stress) and Romantic periods. Not only as an author but also as an editor of the influential literary and philosophical journal *Merkur* and as a translator of William Shakespeare, Wieland exerted a profound influence on his contemporaries and on subsequent generations of writers. In the latter years of Wieland's life, the most prominent authors and thinkers of the age paid homage to this grand old man of German letters.

Wieland was extremely bright (possibly a genius), and surpassed the curricula of various schools and teachers with ease. He began writing at a young age and was invited to live with the famous critic Johann Jakob Bodmer in Zürich as a teenager. His excessive enthusiasm for whatever he applied himself to (including romantic encounters with women), combined with his considerable intelligence, sometimes got him into trouble. His 1764 comic novel *Der Sieg der Natur über die Schwämerey, oder die Abentheuer des Don Sylvio von Rosalva: Eine Geschichte, worin alles Wunderbare zugeht* (*Reason Triumphant over Fancy, Exemplified in the Singular Adventures of Don Sylvio de Rosalva: A History in Which Every Marvelous Event Occurs Naturally*) is a Don Quixote parody and is somewhat autobiographical in its hero's pronounced interest in members of the opposite sex. Because of its narratorial intrusions and its descriptions of the marvelous, which had been deemed unacceptable in Enlightenment literature, it is generally considered the first truly modern German novel. Autobiographical elements of Wieland's life also make their way into *Geschichte des Agathon* (*The History of Agathon*, 1766–67), which treats the psychological development of its Greek hero as he learns to curb his excessive enthusiasms and strives to achieve a harmonious balance between his intellect and his emotions (extremes that plagued the author's own life). At the same time, he was also working on his slightly risqué rococo verse tale *Musarion, oder die Philosophie der Grazien* (Musarion, or the Philosophy of the Graces, 1768), which shares similar thematic concerns in its story of the paramour Musarion who leads the young hedonist Phanias to a balanced appreciation of the role of both philosophy and love in a "graceful" life.

When Wieland left Zürich and returned to Biberach in 1760, he began translating Shakespeare's dramas into German, completing a total of twenty-two translations that he published between 1762 and 1766. Wieland considered the English dramatist's language to be at times rather crude, and he simply edited out or rewrote what he found too objectionable for refined tastes. His bowdlerized translations drew outspoken criticism from a number of people, especially from the young German Sturm und Drang generation of authors such as Johann Wolfgang von Goethe and Johann Christoph Friedrich von Schiller. Nevertheless, it was primarily through Wieland's translations that these and many other German authors came to know the work of the English writer whom they considered to be a dramatic genius of passion and power.

Wieland had long held plans for the creation of a German-language literary journal that would be modeled after the older French literary magazine *Mercure de France*. After discussions with colleagues, the new journal was named *Der teusche Merkur* and publication began in 1773. The journal was well received

WIERTZ, ANTOINE JOSEPH   1219

and became one of the foremost venues for publications concerning the German literary scene.

The epic poem *Oberon* of 1780 was first published in *Merkur*. It is a mixture of legendary medieval stories of Charlemagne's knights, elements of Shakespeare's fairies from *Midsummer Night's Dream*, and the story of the true love of two young people, Huon and Rezia. The work was very popular (it was one of Goethe's favorites), and exerted a strong influence on a generation of young English poets, including such luminaries as Lord Byron, John Keats, Percy Bysshe Shelley, and Samuel Taylor Coleridge, who subsequently praised Wieland as the founder of European Romanticism. Its content, the fidelity of the two lovers despite adversity, presents a strongly ethical message and an elevated portrayal of humanity.

Wieland considered his 1781 *Geschichte der Abderiten* (*The Republic of Fools*) to be one of his greatest works. The story of the ancient town of Abdera, the home of quintessential folly, enables the author to satirize the foolishness that he saw in eighteenth-century society. He takes to task the inanities of politicians, professors, lawyers, religious leaders, and the general public, all those people who had annoyed him over the years. It was very successful in German-speaking nations. In his *Geheime Geschichte des Philosophen Peregrinus Proteus* (*Private History of Peregrinus Proteus, the Philosopher*, 1791), Wieland also aimed his keen intellect upon what he felt was an abuse of faith: the various pseudo-occultists and mystics who had become popular in Europe during the late eighteenth century.

Wieland concluded his long career with the editing of his collected works and letters. His enormous literary talent and his emphasis on emotion and an idealized view of humanity exerted a strong influence on a generation of young Romantic writers, both in Germany and abroad.

THOMAS F. BARRY

Biography

Born September 5, 1733 in Oberholzheim, Swabia. Studied at University of Erfurt, 1749, and University of Tübignen, 1750; lived at the home of Johann Jakob Bodmer in Zürich, 1752–54; director of the chancellery in Biberach; professor of philosophy at University of Erfurt, 1769–72. Private tutor to the children of Duchess Anna Amalia in Weimar, 1772–98. Died in Weimar, January 21, 1813.

Selected Works

Novels

Der Sieg der Natur über die Schwämerey, oder die Abentheuer des Don Sylvio von Rosalva: Eine Geschichte, worin alles Wunderbare zugeht. 1764. Translated as *Reason Triumphant over Fancy, Exemplified in the Singular Adventures of Don Sylvio de Rosalva: A History in which Every Marvelous Event Occurs Naturally* by John Richardson. 3 Vols. 1773. Also translated as *The Adventures of Don Sylvio de Rosalva* by Ernest A. Baker. 1904.

Geschichte des Agathon. 2 vols. 1766–67. Translated as *The History of Agathon* by John Richardson. 4 vols. 1773.

Geschichte der Abderiten. 1781. Translated as *The Republic of Fools: Being the History of the State and the People of Abdera in Thrace* by Henry Christmas. 1861. Also translated as *History of the Abderites* by Max Dufner, 1993.

Geheime Geschichte des Philosophen Peregrinus Proteus. 1791. Translated as *Private History of Peregrinus Proteus, the Philosopher* by William Tooke. 1796.

Poetry

Musarion, oder die Philosophie der Grazien: Ein Gedicht in drey Büchern. 1768.

Der neue Amadis: Ein comisches Gedicht in achtzehn Gesängen. 1771.

Oberon: Ein Gedicht in vierzehn Gesängen. 1780. Translated as *Oberon: A Poem from the German* by William Sotheby. 1798. Also translated as *Oberon: A Poetical Romance in Twelve Books* by John Quincy Adams. 1940.

Bibliography

Craig, Charlotte. *Christoph Martin Wieland as the Originator of the Modern Travesty in German Literature.* Chapel Hill: University of North Carolina Press, 1970.

Kurth-Voigt, Liselotte E. *Perspectives and Points of View: The Early Works of Wieland and Their Background.* Baltimore: Johns Hopkins University Press, 1974.

McCarthy, John A. *Christoph Martin Wieland.* Boston: Twayne, 1979.

Starnes, Thomas C. "Christoph Martin Wieland." In *Dictionary of Literary Biography.* Vol. 97. Edited by James Hardin and Christoph E. Schweitzer. Detroit: Gale Research, 1990.

Shookman, Ellis. *Noble Lies, Slant Truths, Necessary Angels: Aspects of Fictionality in the Novels of Christoph Martin Wieland.* University of North Carolina Studies in German Literature. Chapel Hill: University of North Carolina Press, 1997.

Swales, Martin. *The German Bildungsroman from Wieland to Hesse.* Princeton, N.J.: Princeton University Press, 1978.

Van Abbe, Derek Maurice. *Christoph Martin Wieland (1733–1813): A Literary Biography.* London: Harrap, 1961.

WIERTZ, ANTOINE JOSEPH 1806-1865

Belgian painter and sculptor

Born in Dinant, a picturesque small town in the Ardennes and famous as the birthplace of Adolphe Sax (the inventor of the saxophone), Antoine Joseph Wiertz came from a poor background. His parents were working-class and had high professional ambitions for their son, but it was another relative who encouraged Wiertz to begin studying at the Art Academy of Antwerp when he was fourteen years old. Wiertz had a precocious talent. An admirer of Peter Paul Rubens, whose masterpiece *The Descent from the Cross* and other paintings were on display at Antwerp Cathedral, Wiertz took such other artists as Michelangelo and Raphael as his aesthetic reference points, yet, while drawing on such Renaissance and Baroque influences, developed a style that is clearly Romantic, often decadent, sometimes almost surrealist. Théodore Géricault, one of the founding artists of the French Romantic school, was another important influence. During his visits to Paris (1829–32 and 1833–34), Wiertz studied the masters in the Louvre, and he traveled to Italy (1834–37) as did many other nineteenth-century artists, in order to develop his appreciation of classical art. Under the tutelage of Horace Vernet in the Académie de France in Rome, Wiertz learned to copy the style and attention to detail of the old masters. A combination of classical themes, monumental scale, and naturalistic detail are all evident in *Les Grecs et Les Troyens se disputant le corps de Patrocle* (*Greeks and Trojans in Dispute over the Body of Patrocles*, 1835–36), which Wiertz wanted to display at the Paris Salon of 1838. Refused permission to do so, he succeeded in displaying *Patrocles* at the Paris and Brussels Salons of 1839. Far from moderating the scale and style of his works, Wiertz embarked on his own, highly individualistic career as a painter, in which the decision of the Belgian authorities to provide space for his massive canvases—such as *La Révolte des Enfers contre le Ciel* (*The Revolt of Hell against Heaven*, 1841), also known as *La Chute des Anges rebelles* (*The Fall of the Rebel Angels*), and *Le Triomphe du Christ* (*The Triumph of Christ*, 1847–48), displayed in his studio in the rue du Renard—was crucial, for without such workshops and opportunities to display his paintings, Wiertz would have been unable to produce such large-scale works. Eventually, following a series of negotiations between the artist and the Belgian government, Wiertz was provided with his own huge, private studio in the Léopold district of Brussels and granted a budget, in return for which he agreed to donate his paintings to the state; this building is now the Wiertz Museum.

Wiertz's later paintings, such as *L'Enfant brûlé* (*The Burnt Child*, 1849), *Pensées et Visions d'une tête coupée* (*Thoughts and Visions of a Severed Head*, 1853, which is inscribed with an elaborate text, reflecting in prose those thoughts and versions to accompany the grotesque and macabre images), and *Les Choses du présent devant les hommes de l'avenir* (*The Things of the Present before the Men of the Future*, 1855) reveal his desire to tackle social and political, even revolutionary, themes. Yet the quintessential Wiertzian image can be found in such smaller-scale works as *La Belle Rosine* (*Beautiful Rosine*, 1847), also known as *Deux jeunes filles* (*Two Young Girls*), which depicts a voluptuous young woman, very loosely draped in silk material, gazing up at a skeleton identified by a label on the skull as Rosine. Reflecting the vanitas theme in the tradition of Hans Baldung Grien, the work is a mixture of two classical academic genres, the still life and the nude, and Wiertz plays with the spectator's expectations by revealing the identity of the skeleton, but not of the girls. If these and other works reveal Wiertz's indebtedness to the tradition of the baroque, then his influence on, for example, the German artist Max Klinger, and his anticipation of the style of Félicien Rops point to his largely overlooked significance as a figure in the transition from Romanticism to symbolism. In *Pauvre Belgique* (*Poor Belgium*, 1864–65), the contemporary poet and art critic Charles Baudelaire looked askance at Wiertz's desire, expressed in a pamphlet entitled "Bruxelles Capitale, Paris province" ("Brussels as the Capital, Paris as the Province," c. 1840) for Brussels to become "the capital of the world, so that, compared to you, Paris is no more than a provincial town"; Baudelaire dismissed Wiertz as a charlatan, an idiot, and a plagiarist, a "philosophical painter" who shared with Victor Hugo the wish "to save humanity." Although he is still frequently labeled as an otherworldly eccentric, Wiertz nevertheless knew how to acquire large subsidies for his art, by identifying the need of the recently established Kingdom of Belgium for a state artist, and addressing that need. Indeed, the example of Wiertz exemplifies how the solitary genius of Romanticism has, by the mid-nineteenth cen-

tury, transmuted into the flamboyant outsider, bordering (in the eyes of some) on charlatanism. For example, the eighteenth-century connoisseur becomes the loner of effete dandyism, such as Jaris-Karl Huysmans's gourmet aristocrat, Des Esseintes, in *À rebours* (*Against Nature*, 1884), Oscar Wilde's quest after exquisite, albeit perverse, pleasure in *The Picture of Dorian Gray* (1890), or the exhausted, if petulantly defiant, poetic ego of Jules Laforgue's poetry, who says in "La Cigarette" (1902), "Moi, je vais résigné, sans espoir, à mon sort, / Et pour tuer le temps, en attendant la mort, / Je fume au nez des dieux de fines cigarettes" ("As for me, I go with resignation to my fate, / And to kill time, waiting for my death, / I smoke fine cigarettes in the face of the gods").

When Wiertz died he was buried in accordance with ancient Egyptian funeral rites, leaving a museum specially designed to display his works; his unpublished literary output (including essays and articles on aesthetics and individual works of art, including two prize-winning treatises on Peter Paul Rubens and on Flemish art) were published in 1869 by Charles Potvin. Above all, his significance lies in reminding us of the importance attached by the Romantics to the great artists of the past: the self-conception of the Romantic artist as reinventor as well as innovator.

PAUL BISHOP

Biography

Born in Dinant, Belgium, February 22, 1806. Entered the Antwerp Art Academy, 1820. Visited Paris, 1829–32 and 1833–34; awarded Belgian Prix de Rome, 1832. Traveled in Italy, 1834–37. Moved to Liège, 1839, and then to Brussels, 1845; negotiated with government of Belgium for the construction of a studio for his own use, 1850, 1853, and 1861. Died in Brussels, June 18, 1865.

Selected Works

Collection
Œuvres littéraires. 1869.

Correspondence
La Correspondance d'Antoine Wiertz, prix de Rome, au cours de son voyage d'Italie (septembre 1833–juin 1837). 1953.

Bibliography

Beks, Maarten. *Antoine Wiertz: Genie of charlatan*. Oosterbeek: Bosbespers, 1981.

Colleye, Hubert. *Antoine Wiertz*. Brussels: La Renaissance du Livre, 1957.

Fierlants, Éduard. *Œuvre complète de Antoine Wiertz*. Brussels: E. Fierlants, 1868.

Labarre, Louis. *Antoine Wiertz: Étude biographique*. Brussels: Librairie Européene de C. Marquardt, 1866.

Moerman, André A. and Francine-Claire Legrand. *Antoine Wiertz, 1806–1865*. Paris: Galerie de Varenne; Brussels: J. Damase, 1974.

Potvin, Jules. *Antoine Wiertz, l'époque, l'homme, l'œuvre*. Brussels: F. du Nobele, 1912.

Vautier, Dominique. "Wiertz, Antoine Joseph." In *Grove Dictionary of Art*. London: Macmillan; New York: Grove's Dictionaries, 1999.

Wybo-Wehrli, Isabelle. "Le séjour d'Antoine Wiertz à Rome (mai 1834–février 1837)," *Bulletin des Musées Royaux des Beaux-Arts de Belgique/Bulletin van de Koninklijke Museum voor Schone Kunsten van België* 22, nos. 1–4 (1973): 85–146.

WILHELM MEISTERS LEHRJAHRE (WILHELM MEISTER'S APPRENTICESHIP) 1795-1796

Novel by Johann Wolfgang von Goethe

"The French Revolution, Fichte's *Wissenschaftslehre*, and Goethe's *Meister* are the major trends of the age." Thus did Friedrich von Schlegel, foremost literary critic of Germany's emerging *Romantik*, situate Johann Wolfgang von Goethe's groundbreaking romance of personal growth, identity, and destiny. *Wilhelm Meisters Lehrjahre* has usually been considered the prototype of the modern bildungsroman, inspiring novelistic treatments of youthful self-discovery from Ludwig Tieck's *Franz Sternbalds Wanderungen* (1798) to Josef von Eichendorff's *Ahnung und Gegenwart* (1815) and on into modern literature. Through Thomas Carlyle's translation, as *Wilhelm Meister's Apprenticeship* (1824), it reached American and English readers, including George Eliot, for whom German writing would become important in the course of the nineteenth century. Goethe warmly acknowledged Carlyle's translation, corresponding with him in the waning years of his life. Their letters give some idea of the reception of Goethe's work abroad.

Its first volume (of four), incorporating books 1 and 2, was published in an edition of three thousand in Berlin in 1795. It represents a refabrication of scenes from an unpublished earlier project, *Wilhelm Meisters Theatralische Sendung* (1776–77 and after). The containing theatrical concept was retained in the adaptation; the realism of the original, with its rich line of period social observation, was suppressed. Wilhelm Meister, the protagonist, is a prosperous merchant's son with a taste for the theater. In the beginning, he is a rather conventional, sentimental novice with puppet plays in his childhood background. Play-acting is the vehicle of his escape from the confinements of the mercantile world of his Philistine father, who has sold off his own paternal legacy of fine art. Wilhelm extols play-acting as a route to self-understanding; it draws participants out of themselves, then leads them back, along with the differences and nuances of comprehension that experience brings. The author's appreciation of the value of play pervades the theatrical plotting of his eight-book story.

Wilhelm's broken love affair with an actress shadows his errant career as an amateur actor, then as proprietor of an itinerant troupe of players. Mariana's apparent perfidy puts an abrupt end to the first volume, but affords Wilhelm the personal latitude to find his true mate. The process involved in his coming to self-understanding is appropriately tortuous; the process often seems to be the point, and the narrative validates Wilhelm's many misadventures. Thus it turns out that Mariana was a faithful lover, against the plain evidence of his senses. Their natural son, Felix, had become Wilhelm's charge without his father knowing his identity. The coincidence is typical, but true to Goethe's evident intention. The revelations concerned take place in a symbolically charged setting, in a disembodied voice that proclaims Wilhelm's salvation, on a note distinctly reminiscent of the conclusion of *Faust*. Experience is truth, and self-realization the only horizon of transcendence that matters.

The songs of Mignon, the mysterious child who displaces Mariana in Wilhelm's heart, provide poignant accompaniment to the difficulty and loneliness of the quest. Musical settings to some of these lyrics were included in the original volumes. The erratic story line is alleviated by an old harpist and by others. The lyric notes are not always dramatically effective, but they confirm Goethe's aspiration to a complex narrative mode that is more operatic than novelistic. The extensive dramatis personae include the crew of the traveling theatrical troupe, as well as Mignon and Felix, and the company they meet on the road, much of it aristocratic. All are vague; their names and characters are quasi-allegorical. Large mysteries are unraveled in the concluding book, which features the death of Mignon and revelations about her original identity and hard childhood. The figure of the lost child stalks the text.

Bildung, or formation, is at issue from the second book; the formation of the artist is of special concern to Wilhelm, who wonders if the rules apply in the case of genius. *Wilhelm Meisters Lehrjahre* marks an early stage in Goethe's gradual renunciation of the privilege of genius, something for which Novalis took him to task. Yet Bildung is not a uniform progress, and if there are rules they cannot be abstracted from the fabric of living experience. Bildung remains personal and integral to the individual destiny. It is in the realization and acceptance of this destiny that Bildung finds its purpose. But in that case, does such formation have any positive content? Critics have wondered about considering Goethe's narrative as a novel of character formation. Some have even doubted whether Wilhelm can be considered as a character at all. Nicholas Boyle describes him as having "lost any particularity of self—he is now simply the point at which interpretation takes place." What he interprets is not a time and a place, as in the earlier *Theatralische Sendung*, so much as the artist's erratic condition in developing bourgeois society.

The melancholy undertone of Goethe's narrative is related to the sea changes that his players endure. Their rough and ready staging of *Hamlet* has a protracted place in the story in part because the melancholy Dane is a figure of identity for Wilhelm. Like Hamlet he is a predominant idealist, in Samuel Taylor Coleridge's phrase, living in his mind and for his understanding. Goethe's own reckoning with *Hamlet* is fully explored here; his imaginary production of the play involves him in practical criticism of a kind familiar in Coleridge as well as in August Wilhelm von Schlegel. Wilhelm's restless dejection is a chronic condition, as it is for William Shakespeare's hero of self-consciousness. He acknowledges the likeness openly; assuming the role of the melancholy Dane becomes a way of coming to terms with his own disposition.

In narrative counterpoint, the old harpist suffers a severe attack of melancholia. His treatment introduces Wilhelm to the moral persuasion practiced by a country clergyman specializing in the condition. The madness of melancholia is overcome through the talking cure, with revelations about the harpist's past. The effects of melancholia are seen in passing in other characters, inviting speculation about Goethe's deeper motives in the text. Confession is a recurring motif. The confessional attitude is explicitly disowned in slighting remarks about the poor character of public displays of the sort familiar from the recently scandalous *Confessions* of Jean-Jacques Rousseau. But like Thomas De Quincey's similar disclaimer at the outset of his *Confessions of an English Opium-Eater*, this one may camouflage a related, if indirect, confession aimed at ventilating disturbing personal experiences, and so in vindicating the writer through the salvation of his protagonist.

A. C. GOODSON

Text

Wilhelm Meisters Lehrjahre. 4 vols. 1795–96. Translated as *Wilhelm Meister's Apprenticeship* by Thomas Carlyle, 1824. Current translation by Eric A. Blackall with Victor Lange. New York: Suhrkamp, 1989.

Bibliography

Boyle, Nicholas. *Goethe: The Poet and the Age, Vol. 1: The Poetry of Desire*. Oxford: Clarendon Press, 1991.
———. Goethe: The Poet and the Age, Vol. 2: *Revolution and Romanticism (1790–1803)*, Oxford: Clarendon Press, 2000.
Citati, Pietro. *Goethe*. Trans. Raymond Rosenthal. New York: Dial Press, 1974.
Schlegel, Friedrich von. *Schriften und Fragmente*. Edited by Ernst Behler. Stuttgart: Kröner, 1956.
Schmidt, Jochen. *Die Geschichte des Genie-Gedankens in der deutschen Literatur, Philosophie und Politik 1750–1945*. Vol. 1, *Von der Aufklärung bis zum Idealismus*. Darmstadt: Wissenschaftliche Buchgesellschaft, 1985.

WILKIE, DAVID 1785–1841

Scottish artist

David Wilkie's work is at the forefront of the radical changes that occurred in British art in the nineteenth century. In his popularization of rustic genre scenes, he shifted the emphasis from the ideals of history painting in the grand manner, which had been defined by Joshua Reynolds as the highest mode of art, to pictorial stories of domestic life. His images were extremely successful in the form of prints and engravings, but also gained notoriety in the Royal Academy exhibitions themselves, where one of his most famous images, *Chelsea Pensioners Reading the Gazette of the Battle of Waterloo* (1822), was the first picture to be protected by a guardrail. Wilkie anticipated, and arguably instigated, the ascendancy of genre painting in the Victorian period, but his pictures were also part of a tradition that spanned hundreds of years, drawing directly on Dutch and Flemish paintings of the seventeenth century (he was known as the Scottish Teniers) and, closer to his own time, on Hogarthian narrative and the emotional appeal of the French painter Jean-Baptiste Greuze.

The tales that Wilkie tells in his paintings are essentially comic, such as *The Cut Finger* (1809), which shows a grandmother tending to the bleeding finger of a wailing little boy who has been injured in a game of toy boats, but their humor and tenderness in many ways belie the politics of the situations that they depict. Wilkie's frequent setting of his scenes in peasant cottages raises concerns about the living conditions of the rural poor and the relations between classes. This comes to the fore in the painter's most controversial work, *Distraining for Rent* (1815), in which a farmer and his family are being visited by bailiffs. The painting, which Wilkie intended to prove his abilities as a tragic as well as comic painter, was read by many (including Wilkie's aristocratic patrons) as an attack on inhumane landlords who demanded the repossession of their property in the face of extreme poverty. This image was surprisingly radical coming from an artist described by his close friend, the history painter Benjamin Robert Haydon, as a "cautious Tory." The social injustice of the scene is intensified by the empty cradle in the foreground that is placed alongside a spinning wheel, both objects to be confiscated, while the sombre mood of the piece is effectively conveyed in its lighting and the Rembrandtesque use of chiaroscuro. The atmosphere created by the deep brown

shadows in this picture was developed in later paintings and to very different ends. Areas of shadow dapple the sun-drenched hall in *The Penny Wedding* (1818) and they evoke a mood of quiet contemplation in the candle-lit room in *The Cotter's Saturday Night* (1832–37). The asphalt that the artist used to produce this rich brown tinge, however, had disastrous consequences for the preservation of the paintings and has almost ruined some pictures.

As in all of Wilkie's genre paintings, the effectiveness of *Distraining for Rent* lies in the ability of the painter to make legible the situations and emotions of the pictured figures through their environment and body language. It is the human countenance that provides access to the inner workings of the mind. The extent of Wilkie's achievement here is suggested in the scores of sketches and studies of individual figures that he drew before putting brush to canvas, often altering postures and facial expressions. Here the despair of the farmer is suggested in the way that his body is slumped against the table and his hand supports his head; he is oblivious even to the tugs of his little boy at his jacket. While Wilkie's scenes might sometimes appear staged (in his choice of subject matter and the arrangement of his compositions he did, indeed, owe much to the theater), it is his obsession with human nature, the feelings and emotions of the figures on the canvas, that sets him within the Romantic tradition. In his *Remarks on Painting* (published posthumously in 1843) the artist writes with typical Romantic fervor that "It is the representation of man, with all his moods and aspirations, which constitutes, as it were, the soul of art." The psychological realism of the characters that Wilkie paints incites comparisons with contemporary literature, and some of his paintings were actually reproduced in a textual form. William Wordsworth wrote a poem, "The Power of Music," about the violinist who appears in *The Blind Fiddler* (1811). Not only were the incidents that Wilkie depicted concerned with human emotions, but they were intended to produce a similar effect on the viewer, inciting a sentimental and "poetic" response. The painter Charles Robert Leslie reported that Washington Irving wept in front of *Distraining for Rent*.

Despite their popularity abroad and especially in France, Wilkie's paintings were distinctly national and, alongside the literary influence of Sir Walter Scott and Robert Burns, did much to ensure the popularity of Scottish art. With their highland themes, they appeared as records of a way of life that was fast disappearing. Customs like that depicted in *The Penny Wedding*, where guests paid a subscription for food and entertainment and any remaining money went to the newlywed couple, had already been quashed by the church, and this might explain the fact that the figures in this painting are decked in eighteenth-century costume. In its historical setting, *The Penny Wedding* seems to anticipate Wilkie's eventual departure from genre to portraiture and history painting, a move that was motivated by trips the artist made between 1825 and 1828 to Italy, Austria, Germany, and Spain, where he was greatly influenced by the paintings of Bartolomé Esteban Murillo and Diego Rodriguez Velázquez. The pictures that followed were larger and looser in style than his genre paintings, often with lifesize figures (such as *Napoleon and the Pope*, 1836), and, although they lacked the narrative skill and appeal of earlier images, they continued to bear testament to Wilkie's extraordinary powers of observation. They were also more overtly political, with the artist painting scenes from the recent Spanish insurrection against the French.

It is fitting that David Wilkie, whose work spanned the period of the Romantics and pointed forward to Victorian genre scenes, was himself to become the subject of a painting by an-other contemporary artist who was ahead of his time. *Peace—Burial at Sea* (1842) by J. M. W. Turner is a final tribute to an artist who excelled at capturing in paint the liveliness of everyday incidents and the complexities of human emotions.

JULIA THOMAS

Biography

Born in Cults, near Edinburgh, Scotland, 1785. Entered the Royal Academy schools in London, 1805. Exhibited *The Village Politicians* in the Royal Academy, 1806. Elected Associate of the Royal Academy, 1809; Royal Academician, 1811; painter to the King, 1830; knighted, 1836. Died 1841 returning from a trip to the Holy Land.

Bibliography

Errington, Lindsay. *David Wilkie 1785–1841*. Edinburgh: National Galleries of Scotland, c. 1988.

Miles, H. A. D., and David Blayney Brown, eds. *Sir David Wilkie of Scotland*. Raleigh: North Carolina Museum of Art, 1987.

Payne, Christiana. *Rustic Simplicity: Scenes of Cottage Life in Nineteenth-Century British Art*. London: Djanogly Art Gallery in association with Lund Humphries, 1998.

Pointon, Marcia. "From 'Blind Man's Buff' to 'Le Colin Maillard'; Wilkie and his French Audience," *Oxford Art Journal* 7, no. 1 (1984): 15–25.

WILLIAMS, HELEN MARIA 1761–1827

British chronicler, poet, and novelist

Helen Maria Williams is today read chiefly for her remarkable *Letters from France*, a series of epistolary reports on the events during and after the French Revolution. Williams also wrote poetry and fiction, and before the revolution she enjoyed considerable fame as a writer of sentimental literature. Indeed, the poetics of sensibility informs all her writing, as does a streak of idealistic radicalism.

Williams's literary career began when she met the well-known dissenter Andrew Kippis, who helped her to publish her sentimental narrative *Edwin and Eltruda* (1781). Kippis also encouraged Williams to move to London, where her circle came to include such men and women of letters as Samuel Johnson, Elizabeth Montagu, and Anna Seward. Her subsequent literary efforts, *An Ode on the Peace* (1783), *Peru* (1784), and *Poems* (1786), all established her reputation as a first-rate poet of sensibility, even provoking a tender encomium from a young William Wordsworth, entitled "On Seeing Miss Helen Maria Williams Weep at a Tale of Distress." At the same time, Williams's poetry amply demonstrates her pacifist and abolitionist sympathies. Indeed, Williams's politics are closely intertwined with her reliance on the sublime and sentimental: for example, *Peru* is an emotionally vivid attack on the Spanish invasion of Peru, while her *Poems* includes the Gothic "Irregular Fragment," whose sensationalistic account of murder and violence within the British royal family implies a trenchant critique of monarchy.

Williams's tendency to combine sensibility with political comment came into its own with her interest in the events of the French Revolution. In 1790, Williams published her novel *Julia*, inserting, among the sentimental tableaux of romance and friendship, a panegyric to the storming of the Bastille, entitled "The Bastille: A Vision." Thus did Williams begin an involvement with French politics that would last her lifetime. Characteristically, she was initially motivated by personal interests, for her opposition to the ancien régime stemmed from her friendship with Madame Du Fossé, a young Frenchwoman who had suffered by its aristocratic prejudices and injustices.

In 1790, at Madame Du Fossé's invitation, Williams paid the first of several visits to France and, in 1792, she settled more or less permanently in France. Throughout the next decade she was spectator, participant, and reporter of the turmoil of the Revolution and the atrocities of the Terror. She was an eyewitness to the attack on the Tuileries; she established a salon for Girondist leaders and international radicals, playing host to the likes of Joel Barlow, Thomas Paine, and Mary Wollstonecraft; and she was even imprisoned for a month in 1793, when all British citizens were put under arrest. Eventually, she was forced to flee Paris for Switzerland for six months in 1794. Most significantly of all, Williams described all these experiences in vivid and enthusiastic detail. Her *Letters from France*, beginning with a volume of letters on that first visit in 1790, eventually consisted of some five volumes over four years.

For the modern reader, Williams's letters are remarkable for their transgression of boundaries often thought to be static in the Romantic age. She prided herself on straddling the line between English and French nationalisms. Moreover, in reenacting the discussions of national import that took place under her own roof, she framed political events within the insistently intimate and feminine mode of the letter. She also subverted notions of the domestic with her descriptions of the prison as home. Thus, her letters constantly challenge her reader's expectations of what constitutes the private and public, the domestic and political, and, consequently, the feminine and masculine. This last point Williams herself made overt when she applauded the way in which gender norms and protocol disintegrated in the animated discussions on the Revolution that took place in her salon and elsewhere.

All these ruptures served to alienate Williams from her readers as antirevolutionary tendencies took hold in England. So too did Williams's insistence, in the face of Jacobin terror and regicide, that the revolution was fundamentally right. It did not help that Williams's lover, the radical John Hurford Stone, was a married man. Although Stone divorced his wife in 1794 and remained with Williams until his death, it is not known if they ever married.

In 1801, Williams returned briefly to fiction, with a satire entitled *Perourou, the Bellows-Mender*, which became better known as Edward Bulwer-Lytton's stage adaptation, *The Lady of Lyon*. In the main, though, Williams continued her observations on French politics, with *Sketches of the State of Manners and Opinions in the French Republic towards the Close of the Eighteenth Century* (1801). So too did the government maintain its close watch on her. In 1802, Napoleon Bonaparte, suspicious of her overenthusiastic praise of the English in a poetic tribute to the peace at Amiens, had her arrested for a day and kept under surveillance over the next several years. In 1803, her decision to annotate the letters of Louis XVI, which she discovered too late to be forgeries, brought renewed attacks on her politics and her literary reputation. Although she published nothing for the next decade or so, her revolutionary fervor did not abate, as she demonstrated with *A Narrative of Events Which Have Taken Place in France from the Landing of Napoleon Bonaparte . . .* (1815).

Indeed, Williams never abandoned her political principles. Throughout her life she retained a sentimental enthusiasm for what she typically personified as the virtuous but persecuted heroine Liberty. Her work and her life (for the two are inseparable) resonate today for their imaginative and courageous mix of the personal and political.

ADELINE JOHNS-PUTRA

Biography

Born in London, June 17, 1761. Moved to Berwick-on-Tweed, where she was educated at home, 1769; moved to London and became known in London literary circles, 1781. Visited Paris, 1790; settled in Paris, 1792; imprisoned by Maximilien de Robespierre from October to November, 1793. Began to live with John Hurford Stone around 1794; forced to leave France briefly for Basel, Switzerland, 1794; became a naturalized French citizen, 1817. Died December 15, 1827.

Selected Works

Novels
Edwin and Eltruda. 1782.
Julia, a Novel. 2 vols. 1790. Published with an introduction by Peter Garside, 1995.
The History of Perourou, or The Bellows-Mender. 1801.

Poetry
An Ode on the Peace. 1783.
Peru. 1784.

Poems. 2 vols. 1786. Published with an introduction by Jonathan Wordsworth, 1994.

Correspondence
Letters from France, vol. 1 (consisting of *Letters Written from France in the Summer of 1790; Letters from France Containing Many New Anecdotes; Letters from France Containing a Great Variety of Interesting and Original Information*, originally published 1792–96). Published with an introduction by Janet M. Todd, 1975.
Letters from France, vol. 2 (consisting of *Letters Containing a Sketch of the Politics of France 1794; Letters Containing a Sketch of the Scenes Which Passed in Various Departments of France during the Tyranny of Robespierre, and of the Events Which Took Place in Paris on the 28th of July 1794*, originally published 1795–96). Published with an introduction by Janet M. Todd, 1975.
A Tour of Switzerland, or, a View of the Present State of the Governments and Manners of those Cantons: with Comparative Sketches of the Present State of Paris. 2 vols. 1798.
Sketches of the State of Manners and Opinions in the French Republic towards the Close of the Eighteenth Century. 1801.
The Political and Confidential Correspondence of Louis XVI. 1803.
A Narrative of the Events Which Have Taken Place in France from the Landing of Napoleon Bonaparte on the First of March, 1815, Till the Restoration of Louis XVIII, with an Account of the Present State of Society and Public Opinion. 1815.
On the Late Persecution of the Protestants in the South of France. 1816.
Letters on the Events Which Have Passed in France Since the Restoration in 1815. 1819.
Four New Letters of Mary Wollstonecraft and Helen M. Williams. Edited by Benjamin P. Kurtz and Carrie C. Autrey, 1937.

Bibliography

Adickes, Sandra. *The Social Quest: The Expanded Vision of Four Women Travelers in the Era of the French Revolution*. New York: Peter Lang, 1991.
Favret, Mary A. *Romantic Correspondence: Women, Politics and the Fiction of Letters*. Cambridge: Cambridge University Press, 1993.
Jones, Chris. *Radical Sensibility: Literature and Ideas in the 1790s*. London: Routledge, 1993.
Jones, Vivien. "Women Writing Revolution: Narratives of History and Sexuality in Wollstonecraft and Williams." In *Beyond Romanticism: New Approaches to Texts and Contexts 1780–1832*. Edited by Stephen Copley and John Whale. London: Routledge, 1992.
Kelly, Gary. *Women, Writing and Revolution 1790–1827*. Oxford and New York: Oxford University Press, 1993.
Mellor, Anne K. *Romanticism and Gender*. New York: Routledge, 1993.
Richardson, Alan. "Epic Ambivalence: Imperial Politics and Romantic Deflection in Williams's *Peru* and Landor's *Gebir*." In *Romanticism, Race, and Imperial Culture, 1780–1834*. Edited by Alan Richardson and Sonia Hofkosh. Bloomington: Indiana University Press, 1996.
Sha, Richard C. "Expanding the Limits of Feminine Writing: The Prose Sketches of Sydney Owenson (Lady Morgan) and Helen Maria Williams." In *Romantic Women Writers: Voices and Countervoices*. Edited by Paula R. Feldman and Theresa M. Kelley. Hanover, N.H.: University Press of New England, 1995.
Watson, Nicola J. "Novel Eloisas: Revolutionary and Counter-Revolutionary Narratives in Helen Maria Williams, Wordsworth, and Byron," *Wordsworth Circle* 23 (1992): 18–23.
Woodward, Lionel D. *Une anglaise amie de la Révolution française: Hélène Maria Williams et ses amis*. Paris: Librairie Ancienne Honoré Champion, 1930.

WINTERREISE (WINTER JOURNEY) 1827–1828

Song cycle by Franz Peter Schubert

Winterreise (*Winter Journey*) by the Austrian composer Franz Peter Schubert, is one of the earliest and greatest of all song cycles, and one of the most important texts of musical Romanticism. While Ludwig van Beethoven's cycle *An die ferne Geliebte* (*To the Distant Beloved*, 1816) was the first work to be published with the description *Liederkreis* (song cycle) on the title page, Schubert was the composer who effectively defined the new genre.

Schubert completed two cycles, both of which set poems by Wilhelm Müller: *Die Schöne Müllerin* (*The Beautiful Miller Maid*, 1823–24) and *Winterreise*. The two halves of the latter date from the last two years of Schubert's life, and indeed he was correcting the proofs of the second part while on his deathbed. It seems possible that he planned another cycle, or perhaps two separate cycles, based on the settings of poetry by Heinrich Heine and Ludwig Rellstab posthumously published as *Schwanengesang* (*Swan Song*, 1828). The convenience to Schubert of the new genre was the nature of song cycle as a mediation between song, the genre which Schubert had developed to a completely unprecedented level of sophistication and expressivity, and the possibilities afforded by a large, significant work. The twenty-four songs of *Winterreise* comprise more than an hour of intense, complex music, demanding constant emotional involvement and concentration on the part of the listener. It is thus a more substantial and demanding work than many operas, quite apart from lasting longer in performance than any of Schubert's other chamber works, or indeed symphonies—even including the "Great" C Major Symphony (1825).

Both *Die Schöne Müllerin* and *Winterreise* are works based around one of the topoi of early Romanticism, the *Wanderlied* (wanderer's song). Indeed, the very nature of a song cycle, which inevitably presents a sequence of differing anecdotes and scenes, lends itself to the narrative of journeying. The ubiquitous impulse to treat journeying and the figure of the wanderer as metaphors for an exploration of the human psyche means that the purpose or destination of the journey is relatively unimportant by comparison with the events along the way; a feature of countless Romantic journeys from Johann Wolfgang Goethe's *Wilhelm Meister* to William Wordsworth's *Prelude*. However, *Winterreise* is notable for the paucity of event or anecdote contained within it. The narrative is something that must be inferred from the succession of sights and sounds whose unifying features are the frozen landscape, images of departure and death, and the increasing distance from the protagonist's beloved. Comparisons of Schubert's two cycles are inevitable, and indeed may have informed Müller's design of the poems in any case; *Winterreise* appears to begin where *Die Schöne Müllerin* leaves off, with the poet leaving the home of his beloved after an unsuccessful love affair. The opening words, "Fremd bin ich eingezogen, fremd zieh' ich wieder aus" ("A stranger I arrived, a stranger I depart") in a sense encapsulate the entire action of the cycle. The important thing about the protagonist's journey is its point of departure, not any intended destination; and his sense of alienation is entirely unrelieved by experiences along the journey, since everything he encounters links him in one way or another to his lost love. The frozen rivers, seemingly dead trees, faces apparently aged by hoarfrost, and snow melted by tears are of course the landscape of the desolate mind.

The rather "loose" nature of the narrative of the song-cycle is a reflection of some aspects of its origins. As was the case for *Die Schöne Müllerin*, the poems of *Winterreise* were conceived and published as a group by Müller, with the overall title adopted by Schubert. The twelve songs of Schubert's part 1 were published in the Leipzig journal *Urania* in 1823. All twenty-four were published together in 1824, with the additional songs interleaved and appended to the original twelve, in volume 2 of *Gedichte aus den hinterlassenen Papieren eines reisended Waldhornisten* (*Poems from the Posthumous Papers of a Traveling Horn Player*). Since Schubert began to compose part 2 in the month that part 1 was published (January 1828), it seems unlikely he had discovered all twenty-four songs earlier; he simply extracted the twelve additional songs from the longer set, preserving their sequence (except for songs 10 and 11, which he interchanged). Thus the twenty-four songs of *Winterreise* have a different order from the published order of the whole set of poems. This demonstrates Schubert's view that the twelve songs of part 1 belong together as a whole, distinct work, as well as testifying to the latent rather than explicit narrative they contain. Part 1 begins with the protagonist's alienation, and ends with the temporary respite of *Einsamkeit* (solitude); part 2 begins with rushing movement as "Die Post" ("The Post") brings no letter from the beloved, and ends with the protagonist's enigmatic encounter with a hurdy-gurdy player, "Drüben hinterm Dorf" ("There, Beyond the Town"). The occasional experiment by some singers of performing all twenty-four songs in the published order of the poems ignores the manifold and subtle musical links between the songs upon which the aesthetic integrity of the song cycle depends.

Commentators on *Winterreise* have been united in the opinion that there are many musical correspondances between songs, and an overall patterning of keys and motivic detail; and equally divided in opinion concerning the specific details of this patterning. Part 1 originally began and ended in D minor, but Schubert changed the key of song 12 (to B minor) when he added the second half, and the completed cycle does not have a "main key" as such. Much depends on whether the late changes to the keys of songs give Schubert's final view of the work, as Susan Youens believes, or constitute the interference of a publisher, as Richard Kramer argues. The musical links go far beyond the question of keys, however. One of the most impressive aspects of *Winterreise* is the consistency of the musical imagery which it presents. The dialectic between images of journeying, departure, and movement on the one hand, and the stasis of the frozen scenery (and the protagonist's frozen heart), is written into the fabric of the musical composition.

These concerns are reflected above all in the final song of part 2. Although Müller has not by and large been remembered as a poet, apart from the preservation of his work in Schubert's songs, commentators agree that the ending of *Winterreise* is a poetic masterstroke. The poem "Der Leiermann" ("The Hurdy-Gurdy Player") presents a single, haunting image, of the musician who "wankt er hin und her" ("staggers to and fro"), with numb fingers and an empty beggar's cup. The accompaniment alternates two musical figures, one for the voice and one for the piano, each of them constantly varied and yet refusing to progress. The setting is incredibly spare and compressed, and yet the effect is overwhelming—Schubert's "monumental simplicity," as it has been called. Notably, the description also applies to "Der Doppelgänger," which is the final song in the manuscript of what became *Schwanengesang*. The figure of the hurdy-gurdy player has been taken as an allegory of death, a testament to the transcendent power of music, and as a metaphor for society's rejection of the artist. Whatever interpretation one favors, the song sets the seal on *Winterreise* as one of Schubert's greatest achievements.

ROBERT SAMUELS

Bibliography

Gibbs, Christopher. *The Life of Schubert*. Cambridge: Cambridge University Press, 2000.

Kramer, Richard. *Distant Cycles: Schubert and the Conceiving of Song*. Chicago: Chicago University Press, 1994.

Reed, John. *The Schubert Song Companion*. Manchester: Manchester University Press, 1985.

Turchin, Barbara. "The Nineteenth-century *Wanderlieder* Cycle," *Journal of Musicology* 5 (1987): 498–525.

Youens, Susan. *Retracing a Winter's Journey: Schubert's Winterreise*. Ithaca, N.Y.: Cornell University Press, 1991.

———. "Winterreise: In the Right Order," *Soundings* 13 (1985): 41–50.

WOLLSTONECRAFT, MARY 1759-1797

English educational and political theorist and writer

During her short lifetime, Mary Wollstonecraft gained fame as one of the leading English radical writers of her time. After her early death, she was vilified as an emblem of revolutionary excess. Today she is best known as the author of *A Vindication of the Rights of Woman* (1792), a stirring call for the extension of civil and political rights to women and one of the most important documents in the history of modern feminism.

Wollstonecraft spent her childhood and early adulthood in genteel, peripatetic poverty as her father struggled with alcoholism and failed to earn a living as a gentleman farmer; she was only meagerly educated. Her first attempts to earn a living as a single woman—as companion to a well-to-do widow (1778–80), proprietor of a school (1784–86), and governess (1786–87)—proved unprofitable and frustrating. However, she learned valuable lessons about class structure, the shortcomings of fashionable education, and the power of environment to shape character, themes that she explored throughout her career as a writer, beginning in 1787 with the publication of *Thoughts on the Education of Daughters*, which argued for reforms to the fashionable mode of educating girls for ornamental womanhood.

Mary, A Fiction, a loosely autobiographical novel that was "an artless tale, without episodes, [in which] the mind of woman, who has thinking powers is displayed" was published in 1788. It was quickly followed by a children's book, *Original Stories from Real Life*, and a translation from the French of Jacques Necker's *Of the Importance of Religious Opinions*. She also became a regular contributor to the periodical *Analytical Review* (published from May 1788 to June 1799). Though her pace slowed somewhat in later years, Wollstonecraft was one of the first women, in England or elsewhere, to earn her livelihood entirely by writing.

Through her publisher, Joseph Johnson, she developed contacts with a cosmopolitan group of radical thinkers, including William Godwin, Thomas Paine, and Joseph Priestley, and became deeply concerned with contemporary political and social issues.

In late November 1790, *A Vindication of the Rights of Men* was published. It is Wollstonecraft's rebuttal of William Burke's conservative attack on the liberal hopes for political reform, *Reflections on the French Revolution*, the first such to appear. It was followed in 1792 with a volume that has inspired ardent admiration as well as vituperative abuse: *A Vindication of the Rights of Woman*, "the first sustained argument for female emancipation based on a cogent ethical system" (Miriam Brody).

In December 1792, Wollstonecraft went to Paris, in time to see the early promise of the French Revolution devolve into the Terror. While there, she met Gilbert Imlay, an American adventurer, speculator, and would-be writer (his 1793 novel *The Emigrants* is believed to have been written almost entirely by Wollstonecraft), with whom she established an irregular relationship. She registered as his wife with the American embassy in Paris in 1793, although they never married. Their daughter Fanny was born in France on May 14, 1794, the same year that Wollstonecraft published what had been intended to be the first volume of a larger work, *Historical and Moral View of the Origin and Progress of the French Revolution*, covering the early days of agitation and revolt in Paris. She argued that the Revolution was the inevitable result of despotism, brutality, and moral decay, as well as intellectual progress and political advances. Her analysis is ultimately an optimistic one, imbued with liberal hopes for human improvement and social development. Her optimism was at odds with the prevailing conservative English opinion, which ultimately contributed to a marked decline in her popular reputation.

After Fanny's birth, Imlay's business affairs kept them apart, and evidently his affection for her diminished; in the summer of 1795, after a failed suicide attempt and with the relationship in crisis, Wollstonecraft left for Scandinavia. The result was *Letters Written during a Short Residence in Sweden, Norway and Denmark* (1796), in which she combined descriptions of scenic grandeur with sharply observed analyses of the corruptions of power.

After her return to England in the autumn of 1795, driven to despair by Imlay's deliberate infidelity, she again attempted suicide. Recovering, she rejoined her intellectual and social circle in London, renewing her acquaintance with William Godwin, the author of *An Enquiry concerning Political Justice* (1793), whom she had first met in 1787. They began an intimate relationship that resulted in marriage (March 29, 1797), and Wollstonecraft discovered she was pregnant. Unfortunately, she did not survive the birth of her daughter, Mary Godwin, on August 30, 1797, by many days; she died of a fever on September 10, 1797.

Wollstonecraft's powerful critiques of prevailing social and political conventions, unconventional sexual life, and association with radical political reformers meant that for many of her contemporaries, she represented the worst excesses of libertinism, atheism, and Jacobinism: Horace Walpole described her as a "hyena in petticoats." In the years of conservative backlash that followed her death and the publication of William Godwin's revealing *Memoirs of the Author of the Vindication of the Rights of Woman* (1798), repudiating her, notes Harriet Blodgett, "became a public way of declaring the writer's respectability." Rediscovered by twentieth-century scholars, she is now considered to be the first and foremost of the pioneers of modern feminism.

ALISON M. SCOTT

Biography

Born in the Spitalfields district of London, April 27, 1759. Served as paid companion, 1778–80; nursed invalid mother, 1780–82; after mother's death, lived with the family of her dearest friend, Fanny Blood, contributing to household upkeep by doing needlework. From 1784 to 1786, ran schools in Islington and Newington Green with Fanny and sisters Eliza and Everina; governess for daughters of Viscount Kingsborough, 1786–87. Worked as professional author, 1787–97; lives in France from 1792 to 1795; May 14, 1794, daughter Fanny was born in Le Havre; married William Godwin, March 29, 1797; August 30, 1797, daughter Mary was born. The author died September 10, 1797 in London.

Selected Works

Nonfiction

Thoughts on the Education of Daughters: with Reflections on Female Conduct, in the More Important Duties of Life. 1787.
A Vindication of the Rights of Men, in a Letter to the Right Honourable Edmund Burke. 1790.
A Vindication of the Rights of Woman with Strictures on Moral and Political Subjects. 1792.
An Historical and Moral View of the Origin and Progress of the French Revolution: and the Effect It Has Produced in Europe. 1794.

Letters Written during a Short Residence in Sweden, Norway, and Denmark. London, 1796.
Posthumous Works of the Author of A Vindication of the Rights of Woman. Edited by William Godwin. 4 vols., 1798. Includes *The Wrongs of Woman: or, Maria, A Fragment; Letters to Imlay; Letter on the Present Character of the French Nation; Letters to Mr. Johnson, Bookseller; The Cave of Fancy: A Tale; On Poetry, and Our Relish for the Beauties of Nature*; and *Fragment of Letters on the Management of Infants.*

Fiction

Mary: A Fiction. 1788.
The Emigrants, &c or, the History of an Expatriated Family, Being a Delineation of English Manners, Drawn from Real Characters, Written in America. 1793.

Children's Books

Original Stories from Real Life, with Conversations Calculated to Regulate the Affections, and Form the Mind to Truth and Goodness. 1788.

Translations

Necker, Jacques. *On the Importance of Religious Opinions.* 1788.
Cambon, Madame de. *Young Grandison.* 1790.
Salzmann, Christian Gotthilf. *Elements of Morality for the Use of Children*, with illustrations by William Blake. 1790–91.

Anthologies

The Female Reader; or, Miscellaneous Pieces, in Prose and Verse; Selected from the Best Writers, and Disposed under Proper Heads; for the Improvement of Young Women. 1789.

Bibliography

Blodgett, Harriet. *Centuries of Female Days: Englishwomen's Private Diaries.* New Brunswick, N.J.: Rutgers University Press, 1988.
Brody, Miriam. "Introduction" to Mary Wollstonecraft, *Vindication of the Rights of Woman.* New York: Penguin, 1985.
Falco, Maria J., ed. *Feminist Interpretations of Mary Wollstonecraft.* University Park: Pennsylvania State University Press, 1996.
Godwin, William. *Memoirs of the Author of the Vindication of the Rights of Woman.* London, 1798.
Shapiro, Virginia. *A Vindication of Political Virtue: The Political Theory of Mary Wollstonecraft.* Chicago: University of Chicago Press, 1992.
Todd, Janet M. *Mary Wollstonecraft: A Revolutionary Life.* New York: Columbia University Press, 2000.
Tomalin, Claire. *The Life and Death of Mary Wollstonecraft.* Rev. ed. London: Penguin, 1992.
Yeo, Eileen Janes. *Mary Wollstonecraft and Two Hundred Years of Feminisms.* London: Rivers Oram Press, 1997.

WOMEN

The social, legal, and political position of women in the Romantic era remained, to a large extent, as it had been for centuries. Women were denied access to most realms of public life. Their legal identity was defined in terms of their relation to the male members of their family. They were denied the educational opportunities afforded to their male contemporaries and working-class women suffered a double oppression, exploited as both women and as the lowest paid participants in the labor force.

However, in the post-Revolutionary context of the 1790s, the political rights of women began to be discussed seriously and women (and some men) began to challenge these various inequities. Though not always revolutionaries themselves, women in England, such as Mary Hays, Catherine Macaulay, Hannah More, Helen Maria Williams, and Mary Wollstonecraft argued in favor of increased opportunities for women, particularly in the sphere of education. In America, Judith Sargent Murray was one of a number of women calling for a new feminine influence in the new American republic (*On the Equality of the Sexes*, 1790). In France, women involved themselves in public life as never before, joining, and in some cases forming, political societies to further the revolutionary cause. Olympe de Gouges used the philosophy of natural rights to argue for the complete equality of the sexes (*Les Droits de femmes*, 1791). She was a monarchist, however, and was executed for her royalism in 1793.

Women thus contributed to the turbulent politics of the Romantic era in Europe and America and also they began to address a new political agenda as they developed a new vocabulary of women's rights. In addition, the Romantic era witnessed an increase in other forms of intellectual and cultural activity on the part of women. In the French salons, women exerted an influence over European intellectual life, and at the center of this sphere of influence was Madame Anne-Louise-Germaine de Staël. An influential figure, Staël published works that became, in many respects, manifestos for the European Romantic movement. Her *De L'Allemagne* (1810) influenced French and German Romanticism and was suppressed by Napoleon in the year of its publication in England, on account of its perceived anti-France bias. Her 1816 article in the first issue of *Biblioteca Italia* was both influential in terms of the development of Italian Romanticism, and controversial on account of its criticism of Italy's obsession with its classical and Renaissance past. She also wrote several novels, the most acclaimed of which, *Delphine* (1802), was regarded as something of a female version of Johann Wolfgang von Goethe's *The Sorrows of Young Werther*.

In the later French Romantic period, George Sand (Amandine-Aurore Lucille Dupin) achieved fame and some notoriety. She lived an unconventional life, writing to support herself and having relationships with the poet Louis-Charles-Alfred De Musset and most notably the composer Frédéric Chopin. Sand's novels typically championed the right of women to challenge cultural norms, most notably *Valentine* (1832), *Lélia* (1833), and *Mauprat* (1837).

Particularly in Britain, female literary production exploded in the Romantic era, a fact that Marlon B. Ross has termed "one of the most important literary phenomena in British literary history." Many of the most popular and prolific British novelists of the period were women. Indeed, prose fiction was a literary form that British women of this period largely made their own. To some extent this occurrence may be accounted for in terms of the popularity in England throughout the eighteenth century of "literature of sensibility." Sentimental fiction, with its focus upon domesticity and romance, was thought to be the special province of the female writer. Novels of sensibility, moreover, frequently carried explicit moral messages that helped their authors to secure a favorable critical reception at a time when the novel was still somewhat disparaged as a literary form and feminine authorship still tainted with a certain cultural impropriety. However, in terms of women writing in the Romantic era, one of the most significant aspects of the literature of sensibility was the priority that it gave to the subjective experiences and spiritual depth of its protagonists. In the work of Frances Burney, Maria Edgeworth, Elizabeth Inchbald, and Charlotte Smith, for example, the heroine's moral fortitude and feeling heart is frequently pitted against a decadent, unfeeling, and spiritually shallow social world. These writers thus shared common ground with the later Romantics: they were all concerned to some extent with issues of self and society. Gary Kelly has commented upon the degree to which Romantic poet drew upon "elements of the thematic and formal repertoires of sentimental fiction."

This influence has traditionally been somewhat neglected, along with female novelists themselves. With the exception of Jane Austen, women novelists were not, until the late-twentieth century, included in the canon of British Romantic-era literature. Indeed, female participation in European Romanticism has tended to be neglected overall. British Romanticism has been seen to comprise the work of six male poets and, with the notable exception of Staël, French, German, and Italian Romanticism appears to have developed free of female influence. However, there were over three hundred female poets publishing in England between 1760 and 1830, and they published over one thousand first editions. Stuart Curran has dubbed Charlotte Smith "the first poet in England whom in retrospect we would call Romantic." Her work influenced William Wordsworth and Samuel Taylor Coleridge and her *Elegiac Sonnets* (1784) went into their third edition in 1786. In publishing terms, female poets were often more successful than their male contemporaries and they were not restricted in their work to traditionally "feminine" themes. They sought to evoke the sublime; they considered the nature of individual creativity; they wrote on the subject of war and revolution and extensively on the slave trade. In Germany, Karoline Von Günderode wrote poetry that has been said to express a feminine sublime. Bettina von Arnim and Sophie Schubert were both married and in Arnim's case, related to German Romantic poets; both achieved literary recognition in their own right. Like many of her British contemporaries, Arnim eschewed domestic themes to address a range of social and political issues.

Women also figured in the Romantic era as portrait and landscape painters and, to a lesser extent, as sculptors. Anne Seymour Damer was a sculptor of some note working in England in the early Romantic period and French women painters exhibited at several of the salons. Adelaide Labille-Guiard was an important portrait painter in the late eighteenth century, a teacher of art and a champion of the rights of women artists in the intensely conservative environment of the Royal Academy of Paris. Her *Self-Portrait with Two Students* (1793) remarkably challenges conventional understandings of women's relation to art in the Romantic period. The artist sits at work overlooked by two attentive *female* students.

Finally, women of the period often traveled extensively and wrote about travel, participating in the developing genre of Romantic travel literature. Mary Callcot's journals from India and South America formed an important, though neglected, contribution to this genre, as did Helen Maria Williams' record of her travels through postrevolutionary France (*Letters Written in France in the Summer of 1790*, 1790), Ann Radcliffe's A *Journey Made in the Summer of 1794* (1795) and Mary Wollstonecraft's *Letters Written during a Short Residence in Sweden, Norway and Denmark* (1796). Therefore, in spite of the social limitations upon them, women were not entirely isolated and without influence in terms of Romantic era politics, art, and culture.

SUSAN CHAPLIN

Bibliography

Alexander, Meena. *Women and Romanticism*. London: Macmillan, 1989.

Battersby, Christine. "Unblocking the Oedipal: Karoline von Gunderode and the Female Sublime." In *Political Gender: Texts and Contexts*. Edited by Sally Ledger, Josephine McDonagh, and Jane Spence. London: Harvester Wheatsheaf, 1994.

Constable, John. "Romantic Women Poets." *The Cambridge Quarterly* 2, no. 2(2000): pp. 133–43.

Curran, Stuart. *The Poems of Charlotte Smith.* Oxford: Oxford University Press, 1993.

Haefner, Joel, and Shiner, Carol. *Re-Visioning Romanticism: British Women Writers.* Philadelphia: Penn State University Press, 1994.

Homans, M. *Women Writers and Poetic Identity: Dorothy Wordsworth, Emily Brontë, Emily Dickenson.* Princeton, N.J.: Princeton University Press, 1980.

Kelly, Gary. *English Fiction of the Romantic Period.* London: Longman, 1996.

Mellor, Anne K. *Romanticism and Feminism.* Indianapolis: Indiana University Press, 1988.

———. *Romanticism and Gender.* London: Routledge, 1993.

Poovey, Mary. *The Proper Lady and the Woman Writer: Ideology as Style in the Works of Mary Wollstonecraft, Mary Shelley and Jane Austen.* Chicago: University of Chicago, Press, 1984.

Ross, Marlon B. *Contours of Masculine Desire: Romanticism and the Rise of Women's Poetry.* Oxford: Oxford University Press, 1989.

WORDSWORTH, DOROTHY 1771-1855

English journal and travelogue writer; sister of William Wordsworth

It is only since the 1970s that the writings of Dorothy Wordsworth have been widely recognized as important Romantic-era texts in their own right. Before that time, the forms in which she chose to work—journal and travelogue—were not thought to repay the close attention of critics as much as the poetry and prose fiction of the era. Wordsworth herself never sought a literary reputation and would not send anything she wrote to a publisher, though often urged to do so by friends. "I should detest the idea of setting myself up as an Author," she remarked in 1810. Her best-known works are the *Grasmere Journals* (1800–03) and *Recollections of a Tour Made in Scotland* (1803). The *Grasmere Journals* were begun simply to please her brother William and to provide an outlet for her troubled thoughts and feelings during his absence. However, this journal soon became part of the interwoven pattern of literary and domestic labor in the Wordsworth household. William Wordsworth's earliest critics knew that he had incorporated descriptions from Dorothy's journal into his poems, but more recently scholars have realized that Dorothy was herself a writer of exceptional skill, expressing original insights into the rural economy and the scenic beauty of Cumbria, Somerset, and Scotland. The uniqueness of the *Grasmere Journals* as a piece of writing derives from Dorothy's extraordinary skill in finding the right phrase, or simply a surprising but effective verb or adjective, to capture the quickness of her observation: hills "wrapped in sunshine," roses "fretted" by heavy rain. They also document, in starkly factual prose, the harshness of life for their poorest neighbors, in a community where hunger and illness were constant factors. Besides those already mentioned, she is author of several works that deserve to be better known: the *Alfoxden Journal* (1798); *A Narrative Concerning George and Sarah Green* (1808); *Memorials of a Tour on the Continent* (1820); a prose tale for children; and a number of poems.

Born in Cockermouth on Christmas Day 1771, Dorothy Wordsworth was the third child and only daughter of John Wordsworth, an attorney, and Ann Cookson Wordsworth, the daughter of a linen draper. In 1765 John had been appointed law-agent to the landowner James Lowther, later Earl of Lonsdale. After the death of Dorothy's father in 1783, the earl's refusal to pay the Wordsworth family what he owed them had a profound effect on the economic and social prospects of all the Wordsworth children.

Dorothy was devoted to her four brothers, especially to William, born 1770, and John, born 1772, but in the decade after her mother's death (1778) she saw little of them. From the age of six until twelve, Dorothy was brought up by her second cousin, the hardworking and kindly Elizabeth Threlkeld, who ran a haberdashery business in Halifax, Yorkshire. The Threlkelds were dissenters; the Yorkshire dissenting tradition of cheerfulness, honesty, and care for others played a part in forming Dorothy's character. After the death of her father, the two uncles who became guardians of the Wordsworth children decided that in order to save money, some sacrifices had to be made, and Dorothy was removed from the school she was attending. In 1787, she was sent to live with her maternal grandparents at Penrith, and was taught French and arithmetic by her uncle, the Reverend William Cookson. Two years later, while staying with him and his new wife in Norfolk, Dorothy met the abolitionist William Wilberforce, who was impressed by the dedication that she showed in running a Sunday school for the poor of her uncle's parish. The most valued moments of her youth, however, were the school holidays when her brothers were sometimes able to pay her short visits. One important reunion took place in 1788, when she and William, with the Hutchinson sisters, went for walks around Penrith Beacon and other local sights. These walks were commemorated in Wordsworth's *The Prelude* (1850).

Dorothy's main hope throughout the 1790s was that she would be able to settle in a permanent home with William, the most adventurous and radical of her brothers. To take his part against her disapproving uncles showed a significant degree of boldness. Still young, she had decided that marriage was not for her. She and William first set up house together at Windy Brow, near Keswick, in 1794, then at Racedown, near Bristol, from September 1795 to July 1797. Dorothy assumed the role of her brother's housekeeper and literary assistant. At the beginning of July 1797, they learned that a large house at Alfoxden, close to the Somerset village where Samuel Taylor Coleridge lived, was vacant. They moved in and spent two years there. Her *Alfoxden Journal* was begun on January 20, 1798. Its descriptions of landscape are readable and vivid, though occasionally dependent on the vocabulary and taste of William Gilpin and the "picturesque" tradition.

Dorothy also lived with her brother in Germany during the exceptionally cold winter of 1798–99. Homesickness and the need to economize made it a restricted, unhappy time for them, but this period marked the beginning of William Wordsworth's sustained work on the autobiographical poem that became *The*

Prelude, which (like the earlier "Tintern Abbey") conveys glimpses of the crucial role that Dorothy's intense sensibility and love of rugged countryside played in the development of her brother's poetic vision.

Their first really permanent home was the cottage in Grasmere, which they moved into at the very end of 1799. Years later (in a letter dated December 23, 1815), Dorothy wrote of this event, "we were young and healthy and had attained an object long desired, we had returned to our native mountains, there to live." For her, living in Grasmere was the fulfilment of a long-cherished dream, and this has to be taken into account when considering to what extent Dorothy sacrificed the possibility of a more independent life, and of being recognized in her own right as a writer. However, from their residence at Racedown (1795–97) until 1835, when her mental and physical health underwent a catastrophic breakdown, Dorothy's hard work as housekeeper, cook, breadmaker, laundress, nursemaid, copyist, amanuensis, and secretary sustained the literary activities of the Wordsworth household. Some sense of the labor she performed can be gained from the *Grasmere Journals*. This is the text that established Dorothy Wordsworth's twentieth-century reputation as a writer of unparalleled skill in describing the natural world and constructing narratives of rural life.

Critics sometimes describe the prose of the *Grasmere Journals* as objective, imparting little sense of the observer's presence or feelings, but Dorothy's authorial voice is nevertheless a distinctive one that—without foregrounding a strong personality—conveys awareness of the process of observation, as well as the appearance of the thing observed. Take the birch tree seen on a windy November day in 1801, which was "yielding to the gusty wind . . . the sun shone upon it & it glanced in the wind like a flying sunshiny shower—it was a tree in shape with stem & branches but it was like a Spirit of water—The sun went in & it resumed its purplish appearance the twigs still yielding to the wind but not so visibly to us." As the tree's appearance changes in the burst of sunshine, the rhythm of the sentence captures the suddenness of the change. The similes, especially "like a Spirit of water," suit the eeriness and fluidity of the tree's movement. And there is a reminder of the observers' presence in the phrase "not so visibly to us."

In late August 1803, Dorothy accompanied her brother and Coleridge on a tour of Scotland, traveling in a horse-drawn jaunting car. Her *Recollections* were written in the months subsequent to the trip. The more leisured pace of composition reduces the effect of immediacy that is the distinctive achievement of the *Grasmere Journals*, but gives the later work more continuity, and a more consciously crafted literary style. Her account contains many sociocultural observations; she frequently compares not only Scottish and English landscapes but social customs and economic conditions in the two countries.

The unjustly neglected *Narrative concerning George and Sarah Green*, written at William's urging, documents an unhappy episode in which the parents of a large family living near Grasmere both died of exposure, and shows how the community responded to this tragedy. It reflects Dorothy's move toward a "Tory humanist" understanding of the social order, seeking to reaffirm the values she considered peculiar to rural life. The story gives a utopian picture of the economic stability of a farming community, perhaps overemphasizing its cohesiveness and ability to absorb trauma. Yet the *Narrative* is also compelling to read, constructed with real narrative skill and intimate knowledge of Grasmere people.

Dorothy's last major work, *Memorials of a Tour on the Continent*, derives from the summer of 1820 when she accompanied her brother and his wife on a tour of European countries. By this time, her strong desire to preserve the traditions of her "native mountains," particularly a way of life centered on family and community, had brought her to a politically conservative and quite consciously "English" outlook. Yet the *Memorials* show a frank and unalloyed pleasure in the beauty of European cities and towns such as Bruges.

Dorothy composed some thirty lyric poems, mostly about her affection for Grasmere Vale and its inhabitants. A few of these were published alongside her brother's poetry. It cannot be claimed that Dorothy's is a notably innovative poetic voice, but her poems do convey an attractive sense of delight in being an "Inmate" of Grasmere Vale. Sadly, her old age was dominated by illness. After 1835, her faculties deteriorated, and she came to depend on the constant care given by her close family; nevertheless, she continued to write journals, still remarkable for acute observation and vivid phrasing.

Now that the concept of "authorship" has widened, journals and other forms of life writing no longer fall outside the scope of legitimate literary interest. This should secure Dorothy

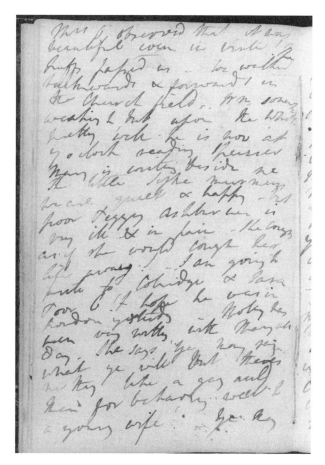

Dorothy Wordsworth, *The Grasmere Journals*. "Mrs. O. observed . . ." Reprinted courtesy of Dove Cottage, The Wordsworth Trust.

Wordsworth a lasting place among writers of the Romantic period.

ANTHONY JOHN HARDING

Selected Works

George and Sarah Green: A Narrative. Edited by Ernest de Selincourt. Oxford: Clarendon Press, 1936.
Journals. Edited by Ernest de Selincourt. 2 vols. London: Macmillan, 1941.
The Collected Poems of Dorothy Wordsworth. In *Dorothy Wordsworth and Romanticism.* Edited by Susan M. Levin. New Brunswick, N.J.: Rutgers University Press, 1987.
Letters. Selected and edited by Alan G. Hill. London: Oxford University Press, 1990.
The Grasmere Journals. Edited by Pamela Woof. Oxford: Oxford University Press, 1991.
Recollections of a Tour Made in Scotland. Edited by Carol Kyros Walker. New Haven, Conn.: Yale University Press, 1997.

Bibliography

Alexander, Meena. "Dorothy Wordsworth: The Grounds of Writing," *Women's Studies* 14, no. 3 (1988): 195–210.
Darlington, Beth. "Reclaiming Dorothy Wordsworth's Legacy." In *The Age of William Wordsworth: Essays on the Romantic Tradition.* Edited by Kenneth W. Johnston and Gene W. Ruoff. New Brunswick, N.J.: Rutgers University Press, 1987.
De Selincourt, Ernest. *Dorothy Wordsworth: A Biography.* Oxford: Clarendon Press, 1933.
Ehnenn, Jill. "Writing Against, Writing Through: Subjectivity, Vocation, and Authorship in the Work of Dorothy Wordsworth," *South Atlantic Review* 64 (1999): 72–90.
Gittings, Robert, and Jo Manton. *Dorothy Wordsworth.* New York: Oxford University Press, 1985.
Heinzelman, Kurt. "The Cult of Domesticity." In *Romanticism and Feminism.* Edited by Anne K. Mellor. Bloomington: Indiana University Press, 1988.
Homans, Margaret. *Women Writers and Poetic Identity: Dorothy Wordsworth, Emily Brontë, Emily Dickinson.* Princeton, N.J.: Princeton University Press, 1981.
Levin, Susan M. *Dorothy Wordsworth and Romanticism.* Douglass Series on Women's Lives and the Meaning of Gender. New Brunswick, N.J.: Rutgers University Press, 1987.
Liu, Alan. "On the Autobiographical Present: Dorothy Wordsworth's *Grasmere Journals,*" *Criticism* 26 (1984): 115–137.
McGavran, James Holt, Jr. "Dorothy Wordsworth's Journals: Putting Herself Down." In *The Private Self: Theory and Practice of Women's Autobiographical Writing.* Edited by Shari Benstock. Chapel Hill: University of North Carolina Press, 1988.
Nabholtz, John R. "Dorothy Wordsworth and the Picturesque," *Studies in Romanticism* 3 (1964): 118–28.
Page, Judith W. *Wordsworth and the Cultivation of Women.* Berkeley and Los Angeles: University of California Press, 1994.
Soderholm, James. "Dorothy Wordsworth's Return to Tintern Abbey," *New Literary History* 26 (1995): 309–21.
Vlasopolos, Anca. "Texted Selves: Dorothy and William Wordsworth in the *Grasmere Journals,*" *A/B: Auto/Biography Studies* 14, no. 1 (1999): 118–36.
Woof, Pamela. "Dorothy Wordsworth's *Grasmere Journals*: The Patterns and Pressures of Composition." In *Romantic Revisions.* Edited by Robert Brinkley and Keith Hanley. Cambridge: Cambridge University Press, 1992.
———. *Dorothy Wordsworth, Writer.* Grasmere: Wordsworth Trust, 1989.
———. "Dove Cottage in 1800," *Wordsworth Circle* 31 (2000): 133–42.
———. "The *Interesting* in Dorothy Wordsworth's Alfoxden Journal," *Wordsworth Circle* 31 (2000): 48–55.

WORDSWORTH, WILLIAM 1770-1850

British poet

William Wordsworth is so synonymous with "Romanticism" that literary histories and anthologies used to designate the era "The Age of Wordsworth." Wordsworth's eighty-year span of life supports the designation: he concludes with the generations "Romantic" as no other next does, born in the year of Oliver Goldsmith's *Deserted Village*, dying at the high noon of the next century, with Victoria as queen and Robert Browning and Alfred, Lord Tennyson the poets of the day. Although an oft-told tale is that "the poet" died long before, some time between 1807 and 1815 (the "great decade" of 1797–1807 yielding the best work), with an afterlife of diminished new verse and repackaged old, the "obituary" does not take adequate measure of Wordsworth's long life as cultural institution and as inescapable reference for poets of the next several generations. This was not just a matter of his honorary degrees in the late 1830s and the Poet Laureateship of his last decade. Wordsworth's poetry was embraced by the public for its power, amid the encroachments of modern life, to evoke a world of sentiment, feeling, and an ideal of "Nature" and as a therapy for the soul, in both its joys and (as John Keats would write to John Hamilton Reynolds, May 3, 1818) its "dark passages." He was, moreover, a "poet" distinctly English, rural, nonaristocratic, the embodiment in life and verse of "plain living and high thinking," at home in the Lake District he made famous, happy in his family, yet devoted to philosophical inquiry. In an unprecedented and perhaps still unrivaled event in English literary history, he worked, intermittently but ceaselessly, on a poetic autobiography. Within just weeks of the end of his breathing life in 1850, his inspired poetic "life" was published—a fourteen-book epic titled the Prelude. Along with Tennyson's *In Memoriam*, it was one of the most widely read poems of the year. Its life, fame, and text expanded across the twentieth century with the serial publication of manuscript versions, from 1826 right into the 1990s, each new edition producing a new "Wordsworth" with which to reckon.

Throughout his life as a writer, Wordsworth sharpened his poetic craft, so that no matter what some felt about the hardening of his sensibility, about his increasingly severe Christian faith, about the betrayal of youthful enthusiasm to conservative politics—the power of the poetry remained compelling. Keats called him a "genius," and Shelley, for all his anger over the political apostasy, could not break his Wordsworthian affiliations of image, tone, language, and even metaphysics. Felicia Hemans typifies the affection of women writers for the paternal, domestic Wordsworth, "The True Poet of Home" (versus the antidomestic alienation represented by Lord Byron). And even Byron, who most often subjects Wordsworth to satire, confessed "reverence" when he met him in 1815. Wordsworth's home in the Lake District, Rydal Mount, became a tourist destination, with visitors journeying from both England and abroad to soak up the sites made famous by the poetry and meet and pay homage to the poet himself.

Wordsworth was deeply rooted in the Lake District, where he was born and bred, one of four children. His father was steward (chief financial manager) to Lord Lonsdale, one of the wealthiest landowners in that part of England. The Wordsworths enjoyed a comfortable middle-class life in the market-town of Cockermouth, and the children reveled in the nearby fields, farmlands, lakes, hills and streams. Yet all this changed with his mother's death when he was eight. A father frequently away on business parsed the family out for care: the boys were "transplanted" (as Wordsworth later phrased it in *The Prelude*) to Hawkshead Grammar School in a distant valley, while their lively sister Dorothy was packed off to live with relatives in a series of situations ranging from comfortable to bleak. Family was a thing of the past, and young William full of energy and dark moods, gave himself to solitary adventures. "I was left alone / Seeking the visible world," he wrote obliquely of this era; "The props of my affections were removed, / And yet the building stood, as if sustained / By its own spirit" (1805, *Prelude* 2.292–96). Although his general mythology locates "the first / Poetic spirit of our human life" in an infant's pre-linguistic intimacy with the mother ("one beloved Presence" 2.250–80), in his particular life, a sensitivity to the world as latent text, a language to be discovered, apprehended, and worked into poetry, seems to have coincided with the solitude that followed the domestic diaspora:

> . . . would walk alone,
> In storm and tempest, or in starlight nights
> Beneath the quiet heavens, and at that time
> Have felt whate'er there is of power in sound
> To breathe an elevated mood, by form
> Or image unprofaned; and I would stand
> Beneath some rock, listening to sounds that are
> The ghostly language of the ancient earth,
> Or make their dim abode in distant winds.
> Thence did I drink the visionary power.
>   (*Prelude*, 1805. 2. 321–30)

From these impulses, Wordsworth implies in this poetic chronicle, emerged his character as a poet, shaped by local intensities, feeling-wrought imagery, and imagination animated by private memory.

The poet who would come to be known in every home in England was, paradoxically, a poet more than half in love with loneliness, withdrawn not only from the social world, but even at times from the entire visual world. This world darkened for the young man with the sudden death of his father, only five years after his mother's, during the Christmas holidays. Lord Lonsdale resisted paying his due to the estate (it was not settled until 1802, by Lonsdale's son, later Wordsworth's patron). Expecting to have to make his own way, Wordsworth entered St. John's College, Cambridge, planning a career in the Church of England. He earned his degree in 1791 but his heart was not in it, Cambridge seeming an unreal world, a forecast of the city life he always found uncongenial, often hellishly alien. "Not seldom had I melancholy thoughts," a "strangeness in my mind, / A feeling that I was not for that hour, / Nor for that place." (3.75–81). It was his travels that impressed him most, especially to the Continent in 1790, one year after the French Revolution. With "France standing on the top of golden hours, / And human nature seeming born again," (6.353–54), he caught the spirit— "Bliss was it in that dawn to be alive, / But to be young was very Heaven!" (10.693–94)—and, like so many of his generation, cherished millenarian hopes of a new era of brotherhood and democracy. The next summer he toured North Wales (climbing Mount Snowdon, an episode that enters the "Conclusion" to *The Prelude*), and then returned to France, reveling in democratic politics, mentored by Michel Beaupuy, an officer in the Republican army, and falling in love with Annette Vallon (whose family was Catholic royalist). Wordsworth's year in France concluded in late 1792, when depleted funds and the emerging Terror forced a return home, leaving behind not only France and French hopes, but also a French family. His and Annette's daughter Caroline was born in December 1792, but with the outbreak of war between France and England, it would be ten years before he saw this family again, on the eve of his marriage to his childhood sweetheart, an English maid of the Lakes, Mary Hutchinson.

The homecoming of 1792 was severe. Caught in conflicting loyalties to England and France, horrified by the bloodbath that had darkened Revolutionary ideals and then the rise of strongman Napoleon and his war of aggression, Wordsworth may have suffered an emotional collapse when, "Sick, wearied out with contrarieties," he "yielded up moral questions in despair" (10.900–01). A domestic reunion with Dorothy, he said later, "maintained for me a saving intercourse / With my true self . . . preserved me still / A Poet" (915–20), but the record of the next few years is mysterious. Wordsworth may have flirted with radical politics at home, may have returned to France to see his lover and their daughter, may have witnessed the guillotining of moderate Girondins whom he knew and admired. A material bounty arrived in 1795, a small legacy of nine hundred pounds from the estate of a tubercular friend that enabled William not only to dream of poetry but to devote himself to the vocation, with Dorothy as encourager, companion, scribe, and housekeeper. He soon met a poet and journalist who had already read and intensely admired his *Descriptive Sketches* (1793), Samuel Taylor Coleridge, who fired and inspired him with a fresh sense of poetic mission and power. In 1797, the three settled in the west country near the Bristol Channel. With comfortable housing, sufficient funds, and good company, Wordsworth thrived on the friendship, the daily walks and talks about poetry. Encouraging and advising each other's endeavors, he and Coleridge were soon collaborating on a venture they hoped would finance a walking tour: *Lyrical Ballads*, first published in 1798 (and then in different editions, and as Wordsworth's sole production, in 1800, 1802, and 1805). This was to prove a landmark event of the "Romantic" movement.

In the heady days of 1798, the company they were keeping with radicals such as John Thelwall and British anxiety about a French invasion through the Bristol Channel put them under suspicion, and their leases were not renewed. They decided to go to Germany for a winter season spanning from 1798 to 1799, to learn the language with an aim of translating the literature for English readers, and to absorb the local culture and philosophy. The trip proved far more enjoyable for Coleridge, happily situated with more financial resources in university towns, while the Wordsworths economized by enduring a miserably cold, lonely winter in the remote town of Goslar. It was in this bleak isolation that Wordsworth generated many of the new poems for a new edition of *Lyrical Ballads*, along with the first fragments of intense recollection that began to coalesce into drafts of a poetic autobiography. He initially thought of this account as a self-authorizing preamble to a major philosophical poem for the new century, taking up the relations of "Man, Nature, and Human Life" in the modern world (Coleridge's abiding vision of his mission). But it was soon clear that his fascination with past, yet hauntingly present "spots of time," as he came to call them (*Prelude*, 11.258ff), was generating an independent venture of life writing (the word *autobiography* had not yet been coined in 1799)—an epic whose composition and revision would occupy the rest of his life.

The trio returned to the Lake District in 1799, Coleridge settling in Keswick, the Wordsworths in the lovely gem of Grasmere village. The second edition of *Lyrical Ballads*, now signed by Wordsworth, appeared in 1800, offering new poems and fronted by an important and subsequently controversial "Preface," declaring such principles as inspiration from "emotion recollected in tranquillity," a bold equation of "all good poetry" with "the spontaneous overflow of powerful feelings," and the assertion that not only can there be "no essential difference" between the language of poetry and the language of ordinary conversation, but that the conversation that is most poetic, most rooted in the essential passions of the heart in relation to nature, is that of rural peasant society. This was in part deliberate mythmaking, a self-promoting break from eighteenth-century poetic principles. But the claims proved so appealing (William Hazlitt saw an advent of "a new style and a new spirit") that they were taken, at the time and increasingly in retrospect, as the mark of a new era. The "Romantic age" has some political starting points (the French Revolution) and prior benchmarks in literary history (William Blake), but its strong definition as a "poetic" movement is routinely keyed to the publication of this influential Preface.

The Wordsworths lived first in Dove Cottage, and then, with William's marriage in 1802 and children swelling the household, in nearby, more commodious residences, eventually settling at Rydal Mount in 1813. This rootedness in a beloved world helped them weather several disasters. John Wordsworth, captain of a merchant vessel whose income was to contribute to his brother's poetic vocation, drowned in a stormy shipwreck off the English coast in 1805; two of the Wordworths' five children died in 1812, and by 1810 Coleridge's opium addiction (not understood then as a medical problem) and his truancy from his own family led to strains and then a bitter alienation not really mended until the late 1820s. Wordsworth's volumes, loved as they were in some quarters, were not best-sellers. *Poems* (1807) was harshly reviewed, and his nine-book epic for the times *The Excursion* (1814) was ridiculed by the leading reviews. Even so, such attention, as well as Wordsworth's assembling of a revised, conceptually categorized *Poems* in 1815, confirmed his emerging fame and importance. Not only did the volumes of 1814–15

present a wealth of work, but the scope of the epic and the sense of mission infusing the corpus fueled Wordsworth's claim as England's most important living poet. Only Byron was a rival, and his sites were more urban than rural, more European than English; indeed, after April 1816, his life in England abruptly ended. Wordsworth received a government patronage position in 1813, and he continued to write and publish poetry in every decade of his long life.

During this lifetime, *The Excursion* was regarded as his major (if not most cherished) work; it was a favorite of Queen Victoria, who appointed him Poet Laureate in 1843. Its first book, *The Wanderer*, with its heartrending story of Margaret's ruined cottage, was widely admired. Yet overall, and especially among poets, Wordsworth's fame and esteem tended to be based on shorter narratives of pathos such as *Michael* and *The Brothers* (tales in which, as he said in his preface to *Lyrical Ballads*, the development of feeling gives importance to the action and situation), the great lyrics of crisis and philosophical reflection such as *Tintern Abbey (1798), Ode: Intimations of Immortality from Recollections of Early Childhood* (1807; 1815), and a substantial body of incomparable sonnets, songs, and lyrics (the "Lucy" poems [1800] and other elegies, *The Solitary Reaper* (1807), the sonnet composed on Westminster Bridge [1802; 1807], and "Surprised by Joy" [1815]). Victorians embraced a "Wordsworth" who could heal the "iron age" of the times, the poet of youth's golden gleam, of "Nature," of unembarrassed sentiment, of memory, of loss and consolation. It was this "healing power" that moved Matthew Arnold to declare in 1879 that Wordsworth bowed only to Shakespeare and Milton in English literature. For many twentieth-century readers it is *The Prelude*—and its extended manuscripts—that is the definitive work, a venture of prescient modernism in its self-inwrought project of writing as a poet about becoming a poet, of exploring and confirming vocation in the event of its practice. Wordsworth virtually defined modern existential subjectivity, elaborating—even as he set out to picture "the discipline / And consummation of a Poet's mind / In everything that stood most prominent" (*Prelude* 13.270–73)—the deep mysteries and dark passages of self-enquiry, forever haunted by a "dim and undetermined sense / Of unknown modes of being." (1.419–20). Yet Wordsworth also provides a compelling and complex measure of his own decades, embodying the multiple, conflicting forces of the Romantic era and their subsequent reverberations.

SUSAN J. WOLFSON

Biography

Born April 7, 1770 at Cockermouth, second son of John Wordsworth (1741–83), steward to Sir James Lowther, later Earl of Lonsdale; sister Dorothy born 25 December 1771 (d. 1855); brothers Richard (b. 1768), John (b. 1772), Christopher (b. 1774). Schooled at Cockermouth until his mother died on March 8, 1778; entered Hawkshead Grammar School (1779–86). First poem, "Lines Written as a School Exercise at Hawkshead" 1785; first publication, 1787, "Sonnet: On Seeing Miss Helen Maria Williams Weep at a Tale of Distress" (*European Magazine*, signed "Axiologus": "worth-words"), the year he entered St John's College, Cambridge. Walking tour in France, Switzerland and Germany with Robert Jones, a close college friend, 1790. Earned bachelor's degree, January 1791, and lived in London until May, then toured North Wales with Jones. After short stays in Cambridge and London, left for France in November 1791. Daughter Caroline was born to Annette Vallon in December 1792, the month he returned to London. Left on a walking tour, from Salisbury to North Wales, summer 1793. *An Evening Walk* and *Descriptive Sketches* published that year. Lived with Dorothy in Yorkshire, 1794, then with Raisley Calvert in the northwest. Calvert died early in 1795 and left a bequest of £900, allowing him to devote himself to poetry. Met Robert Southey, Samuel Taylor Coleridge, and publisher Joseph Cottle, settled in Dorset with sister Dorothy. His play *The Borderers* finished in 1797, then began drafts of *The Ruined Cottage*. Moved to Alfoxden House near the Bristol Channel, and with Coleridge planed *Lyrical Ballads*. 1798: working on *Ballads* and autobiographical verse; visited Tintern Abbey, then moved to moved to London, *Lyrical Ballads* published in September of that year, the month he, Dorothy, and Coleridge left for Germany. At Goslar, Germany, wrote poems for the second edition of *Ballads* and more autobiographical poetry. Returned to England in 1799, arriving, with Dorothy, at Grasmere at the end of the year. Second edition of *Lyrical Ballads*, in two volumes, with preface, published in 1800 (further editions 1802 and 1805).

Composed many of the pieces to appear in *Poems, in Two Volumes* (1807) from 1802 to 1807, and in 1802 wrote the first four stanzas of the "Intimations" Ode, and visited Calais, France, to see Annette Vallon and Caroline before marrying Mary Hutchinson in October of that year. Son John born June 1803; also, toured Scotland with Dorothy and Coleridge that year. Daughter Dora born August 1804. Brother John drowned in the wreck of the merchant ship he captained in February 1805, in May of that year Wordsworth completed the first, thirteen-book draft of *The Prelude*. Visited London in spring 1806; son Thomas born in June. *Poems* published in 1807; began *The White Doe of Rylstone*, later published in 1815. Visited London, February–April 1808; moved to a larger home in Grasmere; daughter Catherine born in September of that year. Published a tract in 1809 on the Convention of Cintra (British treaty for the French withdrawal from Portugal). *Essay on Epitaphs* in Coleridge's periodical, *The Friend*, 1810; son William born; estrangement from Coleridge.

Worked on *The Excursion* from 1810 to 1814. In 1812, daughter Catherine died in June, son Thomas in December. Accepted government patronage post of Distributor of Stamps (official stamped paper for legal documents) for Westmoreland, and then moved to more spacious home, Rydal Mount, near the village of Ambleside and not far from Grasmere, 1813. Toured Scotland, summer 1814; *The Excursion* published in August. First comprehensive collection of *Poems*, 1815. Active in Tory politics, in London and the Lakes District. *Peter Bell* published (parodied before it appears), also *The Waggoner*, 1819. Toured England and parts of Europe with Dorothy in 1820 and published two new volumes (*The River Duddon, Vaudracour and Julia &c*), a collection of *Miscellaneous Poems* and the second edition of *The Excursion*. Further volumes and touring in the 1820s; five-vol. *Poetic Works*, including *The Excursion*, appeared in 1827. Further editions of works appeared throughout the 1830s and 1840s. Received honorary degree from University of Durham (1818) and University of Oxford (1839); resigned stamp distributorship, 1842 and received a Civil List pension of £300. When Southey died in 1843, succeeded him as Poet Laureate. Daughter Dora died 1847. Wordsworth died at Rydal Mount, April 23, 1850.

Selected Writings

The Poetical Works of William Wordsworth. 5 vols. Edited by Ernest de Selincourt, revised by Helen Darbishire. Oxford: Oxford University Press, 1949–59.

Complete textual histories, with valuable annotation, are provided by the Cornell Wordsworth series, general editor Stephen M. Parrish. Includes three major stages of *The Prelude* (1798–99; 1805; 1850), *Lyrical Ballads* and contemporaneous poems, "*The Pedlar and "The Ruined Cottage*," Home at Grasmere, Poems in Two Volumes (1807), Shorter Poems, 1807–1820. Ithaca, N.Y.: Cornell University Press. 1982– .

William Wordsworth: The Poems. Edited by John O. Hayden. New York: Penguin, 1977.

The Prose Works of William Wordsworth. Edited by W. J. B. Owen and J. W. Smyser; Oxford: Clarendon Press, 1974.

The Letters of William and Dorothy Wordsworth. Edited by E. de Selincourt and revised (variously) by Chester L. Shaver, Mary Moorman, and Alan G. Hill. Oxford: Clarendon, 1967–92.

The Prelude (1798, 1805, 1850). With supplementary materials. Edited by Jonathan Wordsworth, Stephen Gill, and Meyer Abrams. New York: W. W. Norton, 1979.

The Prelude: A Parallel Text. Edited by J. C. Maxwell. New York: Penguin, 1971.

Bibliography

Arac, Jonathan. "Bounding Lines: *The Prelude* and Critical Revision," *boundary 2*, vol. 7 (1979): 31–48.

Arnold, Matthew. Preface. In *Poems of Wordsworth*. London: Macmillan, 1879.

Averill, James. *Wordsworth and the Poetry of Human Suffering*. Ithaca, N.Y.: Cornell University Press, 1980.

Chandler, James. *Wordsworth's Second Nature: A Study of the Poetry and Politics*. Chicago: University of Chicago Press, 1981.

Collings, David. *Wordsworthian Errancies*. Baltimore: Johns Hopkins University Press, 1994.

Ferguson, Frances. *Wordsworth: Language as Counter-Spirit*. New Haven, Conn.: Yale University Press, 1977.

Ferry, David. *The Limits of Mortality: An Essay on Wordsworth's Major Poems*. Middletown, Conn.: Wesleyan University Press, 1959.

Friedman, Michael H. *The Making of a Tory Humanist: Wordsworth and the Idea of Community*. New York: Columbia University Press, 1979.

Galperin, William H. *Revision and Authority in Wordsworth: The Interpretation of a Career*. Philadelphia: University of Pennsylvania Press, 1989.

Gill, Stephen. *Wordsworth: A Life*. Oxford: Clarendon Press, 1989.

Harper, George McLean. *William Wordsworth: His Life, Works, and Influence*. New York: Scribners, 1929.

Hartman, Geoffrey H. *Wordsworth's Poetry, 1787–1814*. New Haven, Conn.: Yale University Press, 1975.

Hickey, Alison. *Impure Conceits: Rhetoric and Ideology in Wordsworth's Excursion*. Stanford, Calif.: Stanford University Press, 1997.

Jacobus, Mary. *Romanticism, Writing, and Sexual Difference: Essays on "The Prelude."* Oxford: Oxford University Press, 1989.

Johnson, Barbara. "Strange Fits: Poe and Wordsworth on the Nature of Poetic Language." *A World of Difference*. Baltimore: Johns Hopkins University Press, 1989.

Johnston, Kenneth. *The Hidden Wordsworth: Poet, Lover, Spy*. New York: W. W. Norton, 1998.

———. *Wordsworth and "The Recluse."* New Haven, Conn.: Yale University Press, 1984.

Jones, John. *The Egotistical Sublime: A History of Wordsworth's Imagination.* London: Chatto, 1954.

Kneale, Douglas. *Monumental Writing: Aspects of Rhetoric in Wordsworth's Poetry.* Lincoln: University of Nebraska Press, 1988.

Lindenberger, Herbert. *On Wordsworth's "Prelude."* Princeton, N.J.: Princeton University Press, 1963.

Mahoney, John L. *William Wordsworth: A Poetic Life.* New York: Fordham University Press, 1997.

Manning, Peter J. *Reading Romantics: Texts and Contexts.* New York: Oxford University Press, 1990.

Moorman, Mary. *William Wordsworth, A Biography.* Oxford: Clarendon, 1957–65.

Onorato, Richard. *The Character of the Poet: Wordsworth in "The Prelude."* Princeton, N.J.: Princeton University Press, 1971.

Page, Judith. *Wordsworth and the Cultivation of Women.* Berkeley and Los Angeles; University of California Press, 1994.

Perkins, David. *The Quest for Permanence.* Cambridge: Harvard University Press, 1959.

Simpson, David. *Wordsworth and the Figurings of the Real.* Atlantic Highlands, N.J.: Humanities Press, 1982.

———. *Wordsworth's Historical Imagination: The Poetry of Displacement.* New York: Methuen, 1987.

Wolfson, Susan J. *The Questioning Presence.* Ithaca, N.Y.: Cornell University Press, 1987.

Wordsworth, Jonathan. *William Wordsworth: The Borders of Vision.* Oxford: Clarendon, 1982.

WRIGHT, JOSEPH 1734–1797

English portrait and landscape painter

"Mr. Wright, of Derby, is a very great and uncommon genius, in a peculiar way." Thus pronounced a reviewer in the *Gazetteer* in 1768 at the height of Joseph Wright's career as a painter of people, industry, and light. During his lifetime, Joseph Wright was feted as a painter of the Industrial Revolution, but it would be unhelpful and restrictive to treat him as interested only in depicting rational, scientific, and technological advancements, their inventors and patrons. Wright's oeuvre is more diverse and lyrical than this description suggests. His correspondence, for example, records his passionate interest in the natural sublime and in landscape as genre. His preoccupation with the effects of natural light and artificial illumination could be described as reflecting, literally, Enlightenment attitudes toward progress, but it also makes him a forerunner to John Martin and J. M. W. Turner and their experiments with color and atmospheric effects. Wright's enthusiasm for the eruption of Vesuvius, which he witnessed on a two-year trip to Italy in 1773, and his repeated articulated awe of the grandeur and magnificence of the Lake District are striking evidence of his romantic spirit and enthusiasm for the sublime as defined by Edmund Burke in 1757. On November 11, 1774, for example, he wrote to his surgeon brother, Richard, of Vesuvius, " 'Tis the most wonderful sight in Nature," and later, in 1794, he wrote of the Lake District, "Mountains piled on mountains and tossed together in wilder form than imagination can paint or pen describe." We might, therefore, frame Joseph Wright's work within the contexts of both the Enlightenment and Romanticism, and describe him as a pre-Romantic painter of the Industrial Revolution.

Joseph Wright, styled Wright of Derby, trained as a portrait painter in London under the tutelage of Thomas Hudson (the master of Joshua Reynolds) in the 1750s, exhibiting at the Society of Artists from 1765 onward and at the Royal Academy from 1778. In 1784 he was elected a full member of the academy, but he declined this honor on the basis of some slight he believed he had received. Throughout his career he remained essentially a painter of the provinces. In spite of his London connections, and apart from a trip to Italy in 1773–75 where he made drawings after Michelangelo and the Antique, and two unhappy and unsuccessful years in Bath (1775–77), attempting to follow in the footsteps of the portrait painter Thomas Gainsborough, he lived and worked around Derby and the immediate surroundings of Dovedale and the Derwent Valley, where he made many amicable and profitable contacts. His associations and friendships with leading Midlands industrialists, doctors, scientists, and inventors provided the subject matter for many of his paintings, of which well-known examples include portraits of the businesswoman Mrs. Sarah Clayton (c. 1769), the gentry couple Mr. and Mrs. Coltman (exhibited 1771), the banker Christopher Heath (dated 1781), the clockmaker John Whitehurst (c. 1782–83), and the entrepreneur Sir Richard Arkwright (1789–90). Wright had a wide circle of friends, many of whom were leading luminaries of the Lunar Society (established around 1764–65) such as Matthew Boulton, Erasmus Darwin, Joseph Priestley, James Watt, and Josiah Wedgwood. This society, to which Wright was never actually admitted, met on every Monday nearest the full moon and conducted experiments and debated the various developments in science, medicine, and astronomy. The curiosity in and wonder about the physical world in the late eighteenth century was a favorite theme of Wright's, but no less than light itself. Wright was, above all, interested in the dramatic effects of light and shadow, and these impress us as much as his portrayals of human industry in, for example, his paintings of blacksmiths' shops, iron forges, and cotton mills.

The portrait of *Brooke Boothby*, first exhibited at the Royal Academy in 1781, brings together some of the most striking features of Wright's painting and synthesizes his engagement with both Enlightenment and Romantic ideals. Slightly disheveled and reclining in an autumnal wooded glade, Brooke Boothby, a minor poet and first publisher of Jean-Jacques Rousseau's *Dialogues* (1780), is represented as a figure of both intellectual melancholy and romantic reflection. Like Wright himself, Boothby rests in a space both intellectual and natural. He is at the same time a man of taste and a figure content to be away from the civilized world, and this dualism is dramatized by the natural glow of a setting sun visible through the gap in the trees in the background and the artificial studio lights which illuminate Boothby's expression, fashion, and posture.

Although portrait painting was Wright of Derby's most reliable source of income, he is probably better known for his series of large-scale "Candle Light" paintings and his two major works that dramatically represent the relationship between light and knowledge: *A Philosopher Lecturing on the Orrery* of 1766 and *An Experiment on a Bird in the Air Pump* of 1768. A few critics, most notably Benedict Nicolson, have attributed Wright's interest in candlelight to his study of the work of the Dutch painters Godfried Schalcken and Gerard Honthorst, but this can only be speculative. As Judy Egerton asserts in her authoritative book and catalog of Wright of Derby, "much more work needs to be done on his sources." However, scholars have traced the influence of a number of artists and engravers, including Alexander Cozens, Thomas Frye, Godfrey Kneller, and Benjamin Wilson, on his portraits and landscapes.

JANE DESMARAIS

Biography

Born Derby, September 3, 1734. Apprenticed to Thomas Hudson in London, 1751–53 and 1756–57. First exhibited at Society of Artists, 1765; married Hannah Anne Swift, 1773 and departed for Italy; returned to Derby 1775. First exhibited at Royal Academy in London 1778, elected associate there in 1781 and full member in 1784 (an honor he declined). Exhibited only at Society for Promoting the Arts in Liverpool 1784 and 1787. Died Derby, August 29, 1797.

Bibliography

Bemrose, William. *The Life and Work of Joseph Wright.* 1885.
Cummings, Frederick. "Boothby, Rousseau and the Romantic Malady," *Burlington Magazine* 110 (1968): 659–66.
Egerton, Judy. *Joseph Wright of Derby.* 1990.
Nicolson, Benedict. *Joseph Wright of Derby: Painter of Light.* 2 vols. 1968.
Robinson, Eric. "Joseph Wright of Derby: The Philosopher's Painter," *Burlington Magazine* 100 (1958): 214.

WUTHERING HEIGHTS 1847

Emily Brontë

Wuthering Heights, Emily Brontë's only published novel, was born out of necessity. After she and her sisters failed to sustain a girls' school in their hometown of Haworth, Yorkshire, in order to gain some income for the family, they turned their attentions to something they had been working at since childhood: writing. From a very early age, all of the four surviving Brontë children had been afflicted with what they called "scribblemania," turning out vast quantities of stories detailing the fantastic doings of the inhabitants of two imaginary worlds, Angria and Gondal. Although Branwell and Charlotte were the proprietors of the former and Emily and Anne of the latter, Emily would borrow heavily from one of Branwell's Angrian sagas in 1845 when she took up her pen to write a novel.

By 1846 the Brontë sisters were already published authors, but their pseudonymous *Poems by Currer, Ellis, and Acton Bell* was an utter failure commercially. Even before the appearance of this work, however, they had made the decision to write novels, which were clearly the best-selling works in the literary marketplace. Searching for inspiration for their new endeavors, Charlotte and Emily both turned to the familiar territory of Angria and Gondal, with Emily lifting the idea of a pair of lovers so interdependent and self-involved as to defy death, from Branwell's "The Life of Alexander Percy." This pair she transformed into Cathy and Heathcliff, relocating them to her beloved Yorkshire moors, where they would act out their fates against a backdrop that was the recipient of Emily's truest affections. Her profound connection to the wildness she found there marked her as a true Romantic, and the changes she made to her brother's story resulted in one of the most original and memorable novels of the age.

By the time she came to write *Wuthering Heights*, Emily Brontë had been steeped in the conventions of Romanticism for much of her life, an exposure that produced a sometimes Gothic tale of love that literally embraces death, and a singular hero, Heathcliff, who has more than a touch of the Byronic about him. And she executes the tale of Heathcliff and his female counterpart, Cathy, in a highly sophisticated fashion, moving it beyond convention and morality by relating it through a double frame device, employing two first-person narrators, one who is an outsider and one who is an insider, albeit a conspicuously biased one. Readers are thus drawn into the vortex of love and hate that centers on the house known as Wuthering Heights, while at the same made to keep their distance both from the solipsistic lovers and from those who would pronounce judgment on the pair.

In its basic outlines, the relationship between Cathy and Heathcliff is as irresistibly appealing as that of Romeo and Juliet: two people from different, even antagonistic social backgrounds fall in love so profoundly that nothing can keep them apart. But Emily infuses her hero and heroine with so much passion that they are all too often unappealing. Cathy is frequently petulant and self-indulgent, and for much of the book Heathcliff is savagely bent on avenging himself on those who deprived him in youth of his dignity and his love. Both characters pay little heed to the fates of those around them if these others get in the way of their being together. In the end, everyone, even the skeptical reader, feels an unyielding pressure to surrender to the supreme, naked power of Cathy's and Heathcliff's passion. Theirs is plainly no ordinary love, and it is characterized not so much by self-abnegation as self-annihilation. As Cathy tells her nurse, she loves Heathcliff because " 'he's more myself than I am.' " Then, turning the equation on its head, she feverishly declares, " 'Nelly, I *am* Heathcliff.' "

Into this story of absolute, inevitable connectedness Emily Brontë inserts the tale of another Cathy and another Heathcliff. Catherine Linton, the daughter of Catherine Earnshaw's marriage to Edgar Linton, survives her mother's early death only to be forced by Heathcliff into a mockery of a marriage to his tubercular son, Linton Heathcliff, born of Heathcliff's marriage to Edgar's sister, Isabella Linton. This other love story is played out by two individuals who are but pale imitations of their angry, passionate parental namesakes, who haunt their union. In joining his son with Catherine Linton, Heathcliff hopes to merge his existing control of Wuthering Heights with that of its more refined, substantial neighbor, Thrushcross Grange, ancestral seat of the Linton family. And although he accomplishes this aim, he finds no satisfaction in it. Linton's marriage to Catherine does nothing to resolve the relationship of Heathcliff and his Cathy. Only his own death can quiet his tortured spirit, and only his death will bring about a true alliance between Wuthering Heights and Thrushcross Grange. Heathcliff's death finally frees the younger Cathy, now a widow, to remarry, and the person she chooses as a second husband is Hareton Earnshaw, the true heir to Wuthering Heights and a youth more like Heathcliff than his own son had been.

The complex structure of *Wuthering Heights* leaves one with a sense of inevitability, of forces that oblige humankind to repeat its errors until some final resolution is reached. When Heathcliff finally joins Cathy in death, he insists on being buried beside her, but the configuration of their graves, with Cathy buried between Heathcliff and her husband Edgar, echoes the configuration in life of the Hareton-Catherine-Linton triangle. And when, at the end of the novel, Catherine and Hareton prepare to marry and move to Thrushcross Grange, their old home at Wuthering Heights is left to the spirits of Cathy and Heathcliff, who are said to haunt it. The final word is left to the outside observer of this drama and its sometime narrator, Mr. Lockwood, who has returned to Wuthering Heights out of curiosity. Visiting the graves of Cathy and Heathcliff, he meditates on the benignity of nature and wonders, "how any one could ever imagine unquiet slumbers for the sleepers in that quiet earth."

Wuthering Heights appeared barely a year before Emily Brontë herself died. It sold reasonably well, but was derided for its "low tone of behavior," as was Charlotte Brontë's *Jane Eyre*, published around the same time. Many critics, in fact, believed Charlotte, who wrote under the pen name Currer Bell, to have been the author of both novels. In 1850, offered the opportunity to reprint *Wuthering Heights* together in one volume with Anne's *Agnes Grey* (Anne, too, had by now died from tuberculosis), Charlotte revised the two novels as well as writing a biographical introduction that would, she hoped, clarify the separate identities of Currer, Ellis, and Acton Bell once and for all. Unfortunately, many of Charlotte's changes did not reflect her sisters' intentions, and it was not until 1911, with an edition put together by Clement Shorter, that *Wuthering Heights* was largely rid of the errors that had been introduced by others into both its first and second editions.

LISA PADDOCK

Bibliography

Allcott, Miriam, comp. *Emily Brontë: Wuthering Heights, A Casebook.* London: Macmillan, 1970.

Ardholm, Helena M. *The Emblem and the Emblematic Habit of Mind in Jane Eyre and Wuthering Heights.* Göteborg, Sweden: Acta Universitatis Gothoburgensis, 1999.

Chitham, Edward. *The Birth of Wuthering Heights: Emily Brontë at Work.* Houndsmills, England: Macmillan, 1998.

Knoepflmacher, U. C. *Wuthering Heights: A Study.* Cambridge: Cambridge University Press, 1994.

Goodridge, J. F. *Emily Brontë: Wuthering Heights.* London: Edward Arnold, 1964.

Stoneman, Patsy. *Brontë Transformations: The Cultural Dissemination of Jane Eyre and Wuthering Heights.* London: Prentice-Hall, 1996.

Vogler, Thomas A., ed. *Twentieth Century Interpretations of Wuthering Heights: A Collection of Critical Essays.* Englewood Cliffs, N.J.: Prentice-Hall, 1968.

Willis, Irene C. *The Authorship of Wuthering Heights.* London: Dawsons of Pall Mall, 1967.

Y

YEARSLEY, ANN 1752–1806

British poet, dramatist, and novelist

Ann Yearsley, known also as "Lactilla" or "the Poetical Milk-woman of Bristol," was one of a small number of successful eighteenth-century working-class writers. As such, her life story has become as celebrated as her works. Yearsley (née Cromartie) began her working life selling milk. She was taught to read and write by family members, and developed a taste for John Milton and Edward Young. She married John Yearsley, a poor yeoman farmer, in 1774, and spent the following ten years developing her writing skills while carrying out the onerous duties of a farmer's wife and mother of six children. The severe winter of 1783–84 brought the family close to destitution, and forced Yearsley to take a job collecting pig swill from the home of Hannah More. By August 1784, More had become aware of Yearsley's literary abilities, and she formed a plan to have Yearsley's poems published by subscription, using her considerable aristocratic connections to further the project.

Poems on Several Occasions appeared in 1785 and included poems on comic, tragic, and religious themes. Inevitably, some advertise Yearsley's gratitude toward More (celebrated as "Stella") and More's aristocratic friend Elizabeth Montagu. Many are influenced by Young, with hints toward a grander Miltonic style, but the collection is also thoroughly influenced by the notion of sensibility. Yearsley promotes the view that feeling is antecedent to reason, and she praises the benevolence that flows from the feeling heart as "wisdom temper'd with the milder ray / Of soft humanity." She stresses the importance of a strongly felt response to both personal events and the poet's environment. She invokes sublime landscapes, such as the "terror-striking frown" of Clifton Gorge near Bristol, but is at her best when uniting her emotional engagement with the sublimity of nature with her own social and economic difficulties. She writes,

Beauteous imagery, awak'd
My ravish'd soul to extacy untaught,
To all the transport the rapt sense can bear;
But all expir'd for want of powers to speak.

The poems brought Yearsley a certain measure of fame and fortune. More invested the fortune, around £380, in a trust fund, giving Yearsley a modest annuity of £18. This patronizing, if well-intentioned, scheme angered Yearsley, who felt defrauded. More, in turn, accused Yearsley of ingratitude. The two fell out with a public display of personal acrimony and class misunderstanding. However, Yearsley's writing career was far from over. With the protection and friendship of Frederick Hervey, earl of Bristol and bishop of Derry, she recovered her money and produced a new volume, *Poems on Various Subjects* (1787).

Many suspected that More had rewritten Yearsley's poems, and a desire to refute this allegation motivated the new volume. The tone of obligation to philanthropic superiors, which marks many of her earlier poems, is all but gone, although Yearsley does not advance a politically radical agenda. The first poem, "Addressed to Sensibility," is clearly positioned as a challenge to More, who had published a poem on the same theme in 1782. Here, Yearsley powerfully restates the argument that reason, guided by education, is subservient to untutored emotion. Although this theme runs through many of the poems, the subject and style of the rest of the collection are as varied as its title suggests. For example, a combative poem, "To Those Who Accuse the Author of Ingratitude," immediately precedes two poignant works on the baptism and early death of her son Frederick in 1786. Throughout, Yearsley experiments with form and content, but the greatest experiment appears to be the personal one of finding her own voice, now free from controlling aristocratic patronage.

Over the following decade Yearsley produced occasional poetry. In *A Poem on the Inhumanity of the Slave-Trade* (which some saw as competing with More's poem on the same theme) she entered the public political arena. The campaign for the abolition of the slave trade was at its height in 1788. Yearsley's contribution characterizes the trade as Bristol's shame, and attacks those who defended it with false religion and false sensibility:

> Vap'rous sighs and tears,
> Which, like the guileful crocodile's, oft fall,
> Nor fall, but at the cost of human bliss.

Other poems followed, but in 1789 she changed direction with the performance of *Earl Goodwin, An Historical Play* (published 1791). This dramatizes politics in the reign of Edward the Confessor, but by contrasting the incipient Norman tyranny of Edward with the innate love of liberty exhibited by the "true-born" Englishman, Goodwin, Yearsley addresses contemporary concerns in the revolutionary year of 1789. Dealing more explicitly with French politics is her novel *The Royal Captives* (1795) which, by telling the story of the man in the iron mask imprisoned by Louis XIV, clearly attacks French absolutism, although Yearsley refrains from advocating revolution in Britain. Her style is reminiscent of the sentimental gothic of Ann Radcliffe, but also anticipates the political gothic of William Godwin and Mary Wollstonecraft. *The Rural Lyre* (1796), Yearsley's final collection of poems, and the rarest, marks a retreat from the heartfelt sensibility of her earlier works and lacks the unifying argument, present in her earlier collections, that great poetry can spring direct from the untutored heart. Yearsley was no longer financially reliant on her writing, as in 1793 she had opened a circulating library in Bristol which provided her main income from then until the death of John Yearsley in 1803. In that year she retired to Melksham in Wiltshire, where she died in 1806.

Critical discussion of Yearsley's works has always been closely bound up with the circumstances of her life. Contemporaries saw her either as an example of "natural genius" or as a threat to the social hierarchy. Modern critics have celebrated her achievements as a working woman in the aristocratic and male-dominated world of eighteenth-century England. Her actual writing has often been overlooked, yet, at its best, it is poetry of the mature phase of sensibility and, with its emphasis on individual experience and the power of unconstrained poetic feeling, it can be ranked among the earliest productions of the Romantic movement.

BRYCCHAN CAREY

Biography

Born Clifton Hill, Bristol, 1752, née Cromartie. No formal education, but read what she could while working as a milkwoman. June 1774, married John Yearsley, a yeoman farmer. Summer 1784, her poems came to the attention of Hannah More. June 1785, *Poems on Several Occasions* published. September 1785, dispute with More over profits of the poems. *Poems on Various Subjects*, published, 1787. *Poem on the Inhumanity of the Slave-Trade*, appeared, 1788. *Earl Goodwin, An Historical Play*, performed at Bristol, 1789; *Earl Goodwin* published, 1791. Opened a circulating library in Bristol, 1793. *The Royal Captives*, a novel, 1795; *The Rural Lyre*, 1796. Death of John Yearsley, 1803. Ann retired to Melksham, Wiltshire. Died May 8, 1806.

Selected Work

Poetry
Poems on Several Occasions. 1785.
Poems on Various Subjects. 1787. Facsimile edition; Oxford: Woodstock Books, 1994.
A Poem on the Inhumanity of the Slave-Trade. 1788.
The Rural Lyre: A Volume of Poems, 1796. Reprinted in *The Romantics: Women Poets*. 12 vols. Edited by Caroline Franklin. London: Routledge, 1996.

Other
Earl Goodwin: An Historical Play. 1791.
The Royal Captives: A Fragment of a Secret History. Copied from an Old Manuscript. 4 vols. 1795.

Bibliography

Ferguson, Moira. *Eighteenth-Century Women Poets: Nation, Class, and Gender*. Albany: State University of New York Press, 1995.
Landry, Donna. *The Muses of Resistance: Laboring-Class Women's Poetry in Britain, 1739–1796*. Cambridge: Cambridge University Press, 1990.
Lonsdale, Roger. *Eighteenth-Century Woman Poets*. Oxford and New York: Oxford University Press, 1989.
Waldron, Mary. *Lactilla, Milkwoman of Clifton: The Life and Writings of Ann Yearsley 1753–1806*. Athens, Ga.: University of Georgia Press, 1996.

Z

ZALÁN FUTÁSA (THE FLIGHT OF ZALAN) 1825

Hungarian epic by Mihály Vörösmarty

The Flight of Zalán (1825), by Mihály Vörösmarty, is the most important national epic of Hungarian Romanticism. Its native antecedents are similar verse epics by minor poets such as Endre Pázmándi Horvát and the Transylvanian Sándor Aranyosrákosi Székely, but the general model was provided by Virgil's *Aeneid* and James Macpherson's *Ossian*. Virgil's theme of the refugees from Troy finding a new homeland paralleled Vörösmarty's intention (his main theme was the Conquest of the Carpathian Basin by the tribal alliance of the Magyars) and Ossian was important in setting the elegiac mode of the poem's invocation. Both were translated into Hungarian, though Vörösmarty's Latin was good and he must have read Virgil in the original as well.

The Flight of Zalán was written in hexameters and ten cantos. While Vörösmarty is, according to D. Mervyn Jones, "not primarily an epic poet," he handles the Virgilian hexameter with consummate skill. As for the poet's intent, the thirty-six-lines-long prologue (formally not separated from the rest of the poem) makes it very clear: he wishes to rekindle the flame of Hungarian patriotism by evoking images of the nation's past glory. Already in the prologue the idealized figure of "leopard-skin-clad Árpád" appears; this leader of the Hungarian tribes of the Conquest is as much of a central hero of Vörösmarty's epic as Aeneas of Virgil's epic poem. While the main theme of *Zalán futása* is an episode from the conquest of the Carpathian Basin by the Magyars involving the military defeat of the Bulgarian Prince Zalán, there is a secondary theme in the form of a love triangle. The fair Hajna is courted by two rather different suitors: Ete, "brave destroyer of armies," and the Fairy of the South (Délszaki Tundér).

When Vörösmarty wrote his epic, very little was known about the religion of the ancient Hungarians, though it was suspected to be a shamanistic cult. The poet created two deities; Hadúr (the lord of hosts) was to be the god of the Magyars, whereas their opponents adhere to Ármány (derived from the "Ahriman" of Zoroastrian mythology) and before the final victory of the Magyars *Hadúr* destroys his evil counterpart. This "religious" background, however, is much less important than the struggle of the gods in Homer's or Virgil's epics.

While the poem contains all the usual ingredients of classical epics such as battle scenes and catalogs of heroes, its redeeming feature is the love plot, with its gentle lyrical tone. The Fairy of the South is a purely imaginary character who owns a miraculous pipe and a talking horse, a *táltos*, a creature that appears in many old Hungarian fairy tales. Whether escape to the fairy world indicates a "split between [the poet's] private life and the life of his community" as one modern literary historian István Sötér put it is debatable. To some extent Vörösmarty identifies himself with the Fairy of the South, the rejection of whose love reflects his own hopeless longing for Etelka Perczel, but *The Flight of Zalán* is not so much of a critique of the inertia of the Hungarian nobility as a "clarion call" to the nation to emulate "the beautiful deeds" of the past.

The language of *The Flight of Zalán* is richly expressive. Vörösmarty is the first Hungarian poet who could build on the success of the Language Reform movement: it substantially broadened and increased his vocabulary. Though *The Flight of Zalán* abounds in descriptions of nature, by and large its language is not descriptive but suggestive, achieving its aim with an ingenious use of adverbs and adjectives. It is the lyrical parts of the poem that still have an appeal to the modern reader; already in Vörösmarty's lifetime the poet complained that it was "more praised than read." The prologue, however, has entered the canon of Hungarian poetry.

GEORGE GÖMÖRI

Bibliography

Fried, István. "Jegyzetek a Zalán futásá-hoz." In *Irodalomtörténeti Kozlemények*. 1964.

Jones, D. Mervyn. *Five Hungarian Writers*. Oxford: Clarendon, 1966.

Sötér, István. *A magyar irodalom története, Vol. III*. Budapest: Akadémiai, 1963.

Szerb, Antal. *Gondolatok a konyvtárban*. Budapest: Franklin, 1946.

Trencsényi-Waldapfel, Imre. "Jegyzetek a *Zalán futásá*-hoz." *Irodalomtorténeti Kozlemények*. 1939.

ZHUKOVSKII, VASILII ANDREEVICH 1783–1852

Russian poet, critic, and translator

Vasilii Andreevich Zhukovskii was Russia's first major Romantic poet, translator of Romantic poetry, and aesthetics, and master of the romance and ballad. He wrote most of his poetry before the early 1820s; thereafter he concentrated on translations of German, English, and French poetry. He overcame an early penchant for "sentimental-elegiac" phraseology with a rich musical style and deeply moral content. Long considered a sentimentalist "singer" of disillusionment and religious mysticism, Zhukovskii is now appreciated as an innovator whose work is notable for its striking epithets and metaphors, unprecedented lexicon and phrasing, and ingenious metric and strophic articulations.

For Zhukovskii, inspiration was a "something" from "somewhere" that prompted an inner vision of beauty. Inspiration was revelation, which he variously described as an inexpressible "magic moment," "fleeting vision," "apparition," or his "Creative Spirit" (*Genii*). In "K mimoproletevshemu znakomomu Geniiu" ("To a Fleeting yet Familiar Spirit," 1819), "Iavlenie poezii v vide Lalla Ruk" ("The Appearance of Poetry in the Guise of Lalla Rookh," 1821), "Tainstvennyi posetitel" ("Mysterious Visitor," 1824), and other lyrics, revelation descends from a divine origin and brings "enchantment" to his mundane existence. He could not predict or comprehend the "appearance" of the "captress of my soul," but her existence is a certainty because she left in her wake the poem, alternately characterized by Zhukovskii as a "sign," a "gift of beauty," or a "remembrance."

Zhukovskii feared that the muse would abandon him, but ultimately retained faith in his poetic abilities. In "Ia Muzu iunuiu, byvalo" ("My Youthful Muse, in Days Gone By," 1822 or 1824) he recalls his receptive youth when life and poetry were one. He regrets the loss of inspiration that accompanies growth into adulthood, but concludes that "Thou art still known to me, pure Spirit, Enchantment has not perished, what was, shall be again." However, he continued to struggle with despair generated by the knowledge that he could not adequately express in language emotions developed through contact with nature, memory, and the divine. In "Nevyrazimoe" ("The Inexpressible," 1819) he asks, "What is our mundane language in compare with miraculous nature?" What use is language when "only silence clearly speaks"? This pessimistic poem seems devoid of hope, but the existence of the poem itself denies hopelessness. In its form, the "inexpressible" is beautifully expressed.

Zhukovskii was an orthodox Christian who affirmed the benevolence of God in such concepts as providence, soul, hope, faith, miracle, love, friendship, inspiration, and creativity. These are his semantic-lexical priorities and weltanschauung—that is, his holistic, aesthetic vision derived from a dialectic of moral imperatives. He does not confront contradictions; rather, he seeks to moderate them. This tendency encouraged his reputation as a "passive Romantic." Zhukovskii sought to reconcile opposites, and did so with faith in an ultimate, purposive "Power" who loves humankind. For Zhukovskii, life was a metaphoric journey from darkness toward light. In "Maiskoe utro" ("May Morning," 1797) dawn arrives in light and banishes darkness. In "Pesnia" ("Song," 1818) he asks, "Can I illuminate in a new light / the beauty of a faded dream?" In "Utrenniaia zvezda" ("Morning Star," 1818) the poet's soul strives toward the light of the East.

"More. Elegiia" ("The Sea. An Elegy," 1822) is a conventional pantheistic poem refigured as an intricate lyric, in which vision and sound are in dialectical motion. Vision is an attribute of light, sound of darkness. In the light the sea is mute. It shines, and banishes darkness. Peace is an attribute of light, thus darkness destroys peace. When storm clouds gather, the sea rages at the hostile darkness. This dialect of sight, sound, and motion achieves an active synthesis. Peace and turbulence, light and dark, and sound and silence are reconciled by the beauty of vital nature.

Zhukovskii's poetry does not concern itself with the future. Memory and the past are more essential elements of his work. In "Vospominanie" ("Remembrance," 1816) the poet mourns, "You've gone, you've gone, my days of enchantment . . . Your only trace is in the sadness of my memory!" Nostalgia, longing, and regret are powerful emotions in his poems. The contrast between past and present is prominent in this and other poems, although the poet's attitude toward each era is ambiguous. Happiness on earth has been lost and now exists only in recollection. But the memory of such happiness taints the present.

Hope and beauty come to Zhukovskii through memories, often in the form of dreams. Dreams interact with recollection in a dialectic of "seeming" and "being." In another "Pesnia" the poet's soul strives "To the east, ever to the east" in search of a beauty who visited him from a distant past. The Beautiful does not "appear" to the poet; rather, it "seems" that "she used to appear" to him. He "dreams" that "Far off there to the east . . . Resides the Beautiful." He senses that he previously knew "her": "A beautiful legend Of a wondrous past" that appeared "Sometime in ancient days" and left behind nothing "but a blissful dream." The past is both forgotten and remembered. In "Elizium" ("Elysium," 1812) Psyche bows her head to the waters of Lethe and partakes of oblivion. A memory, or a "seeming," of a distant past suggests a previous existence followed by oblivion or a "forgetting."

Zhukovskii's religiosity, especially his love of light and his belief that commune with nature is commune with God, aligns him with William Wordsworth. He admired Lord Byron's musicality. He shared Edward Young and Thomas Gray's attraction to night and the grave. He carried over work on seasons to his translation of parts of James Thomson's *Seasons* in "Gimn" ("Hymn," 1808–09). His translations of Gottfried August Bürger's ballad "Lenore" ("Liudmila," 1808, "Svetlana," 1808–12) are canonical. Schillerism was an order he adhered to throughout his life. His love of Oriental fancy came to him from Thomas Moore, whose *Lalla Rookh, An Oriental Romance* (1817) was popular throughout Europe. It is difficult to think of any Romantic German or English poet he did not translate. He is known as the Russian balladeer not so much for his five original ballads as for the originality of the thirty-nine he translated from German and English. His translations of poetry often surpass the original works. Zhukovskii believed that a translator must not literally reproduce an original, but find in his imagination "substitutes" for its "beauties." Zhukovskii's best translations are Gray's "Elegy Written in a Country Churchyard" (1802), Moore's "Paradise and the Peri" (1821), Johann Christoph Friedrich von Schiller's "Die Jungfrau von Orleans" (1817–21), Byron's "The Prisoner of Chillon" (1821), and Homer's "The Odyssey" (1840s).

LAUREN G. LEIGHTON

Biography

Born in Tula Province, January 29, 1783. Illegitimate son of landowner Afanasii Iranovich Bunin whose wife and oldest daughter raised him. Educated at Moscow University Pension of the Nobility, received superior moral-intellectual education based on Masonic principles; member of youthful Literary Friendship Society that propagated "new," "modern" aesthetics, 1797–1801; start of lifelong work as translator from German, English, and French, 1801. Editor and critic, *Russkii vestnik* (*Russian Herald*), 1808–9; established as "Russian balladeer" and translator of German and English ballads, 1808–12; service in Moscow Militia, 1812–13. To Dorpat, hope of marrying his half niece Maria "Masha" Protasova came to an end when she married another, 1817. To Saint Petersburg, tutor to Grand Duchess Alexandra Fyodorovna, new wife of future Nicholas I, 1817–26; tutor to heir to throne, future Alexander II, numerous travels abroad with imperial family, devotion to court enabled him to protect Aleksandr Pushkin and others from political repression, 1826–41, retirement from service to court, 1841. To Baden-Baden, continued work as translator, marriage to daughter of German colleague, children and family life, 1841–52. Died in Baden-Baden, April 12, 1852.

Selected Works

Polnoe sobranie sochinenii. 12 vols. in 4. Edited by Aleksandr Sergeevich Arkhangel'skii. Sankt-Peterburg: Izd. A. F. Marksa, 1902.
Stikhotvoreniia. Poet's Library, Large series, 3 vols. Leningrad: Sovetskii pisatel, 1956.
Sochineniia. Edited by Irina Mikhailovna Semenko. 3 vols. Moscow: Khudozhestrennaia Literatura, 1980.
Selections in *Ardis Anthology of Russian Romanticism*. Edited by Christine A. Rydel. Ann Arbor, Mich.: Ardis Publishers, 1984.
Estetika i kritika. Edited by Faina Zinor'evna Kanunova and Aleksandr Sergeevich Ianushkevich. Moscow: Iskusstvo, 1985.
Selection in *Russian Romantic Criticism*. Translated by J. Thomas Shaw. Edited and translated by Lauren G. Leighton. Westport, Conn.: Greenwood Press, 1987.

Bibliography

Faina Zinor'evna Kanunova, et al., eds. *Biblioteka V. A. Zhukovskogo v Tomsk*. 3 vols. Tomsk: Tomsk University, 1978–84.
Iezuitova, Raisa Vladimirovna. *Zhukovskii i ego vremia*. Leningrad: Nauka, 1989.
Kanunova, Faina Zinor'evna. "O filosofsko-istoricheskikh vozzreniiakh Zhukovskogo (po materialam biblioteki poeta)," In *Zhukovskii i russkaia kul'tura*. Edited by R. V. Iezuitova Leningrad: AN SSSR, 1987.
———, ed. *Voprosy mirovozzreniia i estetiki V. A. Zhukovskogo (Po materialam biblioteki poeta)*. Tomsk: Tomsk University Press, 1990.
Katz, Michael. *The Literary Ballad in Early Nineteenth Century Russian Literature*. Oxford: Oxford University Press, 1976.
Pein, Annette. *Schiller and Zhukovskii: Aesthetic Theory in Poetic Translation*. Mainz: Lieber, 1991.
Semenko, Irina Mikhailovna. *Vasily Zhukovskii*. Boston: Twayne, 1976.
Swensen, Andrew J. *Russian Romanticism and Theologically Founded Aesthetics: Zhukovskii, Odoevskii, and Gogol and the Appropriation of Post-Kantian Aesthetic Principles*. Ph.D. diss., University of Wisconsin-Madison, 1995.
West, James. "Vasilii Andreevich Zhukovskii (1783–1852)." In *Russian Literature in the Age of Pushkin and Gogol: Poetry and Drama. Dictionary of Literary Biography, 205*. Edited by Christine A. Rydel. Detroit: Gale Group, 1999.

ZORRILLA Y MORAL, JOSÉ 1817–1893

Spanish dramatist

A leading figure of Spanish Romanticism of the late 1830s, José Zorrilla y Moral is best remembered for a single work, the play *Don Juan Tenorio* (1844). The general lack of critical interest in Zorrilla today belies a long and prolific career, enthusiastic public recognition by contemporaries of his literary achievements, and an extensive body of work in several genres, largely poetry and drama.

Zorrilla's contemporaries credited him with having liberated Spanish letters, theater in particular, from the influence of French models, most notably Alexandre Dumas and Victor Hugo and their Spanish imitators. Literary historians ascribe to him a conscious effort to distance himself from his predecessors by using Spain's past as his principal source of inspiration. This backward glance was aimed at finding source material in episodes and figures from Spanish history and reworking traditional literary models and themes originally introduced during the Spanish "golden age." It is not surprising, therefore, that Zorrilla's work is both nationalistic in tone and highly religious in spirit. In fact, his writings were noted for a marked rejection of the excesses of other Romantic writers, whose work exhibited exaggerated sentiment and outlandish plots, along with characters who frequently succumbed to cynicism, helplessness, and a fatalistic attitude toward the world around them.

Curiously, despite his instant fame, Zorrilla was destined to lead a life of financial insecurity, if not outright poverty. He came to prominence early, in circumstances quite appropriate to the Romantic tradition he is credited with having renewed. Not yet twenty and unknown in Madrid's literary circles, Zorrilla read an elegy at the funeral of Mariano José de Larra. Larra's high standing as a major literary figure and preeminent Romantic writer and critic assured that the leading writers, artists, and intellectuals of the age were present at his funeral. Upon hearing Zorrilla's eloquent verses, Larra's colleagues welcomed the young poet into their circle; Zorrilla became an overnight sensation, and his long writing career was launched.

Before the end of the same year, 1837, Zorrilla published his first volume of poetry. An extraordinarily creative period followed. In the next two years, he completed several collections of poetry and two plays; he also published several of his highly popular *Cantos de trovador* (*Songs of the Troubadour*), verse renditions of historical episodes and legendary anecdotes from the Spanish past. He would go on to write, in quick succession, several volumes of poetry and numerous poetic compositions of varying length. His achievements were honored years later when he received a small government pension, and was "crowned" Spain's national poet in an elaborate public ceremony held in the city of Granada in 1889.

Abundant as his poetic output was, Zorrilla's fame as a poet did not extend beyond his death. Perhaps because of the speed with which he wrote, his verse is deemed to sacrifice depth of feeling and originality in favor of spontaneous expression and the use of accessible and rich descriptive language of broad appeal. His acknowledged pride in his dual identity as a Christian and a Spaniard imbued his work with a strong current of conservative nationalism, which clearly touched his reading public but has lost much of its appeal today. An excellent example of Zorrilla's style is the narrative poem *Granada* (1852), which is, at the same time, a monument of sorts to traditional Romanticism. The work deals with one of the foundational episodes in the history of Spain, the victory of the Catholic Monarchs at the close of the fifteenth century over the last of the Nazrids of Granada. Thematically and stylistically the poem is the quintessence of a Romantic composition in its artful melding of historical and legendary events, exotic characters, motifs, and locales, rich descriptive language, heightened emotions and sensibilities, and strong national and religious fervor. Similar qualities are evident in the three volumes of *Cantos de trovador*, which Zorrilla published at various stages of his career.

In the 1840s, Zorrilla's reputation as a playwright began to rival his fame as a poet. Stage success came in 1840–41, when the first part of his *El zapatero y el rey* (*The Shoemaker and the King*) premiered in Madrid. Like subsequent dramatic works, the play—whose second part followed in 1842—was inspired by historical figures (in this instance the controversial medieval Castilian king Pedro). It was followed in quick succession by *El puñal del godo* (*The Goth's Dagger*, 1843), *Don Juan Tenorio* (1844), and *Traidor, inconfeso y mártir* (*Traitor, Sinner and Martyr*, 1849). Of his dramatic body of work totaling almost thirty plays, twenty-three were staged in the 1840s. Only *Don Juan Tenorio*, however, has continued to be regularly performed in Spain (annually on November 1) and to attract critical attention; arguably, it is the most popular play in the Spanish repertory.

Zorrilla's *Don Juan Tenorio* revolves around a well-worn story line, namely the adventures and exploits of a Don Juan, a sexual predator whose ruthless seduction of women (aside from what feminist criticism might say about the character) challenges authority and mocks social and religious mores and conventions. Tirso de Molina's *El burlador de Sevilla* (1630), and subsequent renditions of the basic outline of the story by Lord Byron, Alexandre Dumas, Prosper Mérimée, Molière, and Antonio de Zamora, among others, have kept alive in literature the figure of the unrepentant libertine. What distinguishes Zorrilla's vision and gives his play its uniqueness is that his Don Juan is not eternally damned for his sins, as his predecessors had been, but saved through the redemptive power of the love of a good and pious woman, Inés. In writing his *Don Juan*, therefore, Zorrilla managed to reconcile the ideal of romantic love with the possibility of religious salvation. Zorrilla thus reaffirmed traditional Spanish values and rescued the figure of Don Juan from the nihilistic and cynical universe in which the character had always lived. It is not surprising, therefore, that the play should have become such an instant sensation.

In 1880 Zorrilla published *Recuerdos del tiempo viejo* (*Recollections of Times Past*), a memoir; it is one of several prose works in which the author recounts (not always faithfully, according to some) key episodes in his personal and artistic life and accounts of his travels, along with insightful commentary on the politics and personalities of his native Spain.

At the time of his death, in 1893, Zorrilla's reputation as a writer was firmly entrenched. His funeral provided the opportunity for the delivery of heartfelt tributes to one of the country's—and the century's—best-known literary figures.

CLARA ESTOW

Biography

Born in Valladolid, Spain, February 21, 1817. Pursued but did not complete law studies in Toledo and Valladolid, 1833–36; moved to Madrid; acquired instant fame as a poet, 1837; married Florentina O'Reilly, a widow sixteen years his senior, 1839. Spent a year in France studying medicine and meeting several notable French authors, 1845–6; returned to Madrid and was elected to the board of the Teatro Español and the Royal Academy; abandoned his wife and traveled to Paris and London. Sailed for America, and lived in Mexico and Cuba, 1858–66. Appointed court poet and director of the National Theater by Maximilian I of Mexico (1864); returned to Spain upon his wife's death, 1866. Married Juana Pacheco (1869); received several honors and commissions, and in 1889 was named national poet. Died in Madrid following surgery to extract a brain tumor, January 23, 1893.

Selected Works

Poesías. 6 vols. Madrid: Editorial Sancha, 1937–40.
Cantos del trovador. Madrid: Boix, 1940–1.
Obras completes. 2 vols. Edited by Narciso Alonso Cortés, Valladolid: Librería Santarén, 1943.
Recuerdos del tiempo viejo. Madrid: Publicaciones españolas, 1961.
Antología. Edited by Trini González Rivas, Madrid: Coculsa, 1968.

Don Juan Tenorio. Edited by Luis Fernández Cifuentes. Barcelona: Crítica, 1993.

Bibliography

Actas del Congreso sobre José Zorrilla: una nueva lectura. Valladolid: Universidad de Valladolid, Fundación Jorge Guillén, 1995.

Cardwell, Richard A., and Ricardo Landeira, eds. *José Zorrilla (1893–1993). Centennial Readings.* Nottingham: University of Nottingham Monographs in the Humanities, 1993.

Navas-Ruiz, Ricardo. *La poesía de José Zorrilla: nueva lectura histórico-crítica.* Madrid: Gredos, 1995.

Shaw, Donald L. *Historia de la literatura española. El siglo XIX.* Barcelona: Editorial Ariel, 1973.

ZUNZ, LEOPOLD 1794–1886

German-Jewish scholar

Named Yom Tov Lippman by his parents, Leopold Zunz took a Germanized name as part of an overall transformation as he moved from a traditional yeshiva education, to study under the philologist August Boeckh at the University of Berlin, and then to the completion of his doctorate at the University of Halle in 1821. Zunz always remained self-consciously and devotedly Jewish, though the central work of his career was changing the terms of what being Jewish meant.

Zunz's work was crucial in establishing the *Wissenschaft des Judenthums*, the science or scholarship of Judaism and Jewishness. In 1819 Zunz helped found the Society for the Culture and Science of the Jews. The Society limited itself "to the purely scholarly aspects of its objectives." "Jewish intellect (*Intelligenz*)," Zunz emphatically wrote to his mentor Samuel Meyer Ehrenberg, "must be concentrated." The society's task, the statutes explain, was to correct the "faulty relationship" between the "internal condition" of the Jews and their "external position among the nations." The required effort had to derive "essentially and directly from the Jews themselves," specifically the "culturally attuned intellectuals" among them.

Zunz had already begun this work in his *Etwas über die rabbinische Literatur* (*On Rabbinic Literature*, 1819). In this work he opined that, just as German was replacing Hebrew, so *Wissenschaft* had to incorporate the remains of the great tradition in a new Jewish scholarship that fit its age. Moreover, since Hebrew books would be less available in a century, the "development of our *Wissenschaft* in a grand style is duty, one whose weight increases because . . . the complex problem of the fate of the Jews may derive a solution, if only in part, from this *Wissenschaft.*" Self-respecting Jews would contemplate the "better parts" of rabbinic literature and so dismiss the "prejudices usually held against it."

In 1823, he edited the short-lived *Zeitschrift für die Wissenschaft des Judenthums*, which attempted to offer scholarly explanations that were suitable for both laypeople and learned readers. Zunz was self-defensively insistent on its intellectual respectability and used the word *Wissenschaft*, or the adjectival *wissenschaftlich* ("scientific"), eight times in his 280-word foreword. Zunz himself wrote three articles for the first volume of the *Zeitschrift*: one dealt with Jewish place names, a second studied the revered eleventh century commentator Rashi, and a third studied Jewish statistical data. In a private letter, Zunz described these as preparations for future work. In the meantime, he offered his readers vivid, if partial, glimpses of the Jewish scholarship that he foresaw.

These writings were autoethnographic. In moving Jewish identity into the realm of scholarship, Zunz wrote for Jews about Jews in scholarly works produced with methods not generally applied to Jewish topics and contexts. For example, his contextualized studies of Jewish texts were modeled on the kind of philology he learned at Berlin from August Boeckh, as applied to Hellenic classics. Though his journal soon folded, he continued the work that was begun in it. Thus, in 1832, Zunz referred affectionately to the Rashi essay in the foreword to his celebrated *Liturgical Discourses* (*Die gottesdienstliche Vorträge*). This major work was a history of Jewish sermonizing during the time of Ezra, through the late medieval Passover *Hagadah* to the present. The work is in actuality a two-thousand-year history of the Jewish nation since, Zunz insisted, with the loss of sovereign "institutions . . . the synagogue remained the sole bearer of her nationality [*Nationalität*]" even while the "liturgy of the synagogue became the banner of Jewish nationality. . . ." Zunz was writing the history of Jewish public life. This important text anticipated Zunz's trilogy of Jewish religious poetry, *Die synagogale Poesie des Mittelalters* (*Synagogal Poesy of the Middle Ages*, 1855), *Der Ritus des synagogalen Gottesdienstes* (*The Rite of Synagogal Liturgy*, 1889), and *Literaturgeschichte der synagogalen Poesie* (1865).

Zunz was also eager to make Jewish learning available to the intelligent Jewish laity. His 1838 edition of the Hebrew scriptures remained the standard printed Hebrew text until supplanted by the Stuttgart Bible between 1967 and 1977. Less famous but equally illustrative of Zunz's intentions was the German translation of the *Bavli* on which he later collaborated with other modernizing Jewish scholars. However, in 1818, Zunz wrote in literary German with frequently untranslated Latin and unpointed Hebrew quotations. It was as if he wrote for himself. "To those," Zunz said, who do not revere "*Wissenschaft* in its honourable greatness . . . we have nothing to say."

Zunz was also a Jewish educator and, when necessary, a Jewish controversialist. He worked for a new type of Jewish school to educate modern Jews, and in 1820 his efforts were repaid with threatened excommunication (*herem*) by the Vilna rabbinate. From 1841 to 1850 he headed the Berlin Jewish teachers' seminary. He also debated with anti-Semites. He deplored recent defamations such as those in the Berlin Professor Friedrich Rühs's *Paulus*. (As a student, apparently Zunz withdrew from Rühs's Bible course due to the consistently anti-Semitic tenor of the lectures.) In 1830 he wrote persuasively to discredit the *Théorie du judaisme* by the Catholic Abbé Luigi Chiarini.

Zunz was, in a short, an exemplary modern Jewish intellectual. His scholarship showed how one could preserve and revere the Jewish cultural legacy by bringing modern historical criticism to bear on it. This meant, further, that by personal example he showed how the highly educated could remain proudly Jewish without any dulling of their critical faculties. He was, therefore, the founder of modern Jewish studies.

ROBERT SOUTHARD

Bibliography

Bamberger, Fritz. "Zunz's Conception of Jewish History," *Proceedings of the American Academy for Jewish Research* 1 (1941): 1–25.

Meyer, Michael. *The Origins of the Modern Jew*. Detroit, 1967.

Schorsch, Ismar. *From Text to Context: The Turn to History in Modern Judaism*. Hanover, N.H.: Brandeis University Press, 1994.

Index